A WILEY PUBLICATION
IN PSYCHOLOGY

Herbert S. Langfeld

Advisory Editor

Manual of

CHILD PSYCHOLOGY

Contributors

JOHN E. ANDERSON

LEONARD CARMICHAEL

RUTH M. CRUIKSHANK

KARL C. PRATT

HELEN THOMPSON

ARNOLD GESELL

NORMAN L. MUNN

FLORENCE L. GOODENOUGH

DOROTHEA McCARTHY

HAROLD E. JONES

JOHN E. HORROCKS

MARGARET MEAD

VERNON JONES

ARTHUR T. JERSILD

KURT LEWIN

SIBYLLE ESCALONA

CATHARINE COX MILES

LEWIS M. TERMAN

LEONA E. TYLER

CLEMENS E. BENDA

HAROLD H. ANDERSON

GLADYS L. ANDERSON

Manual of CHILD PSYCHOLOGY

SECOND EDITION

Edited by

LEONARD CARMICHAEL

Secretary, Smithsonian Institution

NEW YORK · JOHN WILEY & SONS, INC.
LONDON · CHAPMAN & HALL, LIMITED

Library of Congress Catalog Card Number: 54-5582

PRINTED IN THE UNITED STATES OF AMERICA

PREFACE

It has been said that a most serious need of modern psychology is for advanced scientific manuals to bridge the gap between the excellent and varied elementary textbooks in this field and the scientific periodical literature of psychology. This manual is an advanced-level textbook and is intended to be an addition at just this level to the literature of general as well as child psychology. The book is presented as a series of separate chapters, each written by a recognized authority. Its purpose is to provide an accurate and coherent picture of some of the most important aspects of research in the scientific psychology of human development.

Until comparatively recent years most of those who wrote upon the development of individual mental life elaborated essentially speculative theories. They attempted to describe man's so-called inborn instincts or the allegedly *tabula rasa* character of the mind of the young child. The present book is testimony that today psychologists and other scientists by the use of appropriate techniques have established a large body of important and reliable facts concerning the details of human mental development. This book is a clear demonstration that the speculative period in child psychology is past.

Many practical as well as theoretical gains have resulted from the empirical study of the growth of the human mind. It will be clear to the reader of these chapters that it has been possible to formulate hypotheses concerning many specific aspects of mental development. Many of these hypotheses have been tested in the laboratory or in controlled quantifiable social situations. The conclusions so reached are very different from the vague verbal theories of the prescientific era of child psychology.

One who is interested mainly in securing an understanding of adult mental life can gain many new insights into mental processes in general from a study of these chapters. A knowledge of the way in which adult psychological processes develop in each individual is fundamental to a complete understanding of such characteristics. The manual may thus be considered a factual introduction to the understanding not only of child psychology but also of the psychology of the normal adult human mind and even of the abnormal human mind.

The editor has not attempted any modification of the separate styles or points of view of the individual chapters as they are presented. The chapters appear essentially as their authors prepared them. It is believed that the extensive bibliographical references included will be of real value to advanced students and to research workers.

The authors of all the chapters wrote for serious advanced undergraduate students and graduate students as well as for specialists in psychology and in such related fields as education, psychiatry, pediatrics, and medicine in general.

Both as editor of the manual and as the author of a special chapter, I am indebted to Clark University and to the Clark University Press for their generosity in allowing the reproduction in this book of extensive excerpts and the use of other materials

v

previously published in the *Handbook of Child Psychology, Revised Edition,* which was issued in 1933 by that press.

Both the *Handbook of Child Psychology* and the *Handbook of Child Psychology, Revised Edition,* were edited by Dr. Carl Murchison. I wish to express here my profound appreciation for the pioneer work done by Dr. Murchison in producing these handbooks and other advanced books in psychology. This manual owes much in spirit and content to the foresight and editorial skill of Dr. Murchison.

The years since the presentation of the first edition of the *Manual of Child Psychology* have produced important work in this scientific field. This development has been more active in certain fields related to the study of the child than in others. In this second edition, therefore, more elaborate changes have been made in some chapters than in others. Chapter 18, "The Psychopathology of Childhood," is new. The chapter entitled "The Adolescent" is the contribution of an author not represented in the first edition. An addendum

has been added to Chapter 15, "The Influence of Topological and Vector Psychology upon Current Research in Child Development."

Once again I wish to express my appreciation to the authors who have actively cooperated in writing and revising the chapters as presented here.

The favorable reception that the first edition received not only in America but all over the world is indicative of the growing importance of the study of the phenomena of the growth and development of the child. The translation into French of the entire first edition and its publication by the Presses Universitaires de France is one striking example of the favorable acceptance that has greeted the book.

It is hoped that the present revised edition will be of further value to the student of this fundamental and peculiarly human field.

LEONARD CARMICHAEL

Smithsonian Institution
January, 1954

CONTENTS

CHAPTER 1

METHODS OF CHILD PSYCHOLOGY [1]

JOHN E. ANDERSON

In child psychology, as in any other science, a distinction can be made between *content,* or the facts and generalizations which are welded into a body of knowledge; *methods,* or the techniques and procedures by means of which such content is obtained; and *theory,* or the framework of assumptions within which the science operates. Content, method, and theory can never be completely separated from one another. In the beginning, little concern with method or theory appears because new methods produce results so rapidly that major interest centers upon content. But as science matures, interest in method and in theory grows.

Just as with the human body, a science is composed of many parts which grow at different rates and mature at different times. When a promising method is discovered, one area spurts forward rapidly and engrosses many workers, while another remains relatively inactive. In general, progress is from description to quantitatively formulated relations, and from exploration to principles that subsume wider and wider ranges of fact. As the significant problems are more clearly perceived, designed experiments replace simple observations. At any time the methods in some areas of a science are still exploratory, whereas in others methods are very advanced and precise. Little is gained by thinking of or calling a particular method right or wrong. Rather should we see how better methods give greater insight and more significant generalizations.

In the nineteenth century, so notable for its advance in all fields of science, some observations upon children were made in systematic fashion. The first approach, the baby biography, involved day-by-day recordings of the experiences and behavior of a single child, usually by an interested scientist, himself a parent or close relative. Often simple experiments and measurements were included. Among the many such biographies available, of major historical importance are those of Tiedemann (1787), Darwin (1877), Preyer (1882), the Sterns (1907, 1909), Shinn (1893, 1899, 1900), and the Scupins (1907). Dennis (1949) has summarized some of the beginnings of child psychology.

The next stride forward came with a new method, the questionnaire. Starting with

[1] Because of the limited space available for the discussion of the methods of child psychology, many topics must be given brief and incomplete treatment. To discuss adequately even one section of method, e.g., sampling or indirect measurement, would take as much space as is allotted for this entire chapter. And since the content chapters which follow will, of necessity, to some extent treat method in their particular areas, this chapter in presenting an extensive overview, rather than an intensive analysis of a limited area, suggests sources from which workers can secure information that will help them in scientific work with children.

Difficulty is also encountered in citation and bibliography. To cite all the studies which contribute to method would fill this entire volume. Hence citations are limited to examples or instances, to summaries that integrate substantial amounts of material, and to major contributions to statistical or research methods. It is assumed that several modern comprehensive statistical textbooks are available to the reader.

Hall's (1891) inquiry into the "The Contents of Children's Minds," a deluge of questionnaires advanced the knowledge of children, especially those of school ages (Bradbury, 1937).

With Bolton (1892) and Gilbert (1894), extensive tests of school children were undertaken. Unfortunately, Gilbert, who studied simple functions, obtained low relations with school progress. Had he happened upon complex functions and thus obtained significant correlations, he might have set off what came twenty years later, when Binet and Simon (1905) forged a new method which not only initiated the measurement of intelligence but also gave impetus to the invention of a wide variety of measurement devices in areas such as achievement and personality. Thorndike (1904, 1913, 1914) led in the use of the new techniques with school children and contributed to method in all areas by his emphasis upon statistics. For Watson (1919) the crucial psychological observations are those made upon children, not adults. By stressing objectivity and dismissing introspection, he made infants and children appropriate subjects for psychological investigation, a point of view not held by many of his predecessors.

Although clinical descriptions of defective, abnormal, and delinquent children appeared in the medical and psychological literature almost from the beginning, it was not until Freud's emphasis upon the principle that neurotic symptoms in the adult are the outcome of childhood experience that past histories were studied extensively in order to explain present behavior.

The Gestalt psychologists by directing attention to the origin and change of configurations with experience made studies of children important. Similarly, a biological or organismic point of view based on embryological studies emphasized the genetic history of both the elements and integrated patterns of behavior.

Many of the older discussions on the appropriateness of children as subjects or the need for a special psychological talent for the interpretation of child behavior are now chiefly of historical interest. Discussions of method in child psychology are found in many sources, among which a few of the more extensive are Koffka (1924), Thomas and Thomas (1928), Goodenough and Anderson (1931), Symonds (1931), Anderson (1931, 1933), Lewin (1935, 1936), Jones and Burks (1936), Bühler (1937), Horowitz and Murphy (1937), Murphy, Murphy, and Newcomb (1937), Arrington (1943), Koch (1948), Orlansky (1949), Cattell (1950), and Thompson (1952).

Periodic summaries in the field appear regularly in the *Annual Review of Psychology*, in the *Journal of the American Educational Research Association*, and occasionally in the *Psychological Bulletin*. From time to time the *Yearbook of the National Society for the Study of Education* (1938, 1939, 1940, 1944, 1946, 1947, 1950) brings much material together upon particular topics. Abstracts of current articles can be found in *Psychological Abstracts* and in *Child Development Abstracts*. The *Encyclopedia of Educational Research*, edited by Monroe (1949), is also a very valuable source book.

With the wealth of material upon developmental changes in the behavior of infants, children, and adolescents, and an increased concern with the rôle of the environment in the time dimension, child psychology is coming into its own. Less and less are college or graduate students in the psychological laboratories looked upon as the representatives of the human species for scientific purposes; more and more their behavior is viewed as a phase in a developmental cycle beginning with conception and ending with death.

Childhood is then only a phase of a more general process of growth and development. In child psychology the same human organism is studied as is studied later in adult psychology. Hence, no methods are peculiar to child psychology as such, or to adult psychology as such; instead there are adaptations of particular methods to particular age levels. For example, some of the earlier experiments on children used techniques which previously had been tried on adults. In more recent years methods originally developed with very young children have been extended to the study of adult social groups. There are some advantages in the study of children, in that many of the relations met at the adult level in a very complex matrix are encountered in children at a simpler level that permits the isolation of factors and location of significant relations with less difficulty.

A half century of research has given us a very different picture of the nature of the child from that held in earlier periods. The following brief summary (Anderson, 1944) outlines the essentials of the modern point of view:

1. The child is a growing organism who moves by infinitesimal changes from a single cell to a complex organization of structure and function at an adult level. In this progression, scientists describe the differentiation of new structures and functions, changes in the size and form of structures, and changes in the level and effectiveness of function. They seek underlying principles that will bring understanding of these changes and practical methods of modifying or improving development and function.

2. The child is a spatially separated unit that functions as an organized whole in the situations he meets. This molar characteristic of behavior needs particular emphasis. In the physical and chemical sciences, units of organization can be broken up into component parts, reassembled, and broken up again. As a result, the laws governing organi-zation can be worked out with such precision and exactness as to give exceptional prediction and control. Since neither the child nor his behavior can be broken up and reassembled in the literal sense, difficulties arise in scientific child study. Both the psychological terms and the measuring devices used to analyze behavior into manipulable symbolic units correspond only to functions of the organism as a whole. Thus, when we speak of memory, learning, or emotion, separate acts are classified in terms of similarity, not necessarily on the basis of intrinsic characteristics. Any act may be classified under many different categories, depending upon our scientific purpose. For example, the same act can be classified as sensing, learning, emotion, or memory. This wholeness or functional unity of the child makes necessary methods that seem devious and indirect to the physical scientist.

3. The child lives in a context, itself neither simple nor unitary, which continuously affects his behavior and development. Patterns of stimulation come to him out of this context. And, in turn, by virtue of his own make-up, he selects from that context. At all times there is a reciprocal relation between the human being and this biosocial context. The context can be considered in terms both of the moment and of factors operating in time. Because the child is limited in time, behavior becomes structured, and patterns develop both in the stimulus field and in his own response system. Some stimulus patterns become significant because they modify the developmental stream by affecting practice or social relations. Others remain insignificant because they do not affect this web of relations. Why one pattern is significant and another is not, is a crucial problem.

4. The child is engaged in an ongoing process of development that is not reversible. Because of the interrelations that accrue, neither relations within the child, those within the context, nor their interaction can be reproduced a second time in their exact original form. Behavior at any moment results from the child's history and the stimulation pres-

ent. Hence, concepts of simple or single causes must be replaced by concepts of multiple factors, reciprocal relations, and the progressive recession of causes and the ongoing cumulation of effects.

The Problems of Child Psychology

In approaching the child, the scientist seeks to formulate principles that will bring understanding of children and the prediction of their behavior under various circumstances, in order to surround them with influences and opportunities for better living. The general principles or statements of the relations that exist between and among various factors are expressed in either verbal or numerical symbols, or both, which function as a kind of shorthand to reduce the complexities of life to simpler and more manipulable terms. Note also that these generalizations exist in some form long after the children studied have ceased to be. The children Binet tested have been adults for many years, and some have passed on. What science leaves behind, then, is not a replica or duplicate of what it originally studied, but a series of statements or principles which more or less adequately represent the relations originally studied and which enable others to manipulate and control environments in the present. But the principles when taken together also make some sort of coherent whole. The generalizations are then modified as more data are accumulated. The interactions and combinations of factors are mapped with some accuracy, even though they are only parts of still more complex manifolds. A science is then, in a sense, a series of symbols that represent what can and cannot be done, like the rules of a game. But we do not know the rules in advance; we have to discover them through experience, not casual experience but systematic experience.

These symbols must be clearly defined in order that different scientists may understand each other. In everyday speech, words are defined in terms of themselves, and they become dangerous when they are extended to areas and events to which they have no real reference. To meet this difficulty the scientist wherever possible anchors his concepts and terms to specific measurements and expresses relations in a quantitative way. In some degree, progress in science is a matter of moving from a language which is largely descriptive to a more precise and quantitative language. The problem of method is the problem of how this more precise language can be obtained. In seeking the rules of the game under which life is lived, the scientist assumes that rules exist and that life is itself orderly and coherent in spite of its superficial inconsistencies. As Wiener (1948, pp. 62–63) has well said,

> For the existence of any science, it is necessary that there exist phenomena which do not stand isolated. In a world ruled by a succession of miracles performed by an irrational God subject to sudden whims, we should be forced to await each new catastrophe in a state of perplexed passiveness. We have a picture of such a world in the croquet game in *Alice in Wonderland;* where the mallets are flamingoes; the balls, hedgehogs, which quietly unroll and go about their own business; the hoops, playing-card soldiers, likewise subject to locomotor initiative of their own; and the rules are the decrees of the testy, unpredictable Queen of Hearts. . . . The essence of an effective rule for a game or a useful law of physics is that it be statable in advance and that it apply to more than one case. Ideally it would represent a property of the system discussed which remains the same under the flux of particular circumstances. In the simplest case, it is a property which is *invariant* to a set of *transformations* to which the system is subject.

The psychologist studying children seeks principles of wide scope which will facilitate the understanding, prediction, and control of behavior. He is concerned with (a) the fundamental mechanics and dynamics of the developing person; (b) the effects he produces upon the environment; and (c) the effects the environment produces upon him. Next, he describes the developmental process itself in terms of common trends by (d) a successive cross-section or (e) a genetic-longitudinal approach. Finally, he describes individual behavior by (f) assessing the person at any level; and by (g) obtaining a genetic account of him in his total setting.

The Mechanics and Dynamics of the Organism. In any organization of matter in the world of space and time, science assumes that lawful relations exist which can be determined independently of any particular individual or context; i.e., similar principles can be found which operate in many different individuals and in many different contexts. Knowing such principles we gain control over particulars; without knowing them, behavior appears meaningless. The phenomena and principles underlying Weber's law, the distribution of effort, conditioning, and reinforcement would fall under this head. This is the traditional content of psychology. In this area the designed study or experiment, which isolates or systematically varies factors, is basic.

Understanding and significance increase as (1) factors are permitted to operate within their full range in order to avoid generalizations based on small segments of the relations studied; (2) combinations of factors are studied; (3) attention is given to interlocking principles and their fit into explanatory systems. In child psychology another question arises—that of the extent to which the principles hold in terms of age and development, or the amount and char-

acter of the changes which are associated with age.

The Effect of the Organism upon the Environment. At any moment the child is a highly organized energy system within a field of forces known as the environment. As he moves forward in time, his relations within this field and to the external world are determined in part by his own make-up. Children differ widely in intelligence, musical capacity, motor coordination, energy level, etc. If these characteristics, both singly and in combinations, can be measured early in the life of the individual, children of various levels can be separated out and their subsequent history or impact on the environment studied. Although, unfortunately, most early separations have been made on intelligence, there is no reason, other than the availability of appropriate measuring devices, why other separations should not be made. The classical example is found in Terman *et al.* (1925, 1947), who followed gifted children into adult life. Baller's study (1936) of the adult accomplishments of subnormals tested in childhood concerns the opposite end of the scale. Glueck and Glueck (1934, 1937) have studied the later careers of delinquent children. An unusual study of children in the same family fifty years later is presented by Smith (1952). More significant generalizations can be made if the separations are made early and children are followed than if the scientist separates his group on the basis of adult performance and works backward, only to find his results complicated by selective factors that are difficult to interpret. In this approach, the individual becomes the independent variable, and his accomplishment, or the psychological environment he constructs for himself, the dependent variable.

The Effect of the Environment upon the Organism. In educating children content is deliberately introduced into the child's life in order that he may learn. Similarly scientists deliberately produce conditions in order to discover their effects. Questions arise, such as the more effective methods of teaching reading, how to control temper tantrums, what materials to use in geography, whether motion pictures and visual aids improve learning, and whether early training is more important than late training. Sometimes simple and single factors in the environment are modified; sometimes very complex patterns of stimulation are used. In many instances, parallel groups of children exposed differentially to the factors studied are set up. The single factor with a particular effect is the limiting case at one end, and a total environment with all its effects is the limiting case at the other end. Concern is with all types of combinations of factors and all varieties of complexity. Improved skills in statistical techniques make possible many types of analysis that previously could not be made. In this area generalizations are usually expressed in actuarial terms, with prediction within known limits of error for groups and individuals. In many instances, even though the problems originate at a practical level, important generalizations for the mechanics and dynamics of the organism result.

In the past, many studies in child psychology have worked backward from behavior outcomes to antecedent factors. Thus, the histories and behavior of children already delinquent or nondelinquent, jealous or nonjealous, etc., are compared. Sampling and control are set up in terms of an end result. Many generalizations on the effect of home discipline and management are derived from working backward from problem and normal children to descriptions of the homes and neighborhoods from which they come. But if homes of contrasting disciplinary programs that were equivalent in other respects were chosen in advance, and children's subsequent behavior was measured, more significant results would be obtained. Some scientific information is gained from the backward-working approach, and we use it when information obtained by working forward is not available. Greater progress will come as studies move from context to behavior, not from behavior to context. The environmental factor or context becomes the independent variable and behavior the dependent variable.

Some difficulties arise. Suppose that five contrasting environments in terms of distance from civilization are selected and the children measured (Sherman and Henry, 1933); will equivocal results be obtained? No, because any environment that has existed for a long time has exercised a highly selective influence upon its population.

The child coming into an experiment is a representative of a particular environment or context. The need of controlling socio-economic or cultural status becomes evident as more data on the cultural determiners of psychological processes become available. Anderson (1936), Davis and Dollard (1940), Davis and Havighurst (1947), Centers (1949), Havighurst and Taba (1949), Hollingshead (1949), Stendler (1949), and Warner et al. (1949) have published studies which show the significant influence of background factors on the behavior of children. Care must then be taken either to control background factors or to measure their effects.

Normative Cross-Section Approach. Children at various ages, grades, or other levels can be measured, tested, exposed to materials, or placed in comparable situations and observed. When results are analyzed in terms of age or level, two important outcomes appear: (*a*) information on the growth process is secured, and (*b*) norms or standards with which the performance of other children can be compared are obtained.

As the child moves from infancy to adulthood, growth takes place. The adult is essentially at a maintenance level. For practical and theoretical purposes, determining the rate and manner of change with time or level is necessary and important. Much literature in child psychology pictures development, e.g., the many studies of motor, linguistic, intellectual, and social skills. Despite the present concern with longitudinal studies, the cross-section study has particular advantages, since new samples drawn from the population in similar ways at each level cross-check upon the data at other levels. Moreover, uniform sampling procedures can be used throughout the age or level series, a principle that does not hold for longitudinal studies, in which the original sampling is modified by the disappearance of some children from the investigations.

If the results obtained from comparable samples at successive age or other levels are secured, a scale becomes available for the evaluation of individual children. The child's present performance can be compared with those of children at his own or at lower or higher levels, and his developmental position in quantitative terms obtained. A powerful instrument emerges for the practical guidance and assessment of growing persons. For norms to be of maximum usefulness, particular care must be taken to secure adequate samples at each level in order to eliminate distortion arising from lack of representativeness. Terman and Merrill (1937) restandardizing the Binet tests used paternal occupation, geographical location, and rural-urban residence, in addition to sex, to control their samples.

In psychological studies, means and standard deviations are seldom smoothed, in contrast with physical-growth studies, where smoothing is more common. Since the sample at each age level is a new and independent one, smoothing to increase the precision of the norms is justified. Although many norms are based on chronological age, other designations of level can be used. Often combinations, such as sex-age-height for weight or sex-age for motor development, give a much better appraisement of the individual.

Genetic-Longitudinal Approach. Although the results obtained from successive cross-sections are of great value, they give approximations rather than accurate representations of the developmental process (Jones, 1939). For example, because children grow at different rates and reach similar developmental levels at different times, a cross-section study places together at the thirteen-year age level many girls well past puberty and many girls months away from puberty.

Longitudinal studies measure the same children at successive periods (Freeman and Flory, 1937; Dearborn and Rothney, 1941). While means and standard deviations can be obtained at each age level, as in the cross-section study, the longitudinal study, in addition, permits: (1) an analysis of the development and growth of each individual child; (2) a study of growth increments, both for the individual and the group; and (3) an analysis in detail of the interrelations between growth processes, both maturational and experiential, because all data have been obtained on the same children.

But it, too, has some disadvantages. No matter how carefully a sample is selected at the beginning, whatever limits the original sample, which is drawn but once, will affect all subsequent data. In some studies families of stable position in the community, such as home owners, are used; in others, communities known to have little mobility are used. But this may mean a sample that is not typical from the beginning. Casualties because of death, illness, families moving away, and changes in the cooperation of children and parents with the investigator will further distort the sampling at later ages. The investigator should discard data for the incomplete cases, since their use will not only destroy the advantages gained by the longitudinal method but also may actually distort the results (Anderson and Cohen, 1939).

With longitudinal data, other problems appear. Since a cross-section method lumps all individuals of a particular age level together, irrespective of developmental level, treating longitudinal data as though they were cross-sectional data gives no advantage. Shuttleworth (1939) superimposed the periods of maximal rate of physical growth for early- and late-maturing groups, irrespective of chronological age, and made an analysis by plotting curves. Basic similarities in the growth pattern that were not apparent before this treatment were revealed. Markey's (1928) individual curves for vocabulary growth from the baby biographies differ noticeably from the usual growth curves worked out by cross-section methods. Some evidence is available to the effect that the course of animal learning is predictable when equations are plotted for individuals, not groups. This suggests that some of the statistical methods centering in measures of status, i.e., means, standard deviations, correlation coefficients, etc., which are appropriate for cross-section studies have limited use in longitudinal data, for which treatments concerned with progression, rates, increments, and velocity are more appropriate. Courtis (1950), who has applied the Gompertz curve to cross-section data obtained over a range of ages, feels that even for such data statistical methods for studying growth and prediction can be much improved. Honzik (1938) and Anderson (1939b) found that measures

of intelligence vary in predicting terminal status as measures are separated in time and as the functions measured overlap.

A method of treating longitudinal data in terms of increments that results in good curves of the growth process involves selecting a point at which the maximum number of cases is available, calculating the mean of the measures at this point, then calculating the mean of the increments (or decrements) to the next level, adding (or subtracting) this mean to the mean at the base level, then calculating the mean of the increment (or decrement) to the next level, and adding (or subtracting) it to the base level mean plus the mean of the previous increment, and so on. Standard deviations can also be combined by appropriate formulae. The use of increments eliminates the variance of the individuals in the base at different age levels (Shuttleworth, 1934).

A summary of some of the interpretations of longitudinal data is found in Olson (1949), who developed a method of representing developmental level in what he calls *organismic age*. This is obtained by combining various measures of development which have been scaled in age terms, such as mental age, dental age, carpal age, weight age, grip age, and reading age. Thus when such measures are available for a given child inadequacies of development can be spotted. This assumes, however, that development in its various phases should be uniform and parallel, which may or may not be true. The combination of various dissimilar measures with differing reliabilities into a single scale with equal weights is open to question.

The design of longitudinal studies is simple, unless a control group runs parallel to the longitudinal group. Many more cases must be studied at the beginning in order to allow for selective elimination. Once the children are selected, emphasis is given to the measures to be used and their arrangement in time. Precision is increased by using fixed intervals for testing. Often these come near the child's birthday. In planning, particular care must be taken to anticipate the early data that will be needed for interpretation of later data. Early records should be extraordinarily complete (Macfarlane, 1938) as, once a study is well under way, it is almost impossible to make up deficiencies.

Included under the longitudinal-genetic approach are a number of methods for studying children. The classical baby biography described the development of a single child. Detailed studies of the successive drawings of the same children over a long span of years have been made (Goodenough and Harris, 1950). Descriptive accounts of the development of peculiar or abnormal children are available. More recently extensive and well-planned programs follow the same children for long terms of years and use many methods of measuring and observing the children. With the development of cumulative record systems in schools and clinics, a type of record keeping is coming which should give us many of the advantages of the longitudinal techniques in future studies.

The Assessment of the Individual, or the Horizontal Inventory. At any level an individual can be described as a combination of skills, knowledges, attitudes, emergency reaction mechanisms, etc. For many practical purposes in education, clinical work, and guidance, a horizontal inventory of the child's resources is of value. From the standpoint of science the most satisfactory technique involves plotting his position in each of many areas in terms of established norms or standards on a psychograph. For example, results on intelligence and achievement tests scaled in terms of age can be plotted for a single child. In the absence of standardized instruments, descriptive accounts and ratings are sometimes used or

added to scaled measures. Because of the practical value of the horizontal inventory, child psychologists could well give more attention to establishing norms and standards for many behavior patterns. Some norms in the literature center about unusual performances of a laboratory type not related directly to life situations. But norms or standards for such everyday things as dressing habits, ordinary motor performances, and almost all practical skills, except the school skills represented in the achievement tests, are strikingly lacking. In spite of this lack, the assessment function constantly devolves upon the child psychologist.

One outcome of assessment is its possible use for predicting future development. The intelligence test has been demonstrated to have substantial predictive value. For any other assessment procedure, the limits and possibilities of prediction can be worked out. Although actual achievement at any moment is probably more significant for an adult than is a test of potentiality, for the child the problem of potentiality is one of constant concern.

Genetic Account of the Individual in Terms of the Whole Setting. By this unwieldy phrase is meant those studies which attempt to represent the unique character and quality of the individual. It differs from assessment at any single level in that it seeks the background and genesis of present behavior. In its search for generalizations by studying functions common to many individuals, traditional psychology pulls the person apart. But each person is a unique combination with his own history and particular behavior patterns.

In this classification fall the many studies of individual children by the case history, clinical, and psychoanalytic methods. Two points may be made: (1) whereas effective methods are available for describing an individual in terms of single measurements, little work has been done on combinations and patterns; (2) when achieved, the representation of the pattern, as a whole, may be more accurate, in spite of inaccuracies in single measurements, than the representation in terms of isolated and single characteristics, since the pattern is itself a generalization in which errors may cancel out.

Central Problems of Method

From the recent literature of psychology emerge several problems which bear a significant relation to method in the field of research on children. The first two grow out of the impact of Gestalt psychology, namely, the use of statistical procedures to set up phenotypes rather than genotypes, and the problem of whether prediction in the sense of lawfulness is actuarial or individual. The third problem, that of content, level, and dynamics, creates some confusion in the discussion of measurement, since it is not always clear which of these three aspects of the functioning organism is under consideration; and the fourth grows out of the movement of modern science from exploratory to designed research.

Phenotype and Genotype. Lewin (1935, 1936) criticizes many scientific studies of children on the ground that acts are grouped together because of their similarity when they appear and then treated as though they were distinct and discrete phenomena. Thus Lewin (1935, pp. 15, 16) says:

Present-day child psychology and affect psychology also exemplify clearly the Aristotelian habit of considering the abstractly defined classes as the essential nature of the particular object and hence as an explanation of its behavior. Whatever is common to children of a given age is set up as the fundamental character of that age. The fact that three-year-old children are

quite often negative is considered evidence that negativism is inherent in the nature of three-year-olds, and the concept of a negativistic age or stage is then regarded as an explanation (though perhaps not a complete one) for the appearance of negativism in a given particular case. . . . The statistical procedure, at least in its commonest application in psychology, is the most striking expression of this Aristotelian mode of thinking.

Lewin calls such a mode of classification a *phenotype* and distinguishes it sharply from the *genotype,* in which phenomena antecedent to these appearances are studied. A genotype is a homogeneous context of factors, either simple or complex, that produces effects which may differ widely, whereas a phenotype is a classification in terms of the homogeneity of end results which may have arisen from very different origins. For Lewin the central problem of child psychology becomes the study of genotypes. The *genotype* preserves the natural setting; the *phenotype* separates events from their setting. In actual practice, Lewin's experimental procedures conform to his principle, since he observes the effects on behavior of modifications of the environmental context.

But the Lewin view has its critics. A clear statement is found in Thurstone (1935, p. 44):

The constructs in terms of which natural phenomena are comprehended are man-made inventions. To discover a scientific law is merely to discover that a man-made scheme serves to unify, and thereby to simplify, comprehension of a certain class of natural phenomena. A scientific law is not to be thought of as having an independent existence which some scientist is fortunate to stumble upon. A scientific law is not a part of nature. It is only a way of comprehending nature. [And further, p. 47] Some social scientists have objected because two individuals may have the same attitude score toward, say, pacifism, and yet be totally different in their backgrounds and in the causes of their similar social views. If such critics were consistent, they would object also to the statement that two men have identical incomes, for one of them earns when the other one steals. They should also object to the statement that two men are of the same height. The comparison should be held invalid because one of the men is fat and the other is thin. This is again the resistance against invading with the generalizing and simplifying constructs of science a realm which is habitually comprehended only in terms of innumerable and individualized detail. . . . What is not generally understood, even by many scientists, is that no scientific law is ever intended to represent any event pictorially. The law is only an abstraction from the experimental situation. No experiment is ever completely repeated. . . . There is an unlimited number of ways in which nature can be comprehended in terms of fundamental scientific concepts.

Individual and Actuarial Prediction. A related problem concerns the nature of prediction. Some agree with Allport (1940), who feels that because most psychological generalizations are actuarial, that is, are statements of probability for groups, we must search for principles that make prediction possible in the individual case. For instance, when delinquency is said to occur 5 times as frequently among children from broken homes as among those from normal homes, the statement is one of probability. But, for a particular child from a particular broken home, the chances of delinquency may be 0 or 100 per cent or anywhere between.

Two points may be made in criticism of this view. First, prediction in an individual case depends upon the completeness of knowledge. The more we know about the child and his background, the better we can predict his future. For instance, if we

know the relation between broken homes and delinquency, our prediction for an individual will be right, let us say, 1 out of every 2 times. If we know the effect of another factor, say whether the home was broken by divorce, desertion, or death, our prediction will be right 2 out of 3 times. If we now add the cultural level of the home, we will be right 4 out of 5 times. If we now add knowledge of the character of the remaining spouse, we will be right 9 out of 10 times. Thus, the accuracy of prediction increases and the error in prediction decreases as we know more about the case. Ultimately a point may be reached when prediction will almost be perfect. At some point, the return from additional knowledge of factors becomes so small that any practical gain in prediction may be balanced against the effort necessary to secure the data. This is a problem in many areas of measurement. For instance, in designing a measure of general intelligence, the cutting-off point for additional subtests comes when their use results in only minimal additions to predictive value. Many tests consist of about 6 different types of subtests. No one would deny that with 12 subtests a more accurate prediction would be obtained and that with 20 subtests prediction would be still more accurate. But most of the variance in intelligence is predicted from the first 6 subtests. Without research one cannot tell how much time or how many measures are necessary to establish a stable and firm predictive measure. But it is clear that the practical problem is establishing a terminal point in the face of diminishing returns.

As more is learned about the combination of factors and their relative significance, prediction improves both for groups and for individuals. In this area there have been significant advances in modern statistical methods centering about the design of experiments to analyze the weight and contribution of combinations of factors. These developments have come from two sources: from workers in agriculture statistics, notably Fisher (1925, 1936), and from workers concerned with the prediction of performance in practical situations, as in Army, Navy, Air Force, and industrial testing.

Second, although perfect prediction for individuals is the ideal, it is not reached completely even in the physical and natural sciences. Instead, the limits of prediction come to be defined statistically. Thus, it depends upon the number of decimal places to which the analysis of data is carried and the confidence (in the statistical sense) which can be placed in the prediction. For example, the results of developing a photographic emulsion of known constitution in a developer of known constitution for a definite period of time at a constant temperature seem perfect to the naïve person. But the prediction is accurate only within a certain number of decimal places. With more precise measurement, variations will be discovered. For the everyday purpose of developing a print, the prediction is perfect; for the research workers seeking to improve emulsions and developers, it is far from perfect. In terms of the limits within which predictions can be made, the data available to the psychologist differ only in degree from those in other scientific fields.

Much of the difficulty that is encountered comes in the applications of scientific generalizations in the world of practical affairs. The child psychologist shifts from the viewpoint that science is an explanatory system of generalizations to the view that science is a matter of prediction and control of wide practical and of wide theoretical importance. One difficulty centers in the word "cause." In explanatory science he is concerned with the interdependence of variables and is taught that in this framework antecedence is not necessarily

efficient *cause* but *association*. Then he moves into the practical world, where cause is quite properly used in another sense. For example, a developed photographic print may be said to have turned black because of the absence of a fixing bath. If a second print is fixed and does not turn black, the statement, "The first print was spoiled because it was not placed in a fixing bath," is accurate. Note that here concern is with obviously practical relations in which, by changing a factor or a complex of factors, a specific, particular, and predictable result is obtained. Similarly, when the reading of a child with a high IQ and normal vision who reads poorly is improved when he works with a tutor, the improvement can be described as the result of the tutoring. Again the result is produced by introducing specific and describable factors into the child's environment. In this sense, prediction has meaning, even though it may not literally be perfect.

There are other difficulties in prediction which, although they apply primarily to groups, may seriously affect interpretation in individual cases. One concerns workers in the practical field who generalize predictions from small differences to widespread practical conclusions. As an example, consider the statement, so often made in books on the teaching of children, that children below 5 or 6 years lack the physical and physiological development of the eye necessary for reading. The literature when examined indicates that a small proportion of children at early age levels have eye difficulties which interfere with reading. A significant difference in the statistical sense can be obtained between various age levels. But is this difference of such general significance that widespread practical conclusions as to the location of reading in the curriculum can be based upon it? When the problem is examined from this point of view, it becomes clear that the overwhelming majority of children have good visual sense organs, even at a very early age, and that in its anatomical development the eye reaches an adult level very early. Hence, no universal or general factor, either anatomically or physiologically, exists that would prevent most children from learning to read in early childhood. Moreover, when children's manipulation of objects in their spontaneous play is observed, it becomes clear that they make sharp visual discriminations, some of which are as fine or precise as those involved in reading. Hence, the decision as to whether all 3-year-olds or all 6-year-olds in our society should be exposed to reading materials must be made on other than anatomical or physiological grounds.

A surprising number of predictions are made for total populations on the basis of very small differences. To some degree, the nature of the conclusions reached depends upon the particular aspect of the figures on which the person focuses his attention. For example, a survey in the 1930's (Anderson, 1936) showed that 13.4 per cent of Negro young children are without toys. However important it is to correct this deficiency, it is easy to forget that 86.4 per cent of the children are in homes with toys, and to generalize the deficiency into a striking inadequacy. Two errors arise: one is an overemphasis of the proportion with a deficiency; the other is the failure to consider the data in relation to the time series. While data on adverse situations are significant for a particular point in time, from the practical point of view the significant question is the extent to which figures change with time. Did more children in 1949 have toys available than in 1929 or 1909?

Another difficulty in prediction to a practical situation of some importance is illustrated in studies of social status, in which emphasis can go either to the differences between social levels or to the similarities between them. For instance, in the same study the following figures are cited for the presence of telephones in the homes of various socio-economic classes, moving from VII, the lowest, to I, the highest: VII, 17.4%; VI, 24.6%; V, 46.2%; IV, 53.1%; III, 60.0%; II, 84.6%; I, 80.1%. There is a marked difference in the availability of particular items as we move from one social status classification to another. This material can be interpreted either in terms of the sharp difference between groups or in terms of what is common to the groups. For example, attention can go to the 21.4 per cent differences between Class V and Class VI, or to the fact that only 17.4 per cent of the lowest class have telephones as compared with 80.1 per cent of the highest class. Which is the most important? The difference, the commonalities, or the basic trend? Are such data to be interpreted as indicating a sharply separated class structure or as indicating a society in which basically there is homogeneity with differential but overlapping availability of facilities?

To combat the far-too-common overinterpretation of his statements in the practical world, the scientist shows caution in speaking about individual events. Usually he attaches some restriction or limitation that will indicate the amount of risk or the possible error in his generalizations and will show the range within which his generalizations apply.

Content, Level, and Motivation. As a living person in active relation to an environment, the child responds to stimulation with various amounts of energy, makes certain products, shows various skills and knowledge, and functions at certain levels in comparison with other, similar persons. For scientific purposes, it is often helpful to make a distinction between these aspects of his being by dividing them into content, level, and motivation. If we think of the person for the moment as comparable to a machine manufacturing a product, we can think of motivation as the fuel or energy that goes into the machine to make it run, content as the products made by the machine out of the materials fed into it, and level as the quality of the product. A machine for making cans, for instance, might be motivated by electricity or gas, might produce cans from tin or iron, and might produce cans of poorer quality than another machine, say, of later design.

For persons, content means the retained experience, including both the skills and knowledge, of the person and whatever products result from his action. He draws a house or a barn, spells one word or another, reads a novel or a textbook on physics, produces a play or an opera, speaks English or French, plays cricket or baseball, etc. In measuring content, concern is essentially with the results of his achievement or the products of his activity. Products vary with the culture or environment; i.e., if the child grows up in France he speaks French, if in England he speaks English.

By level is meant the quality or altitude of performance of the person. An expert in any area can turn out products at a high level in comparison with a novice; an older child generally performs better than a younger child. A child with special ability performs better than children without it on a task related to that ability. Since there is always some possibility of a chance production at a high level, the level is usually determined by repeated measurements of the child's performance on the theory that high-level performance manifests itself again and again. Measures of potentiality and the principle of handicapping in sports are based on this theory.

By motivation or dynamics is meant the activity, drive, or energy manifested by the person. A person of high level will not produce in a given situation unless he is motivated. Motivation is measured by placing persons of the same levels in contact with particular contents, materials, and facilities. In general, motivation is also concerned with what is done over a period of time and may involve what is done against pressure or resistance. Content usually can be measured quite directly; level and motivation, which can, in some instances, be measured directly, are usually measured indirectly.

Exploratory and Designed Research. Critics often point out that many research workers collect miscellaneous and unrelated facts, that studies are undertaken without a clear problem in mind, and that much effort goes to the elaboration of the obvious or to reiterating experiments or determining relations that are already known. Sometimes, too, they say that investigators concern themselves with the trivial and do not study the significant problems. Far too often, these critics have in mind an ideal experiment to which no real experiment ever corresponds. Not infrequently, when critics are asked to formulate precisely the general questions they wish answered, their criticisms evaporate because of their inability to put their general questions into a form that makes experimentation possible.

Much effort in modern society goes to counting and tabulating characteristics and events of all types. In the United States the greatest count is made every 10 years at the time of the census. Although careful thought goes into formulating the questions used, census taking is, by and large, a preliminary step in research. The data of the census, once collected, are analyzed in great detail by scientists within and outside the government. In census taking, data are collected first and subjected to later analysis; in designed research, the data collected are limited by the analysis to which they will later be subjected in accordance with the plan of the experiment.

But it also must be made very clear that a science consists not of a few collections of facts or a few experiments but of a great mass of knowledge and principles with many facets and relations collected over many years. Looking backward, it is easy to say that particular results are obvious. In fact, to the scientist of the 1950's, almost any study prior to 1930 seems obvious. But, in terms of its own time and place, the results are far from obvious. Much of the refined, accurate, advanced, and sophisticated research of today would be impossible without the work done before 1930. The most helpful way of viewing this process, both from the standpoint of a single problem and from that of the development of science, is to make a distinction between exploratory studies and designed research.

Implicit in the experimental method is the assumption that certain phenomena will be observed and recorded under controlled conditions. Formerly the experimental method was sharply contrasted with observation; now it is clear that there is a continuum which runs from casual and incidental observation to rigidly controlled experiment. Further, it is clear that experimenters are limited in their approach to problems and their observation of phenomena. Experimentation is often done in terms of categories or assumptions which do not fit behavior as it occurs. This results in only a portion of the pertinent behavior being recorded. Watson (1919), in observing and describing the emotional patterns of infants under controlled stimulation, projected his knowledge of the well-structured patterns of older persons upon them. Sherman (1927) showed the inadequacy of these descriptions and demonstrated that an investigator is likely to pick out of the behavior manifold only what meets his purpose. A simple example of

this principle is found by first outlining a series of categories for social behavior, then using them for the observation of young children engaged in free play. Almost every category will prove inadequate, and much behavior not thought of in advance will appear.

Because the significant aspects of behavior are likely to be missed, it is customary to conduct exploratory or pilot studies on a small group of subjects before the procedure is extended to a large group in order to secure final data. Exploratory research ranging from simple observations to elaborate pilot studies has been done in various research stations for many years. Usually an area or problem is tentatively selected; the procedures are tried out on a small group of children; schedules, ratings, observation blanks, design, etc., are revised; another try-out is made; and so on. Finally the series of procedures and the experimental situation become established. In some instances, investigators begin by observing and recording all that children do in free or controlled situations. These protocols are studied and categories are organized as a basis for further observations. Another procedure involves preliminary experiments on small groups of children at a wide range of ages. For example, an experimenter might work with three 2-year-olds, three 5-year-olds, and three 8-year-olds, in order to discover whether his procedures, instructions, and methods were appropriate at these age levels, and revise in accordance with his experience. Then later the revised procedures would be applied to a large sample of children at each age from 2 to 8 years. Other sampling devices may serve in pilot studies. For example, a few bright, average, and dull children may be selected for the preliminary test of a technique. Another type of exploratory research is commonly used in the design of tests or measuring devices. A very large number of items from different sources are collected, tried on a group of subjects, and then sorted over by a technique of item analysis in terms of either an internal or an external criterion or both in order to eliminate inappropriate or ineffective items before the final measuring instrument is applied to the subjects in the primary investigation.

In World War II the Army Air Force developed a method of critical requirements or incidents for exploratory research (Flanagan, 1950). In some respects this is an advance over the protocols used on children for many years in that much recurring routine behavior is neglected and emphasis goes to what is significant in the particular situation. For the incidents themselves, however, recording is very complete. Once behavior in a large number of incidents has been described, the protocols are analyzed and dimensions and continua of behavior are worked out on the basis of which various categories, schedules, and techniques of observation or experiments can be developed for a more precise study of the major problems. One particular point was emphasized by Flanagan at a symposium at the 1950 meeting of the American Psychological Association. When reports on critical incidents were collected from highly trained workers and checked against actually recorded incidents, such reports based on recall were found to be reasonably accurate up to about 2 weeks after the incident occurred, but thereafter became progressively less accurate, until at the end of a month they were of very little value. This result emphasizes the overwhelming value of good observation and recording at the time behavior occurs, and shows how, even in well-qualified and conscientious observers, a lapse of time produces retrospective falsification. Pyles, Stolz, and Macfarlane (1935) have shown how falsification occurs in mothers' reports.

Exploratory research has many values: (1) it moves a study quickly from the armchair into the world of children; (2) it often reveals frequent or major aspects of behavior that have been overlooked; (3) by making the refinement of instructions and procedures possible in advance, it avoids the error of changing an experiment while it is in process; and (4) by bringing the ideas of the experimenter and of others to the study at different times and under different conditions, it facilitates thinking and thus improves the design of the project.

From exploratory research, which covers many types of descriptive and ecological studies, investigators move on to studies in which a specific question or problem is stated as a hypothesis which can be verified or disproved. In hypothesis research, emphasis goes to preliminary formulation of all the details of the project, including sampling, measuring instruments, procedures, etc., in precise terms.

In the psychological and social sciences many investigations deal with isolated single problems. So much is this true that scientists are bewildered at the task of integrating this mass of facts into a set of related principles. The traditional approach to this problem was to urge all scientific workers to present their material in such a way, by giving precise descriptions of sampling, experimental design, procedures, and results, that other workers could integrate the results and generalizations with their own studies. But attempts at integration are not too successful because of discrepancies in sampling and procedure. Even when attempts are made to replicate earlier studies, serious difficulty is encountered because of the inadequacies in the descriptions of procedures and techniques.

Modern discussions of the integration of scientific material stress the value of considering integration in the planning and design of the study. Many think of experiments as simple determinations of a single relation. Actually, however, in both laboratory and science as a whole, particular studies are only episodes in a long trend. Although the classic work of Ebbinghaus consists of many single experiments on memory in which, one after another, various factors are controlled, i.e., length of list, time interval, etc., his results when considered in sequence make an orderly whole.

Modern contributions to the problem of integration are many and depend in the main upon mathematical, logical, and statistical concepts. Fisher (1937) raises the question of so designing experiments that for a given expenditure of time and energy they will yield maximum returns and, at the same time, systematically, through the design itself, explore all the essential relations. Design in this sense is not a determination of the relation between one variable and another but an analysis of an entire manifold.

Hull and his students (1940), working with memory, concerned themselves with the logical derivatives and implications of the postulates growing out of our present information, and then laid out a whole system of experiments to explore the entire web of relations by crucial experiments to test and verify particular generalizations. This process checks, eliminates, modifies, or enlarges postulates and principles as work goes forward and substitutes an entire system of explanation for the isolated experiment. Although Hull's work has not been directly concerned with child psychology, the forward-looking student of method should be familiar with his approach.

Lewin (1936), who was concerned with theory and methodology in child psychology, worked out a system which, in the formal sense, is not so complete as that of Hull. Nevertheless, it represents a major attempt to put meaning into an entire area.

Both he and his students performed many of the experiments that follow from the basic postulates of the system.

Scientists are now moving from project design to what is coming to be called program design (Marquis, 1948), i.e., planning research in advance for an entire area or region of knowledge. Program design involves a series of hypotheses which are interrelated and interdependent, on the basis of which single projects or experiments can be designed. During World War II, in connection with many military projects, program design was developed in high degree. The procedure usually begins with a careful search and summarization of the relevant scientific literature, followed often by some exploratory research. Then, both through individual effort and group discussion, a series of major postulates and their corollaries are developed. Out of these a series of experiments emerges. As the particular experiments are completed, portions of the underlying conceptual framework are modified and new experiments designed. Systematic planning is substituted for casual and incidental approaches to problems. Elegance and completeness of design are set up as ideals.

But a word of caution is necessary. It has long been recognized that, of two explanations which are equally adequate in explaining behavior, the simpler is to be preferred. This principle, known as the law of parsimony, can be extended from single experiments to a general principle of economy for explanatory systems. If science is a mental shorthand which seeks to minimize mental effort, it follows that any ideal construct is to be accepted or rejected on the basis of the degree to which it facilitates the comprehension of a class of phenomena. Hence, the construct to be accepted as science is the one which has a smaller number of degrees of freedom than the phenomena which the reduction is expected to subsume (Thurstone, 1935). If two constructs are equivalent, that with the fewer degrees of freedom is preferred. Thus, we come to a principle of economy of explanation which is far too often neglected in some of the complex and fanciful explanations given for the behavior of children and of adults as well.

Sources of Material for Child Study

As the child moves through his course of development, he not only affects other persons but also leaves behind him products and records which are more or less complete. His behavior in various situations may be recorded, and tests and measurements may be made from time to time. All these constitute sources of material for the student of child behavior. Following is a list of sources:

1. *The present behavior of the child, both verbal and nonverbal.* This includes the observations, measurements, and records of behavior obtained in test or experimental situations designed to elicit responses for specific research purposes. The free responses of the child to stylized materials or in the unstructured situations of the projective techniques are also included. Direct observations of behavior in play and social situations increase in value for scientific purposes with systematic and planned recording.

The process of recording behavior is facilitated by many modern devices, such as the motion picture with and without sound and the various methods of sound recording by disk, wire, and tape. These devices have been so perfected that it is now possible to get permanent records of almost any kind of behavior. Although some difficulty is encountered with the voices of young children because of their low intensity, microphones can be installed in inconspicuous places and rooms redesigned to insure good records. The problem of analyzing and symbolizing the masses of material obtained by audio-visual recording presents some difficulties. Problems of

interpretation also arise, since what appears overtly may not always indicate what is happening within the person, as shown by a number of the older studies of galvanic response in children.

2. *Products of the child left behind as permanent records.* Such permanent products as drawings, letters written by the child, compositions, and constructions often yield significant data. The value of such products increases as accessory information is available, such as the dates or ages at which the products were made and the conditions which occasioned them.

3. *Records on file in home, school, governmental agencies, health departments, social agencies, etc.* Included are all types of records which are preserved by a variety of agencies dealing with children, such as birth certificates and health records. Of particular value are school records, especially the more recent cumulative records that include much relevant data. Often investigators can save themselves much effort and secure better sampling data, as well as important accessory information, by checking with the schools in the areas in which their studies are undertaken.

4. *Introspections of the child.* Modern investigators pay relatively little attention to this source. They prefer to look upon verbal output as behavior, as in the studies of children's thought processes as revealed in their language (Piaget, 1923). However, modern research has developed many clever indirect devices for getting at the attitudes, tensions, and goals of children which obviate the necessity for introspection.

5. *Memories of the child, or of the adult, of his own earlier life.* Once almost the only source of information on child life, these are now of rather minor importance. They vary both in completeness and accuracy. When checked against records of actual events they are found to be subject to many errors. These errors increase with the passage of time and raise serious question as to the reliance to be placed upon such memories. A central problem is whether such memories reflect the present state of the person or repre-

sent an earlier and real event. Many of the data in psychonanalysis are based upon the childhood memories of neurotic adults. Are these true events or projections of adult difficulties? Modern literature distinguishes two techniques for tapping such measures: (a) recording conscious memories, and (b) locating more deeply buried memories by free-association processes or projective methods.

6. *Memories of the child's life retained by those who have been associated with him.* Here are included the many effects left behind by the child in his relations with others and more or less adequately retained by them. These have little scientific value because they are likely to be very incomplete, haphazard, and biased. Sometimes, however, they are used. As the distance in time between contact with the child and reproduction increases, the data become less and less valuable.

7. *Measures of the parents, siblings, and other relatives of the child or of the environment, culture, or background in which he develops.* Strictly speaking, these sources do not furnish direct information. But they do make possible the analysis of the observations or measurements of the child's behavior. Not only are they clearly necessary for sampling, but they also make possible the determination of many significant relations. Examples of the use of such accessory data are found in the studies of heredity and environment, of which the Freeman *et al.* (1928), Burks (1928), and Leahy (1935) investigations are good examples; the various community studies, in which such matters as the relation of delinquency to city area (Shaw, 1931), or intelligence to rural or urban residence (Baldwin *et al.*, 1930), are analyzed; or the many studies of socio-economic or cultural status.

It has become possible to secure observations or measures on children at the identical ages at which similar observations were secured on their parents many years ago. There is some evidence that resemblance coefficients in the existing literature are underestimations because comparisons were made between persons who were tested at very different developmental levels; for example, scores on intelligence tests on mothers or fathers who are 30 years old are correlated with scores obtained on their children who are 7 or 8 years old. Because of the difficulty of securing data on children and their parents at identical age levels, organizations that have kept records that go back 20 or 30 years could well explore the possibilities of such research.

Techniques for Securing Data

Many persons make incidental or casual observations of behavior without control of conditions. The results stated either in the form of principles or of anecdotes are of little scientific value, whether made by a scientifically trained person or not, since no one knows how precise the observations were, what kind of a sample was observed, or what factors in the situation set off behavior. This does not mean that the observations were not accurate, but rather that they are of little value for scientific generalization.

Two characteristics of the scientific method are the *careful observation of phenomena as they occur* and the *accurate recording of these observations* in order that they may be tabulated and analyzed. A scientist does not depend upon his memory, but records events as they occur in order to eliminate bias and retrospective falsification. Whenever possible he makes permanent records, as when he writes down a reaction time, fills out a test blank, uses a polygraph, or makes a motion picture or sound recording. When he cannot observe directly, he uses indirect methods, such as reports, interviews, questionnaires, and inventories; these he checks with unusual care. Good scientific work involves not only skill in observation and recording, but also insight into what it is important to observe and record.

Classifying the ways of securing data presents difficulty because methods overlap and a variety of methods are used to achieve similar purposes. Following is a classification based upon the manner in which data are obtained.

Systematic Observation without Control of Stimulation. First come the methods in which observation is systematic but stimulation is not controlled. The research worker uses "natural" [1] situations or situations as they occur in the ordinary life of the child as a basis for his research. Barker and Wright (1949, 1951) call these methods "ecological" research or "habitat" research. But the methods involved have been in use for a very long time.

1. *Narrative records and habitat studies.* The earliest use of narrative records came in the baby biographies, in which attempt was made to describe all behavior from day to day. Later, children's social behavior was observed on the playground or in free-play periods. Often elaborate check lists and codes were developed (Thomas *et al.*, 1929) to analyze the narrative accounts.

Barker and Wright (1949, 1951) have given this method new emphasis by using teams of trained observers, each of whom observes a child for a half hour. Children are followed from early morning until late at night through all their activities. Observers are trained in advance, and some time is allowed to permit children to become habituated to the presence of the observer. After a short period the children go about their business as though no observers were present. Despite the training of the observers, it is necessary, in order to secure a complete account, for an inter-

viewer to question the observer in order to bring out details which were not in the records taken on the spot. From the records and the interview the episodes of the half hour are documented and arranged in a time sequence to become the basic record. An episode closes with a new stimulation, as for example the entrance of a new person, or when substantial movement of the child to another location occurs. Episodes are coded and classified to form the basic data for analysis. It is clear that the child is exposed to great quantities of stimulation and that even in a single day there are many learning situations. This leads to a volley or bombardment view of the determination of behavior, with much reiteration, reinforcement, and feed-back, rather than a conception in terms of relatively isolated single stimulus-response situations.

2. *Situational sampling.* Closely related to the narrative accounts are the techniques in which the observer selects recurring situations and systematically records the child's reactions to them. The situations selected may vary from the introduction of deliberately selected stimuli into the natural situation, as when an investigator makes two different types of toys available in a play period and records the number and length of times boys and girls play with each type, to recording the objects in the normal playroom which a child picks up with his left hand and with his right hand. Or the observer may adopt the museum technique developed by Marston (1925), in which exhibits are set up at stations, and the length of time, the number and type of exhibits stopped at, and the pathway of the children who enter are recorded. Or behavior at home may be compared with that at school, free-play periods with teacher-guided periods, social relations when one companion is present with those when three or four companions are present (Jersild and Meigs, 1939). In addition to obtaining

---

[1] The criticism so often made that "laboratory" situations are unnatural might equally well be made of all tests and measurements and even of play and projective techniques. Whether they appear "unnatural" to the child is an open question; certainly many children show high interest and motivation and take them in their stride as very normal events.

narrative accounts, Barker and Wright (1949, 1951) stationed observers in the corner drugstore to record all that went on during the day that involved children.

The value of situation sampling arises out of the fact that much behavior that can be produced under laboratory conditions only with difficulty occurs with some frequency in life. The technique is also used with adults in studies of reactions to museum exhibits, advertising on street cars, conversations on trains and at concerts, etc. In studies of the emotional and social behavior of young children *situation sampling* has been of great value. Data obtained from narrative accounts can also be broken up in terms of the recurring situations. Obviously data are obtained more readily when the situations selected occur frequently rather than rarely.

A modification of the situation sampling technique is found in the recording of critical incidents (Flanagan, 1950) mentioned earlier. It is but a step from using situations which occur naturally to deliberately setting up controlled situations which are uniformly presented to many children.

3. *Time sampling.* In order to permit quantification of observations, a closely related technique, known as *time sampling,* developed by Olson (1929, 1934), Goodenough (1928a), and Thomas *et al.* (1929), came into wide use. A summary of the results obtained by the method and a discussion of its implications are found in Arrington (1943). The technique introduces no control in the natural situation except recording the number of times a selected type of behavior occurs during a time interval which is held constant and systematically spaced. For example, on the first day the social behavior of child A is observed for 2 minutes, then that of child B, then that of child C, and so on. On the next day each child is observed for 2 minutes again, but the children are taken in a different order. By making a series of such observations at successive periods and summating the frequencies a total score can be secured for each child for all the periods in which he is observed. Such scores lend themselves readily to statistical treatment. Reliability can be determined by correlating scores for odd and even periods, and the number of observations necessary to secure stable results can be determined. The scores can also be correlated with other factors. Time sampling works well with behavior that occurs frequently. The length of the period of observations and the number of observations necessary to achieve stable results vary with the type of behavior studied.

4. *Play techniques.* Another variant of the observational method appears in the play techniques used by clinical workers for diagnosis and therapy with children having adjustment problems, which are now coming to be used for research purposes. Of the projective techniques (see p. 22), these are more like narrative studies or situation sampling than are the personality measures, such as the Rorschach or Thematic Apperception Test, in which the stimulation presented to the child is controlled. Since many children cannot or will not verbalize their conflicts, exposing them to play materials in a free and secure situation may lead to spontaneous expression of anxieties, conflicts, insecurities, and wishes. Many materials have been used: dolls, knives, drawing and painting (finger) materials, puppets, etc. (Fries, 1937; Frank, 1939; Despert, 1940; Axline, 1947; and Bell, 1948). Children have also been encouraged to engage in dramatic play. Sometimes the play itself, sometimes the stimulated conversation, is regarded as the significant outcome.

Concern here is not with the use of these methods for therapy but as sources of generalizations that give insight into the nature of children. Although studies of reliability and validity are still needed, play techniques have been used with some success as measurement devices in experiments in which contrasting groups are selected, e.g., the comparison of the aggressive behavior of children whose fathers had been away at war with that of children whose fathers had not (Bach, 1946).

Systematic Observation with Control of Stimulation. The characteristic of these techniques is that the research worker presents children with stimulation which is selected and controlled; i.e., the materials presented are laid out in advance, and the reactions of the children to the materials or stimulation are systematically recorded.

1. *Specific measurements.* This includes the many direct measures based on size, time, movement, work accomplished, amount of material retained, errors, etc., and the many indirect measures and tests of complex functions that have been developed over many years by research workers. Basically all record in some fashion a characteristic response pattern to controlled stimulation in quantities that can be manipulated statistically. Examples are measures of height, weight, speed of reaction to a signal, and recall of a series of memorized digits. Because of the wide variety of measurement devices, the specific limitations of each cannot be discussed here. General principles underlying their use are discussed in the next section (p. 33). Whipple (1924) and Greulich *et al.* (1938) present the procedures for many such measurements, and Shuttleworth's (1949a) *Graphic Atlas* contains many curves based on measurements. Much of the later portion of this book, covering particular topics, is devoted to their consideration.

2. *Psychometric tests.* Psychometric tests involve presenting children with series of items, problems, or questions laid out in advance, from which part or total scores

can be obtained that permit comparison of the child's performance with norms obtained on a standard group. The definition covers a very wide series of measuring devices for capacity, skill, achievement, and personality (Goodenough, 1949a, 1949b). The procedures for conducting the tests are rigorously defined in order to secure constancy of administration from examiner to examiner and from one time to another. Scoring is standardized and is made as independent of the particular examiner's judgment as possible. It is done by counting, by checking against keys, or by consulting a manual in which specific rules for scoring are laid down and illustrated by examples. The result obtained can be checked by other examiners. Hence, the ideal of psychometric techniques would be standardized, objectively scored, consistently administered, and uniformly interpreted measuring instruments which would give consistent results when repeated after a short period of time and which would be independent of place and of the personality of the individual examiner. The most notable example is the intelligence test.

3. *Experiment.* Even though the experiment is discussed in detail later, it should be mentioned here as a technique for securing data in which both the stimulation and the conditions under which it is presented are deliberately controlled in order to secure an answer to a specific question. An experiment is a step beyond psychometric testing in terms of the number and completeness of the controls applied and usually, also, in terms of the length of time over which measurement is made. Moreover, it may use a variety of measurements and systematic observations.

Personality Measures of the Projective Type. In the 1940's appeared within the psychological field a whole series of new techniques listed under the general heading of projective methods (Bell, 1948; Bender,

1952). These seek to assess the person's emotional or personality reactions as a basis for therapy or correction of personality inadequacies rather than his capacities or skills. Examples are found in the play techniques mentioned earlier (p. 21), the Rorschach ink-blots, and the Thematic Apperception Test. With their value for therapy, we are not here concerned. But their use in the analysis and study of behavior development needs some consideration. As with other methods, projective techniques can be used successively to measure development or at any particular time to assess status. They may also be given before and after an introduced experimental condition in order to measure its effects. They may be standardized or not.

In essence, the child is presented with various neutral stylized or indefinite materials, upon which he can project his own feelings and attitudes and indicate by the character of his responses how he feels. Such materials as ink-blots or the pictures in the Thematic Apperception Test have a vague and indefinite outline and are not as precisely and specifically structured as most visual materials. Where more precise formed material is used, it is so stylized that it can be interpreted in many ways. For example, stylized dolls and equipment permit the child to project identifications and other characteristics upon them, and may even permit him to perceive them as if they possessed the projected characteristics. The better the test materials, the wider the range of interpretations that may be made of them.

The chief differences between psychometric and projective measures may be summarized as follows:

1. *Structuring.* Psychometric tests are highly structured both in the situations presented and in the responses permitted, whereas projective techniques theoretically are not. This distinction is, however, not a sharp one, because the situation in which projective methods are used must be laid out with some care. Further, although some discussions of projective techniques emphasize their freedom from the defects of the ordinary psychometric examination, both scoring and interpretation are dependent upon a trained examiner. In many instances, attempts are made to reach high degrees of constancy in scoring and interpretation by the use of frequency tables and directions.

2. *Subject's awareness of situation.* In projective techniques attempts are made to set up very natural situations, often by making the child feel that the examination's purpose is quite different from its real purpose. Ideally, the person examined does not know what is going on, and, in general, the more he lacks awareness, the more effective is the test. On the other hand, the psychometric test can hardly be disguised, except for young children for whom the skilled examiner creates interest in the test that is similar to that in play situations. However, in the psychometric test the situation is explicitly one of testing, whereas in the projective situation the testing aspect is kept incidental.

3. *Test results.* In psychometric tests, the answers to questions are either right or wrong. As a result the examiner has little to do with the outcome beyond making the subject secure, motivating him to his best efforts, and recording results. The directions for giving and scoring responses are so explicit that it is difficult for the examiner to project his own feelings into the interpretation. With projective techniques, however, there are no wrong or right answers. Hence the examiner may project his own feelings into the results and interpret them in the light of his own background. Not only do examiners often differ markedly in their interpretation of results, but also the training in projective techniques is divided among various schools and their disciples who sharply criticize one another and each of which feels that it has the only true technique. With psychometric techniques it is assumed that any person with

training can acquire the methods of administration and interpretation.

4. Relation to social pressure. Some hold that psychometric tests reflect culture, whereas projective techniques are independent of culture and social pressures. For example, an ink-blot can be interpreted by people of widely different cultures. But although many of the projective materials are largely independent of language symbols which vary with culture, it does not follow that nonlanguage materials are independent of cultural effects.

5. Validity and reliability. For psychometric techniques validity and reliability are measurable and known, and results can be treated statistically. High consistencies are obtained when studies are made on comparable populations. For many of the projective techniques the reliability and validity are not known. Moreover, many clinicians fail to realize that, when any technique is used for diagnosis, it enters the area of prediction and thus is to be evaluated by statistical processes. Attempts have even been made to use projective techniques for prediction in skill and capacity areas, for which they are not designed.

6. Best performance vs. typical performance. Goodenough (1949a, 1949b) has pointed out a fundamental difference between the psychometric and the projective methods. In a psychometric method, the best possible performance of the child is sought in order that his future performance may be predicted or his level of attainment measured. Conditions which favor maximum performance are desired. With projective methods, on the other hand, the experimenter is not interested in the limits of performance but in the typical or characteristic reactions of the child. He seeks information on how the child feels or how he reacts to circumstances, not information on what he can do when highly motivated.

Ratings. In the use of ratings it is assumed that behavior has already occurred and that an observer can order or classify such behavior on a continuum. At present many types of behavior cannot be measured directly. But such behavior can be described as better than this or poorer than that and thus be placed at a point on a scale which represents an estimate of the amount or quality of the particular characteristic possessed by the subject. Rating techniques fall into two main types: (1) a comparison of stimuli, situations, persons, or products by assigning each to a position or rank-order with reference to every other, as when children are ranked, *first, second, third,* etc.; or (2) an indication of position in comparison with others by marking the point, either graphically, numerically, or verbally, at which he or the behavior under consideration lies with reference to a designated characteristic, as when the child is rated on cooperativeness by indicating whether he is *often, usually, moderately, seldom,* or *never* cooperative. In ordinary speech many such comparisons are made, as when a 10-year-old speaks of his friend as a good catcher or as the best batter, or even when a person is referred to as pretty, or diligent, or lazy. In such statements the existence both of a scalable trait and of a group with which comparisons can be made is implied. Rating techniques, then, are systematizations and quantifications of procedures in common use.

Whether the rater ranks 10 children in order from the best to the least adjusted, or marks the child's adjustment as *excellent, good, average, poor,* or *very poor,* the essential process is the same. The variants in the type of categories, the form of scales, and the method of summating items into a single score are many. Ratings increase in value with the number of raters. Self-rating scales are also in use. The technique has also been applied to children's products, such as drawings and writing. Extensive discussions of the methodology of ratings are found in Symonds (1931), Weiss (1933), Thorndike (1949), etc. Ratings are also widely employed as criteria against which measuring devices, singly or in pooled form, can be validated.

Conrad (1933) found that the reliability of ratings of young children by nursery school teachers and the agreement between judges vary significantly with (a) the trait judged, (b) the child judged, (c) the estimated significance of the trait for the child in question, and (d) the confidence with which the judge rates the trait for the particular child. The fact that Conrad's results are somewhat higher than those usually published for older children suggests that some unreliability in ratings can be traced to unequal acquaintance and to contact under different circumstances of the raters with those rated. Ratings improve when equal amounts of observation under similar conditions are provided.

An underlying assumption in the use of ratings is that the trait rated is homogeneous and that the categories describing the steps fall into a linear continuum. For instance, children are frequently rated on "cooperation," "adjustment," "honesty," "perseverance," "sympathy," "self-reliance," etc. Are these traits entities, or are they manifolds made up of heterogeneous factors? Often ratings are greatly improved in the ease and accuracy with which rating is done, and in the reliability of the ratings obtained, by breaking up manifolds into parts. For example, it is better to rate adjustment and honesty separately than to combine them in one category. Whenever possible more objective and discriminating measures should be substituted for ratings.

Sociometric Techniques. By sociometric techniques (Moreno, 1934; Jennings, 1948; Proctor and Loomis, 1951; Clark and McGuire, 1952), we refer to methods of plotting the relations in a group of children. The data for plotting sociograms may be obtained in various ways, such as (a) direct observation of social relations, (b) asking

children to name their friends or to choose classmates with whom they should like to sit, or (c), in the "guess who" technique, asking them to choose children who fit a given category or description. If extreme categories only are used, remaining children can be assigned intermediate positions. In sociograms the interrelations between the members of a group are shown by connecting lines which run to and from small triangles and circles which indicate boys and girls respectively. By preliminary inspection, the children who are contacted most often or who are the most frequently mentioned are placed somewhere near the center as more lines come to and from them. Approaches toward or away from a particular child can be indicated by arrowheads of appropriate direction. Various relationships can be indicated by differentiated lines, such as solid, thin, dash, or dotted lines.

When a diagram is plotted for an entire group, a pictorial representation of all the interrelations results. Isolates are children with no lines connecting them with others. Stars are children from whom many lines radiate and toward whom many lines converge. A triangle consists of three children in such close relation to one another that they constitute a subgroup, as shown by many interconnecting lines. A line is a group of children in which relations are consistently in one direction. Subgroups of various size appear with many lines between the members and fewer lines going out to other children.

Another method of diagraming is that of Murphy (1937), who, using squares for boys and circles for girls, placed all the children in two columns arranged from the oldest at the top to the youngest at the bottom. The circle or the square that corresponded to a particular child was placed in the center between the two columns, and lines were drawn from the squares and circles in one column to show approaches made to the child and to the squares and circles in the other column to show approaches initiated by the child. Types of lines are varied with the different social techniques or activities, and direction arrowheads are used.

By plotting group structures, relations that are hard to grasp when presented verbally are presented pictorially. Sociograms are of practical value in working with children's groups as they clearly point out isolated and overlooked children who need attention. But there is some question about their contribution to science. Scores based on observations or ratings must be obtained before plotting, and they may be analyzed statistically, whether or not they are plotted. As scores they possess the advantages or disadvantages inherent in their particular character and are subject to the qualifications of other scores of the same type with respect to validity and reliability. Moreover, there is always some question about the generalizations that can be drawn, since they are relative to the particular group on which they are obtained. Despite this, sociograms, when used at various age or grade levels, have revealed interesting developmental trends and have confirmed results obtained by other methods of studying social behavior.

Reports and Questionnaires. In using reports, questionnaires, and inventories, it is assumed that the person answering is recording what he already knows or feels. The questions asked may vary from single questions to be answered *in extenso* to a highly structured list in which appropriate responses are merely checked or underlined. Items may cover what the person knows or what he thinks or feels about himself or others. He may be asked to rate himself or others or to compare his performance with that of others. The results, when obtained, may be pooled into subscores or total scores and used for the indirect measurement of personality or other general traits (Hubbard, 1942).

1. *Reports.* Reports include all types of factual statements that the respondent is in a position to know on the basis of observation, previous knowledge, available figures, test results, etc. Many items on a face sheet or the questions asked in the beginning of an interview fall in this classification. For scientific purposes it is necessary to know whether the respondent is in a position to know the facts and whether his reports are accurate. Most investigators cross-check or verify such reports.

2. *Questionnaires.* A series of questions arranged more or less systematically and grouped about a main topic is called a questionnaire. There are two types of questionnaires: (1) those which seek facts which are known to the person answering and (2) those which seek opinions about particular situations, modes of behavior, individual characteristics, matters of policy, training, etc.

Much of the distrust of the questionnaire arises because of confusion between matters of fact and matters of opinion. If a group of experts is asked to give an opinion as to the value of motion pictures for young children, their expression of opinion is of value only in so far as they are qualified to express an opinion. Neither individual nor summated group opinions are equivalent to scientific data based on observation, measurement, or experiment except that sometimes opinion is studied in and for itself. When a questionnaire deals with facts collected from those in a position to know, it may have much scientific value. For example, a questionnaire which enlists the cooperation of mothers in recording the sleep of their children would be of greater scientific value than a collection of their opinions about sleep. Sometimes questionnaires cause persons receiving them to make systematic observations or to analyze data already in their possession.

Questionnaires aim to secure from many persons observations or opinions which could not be obtained from a single individual. Their accuracy depends on the skill with which they are made out, i.e., the definiteness, specificity, and practicality of the questions, the capacity of the persons answering, the length of time that has elapsed since the occurrence of the events to be recorded, the sampling of persons to whom the blanks are sent, and, what is even more important, within that sampling, upon the characteristics of the sample of persons that reply. Questionnaires are subject to errors of memory, misunderstanding of terms, and mental sets imposed by the questions. In general, verification by other methods is necessary.

3. *Verbal personality and attitude inventories.* There are many questionnaires, check lists of behavior, and inventories covering such aspects of personality and conduct as adjustment, neurotic tendencies, introversion-extroversion, ascendance and submission, social attitudes, fairmindedness, and vocational interests. All have a common characteristic in that the person answers questions about his own attitudes, interests, etc. The inventory does not seek answers to individual items or questions in and for themselves, but is designed to derive a general measure from the answers to many items which can be used either for practical assessment of the individual or for the study of scientific problems. Some inventories can be administered to groups. Although some inventories are loosely called tests, they differ from tests in that there are no right or wrong answers to the items or questions. Irrespective of the correctness or falseness of the answer in terms of objective fact, the responses may be weighted in any direction because of a demonstrated correlation with the criterion for the function which is measured. Hence, predictive value depends upon symptomatic answers to individual items, upon the various patterns of answers, or upon quotients derived from answers or patterns. When subscores are developed the same answer to an item may be scored in one direction for one subscale and in a different direction for another. Items may be printed seriatim, as is the usual custom, or on individual cards, as in the Minnesota Multiphasic. Because most inventories depend on the ability to read and understand the items, their use is limited to children above 8 or 9 years. In some studies devices presented in verbal test form to older children have been read aloud to younger children.

4. *Pictorial questionnaire.* For younger children, and to some degree for older children, various types of questionnaires in which items are presented pictorially rather than verbally have been developed. Much skill has been shown in adapting a wide variety of test, inventory, and other items to pictorial form. A series of pictures in which various human relations are portrayed has been used, particularly in studies of race relations (Radke, 1949) and of social sensitivity (Gates, 1923; Murphy, 1937). Because the method can be used only when there are marked and visible differences between the persons portrayed, it has distinct limitations. Pictorial material is also the basis of the Rorschach method, about which a substantial literature (Hertz, 1942) is developing. This involves evaluation of the child's responses to ink-blots. The Thematic Apperception Test presents children with a series of pictures of somewhat indefinite outline or equivocal meaning and evaluates children's responses.

Interviews. The interview varies from a systematic entering of information obtained from the person interviewed upon a blank prepared in advance to a completely free situation in which conversation goes forward without any report.

1. *Structured interviews.* Structured interviews usually begin with a face sheet for recording essential sampling and evaluative data, such as name, address, telephone, age, education, occupation of father, and names of siblings. The remaining questions concern the particular area or problem in hand. The advantages of schedules prepared in advance and given systematically are many, especially since the data gathered by haphazard and unplanned interviews are difficult to use for scientific purposes. On a prepared blank the fact that the individual refused to answer, did not have the information, etc., can be checked and appropriate interpretations made in the analysis. But unless this is done, a refusal, a negative answer, or the failure of the interviewer to give the question cannot be distinguished. In interviewing for scientific purposes some record should be made for every question asked. Attention must also be paid to the form of the question and the order in which questions are given (Payne, 1951). An example of an extensive series of interviews laid out by a national committee and obtained from every area of the United States by a planned sampling procedure is found in the White House Conference reports (Anderson, 1936; Burgess, 1934). Research on public-opinion polls and interviews for guidance and for social work are turning the interview technique into a valuable scientific instrument.

2. *Unstructured interviews.* More recently the free or open-end interview has come into wide use, not so much for research as for counseling. But it has research possibilities. If a child is asked, "What is a good boy?" and encouraged to talk freely, a very comprehensive picture of home attitudes on discipline may be obtained. With modern methods of sound recording complete records can be made.

Various methods of evaluating or quantifying the material in such interviews to secure scores that picture the child's image or goals are available. The value of such procedures in exploratory research is obvious: frequently from recorded open-end interviews very good structured blanks for subsequent use can be made. The major difficulty with free interviews arises from the omissions which differ from case to case. Although what appears may be said to be symptomatic of underlying tensions, the free interview itself has a somewhat accidental character and differs widely from time to time and from interviewer to interviewer.

Products and Personal Documents. Either because of his own volition or as a result of his instruction, the child may leave behind various products such as pictures he has drawn, constructions he has made, or compositions or diaries he has written. Recorded conversations and interviews may also be considered products. Such products can be subjected to various types of analysis. If the age or the date at which they were produced is available significant age trends may appear. In the past the main analyses have been: (1) in the area of children's drawings, where developmental scales have been laid out and where drawings or paintings have been used to assess personality characteristics, and (2) in the area of autobiographies or diaries, which are often kept by adolescents and which when collected can be analyzed in various ways. The practice of keeping diaries is more common in Europe than in the United States. Controlled diaries (Anastasi, 1948) may also be kept in particular areas of behavior.

Adolescents and young adults have been asked to write their autobiographies, sometimes as class exercises, sometimes as a preliminary to an interview, sometimes in connection with therapy. These so-called personal documents can be subjected to various types of analysis. Taken at its face value, each such account is the story of a unique individual and, as such, has little or no general significance. But when a number of autobiographies are secured, all written under essentially the same conditions and for the same purposes, it becomes possible to analyze the content. Actually, however, the methods available are still in the early stages of development. A promising method developed by White (1947) and by Dollard and Mowrer (1947) is to go through an autobiography and mark all words or phrases that indicate definite attitudes or responses toward persons, objects, ideas, etc. For example, every phrase that lauds the mother and every one that deprecates her might be marked; similarly every phrase indicating frustration and every phrase indicating aggression might be marked. Since sentences frequently involve clauses which express several relations, the smaller units such as phrases are preferred. While a simple count of the total number of expressions of a particular type is of some value, indices, such as the ratio of the phrases expressing security to those expressing insecurity, or the pleasant expressions over the unpleasant expressions (Anderson, 1952), can be developed and studied. Thus, a series of quantitative measures is secured for which intercorrelations and reliability coefficients can be obtained. Certain difficulties arise, however. Some write short superficial autobiographies concerned with events, not feelings. If a person writes freely and without pressure and describes his reactions rather than objective events, good results are obtained. This happens, particularly, when the autobiography is obtained as part of a counseling or guidance procedure in which the person actively seeks help on his problems.

Similar analyses can be made of a variety of other documents obtained from or about individuals, such as recorded conversations, recorded interviews, case histories, letters, or any exchange in which basic attitudes and feelings appear (Horst, 1941; Allport, 1942). To secure an adequate measure in terms of either an absolute count or the ratio between two counts, the particular phenomenon considered must occur in the recorded material with sufficient frequency to make analysis possible and the figures on which they are based reliable.

Individual Case Study. An individual case study can be used as a source of data for making generalizations. As such, it is to be considered in the light of the *scientific* information it yields. Much material in psychoanalysis and some in the clinical, abnormal, and delinquent fields consists of studies of individual children. Usually a summary of observations and interpretations is presented. The value of the concept of the lawfulness of the individual's own history and the practical value of earlier data in predicting later outcomes for the particular individual is not to be confused with using a single case as a basis for generalization to wide populations. In the former case prediction is justifiable; in the latter the representativeness of the case must be demonstrated, which is literally an almost impossible task. McNemar (1940) says, p. 362, "Surely psychologists have learned that very little light is thrown on, say, delinquent behavior by a minute clinical study of one case, yet we are expected by some to believe that the mysteries of human personality will somewhere be unraveled by an intensive study of just one case."

As an example of the widely varying interpretations that may be given by competent persons to a single case, consult Elkin's 1947 paper. He presented a detailed life history of a delinquent boy to 78 specialists from various fields and found very little consensus in judgments and interpretations.

Under some conditions, however, individual case studies can yield significant scientific information. An example is found in the Neilon (1948) study, which matched personality sketches written for children of 18 months by one examiner with those written for the same children at 18 years by another examiner. The problem Neilon faced of determining the degree to which the matching is above chance is one common to many types of psychological investigations where descriptions, protocols, diagnoses, case histories, ratings, scores, etc., are to be matched. The psychological and mathematical principles involved are discussed in a number of papers: Zubin (1933), Chapman (1935, 1936), Vernon (1936), and Levene (1949).

Several types of individual case studies are found in the literature.

1. *Case history.* A case history is a collection of facts about a child referred to an agency for one reason or another. It includes material from official records, his own story, the accounts of relatives, teachers, and others, and the results of any examinations or interviews. Although such histories are of practical value for guidance, their scientific value is limited by the fact that the data collected are gathered after the referral. What is in a file often depends upon the interests of the case worker rather than upon a systematic attempt at complete coverage.

2. *Cumulative record.* In modern practice some agencies keep cumulative records in which measurements and observations are recorded at various times as the child develops. This is superior to the case history, both because of its greater completeness and because it avoids the errors of interpretation arising when working backward from an end result. With the wide extension of the testing movement, the im-

proved cumulative records kept in school systems, and the cumulative folders which various social agencies maintain, many more data collected in advance of the event that brings the child to the attention of the agency become available. In time, with more complete records and successive observations of the same children, a wealth of research material will be available that will make possible the solution of many problems previously impossible of attack. Because of the long life span of the human being and his slow progress in a short period of time, the need for the preservation of data in order to make follow-up studies is great. The Baller (1936) and Glueck and Glueck (1934) studies are examples. It should be noted, however, that the follow-up should be very complete; otherwise, incorrect conclusions may be drawn because the cases easily found are more likely to be those with which success has been achieved.

3. *Clinical studies.* Clinical studies refer to the descriptions of pathological or abnormal cases which abound in the older medical literature. They usually consist of notes on the progress of the particular abnormality and are often supplemented by objective data.

4. *Personality studies of unusual children in the literature.* Often there come to attention children who are unusual in terms of capacity or extraordinary experience. Sometimes descriptive studies can be undertaken at the moment and ongoing developmental records obtained. Examples are found in Woolley's (1925, 1926) studies.

5. *Psychoanalytic personality studies.* A psychoanalyst after establishing rapport with his subject attempts to tap underlying memories and secure information regarding the origin of complexes and conflicts, etc. Through this process he seeks to re-educate the patient in order that the patient may achieve a balance or integration of his in-

stinctual drives and the demands the world makes upon him. The analyst's primary purpose is therapeutic. But he obtains many data on the early experiences of his patients, on which sweeping generalizations and systems of explanation of behavior are erected. Most of the theoretical and so-called observational material in the psychoanalytic literature relating to children is based upon neurotic adults' descriptions of their childhood experiences, which are obviously subject to retrospective falsification and confabulation (Wallen, 1942). Whether such accounts correspond to real experiences in their lives as children is open to question (Anderson, 1948). Most of the experimental checks made with normal populations of children on the generalizations made about child life by psychoanalysts have given negative results (Sears, 1942; Ellis, 1950). Note clearly that this criticism is not concerned with the generalizations about neurotic adults but with those about child life which are not based on actual observations of the patients as children but upon the memories which the patients who are a peculiar sample of adults retain of their own life as children.

There are books on child analysis, by Anna Freud (1925) and Klein (1932), which present some cases in great detail and others briefly. As one who knows normal young children reads, it becomes clear that the child is approached from a particular theoretical point of view and that the responses are fitted to that point of view. Little attempt is made to evaluate, no statistical or quantitative material is presented, and no complete statements or records of the analyst's speech and actions or of the child's responses are given. Some of the content seems to be directly or indirectly suggested to the child. Younger children are very markedly suggestible. No attempt is made to control the sampling of children subjected to analysis, nor are pre-

cise data over a span of years made available as to the success or failure of the therapeutic treatment. It should be noted that for various types of therapeutic procedures, a control can be obtained by comparing the recovery rate under therapy with the spontaneous recovery rate (Eysenck, 1952). The great difficulty with psychoanalysis as a scientific method lies not so much in its particular theories of behavior as in its acceptance of intuition as a valid method of securing basic data (Ellis, 1950).

One outcome of the psychoanalytic approach is the development of a very complex terminology which is substituted for older and simpler concepts. Although substituting a new term for an older one may give precision to the meaning to be conveyed, the new term in time acquires many connotations and loses its original precise significance. Translating from one set of terms to another disturbs the student. If he will take the trouble to go back to the facts and place the explanations of them in parallel columns, differences in explanation will turn out to be semantic or verbal rather than real. Such a comparison, particularly if age is a factor, may show that some generalizations are impossible. One can contrast the descriptions of the awareness of sex in young children as presented in a number of psychoanalytic studies with the actual findings by Conn and Kanner (1947), who in a direct study of children found that children's concepts of sex develop slowly over many years and follow much the same pattern as other concepts.

Behavior Surveys. A behavior survey seeks to record as much and as wide a range of behavior as can be recorded within the limitations of time and space available. In some of the infant behavior surveys many specific and well-controlled techniques, involving measurements, ratings, systematic observations, interviews and reports, measures of home background, etc., are utilized. Behavior surveys may be either cross-sectional or longitudinal. An early example is found in the Blanton (1917) study of infants, with its rather informal descriptions of behavior in many infants. If compared with the earlier Gesell (1928) surveys, which led to the normative schedules, then with the Shirley (1931, 1933a, 1933b) studies, and the more recent studies of Bayley (1933) and Gesell and Thompson (1934, 1938), the improvement in the descriptions of the procedures and tests, in the use of standard statistical procedures for analyzing the data, and in describing the sampling will be clear. Behavior surveys supplement and are themselves supplemented by the intensive studies of more limited area of behavior. They also often function as exploratory studies which become the basis of designed studies.

Combinations. Actually, in the conduct of any particular investigation, except those which involve very limited segments of behavior, a combination of many techniques for securing data is ordinarily used. From the face sheet describing the child studied, which is a report or questionnaire, through the specific observations used in the study, to the ratings which are often employed as criteria, many combinations are possible. Even the projective techniques, which at first glance seemed not to be usable, have been adapted to experimental projects.

Variations of Techniques with Age

Because of the great changes that take place with growth and development, the techniques for scientific study vary from age to age. Outstanding nodal points are birth which puts the infant into the outside world and makes him available for observation, the appearance of speech which enables the child to report directly on his experiences, and the developing of reading and writing skills which make possible many new and economical varieties of measurement. There follows a summary of the main techniques available by age levels.

Prenatal Behavior. Knowledge of prenatal behavior comes mainly from experimental and laboratory studies of animal fetuses, together with limited experiments and more extensive observations on premature human infants. The difficulties in research are tremendous, and the methods in use constitute almost a science in themselves.

Infants. With infants, experiments, direct measurements, and observations constitute the chief source of material. Because infants' responses are relatively fluid and unstructured, and because the infant lacks language, study in many areas, notably the sensory and perceptual one, is difficult. Numerous ingenious techniques have been developed, such as one-way vision screens, cinema recording, the Gesell observation dome, and the stabilimeter, which is a device for recording the movements of the infant in response to stimulation. A disproportionate number of studies are made on neonates because of their availability in maternity hospitals in large numbers. More than with older children there is a tendency to ignore sampling and take whatever children are available for study. Particular care must be taken to secure complete records, because of the tendency of observers to select only what meets their purpose. For instance, in earlier studies of reflexes, it was assumed that a specific movement in a particular segment would appear in response to stimulation such as stroking the sole of the foot lightly. But later observers who recorded all the responses to such stimulation found much variation and activity in other segments (Jensen, 1932). Most psychologists take some pains to avoid crude anthropomorphic interpretations. But another type of projection, is equally dangerous, namely, the unconscious assumption that the highly organized and precise patterns characteristic of older children and adults are to be found in infants and very young children. Some of them will be found, but they will be imbedded in a much larger response pattern. Hence, for scientific purposes, especial care must be taken to give complete descriptions of the behavior manifold.

Preschool Children. With preschool children methods involving direct observation and experiments occupy a prominent place. Because of the child's limited language responses and his inability to read and write, many tests and measurements available for older children cannot be used. Moreover, there is some difficulty in securing cooperation and motivation. Many persons who have worked with older children and adults expect quick answers and prompt responses from small children. But Goodenough (1935) found that reaction times are slower and much more variable and had much difficulty in getting young children to respond to a simple signal. Because of the lack of structuring, it is difficult to instruct the child in such a way that his responses will be limited to the matter in hand. Hence, many ingenious methods involving setting the stage or situation and then observing "natural" behavior have been developed. These are best illustrated in the studies on social behavior, in which children have been observed in free-play periods, in experimentally modified social settings, etc.

Older Children and Adolescents. With older children and adolescents every type of direct and indirect measurement, observation, and recording can be used. To some degree, paper and pencil tests, inventories, and check lists supplant direct observation. The older child or the adolescent knows how to read and write, and is more easily motivated, more docile, and better acquainted with test or experimental

situations. But he is also more self-conscious and may be very clever at concealing his thoughts and feelings from the observer. Hartshorne and May (1928) developed ingenious methods of offering possibilities of deceptive and honest behavior within a pencil and paper test framework. In recent years methods of observation in "natural" or controlled situations have spread from the preschool field to the older child and offer an antidote to the somewhat excessive concern with pencil and paper tests. In the Lippitt (1940) studies of social atmospheres an excellent example of the use of one-way vision screens and careful recording of direct observations of the group structure and of individual behavior within that structure is found. The sociometric technique of Moreno (1934) and Jennings (1948), which is a combination of interviews, statements of choice, of playmates, dramatic play situations, observations in groups, etc., permits the diagraming of the interrelations and a study of group structures among individuals at all age levels. Since 1940 there has also been much use of the projective techniques.

The Development of Measuring Instruments and the Determination of Their Precision

In the first approach to psychological problems, measures with an obvious and direct relation to the phenomena studied were used. For example, speed of reaction was measured in units of time; memory by the amount retained; learning by reaction time or errors, and the height and weight of children in inches or pounds. These are simple as well as direct measures.

Later "indirect" measures appeared. Because the child as a functional unit cannot be separated into discrete parts, as can a chemical compound or a physical structure, indirect measures become necessary in order to break up various phases of functioning into manipulable units for analysis and prediction. The classical instance is found in Binet's measurement of intelligence. By the use of multiple criteria—increase with chronological age, teachers' ratings, academic grades, and life success—leverage was obtained that separated out a commonality among tests which superficially bear little resemblance to one another. Intelligence does not correlate perfectly with any one of these criteria, but because the tests are positively correlated with each of them, that is, test scores increase with chronological age, ratings of brightness, school grades, and life adjustment, it can be assumed that, when they are combined into a single instrument, a factor common to all but not identical with any of these criteria will be measured. In measuring this common factor, the contribution of the components increases if their intercorrelations are lower than their correlations with the criteria, since this means commonality of measurement in terms of the criteria without identity or great overlapping in the components. If different criteria are used, a different commonality may appear. Indirect measurement then begins with a series of assumptions, which may be explicit and clearly recognized but often are implicit and not recognized, and ends with an instrument which gains its meaning from those assumptions, however it may be labeled. Failure to recognize this fundamental point causes much confusion and no end of argument and controversy.

The purpose for which the measure is employed often determines whether measurement is direct or indirect. For example, the weight of the child may be used directly to measure weight or indirectly as an index of nutrition or health. Although psychologists are sometimes criticized for using indirect measures, in actual practice tracers, indicators, or indirect measures are com-

mon to many sciences. In each instance the relation between the indicator and that which it indicates must be determined. Height is obviously measured by distance on a scale of inches or centimeters, and reaction time in units of time—in fact, for many direct measures the very terms used to designate them describe what is measured. Often direct measures are combined into a team for indirect measurement. For example, an arithmetic test given to measure a child's knowledge of what he was taught the preceding week is direct measurement. But he may be given a standardized achievement test in arithmetic not so much to measure what he knows of what has just been taught as to determine his level of functioning in arithmetic. This is on the borderline between direct and indirect measurement. The questions are indicators or samples of his general level of knowledge. That this kind of test is independent of the particular questions asked is shown by the fact that two alternative forms of a test made up of different items will yield similar scores. Or the arithmetic test may also be a part of an intelligence test battery, as in Army Alpha. Here concern is neither with particular knowledge recently acquired nor with achievement in arithmetic, but with problem solving in arithmetic as an indicator of intellectual level, a still more generalized function.

The details of the measuring devices, both direct and indirect, for the many problems and areas in child psychology cannot concern us here. Their number is legion. However, two interrelated fundamental problems arise in all measurement; one is the problem of *validity,* or the extent to which the device measures what it purports to measure; and the other is *reliability,* or the extent to which consistent results are obtained in successive use of the measuring device.

Validity and the External Criterion. With indirect measures the problem of validity, i.e., the relation between the indicator or tracer and the process of which it is an indicator, becomes of central importance (Guilford, 1946; Stuit, 1947; Anastasi, 1950; Gulliksen, 1950a, 1950b). Ordinarily validity is regarded as the relation between the scores on the measuring device and the scores obtained for some "outside" criterion, or criteria which clearly measure what is purported to be measured. The best criteria are some measures of actual performance over a substantial period of time; the indicator or tests seek to predict this performance from a smaller sample of behavior obtained in a short time. Thus an indirect measure is not identical with a criterion but makes possible its prediction. For instance, if we wished to predict children's ability in drawing, we might collect their drawings for many months in order to get a firm distinction between the poor, the average, and the good drawings by studying all of them. Once the ability of the children in drawing was determined from the many drawings over a period of time, we could then correlate any test of the children with these results, and, if a high positive relation resulted, we might proceed to use the test for predicting drawing without going through the months of observation. In other words, an indirect measure is used because it is more economical than direct measures. If we were to measure intelligence directly in children, hundreds of acts in hundreds of situations would have to be described. For this long process the shorter process of a validated test is substituted. Since a measure is no better than the criteria on which it is based, much time, effort, and money are spent in getting good criteria. To get better tests, measures, and inventories, we need better criteria; in fact, the securing of good criteria is the most important single problem in measurement—

the one upon which all else depends. Once good criteria are available, a whole array of statistical and other techniques are available for refinement and improvement.

A measuring instrument may have as many validities as the criteria with which it is correlated; it may be more valid for predicting some criteria and less valid for predicting others. It may also have a variety of subscores which are used for different purposes and to predict different criteria. Coombs (1948a) showed theoretically how a test can be made to yield six meaningful scores or indices, and he later (1948b) provided a rationale for the estimation of these scores.

A measuring instrument may be validated in a variety of ways. Sometimes the entire distribution of the criteria is used, sometimes extreme or contrasting groups who are widely separated in terms of the criteria, and sometimes even an already developed measuring instrument of known value. For instance, some group intelligence tests have been validated by correlation with Stanford-Binet individual examinations.

In the actual construction of a measuring device each individual item, part, or section of the device is correlated with the criteria, and those items, parts, or sections that show substantial correlations are retained and those that do not are discarded. However, in carrying through this process of item analysis some attention must be given to the intercorrelations of items, parts, or sections with each other, as items that correlate well with the criteria but poorly with each other are better than those that correlate well with the criteria and with each other.

Criterion of Internal Consistency. In developing indirect measures a procedure sometimes referred to as an internal criterion is often added. It is assumed that a total score based on many types of items or subtests measures more of whatever common function is being measured than does any individual item or part. Hence, by a technique of item analysis which involves correlating each item or part with total score, those items or parts that show little correlation with the total can be eliminated and those that show substantial correlation retained (Gulliksen, 1950b; Lindquist, 1950; Davis, 1952). This reduces the length of the instrument to an effective minimum and results in a purer measure of whatever it is that is measured. By factor analysis (Spearman, 1927; Kelley, 1928; Thurstone, 1935, 1947; Guilford, 1936; Thomson, 1939), a similar function can be performed; i.e., it can be determined which test components carry particular loadings and which should be eliminated, purified, or added to in order to increase the effectiveness of the measures of the commonality in question.

Scaling and Standardization. Once a measuring device can be developed and its validity determined, and after it has been purified by means of the criterion of internal consistency, it is modern practice to give the instrument to a new group of individuals to determine the relations between the refined instrument and the criteria. This is often called cross validation. Since such relations obtained on the original data would be spuriously high, the principle that the data from the group used for item selection or validation are not to be used for final validation or standardization is generally accepted. In standardization the instrument is often scaled by giving it to groups of children at various age or grade or other levels which have been sampled from the population in accordance with definite principles and which are large enough to secure stable means and dispersions. With direct measures, the units of measurement are usually definite; the child of 8, on the average, reacts in so many thousandths of a second,

is so many inches tall, and remembers so many words after a lapse of time; the child of 9 makes a larger (or smaller) score. Hence, scaling is comparatively simple. For indirect measures the problem of combining measures often based on different units arises.

In age scaling the mean performances of children at various age levels are determined and used as norms. Reference can be made to the normative group through percentiles or standard scores for the group as a whole or any part of it. A method that comes from the Air Force and which may have wide application in studies of children involves the conversion of scores into stanines, which constitute a 9-point scale with the middle interval or stanine 5 from -0.25 to $+0.25\sigma$ and other stanines at 0.5σ above and below, respectively. Stanines offer a ready method of interpreting results and can be used in combination with age norms to indicate the relative position of the child by three digits as 12–9, to show that the child's score lies in the ninth stanine for 12-year-olds.

Sometimes established cutting points, above or below which the individual is classed as defective or normal, neurotic or adjusted, introverted or extraverted, etc., are used. The classical distribution of intelligence quotients in terms of idiot, imbecile, moron, normal, etc., is an example. Often such cutting points are set by practical, social, or legal demands which make the division of the continuum into discrete classes necessary.

1. *Reliability.* The consistency with which a measuring instrument when used several times within a short space of time places those measured at the same level is known as its reliability. Because the child's height today is so little different from what it was yesterday, the same figures should be obtained today as yesterday in measuring it, unless an extraordinarily delicate

scale is available. When measures are repeated and correlated on the same children after a short interval, the size of the coefficients is said to express the reliability of the measure. The greater the consistency, the nearer the coefficients approach +1.00.

The three methods commonly used for determining the reliability of measures involve correlating (1) scores obtained on repetitions of the same measure; (2) scores on two similar but not identical forms of the measure; and (3) the score obtained by summing the responses on odd items with the score obtained by summing the responses on even items. The first method may be vitiated by a differential carry-over of practice effects; the second method corrects for this but necessitates two or more instruments demonstrated in advance to be equivalent; the third is much used, since no practice effects are involved and no second form is necessary. It is, however, an approximation. The determination of reliability is necessary for any measure used for the prediction of the performance of individuals.

The reliability of a scale and standardized measuring instrument can be readily determined. But many of the data available in child psychology are based not upon tests but upon observations resulting from schedules divided into defined categories. For these a reliability measure (perhaps not strictly comparable with that of tests but nevertheless of great value) is obtained by correlating the results of two observers, usually trained in advance, who record the behavior of the same children under the same conditions. When rating scales are employed, the correlation between independent raters or between successive ratings by the same rater after an interval of time can be used. Some investigators use the percentage of agreement between two raters or observers, or between two successive observations or ratings, as measures of reliability. Since no consistent procedures are followed in calculating these percentages, it is difficult to interpret them. More care should be taken to quantify such data in order to permit the use of established correlational procedures. In any event, the use of interperson reliability often produces significant modifications and improvement in observational techniques.

Where children's products, personal documents, or records in projective tests or situations are available, they can be rated or scored by two or more persons independently, each of whom is at the time of scoring ignorant of the others' scoring. This is now known as *blind analysis* and has been extended to diagnosis and classification as well. Here, too, correlation coefficients are to be preferred to the percentages of agreement so often calculated without reference to error formulae.

2. *Heterogeneity and homogeneity or range.* A serious problem arises in the interpretation of reliability, validity, and intercorrelation coefficients obtained on children. Since the size of a correlation coefficient is a function of the homogeneity or heterogeneity of the population on which it is calculated, and since almost every structure and process in children changes in some degree with chronological age, very high coefficients can be obtained by using a wide age range. Reliability coefficients calculated for a level covering a single year can be raised 20 or more points by calculating them for a 3-year age range. Hence, in determining validity and reliability, careful workers usually calculate the coefficients on a narrow age range, usually a single year, in order to eliminate the heterogeneity due to age. When reliability coefficients from different studies are to be compared, corrections for range should be made or comparisons avoided unless some account is taken of the range. Both readers of the

experimental literature and investigators should watch this problem with some care. √ Heterogeneity also affects the intercorrelations of separate measures. Intercorrelations for different motor performances over a range of 4 or 5 years, particularly at younger age levels, are exceptionally high and indicate the possibility of developing a scale for general motor skills. But, when calculated over a year range, the reliabilities are so low as to indicate that such a scale cannot be developed. Moreover, the reliability coefficients for motor items decrease rapidly with age, whereas those for intelligence items increase. Thus, the effect of age upon intercorrelations varies with the function studied.

3. *Contamination.* Another problem in determining the relations between any two or more variables, including both validity and reliability coefficients, arises out of the manner in which the relation may be contaminated by the presence of undetected and unmeasured factors. For instance, motivation may affect the performance of children. To the extent that children vary in their motivation, scores are modified in such a way that the interpretation of the relations or scores is affected (Rust, 1931). Usually the effect of a contaminating factor in a large sample is to reduce the correlations obtained and thus obscure the real relations. In some instances, however, it may produce a spurious relation, as when both variables are positively related to a contaminating factor. As the phenomenon of contamination has become recognized, there has been developed an actual statistical technique of deliberately utilizing contaminating factors in order to suppress certain relations and to make others stand out in tests with several different types of scores. The phenomenon of contamination leads to a consideration of the conditions under which relations can best be determined. This involves the reduction of variable er-

rors, whenever they occur, to a minimum as well as the elimination or control of constant errors. The size of a correlation coefficient is not always the result of the actual relation between the factors measured; it may also be affected by poor measuring devices with low validity and reliability and by masking or contaminating factors.

From the foregoing it is clear that the construction of a good measuring instrument is a technical job that requires much ingenuity and skill as well as an understanding of basic principles of measurement and of the appropriate statistical procedures. A good instrument opens up many areas of research that previously were inaccessible. It is unfortunate that so many haphazard, poorly standardized, inadequately evaluated, and inappropriately named devices are put forward. Nowhere is this more evident than in the fields of child psychology and educational measurement, where such a host of devices is available that an annual bibliography that fills a volume is necessary merely to catalog them (Buros, 1949). Excellent discussions of the principles, statistical procedures, and techniques for validating, scaling, standardizing, and determining the reliability of measuring instruments are found in a number of textbooks and an extensive literature of articles.

Sampling

Some of the inconsistencies and contradictions in published research grow out of variations in the selection of the cases studied. Whereas psychologists were formerly much concerned with the precision of measures, the years since 1930 have been marked by great interest in sampling problems. For scientific purposes the children studied in any investigation become the representatives of an *infinite* population, whereas in practical relations concern is with a *finite* population. A test of reading proficiency is given to a fifth grade. If the tester's interest is only in the performance of the children in that grade, the results obtained have no significance except that of helping the teacher with these particular children. But, if the test is given to establish norms or to compare one method of instruction with another, the children in this particular fifth grade have become the representatives of the children in fifth grades in our society, both at the moment and for some time to come. Hence, the question whether the children are a good sample of fifth graders becomes of paramount importance. It should be clear, however, that a sample representative of all fifth graders or of all 10-year-olds is not always needed. Sometimes the experimenter seeks a sample representative of a subpopulation which can be explicitly defined, e.g., fifth graders of high intelligence or of low intelligence. A study of instructional methods might give different results for these two subpopulations, which in a sense are "competing" groups. Nevertheless, each is representative in the sense that it has characteristics that can be defined and on the basis of which similar samples can be drawn from the population.

In drawing a sample, care must be taken to define the limiting terms with precision. For instance, to say that "problem children" are studied is virtually meaningless, since at least three definitions of such children are current: (*a*) children selected by teachers as difficult (Haggerty, 1925); (*b*) children referred to guidance clinics, courts, or institutions for delinquents (Ackerson, 1931); and (*c*) normal children passing through a particular phase, as in Olson's study of nervous habits (1929).

The necessity of asking the questions, "Of what population is this group a sample?" and "Is it a good sample?" is not always recognized. Some authors carefully and almost apologetically limit their conclusions to the particular sample studied. One may ask, then, why publish at all? Others make extreme generalizations on samples that are neither representative nor adequate in size. One may ask, why publish until some effort has been made to secure a good sample? If conclusions were examined in terms of sampling procedures, many inconsequential studies would not appear.

Implicit in any discussion of sampling is the problem of *statistical significance.* Since the purpose of research is to generalize from a sample to a population, the question whether the results obtained from a given sample arise by chance or are the outcome of the conditions being studied is pertinent. In modern treatments, the *null hypothesis* is assumed, namely, that whatever appears in any particular sample is the outcome of chance. It becomes the obligation of the investigator to prove that his results are not likely to be chance outcomes but are the results of the introduced condition he is studying. He does this by showing the degree of confidence that can be placed in the differences obtained, or the likelihood that they would not occur by chance alone.

Sampling problems first arose in connection with normative studies, since the value of a standard is clearly a function of the sample. Height-weight tables and intelligence test scales are standards against which thousands of individual children will be checked for diagnostic, and practical purposes. If the standards are inaccurate or inadequate, the usefulness of the instrument is substantially reduced.

Is a random sample of humans possible? At first thought it would seem possible to select children at random, but a moment's consideration shows that this is not possible. The essential condition for a random sample is *that each individual in the population is as likely as any other to appear in the sample drawn.* But human beings are social and live in an environment shot through with selective processes. In cities, families of the same income level live in the same neighborhoods. Each occupation and profession is itself selective. A church, a political group, a social club, a leisure-time activity is selective. Often children in the public schools are thought of as a typical or complete population. Since some children do not enter public school because of mental and physical defects, and others go to private schools, even the kindergarten or first grade is somewhat selective. After school entrance some children progress more and others less rapidly. In a short time the children of a given chronological age are spread out over a number of grades. If one were to study all first-grade children in an area with compulsory education, a better sample would be secured than if seventh or eighth graders in the same schools were tested. Since many children never go to high school and only relatively few get to college, high school and college populations are far from representative. Even the schools and areas within a city are highly selective. Table 1 from Maller (1933) shows the mean IQ's of fifth-grade children in 273 health areas in New York City. The mean IQ for the areas varied from 74 to 120. If a school selected for studying happens to be one with a mean IQ of 74, or with a mean IQ of 119, how typical or valid would the generalizations be?

Stratified Sampling. To meet the problems imposed by the differential selection of human beings by their social environments, various techniques have been evolved for drawing stratified samples from the total population. For example, since the child population of the states varies, an investigator might draw a sample from each state that was proportionate to the total child population of the state. Stratified sampling √ assumes that the total population can be divided into classes in accordance with known

TABLE 1

DISTRIBUTION OF MEAN IQ'S IN 273 HEALTH AREAS IN NEW YORK CITY

(Based on the examination of 100,153 fifth-grade children)

Scale	Frequency
118	2
114	11
110	18
106	42
102	46
98	57
94	40
90	29
86	14
82	7
78	6
74	1
Total	273
Mean	100.43
SD	8.28

and measurable characteristics. Within these classes the size of the sample selected is proportionate to the size of the class in the total population. Stratified sampling has been given great impetus by the development of public-opinion polls in which such sampling is critical. The poll procedures involve the use of sampling criteria laid down in advance by means of which a sample that mirrors a total population can be selected. See Yule and Kendall (1937) for principles of stratified sampling, McNemar (1946) for a critical discussion of opinion polling, and Peatman (1947) and various other statistics textbooks for procedures.

Students often confuse the meaning of random and stratified samples, particularly because of the modern emphasis on random sampling. Some assume that a randomized sample of a population automatically guarantees a good representation of the total population. Actually, such a representation can be guaranteed for a single sample only by stratification, unless the sample is itself a very large proportion of the total population. Inspection of a sampling distribution for any statistic reveals that many particular samples selected at random are far from a correct representation of the relation under study. In industrial work with quality control this problem is met by taking a series of random samples. But in psychological work this is not ordinarily done. However, within stratifications based on known characteristics samples are usually drawn at random, particularly if large populations are available to the investigator.

In the selection of stratified samples of children, the following breakdowns are commonly used.

Age. In many earlier studies the numbers of cases at different age levels varied. In modern studies the problem of age sampling is solved by using the same number of children at each age level, say 100 at 2 years, 100 at 3 years, and so on. Age stratification can be further controlled by testing children on their birthdays, or selecting children within 1 month of their birth date, instead of selecting over a range of a whole year within the age classification. This locates the points on an age curve more precisely, increases the accuracy of the determinations, and gives the same results as a larger sample over a wider age range. Selecting a constant number of children at each age level not only improves sampling; it also simplifies calculations and the determination of various statistical constants.

Sex. Some of the earliest studies on children, even those on physical growth, made no distinction between the sexes. But now, since it has become clear that some developmental phenomena differ in the sexes, the practice of reporting results on boys and girls separately is almost universal. The common practice is to use equal numbers of boys and girls. The age sample of 100 chil-

dren described above would, with sex stratification, consist of 50 boys and 50 girls at each age level. Although an equal sex division is not absolutely representative at all ages of the true proportion of the sexes in the population, it is so close to it that no error is introduced.

Location or Area. In the early standardization of intelligence tests, particular efforts were made to secure children from different areas and parts of the country on the assumption that there was great variation with geographical location. In the past educational standards, the enforcement of school attendance, and the content of the curriculum varied widely. But, as conditions improve in backward areas and as modern means of mass communication develop, these differences tend to disappear. Anderson (1936) found differences with geographical location relatively small in comparison with differences in cultural or socio-economic status. A professional person's son in Alabama lives more like and is more like a professional person's son in Michigan than either is like a laborer's son in either state.

Rural-Urban. One difference in location is of some importance; that of rural or urban residence. Baldwin, Fillmore, and Hadley (1930) found significant differences in intelligence test scores, and the studies of the College Entrance Examination Board have revealed some differences in verbal and problem-solving ability, the former in favor of city adolescents and the latter in favor of rural adolescents. With improved means of transportation, the consolidation and equalization of schools, and the widespread extension of the radio, many of these differences are disappearing. A surprisingly large proportion of all the studies on children that are available in the literature have been done on city children because they are more readily available.

Cultural or Socio-Economic Level. Human societies are divided into strata based on income, educational level, cultural background, and a variety of related factors. Because these strata differ markedly in the facilities and opportunities afforded children, a significant sampling problem arises.

available. One of the most widely used socio-economic devices is the Minnesota Scale of Paternal Occupations (Goodenough and Anderson, 1931; Institute of Child Welfare, 1950), which divides adult males into seven classifications according to their occupations as in Table 2.

TABLE 2

CLASSIFICATION OF OCCUPATIONS OF EMPLOYED MALES IN THE UNITED STATES

	1940 Census		Sample	
	Total	Percentage	100	50
Class I. Professional	922,156	2.71	3	2
Class II. Semi-professional and managerial	2,436,397	7.16	7	4
Class III. Clerical, skilled trades, and retail business	4,808,143	14.13	14	7
Class IV. Farmers	5,192,658	15.26	15	7
Class V. Semi-skilled occupations, minor clerical positions, and minor business	8,129,266	23.89	24	12
Class VI. Slightly skilled trades and occupations requiring little training or ability	4,954,463	14.56	15	7
Class VII. Day laborers of all classes (including agriculture)	7,584,820	22.29	22	11

Various proposals have been made for its solution. The most common involve selection either in terms of a single factor, such as paternal occupation or income level; or in terms of a series of questions covering occupation, income, possessions, etc., as in the Sims' scale (1928) or the very complete scale of Leahy (1936); or in terms of cultural level, as in the studies of Warner *et al.* (1949).

Many modern studies in child psychology control selection in terms of paternal occupation, which has a distinct advantage, since the occupational distribution for any particular area or section or for the country as a whole can be determined from census data. Paternal occupation is one of the few cultural facts for which universal figures are

To set up a sample of 100 children at any age level, knowing the occupation of their fathers, proportions can be matched by rounding the percentages; or by rounding to even numbers the sample can be split in half to permit control of sex as well as of occupation. The third and fourth columns of Table 2 show samples for 100 and 50 cases, respectively. It should be noted, however, that this sampling is concerned with increasing the accuracy of the mean and standard deviation of the whole distribution, not with determining the differences between occupational groups. If differences between occupational groups are to be determined, precautions have to be taken to secure enough cases in each class to give confidence in the comparisons.

If published data are checked, much sampling is found to be far from typical. Children from the extremes are more readily accessible than children in the middle ranges. Parents in the upper three occupational groups, which contain 23 per cent of the population, tend to be more cooperative, more easily reached, more interested in programs of measurement, and more likely to volunteer or take advantage of an agency set up for children. Some parents in classes VI and VII are in close contact with social agencies, day nurseries, etc. A private school with tuition draws its population almost entirely from classes I and II. A day nursery or a settlement house draws its population from classes VI and VII. Thus classes III and V in the urban areas tend to be neglected, and only very few studies contain representatives of the rural groups in classes IV and VII.

The necessity of controlling occupational backgrounds depends upon the correlation of the particular characteristics studied with occupational status. But a very substantial number of traits, environmental conditions, facilities, etc., have been shown to be correlated in some degree with occupational status (Anderson, 1936).

Combinations of Controls in Sampling. In most investigations in which sampling is controlled, a number of controls are used simultaneously. The most common are age and sex; to these, many modern studies add a control of socio-economic or cultural status. School grade is frequently used. Urban and rural residence are less often added. Either mental age or IQ is sometimes used as a control. The selection of controls depends upon the nature of the study and the size and location of the population available for study. In general, the deliberate control of sampling through laying out criteria in advance is the ideal. Failing control of sampling, it is important, especially for the subsequent integration

and interpretation of research findings, to give such complete descriptions of the sampling used in any investigation that the reader will be able to compare the results with other studies and make the integration himself. The minimum is chronological age, sex, socio-economic status, and school grade, with such additional material as mental age and urban and rural residence if it is available.

Use of Readily Obtained Data as a Base for Sampling. Since obtaining a sample which possesses defined characteristics presents difficulties, investigators secure children for study in various ways. One method is to consult school or institutional files and to use the recorded data as a base from which to make a selection. The names of children who meet stated requirements as to age, sex, socio-economic status, intelligence, achievement, etc., can be chosen. Usually a list with at least twice as many names as needed in each defined category is made up. The names are then randomized within the category, e.g., 9-year-old boys of occupational class III, and the children are contacted in order and examined. If a given child cannot be located, the investigator moves on to the next one in the category. Sometimes a large number of available persons are examined, in order to draw a smaller sample which possesses known charactersistics for a more detailed study. For instance, in the Griffiths study (1952) the cooperation of many P.T.A.'s was secured, and thousands of parents filled out a face sheet and a brief inventory of their attitudes toward behavior difficulties. From the face-sheet data a sample meeting defined criteria were selected. The attitudes of the children of these parents toward the same difficulties were obtained, and cross-comparisons of parents and children within various educational and occupational classes were made. By using data on the most readily available large population, much time is saved and a much more meaningful and precise attack can be made on the problem in hand. Although investigators often find it disturbing to throw away data that have been collected, there are instances in which such elimination increases the scientific information gained from a study. Sometimes it is possible to analyze the data in the rigidly controlled sample for some purposes, and to use it plus all the other data for other types of analysis.

Size of Sample. The size of the sample necessary to secure significant results for a particular problem presents a real difficulty. In the 1930's it was assumed that the more cases used the more significant were the results. Although this principle is still sound, provided the sample is adequate in character, nevertheless most scientific workers are under practical limitations of time, money, and availability of subjects. It then becomes desirable so to design and arrange a study that the results will be significant, without undertaking a great amount of unnecessary experimentation. From modern discussions it is clear that a small sample selected in accordance with criteria rigidly laid down in advance gives more significant and meaningful results than does a larger sample the characteristics of which are unknown. The better public-opinion polls and the sampling techniques used in modern industry are based on this principle. But some students assume that small samples have some peculiar virtue of their own and interpret Fisher's work as supporting that position. But Fisher is quite clear that a large sample is to be preferred to a small sample; his discussion is concerned essentially with securing the maximum scientific information from the sample available and with the ineffective use of disproportionately large samples that yield relatively small returns when more effort put into design and less into collecting data on a large and miscellaneous sample would yield much more scientific information. Harris, Horvitz, and Wood (1948) have outlined methods for deciding on sample size in designing experiments in which specified degrees of accuracy are desired in determining confidence intervals, the significance of means, and differences between means.

The size of the sample also varies with the type of problem under investigation. For instance, reaction time can be determined with great accuracy on a small number of cases, whereas measures of more complex processes need a larger number of cases. Further, the size of the sample depends upon the number of relations involved. Where two variables are studied and extraneous factors are rigorously controlled by the experimental set-up, a smaller sample is necessary than when the weight and pattern of many factors contributing to a complex area of behavior are to be studied without rigorous experimental controls. Precision depends also upon the reliability and validity of the measuring instrument. With coarse instruments more cases are needed to establish whatever trends or relations exist. McNemar's (1940) bibliography and article on sampling closes with this statement: "Perhaps the confidence to be placed in the results of a study should vary directly with the amount of information concerning the sampling and experimental techniques rather than inversely with the square root of the number of cases" (p. 363).

The Organization and Design of Studies

Experimental design is a phrase that has been used for a plan or outline of an investigation that (1) states a problem or hypothesis precisely, (2) defines a population or supply, (3) draws from the population a sample for study, and (4) arranges the observations and measurements of single and multiple factors in such a way that maximum information will be obtained (Fisher, 1936, 1937). Information as here used means "scientific information," not merely a collection of facts. It refers to facts and principles, and their interrelations. An essential element in design is the deliberate control of the number of cases, the number of samples, and the replication necessary to secure the information wanted. Design implies that the methods of measurement and control, and the sampling procedures, are laid out in advance and are interrelated. Seriatim and isolated experiments are consolidated into single studies in order to secure more scientific information with a smaller number of cases and to evaluate the interaction of factors statistically in a way impossible in one-factor studies. An ideal of design is the securing of maximum information for a given expenditure of time and energy. Fisher and his followers have also provided new statistical tools with which to determine significance, analyze variance, and study interaction.

Design. The problem of design is an old. one. In laboratories systematic arrangements to control factors have always been used. Although many such designs have neglected sampling criteria for subjects, much concern with the number and character of the observations necessary for generalization has been shown. For example, Melton (1936) presented an extensive discussion of experimental methodology in learning which has important implications for other fields. Brunswik (1947) presented detailed analysis of experiments in physical and social perception.

The term "design" may be broadened to cover all schemata for investigations, laboratory experiments, and control group studies by means of which observations are systematically structured. The sampling controls set up by Fisher may be regarded as particular instances of a more general problem. Past and projected investigations can be examined with respect to their design, and questions regarding their quality or the adequacy of the design can be raised. Is the design such that information will be obtained? Will the maximum information in terms of the amount of time, money, energy, and number of cases available be obtained? Of these questions, the second is the more important because it implies a type of planning that will enable the investigator to know in advance what he may expect from his efforts and assumes some knowledge both of the variables under investigation and of the specific hypothesis involved.

The plan or schema of published or projected studies may be represented in diagrammatic form, as in the chart showing the technique of the control group on page 47. The Latin square is a diagram of an investigation in algebraic form.

Discussions and demonstrations of the manner in which Latin squares can be used in the design and analysis of psychological experiments are found in Grant (1948). It is clear that the theory and practice of experimental design are advancing with great rapidity. Grant's (1950) article and books by Johnson (1949), Edwards (1950), Cochran and Cox (1950), Anderson and Bancroft (1952), and Kempthorne (1952) summarize modern developments. The implications of postulates for a system of experiments may be put in terms of symbolic logic, as in Hull *et al.* (1940), or in topological diagrams, as in Lewin (1936). Methods of representing design in generalized symbolic form are of great value in planning studies and in thinking through to their outcomes, since they abstract in some degree from the material particular to an investigation and lead to the essential features underlying many different studies.

One can hardly engage in this symbolic process without improvement in the specific study undertaken.

Experiment. The phenomena of interest to science seldom occur in isolation or with such high frequency that observations can readily be made. No matter how careful the recording or how unbiased the observation, progress is slow when science has to await natural occurrences in natural settings. Experiment, or the deliberate attempt to isolate phenomena and reproduce them frequently enough under controlled conditions in order to determine their characteristic relations, then, becomes the primary and basic scientific method.

Not all phenomena, however, are equally adaptable to the use of experimental techniques. For instance, because of the long life span of the human, experiments in human genetics are sharply limited. Investigators turn to short-lived animals, such as the fruitfly, which produce many generations in a short time, in order to control and isolate the significant factors. Similarly, the complexity of the human environment and the irreversibility of behavior make many growth, developmental, and social phenomena not readily susceptible to laboratory experiment. But science has and is developing other techniques for securing data and making generalizations in those instances. One result of these methods is that key experiments can be introduced at some points in the complex manifold.

In making experiments two methods are used either singly or together to control various factors: (1) making given factors constant in order that they may not affect the particular factors under observation, and (2) isolating a factor or purifying a substance by eliminating all extraneous material and then studying its nature and effects. In either method the experiment takes the complex phenomena of nature, breaks them up into segments, studies the action and relations of these segments, either singly or in combination, and arrives at appropriate generalizations. Every experiment is an abstraction, since material is pulled out of its individual context. Whatever the method used, the control is deliberate and in a sense artificial. Thus, in a relatively simple experiment, children similarly motivated and free from distracting influences throw a ball at a target from a known distance in a special room in order that learning may be studied. Or, in a complex experiment, a series of difficult tasks may be set before children working individually, in groups without team structure, or in groups as members of teams, and praise may be given to half the children in these varied tasks and withheld from the other half. Thus the effect of individual effort, effort under social facilitation, and effort under competition may be compared both with and without the special incentive of praise. Such a complex experiment involves a systematic arrangement, with rotation of stimulation and groups in order that the weight and nature of various factors may be determined and compared.

However, in most experiments on children a major difficulty is soon encountered. If an attempt is made to use the same subjects over again with the same or different stimulation, the children will have changed because of growth and the incidental and formal learning which constantly goes forward. Hence, control groups become necessary.

The Control Group. In actual practice experiments are enlarged to include a second group of children in which the particular factors under observation are not introduced and which is periodically measured in the same way as the group of children in the experiment, called the experimental group. The use of an experimental and control group permits comparison between children subject to and children not subject to an introduced condition. The method of the control group has many ramifications and many modifications. Figure 1 shows its essential features.

In this diagram periodic tests or measurements are indicated by solid lines, the experimental condition by cross-hatched lines, and the absence of this condition by dash

Such a design can be extended by adding other groups subjected to different conditions. The number of cases used may vary from 2, as in co-twin control, to large populations. Usually in setting up control groups the capacities or present attainments of the children are matched and variations are then introduced into the environment or context. Thus, the experimental

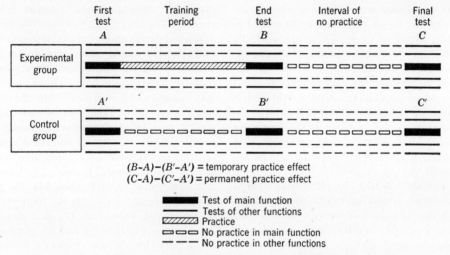

$(B-A)-(B'-A')$ = temporary practice effect
$(C-A)-(C'-A')$ = permanent practice effect

■■■■ Test of main function
──── Tests of other functions
▨▨▨ Practice
▭▭▭ No practice in main function
── ── No practice in other functions

FIGURE 1. Technique of the control group.

lines. The lighter solid lines indicate accessory tests or measurements which might be used to measure transfer or spread because of the introduced condition. Differences between first tests and end tests reveal the immediate effects of the condition introduced, and differences between first tests and final test the permanency of those effects. Measures of the differences between the experimental and the control group can be obtained in a variety of ways, such as dividing the gain in the experimental group by that in the control group or by expressing gains in both groups as percentages of the original score. Such manipulations often clarify thinking about the relations involved.

group may be exposed to typewriters while the control group is not, in order to determine the effect of typewriters upon spelling, reading, and writing (Wood and Freeman, 1932). Or the experimental group may have geography lessons plus motion pictures, and the control group geography lessons without motion pictures. The experimental group may have one type of instruction in reading, and the control group another. The experimental group may be given intensive training in motor, intellectual, or linguistic skills, while the control group moves ahead in its ordinary environment. But the control group may consist of a group of children that differ markedly in a factor under study, as when children of high intelligence are compared with those of low intelligence or children of high musical capacity are compared with those of low musical capacity.

In using a control group an attempt is made to secure a reference line or base from which comparisons can be made. Logically, it seeks to avoid generalizations based upon mere concomitance by taking account of exceptions, that is, by determining whether or not the change occurs in the absence of the particular factor or factors under consideration as well as when they are present. To the naïve observer concomitance often seems of high importance; the scientist must determine whether the concomitance is genuine or accidental. In an only child with a behavior problem, no doubt exists as to the presence of the problem in the particular child. But someone may generalize that "onliness" and "behavior problems" are related.

For the scientist the critical question is how much confidence can be placed in such a generalization—not the fact that the two events occurred together in a particular series of instances. Even additional cases in which only children and behavior problems went together would not eliminate the possibility of bias, sampling errors, or misinterpretation. It is absolutely necessary to secure information on the proportion of only children who do not show behavior problems and on the proportions of non-only children who show and do not show behavior problems. With such a fourfold table based on a sufficient number of subjects the association between being a behavior problem and being an only child can be measured and a generalization made in which the scientist can repose confidence.

Whether control is achieved by artificial and deliberate laboratory methods, by parallel groups, or by statistical analysis, all of which seek to determine net relations, there are three distinct methodological problems.

The *first* is the determination of the relations between and interactions among the variables under consideration. This is a matter of descriptive statistics. The *second* is the determination of the confidence to be placed in the relations as determined. This is a matter of the statistics of inference. Confidence, expressed as a measure of significance or as a fiducial limit, involves disproving the null hypothesis by showing the extent to which the results depart from chance. The *third* is the matter of the psychological significance or meaningfulness of the relations found. This should not be confused with statistical significance. For example, differences in hair color among human beings, which statistically are of great significance, are of almost no psychological significance. Or a difference so small that it requires 1000 cases for its statistical demonstration will have no psychological significance (McNemar, 1940). Psychological significance depends upon (1) the fit of the generalizations within the framework of our existing knowledge, (2) their capacity to reorganize thinking and make meaningful data that did not previously fit, and (3) their usefulness in prediction and control.

The Matched Control Group. In this variation of the control group, the children within a defined group are divided into two groups as nearly alike as possible. Through preliminary measurements their status is determined and the best possible matches made within the framework of the group. With one variable involved, the matching is very simple. By putting the top child on the matching variable in the experimental, the second in the control, the third in the control, and the fourth in the experimental group, and so on, with alternating reversals through the population, the means and the standard deviations of the two groups are equalized. As the number of variables on which matching is done increases, the possibilities of matching within narrow limits is reduced and a much larger population is necessary in order to secure precise matches. In the best applications of this technique the criteria for matching are laid down in advance and then adhered to rigidly. Thus, for example, where matching is done on more than one variable, the sexes can be equalized, socio-economic status matched in terms of parents' occupation, chronological age can be matched within 3 months, and IQ within 10 points.

Usually matching on the variable in which the experimental condition is to be introduced is very precise. The choice of matching factors depends upon this variable. If it is positively correlated with another factor, that factor should be controlled; if there is no correlation, control is not necessary. For instance, in studying motor skills, it is usually not necessary, except with very young children, to control either intelligence or socio-economic status, since the correlations between either of these factors and motor skill for homogeneous age and sex group is very low. But in a study of language, with which both socio-economic status and intelligence are positively correlated, both should be controlled. It might appear that, since the means and deviations for both groups on the original measurements are known, a correction could be applied to take care of differences in intelligence and socio-economic status. Although this is partly true, it is likely that any gain in language ability in the course of the experiment would be differential with respect to both intelligence or socio-economic level. Hence, a spurious difference would be obtained even though a correction had been applied.

There is always the possibility of so completely controlling the variables that little or no variation with the experimental condition is permitted. Sometimes more is held constant than should be. This may

happen with the matching variables but is much more likely to occur within the materials or procedures used in the experimentally introduced condition. Thus, in an educational experiment, materials, textbooks, and exercises were so closely parallel for two groups compared for two different methods of instruction that no differences were obtained. Yet, in the actual practical use of these methods of instruction, the materials, textbooks, and exercises vary with the method of instruction. In experiments evaluating laboratory instruction in science, matching was done on a preliminary examination, but the final testing was done on the lecture material common to both groups and not on the laboratory content. Gates and Taylor (1926) found little or no difference between an experimental and control group as a result of training in a simple motor skill, whereas Mattson (1933), working with skills of three levels of complexity, found that the results obtained in a controlled experiment varied with complexity. And Jersild (1932), who found little change in motor skills of a simple type, with training, found much change in musical ability, that is, the ability to reproduce pitches and intervals. Since these studies suggest that the results obtained in control-group experiments vary with the measures used to test the effect, the complexity of the process itself, and the type or modality of the process, great care must be exercised in interpreting the results.

One source of statistical misinterpretation is found in the use of measures for evaluating the differences between experimental and control groups. Many investigators have used the formula for significance in which the correlational term is absent. When the phenomena studied are positively correlated with the factors by means of which the matching is done, that formula for the standard error of the difference in which the correlation coefficient is present or some modification of it should be used. McNemar (1940) and Peters and Voorhis (1950) discuss the appropriate statistical formulae.

Furthermore, in pairing, controlling a factor such as intelligence also partially controls socio-economic status because of their high positive intercorrelations. McNemar points out that, as one increases the number of variables over which control is exercised, the returns obtained diminish much as do weights in a regression equation, where many overlapping variables are used. Thorndike (1942) points out some of the fallacies in matched group experiments. The question of the number of variables necessary for control for the particular study at hand should be carefully considered in advance, as no rule can be laid down to cover all studies. In most modern studies the variables used for matching are (1) sex, (2) chronological age (or school grade in educational studies), (3) intelligence, (4) socio-economic status, and (5) initial status on the factor investigated.

Solomon (1949) has shown that additional control groups facilitate analysis in experiments in which tests are given before and after an experimental training procedure. In a second control group the pretest is omitted when it might result in an interaction with the training procedure. A third control group, omitting both the pretest and the training procedure, is desirable if an uncontrolled extraexperimental event may affect all groups. The third control group makes pretest effects completely orthogonal to the training effect and permits independent evaluation of the effect of (1) the training procedure, (2) the pretest, and (3) the interaction of pretests and training. (See also Grant, 1950; Canter, 1951.)

Controls Drawn from a Supply. In many studies the individuals in a finite population are paired with children drawn from a supply of cases in the general population.

If the supply from which the control group is drawn is large, very precise matching can be done to meet very narrow criteria. Thus the investigator may be able to match chronological age within 10 days on either side of the birthday, IQ's within 5 points, and socio-economic status, sex, and other factors rigidly. The number of cases necessary to secure pairs increases with the number of matching variables used. Thus, in a study by Goodenough (1928b), in which children were paired with respect to sex, age, IQ, education of father, education of mother, socio-economic status of the father, and the nativity of parents, a supply of more than 300 children was necessary in order to secure matches for an experimental group of 28 children.

Matching after Exposure to Experimental Conditions. Sometimes in a minor variant of the control-group technique one segment of a fairly large population is exposed to experimental conditions and another is used as control, and the matching is done after the collection of data for both segments. It is often more convenient to test all the children in a classroom or school in order not to interrupt the school routine by drawing out the special cases needed. Later, as the matching is done, the irrelevant cases are discarded. Note that here, too, the criteria laid down for matching must be clearly stated, rigidly adhered to, and the matching done on the first measures obtained, not on the end results.

Ex Post Facto Matching and Analysis. When an extensive series of records is available for a large population, it is possible to select groups in accordance with defined criteria on the basis of the records and to compare them in terms of outcomes. This procedure is called by Greenwood the method of *ex post facto* analysis. Both Greenwood (1945) and Chapin (1947) have devoted much attention to its implications and use, as well as to other methods of design for sociological data. Essentially it consists of projecting sampling criteria for control purposes on already existing data and rigorously selecting cases which can be defined with high precision in terms of their original status. There is no theoretical objection to the technique. If, for instance, the records of 100,000 children examined 20 years earlier were available and three groups of 1000 cases each of bright, average, and dull children were selected and their careers followed to the present, the results would be excellent. In fact, the method might even have some advantages in that, since the children did not know that they were being studied for a special purpose, the results would not be distorted by awareness of being in a specially selected group. This method must be sharply distinguished from any selection of cases in terms of end results, a method obviously defective from the standpoint of drawing scientific generalizations.

Co-Twin Control. Because nature does an excellent job of pairing in identical twins, the method of co-twin control offers an unusual opportunity for attacking many scientific problems. One or more pairs of identical twins are selected; one member of each pair is exposed to a particular condition while the other child is not so exposed. Pretests are given, followed by exposure and tests and final tests after an interval. Gesell and Thompson (1929), Hilgard (1933), and Strayer (1930) are good examples of such studies carried on for short periods. In these investigations the twins used in the separate parts of the studies were reversed; i.e., in one, twin A was given the experimentally introduced condition while twin B was held as control, and in the next twin B was given the experimental condition and twin A held as control. In the McGraw (1935, 1939) study of *Johnny and Jimmy,* Johnny was given intensive training in motor skills over many months while Jimmy was not. Periodically both twins were given standard developmental tests, as well as tests in the specific functions in which training was given. Later on the twins were reversed for some training, and still later entirely new test and training situations were given to both. The method of co-twin control also permits many variations, not only in setting up parallel groups but also in setting up contrasting groups, as in the study of identical twins reared apart and the many studies of twin resemblances.

An interesting variation of the control-group technique is found in Kellogg and Kellogg (1933), who reared an infant chimpanzee and a human infant under similar conditions and made comparative tests and observations of performance at various intervals.

Control by Groups Rather than by Individuals. Pairing may be done on the basis of groups rather than individuals. For example, a school in a middle economic district in one city may be paired with a similar school in another city of the same size, and so on. In one half the schools instruction of one type is given, while in the other instruction of another type is given or a particular experimental condition is introduced. An excellent example is found in the Wood and Freeman (1932) study of the influence of the typewriter in the elementary school, in which 21 public schools in 8 cities were used as controls and 22 public schools in 8 cities as experimentals, together with 3 private schools for controls and 8 for experimentals. Some 15,000 children participated in the experiment. In this type of study comparisons may be made in terms of schools, grades, and individual children's performance. It is a question whether results of equal statistical and psychological significance might have been obtained with much less expense, time, and effort by using smaller numbers of children matched for individual performance.

Although the trend of modern statistics is away from large numbers of cases toward small numbers selected in accordance with rigorously defined criteria, there is some difference of opinion in the field of educational research, where large populations are available. Peters and Voorhis (1940), in a chapter on controlled experimentation, stress precise matching of individuals, whereas Lindquist (1940), in an extensive discussion of a variety of control designs for groups, favors the use of schools.

Control by Statistical Devices. In the experiment an attempt is made to isolate or make constant the effect of factors by artificial control of conditions, selection of subjects, etc. By the use of partial correlation a somewhat similar result can be secured. Suppose that the relations among the three variables intelligence, time spent in study, and scholastic success are investigated. After measurements on each of the three variables are secured for a group of children, time of study can be held constant in a partial correlation and the net relation between intelligence and scholastic success determined. Or the obtained variation in scholastic success can be broken down by an analysis of variance into its components and their contribution to the manifold determined after the variation resulting from chance is eliminated. Or two groups of children, one of high the other of low intelligence, can be paired with respect to time spent in study and their scholastic performance can be compared, or the relation between intelligence and scholastic success can be determined for a group of children who vary with respect to intelligence and who are placed under conditions in which all study for equal amounts of time. Thus the same problem is attacked in four different ways, ranging from complex to simple statistical treatments. By

deliberate control of factors much of the subsequent need for complex analysis is eliminated. This brings out a very important point with reference to method; in general, control of conditions in advance is to be preferred to masses of measurement accumulated on many cases without control. Good experimental design may make complex statistical procedures unnecessary. But it should also be clear that, in many manifolds involving complex related variables, the relative weight of various factors and of their interaction can be analyzed only by complex statistical procedures. Hence, experimental and statistical methods complement each other and work toward the same goal of maximum scientific information on the particular problem in hand. A good practical rule is to control whatever variance is possible either by deliberate manipulation of conditions or by stratification and to randomize whatever variance remains in order to minimize its effects on the relations under study.

The Evaluation of a Study

Every advanced student and investigator reads many scientific articles and monographs. Such reports on investigations should not be accepted at their face value but read carefully and critically in order to separate out the firm and stable facts and generalizations. The reader's attention is called to the "Standards for Appraising Psychological Research," prepared by Wolfle et al. (1949).

Following is an outline that has proved of value both in evaluating studies and in checking on studies that are being planned. In a sense it summarizes much of what has been said in earlier pages. Although it could be extended to include many more details, it has been kept as brief and schematic as possible.

1. *Problem.* Is a significant problem attacked? Is an hypothesis that may be supported or refuted by the data collected set up and clearly stated? Or, if it is a normative or survey study, have adequate precautions been taken to insure that the final results will be of value in understanding children? Is sufficient account taken of the results of past studies and of the interrelation of scientific principles to permit the fitting of the results of this study into the framework of scientific understanding?

2. *Design and sampling.* Is the study so planned that it will give an answer to the problem proposed? Can the design be graphed or represented in other symbolic form? Is the number of cases adequate? How are they selected from the total population? Of what total population or supply are they the representatives? Within the limits of sampling established, is the allocation of cases randomized or subject to bias? Are the sampling and design planned with reference to the later statistical treatment and analysis of the data? If the sampling is not representative is it described so completely that the results may be compared and integrated with other studies? Does the description of the sample include chronological age, mental age, sex, grade location, socio-economic status, geographical location, and any other sampling criteria that are important? Can trends with sampling criteria or their combinations be determined? Does the design yield maximum scientific information for the time and energy expended? If not, how could it be modified?

Are the factors which are controlled described? How are control and isolation achieved? In investigations with control groups, is the sampling in control and experimental groups adequately described and similar or identical? How is matching or pairing done? Is the motivation constant for both groups? If not, is motivation checked on another group? Are the effects of incidental practice and indirect stimulation upon the function known or controlled? Are valid and reliable measurements of the level of proficiency in the primary function and in related variables available for the beginning and the end of the experiment, and after a period of elapsed time?

3. *Measurement.* Are the variables studied described in specific terms and clearly differentiated? How are the various measures of the variables obtained? In what units are they expressed? Is quantitative treatment used wherever possible? Are the measures used valid, reliable, and suitable?

4. *Procedure.* Are the procedures used, e.g., apparatus, tests, measuring devices, observational records, clearly and accurately described? Can the study be repeated from the descriptions given of the sampling, design, and measurement procedures? Are data systematically collected? Are adequate and permanent records kept? Is the method of recording uniform throughout? Are omissions and negative instances recorded? Are the procedures laid down followed rigorously without change throughout the study?

5. *Results.* Are the statistical procedures mathematically sound? Are they adapted to the problem? Are all the essential relations studied? Are all the necessary statistical procedures—number of cases, means, dispersion, percentages, measures of significance, correlation coefficients, etc.—used and presented? Are available errors ascertained and reported, or minimized by appropriate procedures? Have the sources and direction of constant error been checked? Is the quantitative material so analyzed as to bring out the essential relationships? Are interactions or interrelations analyzed? Are the data examined for contamination or masking of significant relations? Are the results clearly and succinctly presented? Do the verbal statements agree with the tabular and quantitative findings?

6. *Conclusions and interpretations.* Are the conclusions warranted by the data? Are they too limited in scope, or do they transcend the data widely? Is statistical significance confused with psychological significance? Are spurious relations or artifacts detected? Are significant trends overlooked? Are the results integrated in the general scientific field? Is

the significance of the findings for related fields pointed out?

Conclusion

In child psychology scientific problems are being attacked in a variety of ways by workers who are becoming more and more concerned with methodology. Child psychology, which at first accepted uncritically almost any observations or results obtained from the study of children, has become more mature. It now critically examines its methods and results and deliberately goes about designing experiments. In many areas the study of the child has moved from the exploratory phase to the comprehensive investigation carried on over a long period. In view of the fact that a science is a growing and developing dynamic system, it would be unfortunate if too much concern with a particular method or too narrow a preconception of what child psychology *should be* were to cut off a manifold approach to the complex problems of the developing person. From today's studies, however inadequate, come the highly developed techniques of tomorrow. Science crawls before it walks, and walks before it runs. And science learns from its experience and modifies its own methods, even though progression is often slower and more uneven than we could wish. Methods do not fall into Victorian classifications of right or wrong, of all or nothing. They are tools which are used, modified, and improved as time passes and problems are met. The scientist of today has a great advantage over the one of yesterday, not in his interest or ability but in the better tools that have been forged in the intervening period. Sin in science consists not in the use of a particular method but in failure to use a more adequate method when it is available for a problem in hand. To understand growth and development, which appear

ever more complex as we learn more about them, we need not one but many competent investigators, not one but many and varied investigations.

Bibliography

Ackerson, L. 1931. *Children's behavior problems.* Chicago: University of Chicago Press.

Allport, G. W. 1937. *Personality: A psychological interpretation.* New York: Holt.

——. 1940. The psychologist's frame of reference. *Psychol. Bull., 37,* 1–28.

——. 1942. *The use of the personal document in psychological science.* New York: Social Science Research Council.

Anastasi, A. 1948. A methodological note on the "controlled diary" technique. *J. Genet. Psychol., 73,* 237–241.

——. 1950. The concept of validity in test scores. *Educ. & Psychol. Measm., 10,* 67–78.

Anderson, J. E. 1931, 1933. The methods of child psychology. In C. Murchison (Ed.), *A handbook of child psychology.* Worcester: Clark University Press. 1st ed., pp. 1–27; 2d ed., rev., pp. 3–28.

——. 1939a. The development of social behavior. *Amer. J. Sociol., 44,* 839–857.

——. 1939b. The limitations of infant and preschool tests in the measurement of intelligence. *J. Psychol., 8,* 351–379.

——. 1944. Freedom and constraint or potentiality and environment. *Psychol. Bull., 41,* 1–29.

——. 1948. Personality organization in children. *Amer. Psychol., 3,* 409–416.

——. 1952. Relation of attitude to adjustment. *Educ., 73,* 210–218.

Anderson, J. E. (Chairman.) 1936. *The young child in the home.* White House Conference on Child Health and Protection. New York: Appleton-Century.

Anderson, J. E., and J. T. Cohen. 1939. The effect of including incomplete series in the statistical analysis of longitudinal measurements of children's dental arches. *Child Develpm., 10,* 145–149.

Anderson, R. L., and T. A. Bancroft. 1952. *Statistical theory in research.* New York: McGraw-Hill.

Andrews, T. G. (Ed.) 1948. *Methods of psychology.* New York: Wiley.

Arrington, R. E. 1943. Time sampling in studies of social behavior: A critical review of techniques and results with research suggestions. *Psychol. Bull., 40,* 81–124.

Axline, V. M. 1947. *Play therapy: The inner dynamics of childhood.* Boston: Houghton Mifflin.

Bach, G. R. 1946. Father fantasies and father-typing in father-separated children. *Child Develpm., 17,* 63–80.

Baldwin, B. T., E. A. Fillmore, and L. Hadley. 1930. *Farm children: An investigation of rural child life in selected areas of Iowa.* New York: Appleton.

Baller, W. R. 1936. A study of the present social status of a group of adults who, when they were in elementary schools, were classified as mentally deficient. *Genet. Psychol. Monogr., 18,* 165–244.

Barker, R. G., and H. F. Wright. 1949. Psychological ecology and the problem of psychosocial development. *Child Develpm., 20,* 131–143.

Barker, R. G., and H. F. Wright. 1951. *One boy's day. A specimen record of behavior.* New York. Harper.

Bayley, N. 1933. Mental growth during the first three years: A developmental study of sixty-one children by repeated tests. *Genet. Psychol. Monogr., 14,* 1–92.

Bell, J. E. 1948. *Projective techniques.* New York: Longmans, Green.

Bender, L. 1952. *Child psychiatric techniques.* Springfield, Ill.: Thomas.

Binet, A., and T. Simon. 1905. Méthodes nouvelles pour le diagnostic du niveau intellectuel des anormaux. *Année psychol., 11,* 191–244.

Blanton, M. G. 1917. The behavior of the human infant during the first thirty days of life. *Psychol. Rev., 24,* 456–483.

Bolton, T. L. 1892. The growth of memory in school children. *Amer. J. Psychol., 4,* 362–380.

Bradbury, D. E. 1937. The contribution of the child study movement in child psychology. *Psychol. Bull., 34,* 21–38.

Brunswik, E. 1947. *Systematic and representative design of psychological experiments with results in physical and social perception. Univ. Calif. Syllabus Ser.,* No. 304. Berkeley: University of California Press.

Bühler, C. 1937. Theoretische Grundprobleme der Kinderpsychologie. *Z. Psychol., 140,* 140–164.

Burgess, E. W. (Chairman.) 1934. *The adolescent in the family.* White House Conference on Child Health and Protection. New York: Appleton-Century.

Burks, B. S. 1928. The relative influence of nature and nurture upon mental development: A comparative study of foster parent-foster child resemblance and true parent-true child resemblance. *Yearb. Nat. Soc. Stud. Educ., 27* (I), 219–316.

Buros, O. K. (Ed.) 1949. *The third mental measurements yearbook.* New Brunswick: Rutgers University Press.

Canter, R. J., Jr. 1951. The use of extended control-group designs in human relations. *Psychol. Bull., 48,* 340–347.

Cattell, R. B. 1950. *Personality. A systematic theoretical and factual study.* New York: McGraw-Hill.

Centers, R. 1949. *Psychology of social classes.* Princeton: Princeton University Press.

Chapin, F. S. 1947. *Experimental designs in sociological research.* New York: Harper.

Chapman, D. W. 1935. The generalized problem of correct matchings. *Ann. Math. Statist., 6,* 85–95.

——. 1936. The significance of matching with unequal series. *Amer. J. Psychol., 48,* 167–169.

Clark, R. A., and C. McGuire. 1952. Sociographic analysis of sociometric valuations. *Child Develpm., 23,* 129–154.

Cochran, W. G., and M. Cox. 1950. *Experimental designs.* New York: Wiley.

Conn, J. H., and L. Kanner. 1947. Children's awareness of sex differences. *J. Child Psychiat., 1,* 3–57.

Conrad, H. S. 1933. *The California behavior inventory for nursery school children.* Berkeley: University of California Press.

Coombs, C. H. 1948a. Some hypotheses for the analysis of psychological variables. *Psychol. Rev., 44,* 167–74.

——. 1948b. A rationale for the measurement of traits in individuals. *Psychometrika, 13,* 59–68.

Courtis, S. A. 1950. *Maturation units and how to use them.* Detroit, Courtis.

Cronbach, L. J. 1949. *Essentials of psychological testing.* New York: Harper.

Darwin, C. 1877. A biographical sketch of an infant. *Mind, 2,* 285–294.

Davis, A., and J. Dollard. 1940. *Children of bondage.* Washington: American Council on Education.

Davis, A., and R. J. Havighurst. 1947. *Father of the man.* Boston: Houghton Mifflin.

Davis, F. B. 1952. Item analysis in relation to educational and psychological testing. *Psychol. Bull., 49,* 97–121.

Dearborn, W. F., and J. W. M. Rothney. 1941. *Predicting the child's development.* Cambridge: Sci-Art.

Dennis, W. 1949. Historical beginnings of child psychology. *Psychol. Bull., 46,* 224–235.

Despert, J. L. 1940. A method for the study of personality reactions in preschool age children by means of analysis of their play. *J. Psychol., 9,* 17–29.

Dockeray, F. C., and W. L. Valentine. 1939. A new isolation cabinet for infant research. *J. Exp. Psychol., 24,* 211–214.

Dollard, J., and O. H. Mowrer. 1947. A method of measuring tension in written documents. *J. Abnorm. Soc. Psychol., 42,* 1–32.

Edwards, A. L. 1950. *Experimental design in psychological research.* New York: Rinehart.

Elkin, F. 1947. Specialists interpret the case of Harold Holzer. *J. Abnorm. Soc. Psychol., 42,* 99–111.

Ellis, A. 1950. An introduction to the principles of scientific psychoanalysis. *Genet. Psychol. Monogr., 41,* 147–212.

Eysenck, H. J. 1952. The effects of psychotherapy: An evaluation. *J. Consult. Psychol., 16,* 319–324.

Fisher, R. A. 1936. *Statistical methods for research workers.* 6th ed. (1st ed., 1925.) Edinburgh: Oliver and Boyd.

——. 1937. *The design of experiments.* 2d ed. Edinburgh: Oliver and Boyd.

Flanagan, J. C. 1950. The critical requirements approach to educational objectives. *School and Society, 71,* 321–324.

Frank, L. K. 1939. Projective methods for the study of personality. *J. Psychol., 8,* 389–413.

Freeman, F. N., and C. D. Flory. 1937. Growth in intellectual ability as revealed by repeated tests. *Monogr. Soc. Res. Child Develpm.*, *2*, No. 2.

Freeman, F. N., K. J. Holzinger, and B. C. Mitchell. 1928. The influence of environment on the intelligence, school achievement, and conduct of foster children. *Yearb. Nat. Soc. Stud. Educ.*, *27* (I), 103–218.

Freud, A. 1925. *Einführung in die Technik der Kinderanalyse.* Leipzig, Vienna, and Zurich: Internationale psychoanalytische Verlag. (*Introduction to the technique of child analysis.* Trans. by L. P. Clark, 1928. *Nerv. Ment. Dis. Monogr. Ser.*, No. 48. Pp. 62.)

Fries, M. E. 1937. Play techniques in the analysis of young children. *Psychoanal. Rev.*, *24*, 233–245.

Gates, A. I., and G. A. Taylor. 1926. An experimental study of the nature of improvement resulting from practice in a motor function. *J. Educ. Psychol.*, *17*, 226–236.

Gates, G. S. 1923. An experimental study of the growth of social perception. *J. Educ. Psychol.*, *14*, 449–462.

Gesell, A. 1928. *Infancy and human growth.* New York: Macmillan.

Gesell, A., and H. Thompson. 1929. Learning and growth in identical infant twins: An experimental study by the method of co-twin control. *Genet. Psychol. Monogr.*, *6*, 1–124.

Gesell, A., and H. Thompson, assisted by C. S. Amatruda. 1934. *Infant behavior: Its genesis and growth.* New York: McGraw-Hill.

——. 1938. *The psychology of early growth.* New York: Macmillan.

Gilbert, J. A. 1894. Researches on the mental and physical development of school children. *Stud. Yale Psychol. Lab.*, *2*, 40–100.

Glueck, S., and E. T. Glueck. 1934. *One thousand juvenile delinquents.* Cambridge: Harvard University Press.

——. 1937. *Later criminal careers.* New York: Commonwealth Fund.

Goodenough, F. L. 1928a. Measuring behavior traits by means of repeated short samples. *J. Juv. Res.*, *12*, 230–235.

——. 1928b. A preliminary report on the effect of nursery school training upon the intelligence test scores for young children. *Yearb. Nat. Soc. Stud. Educ.*, *27* (I), 261–269.

——. 1935. The development of the reactive process from early childhood to maturity. *J. Exp. Psychol.*, *18*, 431–450.

——. 1949a. The appraisal of child personality. *Psychol. Rev.*, *56*, 123–131.

——. 1949b. *Mental testing.* New York: Rinehart.

Goodenough, F. L., and J. E. Anderson. 1931. *Experimental child study.* New York: Century.

Goodenough, F. L., and D. B. Harris. 1950. Studies in the psychology of children's drawings: II. 1928–1949. *Psychol. Bull.*, *5*, 369–433.

Grant, D. A. 1948. The Latin square principle in the design and analysis of psychological experiments. *Psychol. Bull.*, *45*, 427–442.

Grant, D. A. 1950. Statistical theory and research design. *Ann. Rev. Psychol.*, *1*, 277–296.

Greenwood, E. 1945. *Experimental sociology: A study in method.* New York: King's Crown Press.

Griffiths, W. 1952. *Behavior difficulties of children as perceived and judged by parents, teachers, and children themselves.* *Inst. Child Welfare Monogr. Ser.*, No. 25. Minneapolis: University of Minnesota Press. Pp. 116.

Greulich, W. W., H. G. Day, S. E. Lachman, J. B. Wolfe, and F. K. Shuttleworth. 1938. A handbook of methods for the study of adolescent children. *Monogr. Soc. Res. Child Develpm.*, *3*, No. 2. Pp. 406.

Guilford, J. P. 1936. *Psychometric methods.* New York: McGraw-Hill.

——. 1946. New standards for test evaluation. *Educ. & Psychol. Measm.*, *6*, 427–438.

——. 1950. *Statistics for students of psychology and education.* 2d ed. New York: McGraw-Hill.

Gulliksen, H. 1950. Intrinsic validity. *Amer. Psychol.*, *5*, 511–517.

——. 1950b. *Theory of Mental Tests.* New York: Wiley.

Haggerty, M. E. 1925. The incidence of undesirable behavior in public school children. *J. Educ. Res.*, *27*, 537–556.

Hall, G. S. 1891. The contents of children's minds. *Ped. Sem.*, *1*, 139–173.

Harris, M., D. G. Horvitz, and A. M. Wood. 1948. On the determination of sample size in designing experiments. *J. Amer. Statist. Assn.*, *43*, 391–402.

Hartshorne, H., and M. A. May. 1928. *Studies in deceit.* Book 1: *General methods and results;* Book 2: *Statistical methods and results.* New York: Macmillan.

Havighurst, R. J., and H. Taba. 1949. *Adolescent character and personality.* New York: Wiley.

Hertz, M. R. 1942. Rorschach: Twenty years after. *Psychol. Bull.*, *39*, 529–572.

Hilgard, J. R. 1933. The effect of early and delayed practice on memory and motor performances studied by the method of co-twin control. *Genet. Psychol. Monogr.*, *14*, 493–567.

Hollingshead, A. B. 1949. *Elmstown's youth: The impact of social classes on adolescents.* New York: Wiley.

Honzik, M. P. 1938. The constancy of mental test performance during the preschool period. *J. Genet. Psychol.*, *52*, 265–302.

Honzik, M. P., J. W. Macfarlane, and L. Allen. 1948. The stability of mental test performance between two and eighteen years. *J. Exp. Educ.*, *17*, 309–334.

Horowitz, R., and L. B. Murphy. 1938. Projective methods in the psychological study of children. *J. Exp. Educ.*, *7*, 133–140.

Horst, P. 1941. *The prediction of personal adjustment.* New York: Social Science Research Council.

Hubbard, F. W. 1942. Questionnaires, interviews, personality schedules. *Rev. Educ. Res.*, *12*, 534–541.

Hull, C. L., C. I. Hovland, R. T. Ross, M. Hall, D. T. Perkins, and F. B. Fitch. 1940. *Mathematico-de-*

ductive theory of rote learning. New Haven: Yale University Press.

Institute of Child Welfare. 1950. *The Minnesota scale for paternal occupations.* Minneapolis: University of Minnesota.

Jennings, H. H. 1948. *Sociometry in group relations.* Washington: American Council on Education.

Jensen, K. 1932. Differential reactions to taste and temperature stimuli in newborn infants. *Genet. Psychol. Monogr., 12,* 361–476.

Jersild, A. T. 1932. Training and growth in the development of children. *Child Develpm. Monogr.,* No. 10. Pp. 73.

Jersild, A. T., and M. F. Meigs. December, 1939. Direct observation as a research method. *Rev. Educ.,* 1–14.

Johnson, P. O. 1949. *Statistical methods in research.* New York: Prentice-Hall.

Jones, H. E. 1939. The adolescent growth study: I. Principles and methods. II. Procedures. *J. Consult. Psychol., 3,* 157–159; 177–180.

Jones, M. C., and B. S. Burks. 1936. Personality development in childhood. *Monogr. Soc. Res. Child Develpm., 1,* No. 4. Pp. vi + 205.

Kelley, T. L. 1928. *Crossroads in the mind of man: A study of differentiable mental abilities.* Stanford University, Calif.: Stanford University Press.

Kellogg, W. N., and L. A. Kellogg. 1933. *The ape and the child: A study of environmental influence upon early behavior.* New York: McGraw-Hill.

Kempthorne, O. 1952. *The design and analysis of experiments.* New York: Wiley.

Klein, M. 1932. *The psycho-analysis of children.* (Trans. by A. Strachey.) New York: Norton.

Koch, H. L. 1948. Methods of studying the behavior and development of young children. Pp. 624–663 in Andrews, T. G., *Methods of psychology.* New York: Wiley.

Koffka, K. 1924. *The growth of the mind: An introduction to child psychology.* (Trans. by R. M. Ogden.) New York: Harcourt, Brace. London: Kegan Paul.

Leahy, A. M. 1935. Nature, nurture and intelligence. *Genet. Psychol. Monogr., 17,* 236–308.

——. 1936. The measurement of urban home environment, *Inst. Child Welfare Monogr. Ser.,* No. 11. Minneapolis: University of Minnesota Press. Pp. 10.

Levene, H. 1949. On a matching problem arising in genetics. *Ann. Math. Statist., 20,* 91–94.

Lewin, K. 1935. *A dynamic theory of personality.* New York: McGraw-Hill.

——. 1936. *Principles of topological psychology.* New York: McGraw-Hill.

Lindquist, E. F. 1940. *Statistical analysis in educational research.* Boston: Houghton Mifflin.

Lindquist, E. F. (Ed.) 1950. *Educational measurement.* Washington, D. C.: American Council on Education.

Lippitt, R. 1940. An experimental study of the effect of democratic and authoritarian group atmospheres. *Univ. Iowa Stud. Child Welfare, 16,* No. 3, 45–195.

Macfarlane, J. W. 1938. Studies in child guidance: I. Methodology of data collection and organization. *Monogr. Soc. Res. Child Develpm., 3,* No. 6. Pp. 254.

Maller, J. B. 1933. Vital indices and their relation to psychological and social factors. *Human Biol., 5,* 94–121.

Markey, J. F. 1928. *The symbolic process.* New York: Harcourt, Brace.

Marquis, D. 1948. Research planning at the frontier of science. *Amer. Psychol., 3,* 430–438.

Marston, L. R. 1925. The emotions of young children. *Univ. Iowa Stud. Child Welfare, 3,* No. 3. Pp. 99.

Mattson, M. L. 1933. The relation between the complexity of the habit to be acquired and the form of the learning curve in young children. *Genet. Psychol. Monogr., 13,* 299–398.

McGraw, M. B. 1935. *Growth: A study of Johnny and Jimmy.* New York: Appleton-Century.

——. 1939. Later development of children specially trained during infancy: Johnny and Jimmy at school age. *Child Develpm., 10,* 1–19.

McNemar, Q. 1940. Sampling in psychological research. *Psychol. Bull., 37,* 331–365.

——. 1946. Opinion-attitude methodology. *Psychol. Bull., 43,* 289–374.

——. 1949. *Psychological statistics.* New York: Wiley.

Melton, A. W. 1936. The methodology of experimental studies of human learning and retention: I. The functions of a methodology and the available criteria for evaluating different experimental methods. *Psychol. Bull., 33,* 305–394.

Monroe, W. S. (Ed.). 1949. *Encyclopedia of educational research.* (Rev. ed.) New York: Macmillan.

Moreno, J. L. 1934. *Who shall survive? A new approach to the problem of human interrelations.* Washington: Nervous and Mental Disease Publishing Co.

Murphy, G., L. B. Murphy, and T. M. Newcomb. 1937. *Experimental social psychology.* (Rev. ed.) New York: Harper.

Murphy, L. B. 1937. *Social behavior and child personality.* New York: Columbia University Press.

National Society for the Study of Education. 1938. The scientific movement in education. *Yearb. Nat. Soc. Stud. Educ., 37* (II).

——. 1939. Child development and the curriculum. *Yearb. Nat. Soc. Stud. Educ., 38* (I).

——. 1940. Intelligence, its nature and nurture. *Yearb. Nat. Soc. Stud. Educ., 39* (I and II).

——. 1944. Adolescence. *Yearb. Nat. Soc. Stud. Educ., 43* (I).

——. 1946. The measurement of understanding. *Yearb. Nat. Soc. Stud. Educ., 45* (I).

——. 1947. Early childhood education. *Yearb. Nat. Soc. Stud. Educ., 46* (II).

——. 1950. The education of exceptional children. *Yearb. Nat. Soc. Stud. Educ., 49* (II).

Neilon, Patricia. 1948. Shirley's babies after fifteen years: A personality study. *J. Genet. Psychol., 73,* 175–186.

Olson, W. C. 1929. The measurement of nervous habits in normal children. *Inst. Child Welfare Monogr. Ser.*, No. 3. Minneapolis: University of Minnesota Press. Pp. 97.

——. 1949. *Child Development.* Boston: Heath.

Olson, W. C., and E. M. Cunningham. 1934. Timesampling techniques. *Child Develpm.*, *5*, 41–58.

Orlansky, H. 1949. Infant care and personality. *Psychol. Bull.*, *46*, 1–48.

Payne, S. L. 1951. *The art of asking questions.* Princeton: Princeton University Press.

Peatman, J. G. 1947. *Descriptive and sampling statistics.* New York: Harper.

Peters, C. C., and W. R. Van Voorhis. 1940. *Statistical procedures and their mathematical bases.* New York: McGraw-Hill.

Piaget, J. 1923. *Le langage et la pensée chez l'enfant.* Neuchâtel and Paris: Delachaux and Nestle. (*The language and thought of the child.* Trans. by M. Warden. 1936. New York: Harcourt, Brace.)

Preyer, W. 1882. *Die Seele des Kindes.* Leipzig: Fernau. (5th ed., 1900.)

——. 1888, 1889. *The mind of the child.* Pt. 1. *The senses and the will.* Pt. 2. The development of the intellect. (Trans. by H. W. Brown.) New York: Appleton.

Proctor, C. H., and C. P. Loomis. 1951. Analysis of sociometric data. *Research methods in social relations: Part Two, Selected techniques.* New York: Dryden Press.

Pyles, M. K., H. R. Stolz, and J. W. Macfarlane. 1935. The accuracy of mothers' reports on birth and developmental data. *Child develpm.*, *6*, 165–176.

Radke, M., *et al.* 1949. Social perceptions and attitudes of children. *Genet. Psychol. Monogr.*, *40*, 327–447.

Rust, M. M. 1931. *The effect of resistance on the test scores of children.* New York: Bureau of Publications, Teachers College.

Scupin, E., and G. Scupin. 1907. *Bubi's erste Kindheit.* Leipzig: Grieben.

Sears, R. R. 1942. *Survey of objective studies of psychoanalytic concepts.* New York: Social Science Research Council.

Shaw, C. R., *et al.* 1931. Delinquency areas: A study of the geographic distribution of school truants, juvenile delinquents, and adult offenders in Chicago. *Behav. Res. Monogr.* Chicago: University of Chicago Press. Pp. xxi + 214.

Sherman, M. 1927. The differentiation of emotional responses in infants. I. Judgments of emotional responses from motion picture views and from actual observation: II. The ability of observers to judge the emotional characteristics of the crying of infants and the voice of an adult. *J. Comp. Psychol.*, *7*, 265–284; 335–351.

Sherman, M., and T. R. Henry. 1933. *Hollow folk.* New York: Crowell.

Shinn, M. W. 1893–1899. Notes on the development of a child. *Univ. Calif. Publ.*, 1. Pp. 424.

——. 1900. *Biography of a baby.* Boston: Houghton Mifflin.

Shirley, M. M. 1931. The first two years, a study of twenty-five babies. Vol. I. Postural and locomotor development. *Inst. Child Welfare Monogr. Ser.*, No. 6. Minneapolis: University of Minnesota Press. Pp. vi + 227.

——. 1933a. The first two years, a study of twenty-five babies. Vol. II. Intellectual development. *Inst. Child Welfare Monogr. Ser.*, No. 7. Minneapolis: University of Minnesota Press. Pp. xvi + 513.

——. 1933b. The first two years, a study of twenty-five babies. Vol. III. Personality manifestations. *Inst. Child Welfare Monogr. Ser.*, No. 8. Minneapolis: University of Minnesota Press. Pp. xi + 228.

Shuttleworth, F. K. 1934. Standards of development in terms of increments. *Child Develpm.*, *5*, 89–91.

——. 1939. The physical and mental growth of girls and boys aged six to nineteen in relation to age at maximum growth. *Monogr. Soc. Res. Child Develpm.*, *4*, No. 3. Pp. vi + 291.

——. 1949a. *The adolescent period: A graphic atlas. Monogr. Soc. Res. Child Develpm.*, *49*, No. 1. Figs. 453.

——. 1949b. *The adolescent period: A pictorial atlas. Monogr. Soc. Res. Child Develpm.*, *49*, No. 2. Figs. 52.

Sims, V. M. 1928. *The measurement of socio-economic status.* Bloomington, Ill.: Public School Publishing Co.

Smith, M. E. 1952. A comparison of certain personality traits as rated in the same individuals in childhood and fifty years later. *Child Develpm.*, *23*, 159–180.

Solomon, R. L. 1949. An extension of control group design. *Psychol. Bull.*, *46*, 137–150.

Spearman, C. 1927. *The abilities of man: Their nature, and measurement.* New York and London: Macmillan.

Stendler, C. B. 1949. Children of Brasstown, *Univ. Ill. Bull.* Urbana: University of Illinois.

Stern, C., and W. Stern. 1907. Die Kindersprache: Eine psychologische und sprachtheoretische Untersuchung. *Monogr. seel. Entwick. Kindes*, Vol. 1. Leipzig: Barth. Pp. 394. (3d ed., rev. 1922. Pp. xii + 434.)

——. 1909. Erinnerung, Aussage und Lüge in der ersten Kindheit. *Monogr. seel. Entwick. Kindes*, Vol. 2. Leipzig: Barth. Pp. x + 160.

Strayer, L. C. 1930. Language and growth: The relative efficiency of early and deferred vocabulary training studied by the method of co-twin control. *Genet. Psychol. Monogr.*, *8*, 215–326.

Stuit, D. B. 1947. The effect of the nature of the criterion upon the validity of aptitude tests. *Educ. Psychol. & Measm.*, *7*, 671–676.

Symonds, P. M. 1931. *Diagnosing personality and conduct.* New York: Century.

Terman, L. M., *et al.* 1925. *Genetic studies of genius.* Vol. 1. *Mental and physical traits of a thousand gifted children.* Stanford University, Calif.: Stanford University Press.

Terman, L. M., and M. A. Merrill. 1937. *Measuring intelligence.* Boston: Houghton Mifflin.

Terman, L. M., M. Oden, *et al.* 1947. *Genetic studies of genius.* Vol. 4. *The gifted child grows up.* Stanford University, Calif.: Stanford University Press.

Thomas, D. S., *et al.* 1929. Some new techniques for studying social behavior. *Child Develpm. Monogr.,* No. 1. Pp. 213.

Thomas, W. I., and D. S. Thomas. 1928. *The child in America.* New York: Knopf. Pp. 928.

Thompson, G. G. 1952. *Child psychology. Growth trends in psychological adjustment.* Boston: Houghton Mifflin.

Thomson, G. H. 1939. *The factorial analysis of human ability.* Boston: Houghton Mifflin.

Thorndike, E. L. 1904. *An introduction to the theory of mental and social measurements.* New York: Teachers College, Columbia University.

——. 1913. *Educational psychology.* Vol. 1. *The original nature of man.* New York: Teachers College, Columbia University.

——. 1913. *Educational psychology.* Vol. 2. *The learning process.* New York: Teachers College, Columbia University.

——. 1914. *Educational psychology.* Vol. 3. *Mental work and fatigue and individual differences.* New York: Teachers College, Columbia University.

Thorndike, R. L. 1942. Regression fallacies in the matched group experiment. *Psychometrika,* 7, 85–102.

——. 1949. *Personnel selection: test and measurement techniques.* New York: Wiley.

Thurstone, L. L. 1935. *The vectors of mind.* Chicago: University of Chicago Press.

——. 1947. *Multiple factor analysis.* Chicago: University of Chicago Press.

Tiedemann, D. 1787. *Beobachtungen über die Entwickelung der Seelenfähigkeiten bei Kindern.* (New ed., ed. by C. Ufer. 1897.) Altenburg: Bonde.

Tryon, C. M. 1939. Evaluation of adolescent personality by adolescents. *Monogr. Soc. Res. Child Develpm., 4,* No. 4.

Vernon, P. 1950. *The structure of human abilities.* New York: Wiley.

Vernon, P. E. 1936a. The evaluation of the matching method. *J. Educ. Psychol., 27,* 1–17.

——. 1936b. The matching method applied to investigation of personality. *Psychol. Bull., 33,* 149–177.

Wallen, R. 1942. Ego-involvement as a determinant of selective forgetting. *J. Abnorm. Soc. Psychol., 37,* 20–29.

Warner, W. L., M. Meeker, and K. Eells. 1949. *Social class in America: A manual of procedure for the measurement of social status.* Chicago: Science Research Associates.

Watson, J. B. 1919. *Psychology from the standpoint of a behaviorist.* New York: Lippincott.

Weiss, L. A. 1933. Rating scales: With special reference to the field of child development. *Psychol. Bull., 30,* 185–208.

Whipple, G. M. 1924. *Manual of mental and physical tests.* Vol. 1. *Simple processes.* Vol. 2. *Complex processes.* Baltimore: Warwick and York.

White, R. K. 1947. Black boy: A value analysis. *J. Abnorm. Soc. Psychol., 42,* 440–461.

Wiener, N. 1948. *Cybernetics, or control and communication in the animal and the machine.* New York: Wiley.

Wolfle, D., R. Likert, D. G. Marquis, and R. R. Sears. 1949. Standards for appraising psychological research. *Amer. Psychol., 4,* 320–328.

Wood, B. D., and F. N. Freeman. 1932. *An experimental study of the educational influences of the typewriter in the elementary school classroom.* New York: Macmillan.

Woolley, H. T. 1925. Agnes: A dominant personality in the making. *Ped. Sem., 32,* 569–598.

——. 1926. Peter: The beginnings of a juvenile court problem. *Ped. Sem., 33,* 9–29.

Yule, G. U., and M. G. Kendall. 1937. *An introduction to the theory of statistics.* (11th ed.) London: Griffin.

Zubin, J. 1933. The chance element in matching. *J. Educ. Psychol., 24,* 674–681.

CHAPTER 2

THE ONSET AND EARLY DEVELOPMENT OF BEHAVIOR [1]

LEONARD CARMICHAEL

Yes,—the history of a man for the nine months preceding his birth, would, probably, be far more interesting, and contain events of greater moment, than all the three-score and ten years that follow it.
—COLERIDGE (1885, p. 301)

The Importance for Psychology of an Understanding of the Early Development of Behavior Patterns

In any complete discussion of child, developmental, or genetic psychology two questions must be asked: When does behavior begin? How does behavior develop during the early weeks, months, and years of life? These two questions may be phrased as one: What is the origin and what is the embryology and early developmental sequence of the behavior patterns which are significant in an understanding of human mental life?

This chapter is written in an effort to deal with these questions. The material brought together here is concerned not only with facts about early human development but also with relevant facts about the development of infrahuman animals. Much more is known in certain respects concerning the early development of life in the animals below man than in man himself, and much of this information has direct bearing upon an understanding of human development.

A knowledge of behavior in prenatal life throws light upon many traditional psy-

chological problems. For example, some of the old questions concerning the relative importance of heredity and environment in the determination of adult human mental life are answered by this study. The contest between empiristic and nativistic theories of perception, the question of whether development is continuous or saltatory, the problem of whether behavior is first general and later specific or first specific and later general, and even the question of the fundamental nature of human learning itself are all illuminated by the facts disclosed in a study of prenatal behavior.

Although reference will be made to learning in this chapter, it is not with learning but with the growth or maturation of behavior that the chapter deals. Howells (1945) has said: " 'Maturation' is simply development in which commonly observed differences between individuals are correlated with previous differences in the inner organism rather than in the environment." Minkowski (1947–1948), one of the great students of the early development of behavior, has considered the problem of the beginning of mental development in the fetus. Here he discusses the relationship between the arousal of the fetal senses and so-called mental development.

In the investigation of the early growth of behavior, it is important to remember that at every stage the scientist is describing some reaction of an organism then living in an environment. At every level of development one must think of the organ-

[1] This chapter is a revision of a chapter in this same field previously published (Carmichael, 1933 and 1946).

ism as maintaining itself in its present environment. This last statement sounds like a truism. Actually, however, a great many errors have been made in the study of the early development of behavior by assuming that later performance is somehow implicit or hidden in earlier types of response. This has been called classically "the error of potentiality" (Lange, 1925, pp. 198–200). For example, one who wishes to describe the linguistic performance of a 5-year-old child must describe that performance as it appears at 5. It is not possible to infer the full character of that performance in any given individual from any study of linguistic performance, for example, in the first year of life. The 5-year-old performance is not implicit in the 2-year-old performance. The environment of the third and fourth years is all-important in determining, for example, whether the child at 5 will speak Spanish or English.

The error of potentiality may be avoided quite simply. It is necessary only to remember that the scientist who is dealing with development must study a series of temporally separated stages of growth. These are his facts. The tendencies or "growth processes" which give meaning to the relationship of these various stages are the scientific inferences that he draws. The question thus becomes not: What adult trait is mysteriously hidden in this or that early behavior pattern? but rather: What is the nature of the many developmental stages which actually were preliminary to the particular adult characteristic which is being studied? In the investigation of the prenatal growth of response, this distinction becomes especially important. The older workers in this field almost always wrote on the basis of a preconceived theory. One such view was the "doctrine of recapitulation." This theory saw in every action of the growing individual a complete parallelism with the action in adult life of an evolutionary ancestor of the individual being studied. This view is now discredited as a universal theory, and so are many other alleged explanations of behavior.

In this chapter an effort is made to deal with growth as the histologist deals with the wax reconstruction of the structure which he is studying. This wax-reconstruction method in microscopical anatomy involves the cutting, mounting, and staining of a series of very thin sections of tissue, and then by appropriate techniques the cutting-out of particular details from each one of these sections in layers of wax of proportional thickness. As these cut-out wax sections are put together, a magnified and truly three-dimensional object emerges. In the dynamic field of behavior a similar procedure is often valuable. Thus behavior as a series of temporal stages can be fully described, and then when these stages are viewed in relation to time a real reconstruction of the growth of behavior may be made. Whenever possible in this chapter, behavioral development will be considered in this way.

One reservation must be made here. In later sections of this chapter it will be seen that structures sometimes mature before a normal environment calls them into function. This may be called the law or principle of *anticipatory morphological maturation.*

When Does Behavior Begin?

Many of the older writers on child psychology, such as Compayré (1896, p. 44), allege that the study of child psychology begins at birth. Throughout the history of biological science, however, the incompleteness of this answer has been obvious to certain writers. Today all agree that we must move into the prenatal period in order to determine what Gesell (1928, pp. 303–306; 1929a, p. 631) has called the "ontogenetic zero." The term *ontogenetic* as used here means development in the individual as contrasted with *phylogenetic* or development in the race, or evolutionary series, of the human and prehuman ancestors of man. Ordinarily, in biology, ontogenetic development is taken as beginning at the time of individual fertilization. Of course, in order that fertilization may take place there is antecedent life in both the ovum and the sperm (at least always in the ovum) before fertilization. Scientifically we must still accept the dictum, "All life comes from previous life." The new individual as such, then, may best be considered as beginning from the processes which are initiated at fertilization.

As just suggested, it is impossible to say that fertilization is in all senses the beginning of a new individual, because the reproductive cells trace themselves back through countless generations. Similarly, it is difficult to distinguish between the dynamic processes of structural development and the processes of the organism which may be called true behavior. Such distinctions can be made only by the use of commonly agreed-upon definitions. Ordinarily the beginning of behavior, and hence the starting point of behavioral psychology, is placed at the point where true receptor-initiated neuromuscular activity begins. It is assumed that this point is the one at which activities of the organism take place which involve sense organs and nervous system as well as muscles. Some writers hold that behavior, instead of beginning at the time of the first sensory-neuromuscular response, really *emerges* at this time. The word "emergence" is used by many writers on developmental psychology. Sometimes this word is given an almost mystical definition. When it is used in this chapter its meaning will be a simple one. Here the word emergence will be used to describe a relationship between events

antecedent in time and a new and different event which is itself also described. For a critique of the definition of the word emergence, see Lovejoy (1926).

It is easy to deal with the emergent or novel creation of behavior in the abstract, but, when one turns to specific experimental studies of this emergence, the difficulty of the problem becomes clearer. Carmichael has studied in some detail, as will be noted below, the very first responses of many organisms. For example, let us take the guinea pig fetus. Logically, it is clear that there must be a time in growth when stimulation of this organism's receptors will not be effective. Then, at an immediately subsequent time, say 1 second later, when such stimulation is given, behavior results. At time A this response is not possible, but after added growth—that is, at subsequent time B—it is possible. The possibility of this first response is considered as dependent upon elaborate changes which include growth and which are taking place in the organism under consideration. Let us trace these changes back in the history of the individual. The processes basic to behavior involve the development of the germ cells in the parents and in the parents' parents. The growth and maturation of the germ cells in the parents are necessary, as are the so-called reduction divisions of the nuclear substance of the germ cells, fertilization, cell division, cell differentiation, cell migration, organ formation, and a whole series of other dynamic changes.

As a result of all this growth, a structure capable of making this first behavioral reaction *emerges*. Without these countless antecedent cellular and subcellular processes, the first external response of an appendage or of the trunk of the living organism could not occur. These processes, moreover, must not be thought of as a simple unfolding of preformed organs This old "preformism view" is no longer held. Rather, at each stage the living organism is now considered to be maintaining itself in a dynamic relationship with the energies and the foodstuffs of its environment. This is not to say that the organism is being formed wholly by its environment, as the other old view, that of "epigenesis," held. Indeed, today it is clear that inheritance and environment always cooperate in development. The old quarrel between preformism and epigenesis is now seen to have been sometimes a battle of words engaged in before the relevant facts were known.

The processes basic to the reproduction of living animals are brought about in a number of different ways. In some animals the egg, after fertilization, continues to develop in protective coverings still within the maternal body. In other animals the egg leaves the body and continues development outside. In many animals the growth of all the fundamental organ systems is complete before hatching or birth. This condition may be considered as characteristic of many vertebrates, some worms, and certain arthropods. In the coelenterates, insects, and vertebrate amphibians, varying stages of growth after the new organism emerges from the egg are the rule. Common usage seems to have established the fact that the first stage of the development of any organism is to be described as *germinal*, the next stage as *embryonic*, and the latest stage preliminary to birth as *fetal*. The word *larval* is used to characterize independent, living, but organically immature organisms.

In describing larval development, two classes of such growth, direct and indirect, have been set up. In the first of these, development is linear—that is, each developmental stage produces an organism which is in most respects more like the adult than was the organism in its preceding stage. In the case of indirect larval development, however, organs often of a high order of complexity are produced which are later destroyed before maturity is reached. The term *metamorphosis* is applied to development of this latter sort. The terms *larval* and *pupal* are applied to describe stages in indirect development. Too little is known concerning the effect of environmental modification during the larval stage upon adult animals. This is a field in which more experimental investigation is almost certain to be done. For example, what influence will certain experimentally induced forms of activity in the wormlike larva have upon the fully developed *imago*, such as an adult butterfly? It is interesting in this connection to notice that among the older writers even on so-called inherited human instinct many examples were taken from types which pass through larval stages. (Cf. Bergson, 1911, pp. 172–176, and McDougall, 1923, pp. 69–71.)

The degree of maturity reached before the new organism begins an independent existence varies markedly from type to type. In so-called *oviparous* species, such as most fish and certain amphibians, eggs are laid as single cells and are subsequently fertilized after they have left the mother's body. In *viviparous* animals, such as certain fish and most mammals, on the other hand, all the early developmental stages are normally passed within the mother's body. Between these two extremes are the so-called *ovoviviparous* organisms, in which fertilization takes place before the egg is laid. Birds are good examples of this type. It is interesting to note that the so-called evolutionary level does not give a clear indication of the sort of reproduction which may be expected of an animal. The common dogfish bears its young inside the body until they are developed so that they may have an independent existence. On the other hand, the monotremes among the primitive mammals lay eggs.

There are, moreover, certain forms in which favorable or unfavorable environmental conditions seem to determine the fact of the hatching of eggs inside or outside the mother's body (Hertwig, 1912, p. 151).

Among the mammals it is also interesting to note that there is a great diversity in the degree of development that has been reached at the time of normal birth. Thus, as will be noted in more detail below, the young of the opossum are born in many respects as relatively early embryos, as contrasted with the newborn guinea pig, in which almost full-grown characteristics are observed (Hartman, 1920; Avery, 1928, pp. 258–265). This fact should be kept in mind at all times as these pages are read. To put this in another way, it may be said that the behavioral age or even the "mental age" of different species of mammals is very different at the time of birth.

Corner (1944) in his admirable book, *Ourselves Unborn: An Embryologist's Essay on Man,* presents a clear description of the anatomical development of man, taking into account its aberrations. He says: ". . . we begin our lives in continuance of a long past and in progression toward an unseen goal; that life is precarious from the first day to the last. . . ."

The Development of Behavior in the Lower Vertebrates

There are stages in the morphological development of the fish, amphibian, reptile, bird, infrahuman mammal, and man which are so similar as to make the study of one form important for a complete understanding of the development of other forms. This fact has long been recognized in anatomical embryology. By analogy, the same may be held to be true of behavior. Care must be taken, however, not to pretend to see homologies of behavior until by direct observation such homologies can

be shown to exist. Figure 1 gives a somewhat too idealized picture of some of these relationships. For example, in certain forms nourishment during the entire fetal period is provided by the yolk of the egg in which the developing organism originated. This means that behavior in connection with alimentation is less important in such types than in others in which at an early developmental stage the ingestion of food is necessary. In spite of this difficulty, the study of fish and amphibians has provided much information of importance to one who would understand the gradual development of behavior. Swenson (1928a) has courageously attempted to set up seven fundamental acts of behavior as basic to the responses of lower vertebrates, mammals, and even man. These forms of behavior are progression, respiration, ingestion, expression, excretion, phonation, and reproduction. The fact that some of these processes can be studied in the amphibian larva as well as in the human infant makes the complete understanding of the simple organism especially important. Coghill (1929c, pp. 1004–1009) and others (Windle and Griffin, 1931, pp. 180–184) have developed this point of view in various papers.

The best history of the development of the study of vertebrate embryos is given by the scientist who did so much for the study of behavior that he may be considered the founder of the experimental study of early behavior. This man is William Preyer, late professor of physiology at Jena. His book, *Specielle Physiologie des Embryo. Untersuchungen über die Lebenserscheinungen vor der Geburt,* published in 1885, may be taken as the starting point for all subsequent investigation in this field. Part of this fundamental work has been translated by Coghill and Legner (1937).

In this basic work Preyer summarizes and reviews a good many observations made on the early movements of fish embryos. Some of these studies were based on the observations of fish embryos growing after definitely dated periods of ferti-

tion. In general, on the day following the first trunk movement the first head movement is noted. Then, in a few days, ener-

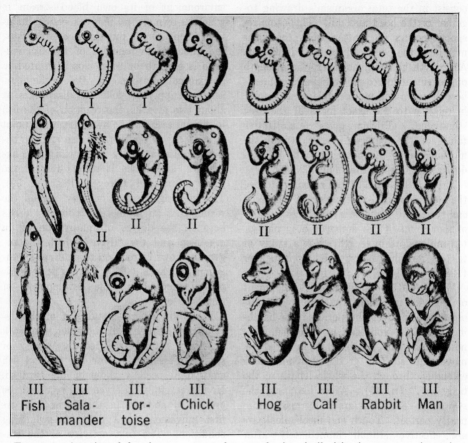

III Fish   III Sala-mander   III Tor-toise   III Chick   III Hog   III Calf   III Rabbit   III Man

FIGURE 1. A series of drawings constructed to emphasize similarities in structure in various embryos at three comparable and progressive stages of development (marked I, II, and III). (From *Darwin, and After Darwin.* Vol. I. *The Darwinian Theory,* by G. J. Romanes. Chicago: Open Court, 1896, 152–153. By permission of the publisher.) This old diagram is presented here as a schematic device only. Research since it was drawn has made some alteration in the relationships demonstrated here.

lization. Slow rotary movements characterize the early behavior of many fish embryos. Fillipi is quoted by Preyer as finding in *Alosa finta* such movements soon after fertilization. In a species of trout Preyer found movement of trunk at a definite number of days subsequent to fertiliza-

getic movements of the whole tiny fish body may be observed. After the liberation of such organisms from their egg coverings, it is found that pressure stimulation on the body surface is followed by responses involving apparently the entire musculature of the trunk. Preyer points out that these movements involve fully developed reflexes (p. 397). He makes this conclusion because the movements described consist in the total organism's drawing together of the head and tail. This same response occurs no matter what the locus may be of the point of pressure stimulation. As growth goes on, however, the strength of movement increases, and the movements become more and more regular and specific in relation to the exact locus of the area stimulated. Preyer gives quantitative tables of the increase in rapidity of the movements of the heart and the gills as development progresses (pp. 398–399).

Paton (1907, 1911) more recently studied the development of behavior in selachian embryos. He demonstrated the possibility of movement in fish embryos only nine or ten millimeters in length. For a study of teleost morphogenesis, see Oppenheimer (1934).

White (1915) describes the development of behavior in brook trout embryos. His observations cover the period from hatching until the yolk sac is absorbed. He notes that "the hatching is initiated by movements starting at the head and later extending through the whole length of the body . . ." (p. 46). After hatching, the swimming reaction is gradually made more nearly perfect. Touch and mechanical jars are effective stimuli immediately after hatching, and, interestingly enough, at this time the head is found to be the region least sensitive to pressure stimuli. Rheotropism, or response to water flow in currents, negative phototaxis, or the avoidance of light, and photokinetic responses, or responses initiated but not necessarily directed by light, are also present at this time. Excess carbon dioxide in the water in which fish are studied is activating up to a point, and then depressing on bodily functions. The dependence of the fish upon the chemical make-up of its external watery environment presents many analogies with the dependence of the higher animal upon the chemical make-up of the liquid internal environment of its own blood stream in which its own central nervous system maintains itself. Or, to put this in another way, the internal environment of the fish embryo is seen to be most closely related to its external environment. Before the nourishment-supplying yolk sac disappears at about two months, the reaction of the fish to stimuli seems to be away from the point of contact. After this, the fish embryo becomes quite suddenly exploratory and aggressive, and hence it moves toward the point stimulated (Preyer, 1885, p. 59). This striking observation may remind the reader that an intimate relationship exists between the degree of maturation of an organism and the "drive" which the organism shows in relation to external stimulation. Nicholas (1927) has applied experimental methods to the development of *Fundulus* embryos.

From the general standpoint of the development of behavior, however, the work of Tracy (1926) is especially worthy of study. This investigator has studied fish embryos, especially those of the toadfish. He has carefully observed and recorded the growth of activity in this form from its first movement to a final free-swimming condition. The first activity of the embryo in this form as in so many others is what may be termed in Parker's sense the preneural and "independent effector" action of the heart (Parker, 1919, pp. 53–63). The first behavioral movement of the fish is the bending of the trunk in the anterior region. At times this movement is to the right, at times to the left. It is probable that the afferent proprioceptor or muscle-sense system is not functional at first. At an early point a spontaneous flutter movement develops. This movement probably is important in freeing the organism from the remaining egg membranes. In general, toadfish larvae when hatched lie at the bottom of the containing vessel in a quiescent state. Then suddenly they move. On the basis of careful study, Tracy concludes that this "spontaneous" behavior is related to cumulative changes in the blood of the organism such that at a certain point the central nervous system is directly stimu- pose as a law is certainly far from regular in this organism, as will be seen in Figure 2. Receptors for light, vibration, chemicals, and body movement (proprioceptors) soon become effective. The behavior initiated by stimulation of these receptors involves jaw movements, trunk movements, and, interestingly enough, rotational and postrotational nystagmus of the eyes.

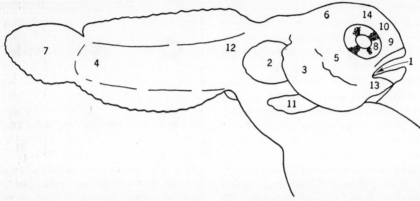

FIGURE 2. Diagram of toadfish larva to show by numbered areas the approximate temporal order of development of tactile reactions from various regions. (From "The Development of Motility and Behavior Reactions in the Toadfish [*Opsanus tau*]," by H. C. Tracy. *Journal of Comparative Neurology*, 1926, *40, 295*. By permission of the Wistar Institute, publisher.) It will be noted that, with some exceptions, this course of development of sensitivity is cephalocaudal, that is, from the head to the tail.

lated or the threshold of the central nervous system is so altered that previously inoperative sensory impulses break over into motor outlets. Thus he concludes that spontaneous movements are the result of metabolites and oxygen deficiency in the blood stream (p. 345). Soon after the onset of such responses, the organism becomes very sensitive to exteroceptive stimuli. The mucous membrane area about the mouth is the first to be sensitized. In general, the spread of sensitivity is from this point toward the tail or possibly to the region that has just become most active. The "cephalocaudal progression" of sensory and motor development which some writers pro- Tracy draws some fundamental conclusions from these studies. He holds that if external conditions could be kept constant the activities of the organism would be determined by its own life processes or metabolism. This would mean that all behavior would be rhythmic, like that of an excised muscle in a balanced salt solution (p. 345). At a later point we shall note that T. G. Brown (1915) holds that early mammalian reflexes may be of this nature. In conclusion, Tracy says: "From the beginning, and more or less continuously during its whole existence, the animal is driven through its environment as a result of stimuli which arise periodically in connection with its metabolic processes" (p. 345). The nature of later behavior may be thought of, he further suggests, as dependent upon neural development and the interference in the intrinsic rhythms of behavior brought about by the stimulation of the special exteroceptors of the organism by external energies. The basic relevance of this observation even for adult human behavior has been considered elsewhere (Carmichael, 1947).

We now turn to the study of the development of behavior in amphibians. Swammerdam, in his *Bibel der Natur* (1752), written before 1685, makes observations on the behavior of frog embryos five days after fertilization and at other periods (Preyer, 1885, p. 392; Swammerdam, edited, 1907). Swammerdam has also recorded observations concerning the development of behavior in snails and other invertebrates. Leeuwenhoek (1697, p. 792) made observations in this same field. Among other early students of behavior in invertebrates may be mentioned Stiebel (1815), Grant (1827), and Home (1827). Bischoff (1842) published a confirmation of the description of movements previously observed by Swammerdam in amphibians. He added a notation of the fact that the rate of these movements is a function of the temperature of the water in which the animals are maintaining themselves. Preyer (1885, pp. 392 ff.) reviewed all this work as well as that of Perschir and Cramer on the amphibian embryo. Preyer himself made elaborate observations on the early movements of frog and salamander embryos. He noted that stimulating the embryo led first to a slight twitch in the anterior portion of the organism. Following this movement in time he noted that the body was bent so as to bring the head and tail nearer together. Reference to Preyer's original drawings, reproduced as Figure 3, as well as to the text of his book,

shows that he considered these C or reverse C movements very important. It is also clear from his drawings that he observed the fundamental S or sigmoid form of reaction. The importance of this S movement in freeing the organism from the egg is pointed out. That this movement is also related to the activity of swimming is an important consideration (pp. 393–394).

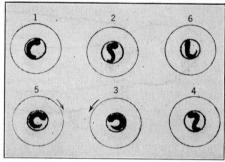

FIGURE 3. Diagram of various positions of frog embryos (*Rana temporaria*) just before emergence from the egg. Note especially the C and S reactions. (From *Specielle Physiologie des Embryo. Untersuchungen über die Lebenserscheinungen vor der Geburt*, by W. Preyer. Leipzig: Grieben, 1885.)

Other students have worked on the relationship between temperature and embryonic movements in larval amphibians (Preyer, 1885, p. 395). Many others have used this convenient laboratory type in work in experimental embryology. Much of this experimental embryology has direct bearing on the problems of this chapter. (See Detwiler, 1920, 1921, 1922, 1923a, 1923b, and the bibliographies given by him.)

If Preyer may be called the father of the scientific study of the development of behavior, the late G. E. Coghill (see references in the bibliography) must always be remembered as the investigator who first charted the relationship between the detailed growth of the nervous system and the consequent alterations which occur in behavior. This investigator is notable also because of the completeness of his work on the salamander *Amblystoma*, as well as on other types. The life of Coghill with his complete bibliography by C. J. Herrick (1949) ably discusses the fundamental contributions of this original scientist to the study of behavior. Coghill's first paper in this field was written in 1902, and from that time until his death in 1941 he published a most important series of papers on the development of behavior in relation to the anatomy of structure. In the course of his many papers, Coghill reported detailed studies of the neural mechanism underlying the first movement and the later sequences of movements as they develop in *Amblystoma*. The first response results from the contraction of muscles just behind the head. As the embryo advances in age, this contraction becomes, after a period of gradual transition lasting for about 36 hours, one which involves the whole animal. The result of this reaction, as pointed out by Coghill, is that the organism assumes a position which may be described as that of a tight coil. This C or exaggerated C coil is sometimes oriented to the right and sometimes to the left. It may reverse instantly. At this point in development, all behavioral activities are initiated in the head region and progress toward the tail.

In commenting upon this sequence, Coghill (1929a) notes that at this time: "Nothing really new has yet been introduced into the behaviour pattern of the animal since its first movement was performed, and the coil reaction gives the animal no locomotor power. Nevertheless the coil has in it the primary locomotor factor: cephalocaudal progression of muscular contraction" (p. 6). The transition from this behavioral level to the S reaction is amazingly simple. One C contraction begins, for example, on the left, but before it has reached the tail another contraction to the right begins.

The components of this movement may be made clearer by consulting Figure 4. As this reaction gains speed, its performance exerts pressure upon the water and thus drives the organism forward. Thus the S reaction becomes the basis of swimming or aquatic locomotion. This fundamental pattern of behavior may well be a peculiarly significant stage in many other types of growing organisms. This same stage is seen clearly in the swimming of the lower vertebrates. It is somewhat obscured in the four-legged mammals and still more obscured in man, but that this S reaction plays its part in the growth of behavior in these higher organisms seems to be an established fact. Five stages in the development of this basic swimming activity have been made out by Coghill (1929a, p. 9). They may be presented as follows: (1) the nonmotile stage, in which direct muscle stimulation by mechanical or electrical means leads to muscular contraction and hence to externally observable response; (2) the early C flexure stage, in which light touch on the skin of any portion of the body leads to a response; (3) the tight-coil stage, in which the contractions noted in stage 2 become more pronounced and the extent of the contraction greater; (4) the S reaction, which is characterized by a reversal of flexure before the previous flexure has been completely executed as a coil, thus leading to the sinuous behavior of the total organism; (5) the speeding-up of the S reaction so as to produce the typical swimming movement of the amphibian larva.

Youngstrom (1937) in studies upon *Anura* (frogs, toads, etc.) concludes that the Coghillian sequence of developing behavior applies with only slight variations to the *Anura* studied. Wang and Lu (1940, 1941), too, have shown that the stages through which the frog passes are similar to those described by Coghill. These investigators have also shown that severance of the spinal cord arrests the development of swimming at about Coghill's stage 4.

As already noted, the salamander has, besides aquatic locomotion, other significant behavior systems. Of these, walking or terrestrial locomotion and feeding require special consideration. The *Amblys-*

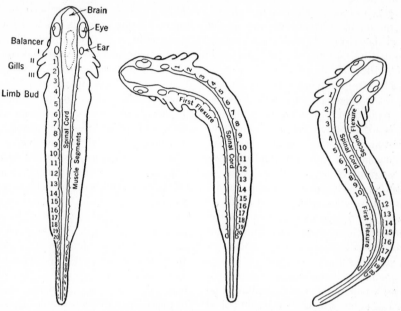

FIGURE 4. Three diagrams of *Amblystoma*. (From *Anatomy and the Problem of Behaviour*, by G. E. Coghill. Cambridge: University Press. New York: Macmillan, 1929, 7–8. By permission of The Macmillan Company.) The diagram at the left shows the organism in an early swimming stage but without indication of muscle contraction. The diagram in the middle illustrates the beginning of a swimming movement as a first flexure by contraction of a number of anterior muscle segments. The diagram on the right illustrates the swimming movement in which the first flexure has passed tailward and the second flexure is beginning in the anterior region.

Coghill studied in great detail the neural structure characteristic of the salamander in each of the five stages noted above. On the basis of these investigations he shows how the known structure of the nervous system may make possible the behavior which has previously been described. It is important to recognize that for the most part Coghill (1929a, p. 13) believed that in young organisms movement is typically away from the point of stimulation.

toma swims before its anatomical development has progressed to the point where it has true limbs. Structurally and functionally the forelimbs are in advance of the developing hindlimbs. In this organism, however, at first both sets of limbs, when they appear, move only in relation to the larger trunk movements described above as those of swimming. Coghill shows why this must be so because of the developing nervous system. Gradually, however, independence of limb action or *individuation* of limb behavior over the dominance of the trunk movements begins (1930e, p. 638). First the forelimbs gain a certain autonomy, and later the hindlimbs also. "It is obvious, therefore," observes Coghill (1929a), "that the first limb movement is an integral part of the total reaction of the animal, and that it is only later that the limb acquires an individuality of its own in behaviour" (p. 19). He then suggests that the forelimb itself may be considered to possess a pattern of development which is comparable to that of the total organism. At first, if movement occurs at all, the whole limb moves. Later, elbow flexion and wrist and digit movement in turn gain independence of the total member. It is important to recognize that during this developmental sequence the time relations of the swimming reaction may be considered as in a way superimposed upon limb activity. Thus one may, if he wishes to, think of the alternate movements of walking in a four-legged organism as a growth out of the basic trunk movements of swimming previously described. Coghill (1929a), indeed, says: "Movement of the trunk in walking is nothing more nor less than the swimming movement with greatly reduced speed" (p. 25). Gradually the sinuous movement of the trunk is reduced as walking becomes more independent, and eventually the characteristic land locomotion of the salamander appears.

The development of the feeding reaction in this same organism has been similarly studied by Coghill (1929a). This response begins with a movement of the trunk; then comes a reaction which involves a sudden lunge of the whole organism; after this there is a gradual correlation between this lunge movement and the activity of the jaws and the muscles of the esophagus. In summarizing this whole development, Coghill (1929a) says: "Behaviour develops from the beginning through the progressive expansion of a perfectly integrated total pattern and the individuation within it of partial patterns which acquire various degrees of discreteness" (p. 38). It should also be noted that as this development continues new senses become important in relation to behavior. Coghill (1930a) believes that "the individual acts on its environment before it reacts to its environment" (p. 345). In considering these beautifully elaborated generalizations of Coghill's, it is important to remember that a different sequence in the development of behavior may well characterize the growth of a mammal and a salamander. One should not forget also that even Coghill's own neurological studies point to specific relationships between the locus of stimulation and the muscles that are caused to respond (1929a, p. 12). In comparing the salamander and the guinea pig, for example, it may be noted that the limbs are quite fully formed before the first behavioral response or reflex takes place in the guinea pig, but in the salamander behavior begins before there is any real morphological forelimb at all.

In a series of papers Carmichael has presented the results of his studies of the development of behavior in *Amblystoma* and the frog under conditions such that experimental groups of animals were raised under unusual environmental circumstances (Carmichael, 1926a, 1927, 1928, 1929). A technique devised by Randolph (1900) and developed by Harrison (1904) was employed. For a consideration of the effect of the anesthetic chloretone on the organism in question, a paper by Matthews and Detwiler (1926) should be consulted. At a period before motility had begun, a large number of developing *Amblystoma* were divided into two groups. The first of these groups was used as a control. The second was used as an experimental group. The experimental group was placed in water containing the anesthetic—a solution of chloretone. The control group was allowed to develop normally in water. Later, at a developmental point previously described by Herrick and Coghill (1915), vigorous responses began in the control group. At this time the experimental group showed morphological development but otherwise remained absolutely inert because of the action of the anesthetic. However, in a short time—often only a minute or two—after the drugged embryos were placed in fresh water, they began to swim well. "In fact, a number of the eighteen *Amblystoma* embryos swam so well in less than one half hour after they had shown the first sign of movement that they could with difficulty, if at all, be distinguished from the members of the control group who had been free swimmers for five days" (Carmichael, 1926a, p. 55).

In later experiments efforts were made to control stimulation in other ways (Carmichael, 1928). As a result of these investigations, the conclusion is drawn that the development of the neural and other mechanisms upon which behavior depends does take place in these organisms whether or not they are as individuals responding to external stimulation. This seems to have a negative implication concerning an extreme interpretation of Child's (1921) environmentalist theory of the causation of growth in the nervous system. Nothing in these experiments is to be taken, however, as invalidating the idea that the growth of the nervous system itself involves activity. Studies such as those of Burr (1932) and P. Weiss (1926, 1939) on this same organism emphasize the dynamic character of such growth processes. For a general consideration of the relationship between neural growth and the development of behavior see Hooker (1950).

Nicholas and a number of collaborators have studied the development of *Amblystoma*, especially in regard to the development of motility in relation to the nervous system. Some of their results show that the sensory component is exceedingly important in coordinating the activity of groups of muscles (Nicholas and Barron, 1935). Nicholas has also carried out a series of studies on limbs of amphibians developed after experimental embryological manipulations so that they have foreign innervation (1924, 1933a). Some of the results obtained in these studies are interpreted as dependent upon the coordination of nerve responses in the central nervous system rather than upon peripheral selection as suggested in the "resonance theory" of P. Weiss (1926, 1939). Nicholas (1929a) published an extensive study of the analysis of the responses of isolated parts of the amphibian nervous system. In this paper an excellent historical summary of the whole field of the innervation of the limbs in developing *Amblystoma* is presented.

In the reptile class comparatively little work has been done, although Preyer (1885, p. 404) reported some occasional observations on snakes. Tuge (1931) also did some very interesting work upon the growth of behavior in the turtle. In this work the sequence of Coghill is seen as modified by the existence of the shell which especially characterizes this form. Smith and Daniel (1947) have also made some interesting observations on the early responses of the turtle.

The Development of Behavior in the Embryos of Birds

From an evolutionary point of view, the bird may be thought of as presenting an interesting comparison with the lower vertebrate and the mammal. The amphibian embryo provides unusually favorable material for developmental study. The growing salamander or frog embryo may be observed, without interference of any sort, through its translucent egg covering and in free life after leaving these coverings. Its egg yolk provides food during a long part of the early developmental period. On the other hand, the study of the development of behavior in the mammal involves relatively complex surgery and, at present at any rate, a certain disturbance of the normal environment of the growing organism. The bird embryo is harder to study than the amphibian but easier than the mammal. It may be studied in a relatively normal environment, but a special technique is necessary to render the development of the bird embryo continuously observable. Down through the years, however, the chicken's egg has been the subject of embryological study. Needham (1931) reviews the use that has been made of the hen's egg in embryology since earliest times. This writer describes the history of the artificial incubation of hens' eggs. He notes also the beginning of systematic observation of embryos taken from eggs in various periods of incubation at the time of Hippocrates (about 460 B.C.). From that time on, the hen's egg has been extensively used in morphological studies of development. Among those who have contributed to this development are Aristotle, Aelian, Pliny, Plutarch, Albertus Magnus, Leonardo da Vinci, Aldrovandus, Fabricius (who made beautiful illustrations of a series of chick embryos), Highmore, Sir Thomas Browne, Harvey, and Malpighi. Today the many admirable manuals on the embryology of the chick, such as those by Patten (1929) and F. R. Lillie (1919), present a large amount of evidence in regard to the structural development of the chick.

Preyer (1885), reviewing certain of these facts many years ago, noted that, whereas the structural development of the chick is comparatively well known, its behavioral development is not. Although advances have been made since that time, this observation is still true. A few casual observations on this development, nevertheless, were made at an early time. Harvey as long ago as 1651 noted that the chick in the sixth day of development showed a bending and stretching of the head (Preyer, 1885, p. 405). About a century later Béguelin noted the heart beat of the small embryo on the third day, and on the sixth day the oscillation of the whole body, and from that point on he records elaborate changes in movement. He records the fact that he was able to observe the development for fifteen days in the same living and developing embryo (Preyer, 1885, p. 405). Home, in 1822, was probably the first to note the movement of the extremities on the sixth day (Preyer, 1885, p. 405). Von Baer, in 1828, published rather extensive studies on the development of behavior in the chick, in which he noted the inception of the pendular movement of the whole embryo as a result of amnion contractions (Preyer, 1885, p. 405). Amnion contractions, he noted, were most marked on the eighth day and were successively less on the succeeding days. This same investigator reported general activity of the embryo on the eleventh, twelfth, and thirteenth days. The amnion contractions of the bird's egg have no complete parallel in other forms. The growing chick seems, as it were, to be tossed in a blanket as it grows. Von Baer also saw what he considered to be the beginning of breathing movements in the 14- to 16-day embryo. Several other investigators are quoted by Preyer as having also made observations upon the development of behavior in the chick. By far the most extensive study up to his time on the development of the bird embryo, however, was made by Preyer himself. The extent of his study may be indicated by the fact that he used some 500 eggs in his experiments.

In this work Preyer gave much attention to the movements of the amnion which have been referred to above. Preyer pointed out that the rhythmic movement of the amnion when at its maximum extent, between the seventh and ninth days, leads to such an agitation of the fetus that no study of fetal activity can be made without taking these contractions into account. The amnion contractions are generally described as independent muscle reactions. They are non-neural. Preyer also describes the gradual development of behavior of the chick embryo from its earliest head movement to the behavior necessary for hatching (pp. 408–416, 555–585). Since the time of Preyer there have been a number of special studies on particular aspects of the fetal and hatching behavior of the bird, such as those by Breed (1911), W. Craig (1912), Clark and Clark (1914), and Patten and Kramer (1933). For the purposes of this chapter by far the most important work is Kuo's, which is presented in a series of papers (1932a, 1932b, 1932c, 1932d, 1932e, 1938, 1939a), and Orr and Windle's (1934).

To collect material for the study of the morphological development of the egg, it is necessary only to open the shells at known periods of incubation. Opening of eggs without special precaution leads to the early death of the embryo, but this is not important if the organism to be studied is placed at once in a fixative to prepare it for the histologist. A number of techniques, however, have been devised to open the shell and still allow the continuous observation of the early development of behavior in the bird. One of these methods, devised by Kuo (1932a), has yielded excellent results. Kuo's method makes possible an uninterrupted study of the developing fetus without interfering in any essential way with the natural membranes

of the egg, or, more important, with respiration of the embryo. Kuo's operation may be described as follows: The shell of the blunt end of the egg is cut off with a fine pair of scissors as far as the inner membrane. The whole inner membrane, however, is allowed to remain intact. A very small amount of melted petrolatum is immediately and rapidly applied to this membrane with a Chinese writing brush. At the temperature of the incubator the petrolatum remains liquid but, when applied by an expert, does not spread. This treatment produces a transparent membranous window through which the embryo and the extraembryonic structures and functions can be observed. This technique renders the membrane so transparent that it is almost as satisfactory as removing the membrane. In the course of observations Kuo uses three incubators, one in which the eggs are kept before they are experimented upon, another in which the operation is performed, and the third a special observation incubator fitted with appropriate glass plates through which a microscope may be used. For a criticism of Kuo's technique, see Becker (1940, 1942).

Kuo has also devised a transparent dial graded in fractions of a millimeter which may be put over the cut end of the egg, thus making the quantitative measurement of fetal movements possible. The writer has collaborated with Kuo in making a moving-picture film of the typical stages of development of the chick embryo. For the most part these pictures were taken through the membrane treated as described above. This procedure has been described (Kuo and Carmichael, 1937). In connection with this technique a consideration of the air space of the hen's egg and its changes during incubation is interesting. (See Romijn and Roos, 1938.)

Using his special technique, Kuo has studied many thousands of eggs, and on the basis of this study he has made definite statements in regard to the developmental sequence of behavior in the chick embryo. This work deserves special consideration in this chapter because it is the work of a scientist who is interested in the psychological significance of behavior and because it places emphasis on the part played by the environment in the determination of the course of behavioral development. The results are also presented in such a way that they are peculiarly applicable to psychological problems.

Kuo has traced the chronology and general nature of behavior in the chick embryo (1932a), the mechanical factors in the various stages leading to hatching (1932b), the influence of prenatal behavior upon postnatal life (1932d), and many other special topics such as the relationship between acetylcholine and the onset of behavior (1939a). In the last-named study Kuo shows that the first true neurally determined responses do not appear until after this substance may be detected. This suggests that there may be a chemical mediation of the first response of the chick. For a review of the general importance of acetylcholine, see Cannon and Rosenblueth (1937). A reference to Figure 1 will show that at one typical stage the embryo of the chick is very similar to the fetus of the reptile and, indeed, to the fetus of man. It must, however, be remembered that the arrangement of the embryo of the bird in relation to its extrafetal membranes is, as suggested above, in a number of ways peculiar. A description of this anatomical relationship may be found in Patten (1929).

Kuo's work on the chick may possibly best be given in summary by indicating briefly something of the observed movement and the time at which the movement was *first* observed. It should be noticed that the writer, by using the time at which the movement was first observed, may do

an injustice in certain cases to the facts as presented by Kuo, because that investigator shows that in many cases the movement does not, on the average, arise until some hours or even days after it was first observed in peculiarly favorable specimens. A summary of the commencement of the passive and active movements characterizing the developmental behavior of the chick may, however, give the best generalized picture of the development of the chick that is possible in the compass of this chapter. The following activities are among those noted: heartbeat, at 36 hours; head vibration, 66 hours; body vibration, 66 hours; head lifting, 68 hours; head bending, 70 hours; trunk movement, 84 hours; amnion contraction, 86 hours; yolk sac movement, 86 hours; swinging, 86 hours; head turning, 90 hours; movement of forelimbs, 90 hours; movement of hindlimbs, 90 hours; movement of tail, 92 hours; movement of toes, 5 days; response to electricity (in an embryo removed from the shell and placed in a physiological salt solution), 6 days; eyelid movement, 6 days; response to pressure, 6 days; movement of eyeball, 7 days; swallowing, 8 days; leg folding, 9 days; fixation of body position, 9 days; bill clapping, 9 days; response to touch (in physiological salt solution), 9 days; first wriggling, 11 days; turning of body, 12 days; protrusion of neck, 16 days; respiratory movement, 16 days; response to rotation, 17 days; tearing of membrane, 17 days; peeping, 17 days; response to light, 17 days; response to sound, 18 days; response to vibration, 18 days; hatching, 19 days. Final leaving of the shell does not typically occur, however, until the twentieth or the twenty-first day (Kuo, 1932a).

Kuo has not been content with a mere passive description of the movements indicated above in their time sequences, but in every case he has attempted to give a description of the mechanical and environmental factors which are important in determining the special movements and the special modifications of movements that he notes. Thus, for example, he points out that the beating of the heart leads to a general rhythmic vibration of the inert fetal body which starts the head into passive mechanical movement. In connection with the heart beat of the chick, it may be noted that the structural and functional change of this organ during growth has been intensively studied by Patten and Kramer (1933). Almost from the first appearance of the cells which are to form the organ, beating may be noted. This passive mechanical movement continues until at length it gives place on the fourth or fifth day to a true active movement. Head movement in the chick begins as an up-and-down bowing. Gradually, as a result of the change of the weight of the head and of associated structures in the egg, this up-and-down movement is changed to a sidewise movement, which is eventually inhibited by the altered relationship between the fetus and the yolk sac.

Kuo makes similar observations in regard to the movement of the appendages and to other special behavioral functions. He notes that during the period of the most forceful amnion activity, from the seventh to the ninth day, the mechanical movement of the fetus so stimulates it that there is a large increase in the active movements of the embryo. These movements are considered significant in the development of further movement. It is also observed that an active movement originating in the embryo may incite further activity of contraction in the temporarily relatively quiescent amnion. Indeed, possibly as a result of this reciprocal activation during the period of vigorous amnion contractions, the movements of the developing chick in this period are almost ceaseless. It thus comes about that every part of the musculature of the embryo has been exercised before half its incubation period is over. This fact led Kuo (1932b) to point out that any correlation which it is desired to make between the development of behavior and the development of the nervous system in the chick must take into especial consideration the changing conditions of response due to morphological growth and increase in weight of the body parts themselves and especially to the changing relationships between these growing body parts and the environment in which the growth is taking place.

It is interesting to note that the specialized movements of the eye and of the eyeball occur as early as the eighth or ninth day but that the first light response of the organism does not ordinarily appear until the seventeenth to the nineteenth day under experimental conditions. Thus the eye reflexes are present in the absence of effective visual stimuli. These early eye movements, indeed, have been found by Kuo to occur in conjunction with movement of the body in space instead of in response to visual stimuli. A similar temporal sequence in mammals and its probable mechanisms as worked out by the writer will be discussed below. Only in the later periods of development do the eyes begin to acquire a relative degree of independence from the rest of the organism. Kuo reports that in general the responses to touch, pressure, and electricity, which may be elicited from at least the tenth day onward, are similar to the normally excited responses which he has observed. In conclusion, Kuo asserts that practically every physiological effector mechanism is thus shown to be in a functional condition long before hatching. Thus the organs begin to function in many cases before they reach adult form; indeed, many function in rudimentary form. He feels that, as is true in the development of structure, too much stress cannot be laid on the fact that the development of behavior is gradual and continual. In Kuo's opinion, the early embryonic movements may be thought of as the elements out of which every later response of the adult bird is built. In this connection he points out that certain of the typical postural attitudes of the adult fowl are but returns to the tonus condition of the attitudes of prehatching life (1932*d*, p. 113). This same observation, incidentally, although too infrequently presented, can be made in respect to mammals and man, and as such will do much to explain the maturation of many allegedly saltatory behavior patterns of postnatal life.

In the carrier pigeon Tuge (1934) has shown that active movements as opposed to passive movements begin at about 105 hours after the beginning of incubation. The first movements observed are extensions and flexions of the head. In 10 additional hours muscles of the neck, trunk, rump, and tail are also involved. "Spontaneous" movements begin before response to chemical or tactile stimuli can be evoked. At about 125 hours in the incubation period the first flexion of the head and neck to tactile stimulation is called out. The reflexogenous zone spreads from the cephalic to the caudal region as development proceeds. Local reflexes of the wings and legs appear at about 155 hours.

Orr and Windle and their collaborators (Orr and Windle, 1934; Windle and Orr, 1934*a*; Windle and Barcroft, 1938; Windle and Nelson, 1938; Windle, Scharpenberg, and Steele, 1938) have studied in detail the development of the bird. In 1934 Orr and Windle reported that the first response to a blunt vegetable fiber needle takes place in the embryonic chick at 6½ to 7 days after the onset of incubation. This first response is a quick movement of the wing away from the trunk, a lateral flipperlike extension. This movement remains local-

ized. The local reflexes of the embryo do not seem to develop from a generalized behavior pattern but rather arise independently. In another paper (Windle and Orr, 1934*a*) these two investigators show that the flexion of the chick fetus which takes place on the fifth day is of a sort which cannot be explained by the spinal cord structure at that time. Probably the mechanism which sets off this behavior is chemical in nature. The motor and sensory sides of the nervous system develop in independence of each other, and the motor side is functional first. For a detailed report of the neural structure of the chick as its behavior develops, the reader should consult Windle and Orr's paper (1934*a*). Windle and his collaborators (Windle and Barcroft, 1938; Windle and Nelson, 1938; Windle, Scharpenberg, and Steele, 1938) have also published a series of papers upon the initiation of respiration and the development of respiration in the duck and the chick.

Kuo has also developed an elaborate theory of the growth of behavior in relation to environmental factors. He points out that the intensity of stimulation must be controlled if one is to make any statement concerning the generality or specificity of an organism's response. In a more recent study (1938) he has pointed out that the physiological *and* behavioral growth of the organism may be summarized in ten stages: (1) cardiac movement, (2) active head movement, (3) trunk movement and response to electric currents, (4) first limb and tail movements and first amnion contraction, (5) head turning and lateral flexion, (6) the hyperactive period from 6 to 9 days, (7) reduction of bodily activities, (8) period of relative quiet (15 to 18 days), (9) prehatching stage, (10) hatching behavior. This is a descriptive procedure much to be preferred to any too easy generalization attempting to summarize the whole course of behavioral growth. Kuo (1939b, 1939c) has also given an interesting review of the whole question of which comes first, total patterns or local reflexes.

As suggested above, the possible importance of chemical mediation in the determination of the onset of behavior requires study. Kuo (1939a) published a paper summarizing his investigations in this field. He found that acetylcholine, the chemical whose presence would most likely be correlated with the onset of activity, was detectable in the embryonic tissues as early as 2½ days after the onset of incubation. Between the fourth and the twelfth days the production of acetylcholine produced per gram of body tissue fluctuates. This substance thus appears before any synapses are present, and it is present in easily detectable quantities before any somatic movement occurs. Kuo has not found any relationship between the acetylcholine development and the development of reflexes.

In considering chemical mediation, it is important not to lose sight of the parallel development of the nervous elements themselves. Windle and Austin (1936) showed in some detail the anatomical growth of the central nervous system of the chick up to five days' incubation.

The Development of Prenatal Behavior in the Infrahuman Mammal

The development of behavior in the infrahuman mammal is in a number of respects more significant for one who would understand the growth of behavior and psychological functions in man than is the consideration of the amphibian or bird presented above. There are peculiar difficulties, however, in studying the development of fetal behavior in mammals. These difficulties can be made clear only by a brief review of the bodily structures and functions involved in the prenatal development

of typical placental mammals, including man. In barest outline, disregarding many differences between various species of such mammals and many consequent qualifications, this process of development may be reviewed as follows:

The tiny fertilized mammalian egg is not at first attached but, probably as a result of ciliary action and the muscular contraction of the tubes, moves from the oviduct where it has been fertilized to the uterus. Parker (1931) has summarized the evidence in this field. During the process of movement, which occupies 4 to 10 days, depending on the type of mammal under consideration, the processes of development have begun which are to form the embryo and its membranes. Two embryonic folds are early formed which join to make up the then enclosing amniotic sac. This sac gradually enlarges. It is filled with a special liquid, the so-called amniotic fluid, which has a very definite chemical make-up and a specific gravity of 1006–1081 (Feldman, 1920, p. 139). The specific gravity of this liquid is thus not far from that of the developing embryo, a fact of great importance in understanding the mechanics of certain forms of receptor–nervous-system–effector action in the fetus at a later period. As growth continues, the sac more and more completely surrounds the embryo.

The embryo thus immersed and supported is relatively independent of most direct mechanical surface contacts. Coincident with this development the other fetal sacs are formed. One of these, the vitelline sac, corresponds to the yolk sac of lower forms, although of course in the higher mammalian types it contains virtually no yolk. In later development of the fetus this sac is relatively much reduced in size, and at the time of birth is known as the umbilical vesicle.

The allantois also makes ts appearance as an outgrowth of the developing digestive tract of the embryo. This saclike structure comes in contact with the previously formed primitive chorion, with which it fuses to make up the true chorion. This doubly derived chorion now rapidly becomes a completely enclosing membranous wall outside the amniotic sac. The chorion continues to be attached to the embryo proper, however, by means of the allantoic stalk, which comes to conduct as well the two allantoic arteries and the two allantoic veins.

As this development has progressed, therefore, the egg has become attached to the wall of the maternal uterus. As the very complex morphological changes, some of which have been suggested above, take place, the circulatory system of the fetus and its membranes continues to develop. This fetal circulatory system is mechanically completely separated from the maternal blood system, but the separation is, in certain areas, only that of a cell wall. By interchange through living membranes, therefore, oxygen and food materials pass from the maternal blood system into the independent embryonic blood system; similarly, carbon dioxide and other metabolites pass in the opposite direction into the maternal blood stream. Typically, in the higher mammals only part of the chorion is thus directly attached to the maternal uterus. This area of attachment is called the placenta. As noted later in the chapter, the exchange of endocrines through the placenta is important. The placenta may best be thought of as involving two parts, one of which is derived from the embryo and the other from the maternal uterus. The part derived from the maternal uterus becomes larger and larger, eventually encapsulating the developing embryo and its membranes, which have just been described. This true maternal membrane, as distinguished from the previously considered fetal membranes, is called the *decidua capsularis*.

In human development, as the fetus grows this decidua capsularis comes to be in contact with the mucous membrane lining of the rest of the uterine cavity, the so-called *decidua vera*. Thus as it grows the fetus is enveloped in an elaborate series of membranes. Figure 5 shows these relationships in very schematic form in the human organism. These developed membranes serve an important function. They provide within the mother's body a strong, many-layered sac in which is maintained an aquatic environment of very constant temperature and remarkably constant physical and chemical constitution. Hsu (1948) has shown that in white rats increasing the temperatures somewhat above normal affects pregnancy. The results suggest that with elevated temperatures the percentage of pregnancies affected is greater when the heat treatment is earlier. This result emphasizes the importance of constant and normal conditions of the uterus during pregnancy.

For an elaborate consideration of fetal development made clear by excellent diagrams, see Spee (1915). See also Barclay, Franklin, and Prichard (1946, 1947) for a consideration of changes in fetal circulation at birth.

By means of the association at the placenta, as just noted, the independently developing embryo is able, parasitically as it were, to receive food materials, oxygen, and other needful substances from the maternal blood supply and to send back into that system the waste products of its own organic life. The extremely important and technical topic of fetal respiration has been intensively studied by Barcroft and his associates and by many other workers. For a review of this literature see Barcroft (1938, 1946), and Windle (1940). The mechanism of the fetal membranes, therefore, makes possible fetal respiration, nutrition, and excretion. It is in a physical world of this sort that we must consider the fetal mammal as developing and in its later stages as actively responding. The nature of this very special environment must not be forgotten in considering every evidence of sensory or behavioral life which the fetus

Birth consists in the rupture of the fetal membranes, often produced by the contractions of the muscular walls of the uterus. The physiology of birth is complex and important. (See Barron, 1940.) A short time after the birth of the young mammal or the child there follows the expulsion of the

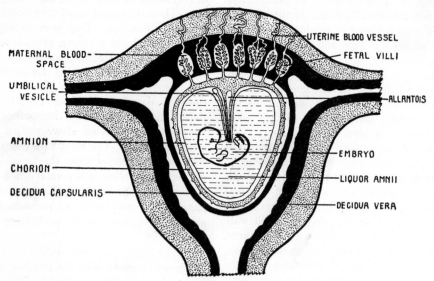

FIGURE 5. Diagram representing the relationship between the uterus, the membranes, and the embryo during early pregnancy. (From "Origin and Prenatal Growth of Behavior," by L. Carmichael. In C. Murchison [Ed.], *A Handbook of Child Psychology*. 2d ed., rev. Worcester: Clark University Press, 1933, 50. By permission of the publisher.)

shows. It must be emphasized, however, that there are great differences in detail in the relationship between fetus and maternal organism in different mammals. As Windle (1940) has pointed out, "Time and again in the study of prenatal physiology it will appear that species variations in the intimacy between maternal and fetal blood streams may explain differences in experimental results" (p. 5).

The relationship between blood flow in the umbilical cord and the rate of fetal growth in the sheep and guinea pig has been studied by Greenfield, Shepherd, and Whelan (1951).

now discarded enveloping membranes. This "afterbirth" consists largely of the remains of the decidua, the chorion, and the amnion. In infrahuman mammals this afterbirth is customarily eaten by the mother (Tinklepaugh and Hartman, 1930). This is an interesting response to be considered in relation to the problem of the special hungers and patterned "instincts" of the organism.

From what has been said, it is obvious that the developing mammal is so well protected that it is difficult to study its growth at different periods, and nearly impossible —although the "impossible" has been accomplished, as will be pointed out below—to observe continuously the development of the same mammalian fetus. A whole series of papers by Nicholas (1925, 1926, 1927, 1929a) demonstrates the possibility of experimental manipulation of the mammalian egg and growing embryo. This work has fundamental implications not only for the "new" embryology but for the whole study of the growth of behavior.

It may still be said that it is "impossible" to study the mammalian fetus under as nearly normal conditions as those under which Kuo has studied the chick. There is real danger in generalizing upon the nature of fetal development on the basis of observations made under abnormal conditions, as Kuo himself (1932c, p. 265) has said. Observations on the mammalian fetus must be abnormal because the protection which is provided by the fetal membranes just considered must be destroyed if direct observation is to be possible.

It will, of course, be unnecessary here to give an account of the development of behavior in all classes and orders of mammals. Indeed, no special studies have been made of most mammalian forms. For example, so far as the writer is aware, no special study has been made of the development of behavior in the fetal monotremes. The study of the development of behavior in these primitive Australian egg-laying mammals would probably provide fundamentally significant facts that might be applied to higher, truly viviparous forms. In both the ornithorhynchus and the echidna, eggs with soft shells, rich in yolk, undergo segmentation in the uterus and are then laid and incubated. The incubation by the ornithorhynchus is in a nest; by the echidna, in a pouch. When hatched, the young of this subclass are nourished by the secretion of great glands possibly more like sweat glands than like the true mammary structures of higher mammals. But a detailed description of behavioral growth in these forms is not, so far as the writer can discover, available.

Study of the development of behavior in what is generally considered the next higher subclass above the monotremes—namely, the marsupials—has been carried on. Indeed, the marsupials are found to be very favorable material for developmental studies. The young of animals in this subclass are born in a condition which can be considered only that of a relatively immature fetus (Langworthy, 1928). In the marsupials, although early development occurs in the maternal uterus, and although the fetus is nourished by secretions from the uterine wall, no true placenta is formed. Possibly for this reason these true mammalian fetuses are born while still at an early period of development and are as yet open to easy continual external observation during most of the important growth stages in which behavior change may be noted. This fact has made this form a favorite one for studies of neurological development by such students as Weed and Langworthy (1925a, 1925b) and Langworthy (1928). After birth the young are cared for by the mother for many weeks in a pouch, the marsupium, into which the mammary nipples open (Hartman, 1920). In certain of the marsupials, indeed, the once independent fetus again becomes functionally but not structurally attached to the mother, as for a long period after the maternal nipple is taken into the mouth the nipple is never removed until the animal is ready to enter upon truly free life (Hartman, 1920, p. 260).

From the standpoint of the student of the development of behavior, the most adequately studied form of this subclass is the Virginia opossum. In a series of complete and brilliant papers, Hartman (1916a, 1916b, 1919a, 1919b, 1920) has brought together the knowledge in regard to the development of the fetus in the opossum and related types. Until his own work was begun, Hartman points out that the birth of the opossum and the behaviorally significant journey of the newborn organisms to the pouch had been observed and described by but one man, Middleton Michel. Michel's observations, which are reprinted by Hartman (1920, p. 252), led to a belief that the mother transferred the newborn animals to the pouch. Hartman's work, however, has shown that the newborn organisms travel directly from the vulva to the maternal pouch without the aid of the mother. He says:

Unerringly the embryo traveled by its own efforts; without any assistance on the mother's part, other than to free it of liquid on its first emergence into the world, this ten-day-old embryo, in appearance more like a worm than a mammal, is able, immediately upon release from its liquid medium, to crawl a full three inches over a difficult terrain. Indeed, it can do more: after it has arrived at the pouch it is able to find the nipple amid a forest of hair. This it must find—or perish [p. 255].

Hartman has further shown that this essential journey is to be considered a negative geotropism, because under experimental conditions embryos can be made to travel away from the pouch if only the skin upon which they are moving is tilted upward. The locomotion of the embryo is described as a kind of overhand swimming stroke in which the head sways as far as possible to the side opposite the hand which is taking the propelling stroke. It is further noted that "With each turn of the head the snout is touched to the mother's skin . . . and if the teat is touched, the embryo stops and at once takes hold" (p. 256).

The conclusion may be suggested, therefore, that this young mammalian organism, less than 2 weeks removed from an un-

fertilized ovum, has already developed to a point of independent ability so far as air respiration, alimentary canal digestion, and the receptor-neuromuscular mechanism of geotropically orientated simple progression are concerned. McCrady (1938) has devoted a book to the description of the development of the opossum, a notable book in many respects but especially because of its beautiful drawings.

McCrady, Wever, and Bray (1937) have studied the electrical responses from the cochlea of the pouch-young opossum. These investigations have correlated reflex startle responses and the electrical output of the ear. The first responses of a startle type were found at 50 days. Nine days later the electrical output showed that the sensitivity of the ear was in about the mid-audible range with 2000 cycles as the maximum. At 82 days the maximum had shifted to 7000 cycles. A linear relationship between intensity of stimulus and electrical response was found. This suggests that these young organisms have a very efficient electrical-acoustical apparatus.

Goerling, in an article also reprinted by Hartman (1920, p. 259), gives an account of the birth of the kangaroo, an animal of the same subclass as the opossum. It has been observed that in the kangaroo the young animal moves through the fur from the opening of the urogenital canal to the pouch. The following observation is recorded in regard to the fetus: "It moved about slowly, very slowly, through the fur upwards, using the arms in its progress, and continually moving the head from side to side . . ." (Hartman, 1920, p. 260). Thirty minutes were required for the passage, but during this time the mother gave no assistance whatsoever. Goerling further notes that the arms of the newborn kangaroo are strongly developed. The small hands open and close like a cat's paws. He says: "By these strong little arms and hands the young one is enabled to labour its way to the pouch, the place of safety and nourishment" (Hartman, 1920, p. 260). It is further pointed out that, so far as the sucking reflex is concerned, once a young kangaroo is removed from the teat which it has taken in its mouth it is apparently unable to reattach itself. Figure 6 shows

FIGURE 6. A so-called mammary fetus of the kangaroo attached to the maternal teat. (From *A Text-Book of Zoology*, by T. J. Parker and W. A. Haswell. London: Macmillan, 1921, Vol. II, 577. By permission of The Macmillan Company.)

the early fetal appearance of the pouch-young kangaroo (Parker and Haswell, 1921, p. 577).

In the series of papers referred to above, Hartman reports his studies of the early embryology of the opossum but without any detailed reference to the onset and development of behavior before the early motility stage in which it is found at birth. It is interesting to note, however, on the basis of the evidence given above, that in the marsupials young organisms which might even still be called embryos are born in what is in many respects a very early fetal condition. Their behavior, as indicated above, is significant at any rate in a number of ways for the general student

of the development of response. Once in the pouch these organisms can be studied without the usual difficulties of disturbed respiration and digestion of higher mammalian fetuses of comparable developmental age which still depend upon the placental circulation. The reports just given suggest that in this organism there is a general conformity with the pattern of development of the amphibian larvae considered above. As in the case of *Amblystoma*, the young opossum moves with a wriggling movement which from the description, "the head swaying as far as possible to the side opposite the hand which is taking the propelling stroke" (Hartman, 1920, p. 256), suggests the double S movement elaborated by Coghill and others as a characteristic of the onset of aquatic locomotion in larval amphibians. It is also significant to note that it is the forelimbs, both in the opossum and even in that characteristically hind-limbed organism, the kangaroo, which are mentioned as the first effective agents of locomotion.

This again at least does not contradict the view that behavior typically develops from the anterior to the posterior segments of the organism. This generalization may be said to be essentially true of behavior growth in invertebrates, amphibians, and bird embryos. Moreover, there is nothing in the development of the feeding reaction which is presented that shows its essential sequence to be different from that already noted in lower types. Langworthy (1925, 1928) and Weed and Langworthy (1925a, 1925b) have studied the development of progression and body posture in pouch-young opossums. They find that decerebration of young opossums does not lead to decerebrate rigidity, but rather to an increase in progression movements. This suggests that at this period the cortex has as yet established little dominance over the other neural determinants of behavior.

Similarly, they note, after giving a complete review of the work on the nervous system of the opossum, that electrical stimulation of the brains of pouch-young opossums gives contralateral leg responses but no other responses for over 50 developmental days (Weed and Langworthy, 1925b, p. 23). These observations are important in regard to the part played by myelinization of the nervous system in behavior and, incidentally, seem to confirm the priority of forelimb progression in the early behavioral repertory of this form. Larsell, McCrady, and Zimmerman (1935) have studied the morphological and functional development of the membranous labyrinth of the inner ear of the opossum. Nerve endings are present around the receptor "hair cells" before the ear is functional. Vestibular reflexes appear at about 43 days after insemination; acoustic reflexes appear at 50 days. Myelin appears on the vestibular nerve fibers at the time reflexes first appear. It increases as the reflexes become more pronounced.

Of all orders of infrahuman mammals, the rodents have probably been most completely studied, so far as the development of behavior is concerned. It is difficult to say when the study of behavioral growth in rodent fetuses began. They are convenient animals to work with, and it is highly probable that some member of this order was used by the classic embryologists, whose work will be historically reviewed below when a discussion of the specific development of behavior in man is given. It is known, at any rate, that the dead embryos of typical rodents—namely, the rabbit, guinea pig, and mouse—besides many other animal forms, were discussed by Hieronymus Fabricius in his monumental work *De Formato Foetu* in 1604 (Needham, 1931, p. 115). It is highly probable that this writer or some of the other great embryologists of the Renais-sance observed the behavior of fetal rodents, because at this time embryology was still much concerned with the Aristotelian problem of the development of the vegetable, sensible, and rational souls in all the forms which were studied.

The first important experimental studies of the development of behavior in this order, however, that the writer has been able to find are those of Bichat (1819, 1827). This eminent early experimental physiologist studied the living embryos of a number of animals, particularly investigating the relationship between the blood stream of the mother and of the fetus. In this work he used the guinea pig extensively. As a result of his studies, Bichat came to a number of interesting, although to some extent unsound, conclusions in regard to the development of behavior in the fetus. He presents a generalized thesis, possibly growing out of the speculations of the Renaissance, that the organism at all stages combines what he calls two lives, one of which is that of sensibility, involving the brain and the senses, and the other that of the vegetative life, involving digestion, circulation, and the like. On the basis of his researches on fetal behavior he concludes that the life of sensibility does not begin before birth, although surprisingly enough he notes and describes in some detail the nature of fetal movements. He alleges that the fetus must be thought of as living in a world virtually devoid of stimulation, as he holds, correctly enough, that an energy, in order to be a stimulus, must change. As the fetus is held in a liquid of constant temperature and properties, he contends that it is virtually unstimulated. He does admit that the sense of touch may be stimulated before birth, but it is not, he further contends, really touch, as every true sensation supposes a comparison between a present and a past state of being.

For this conclusion he is roundly criticized by another eminent French physiologist, Magendie, who later edited Bichat's work. Magendie says in a footnote to Bichat's statements on the sense of touch: "Whatever Bichat may say, it exists in the fetus before birth." Bichat himself (1827), however, points out that touch is to be considered as the most fundamental of the senses and suggests that "philosophers say it is the only one of the senses which always is the agent of truth" (p. 136). Against this sweeping generalization, Magendie, in another footnote, quotes the old experiment of Aristotle upon the illusory localization of the crossed fingers (p. 137). Partly on the basis of his work on guinea pigs, Bichat concludes that the responses of the fetal organism develop continuously from zero to a point of greatest activity just before birth. He supports this conclusion by much anatomical evidence, which includes a discussion of the musculature of the limbs, the brain, the nerves, and the sense organs. He then attempts, it almost seems, to explain away the observations which he has just made, in the light of his own theory. For he at once asserts that the existence of the fetus is not that of an animal but virtually that of a vegetable. This conclusion is based upon the dichotomy which he attempts to establish even in the adult life of man between movements which are dependent upon the will, and hence "animal," as contrasted with such movements as those occurring in sleep, which he alleges are not animal but merely "living."

It is a long step from these early theories and observations to the present knowledge of the development of behavior in rodents, and indeed this step was not taken in a single jump. In 1818 Emmert, an embryologist, published certain incidental observations on the behavioral activity of field mouse embryos (Emmert and Burgätzy,

1818). Zuntz (1877) used fetal rodent material in a series of scientific observations. His work was devoted for the most part to a consideration of the chest movements of the newborn fetus of the rabbit, which was used in part of his study of the development of fetal respiration in mammals.

It was not, however, until Preyer began his series of experiments on fetal guinea pigs and other animals that the modern period of the study of the behavioral growth of the rodent began. In his great summarizing work of 1885, Preyer gives an elaborate history of the study of the development of behavior in each form which he considers. Significantly enough, however, in this treatise, when he deals with the development of mammalian behavior, he begins almost without historical references.

Preyer (1885, pp. 416–428), in his own experiments, however, used a number of different types of mammals and a number of different techniques in his study of the development of behavior. His most significant work was done on the guinea pig. In studying this rodent he used at least six methods:

1. The animal was placed on its back, and the movements of the external abdominal wall of the pregnant mother were observed without interference. He also made such observations on pregnant females on which so-called animal hypnosis or tonic immobility had been induced by an appropriate posture and pressure manipulation. As a result of these types of direct observation he concluded that there are periods of quiescence, lasting sometimes for more than an hour, interspersed with periods of great activity in fetal behavior, at least during the latter part of the pregnancy.

2. In another experiment he placed a long, thin needle directly through the abdominal wall and the fetal sacs of the pregnant female and pressed it into the fetus. This needle was inserted so that, when the

fetus moved, the needle, forming a sort of lever, could be observed to change its position. As a result of these investigations, the frequency of fetal activity was noted. It is all too clear to the modern investigator accustomed to the use of anesthetics in animal experiments that the fetus and the mother could hardly be considered "normal" during these studies.

3. He listened to the fetal movements through a stethoscope and recorded that in the later stages of pregnancy they made a peculiar *Knistern* and *Knacken*.

4. By operation he found it possible to allow a single limb to extrude from the sac in such a way that its movement could be observed.

5. By experimental surgery it proved possible to observe the movements of the fetus still in the mother's body. In this situation he was able to note the effect of changing the blood supply upon fetal behavior and to come to the conclusion that, although deprivation of oxygen did at times lead to general fetal movements, such deprivation was not an essential cause of such movements.

6. He also removed guinea pig fetuses in the air-breathing stage and studied them when supported by blood-warm physiological salt solution and in a warm chamber. In observing the movements of such fetuses he characterized their responses as *"sehr manigfaltig, ungeregelt, asymmetrisch, arhythmisch"* (p. 418).

It is interesting to note below that these are virtually the same words used by Minkowski and many others later in describing early human fetal movements. Preyer also observed certain movements of stretching and of reflex contraction and extension which would be difficult for the fetus while confined in the sac. This phenomenon has been seen many times by the writer, who knows of no evidence that Preyer used any anesthetics in employing any of the methods noted above. The criticism of the more painless work of later investigators, that possibly the fetal material was anesthetized, cannot therefore be urged against this pioneer work of Preyer, which may, however, be criticized on humane grounds.

In one case Preyer (1882) notes that, when his observations were made on a guinea pig in the still intact sac, touching the skin of the face led to a localized brushing movement on the part of the forelimb of the fetus as if to wipe away the offending stimulus which was touching the pad of the vibrissae (p. 212). We shall see that the study of the development of this ability in the fetus may throw light upon certain aspects of the old question as to whether or not the perception of space is natively or empirically determined.

Preyer gives a rather general description of development in the fetal guinea pig. In a fetus 20 to 21 mm. in length no movement was seen, but he adds that this may not be interpreted as assurance that no movement had previously occurred while the organism was in the uterus. In one of 81 to 83 mm., however, opened under blood-warm salt solution, the heart was seen to beat strongly and chest movements were noted. In much larger fetuses, 105 to 111 mm. long, a complete repertory of action almost like that seen in the adult animal was recorded. Many other observations are given on fetuses the lengths of which are not recorded. On the basis of these observations on fetuses, often approximately dated by statements in regard to the hair and teeth condition of the organism, it is possible to say that Preyer noted in the development of behavior in the guinea pig a gradual change in response with growth. The very early movements changed by gradual development until elaborate adaptive responses appeared. Concerning a series of carefully weighed litters in later stages he gives a detailed account of definite responses. These activities include the pinna reflex to sound, now often called *Preyer's reflex*, the pupillary reflex to light, and even the cerebral inhibition of reflexes as a result of antagonistic stimuli (1885, pp. 587–595). He points out that in a 173-gram guinea pig the teeth of the organism were so well developed that they bit his fingernail sharply (p. 423). On the basis of all this observational and experimental work, Preyer turns to his consideration of the development of behavior in the human fetus, to which reference is made below.

The first systematic study of the development of fetal behavior in guinea pigs, from the point of view of genetic psychology, is Avery's (1928), carried out in the Psychological Laboratory of Stanford University. As a background for the study of prenatal development, Avery carefully investigated the responses to stimulation shown by newborn guinea pigs. As contrasted with the naked and almost helpless neonatal marsupials described above, the guinea pig is at birth in many respects structurally and functionally a mature animal. It is born with a sleek coat of fur. Its teeth are well erupted. Its eyes and ears are open. Its heart pulsations and breathing may be quite continuous and regular. It is able to roll from back to side, side to back, and side to haunches. It can crawl, stand, and walk.

To the pinch stimulus applied to the foot it responds by kick or withdrawal of foot. The electrical stimulus elicits a muscular twitch, respiratory gasp, and jump. It can execute the scratch reflex spontaneously or when stimulated in the facial region. Although muscular weakness is evident the patterns of response show good coordination [Avery, 1928, p. 264].

The sensory control of behavior, this investigator points out, has also progressed to a remarkable degree. Lid and pupillary reflexes are present. The newborn animal avoids objects without touching them as it moves about. The ears are functional, and total bodily movements and pinna twitches are elicited by appropriate auditory stimulation. Needle pricks and heated objects lead to quick response. Olfactory stimuli evoke movement of the head. The complex movements of swallowing are well developed. So far as more integrated behavior is concerned, Avery reports that the young run together when separated from each other and run to the mother when separated from her. Somewhat similar observations were also made by Preyer (1882, p. 93). The young lick themselves, swim when placed in deep water, chew shavings, and attempt to disengage a foot held by an observer. No retreat responses were noticed when young guinea pigs were placed with an adult white rat. The prenatal development of behavior of this Minerva-like organism is therefore peculiarly interesting because it is such a complete story.

Avery's work on prenatal development must be strictly evaluated, however, in terms of the rather special conditions which he employed in his experimental study. Abandoning the techniques used by some of the earlier investigators in mammalian behavioral development, Avery removed from the mother each fetus that he studied. He thus, of course, intercepted placental circulation and therefore brought about all the changes which have been found to result from oxygen deprivation and an increasing concentration of metabolites in the fetal blood stream. That is, he often worked with dying fetuses. Thus his work is strictly comparable to most of the work on human fetuses reviewed below. Observations were most often made on a large metal tray placed on a well-lighted observation table. "An electric heater, reflector type, was placed nearby. It served to dry the young and to keep them warm. A temperature of 98° F. was maintained on the observation table" (Avery, 1928, p. 258). This technique provided that, so far as early embryos were concerned, they were studied not only without normal respiration but in what was apparently a continually drying condition.

The results of Avery's pioneer study, therefore, must be considered as a function of these special conditions, because previous studies had shown, and some of the writer's experimental observations adequately demonstrate, that many responses are possible in an aquatic environment which are quite impossible when the organism is placed upon a solid surface in the air. Avery studied animals of gestation ages of 45 to 68 days. The lower point was chosen because, in Avery's opinion, "Prior to this time responses are so slight as to be of little importance for this problem" (p. 270). This decision is in some respects surprising, because Preyer reported movement in fetal guinea pigs of much younger gestation age. Indeed, according to Draper's tables (1920) and Preyer's own estimate (1885, p. 588), the first of Preyer's fetuses moved when they were 26 to 29 gestation days old. The writer has seen movement in a 25-day fetus. Avery's work, therefore, from the standpoint of the general problem of development, must be taken as emphasizing the development of behavior in the later stages of gestation. Indeed, this study is probably most significant in regard to fetuses which have developed to the point that they can, under appropriate conditions, breathe and move without difficulty in an air environment. Bonardi (1946) reported that respiratory movements and raising of the head appeared in fetuses of 60 days or more on touching the nostrils with cold water.

Avery also considered the question of whether or not there is a distinction between the responses of fetuses taken from young and old mothers. He came to the conclusion that there is no significant difference in the maturity of response elicited from the fetuses of young and fully adult mothers (p. 311). This conclusion is unlike that of King (1915) and of Angulo y González (1932b) in regard to the white rat, in which various parental conditions were found to influence fetal development.

By the use of X-rays Avery also ingeniously studied the orientation of the fetuses in the uterus of the guinea pig. This study convinced him that gravitation is apparently not very significant in determining rapid changes in the orientation of the fetus in the uterus. He concludes: "The shifts of the foetuses in utero are inadequate to explain their activity after experimental delivery" (p. 324). As a final conclusion to his study Avery says: "These results substantiate the belief that certain congenital response mechanisms exist in foetal and newborn guinea pigs. Some of these are subject to early modification through experience" (p. 329). For an interesting early study in this field, see Virey (1833).

Carmichael (1934a) studied a large number of fetal guinea pigs in a series of experiments in which as many factors as possible were controlled. This study involved more than 2 years of work and the typing of more than 2000 pages of protocols dictated at the time of the experiments. In most cases motion-picture records of behavior were also made. The apparatus used is shown in Figure 7. A summary of results may be given (pp. 422–466):

1. Heart beat was the only activity observable in the youngest fetuses studied in this investigation. . . .
2. Before any behavior was observed the skeletal muscles of the still immobile

fetus could be made to respond by direct electrical stimulation. . . .

3. In a 28-day fetus behavior involving skeletal muscles response without electrical stimulation was observed. . . .

6. In general, responses at every stage are a function of what were called . . . (a) modes of stimulation and (b) variable conditions of the organism.

7. The first stimulus-released response

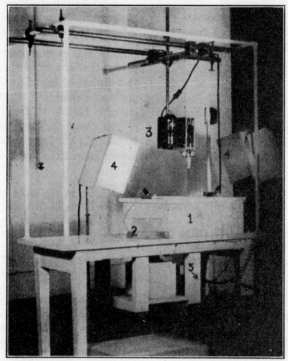

FIGURE 7. Photograph of apparatus. (From "Quantified Pressure Stimulation and the Specificity and Generality of Response in Fetal Life," by L. Carmichael and M. F. Smith. *Journal of Genetic Psychology*, 1939, *54*, 427. By permission of the Journal Press, publisher.) (1) Constant-temperature tank in which is inserted a tray filled with physiological saline solution. Maternal animal is held in this bath by suitable supports and fetal organisms are then exposed for study. (2) Holder and graded series of esthesiometers. (3) Electrically driven motion-picture camera for recording. (4) Reflectors for two 1000-watt lamps used to illuminate the field. (5) Foot-operated switch to start and stop the recording motion-picture camera.

4. The first "spontaneous" movement observed was a lateral flexion of the neck and a synchronous and possibly independent movement of the forelimbs. . . .

5. The first sensory area from which behavior was released in the present study was . . . the concha of the ear. . . .

noted in the study may be characterized, at its first appearance, as a pattern of behavior, which involves a relationship between neck flexion and forelimb movement. . . .

8. Many of the points indicated . . . when stimulated, release behavior from the

first which in spite of very great variability could always be considered as a special "pattern of behavior." . . .

9. Each behavior pattern released by the stimulation of a particular area may be said to undergo a series of changes during fetal life. . . .

10. Photic stimulation of the eye may lead to motor responses of the limbs, etc., before the eyes are normally open in the fetus, when such stimulation is made possible by an operative exposure of the eye. . . .

11. Auditory stimuli released behavior in a 63-day fetus after the liquid had been removed from the external meatus. . . .

12. Needle stimulation ("pain stimuli") in general released responses which were quite comparable to responses released by pressure stimuli rather than to the vigorous responses characteristic of the adult animal when subjected to pain stimulation. . . .

13. Temperature stimuli well above and well below the temperature of the fetus, when applied to the skin, release behavior. . . .

14. In late fetuses compensatory movements during rotation and in the immediate post-rotational period were demonstrated. . . .

15. There is evidence that in late fetal life higher brain centers influence responses which are characteristically called "spinal reflexes." . . .

16. As development progresses, the amount of "motor diffusion resulting from specific receptor stimulation" decreases, at least in certain areas and under certain stimulus conditions. . . .

17. The study does not confirm in detail the specific laws of development, alleging that development is in all respects cephalo-caudal, proximo-distal, or from "fundamental" to "accessory" muscles. . . .

18. It is possible to view most of the typical patterns of behavior released by the stimulation of given areas as capable of securing some end or ends, which during fetal life itself or during subsequent

independent life may serve adaptive needs of the organism. . . .

19. The present study does not give unqualified support to any of the more general theories of the development of behavior, such as those summarized by the words "individuation" or "integration," but suggests rather that the formulation of such generalizations is at present premature. . . .

After this general study it became apparent that a more detailed study of certain aspects of fetal behavior in the guinea pig was important. Bridgman and Carmichael (1935) studied 47 fetal litters *at just about the time that behavior first begins*. As a result of this study the following conclusions were drawn (pp. 262–265):

1. Prior to the onset of behavior in the fetal guinea-pig, myogenic contractions can be elicited from certain muscles. That these early responses are truly myogenic, and not sensory-motor responses, there is little doubt, because of their character, particularly as compared to later movements.

2. Active behavior in the fetal guinea pig begins in the last hours of the twenty-fifth day. Previous observers had placed the onset at least 1 day later than this.

3. True behavior, that is, response that results from stimulation, and which is secondarily induced by nervous discharge, can be elicited 10 to 14 hours before "spontaneous" behavior appears. These stimulated responses are of a sufficiently different character from the earlier myogenic contractions to be classified as active; i.e., involving neural activity. . . .

4. The first active responses of the fetal guinea pig are definite in character, and involve movements of the head, brought about by contraction of the neck muscles, and of the fore leg. The evidence is as yet inconclusive concerning which of these components arises first.

5. It is seen that, from the earliest period, the neck and limb responses occur

sometimes together, and sometimes independently, and that throughout the developmental period studied, independent elements of behavior are present at all times. That is, no gradual progressive "individuation" of the specific responses out of a total pattern is seen. . . .

6. Because of the simple and specific nature of much of the earliest behavior of the fetal guinea pig, it is thought that these responses may advantageously be described as reflexes. Moreover, no need to use such words as "generalized," "totally integrated," or "non-specific" in the description of this behavior has arisen. . . .

The development of temperature sensitivity in the fetal guinea pig has been studied by Carmichael and Lehner (1937). The results of this study are summarized in Figure 8. This figure shows that in fetuses of all ages there is an increase in released behavior as stimuli (drops of water) are used which are either warmer or cooler than the physiological zero (about 37.5° C.) of the organism. The conclusions of this study (pp. 224–226) may be summarized in the following statements:

1. Temperature stimuli . . . are effective in releasing responses during most of the motile fetal period of the guinea pig.

2. At each of three fetal development periods, as these periods were established for the purposes of this study—young, mid, and old—the greater the difference between the temperature of the stimulus and the physiological zero of the organism, the greater the relative number of responses released by that stimulus.

3. At the youngest ages studied, there appears to be a slight tendency for cold stimuli to be relatively more effective than warm stimuli if certain assumptions of equality are made concerning units of measurement.

4. During the "young" period of fetal life, as defined above, there appears to be development of temperature sensitivity.

Sensitivity is greater, that is, in the mid period studied than in the initial period. There is no corresponding increase during the other periods studied. In the last period, the growth of the insulating hair coat unquestionably modifies the effectiveness of the stimuli as applied in this investigation.

5. There is no great change in the percentage of specific and general responses

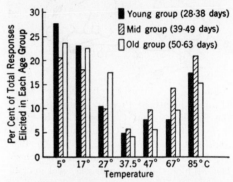

FIGURE 8. Responses of guinea pig fetuses to thermal stimuli. (From "The Development of Temperature Sensitivity during the Fetal Period," by L. Carmichael and G. F. J. Lehner. *Journal of Genetic Psychology*, 1937, *50*, 222. By permission of the publisher.)

released by the stimuli used at any of the three periods studied, nor does the effective intensity of stimulation (as measured by the greater degree of difference from physiological zero) change in a definite manner as development progresses in its efficacy in releasing either general or specific responses. There is a slight preponderance of specific over general responses, as these two words are defined in this paper in each period, but this finding can hardly be considered as statistically significant.

6. There is some shift in the relative sensitivity of the six areas stimulated during fetal development. These data may be considered as supporting the generalization made by previous investigators that the development of sensitivity spreads from the cephalic to the caudal regions of

the body and from the proximal to the distal region of limbs.

Bonardi (1946) has also made observations on the stimulation of the nose with cold and hot water at various fetal ages. At the temperatures used cold water was

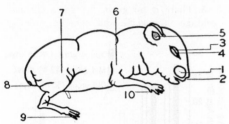

FIGURE 9.   Typical reflexogenous zones. (From "Quantified Pressure Stimulation and the Specificity and Generality of Response in Fetal Life," by L. Carmichael and M. F. Smith. *Journal of Genetic Psychology*, 1939, *54*, 428. By permission of the publisher.) (1) Midpoint of the vibrissae pad on the snout. (2) Inner surface of the vestibule of one external naris (nostril). (3) Midpoint of the upper eyelid. (4) Midpoint of the lower eyelid. (5) Midpoint of the concha of the ear. (6) Skin over the shoulder joint of the pectoral girdle. (7) Skin over the hip bone joint of the pelvic girdle. (8) Anus. (9) Point in medial plantar surface of one hindpaw. (10) Point in medial palmar surface of one forepaw.

more effective than hot water in releasing behavior.

Hooker (1944) and other investigators have emphasized the importance of the use of quantified pressure stimuli in working upon fetal material. Carmichael and Smith (1939) attempted to study this question in detail. (See also Carmichael, 1937.) First they decided to use certain well-established reflexogenous zones as shown in Figure 9. They then prepared a series of calibrated von Frey esthesiometers. In each case the lightest esthesiometer that would elicit a response was used, as well as

one 7 to 9 points higher in the scale of esthesiometers. The quantitative conclusions of this study are shown in Figure 10. An example of the difference in response to the light and heavy stimuli is shown in Figure 11. In summary of this study it may be said that pressure stimuli are like

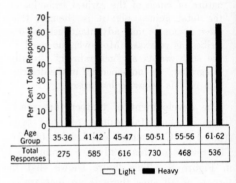

FIGURE 10.   Percentage of responses at each fetal age group studied. (Normal gestation period is 68 days.) (From "Quantified Pressure Stimulation and the Specificity and Generality of Response in Fetal Life," by L. Carmichael and M. F. Smith. *Journal of Genetic Psychology*, 1939, *54*, 431. By permission of the publisher.)

Group 35–36 days		
Total responses 275	Light 36.5%	Heavy 63.5%

Group 41–42 days		
Total responses 585	Light 37.5%	Heavy 62.5%

Group 45–47 days		
Total responses 616	Light 33.6%	Heavy 66.4%

Group 50–51 days		
Total responses 730	Light 38.4%	Heavy 61.6%

Group 55–56 days		
Total responses 468	Light 39.7%	Heavy 60.3%

Group 61–62 days		
Total responses 536	Light 35.4%	Heavy 64.6%

temperature stimuli in the importance of intensity upon resulting response.

Moreover, the present results show that the same relative proportion of general and specific responses seems to be released at all of the typical fetal ages studied. This finding adds further confirmation to the view that specific responses are early developed in fetal life. Thus it becomes more than ever clear that the widely accepted formula that all specific behavior develops from the individuation of previously more general patterns of behavior needs revision. Such revision can come only from continued study of fetal be-

4. Definite though not invariable effects of stimulation on the character of the cortical electrogram have been noted, occurring as early as the 60th day of gestation.

5. The guinea pig brain first exhibits electrical activity at a time when behavioral indications also point to maturation of higher nervous centers.

 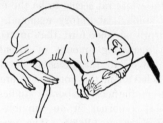

FIGURE 11. Outline tracings from moving-picture film of two postures of 51-day guinea pig fetus. (From "Quantified Pressure Stimulation and the Specificity and Generality of Response in Fetal Life," by L. Carmichael and M. F. Smith. *Journal of Genetic Psychology*, 1939, *54*, 432. By permission of the publisher.) Picture at left shows resting posture of the fetus as stimulated with light esthesiometer. Only response in this case was an eye wink. Picture at right shows one phase of movement elicited by a heavier esthesiometer. In this case, the entire trunk and all limbs are involved in the reaction. Note the precise localization of the stimulated spot by the forepaw.

havior as released by stimuli of quantitatively known character [Carmichael and Smith, 1939, p. 434].

Jasper, Bridgman, and Carmichael (1937) have studied the electrical brain potentials of the fetal guinea pig. Their conclusions (pp. 70–71) are:

1. The brain potentials of the guinea pig first appear when the age of 48–56 days of gestation has been attained.

2. No quantitative ontogenetic trend in the characteristic frequency of potential variation, nor in the total range of frequencies, has been discovered. The appearance of secondary groupings of characteristic frequencies is found more often as age increases.

3. The average amplitude of the characteristic frequencies at any age shows an irregular yet definite increase with age.

In connection with this study it was noted that tying off the umbilical cord abolished most cortical activity but did not for some time abolish the lower reflexes of the fetus.

In another study, using high-gain electrical amplification of bioelectric phenomena in the fetal guinea pig, Rawdon-Smith, Carmichael, and Wellman (1938) have demonstrated that the cochlear electrical response (the so-called Wever-Bray effect) is present in a guinea pig fetus of 52 post-insemination days. The electrical response secured at 52 days had a peak voltage of 1 to 2 microvolts to a stimulus of 600 cycles per second at an intensity of 100 decibels above human threshold. Declining responses were noted to tones below this and above 2000 cycles per second. The rise in electrical output was rapid as development progressed, for by 62 days 100 microvolts was recorded. It is interesting to note that the time of onset of the electrical response of the fetal ear—namely, 52 days—is exactly the same time at which the first overt behavior released by auditory stimuli can be observed in the fetal guinea pig.

Of all rodents, however, not the guinea pig but the white rat seems to be the most generally studied laboratory mammal. It is not surprising, therefore, that in recent years an increasing amount of attention has been given to the prenatal development of behavior in this convenient organism. One of the most elaborate studies of this sort is reported in an unpublished thesis by Swenson (1926). The experimental work for this thesis was done under the direction of Coghill. The thesis is entitled *The Development of Movement of the Albino Rat before Birth*. The operation by which the female is rendered immobile is described by Swenson in a special article (1925). The mother is deeply anesthetized, the neck is opened, and the carotid arteries are ligated as close to their origin as possible. The large left and right external jugular veins are also secured and ligated. Ether is now discontinued, and the skin incision is closed. After the anesthesia has been allowed to pass off, the mother is immersed in physiological salt solution. Each fetus is then in turn shelled out and studied.

Swenson's observation began with fetuses showing absolutely no movement save heart beat and continued at convenient stages to birth. It is difficult to generalize about any such developmental sequence because the omission of any of the details of the onset of behavior is likely to give a prejudiced picture of the total process. It is possible in review here, however, to give a few of the salient points of the growth of behavior in the rat as found by Swenson.

The first movement noticed was a slight lateral bending of the head. This same movement, differently interpreted, may be characterized as a slight cephalic trunk-bending movement. From this early action to the precise adaptive movements of tongue and paws in late fetuses, there is found a continuous quantitative and qualitative change in the movements as observed in litters of increasing gestation age. In the general theoretical discussion of the causal factors concerned in the development of behavior, we shall again refer to the work of Swenson, particularly to the observations which he made upon fetuses with clamped umbilical cords. Clamping of the cord he found to lead to an increase of metabolites in the fetal system and certain characteristic behavioral changes. Abstracts of the thesis noted above, and additional observations, have been published by Swenson (1928*b*, 1929).

Angulo y González (see references in bibliography), also associated with Coghill, has published some very important studies of the development of behavior in the fetal albino rat. He used much the same technique as Swenson in operating on the mother rat and in preparing the fetal material for observation. He selected his material with unusual care. Of the 643 fetuses used in one study, all came from healthy female rats of known stock 110 to 190 days of age, his previous work having indicated that these precautions were necessary in order to obtain scientifically comparable results at various gestation ages. In his work moving-picture records were taken to supplement the written protocols. Angulo y González in his experimental report gives the percentages of fetuses showing each movement at each age. For these detailed conclusions the reader is advised to consult the original papers (1929*a*, 1930*b*, 1932*a*, 1939). This same author, after using the drug *curare*, which alters the physiological relationship of motor nerves and muscles, was able to stimulate muscles directly in young fetuses. This indicates that the first responses of the rat fetus may be purely myogenic.

It is interesting to note that both Swenson and Angulo y González independently first observed movement in the rat fetus in the three hundred and seventy-eighth hour after insemination. Angulo y González' general description of the developmental process, particularly so far as the process of "individuation" of behavior is concerned, may best be given in his own words:

During the early stages of development the appendages move only with the trunk. Thus, upon stimulation of the snout the reaction more frequently obtained is a total mass reaction which involves the trunk and appendages. This total mass reaction we called a total pattern. This total-pattern reaction consists of a primary or basic movement, lateral flexion of the trunk, and a series of secondary movements. Similarly, there develops later a total pattern consisting of a basic movement of head extension and a series of secondary movements. The basic movements, during the early period of behavioral development, assert their sovereignty upon the secondary movements. During the later period of the development of fetal behavior, we find a number of specific reflexes showing what at first seems to be a breaking up of the total patterns into individual and specific reflexes. But close study has convinced me that the process by means of which the individuation and specificity of certain reflexes is attained is not a disintegration or breaking up of the established pattern, but, rather, is due to an inhibitory action by means of which the primary or basic movements are in a large measure arrested. In other words, the total-pattern reaction is never abolished completely, nor is the dominance of the primary over the secondary movements lost [1932a, p. 442].

This same investigator (1933a) has suggested that there are three phases in the development of somatic activity in albino rat fetuses: (1) a myogenic phase in which behavior can be elicited only by direct muscle stimulation; (2) a neuromotor stage in which internal stimuli acting upon the nervous system initiate behavior; (3) a sensory-motor phase in which true reflex action begins.

Angulo y González (1934a) has also shown that the dissolution of the behavioral systems of the fetal rat is in inverse order to its evolution, which is in general cephalocaudal and proximodistal. The relationship of this observation to Hughlings Jackson's generalizations (1884) should be noted. Angulo y González (1934b, 1939, 1940) has studied in detail the change in neural mechanisms which are correlated with behavioral development.

Besides these studies of the whole developmental sequence in the rat there have been a number of investigations devoted to certain aspects of the growth of the activity of the response mechanism in the rat. Lane (1917) has studied the development of the correlation between structure and function of the special senses in the white rat. His method of preparing fetal material consisted in killing the pregnant mother and studying the excised fetuses in a warm chamber. This method is open to the limitations pointed out in the evaluation of Avery's work given above. During the observation period the fetus was bathed in a warm physiological salt solution.

Lane's (1917) observations on the development of the senses in the white rat may be summarized as follows:

Touch. He found no evidence of this sense in 7½-mm. embryos, which are generally agreed to be immobile. Neurologically, at this stage he found both sensory and motor fibers developed. The sensory fibers, however, had not as yet reached the periphery. In 16-mm. embryos, that is, in organisms approximately 17 gestation days old, the tactual sense is reported as present on the flanks and snout, as evidenced by motor response to needle pricks. Lane reports no response to stimulation with a sable brush at this time. This is contrary to the findings of all subsequent investigators and is probably a function of the special condition of the embryos used. In 23- to 28-mm. embryos, that is, embryos approximately 19 to 20 gestation days old, he reports response to stimulation with a fine sable brush as well as with a needle prick. The snout region is most sensitive, although stimulation about the shoulder, upper arm, hip, rump, and thighs also evokes motor responses. He reports that there is a noticeable increase in the number of vibrissae as well as a greater complexity in the neural fiber basket of the vibrissae follicle. In very late fetuses and newborn rats a still better development of the tactual sense is found, responses being elicited by stimulation of any point on the entire body, including the tail. Pain as the result of needle stimulation is at this period shown by squeaks. The fibrillae baskets in the vibrissae follicles are now elongated cylinders, from the base of which neural fibrils in comparatively large bundles are seen to emerge, distad to the base of the follicle itself. In later stages there is no particular advance noted in tactual sensitivity, although the snout region continues to be superior to the rest of the surface in sensitivity.

Equilibrium. In regard to this sense, this investigator found in 7½-mm. embryos that stimulation leads to no behavioral trace whatsoever. Histologically, he reports the semicircular canals to be as yet undeveloped. In the 16-mm. embryo Lane

again found no experimental evidence of the sense of equilibrium, although the semicircular canals are now well developed. In 23- to 28-mm. embryos, Lane still finds no experimental evidence of a sense of equilibrium. Histologically, the differentiation of the cells of the cristae is at this time further advanced than in the previous stage, although the sensory and supporting elements are not yet distinguishable. Slight indications of central connection with the cerebrum are noted. In a 35-mm. fetus the sense of equilibrium was first observed, as seen in the righting responses of the organism when in contact with a surface. Structurally, the semicircular canals are now virtually complete. On the first day after birth, however, the righting responses were better developed, as were the histological and neural connections seen in the semicircular canals. In later stages there was manifested a greater perfection of the sense of equilibrium accompanying an increasing power of coordinated movement. Lane makes no reference to the part possibly played by neck proprioceptors or by other receptor fields in determining these righting responses, nor is any reference made to the analysis of postural reactions suggested by the school of Magnus, to which reference will be made below.

Smell. Lane reports no satisfactory method of smell stimulation in rat embryos from 7½ mm. to 28 mm. in length. Histologically, he says: "During these stages the olfactory apparatus is being gradually laid down, both as regards its sensory and peripheral portions. The histological differentiation of the olfactory epithelium has not advanced sufficiently far to enable the sensory cells proper to be identified" (p. 51). Using a brush placed in an odoriferous substance, Lane obtained no certain response to olfactory stimuli in 35-mm. fetuses. Histological development, however, is noted as continuing. Small's work

(1899) on smell in the newborn rat is quoted, and the statement is made by Lane that "there is on the whole a gradual perfecting of the olfactory sense from day to day" (p. 52). No experimental proof is given of this statement, and it is hard to understand its basis in view of the difficulty reported by Liggett (1928) in dealing with this sense in the white rat.

Taste. In this sense, Lane reports that the 35-mm. fetuses were able to swallow, but neither in these nor in those of any preceding stage were any true evidences of a sense of taste discovered. At no time previous to birth could taste buds or other fully differentiated organs of taste be demonstrated. On the first day after birth, however, he notes that sugar solutions were received with less objection than salt or acid solutions. Lane again makes a generalized statement that in postnatal life this sense is gradually perfected, although no experimental evidence is given to support the view.

Hearing. Here Lane reports that "absolutely no response to sound was noted before the twelfth day after birth," and that "from that day to the sixteenth or seventeenth day there is a gradual increase in the ability to perceive sound" (p. 63). No evidence is given for this conclusion in the monograph, however, save that change is inferred from structure. In his conclusions he says:

> Previous to the twelfth day the portions of the ear concerned with the perception of sound have been undergoing a gradual development, but have not yet reached that degree of differentiation of the organ of Corti necessary for the perception of sound. By the twelfth or thirteenth day the organ of Corti is apparently differentiated for at least part of its extent, though the lumen of the external auditory meatus is not fully opened. The next few days

witness the completion of the differentiation of the apparatus of hearing [p. 63].

For a study of the early growth of the inner ear of the rat, see Wada (1923).

Vision. As far as this sense is concerned, the report of Lane is: "Absolutely no response to light was obtained before the opening of the eyes on the sixteenth or seventeenth postnatal day" (p. 69). This was determined by the use of an electric flashlight. The objection may be raised, on the basis of a good deal of other experimental work, that this stimulus was possibly not strong enough to bring about response. No record is given of the pupillary response which might have been obtained had the eyelids been opened by operation. Histological evidence, however, is given to suggest that there is a neural and receptor development paralleling the reported functional development.

Lane's theoretical conclusions concerning the anatomical basis of early development in the rat fetus and the function of the receptor in the development of the reflex arc will be given at the close of this chapter.

From the report just given of Lane's work, as well as from the incidental observations in the work of Swenson and Angulo y González, it becomes obvious that, of all the sensory fields in the white rat, that of skin sensitivity is apparently earliest and most completely developed during prenatal life. The development of this sense in the fetal rat was quite extensively investigated by Raney, working with the writer (Raney and Carmichael, 1934). In this work the pregnant female was deeply anesthetized and the spinal cord completely transected between the sixth and seventh cervical vertebrae. The result of this operation was to provide an effectively immobilized and, so far as the field of the operation is concerned, a completely desensitized adult organism in which, however, circulation and respiration continue in a virtually normal condition. After a period of one and a half to two hours, the fetuses were shelled out, with placental circulation maintained, into physiological salt solution held at 37.5° C. by thermostatic control. Raney and Carmichael's work was conducted not only in an effort to study the effect of change of skin sensitivity at various fetal developmental ages, but also to consider the origin of what may be called "local sign," at least in so far as such local sign may be demonstrated in the progress of localizing movements of the limbs of the fetus resulting from punctiform stimulation.

Klemm (1914), in his history of space perception, referred to the development of the view that space is perceived in relation to body movement. James (1890, Vol. II, pp. 170–282) also considered the factors leading to this view, and Peterson's experimental work (1926) on local signs as orientation tendencies again emphasized this conception. Raney and Carmichael's work shows that with increasing gestation age the fetus first becomes sensitive to areal stimulation, as, for example, to stimulation with a camel's-hair brush approximately 5 mm. in diameter. Response to punctiform stimulation by a single light hair is observed to begin some time later. The first appearance of sensitivity is in the head region and is observed to pass gradually caudad (that is, toward the tail). The first responses to stimulation are slight movements of the trunk occurring during the sixteenth day, as noted by previous investigators. As development continues, stimulation at any sensitive point may elicit much more complicated behavior, often involving neck, trunk, forelimb, hindlimb, and other muscle movements. The peculiar sensitivity to tactual stimulation of the region from which the vibrissae issue is noted throughout this developmental sequence. The early func-

tion of this tactual organ, as it may be called, is particularly interesting in reference to the full innervation of this area as shown by Lane and in the behavioral observations on the function of the vibrissae in young rats by Small (1899), and especially in the special study of this receptor field by Vincent (1912).

Raney and Carmichael (1934) have found, however, where the mechanical possibility of movement is present, that is, where the limb may touch the surface, that the responses may gradually become more and more precisely related to the point of stimulation. Thus at an early gestation age stimulation of the region of the vibrissae may lead to slight trunk movements. Later such stimulation may lead to the movement of many muscle groups of the fetus, including the limbs. At a still later time, the principal response may be merely that of the forepaw moved ever so slightly toward the point stimulated. If the point touched is on the body wall, the movement may be toward that point. If it is on the nose, it may be toward that point. It must be noted, however, that, even at the best time for such differentiated response in late gestation periods, the stimulation of any point may also bring out very general activity. It is possible that such generalized response is due to interruption of some "spontaneous" movement, or that it is related to the strength of stimulation. The frequency of stimulation or the immediate past activity of the organism may also be important in inducing such activity. The significance of intensity of stimulation in this connection in the guinea pig fetus is explained above. This is not the place for a full consideration of the theoretical implications of Raney and Carmichael's study as it bears on space perception, but the results suggest a certain reformulation of one form of a modified genetic theory of the perception of extension as considered by Boring (1929, pp. 250–262).

Lincoln (1932), also working in collaboration with Carmichael, was able to show in the rat fetus something of the elaborate sensory and behavioral sequences which are antecedent to the sucking reflex as that reflex is seen at birth. The report of this investigation is recorded in library copies of a thesis. This work is especially interesting in relation to Lane's work on the correlation between structure and function in the nursing reflex of the young rat and guinea pig. In Lane's work (1924) especial attention is given to the development of the tongue both as a locus of taste receptors and as a prehensile organ. Further references to the sucking reflex are given below.

Angulo y González (1937) has shown that the sensory system follows the motor system in development. The earliest functional sensory endings develop in the region of the snout as tactile receptors. The receptors in the forelimbs, for example, are later in development than those in the snout. The total arc connections seem to be formed by the growth of collateral fibers which establish functional connections after the sensory and motor systems are complete.

Windle (1934b) has demonstrated that all the spinal reflex arcs are present at 11 mm. but they are incomplete because sensory collaterals are just beginning to enter the mantle layer of the spinal cord. The main difference between the nervous system of motile and nonmotile fetuses lies in the number and length of these elements.

Besides the special studies noted above, there have been a number of other investigations dealing with particular muscle groups or special behavioral characteristics of the white rat fetus. Corey (1931) has studied the causative factors of the initial inspiration of mammalian fetuses, using the white rat as material. In this study it is concluded that the initial respiration of the fetus is normally brought about by a change in the relationship between carbon dioxide and oxygen in the blood in cooperation with the stimulating effect of the drying of the skin. Blincoe (1928a, 1928b) has worked on the development of behavior in the motor system of the forelimb of the rat. He has elaborately studied the anatomy of the limb before the fifteenth day, that is, just before the onset of motility. An effort has also been made to present a correlation between this stage of development in the rat and in man. In the later study he points out that it seems that the arm of the rat shows "the static assembling of many bodily components which await some complementary addition to render them a dynamic whole" (1928b, p. 293). It is suggested that this addition is to be found in functional innervation. In this connection see also a paper by Barron (1934) on the results of his experiments on the peripheral anastomoses between the fore- and hindlimb nerves of albino rats.

Also working with the rat fetus, Windle, Minear, Austin, and Orr (1935) have shown that physiological muscular development may be summarized in the course which it takes. In general this development proceeds from the head to the tail region and distad and ventrad from the dorsal part of the trunk. (See also Windle and Baxter, 1935, 1936.)

Bors (1925), Nicholas (1925, 1926, 1929c), Hooker and Nicholas (1927, 1930), Nicholas and Hooker (1928), and others have performed experimental operations on rat fetuses. Following a very elaborate technique, these students have been able to operate on mammalian fetuses without interrupting pregnancy. In the course of this work they have made a number of incidental observations on the development of motility, and Hooker and Nicholas

(1930) particularly have pointed out the fact that during intrauterine existence "movements are restricted to a large degree and there is also a greater degree of independence of the individual cord segments than is found in later postnatal stages" (p. 431). These observations are significant, for they were made under conditions more nearly approaching those of normal development than any other studies of the development of mammals.

Straus and Weddell (1940) have shown that the earliest visible contractions of the forelimb muscles of the rat appear during the latter half of the fifteenth or the first half of the sixteenth postinsemination day. The extensor muscles are more readily stimulated than the flexor muscles, and if a nerve trunk can be stimulated the response is greater than if the muscle must be directly stimulated. (See also Straus, 1939.)

Corey (1934) has shown that in the fetal rat the cortex is not extensively involved in the production of fetal movements.

A number of studies of special aspects of the development of behavior have been made on the rabbit, to a few of which reference has been made above. Preyer (1885, pp. 418 ff.) made some observations on fetal organisms of this type. Langworthy (1926) has worked on progression in very young rabbits. He points out that in such animals decerebration does not lead to extensor rigidity but to prolonged progression movements. In the more mature newborn guinea pig, however, rigidity follows decerebration. This difference is attributed to the degree of myelinization in the central nervous system. The importance of myelinization, or the formation of the myelin sheaths, on neurons is discussed below. Zuntz (1877) also used the rabbit fetus in his work on respiration. Richter (1925) has observed sucking movements in rabbit fetuses about 20 days old.

Pankratz (1931b) has adapted Swenson's technique to the study of the rabbit. Mechanical stimulation of nose, head, and neck led to response of simple lateral flexion of neck and trunk in 15- to 16-day rabbit fetuses. In a 17-day fetus there was a marked ventrolateral flexion of head and upper trunk, with some movement of the forelimbs. In 20-day-old fetuses, opening and closing of the mouth, active movements of the forelimbs, flexion of the hindlimbs, and lateral flexion of the whole trunk were observed. As the gestation period advanced the movements became more complex.

The cat has proved itself to be an eminently suitable animal for the laboratory study of the development of fetal behavior. Its neuromuscular system is quite highly organized. Its gestation age of over sixty days allows for the development of an organism at birth that is relatively mature. Much is also known as a result of past research concerning its structural development (Hill and Tribe, 1924; Latimer, 1931; Latimer and Aikman, 1931), anatomy, and certain of its adult behavioral characteristics, such as the righting response (Camis, 1930). These factors combine to make the animal peculiarly satisfactory for research upon the development of fetal behavior. The general purposes of this chapter, therefore, demand a rather complete summary of the investigations of fetal behavior in the cat.

Windle and Griffin (1931) reported a study in which a large number of cat fetuses of precisely known or accurately estimated gestation age were experimentally studied. The technique employed by these investigators involved an operation on the brain of the mother cat such that later, without anesthesia, it was possible to study the fetal organisms under warm physiological salt solution with fully maintained placental circulation. The methods of studying the fetuses varied more or less according to age. In all, 34 pregnant cats were used, giving 125 living embryos and fetuses for study. Of the litters of the 34 cats thus employed, 19 were of known age since copulation. The ages of the other fetuses were calculated from their body measurements, a procedure that is not in all respects satisfactory.

These investigators reported that no movement was seen in the 23-day stage or on any day previous to that. In later studies, however, it was established that movement does take place on the twenty-third day (Windle and Becker, 1940a). In the 24- and 25-day stage, what the reader may now begin to consider as the characteristic response of young fetuses, namely, the very slightest slow ventral lateral head flexion, was observed in a number of embryos. This was also independently confirmed by Windle (1930a). The earliest limb reflexes are well-localized movements occurring on the side of stimulation at the twenty-fourth day (Windle, 1934a). In the 26- to 27-day stage, movements were in general more complex and of greater amplitude or duration and strength than those noted previously. Generalized trunk undulations, however, still formed the permanent background of activity, but forelimb flexion had also begun. The investigators have pointed out that, at this stage, rotation of head and trunk appears to be coordinated with older components, but that this activity results in movements which strikingly resemble the righting reflexes seen in later fetal life. At this stage the fetuses seem unresponsive to brush or probe. At 28 days slight flexion of the hindlegs was noticed, and at this time also the first responses to touch, particularly in the head region, were observed. Stimulation of this sort was followed by typical apparently "random" head-trunk-limb undulations. At 30 days the activity recorded was still more complex. Active

flexion of the hindlimbs was noted, and at the same time definite, although sluggish, mouth movements appeared. From this time until birth, continued and progressive increase in the specificity of behavior was noted by these observers.

So far as the development of sensory capacity in these animals is concerned, it has already been noted that no external response to stimulation is found in fetuses of less than 26 mm., that is, of approximately 28 gestation days. These investigators hold that there is evidence, however, of exteroceptive and proprioceptive function even in the first animals that show spontaneous movements. "The fact that the unilateral trunk or neck flexions seemed always to be executed toward the observer and away from the surface on which they rested may indicate that the earliest sensation is one of deep pressure" (Windle and Griffin, 1931, p. 175). So far as behavior at the 26-mm. stage is concerned, it is held that the activity noted may be the result of a "primitive type of proprioception" (p. 175). This would explain the spread of motor response, although there is some possibility that the wavelike progression of muscular contraction noted is due to the function of long association pathways in the central nervous system.

The first so-called cutaneous reflexogenous zone, that is, cutaneous area, in which stimulation can be shown to lead to response included the nose areas and in general most of the head. Pronounced response in the fetuses at 28 days followed stimulation of the nose. Gradually, as fetuses of later ages were considered, the area spread caudally to the neck, pectoral region, forelimbs, trunk, hindlimbs, and finally to the tail. Windle and Griffin point out: "It is interesting to note that spontaneous motor activity always involved a part of the body before responses could be elicited either locally or at a distance from the point stimulated" (p. 175). The strength of stimulation was also reported as significant in determining the nature of response. Usually the light touch of a brush was found to be ineffective in specimens less than 60 mm. long. In a few fetuses a little longer than this a response

75 to 80 mm. marked differences between the responses to light and to strong stimuli were observed, and pain responses were thought to be definitely present.

In the cat, vestibular function probably appears in prenatal life. No absolute evidence of its presence is found until very shortly before birth. It should be borne

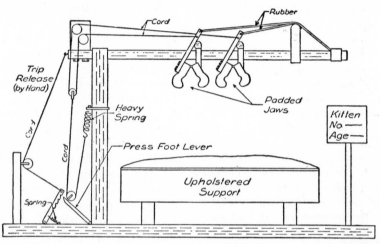

FIGURE 12. Apparatus used in the study of the development of the air-righting reflex in small mammals. (From "A Study of the Development of the Air-Righting Reflex in Cats and Rabbits," by J. Warkentin and L. Carmichael. *Journal of Genetic Psychology*, 1939, *55*, 68. By permission of the publisher.)

was secured when the brush was applied to the nose. It was noticed that a light stimulus which caused no response if once applied was sometimes adequate if repeated several times. This effect of summation of stimuli is noted in many fetal forms under a variety of conditions. Very little difference could be observed between strong innocuous stimulation and stimulation producing observable protoplasmic damage. The authors believe that the primitive type of pressure-touch sensitivity, which they postulate as the characteristic state of the receptor surface of early fetuses, was not replaced by definite touch and pain until relatively late in fetal life. In fetuses of

in mind in all considerations of this sense in fetal life that there are great difficulties in testing it accurately in a squirming fetus. In a later study, however, Windle and Fish (1932) demonstrated by the use of several techniques, including the operative interference with the vestibular apparatus, that the true vestibular righting reflex elicited in animals in contact with a surface probably appears in fetal kittens of 100- to 115-mm. crown-rump length, that is, on about the fifty-fourth day of gestation. These same investigators (Fish and Windle, 1932) considered the onset of rotary and postrotary nystagmus in the eyes of newborn cats.

For an important early study of the developing of the "falling reflex," see Muller and Weed (1916). Carmichael (1934b) and later Warkentin and Carmichael (1939) studied the genetic development of the

of the act. Thus an animal may be able to perform all the behavioral acts needed in air righting before the total pattern in time can be accomplished in the short period allowed by a free fall.

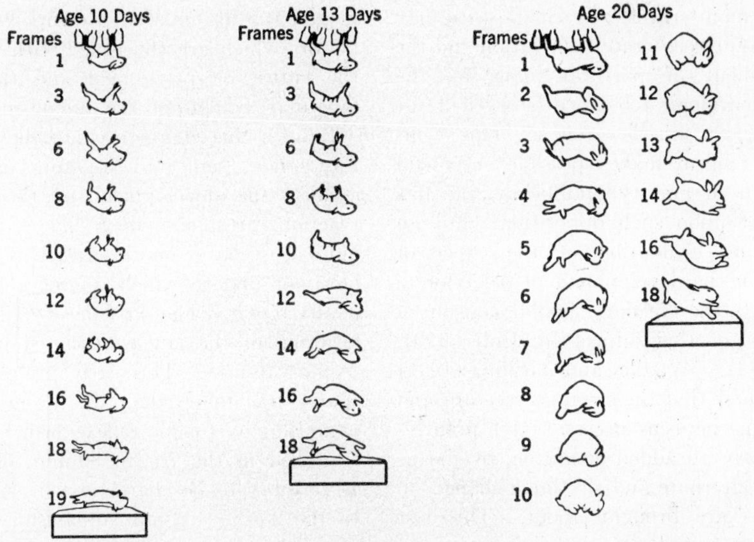

FIGURE 13. Diagrams of movement sequences during falling in a young rabbit at three different ages—10 days, 13 days, 20 days. (From "A Study of the Development of the Air-Righting Reflex in Cats and Rabbits," by J. Warkentin and L. Carmichael. *Journal of Genetic Psychology*, 1939, *55*, 77. By permission of the publisher.) Not every frame is shown. The frames represented are numbered at the left of each diagram, the numbering for each falling sequence beginning with "Frame 1" as the last frame before the jaws opened. Since the film was photographed at the rate of 64 frames per second, and the exposure per frame was about 2 sigma, the time interval from one frame to the next was roughly 15 sigma. All the diagrams are drawn to the same scale; hence the animal is larger at the later ages because of normal gain in size and weight during the days represented.

kitten's capacity to right itself when falling through the air. Rabbits were also used in the second study. The apparatus used to release the animals is shown in Figure 12, and a typical sequence as drawn from high-speed moving-picture films is shown in Figure 13. These studies were correlated with studies on the development of vision in kittens (Warkentin, 1938). They show that there is a genetic relationship between the time sequence of the partial responses making up air righting and the performance

From study of the vestibular sense, Windle and Griffin (1931) turn to a consideration of the development of posture and progression in general. In this study they follow in part the analysis of Hinsey, Ranson, and McNattin (1930). Walking can be shown to require the coordination of several behavioral patterns, including the ability to maintain an erect posture. In this connection the analysis of Magnus (1924, pp. 357 ff.), which shows that posture may depend on impulses from the various receptor groups of the nonauditory labyrinth, from the proprioceptors of the muscles and associated structures, and from the exteroceptors including touch and the distance receptors, is distinctly relevant. In view of the facts it becomes obvious that the maintenance of erect posture may demand quite elaborate stimulation and the establishment of postural tonus by the proper neurological balance between flexor and extensor muscle groups. This complex mechanism makes possible successful opposition to gravity and behavioral acts dependent upon such opposition. For an illuminating evaluation of the effect of gravity on the development of behavior in mammals, the reader should consult a treatment of this subject by Holt (1931, pp. 62–72). Windle and Griffin (1931) further show that the essential receptor and effector mechanisms necessary for progression involve an added condition, by means of which alternate and rhythmic changes in the limbs are brought about. This last component is necessary if balance is to be changed in such a way that stepping movements may be accomplished.

Windle and Griffin report that these mechanisms, which are essential to locomotion, develop at different times during fetal growth. The onset of the righting reflex has just been reviewed. The first positive evidence of rhythmic movement of the forelimbs, involving flexion and extension movements, was seen in a 58- to 60-mm. fetus. At this time the hindleg movements were less rhythmical. Occasionally in a 100-mm. fetus complete stepping movements were observed. In this connection the study of Laughton (1924) on the nervous mechanism of progression in mammals should also be consulted. It is further suggested by Windle and his associates that the unilateral rhythmic flexion-extension of the limb as seen in the scratching reflex may have a relationship to the occurrence

of the alternate rhythms of locomotion. The first indication of the scratch phenomenon was thought to have been observed at the 75- to 80-mm. stage, following ear stimulation. These observations show that the walking movement even as seen in prenatal life involves a complex series of factors which are concerned with virtually the entire receptive field and the entire muscular system of the organism.

Besides this characteristic behavior pattern, these same investigators have also studied the development of the sucking reaction, a response which, like that of locomotion, is characteristic of early vertebrate behavior and to which reference has been made above. The first head raising and lowering of the jaw were noted in 27- to 28-mm. fetuses. This early prefeeding response was followed in the 45- to 50-mm. organisms by tongue reflexes which were so amplified in the 70- to 80-mm. organisms as possibly to be characterized as sucking. In the 95- to 103-mm. organisms, this response had developed so much farther that it was present in virtually its adult form (Windle and Griffin, 1931; Windle and Minear, 1934). Windle and Minear have also shown that the response to faradic shock given to the snout changes with age. At first the reaction is dominantly away from the stimulus (that is, on the opposite side); later, homolateral responses appear. Windle (1937) and his collaborators (Windle, O'Donnell, and Glasshagle, 1933) have also studied the detailed neurology related to the first forelimb responses. At 14 mm., or about 23 days, true reflexes are elicited. At this time the sensory collaterals of the cord are just complete. Windle emphasizes the fact that these responses are not part of a total mass reaction pattern when they first appear. He had previously (1935) shown that the simplest forms of reflex pathways are laid down in the central nervous system before higher integration systems are functional. (See also Windle, Orr, and Minear, 1934.) This same investigator (Windle, 1939) suggests that calcium and potassium deficiencies may account for certain delays observed in the onset of fetal movements.

Another elaborate study of the development of behavior in the fetal cat was undertaken in 1928 by Coronios, working in collaboration with Carmichael and other investigators (Coronios, 1930, 1931, 1933; Coronios, Schlosberg, and Carmichael, 1932). Unlike Windle and Griffin, Coronios used only fetuses from litters whose insemination age he knew accurately. In Coronios' work the pregnant female was prepared for observation under deep ether anesthesia. While the animal was anesthetized the carotid arteries were ligated, a cannula inserted in the trachea, and a complete midbrain section carefully performed. After this section, the anesthetic was immediately discontinued. The decerebrate adult cat was then allowed to remain quiet for 1½ or 2 hours before the fetuses were exposed for observation by an operative technique. Before the observations began, the cat was placed in a specially devised bath apparatus in which physiological salt solution was maintained thermostatically at 37.5° ± 0.5° C. Into this blood-warm liquid the fetuses were shelled out one by one. A summary of the behavior observed at various copulation ages may be found in Figure 14. In a supplement to this chart Coronios (1933) offers the following conclusions:

In the early stages the behavior is diffuse, variable, relatively uncoordinated, and weak. With the increase in gestation age, the reactions become more vigorous, more regular in their appearance, less variable, individualized, and better coordinated. These qualitative changes do not occur abruptly but are continuously progressive modifications in the quality of the observed reactions. Moreover, these quali-

tative changes do not, as it were, "invade" the total organism at once. Rather they seem to follow a general course in their development, beginning at the head region and progressing toward the tail [p. 363].

It is interesting to note in this description of the development of behavior in a highly organized mammalian fetus a marked similarity to the description of the development of behavior noted in *Amblystoma* and virtually all other forms considered above. It must be emphasized, however, that there is danger in making too sweeping generalizations about fetal behavior, but it is impossible to deny that there are certain descriptive terms which accurately characterize the development of behavior in many forms.

As a conclusion to his work, Coronios (1933) makes the following points:

1. Before birth there is a rapid, progressive, and continuous development of behavior in the fetus of the cat.

2. The development of behavior progresses from a diffuse, massive, variable, relatively unorganized state to a condition where many of the reactions are more regular in their appearance, less variable, better organized, and relatively individualized.

3. In the early stages of prenatal development the behavior appears to be progressing along a cephalocaudal course.

4. The development of the sensitivity of the reflexogenous zones passes through a continuous and transitional development from a time when rather vigorous stimulation of any "spot" of the body within a large area serves to elicit variable, diffuse, uncoordinated patterns of behavior to a later time when a weak stimulus becomes adequate, within a much more circumscribed area for precise, well-coordinated, uniform, and less variable patterns of behavior. The direction of such development is cephalocaudal.

5. The "primitive" reactions of breathing, righting, locomotion, and feeding are

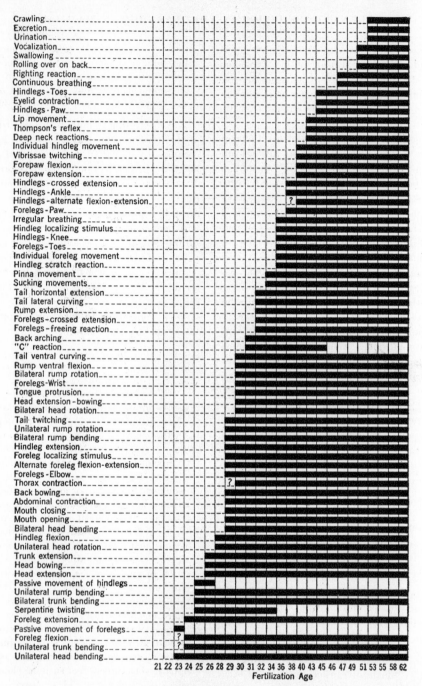

FIGURE 14. A chart constructed to show the development of behavior in cat fetuses of various gestation ages. (From "Development of Behavior in the Fetal Cat," by J. D. Coronios. *Genetic Psychology Monographs*, 1933, *14*, 362. By permission of the Journal Press, publisher.)

the products of a long and continuously progressive course of prenatal development.

6. Behavior development appears first in the gross musculature, and in the fine musculature later.

7. Behavior develops in each of the limbs from a proximal to a distal point; that is, the entire limb is first involved in the response and then gradually the more distal joints become, as it were, independent of the total movement [pp. 377–378].

Each of these generalizations is to be taken as a statement of a typical course of development and not as a specific formula that can be applied to other mammals or man in advance of observation. For example, from the time of Aristotle the anteroposterior course of development has been noted (Needham, 1931, p. 75). This apparently holds true in the primitive gradients of the organism and in the weight of different organs of its developing structure, as well as in the development of "individuated" behavior. This generalization must, of course, be considered descriptive and not explanatory. For further discussion, see Kingsbury (1924, 1926) and Child (1925).

Besides these two elaborate studies of the development of behavior in the fetal cat, there have been a number of incidental studies calculated to investigate some special problem in fetal behavioral growth. T. G. Brown (1914, 1915) reports an experiment on the development of the mechanism of progression in the fetal cat. He used four fetuses of unknown gestation age, the placental circulation being maintained and the observations made in a warm salt solution. The fetuses were studied both before and after decerebration. On the basis of this work he asserts that blood stimulation is very important in eliciting the rhythmic movements seen before birth. He concludes:

It is possible that the "quickening" movements which are a symptom of human pregnancy may be due to similar progression movements in man; and if they are thus evoked by some such accidental asphyxia as that conditioned by pressure upon the umbilical cord they may tend, in an indiscriminate manner it is true, to relieve that pressure [1915, p. 214].

He also suggests on the basis of other observations a phylogenetic theory of the development of locomotion based on Sherrington's view of motor half-centers in the central nervous system.

Langworthy (1929) has also studied the development of behavior in the fetus of the cat. He reported a study on six fetuses near term and a number of kittens of varying ages after natural birth. In these fetuses after decerebration he found behavior that is characteristic of the late cat fetus, although less well-defined hindleg movements were observed than those reported by Brown. The behavior of the fetal and young organisms was then correlated with structural studies of the nervous system. He reported in summary of this work:

Bilateral movements of the extremities begin to coordinate when the ventral commissural fibers of the cord receive their myelin sheath. The animals turn the body at a time when myelinated vestibular fibers reach the spinal cord. The hindleg movements become better coordinated when myelinization becomes marked in the lumbar portion of the cord [p. 169].

The general significance of this correlation of behavior and myelinization will be considered below.

Tilney has prepared a chart showing the stream of behavior reaction in the cat similar to the chart concerning the development of behavior in the guinea pig cited above (Woodworth, 1929, p. 204). In this chart many behavioral acts are shown as appearing in postnatal life which the studies given above show in prenatal life. This is true of "primitive escape," "snatching," and, indeed, virtually all the reactions shown in the chart. The "sudden emergence" of some of these behavior patterns noted below the chart, as in most "saltatory maturation," may seem therefore to involve the reactivation under different environmental conditions of behavior which has had a prenatal developmental history. Similar facts of human fetal development are significant in interpreting the conclusions of Gesell (1929b) and Shirley (1931a, 1931b) concerning human behavioral maturation. Windle and Orr (1934b) have shown that when the fetus is dying there is likely to be a vermiform contraction. These general reactions may appear after the heart has ceased to beat.

A number of special studies have been made on other mammals. Erasmus Darwin (1796, p. 101) quotes an account from Galen of the fetal development of the goat. The fetus, after removal, got to its feet and walked, shook itself, scratched, smelled of objects, and then drank milk. Huggett (1927, 1930) has used this same ungulate in elaborate studies of the onset of breathing reflexes in the fetus, which will be considered below. He used animals 1 or 2 months before full term. The size of the animal made it convenient for operative purposes, but some difficulties which experimenters with small animals are spared may be noted, since a "domestic bath" had to be used to hold the saline solution into which the fetus was delivered (1927).

Scharpenberg and Windle (1938) have now shown that, in the sheep, myogenic responses precede neurogenic ones. Some sensory collateral fibers have grown out from the dorsal funiculus and have reached the internuncial neurones of the cord at the time the first true reflex arcs are established. The most elaborate studies of the fetus of the sheep, however, have been made by Barcroft and Barron (1939). These investigators outline the results of an elaborate series of studies upon this large fetus. In this animal the first spontaneous movements appear on the thirty-fifth day after insemination. These responses involve forelimb, neck, and trunk movements. By the thirty-eighth day the observed movements are more "definite" and the movements are larger and more numerous. Such spontaneous movements are quite transient. Even in a 40-day fetus they may last only 5 minutes after delivery. Maintained posture following movement is seen by the forty-second day. In their study of responses these investigators stimulated by various means the fields related to some of the important peripheral nerves of the body. As a conclusion of the study of the maxillary nerve, for example, they state that the motor response to specific stimulation is at first confined to a few muscles, then more muscles become involved, but at length only those are activated which respond in the adult sheep. Again, in regard to the sensory nerves distributed to the trunk and limbs they conclude that local muscular reactions are first evoked, but with increasing development more and more muscles may be brought into play.

Barcroft and Barron (1936) have also studied the genesis of respiratory movements in the fetus of the sheep. Barcroft, Barron, and Windle (1936) have shown in the same large embryo localized responses to mechanical and electrical stimulation. These writers conclude that behavior may be considered to have its genesis in localized patterns of response. This conclusion is qualified, however, in a later paper by Barcroft and Barron (1937a), in which a neurological distinction is drawn between reflexes and local contractions, for example, of the neck. These same investigators in another paper (1937b) give an excellent description of the movements of the fetal sheep in midfetal life. Barcroft himself gives a more general description of this work in a paper entitled "The Mammal before and after Birth" (1935).

Barcroft's summary of much of this work appears in his excellent volume of Terry Lectures entitled *The Brain and Its Environment* (1938). In this volume brain activity in relation to its internal environment in fetal and neonatal life is brilliantly described. In all of Barcroft's work the importance of the changing internal environment of the fetus subjected to experimental study is emphasized. For a comprehensive evaluation of these problems see Barron (1950) and Windle (1950).

Bolk (1926) has made a comparative morphological study of fetuses of the gorilla, chimpanzee, and man in relation to a theory of development. Tinklepaugh, Hartman, and Squier (1930) have studied fetal heart rate in the monkey. Hines and Straus (1934) have studied the motor cortex of fetal and infant rhesus monkeys. The gestation period of the macaques used was taken as 168 days. Fetuses 85 days old showed good contralateral responses of shoulder and head on cortical stimulation. The fingers gained cortical representation during the first week after birth, as did also the facial areas and lower extremities. It seems that the muscles innervated by the dorsal strata of the limb plexus (extensor system) are the first muscles of the extremities to gain representation in the motor cortex.

Incidental observations on other animal fetuses are given by J. F. Craig (1930) in his revision of Fleming's *Veterinary Obstetrics*. Needham (1931, pp. 484–489) gives tables of the gestation times of hundreds of animals which are valuable for comparative purposes.

General Aspects of Human Fetal Development

Prescientific Study. From one point of view at any rate, all that has gone before in this chapter has been intended to prepare the reader for the consideration of the prenatal development of behavior in human beings. Behavioral development before birth has long been a subject of notice in the human race, but only comparatively recently has it been studied in a systematic and scientific manner.

That the fetus moves before birth is knowledge as old as mankind. Certainly there are references to this phenomenon in the folklore of primitive peoples (Ploss and Bartels, 1927). It is interesting to notice also, so far as the anthropomorphic theory of primitive deities is concerned, that the process of making gods in the image of man even included speculations about god embryos. For a consideration of this topic, see Briffault's work *The Mothers* (1927) and Witkowski (1887). There are references to prenatal development of behavior in Biblical literature and in ancient Indian and Chinese writings. The Egyptians early began the consideration of this matter, as is shown in a hymn to the sun god attributed to Amenophis IV (about 1400 B.C.):

Creator of the germ in woman,
Maker of seed in man,
Giving life to the son in the body of his mother,
Soothing him that he may not weep,
Nurse (even) in the womb.
Giver of breath to animate everyone that he maketh
When he cometh forth from the womb on the day of his birth.
[Needham, 1931, p. 49.] [1]

[1] For much of the historical material given in various parts of this chapter, including the quotation at the head of the chapter, the writer is indebted for actual references and for many interpretations to Needham's illuminating history of embryology (1931). The writer had begun the collection of material in

In pre-Socratic Greek antiquity, among the many who speculated on almost all aspects of nature were those who considered embryology and, apparently, also the beginnings of fetal activity. It was at this time, the very beginning of recorded scientific history, that some of the notions arose in what has been called "theological embryology" which have come down to our own period. At this time some held that the general form of the body is completed in males many days before it is completed in females (Needham, 1931, pp. 51–53). Similarly, Empedocles (about 450 B.C.) began the speculation, which was long to continue, as to whether or not the "life" of the embryo was like the "life" of the independent individual (Needham, p. 51). Plutarch says that Plato (circa 429–347 B.C.) directly asserts that the fetus is a living creature that moves and is fed within the body cavities of the mother (Needham, p. 60).

It was not, however, until the time of Aristotle (384–322 B.C.) that the life and soul of the embryo were considered in detail. In the third chapter of Aristotle's remarkable treatise on embryology, the entrance of the various souls into the embryo is considered. The views there expressed have possibly influenced the laws related to abortion which have appeared since Aristotle's time in canon and civil codes. In transmuted form these ideas appear in both patristic and scholastic philosophy. It is possible that this Aristotelian doctrine is basic to the rules of the church in regard to prenatal baptism, which is considered historically by Witkowski (1887, pp. 133–

this field before Needham's book was published, but when it appeared it proved to be so fruitful in suggestion that it has been used extensively in this chapter. Whenever possible, specific references are given. For a study of the ideas of primitive peoples concerning generation as they have evolved into modern scientific understanding, the reader is urged to consult Meyer's *The Rise of Embryology* (1939).

152). Aristotle taught that the vegetative or nutritive soul existed in the unfertilized material of the embryo. In summary, Aristotle, in the following quotation given by Needham (p. 69), says:

> . . . for nobody . . . would put down the unfertilised embryo as soulless or in every sense bereft of life (since both the semen and the embryo of an animal have every bit as much life as a plant). . . . As it develops it also acquires the sensitive soul in virtue of which an animal is an animal. . . . For first of all such embryos seem to live the life of a plant, and it is clear that we must be guided by this in speaking of the sensitive and the rational soul. For all three kinds of soul, not only the nutritive, must be possessed potentially before they are possessed actually.

During the third century B.C., Herophilus, according to Plutarch, attributes to newborn babies a natural movement, but not respiration. The sinews are the instrumental cause of this movement. Afterward the baby becomes a perfect living animal, and when it is taken forth from the mother's body it inhales air (Needham, pp. 78–80).

Galen is also credited with writing much between A.D. 150 and A.D. 180 upon the subject of developmental embryology. He has especially considered the question of whether the embryo may be described as an animal. A reference to Galen's observations on a goat fetus has already been made.

In the years sometimes called, because of the dominance of the church fathers, the Patristic Period, interest continued in the movements of the fetus. Tertullian (born A.D. 160) held that the soul was fully present in the embryo through uterine life. In his *De Anima* he says:

> Reply . . . O ye Mothers, and say whether you do not feel the movements of the child within you. How then can it have no soul? [Needham, 1931, p. 91.]

Saint Augustine, Bishop of Hippo, apparently did not wholly agree with this, but held that the soul entered the fetus in the second gestation month and sex in the fourth month. Other church authorities followed Saint Augustine in this matter. The council of the church held at Byzantium in 692, however, declared that no distinction could be made so far as infanticide is concerned as to whether the fetus was "formed" or "unformed." Canon law for a time came to recognize the fortieth day for males and the eightieth day for females as the moment of animation, but later the fortieth day was accepted for both sexes (Goeckel, 1911, p. 5). The reader who may wish a modern view of sex differences in development as an exercise in contrasts may well consult Riddle (1927) and Willier (1939).

In the Talmudic writings of the learned Jews between the second and sixth centuries are found a number of views concerning the possibility of stimulating the fetus in the uterus. It is possible that the cutaneous sensitivity of the fetus was understood by these writers (Needham, p. 93). Needham gives a reproduction of a picture from the *Liber Scivias* of Saint Hildegard of Bingen, approximately A.D. 1150, which represents the soul passing down from heaven and entering the body of a pregnant woman and then entering the embryo (p. 96). It is not difficult to believe that the basis for this picture is to be found not only in such embryological knowledge as had come down to this time from antiquity, but also in the direct observations current in all times concerning the quickening of the embryo (Needham, p. 102). The greatest of the Schoolmen, however, Saint Thomas Aquinas (1227–1274), often called "the Angelic Doctor," developed a more elaborate theory of embryonic animation. Needham interprets his views as follows:

He had a notion that the foetus was first endowed with a vegetative soul, which in due course perished, at which moment the embryo came into the possession of a sensitive soul, which died in its turn, only to be replaced by a rational soul provided directly by God [Needham, p. 104].

On the other hand, Duns Scotus (1266–1308), here as in so many other speculations a worthy opponent of Saint Thomas, considered that the embryo contained only a rational soul, which was infused directly into the organism. The views of both these scholastic teachers led to certain theological difficulties. It was difficult to say how the errors intrinsic in man since Adam's fall could be transmitted to each generation if the soul entered the fetus directly from heaven in each generation (Needham, p. 105). This really profound scholastic argument may in certain ways be considered the foreshadowing of some of the present-day arguments concerning the rôles of heredity and environment as determiners of development.

In Dante (1893 edition) it is interesting to note that a neurological theory of the animation of the fetus comes into play. He says:

. . . but how from being an animal it becomes a child, thou seest not yet, moreover this is so difficult a point that formerly it led astray one more wise than thou . . . so that in his teaching he separated the active "intellect" from the soul because he could not see any organ definitely appropriated by it. Open thy heart to the truth and know that as soon as the brain of the foetus is perfectly organised, the Prime Mover, rejoicing in this display of skill on the part of Nature, turns him towards it and infuses a new spirit replete with power into it which subsumes into its own essence the active elements which it finds already there, and so forms one single soul which lives and feels and is conscious of its own existence [Needham, p. 106].

After the Renaissance, books on midwifery began to appear, and in these practical treatises there are a number of observations on fetal movements. For information on these views, see Spencer's *History of British Midwifery from 1650–1800* (1927).

The great William Harvey (Spencer, 1921) combined in himself a knowledge of classical Renaissance embryology, a practical knowledge of midwifery, and a truly scientific ability in observation. A combination of these various advantages makes his writing peculiarly important in this field. He says in one place, according to Needham (p. 139):

> I saw long since a foetus . . . the magnitude of a peasecod cut out of the uterus of a doe, which was complete in all its members & I showed this pretty spectacle to our late King and Queen. It did swim, trim and perfect, in such a kinde of white, most transparent and crystalline moysture . . . about the bignesse of a pigeon's egge. . . .

In all his work Harvey maintained that growth was a process of continual epigenetic development and not the unfolding of something preformed in the eggs of the organisms considered. Harvey also gave a rather elaborate picture of the activity of the human fetus in which he said, in a quotation from Spencer (1921, p. 35):

> For he swimmeth in a water and moveth himself to and fro, he stretcheth himself now this way, and now that, and so is variously inflected and tumbled up and down, in so much that sometimes, being entangled in his own navel string, he is strangely ensnared.

Harvey noted the fact that the mother can feel the kicks of the unborn child in such a way as to assure her that the fetus does not always lie in the same position.

In 1664, Gregorius Nymmanus wrote in support of the proposition that the fetus in the uterus lives a life of its own, evincing its own vital actions, and if the mother dies it not uncommonly survives for a certain period, so that it can sometimes be taken alive from the dead body of its mother. The fetus, he continued, prepared its own vital spirits and the instruments of its own soul, there being no nerve between it and the mother. This is demonstrated by the fact that the fetus *in utero* moves during the mother's sleep (Needham, p. 160).

In the citation just given is seen a combination of the old speculation and the new statement of observation that had become so characteristic of the rebirth of science. This combination of attitudes toward fetal development comes down almost to our own day, but increasingly as the years have passed the problems of embryology have become questions of observation and not of speculation. For a consideration of certain aspects of the triumph of science over surmise in these matters, see Spencer's lecture entitled *The Renaissance of Midwifery* (1924). In the opinion of the writer there is, however, real significance in the fact that during the long centuries of speculation concerning the "besouling" of the fetus, the point of quickening was often considered most important. There is good reason for this. The writer is as convinced as was Tertullian that the quickening of the fetus is significant in the story of the onset of man's most distinctive characteristic—his mental life. Common sense and vulgar tradition are not sure scientific guides, but the observational basis of nonscientific speculation sometimes points to a truth neglected.

One of the problems that grow out of the view that the fetus early comes to have an independent existence is the value placed upon human fetal life. This problem of evaluation is essentially ethical rather than scientific. As such, it continues down to the present time to be significant. It is not, however, a topic within the scope of this chapter. Among the numerous treatments of this topic, the monograph by Goeckel (1911) dealing with the changes that have taken place in the evaluation of the life of the unborn human fetus is important. In this monograph the author reviews primitive opinion and the statements of Roman and old Germanic law in regard to the fetus. He presents an excellent bibliography of Roman Catholic theological pronouncements and of civil legal opinions on the value of the life of the fetus. The legal aspect of prenatal life is also given especial consideration in a paper by Morache (1904). As already noticed, the earlier history of the evaluation of fetal life is fully considered in Witkowski's detailed *Histoire des accouchements chez tous les peuples* (1887). Much of this work, however, seems to be based upon Cangiamila's *Embryologia Sacra* of 1775, which the writer has not seen.

Modern thinking about the value of the fetus is reviewed in such papers as those of Hughes (1905), Arendt (1910), and Glenn (1911), which treat of various aspects of the ethics of dealing with the life of the unborn child.

From early times the belief has been current that the mother's thoughts and experiences directly influence the fetus. For many years, however, this view of prenatal influence has existed in the popular rather than in the scientific tradition. That "thought transference" or some mysterious nervous relationship exists between mother and fetus is not, in general, held today by scientific investigators. Save in the chemical interchange between the two blood streams or in mechanical or infectious transmissions, biology and psychology offer no basis for this view. Compayré (1896, pp.

32–33) gives a brief history of this superstition. He describes the now amusing assertions of Malebranche in regard to the complete intercerebral sharing of all mental processes between fetus and mother and then carries the subject on to the speculations current in nonscientific writings at the end of the nineteenth century. Compayré does not, however, refer to the remarkable assertions of the philosopher Hegel (1894, pp. 28–29) concerning psychological embryology, in which mother and fetus are said to be in undivided "psychic unity." This magic relationship is held to be of the nature of animal magnetism, by which the character and talent of the mother are communicated to the child.

That superstitious views of prenatal influence are still discussed may be discovered by reading articles by the following writers: Coughlin (1905), Walton (1910), Christenbery (1910–1911), Tompkins (1911–1912), Barham (1915–1916), and R. L. Brown (1918). An example of such an observation is the following case described by Morrison (1920). A mother of five healthy children had two teeth removed during pregnancy. She feared that the child would have a harelip. She became obsessed with the idea. The child was born with a harelip. It proved difficult to convince the mother that maternal impressions were not an accepted scientific cause. In this case just given, one is apparently dealing with an unusual coincidence which seems very like a causal connection to those who participate in it emotionally. To the parent such a conclusion may thus be psychologically if not scientifically pardoned. Until new evidence is presented, however, such cases cannot be considered as having scientific significance. We may still say with some assurance that "prenatal influence" in the sense discussed is a superstition.

Scientific Study. We must now turn back in our consideration to the scientific study of the fetus in order to consider what is known about the actual behavioral development of the unborn child. For the human embryos and fetuses 2.1 mm. to 23 mm. in length. The length of each specimen is given in the legend below the figure.

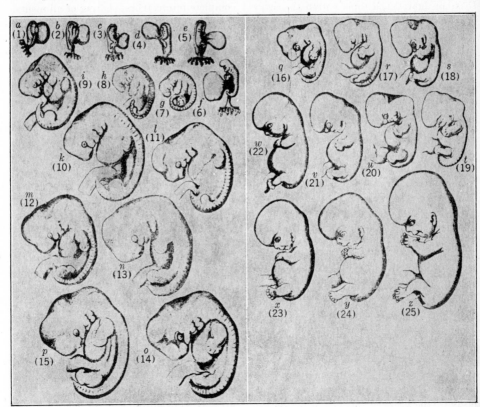

FIGURE 15. The human embryo of His's *Normentafel* as given by Keibel and Elze. (From *Normentafel zur Entwicklungsgeschichte des Menschen*, by F. Keibel and C. Elze. Jena: Fischer, 1908.) The letters designating each fetus, its size in millimeters, and its estimated age in days are: *a*, 2.1, 12–15; *b*, 2.12, 12–15; *c*, 2.15, 12–15; *d*, 2.2, 12–15; *e*, 2.6, 18–21; *f*, 4.2, 18–21; *g*, 4.0, 23; *h*, 5.5, 24–25; *i*, 7.5, 27–30; *k*, 10.0, 27–30; *l*, 9.1, 27–30; *m*, 9.1, 27–30; *n*, 10.5, 31–34; *o*, 11.0, 31–34; *p*, 11.5, 31–34; *q*, 12.5, 31–34; *r*, 13.7, 31–34; *s*, 13.8, about 35; *t*, 13.6, about 35; *u*, 14.5, about 37–38; *v*, 15.5, about 39–40; *w*, 16.0, about 42–45; *x*, 17.5, 47–51; *y*, 18.5, 52–54; *z*, 23.0, 60.

purpose of understanding this prenatal development of human behavior some general idea of morphological development will be found to provide a useful baseline upon which to represent the changing continuum of behavior. Figure 15, taken from Keibel and Elze (1908), shows a selected series of

Many efforts have been made to compile a table from which the ages of fetal human organisms can be estimated on the basis of known physical measurements. Scammon (1927), indeed, estimated that there were 7500 titles on the growth and physical development of the fetus, infant, and child.

The construction of satisfactory norms of growth in prenatal life has proved to be a very hard scientific task because of the difficulties that must be overcome in evaluating the material to be measured. In the first place, even if organisms of truly known age were plentifully available, each age norm would necessarily be stated in terms of some statistical average, because of the many factors such as genetic stock, nourishment, and specific pathology which influence fetal size. For a consideration of some of these factors in infrahuman mammals, see the work of Bluhm (1929).

A greater stumbling block than this variability of size at any true age, however, is found in the fact that it is peculiarly difficult in the human individual to place correctly the starting point of development, even though, in the light of the discussion given at the beginning of this chapter, such point be taken as the moment of fusion of the nuclei of the two parent cells. As a matter of fact, this moment can never be absolutely accurately determined, and therefore many different ways of approximating the zero point of development have been used in the history of human embryology. Even now no complete agreement has been reached as to the most desirable procedure in arriving at this calculation. Of these methods the following are probably most important:

1. *Menstruation age.* In this scale the age of the fetus is calculated from the first day of the last period of menstruation prior to the onset of pregnancy (Mall, 1918).

2. *Mean menstruation age.* This age is similar to the above, except that it is based on the average calculated from many cases. Thus if 51 days is taken as a mean, there is a possible deviation from 40 to 62 days, so far as the relationship to morphological measurement is concerned (Mall, 1918).

3. *Conception age.* The age of the fetus is calculated from the last day of the last menstrual period prior to pregnancy. This is the age used by His and adopted by Minot (1892).

4. *Copulation, or insemination, age.* This age, based upon calculation and upon trustworthy cases of known copulation time, is found to be approximately 10 days shorter than the mean menstrual age defined above (Mall, 1918).

5. *Ovulation age.* This age is calculated from the time of ovulation. It is at present extremely difficult to determine directly the time of ovulation. Determinations are complicated by many factors, such as the observation that it is difficult to know how long spermatozoa may live after entering the female genital tract, and by many other considerations. A complete and critical study of the time of ovulation and the fertile period of the menstrual cycle is given by Hartman (1936) in a book devoted to a consideration of recent data and theories in this field.

6. *Fertilization, or true, age.* This age cannot at present be directly determined, but must be calculated from 1, 2, or 4 above. In general it may be said that the present evidence points to the fact that fertilization occurs in less than 48 hours after copulation (Mall, 1918).

A standard table of age-length equivalents during the prenatal period of development is still further complicated by the fact that the linear measurements of the specimens have been obtained by different methods. The measurements commonly used include the crown-rump length and crown-heel length or standing height. The second of these is really related to the first, that is, it is crown-rump length added to the rump-heel length (Minot, 1903). Besides these two usual measurements, there is the *Näckenlange* of His, that is, the length measured from a particular point in the caudal bend to a particular point in the neck band of the specimen (His, 1880, 1882, 1885).

Of there measurements the crown-rump measurement is possibly best for embryological purposes (Minot, 1903), but in most of the work on the development of behavior the crown-heel length has been employed (Minkowski, 1923, p. 477; 1928a, p. 531; cf. also Scammon and Calkins, 1929).

In a subject so full of possible divergences of opinion, therefore, it is little wonder that many apparently conflicting tables of age-length relationships have been produced. Among the tables frequently referred to are those of C. M. Jackson (1909), Preyer (and the other embryologists summarized by him) given in Minot (1892, p. 381), and the summarizing table from Keith (1913). Instead of giving all these tables and many others to which reference might be made, or of attempting any averaging of the results, it has seemed wise to present Mall's (1910) table, which seems to the writer to be based on excellent evidence. This table, based on Mall's own work and upon the collection of material by Issmer, is given as Table 1. Mall (1918) has reviewed his work subsequent to the publication of this table and finds the table still accurate. It should be noted, however, that particularly so far as the younger stages are concerned there is a possibility of great variability in judging age from such a table as that given. Weight is probably a better index but is seldom given (Minot, 1892, p. 381). Therefore, in all age determinations given in this chapter, it should be borne in mind that the word "approximate" should really be placed in front of almost any statement of fetal age. Streeter (1920) has prepared a series of growth curves of the human fetus based upon most carefully computed data. In his tables and graphs the relationships of weight, sitting height, head size, foot length, and menstrual age of the human embryo are presented. Hooker (1944) has suggested that length and weight provide a

more useful index of behavioral development than does age. Gesell (1928, pp.

TABLE 1

ABBREVIATED DATA FROM MALL TO SHOW RELATIONSHIP BETWEEN VARIOUS AGE DETERMINATIONS OF THE FETUS AND CH (CROWN-HEEL) AND CR (CROWN-RUMP) MEASUREMENTS OF HEIGHT IN MILLIMETERS *

Probable Age in Weeks	Probable Age in Days	Mean Menstrual Age	Mean Length of Embryo (CH)	Mean Length of Embryo (CR)
1	7			
2	14			
3	21	31	.5	.5
4	28	37	2.5	2.5
5	35	43	5.5	5.5
6	42	51	11	11
7	49	59	19	17
8	56	65	30	25
9	63	72	41	32
10	70	79	57	43
11	77	86	76	53
12	84	94	98	68
13	91	100	117	81
14	98	108	145	100
15	105	114	161	111
16	112	121	180	121
17	119	128	198	134
18	126	136	215	145
19	133	143	233	157
20	140	150	250	167
21	147	157	268	180
22	154	165	286	192
23	161	171	302	202
24	168	177	315	210
25	175	185	331	220
26	182	192	345	230
27	189	199	358	237
28	196	205	371	245
29	203	212	384	252
30	210	219	400	265
31	217	228	415	276
32	224	234	425	284
33	231	241	436	293
34	238	248	448	301
35	245	256	460	310
36	252	262	470	316
37	259	271	484	325
38	266	276	494	332
38½	270	280	500	336

* From *Manual of Human Embryology*, by F. Keibel and F. P. Mall. Philadelphia: Lippincott, 1910, Vol. I, p. 199. By permission of J. B. Lippincott Company, publishers.

315 ff.) has considered the problem of human age in relation to infancy.

Arising immediately out of the relationship between growth and age of the fetus is a whole series of studies on the morphological development of the fetus, which of course cannot be reviewed in this chapter. Figure 16 shows graphically the significance of such knowledge for one who thinks of

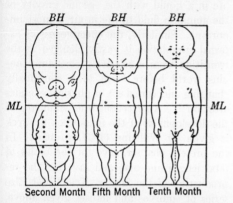

Second Month Fifth Month Tenth Month

FIGURE 16. Changes in body proportions in fetal life. *BH*—body height; *ML*—midline. (From *Premature and Congenitally Diseased Infants*, by J. H. Hess. Philadelphia: Lea & Febiger, 1922, 36. By permission of the publisher.)

the fetus as a "smaller infant." The literature on general fetal development has several times been summarized, the early work having been brought together in an excellent summary by Pinard (1877). In this summary, the work on the morphology, physiology, and pathology of the fetus is treated separately. A bibliography of 870 titles is appended to this treatise. Next to Pinard's summary in importance is Wertheimer's (1904), which brings together the general literature on the fetus to 1904. Probably the most complete summary in English of the anatomical and physiological aspects of fetal development is Feldman's (1920), which, in spite of certain lacunae, should be read by all who are interested in the fetus. Noback and Robertson (1951) have studied the sequence of appearance of ossification centers in the human skeleton during the first 5 prenatal months and have summarized previous work on skeletal development of the human fetus.

As pointed out above, it may almost be said to be necessary, in order to understand the development of behavior, to have some reference line in terms of measurements of anatomical development. It has become a convention by following such a temporal line to divide the prenatal life of the human being into three periods (Feldman, 1920, p. 61; Williams, 1931, p. 163). The first period of 1 or sometimes 2 weeks is spoken of as the *germinal* period. From the third to fifth or sixth week is the *embryonic* period. From the sixth week to birth is the *fetal* period. The normal term of pregnancy is usually placed at 280 days (Williams, 1931, p. 163), although estimates varying between 270 and 284 days have been given by various investigators and summarized by Needham (1931, p. 486). It must be obvious, however, that such figures are meaningless unless the method of calculating true fertilization time is given. The normal length at birth is ordinarily given as 500 mm. in crown-heel, or 320 mm. in crown-rump, length. Sometimes, however, premature infants are born and successfully reared who have passed less than 180 days in the mother's body; but 180 or 181 days is usually taken as the average lower limit below which viability cannot be maintained (Hess, 1922). Claims have been made that much younger fetuses have been raised, but as, for example, in the case of Rodman's fetus which was alleged to have been but 4 months old, there is much doubt of the accuracy of the age estimation (Rodman, 1815; Baker, 1825).

At the other end of the scale the terminal point of postmaturity is also open to great difficulty of estimate. In considering this matter, Ballantyne and Browne (1922) hold that no single index such as fetal length, weight, ossification of the skeleton, placental structure, or cord structural condition is sufficient to date the fetus. They state that the best estimate is obtained by combining a knowledge of the last menstrual period, the date of copulation, the date of the onset of morning sickness, the date of the quickening of the fetus, the size of the uterus, the difficulty of delivery, as well as the evidences of postmaturity such as measurements of length, weight, and ossification. Probably 334 days is the longest period legally considered during which a fetus may be thought possibly to have lived in the mother's body and still be delivered alive (Ballantyne and Browne, 1922, p. 198). Thus, from one point of view at any rate, the human fetal life span that will be dealt with in this chapter must be taken as lasting from fertilization until birth, a time which in the extremest possible cases may vary by as much as 154 days!

In this chapter most of the references to fetal behavior are made to unborn fetuses. It should be kept in mind, however, that the study of correctly dated premature infants may throw light upon the later fetal period. In interpreting the sensory ability or response activity of a prematurely born infant, it is not safe to attribute the same abilities to the unborn fetus of the same age. As suggested in the first part of this chapter, the greatest errors in genetic science are made by suggesting that because environmental conditions of one sort produce behavior of a particular kind in one individual, therefore these same abilities must be "implicit" in an organism living under wholly dissimilar conditions. A normal fetus of the same age as a successfully air-breathing premature infant may act in a very different way from the comparison organism. This is true not only because of mechanical differences of bodily make-up, such as the presence or absence of liquid in the ear, but because of the gross differences brought about by the change from placental respiration to pulmonary respiration and from placental nourishment to alimentary canal nourishment. The sheer mechanical change from life in a liquid with the specific gravity of the amniotic fluid to life in air is most important. Similarly, the effectiveness of external stimulation is vastly changed in the transition from a relatively constant stimulus world before birth to a continually changing and varied set of physical energies after birth. An excellent brief summary of the development of the fetus week by week is given by Williams (1931, p. 163). In the present chapter, save for the tables of fetal length and age, and save for the reproduction of the famous Keibel and Elze series of embryos and fetuses given above, no detailed consideration can be given to gross structural change which occurs during prenatal growth.

An interesting graphic representation of prenatal physical development is that in Figure 17, reproduced from Scammon and Calkins and redrawn by Needham (1931, p. 382), in which the age, height, or weight can, to the limits of accuracy of the original data, be read off if any one of these measurements is known. (See also Streeter, 1920.)

In a paper entitled "Physical Fitness in Terms of Physique, Development and Basal Metabolism" Wetzel (1941) presents a critique of a new method of evaluating individual progress from birth to maturity which suggests that there are types of physique which influence all growth tables. A similar observation could undoubtedly be made of fetal life as well. In this connection a study of body build by Sheldon and his collaborators (Sheldon, Stevens, and Tucker, 1940) should be consulted. For a convenient graphic age conversion scale, see McCarthy (1936).

as possible will be given of the experimental studies on the development of behavior in operatively exposed human embryos. After these lines of evidence of fetal behav-

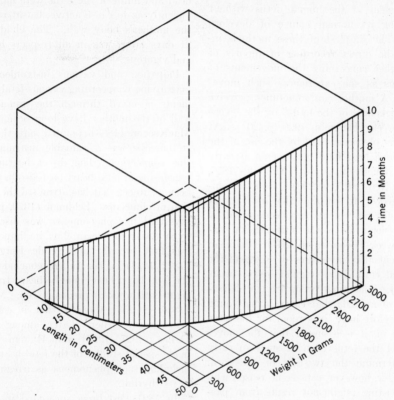

FIGURE 17. Three-dimensional isometric projection from which height, weight, and age of human embryos may be read off if one is known. (From "The Relation between the Body-Weight and Age of the Human Fetus," by R. E. Scammon and L. A. Calkins. *Proceedings of the Society for Experimental Biology and Medicine*, 1924, *22*, 157–161. By permission of the publisher.)

In the paragraphs below a review of the development of behavior in human fetal life without detailed reference to morphology is presented. In this presentation brief consideration will be given to clinical observations made on fetal movements without operation on the mother or the interruption of pregnancy. After this discussion, as accurate and complete a summary

ior have been summarized, a review of the knowledge concerning human fetal sensory life will be presented. A knowledge of sensory development will at once lead to a consideration of the theories that have been proposed to account for the development and control of fetal behavior, and an evaluation of all these observations for human psychology will then be presented.

Nonoperative Studies of Behavioral Development in the Human Fetus

A number of different methods have been used for the scientific study of the development of the human fetus without disturbing its normal course of development. The simplest of these methods involves the direct recording of reports of the mother concerning the movements of the fetus as she experiences such movements. A mother can sometimes perceive the "quickening of the fetus" by the seventeenth week (Feldman, 1920, p. 204). At times the physician may by the use of the stethoscope hear fetal movements as early as the fourteenth week (Mailliot, 1856, p. 258; Neu, 1915, p. 292). It is customary, however, to say that the first time at which such movements can be detected by the physician is in the fifteenth or sixteenth week (Feldman, p. 204). Feldman points out that in fetuses of 8 weeks the umbilical cord shows regular spiral twists (p. 204). Since such twists are not characteristic of animals that carry many young and therefore have little room for the fetus to turn in, it is assumed that the movements of the fetus even at such an early age determine the twisting of the cord. The writer, however, can see no reason why such twisting might not result from passive as well as from active movements.

In later periods of pregnancy, mothers give reports of movement involving part of the body. Sometimes the movements of the extremities or of the trunk alone are noted. Mermann (1887, p. 623), for example, reports a case of rhythmic movement of the fetal back palpated through the mother's abdominal wall in a fetus of 7 months. Whitehead (1867) gives an extended report of a case of violent convulsion of the fetus while still in the uterus. This convulsive condition occurred during the ninth month of pregnancy. The activity of the fetus caused the mother great pain. By palpation and by direct observation it was found that the fetus was in a state of marked hyperactivity. Both the head and limbs of the fetus were moved so violently as to cause active disturbances of the mother's body wall. The child, born 21 days later, was in all respects healthy and vigorous.

Palpation and various instruments for magnifying or recording various fetal movements observed through the intact body wall of the mother have long been in use. MacKeever (1833) pointed out that the stethoscope was a valuable instrument in this connection. The direct hearing and registering of fetal heart beat also have long been a subject that has attracted the attention of clinicians. Feldman (1920, p. 157) says that this phenomenon was discovered by a Swiss physician, but its importance was first brought out by de Kergaradec (1822, 1823). This student concluded that the fetal heart beat could be heard from the eighteenth week of pregnancy on. Mailliot (1856, p. 258) thought that it could be heard much earlier. Later, among others, DeLee (1927, 1928) and Hyman (1930) made special studies of the fetal heart beat, including such phenomena as irregularities in its rhythm.

In 1891 Pestalozza succeeded in taking a cardiograph of the second twin after the first twin had been born (Feldman, 1920, p. 159). In this he was more successful than Hicks (1880), who by the use of an instrument like a cardiograph obtained certain records which were, however, so badly obscured by the rhythmic activities of the mother that they could scarcely be identified. Krumbhaar and Jenks are reported by Feldman (1920, p. 162) as having obtained typical electrocardiographic tracings of the fetal heart. (See also Sachs, 1922.) Maekawa and Toyoshima (1930) have, by the use of amplifiers and a string galvanometer with electrodes placed on the front abdominal wall of the mother, secured excellent electrographic tracings of the fetal heart. After birth the beat of the same heart is also recorded for purposes of comparison.

Stimulated by this work, Carmichael in 1935 attempted, with equivocal results, to record normal fetal heart activity by high-gain amplification. More recently, Mann and Bernstein (1941) and Geiger, Monroe, and Goodyer (1941) have published in this field, and the physiological psychologist D. B. Lindsley (1942) has published a most interesting paper on the heart and brain potentials of human fetuses *in utero*. In this paper a reliable method of recording maternal and fetal electrocardiograms is given. What is even more interesting, however, is the fact that this investigator has also been able to record fetal electroencephalograms. In the latter case, during the seventh and eighth months of human pregnancy electrodes were at times placed on the maternal abdominal wall over the palpated head of the fetus. By suitable amplification and recording, fetal electroencephalograms were secured by this means. The records were typical of those from the precentral region of the brain in the newborn. In all work upon fetal or neonatal heart rate the effect of asphyxia must be considered (Barcroft, 1938). A fall in heart rate that is nonvagal has been demonstrated in fetal rabbits by tying off the umbilical cord (Bauer, 1938).

Among the other early movements of the fetus which are often directly recorded are the so-called *Ahlfeld breathing movements,* or the rhythmic contractions of the fetal thorax felt through the mother's body. These movements should not be confused with uterine contractions occurring after the third month, sometimes called *Ahlfeld's sign,* which incidentally may have something to do with the onset of behavior, if

an analogy with the amnion contraction of the chick noted above may be suggested (Kuo, 1932c, p. 263). In spite of the difficulty of the ancients concerning fetal respiration that involves the intake of no air into the lungs, it has of course long been understood, as Leonardo da Vinci knew, that the fetus does not breathe water (Needham, 1931, p. 108). The gaseous interchange of the mammalian fetus occurs in the placenta between the blood stream of the mother and that of the fetus. The general significance of this process and its detailed consideration have been studied by many physiologists. The history of the early advance of knowledge on this matter is summarized by Starling (1900), and the generally accepted facts about the fetus are brought together by Sarwey (1915) and more recently by Barcroft and Mason (1938). (See also Bylicki, 1921.)

The liquid environment, of course, completely precludes true lung breathing, but at least since 1798 movements of the chest and thorax of the fetus similar to breathing movements have been occasionally noticed. Béclard (1815) observed such movements in various mammalian embryos without removing the amniotic sac through which they were observed. Ahlfeld (1890) has developed a view on the nature and significance of certain irregular but vaguely rhythmic movements of the fetus which seem to be caused by the contraction of the same muscles which will make respiration possible in postnatal life. (See also Kouwer, 1919, and Kellogg, 1930.) Ahlfeld has made graphic records of these movements, which in typical cases vary from 38 to 76 per minute. C. A. Smith (1946) has presented an admirable summary of the fetal aspects of respiration. He discusses the experimental literature in this field. The point is made that respiratory movements of the fetus of animals studied cannot be considered as automatic, constant, and progressive. His view is rather that here again, as in so many other aspects of fetal behavior, we see the setting off of a response pattern under certain conditions which otherwise, although acquired early, is normally held in abeyance for later use.

Teleologically, it has been suggested that these movements may be thought of as preparation for the act of breathing which comes at birth. In the fetus such movements are considered to lead only to the ebbing and flowing of the amniotic fluid in the trachea, but, as movements, they exercise and strengthen the neuromuscular mechanism of breathing. It is possible that this behavior is related to the functional establishment of the rhythmic action of the respiratory centers of the central nervous system. The theory has been proposed, therefore, that birth is not to be considered the point at which the onset of rhythmic respiration occurs. In carrying this idea further, it has been suggested that these prenatal chest movements are initiated, like adult breathing movements, by a change in the concentration of metabolites in the blood stream acting upon the breathing centers of the central nervous system (T. G. Brown, 1915).

In combining the views in regard to fetal breathing movements and their cause, it has been suggested that the active or passive general bodily movements of the fetus may occasionally be such as to impede circulation in the umbilical cord. This mechanical obstruction of the umbilical cord, therefore, leads to an increase in carbon dioxide tension in the blood. This in turn may lead to a facilitation of activity or the activation of appropriate centers in the brain and thus initiate movements whereby the mechanical relationship of fetus and cord is changed in such a manner as to reestablish placental circulation, T. G. Brown, 1915). It has been suggested even more speculatively that not only are the chest

movements of the fetus part of the general movements which bring about a change in the position of the organism but also they act as a supplement to the fetal heart. They thus may act, it is suggested, as a sort of auxiliary pump brought into play as a result of a change in gas tension in the blood acting upon the breathing center (Walz, 1922, p. 334).

If these speculations are in any sense correct, therefore, the so-called first breath of the child may be considered to be just a change in the way in which the same neuromuscular mechanism determines the oxygenation of the blood (Walz, 1922, p. 341). For an excellent popular statement concerning the onset of breathing, see Henderson (1937).

Barcroft and Karvonen (1948) have studied the effects of carbon dioxide and of cyanide on fetal respiratory movements. They conclude that cutaneous sensory stimulation rather than asphyxia is responsible for the commencement of air breathing.

A number of investigators have severely criticized the Ahlfeld concept of prenatal breathing movements. Walz (1922) attributed these objections to the fact that the initial statement of Ahlfeld's view was unfavorably received by the two leading obstetricians of Germany at the time, and that the weight of authority long kept this phenomenon from being correctly evaluated. It should be noted, however, that Huggett (1930) in an experimental study of fetal respiratory reflexes referred to above says: "The exact mechanism suggested by Ahlfeld is not in every sense confirmed."

A good many speculations have been made as to the causes involved in the first intake of air breath. As noted above, many students have held that the increase of metabolites, and especially of carbon dioxide tension in the blood, is one of the essential causes of the first gasp (Corey,

1931). Cohnstein and Zuntz (1884) observed that in a fetal lamb clamping of the umbilical cord led to the first intake of air. Carmichael has noticed this same result in fetal cats, rats, and guinea pigs. Indeed, the procedure of clamping the umbilical cord to study the effect of the blood stimulus on general bodily movements has been part of the experimental technique of several investigators and notably so of Swenson (1926) in his study of the fetal rat. Angulo y González (1933b) reports that in fetuses of 19 postinsemination days in which tactile stimulation of the hindleg aroused no response there was immediate response after ligation of the umbilical cord. The general result of this procedure seems to be an increase in amount and vividness of activity for a time. Pflüger (1877), however, held that some external stimulus, such as cold air, was necessary besides blood change to bring about the first breathing act (cf. Huggett, 1930). Preyer (1885, p. 452) also suggested a relationship between cutaneous stimulation of some sort and the onset of breathing. Corey (1931) holds that an increase in the metabolites of the blood stream and some external stimulus, such as drying of the skin, seem usually to be antecedent to the initial respiratory gasp. It is suggested by Fender, Neff, and Binger (1946) that *asphyxia neonatorum* may play some part in the development of certain cases of epilepsy in human beings. For a general consideration of this problem see Windle (1950).

Snyder and Rosenfeld (1937) have made direct studies of the onset of respiratory movements. They have studied the fetuses of the cat, rabbit, guinea pig, and man. Rhythmic respiratory movements are initiated in all these types in the uterus. Oxygen and carbon dioxide affect fetal breathing movements; a certain level of carbon dioxide, for example, is essential to the maintenance of fetal respiration.

Windle, Monnier, and Steele (1938) and Abel and Windle (1939) show that there are no respiratory movements in cat fetuses less than 13 mm. in length. But in the middle third of the gestation period delicate and rapid rhythms of respiration may begin. Under certain conditions carbon dioxide breathed in by the mother starts such movements. There is no significant increase in blood volume at birth in the pulmonary system. There is a circulation in the lungs during the last part of pregnancy capable of caring for oxygenation when air breathing is established. For a more detailed consideration of the blood gases of the cat fetus, see Steele and Windle (1939), and for a consideration of the physiology and anatomy of the respiratory system in the fetus and newborn infant, see Windle (1941b). See also Potter and Bohlander (1941); Whitehead, Windle, and Becker (1942); and Zettleman (1946).

Besides "breathing movements" there are other movements of the fetus which are indirectly significant in behavior. The movements of the organs of the digestive tract as seen in fetal organisms have been studied by a number of investigators. Yanase (1907a, 1907b) has studied peristaltic intestinal movements in fetal guinea pigs, cats, rabbits, and men. As a result of these studies, he concludes that peristaltic movements may begin long before birth. The status of gastrointestinal activity *in utero* has also been studied, especially in the cat and guinea pig, by Becker, Windle, Barth, and Schulz (1940); Becker (1941); and Becker and Windle (1941). In man such movements are possible in the seventh week. So far as hunger contractions are concerned, Patterson (1914) has shown that hunger contractions are practically continuous in young dogs. As age advances these contractions decrease in magnitude. Carlson and Ginsburg (1915), working on fetal dogs and newborn children, have written: "The empty stomach at birth and in the prematurely born exhibits the typical periods of tonus and hunger contractions of the adult, the only difference between infant and adult being the greater frequency and relatively greater vigor of these periods in the young" (p. 29). For other aspects of the function of the stomach before birth, see Sutherland (1921).

Certainly, in view of the large amount of work on the "hunger drive" as a determiner of activity, part of which is summarized by Warden (1931), the possibility that these stomach and intestinal contractions are stimuli to "random" and "spontaneous" skeletal muscle movement, and indeed to much of the behavior of the premature or full-term infant, cannot be neglected by one who would understand fetal behavior. Such behavior initiated by internal stimulation may well be considered merely the setting into action of inborn neural mechanisms. In this connection, see De Snoo (1937).

The question has often been raised as to whether gross external fetal movements of the various sorts considered above have any part in the rearrangement of the fetus in the uterus in the normal position for delivery at birth. As so often happens when a phenomenon is difficult to explain, it has been alleged that the position of the fetus is governed by instinct (Dubois, 1833). Mechanical and physical explanations have been advanced by Paramore (1909), Barnum (1915), Griffith (1915), McIlroy and Leverkus (1924), and others. Possibly it may be said that no absolutely positive proof has been advanced to show that active fetal movements are essential in determining the normal position of the fetus at the time of delivery. Langreder (1949a and b) has considered the posture of the fetus in relation to fetal reflexes and position at birth.

In the study of the changes of fetal position before birth, much has been learned by the use of the X-ray. We have already seen that Avery attempted to study the changes in position of guinea pigs by the use of roentgenograms. This work of Avery's was directly adapted from human clinical procedures used in the study of the fetus. The use of the X-ray in the study of the fetus has given a new clue to the determination of fetal age by the study of the ossification of the fetal skeleton, although it is by no means an absolute clue. Hess (1918) has brought together much of the literature on this subject and suggests approximate norms of ossification at certain periods. (See also Mall, 1906, and Adair, 1918.) The study by Rudolph and Ivy (1933) on the rotation of the fetal head shows that uterine contractions and the movement of the fetus both contribute to this change in posture. Danforth and Ivy (1938) have shown that uterine activity is in part at any rate a function of calcium. Augmentation of uterine activity is brought about by increasing the calcium present; by decreasing the calcium the action is depressed. In this connection it is interesting to note that Good (1924) has shown that a patient may have the spinal cord completely severed and still give birth to a baby normally and painlessly.

A phenomenon of prenatal and immediately postnatal behavior which has long attracted attention is the first cry of the human organism. Kant (1799) found significance in the first sound uttered by the human infant. Preyer (1893, p. 213), indeed, quotes Kant as saying:

> The outcry that is heard from a child scarcely born has not the tone of lamentation, but of indignation and of aroused wrath; not because anything gives him pain, but because something frets him; presumably because he wants to move, and

feels his inability to do it as a fetter that deprives him of his freedom.

Both Preyer (1893, p. 213) and Compayré (1896, p. 89) have pointed out the futility of such verbal fancies. Such speculation, however, is not as yet entirely dead. An analytical psychiatrist who is quoted by Blanton (1917, p. 458) has written of the cry of the human infant at birth: "It is an expression of its overwhelming sense of inferiority on thus suddenly being confronted by reality, without ever having had to deal with its problems." By operative technique Minkowski (1922, p. 754) has found that crying occurs as early as the sixth month in the prematurely delivered fetus. In clinical practice many cases of *vagitus uterinus*, or fetal crying, have been reported. A typical case is that reported by M. Graham (1919), in which in a difficult delivery, the fetal sac having been ruptured by operative means to assist delivery, the crying of the still unborn fetus could be distinctly heard. Many such cases are reported, but they need not be reviewed here. (See also Feldman, 1920, p. 207.) Fetal hiccup has also been reported by a number of observers. These cases are summarized by DeLee (1928). See also a study by Norman (1942).

All cases of fetal crying reported above seem to be the result of appropriately activated muscles, which bring about the expulsion of air in such a way as to cause it to vibrate. There seems to be no reason to assume that this phonation has any greater mechanistic significance than many of the other random acts of the child. It catches the notice of the observer, however, because from such behavior language develops in later life. This function is, of course, one of the most important aspects of adult human behavior, and an aspect which will in itself come to be, at least in the subvocal stage of "verbal thought," peculiarly important even in strictly introspective psychology.

This concludes the consideration of human fetal behavior of the sort that can for the most part be studied during the normal course of development. In the next pages the study of the development of human fetal behavior in fetuses removed from the uterus before the end of the normal term of gestation will be considered.

The Study of Behavior in Operatively Removed Human Fetuses

Most of the living human fetuses to which reference will be made in the next paragraphs were removed while still alive from the mother's body because some disease of the mother rendered the artificial termination of pregnancy medically necessary. Minkowski's technique (1928a, pp. 518–532) is typical. This investigator and a collaborator removed each fetus that was to be studied by a Caesarean section, usually performing the operation under a local anesthetic. The fetus, placenta, and amnion were removed. The fetus was then placed in a bath of physiological salt solution at normal blood temperature. This meant that such fetuses were cut off from their oxygen supply, and the movements which resulted must be thought of as the movements of increasingly asphyxiated organisms. This is important in the evaluation of the behavior reported, for, as pointed out above, increased metabolites in the blood at first lead to hyperactivity and then to hypoactivity.

The behavioral development of the human fetus as determined in operatively removed cases will be considered here in one series. This has its disadvantages because in certain reports estimated age is given; in others only measurements are presented; but certainly for an understanding of development it is most important to give estimated age. The writer has attempted to make a summarizing table of human fetal development, but he does not feel that such a table gives a correct impression. One who wishes to see this material expressed as well as possible in tabular form should consult Coghill (1929c, pp. 993–996).

The development, then, of human fetal behavior as observed by various investigators in relation to estimated postinsemination age or menstrual age may be given as follows:

Fetuses Less than 9 Weeks Old. In very young human fetuses operatively removed from the mother, the first movement observed is of the beating heart. For several centuries there has been a scientific controversy as to whether the heart beat of the adult individual is to be thought of as primarily determined by direct muscle or by neural stimulation. It now seems that the early embryonic heart beat must be thought of as essentially an independent muscle contraction (Parker, 1919, pp. 50–63). Therefore, in most of the work on the development of behavior the beating of the heart is not considered to mark the onset of "true behavioral life." Pflüger (1877) has demonstrated the beginning of heart beat in the fetus as being in the third week, that is, in a fetus of approximately 4 mm. (See also Strassmann, 1903, p. 951.)

For a consideration of the mechanism of the initiation of contraction in different parts of the heart of a typical vertebrate, see Goss (1937, 1938, 1940) and Copenhaver (1939).

Williams (1931, p. 163) gives an excellent summary of development in this early period. The germinal stage of the human being may be considered to be the first week or two of life. The third week is thought of as the onset of the true embryonic period. At this period the medullary groove begins to be formed. A little later cell structures which make up the

primitive heart are laid down and, as just noted, these cells begin the lifelong beat of the heart. At about this time, also, cerebral and optic vesicles begin to be differentiated and limb buds first appear. The muscles also develop rapidly in fine structure during this period.

In the second month there is continued morphological growth both in total height and weight and in the fine structure of the organs of the growing individual. Windle and Fitzgerald (1937) in a paper on the development of the spinal reflex show that all the elements needed for a reflex are in the central nervous system are laid down during the sixth week but no spinal arcs are complete before the eighth week. Bolaffio and Artom (1924, p. 472) note in this period that isolated limbs torn during delivery can be stimulated directly.

Minkowski (1920b, p. 1202) reports that at the end of the second month cutaneous stimulation elicits response. This finding is not confirmed by Bolaffio and Artom (1924, p. 473), for they point out that at this time the skin is very thin and may involve in its stimulation the activation of receptors in underlying tissues.

Much is known of the structural and minute functional development of the receptors, nervous system, and effectors in this as in all later embryonic and fetal stages. It is not, however, until the fetus reaches the length of 15 mm., or is about 4 weeks old, so far as the writer can discover, that any direct statement can be made in regard to the activity of any part of the response mechanism, and this is a negative statement. In a fetus of this length, Minkowski (1928b, p. 66) reports that it was impossible to bring about muscular response even to an electric current of 40 milliamperes. He made observations on two fetuses of this length, with the same conclusion.

This finding is not entirely unexpected, as Hewer (1927) has shown that histologically the musculature of the fetus develops at uneven rates, the unstriped musculature, which is the first to develop, being clearly formed in an embryo 1 mm. in length. Striped musculature could not be detected in a fetus smaller than 2.5 mm. long, and it did not take on its definitive characteristics in fetuses less than 22 weeks old. Special changes of structure are also noted by this same investigator in regard to heart musculature.

Possibly the youngest human fetus to be observed to move is one reported by Yanase (1907b) in his studies of the development of intestinal movement noted above. In a fetus 20 mm. long and of an estimated age of 6 weeks, one movement involving the right arm is rather casually noted (p. 455). The next youngest human fetus to be reported moving is a fetus 22 mm. long and probably about 6 weeks old described by Strassmann (1903) in a case of extrauterine pregnancy. He observed through a rupture in the tube wall slow movements, backward and forward, of the arms and legs of the fetus (p. 963). In evaluating this observation it should be noted that Strassmann's report is given in such a manner as possibly to lead to a questioning of his observations, since apparently the fetus was observed in such a way that rhythmic mechanical movement of the adult body was possible. Certainly all observers of fetal behavior have had difficulty in deciding whether or not they were seeing something which was not the result of passive external mechanical movement. It should be borne in mind, therefore, that possibly these two earliest observations should be substantiated before they are finally accepted. In a fetus of 30 mm., or an estimated age of 8 weeks, Minkowski (1923, p. 477) observed a wormlike movement of the arms, legs, and trunk.

In Hooker's (1939b) description of his carefully controlled work the statement is made that no response to tactile stimulation has been observed before the eighth week of menstrual age (p. 8). In a 25-mm. fetus of a menstrual age of 8 to 8½ weeks, however, response to tactile stimulation has been recorded. This same investigator has repeated this observation on two other fetuses of approximately the same age. At this stage tactile stimulation is effective only in the area over the mouth and immediately adjacent to that supplied by the mandibular and maxillary divisions of the fifth nerve (p. 9). Hogg (1941) points out that the cutaneous nerves and nerve endings are very immature when responses are first elicited. No encapsulated endings are seen. Excitation is probably dependent upon deformation of the growing tips of the fibers by displacement of the surrounding tissue at this time, according to this author. Stimulation in this area in a fetus of this age led to contraction of the long muscles of the body and neck to produce body flexion. Limb girdle muscles related to both upper extremities were also activated. Rotation of the rump, caused by activation of the pelvic girdle muscles, was observed in very slight degree. Hooker notes that at this period a hair capable of exerting a pressure greater than 25 mg. may cause direct mechanical stimulation. Faradic stimulation at this time is also effective. No spontaneous movements were noted by Hooker at or before this age.

Fitzgerald and Windle (1942) report that in a study of fifteen fetuses 7 weeks to a little over 8 weeks old, fetal movement was seen in only three organisms. These responses were individual reflexes of trunk, arms, or legs when oxygenated blood was still supplied to them. For an excellent summary of the early development of human behavior, see Hooker (1943).

Fetuses 9 Through 12 Weeks Old. In a fetus of 35 mm. (estimated age 8 or 9 weeks) Minkowski (1928*b*, p. 65) reports muscle contraction to galvanic current. Minkowski's work shows that fetuses of 40 to 50 mm. (9 to 10 weeks) sometimes still show this characteristic muscle response possibly without neural activation. This observation coincides with the observations noted above on the fetuses of lower mammals, in which the musculature comes to respond to direct stimulation before true neuromuscular action begins. The most elaborate studies of this sort of muscular response have been made by Wintrebert (1904, 1920). (See also Minkowski, 1924, p. 244.)

Among the many significant observations that might be made at this period, it is interesting to note that the vestibular apparatus seems to be anatomically developed to its full (Minkowski, 1922, p. 753).

A fetus of 42 mm. was removed under operation by Woyciechowski (1928) to interrupt a pathological pregnancy. At the operation a mass was removed from the uterus. As soon as the mass was taken out, a fetus of 42 mm. dropped from the excised sphere of tissue. This fetus, estimated by the operator to be of approximately 2 months' gestation age, was seen to move both arms and legs spontaneously. When it was touched by a finger an energetic "protective movement" began which involved a much stronger moving of the arms and hands and the opening of the mouth. The observations made upon the movement of this fetus were checked by another observer. In spite of cooling, the movements of the fetus lasted in an active form for more than 5 minutes (p. 410).

In fetuses of the 9- to 10-week age period, Minkowski (1921*b*, p. 148; 1922, p. 753) noticed slow, asymmetrical, arrhythmic, noncoordinated movements. He also noted (1922, p. 753) that at this time neu-

rologically the elements of the spinal reflex arc are developed anatomically.

Bolaffio and Artom (1924) studied a fetus of about this same age. They report that dropping the fetus from a height of a few centimeters to a table led to active contractions of the flexor muscles of the limbs. Further, they noted that tapping the table lightly with the fingers elicited responses of energetic movements involving the elevation of the scapulas, movement of the arms, and flexion of the thighs and legs. These movements were elicited for about 3 minutes, after which time they rapidly diminished in intensity and ceased. During the active period, stimulation by a blunt metal rod of the skin of the breast and of the abdomen led to no response. After the cessation of activity, direct brain stimulation led to no muscle response (p. 465).

In a fetus less than 8 weeks old, Minkowski (1922) reports that percussion of the patellar tendon resulted in contraction of the quadriceps muscle. After this contraction had taken place, irradiation followed to other muscles. In this fetus the heart beat was relatively constant at 80 beats per minute, but covering the fetus with normal salt solution at 40° C. led to an increase in the beat of the heart from a basal beat of 80 to 100 beats per minute (p. 752). Extirpation of the cerebral hemispheres in this fetus did not change the reflexes described. Sectioning the medulla just above the cord region, however, abolished the reflexes due to change in the position of the body. In a fetus about 9½ weeks old Hooker (1944) notes that stretch of limb muscles is effective in stimulating proprioceptive organs and initiating response.

In a fetus about 2 months old, Bolaffio and Artom report that stroking and tapping elicited slow local contractions of all the muscles of the limbs. For example, if these stimuli were applied to the palm of the hand, adduction and internal rotation of the corresponding arm were noted; if to the leg, flexion of the corresponding thigh. These investigators state, moreover, that mechanical stimulation of the cortex in this fetus gave a constant movement of elevation of the left shoulder, but no contraction of either of the lower limbs or of the right shoulder. After this same fetus was decerebrated they note a greater vividness (*vivacità*) of the local contractions referred to above and the reappearance of diffusion of movement at a distance from the stimuli which had ceased. In this experiment mechanical stimulation of the medulla led to respiratory movements. They further suggest that even in a fetus of this age removal of the cerebral cortex does remove some inhibition from the lower reflexes. It is interesting to note that during this period the neural and muscular mechanisms basic to sucking are developed so that they may function. A study of the evolution of this mechanism throughout the rest of the fetal period is instructive. For suggestions, see Feldman (1920, pp. 448 ff.) and, for the later period, Irwin (1930).

Bolaffio and Artom report in regard to another fetus about 2 months of age that gentle stimulation of the skin of the whole body was followed by no response, but percussion led to definite responses. Definite percussion blows on the forearm sometimes led to flexion, adduction, and slight internal rotation of the arm. Percussion on any part of the lower limb led to flexion and adduction of the thighs with slight flexion of the legs. If the percussion is rather light, the contractions are limited to the homolateral limbs; if somewhat more energetic, contractions also of the heterolateral limbs are reported. Percussion on the breast and abdomen gave homolateral responses about the pectoral muscles and bilateral responses about the abdominal muscles (pp. 465–466). Hooker (1944, p.

22) reports that in fetuses of about 8 weeks the reflexogenous zone of the cutaneous surface of the infant spreads from a very localized area, including part of the upper lip and the skin about the nostrils, to the whole upper lip, chin, and part of the neck. The responses made at this time are stereotyped and mechanical in nature. That the fetuses are ready for such responses is shown by Windle and Fitzgerald (1937). These workers demonstrate that the elements of the reflex arc are laid down by the sixth week. Spinal cord arcs do not seem to be complete before the eighth week. It should be emphasized that Hooker (1944, p. 25) says in commenting on this stage that "each stimulation in the reflexogenous area evokes a response which, within the limits of ordinary biological variation, is identical with every other one secured."

It is generally thought that even during the third month the cerebral cortex has as yet assumed no functions in relation to the general bodily activity. Bolaffio and Artom, however, report that removal of the cortex in a fetus of this age seems to remove inhibition from the reflexes of the lower limbs. This result is difficult for the writer to interpret. During this period sucking is theoretically possible; that is, the neuromuscular mechanisms necessary to bring about this response have probably already been determined. The reader who wishes a complete consideration of this earliest feeding reaction of the human individual should read the specific references given above to this reaction and then should refer to the summary of the knowledge of the reaction given by Feldman (1920, pp. 448–455). (See also Irwin, 1930.)

After superficial and deep stimulation of numerous points on the body of a decerebrate fetus of 90 mm., Bolaffio and Artom at first recorded very vivid contractions of apparently all muscles. After about 3 minutes, however, the contractions were still bilateral, but limited now to segments and homologous regions of the body. As time passed, the contractions became more and more circumscribed, and after about 3 minutes they were limited to the muscles corresponding to the stimulated point. After 15 minutes every reaction had ceased (p. 466).

During the third month Minkowski (1922, p. 724; 1928a, p. 565) reports labyrinthine reflexes, but Bolaffio and Artom (1924, p. 471), obtaining the same responses that Minkowski reports, interpret them rather as responses elicited as the result of the stimulation of proprioceptors in the neck. Minkowski (1922, p. 723) reports tendon reflexes at this age, but Bolaffio and Artom (p. 473) do not find them until the sixth month. Here once more the decision must be a very difficult one to make, if the writer may judge from his own observations on infrahuman fetuses. Stimulation at the locus of a tendon may lead to a response, but this may be due to several possible forms of stimuli, such as (1) cutaneous stimulation, (2) direct muscle stimulation, or (3) a true tendon-stretch muscle stimulation. Mere observation of the response makes very difficult the decision as to which of these forms of stimulation has been effective. Bolaffio and Artom's careful work, however, seems to indicate that at first muscle sensitivity dominates when the tendons are stimulated, but in later fetuses true tendon reflexes begin gradually to arise.

Hooker (1939a) in summarizing development during this period says that by 9½ weeks of menstrual age responses include rotation of rump and body flexion. The neck-trunk reactions are usually contralateral. At this period "spontaneous" human responses were first observed. This same investigator notes that from 9½ to 12 weeks a "total pattern" of response is dominant. At 11 weeks palmar stimulation causes a quick but incomplete finger closure which

marks the onset of the grasping reflex. Hooker (1938) studied the development of this reflex in great detail. He (1939a) further noted the onset of the plantar reflex during this period. Hooker (1944, p. 27) also noted that by 11 weeks stimulable cutaneous reflexogenous zones have spread over the whole upper extremity, and the sole of the foot has also become stimulable. Patterned eye movements seem to begin at this time.

Fetuses 13 through 16 Weeks Old. By 13 weeks the top and back of the head alone remain insensitive (Hooker, 1944). Minkowski (1922), studying a fetus in the early part of this period (110 mm.), recorded the fact that touching the lower lip or tongue with a blunt probe led to a closing of the mouth, brought about through the lowering and lifting of the jaw (p. 273). He also noticed in the same fetus that reflexes of the trunk and extremities were seen prominently, but after the transection of the cord in the dorsal region the lower reflexes were discontinued at once. This seemed to prove that conduction of activation in this case, at any rate, was through the cord. After this operation, moreover, he noticed that the short reflexes remained unchanged but were themselves abolished after total extirpation of the cord. Destruction of the lumbar and sacral cord abolished the hindlimb reflexes, whereas similar destruction of the cervical cord abolished those of the forelimbs.

The so-called spontaneous movements observed by Hooker at 14 weeks include the activity of most body parts as well as of the "organism as a whole." For the first time these movements, like those at about the same period elicited by tactual stimulation, may be characterized as "graceful" and "delicate." Hooker (1944) points out that by this period, except for movements of respiration and vocalization and the true grasping reflex, the fetus already shows most of the responses that can be elicited in the neonate.

In a fetus of 135 mm. Minkowski (1922, p. 723) notes that a touch on the skin, using a blunt stimulus, led to reactions of diverse parts of the body. Characteristic of such stimulation were the flexion of both arms, the repeated opening and closing of the mouth, and simultaneous retraction of the head. He notes that at this stage of fetal development every part of the skin can act as a reflexogenous zone for various reactions. These reactions, however, tend to spread more or less over the entire fetal organism. Direct muscle excitability still remained at this stage 1 hour after the cord had been extirpated. Total removal of the cerebral cortex did not change the observable responses noted above. Transection at the midbrain, however, seemed to weaken the responses, although they still continued.

In a fetus 160 mm. long Minkowski (1922, p. 723) reports spontaneous dorsal flexion of the great toe, although he could secure no direct response to the touch of the sole of the foot. Distinct contractions of the abdominal walls were evoked in this fetus by brushing. Touching the closed eyelid in this fetus evoked a contraction of the orbicularis muscle.

Erbkam (1837) reports a study of a fetus, accidentally delivered, approximately 170 mm. long. He noted the contraction of both arms and legs and the movement of the head from side to side, "as if to breathe." In this fetus the heart beat for 10 minutes. After that time the water in which the fetus was lying became cool and the heart beat became slower. When more warm water was poured in, however, the heart beat became lively. The eyes of this fetus were closed. The great physiologist Johannes Müller saw the fetus and agreed with the author that it was of approximately 4 months' fetal age.

In a fetus of 180 mm. Minkowski (1923) noted spontaneous movements of all the extremities and the head. These were noted before the umbilical cord was ligated. In this fetus, touching the sole just at the time of delivery led to the dorsal extension of the big toe, the Babinski reflex. Later the plantar flexion followed (1923, p. 486; 1928a, p. 551).

In a fetus 190 mm. long Minkowski (1924, p. 250) obtained definite indication of reciprocal muscle innervation. He also reports at this stage that diagonal reflexes were established; that is, stimulating one foot of the fetus would lead to the movement of the arm on the opposite side. In certain instances the stimulation of the sole of the foot on one side even led to the movement of one finger, the little finger, on the hand of the opposite side of the body. These diagonal reflexes are considered by Minkowski (1922, p. 723) as significant in relation to the trotting reflex noted by a number of students of the genetic development of locomotion.

During this period the sole of the foot reflexes are thought by Minkowski (1928a) to have their connection in the spinal cord and the tegmentum. In terms of response this involves the domination of the response of extension over flexion (p. 551). (See also Dewey, 1935.) For a photographic sequence of the foot reflexes of a 14-week fetus, see Figure 18, from Hooker (1939b). Liesch (1946) has described the stimulation of mucous membrane areas and other cutaneous areas in a fetus 200 mm. in length and of an estimated age of 4 months.

Fetuses from 17 Weeks to Normal Birth Time. In experiments previously referred to, Barcroft (1938) has shown that after about one-third of the normal fetal period has passed in the sheep a remarkable change takes place. At this point the organism which has already developed most

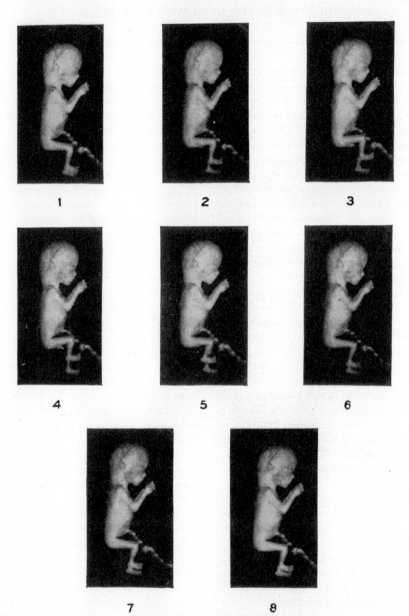

FIGURE 18. Response to tactile stimulation of the sole. Probable menstrual age 14 weeks. (From *A Preliminary Atlas of Early Human Fetal Activity,* by D. Hooker. Privately published, 1939, 91. By permission of the author.) Stimulation was applied by stroking the sole of the right foot with a 2-gram hair (1). The response consisted of the following elements: (*a*) Extreme dorsiflexion of the hallux (2 to 4) and "fanning" of the other toes (3 to 6). The toes, other than the hallux, ultimately show slight plantar flexion (6 and 7). (*b*) Flexion at the hip (2 to 4), slight flexion at the knee (3 to 5), and slight dorsiflexion of the foot (2 to 4). (*c*) Return to normal posture (5 to 8).

of the basic patterns of behavior becomes more quiescent. Spontaneous movements decrease. This is due to the fact that at this time a less adequate supply of oxygen is provided for the fetal central nervous system. At about the sixteenth week Hooker (1944) notes that a similar sluggishness begins in the human fetus. This again gives emphasis to the fact that in the study of the fetus positive evidence that such and such a response can be elicited is much more important than a negative finding when one is seeking for the neurological correlates of behavior.

In several fetuses approximately 200 mm. long, that is, about 17 weeks old, Minkowski found that brushing the sole of the foot led to plantar flexion of the toes, except the big toe, which did not move. This was directly related to Minkowski's elaborate study of the reflexes of the sole of the foot. (See 1922, p. 723; 1923, pp. 478–480; 1928a, pp. 550–556.) Direct mechanical stimulation of the motor roots of the spinal nerve at this stage showed that intersegmental spinal conduction is well established (1922, p. 752). Mechanical stimulation of the cranial nerves at the level of the medulla led to the opening and closing of the mouth. It is presumed by Minkowski that this reaction resulted from the direct stimulation of the facial nerve (p. 752). At this period direct stimulation of the cortex does not lead to response (Bolaffio and Artom, 1924, p. 477), but breathing changes do result from stimulation of the medulla.

In a fetus of 210 mm. Minkowski (1922, p. 723) observed opening and closing of the mouth accompanied by arm movements. The duration of such movements at this period was limited. Maximum responsiveness seldom lasted more than 1 minute at the most. In a fetus of 230 mm. Minkowski (p. 723) noted for the first time continued rhythmic contractions of the sort

often described as Ahlfeld's breathing movements.

In a fetus of this same length Bolaffio and Artom (1924) noted that by employing superficial stimulation they were able to elicit localized muscular contractions in the limbs and other specialized muscle groups. By using strong and deep stimulation on a single segment of one limb, it is possible to elicit flexion of the whole contralateral limb. They also noted that stroking the ridge of the tibia gave vivid adduction of the homolateral thigh. In regard to the development of cortical dominance at this time it is interesting to note that mechanical stimulation of the Rolandic zone of the brain, either through the cranial cap or after its removal, did not call forth any reaction. Nevertheless, removal of the hemispheres did lead to more vivid local responses than in preceding excitations when the brain was intact. Stroking the pectoral muscles called forth adduction of the contralateral limb. In this case also these investigators reported that, if the intensity of the stimuli was increased somewhat, they got contraction of the whole corresponding limb. By stimulating the medulla they were able to call forth violent respiratory movements with active participation of the cervical, thoracic, and abdominal muscles, and those of the diaphragm. These movements were so violent they also led to elevation of the shoulder and adduction of the arms. It is further significant to realize that these investigators found, after repeated successive experiments and as the vitality of the fetus became less, that the muscular contractions disappeared first in the lower limbs and then later in the upper limbs (p. 466).

In a fetus of 240 mm. Krabbe (1912) reported slow movement of the limbs and contraction of the muscles as the result of percussion. He also obtained strong abdominal reflexes as the result of light blows.

The plantar reflex occurred without involving the participation of the big toe. In the fetus which he investigated the heart beat was strong and he was able to elicit a number of reflexes, the abdominal reflex being especially strong. The fetus was a female, but he was unable to elicit the female cremasteric reflex. He felt that both bone and tendon reflexes were present and was able to demonstrate that direct muscle stimulation was possible (p. 434).

In a fetus of 260 mm. Bolaffio and Artom (1924) attempted certain specific neurological experiments. By means of appropriate electric stimuli they explored the cortex but did not obtain any reaction even with intense stimulation. By operation the internal capsule and peduncles of the brain were exposed, but still electric stimulation gave no response. When they reached the pons, however, they got ready and synchronous responses from the muscles innervated by the facial nerve. Finally, stimulation of the medulla gave energetic respiratory movements. Stimulation of the cervical cord led to energetic movements of elevation of the shoulder with flexion of the upper limbs, and stimulation of the lumbar cord gave movements of the lower limbs (p. 466).

In a fetus 270 mm. long Minkowski (1922) noted that from the first the plantar flexion of the toes was present to stimulation of the sole of the foot. Minkowski is of the opinion that at this age the plantar flexion must still be considered as a pure spinal reflex (p. 754).

In a fetus of 280 mm. Minkowski was able to bring about rather elaborate but quite well-differentiated muscular responses to a single electric stimulus. For example, the muscles of the eyelid could be activated with great specificity. After exposure in air this fetus is reported to have made faint sounds (p. 754). These sounds are possibly the earliest observed in a human organism. They may be taken by those who are interested in zero points as the onset of functional activity in the great mechanism which makes human speech possible.

In a fetus of the same length Bolaffio and Artom (1924) observed that every muscle reacted even to quite energetic stimulation, such as percussion, by local contraction. This specificity is more marked in the head region than in the leg region of the fetus. Percussion in front of the ear led to a movement of closing of the eye with elevation of the angle of the mouth and chin. Strangely enough, however, it seems that the deep reflexes are not easily obtained at this age in the arms. Stimulation of the legs shows that the patellar reflex can be called forth bilaterally and the Achilles tendon reflex on one side. No plantar reflex was elicited in one fetus at this age (p. 467).

In a fetus of 310 mm. Bolaffio and Artom further reported the observation of periodic respiration. Breathing was "by fits and starts." The heart beat was regular. At this period all the muscles of the limbs can be excited one by one with percussion, obtaining vivid reaction. Appropriate local stimulation serves to bring out most of the typical percussion reflexes, including minor responses of the fingers, of the toes, and of the sole of the foot. The plantar reflex, however, and some of the others still seem to be absent (p. 467).

In general in the sixth month there is an increased tendency of various receptor-neuromuscular mechanisms to act independently, and this independent contraction is part of the greater vividness of response which characterizes this period as contrasted with earlier periods. Bolaffio and Artom (p. 472) find in this month for the first time tendon reflexes which seem to be assuredly not the result of cutaneous or muscle stimulation. Their judgment on this matter is based on the facts that the specific responses given at this period are not found before this time but continue to increase in strength during the later fetal periods, and that they are the same responses which are elicited in early infancy as true tendon reflexes. Direct stimulation of the mouth and tongue at this age elicited the sucking reflex, according to Bolaffio and Artom. In older fetuses stimulation of the lips alone leads to sucking movements which may or may not be accompanied by the protrusion of the tongue (p. 477). As noted above, Minkowski found this reflex at an earlier period.

These same investigators, using a slightly larger fetus (330 mm.), again reported superficial respiratory movements. These breathing reactions ceased after a minute or two. They reappeared when pressure and percussion of the thorax were used. In this fetus they noted also that with percussion the muscles gave powerful and localized contractions. The tendon reflexes which could be elicited included those of the biceps and triceps and the Achilles reflex. Direct stimulation of the cortex still brought no response. In this fetus it seems that no true cutaneous reflexes could be called forth either before or after the removal of the brain. In another fetus of exactly the same size these same investigators report that the fetus cried weakly and moved about spontaneously but with less strong movements than those characteristic of a fetus at term (p. 468). When death seemed imminent in this fetus the top of the skull was removed and the cortex directly stimulated electrically. All the various zones of the cerebral cortex were stimulated with negative results. Stimulation of lower brain centers, however, led to specific results such as increased breathing rate, shoulder, arm, and finger movements.

Bolaffio and Artom also reported the behavior of a fetus of 340 mm. which appeared to be slightly undernourished. This fetus made weak crying sounds and breathed weakly. After about 2 hours it stopped breathing. During the period before breathing stopped they elicited contractions by tapping one by one the muscles and groups of muscles of the body. In this specimen by stroking the sole of the foot the plantar flexion of the toes was brought out. All these reactions became more vivid just before the death of the fetus (p. 469). This suggests a change in the higher brain centers as a result of a lack of oxygen.

Certain responses noted in the seventh month, while definite, nevertheless are seen to involve synergic muscle groups (Bolaffio and Artom, 1924, p. 481). This finding must be taken into consideration in evaluating statements given in regard to the randomness of activity in the newborn child. It may well be that much of the apparent "mass activity" of the newborn child (Irwin and Weiss, 1930) is not truly diffuse response of the sort found in the early fetus, but rather the activation of groups of synergic muscles in the sense of the term as used by Sherrington and his associates (Creed, Denny-Brown, Eccles, Liddell, and Sherrington, 1932, p. 129). Krabbe, Minkowski, and Bolaffio and Artom all report abdominal reflexes at this period. A number of other specific reflexes are also clearly brought out at this time. The knee jerk is definitely elicited. The plantar reflex, according to Minkowski, now probably involves not only the centers concerned during previous months but also part of the lenticular nucleus and the red nucleus. Bolaffio and Artom feel that at this period the plantar reflex in its typical form is much like that of adult life but that it is still much more variable than it will be at a later period. This leads them to be critical of statistical work on reflexes, such as that of De Angelis (1922). (Cf. also Cesana, 1911.) The corneal reflexes are seen in the seventh month. Direct stimulation of the cornea of the eye leads from this time on to an increasingly strong response. Decerebration in this month was found to lead to increased vividness of most reflexes, but also to a tendency to reflex spread.

In a still larger fetus Bolaffio and Artom reported that with slight percussion of all the muscles of the limbs they observed vivid responses not limited to single muscles. Such responses spread to synergic muscle groups. With percussion of the pectoral muscles they obtained adduction and internal rotation of the arm and flexion of the forearm. They obtained bilaterally the patellar reflex and an extension of the leg, sometimes associated with flexion of the thigh. Associated with this pattern of response was the dorsal flexion of the foot. The Achilles tendon reflexes, however, were not always obtained even in a fetus as old as this one. These investigators also failed to get abdominal reflexes in fetuses of this age. However, the slight excitation of the sole called forth a definite unified toe phenomenon, and then a more energetic stimulation called forth flexion of the toes. The sucking reflex was secured only by stimulating the tongue. They reported that the movement of grasping which they got by applying pressure to the palms of the hand was energetic. These same investigators reported that from the seventh month to birth they investigated 13 fetuses of 7 months, 3 of 8 months, and a large number of mature fetuses. In this study they have not considered protocols of any fetuses which, because of condition of nutrition or on account of the presence of disease, did not present normal situations. They assert that from the end of the sixth month the movements of the fetus

became so powerful and complex as to render very difficult and sometimes impossible detailed and specific report of behavior (pp. 470–487).

During the last 2 months of pregnancy the muscular reflexes decreasingly tend to prevail over the tendon reflexes, according to Bolaffio and Artom (p. 472). By the end of the ninth month the tendon reflexes are so well established that they prevail over special muscular reflexes. All the tendon reflexes are found to be present during this period of fetal life, with the exception of those of certain of the upper limbs which are elicited with difficulty because of the small size of the member. Contralateral adductor reflexes are sometimes called out in this period. Even in the fetuses nearest term, the cremasteric reflex was difficult to elicit (Bolaffio and Artom, 1924, p. 474).

At any prenatal age, including this last period, however, it is noticed that very light stimulation of the hand gives variable and inconstant movements, whereas strong stimulation, possibly involving the muscle or other underlying tissue, leads uniformly to grasping (Bolaffio and Artom, 1924, p. 476). Bolaffio and Artom, therefore, believe that the grasping reflex is not to be thought of as a purely cutaneous reflex in prenatal life. Minkowski (1928a, p. 545) finds this reflex at an earlier period. Iris reflexes are present during the prenatal period (Bolaffio and Artom, 1924, p. 477). The reaction of the iris, however, is slow, and very strong light is needed to call out the response. (See also Minkowski, 1928a, p. 558.) It is difficult to say when the response would begin if stimuli as strong as direct sunlight could always be used. Bolaffio and Artom do not note the fact, but it seems obvious that, with such strong stimulation as they recommend, the danger of independent muscle effector action of the sort described by Parker (1919, p. 53) must be guarded against.

There is some evidence that the cerebral cortex is directly stimulable at this period, although as yet the evidence is not conclusive (Bolaffio and Artom, 1924, p. 480), as will be pointed out below in considering the possibility of fetal learning.

It is possible to add to this consideration of month-by-month fetal development, therefore, some general statements that have been made by those who have been most directly concerned in these investigations. Thus Minkowski holds that one may say that every part of the skin can, as its receptivity is progressively established, serve as a reflexogenous zone for quite variable reactions which tend to spread more or less over the whole fetal organism. In the whole developmental process the gradual acquisition of postural responses and muscle tone is peculiarly important. The development of these responses will be considered below in the section in which the origin and development of the proprioceptive and static senses are considered. Minkowski offers in part explanation of the spread of reflexes during the early periods the fact that the spinal cord tracts as well as the nerve trunks have no medullary sheaths before the fourth month of fetal life. Illustrations of Minkowski's anatomical work on the nervous system are given in several places (1921a, 1928a). There is a suggestion that from this time onward there is an anatomical increase in specificity correlated with the differentiation of the nervous elements in ways possibly involving the nature of protoplasm, neurofibrils, medullary sheaths, synapses, long conduction paths, and other cell changes (Minkowski, 1922, p. 753). These gradual alterations in the nervous system, it is suggested, lead progressively to the possibility of more and more circumscribed and definite response. Compared with the diffuse character of early fetal response, therefore, in the late fetus, Minkowski (1920a) feels that all the well-known special reflexes have more or less been established. The discussion above, however, has shown that the process of development of these reflexes is a complex one and that later in adult life injury to the nervous system may bring about reactions which were characteristic of a previous period, even of a fetal period (Minkowski, 1922, p. 754). For the historical breaking of ground in this connection, see H. Jackson's essay (1884) on the evolution and dissolution of the nervous system.

It must be impossible to read what has gone before in this chapter without realizing that there is a general relationship in sequence of development of behavioral capacities from fish to man. It must be noted, however, that there are peculiar dangers in generalizing from, for example, the amphibian development of behavior, or even the rodent or cat development of behavior, to the growth of adaptive actions in man. For example, it has been shown clearly that in fish, amphibians, and lower mammals the first responses involve a unilateral bending of the trunk. This stage may or may not exist in the human individual, but at any rate no observations have so far been made in which trunk movements unaccompanied by arm movements are observed in early fetuses.

The basic pattern for the development of locomotion and other "individuated" responses, as suggested by Coghill and his students, may be seen in a less typical form in human development than might be supposed, although Coghill (1929c, p. 1009) himself has called attention to the attractive possibilities of the analogy. Little evidence of rhythm in the limbs of the human fetus has been determined. It may well be, therefore, that locomotorlike movements of the limbs do not appear until very late in the human fetal period. Windle and Griffin (1931) have summarized this comparative evidence, and they suggest that the movements observed in the kitten fetuses with which they have worked possibly should not be compared directly to human fetal movements because of the differences between the two in the type of adult locomotion. In a similar way the locomotor mechanisms in fish and amphibians which require a high degree of trunk-muscle integration may be difficult to compare with the conditions obtaining in a mammal that stands erect. Such considerations as this bring up the old problem of the recapitulation in ontogeny of the phylogeny of behavior. This problem is as old as Aristotle (Needham, 1931, p. 69), and yet there seems to be nothing in the present evidence to make this view seem anything but a generalized, and in many details an inaccurate, description, and certainly not an explanation, of development. (See Davidson, 1914; Needham, 1931, pp. 1632–1638.)

Too much emphasis cannot be placed upon the fact that easy generalizations, such as the assertion that all behavioral development occurs from a generalized total pattern of the organism to the specific responses of adult life, must be taken with great caution. While this description may be true in many respects, particularly if the word "pattern" is given an unambiguous meaning, it seems certain on the basis of the specific responses considered above that it cannot be indiscriminately applied. Before generalizations can be made with assurance, there must be a large amount of accurate measurement and the determination of a series of statistical norms in regard to the development of each of the specific developmental stages in each form considered. Typical cross-sections in development in every form and in all responses from significant receptor surfaces must be considered before such a generalization can be made. Certainly the late fetus has an elaborately organized and in some respects quite specific response mechanism. To some stimuli the relatively early fetus makes quite definite responses.

It seems hard to believe that anyone who knows anything of the structure and function of the tracts and centers of the central nervous system can read the report of fetal activity at various developmental levels given above and still feel that there is much to be gained by saying that before birth the organism reacts as a whole, as certain psychologists, possibly under the influence of one form of the *Gestalttheorie*, have suggested. Much of the nervous system may, in some sense, be involved in any partial activity of the system, but this does not mean that the system is not in many respects sharply differentiated. Certain essential relationships between diffuseness and specificity and between individuation and integration of behavior will become clearer after the parts played by the specific senses in fetal life have been considered.

The account presented above from the reports of several investigators gives a picture of the development of behavior in human fetal organisms of estimated ages. No effort has been made to include all known fetuses but only those in which behavior significant for the general problem of this chapter was noted. Minkowski (1923, pp. 486–489) refers to at least 11 fetuses not considered here in which primarily the only reflexes studied were those released by stimulation of the sole of the foot. In the study of this response Bersot (1918, 1919; 1920, 1921) has also considered fetal activity in detail in relation to a study of the development of the clinically significant plantar reflex. This same response has been considered from a scientific and theoretical point of view by

Feldman (1922) and by Minkowski (1926) in work that has been referred to above. For an account of a fetus investigated by Winterstein, see Minkowski (1928a, p. 517).

Hooker has given permission to refer to his *Preliminary Atlas of Early Human Fetal Activity* (1939b), which was first issued for restricted use only. Reference has been made above to this work, but the author wishes to call especial attention to it because it contains very beautiful reproductions of photographs of human fetal material 8½ to 14 weeks of menstrual age. A careful study of this atlas may give a more adequate picture of early human fetal behavior than any other single reference.

The Special Senses in Human Prenatal Life

Historically there has been much speculation in regard to the rôle of the senses before birth. In earlier psychology these speculations centered largely about the question of whether or not some sort of dim conscious awareness exists in the infant before birth. More recently this essentially nonexperimental question has given place to one that may be studied. The question now asked is: How and when does the stimulus control of fetal behavior determined by the activation of the various receptor systems begin before birth, and how do behavior capacities develop? Objective techniques for study of the senses in the premature or newborn infant have been devised, of which those of Canestrini (1913) and A. P. Weiss (1929) are significant examples. These techniques have not only made quantitative study of the senses possible in a new way, but they have also added to the general knowledge of the part that stimulation plays in the subtle alterations of bodily activity. In this chapter, therefore, the various specific senses

will be considered in turn in relation to fetal behavioral or mental life when such behavioral or mental life is considered as including not only experience but also specific receptor-controlled behavior.

After each of the senses has been treated, some generalizations will be made by the author on the significance for psychology of receptor-aroused activity in the fetus. The reader should be reminded that the material presented above on the development of the senses in lower animals and especially the elaborate work on the guinea pig has much relevance in a consideration of the growth of the human senses. In this section, however, the whole emphasis is placed upon human development except where specific reference to infrahuman forms is considered necessary for strictly comparative purposes.

THE CUTANEOUS RECEPTORS

In a consideration of the senses of touch, an effort is made to suggest such differences as have been noted in fetal life between light and deep pressure, temperature, and cutaneous pain. The development of skin in the human fetus has been anatomically described by a number of writers. This work is summarized by Feldman (1920, pp. 233–236). In appearance the skin of the late fetus or early premature infant is very red, owing to the visibility of the vascular system just beneath it. At 2 or 3 months before birth the skin is still quite thin and is covered with *lanugo hairs*, which appear at about the fifth month of pregnancy. The skin of the fetus during midpregnancy is typically much wrinkled, because of the comparative absence of subcutaneous fat. The hair on the scalp at this period is short and poorly pigmented. The nails grow gradually during late fetal life (Hess, 1922, pp. 74–77).

There has been much speculation on the skin as a sensory surface during the uterine life of the fetus. Cabanis is quoted by Genzmer (1882, p. 10) as holding the skin to be a peculiarly important receptor field at this period. Bichat (1827, p. 137) and Magendie, as noted above, discussed the skin sensibility of the fetus. Some casual observations are also reported in relation to the material summarized on a previous page of this chapter concerning the possibility of stimulating the fetus by pressing on the abdominal wall of the mother. Of course, stimulation of this sort may well activate the deep-lying proprioceptors as well as the true tactile receptors. In the review of the literature in the experimental study of the development of fetal behavior in infrahuman organisms, many references have already been made to tactual stimulation. In the human field alone, Minkowski, Bolaffio and Artom, Krabbe, Hooker, and others have considered fetal responses that are released by cutaneous stimulation as indicated above. Hooker has been especially careful to use quantified stimuli. The part played by the sense of touch in animals and man in discrimination and even in responses of equilibration is considered by Kidd (1907).

A. Pressure. In summarizing the work that has been done on human and infrahuman fetuses, the following factors may possibly be isolated as important in a consideration of the pressure sense before birth:

1. Place stimulated. In general, cutaneous sensitivity seems to begin in the oral-nasal region, that is, the region involving the mucous membrane of the nostrils and the red of the lips (Genzmer, 1882, p. 6; Windle and Griffin, 1931, p. 179; Hooker, 1944, p. 22). In rodents the pads of the vibrissae also very early become sensitive (Lane, 1917, p. 34; Raney and Carmichael, 1934; Carmichael, 1934a), and in many animals the regions about the eyes and the openings of the ears are also very early sensitive, as is the anal region (Coronios, 1931). In the human infant Kussmaul (1859, p. 23) found the eyelashes very sensitive, but this was not confirmed by Genzmer (1882, p. 6). Most studies seem to suggest that, with individual variations, skin sensitivity develops by spreading out over the face region and then progressively over the surface of the body. In this development in certain organisms, such as the toadfish, the salamander, the rat, and the cat, a fairly well-worked-out course of temporal difference in the arrival of sensitivity in increasingly caudal segments of the body may be observed. In animals with tails this even goes on out to the end of the tail.

In this general course of development, however, certain exceptions have been made out, as noted above by the writer in a study of the development of the receptive zones of the fetal guinea pig. Sensory development in general has been treated by Minkowski and other investigators as the spreading of what they have termed reflexogenous zones. This term has much to recommend it because at present almost the only method used in the study of fetal sensory capacity on the skin is the recognition of behavior correlated with the experimental stimulation. Windle and Griffin (1931, p. 175) suggest in general that motility precedes the ability of a part to be stimulated. In his consideration of the "reflex circle," Holt (1931, pp. 37–43) has suggested the large part that self-stimulation may possibly play in the development of specific forms of behavior as organisms develop. Certainly no one who has watched an active mammalian fetus can help being struck by the fact that in its movements it stimulates almost its entire body surface by its own moving paws and head. It is peculiarly striking to watch a 48-day guinea pig fetus, for example, stimulate its head and face by appropriately cupped "hands." These scrubbing movements, performed not once but over and over again, are such that the surface must certainly be irritated by the friction.

2. *Areal versus punctiform stimuli.* Minkowski (1922, p. 723), Coronios (1931), Windle and Griffin (1931, p. 175), Carmichael (1934a), Raney and Carmichael (1934), and Hooker (1936) have all apparently noticed that stroking produces stimulation when single punctate stimulation does not bring about response. Following this suggestion, Raney has been able to show that stimulation of a point on the skin by a single hair may not bring about response, but stimulating the same area immediately around such a point with a brush made up of comparable hairs will sometimes do so. (In this connection, see also Kuo, 1932e, p. 507.)

3. *Summation of stimuli.* Carmichael (1934a) and others have noted that a single touch with a light hair may fail to bring out response, but several touches apparently of the same intensity at the same point may be effective in eliciting response.

4. *Weak and strong stimulation.* Genzmer (1882, p. 10) long ago noted that in a premature infant entirely different responses might be elicited to weak and strong cutaneous stimulation. The distinction in terms of the strength of cutaneous pressure is one that has too infrequently been made in studies of fetal development. Thus, as noted above, Bolaffio and Artom disagree with Minkowski as to the point at which cutaneous reflexes begin in the developing fetus. This disagreement may be based on the fact that Bolaffio and Artom (1924, p. 473) indicate the possibility that Minkowski was unwittingly stimulating the underlying musculature and thus that the massive responses which he reports in young fetuses are not cutaneous but are due to the stimulation of deep receptors. The possibility of direct muscle stimulation in such cases must also be remembered. Holt (1931, pp. 40–43) considers that the distinction between strong and weak stimulation is a peculiarly important one in the development of the functional activity of the growing organism. He believes that light stimulation will usually lead to response moving toward the stimulus, or *adiently*, whereas only secondarily does strong stimulation of the same receptor field lead to *abient*, or withdrawal and avoidance, responses. Richter (1925) and others have confirmed this observation. Indeed, Coronios, Schlosberg, and Carmichael (1932) have been able to take moving pictures showing exactly this response as the result of stimulating the paw of a fetal kitten.

Under other circumstances, however, observations have not been such as to confirm this generalization. Thus Coghill (1929a, p. 13) asserts that the first responses of *Amblystoma* are all away from the region stimulated. Windle and Griffin (1931, p. 175) point out that the unilateral trunk or neck flexions of the earliest fetuses seem to be executed toward the observer and away from the surface on which the animal is resting. Kuo (1932e, p. 507) also uses the strength of the stimulus as a peculiarly important part of the theory of development which he has proposed. It seems possible that in responses in which apparently the same receptor field is stimulated first lightly and then more strongly two distinct neural mechanisms may sometimes be brought into play. It might be suggested speculatively that the facts behind the differentiation between the allegedly developmental epicritic and protopathic sensitivity, as proposed by Head and Rivers and especially as explained by Boring (1916) and later by Sharpey-Schäfer (1928), will ultimately provide some clue in the explanation of this diversity of response to different stimulus intensity.

Windle and Griffin (1931, p. 176) also discuss a developmental system of cutaneous receptor mechanisms. The difference in responses to light and heavy tactile stimulation makes peculiarly uncertain the interpretation of results of investigators who do not indicate that they have considered the strength of the stimulus as important in describing the fetal responses which they have elicited in experimental work. It is all the more peculiar that this distinction should not have been continuously made, because of the statement in regard to the difference in responses to weak and strong stimuli made, as noted above, many years ago by Genzmer. As previously reported, Smith and the writer (Carmichael and Smith, 1939) have demonstrated a quantitative relationship between the extent and spread of response and the intensity of punctiform stimulation when calibrated esthesiometers were used.

5. *Localization*. Preyer (1882, p. 110) believes that the first localization response to tactile stimuli is the seeking of the nipple by means of the cutaneous stimulation of the lips. Many specific references have been given above to the motor responses of various fetuses set off by tactual stimulation. It has been suggested in connection with the work of Raney and Carmichael (1934) that such responses possibly develop greater accuracy in localization as age progresses.

6. *Cutaneous reflexes*. As suggested in the preceding paragraphs, the skin may be thought of as a mosaic of points, each spot of which is the locus of stimulation for a more or less specific behavioral response. Many writers have discussed the significance of cutaneous reflexes in adult life. Givler (1921) has suggested the wide significance of the development of one such reflex, that of grasping. Hooker's (1938) careful observations on the grasping reflex show that it develops during fetal life in two phases: finger closing, and gripping. Finger closing appears as a quick flexion of the digits except the thumb at about 11 weeks of menstrual age. Gripping is first observed in the eighteenth week. It is still weak in the twenty-fifth week of menstrual age. In the first 25 weeks of fetal life the thumb seems to play no rôle in fetal grasping.

Minkowski, as noted above, considers in detail the variations in the pattern of the reflexes elicited by the stimulation of the skin of the sole of the foot. Sucking, in its later stages, is possibly conditioned by a number of exteroceptive and interoceptive stimuli, such as the stomach contraction of hunger, but it is in essentials always a cutaneous and mucous membrane reflex. The cremasteric reflex and certain of the abdominal reflexes also result from stimulation of the cutaneous field.

In general, then, it may be pointed out that many of the specific acts of the fetus are induced by stimulation of cutaneous pressure receptors. Mucous membrane reflexes (Minkowski, 1928a, pp. 556–558) are also probably best thought of as involving receptor mechanisms, so far as pressure is concerned, that are similar to cutaneous reflexes. Peiper (1928, p. 92) has tabulated the cutaneous responses seen in newborn children. The writer must here again emphasize his belief that, given a stimulus just above the lower threshold and a quiescent fetus in a standard posture, there is typically *one behavior act* or *reflex* set off by the stimulation of each cutaneous area. These cutaneous "push buttons" are remarkably specific in their behavioral relations when the complexity of the central nervous system is considered.

B. Temperature. Warmth is one of the skin senses attributed by the philosopher John Locke (1849 edition) to the fetus. In spite of this early sanction it is difficult to understand how marked differences in temperature can normally be present in prenatal life. In the study of the temperature sense in the prematurely delivered infant the matter is further complicated by the great variability of body temperature which characterizes the premature infant (Hess, 1922, p. 151; Evensen, 1931, pp. 11–15). Currently accepted views in regard to the mechanism of temperature stimulation start with the assumption that the temperature to which the skin is adapted must be taken as the physiological zero point. From this zero other stimuli are to be considered as above or below; therefore quantified work in regard to temperature in the premature infant is rendered difficult when only absolute temperatures of stimuli are recorded.

Some indications, however, of responses to both warm and cool stimuli in premature infants are given by both Kussmaul (1859, p. 23) and Genzmer (1882, p. 11). For the most part these observations agree with those of the following investigators of the temperature sense of newborn children: Preyer (1882, pp. 111–116), Canestrini (1913, pp. 76–85), Blanton (1917), and Peiper (1928, pp. 28–29). These opinions are criticized by Pratt, Nelson, and Sun (1930, pp. 144–167), who also add their own controlled experimental observations. These three collaborators report that newborn infants react much less strongly to stimuli warmer than the body than to stimuli that are cooler. The writer has described above a study of fetal temperature sensitivity (Carmichael and Lehner, 1937) in which some observations on the temperature responses of guinea pigs were made. In this study unmistakable reactions to temperature both of warm and cool stimuli were obtained under controlled conditions. Drops of blood-warm water call out no response save as they arouse tactile receptors, but cold- or hot-water drops do call out such activities. This sensitivity

has appeared by approximately the middle of the gestation period. Here again the "more intense" stimulus (warm or cold) calls out more active responses than the "less intense" stimulus.

C. Pain. Locke (1849 edition) also attributed the experience of pain to the fetus. Since his speculation there has been little direct experimentation upon the fetal pain sense. A number of casual observations show, however, that the application of stimuli that must have caused gross destruction of skin and protoplasm has not called out very pronounced movements on the part of the fetus. Genzmer (1882, p. 12), on the basis of such observations, holds that the pain sense is very poorly developed in the fetus. On the first day of a premature infant's neonatal life he stimulated it until blood came and got no response. It is certainly true that increase in pressure over that necessary to bring out the typical responses to deep pressure does not always seem in the guinea pig fetus, at any rate, to increase the extent or intensity of response. Thus in certain cases the light pressure of a fine hair may lead to extension and stronger pressure of a heavier hair to retraction, but very strong and even obviously destructive stimulation of the same point may or may not make any observable difference in the elicited response over that noted to strong pressure stimulation. Similar observations have been made on the cat fetus (Windle and Griffin, 1931, p. 176). There can be no doubt that protoplasm-destroying stimuli sometimes bring about violent responses in late fetuses, but even this reaction does not always occur. Speculations on the part played by pain in relation to unpleasantness and discomfort will be referred to in the consideration of the organic senses.

The foregoing paragraphs may be summarized by the statement that there is much evidence that the specialized skin senses have developed to an active functional state long before birth and are able when appropriately stimulated to initiate the release of behavior that is typically precisely related to the point stimulated.

THE PROPRIOCEPTIVE SENSES

The neuromuscular spindles may be taken as typical of the many classes of proprioceptors. They are found in the fourth month of fetal life in practically all muscles, including the extrinsic muscles of the tongue and the external eye muscles (Elwyn, 1929, p. 248). Historically it was not until quite recently that the kinesthetic senses came to be distinguished at all from touch. Carmichael (1926b, pp. 204–209) has described the history of knowledge concerning the "muscle sense." Much that Bichat (1819) wrote about the active touch of the fetus probably referred to the proprioceptive rather than to the cutaneous sense. Kussmaul (1859, p. 32) and Genzmer (1882, p. 8) both refer to responses which must have involved muscle-sense stimulation. Preyer (1885, p. 547) makes similar references. Peterson and Rainey (1910) also hold that not only touch but also the activity of the muscles of the fetus must lay the foundation "under the threshold of consciousness for a sense of equilibrium and vague spatial relationships" (p. 122). In his study of the relationship between local reflexes and posture, Coghill (1929a) comes to the conclusion that ". . . the limb is able to respond very precisely to stimuli arising within the body (proprioceptive) as the result of a particular posture before it can respond to stimuli that arise exclusively from the outside world (exteroceptive) . . ." (p. 21).

In experimental work on operatively exposed human and infrahuman fetal material during the active period, the proprioceptive senses are always much in evidence. Indeed, in the responses in fetal rats both

Swenson (1926) and Angulo y González (1932a) find evidence of this sense in a 16-day fetus. Coronios (1933) and Windle and Griffin (1931, p. 177) deal with this sense in detail. (See also Windle, 1940.) As noted above in the consideration of the cutaneous senses, these investigators report activities that show that the posture of the cat fetus at the time of stimulation seems in certain cases to determine the response that will be elicited. This point is substantiated by many protocols of the experimental studies of fetal behavior that the present writer has recorded. It is possible that this fact alone may be taken as indicating an early onset of proprioceptive control of behavior.

In this connection one must remember the differential gravitational action on the limb and body in air and in the liquid of the amniotic sac. In one of the studies of a very young human fetus—by Strassmann (1903), noted above—it is recorded that the observer pressed against, in a manner which apparently means moved, the limb of the fetus. As a result of this stimulation the experimenter could feel the foot press down on his hand. The writer has noticed this same response in young guinea pig fetuses. Even when very gentle or even relatively strong tactual stimulation would not release a response in the forelimb of the fetus, it not infrequently has happened that a forcible movement of the limb itself by the experimenter gave a specific and direct response. As the skin was not anesthetized in the cases reported, this may not of course be thought of as a wholly proprioceptive stimulus, but, as cutaneous stimulation was ineffective in producing the same response, the facts seem to favor the view that the responses noted were proprioceptively aroused. This conclusion must be taken with reservations because the bending and stretching of the skin which result from he bending of a limb are a very strong pressure stimulus.

There is still other evidence that the proprioceptors are effective very early in fetal development. Hooker and Nicholas (1930) have reported experiments on fetal rats in which the spinal cords were completely sectioned at various levels. After some of these experiments it was found that stimulation above or below the sectioned point of the cord might lead to responses in parts of the body innervated by segments of the cord above or below the cut. The question at once arose as to how these impulses were transmitted. As one of the possible explanations of this transmission, these investigators have suggested the following course of events. An exteroceptive stimulus leads to afferent conduction over peripheral nerves to the cord above the region of the section. From this still intact segment of the cord impulses pass out over efferent peripheral nerves to trunk muscles leading to this response. This response mechanically moves the adjoining musculature and thus directly stimulates the proprioceptors in it. These newly activated proprioceptors then initiate afferent impulses which pass into the cord below or above the region of the cut, as the case may be, and thus in turn activate arcs in the intact region of the cord above or below the section, which in turn lead to responses obviously innervated by connections in the cord beyond the section. (See also Hooker, 1911.)

Windle and Griffin (1931) report many evidences of movement that may be considered on the basis of the analysis of Sherrington and his school of reflex physiologists as at least in part proprioceptively innervated. These investigators report (p. 186) that a quiescent embryo held in the cramped condition of the sac will, on the cutting of the sac, sometimes at once assume an exaggeratedly stretched position.

It seems as though it were attempting to exercise itself after the close confinement of its entire previous existence. It may be remarked that the writer has seen and photographed similar responses. These maintained "extensor thrusts" are in many respects similar to the tonus of decerebrate rigidity as seen in the adult animal and may possibly involve proprioceptive stimulation. The experiments of Weed (1917), Weed and Langworthy (1926), and Langworthy (1928, 1929) give very clear evidence of other reactions involving this receptor system. The writer has sometimes noted when dealing with a late guinea pig fetus that, if the fetus, still wholly immersed in the bath, is held by its own forepaws on a submerged projection, the animal will seem to try to crawl up onto the projection. Correlated movements are here used which seem, to superficial observation, similar to those employed by a swimmer lifting himself out of the water onto a diving raft. This well-integrated and apparently purposeful activity seems to involve complex proprioceptively directed responses.

Most students of the development of fetal behavior agree that locomotion, as, for example, in the first crawling movements of the fetal opossum considered above, sucking, and breathing are three of the earliest essential behavior systems of the newborn animal. It is interesting to note that each of these in its developed form may involve marked proprioceptive stimulation. The geotropic responses of the opossum fetus considered above, occurring less than 2 weeks after copulation, seem, in the light of Crozier's work (1929, pp. 83–98) on geotropism in the rodent, to represent a response in which proprioceptive stimulation plays a part. Hunter (1931) has pointed out in a similar study that the vestibular apparatus and other stimulus factors are probably also important in determining such responses.

As noted above, Minkowski (1922, p. 723; 1928a, pp. 559–560) reports that there are true tendon reflexes in the early fetus. This is questioned, however, by Bolaffio and Artom (1924, p. 472). These latter observers suggest that the responses seen by Minkowski in very early fetuses may have been the result of other forms of stimulation. The mechanism of deep stimulation which they suggest and true tendon-stretch stimulation both involve proprioceptive activity. Indeed, it may be said that the whole study of prenatal behavior in man and in the lower mammals indicates that the proprioceptors in muscles and tendons, and possibly joints, are functional well before birth. By the time of birth these mechanisms have undergone such development that they are among the best-organized receptor fields so far as the initiation and control of behavior are concerned. Much of the "movement of the organism as a whole" which so many writers refer to seems to be the result of rather specific proprioceptive stimulation. Such stimulation often leads to the "spread" of what are really quite delicately timed families of specific responses which can easily be mistaken for "vague" or "diffuse" behavior.

THE RECEPTORS IN THE NONAUDITORY LABYRINTH

Adult posture, righting responses, and other reactions to gravity, tonus changes due to rotation, and other alterations of the body in space are often held to result from stimulation of receptors in the nonauditory labyrinth and associated receptor fields (Camis, 1930, pp. 262–268). As suggested above in a consideration of the development of behavior in the fetal cat, the change of body posture in space has been shown sometimes to involve various combinations of nonauditory labyrinthine, kin-

esthetic, and exteroceptive stimuli. In the fetus it is peculiarly difficult to isolate the part played by the body exteroceptors and muscle proprioceptors from the part played by the receptors in the nonauditory labyrinth. It should be noted that there is some evidence also that in certain types there is an auditory function subsumed by receptors in this *non*-auditory receptor complex.

Historically, comparatively little reference has been made to the static senses in connection with fetal mental life as this life was considered in the older speculative child psychology. Some reference, however, has been made to the part played by these receptors in determining the position of the fetus in relation to gravity. Lane (1917) has noted in his study of the development of the senses in the fetal rat considered above that there is an apparent correlation between the histological development of the semicircular canals and the acquisition of postural righting responses on the part of the fetus. In Lane's work, however, no effort to differentiate between proprioceptive and static stimuli is reported.

The development of the labyrinth has been considered by many writers, including Streeter (1906) and Larsell (1929). (Cf. also Bowen, 1932, and McCrady, Wever, and Bray, 1937.) Minkowski (1922, p. 753), as noted above, has demonstrated from neurological studies that the labyrinth is fully differentiated in a human fetus of 40 mm. As noted above also, Windle and Griffin (1931) report that in very early cat embryos of 26 or 27 days ". . . rotation of head and trunk appeared to be indefinitely coordinated with the older components, namely, lateral and ventral head and trunk flexion. This activity resulted in motions that strikingly resembled the righting reflexes seen in late fetal life" (p. 156). Windle and Fish (1932, p. 95) show that in cat fetuses several days before normal birth true labyrinthine reflexes do appear. These reactions make possible what has been called the first "purposeful" movement of the cat, that is, successful locomotion (Windle and Griffin, 1931, p. 171). This complex behavior act, as already suggested, is held to be a combination of equilibration, body-righting responses, general postural tonus, and rhythmic movement of the limbs.

Coronios and Carmichael have both noticed that, in late cat and guinea pig fetuses, turning the animal over while it is completely immersed in the warm bath does not always lead to righting movements. If the cord is ligated and the same fetus is placed on its side on the experimental table, righting may begin at once. This is possibly to be interpreted as indicating that at this period righting still, at any rate, involves exteroceptive and proprioceptive as well as vestibular functions.

Similarly, Coronios and Carmichael have both been able to elicit typical Magnus reflexes of limb extension as the fetal mammal's neck is turned to the right or the left. These responses are strikingly similar to those of decerebrate mammals and tend to confirm the observation agreed upon by all other investigators that for the most part the young fetus is not under the active control of the cerebral hemispheres. Minkowski (1922, p. 724) reports labyrinthine reflexes in early human fetuses. He suggests that it is not only possible to elicit responses from general labyrinthine stimulation but also possible to distinguish between the reflexes attributed by Magnus and his colleagues to the utriculus-sacculus complex of receptors as contrasted with those attributed to the complex of semicircular-canal receptors. His analysis leads him to believe that most of the fetal responses to nonauditory labyrinthine stimulation are the result of semicircular-canal receptor action.

Minkowski (1922, p. 753) states further that in his opinion the early anatomical development and functional use of the vestibular apparatus in the fetus are probably related to the fact that the fetus is living in a fluid medium the specific gravity of which is almost equal to its own specific gravity. Therefore it is almost "weightless," a condition in which he believes the labyrinthine reflexes may be seen to operate to excellent advantage (p. 753). Minkowski (1928a, pp. 565–568) is careful, however, not to disregard the possibility that the phenomena noted as the basis for attributing labyrinthine function to the fetus may be the result of the stimulation of proprioceptors in the neck and related receptors. Magnus (1924, p. 113), in reviewing this work, seems to emphasize the part of the tonic neck reflexes in such activities.

There is some reason to believe that the first eye movements of the fetus are in response to changes of the bodily position of the fetus in space; that is, the first eye movements are occasioned not by retinal stimulation but as part of the general tonus changes of the body brought about by gross movements in space. This fact is brought out very clearly in Kuo's work (1932a, p. 426). Early eye muscle movements, indeed, may be thought of as specific. These movements take place, however, at the same time that other responses are active and hence may be called part of the "generalized" pattern of responses. Later specific responses are observed which can then be said to differentiate themselves out of the more complex pattern (Minkowski, 1924, p. 253; 1928a, p. 568; Tracy, 1926, p. 283).

There is no reason to believe, however, that these early "postural" responses of the eye muscles are as definitely related to specific aspects of semicircular-canal stimulation as they are in the adult condition so well summarized by Maxwell (1923), Favill (1929), and Holsopple (1929).

Eye movements in adult life that are determined by vestibular function may be modified in various ways (Dodge, 1923). Wellman and Carmichael have made preliminary and as yet unpublished studies of the origin and development of eye movements in the fetal guinea pig. Although these results are still tentative, the following statements may be made, based upon the electrical recording of eye movements in living fetuses: (1) Vestibular stimulation brings about responses before light stimulation is effective in causing eye movements. (2) Optokinetic (that is, light-induced) responses can be called out in the fetal guinea pig which have some of the same characteristics as such responses in older animals. In these experiments a moving field of bars of light and shade gradients is passed near the eyes of the fetus. The resulting reactions show the slow and fast photic responses typical of such stimuli in adult animals.

In conclusion, then, it is difficult to say with assurance the exact part which the labyrinthine senses play in determining behavior before birth, but it is certain that the tonus adjustments of the body muscles in postural responses, including precise adjustments of eye muscles, are among significant prenatal activities. An understanding of these responses in fetal and adult life is important (Magnus, 1925). One of the points, however, at which a knowledge of the development of proprioceptive responses in the fetus is most important is the evaluation of the studies of postnatal life in which the alleged saltatory character of certain responses there noted is observed in the light of the knowledge of prenatal postural responses. Popularly speaking, the postural actions of the fetus

may be considered a fundamental preparation for a diversity of actions in postnatal life. Walking and localizing responses of arms, trunk, and legs can take place only in an organism in which postural mechanisms are developed. It is almost as if these senses provide the essential "gyro-control" necessary before a reaction can be made, just as gyro-apparatus on a warship is necessary if the guns are to be pointed effectively in a heavy sea. In considering the part played by incoming nerve impulses which themselves result from motor reactions one should consider the whole nature of "feed-back" systems in biology as related to similar electronic systems (Wiener, 1948).

THE ORGANIC SENSES

Historically there has been some speculation in regard to the organic senses in the fetus. Some have held that the fetus lives in a perfect world in which hunger, thirst, and all other needs are cared for before they arise (Bichat, 1827, p. 133). Locke (1849 edition), on the contrary, held at an early period in the total story of speculation about fetal life that the unborn child has "perhaps some faint ideas of hunger and thirst." Kussmaul (1859, p. 31) agrees with this view. As noted above, Yanase (1907a, 1907b) has studied the movement of the fetal intestines. In the rhythmic nature of these movements is found a basis for possible organic experience and, indeed, for the indirect activation of the skeletal musculature.

The work of Patterson (1914) and Carlson and Ginsburg (1915) on newborn infants and on dogs delivered before normal time indicates something of the nature of the tonus changes of the stomach which may occur in late fetal life. These changes in these organisms are found under appropriate conditions to be rapid and active. This coincides with the observations of

Preyer (1893, pp. 152–158) and of Peterson and Rainey (1910, p. 121) on the hunger of newborn full-term or even premature infants. Some suggestion of the developmental course of hunger activities and stimulation may be obtained from an observation of Hess (1922, pp. 177–180) that very early premature fetuses are much less able than later premature infants to show the usual signs of needing to be fed. Jensen (1932, pp. 368–375) notes the dependence in the infant of the reflex of sucking, a reflex incidentally too often considered merely tactual, on the concomitance of hunger stimuli and tactual stimuli. Preyer (1893, p. 153) notes the whole sequence of bodily changes, even including those of the eye muscles, which come to be related to the hunger activities of the newborn child.

The theory of "drive" or motivation held by some modern comparative psychologists, which correlates such activities to some extent with organic stimulation, finds support in the observations of the "random" activity of the fetus which is shown by Irwin (1930) and others to accompany hunger stimuli. As noted above, this activity may not be "random" in the ordinary sense of the word but rather the consecutive or concomitant release of a series of already described patterns of behavior. (See Carmichael, 1941.)

This concept of "drive" is closely related to phenomena considered by certain of the older descriptive psychologists as characterizing the motivating power of the affective processes. That is, "drive" is related to the bodily basis of pleasantness and unpleasantness. Thus Preyer (1882, pp. 140–176; 1885, pp. 486–487) and others have discussed reaction related to pleasantness and unpleasantness as apparent before birth or immediately after birth. These conclusions are inferences based on unaided observation of facial expression and on instrumentally recorded bodily changes, such as breathing and directly measured cerebral volume (Canestrini, 1913). Facial expression is reported by Minkowski as beginning in the relatively early weeks of active fetal life, and so it seems that this expressive pattern of so much significance in pleasant and unpleasant situations of later life has had ample opportunity for exercise during the prenatal period.

It may be noted in passing that the rate of fetal heart beat can be modified by external stimulation, thus possibly leading to vascular stimuli of the sort often considered to fall under the heading of "organic experience." The possibility of respiratory experiences, or "feelings of suffocation," is certainly present, so far as may be judged from a knowledge of stimulation and response. But there is, of course, no evidence that any introspective state actually follows such stimulation.

In conclusion, it may be said that there are possibly certain organic changes in the stomach, intestines, heart, and vascular and respiratory systems which occur before birth which may be important in receptor stimulation. It is possible that the stimulation of these receptor systems may lead to fetal activity which does not, of course, have any specific external end in view until, as a result of external stimulation and learning, such stimulation in postnatal life comes to initiate adaptive responses which some wish to characterize as "end-seeking." It may also be noted that no one who has worked with fetal material has failed to see that, after repeated responses, "fatigue" sets in, and for a time stimulation is difficult or impossible (Peiper, 1925).

The question whether fetal quiescence is to be considered as fetal sleep has also been debated (Preyer, 1885, p. 488).

Taste. The histological work on the development of the taste mechanism in the embryo is summarized by Keibel and Mall (1910). Taste buds are said by Parker

(1922) to begin to appear in man during the third fetal month. The taste receptors are also found to be much more widely distributed in fetal life than in adult life. Parker thus points out that there is evidence of a real retraction of the sensory field in man from the late fetal period to the adult state. At first, taste buds are found on the tonsils, hard palate, and parts of the esophagus. Later, functional taste cells are almost always limited to the tongue (1922, p. 110). Here is a striking example of a "reflexogenous" or receptor zone which changes as a function of developmental time.

Historically, there have been several different speculative opinions concerning this sense in prenatal life. The early opinions are summarized by Bichat (1827, p. 136). It is undoubtedly true that the amniotic fluid might serve as a taste stimulus. As change is ordinarily thought of as essential to real external stimulation, however, the question may be debated as to whether or not the change in the amniotic fluid as pregnancy progresses is enough to make it at any point a taste stimulus (Feldman, 1920, p. 139). To the writer this seems unlikely. A safe conclusion seems to be that, although the mechanism for taste is present before birth, there is no adequate stimulation of this sense until after birth. Here again we have an illustration of what the present writer has called the law of *anticipatory morphological maturation.*

Experiments on the sense of taste in newborn children have been carried out by Kussmaul (1859, pp. 16–21), Genzmer (1882, p. 15), and Peterson and Rainey (1910, p. 120), using the method of general observation of facial expression after stimulation. The conclusion of these writers is that sweet is distinguished, even by premature infants, from salt, sour, and bitter. It is difficult to be sure, however, that salt, sour, and bitter are stimuli for be-

havior that is specific. Canestrini (1913) and Jensen (1932) have worked out a method of experimentally recording bodily changes which result from taste. Pratt, Nelson, and Sun (1930) find that under the conditions of their experiment, involving very dilute concentrations, there is not as strong evidence in regard to taste differentiation at birth as had previously been supposed. These later experimenters conclude that the stimulating efficiency of various sapid substances in early life is not only quantitatively but also qualitatively different from the condition in adult life (p. 124). (See Pfaffman, 1936, in this connection.)

In conclusion, it may be said that the receptors for taste are probably never normally activated before birth. The receptor-neuromuscular mechanism, however, has been shown, by work on premature infants, to be ready to function in late fetal life whenever appropriate stimulating conditions are brought to bear upon it. Most experimenters seem to conclude that sweet stands in a class by itself so far as the infant is concerned. Salt, sour, and bitter are apparently distinguishable with greater difficulty. References to the sense of taste in infrahuman fetuses have been given above.

Smell. Bedford and Disse and others quoted by Parker (1922, pp. 23–41) have considered the embryonic development of the receptor cells of the nervous fibers of the olfactory epithelium. Lane (1917, pp. 51–52), as noted above, has studied the development of the olfactory structures in the rat. Feldman (1920, p. 237) points out that the olfactory and tactual parts of the brain were found by Flechsig to be the earliest to be myelinated in the fetus. Historically, save where taste and smell have been grouped together, there seems to have been general agreement, in the early period at least, that while the nasal cavity is filled with the amniotic liquid there can be no *adequate.* olfactory stimulation. Preyer (1885, p. 478) specifically defends this conclusion, basing his statement on Weber's assertion (1847) that substances that could be smelled when vaporized were quite unable to arouse the sense of smell when introduced into the nose as liquids.

A great deal of relevant work in this field has been critically summarized by Parker (1922). This work shows that there is excellent reason to believe "that the olfactory organs of an air-inhabiting vertebrate can be stimulated by ordinary solutions, though this form of stimulation cannot be looked upon as normal" (p. 59). Even though this is true, however, the same difficulty as that met with in the sense of taste must be remembered to exist. Even though the amniotic fluid may be an effective inadequate stimulus for the olfactory receptors, there is little reason to suppose that there would be sufficient change in the liquid to effect significant stimulation during prenatal life.

In this sense field, therefore, the study of smell reactions of prematurely delivered infants will again be very significant in any determination of how the functional development of the olfactory mechanism progresses during late fetal life. Kussmaul (1859, p. 23) found that asafetida and certain other odors, but not irritating substances, led to responses in a 1-month premature infant. He is not sure that he was able to secure responses in earlier premature infants. Peterson and Rainey (1910, p. 121) also found smell reactions in premature infants.

Historically, there has long been a belief that the newborn child could distinguish odors effectively. Feldman (1920, p. 237) asserts that the Jewish sages in the time of the Talmud believed that a blind baby could tell his mother's milk by smell and taste. Rousseau also commented on the sense of smell in newborn infants (Feldman, 1920, p. 237). Preyer (1882, p. 134) reports that an 18-day infant refused a breast nipple on which kerosene had been placed but eagerly took the other odorless breast immediately after the refusal. Preyer (1882, p. 134) also demonstrated that newborn guinea pigs apparently select their food by the sense of smell. He asserted, moreover, that in young animals, including man, the sense of smell in general is most important in determining behavior. Indeed, in infrahuman animals it is suggested that this significant aspect of behavior determination by smell does not come to be neglected to the extent that it is by civilized man.

Experimental work on the sense of smell in newborn infants, which is probably also in general applicable to late premature infants, has been summarized by Canestrini (1913, pp. 86–87), Peiper (1928, p. 27), and Pratt, Nelson, and Sun (1930, p. 143). Canestrini concludes that there has been some exaggeration in regard to the effectiveness of the sense of smell in young animals. He feels that most of the work on smell has been concerned with stimuli which act on the receptors related to the trigeminal cranial nerve components of the nasal receptor surfaces. These trigeminal components are probably best considered as the "common chemical sense" (Parker, 1922, pp. 103 ff.) and not in the usual sense of the term "tactual" as suggested by Pratt, Nelson, and Sun (1930, p. 127). Certainly the trigeminal endings are not "olfactory" in the ordinary sense. Stimulation of the common chemical sense receptors typically sets off violent reactions, such as sneezing. A characteristic irritant of this sort is ammonia. It is significant in this connection to notice that Pratt, Nelson, and Sun found ammonia to be a peculiarly effective "smell" stimulus. Probably the responses of a newborn infant to ammonia should be considered as responses to the common chemical sense rather than to true olfactory stimulation.

In summary: The neural mechanism for olfaction—that is, the mechanism related to the so-called first cranial nerve—is developed before birth, and the possibility of inadequate stimulation exists before birth. It is probably true, however, that olfaction does not generally occur in its normal form until the nasal cavity comes to be filled with air. Premature infants, at least in the last month, are able to smell substances when air enters the olfactory cavity. Much work on smell, however, has probably been vitiated by the fact that the free nerve endings of the trigeminal nerve (the fifth cranial nerve), the receptors for the common chemical sense, have been stimulated rather than the true olfactory spindles.

Hearing. Anatomically the development of the ear in the individual has been extensively studied. This work is summarized by Keibel and Mall (1910, pp. 264–290). Hess (1922, p. 76) shows an original drawing of a section through the ear of a late fetus. Stevens and Davis (1938) have summarized much of the experimental work upon the adult auditory mechanism.

Historical opinion on the sense of hearing in the human fetus is probably best summarized in the words of Kussmaul (1859, p. 27): "Von allen Sinnen schlummert das Gehor am tiefsten." The history of experiment on the sound response of full-term and prematurely born infants is excellently summarized by Pratt, Nelson, and Sun (1930, pp. 78–85). The general conclusion of these authors is in harmony with that of the later investigators, that hearing becomes effective only in the very early part of postnatal life.

Most of the early investigators of the development of audition concluded that the auditory mechanism was developed to a point at which it could be functional before

birth but that the infant remained deaf until by breathing, crying, and possibly yawning the Eustachian tube was opened. Only in this way, they suggested, could the somewhat gelatinous liquid of the fetal middle ear be drained out (Preyer, 1882, pp. 72–96). Peterson and Rainey (1910, p. 118) specifically secured evidence of auditory response in a prematurely delivered infant as soon as there had been an opportunity for the draining of the middle ear. More modern work seems to have offered no reason to differ with this conclusion so far as stimuli of normal intensity are concerned. Preyer (1882, p. 92) also reports that newborn guinea pigs are deaf for ½ hour after birth and are then sensitive to tonal stimuli of a great variety of frequencies (C of third octave to E of eighth). Avery (1928, p. 265) has secured comparable results on late guinea pig fetuses prematurely delivered, as noted above. The experiment of Rawdon-Smith, Carmichael, and Wellman (1938), which shows by electrical methods of recording the onset of functional activity in the cochlea, has already been referred to. This experiment shows that the guinea pig fetus can hear before birth, judging by both electrical and behavioral criteria.

Although there has been some speculation on the fact that the sounds inside the mother's body might act as sound stimuli to the fetus, little evidence has been brought forward to make this seem certain (Preyer, 1885, p. 480). There are experimental findings which suggest that loud auditory stimuli may activate the human fetus. Peiper (1925, p. 237) was led to this study because he noted that in six neonates, very soon after birth, changes in the breathing curve were found in response to a special sound stimulus. The change in the breathing curve is reported as marked. He therefore decided to try to find out whether or not any indication of hearing before birth could be secured. It had been discovered that auditory and other sudden stimuli give two sorts of responses in the newborn—one, a change in breathing rhythm, and the second, a change in the level of general movements. Peiper felt that there was no sure reason to believe that the unborn child would respond differently if it could be stimulated in its auditory receptors. The breathing center in the brain is open to stimulation before birth. He therefore thought of the possibility of using the prenatal "breathing movements" of Ahlfeld as an indicator of sound response. The disadvantage was found, however, that these movements were not always present, and so the number of subjects was limited. But with proper recording apparatus he was able to take records of the general movement of the fetus through the body wall of the mother.

It was obvious that sounds would be much muffled on their way to the fetus. Therefore a very loud sound was chosen as a stimulus, an automobile horn being used. The experimenter waited until the fetus was absolutely quiet and the mother had been prepared so that she would not herself respond to the stimulus. Incidentally, it proved impossible to train all mothers in this way. The stimulus was given in a quiescent interval. In more than a third of the subjects studied, definite fetal reactions were secured to stimulation of this sort. There were, however, individual differences in responsiveness. Sometimes the response was given on one day and not on the next. The movements which the fetus made in response to the stimuli also showed individual differences. Most often, however, the fetus seemed to draw its whole body together. Peiper (1925) comments that it might seem to one who had not been present at the experiments that the movement was a response of the mother and not of the fetus.

He is certain, however, that one who had actually observed the experiment would be convinced that the response was fetal and not maternal. As an additional safeguard, a pneumograph was placed on the mother's chest and her breathing curve taken during the experiment. After a good deal of practice it was possible to train some mothers so that they made practically no response, and thus the fetal response could be recorded. Continued stimulation led to a diminution of the effect. This corresponds to a frequently observed phenomenon of fetuses and neonates, namely, that their responses are easily fatigued or exhausted. Peiper even goes so far as to suggest that this change in response may be thought of as a simple kind of attention. He also states that one mother remarked that she had noticed definite movements of the fetus while attending a concert.

Forbes and Forbes (1927, pp. 353–355) have reported a case of apparent fetal hearing. Thirty-one days before her baby was born a pregnant woman was lying in a metal bathtub full of warm water. A 2-year-old child was playing on the floor beside the tub. Accidentally the child struck the side of the tub with a small glass jar, and at once a sudden jump of the fetus was felt by the mother, which gave a sensation quite unlike the usual kicks or limb movements. A few days later an observer struck the side of the tub below the water line a quick rap with a small metallic object, meanwhile watching the mother's abdomen. A fraction of a second after the rap, a single quick rise of the anterior abdominal wall was clearly visible. The mother at this moment felt the same jump inside her abdomen as previously reported. Her own muscles were entirely relaxed, and she was not at all startled by the noise, nor was she conscious of perceiving any vibration through the skin. The mother's tactual sense later tested showed that the same intensity of vibration could be perceived only by those portions of the skin coming in contact with the tub. In the infant in question, 8 days after birth, it is interesting to note that while the baby was nursing an auditory stimulus occurred which resulted in the flattening of the baby's ear against the side of the head for a few seconds, after which the ear relaxed again. These same investigators also report another case in which concerts attended toward the end of pregnancy resulted in troublesome activity on the part of the fetus. The conclusion of these writers (1927, p. 355) is:

> Good evidence exists that the human fetus 4 or 5 weeks before birth can respond with sudden movements to a loud sound originating outside the body of the mother. It seems probable that this is a true auditory-muscular reflex but the possibility of reception through tactile organs in the skin cannot be excluded.

The response of the fetus to auditory stimulation has been made the basis of several studies of fetal learning, to which reference is made below.

In summary: It may be said that the auditory mechanism seems to be well developed structurally during later fetal life, but in general, possibly because of the closure of the external ear or because of the gelatinous liquid which fills the middle ear, the fetus is probably deaf to sounds of normal intensity before birth and during a short period immediately after birth. Strong sounds, however, especially those which can directly pass through the mechanical blocks noted, seem to be able to bring about auditory stimulation before birth, although it is still possible that such responses are tactual rather than truly auditory.

Vision. The specific morphological cellular changes which are the essential antecedents to the development of the function of the human eye begin in the second or third week of development of the embryonic period, and from that time on an elaborate series of events occurs until, in the normal human individual, binocular convergence and the diverse activities associated with visual space perception and stereoperception develop in the young child. The anatomical aspects of this growth have been summarized by Keibel and Mall (1910, pp. 218–258) and by Mann (1928). Hess (1922, p. 75) has described in some detail the eye of an early premature infant.

So far as the function of sight in normal prenatal life is concerned, there has been general agreement that the absence of radiation of the sort that typically activates the retina makes true sight all but impossible in prenatal life (Preyer, 1885, p. 483). The possibility does exist that under very strong light stimulation, if the head were in just the right place, radiation falling on the mother's abdomen might stimulate the fetal retina, but this seems most unlikely. There is evidence, however, given by Kussmaul (1859, p. 26) that pronounced differences between light and dark bring about specific reactions in an infant born 2 months before term. Peterson and Rainey (1910, p. 118) also found light reactions in premature infants. Genzmer (1882, p. 21) does not confirm this observation. Preyer (1885, p. 485) agrees that adequate stimuli are impossible during fetal life, but he considers the possibility that inadequate stimuli of pressure similar to the stimuli which bring about phosphenes might be effective in prenatal life.

There is evidence that even at normal birth the optic nerve and related structures have not fully developed anatomically (Pratt, Nelson, and Sun, 1930, pp. 44–51). This knowledge has led to speculation in regard to the neural basis of the development of eye muscle function in neonatal life. This whole question has been considered by Preyer (1882, p. 71) in relation to the nativistic and empiristic theories of the visual spatial world, with the conclusion that the evidence is conflicting.

The writer has taken a few records of the eye movements of human babies, using the electrical recording method. These movements were induced by placing the baby's head in a large rotating drum on which there were striations. The results of these experiments showed that it was possible to elicit optokinetic nystagmus in early infants. This technique may also be used as an objective means of determining lower brightness and color vision thresholds in normal or premature newborn infants. For a description of this technique especially as applied to recording of eye wink and eyeball movements see Carmichael and Dearborn (1947).

One of the best indices of the sensitivity of the fetus to light, although possibly not to the full neural mechanism involved in true visual responses, is thought to be the onset of the light-stimulated pupillary reflex. Portal (1818) alleged that responses of the iris diaphragm did not appear during fetal life. Hess (1922, p. 75) and others, however, have shown that in premature infants strong light stimulus leads to contraction of the pupil, followed in 2 or 3 seconds by dilation again. Bolaffio and Artom (1924, p. 476) and Minkowski (1928a, p. 558), as noted above, have been unable to make unequivocal statements about light reflexes in late fetuses. As pointed out in another part of this chapter, care must be exercised, especially when strong light is used, not to confuse the independent non-neurally determined muscular response of the iris to light with the true iris reflex. The development of the pupillary response in postnatal life has been summarized by Peiper (1928, pp. 11–13).

Much of the evidence in regard to the general muscular movements of the eyes in the first days of life has been summarized by Pratt, Nelson, and Sun (1930, pp. 44 ff.). Early eye movements have been carefully studied in the newborn child by Sherman and Sherman (1925). As already noted above, however, there is excellent evidence to show that during fetal life eye movements occur as part of the general tonus change of the body musculature resulting from the spatial reorientation of the entire fetal body. (See Carmichael, 1940b.) Preyer (1882) and many students since his time have discussed the development of function in the auxiliary musculature of the eye, including the mechanism of winking. In general, great differences are noted in the tonus and general behavior of the lids in the newborn child as contrasted with those of the older child. Some hints of the beginning of this development are to be found in the reports on fetal development given by Minkowski. In a fetus of only 160 mm. he found that touching the closed eyelid led to a contraction of the orbicularis muscle (1922, p. 723).

So far as infrahuman organisms are concerned, there is the greatest divergence from type to type in respect to the time of the opening of the eyes. The subject was early investigated, Emmert, one of the first students of fetal mammals, having studied this phenomenon in the mouse (Emmert and Burgätzy, 1818). Certainly no generalizations can be made from form to form in regard to eyelid activities at the time of birth. The guinea pig is born with eyes open and apparently in an adult functional condition, whereas the lids of the rat do not gain their adult condition until the sixteenth or seventeenth postnatal day (Lane, 1917, p. 69). Warkentin and Smith (1937) and Warkentin (1938) have studied the development of a number of visual functions by various techniques in developing animals. (See also Mowrer, 1936, for a general consideration of learning versus maturation in this field.)

In conclusion: Concerning vision in the fetus it can be said that the specific morphological changes that lie behind the development of the visual mechanism occur from possibly the second week after fertilization until well after birth. Light stimuli at intense levels ordinarily do not affect the retina before birth, but in premature infants it can be shown that the eye is probably sufficiently structurally developed before birth to make possible the light or iris reflex and the differentiation between light and dark. The functional development of the neuromuscular apparatus of the eye is also gradual. Indications have been obtained in regard to the relationship between vestibular stimulation and eye movements before birth which suggest that vestibular control is more primitive than visual control. Eyelid reactions are also found to undergo a progressive series of changes before normal birth.

The Senses in General Relationship to the Onset of Mental Life in the Prenatal Period

For the psychologist there are at least two major problems connected with the study of the senses. The first of these is the classic problem of the relationship between the senses and what the philosophers have long called conscious experience. The second is the relationship between receptor activity and the initiation, modification, and control of behavior. As noted above, this control must be considered in certain cases to include a continuous "feed-back" relationship with existing continuous or periodic activity (Wiener, 1948). Many psychologists, on the basis of some excellent reasons, hold that ultimately these two problems reduce to one, as Langfeld (1931)

and others have urged in the interpretation of consciousness in terms of response. Historically, however, and indeed at the present time, the two problems are ordinarily treated as separate, or at any rate as separable. Some prefer to say that consciousness and behavior are aspects of the total functional description of the relationship between the adult (or immature) human organism and its environment. Here, although no attempt will be made to find an ultimate answer to the question whether these problems are really one or two, they will be treated as independent.

A study of the fetal senses contributes little to our knowledge of the so-called introspective psychology of consciousness. There has been some speculation concerning sensory experience before birth, but little of scientific validity has been written. As incidentally noted above, several of the empiristic philosophers concerned themselves with prenatal life. John Locke (1849 edition) did not neglect the possibility that some dim ideas were present before birth. Cabanis (Genzmer, 1882) held that quite elaborate sensory experiences were present in the fetus, even to the consciousness of self. (Cf. Compayré, 1896, p. 40.) Kussmaul (1859, p. 36) held that the child came into the world with a dim perception of an outer world. Preyer (1882, p. 177) also attributed experience of a sort to the fetus. Peterson and Rainey (1910, p. 121) say, "The newborn comes into the world with a small store of experience and associated feelings and a shadowy consciousness."

Such observations could be added to by other excerpts from early psychologists, but on the whole they seem profitless. Compayré (1896, p. 44), more than fifty years ago, summarized the scientific arguments against such speculations as well as against the fancies of the Neo-Platonists that "our birth is but a sleep and a forgetting." The gist of his argument is that there can be no evidence on the matter. With this point of view the writer is in accord.

James (1890) and, more recently, Koffka (1924) and his associates made much of the fact that in early postnatal life specific experiences, like specific acts of behavior, become individuated out of totalities rather than at first synthesized out of discrete elements. Thus James (1890, Vol. I, p. 488) says: "The baby, assailed by eyes, ears, nose, skin, and entrails at once, feels it all as one great blooming, buzzing confusion." And again (p. 487): "Our original sensible totals are, on the one hand, subdivided by discriminative attention, and, on the other, united with other totals." Koffka (1924, p. 131) similarly asserts: "From an unlimited and ill-defined background there has arisen a limited and somewhat definite phenomenon, a quality." Certainly if these descriptions are adequate to the experiential life of the neonate, there is no reason to suppose that they may not also be adequate, although possibly in a still vaguer form, to conscious fetal life. If the writer were asked to make a guess in regard to the matter, he would say that he feels that the description given above by Koffka is probably relatively adequate as a description of the development of fetal conscious experience. It may be pointed out that such experience may parallel reactions to many different and quite specific types of receptor stimuli.

It must be noted, however, that so far as the writer is able to determine, there is no way to prove or disprove the general surmise about "fetal experience" given above. Consciousness of a particular sort must in such cases be assumed from the external observation of the structure and function of an organism in a particular setting. The fetus is of course quite unable itself to give linguistic introspective reports. The general method of introspection as a scientific tool has been severely criticized in the years since the 1920's, and certainly, if the general method is open to objection, the so-called method of indirect introspection is even more vulnerable. But it is only the latter method which may be used in fetal life. As Washburn (1926), one of the ablest exponents of the use of indirect introspection in animal psychology, has said:

We know not where consciousness begins in the animal world. We know where it surely resides—in ourselves; we know where it exists beyond a reasonable doubt —in those animals of structure resembling ourselves which rapidly adapt themselves to the lessons of experience. Beyond this point, for all we know, it may exist in simpler and simpler forms until we reach the very lowest of living beings [p. 33].

So far as the present writer is concerned, there is no objection to applying to ontogeny, that is, growth in the individual, a point of view similar to that expressed above in regard to the growth of consciousness in the development of the animal series. Such judgments must be treated as complex inferences, however, and not as facts of observation. The writer further points out that a scientific definition of the word "consciousness" as commonly used has not yet been presented in a form to win general acceptance.

The second large problem which concerns the psychologist in relation to receptor activity has grown out of the approach to the study of mental life which deals explicitly with the processes of behavior. The problem of the receptor or, possibly better, of stimulus control of behavior is, however, much older than the so-called school of behaviorism. Kussmaul (1859, p. 6) explicitly defended this view in undertaking his study of premature and normal newborn infants. It is related to a much more general position, as is the view expressed by Forel and quoted by Canestrini (1913, p. 100): "Das wahre Baumateriel der Organismen liefern die Reize der Aussenwelt."

It seems more and more certain that, whatever else scientific psychology may do, it must concern itself increasingly with the relationship between the environment external to the receptors, be they extroceptors, interoceptors, or proprioceptors, and to the responses of the organism to such stimulation. In any consideration of fetal psychology, therefore, especial attention should be given to the facts of the stimulus control of behavior. In order to understand this relationship, it will be necessary to review the current status of fact and theory in regard to the causes underlying the beginning and differentiation of activity in the fetal organism. This consideration may well serve as a conclusion to this chapter, because any such discussion will necessarily involve a review of many of those processes of fetal life which are even inferentially significant for general psychology. For an excellent consideration of this general field see Hooker (1942).

In the beginning of this chapter, something was said of the early processes of morphogenesis in the developing organism. It was suggested that the point should be kept continually in view by one who is interested in behavioral development, that the general growth of structure and function always occurs in an organism that is in an environment. Organisms do not live or grow in a physical or biological vacuum. From the first cell division in the developing individual, each process of structural and functional modification is, moreover, to be considered as a complex resultant of activities. Some of these determinants are intrinsic in the cell and are, indeed, in the correct sense of the term hereditary, but such intrinsic determinants always act in a dynamic system which is also subjected to

extrinsic influences. Development is apparently always a resultant of these two sets of forces working *interdependently*. For some of the evidence on this matter, see earlier papers by Carmichael (1925, 1938). Sharp (1926) summarizes this point of view when he says in his consideration of general cytology:

> The cell should not be thought of as a static . . . structure. It is rather a dynamic system in a constantly changing state of molecular flux, its constitution at any given moment being dependent upon antecedent states and upon environmental conditions [p. 58].

If space permitted a review of the present status of that part of scientific embryology which is devoted to developmental mechanics, it would become apparent that the process of growth in the organism involves a most complex series of energy relationships, some of which, it seems probable, have as yet only begun to be unraveled. It is certainly true, however, that, at least since the work in the latter part of the last century by Roux (1896), the older static view of development based on the study of dead histological material has gradually given way to the modern notion of an *Entwicklungsmechanik*. For an evaluation of this change, consult Morgan (1927) and Holt (1931, pp. 8–23). As suggested above in regard to the cell, this study has shown that the process of development in one sense, at any rate, must apparently be considered a dynamic organization of a system of energies. This view of the development of an active organism makes it apparent that growth is not to be thought of as a mere unfolding of preformed materials, but rather as the construction of a new pattern of organized systems and subsystems in protoplasm. Each such system is to be understood only in its particular environment. As Dürken

(1929, pp. 109–113) has well said: "Die Entwicklung ist keine einfache Entfaltung, sondern eine wirkliche Neubildung." And again: "Kurz gesagt, ist daher an der Allgemeingültigkeit des epigenetischen Charakters des Entwicklungsprozesses nicht zu zweifeln." See also Howells (1945).

Many similar statements, and the elaborate evidence upon which they are based, could be found in the rich experimental work of the modern students of developmental mechanics. In such a view, however, it is of course possible, starting with the energy relationships between the organism and its environment, to go beyond the established facts. Whether or not this has been done by Child is difficult for the writer to judge. The following quotation from that student of the physiological development of the nervous system, however, indicates that it is possible for an experimental biologist to consider the external energy relationships of the organism as of the greatest significance in determining development. Child (1921) makes this very definite when he says:

> The organism represents an order and unity in protoplasm which is related at every point to the external world. The development and evolution of organismic integration are essentially the evolution of mechanisms and methods of response and adjustment to environmental conditions [p. 7].

This investigator has developed, on the basis of much experimental work, a concept of various sorts of gradients in the living and developing organism. In certain respects these gradients may in the last analysis be thought of as energy relationships, which are embryologically often precursors of definite organ systems. In so far as the nervous system is concerned, he says:

> . . . the reflex strictly speaking is a specialized behavior pattern depending on the presence of certain morphological mechanisms; but it is physiologically a development from the primary organismic behavior mechanism, the excitation gradient [1924, p. 235].

It may well be, of course, that the relationships between the series of events occurring in the organism and the series of events occurring outside the organism are more elaborate than would be suggested by a relationship "at every point"; that is, that some such view as the "organizer" of Spemann (1927) may supplement the simple intrinsic-extrinsic relationship by what may be essentially a chemical process or other process occurring in time and intrinsic in the organism. Whatever the details of this development may be, however, it seems relatively sure, as the work of many investigators seems to demonstrate, that there is, antecedent to the possibility of functional action in the differentiated nervous system, an elaborate series of processes in the organism some of which involve what are, to the elements of the system, environmental forces. A hypothesis concerning the relationship between a primitive gradient of activity and the beginning and development of true nervous structures and functions has been made especially clear by Coghill (1929a, pp. 39–78). This point of view emphasizes, as Burnham (1917) has well pointed out, that environmental stimulation which is basic in an understanding of adult psychological phenomena is itself in certain respects, at any rate, significant in determining the mechanisms which make such adult responses possible.

In this connection the work of Kappers (1917) and Bok (1917) on the functional activity of neuroblasts in the development of the elements and the relationships of the central nervous system may be mentioned. The theory of neurobiotaxis developed by these writers, which suggests that the growth and arrangements of the nervous components are tropistically determined responses of the elements of the nervous system, has proved to be one of the valuable hypotheses in describing the experimental embryology of the nervous system. The contributions of Ingvar (1920) and others to this point of view are summarized by Child (1921, 1924) and Herrick (1924, pp. 111–112). The brilliant work of Detwiler (1920, 1921, 1922, 1923a, 1923b) and other experimental embryologists on the morphology and energetics of neural development also presents specific evidence on the relationship between external and intrinsic factors in the development of the functional nervous system. (See Sperry, 1951.) For a whole picture of cell activity in the living organism, the reader should consult Gerard (1940).

There seems, therefore, to be excellent evidence for the view elsewhere discussed by the writer (1925) at greater length that, from the moment that growth has begun in the fertilized ovum until senescence or death, development consists in the alteration of existing structures and functions in an organism living in a continually changing environment. It cannot be overemphasized that there is both an external and an internal environment. As elsewhere noted in this chapter, the alterations which take place in the chemistry of the blood stream which supplies the central nervous system are fundamental in altering the way in which this system responds to the afferent neural impulses which come in from its receptors.

In the question of behavior change, it is not possible save for pragmatic reasons to say at any point that growth has stopped and learning has begun, but that the environment plays a part in all "maturation," and maturation plays a part in all learning. The course of this development, however, is apparently almost infinitely complex. It cannot be summarized by any catchword phrase. It does seem, however, that the suggestion made in the introduction to this chapter that even the first receptor-neuromuscular response of the organism is not to be considered in all respects a novel event follows directly from the knowledge that the organism develops in relation to an environment of energies. The processes which have gone on in the organism in order that the first response can occur apparently themselves involve elaborate stimulus-response relationships in narrower environments. Thorndike (1931) has picturesquely said that the life processes of a neuron include (1) eating, (2) excreting waste, (3) growing, (4) being sensitive, conducting, and discharging, and (5) movement. "The neuron thus lives much as would an amoeba or paramecium which had been differentiated to make conduction its special trade and which had become fixed immovably save for a few extremities here and there" (p. 57).

A similar portrait could be drawn of the other cells of the developing response mechanism. Thus it seems probable that the first activity of the total neural arc must be thought of as both old and new. The processes of change that are involved are similar to the processes of its growth in certain respects, but when total activity results, new time relations, if not new polarities, are involved. Thus in a sense an "organismic" response emerges from more discrete and primitive activities. But the function is to be understood completely only if described in terms of the past history of the total mechanism concerned and of the present stimulating situation.

This distinction between *part function* and *total function* which causes so much confusion in biology and psychology is clearly illustrated in the known facts of peripheral nerve regeneration. Sherrington (1922) points out that, when a previously cut nerve is regenerated, what is developed in the nerve, so far as the adaptive function of the total arc is concerned, is useless until total regeneration and end organ attachment are completed. But of course the processes of development are themselves functions of the growing cells and the specific environment of these regenerating cells. Thus the eventual emergence of the so-called property of total arc conduction is in one sense not a saltatory change. So far as the functions of the protoplasmic patterns are concerned, it may be said that they involve a novel temporal and spatial organization of processes that have occurred in other energy relationships during previously described stages, but, from another point of view, with the completed nerve comes a most important and wholly novel emergence of total function. For a suggestion of some of the many factors involved in such development, see Goldstein (1904, 1939).

It seems to the writer, therefore, that the fact that cells and tissues do not develop in isolation, as Irwin (1932b, p. 194) points out in an excellent summary of the so-called *organismic hypothesis* of development, does not necessarily mean, as the same writer asserts, that the "nervous system is a complex dynamic organization which operates as a whole." On the contrary, it seems to suggest that the story of the development of behavior must be written not in any generalized formulae but in terms of the development of minute specific processes, no matter how diffuse or particularized, occurring in individual organisms under definitely described environmental conditions.

The discussion in the last few paragraphs has been presented to prepare the way for the consideration of the psychological aspects of the stimulus control of behavior. In the course of the study of the onset of receptor-neuroeffector behavior, many suggestions have been made for the cause of these first acts. The writer can see no reason to believe that all the diverse causal factors suggested are necessarily mutually exclusive, in spite of some assertions to that effect. Indeed, it seems that, so far as the onset of behavior in the fetus is concerned, the *fallacy of the single cause* has been peculiarly in evidence. As Jennings (1930) well says:

This fallacy is the commonest error of science, making unsound a considerable proportion of its conclusions. Everywhere there is a search for "the" cause of this or that phenomenon; the investigator is not content until he has found "it." Yet natural phenomena—and most emphatically is this true of biological phenomena—merely arise out of the complex situation in which they occur. Many elements of that situation affect them; and all that experimental science can do is to determine what difference is made by altering one or more of these elements; none is "the" cause to the exclusion of the others [p. 208].

In this chapter, therefore, an effort is made to summarize some of the many scientific facts and some of the theories which relate to the onset and development of early behavior in organisms. Here no attempt is made to arrive at one single conclusion, unless that conclusion is that the onset of behavior is most complexly determined.

Fundamental in the writings of most students who have concerned themselves with early development of behavior is the view that the nervous system is basic to the observed responses of the organism. As we have seen above, this view was implicit even in Dante's speculation on the onset of behavior in the fetus. Each advance in the knowledge of the true function of the nervous system has indirectly influenced the thought of those who are concerned with the early development of function in the fetus.

The details of the specific neural changes necessary for the onset and development of behavior have, however, been diversely dealt with. Some students, like Coghill, although not neglecting other factors, emphasize above all else the anatomical relationships in the nervous system of the organisms under consideration as the determiner of behavior. The following quotation from Coghill (1929a) in regard to the neural basis of behavior in *Amblystoma* may be considered typical of this anatomical tendency. It also gives a fair picture of what is at once one of the simplest and one of the most adequately studied of all the neural mechanisms subtending behavior:

> There are therefore in this non-motile *Amblystoma* both sensory and motor nerves in contact with their respective organs, the sensory field on the one hand and the muscles on the other, but the anatomical relations between these systems are such that an excitation cannot pass from the sensory to the motor mechanism. The muscles, while contracting in response to a mechanical stimulus applied directly to them, do not respond to stimuli from the skin, either tactile or chemical. Even when dropped into slowly acting fixing solution, embryos of this stage do not give any evidence of muscular excitation.
> With the ability to respond to tactile or chemical stimulation of the skin there appears a third series of cells. They bridge the gap between the sensory system of one side and the motor system of the other. . . . Their bodies lie in the floor plate of the medulla oblongata and upper part of the spinal cord. . . . In the non-motile stage these cells are unipolar. The one pole of the cell extends either to the right or to the left into close relation with the motor tract on one side only. When they become bipolar they complete the path from the sensory field to the muscle;

and this path leads to the muscles of the opposite side from the stimulus because the conductors from the sensory field pass across the motor path of the same side to establish synapses with the dendrites of the commissural cells in the floor plate . . . [pp. 11–13].

A similar but usually much less completely worked out neural picture could be presented for many of the organisms the development of whose behavior has been considered above. For example, the anatomy of the nervous system of the fetal rat in relation to its behavior has been studied in quite elaborate detail by Angulo y González (1927, 1928, 1929b, 1930c), and this type and many others by Windle (1940) and his associates. But the development of neural structure alone may not explain fully the onset of behavior in any type.

Minkowski (1923; 1928a, pp. 548–556), himself primarily a neurologist, has given in great detail the neural mechanisms which he believes underlie the changes he has observed in the clinically significant reflexes initiated in human fetuses by the stimulation of the sole of the foot.

Although there is almost complete agreement that the nervous system is significant in the onset and development of mammalian behavior, it must be admitted that there is not complete agreement as to the detailed factors of this development. One of the most commonly held views in regard to the basis of functional activity in the nervous system asserts that there is a differing threshold at the synaptic junctures existing between neurons. Sherrington and his associates (Creed, Denny-Brown, Eccles, Liddell, and Sherrington, 1932, pp. 14–15) have reviewed the evidence for such a view, and both Herrick (1924, pp. 103–111) and R. S. Lillie (1932) have dealt with special phenomena basic to an understanding of the synapse. Holt (1931, pp. 24–29) has shown that, in his view at any rate, this theory is adequate, when correctly understood, to explain the complexities of neural-embryonic development, particularly when it is supported by a correct understanding of the functional development summarized in the theory of neurobiotaxis. Lashley (1924) and Irwin (1932a), on the contrary, have raised a number of objections to the synapse, particularly as *the* one and only explanatory factor in the change of behavior. Certainly one must always remember that, in attributing anything to the synapse, one is referring to a *concept* which has been elaborated in part from behavioral data. The danger of a circular argument in "explaining" behavior by the synapse should be remembered. Other views, such as that of nerve fiber density in the spinal gray matter in relation to behavior, have been suggested. (See Windle, 1930b.)

Since the time of Flechsig, there has been a tendency on the part of many neuroanatomists to link myelinogeny, that is, the development of the myelin sheath of neurons, with the onset of differentiated behavior. Flechsig in his later publications even attempted to correlate the degree of myelinization with increase in the complexity of behavior and indeed with psychic life. Tilney and Casamajor (1924), Langworthy (1929), and other students have attempted to show the correlation between myelinization in the central nervous system and the onset of behavior in the newborn and fetal cat, opossum, and other forms. For the most part these investigators point out that this theory must be taken as specific to the particular function and to the particular type considered. Tilney, however, once made the statement in very general terms: "I think there can be no doubt as to the coincidence in the time of myelinization and the establishment of function." (See also Tilney and Kubie, 1931.)

There is, however, evidence of exceptions to this generalization. Probably it is no longer safe, however, to say of this "myelinogenetic law," as Thorndike did (1913, p. 229) on the basis of the experiments of Watson (1903) and others, that it seems "gratuitous and improbable." The evidence for the relationship of myelin and function does not show it as the only cause of the onset of behavior. As Angulo y González (1929a) has shown: "From the point of view of myelinogeny, our studies have proved that myelination is not necessary for function, since all the movements described by Doctor Swenson and by myself in the rat fetus occur many days before myelination could be observed" (p. 461). This same author objects to the observations on behavior made by Tilney and Casamajor, believing that the movements which they observed were really established long before the time at which they were described and hence well before the myelinization which they report. Angulo y González (1929a), moreover, finds that a rat fetus, 19 days after insemination, is capable of discrete reflexes and of showing the inhibitory action of higher centers.

These discrete reflexes, which are specific to a given stimulation, demonstrate a selectivity in the conducting mechanism. Since myelination does not take place until several days after birth, this observation proves that physiological insulation of the conduction path occurs without myelination, and, therefore, that myelination is not a criterion of functional insulation [p. 461].

Windle, Fish, and O'Donnell (1934) have studied the relationship between myelinogeny and the onset of behavior in cat fetuses. They conclude that myelinization in the animals studied is not correlated with function. Myelinization may be considered a consequence of the order of appearance of neurons in the embryo. (See also Langworthy, 1927, 1932.) There are other theories of development besides that of myelinization. For example, following the lead of Paton (1907, 1911) and other investigators, Lane (1917, pp. 15–21) held that the onset of behavior is specifically related to the anatomical development of the neurofibrillae. This investigator advances an elaborate series of arguments to show that the neurofibrillae are possibly to be thought of as the essential basis of functional activity in the nervous system.

If therefore an absolutely conclusive answer cannot now be given to the question of the function of the neurofibrillae, it is most probable, in the light of our present knowledge in this field, that the power of conducting nerve-impulses lies rather in the neurofibrillae than elsewhere. At any rate, the presence of neurofibrillae may be taken as an indicator, a criterion of the functional state of the neurons . . . [p. 21].

After definitely accepting this view, Lane explains the fact that after the neurofibrillae have developed, before the arc can become functional, it is necessary that the receptor develop (pp. 14, 79). In each of the senses he believes that function must wait for the development of the end organ, and that this is the last link to be connected up in the chain between effective environmental stimulation and response. In all the explanations which he offers for the development of this system, he emphasizes intrinsic rather than extrinsic factors (p. 84). In this he is seconded by Avery (1928), who concludes, without further explaining the matter, that fetal behavior is, in part at any rate, caused by and dependent upon "certain response mechanisms which are definitely congenital or innate" (p. 324). Certainly in the general sense of these terms few today will disagree with this conclusion, but it is not an observation which advances "functional knowledge."

Windle (1930a), in studying the spinal cord development of cat embryos 17.5 mm. to 18.5 mm. long in which the first movement—"wormlike, total waves proceeding caudad from an indefinite point in the neck region"—had been observed, notes:

Pyridine-silver preparations of these embryos demonstrate the neurofibrillar structure of the central nervous system. Primitive reflex arcs are distinguishable, afferent, association, commissural, and efferent neurons appearing in proper relationship to each other. . . .

The earliest movements appear in regions where primitive reflex arcs were first distinguishable and not until some time after these have formed [p. 249].

(See also Windle, 1931, 1932.) Herrick (1924), in referring to neurofibrils, says: "They are commonly regarded as the essential conductors of the nervous impulse, but of this there is no direct evidence" (p. 108).

Certain physiologists assert that neural functions and indeed the capacities of the adult organism are related primarily to the time relationships of the neuron (Lapicque, (1926). Or, even more generally, it has been suggested that the facts of the activity of the peripheral nerve fiber, as developed by Adrian, his predecessors, and his associates, may be basic to some aspects of the differentiation and specificity of behavior. For a brilliant exposition of this view, see Erlanger and Gasser (1937). Forbes wrote an article, "The Interpretation of Spinal Reflexes in Terms of Present Knowledge of Nerve Conduction" (1922), in which the suggestion is tentatively made that specificity of behavior and "the evolution of the dominant activities of man" (p. 414) may be thought of as being determined in a system the essential characteristics of which are to be found in a knowledge of the facts of the nervous impulse as it is seen in peripheral nerve fibers. P. Weiss (1926) has studied this relationship from a different and more revolutionary physiological point of view which may well contain within it basic suggestions concerning the onset of those neural activities which make behavior possible.

It is clear that the increasingly detailed knowledge of the specific structure and function of the receptors, the peripheral nervous system, and the various levels of the central nervous system, particularly in regard to the relationships between these processes as brought out by Sherrington and his pupils (Creed, Denny-Brown, Eccles, Liddell, and Sherrington, 1932), must be ultimately taken into consideration in an explanation of the onset and early development of behavior. As indicated many times above, however, this view is almost certainly to be considered in relation to the changes of the chemical make-up of the whole internal environment of the organism.

The function of the endocrines in fetal life is still imperfectly understood. The substances elaborated by the endocrine glands of the body are concerned with growth and metabolism rather than with overt behavior as such.

The principal endocrine function of the pancreas is found in the cells of the islets of Langerhans. There has been much discussion of the part played by this secretion, which is called fetal insulin, in prenatal life. As noted in a previous paragraph some endocrines can pass the placental barrier, and therefore it is difficult to determine what is, for example, fetal insulin and what is maternal insulin in the fetus itself. Windle (1940) has discussed this and related problems. The suprarenals have an interesting history in the fetus. At birth they are about 0.02 per cent of total body weight. In the adult they are only about 0.01 per cent.

Pankratz (1930) has suggested that the onset of behavior is in time, at any rate, related to the beginning of functional action of the secretion of the suprarenal medulla, which possibly causes "an increase in the irritability of the muscular or neuromuscular system, and thus facilitates the beginning of foetal movements" (p. 235). He (1931a) believes that he has experimentally demonstrated in newborn organisms, including man, that there is a temporal correlation between the onset of functional activity in this gland and the first responses of the growing organism.

Willier (1939) has summarized the development of the sex-related hormones in the fetus. Male gonads produce male sex hormones in fetal life. In man this production probably begins about the seventh week. By the eighth week the female ovary is histologically recognizable. The conflict or interrelation between the female sex hormone of the mother and the female or male sex hormone of the fetus, as the case may be, has been the subject of study and speculation.

Wells and Fralick (1951) have studied the production of androgen by the testes of fetal rats. These investigators seem to have demonstrated that the testes of fetal rats produce an andogenic hormone which stimulates the prenatal growth of the accessory reproductive organs of males. Davis and Potter (1948) show that under specific conditions the administration of testosterone propionate to mothers during early pregnancy did not produce demonstrable changes in gonads or genital organs of male fetuses.

Possibly more fundamental than this speculation is the now widely accepted view of the chemical mediation of nerve impulses. Certain aspects of this work have been summarized by Cannon and Rosenblueth (1937). According to this point of view, synaptic function may in certain reflex systems be mediated by acetylcholine or in other systems by an adrenaline-like substance. Kuo (1939a) has demonstrated the presence of acetylcholine in the chick embryo at the time of the onset of motility, and others have also suggested its significance in the mammalian fetus. Nachmansohn (1940) has shown that in the sheep high concentration of choline esterase appears in different parts of the central nervous system at different periods of development. Choline esterase is an enzyme which rapidly alters acetylcholine. Choline esterase is present in the spinal cord in high concentrations between the sixtieth and the eightieth days of gestation, but at that time its concentration in the brain is low. It rises rapidly in the higher centers just before birth, however. These results are in agreement with the activity of the centers involved. Youngstrom (1941) has determined the acetylcholine esterase concentration in typical fetal organisms. This study shows a significant relationship between developing motility and the concentration of choline esterase. A fully satisfactory explanation has not yet, however, been found for the occurrence of greater concentrations of choline esterase in fetal than in adult tissues.

The results just referred to are but a few indications of the modern emphasis on various forms of internal environmental change as related to the onset of activity in the organism. It has become obvious to many investigators that the movements of respiration, as well as other rhythmic movements known to be brought about or facilitated by a "blood stimulus," are important in a total understanding of behavior. For example, it has been reported that the asphyxia of the mother brought about definite movements in a very early fetus (Kussmaul, 1859, p. 31). Preyer (1885) was before his time in considering this problem, as in so many other ways. He considers

the importance of the blood condition in connection with fetal movements on the basis of experiments in which he interfered with the normal respiration of the adult animal (p. 417). As already indicated, Ahlfeld and most of the other students of premature breathing movements have considered the "blood stimulus" to be significant. This sort of activation is also especially considered in the work of Zuntz (1877), T. G. Brown (1915), E. A. Graham (1913–1915), Walz (1922), and Tracy (1926), most of which has been previously reviewed.

Tracy (1926), as explained above, well combines the views of the importance of stimulation and the importance of the development of the nervous system in the determination of the onset of behavior in larval organisms. Thus he says:

. . . The behavior reactions displayed by embryos and larvae of different species at different stages of development are dependent upon the relative time at which efficient connections are established between the various elements of the early nervous system (primitive bilateral motor system, commissural elements, spinal-ganglion cells, Rohn-Beard cells, and receptors) [p. 357].

But he also points out, as noted above, that:

From the beginning and more or less continuously during its whole existence, the animal is driven through its environment as a result of stimuli which arise periodically in connection with its metabolic processes [p. 345].

Barcroft (1938) shows on the basis of elaborate experimental work that, as Claude Bernard said, the constancy of the internal environment is the condition of the free life. The work of Barcroft and his school, indeed, throws doubt upon many experiments in fetal behavior which have been done without continually checking the oxygen tension and other characteristics of the fetal blood. In spite of this vast store of information upon the nature of fetal and maternal blood, it is interesting to note that Barcroft does not make a final judgment concerning the part played by the internal environment in the initiation of behavior (1936). He points out that in a typical reflex the external stimulus is important, and because of the changing cortical oxygenation of blood the center is also important. Thus the two sets of factors should be considered together. Barcroft (1938) does point out, however, that:

> The higher centers await investigation on modern lines; at present there is nothing to be said about them except what is rather obvious, namely, that the foetus of the sheep even up to birth presents few if any signs of consciousness. Within a few minutes of birth . . . the lamb lifts its head and tries to get up. It is plainly awake, and may be sent to sleep once more either by cold or by reducing the amount of oxygen in the blood. These matters must await further investigation; but it is evident that the higher faculties need a higher tension oxygen supply than those of a more vegetative nature [p. 67].

Changes in temperature, oxygen, carbon dioxide, glucose, water, sodium, calcium, and other substances are known as they alter the internal environment to have a part in the changes which result in behavior. These all no doubt contribute to alterations in fetal behavior. (See Carmichael, 1940a, p. 136, and Barcroft and Mason, 1938.)

Sontag (1941) has suggested some important considerations on the significance of fetal environmental differences. He believes that drugs used by women during pregnancy, their nutrition, endocrine status, and even emotional life, may be important in the postnatal life of the children they bear.

Newbery, Pyle, and Champney (1943) have attempted a quantitative study of the ability of mothers to rate the fetal environment in respect to thirteen factors during pregnancy.

Besides such students as Barcroft, who emphasize both the internal and external environment, there are some who emphasize the rôle of the intensity of external stimulation in the onset and development of behavior without much reference to the neural basis of such behavior. Kuo is in certain respects an exponent of such a view. He says:

> . . . As has been previously stated, I am inclined to think that to explain the total behavior pattern in terms of neural anatomy (that is, in terms of certain special connections between neurons) seems unnecessary or far-fetched, since all the neurons in the nervous system are interconnected in some way, and since body parts without direct neural connections may also move together, as in the case of the synchronous movement of the tail with the beak and eyes [1932e, p. 511].

The neurological-minded reader of the above paragraph is probably struck at first by the question of how, if the assertion is true, the observed differentiation in behavior is to be explained. Kuo offers the explanation that local reflexes are determined in part by external environmental influences. In the case of the chick he has ingeniously made many observations, some of which have been presented above, to show that in the fetal organism, growing in a rigidly shell-defined environment, certain mechanical influences interfere with the ease of general movement. For example, as development goes on, head movements come to be interfered with mechanically by the yolk sac, and thus he explains the fact that partial head movements, such as those of the beak, occur in the head region. Kuo (1939a, 1939b) has, as noted above, more recently emphasized other concomitant functions such as the part of acetylcholine in the onset and early development of behavior.

On the basis of elaborate experiments, Lashley (1929) and his predecessors have shown that there was much misunderstanding in regard to the absolute specificity of central nervous system elements which subtend behavior, particularly in the higher centers. (See also bibliography cited by Lashley, 1929.) Lashley's work and the work of many other students make clear that no single brain neuron is probably ever functionally absolutely isolated and that the reflex arc is never so simple as the elementary textbooks a generation ago showed it to be. Indeed, Lashley's brilliant experimental work has revolutionized many of the older conceptions of the specificity of the arcs in the higher centers of mammals.

From these discoveries, however, there is much question whether such writers as Irwin (1932b) are justified in suggesting that "the early form of activity, with its lack of mature specificity and the presence of so few effective coordinations or reaction patterns, probably points to an organismic rather than to a reflex chain theory of behavior." The writer has no wish to disagree with this statement, save only to point out that the "cell theory" and the "reflex theory" that are usually attacked by "organismic" writers are in most such criticisms truly "men of straw." All that has gone before in this chapter seems to suggest that the explanation of behavior will hardly be advanced by saying that the nervous system "operates as a whole." Unquestionably, in the human fetus as in the human adult there are functions which can never be understood in isolation, but only by looking at the *totality* of processes;

but totality alone does not explain the specific long, short, homolateral, and heterolateral skin reflexes, the face, hand, and foot reflexes, the mucous membrane and tendon reflexes, the proprioceptor and static reflexes, and the many other specific responses of the fetus. The fact that an early concept of the reflex arc was inadequate is no reason to assert that there is no truth in the general view that behavior involves discoverable relationships both temporal and anatomical between stimulation and response. Some such responses are more variable and some are more specific than others, but still there are specific patterns of behavior in the growing organism. As Skinner (1931) has effectively said in summary of a paper in which he criticizes current attacks upon the reflex hypothesis:

> The essence of the description of behavior is held to be the determination of functional laws describing the relationship between the forces acting upon, and the movement of, a given system. The reflex is, by definition, the precise instrument for this description [p. 455].

From the paragraphs just given, it is clear that there have been many efforts to explain in simple terms the mechanism which makes the onset of behavior possible. External stimulation is not *alone* important in the development of behavior; nor probably is the change in the synapses, the onset of acetylcholine, or any other factor *alone* the one determinant of all new responses in all organisms at all times. It does seem at present, nevertheless, that so far as the fetus is concerned there can be little doubt that an adequate explanation of its behavior at every stage in its development must be given in terms of the dynamics of its organization in each specific environment. Such dynamics, however, can be expressed only in terms of as detailed a knowledge of the structures and functions of the organism as possible. Any response can be understood only if it is recognized that it may not be the result alone of the most obvious stimulus that is apparently calling it out, but rather that it may be a resultant of the total interoceptive, proprioceptive, and exteroceptive stimulation of the moment in an organism the chemistry of whose internal environment is known in its often rapidly changing characteristics.

In a final understanding of the sensory control of behavior in fetal life, as complete a knowledge of all such relevant factors as possible is important. Seldom apparently during late fetal life can an exteroceptor be stimulated so as to bring about a response that may not be conditioned also by other internal stimuli which may at the same time be tending to drive the organism "at random." This is particularly true of fetuses such as those studied by Minkowski, Bolaffio and Artom, and Hooker, which during observation are always undergoing more and more complete asphyxiation. As suggested above, it must not be forgotten that it may be that at certain periods of development and in certain physiological states the exteroceptors are best thought of as interrupting and directing behavior that is internally aroused. At such times the "drive" of the fetus may be said to be more important than its "knowledge of the external world." In this connection see Minkowski (1947–1948, p. 88). In any case, in a situation of this sort, gradually more and more adaptive behavior develops, which means that the exteroceptors play an increasingly important rôle.

Coghill's well-known formula for behavioral growth is possibly an adaptation of Spencer's famous definition which held evolution to be a passage from "a relatively indefinite incoherent homogeneity to a relatively definite coherent heterogeneity."

Coghill taught that his formula has wide if not universal application in the development of behavior in all vertebrates. He (1929c) states it as follows:

> The behavior pattern from the beginning expands throughout the growing normal animal as a perfectly integrated unit, whereas partial patterns arise within the total patterns and, by a process of individuation, acquire secondarily varying degrees of independence. . . . Complexity of behavior is not derived by progressive integration of more and more originally discrete units [p. 989].

On the basis of what has gone before in this chapter, it seems that this process of *individuation* is certainly *one* important means of describing the process of development, but not the only means of describing such development. On the other hand, concomitantly but not necessarily temporally concomitantly, *integration* has long been recognized as a mechanism of behavior development. As Pavlov (1932) has put it in another context, one must consider the "initial decomposition of the whole into its parts or units, and then the gradual reconstruction of the whole from these units or elements" (p. 102).

In terms of a very broad generalization, the writer believes that an excellent case can be made out for the view that *individuation* is the pattern of all development, including all learning, but certainly in the experimental situation the concept of the *integration* or the combination of responses also provides, at times, a convenient working hypothesis. James (1890, Vol. I, p. 487) said that "psychology must be writ *both* in synthetic and in analytic terms." To the writer this seems to give a satisfactory clue to the expedient way of considering the changes in behavior that occur as fetal and neonatal behavior progresses. As we have seen above, certain responses are early individuated, while others are still quite nonspecific.

New relationships between specific responses, as in the development of the plantar reflex, begin to develop before specification has gone far in certain other bodily acts. Each process must be considered at each level if a false generalization is to be avoided. Hooker (1937) has recently analyzed this problem and suggested three possible sequences of development: (1) At first reflexes are nonspecific. (2) At first reflexes are specific. (3) Specific and total reflexes develop simultaneously. He urges the detailed study of behavior to answer these questions. This chapter suggests that all three are possible descriptions of certain responses, but the writer's own experimental work leads him to believe that (2) above should be emphasized much more than has been "fashionable." For a consideration of a generalized story of functional development of mammalian neuromuscular mechanisms, see Barron (1941).

Genzmer (1882, p. 28), after reviewing the debated question whether the newborn child has intelligence, suggests that the observed movements of the early infant are not the result of intelligence but are rather the material out of which the later intelligence is to be built. If the process of development is one of sheer individuation out of a totality, it would seem that statistical studies of early infancy might well show a high degree of what Spearman calls a "general factor." If the techniques used in the studies of Furfey, Bonham, and Sargent (1930) are satisfactory, however, it seems that the opposite is true. In a study of seventeen responses, such as the plantar and grasping reflexes in newborn children, corrected intercorrelations proved to be zero. These investigators conclude: "These results suggest that there is no mental integration in the newborn child. Integration takes place during the first postnatal month. . . ." Although technical questions may be raised in regard to this study, it certainly seems that, with the use of the same techniques, there is no reason to suppose that the responses of the fetus would show a more general factor than would those of the newborn child.

Minkowski (1924) has considered the part played by the conditioning of reflexes in later development, and certainly the question of the relationship between individuation and integration will be made clearer when it can be said at what ontogenetic level of development true conditioning of responses is possible. Ray (1932) has attempted to condition fetal responses. Spelt (1938), using the auditory response of the fetus described above, has worked on the conditioning of human responses. Marquis (1931), however, has brought about in the newborn child conditioning of the food-taking reaction to the sound of a buzzer. She holds that this may be conditioning at the subcortical level, but in any case it involves what is commonly considered combination rather than individuation of responses. Wenger (1936) and Wickens and Wickens (1939) have also worked in this field. Carmichael (1936) has elsewhere reviewed the work that has been done on early learning in young animals. Here the work of Kasatkin and Levikova (1935a, 1935b) on early conditioning and other studies are reviewed. It is possibly true that at a verbal level all conditioning can be described as individuation, but in such a formulation a generalization of the concept of individuation beyond the point at which it is pragmatically most useful seems required.

It may even be suggested that so-called learning itself always depends upon *maturation* or *growth*. In a trial-and-error sequence the animal must always be able to perform the successful act before learning, that is, the later elimination of maladaptive acts, begins. This same view may even be applied, but less directly, to so-called conditioned response learning. In this connection, see Guthrie (1942). The phenomena of "refractory period" following previous stimulation and the "summation of stimuli" can be demonstrated in fetal organisms (Carmichael, 1934a; Carmichael and Smith, 1939). Both these phenomena show the influence of past activity on present capacity.

In general conclusion, then, in regard to the sensory control of behavior in the fetus and in regard to the related processes of the individuation and integration of behavior, it seems that as yet, at any rate, it is better to record as unambiguously as possible the responses that can be made by a fetus at any stage rather than to attempt to fit all developmental change into one formula. It seems to the writer, nevertheless, that the actually recorded facts of this development of behavior in infrahuman and human fetuses have been shown to throw important light upon certain of the insistent problems of psychology. It has been impossible to consider each of these processes in detail in this chapter. It seems, however, that in the later chapters of this book when, in postnatal life, problems of the development of behavior patterns, heredity and environment, the nature of instinct, the development of perception, the continuity or saltatoriness of development, and the nature of learning are considered, it will be obvious that the facts presented in this chapter will always have a bearing on certain aspects of the answers that are given to such problems. As Tracy (1926, p. 253) has suggested, a study of adult behavior without a consideration of its origin before birth is as incomplete as would be the at present unthinkable study of adult anatomy without reference to the embryology of the structures considered.

The student who wishes further study in this field should consult, besides the detailed references given, papers by Hooker (1936, 1939a, 1942, 1943), which summarize much of the work in this field; the summary of the development of behavior by Dewey (1935); and the important book *Physiology of the Fetus: Origin and Extent of Function in Prenatal Life* by Windle (1940).

The late Sir Joseph Barcroft's important work, to which many references are given in this chapter, is also summarized in a book, *Researches on Pre-Natal Life* (1946). Early development in general is summarized in a chapter, "Ontogenetic Development," by Carmichael in the *Handbook of Experimental Psychology*, edited by S. S. Stevens, 1951.

This chapter may well end with a quotation from Oliver Wendell Holmes (noted by F. C. Irving in his foreword to C. A. Smith's excellent *The Physiology of the Newborn Infant*, 1946):

So the stout fetus, kicking and alive,
Leaps from the fundus for his final dive.
Tired of the prison where his legs were curled
He pants, like Rasselas, for a wider world.
No more to him their wanted joys afford
The fringed placenta and the knotted cord.

Bibliography

Abel, S., and W. F. Windle. 1939. Relation of the volume of pulmonary circulation to respiration at birth. *Anat. Rec., 75*, 451–464.
Adair, F. L. 1918. The ossification centers of the fetal pelvis. *Amer. J. Obstet., 78*, 175–199.
Ahlfeld, J. F. 1890. Beiträge zur Lehre vom Uebergange der intrauterinen Athmung zur extrauterinen. In *Beiträge zur Physiologie, Festschrift zu Carl Ludwig, zu seinem 70. Geburtstage gewidmet von seinen Schülern*, pp. 1–32. Leipzig: Vogel.
Angulo y González, A. W. 1927. The motor nuclei in the cervical cord of the albino rat at birth. *J. Comp. Neurol., 43*, 115–142.
——. 1928. Preliminary report on the motor-cell columns in the cervical region of the albino rat before birth. *Anat. Rec., 38*, 46–47.

Angulo y González, A. W. 1929a. Is myelinogeny an absolute index of behavioral capability? *J. Comp. Neurol.*, *48*, 459–464.

——. 1929b. Neurological interpretation of fetal behavior: The motor-cell columns of the albino rat before birth. (Abs.) *Anat. Rec.*, *42*, 17.

——. 1930a. Endogenous stimulation of albino rat fetuses. *Proc. Soc. Exp. Biol. Med.*, *27*, 579.

——. 1930b. Motion-picture records showing the typical stages in the development of muscular activity in albino-rat fetuses which are used in connection with the corresponding changes in the nervous system. *Anat. Rec.*, *45*, 284.

——. 1930c. Neurological interpretation of fetal behavior: The progressive increase of muscular activity in albino-rat fetuses. (Abs.) *Anat. Rec.*, *45*, 254.

——. 1932a. The prenatal development of behavior in the albino rat. *J. Comp. Neurol.*, *55*, 395–442.

——. 1932b. The prenatal growth of the albino rat. *Anat. Rec.*, *52*, 117–138.

——. 1933a. Development of somatic activity in the albino rat fetuses. *Proc. Soc. Exp. Biol. Med.*, *31*, 111–112.

——. 1933b. Endogenous stimulation of albino rat fetuses. *Anat. Rec.*, Suppl., *55*, 3.

——. 1934a. Functional dissolution of the nervous system in albino rat fetuses induced by means of asphyxia. *Anat. Rec.*, Suppl., *58*, 45.

——. 1934b. Neurological interpretation of fetal behavior: Structural changes in the nervous system of the albino rat and their relation to behavioral development. *Anat. Rec.*, Suppl., *58*, 2.

——. 1935. Further studies upon development of somatic activity in albino rat fetuses. *Proc. Soc. Exp. Biol. Med.*, *32*, 621–622.

——. 1937. Neurological interpretation of fetal behavior: The development of the sensory system in albino rat. *Anat. Rec.*, Suppl., *67*, 4.

——. 1939. Histogenesis of the monopolar neuroblast and the ventral longitudinal path in the albino rat. *J. Comp. Neurol.*, *71*, 325–359.

——. 1940. The differentiation of the motor-cell columns in the cervical cord of albino rat fetuses. *J. Comp. Neurol.*, *73*, 469–488.

Arendt. 1910. Wann ist die Perforation des lebenden Kindes notwendig? *Dtsch. med. Presse*, *14*, 167–168.

Avery, G. T. 1928. Responses of foetal guinea pigs prematurely delivered. *Genet. Psychol. Monogr.*, *3*, 245–331.

Baker, T. E. 1825. Description of a singularly small child. *Trans. Med. Phys. Soc.*, Calcutta, *1*, 364–365. Also in *Edinburgh New Phil. J.*, 1826, October, 398.

——. 1827. Nachricht von einem ausserordentlich kleines Kind. *Z. organ. Physik*, *1*, 260–261.

Ballantyne, J. W., and F. J. Browne. 1922. The problem of foetal post-maturity and prolongation of pregnancy. *J. Obstet. Gynaec. Brit. Emp.*, *29* (New ser.), 177–238.

Barclay, A. E., K. J. Franklin, and M. M. L. Prichard. 1946. *The foetal circulation and cardiovascular system and the changes that they undergo at birth.* Springfield, Ill.: Thomas.

Barclay, A. E., K. J. Franklin, and M. M. L. Prichard. 1947. *The circulation in the foetus.* Springfield, Ill.: Thomas.

Barcroft, J. 1935. The mammal before and after birth. *Irish J. Med. Sci.*, *1*, 289–301.

——. 1936. Fetal circulation and respiration. *Physiol. Rev.*, *16*, 103–128.

——. 1938. *The brain and its environment.* New Haven: Yale University Press.

——. 1946. *Researches on pre-natal life.* Springfield, Ill.: Thomas.

Barcroft, J., and D. H. Barron. 1936. The genesis of respiratory movements in the foetus of the sheep. *J. Physiol. (London)*, *88*, 56–61.

——. 1937a. The establishment of certain reflex arcs in foetal sheep. *Proc. Soc. Exp. Biol. Med.*, *36*, 86–87.

——. 1937b. Movements in midfoetal life in the sheep embryo. *J. Physiol. (London)*, *91*, 329–351.

——. 1939. The development of behavior in foetal sheep. *J. Comp. Neurol.*, *70*, 477–502.

Barcroft, J., D. H. Barron, and W. F. Windle. 1936. Some observations on genesis of somatic movements in sheep embryos. *J. Physiol. (London)*, *87*, 73–78.

Barcroft, J., and M. J. Karvonen. 1948. Action of carbon dioxide and cyanide on fetal respiratory movements; development of chemo-reflex function in sheep. *J. Physiol. (London)*, *107*, 153–161.

Barcroft, J., and M. F. Mason. 1938. The atmosphere in which the foetus lives. *J. Physiol. (London)*, *93*, 22.

Barham, W. B. 1915–1916. Maternal impressions. *Va. Med. Semi-mo.*, *20*, 454–459.

Barnum, C. G. 1915. The effect of gravitation on the presentation and position of the fetus. *J. Amer. Med. Ass.*, *64*, 498–502.

Barron, D. H. 1934. The results of peripheral anastomoses between the fore and hind limb nerves of albino rats. *J. Comp. Neurol.*, *59*, 301–323.

——. 1940. Recent contributions to the physiology of birth. *Sigma Xi Quart.*, *28*, 127–133.

——. 1941. The functional development of some mammalian neuromuscular mechanisms. *Biol. Rev.*, *16*, 1–33.

——. 1950. Genetic neurology and the behavior problem. In P. Weiss (Ed.), *Genetic neurology*, pp. 223–231. Chicago: University of Chicago Press.

Bauer, D. J. 1938. The effect of asphyxia upon the heart rate of rabbits at different ages. *J. Physiol. (London)*, *93*, 90–103.

Becker, R. F. 1940. Experimental analysis of Kuo Vaseline technique for studying behavior development in chick embryos. *Proc. Soc. Exp. Biol. Med.*, *45*, 689–691.

——. 1941. The status of gastro-intestinal activity in utero. *Quart. Bull. Northwestern Univ. Med. School*, *15*, 85 ff.

——. 1942. Experimental analysis of the Vaseline technique of Kuo for studying behavioral development in chick embryos. *J. Genet. Psychol.*, *60*, 153–165.

Becker, R. F., and W. F. Windle. 1941. Origin and extent of gastro-intestinal motility in the cat and guinea pig. *Amer. J. Physiol.*, *132*, 297–304.

Becker, R. F., W. F. Windle, E. E. Barth, and M. D. Schulz. 1940. Fetal swallowing, gastro-intestinal activity and defecation in amnio. *Surg. Gynec. Obstet.*, *70*, 603–614.

Béclard, P. A. 1815. Untersuchungen, welche zu beweisen scheinen, das der Fötus das Schafwasser athmet. *Dtsch. Arch. Physiol.*, *2*, 154–155.

Bergson, H. 1911. *Creative evolution.* (Trans. by A. Mitchell.) New York: Holt.

Bersot, H. 1918, 1919. Variabilité et corrélations organiques. Nouvelle étude du réflexe plantaire. *Schweiz. Arch. Neurol. Psychiat.*, *4*, 277–323; *5*, 305–324.

——. 1920, 1921. Développement réactionnel et réflexe plantaire du bébé né avant terme à celui de deux ans. *Schweiz. Arch. Neurol. Psychiat.*, *7*, 212–239; *8*, 47–74.

Bichat, M. F. X. 1819. *Anatomie générale précédée des récherches physiologiques.* Paris: Brosson, Gabon. 1822. *General anatomy applied to physiology and medicine.* (Trans. by G. Hayward.) Boston: Richardson and Lord.

——. 1827. *Physiological researches upon life and death.* (2d Amer. ed., including notes by F. Magendie. Trans. by F. Gold.) Boston: Richardson and Lord. 1829. *Récherches physiologiques sur la vie et le mort.* (5th ed.) Paris: Gabon.

Bischoff, T. L. W. 1842. *Entwicklungsgeschichte des Kaninchen-Eies.* Brunswick: Vieweg.

Blanton, M. G. 1917. The behavior of the human infant during the first thirty days of life. *Psychol. Rev.*, *24*, 456–483.

Blincoe, H. 1928a. Anatomy of the fore limb of the albino rat at approximately the time in fetal life when muscular movements begin. *Anat. Rec.*, *38*, 40.

——. 1928b. The anatomy of the fore limb of the albino rat at approximately the time in fetal life when somatic movement begins. *Anat. Rec.*, *40*, 277–295.

Bluhm, A. 1929. Über einige das Geburtsgewicht der Säugetiere beeinflussende Faktoren. *Arch. Entwicklungsmech. Organ.*, *116*, 348–381.

Bok, S. T. 1917. The development of reflexes and reflex tracts. *Psychiat. Neurol. Bl. Amst.*, *21*, 281–303.

Bolaffio, M., and G. Artom. 1924. Ricerche sulla fisiologia del sistema nervosa del feto umano. *Arch. sci. biol.*, *5*, 457–487.

Bolk, L. 1926. Vergleichende Untersuchungen an einem Fetus eines Gorillas und eines Schimpansen. *Z. Anat. Entwicklungsgeschichte.*, *81*, 1–89.

Bonardi, G. 1946. Rapporti fra lo sviluppo del riflesso di flessione dorsale del capo e lo sviluppo della respirazione nel feto di cavia. *Bollet. del Soc. Italiana di Biol. Speriment.*, *21*, 833–834.

Boring, E. G. 1916. Cutaneous sensation after nerve-division. *Quart. J. Exp. Physiol.*, *10*, 1–95.

——. 1929. *A history of experimental psychology.* New York: Century.

Bors, E. 1925. Die Methodik der intrauterinen Operation am überlebenden Säugetierfoetus. *Arch. Entwicklungsmech. Organ.*, *105*, 655–666.

Bowen, R. E. 1932. The ampullar organs of the ear. *J. Comp. Neurol.*, *55*, 273–313.

Breed, F. S. 1911. The development of certain instincts and habits in chicks. *Behav. Monogr.*, *1*, No. 1. Pp. vi + 178.

Bridgman, C. S., and L. Carmichael. 1935. An experimental study of the onset of behavior in the fetal guinea-pig. *J. Genet. Psychol.*, *47*, 247–267.

Briffault, R. 1927. *The mothers.* Vol. 1. New York: Macmillan.

Brown, R. L. 1918. Maternal impressions. *W. Va. Med. J.*, *13*, 86.

Brown, T. G. 1914. On the nature of the fundamental activity of the nervous centers; together with an analysis of the conditioning of rhythmic activity in progression, and a theory of the evolution of function in the nervous system. *J. Physiol. (London)*, *48*, 18–46.

——. 1915. On the activities of the central nervous system of the unborn foetus of the cat; with a discussion of the question whether progression (walking, etc.) is a "learnt" complex. *J. Physiol. (London)*, *49*, 208–215.

Burnham, W. H. 1917. The significance of stimulation in the development of the nervous system. *Amer. J. Psychol.*, *28*, 38–56.

Burr, H. S. 1932. An electro-dynamic theory of development suggested by studies of proliferation rates in the brain of *Amblystoma*. *J. Comp. Neurol.*, *56*, 347–371.

Bylicki, L. 1921. À la biologie du foetus. *Gynéc. obstet.*, *4*, 541–543.

Camis, M. 1930. *The physiology of the vestibular apparatus.* (Trans. by R. S. Creed.) Oxford: Clarendon Press.

Canestrini, S. 1913. Über das Sinnesleben des Neugeborenen. (*Monogr. Gesamtgeb. Neurol. Psychiat.*, No. 5.) Berlin: Springer. Pp. 104.

Cannon, W. B., and A. Rosenblueth. 1937. *Autonomic neuro-effector systems.* New York: Macmillan.

Carlson, A. J., and H. Ginsburg. 1915. Contributions to the physiology of the stomach: XXIV. The tonus and hunger contractions of the stomach of the new-born. *Amer. J. Physiol.*, *38*, 29–32.

Carmichael, L. 1925. Heredity and environment: Are they antithetical? *J. Abnorm. Soc. Psychol.*, *20*, 245–260.

——. 1926a. The development of behavior in vertebrates experimentally removed from the influence of external stimulation. *Psychol. Rev.*, *33*, 51–58.

——. 1926b. Sir Charles Bell: A contribution to the history of physiological psychology. *Psychol. Rev.*, *33*, 188–217.

——. 1927. A further study of the development of behavior in vertebrates experimentally removed from the influence of external stimulation. *Psychol. Rev.*, *34*, 34–47.

——. 1928. A further experimental study of the development of behavior. *Psychol. Rev.*, *35*, 253–260.

——. 1929. The experimental study of the development of behavior in vertebrates. *Proc. Papers 9th Int. Congr. Psychol.*, New Haven, 114–115.

Carmichael, L. 1933. Origin and prenatal growth of behavior. In C. Murchison (Ed.), *A handbook of child psychology.* (2d ed., rev.), pp. 31–159. Worcester: Clark University Press.

———. 1934*a*. An experimental study in the prenatal guinea-pig of the origin and development of reflexes and patterns of behavior in relation to the stimulation of specific receptor areas during the period of active fetal life. *Genet. Psychol. Monogr.,* 16, 337–491.

———. 1934*b*. The genetic development of the kitten's capacity to right itself in the air when falling. *J. Genet. Psychol.,* 44, 453–458.

———. 1936. A re-evaluation of the concepts of maturation and learning as applied to the early development of behavior. *Psychol. Rev.,* 43, 450–470.

———. 1937. Stimulus intensity as a determiner of the characteristics of behavior in the fetal guinea pig. (Abs.) *Science,* 86, 409.

———. 1938. Fetal behavior and developmental psychology. *Rapp. et C. R. onzième congr. int. psychol., Paris,* 108–123.

———. 1940*a*. The physiological correlates of intelligence. *Yearb. Nat. Soc. Stud. Educ.,* 39 (I), 93–155.

———. 1940*b*. A technique for the electrical recording of eye movements in adult and fetal guinea pigs. (By title.) *Psychol. Bull.,* 37, 563.

———. 1941. The experimental embryology of mind. *Psychol. Bull.,* 38, 1–28.

———. 1946. *Manual of child psychology.* New York: Wiley.

———. 1947. The growth of the sensory control of behavior before birth. *Psychol. Rev.,* 54, 316–324.

———. 1951. Ontogenetic development. In S. S. Stevens, *Handbook of experimental psychology,* pp. 281–303. New York: Wiley.

Carmichael, L., and W. F. Dearborn. 1947. *Reading and visual fatigue.* Boston: Houghton Mifflin.

Carmichael, L., and G. F. J. Lehner. 1937. The development of temperature sensitivity during the fetal period. *J. Genet. Psychol.,* 50, 217–227.

Carmichael, L., and M. F. Smith. 1939. Quantified pressure stimulation and the specificity and generality of response in fetal life. *J. Genet. Psychol.,* 54, 425–434.

Cesana, G. 1911. Lo sviluppo ontogenico degli atti riflessi. *Arch. Fisiol.,* 9, 1–120.

Child, C. M. 1921. *The origin and development of the nervous system from a physiological viewpoint.* Chicago: University of Chicago Press.

———. 1924. *Physiological foundations of behavior.* New York: Holt.

———. 1925. The physiological significance of the cephalocaudal differential in vertebrate development. *Anat. Rec.,* 31, 369–383.

Christenbery, H. E. 1910–1911. Maternal impressions. *J. Tenn. Med. Ass.,* 3, 274–277.

Clark, E. L., and E. R. Clark. 1914. On the early pulsations of the posterior lymph hearts in chick embryos: Their relation to the body movements. *J. Exp. Zoöl.,* 17, 373–394.

Coghill, G. E. 1902. The cranial nerves of *Amblystoma tigrinum. J. Comp. Neurol.,* 12, 205–289.

———. 1906. The cranial nerves of *Triton taeniatus. J. Comp. Neurol.,* 16, 247–264.

———. 1908. The development of the swimming movement in amphibian embryos. (Abs.) *Anat. Rec.,* 2, 148.

———. 1909. The reaction to tactile stimuli and the development of the swimming movement in embryos of *Diemyetylus torosus,* Eschscholts. *J. Comp. Neurol.,* 19, 83–105.

———. 1913*a*. The correlation of structural development and function in the growth of the vertebrate nervous system. *Science,* 37, 722–723.

———. 1913*b*. The primary ventral roots and somatic motor column of *Amblystoma. J. Comp. Neurol.,* 23, 121–143.

———. 1914. Correlated anatomical and physiological studies of the growth of the nervous system of Amphibia: I. The afferent system of the trunk of *Amblystoma. J. Comp. Neurol.,* 24, 161–233.

———. 1916. Correlated anatomical and physiological studies of the growth of the nervous system of Amphibia: II. The afferent system of the head of *Amblystoma. J. Comp. Neurol.,* 26, 247–340.

———. 1924*a*. Correlated anatomical and physiological studies of the growth of the nervous system in Amphibia: III. The floor plate of *Amblystoma. J. Comp. Neurol.,* 37, 37–69.

———. 1924*b*. Correlated anatomical and physiological studies of the growth of the nervous system of Amphibia: IV. Rates of proliferation and differentiation in the central nervous system of *Amblystoma. J. Comp. Neurol.,* 37, 71–120.

———. 1926*a*. Correlated anatomical and physiological studies of the growth of the nervous system of Amphibia: V. The growth of the pattern of the motor mechanism of *Amblystoma punctatum. J. Comp. Neurol.,* 40, 47–94.

———. 1926*b*. Correlated anatomical and physiological studies of the growth of the nervous system in Amphibia: VI. The mechanism of integration in *Amblystoma punctatum. J. Comp. Neurol.,* 41, 95–152.

———. 1926*c*. Correlated anatomical and physiological studies of the growth of the nervous system of Amphibia: VII. The growth of the pattern of the association mechanism of the rhombencephalon and spinal cord of *Amblystoma punctatum. J. Comp. Neurol.,* 42, 1–16.

———. 1926*d*. The growth of functional neurones and its relation to the development of behavior. *Proc. Amer. Phil. Soc.,* 65, 51–55.

———. 1928. Correlated anatomical and physiological studies of the growth of the nervous system of Amphibia: VIII. The development of the pattern of differentiation in the cerebrum of *Amblystoma punctatum. J. Comp. Neurol.,* 45, 227–247.

———. 1929*a*. *Anatomy and the problem of behaviour.* Cambridge: University Press. New York: Macmillan.

Coghill, G. E. 1929b. The development of movement of the hind leg of *Amblystoma*. *Proc. Soc. Exp. Biol. Med.*, *27*, 74–75.

———. 1929c. The early development of behavior in *Amblystoma* and in man. *Arch. Neurol. Psychiat.*, *21*, 989–1009.

———. 1930a. Correlated anatomical and physiological studies of the growth of the nervous system of Amphibia: IX. The mechanism of association of *Amblystoma punctatum*. *J. Comp. Neurol.*, *51*, 311–375.

———. 1930b. The development of half centers in relation to the question of antagonism in reflexes. *J. Gen. Psychol.*, *4*, 335–337.

———. 1930c. The genetic interrelation of instinctive behavior and reflexes. *Psychol. Rev.*, *37*, 264–266.

———. 1930d. Individuation versus integration in the development of behavior. *J. Gen. Psychol.*, *3*, 431–435.

———. 1930e. The structural basis of the integration of behavior. *Proc. Nat. Acad. Sci.*, *16*, 637–643.

———. 1931. Correlated anatomical and physiological studies of the growth of the nervous system of Amphibia: X. Corollaries of the anatomical and physiological study of *Amblystoma* from the age of the earliest movement to swimming. *J. Comp. Neurol.*, *53*, 147–168.

———. 1936. Integration and motivation of behavior as problems of growth. *J. Genet. Psychol.*, *48*, 3–19.

Coghill, G. E., and W. K. Legner. 1937. Embryonic motility and sensitivity. (Trans. of W. Preyer. *Specielle physiologie des embryo.*) *Monogr. Soc. Res. Child Develpm.*, *2*, 1–115.

Cohnstein, J., and N. Zuntz. 1884. Untersuchungen über das Blut, den Kreislauf und die Athmung beim Säugetierfötus. *Pflüg. Arch. ges. Physiol.*, *34*, 173–233.

Coleridge, S. T. 1885. *Miscellanies, aesthetic and literary.* (Bohn's Standard Library ed.) London: Bell and Sons.

Compayré, G. 1896. *The intellectual and moral development of the child:* Pt. 1. (Trans. by M. E. Wilson.) New York: Appleton.

Copenhaver, W. M. 1939. Initiation of beat and intrinsic contraction rates in the different parts of the *Amblystoma* heart. *J. Exp. Zoöl.*, *80*, 193–224.

Corey, E. L. 1931. Causative factors of the initial inspiration of the mammalian fetus. (Abs.) *Anat. Rec.*, Suppl., *48*, 41.

———. 1934. Effects of brain cautery on fetal development in the rat. *Proc. Soc. Exp. Biol., Med.*, *31*, 951–953.

Corner, G. W. 1944. *Ourselves unborn: An embryologist's essay on man.* New Haven: Yale University Press.

Coronios, J. D. 1930. Preliminary note: Technique for observing and motion-picture recording of fetal behavior (cat). *J. Genet. Psychol.*, *37*, 544–545.

———. 1931. The development of behavior in the fetal cat. (Abs.) *Psychol. Bull.*, *28*, 696–697.

———. 1933. Development of behavior in the fetal cat. *Genet. Psychol. Monogr.*, *14*, 283–386.

Coronios, J. D., H. Schlosberg, and L. Carmichael. 1932. Moving-picture film showing the development of fetal behavior in the cat. (With accompanying booklet.) Chicago: Steolting.

Coughlin, R. E. 1905. Report of two cases of maternal impression. *Brooklyn Med. J.*, *19*, 199–200.

Craig, J. F. 1930. *Fleming's veterinary obstetrics.* (4th ed.) London: Baillière.

Craig, W. 1912. Behavior of the young bird in breaking out of the egg. *J. Anim. Behav.*, *2*, 296–298.

Creed, R. S., D. Denny-Brown, J. C. Eccles, E. G. T. Liddell, and C. S. Sherrington. 1932. *Reflex activity of the spinal cord.* Oxford: Clarendon Press.

Crozier, W. J. 1929. The study of living organisms. In C. Murchison (Ed.), *The foundations of experimental psychology*, pp. 45–127. Worcester: Clark University Press. London: Oxford University Press.

Danforth, D. N., and A. C. Ivy. 1938. Effect of calcium upon uterine activity and reactivity. *Proc. Soc. Exp. Biol. Med.*, *38*, 550–551.

Dante. 1893. *The divine comedy: II. Purgatory.* (Trans. by C. E. Norton.) Boston: Houghton Mifflin.

Darwin, E. 1796. *Zoonomia; or the laws of organic life.* New York: T. and J. Swords.

Davidson, P. E. 1914. The recapitulation theory and human infancy. *Teachers College Contr. Educ.*, No. 65. Pp. 105.

Davis, M. E., and E. L. Potter. 1948. Response of human fetal reproductive system to administration of testosterone propionate during early pregnancy. *Endocrinology*, *42*, 370–378.

De Angelis, F. 1922. I riflessi nel neonato. *Pediatria*, *30*, 1107–1113.

De Kergaradec, L. 1822, 1823. Ueber die Ausculation, angewandt auf das Studium der Schwangerschaft. *Notizen Geb. Natur Heilk.*, *2*, 191, 202–207; *3*, 159.

DeLee, J. B. 1927. Counting fetal heart beat. *J. Amer. Med. Ass.*, *88*, 1000.

———. 1928. *The principles and practice of obstetrics.* (5th ed.) Philadelphia: Saunders.

DeMarsh, Q. B., H. L. Alt, W. F. Windle, and D. S. Hillis. 1941. The effect of depriving the infant of its placental blood. *J. Amer. Med. Ass.*, *116*, 2568–2573.

DeMarsh, Q. B., W. F. Windle, and H. L. Alt. 1940. Effect of depriving newborn of placental blood upon early postnatal blood picture. *Proc. Soc. Exp. Biol. Med.*, *44*, 662–664.

De Snoo, K. 1937. Das trinkende Kind im Uterus. *Mschr. Geburtsh. Gynäk.*, *105*, 88–97.

Detwiler, S. R. 1920. Functional regulations in animals with composite spinal cords. *Proc. Nat. Acad. Sci.*, *6*, 695–700.

———. 1921. Experiments on the hyperplasia of nerve centers. *China Med. J.*, *35*, 95–107.

———. 1922. Experiments on the transplantation of limbs in *Amblystoma:* Further observations on peripheral nerve connections. *J. Exp. Zoöl.*, *35*, 115–161.

Detwiler, S. R. 1923a. Experiments on the reversal of the spinal cord in *Amblystoma* embryos at the level of the anterior limb. *J. Exp. Zoöl.*, *38*, 293–321.

——. 1923b. Experiments on the transplantation of the spinal cord in *Amblystoma*, and their bearing upon the stimuli involved in the differentiation of nerve cells. *J. Exp. Zoöl.*, *37*, 339–393.

Dewey, E. 1935. *Behavior development in infants: A survey of the literature on prenatal and postnatal activity, 1920–1934.* New York: Columbia University Press.

Dodge, R. 1923. Habituation to rotation. *J. Exp. Psychol.*, *6*, 1–35.

Draper, R. L. 1920. The prenatal growth of the guinea-pig. *Anat. Rec.*, *18*, 369–392.

Dubois, P. 1833. Causes de la présentation de la tête, dans l'accouchement. *Arch. gén. méd.*, *1* (2d ser.), 292–295.

Dürken, B. 1929. *Grundriss der Entwicklungsmechanik.* Berlin: Borntraeger.

Elwyn, A. 1929. The structure and development of the proprioceptors. In F. Tilney et al. (Eds.), *The cerebellum: An investigation of recent advances,* pp. 244–280. (*Proc. Ass. Res. Nerv. Ment. Dis.*, 1926.) Baltimore: Williams and Wilkins.

Emmert, A. G. F., and J. J. Burgätzy. 1818. Beobachtungen über einige schwangere Fledermäuse und ihre Eihüllen. *Dtsch. Arch. Physiol.*, *4*, 1–33.

Erbkam. 1837. Lebhafte Bewegung eines viermonatlichen Fötus. *Neue Z. Geburtsk.*, *5*, 324–326.

Erlanger, J., and H. S. Gasser. 1937. *Electrical signs of nervous activity.* Philadelphia: University of Pennsylvania Press.

Evensen, H. 1931. *Entwicklung und Schicksal der zu früh geborenen Kinder.* (Dissertation.) Berlin: Friedrich-Wilhelms-Universität.

Favill, J. 1929. The relationship of eye muscles to semicircular canal currents in rotationally induced nystagmus. In F. Tilney et al. (Eds.), *The cerebellum: An investigation of recent advances,* pp. 530–546. (*Proc. Ass. Res. Nerv. Ment. Dis.*, 1926.) Baltimore: Williams and Wilkins.

Feldman, W. M. 1920. *Principles of antenatal and post-natal child physiology, pure and applied.* London and New York: Longmans, Green.

——. 1922. The nature of the plantar reflex in early life and the causes of its variations. *Amer. J. Dis. Child.*, *23*, 1–40.

Fender, F. A., W. B. Neff, and G. Binger. 1946. Convulsions produced by fetal anoxia; experimental study. *Anesthesiol.*, *7*, 10–13.

Fish, M. W., and W. F. Windle. 1932. The effect of rotatory stimulation on the movements of the head and eyes in newborn and young kittens. *J. Comp. Neurol.*, *54*, 103–107.

Fitzgerald, J. E., and W. F. Windle. 1942. Some observations on early human fetal movements. *J. Comp. Neurol.*, *76*, 159–167.

Forbes, A. 1922. The interpretation of spinal reflexes in terms of present knowledge of nerve conduction. *Physiol. Rev.*, *2*, 361–414.

Forbes, H. S., and H. B. Forbes. 1927. Fetal sense reaction: Hearing. *J. Comp. Psychol.*, *7*, 353–355.

Furfey, P. H., M. A. Bonham, and M. K. Sargent. 1930. The mental organization of the newborn. *Child Develpm.*, *1*, 48–51.

Geiger, A. J., W. M. Monroe, and A. V. N. Goodyer. 1941. Clinical fetal electrocardiography: Its practical accomplishment. *Proc. Soc. Exp. Biol. Med.*, *48*, 646–648.

Gemelli, A., C. Colombi, and R. Schupfer. 1951. L'enregistrement électrique des mouvements oculogyres et ses applications. *Année psychol.*, cinqantième année volume jubilaire, 185–200.

Genzmer, A. 1882. *Untersuchungen über die Sinneswahrnehmungen des neugeborenen Menschen.* (Dissertation, 1873.) Halle: Niemeyer.

Gerard, R. W. 1940. *Unresting cells.* New York: Harper.

Gesell, A. 1928. *Infancy and human growth.* New York: Macmillan.

——. 1929a. The individual in infancy. In C. Murchison (Ed.), *The foundations of experimental psychology,* pp. 628–660. Worcester: Clark University Press. London: Oxford University Press.

——. 1929b. Maturation and infant behavior pattern. *Psychol. Rev.*, *36*, 307–319.

Givler, R. C. 1921. The intellectual significance of the grasping reflex. *J. Phil.*, *18*, 617–628.

Glenn, W. F. 1911. Is a foetus a person? *South. Pract.*, *33*, 117–120.

Goeckel, H. 1911. *Die Wandlungen in der Bewertung des ungeborenen Kindes.* (Dissertation.) Heidelberg.

Goldstein, K. 1904. Kritische und experimentelle Beiträge zur Frage nach dem Einfluss des Zentralnervensystems auf die embryonale Entwicklung und die Regeneration. *Arch. Entwicklungsmech. Organ.*, *18*, 57–110.

——. 1939. *The organism.* New York: American Book.

Good, F. L. 1924. Pregnancy and labor complicated by diseases and injuries of the spinal cord. *J. Amer. Med. Ass.*, *83*, 416–418.

Goss, C. M. 1937. Early development of the rat heart in vitro. *Anat. Rec.*, Suppl., *67*, 20.

——. 1938. The first contractions of the heart in rat embryos. *Anat. Rec.*, *70*, 505–524.

——. 1940. First contractions of the heart without cytological differentiation. *Anat. Rec.*, *76*, 19–27.

Graham, E. A. 1913–1915. The origin and nature of fetal movements. *Trans. Chicago Path. Soc.*, *9*, 123–124.

Graham, M. 1919. Intrauterine crying. *Brit. Med. J.*, *1*, 675.

Grant, R. E. 1827. Beobachtungen über den Bau und das Wesen der *Flustrae*. *Z. organ. Physik*, *1*, 401–418.

Greenfield, A. D. M., T. J. Shepherd, and R. F. Whelan. 1951. The relationship between the blood flow in the umbilical cord and the rate of foetal growth in sheep and guinea pig. *J. Physiol. London*, *115*, 158–162.

Griffith, W. S. A. 1915. An investigation of the causes which determine the lie of the foetus in utero. *Lancet, 2,* 319–325.

Guthrie, E. R. 1942. Conditioning: A theory of learning in terms of stimulus, response, and association. *Yearb. Nat. Soc. Stud. Educ., 41* (II), 17–60.

Harrison, R. G. 1904. An experimental study of the relation of the nervous system to the developing musculature in the embryo of the frog. *Amer. J. Anat., 3,* 197–220.

Hartman, C. G. 1916a. Studies in the development of the opossum *Didelphys virginiana* L.: I. History of the early cleavage. *J. Morphol., 27,* 1–41.

——. 1916b. Studies in the development of the opossum *Didelphys virginiana* L.: II. Formation of the blastocyst. *J. Morphol., 27,* 42–83.

——. 1919a. Studies in the development of the opossum *Didelphys virginiana* L.: III. Description of new material on maturation, cleavage and entoderm formation. *J. Morphol., 32,* 1–73.

——. 1919b. Studies in the development of the opossum *Didelphys virginiana* L.: IV. The bilaminar blastocyst. *J. Morphol., 32,* 73–142.

——. 1920. Studies in the development of the opossum *Didelphys virginiana* L.: V. The phenomena of parturition. *Anat. Rec., 19,* 251–261.

——. 1936. *Time of ovulation in women.* Baltimore: Williams and Wilkins.

Hegel, G. W. F. 1894. *Philosophy of mind.* (Trans. by W. Wallace.) Oxford: Clarendon Press.

Henderson, Y. 1937. How breathing begins at birth. *Science, 85,* 80–91.

Herrick, C. J. 1924. *Neurological foundations of animal behavior.* New York: Holt.

——. 1943. *Biographical memoir of George Ellett Coghill: 1872–1941.* Washington: National Academy of Sciences.

——. 1949. *George Ellett Coghill: Naturalist and philosopher.* Chicago: University of Chicago Press.

Herrick, C. J., and G. E. Coghill. 1915. The development of reflex mechanisms in *Amblystoma. J. Comp. Neurol., 25,* 65–85.

Hertwig, R. 1912. *A manual of zoology.* (Trans. by J. S. Kingsley.) New York: Holt.

Hess, J. H. 1918. The diagnosis of the age of the fetus by the use of roentgenograms. *Ill. Med. J., 33,* 73–88.

——. 1922. *Premature and congenitally diseased infants.* Philadelphia: Lea and Febiger.

Hewer, E. E. 1927. The development of muscle in the human foetus. *J. Anat., 62,* 72–78.

Hicks, J. B. 1880. On recording the fetal movements by means of a gastrograph. *Trans. Obstet. Soc. London, 22,* 134.

Hill, J. P., and M. Tribe. 1924. The early development of the cat (*Felis domestica*). *Quart. J. Micro. Sci., 68,* 513–602.

Hines, M., and W. L. Straus. 1934. The motor cortex of fetal and infant rhesus monkeys (*Macaca mulatta*). *Anat. Rec. Suppl., 58,* 18.

Hinsey, J. C., S. W. Ranson, and R. F. McNattin. 1930. The role of the hypothalamus and mesencephalon in locomotion. *Arch. Neurol. Psychiat., 23,* 1–42.

His, W. 1880, 1882, 1885. *Anatomie menschlicher Embryonen.* (3 vols.) Leipzig: Vogel.

Hogg, I. D. 1941. Sensory nerves and associated structures in the skin of human fetuses of 8 to 14 weeks of menstrual age correlated with functional capability. *J. Comp. Neurol., 75,* 371–410.

Holsopple, J. Q. 1929. Space and the nonauditory labyrinth. In C. Murchison (Ed.), *The foundations of experimental psychology,* pp. 414–433. Worcester: Clark University Press. London: Oxford University Press.

Holt, E. B. 1931. *Animal drive and the learning process.* Vol. I. New York: Holt.

Home, E. 1827. Über die Fortpflanzung der Auster und der Flussmuschel. (Croonian Lecture, 1826.) *Z. organ. Physik, 1,* 391–396. (See also *Phil. Trans. Roy. Soc. London,* Pt. 1, 1827, 39.)

Hooker, D. 1911. The development and function of voluntary and cardiac muscle in embryos without nerves. *J. Exp. Zoöl., 11,* 159–186.

——. 1936. Early fetal activity in mammals. *Yale J. Biol. Med., 8,* 579–602.

——. 1937. The development of reflexes in the mammalian fetus. *Anat. Rec., Suppl., 70,* 55.

——. 1938. The origin of the grasping movement in man. *Proc. Amer. Phil. Soc., 79,* 597–606.

——. 1939a. Fetal behavior. *Res. Publ. Ass. Nerv. Ment. Dis., 19,* 237–243.

——. 1939b. *A preliminary atlas of early human fetal activity.* Privately published.

——. 1942. Fetal reflexes and instinctual processes. *Psychosomatic Med., 4,* 199–205.

——. 1943. Reflex activities in the human fetus. In R. G. Barker, J. S. Kounin, and H. F. Wright (Eds.), *Child behavior and development,* pp. 17–28. New York: McGraw-Hill.

——. 1944. *The origin of overt behavior.* Ann Arbor: University of Michigan Press.

——. 1950. Neural growth and the development of behavior. In P. Weiss (Ed.), *Genetic neurology,* pp. 212–213. Chicago: University of Chicago Press.

——. 1952. *The prenatal origin of behavior.* University of Kansas Press (in press).

Hooker, D., and J. S. Nicholas. 1927. The effect of injury to the spinal cord of rats in prenatal stages. (Abs.) *Anat. Rec., 35,* 14–15.

——. 1930. Spinal cord section in rat fetuses. *J. Comp. Neurol., 50,* 413–467.

Howells, T. H. 1945. The obsolete dogmas of heredity. *Psychol. Rev., 52,* 23–34.

Hsu, C. Y. 1948. Influence of temperature on development of rat embryos. *Anat. Res., 100,* 79–90.

Huggett, A. St. G. 1927. Foetal blood-gas tensions and gas transfusions through the placenta of the goat. *J. Physiol., 62,* 373–384.

——. 1930. Foetal respiratory reflexes. *J. Physiol., 69,* 144–152.

Hughes, H. 1905. Status of the foetus in utero. *N. Y. Med. J., 82,* 963.

Humphrey, Tryphena. 1952. The spinal tract of the trigeminal nerve in human embryos between 7½ and

8½ weeks of menstrual age and its relation to fetal behavior. *J. Comp. Neurol., 97,* 143–210.

Humphrey, Tryphena. 1953. The relation of oxygen deprivation to fetal reflex arcs and the development of fetal behavior. *J. Psychol., 35,* 3–43.

Hunter, W. S. 1931. The mechanisms involved in the behavior of white rats on the inclined plane. *J. Gen. Psychol., 5,* 295–310.

Hyman, A. S. 1930. Irregularities: Phonocardiographic study of the fetal heart sounds from fifth to eighth months of pregnancy. *Amer. J. Obstet. Gynec., 20,* 332–347.

Ingvar, S. 1920. Reaction of cells to the galvanic current in tissue cultures. *Proc. Soc. Exp. Biol. Med., 17,* 198–199.

Irwin, O. C. 1930. The amount and nature of activities of new-born infants under constant external stimulating conditions during the first ten days of life. *Genet. Psychol. Monogr., 8,* 1–92.

———. 1932a. The organismic hypothesis and differentiation of behavior: I. The cell theory and the neurone doctrine. *Psychol. Rev., 39,* 128–146.

———. 1932b. The organismic hypothesis and differentiation of behavior: II. The reflex arc concept. *Psychol. Rev., 39,* 189–202.

Irwin, O. C., and A. P. Weiss. 1930. A note on mass activity in newborn infants. *J. Genet. Psychol., 38,* 20–30.

Jackson, C. M. 1909. On the prenatal growth of the human body and the relative growth of the various organs and parts. *Amer. J. Anat., 9,* 119–165.

Jackson, H. 1884. Evolution and dissolution of the nervous system. *Lancet, 1,* 555–558, 649–652, 739–744.

James, W. 1890. *The principles of psychology.* (2 vols.) New York: Holt.

Jasper, H. H., C. S. Bridgman, and L. Carmichael. 1937. An ontogenetic study of cerebral electrical potentials in the guinea pig. *J. Exp. Psychol., 21,* 63–71.

Jennings, H. S. 1930. *The biological basis of human nature.* New York: Norton.

Jensen, K. 1932. Differential reactions to taste and temperature stimuli in newborn infants. *Genet. Psychol. Monogr., 12,* 363–479.

Kant, I. 1799. *Anthropologie.* Leipzig.

Kappers, C. U. A. 1917. Further contributions on neurobiotaxis: IX. An attempt to compare the phenomena of neurobiotaxis with other phenomena of taxis and tropism. The dynamic polarization of the neurone. *J. Comp. Neurol., 27,* 261–298.

Kasatkin, N. I., and A. M. Levikova. 1935a. The formation of visual conditioned reflexes and their differentiation in infants. *J. Gen. Psychol., 12,* 416–435.

———. 1935b. On the development of early conditioned reflexes and differentiations of auditory stimuli in infants. *J. Exp. Psychol., 18,* 1–19.

Keibel, F., and C. Elze. 1908. *Normentafel zur Entwicklungsgeschichte des Menschen.* Jena: Fischer.

Keibel, F., and F. P. Mall. 1910. *Manual of human embryology.* Philadelphia: Lippincott.

Keith, A. 1913. *Human embryology and morphology.* London: Arnold.

Kellogg, H. B. 1930. Studies on fetal circulation of mammals. *Amer. J. Physiol., 91,* 637–648.

Kidd, W. 1907. *The sense of touch in mammals and birds, with special reference to the papillary ridges.* London: Adam and Charles Black.

Kimel, V. M., and F. Kavaler. 1951. Functional maturation of the motor cortex of the fetal guinea pig as judged by the appearance of muscular responses to electrical stimulation of the cortex. *J. Comp. Neurol., 94,* 257–265.

King, H. D. 1915. On the weight of the albino rat at birth and the factors that influence it. *Anat. Rec., 9,* 213–231.

Kingsbury, B. F. 1924. The significance of the so-called law of cephalocaudal differential growth. *Anat. Rec., 27,* 305–321.

———. 1926. On the so-called law of antero-posterior development. *Anat. Rec., 33,* 73–87.

Klemm, G. O. 1914. *A history of psychology.* (Trans. by E. C. Wilm and R. Pintner.) New York: Scribner's.

Koffka, K. 1924. *The growth of the mind: An introduction to child psychology.* (Trans. by R. M. Ogden.) New York: Harcourt, Brace. London: Kegan Paul.

Kouwer, B. J. 1919. Adembewegingen van de vrucht voor en na de geboorte. *Ned. Tijdschr. Geneesk., 11,* 815–822.

Krabbe, K. 1912. Les réflexes chez le foetus. *Rev. neurol., 24,* 434–435.

Kuo, Z. Y. 1932a. Ontogeny of embryonic behavior in Aves: I. The chronology and general nature of the behavior of the chick embryo. *J. Exp. Zoöl., 61,* 395–430.

———. 1932b. Ontogeny of embryonic behavior in Aves: II. The mechanical factors in the various stages leading to hatching. *J. Exp. Zoöl., 62,* 453–487.

———. 1932c. Ontogeny of embryonic behavior in Aves: III. The structure and environmental factors in embryonic behavior. *J. Comp. Psychol., 13,* 245–272.

———. 1932d. Ontogeny of embryonic behavior in Aves: IV. The influence of embryonic movements upon the behavior after hatching. *J. Comp. Psychol., 14,* 109–122.

———. 1932e. Ontogeny of embryonic behavior in Aves: V. The reflex concept in the light of embryonic behavior in birds. *Psychol. Rev., 39,* 499–515.

———. 1938. Ontogeny of embryonic behavior in Aves: XII. Stages in the development of physiological activities in the chick embryo. *Amer. J. Psychol., 51,* 361–378.

———. 1939a. Development of acetylcholine in the chick embryo. *J. Neurophysiol., 2,* 488–493.

———. 1939b. Studies in the physiology of the embryonic nervous system. *J. Comp. Neurol., 70,* 437–459.

———. 1939c. Total pattern or local reflexes? *Psychol. Rev., 46,* 93–122.

Kuo, Z. Y., and L. Carmichael. 1937. A technique for the motion-picture recording of the development of behavior in the chick embryo. *J. Psychol.*, *4*, 343–348.

Kussmaul, A. 1859. *Untersuchungen über das Seelenleben des neugeborenen Menschen.* Leipzig: Winter.

Lane, H. H. 1917. The correlation between structure and function in the development of the special senses of the white rat. *Univ. Okla. Bull.* (New ser. No. 140) (*Univ. Stud.*, No. 8), 1–88.

——. 1924. A mechanism showing a remarkable correlation between structure and function in connection with the nursing reflex in the young mammal. *Kan. Univ. Sci. Bull.*, *15* (Whole ser. 26), 247–253.

Lange, F. A. 1925. *History of materialism.* (1873.) (Trans. by E. C. Thomas.) New York: Harcourt, Brace. London: Kegan Paul.

Langfeld, H. S. 1931. A response interpretation of consciousness. *Psychol. Rev.*, *38*, 87–108.

Langreder, W. 1949a. Ueber Fotalreflexe und deren intrauterine Bedeutung. *Z. Geburtsh. Gynakol.*, *131*, 236–251.

——. 1949b. Welche Fötalreflexe haben line intrauterine Aufgabe. *Dtsch. Med. Wschr.*, *74*, 661–667.

Langworthy, O. R. 1925. The development of progression and posture in young opossums. *Amer. J. Physiol.*, *74*, 1–13.

——. 1926. Relation of onset of decerebrate rigidity to the time of myelinization of tracts in the brainstem and spinal cord of young animals. *Contr. Embryol., Carnegie Inst. Wash.*, *17*, No. 89, 125–140.

——. 1927. The histological development of cerebral motor areas in young kittens correlated with their physiological reaction to electrical stimulation. *Contr. Embryol., Carnegie Inst. Wash.*, *19*, No. 104, 177–208.

——. 1928. The behavior of pouch-young opossums correlated with the myelinization of tracts in the nervous system. *J. Comp. Neurol.*, *46*, 201–247.

——. 1929. A correlated study of the development of reflex activity in fetal and young kittens and the myelinization of tracts in the nervous system. *Contr. Embryol., Carnegie Inst. Wash.*, *20*, No. 114, 127–171.

——. 1932. The differentiation of behaviour patterns in the foetus and infant. *Brain*, *55*, 265–277.

Lapicque, L. 1926. *L'excitabilité en fonction du temps.* Paris: Presses Université de France.

Larsell, O. 1929. The comparative morphology of the membranous labyrinth and the lateral line organs in their relation to the development of the cerebellum. In F. Tilney *et al.* (Eds.), *The cerebellum: An investigation of recent advances.* (*Proc. Ass. Res. Nerv. Ment. Dis.*, 1926.) Baltimore: Williams and Wilkins.

Larsell, O., E. McCrady, and A. Zimmerman. 1935. Morphological and functional development of the membranous labyrinth in the opossum. *J. Comp. Neurol.*, *63*, 95–118.

Lashley, K. S. 1924. Studies of cerebral function in learning: VI. The theory that synaptic resistance is reduced by the passage of the nerve impulse. *Psychol. Rev.*, *31*, 369–375.

Lashley, K. S. 1929. Brain mechanisms and intelligence. (*Behav. Res. Fund Monogr.*) Chicago: University of Chicago Press.

——. 1951. The problem of serial order in behavior. In L. A. Jeffrees (Ed.), *Cerebral mechanisms in behavior—The Hixon Symposium.* New York: Wiley.

Latimer, H. B. 1931. The prenatal growth of the cat: II. The growth of the dimensions of the head and trunk. *Anat. Rec.*, *50*, 311–332.

Latimer, H. B., and J. M. Aikman. 1931. The prenatal growth of the cat: I. The growth in weight of the head, trunk, forelimbs, and hindlimbs. *Anat. Rec.*, *48*, 1–26.

Laughton, N. B. 1924. Studies on the nervous regulation of progression in mammals. *Amer. J. Physiol.*, *70*, 358–384.

Leeuwenhoek, A. 1697. Part of a letter dated Delft, September 10, 1697, concerning the eggs of snails, the roots of vegetables, teeth, and young oysters. *Phil. Trans.*, *19*, 790–799.

Liesch, E. 1946. La motilità riflessa durante lo sviluppo fetale nell'uomo. *Bollet. del Soc. Italiana di Biol. Speriment.*, *21*, 831–833.

Liggett, J. R. 1928. An experimental study of the olfactory sensitivity of the white rat. *Genet. Psychol. Monogr.*, *3*, 1–64.

Lillie, F. R. 1919. *The development of the chick.* New York: Holt.

Lillie, R. S. 1932. *Protoplasmic action and nervous system.* (2d ed.) Chicago: University of Chicago Press.

Lincoln, A. W. 1932. *The behavioral development of the feeding reaction in the white rat.* Unpublished master's thesis, Brown University.

Lindsley, D. B. 1942. Heart and brain potentials of human fetuses in utero. *Amer. J. Psychol.*, *55*, 412–416.

Locke, J. 1849. *Essay concerning human understanding.* (1690.) Philadelphia: Kay and Troutman.

Lovejoy, A. O. 1926. The meanings of "emergence" and its modes. *Proc. 6th Int. Congr. Philosophy, Cambridge, Mass.*, 20–33.

MacKeever, T. 1833. On the information afforded by the stethoscope in detecting the presence of foetal life. *Lancet*, *24*, 715.

Maekawa, M., and J. Toyoshima. 1930. The fetal electro-cardiogram of the human subject. *Acta Scholae Med. Univ. Imp., Kioto*, *12*, 519–520.

Magendie, F. *See* Bichat, 1827.

Magnus, R. 1924. *Körperstellung.* Berlin: Springer.

——. 1925. Animal posture. (Croonian Lecture.) *Proc. Roy. Soc. London*, *98B*, 339–353.

Mailliot, L. 1856. *L'auscultation appliquée à l'étude de la grossesse.* Paris: Baillière. (German summary by Sickel in *Schmidt's Jb. ges. Med.*, 1857, *93*, 258–260.)

Mall, F. P. 1906. On ossification centers in human embryos less than one hundred days old. *Amer. J. Anat.*, *5*, 433–458.

——. 1910. Determination of the ages of human embryos and fetuses. In Keibel, F., and F. P.

Mall. *Manual of human embryology*, Vol. 1, pp. 180-201. Philadelphia: Lippincott.

Mall, F. P. 1918. On the age of human embryos. *Amer. J. Anat.*, *23*, 397-422.

Mann, H., and P. Bernstein. 1941. Fetal electrocardiography. *Amer. Heart J.*, *22*, 390-400.

Mann, I. C. 1928. *The development of the human eye*. Cambridge: University Press.

Marquis, D. P. 1931. Can conditioned responses be established in the newborn infant? *J. Genet. Psychol.*, *39*, 479-492.

Matthews, S. A., and S. R. Detwiler. 1926. The reactions of *Amblystoma* embryos following prolonged treatment with chloretone. *J. Exp. Zoöl.*, *45*, 279-292.

Maxwell, S. S. 1923. *Labyrinth and equilibrium*. Philadelphia: Lippincott.

McCarthy, D. 1936. A graphic age conversion scale. *Child Develpm.*, *7*, 74.

McCrady, E. 1938. *The embryology of the opossum*. Philadelphia: Wistar Institute of Anatomy and Biology.

McCrady, E., E. G. Wever, and C. W. Bray. 1937. The development of hearing in the opossum. *J. Exp. Zoöl.*, *75*, 503-517.

McDougall, W. 1923. *Outline of psychology*. New York: Scribner's.

McIlroy, A. L., and D. Leverkus. 1924. Changes in polarity of the foetus during the later weeks of pregnancy. *Lancet*, *2*, 267-271. Also in *Proc. Roy. Soc. Med.* (*Sect. Obstet. Gynec.*), 1924, *17*, 89-99.

Mermann. 1887. Ueber eigenthümliche rhythmische Fötalbewegungen. *Cbl. Gynäk.*, *11*, 622-624.

Meyer, A. W. 1939. *The rise of embryology*. Stanford University, Calif.: Stanford University Press.

Minkowski, M. 1920a. Movimientos y reflejos del feto humano durante la primera mitad del embarazo. *Trabajos del Laboratorio de Investigaciones Biologicas, Univ. Madrid*, *18*, 269-273.

——. 1920b. Réflexes et mouvements de la tête, du tronc et des extrémités du foetus humain pendant la première moitié de la grossesse. *C. R. Soc. Biol.*, Paris, *83*, 1202-1204.

——. 1921a. Sur les mouvements, les réflexes, et les réactions musculaires du foetus humain de 2 à 5 mois et leur rélations avec le système nerveux foetal. *Rev. neurol.*, *37*, 1105-1118, 1235-1250.

——. 1921b. Ueber Bewegungen und Reflexe des menschlichen Foetus während der ersten Hälfte seiner Entwicklung. *Schweiz. Arch. Neurol. Psychiat.*, *8*, 148-151.

——. 1922. Ueber frühzeitige Bewegungen. Reflexe und muskuläre Reaktionen beim menschlichen Fötus und ihre Beziehungen zum fötalen Nerven- und Muskelsystem. *Schweiz. med. Wschr.*, *52*, 721-724, 751-755.

——. 1923. Zur Entwicklungsgeschichte, Lokalisation und Klinik des Fussohlenreflexes. *Schweiz. Arch. Neurol. Psychiat.*, *13*, 475-514.

——. 1924, 1925. Zum gegenwärtigen Stand der Lehre von den Reflexen in entwicklungsgeschichtlicher und der anatomisch-physiologischer Beziehung. *Schweiz.*

Arch. Neurol. Psychiat., *15*, 239-259; *16*, 133-152, 266-284.

Minkowski, M. 1926. Sur les modalités et la localisation du réflexe plantaire au cours de son évolution du foetus à l'adulte. *C. R. Congr. Médecins, Aliénistes et Neurologistes de France*, Geneva, *30*, 301-308.

——. 1928a. Neurobiologische Studien am menschlichen Foetus. *Handb. Biol. ArbMeth.*, Pt. V, *5B*, 511-618.

——. 1928b. Ueber die elektrische Erregbarkeit der fötalen Muskulatur. *Schweiz. Arch. Neurol. Psychiat.*, *22*, 64-71.

——. 1947-1948. Zum Problem der ersten Anfänge einer seelischen Entwicklung beim Fötus. *Z. Kinderpsychiat.*, *14*, 87-94.

Minot, C. S. 1892. *Human embryology*. New York: William Wood.

——. 1903. *A laboratory text-book of embryology*. Philadelphia: Blakiston.

Morache, G. 1904. La vie intra-utrine et sa durée. *J. méd. Paris*, *2*, 14-16.

Morgan, T. H. 1927. *Experimental embryology*. New York: Columbia University Press.

Morrison, F. J. 1920. Maternal impressions. *Va. Med. Mo.*, *47*, 127.

Mowrer, O. H. 1936. "Maturation" vs. "learning" in the development of vestibular and optokinetic nystagmus. *J. Genet. Psychol.*, *48*, 383-404.

Muller, H. R., and L. H. Weed. 1916. Notes on the falling reflex in cats. *Amer. J. Physiol.*, *40*, 373-379.

Nachmansohn, D. 1940. Choline esterase in brain and spinal cord of sheep embryos. *J. Neurophysiol.*, *3*, 396-402.

Needham, J. 1931. *Chemical embryology*. (3 vols.) Cambridge: University Press.

Neu, M. 1915. Die Diagnose der Schwangerschaft. In A. Döderlein (Ed.), *Handbuch der Geburtshilfe*, pp. 246-328. Wiesbaden: Bergmann.

Newbery, H., I. Pyle, and H. Champney. 1943. Can mothers rate fetal environment? *J. Psychol.*, *15*, 197-221.

Nicholas, J. S. 1924. Regulation of posture in the fore limb of *Amblystoma punctatum*. *J. Exp. Zoöl.*, *40*, 113-159.

——. 1925. Notes on the application of experimental methods upon mammalian embryos. *Anat. Rec.*, *31*, 385-394.

——. 1926. Extirpation experiments upon the embryonic forelimb of the rat. *Proc. Soc. Exp. Biol. Med.*, *23*, 436-439.

——. 1927. The application of experimental methods to the study of developing *Fundulus* embryos. *Proc. Nat. Acad. Sci.*, *13*, 695-698.

——. 1929a. An analysis of the responses of isolated portions of the Amphibian nervous system. *Roux' Arch. Entwicklungsmech. Organ.*, *118*, 78-120.

——. 1929b. Movements in transplanted limbs. *Proc. Soc. Exp. Biol. Med.*, *26*, 729-731.

——. 1929c. Transplantations of tissues in fetal rats. *Proc. Soc. Exp. Biol. Med.*, *26*, 731-732.

Nicholas, J. S. 1933a. The correlation of movement and nerve supply in transplanted limbs of *Amblystoma*. *J. Comp. Neurol.*, *57*, 253–283.

——. 1933b. Development of transplanted rat eggs. *Proc. Soc. Exp. Biol. Med.*, *30*, 1111–1113.

Nicholas, J. S., and D. H. Barron. 1935. Limb movements studied by electrical stimulation of nerve roots and trunks in *Amblystoma*. *J. Comp. Neurol.*, *61*, 413–431.

Nicholas, J. S., and D. Hooker. 1928. Progressive cord degeneration and collateral transmission of spinal impulses following section of the spinal cord in albino rat fetuses. *Anat. Rec.*, *38*, 24.

Nicholas, J. S., and D. Rudnick. 1934. The development of rat embryos in tissue culture. *Proc. Nat. Acad. Sci.*, *20*, 656–658.

Nissen, H. W. 1951. Phylogenetic comparison. In S. S. Stevens (Ed.), *Handbook of experimental psychology*, 347–386. New York: Wiley.

Noback, C. R., and C. G. Robertson. 1951. Sequences of appearance of ossification centers in the human skeleton during the first five prenatal months. *Amer. J. Anat.*, *89*, 1, 1–28.

Norman, H. N. 1942. Fetal hiccups. *J. Comp. Psychol.*, *34*, 65–73.

Oppenheimer, J. M. 1934. Experimental studies on the developing perch (*Perca flavescens* Mitchill). *Proc. Soc. Exp. Biol. Med.*, *31*, 1123–1124.

Orr, D. W., and W. F. Windle. 1934. The development of behavior in chick embryos: The appearance of somatic movements. *J. Comp. Neurol.*, *60*, 271–283.

Pankratz, D. S. 1930. The possible relations of the development of the suprarenal gland to the origin of foetal movements in the albino rat. *Anat. Rec.*, *45*, 235.

——. 1931a. The development of the suprarenal gland in the albino rat, with a consideration of its possible relation to the origin of foetal movements. *Anat. Rec.*, *49*, 31–49.

——. 1931b. A preliminary report on the fetal movements in the rabbit. (Abs.) *Anat. Rec.*, Suppl., *48*, 58–59.

Paramore, R. H. 1909. A critical inquiry into the causes of the internal rotation of the foetal head. *J. Obstet. Gynec., London*, *16*, 213–232.

Parker, G. H. 1919. *The elementary nervous system*. Philadelphia: Lippincott.

——. 1922. *Smell, taste, and allied senses in the vertebrates*. Philadelphia: Lippincott.

——. 1931. The passage of sperms and of eggs through the oviducts in terrestrial vertebrates. *Phil. Trans. Roy. Soc., London*, *219*, 381–419.

Parker, T. J., and W. A. Haswell. 1921. *A textbook of zoology*. Vol. II. London: Macmillan.

Paton, S. 1907. The reactions of the vertebrate embryo and the associated changes in the nervous system. *Mitt. Zoöl. Stat. Neap.*, *18*, 535–581.

——. 1911. The reactions of the vertebrate embryo and associated changes in the nervous system. *J. Comp. Neurol.*, *21*, 345–372.

Patten, B. M. 1929. *The early embryology of the chick*. (3d ed.) Philadelphia: Blakiston.

Patten, B. M., and T. C. Kramer. 1933. The initiation of contraction in the embryonic chick heart. *Amer. J. Anat.*, *53*, 349–375.

Patterson, T. L. 1914. Contributions to the physiology of the stomach: XIII. The variations in the hunger contractions of the empty stomach with age. *Amer. J. Physiol.*, *33*, 423–429.

Pavlov, I. P. 1932. The reply of a physiologist to psychologists. *Psychol. Rev.*, *39*, 91–127.

Peiper, A. 1925. Sinnesempfindungen des Kindes vor seiner Geburt. *Mschr. Kinderheilk.*, *29*, 236–241.

——. 1928. *Die Hirntätigkeit des Säuglings*. Berlin: Springer.

Peterson, F., and L. H. Rainey. 1910. The beginnings of mind in the newborn. *Bull. Lying-In Hosp. City of N. Y.*, *7*, 99–122.

Peterson, J. 1926. Local signs as orientation tendencies. *Psychol. Rev.*, *33*, 218–236.

Pfaffman, C. 1936. Differential responses of the new-born cat to gustatory stimuli. *J. Genet. Psychol.*, *49*, 61–67.

Pflüger, E. 1877. Die Lebensfähigkeit des menschlichen Foetus. *Pflüg. Arch. ges. Physiol.*, *14*, 628–629.

Pinard. 1877. Fétus, anatomie et physiologie. Fétus, pathologie. *Dictionnaire encyclopedique des sciences médicales.* (Ser. 4.) Vol. II, pp. 472–556. Paris: Masson.

Ploss, H., and M. Bartels. 1927. *Das Weib in der Natur- und Völkerkunde.* (3 vols.) (11th ed.) Berlin: Neufeld.

Portal. 1818. Ueber die Pupillarmembran. *Dtsch. Arch. Physiol.*, *4*, 640–641.

Potter, E. L., and G. P. Bohlander. 1941. Intrauterine respiration in relation to development of fetal lung, with report of two unusual anomalies of respiratory system. *Amer. J. Obstet. Gynec.*, *42*, 14–22.

Pratt, K. C., A. K. Nelson, and K. H. Sun. 1930. The behavior of the newborn infant. *Ohio State Univ. Stud., Contr. Psychol.*, No. 10.

Preyer, W. 1882. *Die Seele des Kindes*. Leipzig: Fernau. (5th ed., 1900.) 1888, 1889. *The mind of the child:* Pt. 1. *The senses and the will;* Pt. 2. *The development of the intellect.* (Trans. by H. W. Brown.) New York: Appleton.

——. 1885. *Specielle Physiologie des Embryo. Untersuchungen über die Lebenserscheinungen vor der Geburt.* Leipzig: Grieben.

——. 1893. *Die geistige Entwicklung in der ersten Kindheit.* Stuttgart: Union. 1893. *Mental development in the child.* (Trans. by H. W. Brown.) New York: Appleton.

Randolph, H. 1900. Chloretone (acelonchloroform): An anesthetic and mascerating agent for lower animals. *Zoöl. Anz.*, *23*, 436–439.

Raney, E. T., and L. Carmichael. 1934. Localizing responses to tactual stimuli in the fetal rat in relation to the psychological problem of space perception. *J. Genet. Psychol.*, *45*, 3–21.

Rawdon-Smith, A. F., L. Carmichael, and B. Wellman. 1938. Electrical responses from the cochlea of the fetal guinea pig. *J. Exp. Psychol.*, *23*, 531–535.

Ray, W. S. 1932. A preliminary report on a study of fetal conditioning. *Child Develpm.*, *3*, 175–177.

Richter, C. P. 1925. Some observations on the self-stimulation habits of young wild animals. *Arch. Neurol. Psychiat.*, *13*, 724–728.

Riddle, O. 1927. Sexual difference in prenatal growth and death. *Amer. Nat.*, *61*, 97–112.

Riesen, A. H. 1951. Post-partum development of behavior. *Chicago Med. Sch. Quart.*, *13*, 17–24.

Rodman, J. 1815. Case of a child born between the fourth and fifth month and brought up. *Edinburgh Med. Surg. J.*, *11*, 455–458.

Romanes, G. J. 1896. *Darwin, and after Darwin:* Vol. I. *The Darwinian theory.* Chicago: Open Court.

Romijn, C., and J. Roos. 1938. The air space of the hen's egg and its changes during the period of incubation. *J. Physiol.*, *94*, 365–379.

Roux, W. 1896. The problems, methods, and scope of developmental mechanics. (*Woods Hole Biol. Lectures*, pp. 149–190.) Boston: Ginn.

Rudolph, L., and A. C. Ivy. 1933. Internal rotation of the fetal head. *Amer. J. Obstet. Gynec.*, *25*, 74–94.

Sachs, H. 1922. Elektrokardiogrammstudien am Foetus in utero. *Arch. ges. Physiol.*, *197*, 536–542.

Sarwey, O. 1915. Anatomie und Physiologie der Schwangerschaft. Pt. 2. In A. Döderlein (Ed.), *Handbuch der Geburtshilfe*, pp. 153–245. Wiesbaden: Bergmann.

Scammon, R. E. 1927. The literature on the growth and physical development of the fetus, infant, and child: A quantitative summary. *Anat. Rec.*, *35*, 241–267.

Scammon, R. E., and L. A. Calkins. 1924. The relation between the body-weight and age of the human fetus. *Proc. Soc. Exp. Biol. Med.*, *22*, 157–161.

——. 1929. *The development and growth of the external dimensions of the human body in the fetal period.* Minneapolis: University of Minnesota Press.

Scharpenberg, L. G., and W. F. Windle. 1938. A study of spinal cord development in silver-stained sheep embryos correlated with early somatic movements. *J. Anat.*, *72*, 344–351.

Sharp, L. W. 1926. *An introduction to cytology.* New York: McGraw-Hill.

Sharpey-Schäfer, E. 1928. The effects of denervation of a cutaneous area. *Quart. J. Exp. Physiol.*, *19*, 85–107.

Sheldon, W. H., S. S. Stevens, and W. B. Tucker. 1940. *The varieties of human physique.* New York: Harper.

Sherman, M., and I. C. Sherman. 1925. Sensori-motor responses in infants. *J. Comp. Psychol.*, *5*, 53–68.

Sherrington, C. S. 1922. Some aspects of animal mechanism. *Science*, *56*, 345–355.

Shirley, M. M. 1931a. A motor sequence favors the maturation theory. *Psychol. Bull.*, *28*, 204–205.

Shirley, M. M. 1931b. Is development saltatory as well as continuous? *Psychol. Bull.*, *28*, 664–665.

Skinner, B. F. 1931. The concept of the reflex in the description of behavior. *J. Gen. Psychol.*, *5*, 427–458.

Small, W. S. 1899. Notes on the psychic development of the young white rat. *Amer. J. Psychol.*, *11*, 80–100.

Smith, C. A. 1946. *The physiology of the newborn infant.* Springfield, Ill.: Thomas.

Smith, K. U., and R. S. Daniel. 1947. Maturational development and integration of response in the sea turtle. (Abstract.) *Amer. Psychologist*, *2*, 266.

Snyder, F. F., and M. Rosenfeld. 1937. Direct observation of intrauterine respiratory movements of the fetus and the role of carbon dioxide and oxygen in their regulation. *Amer. J. Physiol.*, *119*, 153–166.

Sontag, L. W. 1941. The significance of fetal environmental differences. *Amer. J. Obstet. Gynec.*, *42*, 996–1003.

Spee, F. 1915. Anatomie und Physiologie der Schwangerschaft. Pt. 1. In A. Döderlein (Ed.), *Handbuch der Geburtshilfe*, pp. 1–152. Wiesbaden: Bergmann.

Spelt, D. K. 1938. Conditioned responses in the human fetus in utero. *Psychol. Bull.*, *35*, 712–713.

Spemann, H. 1927. Organizers in animal development. (Croonian Lecture.) *Proc. Roy. Soc. London*, *102B*, 177–187.

Spencer, H. R. 1921. *William Harvey, obstetric physician and gynaecologist.* (The Harveian Oration, 1921.) London: Harrison and Sons.

——. 1924. The renaissance of midwifery. (Lloyd Roberts Lecture, 1924.) *Lancet*, *2*, 1049–1056.

——. 1927. *The history of British midwifery from 1650–1800.* London: Bale and Danielsson.

Sperry, R. W. 1951. Mechanism of neural maturation. In S. S. Stevens (Ed.), *Handbook of experimental psychology*, pp. 236–280. New York: Wiley.

Starling, E. H. 1900. The muscular and nervous mechanisms of the respiratory movements. In E. Sharpey-Schäfer (Ed.), *Text-book of physiology.* Vol. 2, pp. 274–312. Edinburgh: Pentland.

Steele, A. G., and W. F. Windle. 1939. Some correlations between respiratory movements and blood gases in cat foetuses. *J. Physiol.*, *94*, 531–538.

Stevens, S. S., and H. Davis. 1938. *Hearing: Its psychology and physiology.* New York: Wiley.

Stiebel, F. 1815. Ueber die Entwicklung der Teichhornschnecken (*Limneus slagnalis*). *Dtsch. Arch. Physiol.*, *1*, 423–426.

Strassmann, P. 1903. Das Leben vor der Geburt. *Samml. klin. Vortr.*, *N. F.*, *Gynäk.*, No. 353, 947–968.

Straus, W. L. 1939. Changes in the structure of skeletal muscle at the time of its first visible contraction in living rat embryos. *Anat. Rec.*, Suppl., *73*, 50.

Straus, W. L., and G. Weddell. 1940. Nature of the first visible contractions of the forelimb musculature in rat fetuses. *J. Neurophysiol., 3,* 358–369.

Streeter, G. L. 1906. On the development of the membranous labyrinth and the acoustic and facial nerves in the human embryo. *Amer. J. Anat., 6,* 139–165.

——. 1920. Weight, sitting height, head size, foot length, and menstrual age of the human embryo. *Contr. Embryol., Carnegie Inst. Wash., 11,* No. 55, 143–170.

Sutherland, G. F. 1921. Contributions to the physiology of the stomach: LVII. The response of the stomach glands to gastrin before and shortly after birth. *Amer. J. Physiol., 55,* 398–403.

Swammerdam, J. 1752. *Bibel der Natur.* Leipzig: J. F. Gleditschens.

——. (Edited.) 1907. Versuche, die besondere Bewegung der Fleischstränge am Frosche betreffend. In *Opuscula selecta neerlandecorrim de arte medica,* Fasc. 1, 82–135. Amsterdam: F. van Rossen.

Swenson, E. A. 1925. The use of cerebral anemia in experimental embryological studies upon mammals. *Anat. Rec., 30,* 147–151.

——. 1926. *The development of movement of the albino rat before birth.* Unpublished doctor's thesis, University of Kansas.

——. 1928a. Motion pictures of activities of living albino-rat fetuses. (Abs.) *Anat. Rec., 38,* 63.

——. 1928b. The simple movements of the trunk of the albino-rat fetus. *Anat. Rec., 38,* 31.

——. 1929. The active simple movements of the albino-rat fetus: The order of their appearance, their qualities, and their significance. (Abs.) *Anat. Rec., 42,* 40.

Thorndike, E. L. 1913. *Educational psychology:* Vol. I. *The original nature of man.* New York: Teachers College, Columbia University.

——. 1931. *Human learning.* New York: Century.

Tilney, F., and L. Casamajor. 1924. Myelinogeny as applied to the study of behavior. *Arch. Neurol. Psychiat., 12,* 1–66.

Tilney, F., and L. S. Kubie. 1931. Behavior in its relation to the development of the brain. *Bull. Neurol. Inst. N. Y., 1,* 229–313.

Tinklepaugh, O. L., and C. G. Hartman. 1930. Behavioral aspects of parturition in the monkey (*Macacus rhesus*). *J. Comp. Psychol., 11,* 63–98.

Tinklepaugh, O. L., C. G. Hartman, and R. R. Squier. 1930. The fetal heart rate in the monkey (*Macacus rhesus*). *Proc. Soc. Exp. Biol. Med., 28,* 285–288.

Tompkins, J. McC. 1911–1912. Influences during pregnancy upon the unborn child. *Old Dominion J. Med. Surg., Richmond, 13,* 219–224.

Tracy, H. C. 1926. The development of motility and behavior reactions in the toadfish (*Opsanus tau*). *J. Comp. Neurol., 40,* 253–369.

Tuge, H. 1931. Early behavior of embryos of the turtle, *Terrapene carolina* (L). *Proc. Soc. Exp. Biol. Med., 29,* 52–53.

Tuge, H. 1934. Early behavior of the embryos of carrier-pigeons. *Proc. Soc. Exp. Biol. Med., 31,* 462–463.

Vincent, S. B. 1912. The function of the vibrissae in the behavior of the white rat. *Behav. Monogr., 1,* No. 5. Pp. 81.

Virey. 1833. Rémarques sur la position du foetus dans l'utérus dans les diverses séries des animaux. *Arch. gén. méd.* (2d ser.), *1,* 295–298.

Wada, T. 1923. Anatomical and physiological studies on the growth of the inner ear of the albino rat. *Amer. Anat. Memoirs, Wistar Inst. Anat. Biol., 10,* 174.

Walton, C. E. 1910. Maternal impressions. *J. Surg. Gynec. Obstet., New York, 32,* 27–29.

Walz, W. 1922. Ueber die Bedeutung der intrauterinen Atembewegungen. *Mschr. Geburtsh. Gynäk., 60,* 331–341.

Wang, G. H., and T. W. Lu. 1940. Spontaneous activity of the spinal tadpoles of the frog and the toad. *Science, 92,* 148.

——. 1941. Development of swimming and righting reflexes in frog (*Rana guetheri*): Effects thereon of transection of central nervous system before hatching. *J. Neurophysiol., 4,* 137–146.

Warden, C. J., *et al.* 1931. *Animal motivation: Experimental studies on the albino rat.* New York: Columbia University Press.

Warkentin, J. 1938. *A genetic study of vision in animals.* Unpublished doctor's thesis, University of Rochester.

Warkentin, J., and L. Carmichael. 1939. A study of the development of the air-righting reflex in cats and rabbits. *J. Genet. Psychol., 55,* 67–80.

Warkentin, J., and K. U. Smith. 1937. The development of visual acuity in the cat. *J. Genet. Psychol., 50,* 371–399.

Washburn, M. F. 1926. *The animal mind.* New York: Macmillan.

Watson, J. B. 1903. *Animal education: The psychical development of the white rat.* Chicago: University of Chicago Press.

Weber, E. H. 1847. Ueber den Einfluss der Erwärmung und Erkältung der Nerven auf ihr Leitungsvermögen. *Arch. Anat. Physiol.,* 342–356.

Weed, L. H. 1917. The reactions of kittens after decerebration. *Amer. J. Physiol., 43,* 131–157.

Weed, L. H., and O. R. Langworthy. 1925a. Decerebrate rigidity in the opossum. *Amer. J. Physiol., 72,* 25–38.

——. 1925b. Developmental study of excitatory areas in the cerebral cortex of the opossum. *Amer. J. Physiol., 72,* 8–24.

——. 1926. Physiological study of cortical motor areas in young kittens and in adult cats. *Contr. Embryol., Carnegie Inst. Wash., 17,* No. 87, 89–106.

Weiss, A. P. 1929. The measurement of infant behavior. *Psychol. Rev., 36,* 453–471.

Weiss, P. 1926. The relations between central and peripheral coordination. *J. Comp. Neurol., 40,* 241–252.

——. 1939. *Principles of development.* New York: Holt.

Wells, L. J., and R. L. Fralick. 1951. Production of androgen by the testes of fetal rats. *Amer. J. Anat.*, *89*, 63–107.

Wenger, M. 1936. An investigation of conditioned responses in human infants. *Univ. Iowa Stud. Child Welfare*, *12*, 7–90.

Wertheimer, E. 1904. Foetus. In C. Richet (Ed.), *Dictionnaire de physiologie*, Vol. VI, pp. 499–634. Paris: Alcan.

Wetzel, N. C. 1941. Physical fitness in terms of physique, development and basal metabolism. *J. Amer. Med. Ass.*, *116*, 1187–1195.

White, G. M. 1915. The behavior of brook trout embryos from the time of hatching to the absorption of the yolk sac. *J. Anim. Behav.*, *5*, 44–60.

Whitehead, J. 1867. Convulsions in utero. *Brit. Med. J.*, 59–60.

Whitehead, W. H., W. F. Windle, and R. F. Becker. 1942. Changes in lung structure during aspiration of amniotic fluid and during air-breathing at birth. *Anat. Rec.*, *83*, 255–265.

Wickens, D. D., and C. Wickens. 1939. A study of conditioning in the neonate. *Psychol. Bull.*, *36*, 599.

Wiener, N. 1948. *Cybernetics, or control and communication in the animal and the machine.* New York: Wiley.

Williams, J. W. 1931. *Obstetrics.* New York: Appleton.

Willier, B. H. 1939. The embryonic development of sex. In Allen (Ed.), *Sex and internal secretions.* Baltimore: Williams and Wilkins.

Wilson, E. E., W. F. Windle, and H. L. Alt. 1941. Deprivation of placental blood as a cause of iron deficiency in infants. *Amer. J. Dis. Child.*, *62*, 320–327.

Wilson, E. E., W. F. Windle, and J. E. Fitzgerald. 1941. Development of the tractus solitarius. *J. Comp. Neurol.*, *74*, 287–307.

Windle, W. F. 1930a. The earliest fetal movements in the cat correlated with the neurofibrillar development of the spinal cord. (Abs.) *Anat. Rec.*, *45*, 249.

——. 1930b. Normal behavioral reactions of kittens correlated with the postnatal development of nerve-fiber density in the spinal gray matter. *J. Comp. Neurol.*, *50*, 479–503.

——. 1931. The neurofibrillar structure of the spinal cord of cat embryos correlated with the appearance of early somatic movements. *J. Comp. Neurol.*, *53*, 71–113.

——. 1932. The neurofibrillar structure of the five-and-one-half-millimeter cat embryo. *J. Comp. Neurol.*, *55*, 315–331.

——. 1934a. Correlation between the development of local reflexes and reflex arcs in the spinal cord of cat embryos. *J. Comp. Neurol.*, *59*, 487–505.

——. 1934b. Correlation between the development of spinal reflexes and reflex arcs in albino-rat embryos. (Abs.) *Anat. Rec.*, Suppl., *58*, 42.

——. 1935. Neurofibrillar development of cat embryos: Extent of development in the telencephalon and diencephalon up to 15 mm. *J. Comp. Neurol.*, *63*, 139–172.

Windle, W. F. 1937. On the nature of the first forelimb movements of mammalian embryos. *Proc. Soc. Exp. Biol. Med.*, *36*, 640–642.

——. 1939. Calcium and potassium deficiency as possible causes of certain delayed fetal movements. *Physiol. Zoöl.*, *12*, 39–41.

——. 1940. *Physiology of the fetus: Origin and extent of function in prenatal life.* Philadelphia: Saunders.

——. 1941a. Development of the blood and changes in the blood picture at birth. *J. Pediat.*, *18*, 538–563.

——. 1941b. Physiology and anatomy of the respiratory system in the fetus and newborn infant. *J. Pediat.*, *19*, 437–444.

——. 1950. Asphyxia neonatorum. Its relation to the fetal blood, circulation and respiration and its effects upon the brain. *Amer. Lecture Ser. Publ. 52.* Springfield, Ill.: Thomas. Pp. 70.

Windle, W. F., and M. F. Austin. 1936. Neurofibrillar development in the central nervous system of chick embryos up to 5 days' incubation. *J. Comp. Neurol.*, *63*, 431–463.

Windle, W. F., and J. Barcroft. 1938. Some factors governing the initiation of respiration in the chick. *Amer. J. Physiol.*, *121*, 684–691.

Windle, W. F., and R. E. Baxter. 1935. Development of reflex mechanisms in the spinal cord of albino rat embryos. Correlations between structure and function and comparisons with the cat and the chick. *J. Comp. Neurol.*, *63*, 189–209.

——. 1936. The first neurofibrillar development in albino rat embryos. *J. Comp. Neurol.*, *63*, 173–185.

Windle, W. F., and R. F. Becker. 1940a. The course of the blood through the fetal heart. An experimental study in the cat and guinea pig. *Anat. Rec.*, *77*, 417–426.

——. 1940b. The relation of anoxemia to early activity in the fetal nervous system. *Arch. Neurol. Psychiat.*, *43*, 90–101.

Windle, W. F., and M. W. Fish. 1932. The development of the vestibular righting reflex in the cat. *J. Comp. Neurol.*, *54*, 85–96.

Windle, W. F., M. W. Fish, and J. E. O'Donnell. 1934. Myelogeny of the cat as related to development of fiber tracts and prenatal behavior patterns. *J. Comp. Neurol.*, *59*, 139–166.

Windle, W. F., and J. E. Fitzgerald. 1937. Development of the spinal reflex mechanism in human embryos. *J. Comp. Neurol.*, *67*, 493–509.

Windle, W. F., and A. M. Griffin. 1931. Observations on embryonic and fetal movements of the cat. *J. Comp. Neurol.*, *52*, 149–188.

Windle, W. F., and W. L. Minear. 1934. Reversal of reaction pattern in the course of development of the snout reflex of the cat embryo. (Abs.) *Anat. Rec.*, Suppl., *58*, 92.

Windle, W. F., W. L. Minear, M. F. Austin, and D. W. Orr. 1935. The origin and early development of somatic behavior in the albino rat. *Physiol. Zoöl.*, *8*, 156–175.

Windle, W. F., M. Monnier, and A. G. Steele. 1938. Fetal respiratory movements in the cat. *Physiol. Zoöl.*, *11*, 425–433.

Windle, W. F., and D. Nelson. 1938. Development of respiration in the duck. *Amer. J. Physiol.*, *121*, 700–707.

Windle, W. F., J. E. O'Donnell, and E. E. Glasshagle. 1933. The early development of spontaneous and reflex behavior in cat embryos and fetuses. *Physiol. Zoöl.*, *6*, 521–541.

Windle, W. F., and D. W. Orr. 1934*a*. The development of behavior in chick embryos: Spinal cord structure correlated with early somatic motility. *J. Comp. Neurol.*, *60*, 287–308.

——. 1934*b*. Vermiform contractions of the musculature of cat embryos at death. *Anat. Rec.*, Suppl., *58*, 92.

Windle, W. F., D. W. Orr, and W. L. Minear. 1934. The origin and development of reflexes in the cat during the third fetal week. *Physiol. Zoöl.*, *7*, 600–617.

Windle, W. F., L. G. Scharpenberg, and A. G. Steele. 1938. Influence of carbon dioxide and anoxemia upon respiration in the chick at hatching. *Amer. J. Physiol.*, *121*, 692–699.

Windle, W. F., M. Sweet, and W. H. Whitehead. 1940. Some aspects of prenatal and postnatal development of the blood in the cat. *Anat. Rec.*, *78*, 321–332.

Wintrebert, M. P. 1904. Sur l'existence d'une irritabilité excito-motrice primitive, indépendante des voies nerveuses chez les embryons ciliés de Batraciens. *C. R. Soc. Biol., Paris*, *57*, 645.

Wintrebert, M. P. 1930. La contraction rhythmée aneurale des myotomes chez les embryons de selaciens: I. Observation de *Scylliorhinus canicula* L. Gill. *Arch. zool. expér.*, *60*, 221.

Witkowski, G. J. 1887. *Histoire des accouchements chez tous les peuples*. Paris: Steinheil.

Woodworth, R. S. 1929. *Psychology*. (Rev. ed.) New York: Holt.

Woyciechowski, B. 1928. Ruchy zarodka ludzkiego 42 mm. *Polsk. Gazeta Lekarska*, *7*, 409–411.

Yanase, J. 1907*a*. Beiträge zur Physiologie der peristaltischen Bewegungen des embryonalen Darmes: I. Mitteilung. *Pflüg. Arch. ges Physiol.*, *117*, 345–383.

——. 1907*b*. Beiträge zur Physiologie der peristaltischen Bewegungen des embryonalen Darmes: II. Mitteilung. *Pflüg. Arch. ges. Physiol.*, *119*, 451–464.

Youngstrom, K. A. 1937. Studies on the developing behavior of *Anura*. *J. Comp. Neurol.*, *68*, 351–379.

——. 1938. On the relationship between the acetylcholine esterase content and the development of motility in *Amblystoma punctatum*. (Abs.) *Anat. Rec.*, Suppl., *70*, 85.

——. 1941. Acetylcholine esterase concentration during the development of the human fetus. *J. Neurophysiol.*, *4*, 473–477.

Zettleman, H. J. 1946. Initial fetal atelectasis. *Amer. J. Obstet. Gynec.*, *51*, 241–245.

Zuntz, N. 1877. Ueber die Respiration des Säugethier-Foetus. *Pflüg. Arch. ges. Physiol.*, *14*, 605–637.

CHAPTER 3

ANIMAL INFANCY

RUTH M. CRUIKSHANK

Historical Introduction

The study of the genetic development of human behavior would not be complete without some reference to and comparison with the ontogeny of behavior in subhuman forms. Accordingly, this chapter has been included in this manual. An analysis of the development of young animals should show in clearly defined ways the general similarities and differences in the development of behavior in man and animals from which general principles can be drawn. Gesell (1928) has very tersely stated this:

> The study of infancy in its broadest sense must therefore be a comparative science. The more general laws of development in the very nature of things will be applicable to all vertebrates not excluding either fish or man. In spite of the bewildering diversity of the behavior traits of the young of widely varying species, it is not improbable that there are certain orders of emergence and sequences of pattern which are common to all. It is conceivable moreover that certain pervading correspondences may even yield to quantitative and qualitative gradations when the infancies of a large array of species are systematically studied from the standpoint of developmental economy [p. 336].

More than this, however, such studies make the contribution of supplying information on problems which may not be readily accessible or even possible for observational and experimental study in the human being. A survey of the preceding chapter by Carmichael as well as of this chapter will suffice to point out certain problems to which studies of the development of the young animal have contributed, or may in the future contribute, additional crucial data. Until complete descriptive accounts of the normal development of young animals have been made, however, progress in the studies whose aim is more than descriptive must remain limited.

Although the young of groups other than the mammals are of interest for any complete survey of this topic, this review is restricted to a consideration of mammalian infancy. Lack of space and, indeed, lack of sufficiently correlated detail make this limitation seem advisable at this time. However, the reader interested in the inclusion of other animals is referred to the accounts of Mitchell (1912) and Pycraft (1913).

That the young as well as the adult of a given species must be observed has probably been considered for some time, although careful and accurate observational studies of young animals in the field or laboratory have not been carried out until comparatively recent times. A statement by Rennie in 1838, quoted by Yerkes and Yerkes (1929), expresses this idea:

> The great interest attached to the chimpanzee, as approaching so nearly to ourselves in the scale of animal life, has induced us to dwell longer upon this part of his history than we had originally intended, but we hope without either wearying the

186

patience or exhausting the curiosity of our readers. A thorough acquaintance with the manners and intelligence of the young animal, as accurately observed and related by zoologists accustomed to such investigations, was besides necessary to enable us to form a just estimate of the habits and economy attributed to the adult in his native forests, and of the degree of credit to which the accounts of different travellers are entitled [p. 209].

John Fiske states the case for an understanding of animal infancy as it is probably most familiar to a student of genetic psychology. His essay, *The Meaning of Infancy*, written in 1883 and republished several times, brought attention to this problem, although post-Darwinian workers in biology, physiology, and psychology had already begun to investigate it. This is Fiske's informal report of how he became interested in the problem:

Well, in the spring of 1871, when Darwin's "Descent of Man" came out, just about the same time I happened to be reading Wallace's account of his experiences in the Malay Archipelago, and how at one time he caught a female orang-outang with a new-born baby, and the mother died, and Wallace brought up the baby orang-outang by hand; and this baby orang-outang had a kind of infancy which was a great deal longer than that of a cow or a sheep, but it was nothing compared to human infancy in length. This little orang-outang could not get up and march around, as mammals of less intelligence do, when he was first born, or within three or four days; but after three or four weeks or so he would get up, and begin taking hold of something and pushing it around, just as children push a chair; and he went through a period of staring at his hands, as human babies do, and altogether was a good deal slower in getting to the point where he could take care of himself. And while I was reading of that I thought, Dear me! if there is any one thing in

which the human race is signally distinguished from other mammals, it is in the enormous duration of their infancy; but it is a point that I do not recollect ever seeing any naturalist so much as allude to [1911 ed., 25–26].

Although at this time a complete historical account of the early studies on the development of behavior in young animals will not be given, it might be well to mention just a few of the more important contributions which have led to our present interest in the subject.

One of the early studies of animal infancy was made by Spalding (1873, 1875), who stressed the necessity for an understanding of the development of young organisms in order to answer certain theoretical questions then prevalent. Spalding's observations were carried out to establish evidence regarding the existence of instincts in the young animal.

Preyer's work (1882) may be taken as pioneer in the experimental study of the psychological aspects of infancy considered in the broad comparative sense. Preyer refers to various behavior items of young animals, comparing them with those of the human infant. His work also includes observations of fetal behavior so that, notwithstanding the fact that his studies are among the first to treat of behavioral development, they do not fall into the error of considering it as a strictly postnatal phenomenon.

Mills (1898) likewise appears to be among the first to attempt a description of the behavior of young animals. Mills enlarges the significance of the study by pointing out the necessity of such a study as part of the total field of psychology. His position is clearly stated:

It must be equally clear to those who, guided by facts alone, untrammelled by tradition and dogma of every kind, com-

pare the psychic status of the young with
that of the mature animal, that psychogenesis is a fact; that the mind does unfold, evolve, develop equally with the body.
And as with the body so with the mind,
each stage in this development can only
be understood in the light of all the previous stages.

This truth is apparently as yet only
dimly comprehended, for, till recently,
studies on psychic history, development or
psychogenesis have been all but unknown,
and as yet, even in the case of man, are
very few and confessedly imperfect [pp.
113–114].

The next important work concerning the
young mammal is Small's (1899). Taking
his lead from Mills, Small made a detailed
study of the development of the white rat.
Small, distinctly recognizing his problem
as one in genetic psychology, introduced
his study as follows:

A study of the psychic development of
any young animal needs no apology. Apart
from the fascination and the self-education
of watching the development of any form
of life from its early protoplasmic simplicity into complex maturity, there is the
solid scientific reason that Genetic Psychology has much to hope from minute
and accurate records of the developmental
periods of young animals of all species. It
may never be possible to reconstruct a
complete psychic organism from the evidence of a single trait—an ideal borrowed
from morphology—but something surely
may be accomplished towards a comparative embryology of the soul. What Preyer
and others have done for the human infant, needs to be done also for the baby-
animal of every species [p. 80].

In 1903, Watson published an experimental study of the psychological development of the white rat correlated with the
growth of its nervous system. Watson did
not repeat Small's work but, testing the
rat in simple learning situations, endeavored

to ascertain the age of psychological maturity for the rodent. This he placed at
approximately 24 days, although the animal learned in simpler situations at an
earlier age.

Allen's work (1904) on the behavior of
the guinea pig was published the next
year. Allen's study was comparable to
Watson's in aim, an examination of another member of the rodent group.

Yerkes' work (1907) on the dancing
mouse contains reference to the development of the young mouse, but it is primarily a study of the mature animal.

More recent work on the development
of behavior in young animals is treated
topically rather than chronologically in
other sections of this chapter.

Behavior of the Newborn Animal

Several references to the behavior of the
newborn animal are to be found in the literature. These studies derive their significance from the fact that birth represents a
stage of transition from one type of environment to another. When such observations are interpreted in light of the
longer developmental history of the organism, they offer valuable data; but when
they are interpreted without reference to
the preceding behavioral development of
the animal, they are extremely misleading.
When the literature on certain topics of
psychological interest such as that of "instinct" is reviewed, the reader is indeed
impressed with this fact.

The developmental levels which mammals have reached in intrauterine life have
been reviewed for the reader in the preceding chapter by Carmichael. Descriptions
of the functional development of the animal at birth are found in succeeding parts
of this chapter. For further discussions
of the development of specific animals at
or soon after birth the reader is referred

to the accounts of: Small (1899), rat; Allen (1904), guinea pig; Goerling (1913), kangaroo; Lashley and Watson (1913), monkey; Blair (1920), chimpanzee; Hartman (1920, 1921, 1928a), opossum; Allesch (1921), chimpanzee; Tilney and Casamajor (1924), cat; Robinson (1925), gibbon; Shaw (1925), Columbian ground squirrel; Johnson (1927), prairie dog; Kao (1927), rabbit; Wade (1927), striped ground squirrel; Avery (1928), guinea pig; Hartman (1928b), monkey; Struthers (1928), Canadian porcupine; Fox (1929), chimpanzee and orangutan; Sturman-Hulbe and Stone (1929), rat; White (1929), chimpanzee; Brown (1930), chimpanzee; Kuroda (1930), monkey; Sherman (1930), bat; Windle (1930), cat; Enders (1931), agouti; Jacobsen, Jacobsen, and Yoshioka (1932), chimpanzee; Tinklepaugh (1932), chimpanzee; Tinklepaugh and Hartman (1932), monkey; Coolidge (1933), gibbon; Coronios (1933), cat; Huestis (1933), deermouse; Foley (1934), monkey; Svihla (1934), deermouse; Tomilin and Yerkes (1935), chimpanzee; Yerkes and Tomilin (1935), chimpanzee; Errington (1939), muskrat; Alcorn (1940), ground squirrel; Fisher (1940), sea otter; Murie (1940), sea otter; Yerkes (1940), chimpanzee; Britton (1941), sloth; Ingles (1941), Audubon cottontail rabbit; Tappe (1941), kangaroo rat; Barrington (1942), pocket gopher; Cooper (1942), lion; Orr (1942), brush rabbit; Richardson (1942a), ring-tailed cat; Hatt (1943), pine squirrel; Richardson (1943), wood rat; Shadle and Ploss (1943), porcupine; Sollberger (1943), eastern flying squirrel; Hamilton (1944), short-tailed shrew; Scheffer (1945), sea lion; Taber (1945), nine-banded armadillo; Smith (1946), bear; McBride and Hebb (1948), McBride and Kritzler (1951), bottle-nose dolphin; Scott and Marston (1950), dog; Tevis (1950), beaver; Liers (1951), river otter; and Pournelle (1952), cotton mouse.

Sensory Development of Young Animals

Vision. The ages at which certain visual responses are observed after birth can be seen by reference to Table 1. A survey of certain studies of the development of visual acuity is made by Warkentin and Smith (1937). They also report the best evidence concerning the development of visual acuity for the young kitten. They give average ages for eye opening (9 days), nystagmus (14 days), visual placing (25 days), acuity of 360-minute visual angle (14 days), acuity of 180-minute visual angle (16 days), acuity of 43-minute visual angle (21 days), and acuity of 11-minute visual angle (25 days). There was no relationship noted between the age of eye opening and the appearance of nystagmus, but a high degree of visual acuity preceded visual placing responses. Concerning the visual acuity of the young chimpanzee and the young child, the Kelloggs (1933) point out that the animal seems to possess very great acuity and notices many finer details than does the child (pp. 89–90). The point needs experimental study.

Turner (1935) has investigated the visual responses of young rats allowed to orient toward a black door in a brightly lighted field. Animals with eyes open perform more efficiently than animals with eyes still closed, and the older animals orient with a greater degree of accuracy, indicating some genetic development of this type of response. This development seems to be correlated with the increased efficiency of the eye mechanism and possibly also with increased learning in the situation. Food deprivation does not seem to have any large effect upon the young rat's orientation to light (Biel, 1939). For a discussion of phototropisms in rats, see Crozier and Pincus (1927a).

TABLE 1

Typical Results from Observations of the Development of Behavior in Young Mammals *

Response	Rat	Guinea Pig	Rabbit	Cat	Dog	Monkey	Chimpanzee
Pupillary response			12 days K † 14th day M	7 days TC 12th day M 7–10 days Wi		(3) days F 2 days LW 2, 3 days HT	1st week JJY
Winking, nonvisual		1 day P	2 days K 14th day M	9 days M	13 days M	(3) days F 1 day LW 1 day HT	1 day JJY
Winking, visual	17 days S	2 days M		11 days M	3d week M	10 days F 8 days HT	10th week JJY
Visual pursuit		2 days M	22 days K 22 days M	14 days TC 14 days M 15 days Wi	18th day M	7 days F 3 days LW 5, 11 days HT	1–2 weeks JJY 1 mo. W
Reaching, visually directed						9 days F 5 days LW	8th week JJY
Responds to sound	17 days S	1 day M 1 day P	11 days K 10 days M	8 days M ?1 day Wi	17th day M	(3) days F 2 days LW 2, 4 days HT	1 day JJY early weeks W
Auditory localization		1 day P		26 days TC 9 days M 21 days Wi	3d–4th week M	12 days LW	
Olfactory responses	1 day S	1 day M 1 day P	4 days K 1st week M	?1 day M	1–2 weeks M	(3) days F 2, 3 days HT	
Gustatory response	1 day S	1 day M 1 day P	2d week M	?9 days M	1 week M		2 days JJY
Tactual responses	?1 day S		1 day M	1 day M	?1 day M	(3) days F 1 day LW	1 day JJY early weeks W
Pain responses	1 day S		1 day K 1 day M	?1 day M	1st week M	(3) days F 1 day LW	1 day JJY

Temperature	1 day S		1 day K ?1 day M	1 day M	1st week M		1 day JJY
Surface righting	1–4 days S		1 day K	1 day Wi		(3) days F 1 day HT	
Air righting			28–30 days Wi				
Scratching	14 days S		1 day K 2nd day M	23 days TC 1 day Wi 16 days M	17th day M	9 days F 12 days LW 7, 14 days HT	3½ mo. W
Crawling	4 days S	1 day M	1 day K 1 day M	1 day TC 1 day M 1 day Wi	1 day M		7–11th week JJY
Swimming				1 day TC 1 day Wi			
Sitting				20 days TC 21 days Wi			12th week JJY
Standing	12–14 days S	1 day M	17 days K 15th day M	14 days Wi 15 days M	?2 weeks M	13 days F 13 days LW 1, 3 days HT	12th week four limb 27th week erect JJY
Walking	12 days S	1 day M 1 day P	6 days K 12 days Hopping 10 days Hopping M	22 days TC 20 days M	2 weeks M	13 days F 13 days LW 1, 5 days HT	13th week four limb 29th week erect JJY
Running	14 days S	1 day M 1 day P		26 days TC 28 days Wi	5th week M		23rd week JJY
Climbing	12–14 days S			31 days TC 4th week Wi 18 days M		(3) days F 24 days LW 1, 2, 4 days HT	25th week JJY

* The chart should be read with recognition of its many sources of error, including (1) observation of the neonatal animal without reference to the fetal animal, (2) casual rather than systematic observations, and (3) variability of developmental ages. Reference for more accurate data for animals whose fetal development has been studied should be made to the preceding chapter by Carmichael.

† Abbreviations: F—Foley (1934); HT—Tinklepaugh and Hartman (1932); JJY—Jacobsen, Jacobsen, and Yoshioka (1932); K—Kao (1927); LW—Lashley and Watson (1913); M—Mills (1898); P—Preyer (1882); S—Small (1899); TC—Tilney and Casamajor (1924); W—White (1929); Wi—Windle (1930).

Investigations of the genetic development of color vision in those mammals which might be expected to have such vision are practically nonexistent. There are to be found investigations of sensitivity to red in the rabbit (Washburn and Abbott, 1912) and in the calf (Kittredge, 1923), a few comments such as those of the Kelloggs (1933, p. 92) concerning the infant chimpanzee, and a study of methods suitable for such work by A. W. Yerkes (1935).

The development of distance perception in young animals, it would seem, might be investigated experimentally with profitable results. Foley (1934) comments that, during the early days for the young monkey he observed, "misjudged distances were the rule rather than the exception" (p. 76). The reactions of the older animal, however, were swift and accurate (Foley, 1935). Kuckuk (1936) reports a number of interesting observations of young bears' recognition of a familiar figure at a distance. In contrast with these observations are those of Lashley and Russell (1934), who found that adult rats reared in total darkness during their earlier life can, without training, discriminate distances and jump with a force well adapted to the distances involved.

We also have some evidence concerning the genetic development of such functions as pattern vision, size discrimination, and brightness discrimination. Hebb's experimental investigations (1937a, 1937b) of the adult rat's discrimination of these variables after being reared in darkness from the age of 6 or 8 days to maturity indicate that for this animal the proficiency of performance does not depend upon previous visual stimulation. When tested at maturity, pattern vision of rats from which the visual cortex had been removed in infancy is lost, according to Tsang (1937b), although discrimination of brightness and relative size persists as it does in adult operates. Tsang

notes a few cases which he believes suggest a primitive type of pattern vision in young operates, which, however, is by no means as delicate as that of the normal animals.

The two chimpanzees reared in darkness to the age of 16 months about which Riesen (1947) reports showed good pupillary responses, startle reaction to sudden changes in intensity of light, and head and eye turning toward the source of light when they were first tested. Blinking at the approach of an object and fixation of an object were not immediately elicitable. Several days of experience in the light were needed before the animals showed visual recognition of an object like the feeding bottle, although this was familiar both tactually and kinesthetically.

Audition. Observational evidence concerning audition in young animals is given in Table 1. Data of this sort are subject to considerable error, but until further evidence is offered they must suffice. Pitch discrimination and intensity discrimination have not been satisfactorily tested. Biel (1939) notes that young animals deprived of food respond to sound stimulation at a significantly later age than do normally fed rats.

Interesting comparisons of auditory localization in the young chimpanzee and the child were obtained by the Kelloggs (1933), who required the blindfolded subject to find the experimenter, whose position could be determined only by his voice. The child at 16 to 17 months made an average error of 40.2 degrees in localizing the sound, whereas the chimpanzee at 13½ to 14½ months made an average error of 25.9 degrees. An 8-year-old child tested in the same way made an average error of 15 degrees. Observations by Kuckuk (1936) on auditory distance perception in young bears are of note.

Olfaction and Gustation. Evidence concerning olfactory and gustatory sensitivity n young animals is given in Table 1 under he appropriate headings. Techniques adequate for measuring olfaction in young animals unable to make decisive motor responses have not been worked out. Pfaffman's technique (1936) for studying gustatory sensitivity in young animals deserves special mention. The number of sucking responses which a young animal makes to various solutions is recorded graphically. Using young kittens, Pfaffman reports differential sensitivity to salt and milk at 1 day. The 10-day-old animal discriminates solutions of salt and bitter and shows some sensitivity to solutions of sweet and sour. Comments upon the responses of the young chimpanzee to gustatory and olfactory stimuli are given by the Kelloggs (1933).

Touch, Pain, Temperature, and Kinesthesis. Since nearly all young animals observed seem to be sensitive to tactile stimulation (see Table 1), a study of the ontogeny of such responses must deal with the fetal organism. It is probable that thigmotactic responses play a large part in the huddling behavior of young animals. James (1952a, 1952b), for example, carefully observed newborn puppies and mechanically recorded their movements toward other puppies, the mother animal, and decoy objects. Tactile stimuli appeared to give direction to their movements.

Few references concerning tactual localization in the young animal appear in the literature. The Kelloggs' (1933) tests, in which a blunt pencil was applied to the body of a young chimpanzee at 10 months, show that the animal makes almost perfect localizing responses. The animal appeared to be very sensitive to tickling. A young chimpanzee which was raised from 4 weeks to 31 months by enclosing the limbs in cardboard cylinders showed, according to Nissen, Chow, and Semmes (1951) some deficiencies in tactual-motor coordination. The animal had difficulty in bringing the fingers to a stimulated region of the body such as the head. It also had difficulty learning to discriminate the position of two widely separated tactual pressure stimuli. In a visual discrimination problem on size, form, and depth, however, the animal performed about as well as a normal animal.

Young animals show definite response to pain stimulation. (See Table 1 and also Anderson and Patrick, 1934.) The chimpanzee examined by the Kelloggs (1933) gave evidence of ability to localize the source of pain when tested at 10 months (p. 118).

Numerous investigators report that they believe temperature variations play a dominant part in the activities of young animals. Huddling in young rats, for example, is considered by Small (1899) to be a manifestation of the need for warmth, and he suggests, as do others, that the need for warmth may be basic in socialization. That variations in temperature influence the amount of spontaneous activity of young animals has been shown by Stier (1930).

Orientation of young animals on an inclined plane has been studied in the rat by Crozier and Pincus (1926, 1927b, 1928, 1929a, 1929b, 1931a, 1931b, 1932a, 1932b, 1933) and by Pincus (1927); in mice by Crozier and Oxnard (1927); in the guinea pig by Upton (1930, 1932) and Elliott and Stavsky (1933); and in the kitten by Stavsky (1932).

Motor Development

A number of observations on the motor development of young animals are summarized in Table 1. For detailed descriptions of the motor development of specific animals the reader is referred to the investigations listed in the section on the behavior of the newborn animal. See also the description of reflexes in puppies

(Bahrs, 1927); other discussions of locomotion in young animals (Hatt, 1931; Kennard, 1938; Beach, 1939); placing reactions in young animals (Tang, 1935; Warkentin and Smith, 1937); air-righting reflexes (Carmichael, 1934; Anderson and Patrick, 1934; Warkentin and Carmichael, 1939); grasping in young animals (Richter, 1931); handedness in rats (Wentworth, 1938); general activity of young rats (Slonaker, 1907, 1912); and persistence of sucking behavior (Lashley, 1914; Richter, 1925; Courthial, 1929; Ross, 1951).

A comparison of the development of motor functions in the infant chimpanzee and the human infant may be made by referring to the table compiled by Shirley (1931), to which Jacobsen, Jacobsen, and Yoshioka (1932) have appended the age of appearance of the behavior item in question for the young chimpanzee they observed. The first number refers to the age of appearance for the human infant, and the second to the age for the chimpanzee. (See Table 2.)

The young chimpanzee raised by the Kelloggs (1933) had passed through the stages of locomotion noted by the Jacobsens and Yoshioka except the final one of erect walking when she was first observed by them at 7½ months of age (pp. 71 ff.). Further development of climbing, jumping, and skipping occurred, and from the descriptions of these activities it appears that they reached a high level of proficiency comparable with the maturation and strength of the young chimpanzee.

The observations of the Jacobsens and Yoshioka (1932) on the development of manipulation in the young chimpanzee are worthy of more elaborate description, for they present a direct comparison with one of the more complex motor developments of the human infant. The young chimpanzee shows reflex grasping at birth, continuation of the ability to hang by one arm

TABLE 2

MOTOR DEVELOPMENT OF HUMAN INFANT AND YOUNG CHIMPANZEE

(From Jacobsen, Jacobsen, and Yoshioka, 1932, as adapted from Shirley, 1931)

1. Progress toward creeping goes through the following stages:
   a. Lifting the head, chin free, when on the stomach; (3/3).
   b. Lifting the head, chest free, when on the stomach; (9/5).
   c. Knee pushing or swimming; (25/7).
   d. Rolling; (29/8–10).
   e. Rocking, pivoting, worming along; method of making progress; (37/11).
   f. Scooting backward by using the hands.*
   g. Creeping forward.*
2. Progress assuming an upright posture goes through the following stages:
   a. Lifting the head when lying on the back; (15/5).
   b. Sitting alone momentarily; (25/12).
   c. Sitting alone; (31/13).
   d. Standing holding to furniture; (42/15).
   e. Pulling self to standing position by means of furniture; (47/15).
   f. Sitting from standing position.*
3. Progress toward walking goes through the following stages:
   a. An early period of stepping.†
   b. Standing with support of a person.†
   c. Walking with help, led by a person; (45/17).
   d. Standing alone; (62/20).
   e. Walking alone; (64/25–29).

* Did not appear for the chimpanzee.
† Adequate tests not made for chimpanzee.

(in contrast with its waning in the human infant), reaching without grasp during the fifth week, hand play and thumb and toe sucking in the seventh week, reaching and grasping during the eighth week, and further development of reaching and grasping during the succeeding weeks. The animal's use of its mouth and its feet in reaching and grasping is noted by the authors. The descriptions of these authors and the comments by the Kelloggs (1933) concerning the very fine manipulations made with the lips by the chimpanzee Gua (p. 59) and the loss of certain skills in foot grasping by Gua after she had worn shoes (p. 237) indicate that under normal conditions the use of these members is more persistent and reaches a higher level of development in the chimpanzee than in the child, although mouth grasping and foot reaching do occur in the human infant. Significant in the manipulations of the chimpanzee is the level of proficiency to which they attain so that the animal is able to perform such skilled acts as guiding a spoon to the mouth (twenty-first week), removing a lid from a small can (twenty-eighth week), holding a nursing-bottle in each hand (thirtieth week), and walking erectly while carrying two small objects (forty-fourth week).

In the series of tests with common objects which the Kelloggs used in comparing the prehension of the child and the chimpanzee, the child excelled the chimpanzee in all but the handling of the envelope, which they both were able to do satisfactorily (pp. 61–62).

Considerable interest has been attached to the development of motor reactions in young animals through correlative neurological studies. It is not intended to treat this topic in detail here, but a few of the studies will be mentioned.

The study of the "electrically excitable" motor areas of the cortex has led to some observations with regard to the correlation of excitability and genetic development of certain motor reactions. The reader is referred to Huber (1934) for an historical review of this problem in which reference is made to the work of Soltmann (1876), Tarchanoff (1878), Ferrier (1880), Paneth (1885), Mills (1898), Michailow (1910),

Bechterew (1911), Weed and Langworthy (1925, 1926), and Langworthy (1927), among others. Most of these studies have indicated that excitability of the cortex occurs some days after birth with the areas associated with the hindlimbs and facial regions excitable later than those areas associated with the forelimbs. The conclusions listed below are ones to be found in the literature.

1. There is a tendency for the appearance of excitability of forelimb areas before hindlimb areas.

2. There is an increase in the number of excitable points with age.

3. The threshold of excitability is higher for younger animals and decreases with age.

4. First movements so elicited are of the whole limb, and movement of discrete segments occurs later.

5. Correlation of development of function with "electrical excitability" of the cortex is difficult to appraise at present.

Although these conclusions probably hold in general, there is good reason to believe that some of the data upon which they are based will be found to be inexact. For example, Henry and Woolsey (1943) have repeated the work on the kitten, using 60-cycle sine-wave stimulation and exploring the cortex of the kitten in greater detail. They find, contrary to results of previous workers, that electrical stimulation elicits responses in the newborn animal from all the principal motor foci which are identifiable for the adult animal. It would seem that crucial data should be sought for the fetal animal. Kennard and McCulloch (1942) have examined the excitability of the cortex of a 3-week-old *Macaca mulatta*. Responses were more easily elicited in the face, less easily in the hand, and not at all in the leg. Relatively high voltages were required, and the responses were characterized as less discrete and slower in execution and cessation than those of an adult animal.

Attempts at correlating behavioral development with the myelinization of the nervous system have not given conclusive results. Watson (1903) and Angulo y González (1929), for example, have not found such a correlation. Tilney and Casamajor (1924) and Langworthy (1929), on the other hand, suggest that myelinization occurs before the functional development of the parts.

Windle (1930) reports an increase in the density of nerve fibers in the spinal cord with increasing motor performance of the kitten.

Studies of the bioelectric phenomena of the central nervous system may in time give additional evidence concerning relationships between behavioral and neural development. Kornmüller's (1935) work and that of Jasper, Bridgman, and Carmichael (1937) are pioneer in this field.

Studies of the effect of brain lesions upon the behavior of the young animal and its subsequent behavior have extended the correlation between neurological and behavioral developments still further. Brooks and Peck (1940), removing the cortex of young rats during the first 5 days of postnatal life, found that ablation of the area of the cortex which for adult rats is the sensory motor area renders the placing and hopping reactions of these animals, when tested several months later, deficient to the same extent that it does those of the adult animal. Kennard (1936, 1938) has observed the effect of lesions made in the motor and premotor areas of the cortex in young monkeys upon their later motor performances. The age of the animal is one of the most important factors determining the deficiencies resulting from the lesion, inasmuch as the loss is not as severe in young animals.

Learning and Memory

As yet the work on the modifiability of response and the permanence of this change in the young animal is somewhat fragmentary, but there are a few problems such as the relationship of maze learning and age which have received more attention, although the results are not completely conclusive.

Incidental Observations. A number of incidental observations of learning in young animals can be found in the literature, but only a few items will be reported here. The feeding situation often provides interesting observations concerning the learning ability of young animals. Dove (1935) notes that the young of animals learn early in life to follow the mother and to eat the same type of food. Foley (1935) comments that, when he entered the laboratory in the morning before feeding time, the sound of his footsteps and the closing of the icebox door would elicit the "hunger-anticipation" cry of the young monkey he observed. The reader will profit from the discussions of the Kelloggs (1933) concerning the incidental learning of Gua in the human environment (pp. 188 ff.). The chimpanzee reared by the Hayeses (1951) since its birth grew up in an environment which, like that of the child, required considerable learning. The baby chimp learned early to grasp the thumb of the hand which held her feeding-bottle and thus pull the bottle toward herself. Later she learned to pull a string to which the bottle was attached. As she grew older, she learned such activities as playing peek-a-boo, imitating adults by blowing a whistle, clapping her hands, stringing a wooden bead on a string, and turning a key.

Maze Learning. There are a number of reports of maze-learning studies in animals of varying ages. Watson (1903) reports that young rats learn a maze more readily than adult animals. Yerkes (1909) found that 1- to 2-month-old mice learned less readily than 10-month-old animals. Hubbert's (1915) results indicate that younger rats learn better than older animals. Liu's (1928) animals 30 and 45 days old made the poorest scores, whereas animals 75 days old made the best scores. Animals older than 75 days performed less well. Stone (1929a, 1929b) reports that young animals 30 to 75 days old make superior scores. Biel (1939, 1940) found in a study of maze learning in young rats 16 to 29 days old that the older animals' performance is significantly superior to that of the younger ones. In an unpublished study of the writer it was found that no large differences in the ability of guinea pigs to run a maze are correlated with age. The younger animals were more active than the older ones, but they did not make consistently superior performances.

Possibly some of the apparent discrepancies in these studies can be explained partially in terms of different motivation at different ages. The investigations of Margolin and Bunch (1940) on the relationship between age and strength of hunger motivation indicated that young rats (30 to 40 days of age) in an obstruction box apparatus crossed the grid a greater number of times than did the postpubescent or the adult animals.

Comparing the maze-learning ability of normal adult rats, adult rats hemidecorticated at 21 days of age, and animals decorticated in adulthood, Tsang (1937a) reports that greater deficiencies exist for the animals older at the time of operation than for the ones which were younger. He reports that a loss of less than 10 per cent of the cortex in the adult animal is as serious as a loss of 40 per cent in the young animal. Hemidecortication in which a diagonal decortication (that is, anterior and posterior quadrants of different hemi-

spheres) was made had a greater detrimental effect than a unilateral decortication.

Other Problems. Golubeva (1939) was able to condition motor responses to acoustic stimuli in newborn guinea pigs. Fuller, Easler, and Banks (1950) were able to condition puppies of 18 to 21 days of age to light, sound, and odorous stimuli. On the basis of conditioned response reactions, they found that light is effective around 16 days, sound about 19 days, and odor and contact at birth.

Yerkes (1909) reports that young dancing mice 1 month old learn to make a white-black discrimination in fewer trials than do animals 4, 7, and 10 months old. Learning of a light-dark discrimination by kittens given differing amount of electrical shock for incorrect choice has been investigated by Dodson (1915). From his results it is indicated that the relationship of strength of stimulus to speed of learning depends upon the difficulty of the problem, so that with a difficult problem a medium shock is superior to a strong one, whereas with a simple problem a strong shock is definitely superior to a medium or a weak one.

Shuey (1932) found little evidence that kittens between 11 and 12 weeks old at the beginning of training can perform a simple alternation problem consisting of pressing two plates of the Jenkins problem box, although one of the nine animals tested seemed to have established a fairly consistent habit. All the kittens tested by Shuey (1931) in the Jenkins problem box learned three steps. A number of other steps were learned by some of the animals, but too few animals were used to show how significant the scores are.

For other observations of learning see Kinnaman (1902), Allen (1904), Hamilton (1911), and Kuckuk (1936).

Some reference is made in the literature to studies of immediate or delayed memory in young animals. The Kelloggs (1933) carried out a delayed-reaction experiment with their son and the young chimpanzee when the subjects were at the approximate ages of 10½ to 12 months and 8 to 10 months, respectively. Under the circumstances of their test situation, they found that the child could delay for 5 minutes, but that at 10 minutes he made errors in about half the trials. The animal, on the other hand, satisfactorily responded to the shorter time intervals and responded correctly in 7 out of 10 trials for an interval of 30 minutes. It appears that the chimpanzee could delay longer than the child in these circumstances. It would be interesting to know the whole course of development for the animal and the child.

Jacobsen, Taylor, and Haslerud (1936) investigated the question of immediate recall after frontal lesions in young monkeys. They found this to be permanently abolished after lesions in the young animal as well as in the older animals.

Effect of Food Deprivation on Learning. The question whether food deprivation in the very young animal has any deleterious effects upon subsequent learning has been studied by several investigators. Biel (1938) examined the effects upon the maze-learning behavior of young animals of severe inanition brought about by subjecting them to reduced food intake. He found no deleterious effect in their learning of the Warden U-maze or the Stone multiple-T maze. Using a multiple-T water maze, he found that rats subjected to food deprivation performed less efficiently at a later age than normally fed rats (1939).

Deprivation of vitamin B is shown by several workers to be detrimental to subsequent maze learning (Maurer and Tsai, 1929, 1930; Bernhardt, 1934; Maurer, 1935a, Poe, Poe, and Muenzinger, 1936, 1937; and Bernhardt and Herbert, 1937). Vitamin B_2 deficiency beginning at 2 weeks

gives less retardation than B_1 or B complex deficit according to Muenzinger, Poe, and Poe (1937), although Maurer (1935b) showed retardation when the deprivation is begun earlier than at 2 weeks of age. The animals show greater deprivation when they are given a diet lacking vitamin B during the nursing period than at a later age. O'Neill (1949) repeated the work on vitamin B deficiency, using controlled amounts of vitamin B_1. He found that larger amounts of thiamine led to improved performance in learning a water maze. If the rats received an excess of B_1, no further improvement was indicated by the addition of other elements of the vitamin B complex.

Biel and Wickens (1941) have shown that rats deprived of vitamin B_1 from approximately 1 week of age were when compared with normal animals at 7 to 10 weeks of age significantly poorer in the conditioning of eyelid responses.

Acute vitamin A shortage does not lead to as severe retardation in nursing rats as a vitamin B deficiency. The number of trials for learning a maze is not significantly different from the learning of normals, although the time scores are reliably different, indicating loss of speed (Maurer, 1935c).

The effects of several other types of food have been studied using young animals as subjects. The maze performance of young rats fed a diet of whole pasteurized cow's milk is not different from that of normally fed controls (Maurer, 1935d). Porter, Griffin, and Stone (1951) found that groups of rats, 29 days and older, fed diets which were chosen to affect glutamic acid metabolism did not show significant differences in performance on an 8-unit Warden water maze. Young albino rats fed a diet arranged to produce an amino acid deficiency learned a simple tunnel maze somewhat better but not significantly so than littermate controls (Bevan and Freeman, 1952). The control animals were fed a standard diet restricted in weight to that of the experimental animals' previous day's diet. On relearning, the control group performed reliably better.

Effect of Electroconvulsive Shock on Learning. According to experiments by Eriksen, Porter, and Stone (1948), the learning of the Stone multiple-T maze by rats given one electroconvulsive shock daily during the age period from 20 to 30 days and trained after a 10- (or 20-) day post recovery period for 15 days on the maze was somewhat inferior to that of litter-mate controls which had received no shock treatment. Although no gross behavioral differences were noted, the differences were statistically significant when the data were analyzed. Animals similarly shocked at the same early age but given 74 to 90 days post-shock rest before being trained on the maze (Porter, Stone, and Eriksen, 1948) were inferior in performance to a control group. Whether the decrement is a function of the age of the animal at the time of shock has not been determined, but, as these investigators point out, the problem should be systematically studied.

Similar results were obtained by Bernberg (1951) with slightly older rats (35 to 44 days) at the time of receiving electroconvulsive shock or electronarcosis treatment. The animals which had undergone either the electroconvulsive shock or the electronarcosis treatment did not learn the Stone multiple-T maze as well as the control animals.

Effect of Anoxia on Learning. Studies on the effect of anoxia at birth or shortly thereafter upon the behavior of animals provide experimental evidence to consider along with clinical studies of human infants. Becker (1950) and Becker and Donnell (1952) found that guinea pigs asphyxiated at birth and tested in a simple alternation maze were less active than litter-mate controls and were inferior to them in learning

ability and retentive capacity. Meier and Bunch (1950) investigated the effect of a 30-minute period of oxygen deprivation undergone within 3 hours of birth upon learning, relearning, and reversing a position habit. In initial learning and relearning when animals were between 75 and 100 days of age, the litter-mate controls performed better but the difference was not statistically reliable. In learning to reverse the position habit, the controls were superior at a 2-day interval, but the anoxic animals were superior in reversing the habit after an interval of 14 days. Armitage (1952) found that offspring of female rats which had been given varying dosages of barbiturates at the time of parturition were inferior in learning and reasoning tests to normal animals when tested at 90 days of age.

Infantile Experiences as Determinants of Adult Behavior. One of the important questions for which partial answers can be supplied from the behavior of animals is the effect of infantile experiences upon later adult behavior. The problem has its significance in that this basic psychoanalytic doctrine can be subjected to controlled experimental analysis. One specific experiment on the topic was carried out by Hunt and his co-workers (1941, 1947) on the effect of infantile feeding frustration upon adult hoarding in the albino rat. In these experiments young rats shortly after weaning were subjected for 15 days to feedings consisting of 10-minute group feedings of a wet mash at irregular intervals varying from 9 to 36 hours. Litter-mate controls had wet mash available to them continuously. After these 15 days the animals were given unlimited food. When the animals were about 7 months old, they were tested by allowing them to obtain and hoard food pellets for 30 minutes on each of 3 successive days. All the animals, including the experimental and the control rats, were given a limited diet (adult feeding frustration situation) for 5 days, which was followed by 4 days of trials of 30 minutes in which they were allowed to hoard. The results showed that the animals hoarded little, even the ones that had been subjected to feeding frustration in infancy. After the adult feeding frustration, the experimental animals hoarded more than the control animals. Hunt (1941) interprets the results in terms of learning theory.

McKelvey and Marx (1951) did not corroborate the earlier results of Hunt. Their two groups of experimental animals, rats deprived of food or water for 15 days just after weaning, did not hoard significantly more than the control animals when they were tested during trial periods after they had reached 130 days of age. Food-deprived males did hoard significantly more on post-deprivation tests than did control males. In an effort to reconcile the conflicting results on infantile deprivation and hoarding, Marx (1952) further tested the hypothesis that increased adult food hoarding in animals deprived during infancy may come about as a result of an increased rate of eating. Significant differences in rate of eating between rats deprived in infancy and control rats were found for the first day of the adult hoarding trials, but by the end of the 7-day deprivation trial period the differences had disappeared. There were no differences in amount of hoarding.

In the experiments of Porter, Webster, and Licklider (1951) it was found that young post-weaning rats (26 and 33 days of age) hoarded very few pellets whereas these same animals after 2 days of food deprivation hoarded on an average almost 10 pellets per 30-minute test. Compared with the scores of older animals, both pre-deprivation and post-deprivation scores are much lower for the young animal. There is an increasing amount of hoarding as the rats are older when first tested.

In Kahn's (1951) experiment on the effect of severe defeat at various age levels on the aggressive behavior of mice, trained fighter mice were allowed to attack non-trained mice. Three groups of mice, 21, 35, and 60 or more days of age, were the experimental animals. Thirty days after the attacks by the fighter mice, both the experimental animal and its litter-mate control were subjected to a test for aggressiveness against another mouse. In general the study indicated that at maturity the aggressive behavior of the animals which were young at the time of the fighter attacks was less than that of the animals which were mature, suggesting that this type of early traumatic experience has more effect upon later behavior than a traumatic experience later in life or at maturity.

Another type of infantile experience and its relation to later behavior are reported by Hall and Whiteman (1951). They studied the effect of an intense sound stimulus administered to mice at the ages of 4 to 7 days by testing them in several different ways at a later age. In the first open-field test the control animals showed markedly fewer signs of emotional reaction than the experimental animals. In the stovepipe test the performance of the control animals was somewhat superior. Both experimental and control animals showed fewer emotional signs with more experience in the test situations. Griffiths and Stringer (1952), giving young rats in their experimental groups intense auditory stimulation, rapid rotation, extremes of temperature, or shock on an electric grid from the first day of life, found no statistically reliable differences between the experimental and control animals. They conclude that "subjection to intense stimulation during infancy does not measurably affect adult behavior in the rat" (p. 305).

Competition for food by adult mice which either had been trained to compete for food when hungry for 7 one-a-day trials beginning at 29 days of age or allowed one single experience in competition at 33 days of age was studied by Fredericson (1951). He found that, when the animals were retested at 72 days of age, they competed over food even though they were not hungry. Littermate controls raised under conditions which did not allow competition for food did not compete for food on similar tests when not hungry.

The effect of early experience on learning and problem-solving behavior is shown in a number of studies which have concerned the effect of a varied or of a limited environment on the animal. Hebb (1947) in exploratory studies showed that animals raised in a limited environment performed more poorly in simple problem-solving tasks than animals raised as pets without as much cage restriction. Animals blinded late in life performed somewhat better in maze learning and problem solving than those blinded early in life. Bingham and Griffiths (1952) concluded that young rats reared in a richer environment (a room containing such items as tunnels and inclined planes) were superior in learning the Warner-Warden maze and an inclined-plane maze to animals reared in small "squeeze" boxes or regular laboratory cages. Forgays and Forgays (1952) likewise found that rats reared in a free-environmental situation from 26 days until about 90 days of age were distinctly superior to rats reared in mesh cages. Rats reared in a free environment which contained "playthings" in the form of simple wooden and metal structures were superior to other animals reared in a free environment. Hymovitch (1952) reported that rats reared in free-environment situations proved superior on a closed-field test given at maturity to animals reared in standard cages, small mesh cages, stovepipe cages, or activity wheels. These groups did not differ significantly in performance on a 10-unit enclosed T-maze. Furthermore, early free-environment experience proved superior to late free-environment experience. Although late-blinded rats performed better on a closed-field test than early-blinded rats, the differences in mean error scores between the groups were not significant.

In summary, the studies described here have confirmed the fact that infantile experiences may affect later behavior. However, this effect is not necessarily inevitable, and it is quite possible that the animal will react after initial readjustment in a manner similar to that of the nonstimulated animal.

Emotional Behavior

Evidence for the development of emotion in young animals will be limited in this review almost entirely to a discussion of emotional development in subhuman primates. Avoidance responses and aggressive responses are, of course, to be noted in other animals. Small (1899), for example, notes that fear in young rats develops considerably after the onset of visual and auditory functions, and he believes that the young give evidence of pleasurable emotions, for they "show signs of satisfaction when hunger and the desire for warmth are satisfied" (p. 98). Kellogg (1931), however, did not find evidence of fear of a moving stimulus in young rats (4 to 5 weeks old).

The aggressive behavior of cats toward rats has often been cited as an instance of instinctive behavior. Early observations showed that kittens do kill rats (Yerkes and Bloomfield, 1910), but more recent studies have shown certain variations in rat-killing behavior in young kittens. Rogers (1932) noted that the young kitten reacts differently to the rat, depending upon whether olfactory, visual, or tactual cues are dominant and whether or not the animal is hungry. The 5-week-old kitten observed by McDougall and McDougall (1927) did kill wild mice, but it did not in the time of the observations kill several white rats with which it was caged from time to time. Kuo (1930) showed that animals reared in isolation killed less frequently than those reared with an adult in a rat-killing environment. Some animals which had previously not killed rats did so after they had seen this done, whereas animals reared with rats did not kill a rat like their cage-mate and, when allowed to watch another cat kill a rat, still failed to make frequent responses of this nature. Studies by Kuo (1938) show that, when kittens were reared together and with two cage-mate rats, they very seldom killed a cage-mate although they frequently ate a shaved rat or the young of the cage-mate rats (as did the adult rats themselves at times).

Young wood rats, according to observations of Richardson (1942b), when their eyes were yet unopened reacted toward snakes as inanimate objects. When the young were 26 days old (eyes open 11 days), they gave an alarm thump when confronted with the snake. Even older animals gave a more typical fear response, although they had had no previous experience with snakes.

The monkey observed by Lashley and Watson (1913) showed avoidance responses to such noises as rustling paper at 3 weeks of age. Tinklepaugh and Hartman (1932) observed that, as long as the young monkeys under 2 weeks of age were clinging to some object, loud noises or stimuli which might lead to fear behavior were not effective. If the animal was prevented from clinging or grasping, however, it showed some fear. Thwarting of the movement of the animal resulted in anger responses. Bingham (1927) reports that one young chimpanzee which he observed gave evidence of fear of the male parent by running to the female parent and clinging to her when the adult male was excited.

Several studies are reported from the Yale laboratories with regard to the development of emotional behavior in the chimpanzee. Jacobsen, Jacobsen, and Yoshioka (1932) report that patterns of fear, anger, mild fear, timidity, and mild excitement may be distinguished for the young chimpanzee. Patterns of fear and anger, although not well differentiated at first, could be observed from birth. The early fear responses were indicated by "clenching of feet and hands, drawing up of the arms and legs, and a tendency to cling to objects; by wrinkling of the face and retraction of the lips; and by a high-pitched crescendo scream" (p. 63). This behavior was elicited according to the authors in several situations: "(1) picking up the infant from the crib, a sudden light touch on various parts of the body, and sudden jarring of the crib; (2) complete removal of support when the infant was held in the arms; and (3) sudden intense noises" (p. 63). Some modifications of the response occurred during the first 3 months, and later, with the development of progression, the animal was able to retreat from the situation.

Anger as a response during the first 6 months was difficult to distinguish from fear. What the authors consider a clear-cut instance of anger was observed during the twelfth week when the animal rejected a nursing-bottle after she had eaten. Thereafter on several occasions the chimpanzee screamed angrily when left alone. Later, anger was often set up by some activity of the animal which was interrupted or forced upon her.

The Jacobsens and Yoshioka differentiate fear from mild fear in that:

(1) Mild fear or timidity did not appear until the fourth or fifth month, when the infant showed marked disturbance if a stranger approached her crib or attempted

to handle her; (2) there was whimpering rather than screaming; (3) while the animal retreated under both conditions, in timidity the retreat was less rapid and less intense; the object was observed more or less continuously during withdrawal in contrast to the headlong flight in fear; (4) timidity was more readily overcome than fear [pp. 69–70].

Mild excitement is described by the Jacobsens and Yoshioka as indicated by

(1) approach toward or manipulation of the stimulating object or person, in contrast to withdrawal in timidity; (2) marked freedom of movement in contrast to the tension of fear and anger; and (3) usually vocalization of a distinctive type, namely, the soft bark which later was replaced upon occasion by rapid inspiration and expiration without laryngeal sound production [p. 70].

Yerkes and Yerkes (1936) observed the behavior of chimpanzees of different ages when a series of animate and inanimate objects were placed before them. The youngest chimpanzees, ranging in age from 1 to 2 years, were in general less responsive than slightly older or adult animals. These workers point out the importance of perceptual development and experience in the genesis of the avoidance response, and they suggest as possible stimulus characteristics predominant in the response: visual movement, intensity, suddenness, and rapidity of change in stimulus.

Haslerud's (1938) study of the effect of animate and inanimate objects in a food-securing situation upon the animals previously observed by Yerkes and Yerkes (1936) indicates that the younger animals showed less avoidance of an inanimate object than they did of an animate object, but the adults showed only slightly less avoidance of the inanimate object than of its animate counterpart.

McCulloch and Haslerud (1939) observed a chimpanzee, reared in isolation, in the food-approach situation. At the first test, at 7 months of age, it was found that only moving objects elicited avoidance responses. Definite avoidance responses were made to a live alligator and a bouncing ball. Some aggression was shown toward a bouncing ball, but on the whole very little response was of the aggressive type. Some months later, at the age of 15 months, the chimpanzee showed more avoidance behavior and more aggressive behavior to a wider range of stimuli. The animal no longer avoided objects on the basis of movement alone, however.

The emotional behavior of the infant ape, Gua, is described by the Kelloggs (1933) as being predominantly fear behavior, but including also evidence of anger, mild anger, jealousy, anxiety, and pleasant emotions. At first the principal conditions for eliciting fear behavior were loss of support and being alone, but later the suddenness or abruptness of occurrence of strange objects or persons presented visually, auditorially, or tactually called forth an avoidance response. Often the animal retreated toward the human person in her environment.

Yerkes and Tomilin (1935) report relatively little behavior of sexual significance on the part of infant chimpanzees. They state that "there are instances, but the surprising limitation in variety as well as in frequency suggests that they are exceptions" (p. 339).

Social Behavior

The study of the development of social behavior in young animals presents a very fertile field for investigations inasmuch as in mammals so many different patterns of adult social behavior seem to exist. To what extent these patterns are modifiable is an interesting question. Since the possibility of many mammals' existing apart from the female adult during the neonatal period is very slight—although a large and well-developed animal such as the guinea pig might occasionally live [1]—complete isolation is not likely. Many mammalian young, however, can be almost completely isolated so that an exact study of the development of the animal under known conditions of social stimulation can be made.

The complexity of social relationships between young and adult animals varies considerably. There are some mammals where the main "social" factors seem to be need for warmth and food on the part of the young, the guinea pig representing this level of development. Still other animals are born in such a weak state that additional "social" factors must be sought in the behavior of the maternal animal, for the offspring are too immature to react in any fashion completely adequate for maintenance of life. On the other hand, some animals, such as the opossum, are extremely immature at birth but are able to make adequate adjustments without the aid of the adult (Hartman, 1920). At later ages the young too give evidence of reactions to the adult which are social in character, although, as soon as self-sufficiency is reached and weaning occurs, there may be no longer any special social bonds between the animals. Still other animals, extremely immature at birth, are cared for by the female until the young are weaned and sometimes longer, but reciprocal social relationships exist for a period of time after this. In contrast to the normal care of the newborn by the adult mother are the statements found from time to time in the literature that the adult mother often kills some or all of the newborn animals. See,

[1] The writer has raised several guinea pigs in isolation without forced feedings of any sort, although food was left within the cage. Mortality is high.

for example, the study of Pearson and Bassett (1946). Instances of maternal care of the young in various species may be found in the surveys of Mitchell (1912), Lang (1925), Yerkes and Yerkes (1929), and Causey and Waters (1936), as well as in many of the references cited previously in the section on the behavior of the newborn animal.

For the typical laboratory animals a number of observations concerning maternal care of the young have been made. The adult female rat makes preparations in the form of nest building before parturition, collects the young into the nest, and hovers over them, allowing them to suckle (Kinder, 1927; Sturman-Hulbe and Stone, 1929; Wiesner and Sheard, 1933). Retrieving behavior occurs for a period of several weeks until the animals start crawling in and out of the nest at about 17 to 20 days of age (Sturman-Hulbe and Stone, 1929). Maternal behavior of rats with cortical lesions is inferior to that of normal animals, according to Beach (1938), but animals operated upon in infancy are usually superior to adult operates.

Other animals, such as the guinea pig, clean the young after birth in a more or less haphazard fashion, allow the young to suckle, but seem to make no attempts to gather the young about them although the young are usually to be found in the near vicinity of the adult. Seward and Seward (1940), in a study of the maternal drive of adult guinea pigs, found that the animal crosses to a litter in a shorter time just after parturition than it does several weeks later. Seward (1940), attempting to analyze more systematically the many factors which go to make up filial behavior in the guinea pig, found that the average time for crossing to the incentive compartment decreases after the animals are 1 week old with little difference in the number of crossings in a period of 10 minutes for either the unfed or the fed group. The difference in time of running to an empty compartment and to the mother is in favor of the adult guinea pig as an incentive. Seward suggests two factors as playing the major part in filial behavior: (1) a biological factor, the need for warmth in addition to food, and (2) a social factor, the result of conditioning to the mother. Evidence fully supporting the theory is not given, but the study is a further step in applying adequate techniques to developmental problems.

Little behavior of the paternal sort has ordinarily been observed in accounts of social behavior, although occasionally observations such as those of Horner (1947) have been noted. But it must be remembered that many of our studies of those animals in which such behavior might be expected have been made under conditions of isolation or under laboratory conditions where natural groupings of the animals did not occur. It is well to remember these limitations in interpreting our knowledge of the normal social development of the young animal. For a discussion of the relationship between parent and offspring in which a wide survey of animal groups is made, see Mitchell (1912), and for a classification of social groupings see Alverdes (1927).

A detailed study of the development, especially social development, of puppies has been reported by Scott and Marston (1950). Seventy-three animals of seventeen litters and seven breeds were observed under very carefully controlled conditions of rearing. For four periods of development, neonatal until opening of eyes, transition until leaving of nest, period of socialization until weaning, and juvenile until maturity, they discuss social development under the general headings: (1) ingestive behavior, (2) eliminative behavior, (3) investigative behavior, (4) et-epimeletic behavior, (5) contactual behavior, and (6)

agonistic or conflict behavior. Allelomimetic behavior and sexual behavior are also included in the last two developmental periods.

Other studies on special aspects of social behavior in puppies include examination of dominance-submission differences in a competitive feeding situation (James, 1949) and social facilitation of eating (Ross and Ross, 1949a, 1949b).

Scott's (1945) observations on the social behavior of a small flock of domestic sheep were made over a period of 4 years under conditions in which there was a minimum of human interference. The early forms of social behavior include such activities as eating-nursing, shelter-seeking, and investigating. Later the young lambs join other lambs in a play consisting largely of immature forms of adult behavior.

Most complete details concerning the social relationships of young and adult subhuman primates come from the work of the Yale laboratories (see, for example, Yerkes and Tomilin, 1935). Carpenter's (1934) observations of young and female howling monkeys in their native habitat show that the young animals cling to and climb upon the adult and that the adult orients the infant toward her and prevents it from climbing too far, retrieves the infant when it falls, and seems to give it a certain amount of tuition as it grows older. The young react fairly specifically to their mothers after they are a few days old. Carpenter suggests that the strength of the social bonds between the adult and young reach their maximum at about 8 to 10 months and decline thereafter. (See also, for descriptions of the young primate, Lashley and Watson, 1913; Allesch, 1921; Bingham, 1927; and Tinklepaugh and Hartman, 1932.)

Evidences of maternal tuition in certain activities of the infant, such as Carpenter (1934) mentions, have been cited by other investigators. Yerkes and Tomilin (1935) comment with regard to this that "effects are achieved, whether or not intentionally, as result of example, request, command, prohibition, prevention" (p. 342).

Very little is known about the relationships among the adult male, adult female, juveniles, and young subhuman primates. Bingham (1927) observed a family of a male, a female, and an infant chimpanzee in its second year. He comments that the male animal neither interfered with the female and the child nor did he assume responsibility for the child. Carpenter's (1934) account of monkeys in their native habitat gives evidence of the concern of all animals in the group at the cries of a fallen young animal. (See also Yerkes, 1936.)

Likewise, little is known about the relationships of young animals to each other in a naturalistic situation. Carpenter (1934) comments upon the attempts of the juveniles in a group of howling monkeys to pull an infant away or to wedge themselves in a position near the adult. Tomilin and Yerkes (1935) report the activities of a pair of infant chimpanzee twins.

The social behavior of animals reared in isolation for a large part of their life is commented upon by Jaocbsen, Jacobsen, and Yoshioka (1932) and by Foley (1935).

Grooming behavior is probably very infrequent for the subhuman primate infant (Yerkes, 1933), but an instance of such is reported by the Jacobsens and Yoshioka (1932) for the chimpanzee in the thirty-ninth week.

Play. Considerable interest in the play of young animals has been evidenced since the publication in 1896 of Groos's *The Play of Animals.* General comments on the subject can be found in Mitchell (1912), Beach (1945), and Schlosberg (1947), and a number of observations are reported below. Many young animals give evidence of play

behavior of the running, jumping, climbing, biting sort. (See, for example, Mills, 1898; Small, 1899; and Allen, 1904.) This type of activity becomes more easily identifiable in the more developed animals. Scott (1945) classifies various sorts of playful behavior in lambs as sexual, fighting, and allelomimetic such as running together, gamboling, and game playing. Foley (1935) reports play behavior in the young monkey consisting of running, jumping, and leaping upon objects. An increase in play behavior occurred after 18 months, when the animal was placed with other animals. Instead of a self-directed play which had previously seemed to be the rule, the animal's activity now seemed to be externally directed. There may be some question whether this transfer resulted from the termination of the isolation of the animal, for Lashley and Watson (1913) noted behavior which Foley considers comparable in a young monkey before 15 weeks.

Carpenter (1934), in his observations of young howling monkeys, notes that the young animals may play alone or with small objects and at a later age may play with other animals in wrestling or chasing types of play. The play activity "rises to a maximum by the time the animal is classed as a juvenile 1, and following a period of development there is a rather sharp decline in the amount of play" (p. 79).

The Jacobsens and Yoshioka (1932) suggest the following analysis of play behavior in the chimpanzee they observed. They note *exploration, manipulation, and simple play,* which occurred infrequently during the first 2 months and developed into a tactile examination of objects during the third month. *Organized play,* "in which the animal organized diverse activities in relationship to a central point" (p. 72), was observed first during the sixth month. A third type of play, *bodily activity as play,* seems to have developed with the motor development of the animal. A fourth type, classed as *play and manipulation essentially social*, was evidenced in such behavior as the threatening and attacking responses with which the animal approached the human observers, a pet dog, and other infant chimpanzees.

Accounts of the play of the young chimpanzee reared in a human environment are given by the Kelloggs (1933) and C. Hayes (1951). The story of the play activities of the animal reared by the Kelloggs begins at the age of 7½ months and is illuminating with regard to the type of play entered into by a chimpanzee and a human child. The ape raised by the Hayeses grew up much as an "only" child in an environment as nearly like that provided for a human being as could be arranged. Both of these animals showed highly advanced play behavior, including physical activities like swinging, playing tag and peek-a-boo, and play with toys and objects appropriated for toys and the like.

For other descriptions of play activities, see Bingham (1927) and Yerkes and Tomilin (1935).

Vocalization. Most of the references to the behavior of young animals include some descriptions of the vocalizations of the animal—the birth cry, the cries of the young when not sucking, the cries occurring during play, startle cries, hunger cries, etc. Descriptions of the vocalizations of monkeys and chimpanzees, with some comment on the possible function of such vocalizations, are to be found in Jacobsen, Jacobsen, and Yoshioka (1932), Kellogg and Kellogg (1933), Carpenter (1934), Foley (1935), and Yerkes and Tomilin (1935). According to Yerkes and Tomilin, the infant chimpanzee's vocalizations include a shrill birth cry, cries of *uh-uh*, barks of *oo-oo*, whimpering, whining, shouting, and screaming. They believe the adult recognizes these cries not so much in terms of

the kind of vocalization as in their pitch, volume, and abruptness. The young animal seems to learn very slowly to react to the sounds and gestures of the adult, but it finally responds differentially to a great many sounds. The observations of the Kelloggs agree with those of Yerkes and Tomilin. Their observations further indicate that the young ape gives no evidence of learning the vocalizations of human beings but that the animal does respond quite definitely to some of the words of the human being.

One of the main projects to which the Hayeses (1950, 1951) devoted their attention was the development of language in the chimpanzee. As a very young animal, the chimpanzee, Viki, brought up in their home seldom made any sounds. Unlike the human infant, she never cried but did make the sound of *oo-oo, oo-oo*, which could turn into a scream if the animal were under severe stress such as falling. At 1 week Viki said the sound *uh-uh-uh-uh*, and she gave a chimpanzee bark at 5 weeks of age. She used the sound described as a food bark at 14 weeks. She also made other combinations of sounds, but these did not compare in frequency or variety with the babblings of babies. At 5 months, training was begun to get Viki to vocalize to the command "speak." At 10 months she made the sound of *ahhh* and reached for food. This was the sound she used in "asking" situations. Later by manipulation of the lips of the animal she was taught three words, *ma ma, papa,* and *cup*.

While Viki's vocalizations of sounds like those of the human adults with whom she lived were very limited, her understanding of sounds advanced much further. To be sure, responses were sometimes dependent upon the situation and did not always occur, even though the animal had previously responded quite correctly. In general, language development in the chimpanzee is limited. Hayes (1950) believes that "the chimpanzee's failure to talk is not due to inadequate speech organs or general intelligence, but rather to a neurological condition similar to aphasia" (p. 276).

Effect of Isolation. In one study on the effect of isolation upon social behavior Bayroff (1936) reared rats in isolation from the twentieth day to approximately the one hundred and fifteenth day. Using a technique designed to test whether the animal displayed any behavior indicating social preference, he found none indicated in his results. The technique used, however, while allowing a response of a social nature, also permitted the establishment of a positional habit on the part of the animal. Accordingly, Bayroff (1940) used another technique which made it necessary for rats swimming under water to reach the escape compartment first in order to be released. No significant differences appeared in the speed of swimming of animals reared in isolation after weaning from that of animals reared together. The experimenter concludes that "the nature of the early life is not the principal determiner of success in the competition" (p. 306).

Descriptive accounts of young primates reared in isolation are given by Jacobsen, Jacobsen, and Yoshioka (1932) and by Foley (1934).

Need for Further Work

The reader who has followed the course of this chapter has probably been impressed by several facts: (1) the accumulation of observations regarding the ontogenetic development of behavior in numerous mammalian groups; (2) the incompleteness of data and possible inaccuracy of some conclusions; (3) the growing number of experimental studies involving the young animal; and (4) the importance of knowledge in this field for the ultimate solution of certain insistent problems in genetic psychology. Considerable work remains yet to be done. Descriptive studies are by no means complete, and experimental studies utilizing precise methods and satisfactory quantitative measurements are relatively few. Yet these basic studies must be made before problems dealing with larger aspects of genetic psychology can be treated successfully.

There have been in the past few years additions to the research on young animals. Some descriptive reports have been made on the genetic development of domestic and typical laboratory animals and also on the growth of animals in their native habitats. Furthermore, more experimental studies have been undertaken, many of these in new areas of investigation, as, for example, the effects of nutritive material on behavior, electroconvulsive shock on later learning, natal anoxia on learning, and early experiences of various sorts upon later behavior. Some of this research has been directly initiated in response to the need for experimental data on topics of great import in child development for which data other than clinical records are not likely to become readily available.

Probably most adequately treated up to now is the development of motor responses in young animals. Here the responses are less difficult to observe, and several groups of scientific workers other than psychologists have been interested in the problem. Relatively lacking in experimental work, but yet providing richly provocative material for research, is the analysis of the perceptual responses of the young animal. Additional work is needed on the problems of learning, memory, and intelligence; and an increased interest and the use of more adequate techniques for observation should contribute further work upon the problems of emotional and social development.

Bibliography

Alcorn, J. R. 1940. Life history notes on the Piute ground squirrel. *J. Mammal., 21,* 160–170.

Allen, J. 1904. The associative process of the guinea pig. *J. Comp. Neurol., 14,* 293–359.

Allesch, G. I. 1921. Geburt und erste Lebensmonate eines Schimpansen. *Naturwiss., 9,* 774–776.

Alverdes, F. 1927. *Social life in the animal world.* New York: Harcourt, Brace.

Anderson, A. C., and J. R. Patrick. 1934. Some early behavior patterns in the white rat. *Psychol. Rev., 41,* 480–496.

Angulo y González, A. W. 1929. Is myelinogeny an absolute index of behavioral capability? *J. Comp. Neurol., 48,* 459–464.

Armitage, S. G. 1952. The effects of barbiturates on the behavior of rat offspring as measured in learning and reasoning situations. *J. Comp. Physiol. Psychol., 45,* 146–152.

Avery, G. T. 1928. Responses of foetal guinea pigs prematurely delivered. *Genet. Psychol. Monogr., 3,* 245–331.

Bahrs, A. M. 1927. Notes on the reflexes of puppies in the first six weeks after birth. *Amer. J. Physiol., 82,* 51–55.

Barrington, B. A., Jr. 1942. Description of birth and young of the pocket gopher, *Geomys floridanus. J. Mammal., 23,* 428–430.

Bayroff, A. G. 1936. The experimental social behavior of animals: I. The effect of early isolation of white rats on their later reactions to other white rats as measured by two periods of free choices. *J. Comp. Psychol., 21,* 67–81.

——. 1940. The experimental social behavior of animals: II. The effect of early isolation of white rats on their competition in swimming. *J. Comp. Psychol., 29,* 293–306.

Beach, F. A., Jr. 1938. The neural basis of neonate behavior: II. Relative effects of partial decortication in adulthood and infancy upon the maternal behavior of the primiparous rat. *J. Genet. Psychol., 53,* 109–148.

——. 1939. Maternal behavior of the pouchless marsupial *Marmosa cinerea. J. Mammal., 20,* 315–322.

——. 1945. Current concepts of play in animals. *Amer. Nat., 79,* 523–541.

Bechterew, W. von. 1911. *Die Funktionen der Nervencentra.* Jena: Fischer.

Becker, R. F. 1950. Behavioral changes produced by asphyxia at birth. *Amer. Psychologist, 5,* 254–255.

Becker, R. F., and W. Donnell. 1952. Learning behavior in guinea pigs subjected to asphyxia at birth. *J. Comp. Physiol. Psychol., 45,* 153–162.

Bernberg, R. E. 1951. A comparison of the effects of electroconvulsive shock and electronarcosis upon the learning ability of young rats. *J. Comp. Physiol. Psychol., 44,* 50–60.

Bernhardt, K. S. 1934. The effect of vitamin B deficiency during nursing on subsequent learning in the rat. *J. Comp. Psychol., 17,* 123–148.

Bernhardt, K. S., and R. Herbert. 1937. A further study of vitamin B deficiency and learning with rats. *J. Comp. Psychol., 24,* 263–267.

Bevan, W., Jr., and O. I. Freeman, Jr. 1952. Some effects of an amino acid deficiency upon the performance of albino rats in a simple maze. *J. Genet. Psychol., 80,* 75–82.

Biel, W. C. 1938. The effect of early inanition upon maze learning in the albino rat. *Comp. Psychol. Monogr., 15,* No. 2. Pp. 33.

——. 1939. The effects of early inanition on a developmental schedule in the albino rat. *J. Comp. Psychol., 28,* 1–15.

——. 1940. Early age differences in maze performance in the albino rat. *J. Genet. Psychol., 56,* 439–453.

Biel, W. C., and D. D. Wickens. 1941. The effects of vitamin B_1 deficiency on the conditioning of eyelid responses in the rat. *J. Comp. Psychol., 32,* 329–340.

Bingham, H. C. 1927. Parental play of chimpanzees. *J. Mammal., 8,* 77–89.

Bingham, W. E., and W. J. Griffiths, Jr. 1952. The effect of different environments during infancy on adult behavior in the rat. *J. Comp. Physiol. Psychol., 45,* 307–312.

Blair, W. R. 1920. Notes on the birth of a chimpanzee. *Bull. N. Y. Zool. Soc., 23,* 105–111.

Britton, S. W. 1941. Form and function in the sloth. *Quart. Rev. Biol., 16,* 13–34; 190–207.

Brooks, C. M., and M. E. Peck. 1940. Effect of various cortical lesions on development of placing and hopping reactions in rats. *J. Neurophysiol., 3,* 66–73.

Brown, C. E. 1930. Birth of a second chimpanzee in the Philadelphia Zoölogical Garden. *J. Mammal., 11,* 303–305.

Carmichael, L. 1934. The genetic development of the kitten's capacity to right itself in the air when falling. *J. Genet. Psychol., 44,* 453–458.

Carpenter, C. R. 1934. A field study of the behavior and social relations of howling monkeys (*Alouatta palliata*). *Comp. Psychol. Monogr., 10,* No. 48. Pp. 168.

Causey, D., and R. H. Waters. 1936. Parental care in mammals with especial reference to the carrying of young by the albino rat. *J. Comp. Psychol., 22,* 241–254.

Coolidge, H. J., Jr. 1933. Notes on a family of breeding gibbons. *Human Biol., 5,* 288–294.

Cooper, J. B. 1942. An exploratory study on African lions. *Comp. Psychol. Monogr., 17,* No. 7. Pp. 48.

Coronios, J. D. 1933. Development of behavior in the fetal cat. *Genet. Psychol. Monogr., 14,* 283–386.

Courthial, A. S. 1929. The persistence of infantile behavior in a cat. *J. Genet. Psychol., 36,* 349–350.

Crozier, W. J., and T. T. Oxnard. 1927. Geotropic orientation of young mice. *J. Gen. Physiol., 11,* 141–146.

Crozier, W. J., and G. Pincus. 1926. The geotropic conduct of young rats. *J. Gen. Physiol., 10,* 257–269.

Crozier, W. J., and G. Pincus. 1927a. Phototropism in young rats. *J. Gen. Physiol.*, *10*, 407–417.

——. 1927b. Geotropic orientation of young rats. *J. Gen. Physiol.*, *10*, 519–524.

——. 1928. On the geotropic orientation of young mammals. *J. Gen. Physiol.*, *11*, 789–802.

——. 1929a. Analysis of the geotropic orientation of young rats: I. *J. Gen. Physiol.*, *13*, 57–80.

——. 1929b. Analysis of the geotropic orientation of young rats: II. *J. Gen. Physiol.*, *13*, 81–120.

——. 1931a. Analysis of the geotropic orientation of young rats: III. *J. Gen. Physiol.*, *15*, 201–242.

——. 1931b. Analysis of the geotropic orientation of young rats: IV. *J. Gen. Physiol.*, *15*, 243–256.

——. 1932a. Analysis of the geotropic orientation of young rats: V. *J. Gen. Physiol.*, *15*, 421–436.

——. 1932b. Analysis of the geotropic orientation of young rats: VI. *J. Gen. Physiol.*, *15*, 437–462.

——. 1933. Analysis of the geotropic orientation of young rats: VII. *J. Gen. Physiol.*, *16*, 801–813.

Dodson, J. D. 1915. The relation of strength of stimulus to rapidity of habit-formation in the kitten. *J. Anim. Behav.*, *5*, 330–336.

Dove, W. F. 1935. A study of individuality in the nutritive instincts and of the causes and effect of variations in the selection of food. *Amer. Nat.*, *69*, 468–544.

Edge, E. R. 1931. Seasonal activity and growth in the Douglas ground squirrel. *J. Mammal.*, *12*, 194–200.

Elliott, M. H., and W. H. Stavsky. 1933. The effect of an upward stress upon the geotropic orientation of young guinea pigs. *J. Gen. Psychol.*, *9*, 216–220.

Enders, R. K. 1931. Parturition in the agouti, with notes on several pregnant uteri. *J. Mammal.*, *12*, 390–396.

Eriksen, C. W., P. B. Porter, and C. P. Stone. 1948. Learning ability in rats given electroconvulsive shocks in late infancy: Part I. *J. Comp. Physiol. Psychol.*, *41*, 144–154.

Errington, P. L. 1939. Observations on young muskrats in Iowa. *J. Mammal.*, *20*, 465–478.

Ferrier, D. 1880. *The functions of the brain.* New York: Putnam's.

Fisher, E. M. 1940. Early life of a sea otter pup. *J. Mammal.*, *21*, 132–137.

Fiske, J. 1883. *The meaning of infancy:* I. *The part played by infancy in the evolution of man:* II. Boston: Houghton Mifflin. (New ed., 1911.)

Foley, J. P., Jr. 1934. First year development of a rhesus monkey (*Macaca mulatta*) reared in isolation. *J. Genet. Psychol.*, *45*, 39–105.

——. 1935. Second year development of a rhesus monkey (*Macaca mulatta*) reared in isolation during the first eighteen months. *J. Genet. Psychol.*, *47*, 73–97.

Forgays, D. G., and J. W. Forgays. 1952. The nature of the effect of free-environmental experience in the rat. *J. Comp. Physiol. Psychol.*, *45*, 322–328.

Fox, H. 1929. The birth of two anthropoid apes. *J. Mammal.*, *10*, 37–51.

Fredericson, E. 1951. Competition: The effects of infantile experience upon adult behavior. *J. Abnorm. Soc. Psychol.*, *46*, 406–409.

Fuller, J. L., C. A. Easler, and E. M. Banks. 1950. Formation of conditioned avoidance responses in young puppies. *Amer. J. Physiol.*, *160*, 462–466.

Gesell, A. 1928. *Infancy and human growth.* New York: Macmillan.

Goerling, A. 1913. *Observations on the kangaroo,* reprinted in C. G. Hartman (1920).

Golubeva, E. L. 1939. [Conditioned reflexes of the newborn guinea pig.] *Ankh. Biol. Nauk*, *54*, 132–142. (*Psychol. Abstr.*, 1939, No. 6113.)

Griffiths, W. J., Jr., and W. F. Stringer. 1952. The effects of intense stimulation experience during infancy on adult behavior in the rat. *J. Comp. Physiol. Psychol.*, *45*, 301–306.

Groos, K. 1915. *The play of animals.* (Trans. by E. L. Baldwin.) (1st German ed., 1896.) New York: Appleton.

Hall, C. S., and P. H. Whiteman. 1951. The effects of infantile stimulation upon emotional stability in the mouse. *J. Comp. Physiol. Psychol.*, *44*, 61–66.

Hamilton, G. V. 1911. A study of trial and error reactions in mammals. *J. Anim. Behav.*, *1*, 33–66.

Hamilton, W. J., Jr. 1944. The biology of the little short-tailed shrew, *Cryptotis parva. J. Mammal.*, *25*, 1–7.

Hartman, C. G. 1920. Studies in the development of the opossum (*Didelphis virginiana* L.): V. The phenomena of parturition. *Anat. Rec.*, *19*, 251–261.

——. 1921. Breeding habits, development, and birth of the opossum. *Smithsonian Repts.*, Publ. 2689, 347–363.

——. 1928a. The breeding season of the opossum (*Didelphis virginiana*) and the rate of intra-uterine and postnatal development. *J. Morphol.*, *46*, 143–216.

——. 1928b. The period of gestation in the monkey (*Macacus rhesus*), first description of parturition in monkeys, size, and behavior of the young. *J. Mammal.*, *9*, 181–194.

Haslerud, G. M. 1938. The effect of movement of stimulus objects upon avoidance reactions in chimpanzees. *J. Comp. Psychol.*, *25*, 507–528.

Hatt, R. T. 1931. Habits of a young flying squirrel (*Glaucomys volans*). *J. Mammal.*, *12*, 233–238.

——. 1943. The pine squirrel in Colorado. *J. Mammal.*, *24*, 311–345.

Hayes, C. 1951. *The ape in our house.* New York: Harper.

Hayes, K. J. 1950. Vocalization and speech in chimpanzees. *Amer. Psychologist.*, *5*, 275–276.

Hayes, K. J., and C. Hayes. 1951. The intellectual development of a home-raised chimpanzee. *Proc. Amer. Phil. Soc.*, *95*, 105–109.

——. 1952. Imitation in a home-raised chimpanzee. *J. Comp. Physiol. Psychol.*, *45*, 450–459.

Hebb, D. O. 1937a. The innate organization of visual activity: I. Perception of figures by rats reared in total darkness. *J. Genet. Psychol.*, *51*, 101–126.

Hebb, D. O. 1937b. The innate organization of visual activity: II. Transfer of response in the discrimination of brightness and size by rats reared in total darkness. *J. Comp. Psychol.*, *24*, 277–299.

———. 1947. The effects of early experience on problem-solving at maturity. *Amer. Psychologist.*, *2*, 306–307.

Henry, E. W., and C. N. Woolsey. 1943. Somatic motor responses produced by electrical stimulation of the cerebral cortex of new-born and young kittens. *Fed. Proc. Amer. Soc. Exp. Biol.*, *2*, 21.

Horner, B. E. 1947. Paternal care of young mice of the genus *Peromyscus*. *J. Mammal.*, *28*, 31–36.

Howell, A. B., and L. Little. 1924. Additional notes on California bats; with observations upon the young of *Eumops*. *J. Mammal.*, *5*, 261–263.

Hubbert, H. B. 1915. The effect of age on habit formation in the albino rat. *Behav. Monogr.*, *2*, No. 6. Pp. 55.

Huber, E. 1934. A phylogenetic aspect of the motor cortex of mammals. *Quart. Rev. Biol.*, *9*, 55–91.

Huestis, R. R. 1933. Maternal behavior in the deermouse. *J. Mammal.*, *14*, 47–49.

Hunt, J. McV. 1941. The effects of infant feeding-frustration upon adult hoarding in the albino rat. *J. Abnorm. Soc. Psychol.*, *36*, 338–360.

Hunt, J. McV., H. Schlosberg, R. L. Solomon, and E. Stellar. 1947. Studies of the effects of infantile experience on adult behavior in rats: I. Effects of infantile feeding frustration on adult hoarding. *J. Comp. Physiol. Psychol.*, *40*, 291–304.

Hymovitch, B. 1952. The effects of experimental variations on problem solving in the rat. *J. Comp. Physiol. Psychol.*, *45*, 313–321.

Ingles, L. G. 1941. Natural history observations of the Audubon cottontail. *J. Mammal.*, *22*, 227–250.

Jacobsen, C. F., M. M. Jacobsen, and J. G. Yoshioka. 1932. Development of an infant chimpanzee during her first year. *Comp. Psychol. Monogr.*, *9*, No. 41. Pp. 94.

Jacobsen, C. F., F. V. Taylor, and G. M. Haslerud. 1936. Restitution of function after cortical injury in monkeys. *Amer. J. Physiol.*, *116*, 85–86.

James, W. T. 1949. Dominant and submissive behavior in puppies as indicated by food intake. *J. Genet. Psychol.*, *75*, 33–43.

———. 1952a. Observations on behavior of new-born puppies: Method of measurement and types of behavior involved. *J. Genet. Psychol.*, *80*, 65–73.

———. 1952b. Observations on the behavior of newborn puppies: II. Summary of movements involved in group orientation. *J. Comp. Physiol. Psychol.*, *45*, 329–335.

Jasper, H. H., C. S. Bridgman, and L. Carmichael. 1937. An ontogenetic study of cerebral electrical potentials in the guinea pig. *J. Exp. Psychol.*, *20*, 63–71.

Johnson, G. E. 1927. Observations on young prairie-dogs (*Cynomys ludovicianus*) born in the laboratory. *J. Mammal.*, *8*, 110–115.

Kahn, M. W. 1951. The effect of severe defeat at various age levels on the aggressive behavior of mice. *J. Genet. Psychol.*, *79*, 117–130.

Kao, H. 1927. *Notes on the congenital behavior of rabbits.* Unpublished Master's Thesis, Stanford University.

Kellogg, W. N. 1931. A note on fear behavior in young rats, mice and birds. *J. Comp. Psychol.*, *12*, 117–121.

Kellogg, W. N., and L. A. Kellogg. 1933. *The ape and the child: A study of environmental influence upon early behavior.* New York: McGraw-Hill.

Kennard, M. A. 1936. Age and other factors in motor recovery from precentral lesions in monkeys. *Amer. J. Physiol.*, *115*, 138–146.

———. 1938. Reorganization of motor function in the cerebral cortex of monkeys deprived of motor and premotor areas in infancy. *J. Neurophysiol.*, *1*, 477–496.

Kennard, M. A., and W. S. McCulloch. 1942. Excitability of cerebral cortex in infant *Macaca mulatta*. *J. Neurophysiol.*, *5*, 231–234.

Kinder, E. F. 1927. A study of the nest building activity of the albino rat. *J. Exp. Zool.*, *47*, 117–161.

Kinnaman, A. J. 1902. Mental life of two *Macacus rhesus* monkeys in captivity: I; II. *Amer. J. Psychol.*, *13*, 98–148; 173–218.

Kittredge, E. 1923. Some experiments on the brightness value of red for the light-adapted eye of the calf. *J. Comp. Psychol.*, *3*, 141–145.

Kohts, N. 1935. [*Infant ape and human child: Instincts, emotions, play, habits.*] *Scientific Memoirs of the Museum Darwinianum in Moscow.* Vol. III. Pp. xvi + 596, c. 145 plates. (Review by A. Gesell, *J. Genet. Psychol.*, 1937, *50*, 465–467.)

Kornmüller, A. E. 1935. Die bioelektrischen Erscheinungen architektonischer Felder der Grosshirnrinde. *Biol. Rev.*, *10*, 383–426.

Kuckuk, E. 1936. Tierpsychologische Beobachtungen an zwei jungen Brunbären. *Z. vergl. Physiol.*, *24*, 14–41.

Kuo, Z. Y. 1930. The genesis of the cat's responses to the rat. *J. Comp. Psychol.*, *11*, 1–35.

———. 1938. Further study on the behavior of the cat toward the rat. *J. Comp. Psychol.*, *25*, 1–8.

Kuroda, R. 1930. Untersuchungen über die körperliche und sinnesphysiologische Organisation eines neugeborenen Affen (*Macacus cynomologus*). *Acta Psychol. Keijo*, *1*, 3–16.

Lang, H. 1925. How squirrels and other rodents carry their young. *J. Mammal.*, *6*, 18–24.

Langworthy, O. R. 1925. The development of progression and posture in young opossums. *Amer. J. Physiol.*, *74*, 1–13.

———. 1927. Histological development of cerebral motor areas in young kittens correlated with their physiological reaction to electrical stimulation. *Contr. Embryol., Carnegie Inst. Wash.*, No. 104, pp. 177–208.

———. 1928. The behavior of pouch-young opossums correlated with the myelinization of tracts in the nervous system. *J. Comp. Neurol.*, 1928, *46*, 201–248.

Langworthy, O. R. 1929. A correlated study of the development of reflex activity in fetal and young kittens and the myelinization of tracts in the nervous system. *Contr. Embryol., Carnegie Inst. Wash.*, No. 114, pp. 127–171.

Lashley, K. S. 1914. A note on the persistence of an instinct. *J. Anim. Behav.*, *4*, 293–294.

Lashley, K. S., and J. T. Russell. 1934. The mechanism of vision: XI. A preliminary test of innate organization. *J. Genet. Psychol.*, *45*, 136–144.

Lashley, K. S., and J. B. Watson. 1913. Notes on the development of a young monkey. *J. Anim. Behav.*, *3*, 114–139.

Liers, E. E. 1951. Notes on the river otter. *J. Mammal.*, *32*, 1–9.

Liu, S. Y. 1928. The relation of age to the learning ability of the white rat. *J. Comp. Psychol.*, *8*, 75–85.

Margolin, S. E., and M. E. Bunch. 1940. The relationship between age and strength of hunger motivation. *Comp. Psychol. Monogr.*, *16*, No. 4. Pp. 34.

Marx, M. H. 1952. Infantile deprivation and adult behavior in the rat: Retention of increased rate of eating. *J. Comp. Physiol. Psychol.*, *45*, 43–49.

Maurer, S. 1935a. The effect of partial depletion of vitamin B (B₁) upon performance in rats: III. *J. Comp. Psychol.*, *20*, 309–317.

——. 1935b. The effect of early depletion of vitamin B₂ upon performance in rats: IV. *J. Comp. Psychol.*, *20*, 385–387.

——. 1935c. The effect of acute vitamin A depletion upon performance in rats: V. *J. Comp. Psychol.*, *20*, 389–391.

——. 1935d. The effect of a diet of pasteurized milk upon performance in rats: VI. *J. Comp. Psychol.*, *20*, 393–395.

Maurer, S., and L. S. Tsai. 1929. Vitamin B deficiency in nursing young rats and learning ability. *Science*, *70*, 456–458.

——. 1930. Vitamin B deficiency and learning ability. *J. Comp. Psychol.*, *11*, 51–62.

McBride, A. F., and D. O. Hebb. 1948. Behavior of the captive bottle-nose dolphin, *Tursiops truncatus*. *J. Comp. Physiol. Psychol.*, *41*, 111–123.

McBride, A. F., and H. Kritzler. 1951. Observations on pregnancy, parturition, and postnatal behavior in the bottlenose dolphin. *J. Mammal.*, *32*, 251–266.

McCulloch, T. L., and G. M. Haslerud. 1939. Affective responses of an infant chimpanzee reared in isolation from its kind. *J. Comp. Psychol.*, *1939*, *28*, 437–445.

McDougall, W., and K. McDougall. 1927. Notes on instinct and intelligence in rats and cats. *J. Comp. Psychol.*, *7*, 145–175.

McKelvey, R. K., and M. H. Marx. 1951. Effects of infantile food and water deprivation on adult hoarding in the rat. *J. Comp. Physiol. Psychol.*, *44*, 423–430.

Meier, G. W., and M. E. Bunch. 1950. The effects of natal anoxia upon learning and memory at

maturity. *J. Comp. Physiol. Psychol.*, *43*, 436–441.

Michailow, S. 1910. Zur Frage über die Erregbarkeit der motorischen Zentra in der Hirnrinde neugeborener Säugetiere. *Pflüg. Arch. ges. Physiol.*, *133*, 45–70.

Mills, W. 1898. *The nature and development of animal intelligence.* London: Unwin.

Mitchell, P. C. 1912. *The childhood of animals.* New York: Stokes.

Muenzinger, K. F., E. Poe, and C. F. Poe. 1937. The effect of vitamin deficiency upon the acquisition and retention of the maze habit in the white rat: II. Vitamin B₂(G). *J. Comp. Psychol.*, *23*, 59–66.

Murie, O. J. 1940. Notes on the sea otter. *J. Mammal.*, *21*, 119–131.

Nissen, H. W. 1931. A field study of the chimpanzee. *Comp. Psychol. Monogr.*, *8*, No. 36. Pp. 122.

Nissen, H. W., K. L. Chow, and J. Semmes. 1951. Effect of restricted opportunity for tactual, kinesthetic, and manipulative experience on the behavior of a chimpanzee. *Amer. J. Psychol.*, *64*, 485–507.

O'Neill, P. H. 1949. The effect on subsequent maze learning ability of graded amounts of vitamin B₁ in the diet of very young rats. *J. Genet. Psychol.*, *74*, 85–95.

Orr, R. T. 1942. Observations on the growth of young brush rabbits. *J. Mammal.*, *23*, 298–302.

Paneth, J. 1885. Über die Erregbarkeit der Hirnrinde neugeborener Hunde. *Pflüg. Arch. ges. Physiol.*, *37*, 202–208.

Pearson, O. P., and C. F. Bassett. 1946. Certain aspects of reproduction in a herd of silver foxes. *Amer. Nat.*, *80*, 45–67.

Pfaffman, C. 1936. Differential responses of the new-born cat to gustatory stimuli. *J. Genet. Psychol.*, *49*, 61–67.

Pincus, G. 1927. Geotropic creeping of young rats. *J. Gen. Physiol.*, *10*, 525–532.

Poe, C. F., E. Poe, and K. F. Muenzinger. 1937. The effect of vitamin deficiency upon the acquisition and retention of the maze habit in the white rat: III. Vitamin B₁. *J. Comp. Psychol.*, *23*, 67–76.

Poe, E., C. F. Poe, and K. F. Muenzinger. 1936. The effect of vitamin deficiency upon the acquisition and retention of the maze habit in the white rat: I. The vitamin B-complex. *J. Comp. Psychol.*, *22*, 69–77.

——. 1938. The effect of vitamin deficiency upon the acquisition and retention of the maze habit in the white rat: IV. Vitamin B-complex, B₁, and B₂(G). *J. Comp. Psychol.*, *27*, 211–214.

Porter, J. H., F. A. Webster, and J. C. R. Licklider. 1951. The influence of age and food deprivation upon the hoarding behavior of rats. *J. Comp. Physiol. Psychol.*, *44*, 300–309.

Porter, P. B., C. S. Stone, and C. W. Eriksen. 1948. Learning ability in rats given electroconvulsive shocks in late infancy. Part II. *J. Comp. Physiol. Psychol.*, *41*, 423–431.

Porter, P. B., A. C. Griffin, and C. P. Stone. 1951. Behavioral assessment of glutamic acid metabolism with observations on pyridoxine and folic acid deficiencies. *J. Comp. Physiol. Psychol.*, *44*, 543–550.

Pournelle, G. H. 1952. Reproduction and early post-natal development of the cotton mouse, *Peromyscus gossypinus gossypinus*. *J. Mammal.*, *33*, 1–20.

Preyer, W. 1882. *Die Seele des Kindes*. Leipzig: Fernau. (2d ed., 1884.)

——. 1888. *The mind of the child*: I. *The senses and the will*. (Trans. by H. W. Brown.) New York: Appleton.

Pycraft, W. P. 1913. *The infancy of animals*. New York: Holt.

Rennie, J. 1838. The menageries. The natural history of monkeys, opossums, and lemurs. In *The library of entertaining knowledge*. London. (From Yerkes and Yerkes, 1929.)

Richardson, W. B. 1942a. Ring-tailed cats (*Bassariscus astutus*): Their growth and development. *J. Mammal.*, *23*, 17–26.

——. 1942b. Reaction toward snakes as shown by the wood rat, *Neotoma albigula*. *J. Comp. Psychol.*, *34*, 1–10.

——. 1943. Wood rats (*Neotoma albigula*): Their growth and development. *J. Mammal.*, *24*, 130–143.

Richter, C. P. 1925. Some observations on the self-stimulation habits of young wild animals. *Arch. Neurol. Psychiat.*, *Chicago*, *13*, 724–728.

——. 1931. The grasping reflex in the newborn monkey. *Arch. Neurol. Psychiat.*, *Chicago*, *26*, 784–790.

Riesen, A. H. 1947. The development of visual perception in man and chimpanzee. *Science*, *106*, 107–108.

Robinson, S. M. 1925. Birth of a white-handed gibbon (*Hylobates lar*) in captivity. *J. Bombay Nat. Hist. Soc.*, *30*, 456–458. (From Yerkes and Yerkes, 1929.)

Rogers, W. W. 1932. Controlled observations on the behavior of kittens toward rats from birth to five months of age. *J. Comp. Psychol.*, *13*, 107–125.

Ross, S. 1951. Sucking behavior in neonate dogs. *J. Abnorm. Soc. Psychol.*, *46*, 142–149.

Ross, S., and J. G. Ross. 1949a. Social facilitation of feeding behavior in dogs: I. Group and solitary feeding. *J. Genet. Psychol.*, *74*, 97–108.

——. 1949b. Social facilitation of feeding behavior in dogs: II. Feeding after satiation. *J. Genet. Psychol.*, *74*, 293–304.

Scheffer, V. B. 1945. Growth and behavior of young sea lions. *J. Mammal.*, *26*, 390–392.

Schlosberg, H. 1947. The concept of play. *Psychol. Rev.*, *54*, 229–231.

Scott, J. P. 1945. Social behavior, organization and leadership in a small flock of domestic sheep. *Comp. Psychol. Monogr.*, *18*, No. 4. Pp. 29.

Scott, J. P., and M. Marston. 1950. Critical periods affecting the development of normal and mal-adjustive social behavior of puppies. *J. Genet. Psychol.*, *77*, 25–60.

Seward, G. H. 1940. Studies on the reproductive activities of the guinea pig: II. The rôle of hunger in filial behavior. *J. Comp. Psychol.*, *29*, 25–41.

Seward, J. P., and G. H. Seward. 1940. Studies on the reproductive activities of the guinea pig: I.

Factors in maternal behavior. *J. Comp. Psychol.*, *29*, 1–24.

Shadle, A. R., and W. R. Ploss. 1943. An unusual porcupine parturition and development of the young. *J. Mammal.*, *24*, 492–496.

Shaw, W. T. 1925. Breeding and development of the Columbian ground squirrel. *J. Mammal.*, *6*, 106–113.

Sherman, H. B. 1930. Birth of the young of *Myotis austroriparius*. *J. Mammal.*, *11*, 495–503.

Shirley, M. M. 1931. *The first two years. A study of twenty-five babies*: I. *Postural and locomotor development*. *Inst. Child Welfare Res. Monogr. Ser.*, No. 6. Minneapolis: University of Minnesota Press. Pp. vi + 227.

Shuey, A. M. 1931. The limits of learning ability in kittens. *Genet. Psychol. Monogr.*, *10*, 287–378.

——. 1932. Some experiments with kittens on the simple alternation problem. *J. Genet. Psychol.*, *41*, 393–405.

Slonaker, J. R. 1907. The normal activity of the white rat at different ages. *J. Comp. Neurol. Psychol.*, *17*, 342–359.

——. 1912. The normal activity of the albino rat from birth to natural death. *J. Anim. Behav.*, *2*, 20–42.

Small, W. S. 1899. Notes on the psychic development of the young white rat. *Amer. J. Psychol.*, *11*, 80–100.

Smith, B. E. 1946. Bear facts. *J. Mammal.*, *27*, 31–37.

Sollberger, D. E. 1943. Notes on the breeding habits of the eastern flying squirrel (*Glaucomys volans*). *J. Mammal.*, *24*, 163–173.

Soltmann, O. 1876. Experimentelle Studien über die Funktionen des Grosshirns der Neugeborenen. *Jb. Kinderheilk.*, *9*, 106.

Spalding, D. A. 1873. Instinct with original observations on young animals. *Macmillan's Mag.*, *27*, 282–293. Reprinted in *Pop. Sci. Mo.*, 1902, *61*, 126–142.

——. 1875. Instinct and acquisition. *Nature*, *12*, 507–508.

Stavsky, W. H. 1932. The geotropic conduct of young kittens. *J. Gen. Psychol.*, *6*, 441–446.

Stier, T. J. B. 1930. "Spontaneous activity" of mice. *J. Gen. Psychol.*, *4*, 67–101.

Stone, C. P. 1929a. The age factor in animal learning: I. Rats in the problem box and the maze. *Genet. Psychol. Monogr.*, *5*, 1–130.

——. 1929b. The age factor in animal learning: II. Rats on a multiple light discrimination box and a difficult maze. *Genet. Psychol. Monogr.*, *6*, 125–202.

Struthers, P. H. 1928. Breeding habits of the Canadian porcupine (*Erethizon dorsatum*). *J. Mammal.*, *9*, 300–308.

Sturman-Hulbe, M., and C. P. Stone. 1929. Maternal behavior in the albino rat. *J. Comp. Psychol.*, *9*, 203–237.

Svihla, A. 1934. Development and growth of deer-mice (*Peromyscus maniculatus artemisiae*). *J. Mammal.*, *15*, 99–104.

Taber, F. W. 1945. Contribution to the life history and ecology of the nine-banded armadillo. *J. Mammal.*, *26*, 211–226.

Tang, Y. 1935. On the development of different placing reactions in the albino rat. *Chin. J. Physiol.*, *9*, 339–346.

Tappe, D. T. 1941. Natural history of the Tulare kangaroo rat. *J. Mammal.*, *22*, 117–148.

Tarchanoff, J. de. 1878. Sur les centres psychomoteurs des animaux nouveau-nés (lapin, chien, cochon d'Inde). *Rev. mens. méd. chir.*, *2*, 826.

Tevis, L., Jr. 1950. Summer behavior of a family of beavers in New York State. *J. Mammal.*, *31*, 40–65.

Tilney, F., and L. Casamajor. 1924. Myelinogeny as applied to the study of behavior. *Arch. Neurol. Psychiat.*, *Chicago*, *12*, 1–66.

Tinklepaugh, O. L. 1932. Parturition and puerperal sepsis in a chimpanzee. *Anat. Rec.*, *53*, 193–205.

Tinklepaugh, O. L., and C. G. Hartman. 1932. Behavior and maternal care of the newborn monkey (*Macaca mulatta*—"*M. rhesus*"). *J. Genet. Psychol.*, *40*, 257–286.

Tomilin, M. I., and R. M. Yerkes. 1935. Chimpanzee twins: behavioral relations and development. *J. Genet. Psychol.*, *46*, 239–263.

Tsang, Y. C. 1937a. Maze learning in rats hemidecorticated in infancy. *J. Comp. Psychol.*, *24*, 221–253.

——. 1937b. Visual sensitivity in rats deprived of visual cortex in infancy. *J. Comp. Psychol.*, *24*, 255–262.

Turner, W. D. 1935. The development of perception: I. Visual direction; the first eidoscopic orientations of the albino rat. *J. Genet. Psychol.*, *47*, 121–140.

Upton, M. 1930. The geotropic conduct of young guinea pigs. *J. Gen. Physiol.*, *13*, 647–655.

——. 1932. The effect of added loads upon the geotropic orientation of young guinea pigs. *J. Gen. Physiol.*, *15*, 333–340.

Wade, O. 1927. Breeding habits and early life of the thirteen-striped ground squirrel, *Citellus tridecemlineatus* (Mitchill). *J. Mammal.*, *8*, 269–276.

Warden, C. J., and T. A. Jackson. 1938. *Development and behavior of the white rat* (Film). 350 ft. 16 mm. New York: Columbia University.

Warkentin, J., and L. Carmichael. 1939. A study of the development of the air-righting reflex in cats and rabbits. *J. Genet. Psychol.*, *55*, 67–80.

Warkentin, J., and K. U. Smith. 1937. The development of visual acuity in the cat. *J. Genet. Psychol.*, *50*, 371–399.

Washburn, M. F., and E. Abbott. 1912. Experiments on the brightness value of red for the light-adapted eye of the rabbit. *J. Anim. Behav.*, *2*, 145–180.

Watson, J. B. 1903. *Animal education: The psychical development of the white rat.* Chicago: University of Chicago Press.

Weed, L. H., and O. R. Langworthy. 1925. Developmental study of excitation areas in the cerebral cortex of the opossum. *Amer. J. Physiol.*, *72*, 8–24.

——. 1926. Physiological study of cortical motor areas in young kittens and in adult cats. *Contr. Embryol.*, *Carnegie Inst. Wash.*, *17*, No. 87, pp. 89–106.

Wentworth, K. L. 1938. The effect of early reaches on handedness in the rat: A preliminary study. *J. Genet. Psychol.*, *52*, 429–432.

White, B. A. 1929. A captive-born chimpanzee. *Sci. Mon.*, *N. Y.*, *29*, 558–565.

Wiesner, B. P., and N. M. Sheard. 1933. *Maternal behavior in the rat.* London: Oliver and Boyd.

Windle, W. F. 1930. Normal behavioral reactions of kittens correlated with the postnatal development of nerve-fiber density in the spinal gray matter. *J. Comp. Neurol.*, *50*, 479–503.

Yerkes, A. W. 1935. Experiments with an infant chimpanzee. *J. Genet. Psychol.*, *46*, 171–181.

Yerkes, R. M. 1907. *The dancing mouse.* New York: Macmillan.

——. 1909. Modifiability of behavior in its relations to the age and sex of the dancing mouse. *J. Comp. Neurol. Psychol.*, *19*, 237–271.

——. 1933. Genetic aspects of grooming, a socially important primate behavior pattern. *J. Soc. Psychol.*, *4*, 3–25.

——. 1936. A chimpanzee family. *J. Genet. Psychol.*, *48*, 362–370.

——. 1939. The life history and personality of the chimpanzee. *Amer. Nat.*, *73*, 97–112.

——. 1940. Laboratory chimpanzees. *Science*, *91*, 336–337.

Yerkes, R. M., and D. Bloomfield. 1910. Do kittens instinctively kill mice? *Psychol. Bull.*, *7*, 253–263.

Yerkes, R. M., and M. I. Tomilin. 1935. Mother-infant relations in chimpanzee. *J. Comp. Psychol.*, *20*, 321–359.

Yerkes, R. M., and A. W. Yerkes. 1929. *The great apes: A study of anthropoid life.* New Haven: Yale University Press.

——. 1936. Nature and condition of avoidance (fear) response in chimpanzee. *J. Comp. Psychol.*, *21*, 53–66.

CHAPTER 4

THE NEONATE [1]

KARL C. PRATT

Birth

Nature and Significance. Birth is the term applied to the transfer of the developing child from the uterine environment to that of the external world. It is accomplished by contractions of the uterus which, by exerting pressure, rupture the fetal membranes and expel the child through the birth canal. This event severs the parasitic connections with the mother and necessitates an autonomy of vegetative functions if the child is to survive. The effects of birth on the infant may be inconsequential and transitory or they may greatly affect the course of subsequent development.

Organismic Changes. In the fetal environment the child leads a parasitic existence. It is dependent upon the maternal organism for external respiration, for digestion of food and the preparation of nutrient materials, for excretory functions, for thermal regulation, and for protection.

During the birth process the circulatory relations with the maternal organism (by way of the umbilical cord and the placenta) are at first disturbed and then broken off. At about this time the crucial vegetative function, external respiration, must appear or the child will be asphyxiated. Clifford (1941) found that over one-half of "live-born" infant deaths are caused by asphyxia.

Up to the onset of the birth cry the lungs have been uninflated and nonfunctional.

Two major theories, according to Fernandez (1918) and Feldman (1920), have been advanced to account for the initiation of pulmonary respiration: (1) that the process is started by external stimuli; (2) that it is brought about by a critical concentration of CO_2 in the blood stream of the infant.

According to the first theory, cutaneous stimuli (contact and thermal) serve to bring about an innervation of the musculature of the thorax while atmospheric pressure inflates the lungs. Relaxation of the muscles produces exhalation. The process is repeated with succeeding inhalations brought about by neural discharges proceeding from the respiratory center. In support of the theory of the excitatory rôle of cutaneous stimuli it is pointed out that the attending physician employs still more intense cutaneous stimuli if the infant has not begun to breathe. The effects of thermal stimuli below physiological zero upon the breathing of newborn infants have been observed by Pratt, Nelson, and Sun (1930), and are a matter of common experience at later age periods.

According to the second theory, pulmonary respiration is started when the CO_2 content of the blood attains the critical concentration which acts directly upon the respiratory center to arouse it to activity. It is said that the birth process, by disturbing the circulatory relations between the maternal organism and the child, increases the CO_2 content of the child's

[1] The writer is indebted to Dr. O. C. Irwin and to Dr. D. M. Trout for suggestions and for criticism in the preparation of this chapter.

blood stream and that breathing starts as soon as the respiratory center is activated. This theory accounts for the Ahlfeld "breathing movements" of the fetus. Doubtless both cutaneous stimuli and those provided by the blood stream cooperate in establishing pulmonary respiration.

Coincidental with the onset of breathing, valves in the heart operate to alter the circulation from the fetal to the natal type. Instead of passing to the placenta for aeration the blood now flows to the lungs.

The interruption and cessation of circulatory relations with the maternal organism mean that no more nutrient materials ready for assimilation are available to the child. Henceforth it must take food, digest it, excrete, egest, and maintain a relatively uniform body temperature despite variations in its thermal environment.

Environmental Changes. Birth transfers the developing child from an environment of relatively few to one of many stimuli; from one in which the conditions for learning are unfavorable, or restricted, to one presenting manifold possibilities; from one devoid of the social factor to one in which it is operative. From the observations of Bersot (1920, 1921) and Langworthy (1933) it seems probable that this postnatal environment not only provides richer opportunities for learning but also stimulates the continuing development of the nervous system.

Birth Trauma. The pressures produced in the birth process sometimes give rise to fractures of bones during passage through the birth canal, but the more common consequences are hemorrhages. They may be of slight extent and quickly absorbed; they may involve vital nerve centers and result in death; or they may permanently affect parts of the nervous system with consequent impairment of function.

In addition to their effects upon general intelligence, birth injuries have transitory or permanent consequences for sense organs such as the ear and the eye. Kutvirt (1912) and Vosz (1923) have correlated lack of auditory sensitivity with prolonged and difficult labor; Sicherer (1907) and Edgerton (1934) have discussed the effect of retinal hemorrhages and other optic disturbances in the neonate.

The psychoanalytical school postulates psychic trauma resulting from the rupture of the fetal relations with the mother. Rank (1929) holds that the primal anxiety state, whence all subsequent anxiety states stem, has its origin during the birth process. This concept is widely accepted as a fundamental facet of psychoanalytic doctrine. Rank, like Ribble (1944), ascribes its formulation to Freud himself. Despert (1946), however, considers it doubtful whether Freud ever regarded it as more than a dubious assumption, and Ruja (1948) asserts that Freud claimed there were no empirical checks by which Rank's thesis could be evaluated. Freud had suggested an investigation of the relation of the crying of newborn infants to the duration of labor of the mothers, but Ruja (1948) did not obtain statistically significant correlations.

Anderson (1948), in a very significant paper, has criticized the dogma, currently popular in psychoanalytic and allied circles, that childhood is a period of extreme susceptibility to trauma or shock. The attempts to locate the traumatic incident have led to a continual but vain regression through adolescence, childhood, infancy, and, finally, to birth. The ultimate, he hints, in such regression would be to place the initial trauma at conception. This, in fact, is where Sadger (1941) was led by his analyses, only to discover that the troubles of some of his patients dated from their *earlier* existence as spermatozoa and ova.

In general, psychoanalytic interpretations of the experience of the child at birth or before show a kinship with the antecedent literary and philosophical treatments of Lucretius, Kant, and others. Sterne, in *Tristram Shandy,* anticipates Sadger's views (1941) by remarking in the famous passage concerning the fate of the homunculus

> Now, dear Sir, what if any accident had befallen him in his way alone!—or that, through terror of it, natural to so young a traveller, my little Gentleman had got to his journey's end miserably spent;—his muscular strength and virility worn down to a thread;—his own animal spirits ruffled beyond description,—and that in this sad disordered state of nerves, he had lain down a prey to sudden starts, or a series of melancholy dreams and fancies, for nine long, long months together.—I tremble to think what a foundation had been laid for a thousand weaknesses both of body and mind, which no skill of the physician or the philosopher could ever afterwards have set thoroughly to rights.

Definitions

Derivation. The term *neonate* is a Graeco-Latin derivative. Its respective Italian, French, German, and English equivalents are *neonato, nouveau-né, Neugeborener,* and *newborn.* The Spanish *recién nacido* has a slightly different but scarcely less indefinite connotation.

Further ambiguity for indices and bibliographies is created by the use of such terms as *child, infant, Säugling, nourrisson, enfant, bambino, lattante,* without restricting adjectives or statements of the age range of the studies.

Duration of the Period. According to McGraw (1932), the child is not a *neonate* until the "umbilical cord is dressed and the baby is taken to the maternity nursery." Before this the just-born child for a period of "about the first 15 minutes of life"

is a *partunate.* This is the period "during and immediately following parturition." In terms of the latter statement the time stated for this period must be grossly inaccurate. Furthermore, it would appear doubtful whether McGraw, in terms of her own definition, is actually reporting the behavior characteristics of *partunates.*

A few authorities hold that the neonatal period extends to approximately the end of the first postnatal week; for others it comprises the first 2 weeks. Still others extend the period to 1 month, with Vinay (1897) going further to an extreme of 3 months. Gundobin (1907) rejects a fixed chronological terminus and instead considers it as ending when complete regularity of assimilation indicates the general integrated functioning of all organs.

Valentine and Dockeray (1936) would differentiate between *newborn infant* ("the first 10 days of life") and *neonate* ("the first 30 days"). There is nothing, however, in the etymology of the terms or in historical usage to warrant such a distinction.

The prevailing usage in the field of infant behavior follows Feldman (1920) and Gesell (1925) in defining the *neonatal* period as extending from birth at full term to the end of the first postnatal month.

General Characteristics. The duration of the period is determined by physiological, medical, and psychological criteria. It is a period of adjustment and perfection of newly acquired vegetative functions. It is marked by the obsolescence of such structures as the ductus Botalli and the umbilical vein, and by the recovery from injuries such as asphyxia, umbilical infections, tetanus, obstetrical paralyses, and hemorrhages incurred during the birth process. It is likewise a period during which certain sensory-motor structures are first activated by adequate stimuli, such stimulation helping to bring about further maturation of the nervous system. This reactivity reveals the effects of fetal maturation but in itself induces no pronounced developmental events, nor does it afford a basis for more than the mere beginnings of learning. In brief, the most important developmental events of the period appear to be those immediately consequent to the incident of birth which ushers in the period.

History of the Study of Neonate Behavior

The Longitudinal Approach. The first more or less systematic attempts to describe the behavior of the newborn infant appeared in the *baby biographies.* Of the fifty or more published during the preceding century and the first decade of this one, the following may be cited as outstanding in content or influence: Tiedemann (1787), Darwin (1877), Champneys (1881), Preyer (1882), Binet (1890), Hall (1891), Shinn (1893–1899), Lowden (1895), and Major (1906). Of these, the biographies by Preyer and by Shinn have had most significance and enduring value for child psychology. Dennis (1936) has compiled a bibliography of baby biographies, and Dennis and Dennis (1937) have made a tabular organization of the temporal incidence of the more important items of behavior as reported in forty such studies.

The serious limitations of the biographical approach to problems of development are well known: a paucity of cases, a probable nonrepresentative selection, and bias because of family ties. Furthermore, the lack of systematically introduced and controlled stimuli together with inadequate provisions for controlling the conditions of observation must result in the inevitable errors of the anecdotal method. The virtue of the "naturalness" of observation as opposed to the "artificiality' of experimentation has, however, been championed by Bridges (1935).

More recently the longitudinal approach to behavioral development has been revived, but with modifications which distinguish it in several respects from the biographical procedure. The investigator pursues the development of a number of children with respect to specific problems. The children are not related to the biographer and are probably not so select a population as that described in the early baby biographies. The observations may be made at fixed time intervals and frequently refer to the performance of children under specific *test* conditions. Notable among investigations of this type are those undertaken by Shirley (1931a, 1931b, 1933a, 1933b), Bayley (1933), Gesell, Thompson, and Amatruda (1938), and other collaborators.

McGraw (1935) and John Dewey, in the introduction to McGraw's account of the nonidentical twins Johnny and Jimmy, have been inclined to characterize all other studies as presenting merely a series of cross-sectional *achievements* and to claim that only her investigations are truly longitudinal. McGraw's conclusions in regard to normal development are, however, not supposed to rest solely upon observations of the one set of twins, but also to depend upon the results of an average of 38 examinations of 68 infants over a period of 2 years. It would thus appear that there is no fundamental distinction in respect to the frequency of sampling of behavioral development, aside from the twins, between McGraw's work and the studies which she has criticized. In a review of McGraw's book, the writer (1936b) has pointed out that all such studies of behavioral development represent time samplings of behavior and that the pursuit of a particular mode of behavior from time section to time section may be described as a longitudinal study, but such usage in no way alters the fact that the pursuit is discontinuous; and hence everything observed in a given time sampling is an "achievement" at the moment regardless of the size of the interval separating the samples.

The Cross-sectional Approach. The ontogenetic progression of behavior may likewise be explored by investigating the response repertory in cross-sections of the population at successive age levels. Because it is difficult to pursue sequential development in a large constant population, most of the data of child development have been obtained from researches of the cross-sectional type, which provide more stable norms and more information regarding individual variation. Almost all investigations of the neonate represent this approach.

Population Controls in Experimentation. In longitudinal studies of development the same population is followed through succeeding age periods. The co-twin control method, devised by Gesell and Thompson (1929) to provide populations with the same hereditary potentialities for the purpose of contrasting the effects of exercise or learning with those due to maturation alone, has as yet not been employed during the neonatal stage. Instead, recourse has been had to the familiar device of control and experimental groups. This is illustrated in Marquis' (1931) attempt to establish conditioned sucking responses in the neonate to auditory stimuli.

In cross-sectional studies which aim to establish the effect of specific stimuli upon the behavior or activity of the infant, as in the researches of Pratt, Nelson, and Sun (1930) and Pratt (1934b), a populational control is in effect when the activity of a given infant is observed and measured not only during an experimental period in which specific stimuli are introduced but also during a control period in which there are no experimental stimuli.

The need for population controls is emphasized further by the fact that the character of a response is influenced by the physiological state of the infant at the time of stimulation. A sampling control may attempt to meet this by varying the position and the order of control and experimental periods. The effects of specific stimuli upon the child must be allowed to subside before other stimuli are applied. When all this is done, however, differences in physiological state remain which seem to necessitate the description and measurement of behavior according to differing physiological conditions. In the field of neonate study Pratt, Nelson, and Sun (1930), Pratt (1934f), Irwin and his students—Weiss (1934), Stubbs and Irwin (1934), and others—and Wagner (1937) have made beginnings in this direction.

Experimentation. Control and measurement are the essence of the experimental method, and they apply to the stimulating conditions, to the nature of the populations studied, and to the responses of the individual organisms.

The rudimentary beginnings of experimental methods may be seen in a few of the baby biographies, in the cross-sectional investigations of Kussmaul (1859), Genzmer (1873), and Kroner (1881) during the past century, and in the studies of Peterson and Rainey (1910) and of Blanton (1917) in the early years of this century. These sometimes involved sizable neonate populations and an extensive survey of the behavior equipment but comprised merely the introduction, without control or measurement, of experimental stimuli, and a more or less uncontrolled observation of the responses elicited. Studies of this type, but confined to some particular response, are illustrated by Engstler's (1905) observations of the plantar responses of 1000 children.

Bechterew (1908) was one of the first students of human behavior to urge that quantitative registration and measurement of responses be substituted for qualitative observation and description. Canestrini (1913) realized this objective by using a pneumograph and a kymograph to register the effect of various stimuli upon respiration. In a similar fashion he recorded circulatory responses by employing a Marey pneumograph attached at the infant's fontanelle. He did not, however, achieve any appreciable control or measurement of his experimental stimuli, nor did he provide an expression, in quantitative terms, of his kymograph records so that central tendency and individual variation might be determined. At about the time of Canestrini's researches, Benedict and Talbot (1914) were using a crib-recorder to afford a continuous registration of the "spontaneous" movements of newborn infants, even for periods of 24 hours.

Peiper, whose researches encompass all aspects of early human behavior (see a partial list of his contributions in the bibliography), employed a modified Morse apparatus to measure reaction times (1925b, 1926a) and devised stimulus controls (1924b, 1926a) for the investigation of thermal and of pain sensitivity. Eckstein and Rominger (1921) measured respiration by means of a facial mask and pneumatic system; Eckstein (1927) improved the earlier crudely instrumentalized study of the sucking response; and Eckstein and Paffrath (1928) employed apparatus to measure the general activity of the neonate. Carlson and Ginsburg (1915) first measured the stomach contractions of the newborn infant.

The problem of emotional patterns of behavior was explored by Sherman (1927a) through the medium of motion-picture photography. At the Yale laboratory Gesell made use of the photographic dome in obtaining motion pictures from different angles, and the subsequent frame analysis of such records provided a remarkable norma-

tive series (1934). The production of instructional films of child development, likewise under his direction, is, as Beck's (1938, 1942) lists indicate, an outstanding contribution.

The comprehensive researches upon neonate behavior undertaken at Ohio State University by Doctor A. P. Weiss (1929) and his students established the groundwork in general technique for many subsequent studies. The activity of the newborn infant was recorded objectively and automatically by an adaptation of the stabilimeter-polygraph apparatus originally designed by Renshaw and Weiss (1926) for the study of postural responses in adults. Pratt, Nelson, and Sun (1930) designed and described an experimental cabinet [1] which would effect some control of the stimuli impinging upon the child. The work of Pratt, Nelson, and Sun likewise represented an advance in the direction of control and measurement or evaluation of many of the stimuli employed. Irwin (1930) made the most extensive studies of neonate activity through 24-hour periods so far attempted. Other major contributions by Weiss and his students are illustrated by Jensen's (1932) remarkably instrumentalized research upon the sucking response, and the first attempt by an American, Marquis (1931), to establish conditioned responses in newborn infants.

After the untimely death of Doctor Weiss the center of significant research upon neonate behavior shifted to Iowa State University, where Irwin and his students not only made the innovations already mentioned but also, in addition to undertaking the solution of new and important problems of neonate behavior, pressed

---

[1] The Pratt experimental cabinet was first modified and improved by Irwin and his students with the introduction of facilities for motion-picture photography, including a "cold" light (1931). Dockeray and Valentine (1939) have redesigned it to meet the original aims more adequately as well as to incorporate the improvements introduced by Irwin.

steadily forward in the setting-up of the best control of all aspects of experimentation that has so far been attained in this field. With Richards (1936), Irwin has demonstrated that the era of uncritical reliance upon the "clinical method" in the investigation of behavioral development must come to an end with realization not only of the inadequacy but also of the personal distortion inherent in the purely observational recording of behavior.

A later research tool employed in investigating the responses of the newborn infant (Hunt, Clarke, and Hunt, 1936) was ultrarapid motion-picture photography as developed by Hunt and Landis (1936). Before their work ordinary motion pictures had been employed for record purposes, for frame analysis of some responses, and for a rough measurement of certain reaction times. With ultrafast motion pictures, however, Landis and Hunt were able to overcome the limitations of our sensorymotor mechanisms and to differentiate responses temporally which heretofore appeared to be overlapping and confused. As Landis and Hunt (1937) point out, what one observes depends in part upon the temporal relations of events, and hence it may become necessary in the future to state the temporal conditions of observation according to which the description of behavior applies.

In the statistical expression of data on infant behavior Bersot (1920, 1921) has been a pioneer. He stressed the need for noting and evaluating the variability of responses. Correlational procedures have been employed by the Shermans (1925) to follow maturational changes or improvement in responses with increasing age; by Furfey, Bonham, and Sargent (1930) to determine whether any general factor runs through all neonate responses; by Pratt (1930) to study the relation of activity to environmental temperatures; and by Irwin

(1932f) to pursue the change in activity from one nursing period to another. The standard error of percentage has been employed by Richards and Irwin (1934c) to determine the prevailing type of toe movements in the plantar response.

Richards and Irwin (1934a) have written the best account of experimental methods in the investigation of neonate behavior, and reviews of the behavior repertory of the infant have been furnished by Peiper (1928, 1930, 1949), Pratt (1933), Hurlock (1933), Stirnimann (1933, 1940), Dennis (1934), Dewey (1935), Munn (1938), and Irwin (1946). A bibliography of the physiology and pathology of the newborn has been compiled by Antonov (1947).

Physiology

Circulation. With the beginning of pulmonary respiration the course of fetal circulation changes to the postnatal type. With increase in age the cardiac rhythm decreases while the blood pressure increases (according to Feldman, 1920, the blood pressure is 60 in the newborn infant and 120 in the adult). Sontag and Wallace (1935a) found that the heart rate averaged 144 beats per minute during the latter part of the fetal period. Murlin, Conklin, and Marsh (1925), as reported by Richards (1935), obtained a basal pulse rate of 117 per minute in the neonate. Halverson's (1941) most comprehensive investigation of the pulse rate under different situations indicates great variation. In *profound sleep* the mean rate was 123.5; during *crying* it was 94.7 beats greater. The velocity of the pulse wave is said by Rominger and Meyer (1932) to increase with age. Bernfeld (1931) has confirmed the Yllpö thesis that the capillary resistance is less at first, particularly among prematures, and that this may be related to a high incidence of hemorrhages during the birth process.

Both rate of heart beat and blood pressure are modified by the various stimuli acting upon the organism. Sontag and Wallace (1935b, 1936) have shown that in the last month before birth vibratory stimuli applied to the mother's abdomen increase the average heart rate by 14.3 ± 0.74 beats per minute. The effects are first demonstrated during the third month before birth. They have also shown that 8 to 12 minutes after the expectant mother begins smoking the fetal heart rate increases 5 ± 0.19 beats per minute.

Canestrini (1913) proved the sensitivity of the neonate to stimuli of different modalities by registering the changes in rate and volume of the pulsations at the fontanelle. Although differentiation of modalities in terms of brain curves is impossible, some stimuli result in a slower pulse rate and others in a faster rate. These are interpreted as indicating, respectively, pleasant and unpleasant feeling tones.

Respiration. According to one view, pulmonary respiration is initiated by intense cutaneous stimulation. Runge (1895) is an exponent of this view. A second theory states that breathing is precipitated by a critical concentration of CO_2 acting upon the respiratory center. Other writers believe that both factors are operative. Peiper (1933a) adheres to the second theory. For him the viability of the premature infant depends upon the level or critical maturation of the respiratory center. In a number of researches he (1933a) and collaborators such as Good (1934) have discovered that the breathing movements of prematures have the characteristics of those which are physiological rather than pathological in lower animals. Creutzfeldt and Peiper (1932) have shown that death from respiratory failure depends upon immaturity of the respiratory center rather than upon its impairment by hemorrhages.

According to Peiper (1933a, 1933b), among the types of breathing indicative of immaturity of the respiratory center are periodic breathing (Cheyne-Stokes), which is sometimes seen in the full-term infant and which is characteristic of the premature, and gasping respiration (*Schnappatmung*), which reveals a still greater immaturity. Breathing of the neonate is of the abdominal type with the thorax becoming more involved when the child assumes an upright posture and begins to walk.

According to Schmidt (1950) and Peiper (1951), observations and motion pictures demonstrate that gasping (*Schnappatmung*) rather than the birth cry is the first respiratory response of the neonate. Schmidt (1950) found gasping to have a duration of 13 to 45 seconds in normal full-term infants, up to 6½ minutes in eighth-month prematures, and up to 12 minutes in difficult births.

Ahlfeld (1905) registered "breathing movements" of the fetus *in utero* of a rate similar to that of the neonate. In the neonate Vormittag (1933) reports the average to be 35 per minute during the first week after birth, and 37.7 per minute during the remainder of the neonatal period. By the end of the first year it has declined to 27.8, and from 10 to 15 years, to 19.1 per minute. Murphy and Thorpe (1931) found an average of 43.1 per minute in the newborn infant, and Peiper (1933a) places it between 35 and 45 per minute. Halverson (1941) reported that the breathing rate alters markedly from one situation to another and from one infant to another. In *sleep before awakening* the mean rate was 32.3; in *crying* it was 133.3 respirations per minute.

Employing a Krogh spirometer, Murphy and Thorpe (1931) found an average minute volume of 721.4 cc. and a mean tidal air of 16.7 cc.

A number of responses deeply involve or are intimately associated with the respiratory mechanisms. Among them are sneezing and coughing, reported as occurring shortly after birth. The birth cry itself is interpreted as a concomitant of the initiation of pulmonary respiration. Peiper (1933a, 1933b) interprets yawning, found even in young prematures, as a breathing movement of a primitive type but having no pathological significance in its persistence. Peiper (1933a, 1939b) has also demonstrated that during the suckling period a relation exists between the respiratory, sucking, and swallowing centers which enables the child to suck, swallow, and breathe at the same time, an ability not possessed by the adult. The rhythm of the swallowing center influences that of the sucking center, and this in turn influences the rhythm of the breathing center. The ratio of swallowing, sucking and breathing movements is commonly 1:1:1, less frequently 2:2:1. Swallowing occurs during the pauses between phases of breathing, according to Peiper (1939b) and Halverson (1944). Halverson (1944, 1946) reported that sucking movements occur simultaneously with breathing movements except during strong sucking, when the strongest sucks come after thoracic inspiration. In general, strongest sucking is accompanied by costal rather than abdominal breathing. Good coordination may be obtained even in premature infants. Peiper (1933a, 1933b) considers crying to be a breathing response.

The rate and amplitude of breathing movements in the newborn are, as Canestrini (1913) proved, modifiable by stimuli of various types and manifest great differences according to the physiological state of the child. As in circulation, the effects of stimuli upon respiration are general and nondifferentiating. Slow and regular breathing movements following certain stimuli are interpreted as revealing a pleasant feeling tone, whereas the heightened respiratory activity consequent to other stimuli is said to indicate unpleasant feeling tones. The effects of specific stimuli are mentioned in other sections of this chapter. Peiper (1933a) emphasizes the contrast in respiratory activity and regularity between sleeping and waking states.

Alimentation. Before birth, nutrient materials ready for assimilation by the fetus are furnished by the maternal organism. The alimentary tract, whose function it is to ingest food, to undertake its digestion, and to egest the indigestible materials, is not functional in the accepted sense of the term. But this does not mean that it is wholly inactive. Bersot (1920, 1921) has emphasized that here, as in respiration, there is preliminary activity during the fetal period. Examination of the contents of the alimentary canal reveals the presence of amniotic fluid which has been swallowed.

From the nutritional point of view it is to be noted that the transition to autonomy in digestion is accompanied by a loss of birth weight until about the middle of the first week, when the child begins to increase in weight and achieves birth weight by the seventh to tenth day. Various and conflicting theories have been developed to account for this loss in birth weight. According to one theory it is caused by scanty milk production. As a general explanation this seems untenable because supplementary feeding does not prevent some loss. This leads to the supposition that imperfect assimilation is responsible. A part of the loss may be mechanical as, for example, a loss of water. Talbot (1917a), however, believes that it arises because colostrum does not meet the energy requirements of the newborn infant.

In most mammals the process of alimentation is served by mouth orientation responses which, elicited by tactual stimulation of the face and lip areas of the young, operate to bring the opened mouth to the nipple. When contact or coupling is thus effected sucking starts, and ingestion of food follows. Salivation takes place and swallowing responses are coordinated with sucking and breathing. Gastric secretion likewise follows. When the stomach fills, the child ceases to nurse and contact is broken. Frequently there is regurgitation, often followed by hiccuping.

The stomach empties in 4 to 5 hours at most; the small intestines in 7 to 8 hours; and the large intestine within 2 to 14 hours. Kahn (1921) has noted that the young suckling differs most in this respect from the adult, who requires 20 to 40 hours for movement of materials through the colon. Proponents of self-demand feedings, such as Trainham and Montgomery (1946), assert that when cow's milk is used the passage through the stomach requires 3 to 4 hours but that with breast milk the duration is from 20 minutes to 1 hour.

Defecation or egestion completes the sequence of activities in the alimentary tract. Halverson (1940) has found that defecation occurs most frequently during the first half hour after feeding. On the basis of 8½ hours of daytime observation he places the median number of defecations in 24 hours at 4.7. Most of the defecations occurred during wakefulness, but, contrary to other observers, he reports that the infants are usually quiet during and after the act.

Aside from the fact that alimentation is a vital process, it is of interest to the student of behavior because it appears to be intimately associated with the two "drives" of "thirst" and "hunger." Simsarian and McLendon (1942, 1945) have stated that on a self-demand schedule of nursings infants were more variable as to frequencies, had a greater number of feedings, and spent more time nursing during the first 10 days after birth than infants under the customarily imposed schedules. Thereafter, al-though still highly variable, the infants' demands approached the 5–6 feedings per day which are characteristic of infant schedules in the culture. The relation of general activity or motility in the neonate to "hunger" has been the object of a number of investigations.

Having correlated the subjective "hunger" in adults with certain muscular contractions of the stomach, henceforth termed "hunger contractions," Carlson and Ginsburg (1915) have demonstrated their presence by means of the balloon technique in infants that have not yet nursed. These contractions differ from those of the adult only in the shortness of periods of quiescence between periods of contraction. According to these investigators, awakening and crying had some relation to the vigor of the contractions.

In more extensive studies R. Taylor (1917) found that the "hunger" contractions of the neonate were more vigorous than those of the adult. In the adult they may be inhibited when taste substances are introduced in the mouth; in the newborn infant no such effects follow. Small quantities of water or of milk introduced into the stomach, however, do produce temporary inhibition of the contractions.

Taylor (1917) describes the sequence of events as follows:

> The first contraction period is apt to be short. After a wait of perhaps twenty minutes a longer and more intense hunger period arrives; then another and another. The infant's sleep becomes lighter. He is more easily awakened by external stimuli or by gastric discomfort. He is put to the breast, nurses vigorously, becomes fatigued or experiences satiety from distention and again goes to sleep.

According to Taylor (1917), increase in reflex excitability is synchronous with the periods of these stomach contractions.

Often the contractions are accompanied by automatic sucking movements. In normal full-term infants "hunger" contractions begin about 2 hours and 50 minutes after nursing, during the first 2 weeks; from 2 to 8 weeks they start in about 3 hours and 40 minutes after nursing. This demonstrates that they arise before the stomach has emptied and are therefore not ascribable to an empty stomach. This particular study offered no evidence that "hunger" is the immediate cause of crying.

These studies, as well as those made of other animals, seemed to indicate that some of the general activity of such organisms is related to events in the alimentary tract. Pratt, Nelson, and Sun (1930) observed the difficulty of obtaining infants who were not crying and were not excessively active as a nursing period approached. They measured general activity in control periods set up to provide a basis for comparison of activity during periods of experimental stimulation.

The most thorough studies of general motility in the neonate are those made by Irwin (1930, 1932c, 1932f) and by Richards (1936a, 1936b). From his 24-hour studies of activity Irwin came to the following conclusion:

The fact that activity usually is greatest toward the end of the observation period, that is, just before nursing, and usually is least at the beginning of the period, just after nursing, suggests that the activity is stimulated probably by hunger contractions. This inference is best illustrated by the exceptional rise of the curve during the long night period when the nursings were eight hours apart. Since the external stimuli were constant, the conclusion seems justified that the activity of these infants is due largely to internal factors, presumably of the alimentary canal.

In a later research involving 73 infants, but with sampling of activity from 2:30 to 5:45 p.m. only, Irwin (1932e) substantiated his earlier findings and demonstrated that there is a significant increase in motility by the fourth to fifth day. Irwin (1932f) also found that general motility correlates .97 ± .04 with lapse of time from one nursing period to another. Contrary to usual belief, he found that more infants were awake during the first 15 minutes than during the last 15 minutes and that more were asleep during the middle 15 minutes of the period. Activity during the first 15 minutes amounted to 17.0 oscillations per minute; during the last 15-minute period it soared to 45.0 oscillations per minute.

Pursuing these studies of motility, Irwin (1933d) found that general motility correlated −.13 ± .008 with Pirquet's index of nutritional status, and .007 ± .08 with Finlay's index. Irwin (1932d) likewise found no significant relations to exist between intestinal area and motility.

Richards (1936c) has attempted to review the evidence bearing upon the nature and origin of the stimuli producing general activity in the newborn infant. He (1936a, 1936b) has conducted experimental researches to determine the relations between motility and muscular activity of the stomach. From the results he has concluded that peristaltic activity increases with the time since feeding. Bodily activity increases similarly but does not result from peristalsis because there is no more bodily activity during strong peristalsis than during gastric quiescence. Furthermore, the presence of the balloon in the infant's stomach inhibits general activity but not peristalsis. This investigator's conclusion, "It is likely that in hunger gastric activity is a specific reaction to the general nutritional state of the organism as expressed, perhaps, by constituents of the blood," leaves the problem of the direct excitant of motility still unsolved.

Excretion. Halverson (1940), on the basis of 8½-hour periods of observation of male infants, has estimated the average number of voidings per 24 hours to be 18.6. The greatest number of micturitions occurred during the first hour after feeding. A wide variation (ranging from 5 to 285 minutes) in the intervals between micturitions was observed. Most voidings took place during wakefulness and while the infant was quiet. The relation of micturition to bathing and to auditory or to other external stimuli appears as yet to have had no systematic study.

Secretion: Duct Glands. Most of the duct glands are functional at birth, although secretion may be limited in amount and restricted to specific stimuli.

Jacobi and Demuth (1923) reported that salivary secretion is difficult to elicit, occurring only during the feeding act. Stirnimann (1936c) also has commented upon the infrequency of salivation of newborn infants to gustatory stimulation. When it does occur to the experimental stimuli he views it as a protective reflex. The ferment concentration of the saliva is greater in the full-term infant than in the adult, according to Hensel (1933).

Nothmann (1909) obtained gastric juice when infants that had not yet nursed were allowed to suck upon an empty bottle. This would seem to indicate innate reflex connections between the sucking act and gastric secretion, but Schmidt (1927) was unable to confirm Nothmann's findings. The premature, as compared with the full-term, infant has a less acid and less stable gastric secretion, according to Schmitt and Móritz (1933).

Sweat and tear glands secrete during the neonatal period, but tears are not an accompaniment of crying. In relation to the protective effects of tear gland secretion Ködding (1940) reported about two spontaneous winks per minute in the neonate as contrasted with six appearing at the end of childhood. The histological studies of Becker (1921) indicate increased tempo of development of the structures in the skin during the neonatal period.

Feldman (1920) accounts for obliteration of the meatus of the ear by the presence of numerous sebaceous glands.

Mammary secretion (witch's milk) of the neonate has long excited popular interest, and an extensive literature has developed on the subject. It is found, regardless of sex, in the majority of newborn infants and is regarded by most investigators as a part of the physiological picture commonly described as the "genital crisis of the newborn." A few, including Feldman (1920), view such secretion as a pathological phenomenon.

Apert (1914), Arteaga (1918), Hoeland (1927), Lorenz (1929), Joseph (1929), and others hold that it first makes its appearance 3 to 4 days after birth. Apert (1914) maintains that it begins to decrease from the eighth day; Jaroschka (1929) that it disappears between 30 and 100 days; and Joseph (1929) that it stops in 3 to 4 weeks. Apert (1914), Hoeland (1927), and Lorenz (1929) report that all stages from colostrum to milk resembling mother's milk are secreted by the mammary glands of the neonate. Apert (1914) has stated the view of those who hold that the phenomenon is produced by placental hormones, whereas Zaharescu-Karaman and Nastase (1931) have demonstrated that intramuscular injection of ovarian sex hormone in female infants is followed by hypertrophy of the mammary glands. Arteaga (1918) found no relation of the dropping-off of the umbilical cord to mammary secretion. Hoeland (1927) and Lorenz (1929) have noted that manual expression of secretion from the glands plays the same rôle in developing and prolonging the period of secretion as nursing does to the maternal breast.

Castro (1930) found such prolongation occurred in only one breast of the infant whom he studied. The hormonal stimulation of mammary secretion has been minimized and criticized by Lorenz (1929). He believes that the times of incidence and maximum secretion are not compatible with theories that such secretion is caused by the presence or by the disappearance of placental or ovarian hormones from the infant's system.

Secretion: Ductless Glands. Indirect evidence indicates the functioning of endocrine glands fairly early in the fetal period. The thymus has been termed the gland of infancy and is said to have an inhibitory effect upon growth, particularly upon sexual development.

The Genital Crisis. During the early part of the neonatal period the infant manifests phenomena which are considered characteristic of puberty. In addition to mammary secretion in both sexes, female infants have enlargement of the uterus, secretion from its mucous membrane, growing follicles and blood spots, according to Hartmann (1932) and other investigators. Hartmann (1932) and Moore (1936) found evidence of stimulation or enlargement of the prostate, and the former investigator reported activity in the testes of male infants. He also held that these phenomena are produced by ovarian hormones and by those of the hypophysis. Litzka (1933) demonstrated that in pregnant guinea pigs these hormones pass through the placenta.

The phenomena of the genital crisis are not, however, to be interpreted as having the sexual significance of puberty. Not only are they transitory but they are also not accompanied by differentiation of receptor organs to make the genital zones highly sensitive to external stimuli. The histological researches of Becker (1933) reveal a marked contrast to the richly endowed oral areas of the neonate.

Similarly, Halverson (1940) found tumescence of the penis in male infants neither to have a sexual significance nor to be ascribable to the factors producing the genital crisis. Studying the time and incidence of the response in relation to micturition and to defecation, he concluded that tumescence was caused by pressure stimulation of the bladder. It is accompanied usually by restlessness and has a frequency of 3 to 11 per day with durations ranging from ½ minute to 66 minutes.

Metabolism. Birth represents an increase in the rate of living of the infant. The neonate's metabolism, in terms of unit surface, is not, according to Carpenter and Murlin (1911), above that of the nursing mother but is above "that of a woman in complete sexual rest."

Talbot (1917a) affirms that the basal energy requirement increases with age from 44 calories per kilogram at 1½ to 6 days to 55 calories at 4 to 5 months. Talbot (1917b) estimates that to maintain normal activity and growth 100 calories per kilogram of body weight is needed as a *total* energy requirement.

Schlossman and Murschhauser (1933) report the basic exchange of newborn infants involves an oxygen consumption of 27.9 cc. per minute with a respiratory quotient of 0.828.

The interrelations of metabolic rates, heat production, body temperatures, pulse rate, specific food, etc., have all received attention.

Benedict and Talbot (1914, 1915) and Talbot (1917a, 1917b) attempted to determine the relation of metabolism and pulse rate and to ascertain what proportions of the food energy are expended to produce activity and growth of infants.

Benedict and Talbot's standards for determining basal metabolism in infants have been confirmed by Levine and Marples (1931), that referring to stature being most reliable. In itself, age has slight relation to metabolism.

The creatinine coefficient is suggested by Paffrath and Öhm (1933) as an index of the level of muscular activity.

Rectal temperatures of newborn infants were discovered by Irwin (1933c) to range from 96 to 101.6° F. Correlation with activity expressed in stabilimeter oscillations per minute was $-.02 \pm .08$. Bayley and Stolz (1937) found a mean rectal temperature of 98.96 ($PE_m = .08$) at 1 month, and at 2 months one of 99.13 ($PE_m = .03$). Imperfect temperature regulatory mechanisms may make the infant slightly poikilothermic for a few hours, according to Herzfeld (1922). Talbot (1917a) maintains that healthy newborn infants tend to maintain their body temperature through increased muscular activity and crying. Levy (1928) indicates that temperature maintenance may be a serious problem in the premature infant.

In a critical survey of the relation of activity in the neonate to metabolic indices, Richards (1935) has concluded that no one index of physiological function correlates highly with bodily activity.

Neuromuscular Physiology. The first responses of the fetus, according to Minkowski (1928), may be idiomuscular rather than neurally aroused. The pioneer researches of Soltmann (1876, 1878), C. Westphal (1886), and A. Westphal (1894) showed that nerve and muscle tissues of newborn mammals are not as irritable as those of adult animals. This view as applied to human neonates is supported by Banu and Bourguignon (1921), by Banu, Bourguignon, and Laugier (1921), and by Rothe (1929). Rothe has stated that irritability is greater to mechanical than to electrical stimulation.

Banu and Bourguignon (1921), Banu, Bourguignon, and Laugier (1921), and Rothe (1929) found that muscle chronaxies

in the newborn infant are greater (2 to 10 times) than those of the adult. In the adult the chronaxies of different muscle groups are sharply differentiated; in the neonate there is little differentiation. In the neonate, proximal chronaxies are greater than distal chronaxies. Banu, Bourguignon, and Laugier (1921) associate this with an alleged greater movement of distal segments of extremities. These observations of movement run counter to those of Irwin (1930) and Shirley (1931a) regarding the order of development of movement.

Muscle chronaxies of neonates differ more than nerve chronaxies from those of adults. Muscle chronaxies approach adult values in 7 to 20 months, nerve chronaxies in about 2 months.

Reaction times are stated in those sections of this chapter which deal with the different types of stimuli.

Hazard (1936) found the slowest reflex conduction rate for the patellar reflex in the newborn infant. The rate increases throughout childhood.

In Smith's (1938a, 1938b, 1939) electroencephalograms of the neonate the pattern derived from the occipital electrodes is a "straight line," but from either post- or precentral regions there are "recurrent, brief, ill-defined series of rhythmic waves of various frequencies." They are present only in sleep and disappear when the child wakes. Ellingson and Lindsley (1949) reported nonpersistent rhythms in the precentral or motor area during the waking state. Persistent alpha rhythms over the sensory zones do not appear until the second postnatal month and are slower than in the adult. Only about 10 per cent of neonates have the sleep spindle-pattern characteristic of adults.

Flechsig's myelinogenetic law, function following myelinization, has been widely accepted even to modern times, as represented by Tilney and Casamajor (1924).

Conel (1939, 1941), in his histological studies of the cortex of the neonate, has employed myelinization as one criterion of differentiation and development of neural tissue but has been careful to point out that it is not known whether the neurones of the cerebral cortex at 1 month after birth are functional in the sense of conducting impulses, nor is it possible to state when the cortex does begin to function. Among the workers in the field of infant development, Bersot (1920, 1921), Minkowski (1922), Peiper (1925a), and Langworthy (1933) have maintained that function may precede myelinization.

Conel (1939, 1941) has mapped the differentiation and development of cells in the cortical areas from birth to the age of 1 month. He has called attention to the fact that the region which shows greatest development, the anterior central gyrus, is the one from which Smith (1938a) first obtained encephalograms of rhythmic waves. Whether these are indicative of anything except metabolic activities is not known.

Reactions to Visual Stimuli

Sensitivity. The ready arousal of various visual reflexes has obviated any serious doubt regarding the existence of visual sensitivity in the newborn infant. The functioning of mechanisms essential to sensory discriminations and to perception is not granted so readily. Thus the presence of retinal hemorrhages, the shape of the eyeball, the alleged nonfunction of accommodatory mechanisms, and so on, would seem to preclude the focusing of clear images upon the retinae, whereas the relative lack of fixation and coordination of the eyes would likewise deprive the child of binocular criteria for depth perception.

Relation to Stimuli. For the adult, visual discriminations vary according to the wavelength, wave amplitude, wave composition, and the duration of the visual stimulus.

According to Munn (1938), there are no unequivocal data indicating the possession by the neonate of differential responses to the wavelength characteristic of visual stimuli. Peiper (1926b), after his discovery of an ocular-neck reflex which is dependent upon the intensity of the visual stimulus, was the first to attack the problem of color vision experimentally in premature infants. According to Peiper, the totally color-blind adult does not manifest the Purkinje phenomenon. Hence, if the infant under dark adaptation can be shown to have the Purkinje shift in brightness, there is good reason to believe that the child reacts differently to different wavelengths of the visual stimulus. From his study of the four prematures Peiper concluded that the Purkinje phenomenon is present at this stage of development, the brightness values of the hues corresponding to those of the adult and thus implying color vision in the young infant.

Smith (1936) showed that even after dark adaptation the long-wave end remained brighter than or as bright as the short-wave end of the spectrum for Peiper's subject. Hence the Purkinje shift of greatest brightness to the short-wave end is not demonstrated. In her own investigation of the brightness values of hues for 20 newborn infants Smith employed three hues (blue, green, and red) of equal energy as transmitted by Wratten filters. Before subjecting the infants to the 5-minute illumination period they were dark-adapted for 5 minutes. The respiration and the activity during the two periods were automatically registered, and observers recorded responses and crying. The percentage of immediate overt responses and the respiratory responses failed to discriminate between the hues. Activity and crying were inhibited most by blue and least by red. Whether

the infant's eyes were closed or open did
not seem to affect this discrimination. In
terms of the means, blue and green—but
not red—inhibit crying and activity in
males, whereas all three hues are effective
for females. This student of the problem
concludes that the reactions of the male
infants conform to the picture presented by
the totally color-blind adult, whereas those
of female infants are compatible with di-
chromatic vision of the protanopic type.
Hence the brightness values for hues of the
same physical energy are not the same for
infants as for adults with complete color
vision.

Peiper (1937b), in commenting upon
Smith's criticism, states that the Purkinje
phenomenon refers to a change in brightness of the hues relative to each other
rather than to white light. He likewise
points out that Smith's subjects were not
completely dark-adapted, and he questions
whether a difference between the means
for the sexes warrants the conclusion that
one sex is color-blind and the other partially color-blind. Smith (1937), in reply,
notes that the crux of the disagreement
rests in conflicting interpretations of what
constitutes the Purkinje phenomenon.

Chase (1937), employing a small moving
spot of color within a larger field of another color but of the same luminosity
value for the adult, found that infants as
young as 15 days showed pursuit movements for all the hues studied but did not
pursue a colorless spot within a colorless
field of a different brightness. This is
taken to mean that the infant has differential reactions to the wavelength characteristics of the visual stimulus.

Stirnimann (1944a) measured the duration of the newborn infant's gaze upon colored papers and found the longest staring
to blue and green, the shortest to yellow.
Red came in between. For him this is proof
that the neonate discriminates hues by its

feelings and that it therefore has color sensations. He has likewise reported color-
contrast responses.

In regard to the Peiper-Smith controversy concerning color discriminations in
newborn infants, Munn (1938) [1] maintains
that the sex differences and brightness values for the different colors found by Smith
are not statistically reliable, but that her
criticism of the inadequacy of Peiper's data
in demonstrating equivalent brightness values of hues for infants and adults is valid.
He says:

> If the brightness value of hues is alike
> for infant and adult, the results of these
> experiments indicate color differentiation
> in very young infants. If the brightness
> value of the various hues is not the same
> for infant and adult, most of the data on
> color vision in infants are equivocal.

This fundamental difficulty in the investigation of color vision in infants had been
anticipated by Pratt, Nelson, and Sun
(1930) as follows:

> It seems that the structure and function
> of the adult eye must be regarded as one
> factor in our definition of luminosity.
> When we speak of the eye of the infant,
> the problem becomes more complex still.

Aside from the factor of duration, the
visible and measurable activity of the neonate seems to depend primarily upon the
intensity characteristic of the visual stimulus. Thus Peiper (1926c) determined the
threshold for the ocular-neck response,
whereas Sherman, Sherman, and Flory
(1936) observed that the rapidity of the
pupillary reflexes depends upon the intensity of the stimulus. Greater sensitivity
with increase in age is shown by a de-

[1] Munn, however, errs in saying that the differences
under discussion are less than three times the PE.
Some are less than three times the standard error of
the difference, but one may well ask whether this is
not primarily a reflection of the small size of the
sample.

crease in the intensity required to elicit the responses. Irwin [1] has repeated certain aspects of Peiper's experiment showing the effects of different intensities of light upon the ocular-neck reflex. The percentage of infants responding and the percentage of responses to stimulation of brief duration (1 second) and ranging in intensity from 5 to 200 foot-candles were recorded. He concluded "that when a brief stimulus is used with a specific reflex the relation is directly proportional, but when a stimulus of continued duration is used with general activity, the effect is inverse."

Greater general activity, according to Irwin and Weiss (1934c), occurs neither under moderate intensities of visual stimulation nor in complete darkness, but under minimal light conditions (0.002 foot-candle). The same investigators, using three intensities of light stimulation (3.9, 0.02, and 0.002 foot-candle), found that activity was greatest under minimal and least under moderate light. Observational records of activity and of crying for the most part corroborated the polygraph recording of the stabilimeter oscillations. Weiss (1934), in the preliminary study of this series using the intensities mentioned, had found that the immediate effects, if any, were excitatory but nondifferential of different intensities. With prolongation of the illumination, however, activity decreased with increase in the intensity of the visual stimulus. The maximal inhibitory effects occurred 2 to 4 minutes after the onset of the stimulus. Maximum differentials occurred when the infants were not close to a feeding period or younger than the fourth day. Females appear to be more sensitive to differences in intensity than males. Irwin (1941a), employing visual stimuli of 5, 25, and 50 foot-candles, demonstrated that general activity

is decreased by these higher intensities also. It was further shown that passage of the infant from an illumination period of 5 minutes' duration and at 5 foot-candles to a period of darkness is followed by an increase in activity.

The relation of intensity and adaptation is discussed in a subsequent section, and the effects upon activity of combining visual and auditory stimuli of some duration are reviewed in the section on the reactions to auditory stimuli.

With the demonstrated uncertainty regarding differential responses in the neonate to the wavelength characteristic of light, it is of course understandable that no investigations of possible reactions to wave composition have been undertaken. Peiper (1926c), Pratt, Nelson, and Sun (1930), Pratt (1934c), and others have reported that visual stimuli of short duration evoke limited reflexes such as the palpebral and the pupillary, or more extensive responses such as the Moro or the "startle." Stimuli of longer duration, as Weiss (1934) has shown, may at the outset produce similar results, but as they persist activity and crying decrease under dim and moderate illuminations.

Infants under low illumination approaching deep twilight conditions do not manifest any appreciable increase in bodily activity during experimental periods of repeated visual stimulation furnished by flashes of light at various time intervals, as contrasted with the activity in control periods.

Visual spot illumination moving within the general visual field may elicit eye and head pursuit movements.

Relation to State of Organism. The general effect of a period of dark adaptation is to increase sensitivity to visual stimuli. Under these conditions Peiper (1926b) found that stimuli of an intensity inadequate for the light-adapted eye are effective

---

[1] Personal communication to the writer upon the results of unpublished research.

in releasing the ocular-neck reflex. Similarly, according to Irwin and Weiss (1934c), there is decreased activity during periods of continuous dim or moderate stimulation, when such periods have been preceded by periods of darkness. Under subsequent minimal intensity of illumination, however, activity is increased. The dark adaptation process from beginning to final stages cannot be differentiated in terms of activity differences. Redfield (1937), employing dark adaptation periods of 1, 5, 10, and 20 minutes and intensities, in the later more extensive study (1939), of 0.5, 1.1, and 4.7 foot-candles in one series, and in another series of 0.04, 00.9, and 0.4 foot-candle, concluded that "increasing sensitivity to light after long as opposed to short periods of dark adaptation is indicated throughout the range of experimental intensities."

The possible alteration of the brightness values of hues and the question whether under dark adaptation the Purkinje phenomenon is produced have been considered in the review of the Peiper-Smith controversy.

In the activity differentials, from minimal to moderate intensities of visual stimulation, Weiss (1934) reported a greater decrease under waking conditions than when infants were asleep. Smith (1936), on the other hand, found no evidence of significant differences in the discrimination of the brightness of hues under these states of the infant.

The palpebral and most other overt responses are elicitable in both waking and sleeping states, but coordinated eye movements in pursuit of a moving light occur apparently only when the infant is awake.

Reaction Times. According to Canestrini (1913) the latent time of the circulatory and respiratory responses to visual stimulation is ½ to 2 seconds.

Types of Response. The responses range from the limited involvement of the accessory muscles of the visual sense organs to the greater involvement of the organism in circulatory and respiratory changes, in movements of the head and eyes, and more rarely of activity of most of the larger segments of the body. Inhibition of general activity appears when stimulation continues.

The *visuopalpebral reflex* (a closing of the eyes or a further tightening or twitch of the eyelids to a flash of light if they are already closed) had been described by Kroner (1881). Preyer (1882) was careful to distinguish this, as he termed it, innate blinking from the protective wink reflex to an approaching object, the latter not being elicitable until about the end of the second month. Pratt, Nelson, and Sun (1930) found that, in point of occurrence to discontinuous stimulation, the visuopalpebral response was the most invariable of those aroused by visual stimuli.

According to the early investigators, Kussmaul (1859), Genzmer (1873), and Kroner (1881), even premature babies manifest a lively *pupillary reflex.* Later investigators such as Guernsey (1929), Beasley (1933b), and Sherman, Sherman, and Flory (1936) seem to have demonstrated that the reflex, although sluggish at birth, rapidly perfects itself during the early part of the first postnatal week. Preyer (1882) and Feldman (1920) reported a consensual pupillary reflex. Gudden (1910) has noted that the pupil of the neonate is smaller than that of the adult during sleep and that there is no sudden dilatation to a maximum upon awakening. The continual play of movement of the margin of the iris, which increases upon external stimulation, was not found by Peiper (1926d) to occur in the neonate.

It is not known whether the ciliary muscle provides any *accommodation* in the early part of the neonatal period. The diameter of the eye, however, according to Peiper (1928), makes it myopic, and retinal hemorrhages would make it even less likely that clear-cut images can be focused upon the retina. Ling (1942) has scrutinized the criteria of fixation and has concluded that neither the focusing of an image upon the retina nor the convergence of the eyes is applicable to newborn infants. For this age the principal criteria of fixation are the immobility of the eye and the inhibition of "spontaneous movements" in response to the stimulus object. Hence fixation may be monocular in type and although not present at birth develop rapidly during the neonatal period.

The convergence of the two eyes to produce *fixation* upon a bright light was observed by Genzmer (1873) and Preyer (1882) in infants shortly after birth. The Shermans (1925) and the Shermans and Flory (1936) find improvement in the response during the first 3 days. Even after coordination has been demonstrated, however, *strabismus* may be observed. Gutmann (1924) had obtained similar results. Peiper (1928) maintains that there is no real fixation during the neonatal period, and Guernsey (1929) states that it is lacking until well into the second month. Beasley (1933b), on the other hand, finds coordination in fixation rather than incoordination to be the general rule. According to Ling (1942), neither convergence nor binocular fixation occurs during the period of the newborn infant.

Kussmaul (1859), Kroner (1881), Preyer (1882), Blanton (1917), and later investigators had observed that a slowly moving light arouses *pursuit movements* of the eye and head. Jones (1926) did not obtain true visual pursuit movements until after the neonatal period. The most completely instrumentalized study of these responses was undertaken by McGinnis (1930). Moving visual stimuli were furnished by a rotating visual field, and motion pictures were made of the eye movements. Under these conditions, successful pursuit (eye movements in the same direction without frequent movements in the opposite direction and with head movements decreasing in frequency) appeared after the second week. Beasley (1933a) and Chase (1937) report that visual pursuit occurs within the first week. Beasley found that vertical and circular pursuit movements appear later than the horizontal, thus confirming the order though not the age of occurrence of these responses as stated by Jones (1926). Morgan and Morgan (1944) have likewise established the earlier appearance of horizontal pursuit movements. According to Beasley (1933a), the optimum rate of movement and distance of the moving light from the eyes varies from infant to infant. This, if confirmed, reveals methodological weaknesses in those experimental techniques wherein these factors were constant from infant to infant. Visual pursuit movements of eye and head are analogous to those observed in young kittens and termed by Tilney and Casamajor (1924) the "oculocephalo-gyric" response.

Conjugate deviation and *coordinate compensatory eye movements* were photographed by Ling (1942) as early as 32 hours after birth.

Optic nystagmus, of the same type found in adults, was observed by McGinnis (1930) to be present in infants a few hours after birth. Catel (1932) reports "physiological" nystagmus in the newborn infant, whereas Bartels (1932) holds that such eye movements resemble those of the blind.

The *ocular-neck reflex,* a bending backward of the head to a flash of light, was shown by Peiper (1926c) to depend upon the intensity of the visual stimulus.

A bright, intense flash of light may evoke, as Peiper (1926c) has noted, a response which some have designated *fear* and others

Moro's Umklammerungs reflex. From the tables of Pratt, Nelson, and Sun (1930) it seems that either this or the "startle" have a higher incidence during the first days of the neonatal period. Dupérié and Bargues (1932), however, were unable to elicit the Moro response by visual stimulation.

According to Canestrini (1913), the respiratory and circulatory responses of the neonate resemble those of the frightened adult.

Weiss (1934), Irwin and Weiss (1934a), and Richards (1936b) have demonstrated that, within certain intensity ranges, general activity decreases as the intensity of the visual stimulus increases.

Learning. According to Denisova and Figurin (1929), visual CR's [1] appear later than auditory CR's and are not set up within the neonatal period. Wenger (1936), pairing visual and electrotactual stimuli for two infants, found some indication of conditioning by the sixth day.

Technique of Investigation. The earlier investigators of the problem of color vision had little or no control over their stimuli and were in no position to determine which aspects of the visual stimulus were related to the observed responses of the infant. The later investigators, employing Wratten filters, have presented visual stimuli of known wavelengths, physical energy, and luminosity value for the human adult.

The problem of the presence or absence of color vision in newborn infants has been approached by attempting to discover whether, under dark adaptation, there is a Purkinje shift in the brightness values of the hues similar to that found in the adult with normal color vision. The differences in duration of fixation of the eyes upon different-colored papers have also been utilized as an approach to the problem.

[1] CR is here used as an abbreviation for conditioned reflexes (or responses).

Another endeavor at solution consists in the movement of a colored spot within a visual field of the same luminosity for the adult, but of a different hue. The ocular-neck reflex has been used as an indicator of change in intensity to stimuli of short duration, and the effects of stimuli of long duration upon general activity have also been determined.

Pursuit movements have been studied in relation to manually produced moving visual stimuli and in relation to control of movement within a given plane.

Respiratory and circulatory responses have been recorded through pneumograph-kymograph systems, whereas general activity has been recorded through stabilimeter oscillations registered upon a polygraph or through electrical counters. Eye movements have been photographed.

Summary. The newborn infant reacts to light, but it is not certain whether any differential responses are made to the wavelength or to the complexity characteristic of visual stimuli. Responses do depend upon the duration and the intensity of the stimuli. Those which are sufficiently intense and of short duration release lid responses, circulatory and respiratory responses, the ocular-neck reflex, and probably the Moro and "startle" responses. If moving spot illumination within the visual field is provided there is some evidence of fixation, of pursuit movements, and of nystagmus. If the stimulus is of sufficient duration the pupillary reflex may be observed, and with continued illumination there is a decrease in general activity. Increasing the intensity, within certain limits, decreases the activity. The effect of a given stimulus intensity is profoundly influenced by the previous conditions of stimulation, that is, as in dark adaptation. Whether newborn infants manifest the Purkinje phenomenon is a matter of controversy.

Reactions to Auditory Stimuli

Sensitivity. From the earliest days of neonate study down to the present there has been a certain amount of controversy regarding the auditory sensitivity of newborn infants. Kussmaul (1859) was convinced that they were insensitive to auditory stimuli, whereas Genzmer (1873) claimed that not only did they possess such sensitivity on the first or second day after birth but that in all probability also the fetus received auditory stimulation from the heartbeats and aortic pulse and from the activities in the digestive tract of the maternal organism.

Kroner (1881) and Moldenhauer—according to Preyer (1882)—reported the early presence of sensitivity but commented upon its great variability. Moldenhauer observed the following reactions to auditory stimuli: quivering of the eyelids, wrinkling of the forehead, head movements, screaming, and awakening from sleep. Repetition of the stimulus either produced no effects or else was quieting. Poli (1893) and Sachs (1893) considered sensitivity to be evidenced by the palpebral reflex, and Sachs also noted the "fear" (*Schreck*) reaction.

Since these early investigations the existence of auditory sensitivity in the neonate has been confirmed by the researches of Koellreutter (1907); Peterson and Rainey (1910); Canestrini (1913); Blanton (1917); Waltan (1921); Peiper (1924c); Pratt, Nelson, and Sun (1930); Irwin (1932g); Pratt (1934b); Weiss (1934); Stubbs (1934); and Froeschels and Beebe (1946). A few writers during this period, namely, Feldman (1920), Löwenfeld (1927), Bryan (1930), and Haller (1932), maintain that there is relative insensitivity during the early postnatal days.

The discovery by Peiper (1924c), later confirmed by the observations and researches of Forbes and Forbes (1927), Ray (1932), Sontag and Wallace (1934, 1935b, 1936), and Bernard and Sontag (1947), that the fetus *in utero* reacts to vibratory stimuli of a rate affecting the auditory receptors of adults would seem to indicate a similar stimulation of the fetal auditory receptors. This may, however, take place through bone conduction, whereas postnatal insensitivity, if present, may depend upon the condition or state of structures normally responsive to air vibrations.

Various explanations have been offered for such alleged insensitivity: (1) mucus in the middle ear (Preyer, 1882); (2) occlusion of the external auditory meatus (Preyer, 1882; Feldman, 1920); (3) tympanic membrane not in a state to respond easily to air vibrations (Feldman, 1920); (4) fixity of auditory ossicles (Compayré, 1896); (5) transitory or permanent birth injuries (Kutvirt, 1912; Vosz, 1923); (6) imperfectly developed auditory nerve (Shinn, 1893–1899; Stern, 1914).

Relation to Stimuli. Auditory stimuli present certain variable characteristics of which the more important are frequency, amplitude, and complexity. As in other stimulus modalities, the duration of the stimulus is likewise of great significance.

There is no indubitable evidence that infants possess either differential responses to varying frequencies of vibration or the possibility of acquiring them during the neonatal period. Moldenhauer claimed that easily observed responses are more likely to occur to high-pitched sounds. This observation has been supported by Sachs (1893), who produced stimuli with tuning forks and Galton whistle; by Waltan (1921), who employed whistles and tuning forks; by Haller (1932), who used an audiometer; and by Muzio (1933) with tuning forks (according to this investigator females react quicker than males). In none of these investigations was there instrumentalized recording of responses.

Stubbs (1934) appears to have been the first to obtain adequate control of the auditory stimulus and at the same time to secure objective records of the responses of infants to it. The effects upon overt activity, recorded by the stabilimeter-polygraph unit, and upon implicit respiratory activity pneumographically registered, were compared when the stimuli were four different frequencies (128, 256, 1024, and 4096 cycles) produced by an audiometer at constant intensity levels in terms of sensation units and with a duration of 10 seconds. Observations were made by two observers, and their reliability was statistically determined. In this research the stabilimeter record disclosed no differences in overt responses to differences in frequency. Nor do the respiratory records reveal any effect of varying frequencies upon respiratory rate, but they do show significantly fewer cases of no response at the lowest as compared with the highest frequency. Of the responses observed, only eyelid opening and decrease in body activity appeared to occur more often at the lower than at the higher frequencies.

In view of Kasatkin and Levikova's (1935a) lack of success in establishing conditioned sucking responses to auditory stimuli before the first half of the second month, it seems unlikely that the conditioned reflex technique will demonstrate any capacity for pitch discrimination in the newborn infant.

The degree of organismic involvement in a response is related to the amplitude of the auditory stimulus. The correlation has been widely noted, but few have carefully investigated it. In the studies by Pratt, Nelson, and Sun (1930) the amount of measurable and observable activity of the neonate did not seem to correspond with the adult ratings of intensity or loudness of the experimental stimuli. The lack of control of the stimulus variables and the undetermined reliability of observations and of measurements render their evidence inadequate for determining the exact relationship of overt activity to the amplitude of auditory stimuli.

Stubbs (1934), who controlled the stimulus by means of audiometer and oscillator, found that with a 10-second duration for each frequency studied the percentage of responses increased as the stimulus intensities ranged upward from 30 through 50, 70 to 85 sensation units. The louder stimuli produced more bodily movements, greater frequency of eyelid closing and respiratory action, and a decrease in crying.

Weiss (1934) investigated the effects of two intensities (50 ± 5 and 75 ± 5 decibels) of a tone with a frequency of 420 cycles for durations of 5 minutes. She measured activity by stabilimeter oscillations and found that under sound-dark conditions the infant exhibited "a significant tendency toward lessened activity with increased sound intensity." In the sound-light experiment visual stimulation reinforced the auditory to bring about an even greater lessening of activity.

The possibility of variation of responses according to variation in the complexity of the auditory stimulus does not seem to have received any experimental study.

Early observations, such as those by Sachs (1893), and all later studies show that overt responses are greater if the stimulus duration is short (as in noises), whereas there may be inhibition of activity or complete lack of response if the stimulus is of longer duration (as in musical tones). These pacifying or inhibiting effects of stimuli of longer duration have been reported by Pratt, Nelson, and Sun (1930). These latter observations should be accepted with caution because the intensities of the stimuli employed were not adequately controlled. Haller (1932) reported that even with a stimulus duration of only 10 seconds the response began with the onset of stimulation and declined or disappeared by the time the stimulus had ceased. Stubbs (1934) used durations of 1, 3, 5, and 15 seconds. The percentage of responses to the longest duration was significantly greater than to the shortest duration of the stimulus. The longer durations operated also to evoke greater bodily activity, increases in rate, and corresponding decreases in amplitude of respiratory responses. The longer durations, such as the 5-minute periods given by Weiss (1934), decrease bodily activity significantly as compared with periods during which no stimuli are presented.

These experiments seem to indicate that the auditory stimulus first releases certain overt responses and thereafter, if the stimulus persists, overt activity subsides and there is less movement than would occur in a period of no experimental stimulation. The continuous stimuli may inhibit the activity which ordinarily results from internal stimuli, or possibly the situation is analogous to the "listening" posture of the adult.

Discontinuous, repeated auditory stimuli produce rapid decreases in the circulatory and respiratory responses, according to the researches of Canestrini (1913). And Peiper (1924c) found that the "fear" response of the fetus *in utero* usually followed upon only the first stimulus. They ascribe this decline to inhibition rather than to fatigue. Pratt (1934b) used relatively constant but unmeasured auditory stimuli to demonstrate that during a period of discontinuous auditory stimulation activity is confined to movements following the discrete stimuli, that the response declines with successive repetitions of the stimuli, and that the amount of activity per stimulation decreases as their frequency is increased within a given period of time.

Relation to State of Organism. Aside from the transitory residual effects of previous stimulation it is known that the response evoked by a given stimulus is also dependent upon the physiological state of the organism. Poli (1893) observed that the cochlear-palpebral reflex (principally closing of the eyes if they are open or further tightening of the lids if they are closed) was most easily elicited during sleep but was most difficult to activate when the child was nursing. Canestrini (1913) noted that the nature of respiratory and circulatory responses depended somewhat upon whether the infant was asleep or awake. Peiper (1925b) obtained a longer reaction time for the "fear" reaction during sleep than during waking, and a number of investigators have affirmed that this "fear" response is best detected in the sleeping infant. That it is invariably followed by awakening is not supported by the data of Pratt, Nelson, and Sun (1930). Stubbs (1934) found that the smallest percentage of responses to auditory stimuli occurred when infants were crying, and the largest when they were awake and inactive.

Reaction Times. Peiper (1925b) reported a longer reaction time for premature infants than for a 2-month-old infant (0.25 second for the latter). Irwin (1932g), with an auditory stimulus of 581 cycles, a duration of 0.07 second, and a constant unmeasured intensity, found that the mean "body startle" reaction time of twelve infants, measured by stabilimeter-polygraph records, was 0.18 ± 0.03. The reaction time of respiratory responses was found by Stubbs and Irwin (1934) to be 0.09 second, with a standard error of the mean of 0.025.

Types of Responses. The overt responses elicited by discontinuous auditory stimuli, according to the intensity of the stimuli and the previous stimulating conditions, range from the minimum involvement of the palpebral reflexes on through to the maximum involvement of most of the large behavior segments. When auditory stimuli are continuous for some appreciable duration, decrease in activity sets in after the initial overt responses.

The *cochlear-palpebral reflexes* may occur in relative isolation when the stimuli are of slight intensity or when the infant has been repeatedly stimulated, as Pratt (1933, 1934*b*) has shown. Moldenhauer was one of the first to observe these in the complex of responses, and Cemach (1920), who gave them particular attention, emphasized their persistence beyond the neonatal period. Irwin (1932*g*) has noted that they are more invariable in occurrence than the "body startle," whereas Landis and Hunt (1939) have maintained that blinking is a component of the "startle" pattern. Froeschels and Beebe (1946) also have reported acoustopalpebral reflexes as the most frequent reaction to auditory stimulation.

Bartels (1910) and Peiper (1928) state that auditory stimuli produce pupillary dilatation in newborn infants, but Peiper observes that there is great irregularity in its occurrence.

When infants are asleep, according to Canestrini (1913), auditory stimuli of some duration, such as musical tones, make breathing slower and shallower and decrease the pulse rate. If the stimuli are intense enough to wake the child the rates of respiration and pulse are increased. Intense stimuli of short duration (such as a pistol shot) result in an immediate increase in the amplitude of respiration, followed by irregular breathing. Stubbs (1934) found that increase in intensity and duration had measurable consequences in respiratory responses and that "respiratory responses were found less often to higher than lower pitches."

The earlier investigators of neonate behavior were impressed with the gross muscular response of the infant to auditory stimuli. Sachs (1893) was one of the first to term these reactions the "fear" (*Schreck*) response, and Watson (1919) made the alleged emotional pattern one of the cornerstones in his theory of three primary emotions. Peiper (1925*a*) was one of the first to liken the fear response, as elicited by auditory stimuli, to the "Moro" response, while granting that there was a difference in latent time. Schaltenbrand (1925) maintained that the Moro response was elicited by sudden sounds. Following these, Irwin (1932*g*), Pratt (1934*b*), Dennis (1934), Richards (1936*a*), and Wenger (1936) have held that the terms "fear," "body jerk," "body startle," etc., are merely different names for a general but variable response which may be elicited by stimuli of various modalities.

Other research workers have insisted that the fear response and the Moro response are distinct, for, according to Dupérié and Bargues (1932), the Moro cannot be evoked by auditory stimuli. They and Gordon (1929) maintain that the responses merely simulate each other, and they agree with Peiper (1925*a*) that in a given stimulus situation the fear reaction precedes the Moro.

Strauss (1929), as reported by Hunt, Clarke, and Hunt (1936), ascribed a "startle" response to intense auditory stimuli which differed not only in pattern but in age of appearance from the Moro response. According to this view, the Moro, but not the startle, is present during the neonatal period. In regard to arm movements, Hunt and Landis (1938) have stressed the extensor characteristic of the Moro as compared with the flexor characteristic of the startle.

Pratt (1937) viewed all these as variants of the Moro, and Wagner (1938*a*) has proposed that they all be called "body jerks." Hunt and Landis (1938) and Hunt (1939) point out that the evidence from ultrarapid motion pictures reveals two patterns of response, one commonly known as the Moro and the other which they, following Strauss, call the startle. They (Landis and Hunt, 1939) assert that both patterns are clearly present at 6 weeks and that after a few months the Moro disappears but the startle remains. They cautiously favor the view that both responses may be present from birth, with the startle somewhat masked by the Moro (for segmental comparison of these see the section on the Moro and startle responses).

Pratt (1933) described variable plantar responses as part of the response to auditory stimuli, and Clarke, Hunt, and Hunt (1937) have photographed them. Pratt, using less intense stimuli than those employed by the three later investigators, noted that toe movements and the palpebral reflexes in many instances persist as other components of the response drop out with successive repetitions of the stimulus.

Waltan (1921), Froeschels and Beebe (1946), and others have claimed that some infants turn the eyes and head toward the source of auditory stimulation.

Learning. The conditioned reflex technique, as a means of studying auditory sensitivity, was suggested by Aldrich (1928). Kasatkin and Levikova (1935a), however, were unable to establish conditioned sucking responses during the neonatal period. Denisova and Figurin (1929), according to Razran (1933), established conditioned food-seeking responses to auditory stimuli during the second month, although natural as opposed to laboratory CR's appeared during the first month. Marquis (1931) stated that conditioned sucking and quietening to auditory stimuli were established during the first ten days after birth. Wenger (1936), despite some masking of the conditioning auditory stimulus by other auditory stimuli, obtained some indication of unstable leg withdrawal and respiratory "gasp" CR's with electrotactual unconditioned stimuli. The Wickenses (1940) attempted, with inconclusive results, to set up auditory-leg movement CR's, with electric shock as the unconditioned stimulus.

Technique of Investigation. Auditory stimuli have been produced with varying degrees of control by tuning forks, Galton and Urbantschitsch whistles, devices providing constant but unmeasured stimuli, and instruments of precise control such as the audiometer. Circulatory and respiratory responses to auditory stimuli have been recorded by means of pneumatic systems (pneumograph and tambour), the kymograph, and the polygraph. Gross movements and increase or decrease of bodily activity have been recorded by means of stabilimeter-polygraph systems or by stabilimeter oscillations through electrical counters. Reaction times have been measured by a modified Morse apparatus, by the stabilimeter-polygraph apparatus, and by ultrarapid motion-picture photography. The patterning of responses and the incidence of responses not registered by mechanical systems have been recorded by some observers and photographed by others.

Summary. The neonate is not deaf, but there is little evidence that it makes pitch discriminations or differential responses correlated with the complexity characteristic of auditory stimuli. Its responses are, however, modified according to the duration and the intensity of the stimuli. If they are of short duration and sufficiently intense, responses such as lid reflexes, circulatory and respiratory changes, and gross muscular patterns of response, such as the Moro and possibly the startle, appear. With successive repetitions of the auditory stimuli the gross muscular components decline in extent of involvement and disappear, leaving the more invariant palpebral reflexes, and frequently responses of the toes. If the stimuli are of long duration their effect is to lessen the activity which would normally occur during the period, and the decrease becomes greater as the intensity of the stimulus is increased.

Reactions to Olfactory Stimuli

Sensitivity. The demonstration of the presence or absence of olfactory sensitivity in the neonate presents such methodological difficulties that the lack of agreement of different investigators is not surprising. Some have held that the sense of smell is important and well developed. Among them are Darwin (1877), Kroner (1881), and Peterson and Rainey (1910). Somewhat less certain of the importance and of the maturity of this sensory field are Ciurlo (1934) and Stirnimann (1936b, 1936c), whereas Disher (1934) is willing to grant that the neonate at least discriminates between odorous and nonodorous substances. Most of the workers in this field, however, have been extremely doubtful whether newborn infants react to olfactory stimuli. Kussmaul (1859), although subscribing to the view that the infant possesses olfactory sensitivity, was one of the first to note that ammonia and acetic acid fumes were most effective in eliciting reactions and to decide that such substances produce their effects as tactile rather than as olfactory stimuli. Preyer (1882) supported this view by saying that such substances irritate the mucous membrane of the nose. Canestrini (1913) found that only such substances affected respiration and circulation. He ascribed these effects to stimulation which set up impulses in the trigeminal nerve. Watson (1919) and Peiper (1928) accept this interpretation, and Tanner (1915), Blanton (1917), Drum-

mond (1921), and Pratt, Nelson, and Sun (1930) likewise hold that olfactory sensitivity is not present or else is poorly developed.

Relation to Stimuli. In the first researches to introduce the principle of a nonodorous air control, a duration control by means of an olfactory pump, and a high degree of saturation of a given volume of air at room temperatures, Pratt, Nelson, and Sun (1930) used acetic acid, ammonia, oil of cloves, and valerian as stimuli. The observers noted the number of responses to stimuli, recorded in code the movements of different segments of the body, and afterward measured the stabilimeter-polygraph records of activity. Although they did not determine the statistical reliability of their observations and measurements, there seems little doubt that of the substances employed only ammonia and acetic acid, as evaluated by the air control, produced unquestionable results. Analysis of the percentage of specific movements of body segments in the responses that did occur to the different stimuli shows that with the air control the body extremities and eyes were most often involved, whereas there were scarcely any head or facial movements. Vocalizations and facial responses had greater incidence to ammonia and acetic acid. Sucking was more conspicuous in the responses to valerian. The infants reacted about as vigorously to acetic acid as to ammonia, whereas adults considered acetic acid much less irritating than the ammonia.

Disher (1934) devised a thermal control and used gas-collecting tubes for her reservoirs of odors. Three different degrees of saturation were obtained by drawing from these and from a pure air source by hypodermic syringes. Stimulation was effected by pushing on the plunger of the syringe while the experimenter counted to 25. Besides the nonodorous air control, odorous substances following Henning's classification, such as violet, asafetida, sassafras, citronella, turpentine, pyridine, and lemon, were employed. Responses were recorded by two observers, and a set of motion-picture records was made. According to this investigator, newborn infants respond significantly in terms of percentage response to stimulation by the odor stimuli as compared with the percentage response to stimulation by pure air. Observation and segmental analysis of the responses, however, disclose no evidence of differential odor discriminations, and the pattern of responses to air alone, when there are responses, is apparently no different from that aroused by olfactory stimuli. Percentage of response and extent of organismic involvement appear to depend upon the degree of saturation of the olfactory stimulus.

Ciurlo (1934), using essence of lavender, valerian, and mint, which, it is supposed, do not stimulate the trigeminal nerve, is reported to have demonstrated by means of graphic records of respiration that the newborn infant differentiates odors as pleasant or unpleasant.

Stirnimann (1936b, 1936c) is of the opinion that volatile substances stimulate not only the olfactory and trigeminal nerves but also the glossopharyngeal nerve. The absence of the olfactory nerve does not lead to lack of response to stimuli which are ordinarily supposed to stimulate the olfactory nerve and to be pleasant. Hence the interpretation that the trigeminal, when activated, gives only unpleasant experiences is unwarranted. Stirnimann holds that differential responses to odorous stimuli are revealed by facial or mimetic responses.

Anise oil involves nasal taste (*gout nasale*) and gives rise to expressions of pleasure and to sucking and licking responses. Oil of chenopodium leads to grimaces of discontent; ammonium carbo-nate produces grimaces and pronounced turning-away of the head from the test tube containing the substance.

Types of Response. The overt responses elicited by ammonia, acetic acid, and so on consist of a throwing-back or turning-away of the head, wrinkling or grimacing of the face, squirming of the trunk, movements of the extremities, and frequently sneezing and crying. Such substances likewise affect respiration and circulation. Other substances, such as anise oil, essence of lavender, valerian, mint, and oil of chenopodium, generally held to be purely odorous stimuli, may give rise to *mimetic* and respiratory responses, supporting a classification into agreeable or disagreeable odors, according to Ciurlo (1934) and Stirnimann (1936b, 1936c). The "pleasant" odors may be accompanied by sucking and licking movements.

Technique of Investigation. The duration, saturation, and temperature of the air in which olfactory stimuli are presented have been controlled by various devices such as the olfactory pump, reservoirs of fully saturated vapor, and pure air source. Responses have been recorded by observers, photographed with the motion-picture camera, and registered by the stabilimeter-polygraph unit. Respiratory and circulatory responses have been graphically recorded by pneumograph-kymograph combinations.

Summary. It seems to be well established that newborn infants react vigorously to such stimuli as ammonia and acetic acid, but whether these rather general reactions of the body musculature are to be ascribed to the sense of smell or of pain is uncertain. According to some investigators, other substances, which are purely odorous for adults, are responded to by infants with mimetic responses indicating "pleasant" or "unpleasant" experiences. Some stimuli lead to avoiding movements; others are followed by sucking and licking responses.

Reactions to Gustatory Stimuli

Sensitivity. Taste was considered by Kussmaul (1859), Preyer (1882), and Peterson and Rainey (1910) to be highly developed in the neonate. Shinn (1893–1899) believed it to be dormant, and Blanton (1917) maintained that taste, smell, and touch are not differentiated at this time. Canestrini (1913) obtained prompt circulatory and respiratory responses to gustatory stimuli but no reactions which would indicate differential responses or discrimination between "sour" and "bitter" stimuli. Pratt, Nelson, and Sun (1930) observed little differentiation, particularly when the percentage of responses evoked was compared with the percentage elicited by distilled water. With increase in age it appears that sucking responses to sugar solutions increase, whereas facial reactions become more pronounced to "salt," "sour," and "bitter" stimuli. Stirnimann (1936b, 1936c) holds that the neonate demonstrates taste discriminations of all four qualities, largely in terms of facial or mimetic reactions. Eckstein (1927) and Jensen (1932) have demonstrated that certain taste substances modify the sucking response.

Relation to Stimuli. The problem of taste sensitivity in the neonate resolves itself into several questions. Does the child make differential responses to taste substances? Are these of the same order or nature as those of the adult? Does the response alter as the strength of the stimulus is changed? The problem is complicated, as in the case of olfactory stimuli, by the fact that other than taste receptors are being stimulated. Also, the area of stimulation is not easily controlled. The arousal of a response may, again, depend upon the intensity rather than upon its specific modality. And, unfortunately, the effective strength of gustatory stimuli cannot be established in terms of equally concentrated solutions. Nor, as Pratt, Nelson, and Sun (1930) found, can it be said that the effective intensity of a taste substance is the same for the infant as for the adult.

Introduction of gustatory stimuli by means of applicator sticks dipped in solutions of salt, sugar, citric acid, and quinine in Pratt, Nelson, and Sun's investigation did not, when compared with similar introduction of distilled water, provide impressive evidence for taste differentiation in infants. Quinine and citric acid solutions appeared to be more effective than salt and sugar solutions. Jensen (1932), using the sucking reflex as an indicator, found differential responses (changes in the sucking response as compared with the control of mother's milk) to air and salt solutions. The approximate limen for the latter is a solution of 0.300 per cent. These differential reactions do not appear until the infant has sucked a few seconds, and therefore the reactions may depend upon the stimulation of other areas than those involved in experiments wherein the taste substance makes immediate contact with tongue areas.

Stirnimann (1936b, 1936c) applied taste solutions to the newborn infant's tongue by means of a nipple-shaped piece of cotton. In his opinion the neonate discriminates all four of the taste qualities, although there are no responses which may be said to be characteristic of each one. The differentiation is evidenced in part by differences in mimetic responses and in part by the sequential order of these in relation to responses of withdrawal, repulsion of the stimulating device, or in relation to sucking responses. The same investigator found that infants reacted more vigorously to a 7 per cent solution of saccharine than to a 7 per cent lactose solution, and again more vigorously to a 16 per cent solution of the lactose solution than to the weaker solution of the same substance. No clear-cut differentiation was made between 0.9, 1.5, and 2.0 per cent salt solutions.

Relation to State of Organism. Jensen (1932) states that the "moderately full baby is a better discriminator than the very hungry infant."

Reaction Times. The responses to gustatory stimuli are varied in nature. From Canestrini's (1913) curves it seems that circulatory and respiratory responses follow quickly upon stimulation. Other responses apparently have a longer latent time.

Types of Response. According to Stirnimann (1936b, 1936c), taste as well as tactual stimuli frequently release a *vasomotor reflex* which produces a tumefaction of the inner surface of the lips. *Sucking responses,* as reported by Pratt, Nelson, and Sun (1930), occur to all taste stimuli. They are more pronounced to sugar solutions and become increasingly so with age. Stirnimann (1936b, 1936c) found these responses to be greatest to lactose, with citric acid a close second, but only of feeble occurrence to stimulation by quinine. Sonohara (1934a) found, as had Stirnimann, that saccharine arouses sucking responses. Jensen (1932) discovered that only salt solutions, among gustatory stimuli, impaired the sucking responses or caused them to cease. This confirms Canestrini's observation.

Movements of the tongue and lips, sometimes termed *defense* or *rejection,* have been observed by Pratt, Nelson, and Sun (1930) and by Stirnimann (1936b, 1936c). Stirnimann noted that muscles of the pharynx are innervated, as in vomiting. Allied to these responses are general activity and even crying. Sonohara (1934b) disagrees with most investigators, who hold that "bitter" stimuli evoke reactions of rejection.

Some have held that facial responses or mimetic reactions—the "wry" face, for example—are rather characteristic to "bitter" stimuli.

The *salivary reflex,* as Stirnimann (1936b, 1936c) and others have noted, is not well established in the neonate.

According to Canestrini (1913), "sweet" stimulation calms the child, salt solutions produce a slight disturbance, and "sour" and "bitter" solutions initiate pronounced irregularity of the *respiratory* and *circulatory* curves.

Technique of Investigation. In most of the investigations the concentrations of the taste solutions have been stated. Responses to these have been compared with those evoked by distilled water and mother's milk as controls. These substances have been introduced into the infant's mouth by applicator sticks or other devices, or have been sucked from a special nursing bottle. The mimetic and other responses have been recorded by observers, while circulatory, respiratory, and sucking responses have been automatically registered by kymographs and polygraphs.

Summary. It is uncertain whether the neonate differentiates all four taste qualities. It appears, however, that in terms of the sucking response salt solutions tend to break up the response, whereas sugar solutions elicit and maintain it. Acid solutions to a lesser extent evoke sucking; quinine solutions seldom do. Facial responses mimetic of "disagreeable" affects are conspicuous responses to the latter. In general, respiration and circulation are least influenced by "sweet," slightly disturbed by "salt," and considerably affected by "sour" and "bitter" solutions. Sucking mounts with age to sugar solutions as do facial responses to quinine. There is some evidence that, beyond the threshold point, responses may be altered by differences in concentration of the taste solution.

Reactions to Thermal Stimuli

Sensitivity. The presence of thermal sensitivity in the newborn infant was noted by early experimenters, Genzmer and Kroner, and has not been questioned in subsequent studies.

The researches which have been undertaken involve either limited areal stimulations (but not punctiform exploration in newborn infants) or activity under different environmental temperatures. There has been no really systematic exploration of the cutaneous surface or other parts of the body to ascertain the differential sensitivity of the various areas. Canestrini (1913) demonstrated that "cold" stimuli applied to the forehead produced prompt and vigorous circulatory and respiratory responses. Pratt, Nelson, and Sun (1930), stimulating the same area with a temperature cylinder (50 sq. mm. application area) at an average temperature of 11 to 12° C., obtained observable responses to 73 per cent of the stimulations. Stirnimann (1939), applying water-filled glass tubes (18 mm. diameter) to the infant's cheeks, found 89 per cent response to temperatures of 43 to 45° C. and 96 per cent response to temperatures of 15 to 17° C. Peiper (1924b), holding constant the contact while changing the thermal stimulation, stimulated the chest with "cold" stimuli and obtained pronounced responses. Stirnimann (1939) stimulated hand areas (hollow of the hand or ball of the thumb) with the temperatures previously mentioned and received no response in 74 per cent of the cases. Application by Pratt, Nelson, and Sun (1930) of the temperature cylinder to the inner surface of the leg at the knee yielded reactions to 91 per cent of the stimulations. Crudden (1937), employing stimuli of ±5° C. or more from the initial neutral (33 to 34° C.) and applying them by Peiper's technique to the dorsal surface of the leg midway between foot and knee, reported some degree of response, as shown by examination of cinema records, to all stimulations. Stirnimann (1939) obtained 94 per cent response to stimulations of the sole of the foot by stimuli of 43 to 45° C., and 100 per cent to those of 15 to 17° C. Although the size of cutaneous areas stimulated and the duration of the stimulation vary in the researches mentioned, they suggest the possibility that leg and foot are more sensitive to thermal stimuli than hand and head areas.

Thermal sensitivity has likewise been demonstrated in the oral cavity. Pratt, Nelson, and Sun (1930) introduced small amounts of distilled water at temperatures ranging from 8 to 53° C. and observed the movements which were elicited. Jensen (1932) measured the alterations produced in the sucking response by milk at temperatures above and below 40° C.

Environmental temperatures likewise give evidence of the thermal sensitivity of the newborn infant. If they are atmospheric, activity tends, as Pratt (1930) has shown, to be negatively correlated with them. Excitatory effects of lowering the temperature of the bath have been noted by Preyer (1882). Exposure of the forehead or of the whole body, or stimulation of the arm by rapid evaporation, had no effect, according to Herlitz (1942–1943), upon pulse rate or blood pressure and produced no consensual skin capillary reactions, but the temperature both of the abdomen and of the rectum fell.

The thermal sensitivity of the neonate has not been compared with that of children in later developmental stages, nor are we able from the work of Peiper (1924b) and Stirnimann (1939) to compare with any certainty the premature with the full-term infant.

Relation to the Stimuli. Temperatures present continuous series, but the "cold" spots respond when some critical point below physiological zero (skin or other body temperature) is reached and again, paradoxically, when a critical point above physiological zero is attained, whereas the "warm" spots respond only when a critical point above physiological zero is reached.

Physiological zero in infants has been given various values by different investigators and according to the area stimulated. It seems clear that oral and anal temperatures will differ from cutaneous temperatures. It is also evident that any thoroughgoing investigation of thermal sensitivity will require the determination of the skin or body area temperature for each neonate before the application of the thermal stimulus.

Pratt, Nelson, and Sun (1930) did not ascertain the temperatures of the areas stimulated. Stimulation of head and leg areas with the temperature cylinder at 33 to 45° C. did not seem to produce appreciable responses, whereas at 11 to 12° C. vigorous responses were aroused. Crudden (1937), on the basis of lack of response in preliminary trials, decided that 33 to 34° ±5° C. was neutral for the area of the leg which he studied.

To oral stimulation, by distilled water applied with a medicine dropper, Pratt, Nelson, and Sun (1930) observed least response at 43° C. among temperatures of 8, 13, 18, 23, 33, 48, and 53° C. From these studies it would appear that the point of least stimulation for this area must lie between 33 and 43° C. Jensen (1932) found no disturbances in the sucking response to mother's milk at 40° C. The higher thresholds or critical points ranged from 50 to 65° C. (median approximately 52° C.); the lower thresholds ranged from 23 to 5° C. (median approximately 19° C.). Physiological zero for mouth areas seems to be within the range 35 to 36° ± 16 to 17° C., and Crudden's (1937) figures show it to be 33 to 34° ± 5° C. for leg areas.

Among early investigators, Preyer (1882), Canestrini (1913), and Peiper (1924b) were impressed with the potency of temperatures below physiological zero as compared with temperatures correspondingly higher. Pratt, Nelson, and Sun (1930) and Crudden (1937) have drawn similar conclusions. Jensen (1932), however, has pointed out that in terms of critical points for the sucking response the lower temperatures employed by Pratt, Nelson, and Sun represent greater deviations than the higher temperatures. Pratt, Nelson, and Sun and Jensen have reported that the incidence and extent of the response depend upon the degree of deviation from the critical thresholds. Crudden found no consistent relationship.

Purely thermal stimulation is difficult if not impossible to set up. In the case of stimuli applied through thermal conduction the only control available is to make the contact stimuli constant while varying the thermal. According to Peiper (1928), Sikorski (1908) reported a turning of the head toward the side stimulated by thermal radiation. Peiper (1928) was unable to confirm this, but Stirnimann (1939), using a *Goldscheiderlampe aus Rubinglas*, found reactions in 85 per cent of the stimulations, with movements toward the stimulus.

Relation to State of Organism. The effect of previous stimulation is illustrated by Crudden's (1937) demonstration of the setting-up of temporary neutral temperatures, in other words, the rapid onset of adaptation.

Pratt, Nelson, and Sun (1930) did not find any clear difference between thermal sensitivity during sleep and waking states, but Crudden (1937) and Stirnimann (1939) are inclined to the view that the threshold is raised in sleep.

The enormous range between the high and low thresholds for thermal effects upon the sucking response, reported by Jensen (1932), may reflect the physiological state of the infant when nursing. Under different conditions the range of thermal neutrality might be considerably reduced.

Reaction Times. According to one of Canestrini's figures (1913), the reaction time of circulatory and respiratory responses to stimulation of the forehead with a cold piece of metal is not more than 0.5 second. Effects upon sucking are shown by Jensen (1932) to be delayed several seconds and to vary with the temperature deviation. Possibly this indicates the dominance of the stimuli producing the sucking response, or it may simply mean that changes in the sucking response await stimulation of other portions of the alimentary tract. With the capsule technique, Crudden (1937) reports reaction times of 2.5 to 11 seconds, with an average of 6.8 seconds to stimulation of the leg area.

Types of Response. Acceleration of breathing, throwing the head backward, gasping, shuddering, increase in brain volume, and irregular pulse follow the application of "cold" stimuli to the infant's forehead. Stimulation of the cheeks with temperatures of 15 to 17° C. leads to a turning-away of the head, whereas those of 43 to 45° C. generally evoke a turning-toward, seeking, or mouth orientation.

Stimulation of leg areas near the knee by the "cold" temperature cylinder produces most commonly flexion of the leg at the hip, with extension occurring only about one-third as often. Stimulation of the calf of the leg produces most frequently general patterns of response with most of the activity confined to the legs and with extension more frequent than flexion. Also,

according to Crudden (1937), there is evidence of a "scratch"-localizing reflex.

Stirnimann (1939) reports that stimulation of the sole of the foot with "warm" stimuli leads to "seeking" movements of the other foot, whereas "cold" stimuli lead to withdrawal movements.

Thermal stimulation of the oral cavity elicits mimetic reactions, mouth movements, head movements, and squirming. It makes the sucking response irregular, and, with sufficient intensity, leads to disorganization and cessation of the response.

General environmental temperatures may give rise to shivering, as related by Blanton (1917), and general activity is correlated $-.205 \pm .024$ with temperature through a range of 74 to 88° F., according to Pratt (1930). Pilomotor reflexes (gooseflesh) to the normal combination of mechanical and thermal stimuli are very fleeting and slight in the newborn but are brought forth by adrenalin according to Hartmann-Karplus (1931).

Technique of Investigation. Cutaneous areas have been explored by thermal stimuli produced by temperature cylinders, evaporation of alcohol, etc. Tactual stimulation has been kept constant through use of a metal capsule attached to some portion of the body, the temperature being varied by changing the water in the capsule by means of inlet and outlet tubes. Radiant heat likewise makes possible a limited study of thermal sensitivity without any tactual accompaniment. The oral cavity has been stimulated with fixed amounts of distilled water at constant temperature, administered with medicine droppers, and by having the baby suck milk at different temperatures.

Jensen (1932) has used a manometer-polygraph combination to record the effects of thermal stimuli on sucking responses. Crudden (1937) has made cinema records, and others have provided verbal descriptions of the responses.

Summary. The newborn infant is sensitive to temperatures that fall below the lower and above the higher thresholds, which appear to vary according to the part of the body stimulated and probably according to certain physiological states. They produce vigorous movements of the parts stimulated by the stimuli deviating most from the thresholds. Respiration and circulation are affected, and the sucking response becomes irregular or even ceases. The response involves more than the segment stimulated, although greatest frequency of reaction occurs in the stimulated member. There may be a localizing reflex of a "scratch" nature. Mild thermal stimuli above the higher threshold may lead to movement toward the stimulus, whereas those below the lower threshold lead to withdrawal movements.

Environmental temperatures appear to be correlated negatively with activity in the newborn infant.

Reactions to Contact or Pressure Stimuli

Sensitivity. A great variety of responses elicitable by contact or pressure stimuli upon the cutaneous areas or within the external cavities of the body leave, as Pratt (1937) has emphasized, no doubt regarding the presence and importance of such sensitivity in the neonate. Phylogenetically and ontogenetically, as Carmichael (1933) has pointed out, this type of sensitivity is the first to appear. It arises first in the oral-nasal region, but the sensitivity is widely distributed by the time the neonatal stage is attained.

There have been no systematic investigations of differences in tactual sensitivity of the cutaneous surfaces of the body. Genzmer (1873) and Preyer (1882), as reported by Peiper (1928), maintain that the face, the hand, and the sole of the foot have greatest sensitivity, whereas the shoulders, the breast, the abdomen, and the back have least sensitivity.

Differentiation of the effects of pressure or contact stimuli from the effects of other stimuli is difficult. The confusion with the effects of thermal, pain, gustatory, and other stimuli presents a difficult problem of control in studying the behavior of the newborn infant.

Another source of uncertainty arises from inadequate control of stimulus intensity so that cutaneous reflexes are confused with those due to deep pressure.

Stimuli which give rise to tickle in the older child produce no analogous vocalization, motility, or facial expression in the young infant, according to Nassau (1938). If it reacts at all it manifests expressions of "unpleasantness" and of withdrawal.

Hartmann-Karplus (1931) asserts that the position of itch as contrasted with pain, thermal, and tactual sensations is not clear. The stimuli producing it are such that perhaps it should be classified by itself, or with pain. Using a commercial itch powder composed of little plant hairs, this investigator reports that during the first 2 weeks there is little or no reaction. When a response does occur its reaction time is about 2 to 3 minutes compared with the 1 minute of older sucklings. The crying and restlessness which are elicited quickly subside. Neither at this time nor during most of the first 6 months is there evidence of localized scratching, although the general activity becomes more pronounced with age. This confirms the basic finding of Szymanski.

Watson (1919), the Shermans (1925, 1936), Peiper (1928), and Crudden (1937) have all reported "defense movements" to continued pressure upon certain body areas.

Relation to Stimuli. The responses evoked from a given body surface by tactual stimuli depend upon their intensity, duration, and whether they are of punctiform or stroking contact application. Summation effects have been noted.

Relation to State of Organism. The nature of the toe movements in the plantar response seems to be altered somewhat in sleep. The mouth orientation and sucking movements are not elicitable after the infant has completed nursing. The plantar response may vary according to postures, possibly determined by preceding stimulation. These are illustrative of various modifications of response which depend upon the condition of the infant at the time of stimulation.

Responses. They range from localized reflexes like the tactuopalpebral to responses which involve much of the body musculature. Many of the responses evoked are commonly described as defense movements. Some are viewed as withdrawal movements; others are supposed to localize and to ward off the stimuli which are being applied. Or they provide a fundamental orientation of the organism, as in the mouth orientation response to contact stimuli of certain facial areas (see section on responses for further description).

Summary. The newborn infant manifests widespread sensitivity to pressure or contact stimuli. The responses aroused constitute much of the neonate repertory and are interpreted by some writers as having a protective utility.

Reactions to Noxious (Pain) Stimuli

Sensitivity. The problem of pain sensitivity in the neonate is twofold: (1) the differences in sensitivity from one body area to another; (2) the degree of sensitivity as compared with later age periods.

In regard to the problem of differential areal sensitivity, Preyer (1882) considered the sole of the foot to be most sensitive, and the Shermans (1925) reported a differential between head and leg areas from birth on, the head areas being more sensitive to repeated needle jabs than the leg areas. Dockeray and Rice (1934), employing one needle jab with $\frac{1}{16}$ inch maximum penetration, found that in terms of vigor and quickness of response head areas were least sensitive, arm areas more sensitive than head areas, and leg areas most sensitive. The Shermans and Flory (1936) in further experiments with minimal intensities of stimuli have confirmed their earlier findings in regard to a cephalocaudal differential in sensitivity. They point out that sensitivity is shown by responsiveness of the organism and not by the amount of activity in the part stimulated.

Whether there is a marked pain insensitivity in the neonate, as compared with later periods, has long been an unsettled question. Genzmer (1873), applying needle pricks to the nose, lips, and hands of premature infants, reported little effect. Newborn infants on the first day manifested similar reactivity, with sensitivity slowly increasing during the first week. Canestrini (1913) noted relative insensitivity to needle pricks and also to faradic and galvanic stimulation. The Shermans (1925) found that an average of 6.5 needle jabs in the head areas was required to arouse a response at 0.5 to 5.5 hours, whereas at 35.5 to 40.5 hours 1.7 stimuli were needed, with 1 stimulation sufficing after 41 hours. The increase in the sensitivity of leg areas is shown by a decrease in necessary needle jabs from 10 at 0.5 to 5.5 hours to 2 at 70.5 to 75.5 hours, with only 1 stimulation required after 76 hours. Peiper (1926a), on the basis of controlled needle stimulation of arm areas, is convinced that there is no marked insensitivity of the premature and the neonate as compared with older sucklings. The sensitivity of normal newborn infants as contrasted with the marked insensitivity of some idiots suggests pain insensitivity as a possible criterion of serious defect. Within the neonatal period Dockeray and Rice (1934) could discover no change in responses with increase in age. McGraw (1941b), on the other hand, found some "hypesthesia" during the first week or 10 days, the intensity of the responses increasing during the first month.

Relation to Stimuli. In studying this field of sensitivity the stimuli commonly employed have been pricks administered with a needle to different cutaneous areas of the body. Whether stimuli usually thought of as falling within some other field, such as those provided by application of ammonia or acetic acid fumes to the nostrils, should be classified as pain or noxious stimuli is not certain. Likewise, whether intense stimuli in such sensory fields as the thermal, the auditory, and the visual, or those involved in holding an infant's nose for a number of seconds, are to be interpreted as pain stimuli is also undetermined.

Relation to State of Organism. Wolowik (1927) observed in a 2-month-old infant that much more intense electrical stimulation was required to evoke crying during nursing than at other times.

Reaction Times. The reaction time (2 seconds) to stimulation of the sole of the foot is longer than that of adults, according to Preyer (1882). Peiper (1926a), applying needle jabs to the volar surface of the arm and measuring reaction times by a modified Morse apparatus, found the reaction time of body movements to range from 0.12 to 0.70 second, and of crying from 2 to 5 seconds.

Types of Response. In general, the responses, if the stimuli are not too intense,

consist of withdrawal movements of the part stimulated and facial reflexes of "discomfort." Dockeray and Rice (1934), however, found only a general mass form of movements regardless of the area stimulated. Crying is a common feature of many of these responses.

Technique of Investigation. Needle jabs administered by the experimenter with more or less control of the penetration provide the stimuli in most investigations. Peiper (1926a) appears to have made this stimulation most constant and automatic. The responses have been recorded by observers, photographed, and their time relations obtained from the records of a Morse apparatus.

Summary. The presence in the neonate of sensitivity to pain stimuli has been demonstrated. Differential sensitivity of the cutaneous areas of the body has not been carefully explored, and there is disagreement regarding the relative sensitivity of the areas which have been investigated. Similarly, there is lack of agreement regarding the degree of pain sensitivity in the just-born infant as compared with that found at later age periods.

Reactions to Movement or Change in Position

Sensitivity. This sensitivity is demonstrated when spatial movements of the body stimulate the static receptors and thus give rise to postural responses. It is likewise manifested by responses aroused by active or passive movement of a part of the body. The sequences in coordinated movements are also said to illustrate the presence of sensitivity of this type.

Some have held that the generalized responses of newborn infants to stimuli may not be touched off directly by the experimental stimulus but that the part first responding produces kinesthetic stimuli which in turn evoke responses in other parts. Givler (1921) has suggested that learning in relation to kinesthetic and tactual stimuli during the fetal period may determine some of the characteristics of the grasping reflex.

Movements of hands and legs toward contact, or other stimuli upon the body, may include kinesthetic stimulation as an essential element in producing the necessary coordinations.

Relation to Stimuli. Peiper and Isbert (1927) and Peiper (1928) provided experimental stimuli by supporting the body in various positions. The postural and other consequences of such positions have also been studied by McGraw (1935). The movements of the infant's head when the child is placed in a prone position constitute the initial step in Shirley's (1931a) schema of sequential development. Jarring of the infant, used by Moro (1918), the withdrawal of support, mentioned by Watson (1919), and the vertical movements produced by Irwin (1932h) provide static stimuli. The effects of turning the head upon the body and limb postures, and of the body upon the head posture, have been investigated by Peiper and Isbert (1927). The effects of rotation upon eye movements (rotational nystagmus) and head movements, with the child in either a horizontal or vertical position, have been reviewed by Peiper (1928), as have the studies of caloric nystagmus. Baldenweck and Guy-Arnaud (1940) asserted that the vestibulary sensory apparatus of the neonate is completely developed. This is demonstrated by the nystagmus, aroused by rotation or by caloric stimulation, which is the same as that of the adult except for a lesser excitability. They relate this development to the active maintenance of equilibrar positions within the liquid environment of the fetus.

Relation to State of Organism. Information on this point is very casual or lacking in the studies reviewed.

Responses. According to Peiper and Isbert (1927) and Peiper (1928), support of the newborn infant at the abdomen only, or at the back on the buttocks, or at the side at the hip shows such complete dominance of gravity that the child is unable to hold its head and trunk upright or in alignment. When placed in a prone position on a table, however, the neonate partially lifts its head. This has also been confirmed by Bryan (1930) and Shirley (1931a).

McGraw (1935, 1941d) has described the process of falling over when the child is placed in a sitting position.

Peiper (1929) demonstrated that, when the newborn infant is held in an erect position with its feet resting upon a surface, alternate or "stepping" movements are made. Peiper made photographs of these and obtained footprint records. Possibly static and kinesthetic, as well as tactual, stimuli are involved in this response. McGraw (1932) has confirmed Peiper's findings.

Inverted suspension (holding the child by the feet, head downward) occasionally produces in the neonate a bending-back of the head as reported by Peiper and Isbert (1927). According to McGraw (1935, 1940b), a flexion of the legs at knee and hip occurs, resulting in an up-and-down movement of the body. Body and head are in general alignment in the vertical plane with arms maintained more or less in the usual flexed position. Irwin's (1936) motion pictures showed that inverted suspension produces in the neonate a momentary backward bending of the head. The reaction, occurring in the cervical region, is designated by him as opisthotonoid.

Jarring or the sudden dropping or raising of the infant evokes, as Irwin (1932h) has shown, the *Moro's Umklammerungs reflex*, which is described in greater detail elsewhere in this chapter.

According to Peiper (1928), it is uncertain whether the *Brudzinski phenomenon* (a drawing-up of the legs when the head is bent forward) is a tonic neck reflex. Peiper and Isbert (1927) found it to be of rare occurrence in the neonatal period. Turning the infant's head to one side with a sudden jerk results in a "fencing" posture of the limbs. Other postural reflexes involving head and trunk consist of movements of the trunk if the head is moved and movements of the head if the body is moved. Mesina (1936) reports that, if one leg of a baby resting upon its back is flexed, the other automatically flexes.

Rotation of the body produces nystagmus and sometimes compensatory head movements arising from stimulation of the static rather than of the visual receptors. Bartels (1910) found that the head movements were in the opposite direction when the child was rotated in horizontal positions; Alexander (1911), that they were in the same direction during rotation, and in the opposite after rotation had ceased. The latter finds no rotation nystagmus, but an after-nystagmus for about 15 seconds. McGraw's (1941a) study appears to support Alexander rather than Bartels. Baldenweck and Guy-Arnaud (1940) were positive that the neonate's nystagmus to both rotational and caloric stimuli is of the same type as that of the adult. Other investigations reviewed by Peiper (1928) present similar contradictory findings. The presence of caloric nystagmus is likewise uncertain.

Summary. Static-kinesthetic sensitivity is demonstrated in the neonate by a variety of responses elicited by movement of the body as a whole, or in part. Beginnings of responses which will lead to upright postures and to walking are discernible.

Reactions to Internal (Organic) Stimuli

Sensitivity. The nature of internal stimuli and the sites of their operation are not well defined or known. But the general motility of the infant, when other stimuli are brought under control or reduced, is accepted by many as evidence that such sensitivity is present in the newborn infant. Indeed, the researches of Pratt, Nelson, and Sun (1930), Pratt (1934b), and especially of Irwin (1930), interpreted from this point of view, indicate that internal stimuli are responsible for most of its activity. As stated elsewhere in this chapter, external stimuli of short duration, although releasing responses which have present or future significance in the life of the child, add little to its total motility. External stimuli of longer duration inhibit activity which otherwise would be aroused by internal stimuli.

The functioning of respiratory and circulatory organs and of other parts of the viscera doubtless do contribute internal stimuli, but the preponderant number are apparently associated with the activities of the alimentary canal and of the excretory systems.

Conditions within or associated with the activities of the digestive tract are known to determine whether contact stimulation will arouse mouth orientation and sucking movements.

Nursing may be followed by *regurgitation*, and this, in turn, by *hiccuping*. Pendleton (1927), studying 40 newborn infants, found that hiccuping started about 10 minutes after regurgitation, lasted 5 to 15 minutes, and had a rate of about 18 per minute. Treatment by rapid administration of fluids soon stopped hiccuping in 72.5 per cent of the cases, immediately in 57.5 per cent of them. This suggests that gastric contents carried into the esophagus by regurgitation provide the stimuli for hiccuping.

Wagner (1938b) has affirmed that

> the hiccough, generally attributed to pressure of a full stomach upon the diaphragm, has frequently been observed in the infant shortly after birth. However, no attempt has been made to proceed further and study the hiccough as an isolated behavior item.

From pneumographic records of 17 neonates she found a duration ranging from 35 seconds to 18 minutes and 20 seconds (mean = 6 minutes, 34 seconds). The mean interval between hiccups ranged from 2.6 seconds to 7.9 seconds (mean of all = 4.5 seconds). This would be at the rate of little more than 13 hiccups per minute as contrasted with Pendleton's (1927) rate of 18. Wagner also found that the number of hiccups per minute tended to decrease throughout the period.

Norman (1942) has reported fetal "hiccups" as early as 125 days before birth, the durations of hiccuping ranging from 1 to 29 minutes (mean duration = 8 minutes) and the frequencies ranging from 10 to 45 per minute. The hiccups apparently occur during periods of heightened activity of the fetus and are accompanied by cardiac acceleration of as much as 30 beats per minute—a phenomenon unobserved in the hiccuping of newborn infants. Anoxemia is suggested as a possible cause of this hiccuping.

The relations of general motility to content and pressure stimuli as well as to the muscular activity of the stomach have received careful study by Carlson and Ginsburg (1915), Taylor (1917), Irwin (1930, 1932f), and Richards (1936a, 1936b, 1936c). It is probable that a great deal of the child's total motility is in some way dependent upon alimentary processes, but whether it is directly related to activity of the stomach or more indirectly produced by some nutritional state is not known (the researches bearing upon these problems are given detailed consideration in the section on physiology).

In the final sequences of alimentation and assimilation, excretion and egestion occur. The excretory aspects of perspiration have no visible connection with general motility. Micturition may, as Pratt (1933) has elsewhere suggested, be preceded by slight activity with quiescence after the act. More activity precedes egestion or defecation. According to Dennis (1932a), the latter presents the following pattern response:

> With each . . . abdominal contraction the legs and toes are extended and raised and the forearms are held to the upper chest. At the same time the infant may grunt and his face often reddens.

Summary. Internal stimuli on the whole are of fairly long duration, and the responses, excepting those involving sphincter muscles, are of rhythmical or periodic incidence. The transition from fetal to postnatal life probably involves an even greater stepping-up of internal than of external stimuli. It is the internal stimuli which account for most of the motility of the infant. The rôle of external stimuli according to type, intensity, or duration is to add variable but negligible amounts to the total activity, or actually to reduce the total which would occur were they not present.

Responses

The Feeding Responses. The responses which orient the newborn mammal to the nipple of the mother's breast and effect an ingestion of milk are among the most fundamental in the young mammal's repertory.

First in the series of these responses are the *head-mouth orientation* movements.

The prerequisite condition for their arousal by contact stimulation is that the infant be approaching a nursing period rather than having just nursed. Pepys (1667) was one of the first to observe that if an infant's cheek is touched the head turns and the mouth opens to grasp the finger. This *"search reflex"* was described very carefully by Kussmaul (1859) and mentioned by Preyer (1882). According to Popper (1921), stroking contact of the cheek may evoke head turning, mouth opening, and snapping movements. Gentry and Aldrich (1948) have applied the term *rooting reflex* to the head-turning and mouth-opening responses. The reflexogenous zone of the *oral* responses has been shown by Minkowski (1928) to be quite extensive early in the fetal period, and Pratt, Nelson, and Sun (1930) have confirmed its extensiveness in the neonatal period. In terms of sucking or mouth responses to contact stimulation they found sensitivity ranging in decreasing order in the following areas: lips, above lips, below lips, cheek. Sensitivity was greater in the waking state and appeared to decrease with age in the cheek areas. Jensen (1932) found the head movements to increase with age upon stimulation of this area.

The nature and the extent of the response depend upon the area which is stimulated. When the cheek is touched the head turns toward the side stimulated and the mouth opens. If the area above the lips is stimulated the head is thrown back and the mouth opens to its widest extent. If contact is maintained, the head may shake vigorously from side to side. Similarly, if the area below the lips is touched the chin drops, the mouth flies open, and the head may bend forward.

These responses have been confirmed by Baliassnikowa and Model (1931–1932) and by Stirnimann (1937a). According to Stirnimann the child must be awake for any except simple reflexes to appear. Halverson (1938) interprets the significance of the response as follows:

> At birth the mouth is superior to the hand in what might be called directed activity and definiteness of function. Upon proper stimulation the mouth can both open and close and with the aid of head and neck movements institute a strenuous search for the stimulating object.

Certainly such coordinations are among the most effective made by the neonate, although in human beings the head and neck or "searching" movements must be regarded as atavistic survivals.

Lip reflexes are coordinated with head-mouth orientation and are more specific to the act of coupling and sucking. This limitation of response progresses as one moves from stimulation of the periphery of the reflexogenous zone toward the lip areas. Head movement decreases or changes character according to the locus of excitation.

Thompson's (1903) lip reflex, consisting of pursing or pouting, is released by tapping the surface of the upper lip. Its relation to the contact-aroused erection of the mother's nipple has been noted. This reflex has been confirmed by Lambanzi and Pianetta (1906), Blanton (1917), Popper (1921), Baliassnikowa and Model (1931–1932), and Stirnimann (1937a), who has found it elicited most frequently by stimulation of the corners of the mouth. Stirnimann (1936a) has also observed a tumescence of the inner surface of the lips.

Sucking and *swallowing* constitute the crucial elements of the feeding responses. Although present at birth, the sucking response increases in vigor during the neonatal period. The response has a long history of objective instrumentalized study from the early researches of Basch (1893), Lifschitz as reported by Bechterew (1908),

Pfaundler (1909), and Barth (1914), in which the infant sucked upon a bottle or the mother's breast through special types of nipple shield, or in which a pneumatic system recorded movements of the chin, to apparatus which measured the changes in pressure set up by the infant's sucking in a closed system such as Kashara's (1916), or manometric set-ups such as those devised by Jensen (1932) and Halverson (1938). The Roentgen kymograph studies of sucking, swallowing, and breathing made by Peiper (1931, 1935b) are likewise a contribution in methodology.

Peiper (1939b) demonstrated that the rhythm of the swallowing center is imposed upon that of the sucking center and this in turn upon that of the respiratory center. Halverson (1944) discovered that the character of breathing alters in the direction of costal movements during efficient sucking, and that good coordination may be present even in the premature infant (1946).

New aspects of the sucking response have been revealed by Balint (1948a, 1948b). The highly sensitive registration of the sucking responses of newborn infants obtainable by the Jacquet polygraph demonstrates the presence of a rhythmical clonus ("quivering") of the tongue. Its frequencies are 6–10 per second. In opposition to other observers he reported little change in the basic sucking rhythm throughout the nursing period. In fact, he was impressed by the stability of each infant's sucking rhythm. Some infants continued at their basic and lowest frequency; others, after a pause in the sucking, resumed at a higher rate, which then gradually subsided to the basic rhythm. In "normal" infants the sucking had greater regularity and the frequencies were lower than in those patterns found in infants suffering from "respiratory" or "intestinal" disorders.

Ribble, according to Norval (1946), asserted that 40 per cent of newborn infants had such feeble sucking movements that they were unable to obtain their nourishment without prompting or assistance. Norval, on the other hand, found only about 4 per cent to have inadequate sucking responses, although the newborn infant's approach is one of "dallying and repetitious trials" rather than of "greediness."

When sucking starts, general activity, according to Jensen (1932), begins to disappear. Salt solutions cause the response to deteriorate or cease, as do certain critical temperatures of milk. Wolowik (1927) has shown that when the 2-month-old child is nursing it requires electrical stimulation over three times as intense to cause crying as at other times. When the infant has stopped sucking, but while contact is yet maintained, other stimuli such as visual stimuli or those afforded by pulling the hair or pinching the big toe will, according to Jensen (1932), again initiate sucking. Under these conditions the organism is, he states, "set" to respond only in this way. Peiper (1938) terms this the dominance of the sucking center and holds (1937a) that this center shows two levels of excitation, one giving periodic sucking and the other regular and rhythmic sucking. The analogy to breathing as well as a developmental relationship are suggested (1939a). The sustained character of the orientation in sucking is striking.

Halverson (1938) considers sucking as arising from pronounced muscle tension. Simultaneous records of sucking pressure, gripping pressure of the hand, and observation of general activity show their maxima at the beginning of sucking, and they decrease together during the course of the feeding period. When the nursing process is hampered there is incidence of penial tumescence which is ascribed to marked abdominal pressure. Peiper (1931, 1935b) and Hofmann and Peiper (1937) found that in the hungry suckling there were between 60 and 80 sucking movements, or 1 or 2 for every inspiration. Neither sucking nor breathing is interrupted by swallowing. Swallowing occurs during the phases between inspiration-expiration or expiration-inspiration.

Some have held that swallowing, as Baliassnikowa and Model (1931–1932) express it, is part of a chain reflex appearing when sucking fills the mouth. Jensen (1932) has observed that sucking, as upon air, may occur without swallowing. And sucking of some substances may be followed by rejection rather than continued swallowing.

Finger sucking is a common response in the neonate, appearing shortly after birth, according to Blanton (1917), Stirnimann (1933), and Kunst (1948). Dennis (1932a) has described the nursing posture of the child.

Peiper's review (1936b) is probably the most comprehensive treatment of the feeding responses which has appeared.

Defense or Protective Reflexes. This classification, although in common usage, is not entirely satisfactory. The terms are usually ill defined and bear the connotation of either conscious intent or unconscious purpose, whereas further study of the responses may disclose that the organism's response is determined by its structure rather than by the precise end which is to be accomplished. Here, as elsewhere, the need is for accurate and comprehensive description of behavior and of the conditions under which it appears and is modified.

There have been attempts to classify responses in terms of movement away from or movement toward the stimulus. Carmichael (1933) has reported the observations of various writers to the effect that the intensity of the stimulus determines the

direction of movement. In terms of the life economy of the infant, however, movement of the part of the organism toward the stimulus or site of stimulation may lead, as in mouth orientation, to continued contact with the stimulus, or it may result in active pushing-away or rejection of the stimulus. Thus it is possible, without any implication of conscious purpose on the part of the infant, to term those responses "protective" which remove it or any part of the infant from stimuli, or those in which some part moves toward and pushes away a stimulus object applied to some part of the body. These latter responses are particularly significant because they demonstrate a certain amount of ability to orient in the environment and to localize the sources of excitation.

With this broad definition, the classification of responses such as the palpebral, pupillary, and mouth rejection as "protective" seems justifiable. The claim that other responses such as the Moro and the grasping reflex are defensive, in terms of the arboreal past of man, should be received with considerable skepticism. Similarly, Babinski's (1922) attempt to classify both extensor and flexor plantar responses as defense movements, the first by virtue of withdrawal of the toes and the latter in terms of "attack," has contributed little toward the understanding of the plantar responses. The purposive interpretation of these movements becomes somewhat difficult in the light of Pratt's (1934d, 1936a) demonstration that stimulation of the upper surface of the foot produces the *same types of movements* of the foot and toes as stimulation of the plantar surface, so that whether it is defense by withdrawal or defense by attack depends upon the location of the stimulus. Considerations such as these should lead to caution in interpreting the purpose of a response.

Among the withdrawal responses not cited elsewhere in this chapter are the spinal and abdominal reflexes described by Galant (1917). In all essentials these consist in a concave bowing or bending-away of the side of the body from stroking contact stimulation. Others, including Peiper, have differentiated between Galant's "spinal reflex" and the abdominal reflexes, but Galant (1930) is of the opinion that they are not different responses but rather the same response released from an extensive reflexogenous zone.

Of even more significance for future development of the infant are those responses in which continuous contact stimulation of some part of the body surface is followed by movement of hand, arm, or leg toward the locus of stimulation. When the infant's nose was held by the experimenter's fingers, Watson (1919) reported defense arm movements. Pratt, Nelson, and Sun (1930), Taylor (1934), and Daniels and Maudry (1935) were unable to confirm this.

The Shermans (1925) and the Shermans and Flory (1936) have reported similar defense movements, improving rapidly during the first few days after birth, to pressure exerted upon the infant's chin. Although Daniels and Maudry (1935) and others have not confirmed the Shermans' findings, the experimental controls of the latter in their later research seem to indicate that some coordinations of this type are present. Indeed such coordinations may mark the early beginning of the hand-mouth movements which play such an important rôle in the subsequent development of the child.

On the other hand, Hartmann-Karplus (1931) found no localizing movements when itch powder was applied to other parts of the body surface.

Crudden (1937) reported a localizing scratch reflex of the contralateral leg to the capsule in his investigations of thermal sensitivity. Peiper (1936a) also, applying curtain clamps to various parts of the body, found, at first, local reactions, followed frequently by movements of hand or foot to the part stimulated. When the infant's hands are each encased in cloths tied at the wrists they move against each other or against the sheet until, according to Stirnimann (1937b), the hands frequently become disengaged. He considers this impulsion toward freedom to be second only to that toward nourishment.

No adaptive movements (hand of the infant striking that of the experimenter) to head restraint were observed by Stoffels (1940–1941) unless the child was on its side, and then only in 5 per cent of the trials.

Stirnimann (1944b) discovered a defense response elicitable by application of the stethoscope over the heart but not over other chest areas. The infant's hand approached and pushed against the stethoscope. The response was not symmetrical like the Moro. It was aroused in 50 per cent of infants on the first day after birth but in only about 15 per cent by the age of 10–14 days.

The Oculo-Cephalo-Gyric Response. The visual pursuit movements described in the section on reactions to visual stimuli constitute further evidence that the newborn infant possesses responses which enable it to orient to some aspects of its environment. These orientations, unlike mouth orientation, have increasing importance among the activities of the organism. Indeed here is an early manifestation of what has been termed attention.

Palmar Response and Arm Movements. The response of the fingers in the palmar response is homologous to that of the toes in the plantar response, save for the variability between extension and flexion of the latter. From the first descriptions given, writers have differentiated between the early neonatal and the later grasping by terming the grasping of the newborn infant involuntary while the adult form is voluntary, except in pathological cases. The voluntary type is said to appear when the involuntary type wanes. Halverson (1937) questions this and argues that there is chronological overlapping of the two. The earlier writers state that involuntary grasping disappears between 4 and 6 months, and Wagoner (1924) considers its persistence a sign of retardation.

Robinson (1891), Buchman (1895, 1900), and Mumford (1897) believed that neonatal grasping proved that, in the past, man or his ancestors lived in trees.

Givler (1921) was one of the first to suggest that the response might be perfected by exercise during the prenatal life and not result entirely from maturation.

The response was described as simian in nature—that is, palm and finger flexion without thumb opposition—by Buchman (1895, 1900). McGraw (1935, 1940a) likewise emphasizes its digital character when the child is partially or completely suspended. Halverson (1937), who has given this response most careful study, reports that the neonatal grasping reflex has two phases: first, closure to light pressure upon the palm; second, gripping or clinging as a proprioceptive response to pull upon the finger tendons. Closure disappears in 16 to 24 weeks, whereas the proprioceptive gripping or clinging disappears after 24 weeks. Closure is a specific or limited response; gripping has associated with it many other movements. McGraw (1940a), following Halverson, also distinguishes between the grasping of a contacted object and that produced by a pull upon the finger tendons, which she characterizes as suspension-grasp behavior.

The strength of the infant's grasp has been expressed most frequently in terms of the time the infant can sustain its own weight with one or both hands. The pioneers, Robinson (1891) and Buchman (1895, 1900), reported times as long as 2½ minutes using both hands, and a few seconds using one hand. Blanton (1917) found the child could support its weight for only a few seconds employing both hands. Richter (1934) suspended infants by both hands from parallel rods and obtained in different infants average suspension times ranging up to 60 seconds, with 128 seconds the longest time obtained. Valentine and Wagner (1934) employed the handle of a dynamometer as a lifting device, and, neglecting the fact that pulling to suspension is not the same situation as suspension of the infant, drew the following conclusion:

It has been generally accepted as a fact that newborn infants are capable of supporting their own weight when grasping with one hand a rod of about the diameter of a lead pencil. The use of the dynamometer in this experiment, where the dynamometer was lifted vertically until the infant released the handle, emphatically disproved such an assumption, for the maximum grasping strength of the strongest subject was 2200 grams, less than the weight of the smallest subject.

The Shermans and Flory (1936) measured the strength of the grasp by the Chatillon Balance and found it to average 1732 grams in the right and 1765 grams in the left hand. A little over 10 per cent of the infants could lift themselves with one hand. Halverson (1937) found the clinging strength of the left hand to be slightly superior to that of the right. At birth the mean strength of the right hand is 1952 grams. Halverson found that infants support more than 70 per cent of their weight with both hands when pulled toward suspension. Of 97 infants less than 24 weeks old, 27, under these circumstances, supported their own weights with both hands, and one at 4 weeks did it with the right hand alone. Halverson states that "it was evident that some of them could have supported considerably more weight than their own mass." The relative strength of the different fingers was also determined by this investigator. Richter (1934) and Halverson (1937) both indicate that the response, measured in terms of suspension time and by the dynamometer, is not so great during the early part of the neonatal period.

The Shermans and Flory (1936) noted, as had earlier investigators, that the grasping reflex is weakest when the infant is asleep, and strongest when the infant is crying. Halverson (1937), testing the gripping pressure upon a small sensitive rubber capsule, found that the strength of the grasp was greatest at the beginning of nursing, decreasing as the infant approached satiety. Thus the grasping response reflects the degree of muscle tension.

The study of handedness in newborn infants has been approached, as we have seen, by measuring the relative strength of the grasping reflex in the right and left hands. The left hand appears at this stage to be stronger. Watson (1919) attempted to determine whether there was preferential motility in arm movements but could discover none. Stubbs and Irwin (1933) reported a significant difference, and Valentine and Wagner (1934) found greater motility in the right arm. This did not appear to be correlated with the later preferential reaching of some of the same subjects.

Reaching toward stimuli acting upon the visual sense organs does not occur during the neonatal period, but, as described in defense movements, there are rather direct movements toward the site of contact stimulation of some areas of the body. Allied to these is the searching-grasp response to stimulation of the dorsal surfaces of the fingers. Stirnimann (1941) states that he obtained it in almost all newborn infants, although Halverson had not observed the phenomenon before the sixteenth week. According to Stirnimann, this is a voluntary rather than a reflex response because it is seldom evoked by anything other than the experimenter's finger or a reasonable facsimile. He interprets this discrimination as an expression of a social impulse or drive.

Postural Responses. The researches upon these responses of the neonate have demonstrated their rôle in the development of the erect position, locomotion, and the complex activity of visual fixation.

Shirley (1933a) in her behavioral silhouettes of the developmental sequence showed that the just-born infant makes contact with the face when placed in the prone position but that by the terminus of the neonatal period the head is lifted so that the chin is raised. Gesell and Ames (1940) held that these postural adjustments of the head and the associated movements of the arms and legs are a segment of the developmental events which will culminate in an upright posture. McGraw (1941e) regarded a righting or rolling response of the infant in the supine position as one of the precursors of the upright posture. No such response was found in the neonate, although the body might be turned from back to side as part of general total movements or in consequence of the Moro response.

During the first three postnatal months the basic postural response, according to Gesell and Halverson (1942), is the tonic-neck reflex. Ling (1942) has stated that it is the characteristic *waking* posture. In this response the head is turned to one side with homolateral arm and leg extension. The contralateral leg and arm are flexed, the arm at the shoulder. The eyes stare upon or in the direction of the extended arm. The relation of flexion of the fingers and toes to the tonic-neck reflex was explored by Pacella and Barrera (1940).

Ames (1942) found that the prevailing leg postures involved either bilateral flexion or extension, with one leg tending to be more active in flexing and extending while the other leg remained flexed. *Locomotor Movements.* The newborn infant possesses no effective means of movement from place to place. From its normal supine, prone, or lateral postures it may shift its position by various responses, but this involves little translation of the body in the horizontal plane.

Bauer (1926) obtained a "creeping phenomenon" when the neonate was placed on its abdomen and contact or resistance offered the soles of the feet. Under these circumstances the infant responds by thrusts of one or both feet, followed by alternate arm movements which tend to raise the body from the supporting surface. At the same time the body bends from side to side. These creeping responses are elicitable during the first 4 months and, according to Bauer, are second only to sucking in their complexity.

Peiper (1928) and Stirnimann (1938) have confirmed Bauer's observations, and Stirnimann, finding it present in an anencephalic subject, decided that it was a subcortical reflex. The creeping phenomenon of the neonate bears some relation to its stepping movements but neither, according to this writer, has any relation to later creeping or walking. McGraw (1941c) has reported greater activity in the lower than in the upper extremities when the infant is placed in the prone position.

Peiper (1929) discovered that, when the newborn infant is supported in an erect posture with the soles of the feet resting upon a table top, the legs extend upon contact and make alternate stepping movements, the length of the double step being about 20 cm. Frequently the leg, on being set forward, crosses in front of the other, preventing further progression. These step-

ping movements differ from later walking in that the activity in the neonate is confined to the lower extremities. The stepping movements are highly variable and uncertain of appearance. In a few months they disappear, and under the same conditions the suckling withdraws its feet. Peiper photographed the stepping movements and obtained footprints by having the infant step upon soot-blackened glazed paper. The discovery of stepping movements of the newborn infant was reported by McGraw (1932). She held that genuine "upright ambulation" is impossible at this period because of an undeveloped equilibratory apparatus. In a later analysis of the problem McGraw (1940c) confirmed some of Peiper's observations. She called attention to the narrow base of the steps. This, of course, contrasts with the wide base of the child that has arrived at the stage of walking without support. Stepping movements have greater incidence from 9 to 14 days than during the first 24 hours, according to Stirnimann (1938). The response disappears in 4 to 5 months.

The Plantar Responses. The literature upon these responses is probably more extensive than upon all other aspects of neonate behavior combined. This is, of course, no indication of a correspondingly important rôle in the life economy of the child, nor are these studies as significant for child psychology as for neurology. Indeed apt is the statement by Richards and Irwin (1934c) that "the popularity which this problem has been accorded may possibly be due to a seeming necessity for the student of infant reactions at some time in his career to do an experiment on infantile plantar phenomena."

In this section no attempt will be made to review the literature in detail. Those who wish to study the problems presented by the plantar responses should consult the following researches and reviews: Bersot

(1920, 1921), Minkowski (1926, 1928), Pratt, Nelson, and Sun (1930), Fulton and Keller (1932), Pratt (1934d), and especially the review by Richards and Irwin (1934c).

Historically, major interest and attention to these responses date from Babinski's (1896, 1898) correlation of extension of the big toe, and sometimes extension and fanning of the toes (1903), with pyramidal tract disturbances in adults and the prediction that such responses would be physiological in infants. Although Leri (1903–1904), Engstler (1905), and many others have reported the Babinski complex to prevail during the neonatal period, others, such as Feldman (1921) and the Shermans (1925), have found a higher percentage of flexion of the toes during this period. Burr (1921) and Wolff (1930) have reported variability so great as to make it seem inadvisable to speak of a "plantar reflex."

In the narrowest sense the term "Babinski" has applied to the limited extension of the big toe alone, but, as already stated, Babinski himself recognized that frequently the other toes were involved in the *signe d'éventail*, and that there was triple retraction of foot, leg, and thigh. Bersot (1920, 1921) and Minkowski (1932–1933) have recognized the necessity of reporting all the behavior segments which are activated by plantar stimulation, and also the necessity for exploring the extent of the reflexogenous zone from which the responses may be evoked.

The work of Richards and Irwin (1934c) indicates that toe extensions occur more frequently than flexions during the neonatal period. This research has additional importance because it demonstrates that one may not place too great reliance in the reliability of the clinical method. Indeed, the lack of agreement in many studies is probably the result as much of errors of observation as of differences in methods or of variability in stimulation. These same considerations have led Pratt (1934d, 1934e), in his studies of the reflexogenous zone and of the patterning of responses, to the belief that no further contributions can be made to the knowledge of plantar responses until frame analysis of motion-picture records is made.

Exploration of the reflexogenous zone tentatively indicates that plantar areas of the leg have greatest sensitivity and that their stimulation results in the greatest generalization of response, whereas stimulation of the hallux results in the most specific response. Leg and thigh segments are more likely and toe and foot segments less likely to be involved when the mesial surface of the leg is stimulated. When toe segments are viewed as one, they are about equally involved in responses, but leg and thigh are less frequently represented. About two-thirds of the toe movements are movements of extension and one-third of flexion. The foot, leg, and thigh manifest mostly flexor movements. Analysis of the responses observed revealed less than 200 different patterns, of which 4, or 2 per cent, accounted for 29 per cent of the observed responses, 6 per cent of the patterns accounted for 50 per cent of the responses, and 15 per cent of the patterns for 75 per cent of the responses. From this it is concluded that no one response pattern may be termed the plantar response. The five most frequent patterns are: foot flexion; extension of toes and foot flexion; extension of the hallux; toes extended, fanning, and foot flexion; hallux extension and foot flexion.

Ontogenetically, the work of Minkowski (1922) and others shows that during the latter part of the fetal period the prevailing response of the toes is flexion. Engstler (1905) and Bersot (1920, 1921) report that this is likewise true in prematures. Babinski (1922) and his associates and Lantuejoul and Hartmann (1923) find flexion the rule during the first few hours after birth.

According to the Shermans (1925), the nature of the response depends upon the previous posture of the toes; repetition of the stimulus will change toe extension to flexion. This dependence upon the posture at the time of stimulation is also affirmed by Richards and Irwin (1934b, 1934c).

In sleep, according to Richards and Irwin's (1934c) research, and as reported by them in other studies, extension of the toe is not so great as when the infant is judged to be awake.

The movements of the segments of the leg in the plantar responses have been viewed by Babinski (1915, 1922) as defense movements. Their alteration with age has usually been correlated with myelinization of the pyramidal tracts.

The Foot-Grasping Response. The Stirnimanns (1940) have reviewed previous reports of a foot-grasping reflex in the newborn infant to light pressure upon the plantar surface near the toes. They report the presence of this tonic reflex in 98 per cent of 800 neonates which they investigated with a special esthesiometer. The toes flex and grasp at a minimal pressure between 40 and 70 grams. Galant (1931) has interpreted plantar flexion of the toes as a rudimentary foot-grasping reflex.

The Moro and "Startle" Responses. The relation or the differentiation of these responses, as noted in the section on reactions to auditory stimuli, is difficult. Moro (1918) himself was aware that stimuli other than jarring would release the response which he described, and that it was suggestive of fear. This identification of responses or at least common elements has come down through Peiper (1925a), Irwin (1932g), Pratt (1934b), Dennis (1934), and others. Strauss (1929), however, followed by Hunt, Clarke, and Hunt (1936),

Hunt and Landis (1938), and Landis and Hunt (1939), differentiated a startle response from the Moro, even though both may be released by the same stimulus or the same types of stimuli.

After testing the Moro response in 250 newborn infants Stirnimann (1943) concluded that, although it resembled the fear reaction, no unpleasantness was involved because no infants cried upon being jarred or shaken. In his opinion the response is not an actual clasping or embrace since the extended arms will not clasp or hold to the experimenter's arm. Hence it should be called the reaction to shaking (Erschütterungsreaktion).

According to Moro (1918), the clasping response to jarring consists of an extension of the arms followed by their bowing and return toward the body. The response is symmetrical and the legs undergo much the same kind of movement. Freudenberg (1921) states that the arms extend, spread, and are adducted to the middle line of the body with the fingers spread and half flexed. The legs are extended, the toes spread and bent. Schaltenbrand (1925, 1928) has furnished essentially the same description with the further notation that it may be elicited not only by jarring but also by sudden noises, rotating the head on the body, or tapping the abdomen. According to Gordon (1929), the Moro simulates the fear response. He observed tremor of the hands in the clasping movement and less participation of the lower extremities. The response is symmetrical except in case of birth injuries. It disappears by the fourth month. Sanford (1931) confined his attention only to arm movements and found that fracture of the child's clavicle resulted in an asymmetrical response. Dupérié and Bargues (1932) have pointed out that the leg responses are highly variable. They were unable to evoke the response by auditory stimuli. McGraw

(1937) has described the movement of the trunk as follows:

Simultaneously there is an extension of the spine, often involving a retraction of the head toward the interscapular part of the spine and a rolling of the body slightly to one side.

Whether the movement of the legs is flexor or extensor depends upon their position at the time of stimulation. She also claims that the response is usually followed by crying. Against this must be set Irwin's (1932h) studies on the effect of vertical elevation of the infant—this did not result in crying. Finally, Richards (1936a) has observed these responses to occur without the application of any experimental stimuli. Dennis (1935) doubts that the response actually disappears at 4 months.

Landis and Hunt (1939) have shown that Peiper's earlier observation of the more rapid fear response preceding the Moro is descriptive of the startle. The primary difference in the two patterns is:

The startle pattern is primarily a flexion response, while the Moro reflex is primarily an extension response. In the latter the arms are extended straight out at the sides at right angles to the trunk, fingers extended, the trunk is arched backward, and the head is extended. Following the primary extension in the Moro reflex there is a secondary flexion response which has been described as a "clasping" response, but it is doubtful whether this is a true clasping response or merely a slow return to normal posture. The primary extension movement seems to be the genuinely significant portion of the response. Despite this gross difference in the two reactions, both Moro reflex and startle pattern may be called forth by many situations involving sudden unexpected stimulation.

Clarke's (1939) genetic studies of the response to auditory stimuli show that first they are typically Moro, then some

elements of the response disappear and the character of movements changes from extension to flexion, giving the "startle."

Vocalization. The birth cry represents the first vocally produced sounds from the newborn infant, but it seems best to regard this as a respiratory response and not a true precursor of speech. Subsequent crying either in response to external or internal stimuli is, according to Schachter (1932a), a part of the generalized behavior which is characteristic of the neonate. It is also closely related to breathing and partakes of its rhythm in continuous crying. As we have seen, activity of this type ceases when auditory stimuli are presented, when the child is swung or rocked, and of course is terminated by sucking.

Although Sherman (1927b) has demonstrated that emotional patterns are not differentiated by differences in crying, it is nonetheless true that this type of activity is the infant's most powerful tool in acting upon its social environment and in thereby obtaining attention and care.

The durations, times, and probable causes of the crying of newborn infants have been tabulated by Aldrich, Sung, and Knop (1945a, 1945b, 1945c). The data were obtained by an observer stationed in the hospital nursery (average number of infants under observation = 20 at one time) and from reports by the individual mothers after they had returned home with their babies. Five probable causes of crying were assigned: hunger, vomiting, soiled diapers, wet diapers, and unknown. Crying ascribed to "hunger" was of longer duration than that resulting from unknown factors. Next in stimulating value came wet, and then soiled, diapers.

Two peaks in crying were noted: one at about 6 p.m. and the other about midnight. The authors consider the first to be produced by an interval between nursings of 5–6 hours. Crying is held to be a manifestation of individual need and not aroused by interstimulation within the nursery community. They believe that a child should not have to cry more than 3 minutes before having its needs satisfied.

The amount of crying increases up to the fourth day, levels off to the sixth, and thereafter declines. During the first 8 days the average total of crying was 117 minutes per day, with a range from 48.2 to 243 minutes. The hourly variation was from 1.3 to 11.2 minutes.

Fairbanks (1942) recorded the cries of an infant when the 2 o'clock feeding was withheld. The mean of the cry was 556 cycles per second, or 1 octave above an adult female and 2 octaves above an adult male speaking voice. The range was 5 octaves, or from 63 cycles to 2631 cycles per second. During the first 6 postnatal months the development was toward higher pitches.

Reviews of the researches upon the vocalization of neonates have been made by Irwin (1941c, 1946), Irwin and Curry (1941), and Irwin and Chen (1943). The most exhaustive studies of the development of vocalization during the early postnatal months have been made by Irwin and his students. Irwin and Curry (1941) ascertained that a behavior unit sample of the sound elements produced during 25 respirations was a more reliable sampling than that obtainable in a time sample. Recording the sounds in the International Phonetic Alphabet, they discovered that during the first 10 days front vowels predominate, with scarcely any middle, and no back, vowels. The crying included the following vowels: æ, ʌ, ɛ, ɪ, u. Consonant sounds were infrequent, the most common being an h with occasionally a w or a k. Chen and Irwin (1946a) found the mean number of vowels to be 4.5, and the mean number of consonants 2.7, during the first 2

postnatal months. Irwin and Chen (1946b) reported that at 1 month the infant produces 7.5 sounds as compared with the 35 sound elements used in adult English speech. In point of frequency vowel sounds occur about five times as often as consonant sounds, according to Irwin and Chen (1946a). Irwin's (1947b) analysis of consonant sounds according to place of articulation discloses that about 98 per cent are velars and glottals, the most frequently used consonants being: k, g, h, and ?. The sounds themselves he found (1947c) were plosives and fricatives.

The problems of the graphic representation of speech sounds have been explored by Irwin (1941b), and the various indices employed in the analysis of infant speech sounds have been evaluated by Chen and Irwin (1946b, 1946c) and by Irwin (1947a). The reliabilities of the data for frequency of speech elements and their patterning have been determined by Irwin and Chen (1941) and by Irwin (1945).

Even during the first 2 months there are, according to Brodbeck and Irwin (1946), statistically reliable differences between the vocalizations of orphanage and nonorphanage children.

Irwin's experimental findings of the course of vowel and consonant development in infants have been interpreted by McCarthy (1949) as illustrations of the "law of developmental direction." Thus she holds that the sequence from the front to back vowels exemplifies the anterior-posterior gradient. The trend of consonantal development from the sounds produced in the back of the oral cavity to those made with lips, tongue-tip, etc., is an instance of proximodistal development.

Lynip (1951) has pioneered in the use of the magnetic recorder and the Sound Spectrograph to pursue the development of vocalization in the child. By these means the subjective appraisal of sounds which is involved in phonetic recording by observers is avoided. The new techniques make possible accurate, quantitative samplings of the vocalization of the child within the home environment.

Facial Responses. "Mimetic" responses of the musculature of the face and head play an important rôle in the anthropomorphism of neonate behavior and in this way serve to control or elicit differential responses from adults. The basis for conditioning of facial expressions is thereby provided.

Peiper (1935*a*), who has made the most detailed study of the origin, types, and significance of facial expressions in early infancy, has divided the responses into those which facilitate further stimulation of the sense organs and those which close or withdraw them from stimulation. Many of the responses are intimately associated with breathing movements.

Spitz and Wolf (1946) have confirmed reports, by Blanton (1917) and others, of the presence of smiling in the response repertory of the neonate. But they emphasize that it is not elicited by any specific external situations and that it does not represent a social response at this stage of development.

Miscellaneous. There are many reflexes of interest to the neurologist which have not been reviewed in this chapter. Among them are the tendon reflexes and the cremasteric reflex. The galvanic skin reflex, reported present during the first year by Jones (1930) and denied by Peiper (1924*a*), has not seemed to offer sufficient data for a detailed inclusion. Veïnger (1950) has reported upon the postnatal ontogenesis of skin galvanic reflexes to visual and auditory stimuli. For a listing of some of the more obscure responses the reader should consult Dennis (1934).

Emotions

Many have inferred, on the basis of "expressive" movements or "mimetic" responses to auditory, olfactory, gustatory, tactual, and other stimuli, that the newborn infant experiences emotions or other affective psychic states.

The gross muscular responses evoked by intense auditory stimuli have been called *fear* from the time of Sachs (1893) on, but it remained for Watson (1919) to elevate the observed pattern into a primary emotion. Other stimuli releasing these responses are those provided by removal of support and by shaking or jarring. Moro (1918) had shown that the latter arouses a characteristic clasping response, and later writers, such as Peiper (1925*a*), Irwin (1932*g*), and Pratt (1933, 1934*b*), came to the conclusion that the Moro response is elicitable by a variety of stimuli, including the auditory. Whether the fear response and the Moro, despite variations, are one and the same response occurring to any sudden stimulus, or whether some of the early responses of the neonate form another pattern, the *startle*, which is an element in adult fears, is not as yet definitely established.

Furthermore, the quick reflexive nature of the responses to auditory stimuli followed by immediate return to quiescence, demonstrated in the researches of Peiper (1924*c*) and Pratt (1934*b*), does not conform to the temporal durations implied in the prevailing definitions of emotional responses. Also, movement in the vertical plane, dropping, or quick elevation did not produce crying or long-continued activity in the infants studied by Irwin (1932*h*).

In Watson's (1919) words, the emotion of fear consists of "a sudden catching of the breath, clutching randomly with the hands (the grasping reflex invariably appearing when the child is dropped), sudden closing of the eyelids, puckering of the lips, then crying." (This should be compared with the descriptions of the Moro and the startle responses.)

Rage is another of the emotions termed primary by Watson (1919). The pattern comprises crying, screaming, stiffening the body, slashing or striking movements of hands and arms, and holding the breath so that the infant's face becomes flushed. These responses are said to come in consequence of hampering or restricting the infant's movements. Pratt, Nelson, and Sun (1930) repeated the experiment of restraining or holding the child's arms—claimed by Watson to be a potent stimulus for rage. Not only did such a pattern of responses fail to appear, but also in most instances no effects followed, or else restraint actually served to quiet the infant. Taylor (1934), who made the most careful attempt to reproduce Watson's experiments, was unable to obtain the patterns described by Watson. Dennis (1940), however, holds that these experimenters failed to elicit rage because they did not employ as intense and prolonged stimulation as Watson. Stoffels (1940–1941) applied restraint to infants in the form of the immobilization of the head or arms but discovered no evidence of a general stiffening of the body or of the adaptive defense movements claimed by some investigators. The responses actually observed started in the immobilized parts of the body and then became generalized. There was no essential pattern which would differentiate "rage" from those responses aroused by other stimulating conditions such as "cold" or "hunger."

Greenacre (1944) believes that the term *restraint*, as applied to infant reactions, should never be left undefined. Thus restraint may involve binding or swaddling to restrict movement; it may differ in intensity; it may vary in the speed or evenness with which it is exerted; or it may differ in regard to the portions of the body which are affected.

The third primary emotion postulated by Watson (1919) is *love*. This consists of a "cessation of crying, smiling, attempts at gurgling and cooing released by stimulation of some erogenous zone, tickling, shaking, gentle rocking, patting and turning upon the stomach across the attendant's knee."

According to Watson, all other emotions appear in consequence of the conditioning of the original innate patterns to other stimuli. This theory had great vogue because of its simplicity but overlooked, as Valentine (1930) was quick to point out, the possibility that some emotional reactions might not be elicitable at birth and yet appear later on as a result of maturation rather than as a product of conditioning.

The validity of the theory suffered most from Sherman's (1927a) demonstration that observers, presumably acquainted with infant behavior, were unable to agree in naming emotional patterns of behavior as observed in motion pictures unless the stimuli were likewise shown.

These researches have resulted in the abandonment of the theory of differentiated emotional patterns in the neonate. Indeed they have led Irwin (1932h), Pratt (1933), Dennis (1934), and Taylor (1934) to abandon the term "emotion" as applying to infant behavior. In its place they advocate a purely descriptive account of the extent of organismic involvement in a response under definite conditions of stimulation, age of the organism, and so on.

Bridges (1932, 1935, 1936), as a result of observational studies, has likewise concluded that the newborn infant does not have differentiated emotional responses but instead an agitation or general excitement from which, partly through maturation and partly through experience, different emotions become differentiated.

Stirnimann (1943, 1944a) and Spitz and Wolf (1946) are inclined, in terms of "expressive movements," to endow infants with emotions in the sense of psychic states. Hence crying and screaming are regarded as indicative of feelings of unpleasantness or of negative emotions. Stirnimann postulates considerable differentiation and specificity of psychic states, whereas Spitz and Wolf hold to two primal emotional attitudes: one of accepting, and the other of rejecting, a stimulus.

Marquis (1943) criticized the Watsonian statement of the exciting conditions for emotions as not descriptive of the usual environment of the newborn infant. Instead she sees frustration of goal responses as the normal cause of emotional behavior. And in our culture this comes about repeatedly as a consequence of the spaced nursing periods arbitrarily imposed upon the infant. There are, however, points which need clarification before we can accept "frustration" as the source of emotional behavior in the neonate. First there should be a clear-cut and limiting definition of emotion in terms of the actual behavior of the infant rather than in terms of stimulus situations. Thus, are crying and generalized activity to be termed emotional behavior? And, if so, do they occur only in situations involving the frustration of goal responses? For example, what goal response is frustrated in the wet-diaper situation? In terms of Irwin's (1932f) correlation of activity with lapse of time from a nursing period it is also pertinent to inquire at what point in the cycle the "frustration" begins. What amount of general activity or what specific pattern of responses must emerge before the infant may be said to have an emotion or to manifest emotional behavior?

In general, students of early infantile behavior are inclined to the view that emotional behavior is represented by generalized rather than specific responses and that upon the acquisition of the specific responses depends the adequacy of the adjustment to the stimulating situation. This is in marked contrast with the position of certain educators who hold that one of the objectives of education is to develop the emotions.

Sleep

Criteria of Sleep and Depth of Sleep. The criteria of sleep in newborn infants are neither well defined nor universally accepted. The oldest and most widely employed, though perhaps naïve, is closure of the eyes. Supporting it is the criterion of decreased irritability and activity. Study of both adults and infants shows that neither is lacking during sleep.

The term *sleep* is usually defined by psychologists in terms of continuous gradations of irritability or of motility rather than in terms of the *either-or* of the two categories, *asleep* and *awake*.

Using this scientific criterion of sleep, Czerny (1892) differentiated gradations of sleep in terms of the strength of electrical stimuli necessary to awaken the infant. Depth of sleep, so expressed, is variable from infant to infant according to the antecedent condition or activities of the child.

Richter (1930) reported that palmar skin resistance increases with the depth of sleep in the neonate. Wenger and Irwin (1935, 1936) suggest that such resistance is basically correlated with muscular relaxation.

The most elaborate attempt to redefine sleep in terms of the degree of motility and of irritability of the newborn infant has been made by Wagner (1937). For her, sleep is a relative term, not antagonistic to the waking state but applying to different degrees of reactivity which express degrees or depths of sleep. Thus:

Now if an infant merely flexes its toes in response to one stimulus and moves its entire body in response to another, should we say it is equally asleep to both stimuli? It seems logical to consider it less deeply asleep to the stimulus to which it makes the greatest response. Taking an infant in any condition whatsoever, then, we can apply various stimuli and observe the responses made, judging the infant as being less deeply asleep to those stimuli to which it responds more.

Relating degree of reactivity (as expressed by extent and duration of responses to pain, tactual, olfactory, and auditory stimuli) to motility patterns, Wagner has set up seven stages of sleep ranging from the most profound, in which the infant is generally quiet, breathing is regular, and there are no eyelid or mouth movements to the shallowest, in which the infant is generally active, with eyes open and with mouth movement. According to her report the extent and duration of responses to the experimental stimuli increase as sleep becomes shallower.

Irwin's (1932f) measurement of motility from one nursing period to another shows, however, that Wagner's motility pattern of least depth of sleep actually is found in the period of least motility, but increased motility is demonstrated in periods manifesting some of Wagner's motility pattern of deeper sleep.

Temporal Incidence of Sleep and Location of Greatest Depth. Canestrini (1913), employing the technique developed by Czerny, placed the greatest depth of sleep at 45 to 60 minutes after falling asleep. In infants 2 months or older Marquis (1933) reported greatest depth (in terms of least temporal periods of activity) of sleep during the first half hour in daytime naps, and during the second hour in night-

time naps. Irwin's (1930, 1932f) studies show that activity is least after nursing, increasing as the next nursing period approaches. Greatest incidence of sleep (eyes closed) occurs about midway between the nursing periods.

The limited time samplings (90 minutes on the average) of Wagner (1937, 1939) and of Reynard and Dockeray (1939) provide an insufficient basis for determining the time of incidence of greatest depth of sleep in either diurnal periods or from one nursing period to another. Irwin (1930) in his 24-hour studies of activity has found greatest motility from 5 to 6 A.M. and least about noon. Similarly, in the measurement of motility between nursing periods least motility is shown immediately after nursing, with increasing activity up to the next nursing period, but Wagner's (1937) seven motility patterns do not agree with the observations made by Irwin. If the fundamental physiological state is most accurately described by actual measurement of general motility, then the duration and disposition of control periods in the researches of Pratt, Nelson, and Sun (1930) and of Pratt (1934b, 1934c) have greater validity than the alleged motility patterns which do not appear to be very well correlated with motility.

Amount of Sleep and Its Periodicity. Among the earlier writers, according to Peiper (1928), it was estimated that the neonate sleeps 20 hours of a day, but that the duration of each period of sleep is no more than 3 hours and is usually less. Pratt, Nelson, and Sun's (1930) records of control periods confirm these earlier estimates.

Wagner (1939) studied the sleep of newborn infants between 2 and 3:30 P.M., and in terms of her own criteria of sleep affirmed that infants are awake 40.3 per cent and sound asleep 12.7 per cent of the time. On the basis of 90 minutes of continuous observation in each 24 hours and with no time samplings at any other part of the day, the author concludes that "Such findings contradict the layman's casual assumption that the newborn infant spends most of its time sleeping."

Age and Sleep. Czerny (1892) found that at later age periods, as contrasted with the neonatal, weaker electrical stimulation awakened the child. According to some writers, as the child grows older the total hours of sleep decrease but the length of sleep periods increases.

Reactivity during Sleep. It is generally believed that during sleep irritability is decreased, reaction times are lengthened, certain responses may not be evoked, and others may be altered. According to Wagner (1937), responses decrease in extent and duration as the depth of sleep increases. Despite the lessened irritability just mentioned, it should be noted that most investigations have taken place under the condition of sleep as expressed by the simplest criterion. In other words, quiescent infants have been selected so that the effects of experimental stimuli would not be masked by activity aroused by internal stimuli.

The postural responses during sleep have evoked considerable interest. Peiper (1928) found a rather well-defined sleep or resting posture in the arms, hands, and legs of the suckling. The legs were flexed upon the body, the fists clenched, and the arms extended so that in the most extreme form the upper arms were at right angles to the body and the forearms parallel to the head. Marquis (1933) reported that during the first year the dorsal posture of the body with the head turned to the right was most frequent among body and head postures. There was likewise bilateral, symmetrical flexion at the elbows. Irwin (1930) also gave a description of postures in the neonate which resemble those found at slightly older age periods. This picture,

in all major essentials, was confirmed by Wagner (1938c). She emphasized that there were many variations of the pattern and that other postures are to be observed.

Canestrini (1913) found it difficult to distinguish waking from sleeping states in terms of curves of respiration and circulation. In his opinion respiratory intervals are longer in sleep and the brain pulsations are decreased.

The effect of sleep on specific responses are discussed in sections dealing with such responses and in those relating sensitivity to different stimulus modes.

Summary. The criteria of sleep, stated in terms of motility, postural or other response patterns, are unsatisfactory so far as the accurate and consistent expression of the physiological state of the organism is concerned. This state is best revealed by the minimal intensity of a given stimulus, typically electrical, necessary to elicit a particular response, and by the amount of measurable motility. The degree of reactivity and the level of motility will define the state of the infant but will not, of course, describe the effects of particular postures or of immediately preceding stimulation upon the responses to experimental stimuli.

In general, reactivity is less during sleep. Some responses are diminished or may not be evoked; others are viewed most easily against a background of lowered general motility. The newborn infant spends the greater part of the day in sleep, in the commonly accepted sense of the term. The child is not, however, immobile most of the time.

Learning

General observations of the neonate in the feeding situation disclose changes in behavior suggestive of learning during the course of the first month. Illustrative of these are the adjustments cited by Feldman (1920), whereby the infant, after a night feeding has been eliminated from his routine, begins to sleep during most of the night. Denisova and Figurin (1929), Ripin and Hetzer (1930), and Marquis (1941) have all reported evidence of early learning in relation to the feeding situation.

The first investigations of the Russian school of physiologists seemed to indicate that conditioned reflexes could not be established before the fifth month. The later research by Denisova and Figurin (1929) revealed that natural CR's of food-seeking movements to originally inadequate stimuli appeared in 23 to 27 days. Experimental CR's, however, were not established until the second month. Then auditory CR's began to appear, but visual CR's followed later in the second month.

Marquis (1931) reported the establishment of conditioned sucking and other responses to auditory stimuli by the fourth to fifth day. The auditory stimuli were produced by a buzzer and had a duration of 5 seconds before insertion of the nipple of the nursing bottle in the infant's mouth and the same duration after the insertion. The infant's responses were recorded by an observer, and the chin movements were registered upon the polygraph tape by means of a pneumatic system under the infant's chin. Conditioning to auditory stimuli in 7 out of 8 of the experimental group was said to be demonstrated by increase in mouth opening and by a decrease in general activity and crying, as contrasted with the nonappearance of such responses in a control group of 4 infants regularly stimulated by the buzzer at feeding times but not with access to the bottle immediately afterward. Near the end of the period of investigation the experimental group was subjected to auditory stimuli produced by a fall hammer striking a tin can, but general activity was not decreased nor was mouth opening elicited. Pratt (1933) has

pointed out that this procedure is invalid because, without any conditioning at all, the neonate responds in a different fashion to stimuli of very short duration from those of longer duration—the latter acting to cause decreased activity. This criticism is reinforced by the results of researches reported by Weiss (1934) and Stubbs (1934).

Marinesco and Kreindler (1933), employing electric shock as the unconditioned stimulus and visual and auditory as the conditioning stimuli, did not establish any CR's during the neonatal period.

Kasatkin (1935) and Kasatkin and Levikova (1935a, 1935b) did not succeed in conditioning sucking or feeding responses to auditory or to visual stimuli in newborn infants. When CR's did appear at a later time the auditory preceded the visual.

Probably, in point of techniques and scope, Wenger's (1936) study of conditioning in the first half of the neonatal period is the most important investigation so far attempted. In some of the experiments, however, the number of infants was very small. Stimuli in the various experiments were well controlled, and responses were recorded by observers and registered by photography or by the polygraph. In one of the experiments eyelid closure conditioned to tactual vibratory stimuli applied to the plantar surface of the foot appeared on the fifth postnatal day, on 3 of which experimentation involving 124 paired stimulations was carried on. In another set of experiments the unconditioned stimuli were electric shocks, applied through an electrode at the plantar surface of the left big toe. This type of stimulus evoked a withdrawal movement described as a flexor twitch of the toes accompanied sometimes by other responses. When tactual vibratory stimuli were used, there was no unequivocal evidence of conditioning in the infant studied. Three out of 5 infants gave clear indication of the conditioning of the flexor twitch and respiratory gasp in response to a pure tone stimulus. Withdrawal responses conditioned to visual stimuli appeared on the sixth postnatal day after 120 paired stimulations had been given. In a third type of experiment regularly intermittent auditory stimulation (buzzer) during feeding gave no evidence of conditioning during 8 weeks of stimulation. Wenger (1936) concluded that conditioning of certain types is possible in some newborn infants but that it is highly unstable.

The Wickenses (1940) applied an electric shock to the sole of the foot as the unconditioned stimulus releasing withdrawal movements, and a buzzer as the conditioning stimulus. Their experimental group of 12 infants received 12 paired stimulations a day for 3 consecutive days, and a control group of 12 infants received 12 shocks alone per day for 3 consecutive days. Both groups manifested the usual evidence of conditioning, but a second control group tested on the first day by the buzzer and again on the third day showed no response.

Kasatkin (1948) is reported to have undertaken conditioned-reflex experiments throughout the following developmental range: fetus, baby, and young child.

From this review of the experimental literature it would appear that the conditioning of newborn infants is difficult and, in fact, that it is not possible to establish such responses in all newborn infants. Spelt (1948), however, has reported that CR's are easily set up in the fetus *in utero* during the last 2 months of prenatal life. Employing a vibrotactile conditioned stimulus and a loud noise as the unconditioned stimulus, CR's appeared after 15–20 paired stimulations. In Wenger's (1936) investigation of neonates, 120 or more paired stimulations were required for the establishment of a conditioned response. There exists, therefore, an unresolved discrepancy between the findings of researches upon the conditioning of newborn infants and those upon the fetus before birth.

Summary. There is some evidence that certain responses may be conditioned to experimental stimuli during the neonatal period. The responses are difficult to establish, highly unstable, and cannot be set up in all infants.

Intelligence

Whether or not one may speak of the intelligence of the neonate depends upon the definition which is adopted. If intelligence is simply the capacity to learn it should be apparent from the researches reviewed in the preceding section on learning that some newborn infants possess this ability. Their learning, however, is confined to simple conditioned responses and is highly temporary. It is possible, as Ray (1932) and Spelt (1938, 1948) claim, that this capacity may be present before birth. Research upon the ability of the viable premature infant to acquire conditioned responses would throw light upon the amount of maturation of its nervous system as compared with that of the full-term infant.

Thurstone (1928), in terms of the mental-growth curves of older children, has calculated that the zero point of intelligence is at birth, or possibly in the fetal period.

If intelligence, however, is to be thought of as a general factor running through all the infant's activities, or as requiring symbolic processes, it is clear that the neonate is devoid of any such manifestations. Thus the correlational procedures of Furfey, Bonham, and Sargent (1930) offer no evidence of a *g* factor in newborn infants.

The usual approach to the problem of intelligence in young infants is to attempt to predict future "mental" growth in terms of norms of motor development. It is assumed that early retardation of motor responses will be followed later by retardation in test performance, and that precocious motor development will be followed by precocious performance on tests. For the period of the neonate Shotwell and Gilliland (1943) have set up a scale of 15 items which are supposed to typify the average child of 4 weeks. Examination of the items of the scale in relation to the data presented in this chapter demonstrates that most of the responses are actually elicitable during the first 10 days after birth and some, such as the palpebral reflexes, are already present in the younger premature infants. Nevertheless, Drummond and Gilliland (1946) claim that in terms of the scale infants show progress from week to week, and that the scale performances of feeble-minded children resemble those of infants from 4 to 12 weeks old.

Gilliland (1948) maintains that the final revision of the Northwestern Infant Intelligence Test employs items which measure an adaptation to the specific environmental situations rather than simple physical development or maturation. IQ's are obtained by assigning 3 points of credit for each point of deviation from the norm for any given age, the norm being evaluated as 100 IQ. The reliabilities furnished are derived from correlation of odd and even item performances. Too few cases have been tested subsequently with the Stanford-Binet to furnish other evidence of reliability. Brunet's (1948) developmental scale of baby tests, drawn from the studies of Bühler and of Gesell, contains some items placed at 1 month which, in actuality, are present, in varying degrees, from birth on.

Irwin (1942) has proposed four criteria or conditions which must be met if an organism is to have intelligent behavior: (1) a functional cerebral cortex; (2) functional distance receptors; (3) an upright posture; and (4) the achievement of substitutive or symbolical behavior. Irwin concluded that the neonate does not meet these conditions. It simply possesses a repertory of motor responses, whereas intelligent behavior must await further maturation.

Even though intelligent behavior is absent in the neonate, it should be possible to determine whether precociousness or retardation of motor responses at this stage is correlated with precociousness or retardation at later stages, either in motor responses or in terms of the scores of intelligence tests. Measurements of physical traits may even be predictive of later motor responses. Thus Norval (1947) has shown that for two newborn babies of the same weight a difference of 1 inch in length means that on the average the longer child will walk 22 days earlier than the shorter child.

Individual, Sex, and Race Differences

The studies of newborn infants which have been productive of quantitative data have for the most part been concerned with the characteristics and the comparisons of *groups*. The aim has been to seek expressions of central tendency and of variability rather than to explore the patterns of *individual* attainments in terms of the measurements secured.

Campbell and Weech (1941), in investigations of those responses of the neonate which were thought to be the forerunners of erect locomotion and of creeping, did not discover any marked differentiation of individuals within the group. The researches of Balint (1948a, 1948b) upon the sucking response were clearly oriented with respect to the disclosure of individual differences in newborn infants. Instead of collecting mass data, wherein the identity of the individual would be lost, he took pains to measure each individual repeatedly throughout the nursing period in order to compare its performance at one time with its performance at another time. In this way he learned that there is considerable consistency or constancy in the rhythm of sucking of a given infant but that the rhythm varies with different infants. The sucking behavior of neonates therefore manifests individual differences. These may be classified or grouped, however, into what is considered "normal" or into what is typical of infants having various disorders. Those suffering from respiratory or intestinal disturbances have higher-frequency rhythms and greater irregularity of sucking than "normal" infants.

Sex. In the "genital crisis," and under other physiological conditions of the newborn infant, reactions characteristic of each sex are observed, although differentiation of these phenomena is not complete because both sexes exhibit mammary secretion. Aside from the studies relating to the genital organs there are few dealing with sex differences in the behavior of neonates.

In terms of bodily and segmental movements reported in observational protocols, Gatewood and Weiss (1930) found that males were less active and had less vocalization than females. Pratt's (1932) comparisons of the activity of these same subjects in terms of percentage of time active, according to the stabilimeter-polygraph records, revealed that males were unreliably less active than females. Halverson (1941) states that "in *Profound Sleep* the boys had a significantly lower pulse rate and a correspondingly lower breathing rate than had girls."

Smith (1936), on the other hand, has found more activity and crying in males. She holds that the brightness values of hues, as determined by their effect upon activity, for males are similar to those of color-blind adults, whereas for females they are similar to those of partially color-blind adults. The sex differences with respect to auditory stimulation discovered by Stubbs (1934) were statistically unreliable.

Feldman (1921) and Richards and Irwin (1934c) have reported conflicting results regarding sex differences in the incidence and nature of toe movements in the plantar response. The differences found are apparently not statistically significant.

Race. Gatewood and Weiss (1930), in their tabulation of observed responses, came to the conclusion that Negro infants are less active than white infants. In terms of percentage of time the infants were active, Pratt (1932) found no significant race differences among these subjects. Bryan (1930) asserted that the Babinski is delayed longer in making its appearance in Negro than in white infants. Beasley (1933a) found a higher percentage of superior visual pursuit movements in Negroes on the first day and reported that these movements improved more rapidly than in the whites.

In summary, there is little unequivocal evidence of sex and race differences in newborn infants.

The Nature of the Neonate Organism

The Neonate as a Man in Miniature. The layman and the literary writer alike regard the newborn infant as a kind of man in miniature or a tabloid version of the adult. It is conceded that the infant is rather helpless, that it cannot talk, get about, or appreciably manipulate its surroundings. Its behavior, however, is anthropomorphized to the emotional, perceptional, and ideational levels of the adult.

The literary man is prone to fix upon quite common items of neonate behavior as symbolically betokening distinguishing idiosyncrasies in later life. Or, waxing poetic in a pessimistic way, the birth cry becomes a wail of anguish at being expelled from the paradise of prenatal life into the terrors of postnatal existence. And, if the poetic philosopher be both disillusioned and sentimental, he may describe all goodness, virtue, and insight as indwelling in the innocence of the babe.

The literary man and the layman err in anthropomorphisms which recognize only a difference in size between the newborn infant and the adult. Their conception of the nature of the neonate is only a popular counterpart of the discarded speculations concerning the homunculus.

The psychoanalytic interpretation of the child is essentially an elaboration of the ideas that have just been described. The typical psychoanalyst evokes the associations of the psychoneurotic patient and attempts, through these, to locate the origin and nature of the traumatic experience. Usually the pursuit carries the practitioner back into the childhood of his patient and leads, almost inevitably, to an evaluation of infancy as mirrored in the psychoneurotic's accounts of his dreams and other experiences. This approach to the nature of the child through study of the adult bears a marked resemblance to G. Stanley Hall's questionnaires upon the earliest memories of adults.

Originally this quest into the ontogenetic past had its terminus in the preschool period (at the age of 2–3 years). When this did not suffice to resolve the difficulties of certain patients the psychoanalytic procedures were continued until the conclusion was reached that the truly original traumatic experience was birth itself. This conception has been imputed to Freud by Rank (1929) and many other psychoanalysts, even though there is evidence that Freud regarded it with considerable skepticism.

For Rank (1929), however, this hypothesis is the key to an understanding of the behavior of both the child and the adult. Before birth the child manifests a "mother libido." Hence birth, which separates the child from the libido object, generates a psychic trauma—the primal or original anxiety state. From this shock ensue these consequences: The childhood of individuals is their *normal* neurosis, which becomes *abnormal* if it continues into adult life; claustrophobia and the fear of the child at being left alone in the dark are produced because the individual is reminded of its separation from the womb of the mother; the fear of large animals arises because the child remembers the state of pregnancy; and fear of beasts of prey comes because of the child's desire to be eaten and hence symbolically return to the mother's womb. In short, infantile anxieties or fears are simply a product of the original birth anxiety.

From all of this it follows, for Rank, that "every pleasure has as its final aim the re-establishment of the intrauterine primal pleasure." Thus the finger sucking of the neonate, for example, represents a substitute for the mother.

The ultimate goal of the psychoanalytic search, according to Rank (1929), is not even the catastrophic event of birth but rather some point in the uterine stage of development. This, in fact, is the position taken by Sadger (1941). According to this psychoanalyst the embryo experiences pleasure *and* pain. These are demonstrated by its "impulsive" movements and by sucking responses before birth. That is, such responses are expressive of "sexual sensations of pleasure" and hence of "mental states" in the embryo. He concedes that the higher psychic functions of "thinking" and "willing" may be absent or present only to a limited extent, but he is positive that "feeling" is hypertrophic. In the continuing life of the individual these mental states are "remembered" as unconscious memories.

During the course of his analyses Sadger (1941) discovered that the source of some psychoneuroses could not be located in the embryonic period. Some of his patients traced their memories to their origins as spermatozoa and ova or even beyond to the preconceptual attitudes of their parents—naturally as sensed by the original germ cells while still within the environment of the parental organism! To Sadger the verbal outpourings of his patients were proof that the germ cells, themselves, are endowed with psychic life and possess the capacity to learn and to remember. As previously noted in the section on birth trauma this is strikingly similar to the fanciful picture drawn by Sterne of the homunculus which was fated to be Tristram Shandy.

According to standard psychoanalytic doctrine the neonate is in an oral-erotic phase of development. Anal and sex-organ eroticism emerge later.

In summary, then, the psychoanalyst considers the young infant to have some of the psychic characteristics of adults. For him childhood and adult life constitute one long series of attempts to resolve the trauma of birth or the shocks or uncertainties of conception. Thus Sadger (1941) differentiates between the origins of guilt or of passive pleasure of the castration type in terms of the circumstances attendant upon the loss of the caudal filament of the spermatozoon when it penetrates the ovum.

The psychoanalytic thesis that nonnutritional sucking is evidence of an initial libidinal oral drive is challenged by the view that such sucking is secondary to, and derived from, the basic "hunger" drive. This is the position of Sears (1948), Davis et al. (1948), and Brodbeck (1950). Their

investigations do not reveal nonnutritional sucking to be increased when infants are deprived of opportunities to nurse. Breastfed and cup-fed babies manifest no difference in the amount of such sucking. In fact, when breast-fed infants are shifted to cup feeding there are significant decreases in nonnutritive sucking. Further, the strength or duration of sucking actually increases in infants that are breast fed.

Although their anthropomorphisms are less extreme, the members of the neoprimitivistic school of child care or development, such as Ribble (1944), Aldrich (1945), Trainham, Pilafian, and Kraft (1945), Frank, (1945), and Trainham and Montgomery (1946), are in agreement with the psychoanalysts that the young organism is very susceptible to emotional shock or trauma. Hence they hail the mother–newborn-infant relationship among so-called primitives as ideal because the child is nursed whenever it cries rather than at definite and fixed times. As neoprimitivists they hold that the mother should be able to differentiate the causes of crying and to nurse the infant when its cries indicate hunger. In the light of Sherman's (1927b) investigation of judgments upon the crying of newborn infants the validity of this hypothesis seems somewhat dubious.

Neoprimitivists subscribe to the doctrine of "felt needs" as the cues for care or training, and oppose any early attempts at cultural patterning with the slogan, "Baby knows best." Immediate and constant gratification of an infant's "needs," as interpreted from its cries, will not fixate crying as the pattern of the "spoiled baby" —the response will wither away of its own accord as the child matures. They relate that a child fed on the self-demand schedule eventually reduces its feedings to the number customarily found in the culture. They neglect to state how the age or time of weaning are to be determined by the "felt needs" of the infant, and some do not adhere to their own expressed principles when they wake an infant in order to get it to feed!

Although the majority of pediatricians now appear, in theory, to adhere to the principle of self-demand feeding, it is, nevertheless, apparent that certain qualifications or reservations are being entertained. These are illustrated in the more temperate recommendations of Glaser (1948), Rowan-Legg (1949), and Weinfeld (1950). And beyond these there are portents of a reaction against the more doctrinaire aspects of the movement.

Orlansky's (1949) able evaluation of the neoprimitivists' theories of infant personality formation discloses their propensity to a maximum of speculation but a minimum of objectively verifiable data. It is indeed clear, as Vincent (1951) has observed, that trends in infant care ideas have a fadlike character and are not well grounded upon an impeccable body of empirical data. The views of the most publicized exponent of the doctrine of "mothering," Ribble, do not stand up factually when subjected to the critical analysis of Pinneau (1950), nor are they supported by Wolfle's (1949) observation that the young infant's means of *escape* from the caress are at first rather ineffectual.

Peiper (1941, 1942–1943, 1949) has judged as inadequate and mistaken those views which hold the infant to be a man in miniature. He has noted that in animal psychology we have learned not to ascribe human characteristics to animals but that in child psychology we are still interpreting infant behavior in terms of the experiences of adults. In the one we demand systematic, objective methods; in the other we are often content to accept the most uncritical anthropomorphisms or, as Spitz and Wolf (1946) phrase it, adultomorphisms.

Interpretations of the psychic life of the infant therefore run the gamut from the naïveté of the complete man in miniature to a more sophisticated appraisal based upon a knowledge of those sensory-motor systems which are functioning. Thus Minkowski (1947) ascribes a primitive psyche to the fetus. At first its responses are to humoral-visceral stimuli and imply a vegetative soul in the sense of Aristotle. Later it has elementary feelings of existence as conditioned by position and movement, and a dull memory of a life in water, warmth, and darkness.

The Neonate as a Recapitulation. The extension by G. Stanley Hall of the doctrine of biological recapitulation in the form of a cultural recapitulation, manifesting itself in childhood, is no longer acceptable to psychologists even though occasionally entertained by the layman.

As we have seen, Buchman (1895, 1900) and Mumford (1897) have cited the neonatal grasping reflex, and Moro (1918) the clasping or embrace reflex, as evidence that man's ancestors led an arboreal existence. McGraw (1939) considers the behavior of the newborn infant to consist in part of atavistic reflexes.

Davidson (1914), in a critical review of the doctrine, has shown that the notion of a precise or complete biological recapitulation of the phylogenetic past is not supported by the data of embryology. This is in no sense a denial that vertebrate animals resemble each other more in early than in later developmental periods.

The Neonate as an Organism Developing Autonomy. From the time of implantation of the fertilized ovum in the uterus until birth the organism leads a parasitic type of existence. At birth the infant achieves autonomy of respiration, digestion, excretion, and the maintenance of body temperature. These are all vital activities which the child must undertake if it is to live.

In the postnatal environment it has greater freedom of movement and the opportunity, by virtue of orienting responses, to react with some selectivity to aspects of a more complicated universe. It responds to some stimuli by movements which prolong stimulation, to others by withdrawal or rejection, and to some it at first responds and thereafter inhibits further motility.

The neonate cannot effectively manipulate its physical environment to provide food, care, and requisite protection. It is possessed of the ability to act upon its social environment by crying and by mimetic responses so that adults minister to its needs. In this manner the environment is effectively manipulated by proxy until the development of voluntary movements, particularly successful reaching to visually perceived objects and directed forms of locomotion, provides still further autonomy of action.

The Neonate as a System of Reflexes. Some neurologists have viewed the behavior of the newborn infant as that of a purely spinal being. Cruchet (1911, 1930), who represents this point of view, states that Virchow was the first to liken the reactions of the newborn infant to those of the decerebrate frog. De Crinis (1932), also, believes that the neonate is a reflex being of a lower type because the cerebral cortex is not functional. Peiper (1925a) holds that a part of the optic thalamus is functional at birth, and that athetoid movements are due to lack of inhibition from the corpus striatum. Langworthy (1933) maintains that "the behavior of the newborn is essentially that of a brain-stem preparation although medullation may extend as high as the upper end of the midbrain." Diffusiveness and lack of coordination of movements are interpreted as due

to a lack of cerebral inhibition. Minkowski (1932–1933) views the newborn infant as a cortical and subcortical spinal being, with emphasis upon the subcortical spinal. Marquis (1931) advanced the idea that conditioning occurs at subcortical levels. The ability of the infant to inhibit responses to successive auditory stimuli is proof, according to Peiper (1930), that it is not a purely "spinal being." Kroh (1926) concurs in this judgment because of persistence of a set or disposition for the few hours elapsing from one feeding period to another.

According to the concensus of present-day theories the neural status of the neonate is essentially, if not entirely, that of a noncortical being. McGraw (1943) has related the observed behavior of the neonate to the data presented in Conel's (1939, 1941) histological studies and has concluded that no cortical influence is operating at this time. Following the neonatal period there is a transitional stage characterized by the onset of cortical function. Then comes the final stage of complete cortical dominance. McGraw (1941b) claims that the first evidence of cortical function is provided by the child's localization of a stimulated area; according to her this is not in the repertory of the newborn infant. Nevertheless, the researches of the Shermans (1925), the Shermans and Flory (1936), Peiper (1936a) and Crudden (1937) all seem to indicate the beginnings of cutaneous localization in the neonate. It is also demonstrated in the mouth-orientation response.

In an important paper on the neurological bases of mental development Peiper (1941) has characterized the newborn infant as a midbrain being because its behavior is essentially the same as that found in infants without cerebrums. It is not, however, the behavior of a purely reflex being. The attempts by extreme environmentalists to account for neonate behavior in terms of prenatally established conditioned responses have been severely criticized by Dennis (1943). He has pointed out that acephalies have the same behavioral equipment as normal newborn infants but that even when they live for some time after birth they make no further progress.

The theory of simple, discrete reflexes as the primary origin of behavior, with the complex responses to be derived from environmental integration of separate, part activities to form coordinated wholes, was championed by Watson (1919). The only exceptions to this process were those patterns of responses termed "primary emotions." This conception of the nature of the neonate organism seems not to be supported by the studies of Bersot (1920, 1921), Minkowski (1928, 1932–1933), Pratt, Nelson, and Sun (1930), Coghill (1930a, 1930b, 1933), Irwin (1932a, 1932b, 1932c), Pratt (1934a), and Delman (1935).

Carmichael and his collaborators, Lehner (1937) and Smith (1939), have demonstrated that the generalization or specificity of a response depends in a given age period of the guinea pig upon the intensity of the stimuli. Coghill (1940), in a summary of basic studies upon the origin and nature of early movements in birds and mammals, states that Carmichael and Smith (1939) did not undertake their experiments during the period of earliest movements.

Without denying a relation between organismic involvement in a response and the intensity of the stimulus, it is still possible to affirm a genetic sequence from generalization to specificity, particularly in view of the fact that there is no good reason to believe that the various researches upon the developing child have been ranged in decreasing order of intensity of the stimuli.

The Neonate as a Developing Organism. In contrast with the view which regards the behavior of the newborn infant as completely describable in terms of simple, discrete reflexes, there is an organismic approach which attempts to describe and to pursue behavioral development ontogenetically. The neonate is considered to be a generalized organism because few of its responses are called forth by just one type of stimuli, few are limited to stimulation of just one sense organ or receptor area, and the responses are not sharply localized in a limited number of effector segments. In its most extreme form the organismic view would appear to neglect the observation of the varying participation of the parts of the neonate and to be content with affirmation that the organism was or was not responding.

From the stage of greatest generalization during the late fetal and the neonatal period, the infant for the most part develops in the direction of increasing specificity of response: stimuli, unless conditioning occurs to effect a generalization, become more "adequate"; the reflexogenous zones for a given response shrink; and there is progressively less involvement of the organism in the response.

Development or maturation does not take place at the same rate in all parts of an organism. Axial trends in the development of behavior are discernible.

Pratt (1937), in analyzing the behavior of the neonate from the stimulus-receptor angle, has shown that many responses such as the circulatory, respiratory, Moro, plantar, and palpebral are released by several types of stimuli acting upon different sense organs. Stimuli which are originally effective for some sense organ may become temporarily or more permanently ineffective; others, because of conditioning, become effective. Learning, as Pratt (1934a) has indicated, may produce a generalization of responses to stimuli which were originally inadequate. Initial generalization of the conditioning stimulus before it becomes specifically restricted in releasing the response was demonstrated in Pavlov's (1928) classic experiments.

Bersot (1920, 1921) and Minkowski (1928) have noted the extremes in extent of reflexogenous zones of various responses during the fetal and neonatal stages of development, and have followed their subsequent restriction, especially in the case of the plantar response. Similarly, Galant (1930) has pointed out the extent of the reflexogenous zone of the spinal reflexes. Reduction of the reflexogenous zone of the sucking response during the first ten days was observed by Pratt, Nelson, and Sun (1930). Stirnimann (1937a) has determined differences in reactivity of the facial areas from which the mouth orientation response may be elicited. Pratt (1934d, 1934e, 1934f) has explored several areas within the reflexogenous zone of the plantar response to determine differences in sensitivity and specificity. Although certain of the reflexogenous zones appear to shrink as time goes on, they do not, according to Bersot (1920, 1921), completely disappear. If the intensity of the stimulus is increased, the responses may continue to be elicited from beyond the standard clinical areas.

The behavior of the newborn infant has frequently been described as random, uncoordinated, or diffuse. This impression has arisen because, even without external stimulation, not only is the infant active much of the time but that activity seems to involve most of the body. This general motility has been described and commented upon by Irwin (1930), Schachter (1932b), and many others. It is usually assumed that the basic cause of this play of activity is a lack of inhibition from the cerebrum. The principal exciting cause is probably organic and appears to be in some way re-

lated to events occurring in the alimentary tract. Gesell (1941) rejected the term "random" as applied to such movements. The infant reacts as it does because of its neuromotor apparatus. Seen in sequence its responses do have "form," possibly describable by the term "vermicular."

The earliest movements of neurogenic origin in the animals studied by Coghill (1929a, 1929b, 1930b) are not simple reflexes but rather movements which initially start with the head and trunk and which apparently involve the grosser musculature. This is followed by differentiation, so that movement of smaller segments, such as the extremities, occurs within the larger total pattern. When individuation is complete, specific responses may appear in relative localization when the total pattern is inhibited.

According to Minkowski's (1928, 1932–1933) analysis of fetal development, stimulation of a given area does not at first result in an active and extensive involvement of the organism. As maturation of the nervous system proceeds, crossed, long, and diagonal reflexes appear. Maximum generalization of response, in the sense of active participation of behavior segments, is then attained.

Irwin and Weiss (1930) set up the descriptive categories of "specific movements" and "mass activity" for neonate behavior. The former are those which are somewhat localized and which occur at a rate slow enough to be noted and recorded by an observer; the latter applies to activity which involves the whole organism at a rate too rapid for analysis. They state that either external or internal stimuli may release such mass activity and that the distinction between such activity and specific movements is quite arbitrary. Following this, Irwin (1932c) has considered "mass behavior" the matrix from which specific responses are later individuated.

Dennis (1932b) and Pratt (1934a) have held that "mass activity" is the result of stimuli operating upon an organism at a time when the development of the nervous system has brought about the functional connection of almost all receptors with almost all effectors, and that, antedating this phase, as indicated by the work of Bersot (1920, 1921) and Minkowski (1928), some of those responses exist in relative isolation and hence should not be considered as individuating from "mass behavior" as the matrix. Irwin (1933a), in reply to Dennis, advances the idea that there is a succession of "mass" patterns, with individuation proceeding from each one.

Carmichael (1934) and Coghill (1940) have also been critical of the concept of "mass behavior," Coghill holding that the term is inappropriate because of its implication of lack of differentiation and lack of organization, whereas organization is implied in the term "total pattern."

Bridgman and Carmichael (1935) and Carmichael and his collaborators, Lehner (1937) and Smith (1939), as a result of researches upon the fetal guinea pig, have come to the conclusion that some of the earliest neurogenic responses of the organism are reflex in nature. For this reason they are inclined to question both the concept of an initial total pattern from which reflexes become individuated and the view that the entire course of behavioral development may be summarized as from-generalization-to-specificity. Fitzgerald and Windle (1942) have objected that Coghill's thesis of development is not applicable to human fetal behavior. According to their researches the "mass reflexes" reported by Minkowski are the result of asphyxia. The earliest responses elicitable are individual or specific reflexes. During progressive anoxia these are the first to disappear; next the mass reflexes to intense stimulation are

extinguished; and last of all the muscle excitability itself vanishes.

Michaels (1944) has contributed an interesting paper to the theory that pathological function in the adult represents a regression to early infantile behavior. He states that the functional symptoms of psychosomatic disorders have the form of responses which were the normal mode at earlier stages of development. Thus

> Just as the activities of the neonate are considered to be of a more generalized and less specific nature, so may the visceral somatic dysfunctions in the adult represent a recrudescence of visceral somatic functions in infancy.

The principal axial trends of development are the cephalocaudad and the proximodistal. The doctrine of development from fundamental to accessory movements, as expounded by Buck (1898), Moore (1901), and Shepardson (1907), is the forerunner of the idea that development proceeds proximodistally. More recently Irwin (1930), Shirley (1931a), and Marquis (1933) have all contributed evidence supporting this principle. Bersot (1920, 1921) has reported that some aspects of the plantar response run counter to this conception, and McGraw (1933) has asserted that, so far as the elements of the grasping reflex are concerned, it is the distal segments which show prior anatomical and functional differentiation. Irwin (1933b), in reviewing the literature, says:

> It would seem that the evidence in regard to the differentiation of vertebrate limbs including morphological structure as well as behavior is convincingly in favor of the proximodistal principle.

The work of the Shermans (1925) and the Shermans and Flory (1936) on pain sensitivity illustrates a cephalocaudad gradient in sensitivity and in rapidity of development. The researches of Irwin (1930) and Shirley (1931a) also lend support to this principle of development in human infants.

The important need in the study of neonatal behavior and development is to obtain increasingly accurate and detailed descriptions of the infant's responses and the stimulating conditions under which they are obtained. This should include further exploration of the possibilities of learning, with particular reference to the comparison of premature and full-term infants. It should likewise make a comparison of the relative learning capacity of full-term infants and of prematures *after* they have attained the *actual* age of full-term infants. The generalizations regarding principles of organization and of development of behavior serve a legitimate end just as long as they do not impede further research or constrain the student to force all observations to fit these frames of reference.

Bibliography

Ahlfeld, J. F. 1905. Die intrauterine Tätigkeit der Thorax- und Zwerchfellmuskulatur. Intrauterine Atmung. *Mschr. Geburtsh. Gynäk.*, *21*, 143–163.

Aldrich, C. A. 1928. A new test for hearing in the newborn, the conditioned reflex. *Amer. J. Dis. Child*, *35*, 36–37.

——. 1945. Physiology of the cry of the newborn infant. *Proc. Mayo Clin.*, *20*, 60–62.

Aldrich, C. A., C. Sung, and C. Q. Knop. 1945a. The crying of newly born infants: I. The community phase. *Proc. Mayo Clin.*, *20*, 347–352.

——. 1945b. The crying of newly born babies: II. The individual phase. *J. Pediat.*, *27*, 89–96.

——. 1945c. The crying of newly born babies: III. The early period at home. *J. Pediat.*, *27*, 428–435.

Alexander, G. 1911. Die Reflexerregbarkeit des Ohrlabyrinthes an menschlicher Neugeborener. *Z. Psychol. Physiol. Sinnesorg.*, *45*, 153–196.

Ames, L. B. 1942. Supine leg and foot postures in the human infant in the first year of life. *J. Genet. Psychol.*, *61*, 87–107.

Anderson, J. E. 1948. Personality organization in children. *Amer. Psychol.*, *3*, 409–416.

Antonov, A. N. 1947. Physiology and pathology of the newborn: Bibliography of the material for the period 1930–1940. *Monogr. Soc. Res. Child Develpm.*, *10*, No. 2. Pp. lx + 217.

Apert, E. 1914. La tuméfaction mammaire et la sécrétion lactée chez le nouveau-né. *Le nourrisson*, *2*, 293–299.

Arteaga, J. F. 1918. El liquido mamario del recién nacido. *Rev. med. cirug. Habana*, *23*, 321–343.

Babinski, J. 1896. Sur le réflexe cutané-plantaire dans certains affections organiques du système nerveux central. *C. R. Soc. Biol., Paris*, *48*, 207–208.

——. 1898. Du phénomène des orteils et sa valeur sémiologique. *Semaine méd.*, *18*, 321.

——. 1903. De l'abduction des orteils (signe de l'éventail). *Rev. neurol.*, *11*, 1205–1206.

——. 1915. Réflexes de défense. *Rev. neurol.*, *27*, 145–155.

——. 1922. Réflexes de défense. *Rev. neurol.*, *38*, 1049–1082.

Baldenweck, L., and Guy-Arnaud. 1940. Valeur fonctionnelle du labyrinthe vestibulaire chez le nouveau-né. *La presse médicale*, *48*, 47–49.

Baliassnikowa, N. J., and M. M. Model. 1931–1932. Zur Neurologie des Saugens. *Z. Kinderforsch.*, *39*, 1–16.

Balint, M. 1948a. Individual differences of behavior in early infancy, and an objective method for recording them: I. Approach and the method of recording. *J. Genet. Psychol.*, *73*, 57–79.

——. 1948b. Individual differences of behavior in early infancy, and an objective method for recording them: II. Results and conclusions. *J. Genet. Psychol.*, *73*, 81–117.

Banu, G., and G. Bourguignon. 1921. Évolution de la chronaxie des nerfs et muscles du membre superieur des nouveau-nés. *C. R. Soc. Biol., Paris*, *85*, 349–352.

Banu, G., G. Bourguignon, and H. Laugier. 1921. La chronaxie chez le nouveau-né. *C. R. Soc. Biol., Paris*, *85*, 49–51.

Bartels, M. 1910. Ueber Regulierung der Augenstellung durch den Ohrenapparat. v. *Graefes Arch. Ophthal.*, *76*, 1–79.

——. 1932. Ueber Augenbewegungen bei Neugeborenen. *Dtsch. med. Wschr.*, *58*, 1477–1478.

Barth, H. 1914. Untersuchungen zur Physiologie des Saugens bei normalen und pathologischen Brustkindern. *Z. Kinderheilk.*, *10*, 129.

Basch, K. 1893. Beiträge zur Kenntnis des menschlichen Milchapparats. *Arch. Gynäk.*, *44*, 15–54.

Bauer, J. 1926. Das Kriechphänomen des Neugeboren. *Klin. Wschr.*, *5*, 1468–1469.

Bayley, N. 1933. Mental growth during the first three years: A developmental study of sixty-one children by repeated tests. *Genet. Psychol. Monogr.*, *14*, No. 1.

Bayley, N., and H. R. Stolz. 1937. Maturational changes in rectal temperatures of 61 infants from 1 to 36 months. *Child Develpm.*, *8*, 195–206.

Beasley, W C. 1933a. Visual pursuit in 109 white and 142 negro newborn infants. *Child Develpm.*, *4*, 106–120.

——. 1933b. An investigation of related problems in the vision of newborn infants. *Psychol. Bull.*, *30*, 626.

Bechterew, W. M. 1908. Ueber die objektive Untersuchung der kindlichen Psyche. *Russki Wratsch*, No. 16. (Abstract in *Folia neurobiol.*, *2*, 362–366.)

Beck, L. F. 1938. A review of 16-millimeter films in psychology and allied sciences. *Psychol. Bull.*, *35*, 127–169.

——. 1942. A second review of 16-millimeter films in psychology and allied sciences. *Psychol. Bull.*, *39*, 28–67.

Becker, J. 1921. Ueber Haut und Schweissdrüsen bei Foeten und Neugeborenen. *Z. Kinderheilk.*, *30*, 3–20.

——. 1933. Ueber periphere Nervenendigungen in den äuszeren Genitalien von Neugeborenen. *Z. Kinderheilk.*, *55*, 264–268.

Benedict, F. G., and F. B. Talbot. 1914. The gaseous metabolism of infants with special reference to its relation to pulse-rate and muscular activity. *Carnegie Inst. Wash.*, Publ. 201.

——. 1915. The physiology of the new-born infant. Character and amount of katabolism. *Carnegie Inst. Wash.*, Publ. 223.

Bernard, J., and L. W. Sontag. 1947. Fetal reactivity to tonal stimulation: A preliminary report. *J. Genet. Psychol.*, *70*, 205–210.

Bernfeld, W. 1931. Experimentelle Untersuchungen über die Capillarresistenz junger, insbesondere frühgeborener Säuglinge (Saugglockenmethode). *Mschr. Kinderheilk.*, *51*, 1–14.

Bersot, H. 1918, 1919. Variabilité et corrélations organiques. Nouvelle étude du réflexe plantaire. *Schweiz. Arch. Neurol. Psychiat.*, *4*, 277–323; *5*, 305–324.

——. 1920, 1921. Développement réactionnel et réflexe plantaire du bébé né avant terme à celui de deux ans. *Schweiz. Arch. Neurol. Psychiat.*, *7*, 212–239; *8*, 47–74.

Binet, A. 1890. Recherches sur les mouvements chez quelques jeunes enfants. *Rev. phil.*, *29*, 297–309.

Blanton, M. G. 1917. The behavior of the human infant during the first thirty days of life. *Psychol. Rev.*, *24*, 456–483.

Bridges, K. M. B. 1932. Emotional development in early infancy. *Child Develpm.*, *3*, 324–341.

——. 1935. Le développement des émotions chez le jeune enfant. *L'Union méd. Canada*, *64*, 15–19; 130–139.

——. 1936. Le développement des émotions chez le jeune enfant. *J. psychol. norm. path.*, *33*, 40–87.

Bridgman, C. S., and L. Carmichael. 1935. An experimental study of the onset of behavior in the fetal guinea-pig: *J. Genet. Psychol.*, *47*, 247–267.

Brodbeck, A. J. 1950. The effect of three feeding variables on the non-nutritive sucking of newborn infants. *Amer. Psychol.*, *5*, 292–293.

Brodbeck, A. J., and O. C. Irwin. 1946. The speech behavior of infants without families. *Child Develpm.*, *17*, 145–156.

Brunet, O. 1948. Baby-tests. Une échelle de développement psycho-moteur pour les enfants du premier âge. *Enfance*, *1*, 250–255.

Bryan, E. S. 1930. Variations in the responses of infants during first ten days of post-natal life. *Child Develpm.*, *1*, 56–77.

Buchman, S. S. 1895. Babies and monkeys. *Pop. Sci. Mo.*, *46*, 371–388.

——. 1900. Babies and monkeys. *Nineteenth Cent.*, *36*, 727–743.

Buck, F. 1898. From fundamental to accessory in the development of the nervous system and of movements. *Ped. Sem.*, *6*, 5–64.

Burr, C. W. 1921. The reflexes of early infancy. *Brit. J. Child. Dis.*, *18*, 152–153.

Campbell, R. V. D., and A. A. Weech. 1941. Measures which characterize the individual during the development of behavior in early life. *Child Develpm.*, *12*, 217–236.

Canestrini, S. 1913. Ueber das Sinnesleben des Neugeborenen. (*Monogr. Gesamtgeb. Neurol. Psychiat.*, No. 5) Berlin: Springer. Pp. 104.

Carlson, A. J., and H. Ginsburg. 1915. Contributions to the physiology of the stomach: XXIV. The tonus and hunger contractions of the stomach of the newborn. *Amer. J. Physiol.*, *38*, 29–32.

Carmichael, L. 1933. Origin and prenatal growth of behavior. In C. Murchison (Ed.) *A handbook of child psychology.* 2d ed., rev., pp. 31–159. Worcester: Clark University Press.

——. 1934. An experimental study in the prenatal guinea-pig of the origin and development of reflexes and patterns of behavior in relation to stimulation of specific receptor areas during the period of active fetal life. *Genet. Psychol. Monogr.*, *16*, 337–491.

Carmichael, L., and G. F. J. Lehner. 1937. The development of temperature sensitivity during the fetal period. *J. Genet. Psychol.*, *50*, 217–227.

Carmichael, L., and M. F. Smith. 1939. Quantified pressure stimulation and the specificity and generality of response in fetal life. *J. Genet. Psychol.*, *54*, 425–434.

Carpenter, T. M., and J. R. Murlin. 1911. The energy metabolism of mother and child just before and just after birth. *Arch. Intern. Med.*, *7*, 184–222.

Castro, F. 1930. Sécrétion lactée du nouveau-né prolongée jusqu'au onzième mois. *C. R. Soc. Biol.*, *Paris*, *105*, 485–486.

Catel, W. 1932. Zum Spontannystagmus des Neugeborenen. *Dtsch. med. Wschr.*, *58*, 1478–1479.

Cemach, A. I. 1920. Beiträge zur Kenntnis der kochlearen Reflexe. *Beitr. Anat., Physiol., Pathol., Therap. Ohres, Nase, Halses*, *14*, 1–82.

Champneys, F. H. 1881. Notes on an infant. *Mind*, *6*, 104–107.

Chase, W. P. 1937. Color vision in infants. *J. Exp. Psychol.*, *20*, 203–222.

Chen, H. P., and O. C. Irwin. 1946a. Infant speech vowel and consonant types. *J. Speech Disorders*, *11*, 27–29.

——. 1946b. The type-token ratio applied to infant speech sounds. *J. Speech Disorders*, *11*, 126–130.

——. 1946c. Development of speech during infancy: Curve of differential percentage indices. *J. Exp. Psychol.*, *36*, 522–525.

Ciurlo, L. 1934. Sulla funzione olfattoria nel neonato. *Valsalva*, *10*, 22–34. (Abstract in *Zbl. ges. Kinderheilk.*, *1934*, *29*, 134.)

Clarke, F. M. 1939. A developmental study of the bodily reaction of infants to an auditory startle stimulus. *J. Genet. Psychol.*, *55*, 415–427.

Clarke, F. M., W. A. Hunt, and E. B. Hunt. 1937. Plantar responses in infants following a startle stimulus. *J. Genet. Psychol.*, *50*, 458–461.

Clifford, S. H. 1941. The effects of asphyxia on the newborn infant. *J. Pediat.*, *18*, 567–578.

Coghill, G. E. 1929a. The development of movement of the hind leg of *Amblystoma*. *Proc. Soc. Exp. Biol. Med.*, *27*, 74–75.

———. 1929b. The early development of behavior in *Amblystoma* and in man. *Arch. Neurol. Psychiat.*, *Chicago*, *21*, 989–1009.

———. 1930a. Individuation versus integration in the development of behavior. *J. Gen. Psychol.*, *3*, 431–435.

———. 1930b. The structural basis of the integration of behavior. *Proc. Nat. Acad. Sci.*, *Wash.*, *16*, 637–643.

———. 1933. The neuro-embryologic study of behavior: Principles, perspective and aim. *Science*, *78*, 131–138.

———. 1940. Early embryonic somatic movements in birds and in mammals other than man. *Monogr. Soc. Res. Child Develpm.*, *5*, 1–48.

Compayré, G. 1896. *The intellectual and moral development of the child*. Pt. 1. (Trans. by M. E. Wilson.) New York: Appleton.

Conel, J. L. 1939. *The postnatal development of the human cerebral cortex*. Vol. I. *The cortex of the newborn*. Cambridge: Harvard University Press. Pp. vi + 117. Plates.

———. 1941. *The postnatal development of the human cerebral cortex*. Vol. II. *The cortex of the one-month infant*. Cambridge: Harvard University Press. Pp. vii + 136.

Creutzfeldt, H. G., and A. Peiper. 1932. Untersuchungen über die Todesursache der Frühgeburten. *Mschr. Kinderheilk.*, *52*, 24–36.

Cruchet, R. 1911. Évolution psycho-physiologique de l'enfant, du jour de sa naissance à l'âge de deux ans. *Année psychol.*, *17*, 48–63.

———. 1930. La mésure de l'intelligence chez l'enfant de la naissance. *J. méd. Bordeaux*, *107*, 951–960.

Crudden, C. H. 1937. Reactions of newborn infants to thermal stimuli under constant tactual conditions. *J. Exp. Psychol.*, *20*, 350–370.

Czerny, A. 1892. Beobachtungen über den Schlaf im Kindesalter unter physiologischen Verhältnissen. *Jb. Kinderheilk.*, *22*, 1–28.

Daniels, E. E., and M. Maudry. 1935. Die Entwicklung der Abwehrreaktionen auf Störungsreize. *Z. Psychol.*, *135*, 259–287.

Darwin, C. 1877. A biographical sketch of an infant. *Mind*, *2*, 285–294.

Davidson, P. E. 1914. The recapitulation theory and human infancy. *Teach. Coll. Contr. Educ.*, No. 65.

Davis, H. V., R. R. Sears, H. C. Miller, and A. J. Brodbeck. 1948. Effects of cup, bottle, and breast feeding on oral activities of newborn infants. *Pediatrics*, *2*, 549–558.

de Crinis, M. 1932. Die Entwicklung der Grosshirnrinde nach der Geburt in ihren Beziehungen zur in-tellektuellen Ausreifung des Kindes. *Wien. klin. Wschr.*, *45*, 1161–1165.

Delman, L. 1935. The order of participation of limbs in responses to tactual stimulation of the newborn infant. *Child Develpm.*, *6*, 98–109.

Denisova, M. P., and N. L. Figurin. 1929. [The problem of the first associated food reflexes in infants.] *Voprosy Geneticheskoy Reflexologii i Pedologii Mladenchestva.*, *1*, 81–88 (Cited in Razran, 1933.)

Dennis, W. 1932a. Two new responses of infants. *Child Develpm.*, *3*, 362–363.

———. 1932b. Discussion: The rôle of mass activity in the development of infant behavior. *Psychol. Rev.*, *39*, 593–595.

———. 1934. A description and classification of the responses of the newborn infant. *Psychol. Bull.*, *31*, 5–22.

———. 1935. A psychologic interpretation of the persistence of the so-called Moro reflex. *Amer. J. Dis. Child.*, *50*, 888–893.

———. 1936. A bibliography of baby biographies. *Child Develpm.*, *7*, 71–73.

———. 1940. Infant reaction to restraint: An evaluation of Watson's theory. *Trans. N. Y. Acad. Sci.*, *2*, 202–218.

———. 1943. Is the newborn infant's repertoire learned or instinctive? *Psychol. Rev.*, *50*, 330–337.

Dennis, W., and M. G. Dennis. 1937. Behavioral development in the first year as shown by forty biographies. *Psychol. Rec.*, *1*, 349–361.

Despert, J. L. 1946. Anxiety, phobias, and fears in young children: With special reference to prenatal, natal, and neonatal factors. *Nerv. Child*, *5*, 8–24.

Dewey, E. 1935. *Behavior development in infants: A survey of the literature on prenatal and postnatal activity, 1920–1934*. New York: Columbia University Press.

Disher, D. R. 1934. The reactions of newborn infants to chemical stimuli administered nasally. *Ohio State Univ. Stud., Contr. Psychol.*, No. 12, pp. 1–52.

Dockeray, F. C., and C. Rice. 1934. Responses of newborn infants to pain stimulation. *Ohio State Univ. Stud., Contrib. Psychol.*, No. 12, pp. 82–93.

Dockeray, F. C., and W. L. Valentine. 1939. A new isolation cabinet for infant research. *J. Exp. Psychol.*, *24*, 211–214

Drummond, M. 1921. *The dawn of mind: An introduction to child psychology*. London: Arnold.

Drummond, M. D., and A. R. Gilliland. 1946. The validation of the Gilliland-Shotwell Infant Intelligence Scale. *Amer. Psychol.*, *1*, 464.

Dupérié, R., and R. Bargues. 1932. À propos des réflexes inconditionnels du nourrison: le réflex de l'étreinte de Moro. *Gaz. hebd. sci. méd. Bordeaux*, *53*, 66–70.

Eckstein, A. 1927. Zur Physiologie der Geschmacksempfindung und des Saugreflexes bei Säuglingen. *Z. Kinderheilk.*, *45*, 1–18.

Eckstein, A., and H. Paffrath. 1928. Bewegungsstudien bei frühgeborenen und jungen Säuglingen. *Z. Kinderheilk.*, *46*, 595–610.

Eckstein, A., and E. Rominger. 1921. Beiträge zur Physiologie und Pathologie der Atmung. Die Atmung des Säuglings. *Z. Kinderheilk.*, *28*, 1–37.

Edgerton, A. E. 1934. Ocular observations and studies of the newborn; with a review of the literature. *Arch. Ophthal.*, *N. Y.*, *11*, 838–867.

Ellingson, R. J., and D. B. Lindsley. 1949. Brain waves and cortical development in newborns and young infants. *Amer. Psychol.*, *4*, 248–249.

Engstler, G. 1905. Ueber den fussohlen Reflex und das Babinski-phänomen bei tausend Kindern der ersten Lebensjahre. *Wien. klin. Wschr.*, *18*, 567–570.

Fairbanks, G. 1942. An acoustical study of the pitch of infant hunger wails. *Child Develpm.*, *13*, 227–232.

Feldman, W. M. 1920. The principles of ante-natal and post-natal child physiology, pure and applied. London and New York: Longmans, Green.

——. 1921. The nature of the plantar reflex in early life and the causes of its variations. *Brit. J. Child. Dis.*, *18*, 24–27.

——. 1927. *The principles of ante-natal and post-natal child hygiene.* London: Bale & Danielsson.

Fernandez, U. 1918. Puericultura post-natal. El recién nacido. Algunos fenómenos fisiológicos inmediatos al nacimento. *Semana med.*, *25*, 115–118.

Fitzgerald, J. E., and W. F. Windle. 1942. Some observations on early human fetal movements. *J. Comp. Neurol.*, *76*, 159–167.

Forbes, H. S., and H. B. Forbes. 1927. Fetal sense reaction: Hearing. *J. Comp. Psychol.*, *7*, 353–355.

Frank, L. K. 1945. The newborn as a young mammal with organic capacities, needs, and feelings. *Psychosom. Med.*, *7*, 169–171.

Freudenberg, E. 1921. Der Morosche Umklammerungsreflex und das Brudzinskische Nackenzeichen als Reflexe des Säuglingsalters. *Münch. med. Wschr.*, *68*, 1646–1647.

Froeschels, E., and H. Beebe. 1946. Testing the hearing of newborn infants. *Arch. Otolaryng.*, *44*, 710–714.

Fulton, J. F., and A. D. Keller. 1932. *The sign of Babinski: A study of the evolution of cortical dominance in primates.* Springfield, Ill.: Thomas.

Furfey, P. H., M. A. Bonham, and M. K. Sargent. 1930. The mental organization of the newborn. *Child Develpm.*, *1*, 48–51.

Galant, J. S. 1917. *Der Rückgratreflex.* Dissertation, Basel. (Abstracted in Peiper, 1928.)

——. 1930. Über die abdominale Variation des Galant'schen Rückgratreflexes (der "abdominale Rückgratreflex") und über die Ausbreitung der reflexogen Zone des Rückgratreflexes bei Säuglingen überhaupt. *Jb. Kinderheilk.*, *129*, 239–241.

——. 1931. Über die rudimentären neuropsychischen Funktionen der Säuglinge. *Jb. Kinderheilk.*, *133*, 104–108.

Gatewood, M. C., and A. P. Weiss. 1930. Race and sex differences in newborn infants. *J. Genet. Psychol.*, *38*, 31–49.

Gentry, E. F., and C. A. Aldrich, 1948. Rooting reflex in the newborn infant: Incidence and effect on it of sleep. *Amer. J. Dis. Child.*, *75*, 528–539.

Genzmer, A. 1873. *Untersuchungen über des Sinneswahrnehmungen des neugeborenen Menschen.* (Dissertation, 1873.) Halle: Niemeyer, 1882. (Abstracted by Peterson and Rainey, 1910; Canestrini, 1913; and Peiper, 1928.)

Gesell, A. 1925. *The mental growth of the preschool child: A psychological outline of normal development from birth to the sixth year, including a system of developmental diagnosis.* New York: Macmillan.

——. 1934. *An atlas of infant behavior: A systematic delineation of the forms and early growth of human behavior patterns.* Vol. I. *Normative series* (with H. Thompson and C. S. Amatruda) Vol. II. *Naturalistic series* (with A. V. Keliher, F. L. Ilg, and J. J. Carlson). New Haven: Yale University Press.

——. 1941. The genesis of behavior form in fetus and infant. The growth of the mind from the standpoint of developmental morphology. *Proc. Amer. Phil. Soc.*, *84*, 471–488.

Gesell, A., and L. B. Ames. 1940. The ontogenetic organization of prone behavior in human infancy. *J. Genet. Psychol.*, *56*, 247–263.

Gesell, A., and H. M. Halverson. 1942. The daily maturation of infant behavior: A cinema study of postures, movements, and laterality. *J. Genet. Psychol.*, *61*, 3–32.

Gesell, A., and H. Thompson. 1929. Learning and growth in identical infant twins: An experimental study by the method of co-twin control. *Genet. Psychol. Monogr.*, *6*, 1–124.

Gesell, A., H. Thompson, and C. Amatruda. 1938. *The psychology of early growth.* New York: Macmillan.

Gilliland, A. R. 1948. The measurement of the mentality of infants. *Child Develpm.*, *19*, 155–158.

Givler, R. C. 1921. The intellectual significance of the grasping reflex. *J. Phil.*, *18*, 617–628.

Glaser, K. 1948. Semi-self-demand feeding schedule for prematurely born infants. *Amer. J. Dis. Child.*, *75*, 309–315.

Gordon, M. B. 1929. The Moro embrace reflex in infancy: Its incidence and significance. *Amer. J. Dis. Child.*, *38*, 26–34.

Greenacre, P. 1944. Infant reactions to restraint: Problems in the fate of infantile aggression. *Amer. J. Orthopsychiat.*, *14*, 204–218.

Gudden, H. 1910. Das Verhalten der Pupillen beim Neugeborenen. *Münch. med. Wschr.*, *57*, 405–406.

Guernsey, M. 1929. A quantitative study of eye reflexes in infants. *Psychol. Bull.*, *26*, 160–161.

Gundobin, N. 1907. Die Eigentümlichkeiten des Kindesalters. *Jb. Kinderheilk.*, *65*, 720–732.

Gutmann, M. I. 1924. Ueber Augenbewegungen der Neugeborenen und ihre theoretische Bedeutung. *Arch. ges. Psychol.*, *47*, 108–121.

Hall, G. S. 1891. Notes on the study of infants. *Ped. Sem.*, *1*, 127–138.

Haller, M. W. 1932. The reactions of infants to changes in the intensity and pitch of pure tone. *J. Genet. Psychol.*, *40*, 162–180.

Halverson, H. M. 1936. Complications of the early grasping reactions. *Psychol. Monogr.*, *47*, 47–63.

Halverson, H. M. 1937. Studies of the grasping responses of early infancy: I, II, III. *J. Genet. Psychol., 51*, 371–449.

——. 1938. Infant sucking and tensional behavior. *J. Genet. Psychol., 53*, 365–430.

——. 1940. Genital and sphincter behavior of the male infant. *J. Genet. Psychol., 56*, 95–136.

——. 1941. Variations in pulse and respiration during different phases of infant behavior. *J. Genet. Psychol., 59*, 259–330.

——. 1944. Mechanisms of early infant feeding. *J. Genet. Psychol., 64*, 185–223.

——. 1946. A study of feeding mechanisms in premature infants. *J. Genet. Psychol., 68*, 205–217.

Hartmann, H. 1932. Zur Anatomie der Geschlechtsorgane Neugeborener. *Arch. Gynäk., 148*, 708–723.

Hartmann-Karplus, D. 1931. Untersuchungen über Juckempfindung, Kratzen und Pilomotorenreflex im Säuglingsalter. *Jb. Kinderheilk., 132*, 140–158.

Hazard, C. 1936. The relation of reflex conduction rate in the patellar reflex to age in human beings. *Univ. Iowa Stud. Child Welfare, 12*, 183–197.

Hensel, G. 1933. Untersuchungen über den Diastasegehalt des Speichels bei Frühgeborenen. *Z. Kinderheilk., 54*, 367–376.

Herlitz, G. 1942–1943. Studien über die konsensuelle Hautgefässreaktion Neugeborener bei Kälteeinwirkung. *Acta Paediat., 30*, 434–448.

Herzfeld, B. 1922. Das neugeborene Kind und seine Eigentümlichkeiten. *Jb. Kinderheilk., 99*, 75–85.

Hoeland, H. 1927. Über die Hexenmilch und die histologischen Veränderungen in den Brüsten des Neugeborenen. *Mschr. Geburtsh. Gynäk., 77*, 114–120.

Hofmann, E., and A. Peiper. 1937. Der Schluckvorgang. *Mschr. Kinderheilk., 70*, 54–56.

Hunt, W. A. 1939. "Body jerk" as a concept in describing infant behavior. *J. Genet. Psychol., 55*, 215–220.

Hunt, W. A., F. M. Clarke, and E. B. Hunt. 1936. Studies of the startle pattern: IV. Infants. *J. Psychol., 2*, 339–352.

Hunt, W. A., and C. Landis. 1936. Studies of the startle pattern: I. Introduction. *J. Psychol., 2*, 201–205.

——. 1938. A note on the difference between the Moro reflex and the startle pattern. *Psychol. Rev., 45*, 267–269.

Hurlock, E. B. 1933. Experimental studies of the newborn. *Child Develpm., 4*, 148–163.

Irwin, O. C. 1930. The amount and nature of activities of new-born infants under constant external stimulating conditions during the first ten days of life. *Genet. Psychol. Monogr., 8*, 1–92.

——. 1931. A cold light for photographing infant reactions with the high-speed camera. *Child Develpm., 2*, 153–155.

——. 1932a. The organismic hypothesis and differentiation of behavior: I. The cell theory and the neurone doctrine. *Psychol. Rev., 39*, 128–146.

——. 1932b. The organismic hypothesis and differentiation of behavior: II. The reflex-arc concept. *Psychol. Rev., 39*, 189–202.

Irwin, O. C. 1932c. The organismic hypothesis and differentiation of behavior: III. The differentiation of human behavior. *Psychol. Rev., 39*, 387–393.

——. 1932d. The relation of body motility in young infants to some physical traits. *J. Exp. Educ., 1*, 140–143.

——. 1932e. The amount of motility of seventy-three newborn infants. *J. Comp. Psychol., 14*, 415–428.

——. 1932f. The distribution of the amount of motility in young infants between two nursing periods. *J. Comp. Psychol., 14*, 429–445.

——. 1932g. The latent time of the body startle in infants. *Child Develpm., 3*, 104–107.

——. 1932h. Infant responses to vertical movements. *Child Develpm., 3*, 167–169.

——. 1933a. Dennis on mass activity: A reply. *Psychol. Rev., 40*, 215–219.

——. 1933b. Proximo-distal differentiation of limbs in young organisms. *Psychol. Rev., 40*, 467–477.

——. 1933c. Motility in young infants: I. Relation to body temperature. *Amer. J. Dis. Child., 45*, 531–533.

——. 1933d. Motility in young infants: II. Relation to two indexes of nutritional status. *Amer. J. Dis. Child., 45*, 534–537.

——. 1936. Qualitative changes in a vertebral reaction pattern during infancy: A motion-picture study. *Univ. Iowa Stud. Child Welfare, 12*, 201–207.

——. 1941a. Effect of strong light on the body activity of newborns. *J. Comp. Psychol., 32*, 233–236.

——. 1941b. The profile as a visual device for indicating central tendencies in speech data. *Child Develpm., 12*, 111–120.

——. 1941c. Research on speech sounds for the first six months of life. *Psychol. Bull., 38*, 277–285.

——. 1942. Can infants have IQ's? *Psychol. Rev., 49*, 69–79.

——. 1945. Reliability of infant speech sound data. *J. Speech Disorders, 10*, 227–237.

——. 1946. Infant psychology. In P. L. Harriman (Ed.), *Encyclopedia of psychology*, pp. 272–286. New York: Philosophical Library.

——. 1947a. Infant speech: The problem of variability. *J. Speech Disorders, 12*, 173–176.

——. 1947b. Infant speech: Consonantal sounds according to place of articulation. *J. Speech Disorders, 12*, 397–401.

——. 1947c. Infant speech: Consonant sounds according to manner of articulation. *J. Speech Disorders, 12*, 402–404.

——. 1947d. Development of speech during infancy: Curve of phonemic frequencies. *J. Exp. Psychol., 37*, 187–193.

Irwin, O. C., and H. P. Chen. 1941. A reliability study of speech sounds observed in the crying of newborn infants. *Child Develpm., 12*, 351–368.

——. 1943. Speech sound elements during the first year of life: A review of the literature. *J. Speech Disorders, 8*, 109–121.

——. 1946a. Infant speech: Vowel and consonant frequency. *J. Speech Disorders, 11*, 123–125.

Irwin, O. C., and H. P. Chen. 1946b. Development of speech during infancy: Curve of phonemic types. *J. Exp. Psychol.*, *36*, 431–436.

Irwin, O. C., and T. Curry. 1941. Vowel elements in the crying vocalization of infants under ten days of age. *Child Develpm.*, *12*, 99–109.

Irwin, O. C., and A. P. Weiss. 1930. A note on mass activity in newborn infants. *J. Genet. Psychol.*, *38*, 20–30.

Irwin, O. C., and L. A. Weiss. 1934a. Differential variations in the activity and crying of the newborn infant under different intensities of light: A comparison of observational with polygraph findings. *Univ. Iowa Stud. Child Welfare*, *9*, 137–147.

——. 1934b. The effect of clothing on the general and vocal activity of the newborn infant. *Univ. Iowa Stud. Child Welfare*, *9*, 149–162.

——. 1934c. The effect of darkness on the activity of newborn infants. *Univ. Iowa Stud. Child Welfare*, *9*, 163–175.

Jacobi, W., and F. Demuth. 1923. Die wahre Acidität der Mundflüssigkeit beim Säugling und Neugeborenen. *Z. Kinderheilk.*, *34*, 293–296.

Jaroschka, K. 1929. Ein Beitrag zur Kenntnis der Sekretionsvorgänge der Brustdrüse von Säuglingen. *Mschr. Kinderheilk.*, *42*, 523–527.

Jensen, K. 1932. Differential reactions to taste and temperature stimuli in newborn infants. *Genet. Psychol. Monogr.*, *12*, 363–479.

Jones, H. E. 1930. The galvanic skin reflex in infancy. *Child Develpm.*, *1*, 106–110.

Jones, M. C. 1926. The development of early behavior patterns in young children. *J. Genet. Psychol.*, *33*, 537–585.

Joseph, S. 1929. Zur Biologie der Brustdrüse beim Neugeborenen. *Mschr. Geburtsh. Gynäk.*, *83*, 219–224.

Kahn, W. 1921. Über die Dauer der Darmpassage im Säuglingsalter. *Z. Kinderheilk.*, *29*, 321–330.

Kasatkin, N. I. 1935. [The development of visual and acoustic conditioned reflexes and their differentiation in infants.] *Sovetsk. Pediat.*, *8*, 127–137. (Abstract 1756, *Psychol. Abstr.*, 1936.)

——. 1948. Rannie uslovye refleksy v ontogeneze cheloveka. (Early conditioned reflexes in human ontogenesis.) Moscow: *U.S.S.R. Acad. med. sci.* Pp. 192. [Abstr. 3741 *Psychol. Abstr.*, 1951, *25*, 372–373.]

Kasatkin, N. I., and A. M. Levikova. 1935a. On the development of early conditioned reflexes and differentiations of auditory stimuli in infants. *J. Exp. Psychol.*, *18*, 1–19.

——. 1935b. The formation of visual conditioned reflexes and their differentiation in infants. *J. Gen. Psychol.*, *12*, 416–435.

Kashara, M. 1916. The curved lines of suction. *Amer. J. Dis. Child.*, *12*, 73–87.

Ködding, I. 1940. Der Lidschlag im Kindesalter. *Mschr. Kinderheilk.*, *84*, 212–223.

Koellreutter, W. 1907. Schwerhörigkeit der Neugeborenen als reine Störung im schallzuleitenden Teile des Ohres. *Z. Ohrenheilk. Krankh. Luftwege*, *53*, 123–138.

Kroh, O . 1926. Die Anfänge der psychischen Entwicklung des Kindes in allgemeinpsychologischer Beleuchtung. *Z. Psychol.*, *100*, 325–343.

Kroner, T. 1881. Ueber die Sinnesempfindungen der Neugeborenen. Breslau: Grass, Barth. (Abstracted in Peterson and Rainey, 1910; Preyer, 1882; and Peiper, 1928.) Pp. 14.

Kunst, M. S. 1948. A study of thumb- and finger-sucking in infants. *Psychol. Monogr.*, *62*, No. 3.

Kussmaul, A. 1859. *Untersuchungen über das Seelenleben des neugeborenen Menschen.* Tübingen: Moser. (Abstracted in Peterson and Rainey, 1910; Preyer, 1882; and Peiper, 1928.) Pp. 32.

Kutvirt, O. 1912. Ueber das Gehör der Neugeborenen und Säuglinge. *Beitr. Anat., Physiol., Pathol., Therap. Ohres, Nase, Halses*, *5*, 249–257.

Lambanzi, R., and C. Pianetta. 1906. Recherches sur le réflexe buccal. *Rev. psychiat. psychol., exp.*, *10*, 148–154.

Landis, C., and W. A. Hunt. 1937. Magnification of time as a research technique in the study of behavior. *Science*, *85*, 384–385.

——. 1939. *The startle pattern.* New York: Farrar and Rinehart.

Langworthy, O. R. 1933. Development of behavior patterns and myelinization of the nervous system in the human fetus and infant. *Contr. Embryol., Carnegie Inst. Wash.*, *24*, No. 139.

Lantuejoul, P., and E. Hartmann. 1923. Note sur le réflexe cutané-plantaire chez le jeune enfant, notamment au moment de la naissance. *Rev. neurol.*, *39*, 387–399.

Leri, A. 1903–1904. Le réflexe de Babinski chez les enfants. *Gaz. malad. inf.*, *5*, 277.

Levine, S. Z., and E. Marples. 1931. The respiratory metabolism in infancy and in childhood: XII. A biometric study of basal metabolism in normal infants. *Amer. J. Dis. Child.*, *41*, 1332–1346.

Levy, S. 1928. Ueber die körperliche und geistige Entwicklung von Frühgeborenen. *Jb. Kinderheilk.*, *121*, 51–85.

Ling, B.-C. 1942. I. A genetic study of sustained visual fixation and associated behavior in the human infant from birth to six months. *J. Genet. Psychol.*, *61*, 227–277.

Litzka, G. 1933. Experimentelle Untersuchungen über den Einfluss der Schwangerschaftshormone auf den Organismus des Fetus und Neugeborenen. *Z. Kinderheilk.*, *54*, 742–757.

Lorenz, E. 1929. Ueber des Brustdrüsensekret des Neugeborenen. *Jb. Kinderheilk.*, *124*, 268–274.

Lowden, T. S. 1895. The first half year of an infant's life. *Post-grad. and Wooster Quart.*

Löwenfeld, B. 1927. Systematisches Studium der Reaktionen der Säuglinge auf Klänge und Geräusche. *Z. Psychol.*, *104*, 62–96.

Lynip, A. W. 1951. The use of magnetic devices in the collection and analysis of the preverbal utterances of an infant. *Genet. Psychol. Monogr.*, *44*, 221–262.

Major, D. R. 1906. *First steps in mental growth: A series of studies in the psychology of infancy.* New York: Macmillan.

Marinesco, G., and A. Kreindler. 1933. Des réflexes conditionnels: I. L'organisation des réflexes conditionnels chez l'enfant. *J. psychol. norm path., 30,* 855–886.

Marquis, D. P. 1931. Can conditioned responses be established in the newborn infant? *J. Genet. Psychol., 39,* 479–492.

——. 1933. A study of activity and postures in infants' sleep. *J. Genet. Psychol., 42,* 51–69.

——. 1941. Learning in the neonate: The modification of behavior under three feeding schedules. *J. Exp. Psychol., 29,* 263–282.

——. 1943. A study of frustration in newborn infants. *J. Exp. Psychol., 32,* 123–138.

McCarthy, D. 1949. Organismic interpretations of infant vocalizations. *Amer. Psychol., 4,* 247.

McGinnis, J. M. 1930. Eye-movements and optic nystagmus in early infancy. *Genet. Psychol. Monogr., 8,* 321–430.

McGraw, M. B. 1932. From reflex to muscular control in the assumption of an erect posture and ambulation in the human infant. *Child Develpm., 3,* 291–297.

——. 1933. Discussion: Grasping in infants and the proximo-distal course of growth. *Psychol. Rev., 40,* 301–302.

——. 1935. *Growth: A study of Johnny and Jimmy.* New York: Appleton-Century.

——. 1937. The Moro reflex. *Amer. J. Dis. Child., 54,* 240–251.

——. 1939. Behavior of the newborn infant and early neuromuscular development. *Res. Publ. Ass. Nerv. Ment. Dis., 19,* 244–246; *Psychol. Abstr.,* No. 3816, 1940, *14,* 390.

——. 1940a. Suspension grasp behavior of the human infant. *Amer. J. Dis. Child., 60,* 799–811.

——. 1940b. Neuromuscular mechanism of the infant. Development reflected by postural adjustments to an inverted position. *Amer. J. Dis. Child., 60,* 1031–1042.

——. 1940c. Neuromuscular development of the human infant as exemplified in the achievement of erect locomotion. *J. Pediat., 17,* 747–771.

——. 1941a. Development of rotary-vestibular reactions of the human infant. *Child Develpm., 12,* 17–19.

——. 1941b. Neural maturation as exemplified in the changing reactions of the infant to pin prick. *Child Develpm., 12,* 31–42.

——. 1941c. Development of neuro-muscular mechanisms as reflected in the crawling and creeping behavior of the human infant. *J. Genet. Psychol., 58,* 83–111.

——. 1941d. Neuro-motor maturation of anti-gravity functions as reflected in the development of a sitting posture. *J. Genet. Psychol., 59,* 155–175.

——. 1941e. Neural maturation of the infant as exemplified in the righting reflex, or rolling from a dorsal to a prone position. *J. Pediat., 18,* 385–394.

——. 1943. *The neuromuscular maturation of the human infant.* New York: Columbia University Press. Pp. 140.

Mesina, R. 1936. [The tonic reactions of the normal child due to position and movement.] *Riv. clin. pediat., 34,* 510. (Abstract 2694, *Psychol. Abstr.,* 1938.)

Michaels, J. J. 1944. A psychiatric adventure in comparative patho-physiology of the infant and adult: With some theoretical suggestions in regard to regression in somatic visceral functions. *J. Nerv. Ment. Dis., 100,* 49–63.

Minkowski, M. 1922. Über frühzeitige Bewegungen. Reflexe und muskuläre Reaktionen beim menschlichen Fötus, und ihre Beziehungen zum fötalen Nervenund Muskelsystem. *Schweiz. med. Wschr., 52,* 721–724; 751–755.

——. 1923. Zur Entwicklungsgeschichte, Localisation und Klinik des Fussohlenreflexes. *Schweiz. Arch. Neurol. Psychiat., 13,* 475–514. (Summarized in Minkowski, 1926.)

——. 1926. Sur les modalités et la localisation du réflexe plantaire au cours de son évolution du foetus à l'adulte. *C. R. Congr. médecins, aliénistes et neurologistes, Geneva, 30,* 301–308.

——. 1928. Neurobiologische Studien am menschlichen Foetus. *Handb. Biol. ArbMeth.,* Pt. V, *5B,* No. 5, 511–618.

——. 1932–1933. Sur le développement, la localisation et la clinique des réflexes. *Bull. soc. roy. méd. Égypte, 10,* 1–20.

——. 1947. Zum Problem der ersten Anfänge einer seelischen Entwicklung beim Fötus. *Z. Kinderpsychiat., 14,* 87–94.

Moore, K. C. 1901. Comparative observations on the development of movements. *Ped. Sem., 8,* 231–238.

Moore, R. 1936. The histology of the newborn and prepuberal prostate gland. *Anat. Rec., 66,* 1–9.

Morgan, S. S., and J. J. B. Morgan. 1944. An examination of the development of certain behavior patterns in infants. *J. Pediat., 25,* 168–177.

Moro, E. 1918. Das erste Trimenon. *Münch. med. Wschr., 65,* 1147–1150.

Mumford, A. A. 1897. Survival movements of human infancy. *Brain, 20,* 290–307.

Munn, N. L. 1938. *Psychological development: An introduction to genetic psychology.* Boston: Houghton Mifflin.

Murchison, C., and S. Langer. 1927. Tiedemann's observations on the development of the mental faculties of children. *J. Genet. Psychol., 34,* 205–230. (See Tiedemann, 1787.)

Murlin, J. R., R. E. Conklin, and M. E. Marsh. 1925. Energy metabolism of normal newborn babies: With special reference to the influence of food and of crying. *Amer. J. Dis. Child., 29,* 1–28. (Reviewed in Richards, 1935.)

Murphy, D., and E. Thorpe, Jr. 1931. Breathing measurements on normal newborn infants. *J. Clin. Invest., 10,* 545–558.

Muzio, O. 1933. Sulla audizione dei neonati. *Ann. laring. ecc., 33,* 105–110. (Abstracted in *Zbl. ges. Kinderheilk., 1934, 29,* 134.)

Nassau, E. 1938. Die Kitzelreaktion beim Säugling. *Jb. Kinderheilk., 151,* 46–49.

Norman, H. N 1942. Fetal hiccups. *J. Comp. Psychol.*, *34*, 65–73.

Norval, M. A. 1946. Sucking response of newly born babies at breast. *Amer. J. Dis. Child.*, *71*, 41–44.

——. 1947. Relationship of weight and length of infants at birth to the age at which they begin to walk alone. *J. Pediat.*, *30*, 676–678.

Nothmann, H. 1909. Zur Frage der "psychischen" Magensaftsekretion beim Säugling. *Arch. Kinderheilk.*, *51*, 123–138.

Orlansky, H. 1949. Infant care and personality. *Psychol. Bull.*, *46*, 1–48.

Pacella, B. L., and S. E. Barrera. 1940. Postural reflexes and grasp phenomena in infants. *J. Neurophysiol.*, *3*, 213–218.

Paffrath, H., and W. Ohm. 1933. Zur Frage der Kreatinurie des Frühgeborenen. *Z. Kinderheilk.*, *54*, 377–379.

Pavlov, I. 1928. *Lectures on conditioned reflexes.* (Trans. by W. H. Gantt.) New York: International Publishers.

Peiper, A. 1924a. Untersuchungen über den galvanischen Hautreflex im Kindesalter. *Jb. Kinderheilk.*, *107*, 139–150.

——. 1924b. Beiträge zur Sinnesphysiologie der Frühgeburt. *Jb. Kinderheilk.*, *104*, 195–200.

——. 1924c. Sinnesempfindungen des Kindes vor seiner Geburt. *Mschr., Kinderheilk.*, *29*, 236–241.

——. 1925a. Die Hirntätigkeit des Neugeborenen. *Jb. Kinderheilk.*, *111*, 290–314.

——. 1925b. Untersuchungen über die Reaktionzeit im Säuglingsalter: I. Reaktionzeit auf Schallreiz. *Mschr. Kinderheilk.*, *31*, 491–506.

——. 1926a. Untersuchungen über die Reaktionzeit im Säuglingsalter: II. Reaktionzeit auf Schmerzreiz. *Mschr. Kinderheilk.*, *32*, 136–143.

——. 1926b. Ueber die Helligkeits und Farbenempfindungen der Frühgeburten. *Arch. Kinderheilk.*, *80*, 1–20.

——. 1926c. Über einen Augenreflex auf den Hals im frühem Säuglingsalter. *Jb. Kinderheilk.*, *113*, 87–89.

——. 1926d. Ueber das Pupillenspiel des Säuglings. *Jb. Kinderheilk.*, *112*, 179–183.

——. 1928. *Die Hirntätigkeit des Säuglings.* Berlin: Springer.

——. 1929. Die Schreitbewegungen der Neugeborenen. *Mschr. Kinderheilk.*, *45*, 444–448.

——. 1930. Sinnesreaktionen des Neugeborenen. *Z. Psychol.*, *114*, 363–370.

——. 1931. Die Nahrungsaufnahme des Säuglings. *Mschr. Kinderheilk.*, *50*, 20–28.

——. 1933a. Die Atmung des Neugeborenen. *Jahreskurse ärztl. Fortbild.*, *24*, 21–25.

——. 1933b. Die Atembewegungen des Unterkiefers. (Ein weiterer Beitrag zum Zerfall des Atemzentrums.) *Jb. Kinderheilk.*, *139*, 117–123.

——. 1935a. Die Entwicklung des Mienenspiels. *Mschr. Kinderheilk.*, *63*, 39–91.

——. 1935b. Röntgenkymographie des Saugvorganges. *Klin. Wschr.*, *14*, 1723–1725.

——. 1936a. Hautschutzreflexe. *Jb. Kinderheilk.*, *146*, 233–239.

Peiper, A. 1936b. Der Saugvorgang. *Ergeb. inn. Med. Kinderheilk.*, *50*, 527–567.

——. 1937a. Die Erscheinung der Dominanz und die Erregungsstufen des Saugzentrums. *Jb. Kinderheilk.*, *149*, 201–206.

——. 1937b. Comments upon J. M. Smith's work, "The relative brightness values of three hues for newborn infants." *Child Develpm.*, *8*, 299–300.

——. 1938. Die Erscheinung der Dominanz bei Reizlöschung. *Jb. Kinderheilk.*, *151*, 1–2.

——. 1939a. Die Saugstörung. *Mschr. Kinderheilk.*, *79*, 241–255.

——. 1939b. Die Führung des Saugzentrums durch das Schluckzentrum. *Pflüg. Arch. ges. Physiol.*, *242*, 751–755.

——. 1941. Die neurologischen Grundlagen der psychischen Entwicklung. *Mschr. Kinderheilk.*, *87*, 179–203.

——. 1942–1943. Die Umwelt des Säuglings. *Arch. ges. Psychol.*, *111*, 1–22.

——. 1949. *Die Eigenart der kindlichen Hirntätigkeit.* Leipzig: Thieme. Pp. xii + 512.

——. 1951. Die Schnappatmung in Filmausschnitten. *Kinderärztliche Praxis*, *19*, 272–279.

Peiper, A., and C. F. Good. 1934. Die Herztätigkeit während des Zerfalles des Atemzentrums. *Jb. Kinderheilk.*, *143*, 1–10.

Peiper, A., and H. Isbert. 1927. Über die Körperstellung des Säuglings. *Jb. Kinderheilk.*, *115*, 142–176.

Pendleton, W. R. 1927. Hiccups among infants. *Amer. J. Dis. Child.*, *34*, 207–210.

Pepys, S. 1667. *Diary.*

Peterson, F., and L. H. Rainey. 1910. The beginnings of mind in the newborn. *Bull. Lying-In Hosp. City of N. Y.*, *7*, 99–122.

Pfaundler, M. 1909. Chapter in P. Sommerfeld (Ed.), *Handbuch der Milchkunde.* Weisbaden: Bergmann. (Abstracted in Eckstein, 1927.)

Pinneau, S. R. 1950. A critique on the articles by Margaret Ribble. *Child Develpm.*, *21*, 203–228.

Poli, C. 1893. L'udito nei neonati. *Arch. ital. otol.*, *1*, 358–364. (Abstracted in *Arch. Ohrenheilk.*, 1896, *41*, 82.)

Popper, E. 1921. Studien ueber Saugphänomene. *Arch. Psychiat. Nervenkr.*, *63*, 231–246.

Pratt, K. C. 1930. Note on the relation of temperature and humidity to the activity of young infants. *J. Genet. Psychol.*, *38*, 480–484.

——. 1932. A note upon the relation of activity to sex and race in young infants. *J. Soc. Psychol.*, *3*, 118–120.

——. 1933. The neonate. In C. Murchison (Ed.), *A handbook of child psychology* (2d ed., rev.), pp. 163–208. Worcester: Clark University Press.

——. 1934a. Specificity and generalization of behavior in new-born infants: A critique. *Psychol. Rev.*, *41*, 265–284.

——. 1934b. The effects of repeated auditory stimulation upon the general activity of newborn infants. *J. Genet. Psychol.*, *44*, 96–116.

Pratt, K. C. 1934c. The effects of repeated visual stimulation upon the activity of newborn infants. *J. Genet. Psychol.*, *44*, 117–126.

——. 1934d. Generalization and specificity of the plantar responses in newborn infants. The reflexogenous zone: I. Differential sensitivity and effector-segment participation according to the area of stimulation. *J. Genet. Psychol.*, *44*, 265–300.

——. 1934e. Generalization and specificity of the plantar responses in newborn infants. The reflexogenous zone: II. Segmental patterning of response. *J. Genet. Psychol.*, *45*, 22–38.

——. 1934f. Generalization and specificity of the plantar responses in newborn infants. The reflexogenous zone: III. The effects of the physiological state upon sensitivity, segmental participation, and segmental patterning. *J. Genet. Psychol.*, *45*, 371–389.

——. 1936a. Problems in the classification of neonate activities. *Quart. Rev. Biol.*, *11*, 70–80.

——. 1936b. Review of McGraw's *Growth: A study of Johnny and Jimmy*. *J. Educ. Res.*, November.

——. 1937. The organization of behavior in the newborn infant. *Psychol. Rev.*, *44*, 470–490.

Pratt, K. C., A. K. Nelson, and K. H. Sun. 1930. The behavior of the newborn infant. *Ohio State Univ. Stud., Contr. Psychol.*, No. 10.

Preyer, W. 1882, 1888, 1889. *Die Seele des Kindes.* Leipzig: Fernau. (5th ed., 1900.) *The mind of the child:* Pt. 1. *The senses and the will;* Pt. 2. *The development of the intellect.* (Trans. by H. W. Brown.) New York: Appleton. (Reprinted ed., 1901.)

Rank, O. 1929. *The trauma of birth.* New York: Harcourt Brace. Pp. xv + 224.

Ray, W. S. 1932. A preliminary report on a study of fetal conditioning. *Child Develpm.*, *3*, 175–177.

Razran, G. H. S. 1933. Conditioned responses in children. A behavioral and quantitative critical review of experimental studies. *Arch. Psychol., N. Y.*, *23*, No. 148.

Redfield, J. E. 1937. A preliminary report of dark adaptation in young infants. *Child Develpm.*, *8*, 263–269.

——. 1939. The light sense in newborn infants. *Univ. Iowa Stud. Child Welfare*, *16*, 107–145.

Renshaw, S., and A. P. Weiss. 1926. Apparatus for measuring changes in bodily posture. *Amer. J. Psychol.*, *37*, 261–267.

Reynard, M. C., and F. C. Dockeray. 1939. The comparison of temporal intervals in judging depth of sleep in newborn infants. *J. Genet. Psychol.*, *55*, 103–120.

Ribble, M. A. 1944. Infantile experience in relation to personality development. In J. McV. Hunt (Ed.), *Personality and the behavior disorders*, pp. 621–651. New York: Ronald.

Richards, T. W. 1935. Gross metabolic changes characteristic of the activity of the neonate. *Child Develpm.*, *6*, 231–241.

——. 1936a. The relationship between bodily and gastric activity of newborn infants: I. Correlation and influence of time since feeding. *Human Biol.*, *8*, 368–380.

Richards, T. W. 1936b. The relationship between bodily and gastric activity of newborn infants: II. Simultaneous variations in the bodily and gastric activity of newborn infants under long-continued light stimulation. *Human Biol.*, *8*, 381–386.

——. 1936c. The importance of hunger in the bodily activity of the neonate. *Psychol. Bull.*, *33*, 817–835.

Richards, T. W., and O. C. Irwin. 1934a. Experimental methods used in studies on infant reactions since 1900. *Psychol. Bull.*, *31*, 23–46.

——. 1934b. Die Veränderung der Fuszsohlenreaktion bei Neugeborenen unter der Einwirken von Reizung und anderen Einflüssen. *Z. Kinderheilk.*, *57*, 16–20.

——. 1934c. Plantar responses of infants and young children: An examination of the literature and reports of new experiments. *Univ. Iowa Stud. Child Welfare*, *11*. Pp. 146.

——. 1936. The use of the clinical method in experimental studies of behavior. *J. Abnorm. Soc. Psychol.*, *30*, 455–461.

Richter, C. P. 1930. High electrical skin resistance of newborn infants and its significance. *Amer. J. Dis. Child.*, *40*, 18–26.

——. 1934. The grasp reflex of the newborn infant. *Amer. J. Dis. Child.*, *48*, 327–332.

Ripin, R., and H. Hetzer. 1930. Früheste Lernen des Säuglings in der Ernährungssitution. *Z. Psychol.*, *118*, 83–127.

Robinson, L. 1891. Darwinism in the nursery. *Nineteenth Cent.*, *30*, 831–842. (Cited by Halverson, 1937.)

Rominger, E., and H. Meyer. 1932. Klinischexperimentelle Untersuchungen zur Kreislaufphysiologie im Kindesalter. *Mschr. Kinderheilk.*, *52*, 421–423.

Rothe, H. 1929. Untersuchungen über die elektrische Erregbarkeit bei frühgeborenen Kindern. *Jb. Kinderheilk.*, *125*, 285–299.

Rowan-Legg, C. K. 1949. Self-demand feeding of infants. *Canad. Med. Ass. J.*, *60*, 389–391.

Ruja, H. 1948. The relation between neonate crying and length of labor. *J. Genet. Psychol.*, *73*, 53–55.

Runge, M. 1895. Der erste Schrei und der erste Athemzug. *Berlin. klin. Wschr.*, *32*, 93–95.

Sachs, R. 1893. Beobachtungen über das physiologische Verhalten des Gehororgans Neugeborener. *Arch. Ohrenheilk.*, *35*, 28–38.

Sadger, J. 1941. Preliminary study of the psychic life of the fetus and the primary germ. *Psychoanal. Rev.*, *28*, 327–358.

Sanford, H. N. 1931. The Moro reflex as a diagnostic aid in fracture of the clavicle in the newborn infant. *Amer. J. Dis. Child.*, *41*, 1304–1306.

Schachter, M. 1932a. Les cris des nourrisons et des petits enfants. *Bull. méd.*, *46*, 637–642.

——. 1932b. Le comportement neuropsychique du nourrisson. *Rev. méd. de l'Est*, *60*, 808–819.

Schaltenbrand, G. 1925. Normale Bewegungs- und Lage-reaktionen bei Kindern. *Dtsch. Z. Nervenheilk.*, *87*, 23–59.

Schaltenbrand, G. 1928. The development of human motility and motor disturbance. *Arch. Neurol. Psychiat., Chicago, 20,* 720–730.

Schlossman, A., and H. Murschhauser. 1933. Gasstoffwechseluntersuchungen bei Neugeborenen und Frühgeborenen. *Z. Kinderheilk., 54,* 301–316.

Schmidt, A. 1927. Über die Beziehungen des Saugreflexes zur Magentätigkeit. *Z. Kinderheilk., 45,* 19–27.

Schmidt, L. 1950. Der "erste" Atemzug. *Mschr. Kinderheilk., 98,* 213–217.

Schmitt, A., and D. v. Móritz. 1933. Magenfunktionsprüfungen bei Frühgeborenen. *Arch. Kinderheilk., 99,* 23–27.

Sears, R. R. 1948. Effects of cup, bottle, and breast feeding on oral drive of newborn infants. *Amer. Psychol., 3,* 264.

Shepardson, E. 1907. A preliminary critique of the doctrine of fundamental and accessory movements. *Ped. Sem., 14,* 101–116.

Sherman, M. 1927a. The differentiation of emotional responses in infants: I. Judgments of emotional response from motion-picture views and from actual observation. *J. Comp. Psychol., 7,* 265–284.

———. 1927b. The differentiation of emotional responses in infants: II. The ability of observers to judge the emotional characteristics of the crying of infants, and of the voice of the adult. *J. Comp. Psychol., 7,* 335–351.

Sherman, M., and I. C. Sherman. 1925. Sensorimotor responses in infants. *J. Comp. Psychol., 5,* 53–68.

Sherman, M., I. C. Sherman, and C. D. Flory. 1936. Infant behavior. *Comp. Psychol. Monogr., 12,* No. 4.

Shinn, M. W. 1893–1899. Notes on the development of a child. *Univ. Calif. Publ., 1.* Pp. 424.

Shirley, M. M. 1931a. The sequential method for the study of maturing behavior patterns. *Psychol. Rev., 38,* 507–528.

———. 1931b. *The first two years, a study of twenty-five babies:* Vol. I. *Postural and locomotor development.* (*Inst. Child Welfare Monogr. Ser.,* No. 6.) Minneapolis: University of Minnesota Press. Pp. vi + 227.

———. 1933a. *The first two years, a study of twenty-five babies:* Vol. II. *Intellectual development.* (*Inst. Child Welfare Monogr. Ser.,* No. 7.) Minneapolis: University of Minnesota Press. Pp. xvi + 513.

———. 1933b. *The first two years, a study of twenty-five babies:* Vol. III. *Personality manifestations.* (*Inst. Child Welfare Monogr. Ser.,* No. 8.) Minneapolis: University of Minnesota Press. Pp. xi + 228.

Shotwell, A. M., and A. R. Gilliland. 1943. A preliminary scale for the measurement of the mentality of infants. *Child Develpm., 14,* 167–177.

Sicherer, O. v. 1907. Ophthalmoskopische Untersuchung Neugeborener. *Dtsch. med. Wschr., 33,* 1564.

Sikorski, I. A. 1908. *Die seelische Entwicklung des Kindes.* (2d ed.) Leipzig. (As reported by Peiper, 1928.)

Simsarian, F. P., and P. A. McLendon. 1942. Feeding behavior of an infant during the first twelve weeks of life on a self-demand schedule. *J. Pediat., 20,* 93–103.

Simsarian, F. P., and P. A. McLendon. 1945. Further records of the self-demand schedule in infant feeding. *J. Pediat., 27,* 109–114.

Smith, J. M. 1936. The relative brightness values of three hues for newborn infants. *Univ. Iowa Stud. Child Welfare, 12,* No. 1, 91–140.

———. 1937. Reply to Peiper. *Child Develpm., 8,* 301–304.

Smith, J. R. 1938a. The electroencephalogram during normal infancy and childhood: I. Rhythmic activities present in the neonate and their subsequent development. *J. Genet. Psychol., 53,* 431–453.

———. 1938b. The electroencephalogram during normal infancy and childhood: III. Preliminary observations on the pattern sequences during sleep. *J. Genet. Psychol., 53,* 471–482.

———. 1939. The "occipital" and "pre-central" alpha rhythms during the first two years. *J. Psychol., 7,* 223–226.

Soltmann, O. 1876. Experimentelle Studien über die Funktionen des Grosshirns der Neugeborenen. *Jb. Kinderheilk., 9,* 106.

———. 1878. Ueber einige physiologische Eigentümlichkeiten der Muskeln und Nerven des Neugeborenen. *Jb. Kinderheilk., 12,* 1–20. (Abstracted by Peiper, 1928, and Eckstein, 1927.)

Sonohara, T. 1934a. Ueber den Einfluss der Saccharinreizungen auf die Leersaugbewegungen bei den Neugeborenen. Eine systematische psychologische Untersuchung von Neugeborenen. 1, 2. *Jap. J. Exp. Psychol., 1,* 1–18. (Abstract 1503, *Psychol. Abstr.,* 1935.)

———. 1934b. (Systematic studies on psychology of human neonates. [1, 3] Reactions to bitter stimuli.) *Jap. J. Exp. Psychol., 1,* 127–141. (Abstract 3798, *Psychol. Abstr.,* 1936.)

Sontag, L. W., and R. F. Wallace. 1934. Preliminary report of the Fels fund. *Amer. J. Dis. Child., 48,* 1050–1057.

———. 1935a. The effect of cigaret smoking during pregnancy upon the fetal heart rate. *Amer. J. Obstet. Gynec., 29,* 77–82.

———. 1935b. The movement response of the human fetus to sound stimuli. *Child Develpm., 6,* 253–258.

———. 1936. Changes in the rate of the human fetal heart in response to vibratory stimuli. *Amer. J. Dis. Child., 51,* 583–589.

Spelt, D. K. 1938. Conditioned responses in the human fetus in utero. *Psychol. Bull., 35,* 712–713.

———. 1948. The conditioning of the human fetus "in utero." *J. Exp. Psychol., 38,* 338–346.

Spitz, R. A., and K. M. Wolf. 1946. The smiling response; a contribution to the ontogenesis of social relations. *Genet. Psychol. Monogr., 34,* 57–125.

Stern, W. 1914. *Psychologie der frühen Kindheit, bis zum sechsten Lebensjahre.* Leipzig: Quelle & Meyer. (4th ed., 1927.)

Stirnimann, F. 1933. *Das erste Erleben des Kindes.* Leipzig: Huber.

———. 1936a. Der Saugwulst der Neugeborenen. *Kinderärztl. Prax., 7,* 210–212.

Stirnimann, F. 1936b. Versuche über Geschmack und Geruch am ersten Lebenstag. *Jb. Kinderheilk., 146,* 211–227.

——. 1936c. Le goût et l'odorat du nouveau-né. Une contribution à la connaissance des réactions du nouveau-né. *Rev. franc. pédiat., 12,* 453–485.

——. 1937a. Die Einstellreaktion beim Neugeborenen. *Jb. Kinderheilk., 149,* 326–329.

——. 1937b. Les réactions du nouveau-né contre l'enchaînement. *Rev. franc. pédiat., 13,* 496–502.

——. 1938. Das Kriech- und Schreitphänomen der Neugeborenen. *Schweiz. med. Wschr., 19,* 1374–1376.

——. 1939. Versuche über die Reaktionen Neugeborener auf Wärme- und Kältereize. *Z. Kinderpsychiat., 5,* 143–150.

——. 1940. *Psychologie des neugeborenen Kindes.* Zürich: Rascher.

——. 1941. Greifversuche mit der Hand Neugeborener. *Ann. Paediat., 157,* 17–27.

——. 1943. Ueber den Moroschen Umklammerungsreflex beim Neugeborenen. *Ann. Paediat., 160,* 1–10.

——. 1944a. Ueber das Farbempfinden Neugeborener. *Ann. Paediat., 163,* 1–25.

——. 1944b. Abwehrbewegungen der Neugeborenen im primitiven Greifraum. *Schweiz. Z. Psychol. u. i. Anwend., 3,* 245–254.

Stirnimann, F., and W. Stirnimann. 1940. Der Fussgreifreflex bei Neugeborenen und Säuglingen. Seine diagnostische Verwendbarkeit. *Ann. Paediat., 154,* 249–264.

Stoffels, M. J. 1940–1941. La réaction dite de colère chez les nouveau-nés. *J. psychol. norm. path., 37–38,* 92–148.

Strauss, H. 1929. Das Zusammenschrecken. *J. Psychol. Neurol., Lpz., 39,* 111–231. (Cited by Landis and Hunt, 1939.)

Stubbs, E. M. 1934. The effect of the factors of duration, intensity, and pitch of sound stimuli on the responses of newborn infants. *Univ. Iowa Stud. Child Welfare, 9,* No. 4, pp. 75–135.

Stubbs, E. M., and O. C. Irwin. 1933. Laterality of limb movements of four newborn infants. *Child Develpm., 4,* 358–359.

——. 1934. A note on reaction times in infants. *Child Develpm., 5,* 291–292.

Talbot, F. B. 1917a. Physiology of the newborn infant. *Amer. J. Dis. Child., 13,* 495–500.

——. 1917b. Twenty-four hour metabolism of two normal infants with special reference to the total energy requirements of infants. *Amer. J. Dis. Child., 14,* 25–33.

Tanner, A. E. 1915. The new-born child. *Ped. Sem., 22,* 487–501.

Taylor, J. H. 1934. Innate emotional responses in infants. *Ohio State Univ. Stud., Contrib. Psychol.,* No. 12, pp. 69–81.

Taylor, R. 1917. Hunger in the infant. *Amer. J. Dis. Child., 14,* 233–257.

Thompson, J. 1903. On the lip reflex (mouth phenomenon) of new-born children. *Rev. Neurol. Psychiat., 1,* 145–148.

Thurstone, L. L. 1928. The absolute zero in intelligence measurement. *Psychol. Rev., 35,* 175–197.

Tiedemann, D. 1787. *Beobachtungen über die Entwicklung der Seelenfähigkeiten bei Kindern.* (First published in 1787. Altenburg Bonde, 1897. (See Murchison and Langer, 1927.)

Tilney, F., and L. Casamajor. 1924. Myelinogeny as applied to the study of behavior. *Arch. Neurol. Psychiat. Chicago, 12,* 1–66.

Trainham, G., and J. C. Montgomery. 1946. Self-demand feeding for babies. *Amer. J. Nurs., 46,* 767–770.

Trainham, G., G. J. Pilafian, and R. M. Kraft. 1945. A case history of twins breast fed on a self-demand regime. *J. Pediat., 27,* 97–108.

Valentine, C. W. 1930. The innate bases of fear. *J. Genet. Psychol., 37,* 394–420.

Valentine, W. L., and F. C. Dockeray. 1936. The experimental study of the newborn, 1926–36. *Educ. Res. Bull., Ohio State Univ., 15,* 127–133.

Valentine, W. L., and I. Wagner. 1934. Relative arm motility in the newborn infant. *Ohio State Univ. Stud.,* No. 12, 53–68.

Veĭnger, R. A. 1950. K vozniknoveniiu kozhnogal'vanicheskogo refleksa pri zritel'nykh i zvukovykh razdrazheniiakh u deteĭ v postnatal'nom ontogeneze. (On the arisal of the skin-galvanic reflex with visual and auditory stimulations in children in postnatal ontogenesis.) *Fiziol. Zh. SSSR, 36,* 653–659. [Abstr. 5461 *Psychol. Abstrs.,* 1952, *26,* 561.]

Vinay, C. 1897. La psychologie du nouveau-né. *Semaine méd., 17,* 33–36.

Vincent, C. E. 1951. Trends in infant care ideas. *Child Develpm., 22,* 199–209.

Vormittag, S. 1933. Untersuchungen über die Atmung des Kindes: I. Atemzahl und Atemform des gesunden Kindes. *Mschr. Kinderheilk., 58,* 249–265.

Vosz, O. 1923. Geburtstrauma und Gehörorgan. *Z. Hals- Nasen- u. Ohrenheilk., 6,* 182–219.

Wagner, I. F. 1937. The establishment of a criterion of depth of sleep in the newborn infant. *J. Genet. Psychol., 51,* 17–59.

——. 1938a. The body jerk of the neonate. *J. Genet. Psychol., 52,* 65–77.

——. 1938b. A note on the hiccough of the neonate. *J. Genet. Psychol., 52,* 233–234.

——. 1938c. The sleeping posture of the neonate. *J. Genet. Psychol., 52,* 235–239.

——. 1939. Curves of sleep depth in newborn infants. *J. Genet. Psychol., 55,* 121–135.

Wagoner, L. C. 1924. A note on the grasping reflex. *Ped. Sem., 31,* 333–336.

Waltan, O. 1921. L'audizione nei neonati. *Il policlinico (sezione pratica), 28,* 1010–1011.

Watson, J. B. 1919. *Psychology from the standpoint of a behaviorist.* Philadelphia: Lippincott.

Weinfeld, G. F. 1950. Self-demand feeding. *Med. Clin. of North America* (Chicago No.), 33–40.

Weiss, A. P. 1929. The measurement of infant behavior. *Psychol. Rev., 36,* 453–471.

Weiss, L. A. 1934. Differential variations in the amount of activity of newborn infants under continuous light and sound stimulation. *Univ. Iowa Stud. Child Welfare, 9,* 1–74.

Wenger, M. A. 1936. An investigation of conditioned responses in human infants. *Univ. Iowa Stud. Child Welfare, 12,* 1–90.

Wenger, M. A., and O. C. Irwin. 1935. Variations in electrical resistance of the skin in newborn infants. *Proc. Iowa Acad. Sci., 42,* 167–168.

——. 1936. Fluctuations in skin resistance of infants and adults and their relation to muscular processes. *Univ. Iowa Stud. Child Welfare, 12,* 141–179.

Westphal, A. 1894. Die elektrischen Erregbarkeitsverhältnisse des peripherischen Nervensystems des Menschen im jugendlichen Zustand und ihre Beziehungen zu dem anatomischen Bau. *Arch. Psychiat. Nervenkr., 26,* 1–98. (Abstracted by Peiper, 1928, and Eckstein, 1927.)

Westphal, C. 1886. Die elektrische Erregbarkeit der Nerven und Muskeln Neugeborener. *Neurol. Zentbl., 5,* 361–363. (Abstracted by Peiper, 1928.)

Wickens, D. D., and C. Wickens. 1940. A study of conditioning in the neonate. *J. Exp. Psychol., 26,* 94–102.

Wolff, L. V. 1930. The response to plantar stimulation in infancy. *Amer. J. Dis. Child., 39,* 1176–1185.

Wolfle, H. M. 1949. The importance of the caress in modern child psychology. *Amer. Psychol., 4,* 249.

Wolowik, A. B. 1927. Ueber die gegenseltige Wirkung der Schmerz und Nahrungsreflexe bei Kindern. *Jb. Kinderheilk., 115,* 185–193.

Zaharescu-Karaman, N., and A. Nastase. 1931. La crise génitale des nouveau-nés provoquée par l'hormone sexuelle ovarienne. *C. R. Soc. Biol., Paris, 107,* 396.

CHAPTER 5

PHYSICAL GROWTH

HELEN THOMPSON

There are important reasons why child psychology should be concerned with the course and characteristics of the child's physical growth. Anderson (1942) has said, "As soon as one works with children he becomes aware that behavior of the moment is an end product determined by many factors, some of which are clearly related to the physical make-up and physiological state of the child. . . . The child development worker . . . quickly becomes concerned with the problems of physical growth, body form, physiological adjustment, appetite, etc., all of which affect the adjustment of the child" (p. 129). Just as child behavior cannot be understood apart from the cultural forces impinging on it, so it cannot be understood apart from the internal stimuli in effect and the physical body through which it perceives, reacts, and functions, and to which others react. It is the child's physical maturity that governs, limits, and to a large extent determines his physical and social environment. A toddler whose eyes are at the level of an adult's knees sees a far different world from that envisioned by an adult; a child whose center of gravity is relatively low will have less difficulty in balance than one whose center of gravity is high. The mechanics of picking up an inch cube presents a different problem to the tiny hand of the 1-year-old from the one presented to the hand of the 5-year-old. Children may suffer emotionally from being a "Shrimp," "Tubby," "Redhead," or "Bucktooth."

The taunt, "Brown eye turn around and tell a lie," can leave permanent personality scars. The adolescent who matures earlier or later than his friends has special social problems (Schonfield, 1950; Jones and Bayley, 1950). So, just as the physician must know how the child's personality and mind grow, the psychologist must know how the child grows physically.

In the conduct of experimental studies in child psychology the problem of equating groups for the purposes of control is a highly important part of the experiment. Should one use chronological age, or anatomical age, or physiological age, or some composite of these? How can such ages be measured? What is the relationship between them? Is it necessary to equate for physical fitness? How can it be judged? And what is the consensus as to body type? All these questions are pertinent in research studies of childhood.

The relationships between physical and mental growth are becoming more apparent as children are studied in greater awareness of the possibilities of interaction between mind and body. For instance, while science has not regressed to the notion of the fetus being marked by maternal impressions, it has progressed to an understanding of how maternal anxieties and fears may so affect fetal life and development as to leave a permanent imprint on the physiological and psychological functions of the child (Sontag, 1946). The effect of deprivation of personal attention and affection on phys-

292

ical development has long been recognized (Bakwin, 1942). Likewise, the undersized, undernourished child who whines and frets may set into action a chainlike series of social percussions and personality repercussions which may be of sufficient social handicap to destroy temporarily, if not permanently, the effectiveness or even the actual development of potential mentality. It may even be a fair prophecy that, in the investigations of individual physical and mental life histories, studies of social behavior and personality may find their fullest realization in the genetic analysis of physical individuality.

Furthermore, the student of mental growth may learn much from a study of physical growth with respect to methods and techniques of study. It is comforting as well as instructive to know that behavior changes from age to age complicate even such an objective determination as height or length. The 6-month-old infant cannot stand, whereas the 2-year-old child resists being placed supine and the 3-year-old assumes distorted and fairly rigid postures in his effort to cooperate. To the student of physical growth these behavior changes are as important to cope with as the changes in physical growth are important to the student of child psychology. Techniques in the one field are suggestive of possible techniques in the other field of study. To secure comparable measures of size, it is frequently necessary to take two measurements at critical ages using the two methods adapted to the younger and older child. Allowance for the change in method can then be made. A similar scheme may be employed to advantage in studies of behavior growth.

Growth is one of the most pervasive problems of child psychology. An understanding of psychological growth can be fostered by studying the laws of growth as revealed by physical growth. The law

of cephalocaudal development, noted first in physical growth, was later studied and confirmed in relation to behavior development.

Surely, then, the child psychologist, as an intelligent scholar, teacher, researcher, or clinician, must know the outstanding facts of physical growth; otherwise his understanding, interpretations, conclusions, and treatment of the child may be delayed, incomplete, biased, or totally false.

Definition

There is considerable confusion about what is meant by the term physical growth. Some authors would use it to denote change in size; others, change in quantity; others, change in quality; and others, any combination of these characteristics. After a careful survey of the literature, Meredith (1945) concluded that the three terms growth, development, and maturation which are used in contradictory ways by different workers serve no "useful and significant distinction" as their proponents had claimed. He proposed using the terms interchangeably, giving preference to growth as being the shortest of the three terms. He defines physical growth as, "The entire series of anatomic and physiologic changes taking place between the beginning of prenatal life and the close of senility" (p. 445). In this chapter the discussion will be limited to anatomic changes and thus will deal with a delimited aspect of physical growth.

The Literature

The literature on the subject of physical growth is vast and widely scattered owing to a variety of scientific, professional, and business interests in the subject. Not only the anatomist, physical anthropologist, biometrist, and psychologist but also the obstetrician, pediatrist, dentist, educator, public-health doctor, actuarian, criminologist, and eugenicist are led to research in this field. Fortunately, adequate summaries are available. For the period up to about 1925, the most useful and complete are those of Baldwin (1921), the Children's Bureau (1927), Scammon (1927a, 1927b), Martin (1928), and Meredith (1936a). Since 1926 the American literature on growth has been systematically reviewed by Brooks (1933), Dawson and Stoddard (1933), Jones (1933, 1936, 1939), Meredith and Stoddard (1936), Meredith (1939a, 1939b), Rothney (1941), Ames and Flory (1944), and Tuddenham and Snyder (1947). Krogman's extensive bibliography (1941b) includes foreign publications. *Child Development Abstracts*, begun in 1927, and *Biological Abstracts*, begun in 1926, cover the most important sources of publication.

In view of the scope of physical growth, a comprehensive summary of the literature cannot be given in the following pages. Instead, references will be selected on the basis of their importance to the child psychologist. No attempt at comprehensiveness will be made. The subject is too extensive.

Historical Summary

Although the first interest in mental development arose in relation to education, the first interest in bodily growth was the concern of the artist. The practical problem of realistically portraying the child led artists to study size and proportion in relation to age. In that early era, beauty values were considered in the absolute sense, and the artist searched for the perfect proportions of youth (Baldwin, 1921). Before 1799, measuring instruments in different centers of learning varied considerably in calibration, as a visit to any museum of physical science will demonstrate. The standard meter bar, constructed in 1799, gradually introduced uniformity. Its construction reflected a deep interest in measurement and served to stimulate further measurement. The human body was a natural subject. Quetelet (1871) was the first to systematize the study of physical growth. He is credited with originating the word *anthropometry*. His figures on body dimensions from birth to maturity are still quoted. Shortly before 1760 there were scientific studies of the weight and physical proportions of the newborn, but it was not until 1779 that the first seriatim study of physical growth was published (Buffon, 1837). This preceded Tiedemann's publication on mental development by only 8 years (Murchison and Langer, 1927).

It was practically 100 years later (Hall, 1896) that physical and mental growth were studied simultaneously, and even then the data were uncorrelated. In the last decade of the nineteenth century and the first decade of the twentieth century, however, there was general interest among psychologists in the relationship between mental and physical traits. Binet (1900, 1910) was concerned with head and face measurements. He attempted to find in them an index of mentality. His failure to establish a close relationship was followed by similar results from the laboratories in London. In this country Porter (1893), Gilbert (1895, 1897), and others were concerned with the relationship between mental and physical traits. Dull children tended to be smaller for their age; bright children tended to be larger. Crampton (1908), studying boys at adolescence, concluded that boys who matured early were better students. Goddard (1912), Binet and Simon (1914), and Doll (1916) were among those who studied the physical growth of the feeble-minded and found them physically inferior to the normal. Baldwin in 1921 stated:

Another experimental study just completed shows that the mental age of the individual bears a direct relationship to the physiological age as indicated by height and weight. The results show that at each chronological age the physiologically accelerated boys and girls have a higher mental age than those of the average or below the average physiological age [pp. 196–197.]

His results were typical of others.

It was generally conceded that physical defects were likely to be associated with mental defects and physical acceleration and well-being associated with accelerated mental growth. Nevertheless, the correlation of mental and physical traits was found to be small, and general interest in the relationship waned. Clinical psychologists routinely noted height and weight but made little use of the data. Researchers in child psychology, to a large extent, lost interest in physical correlates. Two notable exceptions to this generalization are of course the Harvard Growth Study by Dearborn and the Iowa Child Welfare Research Station studies initiated by Baldwin.

Interest in physical development was revived in the middle 1920's with the advent of the various research centers for child development. The whole child, physical, mental, and emotional, as well as his environment and nutrition, became the subject for investigation (Krogman, 1940).

At the same time emphasis was put on longitudinal rather than cross-sectional studies, on individual growth rates and patterns of maturing rather than average growth trends. Again, relationship between the physical and mental was sought but this time in the individual life histories. Data thus accumulated have already yielded many studies, but it will probably be many years yet before the fruits of these researches are fully realized. Rothney (1941), in a summary of research findings, asserts that physical irregularities do not tend to create any particular types of personality or adjustment problems but that suitable or unsuitable educational procedures will probably determine the type of of response which will be made. This, however, may be a premature conclusion. Sontag (1946) concludes, "The unconscious cruelty of children toward anyone of them whose body does not conform to theirs in size, form, and function may be an important factor in the emotional adjustment of children lacking this conformity," and "A child's energy level or constitutional vitality may be very important in determining his response to what he interprets as a hostile environment." Bayley (1951) finds that somatic adrogyny is only one of a multiplicity of factors which influence a person's interest.

Techniques of Measurement

Physical anthropometry is the science particularly concerned with the techniques and instruments for the study of physical growth. Measuring, weighing, and comparing with standard scales might seem to be routine, mechanical procedures which anyone with general scientific training might easily perform. The problem is not so simple as that, however, if the collected data are to have value. For instance, Meredith and Goodman (1941) have shown that routine hospital records of length at birth are seriously unreliable when compared with records made by trained anthropometrists. Not only is the personal error of the novice great, but even among trained workers there is marked individual variation. Lincoln (1930) concludes: "It is apparent that when exact anthropometric measurements on individuals are desired, they must be obtained by methods which include the most careful checking."

The human body is surprisingly elastic and plastic. Boyd (1929) notes:

In spite of common agreement in technique and practice, the human body cannot be measured with a high degree of precision; that height is more reliable than other dimensions; that the living is measured with less precision than the dead; that the degree of precision is different for different dimensions and for different measurements of the same dimension; and that daily physiological linear reduction affects both stature and body stem. . . . [She notes further that error results from] the inaccuracy of the examiner, his instruments and methods; the character of the endpoints of a given measurement; the amount of physiological linear reduction; and the degree to which the child's attitude affects the prescribed position [p. 396].

An appropriate selection of the following references should be consulted *before* initiating a study of physical growth.

Fetal period:
Schultz (1929); Scammon and Calkins (1929).
General techniques:
Baldwin (1921); Davenport (1927); Sullivan (1928); Martin (1928); Franzen (1929); McCloy (1936, 1938); Hrdlička (1939); Potter and Meredith (1948); Krogman (1948).
Infancy and early childhood:
Baldwin (1921); Thompson (1929); Bakwin and Bakwin (1931a); Davenport (1937, 1938); Gesell and Thompson (1938); Baum and Vickers (1941); Boyd (1945).
Skin and subcutaneous fat:
Franzen (1929); McCloy (1938); Reynolds (1950).
Bone, muscle, and overlying tissue by roentgenography:
Stuart, Hill, and Shaw (1940).
Radiographs to predict height:
Bayer and Bayley (1947).
Center of gravity:
Palmer (1944).
Somatotyping:
Sheldon, Stevens, and Tucker (1940); Dupertuis and Tanner (1951).

Whenever physical measurements are reported, it is important to specify clearly how the measures were taken and what precautions were observed to insure their validity and reliability.

Norms of Physical Growth

There is some confusion about the value and purpose of norms. Norms are not criteria for optimal growth. They are statistics for basic comparisons. They are mathematical devices to avoid the error of generalization from isolated cases. They are conclusions of scientific surveys, and as such they are indispensable scientific data which should be groundwork for the systematization and analysis of other data. Norms may be used as control-group data. By comparing experimental data, individual or group, with the norms, conclusions can be reached which will be valid to the extent that the norms and the experimental data have common attributes, except with respect to the variable in question.

Obviously, comparison with norms is valid only when similar techniques have been used in measurement. Theoretically this is so obvious that to mention it seems unnecessary. Practically, however, even psychologists trained in the importance of scientific control will use their own measurement techniques and then search through the literature for comparative norms, using the first figures they find which are measures of the dimension they have taken, forgetting entirely that techniques of measurement may make the comparisons completely invalid.

The more heterogeneous the composition of the group with respect to traits related to the normative trait, the greater will be the number of cases necessary to determine the norm, and the greater will be the variability of the trait as measured. The more highly selective the group on which norms are based, the more precise will be their scientific usefulness. It is generally important to consider race, sex, and locale. Socio-economic status is important but not always easy to define. Individuals obviously atypical should be excluded. Factors which are operating at particular ages must be considered. The inclusion of premature children in a normative study of infancy will shift all values downward.

It was noted above that norms are not criteria for optimal growth. It should be noted also that what is normal for one individual is not normal for another. It is valid to compare an individual with the normal in order to analyze his particular growth pattern, but interpretation of any divergence must recognize individual growth differences. Appraisal of individual growth is most helpful in terms of past growth. A dwarf whose increment in stature is normal for a given period is growing relatively very rapidly considering his growth tempo in the past.

Norms of growth may be in terms of the central tendency and variability of groups, at regularly spaced chronological or other maturity age intervals, or in terms of the statistics of individual growth increments at these ages. Instead of using chronological age as a basis, Boas (1930) and Shuttleworth (1937, 1939) particularly give reasons for evaluating growth according to age at the time of maximum growth. Although this procedure may be highly desirable in the analysis of growth data, it cannot be applied practically at the time of measurement. The same comment applies to appraising growth in terms of size at maturity. It is possible to evaluate growth in terms of some maturity age measurable at the time, such as skeletal age or dental age, but the probable error in measuring these ages is large compared with the probable error of birth age, even considering the

variability of conception age at birth. The use of norms, on any basis, must be tempered with the understanding and judgment required of all interpretive analysis.

It is not practical to give tables of growth norms in this handbook. A few selected norms would tend to emphasize their use when other growth data might be more pertinent. The following list of references will direct the researcher to the more outstanding source material.

NORMS: SELECTED REFERENCES

Body Growth

Fetal period:
Streeter (1920); Schultz (1926); Scammon and Calkins (1929).

Neonatal period:
Taylor (1919); Freeman and Platt (1932); Bakwin and Bakwin (1934a, 1934b); Hess, Mohr, and Bartelme (1934); Meredith and Brown (1939).

Infancy and early childhood:
Woodbury (1921); Freeman (1933); Bayley and Davis (1935); Bayley (1936); Bakwin and Bakwin (1936); Gesell and Thompson (1938); Peatman and Higgons (1938); Davenport (1938); Boyd (1941); Robinow (1942); Meredith (1943, 1946a).

Infancy and late childhood:
Freeman (1933); Simmons and Todd (1938); Vickers and Stuart (1943).

Infancy to maturity:
Bardeen (1920); Baldwin (1921); Baldwin, Wood, and Woodbury (1923); Englebach (1932); White House Conference (1933); Meredith (1935, 1943, 1947); Boynton (1936); McCloy (1938); Pryor (1941); Davenport (1944); Simmons (1944); Reynolds (1948).

Childhood:
Johnson (1925); Wilson, Sweeny, Stutsman, *et al.* (1930); Wallis (1931); Reynolds (1944).

School age to maturity:
Baldwin (1925); Franzen (1929); Gray and Ayres (1931); Palmer and Reed (1935);

Goldstein (1936); Palmer, Riiti, and Reed (1937); Dearborn, Rothney, and Shuttleworth (1938).

Adolescence:

Pryor (1936); Richey (1937); Shuttleworth (1937, 1938, 1939); Stone and Barker (1937); Greulich, Day, Lachman, *et al.* (1938); Greulich, Dorfman, Catchpole, *et al.* (1942); Shuttleworth (1949); Stolz and Stolz (1951).

Head and Face Growth

Wallis (1931); Bakwin and Bakwin (1931a, 1936); Fleming (1933); Bayley (1936); Boynton (1936); Goldstein (1936, 1939); Broadbent (1937); Klein, Palmer, and Kramer (1937); McCloy (1938); Davenport (1940); Boyd (1948).

Dentition

Boas (1927); Cattell (1928); Hellman (1933); Klein, Palmer, and Kramer (1937); Klein, Palmer, and Knutson (1938); Doering and Allen (1942); Robinow, Richards, and Anderson (1942); Hellman (1943); Sandler (1944); Meredith (1946b); Hurme (1948).

Skeletal Development

Graves (1921); Stevenson (1924); Pryor (1925); Baldwin, Busby, and Garside (1928); Sawtell (1929); Camp and Cilley (1931); Hodges (1933); Flory (1936); Kelly (1937); Todd (1937); Shuttleworth (1938); Francis and Werle (1939); Hill (1939); Sontag, Snell, and Anderson (1939); Christie *et al.* (1941); Maresh (1943); Noback (1943); Greulich and Thoms (1944); Reynolds (1945, 1947); Elgenmark (1946); Schmidt (1948); Christie (1949); House (1950).

Subcutaneous Fat

Reynolds (1950).

Head Hair

Trotter and Duggins (1948); Duggins and Trotter (1950); Trotter and Duggins (1950).

Miscellaneous

Surface area:

Boyd (1935); since measurement of surface area is so difficult, formulae have been developed for its estimation—Weinbach (1938).

Vital capacity:

Baldwin (1928); McCloy (1938).

Racial differences:

Weissenberg (1911); Shirokogoroff (1925); Appleton (1927); Godin (1935); Martin (1928); Wissler (1930); Fleming (1933); Steggerda and Densen (1936); Meredith (1939a); Krogman (1941a); Su and Liang (1940); Michelson (1943a, 1943b, 1943c); Goldstein (1947).

Weight (nutrition):

Baldwin, Wood, and Woodbury (1923); Pryor and Stolz (1933); Franzen and Palmer (1934); Royster (1936); Richey (1937); Daniels, Hutton, and Neil (1938); Dearborn and Rothney (1938); McCloy (1938); Peatman and Higgons (1938); Metheny (1939); Stuart, Hill, and Shaw (1940); Pryor (1941); Wetzel (1941); Stuart and Dwinell (1942); Massler (1945).

Center of gravity:

Palmer (1944).

Height predicted from skeletal age:

Bayley (1946).

Growth Trends

The physical growth of the child to be fully appreciated must be considered in relation to growth in general, but that subject would lead us too far astray. Robertson (1923), Davenport (1926b, 1934), Pearl (1928), Robbins, Brody, Hogan, *et al.* (1928), Huxley (1932), Courtis (1932, 1937), the Cold Spring Harbor *Symposium on Quantitative Biology* (1934, Vol. II), Hammett (1936), and Meredith (1945) are among the best sources treating the subject of growth comprehensively and from a theoretical point of view. The search for a theoretical curve of growth generally applicable over any but a relatively short period has not been fruitful (Davenport, 1926*a*, 1926*b*, 1934, 1938; Davenport and Drager, 1936). There are certain mathematical equations which, for certain periods of growth or for general growth trends, are fair approximations, such as the autocatalytic curve suggested by Robertson (1923), the Gompertz curve

neck development, neck development precedes chest growth, chest growth precedes pelvic growth, and arm growth precedes leg growth; also upper-arm growth precedes lower-arm growth, which in turn precedes hand growth; and likewise for the lower extremities. Jackson (1914, 1928), who was the first to formulate this law with respect to human growth, concisely

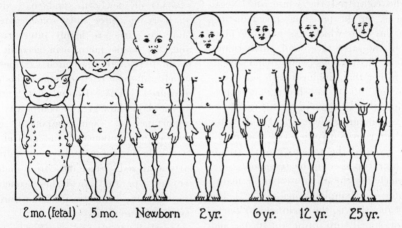

2 mo. (fetal)   5 mo.   Newborn   2 yr.   6 yr.   12 yr.   25 yr.

FIGURE 1. Changes in form and proportion of the human body during fetal and postnatal life. (From "Some Aspects of Form and Growth," by C. M. Jackson. In *Growth,* by W. J. Robbins, S. Brody, A. G. Hogan, C. M. Jackson, and C. W. Green. New Haven: Yale University Press, 1928, p. 118.)

recommended by Courtis (1932), the exponential curve of Huxley (1932), and the more complicated exponential curve of Jenss and Bayley (1937). Medawar (1944), however, has developed a mathematical method for representing the gross changes in the shape of man from the fifth fetal month to maturity. D'Arcy Thompson (1942) approaches the problem graphically in terms of differently timed growth rates of body parts.

The body does not grow as a whole and in all directions at once. Each part must be considered separately. In general, embryonic and fetal growth proceed cephalocaudally and proximodistally. That is, with few exceptions, head development precedes

describes human morphogenesis from its initial differentiation to the adult body. The changes are pictured in Figure 1. Schultz (1926) and Scammon and Calkins (1929) have investigated the changes in body dimensions for the fetal period, that is, from about two months after conception to birth. Both authors note that during this period of growth the changes in bodily dimensions are proportional to the changes in total fetal length. In other words, although there is considerable change in body form during this period, the changes are those initiated in embryonic rather than in fetal life.

The complicated transformations occurring in prenatal life are simply and skillfully described by Gilbert (1938). She ends by describing the anomalies of development as misfortunes of growth at a critical stage. An analogy between physical and behavior growth processes suggests itself to the psychologist.

Racial characteristics appear even in fetal life. Schultz (1926) found distinct racial characteristics in the 5-month-old fetus when he compared the white and Negro specimens, but he noted no racial distinction in the fetus which was not present in adults of the same race; and, furthermore, the racial distinctions were found to increase rather than diminish with age.

Scammon (1930) has shown that in prenatal life the various parts of the body follow a similar growth trend, but after birth their course diverges (see Figure 2). He has grouped the various growth trends under four types: (1) the *lymphoid type,* which includes the thymus, lymph nodes, and intestinal lymphoid masses; (2) the *neural type,* that is, the brain and its parts, the dura, spinal cord, optic apparatus, and many head dimensions; (3) the *general type,* followed by the body as a whole, external dimensions excepting head and neck, respiratory and digestive organs, kidneys, aorta and pulmonary trunks, spleen, musculature as a whole, and skeleton as a whole; and (4) the *genital type,* characteristic of testes, ovaries, epididymis, uterine tubes, prostatic urethra, and seminal vesicles. Nature, however, is never as invariable as man-conceived laws, and Scammon notes divergences from the four types, such as neck circumference, which follows the neural growth curve through early childhood and then follows the curve for general body growth. The suprarenals are even more irregular and atypical. After birth they rapidly diminish in size and then grow slowly until prior to puberty, when they increase relatively rapidly. Other glands have their characteristic curves.

It is the consensus that postnatal growth changes are brought about by a multitude of determining factors, the understanding of which requires carefully controlled and analyzed studies.

The underlying principles of growth have been investigated by the technique of factor analysis. Carter and Krause (1936), analyzing the data of Bakwin and Bakwin (1934a) on newborns, find that, although all body measures show some correlation, "no two parts are highly intercorrelated" and "no single factor can account for a major part of the measured variance when widely different parts of human bodies are measured." They also find that "anthropometric data show greater complexity, lesser importance of each component, greater number of components, and greater specificity" than when mental test data are similarly analyzed. Since data from males and females separately yield these conclusions, the statistics do not result from unreliability of measurements.

Marshall (1936) has used factor analysis to study the growth factors of 18 measurements for the age period from birth to 6 years. He has found four group factors and a number of specific factors. One group factor is identified with subcutaneous fatty tissue, but the other three group factors are not identified in biological terms.

Mullen (1940), using Holzinger's method of factor analysis, which assumes a general factor plus group factors, studied data on girls between 7 and 17 years old. She identified a general size factor related to sexual maturation and two group factors. One factor was concerned with height, span, length of forearm, and lower-leg length. The other factor related to weight, bi-iliac and bitrochanteric diameters, chest girth, width, and depth. These two factors were considered significant with respect to body type.

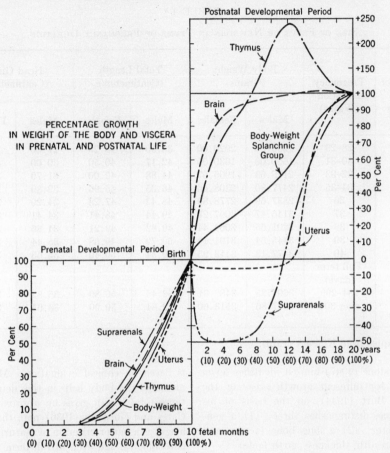

Postnatal Developmental Period

PERCENTAGE GROWTH
IN WEIGHT OF THE BODY AND VISCERA
IN PRENATAL AND POSTNATAL LIFE

Thymus

Brain

Body-Weight
Splanchnic
Group

Uterus

Suprarenals

Prenatal Developmental Period Birth

Suprarenals

Brain Uterus

Thymus

Body-Weight

2 4 6 8 10 12 14 16 18 20 years
(10) (20) (30) (40) (50) (60) (70) (80) (90) (100%)

0 1 2 3 4 5 6 7 8 9 10 fetal months
(0) (10) (20) (30) (40) (50) (60) (70) (80) (90) (100%)

FIGURE 2. Graph showing relative (percentage) growth in weight of the human body and viscera during fetal and postnatal life. (From "Some Aspects of Form and Growth," by C. M. Jackson. In *Growth*, by W. J. Robbins, S. Brody, A. G. Hogan, C. M. Jackson, and C. W. Green. New Haven: Yale University Press, 1928, p. 132.) The horizontal base line (abscissa) indicates age; vertical distance (ordinate) indicates the percentage of the weight at the end of the period, prenatal or postnatal, which has been reached at the corresponding age. (Graph by R. E. Scammon.)

McCloy (1940), using Thurstone's method of factor analysis, and analyzing data on both sexes from birth to maturity, found four subdivisions of Scammon's general body growth: (1) fat growth which may be superimposed on any type of build; (2) general growth seen in the tall, long-limbed, excessively slender; (3) cross-section type

seen in short, very stocky, broad-headed, short-limbed, lateral, or pyknic build; and (4) "Type IV," not definitely identified but most prominent in chest measurement and shoulder width. He concludes: "This would seem to leave us with at least seven types of growth instead of four" (as shown by Scammon).

TABLE 1 *

SIZE OF FETUS OR NEWBORN IN TERMS OF PREGNANCY DURATION

Number of Cases	Pregnancy Duration (Weeks)	Body Weight (Grams)		Total Length (Centimeters)		Head Girth (Centimeters)	
		Males	Females	Males	Females	Males	Females
4	28–29	1255.00	2020.00	38.50	43.25	27.00	31.25
5	30–31	1690.00	1630.00	42.17	40.50	30.00	29.25
11	32–33	2178.63	1906.67	44.88	42.00	31.79	30.00
23	34–35	2477.80	2308.46	46.35	45.96	32.89	31.95
22	36	2837.69	2778.89	48.42	47.28	34.29	33.38
28	37	3146.47	3097.27	49.44	48.41	34.41	34.00
77	38	3201.66	3064.44	49.82	49.21	34.86	34.53
124	39	3445.54	3191.19	50.79	49.38	35.44	34.57
180	40	3477.13	3413.95	50.84	50.40	35.63	35.13
	Full term (days)						
239	284–299	3601.25	3482.81	52.45	50.89	35.82	35.42
52	over 300	3927.86	3513.60	52.84	50.90	36.65	35.47

* Adapted from Kjölseth (1913).

Thurstone (1947) himself identifies seven factors for different growth areas of the body. Burt (1944), on the basis of his technique, distinguishes three: (1) a general factor; (2) a long bone factor; and (3) a breadth, thickness, girth factor.

It is apparent that factor analysis is one approach to the study of body types discussed on page 310.

The Newborn

Usually birth occurs between 270 and 290 days after the beginning of the last menstrual period before conception. If birth takes place earlier, the child is considered prematurely born; if later, postmaturely born. When, as frequently happens, the menstrual history indicates irregularity, or when birth weight is less than 5 pounds, an estimation of the length of term is based on clinical evaluation. Measurements of the body help in this determination; total length gives an approximation. Cates and Goodwin (1936) note that total length is a better criterion of maturity than chronological age even in full-term infants. Table 1, adapted from Kjölseth (1913), gives the average body weight, length, and head circumference according to pregnancy duration. Scammon (1922) finds that the "growth tendency of prematures is in general that of fetuses of the same size and age rather than of full-term children." This finding emphasizes ontogenetic age. Bakwin and Bakwin (1934b) find that newborns from a poverty-stricken environment are smaller in all dimensions measured than newborns from a more favorable environment, but that the infants from different environments are similarly proportioned.

Poor maternal diets are found in conjunction with still births, congenital defects, and functional immaturity as well as small weight and size (Stuart, 1947). Furthermore, these infants, though lighter and smaller, are more likely to be difficult to deliver.

It is a well-established fact that the full-term male infant is larger in all body measurements and weighs more than the full-term female infant. The closest approximation of the sexes is in pelvic width. Cates and Goodwin (1936) report that the weight of the male exceeds the weight of the female by 4 per cent and that the height of the male exceeds the height of the female by 2 per cent. The sex difference finding is consistent with the conclusions of both Schultz (1926) and Scammon and Calkins (1929), who report no sex differences when fetuses are compared in relation to total length rather than age.

Although there are racial differences in birth weight, seasonal variation in temperature has not been found to influence it (Brenton, 1922). Meredith and Brown (1939) have reviewed the literature on the effect of various factors on birth weight and weight gain during the first ten days of postnatal life and present further data from Iowa. They conclude that throughout the period "mean weight is least for first borns, intermediate for infants of second to fourth birth order, and greatest for infants of fifth and higher birth order." They, like Brenton, report no seasonal differences.

Although first borns, at birth, are smaller not only in weight but also in stature and head circumference, they are taller though not necessarily heavier between 1 and 14 years, according to Meredith (1950), who has studied available data. By adulthood, however, Howells (1948) finds no relationship between birth order and body form.

Postnatal Growth

The three composite measures of body growth commonly studied are weight, a three-dimensional measure; surface area, a two-dimensional measure; and height, a linear measure. Scammon (1930) notes that these three functions have the same growth trend except that the curve for surface area has less accentuated inflection points than the curve for weight, and more accentuated inflection points than the curve for length (see Figure 3). The general growth trend of the body as pictured by these curves is characterized by rapid increase in infancy, a slowing-down followed by steady increase in childhood, an increased growth rate beginning between 8 and 10 years and continuing to adolescence, followed by a fairly abrupt tapering-off of growth to maturity.

There is a characteristic sex difference in attaining maturity. Girls are generally more mature than boys of the same age. In early childhood, although girls are more mature, they are smaller. The preadolescent spurt starts earlier in girls than in boys, and, owing to this earlier spurt in growth, the girls temporarily surpass the boys in total size. But the girls' growth spurt is less intense and lasts for a shorter period than the boys' adolescent spurt. Finally, at maturity there is a greater discrepancy in measurements than existed earlier. The characteristic difference is exemplified by the height and weight curves pictured in Figure 4.

The changes in body proportions from birth to maturity are summarized in Section I of the White House Conference publication (1932). It is noted there that, although growth in the first half year after birth is rapid, changes in body proportion are relatively slight. From then to puberty head growth is slow, limb growth rapid, and trunk growth intermediate. In males, from puberty to maturity, growth of the trunk and limbs is at first equal, then there follows a relatively rapid growth of the trunk. Growth in trunk girth continues

to the over-all structure of the pelvis while girls tend to be either absolutely or relatively larger in measurements relating to the inner structure of the pelvis including inlet (Reynolds, 1945, 1947).

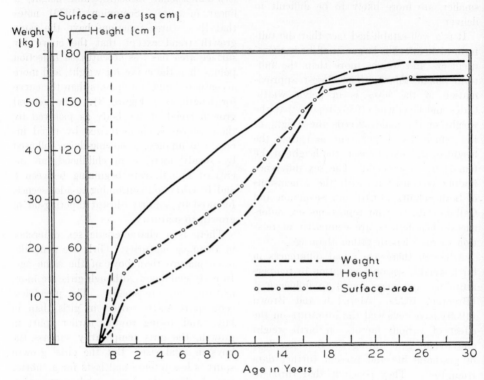

FIGURE 3. Growth curves for height, surface area, and weight drawn according to Quetelet's figures. (Given by E. Boyd in "Growth of the Surface Area of the Human Body," *Institute of Child Welfare Monographs*. Minneapolis: University of Minnesota Press, 1935, No. 10, p. 114.)

longer than growth in length. In females, from puberty to maturity, the trunk elongates in the lumbar region and the pelvis enlarges, while the lower extremities cease to grow in proportion to the trunk. As noted previously, growth in stature ceases earlier in girls, and their increase in trunk width, except in the pelvic region, is less marked during the later part of adolescence.

In infancy and prepuberal childhood, boys are larger in measurements relating

Other sex differences have been noted: Boynton (1936), comparing her study on girls with that of Meredith's on boys (1935), finds that boys are larger than girls in thoracic circumference and girth of forearm throughout the growth years; that girls have a larger thigh than boys from 3 to 18 years; that subcutaneous tissue measurements show a similar pattern for the sexes below 6 years, but from 13 to 18 years girls show a steady increase in this

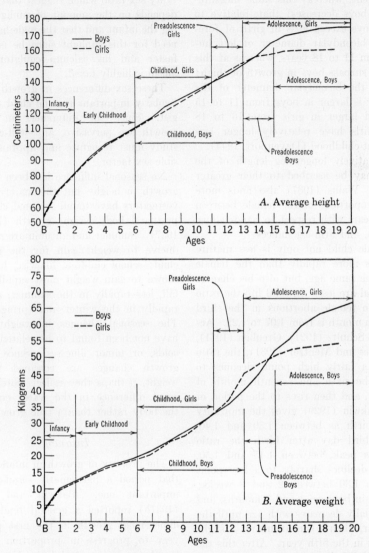

FIGURE 4. Growth of boys and girls from birth to maturity. (From Cole, *The Psychology of Adolescence*. New York: Rinehart and Co., 1948, pp. 18–19.) From age 6 to age 19 these results are based upon F. K. Shuttleworth, "Physical and Mental Growth of Boys and Girls Ages Six through Nineteen in Relation to Age and Maximum Growth," *Monographs of the Society for Research in Child Development, 4*, No. 3, 1939, 248, 249. Below age 6, the curves are averages of several studies, most of which are not longitudinal.

measurement, whereas this same measurement for boys decreases; that, relative to stature, boys exceed girls in girth of forearm and bicondylar diameter of left humerus from 11 to 18 years, whereas at this time girls surpass boys in growth of thigh; and that the bicondylar diameter of the left femur is larger in boys from 11 to 15 years, and larger in girls from 16 to 18 years. Girls have relatively longer legs throughout childhood (Davenport, 1944).

The relatively longer leg length of the females may be ascribed to their greater maturity. Wallis (1931) also finds more mature proportions of the female between 2 and 8 years with respect to hand-radius, trunk-arm, and arm-leg indices.

The male child not only is less mature and grows more rapidly than the female child of the same age, but also his chances for survival are less. In fetal life the ratio of male to female abortions in the third to the fifth month is from 1.07 to 1.22. According to Schultz (1921), Greulich (1931), and Holmes and Mentzer (1931), the ratio starts at a fairly high point, declines to between the sixth and seventh month of pregnancy, and then rises to the period of birth. Bakwin (1929) gives the mortality ratio at birth as between 1.30 and 1.40. On the third day after birth the ratio reaches its peak, between 1.45 and 1.50, and then declines sharply to a low point of 1.20 to 1.30 between 2 and 3 weeks; it rises again between 1 and 2 months, and then gradually decreases with age until the fourth year, when it is near unity. A slight rise occurs in the fifth year. After this the ratio may fall below unity in the teens and in the most active childbearing period.

The findings of Schultz (1921), who concludes that 1.08 to 1.09 males are conceived for every female, would not account for the greater disparity in mortality. Bakwin (1929) points out that there are seasonal and regional differences in the mor-

tality sex ratio which suggest that the ratio depends on the amount of sunlight reaching the infant and that the male has greater need for this sunlight since he is growing faster and his calcium-regulatory mechanism is highly taxed.

These sex differences in growth are particularly important for the child psychologist. Since the differences in physical growth are pervasive, any well-controlled study must recognize and appraise a possible sex factor.

No seasonal influence has been found on growth in height, but the majority of investigators have found seasonal changes in postnatal body weight growth (Marshall, 1937). Summer and autumn are most conducive to weight gain for the preschool child; school children, likewise, have been shown to gain weight most rapidly in the fall, less rapidly in the summer, and least rapidly in the winter and spring months. The seasonal changes in weight growth have not been found to be related to food, colds, or minor illnesses. Since seasonal growth changes are confined to body weight, perhaps they reflect merely a seasonal difference in the water content of the body rather than a true growth trend.

Infancy

The rapidity of growth in infancy makes that period a particularly significant and important one. Bakwin and Bakwin (1931b) reported a general tendency for dimensional growth in the first postnatal year to progress in proportion to total length, as in prenatal life. Nevertheless, when infant growth is studied in detail, modifications in relative growth rate are apparent. Davenport (1938) finds the curve for neck and thigh growth to be highly aberrant and the shoulder and thoracic index changes to indicate special growth adaptations in infancy. Thompson

(1938) reports that between 8 and 56 weeks of age the head and thorax circumferences show a gradually decreasing relative growth rate and lower limb length shows a definitely increasing relative growth rate.

Between birth and 3 years, Bayley and Davis (1935) note, the growth rate in all dimensions decreases, more rapidly at first and then more slowly. They also report that, during the first year, growth ratios show a proportionately increasing width. Thompson (1938) notes that the soles-pubes length relative to total length reaches a critical minimum sometime after birth but before 8 weeks, and thereafter increases rapidly. This finding is in accord with that of Meredith and Knott (1938) with respect to the skelic index, or the ratio of lower limb to stem length. The ratio between lower limb length and total length is an important one because it differentiates the sexes. The females, relatively more mature than the males, have relatively longer lower limbs even as early as 8 weeks.

Cephalic and facial changes in infancy are discussed in the section devoted to face and head growth.

Ponderal growth in infancy follows the general course of growth. Pediatricians rely heavily and probably too exclusively on weight gain as evidence of adequate nutrition. Weight, however, is a sensitive indication of nutrition. Bakwin and Bakwin (1931b) report that infants from poor homes weigh less and are shorter in stature than infants from good homes and that the retardation in bodily dimensions accompanying retardation in weight is greater for the transverse than for the vertical dimensions. They also report (1936) that supervision of a group of infants from poor homes in a pediatric clinic raised the height and weight of these infants to that of the normal group and likewise changed the

relative proportions from relative "linearity" to the normal of the control group.

Although male infants are larger than female infants of the same age (Bakwin and Bakwin, 1931b; Bayley and Davis, 1935; Thompson, 1938; Peatman and Higgons, 1938; and others) and although the growth increment tends to be larger for the male infant, the percentage rate of growth does not in general differ significantly in the two sexes (Thompson, 1938). Dunham, Jenss, and Christie (1939) emphasize the importance of considering both sex and race in studying the growth of infants. Colored infants have long been said to be smaller and to weigh less than white infants (Children's Bureau, 1927; Michelson, 1943a, 1943b, and 1943c; and others). However, Bakwin and Patrick (1944), as well as Scott, Cardozo, Smith, and DeLilly (1950), find no difference between white and Negro infants seen in private practice. They conclude that the slower growth previously reported was due to difference in economic status.

Childhood

During childhood, height and weight progress at a fairly uniform rate (Wallis, 1931). Rate of weight gain is nearly twice the rate of height gain. The lower limbs grow rapidly in proportion to the stem length (Meredith and Knott, 1938). Neither shoulder breadth nor pelvic breadth increases as rapidly as trunk length, but the pelvis broadens more rapidly than the shoulders. The total configurational change is a longer-legged, longer-bodied, and more rectilinear and flatter-bodied child.

Sex difference with respect to skelic index, that is, the ratio between lower extremities and stem lengths, disappears between 5 and 6 years and reappears at 7 years. Females then have the relatively longer legs, despite the fact that they are shorter. This difference continues through the ninth year (Meredith and Knott), 1938).

Other sex differences during childhood have been noted on previous pages.

Adolescence

Adolescence, the second period of rapid postnatal growth, has received special attention. Greulich, Day, Lachman, et al. (1938) have made a well-rounded survey of the methods for studying physical, mental, and social adolescent growth. Shuttleworth (1937, 1939), Greulich, Dorfman, Catchpole, et al. (1942), Bayley (1943a, 1943b), Simmons and Greulich (1943), Greulich and Thoms (1944), and Stuart (1947) have made special studies of the body and skeletal changes occurring at this period. The period is a truly metamorphic one, as shown by the actual growth curve (Davenport, 1926b) and by the marked body changes which complete the differentiation of the sexes.

Girls enter the period of acceleration in height growth, on the average, at about 9 years of age, about 2 years earlier than boys (Boynton, 1936). Girls reach the maximum phase of growth at an average age of about 12.5 years, boys at about 14.8 years (Shuttleworth, 1939). Puberty is demarcated in girls by the menarche and in boys by active spermatozoa which may be found in the morning urine. Puberty is closely related to the age of maximum growth (Shuttleworth, 1939; Simmons and Greulich, 1943). The maximum increase in standing height never occurs after the menarche, and the intervals between the time of maximum growth increment and the menarche is greater in late-maturing girls than in those who mature early (Simmons and Greulich, 1943). Girls of early, average, or late menarche can be differentiated by assessment of their skeletal maturity in advance of their acceleration in height and weight (Simmons and Greulich, 1943).

The menarche normally occurs between 12 and 14 years of age and is preceded by a series of bodily changes. First the breasts enlarge, then pubic hair appears, and a little later axillary hair.

In boys, puberty is preceded by increased growth of the testes and penis, and perhaps a slight swelling of the breasts, then the appearance of pubic hair, followed by the appearance of axillary and facial hair. Voice change usually occurs after the appearance of pubic hair but before its lateral spread. Since the determination of spermatozoa in the urine requires laboratory analysis, the appearance of axillary hair has been used by some as an indication of puberty (Richey, 1937). Greulich, Dorfman, Catchpole, et al. (1942) have defined five stages of somatic sex characteristics in puberal and adolescent boys, giving actual photographs of breasts and genitals, as well as full-length pictures by which individual maturity may be appraised.

Boas and Wissler (1906) noted that the average growth curve minimizes the decline in growth rate in childhood and the increase at adolescence owing to the individual variation in age of growth rate change. Boas (1930, 1932) found that in some individuals physiological development, so far as it is expressed by stature, is rapid, energetic, and short, whereas in others it is sluggish and occupies a much longer period. His statistics for boys show that the earlier the maximum growth, the greater the maximum growth rate; and the taller the initial stature, the earlier the maximum growth rate.

With respect to the individual growth of girls at adolescence, Boas (1932) found that the interval between the moment of maximum rate of growth and the first menses is greater the earlier the maximum rate of growth; and that the earlier the maximum rate of growth, the shorter the total period of growth. He also found that the type of growth curve characteristic of an individual is more closely related to the age of maximum growth than to the date of the first menses; and that individuals who have the same stature at an early age are, as adults, shorter the earlier the age of maximum growth rate.

Richey (1937), investigating growth rates before and after puberty in both sexes, found growth in height and weight slightly accelerated before puberty but more markedly decelerated after puberty. Although the prepubertal spurt in growth increases the disparity in size for children of early, average, and late puberty, the disparity is still more influenced by differences in growth rate after puberty.

The findings of Boas (1932), as well as Shuttleworth's own investigations, led Shuttleworth (1939) to make an extensive study of adolescence in terms of growth increments, relating them to the period of maximum growth. Comparing the growth curves of boys and girls with the same maximum growth age, he finds no crossing of the growth curves but, instead, he finds that at every age the boys are taller than the girls. Also, the growth increments of the boys are greater at every age than those of the girls, but the difference is particularly marked at the age of maximum growth. Analyzing the actual stature difference in terms of accelerating phase, initial decelerating phase, and final decelerating phase, Shuttleworth (1939) finds they contribute 3.67 cm., 5.88 cm., and 3.28 cm., respectively, making a total difference at maturity of 12.85 cm. When he compares children of the same sex but with different ages of maximum growth, he finds that those with later maximum growth ages are only slightly taller at maturity since they have a smaller initial decelerating increment and a smaller final decelerating increment, although their initial deceleration is of longer duration though of less intensity. In other words, the effect of the longer period of growth is canceled by generally less intense growth.

Because of the variability in growth rates associated with the time of maximum growth rate, stature can be predicted more accurately from stature at 6 to 10 years than it can at the following years. In general, Shuttleworth (1939, p. 61) concludes that girls who are tall at any age tend to be tall·at maturity; but girls who are tall at 6 to 9 years are more likely to be taller at maturity (correlation .73 to .83) than girls who are tall at ages 11 and 12 years (correlation .64 to .71). Similarly, correlation in height of boys 6 to 10 years with their adult stature is .72 to .80, whereas the correlation in height of boys 13 to 14 years old with their mature stature is .56 to .61.

Age at puberty appears to be related to body build. Pryor (1936) finds that girls of broad body build menstruate earlier than girls of slender body build, and Bayley's data (1943b) show that early-maturing boys and girls tend to have broad hips and narrow shoulders. She also finds that early-maturing boys have a growth spurt resembling that of girls, and late-maturing girls have a spurt resembling that of boys. Tanner (1947) points out that this, as well as other evidence, supports the notion that the reaction of a tissue to hormonal stimulation depends on its age. Bayer (1940b) finds that disturbances in weight and menstruation are associated with deviations from normal build. Bruch (1941b), however, in a study of more than 200 children, finds that mere obesity is not related to delayed puberty in either boys or girls. Godin (1935) concludes that puberty is a germinal affair, and the maturity of the germ itself is an affair of nutrition. Pryor (1936) suggests that possibly the glandular balance of the broad-built child brings about an optimum nutritional state for pubescence sooner than in the underweight, narrow-built child. Shuttleworth (1937, 1939) tends to emphasize endocrine factors in activating adolescent changes. Greulich, Dorfman, Catchpole, *et al.* (1942, p. 62) from the study of gonadotrophic hormone excretion in adolescent boys conclude, "A likely mechanism for the initiation of puberty is a gradual increase in pituitary secretion, combined probably with an increasing sensitivity of the gonads to the hormone."

Body Types

Mankind tends naturally to order knowledge by generalization. Marked deviations from normal are impressive and foster categorical classifications and artificial pigeonholing. Thus many attempts have been made to separate individuals into physical types. Differences in skin color, shape of head, hair form, ear form, shape of nose (Bean, 1926), stature, span, and weight are commonly recognized as distinctive racial traits. Jackson (1930) points out that these differences do persist from generation to generation and, although there may be some modification, the traits tend to persist even in new environments. He shows, however, by comparing distribution curves of races, that overlapping of the races with respect to any trait is almost complete. Whether the extremes do represent true biotypes is uncertain.

In clinical medicine, abnormal body types are diagnostic of such conditions as acromegaly, acondroplastic dwarfism, mongolism, and cretinism, but even here there are borderline cases which confuse diagnosis. Nevertheless, the concept of type is useful if kept within bounds and not allowed to dominate the analysis and interpretation of data.

Among normal individuals the stout and thin types have long been recognized. Davenport (1923, 1927), particularly, suggests that these are truly types since he finds their distribution bimodal, that they have concomitant differential characteristics, and that they are inheritable traits.

Other suggestions for body type distinctions are Naccarati's (1921) macro- and microplanchnic types, in which the trunk is respectively proportionately larger or smaller than the extremities; Kretschmer's (1925) pyknic type, with round trunk and short extremities; asthenic type, with small trunk and long extremities; athletic type, moderately proportioned; and dysplastic (mixed) type; and Bayer's (1940a) four types of adolescent girls, hypofeminine (Diana), feminine (Venus), hyperfeminine (Rubens), and virile (Amazon), according to their skeletal proportions and covering tissue. Bayley and Bayer (1946) have devised a five-fold classification, based on an appraisal of many sex differences, by which young adults of both sexes may be evaluated according to masculine-feminine type.

Sheldon, Stevens, and Tucker (1940) have developed a promising system of typing somatic adult characteristics according to three components and four second-order variables. The three components are related to the three embryonic tissues, the endo-, the meso-, and the ectoderm. Thus endomorphy is the characteristic of the visceral-dominated body as shown by soft, rounded body regions; mesomorphy is characteristic of the bone-, muscle-, and connective-tissue-dominated body, as shown by a heavy, hard, and rectangularly outlined body; and ectomorphy is characteristically dominated by the central nervous system, as shown by a linear, fragile body with a relatively large surface area. The four second-order variables are: dysplasia, or disharmony between various parts of the

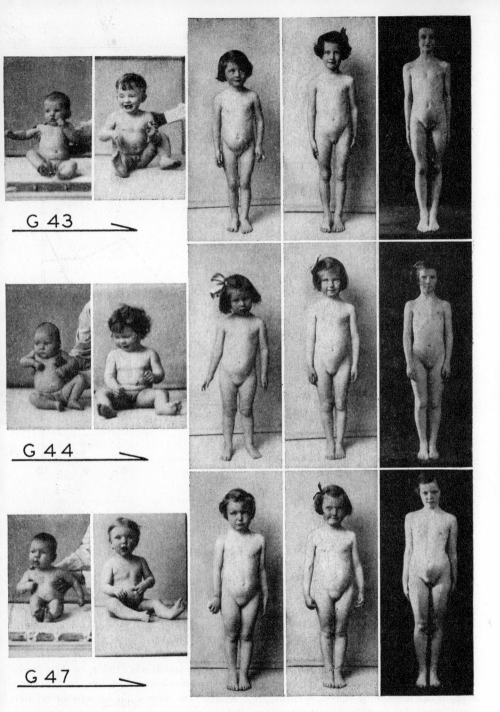

8 WEEKS 1 YEAR 3 YEARS 5 YEARS 9 YEARS

FIGURE 5. Changing body proportions of three girls all taller than average but of different body "types." (Thompson, The Clinic of Child Development, Yale University.)

body; gynandromorphy, or degree of bisex-
uality; texture, or the fineness or coarseness
of structure; and hirsutism, or amount of
body hair. All the above traits are rated
on a seven-point scale by anthropometric
and anthroposcopic methods. Hunt (1949)

such as the stem length:recumbent length
ratio (Hejinian and Hatt, 1929), have
proved valid for certain periods of growth
but lose their significance at other ages.

McCloy (1936), investigating the whole
period of physical growth from birth to

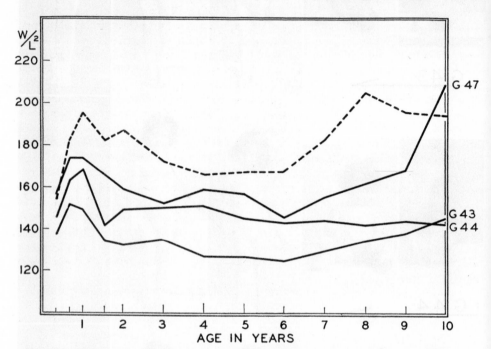

FIGURE 6. Individual changes in weight:length² index with age. (Thompson, unpublished
data.) Girls G43, G44, and G47 are taller than average but of different body build. G43 is
underweight for age and height; legs proportionately long. G44 approximates normal proportions. G47 is overweight for height; pelvis wide for body length. (See Figure 5, p. 311.)
Dotted line represents index changes for short stocky girl.

emphasizes the complex relationship of the
three embryonic layers and their interaction which complicates the theory underlying somatotyping. This may account for
the change in body type with age.

Many complicated formulae have been
devised to classify adults objectively according to type. When the problem of
types is extended to childhood, it is further
complicated by the changing proportions
associated with growth. Certain indices,

maturity by Thurstone's (1935)method of
factor analysis, concludes that the two indices most useful in appraising body type
are weight⅓:height; and chest girth:
height. But even these ratios are unsatisfactory in infancy.

Bayley and Davis (1935), in their study
of the first 3 years of life, find weight:
length ² the most valid measure of relative
chubbiness, or lateral-linear tendencies in
build. But they are unable to predict from

indices at an early age what an individual's body build will be later. The pictures in Figure 5 show clearly the vagaries of growth. Three girls, all taller than average but of distinct body types, are pictured at various stages of growth.

The ratios weight:length [2] for these three children between the ages of 16 weeks and 10 years are plotted in Figure 6. From 28 weeks to 9 years the curves do not cross, but G43 at 28 weeks is more chubby then than G44 at 5 years; and G44 is decidedly more chubby at 28 weeks than G47 is at 5 years. Chubbiness, as Bayley and Davis (1935) find, reaches a peak between 9 and 12 months of age.

Tanner (1947) has shown that Burt's constants, since they provide a continuum rather than a discrete series, are of great value in studying type and the physiological nature of growth. Since individual variations are great, and it is actually a question of degree of type, Tanner's approach, combining as it does D'Arcy Thompson's concept of growth with Burt's concept of factor analysis, is a promising approach for the future.

Weight and Nutritional Status

Weight increase is a correlate of growth, but weight increase is not necessarily indicative of growth. Weight changes may be merely the result of changes in fatty deposits or in water content, both of which may be transitory modifications (Hammett, 1937; Simmons and Todd, 1938). Weight is more variable and more indicative of nutritional status than other physical measurements. Franzen (1929) has devised an instrument for measuring skin and subcutaneous tissue to indicate quantitatively the fatty deposits affecting weight. He and McCloy (1938) have established age and sex norms for this measure on various parts of the body. The norms are

useful for transmuting body dimensions to skeletal dimensions and for thus determining body build more explicitly. Stuart, Hill, and Shaw (1940) have developed a technique for measuring the muscle and overlying tissues of the leg area by roentgenography. Norms for children from birth through 10 years are available (Stuart, Hill, and Shaw, 1940; Stuart and Dwinell, 1942).

Although weight is an acknowledged indication of nutritional status, optimum weight is an individual requirement, since it depends on age, stature, and body build as well as on nutrition. Age norms for weight, which even today are sometimes used, fail to consider that tall children of a given age should generally weigh more than short children of that age. Height-weight norms, which are widely used, account for differences in height but not in body build. Thus height-weight tables have received much criticism from Pryor and Stolz (1933), Royster (1936), Dearborn and Rothney (1938), Simmons and Todd (1938), and others.

Constructive suggestions for more valid nutritional appraisal methods are many. Pryor and Stolz (1933) express the index of nutrition in terms of the percentage deviation of the obtained weight from the weight norm for age, sex, height, and bi-iliac width to this weight norm. They furnish standard tables for ages 6 to 16 years. Franzen and Palmer's (1934) index of nutritional status for children between 7 and 12 years old employs the sum of arm girth with arm flexed, plus arm girth with arm extended, plus chest depth on inspiration, plus chest depth on expiration in terms of age, and bitrochanteric width. Individuals below a certain value are considered undernourished. Royster (1936) has established weight norms for Negro children between 5 and 15 years of age based on age, stature, and bi-iliac diameter. He emphasizes that the Negro child is of a more slender build than the white child and should therefore be appraised only in terms of his own race. McCloy (1938) finds that normal weight is best predicted by four measurements: height, chest circumference corrected for fat, hip width corrected for fat, and knee width. From thirty regression equations, one for each sex and year for ages 4 through 18 years, he has computed tables from which normal weight may be derived. Clayton (1942) finds that McCloy's formula is reasonably accurate except for markedly overfat or emaciated children. Dearborn and Rothney (1938) have derived a formula for normal weight which is a simple function of chest width, chest depth, standing height, and bi-iliac width. It is useful for both sexes between 14 and 18 years of age. Wetzel (1941, 1943) has devised a grid by which a child's position may be determined in terms of his height, weight, and age. This grid carries seven channels. A child's growth curve normally progresses in a particular channel; deviation from this channel is indicative of change in health status. On a supplementary chart are five representative growth curves which include 76 per cent of those of each standard. A child's growth course may be evaluated, thus, in terms of his own standard. It should be noted, however, that this evaluation, no matter how individual, is based only on height, weight, and age. Only to that extent, therefore, can it assess an individual child.

Pyle and others (1948) have offered a method of indicating the variability of an individual's skeletal bone ages, known as the red graph method. It is based on Todd's inspectional method of appraisal. Its use, in combination with the Wetzel grid, is advocated to reveal a more complete appraisal of both skeletal and soft tissue growth (Mann and others, 1948).

Another channel diagram which utilizes calf girth and height in relation to age as an indication of ideal weight is advocated by Massler and Suher (1951). This differs from the Wetzel grid, which they claim merely indicates growth status and trend rather than the ideal.

Daniels, Hutton, and Neil (1938) advocate the use of the creatinine-height index for nutritional appraisal. The determined ratio is the urinary creatinine in milligrams in proportion to height cubed. They claim that this index accounts for poor skeletal development which other indices of nutrition do not measure.

The question of appropriate weight for any child of adolescent age is particularly difficult because of the great variability associated with accelerated, normal, and retarded puberty. At this age, Richey (1937) points out, no statement of overweight or underweight should be made without a consideration of maturity factors.

The underweight and overweight children present special problems for investigation by the child psychologist (McHale, 1926). Bruch (1939, 1940, 1941b) has made highly significant studies showing that obesity, even in severe cases, is commonly a dietary rather than an endocrine problem; that obesity is related to parental overprotection and overfeeding, and to deprivation of satisfying outlets and contacts so that, for the child, food intake assumes inordinate importance. Similarly, Bronstein, Wexler, Brown, and Halpern (1942) conclude that for 35 children whom they studied no endocrine reason could be found for their obesity. Instead, it appeared to be related to sedentary habits, abnormal appetites, parental attitudes, and other environmental factors.

There is the further question of the degree of deviation which a child may show from a method of assessment without being considered under- or overweight.

Metheny (1939) concludes that any child found to be 3 per cent underweight or 10 per cent overweight, in terms of the normal weight predicted by McCloy's formula, should be examined fully. It is the consensus that, in addition to any standard of underweight or overweight, clinical judgment also should be used in appraising any individual child. Krogman (1951) points out the inadequacy of evaluations which do not take into consideration normal and abnormal variation.

Head and Face Growth

Head and face growth has had and will probably continue to have particular interest for the psychologist. It is therefore treated here more extensively than would otherwise be the case.

A comprehensive study of head and face growth has been made by Davenport (1940), who gives longitudinal data on the growth trends and analyzes causes for the irregularities which he finds. He lists an extensive bibliography on the subject and discusses the findings of others in relation to his study. He concludes that a multitude of factors operate to modify the growth trend and that any simple expression of the growth of these parts is inadequate. Some of the factors which influence the external cranial and facial dimensions are uterine pressure in fetal life, gravity at the age of sitting and walking, growth of sinuses and tooth alveoli, possibly masticatory pull, sex, race, and other inherited traits, nutrition, and glandular activities.

The growth centers of the head and face, like those of the rest of the body, have different periods of maximum activity. Todd (1935) comments that:

Brain-case growth is characteristic of infancy and early childhood and with it go the antero-posterior and transverse dimensions of the face, including the zygomata

or malar arches. Vertical or respiratory growth of the face attains maximum velocity in later childhood. Vertical growth of the jaws between floor of the nose and chin reaches its most vigorous phase at and after puberty [p. 262].

He comments further that, since the head and face are sensitive to any factors which affect growth at these ages, defective cranial size must date from infancy, deficient upper facial growth from childhood, and inadequate jaw growth from adolescence. In any individual instance, however, it is difficult to separate growth disturbances from inherited growth tendencies.

THE HEAD

The five most commonly studied head dimensions are length, anteroposterior diameter; breadth, maximum transverse diameter; frontal diameter from temporal bridge to temporal bridge; height, the projected vertical distance from ear to the vertex; and circumference. Landmarks to define these and other dimensions of the head and face are detailed by Sullivan (1928) Hrdlička (1939) and by other authors who discuss method. The cephalic index, the ratio of head breadth to head length, is used to distinguish long from round heads. The tabulated conventional terms are given by Hrdlička (1939) for making the distinctions. He points out that these are arbitrary rather than determined by nature.

Term	Cephalic Index
Hyperdolichocephaly	Below 70
Dolichocephaly	70–74.9
Mesocephaly	75–79.9
Brachycephaly	80–84.9
Hyperbrachycephaly	85 and above

The head and face differentiate early in prenatal life. Even in fetal life they grow more slowly than the body as a whole. Scammon and Calkins (1929) report that at 3 fetal months the total head and face height is nearly one-third of the total fetal length; at 6 fetal months, about one-fourth; and at birth a little less than one-fourth. Absolutely, however, the cranial dimensions all increase rapidly in intrauterine life. Postnatally the head length and breadth continue to increase rapidly for 2 years and then slow down quickly, with a slight spurt at adolescence. Head circumference likewise follows this trend. Meredith (1935) points out that this type of growth characterizes neural growth as described by Scammon (1930). Although head growth has the same growth trend as the brain, it does not follow that cranial measurements are correlated with brain function.

Davenport (1940) expresses the rapid early head growth in terms of percentage of adult head length (190 mm.) at various ages: birth, 63 per cent; end of 6 months, 76 per cent; 1 year, 82 per cent; 2 years, 87 per cent; 3 years, 89 per cent; 5 years, 91 per cent; 10 years, 95 per cent; and 15 years, 98 per cent.

Bayley (1936) reports that head width increases more rapidly in the first 7 months, whereas head length increases more rapidly after 8 months. She found infants relatively dolichocephalic at birth. From birth to 7 months they rapidly become brachycephalic, and after 10 months they again become dolichocephalic. According to Davenport (1940), the head has practically finished its width growth at 3 years, whereas the head continues to grow in length but at a greatly reduced rate. Goldstein (1939), reporting on head growth of the same individuals between 2 and 16 years, finds for length a relatively high annual increment between 2 and 5 years, a sharp drop in the increment until 7 years, followed by pulsations of growth until adolescence. For width, he finds a comparatively high annual increase between 2 and 4 years, with a gradual decline, less steep than for length. Goldstein also finds the

most common individual change in cephalic index to be a drop. Some individuals, however, showed no change and some even increased. Davenport (1940), reporting similarly on individual growth trends, finds that after the first year growth in length was much greater than in width in dolichocephalics, though the reverse was true for brachycephalics.

Absolute cephalic and facial measurements are less in the female than in the male (Davenport, 1940). Bayley (1936) states that the breadth difference tends to increase with age. The cephalic index of the sexes, according to Bayley, does not differentiate them until 11 months of age. Then the mean of the boys is higher than the mean of the girls. Between 5 and 6 years of age, this difference, according to Wallis (1931), diminishes until from 6 to 9 years of age the sexes are equal. Between 9 and 12 years the girls again have longer heads, but at 16 years boys equal and then surpass girls in cephalic index. Bayley (1936) concludes that the cephalic index is unrelated to body build as measured by weight/length ^{2} or stem length/total length, but that cephalic indices of the same children at different ages are fairly consistent.

Head height, particularly after 2 years of age, has a slower growth tempo than head length or breadth. Davenport (1940) reports that its growth is irregular and that decrease in head height is accompanied by increase in head width. Goldstein (1936) notes that head height is definitely greater in man than in the anthropoids.

The frontal breadth of the head grows irregularly. Davenport (1940) reports that it is near its final size at the age of 1 year. He also concludes that "Up to 4 years, as the breadth is increasing, the transverse frontal index decreases; but after that, as the forehead widens, the index increases."

The relative forehead width [1] tends to increase with age in all individuals studied.

Head circumference increases more regularly than other head dimensions. It is not a very reliable measure, however, since it is affected by different degrees of hair growth.

Intelligence and Cranial Dimensions. Psychologists have long sought a relationship between head measurements and intelligence. Hamilton (1936), in a review of the literature, finds a fairly consistently reported correlation of intelligence and cranial measurements of +.05 to +.10. He concludes that a true correlation would not exceed +.15.

Fernald and Southard (1918, 1921), in their macroscopic and microscopic study of the brains of feeble-minded, found a direct relationship with intelligence in only the extreme cases. It is not to be expected then that the external dimensions of the skull would be indicative of intellect. Ashby and Stewart (1933) did report a falling-off in size of the head measurements of the mentally deficient. The smaller measurements were most marked in the idiot region and affected equally head length, breadth, height, and ear-to-ear measurements, but they also found a more marked relationship between body size and IQ than between head size and IQ. Head growth, occurring genetically earlier than body growth, suffered less. This finding, Ashby and Stewart point out, tends to reinforce the notion that feeble-mindedness is an arrest or retardation in intelligence.

At the other extreme, the large head of a hydrocephalic may be associated with feeble-mindedness or normal intelligence.

Head Size and Race. Head length, particularly, varies with race. At 14 years of age the average head length of Negroes is 18.0 mm.; United States Nordics, 180.5

mm.; Jews, 177 mm.; and Italians, 175.0 mm. Although Negroes have the longest heads, the Nordics have the largest post-auricular head segment, the largest ratio of height/length, and the relatively widest foreheads (Davenport, 1940).

THE FACE

Psychologists have not been as interested in face growth as they have been in cranial growth, but, with the present shift in emphasis from intelligence to personality and social behavior, greater interest in facial growth may develop, particularly as far as child psychology is concerned. Study of the face should be encouraged as a potentially profitable field of investigation in relation to behavior-growth studies. The face is easily measured and photographed, and its measurement does not involve disrobing as does measurement of the body.

Dimensions of the face are taken either by direct measurement or from roentgenological records. Some of the commonly studied dimensions are *total height:* the vertical distance from the nasion, which is a point near the depression at the upper part of the nose, to the menton, or anterior lower margin of the chin; *nasal height:* from the nasion to the point where the nasal septum joins the upper lip; *bizygomatic breadth:* the distance between the most lateral aspects of the upper jawbone; *bigonial breadth:* the distance between the lower points at the posterior angle of the lower jawbone; *upper face length:* from the auditory meatus to the nasion; and *lower face length:* from the auditory meatus to the menton. Other landmarks and diameters are used according to the interest of the investigator.

Krogman (1939) points out that normal growth of the face is continuous but not uniform; that different parts alternate in their velocity and intensity of growth. He reports that between birth and 6 years

[1] Head width/total length.

growth is vigorous in all directions, as shown by the figures in Table 2.

TABLE 2

PERCENTAGE OF GROWTH AT VARIOUS AGES

		Age	
Dimension	Birth	2 Years	5 Years
Height	40	70	80
Breadth	60	80	85
Length	70	75	85

Davenport (1940) shows that, in relation to total face height, height of the nose increases most rapidly after birth, and height of the chin next. After 8 or 9 months postpartum he finds that the lower jaw builds up more rapidly than the upper until 2 or 3 years of age. Between 5 and 8 years growth is greater in the lower than in the upper facial measurements (Allen, 1948). From 6 to 12 years of age, according to Krogman (1939), growth occurs principally in height, least in length; from 12 to 20 years the increase is principally in length, and growth in breadth exceeds growth in height. Krogman states further that, in general, length and breadth growth precedes dentition and growth in height, and follows tooth eruption. Hellman (1933) notes that width is the largest dimension, height next, and length or depth least, and that between 5 and 22 years of age the largest dimension increases least and the smallest increases most. Hellman uses the gonion-menton diameter to measure length. He also comments that growth in height and length alternate and that increase in facial depth and width is more in the mandibular than in the zygomatic region and that increase in height is greatest in the ramus or posterior aspect of the lower jaw. Quoting Hellman (1933): "As children grow up . . . there is considerable loss of subcutaneous tissue and an increase

in bony increment beneath it. In females the bony increment seems insufficient to make up for attenuation of the skin" (p. 1123). As a result girls beyond 16 or 17 years show no increase or an actual decrease in facial dimension. In boys the bony growth is greater and the growth trend is progressive.

Davenport (1940) finds that the interpupillary distance increases absolutely as the head enlarges but decreases relatively to bizygomatic width. He also notes that chin height increases differently in different individuals, probably under the influence of special glandular activities, and that the other elements of facial height also vary with individual differences in tooth and sinus development. Todd (1935) notes that generally growth of the female practically ceases at puberty but the male continues to grow for several years following puberty and that hence the majority of women have relatively smaller jaw growth. Although, absolutely, female facial dimensions are all smaller than those of the male, Hellman (1933) reports that the female face is relatively longer and that the male face is relatively deeper.

Many studies have noted the sensitivity of the transverse diameters of the face to disturbances of growth in early childhood. Boas (1911) finds a change in bizygomatic width of children transferred from Europe to the Lower East Side in New York. Bakwin and Bakwin (1931c) find that, relative to body length, infants with such diseases as eczema, tetany, and acute intestinal intoxication are smaller in bimolar and bigonial face widths than healthy infants from the same social environment. Broadbent (1937) also finds face growth affected by nutritional disturbances in childhood. In any individual instance, however, disturbances of growth are not easy to identify except by repeated measurements. The disturbances are imposed on inherited growth tendencies, and to distinguish one from the other is not simple. It is not justifiable to conclude, for instance, that just because a child has a relatively narrow face he is suffering from malnutrition. With repeated measurements, abnormal growth trends can be recognized and, if it seems wise, remedial measures may be employed.

The relationship between facial growth and dentition is discussed under the section on dentition.

Skeletal Growth

Measurements of the external dimensions of the body, using skeletal landmarks, are gross measures of skeletal growth as far as size is concerned. Bone size and maturity, however, are not perfectly correlated. A child may be relatively small yet relatively mature; another child may be relatively large yet relatively immature. It is the differentiation and integration of the bony tissues which reveal the maturity aspect of growth. To understand the distinction it is necessary to review briefly the facts of bone growth.

Bony structure is originated by osteoblasts in either connective tissue or cartilage. The membrane bones of the face and cranium develop directly within the connective tissue, whereas the skeletal bones generally develop in the cartilage. Most bones, especially those formed in cartilage, have more than one center of ossification. In the human body there are over 800 centers of ossification, but half of them do not appear until after birth and centers continue to appear throughout the teens. Fusion begins as early as the eighth lunar month of fetal life and continues to middle age. At birth the infant has about 270 bones. The number increases to about 350 at puberty. This number increases, sometimes beyond the twenties, yet because of the fusion the final mature skeleton has only 206 bones (Arey, 1934). Certain long bones increase in size in the following manner: The cartilage increases in length, while progress in ossification takes place from the center, forming the diaphysis. Secondary ossification centers at the ends of the bone activate to form the epiphyses. When adult length is attained, cartilage proliferation ceases, but ossification continues, epiphyses and diaphysis unite and merge. Maturity is then reached (Arey, 1934, p. 339).

In 1896 the discovery of X-rays and their properties by Roentgen offered a means of studying the growth of the bony structure of the body in the living. Since then great advance has been made in standardization of the techniques of roentgenology and in the appraisal of bone growth. Hodges (1933) has published a most graphic and concise chart depicting the development of the human skeleton in general.

Psychologists have been most concerned with the hand-and-wrist ossification as an index of anatomical maturity. In normal development growth of the bones of the wrist and hand closely parallels general skeletal growth.. Pryor (1925) and others find sufficient lateral symmetry so that in general one hand only need be examined.

The literature up to 1935 is well reviewed by Flory (1936). The first methods of appraisal were naturally inspectional. Then, in an attempt at greater precision, measurement was resorted to. Baldwin, Busby, and Garside (1928) and others published figures for changes in area of the wrist bones from birth to 16 years and also computed anatomical indices which discounted for differences in wrist size. Flory (1936) and Todd (1937) each published an atlas of the osseous development of the hand with age standards. Wallis (1931) measured the width of the diaphysis and epiphysis of ulna and radius and used the ratio of the two measures as an index of anatomical maturity. Both the above-cited publications noted great variability differences in time of first ossification of the carpal bones and warned against using this manifestation as an index of maturity. It is the consensus that matching with a standard series is the most reliable and predictive method of assessing maturity of ossification. According to Todd (1937),

> Maturity determinations in the skeleton are successional changes in outline of shaft ends and in contour of epiphysial ossification centers which mark the progress in skeletal maturation to its final adult form. Dates of appearance of ossification centers, whether in epiphyses or in short bones of wrist and ankle, are not maturity determinators. Like the features of the growing ends they are related to vitamin D activity [p. 40].

It is the different vulnerability of the different centers which causes different patterns of development. More specifically, Todd states:

> The principle of assessment is therefore the utilization of the most advanced centers, not the average of all, as a guide to actual bodily maturity. . . . In the hand it results in reservations on carpal bones and epiphysis of radius, eliminates epiphysis of ulna, and places greatest reliance upon metacarpal and phalangeal epiphyses [p. 15].

Flory (1936) gives very convincing figures to show that a skeletal age rating based on "bone appearance and development, epiphyseal appearance and development, and general developmental characteristics" in terms of a standard age scale is decidedly superior to evaluation in terms of total carpal area or in terms of ossification ratio (p. 105). If the age at which ossification in the hand is complete is used

as a criterion of skeletal maturity, correlations with the criteria and carpal area are approximately .42 at 9 years, .48 at 11 years, .23 at 13 years, and .04 at 15 years, with PE's ranging between .06 and .08; correlations of ossification ratio (the area ossified in relation to a defined area of the wrist) with the criterion are approximately .52 at 9 years, .62 at 11 years, .40 at 13 years, and .33 at 15 years, with PE's between .04 and .08; correlations of skeletal months rating with the criterion are approximately .68 at 9 years, .75 at 11 years, .84 at 13 years, and .86 at 15 years, with a PE between .02 and .06. The greatest advantage of the skeletal age rating is at puberty. Skeletal age is comparable in many respects to mental age, and as such it is of value both in research and practice.

Todd (1937) gives 40 male standards and 35 female standards, spaced at not less than 6-month intervals, from birth up to 19 years. Flory's standards are 20 for each sex at yearly intervals from birth through 19 years. Both Flory and Todd accompany each standard with notes concerning the significance of its various characteristics.

Todd (1930) was enthusiastic in his evaluation of skeletal appraisal. He said:

> Wisely used record of differential maturity, combined with that of differential growth, throws light on vagaries of emotion, on problems of social adjustment, on failure in promotion and a host of problems that beset the teacher of the pre-adolescent grades 4–6.
> . . . Determinations of progress in physical maturation qualifying those of growth in stature and weight differentiate the outsized child, the subnormal child, the superior child of advanced physical development, the physical impress of malnutrition, of respiratory disorders such as hay fever and asthma, of the disharmonically progressing child who is a problem to himself

as well as to those responsible for his guidance and health.

Pyle and Menino (1939) have compared the Todd and Flory standards. They find a correlation of +.87 ±.03 between ratings based on the two standards for 50 unselected 3-year-old children. Skeletal age ratings according to Todd's atlas are more delayed in bone growth than according to Flory's atlas. The more frequent standard intervals of Todd's atlas are considered by Pyle and Menino "clearly advantageous for skeletal age assessments at all age levels below six years of age" (p. 34).

Pyle and others (1948) advocate indicating the degree of variability of skeletal ages of an individual rather than just a composite age. House (1950) found a normal variation of a year below and above the average value for 6-year-old children.

Although the appearance of ossification centers cannot be relied upon to judge maturity, they are sensitive indicators of nutrition. As such they must not be discarded in enthusiasm for the more stable growth phenomena. It is highly important from a psychological point of view to know of environmental disturbances. There is the possibility that they are related to fluctuations in behavior. Variability and probable age of appearance of the carpal bone and the radial and ulnar epiphyses as given by Flory (1936, p. 35) are reproduced in Table 3. The location of these bones in the wrist is shown graphically in Figure 7.

In spite of the general correlation between hand growth and body growth, Sontag, Snell, and Anderson (1939) claim that appraisal of the wrist and hand alone is not sufficient. Using roentgenograms of the left shoulder, elbow, wrist, hand, hip, knee, ankle, and foot, Sontag and his associates have established norms for thirteen

ages from 1 month to 5 years. Their method reduces technical and subjective errors to a minimum. Elgenmark (1946) also finds that one cannot draw definite conclusions regarding ossification generally on the basis of a few isolated areas.

Francis and Werle (1939) charted the appearance of ossification centers for the skeleton in general from birth to 5 years. They give percentages of incidences of ossification separately for the sexes at birth, at 3, 6, 9, and 12 months of age, and at 6-month intervals thereafter. Age standards based on the 80 percentile are given for each ossification center. They conclude that

The reason for variation in date of commencement of ossification and in its progressive development is not some obscure cause inherent in the germ plasm but the result of metabolic disturbance. . . . The centers of ossification appear in sheaves of miscellaneous composition but primary centers are more apt to be delayed in commencement of ossification than are centers appearing in epiphyses [p. 298].

Hill (1939) points out that

In fetal life the record of maturity must depend largely on the appearance of centers since subepiphyseal surfaces are not yet defined and therefore cannot assist identification. . . . [But he also notes that] Because of the protection against nutritional maladies afforded by prenatal existence it may be expected that variability in date of appearance will not be as marked as in infancy [p. 251].

Using crown-rump length as a basis for classification and the 50 percentile as standard, Hill has charted the ossification of bone in fetal life, giving percentages of incidences of ossification for the ten lunar month ages. He also gives a list of stand-

TABLE 3 *

Percentage of Children at Various Ages Whose Carpal Bones and Radial and Ulnar Epiphyses Have Appeared

(Based on more than 6500 records)

Bone	Sex	Age																	Probable Age of Appearance in Months
		B	1	2	3	4	5	6	7	8	9	10	11	12	13	14	15	16	
Capitate	F	8	96	100															6
	M	2	98	100															6
Hamate	F	8	96	100															6
	M	2	98	100															6
Radial epiphysis †	F	0	78	100															9
	M	0	34	98	100														15
Triquetrum	F	0	20	52	79	100													23
	M	0	22	50	57	84	92	93	100										24
Lunate	F	0	0	32	50	80	91	99	100										36
	M	0	8	18	36	64	64	87	98	99	100								42
Naviculare	F	0	0	0	12	30	61	95	99	100									56
	M	0	0	0	4	17	34	51	75	92	99	100							72
M. majus	F	0	0	4	18	53	74	94	99	100									50
	M	0	0	0	4	14	33	51	72	88	96	97	100						72
M. minus	F	0	0	0	15	40	65	95	100										53
	M	0	0	0	4	9	22	48	81	95	98	99	100						73
Ulnar epiphysis †	F	0	0	0	0	0	16	60	99	100									68
	M	0	0	0	0	0	7	27	59	82	98	100							80
Pisiforme	F	0	0	0	0	0	0	0	1	19	50	79	96	100					108
	M	0	0	0	0	0	0	0	0	2	6	22	28	66	95	99	99	100	140

* From Flory (1936, p. 35).

† The radial and ulnar epiphyses have been included here because Carter used both in determining the ossification ratio,

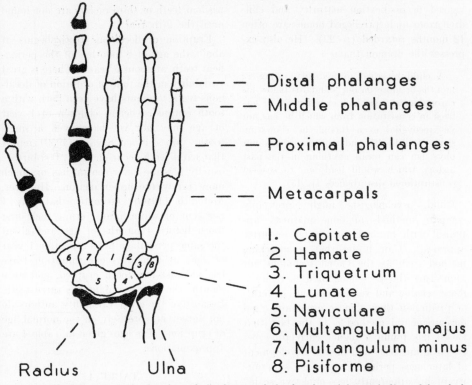

– – – Distal phalanges

– – – Middle phalanges

– – – Proximal phalanges

– – – Metacarpals

1. Capitate
2. Hamate
3. Triquetrum
4 Lunate
5. Naviculare
6. Multangulum majus
7. Multangulum minus
8. Pisiforme

Radius   Ulna

FIGURE 7.   Diagrammatic drawing of the bones of the hand; epiphyses indicated by dark areas. (Adapted from H. Gray, in *Anatomy of the Human Body*. 21st ed., revised by W. H. Lewis. Philadelphia: Lea and Febiger, 1924, p. 230.)

ard degrees of ossification for these ages, basing his standard on the 50 percentile.

Sex Differences in Skeletal Growth

There is a well-defined sex difference in skeletal maturity which according to Flory's data gradually increases with age. There is a readily perceptible difference at birth, practically a year's difference at beginning elementary school age, and approximately a 2-year difference at high school entrance. This is consistent with sex differences in other aspects of physical growth. Female children, although smaller than male children of the same chrono-

logical age, are more mature and reach puberty earlier.

Hereditary factors may play a certain part in determining ossification rate. The correlation between deviations from the norm in ossification ratios are for brothers .62, for sisters .27, and for brothers and sisters .39 (Flory, 1936). Minor fluctuations in ossification rate tend to correct themselves in a year or two and should not be regarded too seriously. Variability in ossification maturity of children in general increases up to late adolescence, after which it decreases to the adult variability. Todd (1937) states that children from privileged homes are approximately 12 months advanced in ossification maturity and children from underprivileged homes are often 12 months retarded (p. 22). He also expresses the opinion that:

A child retarded in maturity rating 12 months or more on our standards below his chronological age has experienced a setback in constitution from which he has not yet recovered even though he shows no signs of ill-health and neither parents nor physician can recall anything in the past history which would lead one to suspect constitutional disturbances [p. 15].

Child psychologists might profitably compare methods of bone maturity appraisal with methods of mental maturity appraisal. Can it be that a matching method such as the Gesell technique for appraising the preschool child is really a more reliable and valid technique in terms of prediction than a more exact and rigid measuremental method? Is the fact that Gesell has found a higher correlation between infant tests and mental development at later ages perhaps due to the superiority of his apparently less objective scale? Certainly the findings in the realm of skeletal growth should give child psychologists cause to reconsider more carefully the problem of behavior-maturity appraisal.

Dentition

The skeleton differentiates from the mesoderm, whereas the teeth develop from both mesoderm and ectoderm: enamel from the ectoderm and dentin; and dentine, pulp, and cement from the mesoderm. Teeth, hair, and nails are similar in that they all develop from skin tissue. Deciduous teeth are formed early in fetal life. The twenty enamel organs and their associated dental papilla of the deciduous teeth are present in the 10-week fetus; those for permanent molars are present at birth; those for the second molars at 6 months; those for the

wisdom teeth or third molars are not found until the fifth year.

Eruption of deciduous teeth begins at about the age of 6 months; of the permanent teeth, at about 6 years. There is great variability in the time of eruption of deciduous teeth. Infants have been born with a tooth erupted, whereas children of 1 year of age may not yet have even a single tooth. Massler and Savara (1950) report that natal teeth occur once in 2,000 births; usually it is the lower central incisor, much more rarely the upper incisor. However, Meredith (1946b) estimates that only 1 per cent of white infants erupt their first tooth before 4 months of age and about the same percentage not until after 1 year of age; at 6 months one infant in three has at least one tooth erupted, and at 9 months the average infant has three teeth. Because of the great variability authors do not agree very precisely on the normal age of eruption. The ages given in Table 4 are approximations.

TABLE 4

DECIDUOUS TEETH: AGE OF ERUPTING AND SHEDDING *

Tooth	Age of Erupting (Months)	Age of Shedding (Years)
Median incisor	6–8	7
Lateral incisor	7–10	8
Canine	17–20	12
First molar	12–16	10
Second molar	18–24	11–12

* Modified from Arey (1934).

Teeth in the lower jaw usually erupt before the corresponding teeth in the upper jaw (Doering and Allen, 1942). There are very few data in the literature regarding sex differences in eruption ages for deciduous teeth. Study of the available data (Meredith, 1946) suggests that there is no appreciable difference in the time of eruption of the first tooth but that, between 9 months and 2 years of age, males are more advanced than females.

Girls, however, are more precocious in shedding their deciduous teeth than boys, perhaps because the permanent dentition of females is more advanced at each age than the permanent dentition of males. Klein, Palmer, and Kramer (1937) give figures based on 4416 boys and girls at Hagerstown, Maryland, which are reproduced in Table 5.

TABLE 5

SHEDDING OF TEETH: NUMBER OF DECIDUOUS TEETH PRESENT

Age in years	6½	8½	10½	12½
Boys: Average number	16.9	11.4	6.0	1.3
Girls: Average number	16.0	10.6	4.3	0.8

Psychologists have been particularly concerned with the effect of thumb sucking on the primary teeth and the dental arch. Lewis (1937), from a study of models made yearly, finds that the type of thumb sucking most damaging to the shape of the arch is that in which the child holds the volar surface toward the palate. A child who persisted in thumb sucking until 3 years old, with resulting deformity, experienced a full correction of the deformity a year and a half after the habit was broken. Another child who broke the habit of sucking the right thumb at 9½ years showed subsequent improvement of the displacement and open bite. Cases where the habit was continued showed no self-correction. There were instances of thumb sucking with no resulting deformity; all such cases broke the habit between the first and second year.

Not only thumb sucking but also tongue pressures are considered important in the development of occlusion (Swinehart, 1950).

The eruption of permanent teeth begins with the eruption of the 6-year molar. The figures given by Klein, Palmer, and Kramer (1937) (Table 6) are derived from the per-

TABLE 6

AVERAGE ERUPTION AGE FOR THE PERMANENT TEETH *

Tooth	Upper Jaw (Years)		Lower Jaw (Years)	
	Boys	Girls	Boys	Girls
Central incisor	7.49	7.20	6.50	6.19
Lateral incisor	8.62	8.15	7.64	7.31
Canine	11.80	11.05	10.70	9.85
First premolar	10.42	10.00	10.75	10.20
Second premolar	11.18	10.82	11.45	11.00
First molar	6.64	6.54	6.44	6.12
Second molar	12.70	12.40	12.20	11.90

* Standard deviations range between 0.70 and 1.77.

centage of children at successive ages who have the designated teeth erupted at the time of examination.

With the exception of the first and second premolars, the teeth of the lower jaw erupt before the corresponding teeth of the upper jaw.

Hellman (1943) points out that there are two active periods of dentition with respect to the permanent teeth, separated by an interval of rest. The period of rest is from about 7 years 9 months to 10 years in females, and from about 8 years 4 months to 11 years in males.

The White House Conference data (1932, 1933) complete the story by giving the average age at which the third molars are beginning to erupt as follows: for boys, 18.59 years; for girls, 20.10 years.

Thus, with respect to permanent teeth, females are more precocious at least up to the teen ages, but by the end of the teens males are again more precocious.

The use of dental age has been suggested as an indication of anatomical maturity (Bean, 1914; Cattell, 1928). The wide variability in time of eruption of the teeth makes an assessment on that basis undesirable. Clinically, however, it is most important to include such an assessment as part of the total examination. As Krogman (1950) points out, problems in dental growth are evidence of more general organic problems.

There are certain ages when the teeth are particularly susceptible to metabolic and cellular disturbances, namely, the neonatal period, about 10 months of age, about 2½ years, and about 5 years of age (Massler, Schour, and Ponchar, 1941).

Naturally there is an intimate relationship between the growth of the face and dentition. The White House Conference (1932, 1933) summarizes three corresponding periods of development as follows:

> The first five years of life, during which the deciduous dentition is completed, and the most intensive antero-posterior growth of the face is taking place. The 10 years following, from 5 to 15, during which the deciduous dentition is shed, all but the third molars are erupted, and the most intensive lateral and vertical growth of the face is taking place. The 5 years following, from 15 to 20, during which the third molars erupt and residual vertical growth is still taking place in females and more intensive growth in males [Part 2, p. 143].

With the eruption and shedding of the first 20 teeth and the eruption of the 32 permanent teeth, together with the accompanying growth of the jaw, there are bound to be associated changes in occlusion. Hellman (1932, 1933) notes that the percentage of normal occlusion in a group of children drops from 70 per cent at 4 years to 22 per cent at 9 years and then gradually increases with age. However, some types of malocclusion are not self-corrective and need orthodontic care.

Normal growth changes in dentition bring many psychological problems. A few examples may be cited. If an infant is being nursed at the age when his first tooth erupts, he may hurt his mother's breast. Her reaction and his are important in establishing their relationship. Similar problems are encountered in the bottle-fed infant. In the older child, teeth used to bite others can become effective though undesirable weapons. If an infant is temporarily indisposed by the eruption of teeth and loses his appetite, this may cause maternal concern because he does not eat. Insistence on his eating may start feeding problems.

When teeth are lost, particularly front teeth, speech becomes difficult; children may be taunted. "All I want for Christmas is my two front teeth" may not be amusing to the 7-year-old! Malocclusion, likewise, is a source of psychological problems due either to unesthetic and malfunctioning teeth or to the uncomfortable and disfiguring corrective braces.

Although these problems are extrinsic to dental growth, they can be avoided or corrected only when normal dental growth changes are understood and considered. The psychological significance of the mouth as a medium of satisfying inner drives and of the teeth as a medium of expressing tension and aggression is surely of sufficient importance to warrant close study of their physical growth by the psychologist.

Conclusion

The physical growth changes discussed in this chapter relate principally to morphological changes which are the outward manifestations of more fundamental growth phenomena. This is a reflection of research interests, knowledge, available techniques for measurement, and sources for research. There is a growing interest in the more physiological, the biochemical, and the electropotential changes with age (Jones, 1947; Sontag, 1947; Clark, 1948). These aspects of growth are more intimately related to functional changes and thence to behavior phenomena. Studied in this way, physical characteristics become as integral a part of an individual's personality as behavior traits. Then the problem of mental and physical relationships changes from an interest in a one-to-one relationship to an interest in a more analytic growth association.

Bibliography

Allen, I. 1948. Facial growth in children of five to eight years of age. Human Biol., 20, 109–145.

Ames, V. C., and C. D. Flory. 1944. Physical growth from birth to maturity. Rev. Educ. Res., 14, 427–437.

Anderson, J. E. 1942. The contribution of child development to psychology. J. Consult. Psychol., 6, 128–134.

Appleton, V. B. 1927. Growth of Chinese children in Hawaii and in China. Amer. J. Phys. Anthrop., 10, 237–252.

Arey, L. B. 1934. Developmental anatomy. Philadelphia: Saunders.

Ashby, W. R., and R. M. Stewart. 1933. Size in mental deficiency. J. Neurol. Psychopath., 13, 303–329.

Bakwin, H. 1929. The sex factor in infant mortality. Human Biol., 1, 90–116.

——. 1942. Loneliness in infants. Amer. J. Dis. Child., 63, 30–40.

Bakwin, H., and R. M. Bakwin. 1931a. Body build in infants: I. The technique of measuring the external dimensions of the body in infants. J. Clin. Invest., 10, 369–375.

——. 1931b. Body build in infants: II. The proportions of the external dimensions of the healthy infant during the first year of life. J. Clin. Invest., 10, 377–394.

——. 1931c. Body build in infants: III. Body build in disease. J. Clin. Invest., 10, 395–403.

——. 1934a. Body build in infants: V. Anthropometry in the newborn. Human Biol., 6, 612–626.

——. 1934b. External dimensions of the newborn. Amer. J. Dis. Child., 48, 1234–1236.

——. 1936. Growth of thirty-two external dimensions during the first year of life. J. Pediat., 8, 177–183.

——. 1939. Body build in infants: IX. Body build in eczema. Human Biol., 11, 269–276.

Bakwin, H., R. M. Bakwin, and L. Milgram. 1934. Body build in infants: IV. Influence of retarded growth. Amer. J. Dis. Child., 48, 1030–1040.

Bakwin, H., and T. W. Patrick, Jr. 1944. The weight of Negro infants. J. Pediat., 24, 405–407.

Baldwin, B. T. 1921. The physical growth of children from birth to maturity. Univ. Iowa Stud. Child Welfare, 1, No. 1.

——. 1925. Weight-height-age standards in metric units for American-born children. Amer. J. Phys. Anthrop., 8, 1–10.

——. 1928. Breathing capacity according to height and age of American-born boys and girls of school age. Amer. J. Phys. Anthrop., 12, 257–267.

Baldwin, B. T., L. M. Busby, and H. Garside. 1928. Anatomic growth of children: A study of some bones of the hand, wrist, and lower forearm by means of roentgenograms. Univ. Iowa Stud. Child Welfare, 4, No. 1.

Baldwin, B. T., T. D. Wood, and R. M. Woodbury. 1923. Weight-height-age tables. Supplement to July issue Mother and Child. Washington: American Child Health Association.

Bardeen, C. R. 1920. The height-weight index of build in relation to linear and volumetric proportions and surface-area of the body during post-natal development. Contr. Embryol., Carnegie Inst. Wash., No. 46, 483–554.

Baum, M. P., and V. S. Vickers. 1941. Anthropometric and orthopedic examinations. Child Develpm., 12, 339–345.

Bayer, L. M. 1940a. Build variations in adolescent girls. J. Pediat., 17, 331–344.

——. 1940b. Weight and menses in adolescent girls with special reference to build. J. Pediat., 17, 345–354.

Bayer, L. M., and N. Bayley. 1947. Directions for measures and radiographs used in predicting height. Child Develpm., 18, 85–87.

Bayley, N. 1936. Growth changes in the cephalic index during the first five years of life. Human Biol., 8, 1–18.

——. 1943a. Skeletal maturing in adolescence as a basis for determining percentage of completed growth. Child Develpm., 14, 1–46.

——. 1943b. Size and body build of adolescents in relation to rate of skeletal maturing. Child Develpm., 14, 47–89.

——. 1946. Tables for predicting adult height from skeletal age and present height. J. Pediat., 28, 49–64.

——. 1951. Some psychological correlates of somatic androgyny. Child Develpm., 22, 47–60.

Bayley, N., and L. M. Bayer. 1946. The assessment of somatic androgyny. Amer. J. Phys. Anthrop., 4 n.s., 433–461.

Bayley, N., and F. C. Davis. 1935. Growth changes in bodily size and proportions during the first three years: A developmental study of sixty-one children by repeated measurements. Biometrika, 27, 26–87.

Bean, R. B. 1914. The eruption of the teeth as a physiological standard for testing development. Ped. Sem., 21, 596–614.

Bean, R. B. 1926. Human types. *Quart. Rev. Biol.,* *1*, 360–392.

Binet, A. 1900. Recherches complémentaires de céphalométrie sur 100 enfants d'intelligence inégale, choisis, dans les écoles primaires du départment de Seine et Marne. *Année psychol., 7,* 375–428.

——. 1910. Les signes physiques de l'intelligence chez les enfants. *Année psychol., 16,* 1–30.

Binet, A., and T. Simon. 1914. *Mentally defective children.* (Trans.) New York: Longmans, Green.

Boas, F. 1911. *Changes in bodily form of descendants of immigrants.* (*U. S. Senate Document 208.*). Washington, D. C.: Government Printing Office.

——. 1927. The eruption of deciduous teeth among Hebrew infants. *J. Dent. Res., 7,* 245–253.

——. 1930. Observations on the growth of children. *Science, 72,* 44–48.

——. 1932. Studies in growth. *Human Biol., 4,* 307–350.

Boas, F., and C. Wissler. 1906. Statistics of Growth. *Rep. U. S. Comm. Educ. for 1904, 1,* 25–132.

Boyd, E. 1929. The experimental error in measuring the growing human body. *Amer. J. Phys. Anthrop., 13,* 389–432.

——. 1935. Growth of the surface area of the human body. *Inst. Child Welfare Monogr. Ser.,* No. 10. Minneapolis: University of Minnesota Press. Pp. 145.

——. 1941. *Outline of physical growth and development.* Minneapolis: Burgess.

Boyd, J. D. 1945. Clinical appraisal of infant's head size. *Amer. J. Dis. Child., 69,* 71–82.

——. 1948. Graphic portrayal of infants' growth with consideration of head size. *Amer. J. Dis. Child., 76,* 53–59.

Boynton, B. 1936. The physical growth of girls: A study of the rhythm of physical growth from anthropometric measurements on girls between birth and eighteen years. *Univ. Iowa Stud. Child Welfare, 12,* No. 4. Pp. 105.

Brenton, H. 1922. Climate and race as factors influencing the weight of the newborn. *Amer. J. Phys. Anthrop., 5,* 237–249.

Broadbent, B. H. 1937. The face of the normal child. Bolton standards and technique in orthodontic practice. *Angle Orthod., 7,* 183–208.

Bronstein, I. R., S. Wexler, A. W. Brown, and L. J. Halpern. 1942. Obesity in childhood. *Amer. J. Dis. Child., 63,* 238–251.

Brooks, F. D. 1933. Mental and physical development in adolescence. *Rev. Educ. Res., 3,* 108–129.

Bruch, H. Studies in obesity in childhood. I. 1939. Physical growth and development of obese children. *Amer. J. Dis. Child., 58,* 457–484. III. 1940. Physiologic and psychologic aspects of the food intake of obese children. *Amer. J. Dis. Child., 59,* 739–781.

——. 1941a. Obesity in childhood and personality development. *Amer. Orthopsychiat., 11,* 467–474.

——. 1941b. Obesity in relation to puberty. *J. Pediat., 19,* 365–375.

Bruch, H., and G. V. Touraine. 1941. The family frame of obese children. *Psychosom. Med., 2,* 141–206.

Buffon, Count de. 1837. Sur l'accroissement successif des enfants; Guéneau de Montbeillard mesure de 1759 à 1776. In *Œuvres complètes,* Vol. III, pp. 174–176. Paris: Furne and Pie.

Burt, C. 1944. The factorial study of physical types. *Man, 44,* 82–86.

Camp, J. D., and E. I. L. Cilley. 1931. Diagrammatic chart showing time of appearance of the various centers of ossification and period of union. *Amer. J. Roentg., 26,* No. 6, p. 105.

Carter, H. D., and R. H. Krause. 1936. Physical proportions of the human infant. *Child Develpm., 7,* 60–68.

Cates, H. A., and J. C. Goodwin. 1936. The twelve-day-old baby. *Human Biol., 8,* 433–450.

Cattell, P. 1928. Dentition as a measure of maturity. *Monogr. Harv. Stud. Educ. Psychol.* Pp. viii + 91.

Children's Bureau. 1927. References on the physical growth and development of the normal child. *U. S. Child. Bur. Publ.,* No. 179.

Christie, A. 1949. Prevalence and distribution of ossification centers in the newborn infant. *Amer. J. Dis. Child., 77,* 355–361.

Christie, A. U., E. C. Dunham, R. M. Jenss, and A. L. Dippel. 1941. Development of the center for the cuboid bone in newborn infants. *Amer. J. Dis. Child., 61,* 471–482.

Clark, L. C., Jr. 1948. The chemistry of human behavior. *Amer. J. Orthopsychiat., 18,* 140–152.

Clayton, M. M. 1942. A study of the McCloy method for determining normal weight. *Child Develpm., 13,* 215–226.

Cold Spring Harbor, New York, Biological Laboratory. 1934. *Symposium on quantitative biology.* Vol. II.

Cole, L. 1948. *Psychology of adolescence.* 3d ed. New York: Rinehart.

Courtis, S. A. 1932. *The measurement of growth.* Ann Arbor: Brumfield and Brumfield.

——. 1937. What is a growth cycle? *Growth, 1,* 155–174.

Crampton, C. W. 1908. Physiological age: A fundamental principle. *Phys. Educ. Rev., 13,* 141–151; 214–227.

Daniels, A. L., M. K. Hutton, and B. Neil. 1938. Relation of the creatinine-height coefficient to various indexes of nutrition. *Amer. J. Dis. Child., 55,* 532–543.

Davenport, C. B. 1923. Body build and its inheritance. *Carnegie Inst. Wash. Publ.,* No. 329.

——. 1926a. Human metamorphosis. *Amer. J. Phys. Anthrop., 9,* 205–232.

——. 1926b. Human growth curve. *J. Gen. Physiol., 10,* 205–216.

——. 1927. *Guide to anthropometry and anthroposcopy.* Baltimore: Waverly Press.

——. 1934. Critique of curves of growth and of relative growth. *Cold Spring Harbor Symposia Quant. Biol., 2,* 203–208.

——. 1937. Some principles of anthropometry. *Amer. J. Phys. Anthrop., 23,* 91–99.

——. 1938. Bodily growth of babies during the first postnatal year. *Contr. Embryol., Carnegie Inst. Wash.,* No. 169.

Davenport, C. B. 1940. Post-natal development of the head. *Proc. Amer. Phil. Soc., 83.*

——. 1944. Postnatal development of the human extremities. *Proc. Amer. Phil. Soc., 88,* 375–455.

Davenport, C. B., and W. Drager. 1936. Growth curve of infants. *Proc. Nat. Acad. Sci. Wash., 22,* 639–645.

Dawson, H. L., and G. D. Stoddard. 1933. Physical growth from birth to puberty. *Rev. Educ. Res., 3,* 130–149.

Dearborn, W. F., and J. W. M. Rothney. 1938. Basing weight standards upon linear bodily dimensions. *Growth, 2,* 197–212.

Dearborn, W. F., J. W. M. Rothney, and F. K. Shuttleworth. 1938. Data on the growth of public school children. *Monogr. Soc. Res. Child Develpm., 3,* No. 1. Pp. 136.

Dodge, C. T. J. 1927. Weight of colored infants. *Amer. J. Phys. Anthrop., 10,* 337–345.

Doering, C. W., and M. F. Allen. 1942. Data on eruption and caries of the deciduous teeth. *Child Develpm., 13,* 113–129.

Doll, E. A. 1916. *Anthropometry as an aid to mental diagnosis.* Vineland, N. J.: Training School.

Duggins, O. H., and M. Trotter. 1950. Age changes in hair from birth to maturity: II. Medulation in hair of children. *Amer. J. Phys. Anthrop., 8,* 399–415.

Dunham, E. C., R. M. Jenss, and A. U. Christie. 1939. A consideration of race and sex in relation to the growth and development of infants. *J. Pediat., 14,* 156–160.

Dupertuis, C. W., and J. M. Tanner. 1951. The pose of the subject for photogrammetric anthropometry, with especial reference to somatotyping. *Amer. J. Phys. Anthrop., 8,* 27–47.

Elgenmark, O. 1946. The normal development of the ossific centers during infancy and childhood: A clinical, roentgenologic, and statistical study. *Acta Paediat., 33,* 1–79.

Englebach, W. 1932. *Endocrine medicine: I. General considerations.* Springfield, Ill.: Thomas.

Fernald, W. E., and E. E. Southard. 1921. Waverly researches in the pathology of the feebleminded. Cases XI–XX. *Mem. Amer. Acad. Arts Sci.,* pp. 133–207. 32 plates.

Fernald, W. E., and E. E. Southard, with the collaboration of A. E. Taft. 1918. Waverly researches in the pathology of the feebleminded. Cases I–X. *Mem. Amer. Acad. Arts Sci.,* pp. 20–128. 20 plates.

Fleming, R. M. 1933. *A study of growth and development.* London: Medical Research Council.

Flory, C. D. 1936. Osseous development in the hand as an index of skeletal development. *Monogr. Soc. Res. Child Develpm., 1,* No. 3. Pp. 141.

Francis, C. C. 1939. Growth of the human tibia. *Amer. J. Phys. Anthrop., 25,* 323–331.

Francis, C. C., and P. P. Werle. 1939. The appearance of centers of ossification from birth to 5 years. *Amer. J. Phys. Anthrop., 24,* 273–300.

Franzen, R. 1929. *Physical measures of growth and nutrition.* New York: American Child Health Association.

Franzen, R., and G. T. Palmer. 1934. *The A C H index of nutritional status.* New York: American Child Health Association.

Freeman, R. G., Jr. 1933. Skeletenwicklung und Wachstum im Alter von 2 bis 18 Monaten, von 2 bis 7½ Jahren und von 8 bis 14½ Jahren. *Anthrop. Anz., 10,* 185–208.

Freeman, R. G., Jr., and V. Platt. 1932. Skeletentwicklung und Wachstum der Säuglinge von der Geburt bis zu einem Monat. *Anthrop. Anz., 9,* 68–78.

Gesell, A., and H. Thompson. 1938. *The psychology of early growth.* New York: Macmillan.

Gilbert, J. H. 1895. Researches on the mental and physical development of school children. *Stud. Yale Psychol. Lab., 2,* 40–100.

——. 1897. Researches on school children and college students. *Univ. Iowa Stud. Psychol., 1,* 1–39.

Gilbert, M. S. 1938. *Biography of the unborn.* Baltimore: Williams and Wilkins.

Goddard, H. H. 1912. The height and weight of feebleminded children in American institutions. *J. Nerv. Ment. Dis., 39,* 217–235.

Godin, P. 1913. *La croissance pendant l'âge scolaire.* Neuchâtel: Delachaux et Niestle.

——. 1935. *Recherches anthropometriques sur la croissance des diverses parties du corps.* Paris: Legrand.

Goldstein, M. S. 1936. Changes in dimensions and form of the face and head with age. *Amer. J. Phys. Anthrop., 22,* 37–89.

——. 1939. Development of the head in the same individuals. *Human Biol., 11,* 195–219.

——. 1947. Infants of Mexican descent: I. Physical status of neonates. *Child Develpm., 18,* 3–10.

Graves, W. W. 1921. The types of scapulae: A comparative study of some correlated characters in human scapulae. *Amer. J. Phys. Anthrop., 4,* 111–128.

Gray, H. 1924. *Anatomy of the human body.* (21st ed., rev. by W. H. Lewis.) Philadelphia: Lea and Febiger.

Gray, H., and J. G. Ayres. 1931. *Growth in private school children.* Chicago: University of Chicago Press.

Greulich, W. W. 1931. The sex ratio among human still births. *Science, 75,* 53–54.

Greulich, W. W., H. G. Day, S. E. Lachman, J. B. Wolfe, and F. K. Shuttleworth. 1938. A handbook of methods for the study of adolescent children. *Monogr. Soc. Res. Child Develpm., 3,* No. 2. Pp. xvii + 406.

Greulich, W. W., R. I. Dorfman, H. R. Catchpole, C. I. Solomon, and C. S. Culotta. 1942. Somatic and endocrine studies of puberal and adolescent boys. *Monogr. Soc. Res. Child Develpm., 7,* No. 3. Pp. 65 + 9 plates.

Greulich, W. W., and H. Thoms. 1944. The growth and development of the pelvis of individual girls during and after puberty. *Yale J. Biol. Med., 17,* 91–97.

Hall, W. S. 1896. The first five hundred days of a child's life. *Child Study Mon., 2,* Nos. 6 and 7, pp. 332–342; 394–407.

Hamilton, J. A. 1936. Intelligence and the human brain. *Psychol. Rev., 43,* 308–321.

Hammett, F. S. 1936. *The nature of growth.* Lancaster, Pa.: Science Press.
——. 1937. Nutrition vs. growth. *Science, 86,* 560–561.
Hejinian, L., and E. Hatt. 1929. The stem-length: recumbent-length ratio as an index of body type in young children. *Amer. J. Phys. Anthrop., 13,* 287–307.
Hellman, M. 1932. Malocclusion as a phase of growth. *Mouth Health Quart., 1,* No. 2, pp. 20–21.
——. 1933. Growth of the face and occlusion of the teeth in relation to orthodontic treatment. *Int. J. Orthod., Oral Surg. and Radiog., 19,* 1116–1146.
——. 1943. The phase of development concerned with erupting the permanent teeth. *Amer. J. Orthod. Oral Surg., 29,* 507–526.
Hess, J. H., G. J. Mohr, and P. E. Bartelme. 1934. *The physical and mental growth of prematurely born children.* Chicago: University of Chicago Press.
Hill, A. H. 1939. Fetal age assessment by centers of ossification. *Amer. J. Phys. Anthrop., 24,* 251–272.
Hodges, P. C. 1933. *Development of the human skeleton: I. Trunk and extremities.* Chicago: University of Chicago Press.
Holmes, S. J., and V. P. Mentzer. 1931. Changes in the sex ratio in infant mortality according to age. *Human Biol., 3,* 560–575.
House, R. W. 1950. A summary of forty-nine radiologists' opinions of the skeletal age limits of apparently normal six-year-old children. *Amer. J. Roentg. Radium Therapy, 64,* 442–445.
Howells, W. W. 1948. Birth order and body size. *Amer. J. Phys. Anthrop., 6,* 449–460.
Hrdlička, A. 1939. *Practical anthropometry.* (2d ed.) Philadelphia: Wistar Institute of Anatomy and Biology.
Hunt, E. E. 1949. A note on growth, somatotyping, and temperament. *Amer. J. Phys. Anthrop., 7,* 79–89.
Hurme, V. O. 1948. Standard variation in the eruption of the first six permanent teeth. *Child Develpm., 19,* 213–231.
Huxley, J. S. 1932. *Problems of relative growth.* London: Dial Press.
Jackson, C. M. 1914. Morphogenesis, in *Morris' human anatomy.* (5th ed.) Philadelphia: Blakiston.
——. 1928. Some aspects of form and growth. In W. J. Robbins, S. Brody, A. G. Hogan, C. M. Jackson, and C. W. Green, *Growth,* pp. 111–140. New Haven: Yale University Press.
——. 1930. Normal and abnormal human types. In J. A. Harris, C. M. Jackson, D. G. Paterson, and R. E. Scammon, *The measurement of man,* pp. 79–113. Minneapolis: University of Minnesota Press.
Jenss, R. M., and N. Bayley. 1937. A mathematical method for studying the growth of a child. *Human Biol., 9,* 556–563.
Johnson, B. J. 1925. *Mental growth of children in relation to the rate of growth in bodily development.* New York: Dutton.
Jones, H. E. 1933. Relationships in physical and mental development. *Rev. Educ. Res., 3,* 150–162.

Jones, H. E. 1936. Relationships in physical and mental development. *Rev. Educ. Res., 4,* 102–123.
——. 1939. Relationships in physical and mental development. *Rev.. Educ. Res., 9,* 91–102.
——. 1947. The relationship of strength to physique. *Amer. J. Phys. Anthrop., 5* n.s., 29–40.
Jones, M. C., and N. Bayley. 1950. Physical maturing among boys as related to behavior. *J. Educ. Psychol., 41,* 129–148.
Kelly, H. J. 1937. Anatomic age and its relation to stature. *Univ. Iowa Stud. Child Welfare, 12,* No. 5. Pp. 38.
Kjölseth, M. 1913. Untersuchungen über die Reifezeichen des neugeborenen Kindes. *Mschr. Geburtsh Gynäk., 38,* 216–298.
Klein, H., C. E. Palmer, and J. W. Knutson. 1938. Studies on dental caries: I. Dental status and dental needs of elementary school children. *Publ. Health Rep., Wash., 53,* 751–765.
Klein, H., C. E. Palmer, and M. Kramer. 1937. Studies on dental caries: II. The use of the normal probability curve for expressing the age distribution of eruption of the permanent teeth. *Growth, 1,* 385–394.
Knott, V. B. 1941. Physical measurement of young children: A study of anthropometric reliabilities for children three to six years of age. *Univ. Iowa Stud. Child Welfare, 18,* No. 3. Pp. 99.
Kretschmer, E. 1925. *Physique and character.* (Trans. by W. J. H. Sprout.) New York: Harcourt, Brace; London: Kegan Paul.
Krogman, W. M. 1939. Facing facts of face growth. *Amer. J. Orthod. Oral Surg., 25,* 724–731.
——. 1940. Trend in the study of physical growth in children. *Child Develpm., 11,* 279–284.
——. 1941a. *Growth of man. Tabulae Biologicae.* Den Haag: Junk.
——. 1941b. *Bibliography of human morphology, 1914–1939.* Chicago: University of Chicago Press.
——. 1948. A handbook of the measurement and interpretation of height and weight in the growing child. *Monogr. Soc. Res. Child Develpm.,* No. 48. Pp. ix + 66.
——. 1950. The growth of the "whole child" in relation to dental problems. *J. Oral Surg., Oral Med., Oral Path., 3,* 427–445.
——. 1951. Abstract 738. *Child Develpm. Abstr. Bibliog., 25,* p. 209.
Lewis, S. J. 1937. The effect of thumb and finger sucking on the primary teeth and dental arches. *Child Develpm., 8,* 93–98.
Lincoln, E. A. 1930. The reliability of anthropometric measurements. *J. Genet. Psychol., 38,* 445–450.
Mann, A. W., S. Dreizen, S. I. Pyle, and T. Spies. 1948. The red graph and the Wetzel grid as methods of determining the symmetry of status and progress during growth. *J. Pediat., 32,* 137–150.
Maresh, M. M. 1943. Growth of major long bones in healthy children. A preliminary report on successive roentgenograms of the extremities from early infancy to twelve years of age. *Amer. J. Dis. Child., 66,* 227–257.

Maresh, M. M., and J. Deming. 1939. The growth of the long bones in 80 infants. Roentgenograms versus anthropometry. *Child Develpm.*, *10*, 91–106.

Marshall, E. I. 1936. A multiple factor study of eighteen authropometric measurements of Iowa City boys aged nine days to six years. *J. Exp. Educ.*, *5*, 212–228.

——. 1937. A review of American research on seasonal variation in stature and body weight. *J. Pediat.*, *10*, 819–831.

Martin, R. 1928. *Lehrbuch der Anthropologie:* Vol. I, *Somotologie;* Vol. II, *Kraniologie, Osteologie;* Vol. III, *Bibliographie, Literaturverzeichnis, Sachregister, Autorenregister.* Jena: Fischer.

Massler, M. 1945. Calculation of normal weight. *Child Develpm.*, *16*, 111–118.

Massler, M., and B. S. Savara. 1950. Natal and neonatal teeth. A review of twenty-four cases reported in the literature. *J. Pediat.*, *36*, 349–359.

Massler, M., I. Schour, and H. G. Poncher. 1941. Developmental patterns of the child as reflected in the calcification pattern of the teeth. *Amer. J. Dis. Child.*, *62*, 33–67.

Massler, M., and T. Suher. 1951. Calculation of "normal" weight in children (by means of normograms based on selected anthropometric measurements). *Child Develpm.*, *22*, 75–94.

McCloy, C. H. 1936. Appraising physical status: The selection of measurements. *Univ. Iowa Stud. Child Welfare*, *12*, No. 2. Pp. 126.

——. 1938. Appraising physical status: Methods and norms. *Univ. Iowa Stud. Child Welfare*, *15*, No. 2. Pp. 260.

——. 1940. An analysis for multiple factors of physical growth at different age levels. *Child Develpm.*, *11*, 249–277.

McHale, K. 1926. Comparative psychology and hygiene of the over-weight child. *Teach. Coll. Contr. Educ.*, No. 221.

Medawar, P. B. 1944. The shape of the human being as a function of time. *Proc. Roy. Soc. London*, No. 867, 133–141.

Meredith, H. V. 1935. The rhythm of physical growth: A study of eighteen anthropometric measurements on Iowa City white males ranging in age between birth and eighteen years. *Univ. Iowa Stud. Child Welfare*, *11*, No. 3. Pp. 128.

——. 1936a. Physical growth of white children: A review of American research prior to 1900. *Monogr. Soc. Res. Child Develpm.*, *1*, No. 2. Pp. 83.

——. 1936b. The reliability of anthropometric measurements taken on eight- and nine-year-old white males. *Child Develpm.*, *7*, 262–272.

——. 1939a. Stature of Massachusetts children of North European and Italian ancestry. *Amer. J. Phys. Anthrop.*, *24*, 301–346.

——. 1939b. Physical growth from birth to maturity. *Rev. Educ. Res.*, *9*, 47–49.

——. 1939c. Techniques of research in physical growth and anthropometry. *Rev. Educ. Res.*, *9*, 80–90.

——. 1943. Physical growth from birth to two years: I. Stature. A review and synthesis of North American research for the period 1850–1941. *Univ. Iowa Stud. Child Welfare*, No. 407. Pp. 237.

Meredith, H. V. 1945. Toward a working concept of growth. *Amer. J. Orthod. Oral Surg.*, *31*, 440–458.

——. 1946a. Physical growth from birth to two years: II. Head circumference. Part I, A review and synthesis of North American research on groups of infants. *Child Develpm.*, *17*, 1–61.

——. 1946b. Order and age of eruption for the deciduous dentition. *J. Dent. Res.*, *25*, 43–66.

——. 1947. Length of upper extremities in *Homo sapiens* from birth through adolescence. *Growth*, *11*, 1–50.

——. 1950. Birth order and body size: II. Neonatal and childhood materials. *Amer. J. Phys. Anthrop.*, *8*, 195–224.

Meredith, H. V., and A. W. Brown. 1939. Growth in body weight during the first ten days of postnatal life. *Human Biol.*, *11*, 24–77.

Meredith, H. V., and L. J. Carl. 1946. Individual growth in hip width: A study covering the age period from 5–9 years based upon seriatim data for 55 nonpathological white children. *Child Develpm.*, *17*, 157–172.

Meredith, H. V., and J. L. Goodman. 1941. A comparison of routine hospital records of birth stature with measurements of birth stature obtained for longitudinal research. *Child Develpm.*, *12*, 175–181.

Meredith, H. V., and V. B. Knott. 1938. Changes in body proportions during infancy and the preschool years III. The skelic index. *Child Develpm.*, *9*, 49–62.

Meredith, H. V., and G. Stoddard. 1936. Physical growth from birth to maturity. *Rev. Educ. Res.*, *6*, 54–84.

Metheny, E. 1939. The variability of the percentage index of build as applied to the prediction of normal weight. *Human Biol.*, *11*, 473–484.

Michelson, N. 1943a. Investigations in the physical development of Negroes: I. Stature. *Amer. J. Phys. Anthrop.*, 1 n.s., 191–213.

——. 1943b. Studies in the physical development of Negroes: II. Weight. *Amer. J. Phys. Anthrop.*, 1 n.s., 289–300.

——. 1943c. Studies in the physical development of Negroes: III. Cephalic index. *Amer. J. Anthrop.*, 1 n.s., 417–424.

Mullen, F. A. 1940. Factors in the growth of girls. *Child Develpm.*, *11*, 27–42.

Murchison, C., and S. Langer. 1927. Tiedemann's observations on the development of the mental faculties of children. *J. Genet. Psychol.*, *34*, 205–230.

Naccarati, S. 1921. The morphological aspect of intelligence. *Arch. Psychol.*, No. 45.

Noback, C. R. 1943. The developmental anatomy of the human osseous skeleton during the embryonic, fetal and circumnatal periods. *Anat. Rec.*, *87*, 29–51.

Palmer, C. E. 1944. Studies of the center of gravity in the human body. *Child Develpm.*, *15*, 98–180.

Palmer, C. E., and L. J. Reed. 1935. Anthropometric studies of individual growth: I. Age, height, and growth in height, elementary school children. *Human Biol., 7,* 319–324.

Palmer, C. E., K. Riiti, and L. J. Reed. 1937. Anthropometric studies of individual growth: II. Age, weight, and rate of growth, elementary school children. *Child Develpm., 8,* 47–61.

Paterson, D. G. 1930. *Physique and intellect.* New York: Century.

Pearl, R. 1928. *The rate of living.* New York: Knopf.

Peatman, J. G., and R. A. Higgons. 1938. Growth norms from birth to the age of five years: A study of children reared with optimal pediatric and home care. *Amer. J. Dis. Child., 55,* 1233–1247.

Porter, W. T. 1893. Physical basis of precocity and dullness. *Trans. Acad. Sci. St. Louis, 6,* 161–181.

Potter, E. L., and F. L. Adair. 1949. *Fetal and neonatal death.* Chicago: University of Chicago Press. Pp. xiv + 173.

Potter, J. W., and H. V. Meredith. 1948. A comparison of two methods of obtaining biparietal and bigonial measures. *J. Dent. Res., 27,* 459–466.

Pryor, H. B. 1923. Differences in time of development of centers of ossification in the male and female skeleton. *Anat. Rec., 25,* 252–273.

——. 1925. Time of ossification of bones of the hand of the male and female and union of epiphyses with the diaphyses. *Amer. J. Phys. Anthrop., 8,* 401–410.

——. 1936. Certain physical and physiological aspects of adolescent development in girls. *J. Pediat., 8,* 52–62.

——. 1941. Width-weight tables (Revised). *Amer. J. Dis. Child., 61,* 300–304.

Pryor, H. B., and H. R. Stolz. 1933. Determining appropriate weight for body build. *J. Pediat., 3,* 608–622.

Pyle, S. I., A. W. Mann, S. Dreizen, H. Kelly, I. G. Macy, and T. D. Spies. 1948. A substitute for skeletal age (Todd) for clinical use: The red graph method, *J. Pediat., 32,* 125–136.

Pyle, S. I., and C. Menino. 1939. Observations on estimating skeletal age from the Todd and the Flory bone atlases. *Child Develpm., 10,* 27–34.

Quetelet, A. 1871. *Anthropometrie.* Brussels: Muquardt.

Reynolds, E. L. 1944. Differential tissue growth in the leg during childhood. *Child Develpm., 15,* 181–205.

——. 1945. The bony pelvic girdle in early infancy. *Amer. J. Phys. Anthrop., 3* n.s., 321–354.

——. 1947. The bony pelvis in prepuberal childhood. *Amer. J. Phys. Anthrop., 5* n.s., 165–200.

——. 1948. Distribution of tissue components in the female leg from birth to maturity. *Anat. Rec., 100,* 621–629.

——. 1950. The distribution of subcutaneous fat in childhood and adolescence. *Monogr. Soc. Res. Child Develpm., 15,* No. 2. Pp. xviii + 189.

Reynolds, E. L., and L. W. Sontag. 1945. The Fels composite sheet: II. Variations in growth patterns in health and disease. *J. Pediat., 26,* 336–352.

Richey, H. G. 1937. The relation of accelerated, normal and retarded puberty to the height and weight

of school children. *Monogr. Soc. Res. Child Develpm., 2,* No. 1. Pp. vi + 67.

Robbins, W. J., S. Brody, A. G. Hogan, C. M. Jackson, and C. W. Green. 1928. *Growth.* New Haven: Yale University Press.

Robertson, T. S. 1923. *The chemical basis of growth and senescence.* Philadelphia: Lippincott.

Robinow, M. 1942. The variability of weight and height increments from birth to six years. *Child Develpm., 13,* 159–164.

Robinow, T. F., T. W. Richards, and M. Anderson. 1942. The eruption of deciduous teeth. *Growth, 6,* 127–133.

Rothney, J. W. M. 1941. Recent findings in the study of the physical growth of children. *J. Educ. Res., 35,* 161–182.

Royster, L. T. 1936. Body type of Negro children. *Arch. Pediat., 53,* 259–262.

Sandler, H. C. 1944. The eruption of the deciduous teeth. *J. Pediat., 25,* 140–147.

Sawtell, R. O. 1929. Ossification and growth of children from one to eight years of age. *Amer. J. Dis. Child., 37,* 61–87.

Scammon, R. E. 1922. On the weight increments of premature infants compared with those of the same gestation age and those of full-term children. *Proc. Soc. Exp. Biol. Med., 19,* 133–136.

——. 1927a. The first seriation study of human growth. *Amer. J. Phys. Anthrop., 10,* 329–336.

——. 1927b. The literature on the growth and physical development of the fetus, infant, and child: A quantitative summary. *Anat. Rec., 5,* 241–267.

——. 1930. The measurement of the body in childhood. In J. A. Harris, C. M. Jackson, D. G. Paterson, and R. E. Scammon. *The measurement of man,* pp. 173–215. Minneapolis: University of Minnesota Press.

Scammon, R. E., and L. A. Calkins. 1929. *The development and growth of the external dimensions of the human body in the fetal period.* Minneapolis: University of Minnesota Press.

Schonfeld, W. A. 1950. Inadequate masculine physique as a factor in personality development of adolescent boys. *Psychosom. Med., 12,* 49–54.

Schmidt, F. 1948. Norm und Variationsbreit der Handwurzelkernentwicklung. *Z. Kinderheilk., 65,* 646–654.

Schultz, A. H. 1921. Sex incidence in abortions. *Carnegie Inst. Wash. Publ.,* No. 275, 177–191.

——. 1926. Fetal growth of man and other primates. *Quart. Rev. Biol., 1,* 465–521.

——. 1929. The technique of measuring the outer body of human fetuses and of primates in general. *Contr. Embryol., Carnegie Inst. Wash. Publ.,* No. 394, pp. 213–257.

Scott, R. B., W. W. Cardozo, A. DeG. Smith, and M. R. DeLilly. 1950. Growth and development of Negro infants: III. Growth during the first year of life as observed in private pediatric practice. *J. Pediat., 37,* 885–893.

Second Conference on Research in Child Development. 1927. Session 6: *Constitution and mental types.* Washington, D. C.: National Research Council.

Sheldon, W. H., S. S. Stevens, and W. B. Tucker. 1940. *The varieties of human physique.* New York: Harper.

Shirokogoroff, S. M. 1925. *Process of physical growth among the Chinese.* Shanghai: Commercial Press.

Shuttleworth, F. K. 1937. Sexual maturation and physical growth of girls age six to nineteen. *Monogr. Soc. Res. Child Develpm., 2,* No. 5. Pp. xx + 253.

——. 1938. The adolescent period: A graphic and pictorial atlas. *Monogr. Soc. Res. Child Develpm., 3,* No. 3. Pp. 246.

——. 1939. The physical and mental growth of girls and boys age six to nineteen in relation to age at maximum growth. *Monogr. Soc. Res. Child Develpm., 4,* No. 3. Pp. vi + 291.

——. 1949. The adolescent period: A pictorial atlas. *Monogr. Soc. Res. Child Develpm., 14,* No. 50. Pp. v + 69.

Simmons, K. 1944. The Brush Foundation study of child growth and development: II. Physical growth and development. *Monogr. Soc. Res. Child Develpm., 9,* No. 37. Pp. vii + 87.

Simmons, K., and W. W. Greulich. 1943. Menarcheal age and the height, weight and skeletal age of girls 4 to 17 years. *J. Pediat., 22,* 518–548.

Simmons, K., and T. W. Todd. 1938. Growth of well children: Analysis of stature and weight, 3 months to 13 years. *Growth, 2,* 93–143.

Sontag, L. W. 1946. Some psychosomatic aspects of childhood. *Nerv. Child, 5,* 296–304.

——. 1947. Physiological factors and personality in children. *Child Develpm., 18,* 185–189.

Sontag, L. W., and E. L. Reynolds. 1945. The Fels composite sheet: I. A practical method for analyzing growth progress. *J. Pediat., 26,* 327–335.

Sontag, L. W., D. Snell, and M. Anderson. 1939. Rate of appearance of ossification centers from birth to the age of five years. *Amer. J. Dis. Child., 58,* 949–957.

Steggerda, M., and P. Densen. 1936. Height, weight and age tables for homogeneous groups with particular reference to Navajo Indians and Dutch Whites. *Child Develpm., 7,* 115–120.

Stevenson, P. H. 1924. Age order of epiphyseal union in man. *Amer. J. Phys. Anthrop., 7,* 53–93.

Stolz, H. R., and L. M. Stolz. 1951. *Somatic development of adolescent boys.* New York: Macmillan. Pp. xxiv + 557.

Stone, C. P., and R. G. Barker. 1937. On the relationship between menarcheal age and certain measurements of physique in girls of the ages 9 to 16 years. *Human Biol., 9,* 1–28.

Streeter, G. L. 1920. Weight, sitting height, head size, foot length and menstrual age of the human embryo. *Contr. Embryol., Carnegie Inst. Wash. Publ.,* No. 274, pp. 143–170.

Stuart, H. C. 1947. Physical growth during adolescence. *Amer. J. Dis. Child., 74,* 495–509.

Stuart, H. C., and P. H. Dwinell. 1942. The growth of bone, muscle and overlying tissues in children six to ten years of age as measured by studies of roentgenograms of the leg area. *Child Develpm., 13,* 195–213.

Stuart, H. C., P. Hill, and C. Shaw. 1940. Studies from the Center for Research in Child Health and Development, School of Public Health, Harvard University: III. The growth of bone, muscle and overlying tissues as revealed by studies of roentgenograms of the leg area. *Monogr. Soc. Res. Child Develpm., 5,* No. 3. Pp. 190 + 23 tables.

Su, T. F., and C. J. Liang. 1940. Growth and development of Chinese infants of Hunan: I. Body weight, standing height, and sitting height during first year. *Chinese Med. J., 58,* 104.

Sullivan, L. R. 1928. *Essentials of anthropometry.* (Rev. by H. L. Shapiro.) New York: American Museum of Natural History.

Swinehart, D. R. 1950. The importance of the tongue in the development of normal occlusions. *Amer. J. Orthod., 36,* 813–830.

Tanner, J. M. 1947. The morphological level of personality. *Proc. Roy. Soc. Med., 40,* 301–308.

Taylor, R. 1919. The proportionate measurements of 250 full term newborn infants. *Amer. J. Dis. Child., 17,* 353–362.

Thompson, D. W. 1942. *On growth and form.* Cambridge: University Press.

Thompson, H. 1929. A measuring board for infants. *Amer. J. Phys. Anthrop., 13,* 281–286.

——. 1938. Body proportions in the growing infant. *Growth, 2,* 1–12.

Thurstone, L. L. 1935. *The vectors of mind.* Chicago: University of Chicago Press.

——. 1947. Factor analysis of body measurements. *Amer. J. Phys. Anthrop., 5* n.s., 15–28.

Todd, T. W. 1930. The roentgenographic appraisement of skeletal differentiation. *Child Develpm., 1,* 298–310.

——. 1933. *Roentgenographic appraisement of developmental growth in the skeleton,* pp. 258–279. (White House Conference on Child Health and Protection, Growth and Development of the Child.) New York: Century.

——. 1935. Anthropology and growth. *Science, 81,* 260–263.

——. 1937. *Atlas of skeletal maturation (hand).* St. Louis: Mosby.

Trotter, M. 1939. Classifications of hair color. *Amer. J. Phys. Anthrop., 25,* 237–260.

Trotter, M., and O. H. Duggins. 1948. Age changes in head hair from birth to maturity: I. Index and size of hair of children. *Amer. J. Phys. Anthrop., 6,* 489–505.

——. 1950. Age changes in head hair from birth to maturity: III. Cuticular scale counts of hair of children. *Amer. J. Phys. Anthrop., 8,* 467–484.

Tuddenham, R. D., and M. M. Snyder. 1947. Physical growth from birth to maturity. *Rev. Educ. Res., 17,* 371–379.

Vickers, V. S., and H. C. Stuart. 1943. Anthropometry in the pediatrician's office. *J. Pediat., 22,* 155–170.

Wallis, R. W. 1931. How children grow: An anthropometric study of private school children from two to eight years of age. *Univ. Iowa Stud. Child Welfare, 5,* No. 1.

Watson, E. H., and G. H. Lowrey. 1951. Growth and Development of Children. Chicago: Year Book. Pp. 260.

Weinbach, A. P. 1938. A simple method for estimating the surface area of the human body from birth to maturity. *Growth, 2,* 303–317.

Weissenberg, S. 1911. *Das Wachstum des Menschen nach Alter, Geschlecht und Rasse.* Stuttgart: Strecker and Schröder.

Wetzel, N. C. 1941. Physical fitness in terms of physique, development and basal metabolism. *J. Amer. Med. Ass., 116,* 1187–1195.

——. 1943. Assessing the physical condition of children: I. Case demonstration of failing growth and the determination of "par" by the grid method. II. Simple malnutrition: A problem of failing growth and development. III. The components of physical status and physical progress and their evaluation. *J. Pediat., 22,* 82–110, 208–225, 329–361.

White House Conference on Child Health and Protection. 1932, 1933. *Growth and development of the child: 1, General considerations; 2, Anatomy and physiology; 3, Nutrition; 4, Appraisement of the child.* New York: Century.

Wilder, H. H., and B. Wentworth. 1918. *Personal identification.* Boston: Gorham Press.

Wilson, C. A., M. E. Sweeny, R. Stutsman, L. E. Chesire, and E. Hatt. 1930. *The Merrill-Palmer standards of physical and mental growth.* Detroit: Merrill-Palmer.

Wissler, C. 1930. *Growth of children in Hawaii: Based on observations by Louis R. Sullivan.* Honolulu: Memoirs of the Bernice P. Bishop Museum.

Woodbury, R. M. 1921. Statures and weights of children under six years of age. *U. S. Child. Bur. Publ.,* No. 87.

CHAPTER 6

THE ONTOGENESIS OF INFANT BEHAVIOR

ARNOLD GESELL

Introduction

Ontogeny is the life history or development of an individual organism. This chapter will concern itself mainly with the first 2 postnatal years of the human life cycle and with that outward aspect of life which goes by the familiar name of *behavior*. Behavior is in a sense more than an aspect; it is the very essence and a culminating manifestation of the life processes of the individual, including the all-pervading process of growth. Biologically —or shall we say semantically—the infant is a growing action system. He comes by his "mind" in the same way that he comes by his body, namely, through the mechanisms of development. Our task is to formulate some of the general principles which underlie the developmental patterning of his total action system.

Comparative Considerations

The individual is a member of a species. His most fundamental behavior characteristics are those which are common to the species as a whole. Less fundamental are those which are peculiar to a breed or stock, differentiated within the species. Some patterns of behavior are so primitive that they are common to a wide range of species. The startle reflex, universal among infants and children, is also found in primates and among lower mammals in types as widely separated as bear and badger. The tonic neck reflex, which plays such a

prominent rôle in the early ontogenesis of infant behavior, has been investigated in the rabbit as well as in man (Magnus, 1924). The lowly *Amblystoma* embodies generic patterns of terrestrial locomotion. This primitive vertebrate in the hands of Coghill (1929) has become a touchstone for elucidating problems of human behavior.

Infancy is the period in which the individual realizes his racial inheritance. This inheritance is the end product of evolutionary processes which trace back to an extremely remote antiquity. But infancy itself is a product of evolution. It was evolved not only to perpetuate a groundwork of racial inheritance, but also to add thereto a contingent margin of specific modifiability. In the more complex orders of life, such as fish, amphibian, reptile, bird, and mammal, the postnatal period of immaturity has become a recognizable part of the individual life cycle and plays an important part in the economy of that cycle. Infancy was evolved to subserve the needs of individual growth. It lengthens as the organism becomes more complex. It varies significantly among different species.

The study of infancy in its broadest sense must therefore be a comparative science. The most general laws of development will prove to be applicable to all vertebrates, not excluding either fish or man. In spite of the bewildering diversity of the behavior characteristics of widely varying species, certain developmental sequences must be common to large groups and orders. Differences in gestation, longevity, size, and growth cycle yield to quantitative comparative study of correlated behavior characteristics. The findings of chemical embryology and of electro-chemistry suggest that there is a general physiology of development. There are far-reaching implications in the fact that the thyroid substance of ox or sheep will profoundly influence the ontogenesis of the behavior of a cretinous infant (Gesell, Amatruda, and Culotta, 1936).

It would take a lengthy syllabus to list and classify resemblances in the behavior of human and infrahuman species. Lashley and Watson (1913) made a valuable pioneering study on the development of a young monkey, reporting the age of appearance in a macaque of such behavior items as creeping, winking, eye following, walking, running, thumb opposition, and grasping. Boutan in 1914 compared adaptation in problem-solving situations of a gibbon and young child; and Yerkes in 1916 contrasted the behavior of a 4-year-old orangutan and a 3-year-old child in a problem-solving situation.

Jacobsen, Jacobsen, and Yoshioka (1932) and Kellogg and Kellogg (1933) each reported on the behaviorial development of a young chimpanzee and compared responses to infant tests in the four fields of behavior—motor, adaptive, language, and personal-social—with those of normal infants at the same ages. Experimental studies of form discrimination (Gellermann, 1933) and responses to problem-solving situations (Brainard, 1930) make direct comparisons between chimpanzees and pre-school children. A. W. Yerkes (1935) has explored the possibility of investigating problems of behavior in chimpanzee infancy.

Riesen and Kinder (1952) report a detailed study on the postural development of infant chimpanzees.

Madam Kohts (1935) compared the behavior of a male chimpanzee during the age period of ½ to 4 years with that of her son from birth to 4 years of age. She sums up her observations as follows:

(1) In the functional biological field: the chimpanzee totally ignores the possibility of walking erect and of freeing his hands for carrying weights. (2) In the sphere of imitation: the chimpanzee is devoid of imitation in so far as human sounds are concerned and generally fails to extend or improve his imitatory behavior. (3) In respect of emotional, altruistic and social behavior: the chimpanzee fails to understand the advantages of friendly sympathetic intercourse with creatures standing on a lower biological level than himself. (4) With regard to habit-forming: the chimpanzee does not improve in the motor habits connected with the use of tools and household implements. (5) In the sphere of playful behavior: he does not indulge in creative constructional play.

On the basis of the foregoing evidence, Madam Kohts concludes: "It is impossible to say that he [the chimpanzee] is 'almost human'; we must go even further and state quite definitely that he is 'by no means human.'"

The comparative study of interspecies resemblances must be approached with critical caution, because many of the similarities are offset by important contextual differences. Similarities often are apparent when differences are hidden and profound. On evolutionary grounds one may expect the highest degree of resemblance in the ontogenesis of anthropoid and of human species. At no phase of the entire life cycle, however, are *Homo* and *Anthropos* the same. Human characteristics are not superadded as a late installment upon a lower primitive stage. They inhere in the very beginnings of fetal and postnatal behavior.

The pre-eminence of human infancy lies in the scope, the depth, and the duration of plasticity. There is a maturation of basic motor patterns as in subhuman species; but this proceeds less rigidly and the total behavior complex is suspended in a state of greater formativeness. This increased modifiability is extremely sensitive to social milieu. In the impersonal aspects of adaptive behavior of the non-language type (practical intelligence) there is a high degree of early correspondence between man and other primates. Some of this correspondence is so consistent as to justify a phyletic and even recapitulatory explanation. Transcending and pervading the interspecies similarities, however, is a generalized conditionability or responsiveness to other personalities which is distinctively human.

Principles of Developmental Morphology

In the comparative study of behavior one cannot escape problems of pattern and form. When Goethe coined the word *Morphologie,* he was interested in the forms of flowers and skulls. To this day the term carries physical connotations. But the concepts of morphology can be extended to the phenomena of behavior. Morphology is the science of form. The dictionary reminds us that form is the shape of anything as distinguished from the substance of that thing. Behavior has shape.

The shapes which behaviors assume can be investigated in their own scientific right. A morphological approach leads to the description and measurement of specific forms, the systematic study of topographic relations and correlations of such forms, their ontogenetic progression and involution, their comparative features among individuals and among species.

"Structure is only the intimate expression of function" was a leading maxim of John Hunter. In a monistic (but not mystic) sense, "the mind" may be regarded as a living, growing "structure" even though it lacks corporeal tangibility. It is a complex, organized, and organizing action system which manifests itself in characteristic forms of behavior—in patterns of posture, locomotion, prehension, manipulation, of perception, communication, and social response. The action systems of embryo, fetus, infant, and child undergo pattern changes which are so sequential and orderly that we may be certain that the patterning process is governed by mechanisms of form regulation—the same mechanisms which are being established by the science of embryology.

Experimental embryology is now one of the most active and flourishing of all the life sciences. It has undertaken the analysis of development, particularly as it affects the anatomy of the organism. Investigators, however, are using functional and behavior criteria increasingly to define the somatic anatomy. This is natural, for, by the principle of hierarchical continuity, there is but one physiology of development. The growth of tissues, of organs, and of behavior is obedient to identical laws of developmental morphology.

It cannot, therefore, be doubted that the general physiology of mental development will find its deeper roots in the same scientific soil which is now intesively cultivated in laboratories of experimental embryology. Already many of the current morphogenetic concepts have more than value analogy to psychical processes: embryonic field, gradient theory, regional determination, autonomous induction, complementary induction, potency, polarity, symmetry, time correlation, etc. Associationism as a psychological tradition has come down from Aristotle and still has considerable vitality, as shown by a prodigious preoccupation with problems of learning and the conditioned reflex. The laws of association deal with the factors of contiguity, assimilation, frequency, primacy, intensity, duration, context, acquaintance, maturity. Needless to say, these laws will some day be reformulated in terms of the biology and physiology of development. The full coordination of animal and child psychology will depend upon such reformulations.

Psychological growth, like somatic growth, is a morphogenetic process. It produces a progressive organization of behavior forms. Our scientific knowledge of this process is still very meager. We lack the grammar and the lexicon for defining form characteristics. We need morphographic as well as mathematical methods which will simplify and generalize form phenomena.

It is possible, however, to define several principles of development which have psychomorphological implications. These principles concern the shaping of the action system and its trends in oriented space and oriented time. The principle of *developmental direction,* for example, recognizes that the action system of the infant does not increase symmetrically like an expanding balloon but is subject to the far-reaching consequences of the biological factor of anteroposterior differentiation.

The very architectonics of the neuromuscular system determines not only a cephalocaudal course but also the relationships between paired and opposed motor organs. We shall propose a principle of *reciprocal interweaving* to characterize this aspect of behavior organization.

Laterality is distinctly a morphological phenomenon, in that it represents a form of dynamic asymmetry. It represents a significant principle of *functional asymmetry.*

During ontogenesis the total action system undergoes specific differentiation in restricted spheres. This orderly specification is governed by a principle of *individuating maturation.*

The growing organism is of necessity in a state of unstable and shifting equilibrium. Also, of necessity, it must restrict the modes and degrees of instability. The oscillations of the organism are self-limited by a principle of *regulatory fluctuation.*

A brief discussion of these five principles may serve to delineate some of the general features of the ontogeny of infant behavior. The several principles are not entirely absolute, and they certainly do not operate independently or in isolation. They overlap and modify each other in interesting and significant ways.

General Sequences of Early Behavior Growth

As a background for the discussion of the several principles of development it will be profitable to take a panoramic glance at the whole domain of behavior development in the first 5 years of life. This domain can be envisaged as four major fields of functional organization: (1) motor behavior, (2) adaptive behavior, (3) language behavior, (4) personal-social behavior.

1. Motor characteristics include postural reactions, prehension, locomotion, general bodily coordination, and specific motor skills.

2. Adaptive behavior is a convenient category for those varied adjustments—perceptual, orientational, manual, and verbal—which reflect the child's capacity to initiate new experience and to profit by past experience. This adaptivity includes alertness, intelligence, and various forms of constructiveness and exploitation.

3. Language embraces all behavior which has to do with soliloquy, dramatic

expression, communication, and comprehension.

4. Personal-social behavior embraces the child's personal reactions to other persons and to the impacts of culture; his adjustments to domestic life, to property, to social groups, and to community conventions. These four major fields of behavior comprise most of the visible patterns of child behavior. They do not, of course, fall neatly into separate compartments. The child always reacts as an integer.

Elsewhere the writer and his collaborators have summarized the ontogenetic trends of development in the four behavior fields at ten age levels from 4 weeks to 5 years (Gesell, Halverson, Thompson, *et al.*, 1940, Chapters III, IV).

Figure 1 depicts the trends and sequences of early behavior growth. The chart includes the fetal period to indicate the continuity of the growth cycle. The ontogenetic organization of behavior begins long before birth. The general direction of this organization is from head to foot, from proximal to distal segments, and from fundamental to accessory control. Lips and tongue lead, eye muscles follow, then neck, shoulder, arms, hands, fingers, trunk, legs, feet. The chart reflects this law of developmental direction; it also suggests that the four distinguishable fields of behavior develop conjointly in close coordination. The motor field of development presents the most evident and extrinsic continuity between the prenatal and postnatal periods (Gesell and Amatruda, 1941).

In terse terms the trends of behavior development are:

In the *first quarter* (4–16 weeks) of the first year the infant gains control of his twelve oculomotor muscles.

In the *second quarter* (16–28 weeks) he comes into command of the muscles which support his head and move his arms. He reaches out for things.

In the *third quarter* (28–40 weeks) he gains command of his trunk and hands. He sits. He grasps, transfers, and manipulates objects.

In the *fourth quarter* (40–52 weeks) he extends command to his legs and feet; to his forefinger and thumb. He pokes and plucks. He stands upright.

In the *second year* he walks and runs; articulates words and phrases; acquires bowel and bladder control; attains a rudimentary sense of personal identity and of personal possession.

In the *third year* he speaks in sentences, using words as tools of thought. He shows a positive propensity to understand his environment and to comply with cultural demands. He is no longer a "mere" infant.

In the *fourth year* he asks innumerable questions, perceives analogies, displays an active tendency to conceptualize and generalize. He is nearly self-dependent in routines of home life.

At *five* he is well matured in motor control. He hops and skips. He talks without infantile articulation. He can narrate a long tale. He prefers associative play; he feels socialized pride in clothes and accomplishment. He is a self-assured, conforming citizen in his small world.

The Principle of Developmental Direction

The principle of developmental direction is reflected in the foregoing summary of developmental trends. The phenomena of polarity and of gradients (electrochemical and otherwise) underlie this principle. The direction of early embryonic growth is determined by the longitudinal gradient of the mesoderm. This gradient governs alike the course of somatic organization and that of behaviorial organization. In the growth of the fetus there is an unmistakable precocity in the development of the anterior end of the organism. At the close of the second fetal month the height of the head rivals the length of the trunk, and the

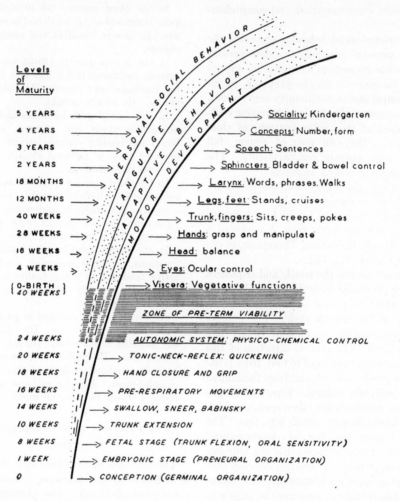

Levels
of
Maturity

5 YEARS	⟶	⟶ Sociality: Kindergarten
4 YEARS	⟶	⟶ Concepts: Number, form
3 YEARS	⟶	⟶ Speech: Sentences
2 YEARS	⟶	⟶ Sphincters: Bladder & bowel control
18 MONTHS	⟶	⟶ Larynx: Words, phrases. Walks
12 MONTHS	⟶	⟶ Legs, feet: Stands, cruises
40 WEEKS	⟶	⟶ Trunk, fingers: Sits, creeps, pokes
28 WEEKS	⟶	⟶ Hands: grasp and manipulate
16 WEEKS	⟶	⟶ Head: balance
4 WEEKS	⟶	⟶ Eyes: Ocular control
{ 0-BIRTH / 40 WEEKS }		⟶ Viscera: Vegetative functions

ZONE OF PRE-TERM VIABILITY

24 WEEKS		*AUTONOMIC SYSTEM: PHYSICO-CHEMICAL CONTROL*
20 WEEKS	⟶	*TONIC-NECK-REFLEX: QUICKENING*
18 WEEKS	⟶	*HAND CLOSURE AND GRIP*
16 WEEKS	⟶	*PRE-RESPIRATORY MOVEMENTS*
14 WEEKS	⟶	*SWALLOW, SNEER, BABINSKY*
10 WEEKS	⟶	*TRUNK EXTENSION*
8 WEEKS	⟶	*FETAL STAGE (TRUNK FLEXION, ORAL SENSITIVITY)*
I WEEK	⟶	*EMBRYONIC STAGE (PRE-NEURAL ORGANIZATION)*
0	⟶	*CONCEPTION (GERMINAL ORGANIZATION)*

FIGURE 1. Ontogenetic trends and sequences of behavior growth. (From *Developmental Diagnosis: Normal and Abnormal Child Development,* by A. Gesell and C. S. Amatruda. New York: Paul B. Hoeber, 1947, p. 9.)

umbilicus is at the level of the cervical vertebrae. The posteriorward migration of the umbilicus is a reflection of the cephalocaudad trend. This trend, however, must not be taken too literally, for the caudad appendage of the embryo, which was prominent in the middle of the second month, is already beginning to regress at the end of that month.

There are many apparent exceptions to the directional rule which do not, however, impair the validity of the general principle. Some of the exceptions arise out of the fact that there are successive head-to-foot sweeps of development so that the trend repeats itself at certain periods appropriate to the ascending levels of organization. We thus expect to find cyclical evidence of the trend in the preneural as well as in the neural stage and in late as well as early stages of infancy.

The principle is well illustrated in the behavior characteristics of the 20-week-old infant. His trunk is still so flaccid that he must be propped or strapped in a chair to maintain a sitting posture. When he is so secured, however, his eyes, head, and shoulders exhibit heightened activity and intensified tonus. The pelvic zone and the lower extremities at 20 weeks are, in comparison, very immature.

Evidence of the cephalocaudad trend will be seen in a later summary of the ontogenetic sequences of prone behavior patterns. The very fact that this sequence converges toward and culminates in the assumption of the erect posture suggests the presence of a unidirectional principle. The principle does not operate with complete simplicity, however, because the mastery of the erect posture depends in turn upon the development of the functions of equilibrium which have a cephalic as well as a caudad status.

Just as neuromotor organization proceeds from head to foot in the direction of the longitudinal axis, so it tends to proceed from the central to peripheral segments. The fundamental axial muscles are among the first to react in a coordinated manner, as shown by the primitive body flexion of the fetus. There is a progressive advance of motor control from the larger, fundamental muscles to the smaller muscles which execute the more refined movements. This trend from fundamental or proximal to accessory and distal control is illustrated in the ontogenesis of postural attitudes, of prehensory approach, manipulation, and prone locomotion.

During the earlier periods of development the arms and also the legs tend to react as wholes, the impulses arising mainly from the shoulder and the pelvic girdles. With advancing maturity, mobility asserts itself at the elbow and wrist joints and at the knee and ankle joints. Forearm, foreleg, hand, and foot show specific segmental activity. The cephalocaudad and the proximal-distal trends overlap and correlate. For this reason, independent activity of the distal segments becomes apparent in the upper extremities before the lower extremities. In the field of prehension, as Halverson (1933) has pointed out, from 16 weeks on, the elbow and digits participate in reaching movements with increasing effectiveness, until at 40 weeks they closely approximate the shoulder in efficiency, whereas trunk and wrist remain functionally retarded.

In the ontogenesis of prehension there is not only a proximal-distal trend but also an ulnar-radial shift. This shift is closely bound up with the growth of thumb opposition. At 20 weeks a crude palmar grasp, often favoring the ulnar aspect of the palm, is evident; but after 28 weeks there is an obvious preference for radial as opposed to ulnar grasp and manipulation. The developmental shift from ulnar to radial grasp is so strong that the infant actually displays a well-defined intolerance as well as motor rejection when an object is pressed against the ulnar aspect of the palm. At 40 weeks he extends his index finger and makes oblique radial approach upon objects which require precise prehension. He brings the volar pad of the thumb against the volar pad of the index (Gesell and Halverson, 1936).

The operation of the cephalocaudad principle in relation to other developmental principles is further illustrated in the summary of the ontogenetic sequence of the prone behavior of the human infant, summarized in Table 1.

The Principle of Reciprocal Interweaving

It is natural that the metaphor of the loom should constantly reappear in the description and interpretation of the developmental process. The products of growth are envisaged as a fabric in which threads and designs are visible. Even at the molecular level the analogy of warp and woof becomes helpful. Wrinch conceives the chromosome as a structure constituted of two elements: long filaments of identical protein molecules in parallel, and a set of ringlike nucleic acid molecules surrounding these filaments and holding them together in a wooflike manner. From such an arrangement and the asymmetric constitution of biomolecules, fabric issues.

The bilateral nature of the anatomy of the human physique and of its musculature suggests that the balance and opposition of its paired organs need to be interrelated in an orderly manner during the long period of ontogenesis. Even single members are bilateral or bivalent in the sense that they have both flexor and extensor activators. Accordingly, in the four-limbed infant there are many double aspect structures (and functions) to be coordinately interwoven: anterior bilateral, posterior bilateral, ipsilateral, crossed lateral, flexor, and extensor.

Flexion and extension are the most fundamental components of muscular movement. Sherrington (1906) has formulated a law of "reciprocal innervation" which shows the functional relationhips of these components in the counteraction of antagonistic muscles. The inhibition of one set of muscles while the opposing muscles are in excitation is a condition for effective movement. Reciprocal innervation is a mode of coordination, a physiological mechanism.

In the ontogenesis of the neuromotor system a complicated integration must likewise be achieved between antagonistic muscles. Appropriate structures for subserving inhibition must be progressively provided. There is a mode of growth which asserts itself in a developmental fluctuation of dominance in flexors versus extensors and also in unilateral and crossed lateral versus bilateral muscle groups. Inasmuch as behavior patterning and structural growth are intimately correlated, we shall describe this developmental principle or mechanism as a reciprocal interweaving process.

Neurologically, this process implies an intricate cross-stitching or involuted interlacing which organizes opposing muscle systems into reciprocal and increasingly mature relationships. Functionally, such a process results in a progressive spiral kind of reincorporation of sequential forms of behavior.

These phenomena of fluctuating dominance and of progressive reintegration can be advantageously studied in the development of prone behavior in the human infant, because the prolongation of human infancy widens the scope and lengthens the cycle of observable motor development. It takes the average infant a full year to acquire the upright posture. We have distinguished at least twenty-three stages in the patterning of the prone behavior which evenuates in standing and walking (Gesell and Ames, 1940). From the standpoint of ontogenesis these stages may be envisaged as a series of postural transformations whereby the infant by slow but sure sequence finally achieves the upright posture. None of the stages or patterns can be dismissed as being merely recapitulatory or vestigial. Each stage, however transient,

TABLE 1

Developmental Stages of Prone Behavior in the Human Infant

(The age at which a given action pattern typically makes its appearance is indicated in parentheses.)

FLEXOR DOMINANCE	EXTENSOR DOMINANCE
1. Passive kneel (1 week) Both arms and both legs are *symmetrically* and sharply *flexed*. Cheek contacts platform, or head may be everted.	
	2A. Passive leg extension (4 weeks) The legs passively assume a *symmetric extended* posture. Arms still *flex*, fists at shoulders. Head lifts slightly less than 45°.
2B. Active kneel (about 4 weeks) Infant spontaneously draws up one knee at a time by *(unilateral) flexion*.	
	3A. Active leg extension (8 weeks) Legs actively assume a *symmetric extended* posture. Arms *flex* slightly forward.
3B. One-knee thrust (about 8 weeks) Infant draws up one knee by *flexion* with an abducted thrust *(unilateral)*. Head lifts from 45 to 90°.	
	4A. Alternate extensor kick (12 weeks) Infant lies with legs well *extended* and kicks in *alternation*. Fists at temples. Head lifts slightly.
4B. Abducted one-knee thrust (about 12 weeks) Infant draws up one knee by *flexion* with increased abduction *(unilateral)*. Head lifts 45 to 90°.	
	5. Swimming (16 weeks) Back arches so that infant's weight rests only on abdomen and lower chest. Arms lift, *flexed symmetrically*. Legs lift, in *symmetric extension*. Head lifts 90°.
6. Simultaneous low creep (20 weeks) Both arms and both legs are *flexed symmetrically*. Face and chest contact the supporting surface but abdomen is lifted.	
	7. Frogging (24 weeks) Arms are *flexed or extended symmetrically*. Legs are *extended symmetrically* in abduction. feet everted. Head lifts 90°.

343

TABLE 1 (*Continued*)

FLEXOR DOMINANCE

EXTENSOR DOMINANCE

8. *Advanced unilateral knee thrust*

9. *Same with foot eversion* (28 weeks)
Both arms *extend symmetrically*, or one *extends* and one *flexes*. Infant draws up one knee by *flexion* with an abducted thrust. (9) Same except that foot is everted. Head lifts 90° or more.

10. *Pivoting* (29 weeks)
Arms alternately *flex and extend*, one after the other, causing trunk to pivot on abdomen. *Symmetrical* leg extension is followed by forward *flexion* of one knee, in abduction. Head lifts 90° or more.

11*A*. *Inferior low creep* (30 weeks)
Arms *flex symmetrically*. One knee flexes forward in adduction. Other knee then *flexes* forward after heel has rotated outward. Weight rests on side of body. Head everted, cheek on platform.

11*B*. *Backward crawl* (31 weeks)
Legs *extend symmetrically* and passively and abdomen rests on the supporting surface. Infant pushes body backward from *symmetrically flexed* arms which come to extension as body pushes away from them. Head lifts less than 90°.

12. *Low creep* (32 weeks)
Both arms are *flexed symmetrically*. Legs *flex* forward in adduction, *one at a time*. Face and chest contact supporting surface but abdomen is lifted.

13*A*. *Crawling* (34 weeks)
Legs *extend symmetrically* and are dragged forward passively. Infant pulls trunk forward by *extending*, then *simultaneously flexing* both forearms. Head lifts 90° or more.

13*B*. Later (34½ weeks) pulls weight forward by *extending* and then *flexing* forearms *one at a time*.

14. *High creep* (35 weeks)
Both arms are *extended* and both legs are *flexed symmetrically*. Knees are forward under trunk in adduction, lifting abdomen and chest from supporting surface. Head is well up from floor and eyes look ahead.

15. *Backward creep* (36 weeks)
Infant is in the high creep position. *Extends* first one leg then the other, lowering abdomen and falling backward. Arms are *flexed symmetrically*.

bilaterally, legs are flexed bilaterally, and each pair of limbs moves alternately. This is classic creeping which all but terminates the ontogenetic sequence. Stages 19 and 20 are transitional to upright posture.

To achieve the exalted status of bipedal locomotion the developmental spiral takes two more short turns at ascending levels, constituting the third and fourth cycles. In both these short cycles there is a partial reversion to immobile bilateral extension, namely, in the plantigrade stance and in standing. Each cycle, however, culminates in locomotion; the third cycle, in plantigrade progression; the fourth, in walking.

It takes the average human infant about 60 weeks to attain independent walking. For a half year he is virtually immobile in the prone position. Before he acquires the upright posture he exhibits a number of primitive and abortive modes of locomotion: rolling, pivoting, forward crawl, backward crawl, regression, rocking, creep-crawling, creeping, and cruising. The very diversity of these activities testifies to the complexity of the process of developmental patterning. Some of the patterns have a recapitulatory suggestion, but they may be mainly regarded as functional expressions of transient but necessary stages in the organization of the neuromotor system.

The general direction of this ontogenetic organization is unmistakably cephalocaudal. The infant can lift his head in the first week of life; not until the end of the first year does he stand on his feet. The expansion of his neuromotor coordination also proceeds in general from proximal to distal segments. Upper arm and upper leg come into postural integration before forearm, foreleg, hands, and feet. The foot is both a caudal and distal terminus, the final fulcrum for locomotion. These directional trends are simple when compared with the intricate interweaving which is essential for functional organization.

Development of Handedness. Detailed long-range studies of the development of handedness in individual infants and children make it evident that the principle of reciprocal interweaving is well exemplified in this field of ontogenesis. Two pairs of opposing trends appear to be in mutual rivalry: bilaterality vs. unilaterality, and right vs. left. This gives rise to many inflections and combinations. These trends are probably not in actual conflict or in true competition but in developmental flux.

In brief, the course of behavior in a right-handed subject in the seated position is typically somewhat as follows (Gesell and Ames, 1947): contact of object unilateral and with the left hand, 16–20 weeks; bilateral contact at 24 weeks; unilateral, usually right hand at 28 weeks; bilateral at 32; unilateral through the rest of the first year with now right, now left, predominating; right-hand dominance 52–56 weeks; marked interchangeability with considerable use of both hands or of left hand at 80 weeks; right hand at 2 years; considerable bilaterality from 2½ to 4 years; right-handedness in general predominating from then on through 10 years.

Directionality of Drawing. Studies of the drawing behavior of preschool children as they copy simple forms indicate that the child's drawing products as well as his actual movements frequently illustrate the developmental mechanism of reciprocal interweaving (Gesell and Ames, 1946). Opposed trends in the child's drawing of a circle are: (*a*) drawing clockwise and drawing counterclockwise, (*b*) starting at the top and starting at the bottom. At 30–36 months of age, the child characteristically draws a circle counterclockwise, starting at the top. At 42 months, clockwise starting at the bottom. At 48 months, counterclockwise, starting at the top. A 60 months, clockwise starting at top or bottom. At

72 months and following, counterclockwise starting at the top as does the average adult.

Visual Behavior. The principle of reciprocal interweaving has proved to be of special significance in the ontogenesis of visual behavior. Human vision is an extremely complex function and does not by any means develop in a uniform, straight-line manner. This development involves complicated interwoven relationships which bring into reciprocal balance the numerous opposed functions of the total visual act. The patterning of vision is thus greatly influenced by the current maturity status of the organism. Developmental optics may be defined as the study of the organization of the visual functions in their dynamic relation to the ontogenesis of the action system.

The eyes take the lead in the conquest and manipulation of space. The baby takes hold of the physical world ocularly long before he grasps it manually. He can pick up a pellet (7 mm. in diameter) with his eyes full 20 weeks before he picks it up with his fingers.

Although an infant stares vaguely into faraway space, his structured visual world begins in the near vicinity of his eyes. For him the space-world is not a fixed, static absolute. It is a plastic domain which he manipulates in terms of the nascent powers of his growing action system. The supine infant, the runabout infant, the sedentary school child, each has his own space-world with a distinctive set of planes of regard. Biological space is a function of the organism. The space-world of the myope differs from that of the hyperope. Every child organizes his space-world in obedience to laws of development, general for the species and unique for himself.

This organizational process operates in three basic functional fields: skeletal, visceral, and cortical. These fields are correlated with the three primary embryological divisions and with the conventional fixation-focus-fusion triad. The *skeletal* component of this functional complex seeks and holds a visual image (optical stimulus); the *visceral* component discriminates and defines the image; the *cortical* unifies and interprets it.

The three functional fields develop conjointly but by no means uniformly. The ratio between skeletal, visceral, and cortical manifestations varies with advancing stages of maturity. In the course of individual development, gradients of performance are built up concurrently but unevenly in the three basic functional fields. Four factors enter into these gradients: (1) *coordination,* which refers to the teaming of the eyes and right-vs.-left dominances; (2) *reach,* which refers to the distance and precedence of the planes of regard; (3) *scope,* which concerns the important relationships between central and peripheral vision; (4) *drift,* which denotes the growth trends signified by the break and recovery span of ocular ductions, the preferred zones of regard, and accommodation and dominant directionalities.

All these variables and gradients are subject to the organizing processes of growth. Accordingly, each age of infancy and childhood affords a distinctive constellation of visual behavior patterns. With so many components and variants entering into the functional complex of the visual system, it is natural that no two children should see exactly alike. The possible constellations of visual components, normal, atypical, and abnormal, are beyond enumeration. The individual variations, however, are governed by a general ground plan of ontogenetic development (Gesell, Ilg, and Bullis, 1949).

Ontogenesis involves many counterpoised functions which must be brought into reciprocal control: peripheral vs. central vision; near vs. far fixation; skeletal vs. visceral adjustments, etc. The developmental resolution of such opposites is accomplished through a reciprocal type of organization.

This ontogenetic principle is so far-reaching that it may be stated in the form of a law as follows:

The organization of reciprocal relationships between two counteracting functions or neuromotor systems is ontogenetically manifested by somewhat periodic shifting of ascendancy of the component functions or systems, with progressive modulation and integration of the resultant behavior patterns.

The Principle of Functional Asymmetry

The principle of functional asymmetry is a special inflection of the principle of reciprocal interweaving and is inseparable therefrom. Bilateral and ipsilateral members must be brought into parallel and diagonal coordination. This takes an enormous amount of dovetailing, which is accounted for by the principle and process of neuromotor interweaving.

But man, in spite of his bilateral, construction, does not face the world on a frontal plane of symmetry. He confronts it at an angle, and he makes his escapes, also, obliquely. He develops monolateral aptitudes and preferences in handedness, eyedness, footedness, and other forms of unidexterity. Perfect ambidexterity, if it exists, would seem to be almost an abnormality, because effective attentional adjustments require an asymmetric focalization of motor set. The behavioral center of gravity always tends to shift to an eccentric position. Unidexterity of hand, foot, or eye does not so much represent an absolute difference in skill as a predilection for stabilized psychomotor orientations.

These orientations are fundamentally postural sets; and they are asymmetric. Ideally reciprocal interweaving operates to preserve harmony and balance; but in actuality there is a superadded ontogenetic deflection to insure the greater efficiency of functional asymmetry.

The tonic neck reflex (t.n.r.) is an asymmetric pattern of behavior, common to man and beast. Magnus, in his classic work, *Körperstellung*, reported an analysis of the postural reaction of decerebrate quadrupeds when their heads were experimentally turned to an extreme right or left position. He found a characteristic response: (1) extension of the forelimb on the side toward which the head was turned; (2) flexion of the opposite forelimb. The reflex occurred in pure form when the labyrinths were extirpated, and it was ascribed to proprioceptive impulses arising in the neck from torsion.

Magnus (1924, 1925) demonstrated the existence of the tonic neck reflex in idiots and patients suffering from extrapyramidal tract lesions; he was unable to induce the reflex in 26 normal infants a few hours to 16 weeks of age. He came to the conclusion that in man the tonic neck reflex is a pathologic phenomenon.

This conclusion is somewhat amazing because we have found the tonic neck response a ubiquitous, indeed a dominating, characteristic of normal infancy in the first 3 months of life. In a clinical sense the response should be regarded as abnormal only when it occurs in children of more advanced age who are suffering from arrest or damage of the central nervous system. In our normative survey of the ontogenetic sequences of behavior pattern, 26 to 49 infants were examined at lunar-month intervals up to the age of 56 weeks (Gesell and Thompson, 1934, 1938). It is a remarkable fact that 100 per cent of the infants at 4 weeks of age, when observed in a free supine posture, spontaneously maintained the cephalic symmetry displaces tonic neck asymmetry. The ontogenetic trends which underlie these transformations of postural pattern are plotted in Figure 3.

The accompanying illustrations show that this attitudinal pattern is clearly evident in the spontaneous waking postures of the

BEHAVIOR ITEMS plotted to show the ontogenetic trends of reactions involving the manifestations and decline of the TONIC NECK REFLEX (TNR).

The infants were observed at lunar month intervals (26 to 49 at each age), in controlled and repeated situations:

    I Spontaneous behavior, in the supine position.
    II Reactions to a dangling ring, in the supine position.

I   SPONTANEOUS
    SUPINE
    BEHAVIOR

    • Su 1 Head predominantly rotated
    ⊙ Su 2 Head predominantly rotated to one given side (right or left)
    △ Su 4 Head maintains midposition
    ▲ Su 7 Rotates head from one side to the other
    × Su 9 Arms predominantly in TNR position
    □ Su 26 Arms in windmill motion
    ⊡ Su 30 Hands predominantly open
    ⊠ Su 35 Hands active in mutual fingering

II REACTIONS TO
    DANGLING
    RING

    ● RD8 Regards ring in midplane (long head)
    ○ RD29 Approaches ring with both hands
    ▲ RD42 Transfers ring from hand to hand

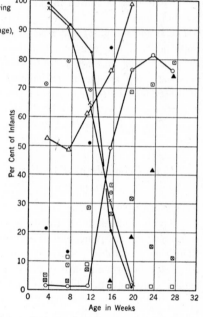

FIGURE 3. Ontogenetic trends underlying tonic neck reflex.

head predominantly rotated to one side; 100 per cent likewise held their arms in characteristic t.n.r. attitudes. We conclude that the t.n.r is a normal and virtually universal feature of neonatal infancy. Indeed, for 8 weeks the t.n.r. holds strong sway; at 12 weeks it is less conspicuous; at 16 weeks it is in transition; at 20 weeks in eclipse, for at 20 weeks 100 per cent of our normative infants maintained the head in midposition. And when the head is predominantly held in midposition, at least one-half of each t.n.r. subsides, and tonic normal infant, whether he lies quiescent or active. Figure 4 illustrates t.n.r. in a rabbit and in a normal infant. The rabbit is adapted from Magnus; the infant is a healthy 8-week-old subject basking in the soft light of the photographic dome. Both are in the right t.n.r. Figure 5 pictures two normal infants, both 6 weeks of age. One is in right t.n.r. and the other in left t.n.r. In each instance the face-arm and face-legs are in extension, the contralateral extremities in flexion. Note the striking semblance to a fencing stance. Figure 6 shows a normal infant who at 1, 6, 8, and 12 weeks of age spontaneously and consistently exhibited a right t.n.r.

Figure 7 pictures the same infant at 24 weeks of age. The spontaneous asymmetry of the earlier ages has been superseded by a symmetric attitude in which both arms flex and the hands engage above the chest

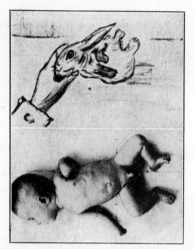

FIGURE 4. Right tonic neck reflex in rabbit and child.

in the midline. This is a lawful developmental sequence. The t.n.r. mechanisms are not extinguished at 24 weeks; they are simply submerged by symmetric bilateral patterns. In another month the bilateral in turn will give way to new unilateral patterns: one-hand reaching, one-handed manipulation, and hand-to-hand transfer, and ultimately to well-defined dextrality or sinistrality. Throughout early human development there is an almost periodic interweaving maturation, now of symmetric and then of asymmetric behavior forms, with corresponding shifts in postural manifestations.

When a large number of normal infants are examined at intervals during the first 3 months, we find that at least one-third consistently assume a right t.n.r.; possibly a third, the left t.n.r.; and the remainder adopt either right or left in a somewhat ambivalent manner. These figures are crude (the problem needs refined study), but they suggest important trends and individual differences in the genesis of laterality. Handedness is a partial and sometimes a misleading index of physiologic unilaterality. It is probable, however, that emphatic, constitutional left-handedness is correlated with a strong infantile left t.n.r.

Morphogenetically, the human t.n.r. should not be envisaged as a stereotyped reflex but as a growing pattern, changing with the maturity and the economy of the

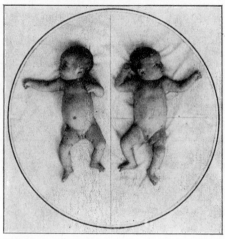

FIGURE 5. Right and left tonic neck reflex in 6-week-old infants.

organism. Torsion of the head to one side in a living fetus 20 weeks old arouses a movement of the arm on that side. This is a rudimentary t.n.r. which becomes better defined and elaborated in the latter half of the prenatal period. Fifteen minutes after the birth of a normal infant, I have detected a greater tonicity in the right as opposed to the left arm (the legs were in equal relaxation). This discrepancy was predictive of a left t.n.r., in which the right or occiput arm tends to show the greater tonus. The infant was kept under continuous observation for 14 days and nights, and, although he was placed in varying postures, he consistently displayed

The submergence of the naïve t.n.r. of early infancy is the result of the ascendancy of cortical controls, probably in the motor and premotor regions, if Bieber and Fulton's (1938) data, regarding ablation, for monkeys and baboons apply to man. This probability is strengthened by our findings in a case of cerebral palsy, in which nec-

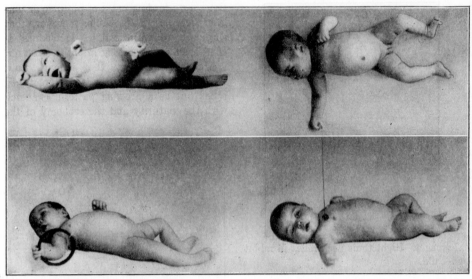

FIGURE 6. Right tonic neck reflex spontaneously and consistently exhibited in infant V. W. at 1, 6, 8, and 12 weeks of age.

a waxing left t.n.r. Another infant, belonging to the right wing, was photographed daily in a standard supine position, from the fifteenth day throughout most of the first year of life. This infant spent approximately one-half of the 834 seconds of cinematically recorded behavior up to the eighty-second day in t.n.r. Sixty-five separate t.n.r.'s were observed; only one of these was leftward.

Figure 8 graphs the incidence of these t.n.r.'s, which fell to zero on the ninetieth day, when the head preferred a midposition and the arms assumed more symmetric and versatile attitudes.

ropsy (at the age of 14 years) revealed a severe but uncomplicated birth lesion of the basal ganglia (status marmoratus). The boy in question, A.C., was afflicted with extreme double athetosis and, although intelligent, could not sit, walk, talk, grasp, or even hold up his head sustainedly. Cinema records of his spontaneous behavior in the supine position were made at the age of 7 years. Subjected to frame-by-frame analysis, these records revealed temporal and spatial patterns remarkably similar to those of the activated t.n.r. of normal infancy. Figure 9 portrays eleven comparable phases in the arm and head movements of the palsied boy, aged 7 years, and of a normal infant, 4 weeks old.

These phases may be envisaged as a slashing windmill reaction emerging out of and returning to a basic t.n.r. attitude. The presence of the t.n.r. was obscured

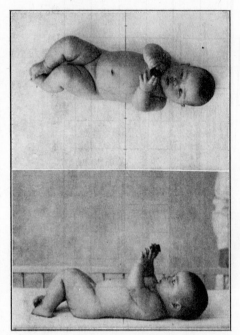

FIGURE 7. Symmetric prehensory and postural patterns at 24 weeks. Simultaneous photographs taken with one camera at zenith and the other at the horizon of the photographic dome.

by lively athetotic movements, but, when the cinema films were quantitatively studied, it was found that this boy was in a t.n.r. posture 41 to 56 per cent of the recorded time at 7, 10, and 13 years of age. The head generally took the lead in initiating the t.n.r. attitude. In no instance was a reversed t.n.r. attitude (head averted to one side with the arm of that side flexed) assumed even momentarily. All this suggests that the proprioceptive stimulus in

the neck was operating to bring about the natural reflex.

The process of transformation from t.n.r. to symmetric postures is extremely complex. It is not a process of simple substitution but one of progressive interlocking so that neither symmetry nor asymmetry gains permanent or complete ascendancy. The addiction of the young infant to t.n.r. postures is both a symptom and a condition of his behavior growth. The infantile t.n.r. represents a morphogenetic stage in which fundamental neurological coordinations are laid down to form the framework for later postural, manual, locomotor, and psychomotor reactions. Indeed, the t.n.r. is part of the ground plan of the organism pervasively identified with its unitary, total action system.

The t.n.r. accordingly has an ecology. More or less directly it subserves adaptations to the environment, prior to birth as well as later. The t.n.r. helps the fetus to accommodate to the conformation of the uterine cavity, and it may even facilitate the longitudinal presentation and orientation of the fetus at the entrance of the birth canal. The t.n.r. of the neonatal infant is well suited to postural attitudes which the child needs to assume when suckled at the breast. The activated windmill t.n.r. of the early weeks with its intensification of grasp responses suggests vestiges of arboreal groping and gripping. The future and formative references of the t.n.r., however, are more significant. The t.n.r. attitude promotes and channelizes visual fixation by the infant on his extended hand; it leads to hand inspection, to eye-hand coordinations, to prehensory approach, and eventually to unidextrality. It contributes to the organization of the diagonal reflexes of prone locomotion. It reduces the hazard of suffocation to the infant and is well adapted to acts of rejec-

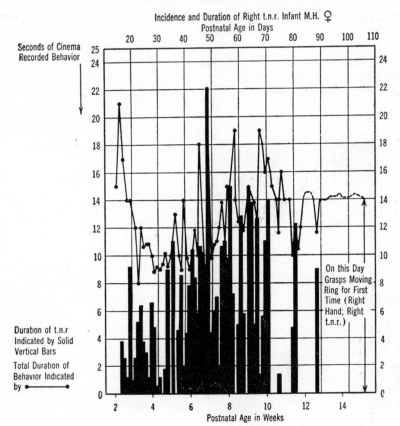

FIGURE 8. Duration and incidence by ages of the right tonic neck reflex in infant M. H. between 2 and 16 weeks of age.

tion, extrication, and withdrawal. Elaborated and inflected, it finally figures in innumerable adult acts of skill, aggression, and extrication. Attitudinal asymmetry always remains in reflex reserve, as well as subject to voluntary mobilization.

The Principle of Individuating Maturation

This principle may help us to recognize the mechanism by means of which the behavioral organism achieves its species characteristicness and yet at the same time makes specific adaptations within its environmental field. From the moment of fertilization, intrinsic and extrinsic factors cooperate in a unitary manner; but the original impulse of growth and the matrix of morphogenesis are endogenous rather than exogenous. The so-called environment, whether internal or external, does not generate the progressions of development. Environmental factors support, inflect, and specify; but they do not engender the basic forms and sequences of ontogenesis.

Even before the human embryo has a nervous system it is a perfectly integrated

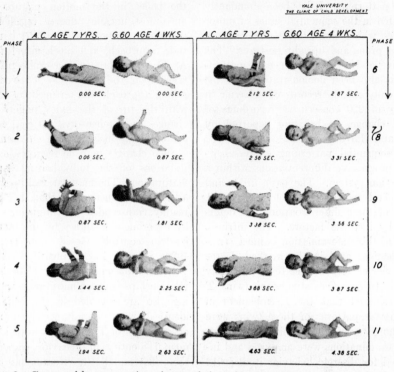

FIGURE 9. Comparable consecutive phases of the athetotic action pattern of A. C., aged 7 years, and of the spontaneous supine action pattern of a normal infant, G60, aged 4 weeks. (From "Correlations of Behavior and Neuro-pathology in a Case of Cerebral Palsy from Birth Injury," by A. Gesell and H. M. Zimmerman. *American Journal of Psychiatry,* 1937, *94,* Plate 3.) Eleven phases, with the elapsed time indicated in seconds, are shown side by side in vertical columns. These phases may be envisaged as a slashing windmill reaction emerging out of and returning to a basic tonic neck reflex attitude.

organism. It changes in shape and dimensions with each passing hour. It grows. This process of growth which derives its fundamental impulsions and directions from the zygote produces continuous reconfiguration. It configures the embryonic vesicle, the blastodermic layers, the skeleton, the skull, the profile of fetal, infantile, and adult nose, and the primary organization of the neuromotor system.

The function of the nervous system is to maintain the integrity of the organism and to anticipate the specific demands of the environment with provisional and preparatory arrangements. These forereference arrangements are not determined by stimulation from the outside world. Experience does not create them. Coghill (1929) has shown that the primary neural mechanism of walking (in *Amblystoma*) is laid down before the animal can respond at all to its environment. The primary attitude of the organism and the initiative of attitude are thus intrinsically determined. We apply the term "maturation" to this intrinsic and prospective aspect of ontogenetic patterning. It has been abundantly illustrated in the sequential series of motor attitudes which characterize the development of prone and upright postures. The pervasive and steady influence of maturation has also been demonstrated with the aid of daily cinema records of behavior in a study of 220 consecutive recordings of diurnal changes in behavior reported by Gesell and Halverson (1942).

The sequential patterning expresses itself in progressive differentiations within a total action system. The basic order and the general modality if not the specific outline of these differentiations are determined by intrinsic factors. The intrinsic nature of this determination is most strikingly demonstrated in the marked degree of behavior correspondence found in highly identical twins. Our studies of twins T and C showed that the resemblances in the behavior patterns of these twins were astonishingly numerous. Thirteen developmental examinations were analyzed and inventoried for discrete behavior items; 612 separate comparative ratings of such items were made. There were 99 items of minor disparity and 513 items of identical or virtually identical correspondence.

In the field of pellet prehension, this parity was very neatly disclosed. A small pellet, 8 mm. in diameter, was placed on a tabletop before each child, within easy reach. At 28 weeks both the twins, being somewhat retarded in their development, were visually unheedful of the pellet, though they definitely regarded a cube. At 38 weeks they addressed themselves in an identical manner to the pellet. The hands were placed in full pronation, the fingers were fully extended and spread apart in a fanlike manner. The thumb was extended almost at right angles. The photographic record of their attack upon the pellet in the motion pictures shows an almost uncanny degree of identity in the details of postural attitude, hand attitude, approach, and mechanism of grasp. At 40 weeks there was a crude raking attack upon the pellet; at 42 weeks this raking approach was replaced by a poking with the tip of the index finger. These changes in prehensory pattern occurred contemporaneously in both children.

Such changes may be regarded as manifestations of the individuating aspect of maturation. The maturational mechanisms are so firmly entrenched that they are not readily transcended by training, as shown by experimental studies by the method of co-twin control (Gesell and Thompson, 1929; Strayer, 1930; Hilgard, 1933).

Maturation and Learning. The intimate relationships between maturation and learning also are revealed in the behavior of identical twins. Simultaneous comparative observations of T and C disclosed a fundamental identity of behavior responses in the pellet and bottle situation at the age of 48 weeks. The twins were in the same crib, seated back to back, and each confronting her own examining table. Two examiners simultaneously held a small 4-ounce glass bottle in view and dropped an 8-mm. pellet into the bottle. Three trials were made with each child. The examiner, having dropped the pellet into the bottle, gave the bottle to the child.

Both children watched this dropping of the pellet with the same transfixed attention. Both children on the first trial, and again on the second trial, seized the bottle, apparently heedless of the contained pellet; but both children on the third trial (without, of course, any influence of imitation) pursued the pellet by poking at it against the glass—identical capacity to profit by experience.

In this instance we find that the correspondence of behavior patternings extends into the minute fields of specific adaptation or of learning. It may be readily granted that maturational factors primarily account for the similarity in capacity and general maturity displayed by these twins. Perhaps these same maturational factors also account for the more detailed correspondences, such as the mode of visual attention, the primary preoccupation with the bottle, and the secondary interest in the pellet. Within a brief span of time we see the spontaneous behavior patterns undergo a specific adaptation and call this adaptation learning. The distinctive criteria of maturation and learning, however, are not easily applied.

Let us assume that on the morrow, in the pellet-and-bottle situation, both children poke immediately with extended forefinger against the side of the bottle. Is this fixation of behavior due to the experience of the previous day? Shall the assimilative processes of the intervening night be regarded as maturation because the modification did not occur in immediate response to the situation; or shall it be called learning because it is virtually a specific adaptation to stimuli recently in the external environment? The fixation of the poking pattern, however, proves to be temporary, because in another lunar month, without specific experience, these same twins adaptively tilt both bottle and hand, and thrust the extended index finger into the open mouth of the bottle in pursuit of the pellet. Is this incremental differentiation of behavior pattern to be attributed to maturation or to learning?

The concept of maturation emphasizes the unity of the organism and the priority of the total pattern of response. The unity of the organism is not to be regarded as a mystical abstraction, but as a reality, namely, the functional unity of the total reaction system. Herrick (1929) identifies it particularly with the diffuse nervous network of

> . . . neuropil which pervades the brain substance and binds it all together as a functional unit. Into this neuropil there is a continuous discharge from every sensory surface of the body, fluctuating from moment to moment but always acting. Here growth is going on as long as learning is possible, here the total pattern expands, and here partial patterns are individuated.

Here also is the anatomic basis for conditioning of the Pavlovian type.

The basic ontogenetic forms of individuation are the result of maturation. Conditioning is superimposed, as it were, upon a maturational substrate. As conceived by Coghill,

> Conditioning of reaction is accompanied by restriction (narrowing) of the zone of adequate stimulation and concomitant restriction in the field of action. The primacy of structural basis for this is in the mechanism of the total pattern.

Which pattern, be it remembered, "is a growing thing."

For this reason all learning involves growth. According to Herrick (1929):

> It involves a change, more or less stable in the anatomical structure of the body, and the neuropil as the most labile part of the nervous system plays the most significant part in this reorganization of the mechanisms of behavior.

Maturation and Acculturation. The individual comes into his racial (and ancestral) inheritance through the processes of *maturation.* He comes into his social inheritance through processes of *acculturation.* These two processes operate and interact in close conjunction. Only through systematic studies of child development, naturalistic, biometric, and experimental, can we gain an insight into the relationship of maturation and acculturation. Here indeed is one of the most comprehensive and crucial problems of the life sciences. In this problem genetic psychology and cultural anthropology have a common stake.

The distinction between maturation and acculturation must not be drawn too sharply, but it must be made. Malinowski (1937) has characterized culture as "a large-scale molding matrix." His meaning is, of course, clear and up to a certain point incontrovertible; but in the interpretation of child development I should prefer to reserve the term "matrix" for the maturational mechanisms which literally establish the basic patterns of behavior and of growth career. A matrix is that which gives form and foundation to something which is incorporated, in this instance, through growth. By growth we do not mean a mystical essence, but a physiological process of organization which is registered in the structural and functional unity of the individual. In this sense the maturational matrix is the primary determinant of child behavior.

Growth is a unifying concept which resolves the dualism of heredity and environment. Environmental factors support, inflect, and modify; but they do not generate the progressions of development. Growth is an impulsion and as a cycle of morphogenetic events is uniquely a character of the living organism. Neither physical nor cultural environment contains any architectonic arrangements like the mechanisms of growth. Culture accumulates; it does not grow. The glove goes on the hand; the hand determines the glove. And the hand, by the way, is a primitive survival, shockingly similar to the hand of the ancient tortoise who swam the seas and walked the earth millions of years before the advent of man.

The Principle of Self-Regulatory Fluctuation

Every living organism is a storer and distributor of energy. The human infant is no exception. His daily cycle of activity and rest reflects the way in which he husbands and expends his energies; it also reflects a method of growth. "Aging and death may be considered to result from the gradual degradation of the original energy which caused the formation of an organism in the environmental field" (Eulenberg-Wiener, 1938).

The living system during the period of active growth is in a state of formative instability combined with a progressive movement toward stability. The so-called growth gains represent consolidations of stability. This opposition between two apparently opposing tendencies results in seesaw fluctuations. The maturing organism does not advance in a straight line but oscillates along a "spiral" course between two self-limited poles.

A spiral kind of organization was also suggested in the phenomenon of reciprocal interweaving. The concept of spirality is not mystical if, in spite of its vagueness, we simply let it denote metaphorically the devious but progressive involutions by which structure and function are jointly matured. The organism at times seems to retreat from a locus of maturity which it had already attained. Temporarily such a retreat may look like an abandonment. It would be abandonment if it continued on one tangent. The course of development, however, being spiral, turns back toward the point of departure; and it does not return precisely to this point. It returns to the same region but at a higher level. The neurological result is an interwoven texture which expresses itself in progressive patterns of behavior. The unity of the ground plan of the organism is preserved. It is a process of reincorporation and consolidation, rather than one of hierarchical stratification.

Many of the ephemeral variabilities of human functioning may be due to fluctuations or inconstancies of internal milieu. On the other hand, advanced forms of adaptive variability may be dependent upon a highly stable milieu and a consolidated developmental organization. Productive modifiability implies stability as well as a certain degree of instability. Stability and variability coexist not as contradictory opposites, but as mutual complements. The relationships are extremely complicated and specific. They may be studied in a dynamic aspect in narrow fields restricted to small periods of duration. They may be studied in a developmental aspect against the broader time frame of the ontogenetic cycle.

Fluctuation is therefore a normal expression of the self-regulatory mechanisms of development. Elsewhere we have presented objective data illustrating the operation of this principle in the development of feeding behavior (Gesell and Ilg, 1937). Detailed observations were made on the spontaneous self-demand schedule of a healthy infant throughout the first year of life. This infant, child J, was fed on the basis of her own carefully observed demands, and with minor exceptions her sleep was not disturbed. Accurate records of times of feeding, food intake, naps, and sleeping were made daily by a physician and a full-time nurse. This undertaking proved to be a long-range experiment which revealed the capacities of self-regulation in an infant who was literally allowed to shape her own behavior day.

Each behavior day was recorded and charted. The entire chart for the period of a year spreads, on ordinary plotting paper, to the formidable length of 7 feet. In the accompanying graphs we reproduce sections of this chart. Figure 10 covers 49 successive days for the age period of 3 to 10 weeks. Figure 11 condenses the total record by plotting 60 successive Thursdays from 3 to 63 weeks. The charts may be read both horizontally and vertically. The shaded areas, read across, show the sleeping periods for a 24-hour cycle. The open circles indicate bottle feedings; a figure in the circle designates ounces of intake.

Lines drawn vertically or obliquely connect these circles and show shifts in the times of feeding. Ages in weeks are ranged in the vertical column at the left. When the chart is examined as a whole, and is scanned from top to bottom, it reveals the process of adjustment by which an infant accomplishes revisions in a schedule of feedings and sleepings.

This process of adjustment is marked by fluctuations, particularly in the first quarter of the year. Compare on the chart the schedules at 3 weeks and at 8 weeks. (The shaded areas represent stretches of sleep; the open spaces, stretches of waking activity, including feeding.) At 3 weeks there are 7 feedings; at 8 weeks there are 5 feedings. This reduction was brought about by following the cues furnished by the infant herself. As early as the age of 4 weeks the chart gives evidence of a readjustment; this infant sleeps for a longer continuous period prior to the early morning and early afternoon bottles; she also sleeps longer in the early night; in so doing she skips her 7 P.M. bottle but demands her 11 P.M. bottle at 10 P.M. The result of this innovation is a 6-bottle day on Thursday of the fourth week. On Friday and Saturday she swings back, with deflections from her usual routine, to a 7-bottle day. On Sunday she advances her adjustment and has only 6 feedings. During the

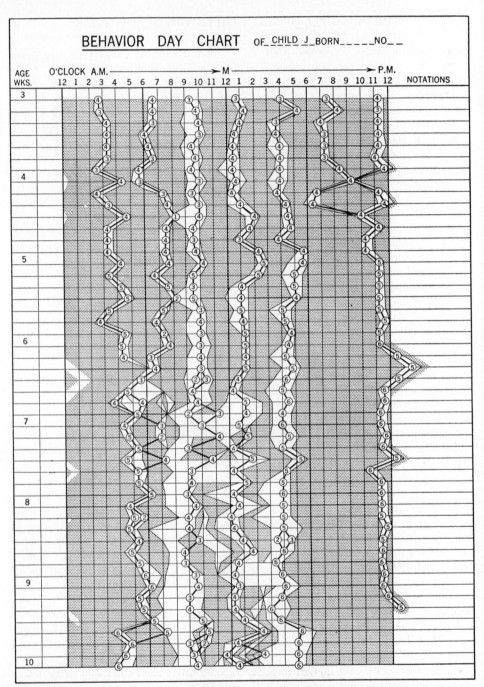

Figure 10. Child J. Feeding schedule from 3 to 10 weeks. (From *The Feeding Behavior of Infants: A Pediatric Approach to the Mental Hygiene of Early Life,* by A. Gesell and F. L. Ilg. Philadelphia: J. B. Lippincott Co., 1937, p. 95.)

360

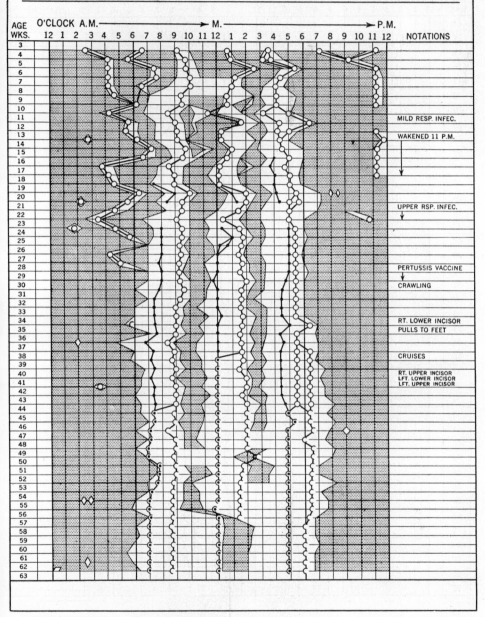

FIGURE 11. Child J. Sleep and feeding for 60 successive Thursdays from 3 to 63 weeks. (From *The Feeding Behavior of Infants: A Pediatric Approach to the Mental Hygiene of Early Life,* by A. Gesell and F. L. Ilg. Philadelphia: J. B. Lippincott Co., 1937, p. 97.)

361

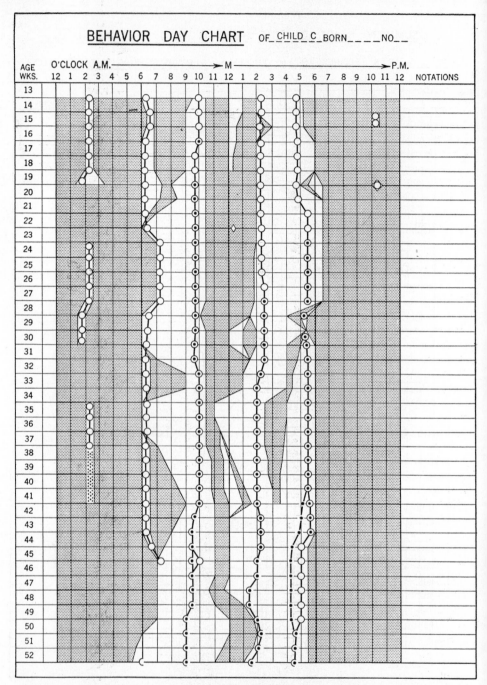

FIGURE 12. Child C. Sleep and feeding from 13 to 25 weeks. (From *The Feeding Behavior of Infants: A Pediatric Approach to the Mental Hygiene of Early Life,* by A. Gesell and F. L. Ilg. Philadelphia: J. B. Lippincott Co., 1937, p. 101.)

next 2 weeks she "settles down" to a relatively steady schedule of 6 feedings. But her morning and afternoon periods of daytime wakefulness are gradually widening, as shown by almost diurnal fluctuations in her schedule.

Superficially, these charted fluctuations seem to be irregular and whimsical. Looked at in perspective, however, they prove to be expressions of a basic mechanism of adjustment. The fluctuations are tentative approaches and approximations to a future schedule. When a future schedule is attained it, too, undergoes fluctuations directed toward a yet more future schedule. This is a growth process; or, if one prefers another concept, this is how the organism "learns."

The range of fluctuation in feeding schedules varies with different infants. In some the coefficient of fluctuation is high; in others, it is low. The latter accommodate themselves most readily to imposed schedules. In this category falls child C, whose feeding schedules are charted in Figure 12. The chart is plotted in terms of weeks rather than days. Although the diurnal variability is somewhat obscured by this condensation, the chart reveals the type of infant who shows a high degree of punctuality in his self-demands.

The almost periodic fluctuation displayed in the acquisition of sleep rhythms is shown in Figure 13. The neonate sleeps most of the 24 hours of day and night. His brief waking periods are largely spent in feeding, but even in these periods he may be in a somnolent stage, suggestive of fetal "hibernation." Sleep is not a reflexive type of reaction which comes to immediate completion with birth. Even in the uterus the infant is "learning" to awake and to sleep. A developmental process of differentiation is already taking place which will sharpen postnatally into rhythmic distinctions between sleep and activity. As early

as 6 weeks the infant may become fussy at evening because he desires sociability or perceptual experience in preference to sleep. Often he quiets if he is allowed to remain in a room where he may watch persons move about or may regard the lights. Physiologically, we may think of this as a method of acquiring the ability to postpone

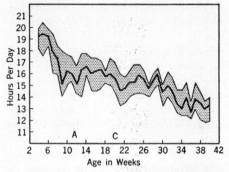

FIGURE 13. Child J. Sleep chart from 4 to 40 weeks. (From *The Feeding Behavior of Infants: A Pediatric Approach to the Mental Hygiene of Early Life,* by A. Gesell and F. L. Ilg. Philadelphia: J. B. Lippincott Co., 1937, p. 99.)

and to channelize sleep, which formerly engrossed almost the entire cycle of the day.

As the infant matures, the total duration of sleep per day constantly fluctuates but steadily diminishes. This is indicated in the accompanying graph (Figure 13), which plots the average hours of sleep per week, and the extremes of variation within each week, for child J from 4 to 40 weeks. It will be noted that the ups and downs show a rhythmic character. But the downs in the end exceed the ups, so that the average amount of diurnal sleep falls from 19 hours in the fourth week to 13 hours in the fortieth week. The number of naps likewise may rise and fall repeatedly but with a trend toward reduction. Usually the early morning and evening naps are the first to shorten and to disappear by merging with the night sleep. The later morning and the afternoon naps persist ordinarily throughout the first year. There is a kind of competition between these two naps. Sometimes as early as 28 weeks the afternoon nap shortens and soon gives way to the morning nap. Typically, however, there is a longer period of fluctuation and readjustment, and the afternoon nap wins out and gains ascendancy in the daily schedule by the beginning of the second year.

Such progressive fluctuations, culminating in a more stable response, are characteristic of all behavior development, including feeding behavior. The fluctuations, instead of being regarded as undesirable or as fortuitous irregularities, should be interpreted as effortful attempts on the part of the organism to accomplish increasingly mature adjustments. From this point of view, fluctuations have a positive function in the economy of growth and learning.

The Individuality of Growth Careers

By virtue of the foregoing principles the human infant shows a strong tendency to develop along well-defined morphogenetic lines characteristic of the species. Inherited engrams, or comparable regulators, not only determine behavior forms common to the race, but they also determine behavior modes and idiosyncrasies peculiar to the individual. The growth career of each individual infant assumes a distinctive pattern.

The range of individual differentiation is wide and diverse. Only in extremely similar monozygotic twins do we find a high degree of developmental correspondence between two individuals. In such twinship the resemblance may extend even to the timing and the minute details of physical and behavioral patterning. A study of twins A and B (Gesell and Blake, 1936)

may be cited here to indicate the precision with which the ontogenetic mechanisms operate.

These twin girls at the age of 12 years presented a duplication of bilateral coloboma involving each of their four eyes. These colobomas were amazingly alike in size, shape, position, and pigmentation. Genetically each coloboma traced back to a defective closure of the fetal ocular cleft. If a single "environmental" adversity caused the notching of the optic cup (in an embryo approximately 7 mm. long) it must have operated coincidentally within an extremely brief and critical interval on four rapidly organizing structures which simultaneously reached identical levels of maturity. This is an excessively remote possibility. It is still more unlikely that four defects of as many choroids, so similar in size, outline, position, and pigmentation, could have occurred at different times in consequence of four separate moments of infection, of irritation, or of damage neatly directed at each of the four eyes. It is, however, conceivable that the original single zygote or the constitutive factors in the twin embryos, which already held the hereditary determiners of all four eyes, held also the specific factors (or mutations) which delimited the development of the choroid. Similar specific factors would likewise account for the persisting remnant of the left hyaloid artery and for the correspondences of the shape and refraction of the four eyes. These eyes were derived from a single cell with one genetic constitution. Similar specific factors must also account for the striking resemblance in the emotional, intellectual, and motor make-up of these twins, including even their handwriting and the spellings and comparable misspellings of simple dictated words, such as *day, eat, sit, let, box, belong, door, yes, low, soft.*

Numerous studies of twins are now available for further analysis of the influence of genetic and epigenetic factors in the production of individuality (Carter, 1940). The medical literature on the pathological correspondences in twins is particularly suggestive with respect to the intrinsic developmental factors involved.

We have studied one highly identical pair of twins at the Yale Clinic of Child Development over a period of 20 years. By repeated physical and mental measurements, by systematic motion-picture records of behavior and experimental observations using the method of co-twin control, we have followed the life careers of these twin girls from infancy to adolescence (Gesell and Thompson, 1941). In the co-twin control studies, we trained one twin (T) and reserved the other twin (C) as a comparative control, to determine the effects of intensive training in such sample functions as stair-climbing, block-building, vocabulary, and manual coordination. These effects proved to be relatively impermanent: the untrained twin attained the equivalent skill as soon as she reached the requisite maturity. Numerous tests at advancing ages revealed an amazing parallelism in their physical and mental growth.

On close analysis, however, even this remarkably similar pair of twins presented consistent individual differences, many of which could be traced back to infancy. The differences are slight but they are durable. Here are some of them. T is quicker, more direct, more decisive; C is more deliberate, more inclusive, more relaxed. T is a bit brighter; but C is more sociable, more communicative. T shows a predilection for straight and angular lines in her drawings of a house, of smoke, of curtains, and of balloon strings. C favors curves. Her curtains are flounced, her smoke curls. In attentional characteristics, T's pick-up is more prompt, she focalizes more sharply, is more alert for details. C's attention is more generally alert, more imaginative, more roving. These differences are slight in degree; but they are permanent in the perspective of 14 years. They are permanent because they are constitutional.

The remarkable correspondences in many instances of twinship serve to emphasize the frequency and diversity of developmental variability among ordinary siblings. Some of the variations can be interpreted in terms of the ontogenetic principles which have just been outlined. Motor ineptitudes, for example, may arise out of exaggerations or defects in the process of reciprocal interweaving; many so-called regressions, likewise. The different modes by which children learn to walk and to run are impressive for variety of style. And often a style of acquiring motor control pervades other fields of behavioral adaptation. It is increasingly clear that many behavior difficulties with accompanying personality manifestations are based upon confused laterality or faulty functional asymmetry. Many forms of abnormality in mental life can be construed, following Coghill's suggestion, as due to excessive individuation. We have already called attention to the wide range of individual differences with respect to the amplitude of self-regulatory fluctuations. A thoroughly healthy individual is not likely to display any extreme deviations or deficiencies in the physiology of development represented by the five ontogenetic principles which have been described.

Nature is infinite in variety and variability. Even identical twins are not perfectly identical. The popular impression that all babies are much alike, especially young babies, cannot be confirmed. This impression has received some scientific support from psychologists who hold that the behavior of infants is chiefly patterned through conditioning processes and through specific learning.

On the basis of the conditioning theory of development, individual differences at birth are slight and increase with age. The investigations at Yale, including the detailed biogenetic studies of twins T and C, of the normative infants and selected subjects of the naturalistic survey all point in a different direction. One study (Gesell, assisted by Ames, 1937) was based upon an analysis of the cinema records of five different infants. The children were photographed under homelike conditions at lunar-month intervals throughout the first year of life. These extensive cinema records embraced the major events of the infant's day—sleeping, waking, bath, dressing and undressing, feeding, play, and social behavior at advancing age levels. Additional cinema records and psychological observations of the same children were made at the age of 5.

A trained and unbiased observer (L.B.A.), *who had never seen the infants*, made a detailed analysis of the cinema records covering the first year of life. On the basis of the objective evidence of the films alone, an estimate of fifteen behavior traits was made and the children were arranged in rank order for each trait. The same children were again studied at the age of 5 and were again rated with respect to the fifteen behavior traits which they had displayed in infancy. The two appraisals were made independently.

Is the strength of a behavior trait in the first year of life predictive of a similar strength in the fifth year? The fifteen traits of behavior individuality which were considered were: (1) energy output, (2) motor demeanor, (3) self-dependence, (4) social responsiveness, (5) family attachment, (6) communicativeness, (7) adaptivity, (8) exploitation of environment, (9) "humor" sense, (10) emotional maladjust-

ment, (11) emotional expressiveness, (12) reaction to success, (13) reaction to restriction, (14) readiness of smiling, (15) readiness of crying.

For each child and for each trait at 1 year and again at 5 years a comparative judgment was made. Out of the 75 comparative judgments, 48 coincided; 21 showed a displacement of 1 rank order only; 5, a displacement of 2; and 1, a displacement of 3 (Figure 14).

Every infant seems to have what may be called a motor habitude or characteristicness which expresses itself in postural demeanor and modes of movement. This characteristicness is difficult of description because it is the compound result of numerous factors, including skeletal frame, disposition of musculature, speed, synergy, smoothness and precision of action.

Some of these factors, however, yield to quantitative study. One of the most accessible of these is laterality. A consistent laterality in both handedness and footedness showed itself in all the children.

In general bodily control and also in manual dexterity, the four children for whom quantitative data were secured readily fell into the following rank order: 1, boy D; 2, boy A; 3, girl B; and 4, boy B.

Several hundred feet of cinema records were available for measuring the prehension time of these children in controlled normative situations. The interval consumed between the zero moment of reaching to the moment of grasp of the test object was computed by counting cinema frames. Each frame has a time value of 0.05 second. The prehension time (that is, the reach-grasp time) increased with the rank order as follows: boy D (rank order 1), 40 seconds; boy A (rank order 2), 47 seconds; girl B (rank order 3), 50 seconds; and boy B (rank order 4), 60 seconds.

In these time values we apparently have a rather basic trait of motor individuality, for this rank order held up with consistency when the patterns of prone progression were measured in detail. For these measurements over 1000 feet of film depicting creeping behavior were available.

a single forward placement of each of the four members. The total time required for one creep advance was determined for each of the subjects in turn. The time values ranged from 0.7 to 1.6 seconds for such a

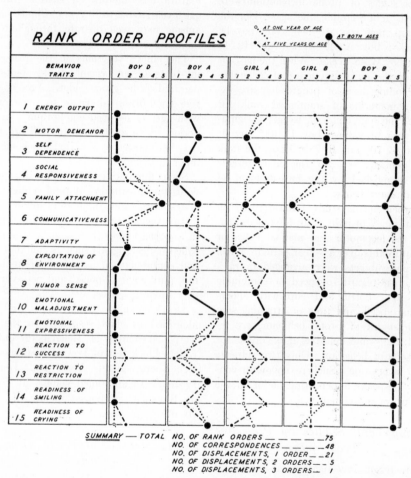

FIGURE 14. Rank order profiles for individuality traits in infancy and at 5 years.

Creeping speed, like prehension time, was measured by counting frames, in this instance the number of frames which recorded a forward movement of a hand or of a leg. A *creep advance* represents a single cycle of progression accomplished by

single creep advance. Once more the resulting rank order was identical with that just given in the preceding paragraph.

In other stages of prone behavior—namely, the *near-step advance* and the *one-step advance*—as well as in simple hands-

and-knees creeping, the time values for the four children retained their characteristic motor rank order.

Another individual difference asserted itself with respect to the age at which the various stages of prone locomotion were attained. For example, the ages when the near-step stage was attained were: boy D, 36 weeks; boy A, 40 weeks; girl B, 48 weeks; boy B, 48 weeks. When the nascent ages for the entire sequence of 23 stages in the ontogenesis of progression are expressed in terms of summated rank for each of the four children, we get a significant series of values: boy D, 38; boy A, 43; girl B, 70; boy B, 78. Again the rank order remains true to the characteristic order established by the measurement of specific motor traits.

Another cinema study (Ames, 1940) on the constancy of individual differences analyzed the locomotor and manual behavior of eight infants over a 3-year period. When the eight subjects were arranged in rank order with regard to speed of combining pellet with bottle and cup with spoon, creeping speed, and time of attaining successive stages of prone behavior, six retained the same relative rank order for each type of behavior. Only two subjects varied in position. Such psychomotor constancy bespeaks a persisting factor in the make-up of individuality.

Developmental Studies by Projective Techniques

More recent investigations at the Gesell Institute of Child Development have demonstrated that projective techniques reveal developmental progressions as well as distinctive traits of individuality. These traits, themselves, evidently undergo maturity changes with growth. The several Rorschach variables (movement responses, color responses, shading responses, and the like) change in a characteristic manner from age to age. Even the general character of the total response at a given age is in some measure predictable. Ames and associates (1952) have shown the presence of maturational factors for each of thirteen age levels from 2 to 10 years. Similar mechanisms may well operate throughout the following decade.

The child's reactions to the Rorschach ink-blots do not become steadily better integrated as he grows older. Ages of relative equilibrium alternate to some extent with ages of lessened equilibrium. An age period which appears to be well organized may be followed by a period which suggests inner disturbance.

Such fluctuations must be interpreted with clinical caution. A total configuration of response, which in an adult might signify disturbance, may be benign or even typical in a young child. The same is true of so-called danger signals such as contamination and confabulation, use of oligophrenic detail, pure color response, and perseveration of a single response.

Developmental trends have also been identified in child responses to the projective technique of Hellersberg and the Kaleidoblock test of Lowenfeld (Ames and Hellersberg, 1949; Ames and Learned, 1952a). An additional volume by Hoeber on Rorschach responses in late life (ages 70–100) is in press.

The Stability of Mental Growth Careers

In illustrating the principles of development, we have most frequently referred to motor and psychomotor characteristics. This is natural because these so-called motor phenomena are the most objective and measurable. It must not be thought, however, that the ontogenetic principles operate only in the motor sphere. It will be well to inquire whether they do not pervade the total domain of psychological growth, including language, adaptive, and personal-social behavior.

Growth is a morphogenetic process of progressive individuation and integration which leads to specific ends. To a considerable extent these ends are inherent in the organism. The organism also displays a prodigious capacity to adapt to circumstances, exigencies, and adversities. In this sense the growth of the individual is plastic and labile. But the individual retains durable characteristicness, and this is the stable aspect of growth.

The writer, in 1928, published the mental growth curves of thirty-three infants and young children whose behavior development had been repeatedly appraised by clinical examinations. We have followed the subsequent careers of thirty of these children, who are now in their teens or older. By comparing the early with the later findings, we can in retrospect determine the predictiveness of the first appraisals, many of which were made during the first year of life.

The group of thirty cases comprised a wide variety of developmental conditions: normal, retarded, mentally defective, superior, premature and postmature infants, a case of cerebral palsy with approximations to normal mentality, cases of cretinism, mongolism, hemihypertrophy, and *pubertas praecox*.

How consistent over a decade and more have been these mental growth careers? In no instance did the course of growth prove whimsical or erratic. In only one case within the period of 10 years was there a marked alteration of trend, namely, from a low average to a high average level (child B.D.). In a few defectives there was a progressive retardation without deterioration. For all others there was a maintenance of the general trend which

was ascertained by the early examinations.

Graphs were plotted for DQ and IQ, but the detailed case records also incorporated after each examination our clinical appraisals, which were by no means always identical with the psychometric quotients. These interpretive clinical judgments, we believe, have more significance than the raw quotients in investigating the consistency and stability of mental growth careers.

Our clinical evidence based on normative determinations demonstrates a high degree of consistency in the trends of early and later growth. Take, for example, the six siblings reported elsewhere (Gesell, 1928) as children D.E., E.F., F.G., G.H., H.I., and I.J. Three of these children over a period of 10 years have clung unmistakably to a normal course of behavior development; the other three, as decisively, to a subnormal course. It took no diagnostic subtlety to distinguish between these two kinds of growth potentiality on the basis of one behavior examination in infancy. The point is that these infant behavior pictures were unambiguously prophetic of the later careers. The predictions, therefore, were accurate. They were safe, also, because nature is never so whimsical as to mix up sectors of the growth curves of two sets of individuals as differently endowed as D.E. and I.J. (Figure 15).

In a similar way the predictive estimates of three distinctively superior children in our group did not miss the mark. The estimates were made before the children could read or write, which means that there was a high degree of indicativeness in the early behavior symptoms.

In less well-defined behavior pictures, equally confident predictions are not forthcoming because we do not have the techniques or acumen to identify and assess the indicators; but a comparable latent predictiveness resides in these pictures as well.

When there is a fairly even balance between the endogenous and the sustaining or exogenous factors, the trends of mental growth, whether subnormal, superior, or mediocre, are likely to be the most con-

to reckon repeatedly in cases of atypical and irregular behavior development. The concept of insurance factors is not mystical. It is derived from experimental embryology and from clinical observation. The surgical excisions, transplantations, and other interferences with the growing

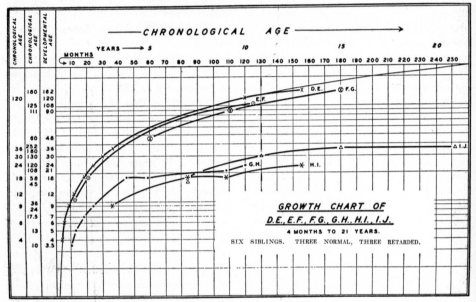

FIGURE 15. Growth graphs of D. E., E. F., F. G., G. H., H. I., I. J. (From *Biographies of Child Development: The Mental Growth Careers of Eighty-four Infants and Children,* by A. Gesell, B. M. Castner, H. Thompson, and C. S. Amatruda. New York: Paul B. Hoeber, 1939, p. 26.)

sistent. Developmental diagnosis and prognosis then come nearest to their mark. When, however, the organism is under stress of distortion because of unfavorable conditions, its ultimate adjustments as expressed in growth characteristics become least predictable. There are too many variables to appraise. External environment can be estimated with some shrewdness; but not so readily the internal developmental reserves.

These hidden reserves are the intrinsic insurance factors with which we have had

tissues of laboratory embryos have demonstrated that the organism is protected with a remarkable fund of reserve mechanisms which promptly or gradually move into every breach and fill it in some way, either through regeneration or compensatory and substitutive growth. If the lesion is too great, the organism dies. If the lesion is not too severe, and the organism not too old, growth may continue in a more or less normal manner.

In the development of the nervous system and in the ontogenesis of behavior, the human organism displays comparable insurance mechanisms. Locked in inner recesses beyond diagnostic scrutiny are reserve factors which may come to the rescue when development is retarded or impaired. As a poison stimulates the formation of antibodies, so certain errors or depressions of development stimulate a regulatory self-correction. These reserve factors, however, are not a single generalized capacity. They are specific biochemical and somatic structures almost infinite in number and variety, and of many degrees of availability. They are present in defective as well as normal individuals. They are probably most abundant in the most vital and best endowed. Vitality is an index of the plenitude and vigor of these very insurance factors. In spheres of behavior they operate not only during the period of growth, but also in old age, at least in the most "vital" individuals.

If there is a principle of uncertainty in the physiology of development it is a biological principle which rests upon important individual differences with respect to these insurance factors. Since they vary in amount, it is difficult to ascertain their strength in those inscrutable infants who present an inadequate and yet not decisively defective behavior picture. Here diagnosis must be wary, sometimes for a whole year or more, because sometimes the insurance factors come tardily and slowly into full force. But if they are present, and if the attendant conditions permit, they will ultimately assert themselves. When there is no counteracting deteriorating process, the tendency of growth will be toward something better and toward an optimal organization of the available equipment.

General Conclusion

Behavior at all stages of development is patterned. Patterning is displayed in the phase of the moment, in the dynamic sequence of specific behavior events, and in the progressive differentiations of the ontogenetic cycle.

The forms of behavior are governed by laws of developmental morphology, and these forms can be analyzed in terms of time and space.

The basic configurations, correlations, and successions of behavior patterns are determined by a process of maturation. The tenacity of this process has been demonstrated by developmental studies of both premature and full-term infants and by experimental studies of monozygotic twins.

The rôle of maturation is most conspicuous in the fetus and infant, but it persists throughout the life cycle until the growth potential completely subsides.

A psychic constitution is more than a general diathesis. It is a structured product of growth. It endures, but it also changes during the life cycle.

The psychic individual is a distinctive entity by virtue of a certain characteristicness in his manifold behavior tendencies and in his secular pattern of growth. Such characteristicness can be investigated from the standpoint of form and can be formulated by morphographic methods. A systematic study of the ontogenesis of behavior thus becomes a psychomorphological approach to the ancient problem of constitution and type.

Bibliography

Ames, L. B. 1937. The sequential patterning of prone progression in the human infant. *Genet. Psychol. Monogr., 19,* 409–460.

——. 1940. The constancy of psycho-motor tempo in individual infants. *J. Genet. Psychol., 57,* 445–450.

——. 1942. Supine leg and foot postures in the human infant in the first year of life. *J. Genet. Psychol., 61,* 87–107.

Ames, L. B., in collaboration with E. Hellersberg. 1949. Responses of three- to eleven-year-old children to the Horn-Hellersberg Test. *Rorschach Research Exchange and Journal of Projective Techniques,* Vol. XIII, No. 4, pp. 415–432.

Ames, L. B., and J. Learned. 1952a. Developmental trends in child Kaleidoblock responses. *J. Genet. Psychol.* (In press.)

——. 1952b. Individual differences in child Kaleidoblock responses. *J. Genet. Psychol.* (In press.)

Ames, L. B., J. Learned, R. Metraux, and R. Walker. 1952. *Child Rorschach responses: Developmental trends from two to ten years.* New York: Hoeber. Pp. xiv + 310.

Bertalanffy, L. von. 1933. *Modern theories of development: An introduction to theoretical biology.* (Trans. by J. H. Woodger.) London: Oxford University Press.

Bieber, I., and J. F. Fulton. 1938. Relation of the cerebral cortex to the grasp reflex and to postural and righting reflexes. *Arch. Neurol. Psychiat., 39,* 433-454.

Boutan, L. 1914. Les deux méthodes de l'enfant. *Act. Soc. linn. Bordeaux, 68,* 3-146.

Brainard, P. P. 1930. The mentality of a child compared with that of apes. *J. Genet. Psychol., 37,* 268-293.

Carmichael, L. 1933. Origin and prenatal growth of behavior. In C. Murchison (Ed.), *A handbook of child psychology* (2d ed., rev.), pp. 31-159. Worcester: Clark University Press.

Carter, H. D. 1940. Ten years of research on twins: contributions to the nature-nurture problem. *Yearb. Nat. Soc. Stud. Educ., 39*(I), 235-255.

Coghill, G. E. 1929. *Anatomy and the problem of behaviour.* Cambridge: University Press; New York: Macmillan.

Dürken, B. 1932. *Experimental analysis of development.* (Trans. by H. G. and A. M. Newth.) New York: Norton.

Eulenberg-Wiener, R. von. 1938. *Fearfully and wonderfully made: The human organism in the light of modern science.* New York: Macmillan.

Gellermann, L. W. 1933. Form discrimination in chimpanzee and two-year-old children: I. Form (triangularity) *per se.* II. Form versus background. *J. Genet. Psychol., 42,* 3-27, 28-50.

Gesell, A. 1928. *Infancy and human growth.* New York: Macmillan.

——. 1938a. *Prone progression in the human infant.* (Film.) New Haven: Photographic Library, Yale Clinic of Child Development. 1000 ft. 35 mm.; 400 ft. 16 mm.

——. 1938b. The tonic neck reflex in the human infant: Its morphogenetic and clinical significance. *J. Pediat., 13,* 455-464.

——. 1938c. *The tonic neck reflex (t.n.r.) in the human infant.* (Film.) New Haven: Photographic Library, Yale Clinic of Child Development. 130 ft. 16 mm.

——. 1939a. The appraisal of mental growth careers. *J. Consult. Psychol., 3,* 73-75.

——. 1939b. Reciprocal neuromotor interweaving: A principle of development evidenced in the patterning of infant behavior. *J. Comp. Neurol., 70,* 161-180.

——. 1940. The stability of mental-growth careers. *Yearb. Nat. Soc. Stud. Educ., 39*(II), 149-160. See also A. Gesell, Some observations of developmental stability, in W. R. Miles (Ed.), *Psychological Studies of Human Variability. Psychol. Monogr.,* 1936, *47,* No. 212, pp. 35-46.

Gesell, A. 1948. *Studies in child development.* New York: Harper. Pp. x + 224.

——. 1951a. *The embryology of human behavior.* A 30-minute, technicolor, 16-mm sound film, which traces the development of behavior patterns in the human infant. Narration by Dr. Gesell. Chicago, Ill.: International Film Bureau.

——. 1951b. *Science in progress.* Vol. VII, Chapter 3. New Haven: Yale University Press.

——. 1952a. *Infant development: The embryology of early human behavior.* (Serves as handbook for film on embryology of behavior.) New York: Harper. Pp. xii + 108.

——. 1952b. Reprinted from: *A history of psychology in autobiography,* Vol. IV, pp. 123-142. Worcester: Clark University Press.

Gesell, A., and C. S. Amatruda. 1941. *Developmental diagnosis: normal and abnormal child development.* New York: Hoeber.

——. 1947. *Developmental diagnosis: Normal and abnormal child development. Clinical methods and pediatric applications.* 2d ed. New York: Hoeber. Pp. xvi + 496.

Gesell, A., C. S. Amatruda, and C. S. Culotta. 1936. Effect of thyroid therapy on the mental and physical growth of cretinous infants. *Amer. J. Dis. Child., 52,* 1117-1138.

Gesell, A., in collaboration with C. S. Amatruda. 1945. *The embryology of behavior: The beginnings of the human mind.* New York: Harper.

Gesell, A., assisted by L. B. Ames. 1937. Early evidences of individuality in the human infant. *J. Genet. Psychol., 47,* 339-361.

Gesell, A., and L. B. Ames. 1940. The ontogenetic organization of prone behavior in human infancy. *J. Genet. Psychol., 56,* 247-263.

——. 1946. The development of directionality in drawing. *J. Genet. Psychol., 68,* 45-61.

——. 1947. The development of handedness. *J. Genet. Psychol., 70,* 155-175.

——. 1950. Tonic neck reflex and symmetro-tonic behavior: Developmental and clinical aspects. *J. Pediat., 36,* No. 2, pp. 165-176.

Gesell, A., and E. M. Blake. 1936. Twinning and ocular pathology. With a report of bilateral macular coloboma in monozygotic twins. *Arch. Ophthal., N. Y., 15,* 1050-1071.

Gesell, A., B. M. Castner, H. Thompson, and C. S. Amatruda. 1939. *Biographies of child development: The mental growth careers of eighty-four infants and children.* New York: Hoeber.

Gesell, A., and H. M. Halverson. 1936. The development of thumb opposition in the human infant. *J. Genet. Psychol., 47,* 339-361.

——. 1942. The daily maturation of infant behavior. A cinema study of postures, movements and laterality. *J. Genet. Psychol., 61,* 3-32.

Gesell, A., H. M. Halverson, H. Thompson, F. L. Ilg, B. M. Castner, L. B. Ames, and C. S. Amatruda.

1940. *The first five years of life: A guide to the study of the preschool child.* New York: Harper.

Gesell, A., and F. L. Ilg. 1937. *The feeding behavior of infants: A pediatric approach to the mental hygiene of early life.* Philadelphia: Lippincott.

Gesell, A., and F. L. Ilg, assisted by J. Learned and L. B. Ames. 1942. *Infant and child in the culture of today. The guidance of development in home and nursery school.* New York: Harper. Pp. iv + 399.

Gesell, A., and F. L. Ilg, in collaboration with L. B. Ames and G. E. Bullis. 1946. *The child from five to ten.* New York: Harper. Pp. xiv + 473.

Gesell, A., F. L. Ilg, and G. E. Bullis. 1949. *Vision: Its development in infant and child.* New York: Hoeber. Pp. xvi + 329.

Gesell, A., and H. Thompson. 1929. Learning and growth in identical infant twins: An experimental study by the method of co-twin control. *Genet. Psychol. Monogr., 6,* 1–124.

——. 1941. Twins T and C from infancy to adolescence. A biogenetic study of individual differences by the method of co-twin control. *Genet. Psychol. Monogr., 24,* 3–121.

Gesell, A., and H. Thompson, assisted by C. S. Amatruda. 1934. *Infant behavior: Its genesis and growth.* New York: McGraw-Hill.

——. 1938. *The psychology of early growth.* New York: Macmillan.

Gesell, A., and H. M. Zimmerman. 1937. Correlations of behavior and neuro-pathology in a case of cerebral palsy from birth injury. *Amer. J. Psychiat., 94,* 505–536.

Halverson, H. M. 1931. An experimental study of prehension in infants by means of systematic cinema records. *Genet. Psychol. Monogr., 10,* 107–286.

——. 1932. A further study of grasping. *J. Gen. Psychol., 7,* 34–64.

——. 1933. The acquisition of skill in infancy. *J. Genet. Psychol., 43,* 3–48.

Herrick, C. J. 1929. Anatomical patterns and behavior patterns. *Physiol. Zoöl., 2,* 439–448.

Hilgard, J. R. 1933. The effect of early and delayed practice on memory and motor performances studied by the method of co-twin control. *Genet. Psychol. Monogr., 14,* 493–567.

Jacobsen, C. F., M. M. Jacobsen, and J. G. Yoshioka. 1932. Development of an infant chimpanzee during her first year. *Comp. Psychol. Monogr., 9,* 1–94.

Kellogg, W. N., and L. A. Kellogg. 1933. *The ape and the child: A study of environmental influence upon early behavior.* New York: McGraw-Hill.

Klüver, H. 1933. *Behavior mechanisms in monkeys.* Chicago: University of Chicago Press.

Köhler, W. 1924. *The mentality of apes.* (Trans. by E. Winter.) London: Kegan Paul; New York: Harcourt, Brace (1925).

Kohts, N. 1935. *Infant ape and human child: Instincts, emotions, play, habits. (Scientific memoirs of the museum darwinianum in Moscow,* Vol. III, pp. xvi + 596, c. 145 plates.)

Kuhlen, R. G., and Thompson, G. G. 1952. *Psychological studies of human development.* New York: Appleton-Century-Crofts. Pp. xiii + 533.

Landis, C., and W. A. Hunt. 1939. *The startle pattern.* New York: Farrar and Rinehart.

Lashley, K. S., and J. B. Watson. 1913. Notes on the development of a young monkey. *J. Anim. Behav., 3,* 114.

Magnus, R. 1924. *Körperstellung.* Berlin: Springer.

——. 1925. Animal posture. Croonian Lecture, *Proc. Roy. Soc., 89B,* 339–353.

Malinowski, B. 1937. Culture as a determinant of behavior, pp. 133–168. In *Harvard Tercentenary Publication: Factors determining human behavior.* Cambridge: Harvard University Press.

Munn, N. L. 1938. *Psychological development: An introduction to genetic psychology.* Boston: Houghton Mifflin.

Needham, J. 1936. *Order and life.* New Haven: Yale University Press.

Riesen, A. H., and Kinder, E. F. 1952. *The postural development of infant chimpanzees.* New Haven: Yale University Press. Pp. xxii + 204.

Sheldon, W. H. 1942. *The varieties of temperament.* New York: Harper. Pp. x + 520.

——. 1940. *The varieties of human physique.* New York: Harper. Pp. xii + 347.

Sherrington, C. S. 1906. *The integrative action of the nervous system.* New York: Scribner's.

Strayer, L. C. 1930. Language and growth: The relative efficacy of early and deferred vocabulary training studied by the method of co-twin control. *Genet. Psychol. Monogr., 8,* 209–319.

Swan, C. 1934. *Postural patterning of the resting infant hand.* Unpublished Master's Essay, Yale University.

Yerkes, A. W. 1935. Experiments with an infant chimpanzee. *J. Genet. Psychol., 46,* 171–181.

Yerkes, R. M. 1916. The mental life of monkeys and apes: A study of ideational behavior. *Behav. Monogr., 3,* No. 1. Pp. 145.

CHAPTER 7

LEARNING IN CHILDREN

NORMAN L. MUNN

Introduction

Learning may be said to occur whenever behavior undergoes incremental modification of a more or less permanent nature as a result of activity, special training, or observation. To say that learning involves an *incremental* modification is to distinguish it from fatigue, which is also due to activity, but with which a performance decrement is associated. By indicating that the learning process involves a more or less *permanent* modification, we differentiate it from sensory adaptation, which disappears soon after removal of the stimulating circumstances. Finally, by including the statement that learning depends upon *activity, special training,* or *observation,* we point to the fact that it differs from modification which depends upon maturation *per se.*

In order to approximate complete coverage of experimental investigations on learning in children, one must take cognizance of conditioning, acquisition of motor skill, memorizing and related mnemonic functions, and problem solving.

Investigations of learning in children, rather than introducing new problems and essentially novel techniques, have followed the leads of animal and adult human psychology. The first investigation of conditioned responses in children (Krasnogorski, 1909) involved modification of the technique of Pavlov, who more than a decade earlier had begun his pioneer investigations

on conditioned salivary response in dogs. Researches on learning of motor skills in children began to appear some time after the experiments of Thorndike (1898) and Small (1899) on animals and those of Bryan and Harter (1897), Swift (1903), and Book (1908) on learning of skills by human adults. The earliest published experiments on learning of motor skills which involved children as subjects are those of Judd (1908) on dart throwing and those of Hicks and Carr (1912) on maze learning. In researches carried out since 1912 the maze technique has figured prominently.

Investigations of mnemonic processes in children began shortly after Ebbinghaus's pioneer study on himself. Jacobs (1887) devised the memory-span test and used it with children. Binet and Henri (1894) worked with the memory span and included memory-span tests in their intelligence scales. Several of the early memorizing experiments (Steffens, 1900; Pentschew, 1903; Radossawljewitsch, 1907) involved children incidentally.

Problem solving, apart from that incidentally involved in the school subjects, has been extensively investigated only in comparatively recent years. Nevertheless, Lindley (1897) studied how children and adults solve various unicursal puzzles. He also, as we shall indicate more fully later, made some pertinent observations on differences in the way in which children and adults attack such problems. Widespread interest in the experimental investigation of problem solving by children has, however, appeared only since publication of Köhler's (1925) researches on problem solving in apes. Investigations of the rôle of incentives and of various other factors relating to economical learning have also followed leads given by animal and adult human psychology.

In many investigations of learning, inclusion of children has been merely incidental. Early students of child development, although they investigated many other problems with children directly, tended, as far as learning was concerned, to accept and apply results obtained with animals and human adults. This accounts, in part at least, for a long delay in the appearance of researches aimed at determining how *children* learn.

The Conditioned Response

During his study of gastric secretion in dogs, Pavlov (1889–1890) observed that stimuli frequently associated with the presence of food become, in themselves, adequate to arouse secretory responses such as salivation. Salivation in response to hitherto neutral stimuli, such as sounds and skin irritation, was later referred to by Pavlov (1903) as a *psychic secretion*. Bekhterev, another Russian investigator, began in 1906 to develop what he termed *associative reflexes* in dogs. In response to shock on the foot or leg, withdrawal or *protective* reflexes were aroused. Bekhterev observed elicitation of similar reflexes by previously *neutral* stimuli after such had been presented in association with shock. Numerous researches based upon the above observations were soon carried out by Pavlov, Bekhterev, and their students.

That conditioned responses are relatively simple habits is doubted by no psychologist. Much of the controversy concerning them hinges upon the claim of Pavlov,

Watson, and others that all learning, no matter how complex, results from conditioning. Habits are referred to by these investigators as chains of conditioned reflexes, or as compound conditioned responses. Our present discussion will avoid theoretical issues by describing the conditioned response in children merely as a type of habit formation. Whether or not all learning may adequately be envisaged in terms of conditioning will be determined only after more data are available. For an excellent discussion of the present status of this controversy the reader is referred to Hilgard and Marquis (1940) and Hilgard (1948).

Prenatal Conditioning. The possibility that certain "reflexes" of the newborn are responses conditioned prior to birth (Holt, 1931) has led several investigators to attempt conditioning of fetuses.[1] The two earliest attempts (Ray, 1932; Sontag and Wallace, 1934) were either unsuccessful or ambiguous in result. However, Spelt (1938, 1948) has reported success. Details of the experiment are reported in the latter publication. Responses of 16 fetuses between the ages of 7 and 9 months were studied through application of tambours to the mother's abdomen and also through maternal responses to felt movement. The recorded data are illustrated in Figure 1 and described in the legend.

A loud clapper elicited movement in all but the youngest fetuses. Before conditioning, there, was never any response to vibrotactile stimulation of the maternal abdomen. In some cases, as few as 15 paired stimulations elicited movement to the tactile vibration alone. From 5 to 11 successive conditioned responses were obtained. One fetus which was studied extensively ex-

---

[1] See Dennis (1943), who discusses this problem in detail and maintains that, despite the views of Holt and others, responses of the newborn are products of maturation rather than conditioning.

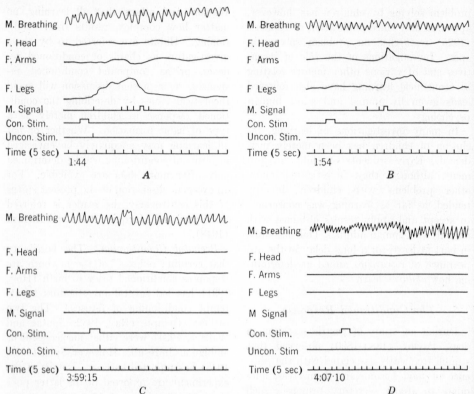

FIGURE 1. Sample kymograph records from fetal conditioning study. (From "The Conditioning of the Human Fetus *in Utero*," by D. K. Spelt. *Journal of Experimental Psychology*, 1948, *38*, 344. By permission of the publisher.) *A*, showing response to both stimuli, and *B*, showing response to *CS*, obtained from same *S*. *C* is a record from a non-pregnant control *S*. *D* shows result of applying *CS* alone in late pregnancy without previous conditioning trials.

hibited retention of conditioning over a period of 18 days. It also demonstrated experimental extinction and spontaneous recovery. Control experiments utilizing the vibrotactile stimulus alone demonstrated that movement to vibration does not develop as a function of age. The conditioned-response procedure applied to non-pregnant subjects produced nothing simulating the results obtained with pregnant subjects. These findings, and the fact that the mothers knew nothing of the nature of the experiment, or indeed that they were serving in an experiment, support the claim that the movements were fetal and not produced by maternal reactions. Although maternal movements, breathing, and sighing, distorted the records, the fetal movements were readily discerned.

Conditioning in Newborn Infants. Conditioning experiments on infants in the first week of life have been reported by Marquis (1931), Wenger (1936) and Wickens and Wickens (1940). In the investigation by Marquis, 10 infants between the ages of 2 and 9 days were stimulated with a buzzer for 5 seconds prior to each feeding period. Within 5 days of training, 8 of these infants began to exhibit sucking and mouth-opening responses to the buzzer. Correlated diminution of crying and of general activity also appeared. Four control infants stimulated with the buzzer, but without associated food, failed to exhibit conditioned responses.

This experiment is criticized by Wenger (1936) on the basis that controls were inadequate and observation of responses too subjective. He failed to obtain conditioned feeding reactions in two newborn infants. That newborn infants may be conditioned, however, is shown by results obtained in his experiments involving eyelid, limb withdrawal, and respiratory responses. In conditioning of eyelid responses the unconditioned stimulus was a flash of light and the conditioned stimulus a tactile vibration of the foot. Tactile vibration preceded light by 3 seconds. During control tests, six 9-day-old infants exhibited lid responses to a tactile stimulation of the foot in 29 per cent of the presentations. The range was from 23 to 34 per cent. Infants with whom conditioning begin on the second day of life, however, reached percentages of 58 to 74 by the ninth day. Acquisition curves showed much daily fluctuation, and Wenger therefore concluded that, although conditioning is undoubtedly present, it is quite unstable.

Wenger also obtained conditioning when the unconditioned stimulus comprised an electric shock which elicited foot withdrawal and respiratory changes. Tactile vibration at the sternum served as the conditioned stimulus. One infant which exhibited no flexion responses to tactile stimulation 2 days after birth was, by the ninth day, making such responses to 50 per cent of the stimulations.

More acceptable evidence of conditioning than could be obtained with tactile vibration at the sternum was disclosed when a tone of 1084 cycles, and having a loudness of 50 decibels above the adult threshold, was substituted. Under these conditions, 3 infants exhibited conditioned flexion and respiratory responses. Two infants trained with a flash of light as the conditioned stimulus also exhibited conditioned withdrawal. They reached a mean percentage of 46 withdrawals. The percentage for controls of the same age was 13. In this, as in all the earlier experiments, conditioning was far from stable.

Wickens and Wickens (1940) criticize the results of the above studies on conditioning in neonates chiefly on the ground that controls were not adequate. Their own study, involving 36 infants younger than 10 days, utilized shock to the right foot as the unconditioned stimulus and the sound of a buzzer as the conditioned stimulus. An experimental group of 12 infants was given 36 paired stimulations of buzzer and shock, 12 each day for 3 days. One control group was tested at intervals with the shock alone. Another was tested with the buzzer alone. This was to check the possibility that maturation might make the infants responsive to the buzzer. In subsequent tests with the buzzer alone, the experimental and first-mentioned control groups gave similar results. This was true in terms of the number of responses to the point of extinction and for spontaneous recovery on the next day. Only 1 infant out of the 12 in the second control group gave any response to the buzzer, thus showing that maturation alone could not account for results with the other groups. A check demonstrated that the results could not be attributed to artifacts of the experimental situation. Two possible explanations of the failure to find a difference in the buzzer-shock and shock alone groups are mentioned. The most likely explanation is that both the shock and the buzzer constituted a *change* in the stimulus complex and that the infants were conditioned to such a change rather than to the buzzer or shock as such. More specifically, it may be that the shock represents a change as well as a stimulus for reflex withdrawal. The sound of the buzzer, especially when presented in the same context as the shock, also represents a change in the same stimulus complex. It does not seem strange, therefore, that withdrawal should occur to the buzzer even though it has not been paired with shock. Such stimulus generalization is perhaps the basis for other examples of pseudo-conditioning (Grether, 1938).

Thus, although the findings are not as clear as one might wish, there seems good evidence for supposing that neonates as well as fetuses are susceptible to conditioning.

Marquis (1941) claims that, whether or not the above studies are accepted as evidence of neonatal conditioning, it is a well-known fact that newborn infants readily adapt to a feeding schedule. She recorded general bodily activity in, respectively, (1) a 4-hour schedule during the period of hospitalization, (2) a 3-hour schedule for 9 days and then a 4-hour schedule, and (3) a self-schedule, i.e., fed only when "hungry." There was clear evidence of adaptation. Adaptation was especially shown in the group shifted from a 3- to a 4-hour schedule. This shift produced a large and statistically significant increase in activity, particularly evident during the last hour before feeding. Marquis claims that this change in activity gives proof of a temporal form of conditioned response, set up according to the law of effect. She claims, moreover, that this sort of modification illustrates the earliest form of human acculturation.

Investigations of Conditioned Responses during Later Infancy. Conditioned feeding reactions in infants between the second and fourth months of life have been investigated by Denisova and Figurin

(1929) [1] and Kantrow (1937). All but 1 of Denisova and Figurin's 11 infants were between the ages of 10 and 23 days at the beginning of the experiment. Natural conditioned responses, consisting of food-getting reactions to previously neutral stimuli, but occurring without experimental training, appeared between the ages of 21 and 27 days. For some of the infants, experimental training comprised presentation of a bell for 15 seconds before and 30 seconds after feeding began. In other cases, the conditioned stimulus was a bell or a bell and light. Feeding reactions to these stimuli appeared at ages ranging from 33 to 77 days, and after 132 to 350 trials.

A more comprehensive and carefully conducted investigation than the one just described is Kantrow's (1937). Sixteen infants aged 44 to 117 days at the beginning of the experiment rapidly developed conditioned feeding reactions to the sound of a buzzer. Sucking movements were recorded by placing over each infant's chin a harness attached to the pen of a polygraph. Other responses, such as crying and general activity, were noted. A control period of variable length (to avoid conditioning to a temporal sequence) preceded onset of the buzzer, which was sounded for 20 seconds. At the end of 5 seconds of stimulation with the buzzer, a bottle, which had been kept outside the visual field, was inserted in the infant's mouth. Stimulation with the buzzer continued for 15 seconds after feeding began. The stimulating sequence and the nature of responses at different stages of conditioning are indicated in Figure 2. Stable conditioned sucking responses appeared within 1 to 5 days, after 3 to 9 experimental feedings and 16 to 72 paired stimulations. An acquisition curve based upon the difference in the means for

[1] This research has been published only in Russian. The present summary is based upon Razran's (1933).

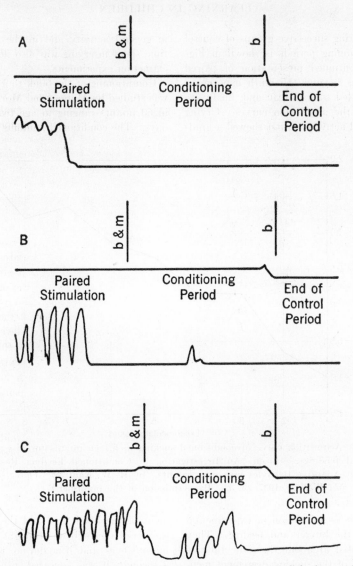

FIGURE 2. Sample sucking records of an infant before and after conditioning to the sound of a buzzer. (From "An Investigation of Conditioned Feeding Responses and Concomitant Adaptive Behavior in Young Infants," by R. W. Kantrow. *University of Iowa Studies in Child Welfare*, 1937, *13*, 11. By permission of the publisher.) Read from right to left. At the end of a control period of variable duration, a buzzer *b* was sounded for 5 seconds, the conditioning period. At the end of this period, the nipple was placed in the infant's mouth and the buzzer continued for another 15 seconds, *b & m*. The lower line in each part of the figure is a record of sucking activity. It was obtained by means of a chin harness attached to the pen of a polygraph. *A*. First experimental feeding, fifth paired stimulation. *B*. Fifth experimental feeding, thirty-second paired stimulation. Note anticipatory feeding reaction. *C*. Eighth experimental feeding, fifty-fourth paired stimulation. Note conditioned sucking activity.

sucking during successive groups of control and conditioning periods is shown in Figure 3. Continued presentation of paired stimulations beyond the ninth experimental session led to a plateau and, finally, to a drop in the acquisition curves. Crying and general activity at first showed a grad-

in general activity and in the amount of time spent in crying was also noted during extinction experiments.

Conditioning of the blink to a puff of air was studied by Morgan and Morgan (1944) in 50 infants ranging in age from 5 to 75 days. The conditioned stimulus was move-

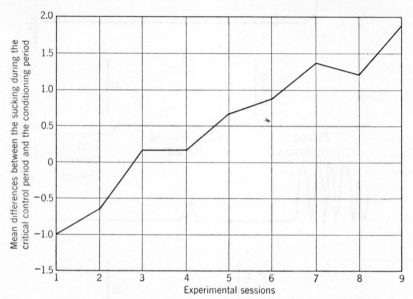

FIGURE 3. Acquisition curve of conditioned sucking in fifteen infants for nine consecutive experimental feedings. (From "An Investigation of Conditioned Feeding Responses and Concomitant Adaptive Behavior in Young Infants," by R. W. Kantrow. *University of Iowa Studies in Child Welfare*, 1937, *13*, 32. By permission of the publisher.)

ual decrease as a function of experimental pairing of the buzzer and feeding. They then increased at about the same time as appearance of the sucking decrement mentioned above. Analysis of the data in terms of degree of hunger at the time of the tests indicated that, unless the infant was hungry, little conditioning appeared. Curves based upon sucking activity during experimental extinction, produced by successive stimulations with the buzzer alone, represent what approximates a mirror image of the curve shown in Figure 3. An increase

ment of the hand that held the bulb. On each trial the bulb was brought before the infant's eyes, and, if he did not wink within 2 seconds, it was squeezed, producing the unconditioned stimulus. Evidence is presented which suggests that the conditioned wink under these conditions cannot be produced before an age of around 45 days.

Conditioned differential sucking activity to tones and to intensities of light has been developed by Kasatkin and Levikova (1935a, 1935b) in infants between 1 and 2 months of age.

Conditioning of emotional responses in infants has been studied by several investigators. Since emotional behavior is the subject of another chapter in this book, however, we shall not undertake a detailed discussion of these studies. It is sufficient to say, at this point, that Watson and Rayner (1920) and H. E. Jones (1930a, 1930b) have succeeded in conditioning fear reactions and galvanic skin responses, respectively, to previously neutral stimuli. Retention of the conditioned responses over periods ranging up to 7 months was noted by Jones. Moss (1924) conditioned two children, the younger of whom was 2 years old, to dislike the sound of a snapper which was associated with squirting of vinegar into the mouth. Bregman (1934) was unsuccessful in her attempt to condition emotional attitudes of 15 infants between the ages of 8 and 16 months. Sounds assumed to be disagreeable were associated with some objects while supposedly agreeable sounds were associated with others. Negative and positive reactions to these objects which might be expected from the nature of associated stimuli did not appear. Although there were no consistent changes in attitude as a result of the conditioning procedure, some infants at times evidenced negative reactions to stimuli associated with the noise. As Wenger (1936) has pointed out, there is no proof of the agreeableness and disagreeableness, for infants, of the sounds used in this investigation. Bregman's claim that conditioning *per se* cannot account for changes in the emotional attitudes of infants seems unwarranted in the light of her results.

Although the restricted data so far available do not justify any extensive generalizations, one may, in summary, say that investigations of conditioning in infants have shown that: (1) sucking, blinking, limb withdrawal, respiration, crying, general activity, galvanic skin responses, and fear reactions may be conditioned to tactual, visual, and auditory stimuli during infancy; (2) although newborn infants may be conditioned, the reactions are often lacking in stability; (3) older infants tend to evidence more stability of conditioned reactions than the newborn; (4) conditioning of the sucking reaction is dependent upon existence of hunger; (5) retention of conditioned responses developed in infancy has in some instances been observed over periods ranging up to 7 months; (6) spontaneous recovery following extinction training has been observed; (7) continued presentation of the paired stimuli may, after conditioning has developed, lead to a decrement in the frequency of conditioned reactions; and (8) the curve of extinction for conditioned feeding reactions approximates a mirror image of the curve of acquisition.

Conditioned-Response Studies with Older Children. Investigations of conditioned responses in children beyond the period of infancy have been numerous. Razran (1933) has summarized more than 30 researches from the Russian laboratories alone. In the following discussion we shall consider only a few studies which are more or less representative of those with children beyond infancy.

As indicated earlier, the pioneer research on conditioned responses in children was Krasnogorski's (1909). In Krasnogorski's initial experiment a child of 3½ years was conditioned so that salivation first elicited only by food occurred in response to a bell. The index of salivary response was swallowing. In later experiments with other children, Krasnogorski placed a tambour over the thyroid cartilage and recorded the swallowing reactions on a kymograph. He also used mouth opening as the response to be conditioned. Later still, saliva was collected by means of suction cups (saliometers) placed over the salivary glands. As Razran's review indicates, the experiments from Krasnogorski's laboratory have, in general procedure, results, and interpretatoin, closely paralleled those of Pavlov on dogs. Krasnogorski (1925) has reviewed in English some of his investigations of conditioning in normal and neurotic children. Mateer (1918), whose research on 50 normal and 14 subnormal children will be mentioned again later, utilized Krasnogorski's general technique. The un-

eleventh trial, however, the foot is partially withdrawn in response to the metronome. A more marked withdrawal appears at the twelfth presentation of the metronome.

Use of this technique has enabled Marinesco and Kreindler to demonstrate clearly, in children between the ages of 15 and 30 months, many of the phenomena of conditioning disclosed in experiments with

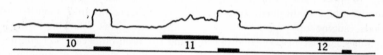

FIGURE 4. Conditioned withdrawal in a child of 26 months. (From "Des réflexes conditionnels: I. l'Organisation des réflexes conditionnels chez l'enfant," by G. Marinesco and A. Kreindler. *Journal de Psychologie*, 1933, *30*, 873.) *Bottom line:* duration of electric shock. *Second line from bottom:* duration of metronome. *Top line:* foot withdrawal.

conditioned stimulus, which elicited mouth opening and swallowing, was chocolate placed in the mouth. Pulling a bandage over the child's eyes just prior to presentation of the chocolate served as the conditioned stimulus.

Still another technique used to develop conditioned responses in children is that of Marinesco and Kreindler (1933). It involves a modification of Bekhterev's general procedure in that the reaction conditioned is withdrawal of a limb from weak electrical stimulation. An electrode is attached to the child's abdomen and another to the foot or hand. The arrangement is such that shock is felt in the limb. A thread attached to the limb and, through a pulley system, to the marker on a kymograph drum serves to record retraction of the arm or leg. The conditioned stimulus is the sounding of a metronome for 50 seconds before onset of the shock, which lasts for 20 seconds. A tracing from part of the record obtained in conditioning a child of 26 months is shown in Figure 4. One will note that there is, in this case, no evidence of conditioning at the tenth trial. At the

animals. The chief phenomena observed in this study were:

1. *Conditioned differentiation of movements.* At first all limbs responded despite the fact that only one was stimulated. During the course of conditioning, however, retraction of limbs other than the one stimulated decreased in amplitude and finally ceased.

2. *External inhibition.* Presentation of a second stimulus, such as light, while the metronome was sounding reduced the amplitude of movements previously made to the metronome.

3. *Trace responses.* When stimulation with shock followed cessation of the metronome by several seconds, the conditioned retraction was delayed for a corresponding interval of time.

4. *Experimental extinction.* Continued presentation of the metronome, without following it with shock, led to diminished conditioned responses and, finally, to their disappearance.

5. *Spontaneous recovery.* After conditioned responses had disappeared as a result of extinction training, they reappeared without further training.

6. *Higher-order conditioning.* After the metronome aroused withdrawal responses it was, with occasional further reinforcement, used as the conditioning stimulus in training with other stimuli to be conditioned.

Changes in semantic conditioning as a function of age have been investigated by Riess (1946), using 68 children ranging in age from 7 to 15 years. After the electrodermal response of each child had been conditioned to certain words, using a buzzer for reinforcement, the magnitude of the EDR to homophones (won, one), antonyms (won, lost), and synonyms (won, beat) was measured. There was transfer from the originally conditioned words to the semantically related words, but the efficacy of the latter types varied with age. The lowest age group (average 7 years, 10 months) responded maximally to homophones, the intermediate group (10 years, 8 months) to antonyms, and the older age group to synonyms.

In a somewhat similar experiment except that purely verbal methods were used, Goodwin, Long, and Welch (1945) found that 8–10 year olds who memorized words at the species level showed a degree of generalization to the genus level. Most subjects vaguely grasped the species-genus relationship.

The studies so far considered in this chapter have dealt with what Hilgard and Marquis (1940) call "classical" as distinguished from "instrumental" conditioning. The latter receives this designation because, in it, the subject's response is instrumental in bringing a reward or escape from punishment. The two studies that we are about to consider fall within the "instrumental" classification because the child gets a reward (piece of candy) by making the response to be conditioned.

Ivanov-Smolensky (1927a, 1927b) was first to use an instrumental technique with children. His general experimental situation is illustrated in Figure 5. The child is seated before the apparatus with a rubber bulb in his hand. As the experimenter, who is in an adjoining room, presses his bulb, food is released and slides down a tube toward the child. Just before release of the food, a bell or other conditioned stimulus is activated. The child observes the food through a small window on the tube and, by pressing his bulb, is able to obtain it. Presentation of the conditioned and unconditioned stimuli and pressing of the child's bulb are recorded objectively by kymographic or other means. Children between the ages of 4 and 15 years have been conditioned in 2 to 88 trials to make stable grasping reactions upon presentation of such conditioned stimuli as the sound of a bell and the flash of a light. Investigations from Ivanov-Smolensky's laboratory are reviewed by Razran (1933). They demonstrate individual differences in susceptibility to conditioning, higher-order conditioning, statistically unreliable differences in the speed with which conditioned grasping and withdrawal responses are developed, and development of reflexes to chains of stimuli. There has also been an attempt to classify children into excitable, inhibitable, labile, and inert types upon the basis of their conditioning behavior. However, only 13 children were used in this study. Bayne, Winsor, and Winters (1929), using the Ivanov-Smolensky technique, found that conditioning to red light was obtained in 8 to 10 trials in two 6-year-old children. A 4-year-old child, however, required over 200 trials to develop grasping responses to the sound of a metronome.

The following study falls within the classification of instrumental responses that Skinner (1938) has designated "operant." This is because the child's response to the lever is "emitted" rather than being elicited by some external stimulus, like the falling candy of Ivanov-Smolensky's study. Pressing the lever occurs as a result of internal processes, not as a response to a stimulus present at the moment of response, as the blink is produced by a puff of air or withdrawal by an electric shock. Skinner designates the latter as "respondent."

obtained with a child whose drive for candy was weak. In this case, periods of rapid response alternated with periods of no response. Curves 2 and 3 were made by children with an intermediate to strong drive for candy. The second curve will serve to illustrate the meaning of such conditioning

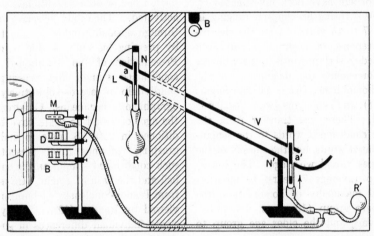

FIGURE 5. Ivanov-Smolensky's method of conditioning. (From "On the Methods of Examining the Conditioned Food Reflexes in Children and in Mental Disorders," by A. G. Ivanov-Smolensky. *Brain*, 1927, *50*, 139. By permission of the publisher.) The experimenter, seated in the room at the left, presses the bulb *R* and causes a piece of chocolate, *a*, on the shelf, *L*, to slide down the tube *N-N'*. As the chocolate passes the window, *V*, in the adjoining room it may be seen by the child, who sits with his hand over the bulb *R'*. By pressing this bulb and thus causing a photographic shutter to move upwards, the child releases the chocolate, which falls into the position *a'*. A Marey tambour, *M*, records the child's grasping response on a kymograph drum. The signal marker, *D*, likewise records release of the chocolate by the experimenter. In conditioning experiments a bell, *B*, or some other stimulus, is presented just before the release of the food and its presentation recorded by the signal marker, *B*. Conditioning is evidenced by grasping at the sound of the bell or prior to observation of food.

Warren and Brown's (1943) investigation is a repetition of the Skinner experiment, but with children rather than rats as subjects. The response of pressing a lever in the playroom was reinforced (rewarded) by the appearance of a pellet of candy in a food tray under the lever. Nine children between the ages of 2 and 5 years completed the experiment. Typical conditioning curves for individual children are shown in Figure 6. The irregular curve (1) was

curves. The child whose lever-pressing is here represented did not press the lever once in the first few minutes. By the eighth minute, however, responses were occurring at the rate of around 20 per minute. The rate of response gradually declined until the thirty-ninth minute. Then the rate increased and remained approximately constant at around 8.2 responses per minute. Each experimental period lasted 22 minutes, but the curves were plotted without showing a break after every 22 minutes.

In addition to demonstrating the Skinner-type operant conditioning in children, this experiment also provides data on experimental extinction, spontaneous recovery, disinhibition, and periodic reconditioning. The experimenters conclude that, within

spectively. These results suggest that, within the age range of 1 to 4 years, and for the type of response involved, susceptibility to conditioning increases with chronological age. The other extensive investigations, however, show results not in agreement with the above. Osipova (1926) conditioned withdrawal reactions in children

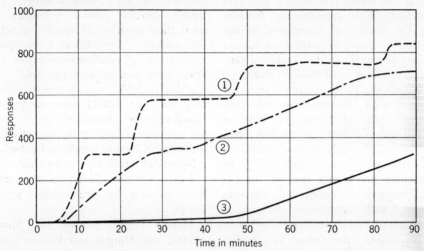

FIGURE 6. The total number of responses emitted is plotted as a function of the length of time elapsed during the initial conditioning periods in which every response was reinforced. The points represent data for single subjects, and the curves are drawn by inspection. (From "Conditioned Operant Response Phenomena in Children," by A. B. Warren and R. H. Brown. *Journal of General Psychology*, 1943, *28*, p. 188.)

certain limitations related to the use of children, their results are similar to those reported for operant conditioning in rats.

Speed of Conditioning as a Function of Age and Intelligence. Mateer's (1918) investigation (see page 382) involved 50 normal and 14 subnormal children between the ages of 12 and 90 months. For normal children the correlation between CA and the number of trials required to produce two successive anticipatory responses was .571 ± .06. The approximate average number of trials required at successive yearly age levels, for the normal group aged 1 to 7 years, was 8, 7, 5, 4, 4, 5, and 4, re-

between the ages of 7 and 19 years. He found that the average number of trials increased with age. The correlation between CA and speed of formation of the conditioned withdrawal response was −.358 ± .033. A biserial correlation based upon 144 cases between 14 and 19 years was −.716 ± .06. Osipova's findings are supported by those of Dernowa-Yarmolenko (1933), who conditioned 1000 subjects between the ages of 8 and 19 years. Each subject was told to raise his hand when the examiner did so. The examiner then tapped on the table with a pencil. Two seconds later he raised his left hand. Ten such paired presentations of the tap and hand raising were presented. Anticipatory hand raising was noted, that is, raising the hand after a tap but before the examiner raised his hand. The percentage of subjects exhibiting anticipatory conditioned reactions within 10 trials was 90 at 8 years. In successive yearly age levels the percentage gradually decreased until, at the upper levels, very few were responding. With increasing age, furthermore, the number of associations of the two stimuli required to produce conditioned reactions increased and the number of conditioned reactions in 10 trials decreased.

In considering the results of Osipova and Mateer, Razran (1935) suggests that conditioning of the laboratory type may be rendered more difficult as an individual grows beyond the early years of childhood, not because of decreased susceptibility to conditioning *per se* but because "instrumental mastery of verbal and conscious processes," with an associated decrease in naïveté, makes him *less willing to submit to the procedure.* Researches by Razran (1936) on adults conditioned indirectly, while they were engaged in other activities, lend support to this view. Mitrano (1939) has attempted to overcome deleterious attitudinal factors by using feeble-minded children and adults as subjects.

Mateer found a correlation of .588 ± .06 between speed of conditioning and MA. Osipova (1926), on the other hand, obtained a biserial correlation of −.540 ± .08 between intelligence and speed of forming the conditioned withdrawal reaction. On the basis of the results so far available, therefore, it would be hazardous to make any generalizations about the relation between speed of conditioning and intelligence. If Razran's view is correct, one might expect a negative correlation between intelligence and the speed of laboratory conditioning.

Solution of Behavior Problems by Conditioned-Response Procedures. Krasnogorski (1925, 1933), Ivanov-Smolensky (1927a, 1927b), Seham (1932), and Gesell (1938) have reviewed applications of conditioned-response procedure to child psychiatry. From the standpoint of indicating actual accomplishment, however, these reviews are quite disappointing. They merely describe general techniques and what these *promise* for solution of behavior problems. Nevertheless, a few specific applications of conditioned-response principles have been made in this field.

Aldrich (1928) and Marinesco, Sager, and Kreindler (1931) have used conditioned-response procedures to determine the presence of hearing in, respectively, a 3-month-old infant thought to be deaf and a 9-year-old functionally mute child.

Jones's (1924a) elimination of a child's fear response by conditioning is well known.

Morgan (1938), Mowrer and Mowrer (1938), and Morgan and Witmer (1939) have been highly successful in eliminating enuresis by a conditioned-response procedure. The problem involved in enuresis is very well stated by Mowrer and Mowrer (1938):

> Learning to awaken to the relatively vague and not very intense pressure created by a filling bladder, while successfully ignoring many other potentially disturbing stimuli, must be for the young child something of a feat, especially in view of the pre-existence of a strictly reflex, subcortical neural mechanism for the autonomic relief of this need [p. 437].

Use of conditioned-reflex procedure here has as its aims, (1) causing the child to associate *getting up* with bladder tension and (2) making the child responsive to bladder tension in its earlier stages, that is, lowering his threshold for this stimulus.

All the above studies have involved essentially the same technique for producing these effects. The child was required to sleep on a mat which, when urination began, short-circuited and rang a bell. Each child was instructed to get up as soon as the bell rang, to open a switch disconnecting the bell, and then to go to the bathroom and finish urinating. All of Mowrer and Mowrer's 30 cases between the ages of 3 and 13 years were cured of enuresis within 4 to 8 weeks. They learned, in other words, to anticipate the ringing of the bell by arising before bladder tension became so great as to cause reflex urination. Morgan and Witmer report that 4 of their 5 subjects were cured of enuresis by this method in 4 to 14 nights. Morgan says that all children who cooperate are readily cured by application of this technique.

The technique just described has been used successfully by Deacon (1939) with feebleminded children at Vineland. Smith (1948) describes this and other conditioned-response methods used by him in the treatment of enuritics.

Learning of Sensorimotor Skills

Acquisition of sensorimotor skills is of singular importance during early childhood. The chief problems of adjustment which confront the infant concern acquisition of skills necessary for manipulation of and orientation with respect to its environment. Some of these skills, such as crawling, walking, and finger-thumb opposition, are probably functions more of maturation than of learning. Even when learning is shown to be involved in the acquisition of such skills, it is, as Dennis (1935) has so aptly pointed out, frequently autogenous. Such learning results from the child's own untutored activities rather than from specific training. On the other hand, there are many skills, such as talking, writing, and buttoning clothes, which fail to develop unless specific training or opportunities for imitation are provided. These skills and the various factors which influence their acquisition will be our prime concern in the following discussions.

The Relative Influence of Maturation and Learning. Acquisition of skill which results from learning is our chief concern, yet we cannot ignore the fact that learning and maturation are concomitant factors in child development. Although some skills develop primarily as a result of maturation and others primarily as a result of learning, the two processes are reciprocally related. This relationship is of especial importance during early childhood when the neuromuscular system is undergoing rapid growth and when, at the same time, there are numerous influences to encourage learning. With increasing age there is a relative decrease in the importance of new maturational factors.

These considerations indicate that investigation of the learning process *per se* in young children must take cognizance of maturation. Failure to control maturational influences has greatly lessened the value of many early, and even some recent, studies on learning in children. In some instances a loose use of the term *learning* has been involved. Thus Kirkpatrick (1899) describes how a child "learns" to walk. Ketterlinus (1931) presents a study which illustrates the ambiguity of interpretation which results when the possible improvement in skill resulting from maturation is ignored. The problem was to determine whether children between 2 and 5 years of age are able to adjust to mirror reversal. The experiment covered a period of 4 weeks, with two trials on a certain day each week. One problem was to pick up objects and put them in a cup. The objects and cup were seen only in a mirror. Age groups of 2, 3, and 4 years were used. Each age group began the experiment with a lower time score than did the preceding one. This may be interpreted as due to the effect of maturation or perhaps to general training which preceded the experiment. Acquisition curves show a decrease in time during the course of the experiment. The *rate* at which a curve dropped, however, was greatest for the youngest group and least for the oldest. This is what one might expect were maturation an important factor. If learning were the chief factor, would one not expect the older, more mature group, to learn faster than the younger group? It might be claimed, on the other hand, that since the 4-year-old group began with the lowest time score it was closer to the physiological limit and thus could not be expected to improve as much as the younger groups.

Such ambiguity of interpretation could have been prevented by using a control group matched with the experimental group in terms of age, sex, intelligence, and initial ability on the tests in question. The same criticism applies to Beebe's (1933, 1934) investigations of *motor learning* in children. Since no control groups were used, the curves obtained cannot be interpreted with any degree of certainty.

Several investigations of learning at the early age levels have used the method of co-twin control or have utilized a trained and an untrained group matched in terms of age, sex, intelligence, and initial performance. The co-twin control investigations of Gesell and Thompson (1929) on climbing and cube manipulation, Strayer (1930) on speech, Hilgard (1933) on walking boards, cutting, and ring tossing, McGraw (1935) on a variety of motor activities, and Mirenva (1935) on jumping, throwing at a target, and rolling a ball toward a target all indicate the strong influence of maturation at early age levels.

Hilgard's (1932) investigation of climbing, cutting, and buttoning activities involved trained and untrained groups of approximately equivalent initial ability. The average time score for a group given 12 weeks of practice in climbing dropped from 18 to 8½ seconds, approximately. Tests at the end of the experimental periods indicated that the average time score of the untrained group had dropped to 13 seconds. Within 1 week of further training, however, the score for this group approximated that of the trained group. Both groups improved in cutting and buttoning, but the untrained group was not able to reach the level of the trained group within an additional week of practice.

Acquisition of skills more complex than the above is also markedly influenced by maturation and nonexperimental training. Hicks (1930a) found that 8 weeks of throwing at a moving target yielded no greater gains than were produced in the control group by "structural growth and general practice which had a direct bearing on the specific skill." The children had an age range of 2½ to 6½ years. In a further report concerning such skills as tracing between two lines and making perforations, Hicks (1930b) obtained similar results. Hicks and Ralph (1931) found that children ranging in age from 24 to 40 months thread the Porteus diamond maze as well without training as they do after 7 weeks of training. The trained and untrained groups began the experiment with a score of 23 points. Two trials per week for 7 weeks yielded the following successive average scores: 27.2, 24.4, 27.9, 26.2, 27.7, 29.7, 29.4. Tests at the eighth week yielded an average score of 31.8 for the trained group. The group which had received no training since the initial tests made an average score of 32.1 Hence the improvement of the trained group was matched by that of the untrained group.

Maturation, and perhaps to a certain degree nonexperimental training, produced as much improvement in skill as did specific training.

Mattson's (1933) investigation with a rolling-ball maze yielded results somewhat like the above when the maze pattern was simple. With more complicated patterns, however, the trained group gave a significantly better performance than the untrained, and the advantage possessed by the trained group increased as the complexity of the maze pattern increased. Since Mattson's is the most thorough investigation of the relative influence of maturation and specific practice in acquisition of a complex skill, we shall consider it in some detail.

The maze patterns used by Mattson are illustrated in Figure 7. Instruction in how to manipulate the maze—that is, press it down in various directions upon its supports so as to make the ball roll in different directions—was given each child at the beginning of the experiment. The goal was then shown and the experimenter said:

This is the house where the marble lives, and this is where we put it [putting the ball at the starting point of the labyrinth]. Do you think you can find the path right down to the little house? Press very hard every time so that the bell rings, and if the gate is shut, and the marble can't go any farther, try another way. Now begin.

The subjects were 24 boys and 26 girls ranging in age from 58 to 72 months. Their average age was 64.7 months, and their average IQ, 103.4. Practice and control groups were matched for age, sex, IQ, and maze scores for the initial 4 days of training. Training was given on all three patterns each day. The order of presentation was such that, in 9 daily trials, each pattern came once as first, once as second, and once as third. Distribution of practice for

the two groups is indicated in Table 1. The two groups, it will be observed from the table, differed only in that the practice

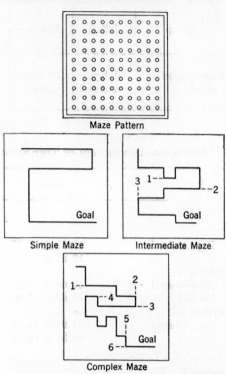

Maze Pattern

Simple Maze   Intermediate Maze

Complex Maze

FIGURE 7. Three maze patterns used to investigate the influence of maturation and learning in acquisition of a complex skill. (From "The Relation between the Complexity of the Habit to Be Acquired and the Form of the Learning Curve in Young Children," by M. L. Mattson. *Genetic Psychology Monographs*, 1933, *13*, 332. By permission of The Journal Press, publisher.) The top view illustrates the rows of screws which made an invisible pathway, through which the ball rolled as the maze was tilted in different directions. Small gates placed at appropriate positions blocked further progress of the ball in certain directions. These gates were placed so that the ball could reach the exit only by rolling along the paths indicated in the remaining diagrams, which show the three degrees of complexity involved.

TABLE 1

DISTRIBUTION OF PRACTICE FOR SUBJECTS

Group	Initial	Practice	Test	Forgetting	Retest	Total Practice
Experimental	4 days	26 days	8 days	60 days	8 days	46 days
Control	4 days	none	8 days	60 days	8 days	20 days

TABLE 2

MEANS AND DIFFERENCES OF TIME SCORES FOR EXPERIMENTAL AND CONTROL GROUPS

Pattern	Mean	Difference	$D/\sigma_{diff.}$
Initial			
Pattern I			
Experimental	17.83 ± 2.17	0.02 ± 0.72	0.03
Control	17.81 ± 2.90		
Pattern II			
Experimental	47.08 ± 8.70	1.52 ± 2.27	0.67
Control	48.60 ± 7.30		
Pattern III			
Experimental	84.98 ± 14.24	0.36 ± 4.11	0.09
Control	85.34 ± 14.78		
Test			
Pattern I			
Experimental	10.84 ± 0.62	2.71 ± 0.40	6.73
Control	13.55 ± 5.12		
Pattern II			
Experimental	18.82 ± 2.85	15.00 ± 1.17	12.80
Control	33.82 ± 5.12		
Pattern III			
Experimental	30.86 ± 6.16	32.94 ± 0.30	14.34
Control	63.80 ± 9.70		
Retest			
Pattern I			
Experimental	11.07 ± 0.71	1.37 ± 0.37	3.73
Control	12.44 ± 1.56		
Pattern II			
Experimental	20.18 ± 7.55	7.09 ± 1.29	5.51
Control	27.27 ± 5.08		
Pattern III			
Experimental	34.00 ± 7.55	20.68 ± 3.08	6.71
Control	54.68 ± 12.32		

TABLE 3

MEANS AND DIFFERENCES OF ERROR SCORES FOR EXPERIMENTAL AND CONTROL GROUPS

Pattern	Mean	Difference	$D/\sigma_{\text{diff.}}$
Initial			
Pattern I			
Experimental	2.43 ± 1.47	0.63 ± 0.355	1.78
Control	1.80 ± 1.01		
Pattern II			
Experimental	10.90 ± 3.48	0.01 ± 0.804	0.01
Control	10.89 ± 2.03		
Pattern III			
Experimental	21.15 ± 5.35	2.30 ± 1.247	1.84
Control	18.85 ± 3.12		
Test			
Pattern I			
Experimental	0.29 ± 0.16	0.19 ± 0.07	2.65
Control	0.48 ± 0.30		
Pattern II			
Experimental	3.14 ± 1.51	4.80 ± 0.584	8.21
Control	7.93 ± 2.50		
Pattern III			
Experimental	7.54 ± 3.04	10.21 ± 1.008	10.13
Control	17.74 ± 4.02		
Retest			
Pattern I			
Experimental	0.37 ± 0.28	0.06 ± 0.096	0.67
Control	0.44 ± 0.36		
Pattern II			
Experimental	3.89 ± 1.96	1.11 ± 0.698	1.60
Control	5.00 ± 2.62		
Pattern III			
Experimental	9.55 ± 3.04	5.82 ± 1.38	4.27
Control	15.36 ± 5.71		

group had 26 more days of tests than the control group.

Progress was measured in time and errors. The means, differences, and reliability of the differences for the two groups on each of the mazes are given in Tables 2 and 3. From the data in these tables it is apparent that, although the practice and control groups began the experiment with approximately equal performances, the subjects who had 26 days of additional practice manifested superior performances on each of the three mazes. This was true in the test at the end of training and also in the retest given 60 days later. It held true for both time and error scores. All these differences except those for time scores on the simple maze in the test period and on the two simpler mazes in the retest were statistically reliable. It is also clearly apparent from the data summarized in Tables 2 and 3 that the advantage of the trained group over the untrained was greater as the complexity of the task increased. A study of relative differences based upon ratios of gain and percentages of gain or loss supported the above conclusions.

This study suggests that earlier investigations in which there was as much gain from maturation and possibly general practice as from specific practice derived their result from the simplicity of the tasks involved. Comparison of learning curves from these studies with those of Mattson for the two complex mazes shows relatively little gain even in the practice groups. One might conclude that, when large gains are made by the practice group, the group left to depend upon maturation will be shown to suffer a disadvantage in later tests.

Learning of Sensorimotor Skills as a Function of Age. Investigations of the relative influence of maturation and learning in acquisition of motor skills have demonstrated that *at early age levels, and for skills that are simple or which show little short-time improvement from either maturation or practice,* the effect of increasing maturation is to make given amounts of practice increasingly effective.

When skills as complicated as manipulating Mattson's mazes II and III are concerned, little if any improvement occurs in the absence of practice. Would older children, however, learn such skills more readily than younger ones? One might expect an affirmative answer for two reasons. In the first place, it seems reasonable to suppose that the older child, having a sensory, neural, and muscular system of greater maturity, should profit more from given amounts of practice than a younger child. In the second place, the older child has a wider previous experience upon which to draw in acquiring new skills and this might be expected to give him an advantage over the younger child.

Since previous experience is a variable and an uncontrollable factor when human beings are concerned, students of the age effect in learning would do well to eliminate the differential effect of experience as much as possible. This was accomplished in Stone's (1929–1930) experiments by using rats which were reared in a relatively constant environment before the tests. If human subjects are used, experiential advantages of the older individual can be reduced to a minimum only by studying the acquisition of skills far removed from those of everyday life. Certain maze problems call for approximately such skills.

The most comprehensive and thorough investigation of the age function in maze learning by children is McGinnis's (1929). Young's (1922) slot maze was used. Each child was required to push a stylus in the form of a shoe along a grooved pathway until the figure of a boy was reached. The subject was instructed to "take the shoe to the boy" as quickly as possible. There were 20 children, 10 boys and 10 girls, in each of three age groups. The average ages were approximately 3, 4, and 5 years. Average IQ's were, respectively, 107.9, 117.5, and 103.8 Each child was given 5 trials daily 5 days per week until a total of 50 trials had been completed. Learning curves based upon median time and error scores are shown in Figure 8. It will be observed that the median time and error scores for the first 5 trials decreased with age. Final levels of performance, however, were similar. The average number of errors for successive age groups beginning with the youngest was: 153.7 ± 19.7, 108.9 ± 10.5, and 78.6 ± 16.4. The difference of 75.1 between average error scores of the 3- and 5-year groups alone approxi-

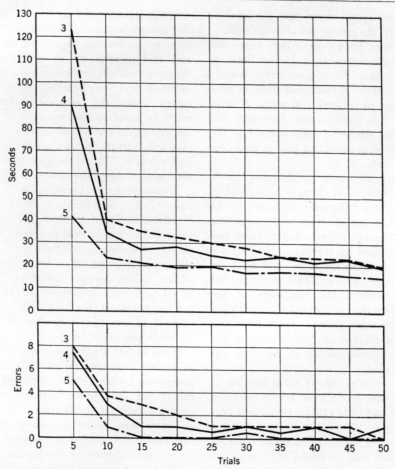

FIGURE 8. Learning curves for time and errors for three age groups. (From "The Acquisition and Interference of Motor-Habits in Young Children," by E. McGinnis. *Genetic Psychology Monographs*, 1929, *6*, 241, 244. By permission of the publisher.)

mated statistical reliability, its critical ratio being 2.9. The average time in seconds for successively older groups was: 2071.2 ± 68.7, 1954.3 ± 51.8, and 1211.4 ± 38.8. Differences between the time scores of the groups showed the older to be superior. However, only the differences between the 4- and 5-year and 3- and 5-year groups were statistically reliable.

Despite better maze performance of the successively older groups, *learning during*

the course of the experiment was similar regardless of age. McGinnis (1929) calculated the differences in time between the initial and final trials for each of the groups. The percentage of gain was similar (91 to 93) for each age group. When averages for the first five trials were compared with those for the last five, the percentage gain was slightly greater for the 3- and 4-year groups (85) than for the 5-year group (75). Analysis of initial and final error scores shows that the *younger* the group the greater the absolute gains.

The older groups, since they began the maze performance at a greater level of efficiency than the younger, were initially closer to their physiological limit in time and closer to perfection in terms of error scores. It is quite possible, therefore, that the actual degree of improvement is not shown by data indicating gain in final over initial scores.

Another approach to this problem is through analysis of changes in variability. Coefficients of variation were larger for the initial than for the last trial, suggesting that intragroup individual differences had been decreased by training. The decrease was greatest for the oldest and least for the youngest group. This suggests that practice reduced the variability of the oldest more than it reduced the variability of the youngest group. Apart from this suggestion there is no clear evidence of differential *learning ability* at the three age levels studied.

Other investigations of maze learning at different age levels have been performed by Hicks and Carr (1912), Gould and Perrin (1916), Wieg (1932), and Wenger (1933). Analysis of the results of these investigations fails to reveal any consistent evidence of age changes in maze-learning ability.

Studies of the effect of age on acquisition of skills other than maze performance also yield results which are either negative or equivocal. Clinton's (1930) study of mirror drawing at yearly age levels from 6 to 17 shows that the average number of lines drawn within a 5-minute learning period increases from 4.7 at 6 years to 30.8 at 17 years for boys and from 2.9 at 6 years to 38.6 at 17 years for girls. On the surface it would appear that there is greater adaptation to the mirror distortion, within the 5-minute learning period, at suc-

cessively higher yearly age levels. Although the author mentions learning curves, he gives no information concerning the initial and final performance at each age level. Without such information one is unable to ascertain how much actual learning occurred within the 5-minute periods. It might be expected that successively higher age groups, as a result of increased experience with mirrors, would start the test with higher scores. This alone may account for the apparent age differences in learning.

Investigations by Dunford (1930), Renshaw (1930), and Renshaw, Wherry, and Newlin (1930) fail to show any evidence that, in learning to localize a point on the skin by touching it with the eyes closed, the rate of learning differs for children and adults. There are age differences in the initial and final accuracies, to be sure, but improvement resulting from a given amount of practice is roughly the same for child and adult groups.

Hicks (1931) studied acquisition of skill in hitting a moving target. No age differences in learning ability appeared. The initial and final scores increased in successive yearly age levels from 3 to 6, but the gains were similar in each group. In this experiment, moreover, a control group to test the influence of maturation gained as much as the trained group.

The only remaining experiments on the influence of age in learning of motor skills by children are those of Eigler (1932) and Langhorne (1933). Eigler studied the problem of learning to synchronize a finger reaction with a recurring flash of light. Twenty-two children between 2 and 6 years and 20 adults were subjects. Age differences in favor of the older groups are suggested. It is apparent, however, that there were differences in the motivation and in the fundamental coordinating ability of the groups. These, rather than differences in learning ability *per se,* could easily account for the observed differences in adaptation. For example, younger children were more afraid of the shocks given for asynchronized responses than were the older children and adults. In Langhorne's experiment groups of children from 7 to 17 years of age were given training in operation of the Renshaw-Weiss pursuitmeter. The problem was to maintain contact between a stylus and a revolving lever arm. Seventy-eight subjects, 45 boys and 33 girls, whose data are treated separately, took part in the experiment. Langhorne does not say how many of each sex were in each group. From the fact, however, that there were groups at 10 different age levels in the boys and at 9 different age levels in the girls, it is apparent that the average size of the groups could not have been greater than 4. Langhorne concludes that there was greater learning ability at successively higher age levels. His results fail to show this. Although the initial and final scores tend to increase with age, the degree of improvement resulting from the amount of practice given is not related to this factor in any definite way. Analysis of the data for boys in terms of percentage of improvement indicates that the age groups from 14 to 17 have higher percentages of gain than the lower age groups. Below 14, however, there is no consistent variation with age. Even less evidence of improved learning ability with age was found in the female groups. In any event, such data are meaningless unless the size of the groups is such as to warrant comparisons.

One is forced to conclude that, if the learning of such motor skills as have so far been studied improves with age, the results fail to show clear evidence of it. Although children of increasing age usually evidence an increasingly high initial level of performance, which may be accounted for on the basis of greater maturity, greater experience, or both, the gross amount and percentage of improvement resulting from given amounts of practice do not appear to change in any consistent way as a function of age. It may be said, of course, that since the older children begin with a higher level of performance (closer to the upper limit) than younger ones, the actual relative accomplishment within the same range of practice is not measured by gross gains. McGinnis (1929) reported decreasing intragroup variability as a function of given amounts of practice at successively higher age levels. This may be an index of the relative gains from training if the groups are sufficiently large to warrant use of the statistical procedures involved. As will be recalled, however, the largest single age group comprised only 20 children.

Sex Differences in Learning of Sensorimotor Skills. Several problems discussed in the preceding section have been used to investigate the influence of sex on learning of sensorimotor skills. In reporting standardization data on his slot maze, Young (1922) mentioned that girls have greater difficulty than boys in completing two trials within the time limit of 5 minutes each. Easby-Grave (1924), using the same test with 6-year-old children, 256 boys and 244 girls, found that of those who failed to complete both tests, 75 per cent were girls. Since only two trials were given, these studies are measures more of initial ability than of learning. The previously mentioned investigation of McGinnis (1929), in which 30 boys and 30 girls were used, showed the same sort of initial advantage for boys as was found in the above studies with the Young slot maze. With continued training, however, this difference disappeared and the girls' final performance approximated that of the boys. In terms of gross improvement as a result of a given amount of training, the girls were thus ahead. We have already men-

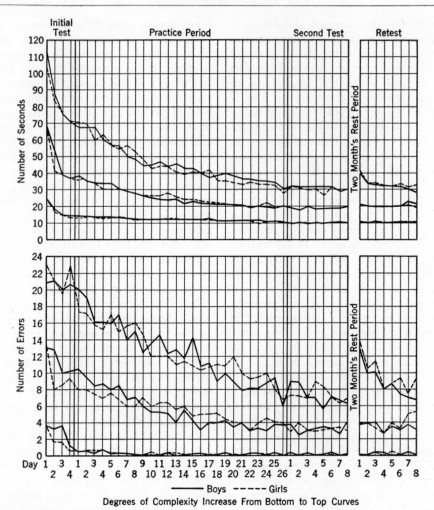

FIGURE 9. Learning curves for time and errors for boys and girls who learned rolling ball mazes of three degrees of complexity. (From "The Relation between the Complexity of the Habit to Be Acquired and the Form of the Learning Curve in Young Children," by M. L. Mattson. *Genetic Psychology Monographs*, 1933, *13*, 369. By permission of the publisher.) For a description of the problem, see page 389 of the present discussion.

tioned the dubious nature of such comparisons.

Wieg (1932) found no difference between the performances of boys and girls in learning her grooved finger and toe mazes. Using a maze through which the subjects walked, Batalla (1936) investigated the

learning ability of 58 boys and 50 girls having an average age of approximately 12 years. Boys began the problem with better scores than the girls and their final performance was still superior, although the gross difference became increasingly smaller as a function of practice. Batalla says that girls required more trials than boys to satisfy the criterion of learning, but he reports no figures to support this observation. The problem is said to be more interesting to boys than to girls, hence there existed a difference in motivation which may have influenced learning.

Mattson (1933), whose study has already received some consideration in this chapter, reports data concerning sex differences in maze performance. Sex comparisons are somewhat questionable owing to the fact that there were only 12 to 13 children of each sex on each of the three mazes. Mattson believes, however, that if sex differences in maze learning existed she should have found at least some suggestion of their presence. The learning curves for time and errors are shown in Figure 9. They are almost identical for the two sexes.

Investigations of other motor skills also reveal little or no evidence of a sex difference in learning *per se*. Hicks (1931) found that, in throwing balls at a moving target, the average initial score of 13 boys was 14, whereas that of 17 girls was 9.9. The average final scores for boys was 14.6, and that for girls, 12.9. On the basis of such data, one might conclude that girls had learned more than boys as a result of an equal amount of practice. Such a conclusion, however, can hardly be justified when it is recalled that so few subjects are involved, that little learning is evident in either group, and that an untrained control group to measure maturational effects improves as much as trained children.

Clinton's (1930) investigation of mirror drawing demonstrated that, although girls make poorer scores than boys at lower age levels, at higher age levels the girls surpass the boys. Learning curves are reported to be more regular for girls than for boys, but they or the data on which they are based do not appear in the article. In her motor-coordination study, Eigler (1932)

found no evidence for a difference in favor of either sex. Langhorne (1933) found no consistent sex difference in his investigation with the Renshaw-Weiss polygraph. At the lower age levels the initial scores of the girls were poorer than those of the boys. At higher age levels, however, there was no difference. The validity of comparisons at any age level in this investigation is, as mentioned earlier, very doubtful because of the smallness of the groups.

Perl (1933) found no significant sex difference in the learning of a simple motor skill, which comprised making small gates (/*/*) as fast as possible. Good learning curves were obtained for 20 one-minute periods of practice. The learning curves for 46 fourth-grade boys and 53 fourth-grade girls of approximately the same IQ were similar in shape and, where they did not overlap, were quite close together. Both raw and T scores yielded similar curves. A slight apparent superiority of the boys was unreliable statistically.

On the basis of these investigations it must be concluded that a differential influence of sex in the learning of simple motor skills such as those investigated has not been disclosed. Although the initial scores of boys have in several studies been higher than for girls, perhaps as a result of previous differences in experience, the gross amount of progress resulting from given amounts of training has been similar for both sexes.

Learning of Sensorimotor Skills as a Function of Intelligence. Investigations of the relation between intelligence test performance and learning of sensorimotor skills in young children agree in forcing the conclusion that, at early ages at least, there is no significant correlation.[1] One study

---

[1] Ruch (1925) presents data for card sorting which indicate a small correlation between intelligence and learning. The correlation decreased in successive practice periods. Correlations between time to sort 100

with adolescents has yielded results not in agreement with those at early and later age levels, hence we shall discuss this last.

McGinnis (1929), training children between 3 and 5 years of age on a stylus maze, found rank-order correlations ranging from $-.280 \pm .291$ to $.600 \pm .202$ between IQ and total time scores. Correlations between IQ and total errors ranged from $.100 \pm .221$ to $.660 \pm .178$. Owing to their large probable errors, few of the correlations for the different groups of subjects can be regarded as reliable. Initial scores and IQ also yielded insignificant correlations. McGinnis concluded that maze performance is not "related very highly to the function which is measured by scores on an intelligence test."

Performance on Mattson's (1933) rolling-ball mazes (see page 389) by children averaging 65 months was likewise unrelated to intelligence test performance. Mean time for 38 days of training yielded correlations with IQ of $-.66 \pm .28$ to $-.28 \pm .12$. Mean errors for the 38 days of training gave correlations with IQ of $-.04 \pm .09$ to $-.06 \pm .09$.

Learning by young children of sensori-motor skills other than maze performance also has little or no relation to intelligence test scores. Goodenough and Brian (1929) trained children in their fourth year to toss quoits over a ring. Rank-order correlation of the number of ringers with results on a battery of intelligence tests was $-.349$. The PE is not reported, but the authors say that this correlation is probably without significance. Hicks (1930a) found a correlation of only .05 between performance in throwing at a moving target and mental age, with CA held constant.

cards and MA (with CA partialed out) went from $.329 \pm .083$ on the first trial to $.107 \pm .092$ on the fifth. Fifty-two seventh- to ninth-grade children were subjects.

The age of the subjects was between 2½ and 6½ years.

Another skill the learning of which has been studied in relation to intelligence is mirror drawing. Wilson (1928) gave 20 boys 20 trials each on a six-pointed star. The ages ran from 8½ to 12¾ years. IQ's ranged from 76 to 148. Separate learning curves were constructed for each boy. These curves indicate no differential influence of intelligence in the acquiring of this skill.

Against all these results suggesting no relation between learning of motor skills and intelligence test scores must be placed data obtained by Knotts and Miles (1929). Two mazes of the Warden multiple-U pattern, one stylus and one raised, were learned by groups of blind and seeing adolescents. For both groups and both mazes, time scores yielded small and unreliable correlations with MA. Insignificant correlations between trials and errors and MA were found on the stylus maze for *blind* and on the raised finger maze for seeing subjects. However, the correlations between MA and, respectively, trials and errors were $-.75 \pm .07$ and $-.75 \pm .07$ for *seeing* subjects on the stylus maze. Data for blind subjects learning the raised finger maze yielded correlations almost as large as these, the correlations being $-.61 \pm .09$ and $-.62 \pm .09$. All four correlations are statistically significant. They therefore suggest that the more intelligent the individual the fewer the trials and errors likely to be involved in mastery of the respective mazes.

The above-mentioned studies force upon us the conclusion that, as far as young children are concerned, learning to thread mazes, to hit a moving target, to throw quoits over a peg, and to overcome effects of mirror distortion in drawing star patterns is unrelated to scores on intelligence tests. The experiment with adolescents is out of line with these findings for younger children and with findings obtained on similar problems with adults. The reason for this discrepancy is not apparent.

Incentives and the Learning of Sensorimotor Skills. Investigations of learning in animals and human adults have shown that the efficiency with which problems are mastered, and in some cases whether or not they are mastered at all, is a function of incentives. Similar investigations on learning in children have been few. Studies by Chapman and Feder (1917) on addition, cancellation, and substitution, Hurlock (1924) on intelligence test performance, Flügel (1928) on addition, Chase (1932) and Anderson and Smith (1933) on squeezing a dynamometer, and Mast (1937) on time required to open a box, although they deal with other factors than learning of motor skills *per se*, show that special incentives such as material rewards, praise, and reproof lead children to increase their effort in the performance of a task.[1]

Abel (1936) has reported a thoroughgoing investigation of the rôle of motivation in learning of a sensorimotor skill by children. She used a raised finger maze of the pattern shown in Figure 10. The subjects were 100 boys between the ages of 9 and 10 years. Their IQ's ranged from 100 to 129. Each child was shown how to proceed from the entrance to the exit of a simple maze by running his index finger along the raised pathway. The subjects were separated into five groups equivalent in CA and MA. They were given 30 trials at a single sitting. Group I received no reward other than that which might be inherent in the situation. The members of Group II received a material reward, a penny, at the end of each trial. A verbal reward, "Good," "Very good," and "Let me see if you can make even fewer mistakes

this time," was given Group III. Group IV received no special reward for the first 15 trials. Beginning with the sixteenth trial, however, each child was given a

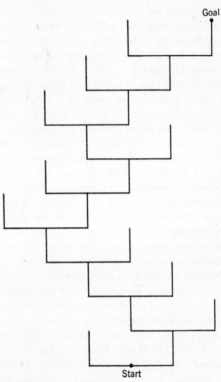

FIGURE 10. The Warden U maze which was used to investigate the influence of different incentives. (From "The Effects of Shift in Motivation upon the Learning of a Sensorimotor Task," by L. B. Abel. *Archives of Psychology*, 1936, *29*, 16. By permission of the publisher.)

penny per trial. Members of Group V received the above-mentioned verbal reward until the sixteenth trial, at which time the material reward was substituted. Abel's aim in adding and in changing incentives at the middle of the training period was to determine whether children, like the rats tested by Tolman (1932) and his students,

[1] For comprehensive reviews of the rôle of incentives in child behavior, see Hurlock (1931), Abel (1936), and Munn (1942).

would show a sharp change in performance following introduction of the different incentives.

As the error curves in Figure 11 indicate, Groups I to III improved. However, the group with no special reward showed least, and that with the material reward most, improvement. In Figure 12 are represented data for the two change-of-incentive groups (IV and V). One will observe that the introduction of a different incentive beginning with the sixteenth trial led to no obvious change in the rate of learning such as was found in experiments of a somewhat comparable nature with rats. Comparison of the mean number of errors in the first 15 as compared with the last 15 trials, however, suggests an increased rate of learning subsequent to the change. When equations for the curves before and after the change were determined and the slope lines compared, it was also apparent that the introduction of new incentives had effected a greater rate of learning.

In order to determine whether the change in mean errors and in slope was greater than could be expected in terms of sampling errors, Abel used a method suggested by Fisher (1930, pp. 75–139). She determined the $P/2$ of the differences in the respective means and slopes. Since 15 trials were involved, a $P/2$ of 0.05 or less would indicate a reliable difference. The $P/2$ of the difference between the means of the first and second halves of both the curves in Figure 12 was 0.00. Change from a verbal to a material reward yielded a $P/2$ of 0.00 for the difference between the respective slopes. However, the two slopes for, respectively, no reward and material reward had a $P/2$ for the difference in slope of 0.39, suggesting unreliability of this difference.

Another method of analyzing the data was to compare the final levels of performance in terms of the mean number of errors in the last 5 trials. The means were: *no reward–reward*, 1.675; *material reward*, 1.675; *verbal reward–material reward*, 1.875; *verbal reward*, 2.325; and *no reward*, 2.625. The differences between the first and third and second and third means are not statistically reliable. The difference between the *verbal and material reward* groups, however, has a critical ratio (D/σ_{diff}) of 3.110, indicating that there are approximately 100 chances in 100 of a difference greater than zero. The difference between the means for the *verbal reward* and *no reward–reward* groups is equally reliable. There are, however, only 99.7 chances out of 100 that the difference in the means of the *verbal reward* and *verbal reward–material reward* groups is also greater than zero. One must conclude, therefore, that *material reward, no reward–reward*, and *verbal reward–material reward* are of approximately equal value as incentives to learning the present maze and that their incentive value is greater than a *verbal reward* or *no special reward*. The latter condition, although it produced learning, was least effective.

Abel points out that it makes no significant difference whether a material reward is given throughout learning or whether it is given only in the last 15 trials. In other words, 15 pennies in the last half of training elicited as much in terms of final achievement as 30 pennies, 1 per trial throughout training. She also suggests that a verbal reward, while stimulating for the first 10 trials or so, gradually loses effectiveness.

In a second experiment with the same maze and following the same method of scoring and analysis, but involving children with lower than average IQ's, Abel determined the effect of giving rewards *only when a certain amount of progress had been achieved*. Whereas the children of the experiment described above received

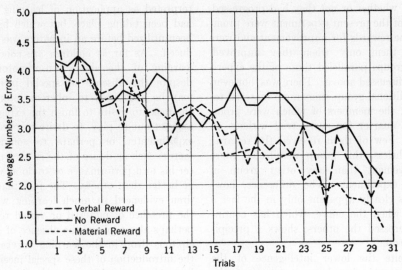

FIGURE 11. Learning curves for children provided with different incentives. (From "The Effects of Shift in Motivation upon the Learning of a Sensori-motor Task," by L. B. Abel. *Archives of Psychology,* 1936, *29*, 22, 23. By permission of the publisher.)

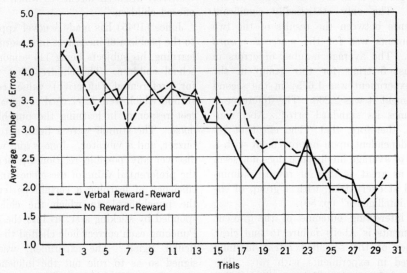

FIGURE 12. The effect of changing incentives. (From "The Effects of Shift in Motivation upon the Learning of a Sensori-motor Task," by L. B. Abel. *Archives of Psychology,* 1936, *29*, 23, 24. By permission of the publisher.)

a reward at the end of each trial, regardless of whether or not they had progressed, those of the present experiment were promised the rewards for improvement and were given them only when they improved. Five groups paralleled those of the experiment discussed above. There was, however, an additional group (maximum material reward), the members of which were promised a quarter for every trial without an error. Few of them received the reward; nevertheless, this group manifested more improvement than any other group in either experiment. The difference, however, is clearly apparent only in the last 5 trials, when the curve, which has continually crossed the others, shows a precipitous drop.

Despite the lower intelligence of the children and the changed nature of the incentives, the results for the other five groups of the second experiment did not differ greatly from those of the first experiment. The only statistically significant difference between the results of the two experiments was for the *material reward* group. The average number of errors in the last 5 trials for this group in the first experiment was 1.675; in the second experiment it was 2.260. The difference is 3.4 times its standard error. Abel concludes, therefore, that "The effect of reward dependent upon improvement with a group of average intelligence does not seem to be as great as that of reward, administered at every trial, with a group of superior intelligence" (p. 50).

An interesting outcome of the present experiments is Abel's failure to find clear evidence of the so-called *latent* learning disclosed in experiments with rats. The unrewarded rats, it will be recalled, failed to show consistent signs of learning before being given a special incentive, such as food or water. When the incentive was introduced there was an extremely rapid drop in the learning curves. This was interpreted as application of learning which had been taking place, but which had not been utilized before an incentive was introduced. As far as children are concerned, learning of the above sensorimotor skill despite the absence of special incentives may be attributed to inherent interest of the task, to desire to finish the experiment and get out to play, to desire to please the experimenter, or perhaps to competitive factors such as desire of the subject to better his own performance or to do as well as or better than others. The fact that children evidenced so much learning without the presence of material or verbal rewards perhaps also explains the absence of a precipitous drop in the learning curves after the introduction of these special incentives. In any event, the rats were hungry or thirsty, and such factors are undoubtedly of much greater motivating value than the relatively artificial incentives which can be offered children.

Jones (1945) has made a novel approach to the problem of incentives in sensorimotor learning, his subjects being 114 junior high school children. The children first rated, for preferential (affective) value, certain stimuli which were later used to signal correct responses in learning the punchboard maze. The stimuli were a light, a tone, a buzzer, and a vibrator. Jones's aim was to discover any possible relationship between the preferential value of these cues and the efficiency of learning a certain pattern on the punchboard, to which the child responded by sticking a stylus into the holes. Punching each correct hole elicited the particular signal. The experiment was designed so as to rule out the influence of every factor but the signaling cue. Jones found, however, that the degree to which the children liked or disliked the respective cues had no bearing upon time or error scores or upon the shape of the learning curve. He says that one can expect no gain from "sugar-coating" a response by providing a "supplementary pleasant experience" to accompany it.

The relative efficacy of praise and reproof in substitution learning was studied by Schmidt (1941) but without results unqualifiedly in favor of either incentive. The person administering positive or negative reinforcement was the most significant variable. Grace (1948), using punchboard learning and different kinds of approval for correct performance, found that the personality of the child was a more significant variable than the kind of approval.

Holodnak's (1943) 6- to 10-year-olds learned a punchboard maze more efficiently when the correct responses were signaled than when the incorrect responses were similarly signaled. The results are interpreted as favoring positive over negative guidance in learning.

Learning of Sensorimotor Skills as a Function of the Training Procedure. Many skills which depend upon specific training for their acquisition will develop regardless of the precise method of training adopted. It is obvious, however, that, some methods of training may be more effective than others. We have already indicated that training which involves certain incentives is more effective than that which involves others. In the present section we are interested in the relative efficacy of different training procedures used under constant conditions of motivation. For example, given a certain motivation, does more or less improvement result when the skill to be acquired is demonstrated frequently? What advantages, if any, will accrue if the child is given manual guidance in the task to be performed? Does faster learning or a higher level of achievement result when the correct procedure is enforced from the start, or is it better to allow the child, by

random trial and error, to find the correct procedure for himself?

Gates and Taylor (1923) have made one approach to this problem. These investigators were interested in determining whether motor control in writing is facilitated by "putting the child through" the various movements to be made. One group, consisting of 21 kindergarten children, was given an opportunity to learn to write the letters *a b c d e* by tracing them through tissue paper.[1] A group of comparable age, motor ability, and intelligence, but consisting of only 14 children, *copied* the letters throughout the learning period. This group was thus free to make many mistakes which the tracing group would not be very likely to make. Five minutes of daily practice for 5 days were given the *tracing* group. In terms of the number of strokes required to write each letter, the mean scores on the 5 successive days were 11.4, 20.6, 20.8, 24.2, and 29.8. In a 5-minute *copying* test, given on the sixth day, the mean score for this group was 8.2. During the 5 days of training in *copying* the same letters freehand, the other group gained in their mean score as follows: 3.7, 7.2, 13.5, 17.6, and 19.5. On the sixth day their copying score was 21.1. In other words, the copying skill of this group, a skill which approximates that called for in everyday life, and which is the aim of training, was more than twice as good as that of the group which was, as it were, put through the appropriate movement with little chance of making errors.

In further training with the letters *e–g* and, later, with the letters *f–j*, both groups continued to improve. When called upon to *copy* letters that they had neither traced

---

[1] This is comparable to the "putting-through" technique used by Carr and his students with white rats. The procedure was not effective as a training technique with rats. See Munn (1933, pp. 342-343) for a brief review of these studies.

nor copied before, both groups had low scores. The mean score of the *tracing* group, however, was only 0.77, as compared with 4.6 for the *copying* group. Thus the transfer value was also greater for the copying than for the tracing procedure.

Melcher's (1934) investigation of stylus maze learning in preschool children who were given visual, manual, and visual and manual guidance indicated that very little learning occurs with such guidance. The learning which did appear may be attributed to the test trials (2 out of every 6 guided trials), during which the children were free to learn by trial and error.

On the basis of the above investigations and those with rats and human adults, one must conclude that more rapid learning of such motor skills as writing and threading a stylus maze occurs when the individual is free to initiate his own movements and to make incorrect as well as correct responses than when he is manually guided in the correct performance.

Goodenough and Brian (1929) determined the relative efficacy of different kinds and amounts of *verbal guidance* upon the learning by 4-year-old children of a ring-toss skill. Although two of the three groups were very small and no statistical analysis of differences is therefore warranted, marked differences in the effectiveness of the methods are clearly suggested. All children, regardless of verbal guidance or its absence, were similarly motivated. They were given praise and encouragement for "ringers" and also received stickers, which changed in nature from day to day, to paste on the wall.

Group A, consisting of 4 boys and 6 girls, was given the following instructions:

This is a game where we try to throw rings over a post. You stand here on this base—be sure both of your feet are in the base all the time—and I'll hand you the rings. Try to throw them on the post over there. Do you see what I mean? All right, go ahead.

No criticism or verbal guidance was given this group.

Group B, comprising 2 boys and 4 girls, was shown how to throw the ring and was given critical verbal guidance throughout the experiment. The initial instructions were like those for the above group except that the experimenter said, "I'll show you how it is done," and then demonstrated. Whenever the child failed to get a "ringer" the experimenter pointed out the source of error, saying, for example, "Not quite so far next time," "A little bit higher so it won't hit the post," etc. These children were also told to hold the ring at the point of juncture of the rope so as to insure better balance. Each chose his own general procedure, some throwing overhand and others underhand, some throwing the ring down onto the peg and some squatting and throwing it up. Within this group the method was changed by the child from time to time, often without adequate test of a given procedure.

Group C, consisting of 2 boys and 2 girls, was required to adhere to a constant method of holding and throwing the ring. Members of this group were instructed to grasp the ring at the point of juncture, to hold it horizontally before them, and, after swinging it a few times, to pitch it forward and upward toward the post. Furthermore, they were given verbal guidance which matched that of Group B.

Twenty trials per day for 50 days were given each child. Scoring was in terms of the number of "ringers" in each 20 tosses. Two children in Group A and 1 in Group B failed to gain. All other children manifested absolute gains ranging from 4 to 56 in Group A, 5 to 47 in Group B, and 21 to 70 in Group C. The corresponding percentage gains ranged from 5 to 287, 24 to 147, and 53 to 175. The median gains for Groups A to C, respectively, were 11.5, or 36 per cent; 17.5, or 66 per cent; and 42.5, or 92 per cent. Until the thirtieth day of the experiment, learning curves overlapped considerably. The highest curve was that of Group C, the next that of Group A, and the lowest that of Group B. If the groups were not so small, we should be justified in concluding that, for this game and for children of this age and intelligence, the best procedure is to enforce from the start a given effective method and to combine this with verbal guidance. In terms of the percentage of gain, if not on the basis of the latter part of the learning curves, we might also be justified in concluding that verbal guidance, even without a standardized throwing procedure, is more effective than leaving the child entirely to his own resources. As the situation stands, however, what might have been a very significant experimental test of the efficacy of verbal guidance is ruined by the fact that groups are too small to warrant any definite conclusions concerning this aspect of the investigation.

In good learners there was a marked tendency for successes to be grouped. This suggests that these children continued to use those responses which they observed to be associated with success. Poor learners showed little evidence of such observation and application. Errors immediately following success were usually due to throws beyond the post. Analysis of individual learning data indicated the following factors to be significant in determining success or failure: overconfidence and undue caution; setting-up of stereotyped undesirable reactions; false association of cause and effect; peculiar associations of meaning with verbal expressions, as when "trying hard" was assumed to be synonymous

with "throwing with great violence"; incorrect focusing of attention, such as looking at arm instead of goal; and random changes in procedure.

Another approach to this problem is Cox's (1933). Thirty-eight boys from the two upper classes of an English elementary school practiced assembling, wiring, and stripping an electric-lamp holder. They were merely told to repeat the operations at top speed until each day's series had been completed. Time required to perform the operations was recorded. Under these conditions no significantly greater progress occurred than was exhibited by a control group of 32 boys given only initial and final tests. Similar results were obtained with adult subjects trained by this technique. In a further investigation with experimental and control groups of adults, initial tests on assembling and stripping were followed, in the experimental group, by 11 days of special instruction and performance of supervised exercises. Under these conditions the experimental group made gains significantly greater than did the control group. The author points out that much more rapid and efficient learning of such operations occurs when, rather than being left to their own resources, individuals are given special exercises and verbal guidance. Undoubtedly the effectiveness of such training would differ for different skills and for individuals of different levels of maturity.

Transfer of Motor Skill.[1] We have already mentioned the fact that Gates and

1 Judd's (1908) study of transfer involved dart throwing, but transfer comprised application of principles to motor skill rather than transfer of skill *per se.* One group of fifth- and sixth-grade boys received instruction in principles of refraction while another, comparable, group received no such instruction. Both groups were then required to hit a target placed 12 inches under water. They were equally successful. Thus knowledge of principles failed to aid the instructed group. When the target was shifted to 4 inches of water, however, boys with a knowledge of

Taylor (1923) found greater transfer from copying the letters *a–e* to copying the letters *f–j* than when the letters *a–e* were merely traced. Since we do not know what success entirely untrained children would have in copying the letters *f–j* under identical conditions, it is impossible to determine the actual transfer in the two cases.

McGinnis (1929) investigated transfer in maze performance. The maze was of the stylus type (McGinnis, 1928), apparently with open alleys. Invisible stops placed at appropriate points limited the movements of the stylus. Four patterns, the paths of which covered the same distance but went in different directions, were used. Since the patterns were not of equal difficulty, scores were equated in terms of their relative difficulty. Four groups, each comprising six 4-year-old children equated in intelligence, received training on the maze patterns in the order AB, BA, ABCD, BADC, respectively. Scoring was in terms of time and errors for 40 trials, in the case of the first two groups, and 50 trials in the case of the others. Positive transfer occurred in every group regardless of the fact that some patterns, by changes in the direction of the goal, were calculated to produce negative transfer. The percentage saved in transferring from one maze pattern to the other ranged from 12.6 to 41.8 seconds and 9.4 to 35.8 errors.

Wieg (1932) investigated bilateral transfer, using a grooved multiple-T maze through which the index finger or big toe could be run. Her aim was to measure transfer from right hand to left hand, from left hand to right hand, from left hand to left foot, from right foot to left foot, from

the principles of refraction made a much more rapid adjustment than did those without such knowledge. As the result of this and other researches, Judd came to the conclusion that "generalization" plays a large part in determining the magnitude and direction (positive or negative) of transfer when such occurs. For a further discussion of transfer, see pages 423–425.

right foot to right hand, and from left foot to left hand. Twenty-four boys and 20 girls, ranging in age from 66 to 78 months, were grouped in sets of 4. These were equated in terms of IQ, CA, socioeconomic status, sex, and initial maze-learning ability. All subjects were first given 3 successive trials with each hand and each foot for 2 days. They were then divided into different groups and given 3 daily trials until they had reached a criterion of not more than 2 errors in 3 successive trials. Time and errors were the bases of comparison. There was, in most cases, a saving in speed and in errors during learning with the transfer limb. The number of cases was too small to allow determination of the reliability of transfer scores. There was, however, a suggestion of greater transfer effects going from a less efficient to a more efficient limb, as from foot to hand or from left to right hand. A greater transfer was apparent in going from the right foot to each of the other limbs than from any one of these limbs to another. A group of adults showed larger transfer scores than children. The reliability of this difference, like that between the various directions of transfer, cannot be determined; hence the results can be regarded merely as suggestive.

Significant transfer from one stylus maze pattern to another was obtained by Jones and Yoshioka (1938) in an investigation with 81 boys and 71 girls, each approximately 13½ years of age. The groups learned different patterns and used different procedures. When these differences were balanced, however, there were lower error scores for the learning of the second than for the learning of the first maze. In different groups the critical ratio ranged from 1.62 to 3.68.

The error curves are shown in Figure 13. One will note that there is an average advantage of 5½ errors in the initial trial with the second maze and that, although this advantage decreases considerably, the two curves remain separated until the fifteenth trial. In accounting for transfer, Jones and Yoshioka (1938) say:

Factors in this transfer probably include an increase in effort to observe and remem-

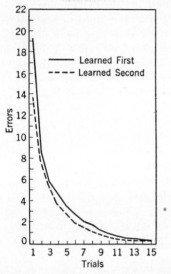

FIGURE 13. Transfer in learning of stylus mazes. (From "Differential Errors in Children's Learning on a Stylus Maze," by H. E. Jones and J. B. Yoshioka. *Journal of Comparative Psychology*, 1938, *25*, 470. By permission of the publisher, Williams and Wilkins Co.)

ber the results of maze exploration, although it may be pointed out that the second order shows fewer errors even on the first trial. The subject is acquainted with both his time and error record on the first test, and commonly seeks to improve his record [pp. 471–472].

The existence of transfer in this experiment is made all the more interesting when it is pointed out that all the subjects had received previous training on stylus and body mazes from time to time. Without such previous training the present transfer would probably have been greater. The experimental results are further analyzed by Yoshioka and Jones (1945) in terms of learning at different stages of practice.

Using sixth- and seventh-grade pupils, Jones and Batalla (1944) found no evidence of transfer from a large alley maze to a stylus maze of the same pattern, or vice versa. They feel that failure to show transfer in this experiment indicates absence of configural and insightful learning. In another maze experiment, Batalla (1943) had previously found absence of insightful behavior.

In this connection one will recall Cox's experiment (1933) which was discussed earlier (page 405). Practice in assembling and stripping electric light holders did not enable a group of 38 boys to do any better in a final test than a control group given only the initial and final tests. The result was similar to that obtained with adults. Specific training, verbal instructions alone and combined with exercises designed to bring important aspects to the learner's attention, did have a transfer value for adults. No children were used under the latter conditions.[1]

Memory

Most experiments in memory deal with learning, recall, recognition, or relearning of symbolic materials such as numbers, words, nonsense syllables, poems, prose passages, and figures. The chief emphasis is upon retention of the effects of previous

[1] Transfer in discrimination learning (the transposition problem) has been studied by Alberts and Ehrenfreund (1951), Hunter (1952), Jackson (1939), Jackson and others (1938, 1939, 1940, 1943), and Kuenne (1946, 1946a, 1948). These studies deal with conditions which contribute to the relational type of response. Alberts and Ehrenfreund found that transposition in older children differs from that in younger children, the difference being attributable to verbalization in the latter. Hunter's (1952) paper deals with theoretical aspects of transposition in children.

stimulation. Retention may be measured in terms of ability to make appropriate responses in the absence of stimuli which originally elicited them (delayed reaction and reproduction), in terms of ability to differentiate old and new stimuli (recognition), or in terms of ability to relearn previous material with a saving of time and effort.

The earliest measurable evidence of a child's ability to respond in terms of absent stimuli comes from tests of the delayed-reaction type. These yield a measure of retentivity prior to the time when conventionalized symbols such as are used in most memory tests have been acquired. Hence we shall begin our discussion of memory in children by considering delayed reaction. This discussion will be followed by a summary of other researches on memory.

Delayed Reaction. The principle underlying delayed-reaction tests is that of presenting stimuli toward which differential responses are required and then removing the stimuli prior to response. In the original Carr-Hunter (Hunter, 1913) method, for instance, the animal was confronted by three compartments, only one of which was lighted in a given trial. The lighted compartment, which offered the only means of escape, varied in position from trial to trial. At first the subject had to learn that escape was possible only through the lighted compartment. The delayed-reaction tests were those in which a differential response to the compartments was required *after the light had been turned off.* The interval between removal of the external differentiating stimulus and the time of response was gradually increased until the subject could no longer remember which door had been lighted.

Instead of escaping through the lighted or previously lighted door, Hunter's child subjects pressed a button corresponding to the position of the door. Since the animals and children in this experiment first had to *learn* that the lighted door was the correct one, this has been called the *indirect* method of testing delayed reaction. The *direct* method, also first used by Hunter (1917), does not require specific training by the experimenter before delay tests are instituted. Hunter and later investigators obtained the child's attention while hiding a toy or some other desirable object in or under one of two or more devices such as boxes, plates, or cups. After an interval, they determined whether the child could locate the hidden object.

In Hunter's investigation, for example, a girl of 13 months was confronted with three similar boxes having hinged covers. A toy with which she had been playing was placed in one of the boxes. When he ascertained that the infant had seen in which box the toy was placed, Hunter disoriented her and, after given intervals, offered an opportunity to find the toy. She located the toy with a high degree of accuracy after intervals between 8 and 12 seconds. At 16 months of age she responded with high accuracy after 24 seconds.

All investigations of delayed reaction in children, except Hunter's first one with animals and children, have involved modifications of the *direct* method just described. Some of these studies have been carried out as routine clinical tests; others have involved intensive experimental investigation.

The most extensive clinical tests of memory in infants are described by Bühler (1930). The earliest test is for infants of 3 months. In this test, the face of the tester appears and then disappears. If it looks for the face or seems disturbed by its absence, the infant is credited with memory. Bühler claims that the 3-month-old infant characteristically searches for, or is disturbed by disappearance of, the tester's face.[1] In a test at the 5-month level, a toy is presented and then removed. The infant is credited with memory if it looks "searchingly" in the direction in which the toy has disappeared.

One of the best delayed-reaction tests of this general type is that devised by Bühler (1930) and Hetzer and Wislitzky (1930) for use with children ranging in age from 10 to 24 months. A ball containing a chicken which pops out is placed in the child's hand. The child plays with the ball, making the chicken appear and disappear. Then the ball is removed and other activity is encouraged. Some time later a ball which looks like the previous one, but does not contain a chicken, is presented. The child is credited with memory if, upon squeezing the new ball, it shows "astonishment," looks "questioningly" at the tester, or puts its finger in the hole when a chicken fails to appear. The maximum delay followed by evidence of memory is about 1 minute at 10 to 11 months, 8 minutes at 15 to 17 months, 15 minutes at 19 to 20 months, and 17 minutes at 21 to 24 months.

Allen (1931) has investigated delayed reaction in 50 boys and 50 girls approximately 1 year old. Each child sat on its mother's lap during the experiment. Three boxes which looked exactly alike were placed on a card table at equal distances from the subject, as shown in Figure 14. Various toys were used as lures. While the mother's eyes were closed (to prevent helpful attitudes), but while the infant was watching, a toy was tapped on a box three times and dropped in, where it was out of sight. The

table was then pulled out of the infant's reach for periods ranging from 10 to 165 seconds. At the end of a delay period, the table was pushed toward the child, who was thus given an opportunity to respond. Three tests in rapid succession, with the toy in a different box each time, were given after 10-, 20-, and 30-second delay periods. For longer delays there were fewer tests, the exact number differing somewhat from

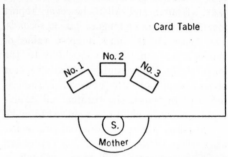

FIGURE 14. Arrangement for measuring delayed reaction in infants. (From "Individual Differences in Delayed Reaction of Infants," by C. N. Allen. *Archives of Psychology*, 1931, *19*, 14. By permission of the publisher.)

one subject to another. Loss of interest during the longer delays was one reason for this variation.

Since there were three possible locations for the toy, chance accuracy would approximate 33 per cent. Accuracy after a 10-second delay was 61 per cent for boys and 66 per cent for girls. After a 20-second delay, it was 65 per cent for boys and 57 per cent for girls. A 30-second delay was followed by accuracy, respectively, of 50 and 48 per cent. With a 45-second delay the percentages were 19 and 36, respectively. The number of cases at longer delays was too small to make the results worthy of consideration. Sex differences were insignificant.

The experiments of Hunter, Bühler, Hetzer and Wislitzky, and Allen all agree

---

[1] Hurlock and Schwartz (1932) have summarized many biographical reports of this type of response in infants. Preyer mentions an infant of 3 months who cried and looked around the room when his nurse disappeared. Shinn reports such behavior in a child of 4 months. Fact and interpretation are so interwoven in such studies that one cannot be sure of their validity. A chance response, occurring once, may be taken as an indication of memory.

in demonstrating that memory of the delayed-reaction type (that is, recall memory) is present during the first year of life. These experiments differ, however, in their findings with respect to the maximum correct delays. The discrepancies with respect to this factor may be attributed to different test situations and to different criteria of successful delay. Bühler and her co-workers, it will be recalled, report maximum delays of *1 minute* as occurring in the first year. Hunter and Allen, however, report maximum delays no longer than *30 seconds*. The "naturalness" and interest value of Bühler's tests perhaps contribute to the longer delays in her studies. Another factor of possible importance, however, is the criterion of response. In Hunter and Allen's experiments, the child was required to make a clear-cut overt differential response, whereas in Bühler's tests facial expression and fingering of the ball were accepted as indicative of memory.

The most extensive investigation of delayed reaction in preschool children is Skalet's (1931). Sixty children between 2 and 5½ years were given tests similar in principle to those discussed above. In the first group of experiments, a child was confronted with three plates under one of which a cooky was placed. After seeing the cooky hidden under a given plate, the subject was taken out of the room. Upon his return to the original situation, the child was required to locate the hidden cooky. If it was located without error, he was allowed to eat it. In successive trials the cooky varied in position in a random manner. Average accuracy of response was 64.8 per cent after delays of 1 to 3 days. After delays of 21 to 29 days, accuracy dropped to 46.2 per cent. Longer delays were followed by merely chance accuracy. The correlation between age and maximum correct delay was .478 ± .077. Skalet points out that verbal symbols enabled the

preschool children to make correct delays after long periods. The great difference in maximum correct delays between the ages of 1 and 2 years may be accounted for partly on the ground that the older child has acquired linguistic substitutes for absent stimuli.

The response required in Skalet's second group of experiments was to select from a random array of figures the one observed in isolation some time previously. She thus obtained a measure of delayed reaction in terms of recognition. In one set of tests, familiar animals were involved. In another, Skalet used geometrical figures of various kinds. Familiar animals gave the best results. For these tests the correlation between maximum correct delay and age was .669 ± .093. Tests with geometrical figures were too difficult for most children.

Two investigations of how certain stimulus factors influence correct delayed reactions in children have been reported. The first deals with the position of the subject, and the second with the position and color of the stimuli. In his original delayed-reaction experiment, Hunter (1913) found that some animals did not perform correctly unless allowed to maintain a fixed bodily orientation during delay. He supposed that a continuing kinesthetic cue was being used. Hunter's findings suggested to Emerson (1931) that the delayed reactions of children might be affected differentially by introducing variations in the degree of bodily orientation during delay. Thirty-two children, ranging in age from 27 to 59 months, were each shown an easel which contained a board with 42 pegs arranged in 7 rows of 6 each. While a child was watching, the experimenter placed a ring over one peg. The child was then required to turn to a similar easel and place a ring over the corresponding peg. In each test the delay was approximately

5 seconds. Nine degrees of orientation were involved. They ranged from stepping to an easel at the side of the stimulus easel to going round to an easel facing in the opposite direction. Scores for correct placement were low throughout. With no disorientation, the average number of correct responses was 17.82. With the first the lure has been hidden or does it represent some *relation* between this and other boxes? Miller refers to his test situations as involving "critical choice delayed reaction." A 10-second delay was used in each situation. Ninety-eight children between 11½ and 162 months of age served as subjects. The first experiment was conducted

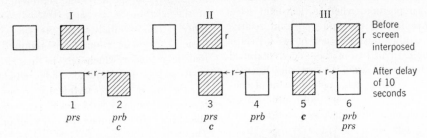

FIGURE 15. Critical tests of cues used in delayed reaction. (From "The Perception of Children: A Genetic Study Employing the Critical Choice Delayed Reaction," by N. E. Miller. *Journal of Genetic Psychology*, 1934, *44*, 327. By permission of the Journal Press, publisher.) The top line represents the original position of the boxes in each of the three tests. The lower line represents the critical choice positions. Each box is dsignated by a number for purposes of reference. *c*, choice on the basis of color; *prs*, response to position of box with respect to the child's own position; *prb*, response in terms of the position of one box in relation to the position of the other box. If the cue were color, boxes 2, 3, and 5 would be selected. Should the cue be position of the box with respect to himself, the subject would respond to boxes 1, 3, and 6. However, if the box presenting two cues were selected, the child would respond to 2, 3, and 6. There are four other theoretically possible cues.

degree of disorientation indicated above, the average score dropped to 6.45. When the positions of the stimulus and the response easels were back to back, the average score was only 1.81. There was an increase in scores with age. The average number of correct placements throughout the experiment correlated $.77 \pm .05$ with CA and $.758 \pm .05$ with MA.

Miller's (1934) investigation concerns the question of how certain exteroceptive stimulus relations affect accuracy of delayed response. His problem may be framed in the following question: When the child makes a delayed response, does the implicit symbol represent the *absolute* position, color, or other aspect of the box in which as follows: A child was seated opposite the experimenter and was asked, "Do you like to play games?" Two boxes of the same size, but one red and the other yellow, were placed in front of the child. The experimenter said: "See the boxes. Now I'm going to hide the dog under a box. Look!" The toy was hidden. A screen was then interposed between the boxes and the child for 10 seconds. At the end of this interval, the experimenter said, "See if you can find the dog." After each response he said, "Fine!," and again hid the toy. The child was then asked, "Can you find it this time?" Various lures besides the toy dog were used.

As soon as the child completed two successive correct responses, critical tests to determine the cues utilized were introduced. The nature of these tests can best be grasped by referring to Figure 15. Three critical tests are represented. The idea was to see whether, in these tests, the child would select a box of the same color as that under which he had seen the lure placed, whether he would select the box having the same relation with respect to his own position, whether he would select the one having the same position relative to the other box, whether he would select on the basis of two of these cues combined, or whether he would select on the basis of some other possible combination of cues. In the critical tests each box contained the toy, although the subject had seen it placed in only one box.

The 11½- to 24-month-old children, of which there were 4, all responded in terms of *position relative to the other box*. In successive age groups, however, there was a gradual decrease in the frequency of this type of response. Response in terms of *color* began, with a frequency of 20 per cent, in the age group of 25 to 36 months. The group contained 11 subjects. Color was an increasingly frequent basis of response until the 5-year level, after which its frequency decreased. *Position relative to the subject* was not a very frequent cue at any age level. Response in terms of the *box with two cues in its favor* was also quite infrequent at all ages. *Unclassified* responses increased with age, reaching a frequency of about 30 per cent at the 120- to 162-month level.

When the distance between the two boxes was doubled, the youngest age group responded 66 per cent in terms of *position relative to the other box* and 33 per cent in terms of *position relative to the subject*. Under these conditions, however, color again became an increasingly important cue in successively older groups.

In a number of further experiments involving principles similar to those of the above tests, use of such cues as position relative to a group of other boxes, different color from a group of boxes alike in color, and combinations of color and position cues was tested. In general, the results of these experiments show that the child below 2 years of age has some representation of the *position of one box relative to another*. This symbol serves as the chief basis of response when he is required to remember under which box he has previously seen a toy placed. Older children, on the other hand, frequently retain a representation of *color*, which symbol enables them to remember the box containing a toy.

Retention after a Single Presentation. Retention of materials seen or heard a single time has been investigated extensively in children. The problem is usually stated more specifically as one of immediate memory or memory span. It was first investigated by Jacobs (1887).[1] Special

[1] Materials used to test the memory span of children have included *digits:* Jacobs (1887), Bolton (1892), Henri (1902), Smedley (1902), Humpstone (1917), Pintner and Paterson (1917), Ide (1920), Town (1921), Starr (1923), Easby-Grave (1924), Gesell (1925), Young (1928), Hallowell (1928), McCaulley (1928), Hurlock and Newmark (1931), Wilson and Fleming (1937), and Terman and Merrill (1937); *letters:* Jacobs (1887); *words:* Kirkpatrick (1894), Henri (1902), Burt (1909), Whipple (1915), Achilles (1920), Stutsman (1926), Hurlock and Newmark (1931), Lumley and Calhoun (1934), and Wilson and Fleming (1937); *objects:* Dewey, Child, and Ruml (1920), Bronner, Healy, Lowe, and Shimberg (1927), and McElwee (1933); *movements:* Baldwin and Stecher (1924), Hurlock and Newmark (1931), Mallay (1935), and Werner (1940); *figures:* Achilles (1920), Allport (1930), Komatsu (1931), Shimidu (1934), Hall (1936); *pictures:* Stern (1904), Squire (1912), Carpenter (1913), Myers (1913), Winch (1914), Town (1921), Baldwin and Stecher (1924), J. A. McGeoch (1925, 1928), Bayley (1926), Conrad and Jones (1929), and Holaday and Stoddard (1933); and *narratives:* Shaw (1896), Yoakum (1921), Bassett (1929), Dietze (1931, 1932), Hurlock and Newmark (1931), Dietze and Jones (1931), Northway (1936), Terman and Merrill (1937), Loder (1937), and Morris (1939).

studies have had as their aims (1) to ascertain how differences in age, intelligence, and sex affect the memory span; (2) to compare the memory span for different kinds of material; (3) to determine the relative efficacy of visual and auditory means of presentation; (4) to observe differences in results obtained when recall or recognition tests of retention are used; and (5), especially in the case of narratives, figures, and pictures, to determine the nature of differences between the original and "recalled" material.

That the memory span of children increases with age has been shown for all kinds of material investigated. The auditory-vocal memory span for digits, as indicated by Starr's (1923) investigation with 2000 children between the ages of 4 and 15 years, is 4 between the fourth and fifth years, 5 between the sixth and eighth years, 6 between the ninth and twelfth years, and 7 beyond the twelfth year. Other studies on auditory-vocal digit span summarized by Hurlock and Newmark (1931), as well as the Terman-Merrill (1937) norms, are in close agreement with these. Although the memory span for words, letters, objects, figures, and ideas in a narrative also increases with age, the particular span is dependent upon the meaning of the materials involved.

Most investigations have shown a positive, but medium, correlation between intelligence and memory span for various types of material. In Bayley's (1926) study, which involved 100 subjects between approximately 3 and 6 years old, correlations between MA and memory span for digits ranged from .40 at the third year to .67 at the sixth year. Correlations between memory span for objects and MA ranged from .44 to .58. Hurlock and Newmark (1931) report the following correlations between the IQ and memory spans of 20 preschool children: *digits,*

.59 ± .11; *syllables,* .72 ± .08; *concrete words,* .52 ± .11; *abstract words,* .55 ± .11; *pictures,* .61 ±.09; *movements,* .59 ± .11; *ideas in a narrative,* .76 ± .07; and *commands,* .64 ± .09. Clark's (1924) investigation suggests that, although there is a positive correlation between intelligence and digit span at early age levels, the correlation is negligible at the high school level.

It is generally claimed that memory spans for boys and girls show a difference in favor of the latter. This view is based, primarily, upon the researches of Kirkpatrick (1894) and Pyle (1920), both of whom measured memory span for words. The developmental range in both studies combined was from about the third grade to the high school level. That a sex difference exists in the memory span for digits is doubtful. Several studies involving both sexes fail to mention a difference, and Pintner and Paterson (1917) and Bryan (1934) found none. Some investigations involving pictures (Shimidu, 1934) and narratives (Shaw, 1896; Bassett, 1929; Dietze, 1932) have disclosed slight superiority of boys. It is of course quite possible that, where meaningful materials of this nature are involved, a sex difference indicates differential acquaintance with the material rather than differences in retentivity.

As reported by Hurlock and Newmark (1931), the average memory span of preschool children for digits is 5 ± 1.00; for concrete words, 4.3 ± 0.65; for abstract words, 3.0 ± 0.30; for syllables in a sentence, 15.1 ± 1.20; for pictures, 1.2 ± 0.35; for movements, 4.3 ± 0.65; for ideas in a narrative, 4.3 ± 0.00; and for commands, 3.3 ± 0.50. Whipple (1915) reports that meaning greatly affects the size of the memory span for words.

Smedley's (1902) results show that the memory span for digits does not differ for auditory and visual methods of presentation until the age of approximately 9 years. After this age the visual span exceeds the auditory. Jones (1927) likewise finds no difference in the digit memory span for visual and auditory presentation. All his subjects were under 9 years of age.

Recognition is apparently easier than recall. Achilles (1920) found that children between 8½ and 11½ years of age recognized an average of 23.95 words and recalled an average of only 5.22 words. For forms, the recognition and recall scores were, respectively, 9.61 and 3.97. Syllables yielded scores of 9.41 and 1.86. An older group exhibited higher scores than these, but the relative difference in favor of recognition as compared with recall scores was similar. In Hurlock and Newmark's (1931) study the memory span for pictures was 1.2 by the recall and 6.1 by the recognition method. Shimidu (1934) reports similar results.

Recall of pictures observed a single time was first investigated extensively by Stern (1904), who framed the problem as one of *aussage* or testimony. He found that children not only fail to report items in the picture but they also add details of their own and, when questioned, respond to suggestions given. The test is thus not one of memory *per se*. Nevertheless, when items fall within the individual's range of experience and vocabulary and when fictitious details are ignored, the number of items reported is fundamentally a measure of recall memory. Winch (1914) tested 200 children, most of whom were between the ages of 3 and 8 years. Stern's picture was used. At successive age levels the average number of items reported was 8.3, 16.1, 26.5, 30.0, and 35.6. The items involved (boy, woman, bread, knife, etc.) were represented in the previous experience of even the youngest child. It is possible, however, that differences in ability to observe and differences in vocabulary, as well as in memory *per se*, con-

tributed to the increments in score at successively higher age levels. Similar experiments have been reported by McGeoch (1925, 1928) with, respectively, normal versus subnormal children and normal children between the ages of 9 and 14 years. Beyond the level of intelligence requisite to observation, intelligence did not affect the number of items reported. Recall scores of normal children increased with age, but increments became small and statistically insignificant at the upper age levels. Conrad and Jones (1929), who tested recall of the contents of three entertaining motion pictures by means of completion and multiple-choice tests involving a simple vocabulary, found that scores increased rapidly between the ages of 10 and 20 years. These studies lead to the conclusion, therefore, that recall of pictures witnessed a single time improves as a function of age. How much of the improved recall is based upon increased adequacy of observation and how much upon increased retentivity *per se* is not apparent.

Allport (1930) and Hall (1936) have investigated changes in reproductions of pictures observed a single time. In Allport's study, 275 children between the ages of 10 and 13 years were shown a simple drawing and then required to reproduce it. Further reproductions were drawn after intervals of 2 weeks and 4 months. Few perfect reproductions appeared. The figures did not, however, lose their identifiability in reproduction. Alterations from the original were chiefly in size, symmetry, and simplicity. Allport suggests that dynamic brain processes "force memory traces into typical lines of change." Hall showed pictures and diagrams to over 200 children between the ages of 9 and 15 years. Each child was told that he would be required to reproduce the picture or diagram after seeing it for a short period (20 seconds). As shown in Figure 16, the general characteristics of the pictures and diagrams were retained while details differed. Naming of the object was a factor in determining the nature of reproductions. A given picture, for example, was referred to by different subjects as "tents," "mountains," "pyramids," and "blades of grass." When called upon to reproduce what they had observed, the subjects were markedly influenced by such verbalizations. Familiar objects tended

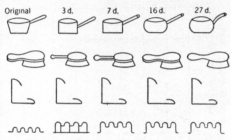

Original   3 d.   7 d.   16 d.   27 d.

FIGURE 16. Examples of successive changes of diagrams and pictures. (From "The Effects of a Time Interval on Recall," by V. Hall. *British Journal of Psychology*, 1936, *27*, 44. By permission of the publisher.)

to change gradually and diagrams suddenly in repeated reproduction.

Studies somewhat comparable to the above, but utilizing narratives instead of visual materials, have been made by Northway (1936) and Wees and Line (1937). Northway's subjects, ranging in age from 10 to 15 years and coming from private and public schools, read a story once and, immediately after doing so, attempted a written reproduction. This reproduction was read by another child who, in turn, attempted to reproduce it. Some reproductions were made after a week's interval. Three stories, each having 250 words, were used. Older children tended to retain the story in its own form more accurately and for a longer time than younger ones. Changes, additions, and omissions were usually such as to recast the story

in familiar phraseology and settings. The more unfamiliar the material the greater was the tendency to recast it. In some instances the story "reproduced" was almost entirely of the child's invention. As one might expect, however, the theme was usually retained with greater accuracy than the details. In Wees and Line's research sixth-grade children read a story and attempted to reproduce it. The same story was presented to different children in changed form. Wees and Line's chief finding is that the nature of the reproduction is determined by the form in which the story is presented.

Memorizing. When materials such as those discussed above are presented repeatedly and retention is measured after each repetition, we have a typical learning experiment. This type of experiment and those considered earlier in the present chapter differ chiefly in that the child is here required to learn symbols rather than movements as such.

The first reported experiment in memorizing in which children were subjects is Steffen's (1900). Children were used only incidentally.[1] In this, as in most of the early memorizing experiments with adults and children, nonsense syllables and poems were learned.

Foster (1928) investigated memorizing of narratives by nursery school children varying in CA from 2 years and 7 months

[1] Other early studies with children are by Pentschew (1903), Radossawljewitsch (1907), Busemann (1911), and Meumann (1913). The number of children included in these investigations was too small to warrant comparison of their memorizing ability with that of the adults involved. In any event, comparison of child and adult learning of symbolic materials may be invalidated by the fact that the symbols have different degrees of meaning for children and adults. Motivation is another possible differentiating factor. Nevertheless, Meumann (1913) discusses alleged differences between the memorizing ability of children and adults. Studies in which memorizing by a single child has been intensively investigated are reported by Winch (1904), Guillet (1909), and Hildreth (1935).

to 4 years and 9 months and in MA from 3 years and 2 months to 5 years and 8 months. Fifteen boys and 16 girls were involved. Stories containing 388 to 472 words were each read to a child 10 times. After the first reading of a story, pauses were introduced at predetermined intervals and the subject was encouraged to continue the narrative as far as possible. His score per repetition was the number of words correctly recalled. Whenever a correct reproduction was made, the experimenter said, "Good." Incorrect reproductions were corrected. After 10 repetitions (9 recall tests) had been given a new story was begun. One repetition was given daily. Twenty-two of the children learned 8 stories in this manner while the rest learned 3 to 4.

A learning curve based upon the mean number of words per child per story for the 8 stories is presented in Figure 17. One notes that the curve is approximately linear, and that the limit of achievement was not reached during the 9 tests. Similarly plotted curves for subjects below a CA of 3 years and 4 months and an MA of 3 years and 10 months, however, show a decided flattening after the eighth repetition. Mean scores of the lowest CA group went from approximately 1 on the first repetition to 8 on the last, whereas the comparable scores of the five oldest children went from 9 to 73. Similarly, the scores of the lowest MA group went from 1 to 8, whereas those of the highest went from 5 to 64. The correlation between CA and total score for all stories was .74; that between MA and total score for all stories, .65. Although the number of subjects was small, the above data all agree in suggesting that the memorizing of narratives by young children increases with age and intelligence. Whether this increase is in mnemonic ability *per se* or in attitudes, previous experience, or the like, cannot be determined. Although girls were

slightly higher than boys in MA, their average scores were lower than those of boys on 7 of the 9 stories. Since the groups were so small, this may not represent a true sex difference.

Several investigators of memorizing in children have used variations of the paired-associates method. The color-naming studies of Lund (1927) and Jersild (1932) are of this variety. Children were shown colors

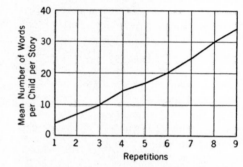

FIGURE 17. Curve for memorizing of stories. (From "Verbal Memory in the Pre-school Child," by J. C. Foster. *Journal of Genetic Psychology*, 1928, *35*, 31. By permission of the publisher.)

and required to recall the appropriate names as quickly as possible. Lund's 5-year-old child and Jersild's 7- to 8-year-old children exhibited an initial rapid increase in speed of naming. This was followed by slow improvement. Jersild used a control group which, despite the fact that it performed only an initial and a final test, also improved. The improvement of this group was less than one half that shown by the trained group. After an interval of 4 months without intervening experimental practice, however, the speed of naming in both groups was approximately equal. Only the control group showed improvement during the interval. It appears that the maturation and/or incidental learning of this group enabled it to approximate what the other group had achieved by experimental practice.

Experiments by Meek (1925) and Kirkwood (1926) also involved paired associates. Meek required 68 children between the ages of 4 and 6 years to associate names of objects with the objects when confusing words (having the first, last, two middle letters, etc., of the key word) were presented simultaneously. Thus the word *ball* appeared on a box containing a ball but, associated with this box were other, empty boxes containing the words *burr, feel, sale, bake,* and *kill.* The other words to be learned in this way were *flag, doll, lion, duck,* and *rose.* Improvement was measured in terms of time, number of corrections, and number of false recognitions in each practice period. Six practice periods separated by intervals of 1 to 30 days were given. Each period was terminated after a specified number of correct recognitions, the number depending upon differences in the training procedure for different groups. Meek's results indicate no conclusive evidence of improvement in memorizing as a function of age. This is perhaps due to the fact that her procedure was not comparable at different age levels. The correlation between MA and time required to learn *ball* to the point of two recognitions ranged, for the age groups of 4 to 6 years, between $.302 \pm .101$ and $.456 \pm .142$. When corrections made in learning all words were correlated with MA the correlations ranged from $-.011 \pm .189$ to $.583 \pm .128$. Correlations increased at each successive age group. The last correlation, based upon data from only 14 children, however, is alone statistically significant. Most of the learning curves show a sharp improvement in the first few periods, followed by little or no improvement. One of the most interesting aspects of this investigation is the analysis of individual cases. This analysis shows that temporary excitement,

boredom, worry over a scolding from the mother given prior to the experiment, daydreaming, etc., lead to marked variations in memorizing.

Kirkwood (1926) investigated association of pictures and blocks having a vague resemblance to each other. Her subjects were 180 preschool children. Twenty blocks and 20 pictures were used. At each practice period the experimenter picked up pictures in random order and asked the child to hand her "the block that goes with this picture." In some instances the block was handed to the child and he was required to select the correct picture. Learning curves based upon the number of correct associations exhibited a rapid rise and then flattened upon approaching the upper limit of 20.

The relation of age and intelligence to memorizing has been the subject of special investigations by Wilson (1931a, 1931b, 1931c) and Stroud and Maul (1933). Wilson found that dull children were, on the average, inferior to bright children in memorizing shorthand characters and descriptive selections. In some individual cases, however, bright children were surpassed by dull children. In Stroud and Maul's study, 172 subjects between the ages of 7 and 11 years, 26 subjects aged 14 years, and 28 subjects aged 18 years were given 10 minutes' practice with nonsense syllables and, on a different occasion, 15 minutes' practice with poems. The number of nonsense syllables and the number of lines of the poems recalled increased with age. Correlations between CA and recall scores, however, decreased from .61 for poems and .49 for nonsense syllables to approximately zero when MA was partialed out. The correlation between MA and recall scores was $.67 \pm .024$ for poetry and $.61 \pm .028$ for nonsense syllables. Stroud and Maul therefore conclude that memorizing ability is significantly related to intelligence, a conclusion supported, it will be recalled, by the data of Meek (1925) and Foster (1928).

The Relative Efficacy of Different Memorizing Procedures. If certain memorizing procedures result in faster learning and in better retention than others, it is important that these procedures be discovered and applied in classroom teaching. A few approaches to this problem have been made in the laboratory and the classroom and with both adults and children as subjects. Use of children in such research was at first incidental. There has been a tendency, however, to investigate the relative efficacy of different procedures with large groups of children as subjects and, at the same time, to approximate schoolroom conditions as closely as possible.

Several investigators have attempted to determine the relative merits of *whole versus part procedures.* Steffens (1900) was the first to investigate this problem. She found that her adult subjects and two children learned poems more rapidly when the poems were read from beginning to end than when verses were learned separately and later connected. Neumann (1907), who required 6 children between the ages of 9½ and 10½ years to associate German and foreign words by whole and part procedures, also found the whole procedure to be superior. He observed, however, that the effectiveness of this procedure increased with increasing intelligence.

Winch (1924) did not find the whole to be superior to the part procedure. He worked under classroom conditions with large groups of children. The children were paired on the basis of age and memory ability as determined by a preliminary test. One child of a pair learned poems by the whole method, whereas his partner learned the same poems by the pure part procedure. Three separate experiments were performed, involving groups of 26 to 38 children ranging in age from 11 years and 8 months to 13 years and 1 month. With the exception of the results for one poem at one age level all data were in favor of the part procedure. Pechstein (1926) found no reliable evidence in favor of either whole or part methods in his investigation with bright and dull children.

The equivocal nature of the above findings led McGeoch (1931) to carry out a further investigation, which appears to be the most thorough yet performed on this problem with children as subjects. Her subjects were 33 gifted and 35 normal children, all approximately 10 years old. The IQ of the gifted group averaged 151 and that of the normal group, 99. The groups were divided equally with respect to sex. Turkish-English vocabularies, nonsense syllable-English pairs, and poems were memorized by whole or part methods. In learning of the last two types of material a progressive part procedure, as well as whole and pure part procedures, was used. The same number of repetitions, in the case of paired associates, and the same time, in the case of poems, were given with each procedure. Scores for paired associates comprised the number of associates recalled upon presentation, singly and in changed order, of the initial members of the pairs. Memorizing of poems was scored in terms of the number of lines recalled.

Data obtained with the Turkish-English vocabulary yielded unequivocal evidence of the superiority of the whole procedure both for gifted and average children. Furthermore, the superiority of this procedure was greater for gifted than for average children. The means, SD's, differences, and standard errors of the differences are given in Table 4. One will observe that all differences between the whole and part procedures for both learning and retention are statistically significant. Nonsense syllable–English pairs

TABLE 4

COMPARISON OF METHODS

Group	No.	Whole		Part		Whole Minus Part		P/W
		Mean	SD	Mean	SD	Diff.	SD$_{diff.}$	
Learning								
Gifted	31	5.06	1.55	2.53	1.27	2.53	0.29	50%
Normal	32	2.42	1.32	1.48	.87	.94	.20	61%
Normal/Gifted		48%		58%				
Retention								
Gifted	31	4.12	1.49	2.17	1.36	1.95	0.26	52%
Normal	32	1.76	1.21	.78	.74	.98	.18	44%
Normal/Gifted		43%		36%				

yielded results in the same direction, but few of the differences were found to be statistically significant. The progressive part procedure gave ambiguous results, in some instances being more effective and in others less effective than the whole method. None of the differences was significant statistically. Poems were learned better by gifted than by average children. However, slight differences between the scores for whole, progressive part, and pure part methods were statistically insignificant. McGeoch concluded that the effectiveness of the whole and part methods depends upon the intelligence of the subjects and the type of material to be memorized.

In a study reported briefly by Northway (1937), poems of varying difficulty, as determined by their "thought content," were memorized by school children. There was no clear superiority of the whole or part procedure. The relative effectiveness of the two procedures differed from one poem to another, and there was no clear relation between the efficiency of the procedure and the difficulty of the poem. It is suggested, however, that poems of intermediate difficulty were learned best by the whole method, whereas those of lesser and greater difficulty were learned about as effectively by either method. Griffiths (1938), as the result of a study involving 14-year-old boys, claims that simple materials are learned with equal efficiency by either part or whole methods but that difficult material should be approached in terms of the whole method at first and then in parts.[1]

The results of researches on whole versus part methods of learning in adults are also conflicting. On the basis of findings so far reported one must conclude that, even for memorizing of a given type of material—for example, poems—findings differ concerning the relative effectiveness of the whole and part procedures. One investigator finds the whole procedure most effective, another the part procedure, and still another finds no difference. Woodworth (1938), after critically evaluating all the literature on whole versus part learning, says that the net result is somewhat as follows:

The parts are easier to learn than the whole and the learner is often happier and better adjusted to the problem when beginning with the parts. He carries over some of the skill and knowledge gained in learning the parts into the subsequent learning of the whole performance. But he finds that putting together the parts is a serious problem requiring much further work. In the end he may have saved time and energy by commencing with the parts —or he may not—much depending on the size and difficulty of the total task and the learner's poise and technique. If he can adjust himself to the whole method and handle it properly, he can learn quite complex performances effectively by the whole method. In a practical situation it is probably best to start with the whole method while feeling free to concentrate at any time on a part where something special is to be learned [p. 223].

The relative efficacy of *massed and distributed practice* has been investigated extensively with animals and adults. Such researches have shown some form of dis-

tribution to be more efficient than massing of practice periods. Similar experiments with children have been few and inadequate.

Munn (1909), in her study of the learning curve, found that short frequent practice periods led to faster learning of a substitution problem by both children and adults than long practice periods. With the exception of this study and a master's thesis, the results of which are summarized by Peterson (1933, pp. 428–430), all reported work with children on this problem has involved memorizing.[2]

Kirkwood (1926) required two matched groups of 11 children each to associate pictures and blocks which were vaguely similar (see page 417). Upon being presented with each of 20 blocks the child was required to select its associated picture. Each day's score was the number of correct associations. One group practiced every day; the other practiced on alternate days. The results are summarized in Table 5. One will observe that the group with a greater distribution of practice not only achieved the criterion of 3 successive correct trials 5 practice periods earlier than the other group, but also attained higher scores at every trial.

Foster (1928) found distributed practice to yield better results than massed practice in the learning of narratives by 29 nursery school children. After one story had been given a single repetition daily for 10 days, another story, assumed to be of approximately equal difficulty, was given 5 daily repetitions for 2 days. The average number of words recalled per repetition was consistently higher for distributed than for

---

[1] Of some relevance in this connection is the study by Hildreth (1942) on solving of jigsaw puzzles by children. The most efficient results were obtained when the children first saw the whole picture.

[2] This thesis, by Long, deals with distribution of practice in dart throwing. There were only 10 boys in each group, the initial ability of the two groups was markedly different, and only a minute statistical analysis, which seems unwarranted in the light of the small number of subjects, discloses any difference in the effectiveness of the two procedures.

TABLE 5

AVERAGE SCORES OBTAINED BY TWENTY-TWO PAIRED CHILDREN IN ASSOCIATING PICTURES WITH
BLOCKS

Practice Periods

1	2	3	4	5	6	7	8	9	10	11	12	13	14

Practice Once Daily

| 10.2 | 14.9 | 16.5 | 18.8 | 19.1 | 19.0 | 19.8 | 19.6 | 19.3 | 20.0 | 19.7 | 20.0 | 20.0 | 20.0 |

Practice on Alternate Days

| 11.3 | 15.2 | 18.9 | 19.6 | 20.0 | 19.8 | 20.0 | 20.0 | 20.0 |

massed practice. A few individuals, however, had higher scores for massed than for distributed practice. Although the trend of Foster's results is in line with that of other researches on distribution of practice, her experiment lacks conclusiveness owing to the fact that a different poem was memorized under each of the conditions.

The advantage of rests between practice periods has been attributed to decreased fatigue, to preservation of neural traces following removal of the stimuli which aroused them, to opportunities for recitation or rehearsal, and to more rapid dropping-out of inhibitory than of facilitory associations during an interval. Any or all of these factors may operate in a given instance. The phenomenon under discussion is also possibly related to better retention of incomplete than of completed tasks (Zeigarnik, 1927) and reminiscence (Hovland, 1938a). For a discussion of this, see pages 425–430.

Another problem concerns the relative efficacy of *recitation and passive reading* of materials to be recalled. It has long been known that retention is poor unless the individual intends to memorize.[1] Myers (1913), for example, found that children and adults fail to remember many items from everyday experience when there has

1 See especially the case cited by Radossawljewitsch (1907, p. 127).

been no intention of recalling them later. On the basis of such facts one should expect recitation to facilitate learning and retention. A specific investigation of this program was undertaken by Gates (1917), whose experiments were carried out under classroom conditions. Forty to 45 children, from grades 1, 3, 4, 5, 6, and 8, were used. The materials to be memorized were lists of nonsense syllables and brief biographies. Each group memorized under each of the conditions of the experiment in such order that all factors other than the relative amounts of recitation and reading were equated. The total time given to memorizing nonsense syllables was divided between reading and recitation so that the percentages of reading were as follows: 100, 80, 60, 40, and 20. Reading comprised going over the material from the beginning to the end without repeating any unit except while looking at it. When recitation was called for, the child was instructed to look over the top of the card and repeat as many units as possible. Only when a unit could not be remembered was he to glance at the card while reciting. More material was given in a lesson than could be memorized in the time limit. A written recall was made after this limit had expired. The results obtained for memorizing of nonsense syllables appear in Table

6.[1] Scores are relative, being derived from average scores by considering the average of each class for all five methods as 100.

TABLE 6

THE RELATIVE EFFICACY OF DIFFERENT PRO-
PORTIONS OF READING AND RECITATION IN
MEMORIZING NONSENSE SYLLABLES

Percentage Reading	100	80	60	40	30
Grade 8					
Relative score	65.40	92.23	99.69	105.45	137.26
PE	2.37	2.69	2.53	2.57	3.35
Grade 6					
Relative score	59.13	88.35	101.34	112.57	136.61
PE	2.74	3.78	2.70	4.09	4.81
Grade 4					
Relative score	63.42	80.53	108.05	113.75	134.42
PE	3.42	2.76	3.36	4.50	4.74

The same general procedure was followed in memorizing of short biographies. Grade 3 was allowed a total of 7 minutes and 30 seconds per biography, whereas grades 4, 5, 6, and 8 were allowed 9 minutes. Added to the proportions of reading and recitation used with nonsense syllables was a 10 reading–90 recitation percentage. Recall scores reduced to a relative basis are given in Table 7. Statistical analysis of these scores discloses that, for all grades, some degree of recitation is significantly superior to reading alone. Taking the average of all scores into consideration, Gates obtained the following relative scores for, respectively, no recitation to 90 per cent recitation: 83.71, 95.32, 101.63, 110.35, 106.67, and 102.30. Considering these data as a whole, it appears that 40 per cent reading and 60 per cent recitation give the best results for this type of material under these conditions.

[1] Results for grade 1 are not included because, owing to differences in technique, they were not comparable with those of other grades.

Tests of retention given 3 to 4 hours after original learning showed trends similar to those found for immediate recall. Relative retention scores for nonsense syllables, averaged for all grades, were, for the successively greater amounts of recitation, as follows: 45.34, 72.96, 93.53, 119.13, and 169.17. Thus an increasing proportion of recitation, within the limits of zero and 80 per cent, led to increasingly better retention of nonsense syllables. For biographical material the comparable scores were: 73.31, 85.44, 110.23, 122.98, 115.65, and 110.82. As in the case of immediate recall, retention scores were highest with 60 per cent recitation.

In repeating these experiments with adults, Gates obtained results essentially similar to those mentioned. His analysis of the process of memorizing suggests that recitation enables the individual to develop with greater facility than is possible in reading alone the requisite "bonds" between items. Where these bonds must be built up by the learner himself, as in learning nonsense materials, recitation seems of most value. In general:

> Recitation leads to greater certainty of one's knowledge. It enables the learner not only to know but to be aware of how well he knows. Fewer blunders and erroneous recalls are made. The material is better organized; it is in more usable form (p. 101).[2]

[2] Investigations on other aspects of economical memorizing in children have been carried out by Dell (1912), on position of items in a series and the relation of this position to ease of learning and recall; by Sullivan (1924), on development of attitudes concerning success and failure; by Meek (1925), on the most effective number of repetitions at different stages of learning; by Jensen and Schrodt (1936), on wording materials so as to bring them within the child's range of comprehension; by Forlano and Hoffman (1937), on the relative adequacy of guessing and telling methods in learning foreign words; and by Adams (1938), on the effect of correcting and repeating errors in serial rote learning.

TABLE 7

THE RELATIVE EFFICACY OF DIFFERENT PROPORTIONS OF READING AND RECITATION IN
MEMORIZING SHORT BIOGRAPHIES

Percentage Reading	100	80	60	40	20	10
Grade 8						
Relative score	87.78	94.62	104.98	105.45	106.80	100.03
PE	3.01	3.64	2.93	2.89	2.09	3.43
Grade 6						
Relative score	89.21	97.58	106.19	104.36	104.77	98.06
PE	4.42	3.48	4.09	4.01	4.83	4.01
Grade 5						
Relative score	80.42	95.15	103.75	108.86	104.57	107.36
PE	2.72	2.93	3.27	3.81	3.41	3.75
Grade 4						
Relative score	86.34	99.94	96.69	111.17	104.13	101.65
PE	4.54	4.60	5.07	4.54	4.13	4.18
Grade 3						
Relative score	74.78	89.29	96.54	121.93	113.12	104.40
PE	3.35	4.21	4.21	3.95	4.81	4.64

Transfer of Improvement in Memorizing. Does memorizing a particular kind of material increase a child's *ability* to memorize? Several investigators have sought an answer to this question.[1]

[1] Although they do not concern memorizing *per se*, the following studies are somewhat relevant. Thorndike (1924) and Brolyer, Thorndike, and Woodyard (1927) investigated the transfer value of various high school subjects. Transfer was measured in terms of improvement in mental-test performance. The small apparent transfer of some subjects, such as mathematics, could be attributed to similarities between subject and mental-test material. The investigators claim that no general transfer occurred. Gordon's (1938) experiment on transfer of training within verbal tests is of interest in this connection. She found that a group of children trained on analogies for 8 weeks following initial tests had significantly higher final analogy scores than did a comparable group given only the initial and final tests. Transfer was probably in terms of an acquired "feeling" for analogy material and perhaps a technique. There is no implication that reasoning ability *per se* had been improved by the training with analogies. On tests which did not include analogies, the two groups performed with equal skill.

Winch (1908) had school children between 10 and 13 years of age memorize poetry on 1 day per week for 3 weeks, after which they memorized history and geography lessons. A control group, equated with the former in terms of initial tests and in terms of teachers' judgments of mnemonic ability, memorized the same lessons after doing sums for 3 weeks. The experiment was repeated with several different groups of children. As an example of the results obtained in these studies we shall cite the data of the initial one, which involved experimental and control groups of 17 children each. The average initial score of each group for memorizing history was 88. The average final score in memorizing history (another lesson of greater length than the first) was 121 for the experimental and 111 for the control group. All experiments yielded results in the same direction. Winch concluded that: "Improvement, gained by practice in memorizing one subject of instruction, is transferred to memory work in other subjects whose nature is certainly diverse from that in which the improvement was gained" (p. 293).

In a further experiment of the same general nature, Winch (1910) found that training in rote memory led to improvement in substance memory. Sleight (1911), who worked with both school children and adults, questioned Winch's techniques and the reliability of his data on transfer from rote to substance memory. Children averaging 12.8 years of age were divided into four groups of equal mnemonic ability as determined by a series of tests. One group learned poetry in rote fashion, one memorized tables, one learned the substance of prose selections, and the fourth, during the same period, did arithmetic problems involving no memorization. These activities occurred 30 minutes daily, 4 days per week, for 3 weeks. All four groups were finally required to memorize nonsense syllables, prose selections, the data of maps, and other materials. In two instances there was a statistically significant difference in favor of the trained group. In memorizing nonsense syllables, the groups which learned poetry and tables gained, respectively, 66 and 85 more points than their controls. The differences had a PE of 11. There was a statistically insignificant drop of 32 points in memorizing prose after learning nonsense syllables and a statistically insignificant increase of 21 to 31 points in going from training with prose to, respectively, literal and substance memorization of prose. Sleight concluded that, where transfer occurs, it is in terms of specific techniques. Subjects developed a procedure which served as well in memorizing one type of material as in memorizing another.

Winch (1911) presents data which seem to indicate transfer from memorizing to inventing stories having a different content. In each case there is a small, but probably insignificant, difference in favor of the trained group. Correlations between memory and invention scores run as high as .623, which is statistically significant.

Gates and Taylor (1925) and Gates (1928) report a transfer experiment involving digit span. Their subjects were 82 children separated into experimental and control groups on the basis of sex, age, intelligence, scholastic maturity, grade, initial memory span for digits, and other mnemonic performances. Children of the experimental group were given 78 days of practice in memorizing series of digits of differing length. The control group was tested for digit span only on the initial and final days of the experiment. The initial digit span of both groups was 4.33. During 78 days of practice the experimental group increased its average digit span to 6.40, a gain of 2.07. The control group had a final score of 5.06, a gain of 0.73. It is apparent that practice in memorizing digits increased the digit span. In a further test 4½ months later, however, both groups exhibited approximately equal spans. Gates assumes, therefore, that "the improvement brought about by training in this case is due to subtle techniques rather than to increased fundamental capacities" (p. 455). An interval of only 4½ months was apparently too long for the techniques to be retained. Both groups were given further practice 8 months after the final tests. On the first day of this practice period the scores of the experimental and control groups were, respectively, 4.73 and 4.83. Twenty-one days of training increased these scores to 5.73 and 5.92. It is again apparent that the 78 days of training 8 months earlier gave the experimental group no superiority over the control group at this later period.

On the basis of the above-mentioned experiments one must conclude that training in memorizing aids further memorizing only in so far as techniques acquired in one situation are applied to further situations. There is no evidence, in other words, that *memorizing ability per se* is improved by training.

children are summarized in Table 8. Some variation from interval to interval is probably due to the fact that relearning took place at different times during the day.

TABLE 8

PERCENTAGE OF NONSENSE SYLLABLES AND POEMS FORGOTTEN

Intervals	5 minutes	20 minutes	60 minutes	8 hours	24 hours	2 days	6 days	30 days	60 days
Syllables	9	15	23	37	28	32	43	66	94
Poems	3	11	23	39	21	29	42	75	85

Forgetting. Ebbinghaus (1885), who was his own subject, found that forgetting of nonsense syllables and poems learned to the point of 1 perfect repetition is at first rapid and then slow. Radossawljewitsch (1907), the first investigator to study forgetting in children, used 11 subjects whose ages ranged from 7 to 13 years. Nonsense syllables and poems were learned to the point of 2 perfect repetitions. These were relearned after intervals ranging from 5 minutes to 60 days. Comparison of the number of repetitions required to learn and to relearn gave an indication of the amount forgotten after each interval.[1] Adults learned and relearned the same materials. Radossawljewitsch found that both children and adults forgot much more slowly than Ebbinghaus. Results for children and adults did not differ in any consistent manner. Data obtained with

1 Forgetting in children has also been measured in terms of recall. Under these circumstances, forgetting after only 10 seconds has been 17 per cent (Vertes, 1931). Experiments by Charles (1929) and Burtt (1932, 1937) have shown that material presented before the second year of life, although beyond recall 6 months (Charles) and 8 to 14 years later, is relearned with large savings in the number of repetitions required for new material. In Burtt's study the savings at 8 years was 30 per cent and at 14 years 8 per cent. Burtt (1941) found no savings at the age of 18. Recall in adulthood of fairy tales heard in childhood has been studied by Brenman (1942), but the results are reported only in a brief abstract.

An interesting forgetting experiment with 60 sixth-grade children has been reported by Klugman (1944b). Each child was shown a sheet of paper which was blank except for a dot. The dot differed in position from child to child and for different memory intervals, but each child served under each of the conditions of the experiment. Each child was asked to reproduce the dot in its proper position. With the dot in a given position, some children reproduced it after .5 minute, others after 1 minute, and others after intervals of, respectively, 2, 4, 8, and 16 minutes. To determine the amount of error, the experimenter superimposed the two sheets and drove a pin through each dot. The deviation was then measured in millimeters. In deriving the forgetting curve shown in Figure 18, Klugman deducted from the memory data the average error made in merely copying the dot from one sheet to the other. The children were equally divided with respect to sex. Half of them were Negro. No sex or race differences were apparent. The serial reproduction method used in this experiment is of only incidental significance. It guaranteed that the dot would be varied in position for each child.

Reminiscence. It is obvious that, when material is completely learned, either retention will be perfect after an interval or there will be decreased retention. Henderson (1903), Ballard (1913), Huguenin

(1914), and several later investigators whose subjects memorized material to a point short of perfection found *better* retention after an interval during which there was no experimental training than immediately after learning. Ballard called this phenomenon *reminiscence*. His re- no further recall. The amount recalled immediately was taken to be 100 per cent. Different groups gave a further recall after intervals of, respectively, 1 to 7 days. Recall of poetry by 6-year-olds improved 38 per cent after the first day, 57 per cent after the second day, 60 per cent after the

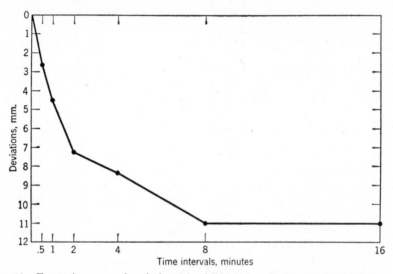

FIGURE 18. Forgetting curve for sixth-grade children, based upon memory for the position of a single dot on a sheet of paper. The copying error has been deducted from the memory error after the respective time intervals. (From S. F. Klugman, "Memory for Position, among Children, as Measured by Serial Reproduction." *British Journal of Psychology,* 1944, *35*, p. 20.)

search has precipitated many further studies and much discussion.

Since reminiscence has been regarded as peculiar to children, and since most of the research has involved child subjects, it warrants careful consideration in any discussion of learning in children.

Ballard's subjects had an age range of 6 to 21 years. In one investigation, involving over 5000 school children, lines of poetry and lists of nonsense syllables were studied for shorter periods than would allow complete learning. A recall was given immediately after the study period and, as far as the subjects knew, there would be

third day, and then began to decline. Only relatively slight improvement (10 to 20 per cent) was evidenced by 12-year-olds. Adults showed decreased rather than increased retention. The scores so far mentioned are based upon *averages* for the various age groups. Ballard also analyzed his data in terms of the *percentage of individuals* showing reminiscence at each age level. Reminiscence was present in 90 per cent at the 6-year level, 75 per cent at the 12-year level, and 30 per cent at the adult level. It is thus apparent that, although average scores indicated improved retention for children alone, some adults also improved. Henderson (1903) likewise found improved retention in adults but greater relative improvement in children. Nevertheless, Ballard's results have been taken as evidence that reminiscence is peculiar to children and more evident in younger than in older children. His results suggest, furthermore, that reminis-

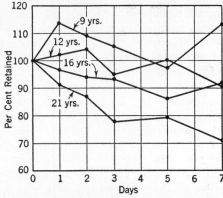

FIGURE 19. Retention of poetry after intervals of 1, 2, 3, 5, and 7 days. (From "A Study of the Phenomenon of Reminiscence," by O. Williams. *Journal of Experimental Psychology*, 1926, *9*, 373. By permission of the American Psychological Association, publisher.) Scores are for correct verbal reproduction of lines from "The Spider and the Fly."

cence is more apparent for poetry than for nonsense material.

Williams (1926) undertook to check Ballard's findings. Four groups, the average ages of which were 9, 12, 16, and 21, studied 40 lines of "The Spider and the Fly" for 5 minutes. They then recalled as much as possible immediately and after periods ranging, for different groups of 100 subjects each, from 1 to 7 days. Disconnected words were also partially learned and recalled. Recall was scored in terms of correct verbal reproduction, reproduction of sense, and reproduction of sense or partial sense. As in Ballard's research, im-

mediate reproduction was scored as 100 per cent. Comparisons were entirely in terms of group averages. Data for retention of poetry by the four age groups after intervals of 1, 2, 3, 5, and 7 days are reproduced in Figure 19. It is apparent that, in terms of averages, reminiscence was exhibited only by the two younger groups. Also apparent is the fact that, even for the older groups, forgetting was initially less rapid than in the experiments of Ebbinghaus and Radossawljewitsch. Data reproduced in the table are for correct verbal reproduction. Other methods of scoring yielded essentially similar results. Scores

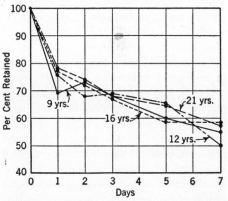

FIGURE 20. Retention of disconnected words after intervals of 1, 2, 3, 5, and 7 days. (From "A Study of the Phenomenon of Reminiscence," by O. Williams. *Journal of Experimental Psychology*, 1926, *9*, 374. By permission of the publisher.) Scores are in terms of correct verbal reproduction.

for retention of disconnected words are reproduced in Figure 20. They indicate no reminiscence and no consistent differences in the retention curves of the different age groups.

More recent studies of reminiscence have attempted to answer questions raised by the researches of Ballard and Williams. One question concerns the claim that reminiscence is more prevalent in children than in adults. Luh and Liang (1933) and Mc-Geoch (1935*a*) found no satisfactory evidence in support of this claim. The former investigators used 11-year-old children and college students. Chinese poetry was studied, then recalled immediately and after an interval. There was no difference in the average amount of reminiscence exhibited by each group. However, a larger percentage of children than of students had scores indicating reminiscence. Mc-Geoch analyzed the original data and found this difference to be unreliable statistically. Her own investigation involved 100 preschool children and 100 college students. Toy animals and common objects were exposed for 30 seconds and then covered.[1] Recall was given immediately and after 24 hours. Small differences in the number of each group reminiscing and in the number of items reminisced were in favor of adults. These differences, however, were not statistically reliable. Adults learned a greater amount of the material than did children; hence McGeoch (1935*b*) decided to determine whether the amount of material learned is in any way related to the degree of reminiscence. Materials comparable with those of the above-mentioned experiment were used. Adults and three groups of children learned, respectively, to the point where they could recall 71, 53, 42, and 29 per cent of the material. In a recall 24 hours later the following percentages of subjects showed reminiscence: 94, 89, 85, and 92. Thus the factor of initial learning did not appear to affect the frequency of reminiscence.

These investigations, and others in which adults have been used exclusively, show that the phenomenon of reminiscence is not

more prevalent in children than in adults.[2] It will be recalled, in this connection, that some of Ballard's adults exhibited reminiscence but group averages obscure this fact. The same may be said of Williams's experiment. For this reason, McGeoch (1935*a*) claimed that the only valid measures of age differences in reminiscence are the percentage of subjects reminiscing and the amount reminisced by these.

May reminiscence be attributed to the effects of intentional review during the interval between immediate and delayed recall?[3] Ballard (1913) claimed that, although reviewing aids reminiscence, it does not account for the phenomenon. Mc-Geoch (1935*c*) investigated this problem in a partial repetition of Williams's study. She used over 400 third- and fourth-grade children. They studied lines of poetry for 5 minutes. Recall was immediate and after 24 hours. After the final recall had been completed, each child was asked whether, before doing the experiment, he had ever heard or read the poem. Seventy-three per cent denied previous knowledge of the poem. They were asked whether they had thought of, or talked about, the poem between the first and second recall. It was made clear that such review was quite permissible and that they should not hesitate to tell about it. Data were then analyzed separately for those who did and those who

---

[1] This method was earlier used with children by Nicolai (1922), who found it to yield higher scores in later than in immediate recall.

[2] See the experiments of Ward (1937) and Hovland (1938*a*, 1938*b*) with adult subjects. Reminiscence (of nonsense syllables) was clearly evident in these studies.

[3] Other approaches to the problem of review are (1) use of material which cannot easily be reviewed (e.g., a maze pattern); (2) use of organisms which, presumably, cannot review; and (3) interpolating activity which interferes with review. McGeoch (1937) found no evidence of reminiscence in maze learning by kindergarten children. On the other hand, Bunch and Magdsick (1933) found reminiscence in maze learning by rats. These studies differed markedly in technique; hence the discrepancy should not be attributed to a difference in subjects. Ward (1937) and Hovland (1938*a*), who used adult subjects, interpolated activity (color naming) between recalls, yet observed reminiscence.

did not report having reviewed. The percentage of subjects who exhibited reminiscence and the amount of material reproduced on the second recall did not differ significantly for the two groups. Scores for verbatim recall of lines were slightly in favor of the review group, whereas these scores combined with those for recall of substance favored nonreviewers. Thus McGeoch concluded that review between the first and second recall does not account for reminiscence or even influence significantly the degree exhibited.

A further question concerns the possibility that reminiscence is due to improvement resulting from the immediate recall. Recall constitutes a review of what has been learned. Even material not recalled immediately may be revived later as a result of an effort to recall it earlier.[1] In her study on maze learning in kindergarten children, McGeoch (1937) controlled this factor by equating the two groups on the basis of initial scores and requiring each to take only one further trial. One group had a further trial immediately; the other group waited for 24 hours. Scores on the last trial were compared to ascertain whether reminiscence had occurred. Reminiscence did not occur. This may be due to factors other than the control instituted, however, for Ward (1937) and Hovland (1938a, 1938b), using nonsense syllables and adult subjects, found reminiscence when similar controls were instituted.[2]

[1] On this point see Woodworth's (1938, pp. 66–68) discussion of research with adults.

[2] Bunch (1938), who stresses the need for matched groups and only one recall by each, believes that the influence of an immediate recall is too small to account for all the improvement found in earlier experiments on reminiscence. In a study with adults, he found only 11 per cent improvement when a second recall was given immediately. A more recent study by Gray (1940) is relevant but inconclusive. Matched groups of children studied words, sentences, and a narrative. One group gave an immediate recall, whereas the other did easy problems in addition to control re-

The phenomenon of reminiscence has been related to the fact that incomplete tasks are recalled more easily than completed tasks. Zeigarnik (1927) required 47 adults and 45 children to perform a series of 18 tasks. They were allowed to complete only one-half the tasks, which were distributed in random order among tasks the completion of which was prevented. Finally, the subjects were asked to recall tasks which they had performed. Significantly more interrupted than completed tasks were recalled. The memorial advantage of interrupted over completed tasks was 90 per cent for adults and 110 per cent for children. Thirty-seven adults and 36 children remembered the interrupted tasks better than the completed. Zeigarnik's results have been verified with children in studies by Pachauri (1935a, 1935b, 1936) and Abel (1938).[3] Martin (1940) reports, moreover, that interrupted tasks yield a greater degree of reminiscence than completed tasks. All his subjects were adults.

Reminiscence has as yet received no satisfactory explanation. Most commonly expressed is the view, first suggested by Ballard, that removal of stimulating circumstances allows neural activity to continue

view. Both groups recalled 24 hours after learning. The first group evidenced an insignificant improvement in recall of the narrative after 24 hours. Otherwise all data for both groups indicated a loss in retention during the interval. Gray regards as important, however, the fact that there was a significantly greater loss in the group which had no immediate recall. This finding perhaps loses significance because the group in question did addition immediately after learning. Although the addition problems were easy, they may have inhibited to some degree what the children had just learned.

[3] Related to this research are studies in which the relative retention of complete and incomplete words and figures has been investigated. A study from Nanking (1935) shows that children retain completed words and pictures better than incomplete ones. Tiernan (1938), on the other hand, finds a slight, but not statistically reliable, advantage for incomplete figures. This tendency was more marked between the ages of 7 and 11 than later.

and bring about further consolidation of what has been learned. Hovland (1938a), who presents an excellent critical examination of several theories, points out that reminiscence appears even when subjects are required to name colors during the period between learning and recall (in his experiment only 2 minutes). Color naming should, he claims, prevent continued activity (perseveration) of the neural traces involved in original learning. Ward (1937) and Hovland (1938a) both favor the view that a rest period after learning weakens "negative excitatory processes" (inhibition), thus facilitating recall. Referring to an apparent relation between reminiscence and distributed learning, Ward says:

It may be that both phenomena are mediated by some more fundamental process or processes. For example, it would theoretically be possible that the different rates of dying out of correct responses or associations on the one hand, and of inhibiting or interfering associations and tendencies on the other hand, could account not only for reminiscence at very short intervals of time, but also for the greater relative economy of practice sessions distributed at intervals of 1 or 2 days. This type of explanation would require the additional assumption that once the interfering associations or tendencies are dropped out they will not return as rapidly with a continuation of learning as do correct responses and associations [p. 56].

It is of course not yet certain that all reported reminiscence phenomena have the same basis, since investigators have used different materials, methods, intervals, criteria, and age levels. Further research will be needed before many points mentioned in the above discussion can be clarified and a satisfactory explanation reached.

There have been several other experiments on retention and forgetting in children. Lyon (1916) and Gillette (1936) both demonstrated that children who memorize quickly tend to be slow forgetters. Gillette controlled the amount learned, as well as the factor of overlearning, yet the quicker learners still demonstrated superior retention. In an experiment with 1000 school children, Houlahan (1941) found retroactive inhibition to be greater immediately after learning than after an interval. She found that increasing the duration of a rest period before introduction of interpolated learning increased the retention score. Studies on the relative retention of pleasant and unpleasant associations have been reported by Rosenzweig and Mason (1934), Carter (1935, 1936, 1937) and Gilbert (1937). In general, such studies have shown that pleasant associations are more adequately retained. However, Carter found that unpleasant words tend to be retained better than indifferent ones. In Gilbert's study, there was equal retention of pleasant and unpleasant words.

Problem Solving

Every learning situation presents a problem of one sort or another. Escaping from a maze, buttoning a coat, hitting the correct keys of a typewriter, and memorizing nonsense syllables or poems are *problems* when confronted initially. As psychologists use the term, however, problem solving refers to activity at a somewhat higher psychological level than is necessitated in learning of sensorimotor and mnemonic skills such as those mentioned. The type of learning designated as problem solving involves attainment of some more or less specific goal under such conditions that observing relations, reasoning, generalizing, "getting the idea," or what the Gestalt psychologists call "insight," greatly facilitate the learning process. Solution of some problems may be achieved only after discovery of an underlying principle, relation, or system of relations. Discovery of a principle is frequently the only immediate goal of the learning process.

Investigators of problem solving in children have utilized materials ranging in complexity from puzzle boxes to tasks calling for abstract reasoning. Many of the relatively simple materials have been patterned after those used in experiments with animals. The puzzle box tests of Healy and Fernald (1911), for example, are similar in principle to those used by Thorndike (1898) and Small (1900) to investigate problem solving in cats, monkeys, rats, and other animals. A large number of researches on problem solving in children take as their point of departure the similar experiments of Hobhouse (1901) and of Köhler (1925) on the use of tools by animals. In these studies the problem is to discover that tools may be used to attain otherwise inaccessible goals. More complicated still are the puzzles used by Lindley (1897) and Ruger (1910) to investigate problem solving in children and adults. J. Peterson's (1918, 1920) rational-learning and mental-maze tests represent another type of problem solving used in investigations with children as well as adults. These devices and several others which involve generalizing are of a predominantly verbal character.

How Children Attack a Problem Situation. Before discussing the solution of problems like those mentioned above it will be enlightening to consider Hamilton's (1911, 1916) observations on how children and other organisms attack insoluble problems. Children and adults were confronted by four doors, only one of which was unlocked. If a given door had been unlocked in one trial it was locked in the next. The problem was to escape from the enclosure. If the unlocked door had always been on the extreme right, on the extreme left, the

second from the right or left, or the right on one trial and the left on the next, the problem could have been solved. Hamilton, however, purposely avoided following such principles. Which door would be unlocked from trial to trial was determined by chance. All subjects exhibited a variety of reactions which he designated as trial and error. Nevertheless, some exhibited a more "logical" trial and error than others. It seemed that they were using *hypotheses* as to the nature of the problem confronting them.[1] From the most to the least logical, the methods of attack were as follows: (A) trying the three inferentially possible doors—that is, those locked in the preceding trial—and avoiding the one previously unlocked; (B) trying all four doors once each in irregular order; (C) trying all four doors in regular order from left to right or right to left; (D) trying a given door more than once with intervening attempts to open some other door; (E) trying on two or more occasions to open a given door without intervening attempts at other doors, or persistent avoidance of a given door while trying all others. An infant of 26 months exhibited 15 per cent A reactions, 5 per cent B reactions, 20 per cent C reactions, 25 per cent D reactions, and 35 per cent E reactions. With subjects of increasing age, however, there was an increase in A and a decrease in E and similarly "illogical" reactions. Human adults exhibited 76 to 85 per cent A reactions and very seldom gave any C, D, or E reactions. The trial and error of young children was quite similar to that of infrahuman animals.

In his experiment with unicursal puzzles —that is, those in which a figure must be traced without lifting the pencil, retrac-

[1] Hamilton did not use the term *hypothesis* in this connection. It was later (1932) used by Krechevsky in reporting his observations of similar trial-and-error behavior in rats.

ing, or crossing lines—Lindley (1897) also found that younger children exhibit a quite inadequate mode of attack. His subjects were from grades 3 to 8. The reactions of children in the lowest grade were, according to Lindley, characterized by lack of circumspection, conventional beginnings, slight and inconsequential variations from one attempt to another, frequent relapses into a former routine, and tardiness in profiting from errors. In older children, these characteristics slowly made way for "greater prevision, more adequate analysis of the design, less conventionality and automatism in procedure, more radical reconstruction of plan in successive trials, all of which led to greater promptness in profiting by mistakes" (p. 469). L. W. Gates (1938), using a multiple-choice situation, likewise observed increasing deliberateness of exploration with increasing age. The ages ranged from 5 to 10 years.

Other investigators of problem solving whose studies will be considered in the following discussions have also noted increasing appropriateness of attack as a function of age.

Puzzle Problems. A variety of puzzle situations have been devised to study problem solving in children. One of the simplest situations, from the standpoint of the psychologist if not of the infant, is the plate-glass test devised by McGraw (1942). Three situations are used. In the first of these the child is on one side of a 30-inch-high piece of plate glass and the lure (bell or other desirable object) is on the other side. The toy can be seen at all times that the child is facing the glass. A baby placed in this situation, if it responds at all, will usually try to reach the toy through the glass. It eventually learns that it must stand up and reach over the partition. In the second of McGraw's tests, the plate glass covers the right or left side of the play pen and the child must reach around

it to obtain the object. The third test is illustrated in Figure 21. McGraw has described her data in detail, particularly pointing out the difficulty of quantifying the results and still doing justice to the process of problem solving. These situations, when applied to children between the ages of 6 and 27 months, elicit marked

FIGURE 21. The lure is obtained by lowering the head and lifting the leg in order to climb between two pieces of plate glass. (From "Appraising Test Responses of Infants and Young Children," by M. B. McGraw, *Journal of Psychology*, 1942, *14*, 95.)

emotional reactions as well as trial and error and sudden insight.

The ability of infants to solve problems by utilizing such implements as rakes, sticks, chairs, boxes, and strings has been studied extensively. We shall shortly discuss these studies in some detail.

A puzzle box frequently used to investigate problem solving in older children was devised by Healy and Fernald (1911). The nature of the problem is illustrated in the diagram and legend of Figure 22. Healy and Fernald used the following instructions:

You see that this box opens by the lid lifting up. The glass is put in so that you can see the way to open it. You can work

*through the holes and use the buttonhook.
Study the box, and if you do the right
things in the right order, it can readily be
opened. Do not break the string or glass.
Open it as quickly as you can.*

The problem is made more difficult by
merely telling the child to open it, using
the buttonhook. He then has to *discover*
that the holes are his only approach to the

of her groups, gives the median time on
the initial trial as 251 seconds at 15 and
153 seconds at 16 years for boys and 436
seconds at 15 and 212 seconds at 16 years
for girls. These results indicate a difference in favor of the older individuals and
the boys. Differences in mechanical skill
rather than in problem-solving ability *per
se* may underlie these differences. After

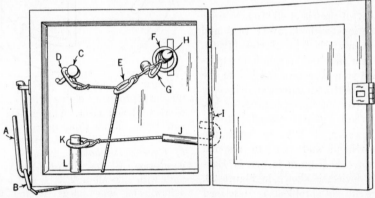

FIGURE 22. The Healy-Fernald puzzle box. (After W. Healy and G. Fernald.) Seven
distinct steps must be followed if the box is to be opened. They are: (1) removing ring K
from post L; (2) pulling out staple J; (3) removing ring I; (4) removing ring F from post
H; (5) removing ring D from arm of post C; (6) removing ring B from hook A; and (7)
removing hook A and opening box.

rings and cords. After the box has been
opened, the subject may be asked to close
it.

The typical mode of attack is by overt
trial and error. Occasionally, however, an
older subject surveys the internal mechanism carefully and, after some delay, opens
the box with no overt trial and error.
When questioned he says that he "figured
out the correct moves." This probably
means that implicit trial and error was the
basis of solution.

Norms for the above problem are re-
ported by Woolley (1926) and Bronner,
Healy, Lowe, and Shimberg (1927).
Woolley, who had over 400 subjects in each

the initial success, time curves drop pre-
cipitously and, within a few further trials,
the box is opened in approximately the
minimum time required for sheer manipulation. Time scores for closing the box are
much higher than for opening it. Healy
and Fernald report that the initial closing
time is approximately twice that required
to open the box.

The sudden drop in the learning curve
for this problem is rather characteristic of
problems the various aspects of which are
all apparent to the subject. Gestalt psychologists claim that such sudden learning
results from a more or less sudden grasping of relations, or *insight*. Where rela-

tions are not apparent, as in the usual maze problem, an individual is obliged to use overt trial and error, perhaps supplemented by implicit processes such as counting or other verbalization.[1] In situations like the present one, however, an individual may attack the problem as he would a maze, or he may, since opportunities are offered, observe the internal relations and so reach a quick solution with perhaps no overt trial and error.[2]

The ability of preschool children to solve puzzle situations without overt trial and error has been studied by Harter (1930). Each problem involved a solution requiring that one step be completed before the next. Overt trial and error would involve moving one part of the apparatus or another until the solution appeared. It was possible, however, to "figure out" the moves beforehand and thus to respond without error. A diagram of one of Harter's puzzle devices is shown in Figure 23. The nature of the problem is described in the legend of this figure.

Ability to solve such puzzles increased with CA and MA. Biserial r's ranged from .54 ± .08 to .73 ± .06 for success and CA, and between .49 ± .09 and .57 ± .08 for success and MA. The amount of overt trial and error, as indicated by the average number of moves, decreased with age. Four yearly age groups from 3 to 6 made the following average number of moves, respectively, on the obstacle peg test: 36.0, 24.7, 20.4, and 17.6. Children who failed to solve the problems made more moves than did successful ones. Only 1 child out

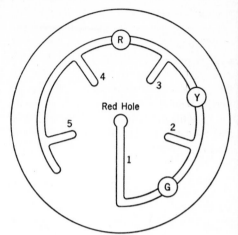

FIGURE 23. Obstacle peg test used to measure problem solving with or without overt trial and error. (From "Overt Trial and Error in the Problem Solving of Preschool Children," by G. L. Harter. *Journal of Genetic Psychology,* 1930, *38,* 362. By permission of the publisher.) A grooved path with side alleys 2, 3, 4, and 5 had red, yellow, and green pegs at the positions marked *R, Y,* and *G.* The pegs were modified styluses with a round knob at the top. They could be slid along the groove but not removed from the apparatus. The experimenter pointed to the red ball between 3 and 4 and told the child to put it in the red hole. If the child pulled at the red knob, he was told to push, not pull. Those who solved the problem used either of the following methods: (1) placing *G* and *Y* in the side grooves and then sliding *R* around to the red hole; or (2) moving the red peg into a side groove, pushing *Y* and *G* back to the blind end of the pathway, and then moving the red peg around to the hole. Ninety per cent of 40 adults and 74 per cent of 53 children used the first method.

of 75 given the obstacle peg test solved it without making any error. Eighteen out of 75 solved a similar type of problem without error. In each case, the average age of the children achieving errorless solutions was much higher than that of those

---

1 Some investigators have used mazes, the entire paths of which are observable. In such instances insight may be apparent. See especially the study by de Sanctis (1931) of observational maze learning in normal and feeble-minded children.

2 For other studies of insight in puzzle solving by children, see Ruger (1910), whose research was primarily on adults but involved four boys, and Wunderling (1935), who used children from the first to eighth grades.

who solved with overt trial and error. On a repetition of the problems, solution was achieved with a marked decrease in moves and an increase in the number of errorless reactions. For instance, 32 out of 50 children given a second trial on the obstacle peg test solved it without overt trial and error as compared to 1 child out of 75 for the first trial. Adults who succeeded on the tests reacted like children who succeeded, but time was greatly reduced.

Problems Involving Utilization of Tools. Tool problems were used by Hobhouse (1901) with animals. Köhler (1925) revived and greatly extended the use of the method in his researches on learning in chimpanzees. It consists, essentially, of confronting the subject with some *lure,* such as food or a toy, which is inaccessible unless certain tools are utilized. These tools may comprise attached strings, a lever with lure attached, a stick sufficiently long to reach the lure if fitted together, a box or number of boxes to be stacked, or some other indirect means of obtaining the lure. The task which confronts the subject is chiefly to learn that the given objects may be used as a means of obtaining the lure.

Richardson's (1932, 1934) investigations dealt with infants between the ages of 28 and 52 weeks. Kellogg and Kellogg (1933) used tool problems with an infant ape and an infant human subject. Researches by Alpert (1928), Brainard (1930), Matheson (1931), Moriya (1937a, 1937b), Sawa (1937), Tagawa (1937), Sobel (1939), and Ling (1946) involved preschool children. Comparative investigations of normal and feeble-minded children have been carried out by Aldrich (1931), Aldrich and Doll (1931a, 1931b), and Gottschaldt (1933). Since several of these investigations have much in common, we shall describe in detail only the most representative ones. Results of related studies will then be summarized briefly.

Since Richardson's investigations deal with infants, they will be discussed first. The two studies were carried out concurrently and on the same infants. In the 1932 article are reported the reactions of 10 boys and 6 girls to string problems given at monthly intervals between the twenty-eighth and fifty-second weeks. The lure was a toy attached to a string. Although the end of the string was within reach, the lure was not. In some tests a barrier prevented the infant from reaching the table top on which the lure and string lay. In others the barrier was removed since, until the age of 44 weeks, it appeared to hinder solution of the problems. Representative string situations are illustrated in Figure 24. Each setting was arranged behind a screen. As soon as this was removed, the experimenter tapped the toy on the table, squeaked it, rocked it, or rattled it, depending on its nature. The reactions of the subject were then observed. If he pulled in the lure, he was allowed to play with it a short time before it was removed. Only settings such as that shown in Figure 24A were used at the earliest age level. Type B was added at 32 weeks. At 36 weeks, type C was added to the tests. From 40 to 52 weeks, all types were used.

The reactions of infants to the above situations suggested five types of *perceptive attitude.* They were: (a) interest in the string rather than in the lure, (b) interest in the lure and apparently accidental contact with the string, (c) awareness of both lure and string without evident purposive utilization of the string, (d) experimentation, and (e) definite utilization of the string as a means to bring the lure into reach. Richardson claims that a and b represent success without insight; c and d, success with incomplete insight; and e, success with insight. The last type was associated with a marked drop in time. Types of response said to involve insight increased in frequency with age. The other types decreased as a function of age. Relative difficulty of the various situations appeared to be determined by the directness with which the dummy string or strings led to the lure. In terms of the percentage of children making initial correct choices, the relative difficulty was in the order shown from A to E in Figure 24.

second week, the percentage had increased to 83. Other criteria likewise indicated increasing ability to perform the problem as a function of age. Part of the improvement was undoubtedly due to greater mechanical ability and better motivation at the higher age levels. As in the string problems, several degrees of "perceptive attitude" or insight could be discerned, and the degree increased with age. Demonstrations failed to influence the infants' grasp of the nature of the situation although,

A   B   C   D   E

Position of Infant

FIGURE 24. Representative string problems used with infants. (From "The Growth of Adaptive Behavior in Infants: An Experimental Study of Seven Age Levels," by H. M. Richardson. *Genetic Psychology Monographs*, 1932, *12*, 230. By permission of the publisher.) In other situations the position of the correct string was the reverse of that shown in these diagrams. The child sat in one half of a crib, and the top of the other half was covered to form a table top on which the settings of the strings were arranged. In some tests a barrier was between the child and the table top; in other tests there was no barrier.

Richardson's second report describes lever experiments carried out with the same infants and under the same general conditions. The experimenter rang a small bell and, while the infant watched, placed the bell on the end of a lever, the short arm of which was within the infant's reach. Turning the short arm of the lever a sufficient number of degrees brought the bell within grasping distance. Two positions of the lever, straight out in the median plane or oblique to the right, were used. A counterclockwise turn of, respectively, 90 to 45 degrees was thus required. If the child failed, a demonstration was given. This was followed by further tests and, if necessary, demonstrations. Between 40 and 44 weeks the percentage of infants succeeding at least once in securing the lure increased from 20 to 67. By the fifty-

after 44 weeks, they appeared to increase motivation.

In problem-solving situations the behavior of individual subjects is frequently more enlightening than group trends. The following protocol is presented by Richardson as representing development of insight in a 44-month infant.[1]

> As soon as the lever board is in place, B gets her hand on the short arm of the lever and tries to tug it toward her. She rotates it about 40 degrees in the counterclockwise direction.
> The lever is returned to its former position by E. The bell is rung. B reaches for it with her left hand as E moves it to the far side of the grill and sets it on the tray. Right hand is also active. B has

[1] Paraphrased from Richardson's (1934) protocols, p. 368.

turned the tray about 20 degrees before the bell is put on the tray. Left and right hands alternately approach short arm, turning it. She does not yet turn it more than 40 degrees in the counterclockwise direction, and occasionally turns it clockwise. As she rotates it back and forth with her right hand, she eagerly watches the bell in the tray. Once she turns the lever as much as 90 degrees, so that the stick is parallel to the grill. After *80 seconds* the tray, following trial rotations, is brought into contact with the grill, and B secures the bell.

E returns the bell to the lever in original position. B, with her right hand, turns the short arm about 40 degrees in the counterclockwise direction. She brings up her left hand. With her right, in a steady movement, she rotates the lever so that *20 seconds* after the beginning of the situation the tray is near the grill. She secures the bell. The bell is removed and set again on the tray. This time the first turn of the short arm is greater. *Five seconds* after the beginning of the situation B has secured the bell and carried it through the grill.

Alpert's (1928) research is representative of those on preschool children. It is a repetition of several situations presented by Köhler to chimpanzees. Forty-four nursery school children 19 to 49 months old were confronted with situations like the following: An object suspended from the ceiling could be reached only by placing a near-by block beneath it in an appropriate position; an attractive toy too far from the play pen to be reached by hand could be obtained if a near-by stick was used to pull it in; a toy placed at a greater distance from the bars of the pen than was the former one became accessible only when two sticks were fitted together and used to angle for it.

The initial responses to such situations were usually of what might be called a trial-and-error nature. There was no grasp-

ing of the fact that the otherwise inaccessible lure could be obtained by the tools lying at hand, even when these were observed and, in some instances, played with. A good example is the behavior of Case 20, a girl of 42 months, in response to the suspended lure.

First exposure. S went up to objective, stared at it, and waveringly raised her left arm halfway up, looking at E; remained thus for 2 minutes, then indicated that she wished her coat taken off. While adjusting her sweater sleeves, caught sight of block, looked long and hard at it, then again partly outstretched her arm toward objective, looking at E, began to chew her nails, still staring at E.

Second exposure. S walked slowly up to objective and tried to reach it with her right hand, looking at E. S remained thus, with arm partly outstretched, gazing around, for 2 minutes. S looked at the block and took a few steps toward it, looking at E; alternated between a step toward block and attempt to reach up for objective; walked off, past the block, looking back at objective several times.

Third exposure. S looked at objective and at E, advanced slowly toward former, arm outstretched, reaching for object in an ineffectual manner as she gazed all around; saw block but continued to reach up. S began to amuse herself with the woodwork on the nearest wall.

Even with two further presentations of this situation, the subject failed to observe that the problem could be solved by using the block. Most children eventually solved the problem. A few solved it very quickly. An example is Case 15, a boy aged 39 months. Only one exposure of 30 seconds' duration was required.

S was much distressed when asked to come with E, but at sight of balloon—objective—he rushed at it trying to reach it with both hands. S turned around to complain to E, spied the block, and announced tearfully that he would get on it; dragged block under objective, got on, and reached up for it but found it rather a hard stretch; jumped off, turned block on its perpendicular side, got on, and swung objective with glee.

A good example of apparent trial and error followed by sudden solution is that or a girl of 38 months reacting to the two-stick problem.

First exposure. S examined one of the sticks and tried to reach objective with it over the top of pen; examined the other stick and used it in the same way, repeating, "I can't" over and over; tried out the stick between the bars, over the top of pen, finally striking it viciously against the floor; complained bitterly, and tried again to reach as before, stretching and straining; tried to climb out and whined, "I can't." E terminated exposure to avoid fatigue.

Second exposure. S reached for objective as above and in 10 seconds said, "Look, I can't," but continued her efforts; fitted sticks up against bars of pen, banged them together, etc. S tried to reach objective with her hand through the spaces, to force her way out, to shake the pen, etc.; said, "Dolly does not want me to get him."

Third exposure. As above, complaining intermittently and finally giving up.

Fourth exposure. S stretched for objective over top of pen, striking out angrily with stick, complaining and asking E to move object closer. S said, "Let's try big stick on little one," picked up the other stick, examined ends carefully and succeeded in fitting them, with a shout of "Bang!" S angled for objective, reached it exultantly, and repeated stunt several times.

Alpert found "exploration and elimination" to be the most frequent behavior of preschool children in responding to the problem situations. Where insight occurred, it tended to be immediate rather than gradual. It was apparent in varying

degrees. Chance operated by bringing about "an optimum constellation of the elements" required for solution. The presence of an optimum constellation, however, did not guarantee that insight would appear. Brainard (1930) carried out similar experiments on a child of 2 years and 7 months whose IQ was 141. Insight was present for some situations but not for others. Similar results are reported by Ling (1946), who used an adaptation of Alpert's technique with 8 preschool children.

Matheson's (1931) investigation differed from the studies of Alpert, Brainard, and Ling in certain significant respects. The subjects were 28 children between the ages of 2 and 4½ years. One problem involved taking a ring off a hook in order to lower a basket containing the lure. Another was of the crossed-string variety, the child being required to pull in a longer string, alone of adequate length. A stick and a box-stacking problem somewhat like those used by Alpert were also involved. Matheson noted 15 types of reaction to these situations, all of which were called out to some extent by each problem. The most frequent of these were "manipulation" and "pointing and reaching," also designated as "trial and error." The rarest responses were "solution without previous manipulation" and "solution for the sake of solution." Only 14 per cent of the children exhibited such responses.

The percentage of children solving the problems went from zero at 2, to 62 at 4 years. The correlation between solution and CA was .464 ± .10; that between solution and MA, .422 ± .107.

Aldrich (1931) and Aldrich and Doll (1931a, 1931b) extended problems like the above to the idiot level of intelligence. The degree of insight attained in stacking boxes, combining sticks, using single sticks, and using a rake to reach a lure is reported to be somewhere between that attained by Köhler's apes and Alpert's preschool children. The importance of strong incentives as a factor in achievement of insight is especially noted in these studies and in one by Sawa (1937) on normal children. Gottschaldt's (1933) investigation involved normal, moron, imbecile, and idiot children. Stick, string, and block-stacking situations were used. The chief contribution of this research is analysis of the behavior in terms of level of aspiration and in terms of field forces, following the lead of Lewin. Gottschaldt found a lower level of aspiration with decreasing intelligence. Feeble-minded children were satisfied with various substitute "solutions." The influence of vectors was brought out in stick problems of the following nature: A short stick lay near at hand and a long one was more distant. The long stick was alone adequate for reaching the lure. In some instances the short stick was secured and played with, the child seeming to forget the long stick and the lure. The presence of a toy near the short stick had a still greater influence upon the "attractiveness" of this inadequate instrument. Whenever an apparently easy, yet inadequate, solution appeared possible, the difficulty of the problem was greatly increased. Such "distraction" was more apparent in feeble-minded than in normal children. Similar principles are involved in detour problems used by Lewin (1935), Sawa (1937), and Tagawa (1937). Theoretical discussions of such problems have been presented by Lewin (1935), in terms of vector analysis, and Hull (1938), in terms of the goal-gradient hypothesis.

Moriya (1937a, 1937b) wished to determine whether preschool children achieve insight into the solution of problems involving the principle of a lever. Only the older of 29 kindergarten children evidenced insight in balancing objects on the flattened

top of a pyramid. In a further problem involving removal of strings from a lever arm in such a manner as to leave it still balanced in the horizontal direction, no insight was evidenced. The author concludes that preschool children use trial and error predominantly in solving problems involving the principle of a lever. Lack of previous experience with levers is, however, probably the real explanation. G. M. Peterson (1932) used somewhat similar lever problems, but on a verbal basis. His subjects were children between the ages of 132 and 168 months. In these, as in many other problems, insight may involve transfer to the new situation of what has been learned previously in somewhat similar situations. The results of a preliminary investigation by Sobel (1939) is of interest here. Sobel found that some children between the ages of 18 and 48 months achieved immediate solution of tool problems. Others solved a given problem only after previous training which involved use of similar implements. The "insight" evidenced in the latter instances was thus known to be based upon transfer.

Solution of Problems by Learning a Principle. To the degree to which problems are solved as a result of implicit rather than readily observed overt activities, the solution is said to result from reasoning. The implicit activity involves "manipulation" of symbols, or substitutes for past stimulation. Such manipulation is often of a trial-and-error nature.[1] When solution of a problem involves learning a principle, we usually speak of the reasoning process as *generalizing.* Several investigations on learning in children have involved problems demanding generalization. Such problems will be considered in the present section.

[1] For a more extensive discussion of the nature of implicit activity such as involved in reasoning, see Munn (1938), pp. 333 ff.

Heidbreder (1927, 1928) used three problem situations to investigate generalizing in 30 children between 2½ and 10 years and in 10 adults. Each problem involved a principle, the discovery of which was the chief task confronting the subjects. In Problem I the child was presented with two boxes, one of which contained a doll. The *right-hand box* always contained the doll, yet it might be closer than the left in one trial and farther away in the next. Problem II utilized plain and flowered boxes. Regardless of its position (right-left, near-far) with respect to the other box, the *flowered* one always contained the toy. Problem III involved boxes with plain figures and boxes with figures having perimeters with red dots. Two boxes of a given kind were used at each trial. If both had plain figures, the doll was in the farther box. On the other hand, if both had dotted figures, *the nearer box* contained the doll. Table 9 shows the

and by six 4-year-olds. Whereas only two 3-year-olds solved Problem II, it was solved by all above this age. The youngest individual to solve Problem III was a 4-year-old. No children of the youngest age group gave a satisfactory reason for selecting a given box. When questioned, they sometimes said that the box was selected because they liked it. Only 5 per cent of the next age group verbalized their solutions. Above the age of 6 years, however, almost every solution was given an adequate verbal formulation.

More difficult of solution than the above is the double-alternation problem used by Gellermann (1931) with 38 children between 3 and 13 years of age. The apparatus was a modification of one used by Hunter with rats and raccoons. Its main features are shown in Figure 25. This is called a "temporal maze" by Hunter to distinguish it from mazes of the spatial variety, that is, those in which the turn in

TABLE 9

Generalizing as a Function of Age *

Age	No.	Problem I		Problem II		Problem III	
		Solutions	Reactions	Solutions	Reactions	Solutions	Reactions
3	10	1	219	2	230	0	216
4	10	6	178	10	23	1	348
6–10	10	10	174	10	23	10	81
Adult	10	10	34	10	16	10	40

* From Heidbreder (1928), p. 525.

number of solutions and number of reactions per problem for subjects at different age levels. One will note that children above the sixth year solved all three problems, and in relatively few trials. The first problem was solved by one 3-year-old

each part may be elicited by stimuli peculiar to this part. The problem which confronted each of Gellermann's subjects was learning to turn *right, right, left, left*, in successive trials, upon reaching the point X. Since the stimuli in the central alley were always alike, and hence could not give differential cues for right or left turns, the subjects were called upon to "figure out" the correct order of turns. They were given no instructions which would in any way suggest the solution. Unless they guessed it, as a matter of fact, the subjects did not at first know that a problem confronted them. They were merely invited to enter the apparatus and to keep moving. Incorrect responses were followed by the closing of a door which prevented

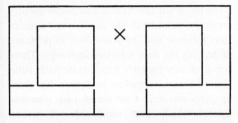

FIGURE 25. A double alternation maze.

progress in the incorrect direction. The subject was, on such occasions, required to retrace and take the correct turn. As soon as the *rrll* response had been made the child was allowed to leave the apparatus. It was readmitted after completion of a trial. This continued until 3 trials in succession without error had been completed. Finally, and without previous intimation, each child was required to give the response *rrllrrll*, that is, to repeat the series without leaving the apparatus. No questions were asked by the experimenter or answered by him while learning was in progress. After completion of the extended series, however, he asked these questions: "What did you think of it?" "How did you learn that [the solution]?"

Whereas adults learned this problem in an average of 6 trials children required an average of 15. Trials to learn ranged from 4 to 37. The average number of errors (incorrect turns) made by children was 30,

almost twice that made by adults. The rank-difference correlation between CA and trials was only .28 ± .11. The two youngest (3- and 4-year-old) children, however, failed to master the problem. From 5 years on, the number of trials and the number of errors decreased with age. The two 5-year-olds failed to extend the series, even after 10 to 12 extension tests. Older children extended the series in 2 to 3 tests.

The nature of the problem which confronts the subjects is perhaps best indicated by their verbal reports. A 10-year-old boy who learned in 14 trials gave the following report:

> First I thought all the walls would close in, and you were going to test my nerve or something like that. Then I found the doors were open, and I kept on walking. I thought there was something to it, because sometimes the doors were closed. After awhile I found you must go around each place twice.

Other reports were of a somewhat similar nature. At first there was no idea concerning what was to be expected, then came the idea that a *problem* was to be learned. Finally, the subjects formulated the problem in some such manner as *"twice to the right and twice to the left."*

The earliest age at which children solve the double-alternation problem has also been investigated by Hunter and Bartlett (1948). These investigators used a double-alternation box apparatus modeled after one earlier used by Gellermann in an experiment with monkeys. Their subjects had an age range of 2 years to 6 years and 9 months. The child sat before two boxes, one to the right and the other to the left. The experimenter, who sat behind the boxes and was hidden by a screen, placed candy in the boxes in the required order, a new piece of candy being placed after each response. Each series consisted of 8 responses in the order *rrllrrll*. If the child opened the wrong box, it could then open the correct one and get the candy. The series was repeated, sometimes 8 times in 1 session. Most children who learned the problem did so within 2 sessions. The criterion of learning was 3 successive correct series, or 24 consecutive correct responses. After the criterion was achieved, an opportunity was given to extend the series from 8 to 12 responses.

The youngest child to achieve the criterion was 3 years and 7 months old. A few children above this age, but younger than 4, failed to reach the criterion. Of those children who failed to reach the criterion, some did perform short series of double alternations. At the earlier ages there was difficulty in controlling motivation. Thus some of the failure at earlier ages may have resulted from insufficient motivation.

There was a positive correlation between trials to learn and, respectively, CA and MA, but there was no correlation between trials to learn and IQ. This is related to the fact that some of the children with the highest IQ's were too young to learn. Children who learned the 8-response series extended the series. Adequate verbalizations were not found below 5 years.

The rôle of verbalization in development of generalizations by children has also been demonstrated in a multiple-choice type of experiment reported by Pyles (1932). Eighty children ranging in age from 2 to 7 years were confronted with 5 figures under one of which a toy was hidden. The instructions were: *"One of these shapes has a toy under it. See if you can find which shape has a toy."* The child tried this shape and that until the toy was discovered. Then the experimenter said, *"Where did you find the toy?"* The child indicated. The experimenter then said, *"Yes, that one had it."* Such comments were made on the first 3 and subsequently on every third trial, the aim being to maintain interest and to stress the importance of having the first selection correct. Three series of experiments were used, with rotation of matched groups to equate for order of presentation. One series had nonsense figures which were unnamed. A second series involved the same figures, but now given a name, "Bokie," or the like. In a third series, well-known animal forms were used. These were named spontaneously by the children. A series was regarded as learned when the child selected the correct figure 4 times in succession.

The results are summarized in Table 10. They indicate that verbalization is an aid to this kind of learning and that, the more familiar the material, the more rapid the learning. The correlation between trials

TABLE 10

COMPARISONS OF SCORES MADE ON THE THREE SERIES WITH ORDER OF PRESENTATION EQUATED

Groups	1–6	1–6	1–6
Series	A. Unnamed	B. Named	C. Animals
Mean number of trials *	21.3 ± 1.95	14.2 ± 1.6	$5.3 \pm .4$
Median number of trials	16.5	7.5	4.0
SD number of trials	22.6	18.1	4.8
Range	1–91	1–76	1–25
Percentage complete failure	15	10	3
Percentage succeeding in 25 trials or less	54	72	96

* Omitting cases of complete failure. From Pyles (1932), p. 111.

and CA ranged from −.19 to −.72; that between trials and MA from −.21 to −.62. The highest correlations were for series *B*, involving the named nonsense figures.

Investigation of ability to respond to different situations in terms of a common principle was made by Roberts (1932) with 43 children between 2 and 5 years of age. The children were confronted by three doors above each of which a colored toy airplane was visible. The experimenter said, *"This house has three doors; all of them open, but only one makes an airplane fall."* Doors and airplanes differed in color. There was, however, always one door with an airplane of the same color above it. This was the correct door. All children solved this problem, but the youngest child giving a statement as to the principle involved was 3 years and 4 months old. At higher age levels there was an increasing frequency of generalizing. All but the 2-year-old subjects reacted appropriately to new situations involving the same principle.

In a second study which was similar, in general principles, to that described, Roberts (1933) used figures of various shapes or sizes instead of colors. In one situation, six lower doors contained squares. Above them, in order, were a triangle, crescent, square, semicircle, octagon, and figure with parallel sides and concave ends. The toy was always hidden behind the figure which matched that above, in this case the square. In some situations, both upper and lower figures differed, but there was always one above which matched the door below. The subjects were 21 children who were aged 4 years and 19 orphanage children between 4 and 8 years of age. These were separated into three matched groups which learned the problems in different orders. Learning of an initial problem was followed by learning of other problems involving different colors, figures, or sizes.

The criterion of learning comprised 4 trials without error. In this study the chief aim was to discover whether a principle learned in one situation would be applied in others. Complete application of the principle would result in absence of errors in the solution of the next problem in the series. When the groups were equated in terms of MA, there was no difference in the learning ability of preschool and orphanage children. The correlation between trials to learn the initial problem and CA was −.40 ± .089. The correlation with MA was −.47 ± .083. With CA held constant, the correlation between trials and MA was reduced to −.30. The percentage of subjects making no errors in achieving the criterion increased with successive problems. On the first problem, for example, no subjects learned without errors; on the second problem, 71 per cent made no errors; on the third problem, 81 per cent made no errors. When the ninth problem was presented, 95 per cent performed without error. Although the children could solve these problems and thus make an overt generalizing response, they were unable to state the principle involved.[1]

J. J. Ray (1936) investigated generalizing in 6 dull, 6 average, and 6 bright 12-year-old children. Pictures were exposed, two at a time, in the aperture of a small

---

[1] This difficulty is perhaps merely linguistic. Hazlitt (1930), in her investigation of concepts such as "exception," found that children between 3 and 7 years of age could *make an exception* in behavior although they did not understand what they were to do when *asked* to make an exception. A child was given a large egg into which various smaller colored eggs fitted. The series of eggs was opened before him and he was asked to put all back into the big egg except the *green* one. The younger subjects either failed to respond or put back all the eggs. When they were asked to put back all eggs *but* the red one, many more children responded correctly. See also Kreezer and Dallenbach (1939), on learning the relation of opposition; Hicks and Stewart (1930), on concepts of size; Graham, Jackson, Long, and Welch (1944), on the concept of middleness; and Lacey and Dallenbach (1939), on the cause-effect relation.

apparatus which was operated manually by the subject. Whenever a key under the *correct* picture was pressed, a green light went on. Pressure on a key under the *incorrect* picture lit a red light. Pressure of either key, in addition to connecting a light, also exposed the next pair of pictures. The child's task was to get a green light every time as soon as possible. Twenty series of problems were used and each involved twenty pairs of pictures. The pictures of a series were repeated until the child responded correctly to the whole series or verbalized the solution. In the simplest problem, the key under the *curved* figure () etc., always lit the green light while that under the straight figure

etc., always lit the red light.

Other series involved animate versus inanimate objects, tools versus playthings, quadrupeds versus nonquadrupeds, and the like. Ability to solve these problems was correlated with intelligence, the dull children solving few and the bright children many series. The nature of the problem confronting the child and some insight into the mode of solution are shown by verbalizations. The verbal responses of only two subjects can be presented here. Subject R responded to the quadruped versus nonquadruped situation, beginning with the eighth pair, as follows:

"Animal." Next pair, "Wait a minute—might be animal with a tail." Second presentation of series, first pair, "I think—wait, let me go through one more time to make sure." Twelve pairs later, "If it's animal it's right, but I think something's wrong." Four series later, "If I'm not mistaken it's an animal that has legs." One pair later, "It's either the largest or a mammal. Wait a minute, let me go

through once more." Two pairs later, "I think it's an animal with four legs. The thing that got me puzzled was the snake and the turtle. Couldn't see any difference hardly."

Thus an implicit trial and error is apparent. Subject K, responding to the animate versus inanimate series, gave evidence of trial and error punctuated with sudden insight. After five pairs had been presented he said:

"I can't get this one." Ten pairs later he said, "I never get this one—I know." After the eleventh pair of the fourth presentation he said, "I believe I've caught on! (Great relief). It's the animal. Easy as pie when I caught on." [1]

Rational Learning. In solving J. Peterson's (1918) "rational learning" problem the subject is required to associate with each of a group of words a number which has been arbitrarily assigned to it. For instance, the letters A, B, and C may be numbered, respectively, 2, 3, and 1. The child is told that the letters A, B, and C are numbered from 1 to 3, but the A may not be 1, B may not be 2, and C may not be 3. He is then asked, *"What number do you think A has?"* He guesses numbers from 1 to 3 until the number 2 is given. Then he is asked to guess the number for B. When he says that it is 3, he is asked the number that goes with C. When he guesses this, the letters are repeated.

[1] Welch (1938, 1939a, 1939b, 1939c, 1940a, 1940b) and Welch and Long (1940a, 1940b, 1942) present a series of studies on development of concepts and generalizations in children. In some respects they are extensions of the early and much more limited studies of Munn and Steining (1931) and Gellermann (1933) on "form" discrimination in children. Limitations of space do not permit an adequate discussion of such investigations in the present chapter, where emphasis must be placed upon learning *per se*. The reader interested in development of concepts and generalizations will find the papers by Welch and by Welch and Long of great value. He should see Welch (1940a) also for an extensive bibliography of related studies.

When he repeats each number correctly as the letters are called, the child is given a longer list of letters.

This problem is believed to involve "rational" learning because, if the subject notes that a number which is correct earlier in the series cannot be used again in the same series, his learning is greatly facilitated. Repetition of an earlier correct number is designated a *logical error*. Likewise, learning will be facilitated if the subject does not repeat a given incorrect number while guessing the numbers which go with a given letter. Such repetitions are designated *perseverative errors*. In Peterson and Harrelson's (1923) study of rational learning in white and Negro children between 7 and 10 years of age, the letters *A* to *E* were used with the numbers 4, 2, 5, 1, and 3, respectively. Learning curves based upon data for 299 white and 314 Negro children were negatively accelerated and very similar to those obtained in learning of sensorimotor skills. Nelson (1936) presents several learning curves for problems involving rational learning of the above-mentioned type.

There was no sex difference for the learning of this problem. The mean score of white children was 1.69 PE units above that of the Negro children. A somewhat similar problem was later used by J. Peterson (1926) to investigate the limits of learning by trial and error in high school subjects.

Maier's Reasoning Problem Adapted for Children. In addition to those problems which involve solution of puzzles, use of tools, learning and application of a principle, and so-called rational learning, there are others not easily classified; Maier's reasoning problem is one of these.

Maier's (1936) investigation is based upon the view that the essence of reasoning is combination of past experiences in solution of a problem. He used the ap-

paratus diagrammatically represented in Figure 26. The child was first made familiar with the entire apparatus. Then the experiment proper was conducted as

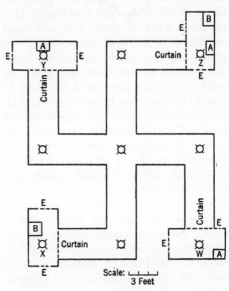

FIGURE 26. Ground plan of an apparatus for testing the ability of children to reason. (From "Reasoning in Children," by N. R. F. Maier. *Journal of Comparative Psychology,* 1936, *21,* 356. By permission of the publisher.) *W, X, Y,* and *Z* represent booths placed at the end of the pathways. *E* represents entrances to the booths. These entrances are covered by drop curtains. Similar curtains also separate the booths from the pathways. *A* represents an adult chair and *B* a nursery school chair. The position of 25-watt electric lights is indicated in the diagram. The apparatus is built of a wooden framework covered with black cloth.

follows: After another brief exploration of the apparatus the child was allowed to emerge through a door of one of the exit booths. This comprised *Experience I.* The child was then led around the apparatus by a devious route until another booth was reached. In this booth it was shown a toy house. When a penny was dropped into the house a tune played. This experience in a specific booth was *Experience II*. Both experimenter and child then left the booth to go in search of a penny by means of which the child could again play the tune. After the penny had been found and the child had been disoriented in the process, he was placed in a third booth and told to go and play the tune. In order to do this without trial and error he would have to utilize Experiences I and II. In other words, if the first experience had been in Y (see Figure 26), the second one in X, and the entrance from which he was to reach X in W, the child would have to think of the fact that W had a given position with respect to X. He could react in such terms only on the basis of his original exploration and the two specific experiences. The starting booth in each test was always the goal booth of the preceding test. Since the child had 3 possible goals in each trial, chance accuracy would approximate 33 per cent.

The subjects ranged in age from 42 to 112 months. They were arranged into groups having average ages of 47.6, 62.3, 70.1, 84.3, and 92.5 months. The size of the groups ranged from 4 to 12. There was an increase in the accuracy of response at successive age levels, the percentages being, respectively, 32.0, 43.6, 58.6, 73.3, and 82.5. The percentage of subjects giving 5 or more correct responses in 10 trials was, respectively, 20.0, 36.3, 71.4, 83.3, and 100. One will note that it was not until the age approximated 70 months that accuracy went far above what would be expected on the basis of chance. Maier says: "The ability to combine the essentials of two isolated experiences in such manner as to reach a goal is rather late in maturing. It is rarely developed in a marked extent in children below 6 years of age." When the data were arranged in terms of mental

age groups, greater than chance accuracy was not apparent below a mental age of 6 years. Scores increased with mental age, as did the percentage of subjects making better than 5 correct responses out of 10.

Problem Solving in the Schoolroom Situation with School Materials.[1] Several investigators have studied problem solving under school conditions and in so doing have utilized arithmetic, geometry, and civics. Donovan and Thorndike (1913) report learning data on addition. Stevenson (1925) outlines some of the difficulties met by children from various grades in solving arithmetical problems. Monroe's (1928) investigation, which also deals with arithmetic, is more analytical than earlier studies. He stated the same arithmetical problems in technical terms, in everyday terms, or in relation to irrelevant material. Equated groups from the seventh grade were tested. Greatest success was achieved when the problems were framed in terms of everyday life. Monroe concludes, however, that a large percentage of seventh-grade children fail to reason in solving arithmetic problems. He claims that they depend upon habit for solution. Some corroboration for this view comes from Henry's (1934) investigation with geometric problems. Only 32 per cent of his group of college students gave evidence of insight in solution of such problems. In 285 test situations, responses of the "Oh, I see" type occurred but 17 times. Brownell (1938) reports that both repetition and insight are involved in learning arithmetic. Stump (1927) plotted curves for the learning of civics problems in terms of the number of "elements" learned. The subjects were high school seniors. Learning curves had a very gradual rise. Although the problems were logical ones, involving development and application of principles, there

[1] For a review of literature on factors which influence learning in school situations, see Stroud (1940).

was little evidence of higher processes than those involved in sheer memorizing. This may be due to the method of presenting the problems rather than to lack of insight in the students.

Social Learning

No doubt much of the learning that occurs in classroom situations at the early grades is motivated by the desire for recognition. The child who gets a star for superior performance is usually not interested in the star so much as in its actual or imagined effect on others. The efficacy of praise and blame probably stems from the same motivation.

The tendency to imitate, which some children learn quite early and which plays a very significant rôle in development of language as well as other skills, is also an important factor in classroom situations. Nor is it unrelated to desire for recognition, for the child tends to imitate those with prestige and not to imitate those with a less desirable status.

One of the most interesting features of the book by Miller and Dollard (1941) is its research on learning to imitate or not imitate. In the first of two experiments on learning to imitate in children, the investigators used 41 first-grade children. Two boxes were set up in a small room. One child (the imitatee) was shown the two boxes and told in which one candy was hidden. This box contained two pieces of which he was to take one. Before the imitatee responded, however, the imitator was brought into the situation. If this child, when told to get candy, copied the other, he also got a piece of candy. In other experiments, with different subjects, the extra piece of candy was in the box other than that in which the model found his piece. Thus the second child was rewarded for not imitating the first. The imitating and non-

imitating situations were repeated until the second child always responded appropriately. Then the situation was changed so that there were four boxes. This was to see whether the imitative or nonimitative tendency already developed would transfer (generalize) to the new situation. Under these new conditions, 75 per cent of the imitators and 100 per cent of the nonimitators responded appropriately.

In the second of their two imitation experiments, Miller and Dollard (1941) investigated the effect on imitation or nonimitation of the "prestige" of the leader. For example, if the subject copied an adult he received a reward, but if he copied a child he received no reward. For some children this was reversed, copying a child being rewarded and copying an adult not being rewarded. Thus the "prestige" of the leader was determined by whether copying his response brought or failed to bring a reward. The subjects were 12 fourth-grade boys, and the apparatus involved a lever to be either rotated or depressed. The reward was candy. The boys soon learned whom to imitate, and they later generalized to a different problem involving different leaders with characteristics like those of the original training.

Learning in Children and Adults

Comparison of learning in children and adults appears especially relevant here, for at the beginning of the present chapter we noted the fact that educators and other students of child development have, until relatively recent years, treated children as though their learning process were in no fundamental way different from that of animals and adults. Were they correct in supposing that principles worked out with animals and adults are also applicable to children? Has the research on learning in children disclosed anything not already apparent?

It should be evident, in the first place, that in so far as investigations on learning in children have been carried out in the classroom, or under similar conditions, they have disclosed the adequacy or inadequacy of given procedures in such situations, something which could not with any degree of assurance have been prognosticated from work with adults in the laboratory. To mention one example, the whole method has not worked nearly so well with children in classroom situations as with adults in the psychological laboratory. In the second place, conditions which serve to motivate adults and children, although alike in certain respects, are sufficiently different to warrant separate investigations. In the third place, so little is known about learning, despite the large amount of research, that we need information from as many sources and from as many levels of development as possible. Finally, it must be acknowledged that learning is dependent upon modification of neuromuscular mechanisms, mechanisms the development of which continues at a rapid pace during the early years of childhood. It is in terms of the growth of these mechanisms that we may expect the learning process in children and adults to differ most fundamentally.

The learning of infants is inferior to that of older children and adults chiefly because of neuromuscular immaturity. There is, of course, no sudden transition at any age level. The growth of learning ability is gradual, and one stage, if we may speak of stages, merges imperceptibly with the next. Nevertheless, when we compare the learning of an infant with that of a school child, the inferiority of the former is glaringly apparent. We see this inferiority in tardiness of development and instability of conditioned responses; in inability to acquire

motor skills readily learned by the older child; in poor retentivity, especially in situations of the delayed-reaction variety; and in lack of ability to attack problems with sufficient effectiveness to allow solution. Not only is the infant handicapped by neuromuscular immaturity, but he is also devoid of the motives which are most effective in impelling the older child to learn, of the background of experience which may be applied to new situations calling for adjustment, and of an effective repertoire of words and other symbols with which external situations can, as it were, be implicitly manipulated.

As a child grows older we are confronted not so much by neuromuscular immaturity as we are by what might, for want of a better term, be called recalcitrance. It is clearly apparent in the conditioned-response experiment. From about the fifth year and thereafter the ease with which conditioned responses may be developed shows a continued decrease despite the fact that the child's nervous system is undergoing further development. As Razran has pointed out, although the child is more capable of modification than at an earlier age he *resists* such modification. He is no longer as docile as formerly. His naïveté has decreased, he has become increasingly critical of his surroundings, he has developed interests and attitudes of which those who would modify his behavior must take cognizance. After the relatively passive stage of infancy is passed, therefore, the psychology of incentives becomes increasingly important. Several investigations mentioned in this chapter have indicated the effectiveness of rivalry and of verbal and material rewards of various kinds in channelizing the efforts of children in learning situations. Lewin's concept of valences may yield fruitful results in this field.

In most of the learning situations considered in this chapter very little difference has been discovered in the modifiability of adequately motivated children and adults. Beyond the early years of childhood, when the handicaps of neuromuscular immaturity have largely been overcome, practically all differences in the learning of children and adults may be attributed to differences in motivation and in previous experience. Our discussion of motor skills, for example, demonstrated that, although older children and adults may begin with higher scores than younger children, the percentage of improvement resulting from a given amount of practice is alike regardless of age. Mnemonic processes show large differences in the ability of children and adults. The writer doubts, however, whether this represents true differences in modifiability and retentivity. In the first place, there is no way, even by use of nonsense syllables, to avoid the fact that increasing age brings increasing acquaintance with symbols and their manipulation. This is a factor of experience, not of neural growth. In the second place, it is difficult, if not impossible, to equate motivation in individuals at different age levels, especially when the levels are as widely separated as those between the first-grade child and the adult. Finally—and this is related to the two previously mentioned factors—mnemonic ability demands good observation as well as good modifiability and retentivity. Because of their wide range of interests and experience, adults are likely to be much better observers than children. Even reminiscence, which was once thought to differentiate child from adult forgetting, has been demonstrated to be prevalent at both levels.

The clearest case of a difference in the learning ability of children and adults could perhaps be made out in the field of problem solving. Even here, however, differences in motivation and in past experience, including familiarity with symbols and their use, rather than in problem-solving ability *per se*, may be the chief differentiating factors. Hazlitt (1930) has particularly challenged the view that a fundamental difference exists between child and adult reasoning. She attributes apparent differences to the type of factors just mentioned.

It seems apparent to the writer that the chief problems relating to learning in children are those of discovering the most adequate motivating conditions and the most effective procedures for the situations in which children must develop. The practical outcome of researches on learning in children will lie in these directions.

So far as discovering anything fundamentally new concerning the learning process is concerned, the investigations on learning in children have failed. One possible reason for this is that such investigations have from the first been patterned too much after the lines of earlier research with animals and adults in the laboratory. A more likely reason, however, is that the phenomenon of learning is fundamentally the same whether studied in the animal, child, or adult. Differences may be attributed to variations in neuromuscular maturation, in motivation, and in previous experience but not, apparently, to a different kind of learning process in each.

Bibliography

Abel, L. B. 1936. The effects of shift in motivation upon the learning of a sensori-motor task. *Arch. Psychol., N. Y., 29,* No. 205.

Abel, T. M. 1938. Neuro-circulatory reaction and the recall of unfinished and completed tasks. *J. Psychol., 6,* 377–383.

Achilles, E. M. 1920. Experimental studies in recall and recognition. *Arch. Psychol., N. Y., 6,* No. 44.

Adams, L. 1938. Five methods of serial rote learning: A comparative study. *Arch. Psychol., N. Y., 31,* No. 221.

Alberts, C. A., and D. Ehrenfreund. 1951. Transposition in children as a function of age. *J. Exp. Psychol., 41*, 30–38.

Aldrich, C. A. 1928. A new test for hearing in the newborn, the conditioned reflex. *Amer. J. Dis. Child., 35*, 36–37.

Aldrich, C. G. 1931. Experimental studies of idiot behavior. *Train. Sch. Bull., 28*, 151–159.

Aldrich, C. G., and E. A. Doll. 1931*a*. Problem solving among idiots: The use of implements. *J. Soc. Psychol., 2*, 306–336.

——. 1931*b*. Problem solving among idiots. *J. Soc. Psychol., 12*, 137–169.

Allen, C. N. 1931. Individual differences in delayed reaction of infants. *Arch. Psychol., N. Y., 19*, No. 127.

Allport, G. W. 1930. Change and decay in the visual memory image. *Brit. J. Psychol., 21*, 133–148.

Alpert, A. 1928. The solving of problem-situations by preschool children. *Teach. Coll. Contr. Educ.*, No. 323.

Anderson, H. H. 1936. Motivation of young children: Further studies in success and failure, praise and blame. *Child Develpm., 7*, 125–143.

Anderson, H. H., and R. S. Smith. 1933. Motivation of young children: The constancy of certain behavior patterns. *J. Exp. Educ., 2*, 138–160.

Arps, G. F., and H. E. Conard. 1916. An experimental study of economical learning. *Amer. J. Psychol., 27*, 507–529.

Baldwin, B. T., and L. I. Stecher. 1924. *The psychology of the preschool child.* New York: Appleton.

Ballard, P. B. 1913. Obliviscence and reminiscence. *Brit. J. Psychol. Monogr. Suppl., 1*, No. 2. Pp. 82.

Bassett, S. J. 1928. Retention of history in the sixth, seventh, and eighth grades with special reference to the factors that influence retention. *J. Hopkins Stud. Educ., 12.*

——. 1929. Factors influencing retention of history in sixth, seventh, and eighth grades. *J. Educ. Psychol., 20*, 683–690.

Batalla, M. B. 1934. An experimental study of children's behavior in a spatial complex. *J. Genet. Psychol., 44*, 127–138.

——. 1936. The learning curve and the reliability of learning scores in a body maze. *Univ. Calif. Publ. Psychol., 6*, 153–162.

——. 1943. The maze behavior of children as an example of summative learning. *J. Genet. Psychol., 63*, 199–211.

Bayley, N. 1926. Performance tests for three, four and five year old children. *Ped. Sem., 33*, 435–454.

Bayne, T. L., A. L. Winsor, and E. S. Winters. 1929. Conditioned motor responses in children. *Proc. Soc. Exp. Biol. Med., 26*, No. 4.

Beebe, E. L. 1933. Motor learning of children in hand and eye coordination with introduction of prismatic deflection. *Child Develpm., 4*, 6–25.

——. 1934. Motor learning of children in equilibrium in relation to nutrition. *Genet. Psychol. Monogr., 15*, 99–243.

Binet, A., and V. Henri. 1894. La mémoire des mots et la mémoire des phrases. *Année psychol., 1*, 1–23; 24–59.

Boggs, L. P. 1905. How children learn to read: An experimental study. *Ped. Sem., 12*, 496–502.

Bolton, T. L. 1892. The growth of memory in school children. *Amer. J. Psychol., 4*, 362–380.

Book, W. F. 1908. The psychology of skill. *Univ. Mont. Publ. Psychol.*, No. 1. Reprinted under same title in 1925, New York: Gregg.

Bott, E. A., W. E. Blatz, N. Chant, and H. Bott. 1928. Observation and training of fundamental habits in young children. *Genet. Psychol. Monogr., 4*, 1–61.

Brainard, P. P. 1927. Some observations of infant learning and instincts. *Ped. Sem., 34*, 231–254.

——. 1930. The mentality of a child compared with that of apes. *J. Genet. Psychol., 37*, 268–293.

Bregman, E. O. 1934. An attempt to modify the emotional attitudes of infants by the conditioned response technique. *J. Genet. Psychol., 45*, 169–198.

Brenman, M. 1942. The recall of fairy tales in normal and hypnotic states. *Psychol. Bull., 39*, 488–489.

Brolyer, C. R., E. L. Thorndike, and E. Woodyard. 1927. A second study of mental discipline in high school studies. *J. Educ. Psychol., 18*, 377–404.

Bronner, A. F., W. Healy, G. M. Lowe, and M. E. Shimberg. 1927. *A manual of individual mental tests and testing.* Boston: Little, Brown.

Brownell, W. A. 1938. Two kinds of learning in arithmetic. *J. Educ. Res., 31*, 656–664.

Bryan, A. I. 1934. Organization of memory in young children. *Arch. Psychol., N. Y., 24*, No. 162.

Bryan, W. L., and N. Harter. 1897. Studies in the physiology and psychology of the telegraphic language. *Psychol. Rev., 4*, 27–53.

Bühler, C. 1930. *The first year of life.* New York: Day.

Bunch, M. E. 1938. The measurement of reminiscence. *Psychol. Rev., 45*, 525–531.

Bunch, M. E., and W. K. Magdsick. 1933. The retention in rats of an incompletely learned maze solution for short intervals of time. *J. Comp. Psychol., 16*, 385–409.

Burt, C. 1909. Experimental tests of general intelligence. *Brit. J. Psychol., 3*, 94–177.

Burtt, H. E. 1932. An experimental study of early childhood memory. *J. Genet. Psychol., 40*, 287–295.

——. 1937. A further study of early childhood memory. *J. Genet. Psychol., 50*, 187–192.

——. 1941. An experimental study of early childhood memory: final report. *J. Genet. Psychol., 58*, 435–439.

Busemann, A. 1911. Lernen und Behalten. *Z. angew. Psychol., 5*, 211–271.

Carmichael, A. M. 1939. Identification of the occasion as a factor in learning. *J. Appl. Psychol., 23*, 741–743.

Carpenter, D. F. 1913. Mental age tests. *J. Educ. Psychol., 4*, 538–544.

Carter, H. D. 1935. Effects of emotional factors upon recall. *J. Psychol., 1*, 49–59.

Carter, H. D. 1936. Emotional correlates of errors in learning. *J. Educ. Psychol., 27*, 55–67.

——. 1937. Emotional factors in verbal learning: IV. Evidence from reaction times. *J. Educ. Psychol., 28*, 101–108.

Chapman, J. C., and R. B. Feder. 1917. The effect of external incentive on improvement technique in addition. *J. Educ. Psychol., 11*, 469–475.

Charles, J. W. 1929. An experiment in teaching reading. *J. Genet. Psychol., 36*, 591–594.

Chase, L. 1932. Motivation of young children: An experimental study of the influence of certain types of external incentives upon the performance of a task. *Univ. Iowa Stud. Child Welfare, 5*, No. 3.

Clark, A. S. 1924. Correlation of the auditory digit memory span with general intelligence. *Psychol. Clin., 15*, 259–260.

Clinton, R. J. 1930. Nature of mirror drawing ability: norms on mirror drawing for white children by age and sex. *J. Educ. Psychol., 21*, 221–228.

Conrad, H. S., and H. E. Jones. 1929. Psychological studies of motion pictures: III. Fidelity of report as a measure of adult intelligence. *Univ. Calif. Publ. Psychol., 3*, No. 7, pp. 245–276.

Cowan, E. A. 1928. Results of motor reconditioning methods used in training a backward child. *J. Genet. Psychol., 35*, 98–104.

Cowan, E. A., and M. Foulke. 1934. Variation in susceptibility to the conditioning of inhibition as an index of constitutional type. *Child Develpm., 5*, 201–236.

Cox, J. W. 1933. Some experiments on formal training in the acquisition of skill. *Brit. J. Psychol., 24*, 67–87.

Davidson, H. P. 1931. An experimental study of bright, average, and dull children at the four-year mental level. *Genet. Psychol. Monogr., 9*, 119–289.

Davis, F., and M. B. Batalla. 1932. A life-size alley maze for children. *J. Genet. Psychol., 41*, 235–239.

Davis, R. A., and Rood, E. J., 1947. Remembering and forgetting arithmetical abilities. *J. Educ. Psychol., 38*, 216–222.

Deacon, J. R. 1939. The conditioned habit treatment of nocturnal enuretics. *Proc. Amer. Ass. Ment. Def., 44*, No. 2, 133–138.

Dell, J. A. 1912. Some observations on the learning of sensible material. *J. Educ. Psychol., 3*, 401–406.

Denisova, M. P., and N. L. Figurin. 1929. The problem of the first associated food reflexes in infants. *Vopr. Genet. Refl. Pedol. Mladen., 1*, 81–88. (*See* Razran, 1933.)

Dennis, W. 1935. The effect of restricted practice upon the teaching, sitting, and standing of two infants. *J. Genet. Psychol., 47*, 17–32.

——. 1943. Is the newborn infant's repertoire learned or instinctive? *Psychol. Rev., 50*, 330–337.

Dernowa-Yarmolenko, A. A. 1933. The fundamentals of a method of investigating the function of the nervous system as revealed in overt behavior. *J. Genet. Psychol., 42*, 319–338.

de Sanctis, S. 1931. Visual apprehension in the maze behavior of normal and feeble-minded children. *J. Genet. Psychol., 39*, 463–468.

Dewey, E., E. Child, and B. Ruml. 1920. *Methods and results of testing school children.* New York: Dutton.

Dietze, A. G. 1931. The relation of several factors to factual memory. *J. Appl. Psychol., 15*, 563–574.

——. 1932. Some sex differences in factual memory. *Amer. J. Psychol., 44*, 319–321.

Dietze, A. G., and G. E. Jones. 1931. Factual memory of secondary school pupils for a short article which they read a single time. *J. Educ. Psychol., 22*, 586–598; 667–676.

Donovan, M. E., and E. L. Thorndike. 1913. Improvement in a practice experiment under school conditions. *Amer. J. Psychol., 24*, 426–428.

Dunford, R. E. 1930. The genetic development of cutaneous localization. *J. Genet. Psychol., 37*, 499–513.

Easby-Grave, C. 1924. Tests and norms at the six year old performance level. *Psychol. Clin., 15*, 261–300.

Ebbinghaus, H. 1885. *Über das Gedächtnis.* Leipzig. 1913. *Memory: A contribution to experimental psychology.* (Trans. by H. A. Ruger and C. E. Bussenius.) (*Teach. Coll., Educ. Reprints*, No. 3.) New York Teachers College, Columbia University.

Eigler, P. 1932. The effect of unusual stimulation on motor coordination in children. *Child Develpm., 3*, 207–229.

Emerson, L. L. 1931. The effect of bodily orientation upon the young child's memory for position of objects. *Child Develpm., 2*, 125–142.

Fisher, R. A. 1930. *Statistical methods for research workers.* (3d ed.) London: Oliver and Boyd.

Flügel, J. C. 1928. Practice, fatigue, and oscillation. *Brit. J. Psychol. Monogr. Suppl.*, No. 13. Pp. 92.

Forlano, G., and M. N. H. Hoffman. 1937. Guessing and telling methods in learning words of a foreign language. *J. Educ. Psychol., 28*, 632–636.

Foster, J. C. 1928. Verbal memory in the preschool child. *J. Genet. Psychol., 35*, 26–44.

Freeland, G. E. 1921. A year's study of the daily learning of six children. *Ped. Sem., 28*, 97–115.

Gates, A. I. 1917. Recitation as a factor in memorizing. *Arch. Psychol., N. Y., 6*, No. 40.

——. 1928. The nature and limits of improvement due to training. *Yearb. Nat. Soc. Stud. Educ., 27*(I), 444–461.

Gates, A. I., and G. A. Taylor. 1923. The acquisition of motor control in writing by preschool children. *Teach. Coll. Rec., 24*, 459–468.

——. 1925. An experimental study of the nature of improvement resulting from practice in a mental function. *J. Educ., Psychol., 16*, 583–592.

Gates, L. W. 1938. The genetic development of rational learning in children. *Psychol. Bull., 35*, 713.

Gellermann, L. W. 1931. The double alternation problem: II. The behavior of children and human adults in a double alternation temporal maze. *J. Genet. Psychol., 39*, 359–392.

——. 1933. Form discrimination in chimpanzees and two-year-old children. *J. Genet. Psychol., 42*, 3–27.

Gesell, A. 1925. *The mental growth of the pre-school child.* New York: Macmillan.

Gesell, A. 1938. The conditioned reflex and the psychiatry of infancy. *Amer. J. Orthopsychiat.*, *8*, 19-30.

Gesell, A., and H. Thompson. 1929. Learning and growth in identical infant twins: An experimental study by the method of co-twin control. *Genet. Psychol. Monogr.*, *6*, 1-124.

Gilbert, G. M. 1937. Age differences in the hedonistic tendency in memory. *J. Exp. Psychol.*, *21*, 433-441.

Gillette, A. L. 1936. Learning and retention: A comparison of three experimental procedures. *Arch. Psychol.*, *N. Y.*, *28*, No. 198.

Goodenough, F. L., and C. R. Brian. 1929. Certain factors underlying the acquisition of motor skill in pre-school children. *J. Exp. Psychol.*, *12*, 127-155.

Goodwin, J., L. Long, and L. Welch. 1945. Generalization in memory. *J. Exp. Psychol.*, *35*, 71-75.

Gordon, M. A. 1938. General and specific factors in transfer of training within verbal tests. *Arch. Psychol.*, *N. Y.*, No. 227.

Gottschaldt, K. 1933. Der Aufblau des kindlichen Handelns. *Z. angew. Psychol., Beih.*, No. 68.

Gould, M. C., and F. A. C. Perrin. 1916. A comparison of factors involved in the maze learning of human adults and children. *J. Exp. Psychol.*, *1*, 122-154.

Grace, G. L. 1948. The relation of personality characteristics and response to verbal approval in a learning task. *Genet. Psychol. Monogr.*, *37*, 73-103.

Graham, V., T. A. Jackson, L. Long, and L. Welch. 1944. Generalization of the concept of middleness. *J. Genet. Psychol.*, *65*, 227-237.

Gray, S. 1940. The influence of methodology upon the measurement of reminiscence. *J. Exp. Psychol.*, *27*, 37-44.

Grether, W. F. 1938. Pseudo-conditioning without paired stimulation encountered in attempted backward conditioning. *J. Comp. Psychol.*, *25*, 91-96.

Griffiths, M. M. 1938. *Part and whole methods of presentation.* (*Aust. Comm. Educ. Res. Ser.*, No. 52.) Melbourne: Melbourne University Press.

Guillet, C. 1909. Retentiveness in child and adult. *Amer. J. Psychol.*, *20*, 318-352.

Hall, V. 1936. The effects of a time interval on recall. *Brit. J. Psychol.*, *27*, 41-50.

Hallowell, D. K. 1928. Mental tests for preschool children. *Psychol. Clin.*, *16*, 235-276.

Hamilton, G. V. N. 1911. A study of trial and error reactions in mammals. *J. Anim. Behav.*, *1*, 33-66.

———. 1916. A study of perseverance reactions in primates and rodents. *Behav. Monogr.*, *3*, No. 2. Pp. 65.

Harter, G. L. 1930. Overt trial and error in the problem solving of pre-school children. *J. Genet. Psychol.*, *38*, 361-372.

Hazlitt, V. 1930. Children's thinking. *Brit. J. Psychol.*, *20*, 354-361.

Healy, W., and G. M. Fernald. 1911. Tests for practical mental classification. *Psychol. Monogr.*, *13*, No. 54. Pp. 54.

Heidbreder, E. F. 1927. Reasons used in solving problems. *J. Exp. Psychol.*, *10*, 397-414.

Heidbreder, E. F. 1928. Problem solving in children and adults. *J. Genet. Psychol.*, *35*, 522-545.

Henderson, E. N. 1903. A study of memory for connected trains of thought. *Psychol. Monogr.*, *5*, No. 23. Pp. 94.

Henri, V. 1902. Education de la mémoire. *Année psychol.*, *8*, 1-48.

Henry, L. K. 1934. The rôle of insight in the analytical thinking of adolescents. *Univ. Iowa Stud. Educ.*, *9*, No. 5, pp. 65-102.

Henry, N. B. (Ed.) 1950. *Learning and instruction.* 49th Yearb. Nat. Soc. Stud. Educ. Part 1. Chicago: University of Chicago Press. Pp. xii + 352.

Hetzer, H., and S. Wislitzky. 1930. Experimente über Erwartung und Erinnerung beim Kleinkind. *Z. Psychol.*, *118*, 128-141.

Hicks, J. A. 1930a. The acquisition of motor skill in young children. *Child Develpm.*, *1*, 90-105.

———. 1930b. The acquisition of motor skill in young children: II. The influence of specific and of general practice on motor skill. *Child Develpm.*, *1*, 292-297.

———. 1931. The acquisition of motor skill in young children: An experimental study of the effect of practice in throwing at a moving target. *Univ. Iowa Stud. Child Welfare*, *4*, No. 5.

Hicks, J. A., and D. W. Ralph. 1931. The effects of practice in tracing the Porteus diamond maze. *Child Develpm.*, *2*, 156-158.

Hicks, J. A., and F. D. Stewart. 1930. The learning of abstract concepts of size. *Child Develpm.*, *1*, 195-203.

Hicks, V. C., and H. A. Carr. 1912. Human reactions in a maze. *J. Anim. Psychol.*, *2*, 98-125.

Hildreth, G. 1935. An individual study in word recognition. *Elem. Sch. J.*, *35*, 606-619.

———. 1942. Puzzle-solving with and without understanding. *J. Educ. Psychol.*, *33*, 595-604.

Hilgard, E. R. 1948. *Theories of learning.* New York: Appleton-Century-Crofts. Pp. vi + 409.

Hilgard, E. R., and D. G. Marquis. 1940. *Conditioning and learning.* New York: Appleton-Century.

Hilgard, J. R. 1932. Learning and maturation in preschool children. *J. Genet. Psychol.*, *41*, 31-56.

———. 1933. The effect of early and delayed practice on memory and motor performances studied by the method of co-twin control. *Genet. Psychol. Monogr.*, *14*, 493-567.

Hobhouse, L. T. 1901. *Mind in evolution.* New York: Macmillan.

Holaday, P. W., and G. D. Stoddard. 1933. Getting ideas from the movies. In W. W. Charters, P. W. Holaday, and G. D. Stoddard. *Motion pictures and youth.* New York: Macmillan.

Holodnak, H. B. 1943. The effect of positive and negative guidance upon maze learning in children. *J. Educ. Psychol.*, *34*, 341-354.

Holt, E. B. 1931. *Animal drive and the learning process: An essay toward radical empiricism.* Vol. I. New York: Holt.

Houlahan, F. J. 1941. Immediacy of interpolation and amount of retention. *J. Educ. Psychol.*, *32*, 37-44.

Hovland, C. I. 1938a. Experimental studies in rote-learning theory: I. Reminiscence following learning by massed and by distributed practice. *J. Exp. Psychol., 22,* 201–224.

Hovland, C. I. 1938*b*. Experimental studies in rote-learning theory: II. Reminiscence with varying speeds of syllable presentation. *J. Exp. Psychol., 22,* 338–353.

Huguenin, C. 1914. Reviviscence paradoxale. *Arch. Psychol., Genève, 14,* 379–383.

Hull, C. L. 1938. The goal-gradient hypothesis applied to some "field-force" problems in the behavior of young children. *Psychol. Rev., 45,* 271–300.

Hull, C. L., and B. I. Hull. 1919. Parallel learning curves of an infant in vocabulary and in voluntary control of the bladder. *Ped. Sem., 26,* 272–283.

Humpstead, H. J. 1917. *Some aspects of the memory span: A study in associability.* Philadelphia: Psychological Clinic Press.

Hunter, I. M. L. 1952. An experimental investigation of the absolute and relative theories of transposition behavior in children. *Brit. J. Psychol., 43,* Pt. 2, 113–128.

Hunter, W. S. 1913. Delayed reaction in animals and children. *Behav. Monogr., 2,* No. 6. Pp. 86.

———. 1917. The delayed reaction in a child. *Psychol. Rev., 24,* 75–87.

Hunter, W. S., and S. C. Bartlett. 1948. Double alternation behavior in young children. *J. Exp. Psychol., 38,* 558–561.

Hurlock, E. B. 1924. The value of praise and reproof as incentives for children. *Arch. Psychol., N. Y., 11,* No. 71.

———. 1931. The psychology of incentives. *J. Soc. Psychol., 2,* 261–290.

Hurlock, E. B., and E. D. Newmark. 1931. The memory span of pre-school children. *J. Genet. Psychol., 39,* 157–173.

Hurlock, E. B., and R. Schwartz. 1932. Biographical records of memory in preschool children. *Child Develpm., 3,* 230–239.

Ide, G. G. 1920. The educability of five year old children. *Psychol. Clin., 13,* 146–172.

Ivanov-Smolensky, A. G. 1927*a*. Neurotic behavior and the teaching of conditioned reflexes. *Amer. J. Psychiat., 84,* 483–488.

———. 1927*b*. On the methods of examining the conditioned food reflexes in children and in mental disorders. *Brain, 50,* 138–141.

Jackson, T. A. 1939. Studies in the transposition of learning by children: III. Transpositional response as a function of the number of transposed dimensions. *J. Exp. Psychol., 25,* 116–124.

Jackson, T. A., and K. Dominguez. 1939. Studies in the transposition of learning by children: II. Relative vs. absolute choice with multidimensional stimuli. *J. Exp. Psychol., 24,* 630–639.

Jackson, T. A., and M. E. Eckhardt. 1940. Studies in the transposition of learning by children: V. The number of stimuli in the training series as a factor in generalization. *J. Exp. Psychol., 27,* 303–312.

Jackson, T. A., and E. A. Jerome. 1940. Studies in the transposition of learning by children: IV. A preliminary study of patternedness in discrimination learning. *J. Exp. Psychol., 26,* 432–439.

Jackson, T. A., and E. A. Jerome. 1943. Studies in the transposition of learning by children: VI. Simultaneous vs. successive presentation of the stimuli to bright and dull children. *J. Exp. Psychol., 33,* 431–439.

Jackson, T. A., E. Stonex, E. Lane, and K. Dominguez. 1938. Studies in the transposition of learning by children: I. Relative vs. absolute response as a function of amount of training. *J. Exp. Psychol., 23,* 578–600.

Jacobs, J. 1887. Experiments in "prehension." *Mind, 12,* 75–79.

Jensen, M. B., and M. Schrodt. 1936. Language difficulty in learning: The relative effectiveness of a series of study sheets of graded difficulty as teaching devices with children in the 6A grade. *J. Genet. Psychol., 49,* 451–467.

Jersild, A. T. 1932. Training and growth in the development of children: A study of the relative influence of learning and maturation. *Child Develpm. Monogr., 10,* p. 73.

Jones, A. M. 1927. An analytical study of one hundred and twenty superior children. *Psychol. Clin., 16,* 19–26.

Jones, H. E. 1930*a*. The galvanic skin reflex. *Child Develpm., 7,* 106–110.

———. 1930*b*. The retention of conditioned emotional reactions in infancy. *J. Genet. Psychol., 37,* 485–498.

———. 1931. The conditioning of overt emotional responses. *J. Educ. Psychol., 22,* 127–130.

———. 1934. The laws of emphasis and effect in children's learning. *Psychol. Bull., 31,* 597–598.

———. 1945. Trial and error learning with differential cues. *J. Exp. Psychol., 35,* 31–44.

Jones, H. E., and M. Batalla. 1944. Transfer in children's maze learning. *J. Educ. Psychol., 35,* 478–483.

Jones, H. E., and D. Dunn. 1932. The configural factor in children's learning. *J. Genet. Psychol., 41,* 3–15.

Jones, H. E., and J. G. Yoshioka. 1938. Differential errors in children's learning on a stylus maze. *J. Comp. Psychol., 25,* 463–480.

Jones, M. C. 1924*a*. The elimination of children's fears. *J. Exp. Psychol., 7,* 382–390.

———. 1924*b*. A laboratory study of fear: the case of Peter. *Ped. Sem., 31,* 308–315.

Judd, C. H. 1908. The relation of special training to general intelligence. *Educ. Rev., 36,* 28–42.

Kanaev, I. 1941. On the question of lability of conditioned reflexes in twins. *C. R. Acad. Sci. URSS., 30,* 856–858.

Kantrow, R. W. 1937. An investigation of conditioned feeding responses and concomitant adaptive behavior in young infants. *Univ. Iowa Stud. Child Welfare, 13,* No. 3.

Kasatkin, N. I., and A. M. Levikova. 1935*a*. The formation of visual conditioned reflexes and their differentiation in infants. *J. Gen. Psychol., 12,* 416–435.

———. 1935*b*. On the development of early conditioned reflexes and differentiations of auditory stimuli in infants. *J. Exp. Psychol., 18,* 1–19.

Keller, F. S. 1950. Animals and children. *Child Develpm.*, *21*, 7–12.

Kellogg, W. N., and L. A. Kellogg. 1933. *The ape and the child: A study of environmental influence upon early behavior.* New York: McGraw-Hill.

Ketterlinus, E. 1931. Learning of children in adaptation to mirror reversals. *Child Develpm.*, *2*, 200–223.

Kirkendall, L. A. 1938. The influence of certain incentives in the motivation of children. *Elem. Sch. J.*, *38*, 417–424.

Kirkpatrick, E. A. 1894. An experimental study of memory. *Psychol. Rev.*, *1*, 602–609.

——. 1899. Development of voluntary movement. *Psychol. Rev.*, *6*, 275–281.

——. 1909. Studies in development and learning. *Arch. Psychol.*, *N. Y.*, *2*, No. 12.

——. 1914. Experiment in memorizing vs. incidental learning. *J. Educ. Psychol.*, *5*, 405–414.

Kirkwood, J. A. 1926. The learning process in young children: an experimental study in association. *Univ. Iowa Stud. Child Welfare*, *3*, No. 6.

Klugman, S. F. 1944a. Cooperative versus individual efficiency in problem solving. *J. Educ. Psychol.*, *35*, 91–100.

——. 1944b. Memory for position among children, as measured by serial reproduction. *Brit. J. Psychol.*, *35*, 17–24.

Knotts, J. R., and W. R. Miles. 1929. The maze-learning ability of blind compared with sighted children. *J. Genet. Psychol.*, *36*, 21–50.

Köhler, W. 1925. *The mentality of apes.* (Trans. by E. Winter.) New York: Harcourt, Brace.

Komatsu, H. 1931. A study on the reproduction of perceived forms by children. *Jap. J. Psychol.*, *6*, 569–590.

Krasnogorski, N. I. 1909. Ueber die Bedingungsreflexe im Kindesalter. *Jb. Kinderheilk.*, *19*, 1–24.

——. 1925. The conditioned reflex and children's neuroses. *Amer. J. Dis. Child.*, *30*, 753–768.

——. 1933. Physiology of cerebral activity in children as a new subject of pediatric investigation. *Amer. J. Dis. Child.*, *46*, 473–494.

Krechevsky, I. 1932. The genesis of "hypotheses" in rats. *Univ. Calif. Publ. Psychol.*, *6*, 45–64.

Kreezer, G., and K. M. Dallenbach. 1939. Learning the relation of opposition. *Amer. J. Psychol.*, *41*, 432–441.

Kuenne, M. R. 1946a. Experimental investigation of the relation of language to transposition behavior in young children. *J. Exp. Psychol.*, *36*, 471–490.

——. 1946b. Experimental investigation of the relation of language to transposition behavior in young children. *Amer. Psychologist*, *1*, 259–260.

——. 1948. Transfer of response in young children on the intermediate size problem. *Amer. Psychologist*, *3*, 361.

Lacey, J. T., and K. M. Dallenbach. 1939. Acquisition by children of the cause-effect relationship. *Amer. J. Psychol.*, *52*, 103–110.

Langhorne, M. C. 1933. Age and sex differences in the acquisition of one type of skilled movement. *J. Exp. Educ.*, *2*, 101–108.

Lewin, K. 1935. *A dynamic theory of personality.* New York: McGraw-Hill.

Lindley, E. H. 1897. A study of puzzles with special reference to the psychology of mental adaptation. *Amer. J. Psychol.*, *8*, 431–493.

Ling, B. C. 1946. The solving of problem-situations by the preschool child. *J. Genet. Psychol.*, *68*, 3–28.

Loder, J. E. 1937. A study of oral learning with and without the speaker present. *J. Exp. Educ.*, *6*, 46–60.

Long, E. D. 1930. *The acquisition of skill by children as affected by distribution of practice.* Unpublished master's thesis, George Peabody College for Teachers.

Luh, C. W., and B. T. Liang. 1933. Further studies in forgetting and reminiscence. *Yenching Stud. Psychol.*, No. 3, pp. 1–14. (Reviewed by McGeoch, 1935.)

Lumley, F. H., and S. W. Calhoun. 1934. Memory span for words presented auditorially. *J. Appl. Psychol.*, *18*, 773–784.

Lund, F. H. 1927. The role of practice in speed of association. *J. Exp. Psychol.*, *10*, 424–433.

Lyon, D. O. 1916. The relation of quickness of learning to retentiveness. *Arch. Psychol.*, *N. Y.*, *5*, No. 34.

Maier, N. R. F. 1936. Reasoning in children. *J. Comp. Psychol.*, *21*, 357–366.

Mallay, H. 1935. The latent memory span of the preschool child. *Child Develpm.*, *6*, 110–119.

Marinesco, G., and A. Kreindler. 1933. Des réflexes conditionnels: I. L'organisation des réflexes conditionnels chez l'enfant. *J. psychol.*, Genève, *30*, 855–886.

Marinesco, G., O. Sager, and A. Kreindler. 1931. Hystéria et réflexes conditionnels. *Rev. neurol.*, *38*, 721–731.

Marquis, D. P. 1931. Can conditioned reflexes be established in the newborn? *J. Genet. Psychol.*, *39*, 479–492.

——. 1941. Learning in the neonate: the modification of behavior under the feeding schedules. *J. Exp. Psychol.*, *29*, 263–282.

Martin, J. R. 1940. Reminiscence and Gestalt theory. *Psychol. Monogr.*, *52*, No. 235.

Mast, E. T. 1937. Motivating factors in child learning. *Child Develpm.*, *8*, 273–278.

Mateer, F. 1918. *Child behavior.* Boston: Badger.

Matheson, E. 1931. A study of problem solving behavior in preschool children. *Child Develpm.*, *2*, 242–262.

Mattson, M. L. 1933. The relation between the complexity of the habit to be acquired and the form of the learning curve in young children. *Genet. Psychol. Monogr.*, *13*, 299–398.

McCaulley, S. 1928. A study of the relative values of the audito-vocal forward memory span and the reverse span as diagnostic tests. *Psychol. Clin.*, *16*, 277–291.

McElwee, E. W. 1933. Further standardization of the Ellis memory for objects test. *J. Appl. Psychol.*, *17*, 69–70.

McGeoch, G. O. 1931. The intelligence quotient as a factor in the whole-part problem. *J. Exp. Psychol.*, *14*, 333–358.

——. 1935a. The age factor in reminiscence: A comparative study of preschool children and college students. *J. Genet. Psychol.*, *47*, 98–120.

——. 1935b. The factor of degree of learning in reminiscence: A second comparative study of preschool children and college students. *J. Genet. Psychol.*, *46*, 455–462.

——. 1935c. The conditions of reminiscence. *Amer. J. Psychol.*, *47*, 65–89.

——. 1937. Reminiscence in maze learning by kindergarten children. *J. Genet. Psychol.*, *50*, 171–186.

McGeoch, J. A. 1925. Fidelity of report of normal and subnormal children. *Amer. J. Psychol.*, *36*, 434–445.

——. 1928. The influence of sex and age upon the ability to report. *Amer. J. Psychol.*, *40*, 458–466.

McGinnis, E. 1929. The acquisition and interference of motor-habits in young children. *Genet. Psychol. Monogr.*, *6*, 209–311.

McGinnis, J. M. 1928. A child's stylus maze. *Amer. J. Psychol.*, *40*, 313.

McGraw, M. B. 1935. *Growth: A study of Johnny and Jimmy.* New York: Appleton-Century.

——. 1942. Appraising test responses of infants and young children. *J. Psychol.*, *14*, 89–100.

Meek, L. H. 1925. A study of learning and retention in young children. *Teach. Coll. Contr. Educ.*, No. 164.

Melcher, R. T. 1934. Children's motor learning with and without vision. *Child. Develpm.*, *5*, 315–350.

Metraux, R. W. 1944. Auditory memory span for speech sounds: norms for children. *J. Speech Disorders*, *9*, 31–38.

Meumann, E. 1913. *The psychology of learning.* (Trans. by J. W. Baird.) New York: Appleton.

Miller, N. E. 1934. The perception of children: A genetic study employing the critical choice delayed reaction. *J. Genet. Psychol.*, *44*, 321–339.

Miller, N. E., and J. Dollard. 1941. *Social learning and imitation.* New Haven: Yale University Press.

Mirenva, A. N. 1935. Psychomotor education and the general development of preschool children: Experiments with twin controls. *J. Genet. Psychol.*, *46*, 433–454.

Mitrano, A. J. 1939. Principles of conditioning in human goal behavior. *Psychol. Monogr.*, *51*, No. 230. Pp. 74.

Monroe, W. S. 1928. How pupils solve problems in arithmetic. *Univ. Ill. Bull.*, *26*, No. 23.

Morgan, J. J. B. 1938. Treatment of enuresis by the conditioned reaction technique. *Psychol. Bull.*, *35*, 632–633.

Morgan, J. J. B., and S. S. Morgan. 1944. Infant learning as a developmental index. *J. Genet. Psychol.*, *65*, 281–289.

Morgan, J. J. B., and F. J. Witmer. 1939. The treatment of enuresis by the conditioned reaction technique. *J. Genet. Psychol.*, *55*, 59–65.

Moriya, M. 1937a. An observation of problem-solving behavior in preschool children: I. Application

of the principle of a lever. *Jap. J. Exp. Psychol.*, *4*, 63–81.

Moriya, M. 1937b. An observation on problem-solving behavior in preschool children: II. Application of the principle of a lever (continued). *Jap. J. Exp. Psychol.*, *4*, 147–160.

Morris, W. W. 1939. Story remembering among children. *J. Soc. Psychol.*, *10*, 489–502.

Morsh, J. E. 1930. The development of right-handed skill in the left-handed child. *Child Develpm.*, *1*, 311–324.

Moss, F. A. 1924. Note on building likes and dislikes in children. *J. Exp. Psychol.*, *7*, 475–478.

Mowrer, O. H., and W. M. Mowrer. 1938. Enuresis —a method for its study and treatment. *Amer. J. Orthopsychiat.*, *8*, 436–459.

Munn, A. F. 1909. The curve of learning. *Arch. Psychol.*, *N. Y.*, *2*, No. 12, pp. 36–52.

Munn, N. L. 1933. *An introduction to animal psychology.* Boston: Houghton Mifflin.

——. 1938. *Psychological development.* Boston: Houghton Mifflin.

——. 1942. The psychology of learning and its classroom application. *Peabody J. Educ.*, *19*, 257–265.

Munn, N. L., and B. R. Steining. 1931. The relative efficacy of form and background in a child's discrimination of visual patterns. *J. Genet. Psychol.*, *39*, 73–90.

Myers, G. C. 1913. A study in incidental memory. *Arch. Psychol.*, *N. Y.*, *26*.

Nanking Experimental Elementary School. 1935. An experimental study of the trends of memory change. *Kiangsu Elem. Sch. Teach.*, *2*, 936–971.

Nelson, V. L. 1936. An analytical study of child learning. *Child Develpm.*, *7*, 95–114.

Neumann, G. 1907. Experimentelle Beiträge zur Lehre von der Oekonomie und Technik des Lernens. *Z. exp. Päd.*, *4*, 63–101.

Nicolai, F. 1922. Experimentelle Untersuchungen über das Haften von Gesichtseindrücken und dessen zeitlichen Verlauf. *Arch ges. Psychol.*, *42*, 132–149.

Northway, M. L. 1936. The influence of age and social group on children's remembering. *Brit. J. Psychol.*, *27*, 11–29.

——. 1937. The nature of "difficulty"; with reference to a study of "whole-part" learning. *Brit. J. Psychol.*, *27*, 399–402.

Osipova, V. N. 1926. The speed of formation of association reflexes in children of school age. *Nov. refl. Fiziol. Nerv. Sist.*, *2*, 218–234. (See Razran, 1933.)

Pachauri, A. R. 1935a. A study of gestalt problems in completed and interrupted tasks: I. *Brit. J. Psychol.*, *25*, 365–381.

——. 1935b. A study of gestalt problems in completed and interrupted tasks: II. *Brit. J. Psychol.*, *25*, 447–457.

——. 1936. A study of gestalt problems in completed and interrupted tasks: III. *Brit. J. Psychol.*, *27*, 170–180.

Pavlov, I. P. 1889–1890. Innervation der Magendrüsen beim Hunde. *Centralbl. Physiol.*, *3*, 113–114.

Pavlov, I. P. 1903. Psychologie et psychopathologie animale expérimentelle. *C. R. Cong. int. Méd.*, Madrid.

Pechstein, L. A. 1926. The whole vs. part methods in learning. *Yearb. Nat. Soc. Coll. Teach. Educ.*, *15*, 181–186.

Pentschew, C. 1903. Untersuchungen zur Oekonomie und Technik des Lernens. *Arch. ges. Psychol.*, *1*, 417–526.

Perl, R. E. 1933. The effect of practice upon individual differences. *Arch. Psychol., N. Y.*, *24*, No. 159.

Peterson, G. M. 1932. An empirical study of the ability to generalize. *J. Gen. Psychol.*, *6*, 90–114.

Peterson, J. 1918. Experiments in rational learning. *Psychol. Rev.*, *25*, 443–467.

——. 1920. The backward elimination of errors in mental maze learning. *J. Exp. Psychol.*, *3*, 257–280.

——. 1926. Limits of learning by trial and error. *J. Exp. Psychol.*, *9*, 45–55.

——. 1933. Learning in children, pp. 417–481. In C. Murchison (Ed.), *A handbook of child psychology*. (2d ed., rev.) Worcester: Clark University Press.

Peterson, J., and P. V. Harrelson. 1923. Comparative abilities of white and negro children: Part III. *Comp. Psychol. Monogr.*, *1*, No. 5. Pp. 141.

Pintner, R., and D. G. Paterson. 1917. A comparison of deaf and hearing children in visual memory for digits. *J. Exp. Psychol.*, *2*, 76–88.

Pyle, W. H. 1920. *A manual for the mental and physical examination of school children.* (Revised edition.) Columbia, Mo.: University of Missouri.

Pyles, M. K. 1932. Verbalization as a factor in learning. *Child Develpm.*, *3*, 108–113.

Radossawljewitsch, P. 1907. Das Behalten und Vergessen bei Kindern und Erwachsenen nach experimentellen Untersuchungen. Leipzig: Nemnich.

Ray, J. J. 1936. The generalizing ability of dull, bright, and superior children. *Peabody Contr. Educ.*, No. 175.

Ray, W. S. 1932. A preliminary report on a study of fetal conditioning. *Child Develpm.*, *3*, 175–177.

Razran, G. H. S. 1933. Conditioned responses in children. *Arch. Psychol., N. Y.*, No. 148.

——. 1935. Conditioned responses: An experimental study and a theoretical analysis. *Arch. Psychol., N. Y.*, No. 191.

——. 1936. Attitudinal control of human conditioning. *J. Psychol.*, *2*, 327–337.

Renshaw, S. 1930. The errors of cutaneous localization and the effect of practice on the localizing movement in children and adults. *J. Genet. Psychol.*, *38*, 223–238.

Renshaw, S., R. J. Wherry, and J. C. Newlin. 1930. Cutaneous localization in congenitally blind versus seeing children and adults. *J. Genet. Psychol.*, *38*, 239–248.

Richardson, H. M. 1932. The growth of adaptive behavior in infants: An experimental study of seven age levels. *Genet. Psychol. Monogr.*, *12*, 195–359.

——. 1934. The adaptive behavior of infants in the utilization of the lever as a tool: A developmental

and experimental study. *J. Genet. Psychol.*, *44*, 352–377.

Riess, B. F. 1946. Genetic changes in semantic conditioning. *J. Exp. Psychol.*, *36*, 143–152.

Roberts, K. E. 1932. The ability of preschool children to solve problems in which a simple principle of relationship is kept constant. *J. Genet. Psychol.*, *40*, 118–135.

——. 1933. Learning in preschool and orphanage children: An experimental study of ability to solve different situations according to the same plan. *Univ. Iowa Stud. Child Welfare*, *7*, No. 3.

Rosenzweig, S., and G. Mason. 1934. An experimental study of memory in relation to repression. *Brit. J. Psychol.*, *24*, 247–265.

Ruch, F. L. 1934. The differentiative effects of age upon human learning. *J. Genet. Psychol.*, *11*, 261–286.

Ruch, G. M. 1925. The influence of the factor of intelligence on the form of the learning curve. *Psychol. Monogr.*, *34*, No. 160. Pp. 64.

Ruger, H. A. 1910. The psychology of efficiency. *Arch. Psychol., N. Y.*, *2*, No. 15. Pp. 88.

Sawa, H. 1937. A simple detour problem in infants. *Trans. Inst. Child. Stud.* (Japan), *17*, 139–160.

Sawden, E. W. 1927. Should children learn poems in wholes or in parts? *Forum Educ.*, *5*, 182–186.

Schmidt, H. O. 1941. The effects of praise and blame as incentives to learning. *Psychol. Monogr.*, *53*, No. 3, 56–352.

Seham, M. 1932. The "conditioned reflex" in relation to functional disorders in children. *Amer. J. Dis. Child.*, *43*, 163–186.

Shastin, N. R. 1938. The methodology of studying conditioned reflexes in children. *Fiziol. Zh. USSR*, *24*, 1055–1062. (*Psychol. Abst.*, 1939, No. 4067.)

Shaw, J. C. 1896. A test of memory in school children. *Ped. Sem.*, *4*, 61–78.

Shimidu, E. 1934. On the development of immediate memory and perception of children. *Trans. Inst. Child Stud.* (Japan), *16*, 723–740.

Skalet, M. 1931. The significance of delayed reactions in young children. *Comp. Psychol. Monogr.*, *7*. Pp. 82.

Skinner, B. F. 1938. *The Behavior of Organisms.* New York: D. Appleton-Century.

Sleight, W. 1911. Memory and formal training. *Brit. J. Psychol.*, *4*, 386–457.

Small, W. S. 1899. Notes on the psychic development of the young white rat. *Amer. J. Psychol.*, *11*, 80–100.

——. 1900. An experimental study of the mental processes of the rat: I. *Amer. J. Psychol.*, *11*, 135–165.

Smedley, F. 1902. *Rep. U. S. Comm. Educ.*, *1*, 1095–1115.

Smith, S. 1948. *The Psychological Origin and Treatment of Enuresis.* Washington: University of Washington.

Sobel, B. 1939. A study of the development of insight in pre-school children. *J. Genet. Psychol.*, *55*, 381–388.

Sontag, L. W., and R. F. Wallace. 1934. A study of fetal activity: Preliminary report of the Fels Fund. *Amer. J. Dis. Child.*, *48*, 1050–1057.

Spelt, D. K. 1938. Conditioned responses in the human fetus *in utero*. *Psychol. Bull.*, *35*, 712–713.

——. 1948. The conditioning of the human fetus *in utero*. *J. Exp. Psychol.*, *38*, 344.

Squire, C. 1912. Graded mental tests. *J. Educ. Psychol.*, *3*, 363–380.

Starr, A. S. 1923. The diagnostic value of the audito-vocal digit memory span. *Psychol. Clin.*, *15*, 61–84.

Steffens, L. 1900. Experimentelle Beiträge zur Lehre vom oekonomischen Lernen. *Z. Psychol.*, *22*, 321–382.

Stern, W. 1904. *Die Aussage als geistige Leistung und als Verhörsprodukt.* Leipzig: Barth.

Stevenson, P. R. 1925. Difficulties in problem solving. *J. Educ. Res.*, *11*, 95–103.

Stone, C. P. 1929–1930. The age factor in animal learning. *Genet. Psychol. Monogr.*, *5*, 1–130; *6*, 125–202.

Stone, G. R., and Lynn, J. O. 1951. Motor performance of children as a function of inverting their reported scores. *J. Genet. Psychol.*, *78*, 97–103.

Strayer, L. C. 1930. Language and growth: The relative efficacy of early and deferred vocabulary training, studied by the method of co-twin control. *Genet. Psychol. Monogr.*, *8*, 215–317.

Stroud, J. B. 1940. Experiments on learning in school situations. *Psychol. Bull.*, *37*, 777–807.

Stroud, J. B., and R. Maul. 1933. The influence of age upon learning and retention of poetry and nonsense syllables. *J. Genet. Psychol.*, *42*, 242–250.

Stump, N. F. 1927. A classroom experiment in logical learning. *J. Appl. Psychol.*, *11*, 117–125.

Stutsman, R. 1926. Performance tests for children of pre-school age. *Genet. Psychol. Monogr.*, *1*, 1–67.

Sullivan, E. B. 1924. *Attitude in relation to learning.* Unpublished thesis, Stanford University.

Swenson, E. J. 1942. Generalization and organization as factors in transfer and retroactive inhibition. *Proc. Ind. Acad. Sci.*, *51*, 248–255.

Swift, E. J. 1903. Studies in the psychology and physiology of learning. *Amer. J. Psychol.*, *14*, 201–251.

Tagawa, S. 1937. The imitation of the detour problem solved with the stick. *Trans. Inst. Child Stud.* (Japan), *17*, 121–137.

Terman, L. M., and M. Merrill. 1937. *Measuring intelligence.* Boston: Houghton Mifflin.

Thorndike, E. L. 1898. Animal intelligence. *Psychol. Rev. Monogr. Suppl.*, *2*, No. 8. Pp. 109.

——. 1924. Mental discipline in high school studies. *J. Educ. Psychol.*, *15*, 83–98.

Tiernan, J. J. 1938. The principle of closure in terms of recall and recognition. *Amer. J. Psychol.*, *51*, 97–108.

Tolman, E. C. 1932. *Purposive behavior in animals and men.* New York: Appleton.

Town, C. H. 1921. Analytic study of a group of five and six year old children. *Univ. Iowa Stud. Child Welfare*, *1*, No. 4. Pp. 87.

Vernon, M. D. 1951. Learning and understanding. *Quart. J. Exp. Psychol.*, *13*, 19–23.

Vertes, J. O. 1931. Behalten und Vergessen des Kindes. *Z. Psychol.*, *122*, 241–354.

Ward, L. B. 1937. Reminiscence and rote learning. *Psychol. Monogr.*, *49*, No. 220. Pp. 64.

Warren, A. B., and R. H. Brown. 1943. Conditioned operant response phenomena in children. *J. Gen. Psychol.*, *28*, 181–207.

Watson, J. B. and R. Rayner. 1920. Conditioned emotional reactions. *J. Exp. Psychol.*, *3*, 1–14.

Wees, W. R., and W. Line. 1937. The influence of the form of a presentation upon reproduction: The principle of determination. *Brit. J. Psychol.*, *28*, 167–189.

Weinstein, B. 1940. Problem-solving in monkeys and children: choice from sample. *Psychol. Bull.*, *37*, 581.

Welch, L. 1938. A preliminary study of the interaction of conflicting concepts of children between the ages of 3 and 5 years. *Psychol. Rec.*, *2*, 439–459.

——. 1939a. The development of the discrimination of form and area. *J. Psychol.*, *7*, 269–297.

——. 1939b. The development of size discrimination between the ages of 12 and 40 months. *J. Genet. Psychol.*, *55*, 243–268.

——. 1939c. The span of generalization below the two-year age level. *J. Genet. Psychol.*, *55*, 269–297.

——. 1940a. The genetic development of the associational structures of abstract thinking. *J. Genet. Psychol.*, *56*, 175–206.

——. 1940b. A preliminary investigation of some aspects of the hierarchical development of concepts. *J. Gen. Psychol.*, *22*, 359–378.

Welch, L., and L. Long. 1940a. The higher structural phases of concept formation in children. *J. Psychol.*, *9*, 59–95.

——. 1940b. A further investigation of the higher structural phases of concept formation. *J. Psychol.*, *10*, 211–220.

——. 1942. Methods used by children in solving inductive reasoning problems. *J. Psychol.*, *14*, 269–275.

Wenger, M. A. 1933. Path-selection behavior of young children in body-mazes. *J. Exp. Educ.*, *2*, 197–233.

——. 1936. An investigation of conditioned responses in human infants. *Univ. Iowa Stud. Child Welfare*, *12*, No. 1, pp. 7–90.

Wenger, M. A., and H. M. Williams. 1935. Experimental studies of learning in infants and preschool children. *Psychol. Bull.*, *32*, 276–305.

Werner, H. 1940. Perception of spatial relationships in mentally deficient children. *J. Genet. Psychol.*, *57*, 93–100.

Whipple, G. M. 1915. *Manual of mental and physical tests;* Vol. 2. Baltimore: Warwick and York.

Wickens, D. D., and C. Wickens. 1939. A study of conditioning in the neonate. *Psychol. Bull.*, *36*, 599.

Wickens, D. D., and C. Wickens. 1940. A study of conditioning in the neonate. *J. Exp. Psychol., 25,* 94–102.

Wieg, E. L. 1932. Bilateral transfer in the motor learning of young children and adults. *Child Develpm., 3,* 247–268.

Williams, O. 1926. A study of the phenomenon of reminiscence. *J. Exp. Psychol., 9,* 368–387.

Wilson, F. T. 1927. Learning of bright and dull children. *Teach. Coll. Contr. Educ.,* No. 292.

——. 1928. Learning curves of boys of IQ's 76–148. *J. Educ. Psychol., 19,* 50–57.

——. 1930a. A comparison of difficulty and accuracy in the learning of bright and dull children in a motor-memory task. *J. Educ. Psychol., 21,* 507–511.

——. 1930b. Factors of repetition and of directed and indirected attention in the learning of bright and dull children. *J. Genet. Psychol., 38,* 498–504.

——. 1931a. A comparison of difficulty and improvement in the learning of bright and dull children in reproducing a descriptive selection. *Genet. Psychol. Monogr., 9,* 395–435.

——. 1931b. Errors, difficulty, resourcefulness and the speed of learning of bright and dull children. *J. Educ. Psychol., 22,* 229–240.

——. 1931c. Difficulty in the learning of shorthand characters by bright and dull children. *J. Genet. Psychol., 39,* 113–122.

Wilson, F. T., and C. W. Fleming. 1937. Correlations of perception with other abilities and traits in grade I. *Child Develpm., 8,* 223–240.

Winch, W. H. 1904. Immediate memory in school children. *Brit. J. Psychol., 1,* 127–134.

——. 1908. The transfer of improvement in memory in school children. *Brit. J. Psychol., 2,* 284–293.

——. 1910. Transfer of improvement in memory in school children. *Brit. J. Psychol., 3,* 386–405.

——. 1911. Some relations between substance memory and productive imagination in school children. *Brit. J. Psychol., 4,* 95–125.

Winch, W. H. 1914. *Children's perceptions.* Baltimore: Warwick and York.

——. 1924. Should poems be learnt by schoolchildren as "wholes" or in "parts"? *Brit. J. Psychol., 15,* 64–79.

Wingfield, R. C. 1938. A study of alternation using children on a two-way maze. *J. Comp. Psychol., 25,* 439–443.

Woodrow, H. 1917. Practice and transference in normal and feeble-minded children. *J. Educ. Psychol., 8,* 85–96; 151–165.

Woodworth, R. S. 1938. *Experimental psychology.* New York: Holt.

Woody, C. 1936. An analysis of differences in the learning of bright and dull children. *Univ. Mich. Sch. Educ. Bull., 8,* 37–39.

Woolley, H. T. 1926. *An experimental study of children at work and in school between the ages of fourteen and eighteen years.* New York: Macmillan.

Wunderling, R. L. 1935. *Kind und Rätsel.* Frankfurt a. M.: Moritz, Diesterweg.

Yerkes, R. M. 1921. A new method of studying the ideational behavior of mentally defective and deranged as compared with normal individuals. *J. Comp. Psychol., 1,* 369–394.

Yoakum, G. A. 1921. The effect of a single reading. *Yearb. Nat. Soc. Stud. Educ., 20*(II). Chap. 6.

Yoshioka, J. G., and H. E. Jones. 1945. An analysis of children's maze learning in terms of stages of learning. *J. Genet. Psychol., 67,* 203–214.

Young, H. H. 1922. A slot maze. *Psychol. Clin., 14,* 73–82.

Young, M. 1928. A comparative study of audito-vocal digit spans. *Psychol. Clin., 17,* 170–182.

Zeigarnik, B. 1927. Über das Behalten von erledigten und unerledigten Handlungen. *Psychol. Forsch., 9,* 1–85.

CHAPTER 8

THE MEASUREMENT OF MENTAL GROWTH IN CHILDHOOD [1]

Florence L. Goodenough

Historical Orientation

Up to the beginning of the second decade of the present century, the topic of mental growth and its measurement occupied an almost negligible place in psychological literature. Just before the turn of the century, it is true, a number of attempts had been made to relate individual differences in the ability to perform simple motor and perceptual tasks to the differences in scholastic ability that have baffled educators since schools were first established. From the time of his student days in Wundt's laboratory, Cattell's attention had been captured by the idea that the study of differences among individuals in their responses to the same stimuli might be of even greater psychological importance than the study of the typical effect upon people in general of a measured physical change in the stimulus itself. After his return to America, Cattell was one of the most energetic leaders in the development of these early tests. The first scientific use of the term *mental test* is to be found in an article by him that appeared in *Mind* in 1890, in which he described a number of tests of sensorimotor capacities which he was then using with his students at the University of Pennsylvania. The interest

aroused by this article encouraged similar experimentation by a number of other leading psychologists, with the result that at the 1895 meeting of the American Psychological Association a committee, headed by Cattell, was appointed to consider the possibility of a cooperative effort to develop tests that would prove useful in gauging the probability of scholastic success among students entering college. A year later, Cattell and Farrand (1896) published a detailed account of the work of the committee in the form of a long series of tests which they planned to try out on Columbia freshmen. [2]

Although college students continued to make up the great body of subjects for these early experiments, tests for use with children were also devised. By far the most important of the investigations carried on during this period with children as subjects were those of Gilbert (1894, 1897). His studies are of special importance because of his attempt to validate his tests by comparison of the results with teachers' judgments of the ability of their pupils. Inasmuch as the tests used were made up of such items as physical measurements—height, weight, and lung capacity—speed of simple reaction, tonal memory, estimation of distance, sensitivity to pain, rate of tapping, and the like, the modern stu-

[1] Grateful acknowledgment is due the Clark University Press for permission to reproduce herein a number of short sections from the writer's previous chapter. "The Measurement of Mental Growth" in *A Handbook of Child Psychology* (Carl Murchison, Editor), Second Edition. Revised, Worcester, Massachusetts, Clark University Press, 1933.

[2] The results of the Columbia testing were later published by Wissler (1901). Correlations between college grades and standing on the various tests were consistently around zero.

dent will not be surprised to learn that, in spite of a fairly regular improvement with advancing chronological age in most of these functions, their relation to teachers' judgments of the ability of their students was negligible.

The interest aroused by the early tests was short-lived. It soon became evident that the results obtained by their use were of little or no practical value for the understanding and guidance of children. Although, because of Cattell's example, these measurements were commonly known as mental tests, they were evidently not measuring *intelligence,* either in the sense that the word is used by the layman or as it is understood by the psychologist of today. This was a disappointing discovery, which led to a general loss of interest in the problem and a virtual cessation of experimental work in testing in this country for almost a decade.

Meanwhile Binet, in France, had also become interested in the measurement of individual differences in mental ability. From the outset, however, his approach to the problem was radically different from that of most others of his time. Most of his experimental articles were published in the journal that he himself established in 1895, *L'Année psychologique.* A critical reading of these studies in their chronological sequence shows the steady trend of his interest away from the artificially simplified tasks of the formalized laboratory to the more complex and realistic problems encountered in life as it is lived. Over and over again he notes that differences between individuals become increasingly evident as one progresses from the relatively "simple" performances to those that are more complex, and that it is the latter rather than the former type of difference with which we are mainly concerned in everyday life. He admits that the simple mental functions or processes are easier to measure ob-

jectively, but insists that this is a secondary consideration, inasmuch as measurement degenerates into mere busy work unless the results are of some practical use. In this distinction between objectivity of measurement and the significance of the measures when made, Binet foreshadowed the discussions of *reliability* and *validity* that were to occupy so large a place in the literature on mental measurement a quarter of a century later.

Binet's first formalized scale for the measurement of intelligence was a direct outgrowth of his work as a member of the special commission appointed in 1904 by the Minister of Public Instruction in Paris for the purpose of devising means of selecting and segregating in special classes those children who were incapable of benefiting by the regular methods of instruction. This scale was published in collaboration with Simon in 1905. It consisted of 30 tests arranged roughly in order of difficulty. Age standards were not available at that time; as a matter of fact, although Binet, in his discussion of the scale, refers specifically to the desirability of comparing the performance of a child with that of others of his age, it seems improbable that the device of arranging tests in age groups for the purpose of ascertaining the mental age had as yet occurred to him. He does, however, indicate the levels of performance that divide the three classes of mental defectives—the idiots, the imbeciles, and the morons. Needless to say, the distinction as here used applies only to those who have attained their final level of development.

Crude as the 1905 scale was, it nevertheless proved to be sufficiently useful to encourage Binet and Simon in the feeling that they were on the right track. In 1908 they published a revision of the scale and in 1911 a second revision. The great feature of the two later scales lies in the fact that, instead of being arranged merely in order of difficulty, the items are grouped according to the age at which they are usually passed.[1] The selection of items was also improved by the elimination of a number that had proved unsuitable and the addition of others that were more discriminative. The tests for idiots were also omitted as unnecessary in a scale designed for public-school children. The 1911 scale, published just before Binet's death, included tests for the mental age range from 3 years to the adult level.

Both the 1908 and the 1911 Binet-Simon scales were translated into English by Goddard (1910, 1911), with only such minor changes as were necessary to make them suitable for use with American children. After trying them out both with feeble-minded children in the institution at

[1] Binet was not the first to whom the general concept of mental age occurred, nor was he the first to adopt the device of arranging tests in age groups. It is not unlikely that crude comparisons between the behavior of backward adults and that of children have been made by laymen at all times, just as today we often hear such expressions as "No more sense than a baby" or "Has to be looked after like a little child" even from people who have never heard of such a term as *mental age*. Reference to early medicolegal papers discloses a number of instances in which the same idea has been made more or less explicit. It is said that, as early as 1848 at the trial of one William Freeman, who was charged with the murder of four persons without provocation, a psychiatrist called as witness in the case stated that "in point of knowledge the accused was like a child of 3 years" (Hall, 1848).

In 1887 Doctor S. E. Chaille published a series of simple tests for children under 3 years of age. These tests are arranged in groups according to the age at which normal infants may be expected to succeed with them, in order, so the author points out, that parents and others who have to do with children may know whether or not a given child is developing as he should. Although Chaille does not use the term "mental age," it is clear from his discussion that this type of comparison was intended. However, Chaille's scale, which appeared in a medical journal of limited circulation at a date when few people were interested in the question of mental measurement, attracted little or no attention and was soon forgotten. It is Binet, therefore, to whom we are indebted for the development of the mental age concept as a practicable means of expressing test results in a roughly quantitative form.

Vineland, New Jersey, and in the near-by public schools, Goddard became thoroughly convinced of the superiority of the new tests over all other methods of assaying the intelligence of children that had been tried up to that date. His many books and papers dealing with this topic were read with great interest by psychologists and educators throughout the country.

The extraordinary rapidity with which Binet testing was taken up in America can be traced to a number of conditions. Most important is the fact that the tests appeared at an opportune moment. In many states the period of compulsory school attendance was being extended, and compulsory attendance laws were being more strictly enforced. The immediate result was that large numbers of backward children who would formerly have dropped quietly out of school and been forgotten were being herded into the primary grades at small profit to themselves and at the cost of much wasted energy on the part of teachers. Ayres's *Laggards in Our Schools*, which appeared in 1909, did a great deal to arouse public interest in the matter of school retardation, and to point the need for more adequate methods of dealing with the problems involved.

Scientific interest in questions of juvenile delinquency also became active at about this period. The first juvenile court was established in 1910. Inasmuch as the question of individual responsibility for delinquent behavior has been a predominating feature of the public attitude for generations, it was but natural that the idea of utilizing the new instrument as a means of securing more valid information on the mental level of delinquent children should have arisen almost as soon as the tests were introduced into this country. The fact (afterward learned) that the Binet tests as revised by Goddard were incorrectly standardized at the older ages, with the result that the mental ages obtained for adolescents who make up 'the great mass of juvenile delinquents were far too low, gave rise to astounding findings. Pintner (1931) has summarized the results of a number of the most striking of these early studies in which the proportion of "feeble-minded" among institutionalized delinquents is said to be as high as 50 to 90 per cent.[1] It was but natural to conclude that if the problems of mental deficiency could be solved the amount of juvenile delinquency would be greatly reduced.

Consideration of the cost of mental defect in terms of delinquency and of the special educational problems it presents led immediately to questions of causation and prevention. The rediscovery of the early work of Mendel by DeVries, in 1900, had by this time attracted the attention of a number of psychologists, among whom was Goddard. With characteristic energy, Goddard at once set about tracing the family histories of feeble-minded children in the Vineland institution in order to see if there might be evidence for the hypothesis that feeble-mindedness not only tends to "run in families" but is inherited according to strictly Mendelian principles as a "unit character." His three books, *The Kallikak Family* (1912), *Feeble-Mindedness; Its Causes and Consequences* (1914), and *The Criminal Imbecile* (1915) com-

prised what was then regarded by many people as a convincing body of evidence that a large proportion of all cases of mental defect is the direct result of biological inheritance of a defective nervous structure. Although Goddard's investigations, carried on as they were at a time when the technical aspects of the biological study of human beings were but little considered, have been severely and justly criticized,[2] their effect upon psychological thinking and upon social provisions for the care and training of delinquent and defective groups has been profound.

Another factor that gave impetus to the testing movement was the rapid increase of organized agencies for social welfare. Up to about 1910, family social work was largely in the hands of untrained volunteer workers from the various churches. With the appearance on the scene of the professionally trained worker, the coordination of records from different organizations, and the need for a better means of separating the cases for whom there was reasonable hope of rehabilitation from those who were unlikely ever to be able to "manage themselves and their own affairs with ordinary prudence,"[3] the importance of mental testing for improving the efficiency of social welfare work became increasingly apparent.

Two additional social changes that stimulated interest in testing need be mentioned. The first of these was World War I, when the possibility of testing large groups of individuals at one time was clearly demonstrated. The cost of administering individual tests has always proved

---

1 Although modern studies show a much smaller percentage of very low-testing cases, the relative number of young delinquents whose IQ's fall below 70 is many times as great as that in the population at large. Both Glueck and Glueck (1934) who used the 1916 revision and Merrill (1947) who used the 1937 revision of the Stanford-Binet tests report that approximately one-eighth of their subjects did not exceed this level. Other investigators have obtained similar results. The high figures reported by the early investigators can be attributed only in part to errors in the standardization of the tests used by them. Moreover, with increased awareness of the problems of the feeble-minded on the part of schools and social agencies, a greater number of such cases are identified and sent to institutions for the mentally deficient rather than to reformatories.

2 In *The Kallikak Family*, the entire case rests upon the unverifiable story of a casual intimacy alleged to have occurred at the time of the Revolutionary War between a Continental soldier of good family and a "feeble-minded" girl encountered in a tavern.

3 This is Tredgold's criterion for separating the feeble-minded from the normal.

to be a major stumbling block in the way of their application to the rank and file of individuals. With the advent of group testing, mental measurement as an aid to educational administration was at once put on a firm basis.

Finally, the cause of mental testing was materially advanced by the rise of the mental hygiene movement with its modern emphasis upon the establishment of behavior clinics for children. The determination of the mental level as a first step in diagnosis and as a partial guide to the kind of treatment most likely to be helpful rapidly became a part of the standard practice in organizations of this kind.

Looking backward along the path over which we have come, it is apparent that the development of mental testing, like many other scientific procedures of modern times, was by no means a result of the abstract curiosity of the "pure" scientist. First and primarily, mental tests as we know them today are practical instruments, devised to meet some specific and immediate social need. Their use as research implements has in practically all instances been secondary in time as well as in importance; it is only within comparatively recent years that new tests have been devised with the needs of the research worker rather than those of the clinician or educator primarily in mind. It is not unlikely that if the opposite condition had prevailed, if the demand for a practical working instrument had been less insistent, leaving the early workers more time to perfect their instrument before its pattern had crystallized into a tradition, the course of the testing movement might have been very different. In the white heat of early enthusiasm, many scientific blunders were made for which we are still paying the price in terms of mistaken concepts and conflicting practices. Nevertheless, these very blunders, with the spectacu-

lar conclusions to which they led, in many instances served to arouse public interest and support for the tests in a way that might never have been accomplished by an instrument designed for the service of pure science. Whether or not our present knowledge of the course of mental growth would have been greater had we postponed our studies until better techniques of investigation had been devised is at least an open question. We might have been better prepared to make such studies, but we might also have been less strongly urged to do so!

Be that as it may, it is of the utmost importance that students of mental growth continually bear in mind the fact that even the best of our present instruments for measuring mental growth are still fallible, although they have been shown to work surprisingly well in the practical situations for which they were designed. Even as tools for scientific research, they become extremely valuable in the hands of those who understand the basic principles by which they were constructed and their consequent possibilities and limitations, but they are by no means foolproof. That false as well as true conclusions have resulted from their use can hardly be attributed to the tests or to the test-makers, but rather, in great part, to the fact that their apparent simplicity has led many poorly qualified persons to apply them to the solution of problems that neither the tests nor their users were well equipped to handle.

The Present Status of Mental Testing in America

Within the few decades that have elapsed since the publication in 1910 of Goddard's translation of Binet's 1908 scale, the literature on mental growth and its measurement has become so voluminous that a mere listing of titles requires an entire book. Hildreth's 1939 *Bibliography of Mental Tests and Rating Scales* covers 251 pages, exclusive of the indexes, and lists 4279 titles. Her 1945 *Supplement* brings the total that had appeared before October 1 of that year to 5294. Equally long listings have been assembled by South (1937) and by Wang (1940). These bibliographies, moreover, include for the most part only references to actual tests and scales. Had the theoretical and experimental literature dealing with these tests and with their evaluation been included, the number of titles would have been many times as great.

Through his work in the preparation of a series of selected bibliographies on tests and testing methods over a period of years, Buros became convinced that the spate of new tests appearing each year was so great that some method of selecting the wheat from the chaff had become well-nigh essential. He therefore decided that in place of his former series of unannotated bibliographies he would arrange to edit and publish a series of *Mental Measurement Yearbooks* in which each of the important tests that had appeared since the publication of the preceding *Yearbook* would be subjected to critical review and evaluation by at least two competent authorities. Three of these *Yearbooks* have now appeared (1938, 1940, and 1949 [1]).

It is obvious that nothing approaching an adequate covering of this enormous volume of literature can possibly be compressed into the number of pages in this chapter. All that will be attempted, therefore, is to direct the reader to some of the most useful sources for further reference. The remaining space will be devoted to a brief discussion of a few of the more crucial problems in the field of measurement.

[1] The original plan for an annual volume could not be carried out because of financial limitations and the interruption incident to the war.

The most competent account of the early history of testing is to be found in Peterson's *Early Conceptions and Tests of Intelligence* (1925). In spite of its early date, Pintner's little book *Intelligence Testing* (1931) is particularly well adapted to the use of beginning students because of its clear presentation of material and its orderly arrangement. The more recent textbook by Mursell (1947) is written at a somewhat more advanced level with a wider covering of the literature. Many of the statements, however, are inexact or ambiguously worded, and the soundness of some of the discussions is open to question. Freeman's *Theory and Practice of Psychological Testing* (1950) is mainly bibliographical. It lists and describes a tremendous number of tests of all types, many of which are little known or used. It is designed to provide the student who is beginning his course in testing with a guide to the material available for his use. Gulliksen's *Theory of Mental Tests* (1950) deals chiefly with the mathematical theories and procedures underlying test construction with particular emphasis upon the determination of test reliability and validity and the importance of these factors for the interpretation and use of test results. Some knowledge of algebra, analytic geometry, and statistical method is presupposed. Goodenough's *Mental Testing; Its History, Principles, and Applications* (1949) is somewhat broader in scope than either of the two last mentioned, dealing, as it does, with each of the three aspects of the topic indicated by the subtitle. Kent's *Mental Tests in Clinics for Children* (1950) draws its material chiefly from her own long and rich experience in clinical work. It provides a refreshing first-hand view of the behavior of children in the test situation together with many practical suggestions as to methods of observation and record taking.

Annual reviews of the current literature in the field of intelligence testing by F. N. Freeman appeared in the *Psychological Bulletin* during the period extending from 1911 to 1920. The series was resumed by R. Pintner in 1926 and continued through 1935. Annual or semi-annual reviews with annotated bibliographies have appeared in the *Review of Educational Research* from 1932 to the present time.

From the beginning, mental testing has found one of its most important fields of usefulness in the public schools. Several books dealing with the application of test results to educational problems have appeared from time to time. Terman's *Intelligence of School Children* (1919) was one of the earliest. Later treatments of the same topic are to be found in Kelley's *Interpretation of Educational Measurements* (1927), Hildreth's *Psychological Service for School Problems* (1930), *Testing and the Use of Test Results* by Lincoln and Workman (1935), and *Measurement in Today's Schools* (revised edition, 1947) by Ross, as well as in a large number of monographs and periodical articles. Most college textbooks in elementary psychology also include one or more chapters on testing and the use of test results.

This tremendous volume of literature bears witness to the important place now occupied by mental testing in American psychology. As an aid to the objective study of human development and its aberrations and for the analysis and measurement of individual differences and their adaptation to the requirements of a complex social organization, the value of the mental test is well recognized. Not only in the practical guidance of individuals but also as a tool for fundamental research has the mental test amply proved its worth. It is doubtful whether any other psychological instrument is so widely used at the present time, for, regardless of the particular topic

under investigation, unless the mental level of the subjects is known the findings may be hard to interpret. Reports of mental test results are therefore looked upon as a well-nigh indispensable feature of most experimental studies in the field of child psychology.

The Nature and Organization of Intelligence

Because the early use of intelligence tests was largely confined to the diagnosis of mental deficiency, little attention was at first paid to the question of what "intelligence" really is. Up to the middle of the second decade of the present century, attempts at definition were chiefly concerned with descriptions of individuals who were lacking in intelligence. As a result, we had many definitions of mental deficiency couched in terms of what the mentally defective person is like, but few attempts at defining or describing the trait in which he was alleged to be deficient. Although Spearman had formulated his "two-factor theory" of intelligence as early as 1904, it was not until much later, when, as a result of the extension of mental testing techniques to all levels of ability, the question of what the mental testers were actually trying to measure was brought clearly to the fore, that this theory became the matter of spirited controversy that it is today.

In 1921 a number of leading psychologists were asked to express their views on the nature of intelligence, and their replies were published (*Symposium*, 1921). Although at first reading the points of view seem rather diverse, a little consideration shows that in reality the differences are less important than they seem. Some emphasized the ability to profit by experience; others, the ability to adjust to new situations. But since the crucial test of the extent to which an individual has profited by his experience is to be found in his ability to employ the knowledge thus gained in new situations, the two concepts reduce themselves to much the same thing in the end. Thorndike's practical suggestion that intelligence consists in the ability of the individual "to make good responses from the standpoint of truth or fact" is certainly in accordance with everyday practice, both in the judgment of intelligence . from behavior and in the scoring of intelligence tests. However, it does not offer any clue to the types of behavior that make most demand upon intelligence. This, of course, is in line with Thorndike's general point of view that intelligence is not a unitary trait. Terman, on the other hand, makes the distinction very explicitly. According to Terman, "an individual is intelligent in proportion as he is able to carry on abstract thinking." Although some have regarded this definition as too academic, giving too little weight to the more practical and concrete aspects of behavior, nevertheless, as was shown in the early sections of this chapter, most investigators have found so low a correlation between the ability to respond to simple, concrete situations and the ability to handle abstractions, symbols, and relationships, as emphasized by Terman, that it seems doubtful whether anything but confusion can result from the attempt to embrace both within a single measure.

The above principle has been clearly recognized in selecting the material for inclusion in tests of intelligence designed for adults and older children. It is very probable that the low correlation universally found between the results of tests given at the early ages and those of tests of the same individuals at later ages is in large part due to the fact that the tests for infants and young children are so largely made up of simple motor and perceptual items that the type of ability measured by

them may be very different from that measured later on by tests that conform more closely to Terman's definition. The latter tests, as, for example, following complicated directions, solving mathematical problems, or drawing analogies, show a fair amount of intercorrelation with each other. In contrast, even among young children the interrelationships of the abilities measured by such concrete motor performances as maze learning, ring tossing, and completing form boards are not high. Apparently, motor performances such as these are at all ages relatively specific, which means in effect that a test sample that includes only a few of them can by no means be regarded as a reliable indication of "general" ability. If the correlation of one measure with another is sufficiently high, only one of these need be used, since performance on the second can then be predicted from the score on the first with considerable accuracy. It is because the more abstract types of tests do show this characteristic of interlinkage, one with another, over a wide area of differential content that it has been found practically feasible to secure a reasonably dependable estimate of the general ability [1] of any individual by the use of a relatively small number of tests that require not over an hour's time for their completion.

Modern students of the nature of intelligence and of the organization of mental traits tend to lean much more heavily upon mathematical analysis for the verification of theories than did their forerunners. We are moving rapidly from the descriptive

[1] Needless to say, the term *ability*, as here used, has reference only to the area covered by the tests. A measure of *abstract thinking* will not predict standing on a specific type of motor performance any more effectively than the latter will predict the former. The advantage of the *abstract* test is that the mental area for which it affords a useful means of prediction is wide, whereas motor tests, generally speaking, have little or no predictive value for any functions outside the narrow limits of each particular item.

to the quantitative level, not only with respect to our attempts to assay individual differences in general ability but also, through mathematical examination of the interrelationships between various types of ability, with respect to our attempts to gain a more precise knowledge of the nature of mental organization. Space does not permit me to do more than touch upon the large body of experimental work centering about this problem. For a more complete account of the investigations and the conclusions that have emerged therefrom the interested reader should consult the brilliant review of the entire field by Thomson (1939). Here it must suffice to say that four somewhat different hypotheses as to the nature of mental organization have emerged from these studies. At one extreme we have the view expressed by Thorndike, which, briefly stated, is that each mental act is a separate element, to some extent independent of all others but also having features in common with many others. Certain acts have so many of their elements in common that we find it convenient to classify them into separate groups to which class names are applied, such as arithmetical reasoning or completing omitted portions of sentences.

Provided certain basic conditions of measurement are fulfilled, intelligence, according to Thorndike, is a simple aggregate of all the abilities underlying each of these separate acts. Symbolically, it may be regarded as a surface of which the height or *altitude* represents the difficulty of the acts that the individual is able to perform within a certain one of these closely related areas, such as completing analogies, while the *breadth* represents the range or number of tasks that can be solved at any given level of difficulty. According to Thorndike, correlation between performance on different mental tasks is not to be explained in terms of any generalized quality of "mind" but is purely a function of the number of common elements involved in their solution. This leads of necessity to the rejection of the whole concept of *general intelligence* and the substitution therefor of *specific intelligences*, the number of which is purely an arbitrary matter, depending upon how fine a classification is needed in any particular instance. He suggests that for many crude purposes a three-way classification under the headings of *abstract intelligence*, or the ability to deal with words and other symbols, *mechanical intelligence*, or the ability to deal with concrete objects and materials, and *social intelligence*, or the ability to deal effectively with people, will be found sufficient. Most of our modern tests of intelligence are based almost entirely upon the first, neglecting the other two. Thorndike regards this as a good thing as far as it goes, which is to say that he feels that only confusion would arise from mixing them. Better tests for the other forms of intelligence, rather than a combination of all three, are needed. He also points out that each of these may be divided almost indefinitely. This is illustrated in the case of abstract intelligence by his famous CAVD test (1926) in which each letter stands for a particular kind of performance.[1] These four tests, needless to say, are not to be thought of as covering the whole area of abstract intelligence; they represent only certain segments of it. However, because of the fairly high intercorrelation of all measures within this area, the remaining portions can be estimated from scores on the measured portion with a degree of accuracy that is sufficient for many purposes.

The other two types of ability may be subdivided in a similar manner. Social ability unquestionably varies with the age, sex, social status, intelligence, and so on,

[1] Sentence completion, arithmetic reasoning, vocabulary, following directions.

of the persons to be dealt with. Some people are very effective in handling children but are awkward and constrained in the company of adults; some get on well with their own sex but not with the opposite sex; some appear to be "born leaders,"[1] others are happiest and most effective when someone else assumes the leading rôle. The limit of divisibility is reached only when the separate act can no longer be subdivided without losing its identity.

Moving upward in the organizational scale from Thorndike's view that the system of organization is external, inherent in the task rather than in the individual we come to the theory of orthogonal traits proposed by Kelley (1928, 1935).[2] By means of a statistical analysis of the intercorrelations between performances on many different kinds of tests, Kelley arrived at the conclusion that all the varying abilities of an individual can be accounted for on the basis of a relatively small number of independent traits or separate abilities that are completely unrelated to each other. In everyday life, as in test performance, a given act usually calls for the simultaneous exercise of more than one of these abilities, and in varying degree. It is because of the almost infinitely great number of combinations and permutations thus made possible that mental abilities appear to be so diverse, inasmuch as it is only by mathematical analysis that a given ability can be "purified" and known for what it is. Nevertheless, the principle, if true, is not devoid of its practical applications, for, if

we once knew what these abilities are and, furthermore, if we were able to ascertain the kind of measurable acts in which a given ability exercises the dominant rôle, we should be able to develop a series of tests that would be more nearly exact measures of these separate functions even though they might not be completely freed from intermixture.

Thurstone (1938), whose theories rank next in our organizational scheme, has attempted to do that very thing. Like Kelley, Thurstone (1935, 1947) developed his theory of mental organization by means of a factorial analysis of tables of intercorrelation. His mathematical approach, is however, somewhat different, and, although, like Kelley, he emerges with a theory of separate and independent mental traits, he differs from Kelley in that he considers these traits to be ranked in order of generality and, hence, we may say, in terms of their importance in individual mental life. Mathematically speaking, these traits, or *factors*, as the mathematicians prefer to call them, are indeterminate, by which is meant that there is nothing in the nature of the analysis itself that tells what a given factor is like. They are simply Factor I (the most nearly general), Factor II, and so on. But it is possible to determine mathematically the part played by any single factor in determining the intercorrelations between tests. By comparing the subject matter of tests in which these *factor loadings* are markedly different, as, for example, tests that have a high loading for Factor I but a low loading for Factor II with those weighted in the opposite direction, hypotheses that are at least in accordance with common sense as to the probable nature of these factors may be drawn up[3] and the factors may then be named in everyday language.

[1] This statement must, of course, not be taken literally. There is evidence that social abilities are at least in part the result of individual experience and training. The extent to which inborn characteristics may also be involved is unknown, though it is probable that they play some part in the matter. The expression is used here in the popular rather than the scientific sense.

[2] Kelley's method is a modification of that proposed by Hotelling (1933). The results obtained are identical but the procedures differ.

[3] The particular set of weights comprising the "factor pattern" for any given series of intercorre-

In the attempt to develop tests that are more nearly "pure" measures of these factors, or *primary mental abilities*, as Thurstone has named them, the procedure followed is essentially a cut-and-try matter in which the guiding principle is finding tasks that differ as much as possible from all those in which the loading for the factor in question is low, and most of all from those in which it is lowest, and which at the same time resemble most strongly those for which this loading is high. By repeating this process a sufficiently large number of times it should be possible, at least on theoretical grounds, to come out eventually with a series of tests by which all the abilities of an individual may be measured with a minimum of wasted time and effort. Within a somewhat less ambitious range,[1] this is what Thurstone has attempted to do in his Primary Abilities Test (1938). By means of a procedure essentially similar to that just described he arrives at the conclusion that individual differences in human mental abilities can be measured and described in terms of only twelve basic abilities, each of which may be possessed

lations is not, however, arrived at by any simple or unequivocal method. In order to obtain such a pattern, axes must be rotated until the resulting factorial structure is reduced to the simplest possible terms. Students of factor analysis are not in complete agreement as to the criterion to be used in determining when "simple structure" has been attained. Thurstone, whose methods are more widely used than those of any other authority, states on p. 181 of his *Multiple Factor Analysis* (1947) that, "If each test vector is in one or more of the coordinate planes, then the combination of the configuration and the coordinate axes is called a *simple structure*. The corresponding factor pattern will then have one or more zero entries in each row." For an account of the basic theory underlying this hypothesis, the reader should consult the original source.

1 Thurstone's primary abilities are not presumed to cover the complete range of human talent. They do not, for example, cover such specialized abilities as musical or artistic talent or motor skills. They involve only the abstract abilities needed for success in the conventional types of intelligence tests and in the academic pursuits of the classroom.

in varying degrees. Seven of these are tentatively named as follows: S = spatial abilities, P = perceptual abilities, N = numerical abilities, V = verbal relations, M = memory, W = words (that is, single unrelated words), and I = induction. With less certainty two others are named as follows: R = reasoning and D = deduction. For the remaining three he is not yet ready to propose names. Thurstone has also developed a battery of tests by which each of the first seven abilities may be measured separately. These tests were originally designed for use with college students and students in senior high schools. Later the procedure was extended downward to the 14-year age level (Thurstone and Thurstone, 1941) and finally to the ages of 5 and 6 years (Thurstone and Thurstone, 1946). Only five abilities were identified at these early ages: verbal, quantitative, perceptual, motor, and spatial. By means of the new series it is possible to draw up a mental profile for each child which will show his comparative proficiency along the following lines: verbal comprehension, word fluency, spatial relations, numerical ability, memorizing, and reasoning. Thurstone states that of these the reasoning or induction factor is most closely associated with the other aspects of ability (that is, is the most nearly general), whereas memorizing is the most nearly independent of the six factors studied.

Spearman, in a series of brilliant books and essays dating from 1904, expounded a theory that calls for an even higher degree of mental organization than that proposed by Thurstone. According to Spearman, all mental activity demands the exercise of a special attribute that he terms *mental energy* because in the realm of mind its place is analogous to that of physical energy in the world of physics. This attribute of mind he designates by the symbol g, or *general* factor, since it is possessed by all individuals, though in varying degree, and enters into all mental activity, though to a varying extent. Because all are to some extent dependent upon g, all measurable forms of truly intelligent behavior, as, for example, the ability to solve arithmetic problems, to complete analogies, to perceive relationships among geometrical forms, or to understand long and complicated sentences, show some degree of correlation with each other. However, individual differences in ability are not wholly traceable to differences in the amount of g. They are also dependent upon other factors, known as s factors, that are more or less specific to particular activities or situations, whereas g is common to all. Some activities involve the g factor to only a slight extent, being chiefly made up of s factors, and these will commonly show only low correlations with other mental acts. Others, in which the g factor is paramount, will intercorrelate highly with one another. Because this theory was the first to be proposed that was based upon mathematical demonstration (although in fairness it must be pointed out that there is not complete agreement among statisticians as to the interpretation of the results), it has attracted much attention and has stimulated a large number of important investigations. Indeed, it was largely the attempt to test Spearman's conclusions that led to the formulation of the three other hypotheses as to the organization of mind that have been described in the preceding pages.

In addition to the g factor, which is primarily intellectual in nature, since, according to Spearman, it involves mainly the "apprehension of one's own experience, the eduction of relations and the eduction of correlates," Spearman has obtained evidence of the existence of other general factors, some of which, as w (volition), appear to be related to what is commonly known as *personality*. Intermediate between these general factors that play a part in all mental activity and the decidedly specific s factors are others of less complete generality but nevertheless common to a rather wide range of mental acts. To these Spearman has given the name *group factors*. He suggests that musical ability and mechanical ability are of this type.

Inasmuch as all these variant hypotheses as to the nature of mental organization have been arrived at by means of different statistical methods applied to the analysis of tables of intercorrelations, it becomes pertinent to ask whether any one of them is more than an artifact of the method employed. This point has been ably discussed in a monograph by Thomson (1939), with which all who are interested in factor theory should be familiar. Because Thomson's treatment of the subject cannot be condensed into a few lines without danger of distortion, no attempt will be made to summarize his conclusions in this chapter. The interested reader should consult the original source.[1]

The Quantification of Intellectual Performance

For some years after the appearance of Goddard's translations of Binet's 1908 and 1911 scales the only way of expressing the amount of acceleration or retardation of an individual child was to state the difference between his actual or chronological age and his mental age. A child was said to "test" so many years "above age" or "below age." But, since the significance of a given number of years' acceleration

[1] For an able discussion of the use of factor analysis in the construction of a scale designed to measure "general intelligence," together with the detailed results obtained from a factorial analysis of the findings for the 1937 revision of the Stanford-Binet, the reader should consult Chapter 9 of McNemar's *Revision of the Stanford-Binet Scale* (1942).

or retardation varies with the age of the child, the use of the *intelligence quotient,* or IQ, first proposed by Stern and popularized by Terman in the Stanford revision of the Binet tests (1916), gained rapidly in popularity. The intelligence quotient, which is the ratio between the mental age and the chronological age, was at first assumed to have a constant meaning regardless of the age of the child. For this reason it was often spoken of as an *absolute* measure of intelligence. More recent work, however, has shown that this is not always the case. Unless certain constant relationships are maintained between the dispersion of test scores at each age and the averages or *norms* for the successive ages, the IQ cannot remain constant either for individuals or for groups. This point has been discussed by a number of different persons, and especially by Freeman (1930). For example, if the curve of mental growth from age to age is assumed to be a straight line, as is done when the tests are arranged in the form of a *year scale* with an equal number of tasks at each age, then the dispersion of mental ages must increase from age to age in a ratio that is proportionate to age. If at the age of 6 the standard deviation of mental ages is 12 months, then at the age of 9 it should be 18 months, at the age of 12 it should be 24 months, and so on. If this condition is not met, then an IQ of 120 earned at the age of 6 will not be comparable in meaning to one of the same apparent value earned at some other age. This is another way of saying that an IQ can have the same meaning at all ages only if its variability is the same at all ages.[1] The amount of error introduced by failure

to conform to this rule increases with the extent of the deviation of a given score from the mean of the group. For example, Terman and Merrill (1937, p. 40) report the standard deviation of the IQ's obtained for Form L of the 1937 revision as 20.6 IQ points at age 2½, 12.5 at age 6, and 20.0 at age 12. For children whose IQ's differ from a constant mean of 100 by only a small amount,[2] say half a standard deviation, the errors introduced by the differences in IQ variability are small. Comparable figures at the three ages specified are 110, 106, and 110. But for those who greatly surpass or fall below the mean, the differences become appreciable. At +3.00 S.D. the 2-year-old would have an IQ of 162, the 12-year-old would rank at 160, and the child of 6 whose actual degree of superiority is identical with that of the other two would apparently rank much lower with an obtained IQ of only 137.5.[3] At −1.5 S.D., an IQ of 81 at age 6 has the same meaning as an IQ of 69 at the ages of 2 or 12 years. Differences in the intercorrelations and in the scattering of success on the items allocated to the several age groups afford the most probable explanation for the difference in variability.

The placement of the items in a year scale such as the Stanford-Binet is by no means a simple matter. The unsophisticated person may think that each item should be placed in the year group at which it is passed by approximately 50 per cent of the cases, but this would be true only if the intercorrelations of all the items at a given age were unity or (what amounts to the same thing) if there were but a single test item for each age. When there are

---

[1] Inasmuch as the IQ is the ratio between the mental and chronological ages, it follows that, if the denominator of the fraction (the CA) is changed, the numerator (the MA) must undergo a proportionate change if the value of the fraction is to remain unaltered.

[2] The means reported by Terman and Merrill also show small differences from age to age, but as the changes do not appear to follow a constant trend they can best be ascribed to irregularities of sampling.

[3] A table of corrective values for the IQ's obtained on this test has been incorporated by McNemar (1942) in his monograph on the standardization of the 1937 revision.

several items at each age level all of which must be passed in order to earn credit for the year and when, furthermore, the problem is complicated by the scattering of successes and failures over several age levels, the allocation of items in age groups becomes an extremely difficult problem, so much so that most constructors of tests who have followed the year-scale method have contented themselves with a cut-and-try procedure, in which items are shifted about from one age placement to another [1] until a satisfactory adjustment has been attained. In a brief but cogent article, Jaspen (1944) points out the issues involved and urges that test makers ascertain and utilize the statistical facts as a guide to the placement of items.

Examination of the available data for other tests indicates that there are relatively few for which the statistical requirements of the IQ technique have been adequately met. The uncritical use of this method for any and all tests for which age standards have been derived has been a regrettably common practice in the past but should certainly be discontinued.

An early study by Kuhlmann (1921), which was based upon a large number of retests of feeble-minded persons by means of his revision of the Binet scale, has been much quoted. In this study it was shown that the IQ's obtained for feeble-minded persons in institutions did not, as was then supposed, maintain a constant level from year to year either for individuals or for the average of the (feeble-minded) group.

Instead, they tended to become lower with advancing age. This study was utilized by Heinis (1926) as a means of verifying his "law of mental development" first proposed in 1924. Heinis, at that time, had been greatly impressed by a series of tests developed by Vermeylen (1922), who had given the series to 10 children at each of the ages from 6 to 12 years. On the basis of Vermeylen's data together with the results obtained by Descoeudres (1921) for children of preschool age and certain unpublished figures of his own, Heinis worked out a curve of mental growth [2] that was presumably calibrated in equal units comparable to the feet and inches on a scale of linear distance. This curve showed marked negative acceleration with rapid growth at the early ages and comparatively small increments at the later ages. The standard deviations of the score distributions also decreased with age. From this curve Heinis derived a measure which he called the "personal constant" or, alternatively, the "personal coefficient" [3] (PC), for which he offers the following definition:

"The personal coefficient of any given individual is equal to the result of the intelligence examination divided by the normal degree of intelligence corresponding to his age, both measures being given in absolute graduation."

The values of the PC bear a superficial resemblance to the IQ but are not directly comparable with it because of the smaller variability, especially at the older ages. Heinis believed that the decreasing IQ's of Kuhlmann's feeble-minded subjects were a necessary consequence of the method of deriving the IQ, and that the IQ's of superior children would show a corresponding tendency to increase with age. He believed that

---

[1] Binet himself observed that the allocation of items to the age at which 50 per cent of the subjects succeed with them results in too low a mental age value. By empirical trial he found that the requirement of 70 per cent passing results on the average in mental ages approximately equal to the chronological ages. This, of course, merely indicates the typical intercorrelation between test items, a factor that varies greatly from one item to another, rendering the adoption of any such general rule hazardous in the extreme.

[2] The formula for this curve will be found on p. 478.

[3] Kuhlmann, Hilden, and others have preferred the term "per cent of average" (P. Av.) as being more explicit.

the PC would yield more nearly constant results. When the new method was applied to Kuhlmann's data, this prediction appeared to be verified. Although Heinis considered this to be sufficient proof of the superiority of the PC over the IQ, not all who have tried the method have obtained equally favorable results. For example, Psyche Cattell (1933) found that the PC was more consistent than the IQ when used with feeble-minded or backward children but that the IQ was more uniform in the case of superior children. Kuhlmann, however, expressed himself as being definitely in favor of the method and made use of it in the final revision of his scale for individual mental examination (1939) published shortly before his death. The PC was also used for expressing the results of some of the earlier editions of the Kuhlmann-Anderson group test, but in the latest edition the IQ derived from the median of the mental ages earned on the ten subtests of which the scale is made up is the measure recommended.

Much of the apparent inconsistency in the attempts that have been made to compare the IQ with the PC has arisen from failure to realize that the units employed in the two measures are not equal in numerical value. As a matter of fact, examination of the tables for converting mental ages or IQ's into PC units prepared by Heinis (1926) or the more convenient arrangement by Hilden (1933) shows clearly that, particularly for ages above those of the primary grades, a given numerical change in the PC is of far greater significance than a similar numerical change in the IQ and that the greater apparent "constancy" of the former has been attained at the cost of lowered discriminative value. McNemar (1942) has given an excellent discussion of this and other factors connected with the Heinis coefficient with particular reference to Kuhlmann's reasons for preferring it.[1]

During the 1940's the *percentile method* of interpreting test scores became increasingly popular. The percentile score, or, as it is often called, the *percentile rank*, is expressed in terms of the percentage of a specified group, usually of the same age, whom the child in question surpasses. The fact that any group may be used for comparison gives the percentile method a degree both of flexibility and of specificity that the methods previously described lack. A mental age norm is always, supposedly, representative of children in general of the age in question. A little consideration, however, will show that it is rarely possible, in the actual standardization of a test, to secure the truly representative group that is implied by the term mental age. This difficulty has been recognized theoretically by practically all workers; nevertheless, the idea that the *mental age norms* which have been worked out in the course of the original standardization of a test have some kind of final or absolute value is implicit in most of the interpretations of results obtained for different groups by the use of various tests. Moreover, rarely are we actively concerned with a comparison between *individuals* in noncompeting groups. Ordinarily we compare college students with other college students, preferably of the same class. We are likely to be more interested in knowing how the 8-year-old daughter of a college professor compares with the 8-year-old offspring of other college professors or with the other children in her class at school than in knowing how she compares with the 8-year-olds in a backward mountain community or with

---

[1] The coefficient of intelligence (CI) proposed by Yerkes and Foster in 1923 is identical with the PC in method of derivation except for the important fact that the scale values were not calibrated in equal units. Like the PC, the CI was obtained by dividing the child's score by the average score of his age group.

the 8-year-old Negroes on a Louisiana plantation. Comparisons between contrasted *groups* of this kind are often interesting, but for this purpose other methods of quantifying test results are more suitable than the quotient methods so often used.

The percentile method has other very obvious advantages. It is easily understood even by the uninformed and is therefore particularly useful in explaining test results to parents, teachers, physicians, and others who may be interested. Since comparisons are made only between individuals of the same chronological age, the implications resulting from assigning equal basic scores to individuals of very different levels of physical maturity and life experience are avoided. An imbecile of 15 with a mental age of 3 is a very different kind of human being from a normal child of 3 years even though he may happen to pass the same number of items on a certain mental test. Even his test score, although it may count up to the same number of items, will usually show decided qualitative differences in the particular items passed and the kind of responses that are made to them. Cunningham (1927) has shown that, even with so carefully standardized a test as the CAVD, differences between the performance of adult imbeciles and normal children between the ages of 2½ and 6 years on the separate items of the test are in some instances as great as 10 times the standard error. Merrill (1924) found decided differences in the performance of gifted, average, and subnormal children of the same mental age on the different items of the Stanford-Binet. The groups also differed considerably in the amount of *scatter* on this test, that is, in the range which it was necessary to cover in order to meet the usual conditions of complete testing. Both the gifted and the subnormal groups "scattered" decidedly more than the group of average ability. Aldrich and Doll (1931) matched normal children of 19 to 38 months with idiot boys of corresponding mental ages and compared their performances on the Gesell developmental items and on the Merrill-Palmer series of performance tests. The idiots were markedly inferior to the normal children on all tests involving language but were superior in the tests involving experience and the use of concrete materials.

Although, when properly used and interpreted, the method of percentile ranks is a simple and valuable device for reducing test scores to meaningful quantitative terms, it must not be forgotten that, unless the distribution of test scores takes the form of a rectangle instead of the usual normal curve, the distances between successive percentiles cannot be equal. Instead, their values will increase steadily toward each extreme. This is easily understood if it is remembered that the percentiles are computed on the basis of the percentage of cases making each successive score, that is, in terms of the areas of successive segments above the base line of the curve. If the distribution of scores approximates the usual bell-shaped form, equal areas will subtend longer and longer segments of the base line as the extremes of the distribution are approached. The difference in score value between the ninety-seventh and the ninety-eighth percentile will be far greater than that between the fifty-seventh and the fifty-eighth. Percentile ranks, therefore, while they are useful methods for expressing individual standing within a specified group, should never be used as media for further computation. They cannot, justifiably, be added or subtracted or averaged. Neither do they lend themselves to the conventional forms of graphic expression such as bar diagrams or histograms. They are interpretative measures only.

Another method of expressing the test standing of an individual is in terms of the number of standard deviations by which he falls below or surpasses the mean standing of his group. As in the case of percentiles, the group may be defined in any way desired. If age is taken as a basis for the definition, however, the range of ages used for determining the standard deviation should equal those used in defining the age of an individual child. That is, if the ages of the children are taken to the nearest month, then the standard deviations used in computing the scores should be calculated within the limits of dispersion shown by children whose ages vary only within a month's range. The point is a rather obvious one, and is mentioned only because it has frequently been disregarded when this method of expressing scores has been used.

The direct expression of test results in terms of untransformed standard deviation units has two practical disadvantages. Such scores involve the use of a decimal point, and they may be either negative or positive in sign. Both these factors make for errors in reading and recording. A device for overcoming this difficulty is rapidly gaining in popularity. It consists in setting the mean of every test or measure used at 50 and the standard deviation at 10. The score of each individual on any type of mental or physical measure thus becomes

$$\text{Converted score} = 50 + 10x$$

where x is the number of standard deviations (plus or minus) by which he deviates from the mean of his group.

Goodenough and Maurer (1942) have suggested a modification of this formula which is designed to make the numerical results correspond to the values which have already been made familiar through the use of the ordinary intelligence quotients. By a simple substitution of constants, the formula becomes

$$\text{Converted score} = 100 + 17.5x$$

This procedure has been used in the derivation of interpretative units for the Minnesota Preschool Scales. The values so obtained have been called IQ equivalents to distinguish them from IQ's obtained in the usual manner. It should be noted, however, that the significance of the two is the same, and the procedure itself is not subject to some of the criticisms often made of the intelligence quotient when calculated in the usual manner.[1]

The use of either percentiles or standard deviation scores (the latter are often called "sigma" scores) is based upon the implicit assumption that the items making up the tests are equally spaced for difficulty. But in few, if any, of the group tests in common use has this requirement been fulfilled. Generally speaking, all that has been done is to arrange the items in an approximate order of difficulty, and then count the number passed by each child. This procedure commonly yields very unequal steps, particularly at the extremes. The irregular overlapping resulting from the unequal spacing made it impossible that interpretative measures such as intelligence quotients or sigma scores calculated from these tests should have equivalent meanings at different levels, even within the limits of the same test. When different tests were used the discrepancies were likely to be even more glaring. A number of scaling procedures designed to overcome those irregularities have been worked out and applied both to the older tests first standardized on the basis of a simple item count and to newly devised tests. Thus far, scaling methods have been more generally applied to the educational tests for the measurement of accomplishment in the

---

[1] In the Army General Classification Test used in World War II a similar method of deriving interpretative scores was used but with the variability constant set at 20. The formula thus becomes:

$$\text{Converted AGCT score} = 100 + 20x$$

different school subjects than to intelligence tests, but work on the latter is well under way, and it is to be expected that in the future the question of scaling will be given much more attention in the construction of tests of all kinds than has been done in the past.

Among the tests in present use for which norms are given in terms of scale values, the Arthur Performance Scale (1930) and the Minnesota Preschool Tests (Goodenough, Maurer, and Van Wagenen, 1940) may be mentioned. The procedure used in deriving the scale values for the Arthur tests is the so-called discriminative value method (D.V.) proposed by Arthur and Woodrow (1919). In scaling the Minnesota tests the C-score method used in a number of educational tests was used. Thorndike's work on the CAVD tests has already been mentioned. This is one of the most thoroughgoing pieces of methodological work that has appeared, and it merits careful study. In the same volume, scaled values for a number of the leading intelligence tests originally standardized on an item count basis are also given.

Although the question of scaling is so fundamental a problem in all attempts at mental measurement, there is as yet no general agreement as to which of the various methods that have been employed will yield the most consistent results. Thurstone (1925, 1928a, 1928b), who has developed a method of scaling based on the overlapping of scores at successive age levels, is very critical of any method which takes account of variability only within a single age group. His method results in scale values which appear to yield an approximately linear relationship between age and variability, a condition which, as was pointed out in an earlier paragraph, is necessary if quotients are to have the same relative significance from one age to another. Although the true linearity of this relationship has been called into question by Holzinger (1928), the error appears to be much smaller than that which would result if scores derived from a single age group were used as the basis for scaling, as Holzinger recommends.

Since the values derived from the so-called absolute scaling methods will vary according to the method employed and the extent to which the empirical data correspond to the assumptions under which these methods have worked out, it is evident that at best the equality of spacing that these methods are presumed to yield is only approximate.[1] It is undoubtedly an improvement over the old item-count method, but much further work needs to be done before we can be certain how and to what extent the results are affected by variations in the conditions of testing and in the sampling of subjects upon whom the test was standardized. All methods of scaling derive their units from the proportion of children at each age who pass each test item. Although the matter has not been adequately tested, it seems highly improbable that scale values can maintain their equality of spacing except for groups that are reasonably similar to the one on which the values were derived. This point has been recognized to some extent. Thurstone (1928a, p. 178), for example, specifically states that "the social and intellectual factors of selection must operate more or less uniformly for the several age-groups" if the conditions requisite for his method of scaling are to be observed.

Thorndike (1926) has pointed out additional sources of error. The ordinary criterion of test difficulty is the relative frequency with which an item is passed. A test that is passed by few children at a given age is regarded as more difficult than one which the majority can answer. The frequency of passing, however, is deter-

[1] See the discussion of this point by McNemar (1942, Chapter XI).

mined not only by intrinsic difficulty but also by the extent to which the fact in question has become a matter of general knowledge, that is, the likelihood that all or most of the children will have had opportunity to become acquainted with it. The word "broccoli" is not intrinsically more difficult than the word "spinach" or "cabbage," but until the last few years at least it would unquestionably have been classed much higher in a vocabulary test. Whether or not the concepts of elementary algebra are intrinsically more difficult than the concepts of long division is uncertain, but because most schools teach long division before elementary algebra more children will succeed with division problems than with algebra problems. Probably more city children than country children of the same age will be able to give a correct answer to the question. "What must you do if you are going some place and miss the streetcar?" but if the question were, "What must you do if the cows break into the wheatfield?" the opposite tendency might be shown. Sherman and Key (1932) report that many of the mountain children whom they studied were unable to give their family name, identifying themselves simply as " 'Lizy's Tom" or "Moses' Joe." Giving the family name is a test for 3-year-olds in the 1916 Stanford revision of the Binet, but if the 3-year-olds upon whom this test was standardized had been asked to give their father's or their mother's first name, they might have been no more successful than the mountain children were in giving the family name. The difficulty of a task for any group is in part a matter of its familiarity or strangeness for that group. It follows that *scale values*, though they may be equally spaced for a particular group, are likely to be quite unequally spaced for another group of similar intelligence but different experience.

No matter what method of quantifying test results is used, the standards obtained cannot safely be applied to other groups unless it has been shown that they are reasonably similar to the standardization group in all matters that may be expected to affect the relative value of the scores. In order that such comparisons may be made, it is essential that the main characteristics of the group used in standardization be defined as exactly as possible. This means that some information about the home background of each child needs to be obtained. Although elaborate social case histories are usually out of the question and would be difficult to handle in any event, a few simple facts such as paternal occupation and residence (city, town, or rural) are easy to ascertain. If these were uniformly classified and reported as a part of the routine information concerning every test that is worked out, many of the discrepancies that result from the use of differently standardized tests could be explained and the suitability of a particular test for use with a given group of children could be more safely judged. The relationship between socio-economic status and mental test standing will be considered further in a later section.

Mental Growth Curves

A natural outgrowth of the attempts to calibrate mental tests in truly equal units is the plotting of the results thus obtained in the form of growth curves. Inasmuch as there is as yet no general agreement as to the method best suited for calibrating the items making up the tests, it is not surprising to find that even when the same procedure is used for plotting the growth curves the "form of the mental growth curve" derived from one test may be radically different from that derived from another test. Dissimilarity of test content, not only from one test to another but also at successive age levels within the same test, also confuses the picture. Dissimilarity of the sampling of subjects used, particularly when the selective factors resulting in a biased sampling have differed from one age level to another, is a further complicating factor.[1] And, finally, there is the fact that the statistical procedures used for plotting the growth curves have varied from one investigator to another.

Courtis (1930) believes there is no single type of growth curve that can adequately express the pattern of growth represented by a conglomeration of items varying irregularly as to both kind and level of difficulty, such as in included in the usual mental test. Such curves lack stability of form because they do not measure a uniform function in a uniform manner. Courtis insists that any adequate plan for the study of mental growth must take its origin from a consideration of the developmental progress in the performance of a single act. After plotting curves for many forms of biologic growth, ranging from the growth in weight of a pumpkin to the increase with age in the percentage of men who are married, he derived a unit called the *isochron*, which is defined as the percentage of the total period of maturation that has been attained by any individual at any time. Isochronic units, so Courtis thinks, have uniform significance for all forms of growth whether of structure or function. The idea is an interesting one but requires further confirmation.

Most present-day students of human development accept the theory that mental growth proceeds most rapidly during infancy and early childhood. This is equivalent to saying that the curve of mental growth is negatively accelerated. No general agreement has been reached, however,

[1] This point is discussed by Anderson in Chapter 1 of this book.

as to the most nearly correct formula for this curve. Gesell (1928) assumed a logarithmic form. Thurstone (1928a and b), after applying his method of scaling to the items of a number of well-known intelligence tests, found that the resultant curves varied with the tests from which they had been derived and (presumably) with the character of the groups to whom the tests had been given. However, when the various curves were extrapolated at the lower end, he found that for all the tests examined the point of "zero" intelligence was located at birth or shortly before birth. Heinis, whose study was mentioned in the preceding section, by applying a logarithmic transformation to Vermeylen's data, derived the following formula which he believed to be an absolute expression of the law of mental growth:

$$Y = 429(1 - e^{x/6.675})$$

where Y = the height of the curve at the age in question.

x = the chronological age.

e = the base of the natural logarithm.

Though the principle involved is arbitrary, since no one knows whether or not mental growth actually conforms to a logarithmic scale, the curve itself is not out of line with modern hypotheses and observations concerning mental progress. The constants used, however, were derived from so few cases (10 at each age) as to render their validity open to serious doubt.

According to Heinis, the midpoint of mental growth is reached at the age of 5 years. Thorndike *et al.* (1926), utilizing the data and the scaling procedure of the CAVD test, arrived at the conclusion that the curve for CAVD altitude is parabolic in form, rising from zero at birth to a mid-value around the age of 3 years and attaining its final height at about the age of 21.

It is interesting to note that, although independently derived, this curve shows fairly close agreement with that for growth in brain weight. Although at first thought the idea that one-half of an individual's ultimate mental stature has been attained by the age of 3 years may seem a bit startling, the following exercise which the writer has repeatedly tried both with university students and with laymen may put the matter in a somewhat different light. The instructions given are:

> First, try to forget all that you may have learned about mental tests.[1] Think only of children as you have known them.
>
> Now try to get the clearest picture that you can of a newborn baby. Go over his abilities and inabilities in your mind in considerable detail. (A few moments' time should be allowed for this.)
>
> Now turn your mind to the adults whom you have known. Consider in detail the things that they are able to do, especially the things that we commonly think of as indicating "intelligence." (Pause.)
>
> Now go back once more to the newborn baby. Holding in mind these two points of reference—the newborn and the adult—move slowly up the age scale, asking yourself at each point, "Is the typical child of this age more nearly like the adult or the newly born infant in respect to the things he is able to do?" Continue this process until you reach an age at which, in your judgment, the resemblances and differences are so evenly balanced that you can no longer come to a decision. If your judgment is sound, that age will fix the halfway point in postnatal mental growth.

[1] This caution is necessary because of the strong tendency on the part of those who have been taught that mental maturity is attained at some specified age, as 16 years, to assume that the midpoint of growth in ability would of necessity correspond with one-half the time span covered between birth and maturity. This, of course, is circular reasoning. The mere length of time required to accomplish something tells nothing whatever about the evenness or unevenness of the rate of accomplishment.

When this exercise has been tried with fair-sized groups who have thoroughly grasped the idea that what they are seeking is a point of balance, equally far removed from the two terminal points in the matter of resemblance, the mean estimate is, as a rule, not far from that set by Thorndike. The distribution of judgments tends to be skewed toward the lower ages, which is, of course, just what would be expected if the true form of the growth curve were parabolic in shape.

The Prediction of Later Status from Earlier Status

The idea that mental tests not only provide a measure of the present mental level of the individual but also yield some indication of his potentialities for further development has from the outset been implicit in the uses to which they have been put. Shortly after the IQ method of expressing test results had been popularized by Terman, the extent to which this measure tended to remain constant for the individual child became a popular subject of investigation. Until the late twenties, however, these studies dealt almost exclusively with children of school age. The few studies based upon younger children that had appeared up to that time usually included only a small number of cases, with little or no attempt at experimental control either of the sampling of subjects or of age at initial and final testing. Sometimes even the results from different tests were thrown together in a single grouping. Only within comparatively recent years have sufficient data been accumulated to provide a tentative answer to this important question: With how great a degree of assurance may we predict the mental level likely to be attained by any child at maturity (or at any other specified age) on the basis of tests given at some stated earlier age?

Both the empirical evidence and the underlying theories on this topic have been summarized by Anderson (1939). His conclusion is essentially the same as that expressed by the writer in Murchison's *Handbook of Child Psychology* (1933, p. 322). Briefly stated, the conclusion is that, *the younger the child at time of first testing, or the longer the interval between tests, the less accurate will be the prediction of later status from earlier status.*

Findings for the Minnesota Preschool Scales by Goodenough and Maurer (1942), however, make it appear that the effect of interval between testings may be actually far smaller than that of the age at first test. The reason for this apparent exception to the results of other investigators is not clear. It may be a function of the particular scale used or of the unit of measurement employed. On the other hand, it is possible that certain functions of the human mind, although measured with very unequal accuracy at different ages, nevertheless remain relatively constant from early childhood to maturity. This hypothesis would be encouraging if true, but much further evidence is needed before we can be warranted in accepting it at its face value. No study that has yet appeared has shown more than a moderate relationship between the results of tests given before the age of 6 and those administered in later childhood or at maturity. Bradway (1944) in a carefully controlled study of the predictive value of the preschool tests in the 1937 Stanford-Binet re-examined 138 of the children used in the original standardization of the scale 10 years after the initial testing. Fifty-two of the subjects had been under 4 years of age when first tested; the remaining 86 had been between 4 and 6 years. Correlations between original and later IQ's on the same scale were +.66 for the younger and +.67 for the

older group. This difference, however, is greater than appears from the *r*'s since the younger group was more variable, the SD's being respectively 17.1 and 14.1 IQ points. The mean change in IQ was 12 points for the younger and 10 points for the older group. Changes of 15 points or more occurred in approximately one-third of the younger and one-fourth of the older subjects. Bradway's conclusion that "an individual IQ obtained prior to the age of 6 years must be interpreted with discretion" seems well justified.

In a later study (Bradway, 1945), an attempt was made to identify factors related to IQ change. Few of the items studied proved to be reliably associated with the differences found.[1] The highest relationship was for a "measure of ancestral intelligence" based upon a composite of such factors as mid-grandfather's occupational status and mother's vocabulary. This, as Bradway correctly points out, may have operated either as an environmental influence or as a hereditary factor not completely realized at the time of the first test. Of possible significance, however, is the fact that the cases for whom large changes in IQ occurred were usually those whose initial IQ's had shown large deviations from the values to be expected on the basis of ancestral intelligence.

Bayley (1933), Honzik (1938), Furfey and Muehlenbein (1932), Shirley (1933), and others who have followed the development of infants from early infancy up to the period at which mental tests show reasonable stability of results from one testing to another, all report an absence of relationship between mental test standing

---

[1] It should be noted that the significance of the differences found by Bradway is less than she reports inasmuch as the statistical methods appropriate for large samples rather than the small-sample techniques were employed throughout the study.

before the age of 18 months and later test performance. After the appearance of speech, the tests begin to have predictive value, although the amount of confidence that can be placed in the results as indices to the child's ultimate level of development continues to be small up to the age of 6 or 7 years. Both Goodenough (1933) and Anderson (1939) have pointed out that the amount of overlap between earlier and later testings is a factor of major importance in determining the degree of relationship between the results of successive testings of the same individuals.

In an article of basic importance for all students of mental growth, Bayley (1940) has shown that, when the same individuals are retested at regular intervals over a period of years, characteristic differences appear in the rate and pattern of their mental growth. Out of a total of 48 cases who were followed over a period of 9 years, 8 maintained fairly constant positions near the mean of the group as a whole throughout the entire period; 8 showed relatively slow rates of growth, with continued tendency to lose in standing when compared with the other members of the group; 8 showed the opposite tendency with continued gain in test standing as age advanced; 8 displayed a tendency to lose in standing during infancy and early childhood but later shifted to an accelerated rate whereby the early loss was regained; and, in contrast to these, another group of 8 cases showed early rapid growth with subsequent loss. The growth curves of the remaining 8 were not classified as to form, since the patterns appeared not to fall into any easily recognized class. These findings are in fairly close general agreement with those obtained by Goodenough and Maurer (1942) in a 12-year study carried out at the Institute of Child Welfare at the University of Minnesota.

Relationship of Intelligence Test Standing to Other Factors

That more than chance relationship exists between the scores made by a given individual on standardized tests of intelligence and his scores on many instruments designed to measure other mental and physical traits is well known. In many instances, however, it is not wholly clear to what extent the relationships found may be ascribed to biological or social factors and to what extent the issue is in reality a matter of semantics. We know, for example, that practically all measures of language development, such as size of vocabularly, mean length of sentence used, and complexity of sentence construction, show fairly high correlation with measures of intelligence. Whether this relationship between *scores* indicates a genuine tendency for two *different* aspects of mental development to vary together or is merely a necessary result of measuring the same thing twice by slightly different instruments and calling the results by different names, is a question about which opinions differ. When greater agreement with respect to factorial procedures has been attained, an answer may perhaps be reached. For the present we shall avoid the issue by specifying that, in the discussion to follow, we are dealing only with relationships between the results of tests *designed* to measure general intelligence and those of measurements *designed* for other purposes.

Although in many instances the correlations are too low to have practical utility, it is nevertheless true that standing on recognized tests of intelligence is positively related to standing on practically all other measurements of socially desirable traits. Even physical measurements such as height and weight have been found to conform to the general rule, although the relationships are not high and in many of the reported studies heterogeneity of race and the inclusion at the lower end of the intelligence scale of special clinical types such as Mongolian imbeciles have operated to make the apparent relation higher than would be the case had a truly representative selection of subjects been used. (See Paterson, 1930.)

That performance on intelligence tests varies according to the social class from which the subjects are drawn has been recognized since the days of Binet. That the relationship is not one of simple cause and effect is demonstrated by the fact that every level of intelligence can be found within each social level, though not in equal proportion. A greater percentage of the very bright come from families of superior socio-economic status, whereas the frequency of backward children is proportionately greater among the lower social classes. The relationship is sufficiently marked to bring about a difference of 20 to 30 IQ points in the mean test standing of children of college professors and those of day laborers.

This relationship between socio-economic status and intelligence must always be kept in mind when considering statistical findings on the correlation of intelligence test scores with other factors such as juvenile delinquency, social behavior, standing on the pencil-and-paper "tests" of emotional stability, and the like. Undoubtedly, children of the upper social classes have fewer incentives to delinquent behavior than those who live in the slums. Undoubtedly, too, their offenses are more likely to be handled privately by cooperation between parents and police than are corresponding offenses by children from homes where little parental assistance can be expected. All this makes for a greater percentage of low-testing individuals among institutionalized delinquents than among children not classified as delinquent, but in all probability a large share of this difference is attributable to the socio-economic factor rather than to intelligence *per se*.

Likewise, the finding that children of superior intelligence are on the average more popular with their mates than those of low intelligence might be considerably modified if the socio-economic factor (which, particularly among older children, involves some degree of prestige, as well as the means for providing little treats or toys for group use) were made equal for all. In the paper-and-pencil tests designed to measure various nonintellectual traits, the almost uniformly positive correlations between scores on these tests and scores on intelligence tests may be interpreted in either of two ways. There may be a true relationship between intelligence and the social or emotional traits presumably measured by these tests, or, on the other hand, the obtained correlations may result wholly or in part from the greater ability of bright children to select the more socially acceptable responses.

The question of sex differences in intelligence has been a matter of active controversy for many decades. That there are differences in the type of intellectual skills in which each sex excels has been thoroughly established. At all ages, males outrank females in general information, especially along scientific lines. They also have better insight into mathematical and mechanical relationships. Females excel in linguistic and perceptual skills and in certain types of rote memory. As might be expected, intelligence tests will therefore show some advantage of one sex over the other according to the kind of items with which they are most heavily weighted. In the standardization of most tests, however, particularly those intended for use with school children, items have usually been so chosen as to keep the sex differences at a minimum. On the average, girls make slightly better school records than boys and are more often ranked superior in intelligence by their teachers in the elementary grades, but it is likely that greater docility and better application to their studies, rather than a genuine difference in ability, are responsible.

That males greatly exceed females in the number who achieve fame is an incontrovertible fact. More males than females are also found among the inmates of institutions for the feeble-minded and in the special classes for mentally retarded children in the public schools. This raises the question of a possible sex difference in intellectual variability. Regardless of the equality of the means, if one sex is more variable than the other, that sex will show a greater proportion at the extremes of the distribution. Because of social and industrial conditions that make it difficult or impossible to examine large and equally representative groups of adults, the answer to the question can best be sought among children.

Perhaps the most crucial data thus far available, as far as the upper extreme is concerned, are to be found in the records of the Stanford University study of intellectually gifted children, which was initiated by Dr. L. M. Terman in 1921. Later careers of well over 95 per cent of the subjects have been studied by means of follow-up tests, interviews, and mailed questionnaires up to the present time. Children were originally chosen for inclusion in the study if their Stanford-Binet IQ's were 140 or higher. In spite of the fact that the method of selecting the children for testing [1]

1 Lack of sufficient funds made it impossible to examine all the school children in the California cities covered by the survey. Teachers were therefore asked to name the two or three children in their classes whom they thought to be most intelligent. The name of the youngest child in each class was also called for. These children were then given a group intelligence test, and all who attained a certain standing were later given an individual Binet test. Since the initial selection was based on teachers' judg-

was such as might possibly favor the girls, the actual sex ratio among the 1070 elementary school children selected on the basis of their standing on the Stanford-Binet was 116.4 boys to 100 girls. Among the 428 high school children who were given the Terman Group Test, the sex ratio of 163.2 boys to 100 girls is even higher [2] (Terman and Oden, 1947).

Unquestionably the most nearly perfect sample of the abilities of a specified group that has ever been obtained comes from Scotland (Macmeeken, 1939), where *all but one* of the 875 children born in Scotland on 4 selected days of the year 1926 and who had survived until the age of 10 were located and tested by means of the Stanford Revision. The mean IQ of the boys was found to be 100.5; that of the girls was 99.7. The corresponding SD's were 15.9 and 15.2 respectively. Although these differences appear small, they would nevertheless, if valid, result in large discrepancies in the proportion of the sexes found at the extremes. Terman has calculated that the sex ratio among those who attain an IQ of 140 or higher would, under these circumstances, be approximately 158 boys to 100 girls, or, if the small difference in the means is disregarded and variability alone considered, the ratio would be 134 males to 100 females.

Data on the sex ratio among the feeble-minded also show an apparent excess of

ments of ability, the possibility that the excess number of boys among those who qualified might be due in part to sex favoritism called for investigation, even though the difference in this case ran contrary to the usual finding. The crucial test of bias is the sex ratio among those named who failed to qualify. This ratio was found to be 103.7 boys to 100 girls, which compares with a ratio of 104.5 boys to 100 girls in the elementary school population as a whole. This difference is too small to be reliable, but at least it does not suggest that biased selection can account for the greater proportion of boys in the gifted group.

2 These figures do not correspond exactly to those given in Vol. I of the Stanford report (Terman et al., 1925) because of different classification of the groups.

males. These figures, however, are subject to a number of sources of misunderstanding that operate little or not at all at the upper extreme. Certain organic factors, such as cerebral birth palsy, are very unequally distributed between the sexes. Sociological and economic conditions are also influential in placing a greater number of males than females in institutions for the feeble-minded. Financial pressures bear most heavily upon the boy, who is expected to become an active breadwinner, whereas the moron girl who is docile and industrious can often satisfy all requirements by helping about the home. Eventually marriage may provide her with some degree of economic security. For her brother, on the other hand, marriage merely adds to his economic responsibilities. The greater aggressiveness of the male is another factor, since it often leads him into difficulties that expose his mental backwardness. These and other circumstances of a similar nature are in all probability partially responsible for the large excess of males over females that has been reported by most institutions for the feeble-minded, but a genuine difference in variational tendency may also play a part.[1]

Considering all the evidence, the hypothesis that the distribution of male intelligence has a wider spread than that of females is a reasonable one, even though it has not yet been definitely established as fact. If verified, such an assumption would account for many of the established facts concerning sex differences, including the greater number of males who attain eminence as well as the greater number found in institutions for the feeble-minded. Although the importance of the standard

deviation has frequently been pointed out by students of sex differences, the extent to which even a very small inequality in the variance of the sexes can affect the proportions at the extremes has not, as a rule, been completely realized. The majority have centered their attention upon the means of the groups, rather than upon their relative dispersion.

The question of racial differences in intelligence, like that of sex differences, is still a controversial issue in spite of the large body of data that has been accumulated on the subject. Differences in interpretation, rather than the figures actually obtained, are in the main responsible for the variant opinions that have been expressed, since the test results reported in most of the published investigations are in fair agreement with one another. In spite of many brilliant exceptions to the rule, Negroes and immigrants to this country from the south of Europe and the Spanish-American countries, together with their children, have been found to rank distinctly lower, on the average, than North American whites on tests designed for the latter. Whether this reflects a genuine biological difference in the distribution of intellect among the races or whether it results wholly or in part from the use of measures that are poorly suited to the appraisal of the mental capacity of subjects whose experiential background differs in many ways from that typical for those upon whom the tests were standardized is uncertain. It is also possible, as some believe, that the growth of intelligence is dependent upon environmental stimulation, and that the members of the groups in question are likely to be truly unintelligent, not because they were originally incapable of intellectual development but because they lacked the opportunities and incentives that make for mental growth. Perhaps future investigators will devise some really crucial tests

---

[1] Although there is evidence that the distribution of intelligence conforms fairly closely to the normal curve, it is by no means certain that the correspondence is exact or that it is identical for both sexes. The small differences in variability that have been reported could be the result of differential skewing at one or the other extreme.

of these hypotheses, but the attempts that have been made so far leave so much room for biased interpretation and conclusions that not much weight can be assigned to them.

Studies of racial differences are particularly liable to bias in the selection of subjects. That immigrants to this country are not representative of the total population of the parent country is more than a possibility. It is likely, too, that the factors leading to emigration have differed from country to country and at different periods of time within the same country. The evidence on these points has been ably reviewed by Tyler in Chapter 5 of her *Psychology of Human Differences* (1947) and will not be repeated here. Her conclusion that the difficulties involved in racial or nationality studies are great and that many of the published studies are of little or no worth because of the want of essential information with respect to the sampling of subjects, the use of unsuitable tests, and other technical faults is certainly well grounded.

The Modifiability of Intelligence

Few, if any, questions relating to mental growth crop up so persistently or have provoked more intensive study than those relating to its possible modification. The obvious practical importance of the problem and the occasional, though by no means universal, improvement in mental level that has been brought about through thyroid treatment in cases of cretinism or by other types of glandular therapy in analogous conditions of endocrine malfunctioning have served as constant examples of the mental gains that can be accomplished when the basis for the original deficiency is once understood. It is but natural, therefore, that theories on the etiology of mental differences should lead by the short-est possible route to theories as to the extent and manner by which these differences may be modified. Because the most obvious indications of mental superiority or inferiority have to do with the learning process, it is not strange that many should question whether differences in learning ability have any constitutional bases at all, or whether they might not better be ascribed to lack of opportunity or stimulation to learn, or to the failure to acquire proper techniques of learning.

Two of the *Yearbooks of the National Society for the Study of Education* (1928, 1940) as well as a large number of separate articles and monographs have been devoted entirely to a consideration of this topic. As yet, however, no general agreement on the basic question involved has been reached, although the weight of evidence when all the large number of investigations reported in the *Yearbooks* and elsewhere is taken into account certainly does not support the view that the intellectual development of children is as readily modified by experience as many wishful thinkers would like to believe. Woodworth (1941) has given us a painstaking and eminently fair critique of the evidence available up to that date, with particular reference to that dealing with the development of twins separated in infancy and of children reared in foster homes. Like many others he noted that, in a number of the studies which have apparently shown that marked changes in intellectual status have resulted from an altered environment, the conclusions reached have been based upon the faulty results of erroneous statistical techniques.

That children reared from infancy in environments where intellectual opportunity is not lacking and where the incentive to intellectual achievement is high are likely to reach a higher level of achievement than others of equal original endowment for whom both opportunity and incentives are poor is conceded by practically all who have considered the matter. But this is not equivalent to saying that either opportunity or incentive will bring about charges that go beyond the limitations set by the germ plasm. "Men do not gather grapes from thorns nor figs from thistles." Such amazing results as those reported by Schmidt (1946) on the changes brought about in the intellectual status of a group of low-grade feeble-minded subjects by means of a not unusual type of educational program should be viewed with considerable skepticism, particularly when the large number of arithmetical errors in her published tables and the questionable accuracy of her original data as investigated by Kirk (1948) are taken into account.

The principle involved may be stated as follows: In respect to every human or animan trait, whether physical or mental, heredity sets limits to individual variability. For some characteristics the range of possible variation for the individual is wide, approaching that for the race. In most cases, however, it appears to be more or less restricted. Just how far the latitude extends in the case of intellect we do not know, nor are our present instruments sufficiently free from inherent sources of error to permit a final answer to the question, for a given change in measured IQ does not always and of necessity connote a similar change in the trait that the test is presumed to measure. If it did, a relatively small amount of coaching on the items of an intelligence test, which may temporarily raise the obtained results by as much as 20 to 30 IQ points with some residual effects as much as 3 years later (Greene, 1928), would richly repay the time and funds required for it! Greene also showed that training on material similar to but not identical with that included in the tests also had a measurable effect upon the results. That changes such as these are superficial rather than genuine indicators of intellectual differences can hardly be doubted. They suggest, however, that divergences in the IQ's of children reared under varying conditions of opportunity and training may likewise result wholly or in part from the fact that the intelligence tests in present use are indirect rather than direct measures. They deal with the results of learning, from which capacity to learn is inferred. When opportunity and incentives have been reasonably similar, the inference is sound, but its validity may well be questioned when a comparison is to be made between two or more groups for whom these factors have been markedly different. Failure to take account of the possible effect of a specified type of experience upon the validity of *test scores* as indicators of the kind of ability which they are presumed to measure may perhaps account for some of the differences in the opinions reached by those who have attempted to study the effect of experience upon mental capacity.

An additional source of disagreement is unquestionably to be found in unclear thinking about the real nature of the point at issue. In the scientific world it is idle to ask the cause of a present condition since causes lie in a past that cannot be reinstated. Our knowledge of causal factors is always derived by inference; we check the accuracy of these inferences by instituting anew the conditions or factors that we hypothesize as necessary antecedents of the present facts and wait to see whether similar consequences result. Because of the exceedingly complex nature of most biological phenomena, modern scientists are wary of accepting at their face value any etiological theories that fail to meet the following generally accepted criteria:

1. Have the experimental conditions necessary for testing the hypothesis been de-

scribed with sufficient detail and accuracy to enable others to make the same tests? That is, is the hypothesis susceptible of experimental validation?

2. When independent tests are made, are similar results obtained?

Whether it is theoretically possible *by any conceivable means* to modify the course of mental growth to any specified extent is an unanswerable question since no one knows what scientific discoveries the future may bring. Whether a method has now been found that can be described in such terms that others may profit by its use is a question that permits a straightforward answer. It is the second rather than the first question that the reader of the literature on this highly controversial issue must hold steadily in mind if he is to avoid becoming hopelessly entangled in a web of conflicting figures. The question involved is not, as many have been led to think, determining the factors that caused the present differences in mentality that we observe in children. That question cannot be answered because too many unknown variables are involved. The question is: has a practicable method been discovered by which the course of a child's mental development can be materially altered? And, if so, *in precisely what respects does this method differ from others that have proved ineffective?* To date, no useful description of such a method has been given us.

Concluding Discussion

In the treatment of this topic more emphasis has intentionally been placed upon the inadequacies and imperfections of our present methods of mental measurement than upon their positive values. These values have been thoroughly demonstrated. In spite of minor inaccuracies, in spite of disagreement as to exactly what it is that we are trying to measure and uncertainty as to what units we shall employ for expressing the results of our measurement, the fact remains that for most purposes and in most cases the tests work amazingly well. In the schoolroom, the behavior clinic, the offices of the vocational counselor, the juvenile court, or the child-placing agency, their practical value has been shown repeatedly.

In one sense it may be said that in the success with which they have been used lies their greatest weakness, for too often this successful use has engendered a blind faith in all test results to which some kind of numerical score is attached. Figures are likely to have a hypnotic effect upon most of us. Although we may know that the significance of a test score varies with the test used, the conditions under which it is given, and the age of the child tested, even the well-informed are often far too prone to feel that, once it has been calculated, an IQ is an IQ with fixed and absolute meaning. This attitude has led to two unfortunate errors in thinking. On the one hand, we have those who, on the basis of a single test, even when given at a tender age, are ready to "diagnose" the child's present mental level, make predictions as to his future, perhaps even take action with respect to matters of vital importance for his future. On the other hand, we have those who, with equally naïve confidence in the accuracy of the tests, regard every fluctuation in standing as indicating a "real" change in the child's mental level. Even a casual reading of the experimental literature on the extent and frequency of changes in IQ upon retesting children of different ages and after varying intervals of time should demonstrate the lack of scientific basis for either of these extreme views. Fortunately, the number who still adhere to them appears to be diminishing. A critical examination of the literature that has appeared since the publication of Goddard's translation of Binet's 1908 scale shows an encouraging shift from the wholesale production of new and half-tried testing devices to the critical examination of the significance and accuracy of those already in use. Improved statistical methods have been applied to problems of scale construction as well as to the investigation of sources of error in measurement. The day is past when a simple statement of the "reliability" and "validity" of a test was thought to provide sufficient information as to its effectiveness.

Bibliography

Aldrich, C. G., and E. A. Doll. 1931. Comparative intelligence of idiots and of normal infants. *J. Genet. Psychol., 39,* 227–257.

Allen, C. N. 1931. Bibliographies in child study and developmental psychology. *Psychol. Bull., 28,* 277–296.

Anastasi, A. 1936. The influence of specific experience upon mental organization. *Genet. Psychol. Monogr., 18,* 245–355.

Anderson, J. E. 1939. The limitations of infant and preschool tests in the measurement of intelligence. *J. Psychol., 8,* 351–379.

Arthur, G. 1930. *A point scale of performance tests:* Vol. I. *Clinical manual.* New York: Commonwealth Fund.

Arthur, G., and H. Woodrow. 1919. An absolute intelligence scale: A study in method. *J. Appl. Psychol., 3,* 118–137.

Asher, E. J. 1935. The inadequacy of current intelligence tests for testing Kentucky mountain children. *J. Genet. Psychol., 46,* 480–486.

Atkins, Ruth E. 1931. *The measurement of the intelligence of young children by an object-fitting test.* Minneapolis: University of Minnesota Press.

Ayres, L. P. 1909. *Laggards in our schools.* New York: Russell Sage Foundation.

Bayley, N. 1933. Mental growth during the first three years: An experimental study of sixty-one children by repeated tests. *Genet. Psychol. Monogr., 14,* 1–92.

——. 1940. Mental growth in young children. *Yearb. Nat. Soc. Stud. Educ.,* 39(II), 11–47.

Binet, A. 1911. Nouvelles recherches sur la mesure du niveau intellectuel chez les enfants d'école. *Année psychol., 17,* 145–201.

Binet, A., and T. Simon. 1905a. Sur la nécessité d'établir un diagnostic scientifique des états inférieurs de l'intelligence. *Année psychol., 11,* 163–190.

——. 1905b. Méthodes nouvelles pour le diagnostic du niveau intellectuel des anormaux. *Année psychol., 11,* 191–244.

Binet, A., and T. Simon. 1908. Le développement de l'intelligence chez les enfants. *Année psychol., 14,* 1–94.

Boardman, H. 1917. *Psychological tests; a bibliography.* New York: Bureau of Educational Experiments.

Bradway, K. P. 1944. IQ constancy on the revised Stanford-Binet from the preschool to the junior high school level. *J. Genet. Psychol., 65,* 197–217.

——. 1945. An experimental study of factors associated with Stanford-Binet IQ changes from the preschool to the junior high school. *J. Genet. Psychol., 66,* 107–128.

Bronner, A. F., W. Healy, G. Lowe, and M. Shimberg. 1927. *A manual of individual mental tests and testing.* Boston: Little, Brown.

Buros, O. K. 1936. Educational, psychological and personality tests of 1933, 1934 and 1935. *Stud. Educ., Rutgers Univ. Bull., 13,* No. 9.

——. 1937. Educational, psychological and personality tests of 1936. *Stud. Educ., Rutgers Univ. Bull., 14,* No. 11. Pp. 141.

——. (Ed.) 1938. *The 1938 mental measurements yearbook.* New Brunswick, N. J.: Rutgers University Press.

——. 1941. *The 1940 mental measurements yearbook.* Highland Park, N. J.: Mental Measurements Yearbook.

——. 1949. *The 1949 mental measurements yearbook.* New Brunswick, N. J.: Rutgers University Press.

Cattell, J. McK. 1890. Mental tests and measurements. *Mind, 15,* 373–381.

Cattell, J. McK., and L. Farrand. 1896. Physical and mental measurements of the students of Columbia University. *Psychol. Rev., 3,* 618–648.

Cattell, P. 1933. The Heinis personal constant as a substitute for the IQ. *J. Educ. Psychol., 24,* 221–228.

——. 1940. *The measurement of intelligence of infants and young children.* New York: Psychological Corporation.

Chaille, S. E. 1887. Infants, their chronological progress. *New Orleans Med. Surg. J., 14,* 893–912.

Courtis, S. A. 1930. *The measurement of growth.* Detroit: Author.

Cunningham, K. S. 1927. The measurement of early levels of intelligence. *Teach. Coll. Contr. Educ.,* No. 259.

Dearborn, W. F. 1928. *Intelligence tests: Their significance for school and society.* Boston: Houghton Mifflin.

Descoeudres, A. 1921. *Le développement de l'enfant de deux à sept ans.* Neuchatel: Delachaux et Niestlé.

Flanagan, J. C. 1935. Factor analysis in the study of personality. Stanford University, Calif.: Stanford University Press.

Freeman, F. N. 1911. Tests. *Psychol. Bull., 8,* 21–24.

——. 1912. Tests. *Psychol. Bull., 9,* 215–222.

——. 1913. Tests. *Psychol. Bull., 10,* 271–274.

——. 1914. Tests. *Psychol. Bull., 11,* 253–256.

——. 1915. Tests. *Psychol. Bull., 12,* 187–188.

Freeman, F. N. 1916. Tests. *Psychol. Bull., 13,* 268–271.

——. 1917. Tests. *Psychol. Bull., 14,* 245–249.

——. 1919. Tests. *Psychol. Bull., 16,* 374–381.

——. 1920. Mental tests. *Psychol. Bull., 17,* 353–362.

——. 1930. Mental indices. In *Proceedings of the first conference on individual differences in the character and rate of psychological development.* Washington: National Research Council. Pp. 8.

——. 1939. Mental tests: their history, principles and applications. (Rev. ed.) Boston: Houghton Mifflin.

Freeman, F. S. 1950. *Theory and practice of psychological testing.* New York: Holt.

Furfey, P. H., and J. Muehlenbein. 1932. The validity of infant intelligence tests. *J. Genet. Psychol., 40,* 219–223.

Gambrill, B. L. 1927. *An analytical list of kindergarten-primary tests.* New Haven: Whitlock's Book Store.

Gesell, A. 1928. *Infancy and human growth.* New York: Macmillan.

Gilbert, J. A. 1894. Researches on the mental and physical development of school children. *Stud. Yale Psychol. Lab., 2,* 40–100.

——. 1897. Researches upon school children and college students. *Univ. Iowa Stud. Psychol., 1,* 1–39.

Glueck, S., and E. Glueck. 1934. *One thousand juvenile delinquents; their treatment by court and clinic.* Cambridge: Harvard University Press.

Goddard, H. H. 1910a. A measuring scale for intelligence. *Train. Sch., 6,* 146–155.

——. 1910b. Four hundred feeble-minded children classified by the Binet method. *Ped. Sem., 17,* 389–397.

——. 1911a. Two thousand normal children measured by the Binet measuring scale of intelligence. *Ped. Sem., 18,* 232–259.

——. 1911b. The Binet measuring scale for intelligence. (Rev. ed.) Vineland, N. J.: The Training School. (Manual and record forms.)

——. 1911c. A revision of the Binet scale. *Train. Sch., 8,* 56–62.

——. 1912. *The Kallikak family.* New York: Macmillan.

——. 1914. *Feeble-mindedness: Its causes and consequences.* New York: Macmillan.

——. 1915. *The criminal imbecile.* New York: Macmillan.

Goodenough, F. L. 1926. *The measurement of intelligence by drawing.* Yonkers-on-Hudson: World Book.

——. 1928. *The Kuhlmann-Binet tests for children of preschool age; a critical study and evaluation.* Minneapolis: University of Minnesota Press.

——. 1929. The relation of the intelligence of preschool children to the occupation of their fathers. *Amer. J. Psychol., 40,* 284–294.

——. 1942. Studies of the 1937 Revision of the Stanford-Binet Scale: I. Variability of the IQ at successive age-levels. *J. Educ. Psychol., 33,* 241–251.

——. 1949. *Mental testing; its history, principles, and applications.* New York: Rinehart.

Goodenough, F. L., and K. M. Maurer. 1942. *The mental growth of children from two to fourteen years: A study of the predictive value of the Minnesota preschool scales.* Minneapolis: University of Minnesota Press.

Goodenough, F. L., and K. M. Maurer, and M. J. Van Wagenen. 1940. *Minnesota preschool scale.* Minneapolis: Educational Test Bureau.

Greene, K. B. 1928. The influence of specialized training on tests of general intelligence. *Yearb. Nat. Soc. Stud. Educ.,* 27(I).

Gulliksen, H. 1950. *Theory of mental tests.* New York: Wiley.

Hall, D. F. 1848. The trial of William Freeman. *Amer. J. Insanity, 5,* 34–60.

Heinis, H. 1924. La loi de developpment mental. *Arch. Psychol.,* No. 74, 97–128.

——. 1926. A personal constant. *J. Educ. Psychol., 17,* 163–186.

Hilden, A. H. 1933. *Table of Heinis' personal constant values.* Minneapolis: Educational Test Bureau.

Hildreth, G. 1930. *Psychological service for school problems.* Yonkers-on-Hudson: World Book.

——. 1939. *A bibliography of mental tests and rating scales.* New York: Psychological Corporation.

——. 1945. *Supplement* to above. New York: Psychological Corporation.

Holzinger, K. J. 1928. Some comments on Professor Thurstone's method of determining the scale values of test items. *J. Educ. Psychol., 19,* 112–117. Comment by Professor Thurstone, *ibid.,* 117–124. Reply to Professor Thurstone, *ibid.,* 124–126.

Honzik, M. P. 1938. The constancy of mental test performance during the preschool periods. *J. Educ. Psychol., 24,* 417–441; 498–520.

Hotelling, H. 1933. Analysis of a complex of statistical variables into principal components. *J. Educ. Psychol., 24,* 417–441; 498–520.

Jaspen, N. 1944. A note on the age-placement of Binet tests. *Psychol. Bull., 41,* 41–42.

Kelley, T. L. 1927. *Interpretation of educational measurements.* Yonkers-on-Hudson: World Book.

——. 1928. *Crossroads in the mind of man.* Stanford University, Calif.: Stanford University Press.

——. 1935. *Essential traits of mental life. The purposes and principles underlying the selection and measurement of independent mental factors, together with computational tables.* Cambridge: Harvard University Press.

Kent, G. H. 1950. *Mental tests in clinics for children.* New York: Van Nostrand.

Kirk, S. A. 1948. An evaluation of the study by Bernadine G. Schmidt entitled "Changes in personal, social, and intellectual behavior of children originally classified as feeble-minded." *Psychol. Bull., 45,* 321–333.

Kuhlmann, F. 1921. The results of repeated mental re-examination of 639 feeble-minded over a period of ten years. *J. Appl. Psychol., 5,* 195–224.

——. 1939. *Tests of mental development: A complete scale for individual examination.* Minneapolis: Educational Test Bureau.

Kuhlmann, F., and R. G. Anderson. 1940. *Kuhlmann-Anderson intelligence tests.* (5th ed.) Minneapolis: Educational Test Bureau.

Lincoln, E. A., and L. L. Workman. 1935. *Testing and the use of test results.* New York: Macmillan.

Macmeeken, A. M. 1939. *The intelligence of a representative group of Scottish children.* London: University of London Press.

McNemar, Q. 1942. *The revision of the Stanford-Binet Scale. An analysis of the standardization data.* Boston: Houghton Mifflin.

Maller, J. B. 1933. Vital indices and their relation to psychological and social factors. *Human Biol., 5,* 94–121.

Maurer, K. M. 1946. *Intellectual status at maturity as a criterion for selecting items in preschool tests.* Minneapolis: University of Minnesota Press.

Merrill, M. A. 1924. On the relation of intelligence to achievement in the case of mentally retarded children. *Comp. Psychol. Monogr., 11.* Pp. 100.

——. 1947. *Problems of child delinquency.* Boston: Houghton Mifflin.

Murchison, C. (Ed.) 1933. *A handbook of child psychology.* (2d ed., rev.) Worcester: Clark University Press.

Mursell, J. L. 1947. *Psychological testing.* New York: Longmans, Green.

Paterson, D. G. 1930. *Physique and intellect.* New York: Century.

Peterson, J. 1925. *Early conceptions and tests of intelligence.* Yonkers-on-Hudson: World Book.

Pintner, R. 1926. Intelligence tests. *Psychol. Bull., 23,* 366–381.

——. 1927. Intelligence tests. *Psychol. Bull., 24,* 391–408.

——. 1928. Intelligence tests. *Psychol. Bull., 25,* 389–405.

——. 1929. Intelligence tests. *Psychol. Bull., 26,* 381–396.

——. 1930. Intelligence tests. *Psychol. Bull., 27,* 431–457.

——. 1931. *Intelligence testing.* (2d ed.) New York: Holt.

——. 1932. Intelligence tests. *Psychol. Bull., 29,* 93–119.

——. 1933. Intelligence tests. *Psychol. Bull., 30,* 488–504.

——. 1934. Intelligence tests. *Psychol. Bull., 31,* 453–475.

——. 1935. Intelligence tests. *Psychol. Bull., 32,* 453–472.

Pintner, R., and D. G. Paterson. 1923. *A scale of performance tests.* New York: Appleton.

Rand, G. 1925. A discussion of the quotient method of specifying test results. *J. Educ. Psychol., 16,* 599–618.

Review of Educational Research. Annotated bibliographies and reviews for years 1932, 1933, 1935, 1936, 1938, 1939, 1941, 1944, 1947.

Ross, C. C. 1944. (Rev. ed. 1947.) *Measurement in today's schools.* New York: Prentice-Hall.

Sandiford, P. 1928. *A bibliography of intelligence and educational tests.* Toronto: University of Toronto Press.

Sangren, P. V. 1929. Comparative validity of primary intelligence tests. *J. Appl. Psychol., 13,* 394–412.

Scheinfeld, A. 1943. *Women and men.* New York: Harcourt, Brace.

Schieffelin, B., and G. Schwesinger. 1930. *Mental tests and heredity: Including a survey of non-verbal tests.* New York: Galton Publishing Co.

Schmidt, B. G. 1946. Changes in personal, social, and intellectual behavior of children originally classified as feeble-minded. *Psychol. Monogr., 60,* No. 5. Pp. 144.

Scupin, E., and G. Scupin. 1907. *Bubi's erste Kindheit.* Leipzig: Grieben.

Sherman, M., and C. B. Key. 1932. The intelligence of isolated mountain children. *Child Develpm., 3,* 279–290.

Shinn, M. 1900. *The biography of a baby.* Boston: Houghton Mifflin.

Shirley, M. 1933. *The first two years: A study of twenty-five babies.* Vol. II. *Intellectual development.* Minneapolis: University of Minnesota Press.

South, E. B. 1937. *An index of periodical literature on testing, 1921–1936.* New York: Psychological Corporation. 5005 titles.

Spearman, C. 1904. "General intelligence" objectively determined and measured. *Amer. J. Psychol., 15,* 201–292.

——. 1927. *The abilities of man.* New York: Macmillan.

Stutsman, R. 1931. *Mental measurement of preschool children. With a guide for the administration of the Merrill-Palmer Scale of mental tests.* Yonkers-on-Hudson: World Book.

Symposium. 1921. Intelligence and its measurement. *J. Educ. Psychol., 12,* 123–147; 195–216.

Terman, L. M. 1916. *The measurement of intelligence.* Boston: Houghton Mifflin.

——. 1919. *The intelligence of school children.* Boston: Houghton Mifflin.

Terman, L. M., et al. 1925. *Genetic studies of genius.* Vol. I. *Mental and physical traits of a thousand gifted children.* Stanford University, Calif.: Stanford University Press.

Terman, L. M., and M. A. Merrill. 1937. *Measuring intelligence: A guide to the administration of the new revised Stanford-Binet tests of intelligence.* Boston: Houghton Mifflin.

Terman, L. M., and M. H. Oden. 1947. *Genetic studies of genius.* Vol. IV. *The gifted child grows up.* Stanford University, Calif.: Stanford University Press.

Thomson, G. H. 1939. *The factorial analysis of human ability.* London: University of London Press.

Thorndike, E. L., et al. 1926. *The measurement of intelligence.* New York: Teachers College, Columbia University.

Thurstone, L. L. 1925. A method of scaling psychological and educational tests. *J. Educ. Psychol., 16,* 433–451.

Thurstone, L. L. 1928a. The absolute zero in intelligence measurement. *Psychol. Rev., 35,* 175–197.

——. 1928b. Scale construction with weighted observations. *J. Educ. Psychol., 19,* 441–453.

——. 1935. *The vectors of mind: Multiple-factor analysis for the isolation of primary traits.* Chicago: University of Chicago Press.

——. 1938. *Primary mental abilities.* Chicago: University of Chicago Press.

——. 1940. Current issues in factor analysis. *Psychol. Bull., 37,* 189–236.

——. 1947. *Multiple factor analysis; A development and extension of "The vectors of mind."* Chicago: University of Chicago Press.

Thurstone, L. L., and L. Ackerson. 1929. The mental growth curve for the Binet tests. *J. Educ. Psychol., 20,* 569–583.

Thurstone, L. L., and T. G. Thurstone. 1941. Factorial studies of intelligence. *Psychometr. Monogr.,* No. 2. Pp. 94.

——. 1946. *Tests of primary mental abilities for ages 5 and 6. Examiner's manual and test blanks.* Chicago: Science Research Associates.

Tredgold, A. F. 1929. *Mental deficiency (amentia.)* (6th ed., rev.) New York: Wood.

Tyler, L. E. 1947. *The psychology of human differences.* New York: Appleton-Century-Crofts.

Vermeylen, G. 1922. *Les debiles mentaux. (Étude experimentale et clinique.)* Paris: Bulletin de l'Institute General Psychologie, No. 4–6.

Wang, C. K. A. 1940. *An annotated bibliography of tests and scales.* Vol. I. Peiping, China: Catholic University Press. (In English.)

Wechsler, D. 1944. *The measurement of adult intelligence. Revised edition with standards to age six.* Baltimore: Williams and Wilkins.

Whipple, G. M. 1914–15. *Manual of mental and physical tests: A book of directions compiled with special reference to the experimental study of school children in the laboratory or classroom.* (2 vols.) (2d ed., rev.) Baltimore: Warwick and York.

Whipple, G. M. (Ed.) 1928. Nature and nurture: Their influence upon intelligence. *Yearb. Nat. Soc. Stud. Educ., 27*(I).

——. 1940a. Comparative and critical exposition. *Yearb. Nat. Soc. Stud. Educ., 39*(I).

——. 1940b. Original studies and experiments. *Yearb. Nat. Soc. Stud. Educ., 39*(II).

Wissler, C. L. 1901. The correlation of mental and physical tests. *Psychol. Rev. Monogr.,* Suppl., *3,* No. 6. Pp. 62.

Woodworth, R. S. 1941. *Heredity and environment: A critical survey of recently published material on twins and foster children.* New York: Social Science Research Council.

Yerkes, R. M., and J. C. Foster. 1923. *1923 Revision: A point scale for measuring mental ability.* Baltimore: Warwick and York.

Young, K. 1924. The history of mental tests. *Ped. Sem., 31,* 1–48.

CHAPTER 9

LANGUAGE DEVELOPMENT IN CHILDREN

DOROTHEA MCCARTHY [1]

Introduction

The amazingly rapid acquisition of an extremely complex system of symbolic habits by young children is a phenomenon which has increasingly attracted the attention of child psychologists as well as linguists in recent years. This area of child development is one of the most important for the child psychologist, not only because the possession of the ability to speak is one of the distinguishing characteristics which sets man apart from the lower animals, but also because of the intimate relationship which exists between language and thought. The increased interest in language development since 1925 appears to be due to the realization of the valuable insights which can be gained into the content of the child's mental life through the study of his linguistic expression, to the dependence on some form of verbal expression in introspective technique as well as in the adequate measurement of intelligence and other psychological traits, and to a recognition of the limitations of psychological observations of infancy, when language responses are not a part of the child's observable repertoire of behavior. There has also been in more recent years an increasing recognition of the important clues that can be gained as to the nature of an individual's personality adjustment

from a study not only of the content but also of the manner of his speech and the form of his verbal expression both oral and written.

The word *language* has a wide variety of meanings, but in the present review emphasis will be placed on the ontogenetic development of spoken language in normal children. Some attempt will be made to show the setting of this aspect of language development in its broader relationships and to show the relationships of normal speech development to the acquisition of the secondary forms of language development in reading and writing and to personality adjustments. Only brief mention will be made of the fields of speech pathology, the physiology of speech, phonetics, linguistics, and semantics, which are much too highly specialized areas for any detailed treatment in the present review.

Excellent discussions of the various definitions of language are to be found in DeLaguna (1927), Pillsbury and Meader (1928), Esper (1935), McGranahan (1936), Eisenson (1938), Lewis (1948), and Miller (1951). In general, the various theories that have been advanced place the emphasis on different aspects of this tremendously complex process, and some recognize its plurality of function. Wundt (1901, 1911–1912) emphasized the expression of mental content, including both ideas and feelings, through language and considered that communication was only a secondary function of language. Pillsbury and

[1] The writer makes grateful acknowledgment to her husband, Robert T. Rock, Jr., for invaluable bibliographical assistance and encouragement in the preparation of this chapter.

492

Meader (1928), however, stress the function of communication in language. In 1927 DeLaguna, after seriously criticizing Wundt's point of view, claimed that a fresh conception of speech as an essential activity of human life was needed. She thereupon advanced a social-behavioral view of the nature of language which has become rather popular with the increasing emphasis on the function of language in the total stimulating situation. J. Dewey (1926) also pointed out that "the heart of language is not 'expression' of something antecedent, much less expression of antecedent thought. It is communication; the establishment of cooperation in an activity in which there are partners and in which the activity of each is modified and regulated by partnership" (p. 179). Esper (1935) states: "The exclusive preoccupation with 'ideas' which are held to be 'expressed' by speech leads to a neglect of the behavior and concrete environment to which the speech is related."

K. Bühler (1934) distinguishes three functions of spoken language: representation, expression, and appeal. McGranahan (1936) points out that a speech phenomenon may be considered (a) in relation to the person who produces it, (b) in relation to the person or persons who hear it, and (c) in relation to the objective fact represented by it. Although Bühler recognized these three aspects, he was more interested in the speech phenomenon itself than in the social-psychological situation. Gardiner (1932) emphasizes four factors: the speaker, the listener, the words said, and the things referred to or spoken about. Much theory has been concerned with the speaker and with the words, but little attention has been paid to the listener and the things spoken of.

Linguists, who in the past have been concerned chiefly with descriptive and historical accounts and comparative details of the grammar of various languages, have become increasingly interested in problems of phonology and semantics. When the linguist thus raises the question of meaning he is led directly into the field of psychology, for he finds that meaning must be explained in terms of the situation in which the word is used. E. Horn (1942) considers that significant trends which have emerged in theory involve a greater recognition of the importance of language in all human culture, rejection of the view that language is the external reflection of psychical processes, as well as an acceptance of the fact that verbal symbols have a predominant function in thinking. Newman (1939) emphasizes the affective aspects of language and considers that they supersede in importance the intellectual and social aspects which continue to be stressed in the literature, especially by Lewis (1948) in his volume entitled *Language and Society*.

In order to realize the importance of language in the psychological development of the child, one needs only to consider the comparative mental vacuum in which the young deaf-mute lives before any means of communication have been established (Baldrian, 1940) and to compare his mental state with that of the normal child who not only can acquire a wealth of information through his understanding of the language of others but also can use language to express his ideas, needs, and wants, as well as to influence the behavior of others. The intimate relationship which most writers claim exists between language and thought is further evidence of the importance of this aspect of the child's development. Language, although perhaps not essential for all thinking, is so frequently involved in thought, and especially in making abstractions and fine distinctions and shades of meaning, as well as in communicating to others the results of one's thought processes, that a certain basic level of attainment in linguistic skills is practically an essential prerequisite to the child's formal education. Vigotsky (1939) makes very provocative distinctions among external or vocalized speech, inner speech, and thought, and concludes that "Without a correct understanding of the psychological nature of inner speech there is no way of explaining the relation of thought to words in all its complexity," and that "thinking and speech are the key for understanding the nature of human consciousness" (p. 37).

As will be shown in this review, a basic mastery of spoken language is normally acquired very rapidly during the preschool years usually between the ages of 1 and 5 years, and the child whose language development is seriously delayed for any reason labors under an almost insurmountable handicap in his social and academic relationships. The earlier a child can acquire facility in linguistic expression, the sooner he is free to reap the benefits of the use of this valuable tool in all his social and intellectual pursuits.

Characteristics of the Literature

As in all aspects of child psychology, the study of language development began with the rather casual observation of isolated cases which were reported in the early biographical literature. Because linguistic development lends itself so readily to the method of direct observation without the use of instrumentation, it played a large part in the studies of the period of the child study movement in the 1890's. Most of these early biographical studies were concerned chiefly with the acquisition of vocabulary from the time of the appearance of the first word up to the fourth or fifth year, when the data tended to become unwieldy. A few dealt with the prelinguistic utterances of early infancy, usually without

benefit of phonetics; and others attempted analyses of all-day conversations extending into the fourth and fifth years of life. Although this wealth of observational material proved stimulating and suggestive for later research workers, it has little scientific merit, for each of the studies employed a different method; the observations were for the most part conducted on single children who were usually either precocious or markedly retarded in their language development; the records were made under varying conditions; and most of the studies were subject to the unreliability of parents' reports. Since the 1930's there has been a revival of interest in the biographical method, with the employment of more refined techniques and special safeguards of objectivity (Lewis, 1951; Low, 1936; Grégoire, 1937, 1947; and Leopold, 1939, 1947, 1949a, b).

Since the 1940's there have emerged two main types of studies, first those dealing with the vocalizations of infants and utilizing phonetics and recording devices, and secondly those in the clinical literature emphasizing the genetic approach to language disorders; so that there seems to be a merging of the clinical and the genetic points of view. Studies of language deviates have become more concerned with the total personality and the dynamics of the disorders. They have ceased to treat symptoms and are more concerned with total syndromes and the search for causes. Thus, once more in this field there is evidence of the study of the abnormal throwing light on the course of normal development.

Previous Reviews. The literature in the field has been brought together from time to time by various authors. In 1833 Feldmann reviewed the reports of the vocabularies of 33 children, and in 1883 Sikorski gave a brief review of studies in foreign languages. In 1899 Franke surveyed about 200 titles for the German *Handbook on Education,* edited by Reins. Preyer (1889a) compared his son's progress in speech with that reported by Sigismund (1856), Lindner (1882), and others. Tracy (1893) presented an excellent summary of the studies of children's language up to 2 years of age, and Meumann (1908) discussed the early anecdotal accounts in the foreign literature with emphasis on the work of Lindner (1882), Ament (1899), and Gheorgov (1905). In 1907 appeared the classic volume, *Die Kindersprache*, by Clara and William Stern, in which they presented detailed observations on their own 3 children and compared their studies with those previously reported in the literature. Between 1907 and 1920 tabular summaries of vocabulary studies were published by Doran (1907), Pelsma (1910), Grant (1915), Gerlach (1917), and Magni (1919). Doran (1907) compiled a summary table of the vocabularies of 98 children between 8 and 72 months of age, and Bateman (1917) summarized all the published reports on the first word. Dale (1949) classified 1855 titles of vocabulary studies and recognized 25 categories. His list is very exhaustive and cites many unpublished studies. In 1948 Lewinski published a review of studies dealing with vocabulary and mental measurement. Leopold (1952) has published an annotated bibliography of child language containing approximately 1200 titles. It combines references from several areas principally from the linguist's and the psychologist's points of view. The psychological references are borrowed with acknowledgment chiefly from the 1946 edition of this manual.

The *Twenty-eighth Yearbook of the National Society for the Study of Education* (1929) included abstracts of 123 published studies on language development in preschool children and 20 researches in progress at that time. The May, 1929, issue of the *Psychological Bulletin* was a "Special Language Number," but it placed little emphasis on linguistic development in the early years. In 1933 a special volume of the *Journal de Psychologie* consisted of a symposium by a number of well-known French psychologists and linguists on "Psychologie du Langage." Most of these articles, however, deal with theoretical problems of the origin of language and of the relationship between thought and language, as well as with problems of imagery and phonetics. Only two, those by Grégoire and Cohen, deal with the acquisition of language by children. The former is concerned primarily with phonetics in the first 2 years and the latter with the effect of infantile speech on the history of a language. McCarthy (1929b), reviewed the reports on infants' vocalizations up to and including the appearance of the first word, and later published more extensive reviews in the *Handbook of Child Psychology* edited by Murchison in 1931 and 1933. A rather comprehensive review of 162 titles by Decroly was published posthumously, about 1934. E. Dewey (1935) devotes about 40 pages of her survey of the literature on the period of infancy to a discussion of studies of language development which appeared between 1920 and 1934. Arsenian (1945) summarized investigations on bilingualism, and Eames (1950) reviewed 24 studies dealing with the relationship of reading and speech difficulties. Some of the more recent investigations on infant vocalizations are summarized in Thompson (1952).

Whereas in 1930 scarcely more than an isolated paragraph or two on language was to be found in textbooks in psychology, nearly all the textbooks in child psychology which have appeared since then include a major chapter on this aspect of the child's development. Some of the best chapters on language appear in textbooks by Stoddard and Wellman (1934), Brooks and Shaffer (1937), Munn (1938), Goodenough (1945), Jersild (1947), Breckinridge and Vincent

(1949), Merry and Merry (1950), Miller (1951), and Thompson (1952).

Irwin (1941a) summarized literature dealing with the speech sounds of the first 6 months of life, and Irwin and Chen (1943) presented a comprehensive review of studies of speech sounds occurring in the first year. Fifty-five titles dealing with children's questions have been summarized by Fahey (1942), and Leopold (1948) has presented a highly critical, but not too informative, review of studies dealing with infant bilingualism with emphasis on German studies and those employing the case study method. A fairly comprehensive annotated *Bibliography of Speech Education* by Thonssen and Fatherson appeared in 1939. It is restricted to materials written in English and directed primarily toward the interests of those in the field of speech education. Part IV, however, deals entirely with language and phonetics, and one section of this part is devoted to references on language development. Froeschels (1948) edited a brief and rather superficial handbook for speech correctionists called *Twentieth Century Speech and Voice Correction* in which scattered bits of information on language development appear.

Quantitative Studies. The years since 1925 have seen the appearance of a series of interesting major studies on large numbers of children, which have employed scientific controls in the observation of more nearly representative groups. M. E. Smith (1926) standardized a vocabulary test for preschool children on 273 children ranging in age from 8 months to 6 years. She employed test words selected from the Thorndike (1921) word list which she elicited by the use of objects, pictures, and questions. In another part of this same study, she analyzed sentence structure in 1-hour records of the conversations of 88 children taken in free play situations. Her vocabulary test was revised by Williams and McFarland (1937). Another vocabulary test by Van Alstyne (1929) measured only the understood vocabulary of 3-year-olds.

In 1930 the writer published a study based on the recording of 50 consecutive verbal responses from each of 140 children ranging in age from 18 to 54 months. A representative sampling of the population was secured by using paternal occupation as a criterion of selection. The data were subjected to four major types of analysis according to (1) the length of response, (2) the complexity of sentence structure, (3) the function of the response, and (4) the proportions of the various parts of speech. Each of these analyses was carried on in relation to age, sex, paternal occupation, mental age, and age of associates. This monograph was condensed and appeared as Chapter 7 in Barker, Kounin, and Wright (1943), *Child Behavior and Development.*

A major investigation by Templin is nearing completion at this writing. Its purpose is to provide normative data over the developmental period from 3 to 8 years on the interrelationships of language skills. Data are being obtained from 480 representative subjects on vocabulary, sentence structure, length of sentence, and articulation of speech sounds. The same investigator is conducting a longitudinal study of articulation following the same children from 2½ to 6 years of age.

The general plan and methods used by McCarthy (1930) have been followed with minor variations by Day (1932), who duplicated the study on 80 pairs of twins, and by E. A. Davis (1937a), who extended the work to higher age levels, and who compared single children with siblings, twins, and only children. Fisher's (1934) study of 72 children of superior mental ability uses larger samples of conversations, but her analyses have much in common with the approaches of the above-mentioned studies. Later studies by M. E. Smith

(1933*b*, 1935*a*, 1939), Young (1941), and Shire (1945) also yield data which are fairly comparable with these investigations.

Piaget (1924), who attempted to study the child's thought processes through a study of his language, pointed out that the child's language was largely egocentric. His stimulating approach served as a point of departure for the functional analyses employed in these major American studies. His claims have not been verified by most of these studies when his method was taken literally. Much interest has centered around the interpretation of, and the attempt to harmonize, these apparently conflicting findings.

Some of the most valuable material on the development of the language sequence has appeared in the longitudinal studies of infant development by Shirley (1933*a*, 1933*b*) and by Bayley (1933). The normative studies of Gesell (1925, 1928), Gesell, Thompson, and Amatruda (1934, 1938), Gesell, Halverson, Thompson, *et al.* (1940), and those of C. Bühler (1930), C. Bühler and Hetzer (1935), and Cattell (1940) have also yielded significant findings regarding linguistic development. These observations made under standardized conditions on large numbers of cases have superseded the earlier biographical reports because of their greater scientific value.

The most elaborate attempt to study the development of articulation in young children was made by Wellman, Case, Mengert, and Bradbury (1931). Tests of language achievement were developed by Descoeudres (1921) in France, and more recently Williams (1937*a*) and his associates at Iowa (Little and Williams, 1937) have developed a language achievement test and have attempted to discover something of the interrelationships of the various aspects of linguistic development. A study by Young (1941) presents the results of records of 360 minutes of conversation per child on 74 children in four different situations. Half of the subjects were from families on relief and half were from upper socio-economic levels. Analyses are conducted on length of response, amount of talking, and the proportions of the various parts of speech. Rigorous grammatical rules, formulated by Jespersen (1933), were employed in the parts-of-speech analysis, and the results are related to the findings of six other similar studies.

An excellent study of written composition was conducted by LaBrant (1933), who used over 1000 subjects ranging from fourth-grade children to adult scientific writers. Although primarily interested in a comparison of deaf and hearing children, Heider and Heider (1940*b*) give data for a hearing group of 817 children, ranging in age from 8 to 14, which constitute one of the most valuable contributions on children's sentence structure in written language.

Goldstein's (1948) *Language and Language Disturbances* is concerned chiefly with problems of aphasia. Only about 10 pages are concerned with language development, and articulatory defects and stuttering are merely mentioned.

As will be seen in the next section, when appropriate allowances are made for selective factors as well as for differences in method and classification, a remarkable degree of uniformity emerges from these research projects regarding most of the important developmental sequences and group differences.

Developmental Stages

From the mass of data which has been collected on children's development during the past two decades in the various research laboratories, it seems as if it should now be possible to sketch an adequate picture of the child's linguistic development.

The various major longitudinal studies mentioned above were much broader investigations and observed language as only one aspect of the development of the whole child. They yield data on language, however, which are of considerably more value than the materials previously available. In the first place, they all involve fairly large numbers of cases (from 25 to over 100) per age level. There is some attempt to have moderately representative groups of children; the observations have all been made under identical conditions within each study; and the authors have in each case been consistent in the criteria which they have employed for the various items at different age levels. Furthermore, all these observations have been made by trained observers who were unrelated to the children examined and who could presumably be objective about the observations. In all the above respects, then, these data are far superior to the earlier isolated biographical studies.

On the other hand, a careful analysis of the material which emerges from such a group of comprehensive studies reveals a number of shortcomings. Since language development was only one aspect of the development observed, it has not been studied at regular intervals throughout the developmental period except by Gesell, who includes language items at all levels. Many writers leave gaps of several months, during which they evidently were more interested in motor, sensory, social, or emotional aspects of the children's development, and for which no language items appear in their scales. It is only by dovetailing the results of several studies, as the writer has done in compiling Table 1, that it is possible to fill in the developmental sequence for language during periods when this aspect of development is probably being obscured by some other aspect which is developing in a more spectacular manner and thus attracts the attention of observers. On a few points many writers have reported data which are apparently in marked agreement. Many items were noted by only one author and hence cannot be compared with the results of other investigations. On other items there is considerable agreement, but, since most of these studies were carried on almost simultaneously, it was not possible for later writers to adopt the terminology of earlier ones and to make their data comparable. The reader is thus confronted with a confusion of terms which appear to be similar but which do not guarantee that the various observers were actually noting the identical behavior in similar situations.

In this table the writer has assembled 126 items of linguistic development which have been reported in eight major infant studies covering the first 2 years. All items which involve vocalization on the part of the child have been included, as well as responses to the human voice, responses to verbal commands, and all responses which are indicative of the comprehension of spoken language. A few items listed by the authors as linguistic were omitted either because they were negative items, such as the report of absence of vocalization or because they did not involve vocalization on the part of the child and could just as reasonably be classified in a social development sequence. The entries in the table have been retained in the terminology of the original authors, and all ages have been converted into months to render them directly comparable. The items are arranged roughly in the order of their appearance. Tentative groupings, which seem reasonable on the basis of similarity of terminology have been made and are indicated by the horizontal lines which mark off groups of items describing almost identical behavior noted by different authors at about the same period. It will be seen that the range in months reported for the different

TABLE 1

Composite Table Showing Age in Months at Which Selected Language Items Are Reported in Eight Major Studies of Infant Development

		Strictly Longitudinal		Principally Cross-Sectional					
		Bayley (1933)	Shirley (1933)	C. Bühler (1930)	C. Bühler and Hetzer (1935)	Gesell, Thompson, and Amatruda (1938)	Gesell and Thompson (1934)	Gesell (1925)	Cattell (1940)
1	Vocal grunt		0.25						
2	Differential cries for discomfort, pain, and hunger						1		
3	Vocalizes small throaty noises					1.3			
4	Vocalizations	1.5							
5	Makes several different vocalizations						2		
6	Makes several vocalizations							4	
7	One syllable		2						
8	Vocalizes *ah, uh, eh*					1.3			
	See Items 26–33.								
9	Attends readily to speaking voice						2		
10	Reacts positively to human voice				2				
11	Responds to voice	1.3							
12	Turns head on sound of voice					4			
13	Voice, attends (supine)								2
14	Voice, turns to (sitting)								4
15	Cooing			2	3				
16	Coos					3		4	2
17	Babbles or coos								
18	Returning glance with smiling or cooing			3					
19	Coos to music							6	
	See Item 22.								
20	Two syllables		3						
21	Gives vocal expression to feelings of pleasure						3		
22	Actively vocalizes pleasure with crowing or cooing						6		
23	Vocalizes pleasure	5.9							
	See Items 15–19, 36–37, 43–44								
24	Vocalizes to social stimulus	3.1							
25	Responds vocally when socially stimulated						4		
	See Items 38, 60.								
26	Vocalizes in self-initiated sound play						4		
27	Articulates many syllables in spontaneous vocalizations							6	
28	Vocalizes several well-defined syllables						6		
29	Says several syllables	6.3							
30	Vocalizes *ma* or *mu*					6.5			
31	Vocalizes *da*					7			
32	Two syllables—2d repetition of 1st—*mama* or *dada*	8				7			
33	Says *da-da* or equivalent	8.5					9		
34	Gives vocal expression of eagerness						5		
35	Vocalizes eagerness	5.6							

TABLE 1 (*Continued*)

COMPOSITE TABLE SHOWING AGE IN MONTHS AT WHICH SELECTED LANGUAGE ITEMS ARE REPORTED IN EIGHT MAJOR STUDIES OF INFANT DEVELOPMENT

	Strictly Longitudinal		Principally Cross-Sectional					
	Bayley (1933)	Shirley (1933)	C. Bühler (1930)	C. Bühler and Hetzer (1935)	Gesell, Thompson, and Amatruda (1938)	Gesell and Thompson (1934)	Gesell (1925)	Cattell (1940)
36 Vocalizes displeasure on withdrawal of coveted object 37 Vocalizes displeasure	5.9				5			
38 "Talks" to a person See Items 25, 60. 39. Distinguishes between friendly and angry talking		6	6					
40 Imitating sounds *re-re-re*—immediate or delayed response 41 Imitates sounds 42 Incipient or rudimentary imitation of sounds See Items 65, 66, 68.			6			10		9
43 Vocalizes satisfaction 44 Vocalizes satisfaction in attaining an object See Items 21–23.	6.5					7		
45 Singing tones		7.3						
46 Vocalizes recognition 47 Gives vocal expression to recognition	7.4					8		
48 Single consonants See Items 30, 31.		8						
49 Adjusts to words See Items 55, 62.					8			9
50 Vocalizes in interjectional manner 51 Vocal interjection	8.1					8		

52 Listens to familiar words
   See Item 61.
53 Listens with selective interest to familiar words
   See Item 62.
	8.5					9		

54 Understands gestures 55 Responds to *bye-bye* 56 Can wave *bye-bye* and often can say it			9		9		12	
57 Expressive sounds 58 Expressive jargon 59 Uses expressive jargon 60 Uses jargon conversationally	13.5	9				15 18		

61 Differentiates words
   See Item 52.
62 Makes conditioned adjustment to certain words
   See Items 69–77.
	9.8					10		

63 Vocalizes in cup-spoon situation 64 Vocalizes in 2-cube situation					10 10			

TABLE 1 (*Continued*)

COMPOSITE TABLE SHOWING AGE IN MONTHS AT WHICH SELECTED LANGUAGE ITEMS ARE REPORTED IN EIGHT MAJOR STUDIES OF INFANT DEVELOPMENT

		Strictly Longitudinal		Principally Cross-Sectional					
		Bayley (1933)	Shirley (1933)	C. Bühler (1930)	C. Bühler and Hetzer (1935)	Gesell, Thompson, and Amatruda (1938)	Gesell and Thompson (1934)	Gesell (1925)	Cattell (1940)
65	Imitating syllables, *mama, papa, dada*			11					
66	Imitates words See Items 40–42, 68.	11.7							
67	One word		14						11
68	First imitative word (*bow-wow*, etc.) See Items 40–42, 65, 66.		15						
69	Adjusts to commands					10			
70	Inhibits on command	11.5							
71	Adjusts to simple commands						12		
72	Places cube in or over cup on command						12		
73	Comprehends simple verbal commissions							12	
74	Understanding simple commands				13–15				
75	Understanding a demand ("Give me that" with gesture)			15–17					
76	Understanding a command ("Sit down" or "lie down" or "stand up" with gesture)			21–23					
77	Putting watch to ear on command See Items 62, 95.			21–23					
78	Responds to inhibitory words					12			
79	Understanding a prohibition				16–18				
80	Understanding a forbidding			18–20					
81	Says 2 words	12.9					12		12
82	Says 2 words or more					12			
83	Says 2 words besides *mama* and *dada*							12	
84	Vocalizes when looking in mirror					12			
85	Says 3 words or more					13			13–14
86	Says 4 words or more					13	15		
87	Words, 5						18	18	15–16
88	Names 1 object (ball, pencil, cup, watch, scissors)	17.4							
89	Names picture in book (dog)		19						
90	Naming 1 object or more				19–24				
91	Names 1 picture	18.7					21		
92	Names picture in book (baby)		22.5						
93	Asks with words See Items 101–103.								17–18
94	Says "Hello," "Thank you," or equivalent							18	
95	Points to nose, eyes, or hair						18	18	
96	Comprehends simple questions See Items 69–77.							18	

TABLE 1 (*Continued*)

COMPOSITE TABLE SHOWING AGE IN MONTHS AT WHICH SELECTED LANGUAGE ITEMS ARE
REPORTED IN EIGHT MAJOR STUDIES OF INFANT DEVELOPMENT

		Strictly Longitudinal		Principally Cross-Sectional					
		Bayley (1933)	Shirley (1933)	C. Bühler (1930)	C Bühler and Hetzer (1935)	Gesell, Thompson, and Amatruda (1938)	Gesell and Thompson (1934)	Gesell (1925)	Cattell (1940)
97	Names Gesell watch on fifth picture See Item 113.	19.4							
98	Names 2 objects	19.6							
99	Repeats things said						21		
100	Repeats 4 syllables (2 words)				30				
101	Joins 2 words in speech						21		
102	Words, combines								21–22
103	Uses words in combination See Item 93.						24		
104	Names 3 pictures	21.2							
105	Picture vocabulary 3								23–24
106	Names 3 objects	21.5							23–24
107	Names 3 objects in picture							36	
108	Identifies 4 objects by name								23–24
109	Names 3 of 5 objects See Items 104-107.						24		
110	Names familiar objects like key, penny, watch							24	
111	Points to 5 objects on card						24		
112	Names 5 pictures	24.4					30		
113	Names Gesell watch and picture See Item 97.	24.5							
114	Points to 7 of 10 simple pictures							24	
115	Points to 7 pictures	25.1					30		28–30
116	Picture vocabulary 7 (1937 Stanford-Binet)								25–27
117	Names 7 pictures	32.9							25–27
118	Pictures, points to 6								25–27
119	First pronoun		23						
120	Uses pronouns past and plural							36	
121	First phrase See Items 124–126.		23						
122	First sentence		23						
123	Uses simple sentences and phrases							24	
124	Distinguishes *in* and *under*							24	
125	Understands 2 prepositions	25							
126	Understands 3 prepositions	28							

items is rather narrow within the horizontal lines. Occasional items noted by only one author appear in isolation in their proper chronological place. The few exceptions, in which items which appear on logical grounds to belong together but where there is considerable divergence in the age at which the behavior is reported, have been cross-referenced. Such discrepancies can usually be understood if one examines the criteria employed by the various authors for crediting the particular items.

Although the writer holds no brief for the tentative groupings which have been indicated in this table summarizing data on the language sequence, the table appears to have some interpretative value in suggesting possible groupings for future investigators who may be able to employ more uniform terminology and criteria in order to clarify this still obscure picture. Additional items are available up to 60 months of age in this group of studies, but they consist largely of the familiar intelligence test items, such as naming parts of the body, naming objects, naming objects in pictures, picture vocabulary and action-agent tests, as well as repetitions of sentences of various lengths. The objects and pictures employed take on variety so that the increasing numbers of things named have little or no significance from one investigation to the other. These difficulties begin to appear in the latter part of the table, but, as the first few items named are probably more nearly comparable from study to study, and since several authors have data up to 24 months of age, it was arbitrarily decided to terminate this analysis with the last group of items for which the earliest entries occurred in the twenty-fourth month.

At first inspection of the array of items in this table the reader may be impressed with the length of the list and the amount of detail. If, however, he will mentally cross out all the items which are appar-

ently duplicates, and list on a single line many of the items between pairs of horizontal lines, the amount of available information on the language sequence from the major normative studies will shrink appreciably. The reader will probably be impressed also with the striking degree of uniformity which is noticeable for the age at which similar items are reported in many instances where more than one author has observed the same or similar behavior with the same or almost the same criteria. Items 1 to 8 are, in general, descriptive of the utterances and syllabic vocalizations observed by most of the authors in the first few months. From the second to the fourth month are clustered all the reports of the infant's response to the human voice; the group of observations of cooing appears during this same time. Observations of vocalizations expressive of pleasure are reported by Bayley [1] and Gesell from the third to the sixth and seventh months, and of recognition in the seventh and eighth months. Variety in syllabification is heard apparently from the fourth to the sixth months and some rudimentary imitation of sounds from the sixth to the tenth months. Interjectional vocalizations are reported at the eighth month and listening to familiar words from the eighth to the ninth months. Response to gestures and to "Bye-bye" occurs from the ninth to the twelfth months.

The greatest discrepancies appear in the group of items from 57 to 60, in which the behavior is described in rather vague terminology and in which the various investigators may have employed different criteria for what constitutes "expressive sounds" and what constitutes "jargon." Differential responses to different words are reported by both Bayley and Gesell in the ninth and tenth months, and C. Bühler and Bayley agree in noting imitation of syllables and

[1] For bibliography references in this section, see headings of Table 1.

words in the eleventh month. Only two of these studies, those by Shirley and by Cattell, report data on the first word. Here, there is an apparent discrepancy, for Cattell notes a vocabulary of 1 word at 11 months, whereas Shirley notes it at 14 months. Shirley, however, recorded only words actually spoken in the presence of the examiner, although the mothers heard the first words considerably in advance of the time at which they were elicited during the examination. Cattell, however, accepted the mothers' reports of the occurrence of the first word. With the exception of C. Bühler,[1] all investigators report responses to commands of various sorts from the tenth to the twelfth months. Two words or more are reported quite uniformly at the twelfth month, with the third and fourth words following very shortly. The naming of single objects and pictures appears quite consistently in the latter half of the second year, as do responses to questions. According to the data available from this group of studies, children begin to combine words in the last quarter of the second year, and, as the vocabulary increases and the child enters upon the naming stage, there is a steady increase in the number of items named and objects pointed to in pictures on verbal request. Such items, numbered 104 to 126, are all clustered from the twenty-first to the thirty-sixth months with the majority of the reports occurring at about 24 months. The first phrases, sentences, pronouns, and prepositions occur in the twenty-third and twenty-fourth months and round out the most advanced accomplishments of the second year of life.

It is somewhat surprising that the same sequence of behavior should be described so differently by these authors, and even by the same author from time to time. It is

also surprising that some items which are readily observable and which one might expect to find reported by all investigators as landmarks are so often overlooked. Inspection of Table 1 for single entries reveals an amazing number of items on which only one of the writers reports data. Inspection of vertical columns of this table also reveals that it is entirely possible for writers to conduct apparently very thorough studies of infant behavior of the inventory type and yet to have serious gaps of several months without the notation of a single language item. For example, Bayley does not have any language items from the twelfth to the seventeenth months, Shirley has none between the ninth and fourteenth months, and C. Bühler has none from the sixth to the ninth months or from the eleventh to the fifteenth months.

Another limitation of this group of normative studies is that none of the observers was trained in phonetics or employed any kind of recording aids, and none gives data on the reliability of observation.

Lewis (1951) working in England and Grégoire (1937, 1947) in France used the phonetic approach to the problem of infant speech, employing the International Phonetic Alphabet and a comparative case study method. Their techniques overcame the earlier difficulties of spelling notation and the use of diacritical marks, but still they dealt with only a few selected infants.

In her review on the period of infancy, in which the section on language is based largely on Decroly's (c. 1934) survey, E. Dewey (1935) states:

> The literature is in general agreement that the first sounds of the newborn infant are the overt elements from which speech develops; that vocalizations are used as means of communication before words proper are used; that comprehension appears before the use of words; that the normal child has a repertoire of a very few

---

[1] Bühler's group was definitely underprivileged and probably was a retarded group of infants, living in institutions.

words by one year of age; that development is slow in the first months of the second year, but that toward the end of that year a great increase in the speed of progress appears; that words are first used in a generalized sense, and that their use for specific meanings is a developmental process; that name words appear first, verbs and adjectives later, relational words still later, and pronouns are just beginning to be used by the most advanced children by the end of the second year; that the first words have the force of a phrase or sentence, and combinations of words do not begin for some time [p. 251].

Prelinguistic Utterances of Infancy

Students of child development have always recognized the tremendous importance of the period of infancy, which is perhaps most often described as the period preceding the assumption of the erect posture. Strictly speaking, however, the word *infancy* means the period *without speech,* since the word itself is derived from the Latin words *in* (meaning without) + *fari* (to speak). The derivation was pointed out in 1880 by Schultze, but this interpretation of the meaning of the period of infancy is rarely encountered in the modern child development literature, and one finds that the derivation of the word is overlooked and emphasis placed on the more dramatic and more readily observable change in motor behavior which happens to occur at about the same time as the onset of speech.

Research in this period when utterances are incomprehensible is fraught with many methodological difficulties, described by McCarthy (1929*b*). There is the problem of hearing correctly the fleeting meaningless sounds and of using phonetic notation correctly in order to record them accurately. Although much progress has been made in mechanical and electrical recording, little

has been done to apply these techniques in the study of infant speech.

The most promising of the more recent developments in apparatus for use in this work are the spectrograph and Sonalator developed by the Bell Telephone Laboratories and described by Koenig and Rappel (1948), Kersta (1948), and by Koenig, Dunn, and Lacy (1946). These devices are sufficiently sensitive to give differentiable graphic records of consonant sounds, but practical research on infant sounds apparently will have to await development of motion-picture recording from the Sonalator.

Carmichael (1946) cites Minkowski's report of faint sounds uttered by a 5-month-old fetus (280 mm.) on exposure to the air as the earliest sounds observed in the human organism. Weak cries and spontaneous movements, more feeble than those of an infant born at term, were reported in a fetus of 330 mm. by Bolaffio and Artom (E. Dewey, 1935, p. 50). Thus, although the mechanism for the production of vocal sounds is ready to function considerably before birth, it is necessary to have the auditory and environmental social stimulation for language itself to emerge.

The Birth Cry. The birth cry is of significance for the development of language because it constitutes the first use of the delicate respiratory mechanisms which are to be involved in speech. Its function is entirely physiological, having to do with the establishment of normal respiration and the oxygenation of the blood. It is also the first time that the child hears the sound of his own voice and, as such, has significance for language development. The earlier interpretations of the child's first cry as having intellectual or emotional significance have largely been discarded and are now no longer held in the scientific literature.

Palmer (1940) reports briefly on a project involving the recording of the birth cry and of further recordings in the first 2 weeks of life. He found that children damaged at birth or prenatally have cries different from the cases delivered normally in pitch, rhythm, accentual character, and volume. Lynip (1951) reports the first graphic recordings of 2-second samplings of the birth cry of one child by means of a "sound spectrograph" developed by the Bell Telephone Laboratories. His pilot investigation on one infant involved taking weekly recordings for the first 13 months. Graphic records of selected utterances were obtained covering only 2.4 seconds' duration. These then require elaborate statistical analysis (not done in this study) of pitch fundamentals, resonances, intensities, etc. The method is an important step forward but needs considerable refinement before large-scale investigations will be feasible. The works of Cowan (1936) and of Hanley (1951) offer promising leads on methodology in this connection.

Later Sounds. It is almost universally agreed that the first utterances of the child are vowels of some sort. Observations in support of this are presented by Taine (1876), Preyer (1893), Tracy (1893), O'Shea (1907), Blanton (1917), Gesell (1925), Bean (1932), Shirley (1933a, 1933b), Lewis (1951), Irwin (1941a), Fisichelli (1950), and Lynip (1951), but from this point on there are divergent reports as to the order of appearance of the various speech sounds. The cruder observational studies were almost unanimous in reporting *m*, *p*, and *b* as the first consonants to appear and to modify the early vowel sounds into syllables.

Schultze (1880) states that the evolution of *lallation* is subject to the law of least physiological effort and that infants' phonetic utterances evolve from labial phenomena to sounds requiring greater effort,

namely, guttural sounds. Ombredane (1935), however, disagrees with this early observation and, in harmony with Irwin, points out that development proceeds from phenomena involving strong muscular tension (the glottic) to those having weak tension but which are uttered by the lips, the most mobile speech organs. He considers that the pre-eminence of the labial phenomenon marks the beginning of cortical functioning and the approach of the period of imitation.

In spite of the former general acceptance of the early appearance of labial sounds which have been said to be formed quite naturally when the child closes his lips while uttering a vowel sound, there is an accumulation of evidence which seems to indicate that the front consonants probably are not the most frequent early sounds.

Lewis (1951), who presents one of the most detailed phonemic studies based on only one child, but carefully integrated with earlier reports of infant vocalizations, is also in substantial agreement with the findings of Irwin and his associates. Lewis makes the interesting distinction between sounds uttered in comfort and sounds uttered in states of discomfort. He groups all the back consonants of *g*, *x*, *g*, *k*, and *r* as the early consonants uttered in comfort and the front consonants, both nasal and oral, as later consonants which are usually uttered in comfort. With regard to the front consonants Lewis (1951) states:

> Many observers have noted the occurrence of the characteristic labial and dental consonants. In Stern's summary of the records we find that they appear after the back consonants and that the nasals (*m* and *n*) occur chiefly in states of discomfort [p. 26].

Lewis (1951) traces an interesting relationship between the child's movements which are characteristically made with the vocal apparatus in typical states of comfort, usually after feeding, and in states of discomfort, usually in anticipation of feeding. The back consonants, which appear early and are said to be typical of periods of comfort, are associated with the swallowing and belching movements which usually follow feeding. In the prefeeding period the child typically makes mouthing movements with tongue and lips in anticipation of feeding which are most likely to result in the later m, p, and b sounds. It is obvious, however, that the infant needs some weeks of preliminary experience in the feeding situation in which to learn to make these anticipatory movements. It is probable that the earlier writers, who claimed that these labial and dental sounds appeared first, did not make their observations early enough in the neonatal period to get the first utterances. Hazlitt (1933) points out that no crying occurs in a state of comfort and that babbling occurs only in states of comfort. In general, the phonetic grouping of sounds for purposes of research in infant vocalizations appears promising. The reader who is interested in more detailed accounts of the phonetics of infant babblings should consult the works of Lewis (1951), and Grégoire (1937, 1947), Leopold (1947, 1949a, b), Fisichelli (1950), and Lynip (1951).

After the first acquisitions of sounds, there seems to be a rather rapid increase in the variety of sounds, so that by the third month most observers of infant behavior report cooing and babbling, which continue until about the end of the first year, when the first words are heard. K. C. Moore (1896) reports that her son had used all the sounds which occur in English by the fourth month. Lewis (1951) maintains that the child's first comfort sounds are really expressive and that they are subsequently transformed into playful babbling, that is, sounds uttered for the mere delight of uttering them.

Major experimental contributions to language development of infants have been made by Irwin and his associates at the University of Iowa. This reviewer has been able to locate a total of thirty articles by these writers scattered in various journals. Typically they consist of two- or three-page presentations of one or two facts, with emphasis on mathematical curve fitting and with a minimum of interpretation or discussion of the relation to child development or theory of language development. Four of them are reviews of the literature on infant vocalization (Irwin, 1941a; Irwin and Chen, 1943; Irwin, 1946b; and Irwin, 1949).

The most popular presentation appeared in the *Scientific American* in 1949, and the most technical of these reviews appeared in the *Journal of Speech Disorders* in 1943. At that time the authors concluded that it was quite obvious that a systematic knowledge of speech-sound status throughout the first year of life had not yet been achieved, and they characterized the literature as "spotty, meagre, and unscientific." Summarizing the reports for the first 6 months, they stated that during the second quarter of the first year of life infants produce most of the vowel elements and about half of the consonants. Contrasting the results of this period with the reports for the first month of life in which only about half of the vowels and very few consonants are present, they noted that a great expansion in the mastery of sounds occurs in the first 6 months of life (Irwin and Chen, 1943).

Three of their studies are concerned primarily with methods and the reliability problem (Irwin, 1941a; Irwin and Chen, 1941; and Irwin, 1945), and two are concerned entirely with variability (Irwin, 1947b, c). These authors use the International Phonetic Alphabet to transcribe the speech sounds uttered during 30 breaths. The respiration unit was found more satisfactory than time units or speech samples of specified length for this type of research (Irwin and Curry, 1941). They use either consecutive or nonconsecutive breaths, during which crying occurs, in the studies of the newborn. Noncrying sounds are reported to be rare in newborns. It cannot be determined from the reports whether the "speech sounds" attributed to older children are also heard during crying or not, and in none of these reports do they give any information as to how long a time was required to secure vocalization during 30 breaths. The descriptions of method are so brief that it is difficult or impossible for others to duplicate the procedure. No descriptions are given of the conditions under which the observations were made.

Irwin was able, after taking all the phonetics courses offered at Iowa, and after considerable intensive training in phonetics under several phoneticians, and by keeping in practice himself, to train Curry and Chen to agree with him in the recording of the vowel utterances of newborn infants with percentages of agreement over 90. This was based on the speech sounds collected in 30 breaths for 18 infants. Continued observational practice did not improve observer reliability appreciably. It should be pointed out that the reliability data presented in the 1941 studies were limited to *vowels* in the *crying of newborn infants*. It is not surprising that high observer reliabilities can be obtained in the newborn period, when there are so few sounds to be discriminated, when the data are limited to vowels which have greater duration than consonants, and when crying, rather than noncrying, sounds are used, in which the sounds are sustained. A further study on the reliability of speech sounds, both vowels and consonants, appeared in

1945. This, however, deals with odd-even reliability and with different samples, and not with observer reliability. The reliabilities are very high, from .93 to .99 for vowels and from .88 to .97 for consonants, indicating high internal consistency when very wide age ranges contribute to the heterogeneity of the data.

The measures used in the Irwin studies are: (1) simple frequencies of the occurrence of each of the vowel and consonant phonemes, counting duplicates; (2) "types" of vowels and consonants, i.e., number of different sounds, or variety; (3) ratios of consonant to vowel frequencies; (4) ratios of consonant to vowel types; (5) type-token ratio (TTR), which is the ratio of the variety of sounds to the frequency of use; and (6) two indices based on the difference between the number and percentage of phonemes in infant and adult speech. In addition, some of these studies utilize a profile technique (Irwin, 1941b) in which a series of single phonemes or groups of phonemes, such as labials or dentals, are arranged along a base line and histograms are erected to indicate their frequencies in per cent. Comparisons of such profiles from age to age or from group to group are helpful and informative.

The earlier articles (1941) are based on 40 infants in the first 10 days and on some small groups of 10 to 15 infants in the first 6 months. The later articles (1946–1948) are all different analyses of the same basic data from 95 children in the first 30 months of life. The original plan was to visit each child twice a month in a longitudinal study, but owing to the war many cases were lost. There are many retests of the same babies in the data. The largest number of subjects at any bimonthly age group is 80, and the numbers dwindle after 20 months, the smallest number, 19, occurring at the 29–30 month age level. The number of records per age level ranges from 27 to 181. The basic data from seven articles are summarized in Table 2. The articles themselves present growth curves for each of these functions, together with the mathematical equations for the curves. In evaluating the data it must be kept in mind that these studies are not independent but are based on the same records from the same babies, observed by the same workers, with similar training, who worked together.

The main points of developmental significance in the data of these studies are: (1) The frequency of vowel sounds is greater than that of consonant sounds in the first 30 months. (2) There is a steady increase in the frequency of vowel sounds until 2 years of age, but then there is a rapid spurt in the curve for vowel frequency as soon as real speech emerges. (3) In early infancy vowel sounds are about 5 times as frequent as consonant sounds. (4) The curve for consonant frequency in this period is parabolic. (5) Consonant frequency does not equal vowel frequency until about 2½ years of age. (6) In the first 2 months children used on the average 4.5 different vowel sounds and only 2.7 different consonants. (7) The number of vowel types exceeds the number of consonant types throughout the first year, but at this time, when the first words usually emerge, the two curves for vowel and consonant types cross, and the number of consonant types exceeds the number of vowel types at all later ages observed. (8) By 2½ years the child uses practically all of the vowel sounds, but only 16, or about two-thirds, of the consonants he will use as an adult (Irwin and Chen, 1946a; and Chen and Irwin, 1946a). (9) During the first 2 months the child's phonemic repertoire consists of 7.5 different phonemes, and by 29–30 months it includes 27 of the 35 phonemes present in adult speech (Voelker, 1935), the progress being greater in the first

year of life than in the succeeding year and a half (Irwin and Chen, 1946a). (10) Sex differences do not emerge until the 26–27 month age level when, at about the age for the onset of true speech, the curve for the girls forges ahead of that for the boys. (11) When consonants are considered from the point of view of manner of articulation, the nasals show a marked increase with age, and the fricatives decrease with age in the first 30 months. (This may conceivably be related to the shift from the lying to the erect posture which occurs during the age span covered.) (12) When consonants are considered according to the place of articulation, back consonants, especially glottals, predominate at first, constituting 87 per cent of the consonants. These and the velars account for 97 per cent of the few consonants used in the earlier months. As the other types of consonants made with the forward parts of the oral cavity, namely the post-dentals, dentals, and labials, emerge the glottals drop to only 8 per cent of the consonants by 30 months of age. (13) When vowels are analyzed according to place of phonation a reverse situation is observed, for the front vowels decrease from 72 to 47 per cent and the back vowels increase from 2.3 to 37 per cent by 2½ years of age. (14) Initial consonants yield a linear curve in the age range studied and exceed medial and final ones. (15) Final consonants are negligible in the first ½ year and are then mastered at an accelerating rate, though they never exceed the initial or medial consonants.

In an unpublished doctoral dissertation under the writer's direction Fisichelli (1950) obtained high-fidelity tape recordings of ½-hour vocalizations of 100 institutionalized infants. There were 20 children at each of five discrete age levels from 6 to 18 months. In general her findings in regard to consonant development agree very well with Irwin's investigations although

TABLE 2

SUMMARY OF BASIC DATA IN SEVEN IRWIN STUDIES

Age in Months [1]	No. of Sub-jects	No. of Rec-ords	Mean No. of Pho-nemes [1]	Mean No. of Vowel Types [2]	Mean No. of Conso-nant Types [2]	Mean Vowel Fre-quen-cy [3]	Mean Conso-nant Fre-quen-cy [3]	Mean Ratio of Consonant Types [4] Vowel Types	Mean Ratio of Consonant Frequency [4] Vowel Frequency	Type-Token Ratio in 100 Sounds [5]	Relative Frequency of Vowel Sounds Classified by Place of Articulation [6]			Relative Frequency of Consonant Sounds Classified by Place of Articulation [7]				
											% Front	% Mid-dle	% Back	% Labials and Labio-Den-tals	% Lin-gua-Den-tals	% Post-Den-tals	% Ve-lars	% Glot-tals
1– 2	62	125	7.2[8]	4.5[8]	2.7[8]	49.0[8]	11.3[8]	63	25	7.5[8]	72.4[8]	25.2[8]	2.3[8]	0.6[8]	—	0.7[8]	11.6[8]	87.1[8]
3– 4	80	181	11.1	6.6	4.5	52.8	14.3	70	29	10.0	60.6	25.8	13.6	3.7	0.8[8]	5.4	14.7	75.4
5– 6	75	166	12.3	7.1	5.2	56.3	17.6	76	36	11.4	62.1	23.7	14.3	8.1	0.7	4.5	12.6	74.3
7– 8	64	170	15.1	8.1	7.0	55.2	21.2	89	40	11.7	63.3	19.8	16.7	13.3	0.8	11.3	8.3	66.3
9–10	62	147	16.0	8.3	7.7	56.4	24.7	95	46	13.5	62.2	17.0	20.8	20.8	1.6	24.3	6.1	47.1
11–12	62	149	18.6	8.9	9.7	58.0	33.5	110	59	15.4	62.1	16.4	21.5	22.9	1.2	34.9	6.7	34.3
13–14	57	127	18.8	10.0	9.8	56.6	32.6	109	57		60.0	17.0	23.1	25.4	1.1	33.9	7.6	32.0
15–16	55	128	20.4	9.7	10.8	56.5	36.1	111	65		59.8	15.9	24.3	25.3	0.7	36.6	8.6	28.8
17–18	50	106	21.0	10.1	10.9	60.0	37.6	109	63		54.0	16.5	29.5	29.6	0.7	39.7	8.1	21.9
19–20	41	84	22.5	10.2	12.4	57.2	40.1	126	70		49.4	17.2	33.4	29.6	0.9	42.4	9.0	18.1
21–22	37	68	23.0	10.3	12.7	58.2	48.9	122	83		46.0	16.2	37.8	33.2	0.7	44.3	10.8	10.9
23–24	31	52	24.4	10.7	13.7	59.9	53.0	128	89		50.3	14.2	35.5	28.4	1.0	48.7	7.7	12.8
25–26	32	51	25.8	11.0	14.8	70.6	67.2	134	93		47.3	14.6	38.1	28.4	0.7	51.9	11.0	8.0
27–28	24	41	26.1	11.0	15.1	73.0	67.4	135	90		49.6	14.6	35.7	24.5	0.7	56.0	10.4	8.4
29–30	19	27	27.2	11.4	15.8	75.3	73.5	139	98		46.6	16.7	36.7	26.0	1.8	52.9	11.5	7.7

[1] Irwin, 1947a.
[2] Chen and Irwin, 1946a.
[3] Irwin and Chen, 1946b.
[4] Irwin, 1946a.
[5] Chen and Irwin, 1946b.
[6] Irwin, 1948a.
[7] Irwin, 1947d.
[8] All values have been rounded to one decimal place.

the institutionalized children showed retardation in comparison with his subjects living with their own families. Fisichelli, too, found regular increases with age in consonant/vowel ratios. When the aspirate h phoneme is omitted (some phoneticians class it as a vowel) she also found a decline in back consonants and an increase in front consonants with increase in age. These measures seem to be of real developmental significance. Vowel data from this study and from the Irwin investigations are, however, more difficult to harmonize. This is probably due to differences in phonetic transcription. The Iowa workers observed the babies directly and undoubtedly were influenced in their notations by lip-reading techniques, whereas in the Fisichelli data transcriptions were done directly from the tape recording so that only auditory cues were used. Then, too, the dialects spoken by middle westerners differ from those of the eastern-seaboard transcribers probably so as to affect the vowel notations especially. Subsequent work by Curry (1950) and by Siegenthaler (1950) shows the difficulties involved in correct identification of vowels without the aid of context, as is necessary in dealing with the utterances of infants. Future workers in this field would do well to heed the warnings stated by the famous linguist Sapir (see Mandelbaum, 1949) in an article entitled "The Psychological Reality of Phonemes."

A few additional points in the Irwin studies concerning relationships to intelligence, socio-economic status, size of family, and institutional experience will be discussed in the appropriate sections. It is to be hoped that these authors will some day integrate this material in monograph form with suitable interpretation and that their promising techniques can be mastered by others, so that such basic investigations can be verified and the findings related to other aspects of child development.

Thompson (1952) is the first to summarize these studies in a major text.

As more objective and more refined observations on the vocalizations of infants begin to appear in the literature it is possible to fit various aspects of the puzzle together and to see an emergent pattern in the prelinguistic utterances. Much of the confusion in the literature is undoubtedly due to the tendency of authors to speak of "sounds" and not to differentiate between vowel and consonant sounds, which Irwin's investigations show have directly opposite developmental trends. Another difficulty is attributable to failure to distinguish between sounds uttered in crying and noncrying vocalizations. In the Irwin and Curry (1941) study approximately 50 per cent of the consonants of newborns were the aspirate sound h. It occurred in their data 4 times as often as the next most frequent consonant. Other writers who report h as among the earliest sounds are Blanton (1917), Fenton (1925), Bean (1932), and Shirley (1933a, b). Lewis (1951) also gives an explanation of the early appearance of the h sound, which he says "is the sound heard if the voice is momentarily withheld in the act of uttering any vowel" (p. 30). It must be remembered in interpreting observations such as this that the organs used in speech are also used for respiration, which biologically is their primary function, and only later are they used for speech, for the essential accomplishment of the newborn, if he is to survive, is breathing. It should not be surprising, therefore, that the young infant, whose breathing is just becoming established, and whose early utterances are almost all in crying states, should have the most frequent consonant sound designated by the letter h which in its Greek origin meant "rough breathing." The frequency of occurrence of this aspirate sound, h, and its classification as a consonant, contributes heavily to the generalization that consonant development proceeds from back to front, in contrast to the front to back development of the vowels.

Evidence has been mounting in the direction of what Goldstein (1948) aptly terms an "organismic" approach to language development, as opposed to the earlier conceptions which he characterizes as "atomistic" theories. He considers that "every individual speech performance is understandable only from the aspect of its relation to the function of the total organism in its endeavor to realize itself" (p. 21). He stresses the importance of the meaningfulness of sounds uttered in each situation. In order to understand the organismic concept of language development it is well to keep in mind some of the principles of organismic development as they have emerged from studies of physical and motor development (McCarthy, 1952c). Certain of the more recent theories in the literature seem to fit in with the laws of developmental direction, that the development of the organism proceeds from anterior to posterior parts of the body and from medial to more peripheral organs. The ideas on language development seem to harmonize also with the theory of motor development proceeding from mass activity through control of gross muscles to the finer muscular coordinations, and these concepts, in turn, enable interpretation in terms of the total organism and make possible an understanding of the triple functioning of the organs of speech in breathing, eating, and speaking (McCarthy, (1952c).

Shohara (1935) points out that both food-getting movements and speech movements serve the same purpose of advancing the general welfare of the organism through facilitating its direct or indirect integration with the environment. The thesis is presented that speech movements of oral and pharyngeal structures are modifications of the various movements involved in eating, namely, sucking, swallowing, and chewing. Shohara claims that aside from the articulatory movements, no movements of oral and pharyngeal structures are known to exist which cannot be shown to be concerned with providing food, including gaseous food or oxygen. This author goes so far as to state that in the articulation of the various consonant sounds the specific action of each muscle or muscle group bears "a close resemblance to, or even identity with, sucking, swallowing, and chewing." It is interesting to note that speech does not emerge in the normal child until after breathing is well established and has become automatic, the child has assumed the erect posture for most of his waking time, and has had some experience with solid food which affords exercise of jaw muscles in chewing (McCarthy, 1949c and 1952c). Shohara points out further that over 80 per cent of the consonants in Indo-European languages are made with the lips and tip of the tongue, and then traces the origin of consonant development from movements of the tongue in sucking, chewing, and grinding. In vowels, however, an opposite situation is noted as they are formed by the contraction of the muscle fibers in the posterior part of the dorsum and root of the tongue, which are the muscle groups used in swallowing. Is there not a parallel here between this theory of Shohara (1935) and Irwin's findings that vowel development proceeds from front to back of the oral cavity and that consonant development proceeds from back to front? May there not be a parallel between the mass activity of the newborn and vowel development? Vowel sounds are made by the stream of breath passing over the vocal cords into an oral cavity of varying shapes at varying times. This oral cavity is smallest when front vowels of i, I, etc., are being made, and these are the vowels which appear first. Then the cavity gradually becomes larger as the mouth is opened wider and the tongue is retracted, for after birth the child no longer needs to use it as a valve to keep out amniotic fluid and is able to live in the medium of the air. This probably is the raw stuff out of which more specific speech sounds, particularly syllables, are individuated.

The consonants however, which result from control of tongue and lip movements, particularly in the anterior regions, develop later, and this development progresses from the back of the oral cavity toward the front. The aspirate *h* and the guttural and velar sounds are first among the consonant group when the young infant is just establishing breathing and when he is learning to suck and to swallow. Vowels predominate during the early months while the infant is still a nursling and remains in a dorsal or prone position most of the time. This theory, it seems, could eventually be harmonized with the observations of regular sequences in the appearance of the various phonemes (Grégoire, 1937, 1947) and with Jakobson's (1941) contributions on comparative linguistics, which show, as Goldstein (1948) puts it, a "constancy in the sequence of the occurrence of sounds [which] indicates that we are dealing with a fundamental phenomenon characteristic of man." Goldstein (1948), however, was not familiar with the Irwin investigations and, going only on the cruder observations of the biographical studies, found it necessary to omit the babbling period in order for his organismic point of view to hold. He rightly points out that Schultze's law of least physical effort is difficult to validate because we do not know which movements are "easier" to make than others. It seems highly probable that in the near future all these points of view can be harmonized to include the babbling period in the developmental sequence.

As McCarthy (1952c) points out, there are five important changes which occur in infancy before the onset of true articulate speech involving syllabic utterances which combine vowels and consonants in meaningful units. After the survival of the infant is fairly well established by the successful maintenance of respiration and ingestion of food, the two primary uses of the organs of speech, he assumes the erect posture. He sits up at about the time he enters into the babbling stage. This postural change must affect the shape of the oral cavity, especially by affecting the normal position of the soft palate, which undoubtedly accounts at least in part for the forward movement of the control of muscles involving the later-appearing consonants. Two other changes, which follow shortly in the last quarter of the first year of life, are the experience with solid food, which stimulates chewing and exercises jaw muscles, and dentition. As chewing activity increases and nursing and suckling activity decrease, the sucking pads in the cheeks of the infant become absorbed, which again alters the shape of the oral cavity. He also acquires front teeth, usually 4 upper and 4 lower ones by the end of the first year, which give a new front wall to the oral cavity and make possible dental and postdental consonant sounds. It is only after respiration has been satisfactorily established, after the child has assumed the erect posture, has ceased to be nursed, has begun to use solid food, and after the frontal incisors have erupted, that the onset of true speech is observed. As control of tongue and lips proceeds and dentition provides the frontal wall of the oral cavity, cortical control of speech sounds begins, and the infant voluntarily imitates the speech of others and imitates his own speech sounds. According to Berry and Eisenson

(1942), "The spinal cord subserves speech directly only in breathing." Swallowing, sucking, and chewing are innervated chiefly through the medulla, and many writers have attributed cortical control to the tongue tip and lip movements involved in the later-developing front consonants. Thus, the gross features of infant behavior, involving the use of the musculature of the organs of speech, appear to follow a neurological sequence from lower to higher centers of the central nervous system.

Other aspects of early infantile experience in oral activity, which should be mentioned for a full appreciation of the significance of this early period, are that the mouth is pre-eminent in the domain of touch in the newborn and that during this early period everything is explored with the mouth, when the palate is extremely sensitive. Also, hand-to-mouth reactions are one of the main ways in which the infant explores his environment. This oral exploration does not wane until after voluntary reaching and grasping and eye-hand coordinations are well established. It is possible that further study of some of these relationships may reveal facts of importance in the genesis of handedness and eyedness which are often found to be disturbed in cases manifesting clinical syndromes of language disorder at higher ages. Of interest in this connection is the fact that hand preference usually begins to be manifested at about the same age as the onset of true speech.

T. K. Davis (1938) stresses that the primitive sounds are not only action but emotion in action, and Ribble (1943) emphasizes the importance of the pleasure value of the sucking activity which relieves tension and establishes a vital relationship with the mother as the giver of this pleasure. Ribble considers that the sucking activity alone is satisfying and pleasurable to the child whether much food is ingested or not. T. K. Davis points out that the organs of the oral cavity have developed from the embryological "primitive gut" and that sounds have greater vital significance the closer their activating organs are to the visceral regions. He considers that the lips which are the most peripheral of the organs of speech and which have already been indicated as probably being under cortical control dominate the expression of ideas rather than the expression of emotions. These suggestions have interesting implications for the study of the emotional tone of many of the child's early sentences (McCarthy, 1930) and for the importance of the mother-child relationships in many of the language disorders (McCarthy, 1946, 1947, and 1952c).

Sherman (1927) showed that adults had little success in judging the emotional accompaniment of infants' cries when the stimuli were not known. Interpretations of the cries were most often based on what was known regarding the stimulating situation and not on any peculiar characteristics of the cries themselves. Blanton (1917), who was the first to observe as many as 25 babies during the first month of life, states: "There were differences of vowels and consonants, of timbre and degree, but no one was used as response to one set of circumstances that was not at the same time used to others—the cry of colic was the one exception." She also states that the other cries of the infant in the first month of life in response to hunger, pain, and cold differ from each other only in intensity.

Lynip (1951) in his spectrogram analysis of the "hunger" and "attention getting" crying of one girl infant states that it was impossible to find sound values corresponding to the interpretations attributed to the various "types" of crying. The designations of "hunger" and "attention" given the cries by the mother and the experimenter were in terms of probability favoring one designation over another because it preceded or followed a feeding period. This author reports that "crying samples differed even though the observable stimuli remained the same" and, further, that "there was some partial resemblance in certain crying when stimuli differed."

Most writers agree that children's speech sounds are much less precise and definite than those of adults, and that during this preliminary babbling period of infancy there occurs increasing definiteness of utterance of various syllables. The often-reported observations that young infants at first use only a few vowels and later add more and more sounds to their verbal repertoire, and the frequent observation of the persistence of baby-talk which is gradually outgrown, have led many writers to assume that the speech sounds are acquired very gradually and that the complex sounds are built up from the simple ones. A number of articles, however, tend to bring this theory of the learning of language into question, for many writers have indicated that they find a tremendous variety in the vocal repertoire of the infant and that they hear many sounds which defy spelling in our alphabet.

McGranahan (1936) says that there are two main types of theories of the evolution of language. One which was popular in the nineteenth century conceived of the development of language as a building-up process involving the progressive combination and integration of a number of elementary units called *roots*. The other more recent theory championed by Jespersen (1922) considers the process of evolution to be one of progressive differentiation of a number of primitive mass units. McGranahan (1936) further points out:

These two theories of linguistic development have interesting counterparts in modern physiological and psychological theories of development. The root theory, for example, corresponds to the reflex theory of behavioral development, according to which more mature and complex behavior results from the combination and integration of a number of elementary reflexes; and the mass theory to the modern psychological conception of behavioral development as the progressive differentiation of original mass activity.

Children whose mother tongue is to be English, and who are hearing only English, often use sounds resembling German umlaut sounds, French guttural *r*'s, and a wide variety of sounds which it is difficult or impossible to describe. These phenomena are usually attributed to the plasticity of the child's speech organs; and, since any child regardless of his parentage learns the language which he hears spoken by those in his environment, it is claimed that the sounds needed for any particular language which the child is to learn are selected from this extensive repertoire and are singled out for practice because they are heard so frequently. Latif (1934) states that out of this astonishingly rich and varied repertoire of sounds those which are used by the child's elders are reinforced and become habitual and others cease to be uttered. He goes on to state:

Almost as soon as sounds begin to be produced at all they begin to be repeated rather slowly and monotonously. . . . This *repetition,* or *reduplication,* may well be considered the final step in that process by which the mere vocalizations become organized into language. It is here that explanation of the development of language must begin [p. 62].

Children's babbling often consists of repetition of identical or similar syllables so that the first vocal utterances to acquire meaning are usually reduplicated monosyllables such as *mama, dada, nana, bye-bye, tick-tick, choo-choo,* and the like. Writers who hold to slow acquisition of sounds and the building-up of the repertoire of speech sounds by imitation, and the gradual perfection of each, stress the difficulty of the sounds from the motor aspect and claim that the sounds which are late in appearing are more difficult to execute. As Goldstein (1948) brings out, however, we do not know the relative difficulty of executing the various speech sounds. It has to be inferred from the time of their appearance.

Others, who see extreme variety in the plasticity of the vocal organs, take the point of view that the child can make the various sounds necessary for the acquisition of any language at a very early age, but they stress the sensory and perceptual difficulties of the acquisition of speech. E. Dewey (1935), in summarizing the literature on this point, says:

> There are a number of theories as to the way in which speech develops from the early vocalizations. In general, two opposing points of view appear: one, that learning goes on by a very gradual process of building up the complex from the simple; the other, that the original phonetic equipment of the individual is very large and that learning takes place by a process of adjusting, and eliminating, the sounds used to the language learned. . . . Grégoire, on the other hand, believes that the sound repertoire of the young infant is phonetically great and that a particular language evolves by the elimination of some sounds. The first sounds the infant makes are uncoordinated, and precision is gained gradually. In the beginning, the infant tries hard to express himself without awareness of trying to use words. He usually ends by crying. Later, about the ninth month, the combination of syllables begins. This sounds in its rhythm like an imitation of adult speech, and in the tenth month he begins to imitate the rhythm of the language of his country. Before the

question can be decided we must have more exact, complex, and phonetically correct records of all sounds made by infants, from the time of birth to the appearance of speech [p. 252].

If Grégoire's theory of the beginnings of speech is substantiated by further investigation, it will be interesting to relate it to the known facts about the development of the gross motor skills in which there occurs individuation of specific movements from the random mass activity manifested by the newborn child. Irwin's researches summarized above appear to be the first steps in the demonstration that some such individuation occurs in the motor responses involved in the development of speech. McCarthy's (1952c) organismic interpretation attempts to relate some of Irwin's findings to certain physical and motor development patterns.

Grégoire (1937, 1947), Lewis (1951), Irwin and his associates, and Fisichelli (1950) have done the most extensive work using the International Phonetic Alphabet. Lynip (1951) questions the validity of this approach, however, for he claims that crying utterances of infants "cannot be expressed in sound values used to describe an adult's language sounds" and that "there exist no symbols representative of sounds made by infants before they learn to talk." He finds only "dim outlines of future sound forms in the spectrograms of babbling." This he attributes to the differences in size and shape of the articulating mechanisms of the child and of the adult. He finds a "similarity" of child utterances to adult speech sounds, but says that they are "lacking in clarity." He found in the child he observed that "a series of changes took place in the infant's sound production until, at the thirteenth month, a remarkable similarity could be observed between the infant's utterances and those of its mother." These sounds, however, were only approximately the equivalents of adult vowels and consonants.

✓ *The Rôle of Imitation.* The mere fact that the child learns the language of his environment is evidence of the importance of imitation. Children imitate all aspects of the behavior of others. This is especially apparent in motor and verbal areas. The fact that the congenitally deaf child does not learn to speak because he is deprived of the opportunity to imitate others also bears witness to the important rôle of this factor. Imitative behavior is reported most often after the ninth month and is especially prominent around the end of the first year and the beginning of the second year when language proper is just beginning to emerge. Champneys (1881) said, "From 9 months the child distinctly imitated the intonation of the voice when any word or sentence was repeated several times." C. Bühler (1930) reports some elemental imitation of sounds as early as 6 months, whereas Cattell (1940) reports imitation of words as a test item at 9 months, and Gesell (1928) at 10 months. C. Bühler (1930) reports imitation of syllables such as *mama, papa,* and *dada* at the eleventh month and Bayley (1933) finds her group of infants imitating words at 11.7 months. Shirley (1933a, 1933b) reports the first imitative word heard in the presence of the examiners in the fourteenth month, although the mothers of the children in her group had reported such behavior considerably earlier. (See Table 1.)

The term *imitation* has been used in several different ways in the literature. Decroly (c. 1934) distinguishes the following forms of imitation (p. 88):

1. Imitation with and without intention to imitate which is sometimes designated as spontaneous or voluntary imitation.
2. Imitation with or without comprehension.

3. Immediate or deferred imitation.
4. Exact and inexact imitation.

It is over the last of these that so much controversy has centered. The most limited use of the term refers only to exact mimetic reproduction of the identical sounds said to the child as a model. Although this sort of reproduction undoubtedly does occur, it is much more rare than the second type, by which is meant the attempt to reproduce sounds heard, regardless of the accuracy of the accomplishment. Most present-day psychologists seem to agree with the opinion of Taine (1876) that new sounds are not learned by imitation of the speech of others, but rather that they emerge in the child's spontaneous vocal play as a result of maturation, and that the child imitates only those sounds which have already occurred in its spontaneous babblings. This view holds that imitation of the speech of others serves only to call attention to new combinations of sounds already used.

Curti (1938) also states:

> By repeating to the child other sounds which he has already spontaneously practiced, adults may evoke the sounds again and again and thus lead to facility in their use. No sound, however, will be thus repeated which the child has not already used [p. 261].

Shirley (1933a, 1933b) calls attention to the fact that there is a marked tendency to imitate the intonations and inflections of the voice regardless of the specific sounds. Valentine (1942) distinguishes two types of imitation noted in his observations of his 3 children; first, the imitation of sound-making in general, which he called a "talking back" stage, occurring at about 2 months, and the later type consisting of distinct efforts to imitate specific sounds. He stresses "readiness to imitate" and describes efforts on the part of 2 of his children "to imitate difficult words—combinations of sounds which they probably had not uttered spontaneously *as* combinations." An excellent discussion of the problem of imitation appeared in Guillaume (1925), which is well summarized in French by Decroly (*c*. 1934) and in English by Lewis (1951).

Lynip (1951), who was the first to obtain graphic recordings of an infant's utterances, states that as one listens to recordings of early imitations they appear to match the mother's sounds, but that "although there is a similarity, there is a lack of clarity to the infant's utterances." He states that exact mimetic imitation was not found, but neither was the child observed to produce the same sounds heard in previous weeks. The tendency to echo adult sounds was found, but the infant's utterances were constantly changing, successive modifications tending to approximate adult sounds more and more closely. The subject of his investigation did not produce any vowel or consonant sounds comparable to those of adults until the thirteenth month, and even then only approximations of adult sounds were noted.

When the child accidentally, and later purposefully, reproduces sounds which he himself has made, the adults in the environment usually say a real word which the child's sounds appear to approximate. This tends to give auditory reinforcement to the sounds the child has just made, at the same time making for more precise perception and rendition of the approved sound groups. Thus there occurs a progressive elimination of errors and a selection of movements which give the best approximation to the real word heard in the speech of adults. Continued practice thus results in the fixation of the sound groups, which come to be uttered habitually.

Basing his point of view largely on Guernsey's (1928) intensive study of 200 children between the ages of 2 and 21 months, Lewis (1951) outlines three stages of imitation. He cites the child's tendency in the first 3 or 4 months to respond to human utterance by making sounds as a rudimentary form of imitation. Most writers do not classify this early vocalization as imitation, but Lewis points out that it is really a question of the criterion of imitation to which one subscribes. He then notes a pause during which there is a "diminution, if not an entire cessation, of the vocal responses to speech typical of the first stage." The third stage which he recognizes is that which most writers report at about 9 months of age. He says: "There can be no question that in the second and third months children normally respond vocally to speech as speech." He argues for the imitative nature of these early sounds, which have been reported in the literature, on the grounds that "first, they most readily occur when the child is attentive to the speaker; secondly, the child's utterance is specially evoked by hearing adult speech; and, thirdly, this utterance consists of his own familiar sounds" (p. 73). He cites the Sterns (1907), the Hoyers (1924), Guillaume (1925), Valentine (1930), and C. Bühler (1931) as showing similarity of phonetic form between the vocalizations of the first 2 or 3 months and sounds spoken to the child by adults. He points out, however, that sometimes the child's responses do not resemble what he hears either in intonation or phonetic form and concludes:

> It would appear, then, . . . that the child's vocal response to adult speech in his earliest months consists of his own familiar sounds; when he hears a sound drawn from his own repertory, his response may occasionally resemble it in intonational and phonetic form.

Three different explanations of the phenomenon of imitation have been advanced in the literature and are well summarized by Lewis (1951) as follows: "First, that there is an innate tendency for the child to respond to speech by speech; secondly, that the child responds by expression to expression; and, thirdly, that vocal responses to speech arise from intervention of the adult into the child's activity of babbling" (p. 76). In discussing the third of these explanations, Lewis points out that this is J. M. Baldwin's (1895) hypothesis of *circular reaction*, which has been accepted by such writers as the Sterns (1907), Bekhterev (1913), F. H. Allport (1924), Koffka (1924), Guillaume (1925), and McDougall (1931), and Allport's description of the circular reflex, which has been followed by Markey (1928), Lorimer (1929), and many others.

The general principle is that "in the course of repetitive babbling, a pattern of alternating hearing and utterance is set up; if an adult repeatedly imitates one of a child's own sounds while he is babbling, the heard sound becomes a part of the pattern of alternation, so that ultimately it remains effective in evoking speech which may resemble the stimulus both in phonetic and in intonational form" (p. 79). Lewis (1951) goes on to point out, however, that Baldwin's (1895) hypothesis which has been so widely accepted cannot by itself account for the child's learning of language through imitation, for the Sterns (1907), Koffka (1924), Guillaume (1925), and McDougall (1931) "have found it necessary to supplement Baldwin's (1895) principle by accepting at the same time the principle of a general tendency to respond to speech by speech."

Lewis (1951) believes he is the first, however, to point out that "the actually observed facts of early babbling and imitation demand that Baldwin's principle shall be modified and supplemented." He concludes then that "our only alternative is to recognize that the hearing of the adult word can merely stimulate the child to the utterance of his *own* babbling sounds and that from this the child may become trained to respond with a particular sound to a particular heard sound" (p. 80).

Training experiments in language presuppose imitation as a basic factor. One of the most conclusive experiments on this point was made by Strayer (1930) in which one member of a pair of identical twins was given intensive training in naming objects, etc., for a period of 5 weeks, whereas the other twin was deprived of all opportunity to hear language during that period. After this initial experimental period, similar training was given to the other twin. The author concludes:

A maturational difference of even 5 weeks has a definite influence on the relative effectiveness of training. . . . Not only was training which was begun with a maturational advantage of 5 weeks more effective than earlier training, but the pattern of response was more mature. Training cannot transcend maturational level.

She adds that the typical stages in the learning process were strikingly alike for both children. Sommer (1932), who found a 28 per cent improvement in an untrained kindergarten group in articulation, also tends to show the influence of maturation, although her trained group showed a 57 per cent improvement due to the effects of both maturation and the training given in articulation.

Decroly (*c.* 1934) calls attention to a controversy in the literature on the problem of the relationship between imitation and comprehension of language. He points out that Compayré (1896), Sully (1908), and Meumann (1908) consider that vocal imitation comes before true language but that Preyer (1900) contends that imitation does not precede comprehension. His son did not imitate the word *papa* until about the second year although he gave considerable evidence of understanding language in the period from 12 to 18 months. The Sterns (1907) are cited as pointing out, in contradiction to Preyer (1900), that sound groups are imitated long before the appearance of comprehension and that the imitation observed in their 3 children at about the ninth month was only imitation of gestures, inarticulate sounds, and intonations of the voice. Imitation of the combinations of articulate sounds did not appear until the end of the second year, at which time many words were understood and some pronounced correctly. As E. Dewey says:

Decroly (*c*. 1934) concludes that auditory differentiation must precede speech and is a necessary element in imitation, and that development of comprehension and auditory perception are inseparable. He says that words do not have a purely tonal or musical interest for the child, and that he distinguishes only those to which he gives a meaning. Therefore, imitation cannot precede understanding; for function must not only be within the capacity of the individual, it must also serve some individual need or interest [p. 260].

Leopold's (1949*a*) third volume on the language development of his bilingual daughter is replete with illustrations of what he terms "mechanical imitation" especially in the use of interjections and in the 1-word-sentence stage. He stresses, however, the selectiveness of the child's imitation and points out that imitation is not a passive process but requires active cooperation on the part of the child and that the child is the one who chooses what he will imitate.

Language Comprehension. Most writers agree that the child understands the language of others considerably before he actually uses language himself. Abundant evidence for this appears in the anecdotal

accounts in the early biographical studies indicating children's responses to commands and questions. Some of these incidents are subjective and are inadequately reported without complete description of the circumstances in which the utterances were made. From the normative studies included in Table 1 it would seem as if the child usually gives objective evidence in his overt behavior of his comprehension of the speech of others at about the end of the first year. There may, however, be a dawning comprehension at about the ninth month, when the child is reported as paying close attention to words and making differential responses to them.

Decroly (*c*. 1934) begins the discussion of the problem of language comprehension with a consideration of the child's earliest responses to sounds, especially to the sound of the human voice, and agrees that the first influence of heard words is affective in nature. He also discusses the problem of the length of the interval between the child's first comprehension of language and his actual use of linguistic expression. The Sterns (1907) are cited as maintaining that there is a relatively short interval between the time when the child first shows that he comprehends speech and his actual use of speech. Schäfer (1921), who took up this problem in detail, claims that most children show an interval of about 3 months between linguistic comprehension and expression.

Bean (1932) states that long before his child could pronounce a word he knew the meanings of a great many words. As a training method, he attempted to converse with the child in single words or short phrases at this period and secured 3 repetitions per item as evidence that "association links" had been formed between 152 words and phrases and the objects or acts to which they belonged. The process of training in the comprehension of language is outlined by Lewis (1951) as follows:

, The child responds affectively both to the intonational pattern of what he hears and to the situation in which he hears it. And at this very same time he hears a phonetic pattern, inextricably intertwined with the intonational pattern and—in many cases—linked expressively or onomatopoetically with the situation. Then his affective response fashions a new whole out of these experiences, this new whole including the intonational pattern, the situation, and the phonetic pattern. When at last the phonetic pattern acquires dominance so that irrespective of the intonational pattern it evokes the appropriate response from the child, we say that he has understood the conventional word. Finally, there comes a time when the child on hearing the particular word refers to a particular object [p. 122].

Gesture Language

It is quite generally agreed that the child understands gestures before he understands words and, in fact, that he uses gestures himself long before he uses language proper. He looks for objects he has dropped, he reaches for objects, etc., long before he can ask for them. These and other overt bodily movements which are used as means of early expression and communication are often accompanied by early vocalizations. It has been claimed that words constitute substitutes for actual gross motor activity. The extreme point of view in this direction is represented by the behaviorists, who hold that the laryngeal movements involved in speech are actual substitutes for overt bodily movements.

An interesting analysis of gesture language is presented by Latif (1934), who says: "It is through the intervention of its elders that the general movements and postures of an infant gradually pass into sym-

bolic gestures." He describes the hungry child seeking his bottle as manifesting "*whole-body* language, since the attitude and activity of its whole body convey meaning to an onlooker," but he goes on to point out:

This whole-body language of the infant soon comes to be abbreviated, through the solicitous participation of the mother. As soon as the infant shows a nascent attitude of food-adience, the mother brings the bottle and thus cuts short the adient efforts of the infant. Whenever it stretches out its hand toward an object, the attentive mother is there to put the object in its hand. Such cooperation on the part of the mother soon reduces the whole-body language of the infant to mere ("conventional") gesture, in which *only a part* and that the earliest part of an action is substituted for the entire action. The responses of the infant thus become merely symptomatic, i.e., symbolic [pp. 76–77].

It is evident that just as the child's gesture may become reduced from the whole-body language to the merely conventional gesture, so those actions which are originally accompanied by vocalization may drop out entirely and the reduction of effort may limit the child's activity to only the vocalizations which come to have symbolic meaning. Latif (1934) also points out that "the child's understanding of the behavior of others does not begin with its appreciation of words; it begins with an appreciation of its elders' actions and gestures" (p. 79). And he states further: "As vocal language (tonal or verbal) develops, the gesture language recedes into the background. But not even at the highest levels of vocal communication do gestures ever entirely disappear" (p. 81).

Witte (1930) conducted some interesting experiments on gesture language in which he attempted to determine what are the limitations of gestures. He finds that concrete ideas and things within the visual field can readily be expressed in gestures, as can commands, questions, and negations. Many verbs and adjectives he finds can be gesticulated, but equality and similarity, the pronoun *it*, and auxiliary verbs are difficult to express in this way.

Much of the literature is obscure on the comprehension of adult gesture and language by children, for so much of it involves notation of the child's responses to commands. Often it is not stated whether the commands are accompanied by gestures or not. As may be seen in Table 1, C. Bühler (1930) specifies in items 75 and 76 that the commands were accompanied by gestures. Other investigators, however, report responses to commands at much earlier ages than she does, and they do not specify that gestures accompanied the commands, although it is rather likely that some gestural cues were employed; undoubtedly the authors would have specified any artificiality introduced into the situation by experimental controls. In all probability the discrepancy in ages is due to differences in the selection of cases.

Studies on the use of gesture language have appeared by Critchley (1939) and by Schäfer (1934). The latter author conducted several experiments in which he instructed children to communicate ideas by gesture only. Children described as of normal intelligence, and presumably normal hearing, interpreted the gestures correctly 67 per cent of the time. Children described as of retarded mentality and assigned to special classes, however, interpreted the gestures of their classmates 86 per cent of the time. As some older children were included in the retarded group, however, and as nothing is given regarding their hearing, caution must be taken in interpreting the author's conclusion that the lower the intelligence the greater is the tendency to use gesture. He considered that normal chil-

dren inhibit gesture in favor of spoken communication. Valentine (1942) also claims that the part played by gestures in communication seems to be very slight in intelligent children who are encouraged by their parents in the use of speech. Since the essence of communication is the conveying of ideas to others, these findings if corroborated by more carefully controlled investigations may have interesting implications for education which characteristically places such a premium on verbal communication. Perhaps the use of more gesture and pantomime in the instruction of those less well endowed with verbal ability would prove helpful.

In discussing gesture theories of the origin of language, McGranahan (1936) says that kinesthetic experience is often proposed as the basis of natural representation, and he cites Paget's (1930) theory which claims that the origin and development of all language are based upon certain positions and movements of tongue, jaws, and mouth which instinctively imitate the events and objects of the outside world. The speech sound which comes from a particular imitative oral gesture is claimed to evoke the same gesture in the hearer and thereby to symbolize the referent of which the gesture is an imitation.

Lewis (1951) takes issue with the Sterns' (1907) view that "the early responses of the child to heard speech are fundamentally built up on natural gestures, whether of the speaker or of the child himself," and he says that "the child responds first to a gesture, then to the gesture accompanied by words, finally to those words in themselves." Lewis (1951) considers that such a description leaves out of consideration the child's early responses to the human voice, for it is evident that the child is quieted by talking and that he distinguishes between friendly and angry talking, and in general is responsive to affective intonations of the voice long before he gives evidence of understanding gestures or of showing differential response to phonetic patterns of words.

Whereas the Sterns and others have accepted the point of view that it is easier for the child to understand the gestures than the language of others, Lewis points to the findings of Bühler and Hetzer (1935), who report that before 6 months of age no child observed by them responded to coaxing or threatening gestures and that an additional 2 months of maturity seemed necessary before such response could be elicited, but that specific responses to differences in the intonation of the voice were definitely established in these same children as early as the sixth month. Lewis (1951) concludes, therefore:

> What we cannot accept is Stern's suggestion that the response to gestures is prior to the response to the intonational patterns of speech. The child responds to both; each indeed may facilitate the effect of the other. Together they evoke an affective response from the child, initiating or inhibiting his acts [p. 121].

The First Word

Although it might seem as if it would be very easy to determine the actual onset of speech by noting the child's first word, there are a number of difficulties surrounding the determination of the exact age at which the child uses his first word. The first use of sound with meaning is usually considered to constitute the child's first word. This event is so eagerly anticipated by parents that they often read meaning into the child's early babblings which happen to coincide with the presence of certain persons, objects, or events in the environment. If the child habitually uses *da-da* in his babbling, and sometimes uses it in the presence of his father, when can it be said that "Daddy" is uttered to designate his father? If the criterion of using the word to mean only one person, and not using it in any other situation, is accepted, it is necessary to observe over a period of time, to note consistency of usage, and to see that the sounds are not used in other situations. This is rather a negative way of establishing the fact that the word is used with meaning, and it does not indicate positively the *first* time the word is *used with meaning*.

Other criteria are accompanying gestures which may make the interpretation of the child's usage more certain and observation over a period of time for recurrences of the sound in similar situations. Some observers consider the child's first word to be his first spontaneous utterance of a word with meaning (meaningfulness being inferred by the adult with little or no objective evidence as to the correctness of the inference); others consider it to be the first word that the child gives evidence of understanding; and still others consider it to be the speaking of a word in imitation of an adult's speech. With such varying criteria it is necessary to employ caution in interpreting data which have been reported on the appearance of the first word.

As Lewis (1951) puts the same problem:

> To discover how reference develops, we have to notice, by considering the child's behavior at times when he is speaking or responding to words, what is the function of a given sound-group both before and after he first appears to attach it to a given object. In other words, we have to judge of the meaning of a word by noticing its place in the child's activity.

Lorimer (1929) points out that "because of the variety of factors involved in the origin of words it is rather artificial to attempt ever to say exactly what is the child's 'first word.'"

Leopold (1939, 1947, 1949a, b), a linguist, who has written four volumes on the acquisition of speech by his daughter, gives four possible ages (8, 9, 16, and 17 months) as the age of her first word, stating: "The hesitation concerning the starting-point (of the 1-word sentence stage) arises from the question whether the interjection listed as the first word 0:8 is recognized as a word or not" (Vol. III, p. 2).

Earlier sections on imitation and on language comprehension have already indicated the chief points of view which have been set forth as to how the child's utterances come to have meaning for him. There is a tremendous psychological gap which has to be bridged between the mere utterance of the phonetic form of a word and the symbolic or representational use of that word in an appropriate situation. As Sapir (1921) says in speaking of sound elements in speech: "What distinguishes each of these elements is that it is the outward sign of a specific idea," and again: "The mere phonetic framework of speech does not constitute the inner fact of language" (p. 43).

As may be seen from inspection of Table 1, only two of the authors (Shirley and Cattell) included in this group attempt to assign an age level to the stage of linguistic development characterized by the use of a single word. Cattell (1940), who accepts the mothers' reports for this item, places it at 11 months, and Shirley (1933a, 1933b), who reports on the first comprehensible word spoken in the presence of the examiners, places it at the fourteenth month. She states, however, that most of the mothers reported that the babies had a vocabulary of 2 or 3 words at 1 year, but that speech did not occur so early during the tests as it did spontaneously in the presence of the mothers. Thus these two studies are probably in fairly close agreement that the first word actually does occur shortly before the end of the first year of

life. C. Bühler (1930) reports the imitation of syllables such as mama, dada, and the like at 11 months, and Bayley (1933) reports imitation of words at 11.7 months.

In Smith's (1926) study none of the 13 children studied at 8 months had begun to talk. The 17 children whom she observed at 10 months had an average vocabulary of 1 word, and 52 children at 1 year of age had an average vocabulary of 3 words. Castner (in Gesell, Halverson, Thompson, et al., 1940), however, points out that Smith's group was probably somewhat precocious.

The scattered reports on the appearance of the first word in the biographical studies have been collated from time to time by various writers. Feldmann (1833) gave statistics on 33 cases in which the mode for the appearance of the first word was at 16 months. Bateman (1917) summarized 35 cases, 18 of whom were English-speaking, 12 German-speaking, and 5 Polish and Bulgarian. Since all these cases were children whose parents were sufficiently interested to write articles on their linguistic development for scientific journals, it is probable that they represent a highly selected group. The age range in this group is from 8 to 15 months, with 43 per cent of the cases using the first word between 10 and 11 months of age. The boys usually reached this stage somewhat later than the girls, and the English-speaking children somewhat in advance of those speaking other languages, with the Polish and Bulgarian children considerably later than other nationality groups. The Sterns (1907) also summarized 26 biographical reports, but most of these are included in Table 3, taken from C. Bühler (1931), who presents data on 49 cases. The 3 cases reported as not using the first word until 20 months of age are reported by Bühler to be definitely pathological. Decroly (c. 1934) reproduces this table of Bühler's with the addition of an-

TABLE 3

TABULATION OF AGE OF APPEARANCE OF FIRST
WORD

(After C. Bühler, 1931)

Age in months	8	9	10	11	12	13	14	15	16	17	18	19	20
Number of cases	3	7	13	6	5	5	4	1	1	1	0	0	3

other case at 11 months. For these data on children drawn largely from superior socio-economic backgrounds the mode for the use of the first word is at 10 months. The median for all cases is at 11 months of age. This agrees with the average age of talking reported by Terman *et al.* (1925) for his gifted group. His data were collected from the parents in retrospect after the children had been located as gifted children in school. Mead (1913), using rather crude techniques of parents' retrospective reports, gives the average age for beginning to talk as 15.3 months for normal children and 38.5 months for a group of feeble-minded children. The significance of these findings will be discussed in the section on the relationship between language development and intelligence.

In regard to the form of the first word there is rather striking agreement in the literature that it is usually a monosyllable or a reduplicated monosyllable such as *byebye, mama, dada, bebe, tick-tick,* and the like. Certainly the commonest words heard in the nursery of the child who is just beginning to talk are of the reduplicated monosyllable type. Perez (1889), the Sterns (1907), Kroeber (1916), and Shirley (1933a, 1933b) are among the many writers who call attention to this phenomenon. The frequently occurring syllables, which are heard again and again in the child's babble, readily become the familiar appellations of babyhood as soon as adults begin to note the child's consistent use of them in specific situations and begin to use them in talking to the child. The Sterns (1907) also point

out how often these words are of an onomatopoeic character, having a natural connection between sound and meaning, such as *moo-moo* and *tick-tick.* Shirley (1933a, 1933b), who terms these "childish imitative words," states that they are apparently picked up from parents or older children in most cases rather than invented by the babies themselves.

Lewis (1951), after making a phonetic analysis of the first words of the 26 children reported on by the Sterns (1907) and observing his own son, states:

> The great majority of the earliest words are of a definite phonetic form: they consist of single or duplicated syllables in which the consonants are either labials (*p, b, m, w*) or labio-dentals (*f, v*) or tipdentals (*t, d, n*); they are made with both lips or lip against teeth or tongue-tip against teeth (or gum ridge). . . . No less than 83 out of 110 (or 75 per cent) contain only front consonants, while 12 per cent contain one front consonant. Further, 85 per cent of the total are either monosyllabic or reduplicated (39 per cent of the former and 46 per cent of the latter) [p. 125].

These observations, it may be noted, agree with the data from the Irwin investigations and with the idea that sounds made with lips and tongue tip are associated with the onset of true speech and with the development of cortical control.

It is difficult to say exactly what part of speech the first words usually are since they are used in isolation for lack of supporting vocabulary. Frequently these words function as 1-word sentences (Lukens, 1894; the Sterns, 1907; Pelsma, 1910; Koffka, 1924; Bean, 1932; Brigance, 1934; and Leopold, (1949a). However, if only the form of the words is considered and the most frequent occurrence of the forms noted, the first words are characteristically nouns or interjections. Markey (1928) and Leopold (1949a) give detailed accounts calling attention to the verbal function of many of the early nouns. By the use of gestures and intonations of the voice the child often uses a single word to convey a variety of meanings in different situations. The single word "ball" may mean "There is the ball," if uttered in the presence of a ball, accompanied by a pointing gesture; or it may mean "Where is the ball?" or "I want the ball," if uttered with a questioning or demanding inflection and accompanied by searching behavior. Meumann (1908) has stressed the point that first words are strongly affective and that they express wishes, feelings, and needs. He claims that if these early words do designate object names at the same time, such function is secondary to that of expressing the emotional relation between the child and the object.

The Growth of Vocabulary

After the appearance of the first few words used consistently with meaning in appropriate situations, there occurs a rapid increase in vocabulary as the child acquires the raw material of language which he is to utilize later in various combinations to express all degrees and shades of meaning. Many of the early biographical studies began with the appearance of the first word and proceeded to list cumulatively all new words as they were first heard in the child's speech. This method has proved moderately satisfactory for studies of the earliest stages of vocabulary growth, but soon the vocabulary becomes so extensive that the lists become unwieldy and adults find it increasingly difficult to detect the new words. Most such records have been kept on precocious children, and the various authors have not employed the same methods in counting plurals, inflections of verbs and adjectives; some counting the root word

only once and others counting all derivatives as separate words, so that comparisons of the total vocabulary counts are almost impossible to interpret correctly. Other difficulties of interpretation arise, as Dale (1931) has pointed out, from the facts that various writers use different lengths of observation periods and employ different criteria for considering that a child "knows" a word. Some investigators recorded only words heard in spontaneous conversation, others recorded "words understood," some kept running cumulative accounts, others recorded all words heard within a week of the child's birthday, and some excluded words which had been in active use a few months before, but which appeared to have dropped from active use according to the latest sample.

The studies of vocabulary may be grouped into several types: (1) estimates of total vocabulary at specified ages (usually of single children); (2) analyses of total vocabularies according to parts of speech; (3) analyses of total vocabularies for subject matter; (4) analyses of the occurrence of the various parts of speech in samples of conversation; (5) analyses of the occurrences of the various parts of speech in compositions; (6) estimates of total vocabularies of groups by the use of the free association technique; (7) estimates of total vocabularies by the use of vocabulary tests; and (8) word frequency counts. The vocabulary tests have all been devised by employing different methods of sampling, so that serious methodological problems are raised. Some of the tests require the actual eliciting of the words, whereas others involve merely pointing to pictures and thus reveal only understood vocabulary.

Summaries of the vocabulary studies of preschool children have been attempted by Tracy (1893), Doran (1907), the Whipples (1909), Waddle (1913), M. D. Horn (1926–

1927a), and others. Outstanding among individual vocabularies recorded are those by Deville (1890), the Gales (1906), the Whipples (1909), Boyd (1914), Bateman (1914), Nice (1915, 1917), the Brandenburgs (1916), Haggerty (1930), and Brigance (1934). Dale (1949) has published an exhaustive bibliography of vocabulary studies. Attempts at complete enumeration of vocabulary have of necessity been confined to the preschool period, and at higher ages some form of sampling has been employed in the efforts to ascertain total vocabulary.

These studies indicate that there are marked individual differences in the size of vocabulary at any age. Shirley (1933a, 1933b) reports that on the average each baby in her group had spoken 36.9 different words in the presence of the examiners by the age of 2 years, the range being from 6 to 126 words. These figures are undoubtedly low estimates, for the sampling secured during the periodic visits of the examiners was probably much smaller than mothers would have reported for these same children had they kept complete records. Although tabular summaries of reported vocabularies have been compiled by some, they are not presented here because of the lack of comparability of the data from one study to another. For estimates of the probable normal vocabulary at various preschool ages the reader is referred to Table 4, from Smith (1926), in the section on vocabulary tests (p. 533).

The vocabulary appears to increase rather slowly at first, then quite rapidly throughout the preschool period, and then more slowly at least until mental maturity. It probably never stops increasing, as the individual is constantly learning the meanings of new words and learning new usages of familiar words throughout life. The age at which the rapid increase in vocabulary occurs is probably related to the age of walking in individual children, for Shirley (1933a,

1933b), Brigance (1934), and others report that there seems to be a plateau in language development during the mastery of a new motor skill, especially that of walking. Although there is enormous variation in the age of onset of both developmental phenomena, most normal children begin to walk before they talk. In many cases, however, especially among girls and among children who are more precocious in their intellectual development, talking precedes walking. In such cases there is likely to be observed a slowing-up of rate of improvement in vocabulary while the child is devoting most of his attention to mastery of the skill of walking. After such a plateau, rapid progress in vocabulary is likely to be made. (See section on relation to motor development, pp. 597–598.) Drever (1915–1916), Brigance (1934), and others report rapid vocabulary development associated with a vacation or trip to the seashore. With the broadening of the child's experience through travel there appears a marked increase in vocabulary. (See section on effect of environment, pp. 584–597.)

This is undoubtedly the same sort of thing that progressive educators attempt to do when they broaden the experiences of primary children in order to develop reading readiness. (See Strickland, 1951; and the National Council of Teachers of English volume, *The English Language Arts*, 1952.) Behrens (1939) stresses conditioning as the essential element in the acquisition of meaning and brings out the importance of supplying the child with a rich variety of experiences in order to increase his knowledge of meanings.

Analyses of vocabularies for content or for listing concepts known to children at various ages are of some value at early ages, but at later ages selective factors are probably operative to such an extent that generalizations based on such data are of little value. One of the most interesting studies of this type is by Shirley (1938), in which verbatim records were made for 336 children from 2 to 5 years during a play period of 30 to 45 minutes. It was found that the four most common concepts related to the mother, home, father, and siblings. The eleven most frequently used word concepts all seemed to carry an emotional tone for the children. At least half the concepts seemed to arise out of common needs of children and another 20 per cent were largely expositional. These findings are of interest when the affective nature of infants' vocalizations is recalled as well as the high frequency of interjectional speech in the earliest words. It tends to emphasize the importance of the function of language to express feelings, wants, and desires.

The study of vocabulary is fraught with methodological problems. Some of the difficulties inherent in vocabulary research may be appreciated from a consideration of Vigotsky's (1939) comments to the effect that a word deprived of meaning is not a word but only an empty sound. Meaning he considers to be a basic constituent criterion of the word itself. He stresses, however, that meaning is not a static property of words but that the meaning of words develops. Werner and Kaplan (1950) have published an interesting experimental study which demonstrates with nonsense "words" how words acquire meaning through usage in various contexts.

Three basic difficulties which have contributed much to the confused state of the literature on children's vocabularies may be mentioned. The first is the difficulty of deciding on the proper criterion for *knowing* a word. Dale (1931) points out in reference to this matter that *know* is a relative term, since there are accretions to the meanings of words throughout life. He argues, therefore, that the *knowing* of a word should be defined in terms of the specific reactions

one is able to make to a word. For example, is the child able to understand the word when he hears it spoken, or is he able to use it in his spontaneous speech, or is he able to read it? How many different shades of meaning does he know for the word, and in what variety of situations can he use it? Is he able to define the word, and, if so, how well can he do it? Such questions about the degree of *knowing* a word are carefully brought out in the study of Bear and Odbert (1941). They serve to show the psychological artificiality which enters into all vocabulary tabulations.

The second basic difficulty in vocabulary measurement, which has been stressed by Seashore (1933), Seashore and Eckerson (1940), and M. K. Smith (1941), involves failure to define *the word* as a unit of measurement. Seashore cites particularly in earlier estimates such as those by Kirkpatrick (1891), Brandenburg (1918), and Holley (1919) the failure to distinguish adequately: (1) among spoken, written, and recognition vocabularies; (2) between root and derivative words, which he says occur in the proportion of 1 to 3.4 words; (3) between commonest and multiple usages of words; as well as (4) among differences in policy regarding inclusion of special terms such as proper nouns, technical, foreign, obsolete, and provincial terms; and (5) among differences associated with various criteria of knowledge of a word. Seashore states that methods of sampling word lists from dictionaries gave very stable proportions of each type of word. Seashore and Eckerson estimated by the use of a four-choice recognition vocabulary test, considering the commonest meaning as correct, that the average college undergraduate recognized 35 per cent of the common basic words in the sample, 1 per cent of the rare basic words, and 47 per cent of the derivative words in the test which was based on a numerical sampling of the items in the Funk and Wagnalls unabridged dictionary. The total vocabulary of college undergraduates, therefore, would be estimated at 155,736 words, the range being from 112,100 to 192,575 for the group studied. Comparisons of the various criteria employed to indicate different degrees of knowledge of a word showed high intercorrelations and yielded estimates of total vocabulary for a group within a range of 8 per cent.

On the third issue basic to the methods of vocabulary studies, Williams (1932) sounds a much-needed and wholesome note of warning to the makers of vocabulary tests regarding the methods of selecting words from the dictionary. Since all vocabulary estimates at higher ages are based on prediction from small samples, it is important that great care be exercised in the selection of the words to be used in the test. Williams points out that all available vocabulary tests have selected the test words by the page method, that is, by taking the last word on alternate pages or according to some such plan. He determined the expected frequency of children's words in the International Kindergarten Union (1928) list of 2500 words and found that the actual number of words of high frequency selected by the page method greatly exceeded the expected proportion. He also found that the larger the dictionary used in the selection the greater was the likelihood of the selection of these very common words for vocabulary tests. He attributes this phenomenon to differences in spatial allotment which favor the words in most common use and those which have the greatest richness of meaning. Naturally such words receive relatively more space in large than in small dictionaries. Williams recommends that the selection of test words in future vocabulary tests be based on the actual counting of ordinal position

in the dictionary, taking every fifth or every tenth or every hundredth word. This appears to be a fundamental criticism of all previous vocabulary tests with the exception of the one just mentioned by Seashore and Eckerson (1940). Their change in sampling method, as well as their use of an unabridged dictionary, undoubtedly accounts for the unusually high, but probably more nearly correct, estimates.

The Seashore-Eckerson vocabulary test published by the authors at Northwestern University is available for grades 1 through 12. Norms have been established on 867 children by M. K. Smith (1941), who devised special adaptations of procedure for the lower grades. The odd-even reliability for this test was above .90 for grades 5 to 9, inclusive, but was less satisfactory at higher and lower ranges. For grade 1 the average number of words in the total vocabulary was 23,700 with a range of 6000 to 48,800, and for grade 12 it was 80,300 with a range of 36,700 to 136,500.

Although the estimates of total vocabulary obtained by Seashore and Eckerson (1940) and M. K. Smith (1941) are much larger than those previously noted in the literature, Hartmann (1941) in his critique of the common methods of estimating vocabulary size considers that even these may be gross underestimates by as much as 100,000 words. He used four lists of varying lengths from a single dictionary and found that all members of a group of normal-school graduates had vocabularies in excess of 200,000 words.

Part I of the Seashore-Eckerson test was given to all 16-year-olds in a typical midwestern community by Schulman and Havighurst (1947). Their results agreed closely with those reported by M. K. Smith (1941). Lovell (1941) and Odbert (1948) both report multiple-meaning vocabulary tests. Lovell (1941) concludes that intensity or richness of vocabulary is fairly closely related to knowledge of single commonest meanings.

Bear and Odbert (1941) studied the degree of insight which pupils have into their knowledge of words and found the often-used method of checking known or unknown words unsatisfactory as pupils identified as unknown fewer than half the words they missed on a vocabulary test. Those having the poorest vocabularies had least insight into their own limitations.

Another vocabulary test for grades 3 through 8 was devised by Gansl (1939). It consists of 100 items of the sentence type of multiple-choice questions. It has a reliability of .94 for 190 eleven-year-old boys, and norms are based on 3306 children. Items were carefully selected from among those of 22 current vocabulary tests; frequencies were determined on the basis of the Thorndike Word List (1931–1932), and the order of difficulty was empirically determined. The author seriously questions "the naïve acceptance in many former tests of the frequency ratings as measures of difficulty," which she found to be wholly unwarranted. The test yields raw and derived, or "D scores," but no estimates of total vocabulary. The curve for vocabulary growth from age 8 to 13 was approximately a straight line with a tendency toward negative acceleration from 12 to 13 years.

Recognition of the multidimensional nature of vocabulary has been revealed in several studies. Feifel and Lorge (1950) published a qualitative analysis of the responses of 900 children ranging from 6 to 14 years of age to the vocabulary test of the Stanford-Binet Form L Scale. The younger children more often employed the use, description, illustration, and demonstration types of definition as well as inferior explanation and repetition responses. Older children significantly more often used synonym and explanatory responses. The younger children were found to perceive

words as "concrete" ideas, whereas older children stressed the abstract or "class" features of a word. Similar tendencies were brought out in regard to the Wechsler-Bellevue vocabulary scale by Gerstein (1949).

Parts of Speech. In the analyses according to the various parts of speech three approaches have been used which yield quite different results. The first, which is suitable only for the vocabularies of very young children where there may be some reasonable expectation of approximating the total vocabulary, is to calculate the proportions of the total number of words in the entire vocabulary, however defined, which belong in each category of the various parts of speech. This method always yields a very large proportion of nouns, merely because nouns are predominant in the language and hence are most numerous in any dictionary. The samples taken for very young children also yield an unusually high proportion of words usually classified as nouns, because during the early acquisition of vocabulary the child goes through the naming stage in which, after making the important discovery that everything has a name, he asks many "what questions" in order to learn the names of the various objects in his environment. As has been pointed out above, however, merely because a word used by a child has the form of a noun does not mean that it always functions as a noun in the child's usage, for he may use what appears to be a noun with a variety of meanings, and it may actually function as a verb, an adjective, an interjection, or even as a whole sentence in itself. (See Leopold, 1949a.) Thus it is difficult, if not impossible, to arrive at a satisfactory answer as to the relative proportions of the various parts of speech in a child's total vocabulary, first because of the difficulty of determining when a child *knows* a word, second because of the difficulty of determining the total vocabulary, third because of the difficulty in classifying the word according to the part of speech it actually functions as in the child's usage, and fourth because of the difficulty of classifying the same word form according to different functions.

In the second type of study of the parts of speech, no attempt is made to determine total vocabulary, but a fairly long sample of running conversation (or sometimes compositions or letters) is taken, and an attempt is made to determine the relative importance of the various parts of speech in the child's running language. After the child has passed beyond the naming stage and has ceased his early use of interjections, about the end of the second year, and when he has begun to combine words into sentences, the relative proportions of the various parts of speech are determined to a large extent by the limitations imposed upon the speaker by the conventional forms of sentence structure. Thus, whereas a child may have a high percentage of nouns in his "total vocabulary," roughly 60 per cent perhaps, at 2 years of age in the first type of analysis, in this second type of analysis he will probably have only about 20 per cent of the words in his running conversation consisting of nouns. This does not mean that he does not have the variety of nouns in his vocabulary, but merely that because he is speaking in sentences he does not need to draw heavily on his store of known nouns, since each simple sentence requires only one noun for the subject. In order to say anything about that noun, however, it is necessary for him to use a verb, and perhaps an adjective or an adverb; at least for every clause involving one noun he is forced by the rules of sentence structure (which he comes to know by the example of others) to use other parts of speech with it. It is also obvious that since such figures are relative, and are expressed in percentages, any

change or trend in one part of speech will upset the balance, and there may be an apparent trend in some part of speech which is really only an artifact and a reflection of the tendency already noted in another part of speech. Which trend is more significant psychologically is usually a matter for interpretation.

The third type of analysis according to parts of speech is that which is based not on the total number of words in a given sample of running conversation or writing but upon the total number of different words appearing in such a sample. A comparison of this method with that of the previous one immediately reveals the fact that the great bulk of language is made up of a small number of frequently recurring words, and that there is relatively infrequent use of the great majority of words in the total vocabulary. Zyve (1927), who recorded the conversations of third-grade children during a 15-minute story period for about 3 months, used both these methods of tabulation and obtained strikingly different results with the two procedures. Nouns constituted 51 per cent of the number of different words and only 15 per cent of the total number of words used. Verbs represented 22 per cent of the number of different words, and they amounted to 27 per cent of the total number of words used. Pronouns also show a striking difference when tabulated by the two methods, as they equaled only 1.5 per cent of the number of different words and 17.2 per cent of the total number of words used. Like the nouns, the adjectives showed a decrease, but the adverbs, prepositions, and conjunctions all showed relative increases when considered according to the total number of words used. The tabulations for the articles bring out clearly the striking artificiality of these methods. There are only 3 different articles in the English language and all 3 of them are used by very young children, yet they represent only 0.1 per cent of the number of different words. These same 3 words recur so frequently in conversation, however, that in Zyve's (1927) data they constituted 7 per cent of the total number of words employed.

Uhrbrock (1936) reports interesting data on this point based on a sample of 24,000 words dictated into an Ediphone by a little girl during the 6 weeks immediately preceding her fifth birthday. He found that three-quarters of the dictated material involved the use of 141 different common words, each of which occurred 20 times or more in his sample. Forty per cent of the total number of different words (750) occurred only once. Separate samples of 1000 running words of dictation never contained fewer than 258 different words or more than 331, with the average number of different words at 290 per 1000 words dictated. Some idea of the difficulty of determining total vocabulary for a 5-year-old may be seen in Uhrbrock's report that 52 new words, not previously encountered in the data, appeared in the twenty-fourth thousand.

Another approach to this problem has involved the "type-token ratio" or TTR. W. Johnson (1944) and his co-workers at Iowa reported several studies employing this measure, which is the ratio of the number of different words (types) to the total words (tokens) in a sample of language. It was also applied to infant vocalizations by Chen and Irwin (1946b) (see Table 2). This measure is sometimes considered to indicate degree of variability or flexibility of language usage. Chotlos (1944) who applied it to extensive samples of the written language of 108 children considers that this index shows the greater differentiation of language structure in older and more intelligent children.

Jersild and Ritzman (1938), using extensive samples of the conversation of a group of very superior preschool children, report that there is a tendency for younger children to use a higher proportion of different words in relation to the total number of words spoken. Roughly every fourth word in their data was a "new" word, and one 3-hour period yielded only about half as many different words as three periods of 3 hours each.

Vocabulary Tests for Preschool Children. The first serious attempt to devise a vocabulary test for young children was made by M. E. Smith in 1926. In this test 203 words were selected by a systematic sampling of the Thorndike (1921) 10,000-word list which had been checked against the vocabularies of a large number of children in order to eliminate words which these young children were almost certain not to know. Most of the words were elicited from the child by means of pictures, although no standard pictures were provided. It is quite likely that the materials gathered by other investigators in attempting to elicit the words of the Smith battery differ widely from those used in the normative work. If the child failed to say the word in response to the appropriate pictures and questions, the examiner then asked another type of question in which the test word was used in such a way that the child could not answer the question unless he understood the word involved. Credit for "knowledge" of the word was allowed if the child responded by using the word in the first type of test, or if he answered the second type of question correctly. Thus the score on the test was made up of a composite of items, on some of which credit was allowed for recalling and speaking the word in the test situation, and on others of which credit was allowed for mere indirect evidence that he "understood" the word. On quite a large number of the test words no second form of the question is provided, however, and the word actually must be said by the child before credit is allowed. Smith reported a split-half reliability of .97 for a 2-year level with this test. On the basis of the fact that actual known total vocabularies were predicted fairly accurately by multiplying the total score by an appropriate multiplier, she argues that total vocabulary can be estimated with this test.

Williams and McFarland (1937) point out, however, that such estimates are really only fair predictions of the total number of known words in the Thorndike list of 10,000 words rather than accurate estimates of total vocabulary. M. E. Smith (1926) reports correlations of +.88 and +.84 with Descoeudres' (1921) tests of language and Cobb's (1922) rearrangement of the Stanford-Binet vocabulary test as evidence of validity of the test. The figures given by Smith as the total vocabularies of 278 preschool children ranging in age from 8 months to 6 years are widely quoted as the best available material on vocabulary estimates at these ages, although it must be remembered in interpreting them that they are subject to the above-mentioned limitations. (See Table 4.)

M. E. Smith's vocabulary test was revised by Williams and McFarland (1937), who overcame a number of these limitations. It is now known as the Smith-Williams Vocabulary Test, and materials are available for two equivalent forms of 42 words each. It has been applied in several of the investigations reported later in this chapter. The revision considerably reduces the administration time, yet a satisfactory reliability of +.96 is reported by the authors between Forms I and II for 359 children from 2 to 6 years of age. The procedure has been modified to make for more rigid control of the recall method, and the test is given first as a recall test and later as

TABLE 4

INCREASE IN SIZE OF VOCABULARY IN RELATION TO AGE

(From M. E. Smith, 1926)

Age			Average	Number	
Years	Months	N	IQ	of Words	Gain
	8	13		0	
	10	17		1	1
1	0	52		3	2
1	3	19		19	16
1	6	14		22	3
1	9	14		118	96
2	0	25		272	154
2	6	14		446	174
3	0	20	109	896	450
3	6	26	106	1222	326
4	0	26	109	1540	318
4	6	32	109	1870	330
5	0	20	108	2072	202
5	6	27	110	2289	217
6	0	9	108	2562	273

a test of verbal recognition. This separates the administration of the two methods for the same word by the length of the test. Results are reported for 242 children who attended the Iowa preschool laboratories and for 64 orphanage children, but, since the authors emphasize that the original and also the revised tests are only relative measures and do not yield absolute figures on total vocabulary, no figures comparable with Smith's data are provided. The two groups tested could hardly be considered adequate normative samples since they had mean IQ's of 124 and 84. Grigsby (1932), using apparently a prepublication edition of the Smith-Williams Vocabulary Test on 83 subjects between the ages of 2 years 8 months, and 6 years 4 months, reports the mean vocabulary at 3 years as 1507, at 4 years, 2148, at 5 years, 2527, and at 6 years, 3054. These estimates are somewhat higher than those reported by M. E. Smith (1926).

Another approach to the measurement of vocabulary was made by Van Alstyne (1929). This test, which takes 15 minutes to administer, is entirely a picture-vocabulary test involving a series of pen-and-ink drawings with four items to a card. It is limited to 3-year-olds with regard to norms, and if children of other age levels are tested with it interpretations have to be made in terms of the 3-year-old norm. The child is expected only to point to the one object out of the four on each card which is named by the examiner and is not expected to speak the words. The test is thus limited to "understood" vocabulary. The reliability reported by the author is +.87 for split halves after using the Spearman-Brown prophecy formula.

Ammons and others (1948, 1949a, b, 1950a, b), basing their work on Van Alstyne's (1929) technique, published a series of studies presenting the standardization of a "full-range picture vocabulary test." It is available from the author in two forms which are reported to have high reliability (from .93 to .987). Norms were based on 30 representative cases per age level from 2 to 17 years from both urban and rural areas. Ammons, Larson, and Shearn (1950b) reported vocabulary figures for a group of adults with this same test. Although responses were entirely nonverbal the results correlate .83 to .85 with the vocabulary test of the Stanford-Binet Form L.

Word-Count Studies. Closely related to the general problem of vocabulary are the various word-count studies and frequency lists of words which have been published for various purposes. The most widely used is Thorndike's *Teacher's Word Book,* which as originally published in 1921 listed the 10,000 words most frequently encountered in extensive samplings of adult writing, including large samplings of children's literature. This list was revised and extended in 1931–1932 to include 20,000 words. The tables indicate in which thousand the words fall, and, in the first 5000 words, whether they fall in the first 500 or the second 500 of each 1000.

In 1944 Thorndike and Lorge published an extension to include the 30,000 most frequently occurring words using five different samplings covering a count of 120 juvenile books such as are approved in schools and libraries. The occurrences of these words were tabulated as they appeared in written material of various sorts and were not those actually used by children as in the International Kindergarten Union List. However, as Gansl (1939) and others indicate such lists serve as guides to the relative difficulty of the vocabularies in various materials and have become standard research tools. Wesman and Seashore (1949) point out that there is a great difference between frequency of occurrence of words as revealed in the Thorndike-Lorge word list and the difficulty of the concepts involved in such vocabulary tests as those of the Stanford-Binet and the Wechsler-Bellevue scales.

A valuable list by Eaton (1940) has appeared, the *Semantic Frequency List for English, French, German, and Spanish.* It is based on the first 6000 concepts, rather than word forms, in frequency lists which have been compiled for the four languages separately and then combined. It was issued by the Committee on Modern Languages of the American Council on Education.

Other word lists which have been devised especially as spelling lists include the lists of Ayres (1915), E. Horn (1925), and many others. Of greatest interest to the child psychologist, however, are: the list of M. D. Horn (1926–1927a), sometimes spoken of as the International Kindergarten Union List, which is based on words actually used orally by children before entering the first grade; Fitzgerald's (1934b) list, based on the letters written by elementary school children in life outside of school; and Rinsland's (1945) list of over 25,000 words used by children in the first 8 grades in their conversations and compositions. Perhaps the most useful single source book on frequency word lists is that by Buckingham and Dolch (1936) called *A Combined Word List*, which presents data showing the degree of overlapping and disagreement on the frequencies of words in seven different word-count studies. A comparison of the Dale, Dolch, and Rinsland word lists has been published by Hildreth (1948).

Zipf (1935) in his *The Psycho-Biology of Language* points out that the words which occur most frequently are quite short and that longer words are much more rare. After elaborate word-count investigations he proposes a theory of linguistic change based on economy of time and effort. He has subsequently (1942) analyzed the records from Fisher's (1934) study as well as Uhrbrock's (1936) data and finds that his theory is substantiated in the oral language of young children. Skinner (1936) confirms Zipf's law with his use of the verbal summator, which has interesting possibilities as a projective technique. Carroll (1938) suggests that the diversity of a small vocabulary sample has a definite relation to the total vocabulary.

Hockett (1950), a linguist, considers that the fundamental speech habits of the individual are firmly established by the age of puberty and that the most important force shaping the dialect is the speech of other children. He believes that phonetic change occurs in a language through the continuity of tradition in successive generations of children. He indicates that the earliest speech of the child consists of a phonemic system much less fully differentiated than that of the adult, and that it develops by splits and contrasts until a reasonable facsimile of the adult phonemic system heard in the environment is attained. He finds a loss of linguistic flexibility at puberty when the sounds of one's own language sound "right" or "wrong" according to how closely they resemble those used by the peer group. If these claims are correct the implications for bilinguals and for foreign language teaching are indeed far reaching.

Baker (1950) studied the pattern of various languages, and, in harmony with Zipf (1935), found that the more frequently words are used in a language the shorter they become. He also showed that the shorter the words the greater is the number of meanings they acquire. Thorndike (1937, 1938), while agreeing in general with the correctness of Zipf's (1935) observations, questions some of his interpretations. G. W. Allport (1936) in his review criticizes the saving of time and effort theory and feels that the more universal process of cue reduction in learning is more important. He considers hearer needs rather than ease for the speaker to be the more important factor. Although he is not satisfied with Zipf's interpretations, he admits that psychologists have nothing better to offer as interpretations of the mental counterparts of linguistic change.

Of the studies which employ the free association technique those by Dolch (1927) and by Prescott (1929) are typical. Elementary school children were asked to write all the words they could think of in 15 minutes. The Prescott study showed an increase in the average number of words given from 35 at 7 years to 157 at 13 years, whereas the Dolch study showed a steady increase from 73 words for the average second-grade child to 191 in the eighth grade. Shambaugh and Shambaugh (1928) used 400 stimulus words with 50 children in each grade from the fourth to the eighth inclusive. The stimulus words were chosen because of their close association with the daily lives of the children. The words were arranged in lists of 50, and no group of children responded to more than one list of words. In all, 1851 children participated and were asked to write in 4 or 5 words which they associated most closely with the stimulus word. The total number of words given ranged from 32,905 in grade 4 to 46,505 in grade 8, a total of 230,631 being given in all grades. The number of different words listed ranged from 2102 in grade 4 to 3017 in grade 7, there being a marked drop in the eighth grade probably due to selective factors. In all grades a total of 4515 different words was given, 1309 of which were common to all grades. Interesting comparisons are made with the Thorndike and Horn lists. For example, 51 per cent of these 1309 words common in the free associations of all grades from fourth to eighth were not found in Horn's first 3000 words. Shambaugh and Shambaugh (1928) also found 98 words which occurred in their data with a frequency of 500 or more, 61 of which did not appear in Thorndike's first 500 words, 15 of which were not in his first 1000, and it was necessary to go into the third 1000 of the words most frequently used in the Thorndike 10,000 word list to include all 98 words which occurred with a frequency of 500 or more in the free association data. This study is cited in detail to illustrate the elusive nature of frequency word lists and the difficulty of making valid comparisons among them. Tinker, Hackner, and Wesley (1940) found that those who have higher vocabularies also have more rapid word associations. There was a correlation of +.83 between the quality of the associative response and vocabulary score.

This type of approach appears in a more modern version in the "Studies in Word Fluency" by Gerwitz (1948a), who constructed a series of eight tests for word fluency involving rhyming, alliterations, thing names, word output, etc.

Comprehensibility of Speech

Adults usually have considerable difficulty in understanding the speech of young children. The degree of comprehensibility of the speech varies with a number of factors, especially with the child's accuracy of sound reproduction, his voice quality, the hearer's familiarity with children in general and with the individual child in particular, as well as with the stage of the child's linguistic development, and with the amount of baby-talk used by adults in the child's environment, which often makes for perseveration of infantile speech habits. This means that there are varying amounts of children's speech which either go unrecorded in the studies which employ longhand or stenographic accounts of oral language, or that varying percentages of the flow of language are subject to separate treatment, owing to incomprehensibility. On the other hand, in spite of very poor pronunciation, there is much in children's speech that can be understood and interpreted correctly by adults who are familiar with children.

Since most of the major investigations of children's spoken language have been made by longhand recording, the degree of comprehensibility, as well as the speed and accuracy of the recorder, is a vital problem in methodology. Day (1932) obtained quite high coefficients of correlation for most indices among the records made by three examiners who noted children's speech simultaneously. These satisfactory degrees of agreement were obtained for indices based on samples of 25 responses. Even though the recorders did not always record the identical responses, errors, which were chiefly those of omission, did not appear to be constant and did not appreciably affect the measures used which were based on the total sample. Betts (1934), however, using the strict criterion of an electrical record of grade-school children's oral compositions compared the relative completeness and accuracy of four types of recording: that of court reporters, longhand recorders, shorthand recorders, and phoneticians. Although the court reporters made the most complete records, they obtained only 80.4 per cent of the material. This was secured with an accuracy of 84.9 per cent. Shorthand reporters had the next most complete records with only 53.3 per cent of the material, and their accuracy was 82.9. Longhand recording yielded only 32 per cent of the flow of speech, but the accuracy remained high (83.9 per cent). Phoneticians had the most incomplete records, but the most accurate, as they noted only 14.9 per cent of the material with an accuracy of 87.6 per cent. The incompleteness of all these types of record is probably very significant from the standpoint of methodology. It is all the more important when it is remembered that the oral compositions were by fourth-, fifth-, and sixth-grade children whose speech undoubtedly was much more comprehensible than that of preschool children, and that the compositions had common content, being based on a short motion picture which the children had seen in school. The greater length of the sentences found at this age level, however, probably operated to reduce the completeness and accuracy in comparison with records on younger children.

Some investigators of children's language development do not mention the incomprehensibility of children's speech, yet from the percentage of incomprehensible responses reported by other authors at the same ages it seems unlikely that any investigators could have understood 100 per cent of what the children said. Such studies should probably be interpreted as having recorded only comprehensible responses. Shirley (1933a, p. 293) states that "incomprehensible vocalization attained its highest frequency in the period between 12 and 18 months; after 82 weeks it reached a low level and thereafter (up to 2 years of age) varied around 10 per cent." McCarthy (1930) found 26 per cent of the responses of her 18-month-old children were comprehensible, 67 per cent of the responses of the 2-year-olds, 89 per cent at 2½ years, 93 per cent at 3 years, and practically all responses from 3½ years on. At most age levels the speech of the boys was much less readily understood than that of the girls. Day (1932) found about 35 per cent of the responses of the 2-year-old twins incomprehensible and only about 7 per cent of the responses of the 3-year-olds. Fisher (1934) reports that 8.1 per cent of the responses of her superior group, ranging in age from 18 to 60 months, consisted of "non-verbal speech." Young (1941) reports her data in terms of the mean number of comprehensible words spoken per 10-minute period. The results are in close agreement with Smith's (1926) figures, showing increases from about 20 words at 30 months to about 70 at 54 months.

Articulation. Wellman, Case, Mengert, and Bradbury (1931) report a correlation of +.80 between age and the ability to give sounds correctly in their very detailed examination of 204 preschool children. They report that at 2 years approximately 32 per cent of the total number of sounds were given correctly, at 3 years 63 per cent, at 4 years 77 per cent, at 5 years 88 per cent, and at 6 years 89 per cent. The most marked increases in accuracy of articulation of all types of sounds appeared between 2 and 3 years of age. E. A. Davis (1937a) used a crude seven-point rating scale in conjunction with her very extensive investigation and reports that 75.7 per cent of the 5½-year-olds, 90.9 per cent of the 6½-year-olds, and 90.4 per cent of the 9½-year-olds had "perfect articulation" in a representative group of 173 singletons with siblings.

Poole (1934) tested 140 preschool children for the ability to articulate 23 consonant sounds in words by evoking isolated words as responses to objects, pictures, and questions, but she does not describe the test itself or supply the materials and questions. She reports that the sounds that the child uses most often in his everyday conversation are the ones in which he shows the greatest ability in articulation. Slightly over 64 per cent of the sounds that appear most often in the words of these children's conversations are articulated correctly before the age of 4½ years. The median child at 6½ years articulated all 23 consonant sounds correctly. Poole states that a normally developing child should be able to articulate all sounds by at least 8 years and that failure to make notable progress in articulation at 6 years indicates that a speech therapist should be consulted. In another briefly reported study by Templin and Steer (1939) an apparently good articulation test was used, although the vocabulary load cannot be determined since the test words are not published. It tests for 84 sounds with one sound per word being tested. The test takes from 7 to 40 minutes to administer and was given to 93 children ranging in age from 1 year 11 months to 4 years 9 months.

Approximately 2000 children in grades 1 to 6 were tested for 66 consonants and consonant blends with a modification of the Detroit Articulation Test in a study by Roe and Milisen (1942). The mean number of errors per child dropped markedly from 13.30 in grade 1 to 7.62 in grade 4, but showed no significant change from grades 4 to 6. Single consonant sounds arranged from most to least difficult were: z, ʍ, θ, $dʒ$, d, s, g, $ð$, v, t, b, $tʃ$, r, k, $ʃ$, f, p, l, $ŋ$, w, and the most difficult consonant blends were, in order, st, str, sk, dr, and fl.

Sayler (1949) carried the work of Roe and Milisen (1942) through grades 7 to 12 testing individually 1998 children with a test of 56 sentences which were read orally. She found very little improvement in articulation in grades 7 to 10, some improvement in grades 10 and 11, but articulation in grade 12 was no better than in grade 11. More boys than girls made articulatory errors in all grades but the twelfth. Consistent improvement was noted in the f, d, and t sounds. The phonemes showing the most improvement were the $ð$, f, z, and t.

A group of 207 children from 18 to 54 months was studied by Metraux (1950) using phonetic transcripts. She found vowel production to be more than 90 per cent correct by 30 months of age, but this level of correctness was not attained in consonant production until 54 months. She gives splendid brief descriptions of the speech of a typical child at each of seven age levels, treating pronunciation, voice, repetitions, relation of language to activities and to other people, as well as manifestations of tensional outlets and illustrative excerpts.

Spriestersbach and Curtis (1951) summarized several unpublished M.A. dissertations done under their direction at Iowa which involved detailed testing for the discrimination and articulation of certain speech sounds in approximately 400 children from kindergarten to sixth grade. They conclude that children who misarticulate speech sounds do so inconsistently and that the inconsistencies can be accounted for on a lawful basis. Sound discrimination errors were only about one-third as frequent as articulatory errors. Older children tended to be more consistent in their misarticulations than younger ones.

A speech-defective group was found by Metraux (1942) to be inferior in the oral reproduction of consonant sounds heard on a record, whereas there was no difference between them and a group of normal speakers on reproduction of the vowel sounds. Boys had a higher auditory memory span than girls in this study. Sheridan (1945), who studied the speech of 650 children under 5 years of age, believes that articulatory defects are due to auditory confusions and not to muscular incoordination.

Templin (1943), testing more than 300 elementary school children on speech sound discrimination, found practically no correlation with degree of hearing loss. Correlations of approximately −.20 with various measures of achievement were obtained. In all grades more errors occurred with sounds in the medial and final positions than in the initial position. Sheridan (1945) reported that initial consonants appear before central and terminal ones. Reid (1947), using similar techniques, concluded that the ability to distinguish between speech sounds is the outstanding factor related to articulatory defects and to the responsiveness to special speech training.

In Templin's elaborate cross-sectional study the mean per cent of correct articulation scores yielded steady growth curves and increased from 56.6 [1] at 3 years to 94.8 at 8 years. Most of the improvement was in the consonants, especially in the consonant blends. She too found that initial consonant sounds were mastered first and final consonants were perfected last.

The most elaborate attempt to test for all the phonetic elements in all positions is by Wellman, Case, Mengert, and Bradbury (1931). This test, however, is extremely long, involving 583 sounds to be tested for by eliciting 352 test words with a variety of unstandardized pictures and questions. Only 75 per cent of the test words occur in the first 2000 words of the Thorndike Word List, and 7 per cent of them are not listed in Horn's 2500 words most commonly used

by children of kindergarten age. Many of the sounds tested for are of rare occurrence in the language and hence are relatively unimportant as far as a child's articulation is concerned (McCarthy, 1935). Similar criticisms can be made of the West Test (1933), the Detroit Test by Stoddard and Languin (1934), the Voegelin-Adams Test (1934), and to a lesser extent of the Blanton-Stinchfield Test (1926), which tests for 100 sounds with 100 test words with standardized pictures.

Henrikson (1948) criticized Wood's (1946) articulation test which he says assumes that the various consonants occur in the three positions with equal frequency. He finds that this assumption is only approximately satisfied for no more than three infrequently occurring phonemes. Significant variations from the expected frequencies occurred for all other phonemes.

As part of the development of their language achievement scale, Little and Williams (1937) modified the speech sounds test originally devised by Wellman and her collaborators (1931). They eliminated the testing for all sounds in medial positions and included only those sounds which occur in the first 1000 of the International Kindergarten Union List. The revised list of speech sounds was divided into seven steps according to level of difficulty as established by Wellman et al., and a child was given 1 point for any 3 sounds pronounced correctly at each of the seven levels of difficulty, with 7 the maximum score. They also devised a measure of intelligibility of children's speech by securing a sample of 50 syllables which Williams had previously found had a predicted reliability of +.94. The child is assigned a score of 2 points for each syllable pronounced correctly, 1 point for each syllable mispronounced but intelligible to an observer not familiar with the child's idiosyncrasies, and 0 for syllables not intelligible to an observer who was not

---

[1] From prepublication data made available through the courtesy of Dr. Templin.

accustomed to the child's speech. Data are presented on 285 cases in which rapid improvement in speech sounds and intelligibility scores were found up to the forty-eighth month, at which time there occurred a leveling-off of the curve for both these functions when the children had attained almost maximum scores.

McCarthy (1935) made a preliminary report on the development of an articulation test for young children designed to overcome many of the difficulties of previously published tests. It is based on the frequency of English speech sounds as they occur in the count of 100,000 words by G. Dewey (1923), who employed the Fonetic Key Alfabet approved by the Simplified Spelling Board. It is designed to elicit 46 test words which include 95 test sounds accounting for 94 per cent of the total number of sounds in the Dewey sample of adult language and for 90 per cent of the sounds occurring in the Horn list. All the test words are taken from the first 1000 words used by kindergarten children, and hence should not place a serious vocabulary burden on children of 3 and 4 years.

A so-called "nondiagnostic articulation test" devised by Templin (1947b) appears to have considerable promise. It tests for 50 sounds, selected as important for articulatory development, in 40 words or in 19 sentences. Reliabilities obtained by the retest and intertest methods were all above .89. Correlations with CA were +.64 and with MA +.71. The test is still in the process of standardization.

There has been considerable difference of opinion among workers in this field as to whether articulation tests should employ the method of eliciting the words in the child's spontaneous manner by showing pictures or asking appropriate questions, or whether the examiner may pronounce the test words for the child in an effort to elicit them. Most writers have scrupulously avoided say-

ing the word for the child, fearing that immediate imitation might occur which would fail to reveal habitual faulty sounds. Morrison (1914–1915) and others, however, have reported that when the children are asked to repeat sounds as well as they can in imitation of the examiner, practically none of the sounds are pronounced correctly simply from hearing the correct form.

Templin (1947a) administered an articulation test to 100 preschool children. She found no difference in measured articulation scores when words were uttered spontaneously and when they were repeated in imitation of the examiner. She also found that it made little difference what word was used to test for a specific sound. It appears, then, that if the child habitually mispronounces a sound he will give only his own approximation to the sound in the test situation, even though he has just heard the correct form. Certain forms of careless speech might be eliminated in such a method, but if the child is actually unable to pronounce the correct forms or habitually fails to use them, the imitative method should reveal such defects just as readily as the eliciting of the child's natural way of saying the word independent of the immediate example of the examiner.

In general, all these tests are very long and they test for rarely occurring sounds with words which involve an excessive vocabulary burden for young children. The two exceptions to this appear to be those devised by Little and Williams (1937) and one reported by Templin (1947b).

Fairbanks et al. (1949a, b) studied voice breaks in oscillograph recordings of the voices of 7-, 8-, 10-, and 14-year-olds. They found 1 voice break for every 14 words. The pitch levels were about one octave above the usual level for adult males. The voice breaks occurred in girls as well as in boys and appeared in the voices of both pre-adolescents and adolescents.

Studies of the incidence of speech defectives vary greatly in that they all employ different criteria of what constitutes a speech defect. Some are concerned only with articulatory difficulties exclusive of stuttering; others emphasize cases of stuttering to the exclusion of other problems. The methods of determining whether or not the child has a speech defect vary greatly, and much depends upon teachers' sensitiveness to such matters. Some teachers are much more aware of minor speech difficulties than others, and this results in percentages varying from about 2 to 25 per cent. Many of the studies report only the total number of speech defectives located without giving the size of the population from which they were drawn.

The whole area of speech defects is such an important, extensive, and highly specialized field that no attempt can be made within the compass of this chapter to treat it adequately. However, one very important problem which arises for the child psychologist is determining whether a child is or is not a speech defective, and when the aid of a speech therapist is indicated. As has already been shown, the vast majority of children go through a period of baby-talk. For many children this is relatively brief and the articulatory imperfections are comparatively unimportant, for the children usually develop correct speech habits quite early. On the other hand, a fairly large number of children have quite marked articulatory defects in their baby-talk which for various reasons persist for some time, even well into the elementary school period. It is an important practical problem for the clinician to be able to distinguish between the children who are likely to outgrow their infantile speech patterns at a reasonably normal age and those who

need speech training from a specialist in order to overcome their articulatory defects. Too early introduction of formal speech training of young children who may outgrow their infantile speech without help, or whose speech infantilisms are only a symptom of general emotional immaturity, may make these children speech-conscious and result in their refusal to talk. With such children, practice in talking may be more essential than drill on correctness of articulation for a time. Gain in self-confidence, increased independence, and social contacts often do much to improve the speech difficulties.

For the few children whose speech is so defective that they are not likely to overcome the difficulty without special training, it is desirable to have a measuring instrument to evaluate and diagnose the seriousness of the articulatory defect. A study by Sommer (1932) indicated that group training was quite effective with nursery school and kindergarten children. Her experimental group which received training improved 57 per cent, as compared with the control group which improved 28 per cent without training. This shows that, whereas in a group of children certain improvement occurs with maturation alone, speech training such as Sommer gave brings about twice as much improvement.

Springob (1930) selected as speech defectives children whose errors as detected with the Blanton-Stinchfield Articulation Test were 20 or more after the age of 4 years. A plot of the number of speech errors against age shows a distinct dropping-out of errors in his 5- and 6-year groups with a few exceptional cases persisting in a large number of errors at these ages. These apparently are the children in need of therapy. Town (1921), after analyzing the speech of 42 children for speech defects, states:

It was found impossible on the basis of the examination results to divide the class into two groups, one of which contained children with perfect speech, and the other of which contained children with defective speech. In speech, as in other abilities, the transition is so gradual from normal performance to defective performance that it does not permit of an absolute dividing line.

However, 10 of her 42 cases were judged to have sufficiently defective speech to need corrective work.

Fuller (1936) showed that when kindergarten children with foreign-language handicaps were given speech training there were fewer failures of promotion in the early grades and that IQ's were apparently increased as much as 10 points by two semesters of speech training.

It appears, however, that speech correction with children of functional articulatory defects operates on the level of treating symptoms rather than causes. If the basic causes are still operative, little will be accomplished in the way of permanent cure. If results are not evident fairly promptly, group or individual psychotherapy and general improvement of the child's mental health should be undertaken. (See the study by Wood (1946) in the section, "Language Disorder Syndromes and Personality Development," p. 608.) The field of speech correction was summarized for educators by W. Johnson *et al.* in *Speech Handicapped School Children* (1948). A more popular presentation for parents of speech-defective children is *Speech Problems of Children* (1950) also edited by W. Johnson.

Quantitative Measures

There are two types of studies which undertake to determine only quantity and rate of speech output without reference to the quality of the expression or to any details of the complexities of sentence structure. These studies are limited in scope but have the advantage of objectivity. Studies of the amount and rate of talking are involved here as well as studies presenting data on length of response. The latter, however, are usually more elaborate studies in which length of response is only one aspect of linguistic development measured.

Amount and Rate of Talking. Gesell (1925) reported on the results of a complete 24-hour record of the vocal activities of a 6-month-old child who spent 3 per cent of its waking time in vocal activity. He says: "There were 104 separate moments of vocalization during the day, varying in complexity from 1-letter sounds to 32 repeated syllables; 75 sounds and combinations of sounds were used." The Brandenburgs (1919) reported on a child who at the age of 40 months used 11,623 words in a day, or an average of 950 words per hour, and by 52 months of age this same child used 14,930 words in a day. They compare these data with a study by Nice (1917) in which a child of 63 months used 10,500 words in a day and with one by Bell (1903) in which a child at 3½ years used 15,230 and another at 4 years used 14,996 words in a day. These are undoubtedly reports on children who were very precocious in linguistic development and who were undoubtedly encouraged to converse freely at home, but they serve to show the important rôle that conversation can play in the life of a young child.

There are very marked individual differences in loquacity, for McCarthy (1930) found that among 140 children observed under similar conditions the time required to record 50 consecutive responses varied from 7 to 50 minutes. Fisher (1934), who recorded the responses of a group of 72 children with a mean IQ of 132.6 for 9 hours of free play, found that the average number of remarks per hour ranged from 23 to 192, with a mean at 92. There was a correlation of +.56 between CA and the number of remarks per hour. M. E. Smith (1926) recorded children's responses for 1 hour during free play. This measure showed a steady increase from a mean of 78 words per hour for 2-year-olds to 400 words per hour at 4 years of age, with practically no change from 4 to 5 years. She states:

> The average total number of words used to the hour shows a regular increase with age; but the variability is too great from child to child for it to be an adequate criterion. In fact, this number ranges from 0 to 1100 words for the entire group studied. The length of sentence, that is, the number of words to the sentence, seems to be a much better measure [p. 17].

A study by Olson and Koetzle (1936) presented a technique for securing a quantitative statement of the amount and rate of talking. The groups they used were small and highly selected, so the study is chiefly of value from the methodological standpoint. It involves the use of a mechanical hand tally and a time-out stopwatch in a modification of Olson's (1929) short-sample technique of observation. Records were made for two 1-minute periods per day for 15 days. The examiner actuated the counter for each word heard and started and stopped the stop-watch as the child talked until a whole minute of continuous talking had elapsed. Measures of rate of talking were made in similar fashion, using 6 samples of 30 seconds each distributed over 6 weeks. Observers checked the reliability of the method against reading aloud and found a correlation of +.99 between the number of words recorded and the actual number of words in the passages read from a book. The mean

error was 1.4 words in 12 samples of 144 words each, and the errors were in the direction of omission. The reliability of the amount records as measured by comparison of odd and even observations was +.93 after application of the Spearman-Brown prophecy formula. Rate samples were quite unreliable, but the authors believe that the reliability could be made satisfactory by increasing the number and length of the observation samples. It was found that the child who talked most talked seven times as much as the child who talked least, and that the most rapid talker spoke 1.4 times as fast as the slowest. Amount scores correlated +.40 in the nursery school and +.73 in the kindergarten with teachers' ratings of the quantity of the child's verbal output as measured on a five-point graphic rating scale. Amount scores showed a correlation of only +.14 and rate scores a correlation of only +.02 with IQ on the Kuhlmann-Binet. The two types of scores correlated only +.13 with each other.

Jersild and Ritzman (1938) reanalyzed the same data used by Fisher (1934) with the addition of 16 more cases. They state that the increase in sheer quantity of speech is perhaps the most obvious indication of the rapid development of language in the early years of childhood. They also note a decelerating rate of increase around 4 to 5 years. The average half-yearly increase in amount of talking between 24 and 48 months for these bright children was 66 per cent.

Young (1941) determined the number of comprehensible words spoken per 10-minute period. This measure showed a steady increase up to 60 months of age and reflected all the group differences, such as difference in sex, socio-economic status, and situation which were revealed in the other analyses in her study.

Gerwitz (1948a, b) measured "word fluency" in a group of 38 children 5 and 6 years of age by means of a free association technique. As might have been anticipated, he found a higher relation to MA than to CA, substantial correlations (.67) with other measures of vocabulary, and low insignificant correlations with a wide variety of other measures. As the numbers were small and reliability was determined on only one variable, the elaborate statistical treatment hardly seems warranted.

Length of Response. As noted earlier, the child uses his first words as whole sentences, but with the increase in vocabulary which soon follows he begins to combine words in varying numbers. One of the most objective and easily determined indices of language growth is the increase in length of response which has been reported by most investigators. A number of the studies on speech development in preschool children have employed similar methods and hence have yielded fairly comparable results, which are shown in Table 5. In general this table reveals quite striking agreement among a variety of workers, each employing a different group of subjects and slightly varying methods. Most of the discrepancies which appear can be accounted for in terms of known selective factors or by differences in the methods of recording and analysis.

The data reported by McCarthy (1930), those on E. A. Davis's (1937a) singletons, and those reported by Templin (1953a) are the most comparable since they were selected so as to be representative of the population on the basis of paternal occupation. Fisher's (1934) group, being a gifted group intellectually, yields much higher mean length of response at all ages. Day (1932) found that her twins, selected by the same criteria as used in the McCarthy study, were seriously retarded in this aspect of language development, and Howard (1934) found a group of 5-year-old triplets also seriously retarded in language development. In this connection it is interesting to note that the reports available on the language development of the Dionne quintuplets reveal that they were more seriously retarded in language development than twins and perhaps more so than triplets. It is indeed unfortunate that the data were not recorded and reported in such a manner as to make the results on the quintuplets directly comparable with this accumulated body of knowledge. (See section on effects of environmental factors, pp. 584–597.)

The results from the McCarthy (1930), Day (1932), Shirley (1933a), E. A. Davis (1937a), and Shire (1945) studies, and the data from the adult situation in the M. E. Smith (1935a) study, as well as from the Hahn (1948) and Templin studies, were taken when the child was alone with the examiner. In the M. E. Smith (1926) study, the Fisher (1934) study, the child-child situation data from the M. E. Smith (1935a, 1939) studies, and in the Young (1941) study all records were taken while the children were engaged with other children in free play situations in nursery schools. As may be seen by a comparison of the adult and child situations (Smith, 1935a), children appeared to use somewhat longer sentences when alone with an adult than when engaged in conversation with other children, but since different numbers of cases were used in the two groups the comparison is obscured. The situation is reversed, however, when the children have an audience of other children, as in the first-grade "show-and-tell" classroom situation of Hahn's (1948) investigation. The same children used sentences averaging 10.4 words before a group but only 6.9 words per sentence on the average when conversing with an adult.

The data reported by Shirley (1933a) are really longitudinal and represent the same measures taken on the same group of children at successive ages. All the other studies are of the cross-sectional type. In the E. A. Davis (1937a) twin group quite a number of the cases at 5½ and 6½ years are the same cases used at an earlier age by Day (1932), although the exact amount of overlap is not specified. In some of M. E. Smith's studies the same children have contributed records at various ages, but it is difficult if not impossible to determine the number of overlapping cases from age to age. In Fisher's (1934) data 10 of her 72 records were obtained by having two records on the same cases about 1 year apart.

In M. E. Smith's (1926) study data were based on 1-hour conversations in the free play situation. In Fisher's (1934) study the data represent 9 hours of recording of spontaneous conversation during free play taken in 3 periods of 3 hours each, and in Young's (1941) study they are based on 28 periods of 10 minutes each distributed over four different types of situations in the nursery school. These two studies may be thought of as the most intensive since they have the largest samples of conversation per child. The McCarthy (1930), Day (1932), Shirley (1933a), M. E. Smith (1935a, 1939), E. A. Davis (1937a), Shire (1945), and Templin (1953a) studies employed 50 responses which have proved to be a sufficiently reliable sample for most purposes, provided the situation remains constant. Young's study was primarily concerned with a comparison of relief cases and privileged nursery school children, so her data are necessarily broken according to socio-economic level. It should also be mentioned at this point that the Davis, Day, McCarthy, and Smith (1935a) studies found marked and consistent differences in length of sentence with change in socio-economic level. This matter will be discussed in more detail in a later section. (See pp. 586–587.)

The Templin investigation has data on the largest number of children over the widest age range of any of the major language investigations. Furthermore, it provides data on vocabulary, articulation, and sentence structure for the same children. The study by Anastasi and D'Angelo (1952), reported in Table 5, is significant as it is the first study giving data on length of sentence by Negro and white children equated in age, sex, socio-economic status, and intelligence. In this study 60 responses were recorded for all subjects and the results were based on the last 50 because McCarthy's (1930) data showed that the first 10 responses were slightly shorter on the average than later groups of 10. The findings will be discussed in more detail in the section on racial differences. (See pp. 586–587.)

Shire (1945), in an unpublished doctoral dissertation at Fordham University, studied 300 first-grade parochial school children having an average IQ of 108 at an average age of 6½ years. Her method of gathering data for measuring language maturity in the prediction of success in first-grade reading was comparable to that of McCarthy, Day, and Davis. Shire's procedure differed from that of Davis's in that she used play materials of equal interest value to both boys and girls. It may be seen from Table 5 that Davis's and Shire's data are in close agreement in regard to length of response, although in this measure and in others Shire's group seems somewhat advanced in comparison with Davis's and appears more like an upward extension of the McCarthy (1930) data. Templin's group seems even more accelerated in length of response. A possible explanation may lie in the greater permissiveness and lessened rigidity in parental methods of child care in recent years. It is probable that Davis's penalizing of the girls in her choice

TABLE 5

MEAN LENGTH OF SENTENCE IN SPOKEN LANGUAGE AS SHOWN IN FOURTEEN INVESTIGATIONS

Author and Type of Study	Date	Group	N	1½	2	2½	3	3½	4	4½	5	5½	6	6½	9½
M. E. Smith * One-hour conversations in play situation. Miscellaneous cases. Not discrete age groups.	1926	Boys	64		1.3	2.2	3.3	4.4	4.1	4.8	4.7				
		Girls	60		2.2	2.4	3.5	3.8	4.4	4.7	4.6				
		All	124		1.8	2.2	3.4	4.3	4.2	4.7	4.6				
McCarthy Representative group. Fifty responses with adult.	1930	Boys	67	1.0	1.4	3.2	3.1	4.2	4.3	4.6					
		Girls	73	1.3	2.1	3.1	3.8	4.4	4.4	4.7					
		All	140	1.2	1.8	3.1	3.4	4.3	4.4	4.6					
Day Representative group of twins. Fifty responses with adult.	1932	Boys	79		1.3		2.5		3.0		2.9				
		Girls	81		1.7		2.5		3.0		3.5				
		All	160		1.5		2.5		3.0		3.2				
Shirley Fifty responses with adult. Longitudinal infant study.	1933	All	23		1.7	2.7	4.2	4.5							
Fisher Gifted group. Three 3-hour samples in play situation.	1934	Boys	35	3.4	4.7	3.4	5.0	8.4	6.9	10.1					
		Girls	37	3.9	4.8	5.3	6.3	5.6	7.6	8.3					
		All	72	3.7	4.8	4.7	5.6	6.9	7.2	9.5					
Howard † Triplets.	1934	All									3.0				

Study	Description	Year	Group	N	1	2	3	4	5	6	7	8	9	10	11
M. E. Smith ‡	Miscellaneous cases. Overlapping in child-child and adult-child situations.	1935a	All	305	1.2	1.8	2.5	3.5	4.3	4.6	4.9	5.0	5.1	4.7	6.0
			Boys	153	1.2	1.5	2.4	3.3	4.3	4.4	5.0	4.9	5.4	5.4	7.0
			Girls	152	1.3	2.0	2.6	3.8	4.2	4.7	4.9	5.0	4.7	5.0	6.5
			All w. adult	198	1.3	2.1	2.8	3.6	4.8	5.1	5.6	6.1	5.7		
			All w. child	107	1.1	1.6	2.4	3.4	4.0	4.3	4.6	4.6	4.8		
E. A. Davis	Representative groups. Fifty responses with an adult.	1937a	Singletons Boys	86									4.4	5.5	6.3
			Singletons Girls	87									4.4	5.3	6.1
			Singletons All	173									4.4	5.4	6.2
			Twins Boys	83									4.5	5.1	7.4
			Twins Girls	83									4.4	5.9	7.2
			Twins All	166									4.4	5.4	7.3
			Only Boys	49									4.7		
			Only Girls	48									5.6		
			All	97									5.1		
M. E. Smith	Bilingual groups in Hawaii. Fifty responses at play with children.	1939	All	1000		1.9		3.0		3.4		3.6	3.7		
Young	Regular nursery school and relief nursery school cases. Large samples. Four situations.	1941	Relief boys	20			2.8	3.0	3.9	4.2	4.3	4.5			
			Relief girls	17			3.1	3.7	4.3	4.4	4.6	5.0			
			Regular boys	20			3.3	3.6	4.4	4.9	5.0	5.2			
			Regular girls	17			3.4	4.1	4.8	5.1	5.4	5.9			
			All boys	37			3.1	3.3	4.2	4.6	4.7	4.9			
			All girls	37			3.3	3.9	4.6	4.8	5.0	5.5			

* Data from M. E. Smith's 1926 study have been recomputed from raw data presented in the appendix because of discrepancies between her Tables I and XII. Actually based on 124 records from only 88 children.

† As reported by E. A. Davis (1937a).

‡ Data from two situations have been grouped in the analysis according to sex.

TABLE 5 (*Continued*)

MEAN LENGTH OF SENTENCE IN SPOKEN LANGUAGE AS SHOWN IN FOURTEEN INVESTIGATIONS

Author and Type of Study	Date	Group	N	1½	2	2½	3	3½	4	4½	5	5½	6	6½	7	8
Shire Fifty responses with adult. First graders from three parochial schools.	1945	Boys Girls All	150 150 300											5.0 5.7 5.4		
Hahn Short samples (med. 70 words) with adult. 80% upper and middle class.	1948	All	116											6.9		
Short samples (med. 48 words) in first grade. "Share and tell" situation same group as above.			116											10.4		

Study	Year	Group	N				
Anastasi and D'Angelo. Fifty responses. Matched Negro and white groups from mixed and unmixed neighborhoods. Lower socio-economic levels.	1952	Negro boys mixed	14	4.53			
		Negro girls mixed	11	4.48			
		All mixed Negroes	25	4.51 †			
		White boys mixed	15	4.39			
		White girls mixed	10	4.75			
		All whites mixed	25	4.53 †			
		Negro boys unmixed	11	4.60			
		Negro girls unmixed	14	3.86			
		All unmixed Negroes	25	4.19 †			
		White boys unmixed	11	4.58			
		White girls unmixed	14	4.85			
		All whites unmixed	25	4.73 †			
Templin * Fifty responses with adult. Representative group.	1953a	Boys	120	5.35	6.73	7.34	7.25
		Girls	120	6.11	6.35	7.16	7.85
		All	240	5.74	6.53	7.26	7.55

* Figures made available by the courtesy of Dr. Templin. When complete study is published data will be presented for 480 cases from 3½ to 8 years.

† Means for total groups combined computed from data supplied in Anastasi and D'Angelo (1950).

of toys lowered her averages for the total age levels.

In general, it may be seen that the child of 18 months is still essentially in the 1-word-sentence stage and that he is just beginning to combine words. A year later, sentences of 2 or 3 words are most typical, and by 3½ years complete sentences averaging about 4 words each are used. By 6½ years the mean length of sentence is about 5 words, and by early elementary school years it appears to level off at about 7 words. Note should be made at this point regarding sex differences in length of response in favor of girls which appear fairly consistently in Table 5. More de-

This same measure has been applied to written language as well as to spoken language. The best available data on the length of sentence in written compositions are supplied by Heider and Heider (1940*b*), who present data for 817 normal cases aged 8 to 14 years who wrote compositions based on a short movie they had seen. It is interesting to compare these figures with those by Stormzand and O'Shea (1924) based on 10,000 sentences collected from children's compositions and letters in various grades as well as with length of sentence in adult writing as represented by the works of such writers as Macaulay, Stevenson and others. (See Table 6.)

TABLE 6

MEAN NUMBER OF WORDS PER SENTENCE IN WRITTEN COMPOSITIONS BY AGE AND SCHOOL GRADE

Age Grade	8 3	9 4	10 5	11 6	12 7	13 8	14 9	10	11	12	College Freshmen	College Upper Classmen	Adults
Heider and Heider	10.2	10.9	11.1	11.1	12.8	13.7	13.9						
Stormzand and O'Shea		11.1		12.0	13.5	15.2	17.3	17.8	18.0	19.8	19.9	21.5	20.9

tailed discussion of this problem will be presented in the section on sex differences. (See pp. 577–581.)

The measure of sentence length was first suggested by Nice (1925), who described four stages of sentence development. The complete sentence stage, she said, did not appear until after 4 years of age. Nice pointed out that the complete sentence usually consisted of 6 to 8 words and was characterized by mastery of inflections. These conclusions, based on observations of only a few children and made before any of the quantitative studies had appeared, afforded a fairly accurate forecast of what was in store for later investigators.

J. E. Anderson (1937) also reports data on sentence length for 150-word samples from the compositions of college students; he obtained a mean length of written sentence at the college level of 20.4 words. He reports, however, that such short samples do not yield adequately reliable measures.

Apparently, then, sentence length is a measure which continues to show increase in normal children until maturity. The use of the measure has been criticized by some writers, and a few substitute measures have been suggested, but none seems to have superseded the mean length of sentence for a reliable, easily determined, objective, quantitative, and easily understood measure of linguistic maturity.

LaBrant (1933) used the mean length of clause in her study, for she argued that division into sentences may be rather arbitrary, especially in the compositions of children who have not mastered punctuation and who may write several run-on clauses as a single sentence. LaBrant argues that the counting of predicates is easier, more objective, and psychologically more sound. The length of clause she found remains fairly constant in grades 4 to 12, although the subordination index, or ratio of subordinate to coordinate clauses, shows an increase. Apparently length of clause is somewhat controlled or restricted by the structure of the language, and whatever increase in sentence length occurs at higher age levels is brought about largely through the addition of more subordinate clauses. J. E. Anderson (1937) determined subordination indices for samples of 150 words each, taken from four different compositions written by college students, and found very low reliabilities averaging only +.07. Subordination indices based on two successive samples of this length taken from the same compositions correlated only +.23. The mean number of words to the sentence yielded reliabilities of only +.31 and +.35 when similarly treated. E. A. Davis (1941) found that the index of subordination was slightly higher in written than in oral products.

E. A. Davis (1937b) also compared the relative merits of the longest sentences with the mean length of all sentences. The measures of the longest sentence and that of the five longest sentences she found exaggerate developmental trends and group differences and tend to throw them into relief. Although they undoubtedly are a better indication of the child's maximum linguistic capacity at the time than the mean of all the sentences, they do not afford as reliable measures, especially at lower ages, as the mean length of all sentences. The longest sentence and the mean of the five longest sentences in a sample have the advantage of ease of computation, but there is considerable sacrifice in reliability when either of these short-cut methods is employed, which is more serious at younger age levels. Davis advocates the use of the mean of the five longest sentences, but the writer is of the opinion that the use of this measure should be restricted to rough group comparisons.

Sentence Structure and Grammatical Form

Most students of children's language development have been concerned not only with the quantitative approach in terms of length of responses, but they have also attempted some form of qualitative analysis to reveal the improvement in sentence structure which takes place as the child develops.

Emphasis has been placed on sentence structure because of the necessity of guiding children's writing and because of the rôle of grammar in the school curriculum. Symonds and Daringer (1930) state:

> Sentence structure in a language is a key to the logic and structure of thinking, inasmuch as the sentence is the smallest complete unit of thought. Growth in the power to form complete, concise, balanced, consistent sentences is an index of the growth in clear and accurate thinking.

The biographical studies usually give anecdotal accounts of the first sentence, but make little or no attempt to trace sentence formation further. According to a summary of these observations in the *Twenty-eighth Yearbook of the National Society for the Study of Education*, the time of the appearance of the first sentence is reported from the fifteenth to the twenty-sixth month by Moore (1896), Bateman (1914), Drummond (1916), Nice (1925), Guillaume (1927a), and Stern (1930). Nice (1925) reports the average age of the appearance of the first sentence for 20 children as 17.5 months. Shirley (1933a, 1933b) calls attention to the marked perseverative tendency which is apparent in the first sentences and suggests that possibly the variety of sentences would afford a better measure than the total number of sentences at the earliest stages. More detailed analyses of sentence structure are reported by Pollock (1878), Moore (1896), Boyd (1913), and Nice (1925). Nice outlines the various stages in sentence formation as follows: (1) the single word stage from 4 to 12 months; (2) the early sentence stage from 13 to 27 months, with an average at 17.5 months, lasting from 4 to 7 months, and characterized by a preponderance of nouns, lack of articles, auxiliaries and copulative verbs, prepositions, and conjunctions; (3) the short sentence stage, which consists of sentences 3.5 to 4.5 words in length and having the same characteristics as the preceding stage, but to a lesser degree; inflections are not yet mastered, and only 1 or 2 sentences out of 50 are compound or complex; (4) the complete sentence stage, which appears at about 4 years and consists of sentences of 6 to 8 words, characterized by greater definiteness and complexity as shown by an increased use of relational words and a fairly good mastery of inflections.

The studies which have presented the most elaborate analyses of sentence structure, and which used almost comparable classifications, are those by McCarthy (1930), Day (1932), E. A. Davis (1937a), Shire (1945), Hahn (1948), Anastasi and D'Angelo (1952), and Templin (1953a). Day's figures are somewhat different from McCarthy's because of the general retardation which Day found in the language

development of twins. The construction analyses of five of these studies are compared in Table 7. Davis's (1937a) groups represented an extension to higher age levels using similar samples from the same geographical area. Shire (1945) and Hahn (1948) supplied additional data for comparison with Davis's 6½-year age level. Considering the variation in method explained in the footnotes there are a number of close parallels. Apparently Shire secured greater spontaneity and had fewer elicited responses than the other authors, as remarks which have to be elicited often fall in the functionally complete category. It is particularly interesting to note the increase in complexity of sentence structure that Hahn's first-grade children used when in an audience situation in the classroom. In spite of her more strict criterion for elaborated sentences her first graders said more elaborated, compound and complex sentences when speaking to other children than when speaking to an adult, even more than Davis's 9½-year-olds used with an adult.

Other studies which have been concerned with construction analysis cannot be compared with this group of studies for various reasons. Fisher's (1934) data are presented only for her total group and are not separated by age levels. In the series of studies by M. E. Smith (1926, 1935a, 1939) totally different classifications are employed, so that the figures are not comparable. In work of this sort change in one category affects the percentages in other categories if the authors have used classifications that account for 100 per cent of the responses. Smith reports on the percentage of complete sentences, simple sentences, and "yes" and "no" only; and the rest of her classification in all three studies is based on the functional classification of sentences into declarative, interrogative, imperative, and exclamatory, which makes the

TABLE 7

MEAN PERCENTAGES OF TOTAL RESPONSES IN EACH CONSTRUCTION CATEGORY AT VARIOUS AGE LEVELS IN THREE COMPARABLE STUDIES

Age in Years	Investigator	Functionally Complete		Simple		Simple with Phrase		Compound and Complex		Elaborated		Incomplete	
		Singletons	Twins	Singletons	Twins	Singletons	Twins	Singletons	Twins	Singletons	Twins	Singletons	Twins
1½	McCarthy	78.4		9.6		0.0		0.0		0.0		11.9	
2	McCarthy	Day *	53.8	70.0	17.3	7.5	1.4	2.0	.9	.2	.6	0.0	25.1	19.7
2½	McCarthy	35.3		38.7		5.3		1.5		1.2		18.1	
3	McCarthy	Day	27.2	48.0	45.1	23.0	8.7	4.0	1.5	.5	1.3	.3	16.2	24.6
3½	McCarthy	30.6		35.3		11.4		6.5		2.3		13.9	
4	McCarthy	Day	32.0	48.0	39.4	28.0	10.9	7.5	6.1	1.5	4.5	.9	6.8	13.3
4½	McCarthy	31.2		36.5		10.4		7.0		5.9		8.8	
5	Day	49.0		24.0		7.0		3.6		1.0		15.4	
5½	E. A. Davis	39.4	38.0	29.4	31.4	7.8	7.8	4.6	4.6	3.6	2.8	15.0	15.4
6½	E. A. Davis	32.0	28.6	30.8	32.2	9.8	10.8	5.4	7.4	5.6	5.8	16.4	15.2
6½	Shire	16.4		29.7		21.3		8.4		8.2		15.8	
6½	Hahn												
	Adult situation	22.0 †		33.2		17.0 ‡		25.5		2.4 ‡		†	
	Class situation	3.3 †		27.8		23.2 ‡		34.8		10.9 ‡		†	
9½	E. A. Davis	33.6	34.8	18.8	22.2	11.4	10.8	6.8	5.4	10.0	10.2	19.4	16.6

* Figures from Day have been estimated from graphs.

† Hahn uses only the category of "non-sentences" which probably includes both incomplete sentences and functionally complete ones here classed as functionally complete.

‡ Hahn's elaborated sentences involved two or more independent units with one or more subordinate clauses. Cf. McCarthy's definition (1930, p. 44).

data more comparable with the functional analyses of many of the other studies. She does not provide a classification for incomplete [1] or fragmentary responses which often occur in records of conversation, so it is difficult or impossible to determine whether or not her classification covers 100 per cent of the data. If various types of sentences have merely been counted without necessarily accounting for all sentences, it is dif-

1 Incomplete sentences were considered "grammatically wrong." Imperatives not requiring a subject in adult language were not counted incomplete. (Personal communication to the writer.)

ficult to ascertain what was used as the base in determining percentages. Young's (1941) study, which in many respects is comparable with the group of studies in Table 7, does not attempt any analysis according to sentence structure.

Shire's (1945) figures, which are comparable with those of Davis on 6½-year-olds, agree closely with hers in the percentage of simple sentences and in the percentage of incomplete sentences. The greatest discrepancy was in the category of functionally complete although structurally incomplete sentences, which were only half as frequent as in Davis's study. This factor may have been due, at least in part, to differences in quality of rapport. Shire (1945) found almost twice as high a percentage of simple sentences with phrases, 3 per cent more compound and complex sentences, and 3 per cent more elaborated sentences.

Hahn (1948) reported on construction analysis of data from 116 first-grade children, who probably represent a more highly selected group than those in the other studies included in Table 7. She used two situations, one an adult-child situation comparable to those of the other investigators. In examining Table 7 for developmental trends the data of Hahn (1948) should be interpreted with caution for two reasons. In the first place her samples are much smaller than the 50 sentences employed in the other studies, as her median sample in the adult situation was only 70 words, or about 10 sentences, and only about 4 sentences in the class situations. Thus, a shift of 1 or 2 sentences from one category to another would make a large shift in percentages, and the data are less dependable because of the small sampling. The large percentage of compound and complex sentences in her data in comparison with the other studies might be due to the fact that approximately 80 per cent of her cases came from upper and middle class homes. Considering the different sampling and slight differences in classification, her figures are in remarkable agreement, however, with those of Davis (1937a) and of Shire (1945), who also report on 6½-year-old children. The greatest discrepancy is in the "compound and complex" category. This is probably due to her more strict interpretation of the elaborated sentences.

Examination of Table 7 for developmental trends reveals that in general there is a decrease in the functionally complete but structurally incomplete sentences, although even at the 9½-year level they continue to constitute about one-third of the speech of the children studied by E. A. Davis (1937a). Simple sentences without phrases show an initial increase, followed by a decrease as the more elaborate forms of sentence structure begin to appear. Simple sentences without phrases constitute 9.6 per cent of the comprehensible sentences at 18 months, and they practically double in number every half-year up to 2½. They appear to reach a peak in the latter part of the preschool period and then decrease. The decrease is much later among twins in accordance with their general linguistic retardation, as this peak is not reached by twins until 6½ years of age. Phrases are first reported in small numbers—about 1 or 2 per cent—at 2 years, and show a steady increase with age in both twins and singletons, although they never exceed about 10 or 11 per cent even by 9½ years of age except in the Shire and Hahn data, where they are found in about one-fifth of the sentences of 6-year-olds. Phrases are comparatively infrequent in the speech of twins until after school age.

Compound and complex sentences also first appear in very small numbers at 2 years of age. Among singletons they quickly rise to 6 and 7 per cent of the total number of comprehensible sentences between 3½ and 4½ years and remain at about this level in the speech of the 9½-year-olds. The extremely high figures for this category in Hahn's data are probably due to the highly selected group and to the stricter definition of elaborated sentences. The emergence of compound and complex sentences appears to be considerably slower in the preschool period for twins, but they seem to catch up in the use of the more complex forms after exposure to the school environment. The category of elaborated responses, first suggested by the writer, which consists of sentences containing two phrases, two clauses, or a phrase and a clause, proved to be a good developmental index for later linguistic development. Such sentences were rare in the speech of the preschool children, and reached a maximum of about 6 per cent at 4½ years. However, they increased to 10 per cent by 9½ years. The same trend appeared, although much more slowly, among the twins. Incomplete sentences, which were nevertheless sufficiently complete to enable the scorer to detect omissions, decreased in McCarthy's data from 25 per cent at 2 years to about 8 per cent at 4½ years. For some unaccountable reason the percentage of incomplete sentences did not show similar decreases with age in the data of Day and Davis, as they continue to constitute 15 or 16 per cent of the responses even up to the 9½-year level.

Shire (1945) found that several measures of linguistic maturity when combined were quite helpful in predicting success in first-grade reading. The measure of linguistic maturity which correlated best with reading achievement was the number of elaborated sentences in a sample of 50 responses. She points out that children who did not make satisfactory progress in two semesters of first-grade reading showed linguistic immaturity, particularly by the absence of elaborated sentences, the shortness of their average sentence, lack of connectives, and lack of variety in their vocabularies as indicated by a comparatively small number of different words in the sample of 50 sentences. Multiple correlations for several combinations of language variables and intelligence test scores in the prediction of first-grade reading ranged from .45 to .63, the number of elaborated sentences and the number of nouns adding most to the intelligence test scores in the prediction. It would seem that kindergarten and first-grade teachers could be taught to record the spontaneous speech of their pupils in the determination of reading readiness.

Williams (1937a) has attempted to quantify the complexities of sentence structure by assigning arbitrary scores to certain types of structure for his language achievement scale. He gives a score for completeness of the expression unit in which a response has subject, verb, and object expressed if the verb requires an object. A score of 2 is given for a complete unit, 1 for an incomplete unit, and 0 for unintelligible responses. He also assigns weights for complexity of sentence as follows: unintelligible, 0; simple sentence, 1; compound, 2; complex, 3; and compound-complex, 4. In addition he has devised a score for word usage composed of the number of words given in conventional usage per 50 running words. These appear to be quite objective and easily applicable techniques which are deserving of further experimentation. They have the advantage of permitting correlational treatment of some dimensions of language development which have heretofore been restricted to treatment in terms of percentages of various types of response. They enable the investigator to assign a single quantitative score for several important dimensions of language development instead of depending on inspection of a series of categories.

The two studies by Stormzand and O'Shea (1924) and by Heider and Heider (1940b) yield valuable data on sentence structure in written composition, as may be seen in Table 8. In written language, sentences are much more likely to be complete, and hence there is not the necessity of providing a category for fragmentary responses as in the records of oral responses of younger children. Stormzand and O'Shea report their data in terms of school grades, whereas the Heiders' material is in terms of ages. However, the results of the two studies have been aligned in Table 8 so

TABLE 8

Comparison of Percentages of Different Types of Sentence Structure in Two Studies of Written Language

Type of Sentence	Heider and Heider * / Stormzand and O'Shea †	Age 8	Age 9 / Gr 4	Age 10 / Gr 5	Age 11 / Gr 6	Age 12 / Gr 7	Age 13 / Gr 8	Age 14 / Gr 9	Gr 10	Gr 11	Gr 12	Freshmen	Upper Classmen	Adults
Simple	Heider and Heider	53	45	40	36	30	27	27						
	Stormzand and O'Shea		48		59	46	48	38	44	39	38	30	22	37
Compound	Heider and Heider	31	36	38	38	41	42	43						
	Stormzand and O'Shea		25		6	13	14	18	18	17	20	18	23	13
Complex	Heider and Heider	8	9	12	13	13	14	12						
	Stormzand and O'Shea		27		37	41	37	44	38	44	42	52	55	46
Compound-complex	Heider and Heider	8	10	10	12	15	17	18						

* N = 817 children who wrote short compositions on a movie they had seen in class.

† Based on 10,000 sentences selected from essays, newspaper articles and editorials, modern light fiction, adult letters, and compositions of university, high school, and fourth- to eighth-grade pupils.

as to compare the 9-year-olds with the fourth graders, etc., assuming that the children were normally placed in school for their ages. It is difficult to evaluate the developmental significance of such data, however, without any adult norm for the expected level at maturity. The nearest approach to such material is provided in a study by Thorndike, Evans, Kennon, and Newcomb (1926–1927), in which 45 samples of writing were analyzed for grammatical construction. There were 18,113 occurrences of the simple sentence in the sampling, and 438 other types of sentence construction were listed with their frequencies per 100,000 sentences. LaBrant's (1933) material is treated using the clause as the unit rather than the sentence, so again comparisons are impossible.

It is indeed unfortunate that more direct comparisons cannot legitimately be made among these various studies. The similarity of the labels of many of the categories is likely to mislead the naïve reader, who has not handled data of this sort, into thinking that many figures are comparable which actually are not because of differ-

ences in methodology, and the counterbalancing effect of the treatment in terms of percentages is likely to be confusing.

Various investigators have been concerned with the incidence of the different parts of speech as they occur in the running conversation of children. The most detailed study of this sort is by Young (1941), who presents, in addition to her own data on 74 cases, the results of six other investigations. Young is chiefly concerned with reconciling certain differences which appear in the literature which she interprets to be due to difference of definition of grammatical terms. She adheres strictly to the definitions in Jespersen's *Essentials of English Grammar* (1933). In the opinion of the present writer, such analyses are of significance for child development only in the very early stages of sentence formation before all the various parts of speech have come into active use. As Young herself states: "The proportions of the parts of speech changed most rapidly before the age of 3, and after that age the rate of change tended to be slower" (p. 87). As soon as the child begins to use full and complete sentences which are grammatically correct, the percentages of the various parts of speech become more or less set by the conventions of the language. The beginnings of the use of modifiers and of prepositions and connectives are probably quite significant and mark important milestones in the development of the child's speech, but as soon as they are employed characteristically their developmental significance becomes submerged in a number of other factors. In addition to being controlled by the demands of conventional usage, they are definitely related to the situation in which the language sample is taken, as Goodenough (1938) has shown in her excellent study of pronouns, in which she states:

> Proportions of the various parts of speech in the language of children are frequently quoted in a fashion that might lead the reader to think that these proportions depend almost wholly upon the child's level of development and vary but little with the conditions of observation. The unsoundness of this point of view will be apparent from an examination of the data here presented. As a matter of fact, while most of the pronouns here listed show a distinct difference in frequency of usage according to the immediate situation under which they are used, age differences are not always apparent, even when no allowances are made for the increasing length of the sentence [p. 338].

More promising leads are afforded by additional indices of improvement in sentence structure as reflected in specific changes in various types of grammatical forms. Such approaches lead the investigator into more detailed treatment and classification. Verb forms, especially the use of past and future tenses, have been studied by Lewis (1951), Adams (1938), M. E. Smith (1939), and Ames (1946). The understanding of prepositions has been

described by Grigsby (1932), and their use in written language has been treated by Heider and Heider (1940b). Connectives have received special treatment from E. A. Davis (1937a) and also from the Heiders. A study of determining and numerating adjectives has been presented by Carroll (1939), and pronouns have received detailed treatment from Goodenough (1938), E. A. Davis (1938a), and Young (1942b). Infinitives have been studied by E. A. Davis (1937a), Young (1941), and Heider and Heider (1940b), and the various types of clauses which were brought to the fore by LaBrant (1933) have also been analyzed in greater detail by E. A. Davis (1937a, 1941), and by the Heiders.

Lewis (1951) brings out that at first the language of the child is concerned exclusively with the immediate situation in which it is spoken and that gradually it begins to deal with things that are absent. This matter of reference to things absent has also been emphasized by both K. and C. Bühler (both, 1930). Lewis relates the child's use of past and future tenses to the functions of his earlier undifferentiated speech. It is because of the child's use of speech as an instrument to draw others into his social circle that he begins to speak of absent things and events. Lewis points out that the child uses a word manipulatively in an effort to call attention to an object which he wishes brought into the present situation. In such instances he claims that the child's utterance is much more an expression of his needs within the present situation than a reference to an absent object. The adult's conversation with the child then becomes a potent factor in the emergence of the use of past and future tenses.

Ames and Learned (1948) studied children's verbalizations in regard to space and found that the largest number of new words relating to space are added to the child's vocabulary between 2 and 2½ years. Children were found to respond first to a space word, then to say it spontaneously, and later to use it in answering a question. Looking and pointing definitely preceded verbalization. A further sequence from general to specific and then to somewhat more general responses was noted. For example, a child when asked, "Where do you sleep?" at first answers, "Home"; later he is likely to say, "In my crib"; but at a still later age, "In my room." The child's use of space words seems to parallel the increasing expansion of his spatial experience.

Quantitative expression in the use of such words as "some," "any," "several," and "two" was studied by Martin (1951) in 150 representative children of both sexes from 3 to 7 years of age. The median number of different quantitative words used increased from 4.0 at 3 years to 9.0 at 7 years.

Adams (1938) approached the problem of verb forms by using the records of the speech of twelve 4-year-olds taken during nursery school activities. He tabulated the first 50 verbs in each child's record and compared them with those in 100 consecutive sentences of adult spoken language. He found that 59 per cent of the adult speech and 56 per cent of the children's speech was in the present tense. The adult speech was found to contain a larger percentage of sentences in the compound tense than the children's, and the children's speech to contain a greater percentage of sentences in the present and present-progressive tenses. He found that at 4 years the future tense has come into common use and occurs 10 per cent of the time, and the preterite or simple past is employed about as often as in adult speech. As the verb takes on past and future forms, the times referred to are immediate rather than remote. Only 4 children made reference to any time earlier than the previous day.

Children's use of future tense nearly always involved reference to the future of the day of speaking.

Ames (1946) reports that children first speak of the present, then of the future, and that references to the past occur later. They first react to time words by ability to wait, then by the use of time words, and not until later are they able to answer questions dealing with time. Leopold's (1949a) third volume on the development of speech in his bilingual daughter presents an interesting section on the development of syntax in the first 2 years from the linguist's viewpoint.

The data available on the use of various types of clauses and on the use of infinitives and auxiliary verbs are almost impossible to summarize. Much of this work has been done on written language, LaBrant (1933) using school compositions on different topics from grade 4 to the adult level, and the Heiders (1940b) using compositions in response to a standardized situation. In the latter study emphasis is placed on the comparison of groups of deaf and hearing children rather than on the developmental trends in either the experimental or hearing group. E. A. Davis (1937a) attempted similar analyses on the oral language of her subjects recorded in a standardized situation on younger children. In most of these analyses she reports data only for the total group, although each age level is heavily weighted with twins and only children, both of which groups showed significant and contrasting differences from the singletons in all other aspects of language development. Her samples are short for each individual, and the more complex and elaborate forms occurred so rarely as to make the means unreliable. In a later study (1941) she reported further analysis of the same data. Only the brightest and linguistically most advanced children were able to place a subordinate clause early in the sentence. This ability emerges in the brightest children at the kindergarten level. Younger children were reported to use the interrogative in indirect discourse more than older children.

J. E. Anderson (1937) pointed out in his study of indices of linguistic development that it is not possible to get an adequate sample for detailed analysis of written language in a passage of only 150 words. This is probably even more serious for oral language in which fragmentary remarks are likely to be more frequent, and hence samples of a given length are likely to yield fewer of the more complex forms in complete sentences for statistical treatment. Goodenough (1938) also states on the basis of her study of pronouns: "A sample of 50 responses is not sufficient for the study of individual differences in the use of separate pronouns, but the consistency of the group trends . . . is evidence of their validity as group measures." A more detailed index, however, was the percentage of pronouns in the total sample, which showed little consistent change with age or sex after 3 years; nevertheless, certain specific groups of pronouns showed very pronounced changes with age and with the conditions of observations. The chief trends noted in this analysis indicated that there was an increase with age in the use of the first personal pronoun and that it is used more frequently during play with other children than in conversing with an adult.

Shire's (1945) analysis of pronouns confirmed Goodenough's results. In comparison with Goodenough's 5½-year-old group, Shire's 6½-year-olds showed an increase in the number of pronouns used in a sample of 50 remarks. On the average about five more first person singular pronouns were used and there were about twice as many occurrences of *we, us,* and *ours.* The third person singular personal pronouns practically doubled, whereas there was practically

no change in the use of third person plural pronouns or the impersonal pronouns. Young (1942b) found greater age, sex, and socio-economic differences in the use of possessive than personal pronouns. Marked decreases in the use of possessive self pronouns were accompanied by increases in the use of possessive pronouns referring to others. Valentine (1942) notes that both pronouns and prepositions are used by young children of 2 to 2½ years in certain specific situations in which they have been learned and not in others, and that the use of these parts of speech does not become generalized until a later period.

Gheorgov (1905) pointed out that the child has a fairly well-developed awareness of self long before he begins to express himself in language, but that it is only with the use of words that the higher types of concepts can be differentiated, such as the *I*, the *self*, and the *mine*. He also calls attention to the familiar phenomenon of the child's designation of himself by his own name which he hears others use when speaking or referring to him. This use of the own name often precedes the correct use of the first personal pronouns and is regarded by some as a sign of immaturity in speech. Goodenough (1938) also found that, contrary to popular opinion, the absolute number of pronouns shows no increase with age after the maximum has been reached at 3½ years, and in proportion to the total number of words used the number of pronouns actually declines. Young (1942b) also conducted a detailed study of the personal and possessive pronouns occurring in her major investigation. She found that they constituted 28 per cent of all the comprehensible words spoken by the nursery school children. The first person singular pronouns *I, me,* and *mine* constituted 36 to 39 per cent of the total, whereas the impersonal *it* accounted for 19 per cent. In face-to-face situations, *you* accounted for 15 per cent of the pronouns and the plural forms of *we* or *us* accounted for only 5 per cent.

Symonds and Daringer (1930) report that in written compositions the use of pronouns is high up to the ninth grade but that thereafter it decreases as the writing takes on a more impersonal and more abstract nature. Goodenough (1938) concludes from her study that the use of an unusually large number of pronouns after the age of 3½ years may be interpreted as evidence of linguistic immaturity. As the vocabulary increases the use of the third person neuter pronoun declines, for proper and common nouns come to be substituted for it as the child is able to be more specific in his speech. In conclusion, Goodenough (1938) brings out a very important point for methodology in future research on language development, for she says:

> Many of the formal grammatical classifications of adult usage are inadequate to bring out significant developmental trends in the speech of children. The very marked changes that occur in the use of pronouns, for example, are almost wholly obscured when all pronouns are grouped into a single class. Developmental processes are qualitative as well as quantitative, and in devising systems for classifying behavioral manifestations it is necessary to keep these qualitative changes in mind if the systems are to be useful. It is suggested that in the study of children's language, too much attention has been paid to the type of grammatical analysis used by adults and too little to the developmental changes in conceptual thinking and social drives that lie back of the verbal expression [p. 344].

Carroll (1939) made a special study of determining and enumerating adjectives in children's speech, and he recommends the study of adjectives as an easy approach to the minute details of syntax because they occur frequently and constitute a relatively large part of the total number of words (about 15 per cent). Shire (1945) found that adjectives constituted 12.3 per cent of the total number of words used by her 6½-year-olds.

According to Carroll (1939) numeratives are very infrequent at 2½ years and occur much more frequently at later ages. Both definite and indefinite adjectives excluding articles show increases with age, although there are relatively fewer definite adjectives and more indefinite adjectives as age increases. The growth curve for the use of the indefinite article, *a*, levels off between 3½ and 4½ years, but for *the*, the curve shows a sharp rise throughout the age range studied, namely, from 2½ to 4½ years. This appears to be in accordance with Young's (1941) finding of a steady increase in the use of articles from 30 to 60 months. The use of articles was found by Loomis and Moran (1931) to be a better index of mental ability than the use of any other part of speech ($r = +.52$). It also correlated $+.51$ with average school grade and $+.32$ with paternal occupation. This detail has been overlooked in most earlier work because articles have seemed like such insignificant words that most previous investigators have grouped them with adjectives and have not treated them separately. The use of many verbs was slightly negatively correlated with intelligence. All these results challenge research workers to comb the field of language development for other significant indices.

Another interesting measure which thus far has received little attention was suggested by Busemann (1925), who used a ratio of the activity words to the qualitative words. It really amounts to an activity quotient determined by dividing the total number of verbs by the total number of adjectives. Busemann claims that this index shows a rhythmical cycle of alternating action and qualitative periods throughout the life cycle. His data, however, do not appear adequate to support these claims, as the results he reports could be accounted for on the basis of sampling. He claims that high activity quotients are related to periods of emotional instability in the child's life. This index has been used by Boder (1940) on various types of adult writing, and he finds that it varies with the subject matter, scientific writing yielding the highest quotients, with fiction, legal writing, and plays following in the order named. He claims to find alternating activity quotients in the writings of Emerson.

Feldman and Cameron (1944) used activity quotients obtained from 3 children, 17 normal adults, and 28 seniles. The ratios were highest for the seniles (2.99) and lowest for adults (1.52), with the children intermediate (1.83).

Ellsworth (1951) analyzed parts of speech in written language of children, normal adults, and schizophrenics. The percentages of the parts of speech obtained on the adult schizophrenic groups resembled those of the fifth graders (youngest group) most closely. These groups used relatively high percentages of nouns and pronouns and relatively low percentages of verbs and adjectives. Ellsworth interprets this as a regressive pattern for the schizophrenics. Both children and schizophrenics, he says, know what they are talking about and assume that others will understand them. They therefore see no need to refine their language. He relates the greater use of pronouns to the egocentricity of children and schizophrenics, but found that the schizophrenics revealed their tendency to project on others more in their greater use of third person pronouns.

The educational and English journals are replete with minor articles on the incidence of various types of grammatical errors in the oral and written language of school children. Most of them are poorly controlled with errors often being jotted down at the whim of the teacher at odd moments during the school day. In general they are extremely pessimistic and stress the fact that errors continue in the speech and writings of children throughout the school period in spite of the educational influences aimed to overcome them. One of the better studies on written language is by Symonds and Daringer (1930), in which the authors report that in the fourth grade there are on the average about 2 errors to every sentence, and that this ratio shows a gradual decrease until about the eighth or ninth grade, when there is about 1 error per sentence in children's writings.

Carlton and Carlton (1945) studied the errors made in oral English by mentally defective adolescents and normal children of the same mental ages. They were shown picture sequences and asked to tell stories about them until samples of approximately 60 clauses were secured. The mental defectives made more errors in oral expression than the normal cases of the same mental ages. Only four kinds of errors accounted for approximately half of the total errors in all groups, and among the normals seven errors accounted for over two-thirds of all errors. The most common errors were not the ones that were most common 2 or 3 decades ago, and these authors make a plea for curriculum adjustment in the light of modern research. Such revision of the curriculum is being planned by the National Council of Teachers of English Curriculum Commission, which has a series of four volumes in preparation on this topic.

One of the soundest and the most optimistic articles on the study of errors is by E. A. Davis (1939). She points out that reports based on frequency of error alone are inaccurate and misleading, and that it is necessary to take into account the frequency of occurrence of a given construction in a given sample of language before it can be properly evaluted. Most teachers, she states, find it easier to note errors than correct usage. In an analysis of the most frequently occurring grammatical errors in her major study (1937a), she points out that a pronoun is inflected correctly once for every 16 words and incorrectly once for every 873 words. Adjectives, however, are compared correctly once for every 407 words and incorrectly once for every 16,211 words. The opportunity to inflect a pronoun occurred approximately 17 times for each child, whereas adjectives were compared less than once per child in the data analyzed. She tried a variety of measures of error approached from the positive rather than the negative angle and found that the mean occurrence per child, the number of occurrences per 1000 words, the ratio to the total words used, ratio of times correct to times incorrect, percentage of correct usage, and errors per 1000 chances to use the construction all revealed definite improvement with advancing age. In general, she found that the number of correct usages increased, and the number of incorrect usages decreased, with advancing age, both absolutely and when studied in relation to the total number of words used. For some constructions there was a marked difference in the children coming from the upper and lower socio-economic levels, those from upper levels presumably having the better example and hence fewer errors. It is also interesting to note that the greatest improvement in the elimination of errors occurred in the less privileged group during the early school years.

The Functions of Language in the Child's Life

Of considerably more interest to the child psychologist than the use of various types of word forms are the analyses which attempt to answer the questions of why the child talks, what motivates him to use language in certain situations, what needs he satisfies by the use of language, and what functions language fulfills in the child's life. The early biographical studies approached this problem by classifying responses as declarative, interrogative, exclamatory, and imperative sentences in accordance with the formal classifications of conventional grammar. As has already been pointed out, however, this system does not lend itself well to the psychological analysis of the language of young children. These categories have been designed to fit written discourse but prove unsatisfactory for the conversation of adults and especially unsuitable for the conversations of children.

Snyder (1914) was one of the first to point out this inadequacy and modified the usual grammatical classifications in her study of a 2½-year-old boy. M. E. Smith followed Snyder's classification of sentences in her 1926 study in which several subdivisions and variations of the usual categories were provided. In that analysis she reported:

> There are more declarative sentences, at all ages, than any other type. Also the proportion of imperative sentences, including variations, is probably significantly greater than the proportion of questions at 2, 3, and 4 years.

The appearance of Piaget's (1926) *The Language and Thought of the Child,* which presented an entirely new approach to the study of the functions of the child's language, stimulated much further research and controversy in the field. Piaget was chiefly interested in the child's language as a means of revealing his thought processes. He recognized two major types of speech in the child's language: first, egocentric speech and, second, socialized speech. Piaget was the first to emphasize the rôle of egocentricity in the child's life. He claimed to have discovered its importance through a functional approach to child language. In egocentric speech, as Piaget defined it, "the child does not bother to know to whom he is speaking nor whether he is being listened to. He talks either for himself or for the pleasure of associating anyone who happens to be there with the activity of the moment. . . . He does not attempt to place himself at the point of view of his hearer." Socialized speech, on the other hand, is speech "in which the child addresses his hearer, considers his point of view, tries to influence him or actually exchanges ideas with him." Piaget recognized three types of egocentric speech, namely, echolalia, monologue, and dual or collective monologue. He subdivided socialized speech into: (1) adapted information, which occurs when "the child really exchanges his thoughts with others," (2) criticism, (3) commands, requests, and threats, (4) questions, and (5) answers. He reported data consisting of about 1500 remarks recorded for each of 2 children 6½ years of age taken down during free play in La Maison des Petites in Geneva. About 38 per cent of the child's remarks fell in the egocentric categories, and only about 45 per cent were spontaneous socialized speech with an additional 17 per cent made up of answers, which were classed as socialized remarks, making a total of 62 per cent socialized speech. Piaget reported a higher percentage of egocentric remarks at ages from 3 to 5 and stated that there occurs a definite

socialization in the child's speech at 7 to 8 years of age. He implied that adult conversation is highly socialized and that this egocentrism is a symptom of psychological immaturity, which is outgrown with age.

McCarthy (1930), in seeking a more satisfactory method of treating children's language from the functional point of view, applied Piaget's categories to her data. Although the method at first appears quite subjective, she found that it possessed a fairly satisfactory degree of reliability, for when four scorers attempted to classify identical responses in the various categories of the functional analysis after studying Piaget's definitions, the average intercorrelation was +.78, and this value would have been +.88 if only three scorers were included, as one of the scorers, who was obviously less interested in the task, had consistently lower correlations with all the others. It appears, then, that really conscientious scorers can classify the responses of preschool children into these categories with a satisfactory degree of agreement. In the application of this classification scheme to her data McCarthy adhered to a literal interpretation of Piaget's definitions of the terms for each category. Piaget's examples often do not fit his definitions, but where confusion occurred the definition was used as the criterion rather than an isolated example. It was necessary to modify the classification slightly in order to make it include all the responses in McCarthy's data. She therefore added two classes, namely, social phrases and dramatic imitation. For convenience, and in order to make it cover a few other responses not included in Piaget's group, his category of "commands, requests, and threats" was termed "emotionally toned responses" and made to include wishes and desires as well. The category of adapted information accounted for such a large percentage of the responses that it was broken into four subheads as follows: naming, remarks about the immediate situation, remarks associated with the situation, and irrelevant remarks.[1]

Egocentricity of Children's Speech. As a result of this analysis McCarthy (1930) found a much smaller percentage of egocentric responses than that reported by Piaget, as all egocentric categories together never exceeded 6.5 per cent at any age level; the average for all age levels was only 3.6 per cent. This seeming discrepancy, which is probably much more apparent than real, has aroused considerable interest and controversy. A number of other writers have since attempted to apply some sort of functional analysis suggested by the Piaget classification. None of the American writers has found his classification usable in its exact form, but unfortunately several investigators have made their own versions in modifying the classifications, so that direct comparisons are difficult if not impossible.

In general, the studies employing a functional approach are of two types. Those studies which attempt to classify on the basis of a literal interpretation of Piaget's definitions invariably emerge with a much smaller percentage of egocentric responses, as did McCarthy's. The second group of studies, particularly those by Rugg, Krueger, and Sondergaard (1929), Adams (1932), and Fisher (1934), who definitely set out to look for egocentrism as it is found in the speech of children, and devised their own definitions of egocentrism, usually in terms of the subject of the sentence, invariably find a high percentage of egocentrism which agrees rather closely with that reported by Piaget. The former group of studies have been summarized in Table 9,

[1] For more detailed description of these categories, see McCarthy (1930, pp. 37–42).

which represents the percentages found in each of the studies by McCarthy (1930), Day (1932), Smith (1935a), and E. A. Davis (1937a), for five of the major categories in the functional analysis.

These figures must be interpreted with extreme caution because of the varying circumstances pointed out in the footnotes to Table 9. Day used the identical method employed by McCarthy, but her subjects were twins and showed marked linguistic retardation and immaturity throughout. The data reported in this table from Davis's study are those given for singletons with siblings, since that group is most nearly comparable with McCarthy's and Smith's data. Davis unfortunately placed all criticism in the same class with adapted information, which would tend to raise the percentage in that category by 1 or 2 per cent. She also treated all expressions of liking and desire, which the other authors treat as emotionally toned responses, under adapted information. Smith collected her data, which are shown in Table 9, in two different situations, one in which the child conversed with the experimenter as in the other three studies, and the other in which data were collected during the free play situation in a nursery school where the child was conversing with other children. Smith used a category called "monologue" and then grouped under "collective monologue" remarks about the immediate situation, remarks associated with the situation, and irrelevant remarks. These were all considered to be types of adapted information and were classed as socialized speech in McCarthy's investigation. Without defining her interpretation of egocentrism Smith computed coefficients of egocentrism which decreased from 40 at year 2 to 26 at year 5. Thus, Smith agreed with Piaget's findings but did not specify how she interpreted his categories or exactly

TABLE 9

PERCENTAGES OF RESPONSES IN MAIN CATEGORIES OF THE FUNCTIONAL ANALYSES IN FOUR MAJOR STUDIES

(The four subcategories Emotionally Toned, Adapted Information, Questions, and Answers make up "Socialized Speech.")

Age	Egocentric Speech				Emotionally Toned				Adapted Information				Questions				Answers			
	McCarthy (1930)	Day* (1932)	Davis† (1937a)	M.E. Smith‡‖ (1935a)	McCarthy (1930)	Day* (1932)	Davis† (1937a)	M.E. Smith‡‖ (1935a)	McCarthy (1930)	Day* (1932)	Davis*§ (1937a)	M.E. Smith‡‖ (1935a)	McCarthy (1930)	Day* (1932)	Davis† (1937a)	M.E. Smith‡‖ (1935a)	McCarthy (1930)	Day* (1932)	Davis† (1937a)	M.E. Smith‡‖ (1935a)
1½	3.1				14.6				60.6				10.8				0.3			
2	6.5	16		40	18.3	30		32	40.8	37		17	13.9	2		5	16.6	13		3
2½	4.0				14.2				57.7				3.5				14.6			
3	3.6	1		33	9.4	18		30	50.9	52		20	13.2	7		8	19.1	19		6
3½	4.7				9.4				53.2				9.7				20.4			
4	1.3	1		26	6.5	15		28	45.2	51		23	12.1	8		12	31.0	22		9
4½	2.2				6.4				54.6				8.2				26.0			
5		2		26		14		22		50		25		9		16		21		7
5½			.4				3.8				59.7				10.6				25.5	
6½			.2				3.3				66.8				9.4				22.7	
9½			.7				1.4				60.7				3.8				37.1	

* Day's subjects were twins markedly retarded in all aspects of language development. Classification was identical with McCarthy's. Figures estimated from graph.

† Davis's data for singletons with siblings. She classed criticism and expressions of liking and desire with adapted information, whereas McCarthy and Day classed them as emotionally toned responses.

‡ M. E. Smith's figures given in this table are based on a grouping of data from two types of situations. The adult-child situation which showed fewer egocentric and emotionally toned responses is comparable to the other studies. Smith did not use discrete age groups as was done in the other three studies.

§ Adapted information not given separately by Davis for different experimental groups. These figures probably include data from twins and only children as well as from singletons.

‖ Figures from Smith under emotionally toned responses in this table were classed by her as "imperative sentences."

how she classified her data.[1] She also compared data on 84 cases whose remarks were recorded during conversation with an adult in a situation similar to McCarthy's study with data from 175 children who were playing in a free play situation in a nursery school and conversing with other children. She found no difference in the amount of egocentrism in the two situations, but the data have been grouped so as to mask any real trends which might appear, since age, sex, and occupational group differences were also operating to unknown degrees in the two sets of data being compared for situation.

In regard to the egocentrism controversy McConnon's (1935) data are of particular interest, for she found an average intercorrelation of only +.17 between the number of egocentric remarks recorded in various situations. She used McCarthy's classification and interpretation of Piaget's categories. The correlation between the home situation and the table-play situation, which probably were most comparable with the McCarthy and Piaget situations, respectively, was only −.135. In her critical ratio analysis the measure of egocentrism yielded the largest number of significant differences when the home situation was compared with the various nursery school situations.

In the study by Williams and Mattson (1942), in which children's language responses in different social groupings were studied, it was found that as the group becomes larger the language becomes more social and less egocentric. Only 1 of their 6 subjects indulged in speech while playing alone, and social speech was found to account for 60 to 78 per cent of the sentences, with the remainder being classified

as parallel speech in their social usage analysis. When they used Piaget's analysis, however, the amount of egocentric speech ranged from 42 to 58 per cent in the various situations.

In another study McCarthy (1929a) compared two methods and found an appreciably higher percentage of egocentric responses in the free play situation (6.32 per cent) than in the adult situation (3.35 per cent). M. E. Smith's (1935a) findings on larger numbers of cases are also in the same direction. Unfortunately, however, for purposes of comparison, she grouped the data obtained by these two methods by age levels separately, which are the figures necessarily reported in Table 9. When she compared the two methods of recording responses in the two different situations she put all age levels together, and this rendered the material incomparable with other available data. The figures given in Table 9 for E. A. Davis's (1937a) data on adapted information were not given by her separately for singletons, twins, and only children, and hence the figures reported here probably include her total group, which was heavily weighted with twins and only children, both of which are deviate groups in linguistic development.

It thus appears that the data of Table 9 are very difficult if not impossible to interpret. In spite of similarity of purpose and methods of collecting data, presentations of the results have varied from study to study to such a degree that comparisons of data which should be comparable are rendered impossible.

Another study, which is presented very briefly so that figures could not be added to the above table, is that by Johnson and Josey (1931), who attempted to repeat some of Piaget's work on 55 children. They state that their results "substaniate few of Piaget's claims" and that

---

[1] In personal communication to the writer, M. E. Smith (June, 1947) stated that she "attempted to follow Piaget's definitions as explained by his *examples.*" These examples often do not fit the formal definitions.

instead of finding them egocentric we found them socially minded, willing and able to assume the position of another and even that of an hypothesis. They were quite able to make themselves understood. . . . Six-year-olds, he [Piaget] tells us, cannot reason because they are too egocentric. We found nothing in our investigation to support this view. On the contrary we found all of our children to be socially minded and in no manner dominated by an egocentric attitude.

Valentine (1942) also takes issue with Piaget, particularly in his definition of collective monologue. He raises a number of questions concerning the social situation in which egocentric speech occurs. However, when elementary school children's contributions to oral discussions were studied by Baker (1942), it was found that as the children grew older they devoted less time to talking about their own activities and more time to discussion of "current happenings." Personal activity percentages decreased from 61 per cent in grade 2 to 18 per cent in grade 6. In the higher grades the children's oral contributions became more frequent, shorter, and more to the point.

The most significant American study which has apparently confirmed Piaget's findings with regard to egocentricity of language is that of Fisher (1934). Although she took the work of Piaget (1926) as her point of departure in the search for the degree of egocentricity in the child's language, she did not follow his classification in arriving at her coefficient of egocentrism. Instead she set up a much simpler and more objective method based on the proportion of the total remarks having the self as subject. Her coefficients of egocentrism obtained by this method were in striking agreement with those reported by Piaget; but, with the marked difference in method, the validity of a direct comparison of these indices bearing identical names is somewhat questionable. One of the chief difficulties is that the classification of the same set of remarks on the basis of Fisher's classification and on the basis of Piaget's would in all probability lead to quite different results, since many remarks can be about the self and yet be directed toward a hearer, require a response from the hearer, and in every other way qualify as a socialized response according to Piaget's definitions. Fisher found that 34 per cent of the remarks were about the self, and she concluded that a high degree of concern with self is characteristic of the preschool child. She did not, however, find any relationship between age and remarks about the self. Adams (1932), who also recorded language in a nursery school setting, defines egocentric remarks as remarks which contain self-references. He used separate categories for monologue and social monologue which were subheads under egocentric remarks in Piaget's original classification. His egocentric remarks show a regular increase with age from 13 per cent at 2 years to 41 per cent at 4 years. It is not surprising that workers using such criteria should find results indicative of a relatively large percentage of egocentrism, for in the M. D. Horn (1926–1927a) list of the words most frequently used by kindergarten children the word *I* is by far the most frequent, with *my* occurring as the ninth and *me* as the twenty-fourth word in order of frequency.

Another investigation which apparently supports Piaget's conclusions, but arrives at the result by different methods, is that by Rugg, Krueger, and Sondergaard (1929). They found that 40.8 per cent of the remarks of kindergarten children were self-assertive. However, their definition of this category did not exclude socialized responses as was done in Piaget's classification, since self-assertive remarks could at the same time be highly socialized.

Those who have disagreed with Piaget's findings when they employ his classifications are not all American investigators so the differences probably should not be explained on the basis of nationality. Ohwaki (1933), who studied her own 2 Japanese daughters, reports that at about the age of 2 years social expression was as frequent as monologue. She attempted to harmonize her findings with those of Piaget by pointing out that if all sentences not directed toward other people are considered as egocentric, talking with animals and the like would be considered egocentric. She thinks, however, that this kind of talking should be considered as very social, since animals are often real companions to children. Huang and Chu (1936) recorded a total of 1500 sentences from 21 nursery school children from 2½ to 5 years of age in the everyday environment and found 80 per cent of their speech socialized and 20 per cent egocentric. Language about other persons was 12.5 per cent of the total, language about the self classified as socialized was 11.6 per cent, and language about the group constituted only 3.3 per cent. Kuo (1937) recorded spontaneous language of 4 Chinese children from 3 to 5 years of age and found that egocentric speech occupied only from 10 to 20 per cent of children's conversation and that it decreased with age.

In her third edition of *Kindheit und Jugend*, published in 1931, C. Bühler discussed this problem in some detail and referred to some unpublished German studies which have not found their way into American literature. She states that Piaget's stimulating investigations were refuted by many different child psychologists, at least in regard to their main thesis (egocentricity). She said that W. Stern always pointed out that the egocentric behavior of the children observed by Piaget was fur-

thered by the special environmental conditions prevailing at La Maison des Petites, which she described as a Montessori preschool in which each child was encouraged to work alone on an individual basis with relatively little social intercourse being developed within the group. She also states that, at the suggestion of Doctor Stern, M. Muchow tested the egocentricity coefficients in a preschool in Hamburg and found completely different ratios from those reported by Piaget.

Another unpublished study by Elsa Köhler resulted in 82 per cent of the speech of preschool children being classified as socialized. This is, of course, much more in line with the American investigations which have employed Piaget's classifications. C. Bühler (1931) herself gives the interesting interpretation that the flow of speech which often accompanies a child's activity is really an expression of a need for social contact. She feels that much of the speech classed as monologue is merely expressing a desire to feel close to others and that it is only secondarily to be considered as playful monologue. She believes that Piaget found reason to emphasize the egocentric aspects of children's language because of the rather peculiar characteristics of the play situation in which the children were observed and because records were taken in only the one type of life situation. Although the drive for social contact may be interpreted as egoistic, the very striving for contact, she says, drives the child away from himself and toward others.

An article by Henle and Hubbell (1938) on egocentricity in adult conversations has occasioned some challenging re-evaluations of the significance of Piaget's work. Heretofore the implication had been that as the child grows older his speech becomes more socialized and that the adult uses relatively little egocentric speech. The high degree of socialization of adult speech has always been implied but never demonstrated. Henle and Hubbell undertook to determine the amount of egocentric speech in adult conversations. They also set up their own criteria of egocentricity. Criticizing the artificiality of Fisher's (1934) technique they proceeded to classify sentences from the point of view of their meaning as ego-related sentences. In this category they include statements of the activities of the speaker, of his feelings and emotions, his ambitions, desires, and interests, as well as all opinions, attitudes, criticisms, and all evaluative and normative statements. The remarks classified were those of college students and other adults and were recorded by a variety of eavesdropping techniques in order to avoid artificiality and to assure spontaneity. They found 40.7 per cent of all the adult remarks fell in the ego-related category. Perhaps individuals of all ages are egocentric in about 40 per cent of their responses, if one uses a somewhat subjective classification scheme based on meaning rather than on the manner of utterance and attendant circumstances, as in Piaget's definitions. If this is true, it may be that the great concern of child psychologists regarding the developmental significance of the supposed outgrowing of the egocentrism of early childhood has been exaggerated in its importance.

Piaget's concept of egocentric speech has been seriously challenged by Vigotsky (1939). He considers that egocentric speech is midway between socialized speech and inner speech. The disappearance of the externalized or vocalized aspect of speech is only an illusory disappearance, he claims. Vigotsky considers that, basically, egocentric speech is the key to inner speech, for it is still subject to observation because it is uttered aloud. It is a form of speech which aids the child's thought processes in

a most intimate way, but, rather than waning during childhood and going through an involution, Vigotsky claims that it goes through an evolution with inner speech and thought as the end products. In support of this contention he points out that it is in conformity with the observed facts that the external expression of egocentric speech decreases with age and that it increases when difficulties arise which require conscious reflection.

According to Vigotsky (1939) the functional and structural qualities of egocentric speech and speech for communication with others are not different from each other in the 3-year-old child, but there is a gradual differentiation of the two speech functions so that by 7 years of age the structure and function of the egocentric speech have taken on more the nature of inner speech and have become differentiated from socialized speech. He designed a series of experiments to test his hypotheses regarding the nature of egocentric speech in which he experimentally weakened and strengthened the social demands of the situation. He first obtained children's coefficients of egocentrism according to the methods of Piaget when they were in free play situations in the presence of other children. He seems to have no difficulty in the quantitative aspect of the problem, as he apparently obtains coefficients of egocentrism of the same order of magnitude of those of Piaget. His quarrel is with the interpretation and significance of egocentric speech. After obtaining coefficients of egocentrism in the usual way, he then diluted the social nature of the situation in an effort to destroy the "illusion of understanding" by others, by putting these children in a situation with deaf-mute children, and also by putting them in a situation with total strangers, or alone at a table in a corner of a room which the experimenter observed from outside. In all these experiments which lessened the social nature of the situation, the coefficient of egocentrism decreased markedly. It also decreased when an orchestra drowned out the child's speaking voice, as well as when the children were told to speak only in whispers. Vigotsky claims that all these experiments prove his hypothesis that egocentric speech partakes first of the nature of social speech and represents a transition from speech for others to inner speech for oneself. Goldstein (1948) supports Vigotsky's point of view, for he considers the evidence convincing and in harmony with existing knowledge of child development.

In summary, it appears that the controversy over egocentrism is more apparent than real and that many of the quantitative discrepancies can be accounted for in terms of (1) differences in definition and interpretation of terms by various authors, (2) the situation in which responses are recorded, and (3) individual differences in the personality characteristics of the children observed. The writer is inclined to the belief that these three factors are of considerably more importance than the factor of nationality which has been stressed by some. It is evident that there is a high degree of egocentrism (about 40 per cent of all remarks) in the speech of young children if one sets out to look for its manifestations without artificial restraints imposed by a rigidly defined classification system (Rugg, Krueger, and Sondergaard, 1929; Adams, 1932; Fisher, 1934). It should be pointed out, however, that even the highest estimates of egocentrism rarely exceed 50 per cent, and hence the enthusiastic statements one occasionally finds regarding the *predominance* of egocentrism in the speech of young children are quite unfounded. If, however, one accepts Piaget's definitions and adheres to them strictly, much smaller amounts of speech are classified as egocentric in any situation, although more egocentric responses are found in free play and in child-child situations than in adult-child situations. Whether or not egocentrism such as is found in studies reporting high incidence of it is characteristic of childhood, and whether it is outgrown with added maturity, is still an open question. The work of Henle and Hubbell (1938) points to the interpretation that perhaps the degree of egocentrism first called to attention in the speech of young children may be a characteristic of human nature which is merely somewhat more subtly manifested in adulthood. Vigotsky's (1939) ingenious experiments are certainly worthy of repetition, and his challenging interpretations lend added emphasis to the key position of language in the study of the higher thought processes.

Socialized Speech. All the studies which have been cited in the preceding section have been concerned with socialized speech as opposed to egocentric speech. The absolute percentages of socialized speech are the complements of the percentages of egocentric speech. Hence all the factors which influence the percentages of egocentrism also affect the percentages of socialized speech. As has already been pointed out, each author has made slight modifications of the classifications, and each of these changes upsets the balance of percentages in a closed system so that the actual figures available on the various categories of socialized speech are not readily comparable except in the few studies which have employed identical methods. In general, those who have duplicated McCarthy's techniques have confirmed her findings in regard to the main trends. The percentage of answers varies with the amount of participation of the adult to stimulate conversation and with the degree to which the observer waited for spontaneous remarks in the adult-child situations. As may be seen from Table 9 roughly one-fourth of the responses are answers in the data of McCarthy (1930), Day (1932), and E. A. Davis (1937a), whereas M. E. Smith (1935a) has only 9 per cent or less in this category at all ages.

The largest single category of socialized speech in most studies which have used this classification is adapted information which amounts to 40 to 60 per cent at the various age levels. It constitutes by far the bulk of the conversation and as a total category shows no definite trend with age. M. E. Smith's (1935a) figures are lower than those of other investigators because she classed remarks about the immediate situation and remarks associated with the situation as collective monologue rather than as adapted information. The most interesting trend in the subgroup of adapted information is that naming is very prominent in the speech of young children, dropping from about 50 per cent of the comprehensible responses of McCarthy's (1930) 18-month-old children to about 10 per cent at the age of 4½. E. A. Davis (1937a) reports only 6 to 8 per cent naming in the 5½- to 9½-year-old children studied by her. Corresponding to the decrease in the amount of naming there is an increase with age in the number of remarks associated with the situation. The child is able to recall information, to bring his past experiences to bear on the present situation, to look ahead into the future, and to talk about related items as he grows older and gains in experience and in his ability to integrate his experiences and to verbalize about them.

Another striking trend which has emerged quite consistently from a number of investigations is that very young children usually begin to talk about things which have emotional content for them. The first word is often an interjection, and even words which are usually used as nouns

are often uttered with exclamatory or interjectional inflection. Apparently young children are motivated to use language in the beginning to satisfy their needs, wants, and desires and to control their environment in accordance with their needs and wants, for the category of emotionally toned responses including commands, requests, threats, and desires constitutes a fairly large percentage of the responses of the youngest children, and this category dwindles in importance with increase in age (Table 9).

In seeming conflict with these findings are those of Young (1942a), who reports children over 48 months using more exclamatory expressions than younger children. This apparently is due to the different situations in which her data were collected, as she also finds more commands given to other children than to adults, and an increasing tendency to use verbal expressions instead of physical contact. This latter is undoubtedly due to nursery school training and to the fact that her data were collected in the nursery school situation.

It has been pointed out by Leopold (1949b) that emotions, wishes, questions, and statements cannot be completely separated during the 1-word sentence stage. He stresses the highly emotional character of the earliest words and states that this affectivity decreases slowly and never completely disappears, for he states that no objective statement is ever made entirely dispassionately. Rostand (1950) gives an interesting psychoanalytic discussion of the relation between affectivity and the child's progress in the use of various grammatical forms. Sanford's (1942) study on adults is also of interest in this connection.

The figures given by E. A. Davis (1937a) on emotionally toned responses are much lower than those of McCarthy (1930) and Day (1932) and really are not comparable with theirs because she classed expressions of liking and desire under adapted information while retaining the category of emotionally toned responses only for exclamations and definite commands. The figures reported for Smith under the heading "Emotionally Toned" in Table 9 are actually classed by her as imperative sentences, but in all probability these are emotionally toned in the sense that the other investigators employed this term. It is interesting to note the decline in the percentage of such responses as the child gains in socialization and in facility of expression. There is also the possibility that the large amount of emotionality in early speech is an accompaniment of the early stage of learning to talk, for the child who understands the speech of others much better than he can express himself may go through a period of emotional stress comparable to the emotional accompaniment which has often been noted in the early stages of learning many motor and other skills.

The category of children's questions has received considerable attention from investigators in recent years, for it has been treated as a separate category in the major studies of language development and it has also received more detailed analysis in studies by Piaget (1926), E. A. Davis (1932), M. E. Smith (1933b), and Lewis (1951). This area has been reviewed by Fahey (1942). In most studies of preschool children, questions seem to make up 10 to 15 per cent of the conversation. There seems to be a slight, although irregular, tendency for the number of questions to increase with age, but by 9½ years Davis (1937a) reports a marked falling off. Smith (1933b) found a slightly larger percentage (16 per cent) of questions asked in the adult-child situation than in the child-child situation (12 per cent), although it must be remembered that the two records were not taken from the same group of children and hence may be affected by sampling errors. McCarthy (1930) and Davis (1937a) found that children of the upper socio-economic classes ask a much larger number of questions than children of the lower socio-economic levels. This is undoubtedly due in part to the intellectual factor, but is probably also related to the satisfaction that the children are likely to get when they ask questions. A child from a superior home is somewhat more likely to get a satisfactory answer to his questions and hence will be encouraged to ask more. Davis (1937a) found that only children tend to ask more questions than singletons or twins. This can probably be explained on the same grounds as the occupational group differences.

Piaget (1926) was interested in children's questions chiefly for the light they might shed on the development of child logic. He devotes an entire chapter in *The Language and Thought of the Child* to a treatment of 1125 questions asked by one child of one adult over a 10-month period between 6 and 7 years of age. He points out that early *why* questions appear at about 3 years, but, classifying the questions according to the type of answer he thinks is expected by the child, he claims that these are not actually questions demanding causal explanations. He states that the earliest *whys* are affective rather than intellectual, and he postulates the hypothesis of precausality. He claims that children do not ask questions of causal relationship until 7 or 8 years of age.

Lewis (1951) is in essential agreement with this point of view, although he tends to emphasize the social function of the child's questions. He attempts to show

that the growth of a child's questions is determined by social cooperation working upon two powerful tendencies in the child —namely, to use language as play and as a means of satisfying his vital needs. . . . Throughout, the growth of the various categories of questions depends very largely upon the replies that the child receives; that is, upon social cooperation.

This is in line with the hypothesis suggested above that the occupational group differences in the frequency of questions may depend upon the degree to which they are answered. Lewis stresses the fact that the child at first tends to use language as a form of play and in an attempt to satisfy his needs. The play is the game of question and answer in which the child calls upon another person to help satisfy his needs. Lewis points out that it gives the child pleasure to speak merely in order to be spoken to. Apparently children learn very early that they can gain the attention of adults and control others by the technique of asking questions. Lewis also points out that children often ask questions to which they already know the answers, often because they are learning to make formulations of events in words and seek social sanctions for these formulations. In building up his system of knowledge the child is said to begin by making tentative statements which, having an interrogative form, invite corroboration or rejection by others. He thinks that whereas there may be some rudimentary notion of causality in the early *why* questions, the child's real notion of causality develops only out of his constant experience with the causal answers that he receives from others.

E. A. Davis (1932) had mothers of 73 children record samples of 50 consecutive questions, totaling 3650 questions. These were classified and analyzed for form, length, and content. The questions were from children in the upper socio-economic brackets, were subject to the unreliability of maternal report, and were not consecutive samples. Adequate tables on the fre-

quency of the various types of question forms were not provided, although the author discussed this point at some length and presented a few critical ratios. When in her later study (1937a) she analyzed over 2000 questions, many of the categories showed discrepancies with the earlier results.

M. E. Smith published (1933b) a separate article based on the 3095 questions recorded in running conversations of preschool children. Most of the analyses involve comparisons of responses recorded in the adult-child and child-child situations, but, as mentioned above, the two situations are not comparable, owing to the differences in selection of cases. She found, however, that *what* questions constituted 12 per cent of all questions and *where* questions 11 per cent, both of these categories showing increase with age. *Who, whose,* and *which* questions accounted for only 2 per cent and showed no relation to age. *How* questions were 6 per cent, *when* 1 per cent, and *why* questions amounted to 4 per cent. None of these groups showed significant change with age. Causal questions she found amounted to 8 per cent of all questions, questions of place 13 per cent, being most frequent at 2 years of age and showing a decrease with age. Questions of fact, time, and invention, showed an increase with age. The category accounting for the largest percentage of the questions was that involving questions concerning human actions and intentions, which included 46 per cent of all. Of interest in connection with the recognition of the naming stage and the increase in nouns in the early vocabulary is the finding that questions asking for the name of an object or person constituted one-fifth of all the questions asked by 2-year-olds and were third in frequency. She also reports that 94 per cent of all questions were concerned with some object, action, or person either in the immediate situation or desired to be there.

Interrelationships of Various Measures of Language Development

As is evident from the foregoing discussions, there is a wide variety of measures and indices of language development which have been employed and traced throughout childhood. Probably the two most widely used measures are those of vocabulary and of length of sentence, the latter having proved to be the most objective and reliable single index. However, comparatively little has been done in an attempt to determine the relative importance of the various aspects of linguistic development or to arrive at any single index of development in this tremendously complex function. One may still ask what is the relative importance of vocabulary, clearness of articulation, length of sentence, completeness and complexity of sentences, and the coefficient of egocentrism. So many of the analyses to which language development has been subjected, particularly the structural, functional, and parts-of-speech analyses, involve classification into percentages within closed systems that relationships can only be inferred from some of the shifts which occur in the percentages. One change or trend in such a system inevitably affects the other proportions, since all figures are relative. The result is that, upon completion of any one type of analysis, a set of values is obtained rather than a single index of the child's level of sentence structure or some other measure which can be correlated with other indices.

Williams (1937a) attempted to shed light on this vital question in "An Analytical Study of Language Achievement in Preschool Children." Measures were obtained of ability to make speech sounds by the use of a modification and shortened form of the articulation test of Wellman, Case, Mengert, and Bradbury (1931), of the correctness of word usage, of the development of the sentence or expression unit, and of vocabulary. Word usage was measured by the number of words spoken correctly per 50 running words of conversation. Development of the expression unit was studied for length, completeness in terms of subject-predicate-object relationship, and in terms of complexity of grammatical construction. The scoring was entirely arbitrary and somewhat crude, yet it served to reveal individual differences in each of these measures in quantitative form with considerable reliability. Odd-even reliabilities for the several measures ranged from +.84 to +.91. Vocabulary was measured with the Van Alstyne Vocabulary Test (1929) and a modification of the M. E. Smith Vocabulary Test (1926), described above in the section on vocabulary tests (see pp. 532–534).

Seventy children, ranging in chronological age from 30 to 78 months and considerably advanced in mental age, were used. Unfortunately not all children had all the tests, so the complete tables of intercorrelations are based on only the 38 three- and four-year-olds for whom all measures were available. A condensed tabulation of intercorrelations and the second-order partial correlations reported by Williams (1937a) is given in Table 10. The reliabilities obtained by the odd-even method are shown in the diagonal cells. All the original intercorrelations are shown above and to the right of the diagonal, and the partial correlations holding chronological and mental age constant are shown below and to the left of the diagonal. As may be seen, there is a rather strong positive relationship among the various language measures with the exception of vocabulary measures, which appear to be relatively independent of the

TABLE 10

CORRELATIONS OF SEVERAL LANGUAGE INDICES WITH CA AND MA, AND INTERCORRELATIONS AMONG THE LANGUAGE VARIABLES

(After Williams 1937a)

N = 38	MA	Speech sounds	Word usage	Length of unit	Complete-ness	Com-plexity	Van Alstyne vocabulary	Smith-Williams vocabulary
CA	.56	.31	.43	.54	.41	.45	.36	.16
MA		.12	.49	.78	.55	.59	.52	.47
Speech sounds		.91	.64	.60	.61	.62	.16	.01
Word usage		.60	.94	.62	.80	.57	.36	.27
Length of unit		.69	.42	.86	.65	.80	.56	.37
Completeness		.58	.66	.41	.89	.74	.41	.21
Complexity		.60	.38	.67	.61	.87	.56	.41
Van Alstyne vocabulary		.57	.13	.28	.16	.36	.84	.59
Smith-Williams vocabulary		.08	.09	.04	−.02	.22	.76	.87

Reliabilities are shown on the diagonal. Zero order r's above and to the right. Partial correlations holding CA and MA constant below and to the left

others. These relationships are maintained at fairly high levels even when the influences of chronological and mental age are eliminated. Of particular interest is the strong degree of relationship which appears between the accuracy of speech sounds and the various measures of length, completeness, and complexity of the expression unit.

Such results are quite in accord with E. A. Davis's (1937a) conclusion that "a child's mastery of articulation is closely related to other phases of language development." She found that faulty articulation, if unduly prolonged, may become a major handicap preventing both adequate command of language and wholesome development of the personality. This is based on a comparison of a group of 160 cases rated as having "perfect articulation" with a group of 88 cases rated as having "faulty articulation." Those with perfect articulation had a mean length of sentence of 4.85 as compared with 4.00 for those with faulty articulation, and the former used 102.2 different words as compared with only 82.5

different words used by the group having faulty articulation. In Part IV of a monograph by Little and Williams (1937) there appears a description of "An Analytical Scale of Language Achievement," with instructions in the appendix for the administration of the scale.

Yedinack (1949) reports interrelationships among several measures of linguistic maturity in four different groups of second-grade children. Length of response correlated with complexity of sentence from +.88 to +.93, being higher in the group having defective articulation than in normal speakers. Correlations of length of response with completeness of response were lower, but also positive, ranging from +.54 to +.68. Complexity and completeness of response correlated +.63 to +.74 in the various groups. Vocabulary yielded very low correlations with these measures in all groups studied. Schulman and Havighurst (1947) gave correlations of vocabulary as measured with the Seashore-Eckerson vocabulary test with Thurstone's V factor of

+.79 and of +.46 with the Iowa Silent Reading Test for a group of 16-year-olds.

The eight measures of word fluency devised by Gerwitz (1948a, cf. p. 536) were compared with scores earned by the same 38 children 5 to 6 years of age on the Smith-Williams vocabulary test. Different correlational patterns were formed between the various tests of "word fluency" and the recognition and recall types of vocabulary. Gerwitz suggests that two types of abilities may be involved in word fluency and that they probably are related to the restrictiveness of the stimulating situation.

Factor analysis techniques were employed by Harris (1948) in a study of the language skill patterns of 200 fifth-grade Indian children. Scores were based on the Gates Basic Reading Test, the Pressey English Test, and five variables involving ratings of written composition. Findings regarding bilingualism and sex differences will be discussed in the appropriate sections (see pp. 591–594 and 577–581).

When completed Templin's investigations will afford ideal data for a study of the interrelationships of vocabulary, articulation, and length and complexity of sentence in the largest cross-sectional study of representative children over the widest age range (3 to 8) yet studied. She will also present longitudinal data on a smaller group of children who were followed from 2 to 5 years of age.

Investigations dealing with the interrelationships of speech and reading have been contributed by Gaines (1941), Shire (1945), Yedinack (1949), Rossignol (1948), and Artley (1948). Gaines (1941) reviews thirteen other studies most of which used poor techniques. Eight of them showed that there was a relationship between speech defects and reading disability, three showed little or no such relationship, and two were inconclusive. Artley also reviews a number of studies in this area. The conclusion is that speech and reading defects are to a substantial degree associated, especially in oral reading, but that there is no agreement as to the causation or the extent of the relationship. Huyck (1940) cites a summary by Rutherford which states that 25 per cent of dysphemia cases have reading and writing defects or other speech difficulties and that 18 per cent of dysarthria cases also have such defects, whereas 16 per cent of children classified as having good speech also had reading, writing, or other language defect. Yedinack (1949) found that 40 per cent of a group of 67 second-grade children identified as poor readers also had articulatory defects and that of 71 cases identified as having articulatory defects 38 per cent also had reading disabilities. She concludes that children with functional articulation defects are significantly inferior in both oral and silent reading to children with normal speaking ability and that there is a tendency for children with articulation and/or reading defects to be inferior to normal speakers in vocabulary. It thus appears that, as investigations are directed more and more to the study of the whole child, more reports are appearing in which language disability syndromes are being identified, and children are not so frequently labeled on the basis of one outstanding symptom as they were formerly.

Individual Differences

Racial and Nationality Differences. Data comparing children of different races in language development are meager. Gatewood and Weiss (1930) reported greater frequency of vocalization among white than among Negro neonates, although Irwin (1949) reports no appreciable difference. Anastasi and D'Angelo (1952) studied 50 Negro and 50 white children among whom there was equal representation of each sex.

Socio-economic factors, and parental education were fairly well equated. They studied mean sentence length and complexity of sentence structure. There were slight but statistically insignificant differences in favor of the white groups. Harris's (1948) study dealing with two groups of American Indians is concerned only with intra- rather than inter-racial comparisons, and the various studies of M. E. Smith (1935b, 1939, 1940, 1949) dealing with Chinese have involved the problem of bilingualism which obscures comparability of data.

It should be pointed out, however, that strikingly similar developmental trends are to be found in biographical studies from various countries regardless of the language being learned. There is certainly observable a common developmental core in reports from the United States, England, France, Germany, Switzerland, Belgium, Japan, Hawaii, and Australia which would seem to indicate that the process of language learning is essentially the same the world over. The rates of its acquisition of course vary with the native endowment of the children, the sampling observed, and the environmental stimulation they receive. Goldstein (1948) states in speaking of sound acquisition in infancy: "Whatever language we consider, we observe, in the acquisition of sounds, the same sequence in time" (p. 36). He cites Jakobson as having confirmed this in Swedish, Norwegian, Danish, Slavic, Russian, Polish, Czech, Serbocroatic, Bulgarian, Indian, German, Dutch, Estonian, and Japanese. Such observations from the field of comparative linguistics tend to support an organismic theory of language development. (See McCarthy, 1952c.)

Sex Differences. One of the most consistent findings to emerge from the mass of data accumulated on language development in American white children seems to be a slight difference in favor of girls in nearly all aspects of language that have been studied. Although Irwin and Chen (1946a) found no sex differences in mean number of phoneme types in infancy, the girls began to surpass the boys by about the tenth month of age. Gatewood and Weiss (1930) report greater frequency of vocalization among girls even in the neonatal period, and Hess, Mohr, and Bartelme (1934), in their intensive study of premature infants, report the mean age of onset of speech (use of words) among 86 prematurely born girls was 17.5 months, whereas 65 prematurely born boys did not use words until a mean age of 18.3 months. Of those who used sentences before 2 years, 7 were girls and only 3 were boys, and approximately twice as many girls as boys began to use sentences in the third year of life. Karlin (1947) attributes the observed sex differences in speech development to later myelination of the neural pathways in boys.

Whenever groups of boys and girls are well matched in intelligence and socio-economic background, and when the situation in which responses are recorded does not tend to favor the interests of one sex or the other, there appear slight differences in favor of girls. Whenever such sex differences fail to appear, or in rare instances are reversed, the result can nearly always be accounted for, when the data are available, in terms of selection on the basis of one of the aforementioned factors. The most clear-cut example appears in Table 5, where the mean length of response, which is the most objective single measure so far available, is shown for the sexes separately as obtained in 14 major studies. In this table there appear 64 comparisons of the two sexes for children of the same age groups. Of these, 43 favor the girls, 3 are identical for the two sexes, and only 18 favor the boys. Two of the figures where the sexes are equal come from Day's (1932) study of twins and 1 from E. A. Davis's (1937a) study, whereas 4 of the differences favoring boys come from the Davis study, which presented a situation that definitely favored boys' interests and 3 involved her twin groups.

The toys used by Davis are described by the author as "a motley collection of little covered wagons with detachable oxen, lassoing cowboys, buffalo hunters, scouts, Indians in attitudes of hostility, flight, or pursuit, and various animals and trees" (p. 20). It is difficult to understand the following justification for this choice of toys by a scientific investigator who is seriously interested in making valid comparisons with other available data on the matter of sex differences in language development. She states:

> Since no play object or situation was discovered which was of equal appeal to boys and girls of the ages studied, it was decided to choose objects known to be of especial interest to boys. This was done because (1) boys of 5 years are already "conditioned" against girls' toys, but girls if given the opportunity ordinarily enjoy boys' toys; (2) even if they are not interested in the toys, girls can easily be induced to cooperate in the experiment; and (3) since the language development of girls is slightly in advance of that of the boys, it is only fair that the advantage, if any, of a high degree of interest in the situation should be given to the boys. If the findings still show superiority on the part of girls, the significance becomes all the greater [p. 20].

It should also be noted that in Davis's procedure picture books were shown "only when the toys had failed of their purpose," namely, to stimulate spontaneous language. Toys were considered to have "failed of their purpose" if the child volunteered no remarks after 10 minutes and could not be induced to enter into conversation. Davis

herself admits, however, that "roughly about twice as many girls as boys were shown the books," and this following 10 minutes of silence; and that "at all ages boys show slightly more interest in the toys than do girls" (p. 21). "Boys are less likely to be shy than girls. . . . Boys were slightly less negativistic than girls . . . [and] girls were somewhat more distractible than boys, perhaps because they were less interested in the situation," and ratings on talkativeness revealed "a consistent tendency toward greater talkativeness in boys than in girls. . . . The mean time is slightly greater for girls than for boys" (pp. 25–26) (that is, to secure the same number of responses), and "greater spontaneity of speech is unquestionably characteristic of boys" (p. 67).

In view of these circumstances it does not appear that anyone should take seriously, as valid comparisons, the data on sex differences from Davis's investigation. The wonder is that, in spite of the very unequal conditions, the girls maintained their superiority in length of response in 4 of the 9 comparisons and were equal to the boys in a fifth instance on length of response, and showed decided superiority on a number of other measures. The reversal of the usual trend seen in McCarthy's 2½-year-old subjects can be attributed to sampling errors, as the girls of that age group came in undue proportion from the lower socio-economic levels. The reversals occurring in M. E. Smith's (1926) data can be accounted for on the basis of age differences as the boys are about 1½ months older than the girls at the ages at which they excel. In Young's (1941) study in which groups relatively homogeneous with respect to socio-economic level were used, there was not a single exception to the general trend toward a slight superiority of girls in length of sentence.

Of particular interest, however, is the report of sex differences favoring the boys in the two Negro groups studied by Anastasi and D'Angelo (1952). This may be due to racial differences or it may be associated with differential attitudes towards the two sexes reflected in different child-caring practices in the two cultural groups. Among the 18 of the 64 differences which favored boys in length of response, 10 can be accounted for on the basis of age, socio-economic level, twinship, or racial factors. (See McCarthy, 1953.)

Although length of sentence is the most objective and the most reliable single quantitative measure to use for comparison of the sexes, almost all other measures which show developmental trends with age also reveal a slightly more rapid linguistic maturity for girls. Mead (1913) found that feeble-minded girls talked earlier than feeble-minded boys, and Sirkin and Lyons (1941) report speech defects to be twice as frequent among mentally defective males as among defective females. I. P. Davis (1938) reports that girls reach maturity in articulation about a year earlier than boys, first-grade girls having about the same articulatory patterns as second-grade boys. Terman et al. (1925) found that gifted girls used short sentences at a slightly earlier age than the gifted boys. Doran (1907), after an extensive survey of the literature on vocabulary, reported that girls have larger vocabularies than boys of the same ages but that the differences were smaller among older children, and M. E. Smith (1926) confirmed this in her vocabulary study.

Sex differences in favor of the girls appear in the comprehensibility of the speech at early levels. In McCarthy's (1930) study boys had only 14 and 49 per cent comprehensible responses at 18 and 24 months as compared with 38 and 78 per cent for girls of the same ages. Similar differences were found throughout the age range studied. Fisher (1934) also found a higher percentage of incomprehensible speech among the boys. They tended to repeat identical speech patterns more often. In the McCarthy (1930), Day (1932), M. E. Smith (1935a), E. A. Davis (1937a), Young (1941), and Shire (1945) investigations, all other analyses, particularly functional and construction analyses, revealed that, when categories are studied for sex differences which reveal increasing or decreasing trends with age, the trend is evident at an earlier age among the girls. The one significant exception seems to be the report of Anastasi and D'Angelo (1952) in which the Negro boys surpassed the Negro girls not only in length of response but in complexity of sentence structure as well.

Davis summarizes the findings of her own study, which revealed sex differences in favor of girls in spite of a situation which was unfavorable to them, as well as that of other investigators as follows:

> In nearly every phase of language studied, girls were found to retain up to the 9½-year level the superiority which has been previously demonstrated for the pre-school period. This is true of articulation, word usage, and length, complexity, and grammatical correctness of sentences. Girls use more personal pronouns and conjunctions than boys, and less slang.

It is interesting to note that both Davis (1937a) and Young (1941) agree in finding the sex differences more marked among children of the lower socio-economic levels than among those from superior homes. Fisher (1934), whose group was the most highly selected, found the smallest sex differences. This might seem to point to an early differential effect of the environment on the two sexes as revealed in linguistic development. In this connection it is of interest that in Davis's study twin boys who had twin sisters, rather than twin brothers, were less seriously retarded in language. One hypothesis which she suggests is that:

> The twin sister, developing a little faster than the boy, may act as a pacemaker for him; but it is equally possible that unlike-sex twins because of parental attitude or differing interests are less dependent on each other than twins of the same sex and more likely to seek out the wider contacts which stimulate and facilitate attempts at articulate speech [p. 126].

Wellman *et al.* (1931) also found that girls articulate consonant elements better than boys.

The proverbial claim that the female is the more talkative is in general borne out by the results of scientific investigations and apparently is evident at a very early age. Jersild and Ritzman (1938) found that girls excel boys in the number of words spoken and in the number of different words used, but some might be surprised at the report by Olson and Koetzle (1936) that, although boys tend to speak less than girls during given periods of time, when they do talk, it is at a slightly more rapid rate. Jersild and Ritzman state: "In summary, then, the present findings with regard to sex differences in verbosity and vocabulary indicate that girls tend quite consistently to surpass the boys, but not to a degree that is statistically significant."

The writer has previously pointed out that the magnitude of the sex differences usually found in young children's language is not large enough to yield statistically significant differences when the usual criterion is employed. It is probable that these differences have not proved significant because of the small numbers of cases usually employed at a given age level, and also because so many analyses have been done in terms of percentages, which are rather unreliable indicators. It should further be pointed out that two methods seem to be employed by writers in the field for determining the significance of a difference although all claim to be using the critical ratio. Some use the number of children observed as the N in the formula, and others use the total number of sentences representative of the age level. Obviously, a large number of sentences from a small number of children would yield more significant differences if the latter method is employed than if N is taken merely as the number of children observed. There is need for clarification of methodology on this point and for uniformity of procedure. Young (1941) obtains many large critical ratios in various comparisons of subgroups by virtue of the fact that she employs the total number of cases in the study (74) when comparing data based on smaller subgroups. It seems to the writer that the correct procedure is to use the number of children being studied in the particular subgroups as the N. When such a method is employed the sex differences seldom prove statistically significant.

The vast accumulation of evidence in the same direction from a variety of investigators working in different parts of the country, employing different situations and methods of observation, and employing different analyses and linguistic indices, certainly is convincing proof that a real sex difference in language development exists in favor of the girls. Critical ratios and t values are employed and are interpreted to mean that if the ratio is sufficiently large it is practically certain that if the experiment were repeated the difference would occur in the same direction again. In the array of data cited above there is presented experimental, rather than statistical, evidence of the reality of the differences, small though they may be; and when experimental trends check in study after study there appears to be little need for the reassurances of statistical significance.

Apparently these small differences in the two sexes in linguistic development are related to later academic success in verbal skills. LaBrant (1933) found, for example, that girls used 148.3 words per theme, whereas the boys used only 124.7 words per theme. The boys in general wrote between 83 and 86 per cent as much as the girls.

Shire (1945) also found sex differences in favor of girls in success in beginning reading, and there were more boys than girls in her lowest decile in first-grade reading. Bennett (1938) in reviewing the literature on reading disability presented a summary table showing 17 groups of cases requiring remedial reading work. The proportion of boys in all these reports is striking, ranging from 60 to 100 per cent of the total groups in the various studies. Is it not possible that exposure to the reading experience at the same chronological age, but at an earlier stage of linguistic maturity, may be partly responsible for the greater toll of reading disability cases among boys? Ley (1930) stated that all forms of difficulty in the development of language occur much more frequently in males than in females, and the higher incidence of stuttering and other speech defects among them is well known. Azoy (1935) found 202 boys to 119 girls in a group of speech defectives and 43 boys and only 22 girls in a group of 65 stammerers. He reported that the sex distribution is the same as that found in Germany. It is probable that this slight though apparently basic difference between the sexes is also partly responsible for the consistent reports of better scholarship among girls in high school and college.

With these data in mind it would be well to re-examine the data on sex differences in intelligence as reported in Terman (1916, 1925), Goodenough (1927, 1928), Monroe (1932), and others which show slight superiority of girls in intelligence as measured with the usual tests having a preponderance of verbal items likely to favor the girls. An unpublished study by Seidl (1937) showed that the Stanford-Binet scores of bilingual girls are apparently more depressed in comparison with their scores on the Arthur Point Scale of Performance Tests owing to their bilingualism than are the scores of a similarly selected group of bilingual boys. It would seem then that bilingualism was a greater handicap to girls than to boys in the intelligence test as they characteristically tend to earn a greater proportion of their scores on verbal items.

Language Development in Handicapped Children. In certain groups of handicapped children, such as the deaf and the blind, sensory handicaps result in a definite restriction of the child's experiences which is often reflected in their language. Maxfield (1936) studied the language development of a group of 8 totally blind preschool children, employing methods similar to those of McCarthy (1930), Fisher (1934), and M. E. Smith (1935a), in an exploratory investigation. Although conclusions were necessarily tentative on such a small number, Maxfield demonstrated that the method employed in these other studies of normal children is directly applicable to young blind children. There was an abundance of language among these children with about twice as high a percentage of their remarks being about things as occurred in Fisher's data. The blind children, as a group, asked many more questions, gave fewer commands, and had unusually high percentages of emotionally toned responses. They used fewer nonverbal responses, but more incomplete responses, and had an unusually high incidence of proper names. As Maxfield stated:

It may be that the trends which have appeared in connection with some of the questions [raised in her study] will be found to group themselves around some fundamental need of the growing blind child. For instance, it seems reasonable to assume that the totally blind preschool child is satisfying his need for a feeling of security through talking a great deal, asking many questions, and using proper names frequently. . . . The trends disclosed . . . probably stand for the blind child's attempt to gain that assurance regarding his environment which seeing children obtain through visual observation [p. 85].

It is also probable that the blind child's greater need for constant supervision provides an environment which is linguistically more stimulating.

Hawk (1937), on the other hand, reports that visually handicapped and blind children show a history of delay in walking and talking and concludes, without controlling intelligence, that visual as well as auditory stimuli play a part in the development of speech. Goldstein (1948) also brings out that there is earlier fixation of sounds which can be observed visually, i.e., by noticing lip formations. This same factor probably accounts for Valentine's (1942) observation that his son B was able to get consonants by imitation, but not vowels. Further investigation of speech and personality factors among blind children has been reported by Brieland (1949).

Thus, although the handicap of blindness does not appear to have a seriously retarding effect upon the child's linguistic development, and may on further investigation actually prove to have a stimulating effect, since the handicap itself forces dependence upon others and requires an abnormal amount of adult attention, the patterns of the functional analysis may be very different in a group of children having atypical needs.

The handicap of deafness, of course, has a much more direct and more serious retarding effect upon language development, for the child who is totally deaf from birth does not acquire language in the normal way and has to be taught to speak by artificial techniques. Children with adventitious deafness, or hard-of-hearing children having various amounts of residual hearing, are much less seriously handicapped, the degree of linguistic retardation being a function of the age at onset of the acoustic handicap, and of the amount of residual hearing, as well as of the type of education and the age at which it was begun. Most of the literature in this field consists of reports of isolated cases, surveys of incidence and causes of hearing loss. There are reports of results obtained with specific educational techniques of interest to teachers of the deaf, and most of the studies of a psychological or educational nature are concerned with problems of the measurement of intelligence in the deaf and with the measurement of their academic achievement. Work being carried on with deaf and hard-of-hearing subjects by Doctor and Mrs. Heider and their associates in the Psychological Division of the Clarence W. Barron Research Department at the Clarke School for the Deaf led to the conclusion by Eberhardt (1940) which states:

The experiments show that the world of the young deaf child is already organized beyond the perceptual level and that this organization closely follows that of speaking people. They show clearly that language is not essential for organized conceptual thought, at least during its first stages. They are interesting, from an educational point of view, in showing that much of the first language development of the young deaf child in school consists in the learning of words for ideas that he already knows and uses in his everyday life. . . . Of course there are many instances in which a new word introduces a new conceptual relationship, but this is also true for hearing persons [pp. 4–5].

Heider and Heider (1940b) point out:

The deaf child usually does not begin to learn language until he has reached an age at which the hearing child has already mastered most of the forms used in adult expression. The whole process by which he learns language is necessarily different from that of a hearing child. From the beginning it is based to a certain extent on the presentation of carefully selected examples from which rules can be derived, while the hearing child learns by free selection from a wealth of language forms.

They analyzed 1118 compositions consisting of accounts of a short motion picture written by 301 deaf and 817 hearing children of seven different age groups. The hearing children were from 8 to 14 years and the deaf from 11 to 17 years, the youngest children in each age group being the youngest children who were able to write the whole story. A very detailed analysis on complexity of sentence structure was conducted. Among the more significant findings were the facts that the sentences of the deaf were shorter both in number of words and number of clauses than those of the hearing, the deaf used relatively simpler and fewer compound and complex sentences, fewer verbs in coordinate and subordinate clauses, relatively more infinitives, and relatively more prepositional phrases. The authors report, that, in all these, except those of the infinitive and prepositional phrase, the performance of the deaf resembled that of the less mature hearing children. It appeared that the deaf used relatively simple language units, shorter sentences, and relatively few forms requiring precision of use. These differences were found even though the deaf children were approximately 3 years older than the hearing children with

whose compositions their work was being compared.

This is in disagreement with results reported by Templin (1950), who found large groups of defective hearing children using longer sentences than normal children in written explanations of scientific phenomena. She interprets this as probably due to their need to use long circumlocutions in sentence structure, as is done in Basic English, because of their meager vocabularies. She also found (1948) fewer spelling errors made by deaf children probably associated with the different learning techniques they must employ and the lack of guesswork based on auditory cues which often lead normal children into spelling errors.

Hudgins and Numbers (1942) analyzed phonographic records of the speech of 192 deaf pupils between the ages of 8 and 20 years who had been taught by the oral method. Teachers of deaf children served as auditors, and a reliability of +.90 was obtained for the method of analysis. Results were chiefly in terms of vowel and consonant errors and errors in rhythm. Approximately 21 per cent of all consonants and 12 per cent of all vowels were malarticulated by the deaf children. Correct rhythm was revealed to be an extremely important element contributing to the intelligibility of the speech of the deaf. The authors concluded:

Speech is a dynamic process; it cannot be broken down into static positions and isolated movements. An *analytic* method of speech teaching of itself, therefore, violates basic physiological and phonetic principles. A synthetic method in which the basic phonetic unit is the syllable is in keeping with these physiological and phonetic principles; it is the natural method by which hearing children acquire speech.

They therefore advocate a basic revision of the methods which have heretofore been employed in the teaching of speech to the deaf.

The study by Hughson and others (1942) involved a detailed analysis of the voice and speech characteristics of 367 children resident in the Pennsylvania School for the Deaf, of whom 249 had never received auricular training and 118 were enrolled in auricular classes, that is, classes using group hearing aids for children with residual hearing. Electrical transcriptions were employed. Children receiving auricular training in speech were found distinctly superior to those taught by the traditional oral method. Their superiority was independent of the amount of residual hearing and age of onset of deafness. They estimate a 2-year shortening in the education of the deaf child by the use of this method. The previously cited study by Hudgins and Numbers (1942) agrees that children having auricular training have more intelligible speech than those taught by the oral method.

Effects of Environmental Factors

Institutionalization. Some of the most challenging results have appeared in the recent studies dealing with the effects of environmental deprivation in institutional, orphanage, or hospital environments. It is indeed amazing to note how early this is manifested and to see how lasting are the effects.

Aldrich, Sung, and Knop (1945a, b, c) and Aldrich, Norval, and Knop (1946) present a series of studies on infant crying. Babies were observed 24 hours a day for the first 30 days in a hospital nursery. Comparisons were made with the amount of crying under conditions of home care and after increased nursing care in the nursery. In the hospital the average baby cried 117 minutes per day and had 11.9 prolonged crying spells (i.e., over 3 minutes). In the home situation there were

only 4 such crying spells per day. When nursing care was increased in the hospital nursery from 0.7 hour per child per day to 1.9 hours per child per day, there was a 51.4 per cent decrease in the amount of crying. Such findings must have important implications for speech and for emotional development.

Brodbeck and Irwin (1946) compared the frequency and variety of phonemes uttered by a group of orphanage children with those heard among a group living with their own families. Statistically significant differences were obtained in favor of the children who enjoyed the stimulation and the affectional relationships of normal family environments. The differences indicating the handicap of the orphanage group were evident as early as the first 2 months, and the discrepancies between the two groups became more marked by the fourth and sixth months of life. The orphanage groups, however, were already markedly below the children from the homes of unskilled laboring groups, even in the first 6 months, and in spite of the fact that feeble-minded children were not included in the orphanage group. (Cf. Irwin 1948b and c.) Fisichelli (1950) also found that institutionalized infants were much more retarded than Irwin's subjects, who lived with their own families, in all measures of their prelinguistic utterances that showed developmental trends with age.

Goldfarb (1943a, b, 1945, 1946) in an interesting series of studies evaluated the language of children who spent their first 3 years in an institution. He compared them with foster children who lived in foster homes from early infancy (approximately 4 months). Comparisons were made on speech sounds, intelligibility of speech, and level of language organization, using the Williams, McFarland, and Little Language Achievement Scale, and picture vocabulary as measured with the Stanford-Binet Form L. Retests were made after 7 months in foster homes, at 6 to 8 years of age, and again in adolescence. The children reared in an institutional environment showed marked language deficiency in all areas measured. The author characterizes their behavior as passive and apathetic and their personalities as impervious to environmental stimulation. The implication is that the institutional deprivation in the first 3 years produced permanent harm to the intellectual, linguistic, and personal-social development of these children. Further studies on this topic are needed, as only 15 to 20 cases entered into the above comparisons, and the marked difference between foster children and institution children in IQ (28 points) before placement is difficult to interpret. It is impossible to say whether the institutional environment produced the intellectual deficit measured with a verbal test or whether the brighter children were placed earlier, and only the duller and generally more retarded children remained in the institution as long as 3 years. The early age of placement of foster children, however, would seem to preclude the possibility of selective placement.

Freud and Burlingham (1944) in England also found retardation in their studies of *Infants without Families* during World War II. This retardation did not appear until the second year of life. This may have been due to insensitive techniques or to the circumstance that for many of the children in their group the deprivation was deferred until later in infancy.

Similar reports also come from France, where Roudinesco and Appell (1950) note the severe developmental retardation of infants raised in institutional environments. Among those who had been institutionalized for a long period of time only 13 per cent had Gesell developmental quotients of 85 or above, whereas 55 per cent were seri-ously retarded with developmental quotients below 70, the retardation being most marked in the language areas of the test. After 18 months of an improved regime designed to have nurses and other attendants give more individualized attention to the children, marked improvement in motor, social, and adaptive behavior occurred, but the least improvement was brought about in language development.

Gesell and Amatruda (1941) give a good description of the dynamics of this environmental deprivation and stress that it operates by "attrition" as well as by "impoverishment" and that the results tend to be cumulative. Gatewood and Weiss (1930) report that vocalizations were less in a situation in which newborn infants were "allowed to lie naturally without any external stimulation" than in an experimental situation in which they were stimulated by various forms of controlled stimuli such as light, sound, temperature, odor, and holding the nose. Apparently the sheer monotony, and impersonal character, of the institutional environment lessens vocalization in comparison with the variety and warmth of a normal home environment. Such factors are apparently operative even in the neonatal period.

Williams and McFarland (1937) applied the Smith-Williams vocabulary test to 64 orphanage children who were compared with a large group of children living in their own homes. The orphanage children were markedly inferior in vocabulary scores, much more so than could be accounted for on the basis of socio-economic level or IQ. Moore (1947) used the same vocabulary test and analyzed 2-minute samples of oral language on orphanage and nonorphanage children. In all measures of language she found the orphanage group markedly retarded. She held CA and MA constant and conducted an analysis of variance which showed a statistically significant difference attributable to environmental influences.

All this evidence should lead to a serious re-evaluation of traditional child-caring practices in institutions and agencies. In fact, such studies have already led many forward-looking social agencies to increase their use of foster homes whenever possible and to place children at earlier ages than formerly. The need for making due allowances for early environmental deprivation when interpreting infant intelligence tests also becomes imperative in the light of such findings.

Occupational Group Differences. There is considerable evidence in the literature to indicate that there exists a marked relationship between socio-economic status of the family and the child's linguistic development. Chamberlain (1900) states that as early as 1847 Degerando reported that "the child of the rich understands more words and less actions, and the child of the poor less words and more actions." This early observation regarding the linguistic superiority of the privileged child has since been confirmed by a number of recent experimental studies. Chamberlain (1900) also reports a study by Lombroso in which 50 children of well-to-do and educated families were found to have much larger vocabularies than 100 children from poor families. In reviewing this study Markey (1928) states: "Both in the precocity with which they interpret the words and in the exactness reached, the children of the former families exceeded those of the poor in the proportion of two to one."

Descoeudres (1921) studied 300 children of the upper and lower classes as they were distinguished by attendance at private or public schools and found that on practically every item of her extensive battery of tests, nearly all of which involved language, the children of the upper social classes were decidedly superior to those of

the lower social classes. Stern (1930), who reworked these data, calculated that the difference between the educated class and the working class would be equivalent to about 8 months in linguistic development.

C. Bühler (1931) reported that children from a neglected milieu show retardation in all aspects of their development, but that the retardation is more evident in language than in other aspects of development. She reported data of Hetzer and Reindorf, who compared a group of children from a "good" environment with a group from an "underprivileged" environment. The children from the more favored environment used more words meaningfully at earlier ages, a larger percentage of them were using 2- to 3-word sentences at earlier ages, and the same differences were revealed when syntax, inflection, and sentence structure were analyzed.

The extremely early age at which these differences manifest themselves is evident from the work of Irwin (1948*b*, *c*), who studied phoneme frequency and types of phonemes in relation to the occupational status of the family in the first 2½ years of life. Although the types of phonemes show no relation to occupational status, and frequencies of phonemes are not related to paternal occupation in the first 1½ years, such a relationship does appear to emerge after 18 months of age, or at approximately the average age of onset of true speech.

In the McCarthy (1930), Day (1932), and E. A. Davis (1937*a*) studies paternal occupation was used as a criterion of selection in efforts to secure representative samplings. In all these studies occupational group differences are consistent and strikingly in favor of the upper socio-economic levels in all types of analysis. The children from the upper social levels not only use longer sentences but also use more mature sentence forms at earlier ages. Functional categories, especially questions, which show trends with age, also reveal more rapid development of children from the more favored homes. In McCarthy's word analysis, children of the lower classes continued to use larger percentages of nouns up to higher age levels, which is probably indicative of linguistic immaturity. In Davis's study 73 per cent of the children from upper socio-economic levels were rated as having "perfect articulation" at 5½ years, but only 58 per cent of the children of the lower levels received similar ratings on articulation at that age. It will be recalled that Fisher's (1934) cases which showed the greatest superiority in linguistic development came, nearly always, from the families of professional men. McCarthy (1930) and Day (1932) found a tendency for the differences between the occupational groups to increase with increase in chronological age, but this was not borne out by Davis's data on school age subjects.

In the study by Young (1941) 6-hour language records were made on 74 cases, half of whom attended the nursery school at the University of Georgia during a period when tuition was charged and half of whom attended when the nursery school was run as a Federal Emergency Relief Project and served only families on relief. Comparisons are made between the "regular" and "relief" cases attending the same school in different years. It was found that the regular group surpassed the relief group in all aspects of language that were analyzed. Relief boys were by far the poorest in language development and regular girls the most advanced.

Worbois (1942) compared the language of children from a one-room rural school and from a consolidated rural school. The groups were matched on IQ, age, home cultural index, and midparent education. Significant differences on the Stanford-Binet vocabulary test and on a verbal effectiveness test were found in favor of the group in the consolidated school. They also used almost twice as many words and half again as many different words in describing the pictures in the Stanford-Binet scale as the children from the one-room school. The principal environmental difference which seemed to be associated with these factors was the education of the teachers, for in the one-room school they had had on the average only 0.6 of a year beyond high school, whereas those in the consolidated school had had an average of 3.0 years of education beyond high school. In their vocabulary study of 16-year-olds Schulman and Havighurst (1947) found statistically significant differences from one socio-economic group to another on the Seashore-Eckerson English Recognition Vocabulary Test, Part I.

Kinds of Experience. Several investigators have reported that travel and events which broaden the child's experiences are accompanied or followed by increases in vocabulary. Drever (1915–1916), after comparing the vocabularies of his own 3 children, who had had a broad environment with considerable travel, and those of slum children, concluded: "Expansion of a child's environment always tends to increase nouns relatively to other parts of speech. Conversely, with a constant or relatively constant environment, the other parts of speech will increase relatively to the nouns."

This is in agreement with Bean's (1932) observation that periods of rapid increase in vocabulary coincided with the widening of the child's experiences through travel and that periods of sentence building paralleled uneventful interim periods. Most of these reports are on isolated cases, yet it is conceivable that the occupational group differences which have been found so consistently in the larger scale studies may be due in some measure to the more restricted environment usually experienced by children of the lower socio-economic classes. Parents of children in the lower classes are presumably less gifted linguistically than parents of children in the upper classes, and hence not only afford a poorer example of language for a model but also probably provide less verbal stimulation.

An extremely challenging study by Milner (1951) selected contrasting groups of first-grade Negro children on the basis of "language IQ" obtained with the California Test of Mental Maturity. Patterns of parent-child interaction were studied for the children who were "high" and "low scorers" on a language criterion similar to reading readiness tests. These children were drawn from widely divergent socio-economic levels. Striking differences were found in the patterns of family life between the "high scorers" and the "low scorers." The families of "high scorers" usually have breakfast together and engage in general two-way conversation at breakfast and before school as well as at supper, the children actively participating in such conversation. Children scoring high on the language tests were also the recipients of more overt expressions of affection from significant adults in the home than the children who earned low scores on the language tests as first graders. On the other hand mothers of "low scorers" do not eat breakfast with their children, do not talk to them during breakfast or before they start for school (except for occasional orders and cautions). These children do not talk to anyone at breakfast or before school. Neither do they have any two-way conversation while eating their supper. These factors tend to be concomitant with variations in socio-economic status which has so often been shown to be related to language development. However, since these circumstances are so much more dynamic from the standpoint of language learning and familial attitudes towards chil-

dren and their patterns of living, it appears that parental attitudes towards children and habits of family life are the really significant factors for language development and that they happen to vary with socio-economic class as well.

There have been a number of interesting facts revealed on the relationship between the age of the child's associates and his linguistic development. The Gales (1906), whose second and third children used twice as many words as the first child at the same age, claimed that "the later children have an advantage in learning much from contact with the older child." Others hold, however, that children understand each other much better than they do adults who are too far above their level. G. S. Hall (1891a), in speaking of children of approximately the same age, said: "Their noises are too well understood by each other, the younger holding the older back."

McCarthy (1930) found that the median percentile rank on length of response of the children in her experimental group who associated chiefly with adults was 70. For those who associated with older children it was 42.5. This latter group was drawn chiefly from large families who usually came from lower socio-economic levels. The children who associated chiefly with younger children had a mean length of response very close to the median for their ages, namely, 52.5. It appears, then, that association with adults is likely to be accompanied by linguistic acceleration. Further evidence comes from M. E. Smith's (1935a) study in which children were shown to use longer sentences and to use more advanced patterns of language development during the situation in which they conversed with an adult than in the situation involving conversation with other children. If association with adults is frequent in the child's experience, and he follows the pattern found by M. E. Smith, he will get more practice in using more mature language in situations which are conducive to better language usage. However, Hahn (1948) found that a group of children serving as an audience stimulated even more mature language expression on the part of her 6½-year-olds than one adult did.

Another striking fact which fits into the picture on age of associates is the marked superiority of only children. Of all the groups studied, only children, especially only girls, seem to be the most precocious in all aspects of language development. It is true that only children most frequently come from homes of the upper socio-economic levels and are somewhat higher in intelligence, but their linguistic superiority appears to be out of all proportion to what would be expected on the basis of their age, sex, mentality, and socio-economic status. Because of the nature of the family pattern, only children usually have more adult contacts than other children. Although these children are undoubtedly of superior native endowment, it must be remembered that their environments differ from those of other children chiefly in affording greater association with adults, broader experience, and greater opportunities for practice in the use of language under optimum conditions.

At the opposite extreme, children in orphanage and institution environments, as shown above, are the most seriously retarded group in language development. Little and Williams (1937), Skeels, Updegraff, Wellman, and Williams (1938), and Flemming (1942) have found marked retardation in vocabulary development among institution children. Although the children of this group undoubtedly come from lower socio-economic levels, are somewhat below the average in native ability, and probably have had restricted environmental experiences, their retardation appears so marked that it is necessary to look for other factors to account for the magnitude of the differences found. Even when Little and Williams (1937) matched cases on mental age, the institution children were much more retarded in vocabulary than non-institution children of the same mental age. If these data are fitted into the picture on age of associates it appears that children living in an orphanage have the maximum amount of association with other children and a minimum of association with, and attention from, adults. If, therefore, association with adults is a facilitating factor in language development, it is understandable why this group of orphanage children should show such marked retardation in linguistic development.

Dawe (1942) reported an educational program emphasizing the understanding and use of language symbols by a group of children in an orphanage. It involved about 50 hours of individual and small-group training in understanding words, looking at and discussing pictures, listening to poems and stories, and going on short excursions. These are the kinds of enriching experiences that the good home in the upper socio-economic brackets usually affords and the kinds of experiences that schools find it necessary to provide in reading readiness programs for underprivileged or immature children. In Dawe's experiment 11 pairs of children were matched on age, sex, school group, MA, IQ, and score on the Smith-Williams vocabulary test. One member of each pair received the training, and the other served as a control. Gains which were significantly greater for the experimental group at the 1 per cent level of confidence were found in all language measures except intelligibility of speech and complexity of organization. Sentence length increased from 5.34 to 6.14, and vocabulary scores increased 17.5 points in contrast to 10.0 points for the control group. Although there was no direct coaching on test items, these language training gains were reflected in an increase in average IQ from 80.6 to 94.8 as a result of the 50 hours of training over a 92-day period. The control group decreased from 81.5 to 79.5 in the same interval in the unenriched orphanage setting. The implications of such findings, if substantiated on larger groups, are indeed far reaching for both education and psychometrics.

In the study by Anastasi and D'Angelo (1952) half of the Negroes lived in a housing development tenanted by both Negroes and whites, whereas the other half were in a segregated housing development. The differences in favor of the whites were more marked in the segregated groups. Where there was opportunity for Negro and white children to mingle freely in social activity their language development was more similar. However, there may have been selective factors operating so that brighter Negroes and duller whites representing the same broad socio-economic brackets may have been living in the mixed situation. Negro boys were superior to Negro girls in the unmixed neighborhood, but girls were superior in both mixed and unmixed white groups. (See Table 5.) This reversal of the sex differences usually found in white groups suggests the possibility of a cultural difference in attitude toward the two sexes or differences in child-caring practices which may be operative.

Effect of Multiple Births. Another line of evidence on the effect of environment comes from studies of children whose environment differs from the normal by reason of multiple birth. Day (1932), who duplicated McCarthy's (1930) techniques with 80 pairs of twins, using the same criteria of selection, found that the twins were markedly retarded in all aspects of language development when compared with McCarthy's singletons. She reported that "the mean length of response for 5-year-old twins is slightly below that of 3-year-old singletons," and a comparison of the yearly gains indicated that the rate of increase in length of response among singletons was about double that found among twins. She attributes the differences to the peculiar social situation of the twin, stating, "One surely could not learn as much or as rapidly, from companionship with an individual so nearly on his own plane, as from one in advance. Satisfactions from this companionship may be adequate to the twin . . . whereas the single child . . . may be motivated to gain his satisfactions from a wider field."

Following up these results, E. A. Davis (1937a) compared twins, singletons, and only children at higher age levels. She found the twins retarded in language as compared with the other groups, but the discrepancy between their linguistic status and that of singletons was not nearly so great after the age of school entrance as Day found at the preschool period. It seems that the home situation of the twins during the preschool period is not likely to promote normal linguistic growth, but that after school experience begins, with its opportunities for wider social contacts, much of the initial handicap is overcome. The twins of the upper socio-economic groups made most of the linguistic gains after school entrance, whereas those in the lower economic brackets made comparatively little progress. A study by Howard (1946) on a large number of triplets revealed even more serious linguistic retardation than Day found among twins, for the 5-year-old triplets had a mean length of sentence of only 2.98 words, which is about equal to Day's 4-year-old twins and to McCarthy's 2½- to 3-year-old groups.

Interestingly enough, the Dionne quintuplets showed even more marked linguistic retardation. Blatz, Fletcher, and Mason (1937) reported that Annette, who was the most advanced of the five in language, began to use words by the nineteenth month and that all the children were using a few words by the twenty-second month. They compare the *total vocabularies spoken* by the quintuplets with McCarthy's (1930) and Day's (1932) data showing the *mean number of words used in a sample of 50 consecutive responses* by singletons and twins, and state that the quintuplets are about 16 to 18 months retarded as compared with the normal children. The *real* comparison which should be made indicates even more serious retardation, since the figures for the quintuplets represent the total cumulative vocabulary ever heard before that age. Obviously, if a short sample of 50 responses recorded in 15 or 20 minutes yielded 66 words for McCarthy's singletons and 55 for Day's twins and the quintuplets did not have as many words in their entire known vocabularies until 32 or 33 months, their retardation in language was indeed serious at that age. It must be remembered also that they were living in a bilingual environment, but up to the time of the report cited above they had used only French and were just about to begin to learn English. It is difficult to explain this retardation entirely in terms of the social situation, since the quintuplets had so much individual attention from adults during their preschool years that it should compare favorably with the amount of adult time and attention which children in smaller families normally receive, unless, perhaps, their environment was psychologically more nearly comparable to that of institution children.

Bilingualism. Another environmental factor which is of prime importance in the acquisition of language by the preschool child is bilingualism. In adulthood the ability to use a second language is a decided cultural advantage, and considerable time and effort are spent in secondary school and college to acquire even a rudimentary knowledge of another language; yet a young child can acquire two languages during the preschool years with apparently little difficulty. However, there are many examples of confusion which children who hear two languages are likely to experience. The usual situation for bilingual children in this country is to hear a foreign language in the home and English at school, and in such instances educational experience reveals that the bilingualism is a handicap to the child's school adjustment and academic achievement. Parents who can speak two languages often ask whether it is advantageous or detrimental to permit the child to hear and speak two languages during the preschool years, when language development normally is progressing so rapidly, and whether a certain mastery of one language should be attained before the second one is introduced. Scientific evidence on these very practical and important problems has been seriously lacking. Most of the studies on bilingualism have been concerned with the effect of this factor on intelligence as measured with verbal tests. Seidl (1937) found that bilingual Italian children usually test on the average 5 or 6 points below average in verbal intelligence and that their scores on performance tests generally run 10 or 12 points higher than on verbal tests. Few studies have been concerned with the effect of bilingualism on the development of the child's language.

Travis and Johnson (1937) studied the relationship of bilingualism to stuttering in 4827 children from 4 to 17 years of age of whom approximately half were monolingual and the other half bilingual. They found that 2.8 per cent of the bilinguals stutter and only 1.8 per cent of the monolinguals stutter. Although, of course, 97.2 per cent of the bilinguals did not stutter, there are 98 chances in 100 that the difference obtained between the two groups is a real one.

Leopold (1939, 1947, 1949a, b, c), a linguist, has conducted one of the most careful and detailed studies based on diary records, phonetic transcriptions, and vocabulary accounts of his daughters, who were brought up hearing both English and German. He reported (1949c) that at first his daughter tried to forge a single-language instrument from the twofold presentation and only considerably later did she separate them into two language systems. He reviewed the literature on bilingual children in 1948 with emphasis on case study reports.

M. E. Smith (1935b) studied the language development of 8 children in the same family who had varied experiences with English and Chinese. On the basis of this study she concluded that it is probably better for young bilingual children to receive their two languages from quite separate sources, each adult in the home using one language consistently, and that change from a monolingual to a bilingual environment has a more serious effect on the child's language than change from a bilingual to a monolingual environment. Such changes she thinks are more difficult for infants from 12 to 18 months of age than for children who have acquired greater facility in the use of speech. It does not appear to delay the first use of words but does seem to have a handicapping effect at later ages.

In 1939 Smith published a most comprehensive investigation on the effect of bilingualism on language development. She studied 1000 children of varying racial backgrounds and varying amounts of bilingualism in Hawaii. The major findings were that in general these children preferred to use English. The Japanese children who heard the least English used 50 per cent English words, but the total group used about 88 per cent English words. In comparison with *haole* [1] children and those who were studied on the mainland, Island children were seriously retarded in the use of the English language, a retardation which is not compensated for by greater advancement in other languages used. The more bilingual groups use more nonverbal sentences and shorter sentences than childrn in a less polylingual environment. They are found to use more exclamatory and fewer interrogative sentences, and to use compound and complex sentences much less frequently. The bilingual groups were also retarded in the use of connectives and pronouns and in the use of the copula and inflected forms, and showed the expected decrease in the use of interjections. When a language is disappearing in competition with a new language, nouns and interjections (which, it will be recalled, are the first to be acquired) persist for the longest time. Those words that pertain to intimate aspects of family life and to eating are the last to be abandoned. In general, it was found that the children of Hawaii from *nonhaole* homes are retarded in language development at the time of school entrance to a degree so marked that, on most criteria, they are at about the level of 3-year-old children from a less polyglot environment. Smith considers that this retardation is due to the bilingualism of many homes and the prevalent use of pidgin English in the Hawaiian Islands.

There is need for further study of bilingualism in the United States, with other languages as the foreign language, and uncomplicated by the presence of a mutilated form of English. Most of the studies are seriously obscured by the factor of socioeconomic status, for most bilingual children either come from highly cultured homes of

---

[1] *Haole* is an Hawaiian word for almost all Caucasians except the Portuguese.

the upper social levels where the language is being deliberately preserved for cultural reasons, or they come from the lower socio-economic levels where the parents have not been sufficiently intellectual to acquire the second language. On the other hand, there are a number of children whose parents remain in lower socio-economic brackets than those in which they would be found in their native countries because the very fact of a language handicap has necessitated their remaining at manual occupations rather than undertaking more verbal or more intellectual tasks. In McCarthy's (1930) study 10 per cent of the cases were bilingual. These children were more advanced than would be expected on the basis of their age, sex, and paternal occupation as measured by mean length of response. It may be that the handicap is more readily detectable in articulation and in quality of speech than in quantitative measures like length of response. Numerous reports seem to indicate that as far as pronunciation is concerned there is a definite advantage to learning the second language at an early age. Yoshioka (1929), however, states on the basis of meager data that older children can handle two languages better than younger ones and that bilingualism seems to require a certain degree of mental maturation for its successful mastery.

Smith (1949) studied the vocabularies of 30 bilingual children of Chinese ancestry in Hawaii who ranged in age from 37 to 77 months. They were as a group somewhat above average in paternal occupation. Her test was given in English on one day and in Chinese on another day by a Chinese examiner conversant with both languages. In either language taken alone the group had below-average-sized vocabularies for children of their ages. Even when the vocabularies of the two languages were totaled only two-fifths of the children exceeded the norm. When words of duplicate meaning were subtracted only one-sixth of them exceeded the norm. Smith concludes that only the superior bilingual child is capable of attaining the vocabulary norms of monoglots, that it is better to have one name for each of many concepts than two names for a smaller number, and that it is therefore "unwise to start any but children of superior linguistic ability on a second language unnecessarily during the preschool years." She also cites an unpublished study by Motoyma in which 50 bilingual Chinese children had English vocabularies only 40 per cent as large as the average monolingual child at entrance into kindergarten. After a year of kindergarten they had vocabularies 62 per cent of the norm. Two of the most careful studies showing the effect of bilingualism on the measurement of intelligence with both verbal and nonverbal tests are those by Seidl (1937) and by Darcy (1946), both of which show that the bilingual child is penalized in the usual measures of intelligence that best predict his functional intellectual level. Studies on bilingualism have been reviewed by Arsenian (1945). Thompson (1952) in concluding his discussion of this topic states:

> The "functional" intelligence of bilingual children is severely impaired in a cultural sense. . . . There can be no doubt that the child reared in a bilingual environment is handicapped in his language growth. One can debate the issue as to whether speech facility in two languages is worth the consequent retardation in the common language of the realm. There is no research evidence that might help answer this important question [p. 367].

In Harris's (1948) study of fifth-grade Indian children's compositions the Montana children, two-thirds of whom heard only English before school entrance, wrote shorter compositions than the Pueblo children, three-fourths of whom heard only Indian before school. Error scores were higher for the Pueblo children, but this may have been a function of the greater opportunity for errors in the longer specimens of their writing. It cannot be determined from the data presented whether the differences are racial or due to bilingualism.

It is becoming increasingly urgent that we have adequate information on this problem of the effect of bilingual experience at various ages, for more and more families are having to spend periods of time in foreign countries in government service and are puzzled as to how best to handle the second language to the children's advantage rather than to their detriment. Furthermore, with the increase in air travel in this shrinking world there is great need for more individuals who can communicate in more than one language, and of course there is the ever-recurrent interest in the various forms of a universal language such as Basic English or Esperanto. It is evident that a thorough re-evaluation of the methods of foreign language teaching in secondary schools and colleges is needed.

Effect of the Situation. Considerable interest has been shown concerning the effect of the immediate situation in which language responses are recorded on the general pattern of results. Attention was called to this factor by McCarthy (1929a), who in an effort to reconcile the results of her major study with those of Piaget (1926) recorded the language of the same children in a situation in which the child was conversing with an adult and also in a nursery school free play situation. Although the odd-even reliability of length of response samples of 50 responses taken in the adult-child situation was +.91, the correlation found between mean length of response for samples taken in the two different situations was only +.54. Some children who were somewhat shy and restrained in the adult situation talked more freely on the playground, and others who were talkative with adults talked relatively little in this group, thus tending to lower the correlation.

McConnon (1935) conducted a study of 28 nursery school children in which two samples of conversation were recorded in each of six different situations; lunch, morning outdoor play period, indoor free play situation, table-play, afternoon outdoor play, and an outdoor play situation at home. Twenty-five responses were recorded in each situation for the same group of children. McCarthy's (1930) methods of recording and analysis were followed quite closely although no construction analysis was conducted. Surprisingly low coefficients of agreement between the two observations in each situation were found, the quantitative analyses yielding the highest mean coefficient of only +.431, the functional analysis yielding a mean correlation coefficient of only +.289 between various situations, and the parts of speech analysis one of only +.072. The two reasons which obviously account for the differences found here are, first, that the quantitative measures, such as length of response and total number of words, are more objective and do not involve judgment and classification by the experimenter, and, second, that they are based on the total sample while the functional and parts-of-speech analyses are based on only parts of the sample, in some instances certain categories being represented by a relatively small number of responses. On the whole, McConnon reports, the home situation yielded the greatest consistency from one occasion to the next. The category of emotionally toned responses yielded the highest consistency coefficient from one situation to another. Of the various nursery school situations, the lunch period apparently offered more controlled conditions than the other school situations. The two outdoor situations both showed low consistency, as did also the indoor play situations.

An inquiry by Janus (1943) on the relationship between children's language and their play is so inadequately controlled that the conclusions should be disregarded. Space does not permit detailed criticism here, but the article has been severely criticized in print by Dennis (1943).

Williams and Mattson (1942) studied the effect of different social groupings on the language of 6 nursery school children. A Fonda recorder enabled them to secure responses for several children at one time. Records were taken when the child was alone, with the experimenter, and with the experimenter and 1, 2, and 3 other children. Most talking and the most social speech occurred with the largest social group, but the mean length of sentence remained fairly constant for the various social situations. The data were also analyzed for parts of speech and according to Piaget's analysis. All the intercorrelations among the various situations were low. For the quantitative indices they averaged $+.31$ to $+.40$, for the functional indices $-.05$ to $+.20$, and for the parts of speech only $-.07$ to $+.23$. The same children used longer responses and more words in samples of conversation taken in an outdoor home situation than in any of the nursery school situations studied.

Further light on the effect of the situation on language records is afforded by Hahn's (1948) study on 116 first-grade children from upper and middle class homes. Recordings were made of voluntary speeches given by these children in the daily "show-and-tell" situation in the classroom where teacher and classmates

were the audience; and 8 days later records were taken in an adult-child situation such as has been employed in most of the major studies. The classroom speeches averaged about 5 or 6 sentences (median 48 words), with a mean sentence length of 10.37 words, as shown in Table 5. In the adult-child situation, although the sample was longer (median 70 words), the mean length of sentence was only 6.85. She found that 6½ times as many "nonsentences" occurred in the situation with the adult as in the group audience situation. She makes the interesting observation that, when an object and an event are not shared visually, longer sentences are required, as when a child told in class of family trips or events at home. Highly personal and family activity stories produced the longest total responses.

In a study by Van Alstyne (1932) it was found that over half the time preschool children tended not to talk to other children while working with play materials. Certain materials appeared to have considerably more "conversation value" than others. Doll play, blocks, crayons, and clay ranked high for percentage of time that their use was accompanied by conversation, whereas painting, scissors, and books were low in conversation value. It is interesting, in view of the sex differences previously shown, that the doll-corner activities and dishes, which are typical girl activities, were among the highest in conversation value. It might be concluded that certain differences in language are due to the effect of the situation, but it must also be remembered that certain situations may attract children of different levels of language development.

It appears from McConnon's investigation that the results of language analyses are dependent upon the situation in which the data are gathered and on the type of index of language development employed.

It is extremely important, therefore, in comparing language studies and in setting up experimental situations for future investigations, to control the situation with great care, to make comparisons only of situations which have been shown to be comparable, and to generalize regarding language development only for the specific situation in which the data have been collected. Apparently there are sufficient differences in the same children's use of language from one situation to another to make it extremely hazardous to infer that a given sample is representative of a child's language development in general.

M. E. Smith (1935a) also attacked this problem by comparing children's language recorded in a nursery school free play situation and in the adult-child situation, but since the personnel of her groups differed it is difficult to interpret her findings. She claims superior language usage by children in the adult-child situation. However, as McConnon concludes: "If a typical picture of the child's behavior is to be obtained, a number of situations must be sampled. Observational studies cannot continue to ignore the situational factor in response if the results are to have significance for child development." She further points out: "In order to obtain a stable index of the child's language responses it is necessary to take a number of samples in a number of situations."

In the study by Young (1941) samples of language in four different nursery school situations were obtained. Each child was observed for 10-minute periods totaling 6 hours of observation during about 15 days. The situations studied were outdoor play, indoor play, dinner, and a period in which the children were looking at picture books. It was found that the setting in which the responses were collected had a marked relation to the amount of language obtained in a given time.

In length of response, however, twelve correlations between compared situations ranged from +.90 to +.94. These and all other intersituation correlations reported by Young are unbelievably high considering the degree of reliability which is usually found for data of this type. They are all the more surprising when one considers the small homogeneous groups upon which they are based. Barring computational errors, the only possible explanation of them seems to be in the relatively longer samples employed, which may have yielded more reliable data. These correlations seem to indicate that sentence length in any one setting tends to be markedly similar to that used by the subjects in the other situations studied. However, Young states:

> Apparently the four groups were not identically affected by the four different settings in which they were placed . . . a situation somewhat similar to that used by McCarthy, may be expected to yield findings representative of those which would be secured in any of the other three settings, if the subjects are of both sexes and come from widely differing socio-economic levels, as in the present investigation. If, however, a relatively homogeneous group is being studied it seems advisable to secure responses in several different types of situation. This appears to be especially important if the subjects are of low socio-economic status [pp. 43–44].

The analysis for parts of speech showed rather marked differences from setting to setting corresponding to the changes found in amount of comprehensible verbal behavior. It seems as if this contribution to methodology should be helpful to future investigators in this rapidly expanding field.

An interesting study by Chapin and Corcoran (1947) reported remarkable success in bringing out speech in a group of 16 "speech-inhibited" children of about 5 years of age through play-group techniques, and several writers, particularly Blanchard (1933), Russell (1944), Werner (1945), Harle (1946), and Allen (1947), report case studies in which children with delayed speech were helped by play therapy or group play contacts of a nursery school. (See section on delayed speech, pp. 606–8.)

However, for most children of the upper socio-economic levels, nursery school experience results in more child contacts and fewer adult contacts, and in the light of the evidence presented earlier it would not be surprising if in some cases there were revealed a retarding effect of nursery school experience, especially for only children of upper socio-economic levels. This possibility, even if later demonstrated, however, should not be interpreted as an indictment of nursery school experience, because such factors need to be evaluated in the light of the child's total development.

Language and Motor Development

As none of the studies conducted so far has devised any single index of language development or measure of linguistic maturity, there are not many satisfactory indications of the relationship of language development to other aspects of the child's development. Language is usually considered to be a substitute or short-cut type of behavior for overt bodily responses, as it is well known that gestures accompany language in the early stages. As was pointed out earlier (see section on gesture language, pp. 521–3), gestures precede the appearance of language and constitute a more primitive form of communication. As language develops and becomes more precise, fewer gestures are needed, and it has often been noted that if a child develops an unusually effective gesture language his development of true language may be delayed for some time. Cases of language retardation are often attributed to the fact that the child develops an elaborate system of gesture language which is so well understood by adults in the child's environment that his wants and needs are satisfied without his having to make the effort to learn to talk. If, in a particular case, it can be shown that such is the cause of linguistic retardation, a refusal on the part of the adults in the environment to understand and respond to the child's gesture-language is usually effective in bringing about the emergence of true language.

Shirley (1933a, b), who made a careful analysis of the motor development of the same 25 children on whom language records were kept, reported a cyclical relationship between linguistic development and the appearance of certain gross motor skills. Children's vocalizations decreased in frequency during periods when reaching for objects, sitting alone, and walking were being mastered. She found correlations between developmental scores on locomotion and vocalization which were all low or negative tending to "confirm the theory that speech development is held in abeyance at the time when motor progress is most rapid." She states further that, although the evidence is meager, "it points in the direction that early vocalization is held in check by rapid motor progress and that babbling is a type of behavior which a baby resorts to when there is nothing better to do, or when the novelty of a new type of motor activity has worn off. This phenomenon was pointed out as early as 1880 by the German observer Schultze, who said that children appear to learn only one thing thoroughly at a time and that while the child learns to walk he pushes aside the development of speech almost entirely and resumes his linguistic task only after the locomotor one has been finished. It is possible that the slowing-up in rate of gain in vocabulary as shown in M. E. Smith's (1926) data (Table 4) at the age of 15 months, which was the age of learning to walk in Shirley's group, is another instance of this same phenomenon. Brigance (1934) also noted it in one child who showed a plateau in vocabulary development during the period of learning to walk. After walking became well established this child showed a rapid spurt in vocabulary development. It is relationships of this sort that are all too meager in the literature of child psychology. In all probability many interesting interrelationships such as these are being overlooked because of the methodology which characterizes so many current studies in child psychology.

Wellman, Case, Mengert, and Bradbury (1931), who give detailed tabulations on the ability of preschool children to articulate various sounds, report correlations of $+.67$ and $+.65$, respectively, between scores on a tracing path test and the total number of sounds and the number of consonant blends articulated. Bilto (1941) studied 90 speech-defective cases ranging in age from 9 to 18 years and found them to be definitely inferior as a group on three sets of motor ability tasks. Since articulation is so largely a motor function, this may be indicative of a general motor ability. Both articulation and motor ability are undoubtedly related to CA and probably to a third factor such as emotional security. Shirley (1933b) found a moderate positive relationship between fine motor coordinations and language development after the age of 45 weeks. H. M. Johnson (1928) reports that nursery school children under 3 years of age frequently use rhythmic vocal accompaniments to their physical activity; Fisher (1934) reports a correlation of $+.86$ between the use of things by nursery school children and talking about things; and Goodenough (1930) reports a low positive correlation of $+.17$, with age constant, between talk-

ativeness and physical activity in nursery school children. These observations are interesting in relation to Vandel's (1947) report that higher apes often utter vocalizations in accompaniment to their actions.

Language and Intellectual Development

Language is an area of the child's development in which more marked and more striking degrees of individual variation can be observed than in almost any other. From the idiot who grows to physical maturity without learning to talk, to the gifted child who begins to use words at 8 months and sentences by the end of the first year of life, there certainly is a wide span which is of considerable developmental significance. Individual differences in linguistic development closely parallel the differences which have been shown to exist in intellectual development, and certainly equal and perhaps even exceed them in magnitude. It is also quite certain that language development has contributed heavily to the variations in intellectual differences as they have thus far been measured. Whether or not this is an artifact due to the highly verbal nature of most of the more satisfactory intelligence tests, or whether there is a more basic fabric of intellectual development consisting largely of linguistic maturation, is something which has not as yet been determined. The facts that thus far no satisfactory intelligence test has been developed for age levels before the emergence of language, and that all the intelligence tests which have proved to have a satisfactory degree of validity are heavily weighted with verbal factors, bear witness to the importance of language in mental development.

The age of onset of talking has often been regarded as symptomatic of the child's later intellectual development. One often hears favorable prognoses regarding the intellectual development of children who talk early, and mothers often become concerned over failure of their children to talk at least by the second birthday. From the scientific evidence available there appears to be some justification for these popular beliefs although the relationship is far from perfect, and the layman accepting such a generalization is quite likely to make serious errors in predicting a child's future mental development merely from a knowledge of the age at which he begins to talk. An idiot never learns to talk, and Terman et al. (1925) found that gifted children with IQ's above 140 talked on the average at about 11 months or approximately 4 months earlier than the average child. However, there were in this group of gifted children some who did not talk at all until 2, 2½, and even 3 years of age. So it is by no means certain that a child who is late in talking will be mentally retarded. However, in general, feeble-minded children usually talk much later than normal or superior children. The average age of talking of a group of feeble-minded subjects is reported by Mead (1913) as 38.5 months as compared with the normal age of 15.3 months. (See also Town, 1912–1913.) It thus appears that feeble-minded children are always late in beginning to talk, and a child who talks early is quite likely to be above average in intelligence. However, although delayed onset of speech is often due to general mental retardation, there are many other causes of delayed speech (see pp. 606–8), and a diagnosis of mental retardation should never be made on the basis of delayed speech alone.

After sketching in a descriptive account of ten stages in a linguistic sequence which he says appeared in all 3 of his children, Valentine (1942) notes that the child Y who showed spontaneous cooing at 4 weeks was the most accelerated in each of the stages, B who cooed at 5 weeks was next, and A who did not coo until 7 weeks was the most retarded in all other linguistic manifestations up to 2 years of age. This corresponded well with their later IQ's as Y and B tested about 145 IQ and A only about 110.

Abt, Adler, and Bartelme (1929) report data on age of onset of speech in a group of 1000 cases with an average IQ of 81. The correlations for age of onset of speech and intelligence were −.41 and −.39 for the two sexes separately.

Irwin (1942) has thrown further light on this problem by showing that the speech sounds made by 10 low-grade feeble-minded children, none of whom was using real language (average age 4 years and average IQ 29), approximate those of normal children 1 year of age in such characteristics as vowel ratio, vowel-consonant ratio, and distribution of consonants. Sirkin and Lyons (1941), who examined 2500 institution mental defectives, report that only one-third speak normally and that the lower the intelligence rating the lower is the incidence of normal speech. Speech correction with these cases was found to be unsuccessful below the moron level, and they consider that a minimum mental age of 5 years 6 months combined with a cooperative attitude is essential to successful speech therapy.

In an analysis of the articulatory defects of a group of 53 feeble-minded cases (physical defectives eliminated), Bangs (1942) concluded that MA is 4.9 times as significant as CA in influencing speech proficiency. The sounds avoided by the feeble-minded were no different from those avoided by the normals. However, omissions of sounds which constituted 35 per cent of all errors in the feeble-minded seemed to be one of the most significant characteristics of their speech. They more frequently omit final sounds. Otherwise their speech corresponds closely to that of normals of the same MA.

In 1945 Irwin and Chen compared a number of their speech sound indices with the results of the Kuhlmann Test of Mental Development and concluded that speech "sound development for the first 2 years of life is independent of intelligence test scores." However, most intelligence tests which are satisfactory at upper ages are highly verbal in nature. Those so far available at the infant level have neglected linguistic development because of methodological problems and have yielded disappointing results. The phonetic approach to infants' vocalization, introduced by Irwin and his co-workers, yields regular trends with chronological age (see Table 2), shows occupational group differences (Irwin, 1948b, c), and differences between institutional and noninstitutional cases (Brodbeck and Irwin, 1946; and Fisichelli, 1950) in the same direction as intelligence tests do at higher age levels.

Investigators have not been very successful in their attempts to measure intelligence until the child is able to talk or at least to respond to verbal commands, in other words, to participate in verbal tests. It is strange that we have gone on blindly expecting sensori-motor items to reveal intellectual development in infants, simply because they are easy to observe, when they are not related to intelligence at other age levels. A pilot study undertaken by Catalano (1952) under the writer's direction involved follow-up intelligence testing with the Stanford-Binet scale of 23 of the cases 4 years of age previously used in Fisichelli's (1950) investigation of infants. A correlation of +.38 was obtained between consonant/vowel frequency ratio in infancy and later IQ. When corrected for age at time of original testing this value was raised to +.41. Consonant types in infancy correlated +.45 with IQ at 4

years of age. It may very well be that phonetic analysis of infants' vocalizations will yield some of the most valid intelligence test items for the infant scales of the future.

In the studies of McCarthy (1930), Day (1932), and E. A. Davis (1937a) the same relationships which were traced with relation to CA also appeared when the data were analyzed according to MA. The marked linguistic superiority of Fisher's (1934) subjects whose average IQ was 132 is significant in considering the relationship between intellectual development and language development. It is also interesting to note that there are differences in intellectual status paralleling the differences in linguistic development, there being slight superiority of girls over boys, of singletons as compared with twins, and of children from the upper as compared with the lower socio-economic levels. This brings up a very interesting problem on which there are not sufficient data for a final answer, namely, whether the more precocious development of language among these groups is due to their greater intellectual endowment or whether their higher scores on the intelligence tests, which are chiefly verbal in nature, are due to the more precocious linguistic development. Shirley (1933b) reports quite high correlations (5 out of 6 between +.63 and +.76) between Minnesota Preschool Test scores and cumulative vocabulary, number of different words used per examination, and vocalization scores, all of them being higher at 2 years than at 18 months.

Two studies have attempted to separate the factors involved in this relationship. Day (1932), in an effort to account for the differences which she found between twins and singletons in language development, matched her 4-year-old group of twins with singletons in regard to total test score, CA at time of testing, sex, and occupational class. The percentages of the total score which each group earned on verbal and nonverbal items of the test were then calculated and were found to match almost exactly. Day (1932) concludes therefore that "the language retardation of these 4-year-old twins does not seem to have been a factor in reducing the total test score and thus lowering the IQ." She also determined "language quotients" for her twins by obtaining ratios between the mean length of response of singletons and of twins of the same ages. The results indicate that "the language retardation is so significantly greater that factors other than 'below average general intelligence' must be responsible for it. The language quotient decreases rapidly as age increases in spite of the fact that the intelligence quotient does not." It thus appears that differences in intelligence do not account entirely for the language retardation of twins, nor does the verbal element in intelligence tests appear to penalize the twin sufficiently to account for the differences in intelligence as measured.

A second study in which an attempt has been made to separate these two influences is that by Williams and McFarland (1937), referred to previously, in which a vocabulary test was given to 242 Iowa City children and to 64 orphanage children. The two groups showed marked contrast in both vocabulary and IQ. When orphanage and noninstitutional children were matched on MA and IQ, there still remained a marked discrepancy between the vocabularies of the two groups, the vocabulary ratios of the orphanage children being only .48 to .68. The authors therefore state: "Thus the orphanage children have vocabularies which are inferior not only to those of children of the same chronological or mental age, but higher IQ, but also to those of children matched for IQ level as well." For the group living in the community the

correlation between vocabulary and MA, with CA held constant, was +.43, whereas for the orphanage group it was +.65.

Another approach to this problem comes from learning studies in which subjects learn more readily when they have names for the learning materials. It is well known that meaningful paired associates are learned more readily in the laboratory than nonsense syllables in the same type of learning situation. Pyles (1932) in an interesting study of the factor of verbalization in learning found that, when young children were given names for nonsense molds which covered rewards, 44 per cent solved the problem in 25 trials or less, whereas only 14 per cent solved it when the molds remained unnamed. This brings up the problem of the relationship between thought and language. Carmichael, Hogan, and Walter (1932) demonstrated that in many cases merely saying a word before the presentation of a visual form definitely influences the manner in which the form is apprehended as well as the readiness with which it is recalled. It was also shown by Goodenough and Brian (1929) that verbal instructions were of considerable help to preschool children in acquiring a simple motor skill.

Language and Social Development

During the early preschool period when the child's language is not yet very useful as a means of social communication, he is still definitely an individualist, and it is probably significant that a marked degree of socialization of his behavior occurs during the later preschool period when language itself is becoming a more efficient means of intercommunication. Every nursery school teacher is familiar with the increased facility in controlling a child's behavior which comes as soon as his understanding of spoken language improves and with the marked change in social behavior which occurs when a child learns to make verbal instead of physical contacts with his playmates. A child who talks very little is often solitary even in a group situation, and a spurt in his linguistic development sometimes appears to facilitate his social contacts so that a previously solitary child may develop friendships as soon as he begins to talk and make verbal approaches to other children.

As indicated above, language responses have been shown to differ from one play situation to another. Further study should be made in order to determine whether the child's stage of linguistic development determines the types of companions he finds congenial and the sorts of play situations in which he will engage or whether the situations themselves determine his linguistic pattern. Schmidt (1941) has shown that speech therapy given to mental defectives facilitates their social adjustments and stimulates them to more gregarious behavior. A positive correlation between maturity of articulation and acceptable social behavior, as measured with the Haggerty-Olson-Wickman Behavior Rating Schedule B, was found in a study by I. P. Davis (1938). This, she considers, may indicate that the factors which retard a child's speech also retard his social development or that the speech difficulty may, in itself, contribute to the retardation in social adjustment. McCarthy (1929a) found no very marked correlations between the Marston extroversion-introversion scale ratings and various linguistic measures for nursery school children observed in free play and in the controlled situation with an adult.

Portenier (1937) found that it took longer to elicit a specified number of responses from a group of children who were rated by their nursery school teachers as poorly adjusted than from a group rated as well adjusted. Hahn (1948) reports that 32 per cent of the first-grade children who volunteered speeches before the class in a "show-and-tell" period were leaders, 51 per cent "sometimes lead," and only 17 per cent of them were classed as "usually followers."

Several writers, particularly Despert (1938) and Bradley (1941), have called attention to the seclusiveness and schizoid tendencies of many children who manifest serious lack of speech in spite of normal hearing and normal mentality. McCarthy (1947, 1949a, and 1952b) and others have called attention to the fact that social adjustment is usually very poor in older children who manifest serious language disorder syndromes. Such children seem to be either very shy or very aggressive and to have no wholesome friendships with their peers. The favorable response of some of these cases to the socializing influence of a nursery school environment will be shown in the next section.

Language Disorder Syndromes and Personality Development

The identification of certain clinical syndromes among cases manifesting language disorders of various types is one of the most interesting trends to appear, and it does much to throw light on the problem of the rôle of language in the adjustment of the total individual, on the dynamics of personality, as well as on the genesis of speech, and on the etiology of the various disorders of the language function.

Most of the evidence comes from the study of those who have failed to develop normal speech and who suffer from some form of language disorder such as delayed speech, infantile speech, or other articulatory defect, or who stutter, or who later manifest a syndrome of reading, writing, and spelling disabilities. There seems to be a new appreciation of the factors of psychological adjustment among workers in the field of speech correction who are coming to realize that they have largely been treating symptoms and have not been removing causes. Among educators, who are baffled by persistent reading, writing, and spelling disorders and by the slow learning of some gifted individuals, there is considerable concentration on methodology and diagnostic and remedial programs in the basic tool subjects. The constructive approach to the teaching of reading has made notable progress in concentrating on the development of the whole child, in recognizing the immaturity of the beginner through measures of reading readiness, by the expansion of preprimer experience, and through intensive efforts to integrate the learning of the various language arts with the total life experience of the child. Outstanding contributions in this area are Betts's (1946) *Foundations of Reading Instruction* and Strickland's (1951) *The Language Arts in the Elementary School.* An overview of trends in this field is available in the first of a series of volumes prepared under the auspices of the Curriculum Commission of the National Council of Teachers of English (1952) and entitled *The English Language Arts.*

When the broad concept of language disorder is utilized to include such varied manifestations as delayed speech, stuttering, functional articulatory defects, and reading disabilities, it appears that various forms of language disturbance occur much more often in combination in the same individuals than would be expected by chance on the basis of the incidence of any one of them in the population (Gaines, 1941; and Yedinack, 1949).

It has also been shown in a variety of studies (see Johnson *et al.*, 1948) that language disability syndromes seem to appear more frequently among males, to run in families, and to occur more often in families

in which twinning occurs, and that these families also produce many individuals who manifest some sort of confusion in lateral dominance as indicated by ambidexterity, mixed eyedness and handedness, and reversal tendencies in reading and writing.

All these lines of evidence have built up in the minds of most investigators, and especially among speech correctionists, a hereditary explanation or some sort of neurological theory in regard to speech, reading, and lateral dominance disturbances (Travis, 1931; Bryngelson, 1935; Orton, 1937; Berry, 1938; and Cole, 1942). This attitude leads to excusing the deficiencies and contributes to their stubborn resistance to treatment. It tends to relieve the individuals and their families from active participation in the overcoming of the disorder, since they come to believe themselves somehow different by native endowment and that hence normal learning in these areas is precluded for them.

The following section presents a summary of a number of significant contributions in this area which the writer believes point to an emotional and functional explanation of most of the language disorder syndromes and indicate that these emotional disturbances are for the most part environmentally determined, but are passed along in families from generation to generation in the form of attitudes toward children and in cultural child-caring patterns which appear to give superficial support to hereditarian explanations.

Studies of Infants. A wealth of material seems to have emerged since the early 1940's centering on the broad area of the relationship of language development to emotional adjustment and normal personality growth, with emphasis on the importance of proper parent-child relationships for normal growth in language and personality. Evidence has been presented in the section on environmental factors of the devastating effects of environmental deprivation (Gesell and Amatruda, 1941; Goldfarb, 1943a, b, 1945; and Brodbeck and Irwin, 1946) in orphanage situations where the child lacks close personal contact with the mother or mother-substitute in early infancy. Ribble (1943) and Spitz (1946) have also described the retarding effects of "hospitalism" on young children, and we are now witnessing a marked emphasis on infant psychiatry leading to changes in the practices of some of the most advanced maternity hospitals which are introducing the "lying-in" arrangement advocated by Gesell and Ilg (1943) for newborn babies in an effort to establish closer mother-child relationships in the first few days of life.

In the discussion of the organismic theory of infant vocalization (McCarthy, 1952c) it has been pointed out that the organs of speech are first used for the establishment of breathing and feeding, the two most vital physiological processes. The emotional tone of the mother-child relationship which is established in those early days, the security provided by the mother's arms while nursing the child, the tone of her voice, and her facial expression probably have much to do with determining the child's first social contacts and the adequacy of his interpersonal relations. It appears from the clinical literature, which is too voluminous to cite here, that, if these early experiences are warm and satisfying and tend to give the young infant security, breathing, feeding, vocalization, and other vital processes are established normally. There seems to be evidence to indicate that the mother who is emotionally mature, free from fears, and ready to accept the responsibilities of motherhood has a better chance of having a normal delivery and of starting the infant off adequately in these important areas (McCarthy, 1952a and 1953).

In an interesting article on "echo-reactions" in young children Stengel (1947) points out that in echoing words the child identifies with persons in the environment, especially with persons to whom he is emotionally attached. Stengel claims that the game of repeating words is one of the means by which the child identifies himself with his models. This author stresses the essentially social nature of these early echo-reactions and their dependence on personal rapport, and considers that the underlying psychological mechanism is identification on a primitive level. Wyatt (1949) also presents an article which emphasizes the importance of the mother-child relationship in this early period. She points out that it is the mother who first brings the language of her social group before her child and that she thus serves as a temporary interpreter for a permanent medium of the culture which has its own set of rules. She stresses that the learning of the mother's speech is deeply emotional, and is achieved through the process of unconscious identification. Since, however, the language is more or less rigid, it imposes early rules, regulations, and frustrations together with gratifications and rewards, and in this process the mother "mediates" between the language and the child but does not "inflict" language upon him.

Goldfarb (1945) points out that infants form strong emotional attachments within the first year of life, probably within the first 6 months. Brodbeck and Irwin (1946), Freud and Burlingham (1944), Roudinesco and Appell (1950), and Buxbaum (1949) also stress the importance of the process of identification with an affectionate adult in the establishment of babbling and word formation. Buxbaum (1949) states that "severely neglected children and those whose attachments to adults are interrupted and infrequent . . . are slow in learning to speak and may remain retarded in speech throughout their lives." These children she describes as "anxious, insecure, inhibited children who were punished for self-expression or suffered the pangs of hunger, cold, and loneliness." It may be that mothers' attitudes towards boy babies are often different from their attitudes towards girl babies, for girls are more in demand for adoption in our culture, and boys are more likely to be active and to require more restraint and are generally considered harder to train and raise (Goodenough, 1931). Boys in our society have little opportunity to identify with fathers, and even when they have the opportunity, there is such a marked difference in the voice quality of the young infant and that of the adult male that it certainly would make the echo-reaction stage much less satisfying to the boy than to the girl whose voice more nearly approximates that of the mother. If the affectional bond with the mother is so vital to the establishment of a proper groundwork for normal speech, may we not have here a partial explanation of the retardation of twins and other multiple-birth children who have to share the mother during infancy and who never do experience a period in which they have her undivided attention to the extent that a singleton has? This idea could also be expanded to include the precocity of the only child reported by Davis (1937a), for only children have longer periods of being the center of the mother's affection. It would also fit in with the frequent observation of marked sibling rivalry in cases manifesting language disorders (McCarthy, 1947 and 1949a) and with the frequently observed onset of stuttering and reading failure after the arrival of a younger sibling (Missildine, 1946).

Fowler (1947) stresses the importance of the rôle of the adult in helping the child build meaning into words. She brings out that the extent to which the child makes a connection between words and actions is dependent on the accuracy and consistency with which parents use words in everyday situations. In teaching the child the word "come" the parent should not only say the word but should also help the child to come, give approval and satisfaction, and be consistent in the application of such techniques. In an observational investigation carried on in the home, Lafore (1945) found that the largest number of the parents' positive contacts were directed toward the child's intellectual development and a comparatively small number toward his emotional development. However, out of a total of 913 practices directed at the child's intellectual development, the smallest category involved encouraging the child in the acquisition of language. Yet, in the light of what is known about the importance of language development for intellectual growth and as preparation for the highly verbal situation of the school, what better practices could the parents of preschool children use, who are ambitious for the child's intellectual growth and academic success, than to encourage and assist them in the acquisition of language?

Allen (1947) has a splendid article summarizing a pediatrician's 20 years of experience in dealing with speech-defective children, which stresses that speech must be regarded as a function of the whole child. He says that any speech defect must be regarded as only a presenting symptom and as one feature of some more widespread condition in the child. After eliminating various physical defects, such as defects of the organs of speech, hearing defects, and mental deficiency, he describes a group in which the speech defect is due to mismanaged emotional factors in otherwise physically and mentally normal children. In this main category he recognizes four types: (1) the delay in learning to speak of the "protest child," who has rejected food in his infancy and who has always been difficult to manage; (2) the continuation of babylike speech in the overprotected child; (3) variations in speech function due to being deprived of a position of emotional dependence; and (4) stammering, in which an emotion is mismanaged by being "throttled down." There results an interference with motor impulses involved in breathing. According to Allen, in various emotional situations such as displacement in the family group, illness, or accidents, the motor impulse in the act of breathing "is prevented from reaching those muscles which should contract first and is transmitted to those muscles which should relax first." With the resulting lack of control over expiration, there is "failure to produce vowel sounds with a repetition of the consonant sounds which precede them." Thus, it is evident that speech disturbances are often associated with disorders in breathing and feeding and probably have their roots in very early infancy when control of these processes is being established.

As will be shown in subsequent paragraphs there are a number of studies which indicate that, in children of preschool age who present speech disorders, other behavior difficulties are common accompaniments. *Delayed Speech.* An investigation by Beckey (1942) involved detailed clinical study of 50 children who were delayed in the onset of speech with 50 who talked at the normal age. Factors in the family stock which were found to be associated with delayed onset of speech were speech defects, left-handedness, and mental deficiency. Among prenatal factors considered, those which seemed to be related to delayed speech were age of the mother below 18 years, and asthenia, nervousness, edema, and kidney and heart disorders during pregnancy. Prolonged labor or other abnormal conditions at birth were also significantly related to late speech, as well as asphyxia in the newborn. Poor motor coordination, ambidexterity, and a tendency

to respiratory diseases, especially measles and whooping cough, poor health, and glandular disturbances were also more frequent among the late speakers. Retardation in age of walking and dentition, as well as diseased or early removal of tonsils and adenoids, were more frequent in the group of children who talked late. Children with delayed speech were more likely to be boys than girls and more likely to have parents who were less well educated and came from lower occupational levels than those of children who began to speak at the normal age. Environmental factors which appeared to be significantly related to delayed speech were isolation of the child, severe frights, and habitual anticipation of the child's wants by the parents. Beckey also found that children with delayed speech cried easily, played alone, and did not want attention as much as children with normal speech. Significantly larger percentages of children in the delayed-speech group made excessive use of gestures and used defective articulation. It should be remembered in this connection that many children make excessive use of gestures before the onset of true speech and that most of the early sentences are emotionally toned in content (McCarthy, 1930).

Goldenberg (1950) discusses 14 children tentatively diagnosed as "idiopathic language retardation" cases. These were carefully examined with the Nance (1946) battery of tests for differential diagnosis of aphasia in children. He states that 4 of his cases placed in the "idiopathic language retardation" category are probably mental defectives, 3 others he considers to be probably suffering from minor brain injuries because of evidence of disturbed perceptual-motor functioning, and 2 had severe hearing loss. He considers that this nosological category may be a group of known and disparate disorders which have merely been classed together because of the common language symptoms, or that it may be a group of similarly based defects belonging to a more general classification of disorders, or that it may be a group whose common lack of speech is the symptom of a general organismic defect.

Salfield (1950) reports a case of a 7-year-old boy suffering from what he terms "elective mutism." He considers that this condition may be "a part reaction to parental coerciveness." He cites Kanner and Schumacher in support of his claim that some sensitive children develop "elective mutism" as a "fixation at an early infantile level on which an apprehended danger situation is met by a refusal to speak." Werner's (1945) case study of an unwanted child who did not talk until after 5 years of age is of interest in this connection.

Delayed onset of speech in young children whose general behavior seems to rule out mental deficiency and who give evidence of ability to hear may occur on a purely neurotic basis for fairly long periods of time. It should always be given serious consideration, for Bradley (1941) cites several authors who consider speech disturbances, especially mutism, as highly significant in the diagnosis of childhood schizophrenia. Despert (1938) considers it a capital symptom, especially in younger schizophrenic children. These findings, coupled with the frequent clinical observations on speech disturbances in adult schizophrenics (Kasanin, 1944; White, 1949; and Feifel, 1949), certainly would seem to warrant further investigation. They are interesting when considered in conjunction with Beckey's findings that the children with delayed speech played alone and did not seek or want attention. An unpublished study by Sutter is cited by Beckey (1942) in which 13 children with delayed speech were compared with a control group on 96 different traits. The delayed-speech group approxi-

mated the normal in only 10 of these traits. Sutter also noted the tendency of such children to play alone, to make few vocalizations, and to be unusually active physically.

Chapin and Corcoran (1947) describe a highly successful program conducted with 16 "speech-inhibited" children averaging 5.6 years in age who were virtually without speech. After an average of 34 play sessions in a regular nursery group in which they were expected to talk and were treated just like speaking children, and during which intensive observations and individual and group therapy were carried on with the mothers, all the children began to talk, and 12 of the 16 were discharged as speaking normally for their ages or as able to go on to regular school. These results were accomplished over a 5-month period.

In discussing a paper presented by Kanner (1946) on autistic children, Despert points out one characteristic which seems to be common to all young schizophrenic children, regardless of the presenting peculiarities of their speech, and that is the unnatural peculiar voice quality and lack of expressiveness, which makes it hardly seem to belong to the personality. She claims that what Pichon called "la fonction appetitive" or the desire to communicate with others, which manifests itself in infants long before true language emerges and which seems to be associated with emotional tone, is apparently lacking in schizophrenic children.

Several writers, Blanchard (1933), Bender (1940), Russell (1944), Werner (1945), Harle (1946), and Allen (1947), to mention only a few, have reported case studies in which play therapy, nursery school, and kindergarten experiences helped to overcome problems of delayed speech; and many have commented on the tendency to seclusiveness and withdrawal which apparently, in its most extreme form, is the mutism of the child schizophrenic mentioned by Bradley (1941) and by Despert (1938).

Articulatory Defects. In a study by Stinchfield, cited by Beckey (1942), the speech-defective group also presented problems of food finickiness, constipation, sleeplessness, and enuresis. Lack of a speech symbol to express need could account for the enuresis, but both could also be caused by an emotional problem.

Wood (1946) studied 50 children having articulatory defects which were not associated with mental deficiency or organic or hearing involvement, together with their parents, who also were of normal intelligence and hearing. The parents of these children having articulatory defects were found to be much more neurotic than the normative groups on the Bernreuter personality inventory and on the California Test of Personality. The children were not significantly different in personality when measured with the California Test of Personality or with the Pintner Aspects of Personality, but those given Thematic Apperception Tests revealed considerable evidence of frustration, withdrawal, lack of affection, elements of anxiety and insecurity, lack of achievement, aggressiveness, hostility, and escape. In nearly all, these evidences were well substantiated by factual material obtained in case histories. All 50 children received speech therapy, and all improved in their scores on an articulation test. However, the mothers of 25 of the cases received psychotherapy and were assisted to overcome their neuroticism and to develop more social outlets and insight into the children's problems. The children whose mothers received psychotherapy made statistically significantly greater gains in their articulation test scores than the children who merely had speech therapy but whose mothers were not treated.

Stuttering. The repetitions in the speech of 62 young children from 2 to 5 years of age were the subject of detailed study in a series of articles by D. M. Davis (1939, 1940a, b). The repetitions in 1-hour verbatim records in a free play situation were employed. The data indicated that all children of this age range do repeat some words. The distribution of percentages of repetition ranged from 6.2 to 43.9. The author states that, "a child whose speech is such that approximately 1 word in 4 is repeated either in part or in whole in a word or phrase repetition is not presenting any abnormality in speech but is talking 'normally.'" In this connection it should be recalled that first words and many baby words are reduplicated monosyllables and are well accepted by most parents. The data for syllable repetition, however, in D. M. Davis's study revealed a very skewed distribution with 16 of the 62 children showing no syllable repetition. Apparently this type of repetition is more significant for the genesis of stuttering than word or phrase repetition. The types of repetition showed very low intercorrelations ranging from $+.03$ to $+.35$. Syllable repetitions were found to decrease with age, and boys repeated more than girls. A composite measure of all repetitions was negatively correlated with CA $(-.48)$ and with MA $(-.44)$. Correlations of repetitions with mean length of response were $-.48$, and with vocabulary $-.47$. All these relationships approached zero when the measure of repetitions was restricted to syllable repetition, which was the one which seemed to be most related to the genesis of stuttering.

Kastein (1947) also mentions this tendency towards repetition in the speech of normal children. She states that for a period of several weeks or months between 2 and 3 years of age every child is inclined to repeat syllables or words. This tendency she interprets as due to a discrepancy between the thought tempo and the speech tempo. When the child is helped to increase his vocabulary normally, this discrepancy gradually narrows and the repetition disappears. It is apparently at this period that overanxious parents with high standards for their children, and perhaps undue concern over speech because of speech problems in other members of the family, become alarmed at the child's normal repetitiveness and call attention to it. The child thus discovers that this manner of speech is a means of getting attention or of punishing the parents, and a fixation on this level may be created and labeled or diagnosed as stuttering by the parents.

Johnson (1942) studied 46 stuttering children who were compared with a group of 46 nonstutterers between 2 and 9 years of age. He found that in three-fourths of the cases the original diagnosis of stuttering was made by the parents and that with 92 per cent of the stutterers the first phenomena so diagnosed were "beyond doubt essentially effortless repetitions of words, phrases, or the first sounds or syllables." Such repetitions also occurred in the speech of the nonstutterers but were not so labeled by parents who were more relaxed about the onset of speech. In Johnson's study the typical hypertonicity, facial grimaces, etc., of the stutterer were not present at the onset, in his stuttering group, but appeared only later.

In McCarthy's (1947) study several stutterers had to accept the arrival of a younger sibling, of whom they were very jealous, at about 2 years of age, or at just about the time they were probably beginning to combine words into sentences and to attract parental attention with their language. Another frequent age of onset of stuttering is the age of school entrance, which is one of the most serious steps in the emotional weaning of the child. This is the time when he has to accept a parent substitute and at which he makes the tremendously important psychological transition from adjustment to the immediate family circle to the larger world of the school.

Glasner (1949) studied 70 young stutterers between 2 and 5 years of age. Fifty-four per cent of them had feeding problems, 27 per cent were enuretic, and 20 per cent suffered from exaggerated fears or nightmares. He identifies three kinds of stutterers: (1) the relatively healthy child whose environment is confused, (2) the severely disturbed child with stuttering as only one symptom, and (3) the dependent, confused, fearful, shy, anxious, and restless child. The third type he finds by far the most numerous and points out that these children have a background of overprotection and pampering and obsessively perfectionist parents.

Similar conclusions emerge from Moncur's (1951) study, in which 48 stutterers between 5 and 8 years of age were compared with a matched group of nonstutterers. In this study "every stuttering child exhibited several symptoms of maladjustment." A questionnaire given to the mothers of both groups yielded many significant differences between the groups. More mothers of stutterers employed harsh disciplinary measures, threats, shame, humiliation, or corporal punishment. They admitted more inconsistency in discipline from time to time and greater disagreement with the fathers on disciplinary matters. They were more indulgent and pampering especially in regard to eating habits, and there were more illnesses, accidents, and unfortunate health conditions affecting the households of stutterers.

Stein (1949) reports that many of the symptoms observable in stutterers succeed each other in the reverse order in which they appear in infantile speech development. Duncan (1949) found five questions on the Bell Adjustment Inventory which differentiated stutterers from articulatory cases. All the items were indicative of disturbed parent-child relationships.

Reading Disability. By school age the language disorder syndromes have a more widespread manifestation because by this time the child is expected to acquire the secondary forms of language, namely reading and writing, and, as pointed out, because the adjustment to school life is the next big step in the psychological or emotional weaning of the child from the mother. Unfortunately there seem to be ever-increasing numbers of children who fail to learn to read by any of the usual methods of instruction. Schools are continually confronted with the problems of the reading disability case, the poor learner of normal mentality, the mirror reader, and the mirror writer; and remedial programs are having to be provided throughout educational systems to try to meet the problems presented. The approach through remedial methods and techniques is often discouraging until the emotional difficulty is overcome (McCarthy, 1949a).

The argument is often presented that the children who suffer from reading disability problems and other language disorder syndromes are disciplinary problems because of school failure and discouragement (Preston, 1940). This is undoubtedly true, but it is often only a secondary factor. The question is seldom asked why these children failed to learn to read in the first place. Studies of their preschool histories usually reveal that they presented personality problems before the attempt to teach them to read. Delinquents as a group are usually very much retarded in reading and related skills, and, as Gates (1936), Witty and Skinner (1939), and Rogers (1942) have pointed out, children

who cannot read rarely make a constructive adjustment.

McCarthy (1947, 1952b and c) as a result of clinical treatment of approximately 50 cases of language disorder, identified two behavior syndromes usually found among poor readers. One group manifested an aggressive personality syndrome which probably represents the older "protest child" mentioned by Allen (1947) at the preschool level and the delinquent non-readers at higher age levels. The other group manifested a submissive syndrome of infantile behavior. In tracing the aggressive syndrome McCarthy found that it was usually associated with marked parental rejection of the child, harsh disciplinary methods, and unfavorable comparisons with siblings. The submissive group, on the other hand, seemed to be composed of those who were at least superficially, severely overprotected by their parents. This syndrome seems to be associated also with bad health histories, undue concern about health, and a variety of psychosomatic complaints (Despert, 1946b; Krugman, 1946). These children seem to get little expression of real love and affection from their parents except when they are sick, and the parents then manifest undue concern. The basic dynamism seems traceable to emotional insecurity stemming from unwholesome parental attitudes of rejection and overprotection (often inverted rejection due to guilt feelings). The submissive child with overprotective parents seems to be more amenable to psychotherapy and remedial work than the aggressive one and is more likely to be found in a remedial program. The really overprotective mother can be helped to show her love more wisely and to release the child for normal growth without arousing guilt feelings, and the immature child can be helped to grow, whereas it is difficult to make the aggressive child sufficiently secure for learning to progress if there is no basic parental love on which to build.

Sobel (1948) reports that work with children having school difficulties invariably reveals "related if not causative emotional factors" which are often secondary to early warping experiences with significant adults. This ties in well with the study by Milner (1951) cited in the section on the effects of the environment (p. 588).

Stewart (1950) studied 30 bright children from 8 to 12 years. They were divided into contrasting groups on the basis of reading achievement, but the groups were similar in age, intelligence, grade level, and socio-economic background. He found no *single* trait characteristic of all inferior readers or all superior readers. He admits, however, that the parents of many of the inferior readers are "more indulgent, overprotective, and capricious than they are rejecting." This study is obscured by the fact that the control group of good readers was also drawn from the clinic files of maladjusted children who did not happen to show the nonreading symptom as part of their clinical syndromes. It was also handicapped by the search for a single trait rather than for one or more syndromes such as McCarthy (1947) noted.

Carefully matched groups of over 200 "problem readers" and "nonproblem readers" in the parochial schools of Cleveland were studied by Sister Mary Vera (1942). Using the California Test of Personality she found that the "problem readers" had poorer personality adjustment manifesting significantly greater feelings of inferiority, poorer school relations, and greater withdrawal tendencies. This particular group was not characterized by greater neuroticism or by antisocial trends as measured with the group pencil-and-paper test employed. One cannot help wondering, however, how valid are the personality measures obtained when such an instrument is given to the more seriously retarded of the "problem reader" group.

Missildine (1946) studied 30 children with reading disabilities and found that 20 came from homes where the mothers were overtly hostile or of a coercive, perfectionist nature. Only 2 in his group were overprotected. Nearly all his cases harbored severe affective disturbances involving some member or members of their families. He also found the contrasting syndromes, however, for some were described as "restless, indifferent, happy-go-lucky" whereas others were "crushed, unhappy, and inadequate." This author concludes that children who do not respond readily to specific remedial techniques should have a psychiatric examination and that real harm may result if the reading disability is regarded as the primary issue and the basic affective disturbances go untreated. Unfortunately, however, many psychiatrists seize upon the reading failure and are concerned only with the secondary symptoms following prolonged reading failure (Robinson, 1946).

Nondirective therapy was employed by Axline (1947) with 37 second graders who were selected as seriously maladjusted in reading at the end of the first semester. Every child was found to have a serious problem of one kind or another which created anxiety. No remedial instruction was given in reading, but the children were made to feel secure in the classroom situation and were encouraged to talk out their problems while painting or engaging in other creative work. Marked gains in all measures of reading achievement occurred for nearly every child after 3½ months of such therapy. Similar results were obtained by Bills (1950) with 8 retarded readers who received play therapy. The implications of such studies for teaching are indeed challenging.

A very significant evaluation of a therapeutic program was published by Redmont (1948) in which he studied the intensive 6-week summer remedial reading program at Pennsylvania State College. Twenty-four severe reading disability cases were in residence, and each was assigned to a student tutor. Blind Rorschach tests were given to the children and to their tutors before and after the therapy. The nonreading children were insecure, withdrawing, anxious, and rigid, similar to McCarthy's (1947) submissive syndrome. The most striking and probably the most significant finding in Redmount's study was that there was a positive relationship between the quality of the personality organization of the tutor and the amount of improvement in the child in 70 per cent of the cases. The better the teacher adjustment as revealed by the Rorschach, the greater the likelihood of improvement in the child. Although good personality adjustment of the teacher was no guarantee of improvement in the child, teacher maladjustment was definitely associated with adverse or indifferent results for the children in both reading and personality adjustment.

If this emotional insecurity explanation of language disorder syndromes is correct, it is not surprising that there are currently such large numbers of children manifesting basic learning difficulties, for the schools of today are populated entirely with children who have known only depression, war, and post-war years with their accompanying tensions, deprivations, and frustrations exaggerating the insecurity of both adults and children and making it more and more difficult for adults to want, welcome, love, and nurture children in wholesome patterns of family life.

The study of speech in relation to personality has also yielded some interesting trends in the clinical literature on older subjects and adults. There is an increasing recognition among psychologists not only of the importance of language and speech in themselves, as communication, and for intellectual growth and experience but also of the fact that *how* a person speaks and expresses himself in writing is often as important or perhaps more significant for indicating personality adjustment than *what* is said (Lloyd, 1941; Feldman, 1948; Freestone, 1948; and Buxbaum, 1949). Analysis of verbal responses to projective techniques and of sentence completion and association tests have contributed to this trend, for, as Breckenridge and Vincent (1949) state, speech is "a thermometer of the emotions." Gunderson (1942) did an experiment with young school children asking them to name "pretty" words or "kitchen" words, etc., and concluded that for young children words have associations rather than generalized meanings. Skinner (1936) has described the verbal summator which has possibilities as a verbal projective technique, and Sanford (1942) conducted an intensive analysis of the samples of the speech of 2 adults by means of 234 "mechanical," grammatical, "psychogrammatical," and lexical categories. Rostand (1950) has written on grammar and affectivity, and Templin (1938) reported a study of the relationship between aggressiveness and various types of speech defective adults.

There has been a vast expansion since 1944 in the field of semantics which it is impossible to evaluate here. Readers who are interested in this aspect of the problem of language are referred particularly to Walpole (1941) *Semantics,* Johnson (1946) *People in Quandaries,* Seegers (1943), Murray (1941), and Rapaport (1952). Seegers (1943) brings out that as civilization has grown we have complicated communication and increased our dependence on symbols without being sure we know what those symbols mean and that we often forget that two people may use the same word with entirely different meanings. Heinemann (1949) described a homonym test which differentiated between equated delinquent and nondelinquent boys. One outstandingly good item involved association to the homonym "no" "know," the delinquent boys giving associations to the former meaning much more frequently than the normal boys, who tended to associate with the "know" meanings.

Newman (1939) presented case material which shows the affective implications of many of the phenomena of speech, yet he pointed out that, in spite of the clear demonstration of the importance of the affective aspects, "the dogma that the function of language is intellectual and collective still persists." Murray's (1941) brief article harmonized these aspects of language rather well at the same time stressing the importance of language for the betterment of human relations. Although he considered that the function of speech is to facilitate the meeting of ideas and purposes as related to facts and reality, he emphasized that "a corporate part of this process is an increased warmth in the human relations. Security and confidence take the place of fear and anxiety; good fellowship and affection take the place of anger and hostility; respect, mutual support, and cooperation take the place of envy, jealousy, withdrawal, and disruption." Murray also said that any remaining infantilism or residue of childhood egocentrism may come out in speech to mar human relations. He even went so far as to state that "contributing to every breakdown in human relations has been unmeasured poor speech—speech reflecting the symptoms of immaturity." He considers that, as the semanticists constantly

emphasize, there is a large proportion of the population who respond to words as if they were the realities instead of mere symbols of them, and these semantic difficulties permit the feelings rather than the intellect to dominate much of human behavior.

Bibliography

Abt, I. A., H. M. Adler, and P. Bartelme. 1929. The relationship between the onset of speech and intelligence. *J. Amer. Med. Assn.*, *93*, 1351–1355.

Adams, S. 1932. A study of the growth of language between two and four years. *J. Juv. Res.*, *16*, 269–277.

——. 1938. Analysis of verb forms in the speech of young children, and their relation to the language learning process. *J. Exp. Educ.*, *7*, 141–144.

Adams, S., and F. F. Powers. 1929. The psychology of language. *Psychol. Bull.*, *26*, 241–260.

Aldrich, C. A., M. Norval, C. Knop, and F. Venegas. 1946. The crying of newly born babies: IV. Follow-up study after additional nursing care had been provided. *J. Pediat.*, *28*, 665–670.

Aldrich, C. A., C. Sung, and C. Knop. 1945a. The crying of newly born babies: I. The community phase. *J. Pediat.*, *26*, 313–326.

——. 1945b. The crying of newly born babies: II. Individual phase. *J. Pediat.*, *27*, 89–96.

——. 1945c. The crying of newly born babies: III. The early period at home. *J. Pediat.*, *27*, 428–435.

Allen, I. M. 1947. Defect of the speech function in childhood. *New Zealand Med. J.*, *46*, 297–307.

Allport, F. H. 1924. *Social psychology.* Boston: Houghton Mifflin.

Allport, G. W. 1936. Book review of G. K. Zipf. *The psycho-biology of language.* (Boston: Houghton Mifflin, 1935.) *Psychol. Bull.*, *33*, 218–221.

Ament, W. 1899. *Die Entwicklung von Sprechen und Denken beim Kinde.* Leipzig: Wunderlich.

Ames, L. B. 1946. The development of the sense of time in the young child. *J. Genet. Psychol.*, *68*, 97–125.

Ames, L. B., and J. Learned. 1948. The development of verbalized space in the young child. *J. Genet. Psychol.*, *72*, 63–84.

Ammons, R. B., and H. S. Ammons. 1948. The full-range picture vocabulary test. Author, New Orleans. Pp. 2.

Ammons, R. B., P. R. Arnold, and R. S. Herrmann. 1950a. The full-range picture vocabulary test: IV. Results for a white school population. *J. Clin. Psychol.*, *6*, 164–169.

Ammons, R. B., and R. W. Huth. 1949a. The full-range picture vocabulary test: I. Preliminary scale. *J. Psychol.*, *28*, 51–64.

Ammons, R. B., and J. C. Holmes. 1949b. The full-range picture vocabulary test: III. Results for a pre-school age population. *Child Develpm.*, *20*, 5–14.

Ammons, R. B., W. L. Larson, and C. R. Shearn. 1950b. The full-range picture vocabulary test: V. Results for an adult population. *J. Consult. Psychol.*, *14*, 150–155.

Anastasi, A., and R. D'Angelo. 1952. A comparison of Negro and white preschool children in language development and Goodenough draw-a-man IQ. *J. Genet. Psychol.*, *81*, 147–165.

Anderson, I. H., and G. Fairbanks. 1937. Common and differential factors in reading vocabulary and hearing vocabulary. *J. Educ. Res.*, *30*, 317–324.

Anderson, J. E. 1937. An evaluation of various indices of linguistic development. *Child Develpm.*, *8*, 62–68.

——. 1939. The development of spoken language. *Yearb. Nat. Soc. Stud. Educ.*, 38(I), 211–224.

Anon. n.d. Speech retardation: A case study. *Child Res. Clin. Ser.*, *1*, No. 1.

Anon. n.d. Language development in a nursery school child: A case study. *Child Res. Clin. Ser.*, *2*, No. 4.

Arlitt, A. H. 1930. *Psychology of infancy and early childhood.* 2d ed., Ch. XIII, pp. 276–293. New York: McGraw-Hill.

Arsenian, S. 1945. Bilingualism in the post-war world. *Psychol. Bull.*, *42*, 65–86.

Artley, A. S. 1948. A study of certain factors presumed to be associated with reading and speech difficulties. *J. Speech Hearing Disorders*, *13*, 351–360.

Axline, V. 1947. Nondirective therapy for poor readers. *J. Consult. Psychol.*, *11*, 61–69.

Ayres, L. P. 1915. *A measuring scale for ability in spelling.* New York: Russell Sage Foundation.

Azoy, A. 1935. [Results of the investigation of speech defects among the school children of Barcelona.] *Rev. Psicol. Pedag.*, *3*, 265–266.

Bain, R. 1936. The self-and-other words of a child. *Amer. J. Sociol.*, *41*, 767–775.

Baker, H. V. 1942. Children's contributions in elementary school discussions. *Teach. Coll. Child Develpm. Monogr.*, No. 29.

Baker, S. J. 1950. The pattern of language. *J. Gen. Psychol.*, *42*, 25–66.

Baldrian, K. 1940. Ueber das Verhältnis zweichen Denken und Sprache (bei Vollsinnigen, Geistesschwachen und Taubstummen). (Beitrag zur Wertung der Sprache und ihres Trägers Persönlichkeit.) *Archiv. ges. Psychol.*, *105*, 478–481.

Baldwin, B. T., and L. I. Stecher. 1924. *The psychology of the preschool child.* New York: Appleton.

Baldwin, J. M. 1895. *Mental development in the child and the race: Methods and processes.* (3d. ed., 1906.) New York: Macmillan.

Ballenger, H. L. 1931. The validation of the Iowa Elementary Language Tests. *Univ. Iowa Stud. Educ.*, *6*, No. 3.

Bangs, J. L. 1942. A clinical analysis of the articulatory defects of the feebleminded. *J. Speech Disorders*, *7*, 343–356.

Barker, R., J. S. Kounin, and H. F. Wright. 1943. *Child behavior and development: A course of representative studies.* New York: McGraw-Hill.

Barnes, W. 1930, 1931. Language as behavior. *Elem. Engl. Rev.*, *7*, 241–245; *8*, 14–17, 24, 44–46, and 48.

——. 1937. Language as social behavior. *Educ. Meth.*, *16*, 275–288.

Bateman, W. G. 1914. A child's progress in speech. *J. Educ. Psychol.*, *5*, 307–320.

——. 1915. Two children's progress in speech. *J. Educ. Psychol.*, *6*, 475–493.

——. 1916. The language status of three children at the same ages. *Ped. Sem.*, *23*, 211–240.

——. 1917. Papers on language development: I. The first word. *Ped. Sem.*, *24*, 391–398.

Bayley, N. 1933. Mental growth during the first three years. *Genet. Psychol. Monogr.*, *14*, No. 1. Pp. 92.

Bean, C. H. 1932. An unusual opportunity to investigate the psychology of language. *J. Genet. Psychol.*, *40*, 181–202.

Bear, R., and H. Odbert. 1941. Insight of older pupils into their knowledge of word meanings. *Sch. Rev.*, *49*, 754–760.

Beck, R. L. 1933. A natural test of English usage. *J. Exp. Educ.*, *1*, 280–286.

Beckey, R. E. 1942. A study of certain factors related to retardation of speech. *J. Speech Disorders*, *7*, 223–249.

Behrens, H. D. 1939. How children derive meaning. *Educ. Adm. Supervis.*, *25*, 364–369.

Bekhterev, W. M. 1913. *La psychologie objective.* (Trans. from the Russian by N. Kostyleff.) Paris: Alcan.

Bell, S. 1903. The significance of activity in child life. *Independent*, *55*, 911–914.

Bender, J. F. 1940. A case of delayed speech. *J. Speech Disorders*, *5*, 363.

Bennett, C. C. 1938. An inquiry into the genesis of poor reading. *Teach. Coll. Contr. Educ.*, No. 755.

Bentley, M., and E. J. Varon. 1933. An accessory study of "Phonetic Symbolism." *Amer. J. Psychol.*, *45*, 76–86.

Berry, M. 1938. A study of the medical history of stuttering children. *Speech Monogr.*, No. 5.

Berry, M. F., and J. Eisenson. 1942. *The defective in speech.* New York: Crofts. Pp. 426.

Betts, E. A. 1934. An evaluation of certain techniques for the study of oral composition. *Res. Stud. Elem. Sch. Lang.*, No. 1, *Univ. Iowa Stud. Educ.*, *9*, No. 2, 7–35.

——. 1946. *Foundations of reading instruction.* New York: American Book Co. Pp. xiii + 757.

Betzner, J. 1930. Content and form of original compositions dictated by children from five to eight years of age. *Teach. Coll. Contr. Educ.*, No. 442.

Beyer, T. P. 1915. The vocabulary of two years. *Educ. Rev.*, *49*, 191–203.

——. 1916. The vocabulary of three years. *Educ. Rev.*, *52*, 478–489.

Bills, R. E. 1950. Nondirective play therapy with retarded readers. *J. Consult. Psychol.*, *14*, 140–149.

Bilto, E. W. 1941. A comparative study of certain physical abilities of children with speech defects and children with normal speech. *J. Speech Disorders*, *6*, 187–203.

Blachly, M. E. O. 1922. Further notes on eighteen months vocabularies. *Proc. Okla. Acad. Sci., 2 (Univ. Okla. Bull.,* N.S., No. 247), 106–108.

——. 1923. A comparison of the sizes of vocabularies of fifty children of the same age. *Proc. Okla. Acad. Sci., 3 (Univ. Okla. Bull.,* N.S., No. 271), 151–155.

Blanchard, P. 1933. The child with difficulties of adjustment. In C. Murchison (Ed.), *A handbook of child psychology* (2d ed., rev.), Ch. XXII, pp. 858–881. Worcester: Clark University Press.

Blanton, M. G. 1917. Behavior of the human infant during the first thirty days of life. *Psychol. Rev., 24,* 456–483.

Blanton, M. G., and S. Blanton. 1920. *Speech training for children.* New York: Century. Pp. xv + 261.

Blanton, M. G., and S. M. Stinchfield. 1926. *Articulation Test A.* Chicago: Stoelting.

Blanton, S., and M. G. Blanton. 1927. *Child guidance.* New York: Century.

Blatz, W. E., M. I. Fletcher, and M. Mason. 1937. Early development in spoken language of the Dionne quintuplets. In W. E. Blatz *et al., Collected studies on the Dionne quintuplets. Univ. Toronto Stud. Child Develpm. Ser.,* No. 16.

Bloch, O. 1921. Les premiers stades du langage de l'enfant. *J. Psychol. norm. path., 18,* 693–712.

——. 1924. La phrase dans le langage de l'enfant. *J. Psychol. norm. path., 21,* 18–43.

Bloomfield, L. 1933. *Language.* New York: Holt.

Boder, D. P. 1940. The adjective-verb quotient: A contribution to the psychology of language. *Psychol. Rec., 3,* 310–343.

Bohn, W. E. 1914. First steps in verbal expression. *Ped. Sem., 21,* 578–595.

Boyd, W. 1913. The beginnings of syntactical speech: A study in child linguistics. *Child Study, 6,* 21–24, 47–51.

——. 1914. The development of a child's vocabulary. *Ped. Sem., 21,* 95–124.

——. 1927. The development of sentence structure in childhood. *Brit. J. Psychol., 17,* 181–191.

Bradley, C. 1941. *Schizophrenia in childhood.* New York: Macmillan. Pp. 152.

Brandenburg, G. C. 1915. The language of a three-year-old child. *Ped. Sem., 22,* 89–120.

——. 1918. Psychological aspects of language. *J. Educ. Psychol., 9,* 313–332.

Brandenburg, G. C., and J. Brandenburg. 1916. Language development during the fourth year. *Ped. Sem., 23,* 14–29.

——. 1919. Language development during the fourth year: The conversation. *Ped. Sem., 26,* 27–40.

Breckenridge, M. E., and E. L. Vincent. 1949. *Child Development. Physical and psychological growth through the school years,* Ch. 11, pp. 393–426. Philadelphia: Saunders.

Brieland, D. M. 1949. Speech and personality factors in the education of the blind. *Amer. Psychol., 4,* 291–292. (Abstract.)

Brigance, W. N. 1934. The language learning of a child. *J. Appl. Psychol., 18,* 143–154.

Brodbeck, A. J., and O. C. Irwin. 1946. The speech behavior of infants without families. *Child Develpm., 17,* 145–156.

Brooks, F. D., and L. F. Shaffer. 1937. *Child psychology,* Ch. 7, pp. 173–206. Boston: Houghton Mifflin.

Brown, M. S. 1935. Study of the vocabulary used in oral expression by a group of fourth grade children. *Educ. Meth., 15,* 39–44.

Brueckner, L. J. 1939. Language: The development of oral and written composition. Child development and the curriculum. *38th Yearb. Nat. Soc. Stud. Educ.,* pp. 225–240. Bloomington, Ill.: Public School Publ. Co.

Bryngelson, B. 1935. Sidedness as an etiological factor in stuttering. *Ped. Sem. and J. Genet. Psychol., 47,* 204–217.

Buckingham, B. R., and E. W. Dolch. 1936. *A combined word list.* Boston: Ginn.

Bühler, C. 1930. The first year of life. [Trans. by P. Greenberg and R. Ripin from the following three German publications: C. Bühler and H. Hetzer, Inventar der Verhaltungsweisen des ersten Lebensjahres *(Quell. Stud. Jugendk.,* No. 5), Jena: Fischer, 1927, pp. 125–250; H. Hetzer and K. Wolf, Babytests, *Zsch. Psychol.,* 1928, *107,* 62–204; H. Hetzer and L. Koller, Vier Testreihen für das zweite Lebensjahr, *Zsch. Psychol.,* 1930, *117,* 257–306.] New York: Day.

——. 1931. *Kindheit und Jugend.* (3d ed.) Leipzig: Hirzel.

Bühler, C., and H. Hetzer. 1935. *Testing children's development from birth to school age.* New York: Farrar and Rinehart.

Bühler, K. 1930. *Die geistige Entwicklung des Kindes.* (6th ed.) Jena: Fischer. (1st ed., 1918.) (*The mental development of the child.*) New York: Harcourt, Brace; London, Kegan Paul.

——. 1934. *Sprachtheorie.* Jena: Fischer.

Burtt, H. E. 1932. An experimental study of early childhood memory. *J. Genet. Psychol., 40,* 287–295.

——. 1937. A further study of early childhood memory. *J. Genet. Psychol., 50,* 187–192.

Busemann, A. 1925. Die Sprache der Jugend als Ausdruck der Entwicklungsrhythmik: Sprachstatistische Untersuchungen. *(Quel. Stud. Jugendk.)* Jena, Verlag von Gustav Fischer.

Bush, A. D. 1914. The vocabulary of a three-year-old girl. *Ped. Sem., 21,* 125–142.

Buxbaum, E. 1949. The role of a second language in the formation of ego and superego. *Psychoanal. Quart., 18,* 279–289.

Campbell, C. V. 1901. Two recent studies of children's vocabularies. *Child Stud. Mo., 6,* 277–280.

Card, M. S., and F. L. Wells. 1936. Vocal symbol formation as a function of reading ability. *J. Genet. Psychol., 48,* 149–176.

Carlton, T., and L. E. Carlton. 1945. Errors in the oral language of mentally defective adolescents and normal elementary school children. *J. Genet. Psychol., 66,* 183–220.

Carmichael, L. 1933. Origin and prenatal growth of behavior. In C. Murchison (Ed.). *Handbook of child psychology* (2d ed., rev.), pp. 31–159. Worcester: Clark University Press.

Carmichael, L. (Ed.) 1946. *Manual of child psychology.* (1st ed.) The onset and early development of behavior., Ch. 2, pp. 43–166. New York: Wiley.

Carmichael, L., H. P. Hogan, and A. Walter. 1932. An experimental study of the effect of language on the reproduction of visually perceived forms. *J. Exp. Psychol., 15,* 73–86.

Carroll, J. B. 1938. Diversity of vocabulary and the harmonic series law of word-frequency distribution. *Psychol. Rec., 2,* 377–386.

——. 1939. Determining and numerating adjectives in children's speech. *Child Develpm., 10,* 215–229.

Catalano, F., and D. McCarthy. 1952. Infant vocalizations as predictors of intelligence. Unpublished study, Fordham University.

Cattell, P. 1940. *The measurement of intelligence of infants and young children.* New York: The Psychological Corporation; Lancaster, Pa.: Science Press.

Chamberlain, A. F. 1900. *The child: A study in the evolution of man.* New York: Scribner's; London: Scott.

Champneys, F. H. 1881. Notes on an infant. *Mind, 6,* 104–107.

Chapin, A. B., and M. Corcoran. 1947. A program for the speech-inhibited child. *J. Speech Disorders, 12,* 373–376.

Chen, H. P., and O. C. Irwin. 1946a. Infant speech: Vowel and consonant types. *J. Speech Disorders, 11,* 27–29.

——. 1946b. The type-token ratio applied to infant speech sounds. *J. Speech Disorders, 11,* 126–130.

Chess, S. 1944. Developmental language disability as a factor in personality distortion in childhood. *Amer. J. Orthopsychiat., 14,* 483–490.

Chipman, C. E. 1935. The vocabulary of mental defectives. *Proc. Amer. Ass. Stud. Ment. Def., 40,* 485–503.

Chotlos, J. W. 1944. Studies in language behavior: IV. A statistical and comparative analysis of individual written language samples. *Psychol. Monogr., 56,* 77–111.

Christian, A. M., and D. G. Paterson. 1936. Growth of vocabulary in later maturity. *J. Psychol., 1,* 167–169.

Ciampi, L. 1933. La patología del lenguaje en la edad evolutiva. *Bol. Inst. Psiquiat., 5,* 147–163.

Cobb, M. V. 1922. Tentative order of difficulty of the Terman vocabulary with very young children. *J. Educ. Psychol., 13,* 357–362.

Cohen, M. 1933. Observations sur les dernières persistances du langage enfantine. *J. Psychol. norm. path., 30,* 390–399.

Cole, E. M. 1942. The neurologic aspects of defects in speech and reading. *New England J. Med., 226,* 977–980.

——. 1947. Neurological aspects of learning. *Amer. J. Orthopsychiat., 17,* 388–391.

Comas, J. 1931. Contribución al estudio de la génesis psicobiológica del lenguaje hablado. *Rev. de Ped., 10,* 484–490.

Compayré, G. 1896. *The intellectual and moral development of the child:* Pt. 1. (Trans. by M. E. Wilson.) New York: Appleton.

Conradi, E. 1904. The psychology and pathology of speech development. *Ped. Sem., 11,* 328–380.

——. 1912. Speech development and intellectual progress. *J. Educ. Psychol., 3,* 35–38.

Cooley, C. H. 1908. A study of the early use of self-words by a child. *Psychol. Rev., 15,* 339–357.

Cooper, C. A. 1942. Discussion on the relationship between speech disorders and personality defects in children, and how stuttering may unfavorably affect children's personality development. *J. Pediat., 21,* 418–421.

Cornioley, H. 1935. *Die sprachliche Entwicklung eines Kindes von ihren Anfängen bis zum dritten Lebensjahr.* Bern: Lang.

Court, S. R. A. 1910–1920. Linguistic creativeness of a child. *Proc. Okla. Acad. Sci., 1 (Univ. Okla. Bull., N.S., No. 220),* 70.

——. 1926. Some sentences of a boy three years, eight months. *Proc. Okla. Acad. Sci., 6,* Pt. II *(Univ. Okla. Bull., N.S., No. 348),* 334–343.

——. 1927. The growth of a small boy's linguistic interest. *Proc. Okla. Acad. Sci., 7 (Univ. Okla. Bull., N.S., No. 409),* 224–234.

Cousinet, R. 1936. Le monologue enfantin. *J. Psychol. norm. path., 33,* 28–39.

Cowan, M. 1936. Pitch and intensity characteristics of stage speech. *Arch. Speech.* I. Suppl.

Critchley, M. 1939. *The language of gesture.* New York: Longmans, Green; London: Edward Arnold. Pp. 128.

Cuff, N. B. 1930. Vocabulary tests. *J. Educ. Psychol., 21,* 212–220.

——. 1935. Social status and vocabulary. *J. Genet. Psychol., 46,* 226–229.

——. 1937. *Child psychology,* Ch. IX, pp. 160–180. Louisville: Standard Printing Co.

Curry, E. T. 1950. An experimental study of the relative identification thresholds of nine American vowels. *Speech Monogr., 17,* 90–94.

Curti, M. W. 1938. *Child psychology.* (2d ed.) New York: Longmans, Green.

Dale, E. 1931. Difficulties in vocabulary research. *Educ. Res. Bull., 10,* 119–122.

——. 1949. *Bibliography of vocabulary studies.* Bureau of Educational Research, Ohio State University. Pp. v + 101.

Daniels, E. M. 1940. An analysis of the relation between handedness and stuttering with special reference to the Orton-Travis theory of cerebral dominance. *J. Speech Disorders, 5,* 309–326.

Darcy, N. T. 1946. The effect of bilingualism upon the measurement of the intelligence of children of preschool age. *J. Educ. Psychol., 37,* 21–44.

Darwin, C. 1877. Biographical sketch of an infant. *Mind, 2,* 285–294.

David, D. 1925. The development of language habits. *J. Educ. Meth., 5,* 155–160.

Davis, D. M. 1939. The relation of repetitions in the speech of young children to certain measures of language maturity and situational factors: Pt. I. *J. Speech Disorders, 4,* 303–318.

Davis, D. M. 1940a. The relation of repetitions in the speech of young children to certain measures of language maturity and situational factors: Pt. II. *J. Speech Disorders, 5,* 235–241.

——. 1940b. The relation of repetitions in the speech of young children to certain measures of language maturity and situational factors: Pt. III. *J. Speech Disorders, 5,* 242–246.

Davis, E. A. 1932. The form and function of children's questions. *Child Develpm., 3,* 57–74.

——. 1937a. *The development of linguistic skill in twins, singletons with siblings, and only children from age five to ten years.* (Inst. Child Welfare Monogr. Ser., No. 14.) Minneapolis: University of Minnesota Press. Pp. ix + 165.

——. 1937b. Mean sentence length compared with long and short sentences as a reliable measure of language development. *Child Develpm., 8,* 69–79.

——. 1937c. Development in the use of proper names. *Child Develpm., 8,* 270–272.

——. 1937d. The mental and linguistic superiority of only girls. *Child Develpm., 8,* 139–143.

——. 1938a. Developmental changes in the distribution of parts of speech. *Child Develpm., 9,* 309–317.

——. 1938b. Basic English in the speech of American children. *Sch. and Soc., 48,* 665–668.

——. 1939. Accuracy versus error as a criterion in children's speech. *J. Educ. Psychol., 30,* 365–371.

——. 1941. The location of the subordinate clause in oral and written language. *Child Develpm., 12,* 333–338.

Davis, I. P. 1938. The speech aspects of reading readiness. *Newer Practices in Reading in the Elementary School. In Seventeenth Yearb. Dept. Elem. Sch. Prins.* Washington, D. C.

Davis, T. K. 1938. Sounds in language. *J. Nerv. Ment. Dis., 88,* 49–99.

Dawe, H. C. 1942. A study of the effect of an educational program upon language development and related mental functions in young children. *J. Exp. Educ., 11,* 200–209.

Day, E. J. 1932. The development of language in twins: I. A comparison of twins and single children. *Child Develpm., 3,* 179–199.

Dearborn, G. V. N. 1910. *Moto-sensory development: Observations on the first three years of childhood.* Baltimore: Warwick and York.

Decroly, O. 1930. *Le développement du langage parlé chez l'enfant.* Liège: Edition Biblio.

——. c. 1934. *Comment l'enfant arrive à parler.* Vols. I and II. Cahiers de la Centrale. (Revu et complété par J. Decroly et J. E. Segers.) *Cent. du P.E.S. de Belgique,* Vol. 8.

Delacroix, H. 1930. *Le langage et la pensée.* (2d ed.) Paris: Alcan.

DeLaguna, G. A. 1927. *Speech: Its function and development.* New Haven: Yale University Press.

Della Vallee, G. 1931. Le prime fasi dello sviluppo del linguaggio infantile. *Riv. ped., 24,* 1–35.

Dennis, W. 1943. Mr. Janus on children's language. *J. Genet. Psychol., 63,* 183–185.

Descoeudres, A. 1921. Le développement de l'enfant de deux à sept ans. Neuchâtel et Paris: Delachaux et Niestlé.

——. 1924. La mesure du langage de l'enfant. *J. Psychol. norm. path., 21,* 43–47.

Despert, J. L. 1938. Schizophrenia in children. *Psychiat. Quart., 12,* 366–371.

——. 1946a. Anxiety, phobias and fears in young children. *Nerv. Child, 1,* 3–15.

——. 1946b. Psychosomatic study of fifty stuttering children. *Amer. J. Orthopsychiat., 16,* 100–113.

Deville, G. 1890. Notes sur le développement du langue. *Rev. linguistique et philol. comp., 23,* 330–343.

Dewey, E. 1935. *Infant behavior.* New York: Columbia University Press.

Dewey, G. 1923. *Relativ frequency of English speech sounds.* (Harv. Monogr. Educ., IV.) Cambridge: Harvard University Press. Pp. xii + 148.

Dewey, J. 1894. The psychology of infant language. *Psychol. Rev., 1,* 63–66.

——. 1926. *Experience and nature.* New York: Norton.

Dolch, E. W. 1925. *Reading and word meanings.* Boston: Ginn.

——. 1927. Grade vocabularies. *J. Educ. Res., 16,* 16–26.

Doran, E. W. 1907. A study of vocabularies. *Ped. Sem., 14,* 401–438.

Drever, J. 1915–1916. A study of children's vocabularies: I, II, and III. *J. Exp. Ped., 3,* 34–43; 96–103; 182–188.

——. 1919. The vocabulary of a free kindergarten child. *J. Exp. Ped., 5,* 28–37.

Driggs, H. W. 1934. The vocabulary of letters of boys and girls 12 to 15 years of age inclusive. *J. Exp. Educ., 2,* 339–354.

Drummond, M. 1916. Notes on speech development: I. *Child Study, 9,* 83–86.

——. 1925. *Five years old or thereabouts.* London: Edward Arnold.

Duncan, M. H. 1949. Home adjustment of stutterers versus non-stutterers. *J. Speech Hearing Disorders, 14,* 255–259.

Eames, T. H. 1950. The relationship of reading and speech difficulties. *J. Educ. Psychol., 41,* 51–55.

Eaton, H. S. 1940. *Semantic frequency list for English, French, German, and Spanish: A correlation of the first six thousand words in four single-language frequency lists.* Chicago: University of Chicago Press.

Eberhardt, M. 1940. A summary of some preliminary investigations of the deaf. *Psychol. Monogr., 52,* No. 1, 1–5.

Egger, M. E. 1879. *Observations et reflexions sur le développement de l'intelligence et du langage chez les enfants.* Paris: Picard.

Eisenson, J. 1938. *The psychology of speech.* New York: Crofts. Pp. 280.

Eisenson, J., and M. F. Berry. 1942. The biological aspects of stuttering. *J. Genet. Psychol., 61,* 147–152.

Ellesor, M. V. 1934. The relation between situation

and response in vocalization of a three-year-old child. *Child Develpm., 5,* 158–164.

Ellsworth, R. B. 1951. The regression of schizophrenic language. *J. Consult. Psychol., 15,* 387–391.

Esper, E. A. 1921. The psychology of language. *Psychol. Bull., 18,* 490–496.

——. 1925. A technique for the experimental investigation of associative interference in artificial linguistic material. *Lang. Monogr.,* No. 1. Pp. 46.

——. 1933. Studies in linguistic behavior organization: I. Characteristics of unstable verbal reactions. *J. Gen. Psychol., 8,* 346–381.

——. 1935. Language. In C. Murchison (Ed.), *A handbook of social psychology,* pp. 417–460. Worcester: Clark University Press.

Fahey, G. L. 1942. The questioning activity of children. *J. Genet. Psychol., 60,* 337–357.

Fairbanks, G., E. L. Herbert, and J. M. Hammond. 1949a. An acoustical study of vocal pitch in seven- and eight-year-old girls. *Child Develpm., 20,* 71–78.

Fairbanks, G., J. H. Wiley, and F. M. Lassman. 1949b. An acoustical study of vocal pitch in seven- and eight-year-old boys. *Child Develpm., 20,* 63–70.

Feifel, H. 1949. Qualitative differences in the vocabulary responses of normals and abnormals. *Genet. Psychol. Monogr., 39,* 151–204.

Feifel, H., and I. Lorge. 1950. Qualitative differences in the vocabulary responses of children. *J. Educ. Psychol., 41,* 1–18.

Feldman, F., and D. E. Cameron. 1944. Speech in senility. *Amer. J. Psychiat., 101,* 64–67.

Feldman, S. S. 1948. Mannerisms of speech; a contribution to the working through process. *Psychoanal. Quart., 17,* 356–367.

Feldmann, H. 1833. *De statu normali functionum corporis humani.* Dissertation, Bonn.

Fenton, J. C. 1925. *A practical psychology of babyhood.* Boston: Houghton Mifflin.

Firth, J. R. 1930. *Speech.* London: Benn.

Fisher, M. S. 1932. Language patterns of preschool children. *J. Exp. Educ., 1,* 70–74.

——. 1934. Language patterns of preschool children. *Child Develpm. Monogr.,* No. 15. Pp. xvi + 88.

Fisichelli, R. M. 1950. A study of prelinguistic speech development of institutionalized infants. Unpublished Ph.D. dissertation, Fordham University.

Fitchen, M. 1931. Speech and music development of a one-year-old child. *Child Develpm., 2,* 324–326.

Fitzgerald, J. A. 1934a. Letters written outside the school by children of the 4th, 5th, and 6th grades: A study of vocabulary, spelling errors and situations. *Univ. Iowa Stud., 9,* No. 1, 9–50.

——. 1934b. The vocabulary of children's letters written in life outside the school. *Elem. Sch. J., 34,* 358–370.

——. 1936. The overlap of child and adult vocabularies. *J. Exp. Educ., 4,* 364–367.

——. 1938. The vocabulary and spelling errors of third grade children's life-letters. *Elem. Sch. J., 38,* 518–527.

Flemming, V. V. 1942. A study of Stanford-Binet vocabulary attainment and growth in children in the city of Mooseheart, Ill., as compared with children living in their own homes. *J. Genet. Psychol., 60,* 359–373.

Foulke, K., and S. M. Stinchfield. 1929. The speech development of four infants under two years of age. *J. Genet. Psychol., 36,* 140–171.

Fowler, M. B. 1947. The role of language in early child development. *Childhood Educ., 17,* 247–252.

Franke, C. 1899. Sprachentwickelung der Kinder und der Menschheit. In Reins (Ed.), *Encyklopädischem Handbuch der Pädagogik.* Langensalza: Beyer.

Frankel, L. R. 1936. The theory of regression. *J. Speech Disorders,* 1, 107–112.

Freestone, N. W. 1948. The wish for defective speech. *J. Speech Hearing Disorders, 13,* 119–130.

Freud, A., and D. T. Burlingham. 1944. *Infants without families.* New York: International Universities Press. Pp. 128.

Friedrich, G. 1906. Psychologische Beobachtungen an zwei Knaben: Beiträge zur Kinderforschung und Heilerziebung. *Beih. z. Kinderforsch.,* No. 17.

Fries, C. C., and A. A. Traver. 1940. *English word lists: A study of their adaptability for instruction.* Washington, D. C.: American Council on Education.

Froeschels, E. (Ed.) 1948. *Twentieth century speech and voice correction.* New York: Philosophical Library.

Fuller, L. 1936. The effect of kindergarten speech training on primary grade progress and achievement of children with foreign language handicap. *Calif. J. Elem. Educ., 4,* 165–173.

Gaines, F. P. 1941. Interrelations of speech and reading disabilities. *Elem. Sch. J., 41,* 605–613.

Gale, H. 1902. The vocabularies of three children in one family at two and three years of age. *Ped. Sem., 9,* 422–433.

Gale, M. C., and H. Gale. 1901. Children's vocabularies. *Pop. Sci. Mo., 61,* 45–51.

——. 1906. Vocabularies of three children in one family to two and one-half years of age. *Psychol. Stud., Univ. Minn.,* No. 1, pp. 70–117.

Gansl, I. 1939. Vocabulary: Its measurement and growth. *Arch. Psychol., N. Y.,* No. 236.

Gardiner, A. H. 1922. The definition of the word and the sentence. *Brit. J. Psychol., 12,* 352–361.

——. 1932. *The theory of speech and language.* New York: Oxford University Press.

Garrison, K. C. 1930. The relationship between three different vocabulary abilities. *J. Educ. Res., 21,* 43–45.

Garrison, K. C., and M. Thomas. 1930. A study of some literature appreciation abilities as they relate to certain vocabulary abilities. *J. Educ. Res., 22,* 396–399.

Garrison, S. C., and K. C. Garrison. 1929. *The psychology of elementary school subjects,* pp. 207–266. New York: Johnson.

Gaskill, H. V. 1941. Language responses and intelligence. I. Verbalization and intelligence. *J. Genet. Psychol., 58,* 407–417.

Gates, A. I. 1935. A reading vocabulary for the primary grades. (Rev. ed.) New York: Teachers College, Columbia University.

Gates, A. I. 1936. Failure in reading and social maladjustment. *J. Nat. Educ. Ass., 25*, 205–206.

——. 1941. The role of personality maladjustment in reading disability. *J. Genet. Psychol., 59*, 77–83.

Gatewood, M. C., and A. P. Weiss. 1930. Race and sex differences in newborn infants. *J. Genet. Psychol., 38*, 31–49.

Gerlach, F. M. 1917. *Vocabulary studies.* (*Stud. Educ. Psychol.*, No. 1.) Colorado Springs: Colorado College.

Gerstein, R. A. 1949. A suggested method for analyzing and extending the use of Bellevue-Wechsler vocabulary responses. *J. Consult. Psychol., 13*, 366–370.

Gerwitz, J. L. 1948a. Studies in word-fluency: I. Its relation to vocabulary and mental age in young children. *J. Genet. Psychol., 72*, 165–176.

——. 1948b. Studies in word fluency: II. Its relation to eleven items of child behavior. *J. Genet. Psychol., 72*, 177–184.

Gesell, A. 1925. *The mental growth of the preschool child: A psychological outline of normal development from birth to the sixth year, including a system of developmental diagnosis.* New York: Macmillan.

——. 1928. *Infancy and human growth.* New York: Macmillan.

——. 1940, 1941. *Wolf child and human child: Being a narrative interpretation of the life history of Kamala, the wolf girl.* New York: Harper.

Gesell, A., and C. S. Amatruda. 1941. *Developmental diagnosis normal and abnormal child development, clinical methods and practical applications.* New York: Hoeber, Med. Book Dept. of Harper. Pp. xiii + 447.

Gesell, A., H. M. Halverson, H. Thompson, F. L. Ilg, B. M. Castner, L. B. Ames, and C. S. Amatruda. 1940. *The first five years of life, a guide to the study of the preschool child.* Ch. VIII, by B. M. Castner. New York: Harper.

Gesell, A., and F. L. Ilg. 1943. *Infant and child in the culture of today.* New York: Harper. Pp. xii + 399.

——. 1946. *The child from five to ten*, pp. 395–399. New York: Harper.

Gesell, A., and E. Lord. 1927. A psychological comparison of nursery-school children from homes of low and high economic status. *J. Genet. Psychol., 34*, 339–356.

Gesell, A., and H. Thompson, assisted by C. S. Amatruda. 1934. *Infant behavior: Its genesis and growth*, pp. 243–257, 286–291. New York: McGraw-Hill.

Gesell, A., H. Thompson, and C. S. Amatruda. 1938. *The psychology of early growth.* New York: Macmillan.

Gheorgov, I. A. 1905. Die ersten Anfänge des sprachlichen Ausdrucks für das Selbstbewusstsein bei Kindern. *Arch. ges. Psychol., 5*, 329–404.

Gilkey, B. G., and F. W. Parr. 1944. An analysis of the reversal tendency of fifty selected elementary-school pupils. *J. Educ. Psychol., 35*, 284–292.

Glasner, P. J. 1949. Personality characteristics and emotional problems in stutterers under the age of five. *J. Speech Hearing Disorders, 14*, 135–138.

Goldenberg, S. 1950. An exploratory study of some aspects of idiopathic language retardation. *J. Speech Hearing Disorders, 15*, 221–233.

Goldfarb, W. 1943a. Infant rearing and problem behavior. *Amer. J. Orthopsychiat., 13*, 249–265.

——. 1943b. The effects of early institutional care on adolescent personality. *J. Exp. Educ., 12*, 106–129.

——. 1945. Effects of psychological deprivation in infancy and subsequent stimulation. *Amer. J. Psychiat., 102*, 18–33.

Goldstein, K. 1948. *Language and language disturbances.* New York: Grune & Stratton. Pp. xii + 374.

Goodenough, F. L. 1927. Consistency of sex differences in mental traits at various ages. *Psychol. Rev., 34*, 440–462.

——. 1928. *The Kuhlmann-Binet tests for children of preschool age: A critical study and evaluation.* (*Inst. Child Welfare Monogr. Ser.*, No. 2.) Minneapolis: University of Minnesota Press. Pp. viii + 146.

——. 1930. Interrelationships in the behavior of young children. *Child Develpm., 1*, 29–47.

——. 1931. *Anger in young children.* (*Inst. Child Welfare Monogr. Ser.*, No. 9.) Minneapolis: University of Minnesota Press. Pp. xiii + 278.

——. 1938. The use of pronouns by young children: A note on the development of self-awareness. *J. Genet. Psychol., 52*, 333–346.

——. 1945. *Developmental psychology*, pp. 248–259. New York: Appleton-Century-Crofts.

Goodenough, F. L., and C. R. Brian. 1929. Certain factors underlying the acquisition of motor skill by preschool children. *J. Exp. Psychol., 12*, 127–155.

Goodenough, F. L., K. M. Maurer, and M. J. Van Wagenen. 1935, 1940. *Minnesota preschool scale manual*, Forms A and B. Minneapolis: Educational Test Bureau.

Goodman, M. 1936. Language development in a nursery school child. *Child Res. Clin. Ser., 2*, No. 4.

Grabo, R. P. 1930. *A study of comparative vocabularies of junior high school pupils in English and Italian speaking homes.* Schenectady, N. Y.: Public Schools.

Graff, W. L. 1932. *Language and languages.* New York: Appleton.

Granich, L., and G. W. Pangle. 1947. *Aphasia: A guide to retraining.* New York: Grune & Stratton. Pp. v + 108.

Grant, J. R. 1915. A child's vocabulary and its growth. *Ped. Sem., 22*, 183–203.

Gray, L. H. 1939. *Foundations of language.* New York: Macmillan.

Gray, M. 1940. The X family: A clinical and laboratory study of a "stuttering" family. *J. Speech Disorders, 5*, 343–348.

Grégoire, A. 1933. L'apprentissage de la parole pendant les deux premières années de l'enfance. *J. Psychol. norm. path.*, *30*, 375–389.

——. 1937. *L'apprentissage du langage: les deux premières années*. Paris: Droz.

——. 1947. *L'apprentissage du langage: II. La troisieme année et les années suivantes*. Liege-Paris: Droz. Pp. 491.

Grigsby, O. J. 1932. An experimental study of the development of concepts of relationship in preschool children as evidenced by their expressive ability. *J. Exp. Educ.*, *1*, 144–162.

Guernsey, M. 1928. Eine genetische Studie über Nachahmung. *Z. Psychol.*, *107*, 105–178.

Guiler, W. S. 1926. Analysis of children's writings as a basis for instruction in English. *J. Educ. Meth.*, *5*, 258–264.

Guillaume, P. 1925. *L'imitation chez l'enfant*. Paris: Alcan.

——. 1927a. Les débuts de la phrase dans le langage de l'enfant. *J. Psychol. norm. path.*, *24*, 26–77.

——. 1927b. Le développement du langage chez l'enfant. *J. Psychol. norm. path.*, *24*, 203–229.

Gunderson, A. G. 1942. Young child and word meanings. *Elem. Engl. Rev.*, *19*, 51–54.

Haggerty, L. C. G. 1930. What a two-and-one-half-year-old child said in one day. *J. Genet. Psychol.*, *38*, 75–100.

Haggerty, M. E., and H. B. Nash. 1924. Mental capacity of children and paternal occupation. *J. Educ. Psychol.*, *15*, 559–572.

Hahn, E. 1948. Analyses of the content and form of the speech of first grade children. *Quart. J. Speech*, *34*, 361–366.

Hall, G. S. 1891a. Notes on the study of infants. *Ped. Sem.*, *1*, 127–138.

——. 1891b. The contents of children's minds on entering school. *Ped. Sem.*, *1*, 139–173.

Hall, Mrs. W. S. 1896–1897. The first 500 days of a child's life: V. *Child Study*, No. 2, 586–608.

Hamill, R. C. 1941. Speech as a pattern of behavior. *Arch. Neurol. Psychiat.*, *46*, 543–544. (Abstract.)

Hanley, T. D. 1951 An analysis of vocal frequency and duration characteristics of selected samples of speech from three American dialect regions. *Speech Monogr.*, *18*, 78–93.

Harle, M. 1946. Dynamic interpretation and treatment of acute stuttering in a young child. *Amer. J. Orthopsychiat.*, *16*, 156–162.

Harris, C. W. 1948. An exploration of language skill patterns. *J. Educ. Psychol.*, *39*, 321–336.

Hartmann, G. W. 1941. A critique of the common method of estimating vocabulary size, together with some data on the absolute word knowledge of educated adults. *J. Educ. Psychol.*, *32*, 351–364.

Hawk, S. S. 1937. Moto-kinaesthetic speech training for children. *J. Speech Disorders*, *2*, 231–237.

——. 1938. Does the intelligence quotient change with speech training? *West. Speech*, *2*, 1, 4.

Hawthorne, J. W. 1934. An attempt to measure certain phases of speech. *J. Gen. Psychol.*, *10*, 399–414.

Hazlitt, V. 1933. *The psychology of infancy*. Ch. V, pp. 49–63. New York: Dutton.

Heidbreder, E. 1936. Language and concepts. *Psychol. Bull.*, *33*, 724.

Heider, F. 1935. The rôle of language in the psychological situation of the child: A comparative study of free play among deaf and among hearing children of preschool ages. *Psychol. Bull.*, *32*, 728–729.

Heider, F. K., and G. M. Heider. 1940a. A study of phonetic symbolism of deaf children. *Psychol. Monogr.*, *52*, No. 1, 23–41.

——. 1940b. A comparison of sentence structure of deaf and hearing children. *Psychol. Monogr.*, *52*, No. 1, 42–103.

Heilig, M. 1913. A child's vocabulary. *Ped. Sem.*, *20*, 1–16.

Heinemann, R. 1949. The differentiation of delinquent from non-delinquent boys by means of a homonym free association test. Unpublished M.A. dissertation, Fordham University.

Henle, M., and M. B. Hubbell. 1938. "Egocentricity" in adult conversation. *J. Soc. Psychol.*, *9*, 227–234.

Henrikson, E. H. 1948. An analysis of Wood's articulation index. *J. Speech Hearing Disorders*, *13*, 233–235.

Hess, J. H., G. J. Mohr, and P. E. Bartelme. 1934. *The physical and mental growth of prematurely born children*. Chicago: University of Chicago Press. Pp. 449.

Hetzer, H., and B. Reindorf. 1928. Sprachentwicklung und soziales Milieu. *Z. angew. Psychol.*, *29*, 449–462.

Hildreth, G. 1948. A comparison of the Dale, Dolch, and Rinsland word lists. *J. Educ. Psychol.*, *39*, 40–46.

Hills, E. C. 1914. The speech of a child two years of age. *Dialect Notes*, *4*, 84–100.

Hinckley, A. C. 1915. A case of retarded speech development. *Ped. Sem.*, *22*, 121–146.

Hockett, C. F. 1950. Age grading and linguistic change. *Language*, *26*, 449–457.

Holden, E. S. 1877. On the vocabularies of children under two years. *Trans. Amer. Philol. Assn.*, *8*, 58–68.

Holley, C. E. 1919. Holley sentence vocabulary scale. Bloomington, Ill.: Public School Publishing Co.

Hollingworth, H. L. 1927. *Mental growth and decline*. New York: Appleton.

——. 1938. Verbal Gestalt experiments with children. *J. Exp. Psychol.*, *23*, 90–95.

Holmes, U. T. 1926–1927. The phonology of an English child. *Amer. Speech*, *2*, 219–225.

Hoppes, W. C. 1934. Considerations in the development of children's language. *Elem. Engl. Rev.*, *11*, 66–70.

Horn, E. 1925. The commonest words in the spoken vocabulary of children up to and including six years of age. *Yearb. Nat. Soc. Stud. Educ.*, 24(I), 186–198.

——. 1926. A basic writing vocabulary. *Univ. Iowa Monogr. Educ.*, 1st Ser. No. 4.

Horn, E. 1942. Language and meaning. *Yearb. Nat. Soc. Stud. Educ.,* 41(II), 377–413.

Horn, M. D. 1926–1927a. The thousand and three words most frequently used by kindergarten children. *Child. Educ., 3,* 118–122.

——. 1926–1927b. Sectional differences in the vocabulary of kindergarten children. *Child. Educ., 3,* 180–182.

Howard, R. W. 1946. The language development of a group of triplets. *J. Genet. Psychol., 69,* 181–188. (See also unpublished study, 1934, on this topic on file at the University of Minnesota.)

Hoyer, A., and G. Hoyer. 1924. Ueber die Lallsprache eines Kindes. *Z. angew. Psychol., 24,* 363–384.

Huang, I., and Y. J. Chu. 1936. The social function of children's language. *Chung Hua Educ. Rev., 23,* No. 7, 69–94.

Hudgins, C. V. 1934. A comparative study of the speech coordination of deaf and normal subjects. *J. Genet. Psychol., 44,* 3–48.

——. 1939. Report of the Clarence W. Barron Research Department: Experimental phonetics. *A. R. Clarke Sch. for the Deaf, 72,* 31–39.

Hudgins, C. V., and F. C. Numbers. 1942. An investigation of the intelligibility of the speech of the deaf. *Genet. Psychol. Monogr., 25,* 289–392.

Hughson, W., A. Ciocco, E. G. Witting, and P. S. Lawrence. 1942. Studies of pupils of the Pennsylvania School for the Deaf: III. An analysis of speech characteristics in deafened children with observations on training methods. *Child. Develpm., 13,* 131–158.

Hull, C. L., and B. I. Hull. 1919. Parallel learning curves of an infant in vocabulary and in voluntary control of the bladder. *Ped. Sem., 26,* 272–283.

Humphreys, W. 1880. A contribution to infantile linguistics. *Trans. Amer. Philol. Assn., 9,* 5–17.

Huyck, E. M. 1940. The hereditary factors in speech. *J. Speech Disorders, 5,* 295–304.

International Kindergarten Union. 1928. *A study of the vocabulary of children before entering the first grade.* Baltimore: Williams and Wilkins.

Irwin, O. C. 1941a. Research on speech sounds for the first six months of life. *Psychol. Bull., 38,* 277–285.

——. 1941b. The profile as a visual device for indicating central tendencies in speech data. *Child Develpm., 12,* 111–120.

——. 1942. The developmental status of speech sounds of ten feeble-minded children. *Child Develpm., 13,* 29–39.

——. 1945. Reliability of infant speech sound data. *J. Speech Disorders, 10,* 227–235.

——. 1946a. Infant speech equations for consonant-vowel ratios. *J. Speech Disorders, 11,* 177–180.

——. 1946b. In P. L. Harriman (Ed.), *Encyclopedia of psychology,* pp. 274–276. New York: Philosophical Library.

——. 1946c. Speech sound mastery during infancy. *Amer. Psychol., 1,* 252. (Abstract.)

——. 1947a. Development of speech during infancy: Curve of phonemic frequencies. *J. Exp. Psychol., 37,* 187–193.

Irwin, O. C. 1947b. Infant speech: The problem of variability. *J. Speech Disorders, 12,* 173–176.

——. 1947c. Infant speech: Variability and the problem of diagnosis. *J. Speech Disorders, 12,* 287–289.

——. 1947d. Infant speech: Consonantal sounds according to place of articulation. *J. Speech Disorders, 12,* 397–401.

——. 1947e. Infant speech: Consonant sounds according to manner of articulation. *J. Speech Disorders, 12,* 402–404.

——. 1947f. The mastery of vowel and consonant sounds during the period of infancy. *Amer. Psychol., 2,* 314. (Abstract.)

——. 1948a. Infant speech: Development of vowel sounds. *J. Speech Hearing Disorders, 13,* 31–34.

——. 1948b. Infant speech: The effect of family occupational status and of age on use of sound types. *J. Speech Hearing Disorders, 13,* 224–226.

——. 1948c. Infant speech: The effect of family occupational status and of age on sound frequency. *J. Speech Hearing Disorders, 13,* 320–323.

——. 1948d. Speech sound development of sibling and only infants. *J. Exp. Psychol., 38,* 600–602.

——. 1949. Infant speech. *Sci. Amer., 18,* 22–24.

——. 1951. Infant speech: Consonantal position. *J. Speech Hearing Disorders, 16,* 159–161.

Irwin, O. C., and H. P. Chen. 1941. A reliability study of speech sounds observed in the crying of newborn infants. *Child Develpm., 12,* 351–368.

——. 1943. Speech sound elements during the first years of life; a review of the literature. *J. Speech Disorders, 8,* 109–121.

——. 1945. Infant speech sounds and intelligence. *J. Speech Disorders, 10,* 293–295.

——. 1946a. Development of speech during infancy: Curve of phonemic types. *J. Exp. Psychol., 36,* 431–436.

——. 1946b. Infant speech: Vowel and consonant frequency. *J. Speech Disorders, 11,* 123–125.

Irwin, O. C., and T. Curry. 1941. Vowel elements in the crying vocalization of infants under ten days of age. *Child Develpm., 12,* 99–109.

Irwin, R. B. 1946. Speech comes to a five year old boy. *J. Speech Disorders, 11,* 197–203.

Jackson, J. 1944. A survey of psychological, social and environmental differences between advanced and retarded readers. *J. Genet. Psychol., 65,* 113–131.

Jakobson, R. 1941. *Kindersprache, Aphasie und allgemeine Luntgesetze.* Upsala: Almquist & Wiksell.

Janus, S. Q. 1943. An investigation of the relationship between children's language and their play. *J. Genet. Psychol., 62,* 3–61.

Jegi, J. I. 1901. The vocabulary of the two-year-old child. *Child Stud. Mo., 6,* 241–261.

Jenkins, F. 1915. A test of the ability of children to use language forms. *J. Educ. Psychol., 6,* 335–344.

Jenkins, R. L. 1941. The rate of diadochocinetic movements of the jaw at the ages from 7 to maturity. *J. Speech Disorders, 6,* 13–22.

Jersild, A. T. 1947. *Child psychology.* (Rev. and enlarged.) New York: Prentice-Hall.

Jersild, A. T., and R. Ritzman. 1938. Aspects of language development: The growth of loquacity and vocabulary. *Child Develpm., 9,* 243–259.

Jespersen, O. 1922, 1923. *Language: Its nature, development and origin.* New York: Holt; London: Allen and Winous.

——. 1933. *Essentials of English grammar.* New York: Holt.

Johnson, E. C., and C. C. Josey. 1931. A note on the development of the thought forms of children as described by Piaget. *J. Abnorm. Soc. Psychol., 26,* 338–339.

Johnson, H. M. 1928. *Children in the nursery school.* New York: Day.

Johnson, W. 1939. Language and speech hygiene: An application of general semantics. *Monogr. Inst. Gen. Semantics,* No. 1. Pp. 54.

——. 1942. A study of the onset and development of stuttering. *J. Speech Disorders, 7,* 251–257.

——. 1944. Studies in language behavior: I. A program of research. *Psychol. Monogr., 56,* 1–15.

——. 1946. *People in quandaries.* New York: Harper. Pp. 532.

Johnson, W. (Ed.) 1950. *Speech problems of children.* New York: Grune & Stratton. Pp. xxii + 265.

Johnson, W., S. F. Brown, J. F. Curtis, C. W. Edney, and J. Keaster. 1948. *Speech handicapped school children.* New York: Harper. Pp. xv + 464.

Joos, M. 1948. Acoustic phonetics. Supplement to *Language,* Linguistic Society of America, *24,* No. 2. Pp. 136.

Kanner, L. 1946. Irrelevant and metaphorical language in early infantile autism. *Amer. J. Psychiat., 103,* 242–246.

Kantor, J. R. 1928. Can psychology contribute to the study of linguistics? *Monist, 38,* 630–648.

Karlin, I. W. 1947. A psychosomatic theory of stuttering. *J. Speech Disorders, 12,* 319–322.

Karlin, I. W., and A. E. Sobel. 1940. A comparative study of the blood chemistry of stutterers and non-stutterers. *Speech Monogr., 7,* 75–84.

Kasanin, J. S. (Ed.) 1944. *Language and thought in schizophrenia.* Berkeley: University of California Press. Pp. 133.

Kastein, S. 1947. The chewing method of treating stuttering. *J. Speech Disorders, 12,* 195–198.

Katz, D., and R. Katz. 1927. *Gespräche mit Kindern (Untersuchungen zur Socialpsychologie und Pädagogik).* Berlin: Springer.

Kaulfers, W. 1928. The prognostic value of general language. *Sch. & Soc., 28,* 662–664.

Kawin, E. 1934. *Children of preschool age.* Chicago: University of Chicago Press.

Keilhacker, M. 1933. Beobachtungsbagen über sprachliche Entwicklung im Schulalter. *Z. Pädag. Psychol., 34,* 286–289.

Keller, H. 1904. *The story of my life.* Garden City: Doubleday Page. (New ed., 1922.)

Kelley, G. A. 1932. Some common factors in reading and speech disabilities. *Psychol. Monogr., 43,* 175–201.

Keneyers, E. 1927. Les premiers mots de l'enfant et l'apparition des espèces de mots dans son langage. *Arch. Psychol. norm. path., 20,* 191–218.

Kenyon, E. L. 1940. The etiology of stammering: An examination into certain recent studies with a glance into the future. *J. Speech Disorders, 6,* 1–12.

——. 1942. The etiology of stammering. *J. Speech Disorders, 7,* 97–104.

Kern, A. 1929. Vom innern Sprechen. Eine experimentelle Studie. *Z. Kinderforsch., 35,* 420–447.

Kern, E. 1933. Die Sprechmotorik des beschulten Taubstummen. Eine experimentelle Untersuchung. *Z. Kinderforsch., 41,* 503.

Kersta, L. G. 1948. Amplitude cross-section representation with the sound spectrograph. *J. Acoust. Soc. Amer., 20,* 796–801.

Kirkpatrick, E. A. 1891. The number of words in ordinary vocabularies. *Science, 18,* 107–108.

——. 1903. *Fundamentals of child study.* New York: Macmillan.

Koenig, W., H. K. Dunn, and L. Y. Lacy. 1946. The sound spectrograph. *J. Acoust. Soc. Amer., 18,* 19.

Koenig, W., and A. E. Rappel. 1948. Quantitative representation in sound spectrographs. *J. Acoust. Soc. Amer., 20,* 787–795.

Koffka, K. 1924. *The growth of the mind: An introduction to child psychology.* (Trans. by R. M. Ogden.) New York: Harcourt, Brace; London: Kegan Paul.

——. 1935. Psychology of learning, with reference to the acquisition of language. *Engl. J.* (Coll. ed.), *24,* 388–396.

Kopp, G. 1934. Metabolic studies of stutterers. *Speech Monogr., 1,* No. 1.

Kopp, H. 1946. Psychosomatic study of fifty stuttering children: I. Ozeretzky tests. *Amer. J. Orthopsychiat., 16,* 114–119.

Kroeber, A. L. 1916. The speech of a Zuni child. *Amer. Anthrop., 18,* 529–534.

Krugman, M. 1946. Psychosomatic study of fifty stuttering children. Round table: IV. Rorschach study. *Amer. J. Orthopsychiat., 16,* 127–133.

Kuhlmann, F. 1939. *Tests of mental development.* Minneapolis: Educational Test Bureau.

Kuo, H. H. 1937. [A study of the language development of Chinese children.] *Chinese J. Psychol., 1,* 334–364.

LaBrant, L. L. 1933. A study of certain language developments of children in grades four to twelve inclusive. *Genet. Psychol. Monogr., 14,* 387–491.

——. 1934. Changing sentence structure of children. *Elem. Engl. Rev., 11,* 59–65; 85–86.

Lafore, G. G. 1945. Practices of parents in dealing with preschool children. *Child Develpm. Monogr.,* No. 31. New York: Bureau of Publications, Teachers College, Columbia University. Pp. xiv + 150.

Lange, G., and W. Neuhaus. 1934. Der Strukturwandel der Kindersprache während der Zeit vom 6. bis 9. Lebensjahr. *Arch. ges. Psychol., 91,* 200–228.

Langenbeck, M. 1915. A study of a five-year-old child. *Ped. Sem., 22,* 65–88.

Latif, I. 1934. The physiological basis of linguistic development and of the ontogeny of meaning: I, II. *Psychol. Rev.*, *41*, 55–85; 153–176.

Lemaitre, A. 1902. Le langage intérieur chez les enfants. Recherches Pedologiques extrait de l'Educateur, *38*. Pp. 22.

Leopold, W. F. 1939. Speech development of a bilingual child: A linguist's record. Vol. I. Vocabulary growth in the first two years. *Northw. Univ. Stud. Human.*, *6*.

———. 1947. Speech development of a bilingual child: A linguist's record. Vol. II. Sound-learning in the first two years. *Northw. Univ. Stud. Human.*, *11*.

———. 1948. The study of child language and infant bilingualism. *Word*, *4*, 1–17.

———. 1949a. Speech development of a bilingual child: A linguist's record. Vol. III. Grammar and general problems in the first two years. *Northw. Univ. Stud. Human.*, *18*.

———. 1949b. Speech development of a bilingual child: A linguist's record. Vol. IV. Diary from age two. *Northw. Univ. Stud. Human.*, *19*.

———. 1949c. A child's learning of numerals. *Quart. J. Speech*, *35*, 202–209.

———. 1952. Bibliography of child language. *Northw. Univ. Stud. Human.*, *28*. Pp. 115. Evanston, Ill.: Northwestern University Press.

Lewinski, R. J. 1948. Vocabulary and mental measurement: A quantitative investigation and review of research. *J. Genet. Psychol.*, *72*, 247–281.

Lewis, M. M. 1948. *Language and society.* New York: Social Sciences Publishers. Pp. 248.

———. 1951. *Infant speech: A study of the beginnings of language.* (2d ed. with additional chapters and appendices.) New York: Humanities Press; London: Routledge and Kegan Paul. Pp. xii + 383.

Ley, J. 1930. Les troubles de développement du langage. *J. Neurol. Psychiat.*, *30*, 415–457.

Lindner, G. 1882. Beobachtungen und Bemerkungen über die Entwicklung der Sprache des Kindes. *Kosmos*, *9*, 321–430.

———. 1898. *Aus dem Naturgarten der Kindersprache. Ein Beitrag zur kindlichen Sprach- und Geistesentwickelung in den ersten vier Lebensjahren.* Leipzig: Grieben.

Linfert, H. E., and H. M. Hierholzer. 1928. A scale for measuring the mental development of infants during the first year of life. *Stud. Psychol. Psychiat. Cathol. Univ. Amer.*, *1*, No. 4.

Little, M. F., and H. M. Williams. 1937. An analytical scale of language achievement. *Univ. Iowa Stud. Child Welfare*, *13*, No. 2, 49–94.

Lloyd, W. 1941. Some aspects of language as significant of personality. *Psychol. Bull.*, *38*, 746. (Abstract.)

Loomis, C. P., and A. M. Moran. 1931. Relation between use of different parts of speech in written composition and mental ability. *J. Educ. Psychol.*, *22*, 465–475.

Lorimer, F. 1929. *The growth of reason: A study of the rôle of verbal activity in the growth of the structure of the human mind*, pp. 32–77. New York: Harcourt, Brace.

Lovell, G. D. 1941. Interrelations of vocabulary skills: Commonest versus multiple meanings. *J. Educ. Psychol.*, *32*, 67–72.

Low, A. A. 1936. *Studies in infant speech and thought.* (*Ill. Med. Dent. Monogr.*, *1*, No. 2.) Urbana: University of Illinois Press. Pp. 71.

Lukens, H. 1894. Preliminary report on the learning of language. *Ped. Sem.*, *3*, 424–460.

Lull, H. G. 1929. The speaking and writing abilities of intermediate grade pupils. *J. Educ. Res.*, *20*, 73–77.

Luria, A. R. 1930. *Language and intelligence in the city child, the country child and the child without a home.* Moscow: Gosizdat.

———. 1932. *The nature of human conflicts.* (Trans. by W. Gannt.) New York: Liveright.

Lyman, R. L. 1929. *Summary of investigations relating to grammar, language and composition.* (*Suppl. Educ. Monogr.*, No. 36. Pp. viii + 302. Ch. III.) Chicago: University of Chicago Press.

Lynip, A. W. 1951. The use of magnetic devices in the collection and analyses of the preverbal utterances of an infant. *Genet. Psychol. Monogr.*, *44*, 221–262.

Mabie, E. 1931. A study of the conversation of first grade pupils during free play hours. *J. Educ. Res.*, *24*, 135–138.

———. 1933. Language ability and personality adjustment. *Elem. Engl. Rev.*, *10*, 165–168.

MacDougall, R. 1912, 1913. The child's speech. *J. Educ. Psychol.*, *3*, 423–429, 507–513; *4*, 29–38.

Magni, J. A. 1919. Vocabularies. *Ped. Sem.*, *26*, 209–233.

Major, D. R. 1906. *First steps in mental growth: A series of studies in the psychology of infancy.* New York: Macmillan.

Malinowski, B. K. 1923. The problem of meaning in primitive languages. In C. K. Ogden and I. A. Richards, *The meaning of meaning*, pp. 451–510. London: Kegan Paul.

Mandelbaum, D. G. (Ed.) 1949. *Selected writings of Edward Sapir in language, culture and personality.* Berkeley: University of California Press. Pp. xv + 617.

Mandell, S. 1931. Relation of language to thought. *Quart. J. Speech*, *17*, 522–531.

Mandell, S., and B. Sonneck. 1935. Phonographische Aufnahme und Analyse der ersten Sprachäusserungen von Kindern. *Arch. ges. Psychol.*, *94*, 478–500.

Markey, J. F. 1928. *The symbolic process and its integration in children.* New York: Harcourt, Brace.

Martin, W. A. 1951. Quantitative expression in young children. *Genet. Psychol. Monogr.*, *44*, 147–219.

Mateer, F. 1908. The vocabulary of a four-year-old boy. *Ped. Sem.*, *15*, 63–74.

Maxfield, K. E. 1936. The spoken language of the blind preschool child: A study of method. *Arch. Psychol.*, No. 201.

McCarthy, D. 1929a. A comparison of children's language in different situations and its relation to personality traits. *J. Genet. Psychol.*, *36*, 583–591.

———. 1929b. The vocalizations of infants. *Psychol. Bull.*, *26*, 625–651.

McCarthy, D. 1930. *The language development of the preschool child.* (*Inst. Child Welfare Monogr. Ser.*, No. 4.) Minneapolis: University of Minnesota Press.

———. 1931. Language development. In C. Murchison (Ed.), A handbook of child psychology, pp. 278–315. Worcester: Clark University Press.

———. 1933. Language development. In C. Murchison (Ed.), *A handbook of child psychology* (2d ed., rev.), pp. 329–373. Worcester: Clark University Press.

———. 1935. A preliminary report on a new articulation test for young children. *Psychol. Bull.*, *32*, 699.

———. 1943. Language development of the preschool child. Ch. VII in R. G. Barker, J. S. Kounin, and H. F. Wright (Eds.), *Child behavior and development*, pp. 107–128. New York: McGraw-Hill.

———. 1946. Language development in children. In L. Carmichael (Ed.), *Manual of child psychology*, pp. 476–581. New York: Wiley.

———. 1947. The psychologist looks at the teaching of English. *Indep. Sch. Bull.*, May, Ser. of 1946–1947, No. 5, 3–11.

———. 1949a. Personality and learning. In *Amer. Counc. Educ. Stud.*, Ser. I, No. 35, 93–96.

———. 1949b. Language development. In W. S. Monroe (Ed.), *Encyclopedia of educational research.* (Rev. ed.) New York: Macmillan.

———. 1949c. Organismic interpretations of infant vocalizations. *Amer. Fsychol.*, *4*, 247. (Abstract.)

———. 1952a. Factors that influence language growth: home influences. *Elem. English*, *29*, 421–428, 440.

———. 1952b. Language and personality development. *The Reading Teacher*, *6*, 28–36.

———. 1952c. Organismic interpretations of infant vocalizations. *Child Develpm.*, *23*, 273–280.

———. 1953. Some possible explanations of sex differences in language development and disorders. *J. Psychol.*, *35*, 155–160.

McConnon, K. 1935. *The situation factor in the language responses of nursery school children.* Unpublished Ph.D. dissertation, University of Minnesota.

McDougall, W. 1931. An outline of psychology. (5th ed.) London: Methuen.

McDowell, E. 1928. Educational and emotional adjustments of stuttering children. *Teach. Coll. Contr. Educ.*, No. 314.

McGranahan, D. V. 1936. The psychology of language. *Psychol. Bull.*, *33*, 178–216.

McGraw, M. B. 1935. *Growth: A study of Johnny and Jimmy.* New York: Appleton-Century.

McKee, P. 1937. Vocabulary development. *Yearb. Nat. Soc. Stud. Educ.*, 36(I), 277–302.

Mead, C. D. 1913. The age of walking and talking in relation to general intelligence. *Ped. Sem.*, *20*, 460–484.

———. 1916. The relation of general intelligence to certain mental and physical traits. *Teach. Coll. Contr. Educ.*, No. 76.

Merry, F. K., and R. V. Merry. 1950. *The first two decades of life.* New York: Harper. Pp. xiii + 600.

Metraux, R. W. 1942. Auditory memory span for speech sounds of speech defective children compared with normal children. *J. Speech Disorders*, *7*, 33–36.

———. 1950. Speech profiles of the pre-school child 18–54 months. *J. Speech Hearing Disorders*, *15*, 37–53.

Meumann, E. 1908. *Die entstehung der ersten Wortbedeutungen beim Kinde.* (2d ed.) Leipzig: Engelmann.

Miller, G. A. 1951a. Speech and language. In S. S. Stevens (Ed.), *Handbook of experimental psychology*, pp. 789–810. New York: Wiley.

———. 1951b. *Language and communication.* New York: McGraw-Hill. Pp. xiii + 298.

Miller, G. F., F. D. Miller, and M. M. Nice. 1923. A boy's vocabulary at 18 months. *Proc. Okla. Acad. Sci. 3 (Univ. Okla. Bull.*, N.S., No. 271), 140–144.

Milner, E. 1951. A study of the relationships between reading readiness in grade one school children and patterns of parent-child interaction. *Child Develpm.*, *22*, 95–112.

Missildine, W. H. 1946. The emotional background of thirty children with reading disabilities with emphasis on its coercive elements. *Nerv. Child, 5*, 263–272.

Moncur, J. P. 1951. Environmental factors differentiating stuttering children from non-stuttering children. *Speech Monogr.*, *18*, 312–325.

Monroe, M. 1932. *Children who cannot read: the analysis of reading disabilities and the use of diagnostic tests in the instruction of retarded readers.* Chicago: University of Chicago Press.

Moore, C. E. A. 1938. Preliminary study of the emotional effects of letter sounds. *Quart. J. Speech, 24*, 134–149.

Moore, J. K. 1947. Speech content of selected groups of orphanage and non-orphanage preschool children. *J. Exp. Educ.*, *16*, 122–133.

Moore, K. C. 1896. The mental development of a child. *Psychol. Rev. Monogr.*, *1*, No. 3. Pp. 150.

Morgan, J. J. B. 1934. *Child psychology.* Ch. IX, pp. 270–308. New York: Farrar and Rinehart.

Morrison, C. E. 1914–1915. Speech defects in young children. *Psychol. Clin.*, *8*, 138–142.

Müller, M. 1862, 1865. *Lectures on the science of language.* (2 vols.) New York: Scribner's.

Munn, N. L. 1938. *Psychological development.* Ch. XII, pp. 372–398. Boston: Houghton Mifflin.

Murchison, C., and S. Langer. 1927. Tiedemann's observations on the development of the mental faculties of children. *J. Genet. Psychol.*, *34*, 205–230.

Murray, E. 1941. Speech personality and social change. *J. Higher Educ.*, *12*, 185–190.

Nance, L. 1946. Differential diagnosis of aphasia in children. *J. Speech Disorders*, *11*, 219–223.

National Council of Teachers of English, Curriculum Commission Series. 1952. Vol. I. Dora V. Smith (Ed.), *The English language arts.* New York: Appleton-Century-Crofts.

National Society for the Study of Education. 1929. Preschool and parental education. *Yearb. Nat. Soc. Stud. Educ.*, *28*, Ch. III, pp. 495–568.

Nausester, W. 1904. Das Kind und die Form der Sprache. *Geb. Pädag. Psychol. Physiol., 7*, No. 7.

Newman, S. S. 1933. Further experiments in phonetic symbolism. *Amer. J. Psychol., 45*, 53-75.

——. 1939. Personal symbolism in language patterns. *Psychiatry, 2*, 177-184.

Nice, M. M. 1915. The development of a child's vocabulary in relation to environment. *Ped. Sem., 22*, 35-64.

——. 1915-1916. Speech of a left-handed child. *Psychol. Clin., 9*, 115-117.

——. 1917. Speech development of a child from eighteen months to six years. *Ped. Sem., 24*, 204-243.

——. 1918. Ambidexterity and delayed speech development. *Ped. Sem., 25*, 141-162.

——. 1920. Concerning all-day conversations. *Ped. Sem., 27*, 166-177.

——. 1922. A child that would not talk. *Proc. Okla. Acad. Sci., 2 (Univ. Okla. Bull.*, N.S., No. 247), 108-111.

——. 1924. The speech development of a little girl. *Proc. Okla. Acad. Sci., 4 (Univ. Okla. Bull.*, N.S., No. 322), 147-168.

——. 1925. Length of sentences as a criterion of a child's progress in speech. *J. Educ. Psychol., 16*, 370-379.

——. 1926. A child's vocabularies from fifteen months to three years. *Proc. Okla. Acad. Sci., 6*, Pt. II *(Univ. Okla. Bull.*, N.S., No. 348), 317-333.

——. 1926-1927. On the size of vocabularies. *Amer. Speech, 2*, 1-7.

——. 1932. An analysis of the conversation of children and adults. *Child Develpm., 3*, 240-246.

——. 1933. A child's attainment of the sentence. *J. Genet. Psychol., 42*, 216-224.

Noiré, L. 1917. *The origin and philosophy of language.* Chicago: Open Court.

Norsworthy, N., and M. T. Whitley. 1933. *The psychology of childhood.* (Rev. ed.) Ch. XII, pp. 243-264. New York: Macmillan.

Odbert, H. S. 1948. An approach to language behavior through a test of word meanings. *Amer. Psychol., 3*, 274-275. (Abstract.)

Ogden, C. K. 1930. *Basic English.* London: Kegan Paul.

Ogden, C. K., and I. R. Richards. 1923, 1929. *The meaning of meaning.* London: Kegan Paul; New York: Harcourt, Brace.

Ohwaki, Y. 1933. Die ersten zwei Jahre der Sprachentwicklung des japanischen Kindes. Ein Beitrag zur Psychologie der Kindersprache. *Tohoku Psychol., 1*, 71-110.

Olson, W. C. 1929. *The measurement of nervous habits in normal children.* (Inst. of Child Welfare, Monogr. Ser. No. 3.) Minneapolis: University of Minnesota Press. Pp. 97.

Olson, W. C., and V. S. Koetzle. 1936. Amount and rate of talking of young children. *J. Exp. Educ., 5*, 175-179.

Oltuszewski, W. 1897. *Die geistige und sprachliche Entwicklung des Kindes.* Berlin: Fischer's Medic. Buchhandlung, H. Kornfeld.

Ombredane, A. 1935. Études sur le langage. Sur les premières manifestations du langage enfantine et sur la prétendue loi de Fritz Schultze. *Hyg. Ment., 30*, No. 4, 69-89.

Orton, S. T. 1937. *Reading, writing and speech problems in children.* New York: Norton.

O'Shea, M. V. 1907. *Linguistic development and Education.* New York: Macmillan.

Paget, R. 1930. *Human speech.* New York: Harcourt, Brace.

Palmer, M. F. 1940. The speech development of normal children. *J. Speech Disorders, 5*, 185-188.

Paterson, D. G., and T. A. Langlie. 1926. The influence of sex on scholarship ratings. *Educ. Adm. Supervis., 12*, 458-468.

Payne, C. S. 1930. The mispronunciation of words. *J. Genet. Psychol., 38*, 427-444.

Pelsma, J. R. 1910. A child's vocabulary and its development. *Ped. Sem., 7*, 328-369.

Perez, B. 1878, 1885, 1889, 1894. *La psychologie de l'enfant: Les trois premières années.* Paris: Alcan. (5th ed., 1894.) *The first three years of childhood.* (Ed. and trans. by A. M. Christie.) London (1885); Chicago: Marquis (1885); Syracuse, N. Y.: Bardeen (1889). (1889 ed. used in preparing this chapter.)

Piaget, J. 1924. *Le langage et la pensée chez l'enfant.* Neuchâtel and Paris: Delachaux & Niestlé. *The language and thought of the child.* (Trans. by M. Warden.) New York: Harcourt, Brace; London: Kegan Paul (1926).

——. 1928. *Judgment and reasoning of the child.* New York: Harcourt, Brace.

Pichon, E. 1932. Aperçu sur le développement moteur et psychique de l'enfant. *Paris Méd. 22*, 38-44.

Pillsbury, W. B., and C. L. Meader. 1928. *The psychology of language.* New York: Appleton.

Pollock, F. 1878. An infant's progress in language. *Mind, 3*, 392-401.

Poole, I. 1934. Genetic development of articulation of consonant sounds in speech. *Elem. Engl. Rev., 11*, 159-161.

Portenier, L. G. 1937. Factors influencing the social adjustment of children of preschool age. *J. Genet. Psychol., 51*, 127-139.

Pos, H. J. 1934. Het affect enzijn uitdrukking in de taal. *Ned. Tijdschr. Psychol., 5/6*, 209-238.

Potter, R. K., G. A., Kopp, and H. C. Green. 1949. *Visible Speech.* New York: Van Nostrand. Pp. 458.

Powers, F. F. 1929. Psychology of language learning. *Psychol. Bull., 26*, 261-274.

Prescott, D. A. 1929. Le vocabulaire des enfants des écoles primaires de Genève. *Arch. Psychol., Genève, 21*, 225-261.

Pressey, S. L. 1925. A statistical study of children's errors in sentence structure. *Engl. J., 14*, 529-535.

Preston, M. I. 1940. Reading failure and the child's security. *Amer. J. Orthopsychiat., 10*, 239-252.

Preyer, W. 1882, 1889, 1900. *Die Seele des Kindes.* Leipzig: Fernau. (5th ed., 1900.) *The mind of the child: Pt. 2. The development of the intellect.*

(Trans. by H. W. Brown.) New York: Appleton (1889). (Only 1900 ed. consulted.)

Preyer, W. 1889a. *The soul of the child*. (Trans. by E. Marwedel.) Pt. 2 of E. Marwedel, *Conscious motherhood*. Boston: Heath.

———. 1893. *Die geistige Entwicklung in der ersten Kindheit*. Stuttgart: Union. *Mental devleopment in the child*. (Trans. by H. W. Brown.) New York: Appleton.

Probst, C. A. 1931. A general information test for kindergarten children. *Child Develpm.*, *2*, 81–95.

Putchkowsky, M. A. 1931. ["Lalling" and its role in the development of children's speech.] *Sovietskaya Psikhonevrol*, No. 2–3, 103–106.

Pyles, M. K. 1932. Verbalization as a factor in learning. *Child Develpm.*, *3*, 108–113.

Rand, W., M. E. Sweeny, and L. Vincent. 1930. *Growth and development of the young child*. Philadelphia: Saunders.

Rapaport, A. 1952. What is semantics? *Amer. Sci.* *40*, 123–135.

Rasmussen, V. 1920, 1921, 1923. *Child psychology:* Vol. I. *Development in the first four years*. (Trans. by G. C. Berry.) London: Gyldendal (1920); New York: Knopf (1923). Vol. II. *The kindergarten child; its conception of life and its mental powers*. Vol. III. *Thought, imagination and feeling: Will and morale*. (Trans. by D. Pritchard.) London: Gyldendal (1921); New York: Knopf (1923).

Redmont, R. S. 1948. Description and evaluation of a corrective program for reading disability. *J. Educ. Psychol.*, *39*, 347–358.

Reid, G. 1947. The etiology and nature of functional articulatory defects in elementary school children. *J. Speech Disorders*, *12*, 143–150.

Remer, L. L. 1932. Handicaps of school entrants. *Univ. Iowa Stud. Child Welfare*, *6*, 195–207.

Ribble, M. 1943. *The rights of infants*. New York: Columbia University Press. Pp. 118.

Richardson, LaV. H. 1944. The personality of stutterers. *Psychol. Monogr.*, *56*, 1–41.

Richter, F. 1927. *Die Entwicklung des psychologischen Kindersprachforschung bis zum Beginn des 20 Jahrhunderts. Ein Beitrag zur Geschichte der Kinderseelenkunde*. Münster: Münsterverlag.

Rickard, G. E. 1935. The recognition vocabulary of primary pupils. *J. Educ. Res.*, *29*, 281–291.

Rigg, M. G. 1938a. A superior child who would not talk. *Child Develpm.*, *9*, 361–362.

———. 1938b. The international Kindergarten Union Word List compared with eight spoken vocabularies. *Child Develpm.*, *9*, 363–364.

Rinsland, H. D. 1945. *A basic vocabulary of elementary school children*. New York: Macmillan.

Robinson, E. W., and H. S. Conrad. 1933–1934. The reliability of observations of talkativeness and social contact among nursery children by the short time sample technique. *J. Exp. Educ.*, *2*, 161–165.

Robinson, H. M. 1946. *Why pupils fail in reading*. Chicago: University of Chicago Press. Pp. xiii + 257.

Roe, V., and R. Milisen. 1942. The effect of maturation upon defective articulations in elementary grades. *J. Speech Disorders*, *7*, 37–50.

Rogers, C. R. 1942. The criteria used in a study of mental health problems. *Educ. Res. Bull., Ohio State Univ.*, *21*, 29–40.

Rossignol, L. J. 1948. The relationships among hearing acuity, speech production and reading performance in grade 1A, 1B and 2A. *.Teach. Coll. Contr. Educ.*, No. 936.

Rostand, F. 1950. Grammaire et affectivité. *Rev. franç. psychanal.*, 299–310.

Roudinesco, J., and G. Appell. 1950. Les repercussions de la stabulation hospitalière sur le développement psychomoteur des jeunes enfants. *Sem. Hôp.*, Paris, *26*, 2271–2273.

Rowe, E. C., and H. N. Rowe. 1913. The vocabulary of a child at four and six years of age. *Ped. Sem.*, *20*, 187–208.

Rowland, E. H. 1907. The psychological experiences connected with different parts of speech. *Psychol. Rev. Monogr. Suppl.*, *8*, No. 32, 36–37.

Rugg, H., L. Krueger, and A. Sondergaard. 1929. studies in child personality: I. A study of the language of kindergarten children. *J. Educ. Psychol.*, *20*, 1–18.

Russell, C. M. 1944. Personality factors in a motor speech delay case. *Amer. J. Ment. Def.*, *49*, 171–176.

Salfield, D. J. 1950. Observations on elective mutism in children. *J. Ment. Sci.*, *96*, 1024–1032.

Salisbury, A. 1894. A child's vocabulary. *.Educ. Rev.*, *7*, 289–290.

Sanford, E. C. 1891. Notes on studies of the language of children. *Ped. Sem.*, *1*, 257–260.

Sanford, F. H. 1942. Speech and personality. *Psychol. Bull.*, *39*, 811–845.

———. 1942. Speech and personality: A comparative case study. *Character and Personality*, *10*, 169–198.

———. 1948. Speech and personality. In L. A. Pennington and I. A. Berg, *Introduction to clinical psychology*, Ch. VIII pp. 157–177. New York: Ronald.

Sapir, E. 1921. *Language, an introduction to the study of speech*. New York: Harcourt, Brace.

———. 1927. Language as a form of human behavior. *Engl. J.*, *16*, 421–433.

———. 1933. Language. In E. R. A. Seligman (Ed.), *Encyclopedia of the social sciences*, Vol. IX, pp. 155–169. New York: Macmillan.

Sayler, H. K. 1949. The effect of maturation upon defective articulation in grades seven through twelve. *J. Speech Hearing Disorders*, *14*, 202–207.

Schäfer, P. 1921. Die kindliche Entwicklungsperiode der reinen Sprachverständnisses nach ihrer Abgrenzung. *Z. pädag. Psychol.*, *22*, 317–325.

———. 1922. Beobachtungen und Versuche an einem Kinde in der Entwicklungsperiode des reinen Sprachverständnisses. *Z. pädag. Psychol.*, *23*, 269–289.

Schäfer, T. 1934. Ueber gebärdliche Verhaltensweisen, insbesondere bei Kindern (Concerning modes of gesture, especially with children). *Arch. ges. Psychol.*, *91*, 1–48.

Schmidt, B. G. 1941. Language development as an aid to the social adjustment of mental defectives. *Ment. Hyg.*, *25*, 402–413.

Schulman, M. J., and R. J. Havighurst. 1947. Relations between ability and social status in a midwestern community: IV. Size of vocabulary. *J. Educ. Psychol.*, *38*, 437–442.

Schultze, F. 1880. *Die Sprache des Kindes: Eine Anregnung zur Erforschung des Gegenstandes.* Leipzig: Ernst Gunther's Verlag.

Seago, D. W. 1925. An analysis of language factors in intelligence tests. *Ment. Meas. Monogr.*, *1*, No. 1. Pp. 125.

Sears, I., and A. Diebel. 1917. A study of the common mistakes in pupils' oral English. *Elem. Sch. J.*, *17*, 44–54.

Seashore, R. H. 1933. The measurement and analysis of extent of vocabulary. *Psychol. Bull.*, *30*, 709–710.

Seashore, R. H., and L. D. Eckerson. 1940. The measurement of individual differences in general English vocabularies. *J. Educ. Psychol.*, *31*, 14–38.

Sechehaye, A. 1917. Les problèmes de la langue. *Rev. Phil.*, *84*, 1–30.

Seegers, J. C. 1943. Language development and meaning. *Rev. Educ. Res.*, *13*, 102–109.

Segalla, F. L. 1934. Writing vocabularies of Negro and white children. *Sch. Rev.*, *42*, 772–779.

Seidl, J. C. G. 1937. *The effect of bilingualism on the measurement of intelligence.* Unpublished Ph.D. Dissertation, Fordham University.

Seth, G., and D. Guthrie. 1935. *Speech in childhood: its development and disorders.* London: Oxford University Press.

Shambaugh, C. G., and O. L. Shambaugh. 1928. An association study of vocabularies of grade children. *J. Educ. Res.*, *18*, 40–47.

——. 1929. A core vocabulary for elementary school pupils. *J. Educ. Res.*, *19*, 39–46.

Sheridan, M. D. 1945. The child's acquisition of speech. *Brit. Med. J.*, *1*, 707–709.

Sherman, I. 1935. *Articulation test with reading disability feature.* Winona, Minn.: Winona Public Schools. (Mimeographed.)

Sherman, I., and B. Kenevan. 1935. *Kindergarten-primary articulation test.* .Winona, Minn.: Winona Public Schools.

Sherman, M. 1927. The differentiation of emotional responses in infants: II. *J. Comp. Psychol.*, *7*, 335–351.

Shinn, M. W. 1893. Notes on the development of a child: I. *Univ. Calif. Publ. Educ.*, *1*, 1–178.

——. 1900. *The biography of a baby.* Boston: Houghton Mifflin.

Shire, Sister Mary Louise. 1945. The relation of certain linguistic factors to reading achievement in first-grade children. Unpublished Ph.D. dissertation, Fordham University.

Shirley, M. M. 1933a. *The first two years: A study of twenty-five babies:* Vol. II. *Intellectual development.* (*Inst. Child Welfare Monogr. Ser.*, No. 7.) Minneapolis: University of Minnesota Press. Pp. xvi + 513.

——. 1933b. *The first two years: A study of twenty-five babies:* Vol. III. *Personality manifestations.* (*Inst. Child Welfare Monogr. Ser.*, No. 8.) Minneapolis: University of Minnesota Press. Pp. xi + 228.

Shirley, M. M. 1938. Common content in the speech of preschool children. *Child Develpm.*, *9*, 333–346.

Shohara, H. 1935. The genesis of the articulatory movements of speech. *Quart. J. Speech*, *21*, 343–348.

——. 1942. A contribution to the genesis of speech movements and the etiology of stuttering. *J. Speech Disorders*, *7*, 29–32.

Siegenthaler, B. M. 1950. A study of intelligibility of sustained vowels. *Quart. J. Speech*, *36*, 202–208.

Sigismund, B. 1856. *Kind und Welt. Vätern, Müttern, und Kinderfreunden gewidmet:* I. *Die fünf ersten Perioden des Kindesalters.* Braunschweig: Vieweg.

Sikorski, M. 1883. Du développement du langage chez les enfants. *Arch. Neurol.*, *6*, 319–336.

Sims, V. M. 1929. The reliability and validity of four types of vocabulary test. *J. Educ. Res.*, *20*, 91–96.

Sirkin, J., and W. F. Lyons. 1941. A study of speech defects in mental deficiency. *Amer. J. Ment. Def.*, *46*, 74–80.

——. 1942. Treatment of speech defects in a state school. *Psychiat. Quart.*, *16*, 333–340.

Sister Mary Vera. 1942. A critical study of certain personality factors as determining elements in a remedial reading program. *Cathol. Educ. Rev.*, *40*, 145–161.

Skeels, H. M., R. Updegraff, B. L. Wellman, and H. M. Williams. 1938. A study of environmental stimulation: An orphanage preschool project. *Univ. Iowa Stud. Child Welfare*, *15*, No. 4. (Ch. V, pp. 75–121.)

Skinner, B. F. 1936. The verbal summator and a method for the studying of latent speech. *J. Psychol.*, *2*, 71–107.

——. 1937. The distribution of associated words. *Psychol. Rec.*, *1*, 71–76.

Smith, L. Z. 1930. An experimental investigation of young children's interest and expressive behavior, responses to single statement, verbal repetition and ideational repetition of content in animal stories. *Child Develpm.*, *1*, 232–247.

Smith, M. E. 1926. An investigation of the development of the sentence and the extent of vocabulary in young children. *Univ. Iowa Stud. Child Welfare*, *3*, No. 5.

——. 1931. A study of five bilingual children from the same family. *Child Develpm.*, *2*, 184–187.

——. 1932. The preschool child's use of criticism. *Child Develpm.*, *3*, 137–145.

——. 1933a. A study of language development in bilingual children in Hawaii. *Psychiol. Bull.*, *30*, 692–693.

——. 1933b. The influence of age, sex, and situation on the frequency, form, and function of questions asked by preschool children. *Child Develpm.*, *4*, 201–213.

——. 1933c. Grammatical errors in the speech of preschool children. *Child Develpm.*, *4*, 182–190.

——. 1935a. A study of some factors influencing the development of the sentence in preschool children. *J. Genet. Psychol.*, *46*, 182–212.

Smith, M. E. 1935b. A study of the speech of eight bilingual children of the same family. *Child Developm., 6*, 19–25.

——. 1939. Some light on the problem of bilingualism as found from a study of the progress in mastery of English among preschool children of non-American ancestry in Hawaii. *Genet. Psychol. Monogr., 21*, 121–284.

——. 1940. A comparison of the English vocabulary used by children of non-American ancestry in Hawaii before they reach the age of seven years with that of kindergarten children in continental United States. *J. Exp. Educ., 9*, 121–132.

——. 1949. Measurement of vocabulary of young bilingual children in both of the languages used. *J. Genet. Psychol., 74*, 305–310.

Smith, M. K. 1941. Measurement of the size of general English vocabulary through the elementary grades and high school. *Genet. Psychol. Monogr., 24*, 311–345.

Snyder, A. D. 1914. Notes on the talk of a two-and-one-half-year-old boy. *Ped. Sem., 21*, 412–424.

Sobel, F. S. 1948. Remedial teaching as therapy. *Amer. J. Psychother., 2*, 615–623.

Solomon, M. 1939. Stuttering as an emotional and personality disorder. *J. Speech Disorders, 4*, 347–357.

Sommer, A. T. 1932. The effect of group training upon the correction of articulatory defects in preschool children. *Child Develpm., 3*, 91–107.

Spitz, R. A. 1946. Anaclitic depression. An inquiry into the genesis of psychiatric conditions in early childhood: II. in A. Freud *et al.* (Eds.), *The psychoanalytic study of the child.* New York: International Universities Press.

Spriestersbach, D. C., and J. F. Curtis. 1951. Misarticulation and discrimination of speech sounds. *Quart. J. Speech, 37*, 483–491.

Springob, J. R. 1930. *Factors influencing the incidence of articulatory speech defects in preschool children.* Unpublished M.A. thesis, University of Minnesota.

Stalnaker, E. 1933. The language of preschool children. *Child Develpm., 4*, 229–336.

Stein, L. 1949. The emotional background of stammering. *Brit. J. Med. Psychol., 22*, 189–193.

Stengel, E. 1947. A clinical and psychological study of echo-reactions. *J. Ment. Sci., 93*, 598–612.

Stern, C., and W. Stern. 1907. *Die Kindersprache: Eine psychologische und sprachtheoretische Untersuchung.* (*Monogr. seel. Entwick. Kindes,* Vol. I.) Leipzig: Barth. (3d ed., rev., 1922.) Pp. xii + 434.

Stern, W. 1930. *Psychologie der frühen Kindheit, bis zum sechsten Lebensjahre.* (6th ed., rev.) Leipzig: Quelle and Meyer. (1st ed., 1914.) *Psychology of early childhood: Up to the sixth year of age.* (Trans. from the 3d German ed. by A. Barwell.) New York: Holt; London: Allen (1924). (2d ed., rev., 1930.)

Stevenson, A. 1893. The speech of children. *Science, 21*, 118–120.

Stewart, R. S. 1950. Personality maladjustment and reading achievement. *Amer. J. Orthopsychiat., 20*, 410–417.

Stinchfield, S. M. 1924. The formulation and standardization of a series of graded speech tests. *Psychol. Rev. Monogr., 33*, No. 149. Pp. 54.

——. 1928. *The psychology of speech.* Boston: Expression Co.

Stinchfield, S. M., and E. H. Young. 1938. *Children with delayed or defective speech: Motor-kinesthetic factors in their training.* Stanford University, Calif.: Stanford University Press.

Stoddard, C. B., and H. K. Languin. 1934. *Articulation Test I. Speech improvement.* Detroit: Board of Education, City of Detroit.

Stoddard, G. D., and B. Wellman. 1934. *Child psychology.* New York: Macmillan.

Stormzand, M. J., and M. V. O'Shea. 1924. *How much English grammar?* Baltimore: Warwick and York.

Stoutemyer, J. H. 1930. Some psychological aspects of language. *Kadelpian Rev., 9*, 331–337.

Strang, R. 1938. *An introduction to child study.* New York: Macmillan.

Strayer, L. C. 1930. Language and growth: The relative efficacy of early and deferred vocabulary training studied by the method of co-twin control. *Genet. Psychol. Monogr., 8*, 209–319.

Strickland, R. G. 1951. *The language arts in the elementary school.* Boston: Heath. Pp. xiv + 370.

Stumpf, C. 1900. Eigenartige sprachliche Entwicklung eines Kind. *Z. pädag. Psychol., 2*, 1–29.

Stutsman, R. 1931. *Mental measurement of preschool children.* Yonkers-on-Hudson: World Book.

Sukhov, G. D. 1939. [The acquisition of speech by the child in the play process.] In *Psikhologitchni doslidzennia. Naookovi zapiski.* Kharkov: Derj. Ped. Inst.

Sully, J. 1896, 1908. *Studies of childhood.* London and New York: Appleton. (New ed., 1908.) (The 1908 ed. consulted.)

Sunne, D. 1933. The effect of locality on language errors. *J. Educ. Res., 8*, 239–251.

Sykes, J. 1940. A study of the spontaneous vocalizations of young deaf children. *Psychol. Monogr., 52*, No. 1, 104–123.

Symonds, P. M., and H. F. Daringer. 1930. Studies in the learning of English expression. IV. Sentence structure. *Teach. Coll. Rec., 32*, 50–64.

Symonds, P. M., and B. Lee. 1929. Studies in the learning of English expression. III. Vocabulary. *Teach. Coll. Rec., 31*, 50–58.

Symposium. 1920. Is thinking merely the action of language mechanisms? *Brit. J. Psychol., 11*, 55–104.

Taine, H. 1876. Note sur l'acquisition du langage chez les enfants et dans l'espèce humaine. *Rev. Phil., 1*, 3–23. (Trans. in *Mind,* 1877, *2*, 252–257.)

Tanner, A. E. 1904. *The child, his thinking, feeling and doing.* Chicago; New York; London: Rand, McNally.

Templin, M. C. 1938. A study of aggressiveness in normal and defective speaking college students. *J. Speech Disorders, 3*, 43–49.

——. 1943. A study of sound discrimination ability of elementary school pupils. *J. Speech Disorders, 8*, 127–132.

Templin, M. C. 1947a. Spontaneous versus imitated verbalization in testing articulation in preschool children. *J. Speech Disorders, 12,* 293–300.

——. 1947b. A non-diagnostic articulation test. *J. Speech Disorders, 12,* 392–396.

——. 1948. A comparison of spelling achievement of normal and defective hearing subjects. *J. Educ. Psychol., 39,* 337–346.

——. 1950. The development of reasoning in children with normal and defective hearing. (*Inst. Child Welfare Monogr. Ser.,* No. 24.) Minneapolis: University of Minnesota Press. Pp. xii + 143.

——. In preparation, 1953a. *The development and interrelations of language skills in children.* (*Inst. Child Welfare Monogr. Ser.*) Minneapolis: University of Minnesota Press.

——. In preparation, 1953b. *A longitudinal study of the development of articulation.*

Templin, M. C., and M. D. Steer. 1939. Studies of growth of speech in preschool children. *J. Speech Disorders, 4,* 71–77.

Terman, L. M. 1916. *The measurement of intelligence: An explanation of and a complete guide for the use of the Stanford revision and extension of the Binet-Simon intelligence scale.* Boston: Houghton Mifflin.

Terman, L. M., *et al.* 1925. *Genetic studies of genius:* Vol. I. *Mental and physical traits of a thousand gifted children.* Stanford University, Calif.: Stanford University Press.

Thompson, G. G. 1952. *Child psychology: Growth trends in psychological adjustment.* Boston: Houghton Mifflin. Pp. xxxiii + 667.

Thonssen, L., and E. Fatherson. 1939. *Bibliography of speech education.* New York: Wilson.

Thorndike, E. L. 1921. *The teacher's word book.* New York: Teachers College, Columbia University.

——. 1931–1932. *A teacher's word book of the twenty thousand words found most frequently and widely in general reading for children and young people.* New York: Teachers College, Columbia University.

——. 1937. On the number of words of any given frequency of use. *Psychol. Rec., 1,* 399–406.

——. 1938. Studies in the psychology of language. *Arch. Psychol.,* No. 231.

Thorndike, E. L., A. L. Evans, L. H. V. Kennon, and E. I. Newcomb. 1926–1927. An inventory of English constructions with measures of their importance. *Teach. Coll. Rec., 28,* 580–610.

Thorndike, E. L., and I. Lorge. 1944. *A teacher's word book—30,000 word list.* New York: Teachers College, Columbia University. Pp. xii + 274.

Tinker, M. A., F. Hackner, and M. W. Wesley. 1940. Speed and quality of association as a measure of vocabulary knowledge. *J. Educ. Psychol., 31,* 575–582.

Tögel, H. 1905. 16 Monate Kindersprache. *Beih. Z. Kinderforsch.,* No. 3.

Town, C. H. 1912–1913. Language development in 285 idiots and imbeciles. *Psychol. Clin., 6,* 229–235.

Town, C. H. 1921. An analytic study of a group of five- to six-year-old children. *Univ. Iowa Stud. Child Welfare, 1,* No. 4.

Tracy, F. 1893. The language of childhood. *Amer. J. Psychol., 6,* 107–138.

Travis, L. E. 1931. *Speech pathology.* New York: Appleton.

——. 1940. The need for stuttering. *J. Speech Disorders, 5,* 193–202.

Travis, L. E., and W. Johnson. 1937. The relation of bilingualism to stuttering. *J. Speech Disorders, 2,* 185–189.

Trettien, A. W. 1904. Psychology of language interest in children. *Ped. Sem., 2,* 113–177.

Uhrbrock, R. S. 1936. Words most frequently used by a five-year-old girl. *J. Educ. Psychol., 27,* 155–158.

Underwood, A. 1931. Investigations in the study of language. *J. Educ. Res., 23,* 162–164.

Valentine, C. W. 1930. The psychology of imitation. *Brit. J. Psychol., 21,* 105–132.

——. 1942. *The psychology of early childhood. A study of mental development in the first years of life,* Ch. XX, pp. 392–448. Cleveland: Sherwood Press.

Van Alstyne, D. 1929. The environment of three-year-old children: Factors related to intelligence and vocabulary tests. *Teach. Coll. Contr. Educ.,* No. 366.

——. 1932. *Play behavior and choice of play materials of preschool children.* Chicago: University of Chicago Press.

Vandel, A. 1947. Le langage animal. *J. Psychol. norm. path., 40,* 129–153.

Vasey, F. T. 1919. Vocabularies of grammar school children. *J. Educ. Psychol., 10,* 104–107.

Velten, H. V. 1943. The growth of phonemic and lexical patterns in infant language. *Language, 19,* 281–292.

Vendryes, J. 1921. *Le langage: Introduction linguistic à l'histoire.* Paris: Renaissance du Livre.

Vigotsky, L. S. 1939. Thought and speech. *Psychiatry, 2,* 29–54.

Vigotsky, L. S., and A. R. Luria. 1929. The function and fate of egocentric speech. *Proc. and Pap. 9th Int. Cong. Psychol.,* 464–465.

Voegelin, C. F., and S. Adams. 1934. A phonetic study of young children's speech. *J. Exp. Educ., 3,* 107–116.

Voelker, C. H. 1935. Technique for a phonetic frequency distribution count in formal American speech. Extract from *Arch. néerl. Phon. exp., XI,* 69–72.

Waddle, C. W. 1913. *An introduction to child psychology.* Boston: Houghton Mifflin.

Wagoner, L. C. 1933. *The development of learning in young children,* Ch. XII, pp. 181–197. New York: McGraw-Hill.

Walpole, H. 1941. *Semantics. The nature of words and their meanings.* New York: Norton. Pp. 264.

Waring, E. B. 1927. The relation between early language habits and early habits of conduct control. *Teach. Coll. Contr. Educ.,* No. 260.

Watts, H. F. 1947. *The language and mental development of children; an essay in educational psychology.* Boston: Heath.

Weiss, A. P. 1925. Linguistics and psychology. *Language, 1,* 52–57.

Wellman, B. L., I. M. Case, I. G. Mengert, and D. E. Bradbury. 1931. Speech sounds of young children. *Univ. Iowa Stud. Child Welfare, 5,* No. 2.

Werner, H., and E. Kaplan. 1950. Development of word meaning through verbal context: An experimental study. *J. Psychol., 29,* 251–257.

———. 1950. The acquisition of word meanings: A developmental study. *Monogr. Soc. Res. Child Develpm., XV,* Ser. 51, No. 1.

Werner, L. S. 1945. Treatment of a child with delayed speech. *J. Speech Disorders, 10,* 329–334.

Wesman, A. G., and H. G. Seashore. 1949. Frequency vs. complexity of words in verbal measurement. *J. Educ. Psychol., 40,* 395–404.

West, R. M. 1933. *Disorders of speech and voice.* (2d ed.) Mimeographed by College Typing Co., Madison, Wis. Pp. 141.

Whipple, G. M., and Mrs. G. M. Whipple. 1909. The vocabulary of a three-year-old boy with some interpretive comments. *Ped. Sem., 15,* 1–22.

White, M. A. 1949. A study of schizophrenic language. *J. Abnorm. Soc. Psychol., 44,* 61–74.

Wilke, W. H. 1938. Development and application of a scale for measuring diction. *Quart. J. Speech, 24,* 268–281.

Williams, H. M. 1932. Some problems of sampling in vocabulary tests. *J. Exp. Educ., 1,* 131–133.

———. 1937a. An analytical study of language achievement in preschool children. Part I of Development of language and vocabulary in young children. *Univ. Iowa Stud. Child Welfare, 13,* No. 2, 9–18.

———. 1937b. A qualitative analysis of the erroneous speech sound substitutions of preschool children. Part II of Development of language and vocabulary in young children. *Univ. Iowa Stud. Child Welfare, 13,* No. 2, 21–32.

Williams, H. M., and M. L. McFarland. 1937. A revision of the Smith vocabulary test for preschool children. Part III. Development of language and vocabulary in young children. *Univ. Iowa. Stud. Child Welfare, 13,* No. 2, 35–46.

Williams, R. M., and M. L. Mattson. 1942. The effect of social groupings upon the language of preschool children. *Child Develpm., 13,* 233–245.

Willoughby, R. R. 1932. The functions of conversation. *J. Soc. Psychol., 3,* 146–160.

Wilson, F. T. 1937. Correlations of vocabulary knowledge with other abilities and traits in Grade I. *Elem. Sch. J., 37,* 451–457.

Wilson, G. M. 1922. Language error tests. *J. Educ. Psychol., 13,* 341–349.

Witte, O. 1930. Untersuchungen über die Gebärdensprache. Beiträge zur Psychologie der Sprache. *Z. Psychol., 116,* 225–308.

Witty, P. A., and M. Fry. 1929. The vocabulary content of compositions written by college students. *J. Educ. Res., 19,* 135–138.

Witty, P. A., and L. L. LaBrant. 1930. Vocabulary and reading. *Sch. and Soc., 31,* 268–272.

Witty, P. A., and C. E. Skinner. 1939. *Mental hygiene in modern education.* New York: Farrar & Rinehart. Pp. 299.

Wolfe, H. K. 1917. On the color vocabulary of children. *Nebraska Univ. Stud., 1,* No. 3, 205–234.

Wölfflin, E. 1901. Reduplikation in der Kindersprache. *Z. dents. Wortforsch., 1,* 263.

Wood, K. S. 1946. Parental maladjustment and functional articulatory defects in children. *J. Speech Disorders, 11,* 255–275.

Worbois, G. M. 1942. Language development of children in two different rural environments. *Child Develpm., 13,* 175–180.

Wundt, W. 1901. *Sprachgeschichte und Sprachpsychologie.* Leipzig: Engelmann.

———. 1911–1912. *Völkerpsychologie:* Vol. I. *Die Sprache.* (3d ed., two parts.) Leipzig: Engelmann (Kroener).

Wyatt, G. L. 1949. Stammering and language learning in early childhood. *J. Abnorm. Soc. Psychol., 44,* 75–84.

Yedinack, J. G. 1949. A study of the linguistic functioning of children with articulation and reading disabilities. *J. Genet. Psychol., 74,* 23–59.

Yoakum, C., and R. M. Yerkes. 1920. *Army mental tests.* New York: Holt.

Yoshioka, J. 1929. A study of bilingualism. *J. Genet. Psychol., 36,* 473–479.

Young, F. M. 1941. An analysis of certain variables in a developmental study of language. *Genet. Psychol. Monogr., 23,* 3–141.

———. 1942a. Certain social indices in the language of preschool subjects. *J. Genet. Psychol., 61,* 109–123.

———. 1942b. Development as indicated by a study of pronouns. *J. Genet. Psychol., 61,* 125–134.

Zagorovskii, P. L. 1928. [Clinical methods of investigating the speech reaction of children.] *Z. Psikhol. Ped. Psikhotekh., 1,* 96–106.

Zaporoshetz, A. V. 1939. [The role of elements of practice and speech in the development of thinking in children.] In *Psikhologitchni doslidzennia. Naookovi zapiski.* Kharkov: Derj. Ped. Inst.

Zerov, V. 1930. [The evolution of written language in primary school children.] *Pedologiya* (Russian), 683–697.

Zipf, G. K. 1935. *The psycho-biology of language.* Boston: Houghton Mifflin.

———. 1942. Children's speech. *Science, 96,* 344–345.

Zyve, C. I. 1927. Conversation among children. *Teach. Coll. Rec., 29,* 46–61.

CHAPTER 10

THE ENVIRONMENT AND MENTAL DEVELOPMENT

HAROLD E. JONES

The Nature of Mental Ability

The studies reported in this chapter are based primarily upon results from the use of standard intelligence tests. Although the deficiencies of our current tests as scientific instruments have been frequently noted (see, for example, Thomas, 1942; Loevinger, 1947), up to the present time we have devised no better way to observe the influence of environment on mental ability.

A mental test has not one but many levels of validity, according to the characteristics of the group to which it is applied; the validity may become very low when it is used with subjects who fall outside a specific cultural or educational range. In such cases it is especially clear, as Stoddard (1951) has pointed out, that intelligence test scores represent not a maximum but a minimum estimate of a child's intelligence.

This is also implied in Hebb's (1949) concept of two kinds of intelligence: the innate potential determined by brain structure and neural metabolism, and the average level of performance which has been built up through previous learning. The two kinds of intelligence show varying degrees of correspondence; it is chiefly the second kind which, from an empirical and functional point of view, is represented in mental tests.

On the basis of perceptual theory it has been argued (Combs, 1952) that we tend to underestimate the margin of difference between performance and capacity. Self concepts of capacity, and teachers' and parents' estimates, often tend to achieve a static and mutually verifying expression in behavior. This may be associated with a high *predictive* validity of mental tests, but it leaves us uncertain of what a person's attainments might be under different demands, with different goals, and with enriched perceptual fields.

If there is a wide margin of error in inferring capacity from mental test performance on the basis of any single score, there must be similar error in defining the extent to which environmental variations have affected this score. Nevertheless, for massed data as well as for cumulative records of the same individuals an ingenious variety of methods can be used to illuminate the complex problems of environmental influence.

Individual differences in mental ability have been discussed by E. L. Thorndike *et al.* (1927) as involving three principal aspects: *level, range,* and *speed.* The level of ability that a person reaches is defined by the difficulty of mental tasks which he can perform; the range, or breadth, of ability is defined by the number of different tasks which he can perform at various levels. Speed, or rate of work, is also a factor in mental efficiency, although probably of less direct importance than the other aspects of ability. A useful line of inquiry would be the study of the effects of environment upon specific aspects of intelligence, as represented, for example, in level, range, or speed scores, or in scores from multiple-aptitude tests, or in component scores derived from factor analysis. In this field, however, few attempts have been made to deal analytically with constituent factors; the principal studies are limited chiefly to general measures of mental function. These general measures, concerned with the capacity to utilize symbols and to acquire *intellective* adaptations, are ordinarily expressed in terms of a composite score, such as the IQ.

The Nature of Environmental Influences

The individual organism comes into being and develops in a maternal environment which supplies nourishment and other biological needs and also provides both protective shielding and some opportunity for functional stimulation. These environmental supports are essential if the organism is to grow, or even to survive. In this connection, no one asks the question, "Which is more important, nature or nurture?" for both are obviously indispensable. Structural and, ultimately, functional development is an outcome of (1) the interaction of genes with their intracellular environment, (2) the interaction of cells, and (3) the interaction of the organism with its surroundings. The hereditary "determiners" or genes cannot function unless the various aspects of the environment play their necessary rôles. On the other hand, the influence of environmental factors is subject to very definite limitations, for, to cite an extreme example, no normal environmental force can change an individual with chromosomes of one species into an individual with the characteristics of a different species. Developmental differences large enough to distinguish species are thus hereditary effects which extrinsic factors cannot (in any given individual) wholly simulate or counteract.

The problem of environmental influences becomes less a matter of general principles, and more a matter for specific analysis, when we turn our attention from the growth of the single individual to the factors which affect individual differences. In this area we may with reason ask, "Which is more important, nature or nurture?" If, however, we attempt to reply to the question (as applied to mental abilities) with an over-all generalization we shall immediately find ourselves in logical difficulties. Suppose that we address ourselves to the task of determining the causes of illiteracy. Haldane (1938) has pointed out that, among adults in England under 40 years of age, illiteracy is probably most often due either to mental deficiency or to blindness. But among adults in Elizabethan England, or in India today, illiteracy may be attributed primarily to the lack of educational opportunity.

Thus we are led to say that hereditary and environmental influences on intelligence do not constitute a single problem for which a single quantitative answer can be found, but a family of problems, each with its own relatively complicated answer.

Quantitative Approaches

Hogben (1933), in a book rich with illuminating examples of the interaction of heredity and environment, points out that statistical methods are useful in detecting the *presence* of either sort of influence, but he questions the meaningfulness of attempts to *quantify* the relative influence of genetic and nongenetic causes of variations. "No statement about a genetic difference has any scientific meaning unless it includes or implies a specification of the environment in which it manifests itself in a particular manner" (p. 14).

Several well-known investigations, however, have had a more ambitious aim.

Methods designed to specify quite exactly the proportional influence of causal factors have been applied to studies of foster children by Burks (1928b), Leahy (1935), and Wallis (1936), and to studies of twins by Newman, Freeman, and Holzinger (1937). Leahy's computation gave the home environment the very meager credit of determining not more than 4 per cent of the variance in mental ability. A more liberal estimate by Burks was 17 per cent. Wright (1931) and Shuttleworth (1935) have reworked the data of these investigators, applying statistical corrections which give results differing somewhat from each other and from the original studies.

In an early study Fisher (1918) developed statistical techniques by means of which, granted the applicability of certain assumptions, "it is possible to calculate the numerical influence not only of dominance but of the total genetic and nongenetic causes of variability" (p. 433). These methods were used by Conrad and Jones (1940) to test hypotheses concerning the nature of hereditary transmission of intelligence but not for the purpose of calculating the numerical influence of nature and nurture.

One of the earliest and most widely criticized quantitative statements was Burt's (1921) regression equation for predicting Binet mental age from schooling, "reasoning ability," and chronological age. Both Holzinger and Freeman (1925) and Burks (1928a) have demonstrated the error in direct inference from regression coefficients to proportional contributions, and Loevinger (1943), in an able critique, has gone considerably further in questioning the nature-nurture statistics based on the assumption of additive factors.

For our present purpose, it is chiefly important that we understand the following limiting conditions of work in this area: (1)

The proportional contribution of heredity and environment does not refer to the make-up of individual IQ's or to the general level of intelligence, but either to average effects upon individual differences or to differences between groups. (2) Existing studies are based on fallible and incomplete measures both of intelligence and of the environment; this fact should be remembered when the data are being manipulated to yield an apparently highly exact result. (3) Even if it is ever logically feasible to seek a single value for the effect of environment, the particular value reported in a given study may not apply in samples involving (a) a different environmental level, (b) a different hereditary selection, (c) a change in variability of either of the above factors, or (d) a change in any special conditions which may affect the interaction of these factors.

The remainder of this discussion will be concerned with results from several different types of approach. Each of these contributes in its own way to our understanding of what environment can and cannot do; each provides some clue as to the relative importance of environmental factors under specified circumstances. For the time being, however, we must think of these results as rough approximations rather than as precise and final statements.

Mental Growth Curves

One approach to the analysis of environmental influences is based on the study of mental growth curves. If the intelligence of children (relative to age) were generally found to be constant throughout childhood, few questions would be raised about the rôle of differential environmental factors, except perhaps as these may be assumed to operate in the prenatal period or in early infancy.

If, on the other hand, mental development of individuals is marked by variable or systematic changes (that is, by fluctuations or age trends, relative to the group), the extent of possible environmental influence becomes an issue of some interest. Such changes, if registered, are not necessarily due to the environment or subject to educational controls. They may be attributable to errors of measurement, to normative defects of the test, or to changes in the composition of the test, or of intelligence, at different levels. They may be due to variations in the temporary state of the subject, dependent upon physical condition, rapport, motivation, or disturbing emotional factors. They may express a neurophysiological growth pattern differing in rate of evolution for different children; such maturational changes are well established in the patterns of physical growth for various organs and for the body as a whole. Any of these factors, in any combination, may conceivably operate to alter the apparent or actual course of mental development. One of our first problems, therefore, is to ascertain the facts as to the regularity of growth, and then to attempt an assessment of the various agencies which may be responsible for irregular or unpredicted variations.

Growth in Terms of Averages. An implicit belief in the lawfulness and uniformity of mental development has at times accompanied the acceptance of IQ and mental age as indices of intelligence most convenient for general use. For any group of children with an average IQ of 100 at age 10, the average will remain substantially the same at 11 and at 12 years if we allow for slight practice effects which tend to increase the IQ, and slight standardization errors which in our present instruments sometimes tend to decrease it. This constancy, however, is the necessary outcome of a scale conceived in terms of mental age.[1] In such a scale, a gain of 1 year in mental age is that increment which occurs (on the average) in 1 chronological year, and the average rate of development during childhood must appear to be constant since it is expressed in terms of constant and equal increments of mental age. It is, of course, now generally understood that such a picture of growth is merely a convenient artifact—convenient largely because of its adaptability for use in connection with an educational grade system based on chronological age.

One approach to the problem of mental growth pattern is through determining the overlapping of distributions of scores at successive ages. In a somewhat selected group, Bayley (1933) has shown that in early childhood overlapping is very small even when retests are given at short intervals. Thus, at 5 months no cases in her sample equal or exceed the average mental score attained at 6 months. At 5 years, on the other hand, evidence of age changes can hardly be seen within a period so short as a month; the distributions for tests given at monthly intervals overlap to such an extent that they are almost identical.

When raw scores are transformed into "absolute" measures, it is possible to compare the data from different scales by computing mean scores at each age as a percentage of the adult mean. This is illustrated in Figure 1, from Jones and Conrad (1944). The three studies represented involve, respectively, a clinic sample from Illinois, tested by the 1916 Stanford-Binet (average IQ approximately 80); the chil-

[1] Heinis (1926) derived a logarithmic formula for mental growth and proposed the use of a "personal constant," based on the logarithmic equation, to avoid alleged arbitrary features on the mental age scale. This proposal has been analyzed in a definitive discussion by Bradway and Hoffeditz (1937). Gesell (1928), in plotting developmental age, has also used a logarithmic method to express the relative rate of what is "arithmetically implicit" in an age scale.

dren of the Harvard Growth Study, tested longitudinally with a variety of group tests, and a cross-sectional public school sample used in standardizing a group mental scale. The almost identical parameters of mental growth exhibited in different samples and through different tests suggests a lawful pattern of development in which the indi-

The phenomena of differential mental growth (Conrad, Freeman, and Jones, 1944) are also of interest in this connection. Different mental functions exhibit differences in the rate, peak, and total magnitude of growth and in the pattern of decline (Jones and Kaplan, 1945) after the peak is reached. Cumulative environmental effects are partly

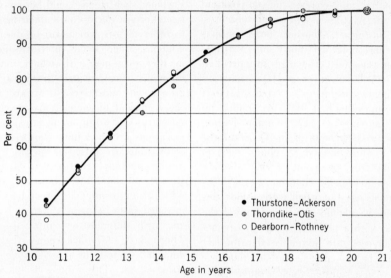

FIGURE 1. Mental growth curves in terms of percentage of mature status. (After Jones and Conrad, 1944, p. 153.) Reproduced by permission of the National Society for the Study of Education.

vidual's response to his environment is influenced by innate or organic limitations.

A theory of environmental influence must be able to deal with the fact that in terms of units other than mental age the growth of intelligence is not linear but with increasing age exhibits a decreasing rate of change. If environment were the predominant factor in mental growth, we might reasonably expect a positive rather than a negative acceleration in later childhood and adolescence, since individual development involves a multiplication of environmental contacts and also an increasing scope of response to the environment.

responsible for these differences, as expressed for example in the long-continued growth of functions based on information and on size of vocabulary. But in general the varying patterns admit of no easy explanation in terms of extrinsic factors.

The foregoing may suggest some of the limitations in the portrayal of mental growth in Figure 1. The analysis of overlapping distributions in successive ages, and the techniques for transforming raw scores into absolute scores, appear to justify confidence in the general form of the curve as shown. But it is well known that the same or similar scores may be obtained through different patterns of item performance. Jones (1931) showed that children and adults matched for mental age perform very differently on various items of the Stanford-Binet.[1] The differential difficulty values of items, in relation to age, signifies that the growth of total scores in an intelligence test involves not merely quantitative changes but also changes in composition, i.e., in the relative weighting of subscores.

IQ Constancy. Another source of evidence concerning variability in growth is based on the study of changes in individual scores. Although average IQ's maintain approximate constancy by force of standardization, individual IQ's are under no such requirement. The common finding that the probable error of an IQ (Stanford-Binet) is approximately 5 points appears reassuring from the point of view of those who wish to classify children on the basis of a single test, but when we consider this statement we should also bear in mind the fact that with a probable error of 5 points (if differences are normally distributed) one child in five may deviate as much as 10 points in a retest.[2] Such a difference is of sufficient practical importance to justify an inquiry into its possible causes.

As would be expected, greater average shifts in IQ are found over longer periods. Bradway (1944), for example, reported results with 138 children who were tested in the preschool period with both forms of the 1937 Stanford-Binet and retested 10 years later with Form L; the mean IQ changes were from 10 to 13 points in different subgroups.

Predictive Correlations. IQ differences on retests may be influenced not merely by changes within the group but also by upward or downward trends of the group as a whole; such trends could be due to practice effects, to errors in standardization, or to other factors which will be discussed in a later section. If our interest is primarily in the constancy with which individuals maintain their relative rate of mental growth, the most straightforward index is the coefficient of correlation between mental status on two different occasions.

Various reviews[3] have shown that retest correlations are rarely as high as .95, and most commonly fall between .80 and .90. Reports on this subject, however, are often difficult to interpret, since they have usually included cases at many different age levels and with different test intervals. R. L. Thorndike (1933) has shown that on an immediate retest the most probable correlation is .89. This value falls to .87 at 10 months, .81 at 30 months, .70 at 60 months. It is recognized, however, that age as well as test interval may influence the results. If the first test is given as late as the tenth year of age, prediction may be better than Thorndike's estimate; thus, in a study by Byrns and Henmon (1935), 250 college students were located who had been tested 8 to 10 years previously. For this selected group the initial IQ (National Intelligence Test) correlated .81 with a group test score obtained in college. On the other hand, if the initial test is given before 2 years of age, correlations with later status may approach zero.

---

[1] See also Laycock and Clark (1942). Kounin (1943) has proposed that the difference in performance between younger and older persons of the same mental age is due to an increase in "intrapersonal rigidity." This is not supported by Thompson and Magaret (1947), who find that the chief source of handicap for the older subjects is in the degree to which items are saturated with the general intelligence factor.

[2] The probable error of the IQ is not a fixed value but may vary according to the age, intelligence level, and test experience of the subject. In the Terman and Merrill (1937) standardization, the average difference between IQ's on Forms M and L was 5.9 for cases with IQ of 130 or above, decreasing to 2.5 for cases with IQ below 70.

[3] The best of these are by R. L. Thorndike (1933, 1940). For longer intervals Bradway (1944) summarized results from eight studies involving constancy correlations between IQ's in the preschool ages and in later childhood.

Retest correlations at 3-year intervals are given in Table 1 from two longitudinal studies. The first of these was based on

TABLE 1

RETEST CORRELATIONS AT 3-YEAR INTERVALS

	Ebert and Simmons (1945)	Honzik et al. (1948)
	r	r
Age 2 by 5		.32 ± .06 PE
Age 3 by 6	.56 ± .04 PE	.57 ± .03
Age 4 by 7	.55 ± .04	.59 ± .03
Age 5 by 8	.70 ± .03	.70 ± .02
Age 7 by 10	.76 ± .02	.78 ± .02
Age 9 by 12 or 13		.85 ± .01

181 children in Cleveland, Ohio; the second, on 113 children at age 2 and on approximately 200 at subsequent ages, in Berkeley, California. Lower predictive coefficients are shown in the earlier years. Going back to still younger ages, the evidence from tests at around 1 year indicates that, when pathological retardates are excluded, later mental status cannot be predicted from existing mental scales. Moreover, we seem to have little prospect of significantly improving predictions from this age level through new items or item weightings. This is not due to lack of reliability in the early tests. With items involving problem solving, imitation, memory, and other forms of adaptive reaction, Bayley (1940a) obtained a reliability coefficient of .94 by combining scores obtained at 7, 8, and 9 months; these measures correlated .81 with mental scores 3 months later, but only .39 with scores at around 21 months, .22 with scores at around 30 months, and practically zero with all later measurements to 6 years and beyond. Although other studies have not covered this age range, similar results have in general been reported between mental tests given at 1 year and 3 to 4 years later.[1]

[1] For 91 cases, L. D. Anderson (1939) reported a correlation of .06 between Gesell scores at 1 year and the

From such results, it might be expected that, in the case of mental scores obtained still earlier in infancy, the correlations with later status would also vary around zero. It is interesting to note, however, that Furfey and Muehlenbein (1932), L. D. Anderson (1939), and Bayley (1940a) all report negative correlations between test scores obtained at 6 months or earlier and test scores obtained at 4 years or later. Although the prediction indices found in these studies are not statistically significant, they are sufficiently consistent to suggest that in a normal sample early status and later growth rates may be negatively related. Speculation on this point may well be reserved until the findings are confirmed by other studies. Of possible relevance is the investigation by Dubnoff (1938), who tested 489 infants in Kazan, U.S.S.R., by the California First Year Mental Scale. Approximately one-third of the group was of Tatar extraction; one-half was tested in homes, and one-half (factory workers' children) in crèches or factory nurseries. Scale scores during the first year favor the Kazan group; in terms of the variability of the Kazan group, the difference is about 2 SD at 1 month. From the fourth to the eighth month the difference drops to about 1 SD, and by the tenth month the averages become approximately equal in the two groups. It could be contended that the relative gain of the California group from 1 to 10 months is due in part to a more favorable environment with regard to medical care, diet, sunlight, and to a more intelligent régime of care by the mother. Dubnoff comments:

Stanford-Binet at 5 years. Furfey and Muehlenbein (1932) found a correlation of −.20 between mental scores at 12 months on the Linfert-Hierholzer scale and Stanford-Binet IQ's given at an average of 4.8 years. For 150 cases, Wittenborn (1953) correlated a general maturity quotient (Gesell), obtained in infancy, with the Stanford-Binet and the Arthur Performance Scale given from 4 to 7 years later; the coefficients were .05 and .12 respectively.

Due to the cold winters, the Kazan child is heavily clothed, and often wrapped in blankets which prevent freedom of movement. Except for about 2 months of the year he is never exposed to sunlight. Rickets is prevalent. . . . The level of education of the parents is very markedly lower than that of the California sample [p. 70].

Environmental factors, however, cannot be adduced to explain the initial superiority of the Kazan infants. Dubnoff's work, together with other related studies, may lead to the speculative suggestion that between natio-racial groups, as within a given group, a slight tendency exists for early precocity to be associated with a slower mental growth at later ages and perhaps with a lower average intelligence level at maturity. A parallel situation may be noted when we compare different animal species; among the primates, for example, the maturity of performance at a given age in infancy can be used inversely to predict the general level of adaptive ability that will be attained at the end of the growth span. Another interpretation, applicable to human infants, is in terms of the greater amount of social stimulation received by infants living in crowded homes; Gilliland (1949) believed that this might account for results in three studies in which he found slightly higher scores for Negro than for white infants, but it is still an open question as to whether, within a normal range, the mental growth patterns are significantly modified by such factors.

To summarize the foregoing, we have noted an apparent slight tendency for mental scores in early infancy to be negatively correlated with mental scores at 4 years or later. At 12 months of age the correlation is close to zero.[1] Beyond that point, however, a positive relationship emerges. Figure 2 shows the smoothed-curve relationship, in terms of the z transformation, between intelligence scores at 18 years and at successive earlier years. The upper curve is based on Bayley's (1949) data from the Berkeley Growth Study ($N = 40$–50), the lower curve on another longitudinal study in Berkeley ($N = 140$–153) reported by Honzik, Macfarlane, and Allen (1948). Both investigations used the Wechsler-Bellevue at age 18 and a variety of individual tests at earlier ages (chiefly the Stanford-Binet, and below age 6 the California Preschool Schedules). In each of the groups, it is apparent that at as early as 2 years of age individual differences are beginning to appear which carry forward to some extent into later childhood. The rate of increase in predictive power is more rapid in the preschool period than later (differences in the level of the two curves are due primarily to differences in variability of the two samples).

The Age Ratio. J. E. Anderson (1940) has pointed out that as we go up the age scale the prediction of later from earlier status involves an increasing proportion of similar elements. The 10-year tests are in content more similar to the 9- than to the 8-year tests. Moreover, the cumulative composites of performance which are represented in test scores are more similar between adjacent than between separated age levels. They become increasingly similar for adjacent levels as maturity is approached, and the increment from 1 year to another has a proportionately smaller effect upon total scores.

Figure 2 is, of course, based upon actual scores (point scores or mental ages). An individual's performance changes from year to year as a result of successive increments of growth-and-learning, as well as from er-

[1] Apparently the only instance of a higher correlation is in a small sample of lower middle class children studied by Cattell (1940). An r of .18 between scores at 9 months and Stanford-Binet at 3 years, and of .57 between 12 months and 3 years was reported.

ror factors. What would be found if we were to set up an artificial series in which the increments for each year were cumulated at random? Thus, at 3 years individual A would be given an arbitrary measure consisting of his own score at 2 years

in any event we must expect that during the first few years of life the predictive power of our tests will be proportionate to the age of testing. It will also be inversely proportionate to the length of the interval over which prediction is attempted. Honzik

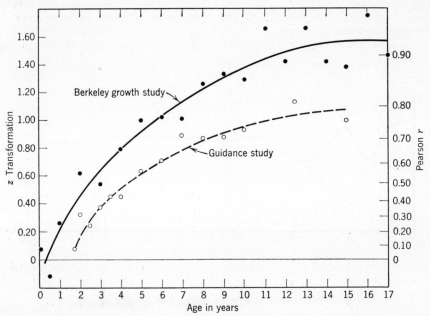

Figure 2. Correlations of intelligence scores at 18 years with scores at successive earlier ages

plus B's increment from 2 to 3 years. The resulting 3-year score could then be added to C's actual increment from 3 to 4 years, in order to obtain an arbitrary 4-year score for A. Such a series (as Anderson has shown by cumulating random numbers) would neecssarily result in a curve of relationship somewhat similar to that actually obtained in Figure 2. Several factors might operate to produce differences in the two curves. For example, if actual mental growth involves greater annual increments for those who already have higher status, then the correlation curve for actual scores, other things being equal, will be higher than that based on arbitrary cumulations. But

(1938) has proposed the concept of the *Age Ratio*

$$\left(\frac{\text{CA at Test 1}}{\text{CA at Test 2}}\right)$$

to express both these factors. The Age Ratio shows a high positive correlation with retest coefficients during the first 6 or 8 years; in later years retest coefficients tend toward greater uniformity even with wide variations in the age span.

Two implications of the Age Ratio concept may now be pointed out. If hereditary components in mental ability are more fully manifested at maturity than at earlier ages, children whose eventual status is to be either high or low will tend to fall nearer the mean in earlier tests and in later tests will gradually approximate their final position.[1]

Individual Growth Curves. The foregoing argument should also be considered in relation to statements about the "plasticity" of early childhood (susceptibility to environmental influences). Figure 3 illustrates an individual growth curve of a fairly

The mental growth [2] of the individual represented in Figure 3 is marked by some irregularities during the first 4 years. At 4, however, he achieves a fairly even, stable position which is maintained with only very minor changes to 10 years. Such a growth pattern has been variously interpreted as due to the changing nature of early tests, to a fundamental instability in early growth (related to physiological instability), and to

SIGMA
SCORES

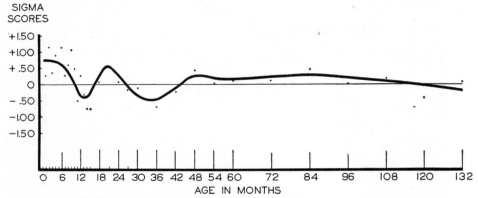

FIGURE 3. An individual mental growth curve based on sigma scores. (From original data, Berkeley Growth Study.)

typical or normal form. The curve is based on sigma or standard scores and is smoothed, the actual points also being shown. It may be noted that this is a relative, not an absolute, growth curve. A horizontal line indicates that the child is maintaining his position in the group; an ascending or descending line indicates that he is growing faster or slower than the group average.

1 This appears to be illustrated in a study by P. Cattell (1937), who made ability classifications of children on the basis of an average of initial tests and retests (thus eliminating changes within extreme groups due to regression). Children of superior average ability tended to increase in IQ on the retest. Among mental defectives, on the other hand, Roberts, Norman, and Griffiths (1938) have reported an average downward shift of about 2 IQ points per year in the age range from 10 to 14 years. It is, of course, possible that this latter finding is associated with an earlier limit of growth in the feeble-minded. See also Sloan and Harmon (1947).

a sensitive response to environmental changes. Although these factors cannot be wholly excluded, it may be pointed out that, in terms of the previous analysis of the Age Ratio, curves of this general type would be expected to be fairly common even in a constant environment or in a function insensitive to differential environmental factors. We should be cautious in attributing greater retest changes in early childhood to some inherent factor of modifiability if it is possible that they are chiefly

2 Standard score curves indicate changes in status, relative to the group, from one measurement to another. They do not provide a direct measure of growth, and, since they are usually based on unanalyzed composite scores, they do not permit inferences as to the composition or dynamics of growth. From this point of view, it may be more appropriate to speak of them as "status curves" than as growth curves.

due to a statistical factor, namely, to a relatively small proportion of similar elements in successive tests.

The growth stability manifested by the individual in Figure 3 is by no means found in all cases. Goodenough and Maurer (1942), in an able analysis of retest data from Minnesota studies, present a number of individual mental growth curves, some of

Case 553 is a boy whose mental test scores increased from a preschool sigma score of −2 to later sigma scores of +2.4 in spite of a bad physical history. He is small-statured, thin, with very poor musculature, and presents a history of early ear infections and chronic bronchitis from infancy, headaches (early glasses), stomach pains (appendectomy); he has had three operations and three serious accidents.

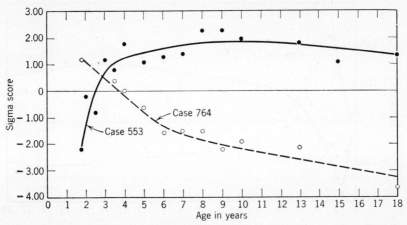

Figure 4. Individual mental growth curves: two contrasting cases. (After Honzik *et al.*) *Journal of Experimental Education.*

which exhibit IQ changes of 20 to 50 points in a span of 8 or 9 years. Unable to demonstrate associated environmental changes or cumulative environmental effects which might account for such extensive shifts in IQ, these writers are inclined to emphasize the rôle of inherent factors in determining mental growth patterns. In another longitudinal study covering a 16-year span Honzik, Macfarlane, and Allen (1948) analyzed IQ changes for varying intervals; between 6 and 18 years variations of 30 or more points occurred in 10 per cent of a sample of 222 Berkeley children. Two of these, a case showing large gains and a case showing large losses, are illustrated in Figure 4. A brief description of these cases follows:

Only one 6-month period in his life has been free of illness. In spite of a frail frame, which has suffered many serious indignities, an early strained family situation, and relatively low mental test scores in his early preschool years, his tested ability steadily increased until 9, from which time he has maintained high and fairly stable scores. His mother is a normal-school graduate; his father completed high school. His greatest security lies in his intellectual interests and achievements, but he has made good social adjustments and an amazingly good adjustment to his handicaps.

Case 764 is an example of a gradual lowering of IQ from 133 to 77 and of sigma scores from +1 to −3. She is an only child born when the mother was 44, the father 37. The estimated IQ of the mother is 65 to 70. The father is a skilled mechanic. The parents went to school until age 14.

Obesity began in late preschool years and increased steadily until therapy was instituted at age 14. Weight was normal at 17. There were, however, no IQ variations in relation to these physical changes. She was always overindulged by the mother, who lived to feed her and keep

the trends as produced solely by intrinsic growth changes. They are discussed here not as providing conclusive evidence for one view or another but as illustrating the extremes (within normal samples) which must be taken into account in mental growth theory.

Group Constancy over Long Periods. The relative stability of the "average" in-

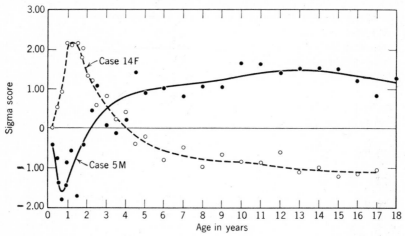

FIGURE 5. Individual mental growth curves: two contrasting cases. (From original data, Berkeley Growth Study.)

her young and who was always complaining that her daughter never gave her enough affection.

Even more striking contrasts in growth pattern are illustrated in Figure 5, showing two cases from the Berkeley Growth Study.

Age trends of such magnitude may usually be expected not oftener than in 3 or 4 per cent of the cases in a normal sample. It is obvious that to a great extent they represent a genuine shift in abilities and are not an artifact of the measuring instruments. To interpret systematic changes of this nature as due to environmental factors raises the question, "What environmental factors?" The case histories have usually failed to disclose significant clues. It is equally hypothetical, however, to regard

dividual is illustrated by the stability of groups in relative intelligence level. In a long-interval study concerned with IQ's in relation to later attainment, Embree (1948) found that the mean IQ in childhood of those later entering college was 118. The means for other groups were: college graduates, 123; those with advanced degrees, 126; honors graduates, 133; Phi Beta Kappa, 137.

The now rapidly developing field of gerontological research will eventually provide us with mental test data covering the whole span of life, and the current problems of development and environmental influence will then be seen in a much longer perspective. Already, however, we are beginning to get results from quite extended programs. Terman and Oden (1947) reported a quarter-century follow-up of the Stanford study of gifted children, first tested in 1921. In various aspects of adult attainment the record of this group has not been disappointing. Originally selected as in the ninety-ninth percentile of mental ability, in the latest measurements they were estimated by R. L. Thorndike (1948b) as falling close to the ninety-sixth percentile of the general population; this is on the basis of an ingenious series of comparisons using as a reference the norms on a vocabulary test administered to a Gallup poll sample.

A Classification of Factors Influencing Changes in Test Scores

In order to assess the importance of extrinsic factors in mental growth, we should attempt to gain some conception of the range and magnitude of other influences which affect test scores. These were briefly indicated on page 632 and are here discussed in greater detail.

Changes in Test Composition. Changes due to the measurement of different abilities cannot be attributed to "chance" factors and yet are not true variations in the growth rate of any one function. For example, consider two children, one possessing unusual motor aptitudes but poor at verbal tasks, the other showing an opposite pattern. In the preschool years the first child may stand relatively high, but these positions may be reversed at later ages when intelligence tests become more verbal in content.

Variability Changes. Contrary to common belief, the variability of mental scores does not always show a regular increase with age but may exhibit cyclical changes. Bayley (1949) has summarized evidence from a number of studies in which variability tends to be greater between the ages

of 10 and 12 years than either before or immediately after. She postulates that scores are relatively homogeneous in the early and also in the late stages of the development of a function and more dispersed during periods of rapid growth when individuals are at varying stages of maturity. Variability changes may, therefore, reflect test composition and the growth characteristics of component functions. The effects of these changes upon IQ will be especially marked for individuals toward the upper end of the IQ distribution.[1]

Changes in the Standardization Sample: Errors in Norms. A child whose IQ is constant in relation to a constant sample may exhibit an *apparent* variation if the standardization sample varies. Bayley (1949) has demonstrated this very clearly in comparing standard scores (in a longitudinal study) with test standardization IQ's. In individual cases the two sets of scores show discrepancies in trends; e.g., standard scores may remain approximately constant over parts of the age span in which the IQ's are increasing or decreasing.

Administrative Factors. "Error" factors in administration are of many sorts, pertaining to the test situation, test scoring, and the "personal equation" of different examiners. This last was apparently a negligible factor in studies by Goodenough (1928a) and Kawin (1934) but has been emphasized by P. Cattell (1937) in connection with the interpretation of mental test data from the Harvard Growth Study.

An experiment by Lantz (1945) indicates that the experience of failure tends to reduce scores and that, to a lesser degree, the

[1] The substitution of IQ equivalents (computed from the standard deviation) for the more usual IQ has often been suggested as a means of reducing apparent IQ changes, particularly when the retest involves a different test instrument. This will not, however, control IQ changes due to irregular age trends in variability unless the table of equivalents is adjusted to take account of this phenomenon.

experience of success leads to improved test performance. A possible implication is that test scores may be influenced to some extent by the examiner's attitude, according to his emphasis upon successful or unsuccessful aspects of a subject's responses. This is a complex matter, since learning experiments, such as those of Postman and Brown (1952), have shown that success and failure may affect performance not only directly but also indirectly through raising or lowering the aspiration levels. As might be expected, however, some subjects are much more vulnerable than others to effects of this nature; Mandler and Sarason (1952) demonstrated this when they classified subjects (college students) in high-anxiety and low-anxiety groups. On mental test items, the former were more variable, and more likely to be handicapped by knowledge of failure. Other experiments (see, for example, Beier, 1952) have shown that persons who are faced with a threatening situation may show measurable losses of flexibility and efficiency in mental performance, and that these effects may extend through various levels of functioning, from motor coordination to abstract thinking. Whether a mental test is regarded as a threat, a pleasurable challenge, or as something in between may depend upon many subtle factors in the management of the test situation.

Negativism. Among preschool children, even when testing conditions have secured generally good cooperation, negativistic responses may occur on individual items, with a small to large effect upon test scores.[1] Of several studies on this subject, Mayer's (1935) report on negativism en-

[1] Whereas error factors are frequently susceptible to environmental changes, and thus operate to reduce constancy coefficients, it may be noted that retest correlations may be spuriously raised if an error factor occurs systematically, for example, if children negativistic on one occasion tend also to be negativistic on succeeding tests, with similar effects upon scores.

countered in the normative group of the Revised Stanford-Binet is probably most comparable with the ordinary test situation, since the effort was directed primarily toward getting the best possible response, with the study of negativistic responses only a secondary aim. Under good testing conditions and with highly trained examiners, the average number of negativistic responses per child ranged between 4 and 7, at ages 2½ to 4½ years. About 75 per cent of the cases in that age range gave at least 1 negativistic response in one of the two testing periods. At 2 years of age less than 25 per cent of the total negativism could be overcome by adroit management, but at 5½ years 90 per cent was overcome. This last level could be reached only with skilled examiners, however, and it is possible that at these ages slight differences in examining technique may be of critical importance to test scores.

Practice Effects. Practice and special training on the part of the subject may introduce spurious changes in mental test scores. According to Terman and Merrill (1937), the *average* gain from a first to a second test is, at different age levels, from 2 to 4 IQ points. Successive additional tests produce smaller gains. An experiment by McIntosh (1944), involving weekly retests for 6 weeks, showed no significant differences beyond the second test and no relation between the practice effect and ability level, although Peel (1951) in a single retest reported greater gains among brighter children. Analyzing results from several group tests, Adkins (1937), following Thorndike, has suggested that the improvement of scores on retest with the same examination may be largely a matter of increased speed on tasks previously solved. If this is so, work-limit tests would be of greater value than time-limit tests in longitudinal studies. The reader interested in the earlier literature on practice effects and other conditions of testing will find a list of such studies in a review by R. L. Thorndike (1940).

Coaching. One special case of practice effect which deserves separate mention is the effect of coaching or specialized training.[1] Although our present studies in this field point to no very clear-cut conclusion, they suggest, as might be expected, that training is most effective when devoted to material similar to that in the test, and that the effects of training are, characteristically, to produce a temporary but not permanent rise in IQ. The application of these findings is greatest at the preschool ages, when test materials are relatively similar to everyday playthings. Earlier reports on the effects of coaching have been reviewed by Burks (1928c).

Intrinsic and Extrinsic Factors. All the factors discussed above may be regarded as involving errors in measurement. In addition to these error factors, mental growth may be conceived as involving actual changes, which have an origin in either intrinsic or extrinsic forces. Intrinsic alterations may arise from specific or general changes in the rate of growth. Relevant factors are the form of the growth curve, with reference to possible cyclical changes, and the age of completion of growth; a neurophysiological basis is implied.

Extrinsic influences on mental growth are roughly of two sorts, social and personal. The social factors include general environmental conditions, such as socio-economic factors in the home and neighborhood and specific educational régimes. What are here called personal factors are those nonability aspects of a person's make-up which ac-

tually affect the course of growth in ability rather than merely modify the score at a particular test period. The personal factors, if traumatic, such as physical diseases or extreme emotional episodes, may affect mental growth fairly directly. The more permanent aspects of physical and mental constitution may influence mental development by virtue of the fact that they comprise part of the equipment through which the individual assimilates the environment.

In evaluating extrinsic relationships, one of the first facts with which we are confronted is that in the preschool period the prediction of later intelligence can be improved by taking into account a measure of the home environment. The varying interpretations of this finding will be discussed in the ensuing section.

Relationships to Cultural-Economic Factors

Education of the Parents. Figure 6, from Bayley's (1953) data, shows at successive ages the relationship between mental scores of children and the education of their parents (in terms of the average years of schooling of father and mother). This is an admittedly imperfect index of the cultural status of the parents and an even less perfect index of the extent to which cultural factors actually enter into the child's environment. Nevertheless, if we compare Figures 6 and 2, we can see that the parents' education (obtained before the birth of the child) yields a much better prediction of the child's intelligence at 18 years than does the child's own test score at ages below 2 years. The relation of parents' education to the child's test score is negative in infancy (a fact consonant with the discussion on page 637). It increases sharply during the period from 1 to 2 years and thereafter shows only minor changes. Somewhat similar corre-

---

[1] The studies of Greene (1928) and Casey, Davidson, and Harter (1928), reported in the *Twenty-seventh Yearbook of the National Society for the Study of Education,* are particularly relevant to this problem.

lation curves have been reported by Bayley and Jones (1937) for other measures of social and economic factors.[1]

For such findings the most obvious interpretation is that better-educated parents provide environments more stimulating to mental growth and that in general children tend to acquire the intellectual status characteristic of the environment to which

eventual intelligence level, they manifest the degree of relationship to parents' intelligence (or to other factors correlated with parents' intelligence) that would be expected on the basis of the inheritance of abilities.

The hypothesis that mental growth involves growth toward hereditary levels is supported by analogous findings from

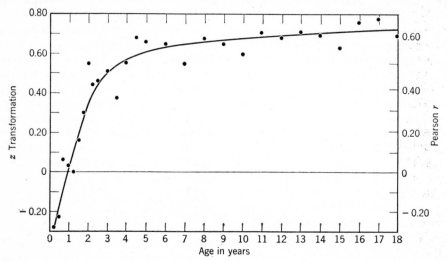

FIGURE 6. The relationship of midparent education to children's mental scores at successive ages. (After Bayley.) *Journal of Educational Psychology.*

they are exposed. Equally reasonable, however, is an interpretation based primarily on the maturing of hereditary potentialities. As a corollary to the discussion of the Age Ratio, the argument has been advanced that, as children approach their

1 Correlations with social status are usually lower than with measures of parent education. Stroud (1928) reported an *r* of .25 between IQ and tax assessments; Chapman and Wiggins (1925), an *r* of .32 between IQ and the Chapman-Sims Scale of Socio-Economic Status. These studies were based on large samples. When cultural items are included in a home rating or an environmental scale, Burks (1928b) found a correlation of .42, and Leahy (1935) one of .53, with intelligence measures. In interpreting correlational data in this field, attention must be given to the characteristics of the socio-economic measures, particularly with regard to skewness of the distributions.

studies of physical growth. Bayley (1953) has reported, for successive ages in childhood, increasing correlations between the heights of boys and their fathers, and increasing correlations between body-build measures of daughters and their mothers. In the case of boys, a gradual upward trend in the correlation of the child's height with the midparent height, from .22 at 2 months to .50 at 5 years and .77 at 17 years, is probably only in small part explainable in terms of environmental factors.

The relationship curve as given in Figure 6 presents us with hypotheses rather than with definitive evidence of causal relationship. Each of these hypotheses may serve as a partial explanation of the facts as obtained, but their relative cogency cannot be estimated unless we turn to evidence involving some form of experimental design. Such evidence will be presented in connection with a discussion of studies of foster children.

Perhaps the most elaborate study employing correlational methods is by Van Alstyne (1929), who examined the relationship between children's intelligence (Kuhlmann-Binet) and various factors in the home environment. The sample, consisting of seventy-five 3-year-old children, was drawn from very diverse environments in New York City, and the correlations may tend to be higher than in a more representative group. Table 2, showing r's and PE's, presents illustrative results from this study.

TABLE 2

THE MENTAL AGE OF CHILDREN AS RELATED TO ENVIRONMENTAL FACTORS

(From Van Alstyne [1929].)

Child's MA by:	r
Mother's education	.60 ± .05
Father's education	.51 ± .06
"Opportunity for use of constructive play materials"	.50 ± .06
"Number of hours adults spend daily with child"	.32 ± .07
"Number of playmates in home"	.16 ± .08
"Number of hours father reads to child"	.06 ± .08
Nutrition index	− .03 ± .08

In general, environmental factors that might reasonably be expected to have some bearing upon mental development yielded no higher correlations than those found for less relevant factors (e.g., a biserial r of .54 ± .08 was found between the child's MA and whether or not he slept alone in his own bed). Both groups of factors illustrate in similar degree the general re-

lation between socio-economic status and intelligence.

The relationship of environmental factors to IQ change has been examined by Bradway (1945) in the case of 50 California children showing especially marked increases or decreases in a retest after 10 years. Initial and retest IQ means for contrasting groups were: 107, increasing to 126; and 113, decreasing to 96. Bradway called attention to the fact that direct measures of the children's environments, such as home status indices, yielded smaller differences for the two groups than measures of parental and grandparental characteristics, such as intelligence scores based on vocabulary or on occupation.

Occupation and "Social Class." The principal earlier sources of material on the relationship of intelligence to socio-economic factors include a volume by Schwesinger (1933) and one by Lorimer and Osborn (1934). Subsequent reviews or critical summaries have been published by Neff (1938), Loevinger (1940), Herrick (1951), and McCandless (1952). Neff pointed out that in various studies of school children a range of about 20 points in IQ has been found between children of the highest and lowest socio-economic groups. This also holds among preschool children, as shown in Table 3. The differences commonly reported are sometimes more marked for verbal tests but are not limited to verbal tests. Thus, Havighurst and Breese (1947) found that children of higher family social status were significantly superior to those of lower status in each of the Thurstone tests of primary mental abilities. In another study, Janke and Havighurst (1945) obtained significant social class differences for each of a series of verbal and nonverbal tests, with the exception of the Minnesota Mechanical Assembly Test.

TABLE 3

MEAN IQ'S OF PRESCHOOL CHILDREN, CLASSI-
FIED BY FATHER'S OCCUPATION *

Father's Occupation	Goode-nough (1928b)	Terman and Merrill (1937)
I. Professional	116	116
II. Semiprofessional and managerial	112	112
III. Clerical and skilled trades	108	108
IV. Semiskilled and minor clerical	105	104
V. Slightly skilled	104	95
VI. Unskilled	96	94

* Goodenough's sample consisted of 380 Minneapolis children between the ages of 18 and 54 months the Kuhlmann-Binet was given twice to each child, the means reported in Table 3 being based on the initial test only. The Terman and Merrill sample consisted of 831 children, ages 2 and 5½ years, in the standardization groups for Forms L and M of the revised Stanford-Binet. In this latter sample, an additional classification of "rural owner' was included, with a mean IQ of 99.

Similar occupational and social class differences are observed when other criteria are employed. If, for example, we examine the percentage distribution of the parents of gifted children, or the parents of persons listed in *Who's Who in America*, we find a very disproportionate number in the higher occupational brackets. On the other hand, parents of children admitted to feeble-minded institutions tend to cluster in the lower brackets. If we turn to results from item analyses, Herrick (1951) has summarized nine studies with reference to items which show large or small social status differences. Although there are some inconsistent findings, several studies indicate that high-status children are relatively more proficient in linguistic tests (especially those involving thinking or reasoning) and do relatively less well in tests emphasizing rote memory and perceptual functions.

The assertion has been made by Neff (1938) that the occupational hierarchy in IQ can be accounted for entirely in environmental terms. This would seem to be implied in Pieter's (1939) suggestion of a "coefficient of innate intelligence," to be obtained through dividing the IQ by an environmental index. A somewhat similar line of argument is advanced by Davis (1948) and Davis and Havighurst (1948). These writers criticize existing intelligence tests as being too narrowly limited to problems of an academic type, which are not equally relevant, comprehensible, or motivating among children of different social classes. Support can readily be found for the argument that current testing methods emphasize subject matter, problems, and tasks which are more compatible with middle-class than with lower-class goals and experiences; such tests tend to underpredict the educability of lower-class children. We cannot, however, jump to the conclusion that these biasing factors account for all or even a major part of the social class differential. Davis's criticisms incur special difficulty with nonverbal tests and with the mental test differences found in the preschool period.

It may be useful to repeat once more the generally acknowledged fact that the validity of mental tests diminishes when we apply them to groups deviating in cultural norms from the original standardization group. Davis (1951), however, goes so far as to deny that genetic factors (although influencing individual mental development) are in any important way related to social level or are segregated by socio-economic conditions.

The hypothesis that the intelligence differential between the social classes is to some extent a hereditary sampling difference emerges from two assumptions: (1) individual variations in intelligence are, in part, genetic in origin; and (2) differences in the selection of occupations and in occupational success are in part determined by intelligence. These differences, moreover, tend to be confirmed both through assortative mating and segregation and, in a competitive society, through the tendency for the more intelligent to rise and the less intelligent to sink in the social scale. This vertical mobility is, of course, incomplete and resisted by considerable inertia; [1] we cannot doubt that it occurs, although up to the present time most studies of interclass migration have failed to utilize measures of mental abilities.

The monograph by Eells, Davis, *et al.* (1951) is an important contribution to the literature on social status. Approximately 5000 children, ages 9 and 10, and 13 and 14, were given five standard tests. Correlations with social status indices (based on parental occupation and education, housing and dwelling area) ranged as high as .43 with Terman-McNemar IQ and as low as .20 to .28 with the Thurstone Spatial and Reasoning Tests, and the Otis Nonverbal IQ. Status differences on individual items were analyzed in greater detail than in any previous study; an additional item analysis would, however, be desirable, comparing social groups not by age but by mental age or IQ. In general,

the results supported previous studies in showing a relation between status differences and verbal symbolic content. The concluding statement refers to "the substantial number of items showing large status differences for which no reasonable explanation can be seen. This may, of course, merely reflect lack of insight on the part of the writer. The presence of such a large proportion of unexplained differences should, however, lead to caution in accepting the idea that all status differences on test items can be readily accounted for in terms of the cultural bias of their content" (p. 357).

Another approach to environmental correlation is found in the study by Thorndike and Woodyard (1942) of the average intelligence of sixth-grade children, in communities of 20,000 to 30,000 population, as related to average income and "general goodness" of community life. Income was estimated from such data as teacher salaries, wages, and median rentals; "general goodness," from expenditures for education, community health, and various economic and social items. For 30 communities, a correlation of .78 was reported between intelligence and income, and .86 between intelligence and "general goodness." [2]

McGehee and Lewis (1942) have stated the intelligence-environment relationship in still another way by computing, for a large sample of children in 36 states, the ratio of superior and retarded children to "normal expectancy." The results, according to

---

[1] Since the members of lower classes have a reduced educational opportunity, it is here that we must look for the greatest discrepancy (in terms of the number of individuals) between potential and realized attainment. One illustration of this is to be found in a study by Goetsch (1940), who examined the college records of a sample of over 1000 high school graduates all of whom had IQ's of 117 or above. In spite of an intelligence adequate for college work, only about one-quarter of these attended college full-time if the parental income was under $2000 a year. Where the parental income was $5000 or above, more than 90 per cent attended college full-time.

[2] These are, of course, correlations between averages. The level of such environmental correlations may be expected to vary considerably in relation to the selection of communities; a later study by R. L. Thorndike (1951) obtained markedly lower coefficients. It is of special interest that in this instance environmental correlations with intelligence were higher than with achievement; Thorndike explains this on the assumption that differences between communities are chiefly in nonschool factors, and that schools tend to introduce a standardizing influence.

parents' occupation, are shown in Table 4. Although the proportion of high IQ children is larger in the higher socio-economic

TABLE 4

RATIOS OF EXCEPTIONAL CHILDREN TO NORMAL EXPECTANCY

Social Class	Superior	Retarded
Professional	2.40	.14
Semiprofessional and business	1.62	.49
Skilled workmen	.88	.98
Semiskilled	.92	1.39
Unskilled	.30	1.53

levels, the great bulk of superior children is to be found in the much larger total membership of groups lower in the social scale. The social and educational implications of this fact have been developed at some length by Warner, Havighurst, and Loeb (1946).

Special interest attaches to the fact that the social differential in intelligence is well established as early as 2 or 3 years of age and is relatively constant in later childhood. From the public school data of the Harvard Growth Study, Shuttleworth (1940) has shown that from 8 to 18 years the mean IQ of children in white collar groups remains fairly constant around 108; the mean IQ was similarly constant around 96 in families where the father was an unskilled or semiskilled laborer. If the social differential is due to family (and neighborhood) environmental effects acting directly, one would expect it to be small in early childhood and to increase gradually with age. The constancy of the difference appears to be more difficult to explain on an environmental than on a primarily hereditary basis.

An additional line of evidence, contrary to the environmental hypothesis, has been supplied by Lawrence (1931), who showed a relationship between children's IQ and the occupational status of their parents, even where environmental differentials were ruled out (in the case of children removed from their homes in infancy and brought up in an institution). D. C. Jones and Carr-Saunders (1927) added a further relevant finding in comparing the intelligence of children of different social origins who lived in an orphanage for varying lengths of time. Continued residence in this less differential environment apparently had little or no effect in reducing or "leveling" the original social differential in intelligence.

A study by Outhit (1933) provides an interesting comparison between the intelligence of children and their parents. Fifty-one families were represented, with 4 or more children in each family. The Army Alpha was used with adults and with children above 12, scores being transformed into IQ's for comparison with the Stanford-Binet IQ's of the younger children. Figure 7 indicates a tendency toward a greater occupational differential among parents than among children or, in other words, a tendency for children of either superior or inferior parents to regress toward the mean of the total group. This result would be predicted on the basis of genetic factors, but, so far as home environments are concerned, it is by no means clear that environmental theory would lead to the same expectation.

Rural-Urban Studies. That rural children in the United States attain lower average IQ's than urban children has been confirmed in numerous reports. The choice of tests is an important factor in this connection. Tests are usually devised by city dwellers and validated on city children; it is reasonable to expect that their content and perhaps also their time limitations will tend to handicap rural children. Attitudes and incentives important for efficient test performance may be stimulated in varying degrees by different school systems; in general, rural children probably receive less practice than urban children in working at high pressure under speed and accuracy requirements. Shepard (1942) has shown that rural children, inferior to urbans on verbal tests and on tests involving speed of performance, were definitely superior in mechanical assembly and in error scores in

Numerous investigations have reported not merely a low IQ for rural children but also an IQ diminishing with age. Among these are: (1) the often-cited report by Gordon (1923) on English gypsies and canal boat children, showing marked negative correlations between age and IQ; (2) Asher's (1935) study of children in the east

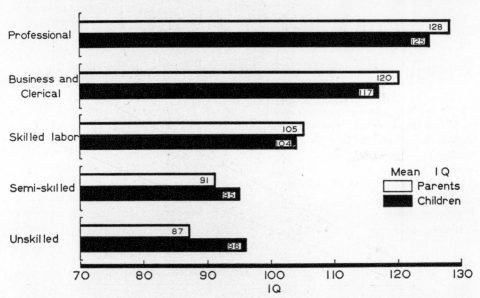

FIGURE 7. Parents' and children's intelligence, in different occupational classes. (After Outhit.) *Archives of Psychology.*

spatial relations tests. Environmental demands and practices must be assumed to have some part in determining such differences.

As long ago as 1929 Shimberg demonstrated that the urban superiority on an information test could be reversed if the test were originally scaled from items supplied by rural teachers and standardized on a rural group. A similar experiment has not been attempted with other types of material; it is probable that a distinctive "urban" and "rural" content is more apparent in an information test than in other tests.

Kentucky mountains (in this group the median IQ dropped steadily from 84 at 7 years to 60 at 15 years); (3) a report by Edwards and Jones (1938) on school children in the mountains of north Georgia (IQ's dropped from around 100 at ages 7 to 9 years to 76 at age 14, and 70 for those older); (4) Jordan's (1933) study of the children of mill workers in a North Carolina town (IQ's decreased from 100 at age 6 to 85 at 13 years); (5) studies of Iowa children by Baldwin, Fillmore, and Hadley (1930) and by Skeels and Fillmore (1937). In the last report, children from underprivileged homes (either rural or urban) were examined at the time of entrance to an orphanage; the mean IQ diminished from 93 at age 4 to 80 at age 14.[1]

Representative results from a group test survey are shown in Figure 8. Chapanis and Williams (1945) administered the Kuhlmann-Anderson test to 4311 children in "a fairly rich agricultural area" located near

were tested. It seems probable that, since the survey was based on children in schools, a somewhat superior selection of children in the county was obtained at the upper ages. Nevertheless, the mental ages of all groups exhibit a somewhat regular divergence from the norm, and the mean IQ's for all cases decrease from 94 at age 6 to 76 at age 15.

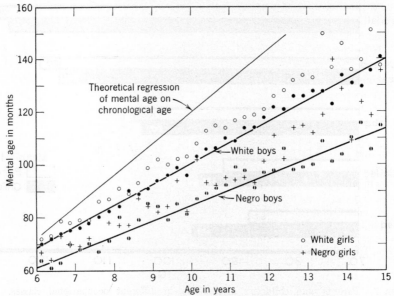

FIGURE 8. Mental growth of rural groups. (After Chapanis and Williams.) *Journal of Genetic Psychology.*

the center of Tennessee. Approximately 90 per cent of the white children and 73 per cent of the Negro children in the county

[1] Speer (1940a, b) and a number of other investigators have utilized similar material from children referred to institutions because of conditions in their own homes. Older children, who have lived longer in homes characterized by poverty and frequently by other undesirable factors, have lower average IQ's than younger children from similar environments. It must be noted, however, that these test scores are not based on cumulative records or on sibling comparisons, but on different samples which may have been subjected to different selective factors. Thus it seems likely that among the older children in very inferior environments some of the brighter ones have already been removed by relatives or by placement agencies.

Results of this nature have been variously interpreted as due to (1) the "retarding effect of poor homes on mental development" (Skeels and Fillmore, 1937), (2) the effect on the Stanford-Binet of "continued existence at a critically low level of social and cultural status" (Neff, 1938), or (3) the effect of using tests which at higher age levels become increasingly inappropriate for the groups to which they are applied (Asher, 1935).

The first of these interpretations, in line with other Iowa studies, proposes an actual psychological handicap resulting from a poor environment. The second and third interpretations are more purely psychometric, although the second seems to imply some actual cumulative handicap in mental test abilities, whereas the third is concerned primarily with an age differential in the tests which lowers their validity.

It would be permissible to hold all these interpretations simultaneously, but they would still fail to give an adequate picture of the complex situation involved in the comparison of different cultural groups. In studying the possibility of differential environmental handicap on different test items, Jones, Conrad, and Blanchard (1932) made an item analysis of test results for 351 New England rural children, aged 4 to 14, as compared with 905 children in the 1916 Stanford-Binet standardization and also with 212 children from a relatively homogeneous urban sampling which was highly superior in socio-economic status. The three groups had mean IQ's of 92, 101, and 117, respectively.

Several individual items were identified as showing very different levels of difficulty in the three groups, with a tendency for the differences to increase with age. These were all verbal items, again illustrating the principle that items which in a common environment may be a good index of intelligence may in widely differing environments become predominantly a good index of the environment.

Under such conditions the resulting IQ's will require reinterpretation, and in this particular study the authors estimated that social and educational factors could on the average account for about half the mean difference of 10 points in IQ between the rural and the normal urban groups. These environmental handicaps, however, appeared to be specific to certain test items, rather than general. As would be expected if the rural-urban difference is in part due to a difference in hereditary

capacities, certain types of tests were found with a marked difference which could not readily be explained in terms of differential opportunities for special training, or differential interest or motivation.[1] On the basis of this item-and-age analysis, the conclusion was offered that the rural group (although representative for the communities studies) presented an inherently poorer selection than the urban comparison groups.

The study of selective rural migration (selective drainage into urban centers and urban occupations) may in the future result in a fuller understanding of rural-urban differences. It is interesting that both in the study discussed above and in an English study by Thomson (1921) fewer high IQ's were found in rural communities accessible to city districts than in comparable communities more remotely located. Areas supplied by good transportation and near a growing urban center are probably in some regions more subject to selective drainage. Similar interpretations may apply to results obtained by Bickersteth (1919) in the Yorkshire dales and by Macmeeken (1939) in isolated rural and coastal sections of northern and western Scotland. It is hard to see how the children in these remote localities could have acquired relatively high average IQ's on the basis of superior cultural opportunities. Economic factors are important in determining the nature of selective migration. Lorimer and Osborn (1934) have cited a number of surveys indicating that in relatively prosperous rural areas the cities attract from both the upper and lower extremes of social status. In depressed rural areas, on the other hand, a survey by Gee and Corson (1929) indicated that the less intelligent

---

1 These included the ball-and-field test, memory for designs, digit memory, picture description, and comprehension.

Results which are in general similar to those of this study have been obtained by Bruce (1940) in a Virginia survey of rural white and Negro children.

are more frequently "bound to the land," whereas those of higher social, educational, and intellectual status tend, in greater proportions, to migrate to urban centers. This is supported by Mauldin (1940) and Sanford (1940) on the basis of data from small southern communities.[1]

Rural-urban differences are maintained into high school and beyond; Nelson (1942), testing over 1000 students entering the State College of Washington, found higher average scores for urban students in all parts of the ACE test. Similar differences were found for (a) test materials which might be expected to be especially vulnerable to environmental influence and (b) subtests (such as figure analogies) regarded as more "culture-free." This would seem to point to the probability of a difference in selection.

In concluding this section, the interpretation of rural handicap as due to lack of cultural privilege is seen to provide only a partial explanation. Commenting on the lack of schooling of southern mountain children,[2] Goodenough (1940a) pointed out that our pioneering New England ancestors did not find schools ready made in the wilderness.

They made schools, and it did not require two centuries of residence for them to do so. Accordingly, I find it hard to accept the idea that the low IQ's of the mountain children are to be explained solely on the basis of educational depriva-

[1] For other studies of rural groups, see Clark and Gist (1938), who reported the occurrence of selective migration in Kansas, and Klineberg (1938), who reported its occurrence in a study in southern Germany but found no evidence for it in a parallel investigation in New Jersey. Conflicting evidence in this field is an indication not of inadequacy in the studies involved but rather of the varying balance of the complex factors influencing selection. For a critical discussion of earlier research, see Thomas et al. (1938, pp. 110 ff.).

[2] See Sherman and Key (1932) and Sherman and Henry (1933).

tion. One is forced to ask: Why were they so deprived? [P. 329.]

The principal outcome of the socio-economic and rural-urban studies is to emphasize the fact that, among groups as among individuals, differences cannot be explained in terms of a fixed structure of relationship. With changes in any of the related factors (test composition, hereditary selection, or environment) group or individual differences will represent varying degrees of hereditary or environmental influence.

"Hospitalism." Another form of environmental deprivation is that experienced by institution children, who may receive less adult attention and less language stimulation than children in normal homes. A number of writers, particularly Spitz (1945, 1946) and Fischer (1952), have emphasized the conception that the child in an institution is frustrated in his attempts to form a libidinal object-relation with a mother or mother-substitute. This relationship is held to be essential to normal mental development, particularly in the third to sixth month of infancy.

Alleged effects of hospitalism, leading to severe mental retardation, have been described for individual children and for small groups, but as yet no studies with appropriate control groups have been conducted. At the present time there may be some question as to whether the conclusions rest primarily on empirical findings, or on deductions from psychoanalytic theory.

It would not be surprising if institutional life were found to involve developmental handicaps. So far as mental functions are concerned, we would not expect this handicap to be clearly shown during the first 6 months of life, or to be of great magnitude in later months. It is often difficult, however, to make proper allowance for sampling factors when the effects of institutional life are being studied.

Racio-Cultural Comparisons. Comparative studies of Negroes and whites have frequently reported a difference between average IQ's with a tendency for the amount of difference to increase with age. Several studies have also indicated, among mixed bloods, a relationship between intelligence and the degree of white admixture. In these comparisons, however, educational factors and social status have usually been uncontrolled. Until further, more crucial evidence is supplied, we must remain in some doubt as to the bearing of Negro-white investigations upon the nature-nurture problem.

Another approach which has given suggestive results is represented in the well-known work of Klineberg (1935), who studied the intelligence of Negro migrants from the South in relation to their length of residence in New York City. The average IQ for children newly arrived was 81.4 (Stanford-Binet), as compared with 84.5 for those who had been in New York 2 to 3 years, and 87.4 for those in residence longer than 4 years. It is reasonable to interpret this as an environmental effect (including greater test sophistication), provided that similar selections of migrants arrived in successive years, and provided also that no selective factors have operated with regard to continued residence in New York. Could an educationally improved environment, exerting its effects early enough and long enough, bring the average IQ of these children not merely to 87 but to the norm of 100 or even higher? An affirmative conclusion is an inviting one but is perhaps a premature "extrapolation" from the facts now available.

Numerous studies of American Indians have obtained somewhat lower means for Indians than for whites. This may be a special case of rural-urban and social class difference. As contrasted with verbal tests, performance tests are sometimes reported as yielding little or no difference. A study illustrating this is one by Havighurst and Hilkevitch (1944). With careful attention to representative sampling, they found among 660 Indian children a mean score on the Arthur Performance Scale approximately equal to the norms. It is of special interest, however, that marked intertribal differences were discovered. These could not readily be assigned to cultural influences from contact with whites; the Shiprock Navajo, for example, with considerable contact with white culture, obtained a mean IQ of 95, whereas the Oraibi (Hopi), with only moderate contact with white culture, registered a mean of 113 (about 90 cases in each sample). The evidence from this study suggests that the verbal factor, but not the speed factor, is a handicap in Indian test performance. Here, as in some other racio-cultural as well as in some social class comparisons, bilingualism may be one of the sources of difficulty. A survey of studies on this topic will be found in Chapter 9, Language Development in Children.

F. S. Freeman (in a volume edited by Skinner, 1936) has very properly emphasized the fact that the comparison of North American Indians and Negroes with others is hindered at almost every turn by social, educational, economic, and hygienic disparities.

> It remains for the future to demonstrate whether North American Negroes and Indians are by nature intellectually inferior to the whites; and such may or may not be the case. What present data do show is that, under existing conditions of environment inequality, they have, as groups, failed to reach the levels attained by contemporary whites [pp. 419–420].

No attempt will be made in this chapter to cover the enormous (and highly controversial) literature concerning "race" differences. With ethnic groups other than those mentioned above, we are constantly faced by questions of intragroup selection (selective migration) as well as by questions bearing on environmental handicaps and the appropriateness of tests. On the basis of tests ordinarily accepted for measuring intelligence, the weight of evidence points to the probability of a difference, in terms of averages, between American citizens of north European and south European descent. It is possible, but not certain, that this difference would wholly disappear if a correction were made for social status and educational differences. The effect of such a correction can hardly be predicted, for no one as yet has conducted an experiment in which controlled selections of children varying as to racial background have been reared under similar environmental conditions.

Educational Opportunity. The differences discussed in the preceding sections are undoubtedly influenced at many points by differences in formal schooling. Relevant but not entirely satisfactory evidence on this problem is available from studies of adolescents in and out of school. In a report entitled "Schooling Makes a Difference," Lorge (1945) examined at age 34 the intelligence test scores of 131 men who had been tested 20 years earlier. For individuals roughly comparable in IQ at age 14, retest scores proved to be higher for those who completed more grades in school. It seems reasonable to assume that those remaining in school longer developed a continuing pattern of interests and attainments which tended to give them an advantage in later tests. But, in the absence of more complete experimental data, explanations can rarely be as simple as this. For example, we cannot ignore the possibility of differential mental growth rates and differ-

ential growth limits reflected both in educational attainment and in later test scores.

IQ changes over a 10-year period were examined by Husén (1951), who compared tests given at induction into military service with test scores obtained in the third grade, for 613 Swedish boys. Gains (found in all groups except those with the smallest schooling) were related to the number of school grades completed. The amount of schooling correlated .80 with the final test scores, but also correlated .61 with the *initial* test score, suggesting that this is another example of the effects of intrinsic difference in growth pattern, reinforced in varying degrees by differences in educational opportunity. Children with initially high IQ's tended to retain their level even when environmentally underprivileged.

Another European study which may bear on this problem is that of de Groot (1948, 1951) who analyzed IQ changes in successive groups of applicants to an industrial training school in the Netherlands. Applicants showed a decline in IQ during the war period, and a subsequent return to the prewar level. Although de Groot attributed this to schooling deficiencies during the war, it is obvious that many other factors, including sampling variations, may have contributed to the trends which he demonstrated.

Vernon (1948) showed that, after the age of 17, boys not attending school declined in ability measures related to scholastic activities but continued to gain in mechanical and spatial abilities. It is reasonable to suppose that the early cessation of schooling may handicap performance in tests which were originally designed to predict scholastic aptitude. On the other hand, the question may be raised whether some of those who leave school early may not do so because of a different pattern of abilities or an early tapering-off of growth in some functions.

Effective gains in intelligence test scores beyond the age of 19 or 20 are not easy to demonstrate in a representative sample but can usually be found in a college population (Livesay, 1939; R. L. Thorndike, 1948a). Here again we are confronted with an unsolved question whether the more intelligent enjoy a longer span of intrinsic growth or whether the better-schooled improve their scores through a piling-up of educational experiences. Perhaps the two alternatives have a common denominator in intellectual stimulation and practice. It would be foolish to deny that longer schooling is a factor of advantage in mental test performance; however, the advantage is not without limits, as can be seen in studies of mental decline among adults. Evidence is contradictory as to whether the rate of decline is related to education, but we cannot doubt that some decline does often occur, probably well before the age of 60, even among those who are continuously engaged in scholarly activities (Jones and Kaplan, 1945).

Another interesting line of evidence concerning presumptive educational effects is to be found in studies of secular trends; what changes can be demonstrated over a period of years in comparable samplings when improvements have occurred in educational factors? The most important body of data bearing on this problem is in the comparison of Scottish 11-year-olds in 1932 and 1947. In the later testing, involving over 70,000 cases, Thomson *et al.* (1949) found slight gains, contrary to the hypothesis of a loss based on differential fertility. Similarly, R. B. Cattell (1950), in a comparison of 10-year-old children in the city of Leicester, found after a 13-year interval a slight but significant increase in a nonverbal test. Since he had previously (Cattell, 1940) predicted a decrease of 1 IQ point in each 10 years, he suggested

the possibility that the predicted fall in intelligence actually occurred but was masked by an advance in education and test sophistication. The British investigators have also speculated on the possibility of selective reproduction within social classes, and of genetic mechanisms which may serve to resist gene loss in a population, in spite of differential fertility. It may be noted that predictions, made early in this century, of declining average height have also failed and have in fact been quite wide of the mark, since in many comparative studies average heights have shown well-defined increases.

Several investigations in this country have given rather striking evidence of gains in mental test scores. Tuddenham (1948) compared World War I draftees with a sample of 768 men selected as representative of the World War II draft population. On comparable revisions of the Army Alpha, he found that the World War II median could be estimated as falling at about the 82 percentile of the World War I distribution. In interpreting this very substantial gain, we need to bear in mind the possibility that the earlier distribution, obtained in the infancy of group testing, may have included more cases for whom the tests were inappropriate or improperly administered. It is also possible that the World War II draftees were more carefully screened in the initial selective procedures. With regard to educational differences, the later sample had, on the average, 2 years more of schooling; it was a more urban sample, with greater exposure to modern media of communication.

Tuddenham's conclusion that a large proportion of the gain is "a consequence of more and better education for more people" deserves serious consideration but leaves us with the usual problem when mental tests on different populations are compared; i.e., to what extent are the differences psychometric and to what extent do they represent genuine increments in mental power? A genetic theory to account for changes of this nature might be that improved communication and increased urbanization reduce the number of retarded children by dispersing recessive gene pools in isolated communities. It is difficult, however, to see how this could account for more than a very minor average gain in IQ within a single generation.

Another example of an apparent secular trend is to be found in Wheeler's (1942) study of Tennessee mountain children, based on 3252 subjects in 40 schools. As compared with results from the same region obtained a decade earlier, the mean IQ (while still well below 100 at nearly all ages) had increased approximately 10 points. Table 5 presents the results for

TABLE 5

IQ GAINS OVER 10 YEARS IN COMPARABLE GROUPS OF TENNESSEE MOUNTAIN CHILDREN

	Mean IQ	
Age	1930	1940
6	94.7	102.6
8	83.9	99.2
10	84.3	91.4
12	81.4	90.2
14	74.7	85.1
16	73.5	80.0

the even years tested. It seems very improbable that the consistently higher level in the later testing could be due to a selective factor affecting all age levels in a uniform manner; to a considerable degree the same families were represented in the two surveys, and there was little evidence of population shifts due to in or out migration. Wheeler attributes the gains to better schools, greater school attendance,

and improved contact with the outer world through better roads. It is a little surprising, however, that the rate of decline in IQ is not affected by the changes which have produced a generally higher level.

Increases in test scores over a period of years are also shown in a remarkable study by S. Smith (1942), who compared the test performance of Honolulu children in 1924 and 1938. Care was taken to obtain comparable samples of all public school children between the ages of 10.0 and 15.0. The writer has computed results in terms of the averages [1] and SD's for the 1924 10-year-old group. Figure 9 exhibits gains which are highly significant in each test and at each age level. The greatest change is in the nonverbal test, in which the 10-year mean for 1938 exceeds the 12-year mean for 1924. When the various racial groups in Honolulu were compared very significant differences were found in each testing. In general, the "whites," Japanese, Chinese, and Koreans obtained high scores, whereas the Hawaiians, Filipinos, Puerto Ricans, and Portuguese scored much lower. Some curious results emerged, however, in comparing results across a time interval. In the nonverbal tests, for example, a critical ratio of 8.5 was found in 1924 for the difference between whites and native Hawaiians. By 1938 an improvement in the nonverbal scores of the Hawaiians brought them nearly to the white average for 1924. Nevertheless, the differentiation of the groups still remained and in fact increased, since the higher-scoring groups tended to make even greater gains in all tests. It has been suggested that this is what would be expected if the original differences are innate, since the more capable groups would presumably take greater advantage of improved educational opportunities than the

1 Smith presents the nonverbal means and (because of skewing) the medians for the two verbal tests.

less capable groups. The author of this study, however, is careful to point out that the results may be complicated by selective factors in migration as well as by various cultural factors, so that it is hardly permissible to use these data for any conclusive statements about differences between races.

As a concluding note on secular trends, mention may be made of a study by Klat-

Mental and Physical Relationships [1]

One of the more competent studies is by Abernethy (1936), who found positive correlations between intelligence and various physical measures at all ages from 8 to 17 years; in the case of height the average r was .26 for boys and .22 for girls in the age range from 2 to 8 years.

The relevance of this topic to the present problem is in part indicated by Sanders'

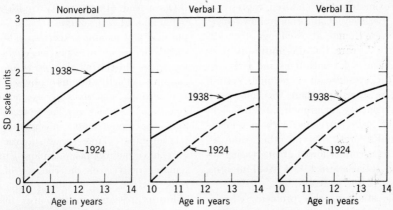

FIGURE 9. Mental growth curves in comparable samples, in 1924 and 1938. (After Smith.) *Journal of Genetic Psychology.*

skin (1952) in which a sample of infants around a year of age was given the Cattell Infant Intelligence Scale. As compared with the norms, superior performance was shown on most items, except vocabulary. Klatskin considered that the score differences provide evidence for a trend in the direction of more precocious development, related to changes since the 1930's in infant care. This trend is described as most apparent in the motor components of infant mental tests, resulting from a régime of greater stimulation and exercise, greater parental attention, and less confining clothes. This can hardly be regarded as more than a hypothesis, however, until additional studies are made, with careful sampling controls.

(1934) discussion of differential physical growth:

> Evidence of differential growth, or its end result—differential size—shows that everywhere children with a superior socio-economic environment are on the average heavier and taller than their age-mates exposed to a less favorable environment. . . . The study does not dispute the fact that in all probability there are inherent differences between the various socio-eco-

[1] The best-known earlier treatise on this topic is Paterson's *Physique and Intellect* (1930). Jones (1933b, 1936, 1939), in a series of reviews, summarized approximately 300 studies, and later reviews by Shock (1939a, 1944, 1947), Carmichael (1940), and Shock and Jones (1941) give a representative account of research on physiological relationships. Perhaps owing to the generally small or zero relationships found, research in this field has diminished in subsequent years.

nomic classes. Its one and only contention is that the rôle of environment cannot be overlooked. . . . And, if environmental differences are important enough to affect physical growth, it is most probable that they affect psycho-social adaptations and behavior as well [p. 299].

The hypothesis implied in the foregoing was subjected to a test by Honzik and Jones (1937), who examined the relationship of height to intelligence in a group of approximately 200 children representative of Berkeley, California. Low correlations were found at each age from 21 months to 7 years, but the uniformly positive coefficients for both boys and girls suggested the presence of a genuine, even if meager, relationship; there was, moreover, a slight tendency for growth rates in height or weight to be correlated with increments in mental scores. As in other samples, mental test scores showed an increasing relation to social status [1] (.04 at 21 months, rising to .42 at 7 years).

In the study of this problem, correlational procedures, dealing with average relationships in a total group, may be less effective than the comparative study of individual growth curves. Honzik and Jones have presented such curves for height, weight, and intelligence, with raw measurements transformed into sigma scores to permit direct comparison as to changes in status in the group. Although some cases showed independent or even diverging curves, a number exhibited a striking concomitance in trend. The suggestion has been made that mental-physical relationships are due to a common influence of the social environment, acting upon intelligence through social example and education and upon physical factors through nutrition and hygiene. In this study, however, the relationship between height and intelligence

[1] A socio-economic index based on parent education, occupation, income, and social ratings.

was found to be independent, or nearly so, of the measured factors in the environment, since the correlations changed very little when social status was held constant. For the sample in question it seems probable that genetic factors, and the association of traits in assortative mating, are more important than cultural-economic factors in determining the fact that brighter children tend to be taller and heavier than children of below average intelligence.

Olson and Hughes (1950) also present individual growth curves for a series of physical and mental measures. The curves show a degree of correspondence which they regard as illustrating the "unity of the organism." Partly because physical-mental relationships sometimes involve a time lag, longitudinal studies may be more successful than cross-sectional ones in depicting growth relationships. Time series statistics, however, have not yet been employed in a systematic analysis of the concept of organismic unity.

Future research in this area may lead to greater interest in physical *patterns* than in single variables. On the basis of preliminary evidence (Sheldon and Stevens, 1942), it would appear that a small positive relation may be expected between intelligence and "ectomorphy," or linear build, and a small negative relation between intelligence and "mesomorphy," or athletic build. If these relations are confirmed, however, it is likely that they will be found to rest at least in part on a differential development of interests and activities in individuals of differing physique.

Health and Physical Defects. If physical condition exerts a direct effect upon mental functioning, it may perhaps be expected that intelligence will show a closer relation to measures of health than to measures of physical size or of body form. Our concern here is with studies of general health, nutritional status, or minor physical defects, and not with neurological or endocrine disorders, or psychopathologies. In one of the earliest studies in this field, Ayres (1909) determined the incidence of physical defects in three groups of children classified as dull, normal, and bright on the basis of progress in school. The sample consisted of 3304 children. The percentage of each type of defect is given in Table 6.

TABLE 6

PERCENTAGE INCIDENCE OF PHYSICAL DEFECTS
IN THREE GROUPS

	Bright	Normal	Dull
Defective teeth	34	40	42
Adenoids	6	10	15
Enlarged tonsils	12	19	26
Enlarged glands	6	13	20
Defective breathing	9	11	15
Defective vision	29	25	24
Other defects	11	11	21
Average number of defects per child	1.07	1.30	1.65

Similar findings have been reported by later investigators. Where relationships have been analyzed in terms of correlation, coefficients are approximately of the same order as for other physical traits such as height or weight. Among the highest r's reported are those found by Dayton (1928–1929) for approximately 14,000 retarded school children in Massachusetts ($-.29 \pm .01$ for boys, $-.25 \pm .01$ for girls, IQ by physical defects). These correlations, similar to those found for other physical-mental relationships, serve merely to illustrate the fact that physical and mental handicaps are associated in the same samples. We cannot conclude that one type of handicap has caused the other, although to a very small degree such causal relationships may be present.[1]

[1] In a study of fifth-grade children in New York City schools, Maller (1933) determined the correlation

Studies of developmental disturbances during the prenatal period and of neonatal damage (as in the case of newborn infants suffering from anoxia or from erythroblastosis) have emphasized the extensive nature of the injury that may be produced by these conditions. This injury is sometimes not clearly apparent until a number of months or even years after birth, but the incidence of difficult births among children later classified as mental defectives (Benda, 1943) is sufficiently high to call attention to the hazards involved in the child's first direct contact with the external environment. Difficult birth conditions, however, are not always associated with later measurable impairment. When Usdin and Weil (1952) compared children who had been apneic for 3 or more minutes at birth with a control group who had breathed spontaneously, no IQ differences could be demonstrated between the two groups.

In such defects as infected tonsils, a quasi-experimental approach is possible through studying the mental test performance of children before and after surgical removal of the infection. It has not been possible to show that the focal infections progressively impair mental ability or that their removal has a beneficial effect upon the intelligence (see reports by Rogers, 1922; Lowe, 1923; and Richey, 1934).

between the mean IQ for each school and the percentage in each school having a given defect. The coefficients were $-.50$ for defective teeth, $-.40$ for visual defect, $-.28$ for malnutrition. These relatively high correlations are due to the use of averages and can be applied to predictions about populations rather than about individuals. It is clear that districts with better health records tend to have higher average IQ's; these districts also have superior socio-economic status, as shown by a correlation of .50 between average IQ and average rentals. Although Maller's results are of unusual interest in describing important aspects of urban social structure, they of course give no indication as to the source of the relationships.

A study of the effects of poliomyelitis deserves some attention with regard to method. Phillips, Berman, and Hanson (1948) located through a Minneapolis clinic 101 children who had had poliomyelitis in the 1946 epidemic and whose earlier Stanford-Binet IQ's were on file in school records. Retests were administered in 1947 to these cases and to a carefully matched control group. Earlier studies on this problem have usually yielded negative results; in the present instance about all that could be shown was that on the average the controls held constant or increased slightly in IQ, whereas the clinic cases held constant or decreased slightly; differences were significant for the younger children and for boys. A further study of 22 clinic cases with an extreme IQ loss (averaging 19 points) indicated that the illness had been relatively severe among these children. However, it is not as yet known whether the retardative effects have a basis in organic brain damage or in some more temporary psychological or educational sequelae of the illness. The mental effects of specific diseases have sometimes been studied through sibling controls. Thus, Gerver and Day (1950) were able to show that children who had recovered from erythroblastosis had significantly lower IQ's than their unaffected siblings. This method of inquiry can be recommended only for those conditions which quite surely involve no differential susceptibility in relation to intelligence.

In a few studies, evidence is available concerning the effect of an improved physical régime upon mental functions. Westenberger (1927) selected the poorest 10 per cent, with regard to physical defects, from a sample of approximately 400 school children in Wisconsin. Medical and surgical treatment was provided over a 9-month period, but without observable effects upon mental development. The investigator concluded: "The influence of defects upon academic performance and intelligence has been somewhat exaggerated in the past." Similar negative results were obtained by Hoefer and Hardy (1928) in a carefully planned 3-year study of the effect of health education.

Effects of changes in physical condition are more likely to be noted in school achievement than in measures of intelligence. Thus, in later reports Hardy (1936) and Hardy and Hoefer (1936) showed that children participating in a health instruction program improved in their school work to a greater degree than members of a control group. Even these gains, however, are not entirely attributable to changes in health régime, since the special attention given to the experimental cases may have had not merely indirect psychological effects, but also more direct effects through changes in motivation. One interpretation of the relationship of physical factors to intelligence is suggested by Halstead (1945), who proposes a physiological energizing factor which may be affected by brain injuries and certain other physical conditions. The *usable* intelligence may thus be impaired without direct impairment of basic mental abilities.

Nutrition. It is to be expected that small positive coefficients will be obtained when measures of nutritional status are correlated with IQ. These correlations arise from the same causes that determine a positive relationship between socio-economic status and IQ (see pp. 645ff.) and tend to disappear if nutritional variations are examined within a single social group. An exception to the last statement may be found in cases close to a subsistence margin. Thus, among 293 children from slum areas, O'Hanlon (1940) found a significant correlation (.18 ± .04) between nutritional condition and IQ.

A more satisfactory approach to this problem is through an experimental procedure, as illustrated in the following two examples. Twenty-five children selected by Smith and Field (1926) as markedly underweight were given school lunches over a 6-month period, together with health lessons and various motivational devices designed to bring about physical improvement. As compared with normal controls, striking gains were shown in weight but mental development appeared to be unaffected. A similar experiment was conducted by Seymour and Whitaker (1938) in a group of 25 underprivileged children (6½ years old) matched with a control from a similar social selection. The experimental group was given daily breakfasts in school, adequate as to variety and amount, whereas the control group received their usual inadequate breakfast of bread and tea at home. Differences between the two groups began to appear on standardized tests (such as cancellation) by the tenth day, but the superiority of the experimental group diminished after the breakfasts were discontinued. Neither of these two experiments points to any actual change in mental growth as a result of nutritional gains.

More positive results have been reported by Poull (1938) and by Kugelmass et al. (1944) in a comparison of IQ's of poorly nourished children before and after nutritional therapy. Marked IQ gains were noted for both mental defectives and normals, the amount of gain being greater for the younger children. The writers infer that prolonged malnutrition may involve irreversible effects upon mental development but that in early childhood mental retardation (of nutritional origin) is more readily overcome. If future experiments, coupled with longitudinal studies, confirm these findings, the implications for child development in economically backward areas may be of great importance. We still lack information, however, about the degree of malnutrition which is critical and the specific factors responsible.

A number of studies have dealt with the effects of specific vitamin administration. Although the greater part of the work in this field is still very preliminary, results are available from an impressive study by Harrell (1946), who conducted a controlled experiment with 55 matched pairs of orphanage children over a period of 1 year. The experimental group received 2 mg. of thiamine daily; the control group received a placebo. Neither the children nor their caretakers in the orphanage knew how the groups were divided or the nature of the treatment. The experimental group showed significantly greater gains in a number of mental functions and in educational achievement; these results were confirmed in a second experiment with 20 pairs of children.

In the years following 1945 considerable attention was given to the possibility of stimulating mental development through the use of glutamic acid in one of several forms. Apparent positive effects have been interpreted as due to changes in neural tissues, favoring more efficient oxidation. The clearest indication of favorable results has been obtained with the mentally retarded, and in the first six months of treatment.[1] Experiments of this nature, however, require attention to the use of matched groups, or if possible matched pairs, and to an administrative procedure in which the mental testers do not know which subjects received the experimental treatment and which subjects received the placebo. Studies utilizing careful controls have as a rule yielded

---

[1] See Zimmerman et al. (1946), Zimmerman (1949), Quinn and Durling (1950), Schwobel (1950), and Harney (1950). Gadson (1951) has summarized the work on glutamic acid and mental deficiency.

negative results. The only significant difference found by Ellson *et al.* (1950) was in a motor coordination test, suggesting (as in some animal studies) that if glutamic acid has any behavioral effect it may be upon overt activity patterns. Loeb and Tuddenham (1950) present a detailed comparison of their results and those of previous investigators, showing the probable methodological reasons for the differences in conclusions.

It has frequently been noted that the relationship of mental and physical traits is more readily demonstrated among the feeble-minded than among normals. This may be due in part at least to a larger proportion of the feeble-minded who suffer, in various degrees, from the effects of organic handicaps expressed both in physical structures and in mental function. Stout (1937) has summarized a study of 10-year-old children by the statement: "The fact that a child is normal in intelligence gives little or no clue as to what his health or physical condition may be." On the other hand, among the 2 per cent at the lowest extreme in intelligence it is clear that we have a disproportionate incidence of many different types of physical defects.

Seasonal Factors. An interesting subsidiary problem has been raised by a number of investigations showing a relationship between IQ and month of birth. These studies, principally by Pintner and his associates but supported by other investigators, purport to show that both in the northern and southern hemispheres children born in the late spring, or summer, have slightly higher average IQ's than children born in the winter months. Of 13 studies summarized by Pintner and Forlano (1943) the season of birth with the highest average IQ was either spring or summer in 11 instances; the lowest average IQ was predominantly in children

born in the winter. These differences have been, hypothetically, related to the greater amount of sunlight and the lower incidence of illness in the warmer as compared with the colder months.

In the case of children of exceptionally high intelligence the most favorable month of birth appears to be slightly different than for the total population. For children with IQ's above 130, and also for individuals of distinction listed in the *Dictionary of American Biography*, Huntington (1938) has reported a high rate of births in the late winter or early spring months. In conformity with his theories of climatic influence, he has argued that children born from February to April have a maximum developmental advantage due to the fact that the early months of the pregnancy fall in the preceding late spring and summer. It is these months, he believes, that provide the most favorable extrinsic conditions for promoting physical vigor and general development. Huntington has been criticized for failing to account for the complex operation of cultural factors influencing conceptions and abortions. "The various seasonal trends in births cannot be denied, but their explanation in terms of meteorological and resulting physical factors must be subject to doubt until more direct evidence is obtainable" (Jones, 1939, p. 99).

In this connection, Goodenough (1940c) later showed for a sample of over 3000 cases that seasonal differences in the frequency of births occur in the higher but not in the lower occupational groups. Since the children at the higher socioeconomic levels also average higher in IQ, the birth-month factor in intelligence can apparently be fully accounted for on the basis of selective planning or other conditions related to cultural status. This argument is supported by the fact that in samples presenting a restricted socio-economic range, as in studies of college students (Clark, 1939; Held, 1940; Forlano and Ehrlich, 1941), intelligence differences related to birth month are either reduced or eliminated.

A different aspect of seasonal variation is considered in studies which have dealt with IQ changes in young children in relation to the month of testing. Wellman (1934) has reported that children in the University of Iowa Nursery School tend to show higher IQ's in the spring than in the fall. She attributed this to the effect of nursery school attendance. However, Lodge (1938) and Jones (1941) obtained similar results among children not in nursery school. In the Jones study, data for 1798 tests, given to children between the ages of 2 and 5 years, were examined with reference to the month of testing. The cases were balanced in such a way as to eliminate the influence of age and of test practice. The highest average IQ's were found in November, December, and January; the lowest in May, June, and July. Several alternative interpretations were offered for these results in terms of (1) the influence of climatic factors (such as periodic storms) upon mental performance, (2) the influence of climatic factors upon basic rates of mental growth, and (3) seasonal variations in play activities which have a positive transfer in mental test performance. Further studies are needed in different geographic areas in order to confirm these findings and, if they are confirmed, to provide an adequate explanation of the results.

Physiological Maturing. Chronological age is not always a good index of the *physiological time* through which a child has lived. In a group of the same age, wide individual differences will occur in the level of maturity assessed by physiological methods. These developmental indications include dentition, pubescence, the age of menarche, skeletal age assessed from X-rays, and anatomical age assessed from physical growth patterns. It has been suggested that a child's IQ at any given time should be computed by referring mental age to physiological rather than chronological age $\left(IQ = \dfrac{MA}{PA} \text{ rather than } \dfrac{MA}{CA} \right)$.

This is illustrated in Figure 10. Case 9M presents a mental growth curve, in terms of raw scores, consistently superior to the average of the total group. He is, however, somewhat retarded in physiological maturing, and if allowance is made for this we find that his growth curve (plotted against skeletal age) is even further above the group average. Case 25M has a mental growth curve which agrees very closely with the average, but in skeletal development he is markedly accelerated. In terms of the number of *physiological years* he has lived, we note that his mental development lags considerably behind expectation. When data are treated in this way, it is possible that clues will sometimes be uncovered which will be useful in interpreting deviate mental growth curves or even in improving the prediction about subsequent growth.

Unfortunately, however, the concept of physiological age has as yet been put to little effective use except in a few research centers. The various measures of physiological maturity do not agree perfectly with each other, and a satisfactory composite measure has not been achieved. When we correlate a single index, such as skeletal maturity, with mental age, the coefficients (at a given level of chronological age) are usually too low to command special interest.[1] In one of the most comprehensive

---

[1] Abernethy (1936) and Bayley (1940b) have reported correlations which at most ages are positive but close to zero. Higher correlations were obtained by Severson (1920-1921) and by West (1936), although West found that coefficients dropped with increasing age.

studies yet reported, Gates (1924) obtained a measure of skeletal age as well as height and some other physical measurements; the multiple r of these with mental age was only .21. In the same sample, mental age predicted educational achievement to the extent of a correlation of .60;

Several studies have investigated mental test performance in relation to the age at puberty. In general, these have led to the tentative finding that IQ's are on the average lower in late-maturing individuals and higher in the early-maturing.[1] If these indications are confirmed, they can be inter-

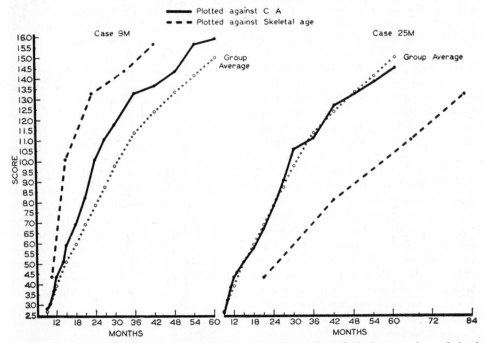

FIGURE 10. Individual mental growth curves, based on chronological age and on skeletal age. (From original data, Berkeley Growth Study.)

when the physical measures were added, this correlation was increased only to .63.

Zuck (1936) and Todd (1938) have sponsored the belief that environmental influences acting through illness or nutritional disturbance have a direct effect upon mental development and that in such cases prior changes are often to be noted in X-rays of the skeleton. Individual cases can no doubt be found to support this view, but the general importance of such relationships remains to be demonstrated.

preted as due either to a stimulating effect of sexual maturing upon mental growth or to a tendency of early-maturing individuals to represent a superior selection. The first interpretation would lead us to look for

[1] A review by Shock (1939a) has summarized a number of investigations in which positive results were obtained. See also Conrad, Freeman, and Jones (1944). Negative results, as by Reymert (1940), have occasionally been reported. It is, of course, well known that at the pathological extreme exceptionally early maturing (pubertas praecox) often occurs without corresponding precocity in mental functions (Keene and Stone, 1937).

a spurt in the rate of mental growth accompanying the increased physical growth in adolescence; this has never been clearly demonstrated.[1] The second and more probable interpretation might rest upon one or several selective factors. It is possible, for example, that (for quite different reasons) the lower socio-economic groups are more heavily weighted with late-maturing individuals as well as with those of lower intelligence (see p. 659).

A readily measured aspect of physical condition is basal metabolism. At the pathological extremes, with which we are not here directly concerned, striking evidence of correlated physical and mental effects can be found in such conditions as cretinism and myxedema, with equally striking evidence of mental improvement after thyroid treatment in certain cases. It is reasonable to inquire whether thyroid function, measured through basal metabolic rate, is related to intelligence in a normal range of cases. This is important for our present topic, since within this normal range thyroid functioning may be disturbed by illness and other extrinsic factors and may also be controlled to some extent by appropriate régime and treatment. Shock and Jones (1940), however, for a school sample of approximately 90 children at an average age of 12 and 14 years, have at each of these ages and for each sex found no demonstrable relationship between highly reliable measures of intelligence and of basal metabolism.[2] This

[1] The Harvard Growth Study, summarized by Dearborn and Rothney (1941), contains a large body of material pertinent to this hypothesis. No relation was found between the physical growth cycle and performance on intelligence or achievement tests.

[2] Similar results have been obtained in other investigations reviewed by these writers, with the exception of two reports by Hinton (1936, 1939) asserting correlations ranging from .80 at age 6 to .53 at age 15 between IQ and basal metabolic rate. The study is difficult to evaluate because complete data are not furnished.

is another instance in which correlations that are quite clear in pathological cases vanish or become obscured when sought in a normal representative group. The authors suggest that "slight variations in functional activity of the thyroid gland are not reflected in changes in mental capacity because in most individuals other adaptive mechanisms are present which may compensate for this thyroid deficiency" (p. 374). To carry over this conception to the general problem of environmental influence, it is a reasonable hypothesis that intelligence itself involves an adaptive mechanism which can to some degree compensate for variations in the environment, at least within an ordinary range of social and physical conditions.

Environmental Factors in the Family Constellation

Birth Order. The hypothesis has been advanced that children who are the firstborn in their families suffer, on the average, a handicap in mental development due to both physical and social disadvantages. The fact of physical disadvantage is well established. Many studies have shown that the first-born are on the average smaller and lighter at birth than later-born in the same families. They include more prematures and more cases of abnormal confinement. Jones and Hsiao (1933), in a study of 310 pairs of pregnancies, found among the first-born a greater proportion of instrumental delivery and of cases marked by poor physical condition after birth. A smaller proportion of the first-born receive normal breast-feeding (Schlesinger, 1923). Studies of later health and physical development [3] have not yielded consistent results; there is, however, a tendency to report a higher incidence of tuberculosis among the first-born.

[3] Summarized by Hsiao (1931).

The educational and social handicaps of the first-born are a matter of speculation rather than of direct proof. It is argued that first-born have the disadvantage of less experienced nurture by the parents, of less social stimulation (from older sibs), and frequently also of a less well-established economic security. However great or little these environmental differences may be, it is apparent that even in combination with a certain degree of physical handicap the average effects upon mental development are negligible.

It is unfortunate that investigators of this problem have been deceived by a number of errors of interpretation, the most important of which arises from the relation between birth rate and social status. Since families of higher social status tend to have fewer but, on the average, more intelligent children, in a mixed population the first- or second-born, for example, will have higher average IQ's than third or fourth children. This, of course, is not actually a consequence of order of birth but is due merely to the fact that the earlier birth orders are weighted with children from small families, who constitute a superior selection. If we attempt to remedy this difficulty by limiting our comparisons to children of the same family, a new difficulty arises from the fact that many intelligence tests are so standardized that the IQ tends to drop slightly with age. This artifact produces a lower average IQ among children of the earlier birth orders (since they are, on the average, older when tested). Another factor to be considered is the unfavorable weighting of late birth orders due to maternal age. It has been clearly shown that the offspring of mothers near the end of the childbearing period are marked by a slightly greater incidence of certain types of mental defect, including mongolism.

In an earlier critique (Jones, 1933a) of research in this field evidence has been given that when these and other methodological difficulties are properly controlled no birth-order differences in intelligence occur in normal samples. So far as this problem is concerned, we must then dismiss the environmental arguments as having little net weight. Atypical results, however, have been encountered in certain highly selected samples. Studies of gifted children by Terman et al. (1925) and of eminent men by Ellis (1926), Cattell (1927), and Huntington (1938) have shown a distribution of birth orders differing from chance expectation and strongly favoring the first-born (see Figure 11). No satisfactory explanation of this finding has been given. It is possible that the first-born more often become eminent because of greater incentive, but one would hesitate to apply this interpretation to the Terman material. An explanation in terms of differential educational opportunity would have even greater difficulty in including Terman's results with children. At least for this latter study, which is the only one dealing directly with intelligence test data, it is likely (as suggested by Terman) that the true explanation will involve some selective factor, such as the greater tendency to locate older than younger members of incomplete families in a restricted age range.

Sibling Resemblance. To illustrate the meaning of an *r* of .50, an example often used is "that degree of resemblance which is ordinarily found among brothers and sisters living in the same family." This order of relationship is now so well established that a study reporting a markedly lower sibling correlation in intelligence would be immediately suspected of an inadequate sampling or of tests deficient in reliability or validity.[1] E. L. Thorndike (1944), on the basis of sibling coefficients of the usual magnitude, has proposed corrections for range and for attenuation. He concluded that in the general population the true sibling r is probably above .70, "implying a greater hereditary factor than has ordinarily been assumed." This may, same degree as those in physical traits such as height, eye color, span, and head measurements. From this he inferred: "We are forced . . . to the conclusion that the physical and psychical characters in man are inherited within broad lines in the same manner and with the same intensity" (p. 204). Two considerations, however,

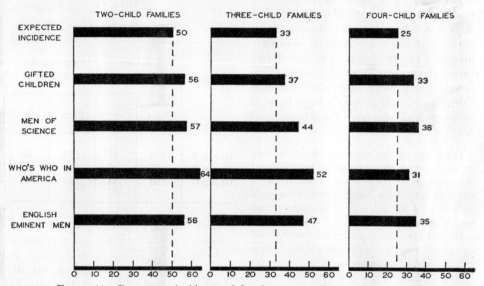

FIGURE 11. Percentage incidence of first-born, according to size of family.

however, represent an overcorrection, since sibling r's not far from .50 have been found in quite representative samplings with adequately reliable tests. One illustration is a study in Scotland, in which Roberts (1941) tested in a given community all of the children whose birth dates fell within certain limits. All their siblings of school age were also tested; the sibling correlation, for 650 pairs, was .53.

In one of the earliest studies in this field Pearson (1903) reported that family resemblances in mental traits were of the

must lead us to a more cautious interpretation of the evidence. First, our present knowledge of genetic mechanisms suggests that if intelligence has a hereditary basis it is genetically more complex than a trait such as eye color; differences in genetic composition might well be expected to produce differences in family resemblance coefficients. Second, a given degree of resemblance may (theoretically) be attained not only through the influence of a common heredity but also through the effects of living in a common environment.

Still another consideration involves the degree of selective mating in the popula-

[1] See Schwesinger (1933) for a summary of earlier investigations.

tion. Pearson, in his theoretical calculations, assumed that the correlation between husband and wife in intelligence was close to zero, but more recent studies show that the husband-wife coefficient tends to be as high as, if not higher than, the sibling coefficient.[1] Differences in selective mating with respect to different traits would be expected to have important effects upon family resemblances in these traits. We must conclude, then, that from a given degree of sibling resemblance no *immediate* inferences can be drawn as to causal factors. The pattern of sibling correlations, however, may prove significant when considered in relation to certain hypotheses of environmental influence. These hypotheses are:

I. Siblings of the same sex share, on the average, a more common social environment than siblings of opposite sex. Hence on an environmental basis higher correlations could be predicted for brothers or for sisters than for brothers-and-sisters.

II. Siblings close together in chronological age share a more similar environment than children widely separated as to age. Changes in social and economic status of the family, in home and neighborhood, and in the age and personal characteristics of the parents, as well as differences in schools and teachers, might be expected to have some average effect in lowering correlations for siblings with a wide natal interval, that is, separated by several years in age.

III. Older siblings have lived together longer than younger siblings and hence share a greater accumulation of environmental influences. It may also be assumed that as children grow older they become responsive to a wider range of environmental factors; in these factors families are more diverse than in factors to which younger children are sensitive. The effect of a greater variability in family environments should (on an environmental hypothesis) be to increase sibling correlations.

Each of these hypotheses may, at certain points, be questioned on theoretical grounds, but they have a sufficient common sense basis to justify an empirical test. Table 7 gives data relevant to the

TABLE 7

SIBLING CORRELATIONS

	Like-Sex Siblings		Opposite-Sex Siblings	
	Pairs	r	Pairs	r
Group A	159	.47	153	.55
Group B	178	.40	144	.55
Group C	158	.44	169	.46

first of these hypotheses from a study by Conrad and Jones (1940). A representative sample of 777 pairs of children in New England rural communities was divided into three groups, on the basis of the tests used. Sibling correlations [2] varied around .50, with no tendency for like-sex siblings to show higher r's. As a comment on this finding, it has been suggested that the family constellation involves individual rôle-choices which may have a differentiating effect upon intellectual functions among like-sex siblings. Such factors, if they are conceived as influencing the development of basic mental abilities, may tend to balance out other factors associated with the more common environment of children of the same sex. On the present evidence, however, it is apparent that a defense of Hy-

---

[1] Reviewed by Jones (1929) and H. M. Richardson (1939).

[2] Studies by Willoughby (1927) and S. K. Richardson (1936) also report no significant differences in the coefficients for like-sex and opposite-sex siblings.

pothesis I will require ambitious ventures into speculation.

Data relevant to Hypothesis II have been supplied by Conrad (1931) for a sample of 778 pairs of siblings. Correlations were calculated for three different age groups and for siblings who were (1) less than 3 years apart in age and (2)

tested at similar ages (on the average, 6 months apart in age) and at separated ages (on the average, 3½ years apart). For 101 cases in each group, identical coefficients (.49) were obtained. It is evident that the environmental influences associated with age differences of siblings are (on the average) without perceptible effect.

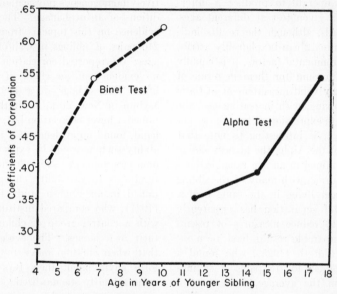

FIGURE 12. Sibling correlations, according to age of the younger sibling.

more than 3 years apart. The coefficients varied around .50, and no comparisons yielded significant differences. The natal interval problem may be approached also by correlating the score difference (IQ, or sigma score) of each sib pair with the age difference (natal interval) of the pair. A positive correlation would be expected if a greater age separation of siblings is accompanied by a greater difference in IQ. For large samples, Conrad in the above-mentioned study and Finch (1933) found all correlations unreliably different from zero. The temporal factor has been examined by S. K. Richardson (1936) in a different way by determining correlations for siblings

With regard to Hypothesis III, Figure 12 presents evidence as to increase of sibling correlation with age. This material, from unpublished data of Jones and Conrad, is based on a sample of 225 pairs of rural children tested with the Stanford-Binet and 210 pairs tested with the Army Alpha. For each subgroup, the maximum age interval between each pair of siblings is 5 years. In each test, the correlations show a definite tendency to increase with age. Although this is consonant with the hypothesis of increasing or cumulative environmental influence, it is unfortunately impossible to eliminate other factors which may also contribute to the age trend.

One might inquire why the correlation drops so sharply when we shift, at around 10 years, from the Stanford-Binet to the Army Alpha. The Stanford-Binet is not more reliable than the Alpha at this age, but it is probably more valid. The difference between these two tests at the same age may be due to much the same validity factors that operate to produce a difference within a given test at different ages. In other words, although the results indicated in Figure 12 can be plausibly attributed to environmental factors, it is equally plausible to account for them in terms of an increasingly valid measurement of basic abilities involving, with increasing age, the more complete expression of hereditary potentialities. It is interesting to note that in the case of the Alpha the highest sibling r (.54) is obtained in an age range extending into maturity, with many of the sibling pairs no longer living in the same homes. Environmental separation has apparently not tended to reduce measures of resemblance. Comparable results have been reported by Hildreth (1925), who found a correlation of .49 for 78 pairs of siblings separated, on the average, from 4 to 5 years.[1]

Before leaving this topic, reference should be made to one other type of sibling study which is of considerable interest for the present problem. This involves the measurement of resemblance among siblings reared in an institutional environment. If the similarity of brothers and sisters is due in part to the fact that they are reared in the same homes, the correlations would be expected to drop not merely when they are separated in different homes but also when they are brought together into the relatively homogeneous physical and social conditions of an orphanage. The best-known evidence on this topic is from a study of 216 pairs of siblings in California orphanages; the reported correlation (.53) shows no evidence of an effect of institutional life.[2] For siblings in a Hebrew orphan asylum in New York, Hildreth (1925) obtained a lower correlation but, on the other hand, found no evidence of a reduced variability such as would be expected if a common environment were influential. Similar results as to variability changes were obtained in an English study by Lawrence (1931), who compared institution children with a control group of children living in their own homes. The evidence suggests that when children move to a more uniform environment their IQ's do not become similarly standardized.

In a smaller number of studies, correlations have been reported between *unrelated* siblings living in the same homes. This is a promising method for examining the effect of the environment provided the original placement has not been made with reference to any social factor related to intelligence. Perhaps the best evidence on this problem is given by Freeman, Holzinger, and Mitchell (1928), who measured the intelligence of 112 pairs of unrelated children living in the same homes. On a

---

[1] In the well-known Chicago study by Freeman, Holzinger, and Mitchell (1928) incidental data were reported for 130 pairs of siblings who had been separated for at least 4 years in different foster homes. The sibling correlation was .25, a diminished resemblance which may have been due to the reduced similarity in their environments. Burks (1928b, p. 321), however, has shown that this correlation rises toward the customary value if cases are omitted below 5 and above 14 years of age, eliminating individuals who are less adequately measured by the Stanford-Binet scale. In future studies, it will be desirable to know the sibling correlation before as well as after separation. If adoptive children are for any reason selected members of their families, and if the families themselves are a selected group, initial as well as the final correlations may be low because of reduced variability.

[2] Originally reported by K. Gordon (1918-1920, 1919), the data were reanalyzed by Pearson (1918-1919) and Elderton (1923) in order to control age factors and also to render the correlation tables symmetrical. In correlations of siblings and of twins, the recommended procedure is to plot each pair of cases twice, transposing the axes (Fisher, 1930, pp. 178 ff.).

genetic basis alone, the correlation would be expected to be zero, whereas the coefficient actually obtained was .25. Although significantly lower than for true siblings, it suggests that a common environment tends to produce some degree of resemblance among individuals living together. However, a part of this relationship must be assigned to a selective rather than to an environmental factor, since the evidence concerning foster-child studies (see p. 684) indicates that placement agencies tend to locate children with some regard to the social and educational status of their true parents.

Twins. Studies of twins offer unusual advantages in the assessment of environmental influence, but up to the present few "crucial" results can be reported from investigations in this field. The following types of comparisons have been employed:

1. *Fraternal twins versus ordinary siblings.* On a genetic basis, fraternal twin correlations should be of the same order as coefficients for sibling resemblance (approximately .50). In fact, however, they tend to range slightly above this figure, occasionally being reported as high as .70. This difference in correlation, if genuine,[1] may be attributable to the more common environment shared by twins. In line with this interpretation are the results from an ingenious study by S. K. Richardson (1936), who artificially "twinned" siblings by recording their IQ's for tests given at the same ages. Under these conditions (as noted in a previous section), the sibling correlations were the same as when computed with the ordinary age intervals (.49 in each computation). On the other hand, true twin correlations tended to diminish when control measurements were employed for different ages (for example, one twin recorded at 8 years and the other at 10). Richardson concluded that "the environment of twins from birth is so similar that it tends to increase their natural resemblance" (p. 197). The twin correlation in this case was .73 for 92 pairs; the correlation for twins as of different ages was .57 for 45 pairs. This difference is not fully significant and would, moreover, be considerably diminished if Richardson had corrected for variability differences. The procedure is nevertheless a promising one and should be applied in further study with a larger number of cases.

2. *Younger versus older twins.* In the earliest twin study using mental test data, E. L. Thorndike (1905) found that in various traits twins 12 to 14 years of age exhibited correlations no higher than those of twins 9 to 11 years of age. He argued that if twin resemblance is due to environment, correlations ought to increase with age. We have here a possibility of a more sensitive test of hypothesis III, discussed on page 670, but still with difficulties in interpretation. Thorndike's negative results (supported, in general, by later studies) have suggested to some writers that small environmental factors may be acting in opposite directions. The effect of longer residence in the same home may make for greater resemblance; but, on the other hand, with increasing age twins may become more independent in their choice of activities.[2]

3. *Fraternal versus identical twins.* More definitive results have been expected in this than in the preceding types of analysis, since we have a comparison in which

---

[1] Twin correlations are subject to spurious inflation because of defects in test standardization, producing slightly lower average IQ's at higher ages. Some investigators have not understood the necessity of partialing out CA in order to control this factor.

[2] This can also be expressed by saying that interfamilial variations (differences among families) may tend to produce correlated changes in twins, with an increasing degree of resemblance, whereas intrafamilial variations may lead to uncorrelated or even negatively correlated changes.

environmental factors have been assumed to operate in a similar manner while genetic factors vary. The genetic difference consists in the fact that identical twins share the same gene determinants, whereas fraternal twins share a similar heredity only to the extent of ordinary brothers and sisters. Investigations have agreed that identical twins are on the average much more similar in intelligence than fraternal twins. Table 8 shows the twin correlations obtained in two representative studies.

TABLE 8

RESEMBLANCE OF IDENTICAL AND FRATERNAL TWINS IN INTELLIGENCE

(Stanford-Binet IQ, corrected for age.)

Investigator	Fraternal Twins		Identical Twins	
	N	r	N	r
Stocks and Karn (1933)	119	.65	68	.84
Newman, Freeman, and Holzinger (1937)	52	.63	50	.88

Newman, Freeman, and Holzinger found a mean IQ difference of 9.8 for pairs of siblings, of 9.9 for pairs of fraternal twins, and of 5.9 for pairs of identical twins. This latter difference, it will be noted, is similar to that reported on page 636 in connection with studies of the constancy of the IQ.[1]

[1] Assuming that in representative samples identical twins correlate .90 in intelligence, ordinary siblings .50, and random pairs .00, Page (1941) has applied a formula predicting that the average intrapair IQ difference will be approximately 6 points for identical twins, 13 for siblings, and 19 for unrelated pairs, in terms of the 1916 Stanford-Binet.

Such results would be expected if twin similarities were primarily genetic, but we must also take into account the fact of a greater degree of environmental similarity. Several studies have shown that identical twins spend more time together, enjoy more similar reputations, are more likely to be in the same classrooms, have more similar health records, and in many other respects share a more common physical and social environment than that ordinarily experienced by fraternal twins (Stocks, 1930–1931; Jones and Wilson, 1932–1933; Wilson, 1934; Lehtovaara, 1938).

Comparisons of twin populations are sometimes made not in terms of resemblance coefficients but more coarsely in terms of intrapair "concordance" or "discordance" as to specified traits. Thus Rosanoff, Hardy, and Plesset (1937) found that among identical twins in whom one member of the pair had been identified as mentally deficient 91 per cent of the co-twins were also classed as deficients. Among fraternal twins this measure of concordance dropped to 47 per cent.

4. *Twin resemblance in contrasted abilities.* Here we are concerned with the comparison of (a) abilities subject to training and (b) traits usually thought to be relatively independent of training. In E. L. Thorndike's (1905) study it was found that the degree of twin resemblance in various traits bore little or no relationship to the susceptibility of traits to training. Hence it could be argued that for both kinds of traits twin resemblance is primarily an expression of genetic factors. Lauterbach (1925) and Wingfield (1928) have also used this method in demonstrating, to their own satisfaction, the relatively minor importance of environmental factors. For identical and fraternal twins combined, Wingfield found twin correlations of .75 for IQ, .76 for educational quotient, .78 for arithmetic scores, and .85 for spelling scores,

with no fully reliable differences. The problem is one of great complexity, however, and many factors affecting (*a*) the incidence of training and (*b*) the genetic constitution of the trait in question may operate to produce results which make direct comparisons difficult between different traits.

5. *The method of co-twin control.* Technically superior to the preceding method is a procedure limited to identical twins, in which one member of a twin pair receives specific training while the other is reserved as a control. During the experimental period both twins undergo mental growth owing to intrinsic maturation and to general functioning, and any residual difference between the twins must be attributed to the experimental factor in the environment. First introduced by Gesell in the study of motor traits, the application of this method by Strayer (1930) in studying language development, and by Hilgard (1933) in connection with memory tests, has led to conclusions emphasizing the importance of intrinsic factors. A co-twin study covering a limited age period can, however, yield no general statement as to the comparative rôle of training and maturation. Its results will apply *only* to that particular age level and to the *specific functions* which are experimentally trained.

During the 1920's and 1930's a number of investigators in the U.S.S.R. employed the co-twin method with reference to various traits including intelligence (reviewed by Levit, 1935). This promising line of research, not wholly in harmony with Marxian theory, appears now to have been abandoned.

6. *The comparison of identical twins reared apart.* In the absence of opportunities for the experimental separation of twins, the next best thing is to make use of separations which have occurred as a result of adoption in different homes. Here also reports have usually dealt with a single pair of twins, but in the well-known volume by Newman, Freeman, and Holzinger (1937) results have been assembled for a total of 19 pairs. The sample is, of course, a heterogeneous one, consisting of twins separated at ages ranging from 2 weeks to 6 years; at the time they were studied, their ages ranged from 12 to 60 years.

Ratings of the differences in the educational environments of the twins were made by five judges, three of whom knew only the case histories and two of whom also knew the twins. For all except 6 pairs of twins, the differences in ability were of about the same size as are found among identical twins reared together. Twelve pairs had small or negligible differences both in ability and in educational environment; for 1 pair there was no marked difference in ability even though a large difference in formal schooling had occurred. One pair with similar schooling showed a marked difference in ability corresponding to other differences in cultural opportunity; the remaining 5 pairs had experienced large or fairly large differences in education and showed corresponding differences in ability. Correlations for the 19 pairs were below the usual coefficient for identical twins, but higher than the usual coefficients for siblings reared together (.67 for the Stanford-Binet IQ, .73 for the Otis IQ). Conclusions from this research, emphasizing environmental factors more strongly than in most twin studies, have been challenged in a number of reviews.[1] The method remains, however, a most important one, and,

1 Burks (1938*a*), McNemar (1938), and Woodworth (1941). Woodworth has emphasized the fact that, when twins of identical heredity are subjected to environments differing about as much as those of the children in an ordinary community, the twins nevertheless remain much more similar than random pairs of children in such a community. This would suggest that interfamilial and general educational differences are not of primary importance in determining variations in IQ in the general population.

following the lead of Newman, Freeman, and Holzinger, we may expect significant results from a gradual accumulation of further cases of twins reared apart. An additional 4 cases reported by Burks and Roe (1949) unfortunately add little to our data on mental development, because of abnormalities in 3 of the 4 pairs.

7. *Longitudinal studies of twins.* Psychological case studies of twins have been exemplified not only in the work of Freeman and his associates but also in an interesting report by Koch (1927) on a pair of Siamese twins and in several studies by Carter (1934) on mature identical twins. These have been based on cross-section and retrospective records rather than on cumulative data. Detailed studies are greatly needed in which the year-to-year development of twins is examined with reference to the relationship of developmental and environmental changes, the consistency of small differences, and the interrelationship of differences. With cumulative observations it is possible to examine the rôle of factors which are usually inaccessible to experimental techniques (illness, accidents, and various "crises" of development).

The most careful longitudinal study of a single pair of twins is reported in a monograph by Gesell and Thompson (1941), covering a period from infancy to adolescence. Blatz *et al.* (1937) in a report on the development of the Dionne quintuplets during the first 3 years also present mental growth material of unusual interest which, it is hoped, may eventually be related to data obtained at later ages.

More complete reviews of twin research have been made by several investigators.[1] Although frequently exploited in journalis-

tic treatments, it is clear that twin studies are not merely a scientific "stunt," but deserve continued serious attention as a basic approach to nature-nurture problems. Certain safeguards, however, must be maintained with regard to the following difficulties in twin research:

1. *Number of cases.* Plural births occur only in the proportion of about 11 per 1000.[2] A large population must be covered in order to establish an adequate sample. Thus, in locating approximately 500 pairs of twins, Wilson and Jones (1931) found it necessary to survey a school enrollment of over 75,000 pupils.

2. *Sampling methods.* The best method of locating twins is through birth records or by a questionnaire placed in the hands of all members of the group that is to be sampled. If reliance is placed on a census of twins by teachers, this method may lead to reporting all fraternal twins who are sufficiently similar to be in the same classrooms but may fail to place on record the fraternal twins who, being less similar, are located in different grades or different schools. Such a factor would spuriously increase coefficients of twin resemblance among fraternals, and it may be responsible for unexpectedly high correlations reported by some investigators. A representative sample of twins may ordinarily be expected to include about one-quarter identicals and three-quarters fraternals.

3. *The classification of twins.* In classifying twins as fraternals or identicals, various methods have been used, including reference to obstetric data on fetal membranes; physical measurements; skeletal X-rays; finger prints and palm prints; hair color, form, and distribution; eye color and the pattern of iris pigmentation; mi-

[1] Some of the best-known treatments are by Dahlberg (1926), Hirsch (1930), Gesell (1931), Levit (1935), Newman, Freeman, and Holzinger (1937), Carter (1940), and Newman (1940). Especially valuable is an analysis of twin and foster-child studies by Woodworth (1941).

[2] Triplet births occur in the proportion of approximately 1 per 8000. Several publications have appeared dealing with small samples of triplets. The best known of these is by Anderson and Scheidemann (1933).

croscopic capillary examination; blood ag-
glutination grouping; and also more subjective methods based on the impression of
similarity in general appearance. No one
of these methods provides an infallible
means of diagnosing identical twins, but
with the application of a variety of methods a very high degree of agreement can
be obtained in independent assessments by
different investigators. In studying a given
trait, such as intelligence, it is unsafe to
use this trait as a part of the basis for
diagnosis. Thus Hirsch (1930) selected
identicals in terms of criteria which included mental similarity, a procedure
which may have had the effect of exaggerating differences in correlations between
the two types of twins. In general, however, errors in diagnosis will spuriously
reduce the difference between identical and
fraternal twin correlations. It is sometimes a wise policy to exclude a small percentage of cases as "undetermined" if these
cases show a conflict in the objective criteria employed for classification.

4. *General selective factors.* Twins are
subject to a heavier infant mortality than
the single-born. The effect of this upon
the selection of surviving twins is not fully
known. One would expect it to improve
the selection slightly; but, if this is so,
then the prenatal or circumnatal factors
affecting the development of twins must
impose a decided handicap, for those surviving into school age are on the average
slightly inferior to single-born in terms of
a number of physical and mental criteria.
This factor may also operate to eliminate
divergent members of twin pairs, with the
effect of increasing our measures of resemblance for those that survive.

An additional factor to be considered in
interpreting research findings is that twins
live in a very special social environment.
Except in the case of twins reared apart,
general conclusions from twin studies may

not be immediately applicable to other selections of cases or other types of environment.

Parent-Child Resemblance. Chiefly because of the difficulty of obtaining intelligence test data for adults, relatively few
studies of parent-child resemblance have
been reported. In an early investigation,
Pearson (1910) obtained a correlation of
.49 between father and son, using ratings
of mental ability. Subsequent studies employing intelligence tests have in general
supported his finding that the resemblance
of parents and children is of the same
order as that of brothers and sisters.[1] This
is not unexpected on the basis of hypotheses of genetic causation, but on an environmental hypothesis one would expect
the sibling correlation to be higher, since
the conditions under which brothers and
sisters are reared, in a given family, are
more similar than the conditions under
which the members of two different generations are reared. It is a matter of unusual interest that these markedly different factors in childhood environments
seem unable to exert any distinguishable
effect upon the family coefficients.

The suggestion has sometimes been made
that, since the mother spends more time
with her children during early childhood
and has more direct supervision over their
activities, a greater resemblance might be
expected between mother and child than
between father and child. So far as mental abilities are concerned, this does not
appear to be the case. With the largest
sample reported to date, Conrad and Jones
(1940) found no differences in parent correlations. In this study the parents and

[1] Somewhat lower coefficients have been reported by
Willoughby (1927) and Freeman, Holzinger, and Mitchell (1928), but Pearson's results agree closely with
those of Burks (1928*b*), Jones (1928), Banker (1928),
Outhit (1933), Leahy (1935), and Conrad and Jones
(1940). A review of earlier studies may be found in
Carter (1932).

children over 14 years of age were tested with the Army Alpha; between 10 and 14 either the Alpha or Stanford-Binet was used; and below 10 the Stanford-Binet was used exclusively. Table 9 summarizes the result.

TABLE 9

PARENT-CHILD CORRELATIONS

	Stanford-Tested Offspring		Alpha-Tested Offspring	
	N	r	N	r
Father	232	.49	196	.49
Mother	269	.49	245	.48

The striking uniformity in these results would of course be predicted on a genetic basis, since on the average the two parents play an equal rôle in transmission of hereditary characters. The greater rôle of the mother in the intimate determination of the child's early environment appears to have no differentiating effect with regard to intelligence. An alternative interpretation, however, might be that such an effect, if present, is balanced out by some other environmental factor.

Like sibling coefficients, parent-child correlations tend to increase with age during the preschool period. This is illustrated in Table 10, based on data from a representative sample of children born in Berkeley, California (Honzik, 1950). The correlations are between children's scores on the California Preschool Schedules and ratings of mothers' intelligence made by two psychologists at the beginning of the study. The results, shown in Table 10, are of course not "crucial," since an increase in correlation would be expected on the basis of both environmental and hereditary hy-

TABLE 10

CORRELATIONS OF CHILDREN'S MENTAL TEST SCORES AND RATINGS OF MOTHERS' INTELLIGENCE

Age	N	r
1.75	116	.11
2.0	112	.08
2.5	113	.06
3.0	115	.17
3.5	107	.39 ± .06PE
4.0	105	.38 ± .06
5.0	103	.53 ± .05

potheses, and also as a result of any increase in the reliability and validity of the tests.

We have seen that studies of family resemblance have frequently led to ambiguous results as to the relative importance of environmental factors in mental development. In general, however, they have emphasized interfamilial differences in heredity as somewhat more potent than differences in family environments, for a normal range of subjects. These studies not only have their own implications but are also of value in providing a normative background for the interpretation of results from a quasi-experimental type of investigation in which "true" family resemblance is compared with the degree of resemblance achieved in foster relationships (see the section on children in foster homes, page 683).

The Effects of Schooling

The theory of intelligence or capacity measurement implies a curvilinear relationship between education and test scores (for children of a given age). Children of school age with no education will make low scores, regardless of their natural talents or "educability." But it is assumed that, beyond a certain level of educational advance, and within a normal range of school opportunities, increments in training will not be accompanied by corresponding increments in mental test score. To assume otherwise would be to regard intelligence tests merely as tests of schooling. We know, however, that in groups relatively homogeneous as to education wide differences occur in test performance and that these differences persist even after extended exposure to a similar educational environment.

If it is maintained that mental growth can be controlled within narrow limits by educational factors, the burden of proof rests with those making this claim. It would appear to be a simple matter to set up an experiment in which an adequately large group is given experimental training of a type regarded as basically stimulating to mental development, and to compare the subsequent mental test records of this group with records obtained from a carefully matched control. In such an experiment, however, numerous precautions need to be taken. It is unfortunately true that in previous work these precautions have rarely been observed in their entirety:

1. The experimental and the control group should consist of matched pairs from the same population, one member of each pair being assigned at random to the experimental or the control procedure. It usually happens that the experimental group is already "given" to the experimenter in the membership of a specific school sample. He must then make a search for suitable controls. Unless he is fully conversant with the factors which have determined the selection of the experimental sample, it is unlikely that he will succeed in matching this selection completely. Thus, if exceptional intelligence of the parents is a factor determining the placement of children in nursery schools, a matching on the basis of children's IQ will be unsatisfactory, since the children in the experimental group will show dif-

ferential gains merely as a result of increasing approximation to the level of ability characteristic of their families.

2. In the selection of cases, homogeneous groups are needed. In the nursery school, for example, it is possible that educational experiences provided in the school exert differing effects according to the age and cultural background of the children concerned. The mixture of cases of various ages and various social groups(as usually occurs) may yield results extremely difficult to interpret. An additional factor to consider in selection is the much-discussed phenomenon of statistical *regression to the mean*. If, for example, a group of children of below-average ability is selected for special educational attention, retests will probably show a movement toward the mean not necessarily because of true changes but because of compensation for errors of measurement which influenced the original selection. These difficulties, as well as other ambiguities, can be reduced by increasing the reliability of the measurements, as, for example, by the procedure of basing all scores on the average of two tests on successive days.

3. The criteria for matching the experimental and control pairs should include chronological age, initial IQ, and physical status of the children, intelligence (or, at any rate, education) of the parents, and a socio-economic index for the home. It is insufficient to match merely on the basis of the children's IQ's, since changes in the nature of the tests may lead to later IQ differences arising from unmatched factors in the original selection and not from the experimental procedure.

Attention must also be given to the maintenance of comparable conditions in the initial testing. Thus, if the nursery school children are tested in the stress of their first attendance at school and the control children are tested under familiar conditions at home, the experimental group may show larger gains on a second test, owing chiefly to gains in rapport. With young children, attention should be given to assessments of effort, cooperation, freedom from inhibition, response to success or failure, and other motivational factors considered with reference to possible effects upon test performance. It would, of course, be desirable to establish controls on the basis not merely of a single period but of a series of tests representing a segment of the growth curve prior to the beginning of the experiment. Children are sometimes given superior educational opportunities because their mental growth appears to be temporarily restricted. This apparent restriction, however, may be due to any of the intrinsic or extrinsic factors discussed on pp. 643ff. Later gains, giving the impression of an improved rate of growth, may represent changes in these factors rather than the effects of the nursery school experience.

4. The experimental situation should be analyzed and described in detail. Investigations which give a vague report of positive effects from undefined "school experience" can neither be interpreted nor repeated unless the specific basis of these effects is made known. Such information is also necessary in order to determine whether the effects are (a) merely specific transfers to certain kinds of test items, (b) the result of attitude changes or increased incentive, or (c) a more generalized change in mental efficiency.

5. Subsequent test comparisons of the experimental control pairs must involve equal amounts of test practice, comparable tests, and comparable conditions in testing. If retests are made by persons who are strangers to the control group but (as teachers or staff members) are well known to the children in the school, differential apparent gains may occur as a result of

this factor.[1] These considerations lead to a further requirement namely, that, when a test is given, the examiner should not be familiar with the results of previous tests and should not know whether the child is in the experimental or in the control group. Subjective factors in the administration and scoring of such a test as the Stanford-Binet may lead to a conscious or unconscious biasing of the results by examiners who think they know how the results "ought" to turn out. Krugman (1939) and Goodenough (1940b) have discussed the possible rôle of these subjective factors in determining basal and final ages and in reaching decisions as to the scoring of marginal successes or failures.

6. The test program should be continued for several years, in order to determine whether possible effects are temporary (and specific to certain test items at certain ages) or whether they are expressed in more lasting effects upon mental development.

7. Finally, since any obtained effects are likely to be small in magnitude, a substantial number of cases is needed in order to reach a well-founded decision as to the significance of differences.

The reports on the effects of nursery school training should be examined in the

[1] In the report by Barrett and Koch (1930) the nursery school cases making the greatest IQ gains were also those regarded by the teacher as showing the greatest improvement in personality traits. Krugman (1939), in difficult clinical cases, attributed the largest changes in test performance to changes in rapport or cooperation. The following comment by Black (1939) is also illuminating:

"In our experience at the Harriet Johnson Nursery School we have found resistance and shyness to be far less characteristic of the nursery school than of the nonnursery school child, regardless of age. The school situation itself tends to produce rapport between examiner and child before the examination begins. Freedom, a feeling of security in the school situation, and in increasing sense of the friendliness and trustworthiness of adults recognized as belonging to the school make the test situation relatively easy for the child and the examiner" (p. 164).

light of the foregoing experimental criteria. An early study by Woolley (1925), with inadequate controls, reported an apparent effect of preschool education upon mental development. Similar results were obtained a few years later by Barrett and Koch (1930) in an orphan asylum group. Because of the small numbers of cases and the lack of adequately defined experimental conditions, and also because of negative evidence in two other studies (Hildreth, 1928; Goodenough, 1928a), the majority of workers in this field turned from the problem as presenting little hope of further reward. It is to the credit of the Iowa group of investigators that they maintained a persistent interest in the possible effects of nursery school education and formulated an extensive and versatile program of research. In general, this research has been interpreted by Wellman and her associates as indicating potency of the preschool environment in generating marked and persistent changes in mental growth. The *Thirty-Ninth Yearbook of the National Society for the Study of Education* (Stoddard et al., 1940) contains a summary of the Iowa studies, together with reports on 9 other preschool investigations, the majority of which were stimulated, in 1938 and 1939, by the strikingly positive findings reported from Iowa. A later summary by Wellman (1945) covers results on 22 preschool groups.

Partly in answer to statistical criticisms, Wellman and Pegram (1944) have reexamined earlier data, with analyses of variance applied to records from an orphanage project in which half of the children of preschool age were enrolled in a nursery school. They concluded, as in a previous report by Skeels et al. (1938):

(a) that the control environment (of the orphanage) produced substantial losses in IQ when experienced for long periods, (b) that preschool education supplementing the control environment counteracted such losses, (c) that whether or not the preschool environment produced gains depended upon the amount and consistency of preschool attendance [p. 263].

McNemar (1945) has also reanalyzed the same data, pointing out the advantage of a covariance method and finding that, whereas gains are demonstrable for the preschool group, losses in the control group are apparently due to selective factors. He therefore rejected conclusions (a) and (b) above. Conclusion (c) is supported by significant positive correlations between IQ gains and amount of school attendance, but McNemar noted that statistical analysis cannot determine whether the changes are due to mental gains from preschool learning or to some factor such as increased rapport. These difficulties in interpreting a given body of data suggest that our chief need in this field is not for statistical methods of greater power and subtlety but for more rigorous experimental procedures with larger numbers of cases.

It may be observed that for the most part the various studies present a negligible relation between IQ change and length of attendance in nursery school. With a few exceptions they agree in showing a slight difference in favor of nursery school groups when these are compared with control groups.[1] Although the difference often fails to be statistically significant, the findings are sufficiently consistent to be of interest. At the present time disagreement exists as to the extent to which errors of measurement, of experimental procedure, and of statistical treat-

[1] The highly controversial literature on this topic includes discussions by McNemar (1940), Goodenough (1940a), R. L. Thorndike (1940), Stoddard and Wellman (1940), Wellman, Skeels, and Skodak (1940), and Stoddard (1943).

ment may be responsible for results which have been so enthusiastically advocated as evidence that mental growth responds promptly and permanently to educational influences in the nursery school.

In our discussion of IQ constancy and the mental growth curve it was shown that with many children the preschool period is marked by a considerable degree of irregularity or variation in mental growth. It is tempting to the educator to believe that these variations are readily subject to his management and control, but as yet he cannot regard the evidence in this field as satisfactory. No one doubts, however, that the nursery school presents opportunities for promoting development in traits more directly amenable to environmental influence and perhaps more essential for adjustment at this age level. In commenting on the Iowa studies, Burks (1939) has stressed the importance of such factors:

> The preschool ages constitute the period *par excellence* not only for developing constructive attitudes toward tasks but for integrating these with a sense of personal value and with feelings of security in social relationships. To accomplish this integration, however, would not necessarily mean that maximal mental growth during the preschool years was necessary or even desirable for all children. Rather, it would seem that the growth of adaptive behavior should be stimulated and guided—often in special instead of in all areas—so as to achieve an harmonious balance with the expanding personality needs of each particular child [p. 555].

It seems probable that such gains in IQ as have been reported are not too large to be accounted for in terms of (1) the effect of personality improvement upon mental functioning and (2) the effect of the nursery school experience upon the reliability and validity of measurement.

In some studies in which the initial test was given before or shortly after entering school, subsequent gains are often more apparent than real. The initial test "undermeasures," in part owing to the strangeness of the situation and unfamiliarity with the examiner, and in part owing to other psychometric handicaps (inappropriateness of test procedures), which may be controlled after a short period of school experience; this is illustrated for both verbal and nonverbal tests in two studies by McHugh (1943, 1945).

It is quite reasonable to expect some IQ gains among children released from a static and unstimulating environment, whether this release is provided by a nursery school, a foster home, or other environmental change.

Wellman and McCandless (1946) have attempted to examine some of the other aspects of preschool experience which can be hypothesized as related to IQ gain; their results are for the most part inconclusive, although opening an interesting area for further research.

Environmental factors in later schooling have been considered in connection with general studies reviewed on p. 656. The evidence in this area is even less satisfactory than in the nursery school investigations, chiefly because of the lack of data from appropriate comparison groups in definitely contrasting educational situations. Goodenough (1940a) has summarized the relevant work in this field through the year 1939, concluding that "the attempts to demonstrate the differential effects of different kinds of school practice upon child achievement have been disappointingly meager when suitable controls have been employed," and that differential effects upon intelligence are even harder to demonstrate by methods used up to this time (p. 330). This should not be taken to imply that the problem has already been answered in the negative but rather that our present need is for more definitive research.

During the 1940's the study in this field receiving the greatest attention is reported in a monograph by Bernardine Schmidt (1946). Of 195 subnormal children retested at the end of 6 years, more than half were asserted to have made gains in excess of 30 IQ points. A control for a part of this group showed average losses of 3.6 points. Kirk (1948) has analyzed the Schmidt materials in connection with a restudy of some of the original data in the Chicago public schools. So many disturbing points have been raised by Kirk and others that the conclusions of the study now seem in considerable doubt.

Children in Foster Homes

Only a limited view of the possible effects of environmental influence can be given through the experimental control of the school environment. Unfortunately, no studies have been made of a representative sample of children observed under conditions involving an experimental, and parallel, modification of factors both in the home and in the school. Such a study would require the random separation of pairs of siblings (or, preferably, identical twins) and their rearing in homes and schools possessing certain specified differences. We do, however, have a number of investigations of children placed in foster homes. These, though limited in a number of respects, provide us with some of our most penetrating evidence concerning the nature-nurture problem.

Studies of foster children have been discussed in reviews by Goodenough (1940a) and Loevinger (1940) and need not be presented here in detail. The two researches that are most comparable as to procedure are by Burks (1928b) in California and by Leahy (1935) in Minnesota. Each investigated approximately 200 children placed in foster homes before 12 months of age. Each obtained intelligence tests of the foster parents, a cultural-economic assessment of the home environment, and a record of the foster child's IQ after he had reached school age (between 5 and 14 years). Moreover, in each investigation a "true child" control group was set up which would permit comparisons of parent-child relationship with and without the presence of a systematic hereditary factor.

It is often found that the selection of children available for adoption in official placement agencies is slightly superior in average intelligence; for Burks's 204 cases the mean IQ was 107.4, and for Leahy's 194 cases (all of whom were illegitimate) the mean IQ was 110.5. Figure 13 presents some of the more important results of these studies. In this figure r has been converted to r^2 in order to indicate the percentage of the variance of children's test scores "accounted for" by a given correlation. Thus, in the Leahy study intelligence of the mothers may be said to account for 26 per cent of the variance of own children but for only 4 per cent of the variance of foster children. From the results shown in this figure the inference can be drawn that the correlations with home environment which have been found in the case of true children are due primarily to the common factor of the parents' intelligence rather than to the environment acting as a causative agent. That is to say, the intelligence of the parents finds expression both in the culture of their home and in the IQ's of their children. What, now, will happen when the hereditary factor is eliminated from parent-child correlations (through the use of foster children)? Should we not expect that this elimination will also directly affect the correlation of the child's IQ with measures of the (foster) home environment? These correlations do actually drop to low values, ranging from .07 to .21. That they remain higher than zero can perhaps be ascribed in part to the tendency for adopted children to shift toward the level of the homes in which they are placed. However, an

to the home" will result in an increased likelihood of selective placement. This appears to have been a factor in the study of Freeman, Holzinger, and Mitchell (1928) of 401 children in Illinois who were placed at an average age of 4 years, 2 months. When tested at around 11 years, the cor-

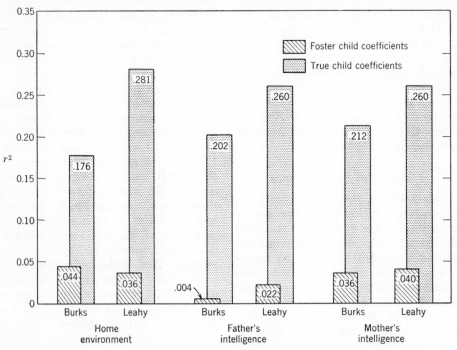

FIGURE 13. A comparison of foster child and true child correlations.

additional factor is present in that the placement of children is rarely experimentally random. In other words, when placement officers have knowledge of the cultural circumstances of the true parents, this is likely to influence their choice of foster homes. Even with elaborate precautions against selective placement, a positive relation has been shown to exist between the occupations of true and foster parents.

When children are placed at ages later than infancy, the aim of "fitting the child

relation with a measure of the foster home [1] was .48. This value, as high as would be expected in a "true child" sample, was apparently influenced somewhat by a choice of foster homes appropriate to the intelligence or to the family origins of the children. If this choice were made without including intelligence tests of the true parents, the subsequent correlation of children's IQ with foster parents' intelligence would

[1] Based on ratings of the material environment, evidences of culture, education of the parents, occupation of the father, and social activity of the parents.

be expected to be lower than for true parent-child relationships. This proved to be the case; for 255 mothers and 180 fathers who were tested when the children were 11 years of age, on the average, the correlation with the foster child's IQ was .28 for the mothers and .37 for the fathers. For a subgroup of 74 children another and more direct type of analysis was possible since tests were available both before and after the children had been in a foster home. The average age of the children at placement was 8 years; at the time of the retest, approximately 12 years. A significant average gain in IQ was shown for children placed in superior homes, and a less significant gain for those placed in poorer homes.

Similar results have been reported in a number of studies in which children were removed from bad home situations and placed in an orphanage or a boarding home (Lithauer and Klineberg, 1933; Wells and Arthur, 1939; Skeels, 1940; Speer, 1940a, b). In such cases, apparent gains are suspect because of difficulties in obtaining a valid test at a time when a child's home is broken or when emotional factors may be present from previous home conditions. Poverty, drunkenness, sex delinquency, inadequate food and housing, and many other disturbing factors are frequently cited as characteristic of the true homes and as giving rise to the need for placement elsewhere. It is difficult or impossible to appraise IQ gains in foster homes unless the initial tests are given under conditions in which test performance can genuinely register the child's ability. A further, and perhaps the chief, explanation of differences between the results of this study and those of Burks and Leahy can be sought in terms of random sampling differences.

An incidental outcome of the Freeman, Holzinger, and Mitchell study has been pointed out by Lorimer and Osborn (1934).

For 156 children classified as members of good, average, and poor foster homes, mean IQ's were obtained of 111, 103, and 91. These differences could be attributed both to environmental influence and to selective placement. However, when the group was subdivided into legitimate and illegitimate children, the former were found to have a mean IQ of 95 and the latter of 106, with similar differences present in each grade of homes. The illegitimate children apparently represent a superior hereditary selection, and this superiority has by no means been obliterated by removal from their true parents.

Similar inferences can be drawn from a report by Stippich (1940) involving a comparison between 48 children whose mothers were feeble-minded, and 29 children of normal mothers; all had been placed in boarding homes before 12 months of age. On the basis of tests given after they were 3 years old, marked differences were noted between the two groups, although they were developing in apparently comparable environments. Twenty-one per cent of the experimental group (children of mentally deficient mothers) and none of the control group fell below 75 IQ. Here, again, the ubiquitous problem of selective placement must be considered. Comparability of the two groups of foster homes appears to be more a matter of assertion than of proof; if there was any tendency to place the children of feeble-minded mothers in less adequate homes this might to some extent account for the results obtained.

Somewhat different results have been reported by Skeels (1941) for a sample of 87 children of mothers who were mentally retarded. After placement in adoptive homes the children attained a mental level "equaling or exceeding that of the population as a whole." For the present purpose, comparisons of small samples of children of feeble-minded and normal mothers are unsatisfactory unless there is adequate information about (1) the diagnosis of the mothers, (2) the conditions of placement, and (3) the mental status of the fathers. Cases should be ruled out in which the mothers' mental deficiency is of clearly secondary origin, as from injury or disease, and in which there is no other record of mental defect in the family. It is also important to know whether the children who have become available for adoption represent a genuinely unselected sample for the families considered. Results would be extremely difficult to interpret if the more retarded children of a defective mother are kept at home or sent to an institution, whereas the more normal offspring are accepted by foster homes. Finally, the mental status and family origins of the fathers cannot be neglected. In the case of illegitimate children of feeble-minded mothers, the ordinary principles of assortative mating may not be operative. It is obvious that "crucial" findings cannot be expected if a substantial proportion of the true fathers are of normal intelligence or derive from families of normal intelligence.[1]

A more recent foster child study is that reported by Skodak and Skeels (1949) on the basis of a fourth and final testing of 100 children placed in adoptive homes some 15 years earlier.[2] In each case placement

was made before the age of 4 months. Table 11 gives the average results for successive tests, based on the Kuhlmann-Binet

TABLE 11

Test	Mean Age	Mean IQ
I	2.2	116.8
II	4.3	112.4
III	7.0	114.8
IV	13.5	107.1

for foster children under 3 years and on the 1916 Stanford-Binet for older children. Subdivided further by age, the highest mean IQ was obtained at 1 year (120.1) and the lowest, in comparable groups, at 14 years (102.4).

The conclusion was offered that the effect of superior foster home environment is shown in the results and also that in general the children exhibit higher test scores than would be expected on the basis of their familial origin. It is undoubtedly true that the foster parents are on the average superior to the true parents in social and educational status. But the true fathers are representative of Iowa males in educational attainment and perhaps not markedly inferior in occupational status if allowance is made for age factors. The chief stigma of the true parents seems to be in the IQ of the mothers. Intelligence measures available for 63 cases show a mean IQ of 86, or slightly more than 1 SD below that of their adolescent children. Factors to be considered in interpreting this discrepancy are (1) the validity of the mothers' tests, administered at a time of probable emotional stress, (2) regression of the children to the mean, and (3) the probability that the sample of mothers includes some cases of mental retardation of secondary origin. If it is assumed that the difference between true mothers' and chil-

---

1 Foster-child studies have not as yet utilized intelligence scores for true fathers. The first study making use of test scores for true mothers was carried out by Skeels (1936). Snygg (1938) reported results from Stanford-Binet IQ's of 312 true mothers and adopted children, in a Toronto study. Parent-child correlations in these two investigations were .09 and .13, respectively; mean IQ's of the mothers were, respectively, 84 and 78, and of the children, 115(?) and 95. These results are not in line with those based on our most carefully controlled and most fully reported foster-child studies. Unfortunately, a further interpretation is difficult because sufficiently complete data have not been presented concerning methods of sampling and conditions of testing.

2 Earlier reports in this series are by Skodak (1939), and Skodak and Skeels (1945). The terminal report in 1949 is especially to be commended for the presentation of the original data in complete form.

dren's IQ's can be attributed wholly to the superior educational opportunities of the foster homes, this effect is apparently consummated in early infancy, since the children's IQ's tend to diminish rather than to increase after 1 year of age.

the Burks and Leahy studies. For this sample, Honzik (1952) has examined age trends in the correlation of children's IQ with the education of their own mothers (from whom they had been separated since early infancy). In Figure 14 these age

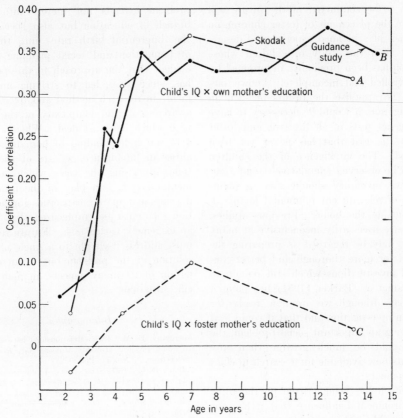

FIGURE 14. Correlations with mother's education, in two studies. (After Honzik.)

The correlational data furnished by Skodak and Skeels are easier to interpret than the data on IQ means. The children's IQ's show approximately zero correlations with measures of the foster parents' education. But the correlation with true mother's intelligence is significant at all ages beyond infancy, and in adolescence is of the order of .4, or only slightly lower than that in

trends (A) are compared with similar correlations (B) for a sample of approximately 200 Berkeley children living in their own families. The third curve, C, presents correlations between the adopted children's IQ and the education of their foster mothers. The framework of environmental theory within which the Skodak and Skeels study was conducted would lead us to expect A to be markedly lower than *B* and perhaps also lower than *C*. The obtained results, however, provide added evidence as to the relatively small weight of environmental factors in producing parent-child resemblances in the variables studied.

One of the most important types of research to be conducted in the future will involve the placement of foster children on the basis of a planned experimental design, rather than the study of children whose location has been previously determined by uncontrolled and incompletely known factors. To appraise the results of such an investigation, it would be necessary to have intelligence tests of all the true and foster parents, a goal that has never yet been reached. The intelligence of the children should be observed cumulatively, and a cumulative inventory should also be maintained of relevant environmental factors in and outside the home. Previous studies, which are necessarily inconclusive at many points, may be regarded as preparing the ground for more thorough and better-controlled investigations which still remain to be conducted. Barker (1951) has pointed out that although we are now ready for such an investigation and that it could lead to solving an important social problem, the cost would be much greater than any amounts now available for research in child development.

So much has been written on the topic of environmental influence that it has not been possible within a single chapter to review all the significant reports and discussions or even to refer to all the principal methods of approach. Little mention has been made, for example, of studies of feeble-minded or gifted children, of the mental growth of institutionalized children, or of mental growth or achievement gauged in other ways than by intelligence tests. Reference has been given, however, to numerous other sources in which further materials can be found. A topic as yet very incompletely studied involves the relationship between intelligence and personality and the effect of variations in emotional adjustment and personal integration upon the nature and the efficiency of mental functioning.[1]

In its social import the nature-nurture problem extends not merely into every branch of education but also (because of the differential birth rate) into the field of population and social planning. It is evident that the approach to this problem has, since 1930, led to striking improvements in research method and to a clearer awareness of the complexity of the issues with which we must deal. When we seek a better understanding of human potentialities in intelligence, we are at the same time appraising the rôles which environmental factors can play in the functional development of our capacities for adaptation. It must be emphasized that this is an extremely varied task. Future research must address itself not to a single ultimate solution of the problem but to an examination of its many aspects, in many specific situations.

Bibliography

Abernethy, E. M. 1936. Relationships between mental and physical growth. *Monogr. Soc. Res. Child Develpm., 1*, No. 7. Pp. 80.

Adkins, D. C. 1937. The effects of practice on intelligence test scores. *J. Educ. Psychol., 28*, 222–231.

Anderson, F. N., and N. V. Scheidemann. 1933. A study of triplets. *Genet. Psychol. Monogr., 14*, 93–176.

Anderson, J. E. 1940. The prediction of terminal intelligence from infant and preschool tests. *Yearb. Nat. Soc. Stud. Educ., 39*(I), 385–403.

Anderson, L. D. 1939. The predictive value of infancy tests in relation to intelligence at five years. *Child Develpm., 10*, 203–212.

Asher, E. J. 1935. The inadequacy of current intelligence tests for testing Kentucky mountain children. *J. Genet. Psychol., 46*, 480–486.

Ayres, L. P. 1909. The effect of physical defects on school progress. *Psychol. Clin., 3*, 71–77.

[1] Cf. discussions by L. S. Hollingworth (1940), Lorge (1940), Lund (1940), and Conrad, Freeman, and Jones (1944).

Baldwin, B. T., E. A. Fillmore, and L. Hadley. 1930. *Farm children: An investigation of rural child life in selected areas of Iowa.* New York: Appleton.

Banker, H. J. 1928. Genealogical correlation of student ability. *J. Hered., 19,* 503–508.

Barker, R. G. 1951. Child psychology. *Annual Rev. Psychol., 2,* 1–22.

Barrett, H. E., and H. L. Koch. 1930. The effect on nursery-school training upon the mental test performance of a group of orphanage children. *J. Genet. Psychol., 37,* 102–122.

Bayley, N. 1933. Mental growth during the first three years. A developmental study of 61 children by repeated tests. *Genet. Psychol. Monogr., 14,* 1–92.

——. 1940a. Mental growth in young children. *Yearb. Nat. Soc. Stud. Educ., 39(II),* 11–47.

——. 1940b. Factors influencing the growth of intelligence in young children. *Yearb. Nat. Soc. Stud. Educ., 39(II),* 49–79.

——. 1949. Consistency and variability in the growth from birth to eighteen years. *J. Genet. Psychol., 75,* 165–196.

——. 1953. Some increasing parent-child similarities during the growth of children. *J. Educ. Psychol.* (in press).

Bayley, N., and H. E. Jones. 1937. Environmental correlates of mental and motor development: A cumulative study from infancy to six years. *Child Develpm., 8,* 329–341.

Beier, E. G. 1951. The effect of induced anxiety on the flexibility of intellectual functioning. *Psychol. Monogr., 63,* No. 365. Pp. 26.

Benda, C. E. 1943. Prevention of mental deficiency from the viewpoint of neuropathology; with special reference to the frequency and significance of birth injuries. *Amer. J. Ment. Def., 48,* 33–45.

Bickersteth, M. E. 1919. The application of mental tests to children of various ages. *Brit. J. Psychol., 9,* 23–73.

Black, I. S. 1939. The use of the Stanford-Binet (1937 revision) in a group of nursery school children. *Child Develpm., 10,* 157–171.

Blatz, W. E., N. Chant, M. W. Charles, *et al.* 1937. *Collected studies on the Dionne quintuplets.* Toronto: University of Toronto Press.

Bradway, K. P. 1944. IQ constancy in the revised Stanford-Binet from the preschool to the junior high school level. *J. Genet. Psychol., 65,* 197–217.

——. 1945. An experimental study of factors associated with Stanford-Binet IQ changes from the preschool to the junior high school. *J. Genet. Psychol., 66,* 107–128.

Bradway, K. P., and E. L. Hoffeditz. 1937. The basis for the personal constant. *J. Educ. Psychol., 28,* 501–513.

Bruce, M. 1940. Factors affecting intelligence test performance of whites and Negroes in the rural south. *Arch. Psychol., N. Y.,* No. 252. Pp. 100.

Burks, B. S. 1928a. Statistical hazards in nature-nurture investigations. *Yearb. Nat. Soc. Stud. Educ., 27(I),* 9–33.

Burks, B. S. 1928b. The relative influence of nature and nurture upon mental development: A comparative study of foster parent-foster child resemblance and true parent-true child resemblance. *Yearb. Nat. Soc. Stud. Educ., 27(I),* 219–316.

——. 1928c. A summary of literature on the determiners of the intelligence quotient and the educational quotient. *Yearb. Nat. Soc. Stud. Educ., 27(II),* 248–353.

——. 1938a. Review of twins: A study of heredity and environment. *J. Abnorm. Soc. Psychol., 33,* 128–133.

——. 1939. Review of *Children in foster homes: A study of mental development,* by Marie Skodak. *J. Educ. Psychol., 30,* 548–555.

Burks, B. S., and A. Roe. 1949. Studies of twins reared apart. *Psychol. Monogr., 63,* No. 300. Pp. 62.

Burt, C. 1921. *Mental and scholastic tests.* London: King.

Byrns, R., and V. A. C. Henmon. 1935. Long range prediction of college achievement. *Sch. and Soc., 41,* 877–880.

Carmichael, L. 1940. The physiological correlates of intelligence. *Yearb. Nat. Soc. Stud. Educ., 39(I),* 93–155.

Carter, H. D. 1932. Family resemblances in verbal and numerical abilities. *Genet. Psychol. Monogr., 12,* No. 1. Pp. 104.

——. 1934. Case studies of mature identical twins. *J. Genet. Psychol., 44,* 154–174.

——. 1940. Ten years of research of twins: contributions to the nature-nurture problem. *Yearb. Nat. Soc. Stud. Educ., 39(I),* 235–255.

Casey, M. L., H. P. Davidson, and D. I. Harter. 1928. Three studies on the effect of training in similar and identical material upon Stanford-Binet test scores. *Yearb. Nat. Soc. Stud. Educ., 27(I),* 431–439.

Cattell, J. McK. 1927. *American men of science.* (4th ed.) Garrison, N. Y.: Science Press.

Cattell, P. 1937. Stanford-Binet IQ variations. *Sch. and Soc., 45,* 615–618.

——. 1940. *The measurement of intelligence of infants and young children.* New York: Psychological Corp. Pp. 274.

Cattell, R. B. 1940. Effects of human fertility trends upon the distribution of intelligence and culture. *Yearb. Nat. Soc. Stud. Educ., 39(I),* 221–233.

——. 1950. The fate of national intelligence; test of a thirteen-year prediction. *Eugen. Rev., 42,* 136–148.

Chapanis, A., and W. C. Williams. 1945. Results of a mental survey with the Kuhlmann-Anderson intelligence tests in Williamson County, Tennessee. *J. Genet. Psychol., 67,* 27–55.

Chapman, J. C., and D. M. Wiggins. 1925. Relation of family size to intelligence of offspring and socio-economic status of family. *Ped. Sem., 32,* 414–421.

Clark, C. D., and N. P. Gist. 1938. Intelligence as a factor in occupational choice. *Amer. Sociol. Rev., 3,* 683–694.

Clark, E. L. 1939. Significance of month of birth as judged by test scores and grades. *Psychol. Bull.*, *36*, 629 (abstr.).

Combs, A. W. 1952. Intelligence from a perceptual point of view. *J. Abnorm. Soc. Psychol.*, *47*, 662–673.

Conrad, H. S. 1931. *Sibling resemblance and the inheritance of intelligence.* Ph.D. Dissertation, University of California.

Conrad, H. S., F. N. Freeman, and H. E. Jones. 1944. Differential mental growth. *Yearb. Nat. Soc. Stud. Educ.*, 43(I), 164–184.

Conrad, H. S., and H. E. Jones. 1940. A second study of familial resemblance in intelligence: Environmental and genetic implications of parent-child and sibling correlations in the total sample. *Yearb. Nat. Soc. Stud. Educ.*, 39(II), 97–141.

Dahlberg, G. 1926. *Twin births and twins from a hereditary point of view.* Stockholm: Bokförlags-A.-B. Tidens Tryckeri.

Davis, A. 1948. *Social-class influences upon learning.* Cambridge: Harvard University Press.

——. 1951. What are some of the basic issues in the relation of intelligence tests to cultural background? In K. Eells, A. Davis, et al., *Intelligence and cultural differences*, pp. 22–28. Chicago: University of Chicago Press.

Davis, A., and R. J. Havighurst. 1948. The measurement of mental systems. *Sci. Mon.*, *66*, 301–316.

Dayton, N. A. 1928–1929. The relationship between physical defects and intelligence. *J. Psycho-Asthenics*, *34*, 112–139.

Dearborn, W. F., and J. W. M. Rothney. 1941. Predicting the child's development. Cambridge, Mass.: Sci-Art Publishers.

de Groot, A. D. 1948. The effects of war upon the intelligence of youth. *J. Abnorm. Soc. Psychol.*, *43*, 311–317.

——. 1951. War and the intelligence of youth. *J. Abnorm. Soc. Psychol.*, *46*, 596–597.

Dubnoff, B. 1938. A comparative study of mental development in infancy. *J. Genet. Psychol.*, *53*, 67–73.

Ebert, E., and K. Simmons. 1943. The Brush Foundation study of child growth and development. I. Psychometric tests. *Monogr. Soc. Res. Child Develpm.*, *8*, No. 2. Pp. 113.

Edwards, A. S., and L. Jones. 1938. An experimental and field study of north Georgia mountaineers. *J. Soc. Psychol.*, *9*, 317–333.

Eells, K. 1951. What is the problem? In K. Eells, A. Davis, et al., *Intelligence and cultural differences*, pp. 3–9. Chicago: University of Chicago Press.

Eells, K., A. Davis, et al. 1951. *Intelligence and cultural differences.* Chicago: University of Chicago Press.

Elderton, E. M. 1923. A summary of the present position with regard to the inheritance of intelligence. *Biometrika*, *14*, 378–408.

Ellis, H. 1926. *A study of British genius.* (New ed., rev.) Boston: Houghton Mifflin.

Ellson, D. G., P. R. Fuller, and R. Urmston. 1950. The influence of glutamic acid on test performance. *Science*, *112*, 248–250.

Embree, R. B. 1948. The status of college students in terms of IQ's determined during childhood. *Amer. Psychologist*, *3*, 259 (abstr.).

Finch, F. H. 1933. A study of the relation of age interval to degree of resemblance of siblings in intelligence. *J. Genet. Psychol.*, *43*, 389–404.

Fischer, L. K. 1952. Hospitalism in six-month-old infants. *Amer. J. Orthopsychiat.*, *22*, 522–533.

Fisher, R. A. 1918. The correlation between relatives on the supposition of Mendelian inheritance. *Trans. Roy. Soc. Edinburgh*, *52*, 399–433.

——. 1930. *Statistical methods for research workers.* (3d ed.) London: Oliver and Boyd.

Forlano, G., and V. Z. Ehrlich. 1941. Month and season of birth in relation to intelligence, introversion-extroversion and inferiority feelings. *J. Educ. Psychol.*, *32*, 1–12.

Freeman, F. N., K. J. Holzinger, and B. C. Mitchell. 1928. The influence of environment on the intelligence, school achievement, and conduct of foster children. *Yearb. Nat. Soc. Stud. Educ.*, 27(I), 103–217.

Furfey, P. H., and J. Muehlenbein. 1932. The validity of infant intelligence tests. *J. Genet. Psychol.*, *40*, 219–223.

Gadson, E. J. 1951. Glutamic acid and mental deficiency—a review. *Amer. J. Ment. Def.*, *55*, 521–528.

Gates, A. I. 1924. The nature and educational significance of physical status and of mental, physiological, social and emotional maturity. *J. Educ. Psychol.*, *15*, 329–358.

Gee, W., and J. J. Corson. 1929. Rural depopulation in certain Tidewater and Piedmont areas of Virginia. *Univ. Va. Inst. Res. Soc. Sci. Monogr.*, No. 3.

Gerver, J. M., and R. Day. 1950. Intelligence quotient of children who have recovered from erythroblastosis fetalis. *J. Pediat.*, *36*, 342–348.

Gesell, A. 1928. *Infancy and human growth.* New York: Macmillan.

——. 1931. The developmental psychology of twins. In C. Murchison (Ed.), *A handbook of child psychology*, pp. 158–203. Worcester: Clark University Press.

Gesell, A., B. M. Castner, H. Thompson, and C. S. Amatruda. 1939. *Biographies of child development. The mental growth careers of eighty-four infants and children.* New York: Hoeber.

Gesell, A., and H. Thompson. 1941. Twins T and C from infancy to adolescence: A biogenetic study of individual differences by the method of co-twin control. *Genet. Psychol. Monogr.*, *24*, 3–122.

Gilliland, A. R. 1949. Environmental influences on infant intelligence test scores. *Harvard Educ. Rev.*, *19*, 142–146.

Goetsch, H. B. 1940. Parental income and college opportunities. *Teach. Coll. Contr. Educ.*, No. 795. Pp. ix + 157.

Goodenough, F. L. 1928a. A preliminary report on the effect of nursery school training upon the intelligence test scores of young children. *Yearb. Nat. Soc. Stud. Educ.*, 27(I), 361–369.

Goodenough, F. L. 1928*b*. *The Kuhlmann-Binet tests for children of preschool age: A critical study and evaluation.* (*Inst. Child Welfare Monogr. Ser.*, No. 2.) Minneapolis: University of Minnesota Press. Pp. 146.

——. 1940*a*. New evidence on environmental influence on intelligence. *Yearb. Nat. Soc. Stud. Educ.*, 39(I), 307–365.

——. 1940*b*. Some special problems of nature-nurture research. *Yearb. Nat. Soc. Stud. Educ.*, 39(I), 367–384.

——. 1940*c*. Intelligence and month of birth. *Psychol. Bull.*, 37, 442 (abstr.).

Goodenough, F. L., and K. M. Maurer. 1942. *The mental growth of children from two to fourteen years; a study of the predictive value of the Minnesota Preschool Scales.* Minneapolis: University of Minnesota Press.

Gordon, H. 1923. Mental and scholastic tests among retarded children: An enquiry into the effects of schooling on the various tests. *Educ. Pamphlets, Bd. Educ., London*, No. 44.

Gordon, K. 1918–1920. The influence of heredity on mental ability. *Rep. Children's Dept., State Bd. Control, Calif.*

——. 1919. Report on psychological tests of orphan children. *J. Delinq.*, 4, 46–55.

Greene, K. B. 1928. The influence of specialized training on tests of general intelligence. *Yearb. Nat. Soc. Stud. Educ.*, 27(I), 421–428.

Haldane, J. B. S. 1938. *Heredity and politics.* New York: Norton.

Halstead, W. C. 1945. A power factor (*P*) in general intelligence: The effect of brain injuries. *J. Psychol.*, 20, 57–64.

Hardy, M. C. 1936. Improvement in educational achievement accompanying a health education program. *J. Educ. Res.*, 30, 110–123.

Hardy, M. C., and C. H. Hoefer. 1936. *Healthy growth: A study of the influence of health education on growth and development of school children.* Chicago: University of Chicago Press.

Harney, Sister Maureen. 1950. *Some psychological and physical characteristics of retarded girls before and following treatment with glutamic acid.* Washington, D. C.: Catholic University of America Press. Pp. 64.

Harrell, R. F. 1946. Mental response to added thiamin. *J. Nutrition*, 31, 283–298.

Havighurst, R. J., and F. H. Breese. 1947. Relation between ability and social status in a midwestern community: III. Primary mental abilities. *J. Educ. Psychol.*, 38, 241–247.

Havighurst, R. J., and R. R. Hilkevitch. 1944. The intelligence of Indian children as measured by a performance scale. *J. Abnorm. Soc. Psychol.*, 39, 419–433.

Hebb, D. O. 1949. *Organization of behavior.* New York: Wiley. Pp. 335.

Heinis, H. 1926. A personal constant. *J. Educ. Psychol.*, 17, 163–186.

Held, O. C. 1940. The influence of month of birth on the intelligence of college freshmen. *J. Genet. Psychol.*, 57, 211–217.

Herrick, V. E. 1951. What is already known about the relation of the I.Q. to cultural background? In K. Eells, A. Davis, *et al.*, *Intelligence and cultural differences*, pp. 10–15. Chicago: University of Chicago Press.

Hildreth, G. H. 1925. The resemblance of siblings in intelligence and achievement. *Teach. Coll. Contr. Educ.*, No. 186.

——. 1926. Stanford-Binet retests of 441 school children. *Ped. Sem.*, 33, 356–386.

——. 1928. The effect of school environment upon Stanford-Binet tests of young children. *Yearb. Nat. Soc. Stud. Educ.*, 27(I), 355–359.

Hilgard, J. R. 1933. The effect of early and delayed practice on memory and motor performances studied by the method of co-twin control. *Genet. Psychol. Monogr.*, 14, 493–567.

Hinton, R. T. 1936. The rôle of the basal metabolic rate in the intelligence of ninety grade school students. *J. Educ. Psychol.*, 27, 546–550.

——. 1939. A further study of the basal metabolic rate in the intelligence of children. *J. Educ. Psychol.*, 30, 309–314.

Hirsch, N. D. M. 1930. *Twins; heredity and environment.* Cambridge: Harvard University Press.

Hoefer, C., and M. C. Hardy. 1928. The influence of improvement in physical condition on intelligence and educational achievement. *Yearb. Nat. Soc. Stud. Educ.*, 27(I), 371–387.

Hogben, L. 1933. *Nature and nurture.* London: Allen and Unwin.

Hollingworth, L. S. 1940. Intelligence as an element in personality. *Yearb. Nat. Soc. Stud. Educ.*, 39(I), 271–275.

Holzinger, K. J., and F. N. Freeman. 1925. The interpretation of Burt's regression equation. *J. Educ. Psychol.*, 16, 577–582.

Honzik, M. P. 1938. The constancy of mental test performance during the preschool period. *J. Genet. Psychol.*, 52, 285–302.

——. 1950. Unpublished data from the Institute of Child Welfare, University of California.

——. 1952. A developmental study of the relation of family variables to children's intelligence. Unpublished manuscript reported at meeting of Western Psychological Association.

Honzik, M. P., and H. E. Jones. 1937. Mental-physical relationships during the preschool period. *J. Exp. Educ.*, 6, 139–146.

Honzik, M. P., J. W. Macfarlane, and L. Allen. 1948. The stability of mental test performance between two and eighteen years. *J. Exp. Educ.*, 18, 309–324.

Hsiao, H. H. 1931. The status of the first-born with special reference to intelligence. *Genet. Psychol. Monogr.*, 9, 1–118.

Hunt, W. A., and I. Stevenson. 1946. Psychological testing in military clinical psychology: I. Intelligence testing. *Psychol. Rev.*, 53, 25–35.

Huntington, E. 1938. *Season of birth; its relation to human abilities.* New York: Wiley.

Husén, Torsten. 1951. The influence of schooling upon IQ. *Theoria, 17,* 61–88.

Janke, L. L., and R. J. Havighurst. 1945. Relations between ability and social status in a midwestern community: II. Sixteen-year-old boys and girls. *J. Educ. Psychol., 36,* 499–509.

Jones, D. C., and A. M. Carr-Saunders. 1927. The relation between intelligence and social status among orphan children. *Brit. J. Psychol., 17,* 343–364.

Jones, H. E. 1928. A first study of parent-child resemblance in intelligence. *Yearb. Nat. Soc. Stud. Educ., 27*(I), 61–72.

——. 1929. Homogamy in intellectual abilities. *Amer. J. Sociol., 35,* 369–382.

——. 1931. The pattern of abilities in juvenile and adult defectives. *.Univ. Calif. Publ. Psychol., 5,* 47–61.

——. 1933a. Order of birth. In C. Murchison (Ed.), *A handbook of child psychology,* pp. 551–589. (2d ed.) Worcester: Clark University Press.

——. 1933b. Relationships in physical and mental development. *Rev. Educ. Res., 3,* 150–162; 177–181.

——. 1936. Relationships in physical and mental development. *Rev. Educ. Res., 6,* 102–123; 146–152.

——. 1939. Relationships in physical and mental development. *Rev. Educ. Res., 9,* 91–103; 134–137.

——. 1941. Seasonal variations in IQ. *J. Exp. Educ., 10,* 91–99.

Jones, H. E., and H. S. Conrad. 1944. Mental development in adolescence. *Yearb. Nat. Soc. Stud. Educ., 43*(I), 146–163.

Jones, H. E., H. S. Conrad, and M. B. Blanchard. 1932. Environmental handicap in mental-test performance. *Univ. Calif. Publ. Psychol., 5,* No. 3, 63–99.

Jones, H. E., and H. H. Hsiao. 1933. Pregnancy order and early development. *Child Develpm., 4,* 140–147.

Jones, H. E., and O. J. Kaplan. 1945. Psychological aspects of mental disorders in later life. In O. J. Kaplan (Ed.), *Mental disorders in later life,* pp. 69–115. Stanford University, Calif.: Stanford University Press.

Jones, H. E., and P. T. Wilson. 1932–1933. Reputation differences in like-sex twins. *J. Exp. Educ., 1,* 86–91.

Jordan, A. M. 1933. Parental occupations and children's intelligence scores. *J. Appl. Psychol., 17,* 103–119.

Kawin, E. 1934. *Children of preschool age.* Chicago: University of Chicago Press.

Keene, C. M., and C. P. Stone. 1937. Mental status as related to puberty praecox. *Psychol. Bull., 34,* 123–133.

Kirk, S. A. 1948. An evaluation of the study by Bernadine G. Schmidt entitled: Changes in personal, social, and intellectual behavior of children originally classified as feeble-minded. *Psychol. Bull., 45,* 321–333.

Klatskin, E. H. 1952. Intelligence test performance at one year among infants raised with flexible methodology. *J. Clin. Psychol., 8,* 230–237.

Klineberg, O. 1935. *Negro intelligence and selective migration.* New York: Columbia University Press.

——. 1938. The intelligence of migrants. *Amer. Sociol. Rev., 3,* 218–224.

Koch, H. L. 1927. Some measurements of a pair of Siamese twins. *J. Comp. Psychol., 7,* 313–333.

Kounin, J. S. 1943. Intellectual development and rigidity. In R. G. Barker, J. S. Kounin, and H. F. Wright (Eds.), *Child behavior and development,* pp. 179–198. New York: McGraw-Hill.

Krugman, M. 1939. Some impressions of the Revised Stanford-Binet Scale. *J. Educ. Psychol., 30,* 594–603.

Kugelmass, I. N., L. E. Poull, and E. L. Samuel. 1944. Nutritional improvement of child mentality. *Amer. J. Med. Sci., 208,* 631–633.

Lantz, B. 1945. Some dynamic aspects of success and failure. *Psychol. Monogr., 59,* No. 1. Pp. 40.

Lauterbach, C. E. 1925. Studies in twin resemblance. *Genetics, 10,* 525–568.

Lawrence, E. M. 1931. An investigation into the relation between intelligence and inheritance. *Brit. J. Psychol. Monogr. Suppl., 16,* 1–80.

Laycock, S. R., and S. Clark. 1942. The comparative performance of a group of old-dull and young-bright children on some items of the Revised Stanford-Binet Scale of intelligence, Form L. *J. Educ. Psychol., 33,* 1–12.

Leahy, A. M. 1935. Nature-nurture and intelligence. *Genet. Psychol. Monogr., 17,* 236–308.

Lehtovaara, A. 1938. *Psychologische Zwillingsuntersuchungen.* Helsinki: Academiae Scientiarum Fennicae.

Levit, S. G. 1935. Twin investigations in the U.S.S.R. *Character and Pers., 3,* 188–193.

Lithauer, D. B., and O. Klineberg. 1933. A study of the variation in IQ of a group of dependent children in institution and foster home. *J. Genet. Psychol., 42,* 236–242.

Livesay, T. M. 1939. Does test intelligence increase at the college level? *J. Educ. Psychol., 30,* 63–68.

Lodge, T. 1938. Variation in Stanford-Binet IQ's of preschool children according to the months in which the examinations were given. *J. Psychol., 6,* 385–395.

Loeb, H. G., and R. D. Tuddenham. 1950. Does glutamic acid influence mental function? *Pediat., 6,* 72–77.

Loevinger, J. 1940. Intelligence as related to socioeconomic factors. *Yearb. Nat. Soc. Stud. Educ., 39*(I), 159–210.

——. 1943. On the proportional contributions of differences in nature and nurture to differences in intelligence. *Psychol. Bull., 40,* 725–756.

——. 1947. A systematic approach to the construction and evaluation of tests of ability. *Psychol. Monogr., 61,* No. 4. Pp. 49.

Lorge, I. 1940. Intelligence and personality as revealed in questionnaires and inventories. *Yearb. Nat. Soc. Stud. Educ., 39*(I), 275–281.

Large, I. 1945. Schooling makes a difference. *Teach. Coll. Rec.*, *46*, 483–492.

Lorimer, F., and F. Osborn. 1934. *Dynamics of population.* New York: Macmillan.

Lowe, G. M. 1923. Mental changes after removing tonsils and adenoids. *Psychol. Clin.*, *15*, 92–100.

Lund, F. H. 1940. Intelligence and emotionality. *Yearb. Nat. Soc. Stud. Educ.*, 39(I), 282–285.

Macmeeken, A. M. 1939. *The intelligence of a representative group of Scottish children.* London: University of London Press.

Maller, J. B. 1933. Vital indices and their relation to psychological and social factors: A study of 310 health areas in New York City with reference to birth rate, death rate, juvenile delinquency, school progress, and intelligence. *Human Biol.*, *5*, 94–121.

Mandler, G., and S. B. Sarason. 1952. A study of anxiety and learning. *J. Abnorm. Soc. Psychol.*, *47*, 166–173.

Mauldin, W. P. 1940. Selective migration from small towns. *Amer. Sociol. Rev.*, *5*, 748–758.

Mayer, B. A. 1935. Negativistic reactions of preschool children on the new revision of the Stanford-Binet. *J. Genet. Psychol.*, *46*, 311–334.

McCandless, B. 1952. Environment and intelligence. *Amer. J. Ment. Def.*, *56*, 596–597.

McCulloch, T. L. 1950. The effect of glutamic acid feeding on cognitive abilities of institutionalized mental defectives. *Amer. J. Ment. Def.*, *55*, 117–122.

McGehee, W., and W. D. Lewis. 1942. The socioeconomic status of the homes of mentally superior and retarded children and the occupational rank of their parents. *J. Genet. Psychol.*, *60*, 375–380.

McHugh, G. 1943. Changes in IQ at the public school kindergarten level. *Psychol. Monogr.*, *55*, No. 2. Pp. 34.

——. 1945. Changes in Goodenough IQ at the public school kindergarten level. *J. Educ. Psychol.*, *36*, 17–30.

McIntosh, D. M. 1944. The effect of practice in intelligence test results. *Brit. J. Educ. Psychol.*, *14*, 44–45.

McNemar, Q. 1938. Special review: Newman, Freeman and Holzinger's *Twins: A study of heredity and environment. Psychol. Bull.*, *35*, 237–249.

——. 1940. A critical examination of the University of Iowa studies of environmental influences upon the IQ. *Psychol. Bull.*, *37*, 63–92.

——. 1945. Note on Wellman's re-analysis of IQ changes of orphanage preschool children. *J. Genet. Psychol.*, *67*, 215–219.

Neff, W. S. 1938. Socioeconomic status and intelligence: A critical survey. *Psychol. Bull.*, *35*, 727–757.

Nelson, C. W. 1942. Testing the influence of rural and urban environment on ACE intelligence test scores. *Amer. Sociol. Rev.*, *7*, 743–751.

Nelson, V. L., and T. W. Richards. 1938. Studies in mental development: I. Performance on Gesell items at six months and its predictive value for performance on mental tests at two and three years. *J. Genet. Psychol.*, *52*, 303–325.

——. 1939. Studies in mental development: III. Performance of twelve-months-old children on the Gesell Schedule, and its predictive value for mental status at two and three years. *J. Genet. Psychol.*, *54*, 181–191.

Newman, H. H. 1940. *Multiple human births.* (*Publ. Amer. Ass. Adv. Sci.*) New York: Doubleday-Doran.

Newman, H. H., F. N. Freeman, and K. J. Holzinger. 1937. *Twins: A study of heredity and environment.* Chicago: University of Chicago Press.

O'Hanlon, G. S. A. 1940. An investigation into the relationship between fertility and intelligence. *Brit. J. Educ. Psychol.*, *10*, 196–211.

Olson, W. C., and B. O. Hughes. 1950. Growth patterns of exceptional children. *Yearb. Nat. Soc. Stud. Educ.*, 49(II), 61–82.

Outhit, M. C. 1933. A study of the resemblance of parents and children in general intelligence. *Arch. Psychol., N. Y.*, No. 149. Pp. 60.

Page, J. D. 1941. Twin, sibling, and chance IQ differences. *J. Educ. Psychol.*, *32*, 73–76.

Paterson, D. G. 1930. *Physique and intellect.* New York: Century.

Pearson, K. 1903. On the inheritance of the mental and moral characters in man, and its comparison with the inheritance of physical characters. *J. Anthrop. Inst.*, *33*, 179–237.

——. 1910. *Nature and nurture.* (*Eugen. Lab. Lect. Series*, 1910, *6*.) London: Dulau.

——. 1918–1919. The inheritance of psychical characters. *Biometrika*, *12*, 367–372.

Peel, E. A. 1951. A note on practice effects in intelligence tests. *Brit. J. Educ. Psychol.*, *21*, 122–125.

Peterson, J. 1928. Methods of investigating comparative abilities in races. *Ann. Amer. Acad. Sci.*, *140*, 178–185.

Phillips, E. L., I. R. Berman, and H. B. Hanson. 1948. Intelligence and personality factors associated with poliomyelitis among school age children. *Monogr. Soc. Res. Child Develpm.*, *12*, No. 2. Pp. 60.

Pieter, J. 1939. Intelligence quotient and environment. *Kwart. Psychol.*, *11*, 265–322.

Pintner, R., and G. Forlano. 1943. Season of birth and mental differences. *Psychol. Bull.*, *40*, 25–35.

Postman, L., and D. R. Brown. 1952. The perceptual consequences of success and failure. *J. Abnorm. Soc. Psychol.*, *47*, 213–221.

Poull, L. E. 1938. The effect of improvement in nutrition on the mental capacity of young children. *Child Develpm.*, *9*, 123–126.

Quinn, K. V., and D. Durling. 1950. Twelve months' study of glutamic acid therapy in different clinical types in an institution for the mentally deficient. *Amer. J. Ment. Def.*, *54*, 321–332.

Reymert, M. L. 1940. Relationships between menarcheal age, behavior disorders, and intelligence. *Character and Pers.*, *8*, 292–300.

Richards, T. W., and V. L. Nelson. 1939. Abilities of infants during the first eighteen months. *J. Genet. Psychol.*, *55*, 299–318.

Richardson, H. M. 1939. Studies of mental resemblance between husbands and wives and between friends. *Psychol. Bull.*, *36*, 104–120.

Richardson, S. K. 1936. The correlation of intelligence quotients of siblings of the same chronological age levels. *J. Juv. Res., 20,* 186–198.

Richey, A. 1934. The effects of diseased tonsils and adenoids on intelligence quotients of 204 children. *J. Juv. Res., 18,* 1–4.

Roberts, J. A. F. 1941. Resemblances in intelligence between siblings selected from a complete sample of urban population. *Proc. Int. Genet. Congr. Edinburgh, 7,* 25 ff.

Roberts, J. A. F., R. M. Norman, and R. Griffiths. 1938. Studies on a child population: IV. The form of the lower end of the frequency distribution and the fall of low intelligence quotients with advancing age. *Ann. Eugen., Cambridge, 8,* 319–336.

Rogers, M. C. 1922. Adenoids and diseased tonsils; their effect on general intelligence. *Arch. Psychol., N. Y.,* No. 50.

Rosanoff, A. J., L. M. Hardy, and I. R. Plesset. 1937. The etiology of mental deficiency with special reference to its occurrence in twins. *Psychol. Monogr., 48,* No. 4. Pp. 137.

Sanders, B. S. 1934. *Environment and growth.* Baltimore: Warwick & York.

Sanford, G. A. 1940. Selective migration in a rural Alabama community. *Amer. Sociol. Rev., 5,* 759–766.

Schlesinger, E. 1923. Die Kinder des kindereichen Familien. *Arch. Kinderheilk, 73,* 50–68.

Schmidt, B. G. 1946. Changes in personal, social, and intellectual behavior of children originally classified as feeble-minded. *Psychol. Monogr., 60,* No. 5. Pp. 144.

Schwesinger, G. C. 1933. *Heredity and environment.* New York: Macmilan.

Schwöbel, G. 1950. Investigations concerning the influenceableness of psychic functions by glutamic acid. *Nervenarzt., 21* (9), 385–393.

Severson, S. O. 1920–1921. The relation of the anatomical age to the chronological, pedagogical, and mental ages with special reference to sex differences. *J. Psycho-Asthenics, 25,* 150–170.

Seymour, A. H., and J. E. F. Whitaker. 1938. An experiment on nutrition. *Occup. Psychol., 12,* 215–223.

Sheldon, W. H., and S. S. Stevens. 1942. *The varieties of temperament: A psychology of constitutional differences.* New York: Harper.

Shepard, E. L. 1942. Measurement of certain non-verbal abilities of urban and rural children. *J. Educ. Psychol., 33,* 458–462.

Sherman, M., and T. R. Henry. 1933. *Hollow folk.* New York: Crowell.

Sherman, M., and C. B. Key. 1932. The intelligence of isolated mountain children. *Child Develpm., 3,* 279–290.

Shimberg, M. E. 1929. An investigation into the validity of norms with special reference to urban and rural groups. *Arch. Psychol., N. Y.,* No. 104. Pp. 84.

Shock, N. W. 1939a. Physiological factors in mental development. *Rev. Educ. Res., 9,* 103–110; 137–139.

———. 1939b. Some psychophysiological relations. *Psychol. Bull., 36,* 447–476.

Shock, N. W. 1944. Physiological aspects of development. *Rev. Educ. Res., 14,* 413–426.

———. 1947. Physiological factors in development. *Rev. Educ. Res., 17,* 362–370.

Shock, N. W., and H. E. Jones. 1940. The relationship between basal physiological functions and intelligence in adolescents. *J. Educ. Psychol., 31,* 369–375.

———. 1941. Mental development and performance as related to physical and physiological factors. *Rev. Educ. Res., 11,* 531–552.

Shuttleworth, F. K. 1935. The nature *versus* nurture problem: II. The contributions of nature and nurture to individual differences in intelligence. *J. Educ. Psychol., 26,* 655–681.

———. 1940. The cumulative influence on intelligence of socioeconomic differentials operating on the same children over a period of ten years. *Yearb. Nat. Soc. Stud. Educ.,* 39(II), 275–280.

Skeels, H. M. 1936. Mental development of children in foster homes. *J. Genet. Psychol., 49,* 91–106.

———. 1940. Some Iowa studies of the mental growth of children in relation to differentials of the environment: A summary. *Yearb. Nat. Soc. Stud. Educ.,* 39(II), 281–308.

———. 1941. Children with inferior social histories: Their mental development in foster homes. *Psychol. Bull., 38,* 594 (abstr.).

Skeels, H. M., and E. A. Fillmore. 1937. Mental development of children from underprivileged homes. *J. Genet. Psychol., 50,* 427–439.

Skeels, H. M., R. Updegraff, B. L. Wellman, and H. M. Williams. 1938. *Univ. Iowa Stud. Child Welfare, 15,* No. 4. Pp. 191.

Skinner, C. E. (Ed.). 1936. *Educational psychology.* New York: Prentice-Hall.

Skodak, M. 1939. Children in foster homes: A study of mental development. *Univ. Iowa Stud. Child Welfare, 16,* No. 1.

Skodak, M., and H. M. Skeels. 1945. A follow-up study of children in adoptive homes. *J. Genet. Psychol., 66,* 21–58.

———. 1949. A final follow-up of one hundred adopted children. *J. Genet. Psychol., 75,* 85–125.

Sloan, W., and H. H. Harmon. 1947. Constancy of IQ in mental defectives. *J. Genet. Psychol., 71,* 177–186.

Smith, A. J., and A. M. Field. 1926. A study of the effect of nutrition on mental growth. *J. Home Econ., 18,* 686–690.

Smith, S. 1942. Language and non-verbal test performance of racial groups in Honolulu before and after a fourteen-year interval. *J. Genet. Psychol., 26,* 51–93.

Snygg, D. 1938. The relation between the intelligence of mothers and of their children living in foster homes. *J. Genet. Psychol., 52,* 401–406.

Speer, G. S. 1940a. The mental development of children of feeble-minded and normal mothers. *Yearb. Nat. Soc. Stud. Educ.,* 39(II), 309–314.

———. 1940b. The intelligence of foster children. *J. Genet. Psychol., 57,* 49–56.

Spitz, R. A. 1945. Hospitalism: an inquiry into the genesis of psychiatric conditions in early childhood. In *The psychoanalytic study of the child*, Vol. I. New York: International University Press.

——. 1946. Hospitalism: a follow-up report. In *The psychoanalytic study of the child*, Vol. II. New York: International University Press. Pp. 113–117.

Stippich, M. E. 1940. The mental development of children of feeble-minded mothers: A preliminary report. *Yearb. Nat. Soc. Stud. Educ.*, 39(II), 337–350.

Stocks, P. 1930–1931. A biometric investigation of twins and their brothers and sisters. *Ann. Eugen., Cambridge*, *4*, 49–108.

Stocks, P., and M. N. Karn. 1933. A biometric investigation of twins and their brothers and sisters. *Ann. Eugen., Cambridge*, *5*, 1–55.

Stoddard, G. D. 1943. *The meaning of intelligence.* New York: Macmillan.

——. 1951. Croissance et mésure d'intelligence. *Année psychol.*, *51*, 17–25.

Stoddard, G. D., *et al.* 1940. Intelligence: Its nature and nurture. Part I. Comparative and critical exposition. Part II. Original studies and experiments. *Yearb. Nat. Soc. Stud. Educ.*, 39(I), 39(II).

Stoddard, G. D., and B. L. Wellman. 1940. Environment and the IQ. *Yearb. Nat. Soc. Stud. Educ.*, 39(I), 405–442.

Stout, H. G. 1937. Variations of normal children. *J. Exp. Educ.*, *6*, 84–100.

Strayer, L. C. 1930. Language and growth: The relative efficacy of early and deferred vocabulary training, studied by the method of co-twin control. *Genet. Psychol. Monogr.*, *8*, 209–319.

Stroud, J. B. 1928. A study of the relation of intelligence-test score of public-school children to the economic status of their parents. *J. Genet. Psychol.*, *35*, 105–110.

Terman, L. M., *et al.* 1925. *Genetic studies of genius.* Vol. 1. *The mental and physical traits of a thousand gifted children.* Stanford University, Calif.: Stanford University Press.

Terman, L. M., and M. A. Merrill. 1937. *Measuring intelligence.* Boston: Houghton Mifflin.

Terman, L. M., and M. H. Oden. 1947. *Genetic studies of genius.* Vol. IV. Stanford University, Calif.: Stanford University Press.

Thomas, D. S., *et al.* 1938. *Research memorandum on migration differentials.* New York: Social Science Research Council. Pp. 423.

Thomas, L. G. 1942. Mental tests as instruments of science. *Psychol. Monogr.*, *54*, No. 3. Pp. iii + 87.

Thompson, C. W., and A. Magaret. 1947. Differential test responses of normals and mental defectives. *J. Abnorm. Soc. Psychol.*, *42*, 285–293.

Thomson, G. H. 1921. The Northumberland mental tests. *Brit. J. Psychol.*, *12*, 201–222.

Thomson, G. H., *et al.* 1949. *The trend of Scottish intelligence: A comparison of the 1947 and 1932 surveys of the intelligence of eleven-year-old pupils.* London: University London Press. Pp. xxviii + 151.

Thorndike, E. L. 1905. *Measurement of twins.* New York: Science Press. (Also in *J. Phil., Psychol. and Sci. Meth.*, *2*, 547–553.

——. 1944. The resemblance of siblings in intelligence-test scores. *J. Genet. Psychol.*, *64*, 265–267.

Thorndike, E. L., *et al.* 1927. *The measurement of intelligence.* New York: Teachers College Press, Columbia University.

Thorndike, E. L., and E. Woodyard. 1942. Differences within and between communities in the intelligence of children. *J. Educ. Psychol.*, *33*, 641–656.

Thorndike, R. L. 1933. The effect of the interval between test and retest on the constancy of the IQ. *J. Educ. Psychol.*, *24*, 543–549.

——. 1940. "Constancy" of the IQ. *Psychol. Bull.*, *37*, 167–186.

——. 1948a. Growth of intelligence during adolescence. *J. Genet. Psychol.*, *72*, 11–15.

——. 1948b. An evaluation of the adult intellectual status of Terman's gifted children. *J. Genet. Psychol.*, *72*, 17–27.

Todd, T. W. 1938. Objective ratings of the constitution of the growing child: Based on examination of physical development and mental expansion. *Amer. J. Dis. Child.*, *55*, 149–159.

Tuddenham, R. D. 1948. Soldier intelligence in World Wars I and II. *Amer. Psychologist*, *3*, 54–56.

Usdin, G. L., and M. L. Weil. 1952. Effect of apnea neonatorum on intellectual development. *Pediatrics*, *9*, 387–394.

Van Alstyne, D. 1929. The environment of three-year-old children. Factors related to intelligence and vocabulary tests. *Teach. Coll. Contr. Educ.*, No. 366.

Vernon, P. E. 1948. Changes in abilities from 14 to 20 years. *Adv. Sci.*, *5*, 138.

Wallis, W. D. 1936. Observations on Leahy's *Nature-Nurture and Intelligence. J. Genet. Psychol.*, *49*, 315–324.

Warner, W. L., R. J. Havighurst, and M. B. Loeb. 1946. *Who shall be educated?* New York: Harper.

Wellman, B. L. 1934. Growth in intelligence under differing school environments. *J. Exp. Educ.*, *3*, 59–83.

——. 1945. IQ changes of preschool and nonpreschool groups during the preschool years: A summary of the literature. *J. Psychol.*, *20*, 347–368.

Wellman, B. L., and B R. McCandless. 1946. Factors associated with Binet IQ changes of preschool children. *Psychol. Monogr.*, *60*, No. 2. Pp. 29.

Wellman, B. L., and E. L. Pegram. 1944. Binet IQ changes of preschool orphanage children: A reanalysis. *J. Genet. Psychol.*, *65*, 239–264.

Wellman, B. L., H. M. Skeels, and M. Skodak. 1940. Review of McNemar's critical examination of Iowa studies. *Psychol. Bull.*, *37*, 93–111.

Wells, J., and G. Arthur. 1939. Effect of foster-home placement on the intelligence ratings of children of feeble-minded parents. *Ment. Hyg., N. Y.*, *23*, 277–285.

West, E. D. 1936. Stage of ossification as a measure of growth and its relation to intelligence-test score. *Harvard Teach. Rec.*, *6*, 162–168.

Westenberger, E. J. 1927. A study of the influence of physical defects upon intelligence. *Cath. Univ. Amer. Educ. Res. Bull.*, *2*, No. 9.

Wheeler, L. R. 1942. A comparative study of the intelligence of East Tennessee mountain children. *J. Educ. Psychol.*, *33*, 321–334.

Whipple, G. M. 1928. Nature and nurture: Their influence upon intelligence and upon achievement. (Selected papers read at the Boston meeting of the Nat. Soc. Stud. Educ.) *J. Educ. Psychol.*, *19*, 361–409.

Willoughby, R. R. 1927. Family similarities in mental-test abilities. *Genet. Psychol. Monogr.*, *2*, 235–277.

——. 1928. Family similarities in mental-test abilities. *Yearb. Nat. Soc. Stud. Educ.*, 27(I), 55–59.

Wilson, P. T. 1934. A study of twins with special reference to heredity as a factor determining differences in environment. *Human Biol.*, *6*, 324–354.

Wilson, P. T., and H. E. Jones. 1931. A study of like-sexed twins. I. The vital statistics and familial data of the sample. *Human Biol.*, *3*, 107–132.

Wingfield, A. H. 1928. *Twins and orphans: The inheritance of intelligence.* London and Toronto: Dent.

Wittenborn, J. R. 1953. *The development of adoptive children* (in press).

Woodworth, R. S. 1941. *Heredity and environment: A critical survey of recently published material on twins and foster children.* New York: Social Science Research Council.

Woolley, H. T. 1925. The validity of standards of mental measurement in young childhood. *Sch. and Soc.*, *21*, 476–482.

Wright, S. 1931. Statistical methods in biology. *J. Amer. Statist. Ass.*, *26*, 155–163.

Zimmerman, F. T. 1949. The glutamic acid treatment of mental retardation. *Quart. Rev. Psychiat. Neurol.*, *4*, 263–269.

Zimmerman, F. T., B. B. Burgemeister, and T. J. Putnam. 1946. *Arch. Neurol. Psychiat.*, *56*, 489–506.

Zuck, T. T. 1936. The relation of physical development to mental expansion. *Proc. 3d Inst. Except. Child, Child Res. Clin. Woods Schs.*, 6–15.

CHAPTER 11

THE ADOLESCENT

JOHN E. HORROCKS

Historical Background

There are many possible approaches to the study of human development. The approach may be that of the psychologist, the sociologist, the anthropologist, the biologist, the physician, or the educator. Within each of these disciplines, in turn, are different ways of considering development, depending upon the bias of the investigator and his purposes in engaging in its study. Consideration may be in terms of a large and significant area of growth and development as personality, social behavior, intellectual growth and decline, physical increment, or physical or physiological functioning. Customarily, the modern study of development has tended to become segmented into the study of chronological age groups in terms of growth, behavior, and problems of a given age group as the neonate, the preschool child, the "middle child," the preadolescent, the adolescent, the adult, and the senescent. It has been recognized, however, that such age distinctions are at best arbitrary, that there is much overlapping, and that no one age group may be fully considered without recognizing its antecedents in an earlier age or its implications for a later one. Still, for pragmatic as well as research purposes large age divisions have been found a practical method of approaching the study of development. Children of a given age range, for example, are usually to be found in school together, associating with each other, and confronted by many common physical and culturally engendered problems.

Adolescence has been one of the major age areas widely studied by those interested in development. Historically, in all cultures and in all eras adults have been exceedingly interested in the activities and welfare of their children. This interest has partly stemmed from a concern with the immediate welfare of children. It has also been a product of the longer national and cultural desire for perpetuation and recognition that children must some day assume the responsibility of carrying forward the tasks begun and the institutions erected by their elders.

From earliest historical times one finds discussions and descriptions of the second decade of life. Aristotle described the advent of puberty and its associated physical changes. In his *Rhetoric* he dwelt at length upon the psychological aspects of the period, particularly as they offered a contrast to the characteristics of people of more mature years. In his *Historia Animalium* he discussed puberty specifically in terms of its physical concomitants, including an extended description of the appearance and effect of secondary sex characteristics. Following Aristotle various authors discussed the period of puberty, although their accounts, like his, whereas often observational, were subjective and speculative and led to generalizations that were never subjected to experimental or other objective verification. Also, while in many cases the period of

697

puberty was not actually written about, it was officially observed and celebrated in cultures ranging from the most primitive to the most advanced. The Roman feast of the *liberalia* during which 16-year-old males assumed the *toga virilis*, and the later Christian custom of confirmation during the period of puberty, are cases in point.

Writers have accorded youth a prominent place in romance and poetry, in biography, and even in philosophy. Plato in his *Dialogues*, although primarily concerned with adults, includes discussions that embody the point of view of youth. Socrates' talk with Lysis in which Lysis complains to him that even his father's servants are allowed to drive the family horses while he is not allowed to do so is reminiscent of the present-day youth who has a similar grievance about the family car. Playwrights and novelists, interested observers of their times, have included descriptions of youth down through the ages, ranging from the lengthy story of Telemachus, the only son of Ulysses, which is told in the first four books of the *Odyssey*, to the more modern writings of Tarkington (1916), Remarque (1928), Marks (1936), and Maxwell (1945). Libby (1901) in a study of the incidence of adolescents in Shakespeare estimates that there are "seventy-four interesting adolescents among the comedies, forty-six among the tragedies, and nineteen among the histories." He notes that there are in particular "thirty characters who, either on account of direct references to their age, or because of their love stories, or because they show the emotional and intellectual plasticity of youth, may be regarded as typical adolescents."

Such considerations of adolescence were, of course, literary or speculative and were neither scientific nor systematic in nature, nor did they approach the problem from the framework of any discipline such as psychology. The nearest approach to a consideration of adolescence from a systematic point of view within an organized area of knowledge occurred in the work of educators or people interested in the education of youth. Francke during the seventeenth century delivered a series of lectures at the University of Leipzig under the title "The education of boys and pubescents" (*De informatione aetatis puerilis et pubescentis*). Rousseau, probably influenced by his own youth, showed considerable interest in the time of pubescence and recognized clear-cut periods of development. He noted that the most crucial event in ontogenesis is the emergence of sex, and he wrote at length in *Emile* upon the period from 12 to 15, which he called "The Age of Reason." Herbart in the early years of the nineteenth century, noting that the ages from 10 to 17 constitute the period of greatest susceptibility to instruction, pointed out that the development of the individual recapitulates not only the phylogenetic stages of development but the cultural ones as well.

The real impetus to the study of development, however, grew out of the work of the nineteenth century evolutionists following Darwin, who, seeking all available evidence to support their theories, felt that in the study of childhood would be found the needed evidence. G. Stanley Hall, after Herbert, was one of the first psychologists to give really serious and prolonged consideration to adolescence as such. His two-volume work *Adolescence* summarized his own thinking and extant research and set the pattern for whatever work was done on adolescence for the quarter-century following its publication in 1904.

The possibility of a two-volume treatise on adolescence in 1904 indicated that a field already existed and that much prior work had been accomplished. Such was the case, for an examination of the literature for the 15 years immediately preceding Hall's book reveals a respectably large group of publications on adolescence. Of this material a great deal, although by no means all, was due to the work of Hall and various of his students. In 1882 in an article on the moral and religious training of children Hall had indicated the psychological nature of the adolescent and stressed the importance of a careful study of the period. Following a similar line of reasoning Burnham wrote in 1891 that "a study of the psychology of adolescence should form a part of the education of every teacher in the higher institutions. The subject should be studied scientifically from the standpoint of physiology, anthropology, neurology, and psychology, and in its ethical, social, and pedagogical foundations." Burnham in his 1891 study used questionnaires, diaries, and autobiographical accounts in studying subjects' reactions as to the kind and nature of problems which they encountered during adolescence.

In 1893 Daniels described what he believed to be the psychological aspects of adolescence, anticipating a present-day trend with a description of puberty ceremonies in primitive cultures. In 1897 Lancaster approached the study of adolescence through an analysis of published biographies and the administration of questionnaires. Starbuck in 1899 published a book, *The Psychology of Religion,* which, although only incidentally concerned with adolescence, did advance the hypothesis that a close relation exists between the advent of adolescence and religious conversion.

A great many of those writing on adolescence were following Hall's lead. Like his, their early work was often speculative and observational or dependent on a normative survey of a selected sample. There was often a tendency to attempt to fit what was observed into the pattern of evolutionary theory or to interpret data in terms of an a priori point of view. Under such a system errors of judgment and of

fact sometimes occurred, some of which were for many years perpetuated in the textbooks, like the "rebirth" theory of adolescence, the *Sturm und Drang* hypothesis, and the preoccupation with proving that "ontogeny recapitulates phylogeny." Describing the inception of adolescence Hall (1904) wrote: "Adolescence is a new birth, for the higher and more completely human traits are now born. The qualities of body and soul that now emerge are far newer. The child comes from and harks back to a remoter past; the adolescent is neo-atavistic and in him the later acquisitions of the race slowly become prepotent." Among the earliest means of investigating adolescence, growing out of the Hall tradition, were the study of the biographies of the great (Yoder, 1894; Swift, 1903), direct conversations with adults about their childhood experiences and impressions (Lancaster, 1898), analyses of the experience of adolescents in literature (Libby, 1901), and, of course, the ubiquitous normative survey.

However, some of the most objective and carefully controlled published work on the adolescent period antedated Hall in its origins, although its interest was a specific aspect of biogical development rather than the wider and interrelated picture that was of interest to Hall and his associates. An example of this specific interest was the attention given to the phenomenon of puberty in women on the part of a group of French medical workers during the first half of the nineteenth century. Various monographs appeared which dealt with feminine puberty from a medical and physiological point of view, although even such sources were not free from a tendency to overgeneralize. The most prolific writer on this topic, however, was Roberton, who published a series of articles on the advent of puberty in women. Although Roberton's identification technique, that of direct questioning, would not be acceptable as a method today, his results more nearly approximated modern findings than anything published to that time. After establishing, by direct questioning of a large sample of women, the age of advent of puberty as 13.75 with a range from 11 to 20 years of age (1831), he published comparative data on the advent of puberty in various cultures (1842, 1845a, 1845b, 1846, 1848). In these studies he challenged the then prevalent opinion that the advent of puberty in tropical countries is earlier than it is in nontropical countries. Roberton's findings on climatic relationships with the age of sexual maturity have since been verified by studies such as those of Mueller (1932) and Mills (1937) which indicate that factors of nutrition and a generally favorable environment rather than climate are the decisive factors tending to hasten the onset of puberty.

Correspondingly, many of the conclusions and points of view of Hall and his students at the turn of the century have also been confirmed by later objective studies, although many of them have not. The comparison is not too adverse, however, when it is realized that Roberton was considering one aspect of adolescence and that in very specific terms, whereas Hall and his associates were trying to interpret and explain all of human behavior as it occurred in individuals during the second decade of life. It is characteristic of any science that later investigators are able to profit by new and improved techniques, a greater amount of knowledge, and whatever mistakes their predecessors may have made.

Present-Day Trends

In the years following 1904 Hall's work continued to set the pattern for work on the psychology of adolescence. Later work tended to differ mostly in refinement of research techniques, in a more objective approach, and in the gradual replacement of the old storm and stress theory with the point of view, initially supported largely by anthropologists such as Mead (1928a, b), that adolescence is not necessarily a time of storm and stress unless the adolescent finds himself in an environment which presents continuing restrictions and frustrations for which the individual is unprepared and for which he has no ready solution. Modern psychology takes the position that adjustment and freedom from storm and stress is a matter of a facilitating environment. If the environment is such that the adolescent can gradually be inducted into experiences for which he is prepared and with which he is able to cope, if he is allowed to assume responsibility and play a mature rôle when he is ready to do so, and if there is a real effort on the part of adults to accept his interests and, where possible, to meet his needs, the adolescent will find his transition into maturity comparatively smooth and uncomplicated. Modern psychology equally recognizes, however, that the adolescent is a human being before he is an adolescent. It is recognized that the adolescent will encounter problems and difficulties as any human does, but in this he has the company of people of all ages. The point of view is that any period of life has its problems and that no one period may be selected as more peculiarly a time of involvement than any other period, unless the culture makes that particular period one that is beset by culturally engendered problems to which it is especially difficult to adjust. This point of view does not deny, however, the fact that an adolescent is undergoing very definite physical changes, that those changes do lead to new feelings and ways of life, and that they do pose problems to which the individual must adjust. One of the earliest full-length statements of this point of view as a psychologist interprets it appeared in a book written by Leta Hollingworth in 1928, and although her statements were largely undocumented by research the point of view has had ample confirmation in numerous studies, of which Dimock's (1937) represents a good example.

Today studies of adolescence typically tend to be concerned with the relation of age and various behavioral characteristics, the subjects being rather few and selected more or less upon the basis of availability. Adequate sampling is rare. Replication seldom occurs, and investigators tend not to relate their studies to others already made in the aspects of adolescence which they are studying, although this last is more likely to be true of studies concerned with activity and interest than of studies in the area of physical development.

Among psychologists engaged in the study of adolescence there have tended to appear two contrasting interests. One confines itself largely to the study of development with particular reference to linear, areal, and ponderal increments, skeletal growth, physiological change, and capacity for physical endeavor. The other is chiefly interested in problems of personality and social and emotional growth. A third group, borrowing freely from the first two, has been particularly interested in the adolescent's learning and intellectual problems in school and elsewhere. There is, of course, great overlapping in these three areas. Except for a few psychologists the distinctions have never been clearcut, but it may fairly be said that most workers in the area represent one of the three biases of approach no matter how much they may recognize and respect the validity of the other two. As a matter of fact, in many studies such as those by H. E. Jones (1943, 1949) there is a deliberate effort to integrate the three approaches and to show their interrelationships. Such integrations have been made possible particularly by long-term studies

such as the California and Harvard Growth Studies and the longitudinal research carried on by the Fels Foundation.

In terms of data collection the two most often-used approaches to the study of the adolescent period are the longitudinal and the cross-sectional. It is recognized that the longitudinal approach is for many purposes the superior technique, but for reasons of expense and time the majority of studies are cross-sectional and are for the most part confined to normative surveys or studies of relationships. The longitudinal approach probably finds its most frequent use in large research centers where funds and facilities are available, although a number of short-duration longitudinal studies, restricted usually to one or two variables, have been made by private investigators and by graduate students doing thesis research. Occasionally a time span longitudinal study of a psychological variable which uses a series of cross-sectional samples of individuals of the same age appears. An example of this approach is Pressey's (1946) study of changes in college and high school students' fears and worries with the passing of historical time. An increasing number of community-wide studies of youth have been appearing in the literature, such as those by Stendler (1949), Hollingshead (1949), and Reed (1950), following the earlier pattern set by the Lynds in 1929 and 1937.

Ordinarily research in adolescent psychology is prosecuted without reference to systematic theory. The proposed Wright-Barker study (1950), partly based on Lewinian concepts, is in contrast to this, however. As a rule, also, research on adolescence has seldom appeared in the form of the classic experimental design of comparison of an equated control and experimental group following an interpolated situation. A survey of the current literature of adolescence reveals a tremendous number of more or less interrelated facts, many of them based on exceedingly dubious research, a number of more or less tested generalizations, and a lack of integration and verification of existing findings in the area. Two of the most pressing needs for future research on adolescence are the selection of adequate and representative samples and the replication of studies.

A complicating factor in research on the adolescent period is the frequency with which findings become "dated" as changing times present new situations and new problems. In the quarter of a century that followed 1925 the adolescent living in the United States experienced a most extraordinarily wide and varied sequence of environmental changes. Immediately following 1925 he lived in a country characterized by prosperity and pervaded by optimism and the last dregs of the "jazz and gin" era. World War I was close enough in the past to be more than a mere historical memory, and the future held great promise as most people interpreted it. The early 1930's reversed this trend as the country found itself beset by a depression, and, with full justification, pessimism and uncertainty filled the air. Those were the days of youth movements, the CCC, the WPA, all shades and varieties of liberalism, the Lincoln Brigade, and wandering gangs of homeless and hopeless youth. It seemed to many people at the time that there could be no future worth living. Certainly the old securities and many of the old ways of life were gone. Then came the increasingly good times of the late 1930's with dawning hope for the future, marred, however, by increasing international tension. By the early 1940's the international situation had deteriorated to the point where the future, particularly for the younger members of the population, became once more a time of uncertainty and fear. World War II brought for youth, whether they were in military service or too young to serve, new ways of life, new values, and new problems of adjustment. Increased mobility, deterioration of family life, death, and, for many, new sources of wealth posed their problems. It was a time when American youth at Guadalcanal and on many another battlefield answered the contemptuous charge of "softness" and "indecision" that their upbringing was supposed to have engendered. Peace in 1945 brought new hope, and a fine future appeared to stretch optimistically ahead. Times were good, education was made possible for many, and the "veteran problem" seemed possible of solution. The dream faded in the midst of gathering international tension, and as youth faced a national draft and universal military service the future again became uncertain as Americans once more existed in a period of tension complicated by a new kind of prosperity.

It should not be assumed that youth living in the United States were alone in the transitions and difficulties which have been described. Youth all over the world have faced crises of the same period of history, and in many countries their problems have made those of children in the United States look simple and uncomplicated.

Of course, no single person was an adolescent during this whole 25 years of change and counterchange, but large numbers of living Americans as well as others all over the world did pass their years of adolescence in one or more of these periods and may be thought of as products of their times. Certainly the literature on adolescence since the 1920's records the impact of the times upon the children who lived during them. For that reason, much of the literature on adolescence is dated, and one must interpret it in terms of generalities rather than specifics. Thus, an article on adolescent attitudes written in 1932 has comparatively little significance for the present except to indicate that "things are different." Such an article does, however, have a general significance, if one interprets it as a generalization as to how a given period or situation may affect behavior and attitude. On the other hand there are also many articles that cover aspects of adolescence little affected by time or condition, for example, interest in the opposite sex and various growth phenomena. It must be remembered, though, that even such apparently stable phenomena may assume new forms and means of expression, as in the case of interest in the opposite sex and the effects of changed diet and environmental conditions upon growth and development.

For these reasons the present discussion has attempted, wherever possible, to base its points upon the literature appearing after 1940. Earlier studies are used only because of certain insights and interpretations they provide in considering youth today, because comparable studies have not been made in recent years, or because they represent recognized landmarks in the literature. As a matter of fact the writer believes that a complete psychology of adolescence could be based entirely on studies made subsequent to 1945.

Definition of Adolescent Psychology

Adolescence has been defined as that time of life when an immature individual in his teens approaches the culmination of his physical and mental growth. Physiologically an individual becomes an adolescent with the advent of puberty and the ability to reproduce his kind. Chronologically puberty generally occurs in girls between the twelfth and the fifteenth years with a range of about 2 years on either side of these figures. For boys puberty tends to occur from 1 to 2 years later than it does for girls. Investigators differ in measures

of variability and central tendency which they cite depending upon the nature and circumstances of their sample (Ellis, 1948, 1947; Hogben, Waterhouse, and Hogben, 1948; Crampton, 1944; Schonfeld, 1943; Dearborn and Rothney, 1941; Shuttleworth, 1937, 1939; Dimock, 1937; Hardy and Hoefer, 1936). Psychologically and chronologically adolescence ends with the attainment of a consistent and comparatively widespread level of maturity. The development of such maturity is a slow process, and there now exists no means whereby it is possible to measure whether an individual has attained such a level. It is ordinarily assumed that most individuals have attained at least a moderate degree of psychological maturity by the time they are in their early twenties and that they are then adults rather than adolescents. For some people, however, psychological maturity never does arrive, with the result that they extend their adolescence throughout their later years.

Hence, the beginning of adolescence is defined in physiological terms and its duration and cessation in psychological terms. However, since the definition and implications of psychological maturity are controversial and display wide variations from individual to individual it is unsafe to make generalizations about the end of adolescence. The permissive limits seem to rest on the assumption that most individuals can be expected to attain the necessary integration of maturity by the time they are well into their twenties.

As a matter of fact, the cessation of adolescence is in reality governed by the culture in which an individual lives. If the culture is such that it allows the individual to exercise responsibility early and to assume the rôle of an adult, then his maturity is hastened. If the culture is such that it denies responsibility and shelters the individual throughout his teens, then maturity tends to be retarded, at least for the majority. In western culture people tend to attain maturity at a much later date than in less sheltered cultures or in earlier historical times when children assumed adult responsibilities at what today appears a fantastically early age.

Considerable psychological and anthropological writing has attempted to draw parallels between western culture and the various primitive cultures of the South Seas, Africa, the American Indians, and various other peoples. Such studies usually take as their base an investigation on a specific primitive culture which is then contrasted with selected aspects of western culture (Whiting, 1941; Lee, 1940; Erikson, 1940; Boas, 1938; Mead, 1928a; Malinowski, 1927). Such parallels began by drawing analogies between cultures and later were used negatively to question psychological assumptions growing out of observations of western culture. It became fashionable to speak broadly of "western culture" vs. "primitive culture." A danger in such broad comparisons was pointed up by studies such as those of Beaglehole (1940) and Evans-Prichard (1934), which emphasized the great complexity and diversity of primitive or preliterate cultures. One cannot properly speak of primitive culture per se but only of a specific localized aspect of a given primitive culture. Such is equally true for western culture. One cannot properly assume, for example, a given situation as being true of *all* the United States any more than one can assume a situation to be true of *all* Europe. Contrasts between American youth and German youth, for instance, are probably too broad. Intracultural differences may well be greater than intercultural differences among western culture as well as among primitive cultures.

Major Aspects of Adolescence

In general, wherever adolescents are to be found there are five major focal points around which problems of behavior and adjustment tend to cluster. They may be thought of as points of reference from which to view adolescent growth and development and may be summarized as follows:

1. Adolescence tends to be a time of seeking status as an individual. There is a tendency to attempt emancipation from childish submission to parental authority and in general a struggle against relationships with adults in which the adolescent is subordinated on the basis of inferiority in age, experience, and skill. It is a period of emerging and developing vocational interests and of striving toward economic independence.

2. Adolescence tends to be a time when peer group relations become of major importance. The adolescent is usually most anxious to attain status with, and recognition by, his age mates. He tends to desire intensely to conform to the actions and standards of his peers. It is also a time of emerging heterosexual interests that bring complexity and sometimes conflict to emotions and activities.

3. Adolescence is a time of physical development and growth that forms a continuous pattern common to the race, but idiomatic to the individual. During this period there is a rapid altering of the body and a revision of the body image and habitual motor patterns. It is during this time that physical maturity is attained.

4. Adolescence tends to be a time of intellectual expansion and development and of academic experience. The individual finds himself in the position of having to adjust to increasing academic and intellectual requirements. He is asked to acquire many skills and concepts useful at some future time but often lacking immediate motiva-

tion. It is a time when an individual is gaining experience and knowledge in many areas and is interpreting his environment in the light of that experience.

5. Adolescence tends to be a time of development and of evaluation of values. The quest for the controlling values around which the individual may integrate his life is accompanied by an increasing awareness of "self," a development of self ideals, and an acceptance of self in harmony with those ideals. It is a time of conflict between youthful idealism and reality.

In considering the foregoing points of reference it is well to recall that, even though the growth and development of all people follow a similar pattern, there are wide individual variations within the pattern. Such individual variations are often the most significant aspects in the consideration of any given individual.

Biological Aspects of Adolescence

Adolescence is a time of growth and differentiation. In some areas of development, it is just as much a time of cessation of growth or the initial attainment of maturity. For most of the growth processes, rapid growth in infancy and early childhood is followed by a plateau or a period of slow growth until just before pubescence. At that time there is usually a spurt of rapid growth succeeded by less rapid growth and gradual deceleration of the growth curve until middle or late adolescence. In late adolescence most growth curves reach an asymptote or in the case of functions such as mental development start a long, gradual decline that progresses throughout maturity. In some cases, such as the thymus, the decline is extremely rapid.

Physical changes have a great deal of influence upon social and psychological behavior. If physical change were simply a matter of changing structure and function,

one could describe them and pass on to other topics. From the point of view of behavior, however, the matter is not so simple; actual structural or functional change is only the beginning, from which stem considerable changes in social behavior, in attitude toward self and others, and in those things which the adolescent feels have value for him. Bayley (1941) and H. E. Jones (1949) have indicated the effects of the rate and direction of maturing and of the development of strength upon an adolescent's social acceptance and status and upon his personal adjustment.

Various studies have revealed over-all patterns of growth and have cited their findings in terms of curves of growth and decline. One may speak of general curves of growth, as for example, height or weight, and even describe their course and general nature. However, there are great individual differences, and these differences are to be found not only in persons but also in groups. Studies sometimes cite growth patterns for a general population group and sometimes for a sample selected from a group of individuals deviate in one or more growth factors. Shuttleworth (1938, 1939) and Dearborn, Rothney, and Shuttleworth (1938) in the Harvard Growth Study divided their sample into a number of homogeneous groups in respect to the advent of first menstruation. In the analysis of data they considered each of these homogeneous groups as a separate and distinct population. Bayley (1943a, 1943b) and H. E. Jones (1949, 1939) in the California Growth Study dealt with early- and late-maturing samples based on skeletal age. Other investigators have used similar devices.

Findings indicate that there is no one standard growth curve. Different organs and different parts of the body grow and develop at different rates of speed, and the curves of their growth take different forms, with considerable variations occurring from person to person. In twenty-two dimensions of growth used in the Harvard Growth Studies, Shuttleworth (1939) noted that each generated a characteristic pattern which was in most cases unmistakably different from the pattern of every other dimension. He further noted that the growth pattern for each dimension was recognizably similar for both sexes, for all menarcheal and age of maximum growth groups, and for children of North European or Italian stock. Certain common elements did exist in the growth curves of all twenty-two dimensions studied. Most important of these was the existence in each dimension of two major growth cycles consisting of accelerating and decelerating phases. However, the growth trends of the twenty-two dimensions were not synchronized in that the growth phases of the first cycle were initiated at different ages and were of different durations.

Physical growth has commonly been studied by measuring growth increments in the various internal and external organs of the body. Most common of the measurements is the linear measurement of the length and width of growth increments or dimensions. Such linear growth may be most clearly observed and compared in measurements of standing height and sitting height. Second of the measurements is areal or cross-sectional measurement, which concerns itself with areal increments or increases in body mass or volume. Such measurements most commonly include the areas of various surfaces of the body, chest dimensions, and girth of arms, legs, and hips. Third is ponderal measurement, which is concerned with growth in body or single-organ weight and mass. Over-all weight is an example of such measurement and is considerably influenced by deposits of fatty tissue.

Quite specific differences in growth patterns are observed when they are considered from the aspect of areal as compared to linear or ponderal growth. One of the more outstanding contrasts occurs in increases (in relative postnatal increments) which take place between birth and early maturity. For example, growth in stature, which is one-dimensional, is 3.5 fold; that is, an individual increases in height 3.5 times his height at birth. In surface area, which is two-dimensional, growth is 7 fold. And finally, in weight, which is three-dimensional, the increase is 30 fold.

Growth in Height and Weight. When ponderal increments of body weight are compared with linear increments of standing height, much the same course of growth is presented. Boys tend to be somewhat taller than girls and remain so until about 10 years of age, at which time girls begin to forge ahead, and from 11 to 14 girls are taller than boys of the same age. But from shortly after 14 boys begin to forge ahead, and they maintain their superiority in height from that time on. This is, of course, the average picture. There are always some boys who are shorter than some girls, and vice versa. There are also considerable differences in the ages at which different children have their growth spurts or attain maximum growth. In general there is an acceleration in growth about 6 months before the advent of puberty. In studies since the 1920's there has been a tendency to categorize subjects as early-, average-, and late-maturing, and to present data in those terms as being more representative of true individual growth patterns. Late-maturing children do not grow so fast as early-maturing children in terms of increments per year, but their growth period does extend over a longer period and continues after the growth of early-maturing children has ceased. There appears to be no correlation between final size and rapidity of growth either during the period of adolescence or before (Friend and Bransby, 1947;

Bayley, 1946; Bunak, 1940; Shuttleworth, 1939; Meredith, 1935; Boas, 1932; Davenport, 1926). Figure 1 presents average yearly increments of growth in standing height for early- as compared to late-maturing boys and girls.

1934; Collins and Clark, 1929; Pfuhl, 1928). Figure 2 presents the average weight of a sample of American boys and girls from a study by Shuttleworth (1939).

Thus, it may be seen that linear and ponderal curves of growth present a number of

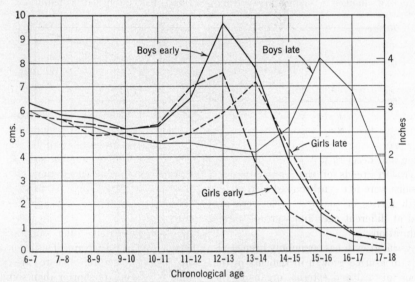

FIGURE 1. Average yearly increments of growth in standing height for early- as compared to late-maturing boys and girls (late and early categories determined by age of maximum growth). Adapted from F. K. Shuttleworth. The physical and mental growth of boys and girls aged 6 through 19 in relation to age of maximum growth, *Monogr. Soc. Res. Child Develpm.*, *4*, No. 3, 1939, pp. 245-247.

In respect to weight, boys and girls tend to follow the same general course of growth, but girls tend to be lighter than boys to prepuberty. In the early part of puberty girls become heavier than boys, after which boys once again become heavier, and they maintain their advantage of weight throughout maturity. The same prepubescent growth spurt occurs in both boys and girls, with girls averaging 1 to 2 years in advance of boys at that time. With weight as with height, age of maximum growth is an important factor in assessing a given individual's relative status (Ellis, 1947; Ni, 1947; Shuttleworth, 1939; McCloy, 1938; Wetzel,

similarities. They both tend to follow the same double sigmoid curve of growth, but in ponderal growth there is a greater increase in rate and a number of minor variations preceding puberty. With both height and weight there are great individual differences. One may not predict any given individual's height or weight from his age, but it is possible to cite average heights and weights for any given age. It is the individual that deviates markedly from the norm who is most likely to experience difficulties of adjustment.

In addition to studies of standing or overall body height and of weight previously cited, a number of investigations have been made of growth of sections of the body such as the arms, legs, trunk, neck, head, chest, hips, and thighs. Many of these studies are linear, but a number of them are areal; that is, they attempt to discover actual changes in surface area rather in another. A further difficulty is that different investigators may use different techniques of measurement, which make their findings show differences that would not actually exist if the same measurement technique was being used by all. Krogman (1950) has published a handbook which

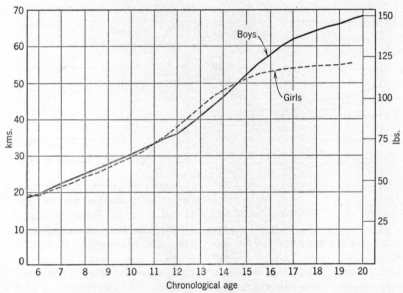

FIGURE 2. Average growth trends in weight of 1458 boys and girls from the Harvard Growth Study. From F. K. Shuttleworth. The physical and mental growth of boys and girls aged 6 through 19 in relation to age at maximum growth, *Monogr. Soc. Res. Child Develpm.*, *4*, No. 3, 1939, pp. 248–249.

than in height or in width alone. Such areal studies are two-dimensional in contrast to one-dimensional linear studies.

Two things are to be remembered in interpreting studies of height and weight. One, as Gould (1938) points out, is that growth curves plotted from averages of different sets of individuals mask individual spurts and cessations of growth. A second is that it is dangerous to generalize from one sample to another since both height and weight are conditioned by many environmental as well as internal variables which may be present in one sample and missing

explains how height and weight measurements may be made and interpreted.

Relationships between Various Bodily Dimensions. In considering the course of general growth a number of different parts and dimensions of the body are involved and must be taken into consideration. Bayley and Tuddenham (1942) note in their discussion of adolescent body build that the relative proportions of the different parts of the body which determine body form or body build are of as great interest to the psychologist as such characteristics as height or weight. They cite the possibility of relationships between physique and the various components of personality and point out that "as a measure of nutrition, weight in relation to height does not take into account the wide differences which exist in skeletal build and in the proportions of the body and its extremities."

There have been various attempts at classification of body build, ranging from the *habitus phthisicus* and *habitus apoplecticus* of Hippocrates to the somatotypes and measurement ratios of modern workers. McCloy (1938) notes that such classifications generally attempt to arrange individuals along a continuum from a relatively tall, slender type at one extreme through an intermediate or "normal type" to a relatively short, stocky type at the other extreme. McCloy cites four general methods of classifying body builds which have found acceptance at one time or another. First is a general index number of body build derived by setting up a ratio between two different measures, usually with a measure of sitting or standing height as the denominator; for example: (chest circumference)/height, (head length)/height, weight/height, (weight ⅓)/height, (stem length)/height, (hip width)/height.

The second type of classification attempts to group individuals into two or more clear-cut categories. An example of this type of subjective classification is that of Stockard (1922–1923), who proposes three categories: linear, intermediate, and lateral. Classifications based upon such arbitrary, discrete categories differ markedly from those of the ratio type. The ratio type are subjectively arrived at, and presuppose that body type may not be categorized into a few separate types but exist along a continuum, and thus form a continuous distribution from one extreme to the other.

The third type of classification, according to McCloy, is that of Kretschmer, who proposes a thin type called asthenic, a stocky type called pyknic, and various mixed or intermediate types. Kretschmer also proposes a deviate type which he calls athletic. The Kretschmer classifications have exercised considerable influence in sociological and psychological thinking, although this type of classification no longer finds acceptance among scientific workers in the field of growth and development.

The fourth type of classification is that of Draper (1930) and of Draper, Dupertuis, and Caughey (1945), who attempt to classify individuals on the basis of predisposition to various kinds of diseases. Draper speaks of a tubercular type, a gastric-ulcer type, a gall-bladder type, and a pernicious-anemia type. Draper's system is a medical one and has not found use among psychologists in their studies of growth and development.

Typical of present classification systems are those of Sheldon, Stevens, and Tucker (1942) and of Reynolds and Asakawa (1948), Sheldon's endomorphic, mesomorphic, and ectomorphic classification being probably the best-known system since Kretschmer's. There are also various methods of appraising physical fitness which use physical-relationship categories such as the Wetzel grid, the Baldwin-Wood age-height-weight tables, the Franzen and Palmer ACH index, and the Pryor and Stolz age-height-hip-weight standards. In an evaluation of the various appraisal procedures in the use of body measurements in a school program Stuart and Meredith (1946) cited weight, stature, pelvic breadth, chest circumference, calf circumference, and subcutaneous tissue thickness as constituting the most useful indicators of physical status and growth progress.

Although the various body classification types have found specific diagnostic uses from time to time, the consensus appears to be that body typing is either not possible or is at best misleading and impractical. There is serious danger that our confidence in the validity of body typing and overgeneralization from data so obtained may lead to extremely unfortunate results. Bayley and Tuddenham (1942) observe that the quantitative treatment of body measures of large populations does not result in a series of discrete "types" but rather that such measures are "distributed normally throughout a range of magnitudes for any dimension measured." They further observe that, although there is a correlation among the various dimensions of the body, the correlation is "by no means perfect," and accurate predictions of an individual's proportions on the basis of a "type" classification is not feasible. From the psychologist's point of view the most profitable procedure is that of observing individual deviations from the average in terms of their effects, for that person, on behavior and social acceptance.

Interrelationships in Body Growth. In common with previously cited measures of the growth of weight and height, a marked prepubescent spurt is observed in the growth of many other bodily dimensions, a spurt which is characterized by sexual differentiation in the earlier and more rapid growth of girls. In girls there is greater growth in hip width, accompanied by sex differences in the distribution of fatty deposits, and the appearance of secondary sex characteristics. Boys, on the other hand, despite a slow start, soon exceed girls in shoulder width; this fact is partly responsible for the greater strength commonly possessed by boys, since their larger bony framework provides greater leverage for the operation of muscles. As previously mentioned, the tendency is to present growth data in terms of whether the individuals being studied mature late, early, or at about the average time. Studies report that different developmental rates and sequences exist where the rate of maturity is markedly accelerated. This appears to be particularly true of boys where bodily proportions are concerned, including the relation of sitting height to standing height, of width to length, and of hip width to shoulder width. The proportion of hip width and shoulder width is different for boys and girls. Girls are quite broad hipped; whereas the ratio between height and hip width in boys remains relatively constant, boys who mature late tending to have narrower hips than those who mature early. There appear to be no differences among girls in terms of the relation of early or late maturity to hip width, although quite definite differences exist between early- and late-maturing boys and girls in the relationship between shoulder and hip width. Late-maturing individuals tend to have broader shoulders than early-maturing individuals, although this tendency is more marked in boys than in girls. Hence, one finds broad-shouldered, narrow-hipped late-maturing boys as compared to narrow-shouldered, broad-hipped, early-maturing boys (Muhsam, 1947; Dublineau, 1944; Bayley, 1943a, 1943c, 1941; Simmons and Greulich, 1943; Schmidt-Voight, 1942; Bayer, 1940; Zeller, 1939; Stone and Barker, 1937; Carey, 1936).

Strength and Physical Development. Closely associated with an individual's growth and development are his physical fitness, physical coordination, and motor development. Such matters are of great importance to adolescent males. The typical adolescent boy is expected to fit the "manly," physically active, physically adept stereotype of boyhood. He stands to gain prestige and social acceptance through athletic ability in competitive sports. It is expected that a boy will be interested in participating in sports and physical activities and that he will have the stamina and ability to implement his interest. An adolescent who lacks such interest, ability, and stamina is confronted by many difficulties of acceptance in his peer relationships and even in many of his relationships with adults. Where physical activity and interest are lacking the adolescent boy must compensate strongly in other directions, but such compensations have their limitations and overcompensation may even militate against him. Various investigators (H. Jones, 1948; Bower, 1940; Cowell, 1935; Thrasher, 1927) have pointed out the social acceptance value for boys of athletic skill, "gameness," strength, etc.

Various Means of Assessing an Individual's Physical Fitness and Strength Potential. Such measures are usually summed up in a descriptive index number representing an over-all picture of physical status or potential. Typically included are measures of grip, leg strength, push and pull, jumping, running, and other tasks which involve moving either the whole body or a part of it. Among such attempts at measurement have been those of Larson (1941), Cozens (1936), MacCurdy (1933), McCloy (1932), Brace (1927), Rogers (1927), Garfiel (1923), and Sargent (1921). No single test of physical fitness appears to offer a satisfactory index. Present procedure favors a combination of tests with emphasis upon dynamic measures such as field and track events.

Strength normally increases at a rapid pace during the first 20 years of life, but at varying rates from year to year. In general it is particularly accelerated after the sixth year. H. E. Jones (1949) notes that the development of strength during childhood and adolescence is more conspicuous than any other aspect of physique and that, whereas one-third of an individual's height is acquired after his sixth year, approximately four-fifths of his strength is acquired after that time. Jones hypothesizes that such rapid changes in strength possibly indicate that strength will show

sensitive responses to accelerant growth factors in adolescence and may well have practical use as partial indicators of the status of other growth factors. Meredith (1935) notes that in the Iowa studies, with the exception of weight, strength possessed a coefficient of variation some 2 to 5 times greater than any other measures used.

In speaking of the acceleration of the growth curve for boys. H. E. Jones (1944) notes that boys are twice as strong at 11 as they are at 6, and that their manual strength increases 100 per cent from 11 to 16. This growth picture has been characteristic of most of the studies made of the development of strength of grip (H. E. Jones, 1949; Meredith, 1935; Metheny, 1941). In so far as the various studies reveal differences, the differences tend to be in levels of strength achieved at various ages rather than in the course and nature of the growth curve itself.

There appears to exist a general curve of growth for strength. Not only do the various measures of strength tend to show similar curves of growth, but there are also high correlations between the course of development of strength and the development of other physical features of the body. This last is not unexpected when it is remembered that strength depends upon the tangible physical features through which it operates and without which it would remain nonexistent. Meredith's (1935) finding, for example, that both strength of grip and weight displayed marked acceleration when the boys he studied reached 13 years may be taken as evidence of a functional relationship.

Since strength may be thought of as a function potential depending on various factors in addition to muscle size, it is reasonable to expect that knowledge of the anatomical growth of an individual's muscles alone would not yield a proper index of his strength. As a matter of fact, because of the accelerated growth of the body generally around the time of pubescence, it has been found that strength tends to increase faster than the anatomical growth of muscle. Sex differences in the growth of strength are, of course, partly due to differences in weight, musculature, and the skeletal framework of boys as compared to girls, but they may also be due in part to the more frequent and vigorous use of the muscles which results from the customarily greater physical activity of boys. In this connection it is interesting to note that, at the age when differences in strength between boys and girls begin to increase markedly, girls are entering upon a more feminine cultural phase, during which their activities assume a more sedentary character than those of boys.

A summary of survey evidence (H. E. Jones, 1946; Bayley and Espenschade, 1944, 1941; Espenschade, 1940; Carpenter, 1938; Dimock, 1935; Atkinson, 1925, 1924) indicate that children who are taller, heavier, and older tend to be stronger and to display greater motor and physical proficiency than shorter, lighter, and younger children. It appears, although the evidence is as yet incomplete, that physiological maturity goes hand in hand with increases in strength and motor performance, and that the age of maximum growth, of physiological maturity, and of anatomical and skeletal maturity is more important than chronological age in this area. Body build as such has exhibited low correlations with motor performance during the years of adolescence. Differences in measures between the sexes are usually found, with the characteristic early development and early cessation of growth in girls contrasting with the later development and later cessation of growth in boys. In general, increases in motor performance tend to cease at about 17 or 18 for boys and at about

15 for girls. So far as sexual maturity is concerned there is a definite positive relationship with strength.

Physiological Development

Advent of Puberty. The phenomenon of sexual maturity with its accompanying behavioral changes and attitudes is one of the chief landmarks in the developmental sequence. The advent of puberty or sexual maturity is the most clear-cut and most dramatic line of demarcation between the child and the adolescent. Puberty is defined as that time in the life cycle when functional maturity is attained by the reproductive organs and the individual becomes capable of reproducing his kind. In girls puberty is marked by the gradual appearance of secondary sex characteristics. A gradual change in figure occurs which includes the deposition of fat on the hips, development of the breasts, a widening of the pelvis, and the appearance of hair on the pubes and axillae. The advent of puberty is generally judged in girls by the appearance of first menstruation. Before first menstruation a girl is classified as prepubescent; following that time she is classified as pubescent. However, the irregularity of the menstrual cycle in young girls indicates a certain amount of caution in using first menstruation as the only criterion of puberty. Greulich (1944) notes that, properly speaking, menstruation is a reflection of a physiological state which usually precedes the capacity to reproduce and which may occur in different individuals at different times during the pubertal cycle. Despite this caution, however, psychologists in their studies customarily accept menstruation as an indication of the advent of puberty and classify and analyze their data on that assumption.

A review of studies citing the average age of first menstruation indicates that findings disagree, sometimes to the extent of 2 or more years. Such differences may be due to problems of inadequate or highly selected sampling, or to variations in techniques adopted by various investigators. The differences may, however, reflect real long-term changes in the entire population. There is evidence (Gould and Gould, 1932; Mills, 1937; Schaeffer, 1906; Neurath, 1932; Bolk, 1923) that average menarcheal age is decreasing in the United States as well as in central and northern Europe. Such general changes, if continuing over a period of time, may have important implications for education and problems of social and heterosexual adjustment where adolescents are concerned.

There is also evidence that environmental factors are related to some degree to the age of onset of adolescence. Greulich (1944) has pointed out that food and feeding habits, nutritional status, illness, and a favorable or unfavorable environment all operate to hasten or retard the onset of puberty. It would not be surprising to find a comparatively retarded average age of first menstruation in underprivileged as compared to highly privileged samples, or in inhabitants of a country suffering severe nutritional difficulties as compared to one which is more fortunately endowed. Two studies whose contrasted findings may offer partial evidence that the concomitants of socio-economic status affect age of first menstruation were made by Shuttleworth (1937) with a sample of higher socio-economic level girls living in Cleveland, Ohio, and Engle and Shelesnyak (1934) with a sample of low socio-economic level girls living in an orphan asylum in New York City. In his study Shuttleworth cited 12.5 years as the average age of menarche for his sample, whereas Engle and Shelesnyak cited the average age of menarche as 13.5. Of course, differences other than socio-economic status may have been operating, but

the differences between these two studies represent a pattern that has been reported in numerous other studies.

Within the United States racial differences do not yield advent-of-puberty differences when groups are equated (Mills and Ogle, 1936; Boas, 1932; Engelmann, 1901), nor does the former belief that warm climate has a considerable effect upon the acceleration of sexual maturity seem tenable either in or out of the United States (Mills, 1937; Mueller, 1932). As a matter of fact Mills (1937) notes that "nowhere on earth do girls mature so early as they do in the central part of North America," and that, as one proceeds "south toward the Gulf of Mexico, east toward the Atlantic coast, or northeast into Canada, the menses tend to begin at later ages," and that a comparison of North and South America reveals an average retardation of 1 full year on the latter as compared to the former continent. Here, again, one might hypothesize environmental and nutritional rather than climatic factors. All investigators agree in reporting individual differences of several years in the attainment of puberty. In general it may be accepted that the average age of onset of puberty in girls in the United States is somewhere between the 12.5 years reported by Shuttleworth (1937) and the 13 to 14 years reported by Gould and Gould (1932), Boas (1932), and Lintz and Markow (1923).

The problem of determining the age of advent of puberty is more difficult for boys than for girls. The clear-cut line of demarcation provided by first menstruation in girls is missing, and the various physical or physiological landmarks by which the pubescent status of boys is determined tend to develop at different times. Dimock (1937), in a study of 1406 boys in a summer camp, reported the average age of pubescence as 13 years, 1 month, on the basis of the Crampton Criteria. The Crampton Criteria determine pubescence partly on the basis of the appearance of pigmented hairs in the pubic region and the gradual appearance of a kink or twist in the pubic hair and a wrinkled scrotum. Of Dimock's 1406 cases, 260 were pubescent. The 260 were from 10 to 16 years, with 1 per cent in their eleventh year, 14 per cent in their twelfth, 76 per cent in their thirteenth, fourteenth, and fifteenth years, and 8 per cent in the sixteenth year. Carey (1936) using the same Crampton Criteria reported that 49 of 259 boys from 11 to 18 years at St. Mary's Industrial School in Baltimore were pubescent. The mean chronological age of the pubescent group was 14 years, 3 months, with a standard deviation of 12.1 months. Most investigators (Schonfeld, 1943; Schonfeld and Beebe, 1942; Westbrook, et al., 1934; Baldwin, 1916; Starbuck, 1899) cite the average age for the advent of puberty in boys as occurring somewhere between the fourteenth and sixteenth years, although occasional investigators (Dimock, 1937; Crampton, 1908) cite 1 year earlier.

In a study of sexual behavior in boys Kinsey, Pomeroy, and Martin (1948) cited the date of first ejaculation as the major criterion of the onset of puberty in boys, although they note that whenever there is "any development of any physiologic or physical character that pertains to adolescence" the investigator must recognize it as symptomatic of the onset of adolescence. They note that, when the year of first ejaculation is considered in conjunction with the appearance of pubic hair, the onset of rapid growth in height, and with the appearance of certain secondary sex characteristics, a definitive picture of pubescent status is obtained. Kinsey feels that, if physical development seems to be some years in advance of first ejaculation, it is better to determine the date of puberty by

exterior physical changes rather than by the date of the first ejaculation. In the Kinsey study, however, 85 per cent of the subjects reported simultaneous acceleration in physical development and first ejaculation.

Kinsey, Pomeroy, and Martin (1948) also reported a positive relationship between social or educational level and date of first ejaculation with nearly a year's variation between different educational levels. The means cited were 13.71 for boys who go on to college, 13.97 for boys who do not go beyond high school, and 14.58 for boys who do not go beyond the eighth grade. They note that differences may well be due to nutritional differences, as they seemed to be in the case of female differences in mean age at menarche.

In addition to first ejaculation, puberty is also marked, as the previous discussion has implied, by the gradual appearance of secondary sex characteristics. In boys the larynx enlarges with an accentuation of the prominence called the "Adam's apple," the voice changes, hair makes its appearance on the pubes, the axillae, and the face, and the external genitals begin a period of rapid growth.

In summary, the time of the advent of puberty is a matter of individual growth. Differences are determined to some extent by heredity and to some extent by environmental factors including nutrition and disease. In general girls reach puberty before boys, the difference averaging from 1 to 2 years. As has been indicated, the exact age for the attainment of puberty depends upon environmental factors such as nutritional opportunities and disease incidence, and upon biological-genetic factors such as race, rate of anatomical growth, and state of health. In general girls reach puberty somewhere between the ages of 9 and 17, and boys between the ages of 11 and 18. Thus, although at 13 boys are found who are already pubescent and girls who are still prepubescent, their number will be smaller than the number of 13-year-old pubescent girls.

Endocrine Aspects of Adolescence. Puberty is part of the normal growth process, closely associated with all the other factors and phenomena of growth. Among these factors are the glands of internal secretion, which are of considerable importance in preparing an individual for sexual maturity as well as in promoting other aspects of growth. Nathanson *et al.* (1941) note that the glands of internal secretion have three main functions: "to stimulate growth, to influence metabolic activities, and to regulate the physical metamorphoses of children." In general, it appears that some time before the onset of puberty the anterior lobe of the pituitary gland produces a gonadotrophic hormone (follicle stimulating hormone, FSH, prolan A) which tends to stimulate the growth of the immature gonads. Under the stimulation of the gonadotrophic hormone the gonads (ovaries in females, testes in males) accelerate their growth and the individual attains sexual maturity. At this point the gonads produce mature sperm and ova, as well as estrogenic (female) and androgenic (male) sex hormones. It is well to note, however, as Shock (1944a) points out, that relatively small amounts of hormone secretion do occur prior to the time the gonads begin their accelerated growth. Shock (1944a) notes that the initiation of puberty has as a probable mechanism "a gradual increase in pituitary secretion coupled with an increasing sensitivity of the gonads to the hormone." In both boys and girls estrogens and androgens (17-ketosteroids) may be traced in constantly enlarging amounts from the third year through puberty.

It may be observed that both androgens and estrogens are excreted by both sexes, but the excretion of androgen is more characteristic of males than of females, whereas the excretion of estrogens is more characteristic of females. However, an excessive secretion of the major hormone of the opposite sex in a boy or girl will tend to lead to at least a partial assumption of some of the secondary sex characteristics of members of the opposite sex. A drastic increase of the sex hormone appropriate to one's sex follows the ninth year, although androgen is secreted in relatively larger amounts than estrogen.

The amount of hormones present at any point in the growth cycle of an individual, and, by analogy, the rate of activity of the glands from which the hormones are secreted, may be determined by a quantitative analysis by measuring the amounts of pituitary, adrenal, and sex hormones to be found in the blood and urine. The methods used are still comparatively crude, and there appears to be no accurate way of determining the presence of sex hormones in the blood stream, although it is possible through chemical analysis to measure the amounts of the hormones secreted in the urine. Because this is a new field with uncertain techniques, there have been comparatively few studies in the determination of hormone levels in the urine and even fewer attempts to correlate the information derived to the human growth sequence. Most of the studies have utilized animals or very small samples of available children. One of the more important studies in this area is that of Nathanson, Towne, and Aub (1941), who used 104 normal children and made a total of 1100 hormone determinations. Other discussions and studies, all appearing after 1930, include those of Greulich, Dorfman, *et al.* (1942), Catchpole and Greulich (1940), Catchpole *et al.* (1938), Gustavson, Mason, *et al.* (1938), Frank (1935), Katzman and Doisy (1934), Neumann and Peter (1931), and Schörcher (1931). The results of the studies are usually not strictly comparable because of differences in the samples used, but there is general agreement that hormone secretion increases with the advent of sexual maturity.

Other Physiological Changes. Among the many physiological changes taking place during adolescence are those in circulation, pulse rate, blood pressure, and the chemical composition of the blood; changes in energy metabolism and respiration; and changes in the excretory function. During adolescence the pulse rate tends to diminish, and though there is an increase following exercise, the rate of increase diminishes with age. The increase, however, tends to be greater in boys than in girls. Shock (1944a) notes that early-menstruating girls and children who experience an early adolescent growth spurt have a pulse rate which is characteristic of more mature girls. Among the studies of pulse rate are those of Shock and Schlatter (1942), Tuttle (1931), and Sutluff and Holt (1925).

In general, blood pressure tends to rise with age, although there is a tendency for a decrease to occur in girls after 16. Richey (1931) reported intercorrelations between systolic, diastolic, and pulse pressure at all ages. The correlation between systolic and diastolic pressure was positive; between systolic and pulse pressure, positive; and between diastolic and pulse pressure, negative. The correlation between systolic and diastolic pressure decreased with age whereas that between systolic and pulse pressure increased with age. Richey also found significant sex differences in actual pressures recorded. Between the ages of 10 and 13 the average systolic pressure was higher for girls than for boys. After 13 the systolic pressure for boys was greater, the amount of difference increasing with age. The average diastolic pressure was higher for girls than for boys between the ages of 11 and 16. The average pulse pressure for boys was higher than for girls after 13, the difference increasing with age. However, Richey notes that the blood pressure of normal children varies between wide limits, suggesting that the normal blood pressure for any age group might best be described as a continuum. Downing (1947) and Greulich, Day, *et al.* (1938) also mention wide day-to-day fluctuations. In studying blood-pressure changes as a function of exercise, Shock (1946) found that an increase in systolic pressure after exercise was greater in boys than in girls. Girls showed little or no change with age, whereas in boys the maximum systolic pressure increased with age. He also found that the rise in systolic pressure after exercise was greater in younger than in older children. There was a marked decrease in diastolic pressure after exercise which disappeared with increasing age.

Nylin (1935) sums up the situation with regard to respiratory changes when he notes that the total respiratory volume increases during adolescence. In a summary of the literature, Greulich, Day, *et al.* (1938) report that the average vital capacity increases about 3 times between the ages of 6 and 16 years. The volume of air in the lungs and respiratory passages at the end of a normal expiration (functional residue) increases during adolescence. The volume of tidal air (inspiration) increases during this period while the rate of respiration decreases. Shock and Soley (1939) found that the minute respiratory volume in boys increases between the ages of 12 and 14. This is attributed to an increase in body size. In boys aged from 14 to 16, respiratory rate decreases, tidal volume increases, concentration of expired air decreases, and expired carbon dioxide increases. In girls aged from 12 to 14, respiratory volume and tidal volume increase whereas in the age range from 14 to 16 changes are taking place that are not clearly defined. Shock and Soley (1939) also note an increase in oxygen consumption in both sexes from 12 to 16 years. However, when this increase is considered with respect to body size, there is an actual decrease in oxygen consumption. They report that in 16-year-old girls most of the respiratory functions were similar to those in adult females. In contrast, 16-year-old boys breathed faster, had a smaller tidal volume, a higher concentration of oxygen and a lower concentration of carbon dioxide in their expired air and total oxygen consumption than did adult males.

During the adolescent period basal metabolism tends on the average to diminish following what Bruen (1933) calls "an independent pubertal metabolic acceleration." Greulich, Day, et al. (1938) in their summary also note a prepubertal change and state that such changes in metabolic rate are necessary for the maintenance of temperature. Shock (1943) notes that metabolic changes with age are greater in adolescent girls than in boys. Girls appeared to be more variable than boys. Shock reports that a rapid decrease occurs with the beginning of menstruation and that this decrease is more closely associated with menarche than with chronological age. Many other bodily changes take place during the adolescent period, including replacement of vellus by terminal hair in the pubic region with axillary hair making its appearance somewhat later. Immediately before adolescence there is also an increase in the secretory activity of the sweat glands located in the axillary region.

In discussing physiological changes, Shock (1944b) makes the point that an analysis of the growth curves for physiological variables presents two characteristics: "(a) In individual children sudden and rapid changes in physiological characteristics are frequent, and (b) the rate of physical maturation differs greatly for different changes." One difficulty in considering such curves is the fact that average growth curves of physiological variables tend to be smooth, thus concealing and averaging out the considerable individual variations present. It is also not enough to consider physiological functioning apart from other aspects of physical activity indulged in by the adolescent. One of the penalties of growing older appears to be slower recovery to a state of physiological and physical balance after exertion. Shock (1946) conducted a longitudinal study of the results of severe exercise upon a group of 100 children as they proceeded through the adolescent years. Recovery curves were plotted for pulse rate, respiration rate and volume, oxygen intake, and carbon dioxide elimination. Shock found that, whereas work output increased with advancing age, the rate of recovery with respect to the physiological factors studied decreased with advancing age.

For the most part, the outward manifestations of physiological change are acceptable enough in our culture for the average adolescent to adjust to them. One exception is acne, which often appears during adolescence and tends not only to cause embarrassment to the adolescent himself but sometimes calls forth an unfortunate reaction of distaste from those with whom he comes in contact. Lawrence and Werthessen (1942), Hamilton (1941), and others have attributed acne during adolescence to an imbalance between male and female sex hormone secretion and report successful treatment by use of hormones. Jolliffe, Rosenblum, and Sawhill (1942) and Straumfjord (1943) report dietary regulation and the administration of the B-complex vitamins as successful in the regulation of acne. Greulich (1944) notes that the increased activity at puberty of the sebaceous glands which appear in the skin and which are particularly large on the wings of the nose may be an important factor in causing acne.

Skeletal Analysis. A number of measures, including chronological age and advent of puberty, have been used in determining an individual's level of maturity. There has, however, been a quest for a more meaningful basis of classification. Of the methods proposed, skeletal analysis has proved one of the more accurate. By the method of skeletal analysis the progress or status of ossification is recorded by means of X-ray pictures. Skeletal analysis has the advantage of providing a comparatively exact estimate of the individual's level of maturity at any point in his life span.

Unfortunately a problem arises in finding a standard with which to compare skeletal X-rays. There have been a number of attempts to formulate such standards, but those presently available are not in entire agreement, with the result that indices and ages computed by different systems are not directly comparable. The most widely used standards are those proposed by Flory (1936) and Todd (1937).

Todd (1937), in an X-ray study of a sample of over 1000 children, reported that in the period from 5 to 13 there appeared for girls a "minor progressive acceleration of female skeletal maturation" between the ages of 6 and 8, with a slowing up between 8 and 9, so that at 9 the maturation of males tended to catch up with that of females. At 10 years of age girls again accelerated, and by the time they were 13 they had arrived at a state of maturation not attained by boys until they reached their fifteenth year. There is a definite slowing down of skeletal maturation in girls following their thirteenth year, until, by the sixteenth to the seventeenth year boys have caught up with them. Todd reported increasing stabilization from 17 on in both sexes. Baldwin,

Busby, and Garside (1928), after a longitudinal X-ray study of children from birth to maturity, also reported sex differences in times of acceleration and arrival at final maturity. Bayley (1943a, 1943b) reported similar findings. Sawtell (1929) noted a definite relationship between ossification and gross body size, and an even greater correlation between weight and height in relation to actual bone growth. Flory (1936) reported a definite relationship between ossification and puberty and noted that acceleration in skeletal development is generally accompanied by an earlier arrival at puberty. The relationship between rate of ossification and physical conditions, such as thyroid deficiency, metabolic disturbances, nutritive deficiencies, have been noted by Francis (1939), Sontag and Pyle (1941), Roberts *et al.* (1939), and Mac-Nair (1939).

Intellectual Growth and Development

Age of Cessation of Mental Growth. The age of cessation of mental growth has occupied considerable space in psychological research. Early investigators estimated that the age of cessation of mental growth occurred sometime in the neighborhood of the thirteenth or fourteenth year of life. Later investigators, particularly since 1924, have gradually raised the estimate for age of cessation upward toward the early twenties. Most investigators agreed, however, that the increments of growth following the sixteenth year were relatively minor. Hart (1924), using the Army Alpha, reported growth approaching a point of cessation at 16 or 17 years. Dearborn and Cattell (1930) found mental ages and point scores on the Dearborn test greater at 18 than at any previous age. Sudweeks (1927) reported scores on the Terman group test increasing until age 19, and Burks, Jensen, and Terman (1930) reported scores at each age to 19 higher than the preceding years. Woodrow (1928), testing the entire school population of a small town, reported no cessation of increase in test scores "at any rate up to 18.5 years." In a community-wide study H. E. Jones and Conrad (1933) reported that the curve of mental growth rose to about 16, displayed a negative acceleration after 16, and reached its highest point between 19 and 21 years. After 21 a long, slow decline began so that scores recessed to about the 14-year age level in the middle fifties. The Jones and Conrad study was particularly adequate in that it contained sufficient subjects in the late teens and in maturity to present a complete picture of growth. The majority of studies of intellectual growth have tended to include subjects of an age range that did not include people of late adolescent and adult status. The final answer is not yet certain, but present evidence agrees that the age of cessation of the growth of intelligence is certainly beyond the teens.

The implication of the age of cessation of mental growth for the education of adolescents is that in terms of mental ability or power the adolescent is nearing his peak. By the time he is 18 he has either already reached his peak or will show only a slight increase from that point on. Under the circumstances his learning ability is potentially as great as it will be during his adult years, and he may profitably be subjected to learning experiences that will challenge his capacities. The reason for withholding certain types of learning experience from an adolescent is not that he is not potentially capable of profiting from them, but that he may have had insufficient previous experience or training.

Rate of Mental Growth. The rate of mental growth has been studied by numerous investigators including Brooks (1921), Baldwin (1933), Jones and Conrad (1933), Freeman and Flory (1937), and Freeman (1938). The growth of intelligence does not proceed at a constant rate throughout its period of development. Mental ability grows rapidly during childhood and begins to decelerate in adolescence. In general, curves of rate of growth of intelligence show a much greater rate of development in early than in later years. The curve tends to show a diminishing rate from 8 to 15 with a greater reduction after 15, so that acceleration is negative in the middle or late teens. The rate varies at different ages in no predictable manner, but it is not highly variable or erratic despite the fact that each child tends to show a distinctive growth pattern. There appear to be no statistically significant differences in rate changes as the result of the onset of puberty, although Stone and Barker (1939, 1937b) reported intelligence test scores and IQ's of post- as compared to prepubescent girls somewhat higher.

Interpersonal Relations

Social Adjustment. One of the most striking tendencies of the adolescent is the great importance which he attaches to the attitudes and opinions of others, particularly those of his own age. The adolescent usually finds his social rôle a difficult one. He has recently passed through stages in social development during which both his accepted personal rôle and the rôle others expected of him were considerably different from the rôle he is now expected to play. He is an individual with limited experience, still in fact a child, who finds himself in what is to him a rapidly expanding adults' world. He finds himself with new physical urges, new physical growth, new interests and values, and new concepts of self. He finds that, unwittingly, he has turned his back on much that used to be important to him. The process of growing up is both difficult and strange, particularly in the adolescent's relations with others, either contemporaries or adults. From his social explorations he must finally emerge with mature and adequate social attitudes, standards, and skills if he is to find any degree of social adjustment as an adult.

As an individual moves from childhood toward maturity his social development is a progression from the great egocentricity of a very young child to the outlook of a mature adult, who no longer regards himself as the center of the universe. This progress is marked by an increasing awareness and acceptance of others and by a redefining of a personal rôle to conform to a society where workable interpersonal relations are essential for economic and social survival and effectiveness. As the individual proceeds through the years of his adolescence he must expand his social consciousness to a point where he is sensitive to the rights and desires of others, and where he is willing, when it is appropriate, to subordinate his own wishes to the greater good of the greater number. Above all he must learn the techniques, the taboos, and the facilitations of social intercourse. Not all persons are successful in this phase of social development, and to the extent that they are not they will tend to encounter increasingly difficult problems as they grow older.

The older a child grows, the more he widens his social contacts, not only in terms of the greater numbers of persons with whom he comes in contact but also in the diversity of situations under which these contacts take place. Anderson (1939) has noted the fact that "one of the striking characteristics of normal development is an ever-widening circle of attachments." He also notes the "increasing differentiation with respect to social organization" with which the child must become familiar and in which he must learn to operate successfully. A central problem of adolescence is the fact that an adolescent often finds himself in social situations in which he must behave as an adult before he knows exactly how to behave. He has developed a sense of values which tends to overstress the social importance of certain aspects of conduct or appearance, and he may overreact to them if he cannot meet the standards set by himself or his group, because of either physical or monetary limitations.

The problems that present-day adolescents encounter in their social relationships have been reported, among others, by Lawton (1949), Remmers and Shimberg (1949), Wall (1948), Tramer (1947), Moraitis (1946), Partridge (1945), Fleege (1945a), Wolberg (1945), Howard (1941), Frank (1941), McGill and Matthews (1940), Curran and Schilder (1940), Butterfield (1939), Wexberg (1939), and Taylor (1938). Cheney (1949) has described a useful method for identifying problems of high school youth.

The Peer Group. The place in which the adolescent has his greatest opportunity of finding social acceptance or rejection and where it is essentially important to him is in the peer group. Acceptance is easier for the conforming adolescent and more difficult for the nonconforming. Adolescents tend to be clannish, to have fairly definite value judgments, and to sharply reject those persons who deviate from their patterns of behavior, dress, and systems of values. For that reason an adolescent who wishes to find acceptance must conform to the mores and the values of his peer group. Deviation means overt nonacceptance, or at best noninclusion or grudging inclusion, in the group's activities. With the great value an adolescent places upon group acceptance such rejection is very disturbing. In his endeavors to gain, to regain, or to hold the esteem of his fellows, the adolescent will often go to lengths that seem extreme to adults. Continued rejection will often lead to aggression, possibly eventual withdrawal, and sometimes to overcompensation in some other activity where group acceptance is not an issue. But, whatever he may do, the peer-rejected adolescent tends to be unhappy and to be placed in a position where he loses many social contact opportunities that are important to him as a developing individual.

Most studies agree that the personal qualities required for acceptance in the adolescent peer society are multiple. Williams (1923) in a study of delinquent boys cited the following as instrumental in the selection of friends: that the individual be of similar chronological age, be of about the same mental age, be fair, be fun to be with, be sportsmanlike, be athletic, be loyal to his friends, and never "tell tales" to those in authority. Dimock (1937) reported that boys tended to be acceptable to each other if they were cooperative, helpful, courteous, considerate of others, honest, unselfish, and self-controlled; if they never or rarely showed off, bluffed, bullied, quarreled, carried grudges, thought they were "picked on," alibied, made excuses, acted superior or domineering, or showed overdependence on others. Anastasi and Miller (1949) list in order of frequency the following six characteristics as being most preferred in friends for both college-entrance and noncollege-entrance high school groups: has many friends, is friendly, well mannered, cooperative in a group, enjoys hearing or telling jokes, and is loyal to friends. Differences occurred in some of the characteristics best liked in friends by the noncollege as compared to the college group. The characteristics chosen with greater frequency by the precollege group were: serious-minded, talkative, talented in arts and crafts, enjoys working on his own hobbies, enthusiastic. The noncollege group more often picked: good listener, athletic, enjoys practical jokes,

"peppy," neat in appearance, grown-up, hail-fellow-well-met. Males preferred their friends to be grown-up and neat in appearance, to enjoy working on their own hobbies, and to enjoy practical jokes. Females preferred their friends to be serious-minded, assured with adults, and cooperative with a group.

In a comparison of the similarities and dissimilarities between pairs of friends of junior high school girls and boys, Wellman (1926) reported greatest similarities among girls in scholarship and least in height. Boys were most similar in height, IQ, and chronological age, and least alike in extroversion, scholarship, and mental age. Vreeland and Corey (1935) in a study of 30 pairs of "very" close friends reported high correlations in degree of neuroticism and social intelligence, but low correlations in social attitude. Both Hartshorne and May (1928) and Dimock (1937) found close similarity in moral insight and knowledge of mutual friends. Dimock reported low intelligence correlations between mutual friends, in contrast to an earlier study by Warner (1923), who felt that similarity of mental ability was the factor that maintained friendship between boys even though it was not important in bringing them together in the first place. Fleming (1932), Van Dyne (1940), and Allport (1920) have also discussed personality correlates of mutual friends. The foregoing studies present to some extent a picture of disagreement, probably due to different samples and instruments used. Possibly a more fruitful approach would be to study differences between popular and unpopular adolescents with more adequate samples. Kuhlen and Lee (1943) in a comparative study of least and most popular boys and girls note that age is an important factor in determining what characteristics will find acceptance or rejection in the peer group. For example, among sixth grade boys, being active in games was important for acceptance, whereas liking the opposite sex was much less important. Among twelfth grade boys, liking the opposite sex had become important and being active in games had become considerably less so. However, more popular boys in both grades showed greater social interest than did the less popular members of the same grades. Girls presented a similar picture, although age changes, as compared to boys, appeared to have less important implications. Kuhlen and Lee make the point, however, that there is a danger of emphasizing such differences "at the expense of essential similarities." In their study, for girls, three of the five traits (friendly, enthusiastic, popular) which characterized the most popular girls in the sixth grade also characterized girls in the twelfth. For boys, four of the five highest traits in the sixth grade (cheerful, enthusiastic, popular, friendly) retained their position in the twelfth grade.

Group behavior of children during adolescence has been studied by Cunningham et al. (1951), Hollingshead (1949), Furfey (1940), Dimock (1937), Punke (1936), and Partridge (1934). In general it has been found that adolescents who belong to peer groups tends to merge into the group and to assume the attitudes and points of view held by the group. However, participation in the activities of a group does not mean acceptance of the individual participating, nor does status in any given group mean equal status in other groups. There appear to be many different kinds of adolescent groups.

Some investigators report a trend toward the formalization of adolescent group activities, but the majority of adolescents still confine most of their activities to informal as compared to formal groups. The lower the socio-economic class, the less the likelihood of formal organization.

Most popular among group activities are watching and celebrating high school athletic contests, sitting and talking in soda fountains or other gathering places, going to movies, visiting, and dancing. In all these activities, but more especially in respect to dancing and visiting, considerable differences are to be observed between boys and girls, in school and out-of-school youth, and among socio-economic classes. Spontaneously formed groups tend to be more cohesive than artificially formed ones. The multiple-purpose group tends to have more cohesiveness than the single-purpose group. The size of the group appears to be important in group cohesiveness—more important than age, although advancing age appears to make for less intragroup cohesion. Definite sex differences appear in the solidarity patterns presented by male and female groups, although there are numerous similarities.

The study of leaders and followers appears to have been a major preoccupation of those investigating adolescent groups. In general, successful adolescent leaders use different methods of control from those used by child group leaders. The leader who takes into account the wishes and needs of his group is most successful. His methods must be comparatively subtle and must not depart too markedly from acceptable adolescent patterns of behavior. Typical of studies of adolescent group leaders and followers are those by Carter and Nixon (1949), Zeleny (1940), Remmlein (1938), Smith and Nystrom (1937), and Brown (1933).

A problem of concern to those interested in adolescent behavior is the formation of the gang, or the transition of existing adolescent groups into gangs. The gang, in contrast to other adolescent groups, is more highly organized and is usually the result of conflict or outside pressures against its members which throw them together for mutual aid and support. Gangs have been reported as most likely to appear among more recent immigrant groups or in sections where there are racial or national tensions. A good proportion of juvenile delinquency finds its inception in the gang. The reasons for joining a gang are often similar to those for becoming a juvenile delinquent. Gang membership is frequently a normal process rising out of environmental difficulties. Not all gangs are antisocial, but their chances of turning eventually in antisocial directions are greater than those of the clique or the crowd. Studies of gang behavior range all the way from the pioneer studies of Puffer (1905) and Thrasher (1927) to the present-day studies of H. Jones (1948) and Crawford *et al.* (1950).

Heterosexual Relations. One of the outstanding aspects of an adolescent's social development is his gradually growing interest in members of the opposite sex, an interest which normally leads him into expanding heterosexual activities after puberty. A complication of this process, as Stolz, Jones, and Chaffey (1937) note, is the acceleration of girls by 1 to 2 years over boys. During this period girls tend to make overtures to the point where the "dominant" male finds his rôle reversed and discovers attempts to drag him into heterosexual activities before he really wishes to participate. This developmental contrast is most apparent in the ninth grade, where, for probably the last time, girls are clearly placed in the dominant social rôle. Studies such as those of Kuhlen and Lee (1943) and Hildreth (1933) clearly reflect the increasing interest of adolescents in members of the opposite sex. Such new interests bring with them many questions and many problems. Adolescents are very much interested in finding out all they can about members of the opposite sex (Davenport, 1923; Blos, 1941), but the answers they receive are unfortunately limited and often from the wrong sources (Ramsey, 1943; Bell, 1938). Many problems of social procedure and facilitation arise. Hutson and Kovar (1942) report that many adolescents are not able to participate in heterosexual activities because of parental restrictions, geographical location, lack of money and suitable clothing, feelings of inferiority, and feelings of not belonging. Problems growing out of dating are many and complex, with many adolescents simply not knowing what to do, although there is evidence that this is not true of all or perhaps even the majority of adolescents, many of whom display more sophistication than adults ordinarily realize (Hollingshead, 1949; West, 1945; Blos, 1941; Lynd and Lynd, 1937; Finger, 1947).

Family Relationships. The adolescent's family is both a source of security and a difficult problem. It is a source of security in that it offers a refuge, a place of acceptance, and a place where material needs are cared for. It is a problem in that it interposes a barrier which retards acceptance as an adult and offers a fertile ground for difficulties of interpersonal relations. The adolescent's relationship to adults is a problem which requires, on his part, not only acceptance of a barrier to his own natural desires and strivings but also a certain willingness to subordinate himself to others and to accept their counsels and decisions as wise and just, even though, at any given time, he may be unable to appreciate either their reason or their necessity. This all-pervasive problem centers around the fact that the adolescent is a person who is approaching the culmination of his growth and is, in effect, passing from childhood into adulthood; he is sometimes more a child than an adult, sometimes more an adult than a child, but in reality he is neither one nor the other.

The adolescent is expected to obey and respect his parents; he must go to school and accept the child-adult student-teacher relationship; he is denied an adult's place and responsibility in the community; his sex and social life is circumscribed; and, above all, day after day, he is constantly dependent upon adults and must accept his inferior status, taking and carrying out orders. Much is forbidden him, and he is typically apt to grow impatient or perhaps resentful. Sometimes he may attempt, even overtly, to fight against his rôle and status, particularly as it appears to him to be prolonged against all reason. Thus, a desire and often an overt striving for independence are natural and common aspects of the adolescent period. The process of achieving independence is known as emancipation or psychological weaning.

As has been implied in the preceding discussion, for the adolescent the home represents, in the final analysis, the ultimate and definitive repository of adult authority, and its effect upon him is very great. Bossard (1948) notes that the development of personality is a constant series of choices, that such choices represent a person's values, and that such values "are in large part the result of family conditioning." Stott (1939a) in a study of city, town, and farm children reported that the two most important factors in family living and the social life of the home, as they affected the personality development of the child, were the "confidence, affection, and companionability" pattern and the pattern of "family discord" or "parental misconduct." Children from homes characterized by "good" patterns of family life as contrasted to "bad" were better adjusted and more appreciative of family life and were superior in their general personality development. In a study on the adolescent in the family conducted by the White House Conference on Child Health and Protection (1934) it was concluded that "the outstanding fact emerging from the study is the significance of the home for the personality development of the child." The most significant aspects of the stable home were found to be affection, confiding in parents, trust and loyalty of child to parents, and control by other means than punishment. Baldwin, Kalhorn, and Breese (1945), Symonds (1939), and Fitz-Simons (1935) all point to the importance of the psychological climate of the home, and Baldwin et al. and Fitz-Simons propose methods of identifying and classifying the psychological climate of any given home.

Extremes of parental reaction tend to have unfortunate effects on adolescent behavior. Indulgence up to a point makes an adolescent's adjustment considerably easier and gives him a real sense of security by creating a permissive atmosphere in which he may move toward personal independence and gradual emancipation. When indulgence becomes overindulgence, however, or when overprotectiveness appears, the consequences tend to be unfortunate. Hattwick (1936) notes the vicious circle and behavior ramifications which parental overprotection can engender.

The adolescent whose home history has been one of overprotection and overindulgence experiences greater difficulty than normal in adjusting to the outside world. Outside his home he endeavors, usually without success, to make himself the pampered center of every situation he enters. He constantly seeks parent surrogates in adults whether his teacher, his employer, or the person he eventually marries.

Among the many aspects of an adolescent's home that affect his behavior are whether he comes from a "broken" home (White House Conference, 1934), the number of siblings and his ordinal position in the family (Hayes, 1938; and Stott, 1939b), socio-economic status (Davis *et al.*, 1941; Bossard, 1948), and geographic mobility (Carrington, 1940).

Interests and Activities

Interests. In the study of adolescent interests, play activities have usually been selected as an effective means of showing the kinds of things that appeal to an adolescent when he is "on his own" rather than under the direct supervision of an adult. Play may be thought of as the implementation of interest. It is the activity product of an interest drive, and it becomes a means of demonstrating interests through actually doing something about them. The most-often-cited study in the area of adolescent play interests is the comprehensive one made by Lehman and Witty in 1927.

The first questions in considering adolescent interests are what young people do and, more important, what they like to do. It is fallacious to assume that a normative study of adolescent activities would be an accurate indication of their interests and preferences. Owing to environmental, economic, and adult restrictions and limitations adolescents are often placed in the position of having to participate in activities which are either distasteful or which are, at best, comparatively far down on their preference list. Of course, other things being equal, many activities indulged in by youth are well liked and preferred, but an assumption that such is true for any given activity should be made with considerable caution.

The answers to the questions what adolescents do and what they like to do must, at best, be provisional. The questions might better be phrased, "What youth, when, and where–" Valentine (1943) notes that interests do tend to fluctuate and that there are enough intergroup differences so that one is not justified in treating "a company of youths of a particular age . . . as

a homogeneous group." Pressey (1946), in a study covering a 20-year period, noted considerable changes in likes and dislikes, and reported that certain of these changes differed with age and sex. Horrocks and Thompson (1946), Thompson and Horrocks (1947), and Horrocks and Buker (1951) reported fluctuations in friendships, which, however, tended to grow less with increasing age, but which did exhibit sex and rural-urban differences. Jacobs (1949) in an analysis of secondary school students scores on the *Kuder Preference Record* cites some stability of interests in the latter years of high school but recommends repeated measurements during that period.

The variables which make for differences in interests during the adolescent period range all the way from the obvious differences (age, sex) to the differences caused by the less obvious factors of intelligence, socio-economic status, place of residence, physical endowment, opportunities and experiences, period in history, and parental restrictions and taboos. Snyder (1941) has summarized the findings of various studies of interests during adolescence. Among the studies reporting adolescent interests and activities following the depression of the 1930's are those by Peel (1948), Canonge (1948), Vickery (1946), Hammond (1945), M. C. Jones (1941), and Hotopf (1940).

One of the most frequently used avenues to the study of adolescent interests has been through the investigation of communication media habits, such as reading, listening to the radio, watching television, and attending the movies. In this area, as in perhaps no other area of behavior, conflicting and indefinite results have been obtained by various investigators. Why do studies disagree? A number of factors, none of them operating in isolation, are responsible. Among the most important are the following: the time in history; the season of the year; whether the sample is from rural or small-town communities or from large cities; and, whether the sample accounted for variables (sometimes cited, sometimes ignored) such as sex, race, creed, family upbringing, opportunity, excellence of instruction, intelligence, aptitude, and experience. The conclusion to be drawn is that a normative survey of adolescent interests may impart information that is peculiar to a given time, a given group, or a given location, and hence may not be universally applicable in considering adolescent behavior in general—even within the limitations of a comparatively homogeneous culture.

Sterner (1947) notes that there appears to be little relationship among the various communication media when children's habits and reactions regarding them are considered. She reports that "from a knowledge of a pupil's activity in one medium one cannot predict how much time he will spend on another medium." It is her interpretation that "it is interest rather than the medium which attracts," and that no two media will be utilized to the same extent by a given child to satisfy his needs and interests.

Reading Interests. In general, adventure is popular in all grades (Brink, 1939; Cox, 1929), with reading being more popular in junior than in senior high school (Donahue, 1947). Abbott (1902) reported that although there is a tendency for older children to read more mature books, half of the selections read by high school freshmen were juveniles, humor being popular with both sexes, and action appealing to boys but being rejected by girls. Brink (1939) found that mystery, humor, and drama lost their appeal with advancing age, but Jordan in two studies, one made in 1917 and one in 1926, found that with advancing age fiction became more popular for both sexes. In a third study, in 1935, Jordan reaffirmed

the earlier point of view by noting that there was little change in the reading tastes of high school students between 1918 and 1932. LaBrant and Heller (1939) reported that with increasing age abstract quality began to appeal more than narrative. Pearson and Center (1936) in their sample of 40,000 found that the tenth grade marked one of the most decided changing points in reading interests. They noted a definite increase in nonfiction reading in the upper grades. Pond (1939) feels that little growth is discernible from grade to grade but notes a transition from juvenile to more mature material between the tenth and eleventh grades. Ridout (1938) in his study of juvenile favorites feels that, by and large, children are more interested in the books adults are reading than children of a generation ago. Today's adolescent, as Ridout interprets him, has a critical taste. He is interested in adventure, but real characters are the criterion for every book he reads.

Adolescents appear to be avid readers of newspapers (Feingold, 1944), and their newspaper reading interests tend to be essentially a reflection of the times and hence mirror the focus of natural interest at any given period (Tangney, 1942). There appears to be a steady increase with advancing age in reading of the editorial page and the stories, but for the most part changes tend to be greatest between the tenth and the eleventh years of school, with ninth, tenth, and eleventh graders displaying more intergrade similarities. With advance in grade the daily newspaper is read more thoroughly; the comic section, the front page, and the sports section retain their popularity; although there is a comparative decline of interest in the comics in the twelfth grade, comics remain the most-read part of the paper (Donahue, 1947; Feingold, 1944; Fendrick, 1941; Grumette, 1937).

Possibly the two best-liked media for reading among adolescents are comic books and regular magazines. Both are read widely, and both tend to be preferred to other types of reading matter. Nasser (1941) reported that a sample of 950 high school students read more than 350 different magazines. Of these, the average student read 7.68 magazines regularly. Comic books tend to be less popular with older adolescents, but their appeal continues to be great throughout the teen years.

Radio and Motion Pictures. Youth are very enthusiastic about both the radio and motion pictures and indulge whenever they happen to have the opportunity. In a study of 2000 boys Fleege (1945b) reported that 3 out of 4 boys attended the movies once a week or oftener, the average boy attending 1.2 times per week, or 4.9 movies per month. Sterner (1947) in her study of the various communication media used by children notes that "radio had more titles listed for it than any other medium. This is the medium to which pupils devote most time each day." The popular status of radio with adolescents is particularly significant when one considers that radio is a comparative newcomer. There has been much discussion relative to the total and comparative influence of television. As of 1953 the medium is still too new and research is still too meager to permit any adequate generalizations. Typical of available studies on television are those by Gable (1951), Siepmann (1950), and McDonagh *et al.* (1950).

Vocational Interests. Vocational selection is another crucial point in adolescent development and adjustment. Adolescents, particularly boys, spend a great deal of time thinking and talking about what they will do after they graduate from school. They are continually confronted with the desirability of making a vocational choice.

There is the further fact that for many a vocational decision represents a real step toward freedom from parental control. For some there is also the desire to get married and to be able to support a family. Various studies of the occupational preferences of adolescents have been reported (Myers, 1947; Cawley, 1947; Berdie, 1945; Bradley, 1943; Roeber and Garfield, 1943; Canning, 1941). A considerable amount of fluctuation occurs in vocational choice, although it tends to lessen with increasing age. Older adolescents are likely to become somewhat more realistic in their vocational choices; younger adolescents tend to select more exclusively on the basis of their interests or what they interpret as their interests. Sex differences are apparent. Girls tend to be somewhat more mature in their vocational choices than boys of the same chronological age, and they usually select more sedentary occupations. Proper vocational guidance seems to be desired and tends to lead, where available, to greater stability and more appropriate choices. Various studies have been made of factors related to vocational choice (Myers, 1947; Bradley, 1943; Peters, 1941; Williamson and Darley, 1935; Strong, 1934). Details and superficial selections may change, but basic elements such as curiosity and mastery tend to remain comparatively stable. Factors determining vocational choice are environmentally engendered. Parents and family are usually most influential in determining vocational choice, then friends, and then professional acquaintances. Sons of higher-income parents are more likely to want to follow in their father's footsteps than the sons of lower-income parents. Social prestige is often an important element in the adolescent's vocational choice. But, whatever the adolescent's final decision, personal advice is decidedly of greater importance in influencing choice than information from other sources.

Bibliography

Abbott, A. 1902. Reading tastes of high school pupils. *Sch. Rev., 10,* 585–600.

Allport, F. H. 1920. The influence of the group upon association and thought. *J. Exp. Psychol., 3,* 159–182.

Al-Meligui, A. 1950–1951. Psychology of adolescence through diaries. *Egypt. J. Psychol., 6,* 173–184.

Anastasi, A., and S. Miller. 1949. Adolescent "prestige factors" in relation to scholastic and socioeconomic variables. *J. Soc. Psychol., 29,* 43–50.

Anderson, J. E. 1939. The development of social behavior. *Amer. J. Sociol., 44,* 839–857.

Aristotle. *The works of Aristotle.* (W. D. Ross, Ed. English trans. 1908–1931.) Vol. IX: *Historia animalium;* Vol. XI: *Rhetorica.* Oxford, Clarendon Press.

Atkinson, R. K. 1924. A motor efficiency study of 8000 New York City high school boys. *Amer. Phys. Educ. Rev., 29,* 56–59.

——. 1925. A study of athletic ability of high school girls. *Amer. Phys. Educ. Rev., 30,* 389–399.

Baldwin, A. L., J. Kalhorn, and F. H. Breese. 1945. Patterns of parental behavior. *Psychol. Monogr.,* No. 58.

Baldwin, B. T. 1916. A measuring scale for physical growth and physiological age. *15th Yearbook,* Pt. I, N.S.S.E., 11–51.

Baldwin, B. T., L. M. Busby, H. V. Garside. 1928. A study of some bones of the hand, wrist, and lower forearm by means of roentgenograms. *Univ. Iowa Stud. Child Welfare,* 4.

Baldwin, O. B. 1933. The maturation of the college student as evidenced by retests with the national council tests. *Psychol. Monogr., 44,* 233–262.

Bayer, L. M. 1940. Weight and menses in adolescent girls with special reference to build. *J. Pediat., 17,* 345–354.

Bayley, N. 1941. Body build in adolescents studied in relation to rates of anatomical maturing, with implications for social adjustment. *Psychol. Bull., 38,* 378. (Abstract.)

——. 1943a. Size and body build of adolescents in relation to rate of skeletal maturing. *Child Develpm., 14,* 47–90.

——. 1943b. Skeletal maturing in adolescence as a basis for determining percentage of completed growth. *Child Develpm., 14,* 1–46.

——. 1943c. Size and body build of adolescents in relation to rate of skeletal maturing. *Child Develpm., 14,* 51–89.

——. 1946. Tables for predicting adult height from skeletal age and present height. *J. Pediat., 28,* 49–64.

Bayley, N., and A. Espenschade. 1941. Motor development from birth to maturity. *Rev. Educ. Res., 11,* 562–572.

——. 1944. Motor development from birth to maturity. *Rev. Educ. Res., 14,* 381–389.

Bayley, N., and R. Tuddenham. 1942. Adolescent changes in body build. In *43rd Yearbook N.S.S.E.,* 33–55. Chicago: University of Chicago Press.

Beaglehole, E. 1940. Psychic stress in a Tongan. *Proc. Sixth Pacific Science Congress, 4,* 43–52.

Bell, H. M. 1938. *Youth tell their story.* Washington: American Council on Education.

Berdie, R. F. 1945. Range of interests. *J. Appl. Psychol., 29,* 268–281.

Blos, P. 1941. *The adolescent personality.* New York: Appleton-Century-Crofts.

Boas, F. 1932. Studies in growth. *Hum. Biol., 4,* 307–350.

——. 1938. *The mind of primitive man.* New York: Macmillan.

Bolk, L. 1923. The menarche in Dutch women and its precipitated appearance in the younger generation. *Konin. Akad. van Wetenschappente Amsterdam, 26,* 650–663.

Bossard, J. H. S. 1948. *The sociology of child development.* New York: Harper.

Bower, P. A. 1940. The relation of physical, mental, and personality factors to popularity in adolescent boys. *Doctors' Dissertation.* Berkeley: University of California Press.

Brace, D. K. 1927. *Measuring motor ability.* New York: Barnes.

Bradley, W. A. 1943. Correlates of vocational preferences. *Genet. Psychol. Monogr., 28,* 99–169.

Brink, W. G. 1939. Reading interests of high school pupils. *Sch. Rev., 47,* 613–621.

Brooks, F. D. 1921. Changes in mental traits with age: Determined by individual retests. *Teach. Coll. Contrib. Educ.,* No. 116.

Brown, M. 1933. Leadership among high school pupils. *Teach. Coll. Contrib. Educ.,* No. 559.

Bruen, C. 1933. Variations of basal metabolic rate per unit surface area with age. II. The pubertal acceleration. *J. Nutrition, 6,* 683–695.

Bunak, V. V. 1940. Typology of growth curves of the human body. *J. Phys. Anthrop., 26,* 69–85.

Burks, B. S., D. W. Jensen, and L. M. Terman. 1930. The promise of youth. *Genetic studies of genius, 3,* Stanford University: Stanford University Press.

Burnham, W. H. 1891. The study of adolescence. *Ped. Sem., 1,* 174–195.

Butterfield, O. M. 1939. *Love problems of adolescence.* New York: Emerson.

Campbell, W. J. 1952. The influence of home environment on the educational progress of selective secondary school children. *Brit. J. Educ. Psychol., 22,* 89–100.

Canning, L. B. 1941. Permanence of vocational interests of high school boys. *J. Educ. Psychol., 32,* 481–494.

Canonge, F. 1948. Intérêts et curiosités des élèves de centres d'apprentissage. *Enfance, 1,* 304–315.

Carey, T. F. 1936. The relation of physical growth to developmental age in boys. *Monogr. Cent. Res. Child Develpm.* Washington, D. C.: Catholic University.

Carpenter, A. 1938. Strength, power and "femininity" as factors influencing the athletic performance of college women. *Res. Quart. Amer. Phys. Educ. Ass.*, *9*, 120–127.

Carrington, E. M. 1940. The family in a changing social order. *Educ. Forum.*, *4*, 191–197.

Carter, L., and M. Nixon. 1949. Ability, perceptual, personality, and interest factors associated with different criteria of leadership. *J. Psychol.*, *27*, 377–388.

Catchpole, H. R., and W. W. Greulich. 1940. Excretion of gonadotropic hormone by pre-pubertal and adolescent girls. *Amer. J. Physiol.*, *120*, 331.

Catchpole, H. R., W. W. Greulich and R. T. Sollenberger. 1938. Urinary excretion of follicle stimulating hormone in young and adolescent boys. *Amer. J. Physiol.*, *123*, 32.

Cawley, A. M. 1947. A study of the vocational interest trends of secondary school and college women. *Genet. Psychol. Monogr.*, *35*, 166–175.

Cheney, T. 1949. A method of identifying problems of high school students. *Occupations*, *27*, 387–390.

Collins, S. D., and T. Clark. 1929. Physical measurements of boys and girls of native white stock in the United States. *U. S. Pub. Health Reports*, *44*, 1059–1083.

Cowell, C. C. 1935. An abstract of a study of differentials in junior high school boys based on the observation of physical education activities. *Res. Quart.*, *6*, 129–136.

Cox, R. M. 1929. The individual and the reading course in a two-year technical high school. *Teach. Coll. J.*, *1*, 35–48.

Cozens, F. W., et al. 1936. *Physical education achievement scales for boys in secondary schools.* New York: Barnes.

Crampton, C. W. 1908. Physiological age. *Amer. Phys. Educ. Res.*, *13*, 144–154, 214–227, 268–283, 345–358.

——. 1944. Physiological age—a fundamental principle. *Child Develpm.*, *15*, 3–52.

Crane, A. R. 1952. Pre-adolescent groups: a topological interpretation. *J. Gen. Psychol.*, *81*, 113–123.

Crawford, P. L., D. Malamud, and J. R. Dumpson. 1950. *Working with teen age gangs.* New York: Welfare Council of New York City.

Cunningham, R., et al. 1951. *Understanding group behavior of boys and girls.* New York: Teachers College, Columbia University.

Curran, F. J., and P. F. Schilder. 1940. Problemas de la infancia y adolescencia. *Index Neurol. Psiquiat. B. Aires*, *2*, 91–111.

Daniels, A. D. 1893. The new life; a study of regeneration. *Amer. J. Psychol.*, *6*, 61–106.

Davenport, C. B. 1926. Human metamorphosis. *Amer. J. Phys. Anthrop.*, *9*, 205–232.

Davenport, F. I. 1923. Adolescent interests. *Arch. Psychol.*, No. 66.

Davis, A., B. Gardner, and M. Gardner. 1941. *Deep south.* Chicago: University of Chicago Press.

Dearborn, W. F., and P. Cattell. 1930. The intelligence and achievement of private school pupils. *J. Educ. Psychol.*, *21*, 197–211.

Dearborn, W. F., and J. W. M. Rothney. 1941. *Predicting the child's development.* Cambridge: Sci-Art.

Dearborn, W. F., J. W. M. Rothney, and F. K. Shuttleworth. 1938. Data on the growth of public school children. *Monogr. Soc. Res. Child Develpm.*, 3.

Dimock, H. S. 1935. A research in adolescence: I. Pubescence and physical growth. *Child Develpm.*, *6*, 176–195.

——. 1937. *Rediscovering the adolescent.* New York: Association Press.

Donahue, E. F. 1947. Leisure-time reading interests of Catholic high school boys. *Cath. Educ. Rev.*, *45*, 523–533.

Downing, E. 1947. Blood pressure of normal girls from three to sixteen years of age. *Amer. J. Dis. Child.*, *73*, 293–316.

Draper, G. 1930. *Disease and man.* London: Kegan Paul.

Draper, G., C. W. Dupertuis, and J. L. Caughey. 1945. *Human constitution in clinical medicine.* New York: Hoeber.

Dublineau, J. 1944. Evolution morphologique de l'adolescent. *Ann. Med. Psychol.*, *102*, 286–388.

Eells, K., et al. 1951. *Intelligence and cultural differences.* Chicago: University of Chicago Press.

Ellis, R. W. B. 1947. Growth in relation to maturity. *Edinb. Med. J.*, *54*, 269–283.

——. 1948. Puberty growth of boys. *Arch. Dis. Child.*, *23*, 17–26.

Engelmann, G. J. 1901. Age of first menstruation on the North American continent. *Trans. Amer. Gynecol. Soc.*, *26*, 77–110.

Engle, E., and M. Shelesnyak. 1934. First menstruation and subsequent menstrual cycles of pubertal girls. *Hum. Biol.*, *4*, 431–453.

Engstrom, W. W., and P. L. Munson. 1951. Precocious sexual and somatic development in boys due to constitutional and endocrine factors. *Amer. J. Dis. Child.*, *81*, 179–192.

Erikson, E. H. 1940. Problems in infancy and early childhood. In *Cyclopedia of medicine, surgery, and specialties.* Philadelphia: Davis.

Espenschade, A. 1940. Motor performance in adolescence. *Monogr. Soc. Res. Child Develpm.*, 5.

Evans-Prichard, E. E. 1934. Lévy-Bruhl's theory of primitive mentality. *Bull., Facul. of Arts, Univ., Egypt, Cairo*, 2, Pt. I.

Feingold, G. A. 1944. Newspaper tastes of high school pupils. *Sch. & Soc.*, *59*, 316–319.

Fendrick, P. 1941. Newspaper reading interests of high school and college students. *J. Educ. Res.*, *34*, 522–530.

Finger, F. W. 1947. Sex beliefs and practices among male college students. *J. Abnorm. Soc. Psychol.*, *42*, 57–67.

Fitz-Simons, M. J. 1935. Some parent-child relationships as shown in clinical case studies. *Teach. Coll. Contrib. Educ.*, No. 643.

Fleege, U. H. 1945a. *Self-revelation of the adolescent boy.* Milwaukee: Bruce.

Fleege, V. H. 1945b. Movies as an influence in the life of the modern adult. *Cath. Educ. Rev.*, *43*, 336–352.

Fleming, E. G. 1932. Best friends. *J. Soc. Psychol.*, *3*, 385–390.

Flory, C. D. 1936. Osseous development in the hand as an index of skeletal development. *Monogr. Soc. Res. Child Develpm.*, 1.

Francis, C. C. 1939. Factors influencing appearance of centers of ossification during early childhood. *Amer. J. Dis. Child.*, *57*, 817–830.

Frank, L. K. 1941. General considerations: Certain problems of puberty and adolescence. *J. Pediat.*, *19*, 294–301.

Frank, R. T. 1935. Sex-endocrine factors in blood and urine in health and disease. *J. Amer. Med. Ass.*, *104*, 1991–1997.

Freeman, F. N. 1938. Intellectual growth based on longitudinal studies. *Bull. Sch. Educ.*, *14*, 33–34. Bloomington, Ind.: Indiana University.

Freeman, F. N., and C. D. Flory. 1937. Growth in intellectual ability as measured by repeated tests. *Monogr. Soc. Res. Child Develpm.*, 2.

Frenkel-Brunswik, E., and J. Havel. 1953. Prejudice in the interviews of children: I. Attitudes toward minority groups. *J. Gen. Psychol.*, *82*, 91–136.

Friend, G. E., and E. R. Bransby. 1947. Physique and growth of schoolboys. *Lancet*, *253*, 677–681.

Furfey, P. H. 1940. The group life of the adolescent. *J. Educ. Sociol.*, *14*, 195–204.

Gable, M. A. 1951. The viewers' views on classroom TV. *Educ. Screen*, *30*, 226–227.

Gallagher, J. R. 1950. Various aspects of adolescence. *Yale J. Biol. Med.*, *22*, 595–604.

——. 1951. Various aspects of adolescence. *J. Pediat.*, *39*, 532–543.

Garfiel, E. 1923. The measurement of motor ability. *Arch. Psychol.*, 9.

Gould, H. N. 1938. Increase in stature of women in college, based on repeated measurements of the same individuals. *Amer. J. Phys. Anthrop.*, *23*, 493.

Gould, H. N., and M. R. Gould. 1932. Age of first menstruation in mother and daughters. *J. Amer. Med. Ass.*, *98*, 1349–1352.

Greulich, W. W. 1944. Physical changes in adolescence. In *Adolescence, 43rd Yearbook N.S.S.E.* Chicago: University of Chicago Press.

Greulich, W. W., H. G. Day, S. E. Lachman, J. B. Wolfe, and F. K. Shuttleworth. 1938. A handbook of methods for the study of adolescent children. *Monogr. Soc. Res. Child Develpm.*, 3.

Greulich, W. W., R. I. Dorfman, H. R. Catchpole, C. I. Solomon, and C. S. Culotta. 1942. Somatic and endocrine studies of pubertal and adolescent boys. *Monogr. Soc. Res. Child Develpm.*, 7.

Griffiths, W. 1952. *Behavior difficulties of children.* Minneapolis: University of Minnesota Press.

Grumette, J. 1937. Investigation into the newspaper reading tastes and habits of high school students. *High Points*, *19*, 5–10.

Gustavson, R. G., L. W. Mason, E. E. Hayes, T. R. Wood, and F. F. D'Amour. 1938. The quanti-

tative determination of estrogenic substances in normal female urine during the menstrual cycle. *Amer. J. Obstet. Gynecol.*, *35*, 115–126.

Hahn, L. 1952. The relation of blood pressure to weight, height, and body surface area in schoolboys aged 11 to 15 years. *Arch. Dis. Child.*, *27*, 43–53.

Hall, G. S. 1882. The moral and religious training of children. *Princeton Rev.*, *10*, 26–48.

——. 1904. *Adolescence; its psychology and its relations to physiology, anthropology, sociology, sex, crime, religion, and education.* 2 vols. New York: Appleton.

Hamilton, J. B. 1941. Male hormone substance; a prime factor in acne. *J. Clin. Endocrinol.*, *1*, 570–592.

Hammond, W. H. 1945. An analysis of youth center interests. *Brit. J. Educ. Psychol.*, *15*, 122–126.

Hanley, C. 1951. Physique and reputation of junior high school boys. *Child Develpm.*, *22*, 247–260.

Hardy, M. C., and C. H. Hoefer. 1936. *Healthy growth; a study of the influence of health education on growth and development of school children.* Chicago: University of Chicago Press.

Hart, H. 1924. The slowing up of growth in mental test ability. *Sch. & Soc.*, *20*, 573–574.

Hartshorne, H., and M. May. 1928. *Studies in deceit.* New York: Macmillan.

Hattwick, B. W. 1936. Inter-relations between the pre-school child's behavior and certain factors in the home. *Child Develpm.*, *7*, 200–226.

Hayes, S. P., Jr. 1938. A note on personality and family position. *J. Appl. Psychol.*, *22*, 347–349.

Herbert, J. F. 1806. *Allgemein Pädagogik: Hauptpunkte der Metaphysik und Hauptpunkteder Logik.* Gottingen: Rower.

——. *A textbook in psychology; an attempt to found the science of psychology on experience, metaphysics, and mathematics.* (Trans. by M. K. Smith, 1891.) New York: Appleton.

Hildreth, G. 1933. Adolescent interests and abilities. *J. Genet. Psychol.*, *43*, 65–93.

Hogben, H., J. A. H. Waterhouse, and L. Hogben. 1948. Studies on puberty, Pt. I. *Brit. J. Soc. Med.*, *2*, 29–42.

Hollingshead, A. B. 1949. *Elmtown's youth.* New York: Wiley.

Hollingworth, L. S. 1928. *The psychology of the adolescent.* New York: Appleton.

Homer. *The odyssey.* (Trans. by A. Pope, published 1942.) New York: Heritage Press.

Horrocks, J. E., and M. E. Buker. 1951. A study of the friendship fluctuations of preadolescents. *J. Genet. Psychol.*, *78*, 131–144.

Horrocks, J. E., and G. G. Thompson. 1946. A study of the friendship fluctuations of rural boys and girls. *J. Genet. Psychol.*, *69*, 189–198.

Hotopf, W. H. N. 1940. Some relations between characteristic interests of school boys. *Adv. Sci.*, *1*, 446.

Howard, E. M. 1941. An analysis of adolescent adjustment problems. *Ment. Hyg., N. Y.*, *25*, 363–391.

Hutson, P. W., and D. R. Kovar. 1942. Some problems of senior high school pupils in their social recreation. *Educ. Admin. and Superv.*, *28*, 503–519.

Jacobs, R. 1949. Stability of interests at the secondary school level. *Educ. Res. Bull.*, *52*, 83–87.

Joffe, N. F. 1951. The prolongation of adolescence in America. *Complex*, *4*, 28–33.

Jolliffe, N., L. A. Rosenblum, and J. Sawhill. 1942. The effects of pyridoxine (vitamin B₆) on persistent adolescent acne. *J. Investigative Dermatol.*, *5*, 143–148.

Jones, H. 1948. Group sentiment and delinquency. *Ment. Health., Lond.*, *8*, 41–44.

Jones, H. E. 1939. The adolescent growth study: I. Principles and methods. II. Procedures. *J. Consult. Psychol.*, *3*, 157–159, 177–180.

——. 1943. *Development in adolescence*. New York: Appleton-Century-Crofts.

——. 1944. The development of physical abilities. In *Adolescence, 43rd Yearbook N.S.S.E.* Chicago: University of Chicago Press.

——. 1946. Motor performance and physiological maturing. *Amer. Psychologist*, *1*, 456.

——. 1949. *Motor performance and growth*. Berkeley: University of California Press.

Jones, H. E., and H. S. Conrad. 1933. The growth and decline of intelligence. *Genet. Psychol. Monogr.*, *13*, 223–298.

Jones, M. C. 1941. The interests of adolescents. *Psychol. Bull.*, *38*, 738. (Abstract.)

Jordan, A. 1926. *Children's interests in reading*. Chapel Hill: University of North Carolina Press.

Jordan, A. M. 1935. Reading interests. *Proc. N. E. A.*, *73*, 342–345.

Katzman, P. A., and E. A. Doisy. 1934. The quantitative determination of small amounts of gonadotropic material. *J. Biol. Chem.*, *106*, 125–139.

Kinsey, A. C., W. B. Pomeroy, and C. E. Martin. 1948. *Sexual behavior in the human male*. Philadelphia: Saunders.

Kramer, D. G. 1885. *A. H. Francke's pädagogische Schriften*. Langensalza: Beyer und Söhne.

Kretschmer, E. (W. J. H. Sprott, trans., 1925.) *Physique and character*. New York: Harcourt, Brace.

Krogman, W. M. 1950. A handbook of the measurement and interpretation of the height and weight of the growing child. *Monogr. Soc. Res. Child Develpm.*, 13, No. 3.

Kuhlen, R. G., and B. J. Lee. 1943. Personality characteristics and social acceptability in adolescence. *J. Educ. Psychol.*, *34*, 321–340.

LaBrant, L. L., and F. M. Heller. 1939. An evaluation of free reading in grades 7 to 12 inclusive. *Contrib. Educ.*, No. 4, Columbus: Ohio State University.

Lancaster, E. G. 1897. The psychology and pedagogy of adolescence. *Ped. Sem.*, *5*, 61–128.

——. 1898. The vanishing character of adolescent experience. *North Western Mo.*, *8*, 644.

Larson, L. A. 1941. A factor analysis of motor-ability variables and tests with tests for college men. *Res. Quart.*, *12*, 499–517.

Latham, A. J. 1951. The relationship between pubertal status and leadership in junior high school boys. *J. Gen. Psychol.*, *78*, 185–194.

Lawrence, C. H., and N. T. Werthessen. 1942. Treatment of acne with orally administered estrogens. *J. Clin. Endocrinol.*, *2*, 636–638.

Lawton, G. 1949. *How to be happy though young*. New York: Vanguard.

Lee, D. 1940. A primitive system of values. *Phil. Sci.*, *7*, 355–378.

Lehman, H. C., and P. A. Witty. 1927. *The psychology of play activities*. New York: Barnes.

Libby, M. F. 1901. Shakespeare and adolescence. *Ped. Sem.*, *8*, 163–205.

Lintz, W., and H. Markow. 1923. Relation of onset of menstruation to environment. *Endocrinology*, 7, 57–60.

Lynd, R. S., and H. M. Lynd. 1929. *Middletown*. New York: Harcourt, Brace.

——. 1937. *Middletown in transition*. New York: Harcourt, Brace.

MacCurdy, H. L. 1933. *A test for measuring the physical capacity of secondary school boys*. Yonkers: H. L. MacCurdy.

MacNair, V. 1939. Effect of a dietary supplement on ossification of the bones of the wrist in institutional children: II. Effect of a codliver oil supplement. *Amer. J. Dis. Child.*, *58*, 295–319.

Malinowski, B. 1927. *Sex and repression in savage society*. New York: Harcourt, Brace.

Marks, P. 1936. *A tree grown straight*. New York: Stokes.

Maxwell, W. 1945. *The folded leaf*. New York: Harper.

McCloy, C. H. 1932. *The measurement of athletic power*. New York: Barnes.

——. 1938. Appraising physical status: methods and norms. *Univ. Iowa Stud. Child Welfare*, 15, No. 2.

McDonagh, E. C., *et al.* 1950. Television and the family. *Sociol. Soc. Res.*, *35*, 113–122.

McGill, N. P., and E. N. Matthews. 1940. *The youth of New York City*. New York: Macmillan.

Mead, M. 1928a. *Coming of age in Samoa*. New York: Morrow.

——. 1928b. The role of the individual in Samoan culture. *J. Roy. Anthrop. Inst. London*, *58*, 481–495.

Meredith, H. V. 1935. The rhythm of physical growth. *Univ. Iowa Stud. Child Welfare*, 11, No. 3.

Metheny, E. 1941. The present status of strength testing for children of elementary school and preschool age. *Res. Quart.*, *12*, 115–130.

Mills, C. A. 1937. Geographic and time variations in body growth and age at menarche. *Hum. Biol.*, *9*, 43–56.

Mills, C. A., and C. Ogle. 1936. Physiological sterility of adolescence. *Hum. Biol.*, *8*, 607–615.

Moraitis, D. 1946. Free composition of an adolescent. *Indiv. Psychol. Bull.*, *5*, 112–118.

Mueller, H. 1932. Enkele waarnemingen omtrent den groei van het beenderenstelsel en omtrent de geslachterijkheid van Javaansche meisjes. *Med-*

edeelengen van den Dienst de Volksgezondheid in Nederlandsch-Indie, *21*, 48–63.

Muhsam, H. V. 1947. Correlation in growth. *Hum. Biol.*, *19*, 260–269.

Myers, W. E. 1947. High school graduates choose vocations unrealistically. *Occupations*, *25*, 332–333.

Nasser, I. 1941. Magazine reading at the junior high level. *Calif. J. Sec. Educ.*, *16*, 485–488.

Nathanson, I. I., L. E. Towne, and J. C. Aub. 1941. Normal excretion of sex hormones in childhood. *Endocrinology*, *23*, 851–865.

Neumann, H. O., and F. Peter. 1931. Die Hormonausscheidungen in Kindesalter. *Kinderheilk.*, *52*, 24–30.

Neurath, R. 1932. *Die Pubertät*. Vienna: Springer.

Newcomer, E. O., and H. V. Meredith. 1951. Eleven measures of bodily size on a 1950 sample of 15-year-old white schoolboys at Eugene, Oregon. *Hum. Biol.*, *23*, 24–40.

Newman, R. W. 1952. Age changes in body build. *Amer. J. Phys. Anthrop.*, *10*, 75–90.

Ni, Tsang-Gi. 1947. Heights and weights of Shanghai school children. *Chinese Med. J.*, *65*, 373–380.

Nye, I. 1951. Adolescent-parent adjustment-socioeconomic level as a variable. *Amer. Sociol. Rev.*, *16*, 341–349.

Nylin, G. 1935. The physiology of the circulation during puberty. *Acta Med. Scand.*, Supplementum LXIX, 1–77.

Partridge, E. D. 1934. Leadership among adolescent boys. *Teach. Coll. Contrib. Educ.*, No. 608.

——. 1945. What has the last decade done to our adolescents? *Nerv. Child*, *4*, 147–150.

Pearson, G. C., and S. S. Center. 1936. *Survey of reading in typical high schools in New York City*. N. Y. C. Ass. Teach. English, First Yearbook.

Peel, E. A. 1948. Assessment of interest in practical topics. *Brit. J. Educ. Psychol.*, *18*, 41–47.

Peters, E. F. 1941. Factors which contribute to youth's vocational choice. *J. Appl. Psychol.*, *25*, 428–430.

Pfuhl, W. 1928. Wachstum und Proportionen in Peter, L., Wetzel, G., and Heiderich, F. *Handbuch der Anatomie des Kindes*, 1. Munich: Bergman.

Plato. *Dialogues* (English trans. by B. Jowett). 2 vols. New York: Random House.

Pond, F. L. 1939. A qualitative and quantitative appraisal of reading experience. *Unpub. doctor's dissertation*. State College, Pa.: Pennsylvania State College.

Pressey, S. L. 1946. Changes from 1923 to 1943 in the attitudes of public school and university students. *J. Psychol.*, *21*, 173–188.

Puffer, J. A. 1905. Boys' gangs, *Ped. Sem.*, *12*, 175–212.

Punke, H. H. 1936. Leisure-time attitudes and activities of high school students. *Sch. & Soc.*, *43*, 884–888.

Ramsey, G. V. 1943. The sex information of younger boys. *Amer. J. Orthopsychiat.*, *13*, 347–352.

Reed, B. H. 1950. *Eighty thousand adolescents*. London: Allen and Unwin.

Remarque, E. 1928. *All quiet on the western front*. Boston, Little, Brown.

Remmers, H. H., and B. Shimberg. 1949. *Problems of high school youth*. Lafayette: Purdue University.

Remmlein, M. K. 1938. Analysis of leaders among high school seniors. *J. Exp. Educ.*, *6*, 413–422.

Reynolds, E. L., and T. Asakawa. 1948. The measurement of obesity in childhood. *Amer. J. Physiol.*, *6*, 475–487.

Reynolds, E. L., and J. V. Wines. 1948. Individual differences in physical changes associated with adolescence in girls. *Amer. J. Dis. Child.*, *75*, 329–350.

——. 1951. Physical changes associated with adolescence in boys. *Amer. J. Dis. Child.*, *82*, 529–547.

Richey, H. G. 1931. The blood pressure in boys and girls before and after puberty. Its relation to growth and maturity. *Amer. J. Dis. Child.*, *42*, 1281–1330.

Ridout, A. K. 1938. Juvenile judgments. *Engl. J.*, *27*, 38–43.

Roberton, J. 1831. Period of puberty in women. *N. Eng. Med. Surg. J.* (abstracted in *Amer. J. Med. Sci.*, p. **513**).

——. 1832. An inquiry into the natural history of the menstrual function. *Edinb. Med. Surg. J.*, *38*, 227–254.

——. 1842. On the period of puberty in Negro women. *Edinb. Med. Surg. J.*, *58*, 112–120.

——. 1843. Early marriage so common in oriental countries no proof of early puberty. *Edinb. Med. Surg. J.*, *60*, 1–18.

——. 1844. On the alleged influence of climate on female puberty in Greece. *Edinb. Med. Surg. J.*, *62*, 1–11.

——. 1845a. On the period of puberty in Esquimaux women. *Edinb. Med. Surg. J.*, *63*, 57–65.

——. 1845b; 1846. On the period of puberty in Hindu women. *Edinb. Med. Surg. J.*, *64*, 423–429; *66*, 56–64.

——. 1848. On the period of puberty in the Negro. *Edinb. Med. Surg. J.*, *69*, 69–77.

Roberts, L. J., et al. 1939. The supplementary value of the banana in institutional diets: I. Effect on growth in height and weight, ossification of carpels, and changes in Franzen indices. *J. Pediat.*, *15*, 25–42.

Roeber, E., and S. Garfield. 1943. Study of the occupational interests of high school students in terms of grade placement. *J. Educ. Psychol.*, *34*, 355–362.

Rogers, F. R. 1927. *Test and measurement programs in the redirection of physical education*. New York: Columbia University Press.

Rousseau, J. J. *Émile ou de l'éducation*. 2 vols. pub. 1932. Paris: Nelson.

——. *Émile*. (English trans. by B. Foxley.) New York: Dutton.

Sargent, D. A. 1921. The physical test of a man. *Amer. Phys. Educ. Rev.*, *26*, 188–194.

Sawtell, R. O. 1929. Ossification and growth of children from one to eight years of age. *Amer. J. Dis. Child.*, *37*, 61–87.

Schaeffer, R. 1906. Über Beginn Dauer, und Erlöschen der Menstruation; statistische Mitteilungen über 10,500 Fälle aus der gynäkologischen Poliklinik.

Monatsschrift für Geburtshilfe und Gynakologie, 23, 169–191.

Schmidt-Voight, J. 1942. Variationen im Erscheinungsbild des schnellreifenden Jugendlichen. *Z. Kinderheilk.,* 63, 356–366.

Schonfeld, W. A. 1943. Primary and secondary sexual characteristics. Study of their development in males from birth through maturity. *Amer. J. Dis. Child.,* 65, 535–549.

Schonfeld, W. A., and G. W. Beebe. 1942. Normal growth and variation in the male genitalia from birth to maturity. *J. Urology,* 48, 759–779.

Schörcher, F. 1931. Zur Physiologie und Pathologie der Prolanauscheidung im Harn bei Kindern und Jugendlichen. *Klin. Wschr.,* 10, 2221–2222.

Sheldon, W. H., S. S. Stevens, and W. B. Tucker. 1942. *The varieties of human physique.* New York: Harper.

Shock, N. W. 1942. Standard values for basal oxygen consumption in girls. *Amer. J. Dis. Child.,* 64, 19–32.

——. 1943. The effect of menarche on basal physiological functions in girls. *Amer. J. Physiol.,* 139, 288-291.

——. 1944a. Physiological changes in adolescence. In *Adolescence, 43rd Yearbook N.S.E.E.,* Chicago: University of Chicago Press.

——. 1944b. Physiological aspects of development. *Rev. Educ. Res.,* 14, 413–426.

——. 1946. Physiological responses of adolescents to exercise. *Texas Rep. Biol. Med.,* 4, 289–310.

Shock, N. W., and M. J. Schlatter. 1942. Pulse rate response of adolescents to auditory stimuli. *J. Exp. Psychol.,* 30, 414–425.

Shock, N. W., and M. H. Soley. 1939. Average values for basal respiratory functions in adolescents and adults. *J. Nutrition,* 18, 143–153.

Shuttleworth, F. K. 1937. Sexual maturation and the physical growth of girls aged six to nineteen. *Monogr. Soc. Res. Child Develpm.,* 2.

——. 1938. Sexual maturation and the skeletal growth of girls aged six to nineteen. *Monogr. Soc. Res. Child Develpm.,* 3.

——. 1939. The physical and mental growth of boys and girls aged six through nineteen in relation to age of maximum growth. *Monogr. Soc. Res. Child Develpm.,* 4.

——. 1951a. The adolescent period: a graphic atlas. *Monogr. Soc. Res. Child Develpm.,* 14.

——. 1951b. The adolescent period: a pictorial atlas. *Monogr. Soc. Res. Child Develpm.,* 14.

Siepmann, C. A. 1950. *Radio, television, and society,* New York: Oxford.

Simmons, K., and W. W. Greulich. 1943. Menarcheal age and the height, weight, and skeletal age of girls ages seven to seventeen years. *J. Pediat.,* 22, 518–548.

Smith, M., and W. C. Nystrom. 1937. A study of social participation and of leisure time of leaders and non-leaders. *J. Appl. Psychol.,* 21, 251–259.

Snyder, W. V. 1941. A survey of recent studies in the measurement of personality, attitudes, and interests of adolescents. *J. Genet. Psychol.,* 25, 403–420.

Sontag, L. W., and S. I. Pyle. 1941. Variations in the classification pattern in epiphyses: their nature and significance. *Amer. J. Roentgenol. Radium Therapy,* 45, 50–54.

Starbuck, E. D. 1899. *Psychology of religion.* New York: Scribner's.

Stendler, C. B. 1949. Children of Brasstown. *Univ. Ill. Bull.,* 46, No. 59. Urbana: University of Illinois.

Sterner, A. P. 1947. Radio, motion picture, and reading interests: A study of high school students. *Teach. Coll. Contrib. Educ.,* No. 932.

Stockard, C. R. 1922–1923. Human types and growth reactions. *Amer. J. Anat.,* 31, 261–288.

Stolz, H. R., M. C. Jones, and J. Chaffey. 1937. The junior high school age. *Univ. High Sch. J.,* 15, 63–72.

Stolz, H. R., and L. M. Stolz. 1951. *Somatic development of adolescent boys.* New York: Macmillan.

Stone, C. P., and R. G. Barker. 1937a. On the relationship between menarcheal age and certain measurements of physique in girls of the ages nine to sixteen years. *Hum. Biol.,* 9, 1–28.

Stone, C. P., and R. G. Barker. 1937b. Aspects of personality and intelligence in post-menarcheal and pre-menarcheal girls of the same chronological ages. *J. Comp. Psychol.,* 23, 439–455.

Stone, C. P., and R. G. Barker. 1939. The attitudes and interests of pre-menarcheal and post-menarcheal girls. *J. Genet. Psychol.,* 54, 27–71.

Stott, L. H. 1939a. Personality development in farm, small-town, and city children. *Agr. Exp. Station Res. Bull.,* No. 114. Lincoln: University of Nebraska.

——. 1939b. General home setting as a factor in the study of the only versus the non-only child. *Character & Pers.,* 8, 156–162.

Straumfjord, J. V. 1943. Vitamin A; its effect on acne: a study of 100 patients. *Northwest Medicine,* 42, 219–225.

Strong, E. K., Jr. 1934. Permanence of vocational interests. *J. Educ. Psychol.,* 7, 49–67.

Stuart, H. C. 1947. Physical growth during adolescence. *Amer. J. Dis. Child.,* 74, 495–502.

Stuart, H. C., and H. V. Meredith. 1946. Use of body measurements in the school health program. *Amer. J. Pub. Health,* 36, 1365–1386.

Sudweeks, J. 1927. Intelligence of the continuation school pupils of Wisconsin. *J. Educ. Psychol.,* 18, 601–610.

Sutluff, W. D., and E. Holt. 1925. The age curve of pulse rate under basal conditions. *Archives Intern. Med.,* 35, 224–241.

Swift, E. J. 1903. Standards of efficiency in school and in life. *Ped. Sem.,* 10, 3–22.

Symonds, P. M. 1939. *The psychology of parent-child relationships.* New York: Appleton-Century-Crofts.

Tangney, H. F. 1942. A study relating to the change in the newspaper reading interests of secondary school students since the entrance of the U. S. into World War II. *J. Exp. Educ.,* 10, 195–199.

Tarkington, B. 1916. *Seventeen.* New York: Harper.

Taylor, K. W. 1938. *Do adolescents need parents?* New York: Appleton-Century-Crofts.

Thompson, G. G., and J. E. Horrocks. 1947. A study of friendship fluctuations of urban boys and girls. *J. Genet. Psychol., 70,* 53–63.

Thrasher, F. M. 1927. *The gang.* Chicago: University of Chicago Press.

Todd, T. W. 1937. *Atlas of skeletal maturation (hand).* St. Louis: Mosby.

Tramer, M. 1947. *Das Seelenleben des Jugendlichen; seine Eigenart und Schwierigkeiten.* Schwarzenburg: Verlag Gerber-Buchdruck.

Tuttle, W. W. 1931. The use of the pulse-rate test for rating physical efficiency. *Res. Quart., 2,* 5–17.

Valentine, C. W. 1943. Adolescence and some problems of youth training. *Brit. J. Educ. Psychol., 13,* 57–68.

Van Dyne, E. V. 1940. Personality traits and friendship formation in adolescent girls. *J. Soc. Psychol., 12,* 291–303.

Vickery, F. E. 1946. Adolescent interest in social problems. *J. Educ. Res., 40,* 309–315.

Vreeland, F. M., and S. M. Corey. 1935. A study of college friendships. *J. Abnorm. Soc. Psychol., 30,* 229–236.

Waite, C. L., and J. A. Rothschild. 1950. The pediatrician and the adolescent: A review of normal growth and development in the adolescent. *Clin. Proc. Child. Hospital, 6,* 344–352.

Wall, W. D. 1948. *The adolescent child.* London: Methuen.

Warner, M. L. 1923. Influence of mental level in the formation of boys' games. *J. Appl. Psychol., 7,* 224–236.

Wellman, B. 1926. The school child's choice of companions. *J. Educ. Res., 14,* 126–132.

West, J. (pseud.) 1945. *Plainville, U. S. A.* New York: Columbia University Press.

Westbrook, C. H., S. G. Lai, and S. D. Hsiao. 1934. Some physical aspects of adolescence in Chinese students. *Chin. Med. J., 48,* 37–46.

Wetzel, N. C. 1934. On the motion of growth. XVI. Clinical aspects of human growth and metabolism with special reference to infancy and pre-school life. *J. Pedia., 4,* 465–493.

Wexberg, E. 1939. Problems of adolescents. *Ment. Hyg. N. Y., 23,* 594–600.

White House Conference on Child Health and Protection. 1934. *The adolescent in the family.* New York: Appleton-Century-Crofts.

Whiting, J. W. M. 1941. *Becoming a Kwoma.* New Haven: Yale University Press.

Williams, P. E. 1923. A study of adolescent friendships. *J. Genet. Psychol., 30,* 342–346.

Williamson, E. G., and J. G. Darley. 1935. Trends in the occupational choices of high school seniors. *J. Appl. Psychol., 19,* 361–370.

Wolberg, L. R. 1945. Adjustment problems in male adolescence. *Nerv. Child, 4,* 129–134.

Woodrow, H. 1928. Mental unevenness and brightness. *J. Educ. Psychol., 9,* 289–302.

Wright, H. F., and R. G. Barker. 1950. *Methods in psychological ecology.* Topeka: Ray's Printing Service.

Yoder, A. H. 1894. The study of the boyhood of great men. *Ped. Sem., 3,* 134–156.

Zeleny, L. D. 1940. Characteristics of group leaders. *Sociol. Soc. Res., 24,* 140–149.

Zeller, W. 1939. *Entwicklung und Körperform der Knaben und Mädchen von vierzehn Jahren.* Berlin: Schoetz.

CHAPTER 12

RESEARCH ON PRIMITIVE CHILDREN [1]
MARGARET MEAD

Introduction

The value of research upon primitive children to students of psychology is part of the whole larger problem of the relationship of researches made among primitive people to the hypotheses and theories of psychology. Therefore, the history of the uses to which psychology has put data about primitive children and data about primitive peoples when constructing theories of developmental psychology is a history of the changing relationship between anthropology and psychology.

The first use to which psychologists put ethnological data was in constructing biogenetic theories in which the postnatal behavior of the child was regarded as recapitulating the past history of the race. In a thorough examination of this position Hallowell (1939) has shown that any such theory involves these untenable positions: (1) an acceptance of the doctrine of acquired characters, (2) a direct equation between the type of culture found among our primitive contemporaries and previous stages in the history of more advanced cultures, and (3) a demonstrable correspondence between the behavior of civilized children and primitive adults. In its crudest form this old biogenetic theory continues to crop up in the literature, and psychologists continue to make investigations to disprove it (Schubert, 1930; Anastasi and Foley, 1936, 1938). More seriously, it lies, as Hallowell has shown, behind much current psychoanalytic thinking and therefore compromises investigations made among

primitive people within the psychoanalytic frame of reference.

All the evidence which we have at the present time suggests that the only situations in which the savage adult can be compared with the child within our society are those in which primitive societies have failed to pattern some aspect of behavior which we have patterned extensively. In those cases, the thinking of the primitive adult, not trained, for example, in scientific logic, may resemble to a certain extent the thinking of civilized children *not yet* trained in the methods of scientific thinking. This resemblance, however, will be negative in terms of slightness of exposure to some cultural patterning and may not be attributed to a greater degree of "primitiveness" in the thinking of the savage adult than of the civilized adult in the sense that primitive means a simpler, a more rudimentary, or an earlier form. Similarly, the drawing of primitive adults who have *never drawn before* often resembles the drawing of civilized children who have *never drawn before*, but when the art of a primitive or non-European society has some positive characteristic—for example, the technique of phenomenal regression instead of perspective—this must be attributed either to the circumstance that the societies have developed and institutionalized different approaches to the problem of representation or to differences

[1] I am indebted to Miss Marion Marcovitz for her collaboration in preparing the bibliography and organizing the tabular statements on unpublished research. M. M.

in the cultural conditioning of perception (Thouless, 1933). There is the further possibility that, since types of thinking or ways of solving problems may tend to appear in a given order in the development of the child, different cultures may select an earlier ontogenetic tendency than others for elaboration (Mead, 1947b). When this occurs we can find elaborations in given primitive cultures of types of behavior manifested for a brief period and within a restricting and limiting frame in our own culture. In such cases there are available to the psychologist data upon ways in which potentialities of human thought, left unexploited or definitely overlaid or distorted in our culture, may develop.

This generalization holds in many fields. We can find cultures which develop the potentiality for animistic thought, as we can also find primitive societies which give their children a training that discourages animistic thought even more rigorously than does our own (Mead, 1932) and cultures which fail either to give encouragement and elaborate channeled forms or to discourage, but leave man's capacity to begin thinking animistically, in childhood, so unpatterned that it will survive merely as an idiosyncrasy in some adults confronted with a new situation (Mead, 1928a).

Róheim (1934b), working within the psychoanalytic frame of reference in the study of primitive children, continues to refer those aspects of primitive culture which are common to all primitive societies to a phylogenetic Oedipus situation, although allowing (Róheim, 1939) more and more for the specific elements in given cultural family situations which account for the particular form that the Oedipus complex takes in the character of members of a given primitive tribe. The most promising attempt to state the relationship between developmental phases in the emerging personality and the institutionalized cultural forms of contrasting societies is to be found in Erikson's (1939) theory of the social implications of *epigenesis*. He applies Freud's theory of pregenital zones and stages to problems of culture by pointing out that the successive emphases upon body zones in early childhood permit the particular modes of these zones to become established as basic social modalities. In a given society the oral-sensory, anal-muscular, and genital-locomotor zones are trained so that their modes (incorporation, retention, elimination, intrusion, and inclusion) become patterned to form a basic social grammar, consisting of such modalities as getting, taking, having, holding, letting go, and giving.[1] Within this theoretical scheme different cultures can be classified according to the extent to which they abbreviate or lengthen these stages, emphasize or deprecate the various modes of behavior associated with given zones, and so produce, as the standard cultural personality, a *monstrum in excessu* or *monstrum in defectu*, stated in terms of developmental possibilities. This approach permits, as did the discredited biogenetic theory, a stimulating cross-comparison between the behavior of children in any given culture, at any given stage, and the behavior of adults in other cultures.

The biogenetic theory and much of the thinking that has replaced it work with the concept of *the primitive*, a synthetic personality, built up partly deductively from a hybrid of sociological, pseudobiological theory and partly through a miscellaneous mass of detail collected and systematized by such comparative writers as Lévy-Bruhl and Frazer. This material was further systematized by psychologists like Freud,

[1] Erikson handled this theory formally in a chart (Homburger, 1937) which was reproduced in the first edition of this manual. It has been omitted here as a much fuller treatment of this chart is included in Erikson's *Childhood and Society* (1950).

Wundt, and Stanley Hall, and "the primitive" as an analogue of "the child" or "the neurotic" or "the psychotic" became a theoretical counter in later psychological research (Piaget, 1924; Storch, 1924). Despite the enormous amount of ethnological research that has been done to demonstrate the great complexity and diversity of preliterate cultures (Evans-Prichard, 1934; E. Beaglehole, 1940) and the untenability of any such concept as "the primitive," this concept still recurs today with monotonous frequency in psychological writing. There arose, however, a counter tendency to document the extent to which primitive man must be regarded as an acculturated adult, subject to the patterning of his culture, and in no sense more archaic, or simple, in his methods of thinking than are we (Boas, 1938). The very great differences between cultures of the world appear then as comparable to the smallest local variations which obtain at home. This approach, in the hands of members of other disciplines, again tended to crystallize a conception of a series of synthetic primitives, as unreal as their single predecessor, members of a given tribe who were just like us except for a few conspicuous details; the Zuñi had a distaste for violence, and the Kwakiutl a freer exaltation of himself. These stereotypes have proved to be almost as mischievous an idea as that of the primitive who thought prelogically and represented the childhood of the race.

Current sophisticated treatments of the reports from primitive society tend to use, in one part of their argument, the data showing that primitive man is just like us in all the respects in which he has been accused of being most different and, in another part of their discussion, discrete items of difference as recorded for particular tribes, who become unreal counters for "nonviolence," "jealousy," "lack of knowledge of paternity," etc. This is the result of combining the generalized rebuttals of the older position, based upon a large number of miscellaneous instances, with a certain amount of data on conspicuous differences.

Neither stereotype is of any genuine use to psychologists; one leads to untenable theory, the other to mere dull disbelief, for the average student who is taught that a given kind of native is just like himself, except for a few conspicuous and striking differences of behavior of which he knows he would be absolutely incapable, very properly rejects the whole argument. To convert these stereotypes it will be necessary for psychology gradually to assimilate and reduce to useful form the more recent findings of ethnologists which stress that a fully acculturated member of a living culture differs in *every respect,* and *systematically,* from members of any other culture (Mead, 1934a; Bateson, 1936; Erikson, 1940; see also Köhler, 1937). Lee (1940) shows, for instance, that the Trobriand lack of recognition of paternity is not merely a prop for matriliny or an isolated piece of illogicality among a people who are just like us but that this nonrecognition stands in a systematic relationship to many other Trobriand ways of thought in a system of thought different from our own.

It is necessary to recognize that the growing child is systematically patterned in every detail, in posture as well as in gesture, in tempo as well as in speech, in his way of thinking as well as in the content of his thinking, in his capacity to feel as well as in the forms which his feeling takes and that only by an understanding of the extent and internal interrelationships of any of these systems of socialization can the psychologist operate usefully with "the Zuñi child" or "the Arapesh child." The use of isolated instances of cultural differences, in the most abstract form possible, so that for the statement "The Mundugumor native feels shame in the outside of his upper arm" the psychologist will substitute "The localization of specific emotions may be introspectively referred to different parts of the body, and parts so identified in one culture may be ignored in another," will enable the psychologist to keep his thinking from becoming culturally limited, but the effect will be negative. Such an abstraction keeps him from making obvious errors of the order of "All children are more animistic than adults," but it does not necessarily stimulate him to say anything new, to advance any more fruitful hypothesis.

Looking at the development of psychology's use of primitive data from another point of view, we find that in the first stage, that of *analogy,* there was an efflorescence of unprofitable and unsound parallels between primitive man and civilized children which led to a dead end in psychological thinking. This period was followed by the period of disproving the assumptions made in the previous period and using primitive material *negatively* to call in question psychological assumptions which had contained a western European premise (Malinowski, 1927a; Mead, 1928b, 1932; Benedict, 1934b). During this period it was further the function of the ethnologist who oriented his work to psychological preoccupations to phrase his material as "Yes, but among the . . . such and such is the case, and so your hypothesis will not hold."

The effect of this type of criticism is to drive the theorist toward higher degrees of abstraction. The Yale frustration-aggression hypothesis (Dollard, Doob, Miller, *et al.,* 1939) is a case in point. The hypothesis states that if a series of acts which would have led to a final satisfying act is interrupted, the subject will either turn toward some other analogous goal (substitution) or he will exhibit aggressive behavior.

The critic replies: "Yes, but the Balinese do not see their own behavior in this way. They see their own behavior either as an infinite continuum leading nowhere or else as separate atomic pieces; they do not see life as we do, as composed of a series of acts punctuated with satisfactions." This criticism calls attention to the whole problem of "time gestalt" and "purpose," and it is now possible to look at the goal seeking and at the aggressive behavior in terms of this new abstraction and to see that both are alike in their punctuation, in that both end in climax. This leads us to the generalization: "If an individual has been conditioned to a certain time gestalt and if a sequence of his acts is interrupted, he will turn toward some other sequence in which a similar gestalt is implicit."

Our criticism has led to a higher degree of abstraction and so to a reduction in the number of entities invoked. In place of the alternative entities, "substitution" or "aggression," we now have only one entity, the "time gestalt" (Bateson, 1941). However, a correction of this order, introduced into a hypothesis which had been carefully framed in an attempt to allow for and rule out the cultural factor, can be introduced only on the basis of an exceedingly detailed study of character formation in other cultures. It is therefore to be expected, in terms of the continual cross-fertilization between psychology and anthropology, that, as the field worker takes more cross-culturally useful frames of reference into the field, he will return with material which will be relevant at a higher level of theoretical abstraction in psychology.

This most recent stage in the application of primitive material to psychological theory has a positive aspect, in which the ethnologist attempts upon the basis of primitive data to develop concepts that could not be derived on the basis of any other data which we possess. The contribution of the ethnologist here may be likened to the contribution which a chemist might have made in discovering a new element *before* the periodic table was constructed. Because our theories of human nature must always be constructed on the basis of subjects who have been socialized, our progress is exceedingly slow in constructing any theoretical picture of the range of human potentialities and the systematic interrelationship of different parts of this range. Until we have enough data to fill in the analogue of the periodic table for human development, it will be necessary to have more and better-detailed studies of the process of character formation and the resulting personality structure in different cultures. Erikson's (1950) chart makes it possible to make an intelligible statement about certain aspects of character formation in about half the primitive societies upon which we have relevant data concerning the way in which the zonal behavior is patterned. Bateson's (1942a) suggestion for the analysis of cultures in terms of types of *deutero-learning*, through which different types of learning identified in learning experiments in the laboratory may be seen to play different rôles in the expectations of members of different cultures, provides us with another such cross-cultural frame of reference, as does his formulation of *end linkage* (1942b). The Gesell-Ilg (Mead, 1947b) spiral concept of development provides another useful cross-cultural model less exclusively preoccupied with affective elements than are those theories of growth which derive from Freudian psychology. Renewed attention to forms of thought of the type which is found extensively in dreams, in schizophrenics, in ritual and art, and in the spontaneous productions of children is introducing new possibilities of cross-

cultural analysis of *primary process* types of thought (Vigotsky, 1939; Schachtel, E. G., 1947; Lowenfeld, 1935). The development of psychosomatic theory has also introduced a new set of concepts within which child development may be seen culturally (Mittlemann, Wolff, and Scharf, 1942; Mead, 1947c; Wolff, 1947). Models for seeing child development in cultural settings as part of a circular system of communication between generations may be expected to come from the newly emerging approach of *cybernetics* (Wiener, 1948; Bateson, 1949; Mead, 1949a). This approach may be opposed to unrewarding discussion of the causal rôle of particular items of child rearing practices (Whiting, MS b; Orlansky, 1949). This newer framework makes it possible to look upon the child as acting within the whole social group and, by making the point of reference the regularities of the human growth process within a social group of all ages, eliminates artificial distinctions between the sequences of growth within the individual organism and the interrelationships among all the human beings within a society (Mead, 1949b).

So the psychologist will continue to demand from material gathered by the ethnologist data for correcting his hypotheses —negative material—and data for amplifying his hypotheses—positive material. Upon the formulation of significant cross-cultural hypotheses which the ethnologist can take into the field will depend the amount of significant materials of this sort which the ethnologist can bring back; and, if the science of human behavior is to proceed at maximum speed, the field ethnologist concerned with psychological problems must be working with hypotheses even before they reach the point of publication and not with the formal psychological statements of some years back.

The Psychologist among Primitive Peoples

We can now turn to the history of the attempts of the psychologist to work in the field, or to set specific problems or provide tests for the use of the field worker. His first contacts with primitive peoples, like his first use of primitive material, were cast in a biological mold. He wanted to study racial differences. Klineberg (1935) and Goodenough (1936) summarize the state of research here. Goodenough says:

> In view of the relatively small amount of information concerning the mental characteristics of various cultural and racial groups that is based upon direct measurement or simple functions, it is greatly to be regretted that up to the present time psychological interest has been so closely centered about the problem of classification on the basis of general broad assumptions the validity of which is uncertain.

The first research was done on the sense organs, and, as Goodenough (1936, p. 6) points out, psychologists were satisfied with the disproof of the extravagant claims of racial differences which had been made and ignored the differences which were found. There was then a very infertile period of applying intelligence tests to primitive children, usually in culture contact environments, which necessitated an equally infertile effort to refute the findings. Efforts are now being made (Porteus, 1937; Cattell, 1940; K. R. Stewart, MS c) to develop tests which can be standardized on the members of preliterate cultures and which will yield positive data on how the individuals think, not merely on how we may classify them. To date, no data have been advanced which actually call into question the basic ethnological assumption of the nonexistence of innate psychological differences between races. The principal importance of this type of research lies in

its background relationship to other problems, for if there were significant and constant differences between all the members of one primitive group and those of another group, then any study of the socialized individual would have to take them into account.

A second attempt on the part of psychologists to collect primitive data has been prompted by problems which they themselves formulated and for which they collected supporting data. Porteus (1937) set out to test the theory that environment was responsible for the poor showing of natives in a culture contact setting. He made a study of primitive people in two differentially difficult *physical* environments, to find that, if anything, the individuals in the harder environment were superior but that, on the whole, the differences were unsystematic. Greater reliance upon ethnological data would have suggested that this investigation, as it was phrased, was not worth undertaking. Dennis (1940a) posed the problem of whether the cradle board affected the age of walking and tested it out in two Hopi communities, one in which the cradle board was still used and one in which its use had been abandoned. Setting aside the reliability of Indian mothers' reports on a problem that involved accuracy in months, the question, like Porteus's, was phrased in a way that tremendously oversimplified the problem. It is to be expected that infants subjected to a type of environmental pressure of which the cradle board is one expression will differ from infants differently reared, but not on such simple items as "age of walking." Rather will they differ in manner of walking, occasions when they walk, significance of walking for the personality, type of balance disturbance to which the individual is subject, etc. It is even probable that most of these effects would remain even if the cradle board itself disappeared, as long as the whole complex of cultural behavior of which the cradle board had been a part survived (Erikson, 1939).

Recent elaborations of this type of earlier approach now occur in reverse. Some single item of behavior which has been described as providing useful clues to the understanding of the acculturation system of a given primitive society, as, for instance, the way in which a pattern of permissiveness or exactingness is expressed in the infant feeding situation, is then assigned hypothetical causal importance, and this hypothesis is either subjected to criticism (Orlansky, 1949) in the light of work done in our own society or uncritically imported as a basis for a pediatric program (Moloney, 1945; Moloney and Cammisa, 1947).

When the emphasis was upon the contribution of research in primitive society as a negative corrective to culturally limited hypotheses, taking a problem into the field, such as the incidence of conflict at adolescence (Mead, 1928b) or the effect of a harsh environment on IQ (Porteus, 1937), seemed to be an effective use of primitive material. From such oversimplified studies, however, we could not expect anything except negative, corrective, precautionary conclusions, and such an approach is now definitely out of date.

Approaches during the Period 1935–1940

These approaches (1935–1940) take as a focusing point, not a simple presence or absence, concomitance or nonconcomitance problem, but instead the investigation of the developing individual within the whole cultural matrix. The older approaches relied upon primitive societies to provide laboratories within which different sorts of children could be found whose behavior could be used to disprove or call in question some hypothesis. The value of primitive socie-

ties was regarded as lying principally in the fact that the culture was a different one and that special sets of conditions, such as cradle boards, prolonged suckling, nonrecognition of paternity, absence of formal schooling, and knowledge of graphic techniques, could be found and their "effects" upon the developing personality studied.

It was later felt that more was to be gained by asking another kind of question, and by utilizing two other aspects of primitive culture: (1) the circumstance that they represented varieties of social systems which we could neither produce experimentally nor derive by extrapolation from known forms and (2) the circumstance that in small groups of preliterate peoples sharing a common culture it is possible to deal with the individual within the whole society, in relation to his total culture, in a way that is not possible in large groups, in a stratified society, characterized by great heterogeneity of culture. The new questions that the psychologist or the ethnologist working in terms of psychology asked were positive questions: What is the mechanism of character formation within the new society? What sorts of learning are emphasized, and what are the results? How is a personality type which places no value on aggression developed, and how do individuals of this sort function within society? Emphasis was laid first upon collecting data upon the total socialization process, and then focal points within that process were studied.

This approach grew out of increased emphasis upon personality and culture (Malinowski, 1927a; Frank, 1931, 1938, 1939a; Fromm, 1933; Benedict, 1934a; Mead, 1934a, 1937; Lasswell, 1935; Bateson, 1936; Dubois, 1937a, 1937b; Horney, 1937; Maslow, 1937; Gorer, 1938) and out of an increasing rapprochement between psychoanalytic findings and cultural studies (Mead, 1930a; Glover, 1932; Róheim, 1932, 1934a, 1934b; Dollard, 1935a, 1935b; Horney,

1935; Mekeel, 1935; Opler, 1935; Erikson, 1939; Kroeber, 1939; Lasswell, 1939; Levy, 1939; Kardiner, 1939, 1945; Schilder, 1940). From this type of investigation we may expect data upon the whole socialization process within a given society which are sufficiently precise to give a greater understanding of specific aspects of socialization, such as types of learning (by conditioned reflexes, by "empathy," by different sorts of identification, by dependence upon verbal or nonverbal cues); patterning of interpersonal relationships in preponderantly symmetrical or asymmetrical terms; utilization of biologically given differences, such as sex differences, in building character; cultural patterning of rhythms of growth; minimization or maximization of hereditary defects or special abilities; development and utilization of symbolic forms; orders of congruence between sorts of character structure and politico-economic forms. Even further illumination is to be expected from using a series of such detailed findings in cross-cultural comparisons which will bring out general tendencies; and on the basis of these tendencies hypotheses, later to be tested in other ways, can be formed.

A first attempt at such a study was made in *Cooperation and Competition among Primitive Peoples* (Mead, 1937). Kardiner (1939) using suggestive data upon some of the formal aspects of culture indicated a series of formal ways in which such investigations might proceed. The most complete field work based upon his frame of reference, and upon which he has drawn in his later work (Kardiner, 1945), is that of Cora Dubois (1944). Whiting (1941) made a similar attempt to illustrate by field materials the applications of learning theory developed by Dollard and Miller (1941).

The period just before the war saw the collection of large amounts of field data, much of which will never be fully published, upon which psychologists, or anthropologists working with questions posed by psychologists, or the two working together may test and explore developing hypotheses.

Developments during World War II and the Postwar Period

Anthropological work was even more affected by the war than other disciplines, because field work became impossible in many of the more primitive areas. Since 1940 work has concentrated along two main lines: (1) the application of projective tests and other standardized testing and observational procedures to groups of children in culture contact situations, principally schooled or partially schooled American Indians, and (2) the application of theory based on previous work on primitive children to the new applied field of studies in national character. The most ambitious attempt at the cross-cultural use of projective tests, in mixed teams of anthropologists, clinical psychologists, and educators, was the work of the Indian Education and Administration Research represented in a large number of publications (Eubank, MS; Hallowell *et al.*, MS; Hassrick, MSS; Havighurst, Gunther, and Pratt, 1946; Havighurst and Hilkevitch, 1944; Havighurst and Neugarten, MS; W. E. Henry, 1945, 1947; Joseph, MS; Joseph, Spicer, and Chesky, 1949; Kluckhohn and Leighton, 1946; Leighton with Adair, MS; Leighton and Kluckhohn, 1947; Macgregor, 1946; Mordy, MS; Rannells, MS; Thompson, 1946, 1948, 1950, MS; Thompson and Joseph, 1944, 1947; Underhill, 1942, MSS; Warner, Havighurst, and Eubank, MS) ranging from discussions of the methodology of the cross-cultural use of a particular test (W. E. Henry, 1947) to reports in which the authors' extensive knowledge of a whole culture is integrated with some of the test results (Leighton and Kluckhohn, 1947;

Macgregor, 1946). Specific results of this very ambitious study, which was planned to meet the standards of cross-disciplinary research in child development, have been contributions to our knowledge of the usefulness and range of the tests employed rather than to the development of new conceptual schemes for dealing with the problems of culture change, for which we at present have no conceptual tools (Mead, 1949c). Cultural insights have been channeled back into the world of projective testing, increasing somewhat the possibilities of the inclusion of cultural concepts in the interpretation and use of the tests, but hardly calling into effective question the original culturally limited concepts on which the tests were developed. The unsatisfactory state of the relationship between Rorschachs and cross-cultural uses is summarized by Abel (1948). Individual anthropologists, particularly Hallowell (1941a, 1941b, 1942) and those working with him (Caudill, 1949; Coelho, MS a and drawings; Watrous, MS), have been able to use the lines of communication with clinical thinking to fertilize their thinking in areas where they already had great cultural knowledge, but the use of these methods, with the emphasis on comparability of method rather than upon cultural patterns, has on the whole yielded great masses of data and little theoretical advance.

The field of national character developed as a wartime measure in which methods based on a combination of anthropological field work and clinical research were applied to attempt to delineate the character of enemies, allies, and native populations. A variety of theoretical formulations were developed (Bateson, 1942b; Gorer, 1943; Mead, 1943b, 1946, 1947f; Levy, 1947; Schaffner, 1948; Leites, 1948; Benedict, 1949; Dicks, 1950). All of them involved hypotheses concerning the importance of regularities in methods of child rearing as a clue to the character structure of members of a culture. They all invoked certain theoretical propositions of the order referred to above [1] about the nature of growth; the significance of certain types of communication (Mead, 1949a) between adults and children, such as those involved in feeding, weaning, teaching of control and bodily autonomy, regulation of bodily functions, etc.; and they drew also upon the theoretical work of learning and Gestalt psychologists. These studies have provided a rich body of hypotheses, the most recent of which are embodied in Gorer's set of hypotheses concerning the rôle of the child rearing practices, particularly swaddling, during the first year of life in the formation of the character of Great Russians (Gorer, 1949; Gorer and Rickman, 1949). But essentially this series of studies, even when made upon exotic cultures such as those of Japan, Burma, and Siam, have not been studies of children but rather studies of cultural practice, as reported by adult observers, which involve children, or deductions about childhood experience from the literary and artistic material or from the anamnestic materials of individual adults. This was inevitable given the conditions under which the material was collected, but the research worker is now left with a set of hypotheses concerning childhood hardly underwritten with any observations on the children of the countries to which these hypotheses apply, producing a period historically analogous to the period when Freudian hypotheses about childhood had as yet no supporting data from child analysis. The older workers in the field of national character have all done field work, but there is serious danger that in the absence of field work opportunities a new group of research workers may develop hampered by a lack of background of ob-

[1] See page 739.

servation of children in a genuinely primitive or exotic cultural setting.

The combination of the national character research and the work done with projective methods, as exemplified in such investigations as Columbia University Research in Contemporary Cultures set up by Benedict (La Barre, 1948), opens up again the possibility of combining data on actual childhood behavior with other types of cultural data from arts, myths, religious ceremonials, and dreams, so as to illuminate the way in which preverbal psychological mechanisms continue to operate throughout life. K. R. Stewart's study of primitive dreams (MSS *f*, *g*) which records and analyzes dreams of children and adults in three native cultures—in a society which interdicts the use of dreams, in a society which neglects dreams, and in a society which turns them into instruments of social control—is a significant field addition to this area. Further analyses of prewar field work on adults and children (Bateson and Mead, E; Belo, E; Tschopik, E) may be expected to provide data on this same set of problems.

The most extensive set of interrelated field studies having at their disposal most of the hypotheses developed during the war are those which have been under United States naval auspices in Micronesia (Barnett, 1949, E; Burrows and Spiro, 1953; Gladwin, E; Joseph and Murray, 1951; Lessa, E; Luomala, E; Rauch and Tolerton, E; Schneider, MSS, E; Spiro, MS, E). These studies should be expected to reflect greater theoretical sophistication in new forms of field observations.

The emphasis upon the study of the total socialization process and the investigation of the development of the personality within the whole culture does not obviate the need for precise psychological studies within the primitive societies which will use more controlled methods for the study of small, delimited problems. Without these basic cultural studies, however, the precise investigations are meaningless. The psychologist who used anthropological data in the past was inclined to pick at random illustrative details torn from the context (Miller, 1928) or recorded in the absence of context, or to content himself with insisting that more precise methods should be used without formulating the interrelationships between the problems which the precise methods were to solve and the delineation of the total socialization process (Bartlett, 1937).

Once this is recognized, it will be possible to take more precise psychological methods into the field. For example, in Bali, it may be observed that the incidence of fatigue seems to be much lighter than in other societies. In the absence of other data, for the psychologist to make a precise determination of the degree of fatigue under different sorts of tasks among the Balinese would get us absolutely no further than the original observational statement. It would back up the original observation but would not add any further understanding. However, a study of the total picture in Bali shows: the way in which learning takes place, by direct manipulation of the learner's body or by participation by the carried infant in the rhythm of the mother's acts, by observing what others do, but with a minimum of verbal teaching of any sort; the way in which the child's behavior is controlled by the affectively toned exclamation accompanied by the invocation of one of an assortment of fear symbols—wildcat, witch, scorpion; the way in which gradual detachment from other persons and a decrease in, and finally the disappearance of, bids for personal attention takes place in the Balinese child whose responsiveness is continually played upon by adults and older children; the absence of overt manifestation of guilt or remorse; the high degree of hypochondria, coupled with a great preoccupation in playing upon one's own body; the way in which a craftsman uses only the particular muscles absolutely essential to a given task, so that there is no spread to total involvement; the premium that the Balinese put upon orientation in space, and their objection to drunkenness; their interruptibility and apparent lack of perseveration; the absence of goal-oriented behavior.

When these and a great number of comparable motifs have been identified and documented, the psychologist skilled in the measurement of fatigue could go in and make significant, precise studies of the amount of fatigue shown by the Balinese in various relevant contexts—in the presence of strangers, in a strange environment, under exhortation to make an effort, in dangerous occupations involving a threat of personal injury, when given verbal instruction as compared with a demonstration of the task, etc.—and from such an investigation a real addition to our knowledge of fatigue might be made.

This general principle holds true of all precise measurements of individuals in primitive society; differences in visual acuity are of merely academic interest and lack any theoretical significance unless they can be correlated with a total behavior picture in which they may be shown to play a systematic rôle. Ability to solve a maze, endurance, perseveration, discontinuity of learning, etc., are important to measure if it is possible to show that these identified mental habits have a systematic relationship to the type of character standardized in that particular culture. (For example, K. R. Stewart (MS b) found that Ainu women showed a definite inability to tackle new problems which could be correlated with the special circumstances of older women's social rôle.)

If the field worker is trained in both psychological and ethnological techniques, both aspects can be developed together; the areas in which precise measurement or contrast groups would be useful can be identified in the field, and the necessary tests given. Alternatively, ethnologists in the field can carry out various suggestions given them in consultation with psychologists, either before they set out or, more fruitfully, after they have identified the foci of their problem. Examples of such cooperation are Nadel working with Bartlett's suggestions (Nadel, 1937a, 1937b); Mead working with the Abel Free Design Test (Abel, 1938); J. Henry and Mirsky working in cooperation with Levy (Levy, 1939; J. Henry, 1940a); and, conversely, K. R. Stewart, as a testing psychologist, using techniques of hypnotism, dream analysis, maze testing, Goodenough test, etc., and working with a knowledge of the cultural background provided by Noone (K. R. Stewart, 1951, E); Erikson making his observations among the Sioux with cultural orientation provided by Mekeel (Erikson, 1939) and among the Yurok with cultural orientation provided by Kroeber (Erikson, 1943); and Dennis making extensive use of the manifold published Hopi cultural material (1940b); as well as the extensive team work of the Indian Education and Administration Research (Thompson, 1948).

With the recent elaboration of technique of recording and observing, single-handed field work is becoming steadily less rewarding, and expeditions in which scientists trained in different disciplines cooperate on the spot will have to take the place of the single worker.

Methods of Research

In discussing methods of field research, certain absolute requirements will be taken for granted and not discussed in detail.[1] In the primitive culture studied, the investigator must have an especially detailed knowledge of the data most immediately relevant to childhood: prenatal care, care of children, family structure, children's play patterns, both formal and informal (Mead, 1931; Flannery, 1936), age grades, initiation system, rituals associated with *rite de passage* (Van Gennep, 1909), etc. He must furthermore have a systematic understanding of the whole culture—the sociopolitical system, the economic arrangements, etc.—so as to be able to place this detailed material in its context. Such an understanding can, of course, be gained in several ways: by direct ethnological research, by the use of existing ethnological sources, by cooperation with an ethnologist in the field, or by working with the cooperation and advice of an ethnologist who has been in the field. Work must be done either in the native language or in a contact language in which the children and the investigator have facility (Mead, 1939a). The direct use of an interpreter is not adequate, but educated natives may be used to give tests, record results, etc. The subjects should be known as individuals, so that at no time will an individual's behavior on a test, in a social situation, or as recorded in a photograph have to be interpreted without reference to that individual's known personality and status within the family, the age group, and the community. As most research on primitive children is highly qualitative and utilizes a very limited number of subjects, this condition is not difficult to meet. The research should be done with a closed group, a village, a clan, a locality, a horde, as the case may be, so that the total social situation within which the individuals live can be accurately stated (Moreno, 1934).

<hr/>

[1] For practical consideration, see Mead (1931).

Observations of "forty Indian children gathered from twelve different tribes at a government school," etc., are relatively valueless until an enormous amount of work has been done on the twelve tribes involved, and then it would still be more rewarding to study forty children within one of the twelve tribes.

We may now consider the more specific methods by which children's behavior can be studied and by which the implications of the cultural setting as expressed in the behavior of the growing child can be evaluated.

The Natural History Approach. This method is based upon careful observation of primitive children within ordinary life situations: infants in their mother's arms; siblings struggling over their mother's breasts; children's behavior at the death of a parent or during a quarrel between their parents; behavior of individuals during initiation; etc. In such an approach the investigator is minimally present, effaces himself or his camera as much as possible, and records the surrounding context of behavior as well as the actual behavior. So a struggle witnessed between an old woman and a child, in which the old woman seems to be putting excessive energy into attempting to drag the child with her, is given retrospective illumination by the circumstance of the old woman's death three hours later (Bali). A child's display of fear in the arms of a young girl nurse which is not paralleled by similar behavior in the arms of a different nurse may be placed against the knowledge that the nurse has just quarreled with her guardian and been expelled from the temple society of unmarried girls (Bali). A child who has never been observed refusing food before may suddenly refuse food from his mother with an accompanying temper tantrum. This behavior becomes relevant if the investigator knows that the child was adopted a short time before, had been taught that his mother was not his mother, and that the adoption arrangement had been abruptly terminated the preceding night as a result of a quarrel among the adults (Iatmul).

There are various stages of refinement with which these methods can be used. The records kept may be taken at random whenever significant behavior is observed (Mead, 1928*b*, 1930*b*; Hogbin, 1931; Firth, 1936; Gorer, 1938); a large enough sample of different types of observation—for example, daughters with fathers in mothers' absence, mimetic play immediately following a cultural spectacle, etc.—may be taken at definite intervals (Bateson and Mead, E, for Bali and Iatmul; Brown, E; Kluckhohn, E, for definite periods, once a year). The records themselves may be *retrospective,* that is, written down after the observations have been completed, or *simultaneous.* Simultaneous records may be of many types: running verbal records of behavior (varying in value depending on whether the recorder has to look at the medium of recording, so that writing methods like touch typing and stenotyping are superior to methods of recording which require visual attenton, such as stenography); records made by one observer or by several observers who concentrate on different aspects of the situation and synchronize against a time scale; records made with a parallel still photographic record, varying from illustrative photographs (Figures 1, 2, 3, 4, 5) giving a general setting to a short series of photographs in a sequence (Figure 6); a sequence of photographs taken with a miniature camera permitting more lavish expenditure of film and automatically giving a permanent sequence record (Figure 7); a sequence taken with a rapid winder, presenting a far more detailed record (Figure 8); or a set of stills taken simultaneously with a cinematograph record. Cinematograph records represent the most complete behavioral record (exclusive of sound), and vary in refinement from short Ciné sequences interspersed with verbal records and short Ciné sequences interspersed with verbal and still records through the final refinement of two 16-mm. Ciné cameras, staggered so as to give a complete record.[1]

There are two further possibilities of obtaining photographic records which have not yet been tried out. The first is the use of a motor-driven camera and the inclusion of a sound recording apparatus. Such a method would be very costly and would require three persons, one for the Ciné camera, one for the sound apparatus, and one to keep a verbal situational record which the sound record would not replace. If it were desired to expand in the direction of equipment rather than in the number of investigators, it is probable that a 35-mm. Ciné camera, equipped with a foot release, a device for taking single frames, and an automatic clock device, might permit a single investigator to approximate, but not to equal, the record kept by two investigators, in which one makes the photographic record, the other the verbal.[2]

1 Bateson, Mead, and Belo have experimented with all the various methods described above. Costs of still photographs are enormously reduced by using bulk film and loading it into cassettes in the field, and by supplementing the use of Ciné film by much less expensive series of stills. The use of two Ciné cameras and two miniature cameras makes it possible to record simple behavioral sequences without any break, if it is possible to have an operator for each Ciné miniature pair. This method, however, necessitates *three* observers, for it has been found that even Ciné records are of very limited value without a complete simultaneous verbal record.

2 All records made by more than one observer must be made against a time scale, and all records, even by a single observer, are enormously improved by the use of a time scale, not only for behavioral sequences but also for single bits of behavior observed out of any known context, as the context may later be filled in or the interval before an observed bit of behavior may become significant.

FIGURE 1. Expression of fear of foreigners by Balinese children. Bajoeng Gede, Bali. G. Bateson. Reading from left to right and from top to bottom:

Doemoen, aged ca. 18 months, in her mother's brother's wife's arms. (Dec. 12, 1936. Leica, 3V-34.)

Patera, ca. one year, in his father's arms. (Dec. 8, 1936. Leica, 3T-9.)

Karbo, 310 days old, in his mother's arms. (Dec. 11, 1936. Leica, 3T-34.)

Badera, girl ca. one year, in arms of a neighbor child. (Oct. 10, 1936. Leica, 3A-21.)

FIGURE 2. Contrasting ways of handling children. Reading from left to right and from top to bottom:

Arapesh, New Guinea. Bischu's ca. week-old baby, carried in a net bag, in which the infant's body gets all-round support as *in utero*. (1932. M. Mead.)

Iatmul, New Guinea. Kalugwaimali's 11-day-old infant on mother's outstretched arm. (May 31, 1938. Leica, 23P. G. Bateson.)

Lepchas, Sikkim. Tafoor's two middle daughters. The Lepcha child spends nearly all waking hours securely fastened to the back, in which position it has to yield passively to every move of the carrier. (1937. G. Gorer. [Gorer, 38 Pl. 23.])

Manus, Admiralty Islands. Ngamel's wife with ca. 8-month-old baby on her back. (1929. M. Mead.)

Pilagá, Argentina. Carrying child in sling. (1936–1937. J. Henry.)

Bajoeng Gede, Bali. Lenjad, carrying her 42-day-old infant girl. Balinese babies are suckled in the sling. (May 6, 1937. Leica, 8E-4. G. Bateson.)

FIGURE 3. Contrasting ways of carrying older children. Mandated Territory of New Guinea. Reading from left to right and from top to bottom:

Mundugumor, Sepik-Aitape District. Kwenda. carrying adopted twin girl, ca. 2 years. Child is given no support by woman whose hands hang idle. (1932. M. Mead.)

Tchambuli, Sepik-Aitape District. Woman of Wompun hamlet carrying child in ceremonial dress. No support given by hands of woman. (1933. M. Mead.)

Arapesh, Sepik-Aitape District. Kamawon, ca. 2-year-old girl, on the back of a young girl, Wadjubel. Both of child's legs supported. (1932. R. F. Fortune.)

Manus, Admiralty Islands. Piwen, aged ca. 2½ years, on the back of her father, Luwil, holding on herself. (1929. M. Mead.)

Figure 4. Sleep postures. Iatmul, Balinese, Pilagá, Pitjentara. Reading from left to right and from top to bottom:

Bajoeng Gede, Bali. Kenjoen, 266-day-old baby girl, in arms of elder sister, Gati, aged ca. 5 years. (Dec. 24, 1936. Leica, 3Wa-35. G. Bateson.)

Iatmul, New Guinea. Pulembelua, seated on a log, with her ca. 3-month-old baby girl on her lap. (Oct. 5, 1938. Leica, 32A. G. Bateson.)

Pilagá, Argentina. Child asleep at breast. (1936–1937. J. Henry.)

Pitjentara, Central Australia. Tuma, wife of Kanakana, demonstrating how mothers sleep over their children. (1929. G. Róheim.)

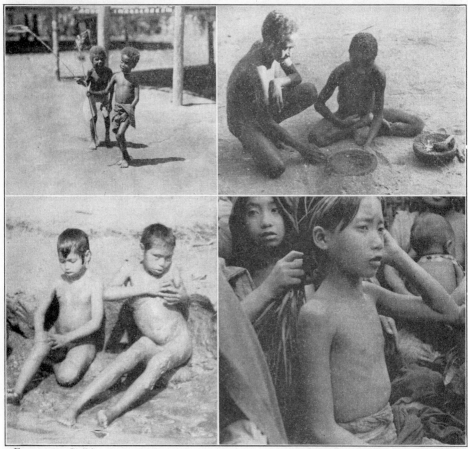

FIGURE 5. Children's symbolic play. Reading from left to right and from top to bottom:

Siwai, Bougainville, Solomon Islands. Girls dancing in imitation of women. (1938–1939. D. Oliver.)

Iatmul, New Guinea. Kowi and Wanggi, boys ca. 12 years old, making play pots by pouring water into mounds of sand. (Aug. 26, 1938. Leica, 29C-45. G. Bateson.)

Pilagá, Argentina. Naicho and Tapeni, girls making themselves clay breasts. (Henry, 1940b.) (1936–1937. J. Henry.)

Bajoeng Gede, Bali. Karni, ca. 10 years, preadolescent girl, with hair still cropped short, wearing false hair made of grass. (April 14, 1937. Leica, 6V-21. G. Bateson.)

FIGURE 6. Child behavior sequences. Reading from left to right and from top to bottom:

Bajoeng Gede, Bali. Raoeh, 312-day-old boy, in mother's arms, while ethnologist medicates his skin. Mother brings child in typical limp fear state; covers his eyes during medication; offers breast to crying child; finally child actively sucks. (Oct. 24, 1936. Leica, 3A-2-5. G. Bateson.)

Pilagá, Argentina. Mother teaching child to walk. Before standing the child up, the mother raises and lowers the baby, never lifting it from the ground, just flexing and unflexing its legs. (1936–1937. J. Henry.)

The most significant cleavage among these methods lies between the *retrospective* and *simultaneous* types of records. As this difference applies both to completely "natural," that is, nonexperimental, situations and to behavior within experimental set-ups, it will be discussed in detail here. Examples of retrospective records are the following:

[Dennis, 1940*b*, p. 145. Observation of 1939 within a contrived set-up among the

Hopi.] Joe seems sleepy and cross. He cries easily. He was sitting on Etta's lap and protested when she tried to get him to sit alone. When he cried, she hugged him and rocked him back and forth. Then she reached to the window and brought along a half-consumed sucker which apparently had been brought along with such a use in view. This quieted him, but he remained on her lap.

[Mead, E 1929. Field notes. Observation in natural set-up on a Manus child,

FIGURE 7. Characteristic teasing situation. Bali. Selection from a sequence of 23 frames (Leica, 5A-3-28), covering about 10 minutes of scenes among wedding guests in Bajoeng Gede. March 1, 1937. G. Bateson. Reading from left to right and from top to bottom:

Karsa, unweaned boy ca. 3 years, crouches laughing behind his mother, Men Singin, who holds her sister's crying baby girl, Meres.

Karsa begins to show anger when his mother gives her breast to the baby.

Mother has returned the baby to her child nurse but is unresponsive to Karsa's continued temper tantrum.

Mother covers her mouth; Karsa still in a temper.

Mother finally picks up Karsa, who pushes her face away.

aged 2½–3 years.] Ponkob, 43–4 (place in numbered households in village census). Ponkob was in a canoe alone, a fairly shallow one, punting. A great pig started to attack the canoe. He screamed with fright, but nevertheless didn't lose his head, and collapsed in the course of their play.] Suddenly, with a shout, Gomma began to scramble off the baobab branch, followed by Zoo, calling out, "Let's swing." For a minute or two they rocked back and forth on the branch and then descended. Now

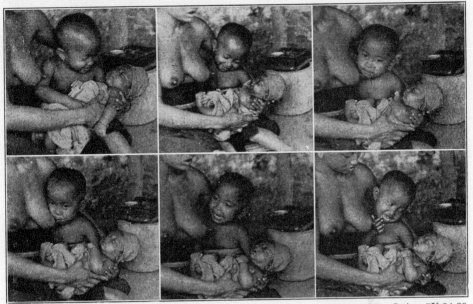

FIGURE 8. Sibling behavior sequence. (Bajoeng Gede, Bali. April 30, 1937. Leica, 7V-34-39. G. Bateson.) Reading from left to right and from top to bottom:

Njawa, girl ca. 3 years, infant brother, aged 30 days, in mother's arms, at a birthday feast for another child. End of a 14-frame sequence. At the beginning of the incident, the mother puts the baby in Njawa's lap, a standard way of making children show off. In the frames shown, the mother's attention wanders and the weaned older child absently steals to the breast, then grins back at the baby.

kept pushing the pig off with his pole and slithering the canoe around for about five minutes. No one came to his aid. Finally the pig gave up, and he, still wailing, made for his house. This happened right behind his own house.

We may compare such records with simultaneous running records of behavior:

[Fortes, 1938, p. 31. Observation of three Tallensi children who had been building a play cattle kraal which had

Gomma remembered his cows. Vehemently he accused his sister of having taken them, and when she denied this challenged her to "swear." "All right," she said placidly. Gomma took a pinch of sand in his left hand and put his right thumb on it. Zoo licked her thumb and pressed down with it on Gomma's thumbnail. He stood still a moment, then suddenly withdrew his thumb. (This is a children's play ordeal.) Gomma examined his sister's thumb and found sand adhering. "There you are," he said, rapping her on the head with a crooked finger.

[E. and P. Beaglehole, 1941. Account of weaning of a Pukapuka child.] Mata, a childless married woman, is minding her sister's baby, William (aged 8 months), for the day, while his mother works in the taro gardens. The child is soon to be weaned and has already started to eat taro and nuts. Mata's keeping the child for the whole day is part of the weaning process. The child gets restless and fretful, so Mata picks it up in her arms and rocks it violently, cuddling it fiercely, bumping it about, and patting it with no gentle hand. To soothe the child further she gives it her dry breast to suck. The baby sucks hard, and then, when he can get no milk, he stands up and suddenly bites Mata's neck. Then he returns to the breast and ends by giving her nipple a severe nip with his teeth. Mata slaps the child on the head. The child cries hard, throws itself about in her lap. It is given some coconut flesh to eat but continues to whimper for some time.

[Mead (Bateson and Mead, E). Field notes. Excerpt from a record called "Karbo and His Parents." Bajoeng Gede, Bali, October 11, 1937. Karbo is 19-months-old; natives speaking Balinese.]

11:32 A.M.
K. comes to step, sits, and wiggles on his bottom.
N. Oera (father of Karbo) rattles some money on the cement.
K. turns and looks at him.
K. drops a piece of banana skin.
K. takes an enormous mouthful (of banana).
N. Oera exclaims in alarm then, "There, chew it."
K. pounds with bracelets on the cement.
K. takes banana and pounds with it.
N. Oera, "Eh! Eh!" (mild exclamation of pain) "Throw it away!"

K. pounds again and throws it away as ordered.
K. pounds another piece.
N. Oera, "Throw it away!"
11:35 A.M.
K. "Away," and throws it away also. (Repeating the last syllable of the Balinese *koetang*, "throw away." This form of syllable clipping is culturally standardized for baby talk, and between intimates.)

A record of this sort can be compared in detail with the following:

[Mead (Bateson and Mead, E). Field notes. Excerpt from "Scaring Children," November 10, 1937, in which Karbo, aged 20 months, is carried by Moespa, a girl of about 11, onto my veranda. Natives speaking Balinese.]

9:50 A.M.
K. reaches toward my papers, out of Moespa's arms.
M., holding him, says, *"Aroh"* (an exclamation of fright or pain), *"aroh,* contains worms."
K. puts a marble into his mouth.
M., "Spit it out. Contains faeces, contains faeces" (omitting the initial *t* in the word *tae,* faeces, standard baby talk).
K. spits it out.
K. puts marble in his mouth again.
I say "Aroh!" as closely imitating Moespa's tone as possible.
K. takes marble out and *then* spits.

We may now consider the advantages of the two types of records. The retrospective type of recording is only as valuable as the questions which were already formulated in the investigator's mind. The investigator selects for later recording certain aspects of the behavior, and later he makes generalizations based upon these illustrations. They may suggest new problems, but they will rarely yield answers to problems which the investigator has not formulated. Therefore, the publication of such protocols, except illustratively to show the type of data used, is hardly justified, in terms of publication costs, because they will already have been squeezed almost dry of theoretical implications. Simultaneous records, on the other hand, although inevitably somewhat affected by the frame of reference also, contain a great deal more spontaneous observation and may yield to analysis and reanalysis not only by the investigator but also by other investigators. Records of this type permit detailed comparisons between many aspects of the behavior of children of the same age, of the same child at different ages, and between children from different cultures. Retrospective recording is an efficient method for solving the negative type of problem which has now been outdated. For the new approach, what we need is a mass of very detailed material about the way in which the individual child develops within his culture; simultaneous records which are ultimately to be made available in full are an absolute requirement.[1]

A further advance in the natural history approach is made when the same situations are recorded for a number of children, for the same child over time, and in different cultures. Advances in this respect have been due to practical considerations which rather limit the number of comparable situations among cultures, for example, bathing a baby, and to theoretical considerations, mainly contributed by various psychoanalytic frames of reference, which have suggested that some situations (suckling, weaning, cleansing after excretion, handling of genitals, sibling rivalry, etc.) were specially significant in the process of character

1 Such records need not necessarily be printed. They may be mimeographed and given a small library circulation, or they may be put on microfilm or microprint. The latter technique, however, is not very fully adapted to methods of detailed cross-comparison between sets of data.

formation and therefore important to observe in detail. Although materials for cross-comparison become immediately much more usable if such standard observations have been made, it is possible to overemphasize the importance of these crucial situations. Erikson's more abstract statement suggests the need for recording tendencies which find many different expressions during the socialization process. Because the simplest way to demonstrate a type of child training is to give a vivid illustration, as Róheim's (1932) illustration of the way in which a Normanby Island mother sings a song as she suckles her child, which is accompanied by pulling the nipple out of the child's mouth at the end of each phrase, it is necessary to guard against the tendency to oversimplify the problem and say that such an experience as this in itself produces the type of character formation observed in the adult (Mead, 1947b).

A more discriminating and accurate way of stating the matter would be to say that in the illustrative incident there are a number of details—for example, the rhythm, the deprivation, the returning of the nipple, etc.—and that of these some one or more are specially significant inasmuch as they are backed up by innumerable other small habitual details of daily life. An identical sort of behavior where, however, it was the rhythm and not the deprivation which was the more typical element, might be found elsewhere, associated with quite different character structure. Similarly, in Iatmul, the nipple is frequently pulled out of the child's mouth in order to transfer the child to the other breast, hoped to contain more milk. Such a deprivation will have a very different effect from that produced by interrupting a child's sucking before it has finished because the mother dislikes suckling, as Mundugumor mothers do (Mead, 1935a). Similarly, in the Iatmul custom by which the mother subjects the child .to a mock weaning, wreathing her nipples with human hair for 15 hours or so, and then going on nursing the child again, until, a month or so later, she finally weans it with a hair wreath, the significant element is the false alarm, which ties up with many other aspects of Iatmul behavior, whereas the use of human hair as a weaning mechanism, although found in many societies, has no very important tie-up in Iatmul.

If we emphasize too heavily a formal set of data, on suckling, weaning, sphincter control, etc., some of the most important nuances are likely to be lost. So, while continuing to collect as much material on these standard situations as possible, in order to assure comparable masses of data, we need to make simultaneous, detailed, and, if possible, multiple-observer and multiple-technique records of large sequences of behavior in normal situations. Such sequences will be valuable in direct proportion to their length, continuity, and the amount of detail recorded. From long records of the interactions of about three human beings in a culturally natural context we may be able to answer great numbers of questions not yet formulated; we can attack such points as cadence and tempo of behavior, proportion of symbolic to nonsymbolic activity at different age levels, and the sequence in which one type of activity is substituted for another.

Recording of Verbal Behavior. The various American schools of anthropology and the Malinowski school have all insisted upon the value of collecting ethnological materials in text, that is, literally recorded in the native language. Text collection has usually been regarded as a corrective for overenthusiastic interpretation, and very little emphasis has been given, except by Malinowski (1935, Vol. II), to the extent

to which a record of words spoken in sequence is a record of behavior. Even without a photographic record of the posture of the individual, and with no formal system for recording tone of voice, large masses of spoken or written (where writing has been introduced) comment from native children is an especially usable form of data.

[Mead, E, 1928–1929. Field notes. Monologue—directed toward the investigator—of a Manus girl, Kawa, aged 4–5 years. February 19, 1929.]

I am called [i.e., someone is calling me].

My tobacco is in the box of Kopal.

There is no paper, but someone will get some in the house of mourning.

Give me some paper to smoke.

Pwailep is at the house of Katu.

Pwailep is the niece [*kaka,* literally, sister's daughter].

Ponap and Posuman have gone to work for the white man.

Topal [her brother] wants to take my tobacco to the Usiai [members of another tribe with whom the Manus trade].

[Someone calls.]

We have no food, it is all in the bush [i.e., not yet traded for].

The ghosts are about. [There has been a death in the village, and the presence of inimical ghosts makes going about, and trading, dangerous.]

We haven't a big canoe.

Ngawa wants to go to make a ceremonial exchange in Dropal.

Do you want to buy it?

[I say "What?"]

Some paper. My tobacco is in the box of Kandra in our [exclusive possessive pronoun] house.

It is also possible to get children from about 9 years to adolescence to dictate material, sometimes quite lengthy texts.

[Mead, 1928b. Portraits of themselves dictated in Samoan by two adolescent girls. 1926.]

I am a girl. I am short. I have long hair. I love my sisters and all the people. I know how to weave baskets and fishing baskets and how to prepare paper mulberry bark. I live in the house of the pastor [p. 255].

I am clever at weaving mats and fine mats and baskets and blinds and floor mats. I go and carry water for all my household to drink and for others also. I go and gather bananas and breadfruit and leaves and make the oven with my sisters. Then we [herself and her sisters] go fishing together, and then it is night [p. 256].

[Bateson (Bateson and Mead, E, Iatmul, 1938). Field notes. Informant Kowi, boy, aged 12. October 22, 1938. In the presence of Mbetna, aged 14.] In the Agamora Reach [of the river] there she went to *undumbu* [Land of the Dead], they took her. They brought [her] to the village. Having put [her] in the house, they wept. Then "turn pancakes" when he had said and looked [and there were none], he hit [her with] adze. Here [holding his own wrist] the spirits put her heart he hit her. She went to *undumbu*. They wept for her. What [shall I say now]? In the morning, going in the top of a malay apple tree he went and hung himself. He —first having tied it badly he fell. Having fallen with a good rattan having tied it he fell. He hanged. Djaneimbuangga [and] Ambwanembindo undid him. They buried him.

Text records of conversations between children and parents, or between children, are also much more valuable than translations, but the problem of getting down more than brief exchanges is very great, whereas in dictated texts or slow, dreamy monologues the recorder has a chance to keep up with the child.

[Mead, E, Manus, 1928-1929. Field notes. Conversation between Kawa, girl, aged 4-5, and Tjokal, boy, aged 11-12, immediately following the monologue recorded above. February 19, 1929.]

Tj. Kawa, your father is calling you.
K. I have no canoe.
Tj. The child-of-Ngandiliu has one, go on.
Tj. [To me.] Her father is calling her. He says: "This evening all the ghosts will emerge."
[Kawa comes back.]
K. We haven't any food in our house. They didn't go to the bush. Tomorrow we'll go.

The Cross-Section Method. The investigator of primitive children is usually limited to a brief period, seldom exceeding a year, and if he wishes to describe the way in which children develop within that culture he must perforce use the cross-section method, that is, construct a picture of the total socialization process by reference to the observed behavior of groups of children at each age level. Many criticisms of the limitations of the cross-section method as it applies specifically to the study of the individual, culturally seen, have been made (Mead, 1928b, pp. 261–262; Dollard, 1935b, p. 4; E. and P. Beaglehole, 1941). Supplemented by the *retrospective* and the *simultaneous* (see below) life history, however, cross-sectional methods are likely to remain one of the principal standbys for the study of children in other cultures. Two methodological devices can increase their usefulness. The first of these is maximum and detailed attention given to the behavior of individuals in periods of maturation, *defined as transitional* for purposes of the investigation. So, if the adolescent girls have been classified by the usages of the culture or by the investigator into groups of preadolescent, adolescent, and postadolescent, there will be certain individuals who stand conspicuously, in physique or behavior or status, whatever the criteria are, at transitional points. The task of the investigator will then be to define the central tendencies in the group which the transition individuals are on the point of leaving and the central tendencies in the group toward which the transition individuals are moving. These individuals will then be observed in the greatest detail, and every alteration or variance of behavior relevant to the defined behavior of the two groups will be recorded, analyzed, and subjected to immediate scrutiny in terms of situational, constitutional, or social-structure factors which might make it atypical.

This transitional behavior will furthermore be utilized to get introspective comments from the preadolescents and adolescents about the behavior, and to get the adults to make retrospective and valuational comments of the order of "I remember when I reached menarche, my mother said . . . ," and "She is just about to reach menarche; she should stop dancing," or "Yes, he refused to carry her even though she had a sore foot because he is not *sapta*" (brave enough to raise a momentarily nubile girl above his shoulder). A year usually provides enough time to study a significant number of transitional cases, whether it be a suckled child through weaning to postweaning, a child with an unpregnant mother through the mother's recognition that she is pregnant, a child with all milk teeth through loss of several milk teeth, a child who is still too young to go anywhere alone through the period when he is entrusted with his first older-boy tasks, etc.

The second method, invented by Lasswell (1937), requires a greater refinement of data and knowledge of age level than are usually available in a small primitive group. It might, however, be applicable to an alien culture with a large population, if the observer had a limited amount of time but almost unlimited resources for observation. By this method the observer keeps under simultaneous observation, in terms of a detailed schedule of behavior items, a series of overlapping age or status groups, so that the transition from *a* to *b* to *c* is recorded for two different groups, when the group in stage *a* is entering *b*, and when the group in stage *b* is entering stage *c*. The detailed utilization of this method is dependent upon knowledge of age of subjects or the substitution of some physiological criteria which are systematically related to behavior, for example, classification according to change of voice in one culture or height in another. Criteria other than age are difficult to handle cross-culturally but would not detract from the adequacy of the method within a given culture. In a general way this method may be utilized in any cross-section study of individuals in a living culture and provides the technique for correcting any error which may come from observing individuals from one point of view; it avoids, for instance, the group in period *b* being thought of more in terms of having left period *a* than as approaching period *c*.

Other Methods Which Can Be Combined with Cross-Section Studies. The field worker is always under far greater pressure than the psychological investigator working within our society. He usually has a definite and very inadequate time allowance; he is working in the medium of a foreign language with subjects unaccustomed to any sort of routine or discipline; and even if the main outlines of the culture are known he has to pay constant attention to the unraveling of the cultural implications of the simplest acts. Furthermore, a great deal of time has to go to subsistence and supporting activities: buying food, medical care of the natives, maintaining rapport, etc. Any techniques which can short-cut this problem are doubly useful.

I shall discuss four: Fortune's handling of *events,* my own method of utilizing the *deviant case,* an adaptation of Levy's method of *pure cases,* and Wolfenstein's method of *paired child-parent interviews.* In the use of *events,* extensively developed by Fortune (1935) and also reported in my Arapesh diary (Mead, 1947a), events of a certain type—illness, misfortunes, quarrels, etc.—are taken as focusing points for the study of the behavior of all individuals involved in that particular situation. This method, applied to the study of children, means that at the end of a field trip one would have a systematic account of the behavior of children of given age and sex when confronted with comparable situations within their households, such as births, death, quarrels, and major *rite de passage* ceremonials. If this method is to be used systematically, a type of event must be chosen which is likely to occur often enough to provide a real sample; for example, quarrels would be a suitable selection for a 6-month investigation among the Iatmul, but no large sample of quarrels could be obtained in a 2-year study of Bali.

In my method of the *deviant case,* individuals who vary from the observed norm, owing to either environment or personality, are selected for study. These cases are analyzed in terms of generalizations already made about the group behavior and the factors identified as significant. For example, individuals from biological families are analyzed to show whether hypotheses made about the influences of large households can be supported (Mead, 1928b, pp. 141–143); or single cases of early weaning are examined to see what light they throw on the rôle of late weaning (Mead, 1935a, p. 38); or the behavior of little boys whose fathers are dead is examined in cultures where the father plays an important part

in education (Mead, 1930b, pp. 112–116). Then, as a related method, deviations in behavior, such as the individual child who has temper tantrums beyond the customary age limit (Mead, 1935a, p. 51) or the girl who bursts out with a suicidal wish at a funeral ceremony in a society where all such outbursts of emotion are disallowed (Bateson and Mead, 1942) or the child who steals in a society where stealing is most unusual (Mead, 1928b, pp. 178–180), are analyzed to discover what elements in the social background or experience of the individual may explain the behavior. The fullest published material on cases of this latter sort is that of J. Henry (1940b), in which three Pilagá children who refused to speak were analyzed to show the emotional deprivation which the children had undergone. A final use of deviant cases is the study of the behavior of individuals whose personality approximates least accurately the type approved by the group for the given age and sex, as a device for illuminating the functioning of the more successfully acculturated individuals (Mead, 1935a).

Levy (1938–1939), in his method of *pure cases,* selects from a large set of full case records a series of cases, all meeting several hypothetically significant criteria, and then analyzes these cases in detail to show a pattern of interaction between the developing personality and the social environment. This method can be applied in the field by making the criteria of "purity" a series of items of conformance to the cultural ideal, for instance, or of conformance to the statistical norm. So a series of cases which are "pure" because they are ideal, or "pure" because they are statistically usual, could be analyzed to show what sort of personality develops under the circumstances which the culture postulates, and under those which actually obtain in the culture. For the Mountain Arapesh, for instance, this would mean studying a series of children from families where the father and mother had been betrothed in childhood, the mother had grown up in the father's parents' home, there had been no other wife, and both father and mother were mild personalities; these would be the pure cases of the cultural ideal. Such a series could be set against children in homes where there were two wives, at least one of whom had not been "grown" by the husband during a child betrothal, which is the statistically usual condition.

Wolfenstein (1946) has developed a method of *paired parent-child interviews,* in which a parent and one or more children are either interviewed along carefully paralleled lines or subjected to the same sort of evocative material, such as a story. This method further localizes the mass of observational data in a situational context and makes it easier to separate out behavior which should be referred to "family culture" or—in dealing with modern ethnic groups within a complex society—to "home ways" (Mead, 1944b) characteristic of subcultural groups within a wider culture. Although an informal use of this method has characterized most field work on primitive peoples, as the field worker inevitably worked with families, it meets many of the requirements, specifically emphasized by Lasswell, for a more precise definition of the observational situation.

The Life History. The significance of the life history in the study of the development of personality within a cultural setting has been most fully stated by Dollard (1935b). Kluckhohn (Gottschalk, Kluckhohn, and Angell, 1945) has systematically discussed the variety of methods used, and I have outlined a further set of problems in my record of the verbal productions of one Arapesh informant (Mead, 1949e). The most satisfactorily annotated published life history of a member of a living native culture is Gorer's life of Kurma (1938).

Radin's *Crashing Thunder* (1926) is still a classic in this field.

It is usual to characterize the life history approach as dynamic and involving time as an active dimension, and the cross-section approach as static, but actually the use of transitional cases in cross-sectional studies shows the individual acting in time, whereas time is merely an implied dimension when the individual relates past events as they appear to him in the present. Life histories may be distinguished in respect to what point in the individual's life is taken as the focus. In the *retrospective* life history, or autobiography, adults relate the story of their lives as they now appear to them; in the *simultaneous* life history a section of the life of an individual capable of introspective comment is recorded, both in terms of actual events and of the individual's comment upon those events. Parallel with this utilization of introspection are *longitudinal* methods, designed especially for the study of young children, in which the behavior of individuals is observed over a period of time or tests are applied at stated intervals with wide gaps throughout a period of development.

Much has been claimed for the *retrospective technique* as restoring the organic locus to the study of personality. It is undeniable that an adult's account of his early memories and childhood experiences furnishes valuable data on the way in which adults see childhood experience, their own and other peoples'. However, these are essentially data upon how the narrator feels and what significance those experiences have for him in the present, not data upon his actual development in the past. This distinction has been lost sight of because for therapeutic purposes a false memory is often as good as a real one. When our object is the study of the growth of personality, data derived from these introspective accounts must be taken with the greatest caution. This is particularly so when the material is gleaned from the memories of survivors of an earlier cultural era and there are no living children against whose experiences these memories can be checked (Eastman, 1902; Michelson, 1918–1919, 1932, 1933; Radin, 1926; Linderman, 1930, 1932; K. R. Stewart, 1951; Devereux, 1937; Landes, 1938).

The survivors of an earlier period may well give a record of their childhood training which jibes perfectly with the data they give on their attitudes as young men and women, with their accounts of cultural values and emphases, and with their present attitudes toward life. There is, however, no guarantee that this internal consistency has not been imposed by the narrators upon the actual facts of their experience; and, whereas consistency among a large number of unrelated observations on individuals of different ages within a living society can be regarded as strengthening the presumption of accuracy for any one observation (if the observations are of such an order that the coherence which might be introduced by the investigator can be ruled out, as in, for example, myths, formal rituals, literal texts, and photographic records), such consistency in retrospective life histories is not of any such value.

The only circumstance under which life histories from members of broken cultures, unsupported by any observational data, can be of value is when there are several histories, with systematic differences among them and sufficient data about the personalities of the narrators so that some day these personalities may be placed in a theoretical frame of reference and we may be able to say, "The formal culture, as seen through the eyes of three individuals of type x, two of type y, three of type z, etc., appears to be of type x, and the differences in the versions given by the various narrators confirm this hypothesis." It is prob-

able that by the time that we know enough to make any such systematic statement we shall not need to reconstruct the childhood experience of members of cultures for which only this very limited kind of data is available. Because there is a possibility that we might need it, however, investigators are urged to get as many data as possible on the present personality of their informants (including moving pictures showing posture and gesture, or at least long continuous portrait sequences; literal records of responses to situations which can be standardized for all informants; disease pictures, if any; performance on projective methods such as the Rorschach).

In the meantime, retrospective life histories are useful mainly in the study of the parents of children who are also being studied, and they may throw valuable light upon the way in which the child's behavior is being interpreted and reacted to by the parent. They are especially valuable if the informants combine memories of their own past with a running comment upon their children's present behavior and if such records can then be put beside observational records of the children's behavior. Children's own accounts of their pasts are even more valuable.

However, such records as these become, in effect, what I propose to call *simultaneous* life histories, in which the emphasis is on the individual's comment, whether it includes retrospective material or not, upon current events, the substance of which is known to the investigator. If such records stretch over several months and are carefully correlated with events in the real life situation, very valuable data can be obtained on the behavior of parents and also on informants' own behavior when the material is gathered from adults' memories combined with their present behavior and comments on that behavior by adolescents and young children. This method was extensively pursued among the Iatmul. Such simultaneous life histories can be continually checked against the events which have stimulated the memories,[1] and the memories themselves can be compared with other individuals' memories of the same event and with the way in which similar situations are being handled in the lives of contemporary children. So an adult's comment on his own adoption, made at a time when he is giving back, in a fit of petulance, a name owned by his adoptive father, may be placed against the actual circumstances under which a child of 3 is at the moment being adopted.

Longitudinal Studies. It is generally recognized that all the above methods—crosssectional studies and various types of life history techniques—are imperfect compromises and substitutes for the on-going life history in which the course of individual lives would be recorded, within the full social setting, from infancy to maturity. The Beagleholes are committed to the absolute necessity of such a measure and, on the basis of a 7½-month study of Pukapuka children (E. and P. Beaglehole, 1941a), assert that, no matter how great the mass of data accumulated in a short-time study, these data cannot be interpreted without a study of selected children over a longer period. I have just completed a study in which I followed a series of Balinese mountain children over a period of a year, with some interruptions over a second 9 months, and during a check-up visit a year later, so that there are records of their behavior over a period of 33 months. Placing the

data of this study against intensive crosssectional studies made in four other cultures, I do not find that the advantages of a longitudinal study are anything like those which the Beagleholes predicted. There is obviously a richer body of material collected over 33 months than over periods of 7 to 9 months (the periods of the other studies), and for purposes of exposition it is useful to be able to show a film of a 33-month spread in the same child's life. An analysis (Mead and Macgregor, 1951) of a longitudinal series of 4000 still photographs of eight Balinese children in terms of the Gesell-Ilg concepts has demonstrated that longitudinal studies, by defining each observed type of behavior in reference to a given individual, increase the certainty with which hypotheses can be constructed. If the proper checks are used in the crosssectional method, as outlined above, and the field worker has a theoretical framework within which individual behavior can be translated into an understanding of the dynamics of socialization, the increased insight to be derived from work in two cultures, rather than from the time spent on a longitudinal study of one, is usually more rewarding. To obtain material from a longitudinal study which will justify the time spent, observations of great precision, of which the most important is either a knowledge of chronological age or detailed physical records of dentition, pubescence, etc., are needed.

Kluckhohn (1939; and Leighton and Kluckhohn, 1947), working on the same assumption as the Beagleholes, has followed the same group of Navaho children over a period of 13 years with consistent observations at intervals of 6 months (except during the war period). For the success of such a plan, consistency and objectivity of records, holding the rôle of the observer constant, and not too great cultural change are all desirable and difficult to attain.

---

[1] This method was used by Gorer (1938, p. 403) in checking on Kurma's belief, not shared by the rest of the group, that his brother had been murdered. The excerpt from Bateson's notes on Kowi's account of his father's suicide (see p. 759) is taken from a check series of eighteen accounts of a suicide in Iatmul, in which the fourteen lengthy and detailed versions fail to agree upon any point except the fact that the man killed his wife and hanged himself, after the rope broke once.

Projective Methods. Projective methods are a suitable form of test for use in the study of primitive children, and the results are excellent expository devices. The general discussions of projective methods (Homburger, 1937; Lerner, 1937a; Frank, 1939b) have to be supplemented by a few further remarks when the methods are to be used not primarily to study children as individuals but to throw light upon cultural processes (Abel, 1948). The projective techniques should be as free from culturally limiting elements as possible. For example, Stewart's metal maze tests (K. R. Stewart, MS d) are less culturally limited than is the Porteus maze test; and the Goodenough "draw-a-man" test, administered flexibly, is more useful than forcing children to draw a white man so as to make it possible to score it. Methods which do not require isolation of the subject are preferable to those that do, for any method, such as Levy's sibling rivalry test, which requires privacy will be definitely ruled out for some cultures. Surprise and bizarre elements are undesirable because the news of the tests will be spread too rapidly through the group, and standards of behavior will be imaginatively elaborated outside the test situation. Tests which require complicated but recordable responses will be valuable in proportion to the amount of response they elicit; tests to which motor responses are important should be avoided unless they can be given in front of a camera, as our vocabulary for describing motor responses is not capable of any sort of cross-cultural accuracy.

At the same time, the simpler the situation to which the children are asked to respond, the more probability there is that the responses will reveal a high proportion of cultural patterning. For example, in the use of toys a small series permits a great number of repeats as every child is likely to use all three or four of the toys presented; a large assortment permits each child to make an idiosyncratic choice, and the underlying pattern is less apparent. As the number of cases will always be few, any test which encourages range is more difficult to deal with. It is also desirable to eliminate tests in which the prompting given by the experimenter is stereotyped.[1] Some projective methods, like the Rorschach, depend for their interpretation upon the compiling of cultural norms for age and sex groups.[2]

The use of projective tests in which a verbal response is expected as in the Rorschach (Abel, 1948) and the Thematic Apperception Test (W. E. Henry, 1947) is less rewarding than the use of tests such as drawing tests, Margaret Lowenfeld's World Test, or her Mosaic Test, in which the actual construction of the child can be kept or reproduced. All tests involving verbal responses introduce misunderstanding by the translation of multidimensional nonverbal thinking into words, by the translation of the words into another language, and, when culturally limited concepts have been incorporated into the method of scoring or interpretation, through the further complication of inapplicable clinical concepts.

Caution must also be observed in interpreting as validation of clinical concepts developed within our own culture what simply amounts to the fact that when field

[1] In giving the Weigl test to Balinese boys, Belo followed the prescribed procedure and stopped the test when they had sorted for form and content, these being the two usual responses for individuals in our society. A later analysis of test results showed that many Balinese used other categories, such as position, and place in a color pattern, as categories of equal importance with form and color, so that, in stopping the test when form and color had been sorted for, a culturally limited "right answer" had been forced upon the subjects.

[2] Doctor Dubois tells me that the analysis of her series of thirty Rorschachs, all on adults, shows this number to be insufficient, and that the collection of Rorschachs on children, when the adult standards are not known, would not in the opinion of her consultants be rewarding.

workers from our culture, making judgments on the "hostility" or "aggressiveness" of a primitive people, agree with a blind analysis made by a Rorschach specialist they are merely demonstrating the fact that Rorschach indicators and other behavioral indicators, when observed in another cultural system, by research workers with the same cultural frame of reference, will be interpreted the same way.

Useful projective methods may be classified by the type of response permitted by the experimental situation, varying from the presentation of a simple situation in which responses are recorded (for example, Japanese paper flowers which open in water, Mead, 1932) through stylized situations, of which the Levy sibling rivalry test is the best example (Levy, 1939; J. Henry, 1940a), to free play with a series of toys.[1]

Children's drawings are perhaps one of the most generally usable projective materials (Figure 9). They are the simplest to collect. It is necessary to keep a record of the composition of each drawing group, the date, the sequence of sheets if a child does more than one, and interpretations, either spontaneously given or systematically elicited. However, the bulk of the data is provided by the children's work, which can be analyzed at leisure out of the field. The material, if white paper and a black pencil or crayon are used, is easily reproduced and very comparable from culture to culture. To make any use of such material, further than to say that each set of drawings betrays a definite style [which shows up sharply in K. R. Stewart's (MS a) enormous collection of Goodenough drawing tests from different tribes], it is necessary

to have a proper record of the adult art style and particular knowledge of the children's own art styles as portrayed in sand drawings, mud sculpture, scratching on walls, etc. With such a collection of drawing types, more positive problems can be attacked than the old biogenetic theory permitted. (Relationship of children's drawings to this theory is summarized in Hallowell, 1939. Compare also Anastasi and Foley, 1936; Schubert, 1930; and Dubois, 1944, Appendix.)

Examples of such problems are the extent to which personalization is characteristic of the children's thought (Mead, 1932), the formation of style (Mead, E; Belo, 1937), emotional attitudes (K. R. Stewart, E, drawings of dreams; Mead, E, "draw a man and woman"), and the identification of basic patterns of symbolism. The contrast between drawings by Balinese and Iatmul children is extremely interesting in this connection. The Balinese way of life is exceedingly formal, stereotyped, and static; interpersonal relations are conducted with a minimum of emotional expression, the minutiae of etiquette govern every act; Balinese children's drawings are full of activity, with free-flowing lines and the depiction of vigorous movement. The Iatmul way of life is in the strongest contrast to the Balinese. Interpersonal relations of great vigor and assertiveness are the rule, quarrels and reconciliations a continual feature of village life. The Iatmul children's drawings, however, are static and scattered aimlessly over the page; there is no movement and no relationship between one design element and another; when told to draw two men fighting they would draw a figure of a man and say, "He is dead." When it is realized that Balinese children are persistently discouraged when they attempt to bring human relations to a climax, whereas Iatmul children are taught to exert maxi-

---

1 In visual terms, these types of specificity are represented by picture interpretation (Mead, 1928a), by the setting of a problem [Draw something you are afraid of (K. R. Stewart, E); draw a man killing a man (Mead, E)], or by cutting the drawing paper to specified shapes (Mead, 1940b), or by permitting the children to draw whatever they like.

FIGURE 9. Children's drawings showing stylistic differences. Reading from left to right and from top to bottom:

Iatmul tribe, Sepik-Aitape District, New Guinea. Man, woman, and animal figures. Gambu-kundiavwan, boy, ca. 12 years. (July 28, 1938. Collected by M. Mead.)

Arapesh tribe, Sepik-Aitape District, New Guinea. Human beings, lizards, trees, houses, moon and stars. Nigimarib, boy, ca. 7 years. (April 4, 1932. Collected by M. Mead.)

Manus, Admiralty Islands, New Guinea. Fishing for turtle from a European schooner. Loponiu. (February 24, 1929. Collected by M. Mead.)

Sajan village, Bali. Two figures from shadow play. I Gandir, boy, ca. 6 years. (1934. Collected by J. Belo.) (Belo, 1937.)

mum personal pressure in order to induce others to satisfy their demands, the importance of these materials becomes evident.[1]

[1] Iatmul children's use of toys in free play is congruent. They construct tableaux and state, for example, that "The snake has killed the child [a female]. The 'possum [who represents the male child] has killed the snake, and the 'possum now mourns [a female activity] over the dead child."

Extensive use of play technique among primitive peoples was first made by Róheim among the Central Australians and on Normanby Island; he found the Australian children dominantly interested in genital play, the Normanby Islanders in mother-child play in which the same characters become alternately mother and child and husband and wife. Róheim, however, controlled the plot of his play situations by interjecting such remarks as "What does the husband do to the wife?" I have used toys among the Iatmul, and J. and Z. Henry (1944) have published a most extensive record for the Pilagá.

All attempts to use projective techniques will be fruitful to the extent that the attention of the invesigator is focused upon the rôle of the culture. He should not merely look for isolated types of behavior similar or different from our own in situations which are experimentally controlled but should try to see the behavior as part of the culture pattern.

Future Research

The general trends in research among primitive children have already been indicated above as being (1) increased emphasis upon the study of the developing child within the culture seen as a whole; (2) possibilities for detailed psychological exploration of aspects of development which a preliminary study of the total situation has shown to be relevant; and (3) accumulation of masses of simultaneous records, verbatim accounts of behavior, photographic records, multiple-observer records, performance on tests of the projective type, etc., which will be amenable to subsequent analysis as our hypotheses become more refined. If problems are to be taken into the field, they should be problems of the constellative type rather than problems which seek to isolate the effects of one factor. The large amount of existing unpublished material on primitive children, some of which is summarized in the table below, provides another source for research. Psychologists may phrase their problems in such a way that field workers may be able to provide relevant material from their existing notes.[1] Nothing, however, is so pressing as more intensive detailed studies of the development of children in living primitive societies. These data are invaluable in extending our knowledge of the possible range of human behavior. Only with this sort of material can we lay the foundations of a psychology free from the limitations of our own cultural bias; and, once the few surviving primitive societies have yielded to culture contact, we shall have no possible way of replacing them.

Work for this revised chapter was begun January, 1949, and completed in early June, 1949. No subsequent additions to the text have been made, so that it describes the state of theory and research at that time. The few bibliographical items bearing a more recent date than June, 1949, are simply those that were in manuscript or in press at the time this chapter was revised and have since been published.

Bibliography

Prefatory Note

Publications in anthropology differ from publications in psychology, where short, formal summaries of masses of concrete observations are the acceptable form for presenting detailed investigations to the student. In anthropological research, a full account of the background against which the individual is studied cannot be omitted in a final statement of the material, and publication is delayed until facilities for complete monograph publication are available. As a result, a large part of the work, sometimes done as much as ten years earlier, may still be unpublished. I have therefore adopted a procedure rather different from that used in other chapters and attempted to gather, by inquiries and questionnaires, material on unpublished work.

Manuscripts to which I have had access are listed in the regular bibliography. Field work on children upon which there are no publications has been listed as Expeditions (E) under the name of the field worker. As an appendix to the bibliography, I have presented a summary table of the information which has been supplied to me in response to these requests. Where the information which I have received is merely that a given worker has used such and such a method in such and such a tribe, but no manuscript or supporting evidence has been forwarded to me, I can only publish this statement without taking any responsibility for the extent and

[1] See Introduction to *Cooperation and Competition among Primitive Peoples* (Mead, 1937) for discussion of this point.

fullness of the results. By including this list of unpublished materials and completed but unorganized field work, I hope to encourage the use of these materials by workers interested in collecting as much comparative material as possible.

Abel, T. M. 1938. Free designs of a limited scope as a personality index. *Character and Pers.*, 7, 50–62.

——. 1948. The Rorschach test in the study of culture. *Rorschach Res. Exch.*, 12, 79–93.

Aberle, D. F. 1951. *The psychosocial analysis of a Hopi life-history.* Compar. Psychol. Monogr., Vol. 21 (Serial No. 107). Berkeley and Los Angeles: University of California Press.

Aginsky, B. W. (E) Skokomish, Pomo.

Anastasi, A., and J. P. Foley, Jr. 1936. An analysis of spontaneous drawings by children of different cultures. *J. Appl. Psychol.*, 20, 689–727.

——. 1938. A study of animal drawings by Indian children of the North Pacific coast. *J. Soc. Psychol.*, 9, 363–374.

Arkin, E. A. 1935. The child and its toy in primitive culture. (In Russian.) Moscow: Zentralny Institut Ochrany Zdorovya Detyei i Podrostkov.

Asch, S. E. 1936. MS. *The social life of the Hopi child.* Address: Swarthmore College, Swarthmore, Pa.

Barnes, F. 1949. The birth of a Ngoni child. *Man*, 49, 87–89.

——. (E) Fort Jameson Ngoni, Northern Rhodesia, 1946–1947. Address: The Close, Headley, Newbury, Berkshire, England.

Barnett, H. G. 1949. *Palauan society.* Eugene: University of Oregon Publications. Chapter V.

——. (E) Palau Islands, 1947–1948. Address: University of Oregon, Eugene, Oregon.

Barnouw, V. 1949. The phantasy-world of a Chippewa woman. *Psychiatry*, 12, 67–76.

——. 1950. Acculturation and personality among the Wisconsin Chippewa. *Mem. 72, Amer. Anthrop. Ass.*

Bartlett, F. C. 1937. Psychological methods in anthropological problems. *Africa* (London), 10, 400–420.

Barton, R. F. 1938. *Philippine pagans: The autobiographies of three Ifugaos.* New York: Routledge.

Bataille, G. 1930. L'art primitif. *Documents*, 7, 389–397.

Bateson, G. 1936. *Naven.* Cambridge: University Press.

——. 1941. The frustration-aggression hypothesis and culture. (Contribution to the symposium on the effects of frustration. Eleventh Annual Meeting, Eastern Psychological Association, April 5, 1940.) *Psychol. Rev.*, 48, 350–355.

——. 1942a. Social planning and the concept of "deutero-learning." In L. Bryson and L. Finkelstein (Eds.), *Science, philosophy and religion* (second symposium), pp. 81–97. New York: Conference on Science, Philosophy and Religion (Country Life Press, Garden City, L. I.).

Bateson, G. 1942b. Morale and national character. In G. Watson (Ed.), *Civilian morale* (Second Yearbook of the Society for the Psychological Study of Social Issues), pp. 71–91. New York: Houghton Mifflin.

——. 1944. Cultural determinants of personality. In J. McV. Hunt (Ed.), *Personality and behavior disorders*, Vol. II, Part V (Determinants of personality—experimental and sociological), pp. 714–736. New York: Ronald Press.

——. 1946. Physical thinking and social problems. *Science*, 103, 717–718.

——. 1947. Sex and culture. *Ann. N. Y. Acad. Sci.*, 47, Art. 5 (Physiological and psychological factors in sex behavior), 647–660.

——. 1949. Bali: The value system of a steady state. In M. Fortes (Ed.), *Social structure: Studies presented to A. R. Radcliffe-Brown*, pp. 35–53. Oxford: Clarendon Press.

Bateson, G., and M. Mead. 1942. *Balinese character: A photographic analysis.* New York: New York Academy of Sciences (Special Publications, Vol. II).

——. (E) Iatmul, New Guinea, 1938; Bali, 1936–1938, 1939.

Beaglehole, E. 1940. Psychic stress in a Tongan village. *Proc. 6th Pacific Sci. Cong.*, 4, 43–52.

——. 1941. Interpersonal theory and social psychology. *Psychiatry*, 4, 61–77.

——. MS. *Aitutaki, Cook Islands: Anthropological and psychological problems.*

Beaglehole, E., and P. Beaglehole. 1941a. Personality development in Pukapukan children. In L. Spier, A. I. Hallowell, and S. S. Newman (Eds.), *Language, culture, and personality*, pp. 282–298. Menasha, Wis.: Sapir Memorial Publication Fund.

——. 1941b. Pangoi, village in Tonga, *Polynesian Soc. Mem.*, 18, 78–88.

——. 1946. *Some modern Maoris.* Wellington: New Zealand Council for Educational Research, pp. 117–178.

——. (E) New Zealand Maori, 1942, 1943, 1944; Aitutaki (Cook Islands), 1948; Samoa, 1949. Address: Victoria University, Wellington.

Beaglehole, P. 1935. Notes on personal development in two Hopi villages. *Mem. Amer. Anthrop. Ass.*, 44, 25–65.

Belo, J. 1937. Balinese children's drawing. *Djawa*, 5 and 6.

——. 1949. *Bali: Rangda and Barong.* Monographs of the American Ethnological Society, XVI. New York: Augustin.

——. MS. *Drawings of children and primitives with reference to the Naskapi.*

——. (E) Andean area; Guatemala; Haiti; Puerto Rico. Address: 405 W. 118th St., New York 27, N. Y.

Benedict, R. 1934a. *Patterns of culture.* Boston: Houghton Mifflin.

——. 1934b. Anthropology and the abnormal. *J. Gen. Psychol.*, 10, 59–82.

Benedict, R. 1938. Continuities and discontinuities in cultural conditioning. *Psychiatry*, 1, 161–167.

——. 1949. Child research in certain European cultures. *Amer. J. Orthopsychiat.*, 19, 342–350.

Berndt, R. M. (E) Boldea, Jaraldi tribe. Address: Sydney University, Sydney, New So. Wales, Australia.

Blackwood, B. 1927. *A study of mental testing in relation to anthropology.* Mental Measurement Monographs, No. 4.

Boas, F. 1938. *The mind of primitive man.* New York: Macmillan.

Brown, G. (E) Hehe, Tanganyika. Address: Temple University, Philadelphia, Pa.

Bunzel, R. (E) Guiché, Guatemala; Chamula, Mexico; Zuni, New Mexico. Address: 62 Perry St., New York 14, N. Y.

Burrows, E. G., and M. E. Spiro. 1953. *The Ifaluk: An atoll culture in Micronesia.* New Haven: Human Relations Area Files. (Behavior Science Monographs.)

Camboué, P. P. 1907. Notes sur quelques coûtumes malagaches. *Anthropos*, 2, 981–989.

Casagrande, J. B. 1948. Comanche baby language. *Int. J. Amer. Linguistics*, 14, 11–14.

Cattell, R. B. 1940. A culture-free intelligence test. *J. Educ. Psychol.*, 31, 161–179.

——. 1941. A culture-free intelligence test: II. Evaluation of cultural influence on test performance. *J. Educ. Psychol.*, 32, 81–100.

Caudill, W. 1949. Psychological characteristics of acculturated Wisconsin Ojibwa children. *Amer. Anthrop.*, 51, 409–427.

Ceballos, R. J. 1942. Caracter de la educacion entre los antiguos Mexicanos. *Revista Mexicana de Sociologia*, 4, 75–80.

Chamberlain, A. F. 1890. Notes on Indian child language. *Amer. Anthrop.*, O. S., 3, 237–241.

——. 1893. Further notes on Indian child language. *Amer. Anthrop.*, O. S., 6, 321–322.

Chao, B. Y. 1947. *Autobiography of a Chinese woman.* New York: Day.

Chemali, B. 1910. Naissance et premier age au Liban. *Anthropos*, 5, 734–747.

Chesky, J. See Joseph, Spicer, and Chesky, 1949: Growing up on the Desert, Part II.

——. (E) Papagos, 1942–1943. Address: 432 Pine St., Halstead, Kansas.

Coelho, R. MS a. *Some psychological characteristics of the Black Caribs of Central America.*

——. MS b. *Couvade among the Black Caribs.* Address: unknown.

——. Ojibwa children's drawings (in possession of A. I. Hallowell, Box 14, Bennett Hall, University of Pennsylvania, Philadelphia, Pa.).

Colson, E. (E) Tonga of Northern Rhodesia, 1946–1947, 1948. Address: Rhodes-Livingstone Institute, Northern Rhodesia.

Cook, P. H. 1942. The application of the Rorschach test to a Samoan group. *Rorschach Res. Exch.*, 6, 51–60.

Cooper, J. M. 1928. Child training among primitive peoples. *Primitive Man*, 1, 10-16.

Copeland, P. MS. *Analysis of peer groups among Red Lake Ojibwa.* MA thesis, University of Chicago.

——. (E) Red Lake Ojibwa (Minn.), 1947. Address: Dept. of Anthropology, University of Chicago, Chicago 37, Ill.

Dazey, E. MS. *Transition from childhood to adulthood among the Klamath.* Address: 933 Richmond St., El Cerrito, Calif.

DeLoria, E. (E) Dakota. Address: Martin, S. Dakota.

Dennis, W. 1940a. The effect of cradling practices upon the onset of walking in Hopi children. *J. Genet. Psychol.*, 56, 77–86.

——. 1940b. *The Hopi child.* New York: Appleton-Century.

——. 1940c. Infant reaction to restraint: An evaluation of Watson's theory. *Trans. N. Y. Acad. Sci.*, Ser. II, 2, 202–218.

——. 1940d. Does culture appreciably affect patterns of infant behavior? *J. Soc. Psychol.*, 12, 305–317.

——. 1941. The socialization of the Hopi child. In L. Spier, A. I. Hallowell, and S. S. Newman (Eds.), *Language, culture, and personality*, pp. 259–271. Menasha, Wis.: Sapir Memorial Publication Fund.

——. 1942. The performance of Hopi children on the Goodenough draw-a-man test. *J. Compar. Psychol.*, 34, 341–348.

——. 1943. Animism and related tendencies in Hopi children. *J. Abn. and Soc. Psychol.*, 38, 21–36.

——. (E) Cochiti, Zuni, New Mexico. Address: University of Pittsburgh, Pittsburgh, Pa.

Dennis, W., and M. G. Dennis. 1940. Cradles and cradling customs of the Pueblo Indians. *Amer. Anthrop.*, N. S., 42, 107–115.

Devereux, G. 1937. Institutionalized homosexuality of the Mohave Indians. *Human Biol.*, 9, 498–527.

——. 1939a. Mohave culture and personality. *Character and Pers.*, 8, 91–109.

——. 1939b. Implications of incest among the Mohave Indians. *Psychoan. Quart.*, 8, 510–533.

——. 1947. Mohave orality: An analysis of nursing and weaning customs. *Psychoan. Quart.*, 16, 519–546.

——. 1948. The Mohave neonate and its cradle. *Primitive Man*, 21, 1–18.

——. 1949. Mohave male puberty rite. *Samiksa: J. Indian Psycho-An. Soc.*, 3, 11–25.

——. 1950. Heterosexual behavior of the Mohave Indians. In G. Róheim (Ed.), *Psychoanalysis and the social sciences*, Vol. II. New York: International Universities Press.

——. MS. Ethnologie des Ha(rhn)de:a(ng) de Tea Ha. To appear in *Trav. et Mém. Inst. Ethnol. Univ. Paris.*

——. Finger-paintings of Indian adolescents. Address: Winter VA Hospital, Topeka, Kansas.

Dicks, H. V. 1950. Some psychological studies of the German character. In T. H. Pear (Ed.), *Psychological factors of peace and war*, pp. 193–218. New York: Philosophical Library.

Dollard, J. 1935a. Mental hygiene and a scientific culture. *Int. J. Ethics, 45*, 431–435.

——. 1935b. *Criteria for the life history.* New Haven: Yale University Press.

Dollard, J., L. W. Doob, N. E. Miller, O. H. Mowrer, R. R. Sears, et al. 1939. *Frustration and aggression.* New Haven: Yale University Press.

Dollard, J., and N. E. Miller. 1941. *Social learning and imitation.* New Haven: Yale University Press.

Dols, P. J. 1908. L'enfance chez les Chinois de la province Kan-sou. *Anthropos, 3*, 761–770.

Dooley, C. T. 1934–1936. Child training among the Wangaru. *Primitive Man, 8*, 22-31; *8*, 73–81; *9*, 1–12.

Dorsey, G. A. 1895. Caddo customs of childhood. *J. Amer. Folk-lore, 18*, 226–228.

Dry, P. D., Mr. and Mrs. (E) Hausa of Zaria Province (Northern Nigeria), 1949–1950. Address: c/o Dr. Meyer Fortes, Dept. of Social Anthropology, Oxford University.

Dubois, C. 1937a. Some anthropological perspectives on psychoanalysis. *Psychoanal. Rev., 24*, 246–273.

——. 1937b. Some psychological objectives and techniques in ethnography. *J. Soc. Psychol., 8*, 285–300.

——. 1944. *The people of Alor: A socio-psychological study of an East Indian island.* Minneapolis: University of Minnesota Press.

Dyk, W. 1938. *Son of Old Man Hat.* New York: Harcourt, Brace.

——. 1947. *A Navaho autobiography.* New York: Viking Fund.

——. MS a. *Son of Old Man Hat,* Vols. II and III.

——. MS b. *Case histories of childhood (autobiographical and biographical).*

——. (E) Navaho, 1947–1948. Address: Brooklyn College, Brooklyn 10, N. Y.

Eastman, C. A. 1902. *Indian boyhood.* New York: McClure.

Edel, M. M. (E) Batciga, East Africa. Address: Brooklyn College, Brooklyn 10, N. Y.

Eggan, D. 1943. The general problem of Hopi adjustment. *Amer. Anthrop.,* N. S., *45*, 357–373.

Eichhorn, E. (E) Haiti (Port-au-Prince and western region, both mountain area and plains). Address: Dept. of Sociology, Ohio State University, Columbus, Ohio.

Eilers, A. 1927. *Die sozialen Beziehungen des Kindes bei den Bantunegern.* Hamburg: Helm und Torton.

Erikson, E. Homburger. (*See also* Homburger, E.) 1939. Observations on Sioux education. *J. Psychol., 7*, 101–156.

——. 1940. Problems of infancy and early childhood. In G. M. Piersol and E. L. Bortz (Eds.), *Cyclopedia of Medicine, Surgery, and Specialties,* Vol. 12, pp. 714–730. Philadelphia: Davis.

——. 1943. Observations on the Yurok: Childhood and world image. *Univ. Calif. Publ. Amer. Archaeol. Ethnol., 35*, 257–302.

——. 1945. Childhood and tradition in two American Indian tribes. In A. Freud et al. (Eds.), *The psychoanalytic study of the child,* Vol. I. New York: International Universities Press.

Erikson, E. Homburger. 1946. Ego development and historical change. In A. Freud et al. (Eds.), *The psychoanalytic study of the child,* Vol. II. New York: International Universities Press.

——. 1950. *Childhood and society.* New York: Norton.

Eubank, L. MS. *Analysis of free drawings of Indian children.* Address: Navaho Mt. Indian School, Tonelea, Ariz.

Evans, J. M. 1932. *Social and psychological aspects of primitive education.* London: Golden Vista Press.

Evans-Prichard, E. E. 1934. Lévy-Bruhl's theory of primitive mentality. *Bull., Fac. Arts, Univ. Egypt* (Cairo), *2*, Pt. 1.

Firth, R. 1936. *We the Tikopia.* London: Allen and Unwin.

Firth, Rosemary. 1942. Child in the home. In *Housekeeping among Malay peasants.* London School of Economics Monographs on Social Anthropology, No. 7.

Flannery, R. 1936. Some aspects of James Bay recreative culture. *Primitive Man, 9*, 49-56.

——. 1937. Child behavior from the standpoint of the cultural anthropologist. *J. Educ. Sociol., 10*, 470–478.

——. 1941. The dearly-loved child among the Gros Ventres of Montana. *Primitive Man, 14*, 33–38.

——. 1952. *The Gros Ventres of Montana: Part I. Social Life.* Catholic University of America Anthropological Series No. 15, pp. 127–170 on infancy and childhood.

——. (E) Lake Nustassini Montagnais, 1944. Address: Catholic University, Washington, D. C.

Foley, J. P., and A. Anastasi. 1938. A study of animal drawings by Indian children of the North Pacific coast. *J. Soc. Psychol., 9*, 363–374.

Ford, C. S. 1939. Society, culture, and the human organism. *J. Gen. Psychol., 20*, 135–179.

Fortes, M. 1938. *Social and psychological aspects of education in Taleland.* Supplement to *Africa* (London), *11*, No. 4 (International Institute of African Languages and Cultures).

——. 1949. *The web of kinship among the Tallensi.* London: Oxford University Press.

——. (E) Nigeria, 1941; Ashanti (Gold Coast), 1945–1946; Bechuanaland, 1948. Address: Oxford University.

Fortune, R. F. 1935. *Manus religion.* Philadelphia: American Philosophical Society.

——. 1939. Arapesh warfare. *Amer. Anthrop.,* N. S., *41*, 22–41.

——. 1942. *Arapesh.* Publ. Amer. Ethnol. Soc. No. 19. New York: Augustin.

Foster, G. M. 1948. *Empire's children: The people of Tzintzuntzan.* Smithsonian Institution, Institute of Social Anthropology, Publication No. 6, pp. 224–247.

Frank, L. K. 1931. The concept of inviolability in culture. *Amer. J. Sociol., 36*, 607–615.

——. 1938. Cultural control and physiological autonomy. *Amer. J. Orthopsychiat., 8*, 622–626.

——. 1939a. Cultural coercion and individual distortion. *Psychiatry 2*, 11–27.

Frank, L. K. 1939b. Projective methods for the study of personality. *J. Psychol., 8,* 389–413.

Friedl, E. MS. *Leadership patterns among the Ojibwa.*

——. (E) Wisconsin Ojibwa, 1942, 1943. Address: Queens College, Flushing, N. Y.

Fries, M. 1941. National and international difficulties. *Amer. J. Orthopsychiat., 11,* 565–567.

——. 1947. Diagnosis of the child's adjustment through the age level test. *Psychoan. Rev., 34,* 1–31.

—— (with C. Kluckhohn and P. J. Woolf). Film: *Family life of Navaho Indians.* New York University Film Library.

Fromm, E. 1933. Die psychoanalytische Charakterologie und ihre Bedeutung für die Sozialpsychologie. *Z. Sozialforsch., 1,* 253–277.

Fuchs, S. 1939. Birth and childhood among the Balihis. *Primitive Man, 12,* 71–84.

Gesell, A. 1946. Some relationships between maturation and acculturation. *J. Nerv. Ment. Dis., 103,* 518–520. (Abstract.)

Gesell, A., and F. L. Ilg. 1943. *Infant and child in the culture of today.* New York and London: Harper.

Gilhodes, P. C. 1911. Naissance et enfance chez les Katchins (Birmanie). *Anthropos, 6,* 868–884.

Gladwin, T. (E) Trukese (E. Caroline Islands), 1947–1948. Address: 9080 Greentree Rd., Bethesda, Md.

Glover, E. 1932. Common problems in psychoanalysis and anthropology. *Brit. J. Med. Psychol., 12,* 109–131.

Goldfrank, E. S. 1945. Socialization, personality, and the structure of Pueblo society (with particular reference to Hopi and Zuñi). *Amer. Anthrop.,* N. S., *47,* 516–539.

Goodenough, F. 1936. The measurements of mental functions in primitive groups. *Amer. Anthrop., 38,* 1–11.

Gorer, G. 1938. *Himalayan village.* London: Michael Joseph.

——. 1943. Themes in Japanese culture. *Trans. N. Y. Acad. Sci.,* Ser. II, *5,* 106–124.

——. 1949. Some aspects of the psychology of the people of Great Russia. *Amer. Slavic and E. European Rev.,* VIII, 155–166.

Gorer, G., and J. Rickman. 1949. *The people of Great Russia.* London: Crosset Press; and New York: Chanticleer Press.

Gottschalk, L., C. Kluckhohn, and R. Angell. 1945. *The use of personal documents in history, anthropology and sociology.* Social Science Research Council, Bulletin 53.

Grimble, A. 1921. From birth to death in the Gilbert Islands. *J. Roy. Anthrop. Inst., 51,* 5–54.

Grinnell, G. B. 1923. *The Cheyenne Indians.* New Haven: Yale University Press.

Gutmann, B. 1932, 1935, 1938. *Die Stammeslehren der Dschagga.* München: C. H. Beck'sche. 3 vols.

Hallowell, A. I. 1939. The child, the savage, and human experience. *Proc. 6th Inst. Except. Child, Child Res. Clin.,* 8–34. [Reprinted in D. Haring (Compiler), *Personal character and cultural milieu,* pp. 349–374. Syracuse, 1948.]

Hallowell, A. I. 1941a. The Rorschach method as an aid in the study of personalities in primitive society. *Character and Pers., 9,* 235–245.

——. 1941b. The Rorschach test as a tool for investigating cultural variables and individual differences in the study of personality in primitive societies. *Rorschach Res. Exch., 5,* 31–43.

——. 1942. Acculturation processes and personality changes as indicated by the Rorschach technique. *Rorschach Res. Exch., 6,* 42–50.

——. (E) Lac du Flambeau Ojibwa, 1946. Address: Box 41, Bennett Hall, University of Pennsylvania, Philadelphia, Pa.

Hallowell, A. I., R. Hassrick, W. E. Henry, A. Joseph, B. Klopfer, and D. C. Leighton. MS. *American Indian personality research.*

Hambly, W. D. 1926. *Origins of education among primitive peoples: A comparative study in racial development.* London: Macmillan.

——. 1947. *Jamba.* Chicago: Pellegrini and Cudahy.

Hanks, L. M., Jr., and J. R. Hanks. 1949. In *Tribe under trust: A study of the Blackfoot Reserve of Alberta,* Chapter VI on youth and age. Toronto: University of Toronto Press.

——. (E) Blackfoot; Arakan Burmese. Address: Bennington College, Bennington, Vt.

Harper, B. W. MS. *Infancy; childhood; adolescence; pregnancy and birth,* Pueblo of Jemez, 1926–1935.

Harris, J. S. (E) South East Nigeria. Address: Trusteeship Council, United Nations, N. Y.

Hassrick, R. B. MS *a. Dakota child personality as evaluated through the Rorschach.*

——. MS *b. Some personality traits of Sioux children as indicated by the Rorschach.*

——. (E) Dakota, 1941–1944. Address: Museum of the Southern Plains, Anadarko, Okla.

Havighurst, R. J. (E) Hopi; Papago; Zuni; Zia; Navaho; Sioux. 1942–1944. Address: Committee on Human Development, University of Chicago, Chicago, 37, Ill.

Havighurst, R. J., M. K. Gunther, and I. E. Pratt. 1946. Environment and the draw-a-man test: The performance of Indian children. *J. Abn. and Soc. Psychol., 41,* 50–63.

Havighurst, R. J., and R. R. Hilkevitch. 1944. The intelligence of Indian children as measured by a performance scale. *J. Abn. and Soc. Psychol., 39,* 419–433.

Havighurst, R. J., and B. Neugarten. MS. *The moral and emotional development of children in five American Indian tribes.*

Hawley, F. (E) Zia Pueblo. Address: University of New Mexico, Albuquerque, N. M.

Heckel, B. 1935. *The Yao tribe: Their culture and education.* University of London Institute of Education, Studies and Reports, No. 4.

Henry, H. 1942. MS. *Collection of drawings by 24 Ramah Navaho children compared with those of 24 Ramah Mormon children of comparable age.*

Radcliffe College A.B. thesis, Peabody Museum Library.

Henry, J. 1936. The personality of the Kaingang Indians. *Character and Pers.*, 5, 113–123.

——. 1940a. Some cultural determinants of hostility in Pilagá Indian children. *Amer. J. Orthopsychiat.*, 10, 111–112.

——. 1940b. Speech disturbances in Pilagá Indians. *Amer. J. Orthopsychiat.*, 10, 362–365.

——. 1942. Symmetrical and reciprocal hostility in sibling rivalry. *Amer. J. Orthopsychiat.*, 12, 252–262.

——. 1947. Environment and symptom formation. *Amer. J. Orthopsychiat.*, 17, 628–632.

——. 1949. The social function of child sexuality in Pilagá Indian culture. In P. H. Hoch and J. Zubin (Eds.), *Psychosexual development in health and disease*, pp. 91–101. (Proceedings of the 38th Annual Meeting of the American Psychopathological Association, 1948.) New York: Grune and Stratton.

——. (E) Otomí Indians (Ixmiquilpan, State of Hidalgo, Mexico), 1941; Tarahumara Indians (Chihuahua, Mexico), 1940. Address: Washington University, St. Louis, Mo.

Henry, J., and Z. Henry. 1944. *The doll play of Pilagá Indian children.* American Journal of Orthopsychiatry Research Monograph No. 4.

Henry, W. E. 1945. Mimeo. *Thematic Appperception Test: A method of analysis.*

——. 1947. The Thematic Appperception technique in the study of culture-personality relations. *Genet. Psychol. Monogr.*, 35, 5–135.

Hilger, I. 1946a. Notes on Cheyenne child life. *Amer. Anthrop.*, N. S., 48, 60–69.

——. 1946b. Ethnological field study of Araucanian Indian child of Chile. *Yearb. Amer. Phil. Soc.* 202–205.

——. 1952a. *Chippewa child life and its cultural background.* Bureau of American Ethnology Bulletin 146. Smithsonian Institution, Washington, D. C.

——. 1952b. *Arapaho child life and its cultural background.* Bureau of American Ethnology Bulletin 148. Smithsonian Institution, Washington, D. C.

——. MS a. *Araucanian child life and its cultural background.*

——. MS b. *The training of the child in several Indian tribes.*

——. (E) Pueblo, 1935; Menomini, 1936; Blackfoot, 1936, 1937; Papago, 1939; Crow, 1940; Navaho, 1941; Arikara, 1942; Sioux, 1942; Cherokee, 1944; Catawba, 1944. Address: St. Cloud School of Nursing, Minn.

Hoernlé, A. W. 1931. An outline of the native conception of education in Africa. *Africa* (London), 4, 145–163.

Hogbin, H. I. 1931. Education at Ontong Jaya, Solomon Islands. *Amer. Anthrop.*, N. S., 33, 601–614.

——. 1943. A New Guinea infancy: From conception to weaning in Wogeo. *Oceania*, 13, 285–309.

——. 1946a. A New Guinea childhood: From weaning to the eighth year in Wogeo. *Oceania*, 16, 275–296.

Hogbin, H. I. 1946b. Puberty to marriage: A study of the sexual life of the natives of Wogeo, New Guinea. *Oceania*, 16, 185–209.

——. 1947. Shame. *Oceania*, 17, 273–288.

——. (E) Solomon Islands, 1943; Huon Gulf (New Guinea), 1944–1949. Address: Sydney University.

Holmberg, A. M. 1950. *Nomads of the Long Bow: the Siriono of Eastern Bolivia.* Smithsonian Institution, Institute of Social Anthropology, Publication No. 10, Washington, D. C.

——. (E) Viru village, Marcará village, Vicos—all in Peru. Address: Dept. of Sociology and Anthropology, Cornell University, Ithaca, N. Y.

Homburger, E. (*See also* Erikson, E. Homburger.) 1937. Configurations in play-clinical notes. *Psychoan. Quart.*, 6, 139–214.

Honigmann, I., and F. W. Underwood. 1947. A comparison of socialization and personality in two simple societies. *Amer. Anthrop.*, N. S., 49, 557–577.

Honigmann, I., and J. J. Honigmann. (E) Kaska Indians, British Columbia and Yukon Territory. Address: New York University, New York, N. Y.

Honigmann, J. J. 1946. *Ethnography and acculturation of the Fort Nelson slave.* Yale University Publications in Anthropology, No. 33, 136–143; 163–165.

——. 1949. *Culture and ethos of Kaska society.* Yale University Publications in Anthropology, No. 40, 176–191.

——. (E) Cree Indians, 1947–1948. Address: University of North Carolina, Chapel Hill, N. C.

Horney, K. 1935. The problem of feminine masochism. *Psychoanal. Rev.*, 22, 241–257.

——. 1937. *The neurotic personality of our time.* New York: Norton.

Hovey, E. O. 1918. Child-life among the Smith Sound Eskimo. *Nat. Hist.*, 18, 361–371.

Hunter, M. 1936. *Reaction to conquest.* London: Oxford University Press.

Joseph, A. MS. *Notes on the Emotional Response and Bavelas Tests of Hopi children.* Address: 24A Garden St., Cambridge, Mass.

Joseph, A., and V. F. Murray. 1951. *Chamorros and Carolinians of Saipan:* Personality Studies; with an analysis of the Bender Gestalt Tests by Lauretta Bender. Cambridge: Harvard University Press.

Joseph, A., R. Spicer, and J. Chesky. 1949. *The desert people: A study of the Papago Indians.* Chicago: Chicago University Press.

Kardiner, A. 1939. *The individual and his society.* New York: Columbia University Press.

——. 1945. *Psychological frontiers of society.* New York: Columbia University Press.

Kidd, D. 1906. *Savage childhood: A study of Kafir children.* London: Black.

Kler, J. 1938. Birth, infancy, and childhood among the Ordos Mongols. *Primitive Man*, 11, 58–66.

Klineberg, O. 1928. An experimental study of speed and other factors in "racial" differences. *Arch. Psychol.*, No. 93.

——. 1935. *Race differences.* New York: Harper.

Kluckhohn, C. 1939. Theoretical bases for an empirical method of studying the acquisition of culture by individuals. *Man, 39,* 98–103.

——. 1946. Personality formation among the Navaho Indians. *Sociometry, 9,* 128–133.

——. 1947. Some aspects of Navaho infancy and early childhood. In G. Róheim (Ed.), *Psychoanalysis and the Social Sciences,* Vol. I, pp. 37–87. New York: International Universities Press.

——. (E) Moencopi Hopi; Ramah Navaho, 1940–1943, 1946–1948. Address: Peabody Museum, Cambridge, Mass.

Kluckhohn, C., and D. C. Leighton. 1946. *The Navaho.* Cambridge: Harvard University Press.

Kluckhohn, C., and C. Chappat Rosenzweig. 1949. Two Navaho children over a five-year period. *Amer. J. Orthopsychiat., 19,* 266–278.

Knops, P. 1938. L'enfant chez les Senenfours de la Côte d'Ivoire. *Africa* (London), *11,* 48–92.

Köhler, W. 1937. Psychological remarks on some questions of anthropology. *Amer. J. Psychol., 59,* 271–288.

Kroeber, A. L. 1916. The speech of a Zuñi child. *Amer. Anthrop.,* N.S., *18,* 529–534.

——. 1939. Totem and taboo in retrospect. *Amer. J. Sociol., 45,* 446–451.

Kuper, H. (E) Swazi (Southeast Africa), 1934–1937, 1942. Address: c/o Dr. A. Beemer, Wroxham House, Jeppe St., Johannesburg.

La Barre, W. 1948. Columbia University research in contemporary cultures. *Sci. Mo., 67,* 239–240.

Labuschagne, A. S. MS. *Perceptual tests for distinguishing difference of ability and temperament among natives of Central Nyasaland.* Master's thesis, University of South Africa.

——. (E) Angoni and Acewa (Central Nyasaland), 1947–1949. Address: Mlanda, P. O. Dedza, Nyasaland.

Landes, R. 1938. *The Ojibwa woman.* New York: Columbia University Press.

——. 1947. *The city of women.* New York: Macmillan.

Lasswell, H. D. 1935. Collective autism as a consequence of culture contact. *Z. Sozialforsch., 4,* 232–247.

——. 1937. The method of interlapping observation in the study of personality and culture. *J. Abn. and Soc. Psychol., 32,* 240–243.

——. 1939. Person, personality, group, culture. *Psychiatry, 2,* 533–561.

Layard, J. (E) Atchin (Malekula); New Hebrides. Address: 17 Parkhill Road, London, N. W. 3.

Lee, D. 1940. A primitive system of values. *Phil. Sci., 7,* 355–378.

——. 1949. Being and value in a primitive culture. *J. Phil., 46,* 401–415.

Leighton, D. C. (E) Zuñi, 1943. Address: 155 E. Main St., Trumansburg, N. Y.

Leighton, D. C., with J. Adair. MS. *People of the Middle Place: A study of the Zuñi Indians.*

Leighton, D. C., and C. Kluckhohn. 1947. *Children of the people: The Navaho individual and his development.* Cambridge: Harvard University Press.

Leites, N. 1948. Psycho-cultural hypotheses about political acts. *World Politics, 1,* 102–119.

Lerner, E. 1937a. New techniques for tracing cultural factors in children's personality organization. *J. Educ. Sociol., 10,* 479–486.

——. 1937b. Constraint areas and the moral judgment of children. Menasha, Wis.: George Banta. Columbia University Ph.D. thesis.

Lessa, W. A. (E) Ulithi (Caroline Islands), 1948–1949. Address: University of California at Los Angeles, Calif.

Levy, D. 1938–1939. Maternal overprotection: I, II, III. *Psychiatry, 1,* 561–562; *2,* 99–109; *3,* 563–597.

——. 1939. Sibling rivalry studies in children of primitive groups. *Amer. J. Orthopsychiat., 9,* 205–214.

——. 1947. *New fields of psychiatry.* New York: Norton.

Linderman, F. B. 1930. *American.* New York: Day.

——. 1932. *Red mother.* New York: Day.

Lindgren, E. J. 1935. Field work in social psychology. *Brit. J. Psychol., 26,* 177–182.

Lipkind, W. (E) Karajá of Brazil. Address: 3 E. 10th St., New York 3, N. Y.

Lowenfeld, M. F. 1935. *Play in childhood.* London: Gollancz.

——. *Mosaic Test.*

——. MS. *World Test.* Address: Institute of Child Psychology, London, W. 11.

Luomala, K., and G. Toffelmier. MS. *Autobiography of a Diegueño Indian witch doctor.*

——. (E) Diegueño; Tabiteuea Island, Gilbert Islands. Address: Dept. of Anthropology, University of Hawaii, Honolulu.

Macgregor, G. 1946. *Warriors without weapons: A study of the society and personality development of the Pine Ridge Sioux.* Chicago: University of Chicago Press.

Malinowski, B. 1927a. *Sex and repression in savage society.* New York: Harcourt, Brace; London: Kegan Paul.

——. 1927b. *The father in primitive psychology.* New York: Norton.

——. 1929. *The sexual life of savages in North-Western Melanesia: An ethnographic account of courtship, marriage, and family life among the natives of Trobriand Islands in British New Guinea.* New York: Liveright; London: Routledge.

——. 1935. *Coral gardens and their magic.* (2 vols.) London: Allen and Unwin.

Mandelbaum, D. 1948. The family in India. *Southwestern J. Anthrop., 4,* 123–139.

——. (E) Kota, India. Address: University of California, Berkeley, Calif.

Marwick, M. G. (E) Cewa (Northern Rhodesia), 1946–1948. Address: S. A. N. C., Fort Hare, via Alice, C. P., South Africa.

Maslow, A. H. 1937. Personality and patterns of culture. In R. Stragner (Ed.), *Psychology of personality,* pp. 408–428. New York: McGraw-Hill.

McPhee, C. 1938. Children and music in Bali. *Djawa*, *6*, 1–15.

Mead, M. 1928a. A lapse of animism among a primitive people. *Psyche*, *9*, 72–79.

——. 1928b. Coming of age in Samoa. New York: Morrow. (Reprinted in *From the South Seas*. New York: Morrow, 1939.)

——. 1928c. The role of the individual in Samoan culture. *J. Roy. Anthrop. Inst.*, *58*, 481–495. [Reprinted in A. L. Kroeber and T. T. Waterman (Eds.), *Source book in anthropology*, pp. 545–561. New York: Harcourt, Brace, 1931.]

——. 1930a. Adolescence in primitive and modern society. In F. V. Calverton and S. D. Schmalhausen (Eds.), *The new generation*, pp. 169–188. New York: Macaulay.

——. 1930b. Growing up in New Guinea. New York: Morrow. (Reprinted in *From the South Seas*. New York: Morrow, 1939.)

——. 1930c. An ethnologist's footnote to "Totem and Taboo." *Psychoanal. Rev.*, *17*, 297–304.

——. 1931. The primitive child. In C. Murchison (Ed.), *A handbook of child psychology*, pp. 669–687. Worcester: Clark University Press.

——. 1932. Investigation of thought of primitive children with special reference to animism. *J. Roy. Anthrop. Inst.*, *62*, 173–190.

——. 1933. More comprehensive field methods. *Amer. Anthrop.*, N. S., *35*, 1–15.

——. 1934a. The use of primitive material in the study of personality. *Character and Pers.*, *3*, 1–16.

——. 1934b. Kinship in the Admiralties. *Anthrop. Papers, Amer. Mus. Nat. Hist.*, *34*, Pt. 2, 183–358.

——. 1935a. Sex and temperament in three primitive societies. New York: Morrow. (Reprinted in *From the South Seas*. New York: Morrow, 1939.)

——. 1935b. Review "The Riddle of the Sphinx" by G. Róheim. *Character and Pers.*, *4*, 85–90.

——. 1937. M. Mead (Ed.), *Cooperation and competition among primitive peoples*. New York: McGraw-Hill.

——. 1939a. Native languages as field work tools. *Amer. Anthrop.*, N. S., *41*, 189–205.

——. 1939b. Researches in Bali, 1936–1939. *Trans. N. Y. Acad. Sci.*, Ser. II, *2*, 24–31.

——. 1940a. Character formation in two South Sea societies. *Proc., Amer. Neurol. Ass.*, *66*, 99–103.

——. 1940b. The mountain Arapesh: II. Supernaturalism. *Anthrop. Papers, Amer. Mus. Nat. Hist.*, *37*, Pt. 3, 317–451.

——. 1941a. Review "The Hopi Child" by W. Dennis. *Amer. Anthrop.*, N. S., *43*, 95–97.

——. 1941b. Review "The Individual and His Society" by A. Kardiner. *Amer. J. Orthopsychiat.*, *11*, 603–605.

——. 1942a. Educative effects of social environment as disclosed by studies of primitive societies. In *Environment and education* (symposium), pp. 48–61. Chicago: University of Chicago Press. (Supplementary Educational Monographs, No. 54, Human Development Series, Vol. 1.)

——. 1942b. Anthropological data on the problem of instinct. In "Second colloquia on psychodynamics and experimental medicine." *Psychosom. Med.*, *4*, 396–397. [Reprinted in C. Kluckhohn and H. A. Murray (Eds.), *Personality in nature, society, and culture*, pp. 109–112. New York: Knopf, 1948.]

Mead, M. 1942c. The comparative study of culture and the purposive cultivation of democratic values. In L. Bryson and L. Finkelstein (Eds.), *Science, philosophy and religion* (second symposium), pp. 58–69. New York: Conference on Science, Philosophy and Religion. (Country Life Press, Garden City, L. I.)

——. 1943a. Our educational emphases in primitive perspective. In C. S. Johnson (Ed.), *Education and the cultural process* (symposium). *Amer. J. Sociol.*, *48*, 5–12.

——. 1943b. Anthropological techniques in war psychology. *Bull. Menninger Clinic*, *7*, 137–140.

——. 1944a. Cultural approach to personality: Anthropological comment on the frame of reference of Andras Angyal. *Trans. N. Y. Acad. Sci.*, Ser. 2, *6*, 93–101.

——. 1944b. Preparing children for a world society. *J. Ass. Child. Educ.*, *20*, 345–348.

——. 1946. The cultural approach to personality. See "Personality" in P. Harriman (Ed.), *Encyclopedia of psychology*, pp. 477–488. New York: Philosophical Library.

——. 1947a. The mountain Arapesh: III. Socio-economic life; IV. Diary of events in Alitoa. *Anthrop. Papers, Amer. Mus. Nat. Hist.*, *40*, Pt. 3, 159–420.

——. 1947b. On the implications for anthropology of the Gesell–Ilg approach to maturation. *Amer. Anthrop.*, N. S., *49*, 69–77. [Reprinted in D. G. Haring (Compiler), *Personal character and cultural milieu*, pp. 418–426. Syracuse, 1948.]

——. 1947c. The concept of culture and the psychosomatic approach. *Psychiatry*, *10*, 57–76. [Reprinted in D. G. Haring (Compiler), *Personal character and cultural milieu*, pp. 427–446. Syracuse, 1948.]

——. 1947d. Age patterning in personality development. *Amer. J. Orthopsychiat.*, *17*, 231–240. [Reprinted in D. G. Haring (Compiler), *Personal character and cultural milieu*, pp. 447–456. Syracuse, 1948.]

——. 1947e. The implications of culture change for personality development. *Amer. J. Orthopsychiat.*, *17*, 633–646. [Reprinted in D. G. Haring (Compiler), *Personal character and cultural milieu*, pp. 457–470. Syracuse, 1948.]

——. 1947f. The application of anthropological techniques to cross-national communication. *Trans. N. Y. Acad. Sci.*, Ser. II, *9*, 133–152. [Reprinted as "A case history in cross-national communication" in L. Bryson (Ed.), *The communication of ideas*, pp. 209–229. New York: Institute for Religious and Social Studies (Harper), 1948.]

——. 1949a. (See Benedict, 1949, pp. 349–350).

——. 1949b. Male and female: A study of the sexes in a changing world. New York: Morrow.

——. 1949c. Character formation and diachronic theory. In M. Fortes (Ed.), *Social structure: Studies presented to A. R. Radcliffe-Brown*, pp. 18-34. Oxford: Clarendon Press.

Mead, M. 1949d. Psychological weaning: Childhood and adolescence. In P. H. Hoch and J. Zubin (Eds.), *Psychosexual development in health and disease*, pp. 124-135. (Proceedings of the 38th Annual Meeting of the American Psychopathological Association, 1948.) New York: Grune and Stratton.

——. 1949e. The mountain Arapesh: V. The record of Unabelin with Rorschach analysis. *Anthrop. Papers, Amer. Mus. Nat. Hist., 41*, Pt. 3, 289-390.

——. 1950. Some anthropological considerations concerning guilt. In M. L. Reymert (Ed.), *Feelings and emotions; the Mooseheart Symposium*, pp. 362-373. New York: McGraw-Hill.

——. 1952. Some relationships between social anthropology and psychiatry. In F. Alexander and H. Ross (Eds.), *Dynamic psychiatry*. Chicago: University of Chicago Press, pp. 401-448.

——. (E) Samoa, 1925-1926; Manus (Admiralty Islands), 1928-1929; Arapesh, 1931; Mundugumor, 1932; Tchambuli, 1933. Also see Bateson and Mead (E). Address: American Museum of Natural History, New York 24, N. Y.

Mead, M., and F. C. Macgregor. 1951. *Growth and culture: A photographic study of Balinese childhood*. New York: Putnam.

Meier, J. 1938. Illegitimate birth among the Gunantuna. *Catholic Anthrop. Conf., Publ. II*, 1-61. (Washington, D. C.)

Mekeel, S. 1935. Clinic and culture. *J. Abn. and Soc. Psychol., 30*, 292-300.

——. 1936. An anthropologist's observations on American Indian education. *Progr. Educ., 13*, 151-159.

——. 1943. Education, child-training and culture. *Amer. J. Sociol., 48*, 676-681.

Mena, R., and J. Jenkins Arriaga. 1930. *Educacion intelectual y fisica entre los Nahuas y Mayas Precolombinos*. Mexico. (Available at the American Museum of Natural History Library.)

Métraux, A., and R. Métraux. (E) Haiti. Address: 305 W. 11th St., New York 14, N. Y.

Michelson, T. 1918-1919. Autobiography of a Fox woman. *Ann. Rep. Bur. Amer. Ethnol., 40*, 291-337.

——. 1932. Narrative of a Southern Cheyenne woman. *Smithsonian Misc. Coll., 87*, 1-13.

——. 1933. Narrative of an Arapaho woman. *Amer. Anthrop., N. S., 35*, 595-611.

Miller, N. 1928. *The child in primitive society*. New York: Brentano.

Miner, H. 1942. Songhoi circumcision. *Amer. Anthrop., N. S., 44*, 621-637.

Mirsky, J. (E) Comanche; Coban, Guatemala. Address: c/o Ginsburg, 273 Hawthorne Ave., Princeton, N. J.

Mittlemann, B., H. G. Wolff, and M. P. Scharf. 1942. Emotions and gastroduodenal function: Experimental studies on patients with gastritis, duodenitis and peptic ulcer. *Psychosom. Med., 4*, 5-61.

Moloney, J. C. 1945. Psychiatric observations in Okinawa Shima. *Psychiatry, 8*, 391-399.

Moloney, J. C., and J. J. V. Cammisa. 1947. Film. *The Okinawan*. Address: Dr. J. C. Moloney, Birmingham, Mich.

Mordy, B. MS. *Content analysis of Indian children's drawing: A method for comparing culture and degree of material acculturation*. Address: c/o Havighurst, Committee on Human Development, University of Chicago, Chicago 37, Ill.

Moreno, F. 1934. *Who shall survive?* Nervous and Mental Disease Monograph Series, No. 58.

Nadel, S. F. 1937a. The typological approach to culture. *Character and Pers., 5*, 267-284.

——. 1937b. Experiments on cultural psychology. *Africa* (London), *10*, 421-435.

Nel, B. F. 1935. *Die Fantasie von Blanke en naturelle Skoolgaande Kindes*. Amsterdam: Swets and Zeitlinger.

Nissen, H. W., S. Machover, and E. F. Kinder. 1935. A study of performance tests given to a group of native African Negro children. *Brit. J. Psychol., 25*, 308-355.

Orlansky, H. 1949. Infant care and personality. *Psychol. Bull., 46*, 1-48.

Oliver, D., and E. Oliver. (E) Siwai, Bougainville. Address: Peabody Museum, Cambridge, Mass.

Opler, M. E. 1935. The psychoanalytic treatment of culture. *Psychoanal. Rev., 22*, 138-157.

——. 1941. An Apache life-way: The economical, social, and religious institutions of the Chiricahua Indians. Chicago: University of Chicago Press.

——. 1946. *Childhood and youth in Jicarilla Apache society*. Publication of the Frederick Webb Hodge Anniversary Publication Fund, Vol. 5. Los Angeles.

——. (E) Jicarilla Apache, Lipan Apache, Mescalero Apache. Address: Cornell University, Ithaca, N. Y.

Parsons, E. C. 1919. Mothers and children at Laguna. *Man, 19*, 148-151.

Paul, B. D. 1950. Symbolic sibling rivalry in a Guatemalan village. *Amer. Anthrop., 52*, 205-218.

Paul, B. D., and L. Paul. (E) San Pedro la Laguna (Guatemala). Address: Harvard University, Cambridge, Mass.

Pearsall, M. 1950. *Klamath childhood and education*. Anthropological Records, University of California (Berkeley), Vol. 9, No. 5.

——. (E) Klamath Indians (south central Oregon), 1946. Address: Dept. of Anthropology, University of California, Berkeley, Calif.

Perham, M. 1936. *Ten Africans*. London: Faber and Faber.

Pettitt, G. A. 1946. Primitive education in North America: Its processes and effects. *Univ. Calif. Publ. Amer. Archaeol. Ethnol., 43*, 1-182.

Piaget, J. 1924. *Le jugement et le raisonnement chez l'enfant*. Neuchâtel et Paris: Delachuaz et Nièstlé. (English translation by M. Warden, *Judgment and reasoning in the child*. New York: Harcourt, Brace; London: Kegan Paul, 1928.)

Pitje, G. M. MS. *Traditional and modern systems of male education among the Pedi and cognate tribes*. MA thesis, University of South Africa.

Porteus, S. D. 1937. *Primitive intelligence and environment*. New York: Macmillan.

Porteus, S. D. 1939. Racial group differences in mentality. *Tabulae biologicae, 18*, 66–75.

Probst, M. 1906. Les dessins des enfants Kabyles. *Arch. Psychol.* (Geneva), *6*, 131–140.

Quick, G. 1933. Arts and crafts in the training of Bemba youth. *Univ. London, Inst. Educ. Stud. Rep.*, No. 4, 43–53.

Radin, P. 1936. Ojibwa and Ottawa puberty dreams. In R. H. Lowie (Ed.), *Essays in anthropology presented to A. L. Kroeber*, pp. 233–264. Berkeley: University of California Press.

Radin, P. (Ed.) 1926. *Crashing Thunder; the autobiography of a Winnebago Indian.* New York: Appleton.

Rannells, E. W. MS. *Drawings by Hopi children.* Address: c/o Havighurst, Committee on Human Development, University of Chicago, Chicago, Ill.

Rauch, J., and B. Tolerton. (E) Mortlock (Nomoi) Islands (Central Carolines), 1947–1948. Address: c/o Dept. of Anthropology, Columbia University, New York 27, N. Y.

Raum, O. F. 1940. *Chaga childhood: A description of indigenous education in an East African tribe.* London: Oxford University Press.

Read, M. H. 1937. Songs of the Ngoni people: Lullabies and initiation songs. *Bantu Studies, 11*, 1–35.

——. (E) Chewa, Northern Rhodesia. Address: London School of Economics.

Róheim, G. 1932. Psychoanalysis of primitive cultural types. *Int. J. Psycho-anal., 13*, 2–221.

——. 1934a. *The riddle of the Sphinx.* London: Hogarth Press and Institute of Psycho-Analysis.

——. 1934b. The study of character development and the ontgenetic theory of culture. In E. E. Evans-Prichard, R. Firth, B. Malinowski, and I. Schapera (Eds.), *Essays presented to C. G. Seligman*, pp. 281–292. London: Kegan Paul.

——. 1939. Racial differences in the neurosis and psychosis. *Psychiatry, 2*, 375–390.

——. 1941. Play analysis with Normanby Island children. *Amer. J. Orthopsychiat., 11*, 524–529.

——. 1943. Children's games and rhymes in Duau. *Amer. Anthrop.*, N. S., *45*, 99–119.

——. (E) Navaho children. Address: 1 W. 85th St., New York 24, N. Y.

Rosenzweig, J. Chappat. MS. *Figure-Plates, a projective test for the study of group attitudes.*

——. (E) Navaho, 1944–1946. Address: 11 Story St., Cambridge 38, Mass.

Sapir, E. 1929. Nootka baby words. *Int. J. Amer. Linguistics, 5*, 118–119.

——. 1934. Emergence of the concept of personality in the study of culture. *J. Soc. Psychol., 5*, 408–415.

Schachtel, A. H., J. Henry, and Z. Henry. 1942. Rorschach analysis of Pilagá Indian children. *Amer. J. Orthopsychiat., 12*, 679–712.

Schachtel, E. G. 1947. On memory and childhood amnesia. *Psychiatry, 10*, 1–26.

Schaffner, B. H. 1948. *Father land: A study of authoritarianism in the German family.* New York: Columbia University Press.

Schilder, P. 1940. Cultural patterns and constructive psychology. *Psychoanal. Rev., 27*, 159–170.

Schneider, D. M. MS a. *Motion pictures as a field technique in social anthropology; A report to the Laboratory of Social Relations.*

——. MS b. *The social organization of Yap.*

——. (E) Yap, 1947–1948. Address: Dept. of Social Relations, Harvard University, Cambridge, Mass.

Schriver, J. L., and E. B. Leacock. 1949. Harrison Indian childhood. In M. Smith (Ed.), *Indians of the urban Northwest*, pp. 195–242. New York: Columbia University Press.

Schubert, A. 1930. Drawings of Orotchen children and young people. *J. Genet. Psychol., 37*, 232–244.

Shimkin, D. B. 1947. *Childhood and development among the Wind River Shoshone.* University of California Anthropological Records, Vol. 5.

Sieber, D., and J. Sieber. 1938. Das Leben des Kindes im Neungli Stamme. *Africa* (London), *11*, 208–220.

Simmons, L. 1942. *Sun Chief: The autobiography of a Hopi Indian.* New Haven: Yale University Press.

Slegtenhorst, H. J. 1930. Karakterologisch Onderzoek van de Rijpere Jeugd in Nederlandsch-Indie. *De Indische Gids*, 970–978.

Spicer, R. (E) Yaqui, 1936–1937, 1941–1942, 1947. Address: Route 4, Box 526, Tucson, Ariz.

Spiro, M. E. MS. *The problem of aggression in a South Sea culture.* Ph.D. dissertation, 1950, Northwestern University.

——. (E) Ifaluk, 1947–1948. Address: Washington University, St. Louis 5, Mo.

Spitz, R. A. 1935. Frükindliches Erleben und Erwachsenenkultur bei den Primitiven: Bemerkungen zu Margaret Mead, "Growing up in New Guinea." *Imago, 21*, 367–387.

Stern, B. 1934. *The Lummi Indians of northwest Washington.* New York: Columbia University Press. (Columbia Univ. Contrib. Anthrop., 17.) (For sale in the United States by Augustin.)

Steward, J. H. 1934. Two Paiute autobiographies. *Univ. Calif. Publ. Amer. Archaeol. Ethnol., 33*, 423–438.

Stewart, K. R. 1951. Dream theory in Malaya. *Complex*, Fall, 1951, pp. 21–33. (In collaboration with S. D. Noone, Perak Museum.)

——. MS a. *The Goodenough "draw-a-man" test.*

——. MS b. *Psychometric studies among the Ainu.*

——. MS c. *A report on the results of Porteus maze tests among some of the racial groups of South-Eastern Asia and the peripheral islands.*

——. MS d. *Stewart ring puzzle test.*

——. MS e. *Stewart emotional response test.*

——. MS f. *Magico-religious beliefs and practices in primitive societies: A sociological analysis of their therapeutic aspects.* Ph.D. thesis, University of London, 1948.

——. MS g. *An adaptation of primitive dream interpretation and reshaping to Western psychotherapy.*

——. MS h. *Multiple voice and the expression and integration of disassociated personality entities.*

Stewart, K. R. (E) Negritos, Luzon; Ainu, Japan; Yami, Botto Tobago; Senoi, Malaya; Ifugao, Philippines. Address: 31 Park Avenue, New York 16, N. Y.

Stewart, O. C. (E) Zuñi, 1940. Address: University of Colorado, Boulder, Colo.

Storch, A. 1924. *The primitive archaic forms of inner experience and thought in schizophrenia: A genetic and clinical study of schizophrenia.* Nervous and Mental Disease Monograph Series, No. 36.

Strong, D. (E) Naskapi. Address: Columbia University, New York 27, N. Y.

Tax, S. (E) Fox, Guatemalan Indians. Address: University of Chicago, Chicago, Ill.

Thompson, L. 1940. *Fijian frontier*, pp. 27–50. San Francisco: Inst. of Pacific Relations, Amer. Council.

——. 1941a. Disciplines and the problem of education in Hawaii. *Hawaii Educ. Rev., 29*, 229–244.

——. 1941b. Report of the social scientist. *Community Survey of Education in Hawaii*, pp. 124–143. (Honolulu.)

——. 1946. Mimeo. *The Hopi crisis: A report of administrators*, pp. 140–208. Office of Indian Affairs, Washington, D. C. (Available from L. Thompson, 26 E. 93rd St., New York 28, N. Y.)

——. 1947. *Guam and its people*, pp. 235–259. Princeton: Princeton University Press (3rd revised ed.).

——. 1948. Attitudes and acculturation. *Amer. Anthrop., 50*, 200–215.

——. 1950. *Culture in crisis: A study of the Hopi Indians.* New York: Harper.

——. MS. *Indian child training patterns.* Indian Administration Research, Final Report. Address: 26 East 93rd St., New York 28, N. Y.

Thompson, L., and A. Joseph. 1944. *The Hopi way.* Chicago: Chicago University Press.

——. 1947. White pressures on Indian personality and culture. *Amer. J. Sociol., 53*, 17–22.

Thouless, R. H. 1933. A racial difference in perception. *J. Soc. Psychol., 4*, 330–339.

Toffelmier, G., and K. Luomala. 1946. Dreams and dream interpretations of the Diegueño Indians. *Psychoanal. Quart., 5*, 195–225.

Tschopik, H. (E) Aymara Indians (Chucuito, Peru), 1940–1942. Address: American Museum of Natural History, New York 24, N. Y.

Turner, S. 1938. Infant life in Yuanling. *Primitive Man, 11*, 1–25.

Underhill, R. 1936. The autobiography of a Papago woman. *Mem. Amer. Anthrop. Ass., 46*, No. 3, Pt. 2.

——. 1942. Child training in an Indian tribe. *Marriage and Family Living, 4*, 80–81.

——. MS a. *Papago morality.*

——. MS b. *The individual in Papago society.* Address: 2623 So. Clayton St., Denver 10, Colorado.

Van Gennep, A. 1909. *Les rites de passage: Étude systematique de rites.* Paris: Librairie Critique.

Vigotsky, L. 1939. Thought and speech. *Psychiatry, 2*, 29–61.

Wagley, C. (E) Guatemala; Taperape; Tenetehara. Address: Columbia University, New York 27, N. Y.

Wagley, C., and E. Galvão. 1949. *The Tenetehara*

Indians of Brazil, pp. 70–88. New York: Columbia University Press.

Walk, L. 1928. Die ersten Lebensjahre des Kindes in Südafrika. *Anthropos, 23*, 38–109.

Wallace, W. J. 1947. Hupa child-training—A study in primitive education. *Educ. Adm. and Super.*, January, 13–25.

——. 1948a. Infancy and childhood among the Mohave Indians. *Primitive Man, 21*, 19–38.

——. 1948b. The girls' puberty rite of the Mohave Indians. *Proc. Indian Acad. Sci., 57*, 37–40.

——. MS a. A bibliography of primitive education.

——. MS b. *The Hupa individual and his culture.*

——. (E) Hupa, 1945–1949; Mohave, 1946. Address: University of California, Berkeley 4, Calif.

Ward, E. 1936. The parent-child relationship among the Yoruba. *Primitive Man, 9*, 56–63.

Warner, W. L. MS. *Autobiography of an Australian aborigine.* Address: Dept. of Sociology, Occidental College, Los Angeles 41, Calif.

Warner, W. L., R. J. Havighurst, and L. Eubank. MS. *The attitudes of Navaho, Zuñi, and Sioux children toward rules of games.*

Watrous, B. G. MS. *A personality study of Ojibwa children.*

——. (E) Lac du Flambeau Ojibwa, 1946, 1947. Address: 854 Ridge Rd., Highland Park, Ill.

Wedgwood, C. 1938. The life of children in Manam. *Oceania, 9*, 1–29.

White, L. A. 1942. The Pueblo of Santa Ana, New Mexico. *Mem. Amer. Anthrop., N. S., 44.* (Memoir 60.)

Whiting, J. W. M. 1941. *Becoming a Kwoma.* New Haven: Yale University Press.

——. 1944. Frustration complex in Kwoma society. *Man, 44*, 140–44.

——. MS a. *The relations of child training practices to magico-religious theories of disease—A cross-cultural study.*

——. MS b. *Child training and hypochondriasis.*

——. (E) Tenino of Oregon; Kwoma, New Guinea; Paiute (Harney Valley). Address: Harvard University, Cambridge, Mass.

Whiting, J. W. M., and S. Reed. 1938. Kwoma culture. *Oceania, 9*, 197–199.

Whitman, W. 1947. *The Pueblo Indians of a changing culture.* New York: Columbia University Press.

Wiener, N. 1948. Teleological mechanisms: Time, communication, and the nervous system. *Ann. N. Y. Acad. Sci., 50*, 197–220.

Wilson, G. 1936. An introduction to Nyakyusa society. *Bantu Studies, 10*, 271–274.

Wilson, G., and M. Wilson. MS. *Nyakyusa age-villages.* Address: Rhodes University College, Grahamstown, South Africa.

Wilson, M. (E) Nyakyusa (S. Tanganyika), 1935–1938.

Wolfenstein, M. 1946. *The impact of a children's story on mothers and children.* Monographs of the Society for Research in Child Development, Vol. 11, Ser. 42. Washington, D. C.: National Research Council.

Wolff, H. G. 1947. Protective reaction patterns and disease. *Ann. Internal Med. 27*, 944–969.

TABLE SUMMARIZING THE RESEARCH METHODS AND MATERIALS REPORTED BY 85 INVESTIGATORS [1]
(The investigators are listed in the bibliography with addresses in case they have not published.)

	Legend (used in questionnaires: 1940, 1949)
General	1. Observations of children in ordinary life situations. 2. Detailed material on the standardized treatment of and training of children. 3. Time samples of child behavior. 4. Studies of group behavior. 5. Tests of any sort. 6. Experimental methods of any sort. 7. Childhood material obtained from adults by life history method. 8. Life history materials obtained from children or adolescents.
Projective Methods	9. Children's drawings, modeling, or carving. 10. Rorschach records. 11. Tests of the Levy Sibling Rivalry Type. 12. Tests involving cognitive processes of the Nadel (1937) type. 13. Intelligence tests used as projective methods, for example, Porteus Maze or Goodenough. 14. Use of free play techniques.
Miscellaneous	15. Collection of children's games and songs. 16. Intelligence tests. 17. Tests of sense perception. 18. Collections of children's dreams.
Photographed	19. Typical treatment of children, for example, suckling position. 20. Standard activities of children's games, etc. 21. Studies of parent-child behavior. 22. Studies of individual children. 23. Studies of series of children in any standard set-up. 24. Body-build pictures.
Language Development	25. Baby talk or special children's language. 26. Records of the way in which children learn a language. 27. Material on the formation of concepts by children.

Aginsky, B. 1, 2, 4, 7, 8.
Barnes, F. 1, 7, 8, 10, 19 (stills), 20 (stills).
Barnett, H. G. 1, 7, 19–21 (stills and Ciné).
Barnouw, V. 7, 10.
Bateson, G. 7, 8, 19–23 (Leicas, Ciné).
Beaglehole, E. and P. 1, 5 (Goodenough "Draw-a-Man," Kohs Block Design, Raven Progressive Matrices, modified Bavelas Test), 9, 10, 13, 16.
Belo, J. 1, 2, 5, 9, 10, 14, 19, 21, 23 (Ciné).

Bunzel, R. 1, 2, 7, 11, 14.
Caudill, W. 1, 5 (TAT), 8.
Chesky, J. 1, 2, 4, 7, 8, 20, 21, 23, 25, 26.
Coelho, R. 1, 2, 7, 9, 10.
Colson, E. 1, 2, 7–9.
Copeland, P. 1, 4, 5 (Sociometric tests), 9, 20, 23.
Dazey, E. 2, 7.
Dennis, W. 1–5 (Dennis and Russel Animism Tests), 9, 15, 25, 27.
Devereux, G. 1, 2, 5 (Finger-painting), 7, 8, 9, 15, 18, 19, 25, 27 (Mohave children's ideas of death).
Dubois, C. 1, 2, 4, 5, 7, 9, 11 (modified Levy Sibling Rivalry Test), 13 (Goodenough "Draw-a-Man" Test), 14.
Dyk, W. 1, 7.
Eichhorn, E. 1, 7, 9, 10.
Flannery, R. 1, 2, 7, 15.
Foley, J. P., and A. Anastasi. 9.
Fortes, M. 1–5, 7, 8, 9, 13–16, 19–24, 26, 27. (Perceptual tests based on Spearman: Lowenfeld Mosaic Test. Sex life and moral development, economic activities of children.)
Friedl, E. 1, 7, 8, 10.

[1] This table was compiled in the spring of 1940, on the basis of a questionnaire sent to all workers in the field, and revised in 1948, when similar questionnaires were sent to the original respondents and to all workers whose names I could obtain by inquiry in those institutions and in those departments most interested in this kind of research. The list of unpublished work is neither exhaustive nor can it be selective, but in an area of research where the need for speed in the development of concepts and methods is paralleled by the speed with which the culture of communities valuable for study is being destroyed this, nevertheless, seems worth doing.

CHAPTER 13

CHARACTER DEVELOPMENT IN CHILDREN—AN OBJECTIVE APPROACH

VERNON JONES

Definition and Distinctions

Any attempt at the objective study of character development is beset with many difficulties, such as the varying concepts as to what is meant by character, the extreme complexity of the phenomenon, and the subtle manner in which nature and nurture exert their influences upon it. Recognizing this, let us attempt at the outset to eliminate as many unnecessary difficulties as we can by delimiting and defining the area of study. The concept of character is related to, and sometimes confused with, such concepts as moral or ethical behavior, temperament, and personality. Impossible as it may be to draw hard and fast boundary lines between these conceptual areas, working distinctions can be made which may help to avoid confusion.

In any strict interpretation of character it is clear that it is not coextensive with ethical or moral behavior. Morality concerns itself with conformity to existing standards of a given time or place. Character does not necessarily imply such conformity. Often in history the individuals who have been rated greatest in point of character have been nonconformists from the point of view of certain existing standards of their day. Moreover, conformity to existing standards sometimes demonstrates not so much character as behavior along lines of least resistance. This does not mean, of course, that character is not related to morality. It means that character is a more dynamic and more inclusive concept. In character development much more attention is given to volitional factors and to individual creativeness in the realm of goals to be achieved than is true in moral or ethical growth. If we add to morality the ability to reconstruct one's values and the volitional powers sufficient to direct conduct progressively toward such evolving values, then we have character as we shall think of it in this chapter.

The area of temperament is perhaps less often confused with character than morality is but illustrations of such confusion are not hard to find. Whether a person is good-tempered, sanguine, phlegmatic, melancholic, or choleric is certainly of interest to anyone rating him for practical purposes of living or working with him, and no claim can be made that such characteristics have no relation to character. Strictly speaking, however, the readiness and capacity of an individual for such relatively prevailing affective experiences are not central to the problem of his character. As Roback (1952) says, the influence of a man's character has a farther reach than his temperament. The value of a man's character, he says, does not fluctuate with our nearness to him in time or space, but his temperament is a matter of only "passing interest." "That Carlyle

781

was bilious, choleric, or grouchy," he says, "is certainly deplorable, but Carlyle's temperament, which counted so much with those he came in contact with, does not determine our estimate of the man from the point of view of character." Whether or not we agree fully with Roback that temperament is of only passing interest, we can readily agree that character is different from temperament in that character concerns itself more with the volitional powers of the individual and the directions and goals of his striving.

Finally we come to the confusion of character with personality. Personality, of course, is a very broad concept, being thought of by Murray and Kluckhohn (1948) as "the organization of all the integrative processes in the brain" of the individual, and as having for its functions self-expression, reduction of aspiration tensions, and the reduction of conflicts by appeasement of major needs and by social conformity and identification. If we may judge by such a formulation and by traditional research emphases in personality, too little interest is manifested in the problems of moral behavior coupled with the allied problems of values and of volition. The student of personality is interested in the adjustments or maladjustments which individuals make to tensions and conflicts, and the goal of his therapy is adjustment. The student of character is not so much interested in the mechanisms of adjustment or maladjustment adopted or in the types of personality developed by the individual who feels frustrated, or deludes himself, or becomes introverted, or develops various stereotypes; he is much more interested in what values underlie the individual's feelings of tension or frustration and stimulate him to attempt to maintain his status and self-esteem by such mechanisms as the students of personality are uncovering.

The main objective of personality development is adjustment to the existing environment; the objective of character development is the growth of the individual toward higher personal and social values and toward conduct consistent with them. Aspiration, striving, and all the volitional factors related thereto are considered to be aspects of character which are never outgrown. Instead of adjustment being an end in the character development of an individual, the kind of adjustment which he makes (whether, for example, by honesty and cooperation, or by deceit and intolerance) is a measure of his character.[1]

In making a distinction between character and personality, we do not wish to give the impression that the two areas can be completely separated. There is, of course, overlapping and interdependence between the two concepts, and the recognition of this is beginning to manifest itself in a rapid rise in attention to the interrelationships between personal values and ethical behavior in individual and social situations, on the one hand, and feelings of acceptance, security, and personal worth—and their opposites—on the other. However, one has only to look at the major research and theoretical interests in personality in the past to see that until recently [2] relatively little interest

[1] For an elaboration of some aspects of this point, see Josey and Snygg (1950).

[2] Interest in these problems, and particularly in the problem of values, has been growing rapidly, as can be illustrated by the writings of certain eminent scholars in neurology, sociology, and psychology, to take only three fields. Space will permit reference to only one representative in each field. Herrick (1946) says that the popular slogan "Science knows no values" is shortsighted and incorrect, for "If science had no interest in human values, there would be no science at all," because science has developed on man's valuing of the search for the truth and demonstrable fact over falsehood and magic. The social sciences must point the way, he believes, to better methods of solving problems of human adjustment in the light of the highest human values. Sorokin (1950) has brought together papers from spe-

has been manifested in the problems of individual and social conduct in relation to values, volition, and the integrity and growth of the self-ideal. These are the very problems in which the student of character is most interested.

If, therefore, character is not coextensive with morality, or temperament, or personality, or the sum total of these, how shall we think of it? Character is the sum total of the attitudes and overt ways of behaving of the individual which are the correlatives of his regulative habits, developing values, and volitional drives. It is a dynamic concept involving inner creativeness and psychocultural determination.[1]

In this chapter on character development, as character is here defined, it will be the aim to include the maximum of experimental data consistent with the attempts to point out integrative threads and with the search for meanings and generalizations. If one is interested in theory construction or in interpreting facts in terms of some theory tentatively accepted, there is ample opportunity for such in the interpretation of the responses of children in situations involving persistence, feelings of guilt, values, and the like. There are, for example, the very difficult but important problems of the source of values and the

cialists in a number of fields, particularly from psychology, on the problem of the value concept of "altruistic love" in its relation to the integration and direction of behavior. Cantril (1950) maintains that man's outstanding characteristics are his capacity to sense values in the quality of experience and his tendency to improve the value aspects of experience. He believes that the value approach in psychology will greatly enhance understanding of individual and social conduct. These writers obviously are not thinking of values as narrowly defined within the framework of existing personality theory. To them values, and their conduct correlates in character, are pervasive and central in human life. They are concerned, therefore, with the study of values and character as basic problems in themselves.

1 For a more detailed treatment of these distinctions and definitions, see Jones (1950).

genesis of volition. With these particular problems little scientific progress has been made. However, it is easy to point to many areas in character development which have been attacked by experimental methods. A variety of devices have been used to study the behavior of children in situations involving cooperation, generosity, honesty, persistence, self-control, truthfulness, levels of aspiration, and the like. Various psychocultural studies have been made which have factual implications for character development. There has also been a large amount of statistical and experimental work done in comparing the responses of delinquent and nondelinquent children. The contributions of various nurtural-cultural and native-biological factors to character development have been studied. It will be the aim of this chapter to bring together the most significant facts from these and similar studies and to interpret them in as meaningful a whole as possible.

Measurement of Character

In an objective approach to character development one of the first problems which arises is that of measurement, for the results of research in a field are no more objective and dependable than the measurements upon which they are based. Are there techniques of measurement, therefore, which are sufficiently valid and reliable in the field of character to supply a factual basis for present evaluation and future study and research? The answer seems to be one calling for cautious optimism. There are several very promising methods which when used with great care have yielded what seem to be dependable results, and newer, more subtle, and more ingenious methods are constantly being devised.

The techniques which have been the most successful in the past and seem most promising for the future can be grouped under eight headings: (1) observation and rating methods, (2) measurement of actual conduct, (3) physiological methods, (4) interview methods, (5) projective techniques, (6) measurement of attitudes, (7) psychodrama, sociodrama, and other rôle-playing devices, and (8) sociometric techniques.

Observation and Rating Methods. One of the oldest and best methods for measure of character is careful observation and rating. The validity and reliability of observations and ratings will, of course, vary with the traits or other aspects of conduct rated and with the training and care of the raters.

The reader who is interested in an extensive review of the methodology of objective observation and rating is referred to Cronbach (1949) and Greene (1952). Suffice it to say here that the best results in character measurement have usually been obtained when the observer-raters have been thoroughly trained, when the ratings were based on aspects of conduct which could be accurately observed, when special attention was given to the avoidance of "halo effects," when final ratings were based on the observations and ratings of several competent judges, and when graphic rating scales and other devices were employed to encourage raters to distribute their ratings widely over the scale range and thus avoid undue bunching of scores.

Test of Actual Conduct. Among the most interesting measures of character have been the tests of actual performance. In such tests the subject does not know that he is being measured in character. Voelker (1921), a pioneer worker in this field, devised several tests which measured the trustworthiness of children. He measured such behavior as the following: whether or not children would return borrowed property and overchange, the degree to which they would cheat in marking

their own test papers, the extent to which they would make overstatements about knowledge possessed and books read, and whether or not they would receive a tip for small favors.

The most extensive work in the devising and using of concealed tests of performance has been done by Hartshorne and May, who worked with large samplings of school children. They employed the best tests available at the time and devised many new ones for the measurement of honesty, self-control, cooperativeness, and allied traits. Extensive statistical data were obtained concerning the validity and reliability of such tests, the intercorrelations among different measures of behavior in these fields, and the relation of various factors, such as intelligence and home background, to such behavior. For detailed discussions of tests of this type, the reader is referred to Hartshorne and May (1928, 1929), Hartshorne, May, and Shuttleworth (1930), Jones (1936), Greene (1952), and Cronbach (1949).

Another trait in which performance tests have been employed is persistence. An extensive review of the methods and results of testing in this field has been made by Ryans (1939a). He (1938a, 1938b) has experimented rather intensively with a test battery including a test of the amount of consecutive effort at a task in learning, endurance in the face of physical discomfort, and the like. French (1948) describes the use of a persistence test in increasing the predictions of school success from a multiple R of .58, based on aptitude and achievement tests, to .65, based on such tests plus the character trait of persistence.

Physiological Methods. In attempts to measure certain character responses, notably truthfulness and deceit, several physiological measures have been tried. Changes in blood pressure, pulse, respiration, and galvanic skin reactions have been the responses most frequently studied in their relation to deception. Lombroso, as early as 1912, refers to his use of the hydrosphygmograph in proving a suspect guilty of stealing. Since that time there has been a gradual development of instruments designed to detect deception by the measurement of several physiological reactions simultaneously. Probably the most successful instruments of this type to date are those devised by Keeler, by Lee, and by a group at the Ohio State University. Results from the Keeler (1934) "polygraph" (or, more exactly, pneumo-cardio-sphygmogalvanograph) were permitted as evidence in a jury trial in Wisconsin in 1935. This was the first time that such physiological measures were accepted as evidence before a jury in the United States, although a few earlier cases are on record where such results had been presented directly to judges in nonjury trials. Imbau (1946) reports that such devices are proving to be increasingly useful instruments in crime detection laboratories.

The key problem in the use of such physiological measures for research or for practical purposes of detection of deception or guilt is one of validity. One question that is particularly significant concerns the probabilities that an honest or innocent person may, in the face of the excitement involved in taking such tests or under suggestion effects from the tester, react as if dishonest or guilty. The measurement of several physiological reactions simultaneously and the use of only thoroughly trained testers are designed to reduce the probabilities of such errors; but the attitude of the more careful experimenters concerning the validity of present instruments is illustrated by Keeler, who said in the Wisconsin case that he recommended his findings as only one element in the evidence and that he would not

convict upon such results alone.[1] Similar caution is suggested by the study of Bitterman and Marcuse (1947), who report certain negative evidence in the use of the Keeler polygraph in an attempt to solve a problem of theft in a college dormitory.

Interview Methods. One of the oldest approaches to the measurement of character is interview methods. Such methods cover a wide range of devices extending from the spontaneous uncontrolled interview to the use of more or less standardized interviews, and more recently to the use of projective techniques like the Thematic Apperception Test and the Rorschach Test, which are sufficiently specialized to demand mention under a separate heading. In character measurement the uncontrolled interview still yields good results in the hands of some clinicians and experimenters. Healy and Bronner (1936, pp. 88 ff.), for example, for a long time have used the "child's own story" among other devices in their study of delinquents. They carefully avoid any claim that these intensive interviews are psychoanalytical in nature, although they use informally some of the same techniques as those used by psychoanalysts for diagnosis.

Havighurst and Taba (1949) use the interview extensively for probing into the impact of the community upon the child's value systems and into his reactions to this impact. Künkel (1938) gives a good demonstration of the possibilities of this method for studying the relation of the character development of a child to the total integration of his mental and emotional life. From such studies we get challenging suggestions as to the possibilities of the use of the intensive interview in evaluating character responses at a depth where such responses

---

[1] See Imbau (1935a, 1935b, 1946). For a good historical treatment of the use of physiological methods for detection of deception and guilt, the reader is referred to Marston (1946).

are viewed not in isolation but in relation to genetic factors and to fundamental patterns of motivation.

Projective Techniques. In the field of personality measurement the projective techniques are attracting a considerable amount of attention, and their use in character measurement is definitely on the increase. There is need in character measurement for techniques which will reveal the dynamics of conduct. In the hands of thoroughly trained and experienced clinical psychologists some of these tests, notably the Thematic Apperception Test by Murray (1943), the Rorschach Test (see Beck, 1945; and Klopfer and Kelley, 1942), the World Test by Bühler and Kelly (1941), and the Rosenzweig (1949) Picture-Frustration Study, may yield valuable insight into basic motivation and frustration of a child or youth as they relate to the present organization and future development of his character.

Measurement of Attitudes. In attempts to measure certain aspects of character, numerous tests of attitudes and opinions have been employed, involving such devices as ranking offenses, marking suggested responses in situations as right or wrong, giving cause-and-effect relations, predicting probable consequences of acts, and the passing of judgment upon nationality or racial groups and upon economic, political, and religious issues. The obvious weakness of such tests is that measures of knowledge and verbally expressed attitudes do not accurately reveal to what extent such knowledge and attitudes will be translated into action. Of course, it might be maintained that such tests are of value because knowledge of, and proper attitude toward, desirable conduct is a prerequisite for such conduct, even though they are not guarantors of it. There is much cogency in this argument, especially as it applies to the use of such tests for revealing points at which education in knowledge and attitudes might be profitably applied. It is quite possible that research in the future may reveal ways of measuring attitudes and aspirations at depths which are nearer the mainsprings of action than present methods which lean so heavily on the verbalized and censored reports of subjects.

Psychodrama, Sociodrama, and Other Rôle-Playing Devices. Among the techniques that purport to measure the individual in relation to others in semicontrolled social situations the psychodrama and sociodrama are proving to be especially interesting and valuable. The psychodrama seeks to measure interpersonal relations and individual attitudes and motivations, whereas the sociodrama deals with intergroup relations and individual-group ideologies. Moreno (1947), to take one example, reports the use of psychodrama in the study and remedy of certain social tensions in a community. By means of this device, not only did the experimenter gain helpful information but also the parents and children who served as subjects gained insight into their own underlying feelings.

As an example of the use of the sociodramatic method, mention might be made of the study and demonstration by Lippitt, Bradford, and Benne (1947), who used the sociodrama as a means of identifying leadership qualities of individuals in a group and as a starting point for leadership training.

The potentialities of both the psychodrama and the sociodrama would appear to be particularly great in the psychocultural investigation which seems destined to play so large a rôle in character research in the near future. Moreno (1943) was one of the first to envisage this possibility in his contributions to measurement methods.

Sociometric Techniques. Sociometric techniques are designed primarily for obtaining peers' evaluations of each other. One of the more interesting of these techniques is the sociogram, developed by Moreno (1934, 1947), which is serviceable for revealing cliques, hierarchies of popularity, leaders, isolates, and the like in social groups. In an assessment program during World War II, the Office of Strategic Services (1948) used sociometric methods extensively to measure personality and character traits of potential officers. The Guess Who Test developed by Hartshorne and May (1929) in the Character Education Inquiry was one of the earliest and simplest of the sociometric methods. Like the sociodrama and the psychodrama these techniques will probably be of increasing interest to the student of character because of their promise as dependable measures of the individual, not in isolation, but in a dynamic social setting—the place where character actually functions.

Violations of Society's Standards. Finally, mention should be made of serious violations of social standards as measures of character. In such social institutions as the law enforcement agencies, the school, the home, and the church, certain minimum standards are set up, and any individual who falls below them is looked upon as a social offender by those interested in maintaining these standards. The standards set up by civil law particularly are quite generally accepted, and consequently any serious violation of these is usually considered indisputable evidence of inferior character development. All studies of juvenile delinquents have proceeded on the assumption that these young people have been measured and found deficient by one of society's most widely accepted tests. We mention this crude yardstick particularly because its verdict is taken so seriously and uncritically by society, when as a matter of fact it is but a rough measure of character and is in need of all the supplementary measures which research with more exact and penetrating methods can reveal.

Individual Differences in Character

One of the first facts which is noted in the inspection of the character responses of children is that the individuals do not fall into dichotomous groups: the strong and the weak, or the persistent and the nonpersistent, or the honest and the dishonest. There are individual differences in character just as truly as there are individual differences in general intelligence or in the knowledge of history. In tests of persistence, for example, Ryans (1938b) and Edmiston and Jackson (1949) find that persistence scores made by a group of subjects spread from very low to very high with no gaps in the distribution. Harris, Gough, and Martin (1950) find prejudice scores among children to vary widely. Similarly in tests of honesty, where dishonesty responses are easily accessible and where motivation for such responses is strong, children have been found to distribute themselves all along the scale. Figures 1 and 2 illustrate this point.

Figure 1 is based on the results of Hartshorne, May, and Shuttleworth (1930) on 21 tests of honesty-dishonesty of children in school and play situations. Figure 2 is based on the original data of Jones (1936) on one test of cheating in school. Both figures represent results for children ranging in age, for the most part, from 12 to 15. It is important to emphasize that the results in both these studies are based not on what children's attitudes toward honesty seemed to be, or on what they said they would do in different situations, but on tests of what they actually did under rather well-controlled conditions. In both figures the distributions are seen to be continuous.

At first glance one might be inclined to say that the individual differences which are spoken of here apply only to the degrees of dishonesty among the dishonest, and that the honest students are still in a class by themselves. This view, although

DISTRIBUTION OF HONESTY SCORES FOR 265 CHILDREN, EACH SCORE BEING MEAN OF 21 TESTS

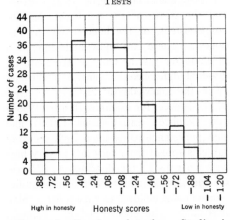

FIGURE 1. Based on data from *Studies in the Organization of Character*, by H. Hartshorne, M. A. May, and F. K. Shuttleworth. New York: Macmillan, 1930, pp. 480, 486.

seemingly logical enough in the case of a given set of data, runs into difficulty when it is found that an individual may be completely honest in one situation, or under one degree of motivation, but he may show a considerable number of lapses from perfect honesty in another situation or under a higher degree of motivation. Gross (1946), for example, found much more dishonesty among seventh grade children in scoring their own test papers when their answers were slightly in error than when the errors were large.

To appreciate the fact that honest-dishonest behavior varies with the nature of

situations and the motivation involved, at least among children, one has only to think how different so-called character traits get in one another's way. Truthfulness at times conflicts with loyalty to one's group; truthfulness to one's host or benefactor may run counter to courtesy or gratitude; truthfulness to the sick may come into collision with tact and helpfulness. Thus, if a child deviates in a given situation from "the truth, the whole truth, and nothing but the truth," shall we think of him and treat him as belonging in a separate category from the honest? It seems more con-

DISTRIBUTION OF SCORES ON MALLER SELF-MARKING (CHEATING) TEST FOR 191 BOYS AND GIRLS IN SEVENTH AND 133 IN EIGHTH GRADE

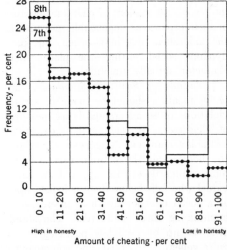

Scores given in percentages, that is, the percentage that the number of cheatings bears to the number of chances to cheat.

FIGURE 2. From original unpublished data of Vernon Jones.

sistent with the experimental facts—and also sounder from the point of view of education and therapy—to say in a case like this that the child's inhibitions against dishonesty and deceit have weakened under the particular motivation or particular conditions of conflict with other "traits," and that in spite of a certain amount of dishonesty some degree of the organization of behavior which we call honesty remains intact. It is in this sense that we may think of a given individual in different situations or different individuals in the same situation as differing in degrees of honesty.

DISTRIBUTION OF TOTAL HELPFULNESS SCORES

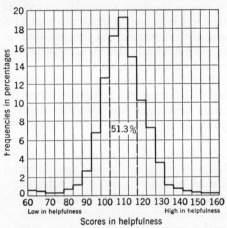

Frequencies given in percentages. Number of cases = 800.

FIGURE 3. Adapted from *Studies in Service and Self-Control,* by H. Hartshorne and M. A. May. New York: Macmillan, 1929, 109. By permission of the publisher.

From the point of view of genetic development of honest behavior in a child, there seems to be much merit in this concept of degrees of honesty, because it is consistent with the basic hypothesis of the gradual development and organization of behavior and it assumes neither a sudden springing into perfection of patterns of behavior, or "traits," on the one hand, nor the sudden and complete collapse of such patterns, on the other.

What has been said about individual differences in honesty seems to apply to all other traits that have been measured. Space, however, will permit the giving of only one more distribution. Figure 3 represents a distribution of scores in helpfulness.

From a study of Figures 1, 2, and 3 it is not possible to generalize about the shape of the different distributions further than to say that they are continuous from the low to the high end of the scale and that the dispersion in all cases is wide. Figures 1 and 3 show a tendency toward normality of distribution, but this is not borne out by Figure 2, where the units of measurement are the simplest. In addition to the statistical fact that the shape of distributions may be affected by the units of measurement employed, it is known that it will vary with different degrees of motivation. It is also quite possible that the shape will differ in groups of different ages and different amounts of training.

The Contribution of Native-Biological Factors to Character Development

Having considered briefly the question of individual differences in character development and their measurement, we come now to the problem of the factors contributing to such differences and to general development. Does a child of a given age show up poorly in character because he is deficient in those biological factors which supply the potential base for character development, or because the conditioning and learning which his environment afforded were faulty? This raises the age-old controversy of nature and nurture, and it raises it in a most complex field of behavior.

If one were starting out, at the present stage of knowledge, to discover the percentage contribution of nature and nurture in accounting for individual differences in character development, he would be doomed to failure. Such a multitude of unmeasurable variables is subsumed under each of these concepts, and they interact in such intricate ways, that the crucial experiment to determine the exact relative influence of each is at present out of the question. However, data are available to indicate that at least intelligence, age or level of maturation, sex, and certain emotional and volitional factors are sufficiently related to development and individual differences in character to justify their discussion, if we can accomplish that difficult task of treating one of these factors at a time without losing sight of the fact that none of them operates singly or in isolation from environmental and cultural forces.

One fundamental thesis of this chapter is that character development of an individual at any given time is an integration based upon certain native and biological factors on the one hand, and upon certain conditionings and learnings stimulated by the environment and the over-all cultural matrix, on the other. It is hoped, therefore, that the following discussion of some of the native factors which influence character development will never become so involved in particulars that it seems to lose sight of this larger framework of inter-relationships.

Influence of Intelligence. The relation of intelligence to character development is probably most readily seen in the rôle which intellect plays in selecting the environment and in orienting the individual in it. The dull and the bright intellectually are not alike in their ability to foresee the consequences of their acts; neither are they alike in their capacity to sense when greater advantages inhere in remote goals than in immediate gratifications. The more able the individual, the better can he select his environment and mold it in accordance with the ends he would achieve. The same

environment does not produce the same total organization of learned conduct and values in the bright and in the dull. Indeed, differences in intellect make of identical physical environments different psychological environments. Of course, this does not mean that superior intellect can so alter inferior environments as to guarantee strong character under any and all circumstances. Good intelligence, however, other things being equal, should enable one to achieve the skills, knowledge, and values that will help him to make the most of a superior environment, on the one hand, or to resist efficiently the restricting effects of a poor environment, on the other.

With these preliminary remarks concerning the meaning of any relation found between intelligence and character development, let us turn now to a consideraton of some of the objective studies. The statistical facts which are available on the relation between intelligence and character can be summarized under three headings: (1) the comparison between intellectually gifted children and unselected children on certain tests of character; (2) the correlation between general intelligence and scores on certain tests of character; and (3) the intelligence of serious offenders or delinquents.

Terman *et al.* (1925) in their classic study, compared a group of 532 children having IQ's over 130 with an equal number of unselected children by means of a battery of 7 tests of character. They found that 85 per cent of the gifted group equaled or exceeded the mean of the unselected, or control, group. The results for each age group are given graphically in Figure 4. It is seen that the gifted boys and girls exceeded the unselected by a significant amount at each age level. Terman also had teachers rate the children of the gifted and the control groups on 25 traits. If we select out of his list those traits most closely related to the problem of character development and compare the ratings assigned to the two groups, we find that 73 per cent of the gifted boys and 74 per cent of the gifted girls exceeded the respective means of the control groups. The five traits upon which the above figures are based are conscientiousness, truth-

MEAN TOTAL SCORES OF GIFTED AND CONTROL CHILDREN, BY AGE, ON SEVEN CHARACTER TESTS

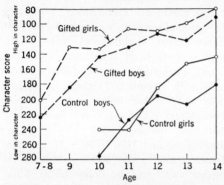

FIGURE 4. Adapted from *Genetic Studies of Genius,* by L. M. Terman, *et al.* Vol. 1. Stanford University, Calif.: Stanford University Press, 1925, 515. By permission of the publisher.

fulness, sympathy and tenderness, will and perseverance, and prudence and forethought.

From the results on the tests and the total ratings, Terman concludes that intellectually gifted children surpass unselected children in tests and ratings of honesty, truthfulness, and similar moral traits. As he points out, the gifted are not free from faults in character development; indeed, he says that one out of five of the gifted has more faults than the average of the general population. However, the average difference between the two groups on the basis of total scores is striking. From it we conclude that children who are gifted

intellectually, and who possess all the other advantages of environment and heredity which go with such giftedness, are placed in a better position to achieve superior character than the less gifted. From the point of view of assessing the relative contribution of intelligence alone to character development, this conclusion is useless; from the point of view of studying the clustering of factors as they affect character development in the realistic interrelations between nature and nurture in the culture in which the child actually lives, it is indicative of thinking in terms of the interaction of the factors of nature and nurture which will characterize this chapter.

A significant point growing out of a detailed analysis of Terman's data which the above composite results do not reveal is that some values in the culture are responded to more strongly than others by the gifted. Terman's data reveal only one such difference, but future research may reveal many. The gifted were found to surpass the average more in traits and values directed to self-success than to traits and values directed to social responsibilities and service. Taken as a group the gifted children exceeded the average in every trait measured, but they exceeded the average most in "will and perseverance" and least in "sympathy and tenderness." In the volitional, aggressive traits 85 per cent of the gifted exceeded the mean of the unselected; in the sympathy-service traits only 59 per cent of the gifted exceeded the mean of the unselected. When one considers the much greater capacity of the gifted to achieve power over others, this difference between their standing on ego-directed and on alter-directed traits takes on considerable social significance. These results of Terman are based on only one investigation and, of course, need verification in other studies before too much stress is placed upon them. However, the results of Spaulding (1938) and of Wilson (1938), working in the field of education, may be interpreted as supplying at least complementary evidence. Spaulding made an extensive study of the social-civic knowledge and attitudes of high school students and found that, whereas the abler students had mastered factual material much better than the average, their insight into and concern about the social problems of their community or nation were far from commensurate with their mental abilities or general scholastic achievements. Wilson, in a similar study, found that young people with high IQ's consistently surpassed the average in comprehension of social terms, knowledge of history, and the like, but that these same students differed from the average very little in knowledge of or attitude toward such community affairs as relief, health, and recreation.

Phillips (1950), in studying intellectual and personality factors associated with social class attitudes of junior high school youth, finds that relative brightness, when coupled with good personality adjustment, tends to be positively associated with acceptance of the typical social class attitudes and behavior patterns of the class group of which the individual is a part.

So much for the relation of intelligence to character development as revealed by studies which contrast the bright and the average. These results can be summarized by saying that the gifted exceed the average on all composite tests and ratings reported, but that there are some definite signs that many gifted children in our present culture are developing their superiority in those character traits making for individual success rather than in those making for social responsibility and progressive social change.

The second line of evidence concerning the influence of intelligence on character development involves results from correlational studies. The most comprehensive investigation of this type to date is that of Hartshorne and May (1928, 1929). They used an extensive battery of tests with elementary school children, and found correlations which average about +.50 between intelligence and honesty in school situations. They attempted to measure the home background of their subjects and to partial out this factor by using the partial correlation technique. The partial r between intelligence and honesty, with home background constant, was found to be +.40. Jones (1936), working with honesty tests similar to those of Hartshorne and May, found correlations ranging from +.32 to +.43 with seventh and eighth grade pupils who were rather homogeneous in home background. The correlation between intelligence and helpfulness was found by Hartshorne and May to be +.16 and that between intelligence and cooperative behavior was found by Jones to be +.09.[1] These are samples of the correlations found between intelligence and tests of actual performance in situations where the subjects did not know that they were being tested in ethical behavior.

If we may judge from the rather wide range of correlations extending from +.09 for cooperation to +.40 for honesty, it seems that intelligence is related in different ways to different aspects of character. Nowhere in the literature do we find the relation to be really close. On the other hand, we almost never find it to be zero or negative.

The third source of evidence on the relation of intelligence to character development is the studies of juvenile delinquency. Healy and Bronner (1926) in their classic

[1] The correlation ratio between the cooperation test and intelligence was found to be +.37. When this is compared with the Pearson r of +.09, it is clear that the regression is curvilinear.

study reported that 13 per cent of the 4000 delinquents examined by them in Boston and Chicago were feeble-minded, that is, below 70 IQ. This should be compared with 1.5 to 2 per cent, which is the percentage of feeble-mindedness in the general population. More recent studies tend to substantiate these findings of Healy and Bronner. Indeed Glueck and Glueck (1934, 1940), working with 1000 delinquents, found exactly the same percentage.

These results on the incidence of feeble-mindedness among delinquents are interesting and relevant as far as they go, but it is clear from the absolute size of the percentages that feeble-mindedness cannot be considered a factor in the large majority of cases. It is the dull and the dull-normal groups, not the feeble-minded, that are the chief sources of juvenile delinquency. Lane and Witty (1935) reported that 80 per cent of their group of 700 delinquent boys were below the average of unselected children in intelligence. Glueck (1935) found 58 per cent of her group of 1000 delinquents to be below 91 IQ as compared with 21 per cent of unselected school children. Armstrong and Heisler (1945) obtained an average IQ of 83 for 200 white delinquent boys in New York City. The average IQ for an equal number of Negro delinquent boys was 79. Owen (1937) made a summary investigation of 21 studies of delinquents and found a mean IQ of 82.4.[1] These are but a few of the many studies of the intellectual status of delinquents, but they give results that are typical.[2]

[1] Eckenrode (1950) reported results based on the testing of 345 delinquent boys on the Stanford Achievement Test from which we estimate that the average educational quotient was 70 or less, indicating that delinquents' efficiency in school is appreciably lower even than their intelligence scores would lead one to expect. Ninety per cent of these boys reported that they disliked school.

[2] For a review of this and certain other correlates of delinquency, see Metfessel and Lovell (1942). The position taken by these writers is essentially

There is no need to multiply the evidence. It shows clearly that intellectual dullness or backwardness is much more frequent in delinquent than in normal populations.

In presenting these three lines of evidence to the effect that intelligence is related to character, care has been exercised to avoid any intimation of a single-line causal relationship. Nothing could be further from the point of view held in this chapter than the concept of superior or inferior conduct, including delinquency, resulting from any single factor or a simple summation of single factors. The systematic position taken here is that such conduct results from a most intricate combination of factors which are usually anything but independent one of another. However, it is believed that the best understanding of this multiple causation can be achieved by a consideration of some of the more important factors, one at a time, and by a gradual approach to the integrations which the evidence seems to justify.

Our first conclusion is that dull and dull-normal children will, on the average, be more likely to be brought before juvenile courts for serious antisocial conduct than average or bright children, if everything else, including the environment, is left alone to work itself out as it will. The second is that, although good intelligence does not guarantee normal or superior char-

the same as that taken in this chapter, namely, that neither feeble-mindedness nor dullness in and of itself produces juvenile delinquency. There are always mediating factors. It is probable, for example, that low mental ability leading to difficulties and frustrations at school is one important mediating factor. It is possible that abilities to foresee consequences of one's acts are dimmed and the capacities to visualize possible punishment ahead are weak as a result of dullness. This may be a second factor. Moreover, when dullness is combined with the inferior home background that ordinarily accompanies it, the training is likely to be defective, the prestige of the family as a restraining force is likely to be negligible, and the individual aspiration level is likely to be low.

acter development, good intelligence, plus all the other advantages and opportunities that usually go with it in our culture, does give one a better chance to avoid or counteract the stimuli leading to inferior character, on the one hand, and to select more worthy stimuli and more socially acceptable goals, on the other.

Influence of Age or Level of Maturation. The influence of level of maturation upon character development, like the influence of intelligence, cannot be studied in isolation from certain other variables. In a strict sense, therefore, it may be maintained that maturation as such cannot be investigated here at all, for it cannot be divorced from improved ability to learn and increased experience. However, the influence of age, coupled with all the attending advantages in ability and learning opportunities, can be studied. Attention can be given, for example, to the problem of whether the manner in which the culture affects the individual is dependent partly on his level of maturation and experience. Attention can also be given to the evidence for physiological and other changes with age in determining the types of drives and motivations which will affect conduct.

Slaght (1928) compared younger and older boys on their ideas as to whether it was wrong "to cheat if you can," "to lie to keep a secret," and "to lie to get even with someone," and found that a significantly greater percentage of the younger children condemned each of these as wrong. Apparently the younger children had not faced the conflict between the virtue of honesty and the virtue of loyalty in some of these questions as squarely as the older ones. Probably, also, the younger boys were more willing to accept the general rule and hand it back as given to them than the older, who may have seen more clearly what the culture actually requires and what exceptions it really makes.

Tudor-Hart (1926), working in collaboration with Bühler, found that lying from a social motive was considered wrong more often by younger children than by older ones. These experimenters also reported that, although selfishness might change in its manifestations, its amount did not seem to decrease with age or advancement in school. In the study of gifted and unselected children, mentioned earlier in this chapter, Terman *et al.* (1925) reported a clearly defined tendency for total character scores, as determined by an average of 7 tests, to increase with age (see Figure 4). A study of the separate distributions for the various tests, however, revealed the interesting fact that the older children obtained their advantage very largely from verbal tests in which knowledge of the most acceptable answer counted most, such as tests of reading preferences and social standards and attitudes. On the tests of overstatement with respect to books read or knowledge possessed, there was no perceptible increase in honesty with age. Also on the "peeping," or cheating, test there was no consistent tendency for the older children to be more trustworthy than the younger. From these and similar results it seems safe to say that the mere process of maturation will not, on the whole, decrease the amount or seriousness of dishonesty and deceit of children. The types of untruthfulness and dishonesty which are practiced at different age levels will be different, but they will vary with the amount of experience and foresight possessed and with the pressures of the peer culture.

The results on tests of moral knowledge and of persistence are more favorable to the older children than are those on tests of honesty and truthfulness. All studies are in agreement that children as they grow older learn better what the accepted standards of society are, both those that are practiced and those that are preached. It also seems definitely established that children, on the average, increase somewhat in persistence as they grow older, at least up to age 14. Hartshorne and May (1929) found a correlation of +.33 between test scores on persistence and chronological age in an elementary school population. Ryans (1939b), however, working with young people ranging in age from 14 to 22, did not find any consistent increases in persistence with age. This indicates that perhaps by early adolescence this trait is pretty well established in the make-up of the average person.

Attending the process of maturation there are frequently definite changes in the manifestations of conduct. With the onset of adolescence, for example, the sex drive influences not only the interests of young people but also their conduct and their inhibitions and controls. Fox (1946) finds several evidences of offenses paralleling certain age ranges among delinquents and criminals.

So much for the sketchy results on the influence of age on character development. They do not tell us what part maturation alone plays. They make no pretense of revealing how much of the difference (or sameness) from age level to age level is due to increased learning ability and experience and how much is due to conscious training by parents, teachers, and others. The results, although unanalyzable along these lines, do indicate conclusively that increase in age, plus all that ordinarily accompanies it, does not produce large improvements in any of the aspects of character that have been investigated, except in moral knowledge. They support the conclusion that children do not "naturally outgrow" their earlier faults as they become older. They lead one to believe that there is no age level which can be properly referred to as the "age of discretion," before

which children's actions may be relatively unsusceptible to training and considered unimportant or insignificant for character development, and after which conduct rather suddenly begins to yield to education and the conditioning of the culture.

Influence of Sex. Our culture does not expect the same character patterns of girls that it expects of boys, and the training that it gives them is different. Whatever differences are found, therefore, in experimental studies between boys and girls in character development should be recognized as not necessarily native. Having granted this, however, we wish to call attention to at least one line of evidence which argues for a biological or native contribution to sex differences in certain aspects of conduct. The glandular systems of boys and girls are obviously different, and there is much evidence to indicate that differences in glandular balance and functioning are related to differences in character and personality. It would take us far afield to attempt to review here the extensive evidence on this, but two very relevant studies will be mentioned in passing. Bize and Moricard (1937) gave injections of testosterone to young boys and found a definite increase in aggressiveness in all social relations. Clark and Birch (1945) administered male and female sex hormones to a male chimpanzee and found that social dominance of the animal was increased by the former hormone and that subordination resulted from the latter. These and many other studies lead to the conclusion that one example of a character difference between the sexes which may result in part from native factors is the greater aggressiveness of the male, other things being equal.

Most of the gross differences that have been found in the comparison of the character development of boys and girls are probably the resultant of a very intricate interaction of a few native differences, such as greater aggressiveness on the part of boys, and a host of environmental differences.

Tudor-Hart (1926) asked a large number of young boys and girls in Austria and in America to name any cases which they could think of where lies were necessary. She found, in comparing the answers of boys and girls, that the girls gave a much larger number of conventional lies, such as "Mother is not at home," "Glad to see you," or "I've had a fine time at your party." An appreciable difference was found in all lies which might be grouped under the heading of social, including lies to keep secrets, to conceal surprises, to protect others, to keep from offending, and the like. Thirty-two per cent of all the lies named by the girls, as compared with 18 per cent of those by the boys, were of this type. Hartshorne and May (1928) found that on the basis of averages on several tests there was no significant difference between the sexes in honesty in school, but the girls cheated more than the boys on a "party test" where cheating consisted of peeping in order to make a good showing in a social situation. Terman et al. (1925) also found, on the basis of a peeping test, that gifted girls were a little more dishonest than gifted boys, although on all honesty tests combined the girls were slightly more honest than the boys. Jones (1936), employing several tests of honesty in school, found no appreciable sex difference at the initial testing, but the girls tended to show somewhat more improvement during 9 months of instruction in character and citizenship than the boys.

With regard to possible sex differences in volitional behavior, the evidence is rather meager and not conclusive, as it is particularly difficult here to control for differences in motivation and early conditioning. In a study of approximately 800 boys and girls, ranging in age from 9 to 16, Sheehy (1938) found that boys are more aggressive, dominant, fearless, and boastful than girls, whereas girls are more suspicious, more fanciful, and more amenable to social controls than boys. Ryans (1939b) found no sex difference in his test in persistence.

On cooperative and "helpful" behavior, Hartshorne and May (1929) reported that boys and girls differ very little on the average, but, wherever small differences do occur, the advantage is usually on the side of the girls. On the average, the girls were found to be consistently more generous than boys in voting money for charitable causes, although in any given social grouping it is not unusual to find that it is a boy who shows the greatest aggressiveness in leadership and action.

In studying the incidence of serious misconduct in school and delinquent behavior among boys and girls, we find the evidence to be conclusive. More boys than girls are found guilty of antisocial behavior. Olson (1930, 1949) found by means of a behavior rating scale that boys have more tendencies toward serious conduct disorders than girls. Rundquist (1938), working with large samples of boys and girls in the first and second grades in school, came to the same conclusion as Olson. It is a well-known fact, of course, that many more boys than girls fall so far below the minimum standards of moral conduct that they run afoul of the law. Schwartz (1949) of the U. S. Children's Bureau reported, on the basis of returns from 76 urban juvenile courts, that the ratio of boys to girls among juvenile delinquents averaged between 6 to 1 and 4 to 1 during the years from 1938 to 1947. In New York Maller (1937) found the ratio to be 7 to 1.

When a study is made of the types of offenses for which boys and girls are arraigned before the courts, significant differences are found. An investigation by the Children's Bureau of the Federal Security Agency (1946) showed the usual results, namely, that girls were referred to the courts most frequently for sex offenses, for running away, and for being ungovernable, whereas boys were arraigned most often for stealing and other crimes against property. (See Table 1.) Dollard *et al.* (1939) inter-

does a "double standard" set by the culture for judging the "morality" of boys and girls. These facts, however, are very relevant to the question of sex differences if we think of them as differences in adequacy of response to situations where this adequacy is judged in terms of existing standards and practices in our present culture.

TABLE 1

OFFENSES AND FREQUENCIES OF OCCURRENCE AMONG 111,939 DELINQUENCY CASES OF 374 COURTS FOR THE YEAR 1945

[Taken from *Social Statistics*, Supplement to Vol. 11 of *The Child* (November, 1946, Supplement), *Juvenile Court Statistics*, 1944 and 1945, U. S. Children's Bureau, Federal Security Agency.]

Reason for Reference to Court	Number			Per Cent		
	Boys	Girls	Total	Boys	Girls	Total
Stealing	38,610	2,269	40,879	42	12	37
Mischief	17,779	1,462	19,241	19	8	17
Traffic violation	9,659	193	9,852	10	1	9
Truancy	6,164	2,517	8,681	7	13	8
Running away	5,652	3,655	9,307	6	19	8
Being ungovernable	5,542	4,298	9,840	6	22	9
Sex offense	2,579	3,411	5,990	3	18	5
Injury to person	2,828	396	3,224	3	2	3
Other reason	3,858	1,067	4,925	4	5	4
Totals	92,671	19,268	111,929	100	100	100

preted such sex differences in crime largely in terms of the greater aggressiveness of boys.

Of course, the facts concerning sex differences obtained from the study of juvenile court cases cannot be interpreted apart from the differences in ethical standards set by society for boys and girls. One might say, for example, that the fact that the greatest percentage of offenses among girls are sex offenses does not represent so much a sex difference in character as it

It is hazardous to attempt to draw any broad generalizations from the above results, but for the purpose of bringing some of the lines of evidence together we submit the following two tentative conclusions.

In the first place, it seems from the results of Hartshorne and May, Terman, Tudor-Hart, Jones, and others that girls may be more submissive than boys and more influenced by what they think is expected of them by adult society. Second, it seems that boys are more aggressive than girls If these two conclusions are correct, we would expect the same degree of lack of socialization in boys and in girls to manifest itself in more serious, aggressive forms among boys. This we find to be the case as mentioned above. We would also expect a larger amount of aggressive leadership for superior conduct among boys than among girls. The evidence on this is not conclusive, but it is at least a possibility that deserves objective testing.

Accidents and Diseases Affecting Brain Functioning—Their Relation to Volition and Certain Other Character Traits. Among the unlearned factors which are known to influence character development at least negatively are injuries and disease which interfere with the normal function of the higher cortical centers. The most interesting point to be emphasized here concerning these studies is that in not a few cases the injury or the disease seems to operate[1] to upset the organized patterns of character responses. If such factors can interfere with the character pattern which had been achieved up to a given point, then we may infer that probably such factors can also retard and set limits to the character development achieved per unit of learning time or cultural exposure in the first place.

Many individual case histories are on record to show that after a cerebral injury the individual has been left not only with reduced intellectual ability but also with greatly altered patterns of inhibition and control. Aita (1948) found among other residuals of brain injury an increase in instability and a disturbance in the

---

[1] Of course not all the total result is necessarily attributable directly to the injury or disease, for important character results may come from an individual's emotional reactions to the injury or disease. The point is, however, that a certain type of injury or disease has these effects whereas others which would seem to be similarly emotionally disturbing do not.

"capacity for interpersonal relations." Newell (1937) made a study of 20 children who had had brain injuries and reported that the most frequent effect of the injury was an increase in irritability with "a general decrease of inhibitory functions." Ten of these children showed neurotic symptoms after the injury and 5 were found guilty of delinquent behavior. Rylander (1937) studied 32 patients after brain operations had been performed. Changes in intellectual ability appeared in 21 of these cases, whereas in 25 cases diminished inhibitions of affective responses occurred, and in 22 notable changes in volitional powers.

In the case of severe mental disease it is well known that changes in the character of the victim occur. Baruk (1947, 1949) finds evidence for believing that disorders of the anterior hypophysis are related to lowered volition powers. Subjects suffering from such disorders, he says, while preserving in large part their judgment of right and wrong, display volitional weakness in the form of nonchalance and lack of control. The disease which has attracted most attention in recent years as a result of its relation to character changes is encephalitis. Many writers, including Greenbaum and Lurie (1948), Levi (1930), Stertz (1931), and Ciampi (1937), have cited cases showing notable changes in character following this disease. Sometimes the change in the behavior occurs soon after the onset of the disease; sometimes it appears in a serious form much later. The chief offenses noted are disobedience, lying, stealing, sex irregularities, cruelty, and violence. These occur in individuals who were, presumably, well adjusted previous to the contraction of the disease. Heersena (1940) stresses the point that the effects of the disease, and any attending infections, are more pronounced in children, whose personality and character are still undergoing rapid development.

Such changes in moral behavior attending disease present interesting theoretical problems. They suggest possible limitations to character development as a result of hereditarily or biologically determined defects. Moreover, if we knew the mechanisms by which satisfactory moral behavior was rather suddenly replaced by definitely unsatisfactory behavior in such cases, then perhaps we should have a better idea about just what happens in the organism in the development of character. Unfortunately, however, the studies shed little light on this. The most promising hint which we get is that the disease may so affect neurological functioning as to throw out of equilibrium, so to speak, the integrations which the individual has achieved. Some evidence for this is presented by Bond and Appel (1931), who state that they find in the postencephalitic condition not only lying and stealing but also heightened feelings of insecurity, stronger regressive tendencies, and more intense introversion or extroversion. We should expect that, attending these signs of increased inner conflict following this disease, the integration in behavior which had been previously achieved would be unsatisfactory and that changes would appear. We should also expect that remnants of old integrations might remain and that the victim might alternate, as he usually does, between the new patterns of conduct and remorse for having forsaken the old.

The Problem of the Inheritance of a Moral Sense. In any discussion of the native, or nonlearned, factors connected with character development, the old question arises as to whether or not a moral sense can be inherited. The intuitionists of the seventeenth and eighteenth centuries postulated an intuitive faculty, presumably hereditary, which could perceive without training what was moral and what was not. The concept of a sort of innate moral deficiency, which is found in the literature from time to time, harks back to this thinking of the intuitionists. This view is illustrated by Betke (1944), who says that delinquency is often due to defective "moral reasoning," and especially by Tredgold (1937), who maintains that a certain proportion of delinquents and criminals are fundamentally lacking in moral sense. The term "moral deficiency" is used frequently in reports of the Mental Deficiency Committee in England.

This concept of a moral sense or moral deficiency is inadequate and misleading; it is mentioned here primarily for the purpose of sharpening the distinction which should be made between saying, on the one hand, that inherited nature affects the substructures upon which character is built and maintaining, on the other, that inheritance affects character directly.

The view represented in this chapter, and the only one which seems consistent with the data presented, is that children do not inherit their character. They inherit capacities for responding to stimuli and for profiting by experience; probably they inherit or biologically develop certain glandular and volitional strengths and weaknesses; and possibly they inherit some propensities toward overdevelopment or underdevelopment of certain impulses or drives. They gradually acquire their character, within the broad limits set by their native make-up, by responding in certain ways in the situations which the environment affords.

The Influence of Nurture

The environmental factors which relate themselves to the character development of a child are legion. Indeed, it would be difficult to name a factor in the environment calling forth a psychological reaction which might not have some relation to character development. All that can be done here is to group under a few headings what seem to be the most potent factors for the majority of children and treat each of these groupings rather generally to illustrate some principles of character development. Those which will be discussed briefly are: home influences, associates, church schools, day schools, recreational activities, and the over-all culture.

Influence of the Home. The first and most important place in a list of environmental factors influencing character development must be assigned to the home. As Groves (1940) says, the home, itself enmeshed in a cultural milieu, is the most powerful transmitter of the culture of the group. It complements such institutions as government, education, sex status, and religion, but it begins its work long before the child is conscious of these other institutions. In the early ages it is in almost complete control of his social acceptance and rejection, of his joys and sorrows. Parental precepts and example get in their conditioning long before conscious teaching of other institutions of society can reach the child, and they are continually reinforced as long as he is under the home influence. Parental acceptance and affection, or the opposite, determine the psychological atmosphere surrounding him before he understands scarcely any of the words spoken in his presence. L. K. Frank (1948) says that it is the family which is the essential agency for the socialization of the young child and for introducing him to the culture in which he is to grow up and live. Lacking the necessary warmth of parental affection, the young child continues too long his egocentricity, develops fears, and begins putting up his defenses in the form of distrustful and revengeful attitudes of mind.

Allport (1950) maintains that children and youth need warm affectionate relationships and at the same time need a respect for and a defense of their own self-esteem. When bids for affection or belonging are rebuffed or self-esteem is threatened, hostility is the usual result in outward conduct while sensitiveness and frustration are the inner correlates.

Liu (1950), in an extensive experimental study comparing Chinese and American children, concludes that strong emphasis on filial piety in the Chinese culture does not seem to interfere with the development of mature and critical judgment in Chinese children in situations involving moral issues. Instead it appears that the close and affectionate family ties, with the patriarchal management in the home, help to provide security and freedom from apprehension for the child or youth.

Stern (1949), in working with uprooted children in Europe in the wake of World War II, concludes that the lack of normal home life and parental identification has prevented many of them from developing their superegos in the normal way, and he senses difficulty in training them to develop proper attitudes of responsibility and service.

Stott (1950) finds juvenile delinquency frequently to be an escape from an emotional situation which is too much for the child, such as domestic disharmony, parental ill health, lack of feeling of security, and emotional estrangement from parents. Cooper (1950) considers inadequate affection in the home and diffidence of parents concerning the social, emotional, and moral development of their children as being the conditions most likely to lead to delinquency. Wallenstein (1937) studied 3000 school children with a battery of character and personality tests to determine the influence of broken homes on measurable conduct. A comparison of the children from such homes with those from normal homes leads him to conclude that inferior development in several aspects of character could be attributed directly to broken homes.

The relation of children's prejudices and idea of right and wrong to those of their parents have been studied by several investigators. Frenkel-Brunswik (1948, 1951) finds a strong positive relationship between the values and prejudices of young people, age 11 to 16, and those of their parents. However, she finds the prejudices of youth to be more flexible and more subject to change by training than those of the parents. Hartshorne, May, and Shuttleworth (1930) correlated children's ideas of right and wrong with the ideas of each of the following: parents, friends, club leaders, day school teachers, and Sunday school teachers. They found the correlation between child and parent to be the highest, with r equaling .55, and that between child and Sunday school teacher to be the least, r equaling .002. Within the home it was found that there is a closer relation between the ideas of child and mother than between those of child and father.

The influence of the size of family on the moral behavior of children has received some attention from experimenters, but no general conclusions can be drawn. If a child gets the impression that he is not wanted by his parents, or if the presence of a younger brother or sister is interpreted as detracting from the affection and attention which he was receiving, he has greater difficulties in making satisfactory personality adjustments. Whether the adjustments finally made, however, will lead to stronger or weaker character development remains an open question. Probably it will depend both upon the individual child and upon the degree to which he feels that he is rejected.

Symonds (1949), after an extensive study of parent-child relationships, came to the conclusion that if one or both parents strongly reject a child he tends to become overaggressive, or hostile, and may resort to truancy, lying, and stealing. If, on the other hand, the parents exercise overprotection with a child, he tends to become overdependent, relatively helpless for his age, and noncooperative in situations requiring give and take. Different observers report different results relative to the reactions of children to overstrictness and overinhibitive treatment in the home. Some report that the child tends to become overaggressive and rebellious; others that he becomes submissive and strait-laced with an overstrong superego. Havighurst (1952) introduces a new note, based on results in an 8-year study, in which he maintains that consistency of discipline is positively related to the development of ethical competence including self-control and self-direction in the child. He advocates teaching children and youth through consistent discipline that there is moral orderliness in the world and that a reasonable degree of social conformity is realistic and desirable.

Several research studies have been made on the effect upon the family situation of one member who is or becomes neurotic or otherwise emotionally disturbed. The study of Berman (1948) is illustrative of this type of investigation. His results indicate that such a person will tend to bring about disequilibrium in the psychological atmosphere of the home. It seems reasonable to expect changes to result in both the emotional adjustment and the character organization of some or all members of the home.

The economic situation in the home is an important factor in the moral development of children when all the other variables correlated with it are considered. If, however, one may judge from the trends in delinquency during the depression years, it seems that the effect of economic status is small when such factors as parental supervision and level of a child's associates are held constant.

Carr-Saunders, Mannheim, and Rhodes (1944), working in England, equated delinquent and nondelinquent children for neighborhood and school district, and Healy and Bronner (1936), working in the United States, paired delinquent and nondelinquent children of the same family. In both studies the attempted equating of home background decreased the apparent importance of formal sociological factors as contributing causes of juvenile delinquency, but such equating did not eliminate the psychological factors. Even in the same home Healy and Bronner found that the delinquent child felt more often discriminated against and thwarted, more often disliked by one or both parents, and more subject to general emotional stress than did the nondelinquent child.

Jones (1932) and Dawson (1938) have shown that in the state of Massachusetts juvenile delinquency did not rise during the economic depression of 1929 to 1937. Adult theft increased, but crime on the part of children and youth below 17 decreased slightly. The Federal Children's Bureau showed a decrease of 16 per cent in the number of juvenile cases handled in a sampling of the courts of the United States from 1929 to 1937. This should be compared, however, with the rapid rise in juvenile delinquency beginning in 1942 when the economic situation in homes was much improved but when the psychologically disrupting conditions attending the war had made themselves felt. After 1945, as Schwartz (1949) has shown, there was a rather rapid decline for a time, which paralleled the improved supervision of children and youth following the war.

Influence of Associates. The influence of home and of associates cannot, of course, be separated because the place where a child's home is located often sets limits to the neighborhood and the range of cultural backgrounds from which he will select his friends. Granting these interrelations, it seems justifiable, nevertheless, to treat the influence of associates separately. Some of the clearest evidence of the influence of associates on character growth or decline comes from the studies of juvenile delinquency. Burt (1925) and Healy and Bronner (1936) stress the fact that there are few other factors comparing in strength with that of intimate companions in determining whether or not an individual will commit a crime, and, if he commits one, what the crime will be.

It is interesting to note in these and in other studies that there has been a shift in the direction of greater emphasis upon intimate friendships as contrasted with larger groups such as boys' gangs. Thrasher (1927) stressed the great power of the gang to mold the conduct of its members, and there is no gainsaying that such effects are very real. There are, however, intimate loyalties and counterloyalties even within the most solidified gang, and many students of delinquency today are stressing particularly the power for good or ill of the relationships among intimate pals— the twos and threes. There is no intention, in stressing this point, of implying that the influence exerted upon a boy by one or two intimate companions detracts from the power of the gang upon him. On the contrary, one may supplement the other. However, some of the influence which was formerly attributed to the gang in molding conduct may really belong to smaller groupings of intimate companions.

Hartshorne and May (1928) have made the interesting, although not surprising, finding that the influence of one's associates upon his conduct is greatest when they are actually with him. They found that the correlation between children's standing on tests of deception and that of their best friends not in the same classroom was .23, whereas the correlation between best friends in the same classroom was .66. These results justify the conclusion that the effect exerted upon one by his companions is greatest when they are present and in a position to influence his behavior through immediate example, suggestion, and favorable or unfavorable reactions to his attitudes and behavior.

This leads to the mention of the influence of group morale. In small intimate groups, the standard of behavior accepted in the group molds the behavior of all its members at least while they are together. This phenomenon is frequently noted in schools and especially in individual classes. If a class group remains fairly well intact for a year or two, certain habits and attitudes toward neatness, cheating, courtesy to teachers, etc., may gradually be developed. These habits and attitudes are usually rather specific, however. A case is known, for example, where a whole school developed a sort of taboo against cheating, but extreme snobbishness was condoned if not actually encouraged by the group. In a given class in school a good group spirit may develop under one teacher and manifest itself in a high degree of honesty and cooperation in her room and in her presence, but under another teacher the conduct of the group may be very different.

Jones (1936) has found that improvement in measurable character made under the conditions of good group morale is largely dependent for its permanence upon the maintenance of the group intact. He used eight classes of seventh- and eighth-grade students in his experiment and gave instruction in character and citizenship over a period of 1 school year. The class

with the best group morale made the greatest gain. But a few months after promotion time, when the previous class groupings had been dissolved, the students of each class were brought together again for testing. It was found that the original gains were maintained most poorly by the students of the class which had developed the best group morale, and they were maintained best by those students who improved in spite of the weakest group morale. The experimenter refers to the gains made under the very favorable conditions of good group morale as *group-linked gains*. They were, in other words, largely dependent for their operation upon the total group and the spirit which welded it together. This concept implies that, if a child rather suddenly shows improved character responses in a social setting where the group morale favors superior conduct, it does not necessarily follow that such conduct has become firmly interiorized at this level. Similarly, if an individual suddenly displays an abrupt drop from his customary level of conduct when in the company of companions where the group morale favors such retrogression, it does not necessarily follow that his individual habits and standards have crystallized at this lower level.

It seems that group-linked gains and losses become interiorized gradually. For education or rehabilitation this would seem to mean that a child who rather suddenly deteriorates under bad influences may be saved from much of his loss by speedy removal from these surroundings. In the case of a child whose conduct has improved under the impetus of superior surroundings, it means that provision should be made for rather protracted exposure to such conditions to allow the gains to become integrated into individual standards and habits.

Influence of Church Instruction. Historically, the problem of ethical instruction has been intimately associated with religious instruction, and no discussion of children's character development would be complete without at least a recognition of this relationship. There is, however, a notable scarcity of objective data on certain crucial questions.

Ligon (1939) has effectively raised many of these questions and has given a plausible account of the influence which well-directed religious education should have upon the character and personality development of children and youth. Theoretically, the opportunities for religious instruction gradually to interiorize the controls of conduct of the individual and to provide emotional toning for such controls would seem very promising, especially if such instruction could be directed more to actual conduct and if it could be integrated more closely with complementing activity in home and school.

A few studies have been conducted in which comparisons have been made between church or church school attendance and character, as measured by resistance to delinquency, by tests of honesty and cooperativeness, and by correlation studies between knowledge of the Bible and character ratings.

Wattenberg (1950) made a study of 2137 delinquent boys to determine the relation, if any, of church attendance to conduct improvement after one offense. He found fewer recidivists among the church-attending boys, and he concludes that church attendance is a part of a mode of living which tends to reduce juvenile misconduct.

Woodruff (1945) found that religious experience has an important effect on the value patterns of young people. Hartshorne and May (1928), working with large numbers of children in public schools, compared the amount of cheating done in a group attending Sunday school and in a group not attending. In their first sam-

pling the percentage of cheating in the former group was 31 as against 40 in the latter group. In their second sampling the percentages were respectively 38 and 43. The same experimenters (1929), working with another group of 84 children, found that those who attended church schools obtained somewhat higher scores on tests of helpfulness than those who did not, and those who were regular in attendance did better than those who were irregular. Maller (1930) found on the basis of objective tests that the honesty of a group of Jewish children increased appreciably during attendance at religious schools.

All these differences are rather small, but they are consistent in their direction. Of course, it can be argued that any differences noted in favor of the groups under church influence may be due not so much to church or church school attendance as to factors in the heredity and homes of children whose parents are sufficiently concerned about their welfare to send them to such schools. Unfortunately, the accuracy of such an argument cannot be proved or disproved because of the past failure, perhaps unavoidable, to measure or control all relevant variables. The fact remains, however, that the children who attended church schools, and who had all the other advantages that might have gone with church school attendance, did better on the tests than those who did not attend.

It would be interesting to determine for homes equated for socio-economic backgrounds whether there was any relation between interest in religion and church attendance on the part of the parents, on the one hand, and the psychological atmosphere of the home for good child upbringing in personality and conduct, on the other. Our hypothesis would be that a positive relation would be found. Manwell and Fahs (1951) maintain that there is a definite relationship between the spiritual and religious health of children and their mental and emotional health. On the problem of interest in religion among college students Allport *et al.* (1948) found in a study at Harvard and Radcliffe colleges a rather high interest in and "expressed need of" religion in relation to development of personal values.

With regard to the influence of Biblical knowledge on the moral conduct of children, it is impossible to draw any definite conclusions at present. Taylor and Powers (1928), working with school children, correlated the results on the Laycock Bible Test with character ratings based on the combined judgments of teachers and found a correlation of .50, whereas the correlation between the character ratings and intelligence was only .24. Hightower (1930), however, made a study of the same problem and found little or no relationship between Biblical knowledge and the different phases of moral behavior tested. The differences in the results of these two studies serve to stress the difficulty of controlling all relevant variables and getting to the bottom of the matter. Until the interrelationships among intelligence, Biblical knowledge, home influence, and various aspects of moral conduct are known, we cannot hope to draw any conclusions about the relation of Biblical knowledge to character.

Influence of the Day Schools. The influence of day schools upon the character and development of children and youth has been studied under three headings: first, the influence of teachers upon individual children and groups; second, the influence of group spirit upon the members of the group; third, the total impact of the school as measured by changes attending advancement to higher grades in the school. Many of the studies have been concerned primarily with the influence of teachers in their contact with individuals and groups.

Space will not permit more than bare mention of this problem. Anderson *et al.* (1946), to take only one example, found that children's behavior in school tended to vary with different teachers. Inferior conduct, however, once begun under one teacher tended to spread over to other situations. The effects upon children of varying degrees of authoritative and democratic classroom management have come in for a good deal of study, but the control of variables in these studies has left much to be desired. It seems probable that the personality and character of the teacher and the manner in which a management method is executed are more important in affecting children's character development than the method as such. The evidence seems clear that in classes or schools where the management is ineffective the attitudes and conduct of the students deteriorate.

The group spirit of a class in which a child is a member is certainly one important condition influencing his conduct. Jones (1936) found this to be the most significant condition differentiating the classes which improved most in conduct from those which improved least in an experimental learning situation. It is impossible to say how much contribution to good class spirit is made by the teacher in his teacher-pupil relations and how much is made by the pupils in their own interrelations, but if we consider these two together we have the sets of factors in the school situation which are most clearly related to character development.

Level of advancement in school in itself does not seem to be a significant determiner of character, at least not in the grade range from 5 to 8, which has been most extensively studied. Jones (1936) found no significant difference in character development between grades 7 and 8 with which he worked, and Hartshorne and May (1928, 1929) found no consistent improvement in grades 5 to 8 which could be attributed to level of advancement alone. Conduct changes in the different grades, but there is no evidence that it systematically improves except under the conditions already noted, namely, through individual teacher leadership and through the establishment of good class spirit supporting certain superior standards of conduct.

Influence of Recreational Activities. The main objective studies in this field have been made on club activities, motion-picture attendance, radio and television entertainment, and reading. Consequently, the discussion here will be confined to these four.

1. *Club membership.* The pioneer investigation of character development employing controlled test situations was made in the field of club activities. This study was conducted by Voelker (1921) for the purpose of determining the influence of Boy Scout work on trustworthiness. He worked with 57 boys, ranging in age from 10 to 14. At the beginning of the experiment he gave a series of performance tests. Then, during an experimental period of 7 weeks, two groups of boys were given intensive work on trustworthiness, and two other groups, having about the same scores on the initial test, were given the regular training prescribed by the Scout organization; two groups not belonging to the organization and receiving no training were held as controls. At the end of the experimental period all six groups were retested with a test battery similar to the initial one. It was found that most progress had been made by the two Boy Scout groups receiving the intensive training, and that the least progress was made by the two groups which received no Scout training. Apparently both the club membership and the special intensive training had some effect. The special training seems, on the surface, to have been the more im-

portant, but the favorableness of the social situation in which the training is given is coming more and more to be recognized as of very great importance, and in this study we have, possibly, an interesting illustration of this point.

Hartshorne and May (1928, 1929), working with their extensive test data, made a comparison of the scores obtained by children who were members of clubs and those who were not. They found that club members, no matter what the organization, were more cooperative than nonmembers; but club members did not consistently exceed nonmembers in honesty.

Numerous results, based on studies of delinquency in urban areas after club activities have been organized or expanded, have appeared to show that clubs providing good recreational programs and capable leadership have accomplished striking results. In such studies, however, the factor or factors accounting for the improvement have not usually been rigorously isolated. Frequently increased club activities in a community are accompanied by better leadership, better housing, etc. It is easy to believe that any opportunities that are provided for children to engage in club activities under supervision and to practice desirable conduct should contribute to their character development, but evidence on just what contributions are made by each of the interlocking variables would require many more controls than have been involved in these studies in the past.

2. *Motion-picture attendance.* The effect of motion-picture attendance on character development of children and youth has been the subject of a considerable number of research investigations. One topic of study has been the frequency of attendance. In urban areas in California, Shull (1940) found, 73 per cent of children between the ages of 9 and 14 attended the movies at least once per week. Fleege

(1945) in a study of boys in 20 Catholic high schools found that 75 per cent attended at least once per week, the average frequency of attendance being 4.9 per month. These results are in close agreement with the earlier results of Dale (1935) in the extensive Payne Fund Study in which it was found that 71 per cent of high school boys attended motion pictures at least once per week. There are, of course, wide variations in different areas of the country and in different sections of a given community. It is interesting to note that in some crowded areas of cities a substantial percentage of children begin rather regular attendance at the movies by or before age 8, and in such sections it is not uncommon to find children attending as frequently as 4 or 5 times a week.

Several studies have been made of what children see at the movies. The studies of Fleege (1945) and of Dale (1935) are good illustrations. One result of these analyses which is of interest in the study of character development is the great frequency of crimes, violent death, overdrawn love and sex scenes, and horror themes. The lack of reality in the films is also emphasized in these studies.

Success is depicted in the movies as coming fast and often easily. In the interest of making the story compelling, there are few normal and average people depicted in average homes. Extremes are the rule. The rich are lavishly rich; the poor are desperately so. Luck and physical strength, beauty and prowess, are out of proportion to their true place in reality. For adults who have experienced life widely, and can easily distinguish between the unreality of a good story and the reality of life, this is not serious. But for children who start their motion-picture attendance at young ages and see life depicted in this manner year in and year out, it may be serious, especially if the home, school, church, or some other institution of society does not correct these warped impressions.

The influence of motion pictures upon emotional responses and upon restlessness during sleep has been studied by Renshaw, Miller, and Marquis (1933). It was found that the restlessness after seeing motion pictures increased 26 per cent on the average with boys and 14 per cent with girls. Using measures of change in pulse rate as a measure of emotional response, Dysinger and Ruckmick (1933) found that while seeing a picture children 6 to 11 years of age displayed responses which averaged three times those of adults.[1] The effect of movies on muscular tension and body temperature was studied by Kleitman (1945), who found that both increased during attendance at many pictures. He says that movie attendance, although looked upon as "relaxation" in the sense of escape from the humdrum of everyday existence, is certainly not always relaxation in the physiological sense.

Many studies have been made to determine the influence of motion-picture attendance on delinquency and crime. The results are conflicting. In general, the investigations which have employed interviewing and questionnaire methods with delinquents have reported that motion pictures were direct causal factors in 10 to 20 per cent of the cases. Blumer and Hauser (1934), for example, have concluded that the movies were important factors in directing 10 per cent of the boys studied and 25 per cent of the girls into delinquent and criminal careers. Cressey and Thrasher (1934) interviewed 139 delinquent boys, age 15 and below, and concluded that 17 per cent of them "were clearly influenced by the movies toward delinquency."

[1] Of course a given change in pulse rate is not so serious with children as with adults, but such wide changes are certainly worthy of note.

On the other hand, such specialists in the study and treatment of delinquents as Healy and Bronner (1936) find much smaller percentages. They are inclined to discount much that delinquent boys and girls say in interviews and questionnaires about the "cause" of their delinquency and seek for objective evidence beyond the delinquent's self-analysis. Healy and Bronner conclude that only about 1 per cent of their cases were clearly motivated in their acts of delinquency by motion pictures.

With such conflicting results before us it is impossible to generalize concerning the percentage of delinquents who were stimulated toward their misconduct by motion pictures. All investigations agree, however, that some motion pictures have deleterious effects on delinquents and near-delinquents. It seems probable that the greatest effects of movies do not appear suddenly and in such ways that they can be accurately measured by existing methods. Probably any detrimental influences are most likely to manifest themselves through gradual and cumulative effects on attitudes over a long period of time, and through supplying to individuals and small groups just enough added stimulation to serve as "trigger action" when they already have rather strong antisocial inclinations or pent-up resentments.

The potentialities of motion pictures for improving standards and conduct have received less attention than their potentialities for harm. However, positive values have not been entirely overlooked. As examples of studies showing gains in moral attitudes and standards, we may mention those of Rosen (1948), Raths and Trager (1948), Thurstone (1931), and Jones (1936). The first two investigators studied the influence of pictures stressing the evils of intolerance. The effects in both studies were in the direction of increased tolerance as measured on attitude questionnaires.

Thurstone found that attitudes toward gambling were changed in a desirable direction as a result of seeing a film. Jones in a study of four films found that ethical standards of children could be raised or lowered as a result of seeing specially selected films. The films which were most effective in raising standards were those which unqualifyingly condemned specific types of undesirable conduct. A large factor in determining whether undesirable conduct was really being condemned in a given picture was the attitude taken toward that conduct by the actor with whom the spectator identified himself.

3. *The radio and television entertainment.* A considerable number of objective studies have appeared concerning the relation of radio to attitudes and conduct of children, but much less material of a conclusive nature has appeared relative to television. Siepmann (1950) has discussed in an extensive report the history and some of the social implications of television and radio, including a chapter on the present and potential use of these media in education and in propaganda. Riley, Cantwell, and Ruttiger (1949) studied matched television and nontelevision homes. They concluded that television is proving to be responsible for new family interests, is providing something for family members to do together, and is stimulating a wider circle of friends in the home.

There is sufficient evidence now available to enable one to say that the radio listening of children and adolescents is very great indeed and that probably most of the programs are neutral in their effect upon the character of children. Some of these programs, such as discussions of current topics, the speeches of prominent leaders, some of the news broadcasts, and the higher grade musical programs, may make positive contributions to the character and citizenship of the listeners. In fairness to the radio as a medium of communication these deserve more attention and investigation. However, the greater number of objective studies have centered on such questionable programs as those with crime, horror, or murder mystery themes to which children listen. On the question as to whether such programs tend, on the average, to throw their weight on the positive or negative side of the scale in the character development of children, we end up with two sets of answers in the main. Some writers, usually with clinical or psychiatric backgrounds, see in such programs desirable outlets for "pent-up emotions" like hate and feelings of aggression. They believe in the beneficial results of emotional release and the cathartic effects of vicariously experiencing the emotions which these programs stimulate.

The other point of view, and one supported by several investigations, is illustrated by Rowland (1944) and DeBoer (1939). Rowland studied the nature and frequency of various crime themes in radio programs and concluded that crime programs distort the truth about crime and the functions and methods of law enforcement agencies. "Crime and violence in drama," he says, "lose their cathartic value when there is a constant habituation to overdoses . . . and may contribute to those frustrations which bring about aggressive behavior." DeBoer reports that such programs as these caused very strong emotional responses in children.

These, and other studies, lead us to conclude that to the extent that children see or listen to overemotionalized, unrealistic, and antisocial programs day after day they are probably subject to cumulative conditioning effects which are not good from the point of view of either mental hygiene or character development.

4. *Reading of books, magazines, and newspapers.* Reading is believed by many writers to be one of the foremost methods which can be employed for character development. The great stress on Bible reading in church schools and the confidence which many writers have expressed in the values of reading biography and great fiction are illustrations of this belief. Jones (1931b, 1952) prepared biographical episodes and tried these out as reading and discussion material in school. In comparing results in trained groups with control groups, he did not find a statistically significant difference on a test of moral knowledge, although subjective judgments seemed to indicate that there may have been some positive gains which the tests were not sensitive or comprehensive enough to detect. Child et al. (1946) have analyzed over 900 stories from third-grade readers and, on the basis of a careful and thorough thema analysis (in Murray's sense), conclude that such reading should if properly arranged encourage the development of certain motives and discourage others on the part of the young child. Gray (1947) has reviewed the literature on the social effects of reading, but he does not so much answer some of our basic questions as reveal that more controlled investigations of various aspects of the problem with children and youth in natural situations are definitely needed.

With regard to the deleterious effects of inferior reading matter, there is more evidence. Healy and Bronner (1936), who base their conclusions on wide experience with delinquents, are very emphatic in their claim that cheap novels and magazines dealing with bandit and underworld life act as a pernicious influence upon the character development of young people. Their conclusion is based on the verified confessions of boys and on the fact that many delinquents were found to have among their possessions a well-fingered book or magazine article which described crimes bearing marked resemblances to the ones committed. In condemning such reading, Healy many years ago made the following insightful statement (which needs expanding to include the newer means of entertainment and excitement of today's youth): "A definite habit and craving for this type of reading is developed just as the individual develops a habit for alcoholic stimulants. The fires of the spirit of adventure are not only kindled but are kept going by this fuel." [1]

Novels and magazine articles are ordinarily sufficiently long and read under such conditions of relaxation as to permit suggestion effects to be at a high point. Particular parts of the written story, as contrasted with the drama, can be turned back to by the reader and reread for more stimulation or specific details. These are doubtless some of the features of the bandit, underworld, and amatory types of stories which contribute to the effects which Healy and others emphasize.

Comic books and strips have come in for considerable study and discussion. The results are rather conflicting. J. Frank (1949) says that comic books follow to some extent the same general pattern that children's cheaper reading has followed in the past except that much crime and horror material has been added. She reports that 50 million copies of comic books are sold monthly and that each copy usually has several readers. She calls for vigilance on the part of parents, teachers, and specialists in child development in scrutinizing marginal material, but sees no occasion for suspecting much, if any, damage from most of the current comics. Hoult (1949) finds what seems to be conclusive evidence that delinquents read more questionable and "harmful" comics than nondelinquents. Bender and Lourie (1941) came to the conclusion that comic-book material often fits

[1] See Healy (1915, p. 305).

the needs of the child in his striving to solve problems involving the attitudes of others toward him and his own impulses toward others. They do not consider the value levels at which some of the more questionable comic books may meet these needs. Jersild (1947) interprets the evidence which is available more seriously. He stresses particularly the point that the comics sometimes act as forces which contradict the teachings of the home and school. The young readers often find ends gained by force and violence in the comics, while they are taught elsewhere to live by more civilized principles; they sometimes find retaliation and cruelty defended, while the home and school try to educate away from such conduct; they sometimes find crime made into adventure and criminals made into heroes of action, while the home and school try to impress them with respect for law and order.

These are illustrations of the state of conflicting opinions and interpretations of the data relative to the effect of the comic book on the character development of children. The studies and discussions of the problem have served to indicate the extent of such reading, to sharpen up the issues involved, and, we hope, to stimulate more research upon it. We suspect that different comic books have very different effects on different children. A few may be actually beneficial to some children. Most are probably neutral for most children from the point of view of character. A few are almost certainly marginal if not harmful to all or most of those who read them. The over-all effect is probably small, except possibly in a cumulative way and in combination with other factors.

The studies of newspaper reading of children and adolescents have centered mainly on their interest in various parts of the paper, on the effects of newspaper reading on knowledge of current events, and on attitudes toward delinquency and crime. Feingold (1944) and Burton (1946), investigated the newspaper tastes of high school students and came to essentially the same conclusions, namely that front-page news, the sport page, and the comic strips ranked highest. The radio section and the motion-picture section were very frequently consulted. Feingold reports that approximately 20 per cent of the students in his study read the crime news very regularly. He also finds that three-quarters of these high school students report that they read the newspaper to keep up with local, national, and international news and that such reading is an advantage to them in their school work. Doob (1948), on the basis of a careful study of propaganda, says that, although some systematic bias undoubtedly exists in newspapers, and is very strong in some, it is usually an outgrowth of the cultural orientation and sincere belief of the owners and editors of the papers or of the reporters or feature writers who write specific articles or stories. He concludes, therefore, that much of the so-called propaganda in most newspapers is in this sense unintentional. However, he advises young and old to read two or more newspapers, each representing a different systematic position, in reaching conclusions on important issues.

The treatment of delinquency and crime in various newspapers differs greatly. Some newspapers feature crime and delinquency and make of the criminal something of a hero and daring adventurer in the minds of children and youth. Some go so deeply into the details of the crime and the methods used by the law in attempts to capture the offender that the delinquent or near-delinquent is educated in the techniques of both crime and escape. Many newspapers see the potential dangers to their communities in such overplaying of crime news and make their reports less sensational and more factual. Baker (1943) described some interesting practical experiments in which editors and publishers of newspapers in certain cities with high delinquency rates agreed to place crime news in the inside pages of their papers and to reduce the headlines. In each case, he says, there was a gradual reduction in the delinquency rate.

Influence of the Culture. Each of the factors discussed thus far in this section are a part of what might be called the *personal environment* of the child. It is a personal environment because within rather broad limits each person has a certain freedom of movement as to the nature and extent of his exposure to each factor. There remains the very important problem of the influence of the totality of the culture in which the child is born and lives. This problem is different only in degree from that of the influence upon the child of, say, the family or the associations of peers in the personal environment where certain norms of conduct are thrown about him and where with only limited consciousness of the existence of any other alternatives he takes these for his standards.

If the group is large enough and the identification with that group as compared with any other is strong enough so that there is only distant or disdainful recognition of other alternatives, then we have the *class stage* in cultural determination. Applying the concepts of class to the problems of character development of children, Havighurst and Taba (1949) have sought to determine what attitudes and values characterize the upper-class child, the middle-class child, and the lower-class child. Working in what seems to have been a prevailingly middle-class city, where there was a considerable amount of mobility in class affiliation, especially in the schools, they have not been very successful in discovering differences except at the extremes.

However, this study is doubtless a precursor of much research that will be directed towards the determination of what attitudes, values, and conduct are held up as the desirable norms and passed on to the children of different groups and "classes" in America. In a study of 1100 white men ranging widely in socio-economic status, Centers (1949) found that those of top occupational and economic strata strongly believed in maintaining the status quo, think that things are about right as they are, and identify themselves with those above them in position or rank. Those in the different levels of the lowest strata have more radical attitudes and identify themselves with those of equal status or with those at levels below them.

Overarching the subgroup or class there is the *over-all culture*. Here the opportunities for mobility and for seeing or accepting alternative standards in other cultures is reduced to practically zero. This is the national or regional culture or civilization typified by such broad cultural designations as "American cultural patterns," "western civilization," "Christian culture," and the like.[1] Every child is born in such an over-all cultural matrix and is influenced by it through every individual and social institution with which he comes in contact. All the factors which comprise the personal environment and all the ramifications of class structure operate within this larger frame of the over-all culture. Customs,

standards of conduct, attitudes, aspirations, and values of every new generation are tremendously influenced by the culture in which it is born and reared.[2] This influence, we believe, is both piecemeal, in the sense of the separate contributions of each of such factors as were discussed under the personal environment, and global in the sense of a totality of orientation.

In emphasizing this sociopsychological approach to character development, we should not overlook the potentialities of the individual human mind in its creativeness to see beyond the culture of a given time and place and set its goals accordingly. But these moments of creativeness are probably rare in the history of individuals and peoples. In the practical problem, therefore, of understanding the most crucial fact about character development of children in different classes and cultures, we can probably do no better than follow the conclusion of Margaret Mead (1949), who says that many of our human frictions in society today arise from a failure to understand differences in culture that make it "natural" for people to think and act differently.

Motivation in Moral Behavior

Up to this point the discussion has been confined largely to phenomena upon which objective data are available, and it is not our intention in this chapter to venture far from such objective material. However, when we come to the question of motivation in character we are confronted with the choice of ignoring the problem altogether or of attempting to discover what the general theories of motivation in psychology have to offer that will apply here. In the face of this dilemma it seems best to adopt the latter course, even though the

[1] Nixon (1952) develops the interesting idea that even truth has meaning only within the framework of an agreed context of fundamental values, and that we lack such a context in some of our thinking today in light of the conflict between democracy and its basic value system, on the one hand, and the enemies of democracy and their value systems, on the other. Dechesne (1950) says that the social institutions functioning in western civilization today have not succeeded in developing and maintaining the altruistic sentiments necessary for their own successful operation and high destiny. He believes that conscious attention to the development of such sentiments is the only solution to the social crisis of our day.

[2] For an extensive discussion of this point see Kuhlen (1952).

limitation of space will necessitate a sketchy treatment.

The points of view found in the literature concerning the dynamics of conduct are varied. There are writers who believe that all behavior springs from many inner drives or urges; there are those who believe in one or two native or biological roots from which all specific motives can be derived; and there are those who deny the theory of innate drives and stress learned wants and the motivating power of the on-going organism in preparatory and consummatory activity.

The clearest and boldest treatment of motivation from the standpoint of innate tendencies has been given by McDougall (1918). "The human mind," he says, "has certain innate or inherited tendencies which are the essential springs or motive powers of all thought and action . . . and are the bases from which the character and will of individuals and nations are gradually developed under the guidance of intellectual faculties" (p. 20). He lists among instincts: curiosity, pugnacity, self-assertion, self-abasement, reproduction, gregariousness, acquisition, etc. The chief difficulties which have been faced by those who hold this view are: first, the inability to demonstrate what tendencies belong in this list of unitary drives and, second, the failure to show the degree to which the manifestation of a tendency which is noted at any given time is native and the degree to which it is acquired. With the advance of the researches on the processes and results of conditioning, on the one hand, and the growing interest in the integrative behavior of the organism, on the other, the belief in an hereditary equipment consisting of rather independent, broad, unitary tendencies to action was appreciably undermined.

In the fields of psychoanalysis and of individual psychology there has been a tendency to look for the dynamics of behavior in two or three native or unlearned roots. Freud (1924) regarded the sex tendency and the self-preservation tendency to be the main elements in human motivation, at least on the side of the "life instincts" as he later called them. The sex tendency encompassed all the direct and indirect derivatives of the sex motive whether conscious or "repressed in the unconscious." The self-preservation tendency included among other things the protection of all of one's moral and social standards. Adler (1927) postulated two universal tendencies: first, a desire for personal power and superiority; and, second, a "social feeling which binds man to man." "With these two points of view," he said, "we can understand how the relation between human beings is conditioned by the relative degree of their social feelings, as contrasted to their strivings for personal aggrandizement, two tendencies which are always in opposition to each other. It is a dynamic game, a parallelogram of forces whose external manifestations are what we call character" (p. 190).

Murphy, Murphy, and Newcomb (1937) suggest for descriptive purposes the following four groups of "human motives": visceral drives, activity drives, aesthetic drives, and emotions. They do not think of these as instinctive, however. They stress the point that there is no separation of the fundamental drives from the means which serve them. The process of motivation they think of as going on unremittingly, and they believe that the patterns of habitual responses are as fully motivated as unlearned responses. Coghill (1936), pointing to the relation of maturation to motivation, holds that as long as the nervous system and brain are changing and developing as a result of maturation there is at least some motivation which must be considered internal. Olson (1949) says that "children, under the influence of appetite and homeostatic mechanisms, tend to seek according to their needs . . . [and] there are strong probabilities that growth has internal factors which constitute drives to action. From the environmental point of view, the child tends to produce in his behavior those things valued by the culture, if they are within the repertoire of possible successful responses. Within a roughly comparable set of values and experiences, there remain differences among children which are too large to be accounted for by nurture" (p. 157).

Numerous other views have been held, such as Dunlap's theory of "fundamental desires," Woodworth's theory of preparatory and consummatory activity as the essential feature in drives, and Stern's concept of pheno-motives and geno-motives. Space will not permit a discussion of these here, but the reader may find a rather extensive treatment of most of them given by Allport (1937).

These conflicting theories serve to illustrate the difficulty of arriving at a comprehensive and integrated concept of motivation in character. However, a few suggestions will be given as proposed guides in the search for such a concept. The first suggestion is that the attempts to reduce the motivation for conduct to two or three pervading tendencies have probably oversimplified the native equipment of man. Such attempts have derived, in what often seems a forced manner, too much from a very few tendencies and have not given sufficient consideration to the possibility that there may be a multitude of unlearned patterns of response, rather than just two or three, which may form the cores for broad tendencies. We know that the child can without training make the responses of sneezing, coughing, and crying to appropriate stimuli. It seems no less certain that the human organism after a certain degree of maturation has an unlearned capacity to experience a tension-expulsion impulse on genital stimulation. This may be the core of the structure which, when elaborated, has been called the sex instinct. Thus it seems quite possible that there is a multitude of fine patterns of actions in the innate structure of individuals and that around these patterns motivations are built up. It is possible also that these patterns differ in strength from individual to individual and that they are integrated in different ways. Thus two children raised under the same evironmental circumstances might not be similarly motivated in the same situation.

A second suggestion to be offered is that the innate tendencies given by McDougall and others, and the "fundamental desires" given by Dunlap, and all the supposedly unitary factors in lists like these, are probably products of an intricate combination, elaboration, and integration of a multitude of simpler urges. The mainsprings of moral behavior are probably not few and simple, but many and complicated, and genetic psychology may in the future show us how these tendencies develop and from what biological nuclei. The more recent work on conditioning and on culture leads us to believe that the influence of training begins much earlier and has much more to do with the manifestation and relative potency of "wants" than the classical treatment of innate tendencies and biological drives has indicated.

Third, motivation for superior and inferior character responses is probably not static, but is evolving. This is, of course, in one sense simply a corollary of the conclusion that the motivation of behavior at any given time is dependent partly on conditioning and training. But, besides this, it seems probable that some of the innate patterns, such as the sex impulse, change with age because of the process of maturation in the nervous system. Such a study as Gesell and Thompson's (1929), which indicated that growth in climbing ability among young children is partly a process of maturation in neural patterns, suggests that such a possibility is well within reason. The change in motivation with age is well illustrated by the work of Piaget (1932), who studied the nature of the rules made and followed by children in their own games and the reasons why they followed them. He distinguished what he calls two moralities among children. One he found in all very young children: an egocentric type of behavior characterized by a tendency to follow rules because they are handed down by elders. He found no tendency for the child, regardless of amount of training, to think of revising rules in games for mutual advantage, and he found nothing upon which he could build a desire on the part of the child to do this or that because of any "mutual respect of child for child." The second type of morality he found to have its beginning later in the life of the child than the first, but not suddenly to replace it—indeed it is not infrequently crowded out or prevented from appearing by the first. It is a morality motivated by a desire to change the rule in a game if in its working some child is not being treated as he himself would like to be. It is the beginning of the desire for creativeness, as opposed to conformity, in character.

No one probably would contend that Piaget's "two moralities," which we have used to illustrate our point of the changing nature of "wants," are due purely to differences in maturation. But Piaget's observation that the second one never precedes the first, coupled with the common observations concerning growth in cooperative play among children and the change in interests of youth with the maturation of the sex functions, leads one to believe that the "wants" of children change not only

through training but also through maturation in neural patterns.

A fourth point which should be made is that motivation for character responses is not some potential power existing somewhere, unrelated to what the organism is doing at the moment, and waiting to be turned on like a starter in an automobile. Woodworth (1934) has particularly emphasized this and has pointed to the fact that any activity in progress may be a motive for the time being. As an illustration of this in the area of character, one would say that a child's motivation for truthfulness or honesty, lying or cheating, at any given time is a part of a chain of on-going activities; that is, his motivation is not unrelated to what he is doing and where he is.

Fifth, emotional conditioning may pronouncedly affect motivation. This is one of the interesting leads in research in character development which has not been followed up by much research. Leeper (1948) has given some careful attention to the interrelation between emotion and motivation in an attempt to achieve a testable theoretical formulation. Bekhterev (1928) has found in working with children afflicted with kleptomania, "in which the emotion of satisfaction is associated with theft," that reconditioning can take place in just a few sittings so that the feeling of extreme annoyance instead of satisfaction is associated with theft. Watson (1926) has found that the emotion of fear may be connected by a conditioning process with situations to which it was not previously connected, and that it may, by the same process, be disconnected from situations to which it was connected. It is surprising that so little attention has been given to this problem in studies of character development, especially in view of the fact that the church has made use of it to such a great extent, as have also primitive tribes, particularly in connection with adolescent initiation ceremonies. It seems probable that one of the chief effects which literature, drama, oratory, and other arts may have upon character development is to link strong emotionally toned reactions to certain motivating forces of the individual.

Our sixth suggestion concerns conscious and unconscious motivation. It is a matter of common observation that very small children misrepresent facts oftentimes not as a result of any conscious desire to deceive but rather as a regular part of their wishful thinking and imagining. Among older children and adults a very large part of their honest behavior is a matter of habit, where it would be impossible to say that they are consciously motivated to refrain from lying or stealing. Moreover, the psychoanalysts have emphasized what they call unconscious motivation in cases where thwartings in certain lines of activity have led to "repressions," which in turn have led to undesirable acts which do not seem to fit in logically with any conscious motivation of the subject. Cases have been cited, for example, where a youth who has been thwarted in certain desires derived from the sex impulse may turn to stealing. From a practical point of view there seems to be no doubt that the genesis of stealing in particular, and other forms of immoral behavior to some extent, may often be traced back to some important conflict or thwarting. It is possible, however, to lay so much emphasis on this type of explanation as to make it seem that almost all character responses are motivated by what "escapes from the unconscious." It would seem a more inclusive and less mysterious explanation to say that conflicts play their part, as do all experiences, in affecting the on-going activity of the individual, but that it is the on-going activity at any given time, including conscious processes, reactions to frustration, and habit mechanisms, rather than some entity in the "unconscious," which provides the motivation for action.

The final suggestion which we wish to make is that verbalized concepts may motivate character responses. This point is implied in much that has been said about activity motivating further activity. Those who subscribe to the view that no behavior, regardless of how much it may benefit society, can be described as moral unless the motive of the agent is consciously moral will say that all motivation in moral behavior *must* depend on verbalized and conscious concepts. This problem has led to an age-old controversy in philosophy which cannot be reviewed here. Suffice it for our purposes to emphasize the contention that verbalized concepts do motivate moral behavior at times. As will be shown later, generalized principles and ideals are gradually built up in accordance with the laws of learning out of experiences which are verbalized. Once these verbalized principles are acquired, they become tools not only for considering the present but also for reconstructing the past and planning the future. Through them, the distant and the past are made a part of the here and now. With them, we build the goals we would achieve. By them, individual characters of the past and present, both great and small, may exert motivating influences upon us.

Such a verbalized concept, for example, as cheating-is-a-form-of-stealing may, under some circumstances, act as one motivating factor for honesty in an examination. In the presence of conflicting motivations the ideal of acting-toward-others-as-we-would-have-them-act-toward-us may become for the individual the prepotent "drive" in the situation. It would be a mistake, of course, to assume that the major part of the motivation in the character of children is dependent upon the prepotency of such a highly complex concept or principle as the last one named. The goal of character development, however, is in that direction. The striking gap which so frequently exists between verbally expressed principles and actions has so impressed some observers that they seem to doubt or belittle the motivating power of ideals. The frequency of the gap must, of course, be granted. However, any account of character development which underestimates the potential motivating power of ideals and other verbalized principles, because they seldom if ever produce action completely consistent with them, would be short-sighted indeed. It would be guilty of discerning nothing in a direction of striving except the goals achieved and of minimizing worthy intentions that do not eventuate in full accomplishment.

Knowledge, Conscience, Aspiration, and Volition in Relation to Ethical Behavior

Knowledge. In popular analyses of ethical conduct it is often assumed that knowledge of "right" and "wrong" and the will to follow the right when it is known are the *sine qua non* of moral responsibility. This assumption is shown most interestingly in attempts made in courts and homes to decide upon punishment for misconduct. Roscoe Pound (1930) says, "Our traditional criminal law thinks of the offender as a free moral agent who, having before him the choice whether to do right or do wrong, intentionally chooses to do wrong." This clearly assumes, in the first place, that the individual knew which act was right and which wrong, and, in the second place, that the individual "willed" to do the wrong. Before the courts, an individual, whether child or adult, is considered to be either responsible for his acts or irresponsible. There are no in-betweens.

If it can be established that an individual's powers have not developed sufficiently for him to know the difference between right and wrong or for him to have adequate "will power" to control his acts, then he is pronounced irresponsible for his acts. In many states, children under 6 or 7 years of age are considered irresponsible if they commit serious offenses, but children slightly older are considered responsible and are punished accordingly. In the home, too, it is sometimes assumed that young children should not be held very strictly accountable for their acts because they have not reached an "age of discretion."

One purpose of this section is to point to the oversimplification in the above concepts. In the first place, there is no point in the development of a child at which he suddenly passes from the age of irresponsibility to that of responsibility. Study after study has shown that children develop gradually in their moral knowledge as well as in conduct. Two or three such studies which deal primarily with moral knowledge may be cited by way of illustration. Written descriptions of 64 childhood situations were presented by Jones (1929a) to 177 children in grades 7 and 8. The instructions were that the proposed action in each situation should be marked as "right," "excusable," or "wrong." There were only 9 situations out of the 64 where as many as 90 per cent of these children agreed as to the rightness or wrongness or excusability of the proposed action. The same situations were presented to several hundred school teachers and prospective teachers, and among these there were only 12 situations where as many as 90 per cent agreed. These findings were subsequently corroborated by Maller (1932).

Even at the college level the question of cheating on quizzes and examinations seems to be a moot issue with many. An intensive study by Katz and Allport (1930), at

Syracuse University, revealed that 26 per cent of the college students examined considered "cribbing" to be as bad as lying or stealing, but that 22.5 per cent definitely condoned it. The remainder took stands in between these two positions. From these and similar studies it seems certain that persons cannot be divided into two categories, those who know the difference between right and wrong and those who do not. There is no time when one is suddenly endowed with ability to discern right from wrong. Strictly, there is no age that can be called "the age of discretion." Throughout life one is continually learning and modifying his views of the right and wrong, or, perhaps more realistically, of the "bests" and the "second-bests," as he faces new situations.

This leads to a second point of oversimplification in many assumptions about character and character development. It is that character is a matter of rather routine conduct and that problem solving and creativeness are not required. This is a serious error in conceptualizing on the problems of character and especially serious in educating for character development. Character cannot properly be conceived of as a mere repetition of learned responses.

New issues must be faced by every developing child, and with increasing maturity he must make his responses more and more independently of parents, teachers, or other counselors. In life, virtues not infrequently run counter to each other, and one has to choose among them. How does the individual arrive at his conception of what is the "right" course of action in a novel situation? The view subscribed to here is that ethical knowledge is derived by a process of generalization from past experience and that, the more the child is taught to generalize from his knowledge and conduct in those stages of development when he has guidance from parents and

teachers, the more will he be able to use effectively the process of problem solving in novel situations. A young child who is properly taught learns that it is wrong to steal jam at home, a pencil at school, and candy in a store, but he may gradually generalize that stealing in any situation is wrong. Thus a hierarchy of values is built up. Any line of activity in a novel situation which in his judgment involves stealing will, therefore, be considered wrong.

As an illustration, consider a boy who for the first time faces the situation of not having his fare collected on a train, owing to the oversight of the conductor. He is confronted with the choice of keeping quiet and retaining his fare or of paying for the service which he is obtaining. In deciding what is right and what is wrong in this new situation, the boy may consider the paying of the fare as linked up with honesty, and the retaining of the money or ticket as associated with dishonesty. If this happens, he is no longer faced solely by the specific choice between paying and not paying, but he is faced by the choice as it has allied itself with the "honesty constellation" or the "dishonesty constellation." If, as a result of development and of training, the honesty constellation is greatly preferred to the dishonesty one, the choice between paying and not paying is largely made. Following this same reasoning there may be further interlinkages. The boy may look upon honest behavior as a sort of subhierarchy in the higher hierarchy of respect for rights of others and dishonesty as a violation of these rights for selfish interest. The simplest choice may be made, therefore, by an individual in the light of his most fundamental values. We call this choosing on "principle." But the principle is not some mysterious and suddenly acquired power for knowing right from wrong; it is an acquired generalization based on specific experiences.

A third oversimplification concerns inferring too much from the oft-repeated observation that knowledge of the right does not insure right conduct. The possible error involved is in underestimating the value of knowledge in character development of children and youth. Granted that knowledge of the right or the best does not guarantee action consistent with it, nevertheless, knowledge is important because one cannot choose the right in a situation except by utter chance if he does not have the proper knowledge or habit patterns. In all conscious choice, knowledge is a prerequisite both to wise and to ethical action. One has as much ethical obligation to keep informed, so that his actions may be rightly geared to changing needs in society, as he has to convert the ethical knowledge which he has into action. It is not alone the converting of ethical knowledge into action that we need in the realm of character and citizenship today; it is the converting of *better* ethical knowledge and values into better action.

Conscience. At this point we come to the crux of the age-old problem of conscience. We cannot hope to do justice to this very complex problem here, but we do wish to recognize it as a problem worthy of psychological study. Most psychologists today are very circumspect about the use of the term *conscience*, but they recognize that tensions accompanying the consciousness of an individual of a serious gap between what he thinks he ought to do and what he does are among the chief sources of personality conflicts.

Freud freely uses the word conscience, and we are indebted to him for what is probably the most systematic attack on tensions growing out of moral values that has been made from the point of view of instinct theory. To Freud, guilt and a sense of inferiority are manifestations of the tensions between the ego and the superego.

But how is this superego or conscience built up? Freud (1930) thinks that the superego develops by the child's gradual "internalizing" certain controls upon himself, motivated by his early helplessness and dependence upon others. Thus, according to Freud, conscience grows out of child-parent relationships which go back fundamentally to instinctive bases. The child identifies himself with the parent and gradually the superego develops, taking over certain controls and exercising the same aggressiveness toward the ego that the father would have exercised toward the child. Out of concepts such as these, Freud builds a systematic structure of urges, controls, and tensions. French, Miller, and Riesman (1950), in discussing the relation of psychoanalysis to ethical values and conduct, maintain that psychoanalysis should aid the patient to find his own moral values. They believe that psychoanalysis contributes to ethical behavior in several ways, in its emphasis on absolute honesty.

In some of the more recent work in anthropology and psychoanalysis less stress is being placed on instincts than characterized Freud's own writings. More emphasis is being placed on early conditioning and cultural influences. Sherif (1948), for example, says that there are acquired motives related to the genetically developing ego values of the child which are not derivations of biogenic needs. "These ego values," he says, "which collectively may be referred to as *conscience*, are incorporated from the prevailing values or norms of one's group; they are imposed by parents, school, church, play group, clique, etc. These ego values thus derived . . . are not, in many cases, conducive to the satisfaction of biogenic needs or the 'derived drives' traceable to them" (p. 36).

Kardiner (1939), maintains that Freud's explanation falls short in that it does not give sufficient recognition to the dependencies, affections, and values which are built up from the earliest age by direct conditioning and learning from the social environment. He says: "In his orientation on instinct, Freud left little room for the operation of societal influences."

Horney (1937) also stresses the cultural basis of many of the wants, values, and aspirations of individuals, and contrasts this approach with the more purely instinctive and biological approach of Freud. This author particularly emphasizes the important rôle played in anxiety and other neuroses by the conflict between what the individual does and what he feels is expected of him, and illustrates (1948), in the case of vindictiveness, how therapy should help the individual to avoid or overcome ethically unacceptable behavior in the interest of his adjustment.

There is much to be said for extending the sources of moral standards, values, and ideals along the lines suggested by Kardiner, Horney, and others. That one has the power to acquire conscience is a gift of nature. The limits to which one's conscience can be made sensitive to intricate and subtle distinctions are probably dependent at least in some measure on native endowment. There may even be certain biological conditions or prepotent impulses which influence the kind of conscience which an individual develops. But, within certain very broad limits, children and adults acquire their consciences by reacting to the stimulation which such factors as the home, friends, church, school, and the over-all culture afford.

Level of Aspiration. The nearest approach which has been made by laboratory experimentation to the above problem is the work on *aspiration level.* Hoppe (1930), who did pioneer research on this problem, defined level of aspiration as the goals, the expectations of a person, or the claims on his future achievement. In his experiments he was not concerned with aspiration in any ethical sense. Some of his results and conclusions, however, like those of others who have worked on the problem, are suggestive in the present discussion. He found, for example, that success on the part of a subject in reaching his aspiration level encouraged him to try harder tasks, whereas failure had the opposite effect.

Child and Whiting (1949), working in real-life situations, also find that success generally leads to a raising of the aspiration level and failure to a lowering. Moreover, they find that shifts in the levels of aspiration of a subject are a function of changes in his confidence in his ability to attain the goals. Weber (1946) adds the finding that excess of level of aspiration over performance is often associated with aggression and emotionality. Gould (1939) concludes that different subjects react differently to the gap between level of aspiration and performance. Some subjects react to feelings of failure by trying to do better; others by becoming discouraged and losing the desire to go on; others by overcoming the consciousness of the gap by dreaming of success, making excuses, etc.; and still others by various combinations of these.

Volitional Factors. In many treatments of character the gap between knowledge of desirable conduct and action consistent with such knowledge is attributed to weaknesses in volitional factors. Indeed, not a few writers consider volition to be the central problem of character and maintain that strong characters are strong primarily in will and that weak characters are weak in will. Stephenson (1935), for example, says that it is "in the sphere of volition and conation that we hope to find the secrets of character." With the concept of character held in this chapter we cannot accept the thesis that character is a function of volition only, but there is no question of the importance of volitional factors in character and in character development.

Attempts to study the phenomenon of volition and to show its relation to conduct fall under two headings: (1) studies involving factor analysis which reveal clusters of related or similar behavior in different situations, and (2) studies of conduct resulting from damage to certain physiological bases of volition due to drugs, toxins, etc. The latter studies indicate the importance of giving attention to the biological and emotional constitution of the individual as well as to his environment in the investigation of character development.

Among the factor-analysis investigations we may mention especially those of Webb, Spearman, Reyburn and Taylor, and Cattell. Applying factor analysis to tests and ratings of character, Spearman (1927) and Reyburn and Taylor (1939, 1943), for example, have obtained evidence for what they call a w or will-character factor. Cattell (1946) gives an extensive review of factor-analysis research and cites many studies as revealing a close clustering or "factor" in this area. Some of the characteristic forms of behavior which are found in a cluster, and on which the individual tends to be consistently high or low, are: persistence, perseverance, stability in pursuit of objective, resistance to distraction, determination to carry through what has been undertaken, resolution, strength of purpose, and the like.

The important point for our discussion here is not so much whether the clustering is close enough to justify the concept of a general factor of w but rather that close clustering has been found indicating a relatively high degree of similarity in the conduct of an individual in different situations involving volitional factors.

In many discussions of volition the implication seems to be that the contributions of early conditioning and general nurture are being underestimated. This is not the implication intended here. Our search is for the factors which, with any appreciable degree of consistency, motivate, limit, guide, or influence character responses of children. Conditioning and other learning influences which affect volitional behavior are recognized here as having already made their contributions to the volitional behavior as we see it at any given time in the life of the child. Any consistency in behavior which is found, therefore, may be as indicative of consistent conditioning and learning of a given individual in his environmental and cultural setting as it is of possible native factors upon which the culture and training operate.

A second line of research in this area to be discussed is that concerned with the physiological bases of volitional behavior and the influence upon such behavior of changes in or disturbances of these bases. Numerous studies have been made which throw light on the effects of drugs such as Benzedrine, Pervitin, sodium amytal, marihuana, and alcohol on persistence, resistance to fatigue, strength of inhibition, and other evidences of willing behavior. One or two illustrations will suffice to indicate the relevance of such researches to the problem at hand. Cuthbertson and Knox (1947) studied the effects of Benzedrine and Methedrine on subjects whose activity had been greatly reduced by fatigue. They found that both drugs increased output on the ergometer under such conditions, Methedrine being the more potent. It was as if certain volitional powers had been increased. We do not know, of course, that the change in behavior was mediated directly by any changes in volitional factors, but the connection is close enough to indicate that investigations of this type should be undertaken by the student of character development for possible clues concerning this important but elusive factor of volition.

Charen and Perelman (1946) have made a clinical study of 60 men addicted to marihuana. They conclude that marihuana weakens the "controls of the superego." Baruk (1949) has experimented with a drug and a toxin and reports that part of their effect is to reduce voluntary powers.

So much for a very brief review of some of the objective results on volitional factors and their relation to character development. That the ground has scarcely been scratched in this complex area is very apparent. It seems safe to say at least tentatively that, on the one hand, physiological and other unlearned factors and conditions of the individual so affect his volitional powers that these can never be ignored in character development; and that, on the other, the volitional habits, the motivations, and the goals of striving which the individual acquires greatly influence the effective strength of his volition and largely determine the directions in which it manifests itself in conduct.

Consistency and Inconsistency in Ethical Behavior in Relation to Trait Theory

One of the most interesting theoretical problems in the study of character is the problem of the consistency or inconsistency in the behavior of an individual in different situations involving honesty, cooperativeness, persistence, and other so-called traits. There is a considerable body of evidence on this problem, most of it consisting of correlational studies in which children's scores on one measure of a "trait" are correlated with their scores on another measure of the same trait. As will be seen from the few typical results on actual performance tests given below, there is relatively good agreement among the statistical results obtained by the different experimenters. Jones (1936), working with 185 seventh-grade pupils, found an average inter-r of .35 among three performance tests of honesty in school situations. Hartshorne and May (1928, 1929), using elementary and junior high school children as subjects, found an average inter-r of .39 among four tests of honesty. Crutcher (1934) reports a median inter-r of .47 among six persistence tests on children ranging in age from 7 to 16.[1] Gross (1946) conducted an experiment involving 229 seventh-grade pupils in honesty under several different conditions and found that only two-thirds of the students who were dishonest on one occasion were dishonest on another. These, we believe, are fair samples of the results that have been obtained, and we need not multiply the evidence.

What does all this mean so far as specificity or generality of traits is concerned? On the face of it, it means that an observer cannot predict very accurately what a child's unanalyzed behavior will be in one situation involving a supposed trait from his behavior in another situation presumably involving the same trait or trait name. For example, a child may be honest on a test where he has a good chance to cheat, and yet he may dishonestly get an advantage over other pupils in a prize contest by peeping when he has promised to compete with his eyes closed. Moreover, a child may cheat under one teacher but not under another.

In studying lying among children, Blatz (1952) distinguishes four types of lies, and the implication is that a child would

[1] It is interesting in passing to compare these inter-r's among different tests within the same "trait" with inter-r's among different "traits." Jones found an average inter-r of .15 between each of his honesty tests and a test of cooperation. Hartshorne and May found an average inter-r of .21 among tests of honesty, helpfulness, self-control, and persistence.

not necessarily behave consistently in situations involving the different types. The types which he mentions are: (1) lies of fantasy, involving imagination and partly unconscious and partly conscious misrepresentation; (2) lies of distortion, including conscious and unconscious omissions, overemphases, and underemphases; (3) lies of loyalty, deriving from the desire to belong, to be accepted, to be loyal to an individual or group; and (4) lies of self-protection involving deceit to avoid the consequences of one's behavior. From such observations and statistical results some are led to question the concept of generality of traits and stress specificity, much as Symonds (1928) has done. "It has been found," he says, "that no one acts perfectly consistently with regard to a trait as would be the case if conduct was an expression of inner traits" (p. 320). He admits that conduct under a given trait name may be generalized by responding to the likenesses and differences in situations, but he concludes that this generalization of conduct does not extend as far as the advocates of a generalized trait theory suppose.

Allport (1937) and Cattell (1946), starting with the same statistical results as Symonds, come out with a very different interpretation from his. Allport calls attention to a correlation of .13, found by Hartshorne and May, between stealing small change and the telling of lies about cheating, and he admits that the "dishonest habit aroused by one of these situations is quite independent of the dishonest habit in the other." He maintains, however, that under this surface specificity there are generalized traits. He admits that a given child who is tested may not steal money and yet may cheat in school and lie about the cheating. But he interprets this as showing not so much the lack of a general trait of honesty as the presence of a general trait of timidity. "Each of these children," he says, "be-

haved as he did toward these tests, not because of specific habits but because he had some deep-lying and characteristic trait" (p. 251). Cattell follows essentially the same line of reasoning in asserting that back of observed inconsistency in behavior there must be a trait. He says: "Just what degree of consistency—i.e., what reliability or consistency coefficient—one should demand in behavior manifestations to justify a trait is an arbitrary matter, best left for discussion when more data have accumulated on trait consistency" (p. 128). This concept of traits is so elusive that any hope of testing its reality in relation to conduct seems very remote.

These are illustrations of the different interpretations based on the same facts. Without ignoring the factual data involved in the low correlations among different aspects of behavior usually classified under the same trait names, it seems possible that we may avoid the morass of complete specificity, on the one hand, and the elusiveness of traits at any cost, on the other, by going back to an analysis of the behavior of the child. First, we should make a distinction between the behavior of a child as seen by an observer or revealed by a test, and the behavior of the child as looked at from his own point of view. If we could put ourselves in the child's place there seems little doubt that we should see much more consistency than his unanalyzed behavior reveals. This would be true because a situation which is designed from the point of view of the examiner to test honesty may not test honesty—and nothing but honesty —from the point of view of the subject. A child, for example, who refrains from cheating with one teacher but cheats freely with another may not think of the two situations as comparable at all. He may not cheat in the one case because he feels that he is on his honor not to try to "put anything over" on someone who treats him fairly and whom he likes; he may cheat in the other because he considers it an opportunity to "steal a march on," or to get even with, someone whom he dislikes or distrusts. As observers of only the honest-dishonest aspects of these situations, we might well conclude that honesty for this child is not very highly generalized. If, however, we view the total situations from the child's position we see more clearly how the behaviors that become classified by adults under a trait name are not necessarily one thing psychologically to the subject but perhaps several things.

Another point to be considered is that generality or specificity of traits probably varies with the age and training of the individual. There is no clear-cut statistical or experimental evidence which can be given here to demonstrate this, but all that we know of early conditioning as well as later learning of children leads us to believe that there should be greater specificity of conduct at the lower levels of learning and greater generality at the higher level.

One of the main theses of this chapter is that development in character should be away from specificity and in the direction of generality. When a child at a very young age makes a response which is judged to be undesirable or wrong in a situation, there come along simultaneously from the parent disapproving gestures, facial expressions, vocal tones, or such words as "no-no," "that's bad," "that's wrong," "that's not yours," "that's being a tattle-tale," "that's dishonest." By repeatedly experiencing annoyance in connection with a response or class of responses the child is conditioned against it. On the other hand, if the child makes a response which is judged to be the proper one, his action is rewarded by a smiling countenance, approving gestures, and such words as "that's a good boy," "that's right," "that's being honest." He has similar experiences on

every side, and, just as he learns gradually the names and uses of objects, he learns that certain acts are looked upon with approval and others with disapproval. This is the beginning of the process of generalizing, but his generalizations are based on only a very few acts which he has learned are not approved of and which he pronounces in a parrotlike fashion to be bad. At this stage of development a child's conduct seems to be highly specific.

But, as time goes on, the child finds that there are approved-of or not-approved-of aspects in a large number of situations; he learns that such words as "right," "wrong," "ought," "mustn't," "truthful," "untruthful," "honest," "dishonest," "loyal," "disloyal" refer to certain common factors in many situations. No other behavior of his is so violently responded to by adults as that where questions of right and wrong are raised, and consequently no other becomes so quickly and so thoroughly emotionally toned. With the increasing ability of the child to use verbalized concepts goes increasing use and understanding of the generalizations of right and wrong, good and bad, honesty and deceit, loyalty and disloyalty. He experiences what is referred to by various trait names in a great variety of situations. Gradually there develops whatever consistency of behavior occurs under trait names for him. These trait names assist him to generalize further, and emotional accompaniments become increasingly attached not only to specific acts but also to classes of acts. This process continues into adulthood.

However, even when an individual reaches his highest stage of maturity we cannot say that his traits are completely generalized in the sense that we can predict with anything like absolute certainty how he will behave in a relatively new situation involving a "trait" in which we rate him highly. When we describe a youth or man as honest, for example, we do not mean that we have observed any unitary or generalized trait of honesty on his part. We mean only that we have observed honest behavior in his case in a variety of situations and that we predict that in further sampling of situations he will respond similarly. This prediction is made partly on the assumption that in new situations involving honesty which he will face he will have systems of detailed habits that will make highly probable such and such conduct and partly also on the assumption that he has a certain orientation, a certain hierarchy of values, which will tend to insure behavior consistent with it.

Unfortunately, experimental facts are not available by which to test the above hypothesis that generality increases with growth in character. Taking all things into account, however, it seems that neither thoroughgoing specificity nor generality is likely to be adequate in any universal sense. The degree of specificity or generality characterizing an individual's conduct will depend, we believe, on his maturity and character development. Thus in attempting to fit our concepts of traits and trait names to the facts of child behavior we conclude that the degree of generality of a "trait" is dependent upon what is subsumed under the trait name and upon the stage of development of the individual.

Some Practical Observations on Character Development

In concluding this chapter a few practical suggestions concerning character development in home, church, and school may be in order.

The Importance of Early and Continuous Training in Character Development. In some of the older doctrines, before the advent of modern research on child development, great faith was placed in sudden changes in the character development of children and youth. The old notion that a child rather abruptly reached an age of moral responsibility after which time he could be "reasoned with" is one illustration of the belief in sudden changes. It is not our purpose here to maintain that rather sudden changes in the values and moral outlook of individuals never occur. Sufficient psychological data are not available on the dramatic cases that are usually cited in support of sudden changes to enable us to judge, but such cases are at least rare in comparison with the multitude of individuals who develop gradually from day to day.

The parent or the teacher who waits for the sudden dawning of an age of discretion seems, in the light of research results on mental growth, to be doomed to disappointment. While parents wait for their small child to be "old enough to understand," certain preliminary orientation of the child is achieved about the relative importance of truthfulness and of not getting caught. Young children have often learned a great deal before their parents stop recounting with amusement their "cute" escapades and "white lies."

Teachers, also, often delay too long or overlook good opportunities in giving early training. Such a simple lesson, for example, as the distinction between mutual helpfulness among classmates and cheating is frequently put off or taught only sporadically until serious confusion develops. The result is that many children in our elementary and secondary schools do not consider cheating an ethical question at all. It is rather a question of what one can "put over on" the teacher and what one can "get by with" in general. What an older child subsumes under the concepts of honor, cheating, tattling, or being a goody-goody or a thief, and what his emotionally toned attitudes toward these are, at any given age, are dependent in no small degree upon his conditioning and learning which began very early. Ethical concepts and behavior are continuously in the process of formation and revision throughout life, of course, but the earlier a child is oriented toward desirable conduct and generalizations, the earlier does he begin to internalize the controls upon him and to evolve his own sense of relative values.

Motivating Character Development. A child learns desirable character responses (1) in accordance with the principles of goal seeking and (2) by experiencing satisfaction in connection with those responses which are ethically and socially acceptable and annoyances with those which are undesirable. Thus meaningful goals, rewards, and punishments are basic in character development as in all learning. Probably in no other form of learning however, is it quite so important that they be adjusted accurately to the stage of development of the child.

Much evidence is accumulating to indicate that reward is usually more effective than punishment in character development. Punishment is being found to be valuable mainly as a deterrent to specific forms of undesirable behavior, since it lacks the constructive qualities to reveal or motivate desirable conduct except in the very simple situations where the right response is the opposite of the wrong. Evidence is also tending to indicate that intensity of rewards and punishments is less important than the promptness and consistency of their occurrence, especially in the early periods of development of the child.

Tangible awards for desirable character responses are sometimes valuable means for making such responses satisfying, but they are ordinarily valuable only in so far as they become progressively unnecessary as the child grows older. If at any age tangible awards tend to establish and perpetu-

ate desirable conduct only as responses to these artificial stimulants, thus failing to internalize the motives, they are to that extent undesirable, as Dimock and Hendry (1929) have interestingly demonstrated.

The types of rewards which seem to be most universal and permanent are those involving social acceptance and approval. Manifestations of genuine approval in the form of compliments, personal acceptance, and added responsibilities are among the strongest satisfactions for a child when they come from an adult or an associate whom he admires.

As an individual becomes older, he never becomes insensitive to social approval, but a more and more important place may gradually be taken by goal seeking and by the satisfaction accompanying the consciousness of self-approval or inner harmony in one's strivings. As Dewey says, "The community without gradually becomes a forum and tribunal within."

Thus, in the most advanced stages of character development, the most important function which the teacher can perform is to show the learner how each new problem in conduct is related to his existing patterns of generalized responses which already have strong emotional attachments and satisfactions connected with them. Once an act is viewed as being in harmony with one's ideals and values, it becomes satisfying in its accomplishment and in its anticipation; once it is viewed as out of harmony, it becomes annoying. Perhaps most of the choices of life are made at lower levels of ethical consciousness than this, but the choices with the greatest significance to character are probably made in this manner. All teaching of youth should make provision for the development of such inner goals and satisfactions. Without such internalized motivation character would always depend upon the short-range stimulation of more or less externally derived rewards and punishments and would lack the sustained pull of goal seeking in the pursuit of ideals and values.

Generalization and Transfer of Training. In character development, as in all other aspects of development where learning plays an important rôle, one of the major practical problems is the degree to which training received in one situation will function outside the narrow confines of that situation. Much research has been directed to this problem, and a review of it would be rewarding, but space limitations prohibit it. Suffice it here, therefore, to draw from this research two observations which bear particularly upon character development. One is that the learner in developing the responses which are called by any trait name should, in the interest of consistency in the application of this trait, be led to practice such responses in a variety of situations. To provide such a variety of situations for the common learnings which society demands, there should be the greatest possible joint planning and cooperation to this end among all the institutions of a community which are concerned with the character development of children.

The second observation is that, in the interest of generalization and transfer, learners should be stimulated and assisted to respond to the *relations* among the various manifestations of a trait in different situations. The potential power of children to generalize has been repeatedly emphasized in this chapter. However in learning honesty, for example, unless the child is assisted in culling out the honesty "element" in a variety of situations and in generalizing the honesty concept, he is left without the most promising bridge between one honesty situation and another, and his concept of honesty is in danger of becoming or remaining an unorganized, unintegrated collection of "do's" and "don't's."

The synthetic process of gradually building up trait concepts and other generalizations, and the analytical process of seeing "elements" in new situations to which these generalizations apply, should go hand in hand. The most realistic and challenging education in character which is supplied by home, school, and church functions largely in the area of stimulating children and youth, on the one hand, to generalize, and thus evolve the goals and values they would achieve, and, on the other, to analyze out of the ever new and increasingly complex problems of their everyday world the ethical issues at stake and to solve these problems in conformity with the highest principles and values which they have attained.

Conclusion

The aim of this chapter has been to raise some of the main psychological problems involved in character development and to present evidence or clues wherever possible toward their solution. Character has been considered as a dynamic concept involving both psychocultural determinants and inner creativeness. It involves the sum total of the attitudes and those ways of behaving of the individual which are the correlatives of his regulative habits, values, and volitional drives.

Both native and environmental-cultural factors have been studied, the central thesis of the chapter being that the child acquires his character in conformity with the principles of conditioning and learning, but that the possibilities for such acquisition and the broad limits thereto are provided by nature. Thus character development has been studied in as naturalistic and realistic a setting as possible. However, it has not been thought of in any narrowly deterministic fashion which rules out the possibilities of creativeness in the evolution of values to which one gives allegiance. The environment conditions but does not control either conscience or values. It is this very independence and creativeness of the human being in passing judgment upon his own conduct and the goals he would achieve that gives character development its chief interest as a field of study and holds out the possibility that it is in this area that the most important integrating and regulating forces of personal and social conduct will be found.

Bibliography

Adler, A. 1927. *Understanding human nature.* (Trans. by W. B. Wolfe.) New York: Greenberg.

Aita, J. A. 1948. Chronic residuals of brain injury. *Nebraska State Med. J., 33,* 163–169.

Allport, G. W. 1937. *Personality.* New York: Holt.

———. 1950. A psychological approach to the study of love and hate. In *Explorations in altruistic love and behavior,* edited by P. A. Sorokin, 145–164. Boston: Beacon Press.

Allport, G. W., J. M. Gillespie, and J. Young. 1948. The religion of post-war college students. *J. Psychol., 25,* 3–33.

Anderson, H. H., J. E. Brewer, and M. F. Reed. 1946. Studies of teachers' classroom personalities. III. Follow-up studies of the effects of dominative and integrative contacts on children's behavior. *Appl. Psychol. Monogr.,* No. 11.

Armstrong, C. P., and F. Heisler. 1945. A note on the attainments of delinquent boys. *Sch. & Soc., 61,* 9–32.

Baker, J. N. 1943. The press and crime. *J. Crim. Law Criminol., 33,* 463–467.

Baruk, H. 1947. Hypophyse: volonté et personalité morale. *Pr. méd.* (Medical Press), *55,* 497–498.

———. 1949. Experimental catatonia and the problem of will and personality. *J. Nerv. Ment. Dis., 110,* 218–235.

Beck, S. J. 1944 and 1945. *Rorschach's test.* Vols. I and II. New York: Grune & Stratton.

Bekhterev, V. M. 1928. Emotions as somatomimetic reflexes. In M. L. Reymert (Ed.), *Feelings and emotions: The Wittenberg Symposium,* pp. 270–283. Worcester, Mass.: Clark University Press.

Bender, L., and R. S. Lourie. 1941. The effect of comic books on the ideology of children. *Amer. J. Orthopsychiat., 11,* 540–551.

Berman, S. 1948. Adjustment of parents to children in the home. *J. Pediat., 32,* 66–77.

Betke, M. A. 1944. Defective moral reasoning in delinquency; a psychological study. *Stud. Psychol. Psychiat. Cathol. Univ. Amer., 6,* No. 4.

Bitterman, M. E., and F. L. Marcuse. 1947. Cardiovascular responses of innocent persons to criminal interrogation. *Amer. J. Psychol., 60,* 407–412.

Bize, P. R., and R. Moricard. 1937. Psychic changes following injection of testosterone in young boys. *Bull. soc pédiat., Paris, 35,* 38.

Blatz, W. E. 1952. What you should know about lying. *Educ. Dig., 17,* 10–13.

Blumer, H., and P. M. Hauser. 1934. *Movies, delinquency and crime.* New York: Macmillan.

Bond, E. S., and K. E. Appel. 1931. The treatment of post-encephalitic children in a hospital school. *Amer. J. Psychiat., 10,* 815–828.

Bühler, C., and G. Kelly. (Eds.) 1941. *The world test.* New York: Psychological Corp.

Burt, C. 1925. *The young delinquent.* London: University of London Press; New York: Appleton.

Burton, P. W. 1946. Newspaper reading behavior of high-school students. *Sch. & Soc., 63,* 86.

Cantril, H. 1950. *The "why" of man's experience.* New York: Macmillan.

Carr, L. J. 1950. *Delinquency control.* New York: Harper.

Carr-Saunders, A. M., H. Mannheim, and E. C. Rhodes. 1944. *Young offenders.* London: Cambridge University Press; New York: Macmillan.

Cattell, R. B. 1946. *Description and measurement of personality.* Yonkers, N. Y.: World Book.

Centers, R. 1949. *The psychology of social class.* Princeton, N. J.: Princeton University Press.

Charen, S., and L. Perelman. 1946. Personality studies of marihuana addicts. *Amer. J. Psychiat., 102,* 674–682.

Child, I. L., E. H. Potter, and E. M. Levine. 1946. Children's textbooks and personality development; an exploration in the social psychology of education. *Psychol. Monogr., 60,* No. 3.

Child, I. L., and J. W. M. Whiting. 1949. Determinants of level of aspiration: evidence from everyday life. *J. Abn. Soc. Psychol., 44,* 303–314.

Children's Bureau, U. S. Federal Security Agency. 1946. *Juvenile court statistics, 1944 and 1945,* Social Statistics, Suppl. to Volume 11 of *The Child.* November.

Ciampi, L. 1937. Postencephalitic ethical defect in children. *Ann. Soc. Argent. Criminol., 3,* 69–88.

Clark, G., and H. G. Birch. 1945. Hormonal modifications of social behavior: I. The effect of sex-hormone administration on the social status of a male castrate chimpanzee. *Psychosom. Med., 7,* 321–329.

Coghill, G. E. 1936. The integration and motivation of behavior as problems of growth. *J. Gen. Psychol., 48,* 3–19.

Cooper, W. M. 1950. Parental delinquency. *Phylon, 11,* 269–273.

Cressey, P. G., and F. M. Thrasher. 1934. *Boys, movies, and city streets.* New York: Macmillan.

Cronbach, L. J. 1949. *Essentials of psychological testing.* New York: Harper.

Crutcher, R. 1934. An experimental study of persistence. *J. Appl. Psychol., 18,* 409–417.

Cuthbertson, D. P., and J. A. C. Knox. 1947. The effects of analeptics on the fatigued subject. *J. Physiol., 106,* 42–58.

Dale, E. 1935. *Attendance at motion pictures and the contents of motion pictures.* New York: Macmillan.

Dawson, L. L. 1938. *The relation of unemployment to certain types of crime in Massachusetts.* Unpublished M.A. thesis. Clark University.

DeBoer, J. J. 1939. Radio and children's emotions. *Sch. & Soc., 50,* 369–373.

Dechesne, L. 1950. The factor of altruism. In *Explorations in altruistic love and behavior,* edited by P. A. Sorokin, 227–248. Boston: Beacon Press.

Dimock, H. S., and C. E. Hendry. 1929. *Camping and character.* New York: Association Press.

Dollard, J., L. W. Doob, N. Miller, O. Mowrer, and R. Sears. 1939. *Frustration and aggression.* New Haven: Yale University Press.

Doob, L. W. 1948. *Public opinion and propaganda.* New York: Holt.

Dysinger, W. S., and C. A. Ruckmick. 1933. *The emotional responses of children to the motion picture situation.* New York: Macmillan.

Eckenrode, C. J. 1950. Their achievement is delinquency. *J. Educ. Res., 43,* 554–560.

Edmiston, R. W., and L. A. Jackson. 1949. The relationship of persistence to achievement. *J. Educ. Psychol., 40,* 47–51.

Educational Policies Commission. 1951. *Moral and spiritual values in the public schools.* Washington, D. C.: National Educational Association.

Feingold, G. A. 1944. Newspaper tastes of high-school pupils. *Sch. & Soc., 59,* 316–319.

Fleege, U. H. 1945. Movies as an influence in the life of the modern adolescent. *Cath. Educ. Rev., 43,* 336–352.

Ford, R. 1939. *Children in the cinema.* London: Allen and Unwin.

Fox, V. 1946. Intelligence, race, and age as selective factors in crime. *J. Crim. Law Criminol., 37,* 141–152.

Frank, J. 1949. Comics, radio, movies and children. *Publ. Affairs Pam.,* No. 148.

Frank, J. D. 1935. Some psychological determinants of level of aspiration. *Amer. J. Psychol., 47,* 285–293.

Frank, L. K. 1948. What families do for the nation. *Amer. J. Sociol., 53,* 471–473.

French, J. W. 1948. The validity of a persistence test. *Psychometrika, 13,* 271–277.

French, T., J. G. Miller, and D. Riesman. 1950. Psychoanalysis and ethics. *Univ. Chicago Round Table,* No. 638, 1–12.

Frenkel-Brunswik, E. 1948. A study of prejudice in children. *Hum. Relat., 1,* 295–306.

——. 1951. Patterns of social and cognitive outlook in children and parents. *Amer. J. Orthopsychiat., 21,* 543–558.

Freud, S. 1924. *Collected papers:* Vol. 1. London: Hogarth Press and Institute for Psycho-Analysis.

——. 1930. *Civilization and its discontents.* (Trans. by J. Rivière.) New York: Cape and Smith.

Gesell, A., and H. Thompson. 1929. Learning and growth in identical infant twins: An experimental study by the mthod of co-twin control. *Genet. Psychol. Monogr., 6.* Pp. 124.

Glueck, E. T. 1935. Mental retardation and juvenile delinquency. *Ment. Hyg., N. Y., 19,* 549–572.

Glueck, S., and E. T. Glueck. 1934. *One thousand juvenile delinquents.* Cambridge: Harvard University Press.

——. 1940. *Juvenile delinquents grown up.* New York: Commonwealth Fund.

Gould, R. 1939. An experimental analysis of "level of aspiration." *Genet. Psychol. Monogr., 21.* Pp. 115.

Gray, W. S. 1947. The social effects of reading. *Sch. Rev., 55,* 269–277.

Greene, E. B. 1952. *Measurements of human behavior.* (Rev. ed.) New York: Odyssey Press.

Greenbaum, J. V., and Lurie, L. A. 1948. Encephalitis as a causative factor in behavior disorders of children: An analysis of seventy-eight cases. *J. Amer. Med. Ass., 136,* 923–930.

Gross, M. M. 1946. The effect of certain types of motivation on the "honesty" of children. *J. Educ. Res., 40,* 133–140.

Groves, E. R. 1940. *The family and its social functions.* Philadelphia: Lippincott.

Harris, D. B., H. G. Gough, and W. E. Martin. 1950. Children's ethnic attitudes: II. Relationship to parental beliefs concerning child training. *Child Develpm., 21,* 170–181.

Hartshorne, H., and M. A. May. 1928. *Studies in deceit:* Book I. *General methods and results;* Book II. *Statistical methods and results.* New York: Macmillan.

——. 1929. *Studies in service and self-control.* New York: Macmillan.

Hartshorne, H., M. A. May, and F. K. Shuttleworth. 1930. *Studies in the organization of character.* New York: Macmillan.

Havighurst, R. J. 1952. The functions of successful discipline. *Understanding the Child, 21,* 35–38.

Havighurst, R. J., and H. Taba. 1949. *Adolescent character and personality.* New York: Wiley.

Healy, W. 1915. *The individual delinquent: A textbook of diagnosis and prognosis for all concerned in understanding offenders.* Boston: Little, Brown; London: Heinemann.

Healy, W., and A. F. Bronner. 1926. *Delinquents and criminals: Their making and unmaking.* New York: Macmillan.

——. 1936. *New light on delinquency and its treatment.* New Haven: Yale University Press.

——. 1948. What makes a child delinquent? *47th Yearb. Nat. Soc. Study Educ.,* 30–47. Chicago: University of Chicago Press.

Heersena, P. H. 1940. Prognosis in postencephalitic behavior disorders. *Med. Clin. N. Amer., 24,* 1179–1190.

Henry, N. B. (Ed.) 1948. *Juvenile delinquency and the schools.* Chicago: University of Chicago Press.

Herrick, C. J. 1946. Scientific method and human values. *Amer. Scientist, 34,* 239–245.

Hightower, P. R. 1930. Biblical information in relation to character conduct. *Univ. Iowa Stud. Char.*, *3*, No. 2.

Hoppe, F. 1930. Erfolg und Misserfolg. *Psychol. Forsch.*, *14*, 1–62.

Horney, K. 1937. *The neurotic personality of our time.* New York: Norton.

———. 1948. The value of vindictiveness. *Amer. J. Psychoanal.*, *8*, 3–12.

Hoult, T. F. 1949. Comic books and juvenile delinquency. *Sociol. Soc. Res.*, *33*, 279–284.

Imbau, F. E. 1935a. Detection of deception technique admitted as evidence. *J. Crim. Law Criminol.*, *26*, 262–270.

———. 1935b. The lie-detector. *Sci. Mon.*, *40*, 81–87.

———. 1946. The lie-detector. *J. Clin. Psychopath.*, *8*, 151–158.

Jersild, A. T. 1947. *Child psychology.* 3rd ed. New York: Prentice-Hall.

Jones, V. 1929a. Ideas on right and wrong among teachers and children. *Teach. Coll. Rec.*, *30*, 529–541.

———. 1929b. Disagreement among teachers as to right and wrong. *Teach. Coll. Rec.*, *31*, 24–36.

———. 1931a. *What would you have done?* Boston: Ginn.

———. 1931b. *Character education through cases from biography.* Boston: Ginn.

———. 1932. Relation of economic depression to delinquency, crime, and drunkenness in Massachusetts. *J. Soc. Psychol.*, *3*, 259–282.

———. 1936. *Character and citizenship gaining in the public school.* Chicago: University of Chicago Press.

———. 1950. *Character and citizenship education—a syllabus for use in teacher training.* Washington, D. C.: National Education Association.

———. 1951. Character and citizenship education. *Phi Delta Kappan*, *33*, 190–192.

———. 1952. *Youth decides—Group guidance in everyday citizenship.* Evanston, Ill.: Row, Peterson.

Jordan, H. W. 1938. Admissibility of deception (lie-detector) tests. *J. Crim. Law Criminol.*, *29*, 287–291.

Josey, C. C., and D. Snygg. 1950. The place of psychology in the development of values. *Personality*, Symposium 1, 1–6.

Kardiner, A. 1939. *The individual and his society.* New York: Columbia University Press.

Katz, D., and F. H. Allport. 1930. *Students' attitudes.* Syracuse, N. Y.: Craftsman Press.

Keeler, L. 1934. Debunking the lie-detector. *J. Crim. Law Criminol.*, *25*, 153–159.

Kleitman, N. 1945. The effect of motion pictures on body temperature. *Science*, *101*, 507–508.

Klopfer, B., and D. M. Kelley. 1942. *The Rorschach technique.* Yonkers: World Book.

Kuhlen, R. G. 1952. *The psychology of adolescent development.* New York: Harper.

Künkel, F. 1938. *Character, growth, education.* (Trans. by B. Keppel-Compton and B. Druitt.) Philadelphia: Lippincott.

Lane, H. A., and P. A. Witty. 1935. The mental ability of delinquent boys. *J. Juv. Res.*, *19*, 1–12.

Larson, J. A. 1932. *Lying and its detection.* Chicago: University of Chicago Press.

Leeper, R. W. 1948. A motivational theory of emotion to replace the "emotion as disorganized response." *Psychol. Rev.*, *55*, 5–21.

Levi, L. 1930. Sul decorso e la prognosi dell'encefalite epidemica nei ragazzi. *Quad. di Psichiat.*, *17*, 89–102.

Ligon, E. M. 1939. *Their future is now.* New York: Macmillan.

———. 1948. *A greater generation.* New York: Macmillan.

Lippitt, R., L. P. Bradford, and K. D. Benne. 1947. Sociodramatic clarification of leader and group roles as a starting point for effective group functioning. *Sociatry*, 1, 82–91.

Liu, C. H. 1950. *The influence of cultural background on the moral judgment of children.* New York: Columbia University, Ph.D. thesis.

Lyons, V. W. 1936. Deception tests with juvenile delinquents. *J. Genet. Psychol.*, *48*, 494–497.

Maller, J. B. 1930. Character growth and Jewish education. *Relig. Educ.*, *25*, 627–630.

———. 1932. Conflicting ideals and their bearing upon character education. *J. Educ. Res.*, *25*, 161–167.

———. 1937. Juvenile delinquency in New York: A summary of a comprehensive report. *J. Psychol.*, *3*, 1–25.

Manwell, E. M., and S. A. Fahs. 1951. *Consider the children; how they grow.* (Rev. ed.) Boston: Beacon Press.

Marston, W. M. 1938. *The lie detector test.* New York: R. R. Smith.

———. 1946. Lie detection—its bodily basis and test procedures. In P. L. Harriman, *Encycl. psychol.*, pp. 354–363. New York: Philosophical Library.

May, M. A., and F. K. Shuttleworth. 1935. The relationship of moving pictures to the character and attitudes of children. (Bound with R. C. Peterson and L. L. Thurstone. *Motion pictures and social attitudes of children.* New York: Macmillan.

McDougall, W. 1918. *An introduction to social psychology.* Boston: Luce.

Mead, Margaret. 1949. Crossing cultural barriers. *Relig. Educ.*, *44*, 67–71.

Metfessel, M., and C. Lovell. 1942. Recent literature on individual correlates of crime. *Psychol. Bull.*, *39*, 133–164.

Moreno, F. B. 1947. Psychodrama in the neighborhood. *Sociatry*, *1*, 168–178.

Moreno, J. L. 1934. *Who shall survive?* Washington, D. C.: Nerv. and Ment. Dis. Publ. Co.

———. 1943. The concept of sociodrama; a new approach to the problem of intercultural relations. *Sociometry*, *6*, 434–449.

———. 1947. Contributions of sociometry to research methodology in sociology. *Amer. Sociol. Rev.*, *12*, 287–292.

Murphy, G., L. B. Murphy, and T. M. Newcomb. 1937. *Experimental social psychology.* (Rev. ed.) New York: Harper.

Murray, H. A. 1943. *Thematic apperception test.* Cambridge: Harvard University Press.

Murray, H. A., *et al.* 1938. *Explorations in personality.* New York: Oxford University Press.

Murray, H. A., and Kluckhohn, C. (Eds.) 1948. Outline of a conception of personality in *Personality in nature, society and culture.* New York: Knopf.

Mutual Broadcasting Company. 1946. *The influence of radio, motion pictures, and comics on children.* New York: Mutual Broadcasting Co.

Newell, H. W. 1937. Effect of head injury on the behavior and personality of children: A study of twenty cases. *Med. Clin. N. Amer., 21,* 1335.

Nixon, C. R. 1952. Vital issues in free speech. *Ethics, 42,* 101–121.

Office of Strategic Services, Assessment Staff. 1948. *Assessment of men.* New York: Rinehart.

Olson, W. C. 1930. *Problem tendencies in children: A method for their measurement and description.* Minneapolis: University of Minnesota Press.

——. 1949. *Child development.* Boston: Heath.

Owen, M. B. 1937. The intelligence of the institutionalized juvenile delinquent. *J. Juv. Res., 21,* 199–206.

Phillips, E. L. 1950. Intellectual and personality factors associated with social class attitudes among junior high school children. *J. Genet. Psychol., 77,* 61–72.

Piaget, J. 1932. *The moral judgment of the child.* (Trans. by M. Gabain.) New York: Harcourt, Brace; London: Kegan Paul.

Pinard, J. W. 1932–1933. Tests of perseveration: Their relation to character. *Brit. J. Psychol., 23,* 5–19.

Pound, R. 1930. *Criminal justice in Cleveland.* New York: Holt.

Raths, L. E., and Trager, F. N. 1948. Public opinion and crossfire. *J. Educ. Sociol., 21,* 345–368.

Renshaw, S., V. L. Miller, and D. Marquis. 1933. *Children's sleep.* New York: Macmillan.

Reyburn, H. A., and Taylor, J. G. 1939. Some factors of personality: a further analysis of some of Webb's data. *Brit. J. Psychol., 30,* 1, 151–211.

——. 1943. Some factors of temperament: a reexamination. *Psychometrika, 8,* 91–104.

Riley, J. W., F. V. Cantwell, and K. F. Ruttiger. 1949. Some observations on the social effects of television. *Publ. Opin. Quart., 13,* 223–234.

Roback, A. A. 1952. *The psychology of character.* 3rd ed. Cambridge, Mass.: Sci-Art Publishers.

Rosen, I. C. 1948. The effect of the motion picture "Gentlemen's agreement" on attitude toward Jews. *J. Psychol., 26,* 525–536.

Rosenzweig, S. 1949. *Psychodiagnosis.* New York: Grune and Stratton.

Rowland, H. 1944. Radio crime dramas. *Educ. Res. Bull., 23,* 210–217.

Ryans, D. G. 1938a. An experimental attempt to analyze persistent behavior: I. Measuring traits presumed to involve persistence. *J. Gen. Psychol., 19,* 333–353.

——. 1938b. An experimental attempt to analyze persistent behavior: II. A persistence test. *J. Gen. Psychol., 19,* 353–371.

Ryans, D. G. 1938c. A study of the observed relationship between persistence test results, intelligence indices, and academic success. *J. Educ. Psychol., 29,* 573–580.

——. 1939a. The measurement of persistence: An historical review. *Psychol. Bull., 36,* 715–739.

——. 1939b. A note on variations in persistence test score with sex, age, and academic level. *J. Soc. Psychol., 10,* 259–264.

Rylander, G. 1937. Personality changes after operations on frontal lobes. *Acta Psychiat. Kbh., Suppl.* 20.

Schwartz, E. E. 1949. Statistics of juvenile delinquency in the United States. *The Annals, 261,* 9–20.

Sheehy, L. M. 1938. *A study of preadolescents by means of a personality inventory.* Washington, D. C.: Catholic University Press.

Sherif, M. 1948. *An outline of social psychology.* New York: Harper.

Shull, C. A. 1940. A study in suitability of motion-picture theatre programs to the needs of the child. *J. Educ. sociol., 13,* 274–279.

Siepmann, C. A. 1950. *Radio, television, and society.* New York: Oxford University Press.

Slaght, W. E. 1928. Untruthfulness in children: Its conditioning factors and its setting in child nature. *Univ. Iowa Stud. in Charact., 1,* No. 4.

Sorokin, P. A. (Ed.) 1950. *Explorations in altruistic love and behavior.* Boston: Beacon Press.

Spaulding, F. T. 1938. *High school and life.* New York: McGraw-Hill.

Spearman, C. 1927. *The abilities of man: Their nature and measurement.* New York: Macmillan.

Stephenson, W. 1935. Perseveration and character. *Character & Pers., 4,* 44–52.

Stern, E. 1949. L'enfant de la maison d'enfants; essai psychologique. *Z. Kinderpsychiat., 16,* 17–24, 33–43.

Stertz, G. 1931. Encephalitische Wesensveränderungen und Mord: Gutachten über dei Zurechnungsfähigkeit. *Mschr. Krimpsychol. Strafrechtsref., 22,* 320–332.

Stott, D. H. 1950. *Delinquency and human nature.* Dunfermline, Fife, Scotland: Carnegie United Kingdom Trust.

Symonds, P. M. 1928. *The nature of conduct.* New York: Macmillan.

——. 1931. *Diagnosing personality and conduct.* New York: Century.

——. 1939. *The psychology of parent-child relationships.* New York: Appleton-Century.

——. 1949. *The dynamics of parent-child relationships.* New York: Bureau of Publications, Teachers College, Columbia University.

Taylor, H. R., and F. F. Powers. 1928. Bible study and character. *J. Genet. Psychol., 35,* 294–302.

Terman, L. M., *et al.* 1925. *Genetic studies of genius:* Vol. 1. *Mental and physical traits of a thousand gifted children.* Stanford University, Calif.: Stanford University Press.

Thrasher, F. M. 1927. *The gang; a study of 1313 gangs in Chicago.* Chicago: University of Chicago Press.

Thurstone, L. L. 1931. Influence of motion pictures on children's attitudes. *J. Soc. Psychol.*, *2*, 291–305.

Tredgold, A. F. 1937. *Mental deficiency (amentia).* (6th ed.) Baltimore: Wood.

Trovillo, P. V. 1939. A history of lie detection. *J. Crim. Law Criminol.*, *29*, 848–881; *30*, 104–119.

Tudor-Hart, B. E. 1926. Are there cases in which lies are necessary? *Ped. Sem.*, *33*, 586–641.

Voelker, P. F. 1921. The function of ideals and attitudes in social education: An experimental study. *Teach. Coll. Contr. Educ.*, No. 112.

Wallenstein, N. 1937. Character and personality of children from broken homes. *Teach. Coll. Contr. Educ.*, No. 721.

Watson, J. B. 1926. Experimental studies in the growth of the emotions. In C. Murchison (Ed.), *Psychologies of 1925*, pp. 37–58. Worcester: Clark University Press.

Wattenberg, W. W. 1950. Church attendance and juvenile misconduct. *Sociol. Soc. Res.*, *34*, 195–202.

Webb, E. 1915. Character and intelligence. *Brit. J. Psychol. Monogr. Suppl.*, *1*, No. 3. Pp. 99.

Weber, C. O. 1946. Levels of aspiration. In P. L. Harriman, *Encyclopedia of psychology*, pp. 45 ff. New York: Philosophical Library.

Wilson, H. E. 1938. *Education for citizenship.* New York: McGraw-Hill.

Woodruff, A. D. 1945. Personal values and religious background. *J. Soc. Psychol.*, *22*, 141–147.

Woodworth, R. S. 1934. *Psychology.* (3d ed.) New York: Holt.

CHAPTER 14

EMOTIONAL DEVELOPMENT

ARTHUR T. JERSILD

INTRODUCTORY

This account draws heavily upon studies of children but it calls upon other sources. The content of this chapter has been influenced by behavioristic and gestalt psychology and by academic psychologists who are not identified with either of these schools (e.g., McDougall), and it represents also an effort to integrate findings of developmental psychology with fruitful developments in psychoanalytic psychology.

The first few paragraphs which follow are not documented in detail. They deal with elementary matters, but they are a necessary introduction to the conceptual framework of the chapter as a whole.

THE MEANING OF EMOTION

To be emotional means to be moved. "Emotion" is a label for a vast range of psychosomatic states. When these states occur, it is by virtue of the fact that something is occurring in the external environment or within the organism itself which thwarts or threatens, furthers or enhances, the process of living.

On the subjective side, an emotion involves *feeling*. The feeling may be quite clearly defined (as when one feels a surge of anger and is aware of it), or it may be vague and difficult to describe (as often is the case when one is anxious). Feelings not only fall on a scale of varying degrees of pleasantness and unpleasantness, but they occur also in indefinitely numerous qualities.

Also on the subjective side, emotion usually involves *perception* or awareness of an event or circumstance which the individual has feelings about or to which he attributes his feelings. It is necessary to say "usually," for strong feelings may occur without a clear perception of what brings them about. This is especially true of feelings that occur by virtue of "hidden" motives and "inner" conflicts and other subjective conditions which the individual is unable clearly to define to himself.

Emotion also involves a more or less clearly defined *impulse* or disposition to action, such as an impulse to fight or flee, or a striving to attain or to sustain a condition that produces joy, or a quick mobilization of one's defenses if something threatens one's pride.

The bodily features of emotional behavior involve *visceral* activities, including a variety of reactions of the glands and of the circulatory, respiratory, and digestive systems, as well as activities of the *skeletal muscles* such as occur when an individual strikes out or retreats or makes subtle postural adjustments, or displays subtle changes in the expression of his face. Muscular activities also include those of the vocal organs that come into play in weeping, outcries, and laughter.

The total response that takes place or that emerges during emotional behavior may be of a highly explosive, *disorganized* character, or it may, at the other extreme, take the form of highly *organized,* well-coordinated behavior that is nicely adapted to cope with a disturbing event or to take advantage of a joyful opportunity.

As already implied, the term emotion, as here used, covers conditions of both a "positive" and "negative" character, conditions in which the organism may be described as being eager, zestful, jubilant, and *moving toward,* as well as conditions in which it is disturbed, distressed, and *moving against* or *away.* It is necessary to emphasize this rather simple point, for often in psychological writings emotion is treated primarily as a form of disorder and distress. Indeed, much of the literature has treated emotion as though it were a rather sinful state, or at least a nuisance.

WHAT GIVES RISE TO EMOTION?

Emotion is involved in the whole business of living. The most obvious occasions for emotion are those involving bodily harm or threat of violence or of being overwhelmed. But emotion may also be elicited by any condition which thwarts or threatens or which furthers or enhances the gratification of a person's needs, as he perceives them, or the realization of his goals, or which blocks or expedites a disposition to action or behavior tendency (recognized or unrecognized, "conscious" or "unconscious") which he has acquired in the process of adapting himself to the demands of life. Emotion is involved in anything in which a person sees himself involved. For this reason, to understand the child's emotion it is necessary to take account not only of the objective stimulus situation and of his overt behavior to this situation but also of the subjective system known as the self which, while not directly observable by others, is to the person himself the most important reality of his existence.

MOTIVES AND NEEDS

To understand emotional development we need a theory of motivation that takes account of elementary needs for safety, sustenance, and shelter which all creatures have in common, and of the particular needs that develop in the life of the individual child because of the capacities he possesses and the kind of person he turns out to be.

Writers in recent years have stressed the need for a broad conception of human motivation. Many of the "propensities" which McDougall (1926) listed before behaviorism was in full cry have stolen back into the literature, although mostly under new names. In addition to primitive needs for sustenance, shelter, and safety, many writers have emphasized tendencies within the organism to realize itself, to utilize its capacities, to exercise its powers. There are just as many potential impulses as there are potential abilities. Goldstein (1947) speaks of the organism's tendency to *actualize* itself as the basic drive. Man does not strive merely for self-preservation but is moved to manifest spontaneity, according to Goldstein.

Murphy (1947) similarly emphasizes the tendency of human beings to utilize their powers by virtue of motivation other than that involved in the need for physical survival. Maslow (1943 and 1948) speaks of needs as arranged in a hierarchy of prepotency, ranging from physiological needs to the needs for esteem and self-actualization. According to Maslow, when the most prepotent need is satisfied, the next higher need emerges, so that man is a "perpetually wanting animal."

In the psychoanalytic field, many writers have stressed a view of human motivation which emphasizes the broad range of human potentiality. Horney (1945), for example, stresses the importance of relationships with others and of the attitudes of others as factors in the development of a person's "real self" and of his fictitious "idealized self" and the intrapsychic needs and defenses which are mobilized in connection with the maintenance of the self-picture. Fromm (1947) speaks of man's efforts to become what he potentially might be. Saul (1947) and Fromm speak of the normal person as one who uses his powers in a *productive* manner. F. Alexander (1948) follows Freud in speaking of both love and play as erotic phenomena, but he goes beyond this to speak of these phenomena as not designed merely to save energy, but to expend it in creative and progressive ways that lead the organism toward new ventures and experiments. The energy children expend in an experimental and playful manner is not simply being used for homeostatic stability or survival.

In listing human motives, the common practice is first to name physiological drives that are directly connected with *physical survival* and *bodily comfort*—the need for *food*, for *drink*, for *air*, for protection from extremes of heat and cold, and the need for excretion of waste.

Another need or drive in this category pertains to sex. Although the sex drive does not reach its "mature" form until puberty, there are many indications, as will be pointed out below, that erotic behavior of some sort is manifested in early infancy and that it appears in various forms throughout childhood years. Later we shall refer to behavior which, according to surface indications, is erotic in character but which functions as a symptom of or vehicle for other motives.

Under this heading, we probably should also include a *parental drive,* although this drive does not define itself as clearly as the hunger drive. Evidence from the study of animals (Warden, 1931), and observations of adults (see, e.g., Thorndike, 1913) indicate that at least on occasion and in certain individuals the drive or drives that lead a parent to be with and to care for an offspring are very powerful. Whatever is "primitive" or visceral about the drive will, of course, in the human being, be embroidered and perhaps even be clouded by other motives. The parental drive cannot, of course, operate in children as it can in a mature person who is capable of begetting children. But the writer believes that, if we grant that such a drive exists at all, we must also assume that it, like other features of human nature that sooner or later emerge in the life process, probably has a developmental history extending back into earlier youth or childhood.

The drives named above have sometimes been called physiological or visceral drives. Some writers have unkindly referred to them as "lower" drives. They have also been called "primary," "vital," or "prepotent" drives.[1] Although we can speak of a person having cravings when hungry, cold, or thirsty, or subject to other visceral needs, there is not a clearly defined set of emotions paralleling each of these drives. However, the way in which the child is permitted to satisfy these needs, and perhaps, to an even greater extent, the rules, restrictions, and restraints which surround these needs, frequently arouse emotional response from early infancy onward. Probably also from a rather early age thwartings or deprivations connected with these drives take on a larger meaning. To a child who is able to formulate an idea of the possible *intentions* of others, denial of food when he is hungry may mean a denial or rejection of *him*.

Apart from drives such as the foregoing which are important for bodily preservation, reproduction, and repair, the organism is equipped also with *activity* drives,

[1] For accounts of motivation, see, e.g., Young (1943), Tolman (1932), Maslow (1943 and 1948), Murphy (1947), O. Klineberg (1940), H. A. Murray (1938).

drives to *use* and *exercise* its capacities. These drives appear in ways too numerous to permit classification, but certain broad categories can be noted.

There is a drive for *muscular activity*. This is especially prominent in young children, who are notoriously "on the go." Muscular activity is the vehicle for many joyful experiences of childhood, and enforced inactivity is a fruitful source of frustration. A drive to use muscular coordination often is especially noticeable when the child is in the process of making a new hurdle in his motor development, such as walking or climbing (Shirley, 1931; Damann, 1941).

There also are drives leading to the use of the *sense organs*. The child feasts upon sights, sounds, cutaneous contacts, and other sensory experiences. In speaking of the "sensory drives," Murphy (1947) points out that they may be intermingled with the "visceral drives," as when appetite for food is influenced by the color of the food.

The gratification of sensory drives probably accounts in part for the emotional content of intense esthetic experiences.

Under the broad heading of activity drives we may also include the *drive to use the intellect*. Moore (1948) states that "Every mental ability, every function, has a native tendency to set itself in action" (p. 108). In due time, the normal child is eager to find out, to explore, to discover. Many children go through a period of avid questioning about the what, how, when, and why of things. We might call this a drive for *cortical activity*, or, in more commonplace language, simply the exercise of curiosity, which is an abundant source of satisfaction. Shand (1920) named curiosity as one of the important impulses on his list. McDougall (1926) listed curiosity as one of the principal instincts and named the

emotion of *wonder* as linked with this instinct.

Needs which overlap those described above have also been referred to in such terms as the need for *achievement*, for *discovery*, for *new experiences*.

Another group of needs which can be observed but which are not easily defined are needs for *love, affection,* and *belonging*. Whether these needs are "primary" in the sense that a child needs love as such, or whether his need for all that love brings and all that it implies springs from his initial helplessness or develops as a "conditioned" product of treatment he receives from loving parents, need not be debated here. Whatever may be the conditions that spur an infant to need love, he shows in countless ways in the process of his development a need for affection as coin that has value in its own right regardless of the source from which it derived its value.

As the child matures, he not only exhibits a need for receiving affection but also manifests affection for others.

Other needs that develop in a child's relations with other persons have been described in various terms, including the need to *belong* and various forms of *gregariousness* which are influenced to a large degree by learning, but which lead a person to be a joiner, cooperator, imitator, dominator, competitor, or a follower or a leader, or, at different times, all of these. Drives connected with his relations with others may also take the form of *need for approval, need for recognition*. These needs pertaining to a child's relationships with others, his link with the society in which he lives, have been emphasized as being of crucial importance in the development of the subjective system known as the self (see, e.g., Mead, 1934; Horney, 1950; and Sullivan, 1947). Sullivan's account of the social (interpersonal) origins of the self are especially persuasive and provocative, and they raise a host of research questions for the worker interested in developmental psychology.

According to some writers (notably Sullivan, 1947) a child is capable of responding emotionally, through a process of empathy, to the attitudes of a significant person who has charge of him. However, this is a speculative matter, and it represents one area, of many, that requires research of a kind that deals not only with the objective environment but also with the subjective environment represented by the child himself.

The needs for approval and recognition overlap with needs associated with the growing child's developing concept of himself. As the child develops and acquires an increasingly differentiated idea of himself, he also acquires a need for satisfactory feelings about himself—a need for self-esteem, a desire, as Maslow (1943) puts it, for a "stable, firmly based, high evaluation of himself . . ." (p. 381). In commenting on this, T. V. Moore (1948) states that whatever convinces one of his excellence and importance ". . . awakens a satisfaction which once experienced is ever afterwards craved and so constitutes a powerful driving force of human nature . . ." (p. 244). Anything that enhances the self-idea may lead to feelings which are experienced as a form of exaltation, or strong feelings of self-confidence, whereas anything that leads in the opposite direction, or threatens so to do, may cause depression, gloom, "feelings of inferiority," discouragement, or fear. McDougall (1926) anticipates these observations on his list of instincts, which includes an instinct of "self-assertion" (or self-display) and, tied to this, a primary emotion of elation or positive self-feeling. We shall have occasion to discuss below conditions that give rise to feelings of joy and satisfaction relating to self, and conditions that lead to gloom or anxiety may occur not only as a

result of a need for approval and esteem in the eyes of others but also, as the child grows older, from a great need for self-approval.

The needs associated with a person's idea and appraisal of himself include both desires for enhancing his self-esteem and also strivings to preserve the integrity or consistency of the self. The classical concepts regarding protection of self originated with Freud, who spoke of the ego and its defenses. The struggles a person may undergo to live up to, preserve, and vindicate an idealized version of himself have been described by Horney (1945, 1950) and others. Snygg and Combs (1949) maintain that the "basic human need" is the "preservation and enhancement of the phenomenal self"—the self of which a person is aware (p. 58). The rôle of the concept of self in emotional behavior has been set forth by several authors, including the writer (Jersild, 1947). The ideas a person has about himself, his attitudes and ideas as to what a person such as he should be expected to like or dislike, do or not do, accept or hate or fear, will be important in determining whether a certain happening is a threat to be warded off or a temptation to be feared or an occasion for joy or a cause for remorse. The position that pleasant and unpleasant emotions are especially likely to occur in connection with circumstances that threaten or challenge or help to unify the self has been set forth in a book by Lecky (1945).

Earlier Accounts of "Primary" Emotions

Many students of emotions have tried to identify what might be regarded as primary or original emotions which all creatures have in common and which might be regarded as providing the basis for the countless mixtures, nuances, and gradations of emotion which we identify in the language of everyday life. Lists of emotions that have been proposed as the primary emotions are of historical interest.

Shand (1920) listed seven emotions: fear, anger, joy, sorrow, curiosity, repugnance, disgust. Ribot (1903) described the "primitive" emotions as fear, anger, affection (from which later are derived the "social" and "moral" emotions), self-feeling or egoistic emotion, and sexual emotion. McDougall (1926) listed seven pairs of instincts and correlative emotions, including: flight–fear; repulsion–disgust; curiosity–wonder; pugnacity–anger; self-abasement (or subjection)–negative self-feeling; self-assertion (or self-display)–elation (positive self-feeling); parental instinct–tender emotion. Watson (1919) and Watson and Morgan (1917) confined the list to three: fear, rage, and love. Hollingworth (1928) suggests that these reactions, as distinguished from the more highly differentiated emotions of later life, might be designated as startle, resistance, and content, and that a fourth form of response, gloom, be added.

Changes in the Conception of What Constitutes an Emotional Stimulus

In connection with past efforts to identify distinct emotional states there have been efforts also to describe what constitutes the primary or original stimulus situation for each emotional state.

One of the simplest and most inadequate formulations was that given by J. B. Watson (1919) when he proposed that the original or natural stimuli for fear were noise and loss of support. Actually it is necessary to take account of the total situation in which the individual finds himself, including both the context in which this or that detail of the *external* stimulus occurs, and, as we have already pointed out, the *internal* situation: the individual's

mental set, his expectations, values, hopes, desires, aspirations, attitudes of defensiveness, and any and all prevailing attitudes toward self and others. The need for taking account of the entire psychological field applies not only to the study of the emotions of a child at a given time but also to the understanding of changes in his reactions as he matures.

EMOTIONS AT BIRTH

According to some psychoanalysts, the child is capable of profound emotional experiences at the time of birth and perhaps even before birth. If we may believe one writer (Sadger, 1941), experience of pleasure and pain, and sensitivity to attitudes of acceptance and rejection by parents, may befall not only the embryo but even the spermatazoon and ovum. Freud (1936) implies that the unborn child is subject to feeling: "The fetus can be aware of nothing beyond a gross disturbance in the economy of its narcissistic libido. Large amounts of excitation press in upon it, giving rise to novel sensations of unpleasure" (p. 96).

The event of being born, according to some writers, represents not only a drastic physical upheaval but also a traumatic psychic experience.

Rank (1932), in speaking of the trauma of birth, maintains that the newborn child is subject to anxiety, and he claims that there is a relationship between the child's earliest phobias and the impression which the birth experience made upon him. Freud (1936) questions this conclusion, but he comments that the human infant "is sent into the world more unfinished" than the young of other animals, and that it is the "biological factor of helplessness . . . [which] brings into being the first situation of danger and creates the need to be loved which the human being is destined never to renounce" (p. 130).

In speaking of the infant, Isaacs (1936, p. 16) says that "knowledge is lacking, understanding has not yet begun: but wants and wishes, fears and angers, love and hate are there from the beginning." According to Bender (1939, p. 582), "When a child comes into the world he comes in lonely, and he is afraid."

Statements such as the foregoing must be regarded as conjectures rather than as descriptions of observed facts. It is interesting to observe how Freud, and perhaps to an even greater extent some of his followers, on the one hand speak of the child's incompleteness at the time of birth and yet, on the other hand, seem to take for granted that the equipment involved in the experiencing of emotion is well developed.

In discussing the beginnings of emotional experience, Stern (1930, pp. 75–76) expresses the opinion that all we can justifiably assume is ". . . the presence of a dull undefined foreshadowing of consciousness in which the sensorial and emotional elements are so inextricably intermingled that they might be designated either as 'sense-emotional states' or 'emotional-perceptive states.'" Whether this describes the situation no one can say. But certainly the notion that the child at birth has (as some writers imply) practically an adult capacity for emotional experience, even though he is very "unfinished" (as Freud puts it) in other respects, can be questioned both on the basis of biological theory and on the basis of observed facts.

It should be recognized that the fact that the cerebral cortex is as yet undeveloped (which means that the cognitive capacity for perceiving danger or thwarting also is restricted) need not, in itself, be regarded as a bar to emotional experience. Observations of apparent emotional excitement as a consequence of direct stimulation of, or interference with, the hypothalamus, suggests the possibility that emotional reactions may occur apart from functioning of the cerebral cortex (see Masserman, 1943; Clark *et al.*, 1938; and a review by Moore, 1948). If such reactions can occur independent of functioning of the cerebral cortex in a mature person, it is conceivable that an infant might experience emotion by way of lower centers before the higher centers are mature. If the hypothalamus can be regarded as a seat of emotion, then, to the extent that the hypothalamus matures and functions earlier in life than the cerebral cortex, the infant might have something in the nature of emotional experiences while his higher centers are yet undeveloped. We would still have to establish a means by which emotional response through the "lower" channels alone might be brought about.

Masserman (1943) summarizes his own work and the earlier work of others by saying that the clinical and pathological data of the rôle of the hypothalamus in emotional experience are inconclusive. It is safest to assign the hypothalamus a rôle in reinforcing and coordinating the mechanisms involved in *expression* of emotion and to leave for further proof the theory that the hypothalamus is the dynamic source or seat of experience of affective states. On the other hand, there is evidence, according to Masserman, which indicates that an emotion is a highly integrated, conative, cognitive, and affective-somatic reaction in which the central nervous system and the entire organism function as a psychobiologic whole.

There are findings which indicate that emotional states may be influenced by drugs (see, e.g., Collins, 1946). But the reactions shown by adults or older children to an abnormal chemical condition (as when drugs are administered) do not tell us what might be the situation as it operates in a normal, immature child.

As it happens, writers who have made the most categorical pronouncements concerning the capacity of the infant to have profound emotional experiences while he is yet in other respects very immature and highly restricted in his capacities for responding have not troubled to make clear what is the medium or machinery, organic or "psychic," which would make such experiences possible.

Studies dealing with the overt response of newborn children to situations designed to produce emotion indicate that emotional behavior at birth is quite diffuse and lacking in differentiation much as is true of the neonate's behavior in general.

OVERT REACTIONS IN EARLY INFANCY

Evidence of Lack of Differentiation

In a study by Sherman (1927) it was found that no clear-cut emotional patterns could be detected in the overt responses of infants to situations such as delay of feeding, sudden loss of support, restraint of head movements, being pricked with a needle. Adult observers, when informed concerning the stimulus that had been applied, tended to name the overt responses of infants in conventional terms. But when they saw motion pictures of the behavior of the children, without knowledge of the stimuli, they failed to guess what the provocation had been or to agree among themselves as to what emotion was being expressed. Adults similarly showed little agreement in identifying the cries of children who, behind a screen, were being subjected to various stimuli calculated to produce hunger, pain, fear, and rage.

Sherman noted that there were no specialized, uniform, or characteristic overt re-

actions or cries on the basis of which one "emotion" could be distinguished from another. Rather, there were was much uncoordinated, unspecialized, and diversified response.

This lack of differentiation in early emotional reactions has been emphasized also by Bridges (1932). Bridges states that the most common response to highly stimulating situations seems to be one of general agitation or excitement.

Investigations of overt reactions soon after birth to provocations that presumably should produce anger tell a similar story. In one such study by the Shermans (1925) restraint of movement was imposed through pressure upon the chins of infants by means of the experimenter's forefinger. No coordinated defense movements appeared during the first 24 hours after birth, but defensive movements did appear by the fifth day.

In a study by Pratt, Nelson, and Sun (1930) of children during the first 2 or 3 weeks of life, infants were observed when their nostrils were compressed in such a way as to prevent breathing (for periods ranging from 5 to 15 seconds), and when their arms were pinned to their sides. The findings did not substantiate Watson's earlier statements regarding defense reactions in the newborn child. It was observed that generalized reactions predominated over specific reactions in early childhood and that distinctive patterns were difficult to detect. Lack of differentiation in early emotional reactions has been emphasized also by Taylor (1934) in a study of 40 children aged 1 to 12 days.

Restraint of movement as such does not produce negative reactions in the newborn, according to observations made by Dennis (1942a), but any form of intense and prolonged stimulation, including rough restraint of movement, can elicit crying and restlessness. In due time stimuli calculated to restrain activity can elicit negative reactions if such stimuli interfere with customary sequences of behavior. In other words, the arousal of emotion depends not simply on the external stimulus as such but upon the impact this stimulus has upon an internal condition.

In most of the voluminous work on emotion in infancy that was precipitated (or influenced) by John B. Watson's pronouncements, attention has been focused almost exclusively on the external stimulus and on overt behavior (except to determine, in advance of stimulation, whether the child was awake or asleep, wet or dry). A vast amount of research on emotional development beyond the infancy period has suffered from this tendency to pay attention primarily to objective and overt features without proper regard for subjective factors which, from the individual's point of view, are the most crucial feature of the psychological field.

Infants in a study by Irwin (1932) were quite placid in a situation which seems rather drastic from an adult point of view. Twenty-four infants under the age of 1 month were observed in a situation that might be expected to produce fear. They were held above the experimenter's head and were dropped and caught after they had fallen a distance of 2 feet. In only 2 instances out of 85 did the infants show the response of crying in reaction to sudden loss of support, and in 12 per cent of the trials no overt responses could be detected. In 46 per cent of the trials in which overt movements were observed these movements were confined to the arms alone.

A more definite pattern of response, which has been designated as the "startle pattern," has been noted by Landis and Hunt (1939), in studies of infants and older individuals by means of high-speed motion pictures. The authors do not describe this as an emotional response but rather as a response that might be called a pre-emotional reaction to sudden or intense stimulation. It is more simple in its organization and expression than the so-called emotions, and it may or may not be followed by emotion proper. The response may be elicited by sudden or intense stimuli from any sense modality but it was found to appear especially as a reaction to sudden, sharp noises.

This startle pattern is described as "a complex, almost invariable, involuntary, innate reflex response." It includes elements such as blinking, closing of the eyes, a thrusting forward of the head and neck, and flexion of the bodily musculature resembling protective contraction or shrinking, involving forward movements of the trunk, contraction of the abdomen, and pronation of the lower arms. Not all the elements of response were found to be present in response to a given stimulus. The response ranges in duration from 0.3 second to 1.5 seconds and is not easily observed with the unaided eye. Landis and Hunt point out that more study is necessary to establish the relationship between the startle pattern and the Moro *Umklammerungsreflex*.

The fact that this startle reaction was revealed by a high-speed motion-picture technique supports M. C. Jones' conjecture in 1933 that finer methods of recording might reveal features or patterns of emotional response early in life that cannot be detected by ordinary observation.

The findings we do have indicate that emotional behavior is highly undifferentiated at birth, and that during the first days or weeks of life many infants not only fail to show a patterned response but even are unperturbed by treatment which, from the point of view of an older person, would seem to be quite provocative or threatening. In addition, the fact that some infants sometimes respond to a certain provocation while others do not suggests that there are large individual differences in susceptibility from the time of birth.

Most of the findings that are based upon empirical research come from studies with a behavioristic slant. Different findings might emerge from studies by psychologists with a different theoretical orientation.

Genetic Studies of Emotional Differentiation during Infancy

As a child matures, emotional responses emerge that correspond roughly to the emotional behavior of adults and to which such labels as anger, fear, and joy, can be applied. Gesell (1928) reports, for example, that at the age of 1 month a child will give different cries for hunger, pain, and discomfort, and that the beginnings of what perhaps might be regarded as delight or pleasure appear in smiles and vocal expressions of apparent feelings of pleasure at the age of 3 months. Blatz and Millichamp (1935) note the progressively expanding repertoire of emotional behavior which becomes more adaptive with age.

Accounts of differentiation of emotional behavior during early months of life have been given by Bühler (1930) and Bridges (1932). At birth, Bühler noted restless, aimless, excited movements which she regarded as signifying "active displeasure." She also observed what she regarded as evidence of fright and actions of flight and defense by way of aimless movements and crying. At 1 month, according to her account, characteristic hunger cries can be noted, as well as further signs of active displeasure. Bridges reports that distress is differentiated from a general state of excitement at about 3 weeks. At 1 month, Bühler notes also signs of "displeased astonishment," and of pleasure (eyes gleaming, corners of mouth drawn up, eyes looking up).

At 2 months the expressions of earlier feeling states show further elaboration, and at this age her infants showed "function pleasure" (a form of response earlier named by Karl Bühler to designate pleasures that accompany the organized course of a succession of movements).

Bridges reports that delight is differentiated at a later time than distress. She found that, under 1 month, the child is either excited or quiescent; he may kick and cry when his feeding is delayed but show calm rather than signs of delight when desired food is given to him. According to Bridges, the beginnings of delight start at 2 months, as manifested by fleeting smiles in response to being nursed, patted, or cared for, but this emotion is more clearly differentiated at 3 months, and more active signs of delight, such as loud laughter, smiling in response to another's smile, and efforts to raise the body in approach to an attentive person, are noted at 4 months.

Additional responses described by Bühler include lively expressions of joy at 5 months and laughing as a general reaction, slapping of the hands, crowing, and smacking and spreading of the fingers at 6 months.

It can be noted that there are many points of similarity in the accounts given by Bühler and Bridges, but there are differences also with respect to the time when some responses are reported as first appearing. Both note what appears to be pleasure in activity or achievement sometime during the first year.

Although these accounts cannot be regarded as definitive, they represent a developmental approach that is much needed in the study of early emotional behavior.

Theories Concerning Emotional Hazards of Infancy

The idea that happenings during the infancy period might have an important bearing upon a person's emotional well-being during the rest of his life has occurred to many observers on contemplating how vulnerable the infant is. He is completely dependent upon others for food, warmth, and physical care. Within a short time after birth he is subject to many frustrations. The satisfaction of his elementary needs is surrounded by restraints. A vast number of regulations are brought to bear upon the child before he is able to see the reason for things and long before he has reached a level of intellectual development that enables him to formulate his experiences in terms that can be remembered in later life. He is called upon at an early age to distinguish between what is approved and disapproved. He has to acquire a vast range of voluntary control. Apart from ordinary trials, he may face special difficulties. He may come into a home where he is unwanted, and, whether wanted or not, he will be subject to the backlash of emotional frictions within the home.

Even if all is quite serene on the surface he may be the victim of the almost endless variety of "mistakes" such as are made by parents who, being human and imperfect, are more or less anxious and uncertain. The tensions, pressures, unresolved problems, and conflicts which have accumulated in the lifetime of his parents will sooner or later, to some degree, directly or indirectly, be visited upon the child. He is bound to be touched by repercussions of the struggles his parents may be undergoing in dealing with their own issues, which may include competitive strivings and power drives; a tendency to sacrifice spontaneity in order to conform to cultural stereotypes; irrational self-rejecting attitudes which they harbor with respect to their own misdeeds, their forebears, their upbringing as children, their social origins, their physical appetites; unrecognized grievances and grudges against their own parents or other authority fig-

ures; an unwitting tendency to project their own feelings upon others; irrational and unperceived endeavors to try to make amends, through their behavior as parents, for circumstances that have struck them as hurtful in their own lives.

Emotional Implications of Infant Care

The bearing which the handling of a child's feeding, weaning, and elimination and his early erotic tendencies might have upon his emotional well-being has received much attention. Studies in child development have emphasized the importance of maturation in determining the level at which children are ready to progress from one mode of behavior to another in their feeding and elimination. Studies of the response of babies to a "self-demand" feeding arrangement have indicated that the child's own desires may provide a good guide to the timing of his feeding and the amount and nature of what he is fed. As already indicated above, psychoanalytic theories have also drawn attention to these aspects of child care.

Theories regarding Early Sexual Hazards. According to the Freudian conception of early development, the infant is faced with possible "aberrations and maldevelopment of the sexual function" (1933, p. 135). Such maldevelopments may occur in connection with what Freud has described as the *oral* and the *anal* phases of *pregenital* development (and also during the phallic phase which comes later). In speaking of the *oral* phase, Freud states that the "erotogenic zone of the mouth dominates what we may call the sexual activity of this period of life" (p. 135). In the *anal* phase, "anal and sadistic tendencies come to the fore," according to Freud (1933, pp. 135–136). Freud and his followers (see, e.g., Fenichel, 1945) have described various outcomes which they regard as likely to occur if the infant is unduly deprived or frustrated in connection with his oral and anal tendencies.

Unfortunately, for a period of many years the followers of Freud were more inclined to reiterate these ideas or to draw logical deductions from them than to bring evidence to bear upon them. There are, however, some statements that can be made that touch more or less directly upon the issues just raised, and related matters.

The importance of various aspects of early sexual development and of various features of child care, including feeding and training for bladder and bowel control, can best be understood if we see each aspect not simply as a segment of development that might have a peculiar significance of its own but as a feature in the larger relationship between the child as a growing self and significant people in his environment. It is by way of their attitudes toward the child's early sex interests, his desire to suck his thumb, his tendency to soil and wet himself—as well as by way of their attitudes toward all other aspects of his development and behavior—that parents communicate approval or disapproval, express their tendency to be prudish, anxious, harsh, perfectionistic, and impatient, or kindly, accepting, and willing to let the child be himself and develop in his own good time.

According to this view, the basic underlying attitude of the parent is more important than this or that practice which they adopt in bringing this attitude to bear in their dealings with sex, or cleanliness, or oral activity, or other aspects of child care.

Oral Activity. From the time of birth, most infants exhibit oral activity beyond what is involved in getting food from the breast or bottle. Many children (perhaps nearly all) suck their thumbs more or less during early months of life.

As time passes, all children use their lips, their tongue, and sometimes their teeth in exploring the world about them. For a time they try to bring almost everything into contact with their mouths. They use their mouths to examine the taste, the texture, the contours, and temperature of things. The mouth is for a time, like the eyes and ears, an important means of exploring the environment.

There clearly is a drive, inherent or early acquired, to use the sucking and mouthing mechanism for purposes other than food-getting. It is reasonable to assume that interference with this absorbing enterprise would be frustrating. To interfere with his sucking and mouthing is a way of blocking self-expression or (in another manner of speaking) a way of opposing his ego. To say also that such oral behavior is related to sexual development is another matter. We can, of course, include oral behavior under the heading of sexuality by the simple linguistic device of defining sexuality so broadly that it arbitrarily includes oral behavior, but that merely begs the question.

It has been observed that an increase in finger-sucking may occur if a child is deprived of the customary amount of sucking that he has enjoyed in connection with getting food, as when a bottle feeding is dropped from a schedule (Levy, 1928). But there are thumb-suckers among children who have been given the freest possible opportunity to suck. Moreover, deprivation of sucking in connection with food-getting does not invariably result in thumb-sucking, as shown in studies reviewed by Orlansky (1949). In other words, in dealing with this aspect of "oral" satisfaction, we are faced with something far more complicated than what is involved in depriving or not depriving a child of oral activity in connection with his feeding.

We do not have to saddle a sexual significance on to oral behavior in order to establish its importance. The very fact that the child undertakes sucking and mouthing so assiduously is enough to establish its importance from his standpoint. And now if we bring sharp disapproval, punishment, and forcible restraint to bear upon the child to curb his eagerness for oral activities we are, to a degree, punishing and thwarting (and perhaps even rejecting) *him*. Something very important in the child's relationships with significant people in his environment occurs by way of their response to his sucking activities. Sucking in a sense becomes the focal point of unpleasant interpersonal relationships (if we may borrow terminology from Sullivan, 1947). Again, a child's sucking activities may become the object or target of the kind of harsh treatment from his elders which may operate as a factor in the causation of anxiety. What thus is done to the child in the context of his sucking activities is the significant thing, this writer believes, whether or not we also choose or refuse to regard oral activity as something tied to a so-called "pregenital" phase of sexual development.

Breast Feeding. According to one school of thought, breast feeding is more conducive to emotional health than bottle feeding. Anna Freud and Burlingham (1944) put it quite simply: "Breast fed babies are, of course, better off than bottle-fed babies" (p. 12). According to Harnik (1930), bottle-fed babies are frequently liable to suffocation during feeding and suffer anxiety as a consequence. In a review of numerous studies bearing upon this problem, Orlansky (1949) points out that, although a baby who receives individual care from his mother has obvious advantages, the assertion that breast-fed babies are invariably better off than bottle-fed babies remains unproved.

It has also been proposed that breast feeding might have a bearing on a child's emotional development on the theory that the practice of cutting out breast feeding might be a form of rejection. The evidence on this matter, as reviewed by Orlansky (1949), is not unequivocal. The fact that a categorical answer is unwarranted on the basis of present evidence is emphasized by findings in a study of 60 babies in three groups of 20 each, one fed by cup, one by bottle, and one by breast, during the first 10 days of life (Davis, Sears, Miller, and Brodbeck, 1948).

If we could get to the bottom of this, we probably would find that it is the overall quality of the parent-child relationship rather than the particular feeding practice as such that is the important thing. It is possible for a breast-feeding mother or a bottle-feeding mother to be affectionate or lacking in affection; she can be relaxed and able to enjoy her child, or tense, anxious, and impatient. The feeding situation, perhaps more than any other single situation, brings the child into frequent close contacts with the parent, and it is by way of contacts that a mother communicates her attitude toward her child, whether the manner of feeding happens to be by breast or bottle.[1]

Weaning. We can assume that weaning must be a frustrating and, at least for the time being, a very unpleasant experience. For this reason, weaning from either breast or bottle might be regarded as possibly having an important bearing on a child's emotional development. According to Pearson (1931), when the breast is withdrawn the nursing infant fears it will never be

[1] One more point regarding this: according to one theory, a woman's refusal to breast-feed (when otherwise all is opportune) may be a symptom of an attitude of rejection of her female rôle and thus a symptom of self-rejection. But in these terms, again, it is the underlying attitude, not the manner of feeding, that is crucial.

returned. In commenting on breast feeding and weaning, Orlansky (1949) speaks of the lack of experimental data.

Training in Bladder and Bowel Control. The work of McGraw (1940) and of Gesell and Ilg (1937) emphasizes the fact that it takes time for the child to mature organically to the point where he is able and ready to exercise voluntary control over his bladder and bowels. In the light of such studies, advice to the effect that toilet training should begin at the age of 3 months or 6 months, or even earlier, is absurd. It is reasonable to suppose that many children have suffered ill effects when parents have tried to establish "early control" by coercive methods. A study by Huschka (1942) of problem children in a hospital suggests that children who have been "coercively" trained might tend to show symptoms such as constipation, fear, and rage more than children who have been trained with better regard for their comfort.

But here (as in connection with feeding and sucking) the effects of methods of training should be considered in the light of the total situation of which they are a part. When we find parents who insist on trying to hurry the child's bowel and bladder control we probably also will find that this is only one detail in a larger pattern of insistence on cleanliness, orderliness, and conformity to a variety of rigid cultural standards. Some such parents probably also try to hurry other features of development. The parent's desire to hurry the child in the process of getting housebroken may represent, for example, an expression of an attitude of self-rejection on the parent's part: he cannot tolerate the part of his nature that is, as he sees it, filthy with excrement, and so he must hurry the child over the hurdle of being a soiled child. Again, the parent's compulsion to hurry the child may be an expression of a larger compulsive tendency to prove that he can get things done in a hurry. It is possible, even, that this pressure may be an expression of a compulsive competitive tendency in the parent: if ordinary babies can get the dry habit by the age of 2 or 3, his child should be able to beat this average by several months.

Mothering. Writings about early development repeatedly reiterate the age-old belief that mother love is an important thing for the child. From the time of birth babies show a desire for human company and human contact beyond the contacts that are incidental to feeding and other aspects of physical care. Levy (1936) has used the expression "primary affect hunger" to denote a child's need for maternal love and other feelings involved in the mother-child relationship. The fact that under certain conditions infants may show extreme symptoms of depression when suddenly separated from their mothers has been noted by Spitz (1946). Studies bearing on the large subject of parent-child relationships will be noted in a later section, but we are interested here briefly in mothering from the point of view of the special hazards of infancy.

The view that lack of proper mothering may have dire consequences in the child's life has been emphasized by Ribble (1943), who reiterates a number of concepts which Freud forcefully set forth several decades ago. Brodbeck and Irwin (1946) found that even during the first 6 months of life children in an orphanage made fewer and less varied speech sounds than children of high or low socio-economic status who were being brought up by parents in their own homes. Other studies, which will be referred to at a later point, indicate that other features of development also are likely to proceed best in a situation in which friendly human relationships prevail.

Moreover, as Bühler (1933) observed and as Spitz and Wolf (1946) later pointed out, there is likely to be an emotional coloring in the infant's first awareness of discrimination of a fellow human being. In connection with the development of auditory perception, according to Bühler ". . . there occurs from two months on a specific reaction to the human voice in all its modifications, and that is smiling. The two-month-old infant, in fact, smiles occasionally at the sound of the human voice, even though at this age he does not smile in response to other stimuli" (p. 376).

In a study by Dennis (1938, 1941) two babies from birth to the age of 7 months were kept under conditions of extreme social isolation. Human contacts were restricted to a minimum, and no one played with the babies, or fondled them, or talked to them. These babies showed a record of early development very much like that of infants in a normal environment. They even responded affectionately when a stolid experimenter came to observe them. A study by Danzinger and Frankl (1934) also suggests that babies may show a high degree of social responsiveness when given the opportunity even though they have spent several months early in life in a situation that provided less human contact than babies usually enjoy in our culture.

The studies just cited leave several questions unanswered but they suggest that the effect on a baby of being deprived of his mother (at an age when he is old enough to notice) may be influenced by several variables. The child's response may depend in part on what he has become accustomed to expect or to go without. The disturbing effect of separation from the mother probably also will be influenced by the extent to which the child already has a disposition to be anxious. Babies seem to differ not only in the extent to which they become accustomed to much or little contact with *one* person (the mother or mother substitute) but also in the extent

to which they are given much or little opportunity, from an early age, to learn to expect affectionate treatment or unkindness when in the care of *many* different persons. The disturbing effect of loss of the person who hitherto has played the mother rôle, as described so movingly by Spitz (1946) and Ribble (1941), should probably be interpreted in this light. It seems to the writer that we need to be guarded in our interpretation of the limited systematic data we have on this extremely important topic.

Important recent contributions concerning the bearing of emotional relationships with others on the emotional health and personality development of the young child have been offered by Horney and Sullivan. We will refer to these later.

Observations regarding Fragility and Hardihood of Infants. The fact that the child is physically weak and helpless is obvious, and many writers take it for granted that he is also *psychologically* more *fragile* than an older person.

The young child is weak, it is true, but there also are certain protective features in his make-up.

He is defenseless against many of the calamities of life, but it is also true that the infant does not have the intellectual ability to perceive their implications to the same degree as does an older person.

While the infant can be aroused to intense excitement by an immediate threat, he can also stage a quicker recovery. He seems to be able to shift more readily than an older person from anger and tears to affection and laughter. Infants do not appear to have as strong a *perseverative* tendency in their emotional behavior as older persons.

Although the infant does not have the ability of an older person to protect himself from harm, it also is probable, on the other hand, that he has a greater capacity for self-repair. Anderson (1948) reviews findings which indicate that the healing rate of physical wounds is faster in children than in adults, and he suggests that there is no reason to assume that the opposite would hold true with respect to psychological wounds.

Moreover, there are many findings which show that the infant, even at a tender age, is not a creature whose emotional life is completely at the mercy of episodes occurring in the environment. Several studies have shown that children show a high degree of consistency in the individual or characteristic ways of responding that mark them as distinct personalities, and that there is a great deal of toughness in their ability to preserve their integrity (see, e.g., Shirley, 1933, 1941; Gesell and Thompson, 1941; and reviews by Anderson, 1948; and Jersild, 1947).

Most important of all, from the point of view of the child's safety, is the dynamic nature of the life he lives from day to day and of the forces of growth that are constantly at work. He is continually interacting with his environment. His life from day to day involves a vast amount of learning, a vast amount of forgetting. New abilities emerge; new experiences befall him; and different currents in his life interact upon each other in changing ways. His curiosity leads him into experiences that bring him to grips with his fears. New impulses that come into play as new abilities emerge make old satisfactions obsolete or give new powers that take the sting out of old frustrations and enable him to satisfy continuing needs in new ways.

While these factors help the child in defending himself against harsh features of his environment, circumstances may interfere with the process of learning by which the child normally revises his emotional attitudes in keeping with the changing realities of life. This can be seen when an emotional attitude keeps persisting even though the occasion which aroused it has long since passed, as when a child retains an attitude of hostility, suspiciousness, and defensiveness even after he has come into friendly hands. Circumstances which produce an overwhelming emotional reaction in early childhood may singly, or cumulatively over a period of time, have a profound and long-continued effect on the child's way of life. At an early age, for example, as documented in a striking manner by observations in an orphanage (by Skeels et al., 1938), children who have to shift for themselves without parental affection and protection may acquire attitudes of distrust and defensiveness which carry over into their responses to friendly people. In observations of older children Redl and Wineman (1951) graphically show how difficult it is for children who have suffered from neglect and abuse to become accustomed to the opportunities offered by a friendly environment.

It seems reasonable to assume that, the more strongly an emotional attitude (such as reacting to others with hostility or fear) has become established, the more difficult it will be to modify it, the more difficult it will be to apply the attitude discriminatingly, and the stronger will be the tendency to take the attitude for granted, to defend or rationalize it, and to build a consistent character structure around it. Moreover, as time passes, a vicious circle is established, for if a child is suspicious and hostile toward other people many of them will respond to him in kind and thus prove (as he sees it) that his defensive attitude is well grounded.

The fact that the experience in infancy may leave a strong trace is shown in studies of animals. J. McV. Hunt (1941) found that rats subjected to feeding-frustration in infancy were more likely to hoard food when again subjected to such frustration as adults than rats which had been frustrated at a later stage of "childhood," or not at all. Effects of infantile experiences on the way adults respond under stress is shown in another study of rats by Wolf (1943). When required to compete for food (after previously being fed individually) animals that had been *deafened* for a time in infancy frequently lost in competition at the adult level when the signal was a *sound,* and those that had been *blinded* for a time frequently lost when the signal was a *light.* In other words, depending upon the kind of limitation they had suffered in infancy, the animals now, under stress, were inhibited in their hearing or seeing. They retreated, so to speak, to an outmoded form of behavior (not seeing or not hearing) which had prevailed for a time during the infancy period.

FACTORS INFLUENCING EMOTIONAL RESPONSE

There are certain broad considerations which must be taken into account in studying the emotions of children at any age level.

Individual Differences

Practically all studies of young children directly or by implication emphasize the fact that children differ greatly in emotional susceptibility and responsiveness. Shirley (1933), for example, describes differences in timorousness and irritability that appear early in infancy and persist throughout later months. A later study by Neilon (1948) of the children originally studied by Shirley indicates that there is a very strong likelihood that temperamental qualities which a person displays in early childhood will continue to characterize him in later years.

The Rôle of Maturation

Many studies have stressed the fact that a child's susceptibilities change as he matures and that the concept of conditioning alone does not explain these changes or the emergence of new or changed emotional responses as a child grows older. Bühler (1930), for example, describes the manner in which new occasions for delight occur as the child becomes able to undertake new performances. Similarly, the development of a child's ability to discriminate and perceive will render him responsive to stimuli to which he was impervious at an earlier time (Shirley, 1933; Jersild and Holmes, 1935a).

Gesell (1929) describes the manner in which fear "waxes and alters with growth"; he maintains that "this pattern is as much the product of organic growth as the various stages in the elaboration and perfection of prehension" (p. 656–657), and he illustrates with a description of reactions shown at different age levels by an infant confined in a small pen. In an earlier study, H. E. Jones and M. C. Jones (1928) noted changes with age in response to a large harmless snake. They point out that ". . . the arousal of fear depends not only upon situational changes, but also upon the individual's general level of development. . . . As a child develops . . . new things startle him because of his new perception of the fact that they are new and unusual" (pp. 142–143).

The varying effects of a given event as children grow older can also be noted in occasional shifts in emotional response. At about 5 to 8 months, for example, a hungry but hitherto relatively calm infant may show signs of anger if there is a momentary delay in his feeding after he has caught sight of the bottle, but at about 8 or 9 months and in the same circumstances a child may show signs of pleasant anticipation rather than anger (Bühler, 1930) if the delay is brief. Other examples of changes that occur in the process of maturing will appear in later sections.

Obviously, learning is one factor in changing reactions such as those described above. The point remains, however, that the reaction to a situation will depend not simply upon the cumulative or spreading effects of specific emotional stimuli that have gone before but upon the changes in capacity and changes in scope of behavior that are associated with growth.

Differentiation of Early Expressions as Related to Growth

The development of facial expression of emotion offers an opportunity to study inherent and acquired features of emotional patterns. In a study by Goodenough (1931a) judges were shown photographs of a 10-month-old child. These photographs were taken under relatively mild conditions designed to elicit various emotional states. The judges correctly identified the situation or emotion depicted by various photographs in 47.4 per cent of the instances, as against a chance expectancy of only 8.3 per cent of correctness. According to Goodenough, "The findings suggest that however greatly the overt expression of emotional states may be inhibited, modified or intentionally assumed in the social relationships of adult life, the language of expression is nevertheless built upon a core of native reaction patterns which appear at so early an age that can hardly be ascribed to training" (p. 101). Findings in keeping with this conclusion are also reported by Goodenough (1932) in a study of a 10-year-old child who had been blind and deaf from the time of birth. Darwin (1913) earlier reported that the expressions of the blind resemble those of persons who can see.

Photographs snapped at opportune moments were utilized by Thompson (1941) in a study of the facial expressions of emotion exhibited by 26 blind and 29 seeing children aged 7 weeks to 13 years. Patterns of emotional response similar to those designated as anger, sulkiness, annoyance, and sadness in seeing children were also exhibited by blind and deaf-blind children, but such responses did not occur as uniformly among the blind as among the seeing. Thompson concludes that the facial expressions exhibited by the blind "seem to be maturational since there is no other obvious way in which they could have been brought about." On the other hand, the effects of mimicry, as distinguished from maturation, appear in certain stylized expressions exhibited by older seeing children.

In a study by Fulcher (1942) brief motion pictures were taken of 118 seeing and 50 blind children while they were voluntarily expressing happiness, sadness, anger, or fear. The seeing differentiated more sharply than the blind between expressions of different emotions, but the differentiations the blind did show were like those shown by the seeing.

The Rôle of Learning

The fact that emotional behavior is modified through learning and that emotional responses become associated with new situations through the process of conditioning is obvious from everyday observation, and it has been emphasized in experimental studies. The classic study in this field is Watson's work (Watson and Rayner, 1920) with a little boy called Albert. When first presented with a white rat, Albert showed interest and curiosity, but as his hand touched the animal a loud noise was sounded which caused Albert to be startled and to withdraw. After several repetitions, Albert no longer reached for the rat but shrank and showed evidences of fear at the sight of the animal.

The concept of conditioning as applied in research work with children so far does not, however, *per se* provide a guide for predicting under what circumstances conditioning is likely to "take" in a laboratory setting or in everyday situations (Valentine, 1930; English, 1929; Jersild and Holmes, 1935a; Bregman, 1934).

Widened Scope of Effective Stimuli

The younger the child, the more his emotions tend to be aroused by tangible events that impinge directly upon him. As he grows older he becomes increasingly responsive to signs and symbols that betoken furtherance or hindrance of his welfare and his wishes, and more and more of his emotional reactions concern anticipated events. Also, of course, as a child grows older, emotions become associated with an enlarging repertoire of activities, plans, and interests, and he becomes increasingly able to entertain lingering or recurrent fears, joys, and resentments. As Lund (1940) puts it, with added maturity there is an increase in objects and situations that have emotional value.

When the child is on the threshold of new experiences or achievements he may for a time react emotionally to situations that subsequently are "laid by." Each new hurdle in the child's development, or in his impact with new environmental conditions, may for a time provide a thrill or offer a hazard.

Differentiation in Expression

Differentiation of overt expressions of emotion is especially noteworthy during the first year of life, but there are many further elaborations after the first year in nuances of facial, vocal, and postural expression.

In the display of anger, for example, Goodenough (1931b) notes that: "With advancing age behavior during anger becomes more overtly directed toward a given end. At the same time the primitive bodily responses of the infant and young child gradually become replaced by substitute reactions of a somewhat less violent and more symbolic character."

The lengths to which the substitution of other forms of expression have gone by the time of maturity are indicated in a study by Richardson (1918), who found that, in about 600 instances of anger reported by 12 adults, no blows were struck "except with those persons who have the correction of children." A shift from overt expression to more subtle or disguised reactions is noteworthy also in the case of fear. As a result of such changes it becomes increasingly difficult to detect and to understand the child's emotions as he grows older.

The fact that a child sometimes will reveal his feelings in make-believe settings or play situations has increasingly been taken into account in the use of projective methods and play technique in the study of children.

The decline with age in frequency of emotional outbursts does not, of course, depend solely upon the development of the inhibitions, gradations, and the substitution of less overt responses. It arises also in part by reason of changes in the character of the emotion. Persisting apprehensions, resentments, and pleasant anticipations cannot so appropriately be expressed by outbursts such as may occur in an episodic response to a concrete happening.

Decline in Crying as an Expression of Emotion. Crying at first usually occurs in connection with bodily movement, but by the age of 6 months crying may occur without the accompaniment of such movements (Bühler, 1930). In a study of 61 children during mental and physical examinations throughout the first year of life, Bayley (1932) found that children cried an average of 15 per cent of the total examination time. In the early months crying resulted mainly from internal causes, but in later months factors in the external environment, such as strangeness of place or persons and continued handling, became increasingly potent.

A sharp decline with age in crying in connection with preschool children's social contacts and in their conflicts with one another has been noted in several studies (Brackett, 1934; Jersild and Markey, 1935). It has also been noted that at the preschool level crying occurs less in response to the child's own falls and bruises than as an expression of anger when a child is hurt or thwarted by someone else (Ding and Jersild, 1932). Ricketts (1934) found in a study of preschool children that crying occurred relatively more often in connection with anger at home than at school. Blatz, Chant, and Salter (1937) found a relatively high incidence of crying in a situation for the feeble-minded where there was less disapproval of crying in public than usually prevails in other situations.

In a study by J. Bell (1943) in which about a hundred children aged 3 to 8 years were observed during dental treatment, crying was displayed by only 25 per cent of the children, and 51 per cent of them smiled or laughed. There were no significant differences between boys and girls in their tendency to cry during dental treatment. At the adult level, however, Landis (1924) found that women cried more often than men in trying experimental situations.

DEVELOPMENTAL CHANGES IN THE INTERLPAY OF THINKING AND FEELING

Although thinking and feeling are intricately interwoven it is useful in studying emotional development to make a distinction between them. One of the most baffling problems in connection with the development of human beings is the problem of achieving a harmonious and productive integration of the individual's intellectual powers and his emotional capacities. Failure to achieve such integration appears, for example, when a person is subject to irrational emotional states, lacks insight into his fears and hostilities, or is governed by "unconscious" forces. In the present chapter we cannot presume to go deeply into this important topic, but we will touch upon certain aspects of it that pertain especially to the growing child.

Theories Regarding the Priority of Thinking and Feeling

Here we may properly elaborate a bit on an issue raised at an earlier point, namely, whether we may regard emotion as the prior and psychologically more primitive form of experience in human development. As noted previously, there are writers who assume that the child has a practically unbounded capacity to feel while he still has a very limited capacity to perceive or to think. Searl (1932) speaks of the child as one who is frequently, easily, and completely overwhelmed by his own feelings before he has anything but a weak sense of any other reality and before explanation or reasoning is possible and while means of communication are lagging behind the strength of his desires. This doctrine is strongly reaffirmed by Isaacs (1933) when she maintains that "the sense of guilt, or, more strictly, the deeper anxieties that represent the primitive forerunners of the sense of guilt, *do* develop spontaneously in the child's mind whatever be the precise nature of his educational experiences . . . in its essence, the sense of guilt is inherent in the fundamental interactions between human mental structure and inevitable early experiences" (p. 371).

The most systematic presentation of the view that the ability to use the intellect by way of sustained thinking, awareness of one's own mental processes, and reasoning in terms of cause and effect lags behind a more primitive form of mental activity in a child's development has been offered by Piaget (1928, 1930, 1932). In accord with Freud, Piaget maintains that *Lustprinzip* is prior to *Realitätsprinzip;* thought serves desire before it serves truth (1928). There is an inborn unconsciousness of thought toward itself, according to Piaget. For many years the child is incapable of detached awareness of his thought processes; he is not bound by logical necessity; he is not conscious of guiding factors in his own thoughts. Piaget distinguishes between *logical* thought, which is *social,* communicable, and guided by a need for adapting to others, and *autistic* thought, which is *incommunicable,* indifferent to truth, and unconscious to itself and of the affective factors by which it is guided, and states that the child's way of thinking occupies a place situated between the autistic and the social (1928, p. 205). Piaget calls this way of thinking "egocentric."

It is not until after the age of 7 or 8 that a child begins to grow conscious of his reasoning process, according to one of Piaget's studies. Until this age the child's picture of the world is always "moulded on his immediate sectional and personal point of view" (1928, p. 248). According to the same report, it is not until age 11–12 that "formal thought" appears when the child "comes to reason about pure possibility" (p. 251). According to Piaget, a child's egocentrism not only makes him unconscious of himself (under the age of 7–8) but also keeps him from being aware of the phenomenon of thought as a subjective phenomenon and it prevents him from establishing the exact limit between his own ego and the external world.

Although Piaget's discussion centers primarily on the nature of the child's logic rather than on the feelings involved, we may probably infer, if Piaget's account is true, that the child would have just as much difficulty, if not more, in understanding his feelings as he has in understanding his thoughts. So construed, Piaget's conclusions lead to a gloomy view of the ability of the human being, in his formative years, to achieve an integration of intellectual awareness and feeling and to bring cognitive processes to bear on forces which influence his way of life.

In discussing what he calls egocentricity in children's thinking, Piaget has identified important truths, but he has overstated them by far. "Egocentric" thinking of the kind described by him occurs in children at all age levels, and also in adults. But, as many investigators have shown, Piaget greatly underestimated the capacity children have for *logical, causal,* and *socially communicable* thinking from a relatively early age (see, e.g., Dennis, 1942*b*; Deshaies, 1937; Deutsche, 1937; Hazlitt, 1929; McAndrew, 1943; Oakes, 1946).

The possibility that a prelogical stage of thinking, such as has been proposed by Piaget, might exist but at an earlier age than Piaget has set or than has been covered by other investigators who have tested Piaget's conclusions was explored by Dennis (1942*b*) in a study of a bright child from the time the youngster began to talk until the age of 6 years. Dennis found that at the age of 3 the child gave many answers concerning the nature and cause of things that conformed to Piaget's expectations, but by the age of 6 many of these had been changed.

In other words, we may conclude that children at an early age (probably from the time when they are able to reveal the nature of their thoughts) are capable of logical and socially communicable thought about things and the nature of things to a far greater extent than Piaget has proposed. These findings do not tell us at what age and to what extent the young child is able to think about his own feelings.

Here is an area where there is great need for research. Stated in broad terms, we might ask, at approximately what level of development is a child able to be aware of himself, able to examine his own feelings, able to begin to bring his intelligence to bear on emotional currents in his life? With this we might raise another question: At about what level of development is it possible to help the child to cultivate his ability to take stock of himself? These questions have fateful implications for human happiness. A vast amount of human misery would be obviated if children could be helped to understand themselves and others—if they could be helped to achieve better understanding of emotional forces in their lives. As matters now stand, a large number of children do not seem to achieve a healthy integration of their cognitive and affective resources. Many from an early age use their intellectual abilities (including their capacity for imagining) to support or defend irrational attitudes of hostility, anxiety, and inferiority. The intellect often serves the purpose of self-deception rather than self-enlightenment.

Lag in Self-Inquiry. Even if we could establish the position that children have more capacity for understanding their feelings than we have generally assumed, we would still have the problem of finding how best this ability might be cultivated and put to use. Elsewhere the writer has set forth the view that in our training of children at home and at school we tend to encourage them to ignore and to evade opportunities for testing and cultivating what-

ever capacity they may have for growth in self-understanding (Jersild, 1951, 1952).

In the normal course of events, it occurs to very few children until about the time of adolescence to mention a desire to understand or to cope with their own emotional problems when they reveal wishes or what they are interested in studying or learning more about (Jersild, Markey, and Jersild, 1933; Jersild and Tasch, 1949). Even at the high school level, an expression of such an interest in self-understanding is rare unless the school has encouraged it. So it is, for example, that even late in childhood it will not occur to children who suffer from troublesome fears to wish for the strength or insight to cope with them or to express an interest in finding out what makes people afraid.

Interaction of Intellect and Feeling. Some writers take the position that emotion is the forerunner, the pacemaker, in intellectual activity. Here again we may cite Isaacs (1933): "It is the child's first experience of instinctual frustration, of unsatisfied longing for food in the intervals between satisfaction, which provides the first stimulus to his appreciation of the external world" (p. 288). This particular statement may be true, but, in the judgment of this writer, it is only part of the truth. A child's emotions influence his perceiving and thinking. But a child's ability to perceive and to think also influence his emotions.

A child's fear of unfamiliar things when he has reached the ability to discern what is strange illustrates the impact of perceptual development on emotional behavior. It might be argued that this illustration is not sound: the response to the stranger may not be in the form of a sequence of perceiving and then fearing, but, rather, the perceiving and fearing perhaps should be regarded as features of a larger unitary response. Even granting this, it would be arbitrary to reverse the order and assume that the primary response to strangeness was fear and out of this arose the perception of strangeness. Children often give evidence of new forms of intellectual discrimination without revealing fear. In other words, unless we arbitrarily read fear into the response, or perform a linguistic trick, we could not state that fear is here antecedent to perception.

Many studies have shown that what a person perceives is influenced by his needs and values. When shown ambiguous pictures a hungry person may see them as pictures of food. The perceiver tends to select or to notice the features that are in line with his attitude. For example, a person who would like to move to another place reads advice from a friend in that place as though it said, "Stay here," instead of the actual words, "Stay there" (meaning where he now is).

Among those who have studied these phenomena are Bartlett (1932) and Edwards (1941). Lund (1925) found high relation between belief that a proposition was true and a wish that it should be true.

According to a summary by McKillop (1952), the following generalizations concerning the effect of attitude seem reasonably well established, at least under certain conditions: (1) perception reflects the individual's attitudes; (2) material that conforms to one's attitude is more easily learned and retained than material that is in opposition to one's attitude; (3) attitude influences one's judgments and one's ability to reason logically; (4) the more ambiguous and unstructured the stimulus, the more important is the rôle of attitude.

In a study of the relationship between the reader's attitude and certain types of reading response, McKillop used 512 eleventh-grade students in 22 classes in three high schools in the New York area, representing a heterogeneous population with people differing in socio-economic status and in racial composition, and she presented passages dealing with Negroes, Communism, and Israel. The topics were presented in a biased way but in a manner that appeared more or less plausible. She found that when the questions in the tests dealt with exactly the specific details presented in the passages the students as a group were able to look for the right answer and to give answers based upon what the passage said. When the questions required the reader to make inferences, to read a little between the lines, most students were still able to answer on the basis of the passage, but exceptions became more frequent and wrong choices tended to be in the direction of attitude. When, however, the questions were so worded that there was no "right" answer and there was an opportunity, for example, to make a judgment regarding the justification for Arab objections to Israel, or to make a prediction concerning the results of overthrow of the Communist government, attitudes of the students became important factors in determining their answers. "Although the spirit of the passages was quite clear with regard to these issues, and although students were directed to answer on the basis of the passage, it became increasingly difficult for the students to distinguish between the general spirit of the passage and how they felt about it" (pp. 80–81).

The influence which emotion may exert over thinking has been expressed very effectively by Murphy (1945), who states that, whenever the task is objective and intelligence free, man can remake the order of his world. "Yet on points concerning his own nature, where his impulses have beclouded the process of his thinking, he still relies on exhorting, moralizing and argument. . . . The towering genius of a great scientist often lapses into childish babblings as he turns to problems in which his personal desires give structure to his thoughts" (p. 2).

Examples of the way in which children's intellectual grasp of a situation influences their emotional response to it are offered by observations concerning the reactions of older and younger children to events connected with war (Kimmins, 1915–1916; Despert, 1942; for a review of other studies, see Jersild and Meigs, 1943). Children of about beginning school age react to war more on a *perceptual* level than do older persons. As children become older, they react increasingly on a *conceptual* level. The older child, for example, is able to appreciate the effects of an air raid not simply in terms of the destruction that lies before his eyes but also as a frightening sign or omen of a policy of destruction which the enemy might carry out in the future.

The bearing of intellectual development on emotional behavior is also shown in the fact that there are certain differences in the emotional behavior of bright and dull children. F. B. Holmes (1935) found that brighter children at the age of 2 or 3 were susceptible to conditions which eventually arouse fear in many children to a greater extent than less intelligent children of the same age. Holmes found correlations ranging from .50 to .53 between IQ and "fear scores" (the more fear shown, the higher the score) in the age range from 24 to 35 months; in the range from 36 to 47 months, the correlation was .18; and at the 4-year level, it was .10. She pointed out that her findings indicate that the more intelligent child seems to develop certain fears earlier than the less intelligent child.

Evidence that brighter children at older levels might also be more sensitive to things that might endanger them is reported in a study by Boston (1939) of children under 9 years of age, including a group with an IQ range of 90 to 104 and another with a range from 115 to 154, whose records were studied from the point of view of a psychiatrist's opinion concerning each child's fantasies and fears. A few of the bright children fitted the theory that superior intelligence is accompanied by greater awareness of danger. Moreover, in the average children, the negative factors in the home that seemed to contribute to fear (such as rejecting or neurotic parents, conflict between parents, frightening experience, or physical factors around which fear centered) were more pronounced and more overtly apparent than in the brighter children.

The relation between intelligence and anger has been examined by Meltzer (1937). He found that anger and intelligence were closely related in a feeble-minded group (the correlation was .65). Imbeciles were more susceptible to anger than idiots, and morons were more susceptible than imbeciles. On the other hand, in a college group with an intelligence range from low-average to near "genius" the correlation was practically zero. The anger reactions of individuals at all levels of intelligence were found to be largely nonadaptive. When after-effects of anger were examined from the point of view of finding trends toward "dissociation" or "integration" the differences between groups at different levels of intelligence were small.

Other things being equal, we might expect the child with greater intellect to have more emotional scope. He is better able to perceive both the tragic and the comic in life about him; more able to sense and to fear the omens of future calamity and more able, also, to anticipate in feeling and in thought the future consummation of his hopes. He is able to acquire a wider range of interests which the circumstances of life may block or bless. But other things are not equal. The bright along with the dull may acquire attitudes at any stage along the course of development which put walls around their intellect. The child with a high IQ, like the professor with a Phi Beta Kappa key, may use his intellect to defend a bias and thus close the door to experiences that might enlighten or enrich his emotional life. Again, the bright person may be as vulnerable as the dull to circumstances which interfere with his spontaneity. Smith (1932) found, for example, that "feelings of inferiority" were quite uniformly distributed through the whole range of intelligence.

These considerations deny the view that the relation between emotion and intellect is one of uniform dominance and priority of the former over the latter. The fact still remains, of course, that a child's emotions may dominate his thoughts, and the fact also remains that he will have emotional experiences in early childhood which he cannot at the time review and examine with his intellect.

Memory of Early Emotional Experiences

Child psychologists and psychoanalysts, alike, have shown much interest in the study of early childhood memories. A "Note on Early Memories" was published by G. Stanley Hall in 1899. In 1893, Miles questioned people concerning the earliest things they were sure they could remember and the age at which these occurred. V. and C. Henri, in 1895, published a questionnaire devoted to early memories. Numerous other studies in this area have been reviewed by Dudycha and Dudycha (1941).

The average age of the person at the time of his earliest remembered experience has varied somewhat in different studies. Dudycha and Dudycha (1933), in a study in which the data consisted only of memories which could be quite accurately placed or traced, concluded that the average age of the earliest memories reported by college students is 3 years, 7 months. Investi-

gators are not unanimous as to the degree to which pleasant and unpleasant experiences prevail in early memories, although earliest remembered experiences usually have an emotional tone. In the Dudycha study cited above, fear was reported in connection with 30.4 per cent of the memories; joy, 27.9 per cent; anger, 10.3 per cent; wonder and curiosity, 8.1 per cent; pain, 5.2 per cent; shame and guilt, 2.6 per cent; miscellaneous emotions, 3.8 per cent; no emotion indicated, 5.2 per cent.

A question might be raised as to what might be the relation, if any, between the number, nature, and timing of a person's earliest memories and his emotional adjustment. Studies by Crook and Harden (1931) and Child (1940) give varying reports with regard to this matter. More intensive clinical investigation would be necessary to provide an adequate answer.

One thing that complicates the study of early memories is the factor of *selective recall*. What one remembers from his past will be influenced not only by what happened in the past, for in the ordinary course of development there is a vast amount of forgetting. Why does a person remember certain things from his early childhood while forgetting so much else? One theory is that some things are remembered not simply because of their intensity or impressiveness, *as such*, at the time of the original experience but because they fit into or are congruent with certain personality tendencies which now exist and which have a history extending back into earlier years. On this theory, a person's early memories may tell us more about his present mood and attitude toward self and others than about the factual events of his childhood. If he is a person who has a strong tendency to feel abused, for example, a tendency to look upon life and fate as being unjustly against him, his early memories may include recollections of times when he was (in reality, or according to his interpretation) treated in a harsh and unfair manner. If he has a strong tendency (now) to disparage and blame himself, he may also have a tendency to recollect experiences in his life when he did something that made him feel especially guilty or unworthy. If he is preoccupied (now) with sexual conflicts or is convinced that sexual difficulties provide the key to human conflicts he is more likely (according to this theory) to have recollections of sexual experiences among his early memories than a person who does not happen to be consciously preoccupied or "unconsciously" troubled by sex to the same degree.

Another factor that needs to be considered has already been alluded to above, namely, the "memory" that is reported may represent something that actually occurred but which at the time involved a great amount of subjective elaboration. There may be an essential element of reality in the "memory" even though the experience was, at the time, subjected to a biased interpretation. In other words, a recollection dealing, say, with sex may mean that a child was actually caught unawares and frightened by a sexual advance from an older person, or it might mean that the child, by reason of already-existing feelings of anxiety or self-disparagement relating to sex, *interpreted* a certain happening (such as being followed) as though it had a threatening sexual significance.

Another factor, in keeping with the foregoing, is suggested especially by Horney's account of ways in which people often tend to "externalize" their inner difficulties. The process of externalizing may take the more or less familiar form of attributing to others (projecting on others) moods or attitudes resident within oneself (as when one who is hostile sees others as hostile but is quite oblivious of his own hostility). Now, one way of externalizing present dif-

ficulties is to project them on to or attribute them to one's own past environment and experiences. To avoid facing himself as he now is, and to avoid taking responsibility, as it were, for his *present* state, the individual may place responsibility upon happenings in his early childhood and he may be able to piece together plenty of "early memories" to support this position. The early memories he reports may, in reality, be true, but they represent only that part of the "truth" which happens to fit the individual's need for finding an explanation for his present problems.

Factors Influencing Recall and Reconstruction of the Past

At a given moment children and adults are likely to be able readily to recall more pleasant than unpleasant events from their immediate past (Wohlgemuth, 1922–1923; Flügel, 1925; Jersild, 1931).

A discussion of the concepts of suppression and repression would be in order here, but these concepts have been applied to the study of children largely on the basis of formulations arrived at through work with adults. The writer has not found any study which deals systematically with suppression and repression in a way that gives an adequate and plausible account of what these processes involve and how they undergo changes at various maturity levels.

Apart from consciously forgetting an episode in its totality, there are processes by which an experience may become modified or distorted in a child's recollection. Northway (1936) has shown, for example, how children, when called upon to recollect stories, tend to recast the contents into familiar terms and settings. She noted further that the younger children (the age range in her study was 10–15 years) by omission and addition molded the materials into a form nearer their interests to a greater extent than did the older children. She found also that, the more foreign the material is to the child's "psychological field," the more he tended to substitute a story of his own invention.

A somewhat similar tendency has been noted in a study by Hildreth (1941, 1944), who found what she called a "difficulty reduction tendency" in children. When children, for example, attempted to reproduce designs they tended to substitute something meaningful for something meaningless, to "close" the design, to add conventional proportions when they were lacking. When confronted with a difficult problem, the child, according to Hildreth, unconsciously remakes it to fit his immature mentality. He reworks it to fit his grasp, getting out of it only what his limited insight and experience permit. This finding is not confined to children, however. Morgan (1944) found that logical thinking of adults may be warped not only by emotional bias but also by simple habit patterns.

Needed Research

The foregoing section touches upon many factors which make it difficult, and in some respects impossible, for the growing child to acquire an intelligent appreciation of what has happened or is happening in his emotional life. We have noted also that children before adolescence and even during that period often show a conspicuous lack of interest in inquiring into the nature and origins of their feelings.

Teachers and even psychologists have a tendency to take this lack of interest in self-understanding for granted, as something obvious, natural, and inevitable. But it is possible that the average child, with proper guidance, could learn, to a far greater degree and at an earlier age, to gain understanding of psychological problems. This is demonstrated in the success which workers have achieved through play therapy, group therapy, and other therapeutic procedures with troubled children at various age levels. The likelihood that children at the preschool level can learn to appreciate, at least to some degree, the psychological nature of some of their problems, and to deal with them, is indicated not only in clinical studies but also in studies conducted in educational settings. Chittenden (1942), in a study of selected nursery school children, found that children showed a decrease in "dominative" behavior (including aggressive methods of domination) without at the same time becoming more inactive or subdued after a training series in which they had a chance to study what happened when dolls used quarrelsome and cooperative methods of handling social problems such as those that arise in the play of young children. Another suggestive finding is reported by Appel (1942), who found that one of the most successful of the techniques used by teachers in dealing with the fights and quarrels of nursery school children was to try to interpret the wishes and feelings that came into play.

Findings such as these suggest that even at the preschool level children probably have a greater capacity for understanding and for using applied psychology than customarily is assumed in connection with their training at school. The studies do not give answer to the queston as to how early and how well a child might learn to bring reason to bear in understanding his own emotional experiences. But the writer ventures the hypothesis that much of the child's lack of understanding of psychological processes which we ordinarily encounter is influenced by cultural factors and is not due solely to constitutional limitations.

The writer (1951b, p. 122) has advanced the theory that human beings, from an early age, have more capacity for learning to face and to understand and to deal constructively with the realities of life than we have hitherto assumed in our psychological theories or in our educational practices. To test this theory would require research of a kind that now is largely lacking in the literature on development. Apart from recognized obstacles within the child himself, many circumstances in our culture, including, in this writer's opinion, many of the things that go under the name of education at school, are calculated to divert and hinder a child from getting into contact with reality.

EMOTIONAL MATURITY

Before going into more detail concerning characteristics of various forms of emotional behavior that emerge as a child matures, it will be well to consider briefly what sort of yardstick or standard we might apply in judging what constitutes more or less "mature" behavior. The concept of "emotional maturity" figures prominently not only in accounts of older people but also in accounts of normal as well as disturbed children. This concept is implicit in the much-used idea of *regression*, or responding to stress by reverting to an earlier, more infantile form of behavior. The concept of emotional maturity is also involved in the idea of emotional *adjustment* and of emotional *stability*. Mitrano (1939) points out that forms of behavior conspicuously shown by children who are judged to be unstable include many "immature" forms of behavior. In line with this observation was a finding by Durea (1937) that delinquent children are emotionally less mature than normal children of similar age.

Many of our prevailing concepts of maturity are colored by cultural expectations which may or may not be well geared to the natural course of development. No-

tions of maturity that are applied to young children when they are urged to be "big," not to cry, not to be so afraid or so angry (which means, in effect, not to *show* that they are afraid or angry) often seem to be very false and very pernicious. Even at the adult level the pose of maturity which some people assume and fear to depart from may be a dangerous sham. But, even so, within broad limits, it would be useful to have a more systematic measuring rod than now is available.

To give meaning to the concept of emotional maturity as applied to children, it would be necessary to take account of maturity at various developmental levels leading up to the mature adult level. Even at the adult level there should be gradations, for as the science of gerontology progresses it probably will be found that there are pronounced differences between a "mature" adult of 25 and a "mature" adult of 45 that are just as truly *developmental* in nature as the differences, say, between the "mature" 6-year-old and the "mature" 10-year-old.

In her classical discussion of emotional maturity, L. S. Hollingworth (1928) calls attention to the fact that many of the tests of fitness for manhood or womanhood in ancient pubic ceremonies were tests of capacity to suffer, carrying the implication that emotional maturity consists of fortitude. In proposing her own criteria, she mentions first that the emotionally mature person is (1) *capable of gradations or degrees of emotional response;* he does not respond in all-or-none fashion. He keeps within bounds. If his hat blows off, he does not blow up. He is also (2) *able to delay his response,* as contrasted with the impulsiveness of the young child. Another indication of maturity is in his (3) *handling of self-pity.* Instead of showing unrestrained self-pity he tries to feel no sorrier for himself than others would feel for him.

The most outstanding mark of emotional maturity, according to Cole (1944), is *ability to bear tension*. Other marks of emotional maturity are an indifference toward certain kinds of stimuli that affect the child or adolescent (such as some of the circumstances that make the child afraid), and an outgrowing of adolescent moodiness and sentimentality.

Both Hollingworth and Cole have ably described some characteristics which we expect, in our culture, to find in a mature person, but their criteria do not provide an adequate theoretical base for the study of emotional maturity. Emotional maturity should be defined in the light of all the resources and powers that come into a person's possession in the process of development. It should not simply emphasize the idea of *controlling* emotions or keeping a lid on them. It should emphasize the idea of using emotional resources in a healthy and spontaneous way. According to this concept, "mature" emotional behavior at any level of growth is that which reflects the fruits of normal development in all the interacting aspects of the child's personality.[1] On this theory, a person who is able to keep his emotions under control, who is able to brook delay and to suffer without self-pity, might still be emotionally stunted and childish.

An adequate theory of emotional maturity must take account of the full scope of the individual's powers and his ability to enjoy the use of his powers.[2]

Below are listed some of the trends and tendencies involved in the process of physical, motor, intellectual, social, and emotional development that have a bearing on emotional maturity:

[1] The discussion here follows rather closely an account written subsequent to, but published prior to, this book (Jersild, 1951a).

[2] This point of view is implicit in Morgan's (1934) account of emotional maturity, and it has been emphasized and elaborated by Saul (1947).

A change from helplessness to a greatly increased capacity for self-help, with a consequent progressive freedom from the frustrations and fears that beset a helpless creature.

A shift from abject dependence on others to increasing balanced independence, with consequent opening of channels for enjoyment of self-help and an increasing degree of psychological as well as physical self-support.

A shift from capacity to appreciate and react only to the immediate present to increasing capacity to encompass the past and to anticipate the future, with resulting changes in anticipation of both good and ill.

Increasing intellectual capacity, including increased capacity for dealing with aspects of life on a symbolic level, increased ability to plan; increased "attention span," bringing increased ability to see beyond and to be immune to momentary or intermediate frustrations; increased intellectual perspective and an increased ability to take a panoramic view of things.

A change from a disposition to be physically very active to an increased capacity during adolescence and later to tolerate and to enjoy sedentary pursuits.

A shift from social life centered only on the parents to a social life that encompasses one's peers and which also includes a capacity not simply to tolerate but to appreciate persons who are considerably older and considerably younger than oneself.

A change from being a creature who at first receives much, gives little, to one who is capable of giving as well as of receiving, and capable of learning to get enjoyment from giving.

Development of capacity to identify oneself with a larger social group, and the ability to participate emotionally in the fortunes of the larger group.

Development from the status of being the child of the family to the status, ultimately, of being able to have children of one's own and, along with this development, a capacity to exercise the feelings and attitudes involved in being a parent psychologically, whether or not one is a parent biologically.

Progressive sexual development and the capacity after puberty for enjoying mature sex experiences.

An increased capacity for bearing the inevitable sufferings and pains connected with life and growth without feeling abused.

An increased capacity for sympathy and compassion as one assimilates the meaning for self and others of the joys and vicissitudes of life.

These are a few of the trends in development that seem to have a bearing on a maturing person's emotional life. We might add the view that if a person has progressed in a healthy manner he will not, at maturity, be involved in hostilities or campaigns of self-vindication that arose in connection with childhood struggles and frustrations or in anxieties pertaining to childhood dangers that no longer exist. [According to Saul (1947), the emotionally mature person's aggressiveness will serve constructive ends.] But this perhaps sets so high a standard of "maturity" that only a few adults could measure up to it. Probably a more realistic way of putting it is that the "mature" adult is not one who necessarily has resolved all conditions that aroused anxiety and hostility but is continuously in process of seeing himself in clearer perspective and continually involved in a struggle to gain a healthy integration of feeling, thinking, and action.

STUDIES OF VARIOUS EMOTIONAL STATES

The ensuing sections will draw upon studies which deal with topics such as anger and hostility, joy, love and affection, and fear and anxiety. Much of the systematic research has been formulated in terms of

these topics. At first glance this might seem like a fractional or atomistic approach, for emotions do not, of course, come in separate bundles that can be examined in the abstract. However, when we deal with these emotional states or with the circumstances underlying them, we actually are not dealing with a segment of experience, for anger and hostility, fear and anxiety, joy and contentment and all other conditions we might name represent an orientation of the organism as a whole. To understand any of these emotional states we must continually take account of the fact that all are intimately linked with the economy of the personality as a whole.

FEAR AND ANXIETY

In this section we will consider apprehensions ranging from episodes of conscious fear in response to a clearly perceived external event to anxieties and phobias which stem from vague or unrecognized tendencies within the individual himself.[1]

The Roots of Fear

Fear is a form of withdrawal or actual or incipient flight from a situation for which the individual has no adequate response. Fear has also been defined, from a purposive point of view, as a form of self-protecting flight from any circumstance which threatens a person's well-being (or what he regards as his well-being). In defining fear we need to encompass more than actual injury or imminent danger, for, almost from the time of birth, fear is often shown in response to stimuli which signalize a *possibility* but not an actuality of danger.

The circumstances in which fear arises even at a very early age, are so diverse that one cannot account for them simply

---

[1] Some of the differences between "fear" and "anxiety," as these terms have been used in the literature, are noted at a later point.

by analyzing the properties of the external stimulus. It is difficult also to find a common psychological ground, or cluster of common subjective or internal factors, that account for the various cases of fear. In a search for factors underlying fear, Hebb (1946) lists three. There are fears which he calls *fears due to "conflict,"* such as those aroused by pain or loud noise which have a "primitive disrupting action, not psychologically analyzable nor dependent on any previous experience" (p. 271). A second class, according to Hebb, consists of *fears due to sensory deficit.* In this class he lists fear of darkness, loss of support, and solitude, all of which "have in common an absence of sensory stimulation" (p. 272). A third class contains *fears arising from constitutional disturbances and maturation.*

This classification by Hebb leaves many questions unanswered but it represents a much-needed effort to bring scientific precision to bear on a subject which has suffered from much loose and oversimplified discussion.

Although fear may be described as a form of flight, the overt response takes many forms other than cringing or fleeing. It may range from apparently quite nonchalant behavior to violent displays of rage.

Psychologists show considerable agreement concerning some fears that appear early in life.[1]

Noise and Loss of Support. As already noted, among the conditions that frequently produce fear during the first days and weeks of life, without prior conditioning, are noises and sudden displacement or loss of support. Fears in the latter category may occur not only when an infant is thrown off balance or actually falls but also as a response to any rapid movement through space, as when carried rapidly

[1] Among the early studies of fear not here reviewed are the works of Calkins (1894–1896); Binet (1895); Mosso (1896); and Hall (1897).

downstairs. These stimuli do not invariably produce fear, and there is need for more investigation, both from the point of view of the properties or characteristics of these stimuli and from the point of view of the larger context in which they occur, before we go further than to say that they are especially potent at an early age.

Other Sensory Stimuli. Apart from noise and displacement, any sudden, intense, abrupt stimulus such as the sudden motion of an object, or an unexpected cutaneous contact, may be a source of primary, unlearned fear.

Fear of the Unfamiliar. Among the primary fears are fears of what is novel, strange, and unfamiliar (strange, that is, from the point of view of the child's previous experience). Somewhere between the age of about 5 and 9 months, many infants show fear of unfamiliar persons (Dearborn, 1910; Shirley, 1933; Jersild and Holmes, 1935a). Fear of strange things and situations has also been observed (H. E. Jones and Jones, 1928; Ellesor, 1933; Valentine, 1930; Bühler, 1930).

Novelty or strangeness has also been observed as a factor in producing fear when combined with other events which separately did not produce fear (Valentine, 1930).

In addition to fears of unfamiliar persons, things, and situations, fears have also been noted as response to unusual or "uncanny" things, including some forms of mutilation such as the detached arm of a doll or the half-decapitated body of a favorite doll (Dearborn, 1910; Valentine, 1930).

Fear of the strange and "uncanny" has also been observed in animals (Köhler, 1925; Hebb, 1946). Chimpanzees, in a study by Hebb (1946), showed numerous instances of fear when confronted with strange or unusual objects, such as a skull with moving jaw, a plaster cast of a chimpanzee visage, a model of an imaginary white grub with long legs. In an earlier study, Hebb and Riesen (1943) had observed fear of strangers in infant chimpanzees. After eliminating, experimentally or otherwise, other variables that might account for this behavior, Hebb concludes that anthropoid fears of inert, mutilated, or dismembered bodies are spontaneous in the sense that avoidance of such objects is not built up by association with a more primitive cause of fear.

When fear of the unfamiliar thus appears as a "primary" fear, without prior conditioning, it does not mean necessarily that this occurs independent of any learning. Learning is involved in such fears to the extent that what is *familiar*, and from which the strange person or thing differs, has become familiar through experience. Whether there is anything corresponding to primitive strangeness, something which in the nature of things will be perceived as strange, apart from any learned kind of awareness, or criterion or standard of familiarity, against which or in contrast with which something is unfamiliar, would be hard to tell. Conceivably there might be experiences arising from organic causes that might be experienced as something intrinsically queer and fear-inspiring.

The foregoing also indicates that, in the course of a child's experience, there are fears that arise by virtue of *lack* of conditioning or lack of familiarization to events that are not intrinsically and universally fear-producing. Six-month-old Charles fears *Jim's* mother because she is strange to him, and 6-month-old Jim fears *Charles's* mother for the same reason. Both might fear their own mothers at 6 months if they had been interchanged at birth and now saw their mothers for the first time.

The unfamiliar confronts a person with something for which he has no prepared response. It represents something which he cannot, at the moment at least, assimilate or take in stride in terms of his accustomed habits of action and perception. It does not fit into his established world; it calls upon him, on a small or large scale, to amend or even to reorganize his "inner" world.

Studies which show the extent to which children outgrow or lay by their fears (see, e.g., Jersild and Holmes, 1935a; Slater *et al.*, 1939) indicate that the process of experience through which the unfamiliar and fearful become familiar and commonplace occurs on a vast scale in the course of development.

But it also is apparent from various studies, as well as from everyday observation, that there may be large gaps and many lags in the process. Many children (perhaps we should say all) reach adulthood with fear of many things *not because these things are intrinsically fearful* but because they have not learned to take them in stride. A genetic study probably would show that fear of the unfamiliar and untried which appears in early infancy has the same paternity, psychologically, as the fear a person shows when he shrinks from new theories in politics and is afraid to face the prospect of getting new or different ideas about himself.

Individual Differences in Scope and Degree of Familiarization. The concept of fear by virtue of lack of familiarity, like the concept of fear through conditioning, greatly enlarges the extent to which it is possible for children to differ in their fears even when they do not have a different inherent tendency to be afraid.

Fear of Animals. Fear of animals usually does not appear as early as many other fears, but once susceptibility to such fears has been established, fear of animals remains prominent during childhood (Hagman, 1932; Jersild and Holmes, 1935a;

Pratt, 1945). As noted in an earlier reference to a study by H. E. Jones and Jones (1928) of fear of snakes, susceptibility to fear of animals changes as a child matures. More children at the age of 2 and at the age of 3 showed fear in response to a dog which was included as one of a number of experimental fear stimuli in a study by Holmes (1935) than to any other situation.

The question whether fear of animals is inherent or acquired has been raised from time to time in the literature. Valentine (1930) is one of the more recent writers who suggests that high susceptibility to fear of animals which he observed in his study suggests that this fear may be innate. On the other hand, Yerkes and Yerkes (1936), in a study of chimpanzees, tentatively conclude that their evidence does not demonstrate a specific fear response prior to or apart from individual experience. In view of findings regarding fears in response to strange things and to sudden, abrupt, or unexpected movements, and to noise, it seems probable, in the judgment of the writer, that fear of animals might occur as an unconditioned fear whether or not fear of the "animalness" of animals as such is innate.

Fear of Darkness. Observers have differed considerably with regard to the inception of fear of the dark. Freud (1936) speaks of being in the dark, being left alone, and finding a strange person in place of the mother as three of the primary anxiety situations in infancy. He believes that all three are "reducible to a single situation, that of feeling the loss of the loved [longed-for] person" (p. 99). Fear of the dark, then, is a feature of "the most basic anxiety of all," which arises in connection with separation from the mother (p. 100).

The evidence from direct observation of children raises doubts concerning this statement with regard to fear of the dark.

The earliest record of fear of the dark in any of the five children observed by Valentine (1930) occurred when one of them was 2 years and 1 month old. J. B. Watson (1924) studied the response of three babies to darkness at about the age of half a year and found no fear, but one child cried when held by a stranger in a dimly lighted room. Dearborn (1910) observed at 176 days what might appear like fear of the dark. Stern (1930) did not record any appearance of fear of the dark in a child he observed until the youngster was 4 years, 2½ months old (p. 514).

The slow appearance of fear of the dark has also been noted by the writer in informal observations of his own as well as in a study in which mothers cooperated (Jersild and Holmes, 1935a). None of the mothers of 8 children who were observed in the age range from birth to a year reported fear of the dark or being alone in the dark (in contrast with many reports of fear of noises, falling, strange situations, etc.). Only 4 instances of fear of the dark, of being alone in the dark, were reported from observations of 23 children aged 12 to 23 months.

According to many observers, then, fear of the dark is rather infrequent during the first year or two as revealed by crying and other signs which the same observers often noted as signs of fear in many other situations during this same period. And, in some of the instances recorded, it was not darkness alone but noise, or a novel circumstance combined with darkness, that seemed to be responsible.[1]

However, as children grow older, darkness is a contributing factor, if not the

[1] On the theory that the flood of new sensory stimuli to which the newborn child is exposed is frightening, one should expect the child at first to be more frightened by any form of illumination than by darkness, and more afraid during the day than during the night, for night time usually brings not only darkness but also less noise.

main cause, in a great many fears. The fact that darkness actually separates a child from others in a psychological sense (as suggested by Freud) by making him and others invisible to one another is an important contributing factor. A state of darkness is often equivalent to a state of being alone. Regardless of the presence or absence of others, darkness makes a person more vulnerable, less able to cope with things. Apart from dangers a person's imagination might conjure up, darkness enhances some actual dangers.

Fear of Solitude and Separation. Freud regarded anxiety with respect to separation from the mother as a basic anxiety. Probably all children sooner or later become susceptible to fear of such loss. It also appears, however, that it takes something more severe and momentous than the ordinary comings and goings of a parent to elicit a fear of being alone or of being abandoned by the parent. In the study cited above (Jersild and Holmes, 1935a), no parents of children under 1 year of age observed fear of being left alone or abandoned during the period of observation. Fear of this sort was reported in 13 per cent of the children at the age level from 12 through 23 months. Perhaps all or nearly all the children might have shown the fear if they had been subjected to separation from their mothers in a drastic manner.

The fact that such separation can be very disturbing is brought out in observations by Edelston (1943) of hospitalized children. He reports a series of 44 cases showing neurotic disturbances of varying degrees. After ruling out physical or physiological interpretations, he concludes that separation-anxiety was the cause of the disturbances. He also points out that such anxiety as a response to hospitalization is not universal, for many children spend time in hospitals without any apparent ill effects. It appears that separation-anxiety, when it occurs, is part of a larger clinical picture.

Disturbing effects of being separated from the home were noted also in studies of children who were evacuated from cities in England during World War II (Isaacs et al., 1941). As interpreted by Isaacs this separation-anxiety is something more sophisticated than a primitive fear. Isaacs states that it is complicated by conflicts involving secret guilt and shame as a result of the child's earlier hate, anger, and defiance toward his parent.

The foregoing observations emphasize that separation from the parent may involve children in intense apprehension, but we need more light on the total context associated with fear-inducing separation before we can conclude that fear of separation as such is one of the earliest spontaneous and practically universal fear reactions.

As far as fear of strangers is concerned, we would conclude, in the light of our earlier discussion, that this cannot be regarded as representing only a fear of separation. Fear of the novel, unhabitual, and strange relate not only to people, as we have seen, but also to situations and things, and it may appear even when a loved person is at hand (as when a child shrinks in apparent fear from a mutilated toy offered to him by his parent).

Later Trends in Children's Fears

Fears in response to events such as those noted above in the infancy period continue to occur quite frequently during preschool years. During the preschool years there is an increase in the everyday display of fear of animals. Fears pertaining to being alone or abandoned also occur, as noted. Many children exhibit fear of dangers associated with imaginary creatures and with darkness. Many of the fears of children of this age also pertain to possible injury through

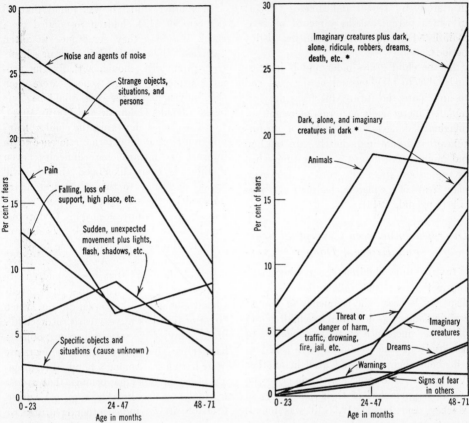

FIGURE 1. Relative frequency of various fear situations as described by parents and teachers, including 146 records of observation of children for periods of 21 days (31, 91, and 24 at the respective age levels), combined with occasional records of 117 additional children (27, 67, and 23 at the respective age levels). (Adapted from "Children's Fears," by A. T. Jersild and F. B. Holmes. *Child Development Monographs,* 1935, No. 20, 54. By permission of the publisher.) Entries followed by an asterisk include a combination of categories some of which are also shown separately.

drowning, fire, traffic accidents, and other physical accidents. Such fears also are relatively frequent during later years.

There are parallels between fears and other features of development during the preschool period [1] and into the elementary period and the period of adolescence. As children grow older they shrink from seeming different or peculiar. At the adolescent period, fears and anxieties relating to physical inadequacies and asymmetries, intellectual inadequacies, and sexual functions may arise (Bonar, 1942; Marsh, 1942).

Figure 1 shows trends in the frequency of various fear situations that were reported

[1] In a study by Dorkey and Amen (1947; see also Temple and Amen, 1944), evidence of "anxiety" in connection with personal relationships between nursery school children was obtained by means of a projective technique which gave the children a chance to use a happy face or a sad face in completing incomplete pictures of children in various situations.

in a study by Jersild and Holmes (1935a) in which parents made a record of fears manifested by their children during 21-day periods.

As the child grows older and is increasingly able to take account of the past and to anticipate the future, his fears are formulated increasingly in terms of remote or imaginary dangers or in terms of misfortunes that do not immediately threaten him but might befall him at a future time when he describes them in words. However, many fears of a concrete character also persist (England, 1946).

Discrepancy between Conceptual Fears and External Danger

By the time children reach school age, and in the years that follow, there is much disparity between the frequency of fear of certain dangers as described by children and the actual incidence of these dangers. In one study in which children were asked to tell about their fears and also, in another part of the same interview, to describe the "worst happenings" of their lives (Jersild, Markey, and Jersild, 1933) it was found, for example, that in the age range from 5 to 12 years 14 per cent of the children expressed fear of animals while only 2 per cent mentioned that they actually had been attacked by animals; 19 per cent expressed fear of ghosts, other supernatural agents, corpses, and the like, while none in actual life had suffered attack from these. In contrast, far fewer mentioned actual bodily injuries and accidents in describing fears than in describing "worst happenings." Interestingly enough, death or loss of relatives was mentioned slightly more often as an actual misfortune than as a recurring fear, and the same held true with respect to a category which included scolding, embarrassment, ridicule, and the like.

In another study, it was found that 53 per cent of 1124 children responded on a check list that they sometimes or often "worried" about "being left back in school" (not promoted), though actually the promotion policies in the schools were such that only about 1 per cent would be "left back" (Jersild, Goldman, and Loftus, 1941). In a situation such as this, the child's "fear" apparently gives an external reference to an internal or "intrapsychic" difficulty: even if there is every likelihood that he will "pass" according to the external standard imposed by the school, he still may regard himself as a failure according to internal standards for his performance falls short of what he thinks he should be able to do.

"Irrational Fears." As suggested above, many of the fears that beset children are "irrational" in the sense that they occur when there is no real external danger. Such "irrational" fears appear early in a child's life. Many of the strange persons, objects, happenings, and situations that he fears are quite harmless. Among a hundred frightening noises or other happenings that arouse fear only one may be a signal of real danger. Probably if we studied other creatures we would find the same: the rabbit is alerted again and again when actually things are safe; the hen runs to cover when the hawk overhead is heading somewhere else; and so on. A great many circumstances which elicit fear are, in effect, signals that danger *might* be afoot. The response anticipates the *possibility* of danger. If we regard such fears as irrational we must go the next step and say that it is natural and normal for children to have irrational fears.

Such irrational fear cannot be regarded, *per se,* as a sign of neurotic tendencies or intrapsychic conflict. But, having recognized this, we still face a question concerning what distinguishes morbid from healthy fears.

"Healthy" and "Morbid" Fears. It would be useful, indeed, if we had a ready way of distinguishing between healthy and morbid fears, between fears that serve a useful function in the normal course of development and fears that persist because something has gone wrong.

To solve this problem we need far more data than now are available from *direct, systematic study* of the personal lives of children over a long span of years. Probably we would need longitudinal studies not in one culture but in several, for cultural conditions influence the fears that arise and they must also be taken into account in judging whether a fear may reasonably be regarded as a response to real danger. In illustrating this point, Horney (1937) points out that a person in a group that has taboos against the eating of meat would, according to his indoctrination, have real cause for fright if he chanced to eat meat, whereas such fright would be unwarranted in someone living under a different set of taboos.

Although the developmental data are inadequate, we may proceed to review some of the efforts that have been made, and theories that have been advanced, in solving the problems raised above.

Anxiety

The concept of anxiety is very important for understanding the emotional life of the child even though there is much diversity, at present, in the definition of anxiety, its origin, and rôle. According to one dictionary definition, anxiety is a painful uneasiness of mind respecting an impending or anticipated ill. Various criteria have been used to distinguish between anxiety and ordinary fear. Generally speaking, it is assumed that the danger or disaster which is involved in anxiety is subjective or internal in nature—it resides within the personality of the anxious person—there are conflicting tendencies and impulses, unfulfilled needs, strivings, obligations, "oughts" and "shoulds" within him that underlie the disturbance known as anxiety.

One difference between ordinary fear and anxiety (as here distinguished) is in clarity and definition, as seen from the point of view of the person who is affected or from an objective standpoint. In fear there is usually a relatively clear *perception of the threatening circumstance* (whether this be external, such as a charging bull, or internal in the form of a sharp pain which makes a person apprehensive about his health). In a state of anxiety, on the other hand, the individual may be unable clearly to define to himself what it is that makes him anxious. "Something" makes him feel uneasy, "sets him off," but this "something" is difficult to recognize.

Also, in a state of ordinary fear the *feeling* is more or less clearly defined. The affected person is frightened and recognizes (if free to give thought to the matter) his feelings as feelings of fright. In anxiety, on the other hand, the feeling states may be quite diffuse, vague, and varied. They may or may not involve an experience of fear. They may involve experiences of being depressed, or tense, or keyed-up, or irritable, or "uneasy," or "under pressure."

There is a difference also in the clarity of the *impulse* that comes into play. The frightened person seeks to avoid or escape, even when he resorts to quite aggressive means of freeing himself from the danger which threatens (as when a frightened child, in desperation, attacks a big bully). But in anxiety the direction of the impulse is usually not so clear. The source or direction from which the danger comes may be perceived so dimly that the anxious person does not know in which direction to flee. So his reaction may appear to be quite indiscriminate and unsuitable.

Moreover, since the source of anxiety consists, by definition, in whole or in part, in a condition within the individual himself, there actually is no clear line of retreat, for a person cannot run away from himself.

Actually, the impulses shown by the anxious person may bear little or no resemblance to an impulse to flee. The anxious person may even seek out rather than shun an external circumstance which symbolizes, in part, his internal conflict (as when a person who is afraid of sex actually seeks out situations which will activate his fears). Again, the impulses connected with anxiety may take compulsive or obsessive forms. Anxiety may be expressed by a compulsion to be good and conforming and at all costs to avoid opposition to others, or a driven tendency to be perfectly neat, punctual, industrious. In older persons, anxiety may express itself by an insatiable drive for prestige, power, or possessions. These are only a few of the means, as described in the literature, by which an anxious person tries to protect and bolster himself.[1]

An illuminating account of manifestations of anxiety in everyday life has been given by Sullivan (1948). He maintains that "man in the process of becoming a person always develops a great variety of processes directly related to the undergoing of anxiety" (p. 3). The situations which arouse anxiety are "almost infinitely varied" but they are generally obscure. The expressions of anxiety that come into play whenever anything goes counter to a person's pride, or prestige, or his conviction that he is worthwhile and respected, or threatens the "self-system" involved in his accus-

tomed way of life, take many forms that bear no resemblance to fear.

The concept of anxiety is useful, according to Sullivan, in explaining "a great many instances of irritation, anger, and unpleasant misunderstanding; all more or less enduring hateful relationships; the welter of belittling, disparaging performances which seem to be almost a national . . . characteristic; . . . the time-destroying more or less obsessional preoccupations which so frequently characterize the gifted; the sad way of the pathologically alcoholic; and a startlingly great proportion of the so-called sexual problems of our times" (p. 11). Sullivan states that resentment often, if not always, includes anxiety in its composition. He sees anxiety also as an element in the condition of many people who are chronically tired. He also regards "feverish overactivity" in work or play (shown by people who, as we say, "work themselves to death") as an expression of anxiety about becoming anxious, or about being discovered to be anxious, or as a means of avoiding awareness of an anxiety-provoking condition.

The inner tendencies and unresolved conflicts which underlie anxiety are quite commonly described as *unconscious* either in the sense that the individual has always been completely blind to them, or in the sense that he has lost sight of happenings within himself.

Other distinctions have also been made between fear and anxiety. The reaction in anxiety tends to be more disproportionate than the ordinary fear response: for example, we may expect a person who is crossing a canyon on an unstable half-rotten plank to be afraid, but it would be much less appropriate for a person to tremble with fear when walking across a well-built bridge.

Another distinction that sometimes is drawn is that anxiety anticipates danger

---

1 For accounts of anxiety, see Freud (1936), Sullivan (1948), Horney (1937, 1945, 1950), May (1950), and Hoch and Zubin (1950). A classical treatment of anxiety which combines a religious orientation with many penetrating psychological insights can be found in Søren Kierkegaard's *The Sickness unto Death* (1951).

and thus serves, in a sense, as a protection against fear.

It has also been observed that the anxiety reaction may be conspicuously indiscriminate and undiscriminating. A person who is frightened by his hostile impulses, may, for example, not only feel panic at the thought of making only a mild criticism but he may go to great lengths later to placate someone whom he actually did not offend (except in his own imagination).

There is disagreement between writers with respect to what they encompass under the term "anxiety." Because of such disagreement, we cannot take findings about anxiety that A has reported and integrate them with the findings of B. For example, anxiety is sometimes treated as a state which fits into a continuum or gradation of fear. Mira (1940) lists phases of fear which begin with prudence and range through precaution, alarm, anxiety, panic, and terror. Goldstein (1947), on the other hand, draws a distinction between anxiety and fear and states that infants in whom the abstract attitude is still in process of developing are much more harassed by anxiety than by fear. Freud and his followers apply the term anxiety (*Angst*) to the earliest infantile levels in a manner that suggests that it should be regarded as a normal feature of development. On the other hand, anxiety is sometimes discussed in terms that have little resemblance to fear but which suggest, rather, a kind of weakness or disturbance in the personality which may express itself through a variety of emotional states.

Concerning the causes of anxiety, as we will note more particularly at a later point, there also is a large difference of opinion.

Phobias. Anxiety may be expressed in the form of phobia. A phobia has variously been defined as an irrational, persistent, and recurrent fear of an object or particular class of objects or situations which in ob-

jective reality represent no danger; as a "morbid fear"; as a fear whose origins have been forgotten.[1] According to Freud's (1933) account, a phobia represents a transformation of an internal danger into an external one: a "neurotic anxiety" is turned into an apparent "objective anxiety" (pp. 117–118).

A classical example of the Freudian conception that a phobia may serve as a transformation of anxiety is given in Freud's (1936) account of little Hans, which we discuss elsewhere in this chapter.

In her account of children's phobias, Isaacs (1933) develops the theme that anxiety is largely allayed by projecting troublesome aggressive wishes on to an external object and so being afraid of it. According to Isaacs, the fear of this phobic object is bad enough but it is not as overwhelming as the internal anxiety and guilt it replaces (p. 308).

As defined above, the fear involved in phobia might be called an *anxious fear* in that it involves hidden and subjective elements.

"Phobias" or "Fears"? The foregoing statements about phobias, like the earlier statements about *anxiety,* raise questions concerning the interpretation of the common varieties of "fear" which children display in their everyday lives, and they also raise a question as to terminology. English and Pearson (1945), in calling attention to findings obtained in studies of children's fears by the writer and his associates (Jersild, Markey, and Jersild, 1933; Jersild and Holmes, 1935a), comment on the "unreality" of a great number of these fears. They express the view that frequently children's expressed "fears" pertaining to wild animals, bad people, conditions associated with darkness, and the like, represent *phobias* rather than simple fears: the con-

[1] Crider (1949) has reviewed numerous writings dealing with the definition and origin of phobias.

scious feeling tone of fear is ascribed to phobic objects which represent a projection of unsolved emotional conflict.

Leaving aside the question as to the nature of the emotional conflict underlying phobias (on which there is considerable disagreement), the writer is of the opinion that this position is partially correct: many of the "fears" that appear in the literature on child psychology are phobias in the sense that they represent something more than a rational fear of an objective danger. We may, however, question the view that all seemingly irrational fears of the sort mentioned above should be regarded as phobias. There probably are many seemingly "unreal" fears that need not be explained as a form of fear due primarily to something else. When a child for a long time is afraid of dogs after actually having been injured and terrorized by a dog, we do not need to assume that this fear represents, say, a displacement of a fear of his father arising out of ambivalent feelings. We face here a problem that is partly a question of the use of words, but largely a problem that can be solved only by more intensive genetic study of normal children.

Factors Contributing to Susceptibility to Fear

In many cases the cause-and-effect relationships in children's fears are relatively clear. The simplest response occurs when a child is frightened by a certain event and fears it when he meets it again. A more complex yet fairly clear sequence occurs when the child fears not only the event that scared him but also events that happen to be directly associated with it. Sometimes the chain of association is more devious and indirect and yet traceable. For example, a child who was frightened when struck by an automobile on the street later not only showed fear of crossing the street

but he also had nightmares involving traffic accidents following which, for the first time, he showed fear of being alone in a dark room (Jersild and Holmes, 1935a). Many fears are not so easily traceable; and, even when fears are traceable, the conditions that render one child more susceptible to fright, and to after-effects of fright, are not easily determined.

Factors that contribute to a child's tendency to be afraid overlap and interact, but for convenience they may roughly be grouped under a few general headings.

Circumstances Involved in Parent-Child Relationships. We have noted earlier that many children, sooner or later, experience fear of being separated from their parents. There are many happenings short of actual abandonment that contribute to a child's apprehensiveness.

One such factor is severe *punishment* or *threats of punishment.* Such punishment may be corporal or it may be psychological in nature, such as punishment by way of being compared unfavorably with others, or by ridicule or by lurid stories. Punishment of a damaging sort may be meted out through a thinly disguised proxy, such as holding over the child the threat that the police will get him, or that he might become sick or paralyzed if he is not good, or that he is headed for hell. When children tell about their fears many of them will specifically describe various forms of threats and intimidation, including various forms of verbal *rejection* (see, e.g., Jersild, Markey, and Jersild, 1933).

Punishment and threats of punishment from the parent or a proxy affect the child in at least three ways which, in turn, may influence his tendency to be anxious. First, punishment may represent a form of rejection or abandonment. Secondly, it may instill the idea that the child is especially *bad* and thereby foster the idea that he is guilty and deserves to come to grief.

Thirdly, the punishment is likely also to arouse hostility toward the person who does the punishing and the child may, in turn, become afraid of his hostile impulses. Anxiety engendered by hostility has been described by Freud and his followers and by Horney.

According to some writers, a child early in life reacts to any form of denial of his wishes by the parents as a form of punishment which might predispose him to anxiety.

Apart from the effects of punishment administered by his elders, a child's tendency to be afraid may be aggravated by circumstances that *threaten to deprive* him of his parents. The coming of a new baby may be construed by the child as such a threat, with resulting apprehensiveness. An example of this appears in one of Holmes's studies of overcoming fear (1936). Here, again, according to psychoanalytical interpretation, the child may become anxious not simply because of the direct threat of loss but indirectly as a reaction against the hostility he feels by virtue of the threat of deprivation. Klein (1932) describes a 4-year-old's fear of being left alone as arising from the child's desire to injure her mother who was pregnant.

A child's disposition to be frightened may also be influenced by the *example of fear shown by his parents*. In a study conducted by the interview method, Hagman (1932) found many similarities between the fears of mothers and the fears of children of preschool age. During World War II, John (1941) found that a young child's fears and the persistence of after-effects following an alarming event, such as an air raid, are likely to be influenced to a marked degree by the extent to which his elders are calm or display terror. When a parent shows fear he tells the child, in effect, that there is danger afoot, and the fact that the parent is afraid perhaps also has the effect of lowering the child's confidence in the parent's ability to protect him from this danger.

Physical Weakness or Handicap. A child's disposition to be apprehensive may be affected by anything that physically weakens him or lowers his capacity, such as *illness* or a *physical handicap*. Stratton (1929) reports that college students who had a history of many illnesses during childhood are likely to exhibit more fear reactions than persons who have been free from serious illness. Not only is illness debilitating in itself but also it may have many psychological consequences by way of overprotection, interference with normal development of independence and self-help, effects on the growing child's ideas about himself and his worth, which indirectly can have a bearing on his anxieties and fears. In a study by Pintner and Brunschwig (1937) *deaf* children of school age reported more fears than children with normal hearing. In a study of *blind* people in the age range from 10 to 21 years, Boutonier and Henri (1946) found that the fears of the blind were aggravated by their difficulty in visually imagining and identifying noises. Their fear of loud noises was aggravated by the fact that such noises mask feebler sounds on which they depend for spatial orientation. They were also subject to shock when suddenly touching something without visual forewarning such as a normal person would have.[1]

Stresses in the Process of Development. Various *hurdles in the process of development* may also involve the child in circumstances that influence his fears. We have already pointed to examples of these.

Conditions contributing to anxiety may occur in connection with the child's *sexual development*. In connection with the prac-

[1] A survey of studies dealing with adjustment to physical handicap and illness has been prepared by Barker, Wright, and Gonick (1946).

tice of masturbation, children are frequently subjected to treatment that arouses shame and guilt and fear concerning their present integrity and future well-being. In a study published in 1937, Pullias found that about 7 out of 10 first-year college boys in his group had received information sometime during childhood or adolescence that the practice of masturbation would lead to serious mental damage, and about the same number had been informed that it would lead to serious physical damage. At the time of the study, over 80 per cent of the college boys stated that they believed that masturbation would produce some form of serious harm either mental or physical or both.

In a survey of the sex practices of boys, Ramsey (1943) found that about 73 per cent reported that they had had experience with masturbation by the age of 12, and about a third reported that they had attempted heterosexual intercourse before adolescence. Many of the boys (exact details are not given) reported that they were worried and afraid by reason of their sex interests. The physical changes that occur in sexual development, notably with the onset of puberty, may also arouse fear. In a study by Landis, Landis, and Bolles (1940) it was found that many women reported that they were emotionally disturbed by their first menstruation, but others were untroubled by this development, or proud of it.

With the onset of puberty some children also are worried by aspects of their physical development that influence their appearance (Stone and Barker, 1939).

According to Freudian theory, there are many other hurdles in the development of sexuality that expose a child to emotional stress. Some psychoanalysts maintain that children are subject to feelings of anxiety or hostility (or both) when they discover the genital differences betwen the two sexes

(see, e.g., Levy, 1940). Findings by Conn (1940) did not reveal that such reactions are typical in normal children.

After-Effects of Severe Fright. After an especially harrowing and frightening event a child (like an adult) may for a time show a heightened tendency to be afraid of the thing that scared him and of other things, besides (John, 1941).

The after-effects of a particular frightening experience probably will be more severe in a child who has a past history of being anxious and emotionally disturbed than in a child who hitherto has been quite stable. In line with this, it was observed in England during the second world war that children who already suffered from anxieties in connection with their everyday home life were more likely to be anxious about being evacuated from home than children who had a happy home life (see, e.g., Burbury, 1941; Davidson and Slade, 1940; Isaacs, Brown, and Thouless, 1941; John, 1941).

Stresses Which Threaten Self-Esteem or Self-Acceptance. Anything that lowers a child's confidence in himself, anything that threatens his self-regard or threatens to disturb the rôle he wishes or pretends to play or threatens to block goals which he regards as important, may increase his tendency to be anxious or afraid.

Blows to Self-Esteem at School. Many of the circumstances that affect a child's self-esteem arise in connection with his life at school. At school, children are exposed to failure, or the threat of failure, on a colossal scale. Even when customary competitive trappings are eliminated, such as public marks and ratings, being labeled as a "slow learner," being "kept back" to repeat a grade, and the like, the academic and the social setting is such that the children become involved in many competitive situations of their own making. School is the situation in which children try themselves out in countless ways, realize their strengths, and discover many of their weaknesses and limitations.

Some schools have standards and policies that foredoom many children to repeated failure. Sandin (1944) has described the emotional impact on children of being officially stamped as failures at school when told that they will not be promoted to the next grade.

Apart from failure in this stark form, the school may function as a proving ground in which the child is plagued by weaknesses and disorders which have arisen in connection with his life at home. In a study by Hattwick and Stowell (1936) it was observed that children who were "pushed" or "babied" by their parents had more social and academic difficulties at school than children who were not subject to such treatment. An especially acute disorder involving fear directed toward the school has been described by several writers as a "school phobia" (Johnson et al., 1941; Van Houten, 1947–1948; Jacobsen, 1947–1948). This phobia has been regarded as a result of emotional conflict which does not originate in experiences in school but is precipitated by something that happens in school. Several writers, in reporting factors associated with this phobia, have mentioned, among other matters, disturbances in the relationships between the children and their mothers, including inconsistency and frustration on the mothers' part, complicated by other happenings in their lives, and, on the children's part, aggressive impulses toward a parent on whom they are very dependent, and a tendency to make demands and to dominate. In a discussion of conditions underlying children's reluctance to go to school, E. Klein (1945) maintains that "all of a child's worries, fears, anxieties, self-consciousness, feelings of inadequacy, his relations to his parents, to his siblings, and to himself tend to gain reflection in the school situation" (p. 263).

The possibility of failure in meeting the demands of the school is mentioned by a large proportion of children when they report what they "worry" about (Zeligs, 1939; Hicks and Hayes, 1938; Pintner and Lev, 1940; Jersild, Goldman, and Loftus, 1941; Pressey and Robinson, 1944).

Conflicting Tendencies and Impulses. Apart from the effects of external threats or reminders of failure and other circumstances that might endanger his self-regard, a child's tendency to be anxious or afraid may be greatly influenced by conflicting tendencies and impulses within himself. In drawing attention to such conflicts and inner defenses, Freud has made a profound contribution to the understanding of human emotions which has wide application whether or not we accept all his theories concerning the nature and cause of conflict.

Theories of Anxiety

The foregoing statements concerning conditions that predispose or contribute to fear or anxiety touch on circumstances which have been emphasized in current prominent theories of the origin of anxiety. But to single out some of the theories for further discussion might help to crystallize certain research issues for developmental psychology. In this area there is great need for direct longitudinal study of children. Much of the theoretical structure underlying present-day concepts of anxiety has been built upon findings gained from work with people in the process of undergoing psychological treatment or from laboratory studies which may or may not duplicate the realities of life as faced by the growing child.

We have already alluded to some features of Freud's (1936) accounts of anxiety. He expresses the opinion that a certain predisposition to anxiety is undoubtedly present in the infant. It is not at its maximum immediately after birth but "first makes its appearance later on with the progress of psychic development" (p. 98). Among "instances of the expression of anxiety in infancy" are those arising in response to the three situations of being left alone, being in the dark, and finding a strange person in place of the one in whom the child has confidence (the mother). And these, according to Freud, are all reducible to a single situation, that of feeling the loss of the loved (longed-for) person (p. 99). He conjectures that the most basic anxiety of all, the "primal anxiety" of birth, arises in connection with separation from the mother (p. 100). He says further in line with this that the situation that the infant appraises as danger and against which it desires reassurance is one of not being gratified. It involves a situation of deprivation. Along the same line he says that "object loss" is the precondition of anxiety, and such a loss appears not only in the early anxiety arising from the loss (separation from the mother) but also in the "next transformation of anxiety," the castration anxiety, which involves a danger of separation from the genital which is "tantamount to a second separation from the mother" (p. 103) for the reason that possession of the genital organ contains a guarantee of reunion with the mother (or a mother substitute) in the act of coitus. And the loss of the organ would mean the loss of this guarantee.

Freud states that in the normal process of development children outgrow their susceptibility to anxiety-producing situations such as a morbid fear of being alone, or of being in the dark, or of strangers. Many phobias of animals likewise are outgrown, according to Freud. But many people continue as adults to remain infantile in their response to danger, continuing to react with anxiety to situations which should have long ceased to arouse it, and "it is

exactly such persons whom we call neurotics" (p. 120).

We have earlier referred to Freud's (1936) classic case of little Hans who had a phobia of horses. He feared that he might be bitten by a horse. Underlying this fear in little Hans was an anxiety stemming from an ambivalent attitude toward his father. He had an Oedipus conflict: he was jealous and hostile toward his father, but he also loved him. He felt hostile, but he also had reason to fear retaliation. His father might punish, might mutilate (castrate) him, and it was "because of castration anxiety that little Hans renounces aggression against his father" (p. 48). His phobia of the horse was an attempt to deal with this conflict. He hit upon a horse as the object of his phobia partly by reason of having once actually seen a horse fall down and he had also seen a playmate fall and hurt himself while playing "horsie." Hans displaced or "detoured" his hostility from the father to the horse. His repressed "instinctual" hostile impulse toward his father was represented in a wish on his part that his father should fall down and hurt himself as had the horse and his playmate. The hidden force behind the repression of hostility toward the father was castration anxiety, and the manifest content of the anxiety, being bitten by a horse, was a "distortion of and substitute for another content, that of being castrated by the father" (p. 49).

Elsewhere Freud says, in more general terms, "anxiety is the reaction to a situation of danger," and the symptoms of anxiety are created in order to avoid the danger situation of which anxiety sounds the alarm (p. 82).

In the foregoing review of Freud's statements, there is the view that anxiety may arise by reason of loss of or threatened separation from the loved object (mother), and also the idea that anxiety may arise because of conflict between incompatible impulses and tendencies (Hans's "instinctual" hostility toward his father clashed with fear of his father). To subsume both of these under one theory, on the ground that the latter, by involving "castration anxiety," also has the meaning of threatened separation from the mother, involves rather complicated speculation.[1] If the two are to be combined it might be better, in this writer's opinion, on the theory that both the separation anxiety and the anxiety arising from hostility toward the father represent conditions which threaten to remove, destroy, or disturb a relationship between the child and someone who is very important to his survival and his development.[2]

We have earlier referred to theories of anxiety set forth by Horney and Sullivan. Although these have not been documented by systematic longitudinal studies of young children, each has the great merit of interpreting anxiety in the context of a systematic theory of personality development and each involves a concept of developmental continuity even though many developmental details need to be filled in or inferred, especially at the early childhood level.

Horney (1939) advances a concept of basic anxiety consisting of a feeling of helplessness toward a potentially hostile world. Anxiety of this kind leads to the development of neurotic defenses and is, in this respect, different from the kind of anxiety which may be aroused by dangers to life and limb, through illness and overwhelming forces of nature. Anxiety develops in an environment which is unreliable, unjust, and cruel, which thwarts the child's free use of his energies and undermines his self-esteem and self-reliance. This is something more comprehensive than Freud's concept, as stated above. According to Horney's concept, the child does not simply fear punishment or desertion because of forbidden drives; rather, a harsh environment as a whole is dreaded as something which is a menace to his development. Such an environment threatens not simply an instinctual desire but the child's individuality, his whole way of life, for his security and his opportunity to develop and to make free use of his resources and to draw upon his potentialities for growth depend upon the adults who have him in their care.[3]

Since it would be dangerous for the child directly to give vent to hostility which is aroused by restrictive treatment, he resorts, according to Horney's account, to certain defenses and strategies in an effort to cope with the world. Depending on a combination of many factors, he may adopt a strategy of trying to assume control over others, a strategy supported by aggressive, expansive, and competitive behavior traits

---

[1] The concept that a boy fears that his father might castrate him represents, it seems to this writer, something even more recondite than the concept of anxiety.

[2] Mowrer (No. 3 in Part I in Hoch and Zubin's *Anxiety*, 1950) has presented a theory of anxiety which takes its lead from Freud's work, but instead of regarding anxiety as arising out of "repressed id" he sees anxiety as representing "repressed superego." Anxiety does not come by reason of repressed instinctual impulses, according to his view. It is "simply the conscious manifestation of unconscious, repressed, repudiated guilt" (p. 28).

[3] The position that frustrations and discrepancies represent the primary source of disturbance in early personality development (as distinguished from early instinctual aggression) has also been set forth by Lauretta Bender (No. 7 in Part IV in Hoch and Zubin's *Anxiety*, 1950). Bender regards anxiety which occurs "as a response to early instinctual aggression" as a matter of secondary importance. She reports that a "serious deformity in personality may occur in a child when there is a critical change in parent relationships before the latter part of the first half-year of life" (p. 121). She regards this as the period when children "first identify their parents and show a definite and individual relationship to people around them" (p. 121). But personality distortion may also be produced, according to her observations, by a very critical break in total family identification during the second, third, and fourth years.

that serve his struggle to vie with others, to go against them, to outdo or rise above. Or he may adopt a strategy of withdrawing within himself, with a predominant tendency to remain aloof and detached. Or he may adopt a self-effacing, compliant, conforming type of behavior. But such strategies (which may appear in mixed forms) provide an expedient and not a solution. To the extent that they are stratagems rather than an authentic expression of the child's nature, they represent something devious and ulterior—a pose, an assumed rôle, rather than the real person. When the individual becomes committed to such an assumed rôle he is, in effect, showing alienation from himself.

In the process of living up to the assumed rôle, defending it and protecting it from being exposed and destroyed, the individual continues and aggravates the process of alienation from self. This condition is burdensome because the realities of life continually threaten the pose that the person has taken.

As the child develops, he will, according to Horney (1939, 1950), acquire a large variety of inhibitions, subsidiary techniques, assumed values, and acquired sensitivities in the service of the strategies he uses in his relationships with other people. The person with a trend toward aggressiveness and competitiveness reacts to others as though they were against him but from an early age he may conceal this tendency under a front of politeness and good fellowship.

The person whose pose is to show a compliant trend has a need to be accepted, liked, wanted, and appreciated, but the "genuine portion" of the urge for affection and approval is "heavily overshadowed by his insatiable urge to feel safe" (p. 51).

The person who takes the way of withdrawal and detachment in interpersonal relationships does not show simply a desire to be alone at times but a form of estrangement from people, a compulsion to put an emotional distance between himself and others, even though he may succeed in putting on an act of getting along very well with others. The detached person eventually develops many forms of behavior in the service of an indiscriminate need not to be influenced, coerced, obligated, or tied to someone else.

These disturbances in *interpersonal* relationships, according to Horney's theory, produce disorders in the *"intrapsychic"* sphere—in the child's own subjective view of himself and relation to himself. In the process of developing artifices and stratagems in coping with others he becomes estranged from himself. In coping with others he is forced to override his genuine feelings, wishes, and thoughts. He is not, as Horney puts it, the driver but the driven. He is divided in the sense that he cannot freely enjoy and freely express his own feelings and thoughts but must subdue them in the interest of safety. He cannot freely be himself. In assuming a front in his relations with others he also adopts a front within himself. Having subordinated his own thoughts and feelings in his defense against others, he has in a sense surrendered the stuff out of which his growing self might develop and evolve.

What emerges is a distorted self different from what might be called the real self. What Horney has called an idealized self comes into being. This represents a kind of pseudo-identity through which the child achieves a false kind of integration and inner rationale for the stratagems and techniques, the "solutions" which he has been driven to adopt in his dealings with others. He needs something that will give him a hold, a feeling of identity, something that would make him meaningful to himself and give him a feeling of significance. Whereas the real or potential self represents all the individual's resources for growth and fulfillment, the idealized self represents what a person is according to an irrational image of what he is or should be. If he feels driven to comply indiscriminately or to be aggressive or detached he does not see these artifices in their true light. He may, for example, see his aggressiveness as a form of strength, as something heroic, marking him with qualities of leadership.

Moreover, according to Horney, the person may even succeed in reconciling (to himself) the contradictory tendencies that occur when trends clash (as would occur when a predominantly compliant person has the impulse to assert himself), and he sees these contradictory tendencies as features of a rich personality—he has the resources not only for being meek and humble but also for being strong.

The idealized image, according to Horney's position, is not a matter of convenience that suddenly comes into being. It develops through time. It serves as a precipitate of the individual's mode of dealing with himself and with others. As one writer has put it, it "consolidates" the individual's defenses, it concretizes them into an integrated whole, "it becomes the epitomy of the defense system" (Gershman, 1950).

Anxiety occurs when this system of defense is tampered with or threatened. Anxiety which originally occurred in the individual's relationship with others now arises by reason of incompatible tendencies within himself. Anxiety is aroused when the neurotic "solution" is threatened. As Gershman (1950) puts it, "the total anxiety of a person is a measure of the discrepancy between the idealized image and the real self."

Some features of this account are easier to verify than others. A child is ignored or harshly punished; he suffers, cringes, feels abused, but is afraid to strike back. So far the process is fairly clear. He adopts a strategy to protect himself from abuse by being, say, very "good" (compliant), and we can see how he can adopt such a strategy without necessarily being very deliberate or conscious of it. But when we move to the next step, as in Horney's account, and bring in the concept of alienation from self, the concept of an idealized image which involves an internal integration of the stratagem or solution the child has adopted to fend for himself in his relations with others, we move from what can be observed and verified to a process which cannot so readily be traced step by step through a series of observable developments. But this difficulty appears, it seems to the writer, in connection with all theories, psychoanalytic or otherwise, which in one way or another attach importance to subjective processes that occur before the child can perceive or formulate in words matters of importance that are happening to him.

This does not negate the truth of a theory, but it does make it more complicated. One trouble about theories of anxiety is that the theories themselves are somewhat anxiety-provoking to those who have to try to express them in their own words. Perhaps this is one reason why so many psychologists for so many years were so easily seduced into following the simplified version of emotional development proposed some decades ago by John B. Watson.

Sullivan's (1947) theory of anxiety likewise is tied to a concept of the developing self and the dependence of the child upon others. According to him, a person comes into being in an interpersonal field. The development of the self in the little child is intimately and intricately tied to the child's relationship with others, especially those nearest to him, the "significant" person or persons in his early life. The self, while it is a highly individual phenomenon, has social origins. The attitudes of the person or persons in whose close care the child lives from hour to hour and from day to day constitute the emotional climate, the psychological environment, in which the process of self-discovery and self-development takes place.

According to Sullivan, the infant feels the approving and disapproving attitudes of significant people in his environment before he is able clearly to perceive what is going on. There is what he calls interpersonal induction of anxiety. Anxiety is induced by the disapproval of people who are significant within the child's interpersonal world. In due time the child is able to perceive approval and disapproval and to recognize the actions or circumstances which bring approval or disapproval, and he becomes alert to signs of approval or disapproval in others. The self-dynamism is built out of experiences of approbation and disapproval, reward and punishment. According to Sullivan, approval brings comfort and satisfaction whereas disapproval brings discomfort, and such discomfort, at a stage of development at which the child is incapable of a clear perception of what is happening to him, may be the origin of a condition of anxiety. The "good mother" is associated with relaxation; the "evil mother," with the undergoing of anxiety (1948, p. 10).

According to Sullivan, the attitudes of significant persons toward the young child have a crucial bearing upon his developing attitudes toward himself. The self is made up of "reflected appraisals." "The child's earliest self-appraisal is in terms of what others think and feel about him. If these appraisals are chiefly derogatory (as they will be for a child with parents who impose unbearable demands on him or otherwise reject him or ignore him), the growing child's attitude toward himself will be chiefly derogatory. The kind of interpersonal re-

lationships that induce anxiety are also the source of intrapersonal anxiety. In the older person, anxiety is aroused by anything that threatens the "self-system." Anxiety intervenes to ward off experiences which might keep a person from living in his accustomed way. Anxiety helps to ward off awareness of tendencies in the individual's personality which have not been integrated with the self the individual conceives and approves. Anxiety, thus conceived, has the effect of safeguarding the morbid condition of the self which arose as a defense against earlier anxiety-producing circumstances, which continue to render a person subject to anxiety. It serves as a defense against the danger of self-discovery.

OVERCOMING FEAR

Numerous methods of dealing with fear have been applied in everyday dealings with children, and many of them have also been tried out under experimental conditions. In a review of such methods, English and Pearson (1945) maintain that they touch only upon the *conscious* aspect of the situation. According to English and Pearson, these measures are only supplemental to the aid the child should have in dealing with the real causes of his phobias.

Probably all would agree that it is important in dealing with fear to try to dispose of both the conscious and the unconscious elements that may be involved. But we need more clarification of how operations on a conscious level might also have an influence on the unconscious level.

In connection with his own studies of fear, the writer has the impression that when a child is helped to overcome a "fear" which a psychiatrist might label as a "phobia" there is also a possibility that the child can gain relief from (or greater strength in dealing with) the condition that underlies the fear or phobia. A child who has with help "overcome" an intense fear of dogs actually may have undergone an experience that extends beyond the mere removal of a symptom. He has faced up against what to him was an objective danger. In the process he may have gained a changed conception of himself and more confidence in his ability to deal with his problems. Any such gain in self-reliance might involve a significant change in the total subjective environment, the self-system. At least, there is this possibility. We can accept this as a possibility in some circumstances and still recognize that in many other situations the steps taken to cope with the conscious or objective aspect of a phobia may have little or no influence on the underlying anxiety.

In an experimental study of methods of eliminating fear, M. C. Jones (1924b) used a number of procedures described as the methods of disuse, verbal appeal, negative adaptation, repression, distraction, direct conditioning, and social imitation. Only the methods of direct conditioning and social imitation proved to be very successful. Hagman (1932) found that when mothers used the method of explanation alone it was unfruitful in a large number of cases, but it was superior to no treatment at all. Explanation was more effective when combined with exposure to the situation. Conn (1941) has described the use of a play-interview technique for helping children to understand and to cope with their fears.

Findings in an investigation by Jersild and Holmes (1935c) by means of interviews with parents and reports by other observers, and results in a later experimental study by Holmes (1935), confirm some of the findings mentioned above and emphasize other procedures.

Greatest success was reported for procedures that helped the child to gain increased competence and skill, aided him in finding practical methods of his own for dealing with the feared situation, and helped him by degrees to have active experience with, or successful direct participation in, the feared situation. Probably, as suggested above, this procedure was effective in some instances because it helped the child to acquire a changed conception of his ability to cope with his weakness and this might entail a changed attitude toward himself.

In an experimental study in which efforts were made to foster active experience with feared situations and skill in handling them, Holmes (1936) worked with 13 children who were afraid to enter a dark room. After 3 to 7 exposures each child in the experiment entered the room alone, without hesitation or requests for company, felt his way through the darkness, turned on the light, and retrieved the ball. Although, as Holmes points out, the results do not indicate whether the gains made by the children would transfer to other situations, the findings, as far as they go, have practical implications.

In another experiment, Holmes worked with 2 children who showed fear of walking across a plank at a height of 4 feet. After 8 exposures, one of the children (aged 39 months) walked the length of the board alone at a height of 6 feet. She also walked happily at the same altitude after 1 exposure to a modified apparatus that was set up in a different situation. The other child also made progress at first, but then reverted to earlier forms of behavior. His problem, as shown by his response to the experiment and by other information, was obviously more complicated than a simple fear of walking on an elevation.

This case emphasizes that direct dealings with a fear which apparently represents an underlying anxiety may fail to have much effect.

Children themselves often are eager to come to grips with fears that impede their everyday activities, and they will sometimes devise quite ingenious ways of their own to gain mastery over a feared situation (Jersild and Holmes, 1935a, 1935c).

A study by Shaffer (1947) of fear and courage during aerial combat confirms and supplements findings from children regarding factors that aggravate and that help to relieve fears. Information was gained from over 4000 fliers after return from combat, practically all of whom reported that they were afraid on every mission. From this study it appears that forewarning about a known danger with ensuing anticipation of it aggravated fear: more showed fear when a mission was known well in advance than when it was announced suddenly. Among the conditions that reduced fear in combat were: confidence and morale (confidence in equipment, crew, etc.) and effective activity (keeping busy, concentrating on the job, on making a good hit, or on other constructive activities). On the other hand, fear increased by helplessness and hopelessness, including inability to fight back, having to be idle while in danger, and being insecure about the future. The finding that helplessness aggravates fear and that ability to control or cope with an anticipated painful event reduces fear also has emerged from experimental work with rats (Mowrer and Viek, 1948).

Overcoming Anxiety through Psychotherapy and Psychoanalysis. We will not in this chapter attempt to review the vast clinical literature dealing with psychotherapy as applied to anxiety or to personality disorders in general. In this area, as in others, there are differences of theory and practical approach, but we will touch briefly on only a few points that are of more or less general interest.

One significant observation, in the writer's opinion, is that concepts which are prominent in current theories in psycho-therapy and psychoanalysis are becoming more and more illuminating when applied to the psychology of everyday life. Many concepts which owe their origin directly or indirectly to the genius of Freud are taking on an added meaning. Theories pertaining to the self (as set forth by writers such as Horney; Rogers, 1942; and Sullivan), concepts pertaining to self-acceptance, self-rejection, the developmental continuity of the self-system, the concept of defenses of the ego (or self), and the concept of alienation from self are as important in understanding children and our everyday adult associates as in understanding the character of a patient.

A great impetus to the understanding of the mature individual also is offered by the concept (explicit in our developmental literature and emphasized also more and more in many psychoanalytic writings) that the *developmental continuity* that links the "mature" personality to early childhood occurs in the form of pervasive trends or tendencies in the total personality structure and not simply by way of an isolated episode or a limited and hidden "traumatic event" or a failure to scale a particular hypothetical hurdle, such as the "oral phase" of "pregenital" development.

The concept of *interpersonal relationships* helps in understanding the great range and variety of factors involved in the social origins of the child's ideas concerning himself (and of self-acceptance and alienation from self).

The concept of *resistance,* long recognized especially in psychoanalytic work, has important implications in connection with the emotional behavior of the "normal" child and the resistance to learning that takes place in the child's life at school and in his relationships with his peers and parents. Lecky (1945) has offered an interesting discussion of this matter. A person seeks to protect and preserve his picture of himself; he strives for self-consistency, and he will resist or try to avoid or reject experiences that threaten to modify or require a re-examination of a cherished view of the self. This concept of resistance helps to throw light on much of the behavior a child shows at home, and it certainly throws light on the vast amount of evasive shadow-boxing in school that goes on under the name of "not being interested" or under the label of "free discussion" at the elementary, high school, college, and post-college levels, and even under the label of "research." This concept also carries with it, the writer believes, the principle that the process of learning involved in revising a concept and attitudes pertaining to the self is likely to be painful. Learning that actually involves an inner revision is likely to hurt, whether the education producing it is offered in the office of a clinical psychologist, or on a psychoanalytic couch, or in the classroom of an ordinary school.

The concept of *transference*, which also has held an important place in psychoanalytic theory, likewise has important ramifications in everyday life. The feelings of hostility, affection, grievance, and the like, which a client or patient projects on to the person who is treating him, may, at moments, be more intense but they are not different in kind from the feelings which a person brings with him into his relationships with people at large.

ANGER, HOSTILITY, AND AGGRESSIVENESS

Anger, like fear, is a response to a threatening circumstance, but in anger the impulse is to move against rather than to move away from the source of the disturbance.

Anger is a response to thwarting under circumstances in which the individual is not completely at a loss or momentarily overwhelmed as in terror.[1] The circumstances that give rise to anger range from those in which a person is restrained from bodily movement to circumstances in which he perceives or believes that his desires, expectations, ideas, or his pride and self-esteem are or might be under attack.

The term *anger*, like the term *fear*, denotes a vast variety and gradation of responses including momentary outbursts of rage, temper tantrums involving a great amount of undirected activity, and more prolonged and recurring states such as those involving chronic feelings of hostility or milder forms of annoyance, sulkiness, and peevishness.[2]

Developmental Changes. The occasions that elicit anger parallel the course of development. A child's susceptibility to anger at any given maturity level is influenced by the *limitations* and by the *urges, strivings*, and *activity tendencies* that are characteristic of that level. As examples, we may note the anger of a young child who wants to put an object in his mouth but lacks the proper motor coordination; the anger of a child who lacks physical strength to dislodge his wagon when it is stuck; the anger of a child who is eagerly "learning" to walk but is hindered; the anger of a school-age child who, as a feature of his social development, has a strong desire to "belong" to a certain group but is blocked by a dominant member; the anger of an adolescent whose urge to make a favorable impression on the opposite sex is thwarted, or who is reminded of his child-

[1] A somewhat more specialized characterization of anger has been offered by Lazell (1929), who maintains that anger afflicts only those who refuse to permit themselves to become conscious of their inferiorities or failures.

[2] Logre and Fouquet (1940–1941) have drawn a distinction between "exasperation" and other emotions such as anger and hysteria. Exasperation, they say, is the "anger of the weak."

ish characteristics when he especially wants to appear mature and independent.

The most systematic evidence concerning anger in young children is provided in a study by Goodenough (1931b) in which parents cooperated in observing and recording anger episodes. In the case of the children who were less than 1 year old, one-fourth of all outbursts arose in connection with routine care such as dressing or bathing. Minor physical discomforts were reported as responsible for about one-fourth of the outbursts. Direct restriction of bodily movements accounted for slightly over 6 per cent of the outbursts.

At 2 years, a large percentage of anger outbursts arose in connection with the establishment of routine physical habits, and second in frequency were conflicts with authority over matters not directly concerned with habit training. Problems of social relationship represented a third important source of difficulty. Provocations arising in connection with matters of self-help or minor physical discomfort or restriction of bodily movement were less prominent.

At the 2-to-3-year level, the three outstanding sources of provocation were conflicts with authority, difficulties connected with the establishment of routine physical habits, and social difficulties with playmates. Between the ages of 3 and 4 years, provocations arising in connection with social difficulties and disagreement with playmates reached their maximum, and conflicts with authority accounted for about one-third of the outbursts that were noted. At 4 years and upward, difficulties arising in connection with social relations continued to represent the most frequent sources of provocation. Next in order came difficulties arising over physical habits and conflicts with authority over matters not connected with physical habits or self-help.

Unfortunately, there are no studies at the school age and adolescent levels similar to the study Goodenough made of younger children. Moreover, the Goodenough study, rich as it is in facts about the young child, offers only a limited amount of information concerning the interplay of anger-provoking situations or episodes (as described above) and the basic or pervasive attitudes of the parent toward his child. Goodenough's observations suggest that situations leading to anger in the child are more likely to occur in his home if parents are inclined to be anxious. From everyday observation one can get the impression that the more a parent is troubled and torn by conflicts the more occasions there will be for the child to be troubled. But even in the most serene home there are bound to be frictions and thwartings leading to anger. It would be helpful if we had a clearer conception of the phenomenon of anger as a frank and inevitable reaction to the robust realities of life as distinguished from the play of irascibility and peevishness which springs from hidden anxieties.

As a child grows older and as his relations with people outside the home become increasingly important to him, there is an increase in frequency of annoyances pertaining to people other than his relatives (Jersild and Tasch, 1949), just as nonrelatives play an increasing rôle in his everyday joys and satisfactions.

In a study of 250 junior high school pupils, aged 11 to 16 years, by means of interviews and other methods, Hicks and Hayes (1938) found that the following circumstances, in order of frequency, most often made the children angry: being teased; people being unfair to them; a sibling taking their property or imposing on them; people lying to them; things not going right; people being sarcastic; and people being bossy (p. 233). Most of these conditions, it can be seen, relate to people and characteristics of people that infringe on the child's comfort, his pride, or his conception of what others have the right to do to him or expect of him. One item on the list indicates that friction between siblings is still an important source of annoyance to children in their early teens.

In a study including both junior and senior high school pupils and dealing specifically with conflicts between children and their mothers, Block (1937) found that 71 per cent of the young people checked an item to the effect that they were disturbed by having their mothers hold brothers or sisters up to them as models of behavior. Many other items pertaining to desires for independence, nagging of various kinds, restrictions of various sorts, were also checked with high frequency. Many children (half of the boys and over four-fifths of the girls) also reported that they had been disturbed because the mother insisted that they must take a brother or sister with them wherever they went.

Findings such as these indicate that the child's need to protect his pride, his independence, and his self-respect represents the most important basis for anger.[1]

At the adolescent level, many children are annoyed not only by specific parental practices but also by parental traits and habits (Stott, 1940).

At the college level, Gates (1926) likewise found that people more often caused anger than things. Meltzer (1933) also found that conditions arising in connection with social relationships were a frequent cause of anger at the college level. Another frequent cause was failure in activities that had been undertaken.

The fact that there are many conditions in everyday life which continue to be an-

noying to people over a wide age range has been brought out in a study by Alexander (1946), who questioned people in the age range from 10 to 50 concerning their antipathies, and in a study by Conrad and Jones (1942), who obtained information concerning the annoyance encountered by a sampling of about 300 children yearly for a period of about 5 years beginning in the sixth grade.

FACTORS CONTRIBUTING TO SUSCEPTIBILITY TO ANGER

Among the circumstances in the environment that made children more susceptible to anger in Goodenough's study were the following: the presence of many adults or many older siblings in the family group; visitors; a tendency on the part of a child's elders to be critical or overanxious or uncertain, or inclined to nag about small matters; a concern about the moral goodness or badness of the child's behavior rather than its appropriateness from a developmental or situational point of view; inconsistency in discipline; past experience in gaining objectives by a show of anger.

Among the organic factors noted by Goodenough (1931b) as contributing to increased irascibility were the child's state of health as indicated by colds, bed-wetting, constipation, etc.; delays in feeding; the presence of fatigue and previous sleeplessness. The influence of factors such as fatigue and hunger on emotional susceptibility has been noted also by Gates (1926) and Young (1937) in studies of college students. Stratton (1929) found that adults who had a history of illness during early childhood tended to be somewhat more subject to anger than persons who had no history of serious illness.

Another factor that directly or indirectly disposes a child to anger is the assignment of tasks that are very difficult or impos-

[1] Hostility associated with sibling rivalry is treated in a separate section below.

sible for him to perform (Dembo, 1931; Keister and Updegraff, 1937); restrictions in space, both psychological and physical, or having to stay within rigid confines may increase tension that leads to aggressive feelings (Lewin, Lippitt, and White, 1939).

Varieties of Expression of Anger and Hostility

The infant's first expressions of anger involve much diffuse, poorly coordinated behavior. The most frequent single expression of anger in early childhood is crying, but this diminishes with age. Goodenough (1931b) observed that before the age of a year the child's outbursts of anger are rather explosive in nature, not well designed to remove a thwarting obstacle or to fight off an offender. As the child grows older his behavior when angry becomes less random and more directly aimed at something or someone. At the age of 4, about half the expressions of anger were found to be aimed at the object of the children's wrath. With this change toward calculated and directed behavior there also was an increase in retaliative behavior of a sort which denoted a desire to get revenge. Goodenough found that threats began to appear between the ages of 2 and 3 and increased in frequency thereafter.

No sooner has a child acquired the ability to direct his anger at the object of his wrath than he comes under pressure to inhibit his expression of anger. For a child to give vent to his anger is uncomfortable and annoying to others and it may even be dangerous to others or to the child himself. The child is not only only under strong and sometimes violent pressure from others to inhibit outward show of anger but he also discovers that if he attacks he is likely to provoke a counterattack. So in the process of development human beings learn a great variety of ways of giving vent to anger and hostility other than in open and direct attack.

Verbal Aggression. At an early age children express their resentment verbally rather than by physical violence. A shift with age toward more bickering and quarreling and less fighting appears notably in connection with children's quarrels at the preschool level. The means of verbal attack which a child is able to learn by the time he reaches maturity are practically endless. They include direct methods, such as calling the other person bad. They include, from an early age, *verbal denial of affection,* which may be expressed directly ("I don't like you"), or indirectly by calling attention to the lovable qualities of someone else.

Verbal aggression may also take the form of assertions of superiority by the aggressor ("I can lick you"; "I've got ten thousand marbles") or by assertions aimed to belittle the offender.

It is largely by verbal means, also, that a large variety of indirect forms of attack are carried out, ranging from simple forms of tattling to gossip and slander designed to injure another person's name.

Teasing. Teasing is a frequent way of expressing hostility, especially in relations between children. Teasing can be developed into such a fine art that the blame is placed on the one who is teased when at last he loses his temper and continues with his fists a fight which his adversary started with words.

Swearing. The function of swearing in relieving the tension associated with aggressive feelings has been examined by Montagu (1942), who notes that social taboos have restricted women from swearing, and when not allowed to swear, women substitute the more infantile reaction of weeping. With increasing social emancipation, according to this line of thought, we may perhaps expect women more and more to renounce weeping in favor of swearing.

There has been no developmental study of swearing, as far as the writer knows. It is a common expectation in our culture that children, like women, will not swear (or, at least, not swear as much as men). Many boys who are destined to do a great deal of swearing do not begin in earnest until they are of adolescent age. It is interesting to note that while swearing is in many respects an infantile form of response, it usually does not appear habitually until the child has "matured" well beyond the infantile level.

Expressions of Hostility in Fantasy and Play. From an early age aggressive impulses occur prominently in children's fantasy and overt make-believe play. Hostile feelings may occur in connection with an imaginary plot or counterattack which includes imaginary scenes in which the individual is superior to the offender, or scores a triumph of wit, or calls him names, or witnesses him actually coming to grief through tripping, stumbling, or some other accident or misfortune. Imaginings of this sort are especially prevalent in connection with anger experiences in adults (Richardson, 1918), and they probably appear, in one form or another, as soon as children are able to pursue an imaginary theme in their own thoughts.

The fact that a child in his play may reveal feelings of hostility (as well as other feelings, such as anxiety and desires for recognition and approval) has made the use of play situations a very productive technique in connection both with research and with therapy with children. When provided with a suitable play setting it has been observed that a large proportion of children will show aggressive behavior of one sort or another. In a study by Baruch (1941) which used dolls representing children's families, 32 of 46 preschool children

within a period of 15 minutes showed aggression in ways such as: separating a single member of the family from others, spanking, burying a member, and calling names.

Although it is an easy matter to provide a play setting in which children will show aggressive behavior, it is not a simple matter to tell what such behavior means. There may be a clear discrepancy between the kind of aggressive behavior a child shows in play and the kind of treatment he receives from his parents. One child who is not spanked by his parents may freely spank the doll he plays with; another who is often spanked may not allow himself to spank the baby doll. There may be a discrepancy also between what the child does in a make-believe setting and what he does in actuality (on the playground with other children, or with his family at home), and what he *says* he does or would do (Fite, 1940).

In a study by Korner (1947), play materials, incomplete stories, and frustrating situations were used with children aged 4 to 6. Expressions of hostility which children revealed included direct expression of hostility; retaliation in kind, such as spanking if the parents spank; open spite; verbal rejection; ridicule. Other, less direct, expressions of hostility included destructiveness; hostility carried out by an external agent, such as having another child in the doll family inflict punishment on the person who causes the frustration; hostility displaced, on to others, such as having the child hit other children rather than the offending father or mother; hostile acts rationalized through identification with the parents, such as having the little boy throw the child who has fought with him out explaining, "My mother throws people out who fight."

Although the children in Korner's study responded rather vigorously to vicarious frustrations imposed in a story-telling situation and to the direct frustration of being kept from using a preferred toy, it was found that there was only a low correlation (.29) between the sum total of hostility tallies in the two experiments. There was also a rather low correlation (.21) between the total of hostility tallies in the story-telling experiments (there were ten story-telling play-material situations) and hostility shown by the children in real-life situations as reported by the parents.

Displaced Hostility. When blocked or inhibited in his impulse to express his anger directly against an offender, a child, like an adult, will frequently center his anger against objects, as when he smashes a toy when angered by his mother whom he hesitates to attack openly. He may direct his anger against animals, as when he hurts the family cat. He may vent his anger upon other persons, as when he "takes it out" on a younger sibling, or turns wrathfully against the milder of his parents when he has been angered by a parent who is stern and whom he fears. He may turn wrath that has been generated at school against his parents. Sometimes there may be a combination of direct or primary anger and projected anger, as when a child is spiteful toward a sibling who has directly annoyed him and who also serves as a scapegoat for anger induced by other frustrations.

Cruelty. The expression of hostile feelings may take the form of recurrent cruelty, as when a child hatches schemes to hurt another innocent person, or sets fire to ant hills, or goes out of his way to kill frogs, toads, and other creatures. The subject of cruelty in children is in need of study from a developmental point of view, for "cruel" behavior may represent varying combinations of hostility, thoughtlessness, and exploratory interest at different developmental levels. The development of marked reactions against cruelty, in the form of irra-

tional solicitude for animals and childish forms of antivivisectionism, also offers a significant field for study. In cases of extreme solicitude for animals it is difficult to tell to what extent it represents pity and sympathy, or an expression of the child's anxieties, or a form of denying or reacting against his own hostile feelings.

Prejudice. Prejudice serves as a means of projecting one's anger on someone else, although this is not its only motivation. While children may incorporate as their own, without feeling very deeply about it, the prejudices held by their elders, the phenomenon of prejudice as a form of displaced hostility sometimes appears at a relatively early age. First graders, for example, sometimes are aggressive toward innocent "foreigners" (the "foreigner" may be a member of a different race or religion, or a different socio-economic level, or simply a stranger or outsider to some or all of the children when he first arrives). In a study of older children, Frenkel-Brunswik (1948) found that those who were notably prejudiced tended, among other matters, to be more punitive in their attitudes than children who were relatively unprejudiced.

Bullying. The aggressive motive behind bullying is usually quite obvious. If a child expresses his hostility primarily or solely by bullying, one may suspect that he not only is hostile but also is subject to anxiety or feelings of inferiority. Bullying as a form of displaced revenge may prevail for a time in children who are abused or persecuted when they first join a new group. In a study of camp children, Osborne (1937) describes a sequence in which a child is first the butt of bullying and teasing, and who then, as he learns to hold his own in the group, for a time bullies others, and then, as he makes further gains in poise and self-confidence within the group, discontinues his bullying.

Antisocial Acts and Ideals. Aggressive impulses may be expressed through various forms of resistance or rebellion against prevailing standards. The most violent forms of expression in this category occur in the form of acts of delinquency and crime. Truancy may also be a gesture of hostility and defiance. Sexual promiscuity apparently also sometimes serves as an expression of resentment or rebellion.

A subtler form of hostile, antisocial behavior occurs when a child harbors ideas or feelings that go markedly counter to the needs or aspirations of the group. In an informal study of children's heroes and ideals by the writer and some of his students it was observed that a few notably rebellious children expressed their aggressive feelings by naming, as their ideals, celebrated criminals. Examples of the manner in which children may show overt sympathy with the enemy during wartime as a way of expressing their hostility toward persons in their environment are described by Escalona (1946).

Self-Inflicted Punishment. From an early age, children occasionally "take out" their anger on themselves. The violent head banging which some children display during temper tantrums is a notable example. Head banging has also been observed as an expression of rage in chimpanzees (Hebb, 1945). As time passes, many additional forms of self-punishment appear, such as when the child unduly blames himself or deliberately courts troubles or accidents that might injure him. This phenomenon of self-inflicted pain, and motives behind it, has been discussed more fully from the point of view of its meaning in adult life than it has been investigated from a developmental point of view.

Psychosomatic Mechanisms. In children, as in adults, the effects of anxiety, hostility, and other disturbing emotional states may appear as physical symptoms. Also, as we have noted elsewhere, a physical weakness or ailment will influence a person's irritability and emotional susceptibility. Both these conditions represent a form of psychosomatic interaction. Emotions may have secondary somatic effects, and a somatic condition may have a pronounced influence on emotion.

Many studies have added to knowledge concerning the interplay of mind and body as revealed in well-known phenomena such as physical disabilities occurring in connection with emotional conflict, as in conversion hysteria; the influence of drugs and toxins on moods and emotions; the occurrence of nausea, voiding of the bowels, and other involuntary physical reactions during times of acute stress.[1]

Sulzberger and Zaidens (1948) have described how emotions may directly involve skin reactions, such as blushing, and gooseflesh, and may also indirectly precipitate skin disorders. Numerous writers have explored the theory that illness may serve as an escape from frustration. The interplay between psychological and biochemical factors in connection with asthma and other allergic reactions has likewise received considerable attention. Among other troubles, arthritis and other rheumatic diseases frequently appear to have a psychogenic origin and represent, according to one theory, a reaction to suppressed hostility.

Probably in instances where such reactions occur there is a physical reason why this particular symptom, and not some other form of somatic reaction, should appear. It is difficult to determine, as one writer puts it, which comes first, the "rheumatic chicken or the emotional egg" (*Time,* June 13, 1949). But, whatever the answer

[1] Readers are referred to the journal *Psychosomatic Medicine* and to various books and articles such as Cannon (1929, 1939); Young (1937); Dunbar (1945); Saul (1947).

to that may be, it is clear that in studying the emotional behavior of children it is important to recognize that a great variety of physical disorders may be symptoms of emotional disorder. This observation includes also physical injuries which may arise, as pointed out in another section, when an emotionally disturbed child deliberately or unwittingly exposes himself to physical accidents as a form of taking revenge upon others or as a means of punishing himself.

Externalization. In many of the expressions of hostility noted above, the hostile person is, in effect, disavowing his anger or avoiding a direct display of it. Such disavowal involves much actual or attempted self-deception.

Anger and hostility are so sharply deplored in most strata of our society that children from a rather early age develop stratagems to conceal their anger from themselves and others and techniques for evading responsibility for their rage. One mechanism is to externalize hostility. The child who has externalized his hostility toward his teacher does not see himself but the teacher as a hostile person, and by this stroke he justifies his grievances against her and is freed from the painful thought that the seat of the difficulty is in him and not in her.

Grievances and Feeling Abused. A common manifestation of externalized hostility appears in the child or adult who is full of grievances.[1] The concept of grievance helps greatly to illuminate many childish arguments, quarrels, complaints, and antipathies, and it is also a great help in understanding much of the recrimination and argumentation that goes on in the name of various "causes" espoused by adults. The person who has managed to develop what to him is a grievance, a "real" reason for feeling abused, possesses a fine device for

[1] For a discussion of the feeling of being abused, see Horney (1951).

placing full blame on others and for removing all blame or responsibility from himself. It is the others who are mean, dishonest, unfair. "They" are against him. "They" are the ones who will seize every opportunity to do him about. At the adult level, there are many symbols and whipping boys representing grievances. We need a "New Deal" because we have been abused by the Old Deal. But to those who feel abused by the New Deal, it is a Raw Deal, so we need a Square Deal, and so on.

An appeal to grievances, an effort (in a political campaign, for example) to play upon the resentments of persons who feel abused, is an especially powerful device because it is directed at something that probably is latent to some extent in all people from early childhood on. It touches upon feelings that have a basis in reality (it is likely that all children actually have experienced mean and unfair treatment from someone and to that extent have a grievance founded in reality). And it touches even more effectively on the irrational attitudes such as those that come into play when an aggrieved person feels hostile toward others and then externalizes hostility, as described above.

While a person's feeling of being abused is directed against others, it may be tied to a person's unrecognized attitudes of contempt and hostility toward himself. On this theory, the person who to a substantial degree predicates his behavior on irrational feelings of being abused lacks integrity in his dealings with himself, and if he plays on these irrational attitudes as a means of manipulating others he lacks integrity also in his dealings with others.

Weakness of "Inner Controls." In an absorbing account of "children who hate," Redl and Wineman (1951) have described difficulties which beset children who have been exposed to severe rejection and abuse. Such children may show a conspicuous lack of the "inner controls" which we expect to find in children who in the course of their character development have had the benefit of friendly relationships with others and have been able to count on others for sympathy, example, and moral support. Among the characteristics observed in such children by Redl and Wineman (1951, pp. 74–140) were: low frustration tolerance; unconstructive stratagems for coping with insecurity, anxiety, and fear; low resistance to temptation; a tendency to become excited and to show "group psychological intoxication" (as revealed, for example, by impulsivity and primitive forms of sublimation); "sublimation deafness"; irresponsibility with regard to property and possessions; a tendency toward panic when confronted with something new; a loss of control over the "traumatic onrush from the past"; disorganization in the face of guilt; lack of insight into self-contributed causal links in a sequence of happenings; lack of a realistic attitude toward time, including lack of a realistic concept of "future consequences" or of "themselves in the future"; considerable blindness to social realities; loss of potentials for learning from experience; greater than normal difficulty in reacting rationally to failure, mistakes, and success; difficulty in reacting constructively to the challenge of competition.

Variations in Culturally Sanctioned Channels of Aggression. The fact that cultural sanctions regarding the expression of aggression operate in varying ways was noted above in a brief comment about swearing, and it has also been emphasized in other observations. In the Saulteaux Indian Society, according to Hallowell (1940), members of the group are under social constraint to cultivate patience, self-restraint, cooperation, and harmony in their dealings with each other and to avoid overt aggression, but closer study shows that strongly hostile feelings still prevail and are expressed through the culturally sanctioned channels of gossip and resort to sorcery and magic. This study suggests that observed differences in aggressiveness between various primitive groups may be more apparent than real, and it also suggests the possibility that a concerted study of many different cultural groups might reveal not only that the problem of aggressiveness prevails in all but also that some groups have solved this problem more constructively than others.

Interplay of Anger and Fear

We have already noted that there is a close relationship between anger and fear. Sometimes a person vacillates between the two. Some circumstances produce both. By virtue of a change in the child, a circumstance which once produced fear (such as a threat by another child) may produce anger (if the threatened child now is older or more confident of his strength). The occurrence of one of the emotions may stimulate the arousal of the other, as when a person is frightened by the violence of his anger, or is angry at himself by reason of the restriction of freedom which his fears impose upon him.

Various studies have shown that there is a correlation between susceptibility to anger and fear. In a study of a group of especially "aggressive" children, Kepler (1933–1934) found that about half of them also showed anxiety in their behavior. In studies of college students, Stratton (1927) and Anastasi, Cohen, and Spatz (1948) found a positive correlation between the frequency of reported experiences of anger and fear. The frequency of reporting both anger and fear might be influenced by the faithfulness and by the perceptiveness of the person who is keeping the record, but it seems reasonable to assume that these emotions would be associated. A person who shows a high incidence of one of them quite likely is vulnerable or irritable or frustrated or harassed to a degree and in a manner that might readily lead to a high incidence of the other.

At the 3-to-5-year level, Felder (1932) found that anger outbursts were far more frequent than displays of fear. It appears that in a well-protected environment it is easier to shield a child from specific events that are likely to frighten him than to eliminate thwartings of the kind that lead to anger. In some instances, however, the higher incidence of anger than of fear may be more apparent than real, since there are children who express their anger quite overtly but conceal their fears or find means of avoiding direct contact with the situations that they dread.

Although passing displays of temper may be more frequent than manifestations of fear, the latter are regarded quite often as constituting a "problem" in behavior of young children (Foster and Anderson, 1930).

Non-Aggressive Responses to Frustration

The subject of frustration overlaps but does not fully coincide with the subject of conditions that give rise to anger and hostility. The term "frustration" as used in current writings has a meaning somewhat broader than the thwarting that elicits anger. In their classic study of frustration, Dollard, Doob, Miller, Mowrer, Sears, et al. (1939) speak of frustration as "an interference with the occurrence of an instigated goal-response at its proper time in the behavior sequence" (p. 7). Other definitions have variously identified frustration as the blocking of or interference with the satisfaction of an aroused need through some barrier or obstruction (Symonds, 1946, p. 51); as a situation in which accustomed re-

actions do not satisfy an aroused motive (Shaffer, 1936, p. 117); as a state of high tension incident to the blockage of a path to a goal (G. Murphy, 1947, p. 145).

Many methods have been used in experiments with frustration, including difficult or insolvable problems or tasks, being denied a favorite toy, having a lure such as chocolate bar suspended just beyond reach, substituting something that has no appeal for something that has much appeal.[1]

Experimentally induced abnormal behavior in animals through the use of frustration techniques has been studied by Maier (1939, see also review of studies, 1948) and others. In Maier's study, rats were placed in a card-discrimination problem situation in which reward and punishment were applied in random order, confronting the animals with an insolvable problem; besides, a jet of air was directed at the rat to force it to react.

Among the responses which frustration may arouse are the following: aggression, regression to a more childish level of behavior, resistance, withdrawal, apathy, expressions of guilt or remorse or shame or embarrassment, nagging, threatening, efforts to evade the issue, efforts to rationalize or explain away the issue. In response to long-continued frustration, the individual may build up mechanisms of self-deception, or he may respond with rigid ritual-like forms of behavior.[2]

As in response to thwartings of a sort that normally produce anger, the response to frustrating situations will depend not only on the source or nature of the frustra-

---

[1] See, e.g., Fajans, 1933; Barker, Dembo, Lewin, 1937; Britt and Janus, 1940; Burton, 1942; Frederickson, 1942; Seashore and Bavelas, 1942; Sherman and Jost, 1942; Korner, 1947; Miller and Bugelski, 1948.

[2] A comprehensive account of various forms of frustration arising both from internal and from external circumstances, and of varying types of response, has been given by Rosenzweig, 1938–1939. Rosenzweig also develops the concept of "frustration tolerance."

tion but also upon habitual tendencies in the child. If he generally tends to be assertive and aggressive, he may respond aggressively; if he is insecure or anxious, he may withdraw or respond with behavior rituals that do not solve the problem. By reason of the fact that response to frustration shows variations of this sort, the particular behavior which the frustrated individual shows may give little or no indication of his needs.

LOVE AND AFFECTION

We have noted earlier that during the first year of life children begin to show affection for others. It would be difficult to determine to what extent the young child's affectionate behavior represents a primary drive or an acquired motive. But we can say, at any rate, that a child's display of affection for others seems to appear spontaneously, and, as Dennis (1938) has shown, it will arise with a minimum of social stimulation from others. The factor of learning will, of course, influence the particular persons and objects to which the child's affections become attached.

Developmental Changes

Most of the written material on affection deals with the child's need for love. It pictures him as one who receives affection without much mention of the fact that he also gives affection. If we could study this matter we probably would find that at a relatively early age the ability to accept and the ability to bestow affection are closely interrelated.

There is very little systematic information concerning the development of affection, concerning the way in which the child's capacity for loving, and the range or scope of his affections, wax and change in the process of development. We know from everyday observation that as time passes the child's affections expand in scope. He shows affection for his parents, immediate members of his family, and, as time passes, for other persons in his environment. Eventually he become capable of a wide range of loyalties that contain an element of affection.

Likewise, from an early age, the child begins to acquire affection for pets and things and places, his doll, his favorite toy, an old blanket, the family cat, the house and grounds wherein he lives, and so on.

With the passing of time there are changes also in the quality of his affection. As he develops, he increasingly gains in ability to appreciate the feelings of others, to sympathize, to feel compassion, to respond to loved persons with thoughtfulness and tenderness, to give to others out of love.

We can also observe in everyday life manifestations of infatuation and romanticized love which some persons show in adolescence but which many exhibit long before adolescence, and others continue to exhibit long after.

We can also observe the manifestations of parental love which may involve a degree of solicitude and tenderness and a degree of self-forgetfulness that mark it off from any other experience in life.[1] This love appears in its fullest form when parenthood is attained, but even this form of love often appears at an early age when a child "mothers" another child, shows a loving, motherly attitude toward a doll, or shows an affectionate, motherly or fatherly attitude toward a parent.

There are findings dealing with one aspect or another of these manifestations, but we

[1] Deutsch (1944–1945) has drawn an interesting distinction between psychological and biological motherhood. A woman can function psychologically as a mother without having borne a child, and the fact that a woman actually has offspring will not necessarily give assurance that she is a motherly person.

have nothing approaching a systematic developmental record of the actual and potential range and scope of a child's affections or of changes in form and quality, or of the dynamic relationship which the development of his own affectional life bears to his personality as a whole. Findings on the last point are limited, for most observers, as we have said, have stressed the child's need of being loved without dwelling on the degree to which it is essential, for his own full development, not only to be loved but to love others. The intimate relationship between love for others and love of self has been discussed by Fromm (1947). The Golden Rule also touches rather trenchantly on this relationship. The relationship between love for self and love for others, acceptance of self and acceptance of others, self-rejection and rejection of others, self-hate and hatred for others is emphasized explicitly or by implication in the writings of Horney (1937 *et seq.*), Rogers (1942), Sullivan (1947), and Sheerer (1949). Love of others and love of self can best be understood when viewed as constituting an intimate and essential interrelationship and not simply a kind of bargaining arrangement.

Impact of Affection on Development

As a matter of common sense, we know that if a child is to thrive he needs to be reared in an atmosphere of affection and that he is under a tragic handicap if he lives in an environment devoid of love. The reason is not simply that love is something nice to have, an added vitamin in the diet, so to speak. The reason goes far deeper and is more pervasive. Love is not just an extra touch—it is something that enters into the quality of the total environment. Where it prevails it affects the nature of all the child's relationships with the people on whom as a helpless person he is

at first abjectly dependent; it is a feature of everything that is involved in the child's nurture.

When a parent genuinely is fond of his child and spontaneously enjoys him as a companion there will be more give and take, more mutual participation in activities through which the child can discover his resources and limitations, less unresolved friction (but not necessarily less friction), less need for evasion and concealment in facing life's problems.

In their relations with their child the loving mother and father communicate affection through all their ways of dealing with him. Love is not offered simply by way of coos and caresses, fond pats and affectionate squeezes (although these are nice at all levels from infancy to old age) but in countless rather prosaic and practical ways. A basic and all-pervasive feature of parental love for a child is that the child is liked for his own sake; he is viewed as something valuable *per se;* he is respected as a personality in his own right. His selfhood is accepted. An outstanding feature of parental love for a child is that it is *unconditional:* the child is worthy as he is; the child is not loved on the condition that he or she is blonde or brunette, or male or female, a "good" baby, a pretty baby, a baby likely to add to the glory of the family name.

Such love for a child has a telling influence on the child's development. The greatest impact is on the development of the self. This position has been advanced most forcefully by Sullivan (1947). Approval and acceptance by others are necessary for the development of self-approval and self-acceptance. The self, according to Sullivan, is made up of "reflected appraisals." As noted earlier, according to this theory, if the appraisals are chiefly derogatory the child's attitudes toward himself will become chiefly derogatory, but if he is accepted and approved by significant people this will influence him in the direction of self-approval and appreciation of his own worth.

There is something emotionally satisfying about being loved, and there also is something very practical about it. The child who is loved for himself is free to be himself. He is free from an early age to manipulate, to explore, to try himself out, to discover his resources and limitations, to test his environment (including the limits of his mother's and father's patience). He has freedom to do the things that lead to learning: to try and err, to make mistakes, to do childish and foolish things, to experiment. Not the least of the factors that help him in learning to realize himself is that the loving parent also has a certain kind of freedom which the unloving parent is not so likely to possess, namely, freedom to be himself in his rôle as a parent; he will not feel a need to put a false face on his own feelings, to act as though he always were chipper and cheerful, full of sweetness and light, with a boundless amount of patience and an inexhaustible capacity for controlling his temper. He does not need to distort his personality by trying to live up to the impossible ideal of being a perfect parent. He will not feel a guilty need to grant the child's every whim or to indulge his every desire for fear that to do otherwise would threaten a precarious relationship between him and his youngster.

A study by Skeels, Updegraff, Wellman, and Williams (1938), earlier referred to, shows impressively how young children, reared in an orphanage without the personal attention which children usually receive at home, may be adversely affected in various aspects of their development, including their capacity for friendly relationships with other people. Goldfarb (1943) found that institutionalized children, as compared with children in foster homes,

showed, among other things, a lower capacity for personal ties and relationships and various symptoms of emotional unresponsiveness. An interesting paper by McCarthy (1953) traces the relationship that might exist between lack of mothering in the mother-son relationship and the frequently observed backwardness of boys as compared with girls in certain aspects of language development.

Zucker (1943) used a story-completion technique and a questionnaire to test the hypothesis that lack of a close emotional tie between children and parents may result in only a superficial assimilation by children of the parents' values and ideas.[1]

The fact that there may be a relationship between an adult's attitudes toward authority, existing institutions, and political and economic issues and his emotional relationships with his parents as a child has been indicated in several studies. Lasswell (1930) reports that attitudes in favor of revolt against established institutional practices were associated in the persons he studied with repressed aggression against the father. Findings obtained by Krout and Stagner (1939) tended to confirm that avowed radicals showed more frequent findings of rejection by their parents and in general more unhappiness in childhood than a control group. In a later study, Stagner

[1] The huge amount of literature dealing with the bearing of parent-child relationships on problem disorders and emotional maladjustment will not be reviewed here except through a brief reference below to parental "rejection" and "overprotection." Among matters associated with maladjustment are the emotional complications involved in living in "broken" families. It is impressive to note that in 1940 it is reported that of the 40,286,770 children under 18 years of age in the United States, 4,518,000 lived in broken homes (Anon., 1944). In 1947 Madow and Hardy (1947) estimated that from available statistics approximately from 11 to 15 per cent of children have broken families before the age of 16. In addition to the homes that are physically "broken" there are uncalculated numbers of homes that are psychologically torn and broken even though they are physically intact.

(1944) found that in a male college population active radicals reported less satisfactory relationships with parents than a control group.

Response to Evacuation. The evacuation of large numbers of children from their homes during wartime has offered opportunities for studying the meaning of normal parent-child relationships in the home. Some observers have expressed the opinion that the immediate effects of evacuation when it involved separation from parents are worse than the immediate effects of air raids, and that it is a greater shock to a child to be separated from his parents than to experience bombardment; other observers voice a contrary opinion (see, e.g., Burbury, 1941; Burt, 1941; Coromina, 1943; A. Freud and Burlingham, 1943; Isaacs, Brown, and Thouless, 1941; John, 1941; Mons, 1941).

Parental Rejection and Overprotection

The term "rejection" and the label "rejected child" have been used to denote the condition of a child who is not loved by his parents (or parent-substitute). The term "overprotection" has been used to designate a parental attitude involving excessive contact and mothering. The term rejection is commonly used to denote the antithesis of a relationship in which there is wholehearted acceptance of the child. However, overprotection and rejection cannot be regarded as opposites, for, as usually construed, overprotection is colored by anxiety and, besides, overprotecting behavior may be one symptom or means of rejecting the child.

Signs or criteria of rejection and overprotection have been discussed by Levy (1943), Symonds (1938, 1939), and Fitz-Simons (1935). Circumstances which might lead a mother to overprotect her child have been discussed by Levy (1943).

One response to maternal rejection is aggressiveness on the part of the child, according to Knight (1933–1934). According to Symonds (1946), the child who is denied love by his parents is thrown back upon himself for love. The fact that rejection by one parent or the other cannot alone account for subsequent behavior is suggested in a study of delinquent children who had received treatment (Glueck and Glueck, 1940). When studied several years after treatment, the same percentage of young persons were reported to have the affection of their fathers in the group that was unreformed as in the group that was reformed.

The concept of rejection is a valuable one for understanding child behavior although it touches on an area of human relationship in which there is need for further research.

A full understanding of the effects of rejection would have to take account of the total social and psychological setting in which practices and attitudes of an apparently rejecting sort operate. Rejection cannot be studied simply by noting the acts, attitudes, and apparent intentions of the person whose affection the child desires. The child who is subject to consistent, strict discipline of an apparently "rejecting" sort may feel less cast off than a child who is subject to inconsistent and unpredictable discipline of a milder sort. Behavior which in itself is not rejecting might have the effect of rejection in a setting in which there is favoritism for one child. The practices that prevail in a given culture or even within a given community will have a bearing on the extent to which parental behavior becomes psychologically equivalent to rejection. A very important factor in determining whether the attitude of a parent or parent-substitute is regarded as rejecting is the attitude already established in a child. A child who feels abused (see an earlier section) probably will interpret the behavior of a parent or teacher as a form of rejection far more readily than would another child. It is likely that a child will have the experience of feeling rejected in many situations which the parent does not regard as rejecting in character. For example, the child who is constantly being pressed to live up to standards that are beyond his reach is being rejected. He will have constant reminders of his imperfection—he is not as clean, or is not as obedient, as quiet, or quick at learning as he should be, and so on.

Whenever a child is measured against a preconceived standard and found wanting (or feels that he is found wanting) it is likely that his experience may be much like that of an openly rejected child.

Emotional Acceptance and Rejection of Children by Persons Outside the Home

Many features of the parent-child relationship in the home are likely to be reestablished in the child's relationship with adults outside the home who serve, to some degree, as substitute parents (the teacher, camp counselor, nurse, and the like). Usually, however, the emotional relationship involved will be far less affectionate and intimate than that which prevails in a good home. In a study by del Solar (1949) in which children were appraised by their parents and also by their teachers (in a school with an avowedly humane philosophy of education) it was found that emphasis on companionship and mutual affection was frequent in the reports of parents but almost completely lacking in the reports by teachers. Teachers also mentioned fewer satisfying qualities in the children than did the parents. This is not at all surprising, but in emphasizing the vast disparity between the emotional ties a child can establish in the home and those

he can expect to establish with adults outside the home, these findings underscore the importance of the former.

In his relations with adults outside the home the child not only is likely to meet aloofness but may even encounter severe rejection. In commenting on psychiatric work with evacuated children in England during World War II, Alcock (1948) states that there often exists in many adults an impulse of hostility, often deeply unconscious, toward children who are not actually or emotionally their own. How widely this statement applies would be difficult to tell. Certainly one can conclude from everyday observation that adults cannot be counted on to be more charitable toward other children by virtue of having children of their own. For this reason, among others, the father or mother of many children may be a poorer guardian of the welfare of children at large than a childless teacher. Indeed, it is only by assuming that Alcock's statement holds true, rather widely in some communities, that we can account for the fury of the attacks that sometimes are made when educators, welfare workers, and others make modest proposals for improving the lot of children.

Actually, in contacts with institutions outside the home, children encounter a vast amount of treatment which, in effect, might well be construed as a kind of rejection. At school large numbers of children who do not happen to possess the kind of intelligence that is necessary for doing average or above average academic work are frequently reminded that they are not much good. The school dispenses failure on a colossal scale, and this sort of failure can readily strike a young person as a kind of repudiation. Moreover, much of this failure is due to questionable standards which require that all children go through certain academic exercises that have little if any meaning to them. It is perhaps only on the assumption that there is a large amount of hostility toward children in our society (as suggested by Alcock's study) that we can explain the fact that our society tolerates the kind of self-derogating treatment to which so many children are constantly being subjected in the name of education.

Emotional Rewards and Penalties of Parenthood

Anything that contributes to the emotional rewards of being a parent and anything that adds to the emotional burden is bound in one way or another to influence the parent-child relationship.

When parents themselves are questioned concerning the emotional rewards of parenthood they place great emphasis upon the friendliness their children show toward them, the companionship they derive from them, the interests they share with them, and other features that represent a loving relationship. In a study in which 554 parents were questioned (Jersild, Woodyard, and del Solar, 1949), items under this general heading of companionship and affectional relationships were mentioned by 72 per cent of the parents. A large proportion of the parents also mentioned satisfaction and pride in their rôle as parents (64 per cent), and an even larger proportion mentioned the pleasure they derived from witnessing the development and manifestations of their children's personalities (82 per cent). A great number of other expressions of appreciation pertained to the relationship existing between the child and the other parent or with relatives (54 per cent). There were many expressions of appreciation also of various features in the child's progress, his development, his relations with people in the community, and the like.

An important factor which influences the composure of parents and which, in turn, may affect the emotions that come into play

in dealings with their children is the factor of physical discomfort and fatigue. Problems and irritations due to crowding and congestion, lack of room space, lack of play space, and the like, were mentioned by large numbers of urban parents in the study cited above. City parents of low economic status especially felt the pinch of congested city life, cramped quarters, and other matters that added to the physical burden of caring for children, and their problem on this score was aggravated by the fact that they not only had less space as a family but also, on the average, had more children to occupy this space. The poorer parents were relatively far more preoccupied with the physical aspects of child care than with the psychological characteristics or psychological needs of their children. Financial poverty, it might be thought, could entail a certain impoverishment of affection, for poor parents would have less time and leisure and perhaps less psychological energy and freedom to enjoy their children. But, as it happened, the poorest group of parents in the study above, in spite of all their complaints about physical hardships, mentioned the companionship of their children as a source of satisfaction just as much as did members of other groups.

SIBLING RIVALRY AND JEALOUSY

One frequent source of thwarting which leads to hostility (and which may also produce grief and anxiety) arises in rivalry between siblings.

Feelings and Impulses Associated with Jealousy. Jealousy has not usually been described as a primary emotion but has been treated as a hybrid. Ribot (1903) notes that the gradations of jealousy range from "mild cases up to madness and homicide" and cites Descartes' definition of jealousy as "a kind of fear related to the desire we have for keeping some possession" (p. 268). Components of jealousy, as described by Ribot, include a pleasurable element related to something desired or possessed, an element of depressing vexation arising through the idea of dispossession or privation, and destructive tendencies, such as hatred and anger directed toward the real or imagined cause of this dispossession or privation. Among the feelings mentioned as components of jealousy by adult subjects in an investigation by Gesell (1906) were anger (which was most frequent, and was sometimes combined with feelings of hatred and with vengeful thoughts), self-pity, grief, sadness and dejection, mortification, fear, and anxiety. The most frequent combinations were anger, self-pity, and grief. These descriptions by adults seem to conform to symptoms exhibited by jealous children, but just what are the feelings of a jealous child would be difficult to appraise, since children are not very articulate about such matters.

Overt Expressions of Jealousy. Prominent among the overt symptoms of jealousy as described by S. Foster (1927) and others are expressions of anger, ranging from open hostility to substitute forms of attack. These may be directed toward the person whom the child looks upon as a rival for affection and attentions which he desires for himself, or they may be directed against the person whose affection is desired. The latter may also be subjected to reproaches and appeals, designed to arouse sympathy. The child who is jealous of a younger sibling may revert to infantile habits, such as demands to be fed and dressed when actually he is able to take care of himself (Sewall, 1930). As a bid for attention he may also exhibit fears that previously did not exist, show relapses in bladder and bowel control, and idiosyncrasies with regard to food. Various expressions of hostility have been described by Levy (1937b) in a study which utilized dolls to represent a mother, a baby, and an older brother or sister.

Among other expressions may appear an unwonted display of affection or helpfulness, or a tendency to lie and tattle, or varying forms of competitiveness. The child may also be very subdued in his behavior, as though he were grieving, or he may resort to vindictive make-believe and fantasies of self-glorification. Children who are afflicted sometimes will show quite contrasting behavior at different times and in different situations, and their reactions to the same person at different times may range from attack to attempts to curry favor. The repertoire of the jealous child is likely to be that of a troubled person who tries many different techniques in meeting a problem.

The label "jealous child" commonly refers to children who exhibit marked symptoms, or whose elders are unusually alert to any symptoms that appear. A systematic study of normal children would no doubt show that all of them exhibit symptoms of jealousy to a greater or lesser degree.

It should be noted that many of the forms of behavior described above may also be exhibited by a child who is not directly competing with a sibling but who is uncertain or troubled about his relations with his parents or teachers or other associates, and many of the struggles of a jealous child resemble those of a person who is uncertain concerning his own worth and seeks to vindicate or prove himself even though he has no visible rival.

Causal Factors. Studies of children who are conspicuously jealous (S. Foster, 1927; Sewall, 1930; Smalley, 1930; Ross, 1931) and of children who show rivalry (Macfarlane, 1938) do not reveal any other single, outstanding factor that distinguishes them from others. Differences in intelligence and age between two siblings may have an influence in individual cases, but more important are the complex factors involved in the relationship between parents and their children, between the father and the mother, and disturbing influences such as friction in the home, favoritism, and rejection of one child.

There probably will be an exceedingly great provocation to jealousy if one of the rivals in the family is used as a foil or scapegoat in a hostile struggle between the father and mother. If, because of the resemblance in appearance or temperament or for some other reason, a child is made the object of a father's or a mother's resentment toward the spouse, the child obviously is in a tough spot, and being barred, as a child, from directing his hostility against the offending parent, he will be under all the more pressure to project his anger and anxiety upon the sibling who is favored by that parent.

Ramifications of Childhood Jealousy. Many writers have maintained that the emotional drama involved in a child's relationships with members of the family, including relationships with his siblings, may have a marked influence on attitudes toward people and toward the world as long as he lives. Many of the disorders that arise between persons and between people in the adult society have their prototype in the family scene when the adults were small.

Benedict (1940) has pointed out that extreme hostility that is engendered within the family is not merely a function of high civilization as such or of the mechanization of industries of the institution of capitalism. It is a condition which may arise within a simple society or a complex one if certain social institutions prevail. Benedict makes this observation in commenting on a study by Henry (1940) which describes the hostility and quarrelsomeness of Pilaga Indian children who experience a great amount of affection and attention during their early

months of life and then later are more and more ignored, until, with the coming of a new child, they are left to their own resources. Within this relatively simple culture the customs are such that the child, after having received much attention, is virtually rejected, and, according to Henry, as a consequence he becomes a "poor, hostile, little flounderer for many years" (p. 119).

By reason of the complexity of the factors involved in rivalry and jealousy, minor expedients for allaying jealousy such as simply announcing to a child that a new baby is coming or a policy of providing "two of everything" to eliminate friction over possessions seem to be of little avail (Sewall, 1930; Macfarlane, 1938).

JOY

Studies dealing with the pleasures and joys of life are very skimpy compared with works that deal with frustration, anger, fear and anxiety, and other forms of unpleasantness. If judged by the preponderance of attention given to painful emotions, psychologists must be regarded as a gloomy lot, and some psychiatrists look even a shade gloomier.

Signs and occasions of joy in infancy were noted in earlier references to Bühler (1930) and Bridges (1932). Available data do not provide the basis for a precise classification of behavior that might be described as joy or pleasure. Even more tenuous are the nuances of feeling, mood, and expression involved in later forms of behavior that are described by such terms as pride, positive self-feeling, pleasant anticipation, interest, contentment, and happiness.

A consideration of the ramifications of the feeling of satisfaction or joy would carry us into the field of children's interests, play activities, and also into the larger field of personality development. In a study based upon compositions written by children in the elementary school grades, Stryker (1898) found that outstanding specific occasions for joy named by the children included gifts, expeditions and excursions, parties and games, and experiences with new places and things.

When children describe what makes them especially joyful, some types of happenings appear quite frequently over a wide age range, whereas others show a decline or an increase with age. Table 1 is a summary, in terms of broad categories, of circumstances named by children at different age-

TABLE 1 *

FREQUENCY OF RESPONSES IN VARIOUS CATEGORIES WHEN CHILDREN DESCRIBED "ONE OF THE HAPPIEST DAYS OF MY LIFE"

(The values represent percentage of children giving one or more responses in each category.)

	Grades 1–3 Ages 6–9		Grades 4–6 Ages 9–12		Grades 7–9 Ages 12–15		Grades 10–12 Ages 15–18	
	Boys	Girls	Boys	Girls	Boys	Girls	Boys	Girls
Number	363	331	309	343	282	290	159	171
Receiving or having or otherwise enjoying material things, gifts, toys, money, living quarters	8.7	8.1	10.4	7.2	10.1	4.5	5.6	3.1
Holidays, festive occasions, birthdays, Christmas, etc.	39.1	40.5	32.4	38.9	6.3	10.1	0.6	6.5
Sports, games, hiking, hunting, bicycling, etc.	10.2	6.4	9.1	5.5	12.4	5.8	13.0	7.3
Going to miscellaneous places of recreation, going to camps, traveling, going to resorts, to parks	9.6	9.0	10.1	11.4	9.7	13.9	30.2	6.9
Self-improvement, success in school, educational opportunity, evidence of vocational competence, getting a job	2.4	2.3	2.9	1.9	4.8	4.1	13.6	15.9
Happenings connected with school, including last day, end of school, going to a certain school	3.6	3.4	5.4	4.3	14.0	11.1	7.0	5.4
Relationship with people (explicitly described), companionship, being with certain friend, return home of relatives, etc.	7.7	15.9	8.0	15.8	10.5	22.0	8.7	19.9
Residing in, moving to, a certain city or community	1.3	1.0	0.8	2.9	0.9	2.9	1.4	5.0
Benefits befalling others, or mankind in general, including end of war	0.6	0.8	3.2	2.8	2.2	2.6	7.9	9.7

* Reproduced, by permission, from Jersild and Tasch (1949). The table omits several categories including hobbies, movies and radio programs, art activities, etc., mentioned by only small percentages of children.

grade levels when they described what they regarded as "One of the happiest days" of their lives.

Young children decidedly more often report a holiday or birthday or other occasion when they receive special attention and tokens of affection by way of gifts as a "happiest day" than do the older children. Older children oftener report as especially joyful occasions on which they are made aware of their own qualities and achievements. The older children place more emphasis than the younger ones on pleasures connected with self-discovery and self-realization. They mention successes and opportunities which involve evidence of or an opportunity for self-improvement or vocational preparation or placement, or experience of greater independence, more often than younger children. Older children also mention more often benefits befalling others. Experiences involving visits with friends, being able to enjoy the companionship of a certain person, and happenings which affect their relationship with members of their families are mentioned by a rather large number of children at all ages. Girls mention joyful events involving relationships with *people* considerably more than do the boys.

The findings here reviewed give only a limited picture of the day-to-day joys of growing children. There is need in this area, as in several others, for more systematic and comprehensive research.

Throughout life, satisfactions will arise from unimpeded activity, successful achievement, and ventures into new activities which give a person a broadened conception of himself. Children will themselves often seek hurdles, including mild forms of danger, for the satisfaction of overcoming them (Valentine, 1930; T. D. Jones, 1939; Gutteridge, 1939).

Prominent among the gratifications of everyday life are, of course, the numerous pleasures derived from ministering to bodily needs and the satisfying of physical appetites, pleasures associated with food and drink, fragrant odors, the comforts of rest and relaxation. To the extent that overt signs may be trusted, it would appear that pleasant, or at least neutral, tones predominate greatly over unpleasant states in normal children, as seems also to be true of normal adults (see, for example, Wohlgemuth, 1922–1923; Flügel, 1925; G. Watson, 1930; Hersey, 1931; Jersild, 1931; Hartmann, 1934–1935; W. B. Johnson, 1937).

LAUGHTER AND HUMOR

Although laughter does not represent any distinct emotion it deserves consideration as an outstanding expressive reaction. References have been made in an earlier section to the accounts by Bridges (1932) and Bühler (1930) of the appearance of laughter during the early months of life. Washburn (1928) noted laughter at 12 weeks in response to a "chirruping" sound as the experimenter bent over the child. The most effective laughter stimulus (at 16 weeks) was the "threatening head."

There have been many theories of laughter and humor which we will not here review in detail, including the theory that it represents the sudden transformation of expectation into nothing, that it represents a sudden release from anxiety or repression, that it represents a form of derision, that it represents relief from aggressive and libidinous tendencies, that it is a response to incongruity, that it represents a happy overflow of animal spirits. Actually, when we observe the variety of conditions that produce laughter, and the fact that different people laugh at different things, we probably have to accept all these hypotheses and more besides to account for all occasions. We probably would also find, on close study, that one theory might fit one person and not another, for, at one extreme, there may be a sour child who laughs only in derision of others and, at the other extreme, one whose laughter is a bubbling expression of friendly mirth.

Several studies at the preschool age have shown that laughter is most likely to appear in association with bodily activity, especially in connection with social play (M. C. Jones, 1925; Enders, 1927; Kenderdine, 1931; Ding and Jersild, 1932; Brackett, 1934). Kenderdine (1931) found that at 2 years laughter in response to motions made by the child himself or others was highest in frequency, and next in order came laughter in response to socially unacceptable situations. At 3 years the latter situations led the former. She also noted laughter in response to circumstances such as grimaces and pleasure in accomplishment and word play. In a study of preschool children, Ding and Jersild (1932) found little evidence for the theory that laughter commonly denotes feelings of derision or superiority. Kenderdine (1931), however, noted some instances of laughter in response to inferiority in others.

Justin (1932), in a study of children aged 3 to 6 years, used a number of situations to represent the following conditions: (1) surprise or defeat expectation; (2) superiority and degradation; (3) incongruity and contrast situations; (4) social smile as a stimulus; (5) relief from strain; (6) play situation. Some children at all age levels laughed or smiled in response to all the experimental situations. Incongruity and superiority and the play situations became somewhat more laughter-provoking as age increased, but the main change noted in relation to age was increased tendency to laugh at more of the specific situations that were used to represent each of the large classes of laughter-provoking stimuli.

Children of high intelligence in the group studied by Kenderdine tended to laugh more than children of average or somewhat above average IQ. Justin also found a positive correlation between IQ and tendency to laugh, especially in response to incongruity. It seems plausible that bright children might be more responsive than less intelligent children to laughter-provoking subtleties; in a study of older children, Brumbaugh (1939) found, for example, that brighter children were better able to recognize absurdities. Other factors in a child's social and emotional adjustment, however, are likely to have a more important bearing upon his disposition to laugh than the factor of intelligence alone.

In a study of children aged 7 to 18 years, Laing (1939) concluded from data obtained through questioning, essays, and reports by the subjects concerning their best jokes that the development of a sense of humor parallels the child's intellectual and emotional development. At 7 to 10 years, the major sources of humor are described as deviation from the normal; and at 11 to 13 years, important sources were the discomfiture of others and deviation from the normal. In the range from 7 to 13 years, situations regarded as humorous were mostly visual, but at 14 to 18 there was an increased appreciation of verbal humor. Herzfeld and Prager (1930) likewise describe changes in children's understanding of the comic as related to intellectual development. They note, for example, that when the child has acquired a grasp of size relationships he finds amusement in inanimate objects that show gross disproportions in size or colors, and at later ages other forms of distortion and incongruity, including human frailties, become effective. Piret (1940) also found that appreciation of humor parallels intellectual development. Brumbaugh (1939), in a study of children in grades 3 to 6, found that incongruity was the most frequent stimulus to laughter and that the children often showed a liking for comedy of the sort that was disapproved by many of their elders.

The fact that one prominent form of children's humor involves play with forbidden ideas appears from a study of the favorite "jokes" of children. In an informal study, the writer found many "off color" items among the favorite jokes written down by several hundred children aged 12–13. A fairly typical item was the following: *Question:* Why did the ram fall over the cliff? *Answer:* He didn't see the U-turn.

SYMPATHY

Sympathy denotes suffering with another, and therefore an account of sympathetic behavior should emphasize feelings that are involved. In young children, such feelings can only be inferred from the child's language and actions.

In a study by Boeck (1909) based upon parental reminiscences and questionnaire returns, the largest number of reported sympathetic responses was directed toward people (358, of which 285 were directed toward the father, mother, sisters, or brothers); 207 responses were directed toward animals; and 65 responses were directed toward other objects.[1]

Berne (1930), in a study that utilized rating scales, found evidence of a slight increase in sympathy at the four-year level as compared with the three-year level.

In a study by L. B. Murphy (1937) of preschool children, sympathetic responses were classified under headings such as helping, comforting, punishing, or removing the causes of distress, protecting, defending, warning, suggesting a solution, anxious or disorganized responses (such as showing an anxious expression, evidences of worry, and crying). Murphy utilized a number of experimental situations that provided an opportunity for the display of sympathy, and also observed children during their free play.

Murphy noted that children 2 and 3 years old did not generally respond sympathetically to black-and-blue wounds, swellings, and other minor distortions of flesh which to an adult would suggest discomfort or illness, or to Red Riding Hood's being eaten up by the Wolf, pictures of accidents, funerals, being crippled, and the like. Three-year-olds responded generally, although not universally, to such evidences of distress as bandages, blindness, injuries colored with iodine, red swellings, and the like; also to crying, accidental falls, attacks by another person, deprivation of toys, of food, or of mother; interferences, such as being caught in a pen or having to stay in bed.

Records obtained during 188 hours of observation of the behavior of one group of children disclosed 318 sympathetic responses and 195 responses that were classified as unsympathetic. In another nursery school group, 398 sympathetic and 60 unsympathetic responses were observed during 234 hours of observation. These frequencies of sympathetic behavior are considerably lower than the frequencies of resistant or combative behavior exhibited by children of this age. Such frequencies are not directly comparable, however, since the number of times sympathy occurs will depend, among other things, upon the occasions that arise for a display of sympathy.

Older children not only responded to a wider range of distress situations but also exhibited more active responses to comfort and defense as distinguished from passive staring or inquiries concerning another's misfortunes. Factors in the personality of the individual children were, however, more im-

1 These statements concerning Boeck's findings are taken from a review by L. B. Murphy (1937).

portant than the factor of age. Murphy describes many such factors. For example, a child who is sympathetic when he himself is disturbed or uncertain of his status in the group may become less sympathetic as he gains in confidence, whereas another child may show the reverse tendency. Again, a child may shift from sympathetic to unsympathetic behavior if his own self-interest is involved. Macfarlane (1938) likewise found that a child was less likely to sympathize with another's distress if the child himself was the cause of the distress.

Compassion

By origin and usage, "sympathy" and "compassion" are similar in meaning, but "compassion" might well be reserved to designate a higher order of emotional maturity. Compassion may be defined as a kind of fellowship of feeling which involves a capacity for kinship with the totality of another's emotional state. As such it involves an appreciation of some of the struggle, the striving, hope, or despair that lies beneath surface manifestations of anger, gaiety, grief, pride, or fear. To be compassionate a person must be able to draw fully upon his own capacities for feeling, for unless he is at home with his own feelings he cannot recognize the feelings of another, nor will he have the incentive to understand the roots from which they spring.

The one who is capable of compassion, so defined, is aware of the self-distrust that lies behind another's overeagerness to please. The compassionate parent recognizes the fear behind the bold front his child assumes when he faces up against a bully, and he senses his child's grim courage as he goes jauntily off to school to face a harsh teacher. But he realizes also that the bully is unhappy and that the harsh teacher suffers too, for otherwise they would not want to inflict pain. The compassionate teacher recognizes the anxiety that is concealed under the insolence of his most troublesome pupil. To be compassionate means to have an ability to mourn with one who mourns but also subtly to console him, for one who is compassionate will probably surmise that the person who grieves is richer than he who has nothing worth grieving about, and it is better to feel sorrow than to feel nothing.

In keeping with this concept, to be compassionate a person must be able to face his own emotions, and that is why compassion here is designated as something "mature." To perceive the anguish behind another's anger, instead of recoiling or striking back, a person must be strong enough to acknowledge some implications of his own hostility. To be able to react sympathetically to anxiety in others as it appears in the form of arrogance or false pride or a show of power or in the countless obsequious contrivances of everyday life he must have the strength to see some of his own anxiety in naked form. And to feel compassion for those who struggle against despair he must have had the courage to perceive the dreadful threat of despair in his own life. While compassion, as here described, involves feeling for others it requires a mature form of self-realization, since compassion for others is possible only if a person is capable of compassion for himself.

In the writer's opinion, it is necessary in our research to explore more adequately than we have in the past the implications of such a concept of the intimate relationship between feelings toward self and feelings toward others if we are to arrive at a mature formulation of emotional development and of what constitutes emotional "maturity."

EMOTIONAL IMPACT OF SEXUAL DEVELOPMENT

A few points should be added to round out the numerous references made in earlier sections to the subject of sex.

Infantile Sexuality. Freud's theory (see, e.g., Freud, 1930) that sex is not something that is visited upon the child at about the time of puberty but is a development which goes back to early infancy can be confirmed by everyday observation, and it has also been underscored by numerous research investigations.

There is sensitivity in the genital areas in early infancy, and many children (probably all, to some degree) in infancy and early childhood manipulate their genitals or use some other form of self-stimulation, apparently to achieve pleasure or relief. Halverson (1940), in observations of 9 male infants aged 3 to 20 weeks, found that tumescence occurred at least once daily in most of the children. Mothers interviewed in a study by Levy (1928) reported that by the age of 3 years 26 of 49 boys involved in the questioning had applied direct manual stimulation, such as holding, stroking, or pressing the genital organ. Manual stimulation was reported also in the case of 4 of 26 girls, but this, as Levy points out, does not take account of the possible occurrence of other forms of stimulation that are difficult to detect, such as thigh-rubbing. Koch (1935), in systematic observations of children of nursery school age, also found a higher incidence of masturbatory activities in boys than in girls. Isaacs (1933), on the basis of direct observation, has presented an impressive collection of anecdotes showing ways in which children of preschool age express an interest in genital functions.[1]

[1] For reviews, or reports of original findings, see Willoughby (1937); Sears (1943); Landis, Landis, Bolles, *et al.* (1940); Ramsey (1943); and Kinsey, Pomeroy, and Martin (1948).

The advantage of systematic, direct observation, such as was employed in some of the studies mentioned above, cannot be exploited with older children. The findings at later levels indicate that there is a wide, and perhaps almost universal, prevalence of varying degrees of interest and curiosity concerning sex in the prepubertal years and a large proportion of children during this period engage in experimentation, manipulation, and sex play. Sex apparently does not take a holiday, such as Freud assumed in his concept of the latency period.

As one would expect, there is an accentuation of such interests and activities at puberty. By the time adulthood is reached, findings in various studies indicate that 90 per cent or more of males and a smaller proportion of females have engaged in masturbation at one time or another with varying duration. Likewise, varying but quite substantial percentages report other forms of sex experimentation ranging from mild petting to intercourse, crushes, love affairs, exposure to mild or major forms of sex aggression, and the like. The study by Kinsey, Pomeroy, and Martin (1948) shows that a large proportion of males have had premarital intercourse. Such endeavors are probably accompanied by varying degrees of placidity and enjoyment, and varying degrees of fear and guilt. The Kinsey Report centers attention primarily on sexual outlet, and does not explore the question as to how often a sexual outlet leads to shame and guilt or pride and joy.

For a large number of young persons there is a long period of sexual unemployment between the time of pubescence and the time when the young people marry. Though findings by Kinsey and his associates, and by others, show that a large proportion of persons rebel against the social codes, many of those who rebel still conform to a great extent, for many of them violate the code only once or twice or a few times—in other words, less frequently than they would if they habitually followed only their own urges. Findings in this area open a vast field for further study. They have shown that many of our laws and attitudes relating to sex are unrealistic, but they have not shown how these problems might be solved.[1] Moreover, a survey of sex practices may show what is "normal" from a statistical point of view without answering questions about the psychological meaning of this norm. Sex behavior may, in one instance, be a part of a spontaneous, self-fulfilling process and, in another instance, a kind of compulsion or an expression of anxiety.

Probably because of the many problems that sex raises, we find that discussions of sex emphasize mostly frustrations such as those named above without dwelling on the fact that sex is a source of satisfaction, enjoyment, and self-fulfillment.

One outstanding development in the psychology of sex is that sex is being viewed less from a segmental, parochial point of view and more from the point of view of its place in the total picture of personality. This view recognizes that sex is a motivational force that has an urgency in its own right, but it recognizes also that much behavior that has an erotic character and which seems to have a sexual motivation may actually be ancillary to a larger motivational pattern. In other words, sexual disorders may be an expression of a more general disorder. Sex behavior, according to this view, cannot be understood when studied solely by itself but must be examined also in the light of the larger entirety of the life pattern of which it is a part.

Sex may be the medium, the vehicle through which other tendencies or forces in the personality express themselves. It may serve, as it were, as the avenue through which attitudes which have an important bearing on self-development are communicated to a child, and it may serve also as the idiom through which the self communicates with others. When parents deal with their child's sex development as something repugnant they may, in effect, communicate to the child that he is a repugnant person.

In a climate of disapproval which leads to self-disapproval, the child may fix upon the sexual aspect of his nature as a convenient symbol and confirmation of his unworthiness. If he has been subject to disparagement of a kind that would make him feel guilty, the sexual part of his nature provides a convenient fixation point for his feelings of guilt.[2]

According to this viewpoint, the sex behavior of the adolescent and older person may express a wide range of symptoms of self-distrust or alienation. The young person who feels emotionally out of touch with people may seek sexual contact as the only means of closeness and emotional intimacy he knows.

If he feels the need for self-vindication and assurance of his own worth, he may resort to sexual conquest as a means of proving himself.

His sexual behavior may be a feature, central or peripheral, of a larger, more inclusive competitive attitude toward people.

If he has hostile and vindictive attitudes toward himself and others he may use sex behavior as a means of inflicting hurt and gaining revenge.

Sex may be the theatre of operations, so to speak, in which a person expresses his contempt for himself or others, or tests himself, strives to achieve a feeling of re-

1 See studies already named and also Pullias (1937) and Hattendorf (1932).

2 Ways in which sex may be a symbol or vehicle for personality tendencies have been discussed by Weiss (1950).

latedness to others, or seeks to find confirmation of his worth. According to this same view, frigidity and impotence in various forms and degrees may be secondary, as it were, to attitudes of contempt toward self (see, e.g., Pinsky, 1950a, 1950b). And a set of inconsistent attitudes toward the opposite sex which enable the adolescent to look upon some girls as fair game while others (close to his family and social circle) are exempt and put on a pedestal of virtue may, according to this view, represent a kind of neurotic duplicity, a lack of integrity within the self even though the person, according to his own lights, views his attitudes as a rational "solution."

AMOROUS BEHAVIOR

A large proportion of children become infatuated or are romantically attracted to a member of the opposite sex before puberty, and the average person, during the course of development, falls in love not once but several times. It is difficult to review the literature in this area, for usually the meanings authors attach to terms such as "love," "love attachment," "falling in love," "being in love," and "love affair" are not entirely clear.

One of the problems is the relation or distinction, if any, between amorous behavior and erotic behavior. A review of studies in this area has been offered by Grant (1948). Writers report distinctions between what has variously been known as amorous enchantment, amorous attachment, erotic attraction, infatuation, "venereal voluptuousness," or feelings of "love" and longings that definitely include a desire to copulate. Reik (1945) notes the difference between the relatively undiscriminating quality of venereal desire and the highly personalized and selective character of amorous attachment, and regards these as representing different categories of experience.

In a population of adults studied by Hamilton (1929), the first experience of falling in love was placed somewhere between the ages of 6 and 11 inclusive by 38 per cent of the women and 40 per cent of the men. Many reported that when they were in love at this early age they did not have conscious sex feelings or desires. S. Bell (1902) earlier compiled numerous records of the presence of the "love emotion" in children between 3 and 8 years of age as shown by behavior such as embracing, sitting close together, grief at separation, giving of gifts, jealousy, and making sacrifices. The pleasure involved in the early stages, according to Bell, is not specifically sexual except in some cases: there may be "love making" in the form of hugging and kissing without physical sensation of being sexually excited and aroused.

In a study of college girls, Ellis (1949) found that the median girl said that she had become infatuated with a male at the age of 12 but had not fallen in love until the age of 17. Ellis found that in adolescence the girls became infatuated and also fell in love more often than prior to adolescence. The median girl reported she had only one infatuation before the age of 12, and that she was infatuated five different times between the ages of 12 and 18. From these and other findings Ellis concludes that the college girls in question had tended to become infatuated considerably earlier than they fell in love; had had more prepubertal infatuations than loves; had more adolescent infatuations than loves; had fewer single but more plural infatuations than loves from the eighteenth year onward.

The emotional characteristics of "being in love" have received some attention from psychologists, but far less than the subject deserves.

According to Reik (1945), when a person falls in love it means that he has become emotionally attached to a person who represents the idealized image of himself. Loving means exchanging the ego ideal, which the person vainly seeks to reach, for an external object. The unconscious process by means of which this is done is in the nature of a projection. Reik's readable account no doubt describes what often happens when people fall in love. But, as far as this writer can discern, Reik is describing a neurotic condition; a person thus in love is in a false position in relation to another person and is in a state of duplicity in relation to himself. The idealized image may be compounded of a variety of unrealistic and irrational elements. Reik himself speaks of it as something impossible of attainment.

A different interpretation of the experience of love as it might strike the healthy young adolescent has been offered by Macmurray (1937), who regards falling in love as a kind of mutual self-discovery. The person in love and the loved person each is appreciated for his own sake. Wenkart (1949) describes how adolescents are prepared for love by a longing to have someone to acknowledge, accept, and appreciate them for themselves, and when members of the opposite sex give each other such assurance they are confronted with a wealth of feeling which they never knew they had and which gives the first love experience an element of revelation. Healthy love, according to Wenkart, involves mutuality, enjoyment of expressing and offering love, and delight in what is reciprocated. It presupposes awareness of self and a desire to grow. It involves self-fulfillment rather than an escape into an idealized image. The healthy adolescent, according to this position, grows in self-realization through his love and does not depend upon the love of another as an external substitute or consolation for his own lack of self-esteem.

It is apparent that being in love means different things to different people. Also, as can be seen from everyday observation, it involves a variety of emotional components. There is erotic attraction. There are feelings of tenderness. There is a desire to be with, to give, to share. These elements may appear in various mixtures and gradations. There may be strong feelings of apprehension somewhere along the way. The person in love may experience strong feelings of resentment at one stage or another in his relationship with the beloved person. He may feel threatened. If he is troubled with guilt and feelings of inferiority, these may be reactivated. If he has many grievances associated with a hostile attitude toward people, he may be in conflict, uncertain as to whether he is capable of a genuine feeling of affection. If he has lived as a withdrawn sort of person, or if he harbors a vindictive attitude toward the opposite sex, stemming from earlier years, the experiences associated with one phase or another of being in love may produce anxiety, for he cannot fall in love and still retain the emotional isolation and aloofness or vengefulness which hitherto has characterized his relationships with other human beings.

There is much else in the situation that might make him uneasy. The beloved person may be wonderful but (unlike Reik's choice) she (or he) may in many ways fall short of the ideal the person had set for himself. So, if he commits himself nonetheless, he must renounce some of his claims, not only upon the loved one but also upon himself. If he can succeed in doing this realistically he probably is ready for the next chapter in his life. But if his illusions remain intact and he is swept along on a romantic wave of self-deception he probably will go through the process again as he turns (in actuality or in his imagination) from one infatuation or from one spouse to another in a futile endeavor to find through another a release from an unhealthy condition within himself.

Bibliography

Abel, T. M. 1932. Unsynthetic modes of thinking among adults: a discussion of Piaget's concepts. *Amer. J. Psychol.*, *44*, 123–132.

Alcock, T. 1948. Conclusions from psychiatric work with evacuated children. *Brit. J. Med. Psychol.*, *21*, 181–184.

Alexander, C. 1946. A correlation between age and antipathy. *J. Soc. Psychol.*, *23*, 229–231.

Alexander, F. 1948. *Fundamentals of psychoanalysis.* New York: Norton.

Anastasi, A., N. Cohen, and D. Spatz. 1948. A study of fear and anger in college students through the controlled diary method. *J. Genet. Psychol.*, *73*, 243–249.

Anderson, J. E. 1927. The dream as a re-conditioning process. *J. Abnorm. Soc. Psychol.*, *22*, 21–25.

——. 1948. Personality organization in children. *Amer. Psychol.*, *3*, 409–416.

Anon. 1944. One child in nine in a broken family. *Statist. Bull., Metrop. Life Insur.*, 25, No. 3, 3–6.

Appel, M. H. 1942. Aggressive behavior of nursery school children and adult procedures in dealing with such behavior. *J. Exp. Educ.*, *11*, 185–199.

Barker, R., T. Dembo, and K. Lewin. 1937. Experiments on frustration and regression in children. *Psychol. Bull.*, *34*, 754–755.

Barker, R. G., B. A. Wright, and M. R. Gonick. 1946. *Adjustment to physical handicap and illness: A survey of the social psychology of physique and disability.* New York: Soc. Science Res. Council.

Bartlett, Sir F. 1932. *Remembering.* New York. Macmillan.

Baruch, D. W. 1941. Aggression during doll play in a preschool. *Amer. J. Orthopsychiat.*, *11*, 252–260.

Baruch, D. W., and J. A. Wilcox. 1944. A study of sex differences in preschool children's adjustment coexistent with interparental tensions. *J. Genet. Psychol.*, *64*, 281–303.

Bayley, N. 1932. A study of the crying of infants during mental and physical tests. *J. Gen. Psychol.*, *40*, 306–329.

Bell, J. 1943. *Psychological aspects of dental treatment of children.* Madison: J. Exp. Educ. Pp. 87.

Bell, S. 1902. A preliminary study of the emotion of love between the sexes. *Amer. J. Psychol.*, *13*, 325–354.

Bender, L. 1939. Mental hygiene and the child. *Amer. J. Orthopsychiat.*, *9*, 574–582.

——. 1950. Anxiety in disturbed children. In P. H. Hoch and J. Zubin (Eds.), *Anxiety*, Chapter 7. New York: Grune and Stratton.

Benedict, R. 1940. Discussion of "hostility in Pilaga children." *Amer. J. Orthopsychiat.*, *10*, 120–121.

Berne, E. V. C. 1930. An experimental investigation of social behavior patterns in young children. *Univ. Iowa Stud. Child Welfare*, *4*, No. 3.

Binet, A. 1895. La peur chez les enfants. *Année psychol.*, *2*, 223–254.

Blatz, W. E., K. D. Allin, and D. A. Millichamp. 1936. A study of laughter in the nursery school child. *Univ. Toronto Stud. Child Develpm. Ser.*, No. 7.

Blatz, W. E., S. N. F. Chant, and M. D. Salter. 1937. Emotional episodes in the child of school age. *Univ. Toronto Stud. Child Develpm. Ser.*, No. 9.

Blatz, W. E., and D. A. Millichamp. 1935. The development of emotion in the infant. *Univ. Toronto Stud. Child Develpm. Ser.*, No. 4.

Block, V. L. 1937. Conflicts of adolescents with their mothers. *J. Abnorm. Soc. Psychol.*, *32*, 193–306.

Boeck, W. 1909. *Das Mitleid bei Kindern.* Giessen: v. Münchow.

Bonar, H. S. 1942. High-school pupils list their anxieties. *School Rev.*, *50*, 512–515.

Boston, M. V. 1939. Some factors related to the expression of fear in a group of average and superior children. *Smith Coll. Stud. Soc. Work*, *10*, 106–107.

Boutonier, J., and P. Henri. 1946. La peur et l'angoisse chez les enfants et les adolescents aveugles. *J. Psychol. Norm. Path.*, *39*, 341–349.

Brackett, C. W. 1934. Laughing and crying of preschool children. *Child Develpm. Monogr.*, No. 14.

Bregman, E. O. 1934. An attempt to modify the emotional attitudes of infants by the conditioned response technique. *J. Genet. Psychol.*, *45*, 169–198.

Bridges, K. M. B. 1932. Emotional development in early infancy. *Child Develpm.*, *3*, 324–334.

Britt, S., and S. Q. Janus. 1940. Criteria of frustration. *Psychol. Rev.*, *47*, 451–459.

Brodbeck, A. J., and O. C. Irwin. 1946. The speech behavior of infants without families. *Child Develpm.*, *17*, 145–156.

Brumbaugh, F. N. 1939. Stimuli which causes laughter in children. Ph.D. dissertation, New York University.

Bühler, C. 1930. *The first year of life.* New York: Day.

——. 1933. The social behavior of children. M. Murchison (Ed.), *A Handbook of child psychology*, 2d ed. Worcester: Clark University Press. Chapter IX, pp. 374–416.

Burbury, W. M. 1941. Effects of evacuation and of air raids on city children. *Brit. Med. J.*, *4218*, 660–662.

Burt, C. 1940. The incidence of neurotic symptoms among evacuated school children. *Brit. J. Psychol.*, *10*, 8–15.

——. 1941. The billeting of evacuated children. *Brit. J. Educ. Psychol.*, *11*, 85–98.

Burton, A. 1942. The aggression of young children following satiation. *Amer. J. Orthopsychiat.*, *12*, 262–267.

Calkins, M. W. 1894–1896. The emotional life of children. *Ped. Sem.*, *3*, 319–330.

Cannon, W. B. 1929. *Bodily changes in pain, hunger, fear and rage.* (2d ed.) New York: Appleton.

——. 1939. *Wisdom of the body.* New York: Norton.

Child, I. L. 1940. The relation between measures of infantile amnesia and neuroticism. *J. Abnorm. Soc. Psychol.*, *35*, 453–456.

Chittenden, G. E. 1942. An experimental study in measuring and modifying assertive behavior in young children. *Monogr. Soc. Res. Child Develpm.*, 7.

Clark, W. E. L., J. Beattie, G. Riddock, and N. M. Dott. 1938. *The hypothalmus.* Edinburgh: Oliver and Boyd.

Cole, L. 1944. *Attaining maturity.* New York: Rinehart.

Collins, W. J. 1946. The effects of certain parasympathomimetic substances on the emotions of normal and psychotic individuals. *Stud. Psychol. Psychiat.*, No. 7, *6*, 37.

Conn. J. H. 1940. Children's reactions to the discovery of genital differences. *Amer. J. Orthopsychiat.*, *10*, 747–755.

——. 1941. The treatment of fearful children. *Amer. J. Orthopsychiat.*, *11*, 744–752.

Conrad, H. S., and M. C. Jones. 1942. Some results from an "annoyance inventory" in a cumulative study of adolescents. *Psychol. Bull.*, *39*, 475–476.

Coromina, J. 1943. Repercussions of the war on children as observed during the Spanish Civil War. *Nerv. Child.*, *2*, 320–323.

Crider, B. 1949. Phobias: Their nature and treatment. *J. Psychol.*, *27*, 217–229.

Crook, M. N., and L. Harden. 1931. A quantitative investigation of early memories. *J. Soc. Psychol.*, *2*, 252–255.

Damann, V. T. 1941. Developmental changes in attitude as one factor determining energy output in a motor performance. *Child Develpm.*, *12*, 241–246.

Danzinger, L., and L. Frankl. 1934. Zum Problem der Funktionsreifung. *Z. Kinderforschung*, *43*, 219–254.

Darwin, C. 1913. *The expression of the emotions in man and animals.* New York: Appleton.

Davidson, M. A., and I. M. Slade. 1940. Results of a survey of senior school evacuees. *Brit. J. Educ. Psychol.*, *10*, 179–195.

Davis. C. M. 1928. Self-selection of diet by newly weaned infants. *Amer. J. Dis. Child.*, *36*, 651–679.

Davis, H. V., R. R. Sears, H. C. Miller, and A. J. Brodbeck. 1948. Effects of cup, bottle and breast feeding on oral activities of newborn infants. *Pediatrics*, 549–558.

Dearborn, G. V. N. 1910. *Motor-sensory development: Observation of the first three years of a child.* Baltimore: Warwick and York.

del Solar, C. 1949. *Parents and teachers view the child.* New York: Horace Mann-Lincoln Institute of School Experimentation, Teachers College, Columbia University.

Dembo, T. 1931. Der Ärger als dynamisches Problem. *Psychol. Forsch.*, *15*, 1–144.

Dennis, W. 1938. Infant development under conditions of restricted practice and of minimum social stimulation: A preliminary report. *J. Gen. Psychol.*, *53*, 149–157.

Dennis, W. 1941. Infant development under conditions of restricted practice and of minimum social stimulation. *Genet. Psychol. Monogr.*, *23*, 143–189.

——. 1942a. Infant reactions to restraint: An evaluation of Watson's theory. *Trans. N. Y. Acad. Sci.*, Ser. II, *2*, No. 7.

——. 1942b. Piaget's questions applied to a child of known environment. *J. Genet. Psychol.*, *60*, 307–320.

Deshaies, L. 1937. La notion de relation chez l'enfant. *J. Psychol.*, *60*, 207–320.

Despert, J. L. 1942. *Preliminary report on children's reaction to the war, including a critical survey of the literature.* New York: Payne Whitney Nursing School of Cornell University Medical College.

Deutsch, H. 1944–1945. *Psychology of women.* Vols. I and II. New York: Grune and Stratton.

Deutsche, J. M. 1937. *The development of children's concepts of causal relations.* Minneapolis: University of Minnesota Press.

Ding, G. F., and A. T. Jersild. 1932. A study of laughing and smiling of preschool children. *J. Gen. Psychol.*, *40*, 452–472.

Dollard, J., L. W. Doob, N. E. Miller, O. H. Mowrer, R. R. Sears, *et al.* 1939. *Frustration and aggression.* New Haven: Yale University Press.

Dorkey, M., and E. W. Amen. 1947. A continuation study of anxiety reactions in young children by means of a projective technique. *Genet. Psychol. Monogr.*, *35*, 139–183.

Dudycha, G. J., and M. M. Dudycha. 1933. Some factors and characteristics of childhood memories. *Child Develpm.*, *4*, 265–278.

——. 1941. Childhood memories: A review of the literature. *Psychol. Bull.*, *38*, 8, 669–681.

Dunbar, F. 1945. *Emotions and bodily changes: A survey of literature on psychosomatic interrelationships.* (3d ed.) New York: Columbia University Press.

Durea, M. A. 1937. The emotional maturity of juvenile delinquents. *J. Abnorm. Soc. Psychol.*, *31*, 472–482.

Edelston, H. 1943. Separation anxiety in young children: A study of hospital cases. *Genet. Psychol. Monogr.*, *28*, 3–95.

Edwards, A. E. 1941. Political frames of reference as a factor influencing recognition. *J. Abnorm. Soc. Psychol.*, *36*, 34–50.

Ellesor, M. V. 1933. Children's reactions to hover visual stimuli. *Child Develpm.*, *4*, 95–105.

Ellis, A. 1949. A study of human love relationships. *J. Genet. Psychol.*, *75*, 61–71.

Enders, A. C. 1927. A study of the laughter of the preschool child in the Merrill-Palmer nursery school. *Pap. Mich. Acad. Sci. Arts, Letters*, *8*, 341–356. (Cited in *Yearb. Nat. Soc. Stud. Educ.*, 1929, *28*, 603–604.)

England, A. O. 1946. Non-structural approach to the study of children's fears. *J. Clinical Psychol.*, *2*, 364–368.

English, H. B. 1929. Three cases of the "conditioned fear response." *J. Abnorm. Soc. Psychol., 24,* 221–225.

English, O. S., and G. H. J. Pearson. 1945. *Emotional problems of living.* New York: Norton.

Escalona, S. K. 1946. Overt sympathy with the enemy in maladjusted children. *Amer. J. Orthopsychiat., 16,* 333–340.

Fajans, J. 1933. Die Bedeutung der Entfernung für die Stärke eines Aufforderungscharakters beim Säugling und Kleinkind. Untersuchungen zur Handlungs und Ajjektpsychologie. *XII. Psychologische Forschung, 17,* 215–267. Herausgegeben von K. Lewin.

Felder, J. G. 1932. Some factors determining the nature and frequency of anger and fear outbreaks in preschool children. *J. Juv. Res., 16,* 278–290.

Fenichel, O. 1945. *The psychoanalytic theory of neurosis.* New York: Norton.

Fite, M. D. 1940. Aggressive behavior in young children and children's attitudes toward aggression. *Genet. Psychol. Monogr., 22,* 151–319.

Fitz-Simons, M. J. 1935. Some parent-child relationships as shown in clinical case studies. *Teach. Coll. Contr. Educ.,* No. 643. New York: Teachers College, Columbia University.

Flügel, J. C. 1925. A study of feelings and emotions of normal subjects in everyday life. *Brit. J. Psychol., 15,* 318–355.

Foster, J. C., and J. E. Anderson. 1930. *The young child and his parents. (Inst. Child Welfare Monogr. Ser.,* No. 1.) Minneapolis: University of Minnesota Press.

Foster, S. 1927. A study of the personality make-up and social setting of fifty jealous children. *Ment. Hyg., N. Y., 11,* 53–77.

Frank, L. K. 1939. Projective methods for the study of personality. *J. Psychol., 8,* 389–413.

Frederickson, N. 1942. The effects of frustration on negativistic behavior of young children. *J. Genet. Psychol., 61,* 203–226.

Frenkel-Brunswik, E. 1948. A study of prejudice in children. *Hum. Relat., 1.* 295–306.

Freud, A., and D. Burlingham. 1943. Monthly reports on Hampstead Nurseries. *Foster Parents Plan for War Children, Inc.,* 55 W. 42 Street, New York, N. Y.

———. 1944. *Infants without families.* New York: International Universities Press.

Freud, S. 1930. Three contributions to the theory of sex. (4th ed., trans. by A. A. Brill.) *Nerv. Ment. Dis. Monogr. Ser.,* No. 7. Pp. xiv + 104.

———. 1933. *New introductory lectures on psychoanalysis.* (Trans. by W. J. H. Spratt.) New York: Norton.

———. 1936. *The problem of anxiety.* New York: Norton.

Fromm, E. 1947. *Man for himself.* New York: Rinehart.

Fulcher, J. 1942. *"Voluntary" facial expression in blind and seeing children.* Ph.D. thesis. New York: Columbia University.

Gates, G. S. 1926. An observational study of anger. *J. Exp. Psychol., 19,* 325–336.

Gershman, H. 1950. The problem of anxiety. *Amer. J. Psychoanal., 10,* 89–91.

Gesell, A. 1906. Jealousy. *Amer. J. Psychol., 17,* 437–496.

———. 1928. *Infancy and human growth.* New York: Macmillan.

———. 1929. The individual in infancy. In C. Murchison (Ed.), *The foundations of experimental psychology* (1st ed.), pp. 628–660. Worcester: Clark University Press.

Gesell, A., and F. L. Ilg. 1937. *Feeding behavior of infants.* Philadelphia: Lippincott.

Gesell, A., and H. Thompson. 1941. Twins T and C from infancy to adolescence: A biogenic study of individual differences by the method of co-twin control. *Genet. Psychol. Monogr., 24,* 256.

Glueck, S., and E. Glueck. 1940. *Juvenile delinquents grown up.* New York: *Commonwealth Fund.*

Goldfarb, W. 1943. The effects of early institutional care on adolescent personality. *J. Exp. Educ.,* No. 143, *12,* 106–129.

Goldstein, K. 1947. *Human nature in the light of psychopathology.* Cambridge: Harvard University Press.

Goodenough, F. L. 1931a. The expression of the emotions in infancy. *Child Develpm., 2,* 96–101.

———. 1931b. *Anger in young children. (Inst. Child Welfare Monogr. Ser.,* No. 9.) Minneapolis: University of Minnesota Press.

———. 1932. Expression of the emotions in a blind-deaf child. *J. Abnorm. Soc. Psychol., 27,* 328–333.

Grant. V. W. 1948. A major problem of human sexuality. *J. Soc. Psychol., 28,* 79–101.

Griffiths, R. 1935. *The study of imagination in early childhood.* London: Kegan Paul.

Gutteridge, M. V. 1939. A study of motor achievements of young children. *Arch. Psychol., N. Y.,* No. 244.

Hagman, R. R. 1932. A study of fears of children of preschool age. *J. Exp. Educ., 1,* 110–130.

Hall, G. S. 1897. A study of fears. *Amer. J. Psychol., 8,* 147–249.

———. 1899. A study of anger. *Amer. J. Psychol., 10,* 516–591.

Hallowell, A. I. 1940. Aggression in Saulteaux Society. *Psychiat. 3,* 395–407.

Halverson, H. M. 1940. Genital and sphincter behavior of the male infant. *J. Genet. Psychol., 56,* 95–136.

Hamilton, G. V. 1929. *A research in marriage.* New York: Boni.

Hartmann, G. W. 1934–1935. Personality traits associated with variations in happiness. *J. Abnorm. Soc. Psychol., 29,* 202–212.

Hattendorf, K. W. 1932. A study of the questions of young children concerning sex: A study of an experimental approach to parent education. *J. Soc. Psychol., 3,* 37–65.

Hattwick, B. W., and M. Stowell. 1936. Relation of parental over-attentiveness to children's work habits and social adjustments. *J. Educ. Res., 30,* 169–176.

Hazlitt, V. 1929. Children's thinking. *Brit. J. Psychol., 20,* 354–461.

Hebb, D. O. 1945. The forms and conditions of chimpanzee anger. *Bull. Canad. Psychol. Assoc., 5,* 32–35.

———. 1946. On the nature of fear. *Psychol. Rev., 53,* 259–276.

Hebb, D. O., and A. H. Riesen. 1943. The genesis of emotional fears. *Bull. Canad. Psychol. Assoc., 3,* 49–50.

Henri, V., and C. Henri. 1895. On our earliest recollections of childhood. *Amer. J. Psychol., 7,* 303–304.

Henry, J. 1940. Some cultural determinants of hostility in Pilaga Indian children. *Amer. J. Orthopsychiat., 10,* 111–119.

Hersey, R. B. 1931. Emotional cycles in man. *J. Ment. Sci., 77,* 151–169.

Herzfeld, E., and F. Prager. 1930. Verständnis für Scherz und Komik beim Kinde. *Z. angew. Psychol., 34,* 353–417.

Hicks, J. A., and M. Hayes. 1938. Study of the characteristics of 250 junior high school children. *Child Develpm., 9,* 219–242.

Hildreth, G. 1941. The difficulty reduction tendency in perception and problem solving. *J. Educ. Psychol., 32,* 305–313.

———. 1944. The simplification tendency in reproducing designs. *J. Genet. Psychol., 64,* 329–333.

Hoch, P. H., and Zubin, J. 1950. *Anxiety.* New York: Grune and Stratton.

Hollingworth, H. L. 1928. *Psychology: Its facts and principles.* New York: Appleton.

Hollingworth, L. S. 1928. *Psychology of the adolescent.* New York: Appleton.

Holmes, F. B. 1935. An experimental study of the fears of young children. In Jersild and Holmes, Children's fears. *Child Develpm. Monogr.,* No. 20, pp. 167–296.

———. 1936. An experimental investigation of a method of overcoming children's fears. *Child Develpm., 7,* 6–30.

Horney, K. 1937. *The neurotic personality of our time.* New York: Norton.

———. 1939. *New ways in psychoanalysis.* New York: Norton.

———. 1945. *Our inner conflicts.* New York: Norton.

———. 1950. *Neurosis and human growth.* New York: Norton.

———. 1951. On feeling abused. *Amer. J. Psychoanal., 11,* 5–12.

Horowitz, R., and L. B. Murphy. 1938. Projective methods in the psychological study of children. *J. Exp. Educ., 7,* 133–140.

Hunt, J. McV. 1941. The effects of infant feeding frustration upon adult hoarding in the albino rat. *J. Abnorm. Soc. Psychol., 36,* 338–360.

Hunt, Wm. A. 1941. Recent developments in the field of emotion. *Psychol. Bull., 38,* 249–276.

Huschka, M. 1942. The child's response to coercive bowel training. *Psychosomatic Med., 4,* 301–308.

Irwin, O. C. 1932. Infant responses to vertical movements. *Child Develpm., 3,* 167–169.

Isaacs, S. 1933. *Social development in young children: A study of beginnings.* New York: Harcourt, Brace.

———. 1936. *The nursery years.* New York: Vanguard.

Isaacs, S., S. C. Brown, and R. H. Thouless. (Eds.) 1941. *The Cambridge evacuation survey.* London: Methuen.

Isaacs, S., *et al.* 1941. *Children in wartime.* New Education Fellowship.

Jack, L. M. 1934. An experimental study of ascendant behavior in preschool children. In L. M. Jack, E. M. Manwell, I. G. Mengert, *et al.,* Behavior of the preschool child, *Univ. Iowa Stud. Child Welfare,* No. 9, *3,* 7–65.

Jacobsen, V. 1947–1948. Influential factors in the outcome of treatment of school phobia. *Smith Coll. Stud. Soc. Work, 18,* 181–202.

Jersild, A. 1931. Memory for the pleasant as compared with the unpleasant. *J. Exp. Psychol., 14,* 284–288.

Jersild, A. T. 1947. *Child psychology.* (3d ed.) New York: Prentice-Hall.

———. 1951a. Emotional development. Chapter 3 in C. E. Skinner (Ed.), *Educational Psychology.* (3d ed.) New York: Prentice-Hall.

———. 1951b. Self-understanding in childhood and adolescence. *Amer. Psychologist, 6,* 122–126.

———. 1952. *In Search of Self.* New York: Bureau of Publications, Teachers College, Columbia University.

Jersild, A. T., B. Goldman, and J. J. Loftus. 1941. A comparative study of the worries of children in two school situations. *J. Exp. Educ., 4,* 323–326.

Jersild, A. T., and F. B. Holmes. 1935a. Children's fears. *Child Develpm. Monogr.,* No. 20, Pp. 356.

———. 1935b. Some factors in the development of children's fears. *J. Exp. Educ., 4,* 133–141.

———. 1935c. Methods of overcoming children's fears. *J. Psychol., 1,* 75–104.

Jersild, A. T., and F. V. Markey. 1935. Conflicts between preschool children. *Child Develpm. Monogr.,* No. 21. Pp. xi + 181.

Jersild, A. T., F. V. Markey, and C. L. Jersild. 1933. Children's fears, dreams, likes, dislikes, pleasant and unpleasant memories. *Child Develpm. Monogr.,* No. 12.

Jersild, A. T., and M. M. Meigs. 1943. Children and war. *Psychol. Bull., 40,* 541–573.

Jersild, A. T., and R. J. Tasch. 1949. *Children's interests and what they suggest for education.* New York: Teachers College Bureau of Publications.

Jersild, A. T., E. S. Woodyard, and C. del Solar. 1949. *Joys and problems of child rearing.* New York: Teachers College Bureau of Publications.

John, E. 1941. A study of the effects of evacuation and air-raids on children of preschool age. *Brit. J. Educ. Psychol., 11,* 173–182.

Johnson, A. M., E. I. Falstein, S. A. Squrek, and M. Svendson. 1941. School phobia. *Amer. J. Orthopsychiat., 11,* 702–711.

Johnson, W. B. 1937. Euphoric and depressed moods in normal subjects. *Character and Pers., 6,* 79–98.

Jones, H. E. 1930. The galvanic skin reflex in infancy. *Child Develpm., 1,* 106–110.
——. 1931. The conditioning of overt emotional responses. *J. Educ. Psychol., 22,* 127–130.
Jones, H. E., and M. C. Jones. 1928. Fear. *Childhood Educ., 5,* 136–143.
Jones, M. C. 1924*a*. A laboratory study of fear: The case of Peter. *Ped. Sem., 31,* 308–316.
——. 1924*b*. Elimination of children's fears. *J. Exp. Psychol., 7,* 382–390.
——. 1925. A study of the emotions of preschool children. *Sch. and Soc., 21,* 755–758.
——. 1933. Emotional development. In C. Murchison (Ed.), *A handbook of child psychology* (2d ed., rev.), pp. 271–302. Worcester: Clark University Press.
Jones, T. D. 1939. The development of certain motor skills and play activities in young children. *Child Develpm. Monogr.,* No. 26. Pp. 180.
Justin, F. 1932. A genetic study of laughter-provoking stimuli. *Child Develpm., 3,* 114–136.
Keister, M. E., and R. Updegraff. 1937. A study of children's reactions to failure and an experimental attempt to modify them. *Child Develpm., 8,* 241–248.
Kenderdine, M. 1931. Laughter in the preschool child. *Child Develpm., 2,* 228–230.
Kepler, H. 1933–1934. Distribution of aggressive and submissive behavior among two hundred problem children. *Smith Coll. Stud. Social Work, 4,* 167–168.
Kierkegaard, Søren. 1951. *The sickness unto death.* Princeton: Princeton University Press.
Kimmins, C. W. 1915–1916. The interests of London children at different ages in air raids. *J. Exp. Pedagogy, 3,* 225–236.
Kinsey, A. C., W. B. Pomeroy, and E. E. Martin. 1948. *Sexual behavior in the human male.* Philadelphia: Saunders.
Klein, E. 1945. The reluctance to go to school. *Psychoanal. Stud. of the Child.* Vol. 1.
Klein, M. 1932. *The psycho-analysis of children.* New York: Norton.
Klineberg, O. 1940. *Social psychology.* New York: Holt.
Kluckhohn, C. 1947. Some aspects of Navaho infancy and early childhood. *Psychoanal. and Soc. Sc., 1,* 37–86.
Knight, E. 1933–1934. A descriptive comparison of markedly aggressive and submissive children. *Smith Coll. Stud. Soc. Work, 4.*
Koch, H. L. 1935. An analysis of certain forms of so-called "nervous habits" in young children. *J. Genet. Psychol., 46,* 139–170.
Köhler, W. 1925. *The mentality of apes.* (Trans. by E. Winter.) New York: Harcourt, Brace.
Korner, A. F. 1947. *Some aspects of hostility in young children.* Ph.D. dissertation, Columbia University.
Krout, M. H., and R. Stagner. 1939. Personality development in radicals. *Sociometry, 2,* 31–46.
Laing, A. 1939. The sense of humour in childhood and adolescence. *Brit. J. Educ. Psychol., 9,* 201.

Landis, C. 1924. Studies of emotional reactions: II. General behavior and facial expression in emotion. *J. Gen. Psychol., 2,* 59–72.
Landis, C., A. Landis, M. Bolles, *et al.* 1940. *Sex in development.* New York: Hoeber.
Landis, C., and W. Hunt. 1939. *The startle pattern.* New York: Farrar & Rinehart.
Lasswell, H. D. 1930. *Psychopathology and politics.* Chicago: University of Chicago Press.
Lazell, E. W. 1929. *The anatomy of emotion: man's two natures.* New York: Century.
Lecky, P. 1945. *Self-consistency.* New York: Island Press Cooperative.
Lee, M. A. M. 1932. A study of emotional instability in nursery school children. *Child Develpm., 3,* 142–145.
Lerner, E., L. B. Murphy, J. L. Stone, E. Beyer, and E. W. Brown. 1941. Methods for the study of personality in young children. *Monogr. Soc. Res. Child Develpm., 6.*
Levy, D. M. 1928. Fingersucking and accessory movements in early infancy. *Amer. J. Psychiat., 7,* 881–918.
——. 1936. Primary affect hunger. *Amer. J. Psychiat., 94,* 643–652.
——. 1937*a*. Thumb or finger sucking from the psychiatric angle. *Child Develpm., 8,* 99–101.
——. 1937*b*. Studies in sibling rivalry. *Res. Monogr. Amer. Orthopsychiat. Ass.,* No. 2. Pp. 96.
——. 1940. "Control-situation" studies of children's responses to the difference in genitalia. *Amer. J. Orthopsychiat., 10,* 755–763.
——. 1943. *Maternal overprotection.* New York: Columbia University Press.
Lewin, K., R. Lippitt, and R. K. White. 1939. Patterns of aggressive behavior in experimentally created "social climates." *J. Soc. Psychol., 10,* 271–229.
Logre, J. B., and P. L. Fouquet. 1940–1941. L'Exaspération étude psychologique et clinique. *J. Psychol. Norm. Path., 37–38,* 346–373.
Lund, F. H. 1925. The psychology of belief. *J. Abnorm. Soc. Psychol., 20,* 63–81; 174–196.
——. 1940. Intelligence and emotionality. 39th NSSE, Part I, 282–285.
McAndrew, M. B. 1943. An experimental investigation of young children's ideas of causality. *Stud. Psychol. Psychiat.,* Catholic University Amer., *6,* No. 2.
McCarthy, Dorothea. 1953. Some possible explanations of sex differences in language development and disorders. *J. Psychol., 35,* 155–160.
McDougall, W. 1926. *An introduction to social psychology.* Boston: Luce.
McGraw, M. B. 1940. Neutral maturation as exemplified in achievement of bladder control. *J. Pediat., 16,* 580–590.
McKillop, A. S. 1952. *The relationship between the reader's attitude and certain types of reading response.* New York: Teachers College Bureau of Publications. Pp. viii + 101.
Macfarlane, J. W. 1938. Studies in child guidance: I. Methodology of data collection and organization.

Monogr. Soc. Res. Child Develpm., *3*, No. 6, Ser. 19. Pp. vii + 254.

Macmurray, J. 1937. *Reason and emotion.* New York: Appleton-Century.

Madow, L., and S. E. Hardy. 1947. Incidence and analysis of the broken family in the background of neurosis. *Amer. J. Orthopsychiat.*, *17*, 521–528.

Maier, N. R. F. 1939. *Studies of abnormal behavior in the rat.* New York: Harper.

——. 1948. Experimentally induced abnormal behavior. *Sci. Month.*, *67*, 210–216.

Markey, F. V. 1935. Imaginative behavior in preschool children. *Child Develpm. Monogr.*, No. 18. Pp. 138.

Marsh, C. J. 1942. The worries of the college woman. *J. Soc. Psychol.*, *15*, 335–339.

Maslow, A. H. 1943. A theory of human motivation. *Psychol. Rev.*, *50*, 370–396.

——. 1948. "Higher" and "lower" needs. *J. Psychol.*, *25*, 433–436.

Masserman, J. H. 1943. *Behavior and neuroses.* Chicago: University of Chicago Press.

May, R. 1950. *The meaning of anxiety.* New York: Ronald Press.

Mead, G. 1934. *Mind, self and society.* Chicago: University of Chicago Press.

Meltzer, H. 1933. Students' adjustments in anger. *J. Soc. Psychol.*, *4*, 285–309.

——. 1937. Anger adjustments in relation to intelligence and achievement. *J. Genet. Psychol.*, *50*, 63–82.

Menninger, K. A. 1938. *Man against himself.* New York: Harcourt, Brace.

Miles, C. 1893. A study of individual psychology. *Amer. J. Psychol.*, *6*, 534–558.

Miller, N. E., and R. Bugelski. 1948. Minor studies of aggression: II. The influence of frustrations imposed by the in-group on attitudes expressed toward out-groups. *J. Psychol.*, *25*, 437–442.

Mira, E. 1940. Analisis estructural del miedo. (Structural analysis of fear.) *Rev. psiquiat crim.*, *5*, 215–226. Original not seen. See *Psychol. Abst.*, 1941, 2162.

Mitrano, A. J. 1939. Preliminary construction of a schedule of emotional stability for children. *Amer. J. Orthopsychiat.*, *9*, 360–367.

Mons, W. E. R. 1941. Air raids and the child. *Brit. Med. J.*, No. 4217, 625–626.

Montagu, M. F. A. 1942. On the physiology and psychology of swearing. *Psychiat.*, *5*, 189–201.

Moore, T. V. 1948. *The driving forces of human nature.* New York: Grune and Stratton.

Morgan, J. J. B. 1934. *Keeping a sound mind.* New York: Macmillan.

——. 1944. Following the path of least resistance in thinking. *J. Educ. Psychol.*, *35*, 27–38.

Mosso, A. 1896. *Fear.* (Trans. by E. Lough and F. Keiɕow.) New York: Longmans, Green.

Mowrer, O. H. 1950. Pain, punishment, guilt and anxiety. In P. H. Hoch and J. Zubin (Eds.), *Anxiety*, Chapter 3. New York: Grune and Stratton.

Mowrer, O. H., and P. Viek. 1948. An experimental analogue of fear from a sense of helplessness. *J. Abnorm. Soc. Psychol.*, *43*, 193–200.

Mullahy, P. 1948. *Oedipus myth and complex.* New York: Hermitage Press.

Murphy, G. 1945. The freeing of intelligence. *Psychol. Bull.*, *42*, 1–19.

——. 1947. *Personality.* New York: Harper.

Murphy, L. B. 1937. *Social behavior and child personality.* New York: Columbia University Press.

Murray, H. A. 1938. *Explorations in personality: A clinical and experimental study of 50 men of college age by workers at Harvard psychological clinic.* New York: Oxford University Press.

Neilon, P. 1948. Shirley's babies after fifteen years. *J. Genet. Psychol.*, *73*, 175–186.

Northway, M. L. 1936. The influence of age and social group on children's remembering. *Brit. J. Psychol.*, *27*, 11–29.

Oakes, M. E. 1946. Children's explanations of natural phenomena. *Teacher's Coll. Contr. Educ.* New York: Teachers College, Columbia University.

Orlansky, H. 1949. Infant care and personality. *Psychol. Bull.*, *46*, 1–48.

Osborne, E. G. 1937. *Camping and guidance.* New York: Associated Press.

Pearson, G. 1931. Some early factors in the formation of personality. *Amer. J. Orthopsychiat.*, *1*, 284–291.

Peller, L. E. 1939. The child's approach to reality. *Amer. J. Orthopsychiat.*, *9*, 503–513.

Piaget, J. 1928. *Judgment and reasoning in the child.* New York: Harcourt, Brace.

——. 1930. *The child's conception of physical causality.* (Trans. by M. Gabain.) New York: Harcourt, Brace.

——. 1932. *The language and thought of the child.* (Trans. by M. Gabain.) New York: Harcourt, Brace.

Pinsky, A. 1950a. *Frigidity in women.* New York: Auxiliary Council to the Assoc. for the Adv. of Psychoanal.

——. 1950b. Impotence in men. See Pinsky, 1950a.

Pintner, R., and L. Brunschwig. 1937. A study of certain fears and wishes among deaf and hearing children. *J. Educ. Psychol.*, *28*, 259–270.

Pintner, R., and J. Lev. 1940. Worries of school children. *J. Genet. Psychol.*, *56*, 67–76.

Piret, R. 1940. Recherches génétiques sur le comique. *Acta Psychol.*, Hague, *5*, No. 2–3, 103–142. Original not seen. See *Psychol. Abst.*, July, 1944, No. 2324.

Pratt, K. C. 1945. A study of the "fears" of rural children. *J. Genet. Psychol.*, *67*, 179–194.

Pratt, K. C., A. K. Nelson, and K. H. Sun. 1930. The behavior of the newborn infant. *Ohio State Univ. Stud., Contr. Psychol.*, No. 10.

Pressey, S., and F. Robinson. 1944. *Psychology and the new education.* New York: Harper.

Pullias, E. V. 1937. Masturbation as mental hygiene problem: A study of the beliefs of seventy-five young men. *J. Abnorm. Soc. Psychol.*, *32*, 216–222.

Ramsey, G. V. 1943. The sexual development of boys. *Amer. J. Psychol.*, *56*, 217–233.

Rank, O. 1932. *Modern education: A critique of its fundamental ideas.* New York: Knopf.

Redl, F., and Wineman, D. 1951. *Children who hate.* Glencoe: The Free Press.

Reik, T. 1944. *A psychologist looks at love.* New York: Rinehart.

——. 1945. *Psychology of sex relations.* New York: Farrar and Rinehart.

Ribble, M. A. 1941. Disorganizing factors of infant personality. *Amer. J. Psychiat.,* 98, 459–463.

——. 1943. *The rights of infants, early psychological needs and their satisfaction.* New York: Columbia University Press.

Ribot, T. 1903. *The psychology of the emotions.* New York: Scribner's.

Richardson, R. F. 1918. *The psychology and pedagogy of anger.* (*Educ. Psychol. Monogr.,* No. 19.) Baltimore: Warwick and York. Pp. 100.

Ricketts, A. F. 1934. A study of the behavior of young children in anger. In L. M. Jack *et al.,* Behavior of the preschool child, *Univ. Iowa Stud. Child Welfare,* No. 9, 3, 159–171.

Rogers, C. 1942. *Counseling and psychotherapy.* Boston: Houghton Mifflin.

Rosenweig, S. 1938–1939. A general outline of frustration. *Character and Pers.,* 7, 151–160.

Ross, B. M. 1931. Some traits associated with sibling jealousy in problem children. *Smith Coll. Stud. Soc. Work,* 1, 364–376.

Sadger, J. 1941. Preliminary study of the psychic life of the fetus and the primary germ. *Psychoanal. Rev.,* 28, 327–358.

Sandin, A. A. 1944. Social and emotional adjustments of regularly promoted and non-promoted pupils. *Child Develpm. Monogr.,* No. 32. New York: Teachers College Bureau of Publications. Pp. 142.

Sargent, H. 1945. Projective methods: Their origins, theory and application in personality research. *Psychol. Bull.,* 42, 257–293.

Saul, L. 1947. *Emotional maturity.* Philadelphia: Lippincott.

Searl, M. N. 1932. Some contrasted aspects of psycho-analysis and education. *Brit. J. Educ. Psychol.,* 2, 136–137.

Sears, R. R. 1943. Survey of objective studies of psychoanalytic concepts. *Soc. Sci. Res. Council Bull.,* 51. New York.

Seashore, H. G., and A. Bavelas. 1942. A study of frustration in children. *J. Genet. Psychol.,* 61, 279–314.

Sewall, M. 1930. Two studies in sibling rivalry: I. Some causes of jealousy in young children. *Smith Coll. Stud. Soc. Work,* 1, 6–22.

Shaffer, L. F. 1936. *The psychology of adjustment.* Boston: Houghton Mifflin.

——. 1947. Fear and courage in aerial combat. *J. Consult. Psychol.,* 11, 137–143.

Shand, A. F. 1920. *Foundations of character.* London: Macmillan.

Sheerer, E. T. 1949. An analysis of the relationship between acceptance of and respect for self and acceptance of and respect for others in ten counseling cases. *J. Consult. Psychol.,* 13, 169–175.

Sherman, M. 1927. The differentiation of emotional responses in infants: II. The ability of observers to judge the emotional characteristics of the crying of infants, and of the voice of an adult. *J. Comp. Psychol.,* 7, 335–351.

——. 1928. The differentiation of emotional responses in infants: III. A proposed theory of the development of emotional responses in infants. *J. Comp. Psychol.,* 8, 385–394.

Sherman, M., and J. Jost. 1942. Frustration reactions of normal and neurotic persons. *J. Psychol.,* 13, 3–19.

Sherman, M. M., and I. C. Sherman. 1925. Sensorimotor responses in infants. *J. Comp. Psychol.,* 5, 53–68.

Shirley, M. M. 1931. *The first two years: A study of twenty-five babies.* Postural and Locomotor Development Institute. Minneapolis: University of Minnesota Press, Vol. I. Pp. 227.

——. 1933. *The first two years:* Vol. III. *Personality manifestations.* Minneapolis: University of Minnesota Press. Pp. 228.

——. 1941. The impact of the mother's personality in the young child. *Smith Coll. Stud. Soc. Work,* 12, 15–64.

——. 1942. Children's adjustments to a strange situation. *J. Abnorm. Soc. Psychol.,* 37, 201–217.

Skeels, H. M., R. Updegraff, B. L. Wellman, and H. M. Williams. 1938. A study of environmental stimulation: An orphanage preschool project. *Univ. Iowa Stud. Child Welfare,* 1. Pp. 156.

Slater, E., R. Beckwith, and L. Behnke. 1939. Studies from the Center for Research in Child Health and Development, School of Public Health, Harvard University: II. Types, levels, and irregularities of response to a nursery school situation of forty children observed with special reference to the home environment. *Monogr. Soc. Res. Child Develpm.,* No. 4. Pp. 148.

Smalley, R. E. 1930. Two studies in sibling rivalry: II. The influence of differences in age, sex and intelligence in determining the attitudes of siblings toward each other. *Smith Coll. Stud. Soc. Work,* 1, 23–40.

Smith, R. B. 1932. The development of an inventory for the measurement of inferiority feelings at the high-school level. *Arch. Psychol.,* 144. Pp. 118.

Snygg, D., and A. W. Combs. 1949. *Individual behavior.* New York: Harper.

Spitz, R. A. 1946. Anaclitic depression. *Psychoanal. Stud. Child.,* 2, 313–342.

Spitz, R., and K. M. Wolf. 1946. The smiling response. A contribution to the ontogenesis of social relations. *Genet. Psychol. Monogr.,* 34, 57–125.

Stagner, R. 1944. Studies of aggressive social attitudes: III. The role of personal and family scores. *J. Soc. Psychol.,* 20, 129–140.

Stagner, R., and N. Drought. 1935. Measuring children's attitudes toward their parents. *J. Educ. Psychol.,* 26, 169–176.

Stern, W. 1930. *Psychology of early childhood.* New York: Holt.

Stone, C. P., and R. G. Barker. 1939. The attitudes and interests of premenarcheal and postmenarcheal girls. *J. Genet. Psychol., 54,* 27–71.

Stott, H. 1940. Adolescents' dislikes regarding parental behavior and their significance. *J. Genet. Psychol., 57,* 393–414.

Stratton, G. M. 1927. Anger and fear: Their probable relation to each other, to intellectual work and to primogeniture. *Amer. J. Psychol., 39,* 125–140.

——. 1929. Emotion and the incidence of disease: The influence of the number of diseases and of the age at which they occur. *Psychol. Rev., 36,* 242–253.

Stryker, M. F. 1898. Children's joys and sorrows. *Child. Stud. Monogr., 4,* 217–225.

Sullivan, Harry Stack. 1947. *Conceptions of modern psychiatry.* Washington, D. C.: The William Alanson White Psychiatric Foundation.

——. 1948. *The meaning of anxiety in psychiatry and in life.* Washington, D. C.: The William Alanson White Psychiatric Foundation.

Sulzberger, M., and S. Zaidens. 1948. Psychogenic factors in dermatologic disorders. *Med. Clin. N. Amer., 32,* 669–685.

Symonds, P. M. 1938. A study of parental acceptance and rejection. *Amer. J. Orthopsychiat., 8,* 679–688.

——. 1939. *The psychology of parent child relationships.* New York: Appleton-Century.

——. 1946. *The dynamics of human adjustment.* New York: Appleton-Century.

Taylor, J. H. 1934. Innate emotional responses in infants. *Ohio Univ. Stud. Contr. Psychol., 12,* 69–81.

Temple, R., and E. W. Amen. 1944. A study of anxiety reactions in young children by means of a projective technique. *Genet. Psychol. Monogr., 30,* 61–113.

Thompson, J. 1941. Development of facial expression of emotion in blind and seeing children. *Arch. Psychol. N. Y.,* No. 264.

Thorndike, E. L. 1913. *Educational psychology:* II. *The original nature of man.* New York: Teachers College, Columbia University.

Tolman, E. 1932. *Purposive behavior in animals and men.* New York and London: Century.

Valentine, C. W. 1930. The innate bases of fear. *J. Genet. Psychol., 37,* 394–420.

Van Houten, J. 1947–1948. Mother-child relationships in twelve cases of school phobia. *Smith Coll. Stud. Soc. Work., 18,* 161–180.

Vernon, M. D. 1941. A study of some effects of evacuation on adolescent girls. *Brit. J. Educ. Psychol., 36,* 457–576.

Warden, C. J. 1931. *Animal motivation; experimental studies on albino rats.* New York: Columbia University Press.

Washburn, R. W. 1928. A study of the smiling and laughing of infants in the first year of life. *Genet. Psychol. Monogr., 6,* 397–539.

Watson, G. 1930. Happiness among adult students of education. *J. Educ. Psychol., 21,* 79–109.

Watson, J. B. 1919. *Psychology from the standpoint of a behaviorist.* Philadelphia: Lippincott.

——. 1924. *Psychology from the standpoint of a behaviorist.* (2d ed.)

——. 1928. *Psychological care of infant and child.* New York: Norton.

Watson, J. B., and J. J. B. Morgan. 1917. Emotional reactions and psychological experimentation. *Amer. J. Psychol., 28,* 163–174.

Watson, J. B., and R. Rayner. 1920. Conditioned emotional reactions. *J. Exp. Psychol., 3,* 1–14.

Weiss, F. A. 1950. Some aspects of sex in neuroses. *Amer. J. Psychoanal., 10,* 27–37.

Wenkart, A. 1949. *Healthy and neurotic love.* New York: Auxiliary Council to the Association for the Advancement of Psychoanalysis.

——. 1950. The self and the process of integration. *Amer. J. Psychoanal., 10,* 91–92.

White, R. W. 1945. Interpretation of imaginative production. In J. McV. Hunt (Ed.), *Personality and the behavior disorders.* New York: Ronald.

Willoughby, R. R. 1937. Sexuality in the second decade. *Monogr. Soc. Res. Child Develpm., 2,* No. 10.

Wohlgemuth, A. 1922–1923. The influence of feeling on memory. *Brit. J. Psychol., 13,* 405–409.

Wolf, A. 1943. The dynamics of the selective inhibition of specific functions in neuroses. *Psychosomatic Med., 5,* 27–38.

Yerkes, R. M., and A. W. Yerkes. 1936. Nature and conditions of avoidance (fear) response in chimpanzee. *J. Comp. Psychol., 21,* 53–66.

Young, P. T. 1937. Laughing and weeping, cheerfulness and depression: A study of moods among college students. *J. Soc. Psychol., 8,* 311–334.

——. 1943. *Emotion in man and animal.* New York: Wiley.

Zeligs, R. 1939. Children's worries. *Sociol. Soc. Res., 24,* 22–32.

——. 1941. Environmental factors annoying to children. *Sociol. Soc. Res., 25,* 549–556.

Zucker, H. J. 1943. Affectional identification and delinquency. *Arch. Psychol.,* No. 286. Pp. 60.

CHAPTER 15

BEHAVIOR AND DEVELOPMENT AS A FUNCTION OF THE TOTAL SITUATION

THE LATE KURT LEWIN

If one wishes to use the facts concerning development, personality, social relations, cognition, and motivation which are discussed in the various chapters of this book for the purpose of understanding, guiding, or predicting the behavior of the child, these data will have to be linked in such a way that they become applicable to a particular child at a particular time. This chapter discusses procedures and concepts which have been found to be instrumental for this purpose. Some of the relevant methodological questions are considered and certain problems of cognition, motivation, and development are treated as examples. Frequently, reference is made to data which are discussed in more detail in other chapters; but no attempt to achieve completeness could be made within the limitations of this chapter.

ANALYSIS, CONCEPTS, AND THEORY IN CHILD PSYCHOLOGY

The Psychological Field

STIMULUS AND SITUATION: THE BASIC FORMULA FOR BEHAVIOR

Scientific procedure is analytical in that it tries to determine or to "isolate" the effect of the various factors. It studies, for instance, the effect on the child of different intensities of light, of different degrees of hunger (Irwin, 1930; Pratt, 1933), of failure or praise. It is widely agreed, however, that the effect of a given stimulus depends upon the stimulus constellation and upon the state of the particular person at that time. The perceived form, size, and color of a visual object corresponding to the same retinal stimulus vary widely according to the visual background and the nature of the rest of the visual field (Gelb, 1938). The toys and other objects in a room may lead to very different reactions of the year-old child when the mother is present and when she is not (MacDonald, 1940). In general terms, behavior (B) is a function (F) of the person (P) and of his environment (E), $B = F(P, E)$. This statement is correct for emotional outbreaks as well as for "purposive" directed activities; for dreaming, wishing, and thinking, as well as for talking and acting.

PERSON AND PSYCHOLOGICAL ENVIRONMENT

In this formula for behavior, the state of the person (P) and that of his environment (E) are not independent of each other. How a child sees a given physical setting—for instance, whether the frozen pond looks dangerous to him or not—depends upon the developmental state and the character of that child (Murray, 1938) and upon his ideology (Mead, 1928). The worlds in which the newborn, the one-year-old child, and the ten-year-old child live are different even in identical physical or social surroundings. This holds also for the same child when it is hungry or satiated, full of energy or fatigued. In other words, $E = F(P)$. The reverse is also true: The state of the person depends upon his environment, $P = F(E)$. The state of the person after encouragement is different from that after discouragement (Fajans, 1933), that in an area of sympathy or security from that in an area of tension (Murphy, 1937), that in a democratic group atmosphere from that in an autocratic atmosphere (Lewin, Lippitt, and White, 1939). The momentary intellectual ability of a child as measured by an intelligence test (MA) is different in an atmosphere of good rapport with the examiner from what it is in one of poor rapport. In regard to the effect of the environment upon development there is a consensus that environment may change intelligence, although opinion differs in regard to how much intelligence can be changed by environment (Terman, 1919; Wellman, 1932–1933; Stoddard and Wellman, 1934; Burks, 1940; Goodenough, 1940). Certainly the ideology, values, and attitudes of the growing individual depend greatly upon the culture in which he is reared (Mead, 1937; L. K. Frank, 1938) and upon his belonging to a privileged or underprivileged group (Dollard, 1937; Lewin, 1940b).

In summary, one can say that behavior and development[1] depend upon the state of the person and his environment, $B = F(P, E)$. In this equation the person P and his environment E have to be viewed as variables which are mutually dependent upon each other. In other words, to understand or to predict behavior, the person and his environment have to be considered as *one* constellation of interdependent factors. We call the totality of these factors the life space (LSp) of that individual, and write $B = F(P, E) = F(LSp)$. The life space, therefore, includes both the person and his psychological environment. The task of explaining behavior then becomes identical with (1) finding a scientific representation of the life space (LSp) and (2) determining the function (F) which links the behavior to the life space. This function F is what one usually calls a *law*.

GENERAL CHARACTERISTICS OF A PSYCHOLOGICAL FIELD

The novelist who tells the story behind the behavior and development of an individual gives us detailed data about his parents, his siblings, his character, his intelligence, his occupation, his friends, his status. He gives us these data in their specific interrelation, that is, as part of a total situation. Psychology has to fulfill the same task with scientific instead of poetic means. The method should be analytical in that the different factors which influence behavior have to be specifically distinguished. In science, these data have also to be represented in their particular setting within the specific situation. A totality of coexisting facts which are conceived of as mutually interdependent is called a *field* (Einstein, 1933). Psychology has to view the life space, including the person and his environment, as one field.

What means are most appropriate for analyzing and representing scientifically a psychological field have to be judged on the basis of their fruitfulness for explaining behavior. In this respect, the following general points should be remembered:

(1) A prerequisite for properly guiding a child or for the theoretical understanding of his behavior is the distinction between that situation which the teacher, the parents, or the experimenter sees and that situation which exists for the child as his life

---

[1] The possibility of treating the factors determining development formally in the same way as the factors determining behavior simplifies psychological theory considerably. I owe this idea to Donald K. Adams.

space. *Objectivity* in psychology demands representing the field correctly as it exists for the individual in question at that particular time. For this field the child's friendships, conscious and "unconscious" goals, dreams, ideals, and fears are at least as essential as any physical setting. Since this field is different for every age and for every individual, the situation as characterized by physics or sociology, which is the same for everybody, cannot be substituted for it. It is important, however, to know the physical and social conditions because they limit the variety of possible life spaces—probably as *boundary conditions* (Lewin, 1936a) of the psychological field.

(2) The social aspect of the psychological situation is at least as important as the physical. This holds even for the very young child.

(3) To characterize properly the psychological field, one has to take into account such *specific* items as particular goals, stimuli, needs, social relations, as well as such more *general* characteristics of the field as the *atmosphere* (for instance, the friendly, tense, or hostile atmosphere) or the amount of freedom. These characteristics of the *field as a whole* are as important in psychology as, for instance, the field of gravity for the explanation of events in classical physics. Psychological atmospheres are empirical realities and are scientifically describable facts (Lewin, Lippitt, and White, 1939).

(4) The concept of the psychological field as a determinant of behavior implies that everything which affects behavior at a given time should be represented in the field existing at that time, and that only those facts can affect behavior which are part of the present field (Lewin, 1936a).

(5) To avoid unnecessary assumptions, one can represent the psychological field scientifically by the interrelation of its parts in mathematical terms without asking what the "essence behind" this field is.[1] Such a mathematical representation of the psychological field and the equations expressing the psychological laws are all that have to be known for predicting behavior.

Theories and Constructs: Law and the Individual Case

THEORIES ARE UNAVOIDABLE

Without theories it is impossible in psychology, as in any other science, to proceed beyond the mere collection and description of facts which have no predictive value. It is impossible to handle problems of conditions or effects without characterizing the *dynamic* properties behind the surface of the directly observable *phenotypical* properties.

The terms *need, association, conditioned reflex, excitatory tendency, gestalt, libido,* and *super-ego* are examples of theoretical constructs with which various psychological schools have attempted to characterize certain underlying dynamical or genotypical facts. It is important to distinguish those facts which are essential for prediction and explanation from their various symptoms. For instance, an emotional state such as anger can lead to a variety of very different symptoms (noisiness, as well as extreme politeness [Dembo, 1931]); tension can lead to aggressiveness as well as apathy (Lewin, Lippitt, and White, 1939). The same personality may manifest itself in practically opposite actions. In other words, a given state of a person corresponds to a variety of behavior and can, therefore, be inferred only from a combined determination of overt behavior and the situation. This is only another way of saying that behavior (*B*) is deter-

---

[1] What here is called *life space* is more or less identical with or closely related to the concept of brain field (Köhler, 1920) or regnancy (Murray, 1938).

mined by the person and the environment $[B = F(P, E)]$ and not by the person or the environment alone.

Psychology has never avoided, nor can it avoid, theory (Reichenbach, 1928; Hull, 1930; Tolman, 1935; J. F. Brown, 1936; Lewin, 1938), but it can try to eliminate those speculative theories which are frequently introduced without clear intent or in a hidden way, and try instead to make use of openly stated empirical theories. The main desiderata for an efficient empirical theory are: (1) constructs which (a) are linked to observable facts (symptoms) by a so-called operational definition or by a number of operational definitions corresponding to the possibilities of observation under different circumstances; and constructs which (b) have clearly defined conceptual properties. These properties are coordinated to certain mathematical (logical) concepts. Such a coordination is a prerequisite for logically strict derivations (Hull, 1930; J. F. Brown, 1936; Lewin, 1938). (2) The laws (that is, the relation between behavior, on the one hand, and the field characterized by certain constructs, on the other, or between various factors determining the field) should be verified by experiment. A law should be accepted as valid only if it is not contradicted by data in any branch of psychology. In this sense, a law should always be general.

GENERAL LAWS AND INDIVIDUAL DIFFERENCES

The problems of general laws and of individual differences frequently appear to be unrelated questions which follow somewhat opposite lines. Any prediction, however, presupposes a consideration of both types of questions.

To give just one example of the linkage between the study of general laws and of individual differences: The velocity with which an activity is satiated increases, according to Karsten (1928) (see p. 825), with the degree to which the activity is psychologically central (as against peripheral). This proposition has the nature of a general law. If correct, it would explain why both agreeable and disagreeable activities are more quickly satiated than relatively neutral ones, and why fashions in women's clothes change faster than in men's clothes. By means of this law one can account for variations in the speed of satiation exhibited by the same person in different states. Certain activities, for example, are more central during menstruum than during intermenstruum and, in accordance with the general law, these activities are satiated more quickly during menstruum. When applied to age differences the law would explain why the velocity of satiation of certain activities is slower in older than in younger children. Finally, it would explain why certain types of problem children who are oversensitive reach the satiation point more quickly than the average child of that age.

This example may show that problems of individual differences, of age levels, of personality, of specific situations, and of general laws are closely interwoven. A law is expressed in an equation which relates certain variables. Individual differences have to be conceived of as various specific values which these variables have in a particular case. In other words, general laws and individual differences are merely two aspects of one problem; they are mutually dependent on each other and the study of the one cannot proceed without the study of the other. This implies that the data about the various age levels provided by child psychology have practical value for the understanding and guiding of individual children only if these data are linked with the concrete situation which is dominating the behavior of a given child at a given time.

LINKING THE VARIOUS PARTS OF PSYCHOLOGY

This example concerning psychological satiation illustrates also that laws should, and usually can, be applied to all parts of psychology. One of the main functions of theories and constructs is to bind together all the various fields of psychology which otherwise would tend to fall apart into a number of unconnected disciplines. Child psychology, which necessarily has to deal with such apparently divergent questions as nutrition, growth, emotions, perceptions, culture, personalities, social relations, actions, and thought (L. K. Frank, 1938), demands the synthetic ties offered by theories and constructs probably more than any other branch of psychology and is a particularly good testing ground for their validity.

Microscopic and Macroscopic Units in Psychology

A problem where prejudices have greatly hampered progress of research is the treatment of units of different sizes. In child psychology we want to know the development of, and conditions for, the movement of the various fingers in the action of grasping (Halverson, 1931) or the movement of the tongue (Gesell *et al.*, 1940), as well as the effect of the home background upon the school work of a child, or the effect of his childhood relations with his parents on his behavior as an adult. Child psychology is concerned with questions regarding time units of a fraction of a second ("reaction of the eyelid, eye movements in the act of reading") and with time units of many years (problems of life history, Dollard, 1935; Allport, 1937; Bühler, 1939).

For instance, the investigation of stuttering involves the study of the position of a sound or syllable in a word (S. F. Brown, 1938*a*), of a word in a sentence (S. F. Brown, 1936–1937; 1938*b*); it involves the study of the importance of the sentence in the text of the paragraph (Johnson and Knott, 1937); the relation of this verbal expression to the immediate social situation—speaking alone or to a small or large audience (Porter, 1939; Barber, 1939); the effect of the family's classification of the child as a stutterer (Gray, 1940); the individual's position in his family—for instance, his position in the rank order of siblings (Rotter, 1939); his position within the population at large (Travis, Johnson, and Shover, 1937); and the general atmosphere of his life space. In other words, it is necessary to investigate units of action of widely different sizes and situations of widely different scope, such as the "immediate situation" and the "situation at large."

Dealing with units of different sizes is common in every science. Physics, for instance, deals with the ion, the atom, the molecule, and the so-called macroscopic physical objects up to units of the size of the stars. Each size of unit has to be approached technically in a somewhat different way and has some characteristics of its own. However, there is no logical reason to call one type of unit—for instance, the smaller one—more real than the other.

In psychology, too, it is possible to obtain objective and reliable observations in regard to units of any size if one uses methods fitted to the various types (Ronald Lippitt, 1940; Barker, Dembo, and Lewin, 1941). The attempt to determine reliably large macroscopic units by observing microscopic units, however, is bound to fail (Thomas, 1932) in psychology as in other sciences. It is technically impossible to describe the movement of the sun by describing the movement of every ion contained in it.

Laws usually are concerned with the relations between various parts of a situation and are independent of the absolute size to a high degree. Without this dependence of laws upon structure rather than upon size, experimentation would be infinitely more difficult.

Constructs Basic for Representing the Psychological Field

It seems to be possible to represent the essential properties of the life space with the help of relatively few (perhaps a dozen) related constructs. To some degree it is a matter of convenience which of a group of interrelated constructs are to be considered the basic ones (Reichenbach, 1928). For the purpose of this representation we shall use mainly the following constructs: psychological force, psychological position, and potency of a situation.

(1) The concept of force in psychology refers to phenomena which have been called *drive, excitatory tendency,* or by any other name expressing "tendency to act in a certain direction." The term *force* intends to express this directed element, attributing to it, in addition, a magnitude (strength of force) and a point of application, without assuming any additional implications (Lewin, 1938).

(2) The position of the person within the total psychological field and the position of the other parts of the field in relation to one another are of prime importance. This holds for the relative position of various areas of activities the child might enter, the relative position of social groups to which the child belongs, or would like to belong, and of areas of security and insecurity. Although it is not possible today to measure psychological distance or direction quantitatively, it is possible to treat some problems of position by means of the qualitative geometry called topology.

(3) Potency refers to the weight which a certain area of the life space has for a child relative to other areas. This concept is particularly valuable in case of "overlapping situations," that is, when the belongingness to two groups or the involvement in two or more activities at the same time is pertinent.

THE BEHAVIOR IN A GIVEN PSYCHOLOGICAL FIELD

Cognitive Structure of the Life Space

THE LIFE SPACE AS A WHOLE DURING DEVELOPMENT

Differentiation of the Various Dimensions of the Life Space. An outstanding characteristic of the change of the life space during development is an increasing differentiation. The importance of this factor has been shown in regard to the development of language (Gesell and Thompson, 1934), knowledge (Tolman, 1932), social interrelations (Murphy, 1937), emotions (Jersild, 1936), and actions (Fajans, 1933).

The life space of the newborn child may be described as a field which has relatively few and only vaguely distinguishable areas (Koffka, 1928). The situation probably corresponds to a general state of greater or less comfort. No definite objects or persons seem to be distinguished. No area called "my own body" exists. Future events or expectations do not exist; the child is ruled by the situation immediately at hand.

Some of the first areas which get a definite character seem to be connected with food and elimination. As early as three to six days the child reacts to being prepared for nursing (Marquis, 1931). A similar increase in size and differentiation of the life space occurs in other respects. The child studies his own body (Bühler, 1939) and his immediate physical surroundings. Within the first few months, certain social relations develop.

The increase of the life space in regard to the psychological time dimension continues into adulthood. Plans extend farther into the future, and activities of increasingly longer duration are organized as one unit. For instance, between two and six years of age the duration of play units increases (Barker, Dembo, and Lewin, 1941).

The differentiation of the life space also increases in the dimension of reality-irreality. The different degrees of irreality correspond to different degrees of fantasy. They include both the positive wishes and the fears. Dynamically, the level of irreality corresponds to a more fluid medium (J. F. Brown, 1933; Erikson, 1940) and is more closely related to the central layers of the person. This fact is particularly important for the psychology of dreams (Freud, 1916; T. French, 1939). Play can be understood as an action on the level of reality closely related to the irreal level (Sliosberg, 1934). The play technique (Homburger, 1937), in the study of personality, makes use of the fact that the irreal level is closely related to the central layers of the person.

The level of irreality in the psychological future corresponds to the wishes or fears for the future; the level of reality, to what is expected. The discrepancy between the structure of the life space on the levels of irreality and of reality is important for planning and for the productivity of the child (Barker, Dembo, and Lewin, 1941). Hope corresponds to a sufficient similarity between reality and irreality somewhere in the psychological future; guilt to a certain discrepancy between reality and irreality in the psychological past. In the young child, truth and lying, perception and im-

agination are less clearly distinguished than in an older child (Piaget, 1932; Sliosberg, 1934; L. K. Frank, 1935). This is partly due to the fact that the younger child has not yet developed that degree of differentiation of the life space into levels of reality and irreality which is characteristic of the adult.

The speed with which the life space increases in scope and degree of differentiation during development varies greatly. A close relation seems to exist between intelligence or, more specifically, between mental age and the degree of differentiation of the person and the psychological environment (Lewin, 1935; Kounin, 1939). If this is correct, differences in IQ should be considered as different rates of increasing differentiation of the life space. Similar considerations apply to motor development (McGraw, 1935) and to social development.

The growth of the life space has a different rate at different times. Such differences are particularly important for the so-called developmental crises, as in adolescence (Dimock, 1937; Lewin, 1939).

Figure 1a and b represents schematically the scope and degree of differentiation of the life space as a whole at two developmental stages. The differentiation concerns the psychological environment as well as the person. The increasing differentiation of needs, for instance, can be represented as an increase in the differentiation of certain intrapersonal regions. The main differences between these developmental stages are: (1) an increase in the *scope* of the life space in regard to (a) what is part of the psychological present; (b) the time perspective in the direction of the psychological past and the psychological future; (c) the reality-irreality dimension; (2) an increasing *differentiation* of every level of the life space into a multitude of social relations and areas of activities; (3) an increasing *organization;* (4) a change in the general *fluidity* or *rigidity* of the life space.

Not all the areas of this life space are accessible to the child. He sees older children engaged in certain activities, which he

tance for behavior and development of the normal and abnormal child (Lewin, 1936*a*).

Regression. A change of the life space as a whole in the direction opposite to that characteristic of development may be called *regression.* Regression may include

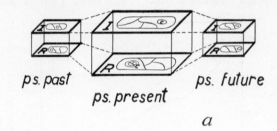

ps. past

ps. present

ps. future

a

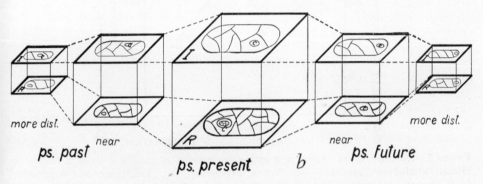

more dist.

ps. past   near

ps. present   *b*

near

ps. future

more dist.

FIGURE 1. The life space at two developmental stages.

Figure 1*a* represents the life space of a younger child. Figure 1*b* represents the higher degree of differentiation of the life space of the older child in regard to the present situation, the reality-irreality dimension, and the time perspective. *C*, child; *R*, level of reality; *I*, level of irreality; *Ps Past,* psychological past; *Ps Present,* psychological present; *Ps Future,* psychological future.

dren engaged in certain activities, which he would like to do himself, but into which he finds he cannot enter because he is not strong or clever enough. Additional limitations of his space of free movements are established by the prohibitions of the adult or by other social taboos.

The relation between accessible and inaccessible regions in the life space, the size of the space of free movement, and the precision of boundary between accessible and inaccessible areas are of great impor-

a decrease in time perspective, dedifferentiation or disorganization, leading to behavior more or less typical for children on a younger age level.

Regression may be either permanent or temporary. It is a common phenomenon and may be due, for instance, to sickness (Jersild, 1936), frustration (Barker, Dembo, and Lewin, 1941), insecurity (Murphy, 1937), or emotional tension (Dembo, 1931; Jersild, 1936). Regression, in the sense of a narrowing-down of the psychologically present area, may result from emotional tension, for instance, if the child is too eager to overcome an obstacle (Köhler, 1925).

Regression may occur not only as a result of such frustration in the immediate situation but also as the result of a back-

THE POSITION OF THE PERSON. BEING INSIDE AND OUTSIDE A REGION

Position, Neighboringness, and Locomotion. The determination of the position of the person within the life space is the first prerequisite for understanding behavior. His social position within or outside of

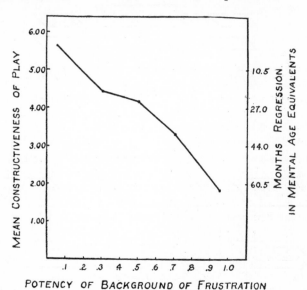

FIGURE 2. Decrease in constructiveness with a background of various degrees of frustration. (From "Studies in Topological and Vector Psychology: II. Frustration and Regression," by R. Barker, T. Dembo, and K. Lewin. *University of Iowa Studies in Child Welfare,* 1941, **18,** 166. By permission of the publisher.)

ground of frustration. Barker, Dembo, and Lewin (1941) have shown that the constructiveness of play of a five-and-one-half-year-old child may regress to the level of a three-and-one-half-year-old child as a result of a background of frustration. This is due to the fact that constructiveness of play is closely related to time perspective, the degree of differentiation within an organized unit of play, and the functional relation between irreality and reality. The amount of regression increases with the potency of the background of frustration (Figure 2).

various groups should be known; his position in regard to various activities, in regard to his goal regions, and in regard to physical areas should be determined. This is fundamental because the region in which the person is located determines (1) the quality of his immediate surroundings, (2) what kinds of regions are adjacent to the present region—that is, what possibilities the individual has for his next step—and (3) what step has the meaning of an action toward his goal and what step corresponds to an action away from his goal.

Most behavior can be conceived of as a

change of position—in other words, as a locomotion of the person. (The other cases of behavior are changes of structure.) In turn, every behavior changes the situation. We shall mention only a few examples of the effect of the region in which the person is located.

"Adaptation" to a Situation. A common phenomenon is what is usually called adaptation in the sense of "getting tuned to the present atmosphere." H. Anderson (1939) found that children of preschool age reacted to an aggressive approach with aggression, to a friendly approach in a friendly manner. Ronald Lippitt's (1940) study on democratic and autocratic atmospheres found similar adaptation of the children to the cultural atmosphere produced by the leader. J. R. P. French, Jr. (1944) found adaptation to group atmospheres in experiments with college freshmen. There are many indications from case studies that the tenseness of the mother easily affects the emotional state of the young child. There are indications that this occurs even during the first few months of life. It is a common observation that children who are learning bladder control may resume bed-wetting if exposed to the sound of running water.

The adaptation to the present region is frequently employed to make a child do something "against his will." A child of a few weeks may be induced to drink at the breast when he does not like to by keeping his head pressed to the breast in the position of feeding. Waring, Dwyer, and Junkin (1939) describe how the child and the adult both commonly use this technique for their own purposes when they differ about the desirability of eating a certain food. The child tries to avoid the pressure of the adult by leaving the eating-situation (for instance, by going to the toilet) or by making the adult leave the eating-situation psychologically (for instance, by starting conversations about noneating topics). On the other hand, the adult frequently uses one of two methods of coercion. He may lower the potency of the eating-situation (see later), and thus the resistance of the child, by "distracting his attention" from the eating (that is, by making the child enter a psychologically different region) and then slip in the food. Or he may heighten the potency of the eating-situation and of his own pressure, and in this way induce the child to eat. In the latter case he frequently uses the "step-by-step method": having the child sit at the table, then putting the food on the spoon, and so on.

J. D. Frank (1944) has found, in an experiment with college students, that the step-by-step method is more efficient in coercing the person to eat than the attempt to make him go the whole way at one step. The effectiveness of the step-by-step method seems to be based on the gradual acceptance of the situation in which the person finds himself so that he resists less the making of the next step. A similar method is frequently used in domestic and international politics. People who are ready to fight against being pushed into a situation may accept the *fait accompli.*

Group Belongingness. Most social goals can be characterized as a wish to belong or not to belong to a certain group. This group may be a group of friends, an athletic organization, or a favorite subgroup within a larger group. It may be a group of only two persons, as with the friendship between mother and child. Belonging or not belonging to the group is equivalent to having a position inside or outside this group. This position determines the rights and duties of the individual and is decisive for the ideology of the individual.

The feeling of belonging to certain groups is a crucial factor for the feeling of security in children of minorities (Dollard, 1937; Lewin, 1940b). MacDonald (1940) found that the security of the child is greatly increased by the presence of the mother. The tendency to enter a certain group and to keep certain children in and

feeling of group belongingness (as expressed, for instance, by the use of the term "we" instead of "I") is stronger in democratic than in autocratic clubs. In the autocratic atmosphere the larger group is actually composed of a number of sub-

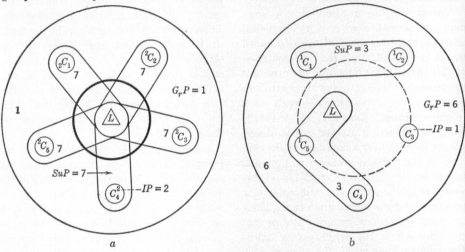

a   b

FIGURE 3. Subgrouping and potency of the group as a whole in (a) an autocratic and (b) a democratic setting. (Derived from "Studies in Topological and Vector Psychology: I. An Experimental Study of the Effect of Democratic and Authoritarian Group Atmospheres," by Ronald Lippitt. *University of Iowa Studies in Child Welfare*, 1940, **16**, 133–135. By permission of the publisher.)

In the autocratic situation two distinct social strata exist, a higher one containing the leader (L) and a lower containing the children (C). (The social distance between these strata is indicated by the heavy black circle.) In democracy the status differences are less marked (dotted line). In the autocratic setting distinct subgroups of two exist containing one child and the leader. Therefore, if the leader is taken away, no strong bond between the members remains. In democracy the subgrouping is varying and less rigid. The potency of the group as a whole (GrP) is higher there than in the autocratic setting where the potency of the individual goal (IP) and of the subgroup (SuP) is relatively higher.

other children out of that group plays a great rôle in the behavior of the nursery school child (Murphy, 1937; Rosemary Lippitt, 1940). This tendency is important for the children's gang (Shaw, 1933). Juveniles in the reformatory who have not fully accepted their belonging to the criminals have a tendency to name as their best friends persons outside the reformatory (Kephart, 1937).

Ronald Lippitt (1940) found that the

groups containing the leader and one child each, whereas in the democratic group the group as a whole has a greater potency (Figure 3a and b). This is one of the reasons why children in these autocracies are more likely to be aggressive against their fellows although submissive to the leader. M. E. Wright (1940) found that friendship between two children increases in certain situations of frustration partly because these situations favor a group structure in which the children see themselves opposed to the adult.

Bavelas (1942a) found that the degree of cooperation between children in a day camp increased after their adult leaders were retrained from autocratic to democratic leadership techniques.

Moreno (1934) has developed a technique which permits an easy determination of group structure and group belongingness under certain circumstances. Other techniques have been developed, for instance, by Bogardus (1933) and by Ronald Lippitt (1940).

The difference between being inside and outside a region is basic not only for social groups but for all goal-seeking activities, and for the problem of frustration. Seeking a certain goal is equivalent to a tendency to enter a region outside of which one is located. We shall take up this question when discussing psychological forces.

CHANGE IN COGNITIVE STRUCTURE

The structure of the life space is the positional relations of its parts. Structure may be expressed by the topology of the life space. Locomotion of the person, that is, the change of his position from one region to another region, can be viewed as one type of change in structure. Other examples are those changes which occur during "insight" or learning. The infinite variety of changes in structure may be classified roughly into (1) an increase in differentiation of a region, that is, an increase in the number of subregions; (2) a combination of separated regions into one differentiated region; (3) a decrease in differentiation, that is, a decrease in the number of subregions within a region; (4) a breaking-up of a whole, that is, previously connected subparts of a region are separated into relatively independent regions; and (5) a restructuring, that is, a change

in pattern without increase or decrease of differentiation.

Detour. Insight. Restructuring of certain areas of the life space can be readily

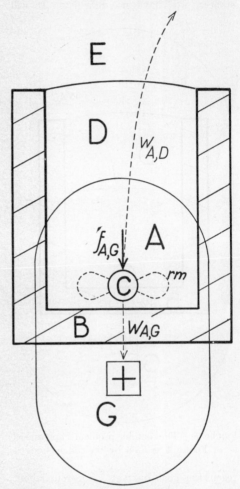

FIGURE 4. A simple detour problem as seen by the young child.

observed in the solution of detour problems. The basic questions can be illustrated by a simple example: A goal G (Figure 4) lies behind a U-shaped physical barrier B. The child C, of a mental age of one year (this may be a chronologically young child, or an older feeble-minded child) is likely to try to reach the goal by an action toward the barrier along the path $w_{A, G}$.[1] A child of five years, under the same circumstances, will have no difficulty. It will

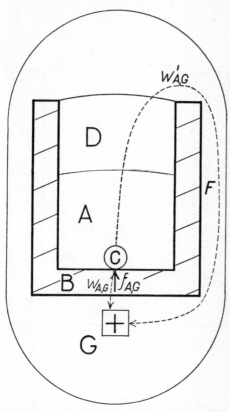

FIGURE 5. The detour problem represented in Figure 4 as seen by the older child.

reach the goal by way of a roundabout route along the path $w'_{A, G}$ (Figure 5). What are the difficulties of the younger child? Both children have the tendency to locomote from their present situation A toward the goal G. (As we shall see later, we can say there exists a psychological

1 A fuller discussion of the problems of direction and path in psychology may be found in Lewin (1938).

force $f_{A, G}$ acting on the child in the direction from A toward G.)

We can understand the difference in difficulties if we consider what "direction toward G" means for both children. For the young child the direction from A to G, $d_{A, G}$, is equal to the direction toward the barrier B, $(d_{A, G} = d_{A, B})$. A movement from A to D along the path $w_{A, D}$ would have, for this child, the meaning of going away from G. In other words, the direction toward D, $d_{A, D}$, is opposite to the direction toward G, $d_{A, G}$ $(d_{A, D} = d_{\overline{A, G}})$. For the older child (Figure 5) the direction toward D, $d_{A, D}$, has not the character of being opposite to the direction but of being equal to the direction to G $(d_{A, D} = d_{A, G})$, because the step from A to D is seen by this child as a part of the roundabout route $w'_{A, G}$ toward G. The difference in the meaning of the direction $d_{A, G}$ toward G is due mainly to two facts:

(1) For the younger child the immediate situation is less extended than for the older one (this is but one result of the fact that the life space of the younger child is smaller in many aspects than that of the older child). It includes only the regions A, B, and G (Figure 4). For the older child, a wider area is psychologically present, including, for instance, the areas D and F. As an effect of this difference in scope of the present situation the younger child sees the areas A and G separated by the impassable barrier B. For the older child, regions A and G are connected by way of passable regions D and F.

Directions in the psychological life space are defined by certain paths as a whole. The older child sees the step from A to D as a part of the path A, D, F, G toward G. The young child sees the step A, D as a part of the path A, E, that is, away from G. The difference in the cognitive structure of the situation for the young and older child leads, therefore, to a different meaning of the direction toward G and, accordingly, to a different locomotion resulting from the same tendencies of both children to reach G.

(2) For the young child, the path $w'_{A, G}$ simply does not exist psychologically. For the older child two paths toward G exist psychologically, namely, the roundabout route $w'_{A, G}$ and the blocked "direct" path $w_{A, G}$. The "direct" direction toward G can be interpreted, in this case, as the direction of looking toward G; the less "direct" direction as that of walking toward G. For the young child, "direction toward G" has not yet been differentiated into these two directions. (This is an example of the lesser degree of differentiation of the life space of the younger child.)

A two-year-old child placed in the same situation may at first have a cognitive structure corresponding to that of the younger child (Figure 4). After a few attempts the structure of the situation may change to that of the older child (Figure 5). These changes frequently occur as a sudden shift. They are an example of what has been called *insight* (Köhler, 1925).

Insight can always be viewed as a change in the cognitive structure of the situation. It frequently includes differentiation and restructuring in the sense of separating certain regions which have been connected and connecting regions which have been separated. For instance, to use a branch of a tree as a stick (Köhler, 1925) for reaching a goal behind a fence (Figure 6) it is necessary to see the branch br as a relatively separate unit instead of a part within the larger unit of the tree Tr. In addition, it is necessary to connect this branch br with the goal G behind the fence.

From the theory of insight in detour problems certain conclusions in regard to factors facilitating insight can be derived. Becoming emotional leads frequently to a narrowing-down of the psychologically existing area. A state of strong emotionality should, therefore, be detrimental to finding intellectual solutions (see p. 815). A distance sufficient to permit a survey of the larger situation helps in the solution of intellectual problems. Katona (1940) discusses the effect of various settings upon the change of the cognitive structure and the ability to find new solutions.

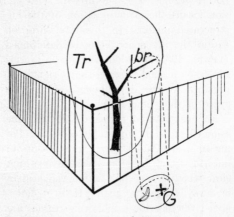

FIGURE 6. Problem solving. A case of change in cognitive structure.

The principles of change in cognitive structure discussed here are as applicable to social and mathematical problems as to physical problems.

Learning. Orientation. Learning is a popular term referring to such different processes as learning to like spinach, learning to walk, and learning French vocabularies, that is, problems of changes of goals or needs, changes of posture and muscular coordination, and changes in knowledge. Therefore, no one theory of learning is possible. Problems of change in goals will be discussed later. Insight is an example of learning in the sense of change of cognitive structure. Learning, in this sense, usually involves several of those types of structural changes which we have mentioned previously, combined with a change in the degree of organization.

A change in the direction of greater differentiation takes place, for instance, when a child gets oriented in a new surrounding. Being in an unknown surrounding is equivalent to being in a region which is unstructured in the double sense that neither the quality nor the subparts of the present region, nor the immediately neighboring regions, are determined. Orientation means the structurization of the unstructured region. In this way, direction within the life space becomes determined (Lewin, 1938). Orientation is a process which, on a smaller scale, shows significant parallels to the development of the life space of the young child.

An unstructured region usually has the same effect as an impassable obstacle. Being in unstructured surroundings leads to uncertainty of behavior because it is not clear whether a certain action will lead to or away from the goal. It is undetermined whether the neighboring regions are dangerous or friendly. Waring, Dwyer, and Junkin (1939) found that children during the meals of the first nursery school day were more ready to acquiesce to the advice of the adult than later on when they felt themselves to be on better-known ground for resisting.

The problem of learning is treated in detail in another chapter (Chapter 8). We shall add, therefore, but one remark about the relation between repetition and learning. Repetition of a certain activity may lead to differentiation of a previously undifferentiated region of the life space, and to unification of previously separated activities. This is frequently the case in motor learning. However, if continued long enough, repetition may have the opposite effect, namely, a breaking-up of the larger units of actions, a dedifferentiation, unlearning, and disorganization similar to

that of primitivation or degeneration. These processes are typical of psychological satiation and oversatiation.

Force and Force Field

FORCE AND VALENCE

Resultant Force, Locomotion, and Force Field. The structure of the life space determines what locomotions are possible at a given time. What change actually occurs depends on the constellation of psychological forces. The construct *force* characterizes, for a given point of the life space, the direction and strength of the tendency to change. This construct does not imply any additional assumptions as to the "cause" of this tendency. The combination of a number of forces acting at the same point at a given time is called the *resultant force.* The relation between force and behavior can then be summed up in the following way: Whenever a resultant force (different from zero) exists, there is either a locomotion in the direction of that force or a change in cognitive structure equivalent to this locomotion. The reverse also holds; namely, whenever a locomotion or change of structure exists, resultant forces exist in that direction.[1]

Psychological forces correspond to a relation between at least two regions of the life space. A simple example is the force $f_{A, G}$ acting on a child C in the direction toward a goal G (Figure 7). This force depends upon the state of the child C, particularly upon the state of his needs, and upon the nature of the region G. If the region G (which may represent an activity, a social position, an object, or any other possible goal) is attractive to the person,

---

[1] We are not discussing here the complicated problems of the alien factors, that is, those physical and social factors which may be viewed as the boundary conditions of the life space (Lewin, 1936a; 1943; 1944). We keep within the realm of psychology.

it is said to have a positive valence $(Va(G) > 0)$.

Such a valence corresponds to a field of forces which has the structure of a positive central field (Figure 7). If no other valences existed, the person located in any region $A, B, D, E \ldots$ would always try to move in the direction toward G. In other words, the valence G corresponds to a force $f_{A, G}, f_{B, G}, f_{D, G},$ etc. The observation of behavior permits not only the

bend his head toward the goal. The older, more differentiated child is likely to react in a more "controlled" way with only a part of the body.

Strength of Force and Distance of Valence. We shall discuss later what factors determine a change of valence. First, let us ask what effect a given valence, or distribution of valences, has on behavior. The strength of the force toward or away from a valence depends upon the strength of

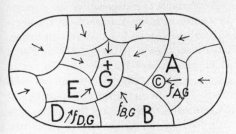

FIGURE 7. A positive central field of forces corresponding to a positive valence.

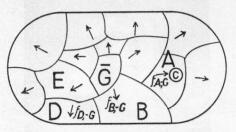

FIGURE 8. A negative central field of forces corresponding to a negative valence.

determination of conscious goals but also of "unconscious goals," as Freud uses the term.

If the person is repulsed, we speak of a negative valence of G $(Va(G) > 0)$, corresponding to a negative central field (Figure 8), which is composed of forces $f_{A, -G}, f_{B, -G}, f_{D, -G},$ etc., away from G.

The effect of forces may be observed from earliest infancy: Movements toward or away from the breast during feeding are noted in the first weeks of life. Looking toward an object (fixation) is another example of directed action. Later on, there is grasping. More elaborate directed actions presuppose a correspondingly higher differentiation of the life space. In a young child a force is more likely to affect directly every part of the child than it is at a later age. For instance, the child of six months reaching out for a toy may move both arms and legs in this direction (Figure 9). He may open his mouth and

that valence and the psychological distance $(e_{A, G})$ between the person and the valence $[f_{A, G} = F(Va(G), e_{A, G})]$.

Fajans (1933) found that the persistence of children (ages 1 to 6 years) trying to reach a goal from various physical distances (8 to 100 cm.) increases with decreasing distance. This may mean that, with increasing distance, either the force decreases or the child sees more quickly that the barrier is insurmountable. If the first factor is dominant, emotional tension should decrease with distance (see p. 815). Fajans found this to be true only for the infants. For the older children, the second factor seems to be dominant, probably because these children view the obstacle as dependent upon the will of the experimenter rather than as physical distance.

In some experiments with rats, the velocity of running toward a goal was found to increase with decreasing distance (Hull, 1932). H. F. Wright (1937) found no consistent indication of such a speed gradient in experiments where nursery school children pulled the goal (a marble) toward themselves. This indicates that the relation between strength of force and bodily locomotion is rather complicated in psychology and that physical and psychological distance may be related quite differently under different circumstances.

FIGURE 9. Action in the direction of a positive valence. (From *Dynamic Theory of Personality*, by K. Lewin. New York: McGraw-Hill, 1935, 82. By permission of the publisher.)

As a particular example, the situation may be mentioned where the person "nearly" reaches a goal. In animals (Hull, 1932), as in children (H. F. Wright, 1937), a marked slowing-down has been observed at the last section before the goal is reached. If the force were related simply to the physical distance, there should be no sudden drop in velocity at this point. Obviously, after the individual is inside the goal region, the force $f_{A, G}$ can no longer have the direction "toward" the goal region but changes to a force $f_{G, G'}$ which properly has to be interpreted as a tendency to resist being forced out of the goal region (for details see Lewin, 1938). Being in the goal region is frequently not equivalent to consumption of, or to bodily contact with, the goal, but it is equivalent

to having the goal in one's power, to being sure of it. This is probably the reason for the slowing-down in the last section before the goal. This also explains the frequent "decrease of interest" after possession, illustrated by the following example. A nine-month-old child reaches out for two rattles lying before him. When he gets one he does not begin to play but is interested only in the rattle he does not have.

An example of a decrease of the strength of a force with the distance from the negative valence can be found in certain eating-situations (Lewin, 1938, p. 117). For a child who dislikes his spinach, the act of eating might consist of a series of relatively separate steps, such as putting the hand on the table, taking the spoon, putting food on the spoon, etc. (Figure 10a). The strength of the force away from eating the disagreeable food and, therefore, the resistance against making the next step increases with the nearness of the step to the actual eating (*Re*). After the child starts chewing, the structure of the situation in regard to this bite usually is fundamentally changed, as shown in Figure 10b. Instead of resisting, the child tries to finish the bite. This is an example of how the direction and strength of the forces acting on the person depend upon the region in which the person is located.

The change of the strength of the force with the distance to the valence is different for positive and for negative valences. The latter usually diminishes much faster (see later, Figure 15). The amount of decrease depends also upon the nature of the region which has a positive or negative valence. It is different, for example, in case of a dangerous animal which can move about, from the amount in case of an immovable unpleasant object.

The effect of temporal distance on the strength of the force seems to parallel that of physical distance in some respects. E. Katz (1938), in experiments with nursery school children, found that the frequency of resumption of interrupted tasks increases with the nearness of the interruption to the completion of the task, but that it drops for interruptions very close to the end. Institutionalized adolescents,

The restraining forces, just as the driving forces, are due to a relation between two regions of the life space, namely, the nature of the barrier region and the "ability" of the individual. The same social or physical obstacle corresponds, therefore, to different restraining forces for different individuals.

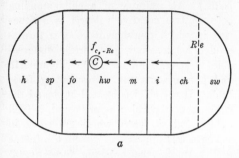 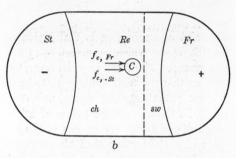

FIGURE 10. (*a*) Eating situation in case of disliked food. (*b*) Change of direction of forces after the child started real eating. (From "The Conceptual Representation and Measurement of Psychological Forces," by K. Lewin. *Contributions to Psychological Theory*, 1938, **1,** 117. By permission of the Duke University Press, publisher.)

(*a*) C, child; Re, real eating; h, putting hand on table; sp, taking spoon; fo, putting food on spoon; hw, bring spoon halfway to mouth; m, bringing spoon to mouth; i, taking food into mouth; ch, chewing; sw, swallowing. Eating has a negative valence; the force away from eating $f_{C,-Re}$ increases stepwise with the decrease of distance between C and Re.

(*b*) C, child; Re, real eating; St, struggle with adults; Fr, freedom; $f_{C,Fr}$, force in the direction of freedom; $f_{C,-St}$, force away from struggle.

like other prisoners, may attempt to escape shortly before they are eligible for release. Frequently they become rebellious (Farber, 1944). Their emotional tension is heightened by the temporal nearness of the goal.

TYPE OF FORCES

Driving and Restraining Forces. The forces toward a positive, or away from a negative, valence can be called *driving forces.* They lead to locomotion. These locomotions might be hindered by physical or social obstacles. Such barriers correspond to *restraining forces* (Lewin, 1938). Restraining forces, as such, do not lead to locomotion, but they do influence the effect of driving forces.

Induced Forces, Forces Corresponding to Own Needs and Impersonal Forces. Forces may correspond to a person's own needs. For instance, the child may wish to go to the movie or to eat certain food. Many psychological forces acting on a child do not, however, correspond to his own wishes but to the wish of another person, for instance, of the mother. These forces in the life space of the child can be called *induced forces,* and the corresponding positive or negative valence "induced valence." (A force acting on the child in the direction to the goal G induced by the mother M may be written $^{iM}f_{C,\,G}.$)

There are forces which psychologically correspond neither to the own wish of the child nor the wish of another person, but have, for the child, the character of something "impersonal," a matter-of-fact demand. We call them *impersonal forces*. It is of great importance for the reaction of the child and for the atmosphere of the situation whether an impersonal request or the personal will of another individual is dominant.

Point of Application. Forces may act on any part of the life space. Frequently, the point of application is that region of the life space which corresponds to the own person. The child may, however, experience that the "doll wants to go to bed," or that "another child wants a certain toy." In these cases the points of application of the forces are regions in the life space of a child other than his own person. Such cases are most common and play an important part, for instance, in the problems of altruism.

CONFLICT SITUATIONS

Definition of Conflict. A conflict situation can be defined as a situation where forces acting on the person are opposite in direction and about equal in strength. In regard to driving forces three cases are possible: The person may be located between two positive valences, between two negative valences, or a positive and negative valence may lie in the same direction. There may be, also, conflicts between driving and restraining forces. Finally, there may be conflicts between own forces and various combinations of induced and impersonal forces. The effect and the development of conflicts vary with these different constellations, although all conflicts have certain properties in common.

Conflicts between Driving Forces. What is usually called a *choice* means that a person is located between two positive or negative valences which are mutually exclusive. The child has to choose, for exam-

ple, between going on a picnic (G^1, Figure 11a) and playing (G^2) with his comrades. (Figure 11 and some of the later figures represent situations where the physical directions and distances are sufficiently important psychologically to be used as frames of reference for the life space. One can speak in these cases of quasi-physical fields.) An example of a child standing between two negative valences is a situation in which punishment (G^1) is threatened if he does not do a certain disagreeable task (G^2, Figure 11b). Figure 11a and b represents the corresponding force fields. If the child is located at A and the strength of the valences are equal, he will be exposed to forces which are equal in strength but opposite in direction. In the first example, the opposing forces f_{A, G^1} and f_{A, G^2} are directed toward the picnic and play. In the second example, the opposing forces $f_{A, -G^1}$ and $f_{A, -G^2}$ are directed away from the task and the punishment.

From these force fields certain differences of behavior can be derived. In the case of two negative valences, there is a resultant force in the direction of "leaving the field" altogether. If the two negative valences are very great, the child may run away from home, or try to avoid the issue. To be effective, the threat of punishment has to include the creation of a set-up which prohibits this avoidance (Lewin, 1935), that is, the creation of a prisonlike situation, where barriers B prohibit leaving the situation in any other way than by facing the task T or the punishment P (Figure 12). If there is a choice between two positive valences, no force in the direction of leaving the field exists. Instead, the child will try to reach both goals if possible.

An example of a conflict due to the presence of a negative and a positive valence is the promise of reward for doing a disagreeable task (Figure 13). Here a conflict is brought about by the opposition of the force $f_{A,R}$ toward the reward R and the force $f_{A,-T}$ away from the disagreeable activity T. The structure of the situation is similar to that characteristic of a

The necessity for setting up a barrier around the reward indicates one of the differences between this method of making the child perform a disagreeable activity T and the methods which try to change the negative valence of T itself into a posi-

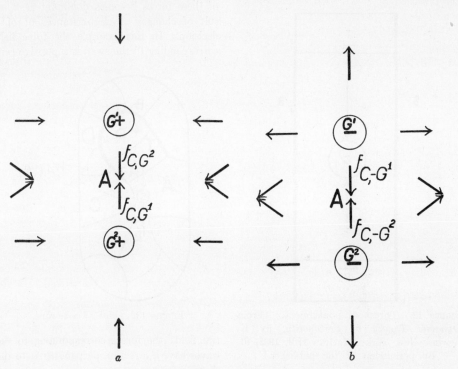

FIGURE 11. (a) Force field corresponding to two positive valences. (b) Force field corresponding to two negative valences.

detour problem. Indeed, the child frequently tries to reach the reward R along a roundabout route $w_{A,C,R}$ without passing through the disagreeable activity. The reward will be effective only if all other paths to R are blocked by an impassable barrier B which permits entrance to R only by way of T. The barriers in this case, as in the case of the threat of punishment (Figure 12), are usually social in nature: The child knows that the adult will prevent certain actions by social force.

tive one. A "change of interest" in T may be brought about by imbedding the activity T (for instance, the disliked figuring) into a different setting (for instance, into playing store), so that the meaning, and consequently the valence, of T is changed for the child. Such a method makes the creation of a barrier unnecessary and secures spontaneous actions of the child toward the previously disliked activity as a result of the newly created positive central field.

Another example of a conflict between a positive and a negative valence can be observed in a setting where a child of three years is trying to seize a toy swan S from the waves W on the seashore (Figure 14). Following the forces $f_{C, S}$, the child will

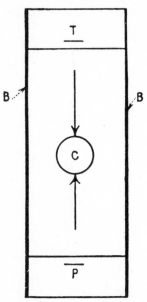

FIGURE 12.   Threat of punishment.   (From *Dynamic Theory of Personality*, by K. Lewin.   New York: McGraw-Hill, 1935, 91. By permission of the publisher.)

T, disagreeable task; *P*, threat of punishment; *C*, child; *B*, barrier preventing the child from leaving the situation through other regions than *T* or *P*.

approach the swan. If, however, he comes too close to the waves W, the force away from the waves $f_{C, -W}$ may be greater than those toward the swan. In this case the child will retreat. The force corresponding to the negative valence of the waves decreases rather rapidly with the increasing distance because of the limited range of the effect of the waves (Figure 15). The forces corresponding to the positive valence of the swan diminish much

more slowly with the distance. There exists, therefore, an equilibrium between the opposing forces at point E where their strengths are equal $(f_{E, S} = f_{E, -W})$. The children may be observed wavering around this point of equilibrium until one of these forces becomes dominant as a result of changes of circumstances or of a decision. In this example the force field corresponding to the swan is a positive cen-

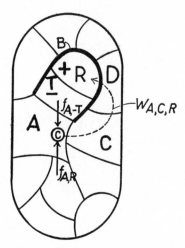

FIGURE 13.   Offer of a reward.

tral field; the forces corresponding to the waves have a direction perpendicular to the shore.

Conflicts between Driving and Restraining Forces. A most common type of conflict arises when a child is prevented from reaching a goal G by a barrier B. Two basic cases may be distinguished: (1) the child is surrounded by a barrier with the goal outside (Figure 12); (2) the goal is surrounded by a barrier with the child outside (Figure 16). The first case is a prison-like situation which gives the child little space of free movement. In the second case, the child is free except in regard to the region G. Each of these cases leads to specific reactions (Lewin, 1935). We shall now discuss in greater detail a sequence of behavior typical of the second case.

At first, a certain amount of change in structure usually occurs: The child tries to investigate the nature of the obstacle with the purpose of finding a sector *s* within the barrier which will permit passage. Such a

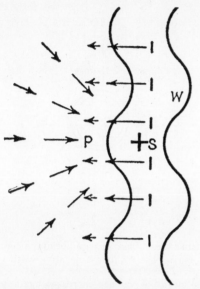

FIGURE 14. Force field in a conflict resulting from a positive and negative valence. (From *Dynamic Theory of Personality*, by K. Lewin. New York: McGraw-Hill, 1935, 92. By permission of the publisher.)

S, attractive toy; *W*, waves perceived as dangerous; *P*, point of equilibrium.

change in cognitive structure is similar to that observed in detour problems. It is very common for a child to be in situations where an obstacle could be overcome with the help of an adult. In these situations the barrier is composed of at least two sectors, one corresponding to the physical obstacle (*ph*, Figure 16), the other to the social obstacle (*sl*). In the experiment of Fajans, mentioned above, practically all children conceived of the

barrier at first as a physical obstacle (as too great a physical distance). For the children above two years, after some time the social aspect of the situation became clear and led to social approaches toward the goal (the children asked the adult for help).

The barrier acquires a negative valence

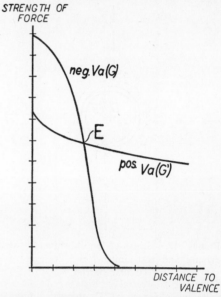

FIGURE 15. Schematic representation of the change of the strength of a force with the distance to a positive and a negative valence.

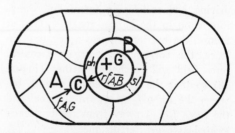

FIGURE 16. Conflict between driving and restraining forces in the case of a physical and social obstacle to a goal.

$f_{A,G}$, driving force; $rf_{\overline{A,B}}$, restraining force; *ph*, physical sector of the barrier (*B*); *sl*, social sector of the barrier.

for the child after a number of unsuccessful attempts to cross it. This change is equivalent to a change in the force field from the structure represented in Figure 17 to that of Figure 18. If the barrier is an obstacle but has no negative valence, the corresponding force field does not reach much beyond the barrier (Figure 17). The

Fajans (1933) has given a detailed report about the form and sequence of events in such a situation. Usually the child leaves the field at first only temporarily. After some time, the forces toward the goal again become greater than the forces away from the barrier, and the child returns. If the new attempts are still unsuccessful,

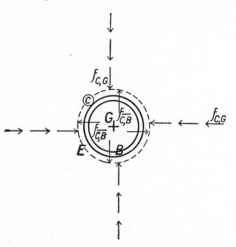

FIGURE 17. Line of equilibrium between driving and restraining forces in case of a circular barrier.

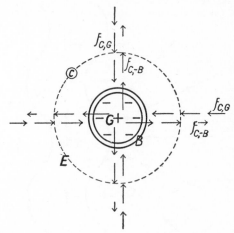

FIGURE 18. Line of equilibrium after the barrier has acquired a negative valence.

restraining forces $rf_{\overline{G, B}}$ merely hinder a locomotion in the direction of the force $f_{G, B}$ without driving the person away from B. The line of equilibrium E between driving and restraining forces lies, therefore, close to the barrier region. If, after failure, the barrier acquires a negative valence, the corresponding negative central force field will reach out farther (Figure 18) so that the line of equilibrium E between the force $f_{G, G}$ toward the goal and the force $f_{G, -B}$ away from the barrier is located at a greater distance.

With increasing failure, the negative valence tends to increase. This enlarges the distance between the line of equilibrium and the barrier until the child leaves the field altogether.

the negative valence increases again until the child leaves. On the average, these later attempts show less duration. Finally, the child leaves the field permanently; he gives up. Barker, Dembo, and Lewin (1941) report similar sequences of behavior in children between two and six years in a slightly different setting of frustration.

Active children, on the average, are more persistent than passive ones (Fajans, 1933). Some active children, however, are particularly quick to leave the situation, probably because they decide soon that the barrier is impassable. A state of equilibrium in such a conflict can lead to passive, gesturelike action toward the goal: The child stays below the goal with his arm erect but he makes no actual attempts to reach it. Children frequently leave the field psychologically without leaving the room bodily. They may try to enter a different activity, may daydream, or start self-manipulation with their clothes or their body (Fajans, 1933; Sliosberg, 1934; Mac-Donald, 1940).

A conflict between driving and restraining forces may also occur if the child is prevented by an obstacle from leaving the field of a negative valence. Such a situation exists, for instance, if a child is oversatiated with an activity but prevented from leaving it, or in any other prison-like situation. The sequence of behavior is, in many respects, similar to that discussed above. Attempts to leave are followed by the giving-up of such attempts as the result of the relation between the strength of the force $f_{A,\,-A}$ away from the region A and the increasing negative valence of the barrier. Frequently a state of high emotional tension results.

Conflicts between Own and Induced Forces. Every one of the conflict situations discussed above might be due to the opposition of two forces corresponding to the child's own needs, to the opposition of two induced forces, or to the opposition between an own and an induced force. Many effects of conflict situations are independent of these differences. Certain effects, however, are typical of conflicts between own and induced forces.

A force induced by a person P on a child C can be viewed as the result of the power field of that person over the child (Figure 19). The person having power over the child is able to induce positive and negative valences by giving orders. By a restraining command, he can change the character of a region which would be passable according to the child's own ability into an impassable barrier. In other words, "the power of P over C" means that P is able to create induced driving or restraining forces $iPf_{C,\,G}$ which correspond to P's will.

A conflict between own and induced forces always permits at least one other solution in addition to those discussed above: The child may attempt to undermine the power of the other person, at least in the area of conflict. The tendency of a conflict between own and induced

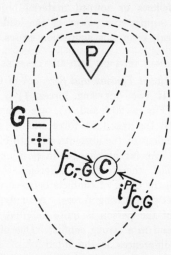

FIGURE 19. Power field.

P, stranger; C, child; G, activity having positive valence for the child and an induced negative valence; $f_{C,\,-G}$, own force away from G; $iPf_{C,G}$, force induced by P in the direction of G. ———, lines corresponding to equal strength of power field.

forces to lead to fights has been observed by Waring, Dwyer, and Junkin (1939) in nursery school children in an eating-situation. Dembo (1931) and J. D. Frank (1944) have observed similar tendencies in students. M. E. Wright (1940) found an increasing aggression against the experimenter in pairs of nursery school children in a setting of frustration induced by the experimenter. The children showed greater cooperation among themselves. This might be interpreted as due partly to the tendency to increase their own power relative to the power of the experimenter. Lewin, Lippitt, and White (1939) found a strong tendency toward aggression in autocratic atmospheres which are dominated much more by induced forces than by forces corresponding to the own needs of the children. This aggressiveness, however, was usually not directed against the supreme powers of the leader but diverted toward their fellows or toward material objects. If the suppressive power of the leader is too great, even this aggression ceases.

EMOTIONAL TENSION AND RESTLESSNESS

Emotional Tension and Strength of Conflict. If two opposing forces, $f_{A, G}$ and $f_{A, D}$ (Figure 20a and b), are equal in strength the resultant force will be zero, independent of the absolute strength of the forces. As far as changes in position are concerned, therefore, no difference should exist in the effect of conflicts between weak and between strong forces. Actually, the state of the person is quite different in a weak and in a strong conflict. One of the main differences is the intensity of emotional tension (*et*), which seems to be a function of the strength of the opposing forces [$et = F(|f_{A, G}|)$] (Sears and Sears, 1940). As mentioned above, greater emotionality is found in infants if the distance to an inaccessible goal is small than if it is larger. This is one of the reasons why increasing incentives favor the solution of detour and other intellectual problems only up to a certain intensity level. Above this level, however, increasing the forces to the goal makes the necessary restructurization more difficult, partly because the person has to move against stronger forces, partly because the resultant emotionality leads to primitivation (regression). Barker, Dembo, and Lewin (1941) found that the frequency of negative emotional behavior increased with the intensity of frustration. The same holds for the amount of regression as measured by the constructiveness of play (Figure 2).

The Form of Restless Movement. One of the simplest expressions of emotionality is restless movements, movements which are not directed to a certain goal but are merely an expression of tension. (Actually, all combinations of undirected expression, such as restlessness and purposeless behavior, occur [Dembo, 1931].) Irwin (1932) found that general activity as meas-

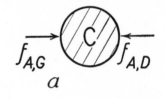

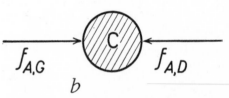

FIGURE 20. Emotional tension in case of (*a*) weak conflict and (*b*) strong conflict.

ured by the stabilimeter increases in infants with the time after the last feeding. This indicates that the amount of undirected activity is a good measurement for the state of tension accompanying hunger at that age level.

Restless movements are usually perpendicular to the direction of the force to the goal, or, more generally, they proceed as much as possible along the line of equilibrium. In the case of the six-month-old child reaching to the goal (Figure 9), restless movements of his arms and legs occur perpendicular to the direction of the goal. Behind a U-shaped barrier (Figure 4), the restless movements are parallel to the barrier along the line *rm*. In a constellation corresponding to Figure 17 or 18 the restless movements will follow the line *E*. This is verified in a situation where a one-and-one-half-year-old child tries to reach a toy G behind a circular physical barrier B. The restless movements of the child take the form of circling around that barrier. (For details see Lewin, 1938.)

The restless movement can be understood as a tendency to move away from the present situation, that is, as a movement corresponding to a force $f_{A, -A}$.

Overlapping Situations

OVERLAPPING SITUATIONS DEFINED. RELATIVE POTENCY

Frequently the person finds himself at the same time in more than one situation. The simplest example is that of divided attention: A child in the classroom listens to the teacher but also thinks about the ball game after school. The amount to which the child is involved in either of these two situations, S^1 and S^2, is called their relative potency, $Po(S^1)$ and $Po(S^2)$.

The effect a situation has on behavior depends upon the potency of that situation. In particular, the effect a force has on behavior is proportional to the potency of the related situation.

OVERLAPPING ACTIVITIES

Barker, Dembo, and Lewin (1941) speak of secondary play, as distinguished from primary play, when the child does not give his full attention to play. The constructiveness of secondary play is decisively below that of primary play. In experiments about psychological satiation (Karsten, 1928; Kounin, 1939), a person who is supposed to do an activity over and over again tends to perform the repetition as a secondary activity on a peripheral level. Activities such as writing may be considered as an overlapping of two activities, namely, (1) conveying a certain meaning, (2) writing symbols. The first has

the nature of a steadily progressing action, the second that of a repetition. The velocity of becoming satiated depends upon the relative potency of the repetitive aspect of the activity. Writing a letter, therefore, may lead more quickly to satiation in a child for whom writing is more difficult. Similarly, walking or other activities which usually have very low potency for the adult may soon lead to satiation in the child (see p. 825).

DECISION

A situation of choice can be viewed as an overlapping situation. The person be-

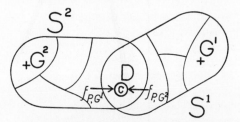

FIGURE 21. State of indecision.

S^1 and S^2, the two possibilities with the corresponding goals G^1 and G^2; D, a region of making a decision.

ing in the process of making a decision D (Figure 21) usually alternates between seeing himself in a future situation corresponding to the one and to the other possibility (S^1 and S^2). In other words, the potency of the various possibilities fluctuates. When a decision is reached, one of these situations acquires the dominant potency permanently. In a choice between activities of different degrees of difficulty, the decision is influenced by the probability of success or failure on each task. Escalona (1940) has shown that this probability is equivalent to the potency of the corresponding future situation.

The decision time increases also, the more the opposing forces are equal in strength (Barker, 1942). B. A. Wright (1942a, 1942b) found, in a study of altruistic and egoistic choices, that eight-year-old children whose choices were all either altruistic or egoistic arrived at a decision more quickly than those who made sometimes the one type of choice and sometimes the other (Figure 22). Cartwright (1941), in experiments on discrimination of figures or of meaning, found the decision time to be longest if the forces in opposite directions were equal. Recently the theory has been elaborated and quantified by Cartwright and Festinger (1943).

Decision time also increases with the importance of the decision (the valence of the goals). Jucknat (1937), in a study of the level of aspiration with children, and Barker (1942), in a study of choices between more or less agreeable or disagreeable foods, found that the choice time increases with the intensity of the conflict.

The decision time is longer in choices between two negative than between two positive valences (Barker, 1942). This latter fact derives from the different equilibria existing in the different constellations of forces (Lewin, 1938). Decision time shows great individual variations. Extreme decision-retardation is typical of certain types of depression (Escalona, 1940; Deri, 1943).

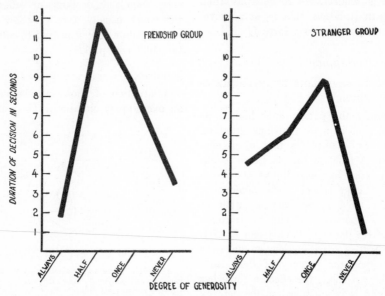

FIGURE 22. Time of decision in various degrees of conflict. (Derived from "Altruism in Children and the Perceived Conduct of Others," by B. A. Wright. *Journal of Abnormal and Social Psychology*, 1942, **37**, 218–233.)

IMMEDIATE SITUATION AND BACKGROUND

The influence which the background of a situation has on behavior can be understood as an overlapping of an immediate situation and of the situation at large (Barker, Dembo, Lewin, 1941). A background of frustration decreases constructiveness of play even if the play itself is not hampered from the outside. The amount of regression increases with increasing potency of the background of frustration (Figure 2).

Sheffield (1937) and others report cases where school work was greatly changed by a change of the home background.

THE EFFECT OF THE GROUP ON THE INDIVIDUAL. THE MARGINAL CHILD

The effect of group belongingness on the behavior of an individual can be viewed as the result of an overlapping situation: One situation corresponds to the child's own needs and goals; the other, to the goals, rules, and values which exist for him as a group member. Adaptation of an individual to the group depends upon the avoidance of too great a conflict between the two sets of forces (Lewin, 1938).

A child usually belongs to a great number of groups, such as his family, the school, the church, friends. Within the family he may belong to a subgroup containing him and his closest sibling. The effect of the various groups, particularly whether or not the child is ruled by the ideology and values of the one or the other, depends on the relative potency of these groups at that time. Schanck (1932) has found that the influence of public or private morale is different at home and in the church. In school children, the tendency to cheat changes with the social setting (Hartshorne and May, 1929).

Many conflicts in childhood are due to forces corresponding to the various groups to which the child belongs. Such conflicts are particularly important for children in marginal positions, that is, for children who are standing on the boundary between two groups. One example is the adolescent who no longer wants to belong to the children's group but who is not yet fully accepted by the adults. Uncertainty of the ground on which the child stands leads to an alternation between the values of the one and of the other group, to a state of emotional tension, and to a frequent fluctuation between overaggressiveness and over-

timidity (Lewin, 1939). The degree to which such adolescent behavior is shown depends upon the degree to which children and adolescents are treated as separate groups in that culture (Benedict, 1934; Reuter, 1937).

A similar effect of marginality can be observed in regard to other types of groups. Emotional tension is high in inmates of reformatory schools as a result of the marginal position of these children between the criminal and the "honest citizen" (Kephart, 1937). Emotional tension diminishes when the child accepts his belongingness to a definite group. A decrease in emotionality was observed in those inmates who accepted their belonging to the criminal class. Marginality is an important problem for the crippled or the otherwise handicapped child (Bartōs, 1932; Dresdner, 1933). Shaw et al. (1929) have shown the influence of residing in marginal sections of a city on criminality of children. Marginality raises important problems for children belonging to minority groups, such as Negroes or Jews (Lewin, 1940b; Frazier, 1940). The effect, in many respects, is similar to that typical of the adolescent.

FACTORS DETERMINING THE FIELD AND ITS CHANGE

In the preceding section we have discussed the results of the cognitive structure and of certain constellations of forces on behavior. We shall now discuss factors which determine the constellation of forces. This second problem is equivalent to the question of how one part or aspect of the life space depends upon other parts or aspects. Of course, both problems are interrelated since any behavior resulting from a certain situation alters the situation to some degree. We shall here limit our discussion to problems related to needs. They refer to the relation between the state of that region in the life space which represents the person and the psychological environment.

Need, Force Fields, and Cognitive Structure

NEED AND VALENCE

During the development of the child, needs are constantly changing in intensity and degree of differentiation. The so-called crises of development are periods of particularly important or particularly quick changes in needs (Dimock, 1937; Bühler, 1939). In addition, there is a change of needs in briefer periods corresponding to the states of hunger, satiation, and oversatiation.

Needs have the character of "organizing" behavior. One can distinguish a hierarchy of needs (Allport, 1937; Murray, 1938; Barker, Dembo, Lewin, 1941). One need or a combination of several needs may set up derived needs (quasi-needs) equivalent to specific intentions.

Needs are closely related to valences. What valence a certain object or activity $[Va(G)]$ has depends partly upon the nature of that activity (G), and partly upon the state of the needs $[t(G)]$ of the person at that time $[Va(G) = F(G, t(G))]$. An increase in the intensity of need (for instance, the need for recreation) leads to an increase of the positive valence of certain activities (such as going to the movies or reading a book) and to an increase in the negative valence of certain other activities (such as doing hard work). Any statement regarding change of needs can be expressed by a statement about certain positive and negative valences.

As a result of the increase in positive valence which accompanies the state of hunger of a particular need, areas of activities which are negative or on a zero level when the need is satiated acquire a positive valence. The hungrier person is usually satisfied with poorer food (D. Katz, 1937).

The valence of an activity is related to its consummatory value for satisfying the need. Not all activities, however, which have positive valence also have satisfaction value in case of consumption; on the other hand, activities with no or even negative valence may have satisfaction value. Valence and satisfaction value should, therefore, be clearly distinguished. It is surprising how frequently valence and value actually go hand in hand. D. Katz (1937) reported an increase in the valence of foods which contain minerals for which deficiencies had been established in chickens. When the deficiency was removed the valence again decreased. Similar results have been claimed for children. Experience may change the valence as well as the meaning which an activity has for the child. The child has to make many important decisions (for instance, in regard to occupation) on the basis of the valence of an activity rather than on the basis of clear knowledge of its satisfaction value.

NEED AND COGNITIVE STRUCTURE

The cognitive structure of the life space is influenced by the state of the needs. Murray (1938) found that faces of other people appear more malicious to children in a state of fear than normally. Stern and MacDonald (1937) found that pictures without definite meanings will be seen according to the mood of the child.

The effect which a need has on the structure of the life space depends upon the *intensity of the need* and upon the fluidity of the related areas of the life space. Dembo (1931) found hallucination-like wish fulfillments in highly emotional situations. If the visual field is sufficiently fluid, its structure may be considerably changed by intention (quasi-need) (Gottschaldt, 1926; Lewin, 1935). Levels of irreality, being more fluid than the level of reality, are, consequently, more easily influenced by both wishes and fears. This is the reason why dreams and daydreams mirror the needs of the child. This also explains why, in fantasy and dreams, needs may come into the open which are kept from "public life" by social taboos.

Sliosberg (1934) has shown that the meaning of objects and events is more fluid in *play* than in nonplay situations. The so-called play technique (Homburger, 1937; Erikson, 1940) and other projective methods (Murray, 1938) make use of this greater flexibility of play to study the deeper desires and suppressed wishes of children. (It should be mentioned, however, that play frequently mirrors the actual home situation rather than the wishes and fears of the child.)

Needs affect the cognitive structure not only of the psychological present but, even more, of the psychological future and past. This is particularly important for the level of aspiration (see p. 830). If the effect of the needs on the psychological future is particularly great, one speaks of an unrealistic person. One form of the influence of needs on the structure of the psychological past is called *rationalization;* other forms are *repression* and *lying.* The lying of the child in the first years of life seems frequently to have the nature of an actual change of the psychological past in line with the child's needs.

There are great individual differences (Davidson and Klopfer, 1938) in the way in which a child sees ink blots (Rorschach test). Unstable problem children are more likely to be carried away by wishes and fears than the average child as a result of their greater fluidity.

Satisfying a Need

A need may be satisfied either by reaching the desired goal or by reaching a substitute goal.

THE EFFECT OF SATISFIED AND UNSATISFIED NEEDS. SATISFACTION THROUGH REACHING THE ORIGINAL GOAL

The intention to carry out a certain action is equivalent to the creation of a quasi-need (Lewin, 1935). As long as that need is not satisfied, a force corresponding to the valence of the goal region should exist and lead to an action in the direction of that goal (Lewin, 1940a).

Ovsiankina (1928) studied the resumption of interrupted activities. She found a high tendency to resume the task (about 80 per cent) if the inner goal of the person was not reached. In some cases, after resumption, the person stopped as soon as a substitute satisfaction was reached. The frequency of resumption depends upon the nature of the task (it is high for tasks with a definite end as against continuous tasks) and upon the attitude (need) of the subject. Children between nine and eleven showed a percentage of resumption (86 per cent) similar to that of adults. Children who had the attitude of being examined and of strict obedience showed little resumption owing to the lack of involvement; they were governed mainly by induced forces (see p. 808). E. Katz (1938), in a study of resumption of interrupted activities on nursery school children, found practically the same frequency of resumption as Ovsiankina (88 per cent). Differences of intelligence, within the normal range, did not affect the resumption significantly.

The tendency to resume is not diminished if the unfinished work is out of sight (Ovsiankina, 1928). On the other hand, the presence of uncompleted work of another person does not lead (or extremely seldom leads) to spontaneous completion in adults (Ovsiankina, 1928) or in children (Adler and Kounin, 1939). Both results indicate that the state of the need of the child is decisive for resumption. Such a need might be instigated if the child becomes sufficiently involved through watching another person doing the work. (The results of Rosenzweig [1933] with children of various ages differ somewhat from those of E. Katz and Adler and Kounin. These differences are probably due to factors peculiar to his situation.)

The forces in the direction of the goal which correspond to a need can be observed in thinking as well as in action. Zeigarnik (1927) studied the effect of quasi-needs on the tendency to recall. She found the quotient of the recollection of uncompleted to completed tasks to be 1.9 for adults and 2.5 for children between five and ten years old. This quotient, like the frequency of resumption, depends on the degree of involvement of the subject. The difference between children and adults is probably due to a greater involvement of the children in the particular type of activity and to a more immediate dependence of thinking upon the valences. Zeigarnik found that certain types of unintelligent children are particularly persistent in their tendency to come back to the unfinished tasks, whereas easily distractable children show a low quotient.

Marrow (1938) investigated the effect of praise and condemnation in a competitive situation on the Zeigarnik quotient. He found that in both cases it rises. This indicates that the strength of the force in the direction of spontaneous recollection is a function of the intensity of the need. When the subject was told that he would be interrupted as soon as the experimenter saw that he could complete the activity successfully, the quotient was slightly be-

low one. The findings of Marrow and Zeigarnik show that the decisive factor for the release of the need tension is the reaching of the individual's goal rather than the finishing of the work as such. Experiments by Schlote (1930), Sandvoss (1933), and Pachauri (1935) generally substantiate Zeigarnik's findings.

Rosenzweig (1933) studied the Zeigarnik quotient under conditions where the interruption created a feeling of failure. Some children recollected more unfinished, others more finished, tasks. The latter children had a higher average rating on pride. In Rosenzweig's setting, the force in the direction of recalling a task, which is due to the need tension, is counteracted by a force away from this task, which is due to the negative valence of failure. For the children who show a high rating in pride, this negative valence should be higher, thus producing Rosenzweig's results.

SUBSTITUTE SATISFACTION

The term *substitution* has been introduced into psychology by Freud (1916). Frequently one activity is called a substitute for another if they show similarity. However, as any two types of behavior show some kind of similarity, this terminology is misleading. Functionally, substitution can be linked either to the valence of an activity or to its satisfaction value.

Substitute Value, Similarity, and Degree of Difficulty. Lissner (1933) studied the value which one activity has for satisfying a need originally directed toward another activity by a technique of resumption. The substitute value is measured by the amount of decrease in resumption of the interrupted original activity after a substitute activity has been completed. The substitute value increases (1) with the degree of similarity between the original and the substitute activity and (2) with the degree of difficulty of the substitute activity. The latter factor seemed to be related to the higher level of aspiration corresponding to a more difficult task.

Substitution on Fantasy Level. If reaching the original goal (for instance, that of attacking another person) is hindered, frequently a substitute action on the level of fantasy or talk can be observed (Doob and Sears, 1939). Freud views the dream in part as such a substitute activity. Have these substitute activities substitute value?

Mahler (1933), using as her subjects children six to ten years old, has studied the substitute value of finishing an interrupted activity by talking or thinking instead of acting. She, too, measured substitute value by the decrease of the frequency of resumption. On the average, the substitute value (2.3) for finishing by action was considerably higher than for finishing by talking (1.2). (Little difference was found between children and adults.) For some activities, such as figuring, however, finishing by talking had a high substitute value. According to Mahler, the same factor which determines the substitute value of actions is decisive for the substitute value of talking, namely, whether or not the individual's goal is reached. For *problem tasks* the intellectual solution is decisive; therefore, talking can have a very high substitute value. For *realization tasks* the building of a material object (such as making a box) is the goal; therefore, talking has practically no substitute value. Thinking through an activity had no measurable substitute value for realization or problem tasks. This finding indicates that frequently a condition for satisfaction value is the creation of a social fact (letting another person know). "Magic" solutions performed in a "make-believe" manner seemed to have a certain amount of substitute value, but only if the subject had accepted the magical nature of the situa-

tion. This was accepted more readily by children than by adults.

Substitute Value and Cognition. Adler (1939) studied the relation between certain cognitive processes and substitute value at three age levels (seven to ten years chronological age). After interruption of the original task, the child had to finish a second task which was physically identical to the interrupted one. For the younger children, building a house for Mary had no substitute value for building a like house for Johnny, although these children were able to see the similarity of the two activities. For older children, too, the substitute value was low in a situation which favored the "concrete attitude" (that is, viewing each house as specifically related to Mary or Johnny). If, however, a *categorical attitude* (that is, if house-building as such) was stressed, the two activities showed considerable substitute value in the older children. For the younger children, the substitute value was low even in the "categorical" situation.

Theoretically, the substitute value of one activity for another depends upon a communication between the two underlying need systems in such a way that satisfying the one also satisfies the other. The results of Lissner, Mahler, and Adler indicate that this communication depends partly on the cognitive similarity of the activities, and this in turn on the nature of the situation and the developmental state of the person. These results are in line with the findings that the more primitive person is more *concrete-minded* (Gelb and Goldstein's [1924] work on patients with brain lesions; H. Werner's [1940a, 1940b] findings concerning the increase of "objectivation and abstraction" during development; Weigl's [1941] experiments on children; common observations of feeble-minded). They support Vigotsky's (1934) theory that "situational" thinking precedes the "abstract, conceptual" thinking in the development of the child. The relatively high age (ten years) at which the "categorical situation" became effective in Adler's experiment indicates, in addition, that the mere ability to see abstract similarities does not necessarily have sufficient weight to establish substitute value for needs.

SUBSTITUTE VALENCE IN PLAY AND NON-PLAY SITUATION

If reaching a goal, that is, satisfying a need in a particular way, is hindered, spontaneous substitute goals may arise. Students who were unsuccessful in their attempts to throw rings over a bottle were found to throw them over near-by hooks (Dembo, 1931). Such spontaneous substitute actions, according to Dembo, have frequently no permanent substitute value. Instead of satisfying, they seem only to heighten the emotional state. This indicates that activities which appeal as substitutes, that is, which have substitute valence, do not need to have satisfaction value. We have mentioned a similar discrepancy between valence and value in ordinary consumption.

Sliosberg (1934) studied substitute valence with children between three and six years in play and in a serious situation. In a serious situation, children would not accept make-believe candy (cardboard) for a piece of chocolate if the make-believe candy was offered after they had started to use real chocolate. If the make-believe candy was offered from the beginning, 17 per cent of three- and four-year-old children accepted it and treated it in a gesture-like way as real candy. Also, make-believe scissors were accepted (in 15 per cent of the cases) for real ones only if they were offered before the real ones.

In a play situation, the children accepted the make-believe chocolate or scissors in almost 100 per cent of the cases (some of them even started to chew the chocolate cardboard). If the make-believe object was introduced without relation to the particular play at hand, the percentage of acceptance decreased slightly to 75. The child was less ready to accept the substitute object if the related need was in a state of greater hunger.

Important for the acceptance or refusal of a substitute is the plasticity of the meaning of the object and of the situation. A toy animal has a more fixed meaning than a pebble or a piece of plasticene and is, therefore, less likely to be accepted as a substitute for something else. The acceptability of substitutes depends more on the plasticity of meaning of the substitute object than on that of the original object. That substitutes are more readily accepted in play is due to greater plasticity of play in respect to social rôles, to the child's own position and goals, and to the meaning of objects.

Changes of Needs and Goals

The emergence of a substitute valence can be viewed as one example of a change of needs or valences. How needs arise in the long-range history of a person and in momentary situations is one of the basic problems of child psychology. New needs, or, more correctly, a change in needs, may result from a great variety of circumstances (Murray, 1938). A child may find out that his friend thinks highly of certain actions and he then comes to value them himself. A change in a social setting, such as attending a children's party, may significantly change the needs of the child in regard to his table manners. Reaching a goal, as well as not reaching it, may change the valences in a momentary or permanent way. During development, new needs may arise by way of differentiation from the previous ones. Behavior in a specific situation usually results from a combination of several needs; in this way, a "derived need" for this behavior may arise. Such a derived need may be kept dependent upon the *source needs* or may become functionally autonomous (Allport, 1937). Some needs seem to die gradually in various periods of the life history of the individual.

Generally speaking, needs may be changed by changes in any part of the psychological environment, by changes of the inner-personal regions, by changes on the reality level as well as on the irreality level (for instance, by a change in hope), and by changes in the cognitive structure of the psychological future and of the psychological past (Lewin, 1942). This is well in line with the fact that the total life space of a person has to be considered as one connected field. The problem of emergence of needs lies at the crossroad of cultural anthropology, developmental psychology, and the psychology of motivation. Its investigation has been hampered by premature speculative attempts to systematize needs into a few categories. In the following pages we shall discuss a few of the related questions.

RESTRAINING FORCES AFFECTING NEEDS

Giving Up. Persistence. We have seen (p. 813) that a failure to reach a certain goal may increase the negative valence of the obstacle until the constellation of forces is changed in such a way that a person will withdraw temporarily or finally. This withdrawal is frequently accompanied by an open or concealed conflict which may show itself in aggressiveness. The withdrawal can, however, go hand in hand with a full acceptance of the inaccessibility of the goal. This is equivalent to an actual giving-up: The inaccessible region ceases to be an effective part of the life space. If the child reaches a state where the in-

accessibility becomes a "matter of fact," he is no longer in a state of frustration or conflict.

What is usually called persistence is an expression of how quickly goals change when the individual encounters obstacles.

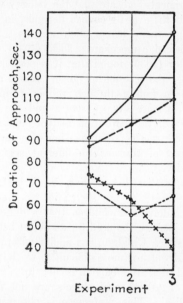

FIGURE 23. The effect of success, encouragement, substitution, and failure upon persistency. ———, success with concomitant encouragement; ————, success; ————, substitute success; ++++, failure. (From *Dynamic Theory of Personality*, by K. Lewin. New York: McGraw-Hill, 1935, 253. By permission of the publisher.)

Fajans (1933) found previous failure to decrease persistence in one- to six-year-old children when they were again confronted with the same type of difficulty. Success led to a relative increase in persistence (Figure 23). When the same task was repeated, a combination of success and praise increased persistence 48 per cent, a success alone 25 per cent; a substitute success led to a decrease of 6 per cent, failure to a decrease of 48 per cent. Similar effects of praise and failure were found by Wolf (1938). We have seen that such a change in goals depends on the change in the cognitive structure and on individual differences (Wolf, 1938) which can be observed even in the infant (Fajans, 1933). These experiments indicate that the velocity with which these goals change depends, in addition, upon the psychological past and the social atmosphere. Jack (1934) and Keister (1936) found that it is possible to change the reaction of nursery school children to failure through proper training. The increase of persistence and the decrease of rationalization and of emotional and destructive reactions showed a certain amount of transfer to different areas of activity.

Difficulties Intensifying Needs. H. F. Wright (1937) has shown in experiments with adults and children that a difficulty may increase the need for an object behind a barrier. Children, like adults, will prefer a goal which is more difficult to reach, provided that the barrier is not too strong and that both goal objects are not fully identical. This preference is observed if the object itself has the nature of a goal, but not if it is merely a means. For instance, the child will prefer (everything else being equal) a toy which is slightly more difficult to reach. If, however, he has to choose between two tools with which to get the same object, he will prefer that tool which is easier to reach. Wright's investigations indicate that the so-called law of parsimony (using the easiest way) holds only for psychological means, but not for ends. This latter fact is closely related to the problem of the level of aspiration (see p. 830).

PSYCHOLOGICAL SATIATION

One can distinguish in regard to all or most needs a state of hunger, of satiation, and of oversatiation. These states corre-spond to a positive, a neutral, and a negative valence of the activity regions which are related to a particular need. Karsten (1928), in experiments with college students, has studied the effect of repeating over and over again such activities as reading a poem, writing letters, drawing, and turning a wheel. She found the main symptoms of satiation to be (1) small variations; (2) large variations; (3) the breaking-up of larger units of actions into smaller parts, loss of meaning; (4) mistakes, unlearning; (5) fatigue and similar "bodily" symptoms.

These results provide one more reason for revising the older theories which explain the genesis of larger units of actions in terms of associations between smaller units established through repetition. Repetition may lead to the combining of smaller units of action into larger ones, but sufficient repetition will break up larger units. This involves, in case of meaningful material such as poems or sentences, a destruction of the meaning. A similar disintegration may also occur for the situation as a whole.

Satiation occurs only if the activity has, psychologically, the character of an actual repetition, of marking time as opposed to making progress. If the character of making progress can be maintained, the usual symptoms of satiation will not appear.

Psychological satiation frequently leads to muscular fatigue or such bodily symptoms as hoarseness. It is frequently the main cause of "fatigue" in children. Like hysterical symptoms, these bodily symptoms cannot be eliminated by voluntary effort, although they are caused by psychological factors and may disappear with the transition to other activities even though the new activity makes use of the same muscles in practically the same way. Imbedding an activity in a different psychological whole so that its meaning is changed has practically the same effect in satiation as shifting to a different activity. The superiority of the method of learning to read and write whole sentences or words rather than single letters is based partly on the fact that the former method is less likely to lead to satiation. The good primer is careful to repeat the same words in such a way that they are imbedded in somewhat different wholes, and that a "progress of meaning" rather than actual repetition occurs.

Repetition not only changes the needs related to the activity which is carried out, but usually also affects the needs related to psychologically similar activities, by way of cosatiation.

The velocity of satiation (that is, how quickly repetition leads to a change in needs) depends, according to Karsten, mainly upon (1) the nature of the activity (particularly the size of its units of action), (2) the degree of centrality, and (3) the individual character and state of the person. Pleasant as well as unpleasant activities are more quickly satiated than neutral activities which in other respects are equivalent. Giving more attention to an activity (without changing its meaning) seems merely to quicken satiation. Freund (1930) found that the velocity of satiation of minute tasks is greater during menstruum. All three results can be interpreted as indicating that the velocity of satiation increases with the centrality of the activity. Frequently a person tries to avoid satiation by doing the activity in a peripheral manner. Automatic activities such as breathing or walking do not become satiated if they are not carried out consciously as mere repetition. The effect of primary and secondary aspects of an activity can be handled with the concept of relative potency (see p. 816).

Children, in line with their lesser degree of differentiation, are likely to be involved in an activity with their whole person. The velocity of satiation should, therefore, vary inversely with mental age. Experimental results seem to confirm this expectation, although they are not univocal (Lewin, 1935; Wolf, 1938). The apparent divergence of findings is probably due to the fact that child psychology treats the problems of satiation under the title of persisting or perseverant behavior and that the term *persistence* is used to refer to dynamically rather different situations (for instance, persistence in overcoming an obstacle and persistence in carrying on an activity without an obstacle). Shacter (1933) found satiation time to be longer for a complex task than for a simpler one, without much age difference between three-, four-, and five-year-old children.

Wolf (1938) studied satiation in situations of praise, competition, and of no incentive with children of four and six years, making a careful analysis of the individual cases. She found the individual goal of the child to be of primary importance and this goal to depend upon the level of aspiration (see p. 830).

Kounin (1939) compared the satiation and cosatiation of normal 7-year-old children with 12- and 30- to 40-year-old feeble-minded persons of the same mental age. He found (Figure 24) that the velocity of satiation (drawings of different patterns) decreased with increasing age. The younger child shows greater cosatiation in spite of the small number of repetitions required for satiating an activity. In other words, the velocity of satiation and the degree of cosatiation decrease with chronological age even if mental age is kept constant. Kounin (1939) and Seashore and Bavelas (1942) found about the same symptoms of satiation in children which Karsten has described with adults.

The phenomena of satiation indicate (1) that there is a close relation between activities and needs, and (2) that an activity can be viewed as a consumption which changes the underlying need and, therefore, the positive valence of the activity into a negative one. As a result of this consumption the valence of "similar activities" also becomes negative, whereas certain different types of activities acquire an increasingly positive valence.

A satiated or oversatiated need, after a

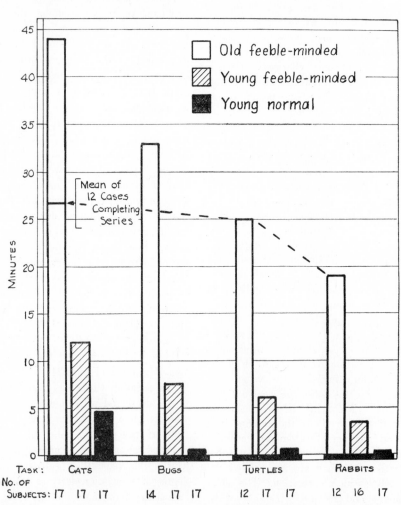

FIGURE 24. Velocity of satiation and cosatiation with individuals of different chronological age and the same mental age. (From *Experimental Studies of Rigidity as a Function of Age and Feeblemindedness*, by J. S. Kounin. Unpublished Ph.D. Dissertation, University of Iowa, 1939.)

lapse of time, frequently changes back into a state of hunger. The conditions of these changes need investigation.

INTENTION

The effect of an intention can be viewed as the setting-up of a quasi-need (Lewin, 1935). A quasi-need is dynamically equivalent to other needs in that it tends to create actions in the direction of satisfying the need with or without the presence of a corresponding goal object. Intentions are made, as a result of a given time perspective, to secure a certain behavior in the future which is expected to bring nearer the fulfillment of one or of several needs. The newly established quasi-need usually remains dependent on these source needs.

Experiments of Birenbaum (1930) show that the tension level of such a quasi-need depends upon the tension level of the more inclusive set of needs of which this quasi-need is a part. An intention will be "forgotten," that is, not carried out, if these source needs have been satisfied in the meantime, or if the state of the person as a whole has become one of high general satisfaction.

NEEDS AS PART OF MORE INCLUSIVE NEEDS. GOAL STRUCTURE

It has been stated that goals or other valences are closely related to needs. Changes of goals depend largely upon the interdependence of needs. Needs may be interdependent in different ways. (a) Two or more needs can be in communication so that their need tensions vary concomitantly. As we have seen, such relation is important for the problem of substitution. (b) The interdependence between needs can be one of ruling and being ruled. For instance, quasi-needs which correspond to intentions are induced by ruling needs. In both cases of interdependence, the need becomes a part of a more inclusive need system.

We have discussed the effect of completion and noncompletion in regard to satisfying or not satisfying the need behind an action. We shall discuss now the effect of those actions on the setting-up of new goals.

Maturity of Aspiration. To a child of six months, lying on his stomach and trying to reach a rattle, it seems to make no difference whether he finally reaches the rattle as the result of his own effort or whether the rattle is brought within his reach by someone else. The child will be satisfied both ways. A child of three, trying to jump down from the third step, may refuse help. He will not be content unless he has reached certain results by his own effort. The very young child seems to know only satisfaction and dissatisfaction but not success and failure. In other words, he has needs and goals but not yet a level of aspiration.

We speak of *aspiration* in regard to an action if the result of this action is seen as an achievement reflecting one's own ability; if, in addition, different degrees of difficulty can be distinguished, we speak of a *level of aspiration.* The level of aspiration is of basic importance for the conduct of human beings and influences most of their goal-seeking. In this connection we have the paradox that the individual may prefer something more difficult to something more easy.

Fales (C. Anderson, 1940) has studied the development, over a period of six months, of aspiration in two- to three-year-old children. She observed such activities as putting on and removing snow suits. Refusing help is probably the best behavioral symptom for the existence of an aspiration in regard to an activity. Such insistence on independence indicates that one's own action has become a part of the goal. Observing manipulations of various degrees of difficulty (such as opening the zipper, getting an arm out of the coat, hanging the cap on the hook), she found that children at this age have an aspiration only in regard to particular activities. One of the determining factors is degrees of "maturity of aspiration," corresponding to different types of goals and procedures in attaining them at various age levels. C. Anderson (1940) developed a scale of maturity of aspiration for children between two and eight years, using

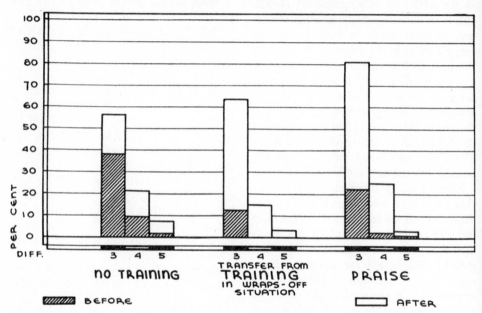

FIGURE 25. Development of aspiration as a function of difficulty of task, training, and praise. (From an incomplete study by Fales, quoted in *The Development of a Level of Aspiration in Young Children*, by C. Anderson. Unpublished Ph.D. Dissertation, University of Iowa, 1940.)

Ordinate refers to per cent of refusal of help.   Numbers on abscissa refer to degrees of difficulty of task.

tivities. One of the determining factors is the ability of the child; he will not refuse help for activities definitely beyond his reach. As he becomes older or is better trained (Figure 25) an aspiration develops in regard to the more difficult actions. Fales also found that social situations or praise (Figure 25) facilitate the rise of an aspiration. This indicates that a social component is important for aspiration from its earliest development.

It is possible to distinguish different de-

activities such as throwing a series of rings over a stick and knocking down tenpins with a ball. A child of eight will consider the series of five throws as one unit and will not, therefore, rethrow single rings which miss the stick before counting his score. Children of the youngest group (three years old) always pick up the single rings after missing the stick and rethrow them or place them directly on the stick (Figure 26). The youngest children do not hold to the rule of standing behind a given place. These and other symptoms indicate that the development of a level of aspiration, the choosing of a goal of a particular degree of difficulty, presupposes (1) that a number of goals are seen as subgoals within a larger goal structure, (2) that the action itself is conceived as a part of the goal, and (3) that the child under-

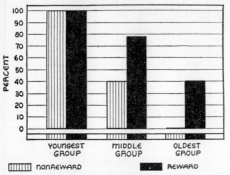

FIGURE 26. Maturity of aspiration at three age levels and amount of regression in case of social pressure (reward situation). (From *The Development of a Level of Aspiration in Young Children*, by C. Anderson. Unpublished Ph.D. Dissertation, University of Iowa, 1940.)

The frequency with which the child places the missed ring on a stick or rethrows the single ring instead of finishing the series of rings is indicated.

stands the meaning of rules and is ready to keep them.

If pressure is brought to bear on a child by offering a reward, the level of aspiration (that is, the degree of difficulty chosen) will decrease. If a lowering of the level of aspiration is made impossible, the maturity of aspiration may regress (Figure 26); that is, a procedure is used which is characteristic of a younger age level. Regression of the maturity of aspiration can be observed in adults in emotional situations.

Level of Aspiration. Level of aspiration has been defined (Hoppe, 1930) as the de-

gree of difficulty of that task chosen as a goal for the next action. One may distinguish two main problems: (1) under what condition the individual experiences success or failure and (2) what factors influence the level of aspiration.

Conditions for the experience of success or failure. The experience of success or failure depends on the level of performance within a frame of reference (Lewin, Dembo, Festinger, and Sears, 1944). This frame of reference can be the level of aspiration (that is, the goal which has been set for that action), the past performance, or the standards of a group. A feeling of success will prevail if a certain level, related to the dominant frame of reference, is reached. What frame of reference will be dominant depends upon a number of factors, one of which is the tendency to avoid the feeling of failure.

It has been shown (Gould, 1939; P. Sears, 1940; Festinger, 1942) that to avoid the feeling of failure after a poor performance the frame of reference is frequently shifted. Other ways to avoid failure are various forms of rationalization (Hoppe, 1930; Gould, 1939), such as blaming a poor instrument for the shortcomings of the performance. In this way the link between performance and one's own ability is cut, which is, as we have seen, one of the conditions for the phenomenon of aspiration.

Jucknat (1937) distinguishes different intensities of the feeling of success and failure. They are to be related to the amount of discrepancy between goal and performance. This holds, however, only within the range of difficulties which is close to the boundary level of ability. "Too easy" and "too difficult" tasks do not lead to feelings of success and failure. This may be the reason why rivalry among siblings is less frequent when there are relatively great differences of age among them (Sewall, 1930).

The relation between the feeling of success and failure, on the one hand, and the boundary of ability, on the other, is operative only if other frames of reference, such as certain group standards, do not become dominant. The mentally retarded child might have permanently the feeling of failure in a group of children of high ability even though the tasks were actually far beyond the limit of his own ability.

Case studies (Kanner, 1935) and experimental data (Fajans, 1933) show that change in group status (for instance, gaining recognition or love or being rejected by an individual or a larger group) is, in many respects, equivalent to success or failure.

Factors determining the level of aspiration. After the experience of success or failure the person may either quit or continue with a higher, equal, or lower level of aspiration. The difference between the level of aspiration for the new action and the level of past performance is called the "discrepancy" between level of aspiration and performance. (For details see Lewin, Dembo, Festinger, and Sears, 1944.)

The factors determining a change in the level of aspiration are manifold. Jucknat (1937) found that with children from nine to fifteen and with adults the direction and the amount of the change in the level of aspiration depend upon the degree of success and failure (Figure 27). In addition, within a given series of tasks, the discrepancy is smaller for the same amount of success and greater for the same amount of failure the closer the previous level of performance comes to the extreme of the series of difficulties.

The level of aspiration is much influenced by social factors. In a situation of competition it might be increased (J. D. Frank, 1935). The knowledge of group standards may affect the level of aspiration (Festinger, 1942). For instance, the

discrepancy between aspiration and performance increases toward a higher level of aspiration if the person learns that his performance is below the standard of his

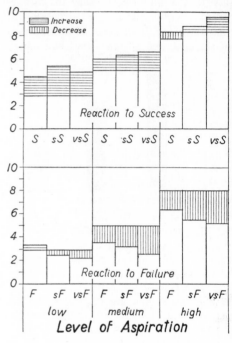

FIGURE 27. Change in the level of aspiration as a function of (a) strength of the feeling of success and failure; (b) the relative difficulty of the previous level of performance. (From "Performance, Level of Aspiration and Self-consciousness," by M. Jucknat. *Psychologische Forschung*, 1937, **22**, 102. By permission of the publisher.)

S, success; sS, strong success; vsS, very strong success; F, failure; sF, strong failure; vsF, very strong failure. Ordinate refers to degrees of difficulty of task.

own group or of a group which he considers to be lower. The discrepancy decreases if the opposite conditions obtain. The level of aspiration is affected also by the degree of realistic judgment about one's own ability (J. D. Frank, 1935). P. Sears (1940) found the average positive discrepancy (that is, the amount by which the level of aspiration exceeds past performance) to be greater in children after failure than after success, indicating a greater degree of realism after success than after failure.

For the same individual, the direction and amount of discrepancy seem to be constant to a certain degree for a number of activities (J. D. Frank, 1935; P. Sears, 1940; Gardner, 1939). P. Sears (1940) and Jucknat (1937) found the discrepancy to be greater in children of poor standing than in children of good standing in school. The degree to which the level of aspiration in one activity affects the level of aspiration in another activity depends upon their similarity and upon how well previous experience has stabilized the level of aspiration in these activities (Jucknat, 1937). The influence of success in one activity on the level of aspiration in another is slight if the child has clearly found out his ability in the latter.

The level of aspiration is closely related to the time perspective with respect to both the psychological past and the psychological future. According to Escalona (1940), the level of aspiration at a given time depends upon the strength of the valence of success and failure and upon the probability of success at that time. By representing this probability as the potency of the future success or failure situation, the basic facts concerning the level of aspiration can be understood (see Lewin, Dembo, Festinger, and Sears, 1944).

INDUCED NEEDS. GROUP GOALS AND INDIVIDUAL GOALS

The needs of the individual are, to a very high degree, determined by social factors. The needs of the growing child are changed and new needs induced as a result of the many small and large social groups to which he belongs. His needs are much affected, also, by the ideology and conduct of those groups to which he would like to belong or from which he would like to be set apart. The effects of the advice of the mother, of the demand of a fellow child, or of what the psychoanalyst calls *super-ego*, all are closely interwoven with socially induced needs. We have seen that the level of aspiration is related to social facts. We may state more generally that the culture in which a child grows affects practically every need and all his behavior and that the problem of acculturation is one of the foremost in child psychology.

One can distinguish three types of cases where needs pertain to social relations: (1) the action of the individual may be performed for the benefit of someone else (in the manner of an altruistic act); (2) needs may be induced by the power field of another person or group (as a weaker person's obedience of a more powerful one); (3) needs may be created by belonging to a group and adhering to its goals. Actually, these three types are closely interwoven.

Sources of Ideology. The frequency with which children named the teacher as a source for praise or scolding of behavior in school remained relatively constant from the fourth to the eighth grade in certain schools (Bavelas, 1942b). An individual classmate (as distinguished from the concept "children") was frequently named as source for evaluation of behavior at the fourth grade (Figure 28); this frequency declined to zero at the eighth grade. The school superintendent was practically never named as source at the fourth grade (Figure 28); he was named with increasing frequency later on, mainly as a source for scolding.

Kalhorn (1944) compared positive and negative values (Figure 29a) and sources of values (Figure 29b) in Mennonite and non-Mennonite children in rural areas. She found differences in the emphasis on such values as individual achievement and religion. In both groups the parents are indicated by the children to have the most dominant influence as a source of values.

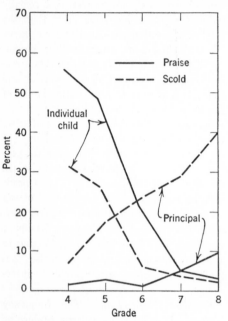

Fig. 28. Frequency with which an individual child and the school principal are given as source for praise or scolding of school conduct at different grades. (From "A Method for Investigating Individual and Group Ideology," by A. Bavelas. *Sociometry*, 1942, **5**, 376. By permission of the publisher.)

The same conduct may have different psychological meaning in different cultures. For instance, going to church is linked with God as the source of approval by the Mennonite children, with everyone by the non-Mennonite children. This indicates that church-going is primarily a religious affair with the former, a social affair with the latter.

Egoism and Altruism. In an experiment by Moore (1931), children between the ages of two and three were asked to share orange juice with a companion who was seated beside the subject. Her results show wide individual differences and no correlation with the degree to which the child respects the rights of others as determined by other methods. Hartshorne and May (1929) studied test situations in which service (altruism, cooperation) of the children could be observed. They claim that the tendency to serve is "specific" rather than "general" in children between ten and fourteen years (for a discussion of the problem of generality of traits see Allport, 1937). McGrath (1923), using a questionnaire technique, reports that an altruistic response to a hypothetical situation increases with age. Piaget (1932) orders his findings on the moral development of children in terms of two psychologically different moralities which are an outgrowth of two types of social relations: up to seven or eight years, there exists a social relation of unilateral respect in which the child is subjected to adult authority. Gradually a relationship of mutual respect is set up in which each member has a more equal part of the control.

B. Wright (1941, 1942a, 1942b) studied children in a situation where they had a choice of keeping a preferred toy or giving it to someone else. The other child (who was not present) was either someone unknown or a best friend. The five-year-old child was practically always egoistic; the eight-year-old child showed considerable altruism, and more so toward the stranger (58 per cent generous choices) than to the friend (23 per cent generous choices). When acting as an umpire between a friend and a strange child in distributing the toys, the five-year-old child favored the friend more frequently than the stranger. The eight-year-old favored the stranger more frequently than the friend.

Praised Conduct

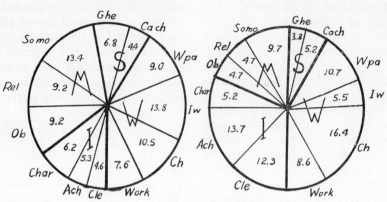

Source for Praise

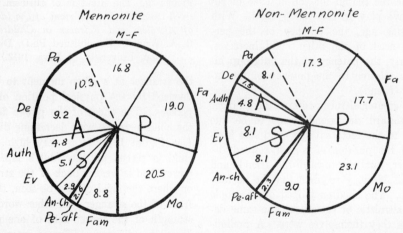

FIGURE 29. (a) Praised conduct. (b) Source for praise. (From "Studies in Topological and Vector Psychology: III. Values and Sources of Authority among Rural Children," by J. Kalhorn. *University of Iowa Studies in Child Welfare*, 1945, **20**. By permission of the publisher.)

(a) *W*, work area (work; *Ch*, chore; *Iw*, intensive work; *Wpa*, work for parents); *S*, social area (*Ca ch*, care of other children; *Ghe*, generalized help); *M*, morality area (*So mo*, social morality; *Rel*, religion and virtues; *Ob*, obedience); *I*, individual area (*Char*, character; *Ach*, individual achievement; *Cle*, cleanliness).

(b) *P*, parents (*Mo*, mother; *Fa*, father; *M-F*, mother and father; *Pa*, parents); *A*, authority (*De*, deity; *Auth*, authority); *S*, society (*Ev*, everybody; *An-ch*, another child; *Pe-aff*, person affected; *Fam*, family).

Theoretically, the altruistic or the egoistic choice can be viewed as the result of the relative strength of forces acting on different regions of the life space and of the potency of various situations. In the life space of child C (Figure 30), a force $f_{C, G}$ acts on his own person in the direction to a goal G. In addition, a force $f_{Ot, G}^{C}$ exists in his life space, acting on the other child, Ot, in the direction of the same goal. (The situation permits only one person to obtain the goal.) This second force, $f_{Ot, G}^{C}$, corresponds to the need of the other child as perceived by the child whose life space is represented and the readiness of the child C to back the goal of the child Ot. Formalistically speaking, the altruistic or egoistic choice depends on the relative strength of these two forces. According to Wright, the need of the other child is not perceived by the very young child. This may be the reason for the absence of cooperative play in the young child. With increasing age, the potency of the perceived need of the other child increases. Similarly, the potency of the outgroup increases relative to the potency of the ingroup (friend).

The greater altruism toward the stranger than toward the friend seems to be due partly to the fact that the child sees himself in the position of a host toward the stranger, but not toward the friend, and that his ideology requires that he be hospitable. The children judged other people to be altruistic or egoistic to the same degree as they themselves were. A preliminary study seems to indicate that adults in a similar setting are more egoistic than the eight-year-old child.

Obedience and Social Pressure. In discussing problems of conflicts we have seen that the force acting on a person in the direction of a goal might be counteracted by induced forces corresponding to the will of another person. In view of the relation between psychological forces and psychological needs we can also speak of *induced needs*. The relation between two persons might be that of friends or that of enemies; the need of each would depend greatly on the power field of the other.

Wiehe (Lewin, 1935) observed children between two and four years of age when a stranger entered the child's room. He found the strength of the power field of

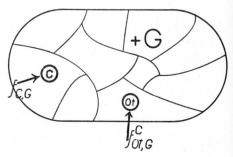

FIGURE 30. The situation of altruism. (Derived from *The Development of the Ideology of Altruism and Fairness in Children*, by B. A. Wright. Unpublished Ph.D. Dissertation, University of Iowa, 1942.)

the stranger at a given moment to be influenced by the physical position of both persons. The effect of the power field on the child increases with decreasing distance (see Figure 19). It is very high if the child is placed on the adult's lap. The power field is weaker back of the stranger, or where the child cannot be seen, than in front of the stranger. In other words, the strength of the power field of one person on another differs for different areas. J. D. Frank (1944), in experiments with students, and Waring, Dwyer, and Junkin (1939) in experiments with nursery school children at the dinner table, also found the effectiveness of the power field for creating induced forces to be greater if the distance between the persons is smaller.

Lippitt and White (1943), in experiments with ten-year-old children, tested the effect of induced needs during the presence and the absence of the inducing power field. They found that the amount of work output in an autocratic group atmosphere dropped very decisively within a few minutes when the leader left the room. This was in contrast to a democratic group

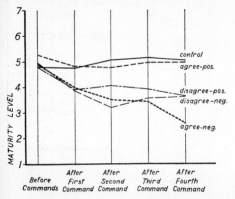

FIGURE 31. The effect of conflicting authorities on constructiveness. (From "Studies in Topological and Vector Psychology: III. The Effect of Conflicting Authority on the Child," by C. E. Meyers. *University of Iowa Studies in Child Welfare,* 1944. By permission of the publisher.)

atmosphere, where the work had been chosen and planned by the group itself, and where the work output was unchanged when the leader left. C. E. Meyers (1944) studied the effect of conflicting adult authority on children of nursery school age. He found that the opposing orders lower the children's constructiveness of play very considerably (from 4½ to 2½ on his constructiveness scale) (Figure 31). The child may stop action altogether (aside from self-manipulation similar to that described by MacDonald, 1940) if he does not find a way to follow the orders of both authorities. Even if the orders of both adults agree, too frequent interference with the child's play lowers his constructiveness

somewhat. Negative commands were more damaging than positive commands, and vague commands more damaging than specific ones.

Induced needs which are opposite to own needs may lead to a permanent state of conflict which is more or less concealed. If such a conflict cannot be resolved by breaking the dominant power field (see p. 814), the child may become aggressive toward less powerful persons. Lewin, Lippitt, and White (1939) found that, on several occasions, one of the children was attacked as a scapegoat in the autocratic group (Figure 32).

Taking Over Foreign Goals. An induced need may slowly change its character in the direction of an own need. In other words, the person not only will follow orders but also "accept" them (in the meaning of taking them over). Waring, Dwyer, and Junkin (1939) have observed changes in this direction with nursery school children.

Duncker (1938) studied changes in food preferences of children from two to five years of age, as affected by a story in which the hero abhorred one and enthusiastically relished the other of two kinds of food. After the story, the children preferred the hero's favorite food, although previously it had been unattractive to them. This effect decreased with time, but could still be detected after six days. Thompson (1940) studied the effect of prejudicial leadership on ten-year-old children. The leader set up an underprivileged minority within a group of children who originally had equal status. After a number of club meetings the children of the privileged majority continued to treat the rest of the children as underprivileged even when the leader left the room. This discrimination, however, was not so strong as in the presence of the leader. This shows both that the presence of the power field of the leader has some influence and that the induced goals have been taken over in some measure.

Lippitt and White (1943), in a study of autocratic, democratic, and laissez-faire values." Children who follow boy values are more sociable among themselves but less obedient at school.

Horowitz (1936) found no prejudices against Negroes in white children under

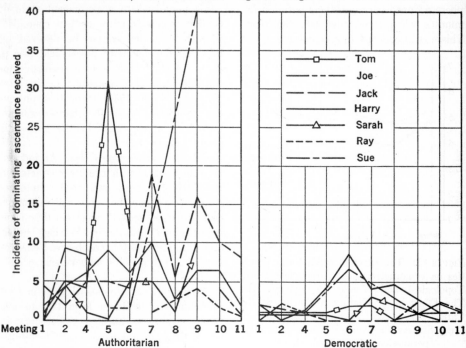

FIGURE 32. The emergence of scapegoats. (From "Studies in Topological and Vector Psychology: I. An Experimental Study of the Effect of Democratic and Authoritarian Group Atmospheres," by Ronald Lippitt. *University of Iowa Studies in Child Welfare*, 1940, **16,** 165. By permission of the publisher.)

The curves indicate that the amount of dominating behavior directed against the various individuals was much greater in autocracy than in democracy. In autocracy two individuals (Tom and Joe) were treated as scapegoats (at the fifth and ninth meetings, respectively).

groups, have found that the readiness of an individual to accept autocracy in the club depends partly upon the home background. A combination of a firm and warm home atmosphere seems to be most favorable to that end; that is, an atmosphere of relative autocracy which, nevertheless, by its warmness, prohibits the child from becoming independent of the family. These children are likely to adhere to "adult values" rather than "boy three years. The prejudices increased between four and six years. This increase was as great in New York as in the South. It was independent of the degree of acquaintance of the children with Negro children, and of the actual status of the Negro child in the class which the white child attended. The prejudices are, however, related to the attitude of the parents of the white child. This indicates that the prejudices against the Negroes are due to an induction and gradual taking-over of the culture of the parents by the child.

A phenomenon which is probably partly due to the acceptance of originally induced needs and partly to the problems of group belongingness (see p. 800) is the hatred against one's own group in persons belonging to an underprivileged group. This hatred against the own group is frequent among the bodily handicapped and among socially underprivileged groups (Davis and Dollard, 1940; Lewin, 1940b). It means that the values and prejudices of the privileged group have been taken over by the members of the socially lower group even if they are directed against their own group. This hatred of one's own group may lead to self-hatred. It is augmented by the need of the individual to raise his status and, therefore, to separate himself from the underprivileged group.

Whether or not an induced need has changed its character and has become an own need is frequently difficult to decide. Lippitt and White (1943) distinguished two types of reaction to an autocratic atmosphere: one called *aggressive autocracy*, and the other *apathetic autocracy*. In the latter case the children seem to work willingly. Signs of discontent or obstruction may be entirely absent. Particularly strict obedience may have the appearance of a voluntary action. This holds also for the behavior of children in institutions. Nevertheless, the effect of the removal of the leader in the experiment shows how great the actual difference in both situations is for the child.

Needs of a Child as a Group Member. As mentioned above, the children in the democratic group studied by Lippitt and White did not decrease the intensity of their work if the leader left. The plan for this work had been decided upon by majority vote after consideration. This shows that under these conditions a need corresponding to a group goal is more like an own need than an induced need. This problem is closely related to the difference between "we"-feeling and "I"-feeling. Lewin, Lippitt, and White (1939) found "we"-feeling, as measured by the verbal expression and the attitude toward the work, to be greater in the democratic group than in the autocratic group where an egocentric attitude prevailed.

One can consider two factors to be basic for the kind and degree of influence which group goals have for the goals of the individual: (1) the degree of dependence of the person on the group; (2) the character of enmity or friendship of this dependence. According to Ronald Lippitt (1940), the power fields of enemies weaken each other in areas where they overlap, whereas the power fields of friends strengthen each other. In addition, friendship as distinguished from enmity includes the readiness to accept and to back up the intention of the other person. According to M. E. Wright (1940), both characteristics can be expressed by the degree of accessibility of one's own power field to the power field of the other person.

Individual Differences

We have seen that it is not possible to determine the specific characteristics of individuals by classifying them according to their overt behavior. Instead, one has to look for factors which can be inserted as constant values into the variables of the equations which represent psychological laws. In this way also the variability of behavior, that is, the difference in behavior of the same individual in different situations, becomes susceptible to treatment. This variability does not mean merely that the absolute frequency or intensity of a certain type of behavior depends upon the situation. Actually, the rank-order of individuals in regard to a certain trait may also be different in different situations. For instance, Lewin, Lippitt, and White (1939) found in clubs of ten-year-old boys that, in regard to some "traits," such as "demanding attention from other club members" and "out-of-field conversation," the rank-order of the individual in different atmospheres remains rather constant ($r = .85$ and $r = .78$). In other traits, such as "dependence upon leader," there is scarcely any consistency of rank-order ($r = .02$). There are more extreme changes in the rank-order in "work-mindedness" than in "aggressiveness." The changes seem to be linked to the differences of meaning of the particular atmospheres to the particular children.

The attempts to link positively problems of individual differences and of general laws are relatively new in psychology. We shall mention but one example, which is related to differences in age, intelligence, and rigidity of the person. Lewin (1935) has outlined a theory according to which differences in mental age are closely related to the degree of differentiation of the person. The variety of states which an organism can assume, and the corresponding variety of patterns of behavior, must logically be conceived of (Barker, Dembo, and Lewin, 1941) as a function of the degree of the differentiation of that organism. Therefore, with increasing mental age, the individual should show an increasing flexibility, in the sense of richness, of behavior. This is in line with empirical observations of individuals of different mental age and with the peculiar pedantry and stubbornness of the young child.

The increase of flexibility with increasing mental age is somewhat counteracted by a decrease in plasticity which seems to go hand in hand with chronological age and which seems to be important for senility. A certain type of feeble-minded-ness is characterized by the fact that these individuals show at the same level of differentiation (the same mental age) less plasticity (Lewin, 1935). If this theory is correct, one should expect less cosatiation in feeble-minded persons than in normal persons of the same mental age. Kounin (1939) demonstrated this with individuals whose chronological ages were 7, 12, or 30, all having a mental age of 7 (see p. 826). One can derive from the same set of premises that feeble-minded individuals should be less able to tolerate overlapping situations. One should expect, therefore, that the feeble-minded person would make fewer mistakes in case of change of habits under certain conditions, that he would show greater difference in speed of performance between overlapping and nonoverlapping situations, and that he would be less able to change the cognitive structure in a test requiring several classifications of the same group of objects. Kounin's experiments substantiate all these derivations. The results of Koepke (Lewin, 1935) and of Gottschaldt (1926) indicate that the readiness of the feeble-minded person to accept or to refuse a substitute is either very small or very great, according to the specific situation. This is in line with what should be expected from a relatively rigid individual.

The coordination of certain individual differences with differences in the degree of differentiation and rigidity of the person makes it possible to link behavior in quite a variety of fields, such as cognition, stubbornness, substitution, and satiation, and to understand apparent contradictions of behavior. A greater rigidity of the feeble-minded person also explains why his development is slower than that of the normal child (that is, the relative constancy of the IQ) and why he reaches his peak of development earlier.

It can be expected that all problems of

individual differences will be linked more and more with the general psychological laws of behavior and development and that in this way a deeper understanding of both the individual differences and the general laws will be possible.

Bibliography

Adler, D. L. 1939. *Types of similarity and the substitute value of activities at different age levels.* Unpublished Ph.D. Dissertation, State University of Iowa.

Adler, D. L., and J. Kounin. 1939. Some factors operating at the moment of resumption of interrupted tasks. *J. Psychol., 7,* 355-367.

Allport, G. W. 1937. *Personality: A psychological interpretation.* New York: Holt.

Anderson, C. 1940. *The development of a level of aspiration in young children.* Unpublished Ph.D. Dissertation, University of Iowa.

Anderson, H. H. 1939. Domination and social integration in the behavior of kindergarten children and teachers. *Genet. Psychol. Monogr., 21,* 287-385.

Barber, V. 1939. Studies in the psychology of stuttering: XV. Chorus reading as a distraction in stuttering. *J. Speech Disorders, 4,* 371-383.

Barker, R. 1942. An experimental study of the resolution of conflict by children. In Q. McNemar and M. A. Merrill (Eds.), *Studies in personality.* New York and London: McGraw-Hill.

Barker, R., T. Dembo, and K. Lewin. 1941. Studies in topological and vector psychology: II. Frustration and regression. *Univ. Iowa Stud. Child Welfare, 18,* No. 1.

Bartõs, A. 1932. Die psychologischen Grundlagen der seelischen Erziehung bei Verkrüppelten. *4. Vers. f. Kinderforsch.,* 244-253.

Bavelas, A. 1942a. Morale and the training of leaders. In G. Watson (Ed.), *Civilian morale,* second yearbook of the SPSSI. Boston: Published for Reynal and Hitchcock by Houghton Mifflin.

——. 1942b. A method for investigating individual and group ideology. *Sociometry, 5,* 371-377.

Benedict, R. 1934. *Patterns of culture.* Boston: Houghton Mifflin.

Birenbaum, G. 1930. Das Vergessen einer Vornahme. Isolierte seelische Systeme und dynamische Gesamtbereiche. *Psychol. Forsch., 13,* 218-285.

Bogardus, E. S. 1933. A social distance scale. *Sociol. Soc. Res., 17,* 265-271.

Brown, J. F. 1933. Über die dynamischen Eigenschaften der Realitäts- und Irrealitätsschichten. *Psychol. Forsch., 18,* 1-26.

Brown, J. F. 1936. *Psychology and the social order.* New York: McGraw-Hill.

Brown, S. F. 1936-1937. Influence of grammatical function on the incidence of stuttering. *J. Speech Disorders, 2,* 207-215.

Brown, S. F. 1938a. A further study of stuttering in relation to various speech sounds. *Quart. J. Speech, 24,* 390-397.

——. 1938a. Stuttering with relation to word accent and word position. *J. Abnorm. Soc. Psychol., 33,* 112-120.

Bühler, C. 1939. *The child and his family.* New York: Harper.

Burks, B. S. 1940. Mental and physical developmental pattern of identical twins in relation to organismic growth theory. *Yearb. Nat. Soc. Stud. Educ.,* 39(II), 85-96.

Cartwright, D. 1941. Decision-time in relation to the differentiation of the phenomenal field. *Psychol. Rev., 48,* 425-442.

Cartwright, D., and L. Festinger. 1943. A quantitative theory of decision. *Psychol. Rev., 50,* 595-621.

Davidson, H. H., and B. Klopfer. 1938. Rorschach statistics: II. Normal children. *Rorschach Res. Exch., 3,* 37-42.

Davis, A., and J. Dollard. 1940. *Children of bondage.* Washington, D. C.: American Youth Commission.

Dembo, T. 1931. Der Ärger als dynamisches Problem. *Psychol. Forsch., 15,* 1-144.

Deri, S. 1943. *The psychological effect of the electric shock treatment.* M.A. thesis. State University of Iowa.

Dimock, H. S. 1937. *Rediscovering the adolescent.* New York: Association Press.

Dollard, J. 1935. *Criteria for the life history.* New Haven: Yale University Press.

——. 1937. *Caste and class in a southern town.* New Haven: Yale University Press.

Doob, L. W., and R. R. Sears. 1939. Factors determining substitute behavior and the overt expression of aggression. *J. Abnorm. Soc. Psychol., 34,* 293-313.

Dresdner, I. 1933. Ueber Körperbehinderung und seelische Entwicklung. *Z. angew. Psychol., 44,* 399-437.

Duncker, K. 1938. Experimental modification of children's food preferences through social suggestion. *J. Abnorm. Soc. Psychol., 33,* 489-507.

Einstein, A. 1933. *On the method of theoretical physics.* New York: Oxford University Press.

Erikson, E. H. 1940. Studies in the interpretation of play: I. Clinical observation of play disruption in young children. *Genet. Psychol. Monogr., 22,* 556-671.

Escalona, S. K. 1940. The effect of success and failure upon the level of aspiration and behavior in manic-depressive psychoses. *Univ. Iowa Stud. Child Welfare, 16,* No. 3.

Fajans, S. 1933. Erfolg, Ausdauer, und Aktivität beim Säugling und Kleinkind. *Psychol. Forsch., 17,* 268-305.

Farber, M. L. 1945. Studies in topological and vector psychology: III. Imprisonment as a psychological situation. *Univ. Iowa Stud. Child Welfare, 20.*

Festinger, L. 1942. Wish, expectation, and group performance as factors influencing level of aspiration. *J. Abnorm. Soc. Psychol.*, *37*, 184–200.

Frank, J. D. 1935. Some psychological determinants of the "level of aspirations." *Amer. J. Psychol.*, *47*, 285–293.

———. 1944. Experimental studies of personal pressure and resistance: II. Methods of overcoming resistance. *J. Gen. Psychol.*, *30*, 43–56.

Frank, L. K. 1938. Cultural control and physiological autonomy. Reprinted from *Amer. J. Orthopsychiat.*, *8*, No. 4, 622–626.

———. 1939. Cultural coercion and individual distortion. *Psychiatry*, *2*, 11–27.

Frazier, E. F. 1940. *Negro youth at the crossways.* Washington, D. C.: American Council on Education.

French, J. R. P., Jr. 1945. Studies in topological and vector psychology: III. Organized and unorganized groups under fear and frustration. *Univ. Iowa Stud. Child Welfare*, *20*.

French, T. 1939. Insight and distortion in dreams. *Int. J. Psycho-Anal.*, *20*, 287–298.

Freud, S. 1916. *The interpretation of dreams.* (Trans. by A. A. Brill.) (Rev. ed.) New York: Macmillan.

Freund, A. 1930. Psychische Sättigung im Menstruum und Intermenstruum. *Psychol. Forsch.*, *13*, 198–217.

Gardner, J. W. 1940. The relation of certain personality variables to level of aspiration. *J. Psychol.*, *9*, 191–206.

Gelb, A. 1938. Colour constancy, pp. 196–209. Article in W. D. Ellis (Ed.), *Source book of gestalt psychology.* London: Kegan Paul.

Gelb, A., and K. Goldstein. 1924. Über Farbennamenamnesie nebst Bemerkungen über das Wesen der amnestischen Aphasie überhaupt und die Beziehung zwischen Sprache und dem Verhalten zur Umwelt. *Psychol. Forsch.*, *6*, 127–186.

Gesell, A., H. M. Halverson, H. Thompson, F. L. Ilg, B. M. Castner, L. B. Ames, and C. S. Amatruda. 1940. *The first five years of life: A guide to the study of the preschool child.* New York: Harper.

Gesell, A., and H. Thompson, assisted by C. S. Amatruda. 1934. *Infant behavior: Its genesis and growth.* New York: McGraw-Hill.

Goodenough, F. L. 1940. New evidence on environmental influence on intelligence. *Yearb. Nat. Soc. Stud. Educ.*, 39(I), 307–365.

Gottschaldt, K. 1926. Über dem Einfluss der Erfahrung auf die Wahrnehmung von Figuren: I. Über den Einfluss gehäufter Einprägung von Figuren auf ihre Sichtbarkeit in umfassenden Konfigurationen. *Psychol Forsch.*, *8*, 261–318.

Gould, R. 1939. An experimental analysis of "level of aspiration." *Genet. Psychol. Monogr.*, *21*, 3–115.

Gray, M. 1940. The X family: A clinical study and a laboratory study of a "stuttering" family. *J. Speech Disorders*, *5*, 343–348.

Halverson, H. M. 1931. An experimental study of prehension in infants by means of systematic cinema records. *Genet. Psychol. Monogr.*, *10*, 107–286.

Hartshorne, H., and M. A. May. 1929. *Studies in service and self-control.* New York: Macmillan.

Homburger, E. 1937. Configurations in play: Clinical notes. *Psychoanal. Quart.*, *6*, 139–214.

Hoppe, F. 1930. Erfolg und Misserfolg. *Psychol. Forsch.*, *14*, 1–62.

Horowitz, E. L. 1936. The development of attitude toward the Negro. *Arch. Psychol.*, *N. Y.*, No. 194.

Hull, C. L. 1930. Simple trial-and-error learning: A study in psychological theory. *Psychol. Rev.*, *37*, 241–256.

———. 1932. The goal gradient hypothesis and maze learning. *Psychol. Rev.*, *39*, 25–43.

Irwin, O. C. 1930. The amount and nature of activities of newborn infants under constant external stimulating conditions during the first ten days of life. *Genet. Psychol. Monogr.*, *8*, 1–92.

———. 1932. The distribution of the amount of motility in young infants between two nursing periods. *J. Comp. Psychol.*, *14*, 429–445.

Jack, L. M. 1934. An experimental study of ascendant behavior in preschool children. *Univ. Iowa Stud. Child Welfare*, *9*, No. 3, 7–65.

Jersild, A. T. 1936. The development of the emotions. In C. E. Skinner (Ed.), *Educational psychology.* New York: Prentice-Hall.

Johnson, W., and J. R. Knott. 1937. Studies in the psychology of stuttering: I. The distribution of moments of stuttering in successive readings of the same material. *J. Speech Disorders*, *2*, 17–19.

Jucknat, M. 1937. Performance, level of aspiration and self-consciousness. *Psychol. Forsch.*, *22*, 89–179.

Kalhorn, J. 1945. Studies in topological and vector psychology: III. Values and sources of authority among rural children. *Univ. Iowa Stud. Child Welfare*, *20*.

Kanner, L. 1935. *Child psychiatry.* Springfield, Ill.: Thomas.

Karsten, A. 1928. Psychische Sättigung. *Psychol. Forsch.*, *10*, 142–154.

Katona, G. 1940. *Organizing and memorizing: Studies in the psychology of learning and teaching.* New York: Columbia University Press.

Katz, D. 1937. *Animals and men.* New York and London: Longmans, Green.

Katz, E. 1938. *Some factors affecting resumption of interrupted activities by pre-school children.* (*Inst. Child Welfare Monogr. Ser.*, No. 16.) Minneapolis: University of Minnesota Press. Pp. 52.

Keister, M. E. 1936. *The behavior of young children in failure.* In Barker, Kounin, and Wright, *Child Behavior and Development.* New York: McGraw-Hill.

Kephart, N. C. 1937. Studies in emotional adjustment: II. An experimental study of the "disorganization" of mental functions in the delinquent. *Univ. Iowa Stud. Child Welfare*, *15*, No. 1.

Koffka, K. 1928. *The growth of the mind: An introduction to child psychology.* (Trans. by R. M. Ogden.) (2d ed.) New York: Harcourt, Brace.

Köhler, W. 1920. *Die physischen Gestalten in Ruhe und im stationären Zustand.* Braunschweig: Germany: Friedr. Vieweg & Sohn.

———. 1925. *The mentality of apes.* (Trans. by E. Winter.) New York: Harcourt, Brace.

Kounin, J. S. 1939. *Experimental studies of rigidity as a function of age and feeblemindedness.* Ph.D. Dissertation, University of Iowa.

Lewin, K. 1935. *Dynamic theory of personality.* New York: McGraw-Hill.

———. 1936a. *Principles of topological psychology.* New York: McGraw-Hill.

———. 1936b. Psychology of success and failure. *Occupations, 14,* 926-930.

———. 1938. The conceptual representation and measurement of psychological forces. *Contr. Psychol. Theor., 1,* No. 4.

———. 1939. Field theory and experiment in social psychology: Concepts and methods. *Amer. J. Sociol., 44,* 868-896.

———. 1940a. Studies in topological and vector psychology: I. Formalization and progress in psychology. *Univ. Iowa Stud. Child Welfare, 16,* No. 3, 7-42.

———. 1940b. Bringing up the child. *Menorah J., 28,* 20-45.

———. 1942. Time perspective and morale. In G. Watson (Ed.), *Civilian morale,* second yearbook of the SPSSI. Boston: Published for Reynal and Hitchcock by Houghton Mifflin.

———. 1943. Defining the "field at a given time." *Psychol. Rev., 50,* No. 3, 292-310.

———. 1945. Studies in topological and vector psychology: III. Constructs in psychology and psychological ecology. *Univ. Iowa Stud. Child Welfare, 20.*

Lewin, K., T. Dembo, L. Festinger, and P. Sears. 1944. Level of aspiration. In J. McV. Hunt (Ed.), *Handbook of personality and the behavior disorders.* New York: Ronald.

Lewin, K., R. Lippitt, and R. White. 1939. Patterns of aggressive behavior in experimentally created "social climates." *J. Soc. Psychol., 10,* 271-299.

Lippitt, Ronald. 1939. Field theory and experiment in social psychology: Autocratic and democratic group atmospheres. *Amer. J. Sociol., 45,* 26-49.

———. 1940. Studies in topological and vector psychology: I. An experimental study of the effect of democratic and authoritarian group atmospheres. *Univ. Iowa Stud. Child Welfare, 16,* No. 3, 45-195.

Lippitt, R., and R. White. 1943. The "social climate" of children's groups. In Barker, Kounin, and Wright, *Child behavior and development.* New York: McGraw-Hill.

Lippitt, Rosemary. 1940. *Popularity among preschool children.* Unpublished Ph.D. Dissertation, University of Iowa.

Lissner, K. 1933. Die Entspannung von Bedürfnissen durch Ersatzhandlungen. *Psychol. Forsch., 18,* 218-250.

MacDonald, J. M. 1940. *The behavior of the young child under conditions of insecurity.* Unpublished Ph.D. Dissertation, Harvard University.

Mahler, V. 1933. Ersatzhandlungen verschiedenen Realitätsgrades. *Psychol. Forsch., 18,* 26-89.

Marquis, D. P. 1931. Can conditioned responses be established in the newborn infant? *J. Genet. Psychol., 39,* 479-492.

Marrow, A. J. 1938. Goal tension and recall. *J. Gen. Psychol., 19,* 3-35; 37-64.

McGrath, M. C. 1923. A study of the moral development of children. *Psychol. Monogr., 32,* No. 2, 1-190.

McGraw, M. B. 1935. *Growth: A study of Johnny and Jimmy.* New York: Appleton-Century.

Mead, M. 1928. *Coming of age in Samoa.* New York: Morrow.

———. 1937. *Cooperation and competition among primitive peoples.* New York: McGraw-Hill.

Meyers, C. E. 1945. Studies in topological and vector psychology: III. The effect of conflicting authority on the child. *Univ. Iowa Stud. Child Welfare, 20.*

Moore, E. S. 1931. The development of mental health in a group of young children: An analysis of factors in purposeful activity. *Univ. Iowa Stud. Child Welfare, 4,* No. 6.

Moreno, J. L. 1934. *Who shall survive? A new approach to the problem of human interrelations.* Washington, D. C.: Nervous and Mental Disease Publishing Co.

Murphy, G., L. B. Murphy, and T. M. Newcomb. 1937. *Experimental social psychology* (rev. ed.). New York: Harper.

Murphy, L. B. 1937. *Social behavior and child personality: An explorative study in some roots of sympathy.* New York: Columbia University Press.

Murray, H. 1938. *Explorations in personality.* London: Oxford University Press.

Ovsiankina, M. 1928. Die Wiederaufnahme von unterbrochener Handlungen. *Psychol. Forsch., 11,* 302-379.

Pachauri, A. R. 1935. A study of Gestalt problems in completed and interrupted tasks: I. *Brit. J. Psychol., 25,* 447-457.

Piaget, J. 1932. *The moral judgment of the child.* (Trans. by M. Gabain.) New York: Harcourt, Brace; London: Kegan Paul.

Porter, H. von K. 1939. Studies in the psychology of stuttering: XIV. Stuttering phenomena in relation to size and personnel of audience. *J. Speech Disorders, 4,* 323-333.

Pratt, K. C. 1933. The neonate. In C. Murchison (Ed.), *A handbook of psychology,* pp. 163-208. (2d ed., rev.) Worcester: Clark University Press.

Reichenbach, H. 1928. *Philosophie der Raum-Zeitlehre.* Leipzig: De Gruyter.

Reuter, E. B. 1937. The sociology of adolescence. *Amer. J. Sociol., 43,* 414-427.

Rosenzweig, S. 1933. The recall of finished and unfinished tasks as affected by the purpose with which they were performed. *Psychol. Bull., 30,* 698 (abstract).

Rotter, J. B. 1939. Studies in the psychology of stuttering: XI. Stuttering in relation to position in the family. *J. Speech Disorders, 4,* 143-148.

Sandvoss, H. 1933. Über die Beziehungen von Determination und Bewusstsein bei der Realisierung unerledigter Tätigkeiten. *Arch. ges. Psychol.*, *89*, 139-192.

Schanck, R. L. 1932. A study of a community and its groups and institutions conceived of as behaviors of individuals. *Psychol. Monogr.*, *43*, No. 2, 1-133.

Schlote, W. 1930. Über die Bevorzuzung unvollendeter Handlungen. *Z. Psychol.*, *117*, 1-72.

Sears, P. S. 1940. Levels of aspiration in academically successful and unsuccessful children. *J. Abnorm. Soc. Psychol.*, *35*, 498-536.

Sears, R. R., and P. S. Sears. 1940. Minor studies in aggression: V. Strength of frustration-reaction as a function of strength of drive. *J. Psychol.*, *9*, 297-300.

Seashore, H. G., and A. Bavelas. 1942. A study of frustration in children. *J. Genet. Psychol.*, *61*, 279-314.

Sewall, M. 1930. Some causes of jealousy in young children. *Smith Coll. Stud. Soc. Work*, *1*, 6-22.

Shacter, H. S. 1933. A method for measuring the sustained attention of preschool children. *J. Genet. Psychol.*, *42*, 339-371.

Shaw, C. R. 1933. Juvenile delinquency—a group tradition. (*Child Welfare Pamphlets*, No. 23.) *Bull. State Univ. Iowa, New Ser.*, No. 700.

Shaw, C. R., et al. 1929. *Delinquency areas: A study of the geographic distribution of school truants, juvenile delinquents, and adult offenders in Chicago.* (*Behav. Res. Monogr.*) Chicago: University of Chicago Press. Pp. xxi + 214.

Sheffield, A. 1937. *Social insight in case situations.* New York: Appleton-Century.

Sliosberg, S. 1934. A contribution to the dynamics of substitution in serious and play situations. *Psychol. Forsch.*, *19*, 122-181.

Stern, W., and J. MacDonald. 1937. Cloud pictures: A new method of testing imagination. *Character and Pers.*, *6*, 132-147.

Stoddard, G. D., and B. L. Wellman. 1934. *Child psychology.* New York: Macmillan.

Terman, L. M. 1919. *The intelligence of school children.* Boston: Houghton Mifflin.

Thomas, D. S. 1932. An attempt to develop precise measurements in the social behavior field. *Sociologus*, *8*, 436-456.

Thompson, M. M. 1940. *The effect of discriminatory leadership on the relations between the more and less privileged subgroups.* Unpublished Ph.D. Dissertation, University of Iowa.

Tolman, E. C. 1932. *Purposive behavior in animals and men.* New York: Century.

——. 1935. Psychology versus immediate experience. *Phil. Sci.*, *2*, 356-380.

Travis, L. E., W. Johnson, and J. Shover. 1937. The relation of bilingualism to stuttering. *J. Speech Disorders*, *3*, 185-189.

Vigotsky, L. S. 1934. Thought in schizophrenia. *Arch. Neurol. Psychiat., Chicago*, *31*, 1063-1077.

Waring, E. B., F. M. Dwyer, and E. Junkin. 1939. Guidance: The case of Ronald. *Cornell Bull. for Homemakers*, No. 418, 1-112.

Weigl, E. 1941. On the psychology of so-called processes of abstraction. *J. Abnorm. Soc. Psychol.*, *36*, 3-33.

Wellman, B. L. 1932-1933. The effect of preschool attendance upon the IQ. *J. Exp. Educ.*, *1*, 48-69.

Werner, H. 1940a. *Comparative psychology of mental development.* New York: Harper.

——. 1940b. Perception of spatial relationships in mentally deficient children. *J. Genet. Psychol.*, *57*, 93-100.

White, R. K. 1940. An analysis of conversation in autocratic and democratic atmospheres. *Psychol. Bull.*, *37*, 476.

Wiehe, F. 1935. *Die Grenzen des Ichs.* Quoted in Lewin (1935).

Wolf, T. H. 1938. *The effect of praise and competition on the persistent behavior of kindergarten Children.* (*Inst. Child Welfare Monogr. Ser.*, No. 15.) Minneapolis: University of Minnesota Press.

Wright, B. A. 1941. An experimentally created conflict expressed in a projective technique. *Psychol. Bull.*, *38*, 718 (abstract).

——. 1942a. Altruism in children and the perceived conduct of others. *J. Abnorm. Soc. Psychol.*, *37*, 218-233.

——. 1942b. The development of the ideology of altruism and fairness in children. Ph.D. thesis, State Univ. Iowa. (Also, *Psychol. Bull.*, *39*, 485-486 [abstract].)

Wright, H. F. 1937. The influence of barriers upon the strength of motivation. *Contr. Psychol. Theor.*, *1*, No. 3.

Wright, M. E. 1940. The influence of frustration upon the social relationships of young children. Ph.D. thesis, State Univ. Iowa. (Also, *Psychol. Bull.*, *38*, 710 [abstract].)

Zeigarnik, B. 1927. Ueber das Behalten von erledigten und unerledigten Handlungen. *Psychol. Forsch.*, *9*, 1-85.

THE INFLUENCE OF TOPOLOGICAL AND VECTOR PSYCHOLOGY UPON CURRENT RESEARCH IN CHILD DEVELOPMENT: AN ADDENDUM

Sibylle Escalona

Behavior and development as a function of the total situation is more than a summary of interrelated research studies; it is the expression of a point of view in psychology which is applicable to perception, thought, or personality as it is to child development. It was Kurt Lewin's expectation that topological and vector psychological concepts would help to break down the barriers between various branches of psychology and help to create a unified theory which would permit integrated treatment of all manner of psychological functions. In a sense Lewin's child psychology aimed at the destruction of child psychology as an independent specialty.

A comparison of representative work in 1953 with that of 1945 reflects a clear trend in the direction of unification. The content of the present volume is witness to the fact that there has been interpenetration and cross-fertilization among all facets of psychological endeavor to the degree that studies of motor learning (Gesell, 1946; Gesell and Amatruda, 1945, 1947) or of language development (McCarthy, 1949) usually imply a theoretical commitment to one among several models of personality theory. Child development, by the very nature of its subject matter, invites convergence of different disciplines from physical growth to cultural anthropology. A survey of the present volume will suggest to the reader the degree to which psychologists have succeeded in comprehending the "child as a whole." The writer believes that the dominant trend toward multidis-

cipline research has succeeded in all but abolishing the isolated study of narrow sections of the developmental process, but that a true integration of concepts and methods has yet to occur. In topological terms child psychology has become a more fluid and more highly differentiated field, but a consistent hierarchical structure to serve as organizing agent has not yet been developed. It is the task of this addendum to summarize the rôle which topological and vector psychology has played in psychological research within the field of child development.

Almost [1] no purely topological and vector psychological studies of children have been conducted since the Iowa work on frustration and aggression (Barker, Dembo, and Lewin, 1941) referred to in the above chapter. Instead, concepts and methods from this source have found their way into research with children which may be characterized as primarily clinical or primarily within the frame of reference of social psychology. It would be more accurate to say that psychologists who were and are identified with topological and vector psychology have since focused their interest on clinical or social psychology (as it applies to child

---

[1] An exception which came to our attention is a master's thesis by William A. Koppe (1944). Experiments with a kindergarten population demonstrated that the "laws" governing the level of aspiration as formulated by others (Escalona, 1948; Frank, 1935; Hoppe, 1930; Jucknat, 1937) are substantially applicable to children at this age level. His results also indicated that level of aspiration is partly determined by a variable not usually controlled, namely, the absolute level of attainment

development) and have found Lewin's systematic position valuable in setting and solving their problems. Below we shall refer to three major studies of this type. The intent is to illustrate the type of inquiry which has remained closest to topological and vector psychological studies.

A second and perhaps more important observation is that many of the principles brilliantly summarized in Lewin's article included in this volume are no longer identifiable as belonging to one school of thought within psychology, so general is their acceptance. For instance, the great majority of child psychologists stress the importance of seeing each behavior episode in context, and, consequently, simple frequency statistics are being replaced by more sophisticated measurements which give expression to the multiple determination of behavior. Similarly, few child psychologists now need to be reminded that the physical "objective" environment is not identical with the child's psychological environment, and that knowledge of the latter is required for an understanding of his actions. The concepts of differentiation and organization as central ones in the description of any developmental process have found universal acceptance. More specific Lewinian formulations of aspects of child behavior have also found application in psychological research which may be remote from topological and vector psychology in general orientation. Among these one might name "detour" problems (as related to intelligence and learning), time perspective as a dimension of psychological functioning which changes with growth, "substitution," and "satiation." These remarks are in here in order to suggest to the reader scarcity of narrowly topological child psychology may indicate approach has proved unpro- years but rather that child

psychology as a whole is changing and that topological and vector psychology has played a significant rôle in determining the nature of this change.

Experiments and Field Studies of Contagion.[1] In a group situation children influence the behavior of one another in two important ways, among others. The more familiar variety of social influence comprises situations where one child communicates his *intention* of changing the behavior of others ("let's play football"). The other variety of social influence has been discussed by Fritz Redl (1949) and others under the heading *behavioral contagion*. In the group treatment of delinquent children Redl noted occasions when the behavior of one child suddenly spread to other group members. Yet it was highly questionable whether the "initiator" had any intention of influencing the others; if so he certainly did not communicate this in an observable manner. As long as it remained unpredictable and somewhat inexplicable, contagious behavior created practical problems in the management of groups.

The effect of various group atmospheres (autocratic, laissez-faire, democratic) upon behavior was studied by Lippitt (1939) and Lewin, Lippitt, and White (1939). These studies resulted in the first of a series of formulations which treat of groups as dynamic wholes with identifiable properties. Both methodologically and theoretically this work found its continuation in action research with adult populations. The study of contagion reported here, which was directed jointly by Ronald Lippitt and Fritz Redl, is the exception in that it concerns child behavior.

1 This project was supported in part by a grant from the National Institute of Mental Health, U.S.P.H.S. Principal investigators: Fritz Redl, Wayne University, and Ronald Lippitt, Michigan University.

A field staff systematically observed 16 children's groups in the setting of summer camps for emotionally disturbed children. Contagion was here defined as a situation where the behavior of one child (the initiator) brought in its wake behavioral changes in other members of the group in the same direction (i.e., the behavior of those susceptible to contagion became similar to that of the initiator), and where the initiator had not overtly indicated an intention to influence the behavior of others. This was distinguished from "direct attempts to influence" in order to see what similarities or differences might be found in the determinants of the two kinds of influence. The most important data consisted of: (a) The recording of instances of contagion and instances of direct attempt to influence throughout the camp season for all groups. (b) Serial assessment of each child's position within the group, and the network of relationships constituting the group, by means of sociometric techniques. (c) Repeated ratings provided by camp counselors for each child assessing relevant variables in terms of the child's behavior and his rôle in the group. It was found that whether or not a child is likely to succeed in initiating contagion does not greatly depend on his more permanent personality characteristics but depends instead upon his perception of his status in the group, and on the group's perception of his position within it. Both these conditions had to be present; the data showed that a child who regarded his position in the group as secure and high in status value but whose actual position was low seldom succeeded in releasing contagious behavior. Conversely, even if highly esteemed by the group, a child was not likely to become an initiator if he was unaware of his "power." Contagion was the more likely to occur the greater the similarity between the goals (and underlying need structure) of the group and the individual initiator (Polanski, Lippitt, and Redl, 1950).

In the planning of therapeutic groups and more generally it has often been assumed that a child's behavior in a group can largely be predicted from an understanding of his personality. These findings, however, seem to show that children's behavior in a group can be predicted, to a surprising degree, solely in terms of functioning group positions. While a diagnostic appraisal of personality is a necessary supplement to prediction of group behavior, it is the more useful the more diagnosis is geared to "group relevant" dimensions of personality. Among these, "social sensitivity" to group atmospheres and standards was found especially important.

From a methodological point of view it is interesting to note that the field study yielded more precisely formulated hypotheses, some of which were then checked in a series of experiments. It had originally been thought plausible that contagion might depend upon the characteristic impulse-balance of the child, i.e., that children whose control of impulses is especially weak would be especially likely to set off or succumb to contagion. The field study showed that generally this is not the case, but in one specifically structured situation impulsivity did predict initiators of contagious behavior more significantly than did group status, namely, if the entire group was in a state of need frustration, but the children were restrained from expressing their reactions to frustration. Using this clue, experiments were designed in which need frustration was induced and restraints against the expression of frustrated needs were also induced, and it was possible to measure susceptibility to contagion under various conditions. It was in this latter phase of the study that topological concepts were used to clarify the psychological processes which allow behavioral contagion to occur (Grosser, Polansky, and Lippitt, 1951).

We shall refer to only those aspects of the experimental procedure which are necessary for an understanding of the theoretical statement. Children were studied in "groups" of two, and, unbeknown to the experimental subject, the second "group member" was in fact a collaborator [1] whose behavior was directed by prearranged signals from the experimenter. The desired conflict between a goal and opposing psychological forces was created in the classical manner. The subject, or as he believed the group of two, was introduced to a highly pleasurable activity (dart throwing), which was interrupted at a high point of motivation. He was then put to the performance of a boring task (filling sheets with figures 8). He was made to feel that unpleasant consequences might ensue were he to neglect the assigned task and return to the dart throwing. The experimenter then left the room, observing through a one-way vision screen and directing the behavior of the child collaborator by means of inconspicuous sounds. In the control situation for each experimental variation the collaborator simply obeyed instructions, i.e., did not initiate behavior which might prove contagious. In the experimental condition he engaged in a graded series of behaviors which corresponded to the frustrated need, from "wriggling fingers," and thus evading the task, to resuming dart play. The design was such as to allow for an analysis of variance. For each condition the behavior of subjects who were exposed to "temptation" was compared with the behavior of subjects whose partner did not violate the rules. Variations

included different degrees of friendliness between the children (induced by the collaborator), different degrees of activity on the part of the collaborator, and a situation in which a variety of pleasurable distractions from the task were available.

It was conclusively demonstrated that the initiating behavior of the collaborating child so changed the experimental child's perception of the situation as to cause him to express the frustrated need in overt behavior, as he did not in the control situations. Neither the degree of friendliness between the group members nor any of the other variables studied exerted an appreciable influence upon susceptibility to contagion. The experimental situation was conceptualized as a conflict between the desire to resume dart throwing (own goal, OG), the induced intention to perform the assigned task (induced goal, IG), the fear of unpleasant consequences of disobedience (restraining force of barrier surrounding task region, $rf_{P, TS}$), and the desire to get out of the increasingly unpleasant task situation (force away from task situation, $f_{P, -TS}$). In the control situation (Figure 1) it could be said that: $f_{P, IG} + rf_{P, TS} > f_{P, -TS} + f_{P, OG}$. An integrated treatment of the statistical data in terms of the topological concepts permitted the derivation that the initiator's actions changed the situation for the experimental child chiefly in two ways, one structural and one dynamic. Seeing the group member fritter away time without working created a new region (F = fidgeting), which was attractive because it offered a way of leaving the field without being an outright violation of the induced rules. Also, in the child's experience the behavior of the initiator led to a decrease in the strength of the barrier surrounding the task region. In situations where the collaborator actually engaged in the "forbidden pleasure," only the second condition was met. As shown

---

[1] As far as we know this is the first time that children (12 to 14 years of age) have by design and with foreknowledge collaborated in an experimental procedure.

in Figure 2, the task was now partially surrounded by a barrier but a path was open to a region of activities outside of the assigned task not in a direction contrary to the induced forces.

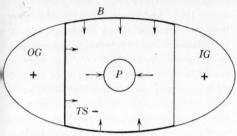

FIGURE 1. Experimentally produced conflict, control situation. OG = own goal; IG = induced goal; TS = task situation; P = person; B = barrier.

In view of the fact that under the sway of contagion children overtly expressed the frustrated needs it may be said that $f_{P, IG} + rf_{P, TS} < f_{P, OG} + f_{P, -TS}$. This state of affairs led, among other things, to locomotion in the direction of region F (fidget-

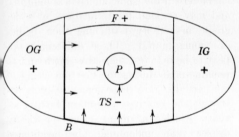

FIGURE 2. Experimental conflict, collaborator has altered child's perception of situation. OG = own goal; IG = induced goal; B = barrier; F = fidgeting; TS = task situation; P = person.

ing), which was unequal in direction to both OG and IG but was in the direction of $f_{P, -TS}$. This direction of the child's behavior was hence due to a change in the strength of the restraining force emanating from the experimenter's instructions.

This study illustrates an integrated approach to one facet of child behavior. The interest in the dynamics of group life is combined with a clinical therapeutic interest in the treatment of behavior disorders by means of group therapy. The underlying problems concerning behavior as a function of the (group) situation and concerning the dynamics of groups-as-a-whole were conceptualized largely in terms of topological and vector psychology.

Earliest Phases of Personality Development: A Non-normative Study of Infant Behavior.[1] Among the early attempts to substantiate (in part) the general theory of development in topological terms was Fajans's (1933) study of goal-directed behavior in infants. A more complex and precise formulation was later presented by Barker, Dembo, and Lewin (1941). Although the second study was based on experimental work with preschool-age children the theory encompasses the total span from infancy to maturity. Both studies were concerned with the general laws of the developmental process; in so far as prediction was used it referred to group differences in the behavior of different age groups under comparable situational conditions.

In more recent years the direct observation and experimental study of infant behavior has come into its own as an important component of child psychology.[2] Unlike the study referred to below, most

[1] This project was supported (in part) by a grant from the National Institute of Mental Health, U.S.P.H.S. Principal investigators: Mary E. Leitch and Sibylle Escalona, both of the Menninger Foundation. Topeka, Kansas.

[2] This statement is based more on the existence of numerous large-scale research projects now under way than on published results. Among others we may mention the Fels Institute at Antioch College, the Denver Child Research Council of the University of Colorado Medical School, and the Child Study Center of Yale University. Each of these groups is currently conducting intensive studies of infant behavior and development.

of these researches have fallen into one of two categories: (*a*) the relationship between one environmental variable (or a constellation of such) present in infancy has been related to subsequent personality development (Spitz, 1945, 1946*a* and *b*, 1949); (*b*) empirical-descriptive data concerning the behavior of young children was systematized in terms of the presence or absence of specific intrapersonal variables which were seen as constitutionally given co-determiners of behavior and development (Fries, 1938, 1944, 1945, 1946; Spitz and Wolf, 1946).

Leitch and Escalona, and their associates, conducted an observational study of the variability of behavior among healthy infants ranging from 4 to 32 weeks in age. Their primary concern was to describe the great variety of behavior adaptations that occur among normal infants and to define some determinants of this variability. The method was substantially that of a field study, but supplemented by some methodological refinements ordinarily employed in experimental research.[1] In brief, the behavior of each of the 128 infants (16 at each lunar month level) was recorded continuously by three trained observers for a period of approximately 4 hours in a natural situation. That is, the infant and his mother were observed as the mother took care of the baby, feeding him, putting him to sleep, dressing him, etc. The detailed behavior observations and extensive interviews with mothers were supplemented by further observations in the babies' homes, by cinema photography, by psychological testing (of the infants), and

[1] It seems notable that all three studies reported here have gone to the field for their data but have brought to the field studies the methods and statistical procedures usually characteristic of laboratory research. All these field studies are explicitly designed to yield hypotheses of such a form that confirmation by the experimental method will ultimately be possible.

by various ratings and simple growth measurements.

The observations made in the course of this study support those made by others (Bayley, 1949; Escalona and Leitch, 1949; Escalona, 1950; Fries, 1938; Gesell and Ames, 1937; and Gesell, 1946) to the effect that the behavior of an infant cannot be understood solely in relation to his environmental experience. Not only do different babies behave quite differently in comparable situations, but it has also been found impossible to explain all differences or communalities in infant behavior in terms of the past experience of these children. Although on the one hand it can often be demonstrated that at each moment the infant is responding to the momentary situation *as he perceives it*, it cannot be plausibly demonstrated that he acquired the characteristics which determine his subjective perception in the course of previous experience. To illustrate, some babies characteristically respond to stimulation by marked bodily activity, others characteristically show much less motility and may respond to stimulation by a decrease in activity (stiffening their bodies or "going limp"). These differences appear to be manifest soon after birth and to remain stable during the first few years of life, at any rate (Escalona, 1950). Although the relative amount of bodily activity which an infant characteristically displays can undoubtedly be heightened or lowered by environmental influences, the observed activity differences under a wide range of environmental circumstances leave little doubt that a spontaneous tendency toward relatively greater or lesser bodily activity is an inherent property of the organism.

The theoretical framework which determined initial hypotheses as well as the analysis of data in this study consisted of an attempt at integration between the content of psychodynamic personality theory and the systematic position of Lewin. In his chapter Lewin indicated the importance of individual differences for the application of general laws of behavior to specific predictions. "It can be expected that all problems of individual differences will be linked more and more with the general psychological laws of behavior and development and that in this way a deeper understanding (of both) will be possible." The familiar formula $B = f(P, E)$, like any general law, is applicable only if certain values can be inserted to specify the nature of P(erson) and E(nvironment) for the fraction of time for which a derivative statement is to be made. This study was, in part, an attempt to delineate the dimensions of P (structure and dynamic state of person) which could be distinguished during the first half year of life. With the systematic inclusion of the physical and social environment it became an attempt to approximate a description of the lifespace (or 128 lifespaces) for the early infancy period. Since personality development may be thought of as a behavior continuum through the life cycle, the above formula should hold for the more stable characteristics called "personality" quite as much as for each momentary behavior episode, $PD^{t_1 \cdots t_n} = f(P, E)^{t_1 \cdots t_n}$ (personality development through time is a function of the person and the environment through time). Written thus, the formula appears to express a circular relationship. However, a dynamic view of personality growth implies interdependence among the three elements of the equation though the geometrical analogy would be a spiral rather than a circle.

Leitch and Escalona applied the lifespace concept to their material by postulating that the psychological environment which determines behavior and development is a function of the relevant nonpsychological factors (biological, physical, and social environment) as modified by, or filtered through, certain possibly constitutional properties of the person. These organismic characteristics may include among others: (a) Perceptual sensitivity and differential distribution of sensitivity over various sensory modalities. For example, infants differ in absolute threshold for sensory stimuli so that some startle or otherwise respond strongly to light, sound, touch, temperature, or other stimuli (low threshold), whereas from other infants the same stimuli elicit mere attentiveness or other minor behavioral responses (high threshold). Similarly, the same baby is thought to be differentially sensitive in various modalities, so that one baby may for instance respond relatively most acutely in the auditory sphere and less so in the visual, whereas the reverse may be true of another. (b) Strength of movement impulse or activity level; this has been referred to above. (c) Tension tolerance, which refers to the degree of tension (or disequilibrium) which the organism can maintain without resulting primitivization of behavior. The investigators saw individual differences in infant behavior, and especially differences in response to similar or identical environmental circumstances, as partly a function of the fact that the world impinges in a different fashion upon differently constituted infants; i.e., the same stimuli are not perceived identically by different babies.[1] It was hypothesized that certain behavior syndromes can be discerned among infants which reflect various styles of infantile adaptation, and which

[1] It goes without saying that organismic characteristics are hypothesized to be only one among several factors influencing the state of the person which in turn influences subjective perception. The kind and intensity of existing needs and other conditions which arose owing to past or present circumstances play a large rôle.

may be found to occur among a wide range of environmental constellations.[1]

As a by-product of this investigation the effects of overstimulation upon infant behavior were explored by the same research group (Escalona and Bergmann, 1949). The behavioral consequences of heightened tension states were investigated by Dembo (1931) and by Barker, Dembo, and Lewin (1941). When changes in infant behavior under perceptual overstimulation were observed it was found that these behavior changes conformed to the coordinating definitions for a "system in a state of tension." In this instance "tension" could not be said to result from psychic conflict (there being no demonstrable conflict between simultaneous goals when infants are stimulated through prolonged exposure to sights, sounds, touch, and social contacts), but there occurred: (a) increased communication between intrapersonal regions; (b) a decrease in the capacity for coordinated behavior (decrease in hierarchical organization), and, finally, in many instances (c) de-differentiation or primitivization of behavior. An experimental situation was filmed [2] in which a heightened tension state was created in infants 4½ to 6 months of age by means of perceptual overstimulation. Primitivization of behavior was assessed through a comparison of the behavior of the same children in response to standard situations adapted from developmental tests before and after exposure to prolonged stimulation.

The Midwest Field Study of Children's Behavior. In one sense the Midwest study of children's behavior parallels the study of infant behavior described above. If the formula $B = f(P, E)$ is the point of departure one might say that in the infant study emphasis was placed on exploration of specific variable properties of P, whereas in the Midwest study emphasis was focused upon a determination of the distribution of variables which go to make up E, at least in one specific sociocultural group. In both investigations interest centered on the *mediation* process by means of which nonpsychological factors are transformed into the "psychological world" of the individual child.

The complex interrelationships between psychological experience and the nonpsychological milieu were formulated by Lewin (1944) and by Heider (1927, 1944). Climatic and geographical conditions, economic and social factors, the actual physical properties of the world about, all enter and determine the lifespace. This is as true for the neonate crying from cold as for the octogenarian smoking his pipe. Yet the same object, or the same bodily sensation, may have different meanings to different persons, or to the same person at different times. Lewin (1944) used the term "psychological ecology" to designate the realm of inquiry which deals with the laws governing the mediation between the nonpsychological environment and the psychological field.

The Midwest project was a large-scale study in psychological ecology (Barker and Wright, 1950; Wright and Barker, 1950a). Under the direction of Roger Barker and Herbert Wright a field staff (most of whom resided in Midwest [3]) developed a complex research design for the precise recording of spontaneous child behavior in a community. The aim was to describe the conditions of life and the behavior of all the children in a small American town (named "Midwest"). Trained observers

---

[1] At the time of this writing some such behavior syndromes have tentatively been suggested, chiefly as a guide to analysis of data. The analysis may or may not succeed in demonstrating their existence.

[2] *Eight infants: Tension manifestations in response to perceptual overstimulation.* New York: New York University Film Library.

[3] "Midwest" is a fictitious name assigned to the actual community where this study was conducted.

accumulated what is probably the largest amount of behavior data ever collected by a single research group. Sampling techniques were used in order to determine the amount of material descriptive of child behavior which was needed in different settings (school, playground, home, church, club meeting, etc.), for different age groups, and the like. In addition, a sizable number of "day records" (Barker and Wright, 1951) were made; these were continuous observations of a single child's day from the moment he arose to the moment he went to bed at night (observers spelling each other off at half-hour intervals).

At the time of this writing results have not appeared in print. A major research contribution, and one that stems directly from a topological analysis of the problem, has been made, however, in terms of a theoretical framework and elaborate methodology (of data analysis) by means of which the overwhelming mass of data can be made comprehensible (Wright and Barker, 1950a). The authors conceptualized the field in which behavior takes place as the *psychological habitat*.[1] This "primary homeland of behavior" envelops the child wherever he goes; it is the things and conditions that make up his world in terms of their subjective *meaning*. The attempt was to reconstruct, by inference, the psychological habitat for each child at each moment under observation by simultaneous recording of the child's surroundings and of his overt behavior. The mediating process between outer and inner world, which determines the aspects of his environment which the child will perceive as goals, as barriers, as tools, as negative or positive regions, etc., was conceptualized in terms of *behavior settings* and *behavior objects*

(see Figure 3 [2]). A behavior setting was defined as a part of the nonpsychological milieu which is perceived by the community as appropriate for a certain range of behaviors. (A drugstore, a church, a back alley, and a river bank are all behavior settings.) Behavior objects were defined as parts of the nonpsychological environment which are perceived by the community as appropriate for a certain range

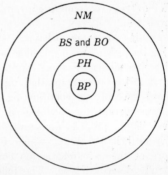

FIGURE 3. Mediation between nonpsychological milieu and psychological habitat. BP = behaving person; PH = psychological habitat; BS = behavior settings; BO = behavior objects; NM = nonpsychological milieu.

of actions. (A baseball bat, a Sunday school teacher, an ice cream cone, and a fountain pen are all behavior objects.) Topologically speaking, a behavior setting is an activity region (Lewin, 1936, 1938); a behavior object is a point region within an activity region. Although it is true that almost anything may happen almost anywhere, the Midwest data furnished impressive evidence to show the coerciveness of behavior settings and behavior objects. All behavior observed in the same setting (over a period of years) showed a striking similarity; behavior in different settings or with different objects showed strikingly

---

[1] The definition is equivalent to those for "psychological environment" or "momentary lifespace" as these appear elsewhere in the literature.

[2] Figure 3 is *not* a topological representation but a diagram intended to save the space which would be required for a full written statement.

consistent disparity. In conjunction with parallel behavior observations the systematized assessment of the child's changing surroundings permitted interesting types of analysis. For instance, a given child on a certain day of his life in Midwest entered 27 different behavior settings and used over 500 different behavior objects in a manner sufficiently overt to enter the descriptive records. Figures such as these could be compared for children belonging to different socio-economic groups, different age levels, etc.

Quantifying on-going behavior without violating its psychological meaning is more complex than doing the same for its outer context. It is at this point that topology, and more especially the coordinating definitions constructing the hodological space (Lewin, 1938), proved important.[1] The analysis of behavior units, which formed the core of this research, is too complex to be fully described here. The following will give some notion of the empirical and theoretical potentialities of this approach to child research.

The largest meaningful unit in the division of a behavior continuum was defined as an *episode*, which encompasses an action from the first step in the direction toward a goal to the last step which is still a part of the same action directed toward the same specific end. Since most behavior is structured in such a way that several subgoals are attained on the road toward the main goal, the unit corresponding to a subgoal which is dynamically dependent upon the major goal and hence in the same direction is designated as a *phase*. By definition, a phase cannot be further subdivided on the level of molar (psychologically

meaningful) behavior. (The rule of thumb by which to distinguish molar from molecular behavior has been to say that those actions which are meaningfully performed by a person are molar, those that are performed by a leg, a set of glands, a finger, etc., are molecular: A *person* walks or reads, a *foot* is lowered to the ground in taking a step, the *eyes* move laterally while the *person* is reading. Therefore, the same set of motions may constitute an action, molar behavior, at one moment, and an actone, molecular behavior, the next. For instance, a deliberate wink may be an action performed by a person; a second later blinking may occur unnoticed.) The phase was further defined by the criterion that its potency must be less than that of the episode of which it is a part.

Each complete episode falls into two *stages*, the translocation and the consummatory stage respectively. This is to distinguish that part of an action which consists of moving toward a goal (translocation) from those activities which ensue once the goal has been reached (consummatory). If the episode is, for instance, the purchase of an ice cream cone, the child's actions up to the point the nickel has been paid and the cone has been grasped fall into the translocation stage, the manner in which he eats the cone falls into the consummatory stage. Behavior is organized not only in terms of a single major goal and a series of subgoals on the way; for instance, the episode "going to school" may be so structured that "crossing Main Street" may be subgoal, yet reaching Main Street may be experienced as falling into several smaller units such as "passing the bakery" and "turning the corner." These and similar subdivisions were taken into account in this behavior analysis, but it will not be necessary to burden the reader with the cumbersome corresponding terminology. Fig-

[1] We thought it interesting to read (Wright and Barker, 1950a) that the investigators experimented with numerous conceptualizations to guide their behavior analyses. After more than a year's work they "rediscovered" Lewin's (1938) formulations and found them appropriate to their needs.

ure 4 is a schematic representation of this mode of analysis.

It is comparatively rare for a person to be engaged in only one situation, or one meaningful action, at a time. More frequently, both episodes and/or phases may overlap (as when children converse while walking to school). Episodes or phases may be interrupted by episodes of quite a different meaning (i.e., direction); sub-

situation were experienced as restricting, coercing, helping, increasing, or decreasing the scope of free movement, etc. Other variables concerned the clarity with which the child perceived the situation, the degree of efficiency and creativity he attained, and the like.

The results of these behavior analyses were entered on Hollerith cards, which permits nearly infinite patterning of results.

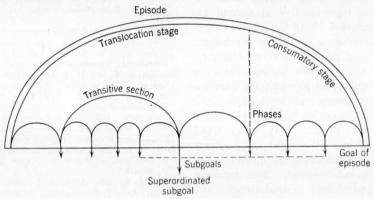

FIGURE 4. Units of analysis for single behavior episode.

sequently they may be resumed, or may remain unfinished (for instance, playing ball on the way to school may temporarily give rise to behavior directed toward goals that have nothing whatever to do with school). It may also happen that what would ordinarily be a step in the direction of a goal may come to be so absorbing in its own right as to be no longer experienced as related to the main goal (this was designated as a "dependent episode").

Comparably complex modes of analysis have been worked out in order to allow for inferences about the quality of each experience and the fate of each episode. On the basis of specified behavior clues, ratings were made concerning such things as how great the child's involvement was, the degree of satisfaction or frustration he experienced, whether other persons in the

For the child population of the community called Midwest it is possible to know what proportion of their actions was successful, and which kinds of actions in what settings, with what objects and in which social situations, tended to be successful most often. In case of failure it is possible to know in what proportion of actions the adult prevented the child from reaching his goal, and where and how this occurred, as well as the proportion of instances where the child's goals were impracticable because of the reality of the outer situation, because of his misjudgment of his own capacities, or for other reasons. For Midwest we may expect to learn in which settings children experienced the least and the most coercion and at whose hands. We can learn about those settings and objects in relation to which children displayed the greatest and the least emotional intensity, and the nature of the emotions they expressed. We may learn the degree to which some children were restricted in terms of settings they were allowed to enter, objects they were allowed to use, etc. Or we may ask for a curve depicting the increasing complexity of goal structure in the behavior of children as a function of increasing age, and so on, ad infinitum.

If the three studies referred to in this section are representative of current research conducted within the general framework of topological and vector psychology, the following may be said in summary. Those adopting Lewin's systematic position tend to think of all psychological phenomena as a continuum, and they tend to search for formulations of lawfulness applicable to all behavior. In conformity with a trend conspicuous in all the social sciences, they therefore work towards an integration of the various subdisciplines (from sociology and social psychology to psychoanalysis and physiology). Their interest has shifted somewhat from the validation of general laws by experimental procedures in laboratory situations to the discovery of constellations of variables as they occur in life situations, by means of controlled observations under field conditions. Furthermore, a marked research interest has developed in the processes of mediation, which is but another way of saying that topologists have broadened their realm by concerning themselves not only with the nature of the psychological situation but also with its genesis and its development through time.

Bibliography

Barker, R. G., Tamara Dembo, and Kurt Lewin. 1941. Frustration and regression: Studies in topological and vector psychology: II. *Univ. Iowa Stud. Child Welfare, 18,* No. 1.

Barker, R. G., and H. F. Wright. 1950. Psychological ecology and the problem of psychosocial development. *Child Develpm., 20,* 131–143.

Barker, R. G., and H. F. Wright. 1951. *One boy's day.* New York: Harper.

Barker, R. G., H. F. Wright, Jack Nall, and Phil Schoggen. 1950. There is no class bias in our school. *Progressive Educ., 27,* No. 4, 106–110.

Bayley, Nancy. 1949. Consistency and variability in the growth of intelligence from birth to eighteen years. *J. Genet. Psychol., 75,* 165–196.

Dembo, Tamara. 1931. Der Ärger als dynamisches Problem. *Psychol. Forsch., 15,* 1–144.

Escalona, S. K. 1948. *An application of the level of aspiration experiment to the study of personality.* New York: Bureau of Publications, Teachers College, Columbia University.

——. 1950. The use of infant tests for predictive purposes. *Bull. Menninger Clinic, 14,* No. 4, 117–128.

Escalona, S. K., and Paul Bergmann. 1949. Unusual sensitivities in very young children. *Psychoanalytic study of the child,* Vol. III. New York: International Universities Press.

Escalona, S. K., and M. E. Leitch. 1949. The reaction of infants to stress. *Psychoanalytic study of the child.* Vol. III. New York: International Universities Press.

Fajans, Sara. 1933. Die Bedeutung der Entfernung für die Stärke eines Aufforderungscharakters beim Säugling und Kleinkind. *Psychol. Forsch., 17,* 215–267.

Frank, J. D. 1935. Some psychological determinants of the "level of aspiration." *Amer. J. Psychol., 47,* 285–293.

Fries, M. E. 1938. Interrelated factors in development. *Amer. J. Orthopsychiat., 8,* 726–752.

——. 1944. Importance of continuous collaboration of all agencies in dynamic handling of the child. *The Nervous Child, 3,* No. 4, 258–267.

——. 1945. Psychosomatic relations between mother and infant. *Psychosom. Med. 6,* No. 2, 159–162.

——. 1946. The child's ego development and the training of adults in his environment. *Psychoanalytic study of the child,* Vol. II. New York: International Universities Press.

Gesell, Arnold. 1946. Some relationships between maturation and acculturation. *J. Nerv. Ment. Dis., 103,* 518–520.

——. 1947. The predictiveness of infant behavior traits. *Science, 106,* 512.

Gesell, Arnold, and C. S. Amatruda. 1945. *The embryology of behavior: The beginning of the human mind.* New York: Harper.

——. 1947. *Developmental diagnosis: Normal and abnormal child development.* 2nd ed. New York: Harper.

Gesell, Arnold, and L. B. Ames. 1937. Early evidences of individuality in the human infant. *J. Genet. Psychol., 47,* 299–361.

——. 1947. The infant's reaction to his mirror image. *J. Genet. Psychol., 70,* 141–154.

Grosser, Daniel, Norman Polansky, and Ronald Lippitt. 1951. A laboratory study of behavioral contagion. *Human Relations, 4,* No. 2, 115–142.

Heider, Fritz. 1927. Ding und Medium. *Symposium, 1,* 109–157.

Heider, Fritz. 1944. Social perception and phenomenal causality. *Psychol. Rev., 51,* 358–374.

Hoppe, Ferdinand. 1930. Erfolg und Misserfolg. *Psychol. Forsch., 14,* 1–62.

Jucknat, Margarete. 1937. Leistung und Anspruchsniveau. *Psychol. Forsch., 22,* 89–174.

Koppe, William A. 1944. The setting of levels of aspiration by kindergarten children with respect to degrees of attainment. Unpublished master's thesis, University of South Dakota.

Lewin, Kurt. 1935. *Dynamic theory of personality.* New York: McGraw-Hill.

——. 1936. *Principles of topological psychology.* New York: McGraw-Hill.

——. 1938. The conceptual representation and measurement of psychological forces. *Contr. Psychol. Theor., 1,* No. 4, 1–247.

——. 1944. Constructs in psychology and psychological ecology. Studies in topological and vector psychology: III. *Univ. Iowa Stud. Child Welfare, 20,* 1–30.

Lewin, Kurt, Ronald Lippitt, and R. K. White. 1939. Patterns of aggressive behavior in experimentally created "social climates." *J. Soc. Psychol., 10,* 271–299.

Lippitt, Ronald. 1939. Field theory and experiment in social psychology: autocratic and democratic group atmospheres. *Amer. J. Sociol., 45,* 26–49.

Littman, R. A., and E. Rosen. 1950. Molar and molecular. *Psychol. Rev., 57,* 58–65.

McCarthy, Dorothea. 1949. Personality and learning. *Amer. Council Educ. Studies,* Series 1, No. 35, 93–96.

——. 1953. Language development in children. In Carmichael, *Child psychology.* 2nd ed. New York: Wiley.

Polansky, Norman, Ronald Lippitt, and Fritz Redl. 1950. An investigation of behavior contagion in groups. *Human Relations, 3,* No. 4, 319–348.

——. 1950. The use of sociometric data in research on group treatment process. *Sociometry,* xiii, 39–62.

Redl, Fritz. 1949. The phenomenon of contagion and shock effect in group therapy. In *Searchlights on delinquency.* New York: International Universities Press.

Redl, Fritz, and David Wineman. 1951. *Children who hate.* Glencoe, Ill.: Free Press.

Spitz, R. A. 1945. Hospitalism—an inquiry into the genesis of psychiatric conditions in early childhood. *Psychoanalytic study of the child,* Vol. I. New York: International Universities Press.

——. 1946a. Part II: Hospitalism—an inquiry into the genesis of psychiatric conditions in early childhood. *Psychoanalytic study of the child,* Vol. II. New York: International Universities Press.

——. 1946b. Anaclitic depression. *Psychoanalytic study of the child,* Vol. II. New York: International Universities Press.

Spitz, R. A., and K. M. Wolf. 1946. The smiling response: a contribution to the ontogenesis of social relations. *Genet. Psychol. Monogr., 34,* 57–125.

——. 1949. Autoerotism. *The psychoanalytic study of the child,* Vol. III/IV. New York: International Universities Press.

Wright, H. F., and R. G. Barker. 1950a. *Methods in psychological ecology:* A progress report. Impression offset for use of interested research workers, Topeka, Kansas.

——. 1950b. The elementary school does not stand alone. *Progressive Educ., 27,* No. 5, 133–137.

Wright, H. F., R. G. Barker, *et al.* 1951. Children at home in Midwest. *Progressive Educ., 28,* No. 5, 137–143.

CHAPTER 16

GIFTED CHILDREN

CATHARINE COX MILES

Foreword

Study of gifted children was largely descriptive and anecdotal until Terman and Hollingworth identified and then analyzed the backgrounds and characteristics of boys and girls of high IQ. Other investigators, among them Witty, Hildreth, and Sumption, confirmed the earlier findings of Terman and Hollingworth and their associates. A number of valuable contributions came from investigators throughout the United States and abroad.

The major study of the gifted, Terman's 50-year project, reached its halfway mark at midcentury. The "composite picture" which emerged from study over a 25-year period of some 1500 gifted children by Terman and his associates stands as a monument to intelligent planning and the devotion of an investigator to an important psychological and educational problem.

In the following pages the study of the gifted is traced from its notable origins. The major scientific findings are presented chronologically down to the middle 1940's. A concluding section is devoted to developments in the period following the second world war in which Terman's 25-year report (1947) was a major event. A summary is attempted of Terman's principal results and other gifted studies of the period are also briefly reviewed. The status of gifted study evaluated in the light of contemporary genetic and biosocial research efforts and results affords a promis-

ing starting point for new research design. Continuing study of Terman's gifted subjects and their children may answer further questions regarding origins and influences in superior adult achievement.

Introduction to the Historical Review

When intelligence tests of the Binet type were first applied to the general population the purpose of measurement was the differentiation of the dull from the average. But the earliest surveys showed quite another possibility, for these tests, found to be singularly effective as indicators of mental power, at once set off a small group of superior individuals whose test scores were as far above the generality as those of the feeble-minded were below it. The rarity of individuals scoring 130 or 140 IQ and higher, and their extraordinary facility in performance, naturally aroused a feeling of wonder and surprise. In the first 1000 children tested, only 1 per cent rated as high as 130, and the 4 or 5 whose IQ's passed the 140 mark seemed indeed phenomenal. It was natural to think of these unusually brilliant test performers as the probable leaders of the future, those among whom the most distinguished personalities, including geniuses of all kinds, were most likely to appear. Furthermore, by assuming an appropriate critical point they could be arbitrarily defined as geniuses or near-geniuses in Galton's special sense of possessing unusually superior mental ability, if this were defined as mental test ability. What the significance of their high competence might be for future attainment could only be surmised.

Research has now shown that children of high IQ maintain their score level relatively well. The superior school achievement of groups rating high in intelligence tests has also been sustained. These results confirm the validity of the IQ test-construction procedures. It should be noted, however, that while predictable results like these have been verified new ambiguities in interpretation have emerged and old problems have appeared in new guise. Conditions for the deviations of individuals and subgroups from total group trends are frequently unclear.

The turning of the research spotlight on the children of high IQ has illuminated more than one dark area. A change in terminology may be mentioned: the terms *genius* and *near genius* have been gradually abandoned in favor of the more acceptable designation *gifted*.

Consideration of the numbers of gifted children in the community indicates their absolute frequency as well as their relative rarity (Table 1). In the public school population of the United States, numbering some 28,000,000, there are probably not less than 110,000 to 140,000 of the very highly gifted children, and somewhere near twice this number who rate as high as 130 IQ. An average American town of 10,000 with a school population of roughly 2000 may be expected to have 20 children with IQ's of 130 or higher, of whom 10 or so rate as high as 140. Certain regions of the United States have relatively more, others relatively less, than the average approximations. Communities and cities vary within themselves in the density of the gifted population. Schools also differ, high schools generally attracting more of the superior intellects than elementary schools, and colleges more than either. Private schools also differ among themselves, some of them having as high populations of gifted children as the average or even the superior college.

Gifted children have many traits in common. It may be difficult to distinguish some 130 IQ's from the 140's, but the gifted group as a whole differs unmistakably from average children of the same age and schooling. Future investigators face the problem of designing research to reveal differences between gifted children and their less high scoring siblings or other associates whose origins and experience appear to have been similar. As other variables besides intelligence become more satisfactorily measurable their significance in these comparisons may be shown in as well-planned studies as those earlier designed to compare the gifted with samples from the general average.

The problem of creative genius has scarcely been touched in the studies of the gifted. However, it now seems more than probable that historical geniuses would, if tested in childhood, have scored high on the IQ scale.

Study of the most superior specimens of a species is of importance for pure and applied science. It is essential for pure science to determine the upper limits of superiority, the nature of the characteristics of the upper deviates, the ways in which they differ from the average, the individual differences among them, and their similarities. It is not to be expected in any biological series that they will prove to be a type, yet there will be certain traits in which they tend to resemble one another more than they resemble, for example, the average of their species or the average of those less superior whose backgrounds and opportunities have apparently resembled their own.

TABLE 1

PERCENTAGE OF GIFTED CHILDREN IN SCHOOL POPULATIONS AS REPORTED BY VARIOUS INVESTIGATORS

(IQ 140 Plus and Upper Centile)

Stanford-Binet Intelligence Test

	Revised	Old Form				
Population	2904	874	905	112	149	100
Investigator	Merrill	Macmeeken	Terman	Terman	Terman	Malherbe
Date	1938	1939	1916	1919	1919	1921
School status	Grades 1–8	Single age	Grades 1–8	Kindergarten	Grade 1	Grades 1–8
Percentage of group rating 140+	1.33	1.03	.55	2.7	1.30	13.0
Percentage of group rating 136+						
Upper 1 per cent	143 IQ+		130 IQ+			
Median IQ of group	100	100	100	106	88	124

Group Intelligence Tests

							Educ. Rec. Bureau	
Population	4925	13,220	27,642	53,751	1295	3522	4075	10,982
Investigator	Pintner	Duff and Thomson	Witty	Cohen and Coryell	Dearborn and Cattell	Rogers	Educ. Rec. Bureau	
Date	1931	1923	1934	1935	1930	1928	1940	
School status	Grades 1–8	Grades 11–12	H.S.	Senior H.S.	Grades 1–8	Grades 1–8	Grades 1–8	Grades 7–8
Percentage of group rating 140+	1.20	.12	.34	3.34	6.3	6.4	3.9	7.4
Percentage of group rating 136+							6.5	11.2
Median IQ of group	96	100	104		119	115	116	117

It is of importance to applied science to know under what circumstances these superior deviates appear. If it should be found that the function of intelligence can be measurably increased through training methods, through environmental influences, and the like, then the hope would be justified that the effective number of the gifted may be considerably enlarged. If, on the other hand, biological elements are chiefly involved, it is not likely, under existing conditions, that the present percentage can be appreciably augmented. The attention of psychologists, which has been directed toward the study of background as well as foreground, is now being turned especially to a consideration of the environmental conditions favorable for the development of gifted children, that is, toward the discovery of opportunities and influences which can stimulate their talents to strong, healthy, optimal growth.

History

Philosophers and other teachers who have tried to work out systematic methods of producing a good human society have given thought to the selection and education of superior children. Plato spoke of the importance of discovering and suitably educating the most able youths for leadership in the state. He suggested that tests of native ability should be the basis of the selection. From his day until the introduction of modern universal school systems, education was, however, generally the prerogative of the children of the well-born and the able, plus a few outstanding minds from the lower economic or social groups. State administrators, teachers, and priests tried to recruit pupils of superior natural gifts who might be trained to carry on community institutions and maintain or extend the group culture. Under the apprentice system skilled specialists tried to attract gifted youngsters apt in learning and capable of superior accomplishment. Practical rather than scientific methods of finding and training gifted children are still in general use today. Ostwald in 1909 formulated his scheme for the selection of gifted university students for advanced research. Present-day personnel methods involve essentially similar problems and procedures. With or without the use of special technical aids, education and industry seek the gifted and train those who are expected to qualify for later leadership (E. L. Thorndike, 1939).

Prescientific Observation of Gifted Children. Parents in all times have been alert to recognize superior competence in their offspring, and it has often been they who discovered and brought to wider attention children with special mental ability. When the parents were themselves teachers they not infrequently attributed the unusual competence of the children to their own superior methods of instruction. Superior children have frequently been reported singly and in interesting collections. One of the more famous prodigies was Christian Heinrich Heineken, who showed remarkable powers of observation and speech at the age of 10 months. Before the age of one year he could recite stories and verses. Under a tutor's instruction he soon learned arithmetic fundamentals, anatomical systems, and world history. At the age of 4 years he could read printed and written German, relate stories in French, and recite 1400 sentences from good Latin authors; he knew all the important places on the map. His knowledge was said to be more than mere memory, for he could discuss what he knew with intelligence. His fame spread through Europe and he was invited to visit the Danish king, who was delighted and amazed by his conversation. Unfortunately, his health failed and he died at the age of 4 years and 4 months. Like Christian Heinrich, some others cited down to our own time (Braun, 1920; Bridgman, 1938) died at an early age and before their unusual promise could show complete fulfillment.

In happy contrast, the life story of Karl Witte gives the sequel to a gifted childhood in terms of superior, highly esteemed adult achievement. Considered to be quite unprepossessing as an infant, he was so carefully trained that at 6 his thinking was logical and his information accurate. He learned foreign languages readily and by the age of 9 was proficient in several. Science, art, and history he acquired by a natural project method devised by his father. Entering the university at 9 he completed a distinguished course in all his subjects and at 14 received the Ph.D. degree. When, at 16, he was appointed university instructor his youthful appearance caused objection and it was suggested by a royal patron that he devote some years to travel. During a residence abroad he was led to the literary study in which he became distinguished while continuing his chosen career in jurisprudence. At 21 he became a university teacher, at 23 a full professor. His long and active life was happy in domestic as well as in wider social relationships. He was devoted to community, professional, and scholarly activities in which, before his death at the age of 83, he had won high honor and distinction.

From many accounts we may conclude that, as in Witte's case, rapid mental development in superior healthy children can further unfold at a high level of adult distinction. On the other hand, precocity due to overtraining may regress to a mean of mediocrity. The one-sided advancement of the emotionally unstable may later deteriorate or end in mental illness. A typical early collection of case studies of historical precocious children is that of Buckley (1853). A more recent report of seven

American prodigies illustrates the late pretest point of view (Dolbear, 1912).

Beginning of Scientific Psychological Observation. Early scientific method was injected into the study of the gifted and a new phase of interest aroused in their investigation by the genetic and statistical researches of Galton (1869) and his contemporaries. These constituted the first quantitative psychological studies of human endowment. DeCandolle (1885) and, subsequently, Ward (1906) introduced scientific method into the classification of the social influences favorable to the appearance of the gifted, contending that these are at least as important as the constitutional endowment in determining achievement. J. McK. Cattell (1915, 1917) combined the two points of view and methods in his studies of *American Men of Science.*

Yoder (1894) included childhood traits in his statistical study of the natural history of fifty eminent men, and Ellis (1904) devoted special attention to interrelationships of precocity and health in the childhood of eminent Britons.

Three studies already referred to, by Terman, belong to the intermediate period in which the methods of psychology as of all natural science were gradually evolving. A study of leadership, suggestibility, and other traits in school children (Terman, 1904) was followed by a summary of contemporary opinion regarding precocity, prematuration, and the new concepts of mental hygiene (Terman, 1905). By laboratory study employing a large variety of early intelligence test items, the abilities of bright and dull boys were compared (Terman, 1906). In the title of this study, "Genius and Stupidity," Galton's concept of genius as superior mental ability was introduced.

In 1905 Binet's mental test scale was published, Goddard's translation appeared in 1911, and Terman's revision in 1916.

Case studies of gifted children soon showed the possibilities of the new methods to discover superior mentality. The first of these utilized mental ratings based on early versions of Binet's scale preceding the Stanford standardization. The author of the earliest report was incredulous (Bush, 1914); the second (Langenbeck, 1915) found in the Binet data gratifying proof of obvious precocity.

Modern Period of Quantitative Study. The small group of children with exceptionally high IQ's revealed by the revised Binet method proved to be neither peculiar nor one-sidedly intellectual as had been suggested in some earlier studies of precocious children. They were found rather to be essentially normal, well-adjusted children (Terman, 1915). Brief reports of four whose IQ's reached 140 or above were included as the highest in a series covering the IQ range and illustrating the measurement of intelligence (Terman, 1916). The definition of 130 IQ as the scoring point exceeded by the highest centile of mental ability was enunciated in the same volume.

The following year Garrison, Burke, and Hollingworth (1917) published the first account of an IQ in the 180's. Rusk (1917) described the test performance of an English child whose repeated Binet scores gave IQ's near 200, and Terman (1917), from biographical data, appraised Galton's childhood IQ as near 200. Other cases described in the first decade of measurement included an IQ of 167 (Coy, 1918); a phenomenally precocious reader (Terman, 1918), later found to have an IQ of 140 (Terman and Chase, 1920); and some 35 individuals in the IQ range from 140 to 184 (Terman, 1919). Besides affording case reports, these 35 gifted children with 14 other top centile individuals were, the subjects of the first group study of the intellectual, educational, and social characteristics of gifted public school children.

Gillingham (1920) reported seven IQ's of 140 and higher in a study of superior private school children with personality handicaps. Whipple (1919) outlined and illustrated methods of selection and instruction for superior, including technically gifted, children, reporting experimental results and norms and appending a bibliography. Clearly the new method of measurement had provided a means for differentiating intellectually able individuals in childhood, and psychologists soon became aware of the possibilities for the further study of individuals and groups thus differentiated.

The period from Henry's "Classroom Problems in the Education of Gifted Children," in the 1920 *Yearbook of the National Society for the Study of Education,* to Whipple's "Education of Gifted Children," in the 1924 *Yearbook* (Part I) of the Society, shows gradually developing systematization in method and presentation. The two volumes mentioned give cross-sections of contemporary interest and knowledge. Their bibliographies are extensive and valuable. Detailed studies of the educational status and progress of superior children in special classes published in this period include Coy (1923), in which the use of the term gifted was first specifically limited to the top centile; Cobb and Taylor (1924); and Stedman (1924). Goddard's monograph in this succession appeared in 1928. Root's (1921) descriptive study of superior children gave an experimental-psychological analysis of the mental processes of 53 cases, 23 of them of IQ 140+. A. M. Jones (1925) reported a detailed classification from clinical and educational data of material confirming for 120 children in Pennsylvania conclusions drawn by Terman for his first group of 59 upper centile Californians. Investigators at this time characteristically grouped their results and summarized the trends indicated by ranges and central tendencies. Their studies of superior children included school or clinic children variously restricted, in terms of IQ level, some extending consideration to include children within the average intelligence range. The researches dealing chiefly with groups of IQ 130+ or 140+ or presenting individual case studies at this level form the material basis for the present review. Other supportive works concerning above-average groups are occasionally referred to briefly.

Yates's account, in 1922, of 25 superior high school students marked the first use of group tests for the selection of notably high intelligence. The assumption that the reported scores corresponded to individual IQ's of 140 or higher is open to question. The upper centile criterion may, however, have been approximately fulfilled in this early work.

Whipple's *Yearbook* in 1924 contained the first statistically developed results from studies of the traits and achievements of large populations of the gifted. In this volume Terman outlined the Stanford study of more than 1000 gifted children with IQ's of 140 or higher. The methods of sifting the population by group and individual tests were described, and results obtained in the first cross-sectional research were briefly enumerated (Terman, 1924*b*). Terman and DeVoss (1924) also presented a preliminary summary of the educational test achievements later reported in detail. Waddle's (1924) case studies included a number of exceptionally high IQ's and reported remarkable achievements. The *Yearbook* researches describing upper centile intelligences and reporting many cases with IQ's 140 and higher include the studies by Hollingworth and Taylor (1924) of physical size and strength, Cobb and Taylor (1924) of achievement test scores, and Patrick (1924) of school achievement and personality traits. Standard educa-

tional tests with the devices of educational ages and quotients had added considerably to the effectiveness of statistical techniques for gifted child study.

In the next six years, 1925 to 1930 inclusive, the essential descriptive and statistical picture of the gifted child as we recognize it today was drawn. The researches of Terman and his associates, frequently referred to in this article as the California or Stanford studies, and Hollingworth's monograph were primarily responsible. Other investigators made valuable additions, generally by way of supporting evidence. Terman's researches were published in 1925 and 1930 as Volumes I and III of his *Genetic Studies of Genius*. These compendia afford the most complete available store of factual data about large groups of gifted boys and girls in childhood and adolescence. The first volume devoted 19 chapters to the history, methods, and results of the Stanford study of 1000 gifted preschool and elementary school children and 300 gifted high school pupils. A brief report of a follow-up study after 2 years and an important review of conclusions and problems completed the work (Terman *et al.*, 1925). In Volume III were reported methods and results in a cross-section follow-up after 7 years, 13 chapters; 86 cases illustrating individual differences and personality problems, 9 chapters; personal histories and achievements of seven gifted juvenile writers, 5 chapters; and a summary of retrospect and prospect in a critical, evaluative presentation, 1 chapter (Burks, Jensen, and Terman, 1930). The work presented in these two volumes is invaluable (1) because of the large number of subjects, representing about nine-tenths of the highest IQ's in a population of 250,000 public school children of their age, (2) because of the combination of longitudinal and cross-sectional study, (3) because statistical treatment is supported by case illustrations, and (4) because the basic data are made available for direct study and comparison.

Hollingworth, in 1926, published her monograph, *Gifted Children*, a general summary presentation of the background and foreground of the field of study. A series of researches by the same author and her associates on special problems concerning gifted children included further, before 1931, a study of the regression of the IQ's of the siblings of the gifted (Cobb and Hollingworth, 1925), measurements of motor functions (Hollingworth and Monahan, 1926), measurements of special musical abilities (Hollingworth, 1926a), a follow-up account 10 years after the first study of an unusually gifted boy, IQ 187 (Hollingworth, 1927), the important evidence of the superiority in school achievement of the more gifted over the less gifted (Hollingworth and Cobb, 1928), and a study of the growth in stature of the gifted (Hollingworth, 1930a).

In the same period Lamson (1930) reported on gifted children studied in the senior high school 7 years after their identification in the lower grades; Gray (1930) contributed a study of young college students; Lehman and Witty (1927) examined the play behavior of gifted school children; and Witty (1930) reported his first research on 100 gifted children with a follow-up after 6 years. The Witty studies covered many of the points studied also by Terman, and their similar findings gave direct support to the larger researches. Baumgarten in 1930 reviewed the studies of precocious children and described, psychologically, children with special artistic gifts.

In the year following the publication of Volume I of the *Genetic Studies of Genius*, Volume II of the series appeared: a study of the early mental traits of historical

geniuses (Cox, 1926). This work belongs in the succession, from Galton through Yoder, Ellis, and Cattell, of quantitative evaluations of historically recorded biographical data concerning persons of eminent achievement. It differs from the older studies in the introduction of the new concept of intelligence measurement. The appraisal of the IQ's of historical persons in childhood as proposed and illustrated by Terman (1917) was here applied to a large number of the most eminent men of the past, including many of the world's greatest geniuses. Previsaged by Terman, this work reported by Cox, from data gathered by her and her associates, approached the problem of the gifted by making available for comparison the IQ ratings, personality trait evaluations, and environmental appraisals from available childhood data for 300 of the most distinguished figures in the history of American and European progress.

In the 1930's and the early 1940's individual and group studies of gifted children contributed many additional details to form the gradually emerging outline picture as it appears in later sections of this chapter. Three reviews and summaries gave the findings and conclusions to date (Terman, 1931; Terman and Burks, 1933; Hollingworth, 1940). Hollingworth's (1942) final volume directed attention to the rare individuals whose childhood IQ's reached 180 or higher. Case studies of 12 such unusual children were here prefaced by a detailed historical section with résumés of the previously published accounts of 19 other children with similarly high IQ's. The book contains also a summary (five chapters), with critical comments and amplifications, of the author's findings and conclusions hitherto available only in scattered periodical form.

Significant contributions of research in these years include (1) the increasing evidence of the persistence in the gifted as they grow older of high intellectual ability and achievement as demonstrated by test performances and academic standing (Hollingworth and Kaunitz, 1934; Lorge and Hollingworth, 1936; Hildreth, 1939; Hollingworth, 1940; Terman and Oden, 1940a; Witty, 1940a; Hollingworth, 1942; Witty and Theman, 1943) and (2) the beginnings of differential study of subgroups of the gifted as in Lewis's (1941) comparison of the traits of gifted children of superior and inferior educational achievement and in Terman and Oden's (1940b) comparison of the most and the least successful of the California gifted group who had reached adulthood.

The more extensive bibliographies for the twenty-five-year period of research include those of Terman and Chase (1920), Henry (1920), Coy (1923), Whipple (1924), Hollingworth (1926b), Terman and Burks (1933), Blair (1938), Hollingworth, Terman, and Oden (1940), and Hollingworth (1942). Bibliographies on the education of the gifted in the 1940's were prepared by Newland (1941) and Hildreth and Ingram (1942).

Emerging Search for Further Defining Traits. A series of essentially duplicate studies tends to follow the elaboration of a new scientific technique. This occurred when the Binet method appeared. Many psychologists sought to discover or verify the presence of high IQ children in populations available for testing. To this primarily scientific interest a practical educational one was joined. Recognition of the desirability of segregating gifted children for educational economy and effectiveness made demands for adequate methods of selection. The mental tests provided a practical and objective basis that was found to be increasingly useful, especially when applied in conjunction with other methods of appraisal.

When the high IQ groups had been segregated, further progress depended on accurate measurement of behavior capacities and personalities. Again two interests converged. The need for scientific knowledge about the accomplishments, abilities, and traits other than the intellectual of the high IQ's was a compelling incentive to research; and the needs of teachers faced with the problems of instructing children 40 to 100 per cent accelerated intellectually gave the problem immediate practical urgency. The results have exceeded early anticipations in their extent and concurrence, and they have raised many new problems demanding further investigation.

With the preliminary publication of the 16-year follow-up of Terman's gifted thousand (Terman and Oden, 1940a, 1940b), research concerning gifted children entered a new phase. Personal characteristics, hereditary factors, school progress, and achievement were here for the first time compared for gifted children, apparently intellectually indistinguishable in childhood, who later became (1) successes or (2) failures in terms of professional, occupational, and economic achievement. The ground was thus cleared for the next step: the identification of those within the gifted groups who are likely to become in terms of total personality the most competent adults. A basis for a more restricted definition of the term gifted may result, or a new classificatory term may be found for the high IQ children of greatest potentiality, the gifted in childhood who in exceptional accomplishment in their maturity realize the rare promise of their youth.

Children who have not only the superior intellects to which the term gifted now attaches, but also the other traits and characteristics in which later superior achievement is rooted, are intrinsically gifted in a broad psychosocial meaning of the word. Whether there are others not so highly gifted in intelligence as the 130 or 140+ IQ's discovered in childhood, nor so precocious in the unfolding of their mental powers, who later display equal or superior success in their mature work, only further research can prove. The indications now available seem to show that it is the integrated totality of personality, with its varying physical, emotional, intellectual, and social components forming more rather than less effective patterns, in which success in contrast to failure is conditioned under appropriate environmental stimulations. Tracing forward the life progress of large groups of gifted children and upper centile children and tracing backward the developmental course of equally successful adult individuals who were not labeled as gifted in childhood must eventually solve the puzzle.

Characteristics of Gifted Children

The understanding, care, and training of gifted children and the theory of their origin and psychological constitution depend on knowledge of their background, their emotional and social traits, and their physical characteristics and on adequate measures of their intellectual endowment. Detailed observation and extensive quantification must precede analysis, and hypotheses are not to be accepted as conclusions. Parents, teachers, even psychologists, may cling to certain prejudices regarding the problems of the gifted which only many facts can ultimately dispel. Some of these are now available and from them parts of the picture of the gifted children can be distinctly discerned; others are still fragmentary and unclear, with contradictory elements. In the following pages the present knowledge is briefly reviewed.

Racial Origin. Gifted children in the United States have been more frequently found in the racial groups in which in the past century economic, social, educational, and professional leadership has been generally centered. Yet exceptions have also appeared, indicating that superiority may occur in any of the races or ethnic groups that have contributed to the American population. In Terman's main group 51 per cent are of British descent; 17 per cent, German and Austrian; 6 per cent, French; 4 per cent, Scandinavian; and 10.5 per cent, of combined Jewish stock. Old American families from New England and the Middle West have contributed substantially more than their quota to the California group, whereas foreign-born parents are numerically less well represented. Whatever groups are in the general population are also represented in the gifted group; Negroes, Mexicans, and Orientals are included in the California studies. In the Middle West (Witty, 1930, 1940a), in Ohio (Cleveland, 1921), and in Pennsylvania (A. M. Jones, 1925), the gifted groups have drawn heavily on the hereditary stocks constituting the more favored and enterprising elements of the population. In New York City, Jewish children are especially in excess in the public school gifted groups (Hollingworth, 1926b).

The racial contributions to the gifted populations in the various studies correspond roughly to the rank order of IQ means of the same stocks in the public schools. They are also in general agreement with the draft army results of 1918. Yet conclusions as to the superiority of parent stocks or future groups of gifted children should not be drawn from results limited geographically, economically, and in terms of migration. Certain elements have never been adequately surveyed, as, for example, children of Irish descent in parochial schools. Indians and Negroes have been insufficiently represented in the public school groups surveyed. When looked for in city Negro communities many high IQ Negro children can be found (Jenkins, 1943; Witty and Theman, 1943), and the degree of giftedness is uncorrelated with the extent of white ancestry (Jenkins, 1936). A Negro girl of 200 IQ has been reported (Witty and Jenkins, 1936). Studies of IQ distributions in England and Scotland show that roughly the same IQ level marks the upper centile in those countries as in the United States (Duff and Thomson, 1923; Macmeeken, 1939). We may say in summary that, although it is true that under existing social conditions certain racial or ethnic groups produce relatively more gifted children than others, no final conclusions about the relation of giftedness and race should be drawn until wider regions are sampled and conditions for the study of social inheritance are more fully understood (Hollingworth, 1940).

Sex Ratio. An excess of boys over girls has been found in the higher IQ brackets in the majority of groups of gifted children so far described. Among elementary school children Terman *et al.* (1925) found a ratio of 121 boys to 100 girls in 643 preschool and elementary school children; A. M. Jones (1925), 135 boys to 100 girls in 120 cases. In contrast, Witty's (1930) 100 numbered 51 boys and 49 girls, and Jenkins's (1936) Negroes showed excess in favor of the girls. In none of these researches, however, was the sex ratio a primary problem, and representative selection had not been attempted. The method of nomination used by Terman and the admission of volunteered subjects are both known to increase the numbers of higher scoring boys, as has been shown, among others, in the Scottish study of 1000 "representative" single age 11-year-olds (Scottish Council, 1933). In proof, the only completely objective sample, a rigid single age group in which all the Scottish children born on certain days were tested, was found to contain 4 boys and 5 girls of IQ 140+ (Macmeeken, 1939). Lewis's (1940) study also shows more girls than boys in the higher IQ categories. His ratio is 46 to 40 for IQ 140+.

Terman's high school group (Terman *et al.*, 1925) of 200 gifted boys and 109 gifted girls selected by nomination and group intelligence test offered an even larger numerical sex contrast than his younger populations, and other comparisons of the sexes with respect to numbers at the highest group test score levels seemed at one time to confirm a disproportion largely increasing with age (Terman and Burks, 1933). However, many of the reported results were drawn from groups unequally selected or were based on tests of unequal difficulty for boys and girls. Data reported for large high school and college populations derived from fairly homogeneous distributions with equal mean scores for the sexes show generally smaller contrasts than the earlier studies. In illustration (Table 2), Witty's (1934) group test results for IQ's 140+ in high school populations are compared with high school seniors' scores reported by Henmon and Holt (1931) and the Thurstones' (1937, 1938) statistics for college freshmen. The ratios show the boys generally but not always outnumbering the girls at the highest levels, but no regular age-sex trend appears consistently.

Causes for lack of agreement in the given results probably include lack of homogeneity in the population samples compared and inadequacy of the tests as measures equally fair to both sexes at the upper extremes even when the means are satisfactorily equated. Essential for fair comparison of superior deviates are sufficiently high "ceilings" in different sections of the tests, equality in population samples, and statistical adequacy of sample size at the gifted level. Appropriate consideration should also be given to the pos-

TABLE 2
SEX RATIO IN TOP RANGE OF GROUP-TEST DISTRIBUTIONS IN HIGH SCHOOLS AND COLLEGES

Investigator and Tests Used	Population Tested	Boys	Girls	Total	Ratio * Boys to Girls
Witty (1934) Terman Group Test	Pupils in high schools: Indiana, Kansas, Oklahoma, Illinois	14,149	13,493	27,642	
National Intelligence Test, etc.	Top 0.34 per cent (140 IQ+)	47	48	95	94 to 100
Henmon and Holt (1931) Ohio State Univ. Psychological Test	Seniors in high schools: Wisconsin	6,458	8,636	15,094	
	Top 0.46 per cent	39	31	70	168 to 100
Henmon and Holt (1931) American Council on Education Test (1929)	Seniors in high schools: Wisconsin	7,503	9,451	16,954	
	Top 1.18 per cent (97th college percentile)	111	90	201	156 to 100
Thurstone and Thurstone (1937) American Council on Education Test (1936)	College students	28,185	25,179	53,364	
	Top 2.71 per cent † (97.3 percentile)	802	643	1,445	112 to 100
Thurstone and Thurstone (1938) American Council on Education Test (1937)	Students in 323 colleges	32,500	26,450	68,899	
	Above 97th percentile ‡	1,207	771	1,978	123 to 100
	Students in private men's and women's colleges	6,787	6,590	13,377	
	Above 97th percentile ‡	417	262	679	161 to 100
	Students in private coeducational colleges	8,951	6,914	15,865	
	Above 97th percentile ‡	379	253	632	116 to 100
	Students in public coeducational colleges	11,355	5,651	17,006	
	Above 97th percentile ‡	283	138	421	101 to 100

* Relative to numbers tested. Calculations made for this table from data reported by investigators as cited.
† Wrenn (1935) gives ave. IQ 140 = 97th percentile A.C.E. ‡ Approximate.

sible involvement of differences beside the intellectual, such as social motivation, physical endurance, and fatigability in learning situations and examinations, and amount of practice and experience with different kinds of subject matter. Such factors may complicate the measurement of intelligence more at the extremes than at the means. The existence of a sex difference or its amount can be indicated certainly only when the secondary factors are eliminated and the comparisons are made with group or individual test techniques equally fair to both sexes at the part of the scoring range involved.

Heredity and Home Background. Gifted children may come from humble or from superior homes. In Terman's group 31 per cent of the fathers were professional; 50 per cent, semi-professional or in business; 12 per cent, skilled laborers; and less than 7 per cent, semi-skilled or unskilled. In Witty's group 64 per cent were in business, 34 per cent were professional. In terms of proportional representation in the general population the professional class has ten times its quota of gifted children; the commercial and public service groups exceed their quota by 50 per cent, whereas the industrial group contributes less than half its share. Even so, the large non-professional general population is so great that its numerical contribution to the gifted group is more than twice that of the professions. Groups of superior, but not gifted, children show relatively similar distributions in occupational and professional homes (Blair, 1938). Rated on the Barr Occupational Scale, the fathers of Terman's children show a much higher average index than the theoretical norm for the general population. And the fathers of two gifted children rate higher than the fathers of one. Witty has pointed out that the average Barr rating for the fathers of high school children, average IQ

111, is approximately halfway between the index of the fathers of gifted children and the estimated theoretical index for the general population.

The good stock producing the gifted is further indicated by the statistics for education and various measures of social value in the parents. The education of the fathers and mothers in the California study averages 12 years; the grandparents had less schooling than this, but more than the average in their day. Witty's Kansas and Missouri mothers also average 12 years of education; his fathers, 13 years. Among the parents of Jones's group, which seems to have been drawn from a university clinic, 55 per cent of the fathers and 24 per cent of the mothers were college graduates. These figures are higher than are generally found for the parents of typical gifted pupils in public schools. In the California group one or both parents of a fourth of all the children held a college degree. In Witty's group 50 per cent of the parents had 2 years or more of college training.

It is characteristic for gifted children to be born in families where positions of honor, trust, and responsibility are the rule rather than the exception. Terman found among the members of 528 families of gifted children more than twice that number of political, religious or fraternal, professional, financial, or executive positions. Witty reports similar results. Eminent relatives are also numerous in the families of the gifted in Terman's group, including 14 members of the Hall of Fame, 25 men and women listed in *Who's Who*, and 57 relatives in the *American Encyclopedia of Biography*, or an equivalent source. The fathers and mothers of the gifted children report a large and varied interest in hobbies (Witty, 1930). Teachers regard gifted homes as probably favorable in 85 per cent of Terman's cases, unfavorable in 9 per cent; in a control group the corresponding figures are 62 and 24 per cent. Further statistics indicate energy and stability in the families of the gifted. The average family containing a gifted child has 3.35 children when completed, showing a relatively small decline from the 3.67 children in the completed families of the parents. The correlation coefficient between the schooling of the parents and the size of the family is −.21 ±.07; between IQ and size of family, −.27 ±.06. Seven per cent of the parents of the gifted have been divorced or separated as compared with an estimated rate in the general population of 8 to 9 per cent. Infant mortality and morbidity rates are low in the families of the gifted; only 8 per cent of the fathers and 12 per cent of the mothers report as much as one or more, often minor, chronic illnesses. In agreement with Cattell's findings for men of science, where there are two or more children in the family, the gifted is likely to be the first-born.

Physical Traits and Health History. Baldwin's study of the California gifted group finds them superior to the age norms in thirty-four anthropometric measurements, including height, weight, general physical development, and muscular energy (Burks, Jensen, and Terman, 1930). Age for age, they exceed the developmental norms for average children. In height and weight they resemble private school children and other select groups drawn from superior population samples and enjoying more adequate physical care than average children (Table 3). At each reported age the gifted boys considerably exceed Shuttleworth's (1939) superior socioeconomic group; they are slightly taller and heavier than Baldwin and Wood's (1923) norms; and they almost equal Gray and Jacomb's (1921) norms derived from exclusively healthy, private school children. Witty's

(1930) results also show better than average bodily development.

Hollingworth and Taylor's (1924) data for 45 gifted Jewish children in New York City are in agreement with the other results with respect to height, and show, in a comparison of their results with norms for average and feeble-minded children, that a positive intelligence-height relationship is present. These children were also especially well nourished, as indicated by height-weight coefficients, and their strength, measured by dynamometer test, was supe-

TABLE 3

HEIGHT AND WEIGHT OF GIFTED AND OTHER GROUPS OF BOYS

Age [*]	Gifted			Baldwin and Wood [‡] (1923)	Faber [‡] California Terman *et al.* (1925)
	Baldwin [†] (1923) Terman *et al.*(1925)	Shuttleworth [‡] (1939)	Gray and Jacomb[†] [§] (1921)		
Height (in Inches)					
7	48.5	46.2	48.1	48	47.1
8	50.6	48.7	52.1	50	49.2
9	52.3	50.8	55.8	52	51.2
10	53.7	52.8	56.0	54	53.3
11	56.2	54.8	56.8	56	54.7
12	57.9	56.6	59.7	58	56.8
13	59.9	58.6	60.1	60	58.8
14	62.6	61.1	62.8	63	61.4
15	64.7	64.6	66.2	65	62.8
Weight (in Pounds)					
7	55.8	47.8	45	53	51.3
8	57.8	53.8	59	58	57.5
9	68.6	59.5	71	64	62.9
10	71.4	65.5	72	71	71.1
11	82.2	71.8	77	78	75.3
12	87.5	79.0	85	85	83.2
13	95.4	86.4	86	94	91.1
14	109.3	97.6	104	111	103.3
15	118.8	114.8	120	123	111.1

[*] Age to nearest birthday.
[†] Net weight.
[‡] Weight with clothing.
[§] Weights read from height-weight table.

rior to that of average and vastly superior to that of dull children of the same age. The height of these children measured year by year for a 6-year period continued on the average about 5 per cent above the norms (Hollingworth, 1926b). Monahan and Hollingworth (1927) found gifted children appreciably superior in neuromuscular capacity as measured in strength of grip, in jumping, and in tapping speed. The early studies of Cleveland (1921), Yates (1922), and A. M. Jones (1925) are in agreement with the more recent and more detailed results in indicating superior physical development and energy with infrequent physical defects. Hildreth's (1939) 50 upper centile elementary school children of Jewish race were superior to a matched control group in energy, physique, activity, and resistance to fatigue. In this connection the exploratory psychogalvanic research of Collmann (1931) is of interest. He found that superior children (average IQ 138) are less disturbed emotionally by an experimentally stimulating situation than average children.

Health histories were secured in Terman's and Witty's studies. The general conclusion from both researches is that gifted children are generally above the average in physical health and strength. The parents of the gifted are in the prime of life when the children are born, the fathers in the early thirties, the mothers in the late twenties, in agreement with Cattell's figures for the parents of 865 men of science. In the California group only 4.4 per cent of the children were born prematurely. The mother's health during pregnancy was rated as poor or very poor in but 7.8 per cent of the cases. The mean birth weight for both the California and Middle Western infants was approximately 12 ounces above the norm as given by Faber and Holt. Of the California gifted children, 57 per cent were breast-fed 8 months or longer as compared with 39 per cent reported by Woodbury in a norm group. In three successive health reports of Witty's gifted, superiority was maintained by upwards of 84 per cent; 90 per cent were reported to have good or excellent health during the first year. Sixty-eight per cent reached or exceeded a control group in health index in Witty's first study. Witty's children cut the first tooth at 6.8 months, Terman's at 7 months, in comparison with the norm range from 6 to 9 months. Terman's group talked at 11.3 months; the boys at 11.74 and the girls at 11.01. The average age for taking the first step was 13.05 months; for the boys, 13.10 and for the girls, 12.87. These results were compared by Terman et al. (1925) with Mead's norms: walking, 13.88; talking, 15.3 months. Talking appears in Witty's and Terman's gifted children to be slightly more precocious than the other activities reported from this early age. Comparison of the California elementary school gifted children with a control school group shows relatively fewer gifted children with defective hearing, mouth breathing, stuttering, headaches, or other symptoms of nervousness. The hours of sleep for the gifted are, age for age, more than those for the control group. Increasing from year 7 the difference amounts to about three-quarters of an hour at 12 and 13 years.

Pubescence was reached somewhat earlier by the gifted than by control children. Thus 100 per cent of Terman's 14-year-old boys were postpubescent as compared to 53 per cent of the control boys; and 48 per cent of 13-year-old girls had reached menarche in contrast to 25 per cent of control girls.

In the California study detailed medical examinations were given by two pediatricians to 783 gifted children. The careful individual appraisals by the physicians led to an expressed impression that major and minor defects are much less common among the gifted than among unselected children, and that "other things being equal there is a direct correlation between physical health and mentality in children when studied in groups." The home care, cleanliness, and health habits of the majority of the children indicated by their diet, hours of sleep, etc., were evidence of the superior intelligence of the parents. The conclusion was reached that, physically, the gifted child ranks above the average child of the community.

School Progress. Early attendance, relatively rapid grade advancement, and more than average interest in the more theoretical subjects characterize gifted children in school. Of the California gifted group in the early 1920's, 3 out of 5 attended kindergarten before entering the elementary grades at the average age of 6 years, 3 months. One out of 5 skipped half the first grade, and 1 out of 10 was immediately entered in the second grade on beginning school. Acceleration tended gradually to increase so that by the time the elementary school course was completed one entire grade had commonly been skipped. Of Terman's children 85 per cent skipped one or more half grades. After skipping, and so missing a segment of the curriculum content, the gifted children were, in the teacher's opinion, entitled to still further advancement, 8 out of 10 deserving additional promotion. Although 4 per cent had actually repeated a half grade, no elementary school child in the California group was retarded in terms of age-grade standards. In terms of mental age and of tested educational accomplishment, however, the group was far below the appropriate placement, a characteristic condition of gifted children in school. The mean progress quotient (grade age divided by chronological age) was 114 for the California group, 116 for Witty's group. If the average gifted child were promoted in terms of mental age, he would be at least 2.8 years advanced at age 7, and at age 11 he would be entitled theoretically to placement in the tenth grade or higher by reason of his 5 or more years of acceleration. It is not, however, suggested that promotion in the regular school should be made in these terms, although the frequently serious misplacement of the gifted is clearly indicated by these figures.

The school work of the gifted is rated subjectively by their teachers as superior to that of their classmates in debating, history, composition, literature, grammar, general science, geography, civics, reading, and arithmetic. The contrast in the quality of the work is most conspicuous in subjects requiring verbal comprehension, usage, and formulation; least so in activity subjects little correlated with intelligence, such as physical training, sewing, drawing, clay modeling, penmanship, manual training, painting, and shopwork. In five elements of musical sensitivity measured by the Seashore tests, Hollingworth (1926a) found 49 gifted children (IQ 135+) undistinguished from a control group of the same age. In speed and quality of penmanship Hollingworth and Cobb (1928) found the performance of the gifted children very close to the norms for their age. Because of their more frequent superiority, the average excellence of the gifted in 29 subjects combined is one step higher on a 7-point scale than that of control children (Terman *et al.*, 1925). Witty's results are in agreement in showing excellence, whether qualitatively or quantitatively measured (Witty, 1940a).

The weaknesses of the gifted appear most often in subjects requiring manual coordination or dexterity; those of the control children, in work requiring abstract thought. For the gifted, 68 per cent of the weaknesses are in writing, art, and handwork, as against 16 per cent for the control. Conversely, 17 per cent of the gifted are reported weak in such subjects as arithmetic, English, and history, whereas 61 per cent of the control children are weak in these subjects (Terman *et al.*, 1925).

Gifted children's school subject preferences correlate with the teachers' estimates of the quality of their work in the different subjects to the extent of .41 (Terman *et al.*, 1925). Witty found the same trends of preference, especially toward the verbal subjects (Witty, 1930). The boys are more alike in their preferences than the girls, and the gifted girls resemble the gifted boys in their choices more than they do the control girls. Subjects rated as easy by the gifted more often than by the control are again the more abstract and verbal: literature, debating, history, and grammar; and the preference and ease ratings correlate to the extent of .59. The normality of the gifted is indicated by their resemblance to control children in giving a high preference rating to games and sports as a school subject (Terman *et al.*, 1925).

Gifted children are regular in school attendance, very infrequently dislike school, and in more than half the cases—54 per cent for the boys and 70 per cent for the girls—have a "very strong liking for school." In the grades they devote on the average two hours of homework per week to school lessons (Terman *et al.*, 1925).

School Achievement. Educational achievement quotients from the Stanford Achievement Tests of gifted groups indicate without exception performance notably above the average, yet these scores age for age are little correlated in gifted children with years of grade school attendance. Intelligence, not formal schooling, largely determines their level (Terman *et*

al., 1925). For the brightest children in regular public school classes they are generally relatively lower than for the moderately superior children (Cohler, 1941; Johnson, 1942). The highest quotients so far reported are those from two New York City groups: (1) two opportunity classes where half the regular school time was devoted to the prescribed grade school curriculum, the other half to an enrichment program; (2) a mixed group of individual pupils in regular classes where no special enrichment had been attempted (Gray and Hollingworth, 1931). The unusually high scores in both groups suggest that exceptional motivation had been elicited through some technique of test administration. Relative to their IQ's, the two groups are closely equated in achievement, thus demonstrating neither advantage nor disadvantage in regular school accomplishment from (1) segregation, (2) shortened time for prescribed subjects, or (3) enrichment in the addition of special subjects. However, the fact that the opportunity class children achieved thus well after spending only half as much time on the subjects should not be lost sight of. Terman's large groups reported in 1925, Witty's 1930 group, and Terman's 11-year-olds from the 1925 group reported in 1930 also show high standing in terms of achievement quotients. But children, especially girls, selected in California for their high IQ's in 1922 and tested in achievement as 11-year-olds 5 to 7 years later show considerable regression in score from the means of those whose achievement was measured near the time of their qualification for the gifted group. Other score series may be compared with these (see Table 4): Patrick's (1924) upper centile opportunity group, Cobb and Taylor's (1924) gifted opportunity groups, Hildreth's (1938b) three IQ levels from regular classes in the Lincoln School, and

TABLE 4

Educational Achievement Quotients of Gifted and Other School Children

Investigator	Terman et al.		Witty	Gray and Hollingworth		Burks, Jensen, and Terman		Burks, Jensen, and Terman		Hildreth			Cobb and Taylor		Patrick	Jenkins		Wood: Educational Records Bureau	
Date	1925†		1930†	1931†		1930†		1930†		1938b*			1924*		1924*	1936†		1929*	
Number of cases	307	259	100	36 P.S.	56 O.C.	68	52	24	29	36	51	50	29	16	25	29	64	72 to 183	55 to 81
Sex	Boys	Girls	Both	Both	Both	Boys	Girls	Boys	Girls	Both	Both		Both		Both	Boys	Girls	Both	Both
Age (years or years and mos.)	6 to 14		Gr. 3 to 7	11-1	11-6	11	11	11	11	11	11	11	9	10	11-3	6 to 14		11-9	9-10
IQ average	151	151	152	151	157	153	155	146	136	147	134	104	152	146	142	135	134	124‡	112‡
Composite EQ			136	150	153	149	148	136	130						133	130	126	121 (90)	118 (55)
Reading	145	145	143	152	152	145	145	143	139	140	139	113	151	145	143	136	135	134 (163)	118 (65)
Arithmetic	138	136	134	153	156	139	137	129	127	140	131	102	142	141	139	124	121	114 (183)	113 (81)
Spelling	140	138	131	149	154	139	140	129	120	129	119	102	150	153	124	126	129	113 (62)	116 (56)
Nature study			132	145	144			134	125						129			115 (72)	114 (34)
Hist. and lit.				152	156	141	147	141	128				147	144	139	133	134	127 (91)	118 (57)
Lang. usage	146	148				151	145	139	142						141			132 (117)	128 (80)
Sci. inform.	151	142				159	156									132	120		
Lang. and lit.	157	152				158	140												
Hist. and civ.	148	138				157	158												
The arts	154	153																	

* Medians reported.   † Means reported.   ‡ Approximate   † Based on group tests.

Woods's (1929) private school children with superior group IQ scores.

The differences in the various series of data raise many questions. To the extent that they are in agreement they show marked superiority in the average scores for the gifted; persistent excellence as compared with superior, but not exclusively gifted, private school pupils. In general, differing IQ levels are seen to maintain their relative status in achievement test scores. Differences in teaching emphasis may be involved in the contrasts and perhaps, as mentioned above, test motivation also. These factors, together with regression, here produce diverse score patterns under varying conditions of age, grade, and school curriculum.

Hollingworth and Cobb (1928), comparing a series of achievement test scores of two gifted groups of 20 children each as they progressed in a special public school opportunity class during a two-year period, found a brighter group, clustering around 165 IQ, maintaining its superior status over a less bright group (145 IQ), although educational opportunity had been the same for both. Results showed the excess for the higher IQ group to be most marked in tests measuring the more complex abilities. The higher IQ group was more than a year in advance of the lower group in all the reading comprehension tests, in spelling, in nature study and science information, and in difficult mathematical processes including fractions and long division. Later Hildreth (1938b), comparing three IQ levels from grade to grade in the same private school classes, also found no tendency for IQ differences to become ineffective under conditions of similar class instruction plus special coaching for the lower IQ's.

Studies of achievement scores have been reviewed by Gray and Hollingworth (1931) and by Terman and Burks (1933). The reported researches are in agreement with those cited here in showing (1) superior school achievement scores of the gifted as compared to their age norms, (2) relative inferiority in most groups of educational age scores as compared to mental age scores, (3) equivocal evidence with respect to the advantages and disadvantages, as measured in available test scores, of special opportunities and programs.

DeVoss (Terman, 1925) made a careful study of the specialization of ability in achievement test terms, which he illustrated with case studies. He concluded that the achievement profiles of the gifted are like those of average children in pattern, but they rate at a much higher level. The score disparities in the various school subjects are similar and the gifted are no more one-sided than average children. Typical good readers tend to be relatively deficient in arithmetical computation, good calculators excel in science information, but are somewhat less capable in the language functions. Good spellers are relatively more successful with exact scientific work, including arithmetic, and less successful in verbal interpretation. In both gifted and control profiles the range from the best to the poorest single performance level is relatively narrow. The unevenness of scores, in younger children especially, can hardly be accounted for by differences in training and is believed to show the influence of innate factors. When measured in terms of standard scores with the intelligence level at 100 per cent, the high achievement level of the gifted is only 62 per cent above the chronological age norm. Measured in terms of educational quotient, the corresponding percentage is 80. Abilities in the various school subjects correlate more closely with general intelligence ratings than with any special ability for which measures were available in the gifted study.

As a corollary to the study of the evenness of achievement, the evenness of mental ability was rated by the teachers for the gifted and a control group with results favorable to the gifted. The question, as stated to the teacher, "Is child's mental ability very even, ordinarily even, rather uneven or very uneven?" may be interpreted in terms of day-to-day stability of performance or in terms of capacity for various types of work.

Extracurricular Pursuits and Interests. Somewhat more than half Terman's gifted group study music, drawing, painting, dancing, language, etc., outside the regular school curriculum. An average of 6½ hours a week is devoted to these studies by those who pursue them. The parents report noting superior ability in special subjects and in general intelligence as indicated in Table 5. It is of interest that 8 per cent of the parents report that they have never observed indications of superior intelligence in their children; 6 per cent more give no response to this item. Those who report recognition of intellectual superiority state that it was first noted just before 3½ years of age in the girls and a little later in the boys. Musical ability is noted on the average at 5 and the other special abilities at 6. The parents enumerate quick understanding, great curiosity, retentive memory, early speech, unusual vocabulary, and extensive information as the most frequent early indicators of superior intelligence.

Approximately 70 per cent of the parents state that they allowed the child to go his own pace in school, 19 per cent encouraged rapid progress, and 9 per cent held the child back. Most of the parents attempted to encourage progress by answering questions and by taking interest in the child's interests; few parents carried out systematic plans of home training.

Approximately half the California gifted children learned to read before starting to school. In Witty's group 38 per cent

TABLE 5

Percentages of Gifted Children Reported by Their Parents as Showing Various Kinds of Superior Ability *

	General Intelligence	Music	Arith. or Math.	Science or Nat. Study	Dramatics	Drawing or Painting	Dexterity, Handwork	Mechanical Ingenuity
Boys	84%	31%	52%	29%	18%	27%	21%	31%
Girls	85%	42%	45%	29%	42%	31%	31%	7%

* From Table 103, p. 278, L. M. Terman *et al.*, *Genetic Studies of Genius*, Vol. I. *Mental and Physical Traits of a Thousand Gifted Children*, Stanford University Press, 1925. By permission of the publishers.

learned to read before the age of 5; and of Terman's children 20 per cent learned at this age, 6 per cent before 4, and nearly 2 per cent before 3. This precocious activity among gifted children is stated to have occurred generally with little or no formal instruction. Learning to read at an unusually early age appears to be a correlate of high IQ in childhood.

Reading is the favorite pastime of the gifted children as well as their best-liked and easiest school subject. Teachers report that 9 out of 10 in a group of 400 read more than the average, and that nearly 60 per cent read very much, in contrast with about 12 per cent of a control group who do so. Parents estimate that their gifted children devote each week 6 hours at age 7 up to 12 hours at age 13 to their favorite pursuit.

A record of two months' reading shows that the gifted read more than twice as many books as control children of the same age. From the age of 9 the gifted exceed the average children of all ages up to 14 in number of books read (Terman *et al.*, 1925). That superiority in this respect is not necessarily a favorable sign of later achievement is shown by the comparison of the reading records of Terman's adult success and failure groups. The members of the failure group had reported in childhood a greater number of books read than had the success group (Terman and Oden, 1940*b*). Excess in this respect may admit of two interpretations beside the appar-

ently favorable one: overstatement may be characteristic of some gifted children, and social withdrawal or flight from reality may be present in some children who read excessively.

Gifted, like control, children prefer, if they are boys, first of all stories of adventure or mystery; if girls, stories of home and school life; but gifted children name also many more works of genuine literary excellence, including two to ten times as many books of poetry and drama, science, history, biography and travel, and definitely less popular, emotional fiction. Another investigation concurs with these results of Terman's in reporting superior quality in a larger proportion (49 per cent) of high IQ than of control (9 per cent) children (Cleveland, 1921). The Californians' best-liked book was a favorite for both gifted and control children; but boys and girls had only 5 of 20 favorites in common.

Gifted children express slightly stronger interest than do unselected children in the various activities that occupy their out-of-school hours. Sex differences rather than intellectual differences largely determine the trend of activity choices, yet a real contrast is shown between the gifted and unselected children in the number of collections made at all ages from 6 to 13. The gifted make about twice as many collections as the control, and the number of these having scientific interest and value is twice as large (Terman *et al.*, 1925).

The vocational ambitions of the gifted as compared to those of control children rate one and a half to two and a half points higher on the Barr Scale, a significant difference for the group as a whole. In the gifted group the preferred occupation rates nearer to the occupational status of the fathers than in the control group. The ambitions of the unselected tend, in terms of their abilities, to be more wishful than realistic, whereas the gifted may in most cases fortunately combine these two trends. Among the gifted, a small fraction chooses in childhood, and subsequently enters, occupations generally followed by people of average intellect and opportunity. Culture and custom limit the choices and the careers of the girls, as in some cases temperament or the lack of social or educational advantages does those of the boys (Terman et al., 1925).

Results from Wyman's (Terman et al., 1925) association test of (1) intellectual, (2) social, and (3) activity interests show characteristic contrasts between gifted and control groups in these interests, at each of four ages from 10 to 13. The largest differences are in the intellectual interests, but the social interest contrasts are also significant statistically. The differences in the activity interests are significant only at ages 10 and 11 for the boys and at 10 for the girls. Measurement by correlation of the relative effect of intelligence and intellectual interests upon school achievement shows that when the factor of intellectual interests is rendered constant intelligence and achievement correlate .76; with intelligence constant, intellectual interests and achievement correlate .49. Intellectual interest, although not so potent as intelligence, is thus found to be a possibly significant factor in school accomplishment. It is significant for all the school subjects except spelling and is greatest in the case of arithmetical reasoning. By a similar method, social interest and activity interest prove to be uncorrelated with school achievement scores.

Play Activities. The play interests, knowledge, and practice of 554 gifted children have been compared with those of 474 control children from the same elementary school grades (Terman et al., 1925). In play knowledge the quotient of the gifted is found to be 136; that is, a 10-year-old intellectually superior child has as much play information as an average 13-year-old child. The boys of both groups somewhat exceed the girls in play information. The gifted express as much liking for games and fondness for playing with others as average boys and girls. The gifted are inclined to prefer playmates who are older than themselves and they show less sex preference in the choice of playmates than do average children of the same age. The average amount of play with other children, 2¾ hours a day for the boys and 2¼ hours a day for the girls, is somewhat less than the time so spent by the average child. Yet the normality of the gifted is indicated by their devotion of more time to play than to reading and study combined (Terman et al., 1925; Coy, 1930). The play interests of gifted and average children are generally similar rather than contrasting. The slight differences appear to be associated with the somewhat greater mental maturity of the gifted. They tend to prefer games played typically by older children, and interest in the childish games wanes with them at an earlier age than in the average. These results derive from ratings on a play maturity scale (Terman et al., 1925).

Lehman and Witty (1927) report 50 gifted and 50 matched control children interested in the same diversity of plays and games. The gifted girls engage in a somewhat larger number of play activities than the average girls; the gifted boys in a slightly smaller number of play activities. The averages of the sexes combined prove to be identical. The gifted less frequently take part in certain kinds of vigorous physical play exercises and more often in games and pursuits in which reading is an element. Aside from reading itself, the best-liked activities are similar for the gifted and the control groups. The like sex intercorrelations of the preference ratings for 90 plays, games, and amusements, based on the children's own expression of attitude and participation, are above .80. This demonstrates that the games enjoyed most and played oftenest by gifted and average children are generally the same active social games, although gifted children prefer thinking games and those that are mildly social and quiet. Boys, whether gifted or average, prefer boys' games, and similarly girls, whatever their mental endowment, generally prefer typical girls' activities.

Personal and Social Character Traits. The traits of gifted children have been appraised by means of various tests and by ratings on elements of behavior defined for the purpose. The results, although lacking the statistical reliability and objectivity of the intellectual and educational measurements, seem to indicate through cumulative agreement that gifted children as a group tend to differ characteristically and favorably from unselected children. A wide range of tests and ratings has been reported by Terman and his associates (1925) for more than 500 gifted children and an equally large unselected control group. Witty's (1930) results for 100 gifted children are corroborative. In a number of other studies top centile or other superior children have been reported whose traits tend to resemble the strictly gifted groups.

When compared with control children in scores on tests of personal and social standards and ideals (Raubenheimer-Cady Series), the gifted children show far more favorable social preferences and social attitudes, more desirable preferences, less boastful exaggeration, less cheating, and considerably greater trustworthiness under stress. Sixty to 80 per cent of the gifted exceed the median scores on the separate tests of the battery (Terman, 1925).

On a total score, combining results for the entire series of tests, the average excess for the gifted children was 85 per cent, and the typical gifted nine-year-olds equaled or exceeded control children through age 14. Although both groups showed wide individual differences with interesting age-sex trends, the characteristic contrasts were maintained between gifted and control children. Witty's 100 gifted children were also superior on three of the same tests.

Freedom from psychopathic trends, as measured by Cady's version for children of the Woodworth Personality Inventory, showed a further superiority of the gifted children, with 67 per cent of the boys and 75 per cent of the girls equaling or exceeding the control median. Emotional stability measured by this test rates for the gifted more than 0.5 SD above the control children's average, a position maintained or slightly increased after four or five years, as demonstrated by retest (Burks, Jensen, and Terman, 1930). The individual consistency in earlier and later test scores (.42) is sufficient to indicate at least some degree of predictability of the characteristics thus measured.

The developmental-maturity quotients of some 50 top centile opportunity class pupils aged 9 to 12 were found by R. L. Thorndike (1940b) to indicate an acceleration approximately equal to that of their school progress. On the Furfey Developmental Scale the boys rated an average quotient of 114; on its adaptation by Sullivan the girls' quotient was 118. Wide item variation was characteristic, with high maturity shown in the choice of books to read, things to think about, and future vocations. Interest and attitude scores on the Pressey Test were reported for a similar group (R. L. Thorndike, 1939). The total test scores of interests and attitudes corresponded more closely to the mental than to the chronological ages of these children. The boys rated as definitely more mature than the girls. Both sexes scored highest in the traits which they admire in others and in their freedom from fears and worries. Judgments of wrong and interests rated as less mature, although above average for both sexes. Individuals showed wide variability in item and subtest scores.

Character trait ratings made by teachers and parents on more than 1000 gifted and control children indicate that the gifted as a group appear normal or better in the estimation of the adults most closely associated with them (Terman et al., 1925). Compared to a control group, their ratings are equal or higher on 25 traits including intellectual, volitional, emotional, moral, physical, social, and special ability traits. Parents and teachers are agreed ($r = +.70$) in ranking the order of superiority from marked excess in the case of the intellectual and volitional traits (difference more than 1 SD) to approximate equality in the physical and social traits. The ratings are found to be discriminative, and the "certainty of judgment" is fairly high. Single traits showing the largest excess for the gifted include common sense, originality, desire to know and to excel, self-confidence, sense of humor, truthfulness, prudence and forethought, conscientiousness, and leadership. In each of these traits 70 per cent or more of the gifted exceed the rated mean of the control children. In fondness for large groups, in freedom from vanity, and in cheerfulness

the gifted differ least from average boys and girls. Although distinguished for leadership, in popularity they are close to the general mean. In ratings made five years later, the gifted still showed excess in the same traits when compared to a control group (Table 6), although the contrast was now not quite so sharply drawn. The rank orders of the trait differences were similar. Parents were inclined to see improvement with respect to conscientiousness and freedom from vanity, whereas teachers reported little change in these respects (Burks, Jensen, and Terman, 1930).

Teachers of New York City gifted children reported their pupils average or superior in a series of desirable traits (Specht, 1919). Reports by 31 teachers of superior children in St. Paul, Minnesota, are in agreement in finding the gifted children above the average in many traits, including courtesy, cooperation, imaginativeness, inquisitiveness, and willingness to take suggestions. These children have a keen sense of humor and are not inclined to become discouraged. Contrary to an older popular opinion, they are not considered especially forward, domineering, egotistical, or self-willed (Johnson, 1923; Laycock, 1933). Hildreth (1939) found 50 upper centile children, including 20 with IQ's in the 140's or higher, superior in personality traits to matched children of average IQ in the same school. Recorded notations for intellectual, personality, and character traits included nearly five times as many favorable entries for the superior as for the control children, whereas the latter showed excess in the unfavorable traits. The superior children excelled in activity and vivacity, independence, and self-assurance, they had more experiences to relate, their sense of humor was more often noted, as was also their willingness to face difficulties.

Simmons (1939) studied the suggestibility of 47 top centile, special opportunity class

TABLE 6

PERSONALITY TRAIT RATINGS OF GIFTED AND CONTROL CHILDREN
(MEANS AND SD'S) *

Trait Names		Teachers' Ratings						Parents' Ratings			
		1927–28 Gifted		1921–22 Gifted		1921–22 Control		1927–28 Gifted		1921–22 Gifted	
		Boys	Girls	Boys	Girls	Boys	Girls	Boys	Girls	Boys	Girls
Traits in which gifted children differ little from control children											
Fondness for groups	M	6.4	5.9	6.2	5.6	6.1	5.9	6.2	5.0	5.5	4.7
	SD	2.2	2.1	2.1	2.2	2.1	2.0	2.7	1.8	2.6	2.2
Freedom from vanity	M	5.9	5.7	5.9	5.4	6.1	5.6	5.1	5.1	5.7	5.9
	SD	2.6	2.5	2.7	2.3	1.9	2.0	2.4	2.4	2.2	2.3
Sympathy	M	5.9	5.6	5.8	5.2	6.3	5.7	4.9	4.3	3.9	3.7
	SD	2.2	2.1	2.1	2.1	1.8	1.8	2.4	2.2	2.3	2.2
Popularity	M	6.5	6.4	6.4	5.7	6.5	6.2	5.6	5.2	5.5	5.2
	SD	2.1	2.2	2.0	2.0	1.8	1.9	2.1	1.5	2.0	2.1
Traits in which gifted children differ significantly from control children											
Leadership	M	6.6	6.3	6.3	5.8	7.2	7.0	5.2	5.0	5.3	4.9
	SD	2.0	2.2	1.9	2.0	2.1	2.2	2.0	2.0	2.2	2.1
Desire to excel	M	5.0	4.2	4.2	3.6	6.1	5.6	4.5	3.6	3.7	3.3
	SD	2.5	2.4	2.2	1.9	2.4	2.0	2.1	1.9	1.9	1.9
Conscientiousness	M	5.0	4.5	4.8	4.0	6.2	5.4	4.2	3.7	4.4	4.3
	SD	2.6	2.4	2.5	2.2	2.3	2.2	2.4	2.2	2.1	2.2
Common sense	M	4.9	4.9	4.2	4.1	6.2	5.9	4.3	4.0	4.4	4.3
	SD	2.0	2.0	1.9	1.9	1.8	1.8	2.1	1.9	2.0	1.9
Perseverance	M	5.1	4.4	4.4	4.1	6.4	6.1	5.2	4.2	4.9	4.1
	SD	2.4	2.3	2.1	1.9	2.2	2.0	2.0	2.2	2.3	2.0
Traits in which gifted children differ largely and significantly from control children											
Desire to know	M	4.6	4.4	3.5	3.9	6.3	6.2	3.5	3.4	2.7	2.8
	SD	2.3	2.4	1.9	2.1	2.0	2.1	2.2	2.0	1.9	1.8
Originality	M	5.0	4.9	4.4	4.5	6.8	6.9	4.1	4.0	4.0	3.9
	SD	2.2	2.2	2.1	2.1	1.9	1.9	2.2	2.1	2.2	2.1
General intelligence	M	4.0	3.8	3.1	3.1	6.4	6.2	3.3	3.3	3.1	3.1
	SD	1.9	1.7	1.6	1.8	1.9	1.8	1.3	1.4	1.6	1.6

* Data rearranged from B. S. Burks, D. W. Jensen, L. M. Terman, *Genetic Studies of Genius*, Vol. III, *The Promise of Youth* (Table 77, p. 190), Stanford University Press, Stanford University, California, 1930. By permission of the publishers.

children, aged 8 to 11, matched for age and sex, with a below-average group. In each of the experimental test situations employed, the group of higher intelligence yielded to fewer suggestions than the lower intelligence group, the differences being statistically reliable. Subjective ratings on independence from others in thinking also showed a reliable difference in favor of the gifted.

Classroom attitudes of high IQ children are found satisfactory and in general superior to the average. The children take active part in class discussions (Johnson, 1923), they respect authority (Woods, 1929), and are responsive to school discipline (Terman, 1925; Witty, 1930). In Root's (1921) study, conformity and traditional orthodox behavior were reported as characteristic of superior as of average children. The favorable conditioning of behavior by home influences is suggested in the conclusions of McGehee and Lewis (1940) from a study of teachers' estimates of the attitudes of their parents toward 45,000 children in 36 different states. Superiority of the parents' attitude was highly correlated with the intelligence of the children. The gifted boys and girls had the advantage of parental attitudes rated as superior in 66 and 61 per cent of the cases as compared with the attitudes toward the normative groups in which 20 and 23 per cent were so rated.

Summary of the Traits of the Gifted. Studies of young gifted children, beginning with Terman's report in 1919 and including the work of Root, Jones, Goddard, and Whipple, are in agreement with the larger, more recent, more strictly defined (IQ 140+), statistically more fully treated results of Terman, Hollingworth, Witty, and their associates, Hildreth, and other contemporary investigators. The various aspects of the background, development, interests, and achievements of gifted chil-

dren are found to be clearly marked by superiority, characteristically greater the more the trait in question is correlated with intellect. Gifted children are superior specimens physically as well as psychologically, and they tend to express a superior energy in their activities. They come from better homes and in many cases have had better educational backgrounds and opportunities. Yet, as we shall see in the consideration of individual cases, superior environments and educational advantages do not insure the production of crops of gifted children, and in capacity and accomplishment individual gifted children generally appear as unique and isolated individuals even against their superior backgrounds. We must, therefore, believe that inheritance of gifted traits is individual and complex and that training can only develop, never create, gifted capacity.

That there is no one-to-one correlation between intelligence and character traits is no surprise in view of the vast complexity of human personality. However, cumulative evidence seems clearly to demonstrate the better endowment of the gifted and their better training and development in social terms, as compared with average children. Techniques for precise measurement of causal relationships in this realm are not available to present-day research.

Progress of the Gifted from Childhood to Maturity

The relatively large populations of gifted children who have been intensively studied by psychologists no doubt include many all-round, highly superior individuals of whom it is reasonable to expect persistent growth at a level demonstrably above average and sustained continuity with respect to behavior and achievement. Because tests are fallible and the range of tested traits is narrow, some individuals who would rate below more broadly defined gifted standards are by current practice necessarily included in the groups selected for study. Moreover, test errors and changes in developmental rate, whether constitutionally or environmentally conditioned, lead to score and rating regressions. However, the subsequent histories of children selected as gifted in childhood indicate that the errors and changes are not sufficient to invalidate the selection technique as a basis for group prediction, and the accumulated results point to the ultimate possibility of individual clinical predictions of fair reliability.

Gifted children were first reported at the elementary school level, where their presence was revealed in the earliest individual test surveys and where the problems of their education appeared most urgent. Studies of older gifted children have included (1) follow-up surveys, after a period of years, of groups investigated in childhood and (2) surveys of various young groups not previously studied, adolescents, and college students, usually selected in terms of group test scores, or of youth in relation to academic status. Duff (1929) and Witty (1940a) have reported the progress of gifted school children in the grades. Terman and Hollingworth and their associates have contributed the majority of studies of gifted adolescents and college students, and the only studies so far reported of gifted young adults. The data from all these researches are in agreement in indicating relative persistence in the characteristic trait patterns of the gifted as they grow older and continued contrast between them and average children in intellectual achievements and superiority of interests. A summary of illustrative results is presented.

In a preliminary follow-up of more than 1000 gifted children made two years after his first study, Terman et al. (1925) found that the typical educational acceleration was continued and the indications of superior ability appeared consistently in the school and home reports. Gains far outweighed losses in deportment, in group activities, in breadth of interests, and in the social adaptability of the group as a whole. Children who had skipped grades were reported to have gained in application and to be more often eligible for further rapid advancement.

In a more detailed follow-up carried out seven years after the first study, data for 900 children were gathered and analyzed (Burks, Jensen, and Terman, 1930). As far as possible the traits and characteristics measured in the first study were again evaluated. Intelligence was rechecked by two individual and two group tests in four population samples. The Stanford-Binet IQ results for children within the appropriate age range disclosed for the boys a small average decrease of 3 points, from 147 to 143; for the girls a sizable loss of 14 points, 149 to 135. The changes were apparently not correlated with age. In the groups of age 13 and under 20 who were given the Terman group test, the boys were significantly superior to the girls in score. The median Terman group test IQ for the retested children was judged equivalent to a Stanford-Binet IQ above 130, thus indicating maintenance of top centile status by 50 per cent of the group. The ninetieth centile was exceeded by 75 per cent. The retest Terman group scores were very little lower than those taken age by age in the high school group tested seven years before. Analysis of factors of environment, personality, health, race, and Stanford-Binet test structure failed to reveal causes of the score decrement. The slight drop in scores for the boys was attributed, in the absence of any other explanation, to a difference in the tests used or to simple regression; for the girls the larger decrement was attributed to these factors or to a change in developmental rate and age of intellectual maturation. A sex difference in social motivation might also have been involved. Roughly paralleling the IQ scores, the Stanford Achievement Test quotients proved to be a little lower than they were in the first survey. For the boys the drop amounted to 6 points, for the girls, 10 points. Here again test standardization and regression factors were probably involved. Yet the scores were still far in excess of those of average children of like age.

Elementary School. The acceleration of the group in school grade status had continued and the projected Ayres-Strayer standards of educational progress showed no case of retardation. In comparison to the earlier acceleration of 67 per cent of the group, a slight gain had resulted in acceleration for 74 per cent of the boys and 84 per cent of the girls. Grade status continued typically above the chronological norm but far below the mental age status. School attendance continued to be regular, although liking for school had become slightly less strong. Attitude toward school was rated by the teachers as favorable for more than 80 per cent of the children. The amount of time devoted to homework had increased steadily with age. The gifted boys graduated from the eighth grade at the early age of 13 years, 1 month; the girls at 12 years, 10 months (Burks, Jensen, and Terman, 1930).

High School. Lamson (1930) studied the high school careers of 56 gifted children who had been identified as of top centile IQ status before the age of 9 years and placed on the basis of their high intelligence in special opportunity classes. They had entered high school from the special classes on the average before the age of 12 and they were about to graduate at age 16. Compared with a control group of 106 students in the same high school

grades, the gifted were significantly superior in scholastic achievement and had a smaller percentage of failures, although in age they were two years younger. The gifted had participated in extracurricular activities to an extent exceeding the control group by 25 per cent. Lack of time and participation in other activities, including the reading of modern current fiction, study of music, and social dancing, prevented greater participation. The gifted impressed their teachers by their intelligence, the general quality of their work, and their sustained effort to an extent significantly in excess of the impression made by the control children. In self-control, general deportment, and appearance, they were rated as somewhat superior to the average pupils; in popularity and in conceit there was little difference between the two groups. In the teachers' estimations general deportment and quality of work improved for the gifted during a 2½-year period. Generally good health was reported for the high school years, and 6 out of 10 of the gifted expressed no regret at having entered high school at an exceptionally early age. Age 13 they considered the most favorable for high school entrance. Four out of five were glad to have had the advantages of the opportunity classes. Reasons for failures, activities participated in, offices held, honors, books read, and attitudes toward scholastic work were reported in detail.

Terman's gifted children (Burks, Jensen, and Terman, 1930) had consistently superior high school reports; a sample of 77 cases won "A" grades in their separate studies about four to eight times as frequently as the unselected high school pupils in the same classes. In every course, including science and mathematics, the gifted girls were given higher average marks than the boys. For the girls the "A" grades amounted to approximately three-quarters of their school work; for the boys, to something approaching half. In the estimation of the teachers about one-third of the group showed remarkable ability in some special subject or subjects, whereas only 15 per cent were rated as weak. Excellence and weakness generally appeared in the same subjects as before. Parents reported specialized ability in something over 60 per cent of all the cases, including for the boys mathematics, science, debating, public speaking, or mechanical ingenuity; for the girls, art, dramatics, dancing, writing, household art, and music.

Tests of high school achievement showed marked superiority of upwards of 150 gifted children reported above the high school norms (Burks, Jensen, and Terman, 1930). In comprehension of literature (Burch Test) the two-years-younger gifted group rated more than 1 SD above the control mean; in algebra problems (Hotz Test) the average difference is .5 SD. In the Iowa Content Examination, including tests of achievement in English, mathematics, science, and history, the girls exceeded the norm by 1 to 1.5 SD; the boys by 1.5 to 2 SD. The high school senior norms for the separate parts of this test were exceeded by 10 per cent or more of the gifted group. In total score 97 per cent of the gifted boys and 100 per cent of the gifted girls exceeded the control mean.

Characteristic sex differences in preference for school subjects were shown by the gifted group, 241 boys tending to prefer the sciences and to show distaste for ancient languages, 196 girls liking art, English, and modern languages and disliking mathematics and civics (Burks, Jensen, and Terman, 1930). The amount of time spent on general reading outside school studies was slightly greater for the girls, with an average of 7.6 hours per week for them in contrast to 7.2 hours for the boys. After 14 the boys spent more time on home study than on general reading, whereas before this age the opposite was true. For the girls this change occurred at 13. Sex and age differences in reading interests continued, and reading was still preferred to all other occupations by both gifted boys and gifted girls. Active games were preferred to those that required little exercise, and games and exercise were next in preference to reading. About a third of the boys and nearly half the girls stated that they had been greatly influenced by a single "person, book, philosophy, or religion." The strongest influence was most often that of one or both parents. Interest in collecting tended to decline after 14, the boys having continued to make on the average more collections, including a larger number with scientific interest.

Acceleration was characteristic, as before. The boys graduated from high school at 16 years, 10 months; the girls two months younger. In high school and also in college the group as a whole was generally about two years younger than the age norm of their class. More than 80 per cent of the gifted group in high school expressed the intention of going on to college.

Characteristics and Aptitudes of Gifted High School and College Students. Social and personality traits (Raubenheimer-Cady series), when remeasured after a lapse of 4 or 5 years, showed little change in mean scores in similar age ranges (Burks, Jensen, and Terman, 1930). The correlation coefficient was .42 for 150 gifted children twice tested. The Wyman test of intellectual, social, and activity interests showed very small changes in average scores for the children retested 5 years after the original study. However, the correlations between the tests of individuals were not very high, ranging from .15 in activities to .37 in social interests and showing only a mild degree of permanence in interest type as measured by this test.

Personality ratings on 12 traits selected from the 25 used in the earlier investigation in general supported the previous findings in indicating marked divergence of the gifted group from unselected children in intellectual traits, moderate divergence in volitional and moral traits, and similarity tending toward equality in social traits (Table 6). Teachers and parents agreed fairly closely in the rank order of ratings and their estimates showed little change from those made 7 years before. Field visitors' appraisals placed the gifted at or above the hypothetical norms as follows: in achievement, boys 98 per cent, girls 99 per cent; in social adjustment, boys 81 per cent, girls 80 per cent; in environmental conditions, boys 95 per cent, girls 91 per cent (Burks, Jensen, and Terman, 1930).

The good looks of gifted children of high school age may contribute to their favorable social adjustment. Hollingworth (1935) reported that 10 judges rating from photographs agreed in finding the faces of 40 gifted children more attractive than those of a control group.

Tests given for the first time in the California study in 1927–1928 were the Watson Test of Fair-Mindedness, the Terman-Miles Masculinity-Femininity Test, and the George Washington University Social Intelligence Test. For each of these, results have been reported in detail for groups ranging in size from 75 to 175 individuals (Burks, Jensen, and Terman, 1930). In fair-mindedness the gifted differ little from other, generally older, groups of similar education. In mental masculinity adolescent gifted boys and girls resemble college men and women more than they do the youth of their own age. The boys differ from college men in more masculine ratings in the two sections of the Terman-Miles test where intelligence is associated with high masculinity of score; in items where culture, domestic sentiment, and literary taste have a feminizing influence on response, the ratings are less masculine than those of the college students. The gifted girls' profile resembles that of college women in showing a masculine score trend where this is generally correlated with high intelligence. In parts of the test where intelligence and intellectual interests exert little influence (Terman and Miles, 1936) gifted girls respond and score like average groups of their sex. On the Social Intelligence Test the median scores for the gifted are high above the age norms and even exceed the college norms. The high correlation known to exist between the scores on this test and intelligence test scores may largely account for these excessive ratings.

The Bernreuter personality profiles of 36 boys and 19 girls, mainly Jewish, of average age 18 years, 6 months, reported by Hollingworth and Rust (1937) are in general agreement with Terman's personality appraisals of the gifted in showing excess for both sexes in the traits of self-sufficiency and dominance and a lower neurotic tendency as compared to college students and adult norm groups. The differences tend to be significant for the boys, although for the girls they are so only in self-sufficiency.

Of 169 boys past 14 who took the Strong Occupational Interest Test (Burks, Jensen, and Terman, 1930) 23 per cent received "A" ratings in their chosen vocation (indicating interests like those of men in the three highest scoring quartiles in the vocation in question), 50 per cent received "B" ratings (resembling the interests of the men in the given vocation who rate within the lower quartile), and 27 per cent received "C" ratings (resembling the lowest 2 per cent of the men in the occupation in question). These results compare favorably with the scores for Stanford University seniors, who rate 32 per cent "A," 50 per cent "B," and 18 per cent "C" in their chosen vocations. Chance ratings give only 5 or 6 per cent "A," 25 per cent "B," and 70 per cent "C." The gifted boys, although considerably younger than the Stanford seniors, have, as revealed by this test, already developed almost to an equal extent the interests characteristic of their probable future vocations. Although this is in part due to the fact that young boys of potential college ability resemble one another in showing the characteristic likes and dislikes of chemists and engineers, yet the presence of fair-sized groups of "A" raters in other "most likely" occupations indicates that there are here probably true occupational interests exhibited by gifted boys at a fairly early age.

Scientific aptitude scores of 41 gifted boys measured by the Zyve Test equal as a group the mean for nonscientific faculty members, rating above the mean for unselected freshmen and very close to halfway between the latter and the high average of graduate students in scientific departments (Burks, Jensen, and Terman, 1930).

That the gifted are by no means characterized by studious reclusiveness is shown in their social and leadership ratings and in their community activities. Both boys and girls report social interests, enjoyment in leadership and in managing other people (Burks, Jensen, and Terman, 1930). Eighty-seven per cent of the boys and 96 per cent of the girls report having held one or more offices or honors in a wide variety of extracurricular activities. It proves to be as likely for them to have won notice in any one of several kinds of extracurricular activities as in scholarship. The girls more often participate in dramatics, the boys in student organization and scout troop activities. Yates's (1922) group numbered more than twice as many gifted (28 per cent) as control (12 per cent) leaders in high school activities. Finch and Carroll's

(1932) gifted high school seniors had held twice as many elective offices as the average high school pupil.

Studies of school and college leaders and leadership support these results by indicating the extent to which intelligence is a factor in social recognition and administrative distinction. High school honor students have been found to be younger, to rate higher in intelligence, and to graduate in less time than the average, although they carry more extracurricular activities (Zeigel, 1927).

In the reported studies there is no conflicting opinion regarding the value of superior intellect for leadership. Emphasis is sometimes laid on the need for due recognition of other desirable traits (Witty, 1930), but these, too, especially wisdom (prudence and forethought), motivation (will and perseverance), truthfulness, cheerfulness, stability of mood, generosity and unselfishness, conscientiousness, and sympathy, are more often found in conjunction with superior intellect than otherwise (Terman *et al.*, 1925).

Good health has persisted in 77 to 90 per cent of the gifted during the six-year period since the first survey. No more than 1 to 5 per cent report "poor health." Colds, headaches, and worry are relatively infrequent, and no more prevalent in the older gifted children than in the control group measured in 1921 and 1922. As compared with themselves in early childhood, fewer gifted boys but somewhat more gifted girls are reported to show signs of nervousness in the adolescent period. Organic disease is infrequent, occurring in only 4 per cent of the boys and 5 per cent of the girls. Serious eye trouble is present in less than 2 per cent of the gifted, and subnormal hearing shows decrease with age to less than 2 per cent of the group. The gifted children sleep less than they did at a younger age, but they continue to sleep more at each age than unselected children; their parents report that 98 per cent of the boys and 95 per cent of the girls sleep soundly. Five deaths, or less than 1 per cent, occurred in the 643 members of the regular group in the seven-year period between the first study and the second (Burks, Jensen, and Terman, 1930).

The Gifted Children in College and After. In their college years the gifted children as a group have maintained their status intellectually, academically, and in social adjustments. Their later occupational and economic careers have also developed on the whole favorably. Six reports give psychological test scores of gifted groups in college. The academic and social adjustments are presented in two confirmatory studies. The college progress of Terman's gifted children was briefly reported in 1930 and again in 1940 for the larger population who had progressed so far (Terman and Oden, 1940a). Gray (1930) studied the scholastic aptitude ratings, scholastic records, physical measurements, and the extracurricular and social activities of 126 boys and 28 girls who entered Columbia and Barnard colleges at 15 years of age or younger. Although these youngsters had not been identified by high IQ's in childhood, we may tentatively group them with the gifted because their Thorndike Scholastic Aptitude Test scores average as high at college entrance as the means reported by Terman for gifted children in California (Burks, Jensen, and Terman, 1930). Special investigations of the intelligence scores at college entrance or later of groups of gifted children have been supplied by Hollingworth and Kaunitz (1934), Lorge and Hollingworth (1936), and Hildreth (1939).

The data from the follow-up reports concerning late adolescent or young adult mental status are in agreement regarding the extent to which the gifted maintain after 6 to 16 years from their first selection their early demonstrated capacity to reach the highest levels of tested intelligence. Eighty-two per cent of Army Alpha scores of 116 top centile children rated 10 years after first identification by Stanford-Binet test reached the adult top centile norm. Of the remainder all were in high centiles, none regressed to the mean. Gifted boys 18 years of age or older all scored above the ninety-seventh centile. Fifty-seven cases with IQ's 150 or above rated without exception in the top centile. About one-third of the 140's scored somewhat lower (Hollingworth and Kaunitz, 1934). In their CAVD scores, cooperative general culture and general science tests, and Army Alpha scores, and in academic accomplishment, 21 individuals identified as gifted in childhood attained as a group the high standing predictable from their early Stanford-Binet and school achievement test scores (Lorge and Hollingworth, 1936). Data for a selection of these appear in Table 7. The scores reported for the science and culture tests fall for the most part within the upper quartile on the college norms. In the CAVD test 18 out of the entire group of 21 score above the seventy-fifth centile for law school freshmen and A.M. candidates in Teachers College, Columbia University.

Hildreth (1939) reports the American Council Psychological Test scores in senior high school of 70 children identified as to Stanford-Binet IQ before the age of 13. On this test, in which children of average eleventh and twelfth grade ability rate near the fiftieth centile, the mean rating for 12 gifted children with early IQ's of 140+ reaches the 97.5 centile for college students the country over. This result is in agreement with a statement by Wrenn (1935), based on results for 39 of Terman's gifted children, that the gifted of 140 IQ status rate at college entrance at the ninety-

TEST SCORES OF HIGHLY INTELLIGENT CHILDREN IN CHILDHOOD AND IN EARLY MATURITY *

| Child | IQ First Stanford Binet † | Stanford Achievement Tests | | | | | | | | Form 8 Army Alpha ‡ | CAVD | General Science Centile | General Culture Centile | Age | Educational Status (College Degrees, Advanced Study, Major Subject, and Scholastic Honors) |
		Reading Par. Mng. EQ	Arithmetic Computation EQ	Arithmetic Reasoning EQ	Nature Study and Science EQ	History and Literature EQ	Language Usage EQ	Spelling Dictation EQ	Composite EQ						
1	190+	163+	168	180	170	164	159	182	171	210	454	93	100	21-0	B.A. +1 yr. med. sch.; Phi Beta Kappa; major, premedical.
2	188+	133	165	197	173	179	175	203	184+	198	439	93	98	19-6	H.S. gr. + part of a semester in college.
E	187+										445	84	100	26-4	B.A., M.A., Ph.D., major hist.; ordained clergyman; Phi Beta Kappa.
3	187+	158	152	185	162	172	151	163	168	204	435	93	93	20-9	B.A., in 1st yr. grad. wk., major, statistics and economics.
D	183+										444	98	98	24-6	B.A. + 3 yrs. grad. wk. in physics; Phi Beta Kappa; research physicist.
E.B.	175	155+	161	149	152	146	146	166	154	192 §	438	80	98	21-1	B.A. + 1st yr. grad. wk.; major, social science.
7	174	150	171	161	167	177	182	171	175	181 §	435	75	98	21-6	B.A., major English.
8	173 or 177	149	173	133	158	190	132	177	193	188	435	98	84	20-5	B.A.
9	172	162	171	163	176	176	173	187	171	191	429	93	84	20-2	B.A., M.A.; chem. and premed. + 1 yr. medical school.
14	168										425			19-7	B.A., major premed. + nearly 2 yrs. med. sch.; Phi Beta Kappa.
15	168	162	155	158	138	152	151	156	154	193	431	50	93	21-8	3 yrs. college; major economics.
16	167	164	151	170	154	163	160	181	164	197	423	80	98	21-0	B.A., major philosophy.
68	145	152	162	130	114	136	129	144	139	159	421	10	84	21-6	B.A. + 1st yr. grad. wk. in political science.
67	145	161	156	153	152	156	159	173	159	193	425	93	93	21-1	B.A., major chemistry.
95	138	144	162	142	123	140	137	162	144	166	412	60	75	22-3	B.A.
115	133									183 §	431	75	93	20-8	B.A., Phi Beta Kappa.

* Data from Lorge, Irving, and Hollingworth, "Adult Status of Highly Intelligent Children," *J. Gen. Psychol.*, 1936, *49*, 215–226, Table 1. By permission of the editor, C. Murchison.

† CA's 5 to 9 years. ‡ CA's 17 to 19. § Form 5.

seventh centile on the A.C.P. examination. Fifty-seven of Terman's gifted girls rated a mean score of 84, and 69 of his boys a mean of 87 on the Thorndike College Entrance Examination as reported in 1930 (Burks, Jensen, and Terman). These scores were approximately 1 SD above the Stanford University average for the corresponding years. In 1940 Terman reported the scores of some 400 gifted as rating 1 SD above the ."highly selected Stanford population and only a few points below the mean of graduate candidates for the Ph.D. degree in psychology." Gray's young Columbia entrants averaged 92, his young Barnard students 84 on this test, the former rating 1 SD above the Columbia College mean, the latter approximately .3 SD above the Barnard mean.

These various scores at college entrance are in approximate agreement.[1] They in-

dicate (1) that gifted children tend to preserve at late adolescence or early adulthood their high centile test competence; (2) that children with IQ's of 140+ in childhood tend to rate within the top 5 to 10 per cent on the national college entrance psychological test norms and to average scores about 1 SD above the mean of highly selected student distributions; and (3) that a tendency to regression toward the college mean occurs in many cases, more often among the girls than among the boys. Hollingworth's conclusion that the gifted. are those at and above the seventy-fifth percentile of college graduates for the country at large perhaps underestimates the Columbia norms and the gifted ability in view of Hildreth's results and Wrenn's conclusion. Further adult scores from larger groups are needed to define more precisely the college and adult test score level of the gifted and to determine the extent, if present, of a regressive tendency in scores from childhood to maturity.

The first large-scale study in adulthood of children identified in childhood as gifted was made by Terman in 1936, sixteen years after his initial cross-sectional survey (Terman and Oden, 1940a). Of 1500 gifted subjects on record 93 per cent were located; and of these 755 males and 555 females cooperated with information deemed unusually adequate and reliable, a high record

[1] *Group Test IQ and Prediction.* Keys (1940), in a study of the college achievement of University of California students who had been given a Terman Group Test during their high school years, found an average IQ of 111 for the entering college group who failed to obtain the qualifying certificate for the third college year, an IQ of 115 for those who obtained the certificate but did not graduate, an IQ of 117 for those who graduated, and an IQ of 125 for honor graduates. A student whose IQ was 140 or higher on the group test proved to have 100 times as many chances of graduating with honors as the student with an average IQ score. Yet there were 6 of 19 honor students from the IQ range 105–119, and 8 from the range 120–139. Traxler (1940) has reported the median group test IQ of 68,899 college students in 323 colleges as 109, Q_3 117, Q_1 101, in terms of Otis equivalents of American Council Test scores.

These and other similar results raise several questions as yet unanswered by experimental evidence: (1) Were the early group test IQ's of the students scoring at relatively low levels, but later achieving university success, inadequate measures of their ability at the time the tests were given? (2) Had a change occurred for them in the rate of development between the time of the test and the time of graduating from college? (3) Can students adequately measured by IQ's no higher than these achieve college graduation and even distinction by reason of the

excellence of nonintellectual personality traits? Terman's 1940 study of the later achievement of gifted children shows that for the top half of 1 per cent in IQ score other factors than the high IQ are involved in young adult success. What then of 130 IQ's, 120 IQ's, and so on? It has been definitely demonstrated by studies such as that of Keys that there are relatively few individuals from the lower levels achieving the more distinguished successes. The formula for the diminishing returns is, however, as yet not determined. Further investigation is needed paralleling Keys' work, also systematic studies for comparison with the gifted and upper centile groups of the personality traits and careers of 130 and 120 IQ's.

in questionnaire response. Parents and teachers added their observations with similar completeness. Two age groups are included in the survey: the elementary school children of 1922 now in their twenties, median age 26; and the high school group of 1922 in the late twenties and early thirties, median age 32. The preliminary report of 1940 combines these in a single group. The reported loss by death, 3 per cent, is probably less than the expectation for a group of this age.

The girls' history is, as would be expected, shorter and less obviously significant than the boys', with only a few exceptional careers to mark the limits of high attainment. Eighty-five per cent of the girls attend college, and of these 90 per cent graduate. Class and student honors are frequent. Of the graduates, one-fifth are elected to Phi Beta Kappa, 3.5 per cent to Sigma Xi; half continue in graduate work, but few go beyond the M.A. degree. A fifth earn part of their college expenses as undergraduates, a third are self-supporting as graduate students. The occupational distribution of the 244 women who have completed their education and are gainfully employed shows 38 per cent in office work or business, 27 per cent in teaching, 9 per cent in music, art, or drama, 5 per cent in library work, 2 per cent in nursing, and 1.6 per cent in medicine. Of those who are not married or gainfully employed a number are engaged in volunteer social work. The average earnings (in 1936) of the high school graduate women are $90 per month; of those who attended college without graduating, $95; of the college graduates, $120. At each level the salaries amount to about half the corresponding income of the gifted boys. Fifty-one per cent of the girls were married at the time of the survey, and of these some 8 per cent had been divorced. The mean age at marriage was just under

23 years. Half the girls married college graduates; and the remaining half, men of more than average education. Four gifted intermarriages have occurred. Inclusion in the gifted groups has not, in their estimation, affected 65 per cent of the girls; 19 per cent record a favorable effect, 11 per cent an unfavorable one, and 5 per cent a mixed influence. The moral record has been good for the group as a whole. Sex delinquencies have been specifically reported for less than 1 per cent; alcoholic excess has been known in a few cases. Marriage and social life rather than intellectual pursuits have, as for girls generally, furnished the goals of the majority of the gifted. A few have achieved the Ph.D. or the M.D. degree or graduate distinction in law or engineering. A small number is carrying on superior administrative, business, or professional work.

Gray's (1930) study of 28 college women of unreported childhood IQ who averaged Thorndike college entrance scores equal to the Stanford gifted girls at the same or a younger age traces a similar picture for the college years. The 28 as a group had fewer college entrance deficiencies than the average student in the same college; three had state scholarship awards as freshmen; 79 per cent graduated, a relatively high percentage; but only 1 girl entered a graduate professional school. General honors were won by 3.6 per cent, special subject honors by 10.7 per cent, and Phi Beta Kappa election by over 21 per cent. One graduate fellowship and one scholarship were granted to members of the group. The health histories were favorable, and physical fitness test scores rated above the college average. In anthropometric tests the 28 were below the college average by reason of being younger; in motor ability, however, they exceeded the norms. They engaged in more athletic and other extracurricular activities than average college women.

Glen

Their responses to an emotionality questionnaire indicated more favorable adjustments than those of the comparable norm group. The later history of these students is not available.

Terman's 755 males surveyed sixteen years after their childhood IQ identification contribute a sketch outline of early adult gifted achievement in present-day educational, domestic, occupational, and economic life (Terman and Oden, 1940a). Nine out of ten enter college, and of these 95 per cent graduate. The gifted college student is three times as likely as the average to win graduation honors. About 16 per cent of the boys are elected to Phi Beta Kappa, 12 per cent to Sigma Xi, and some of the others win departmental distinction. Two-thirds continue in graduate work and of these 25 per cent receive a Ph.D. or M.D. degree, 25 per cent a degree in law, and 30 per cent the M.A. or some other predoctoral degree. Forty per cent are partially self-supporting as undergraduates, 14 per cent earn their entire expenses. The group as a whole earned more than half a million dollars in the undergraduate years. As graduates one-third are wholly self-supporting. A fourth of the entire group has won scholarships, fellowships, and assistantships to the extent of $200,000. The total record in class and student body honors is above average, and the course grade records are superior. Exceptions are attributed to poor work habits, lack of interest, maladjustment, or deliberate neglect of studies in the interest of special projects or social activities.

Forty-six per cent of the group are married, and of these 8 per cent are divorced. The mean marriage age is 24. The education of the spouse is above average with four of every ten of the wives college graduates. Forty per cent of all the married gifted of both sexes have offspring, numbering for the entire group 350. Seventy-three per cent of the gifted boys report no effects from inclusion in the gifted group; 13 per cent state that the effect has been favorable; 5 per cent regard it as unfavorable. The moral record has been above average. Exceptions include for the boys three criminal records and some cases of chronic alcoholic excess.

The occupational accomplishment of the group seems reasonably appropriate. Of the professions in which 50 per cent of the gifted engage, law recruits 13 per cent; engineering and geology, 10 per cent; medicine, 7 per cent; college teaching, 8 per cent; laboratory research, 5.5 per cent; religious or social work, 6 per cent. About 25 per cent enter semiprofessional or higher business pursuits and the remainder are engaged in office work, skilled trades, retail business, and a variety of other occupations. Less than 1 per cent of the employable members of the group were unemployed in 1936, and none was reported on relief. The salaries (in 1936) of the young adult gifted ranged from an average of $122 at 21 or 22 to $250 at 30. Ph.D. and M.A. graduates earned on the average $200 a month, physicians $217. High earnings include those of a lawyer, $12,000; a radio advertising executive, $10,000; an investment expert, $7000; a college professor, $8000; two musicians, $6000 or more. Some of these individuals may be on their way to the top salary class of adults (E. L. Thorndike, 1939). Half the entire group are launched upon careers worthy of their abilities. The arts have claimed several successful devotees, scientific research a number of others now already known for their publications. Bearing in mind that the financial and industrial depression of the 1930's coincided with the entrance of these youths on their mature careers, we find that the record as a whole is favorable.

Gray's (1930) 126 boys are younger

(under 16) at college entrance than Terman's gifted children (age 17). Their Thorndike entrance examination scores rate higher (92) than the mean (87) reported by Burks, Jensen, and Terman in 1930. Thirty-nine of the 126 had state scholarship awards constituting approximately one-quarter of the total number granted to 25,000 Columbia freshmen in the same period. The total group had fewer deficiencies at entrance than the average student. Eighty-four per cent graduated from college, 79 per cent in four years as compared to 72 per cent for Columbia students generally. Sixteen per cent won Phi Beta Kappa honors, 10.3 general honors, as compared to 8 to 10 per cent and 3.1 per cent, respectively, of their classmates thus distinguished. In correlation with their younger age, Gray's boys were shorter, lighter, and inferior in strength as compared to the average college freshmen; however, they exceeded their own age norms in both height and weight. In interclass athletics and in nonathletic extracurricular activities they participated to a larger extent than their classmates and they were more successful in winning recognition. In emotional adjustment scores they rated more favorably than reported norm groups, and they were, according to their own statements, capable of profiting by early college entrance in spite of the difficulties of such a course. About one-fifth of the group expressed the belief that guidance in establishing habits of thought and work was essential for younger college students, and an equal number stated that in their opinion the superior student is neglected by his parents and college.

As a whole the results of the several researches show the level of attainment reached by the gifted under existing social, economic, and educational conditions. The contrast between the careers of the girls and the boys shows a lower level of economic and professional competence in the former and illustrates a well-known sex difference in social expectation and occupational opportunity. Nor can it be denied that a deeper, psychophysiological contrast may also be involved (Miles, 1935; Johnson and Terman, 1940).

Successful and Unsuccessful Adult Achievement of Gifted Children. In a short survey Terman and Oden (1940b) present a fascinating preview of a comparison between the most and the least successful of 600 gifted boys, selected in childhood, and at the time of this survey 23 years of age or older. Success was rated by three judges in terms of the extent to which native intellect had been utilized in life accomplishment. The upper and lower quarters of the resulting distribution were compared with respect to educational and occupational status, intelligence scores, achievement scores and school marks, extracurricular activities, books read, family background, racial differences, marital statistics and offspring, home environment, social adjustment and traits of personality, occupational preferences, masculinity-femininity scores, and pubertal changes. The results are summarized in Table 8. The statistical significance of the enumerated contrasts is not stated in the brief report, but many of the differences seem large enough to be clearly meaningful and the trends revealed by series of small differences may prove cumulatively important.

The successful group had generally the more satisfactory family background in terms of occupational status, marriage permanence, parental education, quality of the home, home instruction, and mental stock as indicated by higher sibling IQ and by fewer cases of abnormality in the relatives. Racially, a relatively small but noteworthy contrast appeared in the greater number of Jews in the success group. In child-

TABLE 8

CHARACTERISTICS IN CHILDHOOD AND AS YOUNG ADULTS OF MOST AND LEAST SUCCESSFUL MEMBERS OF THE CALIFORNIA GIFTED GROUPS *

	A Most Successful	C Least Successful		A Most Successful	C Least Successful
	$N = 167$	$N = 146$		$N = 167$	$N = 146$
Age (1939)	27.6	27.4	A marks in high school	62.5%	28.0%
Binet IQ (1922)	153.6	150.5	Iowa High School Con-		
T.G.T. IQ (1922)	148.5	147.5	tent Examination		
			Score:		
Home instruction	70.4%	52.0%	Above 99th percentile	45.2%	26.5%
Learned to read before			At or below 95th per-		
age 5	45.0%	45.0%	centile	3.2%	20.7%
Read 10 or more books					
in 2 mos. (1922)	56.0%	69.1%	Entered college	98%	70%
AQ (1922)	142.5	138.8	Of these, graduated		
Information Q (1922)	156.8	154.4	from college	90%	50%
			Thorndike Score in col-		
Personality in childhood:			lege	91.4 (57)	90.9 (25)
All traits, teachers'					
ratings	4.77	5.16	Postgraduate study	72.5%	19.4%
Adjustment difficulties	23.5%	33.1%	Phi Beta Kappa	32.5%	1.3%
Teased or thought			Sigma Xi	21.8%	2.8%
queer	7.0%	12.0%	Both	9.9%	0
Nervous symptoms	35.0%	43.0%			
			Self-supporting, half or		
Reported age of puberty	14.3	15.2	more	36.7%	45.8%
Masculinity score	+73	+64			
Paid jobs to age 16	63.0%	75.0%	Scholarships, fellow-		
			ships, etc.	50.0%	10.0%
Occupational preference			Total stipends from		
expressed	82.8%	68.5%	above	$116,000	$5,600
Social adjustment rat-			Mean earned income:		
ings normal or supe-			Age 23–24	$210	$96
rior (1928)	87.1%	74.6%	Age 28	$336	Less than $162
Education of parents:			Age 35	$500	
Post-graduate college	Fa. Mo.	Fa. Mo.	Married (1938)	64.5%	48.6%
work	25.3% 5.3%	14.0% 3.8%	Have offspring	46.0%	46.0%
College graduate	41.0 18.5	22.6 12.0	Wives gainfully em-		
8th grade only	11.6 5.3	19.5 16.3	ployed	10.7%	29.5%
			Divorced	4.6%	14.1%
Divorce or separation of					
parents	11.9%	19.8%	Occupational classifica-		
Mental abnormality in			tion:		
relatives	33.5%	41.0%	I. Professional	70.0%	17.1%
			II. Semiprofessional		
Home environment supe-			or higher busi-		
rior (1928)	90.3%	79.0%	ness	25.6%	11.1%
			III. Clerical, retail,		
Occupational classifica-			skilled trades	3.8%	33.6%
tion of father:			IV to VI. Others	.6%	34.3%
I. Professional	36.7%	21.1%	Unemployed	0.0	3.6%
II. Semiprofessional					
or higher business	23.9%	20.2%			
III to VI. Others	39.4%	58.7%			

* Data from L. M. Terman and M. Oden, "Correlates of Adult Achievement in the California Gifted Group,' *Yearb. Nat. Soc. Stud. Educ.*, 1940, 39(I), 74–84, ed. by G. M. Whipple. Quoted by permission of the Society.

hood the less successful groups learned to read as early as the more successful, reported more books read, and performed approximately as well on school achievement, information, and intelligence tests. Parents and teachers had been able to discern in the successful gifted at a fairly young age slightly more favorable intellectual, social, moral, emotional, and especially volitional traits (Table 9). The successful

cent graduated. The disproportion in the graduate schools is even greater. Somewhat more C's than A's had to earn their expenses in college, but five times as many A's as C's received honor appointments with stipends. The contrast in the amount of financial support thus won and in upper class and senior honors is more than 20 to 1 in favor of the A's. The slump in academic grades may too often be traced

TABLE 9

MEANS OF PARENTS' AND TEACHERS' RATINGS OF (1) THE TRAITS OF 300+ GIFTED BOYS AND 250+ GIFTED GIRLS, COMPARED WITH (2) SIMILAR MEANS OF 167 GIFTED BOYS RATED SUCCESSFUL IN YOUNG ADULT LIFE AND 146 GIFTED BOYS RATED UNSUCCESSFUL, AND (3) THE MEANS OF TEACHERS' RATINGS OF THE TRAITS OF 267 CONTROL BOYS AND 256 CONTROL GIRLS *

Traits	Gifted [1] Boys *	Control Boys †	Girls †	Gifted [1] Girls *	Gifted [2] A Group	C Group
Intellectual	3.66	6.4	6.3	3.70	3.5	3.8
Volitional	4.66	6.4	6.2	4.32	4.4	4.9
Emotional	4.83	5.9	5.8	4.80	4.3	4.7
Moral	4.82	6.2	5.6	4.50	4.4	4.7
Physical	5.53	6.4	6.1	5.42	5.3	5.3
Social	5.79	6.5	6.1	5.38	5.7	6.0
All Traits	4.88	6.3	6.0	4.82	4.77	5.16

* Teachers' and parents' ratings combined.   † Teachers' ratings.

Data derived or computed from [1] L. M. Terman et al., Genetic Studies of Genius, Vol. I, Mental and Physical Traits of a Thousand Gifted Children, Stanford University Press, 1925 (Table 192, p. 542), and [2] L. M. Terman and M. Oden, "Correlates of Adult Achievement in the California Gifted Group," Yearb. Nat. Soc. Stud. Educ., 1940, 39(I), p. 82, (Ed., G. M. Whipple), Public School Publishing Co.

or A group was slightly more accelerated in school than the unsuccessful C's; they reached puberty somewhat younger and during the high school period they showed superiority in school work, school performance tests, and extent of extracurricular activity. The differences in extracurricular activity are large, and they are probably significant in school marks, in Iowa Content Examination scores, and in leadership expressed in terms of the number of activities engaged in. Of the A's 98 per cent entered college, and 90 per cent graduated; of the C's 70 per cent entered and 50 per

to an unsuitable educational régime which retarded the child or youth until he lost interest or forgot how to study.

After college, or in some cases after high school, occupational or professional activity was rewarded by salaries showing a greater than 2-to-1 contrast in the early years and reaching a 3-to-1 difference by age 35. The occupational classification reveals the typical adult contrast of the two groups, with 95.6 per cent of the A's and only 28 per cent of the C's in the two higher brackets. Earning power and general success may be causal in the larger number of marriages among the A's, but so also may be psychophysiological stability and balance. These factors may be involved in the 1-to-3 contrast in divorce frequency. The authors conclude: "The data reviewed indicate that *above the IQ level of 140, adult success is largely determined by such factors as social adjustment, emotional stability, and drive to accomplish.* To what extent these qualities are the product of environmental influences and to what extent they have a genetic basis, no one can say" (Terman and Oden, 1940*b*, p. 84, *Yearb. Nat. Soc. Stud. Educ.*, 1940, 39 (I). Quoted by permission of the Society.)

Individual Differences among Gifted Children

The large statistical studies of the gifted have necessarily stressed group trends, measured by averages, comparing these when possible with norms for unselected groups. Thus the typical traits and behavior patterns of highly intelligent children have been outlined against the background of the generality. However, as Terman, Hollingworth, and Witty have been at pains to emphasize, gifted children as individuals are not adequately represented by this method alone. The gifted, superior deviates as they are, are farthest perhaps from constituting a stereotype. Each individual is unique in the patterns of behavior that express character and in the traits whose vastly complex integration forms the personality. Essential statistical measurements of central tendencies in the intellectual, emotional, and social aspects of individual behavior result in oversimplified generalizations. These are qualified theoretically, it is true, by mathematical measures of dispersion indicating the wideness of contrasts in each separate trait of the gifted. Only acquaintance with

individual gifted children can create the appropriate lively sense of unduplicated human personalities, differing even in the patterns and expressions of their exceptional intellects and in other traits covering the whole wide range of constitutional and functional potentialities.

Well-drawn case studies afford individual illustrations that diversify the interesting individualities whose performance and characteristics furnish the basis for the important statistical studies. Hollingworth, Terman, and others have provided long series of case descriptions indicating some of the possible trait combinations within the gifted group.

Superior mental endowment itself, the qualifying basis for the rating of gifted, may show contrasting characteristics in its expression. Thus the scientific, analytically ingenious, inventive child differs from the literary, generalizing, verbally expressive and retentive, interpretative child. In adulthood the former becomes characteristically the experimental scientist, the latter the writer or lecturer. Hollingworth's D and E illustrate this contrast (Hollingworth, 1926*b*; Burks, Jensen, and Terman, 1930).

Sustained intellectual capacity proved by repeatedly high intelligence test ratings is a characteristic of gifted children. Yet wide individual differences from test to test and large IQ changes are not infrequent with regressive score losses somewhat outweighing gains, especially in the girls. Thus Bertha, in a comfortable superior home and with an IQ of 139, deteriorated in scored IQ to 107 in six years. Clara, a clairvoyant's daughter, showed after six years a drop from IQ 148 to a T.G.T. score far below the gifted mean. In contrast, Terman's Madeline (IQ's 192 and 190) and David (IQ 184, Thorndike score 106) in childhood, and Hollingworth's cases 1 (IQ 190+, CAVD 454) and 20 (IQ 162 and

CAVD 429) in childhood and early adulthood, illustrate persistence in high scoring capacity. Madeline and David, described in detail, are able personalities with varied active interests and achievements (Burks, Jensen, and Terman, 1930).

In school achievement the gifted are superior as a group by whatever measure is applied. Test scores of accomplishment as a whole rate far above the general age norms (Terman and DeVoss, 1924). Yet here also wide individual differences are present in separate subject scores and in the total composite rating. Gray and Hollingworth (1931) have reported subject-quotient ranges for the gifted extending from 100 (average) to the upper test limit (210) and composite-quotient ranges from 119 to 187. The highest and the lowest of these quotients represent vastly divergent performance and competence. Achievement ratios (educational quotient divided by IQ) giving approximate measures of educational capability show extremely wide contrasts in the extent to which gifted children utilize their potential capacity. Lorge and Hollingworth (1936) report 105 and 106 as their highest childhood achievement ratios for 19 gifted children now college graduates, and yet these two scores belong to individuals with IQ's as diverse as 145 and 172. The two lowest achievement ratios, 83 and 85, in the same series, belong to children with IQ's of 162 and 174. Motivation and special influences may make high as well as low intellects more or less effective in the tests and also in the school work they are designed to measure (Tiebout, 1943). Two cases of gifted children with inferior scholarship records illustrate this deviation from the gifted mean. Edwin, IQ 141, failed eight subjects, rated C in sixteen units of work, and was finally asked to withdraw from high school because of his poor standing. His explanation was that he didn't like to work. Glandular

disfunction was suspected by medical examiners. Thomas, IQ 142, had a mediocre school record as a result of devoting his time and effort to music, in which he excelled. In contrast with these rare cases whose performance is distinctly poor are the more characteristic gifted who do well in school, find the work in the lower grades relatively easy, score in the superior range on educational tests, lead the class in high school, and win distinguishing honors. Hollingworth's (1942) C, G, and L and Verda, one of Jensen's gifted juvenile writers, are among these (Burks, Jensen, and Terman, 1930).

In nonintellectual traits the gifted range from high to low in test scores and in behavior. Physical, mental, emotional, and social traits show wide deviations from the typical, superior averages of the group as a whole. Statistical expression generally shows about as great divergences from the highest to the lowest trait measures of the gifted as occur in unselected groups. Case studies again give concrete form to the statistics (see especially Burks, Jensen, and Terman, 1930). Beside the characteristically healthy, strong, well-developed gifted from superior stock and excellent homes there are also a few like Terman's Marshall. Hampered in childhood by physical frailty, lameness, poverty, bad heredity, and sordid environment, he became by 1940 a member of the young adult success group. Although coming generally from superior economic and social backgrounds, the gifted group includes the daughter of a Negro Pullman porter and the sons of an inflexible, Austrian-born laborer. Above the average in emotional stability, they number their share of behavior and adjustment problems, of hampering shyness, self-consciousness and inferiority complexes, of overbearing aggressiveness and conceit, of disobedience, dishonesty, laziness, and even a case or two of "queerness" and psycho-

Homosexuality ??

pathy. Lack of motivation may appear or excessive driving ambition; neurotic avoidance of responsibility, and zealous, single track pursuit of personal objectives. Hollingworth (1931) outlined special sources of personality disability to which the highest IQ's are liable and illustrated the consequences of these under varying conditions (Hollingworth, 1942). Gillingham (1920) described unstable and neurotic children at various high IQ levels. Terman enumerated the emotional adjustment hazards of the most superior deviates (Burks, Jensen, and Terman, 1930). Regensburg (1926) described clinically cases of instability and maladjustment and outlined methods of treatment. Nevill (1937) reported a statistical investigation of maladjusted gifted children referred for clinical diagnosis and guidance. Zorbaugh (1936) has enumerated the specific problems for which gifted children were referred to the New York University Clinic for the social adjustment of the gifted, and which cover the whole range of psychophysiological maladjustment indicators (enuresis, masturbation, stuttering, compulsions and mild obsessions, excessive daydreaming and fantasy, seclusiveness, temper tantrums, quarreling, defiance of discipline, truancy, lying, stealing, sex delinquency, and the like).

Terman described an unstable neurotic girl, IQ 152, a persistently delinquent boy, IQ 143, and a constitutional psychopath, IQ 165, who was finally a suicide. The statistics for high IQ's among neuropsychiatric cases are of interest in this connection. Schott (1931) found 18 patients able to rate a top score on the 1916 Stanford-Binet scale in a tested hospital sampling of 450 cases. The 4 per cent of highly intelligent individuals in this representative psychopathic group roughly equals the expectation as defined by Terman (1916) for the general population.

It is important to recognize that differences and contrasts are present in the superior intellectual trait profiles of the gifted and that these children, like unselected boys and girls, show unfavorable as well as favorable deviations from the group averages in measures of performance and personality. But a well-balanced picture of the gifted as a group shows more successful than unsuccessful members, more who maintain than who lose the superior quality of their intellectual interests and achievements, more who are stable, effective, and well-motivated than unstable, irresponsible, or deficient in ambition and drive. Favorable deviations are more frequent than unfavorable in the scores on tests of accomplishment and ability, whether scientific, literary, or artistic, in scholastic and extracurricular interests, in vocational choices, in indications of mental masculinity-femininity, of fair-mindedness and of social intelligence, of mental independence from suggestibility, of leadership, and of moral responsibility. Case studies of favorable rather than unfavorable deviates among the gifted illustrate the predominating membership of the group as a whole. Many such single cross-sectional pictures are available in which high IQ's are accompanied and supported by superior physical and social traits, excellence in studies and in extracurricular activities, and the favorable opinions of their companions. A few cases studied and described at intervals from childhood to adulthood afford the most striking proof of the persistence of gifted personality. Hollingworth's E, four times described (Lorge and Hollingworth, 1936, and Hollingworth, 1942), and Terman's David, Francis, and Henry Cowell are among the best examples (Burks, Jensen, and Terman, 1930). Adequately representative, in IQ terms, of the group as a whole, they exemplify in personality traits the effective, goal-seeking, eagerly, patiently, and persistently ambitious whose ability is equal to the demands of their objectives and whose objectives are adequate for the realization of their potential talents.

Adjustment Problems of Gifted Children

The special problems of adjustment of the gifted are not, as was at one time supposed, primarily due to an essential emotional instability. Terman's results showed that children of high IQ's are not as a group less stable emotionally than a control population. On the Woodworth-Cady emotional stability questionnaire they rated as more stable than the control children at every age from 7 to 14. The critical ratios for the group differences were 6.11 for the boys (284 gifted, 258 control) and 7.61 for the girls (248 gifted, 275 control). Ratings of emotional traits by parents and teachers showed a statistically significant advantage of the gifted, and this was further indicated by an excess for them (68 per cent) above the control median. In social traits involving emotional elements a further series of ratings showed approximate equality of the group, 58.5 per cent of the gifted scoring as high as or higher than the average control child (Terman et al., 1925).

Comparing superior with inferior school children, Laycock (1933) found that the superior individuals made superior adjustments. Conklin (1940), investigating the infrequent school failures of top centile children, came to the conclusion that in these relatively rare cases personality factors, as yet unanalyzed, were involved. Witty (1940a), following the careers of his 100 gifted children identified ten years earlier, found his group generally superior in poise and stability. Yet exceptions were present, and, although no child was rated as "queer" by his associates, 10 per cent were maladjusted. Of these there were two types: the anxious, withdrawn, insecure, and the indifferent, bored, socially inadequate. The failure of the environment to stimulate maximally and to develop habits of industry was mentioned.

Nevill's (1937) study of behavior problems in gifted children suggests no correlation between IQ and type of emotional difficulty or adjustment, although it does indicate that a high IQ is generally an advantage in accomplishing good adjustment. This research supports the conclusions of Gillingham's (1920) early report in indicating that gifted children, although as a group above average in stability, are not at all as individuals free from emotional and social adjustment difficulties. No conclusion as to relative prevalence of problems can be made from either of these reports, as control group data are not available. That Nevill's gifted cases constitute 12 per cent of her clinical practice indicates the social and intellectual status of the clientele in the private clinic where the study was made rather than the incidence of instability among superior children.

Beside the typical constitutional-emotional problems coincident to nervousness, overanxiousness, sensitivity, and other typical personality disorders, and infrequent social problems such as lying and stealing, conditions now known to be less rather than more frequent among gifted than unselected children, there appear in certain of Nevill's gifted patients handicaps perhaps in part specifically related to their high intelligence. These include excessive quickness, resulting in inaccuracy, awkwardness, and clumsiness in writing and handwork when correlated with the younger life age, and impracticality, associated with lack of experience. Complaint is made in several cases of too much time spent in reading, of being self-centered and bossy, and in a few instances of mixing poorly, being teased easily, solitary, resistant, or bumptious. These problems, more or less closely interassociated in individual children with high IQ's, are similar to those summarized by Hollingworth after years of close personal study of the gifted. Hollingworth's (1936b) classification includes: (1) problems of physique (being weaker and smaller than their classmates); (2) problems of adjustment to occupation (preferring self-direction to direction by others); (3) problems involved in "suffering fools gladly" (difficulty in accepting the dogmatism of lesser intellects); and (4) the tendency to be isolated in interests and goals. When a gifted child is also a sensitive or nervous child his adjustment difficulties naturally tend to increase (Hollingworth, 1942).

Nevill and Hollingworth agree that the difficulties inherent in brilliance do not create maladjustment, although they may predispose to unsatisfactory behavior not infrequently based on a sense of inferiority due to relative backwardness in social and physical development. The gifted become ultracritical, self-sufficient, or mentally lazy as a result of their semi-awareness of mental superiority, insufficient social experience, and incomplete independence in the development of personal responsibility. Successful treatment comes through early recognition of the problems and through cooperation of home and school in (1) creating a relatively normal milieu with appropriate social contacts and without overstimulation and (2) in building the intellectual understanding and the social habits of the child to meet the contrast difficulties that cannot be avoided.

Nevill reports that good adjustment occurs when parents and teachers (1) without expecting too much at first and without exaggerating the child's superiority have built in him a healthy natural pride

in his powers, (2) have treated him as older intellectually while recognizing his emotional immaturity, (3) have encouraged his all-round development, and (4) have taxed his mental powers sufficiently at school. Hollingworth concludes that "intellectually gifted children between 130 and 150 IQ seem to find the world well suited to their development." They are superior in size, strength, health, and beauty, well balanced emotionally, and of good character; they tend to win confidence and to be granted leadership. Above 150 IQ the conditions may be less favorable.

Both Hollingworth and Terman have given attention to the highest IQ level where they find the need of special opportunity classes and special social adjustment most essential in order to avoid a sense of alienation and resulting negativism. The very exceptional children have few congenial playmates in childhood and little opportunity for normal social contacts with their peers. That 10 cases out of 35 IQ's 170+ are reported by Terman as lacking youthful social intercourse or even being seriously maladjusted is not surprising, in view of these considerations. It is perhaps more surprising that the average for this very high scoring group is only half a step below the mean on a five-step scale of social adjustment and that 64 per cent of the group rate as average or better on the same scale (Burks, Jensen, and Terman, 1930). Case studies of the highest IQ children show that their adjustments and satisfactions are mainly achieved in strictly intellectual fields and that these tend generally to be solitary. Their absorption in their interests and their individual emotional stability equations no doubt condition the extent of their comfort in their almost necessarily restricted social relationships. That their experiences have been sufficiently satisfactory and that they hold their own emotionally under the prevailing conditions seem to be indicated by the presence of six of them in Terman's (Terman and Oden, 1940b) adult success group as contrasted with but two in his failure group.

Potentiality and Realization

The report of gifted accomplishment in young adults confirms the view that equality of IQ in childhood does not insure, although it predisposes to, equality of achievement in maturity. Intelligence is an important factor in accomplishment, but it proves to be only one factor among others, perhaps many others. Interrelationships among the factors may be as important for accomplishment as the presence of the factors themselves. The follow-up studies so far made suggest that more effective personalities emerge when heredity and environment are both favorable. No single unfavorable element in the picture has been found to block accomplishment in the gifted if a sufficient number of others are favorable. Similarly, no single favorable element has proved sufficient to insure the realization of potential ability along the many possible lines of gifted accomplishment or even along a single line. The highest IQ's (170 or 180 and above), although more often predisposing to success than to failure, do not necessarily insure the highest achievement. Nor do they, although sometimes associated with serious problems in childhood development, produce a condition of social maladjustment essentially thwarting (Terman and Oden, 1940b; Hollingworth, 1942).

Gifted groups include individuals of many possibilities. Intercorrelations between intelligence and special skills and abilities are generally positive, and the scores of the gifted have been demonstrated as above the average, sometimes far above, in tests and childhood achievements prognostic, under favorable conditions, of later distinguished accomplishment. Both boys and girls are capable of superior literary and artistic work and produce examples of superior merit at an early age, often in the preschool years. However, the social influences of our athletic, industrial, mechanized age are opposed to the cultivation of these gifts in childhood, especially in boys.

History and biography show few examples of high achievement in adulthood along lines requiring special skills of manual or verbal expression where practice has not developed native ability from youth. The economic pressures of our time direct the emphasis of school instruction toward the primary aim of individual self-support. Mechanical invention may be included as an objective in practical education, but the development of literary, artistic, and musical creation is usually secondary and generally occurs only occasionally in individual extracurricular experience. Literary juvenilia of merit in Terman's gifted group were all the work of girls, although boys are known to produce superior literary work in childhood and youth under appropriately stimulating circumstances. Writing has at present little prestige value among boys except occasionally in the homes of successful literary or artistic parents or in schools, generally private schools, where literature is cultivated as a highly valued expression of superior personalities. Lang (1897) believed that youthful literary achievement is a poor indicator of later work of merit, but in the arts the child is father of the man and we are therefore not surprised that Terman's adult gifted include fewer writers than scientists, business administrators, or professional men. It is natural to believe that any sizable group of gifted children probably contains many more who could become successful creative workers than who do, but the means of developing these latent talents are not available and a valuable potential asset is thus usually wasted.

Scientific aptitude is another example of a talent present in the gifted group to a far greater extent than its probable realization in adult achievement. Social influences are opposed to superior scientific education and development in girls, and few of the potential scientists among them will reach a higher goal than high school teaching. Of the boys with this aptitude, the majority become industrial workers and engineers rather than contributors to the advancement of essential scientific progress.

Talents of superior grade in all the fields of human activity are no doubt present in any large group of gifted children. They are suggested or demonstrated by high scores on appropriate tests wherever these have been applied. No single individual, however, can in our complex society carry to a high level of achievement more than one or two human talents even under the most favorable circumstances. Mathematicians are seldom also superior artists or facile linguists, nor are engineers generally able to achieve high rank as poets or musicians even if talent for the necessary skills had been present in childhood. In science a man can today scarcely master more than a single branch, and literature, music, or art require complete devotion. A practical education, a brief apprenticeship, a few years of ill-paid junior business or professional service, the founding of a home, and the rearing of a family give little opportunity for the development of secondary or even primary talents in superior individuals even under favorable conditions. And conditions are frequently not favorable. Poverty, ill health, excessive responsibilities, social limitations, emotional handicaps increase the burdens of the personal, social, and economic life and prevent the realization in many gifted personalities of their potential capacity. For the feeble-minded, society undertakes to lift some of the burdens and cast off the restrictions as far as this may be. The gifted, the potential leaders, discoverers, and creators, however, are usually left to develop their own skills in their own way and in terms of personal initiative alone. Fortunately many of them have the energy, the ability, and the plasticity to make the necessary adjustments, overcome the environmental obstacles, and win the necessary economic support (Bridgeman, 1930). Others, as Terman's (1940) young adult study shows, are more or less exhausted by the struggle and fall by the way. Discovering means of preventing failure and of increasing the effectiveness of the possible life contribution of the gifted is a challenging task. Identifying talent and cultivating it maximally is an essential in the development of the natural resources of a progressive society (Terman, 1939b).

The Education of Gifted Children

Systematic attempts to segregate and specially train gifted children have developed in some of the more progressive localities as a practical consequence of the selection and study of the gifted by mental test methods. Many schools emphasize enrichment and individualized instruction within their regular groups. Before these methods were systematically formulated a few far-seeing educators had tried to meet the needs of the brighter pupils by various administrative plans. These included flexibility in promotion, double or multiple track curricula with varying rates of speed, constant and shifting group systems, promotion on the basis of separate subject mastery, and self-reliant programs with or without preparatory training centers for the rapid advancement of the more successful pupils at certain crucial points in the curriculum. In these procedures and their variations two aspects of individual and group differences in learning may be recognized: (1) diverse rates of advancement are appropriate for children of varying abilities, and the pupils at widely different levels on the intelligence scale can best be accommodated by some form of segregation or system of diversified progress; (2) wide differences in the amount and complexity of content that can be readily acquired by children of differing degrees of competence can be met by some flexible form of curriculum enrichment.

These principles were recognized and methods based upon them were developed by individual teachers of brilliant pupils long before they became the concern of administrative educators. Parents and tutors of able and precocious children developed their own systems of acceleration and enrichment. Karl Witte, Macaulay, and John Stuart Mill were instructed individually at rates of speed far beyond those of even the most superior private schools or opportunity classes, and the curricula devised for them were designed to cover by the age of 10 or 12 the elements and many of the higher aspects of liberal education, including the languages, literature, history, mathematics, theoretical science, and philosophy. Many other children besides, including Lord Kelvin, physicist, his brother James Thomson, engineer, Grotius, founder of international law, and the philosophers Bentham and Schleiermacher, were prepared by tutors or under flexible school plans which permitted college or university matriculation at the age of 11 or 12, followed by long careers of brilliant and active accomplishment. Men who achieve the distinction of inclusion in *Who's Who* and the notable group of starred American men of science have as a rule passed more rapidly through the elementary and college preparatory school years than the average boy. Enrichment of educational content came to them in part through superior private school instruction, in part through the personal interest of public school teachers, tutors, or friends, and in part as a result of personal initiative (Hollingworth, 1926b and 1942; Gray, 1930).

Private schools in the United States and elsewhere are actually carrying on the segregated education of superior pupils. Reports of the Educational Records Bureau (1940, 1943) and other sources indicate that approximately 90 per cent of the children in these schools are average or above in tested intelligence and educational competence, and that 5 to 25 per cent of them are gifted in the technical sense, having IQ ratings of 130+ or 140+. The average rate of learning in private schools is 15 to 20 per cent faster than that in the average public elementary school, an advantage that has generally been utilized in thoroughness and enrichment rather than by accelerated promotion.

Exceptional pupils are not adequately taken care of by the usual routine of the public schools. Often their very presence is not recognized. Thus Terman, among others, found that the more able public school children are discovered more readily in terms of birth date than by teachers' subjective nominations.

Public schools that have adopted multiple track or xyz class systems have partially met the need by their segregation of the average (y) from the dull (z), and the high average and superior (x) from the middle group. The x classes in many public schools enroll pupils approximately equal in ability to private school children. But just as the dull classification fails to meet the needs of the feeble-minded, so the above average group cannot sufficiently adapt its needs to its most gifted members. Children with IQ's of 140 or even 130 and above have quite different learning needs from the group averaging below 120.

Special classes explicitly for gifted children are a development of the mental test period. Race (1918) reported one of the first where selection was based on IQ tests. The pupils, IQ 120+, were described as healthy, stable, and capable of more and better work than the average. Without excessive effort they covered the prescribed course content in half the regular time. Specht (1919) described in similar terms work of children of the same level of superiority in a segregated New York class. Whipple (1919), Coy (1923), and others have also reported success with above average children. Cleveland (1920) stated that the scholastic records of the segregated gifted children and their extracurricular pursuits exceeded, sometimes considerably, the typical student performance of their class group.

From 1920 onward until 1930 there was a gradual increase in the number of special classes. The children were generally chosen early in the elementary school course. Usually, due regard was given to health and personality factors. The teachers were as carefully selected as the pupils and they were given much freedom in the planning and conduct of the work. The cost per pupil was somewhat greater than in the regular classes, and for this reason small school systems with few high IQ children infrequently attempted segregation.

From 1918 to 1923 educational psychologists in Germany as well as in the United States were experimenting successfully with the segregation of superior children for school instruction. Selection by test, supplemented by teachers' appraisals of health, motivation, and personality, gradually took the place of reliance on either test or teachers' judgments alone. Alert, competent, well-adjusted teachers were given charge of the instruction of the gifted (Lämmermann, 1931). In other European countries mental tests have been used as a basis for the granting of scholarships in special schools rather than for segregation within the regular schools.

In the period from 1923 onward attention was directed in the United States chiefly to the curriculum and problems of enrichment. Early considerations were summarized and discussed by Whipple (1919), Freeman (1924), Stedman (1924), Henry and others, in the *Yearbook of the National Society for the Study of Education* (1924), Hollingworth (1926b), Jensen (1927), and Goddard (1928). Later methodology and objectives have been formulated by Adams and Brown (1930), Osburn and Rohan (1931), Dransfield (1933), Cohen and Coryell (1935), and in terms of basic principles by Hollingworth (1942). Bentley (1937), Carroll (1940), Heck (1940), and Garrison (1940) have summarized typical school attitudes and practices in the teaching of gifted children. Bibliographies have been prepared by Newland (1941), Gray (1942), and Hildreth and Ingram (1942).

Intraclass segregation of small groups and individualized project programs are developing where class segregation has proved nonfeasible. Hollingworth (1936c), from experience in special opportunity classes for the gifted, advises enrichment in the regular elementary school curriculum, including (1) courses in the development of civilized culture, using the project method; (2) biography of world leaders; (3) the tools of learning, including foreign languages; and (4) special work in art and music, including an introduction to appreciation. In the high school course Cohen, Coryell, and their associates (1935) emphasize the value and importance of teacher leadership and stimulation. Gifted pupils need to be associated with teachers who are themselves enthusiastic devotees of the subjects they teach and of the culture to which these are essential.

The most usual method of dealing with the rapid progress possibilities of the gifted in the public schools is by the simple expedient of grade skipping. The average gifted child in Terman's group skipped at least one grade, and those who skipped more were reported by their teachers as doing better work than those who skipped less. An unpublished study of Hoskinson is reported by Henry (1924) in which high school and college students who had skipped one or more half grades were found to be characteristically rapid readers, quick learners, industrious, and able to concentrate. They had learned to study independently and they brought from home a good attitude toward school and school work. Eighty-seven per cent believed that the skipping had been advantageous to them. The more recent study of McElwee (1932) in which the personality traits of accelerated children were compared with average and retarded groups finds the traits of the advanced pupils consistently superior. Their attitudes toward school work and their school habits are reported to be especially good.

Results reported by Wilkins (1936) on the high school achievement and social adjustment of accelerated pupils are in harmony with these findings and seem "to give further evidence that the dangers attributed to acceleration (unless of course practiced unwisely) have been largely overestimated."

The United States Office of Education reported, for 1935–1936, 3009 gifted children enrolled in special classes of public school systems in fourteen cities at a cost of $176,672. The enrollment had decreased 25 per cent during the period of financial curtailment beginning in 1930. "The education of gifted children," the report explains, "has always constituted a subject for debate with a rather definite difference of opinion as to the effect of membership in a special class upon their social adjustment. Many fine things are being done for this group without separate organizations for their instruction" (Foster and Martens, 1938, p. 1). In many large cities the xyz systems are now expected to take care of intelligence grouping sufficiently to meet the needs of the gifted at the elementary school level. Enthusiasts for segregation repeatedly emphasize the values of the method in making possible the maximal mental stimulation and better social adjustment of the abler pupils (Orleans, 1940). Enrichment within class groups is said to offer a successful solution without the organizational and administrative complexities of specific segregation. Witty (1940b) effectively re-emphasized the undemocratic trend of gifted segregation in the public schools. He also contends that homogeneous grouping on a mental test basis is impossible. The evidence from the New York and other opportunity classes seems at variance with this view. Myers (1935) believes that the best all-round development of the gifted child results when he works at school at his own rate but in a regular class of normal children.

Research since 1930 has added little more than general confirmation to the earlier findings regarding the benefit of segregation (Heck, 1940). Lamson's (1930) segregated children excelled in high school above the average of their older classmates. Gray and Hollingworth's (1931) segregated gifted children, devoting only half their time to the prescribed curriculum, rated as high on educational achievement tests as nonsegregated children of equal intelligence who were spending full time on the prescribed work. A study of segregated and unselected first-grade children by Dvorak and Rae (1929) led to the conclusion that both segregation and enrichment had positive value. Studies by Danielson and Herschberger (reported by Terman and Burks, 1933) record comparisons of special class gifted children with gifted pupils from the regular grades. The subject marks for the former were higher and their participation in art activities, athletics, dramatics, committee work, and office holding was greater. Teachers' ratings of the two groups were approximately equal on accuracy, dependability, and leadership. The former special class group received the higher ratings in cooperation, initiative, and industry. In answering the question "In which grades have you been the happiest?" the segregated twice as often as the nonsegregated mentioned those grades in which the special class experience occurred. A study by Herr (1937) showed that superior children (average IQ 125) completed the work of the seventh and eighth grades in one year without loss in school marks, achievement scores, or extent of participation in extracurricular activities as compared with groups of equal ability who performed the work in a two-year period. Health and attendance were satisfactory in the accelerated group. Personality ratings showed possibly significant differences which are not necessarily indicators of unfavorable effects from the acceleration.

The experimental work with gifted children in which segregated are compared with nonsegregated groups seems to point to the more favorable progress of the former as compared with the latter. The studies are too few to be completely convincing. Enrichment and intragroup instruction may be almost equally effective. The important finding with reference to the education of the gifted relates to the development of attitude and motivation. Gifted children, like others, require ade-

quate opportunity and stimulation, and this can be more or less successfully given with due planfulness under various systems, so long as diverse rates of advancement are permitted and an adequately enriched curriculum is maintained. If segregation is used, selection in terms of total personality assets and needs is certainly desirable.

The Childhood of Genius

Biographical accounts of the early development of distinguished contemporaries or historic geniuses furnish psychological material of special interest for comparison with the observed and tested behavior of gifted children. Rate of mental development, frequency and type of precocious achievement, personality traits, especially the volitional, family background, educational opportunity, and social environment can be traced in biography and measured by the statistical methods of historiometry. It is true that tradition has not infrequently invested geniuses of the past with phenomenal characteristics and has popularly given them personalities unparalleled in contemporary cross-sectional studies. The factual material of reliable biography, however, can be viewed and weighed apart from exaggeration and excessive eulogy. When so examined the data, although often unfortunately too few, are comparable with current records. Gifted children of today undoubtedly include many of the leaders of tomorrow, and the childhood traits of the leaders of the past objectively evaluated can enlighten us about the most superior contemporary personalities.

Inquiry and controversy in this field have centered in the problems of the mental growth, the heredity, the special interests, the cultural opportunities and development, and the early physical and mental health of world leaders. Popular conclusions about these matters drawn from biased selections of illustrative data have gained a hold on popular opinion that gives way only slowly in the face of careful, objective, statistical studies of large representative populations. The view that ability finds a way to distinction, whatever the social handicaps, probably takes insufficient account of the demonstrable advantages in the environment of successful leaders. On the other hand, the opposite opinion that training and opportunity make the man must finally fall before rigorous comparisons of achievements of the equally schooled but unequally gifted. Fallacious evidence of the presence in geniuses generally of instability, psychopathy, delay in development, and degenerative precocity has been brought forward by the fascinating, subjective method of descriptive anecdote (Lombroso, 1891). Conclusions based on selected data of this kind have no place in a scientific natural history of genius, although they may serve the desirable end of stimulating research for proof or disproof.

The first studies of large samples of objective data were made by Galton, who elaborated a statistical psychobiographical method. The superior hereditary background of eminent men of science, letters, art, and public life was demonstrated in every such study (for example, Galton, 1869; DeCandolle, 1885; and Ellis, 1904). Correlation was demonstrated between the appearance of genius and such factors as social and economic security, educational opportunity, and favorable cultural influences. The importance of environmental stimulation for the emergence of ability and the possible veto power of poverty or educational restrictions were emphasized (Ward, 1906). Reviewing his own results and those of others, Ellis advised caution in the interpretation of cause and effect in the nature-nurture composite of genius.

Sully (1886) and Ellis (1904) found healthy, persistent precocity characteristic of leaders and geniuses. Precocity in the field of special interest was demonstrated by 80 per cent in a group of 287 geniuses representing the principal fields of human endeavor. Mental acceleration was noted by the biographers of one-third of Ellis's cases, and only 4 per cent were said to have been "not precocious." Those who failed to show early mental superiority or strong intellectual interest were not among the more distinguished for original intellectual achievement in maturity. "In order to go far," Ellis concluded, "it is evidently desirable to start early."

The first general statistical survey of the boyhood development of great men was Yoder's (1894) study of fifty geniuses and leaders. The tabulated results minimized the importance of poor health stressed by Lombroso, although they showed how in individual instances, as in the case of Dickens, delicate physique could be of advantage in intellectual pursuits. Yoder's great men were above average in size, born of parents in the period of mature energy, and were normal in childhood development and pursuits, including sports. At an early age they had already displayed strong memories, active imaginations, and many of them had shown a scientific spirit of investigation. "Like ordinary men, they were influenced by their environment."

Characteristic advantages in background and education were enjoyed by 1036 noted American men of science selected by their scientific associates at the instigation of Cattell (1915, 1917), who planned, organized, and interpreted the statistics. The national and racial heredity of the scientists showed trends similar to those of the gifted, with the northern European and British stocks preponderant. Professional men contributed a disproportionate share of members to the group. The sex difference in numbers is commented upon. Contrast in the production of various geographical regions is statistically expressed and interpreted with respect to the influence of universities and great teachers. Thus Massachusetts and Connecticut were, for example, fifty times as likely to rear a distinguished scientist in the period studied as the Southeastern States. Centers of learning where eminent investigators attracted the best students produced many times their share of younger scientific leaders. Thus from Agassiz at Harvard came thirteen first-rank naturalists; from Brünnow at Michigan, a quarter of the leading astronomers of their day. Teaching and inspiration directed the line of study and interest, and the effective expression of native ability was augmented through personal contacts.

The studies from Galton to Cattell showed the importance for achievement of superior innate ability, good heredity, and adequate education. As yet superior ability had been defined in such terms as school achievement, literary or scientific accomplishment, or creative artistic production. These were not interchangeably meaningful. An index of general mental measurement became available in the Binet tests and these, as revised at Stanford, Terman proposed to apply to biographical material for the evaluation of the childhood development of great men. The IQ of Francis Galton thus appraised on the basis of early records proved to be near 200 (Terman, 1917).

To Terman's plan for IQ evaluation the Stanford investigator of the childhood of geniuses added appraisals of heredity, environmental factors, and ratings of personality traits (Cox, 1926). The results may with due caution be compared to the test results and ratings that make up the picture of the gifted children. The subjects of the genius study were 301 persons

objectively rated among the 500 most eminent leaders of history and selected as adequately representing adult human distinction. The data from several thousand biographical works pertaining to the youth of these men, gathered into individual case studies, served as the basis for mental and personality trait ratings and evaluations of background and environment. Résumés of these materials are presented in the published study. Three experienced psychologists rated the items concerning mental behavior on an IQ scale, adding also in each case an appraisal of the adequacy of the data for this purpose. The agreement of the series of ratings is indicated by correlation coefficients of the order of .70. Two psychologists rated the environmental factors. One psychologist and one experienced teacher rated a series of personality traits for a representative third of the group. Tabulations of longevity and of fields of activity and a collection of early literary productions were also included in the published report.

The evidence of superior mental capacity in the subjects of this study is unequivocal. No individual, however meagerly reported by his biographers, was rated below average on the sum total of available childhood information. The three psychologists, advised to rate conservatively on the data alone, and as if the identity of the child were not known, found sufficient indication of superior intelligence to justify the conclusion that the group average IQ lies well within the gifted range. Ratings below 140 IQ resulted from regression of estimate when the data were too few for self-corroboration, or when they were of a sort as yet not adequately indexed in IQ terms (Table 10). Data evaluated as equal in reliability to an abbreviated Stanford-Binet test consisting of as many as two items per year-group gave an average IQ of 152. When the data reached the reliability of a Stanford-

TABLE 10

SCALE OF IQ RATINGS OF GENIUSES IN CHILD-
HOOD AND YOUTH INDICATING INCREASE OF
RATING AS A FUNCTION OF COMPLETENESS OF
THE DATA *

	Average IQ	Relative Coefficient
134 case studies with data equal to ½ to ½ test item per year group	124	.29
32 case studies with data equal to ¾ test item per year group	139	.53
54 case studies with data equal to 1 test item per year group	142	.60
41 case studies with data equal to 2 test items per year group	152	.75
13 case studies with data equal to 3 test items per year group	171	.82

* Based on data in Table 8, p. 53, and Table 18, p. 76,
C. M. Cox, *Genetic Studies of Genius*, Vol. II, *The Early
Mental Traits of Three Hundred Geniuses*, Stanford
University Press, 1926. By permission of the publisher.

Binet test of three items per year-group, the average IQ was 171. Psychological and statistical considerations indicated that if all the facts were available for the genius group the average rating would well exceed 160.

Wide individual differences were present in the mental scores of the members of the group as a whole and even in the smaller numbers of the more completely recorded cases. It was not possible to conclude that a high, narrow IQ range accounted for all. Men eminent as soldiers showed least conclusively the childhood behavior associated with high mental test ratings; yet a fairly satisfactory appraisal of their probable average IQ registered above 140. Adequately reported artists and musicians averaged 160; statesmen and imaginative writers, 165; religious leaders and prose writers, 170; scientists, 175; and philosophers, 180. The lowest uncorrected, individual appraisals based on material sufficient for a single, relatively dependable IQ estimate (reliability coefficient .75) were at 135, the highest reached 200. Among the estimates based on more complete and, hence, for this purpose more reliable material were those for John Quincy Adams, 165; Pope and Chatterton, 170; Coleridge, 175; Voltaire and Macaulay, 180; Grotius, J. S. Mill, and Leibnitz, 190; and Goethe, 200. IQ values statistically corrected to offset the error due to brevity in the records gave Darwin, Scott, and Mozart IQ's of 165; Longfellow, Luther, and Faraday, 170; Agassiz and Kant, 175; Dickens and Hume, 180; Davy and Galileo, 185; Berkeley and William Pitt, 190. The correlation between IQ and the rank order of eminence in the group as a whole was low. Eminence in terms of illustrious achievement qualifying for this particular group, although associated with superior intelligence, was therefore not demonstrably a function of the high IQ as estimated. Other traits or circumstances generally rather obviously accounted for the presence of the intellectually lower-scoring members of the group, for the occasional low scores of some who probably deserve much higher ratings, and for the low eminence ratings of a few whose IQ's were found equal to the highest ever reported. The author was of the opinion that even the statistically corrected values were in many cases too low to serve as fully satisfactory measures of these rare intellects. Yet the purpose of the study had been served in bringing to light the levels of intelligence which had been exceeded by the illustrious, as indicated even in the often scanty reports of their early achievement.

Ratings of the fathers' occupations showed the trends of superior heredity and the advantages of background available to the geniuses; 80 per cent of the fathers belonged to Taussig's two upper economic classes. Ratings of home training and discipline of a representative third of the group averaged two steps higher than the assumed norm on a seven-step scale. Breadth, intensity, and kind of interests also proved superior to the assumed mean for children of equal mental age. Intellectual interests, intensity of a single interest, and breadth of interrelated interests rated especially high. Social and activity interests showed a slight negative correlation with the intelligence rating.

Sixty-seven character traits defined by Webb (1915) were made the basis of a personality profile of 100 of the more fully reported geniuses. Ratings considerably above average for the group as a whole were found (1) in four emotional traits: cheerfulness, imaginativeness, esthetic feeling, and excitability; (2) in three emotional-social traits: family affection, friendship, and loyalty; (3) in eleven social traits: fondness for a small circle of intimate friends, impulsive kindness, kindness on principle, trustworthiness, conscientiousness, desire to be liked, sense of corporate responsibility, sense of justice, religious interest, pure-mindedness, wideness and intensity of influence; (4) in two physical activity traits: energy or restlessness and physical bravery; (5) in all of the five positive self-traits: desire to excel, desire to be a leader, adequate self-confidence, self-esteem, and esteem of his own special talents; (6) in eleven intellectual traits: absence of suggestibility, degree to which action and thought are dependent on reason, keenness of observation, attention to detail, extent of mental work bestowed on studies and on special interests, soundness of common sense, originality and creativeness, strength of memory, quickness and profoundness of apprehension; (7) in four traits of persistence: degree to which he works with distant objects in view, degree of will and perseverance, tendency not to abandon tasks in the face of obstacles, or from mere changeability; (8) in balance; and (9) in strength or force of character as a whole. In Table 11 the

personality traits are listed in which the geniuses are as distinguished or more so than they are in terms of their superior mental ability. In these traits they rate as a group at or above +1.5 on a seven-point scale in which 0 represents the mean and +3 the upper limit.

The conclusions from the data for geniuses support the view that good heredity and good home training are valuable assets for mature achievement and that superior interests are a basis of desirable stimulation. The youths in the genius group were probably without exception endowed with high, many of them with the highest, intellectual capacity of which human beings are capable. All of them had the capacity and the opportunity to develop motivation of a rarely superior order. The composite in their personalities of intellectual and emotional traits was so integrated and functioned so dynamically as to produce original, creative achievement in science, art, literature, philosophy, religion, or statesmanship. If leaders like these appear from among our gifted children they will probably also be found to possess not only high, often the highest, intellectual capacity, but also superior traits of personality, especially motivating power. Moreover, like these geniuses, they will no doubt benefit optimally from whatever favorable circumstances may enhance the effectiveness of their developing capacities.

The mental and physical health in childhood of fifty representative and well-reported members of this same group of geniuses and illustrious persons was rated and reported on by Miles and Wolfe in 1936. The mean physical health ratings showed 12 per cent of the group above average, 58 per cent average, 28 per cent somewhat below average, and 2 per cent with definitely frail health. In mental health 14 per cent were rated above average 64 per cent at the average, 14 per

TABLE 11

High Personality Trait Ratings of One Hundred Geniuses in Childhood*

(Ratings are averages of two raters on a seven-point scale, +3 to −3, when 0 is the assumed average of the general child population.)

Intellectual Traits:

Mental work devoted to routine studies	1.7
Independence of thought	1.8
Keenness of observation	1.9
Strength of memory	2.0
Quickness of apprehension	2.0
Originality, creativeness	2.1
Profoundness of apprehension	2.3
Mental work devoted to special pursuits	2.4

Social Traits:

Trustworthiness	1.7
Conscientiousness	1.7
Wideness of influence	1.7
Intensity of influence on intimates	2.0

Self-traits and Motivation:

Desire to be a leader, to impose his will	1.7
Correctness of his own self-appraisal	1.7
Correctness of self-appraised special talents	2.0
Belief in his own powers	2.0
Force of character as a whole	2.0
Devotion of effort toward distant goals	2.0
Strength of will in perseverance	2.3
Persistence in the face of obstacles	2.3
Steadfastness of effort	2.5
Desire to excel in efforts	2.6

* Data from Table 49, C. M. Cox, *Genetic Studies of Genius*, Vol. II, *The Early Mental Traits of Three Hundred Geniuses*, Stanford University Press, 1930. By permission of the publishers.

cent as showing mental or emotional weakness, and 8 per cent with considerable or serious mental or emotional weakness. In a single case, that of Chatterton, definite emotional disorganization was clearly present, leading at a young age to suicide. Equated with Olson's Schedule B of mental health for children, the ratings of the fifty geniuses show a similar distribution of percentages reaching or exceeding a certain point on the scale (Table 12). In spite of the differences in method of arriving at the results compared in the table, there is a fair agreement between them, and it may be concluded therefore that the mental health of this representative group of the illustrious was on the average no less satisfactory than that of unselected school children today. A relationship subtle or otherwise between genius and insanity is not indicated by this particular comparison.

The apparent contradiction between these results and the conclusions of Lombroso, Lange-Eichbaum, and others who have found mental peculiarity or psychopathy a characteristic of their geniuses is discussed by Miles and Wolfe. The conclusion is reached that the disagreement among investigators regarding the relationship of genius and psychopathy or insanity is largely due to the definition of the term. Many imaginative geniuses have been unstable emotionally. Men of action, on the other hand, have less often shown psychopathic traits. White (1930) had arrived at a similar conclusion from a study of the adult careers of the entire group of Cox's geniuses.

Gifted Children and Genius

Human beings differ with respect to traits and trait constellations. Both capacities and accomplishments are subject to quantitative and to qualitative measurement, and superiority may therefore be of either kind. Economic necessity generally calls for quantity, cultural progress for quality. Objective psychological measurement has differentiated primarily capacities. Evaluation of products is an interpretative function. The correlation be-

TABLE 12

	Below Average			Average			Above Average	
Subjective mental health scale	2	2.5 3	3.5 4	4.5	5 5.5 6	6.5 7
Rating on Olson's Schedule B	116	99	82	73	69 66	48
Percentage of Olson's cases at or above a given percentage	98	91	72	59	52 45	5
Percentage of 50 geniuses at or above a given scale point	100	98	82	62	56 40	16

tween capacity and accomplishment has been assumed to be high. Measures or indices of one have often been accepted as satisfactory substitutes for the other. Recent psychological study attempts the difficult task of comparing capacity with accomplishment. The multiple measurable factors are analyzed in each by the method of intercorrelation.

Gifted children selected on the basis of early test performance represent a capacity group. Geniuses selected on the basis of past careers constitute an accomplishment group. Both are superior human specimens deviating exceptionally from the average. The problem of correlation between the factors contributing to the superiority of these two groups and between the traits of the personalities qualifying for membership in each can be approached only indirectly through descriptive comparisons. Such comparisons can give no final answers. They may, however, clear up certain misconceptions, define the problems more precisely, and throw some light on the larger relationships. Perhaps we may better understand what gifted children are and what is meant by genius if we attempt some consideration of their similarities and differences.

The term *genius* is popularly applied to a human being when he has accomplished altogether original creative work of the highest quality, such as is recognized as extraordinary in some valued field of human enterprise. The genius has been most often identified in the arts and in scientific discovery, because here individual origination and independent creation were most obvious. Political leadership has sometimes been recognized as possessing the individual quality essential to genius. Originally restricted to a few fields, the term has been used more and more to designate the individuals endowed with the power for whatever extraordinary feats the culture of the period chose to value as most significant.

In the early development of the genius concept the extraordinary accomplishment was attributed not to human capacity but to divine inspiration. This was the mystical or supernatural theory of genius. Its significance is idealistic and religious; its basis is emotional. It persists even at the present day, though its objects are generally historically remote. It has, unfortunately for the scientific use, tinged the word *genius* emotionally and subjectively, while popularly and poetically emphasizing in a desirable way the high value of original creative activity. The repudiation by some psychologists of the use of the term *genius* or *near-genius* as applied to gifted children may originate in the experience of contrast when elementary school boys and girls, even the brightest of them, are compared with the idealized characters whom we identify as the great men of history (Lange-Eichbaum, 1928, 1931).

While poets and popular philosophers perpetuated the subjective interpretation of genius, scientists attempted to objectify the picture. The rationalists said genius can be developed through training, but it will be recognized as genius only if it is expressed in production at the right time and place. The sociologists further developed this view, emphasizing environmental influences in the development of the product of genius and in the readiness of the world to accept it (Ward, 1906). Social conditions, they said, not individual accomplishments, are responsible for works of genius. Men of ordinary gifts may, according to this hypothesis, become leaders and be acclaimed as great. This view valuably emphasized the importance of social influences for the development of superior achievements, and in this it is amply supported by results from the studies of gifted children. However, the further conclusion that great leaders are men of mediocre capacity has not been substantiated by scientific evidence at least with respect to intelligence, although it does appear to be true that a rather wide range of superior ability is represented in the world's leadership group (Cox, 1926).

The contributions of clinical psychiatry include the various explanations of genius as abnormal personality function. The attempts to relate genius to insanity have classical roots and show also the influence of the subjective, unique quality interpretation. Pathological material especially available in the biographies of literary geniuses has given support to these efforts. The psychoanalysts belong to the clinical group in their identification of genius as a neurosis or as a compensatory reaction. A valuable contribution from the psychiatric point of view is in the emphasis on the total dynamic function of the personality with its complex factors and deeply conditioned impulses (Reid, 1911–1912; Witty and Lehman, 1930; Schott, 1931).

The relatively small number of insane geniuses in representative groups of the illustrious suggests that the relationship between genius and mental abnormality has been exaggerated (White, 1930). Also the fact that among gifted children, who, however, may not especially include those with subjective and creative gifts, mental as well as physical health has generally rated above the average seems to point in the same direction (Burks, Jensen, and Terman, 1930). It is not known whether this is simply the result of a sound mental hygiene in superior families or a consequence of the repression of subjective factors by the more intelligent children, or a consequence of unintentional exclusion from the studies of psychopathic gifted children.

That many geniuses have shown eccentric traits has been mentioned by Ellis, Galton, and others. How much more eccentric they were than average men has never been stated exactly. The eccentricities of the great have always been of interest to people of lesser accomplishment, and they may be more often reported or weighted with more serious consideration than those of the generality. The evidence from the childhood of eminent men fails to support the view of frequent idiosyncrasy except in the subjective, sensitive individuals already mentioned. Among the gifted children queerness and peculiarity are infrequent. Deviation from the typical, mentally healthy average is not regarded with favor by parents and teachers today. Capable self-control is the popular ideal, and children are encouraged not to be "different." The children who have shown unfavorable emotional developments have not been those among whom later distinction seemed probable (Witty, 1940b).

Genius as Most Superior Native Ability

The position of genius at the top level on a scale of ability was first suggested by Galton. His theoretical ability scale, constructed according to the requirements of the normal probability curve, differentiated levels of competence from the lowest (idiocy) to the highest (the genius level) in terms of frequency of occurrence and the correlated statistical measures of deviation from the mean. Although superiority in scale terms was expressed as degree of achievement, Galton emphasized the native capacity factors which made the achievement possible. He devoted much careful research to the definition of scale points as indicators of the statistical frequency of mediocrity, superiority, and eminence, including the high level of distinction of the genius. The lowest level of eminence defined from historical and contemporary statistics of achievement he placed at a point on the scale beyond which not more than one individual in 4000 of the general adult population could rate. Position at this level Galton illustrated in the careers of successful English judges and bishops. Higher levels specifically defined included, first, men of great national reputation, each being as one in 79,000; and, second, the rare illustrious characters of history, who rank as one in a million or more, and include only men of the greatest, internationally recognized distinction. From the life histories of his highest ability groups Galton deduced the basic psychological traits of genius: superior ability, persistent and intense motivation, and great physical power for work. These traits he found in all, but he discovered that they differed in relative weight according to the field of eminent accomplishment.

Galton's ingenious scale is arbitrary and fallible, as are all methods of measuring achievement and capacity. Its merit lies in the application of statistical psychological techniques to the rating and equating of human ability and superiority and in its objectification of the native traits of men of genius as measurable quantities.

The traits of adult genius discovered by Galton have in a relatively recent study been found to characterize illustrious historical personalities in childhood (Cox, 1926). A high general level of accomplishment and versatility which suggested that achievement might have resulted for many in any one of several fields was mentioned by Galton and demonstrated by White (1931) from Cox's data.

Intelligence and ability tests have proved for many specific lines of mental capacity and accomplishment that Galton's theory of the normal distribution of human ability meets the criterion of present-day objective measurement. Terman's results in the study of gifted children show close agreement between the statistics for the distribution of intelligence at the highest levels and Galton's upper segments on the normal curve constructed in terms of the threefold native ability that constitutes "genius." Among Terman's gifted are not a few who possess besides high test intelligence also high motivation and great power for accomplishment. These are especially well represented in the 1940 success group. Had Galton's threefold criterion been applied in the original selection of the California gifted children, there would be statistical grounds for the expectation that somewhere near 4 per cent (about thirty individuals) of those chosen might qualify for classification at Galton's lowest eminence level, a small fraction of 1 per cent (one or two persons) at his second eminence level, but by reason of the relatively small numbers perhaps none at the level of the "illustrious."

In statistical terms the majority of Terman's group may be as far below the level of Galton's "eminence" as the average 100 IQ child is below the child rating at 120 IQ. We may recall that 4 or 5 per cent, but not generally more, 100 IQ children do sometimes later reach the 120 IQ level in test terms (Merrill, 1938), and this analogy may illustrate the possibility of a similar gain in status from a lower to a higher level on a general achievement or eminence scale. The 1940 report of Terman's success group gives reason to suppose that somewhere near the appropriate proportion of gifted boys who are highly superior in motivation and energy as well as in intellect are on their way to the levels of eminence corresponding to Galton's statistical prediction.

Contemporary psychology views personality at every level as vastly complex. Each individual is recognized to be the product of numerous constitutional elements mutually interacting, and at every stage in the course of their development variously stimulated by many combinations of environmental influences. Individual differences occur in every dimension involving every possible combination of the multiple external and internal factors and their relationships. Rare genius offers no exception, nor does the superior segment of intellectual capacity represented by the gifted children (Carmichael, 1934).

Results of Research and Emerging Problems, 1947–1953

In 1947 the study of gifted children reached the end of an important chapter with the publication of Terman and Oden's *The Gifted Child Grows Up*. Before the second world war research with gifted children had attracted numerous investigators.

In 15 years (1927–1941) the *Psychological Abstracts* listed 113 publications in this area, averaging 7.5 studies per year. In the next 5-year period the war influence was no doubt responsible for some reduction in publication. However, in 5 years (1942–1946) 30 publications were listed regarding the gifted, averaging 6 titles per year. Then, in 1947, came Terman's volume, and in the next 5-year period (1948–1952) no more than 10 publications of research results were reported, averaging 2 per year. Perhaps many potential investigators felt that the Stanford study had dealt so broadly and fully with the major problems as formulated that little remained unexplored in the field as previously outlined. The Stanford study had not only built a reliable foundation of sound and dependable factual data, but by careful design this masterpiece of research had now in 25 years of continuing study answered the basic questions posed earlier in the enthusiasm and in the clear light of the psychologies and the statistics of the 1920's. A review at this point of the Terman and Oden report affords the best opportunity for gaining a comprehensive view of the major problems posed, the facts established, and the conclusions and interpretations reached during the important period of research in which study of the gifted flourished as a significant development. Terman was especially qualified by experience and interest to leadership in this period. He was uniquely prepared to utilize effectively mental test instruments from the earliest phase of their development. His sustained enthusiasm, painstaking and indefatigable labor through years of detailed data gathering were shared by his loyal and accurately trained research staff. The gifted subjects, 1528 in number, their parents and other relatives, and their teachers collaborated over the years thoughtfully and effectively. The results present a unique contribution to research.

In the following pages the reviewer attempts to summarize the major conclusions of this important volume. Thereafter, other pertinent research reports of the late 1940's and early 1950's are briefly brought into view. The trends in research suggested and issuing from the combined material emerge to point out possibilities in new directions.

The Terman and Oden volume brings together the available data on which to base an answer to Terman's question formulated in 1921: "In what respects does the typical gifted child differ from the typical child of normal mentality?" If the pertinent question of the 1950's finds a new phrasing one may readily concede that Terman's great work has contributed largely to effective restatement.

No brief review can do justice to the tremendous Terman-Oden study. Its 400 pages of detailed reporting contain a complete report of the work to date. Following the original plan for the research, the composition and social origin of the gifted groups are set forth, and conclusions are briefly and objectively formulated and statistically confirmed from the results of ratings and measures of traits, characteristics, achievements, and interests. Data from the cross-sectional studies of 1921–1923, 1927, 1936, 1940, and 1945 are brought together topically. The subject matter includes the older and the newer material combined in a comprehensive treatment covering background, vital statistics, general health and physique, mental health and adjustment, and intelligence and achievement test results. The distinctly new studies cover intellectual status in adulthood, educational histories, occupational status and earned income, war records, vocational and avocational interests, interest test data, political and social attitudes, marriage and marital adjustment, and information with statistics regarding spouses and offspring. The final emphasis is on status after 25 years of continuing study of this large group selected in childhood in terms of high IQ. Chapters are devoted to the highest IQ's of all (170+), of whom there are 81; to the Jewish gifted, numbering 122; and to a comparison between the most and least "successful" of the gifted men, with an illuminating comparison of some of them with American Rhodes Scholars.

The work of Terman and his associates probably stands alone in the history of research for its accomplishment of a planned study in verification of stated hypotheses, requiring the cooperation of more than 1500 exceptional human subjects in repeated reports and evaluations and extending over a 25-year period. In consequence of the excellence and accuracy of the data gathering and the promptness of reporting, some of the more significant results of this study became a cornerstone in psychology as early as 1925. In 1940 a preview of the adult status outlined the chief conclusions regarding achievement now amply confirmed by the detailed field study of 1945. The whole volume in its thorough coverage and statistical completeness testifies to the objective sincerity of the research.

From the findings the following significant results point up fundamental facts and relationships.

1. School children representative of the top 1 per cent of tested intelligence are as a group superior in other respects as well. They rate far above the average in physique, social adjustment, personality traits, school achievement, play information, and versatility of interests.

2. From childhood to maturity the gifted have continued to rate above average in health. The mortality rate has never

reached the average expectancy for their age. Serious maladjustment has occurred less frequently in this group than in the general population. As adults the gifted are normal or superior in marital status and sexual adjustment. Their social and political attitudes are not deviant. Their war records are creditable, in many cases distinguished.

3. The gifted have been accelerated in school to an extent amounting to 1 year or a little more at high school graduation. Acceleration has proved to be associated with superior academic achievement, with more extensive college training, and with exceptional adult "success." It has not usually proved to be a handicap to social participation or personal adjustment.

4. In school achievement the gifted have been superior at every educational level. Many have remarkable educational records. Yet, as the authors point out, it is noteworthy that, contrary to the general trend, many individuals have failed to achieve academically at the level of their predicted competence.

5. Close to 90 per cent of the gifted have attended college, and almost 70 per cent are college graduates. Of the men 68 per cent and of the women 60 per cent have completed some graduate university work. This record greatly exceeds the average among whom these individuals attended public schools in childhood.

6. In tested intelligence, the group as adults average about 1.0 SD above the average of college students, and about 2.0 to 2.5 SD above the average of the general population. Half of the gifted are very close to (probably within 4 percentiles of) their original top status. Forty per cent have slipped somewhat more, although two-thirds of the group as a whole scored above the ninety-second percentile. Some 10 per cent have regressed to the

eighty-fifth percentile or lower, as compared to adults in general.

7. In excellence in preparation and in vocational achievement the gifted are outstanding. Compared to any like-sized random selection of young adults the group as a whole has now produced many times the expected number of leaders in business and of competent professional men in engineering, law, medicine, college teaching, and other specialties. The least successful fifth of the gifted sample includes a few individuals seriously hampered by poor health or poor personal adjustment. The majority members even of this fifth, although less outstanding than the other four-fifths, compare favorably in their adult accomplishments with average college graduates.

8. The highest IQ's (170+) equaled or exceeded the gifted group as a whole in many respects. In college their records were more distinguished and more of them advanced farther in graduate study. As adults the men of the group achieved more notably. The highest IQ men have been about as well adjusted as the total gifted group; the women, perhaps somewhat less so.

9. The subjects of Jewish descent, although more often coming from homes of lower status than the average among the gifted, have surpassed the gifted Gentiles in achieving higher educational and occupational status. Relatively more of them have reached notable achievement as adults.

The presentation of data and discussions culminating in the important conclusions here briefly summarized is followed by a comparison of the "most successful" fifth of the gifted men with the "least successful." This comparison in terms of adult achievement gives concrete form to Terman's concept of "gifted" and brings his once-designated "geniuses and near-geniuses" into readily understood and easily classified categories of the American economic, occupational, and educational structures. (For definitions and details of the comparison see especially Chapters 13–15, Terman and Oden, 1947.)

The "most successful", Group A, include outstanding young professional men, business executives, and specialists in the creative arts and in industry. They are compared, in many respects favorably, with American Rhodes Scholars of similar age.

scores are relatively high, although significantly lower than those of Group A. Their average is 0.8 SD above the means of Stanford University student samples.[2]

Comparative results for the two groups appear, as reported in 1940, in Table 8 above. Although selected in terms of adult achievement they show some interesting differences in early development, family background, traits, and relationships. Besides many small differences between Groups A and C some important contrasts are as

TABLE 13

STANFORD-BINET IQ's IN CHILDHOOD AND ADULT CONCEPT MASTERY SCORES
OF GIFTED GROUPS

Data from L. M. Terman and M. H. Oden, *The Gifted Child Grows Up*,
Stanford University Press, 1947.

Gifted Groups

	Group A Males *	Group C Males ‡	Jewish Group Males †	Gifted † Total Males	Total Females
No. of cases	96	92	71	577	493
Childhood Stanford-Binet IQ score average	155.0	150.0	152.7	151.5	150.4
CR		3.0			
No. of cases	79	116	56	527	427
Adult concept mastery score average	112.4	94.1	102.9	98.1	93.9
CR		4.2			

Occupational status: * very superior; † superior; ‡ above average.

In adult intelligence score they rate as a group some 2.0 SD above Stanford University students [1] (Table 13).

The "least successful," Group C, are for the most part men of undistinguished achievement, engaged in relatively mediocre pursuits. Their adult intelligence

[1] R. L. Thorndike (1948) further defines this adult intelligence rating by an ingenious comparison utilizing a method of test conversion involving an adult Gallup Poll, a group of students from colleges in New York City ($N = 198$), and a smaller group ($N = 53$) of Co-

follows: The A's rated in childhood as more stable emotionally; their social adjustments and significant personality traits

lumbia doctoral candidates and a few instructors. The gifted men, Group A, rate close to the ninety-eighth percentile of both the poll and the college students. They average in score about 0.5 SD below the mean of the doctoral group.

[2] The average adult score of Group C is above the ninety-sixth percentile of Thorndike's poll and above the ninetieth percentile of his college students. Their mean is about 1.1 SD below that of his doctoral group.

were regarded as more favorable; there are fewer "only" children among them. The personality differences increased in adolescence. In early adulthood appreciably more C's than A's appeared nervous and emotionally unstable. Through the high school years the A's had better scholastic records and engaged in more extracurricular activities than the C's. At college age the educational and activity differences were marked. Although the average physical health ratings of the two groups showed little divergence, the A's rated as more energetic in their interests, and more active in social organizations and pursuits. In educational and occupational accomplishment the A's drew farther and farther away from the C's from the early high school period onward. The C's suffered more background disabilities, especially broken homes including divorce or separation of the parents or death of the father. In marriage and marital adjustments the A's excelled. Their spouses were more intelligent, more highly educated, and came from families of higher educational status. In the appraisals of 1945 the A's (judged by their parents, their wives, and themselves) rated appreciably higher than the C's in absence of inferiority feelings, and significantly so in self-confidence, perseverance, and integration toward goals.

Reviewing these differences it appears that the A's deviate in the same direction from the generality as the total gifted sample, and they deviate somewhat more. They are a fairly homogeneous group of well-adjusted, extremely able adults who were once extremely high IQ children. The C's deviate in the same direction as the gifted sample with respect to high test score in intelligence as children and (though relatively less so) as adults, more advanced schooling, and higher adult employment status. But the C's are apparently a more heterogeneous group. Some are unstable,

with more than average "nervous" signs and ratings of poor adjustment; "only" children are relatively more numerous among them. Handicaps in terms of parental divorce and the early decease of their fathers are more frequent in this group. But the disadvantages associated with lower social home status appear to present the outstanding factor or handicap. Were more of the C's than of the A's overrated in childhood test scores? As youngsters they were quick, and alert mentally in the test situations, but as time has gone on they have not so highly developed the traits of perseverance and integration toward goals characterizing the success Group A. There are implications that some members of Group C are simply well-adjusted lower-middle-class workers who for various good reasons have found congenial skilled or semiskilled employment and have not tried, or have not succeeded if they did attempt, to escape from the social, economic, and domestic groove of their childhood rearing.

In conclusion Terman states that his total sample includes some 20 or 25 men of science "who have either achieved, or appear likely to achieve, a national reputation among their kind"; a number of talented writers; and a dozen or more outstanding medical men and lawyers. Among the currently highly successful financial and industrial operators may be some who will achieve national distinction. With respect to these and others less notable in their accomplishment he has this to say: "We do not . . . know whether they are more happy or less happy than the average person in the generality. We do know that they are better fed, better housed, and better doctored than the average person, that they are in a position to care better for their children, and that they have less reason generally to be anxious about the future."

Investigators familiar with the problems he had to face will agree with Terman that, "considering the scope of the investigation, the limited funds, and the status of psychological methodology at various stages of the research," there is "little to regret regarding the choice of devices, rating schemes, case-history procedures, and other techniques employed." The methods used in selecting subjects "provided a fairly representative population of high IQ's." The methods developed for following the subjects have led to clear-cut and valuable results.

Plans for the future outlined by Terman and Oden include further following of the group, testing all, if possible, of their offspring in intelligence and school achievement, and the gifted themselves at intervals with more adequate intelligence tests than have been hitherto employed. Personality studies are outlined: tests of marital adjustment, psychiatric studies and projective tests, tests of primary personality traits, and somatotypes. The possibilities are great, the authors conclude, and financial limitations should not curtail further essential developments.

The IQ has proved to be an effective selector, and the factual picture of the "gifted" in American culture is viewed by many, especially practical educationists, as a valuable and useful construct. This construct science owes chiefly to the wisdom and perseverance of L. M. Terman. The Stanford data and the goodwill of the gifted subjects afford rich material and possibilities for the further studies projected.

Other Gifted Research

Other investigations reported in the late 1940's and early 1950's follow the same general pattern in emphasizing the superiority of the high IQ's in traits, accomplish-

ments, and promise of adult achievement. Parkyn's (1948) excellent volume reports similar conditions and results for the gifted in New Zealand, adding also suggestive discussion of background factors and an analysis of successes and failures of his superior subject group in the subtests of the Terman-Merrill Binet. Lightfoot's (1951) comparison of superior with retarded children in a New York City school shows the significant advantage of the gifted over the retarded in the traits and conditions measured. This study effectively utilizes Murray's behavioral classification. Ausubel's (1951) well-thought-out development of a technique for measuring prestige motivation indirectly points to general gifted superiority in his group while serving as a pilot effort in the area of social attitude.

R. L. Thorndike (1948) has made a contribution, already referred to, pointing up an inferential corollary of Terman's work: that the gifted label in childhood although favorable is not definitive for superior adult intelligence test status. To Terman's estimate of the regressed mean of the adult gifted as IQ 140 and McNemar's estimate of IQ 134 Thorndike adds his appraisal approximating IQ 128. Thorndike's work brings the Concept Mastery Test developed and employed by Terman into a comparable, if crude, approximation with other scales by equating results for the gifted with other adult intelligence norms. His data afford the basis for a graphic presentation of the score trends in the maturing gifted group. For illustration in this review we have plotted (Figure 1) smoothed approximate paths of score decline from childhood to adulthood of the 30, 50, 67, 87, 99.6, and 99.9 percentiles of Terman's group who when first tested scored within or close to the top 1 per cent on available IQ scales. Position on the Stanford Concept Mastery Test is given in terms of adult test score explicable by

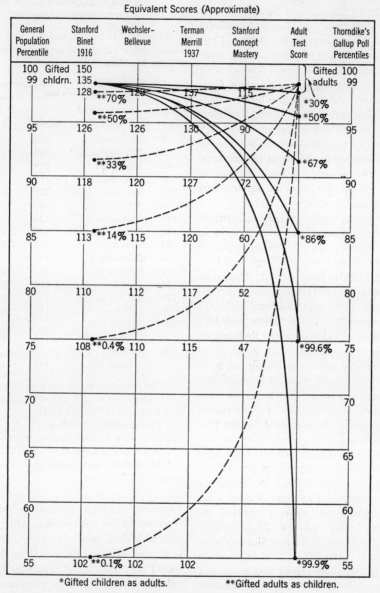

FIGURE 1. Paradigm of gains and losses in IQ from childhood to young adulthood.

comparison with Thorndike's adult Gallup Poll group. Thus, 30 per cent of the formerly gifted children may be said to rate as adults within the top 2 per cent of adults in general, 50 per cent within the top 4 per cent, two-thirds within the top 8 per cent, 86 per cent within the upper 15 per cent. These scale positions on the Stanford Concept Mastery Scale are graphically compared with Stanford-Binet 1916, Wechsler-Bellevue, and Terman-Merrill 1937 IQ's by the use of reported percentile positions on those scales. A paradigm of this type is, of course, crude. Its possible value is in emphasis on the need for further and more dependable measures.

In the same figure hypothetical curves are drawn indicating the possible gain in IQ from childhood to maturity as reported by, among others, Terman, Lorge, and Hollingworth (1936), Keys (1940), Thorndike (1948), and Bayley (1949). These investigators have shown that childhood high IQ's do not account for all the known high IQ's in adulthood. Various causes and factors have been proposed to account for IQ gains with increasing age. Technical faults in test construction, inequalities in social and educational experience, physical and mental changes, and alterations in maturational rates are among the suggested factors producing not only the possibilities for decline demonstrated by Terman but also the perhaps equally important possibilities for rise in IQ from childhood to adolescence or later as suggested in many studies.

Some intelligence ratings reported by Simon and Levitt from the Columbia University Vocational Guidance files are relevant (Table 14). These lend support to some very old assumptions that adult test scores correlate with occupational training, experience, and achievement (sometimes in contrast to childhood ratings) while some individuals of superior test intelligence continue to be found in almost every oc-

TABLE 14

WECHSLER-BELLEVUE IQ's OF ADULT OCCUPATIONAL GROUPS

From L. M. Simon and E. A. Levitt, IQ scores and occupational area, *Occupations*, *29*, 24 and 25, 1950.

No. Cases	Occupational Group	Wechsler-Bellevue Scores		
		Median	Q3	90%
52	Engineers	133	135	140
52	Professional I *	132	134	137
45	Educators †	129	134	137
61	Professional II ‡	128	133	138
421	Teachers	126	132	137
66	Social service	125	132	135
134	Managers	125	130	136
191	Nurses	124	128	132
62	Arts §	124	131	138
153	Salesmen ‖	122	128	132
107	Secretarial	121	125	130
55	Bookkeepers	117	125	129
128	Clerks	116	122	131
62	Office workers	116	123	128
107	Skilled laborers ¶	115	123	127
57	Personal service	106	113	122

* Physicians, dentists, lawyers.
† College deans and instructors, high school and grammar school principals.
‡ Pharmacists, accountants.
§ Singers, musicians, actors, artists, etc.
‖ Wholesale and retail.
¶ Machinists, mechanics, plumbers, electricians.

cupation. Army General Classification Test scores for occupational groups are in line with these results (Stewart, 1947).

Studies of the educational needs of the gifted and reviews of facilities and programs for meeting them complement Terman's findings with respect to the schooling of the gifted, outlining programs to meet some of the conditions his data have so clearly indicated. The *Education of the*

Gifted published by the Educational Policies Commission (1950) reviews problems pertinent to study of the gifted: the rôle of the gifted in a democracy, waste of talent in American life, identification of the gifted, education of the gifted, investment in talent, and an able summing up of the educational challenge in leadership training. The special needs of the "gifted" top percentile and the "moderately gifted" upper 10 per cent are now too often neglected, the Commission specialists conclude. Consideration of the exceptional learning capacity and competence of the groups likely to include many more than their share of specialists and leaders is seen here as essential to increasingly adequate development of human resources.

The Gifted Child edited by Paul Witty (1951) is a useful compendium for teachers of superior children and for educators generally. Prepared under the sponsorship of the American Association for Gifted Children this volume contains 14 reports by individual specialists or groups of educators who present here their conclusions after years of study and experience in dealing with the training of gifted children. The editor outlines the history of the education of the gifted in the United States and surveys current educational practices and provisions for the gifted in elementary and secondary schools. Terman and Oden describe the Stanford Studies, and Pritchard brings together the contributions of Hollingworth. The qualities and preparation desirable in teachers of the gifted are discussed by Ryan, Strang, and Witty. Hobbs writes on community recognition of the gifted, and W. Davis discusses the science talent search. Other topics discussed are methods of identifying gifted children, observations of gifted and talented children in clinics and schools, a high school of science for gifted students, the mental hygiene of gifted children, and school administrative problems in educating the gifted. A summary and recommendations by the editor are followed by an annotated bibliography. Although this volume presents little original research it is a valuable compilation of studies summarizing current attitudes and practices with many thoughtful suggestions and insights from specialists teaching in this field.

Contribution of Research on the Gifted to Related Areas of Investigation

Detailed study of groups of extremely gifted deviates has done more than set up a picture of the "most successful" members of their class. It has, as already noted, verified the usefulness of the IQ technique for early selection of groups likely to include many of those capable of superior development and achievement under existing conditions in our prevailing culture. In doing this it has also indicated that the IQ test does not serve as a magnetized needle, far less as a divining rod, pointing without fail at some innate potential. The studies of the gifted thus lend support to the view that although IQ tests do tend to measure present ability they are probably far from accurate as indicators of native capacity (Cronbach, 1949; Hebb, 1949).

The study of the gifted has further brought to light many of the conditions associated with the appearance of more rather than less high IQ children in a group or community. These results may be compared with the findings of Eells *et al.* (1951) relating IQ scores directly to social class. The high IQ scores of private school children are another indication of the same or a related phenomenon (*Educational Records Bulletin*, 1950). See Table 15. The studies of the gifted have revealed many of the conditions under which, given high IQ's in childhood,

TABLE 15

INTELLIGENCE TEST SCORES OF SCHOOL CHILDREN FROM HIGH AND LOW
SOCIAL CLASS GROUPS *

	Social Class	No. Children	Mean IQ	SD	CR	Per Cent Scoring 130 IQ+
Henmon-Nelson Test (ages 9–10)	1. High status old American	226	115.8	16.2	1 and 2 12.6	19.5
	2. Low status old American	322	98.4	15.7	2 and 3 0.8	1.9
	3. Low status ethnic	143	97.1	15.7	1 and 3 11.0	2.1
Terman-McNemar Test (ages 13–14)	1. High status old American	233	114.9	13.1	1 and 2 18.3	12.9
	2. Low status old American	361	93.0	15.8	2 and 3 0.9	0.8
	3. Low status ethnic	151	91.6	16.3	1 and 3 14.8	0.7
Kuhlmann-Anderson Test (ages 9 and 10)	1. High status old American	228	107.9		1 and 2 11.7	
	2. Low status old American	329	97.3		2 and 3 0.3	
	3. Low status ethnic	146	96.9		1 and 3 9.3	
Kuhlmann-Anderson Test (ages 4–17)	Independent schools 1940–1949	59,708	120.8			23.4

* Data on Henmon-Nelson Test, Terman-McNemar Test and Kuhlmann-Anderson Test (ages 9 and 10) are from Eells *et al.*, 1951. *Intelligence and cultural differences.* University of Chicago Press, Tables 20 and 21. Data on Kuhlmann-Anderson Test (ages 4–17) are from Educational Records Bureau. 1950. 1949 fall testing program in independent schools. *Educ. Rec. Bull.*, No. 53.

high levels of adult achievement are likely to be attained. The evidence that the IQ test becomes an increasingly adequate selector as the favorable or unfavorable factors or conditions accumulate is in line with the view that the intellectual abilities tapped by the test are typical products of the cumulative cultural learning. The results in gifted study are, so far, group results. With respect to individuals the conditions, as in all genetic and child psychology, are seen to be multiple and complex, indicative of intricate biological and social factors, tendencies, and interrelationships.

Further treatment of data already gathered and in part reported may uncover further leads. For example: The Stanford data have been searched and categorized to picture a "success" group reported above and rated in terms of "the extent to which a subject had made use of his superior intellectual ability." These terms were interpreted to include the brilliance of the academic record, the achievement of listing in *American Men of Science* and *Who's Who*, successful professional standing as college teachers, lawyers, medical men, engineers, and business men, with the additional choice of a few outstanding young figures in literature, art, motion pictures, or radio. The specifications are those recognized as describing midcentury American success at the upper economic level perhaps slightly overweighted in the direction of science. Other types of success perhaps less brilliant but no less interesting and potentially valuable might be defined within the gifted group. The gifted who most fully utilize their intellectual abilities and their opportunities to become skilled or semiskilled workers or those whose circumstances and interests lead them into the clerical field may also prove to be significantly identifiable in terms of the conditions of their backgrounds and experience. Even the gifted women offer problems for further analysis in terms of data already gathered. The direction of their interests and efforts toward professional, housewifely, or combined goals may well be associated with factors and conditions already recorded and identifiable.

The studies of the gifted as they now stand and without further amplification lend support to a number of views or hypotheses in four currently active areas of research.

1. Research on the gifted may have somatic implications. Derivation from sound somatic stock, favorable nurture in infancy, the earliest (and later) personal associations and interrelationships with stable and generally well-adjusted people, freedom from nervous symptomatology and personal maladjustment—these are conditions and factors found to prevail among the gifted and to be most frequent among

those who continue to develop favorably from childhood onward. The hypothesis that superior innate somatic potentials will tend to become manifest in identifiably superior child personalities is supported by these data. Confirmation is also rendered to the view that favorable conditions increase the tendency for superior behavior to emerge and to maintain its superior developmental level and direction. Are there individuals of greatly superior innate potentialities who by reason of unfavorable prenatal or postnatal conditions fail to develop, in the behavioral channel available, the abilities that will register as of high IQ level and the personalities generally associated with them? Biological and psychoanalytic studies suggest that the answer is "yes." The gifted studies offer little direct evidence with respect to this aspect of the problem. Relevant to the problem of negative outcome for superior individuals, labeled as gifted, are the case studies of once superior individuals who were eventually disrupted emotionally under adverse conditions and disastrous relationships (Burks *et al.*, 1930; Terman and Oden, 1947).

2. Research on the gifted has implications for social psychology. These studies lend support to the view that rôles and goals associated with superior social class are readily acquired by individuals of high IQ and tend to become for them relatively comfortable and flexible channels for social and vocational behavior. The hypothesis that high IQ is an asset in rôle and goal acceptance and in upward social mobility is supported by the data. The hypothesis that easy access to rôles and goals of high social value is an asset in gifted achievement is also supported. The view that high IQ is always an asset even where rôles and goals conflict, as, for example, in the highest IQ women, is not clearly supported by the data. The hypothesis that for many

gifted individuals familial rôles and goals prevail over high IQ in determining life pattern and achievement is supported (Terman and Oden, 1947).

3. Research on the gifted may have implications for studies in motivation. The identifiable physical and personal adjustment factors favorable for the development of exceptionally high test achievement and gifted behavior plus the social class background and experience in which appropriate rôles and goals are learned may to some readers seem sufficiently to account for the emergence of gifted individuals. But the favorable factors still fail to correlate fully with the observed results. And so further measurable variables are still to be sought. Recorded case studies of individual success and achievement at the gifted level suggest the relevance of subcultural or familial contributions in terms of life patterns with typical goals and motivations. The report of the Jewish gifted in the Stanford study supports a hypothesis of a motivational pattern developed in parent-child interrelationships in American Jewish families with gifted children. The gifted Jewish children although coming from relatively lower social class background than the group as a whole emerge with higher IQ ratings in childhood and eventually with higher adult intelligence scores and higher professional and business status than the Gentile gifted. Individual case studies, Gentile as well as Jewish, illustrate diverse home atmospheres and subcultural goals specific in certain groups and tending to develop motivations favorable perhaps to limitation of objectives and rather certainly to excessive exertion toward ends contributing to high IQ scores, to superior school work, and eventually to superior adult achievement (Terman and Oden, 1947). Attitudes of success and failure have been shown to influence intelligence test scores (Lantz,

1945). Under the impetus of motivation to achieve higher military status above-average groups have raised their standing as much as 22 percentiles (Schlesser, 1950). On the negative side, unfavorable home situations, financial limitations and resulting conflicts, parental rejection, sibling rivalry, and especially lack of favorable parental involvement in the gifted child's progress and welfare have been associated with falling IQ, poor school work, and eventually less than optimal adult achievement (Burks et al., 1930; Carlson, 1945). Favorable personality changes have resulted from understanding guidance at school and from special types of therapy (Margolies, 1946). Favorable parental attitudes, encouragement, and even sacrifice in conditions of poverty, family solidarity, involvement in the child's progress with varying degrees of pressure, development and maintenance of family interests and customs and of a family tradition rooted realistically in shared family experience, thoughtful consideration by the parents of the welfare and the capabilities of the child —various combinations of these tendencies appear to function as stimulators in the learning and the rôle-taking and may eventually operate, sometimes quite powerfully, toward accepted goals of achievement. The Fels researches include in their design attempts to measure some of these variables. Their results suggest that individual parental attitudes and home climate as differentiated from social class rôle-learning and identification can be measured. An early finding in these investigations that parental behavior indicative of freedom, of emotional warmth, and of acceleratory methods are related to early change in developmental status has been supported by further work. The investigators report that a democratic-acceptant attitude is conducive to mental development. When, in addition, the parental attitude is nonindulgent it is conducive to intellectual growth in all its aspects (Baldwin *et al.*, 1945). Measurement of parent behavior by the Fels (Baldwin *et al.*, 1949) or similar scales seems to offer excellent possibilities for defining an additional variable or variables operating in gifted development.

4. Specific situations. The gifted may have achieved their original high IQ scores in consequence of chance factors operating favorably. In the further development of every one of them the special and unique circumstances of their lives continue to operate as stimulators or repressors of the potentials for superior utilization of their superior capabilities, their familial advantages, and their social privileges. In individual instances ill health, financial loss, or a sense of insecurity or inferiority has sometimes acted as a spur to achievement. Detailed biographies and especially autobiographies indicate the varied contributions of innumerable small incidents affecting the course of a life history. In the gifted, so far as reported, the record shows usually cumulative good luck as compared with the generality, but additional specific factors may emerge under further and more detailed scrutiny (Terman and Oden, 1947; Parkyn, 1948). A valuable individual contribution to the understanding of many problems of gifted children is found in the fascinating autobiography of Norbert Wiener (1953). In this volume the cultural and familial background of a prodigy and his remembered experiences in childhood and youth are clearly depicted. Parental forcing is described with sympathetic understanding of a frustrated though able scholar-father who sought self-expression through the achievement of his bright and responsive son. The careers of other contemporary gifted children variously and probably in most instances unreasonably pushed by their parents further illustrate the interaction with precocity of mental and physical vigor, personality traits, and family acceptance of assets and limitations.

The Emerging Personality Patterns of the Gifted

The Stanford gifted as a group are reported living their lives a little more happily and being themselves a little better adjusted, as well as more intelligent, than the average as evidenced in their handling of their personal problems and interrelationships. Otherwise, as far as we know them from Terman, they carry on within the typical American framework and are identified with the typical interests of occupation and social class. Insufficient data are available to trace patterns, styles, or modes of life and development differentiating high IQ variants from other people whom they resemble in social origin, family tradition, etc. Are there tendencies, associated with giftedness, for restriction in some respects and expansion in others of the personality potentials? Roe's studies (1949, 1951) of exceptional adults suggest that by means of projective techniques it may be possible to determine styles of inhibitions and of cultivation of tendencies within accepted rôles characterizing the emerging personalities of people including the gifted, in various walks of life. If and when factor analysis is effectively developed in studies of the gifted and their offspring the results may be expected to clarify the interrelationships of conditions now vaguely perceived.

Research is, of course, limited by the availability of material—in this area, gifted subjects. Terman has achieved access to a large group of gifted individuals, winning their interest and cooperation in a continuing investigation. The protection of individual personal freedom and of anonymity has been an important feature of the relationship. The sharing of interest in the research by the subjects may eventually make possible cooperation in detailed case studies. If these could be prepared at various stages under the direction of specialists from the different areas of research converging in human personality study they would illuminate many aspects in the complex cluster of problems involved. Furthermore, they might suggest leads for new theory. The studies themselves need not be published in early stages of the investigation. They could be preserved and used as confidential material by qualified scientists working together at a center for research on the gifted. Methodological approaches are opening from many directions, and the scientific horizon is widening around the problems of personality. The availability of the gifted group and their offspring should be protected and further utilized.

The problem of terminology is still puzzling. The Stanford group and others studied are largely high IQ groups. Among them the very intelligent (highly able to function in terms of the central factor in the test) have not been differentiated from the pseudo-intelligent (who owe their perhaps equally high scores to a considerable extent to chance successes or to more or less unrelated abilities) (Magaret and Thompson, 1950). The gifted label has been achieved by varying degrees of superiority at different ages (Cronbach, 1949). Children talented in the arts or in manipulative skills have been little studied. The term "gifted" although widely adopted is also widely questioned, as it appears to derive from an assumption of innate potential or potentials still largely inferential. Even granted the assumption, the conditions of emergence, so far as they appear to have been revealed, are so diversely operative that actually the gifted label may be acquired in childhood by only a fraction of those of equal potential ability.

Conclusion

More and less gifted individuals continue to appear in every age group and in every population. It has now been demonstrated beyond question that persons selected by test as of high IQ at a young age will tend to continue to maintain their high status at later ages. IQ sifting is useful. But it is far from final for achievement prediction. Culture, home and school opportunity, health, and motivation have proved to be factors favorable to superior development in intellect and personality. These factors correlate with IQ, but they are, so far, insufficient fully to account for either intelligence score or demonstrated talents. Gifted children as a group are superior to average children in many respects among which high IQ is but one. Further elucidation of the high IQ or the gifted problem will necessitate comparison of groups homogeneous with respect to other traits and differing only with respect to the one in question. In the meantime detailed individual studies will continue to give helpful suggestions as to the factors that may be involved. The most favorable and appropriate opportunities for the development of every child will tend to clarify the problem, while at the same time fostering the emergence of optimal talents in a maximum number of those potentially most highly gifted.

Bibliography

Adams, F., and W. Brown. 1930. *Teaching the bright pupil.* New York: Holt.

Adams, F. J. 1940. College degrees and elementary school intelligence quotients. *J. Educ. Psychol., 31,* 360-368.

Alltucker, M. M. 1924. Is the pedagogically accelerated student a misfit in the senior high school? *Sch. Rev., 32,* 193-202.

Alpern, H. 1939. Educating the superior student in the high schools of New York City. *J. Educ. Psychol., 13,* 112–119.

Atkins, H. A. 1929. The gifted child and his teachers. *Ment. Hyg., N. Y., 13,* 719–739.

Austin, M. 1925. *Everyman's genius.* Indianapolis: Bobbs Merrill.

Ausubel, D. P. 1951. Prestige motivation of gifted children. *Genet. Psychol. Monogr., 43,* 53–116.

Baer, M. V. 1939. How St. Louis schools serve their bright pupils. *Nat. Educ. Ass. J., 28,* 121.

Baisch, H. 1939. Wahrsinn oder Wahnsinn der Genius? *Beih. Z. angew. Psychol.,* No. 85.

Baker, H. J. 1927. *Characteristic differences in bright and dull pupils.* Bloomington, Ill.: Public School Publishing Co,

Baldwin, A. L., J. Kalhorn, and F. H. Breese. 1945. Patterns of parent behavior. *Psychol. Monogr., 58,* No. 268, 1–75.

——. 1949. The appraisal of parent behavior. *Psychol. Monogr., 63,* No. 4, 1–85.

Baldwin, B. T. 1924. Methods of selecting superior or gifted children. *Yearb. Nat. Soc. Stud. Educ.,* 23(I), 25–47.

Baldwin, B. T., and T. D. Wood. 1923. *Weight-height-age tables.* (Tables for boys and girls of school age.) Washington, D. C., American Child Health Association.

Baumgarten, F. 1930. *Wunderkinder. Psychologische Untersuchungen:* VIII. Leipzig: Barth.

Bayley, N. 1949. Consistency and variability in the growth of intelligence. *J. Genet. Psychol., 75,* 165–196.

Beckham, A. S. 1942. A study of social background and music ability of superior Negro children. *J. Appl. Psychol., 26,* 210–217.

——. 1942. A study of social background and art aptitude of superior Negro children. *J. Appl. Psychol., 26,* 777–784.

Bentley, J. E. 1937. *Superior children.* New York: Norton.

Berkhan, O. 1910a. Otto Pöhler, das frühlesende Braunschweiger Kind. *Z. Kinderforsch., 15,* 166–171.

——. 1910b. Das Wunderkind Christian Heinrich Heineken. *Z. Kinderforsch., 15,* 225–229.

Berman, A. B., and A. Klein. 1942. A personality study of maladjusted pupils of superior mentality. *High Points, 24,* 57–63.

Bessen, M. 1934. *Suggestibility of normal and abnormal school children.* Unpublished Master's Thesis, Columbia University.

Biber, B., and C. Lewis. 1949. An experimental study of what young school children expect from their teachers. *Genet. Psychol. Monogr., 40,* 3–97.

Binet, A. 1909. La psychologie artistique de Tade Styka. *Année psychol., 15,* 316–356.

Blair, G. M. 1938. Mentally superior and inferior children in the junior and senior high school; a comparative study of their backgrounds, interests and ambitions. *Teach. Coll. Contr. Educ.,* No. 766.

Boodstein, O. 1909. Frühreife Kinder. Psychologische Studie. *(Beitr. Kinderforsch. u. Heilerziehung, 61.)* Langansalza, Beyer.

Bowerman, W. G. 1947. *Studies in genius.* New York: Philosophical Library.

Braun, O. 1920. *Aus den nachgelassenen Schriften eines Frühvollendeten.* (Ed. by J. Vogelstein.) Berlin: Cassirer.

Bridgeman, D. S. 1930. Success in college and business. *Person. J., 9,* 1–19.

Bridgman, A. S. 1938. *My valuable time.* Brattleboro, Vt.: Stephen Daye Press.

Brim, O. G. 1952. *Ability and achievement: Summary of selected research on gifted children* (mimeographed). Social Science Research Council—Markle Fund Project, Cultural Factors in Talent Development under the direction of F. L. Strodtbeck, Yale University.

Brown, A. W. 1926. The unevenness of the abilities of dull and bright children. *Teach. Coll. Contr. Educ.,* No. 220.

Brown, G. L. 1950. On the constancy of the IQ. *J. Educ. Res., 44,* 151–153.

Brown, M. V. 1949. Teaching an intellectually gifted group. *Elem. Sch. J., 49,* 380–88.

Bruce, J. A. 1911. New ideas in child training. *Amer. Mag., 72,* 286–294.

——. 1912. Lightning calculators. *McClure's Mag., 39,* 586–596.

Bruner, H. B. (Ed.) 1941. Some issues and problems raised by the Conference on Education for the Gifted. *Teach. Coll. Rec., 42,* 432–460.

Buckley, T. A. 1853. *The drawings of genius.* London: Routledge.

Burks, B. S. 1925. A scale of promise and its application to 71 nine-year-old gifted children. *Ped. Sem., 32,* 389–413.

Burks, B. S., D. W. Jensen, and L. M. Terman. 1930. *Genetic studies of genius:* Vol. III. *The promise of youth; follow-up studies of a thousand gifted children.* Stanford University, Calif.: Stanford University Press.

Burnside, L. H. 1942. Psychological guidance of gifted children. *J. Consult. Psychol., 6,* 223–228.

——. 1942. An experimental program in the education of the intellectually gifted adolescent. *School Rev., 50,* 274–285.

Bush, A. D. 1914. Binet-Simon tests of a thirty-nine-month-old child. *Psychol. Clinic, 7,* 250–257.

Carlson, E. F. 1945. Project for gifted children: a psychological evaluation. *Amer. J. Orthopsychiat., 15,* 648–61.

Carmichael, L. 1934. The psychology of genius. *Phi Kappa Phi J.,* 149–164.

Carroll, H. A. 1930. Generalization of bright and dull children: A comparative study with special reference to spelling. *Teach. Coll. Contr. Educ.,* No. 439.

——. 1940. *Genius in the making.* New York: McGraw-Hill.

——. 1940-1941. Intellectually gifted children. *Teach. Coll. Rec., 42,* 212–227.

Carroll, H. A., and L. S. Hollingworth. 1940. The systematic error of Herring-Binet in rating gifted children. *J. Educ. Psychol., 21,* 1–11.

Cattell, J. McK. 1915, 1917. Families of American men of science. *Pop. Sci. Mo., 86,* 504–515; *Sci. Mo., 4,* 248–262; *5,* 368–378.

——. 1927. The origin and distribution of scientific men. *Science, 66,* 513–516.

Cattell, P. 1933. Do the Stanford-Binet IQ's of superior boys and girls tend to decrease or increase with age? *J. Educ. Res., 26,* 668–673.

Cleveland, E. 1920. Detroit's experiment with gifted children. *Sch. and Soc., 12,* 179–183.

——. 1921. Some further studies of gifted children. *J. Educ. Res., 4,* 195–199.

Cobb, M. V., and L. S. Hollingworth. 1925. The regression of siblings of children who test at or above 135 IQ (Stanford-Binet). *J. Educ. Psychol., 16,* 1–7.

Cobb, M. V., and G. A. Taylor. 1924. Standard achievement tests with a group of gifted children. *Yearb. Nat. Soc. Stud. Educ.,* 23(I), 275–289.

Cohen, H. L., and N. G. Coryell. 1935. *Educating superior students.* New York: American Book.

Cohler, M. J. 1941. Scholastic status of achievers and nonachievers of superior intelligence. *J. Educ. Psychol., 32,* 603–610.

Collmann, R. D. 1931. The psychogalvanic reactions of exceptional and normal school children. *Teach. Coll. Contr. Educ.,* No. 469.

Conklin, A. M. 1940. Failures of highly intelligent pupils; a study of their behavior by means of a control group. *Teach. Coll. Contr. Educ.,* No. 792.

Cox, C. M. 1926. *Genetic studies of genius:* Vol. II, *The early mental traits of three hundred geniuses.* Stanford University, Calif.: Stanford University Press.

Cox, C. M. *See also* Miles, C. C.

Coy, G. L. 1918. The mentality of a gifted child. *J. Appl. Psychol., 2,* 299–307.

——. 1923. The interests, abilities and achievements of a special class for gifted children. *Teach. Coll. Contr. Educ.,* No. 131.

——. 1930. The daily programs of thirty gifted children. *J. Genet. Psychol., 37,* 123–138.

Cronbach, L. J. 1949. *Essentials of psychological testing.* New York: Harper.

Cutts, N. E., and N. Moseley. 1953. *Bright Children; a guide for parents.* New York: Putnam.

Danielson, C. L. 1929. A study of the effect of a definite course of reading in general literature upon achievement in content subjects with children of superior mental ability. *J. Educ. Psychol., 20,* 610–621.

——. 1931. Special classes for highly endowed children. *4th Yearb. Psychol. Educ. Res. Div.,* Los Angeles City Schools, 67–87.

Davidson, H. A. 1904. The gift of genius. *J. Ped., 16,* 281–297.

Davidson, H. H. 1943. *Personality and economic background; a study of highly intelligent children.* New York: King's Crown Press.

Davis, H. 1924. Personal and social characteristics of gifted children. *Yearb. Nat. Soc. Stud. Educ.,* 23(I), 123–144.

Dearborn, W. F., and P. Cattell. 1930. The intelligence and achievement of private-school pupils. *J. Educ. Psychol., 21,* 197–211.

DeCandolle, A. 1885. *Histoire des sciences et des savants depuis deux siècles.* Genève: Georg.

Department of Superintendence. 1931. How elementary and secondary schools are meeting the needs of individual pupils. *Yearb. Nat. Educ. Ass., 9,* 107–146.

DeVoss, J. C. 1925. Specialization of the abilities of gifted children. In L. M. Terman *et al., Genetic studies of genius:* Vol. I, *Mental and physical traits of a thousand gifted children.* Stanford University, Calif.: Stanford University Press.

Dolbear, K. E. 1912. Precocious children. *Ped. Sem., 19,* 461–491.

Dooley, L. 1916. Psychoanalytic studies of genius. *Amer. J. Psychol., 27,* 363–417.

Downes, F. E. 1912. Seven years with unusually gifted pupils. *Psychol. Clin., 6,* 13–18.

Drag, F. L. 1941. The gifted child: A report of practices in California cities. *Calif. J. Elem. Educ., 10,* 8–28.

Dransfield, J. E. 1933. Administration of enrichment to superior children in the typical classroom. *Teach. Coll. Contr. Educ.,* No. 558.

Duff, J. F. 1929. Children of high intelligence: A follow-up inquiry. *Brit. J. Psychol., 19,* 413–439.

Duff, J. F., and G. H. Thomson. 1923. The social and geographical distribution of intelligence in Northumberland. *Brit. J. Psychol., 14,* 192–198.

Dunlap, J. M. 1945. Testing the tops. *J. Except. Child., 11,* 142–46.

Durost, W. N. 1932. Children's collecting activity related to social factors. *Teach. Coll. Contr. Educ.,* No. 535.

Dvorak, A., and J. J. Rae. 1929. A comparison of the achievement of superior children in segregated and unsegregated first-grade classes. *Elem. Sch. J., 29,* 380–387.

Dvorak, H. D. 1923. The mental tests of a superior child. *Ment. Hyg., N. Y., 7,* 250–257.

Educational Policies Commission. 1950. *Education of the gifted.* Washington, D. C.: National Education Association of the United States.

Educational Records Bureau. 1940. 1939 fall testing program in independent schools. *Educ. Rec. Bull.,* No. 29.

——. 1943. 1942 fall testing program in independent schools. *Educ. Rec. Bull.,* No. 37.

——. 1950. 1949 fall testing program in independent schools. *Educ. Rec. Bull.,* No. 53.

Eells, K., A. Davis, R. J. Havighurst, V. E. Herrick, and R. Tyler. 1951. *Intelligence and cultural differences.* Chicago: University of Chicago Press.

Ellis, H. 1904. *A study of British genius.* London: Hurst and Blackett.

Ellwood, M. 1938. A descriptive study of a gifted child. *Pittsb. Schs. Bull.*, No. 12, 169–173.

Engle, T. L. 1935. Achievements of pupils who have had double promotions in elementary school. *Elem. Sch. J.*, *36*, 185–189.

Fenton, N., and L. S. Howard. 1924. The challenge of the private school. *J. Educ. Res.*, *9*, 22–28.

Finch, F. H. 1946. Enrollment increases and changes in the mental level of the high-school population. *Appl. Psychol. Monogr.*, *10*, 1–75.

——. 1948. The gifted child. *Understanding the Child*, *17*, 33–64.

Finch, F. H., and H. A. Carroll. 1932. Gifted children as high-school leaders. *J. Genet. Psychol.*, *41*, 476–481.

Foster, E. M., and E. H. Martens. 1938. Statistics of special schools and classes for exceptional children. (Biennial Survey of Education in the United States: 1934–1936, Vol. II, Chap. VI.) [*Bull. U. S. Dept. Interior*, 1937, No. 2 (advance pages)].] Washington, D. C.: Government Printing Office.

Freeman, F. N. 1924. The treatment of the gifted child in the light of scientific evidence. *Elem. Sch. J.*, *24*, 652–661.

French, W. C. 1923. A plan of organization for taking care of bright pupils. *Elem. Sch. J.*, *24*, 103–108.

Galton, F. 1869. *Hereditary genius.* London. (New ed., 1914.) New York: Macmillan.

Garrison, C. G., A. Burke, and L. S. Hollingworth. 1917. The psychology of a prodigious child. *J. Appl. Psychol.*, *1*, 101–110.

Garrison, K. C. 1940. *The psychology of exceptional children.* New York: Ronald.

Garrison, S. C., and G. M. Pullias. 1923. Bright children. *Psychol. Clin.*, *14*, 259–263.

Gesell, A. 1921. *Exceptional children and public school policy.* New Haven: Yale University Press.

Gesell, A., *et al.* 1939. Biographies of child development. New York: Hoeber.

Gillingham, A. 1920. Superior children—their school progress. *J. Educ. Psychol.*, *11*, 327–347.

——. 1923. Educating the gifted child. *Amer. Rev.*, *1*, 401–412.

Goddard, H. H. 1928. *School training of gifted children.* Yonkers-on-Hudson: World Book.

Goldberg, S. 1934. A clinical study of K, IQ 196. *J. Appl. Psychol.*, *18*, 550–560.

Goodenough, F. L. 1926. Racial differences in the intelligence of school children. *J. Exp. Psychol.*, *9*, 388–397.

Graham, B. G., *et al.* 1938. A descriptive study of a gifted child. *Pittsb. Schs. Bull.*, No. 12.

Gray, H., and W. J. Jacomb. 1921. Size and weight in one hundred and thirty-six boarding school boys. *Amer. J. Dis. Child.*, *22*, 259–271.

Gray, H. A. 1930. Some factors in the undergraduate careers of young college students. *Teach. Coll. Contr. Educ.*, No. 437.

Gray, H. A., and L. S. Hollingworth. 1931. The achievement of gifted children enrolled and not enrolled in special opportunity classes. *J. Educ. Res.*, *24*, 255–261.

Gray, W. S. 1942. Education of the gifted child: With special reference to reading. *Elem. Sch. J.*, *42*, 736–744.

Greenberg, B. B. 1939. The education of the intellectually gifted. *J. Except. Child*, *5*, 101–109.

Groszmann, M. P. E. 1917. *The exceptional child.* New York: Scribner's.

Guthrie, L. G. 1907. Contributions from history and literature to the study of precocious children. *Lancet*, *173*, 1592–1596.

Haggerty, M. E. 1925. The incidence of undesirable behavior in public school children. *J. Educ. Res.*, *12*, 102–122.

Hahn, O. 1911. Eigenärtige begabung eines Dreijährigen. *Z. pädag. Psychol.*, *12*, 291–292.

Hall, C. S. 1951. The genetics of behavior. In S. S. Stevens (Ed.), *Handbook of experimental psychology.* New York: John Wiley.

Harley, H. L. 1913. Physical status of the special class for bright children at the University of Pennsylvania summer session, 1912. *Psychol. Clin.*, *7*, 20–23.

Hartlaub, G. F. 1930. *Der Genius im Kinde: Zeichunungen und Malversuche begabter Kinder.* Breslau: Hirt.

Hartshorne, H., and M. May. 1928. *Studies in deceit.* (2 vols.) New York: Macmillan.

Hattery, L. H. 1950. Why waste talent? *Sch. and Soc.*, *71*, 81–84.

Havighurst, R. J. 1949. Culture and the IQ. *Purdue Univ. Stud. Higher Educ.*, No. 69, 42–53.

Hebb, D. O. 1949. *The organization of behavior: A neuropsychological theory.* New York: Wiley.

Heck, A. O. 1930. Special schools and classes in cities of 10,000 and more in the United States. *U. S. Off. Educ. Bull.*, No. 7.

——. 1940. *The education of exceptional children.* New York: McGraw-Hill.

Henmon, V. A. C., and F. O. Holt. 1931. A report on the administration of scholastic aptitude tests. *Bull. Univ. Wis.*, No. 1786.

Henry, T. S. 1920. Classroom problems in the education of gifted children. *Yearb. Nat. Soc. Stud. Educ.*, 19(II).

——. 1924. Annotated bibliography on gifted children and their education. *Yearb. Nat. Soc. Stud. Educ.*, 23(I), 389–443.

Herr, W. A. 1937. Junior high school accelerants and their peers in senior high school. *Sch. Rev.*, *45*, 186–195; 289–299.

Herschberger, M. 1931. *Follow-up of segregated and non-segregated gifted pupils in Pasadena.* Unpublished report.

High school methods with superior students, 1941. *Nat. Educ. Ass. Research Div. Bull.* 19, 155–197.

Hildreth, G. 1938a. Characteristics of young gifted children. *J. Genet. Psychol.*, *53*, 287–311.

Hildreth, G. 1938b. The educational achievement of gifted children. *Child. Develpm.*, *9*, 365-371.

——. 1939. Comparison of early Binet records with college aptitude test scores. *J. Educ. Psychol.*, *30*, 365-371.

Hildreth, G., and C. P. Ingram. 1942. Selected references from the literature on exceptional children. *Elem. Sch. J.*, *42*, 688-705.

Hinkle, B. M. 1923. *The re-creating of the individual.* New York: Harcourt, Brace.

Hinrichsen, O. 1939. Hochbegabung, Erfolg und psychische Krankheit. *Psychiat. neurol. Wschr.*, *41*, 239-242.

Hirsch, N. D. M. 1931. *Genius and creative intelligence.* Cambridge: Sci-Art Publishers.

Hirsch, W. 1896. *Genius and degeneration.* (Trans., 2d ed.) New York: Appleton.

Hirt, Z. I. 1922. A gifted child. *Train. Sch. Bull.*, *19*, 49-54.

Hollingworth, L. S. 1922. The subsequent history of E. *J. Appl. Psychol.*, *6*, 205-210.

——. 1926a. Musical sensitivity of children who test above 135 IQ (Stanford-Binet). *J. Educ. Psychol.*, *17*, 95-109.

——. 1926b. *Gifted children: Their nature and nurture.* New York: Macmillan.

——. 1927. Subsequent history of E: ten years after the initial report. *J. Appl. Psychol.*, *11*, 385-390.

——. 1930a. Do intellectually gifted children grow toward mediocrity in stature? *J. Genet. Psychol.*, *37*, 345-360.

——. 1930b. Playmates for the gifted child. *Child Study*, *8*, 103-104.

——. 1931. The child of very superior intelligence as a special problem in social adjustment. *Ment. Hyg., N. Y.*, *15*, 3-16.

——. 1935. The comparative beauty of the faces of highly intelligent adolescents. *J. Genet. Psychol.*, *47*, 268-281.

——. 1936a. Some suggestions on scholarships. *Ind. J. Columbia Univ.*, *4*, 4.

——. 1936b. The Terman classes at Public School 500. *J. Educ. Sociol.*, *10*, 86-90.

——. 1936c. Development of personality in highly intelligent children. *Yearb. Nat. Elem. Sch. Prin.*, *15*, 272-281.

——. 1936-1937. The founding of Public School 500. Speyer School: *Teach. Coll. Rec.*, *38*, 119-128.

——. 1938. An enrichment curriculum for rapid learners at Public School 500: Speyer School. *Teach. Coll. Rec.*, *39*, 296-306.

——. 1939a. Problems of relationship between elementary and secondary schools in the case of highly intelligent pupils. *J. Educ. Sociol.*, *13*, 90-102.

——. 1939b. What we know about the early selection and training of leaders. *Teach. Coll. Rec.*, *40*, 575-592.

——. 1940. Review of research. *Yearb. Nat. Soc. Stud. Educ.*, *39*(I), 43-66.

——. 1942. *Children above 180 IQ, Stanford-Binet.* New York: World Book.

Hollingworth, L. S., and M. V. Cobb. 1928. Children clustering at 165 IQ and children clustering at 145 IQ compared for three years in achievement. *Yearb. Nat. Soc. Stud. Educ.*, 27(II), 3-33.

Hollingworth, L. S., and H. A. Gray. 1930. Juvenile achievement as related to size. *Teach. Coll. Rec.*, *32*, 236-244.

Hollingworth, L. S., and R. M. Kaunitz. 1934. The centile status of gifted children at maturity. *J. Genet. Psychol.*, *45*, 106-120.

Hollingworth, L. S., and J. E. Monahan. 1926. Tapping rate of children who test above 135 IQ (Stanford-Binet). *J. Educ. Psychol.*, *17*, 505-518.

Hollingworth, L. S., and M. M. Rust. 1937. Application of the Bernreuter inventory of personality to highly intelligent adolescents. *J. Psychol.*, *4*, 287-293.

Hollingworth, L. S., and G. A. Taylor. 1924. Size and strength of children who test above 135 IQ. *Yearb. Nat. Soc. Stud. Educ.* 23(I), 221-237.

Hollingworth, L. S., L. M. Terman, and M. Oden. 1940. The significance of deviates. *Yearb. Nat. Soc. Stud. Educ.*, *39*(I), 43-92.

Honzik, M. P., J. W. Macfarlane, and L. Allen. 1948. The stability of mental test performance between 2 and 18 years. *J. Exper. Educ.*, 309-324.

Horn, E. 1924. The curriculum for the gifted: Some principles and an illustration. *Yearb. Nat. Soc. Stud. Educ.*, 23(I), 73-89.

Horn, J. L. 1924. *The education of exceptional children.* New York: Century.

Jenkins, M. D. 1936. A socio-psychological study of Negro children of superior intelligence. *J. Negro Educ.*, *5*, 175-190.

——. 1943. Case studies of Negro children of Binet IQ 160 and above. *J. Negro Educ.*, *12*, 159-166.

——. 1948. The upper limit of ability among American Negroes. *Sci. Mon. N. Y.*, *66*, 399-401.

Jensen, D. W. 1927. The gifted child. *J. Educ. Res.*, *15*, 34-35; 126-133; 198-206.

Johnson, H. G. 1942. Does the gifted child have a low AQ? *J. Educ. Res.*, *36*, 91-99.

Johnson, O. J. 1923. Teacher's judgments of qualities of gifted pupils as related to classroom activities. *Sch. and Soc.*, *17*, 466-469.

Johnson, W. B., and L. M. Terman. 1940. Some highlights in the literature of psychological sex differences published since 1920. *J. Psychol.*, *9*, 327-336.

Jones, A. M. 1925. An analytical study of one hundred and twenty superior children. *Psychol. Clin.*, *16*, 19-76.

Jones, V. A., and W. A. McCall. 1926. Application of two techniques in evaluating some policies of dealing with bright children. *Teach. Coll. Rec.*, *27*, 825-835.

Keliher, A. V. 1931. A critical study of homogeneous grouping. *Teach. Coll. Contr. Educ.*, No. 452.

Kellogg, R. 1949. Skills instruction for the gifted child in the regular classroom. *Nat. Elem. Prin.*, *29*, 37-40.

Kenworthy, M. E. 1928. Some emotional problems seen in the superior child. *Amer. J. Psychol., 4,* 3.

Kerschensteiner, G. 1905. *Die Entwicklung der zeichnerischen Begabung.* Munich: Gruber.

Keys, N. 1935. Adjustment of under-age students in high school. *Psychol. Bull., 32,* 539.

———. 1940. The value of group test IQ's for prediction of progress beyond high school. *J. Educ. Psychol., 31,* 81–93.

Kik, C. 1909. Die übernormale Zeichenbegabung bei Kindern. *Z. angew. Psychol., 2,* 92–149.

Kluckhohn, C., and H. A. Murray. 1948. *Personality in nature, society, and culture.* New York: Knopf.

Kramer, F., and W. Stern. 1908. Psychologische Prüfung eines elfjährigen Mädchens mit besonderer mnemotechnischer Fähigkeit. *Z. angew. Psychol., 1,* 291–312.

Kretschmer, E. 1931. *The psychology of men of genius.* (Trans. by R. B. Cattell.) New York: Harcourt, Brace.

Kyte, G. C. 1924. Two types of experimental programs in the education of gifted children. *Yearb. Nat. Educ. Ass., Dept. Elem. Sch. Prin., 3,* 395–430.

Lämmermann, H. 1931. Ueber das Verhältnis von Allgemein- und Sonderbegabung und seine Bedeutung für eine organisatorische Differenzierung der Schule. *Z. pädag. Psychol., 32,* 377–391.

Lamson, E. E. 1930. A study of young gifted children in senior high school. *Teach. Coll. Contr. Educ.,* No. 424.

———. 1935. High school achievement of fifty-six gifted children. *J. Genet. Psychol., 47,* 233–238.

Lang, A. 1897. Genius in children. *No. Amer. Rev., 164,* 32–37.

Lange-Eichbaum, W. 1928. *Genie, Irrsinn und Ruhm.* Munich: Reinhardt.

———. 1931. *The problem of genius.* London: Kegan Paul.

Lagenbeck, M. 1915. A study of a five-year-old child. *Ped. Sem., 22,* 65–88.

Lantz, B. 1945. Some dynamic aspects of success and failure. *Psychol. Monogr., 59,* No. 271.

Laycock, S. R. 1933. Adjustments of superior and inferior school children. *J. Soc. Psychol., 4,* 353–366.

———. 1940a. Special classes for gifted children. *Understanding the Child, 9,* 3–6.

———. 1940b. The mental hygiene of exceptional children. *J. Except. Children, 6,* 244–250.

———. 1942. Helping the bright pupil. *School, 30,* 561–565.

Lazar, M. 1935. Reading interests, activities and opportunities of bright, average and dull children. *Teach. Coll. Contr. Educ.,* No. 707.

Lehman, B. H. 1928. *Carlyle's theory of the hero: Its sources, development, history, and influence on Carlyle's work.* Durham, N. C.: Duke University Press.

Lehman, H. C. 1946. Age of starting to contribute versus total creative output. *J. Appl. Psychol., 30,* 460–80.

Lehman, H. C., and P. A. Witty. 1927. The play behavior of fifty gifted children. *J. Educ. Psychol., 18,* 259–265.

Lewis, W. D. 1940. A study of superior children in the elementary school. *Peabody Coll. Contr. Educ.,* No. 266.

———. 1941. A comparative study of the personalities, interests, and home backgrounds of gifted children of superior and inferior educational achievement. *J. Genet. Psychol., 59,* 207–218.

———. 1943. Some characteristics of very superior children. *J. Genet. Psychol., 62,* 301–310.

Lightfoot, G. F. 1951. Personality characteristics of bright and dull children. *Teach. Coll. Contr. Educ.,* No. 969.

Lincoln, E. A. 1933. Preliminary report on the Stanford-Binet IQ changes of superior children. *J. Exp. Educ., 1,* 287–292.

———. 1935a. A study of changes in the intelligence quotients of superior children. *J. Educ. Res., 29,* 272–275.

———. 1935b. The Stanford-Binet IQ changes of superior children. *Sch. and Soc., 41,* 519–520.

Lindley, E. H., and W. L. Bryan. 1900. An arithmetical prodigy. *Psychol. Rev., 7,* 135.

Lombroso, C. 1891. *The man of genius.* London: Scott.

———. 1901. Determining of genius. *Monist, 12,* 49–64.

Lorge, I., and L. S. Hollingworth. 1936. Adult status of highly intelligent children. *J. Genet. Psychol., 49,* 215–226.

Macmeeken, A. M. 1939. The intelligence of a representative group of Scottish children. *Publ. Scot. Coun. Res. Educ.,* No. 15.

MacMurray, D. 1937. A comparison of the intelligence of gifted children and of dull-normal children measured by the Pintner-Paterson Scale, as against the Stanford-Binet scale. *J. Psychol., 4,* 273–280.

Magaret, A., and C. W. Thompson. 1950. Differential test responses of normal, superior and mentally defective subjects. *J. Abnorm. and Soc. Psychol., 45,* 163–167.

Malherbe, E. H. 1921. New measurements in private schools. *Survey, 46,* 272–273.

Margolies, A. 1946. A portrait of George Miles—problem child. *High Points, 28,* 25–30.

Martens, E. H. 1933. Gifted children. Teachers' problems with exceptional children. *Pamphlet 41* (II). Washington, D. C.: U. S. Office of Education.

———. 1946. *Curriculum adjustments for gifted children.* Washington, U. S. Government Printing Office.

Mateer, F. 1936. Clinical problems of bright children. *J. Educ. Soc., 10,* 91–99.

McCandless, B. R. 1939. The effect of enriched educational experiences upon the growth of intelligence of very intelligent children. *Psychol. Bull., 36,* 628.

McElwee, E. W. 1932. A comparison of the personality traits of 300 accelerated, normal, and retarded children. *J. Educ. Res., 26,* 31–34.

McElwee, E. W. 1934. Seymour, a boy with 192 IQ. *J. Juv. Res.*, *18*, 28-35.

McGehee, W., and W. D. Lewis. 1940. Parental attitudes of mentally superior, average and retarded children. *Sch. and Soc.*, *51*, 556-559.

McNemar, Q. 1942. *The revision of the Stanford-Binet Scale.* Boston: Houghton Mifflin.

Mensh, I. N. 1950. Rorschach study of the gifted child. *J. Except. Child*, *17*, 8-14.

Merrill, M. A. 1938. The significance of IQ's on the revised Stanford-Binet scales. *J. Educ. Psychol.*, *29*, 641-651.

Mersand, J. 1936. How should the teacher carry on work for the gifted child? *High Points*, *18*, No. 7, 42-50.

Miles, C. C. 1935. Sex in social psychology. In C. Murchison (Ed.), *A handbook of social psychology.* Worcester: Clark University Press.

Miles, C. C., and L. S. Wolfe. 1936. Childhood physical and mental health records of historical geniuses. *Psychol. Monogr.* (Dodge Commemorative Number), *47*, 390-400.

Miles, C. C. See also Cox, C. M.

Mitchell, F. D. 1907. Mathematical prodigies. *Amer. J. Psychol.*, *18*, 61-143.

Monahan, J. E., and L. S. Hollingworth. 1927. Neuromuscular capacity of children who test above 135 IQ (Stanford-Binet). *J. Educ. Psychol.*, *18*, 88-96.

Moreau, P. 1891. Les enfants prodiges. *Ann. psychiat. et d'hypnol.*, 97-107.

Mort, P. R. 1939. Leadership in democratic living. *Teach. Coll. Rec.*, *40*, 561-564.

Mort, P. R., and F. G. Cornell. 1938. *Adaptability of public school systems.* New York: Teach. Coll. Bur. of Publ., Columbia University.

Murphy, G. 1947. *Personality, a biosocial approach to origins and structure.* New York: Harper.

Musselman, J. W. 1942. Factors associated with the achievements of high school pupils of superior intelligence. *J. Exp. Educ.*, *11*, 53-68.

Myers, G. C. 1935. The social problem of the gifted child. *J. Except. Child*, *2*, 39-43.

National Committee on Coordination in Secondary Education. 1939. Education of gifted children in secondary schools. (Report adopted at Cleveland, Feb. 27, 1939.) *J. Educ. Sociol.*, *13*, 120-126.

Nemzek, C. L. 1932. Constancy of the IQ's of gifted children. *J. Educ. Psychol.*, *23*, 607-610.

Nevill, E. M. 1937. Brilliant children: With special reference to their particular difficulties. *Brit. J. Educ. Psychol.*, *7*, 247-258.

Newland, T. E. 1941. The education of exceptional children: The mentally gifted. *Rev. Educ. Res.*, *11*, 277-287.

Nisbet, J. F. 1891. *The insanity of genius.* London: Paul.

Noonan, N., and D. E. Norris. 1938. Studies of gifted children. *J. Except. Child*, Jan. (extra issue), 46-56.

Olson, W. C. 1930. *Problem tendencies in children: A method for their measurement and description.* Minneapolis: University of Minnesota Press.

Orleans, J. B. 1940. The gifted pupil at George Washington High School: A survey and a forecast. *High Points*, *22*, 17-42.

Osburn, W. J., and B. J. Rohan. 1931. *Enriching the curriculum for gifted children: A book of guidance for educational administrators and classroom teachers.* New York: Macmillan.

O'Shea, M. V. 1911. Popular misconceptions concerning precocity in children. *Science*, *34*, 666-674.

Ostwald, W. 1909. *Groose Männer.* Leipzig: Akademische Verlagsgesellschaft.

Parkyn, G. W. 1948. *Children of high intelligence. A New Zealand study.* New Zealand Council for Educ. Res. New York: Oxford University Press.

Patrick, M. L. 1924. Some attainments of gifted children in segregated classes at Louisville. *Yearb. Nat. Soc. Stud. Educ.*, 23(I), 262-274.

Peachman, M. C. 1942. Attitudes: Their significance in education for the gifted. *J. Educ. Psychol.*, *33*, 83-98.

Peter, R., W. Stern, et al. 1919. Die Auslese befähigter Volksschüler in Hamburg. *Beih Z. angew. Psychol.*, *18*.

Petzoldt, J. 1911. Die Einwände gegen Sonderschulen für hervorragend Befähigte. *Neue Jahrb. Päd.*, *28*, 1-24.

Pintner, R. 1931. *Intelligence testing: Methods and results.* (2d Ed.) New York: Holt.

Poincaré, H. 1914. *Science and method.* (Trans. by F. Maitland.) London: Nelson and Sons.

Pressey, S. L. 1946. Age of college graduation and success in adult life. *J. Appl. Psychol.*, *30*, 226-33.

Race, H. V. 1918. A study of class of children of superior intelligence. *J. Educ. Psychol.*, *9*, 91-97.

Reavis, W. C. 1924. The administration of the superior students in the University of Chicago High School. *Yearb. Nat. Soc. Stud. Educ.*, 23(I), 355-365.

Regensburg, J. 1926. Emotional handicaps to intellectual achievement in supernormal children *Ment. Hyg.*, *N. Y.*, *10*, 480-494.

——. 1931. Studies of educational success and failure in supernormal children. *Arch. Psychol.*, *N. Y.*, *20*, No. 129.

Reibmayr, A. 1908. *Die Entwicklungsgeschichte des Talents und Genies.* Munich: Lehmann.

Reid, E. C. 1911-1912. Manifestations of manic-depressive insanity in literary genius. *Amer. J. Insan.*, *68*, 595-632.

Remmers, H. H. 1930. Distinguished students: What they are and why. Studies in higher education, 15. *Bull. Purdue Univ.*, *31*, 2.

Révész, G. 1916a. *Erwin Nyiregyhazi: Psychologische Analyse eines musikalisch hervorragenden Kindes.* Leipzig: Veit.

——. 1916b. Das musikalische Wunderkind. *Z. pädag. Psychol.*, *19*, 29-34.

——. 1921. *Das frühzeitige Auftreten, der Begabung und ihre Erkennung.* Leipzig: Barth.

Richards-Nash, A. A. 1924. The psychology of superior children. *Ped. Sem.*, *31*, 209-246.

Rigg, M. 1938. A follow-up study of sixteen superior students. *Sch. and Soc.*, *48*, 411-412.

Roe, A. 1949. Psychological examinations of eminent biologists. *J. Consult. Psychol.*, *13*, 225–246.

——. 1951. A psychological study of physical scientists. *Genet. Psychol. Monogr.*, *43*, 121–239.

Roff, M. 1949. A factorial study of the Fels Parent Behavior Scales. *Child Develop.*, *20*, 29–45.

Rogers, A. L. 1928. Educational guidance of pupils in private schools. *Private Sch. Teach. Ass.*, Phila., Pamphlet No. 3.

Root, W. T. 1921. A socio-psychological study of fifty-three supernormal children. *Psychol. Monogr.*, *29*, No. 133. Pp. 134.

Rusk, R. N. 1917. A case of precocity. *Child Study*, *10*, 21–27.

Rust, M. M. 1931. The effect of resistance on the intelligence scores of young children. *Child Develpm. Monogr.*, No. 6. Pp. xi + 80.

Ryans, D. G. 1939. An observation on the changes in variability of high, medium and low "intelligence" groups, etc. *J. Genet. Psychol.*, *54*, 467–470.

Sanguinet, E. H. 1929. What modifications in the technique of instruction should be made for superior children? *Educ. Admin. Supervis.*, *15*, 58–66.

Schlesser, G. E. 1950. Gains in scholastic aptitude under highly motivated conditions. *J. Educ. Psychol.*, *41*, 237–242.

Schneider, D. E. 1950. *The psychoanalyst and the artist.* New York: Farrar, Straus.

Schoenbeck, E. 1922. Die Begabten in deutschen Unterricht. *Prak. Psychol.*, *3*, 223–230.

Schorn, M. 1928. Zur psychologie des frühbegabten Kindes. *Z. Psychol.*, *105*, 302–316.

Schott, E. L. 1931. Superior intelligence in patients with nervous and mental illnesses. *J. Abnorm. Soc. Psychol.*, *26*, 94–101.

——. 1932. School maladjustment of some mentally superior patients in a psychiatric clinic. *Psychol. Clin.*, *21*, 202–207.

Schussler, H., and W. Schwarzhaupt. 1921. Die pädagogische und experimentell-psychologische Auslese der Begabten für die Übergangsklasse. *Z. pädag. Psychol.*, *22*, 188–195.

Schuster, E. 1907. The promise of youth and the performance of manhood. *Eugen. Lab. Mem.*, London, *3*.

Scottish Council for Research in Education. 1933. *The intelligence of Scottish children.* London: University London Press.

Scripture, E. W. 1891. Arithmetical prodigies. *Amer. J. Psychol.*, *4*, 1–59.

Seltzer, C. C. 1946. Body disproportions and dominant personality traits. *Psychosom. Med.*, *8*, 75–97.

Sérouya, H. 1927. Eine frühreife philosophische Hochbegabung. *Z. angew. Psychol.*, *29*, 236–238.

Shaer, I. 1913. Special classes for bright children in an English elementary school. *J. Educ. Psychol.*, *4*, 209–222.

Sherif, M., and H. Cantril. 1947. *The psychology of ego-involvements.* New York: Wiley.

Shields, T. E. 1909. *The making and unmaking of a dullard.* Washington, D. C.: Catholic Education Press.

Shirley, H. F. 1948. *Psychiatry for the pediatrician.* New York: The Commonwealth Fund.

Shuttleworth, F. K. 1939. The physical and mental growth of girls and boys age six to nineteen in relation to age at maximum growth. *Monogr. Soc. Res. Child Develpm.*, *4*, No. 3. Pp. vi + 291.

Simmons, R. McK. 1939. A study of a group of children of exceptionally high intelligence quotient in situations partaking of the nature of suggestion. *Teach. Coll. Contr. Educ.*, No. 788.

Simon, L. M., and E. A. Levitt. 1950. The relation between Wechsler-Bellevue IQ scores and occupational area. *Occupations*, *29*, 23–25.

Slavin, J. S., and F. Griffith. 1942. Scholastic ratings of honor school pupils. *High Points*, *24*, 35–43.

Specht, L. F. 1919. A Terman class in Public School No. 64, Manhattan. *Sch. and Soc.*, *9*, 393–398.

Stedman, L. M. 1924. *Education of gifted children.* Yonkers-on-Hudson: World Book.

Stern, W. 1911. The supernormal child. *J. Educ. Psychol.*, *2*, 143–149; 181–190.

——. 1918. Die Methode der Auslese befähigter Volkschüler in Hamburg. *Z. pädag. Psychol.*, *19*, 132–142.

Stewart, N. 1947. AGCT scores of Army personnel grouped by occupation. *Occupations*, *26*, 5–41.

Strang, R. 1950. Inner world of gifted adolescents. *J. Except. Child*, *16*, 97–101.

Street, R. F. 1937. The mentally superior child. *J. Except. Child*, *3*, 83–86.

Strodtbeck, F. L. 1953. *Implications of the study of family interaction for the prediction of achievement* (preliminary report, mimeographed). Social Science Research Council—Markle Fund Project, Yale University.

Stumpf, C. 1909. Akustische Versuche mit Pepito Arriola. *Z. angew. Psychol.*, *2*, 1–11.

Sully, J. 1886. Genius and precocity. *Pop. Sci. Mo.*, *29*, 469–482, 594–604.

Sumption, M. R. 1941. *Three hundred gifted children. A follow-up study of the results of special education of superior children.* Yonkers-on-Hudson: World Book.

Terman, L. M. 1904. A preliminary study in the psychology and pedagogy of leadership. *Ped. Sem.*, *11*, 413–451.

——. 1905. A study of precocity and prematuration. *Amer. J. Psychol.*, *16*, 145–183.

——. 1906. Genius and stupidity. *Ped. Sem.*, *13*, 307–373.

——. 1915. The mental hygiene of exceptional children. *Ped. Sem.*, *22*, 529–537.

——. 1916. *The measurement of intelligence.* Boston: Houghton Mifflin.

——. 1917. The IQ of Francis Galton in childhood. *Amer. J. Psychol.*, *28*, 209–215.

——. 1918. An experiment in infant education. *J. Appl. Psychol.*, *2*, 218–229.

——. 1919. *The intelligence of school children.* Boston: Houghton Mifflin.

Terman, L. M. 1922. A new approach to the study of genius. *Psychol. Rev., 29,* 310–318.

——. 1924a. The conservation of talent. *Sch. and Soc., 19,* 359–364.

——. 1924b. The physical and mental traits of gifted children. *Yearb. Nat. Soc. Stud. Educ.,* 23(I), 155–167.

——. 1931. The gifted child. In C. Murchison (Ed.), *A handbook on child psychology.* Worcester: Clark University Press.

——. 1939a. Educational suggestions for follow-up studies of intellectually gifted children. *J. Educ. Sociol., 13,* 82–89.

——. 1939b. The gifted student and his academic environment. *Sch. and Soc., 49,* 65–73.

——. 1940. Intelligence in a changing universe. *Sch. and Soc., 51,* 465–470.

Terman, L. M., *et al.* 1925. Genetic studies of genius: Vol. I. *Mental and physical traits of a thousand gifted children.* Stanford University, Calif:. Stanford University Press.

Terman, L. M., and B. S. Burks. 1933. The gifted child. In C. Murchison (Ed.), *A handbook of child psychology.* (2d Ed.) Worcester: Clark University Press.

Terman, L. M., and J. M. Chase. 1920. The psychology, biology and pedagogy of genius. *Psychol. Bull., 17,* 397–409.

Terman, L. M., and J. C. DeVoss. 1924. The educational achievements of gifted children. *Yearb. Nat. Soc. Stud. Educ.,* 23(I), 169–184.

Terman, L. M., and J. C. Fenton. 1921. Preliminary report on a gifted juvenile author. *J. Appl. Psychol., 5,* 163–178.

Terman, L. M., and C. C. Miles. 1936. *Sex and personality.* New York: McGraw-Hill.

Terman, L. M., and M. Oden. 1940a. The significance of deviates: II. Status of the California gifted group at the end of sixteen years. *Yearb. Nat. Soc. Stud. Educ.,* 39(I), 67–74.

——. 1940b. The significance of deviates: III. Correlates of adult achievement in the California gifted group. *Yearb. Nat. Soc. Stud. Educ.,* 39(I), 74–89.

——. 1947. *The gifted child grows up.* Stanford University: Stanford University Press.

Theman, V., and P. A. Witty. 1943. Case studies and genetic records of two gifted Negroes. *J. Psychol., 15,* 165–181.

Thom, D. A., and N. Newell. 1945. Hazards of the high IQ. *Ment. Hyg. N. Y., 29,* 61–77.

Thompson, N. Z. 1949. Education of the gifted in various countries. *J. Except. Child, 15,* 193–208, 239–254.

Thomson, G. H. 1936. *Intelligence and civilisation.* Edinburgh: University Press.

Thomson, G. (Ed.) 1949. *The trend of Scottish intelligence.* London: University of London Press.

Thorndike, E. L. 1939. How may we improve the selection, training, and life-work of leaders? *Teach. Coll. Rec., 40,* 593–605.

——. 1941. Gifted children in small cities. *Teach. Coll. Rec., 24,* 420–427.

Thorndike, R. L. 1939. Responses of a group of gifted children to the Pressey interest-attitude test. *J. Educ. Psychol., 30,* 588–594.

——. 1940a. Constancy of the IQ. *Psychol. Bull., 37,* 167–186.

——. 1940b. Performance of gifted children on tests of developmental age. *J. Psychol., 9,* 337–343.

——. 1941. Problems in identification, description, and development of the gifted. *Teach. Coll. Rec., 24,* 402–406.

——. 1948. An evaluation of the adult intellectual status of Terman's gifted children. *J. Genet. Psychol., 72,* 17–27.

Thorner, M. W., and G. H. J. Pearson. 1940. Behavior disorders of intellectual origin occurring in childhood. *Amer. J. Dis. Child., 60,* 1245–1251.

Thurstone, L. L., and T. G. Thurstone. 1937. The 1936 psychological examination for college freshmen. *Educ. Rec., 18,* 252–273.

——. 1938. The 1937 psychological examination for college freshmen. *Educ. Rec., 19,* 209–234.

Thurstone, L. L., T. G. Thurstone, and D. C. Adkins. 1939. The 1938 psychological examination. *Educ. Rec., 20,* 263–300.

Tiebout, H. M. 1943. The misnamed lazy student. *Educ. Rec., 24,* 113–129.

Tonsor, C. A. 1941. Failure in the bright school. *High Points, 23,* 67–70.

Toops, H. A. 1928. The selection of graduate assistants. *Person. J., 6,* 457–472.

Traxler, A. E. 1940. What is a satisfactory IQ for admission to college? *Sch. and Soc., 51,* 462–463.

——. 1941. Comparison between IQ's on the new edition of the Kuhlmann-Anderson intelligence tests and Binet IQ's. *Educ. Rec. Bull.,* No. 31.

Trow, W. C. 1941. Who are the gifted? *Educ. Digest, 7,* 17–20.

Valentiner, T. 1911. Ein elfjähriger Humorist. *Säemann, 4,* 218–227.

Van Alstyne, D. 1923. A study of ten gifted children whose school progress was unsatisfactory. *J. Educ. Res., 8,* 122–135.

Van Wagenen, M. J. 1925. A comparison of the mental ability and school achievement of the bright and dull pupils in the sixth grade of a large school system. *J. Educ. Psychol., 16,* 186–192.

Varner, G. F. 1922. Can teachers select bright and dull children? *J. Educ. Res., 6,* 126–132.

Waddle, C. W. 1924. Case studies of gifted children. *Yearb. Nat. Soc. Stud. Educ.,* 23(I), 185–207.

Ward, L. F. 1906. *Applied sociology.* Boston: Ginn.

Warner, M. L. 1930. Eugene, a brilliant boy who failed in school. *Psychol. Clin., 19,* 143–155.

Washburne, C. W. 1924. The attainments of gifted children under individual instruction. *Yearb. Nat. Soc. Stud. Educ.,* 23(I), 247–261.

Webb, E. 1915. Character and intelligence. *Brit. J. Psychol. Monogr. Suppl., 1,* No. 3. Pp. 99.

Whipple, G. M. 1913. Supernormal children. In P. Monroe (Ed.), *Cyclopedia of Education,* Vol. V., pp. 464–467. New York: Macmillan.

——. 1919. *Classes for gifted children: An experimental study of method of selection and introduc-*

tion. Bloomington, Ill.: Public School Publishing Co.

Whipple, G. M. 1920. Some features of the education of gifted children. *Sch. and Soc*, *12*, 175–179.

——. 1923. School provision for gifted children in the United States. *Nat. Conf. Soc. Work*, 399–404.

——. 1924. Education of gifted children: historical and introductory. *Yearb. Nat. Soc. Stud. Educ.*, 23(I), 124.

White, R. K. 1930. Note on the psychopathology of genius. *J. Soc. Psychol.*, *1*, 311–315.

——. 1931. The versatility of genius. *J. Soc. Psychol.*, *2*, 460–489.

White, R. W. 1952. *Lives in progress*. New York: Dryden Press.

White House Conference on Special Education. 1931. *The handicapped and the gifted*. New York: Century.

Wiener, N. 1953. *Ex-Prodigy: My Childhood and youth*. New York: Simon & Schuster.

Wilkins, W. L. 1936. High school achievement of accelerated pupils. *Sch. Rev.*, *44*, 268–273.

Williams, T. A. 1911. Intellectual precocity. *Ped. Sem.*, *18*, 85–103.

Wilson, F. T. 1949. A survey of educational provisions for young gifted children in the United States. *J. Genet. Psychol.*, *75*, 3–19.

Witte, K. 1914. *The education of Karl Witte*. (Trans. by L. Wiener.) New York: Crowell.

Witty, P. (Ed.) 1951. *The gifted child*. Amer. Assoc. for Gifted Children. Boston: Heath.

Witty, P. A. 1930. A study of one hundred gifted children. *Univ. Kan. Bull. Educ., State T.C. Stud. Educ.*, *1*, No. 13.

——. 1934. The relative frequency of gifted boys and girls in the secondary school. *Educ. Adm. Supervis.*, *20*, 606–612.

——. 1936. Exploitation of the child of high intelligence quotient. *Educ. Meth.*, *15*, 298–304.

——. 1940a. A genetic study of fifty gifted children. *Yearb. Nat. Soc. Stud. Educ.*, 39(II), 401–408.

——. 1940b. Contributions to the IQ controversy from the study of superior deviates. *Sch. and Soc.*, *51*, 503–508.

——. 1940c. Evidence regarding the nature of intelligence from the study of superior deviates. In *Addresses and Discussions Presenting the 39th Yearbook of the National Society for the Study of Education*. Salem, Mass.: Newcomb and Gauss.

Witty, P. A., and M. D. Jenkins. 1936. Intrarace testing and Negro intelligence. *J. Psychol.*, *1*, 179–192.

Witty, P. A., and H. C. Lehman. 1930. Nervous instability and genius: Some conflicting opinions. *J. Abnorm. Soc. Psychol.*, *24*, 486–497.

——. 1932. A study of the reading and reading interests of gifted children. *J. Genet. Psychol.*, *40*, 473–485.

Witty, P. A., and V. Theman. 1943. A follow-up study of the educational attainment of gifted Negroes. *J. Educ. Psychol.*, *34*, 35–47.

Witty, P. A., and L. Wilkins. 1933. The status of acceleration or grade skipping as an administrative practice. *Educ. Adm. Supervis.*, *19*, 321–346.

Wood, E. P. 1929. The educational achievement and intelligence of independent school children. *Educ. Rec. Bull.*, No. 2.

Woodrow, H. 1919. *Brightness and dullness in children*. Philadelphia: Lippincott.

Woods, E. L. 1917. Provision for the gifted child. *Educ. Adm. Supervis.*, *3*, 139–149.

——. 1929. Personality traits of children of superior intelligence in special classes and in regular classes. *3d Yearb. Psychol. Educ. Res. Div., Los Angeles City Schools*, No. 185, 102–109.

——. 1944. The mentally gifted. *Rev. Educ. Res.*, *14*, 224–230.

Woolley, H. T. 1925. Agnes: A dominant personality in the making. *Ped. Sem.*, *32*, 569–598.

Wrenn, C. G. 1935a. Aiding the fit. *J. Higher Educ.*, *6*, 357–363.

——. 1935b. Intelligence and the vocational choices of college students. *Educ. Rec.*, *16*, 217–219.

Yates, D. H. 1922. A study of some high school seniors of superior intelligence. *J. Educ. Res. Monogr.*, No. 2. Pp. 75.

Yoder, A. H. 1894. The study of the boyhood of great men. *Ped. Sem.*, *3*, 134–156.

Zeigel, H., Jr. 1927. Achievement of high school honor students in the University of Missouri. *Sch. and Soc.*, *25*, 82–84.

Zillig, M. 1929. Zur Psychologie des dichterischschaffenden Kindes. *Z. Psychol,*, *112*, 302–324.

Zorbaugh, H. W. (Ed.) 1936. Gifted and talented children. *J. Educ. Soc.*, *10*, 65–128.

Zorbaugh, H. W. 1940. How may the community utilize its gifted children? *Ment. Hyg., N. Y.*, *24*, 1–16.

Zorbaugh, H. W., and R. K. Boardman. 1936. Salvaging our gifted children. *J. Educ. Sociol.*, *10*, 100–108.

CHAPTER 17

PSYCHOLOGICAL SEX DIFFERENCES

LEWIS M. TERMAN AND LEONA E. TYLER [1]

This chapter is principally concerned with the literature that has appeared from 1920 through 1952. Earlier contributions have not been included since it is generally true that later studies in this area have presented findings that agree with the earlier work but are statistically much sounder. We have confined our attention to studies of children and adolescents, in most cases excluding comparisons of college males and females because of the selective factors which obscure the meaning of the sex differences in this special group. As a rule we have not included studies based on small or obviously biased samples. However, it is the representativeness of the sample and the demonstration of statistical significance, rather than size alone, which has determined how much weight can be attached to any set of results.

The survey is of necessity incomplete. The great majority of the studies summarized have been published in the English language in America or Great Britain. Those from other countries which have found their way into the *Psychological Abstracts* have usually been included, but for most of these only the abstract was read. Material covered here has come largely out of research planned according to the Galtonian tradition, with its emphasis on objective and statistical methods. Much has

been written on sex differences from other viewpoints, philosophical or descriptive. The psychoanalytic writers alone have produced a considerable body of writing on this subject. These discussions we have made no attempt to include.

Since the meaning and origin of the sex differences that have been identified are important considerations, it seemed desirable to follow a "tracing-back" procedure in the organization of the material. Studies to be summarized have thus been arranged roughly according to the ages of the subjects on whom they are based, so that the reader may be able to form some judgment as to how early differences appear. This helps us to draw tentative conclusions as to how fundamental they are in human development.

The Physical Background of Sex Differences

Sex differences have been found for almost every physical variable, including body build, gross and fine anatomy, physiological functioning, and biochemical composition. Indeed, every cell in a human body bears the stamp of its sex. As we are here concerned with psychological sex differences, we shall confine our discussion of physical differences to those which would seem most likely to have correlates in the realm of psychological behavior. The reader who wishes to pursue the matter further may well begin with the excellent

[1] The authors wish to acknowledge the assistance given by Winifred B. Johnson, George Kuznets, and Olga McNemar in reviewing the literature which appeared prior to 1941.

graphic and pictorial atlas compiled by Shuttleworth (1951).

Body Size. In general, it can be stated that males are larger than females, although there is a period, between the ages of 11 and 15, when the situation is modified because of the earlier female preadolescent growth spurt. Mean weight of boys at birth exceeds that of girls by approximately 5 per cent. This superiority continues to about 11 years, then rapidly decreases, until at 14 the direction of the difference is reversed, and the mean for boys is about 5 per cent below that for girls. By 15 or 16 boys have regained their former advantage, and by 20, the mean superiority of males is in the neighborhood of 20 per cent.[1]

Mean body length is slightly higher (1 or 2 per cent) for boys than for girls from birth to about 11 years. From ages 11 to 14, girls average taller, but the greatest difference in this direction is only about 2 per cent. Growth in height rapidly slows down for girls after 15 and almost ceases by 17. Height continues to increase fairly rapidly for boys up to 17 or 18 years, and usually does not cease completely until the early 20's. By this time male superiority amounts to something like 10 per cent.

Vital Capacity. Sex differences in vital capacity are greater than those for height or weight and may be more significant for behavior. Because vital capacity is one of the determiners of the sustained energy output which is possible for an individual, it could be one of the factors underlying sex differences in play interests, drive for achievement, and liking for activity and adventure. The superiority of boys in vital capacity is about 7 per cent by age 6, increasing to 10 or 12 per cent at age 10 and

to about 35 per cent at age 20. It is particularly significant that the *vital index,* or the ratio between vital capacity and weight, is higher for boys at all ages for which measures have been made.

Strength. Muscular strength is another trait in which boys are superior to girls at all ages for which tests have been reported. In strength of grip of right hand the superiority of boys is about 10 per cent at age 7 and increases slowly to age 14. The curve for girls flattens at 16, that for boys about 3 years later. At age 18 the mean superiority of boys is about 50 to 60 per cent. Sex differences in strength of back and legs are correspondingly great and follow a similar course.

Rate of Maturation. Some of the most marked age shifts in the amount or direction of sex differences are largely functions of the more rapid physical maturation of girls. Maturational differences are especially conspicuous in gonadal functioning. Girls of all races precede boys on the average by 12 to 20 months in pubertal development, and their adolescent growth changes are correspondingly accelerated. In skeletal development girls are superior to boys at birth and increase this superiority at a fairly steady rate until growth is complete. At age 6 girls are a year more advanced in this respect than boys; at age 9, 1½ years; and at 13, about 2 years. Flory (1935) finds in girls a correlation of .637 ± .048 between age of first menstruation and skeletal-months ratings taken at age 11. Dentition also proceeds more rapidly with girls, but the sex difference here is less than for skeletal development (P. Cattell, 1928).

Sex Ratio and Viability. It is well known that human beings show an excess of male over female births (Parkes, 1926; Crew, 1927; Bakwin, 1929; Dublin and Lotka, 1936). The ratio differs with race, but is usually between 103 and 107 males to 100

[1] Physical sex differences vary more or less with race and nationality. Unless otherwise noted, the differences referred to in this chapter are for white subjects of predominantly western European descent.

females. For stillbirths the ratio is around 130 or 135, and for miscarriages it is almost 200. Data reported by Bakwin (1929) indicate that the sex ratio for mortality increases with improvement in general health conditions; that is, the more recent the figures and the more favorable the climatic and cultural conditions, the greater the excess of female survivors. Females are more resistant to most infectious diseases. In the period of infancy (under 1 year) seventeen of the eighteen foremost causes of death given by the mortality statistics of the United States showed a mortality sex ratio markedly favoring girls. In childhood and adolescence the girl maintains her superior resistance. The exception at this period is tuberculosis, which shows twice as many female as male deaths in the age period 12 to 27 (Frank, 1933).

Stability of Bodily Function. A number of facts suggest greater stability of bodily function in the male. For example, glandular imbalance is much more common in females, with the possible exception of pituitary disturbance (Rowe, 1928; Dublin and Lotka, 1936; Shuttleworth, 1938). Glandular obesity is usually reported as showing a sex ratio of near 10 to 1. The mental diseases to which females are most prone are those associated with fluctuations of bodily function; mania and depression and involutional mental upset. The male shows less fluctuation than the female in body temperature (Burton, 1939; Murlin, 1939), basal metabolism (Burton, 1939), acid-base balance of the blood (Shock and Hastings, 1934), and level of blood sugar (Rowe, 1928). Females are more prone to flushing and fainting. Girls are more reactive to stress than boys, according to Sontag (1947), but recover more quickly. From such differences it would appear that homeostatic mechanisms operate within narrower limits in the male than in the female. This fact has been proposed (Johnson and Terman, 1940) as a possible explanation of the temperamental or personality differences that have appeared in many studies.

Neuromuscular Tension. There is evidence that the male is geared to muscular reactivity in greater degree than the female. Tics of the muscular-spasm variety seem to be more prevalent in boys than in girls (Terman *et al.*, 1925). At the nursery school level boys exceed girls in motility, according to Goodenough (1930). Hattwick (1937) reports that boys more often jump and squeal excessively, are tense at rest, and stay awake at nap time. Infantile tetany occurs twice as often in boys as in girls (Bakwin, 1929). Gatewood and Weiss (1930), measuring the reactions of the newborn in a stabilimeter, find males more reactive to stimulation as shown by greatly increased respiration rate. This characteristic may also underlie some of the psychological differences in interests and personality traits.

Miscellaneous Physical Differences. In the sensory field the higher incidence of defective color vision among males is well known. With older children and adults auditory defect in the perception of high-frequency tones is more common in males (Beasley, 1938; Ciocco, 1938). Left-handedness, stuttering, and alexia (nonreading) all show a higher incidence for males than for females. (Some believe these three variables to be functionally interrelated.) Epilepsy and mental deficiency are also more common among males (Danby, 1934), though the true difference is probably less than the sex ratio of admissions to state and private institutions would indicate. Scheinfeld (1943) has considered these data with regard to the greater incidence of defects in the male, along with the statistics on viability cited above, as evidence for a general biological superiority of the female.

Overlapping and within-Sex Variability. For all the physical characteristics that have been discussed there is a large amount of variability from person to person within the same sex, and a large amount of overlapping in comparable male and female distributions. Maleness or femaleness is not an all-or-none characteristic, either physically or psychologically. Beach (1948) has summarized the research evidence with regard to sex hormones and their effects. It would seem to indicate that both the neuromuscular mechanisms and the hormonal secretions capable of mediating masculine or feminine behavior are to be found in both sexes. It is the balance between the two which is important. In the male, the masculine pattern is typically much more sensitive and easily brought into action than the feminine; in the female, the reverse is true. Furthermore, there is no polarity or opposition between the effects of the two types of sex hormones. Either androgen or estrogen can increase the responsiveness of the neuromuscular mechanisms for *either* type of sex behavior. It is a problem of *relative* sensitivities. The mechanisms for male behavior are much *more* sensitive to androgen, those for female behavior much *more* sensitive to estrogen.

To what extent the variability we encounter in psychological traits can be accounted for in terms of the variability in physical and physiological characteristics is still an unsolved problem. The evidence available does not tell us how large a proportion of psychological masculinity or femininity in human beings is linked directly with physical factors. Both Beach (1948) and Seward (1946) call attention to the fact that, as we ascend the evolutionary ladder, biological factors are of progressively less importance in determining sex behavior, and social factors are progressively more important.

There is scattered evidence, however, of some relationship between physical and psychological deviations from the sex norms.

Among normal subjects a few low but fairly reliable correlations have been found between physical measures and masculinity-femininity scores on the Terman-Miles M-F test (Terman and Miles, 1936; Gilkinson, 1937). Sheldon (1940) claims to have found significant personality characteristics associated with masculinity and femininity of body build in male college students. Changes in personality in boys with hypogenitalism or adiposity have been reported when injections of testosterone were administered over a period of months. There was an impression of increased aggressiveness shown by a detachment from the family group and a greater tendency to assertiveness (Marquis, 1940). Sollenberger (1940) found a close relationship between the amount of male sex hormone in the urine of adolescent boys and their maturity of interests and attitudes; in fact the correlations reported in this research are so high as to be suspect.

It would seem that both physical and social factors may be involved in producing psychological masculinity and femininity, but the tendency at present is to give the social the greater weight. The method developed by Bayley and Bayer (1946) for the assessment of somatic androgyny (characteristics of the opposite sex) is designed to make possible some definitive research on the subject. So far it has shown (Bayley, 1951) that no consistent relationship between physique ratings and M-F scores on the Kuder Preference Record can be demonstrated for 79 boys and 83 girls in the Guidance and Berkeley Growth studies. Further studies using this technique should clarify the issue.

Sex Differences in Abilities

A tremendous amount of work has been done on differences between the sexes in intelligence and special mental abilities. It would be far beyond the scope of this review to summarize all these separate investigations. We shall rather begin with the generalizations that seem to be warranted by the bulk of the research evidence and then cite some typical studies, particularly the more recent ones, in connection with each statement. These generalizations are as follows:

1. If there is a difference between the sexes in general intelligence, it cannot be identified by means of our present tests, since some types of problem favor males, others favor females, and there is no satisfactory way to decide which ones constitute more valid indicators of general mental ability (McNemar, 1942).

2. Girls tend to excel on verbal types of problem; boys, on quantitative or spatial.

3. School marks almost universally indicate superior achievement for girls, whereas achievement tests show girls superior in all kinds of language material, boys in science and mathematics.

4. Vocational aptitude tests show boys higher in mechanical, girls in clerical, aptitudes.

5. Ability differences are most apparent at the older age levels in children. Most of them do not show up at the preschool period.

General Intelligence. Much of the confusion arising from conflicting reports based on different samples of the population has been cleared up by the Scottish Mental Surveys. The first of these (1933) involved a verbal group test of practically all the children (except the blind or deaf) who were born in Scotland in a given year, totaling over 87,000. The test was administered when the subjects were between 10½ and 11 years of age. The means for the sexes were almost identical. The 1916 Stanford-Binet was given to a subsample of 500 of each sex. After a correction was applied to free the sample from bias due to overrepresentation of superior children there was no reliable difference between the sexes in mean IQ.

In the second Scottish survey (Macmeeken, 1939) the 1916 Stanford-Binet was given to all living children who had been born in Scotland on one of four specified days of 1926 (444 boys and 430 girls). This is the most nearly perfect sampling in the history of psychometrics, for only a single child who should have been tested was missed. Here again the mean IQ's were almost identical for the sexes.

The issue was somewhat confused, however, by the results of the later Scottish survey reported in *The Trend of Scottish Intelligence* (1949). This time a complete sampling of all children born on six specified days in 1936, 1215 in all, gave mean IQ's of 104.387 for the boys and 100.734 for the girls on the Terman-Merrill Revision, Form L. The difference is 3.24 times its standard error. In contrast to these findings, on the group test given to all children born in 1936, the girls scored 1.74 points higher than the boys, a difference which because of the large numbers involved is also statistically significant. These figures would seem to lend further support to the conclusion that the direction and magnitude of sex differences in intelligence depend primarily on what test is used.

Another good sampling was made by Roberts *et al.* (1935), who gave the Otis advanced test to all children of Bath, England, born between specified dates in 1921 and 1924. The sample included 1336 boys and 1217 girls, aged 9½ to 13½ when the tests were administered. The sex difference was minute and unreliable.

The amount and direction of difference on nonverbal and performance tests depend upon the specific nature of the tests used. Data were reported by Pintner (1924) for 924 subjects aged 10 and for 1346 subjects ged 12 given his nonlanguage group test. No reliable sex difference was found. Lincoln's (1927) data on 200 to 400 subjects at each age from 7 to 16 given the Dearborn general examination showed only small and inconsistent differences between the sexes. Goodenough (1926) gave sex comparisons for nearly 1600 subjects, ages 6 to 11 years, on her test of drawing a man. The girls were superior at each age, the critical ratios ranging from 0.5 to 2.7. That this is some function of cultural differentiation is shown by the findings of Dennis (1942) and Havighurst, Gunther, and Pratt (1946) that in some Indian societies boys are superior to girls on the Goodenough Test. The previously mentioned Scottish group, consisting of 444 boys and 430 girls born on specified days in 1926, was given between the ages of 9 and 11 a battery of eight performance tests including a form board, a manikin, two picture-completion tests, cube construction, and Kohs block designs. The difference favored boys (CR = 3.74).

It is possible that the increasing use of primary mental abilities tests based on factor analysis will gradually clarify the reasons for the sex differences on some intelligence tests. Hobson (1947), using as subjects several fairly large groups of eighth-and ninth-grade students, found that girls made higher scores on W (word fluency), R (reasoning), and M (rote memory), whereas boys were higher on S (space), and V (verbal meanings). Havighurst and Breese (1947), who tested all 13-year-old children in a typical midwestern community, found that girls excelled on N (number), W (word fluency), R (reasoning), and M (rote memory), the boys on S (space). They found no difference on V (verbal meanings). It is interesting to note that neither study showed male superiority on N, which we might expect on the basis of the school achievement tests,

and that the well-substantiated verbal superiority of girls would seem to be one of fluency rather than of meanings and concepts. Male superiority on S is in line with the findings on mechanical aptitude (Bennett and Cruikshank, 1942). Lord (1941) showed that boys as young as fifth-graders are superior to girls in locating places and naming the primary directions.

British psychologists have been particularly interested in the space factor because of its relationship to ability to learn practical skills. Smith (1948), who administered nine paper-and-pencil tests of spatial ability to 100 boys and girls ranging in age from 12.5 to 14.5, obtained a significant sex difference on spatial tests when there was none in verbal intelligence tests. Emmett (1949) has re-analyzed data from several large-scale studies to show that there is a special spatial ability that can be identified by the age of 11, and that boys are clearly superior to girls in tests in which it is involved.

The youngest group for which a sex comparison based on factor analysis is available is in a study reported by Mellone (1944). His subjects were 7-year-olds, 218 boys and 196 girls, who were given a battery of picture tests of mental ability. For the girls, one general factor alone accounted for the correlations, but boys showed a separate space factor as well. This study suggests that mental abilities during the course of development may come to be differently organized or related to each other in the two sexes.

That the abilities on which boys and girls differ may be even more narrowly specialized than the factor analysis studies indicate is suggested by results reported by Duggan (1950). Immediate recall tests administered to mixed groups of secondary school students showed girls to be superior at observational noting and remembering words, and boys to be superior in remembering numbers.

A report on sex differences in an entirely different sort of ability from those we have been discussing comes from Witkin (1949), who has been working with perceptual situations in which the subject must separate kinesthetic from visual cues in making judgments of the upright. Pronounced sex differences have been found, males at all ages tested showing superiority in this type of perceptual analysis. With the rod-and-frame test the differences were apparent with children as young as 8. The relationship of these differences in perception to other abilities and personality characteristics is being investigated.

Achievement in the Language Areas. Most of the many studies based on school achievement tests have shown girls to be superior in tasks involving the use of language. Stroud and Lindquist (1942), using large random samples of all students who had been given the Iowa Every-Pupil tests from 1932 to 1939, report for the grade school comparisons that the girls are higher on reading comprehension, work study skills, and basic language skills. High school comparisons, probably reflecting some unknown selective factors with regard to continuation in school, show boys superior on everything *except* reading comprehension. Stalnaker (1941), reporting on the English examination of the 1940 College Entrance Examination Board, shows that there are large and significant differences in favor of girls that cannot be explained in terms of selection, since boys average better on the other examinations and on the Scholastic Aptitude Test.

School surveys using reading tests, if they show any significant difference, usually show higher scores for girls. Moore (1939), giving results from a number of school groups ranging in level from eighth grade to college seniors, reports that girls are consist-

ently superior on the Van Wagenen Rate of Comprehension Test, although not all single differences are significant. In a further study (1940), in which he reports speed scores on the Iowa silent reading test for all white pupils in grades 6, 8, 10, and 12 in two southern towns, the only reliable difference (CR = 2.9) favored the girls in grade 8, and this was accompanied by a reliable difference favoring girls on the Otis test of mental ability (CR = 3.5). Jackson (1944) found that the 300 advanced and 300 retarded readers, grades 2 to 6, whom he picked out for an interview study on the basis of a reading test included a disproportionate number of girls in the high group (59.0 per cent) and of boys in the low group (63.3 per cent). A study carried on by Samuels (1943) of all English-speaking first-graders in Phoenix, Arizona, shows girls reliably superior on the Kuhlmann-Anderson intelligence test, reading readiness at the beginning of the year, and reading achievement at its close. When boys and girls were paired for intelligence and school situation, the achievement differences still favored girls. [The Kuhlmann-Anderson intelligence test is one on which girls of all ages consistently get better scores than boys (Lewis, 1945).]

On the other hand, a number of school surveys have not shown any tendency toward female superiority. Heilman's (1933) data for all 10-year-old children in the public schools of Denver showed no sex difference for either of the reading subtests of the Stanford Achievement Tests. Schiller (1934) found no reliable sex difference from her application of the Gates silent reading test to third- and fourth-grade subjects. Results on the Thorndike-McCall reading test have been reported by Thorndike *et al.* (1934) for 266 boys and 200 girls aged 13 to 15 years, and for 785 boys and 905 girls in the eighth grade of New York City public schools. In the first of these groups there was a reliable difference favoring girls; in the second, a reliable difference favoring boys. McIntyre and Wood (1935) administered tests of reading achievement to approximately 33,000 subjects in Australia. The tests provided separate measures of vocabulary, speed of reading, reading for general meaning, reading for detail, and reading for inference. Only on speed of reading were there consistent and reliable sex differences favoring girls. Millard (1940), in a longitudinal study over the 6-year grade-school period using Courtis growth curves, found some sex differences in the constants in the equations (representing differences in the shape of the curves) but no difference in ultimate achievement. In Jordan's (1937) comparison of high school senior boys and girls in North Carolina on two reading tests, girls were superior to boys, although only one of the differences was statistically significant. On the other hand, score distributions reported by Woody (1937, 1938) on the Traxler silent reading test applied to first- and second-year high school students in a Michigan survey yielded mean differences (computed by Kuznets) that favored boys.

The fact that most of the reading investigations reporting female superiority have been based on speed of reading tests, coupled with the above-cited evidence from the primary mental abilities studies that it is fluency rather than verbal meanings in which girls excel, gives us some clue as to a possible reason for the discrepancies between reported results. This interpretation is substantiated by the work on general vocabulary, in which there appears to be no sex difference. Gansl (1939) used a 100-item multiple-choice test in all regular classes of grades 3 to 8 in two New York City public schools. In one school all the means for ages 8 to 14 favored boys, but only at age 12 was the difference statistically significant. In the other school the

differences were neither reliable nor consistent. Schiller (1934) did not find a reliable sex difference on the vocabulary subtest of Thorndike's CAVD given to 189 boys and 206 girls in the third and fourth grades of a Brooklyn public school. Similarly small and inconsistent differences were reported by Bryan (1934) for 100 boys and 100 girls at ages 5 and 6; by Garrett, Bryan, and Perl (1935) for ages 9, 12, and 15; by Broom (1930) for 600 junior high school subjects of each sex; by Hales (1932) for a large group of 12- to 16-year-old Australian subjects; and by McIntyre and Wood (1935) for Australian children aged 9 to 12. The count made by Smith (1926) of words used by 68 boys and 69 girls under age 2 did not reveal consistent differences in favor of either sex, and a vocabulary test devised by Terman and used with 100 children of each sex, aged 2 to 6 years, showed no reliable sex difference.

On the other hand, even in very young children there would seem to be a sex difference in what might be called verbal fluency. The mean age of learning to talk appears to be slightly lower with girls than with boys. According to mothers' reports on 502 gifted children (Terman *et al.*, 1925) the difference was approximately 3 weeks, or 5.52 times its standard error. In the same study girls were reported as using short sentences earlier than boys, but this difference was not very reliable (CR = 1.71). There is a possibility, of course, that mothers' reports of this kind are subject to a memory bias favoring girls. Smith (1926) and McCarthy (1930) reported the mean length of spoken sentences among preschool children to be slightly greater for girls, although the age-sex groups in both studies were too small to afford reliable differences.

Several studies indicate a slight superiority of girls in articulation, intelligibility, and correctness of speech sounds. In a study of speech sounds of 204 preschool children Wellman *et al.* (1931) found differences in correctness of consonant sounds that were fairly reliable at ages 3 and 4 (CR's = 2.6 and 2.5). Differences in the correctness of vowel sounds were not significant. Little and Williams (1937) in a study of speech sounds, intelligibility, and organization, based on 177 preschool subjects and 155 orphanage children of preschool age, concluded that "there is a general tendency for girls to score higher than boys in all areas and at most age levels." This conclusion, however, was not supported by the data which the authors presented. In 18 sex comparisons of the preschool group 9 favored girls, 8 favored boys, and 1 showed no sex difference. Of 15 comparisons for the orphanage group, 9 favored girls, 6 favored boys. The age-sex groups were small, and tests of significance were not given. On the whole, however, the reported results may indicate greater verbal fluency for girls.

The well-known fact that many more boys than girls are stutterers is consistent with these findings. Schuell (1946, 1947) offers some evidence that the difference in the incidence of stuttering may have an emotional rather than an intellectual basis. A questionnaire on family attitudes and treatment was administered to 134 girls and 156 boys, aged 8 to 14. There were statistically significant differences with regard to punishment and praise at home, attitudes toward school, and things worried about. It raises the interesting possibility that the advantage girls have in verbal fluency in general might be related to their more secure emotional attitude, but considerably more research would be needed to substantiate it.

A study by Anastasi and D'Angelo (1952) brings out another aspect of the problem of sex differences in language skills. Their subjects were comparable groups of 50 white and 50 Negro 5-year-olds in day care centers. Besides giving the Goodenough Draw-a-Man Test, they analyzed various language characteristics shown in the children's speech. Girls in both groups scored significantly higher than boys in the drawing test. On the language measures, however, the direction of the sex difference was opposite for white and Negro children. White girls scored significantly higher than boys, but Negro boys scored significantly higher than girls. The authors do not attempt to account for this reversal of trend except to note that it is difficult to reconcile with purely biological explanations.

Achievement in Science and Related Areas. One of the most clear-cut and consistent sex differences at the high school level and above is the difference in science knowledge and achievement. Edgerton and Britt (1944, 1947) have furnished some valuable evidence on this point. In the Science Talent Search, every year from two to three times as many boys as girls apply, which might lead one to expect that the girls would be more highly selected. Yet, in spite of this fact, the boys have each year obtained higher scores on the test. Differences are unquestionably significant and always in the same direction. Jordan (1937) in his survey of North Carolina high school seniors, which included some 8000 boys and 11,000 girls, reported an astronomically large critical ratio in favor of boys on the science section of the achievement test used (CR = 31.7) Learned and Wood (1938) in their valuable study of the achievement of college students reported achievement scores in natural science for 2992 men and 1410 women. The mean was markedly higher for men, the difference being 24 times its standard error. Some interesting supporting evidence comes from a study by Zapf (1945) in which ninth-grade girls are reported to be signifiantly more superstitious than boys of the same age level.

Studies using elementary school subjects ordinarily show differences in the same direction, but less marked. Terman *et al.* (1925) reported achievement test scores for sex groups of about 560 gifted children and an equal number of unselected children, all n grades 3 to 8. The gifted sex groups were closely equated for IQ. On 110 items of science information the difference in means consistently favored boys in both the gifted and unselected groups, though in a majority of the 13 comparisons the differences lacked statistical significance because of the small N's at a single age. Heilman's (1933) study of unselected 10-year-olds in Denver reported a higher mean for 464 boys than for 482 girls on the nature study and science section of the Stanford Achievement Tests (CR = 2.6). Considering the large numbers in the study, this critical ratio would seem to represent a comparatively small difference.

Studies of primary and preschool children on types of thinking that might be assumed to be related to science achievement report no significant sex differences. Bergen (1943) attempted to find out what procedure or sources of information third-grade children would utilize in solving problems of causal relationships. There seemed to be no consistent sex differences. Dickinson and Tyler (1944) found no sex differences n the ability to form concepts at the second-grade level. McAndrew (1943) obtained no significant sex differences in 3- to 5-year-olds in ideas of causality as shown by their answers to questions and their analysis of "tricks." These findings are consistent with the hypothesis that the difference in science achievement is one which develops during the school period and is related more to a difference in interests than to a difference in basic abilities.

Achievement in Arithmetic. Studies based on achievement tests given in grade school are not entirely consistent, but in general they tend to show a slight male superiority in arithmetical reasoning, and either no difference or female superiority in simple computations. As in the case of science, it appears that, the lower the age group tested, the less significant is the difference. Heilman's (1933) study of 10-year-olds in Denver showed girls superior to boys in the arithmetic computation test of the SAT battery (CR = 2.10) and boys superior to girls in the arithmetic reasoning test (CR = 2.68). In his monumental study of the mental and scholastic achievement of London children Burt (1921) reported sex comparisons in seven phases of arithmetical achievement for about 250 of each sex at each age from 8 to 12 years. In oral arithmetic boys were reliably superior at every age. In "mechanical" arithmetic the differences were unreliable except at age 12, where they favored boys. In arithmetic problems the differences were reliably in favor of boys at all ages and were particularly large at ages 11 and 12. In addition, subtraction, multiplication, and division (five age-sex comparisons for each) there were only two reliable differences, both favoring girls in addition. Schiller's (1934) data for 189 boys and 206 girls in grades 3 and 4 showed no appreciable sex differences in computation, but in arithmetical reasoning boys were reliably superior (CR = 4.17). Cunningham and Price (1935) reported the results of arithmetic tests given to approximately 40,000 children in Australia. In the four fundamental processes the differences were small and inconsistent. In "mechanical" arithmetic the differences all favored boys but were not statistically significant. In "problem" arithmetic the differences all favored boys and were highly reliable. Grossnickle (1937) gave a test of "concepts in social arithmetic" to 667 boys and 670 girls at the end of the eighth grade. The sex difference favored boys and though small in magnitude was statistically significant (CR = 5.4).

At the primary and preschool levels there seems to be little differentiation. Buckingham and MacLatchy (1930) studied the number abilities of approximately 1000 first-grade entrants aged 6 to 6½ years. The subjects were tested in rote counting by 1's and by 10's, counting 20 objects, number selection, and number identification. In all but 2 of 11 comparisons the difference favored girls, the critical ratios ranging from 1.03 to 2.90. Woody (1931) gave an individual inventory test in arithmetic consisting of 205 items to approximately 100 children in kindergartens, 600 in grade 1B, 1800 in grade 1A, and 300 in grades 2B and 2A. Boys were superior in all comparisons, but in no case was the difference statistically significant. The standardization data on which the 1937 Stanford-Binet revision is based afford sex comparisons on concept of 1, concept of 2, concept of 3, concept of 4, counting to 3, counting 13 pennies, counting taps, knowledge of numbers, making change, and arithmetical reasoning. On concepts of 1, 2, 3, and 4, there are 16 sex comparisons by age on percentages passing, of which 11 favor girls and 4 favor boys. In the three counting tests the sex difference favors girls in 11 comparisons, boys in 2. In knowledge of numbers the differences are small and inconsistent. In making change all 6 comparisons favor boys. The most reliable differences are for the test of arithmetical reasoning, the boys being superior in all the age groups.

From the above studies it appears that in arithmetical achievement the sex differences are small at the lower levels represented by routine computation and that they progressively favor boys as we go toward the more complex levels of arithmetical reasoning. In the work reported by Blackwell (1940) there is an interesting suggestion that the mental processes by means of which mathematical problems are solved become differentiated in boys and girls as development proceeds. He made a factor analysis based on a battery of mathematics tests given to 100 boys and 100 girls, aged 13½ to 15 years. The first two factors that emerged were alike for the two sexes, the well-known g and a factor he called o representing the carrying-out of mathematical operations. The third factor v seemed to be more specifically verbal in girls and more like verbal reasoning in boys. A fourth factor was identified for girls but not for boys, a factor which seemed to represent precision or exactness.

Sex Differences in Dispersion. The hypothesis of greater male variability in mental traits has frequently been invoked to explain the preponderance of males among the ranks of both mental defectives and genius. Some supporting evidence has accumulated, but on the whole there is about as much against the idea as in favor of it. Hollingworth (1922) has shown that the excess of males in institutions for the feeble-minded might well be accounted for in terms of biased samplings. McNemar and Terman (1936) made an extensive survey of the most reliable and objective data available on variability of the sexes in physical traits, scholastic achievement, and intelligence. The results for achievement are far from consistent but on the whole afford a slight preponderance of evidence favoring greater male variability. In the less-well-standardized psychological tests the evidence breaks about evenly for the sexes. However, of 33 comparisons based on such standardized tests as CAVD, NIT, the Pressey group test, and the 1916 Stanford-Binet, 29 showed greater variability for males, the mean of the critical ratios being 1.47. This mean is 8.4 times ts standard error. On the other hand, the carefully selected group tested in the standardization of the 1937 Stanford-Binet scales, including about 1500 of each sex, showed no consistent sex differences in dispersion. Perhaps the best data of all come from the Scottish surveys previously mentioned. In the first study, using the group test, the variance ratio is significant at the 1 per cent level. In the second, however, using the Binet test, the variance ratio falls just short of significance at the 5 per cent level. The third (1949) shows a slightly higher standard deviation for girls on the individual test and for boys on the group test. Thus the answer to the question of sex differences in intelligence variability would seem to depend on the nature of the test.

Comparisons of the incidence of gifted boys and girls in the population differ in their findings. A school population of 168,000 in grades 3 to 8 which was sifted by Terman et al. (1925) for children of 140 IQ or higher yielded 352 boys and 291 girls who reached this standard, a ratio of about 6 to 5. Of these, 65 boys and 48 girls reached or exceeded 160 IQ, a ratio of approximately 5.4 to 4. A large high school population sifted by the Terman group test yielded 257 boys and 121 girls whose scores were judged to be the equivalent of 140 IQ or higher on the Stanford-Binet, but differential selective factors in the high school samples of boys and girls would keep us from attaching too much importance to this large difference. Witty (1930), on the other hand, found no difference in the proportions of boys and girls in his high-IQ group, and Lewis (1945), in the largest survey ever made of exceptional children, involving the selection of the top and bottom 10 per cent from 45,000 fourth- to eighth-grade children in 455 schools, 310 communities, and 36 states, reported a sex ratio of 146 girls to 100 boys

in the high group. Differences in the bases for selection probably underlie the discrepancies in these findings. Terman used teachers' judgments for his preliminary screening, and tested those reported to be the brightest in their schools. However, a statistical study of nominations did not suggest that these favored boys because of prevailing stereotypes. Lewis used the Kuhlmann-Anderson test, which appears to be somewhat overly weighted with content favoring girls.

It seems unlikely on the basis of present evidence that the enormous differences in male and female eminence which all studies of genius show can be accounted for by greater male variability alone. Differences in motivation and opportunities appear to be more plausible explanatory factors.

Sex Differences in Motivational and Personality Traits

Interests. In contrast with the small and often inconsistent differences reported with regard to sex differences in mental abilities, the evidence for differences in interests of the two groups is unequivocal. Furthermore, such differences show up with as much clarity in the primary and preschool groups as in those approaching adulthood. This does not in itself argue for a biological explanation, but it does indicate that any social sex typing which occurs must begin very young.

Plays, Games, and Other Activities. Sex differences are prominent in the play and other spontaneous activities of children in cultures ranging from the very primitive to the most advanced. In part these differences reflect the division of activity that prevails between males and females in the adult population, though not all the plays of children, even among primitives, are imitative of adult behavior.

There are certain general types of plays and games that are common to cultures widely separated with respect to the adult occupational activities (Miller, 1928). Endogenous factors that might be expected to contribute to sex differences in children's play activities include physical strength and energy, motor speed and skills, and the temperamental predisposition to given types of emotional and social response.

Hildreth (1933) reported data on the recreational and play interests of 89 boys and 84 girls in the ninth grade and of 52 boys and 51 girls in the twelfth grade enrolled in one public and one private school. Check lists were given out, and subjects were asked to designate the three games they liked best. Rank orders of games and activities differed as between public and private school, showing the need of wide sampling as a basis for generalizations in this field. Football was chosen almost exclusively by boys. Baseball was most popular with boys, but it also ranked among the five games most popular with girls. There was little difference in basketball, handball, or soccer. Bridge, golf, tennis, and croquet rated higher with girls; boxing, chess, and wrestling with boys. Similar data secured for other activities showed swimming and ice skating about equally popular with the sexes. Rating higher with boys were bicycle riding, driving automobiles, fishing, and camping; higher with girls were social dancing, horseback riding, reading, and attending movies. This study illustrates the growing tendency of girls to participate in games formerly monopolized by boys. That adolescent girls, however, are less interested than boys in athletic activities in general is shown by a study by Hammond (1945) in which activities checked by boys and girls on Youth Center enrollment blanks were correlated and factor-analyzed. Boys were higher on the factor representing athletic activities, girls on the factor covering artistic activities dancing, etc. A report by Lund (1944) seems to indicate that interest in athletic activity decreases in girls throughout the high school period. The percentages of boys and girls in a high school presenting medical excuses to enable them to get out of physical education classes were compared for each grade from seventh through twelfth. At the seventh-grade level, 6.7 per cent of the boys and 6.8 per cent of the girls presented such excuses. There was little change from year to year for the boys, but the percentage for the girls increased steadily until, at the twelfth-grade level, 7.6 per cent of the boys and 24.8 per cent of the girls presented excuses. Since it seems extremely unlikely that this represents a deterioration in the health of the girls over this period, the trends must be ascribed to differences in motivation

At the elementary school level also there are marked differences in what boys and girls like to do. In a study of the play interests of 554 gifted and 474 unselected children of grades 3 to 8 Terman et al (1925) reported a "masculinity index" for each of 90 plays, games, and activities. The indices were based on knowledge of, interest in, and time devoted to, the various activities by unselected boys and girls. The masculinity ratings of these 90 activities are here given in terms of standard scores in the order from most to least masculine, the score 13 representing the line of neutrality.

24. Tools.
21. Shooting.
20. Kites, bicycles, marbles, wrestling, boxing, football.
19. Tops, machinery, baseball.
18. Fishing.
17. Bow and arrow, skiing, tug of war, soccer.
16. Stilts, garden work, basketball, pool.

15. Hoops, swimming, rowing, hunting, snap the whip, shinny, racing and jumping.
14. Coasting, hiking, riding, duck on rock, leap-frog, bowling, handball, backgammon, checkers, chess, billiards.
13. (Line of neutrality) Red Rover, pompom pull-away, follow the leader, anty over, roly-poly, fox and geese, croquet, volleyball, dominoes, crokinole, parchesi, tiddledy-winks, snap, cards, history cards, geography cards, word building.
12. Jackstraws, postoffice, blackman, fox and hounds, tennis, authors.
11. Tag, hide and seek, puss in corner, dare base, Simon says, playing church, solving puzzles.
10. Jackstones, skating, drop the handkerchief, blindfold.
9. Ring around the rosy, London Bridge, farmer in the dell, in and out the window, cat and mouse, jumping rope, guessing games, charades.
8. Dancing, sewing, playing store.
7. Knitting or crocheting.
6. Playing school.
5. Cooking, playing house.
4. Hopscotch.
3. Dressing up.
2. Dolls.

An outstanding fact brought out by these masculinity ratings is that nearly all the games that involve strenuous activity are definitely on the masculine end of the scale.

Similar results have been obtained by Lehman and Witty (1927) in a series of surveys on children's play activities involving some 17,000 city children and over 2000 rural children. On a list of 200 play activities the children were told to check anything they had done during the past week just because they wanted to, and to indicate the three things they liked best. The results are difficult to evaluate, as sex differences are shown only in the form of graphs and rank-order lists. However, a number of these differences are evident. In the first place, boys are more variable than girls in their play life. Boys more often engage in the following types of activity: active, vigorous plays and games; those involving muscular dexterity and skill; those involving competition; and the more highly organized plays and games. Girls, on the other hand, are more conservative in their play life; they participate more often in sedentary activities and in activities involving a restricted range of action. On the whole, the largest sex differences occur for ages 8½ to 10½, inclusive. After 10½ the similarities in activities become more and more evident as chronological age increases; at least more activities are common to the sexes and the range of interest of each sex becomes narrower. The authors' data on specific games are similar to Terman's.

J. C. Foster (1930) asked 738 boys and 685 girls in the first six elementary grades of Minneapolis schools to list the games (10 or less) played within the last year, indicating whether the game was played outdoors or indoors. She then classified the games into 11 types, using such headings as (1) catching, throwing, kicking, (6) informal dramatization, and (11) group games of the guessing type, for example. There were no very marked sex differences in preference for these 11 classes of games, although the catching, throwing, and kicking games constituted at every age a larger percentage of those listed for boys than for girls. Girls showed a greater interest in the outdoor jumping and hopping games, and, except for age 6, a greater interest in informal dramatizations. Data for individual games in general corroborate the Terman and the Lehman and Witty findings.

One method of identifying interest differences is through the analysis of choices made from play materials. Honzik (1951), using as subjects 163 eleven-year-olds, 164 twelve-year-olds, and 154 thirteen-year-olds, presented a variety of materials with the request that the child create a dramatic scene for a movie. The boys showed a strong tendency to choose blocks, vehicles, and people in uniform, the girls to choose furniture and people in ordinary dress.

Erikson (1951) has presented some other results from the same study. Not only did these preadolescent boys use blocks a great deal more than the girls did, but they used them in characteristically different ways. There were statistically significant sex differences in the extent to which high structures, ruins, and moving objects momentarily stopped were shown. In these categories, boys were higher. Girls used the blocks to mark off open enclosures, usually the interiors of houses, and they built predominantly static scenes. Erikson analyzes some of the internal evidence suggesting that basic physical and anatomical differences rather than environmental factors underlie these behavior tendencies.

Farwell (1930) tested experimentally the reactions of young children to constructive play materials. The subjects were 125 boys and 146 girls enrolled in kindergarten, first grade, and second grade. The children were taken in small groups to a room equipped with several sets of materials for modeling, building, drawing, painting, sewing, cardboard construction, and paper construction. The time spent by each child on each of the activities during fourteen 30-minute play periods was recorded. The building material gave the largest sex differences, boys at all age levels devoting about 50 per cent of their time to it as compared with 5 per cent for the girls. Girls devoted about 30 per cent of their time to painting and the same amount to modeling. Painting and modeling were also popular with boys, but less so than with girls. In their modeling and painting,

the boys showed more interest in vehicles the girls in articles of furniture. It is interesting to note that a Japanese repor by Oyama and Kido (1939) also state that preschool boys choose to model mov able objects, girls static ones, although i the abstract available there were not enough supporting data to evaluate the statement.

Data on children's collections obtained by Terman (1925), Lehman and Witty (1927), Witty and Lehman (1930), and Whitley (1929) have shown little or no sex difference in the number of collections made, but a strong tendency for boys and girls to collect different things. Boys are more likely than girls to collect stamps, girls more likely than boys to collect dolls or pieces of cloth. There is a wide diversity for both sexes in types of items collected.

Reading, Movie, and Radio Interests. Sex differences in reading preferences are among the most interesting to be found in any field because of the clear indication they give of a fundamental difference in masculine and feminine interests. At home, at school, and in public libraries the books to which children are exposed are largely the same for boys and girls; yet marked sex differences in reading preferences are evident as early as the primary school grades and persist to adult years. These differences can hardly be due to direct adult pressures, for children are notoriously perverse in reading the kinds of books they find interesting rather than those urged upon them by parents and teachers. Whereas there are girls' games that are practically taboo for boys, there is no comparable pressure to keep boys from reading fiction or girls from reading adventure stories. Because the kind of book a child reads is less noticeable than the kind of play he engages in, reading argely escapes censorship so far as separate standards for the sexes is concerned.

Studies at high school and elementary school levels practically all agree that girls read more than boys, and that their choices run to milder stories of home and school as contrasted with the active or violent adventure preferred by the boys. Adams (1936), reporting on the use made of the school library by the 17,616 pupils enrolled in 24 high schools, reported that girls exceed boys in number of books read and in frequency of library attendance. In both junior and senior high schools, boys more often read newspapers, whereas girls spend more time on magazines, books, and poetry. Jordan (1921) studied the reading interests of some 3500 children in grades 6 through 12 in three towns and one city. Each child was asked to name in order of preference the 5 books and the 3 magazines he liked best of any he had ever read. Three categories, as classified by the author, accounted for more than 90 per cent of the book choices of each sex: adventure, novels, and stories. Boys showed a definite preference for adventure; girls, for novels and stories. Percentages of total choices were as follows:

	Boys	Girls
Adventure	58	18
Novels	18	42
Stories	15	35

In the magazines listed by the children, adventure and science titles were more prominent in the boys' choices, woman's arts in the girls'.

Johnson (1932) obtained data on the reading of 888 boys and 968 girls in 19 different Minnesota schools, grades 6 through 11. The children were asked to keep a detailed record of their reading over a period of 1 month. The most pronounced sex differences were for scientific articles in magazines (46 per cent of boys and 17 per cent of girls) and sports sections of newspapers (74 per cent of boys, 34 per cent of girls). More boys than girls read the crime news and the national news. More girls than boys read the children's page, the society news, the home page, and the advertisements. Among the books reported, there was not one common to the boys' and girls' lists of 10 most frequently read. Preferences of boys for adventure stories, and of girls for stories of home, school, and children, were apparent.

Terman and Lima (1926), with a somewhat younger group, aged 9–15, obtained similar results when 511 gifted children and 808 control children were asked to keep 2-month reading records. The girls in both gifted and control groups read 20 to 30 per cent more books than the boys. The girls read enormously more stories of home and school life and decidedly more emotional fiction, whereas the boys read many more stories of adventure or mystery. Percentages of books falling in certain categories were as follows:

	Boys	Girls
Stories of adventure or mystery	56	18
Stories of home or school life	2.5	32
Emotional fiction	3.5	16
Informational fiction, including the classics	15	11
Fairy tales, folk tales, and legends	7	10

The authors also obtained information from 602 gifted and 1225 unselected children as to the books they "had most enjoyed reading last year." As in other, similar studies, all the books receiving most choices were fiction. In the two lists of the 20 most liked by each sex, there were only 5 common titles. These were boys' books that are sometimes read by girls. Boys almost never read girls' books, yet they have a wider range of interests in reading and do less rereading than girls.

Russell (1941), who studied library choices among ninth and tenth graders in Saskatchewan, obtained the same kind of results for this Canadian group as are customarily found in the United States, girls tending to prefer milder adventure and romance, whereas boys chose more active fiction.

Thorndike and Henry (1940) presented a list of fictitious titles to rapid-learning and slow-learning groups in grades 6, 7, and 8, asking them to check those they would like to read. The sex differences in choices were considerably greater than the intelligence differences. The girls, both bright and dull, preferred mild adventure stories about children, love and romance, descriptions of feminine activities, and self-improvement. The boys more frequently chose violent or outdoor adventure, sports, travel, exploration, and war. In some of the other categories the sex differences seemed to depend on the sex of the person mentioned in the title. A similar study by Baumgarten-Tramer (1945–1946) found that 40.1 per cent of the boys' choices were for adventure stories, whereas 52.8 per cent of the girls' choices were for familiar stories, biographies, and "stories of destiny."

The phenomenal popularity of comic books with children has called attention to the fact that there are some reading materials that are very well liked by both boys and girls. Andersen (1948) found in a questionnaire study of 686 seventh- and eighth-grade pupils that for both sexes comic books headed the list of things liked. Witty (1941) and Witty, Smith, ánd Coomer (1942) found that both comic strips and comic books were ranked high by both sexes, grades 4 through 8, and that, though there were some discrepancies in the ratings given specific magazines, the same ones were ranked high and low by both sexes. A study by Butterworth and

Thompson (1951), however, in which the list of comic books used in the questionnaire was based on titles mentioned spontaneously by children in a previous study shows the same type of sex differences for 1256 subjects in grades 5 through 12 that have been obtained using other varieties of reading matter. Boys prefer adventure and sports; girls prefer adolescent activities, romance, and real people.

Studies of radio listening habits show a trend toward high popularity and not much differentiation. Longstaff (1936) Eisenberg (1936), Clark (1940), and Ricciuti (1951) all report data of this sort. Eisenberg shows that, of the 28 programs most popular with boys, all but 8 are found in the 28 most popular with girls and the correlation between order of preference for the two sexes is .88. What difference there is between the two is of the kind one would expect from the reading studies and shows girls giving higher rank to programs of sentiment and emotion, home scenes, and everyday realities, while boys rank higher programs of mystery strenuous adventure, and detection of criminals.

In movie interests we find patterns of sex difference similar to those for reading

	Boys	Girls
Adventure	15.3	6.5
Romance	3.9	19.4
Tragedy	3.3	9.2
War	5.1	1.9
Western	20.4	12.0

Written quizzes given by Mitchell (1929) to about 10,000 children in grades 5 to 12 showed significant differences in five of the ten categories into which choices were classified. The percentages for these were as tabulated. Abbott (1927) analyzed ratings obtained from high school boys and girls of 54 films from the "Selected List" of the National Board of Review, and concluded that both sexes want plot, action, and suspense; that the boys like comedy and dislike romance and too much emotion, whereas the girls like romance and appeal to sympathy, dislike comedy, and show greater sensitiveness to ethical questions. Seagoe (1931) and Hicks and Hayes (1938) report differences of somewhat the same sort.

An approach to the problem of differential interests from a slightly different direction was made by Coleman (1931), who analyzed the subjects chosen for written compositions by 5000 children in grades 7 to 12. The children were given three lists of titles, of 36 each (representing 36 categories), and were allowed to choose one title from each list for a composition. Titles that are reliably more popular with boys fall in such categories as current events, famous people, machines, handwork, modern industries, and outdoor activities. Categories appearing reliably more often in girls' choices include children, home life, personal experience, proverbs, religion, sentiment, sympathy, travel, school, literature, art, and human anecdotes. The sex differences here are strikingly like those found for reading interests.

Preferences for School Subjects. Three studies in widely separated places have reported the same types of sex difference in subject preference at the high school level (Book, 1922; Colvin and MacPhail, 1924; Livesay, 1942). Book's populations included 2300 boys and 3400 girls in Indiana. The populations studied by Colvin and MacPhail included a fifth of all high school seniors in Massachusetts, so chosen as to make a representative sampling. Livesay's subjects were seniors in Hawaii high schools. In all three, the boys named science, mathematics, and history or social studies more frequently than did girls, whereas girls more often listed English,

commercial studies, or languages as preferred.

Hicks and Hayes (1938) secured data on subjects best liked and least liked by 102 boys and 148 girls in a junior high school, grades 7 to 9. The sex differences followed about the same pattern as those found for high school seniors. Boys more often than girls prefer mathematics, science, and the social studies (history, civics, and geography); English is far more popular with girls.

There is evidence that the sex differences are the same for different ability levels. Blair (1938) has reported subject preferences expressed by mentally superior and mentally inferior children in junior and senior high school in the state of Washington. His population included approximately 200 of each sex in both superior and inferior groups, or more than 800 subjects in all. The superior and inferior groups had IQ's respectively 1 standard deviation above or 1 standard deviation below the mean of their class populations, so that there was a large intelligence difference. For each school subject except history and social science the direction of sex difference is the same in both groups, but in mathematics, science, foreign languages, and especially English the difference is greater for the superior than for the inferior group. The patterns of sex difference resemble those for unselected high school populations. Terman et al. (1925), who asked 245 gifted children and 226 control children, aged 11 to 13, to rate 29 school subjects, also found the same preference patterns at both ability levels. The following subjects were rated reliably higher by girls than by boys in both gifted and control groups: drawing, modeling, music (especially singing), dramatics, grammar, folk dancing, and penmanship. Subjects rated higher by boys in both groups were general science and United

States history. However, science, mathematics, and English did not show at this age level the markedly differential appeal for boys and girls that characterizes these subjects in high school.

Another study suggesting that sex differences in preferences are less marked in grade school than in high school has been reported by Sister Columba (1926) for a population of 792 boys and 872 girls in grades 3 to 8 in schools (presumably Catholic) of Washington, D. C. The children were asked to name their best-liked and least-liked subject. On reworking the author's data to take account of varying N's, we find for the total group of six grades only two critical ratios above 2.00 for sex differences on best-liked subjects: more girls than boys named religion (CR = 3.98) and more boys than girls named history (CR = 3.28). On subjects least liked, five differences yielded critical ratios above 2.00: more boys than girls named English (CR = 7.48) and spelling (CR = 2.84), whereas more girls than boys named geography (CR = 3.30), history (CR = 2.89), and arithmetic (CR = 2.36). There was no appreciable sex difference on reading or penmanship. Study of trends from grade to grade showed that there was a moderately consistent trend toward emergence and increase of the sex differences from one year level to another, but every subject showed some irregularities and at least one shift in the direction of the differences. Religion, for instance, was better liked by boys in the eighth grade and much better liked by girls in the seventh; history was more favored by girls in the eighth grade and by boys in the seventh. These larger irregularities could not be attributed to chance factors but would suggest that a subject's appeal to a given sex may be greatly influenced by instructional methods and subject matter content, both of which vary from grade to grade and from teacher to teacher.

Occupational Interests. The numerous studies that have been made of children's occupational preferences show large differences between the sexes at all age levels Information of this kind probably tells us very little about sex differences in real interests, but it does throw some light on the characteristic ways boys and girls see the sex rôles in our society. We shall merely refer the reader to a few typical studies without discussing them.

Douglass (1922), using the questionnaire method, ascertained the prospective occupation and reasons for choice of approximately half the high school seniors in the state of Washington—1186 males 1658 females. Alberty (1925) reported the occupational preferences of 1468 boys and 1507 girls enrolled in high school. For more than 300 of each sex the preferences were obtained in three successive years. Girls showed less change of preference than boys, probably because girls have fewer occupations to choose from. Book (1922) reported sex differences in the occupational preferences of 6000 high school seniors in Indiana. Beeson (1928) analyzed the vocational choices of about 2000 high school students in Colorado. Boynton (1936) obtained information from more than 1500 children of grades 1 to 6 in several southern communities. Personal interview methods were used for the first three grades and the usual questionnaire technique for the others. Lehman and Witty (1931) administered the Lehman-Witty vocational attitude quiz to some 13,000 of each sex, ages 8½ to 18½, in two large cities in Kansas, but their material has not been adequately evaluated for sex differences. Williamson and Darley (1935) analyzed the occupational preferences of all Minnesota high school seniors who entered the University of

Minnesota during the 5-year period 1929–1933. Preferences were classified according to the Brussell occupational scale.

The results of such studies are greatly influenced by geographical location and by the limited knowledge children have about the nature of specific occupations and about their own mental equipment. Information as to how a given child's interests, attitudes, likes, and dislikes resemble or differ from those of persons successfully engaged in particular vocations can best be secured indirectly by means of a vocational interest test such as that devised by Strong. Carter and Strong (1933) administered the test to 34 pairs of unlike-sexed twins and to a group of 100 nontwins of each sex from the same high school. The age range was 12 to 20 years, with a mean of 16 for both twin and nontwin groups. The scores for boys were significantly higher on the scales for engineer, chemist, farmer, physicist, and purchasing agent, and small differences in the same direction were found for doctor, psychologist, and mathematician. The scales showing significant differences in favor of girls were those for journalist, advertiser, life insurance salesman, city school superintendent, and certified public accountant. The scales for artist, teacher, minister, and YMCA secretary gave significant sex differences in favor of the girls for the nontwin cases, but for the twin group these differences were not so great. All but one of the occupational interest scales which show higher scores for boys were in the "science" group, and in general the areas where the girls were higher were marked by the use of language and contact with people. (This research used a test designed specifically for men rather than women, so that the most markedly feminine areas were not included.)

In an effort to help Pittsburgh high school students analyze their own special vocational aptitudes and work interests, Miner (1922) devised a blank eliciting information on specific types of work, classified on the basis of the skill required rather than on vocations as they exist in the industrial framework. The largest differences in favor of the girls were for teaching, welfare work, entertaining, and working with records. Favoring boys were the differences in operating engines, construction work, and scientific work. When students were asked their preferences regarding types of work involving stated characteristics, the boys showed significant preferences for work involving much responsibility, calmness rather than enthusiasm, risk or discomfort with greater pay, outdoor activity, planning, giving directions, and dealing with things rather than people. Girls were significantly higher in the choices they made of work involving little responsibility, enthusiasm, indoor activity, carrying out plans, following rather than directing, and dealing with people rather than things. They were less favorable to work involving risk or discomfort with greater pay. These findings are psychologically meaningful and agree closely with the patterns of sex difference found in other areas of children's interests and in the research on adult men and women carried out by Strong and others.

In the Kuder Preference Record (Kuder, 1946) boys and girls are asked to choose between various alternative activities, selecting out of each combination of three the one they like most and the one they like least. Here too sex differences of the same kind are apparent. High school boys come out consistently higher than high school girls on the scales for mechanical, computational, scientific, and persuasive interests. Girls are higher on the artistic, literary, musical, social, and clerical scales. Differences for college students and for adult men and women are all in the same direction.

Miscellaneous Interest Differences. There have been a few studies of children's drawings that point toward interest differences. Hurlock (1943) analyzed the spontaneous productions of adolescents as salvaged from waste baskets, the margins of class papers, etc. Boys draw many more caricatures than girls, whereas girls draw true-to-life pictures of people, animals, and flowers. Boys draw more printed words and are more likely to choose "show-off" or "smart" phrases to ornament.

In general, comparisons of boys' and girls' drawings at the earlier age levels have not shown significant differences in theme. There are two European studies for which only abstracts were available which may show some trends. Fontes (1946–1947) reported that the drawings of girls were more likely to use religious subjects such as God, the Virgin, and the infant Jesus. Only 0.4 per cent of boys' drawings were of this type as compared with 9.1 per cent of the girls'. Baumgarten and Tramer (1943) reported that when 272 Serbian child refugees, 5 to 12 years in age, in camps in Switzerland, were asked to make drawings, the boys drew airplanes, tanks, and battle scenes, whereas the girls drew churches, flowers, landscapes, and household articles. No statistical evaluation was given in the abstract.

Consistent with this difference in choice of subjects for pictures was the finding in three age levels that boys in this country were much better informed about the war than girls were. Meine (1941) found that junior and senior high boys excelled girls in both news information and news habits. Preston (1942) found higher scores on an information test for boys than for girls at the 8-to-15-year level. Geddie and Hildreth (1944) interviewed 21 first graders using questions about the war. Boys knew much more about it and were more interested. The number is small, and no significance

tests are given, but the difference is very striking. Of the 12 boys, 11 were enthusiastic or excited, 1 indifferent. Of the girls, only 2 were enthusiastic, 7 indifferent.

Another study, difficult to classify (Katz 1944), investigated the choices children in grades 2 to 6 made when presented with pairs of traditional and modern paintings. Though the general trend was for an increasing preference for traditional paintings from year to year, the girls were more likely than the boys to choose the traditional. By the sixth grade level, these sex differences had disappeared.

Dietrich and Hunnicott (1948) also investigated sex differences in preferences for pictures. Their subjects, 40 first and second grade children, generally preferred landscapes to interiors, still life, and people. The boys, however, were more likely than the girls to prefer seascapes to landscapes, and the girls more likely than the boys to prefer people to landscapes.

In a study by Tyler (1951) of the interests of first grade children an oral preference record was used from which scores for four general types of activity could be derived, namely, outdoor play, indoor play, paper-and-pencil activity, and helping adults with work. There were enough sex differences on individual items to make possible the construction of an M-F scoring key. Interest scores were correlated with scores on some of the Primary Mental Abilities tests for boys but not for girls. This suggests that interests may be differently organized in the two sexes even at a comparatively early age, with boys tending more strongly to develop interests congruent with their special abilities and disabilities.

It would be difficult to summarize what these miscellaneous studies show, but their findings in general would seem to substantiate research done at the adult level indicating that masculine interests are broader, ess personal, and more diversified than feminine. Their principal interest for us lies in the fact that they indicate that such differences show up fairly early in children's development and in spite of similarity in the educational environment of the two sexes.

Aggressive and Dominant Behavior. One of the sex differences most universally found, which can be traced back from the adult to the preschool level, is in this area. Measures of dominance or ascendance of the type devised by Allport and by Bernreuter almost invariably yield higher scores for males than for females at the high school and college ages. Sex differences in this direction reported by Bernreuter (1933) have critical ratios of 3.38 for high school subjects, 2.74 for college subjects, and 3.97 for older adults. Carter (1935) found a similar sex difference on the Bernreuter dominance scores of 118 pairs of twins enrolled in high schools. Perry (1934) reported a somewhat similar sex difference on this test in the case of 178 men and 144 women in junior college. Another interesting sex difference reported by Perry is that the dominance and self-sufficiency scores of girls were positively correlated with scholarship, whereas no such relationship was found for boys. Bell (1939) reported for large populations sex differences in social adjustment scores yielded by his adjustment inventory. The inventory is so constituted that high scores indicate the presence of considerable social aggressiveness. These scores were higher for males in four separate groups, the critical ratio of the sex differences being as follows: for 251 high school subjects, 2.03; for 414 college subjects, 2.62; for 148 delinquents, 2.07; for 468 adults, 4.35.

Studies based on ratings and behavior observations show the same kind of difference for younger subjects. In a study of self-ratings by 110 boys and 109 girls in the seventh and eighth grades, Hurlock (1927) reports that more boys than girls describe themselves as daring (18.1 vs. 4.6 per cent), fond of a fight (16.3 vs. 8.2 per cent), or proud (38.2 vs. 19.2 per cent). Boys quarrel more than girls. One of the most marked sex differences found by Macfarlane, Honzik, and Davis (1937) in their reputation study of young children of the first three grades was the greater frequency of quarrelsome behavior among boys. Children also condemn this trait in girls more than in boys: the r between "popular" and "not quarrelsome" is .77 for girls but only .48 for boys. Data by Fuxloch (1930) on 500 children of kindergarten and school age indicate that in their free play boys are more pugnacious and more outstanding in leadership than girls.

These characteristic differences are plainly evident at the nursery school level. Using 1600 time-samplings of the behavior of 40 nursery school children, Green (1933a) reported an average of 13.4 quarrels for boys as against 10.2 for girls. Boys also quarreled with more children. Another analysis by Green (1933b) showed that boys' quarrels were more often physical, girls' more often verbal. Dawe's (1934) detailed analysis of 200 quarrels among nursery school subjects gives 13.5 as the mean number of quarrels for boys as against 9.6 for the girls. Dawe notes that boys are more likely than girls to quarrel over possessions, whereas girls more often than boys quarrel because of interference with an activity. Boys do more striking, girls more pulling and pinching. Boys more often precipitate their quarrels; girls more often take retaliative or objecting rôles. Jersild and Markey (1935) and Roff and Roff (1940) found less sex difference in conflict tendencies at the nursery school level than other investigators have reported.

Goodenough (1931) had mothers keep daily records of the anger outbursts of 26 boys and 19 girls, aged 7 to 82 months. During the period covered the mean number of such outbursts was 45 for boys and 37 for girls. Hattwick's (1937) ratings of 579 nursery school children indicate that in their relations with other children boys more often grab toys (CR = 2.60) and attack others (CR = 2.76), whereas girls more often avoid play (CR = 1.97). The boys exceed girls in all forms of aggressive behavior with the exception of verbal bossing. The author thinks that these sex differences could hardly be due to social pressures, since they were almost equally in evidence from 2 to 4½ years. Caille (1933) also reports more aggressive behavior among boys in a group of 36 nursery school children, aged 19 to 49 months (CR = 2.36). Among 104 children aged 2 to 4 years, Berne (1930) found boys more given to teasing (CR = 3.7) and social conformance more characteristic of girls (CR = 3.2).

Some interesting studies comparing the reactions of boys and girls in a projective doll play situation have been carried out at the University of Iowa. Pintler, Phillips, and Sears (1946), using as subjects 40 boys and 30 girls with an average age of about 4.5, found that the boys showed significantly more aggression in the way they used the dolls and other materials. They were less likely than the girls to use the dolls in the customary stereotyped way. Sears (1951), in a later and more complete report based on equal sex group of 3-, 4-, and 5-year-olds, 150 in all, showed that boys differ from girls not only in the frequency but also in the direction and kind of aggressive acts. They are much more likely to show behavior classified in the "bodily injury" category. Bach (1945) with the same sort of projective situation found highly significant sex differences in 35 preschool children, aged 34 to 64 months. Girls produced a larger amount of doll action than did boys, a higher proportion of

affectionate themes, and more verbal ordering and commanding. A greater proportion of the boys' fantasies were of a socially unacceptable nonstereotyped character and were marked by aggressive hostility. Girls concentrated more on socially approved themes to be acted out in the play (e.g. resting) and boys on disapproved themes (e.g., toilet activity). These Iowa investigators are inclined to explain their findings in terms of a sex-typing process dependent on early learning.

The report by Yarrow (1948) on 60 preschool children ranging in age from 3–0 to 5–7 furnishes corroborative evidence of these findings from another area of the country. Boys were more active and aggressive than girls under all the conditions set up in these experiments.

Delinquency and Behavior Problems. Data from courts, from child guidance clinics, and from schoolrooms substantiate the finding that males are more aggressive than females. Sex differences in delinquency are difficult to interpret for various reasons. The sexes are exposed to different temptations and in different degrees. The criteria of delinquency are not the same for boys and girls, and there is differential treatment of the sexes with respect to arrests and disposal of cases. The available statistics probably minimize the actual amount of delinquency among girls as compared with boys. There is one exception, however, to this tendency: the statistics undoubtedly exaggerate the relative sex delinquency of girls because the social tolerance of sexual misconduct by girls is much lower than it is for boys. Healy and Bronner (1926) gave the sex ratio in two large series of juvenile court cases as 2.3 boys to 1 girl. There was close agreement between the Chicago and Boston series. Fortes (1933) reported 808 boys and 59 girls in the records of probation officers of East London, Connecticut.

This is a ratio of 7.3 to 1. Alper and Lodgen (1936) reported probation data for all but two counties in Pennsylvania. The totals were 2533 boys and 748 girls, a ratio of almost 3 to 1.

Maller (1933) noted a marked change in the sex ratio among juvenile court cases during the three decades beginning in 1902. The ratio was about 8 to 1 in the first decade, 4 to 1 in the second, and 2.7 to 1 in the third. In 30 years the number of boys brought before the juvenile court decreased by 20 per cent, whereas the number of girls more than doubled. Maller believes that this rapid change is not primarily a function of altered court procedure and attributes the increase in delinquency among girls to the increasing incidence of parental divorce, which is supposed to have a worse effect on girls than on boys. We doubt the correctness of this interpretation and suspect that the observed trend is largely due to changes in selective factors.

With all these fluctuations in sex ratio from place to place and from time to time, all statistics show that the incidence of delinquency is much greater in boys than in girls. Statistics from all sources report a higher percentage of boy than of girl delinquents charged with offenses against property, and a higher percentage of girl delinquents charged with sex offenses.

Data on sex differences in the problems encountered by child guidance clinics are also of doubtful value because of the selective factors that may affect clinic populations. On the whole, however, they show the same trends as the other figures from more representative populations. For details the reader should consult the report by Schumacher (1933) on 120 consecutive cases of each sex examined in a child guidance clinic, and Ackerson's (1931) analysis of 5000 consecutive cases exam-

ined at the Institute for Juvenile Research at Chicago. Percentage frequencies of certain personality problems among 2853 white boys and 1739 white girls in Ackerson's population were as tabulated. The

	Boys	Girls
Restless, overactive	19	16
Irritable temperament	19	14
Touchy	13	10
Distractible	12	9
Personal violence	8	4
Request for sanity diagnosis	7	4
Potential sex delinquency	0.1	3

percentages for "potential sex delinquency" illustrate the need for caution in drawing conclusions from such data. Taken at their face value, the figures would suggest that the incidence of potential sex delinquency is 30 times as high for girls as for boys!

Schoolroom studies universally report more problem behavior among boys, but these of course are distorted by the many kinds of bias known to affect teacher attitudes. Haggerty (1925) secured teachers' ratings on the incidence of faults and problem behavior among 800 children in grades 1 to 8. By weighting the faults according to estimated seriousness the author derived a behavior score for each child. The mean scores were higher (more unfavorable) for boys in every school grade. Wickman (1928), who had assisted in the Haggerty study, reported similar scores for 462 boys and 412 girls in Cleveland. Undesirable kinds of behavior that were reported by teachers at least twice as frequently for boys as for girls included truancy, destruction of property, stealing, profanity, disobedience, defiance, cruelty, bullying, and rudeness. The aggressive nature of most of these activities is apparent. The only kind of problem more frequently reported for girls was the writing of obscene notes. Children regarded by teachers as presenting minor behavior problems included 49 per cent of boys and 35 per cent of girls; those judged to have serious behavior problems were 10 per cent of boys and 3 per cent of girls. Olson (1930) reported similar figures for 1473 boys and 1394 girls.

Williams (1933) secured data in 10 cities on 1343 children regarded by their teachers as problem cases. These constituted 2.4 per cent of the school population covered by the survey. In the problem group the ratio of boys to girls was 4 to 1. Types of behavior more common among problem boys than problem girls were "misconduct in school" (46 vs. 22 per cent), disobedience (45 vs. 23 per cent), and annoying other children (48 vs. 31 per cent). The incidence of 37 types of undesirable behavior, as judged by teachers, was reported by Hurlock and McDonald (1934) for 438 boys and 352 girls in a junior high school attended largely by Jewish children. More frequent among problem boys than problem girls were lying, cheating, truancy, disobedience, rudeness, and bullying.

The studies just reviewed are so typical of their kind that it would be a waste of time to cite others. They corroborate the results of better-controlled studies of sex differences in aggressive behavior, but they also reflect to an unknown extent teacher attitudes rather than pupil characteristics. There are a number of indications that some sort of "halo" effect operates to give girls higher ratings in practically everything. This of course might originate in the unfavorable reaction most people show to aggressive behavior. Ratings secured by Terman et al. (1925) for gifted and control groups, each numbering more than 500, showed that under the most careful procedures the ratings contain a "generosity factor" which is differential for sex. Girls were rated significantly higher than

boys on almost everything, including "moral" traits like sympathy, generosity, conscientiousness, and truthfulness, and miscellaneous characteristics such as health, physical energy, persistence, common sense, and freedom from vanity. Only on mechanical ingenuity were boys rated significantly higher than girls.

Hayes (1934) had about 400 of each sex, aged 10 to 15 years, rated on a large number of behaviors. The median rating for girls was higher than for boys at every age, the maximum difference being at 14. Langlie (1937) had 170 high school seniors (85 of each sex) rated by several men teachers, and 135 boys and 300 girls rated by several women teachers, on ability to learn, intellectual initiative, industry, scholastic zeal, dependability, and capacity for college work. Median ratings by both men and women were higher for girls on every trait, although college aptitude tests of these subjects averaged slightly higher for boys. Indicative of the greater halo factor in girls' ratings is the higher intercorrelation found for girls than for boys on the various trait ratings.

Rundquist (1941) has presented evidence which he interprets to mean that the practically universal superiority of girls in school marks is related to this rating factor. Whereas at the grade school level there was little difference between boys and girls in the relationship of marks to intelligence test scores (r's from .75 to .79), in junior high there was a considerable discrepancy. For boys the correlations between marks and tests ranged between .42 and .58. For girls they were from .68 to .77. Behavior factors becoming intensified at adolescence might account for these trends.

In general, the comparisons of the sexes with regard to negativism and resistant behavior in very young children show males somewhat higher in these traits.

Goodenough (1928) reported ratings of 380 nursery school children on degree of shyness, negativism, and distractibility during the administration of Kuhlmann-Binet tests. There was no sex difference on shyness. Negativism was reliably more common among boys, but this difference was present only at the upper occupational levels. The peak of negativism was at 18 months for girls, at 30 months for boys. The second study by Goodenough (1929), based on tests of 990 subjects, confirmed the earlier findings. Mayer (1935) found negativistic behavior among 245 children of ages 2 to 5½ years, during the administration of the revised Stanford-Binet scales, to be slightly more frequent with boys, but the difference approached statistical significance only at age 4 (CR = 2.1). Nelson's (1931) mental test data for 91 three-year-olds showed boys to be slightly, though not reliably, more resistant. On the other hand, Levy and Tulchin (1923), reporting on tests of 983 subjects aged 6 to 63 months, show girls slightly more resistant than boys at all ages except 30 months. This may be because they included in the category of resistant behavior every kind of interference with the progress of the test, including crying and inattentiveness.

A somewhat different type of situation was utilized in the studies by Reynolds (1928) and Caille (1933). Reynolds' procedure was to try to get the child to play with blocks while sitting on the experimenter's lap and to engage in imitative play with the experimenter. The mean score for negativism was slightly but not reliably higher for 105 boys than for 124 girls. The age range was from 2 to 5 years. The mean for girls began to drop at 3 years, that for boys at 4 years. Caille's study of 17 boys and 19 girls summarizes evidence of resistance based not only upon mental tests but also upon

stenographic records of the speech of each subject during two days of nursery school attendance. Again, resistant behavior was found to be more common with boys.

Suggestibility, which may be thought of as the opposite of negativism, was a favorite subject for investigation in the early decades of experimental psychology but has received much less attention of late. Whipple (1915) presents a summary of the older literature, and more recent studies among children have been reported by Aveling and Hargreaves (1921), Lodge (1926), White (1930), Hurlock (1930), Messerschmidt (1933), and Wegrocki (1934). In general, the sex differences disclosed by these studies are small, but the direction consistently indicates that girls are more suggestible than boys.

Neurotic and Emotional Response. A considerable amount of evidence has accumulated that females are more emotional or less stable than males. Much of the work has been done with adult subjects and thus falls outside the scope of this review. Children and adolescents have, however, been studied by means of paper-and-pencil tests and questionnaires and by more or less well-controlled observation, and the findings show some general trends.

With personality questionnaires, older adolescents show sex differences like those in the adult population, differences which are less apparent or fail to show up at all at the younger age levels. Mathews (1923) gave a modified Woodworth Personal Data Sheet to 575 boys and 558 girls, aged 9 to 19 years. For all ages combined the median number of "emotionally unstable" replies was about 25 per cent greater for girls than for boys, a difference that is statistically reliable. However, between ages 10 and 17, the median of unstable responses for boys decreased from 35 to 14, whereas for girls it increased from 24 to 37. Only after age 14 were the scores significantly better for the boys. Schubert and Wagner's (1936) Woodworth scores for 229 boys and 248 girls, all high school seniors, showed a much smaller sex difference, but in the same direction. Bernreuter's (1933) test for neurotic tendency (B 1-N), which has much in common with the Woodworth test, yielded scores which were reliably more "neurotic" for females in all the author's standardization groups. The critical ratio in the high school group was 3.94. Carter's (1935) application of the Bernreuter test to 128 male and 108 female twins aged 12 to 19 years also showed girls reliably more "neurotic" than boys. Emotionality, or neurotic tendency, is one of several aspects of maladjustment measured by the Bell Adjustment Inventory. In high school, college, and delinquent populations this inventory yields higher emotionality scores for females than for males. For high school groups the reported CR is 8.51 (Bell, 1939).

When Hartshorne, May, and Maller (1929) gave the Woodworth test to 393 boys and 382 girls in grades 5 to 8, however, they found no reliable sex differences. Cady's modification of the Woodworth test was given by Terman et al. (1925) to 532 gifted subjects aged 7 to 14 and to 533 unselected subjects aged 10 to 14. In neither group was there a reliable sex difference at any age.

Using his own psychoneurotic inventory F. Brown (1934) found no significant sex differences in a population of 1663 unselected children in grades 4 to 9. Springer (1938) confirmed this finding. In Springer's study, Brown's inventory was given to 800 children of grades 4 to 9, including 190 boys and 137 girls in a slum district and 237 boys and 236 girls in a good district. Girls of both groups tested slightly more "neurotic" than boys, but the critical ratios were only 1.5 and 1.8.

At the age levels where they occur, these sex differences in emotionality score seem not to be confined to any one segment of the population, although not enough special groups have yet been tested to warrant a certain judgment on this point. As stated above, Bell obtained comparable results in delinquent and nondelinquent groups. Maller's character sketches for testing emotional stability showed about the same sex differences for 103 Parisian children as others have found for children in this country (Kinter-Remmlein, 1933). A comparison of blind and sighted high school students by means of the Clark-Thurstone neurotic inventory (P. A. Brown, 1939) yielded even larger sex differences for the blind than for the normal subjects. The CR for the normal group was 3.44; for the blind group, 7.16.

Tests which attempt to get at "affectivity" by asking subjects to check such things as worries and annoyances have not produced entirely consistent results. Sunne (1925) gave the Pressey test to 130 boys and 102 girls in grades 7 and 8 and found that girls checked reliably more worries than did boys. Collins's (1927) data from Pressey tests of 1500 Scotch and English children aged 11 to 15 showed slightly higher affectivity scores for girls with a marked sex difference in the worries test. Zeligs (1939) found that 12-year-old girls checked significantly more worries from a list than did 12-year-old boys. This author also reported (1945) that sixth-grade girls are annoyed by more factors than boys of the same age, and react to a greater degree than boys do to these annoyances. Clear supporting data with significance tests are not provided. On the other hand Kohn (1937), using the X-O test as revised in 1933, found no sex differences in an orphanage high school population of

149 boys and 118 girls. There may, of course, be some selective factors in the orphanage population accounting for this exception to the general trend. Pintner and Lev (1940) report boys more prone than girls to worry about social and personal inadequacy. These authors administered an inventory of 53 worry items to 270 boys and 270 girls in grades 5 and 6. Some of the differences reported are so unexpected as to suggest that errors may have occurred in data tabulation or else that the boys' responses were inspired by a sense of humor. For example, these boys of 11 and 12 years are reported as worrying more than girls about "being late for supper" (CR = 4.31), "not having a pretty home" (CR = 2.67), and "getting married" (CR = 2.44).

In their analysis of sex differences in responses to individual items of the M-F test Terman and Miles (1936) summarized data from 550 subjects on anger, fear, disgust, and pity. The subjects included 250 in the seventh grade, 200 in the eleventh grade, and 100 college students. The inventory called for a rating of degree of emotion aroused in the subject by each of 34 situations for anger, 40 for fear, 36 for disgust, and 28 for pity. In all three populations and for all four types of emotion, the responses of girls indicated greater affectivity than those of boys. However, for a given emotion the direction of sex difference varied according to the specific situation presented. Whether the emotion in question be anger, fear, disgust, or pity, the items that have low affectivity thresholds for boys are largely different from those that have low thresholds for girls. These qualitative differences, too numerous to review here, are psychologically more interesting than the quantitative differences.

The preponderance of evidence from personality inventories thus indicates some-what greater emotionality for females. The amount of sex difference varies from test to test but even when small or nonsignificant is almost invariably in one direction. At the same time caution is necessary in the interpretation of pencil-and-paper tests of emotionality. We cannot be sure that boys and girls are equally willing to confess their emotional reactions or that the individual questions in a personality inventory carry always the same meaning for the sexes. The fact that much larger score differences show up for adolescents than for younger children is consistent with the interpretation that boys and girls gradually become aware of what it is acceptable for them to admit. However, a study by Darley (1937) indicated that the greater emotionality shown by females may not be spurious. When college students who had been given tests of maladjustment were clinically interviewed by two experienced counselors, it was found that the excess of maladjustment among women as compared with men was more marked in the clinical diagnoses than in the test scores. The fact that evidence on children obtained from nonquestionnaire methods points in the same direction is likewise important.

A word of caution is also in order with regard to the common use of the term "emotionality" as synonymous with neuroticism. Even if we assume that the subject who scores high on the usual psychoneurotic inventory is properly described as psychoneurotic or as emotionally unstable, it does not follow, as Landis, Zubin, and Katz (1935) have pointed out, that the extremely low-scoring subject is emotionally stable. He may be, but there is a chance that his hypo-emotionality is indicative of a schizophrenic tendency.

In attempting to get away from the difficulties inherent in work with personality inventories, much use is being made of the so-called projective methods. So far investigations of sex differences by means of the Rorschach test have produced very little in the way of tangible results. Hertz (1942) and Hertz and Baker (1943), after analyzing the records of 41 boys and 35 girls who were given the test at 12 and again at 15, have reported that the girls at both ages show more movement responses than boys, and that at the 15-year level they are also higher in primary C (color predominant over form as a determinant). These differences point toward slightly more introversion and instability in girls than in boys, but both the differences and the groups on which they are based are far from large. Furthermore, the samples seem not to be very representative of the adolescent population. A more satisfactory study from the standpoint of numbers and representativeness is that of McFate and Orr (1949), who have tabulated results from the analysis of 669 Rorschach protocols from 194 adolescents in the California Guidance Study. They too show girls to be more responsive than boys on the Rorschach, both quantitatively and qualitatively. Girls make more use of the color variables, a finding which would seem to fit in with evidence from other sources that emotionality and social responsiveness are feminine traits. The fact that boys are higher on scores ordinarily considered anxiety indicators is not so easily explained, since other types of study have shown girls more anxious than boys. Stavrianos (1942) and Rose and Stavrianos (1943) have reported on younger children, aged 5 to 11, but the data are inadequate to warrant any conclusions. Samples for the separate age groups are too small, important variables such as IQ are uncontrolled, and no significance tests or variability data are given. Further research is obviously needed.

Children's fears have been investigated both by verbal reports and by observational techniques. In general, girls seem to be more fearful than boys at all ages. We have mentioned that Terman and Miles found that girls were higher than boys on the "fears" section of their M-F test. Pintner and Brunschwig (1937) questioned 159 deaf and 345 hearing children of ages 12 to 15 regarding 39 fear situations. Girls of both groups reported more fears than did the boys (CR = 6.15 for the deaf, 4.53 for the hearing group). Pratt (1945), who asked 570 rural children in groups from kindergarten to eighth grade to list fears, found that girls listed significantly more than boys. Jersild, Markey, and Jersild (1933) and Jersild and Holmes (1935) reported interviews with 400 children, 25 of each sex at each age from 5 to 12 inclusive. Twice as many boys as girls reported no fears, and the girls reported a larger number of different fears. In teachers' ratings secured by Wickman (1928) for more than 1600 school children the girls were more often reported as showing oversensitive and fear behavior. Kimmins (1920, 1931, 1937) had 6000 London children, ages 5 to 18, report the last dream they could remember. In the range from 8 to 14 years more fear dreams were reported for boys (19 per cent) than for girls (16 per cent). After 14, fears decreased with boys and increased with girls. Little statistical treatment was presented, so that it is impossible to determine whether these results contradict those obtained by other methods.

Sex differences in fear responses have been reported at the nursery school level. Jersild and Holmes (1935) presented fear situations in the laboratory to 57 boys and 48 girls aged 2 to 5 years. Mean fear scores were higher for girls than for boys (CR = 2.58), and when 29 sex pairs were matched for age the difference was even greater (CR = 3.29). Parental records of children's fear responses, as reported in the same monograph, showed very little difference in number of fears for boys and girls, the averages being 4.9 and 5.2 respectively. There were marked differences in what constitutes a fear situation. Boys were more afraid of kinesthetic catastrophe; girls were more afraid of strangers and of social mishaps. These differences may be related to the greater muscular activity of boys and the greater social concern of girls. Hattwick (1937) had three independent judges record behavior tendencies of 300 nursery school children of each sex, aged 2 to 4½ years. Girls were reported oftener than boys in several categories related to fear. The ones showing the highest statistical significance were "Stays near adult" (CR = 4.50) and "Avoids play" (CR = 1.97).

Another source of data on emotional differences between the sexes has been the observation of various nervous habits in children. Wechsler (1931) reported on the incidence of nail-biting among 3000 New York children ranging in age from less than 3 years to 18 years. Before 11 years, the sex differences were small and inconsistent; from 11 to 13 the incidence was reliably higher among girls; but for ages after 13 it was reliably higher for boys. Wechsler's method of determining presence of nail-biting by a quick glance at the child's hand has been criticized by Olson (1936) as inaccurate. Billig (1941) found slightly more nail-biters among girls than among boys in the intermediate grades, but gives no statistical significance tests. Michaels and Goodman (1934) reported data on enuresis and "other neuropathic traits" for 255 boys and 220 girls, ages 6 to 16, who attended a summer camp. The information was obtained partly from parents and partly from the subjects themselves by observation and questioning. The tabulated percentages were found for various conditions.

	Boys	Girls
Enuresis after age 3	26.1	23.4
Thumb-sucking	17.6	34.1
Nail-biting	45.7	57.1
Speech impediment	23.3	17.0
Tantrums	12.8	16.1
Sleep disturbances	16.1	22.0
Fears	31.1	58.7

The only reliable differences here are the excess of girls with a history of thumb-sucking, nail-biting and fears.

Olson (1929) has made one of the most valuable studies of nervous habits in normal children. His subjects were 225 boys and 242 girls in grades 1 to 6 and 169 children in grades 7 and 8, each of whom was observed during 20 five-minutes periods. The main categories of nervous habits observed gave the following frequencies, in percentages (for 221 boys and 238 girls in the first six grades).

	Boys	Girls	Diff. PE Diff.
Oral	47	60	4.1
Nasal	28	27	. . .
Hirsutal	17	28	4.2
Ocular	11	19	3.5
Aural	13	8	−2.5
Genital	5	3	−1.7

Terman et al. (1925) obtained data from parents, teachers, and medical examinations regarding various nervous conditions in a gifted population of nearly 600, ages 5 to 13. Parents reported 10 per cent of boys and 13 per cent of girls as having "marked fears." Teachers reported "excessive timidity" for 4.9 per cent of boys and 10.5 per cent of girls and "tendency to worry" for 9 per cent of boys and 12 per cent of girls. The medical records of these subjects showed enuresis still present with 20 boys but with only 5 girls. Cummings (1944) analyzed observations made by teachers of 239 children in school, aged 2 to 7. Symptoms of emotional difficulties were in this group more frequent in boys, the greatest differences being for daydreaming, cruelty, aggressiveness, obstinacy, and disturbed sleep. Girls were slightly but not reliably more fearful. The nature of the emotional symptoms observed in this study may partially explain why its findings differ from many of the others, since they include aggressive behavior of various kinds.

Blatz and Ringland (1935) have reported a time-sampling study of "tics," a term used by them to include such a wide variety of habits and mannerisms as to involve practically all the children in a normal group. The subjects were 30 boys and 31 girls enrolled in nursery school, kindergarten, and first grade. The mean number of positive notations per child was somewhat higher for girls. Koch (1935) made time-sample observations of nervous habits of 21 boys and 25 girls attending nursery school. Her data were secured in 400 half-minute periods distributed over 8 months. The only reliable sex difference was for the hirsutal-caputal category, for which the average number observed per child was 1.8 for boys and 8.6 for girls. Brackett (1934) recorded time-sampling observations of crying for 17 boys and 12 girls aged 18 to 48 months. The samples are too small to yield reliable sex differences, but there is a trend toward more crying by girls (CR = 1.1). Macfarlane (1938) reported the incidence of various forms of special behaviors for 60 boys and 60 girls observed at each of the following ages (months): 21, 24, 30, 36, 42, 48, 54, and 60. Nail-biting, thumbsucking, and jealous behavior showed "a small but consistently higher incidence in girls." However, the N's are quite small for the separate categories. On total of extreme behaviors studied there was no appreciable sex difference. Among the 600 nursery subjects studied by Hattwick (1937) the following nervous tendencies were unrelated to sex: enuresis, nail-biting, chew-

ing objects, playing with fingers, picking nose, twitching, holding body tense. Kunst (1948), who made observations on 143 infants in an orphanage, reports more thumbsucking for boys than for girls.

Michaels and Goodman (1939) summarized case-history data on enuresis beyond age 3 for 500 male and 500 female patients in a state psychopathic hospital. In the 193 case histories that were positive, 56.5 per cent were of males and 43.5 per cent were of females, a reliable difference. In 122 cases with whom enuresis persisted after 10 years, 61.5 per cent were males and 38.5 per cent females.

Although there is some disagreement from study to study, if we lump together the numerous kinds of behavior known as nervous habits, it appears that the total incidence of such behavior is probably higher with girls. For enuresis, however, and perhaps one or two other categories it is higher with boys. Unfortunately we do not know enough about the interrelationships of the variables in question to interpret these findings. The fact that they are commonly classed together under a single label is no guarantee that they have the same significance for personality development. It is possible, for example, that enuresis is more of an aggressive attack on a frustrating environment than a simple indication of tension like nail-biting. A factor analysis of time-sampling records might help to clarify the pattern.

There have been a few studies of sex differences in emotional tendencies which are difficult to classify under any of the main topics discussed above. Chrysanthis (1946) questioned 1418 pupils, aged 12 to 18, as to length and depth of sleep, condition after sleeping, and frequency of dreaming. He reported that females dream more frequently and sleep more lightly, but no supporting data were given in the available abstract of the paper. Abel

(1941), using a modified Zeigarnik procedure in which recall was compared for completed and uncompleted tasks, found that girls recalled significantly more incompleted activities than did boys, which would seem to indicate a higher degree of some sort of tension. Child (1946) exposed 298 boys and 305 girls in the first seven grades to an experimental situation which gave them an opportunity to choose between a piece of candy easy to obtain and one difficult to obtain. There was a significant tendency for boys to exceed girls in the choice of the more distant goal. Motivations involved seem to have been drive for achievement, anxiety about being considered lazy, and drive for fun in exercise.

We may summarize the work on emotional responses as a whole by saying that there is fairly clear evidence from a variety of sources that a sex difference exists, that it is in the direction of greater emotional instability in girls, and that differences are identifiable even in the nursery school period. There are still a number of unexplained exceptions to the general trends.

Social Attitudes and Behavior. It is a common belief that one of the characteristically feminine traits is an absorbing interest in persons and personal relationships. That in fact a sex difference exists in this respect is indicated by data from subjects over a wide range of ages. It should be noted, however, that social interest and social participation are by no means the same variable. A number of researches suggest that the female shows more sociality, in the sense of social desire, but that introvertive tendencies and inferiority feelings often inhibit her social participation.

We have already seen that the greater social interests of girls appear in their play activities, in the books they read, and in their occupational preferences. Terman's (1925) sociability ratings of both gifted and unselected children, based on preference for social versus nonsocial plays and games, averaged higher for girls than for boys at every age. Wyman's (1925) word-association test used with these same subjects as a measure of interests also showed girls consistently above boys in social interest and as consistently below them in activity interest.

Symonds (1936) had 784 boys and 857 girls in junior and senior high schools rank 15 "major areas of life concern" according to their interest in reading about or discussing them. The largest sex difference was on personal attractiveness, which had a mean rank order of 5.4 for girls as compared with 8.1 for boys. Manners and getting along with others were also ranked somewhat higher by girls. All these differences indicate greater social interests among girls.

Terman and Miles (1936) found much evidence of the greater social orientation of girls among 550 subjects at the seventh grade, high school, and college levels. From their analysis of sex differences on M-F test items it appears that situations which involve attack on social self-feelings are almost the only field in which girls report more anger than boys. They are more angry at "being socially slighted," "hearing friends unjustly abused," "seeing boys make fun of old people," "seeing someone laugh when a blind man runs into an obstacle," or "seeing a person treated unfairly because of his race." The items expressing care for personal appearance and liking for social gatherings all carried feminine weights in the scoring of this test.

The greater sociality of girls is evidenced even in their dreams. Cason's study (1935) of some 200 subjects ranging in age from 8 years to adulthood showed that girls more than boys dream of home, family, and other persons. Schubert and Wagner (1936) found that among 355 high school seniors 62.6 per cent of girls as against 30 per cent of boys reported dreams about members of the family or about dead people. For 517 younger children, chiefly 4 to 12 years, Foster and Anderson (1936) reported 24.5 per cent of girls but only 9.8 per cent of boys having dreams of strange or bad people.

Interviews with 666 children, aged 5 to 12, by Jersild, Markey, and Jersild (1933) showed 12 per cent of "first" wishes by girls to concern siblings, companions, or friends, as against 3 per cent of wishes by the boys. Questioned regarding the best thing that ever happened to them, 14.9 per cent of girls as against 8.3 per cent of boys mentioned such things as parental relationships and other human contacts. Regarding the worst thing that ever happened to them, 15.6 per cent of girls and 8.0 per cent of boys mentioned people or undesirable traits of people. Asked what they liked best, 31 per cent of girls and 23 per cent of boys replied in terms of people or associations with people.

Davis (1932) had mothers of children aged 3 to 12 record 50 consecutive questions asked in the parental presence by 39 boys and 34 girls. Girls asked more questions on social relations (CR = 3.04), boys on causal explanation (CR = 3.07).

Orgel and Tuckman (1935) found that among 235 boys and 75 girls in a Hebrew orphanage 39.1 per cent of boys' nicknames and only 6.7 per cent of girls' are based upon some physical peculiarity or defect, whereas affectionate forms of nicknames account for 32 per cent of those given to girls as against 3.8 per cent of those given to boys. That is, in bestowing nicknames girls manifest more social sensitivity and more personal affection.

Jealousy is one indication of the value an individual attaches to given social relationships, and studies of jealousy all show that it is more prevalent among girls than among boys. S. Foster (1927) and Sewall (1930) found this to be the case with preschool children. Ross (1931) reported that in an older group, aged 6 to 11 years, sibling jealousy was much more common among girls (17 per cent, as compared to 11 per cent for boys).

The fact that gifted subjects (Burks, Jensen, and Terman, 1930) showed no appreciable sex difference on the Moss test of social intelligence is probably attributable to the inadequacy of the test, for Butler's study (1934) of 1600 subjects in grades 8 to 12 showed that girls greatly exceed boys in knowledge of matters having to do with family relationships and social adjustments. McNiel (1944) tested high school freshmen and seniors on understanding of factors underlying behavior. All comparisons showed girls significantly superior to boys.

Sex differences in sociality have been noted at a very early age. Thus Berne (1930), using a rating-scale technique with 82 nursery school children, found that girls show more responsibility for others, more social conformance, and more motherly behavior than do boys. Hübsch and Reininger (1931) reported that, among kindergarten children in Vienna, boys were more concerned with things, girls with personal relationships.

Spontaneous Social Groupings. There have been a number of studies attempting to find out what boys and girls actually do in social situations. Wellman (1926) made observations of the free groupings of 27 boys and 27 girls in a high school population of 113. She found that boys at this age seek a much wider range of companions than do girls. The mean number of companions was 22.2 for the boys as compared with 16.5 for the girls. Campbell (1939) also showed by means of a modified "guess-who" technique that boys' social relations are less rigidly structured than those of girls. In the ninth-grade group of 75 girls and 77 boys on which his results are based boys associated with more persons than girls, and girls were more given to clique association and more prone than boys to mention unfavorably an acquaintance outside the inner circle. Burks, Jensen, and Terman (1930) reported that at high school age gifted boys often than gifted girls have no close chums.

Adolescent crushes have been studied by Hurlock and Klein (1934). Their subjects included 148 boys and 202 girls in the high school, and 54 men and 155 women who were teachers or counselors. The data secured were memory reports elicited by a questionnaire. More females than males reported having experienced one or more crushes (86.6 vs. 71.6 per cent). Nearly all the homosexual crushes were reported by girls.

Tuddenham (1951, 1952) has studied characteristics related to popularity in first-, third-, and fifth-grade children by means of a guess-who technique similar to that used by Tryon (1939) with seventh and ninth graders. His subjects were 1437 children from 42 classrooms in Berkeley elementary schools. While all good traits included in the test were positively correlated with popularity, giving rise to a large general factor particularly at the first-grade level, among the older age groups the cluster of traits including "real boy," "leader," "good at games," and "takes chances" becomes more closely related to popularity for boys, and the cluster including "quiet," "not a show-off," "not quarrelsome," and "doesn't fight" becomes more closely related to popularity for girls. Girls are rated significantly higher than boys on all good traits, but the sex difference narrows with age.

A series of sociometric studies by Bonney (1942a, 1942b, 1944) have been concerned with popularity and social acceptance among second-, third-, and fourth-grade children. Girls seem to outrank boys consistently in social success. They are chosen more frequently in the various choosing situations and get higher scores for "mutuality of friendship."

Nursery school studies have been concerned with social success and breadth of social contacts among boys and girls and also with the relative participation in unisexual and bisexual groupings. One of the early studies was by Chevaleva-Janovskaja (1927), who analyzed 888 playground groupings of 276 children, aged 3 to 8 years, in Odessa. She reported greater participation in social groups by boys than by girls and a preponderance of unisexual as compared with bisexual groupings among the preschool children. At a later age range girls were found in bisexual groupings more often than in unisexual (56.84 vs. 43.16 per cent). Challman (1932) recorded 7248 social groupings among 17 boys and 16 girls attending nursery school. Girls showed a trend toward more social participation and higher friendship scores than boys. Green's (1933a) time-sampling study of friendships and quarrels among 21 boys and 19 girls in a nursery school indicated that girls make more social contacts than boys in terms of number of children played with, and that unisex groups predominate.

Another time-sampling study of social behavior at the preschool level was made by Parten (1933). Her subjects were 19 boys and 15 girls who afforded 781 groupings for an analysis. Two-thirds of the two-child groups are unisexual. When the data were treated so as to show the five favorite playmates of each child, it was found that 81 per cent of girls' favorites were girls, whereas only 62 per cent of boys' favorites were boys. The most-favored playmate of each girl was in every case of the same sex, whereas this was true for only 12 of the 19 boys. This fits in with Bonney's finding that girls score higher in social acceptance in the early grades.

What these results would seem to show when we put them together is that girls have an advantage in breadth of social contacts at the preschool and primary grade level that they lose to boys by the time adolescence is reached. A few studies throw some light on the process of attitude change through which this comes about. S. Smith (1939) had 1600 children, including 100 of each sex from 8 to 15, express by a vote whether given traits were more characteristic of boys or girls. The age comparisons indicated that boys' opinions of themselves became relatively more favorable with age, girls' opinions of themselves relatively less favorable. Conversely, with increasing age boys had a relatively poorer opinion of girls, whereas girls had a better opinion of boys.

Kuhlen and Lee (1943) studied 700 children in grades 6, 9, and 12 by guess-who and sociometric techniques. There were at all ages the sex differences one would expect to find on the items "restless" "talkative," "active," "attention-seeking," "enjoys fights," and "enjoys jokes" (boys higher than girls), and "acts older" (girls higher). But the more interesting finding was that, with changes in age, boys were more frequently mentioned as "liking opposite sex," "enjoying jokes on self," "being popular," "being willing to take a chance," and "being enthusiastic." It appears that during this period boys gradually take over the social initiative. Tschechtelin (1945), who administered a 22-trait personality scale to 1542 children and to 485 teachers in 140 classes representing all types of Indiana schools, showed that, while girls' self-ratings were much more favorable than those of boys when compared with teacher and classmate ratings, there was a marked trend for the boys' self-ratings to become higher from grade to grade over the 5-year interval covered (grades 4 to 8).

Character and Reputation. It is part of the traditional beliefs with regard to sex differences that females are superior to males in various moral qualities. Evidence from the previous section that girls are more social in their outlook and more interested in the approval of those around them might furnish some basis for such a difference. There have been a few large-scale research studies in this area. Terman *et al.* (1925) gave a battery of seven character tests to the gifted and control children, aged 7 to 14, whom he studied. It included two tests of overstatement, two tests of questionable interests, a test of honesty, and a test of emotional stability. The first five were taken from a battery devised by Raubenheimer (1925), the last two from Cady's battery (1923). Only three of the seven tests were of the performance type: the two overstatement tests and the test of honesty. The other four were indirect measures, although they were shown to differentiate between delinquent and nondelinquent groups. Boys in both gifted and control groups made worse scores than girls on five of the seven tests. Those which were clearly significant in this direction for the gifted group were "overstatement B" (CR = 3.33), "questionable interests: book preferences" (CR = 2.52), "questionable interests: character preferences" (CR = 3.06), and "social attitudes" (CR = 4.73). In the control group boys were significantly lower only on social attitudes (CR = 3.88) although all differences were in the same direction. Girls in both groups made somewhat worse scores in the performance test of honesty, but in neither group was the difference statistically significant. There was no difference in emotional stability. On weighted total score for all seven tests, girls were significantly superior (CR = 3.33 for gifted, 3.07 for control).

The most extensive data on sex differences in character tests are those reported by Hartshorne and May (1928). Their tests were for the most part direct measures (performance tests) of "good" and "bad" behavior. They include numerous tests of deception, of service and cooperation, of persistence and self-control, and of moral knowledge. Deception tests included such things as grading papers wrongly, answering items after time was called, peeping when eyes are supposed to be shut, exaggerating scores on athletic contests, etc. In all but one of eight deception tests, a larger proportion of girls than of boys succumbed to the temptation. Clearly significant sex differences were obtained for grading papers at home (CR = 6.10), peeping when eyes were supposed to be shut (CR = 3.41), peeping in a social game (CR = 4.69), and denying types of deception of which they had been guilty (CR = 3.49). There is evidence also that boys behaved more consistently from test to test than did the girls, which is interpreted by the authors as indicating that boys are better integrated than girls in this area of conduct.

Hartshorne, May, and Maller (1929) found sex differences in the opposite direction in their study of cooperative behavior and persistence at tasks. Five tests of cooperation were given to approximately 400 subjects of each sex in grades 5 to 8. In three of the tests subjects were allowed to choose between keeping and sharing proceeds earned or things given them. Another allowed a choice between doing or not doing tasks for the benefit of hospital children. The fifth tested "endurance in cooperation" by having the subject work at a speed task 12 minutes for himself and a second 12 minutes for his class. The re-

sults showed the girls significantly more cooperative in three tests. On the other two tests the boys were slightly more cooperative but the difference was not reliable. On total score for the five tests, girls were superior to boys, with a critical ratio (1.9) which almost meets accepted standards of statistical significance.

Persistence was measured in the same population by three types of tests. In one test stories were read to the subject as far as the climax, at which point the climax, in a form very difficult to decipher, was given the child to read. The subject could either persist in reading the climax or go on to a new story. In a second test the subject was given two puzzles at the same time and was told which to begin with. Score was time spent on the first before giving up and turning to the other. In one experiment both puzzles were of the mechanical variety; in another they were magic squares. As a third test of persistence the authors used the scores earned in the "endurance of cooperation" already described. In this set of tests also the mean for girls was a little higher (CR = 1.7).

Inhibition (or self-control) was measured in the same populations by four tests: "picture inhibition," "puzzle manipulation," "safe manipulation," and "story inhibition." All these involved work tasks for the subject to do in the presence of interesting distractions. On every test the girls showed greater self-control (CR's ranging from 2.6 to 5.5).

One of the most interesting findings in this group of studies was that, for everything except the inhibition battery, there was much more difference in the *reputations* of boys and girls with respect to the character qualities being measured than there was in their performance on the tests. Reputation scores were obtained from guess-who ratings and a check list filled out by teachers. On cooperation, where the critical ratio for the battery of tests was 1.9, the critical ratio for reputation scores was 7.9. Ratings by teachers and by the children themselves showed the same trend. On persistence, where the critical ratio for the test battery was 1.7, it was 7.6 for the reputation scores. On inhibition, the critical ratio for reputation was 5.0, which was almost exactly the same as the one for performance. It would seem that perhaps females get credit for more moral superiority than they actually possess.

There have been a number of other studies of persistence, but the results are conflicting and confusing, largely because the low intercorrelations between various tests designed to measure persistence throw doubt on whether there is a general factor corresponding to the trait name. A subject's score on any one test depends upon the specific nature of the activity involved, on the appeal it has for him, and on the manner in which the task is set. The reader who wishes to examine detailed results is referred to studies by Ryans (1939), Chapman (1924), Cushing (1929), Pinard (1932), Shacter (1933), R. B. Cattell (1935), and Wolf (1938).

The character test data in general indicate that, although sex differences vary according to the specific situation a test involves, there is a tendency for boys to cheat less than girls and for girls to exceed boys in tests of self-control, persistence, cooperativeness, moral knowledge, and moral opinions.

Level of Aspiration. One study by Walter and Marzolf (1951) has compared boys and girls on level of aspiration as measured by the Rotter aspiration board. The subjects were 10 boys and 10 girls selected at random from each of five grades, the fourth, sixth, eighth, tenth, and twelfth. An analysis of variance showed that the only significant differences in goal discrepancy scores

were those associated with sex. Girls at all grade levels tended to set lower standards for themselves.

Physiological and Cultural Factors in Sex Differences

A complete understanding of sex differences involves evaluation of the factors producing them. Though no general agreement has been reached in this area, there is some evidence upon which tentative conclusions can be based.

As has been stated in our first section, the sexes differ markedly in their anatomical, physiological, and biochemical characteristics. It seems only reasonable to suppose that these differences might result in psychological predispositions toward some kinds of behavior rather than others. In addition to the studies previously cited by Sheldon (1940), Terman and Miles (1936), Gilkinson (1937), Marquis (1940), and Sollenberger (1940) indicating that some relationship between physical and psychological variables exists, the work reported by Stone and Barker (1939) is pertinent. They gave personality tests to a large population of adolescent girls and found reliable differences in the responses of pre-menarcheal and post-menarcheal groups of a given age. Their data suggest that the menarche brings with it behavior tendencies toward quieter living and toward feminine interests and introverted attitudes.

There is also, however, considerable evidence that the cultural environment is actually not the same for boys as for girls. The social influences to which they are subjected differ in countless and subtle ways. The differential pressures begin early and operate continuously. They are omnipresent in such things as clothing, play activities, restrictions of mobility, experience with money, home and school discipline, parental associations, occupational experience, educational exposures, and innumerable ideals of conduct and life satisfactions. Only a few of these things have been given any systematic study as yet.

Parent-Child Relationships. Freudians have given great prominence to this factor, but most of the psychoanalytic contributions on the problem are beyond the scope of a discussion that is concerned primarily with objective evidence amenable to statistical treatment.

There have been a few studies of parent preferences. Simpson (1935) interviewed 500 children, 50 of each sex at each age from 5 to 9 years, each of whom was living at home with both parents. The children were questioned about the favorite parent and were shown pictures of home life which elicited responses throwing additional light on attitudes toward parents. Preferring the mother were 69.6 per cent of boys and 61.2 per cent of girls. The difference is fairly reliable, but a large part of it is accounted for by the marked preference of 5-year-old girls for the father. Greatest mother preference was shown by children whose mothers worked away from home and so had acquired a scarcity value. A number of differences in parental treatment of the children were brought out in the interviews. For example, boys were more often spanked by fathers, girls by mothers. Mott (1937), whose subjects were 67 boys and 57 girls, aged 6, found that both boys and girls preferred the mother about twice as often as the father. Hayward (1935), reporting on 180 unselected children, grades 4 to 9, and 140 delinquent children found no tendency to prefer one parent over another.

Meltzer (1941, 1943) used a free-association technique to get at the attitudes of 76 boys and 74 girls, aged 9 to 16, toward their parents. The mother tended to be preferred by both sexes, but to a larger extent by boys than girls. The author

states that the deviation from a healthy attitude was more likely to be in a direction of overdependence for girls, insecurity and rejection for boys, but gives no significance tests to support the generalization. An evaluation of the feeling tone of the reactions showed that for girls it was more pleasant, more emotional, and more acceptant than for boys. Though the data on parent preference themselves seem to prove very little in any of these studies, Meltzer's findings suggest that phenomenologically there may be considerable difference in home environment for boys and for girls.

Several other studies support this generalization. Terman (1938) found a number of sex differences in the reports given by 792 husbands and 792 wives regarding their childhood experiences. The women reported stronger attachment to the father than did the men, more conflict with the mother, less childhood punishment, more unhappiness in childhood, and more adequate sex education. Similar differences were found in other marital studies (Terman and Buttenwieser, 1935; Burgess and Cottrell, 1939).

Personal history data and several personality test scores reported by Wang (1932) for 358 college students (203 men and 155 women) gave some evidence of sex difference in the correlates of family background. Introversion in women was associated with lax discipline by the mother and with lack of religious training, but neither of these relationships was found for men. Introversion in men was associated with a history of irregular money allowance, extroversion with regular allowance or regular earnings. Stagner (1938), who used 28 men and 22 women college students as subjects in an attempt to discover the relationship between attitudes toward parents and emotional instability, also found that the significant items differed somewhat for the two sexes. A Czechoslovakian study by Jurovsky (1948), based on ratings made of their relationships with their parents by 18- and 19-year-olds being given vocational counseling, indicated that boys showed poorer relationships than girls.

Gardner's (1947) study of items checked on a questionnaire by fifth- and sixth-graders shows boys to be slightly more critical than girls of their fathers, although no significance tests are given. Schuell's (1946, 1947) questionnaire study of 134 girls and 156 boys, aged 8 to 14, showed statistically significant differences between boys and girls in what they had to say about both praise and punishment in their homes. In interpreting this material, we should remember that it is probably not so important whether parents *actually* treat boys and girls differently as whether the children *feel* that there is such a difference, since it is the phenomenological reality that shapes the behavior.

Even in areas of experience provided by parents for both boys and girls, the exact nature of the experience is likely to differ for the sexes. Hanson (1933) found from interviews with 39 boys and 59 girls, all of whom had an allowance and managed their own money, that a larger proportion of boys than of girls had had experience in borrowing (44 vs. 30 per cent), lending (39 vs. 18 per cent), investing (75 vs. 43 per cent), and buying clothes (53 vs. 29 per cent). On the other hand, more girls than boys kept accounts.

Newell (1936) studied the effect of maternal hostility upon 35 boys and 40 girls of ages 4 to 18. Results are compared with those from a control group of 36 boys and 46 girls. The author concluded that boys are more aggressive if there is consistent hostility on the part of one or both parents, and that girls are submissive if the father is protective or ambivalent. These conclusions rest on judgments of a rather subjective nature and need to be checked against more objective evidence.

Cavan (1932), in his study of 900 junior high school children, using the Woodworth test of neurotic tendency, found some evidence that girls suffer more from unsatisfactory home relationships than boys do. The answer to the item on which the subject answers whether or not he sometimes wishes he had never been born seems to afford a single index of the neurotic trends measured by the whole test. More girls than boys answered this affirmatively, and the difference between percentages for children from broken and unbroken homes was considerably larger for girls.

Sensitivity to Environment. There is a fairly general belief that girls are more susceptible to environmental influences in general than boys, but the data available are somewhat conflicting and do not afford any clear check on the hypothesis. Cavan (1932) in the study cited above presented a little evidence that broken homes have a stronger emotional effect on girls than on boys. Spencer (1938) investigated mental conflict among 192 high school students, 88 boys and 104 girls. Although his method of measuring conflict (too complicated to describe here) yielded higher conflict scores for boys, the scores of girls were more closely related to a number of environmental variables, including broken home, irregular church attendance, and being youngest in the family. Engle (1945) states that second- and third-grade girls suffer more from being members of minority groups than boys do, as measured by their deviations from the norms on the California Test of Personality. Neither the differences nor the critical ratios, however, are large enough to carry much weight. Keir (1945), reporting on a questionnaire given to 108 boys and 135 girls, aged 11 to 14, from three London schools that had been evacuated to other places, stated that there is a slight but definite tendency for girls to pay more attention to people in their immediate environment and to show more emotionally-toned responses.

One of the most satisfactory studies was reported by Maddy (1943). He chose as subjects 319 children in sixth grade coming from professional and semi-skilled occupational groups. With this much difference in family background, there were 16.1 IQ points' difference between the averages for the two groups. On the personality tests used, the Pintner *Aspects of Personality* and the Pressey X-O, girls from the professional families were higher than those from the semi-skilled families in dominance, extroversion, and emotional stability. The boys from the two groups differed only in extroversion. The sensed social status had evidently affected girls more strongly than boys.

On the other hand, there are several studies that do not point in the same direction. Terman's (1938) study of 792 marriages reported separately for husbands and wives the relationships between marital happiness and a number of variables having to do with family background. Among the relationships that approached statistical significance there were just as many affecting husbands more strongly as affecting wives more strongly, and there were a number of variables showing no husband-wife difference at all.

In Germany, Busemann and Harders (1932) compared the school grades of 473 children of unemployed parents with the grades of 1154 whose fathers were fully employed. Although the authors concluded that girls suffers more effect than boys from parental unemployment, actually their data showed that this sex difference is unreliably small and that it disappears altogether when the comparison is made separately for three occupational

classes. Springer (1938) gave the Brown personality inventory to 327 slum children and to 473 children of a good district, aged 9 to 15 years. There was no evidence from the sex differences in adjustment scores in the two environments to show that life in a slum district affects one sex more than the other. The adjustment scores reported by Pintner (1940) for 1400 children who were hard of hearing and for a comparable group of normal children indicated that hearing loss affects the adjustment of boys more than that of girls.

It seems, thus, that the broad generalization that girls are more sensitive than boys to *all* types of environmental influence requires some clarification, although the trend of the evidence is indeed in the direction of greater female sensitivity.

The Concept of Sex Rôles. It seems possible that the effects of both physical and cultural factors in producing psychological sex differences can best be understood if we think in terms of sex rôles as they are formulated in any given society and understood and accepted by the individuals who compose it. Physical differences predispose males toward what are considered masculine rôles, and females toward what are considered feminine rôles, but many social factors operate at the same time to determine exactly what pattern of attitudes and behavior any given individual will accept.

A few studies have been concerned with this problem. Milner (1949) made a thorough and intensive study of 30 early adolescents of the lower-middle and upper-lower social classes. She wished to find out how rôles associated with sex and with social status were affecting personality development. The characteristic most typical for boys was difficulty in impulse control. Most typical for girls was a drive for conformity and the absence of close emotional ties. Whether or not an individual showed the typical personality seemed to be related to the closeness with which the mother approximated the feminine personality typical of her social group.

Rabban (1950) used a larger number of subjects, 15 boys and 15 girls at each of five age levels: 36, 48, 59, 72, and 102 months. They were divided into two subgroups, one from an upper-middle-class suburban community, the other from a working-class industrial area. By a technique involving toy choice and questioning he attempted to analyze the extent to which children in each age, sex, and class group were aware of their sex rôles. Not much general awareness of sex rôle was shown at the 3-year level, but it became increasingly apparent at each of the following ages. Boys were clearer than girls as to their sex rôles, and the working class clearer than the middle class. Middle-class girls were the latest to develop the sex-rôle concepts.

Sears, Pintler, and Sears (1946) have reported a well-designed study throwing some light on how the sex-rôle concepts develop. In a standardized projective doll-play situation, 3-, 4-, and 5-year-old children were scored for aggression. As in previous studies, there was a marked sex difference in the total amount of aggression shown. The next step was to compare aggression scores for children whose fathers were at home and children whose fathers were away in the Armed Services. The girls showed no difference in aggression, whether they were from father-present or father-absent homes. But the boys from the father-present homes were significantly more aggressive than the others. Differences were most pronounced in the 3-year-olds. These results are compatible with a sex-typing hypothesis, and it is difficult to think of any other which would account for them. Boys who have fathers at home

develop by age 3 a concept of masculinity permitting a considerable amount of aggression. Boys whose fathers are absent develop the same concept, but more slowly. It is in evidence in their behavior by 5 but not by 3. Sears (1951) also discusses these results.

The task of evaluating the importance of physical and cultural factors has hardly been begun. In the abilities area, the sex differences probably depend largely on whatever cultural factors are now determining sex rôles. The fact that most of the special abilities investigated do not differentiate the sexes at the earlier age levels, and that they are so closely related to interest differences, would seem to support such a conclusion. In the area of motivational and personality traits, the relationships are considerably more obscure. Most of these differences show up at a very early age. Many of them, like activity interests and aggressiveness, are characteristics that could easily be related to physical and hormonal factors. But it is unlikely that any one of them is determined by physical factors alone. If sex-typing can be shown as early as the age of 3 and in a trait like aggressiveness, as the Sears study seems to indicate, there is certainly reason to expect it to operate in connection with most other characteristics. The unraveling of these relationships is a task for the future—an important task, since a large part of any individual's total adjustment and life efficiency depends upon an adequate understanding of the possibilities and limitations which his sex brings with it.

Bibliography

REFERENCES CITED

Abbott, M. A. 1927. A study of the motion picture preferences of the Horace Mann High Schools. *Teach. Coll. Rec., 28,* 819-835.

Abel, T. M. 1941. Measurement of dynamic aspects of behavior among adolescents. *J. Genet. Psychol.*, *58*, 3–26.

Ackerson, L. 1931. *Children's behavior problems.* Chicago: University of Chicago Press.

Adams, E. A. 1936. The use of libraries in junior and senior high schools. *Univ. S. Calif. Educ. Monogr.*, No. 8. p. x + 105.

Alberty, H. B. 1925. The permanence of the vocational choices of high school pupils. *Industr. Arts Mag.*, *14*, 203–207.

Alper, B. S., and G. E. Lodgen. 1936. The delinquent child in Pennsylvania courts. *Ment. Hyg.*, *N. Y.*, *20*, 598–604.

Anastasi, A., and R. D'Angelo. 1952. A comparison of Negro and white preschool children in language development and Goodenough Draw-a-Man I.Q. *J. Genet. Psychol.*, *81*, 147–165.

Andersen, E. M. 1948. A study of leisure-time reading of pupils in junior high school. *Elem. Sch. J.*, *48*, 258–267.

Aveling, F., and H. L. Hargreaves. 1921. Suggestibility with and without prestige in children. *Brit. J. Psychol.*, *12*, 53–75.

Bach, G. R. 1945. Young children's play fantasies. *Psychol. Monogr.*, *59*, No. 2.

Bakwin, H. 1929. Sex factor in infant mortality. *Human Biol.*, *1*, 90–116.

Baumgarten, F., and M. Tramer. 1943. Kinderzeichnungen in vergleichend psychologischer Beleuchtung. Untersuchungen und serbischen Kindern. *Z. Kinderpsychiat.*, *9*, 161–220.

——. 1945–1946. Zur frage der psychischen Geschlechtsunterschiede bei Schulkindern. (On the question of psychic sex differences in school children.) *Criança portug.*, *5*, 261–269.

Bayley, N. 1951. Some psychological correlates of somatic androgyny. *Child. Develpm.*, *22*, 47–60.

Bayley, N., and L. Bayer. 1946. The assessment of somatic androgyny. *Amer. J. Phys. Anthrop.*, *4*, 433–461.

Beach, F. A. 1948. *Hormones and behavior.* New York: Hoeber.

Beasley, W. C. 1938. Sex differences and age variations in hearing loss in relation to stage of deafness. *Nat. Health Surv. Bull.*, No. 6.

Beeson, M. F. 1928. A study of vocational preferences of high school students. *Voc. Guid. Mag.*, *7*, 115–119.

Bell, H. M. 1939. *The theory and practice of personal counseling.* Stanford University, Calif.: Stanford University Press.

Bennett, G. K., and R. M. Cruikshank. 1942. Sex differences in the understanding of mechanical problems. *J. Appl. Psychol.*, *26*, 121–127.

Bergen, C. 1943. Some sources of children's science information; an investigation of sources of information and attitudes towards such sources as used or expressed by children. *Teach Coll. Contr. Educ.*, No. 881.

Berne, E. V. C. 1930. An experimental investigation of social behavior patterns in young children. *Univ. Iowa Stud. Child Welfare*, *4*, No. 3.

Bernreuter, R. G. 1933. The theory and construction of the personality inventory. *J. Soc. Psychol.*, *4*, 387–405.

Billig, A. L. 1941. Finger nail-biting: its incipiency, incidence, and amelioration. *Genet. Psychol. Monogr.*, *24*, 123–218.

Blair, G. M. 1938. Mentally superior and inferior children in the junior and senior high school; a comparative study of their backgrounds, interests, and ambitions. *Teach. Coll. Contr. Educ.*, No. 766.

Blackwell, A. M. 1940. A comparative investigation into the factors involved in mathematical ability of boys and girls. *Brit. J. Educ. Psychol.*, *10*, 143–153, 212–222.

Blatz, W. E., and M. C. Ringland. 1935. *A study of tics in pre-school children.* Toronto: University of Toronto Press.

Bonney, M. E. 1942a. A study of the relation of intelligence, family size, and sex differences with mutual friendships in the primary grades. *Child Develpm.*, *13*, 79–100.

——. 1942b. A study of social status on the second grade level. *J. Genet. Psychol.*, *60*, 271–305.

——. 1944. Sex differences in social success and personality traits. *Child Develpm.*, *15*, 63–79.

Book, W. F. 1922. *The intelligence of high school seniors.* New York: Macmillan.

Boynton, P. L. 1936. The vocational preferences of school children. *J. Genet. Psychol.*, *49*, 411–425.

Brackett, C. W. 1934. Laughing and crying of preschool children. *Child Develpm. Monogr.*, No. 14. Pp. xv + 91.

Broom, M. E. 1930. Sex differences in mental ability among junior high school pupils. *J. Appl. Psychol.*, *14*, 83–90.

Brown, F. 1934. A psychoneurotic inventory for children between nine and fourteen years of age. *J. Appl. Psychol.*, *18*, 566–577.

Brown, P. A. 1939. Responses of blind and seeing adolescents to a neurotic inventory. *J. Psychol.*, *7*, 211–221.

Bryan, A. I. 1934. Organization of memory in young children. *Arch. Psychol.*, *N. Y.*, No. 162.

Buckingham, B. R., and J. MacLatchy. 1930. The number abilities of children when they enter grade one. *Yearb. Nat. Soc. Stud. Educ.*, *29* (II), 473–549.

Burgess, E. W., and L. S. Cottrell. 1939. *Predicting success or failure in marriage.* New York: Prentice-Hall.

Burks, B., D. W. Jensen, and L. M. Terman. 1930. *Genetic studies of genius:* Vol. III. *The promise of youth; follow-up studies of a thousand gifted children.* Stanford University, Calif.: Stanford University Press.

Burt, C. L. 1921. *Mental and scholastic tests.* London: King.

Burton, A. C. 1939. Temperature regulation. *Ann. Rev. Physiol.*, *1*, 109–130.

Busemann, A., and G. Harders. 1932. Die Wirkung väterlicher Erwerbslogikeit auf die Schulleistungen der Kinder. *Z. Kinderforsch.*, *40*, 89–100.

Butler, E. I. 1934. A study of the needs of high school students and the effectiveness of a program of learning in selected phases of child development and family relationships. *Univ. Iowa Stud. Child Welfare, 10,* 169–248.

Butterworth, R. F., and Thompson, G. F. 1951. Factors related to age-grade trends and sex differences in children's preferences for comic books. *J. Genet. Psychol., 78,* 71–96.

Cady, V. M. 1923. The estimation of juvenile incorrigibility. *J. Delinq. Monogr.,* No. 2. Pp. 140.

Caille, R. K. 1933. Resistant behavior of preschool children. *Child Develpm. Monogr.,* No. 11. Pp. xvi + 142.

Campbell, H. M. 1939. Differences in clique formation among adolescent boys and girls revealed by a "guess who" technique. (Abstract.) *Psychol. Bull., 36,* 537.

Carter, H. D. 1935. Twin-similarities in emotional traits. *Character and Pers., 4,* 61–78.

Carter, H. D., and E. K. Strong. 1933. Sex differences in occupational interests of high school students. *Person. J., 12,* 166–175.

Cason, H. 1935. The nightmare dream. *Psychol. Monogr., 46,* No. 209. Pp. 51.

Cattell, P. 1928. *Dentition as a measure of maturity.* Cambridge: Harvard University Press.

Cattell, R. B. 1935. On the measure of "perseveration." *Brit. J. Educ. Psychol., 5,* 76–92.

Cavan, R. S. 1932. The wish never to have been born. *Amer. J. Sociol., 37,* 547–559.

Challman, R. C. 1932. Factors influencing friendships among preschool children. *Child Develpm., 3,* 146–158.

Chapman, J. C. 1924. Persistence, success and speed in a mental task. *Ped. Sem., 31,* 276–284.

Chevaleva-Janovskaja, E. 1927. Les groupements spontanés d'enfants à l'âge pré-scolaires. *Arch. Psychol., Genève, 20,* 219–233.

Child, I. L. 1946. Children's preference for goals easy or difficult to obtain. *Psychol. Monogr., 60,* No. 4.

Chrysanthis, K. 1946. The length and depth of sleep. *Acta Med. Orient. Jerusalem, 5,* 152–155.

Ciocco, A. 1938. Audiometric studies of school children: V. Changes in air conduction acuity after an interval of five years, with particular reference to the effect of age and sex. *Ann. Otol., etc., St. Louis, 47,* 926–937.

Clark, W. R. 1940. Radio listening habits of children. *J. Soc. Psychol., 12,* 131–149.

Coleman, J. H. 1931. Written composition interests of junior and senior high school pupils. *Teach. Coll. Contr. Educ.,* No. 494.

Collins, M. 1927. British norms for the Pressey Cross-out Test. *Brit. J. Psychol., 18,* 121–133.

Columba, Sr. M. 1926. A study of interests and their relations to other factors of achievement in the elementary school subjects. *Cath. Univ. Amer. Educ. Res. Bull., 1,* No. 7.

Colvin, S. S., and A. H. MacPhail. 1924. Intelligence of seniors in the high schools of Massachusetts. *U. S. Bur. Educ. Bull.,* No. 9.

Crew, F. A. E. 1927. *The genetics of sexuality in animals.* New York: Macmillan.

Cummings, J. D. 1944. The incidence of emotional symptoms in school children. *Brit. J. Educ. Psychol., 14,* 151–161.

Cunningham, K. S., and W. T. Price. 1935. The standardization of an Australian arithmetic test. *Aust. Coun. Educ. Res. Ser.,* No. 21.

Cushing, H. M. 1929. A perseverative tendency in pre-school children. A study in personality differences. *Arch. Psychol., N. Y., 17,* No. 108.

Danby, T. A. 1934. The sex incidence of mental deficiency (amentia) with a consideration of mental variation in the sexes. *Ment. Welfare, 15,* 8–16.

Darley, J. G. 1937. Tested maladjustment related to clinically diagnosed maladjustment. *J. Appl. Psychol., 21,* 632–642.

Davis, E. A. 1932. The form and function of children's questions. *Child Develpm., 3,* 57–74.

Dawe, H. C. 1934. An analysis of two hundred quarrels of preschool children. *Child Develpm., 5,* 139–157.

Dennis, W. 1942. The performance of Hopi children on the Goodenough Draw-a-Man test. *J. Comp. Psychol., 34,* 341–348.

Dickinson, A. E., and F. T. Tyler. 1944. An experimental study of the generalizing ability of grade II pupils. *J. Educ. Psychol., 35,* 432–441.

Dietrich, G. L., and C. W. Hunnicutt. 1948. Art content preferred by primary grade children. *Elem. Sch. J., 48,* 557–559.

Douglass, A. A. 1922. Vocational interests of high-school seniors. *Sch. and Soc., 16,* 79–84.

Dublin, L. I., and A. J. Lotka. 1936. *Length of life.* New York: Ronald.

Duggan, L. 1950. An experiment on immediate recall in secondary school children. *Brit. J. Psychol., 40,* 149–154.

Edgerton, H. A., and S. H. Britt. 1944. Sex differences in the Science Talent Test. *Science, 100,* 192–193.

——. 1947. Technical aspects of the Fourth Annual Science Talent Search. *Educ. Psychol. Measmt., 7,* 3–21.

Eisenberg, A. L. 1936. *Children and radio programs.* New York: Columbia University Press.

Emmett, W. C. 1949. Evidence of a space factor at 11 and earlier. *Brit. J. Psychol., Statist. Sect., 2,* 3–16.

Engle, T. L. 1945. Personality adjustments of children belonging to two minority groups. *J. Educ. Psychol., 36,* 543–560.

Erikson, E. H. 1951. Sex differences in the play configurations of pre-adolescents. *Amer. J. Orthopsychiat., 21,* 667–692.

Farwell, L. 1930. Reactions of kindergarten, first- and second-grade children to constructive play materials. *Genet. Psychol. Monogr., 8,* 431–562.

Flory, C. D. 1935. Sex differences in skeletal development. *Child Develpm., 6,* 205–212.

Fontes, V. 1946–1947. Osobrenatural nos desenhos infants. (The supernatural in children's drawings.) *Criança portug., 6,* 71–100.

Fortes, M. 1933. Notes on juvenile delinquency: I. The age of young delinquents in East London. *Sociol. Rev.*, *25*, 14–24.

Foster, J. C. 1930. Play activities of children in the first six grades. *Child Develpm.*, *1*, 248–254.

Foster, J. C., and J. E. Anderson. 1936. Unpleasant dreams in childhood. *Child Develpm.*, *7*, 77–84.

Foster, S. 1927. A study of the personality make-up and social setting of fifty jealous children. *Ment. Hyg., N. Y.*, *11*, 53–57.

Frank, L. K. 1933. *Childhood and youth.* In President's Research Committee on Social Trends, *Recent social trends in the United States.* New York: McGraw-Hill. Vol. II, pp. 751–800.

Fuxloch, K. 1930. Das Sociologische im Spiel des Kindes. *Beih. Z. angew. Psychol.*, No. 53.

Gansl, I. 1939. Vocabulary: Its measurement and growth. *Arch. Psychol., N. Y.*, No. 236.

Gardner, L. P. 1947. An analysis of children's attitudes toward fathers. *J. Genet. Psychol.*, *70*, 3–28.

Garrett, H. E., A. I. Bryan, and R. E. Perl. 1935. The age factor in mental organization. *Arch. Psychol., N. Y.*, No. 176.

Gatewood, M. C., and A. P. Weiss. 1930. Race and sex differences in newborn infants. *J. Genet. Psychol.*, *38*, 31–49.

Geddie, L., and G. Hildreth. 1944. Children's ideas about the war. *J. Exp. Educ.*, *13*, 92–97.

Gilkinson, H. 1937. Masculine temperament and secondary sex characteristics: A study of the relationship between psychological and physical measures of masculinity. *Genet. Psychol. Monogr.*, *19*, 105–154.

Goodenough, F. L. 1926. *Measurement of intelligence by drawings.* Yonkers-on-Hudson: World Book.

——. 1928. The Kuhlmann-Binet tests for children of preschool age. *Inst. Child Welfare Monogr. Ser.*, No. 2. Minneapolis: University of Minnesota Press. Pp. viii + 146.

——. 1929. The emotional behavior of young children during mental tests. *J. Juv. Res.*, *13*, 204–219.

——. 1930. Interrelationships in the behavior of young children. *Child Develpm.*, *1*, 29–47.

——. 1931. Anger in young children. *Inst. Child Welfare Monogr. Ser.*, No. 9. Minneapolis: University of Minnesota Press. Pp. xiii + 278.

Green, E. H. 1933*a*. Friendships and quarrels among preschool children. *Child Develpm.*, *4*, 237–252.

——. 1933*b*. Group play and quarreling among preschool children. *Child Develpm.*, *4*, 302–307.

Grossnickle, F. E. 1937. Concepts in social arithmetic for the eighth grade level. *J. Educ. Res.*, *30*, 475–488.

Haggerty, M. E. 1925. The incidence of undesirable behavior in public-school children. *J. Educ. Res.*, *12*, 102–122.

Hales, N. M. 1932. An advanced test of general intelligence. *Aust. Coun. Educ. Res. Ser.*, No. 11.

Hammond, W. H. 1945. An analysis of youth centre interests. *Brit. J. Educ. Psychol.*, *15*, 122–126.

Hanson, R. L. 1933. An investigation of children's use of money. *Child Develpm.*, *4*, 50–54.

Hartshorne, H., and M. A. May. 1928. *Studies in deceit:* Book I. *General methods and results;* Book II. *Statistical methods and results.* New York: Macmillan.

Hartshorne, H., M. A. May, and J. B. Maller. 1929. *Studies in service and self-control.* New York: Macmillan.

Hattwick, L. A. 1937. Sex differences in behavior of nursery school children. *Child Develpm.*, *8*, 343–355.

Havighurst, R. J., and F. H. Breese. 1947. Relation between ability and social status in a midwestern community: III. Primary mental abilities. *J. Educ. Psychol.*, *38*, 241–247.

Havighurst, R. J., M. K. Gunther, and I. E. Pratt. 1946. Environment and the Draw-a-Man test. *J. Abnorm. Soc. Psychol.*, *41*, 50–63.

Hayes, M. 1934. A scale for evaluating adolescent personality. *J. Genet. Psychol.*, *44*, 206–222.

Hayward, R. S. 1935. The child's report of psychological factors in the family. *Arch. Psychol., N. Y.*, *28*, No. 189.

Healy, W., and A. F. Bronner. 1926. *Delinquents and criminals, their making and unmaking.* New York: Macmillan.

Heilman, J. D. 1933. Sex differences in intellectual abilities. *J. Educ. Psychol.*, *24*, 47–62.

Hertz, M. R. 1942. Personality patterns in adolescence as portrayed by the Rorschach ink-blot method: I. The movement factors. *J. Gen. Psychol.*, *27*, 119–188.

Hertz, M. R., and E. Baker. 1943. Personality patterns in adolescence as portrayed by the Rorschach ink-blot method: II. The color factors. *J. Gen. Psychol.*, *28*, 3–61.

Hicks, J. A., and M. Hayes. 1938. Study of the characteristics of 250 junior high school children. *Child Develpm.*, *9*, 219–242.

Hildreth, G. 1933. Adolescent interests and abilities. *J. Genet. Psychol.*, *43*, 65–93.

Hobson, J. R. 1947. Sex differences in primary mental abilities. *J. Educ. Res.*, *41*, 126–132.

Hollingworth, L. S. 1922. Differential action upon the sexes of forces which tend to segregate the feeble-minded. *J. Abnorm. Psychol.*, *17*, 35–57.

Honzik, M. P. 1951. Sex differences in the occurrence of materials in the play constructions of preadolescents. *Child Develpm.*, *22*, 14–35.

Hübsch, L., and K. Reininger. 1931. Zur Psychologie des Kinderspiels und der Geschlechtsunterschiede im Kindergartenalter. *Z. angew. Psychol.*, *40*, 97–176.

Hurlock, E. B. 1927. A study of self-ratings by children. *J. Appl. Psychol.*, *11*, 490–502.

——. 1930. The suggestibility of children. *J. Genet. Psychol.*, *37*, 59–74.

——. 1943. The spontaneous drawings of adolescents. *J. Genet. Psychol.*, *63*, 141–156.

Hurlock, E. B., and E. R. Klein. 1934. Adolescent "crushes." *Child Develpm.*, *5*, 63–80.

Hurlock, E. B., and L. C. McDonald. 1934. Undesirable behavior traits in junior high school students. *Child Develpm.*, 5, 278–290.

Jackson, J. 1944. A survey of psychological, social, and environmental differences between advanced and retarded readers. *J. Genet. Psychol.*, 65, 113–131.

Jersild, A. T., and F. B. Holmes. 1935. Children's fears. *.Child Develpm. Monogr.*, No. 20. Pp. ix + 356.

Jersild, A. T., and F. V. Markey. 1935. Conflicts between preschool children. *Child Develpm. Monogr.*, No. 21. Pp. xi + 181.

Jersild, A. T., F. V. Markey, and C. L. Jersild. 1933. Children's fears, dreams, wishes, daydreams, likes, dislikes, pleasant and unpleasant memories. *Child Develpm. Monogr.*, No. 12. Pp. xi + 172.

Johnson, B. L. 1932. Children's reading interests as related to sex and grade in school. *Sch. Rev.*, 40, 257–272.

Johnson, W. B., and L. M. Terman. 1940. Some highlights in the literature of psychological sex differences published since 1920. *J. Psychol.*, 9, 327–336.

Jordan, A. M. 1921. Children's interests in reading. *Teach. Coll. Contr. Educ.*, No. 107.

——. 1937. Sex differences in mental traits. *High Sch. J.*, 20, 254–261.

Jurovsky, A. 1948. The relations of older children to their parents. *J. Genet. Psychol.*, 72, 85–100.

Katz, E. 1944. *Children's preferences for traditional and modern paintings.* New York: Bureau of Publications, Teachers College.

Keir, G. 1945. Some sex differences in attitude toward change of environment among evacuated central school children. *Brit. J. Educ. Psychol.*, 15, 146–150.

Kimmins, C. W. 1920. *Children's dreams.* New York: Longmans, Green.

——. 1931. Children's dreams. In C. Murchison (Ed.), *A handbook of child psychology* (1st ed.), pp. 527–554. Worcester: Clark University Press.

——. 1937. *Children's dreams; an unexplored land.* London: Allen and Unwin.

Kinter-Remmlein, M. 1933. *Enquête sur un groupe des petits Parisiens; leur idées sur le bien et le mal; leur réactions de coopération et d'altruisme.* Paris: Rodstein.

Koch, H. L. 1935. An analysis of certain forms of so-called "nervous habits" in young children. *J. Genet. Psychol.*, 46, 139–170.

Kohn, H. A. 1937. Some experiences with the Pressey X-O test using a group of normal orphan children in a superior institutional environment. *J. Genet. Psychol.*, 51, 219–222.

Kuder, G. F. 1946. *Revised manual for the Kuder Preference Record.* Chicago: Science Research Associates.

Kuhlen, R. G., and B. J. Lee. 1943. Personality characteristics and social acceptability in adolescence. *J. Educ. Psychol.*, 34, 321–340.

Kunst, M. S. 1948. A study of thumb and finger-sucking in infants. *Psychol. Monogr.*, 62, No. 3, 1–71.

Landis, C., J. Zubin, and S. E. Katz. 1935. Empirical evaluation of three personality adjustment inventories. *J. Educ. Psychol.*, 26, 321–330.

Langlie, T. A. 1937. Personality ratings: I. Reliability of teachers' ratings. *J. Genet. Psychol.*, 50, 339–359.

Learned, W. S., and B. D. Wood. 1938. The student and his knowledge. *Carnegie Found. Adv. Teaching Bull.*, No. 29.

Lehman, H. C., and P. A. Witty. 1927. *The psychology of play activities.* New York: Barnes.

——. 1931. Further study of the social status of occupations. *J. Educ. Sociol.*, 5, 101–112.

Levy, D. M., and S. H. Tulchin. 1923. The resistance of infants and children during mental tests. *J. Exp. Psychol.*, 6, 304–322.

Lewis, W. D. 1940. A study of superior children in the elementary school. *Peabody Coll. Contr. Educ.*, No. 266.

——. 1945. Sex distribution of intelligence among inferior and superior children. *J. Genet. Psychol.*, 67, 67–75.

Lincoln, E. A. 1927. *Sex differences in the growth of American school children.* Baltimore: Warwick and York.

Little, M. F., and H. M. Williams. 1937. An analytical scale of language achievement. In *Development of language and vocabulary in young children. Univ. Iowa Stud. Child Welfare, 13*, No. 2, pp. 47–94.

Livesay, T. M. 1942. Subject preference as related to test intelligence, intended vocation, college expectation, and race of high school seniors in Hawaii. *J. Educ. Res.*, 36, 178–184.

Lodge, J. H. 1926. The illusion of warmth test for suggestibility. *Forum Educ.*, 4, 180–186.

Longstaff, H. P. 1936. Effectiveness of children's radio programs. *J. Appl. Psychol.*, 20, 208–220.

Lord, F. E. 1941. A study of spatial orientation of children. *J. Educ. Res.*, 34, 481–505.

Lund, F. H. 1944. Adolescent motivation: sex differences. *J. Genet. Psychol.*, 64, 99–103.

Macfarlane, J. W. 1938. Studies in child guidance. I. Methodology of data collection and organization. *Monogr. Soc. Res. Child Develpm.*, 3, No. 6. Pp. vii + 254.

Macfarlane, J. W., M. P. Honzik, and M. H. Davis. 1937. Reputation differences among young school children. *J. Educ. Psychol.*, 28, 161–175.

Macmeeken, A. M. 1939. The intelligence of a representative group of Scottish children. London: University of London Press.

Maddy, N. R. 1943. Comparison of children's personality traits, attitudes, and intelligence with parental occupation. *Genet. Psychol. Monogr.*, 27, 1–65.

Maller, J. B. 1933. The trend of juvenile delinquency in New York City. *J. Juv. Res.*, 17, 10–18.

Marquis, D. G. 1940. Physiological psychology, *Ann. Rev. Physiol.*, 2, 433–461.

Mathews, E. 1923. A study of emotional stability in children. *J. Delinq.*, 8, 1–40.

Mayer, B. A. 1935. Negativistic reactions of preschool children on the new revision of the Stanford-Binet. *J. Genet. Psychol.*, *46*, 311-334.

McAndrew, M. B. 1943. An experimental investigation of young children's ideas of causality. *Stud. Psychol. Psychiat. Cathol. Univ. Amer.*, *6*, No. 2.

McCarthy, D. A. 1930. The language development of the preschool child. (*Inst. Child Welfare Monogr. Ser.*, No. 4.) Minneapolis: University of Minnesota Press. Pp. xiii + 174.

McFate, M. Q., and Orr, F. G. 1949. Through adolescence with the Rorschach. *Rorschach Res. Exch.*, *13*, 302-319.

McIntyre, G. A., and W. Wood. 1935. The standardization of an Australian reading test. *Aust. Coun. Educ. Res. Ser.*, No. 39.

McNemar, Q. 1942. *The revision of the Stanford-Binet scale.* Boston: Houghton Mifflin.

McNemar, Q., and L. M. Terman. 1936. Sex differences in variational tendency. *Genet. Psychol. Monogr.*, *18*, 1-65.

McNeil, B. 1944. Development at the youth level of a conception of the causes of behavior and the effectiveness of a learning program in this area. *J. Exp. Educ.*, *13*, 81-85.

Meine, F. J. 1941. Radio and the press among young people. In Lazarsfeld, P. F., and F. Stanton, *Radio Research*, New York: Duell, Sloan & Pearce, pp. 189-223.

Mellone, M. A. 1944. A factorial study of picture tests for young children. *Brit. J. Psychol.*, *35*, 9-16.

Meltzer, H. 1941. Sex differences in parental preference patterns. *Character and Pers.*, *10*, 114-128.

———. 1943. Sex differences in children's attitudes to parents. *J. Genet. Psychol.*, *62*, 311-326.

Messerschmidt, R. 1933. The suggestibility of boys and girls between the ages of six and sixteen years. *J. Genet. Psychol.*, *43*, 422-437.

Michaels, J. J., and S. E. Goodman. 1934. Incidence and intercorrelations of enuresis and other neuropathic traits in so-called normal children. *Amer. J. Orthopsychiat.*, *4*, 79-106.

———. 1939. The incidence of enuresis and age of cessation in one thousand neuropsychiatric patients: with a discussion of the relationship between enuresis and delinquency. *Amer. J. Orthopsychiat.*, *9*, 59-71.

Millard, C. V. 1940. The nature and character of pre-adolescent growth in reading achievement. *Child Develpm.*, *11*, 71-114.

Miller, N. 1928. *The child in primitive society.* New York: Brentano's.

Milner, E. 1949. Effects of sex role and social status on the early adolescent personality. *Genet. Psychol. Monogr.*, *40*, 231-325.

Miner, J. B. 1922. An aid to the analysis of vocational interests. *J. Educ. Res.*, *5*, 311-323.

Mitchell, A. M. 1929. *Children and movies.* Chicago: University of Chicago Press.

Moore, J. E. 1939. Sex differences in speed of reading. *J. Exp. Educ.*, *8*, 110-114.

———. 1940. A further study of sex differences in speed of reading. *Peabody J. Educ.*, *17*, 359-362.

Mott, S. M. 1937. Mother-father preference. *Character and Pers.*, *5*, 302-304.

Murlin, J. R. 1939. Energy metabolism. *Ann. Rev. Physiol.*, *1*, 131-162.

Nelson, J. F. 1931. Personality and intelligence. *Child Develpm. Monogr.*, No. 4. Pp. 62.

Newell, H. W. 1936. A further study of maternal rejection. *Amer. J. Orthopsychiat.*, *6*, 576-589.

Olson, W. C. 1929. The measurement of nervous habits in normal children. *Inst. Child Welfare Monogr. Ser.*, No. 3. Minneapolis: University of Minnesota Press. Pp. xii + 97.

———. 1930. *Problem tendencies in children: A method for their measurement and description.* Minneapolis: University of Minnesota Press.

———. 1936. The diagnosis of oral habits in children from the condition of the hands. *J. Abnorm. (Soc.) Psychol.*, *31*, 182-189.

Orgel, S. Z., and J. Tuckman. 1935. Nicknames of institutional children. *Amer. J. Orthopsychiat.*, *5*, 276-285.

Oyama, S., and M. Kido. 1939. An experimental study on plastic molding by children. *Jap. J. Psychol.*, *14*, 327-338.

Parkes, A. S. 1926. The mammalian sex-ratio. *Biol. Rev.*, *2*, 1-52.

Parten, M. B. 1933. Social play among preschool children. *J. Abnorm. (Soc.) Psychol.*, *28*, 136-147.

Perry, R. C. 1934. A group factor analysis of the adjustment questionnaire. *Univ. S. Calif. Educ. Monogr.*, No. 5. Pp. xi + 93.

Pinard, J. W. 1932. Tests of perseveration: I. Their relation to character. *Brit. J. Psychol.*, *23*, 5-19.

Pintler, M. H., R. Phillips, and R. R. Sears. 1946. Sex differences in the projective doll play of preschool children. *J. Psychol.*, *21*, 73-80.

Pintner, R. 1924. Results obtained with the non-language group test. *J. Educ. Psychol.*, *15*, 473-483.

———. 1940. An adjustment test with normal and hard of hearing children. *J. Genet. Psychol.*, *56*, 367-381.

Pintner, R., and L. Brunschwig. 1937. A study of certain fears and wishes among deaf and hearing children. *J. Educ. Psychol.*, *28*, 259-270.

Pintner, R., and J. Lev. 1940. Worries of school children. *J. Genet. Psychol.*, *56*, 67-76.

Pratt, K. C. 1945. A study of the "fears" of rural children. *J. Genet. Psychol.*, *67*, 179-194.

Preston, R. C. 1942. Children's reactions to a contemporary war situation. *Child Develpm. Monogr.*, No. 28.

Rabban, M. 1950. Sex-role identification in young children in two diverse social groups. *Genet. Psychol. Monogr.*, *42*, 81-158.

Raubenheimer, A. S. 1925. An experimental study of some behavior traits of the potentially delinquent boy. *Psychol. Monogr.*, *34*, No. 159. Pp. 107.

Reynolds, M. M. 1928. Negativism of preschool children. *Teach. Coll. Contr. Educ.*, No. 288.

Ricciuti, E. A. 1951. Children and radio: a study of listeners and nonlisteners to various types of radio programs in terms of selected ability, attitude, and behavior measures. *Genet. Psychol. Monogr.*, *44*, 69–143.

Roberts, J. A. F., R. M. Norman, and R. Griffiths. 1935. Studies on a child population. *Ann. Eugen., Camb., 6*, 319–338.

Roff, M., and L. Roff. 1940. An analysis of the variance of conflict behavior in preschool children. *Child Develpm., 11*, 43–60.

Rose, A. A., and B. K. Stavrianos. 1943. Sex differences in the perceptual attitude of children. *J. Psychol., 16*, 129–143.

Ross, B. M. 1931. Some traits associated with sibling jealousy in problem children. *Smith Coll. Stud. Soc. Work, 1*, 364–376.

Rowe, A. W. 1928. Studies of the endocrine glands: I. A general method for the diagnosis of abnormal function. *Endocrinology, 12*, 1–54.

Rundquist, E. A. 1941. Sex, intelligence, and school marks. *Sch. and Soc., 53*, 452–456.

Russell, D. H. 1941. Reading preferences of younger adolescents in Saskatchewan. *Engl. J., 30*, 131–136.

Ryans, D. G. 1939. A note on variations in "persistence" test score with sex, age, and academic level. *J. Soc. Psychol., 10*, 259–264.

Samuels, F. 1943. Sex differences in reading achievement. *J. Educ. Res., 36*, 594–603.

Scheinfeld, A. 1943. *Women and Men.* New York: Harcourt, Brace.

Schiller, B. 1934. Verbal, numerical, and spatial abilities of young children. *Arch. Psychol., N. Y.*, No. 161.

Schubert, H. J. P., and M. E. Wagner. 1936. The relation of individual personal data responses and transiency, place among siblings, and academic ability. *J. Abnorm. (Soc.) Psychol., 30*, 474–483.

Schuell, H. Part I, 1946. Sex differences in relation to stuttering. *J. Speech Disorders, 11*, 277–298. Part II, 1947. *J. Speech Disorders, 12*, 23–38.

Schumacher, H. C. 1933. An inquiry into the etiology of children's maladjustment. *Amer. J. Orthopsychiat., 3*, 376–398.

Scottish Council for Research in Education. 1933. *The intelligence of Scottish children: A national survey.* London: University of London Press.

Seagoe, M. V. 1931. The child's reaction to the movies. *J. Juv. Res., 15*, 169–180.

Sears, P. S. 1951. Doll play aggression in normal young children: influence of sex, age, sibling status, father's absence. *Psychol. Monogr., 65*(6).

Sears, R. R., M. H. Pintler, and P. S. Sears. 1946. Effect of father separation on preschool children's doll play aggression. *Child Develpm., 17*, 219–243.

Sewall, M. 1930. Two studies in sibling rivalry: I. Some causes of jealousy in young children. *Smith Coll. Stud. Soc. Work, 1*, 6–22.

Seward, G. H. 1946. *Sex and the social order.* New York: McGraw-Hill.

Shacter, H. S. 1933. A method for measuring the sustained attention of preschool children. *J. Genet. Psychol., 42*, 339–371.

Sheldon, W. H. 1940. *The varieties of human physique.* New York: Harper.

Shock, N. W., and A. B. Hastings. 1934. Sex difference in average pH, bicarbonate, and carbon dioxide tension of blood. *J. Biol. Chem., 104*, 585.

Shuttleworth, F. K. 1938. The adolescent period; a graphic and pictorial atlas. *Monogr. Soc. Res. Child Develpm., 3*, No. 3. Pp. v + 246.

——. 1951. The adolescent period; a pictorial atlas. *Monogr. Soc. Res. Child Develpm., 14*, No. 2. Pp. v + 69.

Simpson, M. 1935. Parent preference of young children. *Teach. Coll. Contr. Educ.*, No. 652.

Smith, I. M. 1948. Measuring spatial ability in school pupils. *Occup. Psychol., Lond., 22*, 150–159.

Smith, M. E. 1926. An investigation of the development of the sentence and the extent of vocabulary in young children. *Univ. Iowa Stud. Child Welfare, 3*, No. 5.

Smith, S. 1939. Age and sex differences in children's opinion concerning sex differences. *J. Genet. Psychol., 54*, 17–25.

Sollenberger, R. T. 1940. Some relationships between the urinary excretion of male hormone by maturing boys and their expressed interests and attitudes. *J. Psychol., 9*, 179–189.

Sontag, L. W. 1947. Physiological factors and personality in children. *Child Develpm., 18*, 185–189.

Spencer, D. 1938. *Fulcra of conflict. A new approach to personality measurement.* Yonkers-on-Hudson: World Book.

Springer, N. N. 1938. The influence of general social status on the emotional stability of children. *J. Genet. Psychol., 53*, 321–328.

Stagner, R. 1938. The role of parents in the development of emotional instability. *Amer. J. Orthopsychiat., 8*, 122–129.

Stalnaker, J. M. 1941. Sex differences in the ability to write. *Sch. and Soc., 54*, 532–535.

Stavrianos, B. K. 1942. An investigation of sex differences in children as revealed by the Rorschach method. *Rorschach Res. Exch., 6*, 168–175.

Stone, C. P., and R. G. Barker. 1939. The attitudes and interests of premenarcheal and postmenarcheal girls. *J. Genet. Psychol., 54*, 27–71.

Stroud, J. B., and E. F. Lindquist. 1942. Sex differences in achievement in the elementary and secondary schools. *J. Educ. Psychol., 33*, 657–667.

Sunne, D. 1925. Personality tests: White and Negro adolescents. *J. Appl. Psychol., 9*, 256–280.

Symonds, P. M. 1936. Sex differences in the life problems and interests of adolescents. *Sch. and Soc., 43*, 751–752.

Terman, L. M. 1938. *Psychological factors in marital happiness.* New York: McGraw-Hill.

Terman, L. M., et al. 1925. *Genetic studies of genius: Vol. I. Mental and physical traits of a thousand gifted children.* Stanford University, Calif.: Stanford University Press.

Terman, L. M., and P. Buttenwieser. 1935. Personality factors in marital compatibility. *J. Soc. Psychol., 6*, 143–171; 267–289.

Terman, L. M., and M. Lima. 1926. *Children's readings.* (1st ed.) New York: Appleton.

Terman, L. M., and M. A. Merrill. 1937. *Measuring intelligence.* Boston: Houghton Mifflin.

Terman, L. M., and C. C. Miles. 1936. *Sex and personality: Studies in masculinity and femininity.* New York: McGraw-Hill.

Thorndike, E. L., *et al.* 1934. *Prediction of vocational success.* New York: Commonwealth Fund.

Thorndike, R. L., and F. Henry. 1940. Differences in reading interests related to differences in sex and intelligence level. *Elem. Sch. J., 40,* 751-763.

The trend of Scottish intelligence. 1949. London: University of London Press.

Tryon, C. M. 1939. Evaluations of adolescent personality by adolescents. *Monogr. Soc. Res. Child Develpm., 4,* No. 4. Pp. x + 83.

Tschechtelin, S. M. A. 1945. Self-appraisal of children. *J. Educ. Res., 39,* 25-32.

Tuddenham, R. D. 1951. Studies in reputation: III. Correlates of popularity among elementary-school children. *J. Educ. Psychol., 42,* 257-276.

———. 1952. Studies in reputation: I. Sex and grade differences in school children's evaluations of their peers. *Psychol. Monogr.,* 66(1).

Tyler, L. E. 1951. The relationship of interests to abilities and reputation among first-grade children. *Educ. Psychol. Meas., 11,* 255-264.

Walter, L. M., and Marzolf, S. S. 1951. The relation of sex, age, and school achievement to levels of aspiration. *J. Educ. Psychol., 42,* 285-292.

Wang, C. K. A. 1932. The significance of early personal history for certain personality traits. *Amer. J. Psychol., 44,* 768-774.

Wechsler, D. 1931. The incidence and significance of fingernail biting in children. *Psychoanal. Rev., 18,* 201-209.

Wegrocki, H. J. 1934. The effect of prestige suggestibility on emotional attitudes. *J. Soc. Psychol., 5,* 384-394.

Wellman, B. 1926. The school child's choice of companions. *J. Educ. Res., 14,* 126-132.

Wellman, B. L., I. M. Case, I. G. Mengert, and D. E. Bradbury. 1931. Speech sounds of young children. *Univ. Iowa Stud. Child Welfare, 5,* No. 2.

Whipple, G. M. 1915. *Manual of mental and physical tests:* Part III. *Complex processes.* Baltimore: Warwick and York.

White, R. S. 1930. Motor suggestion in children. *Child Develpm., 1,* 161-185.

Whitley, M. T. 1929. Children's interest in collecting. *J. Educ. Psychol., 20,* 249-261.

Wickman, E. K. 1928. *Children's behavior and teachers' attitudes.* New York: Commonwealth Fund.

Williams, H. D. 1933. A survey of predelinquent children in ten middle western cities. *J. Juv. Res., 17,* 163-174.

Williamson, E. G., and J. G. Darley. 1935. Trends in the occupational choices of high school seniors. *J. Appl. Psychol., 19,* 361-370.

Witkin, H. A. 1949. The nature and importance of individual differences in perception. *J. Person., 18,* 145-170.

Witty, P. 1941. Reading the comics—a comparative study. *J. Exp. Educ., 10,* 100-104, 105-109.

Witty, P., E. Smith, and A. Coomer. 1942. Reading the comics in grades VII and VIII. *J. Educ. Psychol., 33,* 173-182.

Witty, P. A. 1930. Study of one hundred gifted children. *Kansas Stud. Educ., 1,* No. 13.

Witty, P. A., and H. C. Lehman. 1930. Further studies of children's interest in collecting. *J. Educ. Psychol., 21,* 112-127.

Wolf, T. H. 1938. The effect of praise and competition on the persisting behavior of kindergarten children. *Inst. Child Welfare Monogr. Ser.,* No. 15. Minneapolis: University of Minnesota Press. Pp. vi + 138.

Woody, C. 1931. The arithmetical backgrounds of young children. *J. Educ. Res., 24,* 188-201.

———. 1937, 1938. The sophomore and freshman testing program in the accredited high schools of Michigan. *Bur. Educ. Ref. and Res., Bull., 149,* 150.

Wyman, J. B. 1925. Tests of intellectual, social, and activity interests. In L. M. Terman *et al., Genetic studies of genius.* Stanford University, Calif.: Stanford University Press. Vol. I, pp. 455-483.

Yarrow, L. J. 1948. The effect of antecedent frustration on projective play. *Psychol. Monogr.,* 62(6).

Zapf, R. M. 1945. Relationship between belief in superstitions and other factors. *J. Educ. Res., 38,* 561-579.

Zeligs, R. 1939. Children's worries. *Sociol. Soc. Res., 24,* 22-32.

———. 1945. Social factors annoying to children. *J. Appl. Psychol., 29,* 75-82.

ADDITIONAL SELECTED REFERENCES

Ackerson, L. 1936. On evaluating the relative importance or "seriousness" of various behavior problems in children. *J. Juv. Res., 20,* 114-123.

Allen, C. N. 1927. Studies in sex differences. *Psychol. Bull., 24,* 294-304.

———. 1930. Recent studies in sex differences. *Psychol. Bull., 27,* 394-407.

———. 1931. Individual differences in delayed reactions of infants. *Arch. Psychol., N. Y., 19,* No. 127.

———. 1935. Recent research on sex differences. *Psychol. Bull., 32,* 343-354.

Altmaier, C. L. 1931. The performance level of children in the sixth grade in two Philadelphia public schools. *Psychol. Clin., 19,* 233-257.

Anderson, H. H. 1939. Domination and social integration in the behavior of kindergarten children in an experimental play situation. *J. Exp. Educ., 8,* 123-131.

Armstrong, C. P. 1937. A psychoneurotic reaction of delinquent boys and girls. *J. Abnorm. (Soc.) Psychol., 32,* 329-342.

Barrett, H. O. 1950. Sex differences in art ability. *J. Educ. Res., 43,* 391-393.

Bell, M. A. 1927. On sex differences in nonintellectual mental traits. Unpublished master's thesis, Stanford University.

Bennett, E. E. 1932. What high-school pupils read in school papers. *Sch. Rev.*, *40*, 772–780.

Blatz, W. E., and E. A. Bott. 1927. Studies in the mental hygiene of children: I. Behavior of public school children—A description of method. *Ped. Sem.*, *34*, 552–582.

Block, V. L. 1937. Conflicts of adolescents with their mothers. *J. Abnorm. (Soc.) Psychol.*, *32*, 193–206.

Blumenfeld, W. 1948. Intelligence examinations in Peru with the Lima revision of Terman's Group Test. *J. Genet. Psychol.*, *73*, 251–268.

Britt, S. H., and S. Q. Janus. 1941. Toward a social psychology of human play. *J. Soc. Psychol.*, *13*, 351–384.

Broster, L. R., *et al.* 1938. *The adrenal cortex and intersexuality.* London: Chapman and Hall.

Brown, F. 1937. Neuroticism of institution versus noninstitution children. *J. Appl. Psychol.*, *21*, 379–383.

Brown, P. A. 1938. Responses of blind and seeing adolescents to an introversion-extroversion questionnaire. *J. Psychol.*, *6*, 137–147.

Brumbaugh, F., and F. T. Wilson. 1940. Children's laughter. *J. Genet. Psychol.*, *57*, 3–29.

Bühler, C. 1927a. *Das Problem der Differenz der Geschlechter.* (*Dtsch. Mädchenbildung*, Vol. 3.) Leipzig: Teubner.

——. 1927b. Die ersten sozialen Verhaltungsweisen des Kindes. *Quel. Stud. Jugendk.*, No. 5.

Busemann, A. 1928. Geschwisterschaft, Schultuchtigkeit und Charakter. *Z. Kinderforsch*, *34*, 1–52.

Caldwell, O. W., and G. E. Lundeen. 1934. Further study of unfounded beliefs among junior high school pupils. *Teach. Coll. Rec.*, *36*, 35–52.

Campbell, E. H. 1934. The social-sex development of children. *Genet. Psychol. Monogr.*, *21*, 461–552.

Carpenter, A. 1941. The differential measurement of speed in primary school children. *Child Develpm.*, *12*, 1–7.

Carter, H. D. 1938. A preliminary study of free association: I. Twin similarities and the technique of measurement. *J. Psychol.*, *6*, 201–215.

Celestine, Sr. M. 1930. A survey of the literature on the reading interests of children of the elementary grades. *Cath. Univ. Amer. Educ. Res. Bull.*, *5*, Nos. 2 and 3.

Chauffard, C. 1949. Regidité ou plasticité des aptitudes chez l'enfant. *Enfance*, *2*, 202–221.

Commins, W. D. 1928. More about sex differences. *Sch. and Soc.*, *28*, 599–600.

Conrad, H. S., H. E. Jones, and H. H. Hsiao. 1933. Sex differences in mental growth and decline. *J. Educ. Psychol.*, *24*, 161–169.

Dale, A. B. 1926. Group tests in reasoning ability. *Brit. J. Psychol.*, *16*, 314–338.

Darley, J. G. 1937. Scholastic achievement and measured maladjustment. *J. Appl. Psychol.*, *21*, 485–493.

Dewey, E., E. Child, and B. Ruml. 1920. *Methods and results of testing school children.* New York: Dutton.

Dietze, A. G., and G. E. Jones. 1931. Factual memory of secondary school pupils for a short article which they read a single time. *J. Educ. Psychol.*, *22*, 586–598; 667–676.

Dodge, A. F. 1937. Social dominance of clerical workers and sales-persons as measured by the Bernreuter Personality Inventory. *J. Educ. Psychol.*, *28*, 71–73.

Driggs, H. W. 1934. The vocabulary of letters of boys and girls 12 to 15 years of age inclusive. *J. Exp. Educ.*, *2*, 339–354.

Dublin, L. I., and B. Bunzel. 1933. *To be or not to be: A study in suicide.* New York: Smith and Haas.

Dudycha, G. J., and M. M. Dudycha. 1933. Some factors and characteristics of childhood memories. *Child Develpm.*, *4*, 265–278.

Dunn, F. W. 1921. Interest factors in primary reading material. *Teach. Coll. Contr. Educ.*, No. 113.

Durea, M. A. 1939. A survey of the adjustment of school children. *Child Develpm.*, *10*, 107–114.

Easby-Grave, C. 1924. Tests and norms at the six-year-old performance level. *Psychol. Clin.*, *15*, 261–300.

Ellis, H. 1894. *Man and woman.* 1st ed. London: Scott.

——. 1903. Variation in man and woman. *Pop. Sci. Mon.*, *62*, 237–253. Also in Appendix to *Man and woman.* 6th ed. London: Black, 1926.

Espenschade, A. 1940. Motor performance in adolescence, including the study of relationships with measures of physical growth and maturity. *Monogr. Soc. Res. Child Develpm.*, *5*, No. 1.

——. 1947. Development of motor coordination in boys and girls. *Res. Quart. Amer. Ass. Hlth.*, *18*, 30–40.

Evans, H. M. 1939. Endocrine glands. Gonads, pituitary, and adrenals. *Ann. Rev. Physiol.*, *1*, 577–652.

Ferrell, G. V. 1949. Comparative study of sex differences in school achievement of white and Negro children. *J. Educ. Res.*, *43*, 116–121.

Fischler, D., and I. Ullert. 1929. Contribution à l'étude des tests de mémoire immédiate. *Arch. Psychol., Genève*, *21*, 293–306.

Franklin, E. E. 1926. The permanence of vocational interests after three years. *Sch. and Soc.*, *23*, 438–440.

Garrett, H. E., and T. R. Fisher. 1926. The prevalence of certain popular misconceptions. *J. Appl. Psychol.*, *10*, 411–420.

Gerberich, J. R. 1930. The gifted pupils of the Iowa high school survey. *J. Appl. Psychol.*, *14*, 566–576.

Goodenough, F. L. 1927. The consistency of sex differences in mental traits at various ages. *Psychol. Rev.*, *34*, 440–462.

Greene, E. B. 1937. *Michigan vocabulary profile:* Forms I, II. Ann Arbor: author.

Guilford, J. P., and R. B. Guilford. 1936. Personality factors S, E, and M, and their measurement. *J. Psychol.*, *2*, 109–127.

Guilford, J. P., and H. Martin. 1944. Age differences and sex differences in some introvertive and emotional traits. *J. Gen. Psychol.*, *31*, 219–229.

Hansen, H. C. 1939. Relationship between sex and school achievement of one thousand Indian children. *J. Soc. Psychol.*, *10*, 399–406.

Hanske, C. F. 1931. Sex differences in high-school chemistry. *J. Educ. Res.*, *23*, 412–416.

Hartshorne, H., M. A. May, and F. K. Shuttleworth. 1930. *Studies in the organization of character.* New York: Macmillan.

Henmon, V. A. C. 1929. *Achievement tests in the modern foreign languages.* New York: Macmillan.

Hollingworth, L. S. 1914. Variability as related to sex differences in achievement. *Amer. J. Sociol.*, *19*, 510–530.

Holmes, F. B. 1936. An experimental investigation of a method of overcoming children's fears. *Child Develpm.*, *7*, 6–30.

Holzinger, K. J., and F. Swineford. 1939. A study in factor analysis: The stability of a bi-factor solution. *Suppl. Educ. Monogr.*, No. 48. Pp. ix + 91.

Horton, B. J. 1937. The truthfulness of boys and girls in public and private schools. *J. Abnorm. (Soc.) Psychol.*, *31*, 398–405.

Hurd, A. W. 1934. Sex differences in achievement in physical science. *J. Educ. Psychol.*, *25*, 70.

Jones, H. E. 1947a. Sex differences in physical abilities. *Hum. Biol.*, *19*, 12–25.

——. 1947b. Sex differences in physical abilities. *Hum. Biol.*, *19*, 12–25.

——. 1949. *Motor performance and growth.* Berkeley: University of California Press.

Jones, H. E., and R. H. Seashore. 1944. The development of fine motor and mechanical abilities. *Yearb. Nat. Soc. Stud. Educ.*, *43*, 123–145.

Kamat, V. V. 1939. Sex differences among Indian children in the Binet-Simon tests. *Brit. J. Educ. Psychol.*, *9*, 251–256.

Kamel, M. 1947. Evaluations of adolescent personality by adolescents and adults. *Egypt. J. Psychol.*, *3*, 33–54, 147–152.

Kangley, L. 1938. Poetry preferences in the junior high school. *Teach. Coll. Contr. Educ.*, No. 758.

Kaulfers, W. 1928. Intelligence of one thousand students of foreign languages. *Sch. & Soc.*, *28*, 597–599.

Klopfer, B. 1939. Personality differences between boys and girls in early childhood. (Abstract.) *Psychol. Bull.*, *36*, 538.

Kuznets, G. M., and Q. McNemar. 1940. Sex differences in intelligence-test scores. *Yearb. Nat. Soc. Stud. Educ.*, *39* (I), 211–220.

Landreth, C. 1941. Factors associated with crying in young children in the nursery school and the home. *Child Develpm.*, *12*, 81–97.

Learning, R. E. 1922. Tests and norms for vocational guidance at the fifteen-year-old performance level. *Psychol. Clin.*, *14*, 193–220.

Levy, D. M., and S. H. Tulchin. 1925. The resistant behavior of infants and children: II. *J. Exp. Psychol.*, *8*, 209–224.

Lillie, F. R. 1939. General biological introduction. In E. Allen (Ed.), *Sex and internal secretions*, pp. 3–14. (2d ed.) Baltimore: Williams and Wilkins.

Lockhart, E. G. 1930. The attitudes of children toward law. *Univ. Iowa Stud. Charact.*, *3*, No. 1.

Madsen, I. N. 1924. Some results with the Stanford revision of the Binet-Simon tests. *Sch. & Soc.*, *19*, 559–562.

Maller, J. B. 1929. Cooperation and competition; an experimental study in motivation. *Teach. Coll. Contr. Educ.*, No. 384.

McBee, M. 1935. A mental-hygiene clinic in a high school. *Ment. Hyg., N. Y.*, *19*, 238–280.

McCay, J. B., and M. B. Fowler. 1941. Some sex differences observed in a group of nursery school children. *Child Develpm.*, *12*, 75–79.

McCracken, T. C., and H. E. Lamb. 1923. *Occupational information in the elementary school.* Boston: Houghton Mifflin.

Miles, C. C. 1935. Sex in social psychology. In C. Murchison (Ed.), *A handbook of social psychology*, pp. 683–797. Worcester: Clark University Press.

Morton, D. M. 1936. Number forms and arithmetical ability in children. *Brit. J. Educ. Psychol.*, *6*, 58–73.

Nifenecker, E. A., and H. G. Campbell. 1937. *Review of departmental experience in dealnig with problems of school maladjustment: Part II. Statistical reference data relating to problems of overageness, educational retardation, non-promotion, 1900–1934.* New York: Board of Education, Bureau of Reference, Research and Statistics. (Publ. No. 28.)

Odlum, D. M. 1947. Some observations on the reaction of children to wartime conditions as seen in a child guidance clinic. *Z. Kinderpsychiat.*, *13*, 173–180.

Pearson, K. 1897. *Chances of death.* London: Arnold. Vol. I.

Peck, L. 1935. Teacher's reports of the problems of unadjusted school children. *J. Educ. Psychol.*, *26*, 123–138.

Phillips, A. 1931. Sibship: Intelligence and behavior. *Psychol. Clin.*, *20*, 97–115.

Pintner, R. 1933. A comparison of interests, abilities, and attitudes. *J. Abnorm. (Soc.) Psychol.*, *27*, 351–357.

Pintner, R., J. B. Maller, G. Forlano, and K. Axelrod. 1935. The measurement of pupil adjustment. *J. Educ. Res.*, *28*, 334–346.

Pressey, S. L. 1921. A group scale for investigating emotions. *J. Abnorm. Psychol.*, *16*, 55–64.

Pressey, S. L., and L. C. Pressey. 1933. Development of the interest–attitude tests. *J. Appl. Psychol.*, *17*, 1–16.

Pyle, W. H. 1925. The relation of sex differences to the kind of material used. *J. Educ. Psychol.*, *16*, 261–264.

Remer, L. L. 1932. Handicaps of school entrants: A study of traits which handicap children entering kindergarten and first grade. *Univ. Iowa Stud. Child Welfare, 6,* 197-207.

Riddle, O. 1929. Some interrelations of sexuality, reproduction, and internal secretion. *J. Amer. Med. Ass., 92,* 943-950.

Rigg, M. G. 1940. The relative variability in intelligence of boys and girls. *J. Genet. Psychol., 56,* 211-214.

Ryans, D. G. 1939. The measurement of persistence: An historical review. *Psychol. Bull., 36,* 715-739.

Schmidberger, G. 1932. Über Geschlechtsunterschiede in der Rechnenbegabung. *Z. pädag. Psychol., 33,* 70-85; 104-165.

Sletto, R. F. 1934. Sibling position and juvenile delinquency. *Amer. J. Sociol., 39,* 657-669.

Smith, M. E. 1933. The influence of age, sex, and situation on the frequency, form, and function of questions asked by preschool children. *Child Develpm., 4,* 201-213.

Speer, G. S. 1939. Oral and written wishes of rural and city school children. *Child Develpm., 10,* 151-155.

Stagner, R., and N. Drought. 1935. Measuring children's attitudes toward their parents. *J. Educ. Psychol., 26,* 169-176.

Straker, A., and R. H. Thouless. 1940. Preliminary results of Cambridge survey of evacuated children. *Brit. J. Educ. Psychol., 10,* 97-113.

Symonds, P. M. 1937. Changes in sex differences in problems and interests of adolescents with increasing age. *J. Genet. Psychol., 50,* 83-89.

Thorndike, E. L. 1926. Sex differences in status and

gain in intelligence scores from thirteen to eighteen. *Ped. Sem., 33,* 167-181.

Thurstone, L. L., and R. L. Jenkins. 1931. *Order of birth, parent-age, and intelligence.* Chicago: University of Chicago Press.

Thurstone, L. L., and T. G. Thurstone. 1930. A neurotic inventory. *J. Soc. Psychol., 1,* 3-30.

Touton, F. C. 1924. Sex differences in geometric abilities. *J. Educ. Psychol., 15,* 234-247.

Traxler, A. E. 1935. Sex differences in rate of reading in the high school. *J. Appl. Psychol., 19,* 351-352.

Washburne, C. W., and M. Vogel. 1926. *What children like to read.* Chicago: Rand McNally.

Washburne, J. N. 1932. The impulsions of adolescents as revealed by written wishes. *J. Juv. Res., 16,* 193-212.

Weinberg, D. 1932. Contributions à l'étude expérimentale de quelques différences de caractères chez les garçons et les filles. *Bull Soc. de Sexol., 1,* 57-66.

Wellman, B. L. 1933. Sex differences. In C. Murchison (Ed.), *A handbook of child psychology,* pp. 626-649. (2d ed., rev.) Worcester: Clark University Press.

Wilds, E. H. 1932. Interschool contests in American high schools. *Sch. Rev., 40,* 429-441.

Winkler, J. B. 1949. Age trends and sex differences in the wishes, identifications, activities, and fears of children. *Child Develpm., 20,* 191-200.

Woolley, H. T. 1926. *An experimental study of children.* New York: Macmillan.

CHAPTER 18

PSYCHOPATHOLOGY OF CHILDHOOD

CLEMENS E. BENDA

MENTAL DEFICIENCY

Marginal Forms of Mental Inadequacy

Definitions. In any larger sample of a population, a certain percentage of persons are unable to compete under equal conditions with others of the same age and the same cultural background because of the fact that their mentality is not functioning adequately for the task at hand. If such mental aberrations occur in adolescents or adults who have functioned adequately up to the time of their illness, we speak of mental "illness," a psychoneurosis or psychosis, according to the severity of the disorder and its character. The official definition of mental illness or "insanity" is:

> a condition which renders the affected person unfit to enjoy liberty of action because of the unreliability of his behavior with concomitant danger to himself and others. [Dorland, 1942.]

Though it may be difficult to determine in an individual case whether a mental illness is present, the situation as a whole is quite clear. Everybody realizes also that a mental illness, even of an emotional character, may interfere with the manifestations of what is usually called "intelligence." Nobody will therefore take the outcome of a psychometric examination of intelligence done during a mental illness as a true measure of the degree of intelligence which had been at the disposal of that person under normal conditions, and the testing of intelligence does not serve as a means of differential diagnosis between mental illness and mental "defects."

However, the situation is quite different if we deal with children. Interference with intellectual performance which we may find in children in a variety of disorders of mentation has led to the concept of "mental deficiency" or "feeble-mindedness," and it has been generally assumed for almost one hundred years that a mentally defective person is entirely different from a person with mental illness or "insanity." Although there is no generally accepted definition of mental deficiency, and all regulations dealing with mental deficiency are state and not federal laws, a fairly adequate definition of mental deficiency may be formulated in the following way:

> A mentally defective person is a person who is incapable of managing himself and his affairs, or being taught to do so, and who requires supervision, control, and care for his own welfare and the welfare of the community.

If this definition is compared with that of mental illness, it is obvious that it does not provide an adequate tool to differentiate between the two; and, yet, all legal provisions for the mentally defectives emphasize that the provisions do not refer to "insane" or mentally ill persons.

Historically, the emphasis in definitions of mental deficiency is placed on an impairment of "intelligence." If a mentally disturbed person has sufficient intelligence to perform within the normal range on Stanford-Binet intelligence tests, such person is considered ill but not mentally defective. If, however, the disorder of mentation is severe enough to impair the intellectual performance to a degree outside the average range, the person is usually called mentally

mind existing before the age of 18 years, whether arising from inherent causes or induced by disease or injury.

Although the use of the term "arrested" development seems to offer a useful differentiation to separate persons with defects of mentation from other groups, the term "incomplete" development becomes mean-

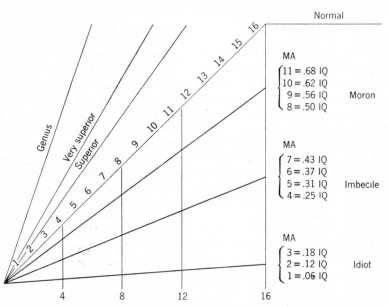

FIGURE 1. Classification of subnormal IQ ratings and corresponding mental ages for adolescent mental defectives of 16 years and above.

defective. It is therefore not surprising that the vast majority of children and young people with any type of mental aberration are considered "mentally defective," and no further differentiation is offered or attempted.

The English law, which offers a standard definition of mental defectiveness based on the *Report of the Mental Deficiency Committee*, or the so-called Wood Report, reads:

Mental defectiveness means a condition of arrested or incomplete development of

ingless if we realize that psychoneurotic or psychotic conditions are also "fixations" or regressions to earlier developmental stages and that any lack of maturity is actually an "incomplete development of the mind."

The psychological classification of the whole group of mental deficiency uses three main categories with the common denominator that a defective person has an IQ rating below 70, taking a mental age of 16 as standard level for the adolescent group. The demarcation between imbecile and idiot is not entirely uniform, and some use an IQ rating of 20 as margin, some of 25. As to the borderline between imbeciles and morons, the line is placed at an IQ level of 50, although 45 would be more feasible in many instances.

In America the expressions "feeble-mindedness" and "mental deficiency" are used synonymously, whereas in England "feeble-mindedness" is reserved for the higher grades which in America are called "morons." It seems preferable that "feeble-mindedness" be reserved for the "marginal" group, or the "moron," because the application of "feeble-mindedness" to the whole field of mental inadequacy implies that we deal with quantitative gradations but not qualitatively different groups. It has to be emphasized that a large percentage of the "feeble-minded" or the marginal group are completely different from persons with severe forms of mental deficiency, the "idiots" or "imbeciles," and the two groups should be kept strictly separate.

It is only in the last few years that it has been recognized more and more that the distinction between mental deficiency and mental illness cannot be maintained unless the term "mental deficiency" or feeble-mindedness is actually reserved for the marginal groups, who are not patients or ill people but persons with an inadequate intellectual endowment. As far as the more severe degrees of mental inadequacy are concerned, an analysis of the group reveals that we are dealing with a great variety of conditions of defective development or diseases of the central nervous system. Although some of the defects and malformations may be relatively stationary, in general there is no true "arrest" of development; and, as long as life proceeds, changes take place which are either an improvement or a progressive disorganization of the nervous system. It is time, therefore, to abandon terms like idiocy or imbecility as diag-

nostic definitions and to realize that the patients with IQ ratings below 50 are suffering from a variety of conditions which interfere with appropriate mental performance. Since in infancy and childhood we deal with a period of rapid growth and differentiation, any interference with development leads to changes in organization and subsequent differentiation. Moreover, the borderline between mental illness on an infectious or metabolic basis and those total personality disorders which we call schizophrenia, the character of which is not yet entirely clear, is so fluid that from a clinical point of view a differentiation cannot be maintained. This author has therefore proposed that the field of psychopathology of childhood be considered as the realm of developmental disorders of mentation, and that each group be considered according to its own merits.

The human personality as a functioning unit is constantly engaged in interaction with its environment. The behavioral patterns show different aspects in which motor behavior and sensory perception, emotional patterns and a rather abstract faculty called "intelligence" can theoretically be distinguished.

It is impossible within the framework of this chapter to discuss the definition of intelligence in more detail. Many other chapters in this book deal with intelligence and its measurement. One of the difficulties of all definitions of intelligence is that some writers consider human intelligence as that which distinguishes mankind from the animal kingdom; and, although it may be agreed that animals reveal manifestations of a faculty called "intelligence," in talking about human intelligence investigators emphasize those aspects that distinguish mankind from other creatures. In such a definition the ability to judge, to adapt to new situations, to learn from experience is usually emphasized as a characteristic of human intelligence, although the last item, to learn from experience, is granted to animals, too. However, if we deal with the concept of human intelligence on a more modest scale, we use those factors which were emphasized by Binet when he established the Binet-Simon test, which is the foundation of all later psychometric measures. Binet wanted to tap the faculty of judgment called "good sense," "practical sense," "initiative," and the faculty of adapting oneself to circumstances. From the viewpoint of psychometric ratings, human intelligence ratings can be represented on a quantitative scale in which is charted the degree of intellect which an individual can command at the time of examination. As Figure 2 shows, if the mean average intelligence is standardized at 100 the average range covers a field of IQ ratings between 70 and 130, or twice the standard deviation of 15, with about 2 to 3 per cent of test results above and below this range within 3 times the standard deviation. It is obvious, however, that the number of persons who test below 70 is much larger than the expected proportion of 2 to 3 per cent. The remaining number is composed of persons with pathological conditions which interfere with human intelligence and create a variety of aberrations of mental performance. However, throughout the whole scale of intelligence, mental illness may interfere with mentation at any level of development, and emotional disorders may also influence human behavior at any level of intelligence.

Psychological Ecology. Mental inadequacy involves not only intricate psychological problems which throw light on the complexity of human intelligence and its developmental anomalies but also sociological, educational, and biological problems which deserve attention. As a matter of fact, human intelligence cannot be separated from its biological and sociological environment,

and psychological ecology is an important science though still in its very beginning.

The fate of the mentally inadequate person depends greatly on the type of family in which he is born. The inadequate child who is the only inferior member in an average or superior family is, from the very beginning, exposed to discrimination as an inferior member of the group. Discouragement, contempt, and neglect enter into the emotional and mental development from early infancy. Unable to respond adequately to his environment and return affection and attention with equal currency, the inadequate child finds himself exposed to early isolation and exclusion. Such a child is often a source of embarrassment to the other members of the family, who react to his presence with shame and may try to hide the fact of his existence. Parents, siblings, and teachers feel that he is "lazy," "dull," or lacking "will," and the child is usually treated with impatience. Thus, he will develop an inferiority complex and will soon slow down in his attempts to cope with his environment. Discouragement in school will often be so complete that the child will not do the things he knows how to do, and will remain a nonreader and will even lag behind his mental age in other subjects.

The reactions to such an unfavorable situation vary with the constitutional character of the individual and the dynamics to which he is subjected. Many withdraw from contact with their surroundings and indulge in excessive daydreaming and fantasy life. Others struggle to maintain a certain amount of self-respect by overactivity and social enterprises which are often far beyond control. Children of this type get into trouble and are sometimes caught stealing or participating in "unnatural" sexual activities or in other misdemeanors. It has been the custom to blame intellectual inadequacy for such be-

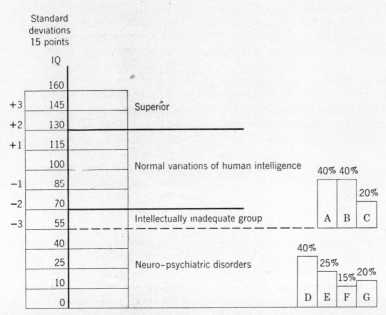

FIGURE 2. Psychological and psychopathological classification of normal and abnormal intelligence scores.

The normal variations of human intelligence are grouped around a mean of 100, and fall into a range ±2 times the standard deviations of 15 points. A certain percentage, about 2.5, of the total falls within 3 times the standard deviations. Theoretically, the normal intelligence falls, therefore, in a range between 55 and 145 IQ rating. The range of intellectually inadequate persons with IQ's between 55 and 70 is composed of three groups:

A. Normal minus variations within 3 times the standard deviations.

B. Genetic oligoencephaly.

C. Accidental cases, due to trauma, infections, metabolic disorders, or emotional disturbances.

The severer forms of mental deficiency, with IQ ratings below a range of 45 to 55, are composed of neuropsychiatric disorders:

D. Prenatal developmental disorders.

E. Traumatic "birth injuries."

F. Infectious diseases.

G. Metabolic disorders; neoplastic malformations; so-called degenerative diseases; and psychoses.

(Taken from C. E. Benda, M. J. Farrell, and C. E. Chipman, The Inadequacy of Present-Day Concepts of Mental Deficiency and Mental Illness in Child Psychiatry. *Amer. J. Psychiat.*, *107*, 721, 1951.)

havior patterns, but the psychoanalytical study of the emotional development of such children clearly indicates that they react like the normal child and that their behavior patterns are the product of psychodynamic factors and not of the fact that their judgment and mental ability are limited. The final fate of the inadequate member of an average family depends very much on the handling and understanding such a person encounters. Many end in institutions or are hidden, usually in inadequate home arrangements, in which they lead a life far below their capacities.

The moron from an inferior family, or from a family where one or both parents are of low mentality, usually has a different life. Not recognized in early infancy or childhood, such a child usually grows up under unsatisfactory home conditions until a social agency finally steps in. The feebleminded mother, unable to manage a family that is often too large, neglects the children by giving them inadequate food and overlooking early infections. She may attempt to escape by being promiscuous or by leaving the home for many hours of the day or night. The father or both parents are frequently alcoholic. The father, if not feeble-minded himself, may desert the home which is beyond his control. The accident rate in such families is high: burns from water boiling over, open flames, or burning houses are frequently found in children from these families. Others suffer from severe infections, chronic running ears, bone infections, or acute illnesses with involvement of the nervous system, which may increase the degree of mental defect. Other children suffer from severe nutritional deficiencies in infancy, their physical and mental development being delayed through malnutrition. Psychologically, an atmosphere of insecurity is created by neglect of the children, illness, death, and accidents. Thus, many

children of this type are never able to develop a firm personality structure.

Lacking physical and psychological mothering, many of these children become psychopathic personalities, with severe emotional disorders lasting over many years, with resultant lack of ability to form any strong emotional attachments. When placed in foster homes through social agencies, they are not likely to make adequate adjustment. Misdemeanors and sexual play, taken in stride by real parents with regard to their own children, are critically judged and condemned in foster children and state wards, and foster parents are often ready to give up a child who does not come up to their expectations or who is not easily handled. Moving from home to home increases the child's feeling of insecurity, and the possibility of making a satisfactory community adjustment vanishes. When near puberty but often before 10 years of age, children of this type are found engaged in delinquencies and attract attention for sexual irregularities. These behavior patterns may be adopted because of the need to please other children, to be accepted as a "regular," as well as to derive primitive libidinous satisfaction from sexual play for themselves. Such activities do not endear the marginal group to the rest of society, and a child of this type finds it increasingly difficult to be accepted. He is, therefore, likely to remain a member of the marginal group throughout life.

The inadequate girl who may be physically well developed is apt to find men who are interested in her, and many girls of this type become public charges because of illegitimate pregnancies. If they marry, they start another family of the same type as that from which they have derived, and the cycle starts another turn, not for "hereditary" reasons or reasons of mere "feeble-mindedness," but by virtue of the complex psychological, sociological, and educational problems which this group presents.

The mentally inadequate male is less likely to find a female mate of superior intelligence, because girls of normal intelligence will spurn these individuals, who are usually unattractive, dull, slow, and unable to support their courting with adequate funds. The inadequate man is, therefore, condemned to fall back on females of lower mentality, and if he marries we usually find marriage of two inferior people who are utterly incapable of managing their own affairs, let alone a large family with many children.

This rather grim picture of the life history of the mentally inadequate group shows the complexity of the situation. Some states believe that sterilization may be an adequate remedy, but no single measure is adequate to cure this situation because even strict sterilization laws cannot interfere with the parent group which remains in the community. These parents may lead a life which is objectionable, but not enough so to justify any interference by law.

A confirmation of the above observations has been provided by a study on ecological data of 100 moron patients at the Walter E. Fernald School by Thomas Lenthall.[1] Of the institutionalized patients, 80 per cent of the male and 58 per cent of the female patients came from broken homes; 24 per cent of the male and 16 per cent of the female patients were illegitimate; in 7 per cent the father had deserted the family, in 4 per cent the mother; in 3 per cent the parents were divorced, in 1 per cent separated. The father had died in 3 per cent, the mother in 8 per cent; 4 per cent of the fathers and 4 per cent of the mothers were in prison, and in 1 per cent both parents; 3 per cent of the mothers were institutionalized in a state school and 3 per cent in a mental hospital.

[1] Unpublished material.

In addition there were a few other data which accounted for the total percentage mentioned above. Abuse of alcohol by the parents was found in 36 per cent of the male and 22 per cent of the female patients; sexual promiscuity and low moral standards in at least one of the parents were found in 44 per cent. Both parents were of low mentality in 4 per cent and feeble-minded in 5 per cent, although the feeble-mindedness of the parents in the male patients was as high as 10 per cent while none of the female patients had both parents feeble-minded. Feeble-mindedness in the mother alone was found in 14 per cent, and low mentality in 10 per cent. In the father group, low mentality was found in 4 per cent but feeble-mindedness in none, confirming another observation reported before that the feeble-minded male has relatively few marriage chances, and the feeble-minded male usually marries a female of lower mentality than his own.

The Marginal Group. The person with marginal intelligence is an individual whose mental maturation lags behind that of his contemporaries. Mental maturation is a process which includes the development of judgment and evaluation of a present situation and the ability to adjust to new situations and to utilize previous experiences. It also calls for a certain standard speed of mental functioning which enables the person to compete with others at the same rate of functioning. Children with mental inadequacy lag in every respect behind their age group, and adults of the marginal group never attain the mental maturation necessary to be entirely self-sufficient, especially in a competitive society under most adverse conditions. Not every child with slow mental maturation is mentally defective, and it must be understood that the status of incomplete maturation must be a permanent condition in order to fulfill the diagnosis of mental deficiency.

Delayed maturation may be caused by many different factors. Some children are slow starters or have been traumatized at birth, but they gradually come up to a normal level. Other children may be greatly handicapped by unfavorable original or social or nutritional conditions, and development is delayed but not permanently handicapped. This type of development is well demonstrated by the following case history, which is selected from a large group of similar records:

Barbara is the third of four children. The father is described as a person of limited intelligence who went to the sixth grade in school and started to work at 14. He had a long list of varied employments and filled every kind of job as an unskilled laborer, but was never able to hold any position very long. His work was irregular, and the family needed public aid. He was quarrelsome, not on speaking terms with his own family, and very weak.

The mother was the brighter of the two but had a very unstable personality. She herself had lost her parents when a small child, and was adopted by her grandparents. She had a very unhappy childhood, was always in poor health, had rheumatic fever and ear abscesses and was anemic. Psychologically she was described as a very aggressive person who dominated the father, and the psychiatrist who worked with the family felt that the mother was a very cold person in relation to her children, whom she rejected. The children suffered both from the turbulent home situation and from the absence of warmth and love from their mother.

Barbara was more or less of a health problem from birth. She had great feeding difficulties and food idiosyncrasies. When a year old, she was placed in a children's hospital for treatment. She had always been underweight, and weighed less than 17 pounds at 9 months. She could not sit alone, and had not cut teeth at 1 year. She showed temper tantrums,

picked up a rattle and hit herself over the head with the result that large bumps began to form. At the children's hospital she was a markedly emaciated, dirty, undernourished baby of 1 year, lying almost lifeless in bed. Her buttocks and back were covered with ulcers. Over her head there were large, hard hematomata. When treated, she gained weight and her mental attitude improved considerably. However, it was difficult to give her an adequate mental rating. There is little known about the history for the following years except that the child had enuresis and temper tantrums, was moody, and started to become a real behavior problem.

The mother became more and more nervous and irritable; she developed cancer, for which she was finally admitted to a hospital. Shortly after the mother had entered the hospital, the house burned down owing to negligence. The neighbors stepped in and provided temporarily for the children, but, when they saw that the father made no plans, the neighbors withdrew and the children were finally taken over by a social agency because of the unbearable conditions in which the family was found.

Placed in a foster home, Barbara wet the bed every night. All sorts of methods were tried to help her but nothing checked the habit. Barbara, in a deep stupor at night which was almost a coma, staggered to the bathroom and back like a person in a daze. One night the child got up herself and walked into the kitchen, probably thinking she was going to the bathroom. Apparently intending to turn on the faucet to get a drink of water, she turned the handles of the gas stove; the gas did not light and the child was nearly overcome by the gas fumes.

During the next year the child improved in her nutritional state and was better behaved except for enuresis. Her school work was poor. Because of her age she was placed in the third grade, and only after it was found that she was completely unable to do what the other children did was the child examined and tested.

Barbara was a slim, cooperative little girl of 9 years 4 months, of fairly average height and weight. The occiput appeared flattened, apparently from early rickets, the lips were dry and bleeding, the teeth poor, and there were scars all over her back from early ulcers. In a psychological test the child, who was friendly and appeared quite happy under test conditions, scored a Stanford-Binet mental age of 8 years, which gave her an IQ rating of 87. She acted in a much more sophisticated manner than one would expect. She had built up a defense against possible failure through a variety of methods for eliciting cue words from the examiner. Often her

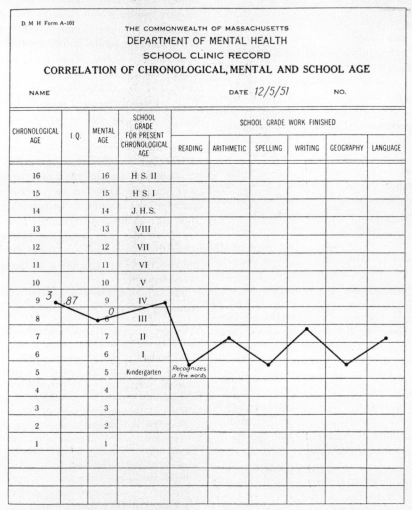

FIGURE 3. Correlation chart as used in the institutions of the Massachusetts Department of Mental Health to demonstrate the relations between chronological age, mental age, expected school grade placement, and actual school knowledge.

pose was that of absentmindedness and she would say, "Oh dear me, what is that word? I know it so well." The word in question was apt to be a most familiar one which supplied the essential point in an answer. The psychologist concluded, "Barbara's behavior resembles that of a child who is forced to capitalize on a disarming personality to protect herself against her inability to meet requirements set for her."

We may observe here a specific personality reaction, often found in psychopathic children who have had no possibility to develop a firm ego structure. This child has chosen the way of submission and of pleasing the other person at any price. It is to be feared that this girl may engage in promiscuous sexual activities when she grows into adolescence, because to be loved is her greatest need to give her self-confidence, although her need for it will outstrip any possible amount of love and satisfaction she will ever be able to receive. This constant frustration drives personalities of this type from one person to another without ever finding satisfaction or being able to give any returns, for she has never learned what love is or what it means to love others.

The psychometric examination of Barbara shows that her IQ rating of 87 places her within the normal range of intelligence, although she is slow and lags in her judgment about 1 year behind the average. Her school examination shows that she does not adequately utilize her capabilities. Her emotional difficulties have prevented her from learning to read and spell, and she is what is called a nonreader. From an educational point of view, she needs remedial reading; in other subjects, like arithmetic, writing, and language, the child is able to do second-grade work. Her writing, mainly good lettering, indicates that she has an adequate perceptual discrimination for let-

ters and words and could, therefore, be taught to read.

Most mentally inadequate children are not recognized as defective before they enter school, though a careful analysis of the group shows that they are often slow in walking, indifferent to toys as play objects, and frequently slow in vocalizing their needs. Even though they are able to talk in single words at a normal age, use of language as a means of communication is delayed and the children only gradually use their small vocabulary in sentences with minor acquisitions at each age level. Physically they are not conspicuously different from other children, and most of them enter school at the age of 5 or 6 years but are unable to cope with the assignments. In smaller communities and schools, these children are usually not recognized as mentally inadequate, and they may either repeat the first grade or be pushed up to higher grades in order to keep them within their age group. Although they actually fail constantly in school, the practice of promoting such children from grade to grade may delay recognition of the degree of inadequacy.

The situation is well demonstrated by the following history:

John was an 11-year-4-months-old boy, of normal height but almost 30 pounds overweight. His overweight was due to voracious eating caused by great emotional insecurity. The psychometric examination showed a mental age of 9 years 1 month, which gave him an IQ rating of 80. The boy offered a great deal of conversation, asked innumerable questions, and showed a great deal of interest which was centered mostly on toys and subjects which would interest a much younger child. His psychological success and failures were scattered over a large range; his basal was at a 5-year level, and he succeeded in some items through 14 years, which was above his chronological age. He showed

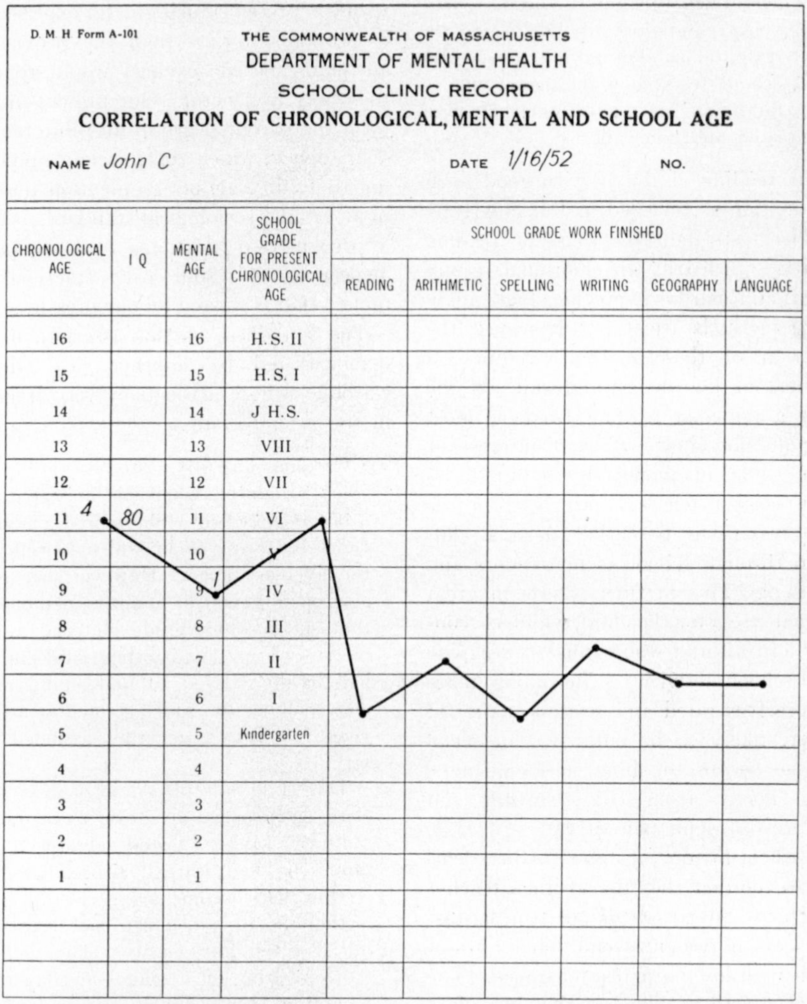

D. M. H. Form A-101				THE COMMONWEALTH OF MASSACHUSETTS DEPARTMENT OF MENTAL HEALTH SCHOOL CLINIC RECORD CORRELATION OF CHRONOLOGICAL, MENTAL AND SCHOOL AGE						
NAME John C							DATE 1/16/52		NO.	
CHRONOLOGICAL AGE	I Q	MENTAL AGE	SCHOOL GRADE FOR PRESENT CHRONOLOGICAL AGE	SCHOOL GRADE WORK FINISHED						
				READING	ARITHMETIC	SPELLING	WRITING	GEOGRAPHY	LANGUAGE	
16		16	H. S. II							
15		15	H. S. I							
14		14	J H.S.							
13		13	VIII							
12		12	VII							
11	80	11	VI							
10		10	V							
9		9	IV							
8		8	III							
7		7	II							
6		6	I							
5		5	Kindergarten							
4		4								
3		3								
2		2								
1		1								

FIGURE 4. The correlation chart of an 11-year-old child who failed completely in school shows that the boy scored an IQ of 80 but was a non-reader and non-speller. In his best subjects he scored on a second grade level instead of a fourth grade level which would correspond to his mental age. Psychiatric examination revealed that the boy was not "feeble-minded," as expected by school authorities and in previous superficial examinations, but was "dull normal" and subject to an emotional disturbance which interfered with normal school progress.

fairly good abstract reasoning and verbal fluency, and good rote recall. According to his mental age, this boy should do fourth grade work (chronologically, he would be expected to be in the sixth grade). His actual school tests showed a great inadequacy far below his mental age. He was a nonreader and nonspeller.

Again, reading disability with good form discrimination as revealed in John's writing and other tests indicates that the reading disability is primarily an emotional refusal to learn, and can be overcome if adequate teaching methods are used. However, the application of these methods requires a great deal of knowledge and skill on the part of a remedial reading teacher; most schools do not show sufficient interest or provide sufficient money to acquire adequate special teachers; and the result is that a great many potentially normal children go through school as nonreaders and nonspellers. This in turn results in great emotional stress for the child, who feels constantly left out and who cannot participate in the school activities. Becoming more and more frustrated and restless, many of them are likely to be entangled in social difficulties because of minor misdemeanors, playing "hooky" from school, stealing, and other forms of delinquency.

The school history of John further demonstrates the fact that the average teacher is not able or prepared to spot reading disabilities or to recognize emotionally upset children with low normal intelligence. The boy was entered in school at the chronological age of 5 years, when he was unable to do anything and should have been refused entrance. At the age of 11 he had 6 years of unsuccessful schooling behind him with an immeasurable amount of frustration and the net result that in reading and spelling he was still on a primer, in other subjects on a second-grade school level, achieved by other children after a single year. The

school's waste of time and effort and the child's loss and frustration in emotional values represent much greater expense, even in economic terms, than the provision of adequate special teachers would represent to society in general. Our present methods push the marginal group into illiteracy and delinquency, which costs society millions of dollars each year, not to mention the losses in moral and sociological standards, whereas a preventive educational and mental hygiene program would cost a fraction of the money that is wasted by our present system.

The soundness of this assertion may be demonstrated by another case, that of Caroline, whose inadequacy was discovered in the second grade.

Caroline was first tested at the age of 7 years 8 months, when she appeared to be a failure in school. She scored a Stanford-Binet IQ rating of 89, which is well within the average range. However, her mental age of 6 years 10 months demonstrated that she was first-grade material in arithmetic, writing, and other subjects. She had hardly started to understand reading and spelling, for which a mental age of 6 years 6 months is generally assumed necessary.

This child was placed in a good special class, with special attention to reading disabilities. When tested almost 5 years later, she had learned to read well and reading had become a better subject than arithmetic, of which she had learned the initial rules quite easily. The child was still operating on a school level below her mental age, and a psychiatric study demonstrated that she was showing severe emotional difficulties. She appeared rigid in her approach, insecure, and somewhat compulsive. She showed regressive tendencies or, rather, rigid adherence to more immature behavior patterns which made her appear silly, undisciplined, and emotionally unstable. She did most bizarre things in an effort to get attention—talked loudly, shrieked in a high-pitched voice—and was

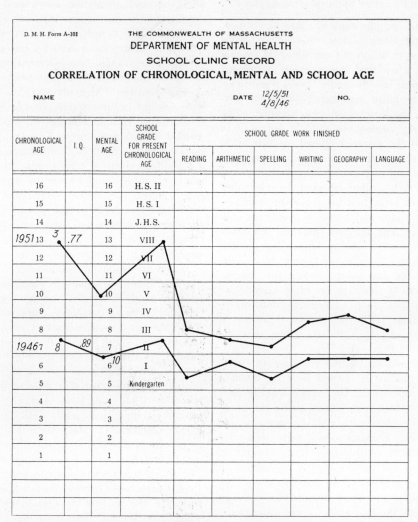

D. M. H. Form A-101

THE COMMONWEALTH OF MASSACHUSETTS
DEPARTMENT OF MENTAL HEALTH
SCHOOL CLINIC RECORD
CORRELATION OF CHRONOLOGICAL, MENTAL AND SCHOOL AGE

NAME   DATE 12/5/51
                                         4/8/46   NO.

CHRONOLOGICAL AGE	I.Q.	MENTAL AGE	SCHOOL GRADE FOR PRESENT CHRONOLOGICAL AGE	SCHOOL GRADE WORK FINISHED					
				READING	ARITHMETIC	SPELLING	WRITING	GEOGRAPHY	LANGUAGE
16		16	H. S. II						
15		15	H. S. I						
14		14	J. H. S.						
1951 13 3	.77	13	VIII						
12		12	VII						
11		11	VI						
10		10	V						
9		9	IV						
8		8	III						
1946 7 8	.89	7	II						
6		6 10	I						
5		5	Kindergarten						
4		4							
3		3							
2		2							
1		1							

FIGURE 5. Correlation chart showing original test results at an age of 7 years 8 months, and retest results at an age of 13 years 3 months. The IQ rating has dropped from 89 to 77. Variations in the outcome of IQ tests within less than 10 points may be of no significance, but the drop in IQ rating from 89 to 77 has to be considered significant and shows that original IQ scores in the marginal group must be taken with caution.

satisfied when she drew attention, regardless of whether approval or disapproval.

Some people consider the practice of pushing along a slow child advantageous because it delays the psychological trauma of being removed from a group and placed in special class or under specific conditions, but the harm and damage done far outweigh the benefits of such handling. The mentally inadequate child is not able to absorb the material offered in class or to play along with his classmates on the playground in extracurricular activities, and these facts cannot be ignored. The other children often take advantage of an inadequate child, and abuse him in many respects. The teachers, parents, and other adults rarely have understanding for the handicapped child, and they blame the child for his failures. For this reason, children of this type are often exposed for many years to psychologically unfavorable conditions until their actual deficiency is recognized. It is in this group that the Stanford-Binet and school tests are most useful and enable the examiner to determine the actual mental level on which a child operates. The application of adequate school tests clearly shows the grade level on which such a child is actually able to work. Examinations of many thousands of children of this type reveal the rather monotonous picture that some children in the age group between 9 and 12 years have mental ages of 5 to 7 years and are not even able to do first-grade work. Sometimes they have been in one grade for many years, unable to do a single subject adequately or to absorb the material that they were expected to learn. Years of frustration and disappointment often bring these children to the verge of delinquency, and it is usually a blessing if a psychometric examination eventually reveals the degree of retardation and permits placement either in

a special class or in a special school where education and orientation are offered according to the mental age level on which the child is able to operate.

Mental maturation is indeed a biological process which cannot be accelerated by artificial means except in certain specific endocrine disorders. Mentally retarded children are, for instance, rarely able to learn to read until their mental age has reached at least 6 years 8 months to 7 years. It is not uncommon, therefore, that children with a chronological age of 8 or 9 years are absolute nonreaders and nonspellers while in other subjects they are not so conspicuously retarded. The ability to read depends upon the ability to discriminate forms and, therefore, on the development of a specific degree of perceptual discrimination, the stages of which are readily recognizable with the Stanford-Binet test; and it is surprising to see that a child may be able to copy a quadrangle but is unable to copy a diamond, which apparently is a very adequate test for the 7-year level of form discrimination. It is obvious that the child who has not reached the necessary stage of perceptual maturity is not able to do adequate school work on grade levels, and, although intensive training may teach a child to remember certain forms, he never will be able to perceive differences until the process of maturation has reached a stage in which such differential perception comes naturally.

Of course, these remarks do not attempt to cover the field of reading disabilities which are specific disabilities that may occur independent of intellectual retardation. Some highly intelligent persons have certain degrees of reading disability, which are often not actual disabilities but incapacities to absorb the offered material in the way the average child learns to read. Some of these persons have a different perceptual capacity and learn more readily from material offered through auditory or kinesthetic methods, and it is often a question of changing the technique of teaching rather than a question of intellectual inadequacy or retardation.

The mentally inadequate child shows not only a slower process of intellectual maturation but also a quantitative limitation in the ability to absorb material and to cope with different situations. Therefore, such a person not only lags behind his age group in judgment but is also unable to deal with the same amount of actual material handled by the average person without difficulty.

Persons of this type are, therefore, limited in the scope of their interest, have a short attention span, and are slow in handling various materials. They are often confused by the complexities of modern urban civilization although they may be able to get along, unnoticed, under the more uniform conditions of rural life. The problems of mental deficiency are much more acute in urban communities than in rural areas, and many mentally defective persons are able to remain in the community and do satisfactory work within the limited field of farm activities although they are absolutely unable to deal with the complex situation to which a modern child is exposed in a city.

Mental inadequacy is a biological phenomenon which actually is not restricted to the sphere of intellectual judgment or what is usually called human intelligence. Slowness in reactions makes people of this type awkward in their motor expressions. Thus, it is a misconception to think that mentally dull people are necessarily able to compensate for their mental inadequacy by special physical or manual skill: the opposite is true. Usually, people with mental inadequacy are also slow and inadequate in physical skills, although it may be easier to develop manual abilities to a satisfactory degree than to improve scholastic achievements.

The Moron Group. Analyzing mental inadequacy on a moron level (Figure 2, *A, B, C*), we may distinguish three different groups. The first is composed of those otherwise fairly normal persons whose mental endowment is below the normal average range of mentality but falls within 3 times the standard deviation of 15. These people are mentally inadequate, "dull," or "morons," but they are fairly normal from a biological point of view, and they form the antithesis to the highly endowed persons of superior intelligence. In any biological sampling the superior variations are counteracted by the so-called minus variations, and any society which accepts its fortunate members must also accept the unfortunate ones and make the most of it. The so-called minus variations or the "subcultural" group form about 2.5 per cent of the average. In reality, however, there is a much larger percentage of mentally inadequate persons, namely about 5 per cent instead of 2.5 per cent. The increase is explained by the presence of pathological types of mental inadequacy, patients who are mentally defective on a genetic basis. The dull intelligence and slowness of mentation are particularities of the "minus-variations," which are otherwise not conspicuous and remain in the community unless social factors make their institutionalization necessary. Those factors have been discussed in the first part of this chapter.

The second group of mentally inadequate persons represents the manifestation of a genetically determined constitutional inadequacy in which mental and physical aberrations are linked together and have become a permanent genetically determined peculiarity. This group may well be designated by the term "oligophrenia vera," or oligocephaly, from the Greek term "oligos," which means little or limited in scope, in contrast to "micros," which refers to an actual deficiency in size as expressed in the

English word "small" or in the medical term "microcephaly." Oligoencephaly is a genetically determined form of mental inadequacy characterized by the combination of intellectual deficiency and more or less physical aberrations from the norm. These persons are not only intellectually but also constitutionally inadequate, and their physical handicaps may manifest themselves in certain anomalies which can be determined in careful physical examinations. The anomalies exist in greater asymmetries between the two halves of the body, asymmetries of the eyes and ears, abnormally high palate, curvatures of the spine, abnormally long and thin fingers, high arched feet, asymmetries between the breasts, unusual flexibility and mobility of the joints, insufficient vascularization of the extremities, and inadequate tonus control of the autonomic nervous system which manifests itself in moist and clammy cold extremities. Anatomical studies by the writer have shown that these anomalies of lateralization are associated with actual anomalies in the development and lateralization of the central nervous system. These aberrations are identical with the condition of myelodysplasia or spinal dysraphism. Anatomical studies of the brain show that the central nervous system is actually less well developed than in the normal average, the size of the brain usually being smaller than normal, the weight less, differentiation less advanced, and the nerve cells of smaller and more irregular structure. Of course, oligoencephaly occurs in all gradations of arrested differentiation, and it is incorrect to limit the diagnosis of oligophrenia to the actual IQ level between 50 and 70. Members of the oligophrenic families cover the whole marginal group; a number of them test within IQ levels of 70 to 80 while in others the IQ may be as low as 45. Within this group, psychometric examinations give an entirely adequate insight into the degree of retardation or maturation which a person has attained. The IQ level in this group remains fairly constant throughout life, and an IQ of 55, 65, or 75 represents a valid measure of the competence and a prognostically valuable standard for determining the future of such an individual. A person with genetically determined oligophrenia is useful in proportion to the IQ rating which he obtains, and the individual can become a useful member of the community according to his capacities and the ability of a society to make use of its members with limited capacities. The problem presented by genetically determined oligophrenia is that these persons are likely to produce offspring in whom, again, a large number of oligophrenic individuals appear. The gradients of oligophrenia may produce more severe defects in later generations, especially if both parents are oligophrenic.

The third group of mentally inadequate persons is composed of those individuals whose development has been impaired through accidental factors. These persons are the unlucky victims of previous prenatal, paranatal, or postnatal diseases which have not been overcome without untoward residues. The degree of limitation depends upon the degree of damage, and the usefulness of such a person depends upon how much compensation can be made for the original damage. From a psychological point of view, such an individual is a member of the mentally inadequate group and deserves the same consideration as other members of this group. From a medical point of view, patients of this type are similar to those in the more severe categories, but are more fortunate because they have been able to overcome some of the orginal damage though some residues have been left.

The Severe Degrees of Mental Deficiency (Imbecility and Idiocy)

The severe degrees of disorders of mentation, which psychologically include the imbeciles and idiots, represent an entirely different group from the one described above as intellectually inadequate. Although the terms "idiot" and "imbecile" may be useful for the psychologist, to indicate the degree of retardation and the mental level on which a person operates, these psychological terms have no medical significance and are only likely to detract the attention from the true problems that are involved.

An analysis of the severe degrees of mental deficiency indicates that the group is composed of persons whose mental development has been interrupted either before birth, at birth, or after birth because of different factors. The differentiation of the disorders according to time has a great value for diagnostic and prognostic reasons, because each type of disorder needs a somewhat different approach. Moreover, it has been increasingly recognized that it is not so much the type of noxious agent which interferes with development as the time in which the noxious factors operate which determines the structural damage and, therefore, the intellectual defect which such an individual manifests. According to time, the disorders of mentation can be classified as:

A. Antenatal.
B. Paranatal.
C. Postnatal.

According to the causes, we may classify the disorders in the following way:

A. Genetic (metabolic) disorders.
B. Exogenous (accidental) disorders.
 1. Traumatic.
 2. Vascular.
 3. Infectious.

4. Metabolic.
5. Degenerative and unknown.
C. Emotional disorders: psychoneuroses.
D. Total personality disorders: psychoses.

As the above classifications indicate, it is impossible to introduce one type of classification which would cover the whole field and give a satisfactory understanding of all the different conditions. The rôle of heredity in the causation of mental deficiency and psychoses has been the subject of many arguments since the 1920's. Some people have stated that the majority of mental defects are due to heredity, but, on the other hand, a wealth of experimental data on the production of malformations in the growing fetus has provided sufficient evidence that practically all prenatal developmental disorders can occur on an exogenous basis. Some of the confusion is due to the rather illogical and unscientific use of the term "heredity." At the zero hour of ontogenetic development, each individual starts its course with a different endowment of genetic determinators which are the product of countless generations of ancestral development as a result of the interaction of the organism and its environment, against which the organism maintains its individual entity. It is generally assumed that the genes are the carrier of genetic patterns. The genes are unit processes or determiners which, in chemical terms, are nucleoproteins of the size of a molecule or smaller. The term "heredity" refers to two different concepts: first, to the general "constitution" with which any individual encounters the environmental stress. There is no doubt that the specific constitution of each individual is determined by genetic factors to a large extent, but at the same time the phenotype is greatly influenced by environmental factors which bring certain genetic possibilities to full development while others are partially suppressed.

Secondly, if one uses the term heredity in pathology, one usually thinks of specific disorders, either true gene mutation, loss of certain genes, or abnormal combinations which cause specific defects either of structural development or of metabolism. Such genetic malformations are, for instance, cleft formations like a cleft palate, spina bifida or cranial dysostosis, or specific metabolic disorders of which gargoylism, amaurotic idiocies, phenylpyruvic oligophrenia, and tuberosclerosis are some outstanding examples.

The Antenatal Developmental Disorders. For the majority of studies and observations, life starts at birth, and the trauma of birth is considered the first major event that may bear decisive biologic and psycholic consequences for the future of an individual. We are accustomed to think that intrauterine life is a rather well-protected period in which the growing child is not exposed to major injuries. Research, however, has provided ample evidence that the 9 months of prenatal development are a period of great biological importance, and many of the developmental disorders which produce dysgenetic behavior patterns and physical anomalies are produced during the prenatal period by a noxious agent operating upon the growing embryo. The prenatal developmental disorders are sometimes genetically determined malformations in which genetically determined processes are not completed: for instance, cleft palate, spina bifida, and cleft formations in the spinal cord or central nervous system. The development of any body organ, including the central nervous system, may be interfered with through defective genes which fail to organize specific processes necessary for the completion of the organism. It is often difficult to determine whether a specific malformation is due to genetic defects or to external factors. The presence of the same malformation in different members of a family is frequently the only clue that a malformation is determined through genetic factors.

On the other hand, experimental teratology [*teras* = malformed (fetus)] and experimental embryology have produced overwhelming evidence that practically all malformations found in human beings can be produced experimentally in animals. These studies indicate that the stage of development in which a defect occurs is of greater importance than the pathogenic factor. Malformations can be experimentally produced through any changes in the environment of the growing fetus, and trauma, chemical factors, temperature changes, radiation, interference with oxygen supply, and nutritional and other factors can be used with equal success. It is the time in which the noxious agent is applied that determines what type of malformation will occur.

The time *in utero* can be divided into the organogenetic and organokinetic periods. In the first, which covers roughly 6 to 8 weeks, the structural patterns are laid out and the embryo develops from the fertilized cell to a human organism which is basically organized in the same way as the child who will be born about 7 months later. This organogenetic period is a period of intensive differentiation, with relatively little growth in size and weight. At the end of the organogenetic period, the embryo measures only about 1 inch, but this organism shows the same structural organization as the later human being. The first 8 weeks are characterized by most intensive differentiation, and any noxious factor interfering for as little as several hours to days may interrupt this process and produce a malformation that remains as a defect throughout life if the organism can survive. These acquired developmental disorders can be arranged as members of a series of stage-specific defects which show transitions from one stage to the next according to the time space under which the teratogenic agents operated. Each malformation also shows a biologic gradient ranging from the full suppression of a specific developmental stage to minor degrees which often may be discovered only if the more severe stages are well known.

It is another established fact that development does not proceed with equal intensity at each part of the organism at the same time. It seems as if the energy of growth is alternately thrown into the various systems and each one attracts the full energy for a period of time until the main force is shifted to another section. Like a game of cards, each player has his turn, and if a chance is missed it may never come again. This definitely irreversible character of development is a fact that many people, including clinicians, shrink from accepting. If one area of development is suppressed the whole balance is altered and the retardation of one part exercises an influence upon other parts which may react either by compensation or retardation, the result being a complex disorder in which the original damage may be obscured.

There is little use in dealing with each malformation in detail if the teratogenic principle is understood. One factor, however, has to be emphasized in relation to any psychological and biological problem dealing with the nervous system: Although the organogenetic phase of the human organism is roughly completed by the third month, and physical malformations due to arrest or defect cannot develop after the completion of this period, the central nervous system is at that time still a mass of undifferentiated ectodermal tissue which completes its major developments not only during the 9 months of gestation but is still quite immature at the time of birth, and important developments take place even after birth.

The stage-specific defects can be marshaled according to the stage through which the organism passes. The migration of the eyes from the lateral aspect of the skull toward a frontal position may be interfered with and the condition of hypertelorism or Greig's disease may occur. The period between the eighth and tenth week, the so-called "neofetal period," seems to be stage-specific for the condition of congenital acromicria (commonly called mongolism), in which again all gradients in the severity of developmental arrest can be found. This stage-specific period of mongolism is identical with the neofetal period of Ballantyne, which is the transitional stage before placental circulation is fully established.

Microcephaly. For the understanding of the psychopathology of mental defect and dysgenetic behavior patterns, it may suffice to outline briefly the gradient of inadequate development of the nervous system. Underdevelopment of the brain runs through the stages of anencephaly to microcephaly, in which the brain itself remains a miniature edition of a normal brain. True microcephaly (microcephalia vera) is a disorder which is often genetically determined, and families with five to seven microcephalic children have been described in the literature. However, microcephaly is by no means always of a genetic nature.

Microcephaly must be divided into the severe degrees of prenatal developmental arrest and those of arrest of skull development occurring after birth. In the latter type, skull circumference and capacity remain below normal but have reached the size of a full-term baby at birth. This type of microcephaly is usually due to paranatal factors, most frequently birth injuries, in which the brain is damaged at that time and arrest of brain development leads to arrest of the growing head. The former type of microcephaly, the true prenatal developmental defect, can be divided into the genetically determined symmetrical underdevelopment of the brain and types of malformations which occur on an exogenous basis.

organization of mentation and, therefore, that the scale of reactions will be maladjusted. Such persons are mentally defective, usually to a severe degree, and score on psychometric tests in the idiot or imbecile range. However, the different organization of the nervous system will also lead to different types of emotional and

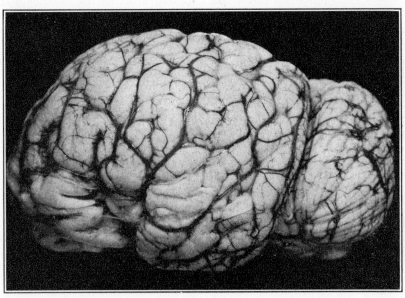

FIGURE 6. Lateral view of brain with agenesis of occipital lobes. The cerebellum is attached to the brain in a horizontal plane similar to some lower animals. This is a manifestation of congenital prenatal anomalies of brain development resulting in microcephaly. (From C. E. Benda, *Developmental Disorders of Mentation and Cerebral Palsies,* figure 29-A, with permission of publisher, Grune & Stratton, New York, 1952.)

The exogenous types of microcephaly include complete lack of fissuration and differentiation of the brain, as found in pachygyria (lissencephaly or the "loaf of bread" brain) and the various types of microgyria, microgyria interna, fissures and clefts as seen in porencephaly, and agenesis of parts of the brain like cerebellar agenesis or certain lobes of the cerebrum, occipital, temporal, or frontal. For the psychologist it is important to know that a person with a different brain structure has a different

motor expression, and the behavior patterns of such a child may be best designated as "dysgenetic." With decreased infant mortality and improved life expectancy of these patients, the microcephalic child is now apt to survive infancy and early childhood, and we see more and more individuals with unbelievably small brains survive and grow into adolescence.

The psychological and motor behavioral patterns of these microcephalic children offer interesting aspects for research in motor behavior. Two factors are striking. Early motor development of the infant does not depend upon the intactness and completeness of the cerebral cortex. Some microcephalic children show surprisingly advanced motor development, and it is a mistake to assume that later intellectual development or expressions of "derivative" intelligence can be judged and tested in the first year of life. The derivative behavioral patterns are by no means identical with early motor patterns of fundamentally subcortical origin. Another aspect is the surprising independence of bodily growth and differentiation from the regulation of the central nervous system early in life. Some children with no brain to speak of, or without function, have a surprisingly good development of their bodies. This, however, is not always true. Many early developmental orders of the nervous system are associated with physical defects of other body parts, and prenatal developmental disorders in general manifest themselves in a variety of biological defects which indicate a general constitutional inadequacy.

Megalo- or macrocephaly. The opposite of microcephaly is not hydrocephaly, as is so often assumed, but megalocephaly or macrocephaly, a rare condition in which the brain attains a much heavier weight than normal. Brain weights of 1770 grams to 2850 grams have been described in the literature, and the author has collected three brains weighing 2615, 2060, and 1930 grams respectively. The heaviness of the brain and increase of mass are not identical with better neurogenic tissue; we deal in macrocephaly with a local gigantism of the nervous system which is a neoplastic malformation.

Hydrocephaly. Internal hydrocephalus is the accumulation of spinal fluid in the ventricular system. This accumulation may assume tremendous proportions; the author has observed a case in which more than a gallon and a pint of spinal fluid were removed at autopsy (1-year-old child, head circumference 28½ inches). The increase of fluid in the ventricular system is associated more or less with complete cortical atrophy. The cortical mantle is pressed against the inner side of the skull, and the skull yields to the pressure by a gradual increase in the size of the head, which may progress rapidly at certain times. In one child of 3 years 5 months, a circumference of 36½ inches was observed.

The main types of hydrocephaly may be divided into four categories: (1) dysgenetic hydrocephaly; vesiculocephaly; hydranencephaly; (2) hydrocephaly due to abnormal production of spinal fluid; (3) hydrocephaly due to obstruction of circulation; (4) hydrocephaly due to abnormal absorption.

The first type is due entirely to early developmental failure of the brain mantle.

The second type is relatively rare and occurs mainly under toxic and infectious conditions associated with what used to be called "meningitis serosa."

Of importance is the third type, in which obstruction of circulation occurs. The main sites of obstructed circulation due to developmental anomalies are in the aqueduct of Sylvius and the exit of the fourth ventricle. Aqueduct stenosis occurs either as a congenital anomaly or, more often, as a result of early infectious ependymitis, gliosis, or tumor formation. The most frequent incidence of hydrocephaly is associated with atresia of the posterior exits of the fourth ventricle, especially the foramen Magendie. The membranous closure of the foramen prevents the spinal fluid from escaping, and the ventricle system is gradually enlarged, leading to atrophy of the cerebrum and a bulging cyst in the posterior cavity of the skull. About 50 per cent of cases of hydrocephaly confirmed by post-mortem examination showed atresia of the foramen Magendie. Other cases showed a combination of spina bifida, meningocele, and a malformation of the cerebellum which is known in the medical literature under the term "Arnold-Chiari malformation."

also caused by organization of subarachnoid hemorrhages, and chronic hematomas usually lead to increased spinal-fluid pressure. The enlargement of the lateral ventricles and increase of spinal fluid due to lack of absorption is not restricted to children but

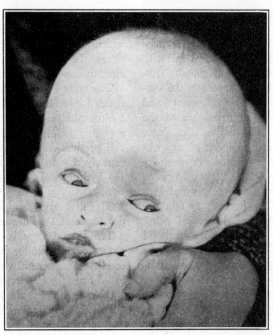

FIGURE 7. Hydrocephaly with increase of head circumference and severe brain atrophy due to increased spinal fluid in the ventricular system.

Hydrocephaly due to interference with the normal absorption of spinal fluid is mainly caused through infectious processes which have primarily caused meningitis and perineuritis, with ensuing fibrotic organization of the meningeal and perineural spaces. Since the spinal fluid escapes through the subarachnoid spaces and is drained partially into the sinus system, the fibrotic organization of these spaces interferes with the adequate absorption, and, therefore, a gradual increase in spinal fluid with enlargement of the lateral ventricles and cortical atrophy will develop. Meningeal fibrosis is

is often found in older people and accompanies senile atrophies.

Cranial dysostoses. Several conditions of prenatal developmental arrest are associated with various types of cranial dysostosis or true tumor formations like tuberosclerosis, von Recklinghausen's disease, cranium bifidum, and other anomalies which are primarily of medical interest.

Congenital Acromicria (Mongolism). Of all the antenatal developmental disorders, congenital acromicria (mongolism) is most important for two reasons. The mongoloid child usually comes from a normal family, with normal parents and normal siblings, and the single incidence of a severe mental defect in a normal family among the average population represents a severe psychological, sociological, and educational prob-

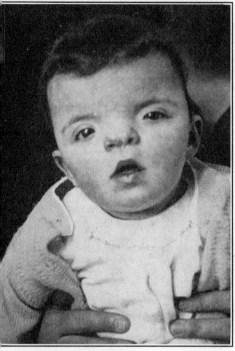

FIGURE 8. Hypertelorism (Greig's disease). *Note* the abnormal distance between the eyes, and duplication of tip of nose, as an expression of abnormal fetal development of the skull.

lem. Secondly, mongolism occurs about 3 to 4 times among 1000 births, and seems to be on the increase. Among all single types of mental deficiency of severe degree, mongolism now takes the first place, with 10 to 25 per cent, as the most conspicuous single morbid entity.

It was only in 1866 that mongolism was discovered as a specific morbid entity. Up to that time, it had been considered a particular manifestation of cretinism, which has

been known in our western civilization for at least 1000 years, if not longer. This situation is still reflected in the remarks of the famous Edouard Séguin in 1866 in *Treatise on Idiocy and Its Treatment by Physiological Method*:

> The lowland cretinism of Belgium, Virginia—with its discrete goiter, its grey and dirty straw-colored skin, bears the same relation to idiocy and imbecility as the more extensive alpine variety. So does *furfuraceous cretinism* with its milk-white rosy and peeling skin; with its shortcomings of all the integuments, which give an unfinished aspect to the truncated fingers

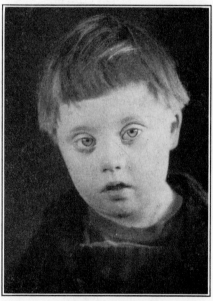

FIGURE 9. Mongoloid boy, 9 years of age. *Note* fine silky hair, slanting eyes, depressed nose bridge, dry lips, open mouth, short neck.

and nose; with its cracked lips and tongue, with its red, ectopic conjunctiva, coming out to supply the curtailed skin at the margin of the lids.

It was in the same year that Langdon Down gave his classical description of mon-

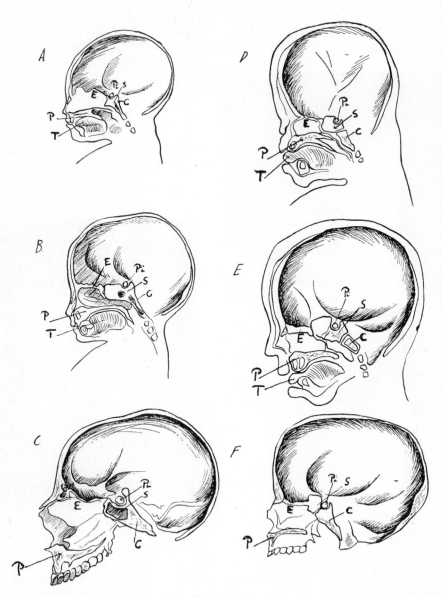

FIGURE 10.

golism, which became the foundation of later research on this condition. However, progress was extremely slow until the late 1930's, when intensive research in the mongoloid malformation was started by this author, which research finally succeeded in discovering the particular pathology which is behind this strange growth disorder.[1]

Mongolism is a combination of mental retardation with a number of physical anomalies which may involve every organ system. Body growth is delayed, and the hands and feet remain small and wrinkled and show abnormal patterns of hand lines and skin ridges. The sex organs are usually underdeveloped, the belly is protruding, and an umbilical hernia is marked. The skin is often primarily soft and puffy; later it often shows a tendency to dermatitis or roughness. The vascular tree is underdeveloped, and marmoration of the skin frequent. The child is usually hypotonic or

[1] *Mongolism and Cretinism,* 1st edition 1947, 2nd edition 1949.

"double jointed," is late in sitting up and standing, and speech often occurs years after the normal child is expected to speak. All these peculiarities would not give rise to the establishing of a specific morbid entity, for similar patterns can be found in other types of mental defect. What establishes the disorder is the anomaly of the head development, which results in a short, somewhat small head, slanting egg-shaped orbit holes with slanting palpebral fissures, and often a fetal skin fold at the internal angle of the eye called "epicanthus." The nose and nasal cavities are short and underdeveloped, the mouth undersized with a peculiarly shaped palate, and the tongue, which may be of normal size, does not find berth in the small oral cavity. Comparative anatomical studies by the writer have shown that the mongoloid visceral and cerebral skull undergoes a deceleration of growth in the neofetal period (eighth to twelfth week) with a definite shortening and abnormal angulation in the

---

FIGURE 10. Comparison of normal skull development (*A, B, C*) and the acromicric growth disorder seen in mongolism (*D, E, F*). [From C. E. Benda, What is Mongolism (Congenital Acromicria)? *International Record of Medicine, 165,* 75, 1952.]

A. Embryo * (47674). Calculated age, 16 weeks. *Note* clivus and sphenoid body with partial ossification; anterior sphenoid and ethmoid with crista cartilaginous; hard palate is firm and partially ossified; tongue within mouth behind maxillary ridge.

B. Embryo * (47706). Calculated age, 19 weeks. *Note* progress in ossification and increase in size of sphenoid and ethmoid bones.

C. Diagram of normal adult skull. *Note* development of sphenoid and frontal sinuses, great increase in development of visceral skull.

D. Mongoloid premature stillborn. *Note* smallness of clivus and sphenoid body, shortness of anterior cavity, upright grading; shortness of visceral skull; short, thick hard palate; tongue too big, protrudes between jaws.

E. Three-months mongoloid baby. *Note* shortness of clivus; abnormal position of sphenoid; shortness of anterior skull cavity; shortness of hard palate, with tongue protruding.

F. Mongoloid skull of patient about 20 years of age (compare with *C*). *Note* shortness of clivus, abnormal position of sphenoid, remnants of cartilage in sphenoid, shortness of anterior cavity, smallness of maxilla, and shortness of hard palate. The configuration of the skull is essentially the same as in the newborn, and the visceral skull has not participated in the extensive postnatal visceral development seen in the normal.

* By courtesy of Dr. Arthur T. Hertig, Lying-in Hospital, Boston, Mass.

skull basis, and an underdevelopment of the visceral skull. This deceleration of growth at this particular period is the cause of the fetal or unfinished appearance of the mongoloid newborn who has some, though extremely superficial, resemblance to the mongolian race. However, a more thorough analysis of the patterns shows that mongolism is not, as Langdon Down thought, a "regression into the mongolian race"; thus, the unfortunate term should be replaced by a more scientific one like "congenital acromicria." Further studies show that the deceleration of growth in mongolism is not restricted to the skull or the bony system but involves the whole dynamics of central growth regulation. The central growth regulation, which is represented in the neuro-endocrine junction at the subthalamic pituitary system, fails to provide adequate growth to the mongoloid infant and child, and the patient remains in his development between 30 and 60 per cent behind the average. A similar deceleration can be seen in the mental development of these patients. Although it is still customary to talk of "mongolian idiots" the mongoloid child is by no means often an idiot, and mongolism ranges over a wide field of mental levels. There are mongoloid children with IQ ratings as high as in the lower 70's, although the majority of mongoloids remain in an IQ range between 40 and 60. In some patients the slowing-down of mental development is so extreme that the child never exceeds a mental level of about 2 years. According to the wide variety of mental scores, mongolism should not be taken as an absolutely uniform entity, and each child needs individual attention according to his capacities.

The mongoloid child usually comes from a normal family. Needless to say, feeblemindedness or genetic inadequacy in a family is no protection against mongolism, but mongolism is a specific biological variant due to interference in development at a specific critical period, and is definitely not due to genetic factors. The reasons for the slowing-down of neofetal development are manifold. It has not escaped earlier investigators that mongolism occurs often in a large family at the end of the birth line or, rather, when the mother is in her 40's. As early as 1886, Shuttleworth wrote:

> It is remarkable that, in my experience, nearly one half of these children are the last born of a long family.

Newer studies have shown that it is not so much the number of preceding pregnancies which causes mongolism as a manifestation of maternal "exhaustion" as the fact that the mother has entered menopause or is near the cessation of menstruation. During the period of "change of life" the incidence of mongolism does greatly increase. Of women who had a mongoloid child in an age group between 41 and 52, 53.9 per cent were actually in the menopause or had menstrual irregularities before pregnancy. In the same age group, 92 per cent had no children for a period of 3 to 16 years and there was an unusually long interval between the last pregnancy and the child who turned out to be a mongoloid. Often it is a first pregnancy around the maternal age of 40 years which will end in the birth of a mongoloid. Though these data suggest that the cessation of the normal menstrual cycle (which is an indication of the declining power of the ovaries) has something to do with the development of mongolism, this is by no means the only cause. More than 45 per cent of all mongoloids are born to mothers under 35 years of age. However, it is worth while mentioning that the percentage of mongolism in the maternal age group from 18 to 28 is about 0.15 per cent and in a maternal age above 45 it is 9.1–12 per cent.

Analyzing the incidence of mongolism in younger maternal age groups, the inability to become pregnant is most remarkable and ranges from 33 per cent in mothers between 18 and 20 years to 81 per cent in the age group between 31 and 40 years. In the age group between 20 and 40, 38.5 per cent of the mothers had been treated for thyroid trouble. In the majority, these thyroid "troubles" were of a nature of hypothyroidism but in a few instances dysthyroidism or even hyperthyroidism may be suspected. It has also been observed that abortions in other pregnancies were more frequent than in the control material, and intrauterine bleedings during pregnancy have often been observed (38–67 per cent in the maternal age group between 18 and 40). These data and numerous preceding abortions have led Engler to emphasize anomalies in the nidation of the ovum. C. E. Benda indicated that mongolism seems to develop when the ovum fails to find a satisfactory nutritional system with the maternal organism. Previous abortions, endometritis, or unfavorable conditions, for instance in a twin pregnancy, are likely to provide inadequate conditions for the nidation of an ovum. These observations also admit the possibility that over-aged ova which lack vitality are not able to achieve a satisfactory nidation or are slow in general differentiation. In a small percentage of cases infectious diseases (including German measles) were found in the prenatal history, having occurred in the third month of the gestation period.

Summarizing the situation, it may be reiterated that mongolism occurs on the threshold of hormonal or nutritional deficiency of the growing fetus. The maternal organism appears to be unable to produce the proper endocrine environment for the embryo. The necessary adjustments are either delayed or insufficient, the result being that the fetus is deprived of a number of nutritional factors (including oxygen) that are essential for its proper development. The maternal condition is due either to the approach of the menopause (women beyond 40 years of age) or to an insufficient response to fertilization (young women, or women over 30 who had no children before). There is a third group of cases in which mongolism occurs because of the fact that an intercurrent illness has rendered the mother temporarily unfit for a pregnancy.

Cretinism. Compared with the complex nature of the mongoloid deficiency, the condition of cretinism is much simpler and more clearly recognizable, although the actual knowledge about the causation of sporadic cretinism is still scant. Cretinism is due to the inability of the thyroid to provide the organism with sufficient thyroid hormones which are contained in the so-called "colloid" of the thyroid (thyroxin). This happens either in a congenital aplasia of the thyroid or in goiterous ethnic groups where specific geographical conditions of soil, water, and air do not provide adequate iodide for the formation of thyroxin. Cretinism on the basis of geographical factors is called "endemic cretinism" and is distributed over the whole earth in certain mountainous or central areas far removed from the ocean. Cretinism is not due to goiter and is frequently fully developed without it. If goiter is present, it is the manifestation of an inadequately functioning thyroid which is attempting to compensate for its inadequate function by a hypertrophy which is inadequate. The cretin's development is almost completely lacking if there is complete thyroid aplasia. Figure 11 demonstrates a cretin of almost 11 years who resembles an infant of 6 months, and neither his physical and osseous development nor his mental growth has made any progress since the first few months of life. Mentally, the untreated cretin remains on the lowest level of possible mentation. However, if treated early in life and if the thyroid deficiency is compensated for by adequate thyroid substitu-

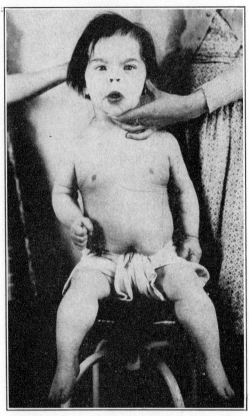

FIGURE 11. Eleven-year-old cretin whose bone age and appearance are that of a child less than 2 years of age. Complete idiocy. No previous treatment. *Note* depressed nose bridge, squinting eyes, thick lips and tongue, pale flabby edematous skin, protruding belly.

tional treatment, he may show a satisfactory physical and mental development and there may be no impairment in IQ ratings at all.

Gargoylism and other metabolic disorders. A number of other metabolic disorders have been discovered which show the importance

of metabolism in the production of disorders of mentation. Of these disorders, gargoylism is of especial interest because the gargoyle looks in many ways like the mongoloid and the cretin, and has been confused with them. Gargoylism is a genetic disorder and, therefore, often occurs in families in several instances. It develops in different forms, starting sometimes soon after birth (infantile form), sometimes late in infancy or even in early childhood. According to the age, the children have a somewhat different appearance and different degrees of mental retardation, but the basic features are a growth deficiency with severe changes in the osseous system, a large belly with an umbilical hernia, and enlargement of the liver (hepatomegaly). The neck remains short, the head becomes larger, increasing in length and width with indications of hydrocephaly of minor degree. There is often a membranous veil in front of the cornea. Anatomical study shows that gargoylism is a metabolic disorder which involves all organ systems of the body, including the brain. The nerve cells degenerate and often contain huge amounts of fat similar to that seen in amaurotic idiocy. Fat droplets and glycogen are found in the liver, lungs, spleen, and many other tissues, indicating that gargoylism is a metabolic disorder in which a specific enzymatic system either has not developed or breaks down.

Gargoylism has some as yet undefined relationship to other forms of abnormal fat metabolism, the so-called lipoidoses, of which the so-called amaurotic idiocies are best known. In amaurotic idiocy a specific metabolic disorder of fat metabolism is present. Amaurotic idiocies occur at different age levels, with different clinical symptoms and different mental manifestations. Although the infantile form is of special medical interest, the so-called juvenile form (which develops in an age group between 8 and 12 years and which starts with epileptic seizures and increasing loss of vision) is of greater interest to the psychologist, physician, and educator because patients with the juvenile form of amaurotic

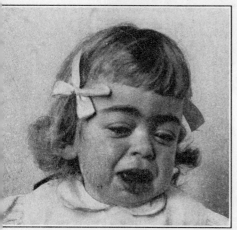

FIGURE 12. Four-year-old child with gargoylism (Hurler's syndrome, lipochondrodystrophy). *Note* strange appearance of child, with enlarged head, depressed nose bridge, thick lips and tongue, short neck. (From C. E. Benda, *Developmental Disorders of Mentation and Cerebral Palsies,* figure 86-A, with permission of publisher, Grune & Stratton, New York, 1952.)

idiocy may have been normal throughout infancy and early childhood before the disorder occurred.

An important disorder of protein metabolism is seen in phenylpyruvic oligophrenia, a metabolic disorder of an amino acid (phenylalanine) which is increased in the blood and secreted in the urine of these patients. For some unknown reason, the enzymatic catabolism of phenylalanine is blocked and a part of this abnormally increased amino acid is excreted in the form of phenylpyruvic acid in the urine. The

easy demonstration of this product in the urine makes it possible to establish the diagnosis of phenylpyruvic oligophrenia rather easily. This disorder, which usually dooms the patient to complete idiocy, is a genetic disorder which may affect several members of a family. It often occurs in perfectly normal families and has been observed in some offspring of highly intelligent people who have made great contributions to our society.

Paranatal Disorders. The majority of conditions described in the previous pages are either disorders of development which took place in the prenatal period or metabolic disorders which are determined by genetic factors. Another large group of disorders of mentation is produced through extrinsic factors which operate at the time of birth. The whole group may be readily summarized under the term "paranatal disorders."

It is well recognized that the time of birth is a critical period for the child and that, therefore, birth is associated with an increased biological risk. Difficulties may start weeks before birth by premature separation of the placenta or abnormalities in circulation which interfere with the nutrition of the unborn. Lack of oxygen and other nutritional factors may produce anoxia of the brain, with severe damage to brain tissue and resulting cystic degeneration of the white matter and anoxic lesions of the gray matter. The actual time of birth multiplies similar dangers, and anoxia or interruption of oxygen supply of the brain, traumatization of the brain through compression, bleedings inside and around the brain, neonatal pneumonia and interference with blood and oxygen circulation due to premature breathing, and anemias with their severe sequelae form the gamut of possible noxious factors which interfere with the health of the newborn child. Few of the children exposed to such conditions escape entirely unimpaired, and in the majority of them motor disabilities manifest themselves so that paranatal disorders are almost identical with the field of *cerebral palsy*. However, some birth-injured children may show little actual mo-

jority of patients the damage to the brain involves large areas, including those integrative fields serving "intelligence," and may range from a slight developmental retardation to a complete incapacity for intellectual adjustment. The application of

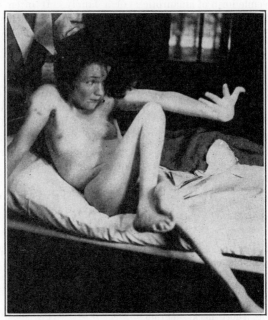

FIGURE 13. Cerebral palsy. *Note* uncontrolled movements of arms (athetoid choreatic movements with flexion and hyperextension of various parts of the extremities, spasticity of lower extremities. This instance of cerebral palsy was due to kernicterus, or the Rh factor. There are many different types of cerebral palsies, mainly due to so-called birth injuries. (From C. E. Benda, *Developmental Disorders of Mentation and Cerebral Palsies*, figure 82-A, with permission of publisher, Grune & Stratton, New York, 1952.)

tor disability, the main damage involving so-called "silent" areas of the brain, that is, areas like the frontal lobes the function of which is not immediately apparent and the lack of which is, therefore, not obvious to the observer.

Cerebral palsy is a disorganization of motor control through damage to the central nervous system. In some individuals the damage does not interfere with "intellectual" development and motor impairment is the only symptom, but in the ma-

psychological ratings like Stanford-Binet mental ages to the child with cerebral palsy is of dubious value and may be useful only for placement in a specific grade or new training program. The brain-injured child manifests a great number of changes in the motor and perceptual fields, and what may appear as "intellectual" deficiency may actually be a perceptual anomaly, as has been demonstrated by a number of investigators (Werner, 1948; Strauss and Lehtinen, 1947; Goldstein, 1936; and others).

To gain a satisfactory insight into the mental abilities of a child with cerebral palsy, one has to observe him on different occasions and retest him at periodic intervals. Any conclusion arrived at in infancy or early childhood may be wrong and misleading, because some brain-damaged children make a very slow start but gain speed after the first years have passed.

Cerebral palsies manifest themselves in different ways, and the neurologist may classify the forms according to certain types of motor disability. Little's spastic rigidity is the most severe type of cerebral palsy, which is often identical with decerebration, in which the cerebrum is severely damaged and the child operates on a lower level of neurogenic integration. On the other hand, traumatism of the cerebellum may lead to ataxia or a form of cerebral palsy which interferes little with intellectual performance. For the psychologist it is most important to realize that motor disability creates a different perceptual climate for the handicapped individual. The inability of the infant and child to conquer the world and to incorporate his environment through the gradual stages of oral, visual, auditory, and tactile exploration creates a different concept of reality, and the child with cerebral palsy therefore needs a substitute for his deprivation in sensual exploration of the world. The child has an increased disability to make a satisfactory emotional contact with his surroundings, and, reciprocally, the environment is easily frustrated and rejects the child who is not able to make any returns in emotional and intellectual gratification. The training of such a child, which has been attracting much interest, is a complex problem which is dependent not only upon the creation of better motor control but also upon the application of a multidimensional approach in which the psychologist, neuropsychiatrist, educator, and, last but not least, parents

and close environment have to collaborate intimately with each child.

Although the majority of children with cerebral palsy suffer from paranatal disorders, infectious diseases of infancy contribute another large group to this category. Most children run through the usual infant infections (measles, scarlet fever, mumps, whooping-cough, pneumonia, and others) without damage to the nervous system, but a small percentage are damaged through noxious factors, either actual virus diseases, toxins, or allergic reactions, which cause a variety of pathological features. If damaged before speech and gait are established, the child may be greatly retarded in the acquisition of these skills and remain without speech for many years, even throughout life. If illness occurs in the second year, speech may be lost and return after a long time or inadequately. Speech defects are, therefore, one of the most characteristic "palsies" of the postinfectious organic syndrome. If no "organic" symptoms are manifest, a disturbance of behavioral patterns is not unusual. The child with postinfectious cerebral palsy often shows overactivity and restlessness, disorganization of behavior, aggressiveness, and emotional instability, and the combination of these symptoms is often so characteristic that the postinfectious child can be recognized even with an indecisive history.

PERSONALITY DISORDERS ON A HIGHER INTEGRAL LEVEL

Emotions and Emotional Disorders (Psychoneuroses)

Although many abnormal mental reactions and illnesses are nowadays recognized as "emotional" disorders, the term emotions is still unsatisfactorily defined and no generally accepted theory of emotions is available. In theoretical physics it is not contested that physical facts are without meaning unless a theory attempts to marshal the wealth of observations. In psychology, however, the necessity for theoretical concepts is still little recognized and is often mistaken for love of speculation. Before any progress in the understanding of emotional disorders can be expected, a clearer understanding of "the emotions" and their rôle is necessary, and in the following paragraphs the attempt will be made to offer such a theory, based on the writer's own observations and data presented by other investigators (Cobb, 1950; Yakovlev, 1948; and Papez, 1937).

If we talk of emotional disorders, we obviously mean to differentiate such disorders from other pathological categories, like disorders of intelligence or "cerebration." In emotional disorders we deal, not with disorders of interpersonal relations which are due to abnormal perceptual functions or abnormal intellectual interpretation of experiences and judgment, but with disorders of affects, moods, and the expression of inward feelings which disturb the normal formation of contacts between an individual and his antagonists. Some investigators still use the term "emotions" only for pathological conditions of rage, terror, inhibition, or depressions—briefly, any pathologic exaggeration or inhibition of normal affects, but there is nothing either in the etymology (e-motion) or in the accepted meaning of the word which would warrant such limitation.

Each living organism automatically registers its own position in relation to its environment by a status of organismal briefing which is inwardly experienced as a certain "feeling" or "affect" (ad-facere) which expresses itself on a somatic level in a certain organization of organismic responses as sensations, and is experienced on a higher integral level as a certain state of changes in tension or mood. Although each feeling has a certain duration, it is dynamic in nature and is related to a previous experience, and it is anticipatory as it is modified by the direction in which the organism moves toward a solution of the present status to reach a condition of lessened tension or equilibrium.

What is experienced inwardly as a feeling may be called the "climate" in which an organism functions. That which is observed as an outward motion (e-motion) is the expressive behavior which the organism activates in order to change its relationship to the environment with which it interacts.

By the term "emotions," therefore, is meant that field of human and animal experiences and behavior which encompasses the immediate responses of a living organism to external and internal stimuli. Although the classical terminology considered emotions an affective state of "consciousness" in contrast to cognitive and volitional states—meaning that any human experience is a part of "consciousness," therefore there cannot be anything actually "unconscious" in our consciousness (though it may be not "focused")—this concept of consciousness has become less and less acceptable to modern psychology. Animals, including man, live through a continuous stream of emotional experiences in which the contact with the outer world is registered in emotional values according to the gratification or lack of gratification which an object of encounter offers. This system of emotional experiences permanently influences any new action and modifies motivations, but it functions on a different level of integration. It has nothing to do with awareness of experiences or motivations, and is not immediately accessible to cognitive consciousness. The field of emotions links nature together on a level of instinctual and libidinous drives, in which animal and man share equally, although each emotion is private and essentially unsharable because each individual finds himself in a different state of needs and satisfaction. The field of cognition or awareness seems to be reserved to man; although we do not know the "language" of animals, we have reason to believe that the use of human language has introduced into nature a new level of interaction: the level of symbolic representation, which is a specific type of human life. It is for this level of human mentality that psychodynamic psychology wishes to restrict the term "conscious" functions.

Whereas the affective state through which an organism passes leads, on a bodily level, to an organization of autonomic responses, the total of sensations and feelings results in a certain "mood" which represents the organization of organismic responses in toto. The affective condition under which an organism operates is its positional briefing for further action. Changes in mood can therefore be described in different terms. One may either deal with the outward or inward direction of an emotional expression like extrovert and introvert, or with degrees of emotional expressive behavior in terms of acceleration, increased intensity, lack of inhibitions, aggressiveness, elation, or the opposite as expressed in inhibitions, retardation, lack of initiative, etc. Stanley Cobb has presented a possible classification of the emotions, arranging them in a circle with the opposite poles of pleasant and unpleasant and least differentiated and most differentiated. Under pleasant emotions are registered joy, elation (mania), and on a more differentiated level companionship, love, and affection; their opposites are fear, terror, sadness, depression, loneliness.

Whatever system of classification of different moods is used, each will register different intensities, different directions, and sensations of a pleasant or unpleasant nature. In each, emotion manifests itself as an unconscious dynamic behavior which characterizes the position in which an individual finds himself in relation to his internal and external environment. While, therefore, on the one hand emotions are reactions to outward stress and stimuli and a specific mood registers the bearing of an organism with regard to outside forces, on the other hand it is evident that the position of each individual is determined by his own "energy" and driving force, by the direction in which an organism moves on account of his instinctual needs, and by the amount of energy that an organism is able to throw into the battle.

One of Freud's most important contributions is the discovery that the emotional life is conditioned by the instinctual drives and that, therefore, emotional reactions are to be understood only in regard to the needed gratification of a specific drive which determines the action of an individual. The emotional life is centered around the gratification principle, and our affects are determined by their emotional value in relation to the possible gratification of some need. Earlier physiology and psychology considered the whole field of sensations, perceptions, and affects as a system of reactions to stimuli in which the individual behaves rather passively while his actions are determined as reactions to outside stimuli. Freud has demonstrated that the individual is activated and conditioned through his primary instinctual needs, which determine the nature of his emotional experience.

The fundamental drives which condition the activity of an individual, and the "energy" which is behind these drives, have been matters of argument between different schools of biologists and psychologists for almost a hundred years. It is obvious that each situation is actually met in a different emotional state, according to the nature of the drive which is behind the action and the motives which determine a specific behavior. The more highly integrated the world of an individual, the more complex is the system of motivations that determine emotional responses in their specific character. However, most scientists, in their scientific endeavor to explain the complexity of phenomena by reducing them to one "causative" factor which is supposed to be behind all of it, felt the need to designate one source as the fundamental force behind the whole life or, at least, the psychological complexities. For the vitalist it was "life" itself, this unknown process which distinguished the living cell from inorganic matter, the entelechy of Aristotle, which Driesch renewed; for Bergson it was the *élan vitale*. For other schools, including Freud, it was a basic "energy," libido, or, finally, sex.

It is one of the weakest points in the monumental work of Freud that he himself and his pupils considered it his greatest contribution that he had "discovered" sex as the driving force behind all human psychological activity. This, however, is not actually a discovery but a bold terminological simplification which is even of dubious value as a heuristic principle. If Freud's sex theory means (and Freud was convinced that he had proved this point) that all the emotional gratifications which an individual seeks on different levels of behavior are identical and "nothing but" the need for sexual gratification, this statement disregards the essential difference between "sex" as it appears at the time around puberty and the infantile emotional cravings which a child manifests. This either makes the use of the term "sex" meaningless by applying it to all emotions, or obscures the essential difference between actual sex behavior and general emotional needs. Freud himself was convinced that his sex theory was able to explain the vicissitudes of various instinctual drives, and

he was proud to have demonstrated, as he thought, that all emotional needs are evolved from sexual libidinous behavior patterns and these original sexual behavior patterns are modified through inhibition and sublimation by the action of the superego. This "theory" does not do justice to the actual facts, and it confuses an arbitrary interpretation with actual observations. The general need for emotional gratification and well-being, and sexual libido, obviously are not the same. Moreover, the sex drive does not precede all instincts so that the emotions derive from sexual drives; on the contrary, the sexual drive differentiates out of a general unspecific contact behavior and represents a specific drive with specific needs. The need for emotional gratification constitutes a large field of psychobiological needs which, in man, are not organized under the dominance of the sexual drive for almost 15 years. Nature has deemed it wise to delay the development of the sex drive for such a long time, during which numerous channels of gratification are offered to the growing child. Only after a relatively firm ego structure has been developed, and selective emotional behavior has had sufficient time to establish a system of ego-near emotional values, is the sex drive permitted to take its powerful and domineering place within the system of driving forces.

Modern psychoanalysts identify Freud's sexual theory more and more with a general theory of emotions, but this modification of Freud's original concept was not intended by him, nor is it a development of psychoanalytical experience. However, most analysts have now accepted the general theory of emotions as a necessary modification of the sex theory, and in this regard there is fairly general agreement between the analytical school of psychology and other genetic psychologists.

Since any contact formation of an individual is colored by the emotional status through which the organism passes, the laws of emotional life are indeed the foundations of psychopathology as far as this science deals with the unconscious interpersonal relations with other organisms. The life experience of each individual, from the day of birth on, is the history of his emotional experiences through contact with the outer world. Any meaningful contact and, therefore, any experience is an affective experience determined by the individual's instinctual needs and the positive and negative emotional values of an object, regardless of whether this object is alive or inorganic matter. The human race has inherited no "instincts" as species memory of adequate behavior patterns. The individual has to collect his own experience by groping acts of trial and error through which the world is gradually incorporated as the specific environment in which the individual moves. This is not an "objective" environment of objects and matter but a subjective, affective environment of an emotional nature because each object is charged with an emotional value in regard to the subject which encounters it. The drives and emotions are specific action patterns in the stage show which the individual puts on to win his point in striving for individual gratification. This drive is constantly corrected and modified by group behavior and its patterns.

Since the history of emotional contacts reveals the true story of psychological patterning of behavior, which is primarily unconscious and not remembered in the form of symbolic representations, it is obvious that the study of the emotional life history needs an entirely different approach from the classical, experimental, or rational-logic one. Through Freud, psychoanalysis offered for the first time a scientific method of approach to the unconscious through the analysis of dreams or other unconscious manifestations of the emotional orientation which is behind unconscious behavior patterns.

Of course, the emotional orientation of behavior is not the only one: though man has no "instincts" as species memory of adequate behavior patterns, man has language through which the "experience" of the race is pumped into each growing child by means of words which are the currency of symbolized experience. Through the word, each individual participates in the common knowledge of his specific cultural group, and shares with it its species and group memories. As a means of communication, language as such is foreign to the individual's own emotional status, which is determined by his own life history. The problem of expressing individual emotional states and evaluations through the common instrument of language is, therefore, a basic problem of all exchange of feelings in literature and common contact between individuals. Psychoanalysis as a science of the unconscious is also greatly handicapped by the basic fact that it deals with a language-foreign material and yet depends for communication on the currency of words.

The Psychoneuroses

It is impossible to discuss the large field of emotional disorders or "the psychoneuroses" in detail within the scope of this chapter. The previous remarks were made in order to enable the reader to understand the principles of emotional disorders and to find his way through this complex field, even if details of the matter have to be neglected.

Emotional disorders can be defined as affect-conflicts and disorientations. The psychoneurotic patient is disoriented in his instinctual behavior patterns because his own emotional experience has devaluated the objects of his instinctual and libidinous attraction, and he finds himself in a conflict between the need for gratification of his drive and his past emotional experience which bars him from attaining the desired gratification. The neurotic's own experience, for instance in regard to love and attitudes toward the other sex, may have been a frustrating one through previous exposure to lovelessness, cruelty, or rejection on the part of the mother or another important person on whom he had to rely and who did not live up to the expected rôle. With such a background, he has difficulties in later life in overcoming the negative experiences and in surrendering without distrust and suspicion to a new experience.

Time and again we see how the behavior of the male adolescent and adult is influenced by the life history of his contacts with the other sex, as well as by the rôle which the father played in early childhood. If a weak father deprived the son of the possibility of a satisfactory identification with a maturer person of his own sex, the son is often unable to find his rôle as a mature person in society. The same is true of the woman. While the female child is anxious to have a gratifying emotional relation to the father, in families where the parents are divorced or the family has been deserted by the father and the female child is left with the mother, such a child often has a difficult time overcoming this primary disappointing experience with a father and representative of the other sex. The emotional relationship to the other sex may be impaired by inherent hostility and distrust, and many girls act out their latent hostility in an ambivalent relationship to many different men. Moreover, they take revenge on their parents by unconventional behavior patterns which often lead to promiscuity. Even birth to an illegitimate child may be given by highly intelligent girls who are obsessed with a desire to spite the world in general and their family in particular.

Since early frustration is usually mixed with helpless hostility and craving for revenge which cannot be satisfied except by day dreaming and unconscious hostility, the emotional relations of the neurotic are usually characterized by striking ambivalence, which means the undifferentiated mixture of antagonistic emotions within the same relationship. It is the complex presence of affection and hatred or hostility at the same time which inhibits the neurotic from experiencing gratification without guilt, and not until this ambivalence has been recognized and dissolved is the neurotic able to live in an undisturbed relationship with those people whom he wants to love most.

The life history of a person reflects the history of his emotional contacts with the outer world from the day of birth. The first instinctual need of the newborn is represented in the need for food, which is satisfied by a mother or her substitute. It is quite obvious that not only must the need for food be satisfied in regard to the necessary calories but also the way in which the need is gratified has a great psychological value and is decisive for the establishment of psychological relations between the newborn and his first contacts. What Margaret Ribble has called "psychological mothering" involves the care of the child, the way it is handled, the amount of attention and love it receives, and the well-being which results from such psychological gratification. The life history of many psychoneurotic patients indicates that the first contact of the baby with its mother was highly unsatisfacory. A cold, rejecting mother who does not like her child may often fulfill her duties by following a meticulous schedule of feedings, but her unconscious hostility and rejection may express itself in a hundred small ways. Unsatisfactory home conditions may be the cause of constant tension, and the infant's first emotional experiences may be associated with great anxiety.

Not only the feeding but also the training of the child is an area in which the personal contact between mother and child is closest and, therefore, most likely to lead to future complications if unsatisfactory. Psychoanalysis has demonstrated the fact that the training period of a child with regard to his excretions is of psychological significance in that at this stage the mother functions in a controlling and often punitive way and the child learns for the first time that it is holding an object of its own which can be used as an object of bargaining to buy emotional gratification in the way of praise, attention, and rewards. Although this phase may easily remain unnoticed for the majority of human beings, the history of many neurotics indicates that the training period was indeed a period of struggle and that an overanxious or overbearing mother had attached undue importance to the excretory functions. Enemas and overmeticulousness are so often mentioned in the history of psychoneurotics who develop what psychoanalysts have called an "anal" character that the fact cannot be denied that the undue attention to the excretory function may create an emotional shift in the individual which often cannot be overcome without special attention (Huschka, 1944).

No doubt the experience of a mother as a cold and unpleasant, unloving person reflects itself throughout life and will tinge later contacts with mothers, wives, and the other sex in general throughout life. On the other hand, a mother may be a very demanding person who talks constantly of the need of being loved, and the need for gratitude because she has "sacrificed" herself and bestowed upon her child such an amount of care. In a growing child with these experiences, a conflict will arise between his actual experience of love which was coldness, rejection, and unfriendliness, and the connotation of the term "love" as a devoted and unselfish attitude, ready to give as much as take, an attitude which does not fit into the emotional experience of the individual. Such a conflict is highly confusing, and the ambivalence of affects may remain throughout life and render such a man unable to love any woman, or vice versa. It is so often found in later life between two persons that his and her love are not the same, which actually means that the experience of what is love in two different individuals is so complex and of such different nature that the two emotional concepts can never be reconciled.

With the growth of the child, his contacts with the outside world become steadily more complex. The relationship to the father as a third person besides mother and child has many potentialities of conflict, especially in families where the relationship between father and mother is not satisfactory. Tension or strife between parents may reflect itself in a competitive fight for the affection of a child, or it may result in rejection, the image of the other parent on whom some of the parental hostility may be centered being seen in the child. A boy striving for the affection of the mother may find himself in a competitive situation with the father, whom the child may wish to displace, a situation which Freud called the "Oedipus complex." This Oedipus situation, the emotional affinity between mother and son and daughter and father, is a natural stage of development which under normal conditions serves to establish attitudes and behavior patterns which are essential for mature relationships. However, abnormal emotional interaction in the Oedipus (and Electra) situation can be the germ of severe neurotic difficulties in later life. A mother who rejects her son as a representant of the male sex, on account of unconscious or conscious hostility toward the father, may prevent a male child from normal development and force such a child either into a confusing cross identification with the other sex in order to please the mother and be accepted, or may breed overhostility against the mother and the other sex, manifested in overt hostility and cruelty which are so often mixed with sexual relations in later life. On the other hand, a mother who utilizes the affection of the boy and bestows overaffection on him may create in him unwarranted tendencies to replace the father and to compete with him at a time when competition is hopeless. The amount of undrained hostility toward the father, and the fear of his revenge, keeps many adolescents in a rôle of dependency on the mother and in fear of competition with other adult men. Adolescents of this type are often extremely gifted and promising but in the moment of success they are not able to take it, and they destroy their own success by not living up to adult behavior patterns. Their unconscious fear of revenge and fear of competing with other men, on account of their unconscious hostility toward them, keeps these boys unduly tied to the mother and to the protective climate of childhood.

Similar conditions are easily demonstrated for the girl. Since the mother represents not only a person with whom the growing girl has to compete in sex but also the moral traditions which are meant to prevent the girl from premature sexual relations, the mother is often considered with a mixture of hostility and affection, and if hostility outweighs love the female child is easily led to actions which are likely to spite the protective mother and that for which she stands.

Freud has called the individual representation of the total of group behavior and experience the "superego," and a psychoneurotic finds himself usually in a conflict between his individual needs and the values which he has incorporated in his superego and which so often represent a set of values that he does not like and that he considers inhibiting factors on his way to gratification.

Other persons in addition to mother, father, and siblings enter the picture, and contacts with these new persons will again color the future emotional evaluations of persons of similar relationship. Moreover, socialization of the growing youth makes it necessary that his behavioral patterns be fitted into the needs of a larger group. The great complexity of emotional relations between members of a family increases constantly as the radius of contacts of a child increases, but it must be admitted that the basic contacts as they develop in the first years of life in relationship to mother, father, and siblings are of fundamental importance. A child whose early life was satisfactory and happy is usually able to meet new contacts with a firmer ego structure, which will enable him to make satisfactory adjustments. When, however, the ego structure never had an opportunity to develop, every new contact represents a possible danger and a weak ego structure may collapse even under minor stresses. Since, however, at present so many psychologists overemphasize the importance of early childhood experiences, it must also be emphasized that life is a dynamic process which continues to require new adjustments throughout its duration but which also offers possibilities of learning and new adjustments at every period. It is by no means true that all emotional difficulties derive from early childhood experiences. Conflicts arise throughout life at every level of maturation, and at every level there are possibilities of maladjustment which can be dissolved much faster and easier if they are of recent origin.

The typical development of a psychoneurosis in adults follows certain laws which, for instance, Franz Alexander has represented in a scheme. Of his six points, only the first three are important for the understanding of psychoneuroses in children:

1. Precipitating factors. The actual situation with which the patient cannot cope.
2. Failure in the solution of actual problems. Unsuccessful attempts at adaptation of shorter or longer duration.
3. Regression. The replacement of realistic effort to gratify needs by regressive fantasies or behavior.

These three factors can readily be recognized in most emotional disorders of childhood. Children who are not able to cope with new situations show regression and mobilize earlier behavior patterns in order to obtain gratification on a more primitive level. One of the most common and relatively harmless psychoneurotic manifestations is the reappearance of bed wetting in a 3- or 4-year-old child who experiences the birth of a new sibling for which he had not been properly prepared. When he notices that he is suddenly losing much of the attention, if not affection, which he previously enjoyed, and the new arrival centers upon itself a great amount of attention and love, the child regresses to behavior patterns which in his previous experience proved powerful in attracting motherly attention. Moreover, the newborn or infant is not scolded for wetting the bed and soiling the diapers, which is accepted as something natural at that stage, whereas he himself has had to go through a period of strict training in order to get rid of these "bad habits." The older child may easily regress into a stage of identification with the younger sibling, in order to obtain the same amount of attention and gratification for his need that he

observes in his younger and often envied sibling. If the sibling is of a different sex, and the increased attention of the mother is not only the natural attention which the more helpless baby requires but is an unconscious preference of the other sex by the mother, either girl or boy, the sibling rivalry may turn into an actual problem of emotional relationships with the other sex.

In children, psychoneurotic conflicts manifest themselves on two levels: first, in so-called "psychosomatic" manifestations; and, second, in behavior disorders with a great variety of expressions. The psychosomatic manifestations are often associated with either disorders of breathing, e.g., in the form of asthma, or disorders in functions of the intestinal tract in the form of persistent constipation or diarrhea. Later in life, the same type of disorder may lead to severe spasms and the development of ulcers. On a higher psychological level, psychoneurotic conflicts are often expressed in children in the refusal to learn to talk and to use language as a common means of communication. During school age, reading and spelling difficulties are often of an emotional nature. In more severe cases, the emotional disorder manifests itself in a regression to stages of earlier development and the patterns of a younger child are adopted. The child either develops excessive dream life and abandons his reality contacts by imaginary gratification through dreams and dealings with dolls and imaginary subjects, or on the other hand, if the ego structure has never incorporated the proper inhibitions of behavior, he may try to compensate for their repression by overactivity and especially aggressive behavior which manifests itself in revolt and hostility, and even delinquency. Of the so-called conversion or hysterical symptoms, blindness or at least difficulty in vision is not too rare. In the field of nutrition, overeating is one of the most common expressions of emotional insecurity, in which children, especially boys, want to become big and strong and like adults by consuming a great amount of food. On the other hand, the need in females for being different from the mother, who may be very stout and fat, may result in loss of appetite and very little eating, which under pathological conditions may result in anorexia nervosa, a very severe neurosis which sometimes has a fatal outcome.

From a general psychological point of view it has to be realized that emotional disorders change the set of motivations of a child, and, therefore, his contact with the outer world may be changed in its essential pattern. Children of school age revolt by refusing to learn what they are supposed to learn, by lack of attention or short attention span, by inability to memorize, and by excessive dealing with dreams, especially in the form of ambitious daydreams. Such emotional behavior may lead to complete failure in school, and many children with emotional difficulties are considered stupid, of inadequate intelligence, or even feeble-minded. The evaluation of IQ tests has therefore to be done with the greatest caution, and a low IQ in an emotionally upset person may by no means represent the actual mental capacities. It has also to be remembered that many children of borderline or somewhat dull intelligence are likely to get involved in severe emotional conflicts. It has been demonstrated in discussing the marginal group that hardly any child coming from the marginal strata is spared from severe emotional conflicts which further interfere with the development of an intelligence which may be somewhat inadequate anyway. In any evaluation of a personality, one has therefore to carefully evaluate the set of motivations and emotional contacts which tinge the human behavior to a great extent.

CHILDHOOD SCHIZOPHRENIA

Whereas the psychoneuroses and affect-disorders involve the field of emotional states or moods which determine the organismic bearing and set the patterns of outward expression of internal states, in schizophrenic psychoses we find a disorganization of behavior patterns which involve primarily the formation of contact with reality. It is one of the major contributions of modern child psychiatry to have discovered that schizophrenia, which is the most important mental disease in adolescents and adults, may occur in childhood and infancy. Children with childhood schizophrenia had previously been considered hopeless idiots, and the psychotic child had constituted that group of "defectives" who differed from patients with organic brain syndromes and yet were not accessible to any education or routine training. The "idiot" of a schizophrenic nature was that patient whose condition clinicians and anatomists used to call "functional" mental deficiency because even at autopsy no significant pathology could be discovered with histopathological means available up to now.

It is only recently that newer observations, based on the behavior of adult schizophrenic patients, have taught us to differentiate between mental defect and childhood schizophrenia. The discovery of childhood schizophrenia may throw new light upon the problem of schizophrenia in general, and may explain what actually happens in the schizophrenic patient, because the occurrence of childhood schizophrenia (that means in patients of much less integrated personality with less "experience") gives a clearer insight into the fundamental process. L. Bender (1942) defines childhood schizophrenia as a clinical entity which reveals pathology in behavior at every level and in every area of integration or patterning within the functioning of the central nervous system, be it vegetative, motor, perceptual, intellectual, emotional or social. Furthermore this behavior pathology disturbs the pattern of every functioning field in a characteristic way. The pathology cannot therefore be thought of as focal in the architecture of the central nervous system but rather as striking the substratum of integrative functioning or biologically patterned behavior.

Despert (1941) considers the early symptoms to be detachment, lack of emotional relationships, and flatness of affect. Children with schizophrenia reveal

excessive dependence on the mother, bizarre behavior, temper tantrums, speech and language deviations (infantile autism, obsessive interest in word forms, neologisms).

What is it that distinguishes the schizophrenic child from the idiot? Observations on children with childhood schizophrenia show that these children are quite intelligent in many respects and that, therefore, the application of the term "idiocy" has no meaning and the application of Stanford-Binet or similar intelligence tests is thoroughly inappropriate. Children with childhood schizophrenia may not talk. As a matter of fact, the majority of them do not acquire speech as a means of communication, and it is the absence of speech which so often first brings the patient to the attention of the physician. The schizophrenic child reveals no contact with his surroundings. He walks along without taking notice, and yet observes keenly. He is often interested in even complicated mechanisms, pulling them apart and sometimes, though rarely, putting them together. He avoids obstacles, climbs skillfully, rushes away, looks after his own needs, but does not respond to emotional contact or care

to deal in any way with outside matters. That such a child can hear is often demonstrated, as he will stop when briskly called; that he understands can be shown by the fact that he often carries out a command if it is given in an authoritative manner, though he will not listen to pleading or reason. Bender has called attention to the fact that these children often maintain infantile motor behavior patterns; for example, by whirling the child around, the examiner placing a hand on the child's head, the child may maintain the motion like a spinning top. This, however, is not always so, and an observation made by me recently may be of interest:

One of the children who was tested in this way by the present writer did not continue the spinning motion but had to "unwind" himself, turning backward the same number of times as he had been turned in the original direction. When he walked out of the front door, he had to return through the front door; if he left through the back door he had to come in the same way. Forceful interruption of these compulsive patterns was answered with increased anxiety. This child walked always on the same path which he trod on the lawn, in a complicated zigzag manner; he was not able to go on a straight line. When forced to do so he showed anxiety, but when left to his own impulses he would return exactly the same way as he had come. There was no speech. If left alone, the child would play for hours with the same piece of string, pulling it apart, or picking flowers and pulling their leaves. This obsessive behavior was only interrupted by continuous masturbation or rocking on a bench, which he would continue for hours. Speech was limited to grunting noises, which were always expressed in a monotonous way without modulation. And yet this child found his way around the house, fed himself, used the icebox independently, and rarely broke or damaged anything around him.

If one observes a larger group of children with schizophrenia, they all show similarities. They are well built, often beautiful children, whose physical appearance belies their severe mental aberration. They show an amazingly good memory, returning to the same places and toys even years later and recognizing familiar persons and subjects without difficulty. They do not speak because they have no capacity for acquiring the great variations in expression, rhythm, and modulation which human speech involves and they have no sense of the meaning which is a part of human verbal communication. If the children learn to talk, they use speech in single words or short commands which either express their wishes or are repetitions of commands given to them. Many schizophrenic children refer to themselves in the third person or in the way their surroundings refer to them. Speech is therefore only a repetition of the sounds which they have heard when carrying out certain motions.

The most characteristic fact in some of the more highly organized children with schizophrenia is their compulsive behavior, which makes them appear extremely insecure and forces them to stick at all costs to familiar behavior patterns which have been tested before and which do not seem to involve new risks. If the schizophrenic child is even more severely disturbed, he appears completely disorganized and will not react to emotional contacts or his material surroundings. Having no relationship with the outside world the child handles all matter without concern, is destructive and aggressive, and shows only the most primitive instincts of self-preservation. If these children are playing with toys, they usually disregard dolls or any symbols of human beings. Sometimes, though rarely, animals may be included in the play activity if the child is familiar with them as a steady part of his mental environment. Mostly the child will play with simple blocks, and higher-grade schizophrenic children who permit some insight into their mental functioning indicate that they use blocks and simple forms as representations of persons and animals with the same facility with which other children would pick actual dolls and symbolic pictures.

Understanding the schizophrenic child has made it possible in some instances to draw a child out of his complete isolation (autism). Some of these children have definitely proved that they have high intelligence and that they experience their surroundings in certain ways without the possibility of achieving actual contact. As in adult schizophrenia, the phenomenon of autism or isolation, the lack of "contact formation," appears to be the fundamental disorder. The difference between neurosis and psychosis rests upon the opposite way in which emotional problems are handled. As Alexander (1948) so aptly expresses it:

> The dynamic relation between the ego and the emotional demands is exactly reversed in psychoses and neuroses. In neuroses the ego overpowers the emotional demands and the neurotic symptom is a protest of the restricted impulses; in psychoses the ego yields to impulses, and hence the apparent lack of repression. In psychoses the impulses overpower the ego and it abandons its acquired function of recognizing reality. At the same time the ego loses its other function of harmonizing the different instinctual demands and turns out to be weak in the face of both external reality and the pressure of the primitive unadjusted instinctual impulses.

In other words, the child with childhood schizophrenia does not learn to handle the reality problem or to make what one calls "contact" with reality and an appropriate adjustment to its demands. It is, therefore, not chance that one group of childhood schizophrenia manifests itself between 1½ and 2½ years, when the normal child makes the transition from the inward stage to reality testing. The schizophrenic child apparently refuses to accept the outside world as something different from his inside dreams and wishes, and makes no differentiation between his own imagination and the so-called "reality." It is for this reason that speech has no meaning. The possibility of contacting the outside and maintaining the individual strength (ego strength) is apparently not a function of the brain itself, but of the strength of the fundamental drives of the organism which are anchored in the organism as a whole rather than in the central nervous system. It is for this reason that some European scholars have come to talk of schizophrenia as "somatosis." Although this term does not seem to be well chosen because it entirely leaves out the importance of derivative mental functions, it is meant to indicate that it is the strength of the organism with its fundamental drives which seems at fault. Other investigators have emphasized the weakness of the vital drives (Vital Triebe), which seem much less firm than in an individual of normal strength. They consider schizophrenia a contact weakness in which the individual is not able to exert the normal pressure and resistance toward the outside world. There can be little doubt that in some individuals this primary contact weakness and the lack of fundamental drives are due to a genetic inadequacy which is not so much an inadequacy of structural cerebral patterns as of the *vis a tergo* which drives an individual toward its environment in order to seek gratification of its natural needs. The inherited weakness prevents the child from making the transition from the inward orientation to an outward drive, and the child, therefore, remains overdependent and en-

capsulated in his own world. His weak ego relies on simple defense mechanisms which are primarily of a compulsive character, repeating time and again the same patterns with a complete inability to shift from one pattern to another and to enter the sphere of "effectuation." [1] Children with inherent contact weakness remain, therefore, in their own world. As Alexander (1948) says:

> the psychotic has, in a sense, no respect for reality. It is easier for him to relinquish his contact with reality than to control his own emotions, and as a result he solves his inner conflicts by changing the picture of reality to suit his subjective demands.

Besides inherited weaknesses, traumatic childhood experiences are certainly able to produce a similar withdrawal from outside contact. Histories of children with infant schizophrenia indicate that some of them have been exposed to a traumatic separation from the mother either through illness or death, or have experienced some other severe traumatism which may not be enough to harm the average child but may be sufficient to inhibit the progress of a weaker organism. Childhood schizophrenia is likely to become manifest during those critical periods when the child is confronted

---

[1] The term "effectuation" was coined by P. Yakovlev, who has distinguished three spheres of motility in a paper, "Motility, Behavior, and the Brain":

1. The sphere of visceral motility, which encompasses the change of state of energy within the organism: cell metabolism, respiration, circulation, secretion, etc.

2. The sphere of motility of the outward expression of internal states covers the gamut of the so-called "emotions," i.e., internal motions brought out.

3. The sphere of motility of effectuation, which creates changes in the world of matter and produces work through which the creature impresses itself upon the world of matter, e.g., locomotes, shapes and handles matter, using his own body and parts of it as tools.

This sphere of effectuation is pathologically affected by those abnormal conditions to which the term "psychoses" is usually applied.

with severe changes in its inner and outer environment. The first critical time, as mentioned, is between 1½ and 2½ years, when the normal child makes the transition toward reality contact. The second critical phase is between 6 and 10, when increased demands of school and social life frighten a weak child from forming and exerting stronger drives. Childhood schizophrenia therefore develops frequently in the prepuberty period before the age of 10, and results in a regression to former infantile behavior patterns which have proved to be safe and are now compulsively repeated and maintained. The third most critical period is at puberty, when the sudden appearance of sexual drives forces the developing individual to face the reality of his own sexual nature, and to face the needs of impressing his own sexual character upon his environment and the other sex. Not only the weakness of the fundamental drives themselves but also the psychological need to face reality as a sexual being forces the individual to command a fairly well-established ego structure, in order to achieve a satisfactory compromise between the reality principle and one's own needs for gratification. A weak ego structure may easily break down at that critical period and regress to former behavior patterns which dispense with the need for an aggressive behavior toward reality.

It has long been established that hallucinations and other phenomena of adult schizophrenia are manifestations of regression into a time when there was little difference between the inner and outer world, and the child was able to move around in his imaginary world without limitations. The close relationship between hallucinatory experiences and dreams shows that the schizophrenic individual returns to a dream world. In childhood schizophrenia, where the separation between ego and the outside world has never been completed, we see relatively few hallucinatory experiences and there is no evidence that young children actually have hallucinations comparable to the hallucinations of adolescents and adults. However, certain behavior patterns of schizophrenic children like grimacing, talking to oneself, looking around with sudden lightning glances, mannerisms, shaking of the head, making significant signs the meaning of which is unknown to everybody except the patient himself, outbursts of aggressive or self-mutilating behavior, indicate that the schizophrenic child has a very active inner life which is, however, difficult to interpret because these patients have not yet progressed to a state of differentiation in which they are able to express their thoughts.

Childhood schizophrenia has to be distinguished from other conditions which may produce some similarities in behavioral patterns. Asphyxiation at birth is a frequent reason why children act in a dreamy, half-conscious manner and take no notice of what is going on about them. They may learn eventually to walk but may not talk. Another illness which has some similarity to childhood schizophrenia, although it should be clearly differentiated from it, is dementia infantilis or Heller's disease which occurs often around the age of 3 years and leads to a rapid loss of speech and progressive deterioration although motor patterns are well maintained and no neurological symptoms can be found. Heller's disease is apparently a degenerative metabolic disorder in which the nerve cells undergo severe degeneration and lobar atrophy of the brain (especially the frontal lobes) occurs. Heller's disease has therefore to be considered a manifestation of "the organic brain syndrome."

It has been mentioned that no univocal histopathological data are available in schizophrenia. After what has been said above, this should no longer surprise the investigator. Schizophrenia is a total personality disorder in which the individual has severed his contact with the outside world and has withdrawn to his own world. Although in many schizophrenics there may be found an undue dependence on a protective environment on account of lack of drives toward the outside world or an organismic weakness which may have a "constitutional" basis of decreased cellular activity and resistance to stress, no one can specify from what sources organismic activity and different rates of vitality derive. We know that the nervous system, the endocrine system, especially the pituitary, adrenals, and gonads, have to do with the phenomenon of vitality, but we also know that no single gland or action is responsible for this basic phenomenon because the action of the glands themselves is a manifestation of basic organismic energy. Although it is, therefore, possible to show anomalies in adrenal or gonadal function, in vasomotor control, or in brain activity (often demonstrable in abnormal electroencephalograms), none of these isolated pathological data can explain the complex phenomenon of behavior patterns as seen in schizophrenia. In childhood schizophrenia the therapeutic problem is primarily that of creating an appropriate environment of a more protective nature, in which the schizophrenic child can develop a stronger ego structure without constant danger.

We have to learn to provide a greater variety of environmental conditions so that a larger number of the population can find facilities for individual development. Our civilization has to make use of all its members according to their own capacities and not according to a fictional "average" where an adequate environment is only pro-

vided for a more or less large group near the center of biological and mental variations.

Bibliography

Alexander, Franz. 1948. *Fundamentals of Psychoanalysis.* (3rd printing.) New York: Norton.

Alexander, F., and H. Ross. (Eds.) 1952. *Dynamic psychiatry.* Chicago: University of Chicago Press.

Ballantyne, J. W. 1905. *Manual of antenatal pathology and hygiene.* 2 vols. New York: William Wood.

Bellak, L. 1948. *Dementia praecox: The past decade's work and present status, a review and evaluation.* New York: Grune & Stratton.

Benda, C. E. 1949a. *Mongolism and cretinism.* (2nd ed.) New York: Grune & Stratton.

——. 1949b. Prenatal maternal factors in mongolism. *J. Amer. Med. Ass., 139,* 979.

——. 1952a. *Developmental disorders of mentation and cerebral palsies.* New York: Grune & Stratton.

——. 1952b. What is mongolism? (congenital acromicria). *Int. Rec. Med., 165,* 75.

——. 1952c. Acromicria congenita or the mongoloid deficiency. *The biology of mental health and disease.* New York: Paul B. Hoeber, p. 402.

Benda, C. E., and D. Durling. 1952. Mental growth curves in untreated institutionalized mongoloid patients. *Am. J. Mental Deficiency, 56,* 578.

Bender, Lauretta. 1942. Childhood schizophrenia. *Nerv. Child., 1,* 138.

——. 1947. Childhood schizophrenia. Clinical study of one hundred schizophrenic children. *Amer. J. Orthopsychiat., 17,* 40.

Bender, Lauretta, and W. R. Keeler. 1952. The body image of schizophrenic children following electroshock therapy. *Amer. J. Psychiat., 109,* 421.

Benedek, Therese. 1949. The psychosomatic implications of the primary unit: Mother-child. *Amer. J. Orthopsychiat., 19,* 642.

Binet, A., and T. Simon. 1916a. *The intelligence of the feeble-minded.* (Trans. by E. S. Kite.) Baltimore: Williams & Wilkins.

——. 1916b. *The development of intelligence in children.* (Trans. by E. S. Kite.) Baltimore: Williams & Wilkins.

Bisch, L. E. 1925. *Clinical psychology.* Baltimore: Williams & Wilkins.

Bleuler, M. 1951. Forschungen und Begriffswandlungen in der Schizophrenielehre, 1941-1950. *Fortschr. Neur. Psychiat., 9/10,* 385-452.

Bossard, James H. S. 1948. *The sociology of child development.* New York and London: Harper.

Brierley, Marjorie. 1951. *Trends in psycho-analysis.* London: Hogarth.

Carmichael, L. (Ed.) 1946. *Manual of child psychology.* (1st ed.) New York: Wiley.

Cobb, Stanley. 1950. *Emotions and clinical medicine.* New York: Norton.

Coleman, J. C. 1950. *Abnormal psychology and modern life.* Chicago: Scott, Foresman.

Crain, Loren, and Heinz Werner. 1950. The development of visuo-motor performance on the marble board in normal children. *J. Genet. Psychol., 77,* 217.

Davenport, C. B., C. E. Keeler, M. Slye, and M. T. Macklin. 1940. *Medical genetics and eugenics.* Philadelphia: Women's Medical College of Penn.

Dayton, N. A. 1939. Report of the mental deficiency committee. Public Document 117, Comm. of Mass.

Dearborn, W. F., and J. W. M. Rothney. 1941. Predicting the child's development. Cambridge: Sci-Art Pub.

Despert, J. L. 1941. Thinking and motility disorders in a schizophrenic child. *Psychiat. Quart., 15,* 522.

Deutsch, Helene. 1944. *The psychology of women.* 2 vols. New York: Grune & Stratton.

Doll, E. A. 1919. The average mental age of adults. *J. Appl. Psychol., 3,* 317.

——. 1921. The growth of intelligence. *Psychol. Monogr., 29,* No. 2. Pp. vi + 130.

——. 1927. Borderline diagnosis. *Proc. Amer. Ass. Stud. Feeble-mind., 32,* 45-59.

——. 1935. The clinical significance of social maturity. *J. Ment. Sci., 81,* 766-782.

——. 1936. The Vineland social maturity scale: Revised condensed manual of directions. *Pub. Train. Sch., Vineland, N. J., Series* 1936, No. 3. Vineland, N. J.: Smith Printing House.

Dorland, W. A. N. 1942. *The American Illustrated Medical Dictionary.* (19th ed.) Philadelphia: Saunders.

Down, J. Langdon. 1887. On some of the mental affections of childhood and youth. London: Churchill.

Dubitscher, F. 1937. *Der Schwachsinn.* Leipzig: Thieme.

Engler, M. 1949. *Mongolism (peristatic amentia).* Baltimore: Williams & Wilkins.

Fernald, W. E. 1912. *Feeble-minded children.* Boston: Geo. H. Ellis.

——. 1917. Standardized fields of inquiry for clinical studies of borderline defectives. *Ment. Hyg., 1,* 211.

Freud, A. 1946. The psychoanalytic study of infantile feeding disturbances. In *The psychoanalytic study of the child, 2,* 119. New York: International Universities Press.

——. 1950. The contribution of psychoanalysis to genetic psychology. Presented at Clark University, Worcester, Mass., *Symposium on genetic psychology,* p. 476.

Freud, S. 1948-1950. *Collected papers.* Authorized translation under the supervision of Joan Riviere, International Analytical Library. Edited by Ernest Jones. 5 vols. Vols. 1-4, 1948; Vol. 5, 1950. London: Hogarth.

Gates, R. R. 1946. *Human genetics.* 2 vols. New York: Macmillan.

Gerard, M. W. 1947. The psychogenic tic in ego development, in *The psychoanalytic study of the child, 2* (1946), 133-62. New York: International University Press.

Gesell, A. 1928. The diagnosis of mental defect in early infancy. *Proc. Amer. Ass. Stud. Feeble-mind., 33,* 211-218.

Gesell, A., B. M. Castner, H. Thompson, and C. S. Amatruda. 1939. Biographies of child development: The mental growth careers of eighty-four infants and children. New York: Hoeber.

Goddard, H. H. 1911. Two thousand normal children measured by the Binet measuring scale of intelligence. *Ped. Sem., 18,* 231-258.

——. 1912. *The Kallikak family: A study in the heredity of feeble-mindedness.* New York: Macmillan.

——. 1919. *Psychology of the normal and subnormal.* New York: Dodd, Mead.

——. 1942. In defense of the Kallikak study. *Science, 95,* 574.

Goldstein, K. 1936. The modifications of behavior consequent to cerebral lesions. *Psychiat. Quart., 10,* 586.

Halstead, W. C. 1947. *Brain and intelligence.* Chicago: University of Chicago Press.

Hammarberg, C. 1895. Studien über Klinik und Pathologie der Idiotie. Nebst Untersuchungen über die normale Anatomie der Hirnrinde. Upsala: E. Berling.

Heller, T. 1908. Ueber dementia infantilis. *Z. Erforsch. jugendl. Schwachsinns, 2,* 17.

——. 1930. Ueber dementia infantilis. *Z. Kinderforsch., 37,* 661.

Huschka, Mabel. 1944. The child's response to coercive bowel training. *Contemporary psychopathology.* Cambridge: Harvard University Press.

Jessner, Lucie, Gaston E. Blom, and Samuel Waldfogel. 1952. Emotional implications of tonsillectomy and adenoidectomy on children. *The psychoanalytic study of the child, 7,* 126. New York: International Universities Press.

Kallman, F. J. 1938. *Genetics of schizophrenia.* New York: Augustin.

Kanner, Leo. 1948. *Child psychiatry.* (2nd ed.) Springfield, Ill.: Thomas.

Keeler, W. R., and Lauretta Bender. 1952. A follow-up study of children with behavior disorder and Sydenham's chorea. *Amer. J. Psychiat., 109,* 421.

Klapper, Zelda S., and Heinz Werner. 1950. Developmental deviations in brain-injured (cerebral-palsied) members of pairs of identical twins. *Quart. J. Child Behavior, 2,* 288.

Klein, M. 1950. *The psycho-analysis of children.* (4th ed.) London: Hogarth.

Kris, E. 1950. Notes on the development and on some current problems of psychoanalytic child psychology, in *The psychoanalytic study of the child, 5,* 24-46. New York: International University Press.

Levy, D. M. 1943. *Maternal overprotection.* New York: Columbia University Press.

——. 1944. On the problem of movement restraint: tics, stereotyped movements, hyperactivity. *Amer. J. Orthopsychiat., 45,* 644.

Masserman, Jules H. 1946. *Principles of dynamic psychiatry.* Philadelphia and London: Saunders.

Myerson, A. (Chmn.) 1936. Eugenical sterilization: A reorientation of the problem. (By the Committee of the Amer. Neur. Ass. for the Investigation of Eugenical Sterilization.) New York: Macmillan.

Papez, J. W. 1937. A proposed mechanism of emotion. *Arch. Neurol. Psychiat.*, *38*, 725.

Penrose, L. S. 1949. *The biology of mental defect.* New York: Grune & Stratton.

Potter, E. L. 1952. *Pathology of the fetus and the newborn.* Chicago. Year Book Publishers.

Ribble, M. A. 1943. *The rights of infants.* New York: Columbia Univ. Press.

——. 1945. Anxiety in infants and its disorganizing effects. *Modern trends in child psychiatry*, 11–25. New York: International University Press.

Roberts, J. A. F., R. M. Norman, and R. Griffiths. 1936. Studies on a child population: I. Definition of the sample, method of ascertainment, and analysis of the results of a group intelligence test. *Ann. Eugen., Camb., 6*, 319–338.

Sartre, Jean-Paul. 1948. *The emotions. Outline of a theory.* (Translated from the French by Bernard Frechtman.) New York: Philosophical Library.

Sears, Robert R. 1950. Effects of frustration and anxiety on fantasy aggression. Presented at Clark University, Worcester, Mass., *Symposium on Genetic Psychology*, p. 498.

Seguin, E. 1907. *Idiocy: And its treatment by the physiological method.* (Reprint of 1866 ed. by Committee on Publication, Teachers College, Columbia Univ.) Albany: Brandow Printing Co.

Shuttleworth, G. W. 1909. *Mongolian imbecility.* London: Brit. Med. J.

Sontag, L. 1944. Differences in modifiability of fetal behavior and physiology. *Psychosom. Med., 6*, 151.

Southard, E. E., and O. J. Raeder. 1921. Waverley researches in the pathology of the feeble-minded. *Memoirs Am. Acad. Arts and Sci., 14*, 3.

Spitz, R. A. 1945. Hospitalism. In *The psychoanalytic study of the child*, Vol. 1, p. 53. New York: International Universities Press.

——. 1946. Hospitalism. *Ibid.*, Vol. 2, p. 113.

——. 1950. Relevancy of direct infant observation. *Ibid.*, Vol. 5, p. 66.

Strauss, A. A., and L. E. Lehtinen. 1947. *Psychopathology and education of the brain-injured child.* New York: Grune & Stratton.

Strauss, A. A., L. E. Lehtinen, and H. Werner. 1941. The mental organization of the brain-injured mentally defective child. *Amer. J. Psychiat., 97*, 1194.

Thorpe, L. P. 1946. *Child psychology and development.* New York: Ronald.

Tomkins, Silvan S. (Ed.) 1944. *Contemporary psychopathology.* Cambridge: Harvard Univ. Press.

Wechsler, D. 1939. *The measurement of adult intelligence.* Baltimore: Williams & Wilkins.

Werner, H. 1948. *Comparative psychology of mental development.* Chicago: Follett.

Werner, Heinz, 1949. Thought disturbance with reference to figure-background impairment in brain-injured children. *Confinia Neurologica, 9*, 255. S. Karger.

Weygandt, Wilhelm. 1936. *Der jugendliche Schwachsinn.* Stuttgart: Ferdinand Enke.

Whipple, G. M. (Ed.) 1928. Nature and nurture: Their influence upon intelligence. *Yearb. Nat. Soc. Stud. Educ., 27* (I).

——. 1940. Intelligence: Its nature and nurture: Comparative and critical exposition. *Yearb. Nat. Soc. Stud. Educ., 39* (I). (See also supplement, Addresses and discussions presenting the Thirty-ninth Yearbook. Salem, Mass.: Newcomb and Gauss.)

Yakovlev, P. I. 1948. Motility, behavior and the brain. *J. Nerv. Ment. Dis., 107*, 313.

CHAPTER 19

SOCIAL DEVELOPMENT

HAROLD H. ANDERSON AND GLADYS L. ANDERSON

Growth and development are included in the titles of eight preceding chapters in this *Manual*. Unlike some of the other chapters, this chapter cannot be based upon studies that have dealt primarily with the defined title of the chapter, "Social Development." Although many studies are reported and catalogued under social behavior, the scope of this chapter is without limit.

The beginnings of emotional behavior—for example, the early differentiations of emotional responses, the studies of anger, hostility, aggressiveness, jealousy, security and insecurity, laughter, pleasure, sympathy, and sex behavior—are properly included in a chapter on emotional development, as, in fact, they are here (Jersild, Chapter 14). However, practically everything that can be written under emotional development is encompassed within the framework of social development. It is obvious that systematic overlapping of reporting is to be avoided, but occasional cross references to studies and to theoretical discussions will be made.

Similarly, in Chapter 15, entitled "Behavior and Development as a Function of the Total Situation," much of the interaction between the child and his psychological environment is not defined differently from his social development. No attempt will be made in this chapter to repeat the detailed, theoretical formulations and the insightful interpretations of Lewin's topologi-cal psychology, though, again, occasional cross references will be made.

Of all the possible areas of overlapping with social development of the child, none could be greater than the area of learning. Since there is a chapter "Learning in Children" (Munn, Chapter 7), no attempt will be made to present a systematic treatment of learning. In all probability much, if not all, social development is inseparable from learning. The mass of research on learning, nevertheless, obliges us to look to the future for the applicability of the principles of learning to human social development.

Even considering the inevitable overlapping, there is to be found in the current psychological literature a vast amount of research and theoretical discussion related to social development that has not been envisaged in the other chapters of this *Manual.*

Under the title of "Social Development" it would be logically possible to outline or to prepare a synthesis of the theoretical structure of all the major works on personality or of all the theories and research reported in the current books on social psychology or to summarize the already "classical" theories concerning social development contained in Freudian psychoanalysis. The writers of this chapter have decided not to undertake such a task. The treatment of social development needs to be consistent with broader areas of overlapping, i.e., it must be consistent with knowledge of the general principles of science, with the facts of the biological sciences and the social sciences, and with the principles of values, of ethics, and of harmonious living.

It does seem possible and worth while to attempt to report in a related and consistent way a wide variety of studies, many of which are not related by their authors to other studies or to theoretical assumptions concerning social development. To do this the writers will present a brief review of a concept of growth, which is emerging in more and more places in the psychological literature, and a crude outline or a structure of levels of growth relationships, which can represent at once psychological growth or social development.

Apart from a swift historical review of trends in psychological thinking since 1900, no effort will be made to review the considerable number of early studies, more static in their orientation but none the less representing valued and necessary steps of imaginative and adventuresome psychologists of their day. These earlier studies, including especially a number of studies of European origin, have been well reported by Bühler (1933). The concept of social development is so all inclusive and the experimental studies so numerous that the large and extensive bibliography following this chapter must be understood as an effort to be representative. Numerous investigations, equally worthy, have not been specifically cited.

Trends in Psychological Thinking

During the period following 1900 certain trends appeared out of which present research in social development has emerged.

1. *Discovery of the Individual Person.* At the turn of this century psychologists discovered the individual person. This discovery, although taken so much for granted today as a simple idea, was epoch making at the time. Using the observational and descriptive methods of the natural scientists, Darwin (1877), Preyer (1882, 1888, 1889), Shinn (1893–1899, 1900), the Scupins (1907), and the Sterns (1907, 1909) published their biographies of infants and small children. These reports are historical landmarks.

Binet (1898, 1902) not only developed the battery of *individual* psychological examinations but, long before the time of Adler's (1923) *Practice and Theory of Individual Psychology,* published reports with *psychologie individuelle* in the title. Even in the field of religion, a psychologist, James (1902), published his *The Varieties of Religious Experience.* This "timely" volume left unquestioned the individuality of religious experience.

In 1909, when the Juvenile Psychopathic Institute was opened in Chicago, the best experts in the land thought that delinquency had its base in psychopathology. Six years later this idea was refuted by the director of the institute in an encyclopedic volume to which its author, Healy (1915a), gave the significant title *The Individual Delinquent.* Healy not only maintained that one should make a thorough study of the individual delinquent but, anticipating another emerging trend, he demonstrated the importance of the "total situation" about the child as contributing to the delinquency.

2. *Freudian Psychoanalysis.* At the same time that the individual person was being discovered in Paris by Binet and in Cambridge, Massachusetts, by James, he was not only being discovered but analyzed by Freud (1896, 1900, 1904) in Vienna. Psychoanalysis developed very slowly and for a number of years in isolation from psychiatry and academic psychology in both Europe and America. G. Stanley Hall brought Freud (1910) to America where he gave at Clark University a series of lec-

tures on "The Origin and Development of Psychoanalysis."

Freud not only introduced a new dynamic conceptual scheme of thinking about behavior and unconscious motivation but formulated the first systematic statement of personality viewed as a developmental sequence. One of the most remarkable features of this sequence as well as a source of its chief defects lies in the fact that Freud constructed his genetic psychology for normal children out of work with the memories and introspections of neurotic adults. Anna Freud (1951), discussing the unavoidable factors in selection of cases, said:

> This situation as it exists in psychoanalytic work for practical reasons is responsible for a particular trend which has become characteristic for psychoanalytic investigations from the very outset, that is, for the tendency to establish and reconstruct the facts of normal psychology from the distortions and exaggerations presented by pathological manifestations [p. 482].

With the slow development of psychoanalysis came inevitable differentiations by Freud himself and by others as the first formulations were tested and reexamined against successive clinical experiences. These differentiations, each an effort to describe and to interpret and explain behavior, beginning with elaborations, refinements, and differences in interpretation by Jung (translated 1916, 1923) and Adler (1907, 1909, 1923), were followed by a long and still growing succession of psychoanalytic writers. Psychoanalytic theories have since been the subject of investigation by, for example, experimental psychologists (Sears, 1943, 1944), psychiatrists using experimental and observational methods with animals and infants (Levy, 1928, 1934; Spitz, 1945; Spitz

and Wolf, 1946; Ribble, 1939, 1943, 1944), learning theorists and anthropologists (Mowrer and Kluckhohn, 1944). Longitudinal studies have also been undertaken (Fries, 1944, 1947; Fries and Lewi, 1938).

Reviewing significant aspects of psychoanalytic development since her father's visit to America, A. Freud (1951) commented:

> Now, after forty years, all this has changed beyond all expectation. There are today more psychoanalysts in the United States than in all other countries of the world put together. There are as many as thirteen Branch Societies of the International Psychoanalytic Association and, linked with them, ten to thirteen Training Institutes for the instruction of future analysts, their number increasing still from year to year. Many scientific periodicals are open to psychoanalytic contributions. Books on the subject are so prolific that even the most diligent worker in the field has difficulty in keeping his knowledge of the literature up to date [p. 477].

3. *Discovery of the Whole Child in the Total Situation.* It is not clear in how many areas nor in what order the awareness of the importance of the child's environment began to emerge. In the study of delinquency and misbehavior Healy has been a pioneer. Healy (1915b) pointed out that dishonesty, like delinquency, was a *situational phenomenon* and not a characteristic of the child himself. He cited cases where dishonesty disappeared when the situational stresses were removed. With the same theme in mind, H. H. Anderson (1929), at the University of Geneva, discussing the work of psychological clinics, devoted a chapter to *L'enfant entier dans la situation entière.*

At a symposium on "The Treatment of Behavior and Personality Problems of Children," Lowrey (1930–1931), chairman, expressed a general consensus: "These groups [psychiatrists, clinical psychologists, and psychiatric social workers] have finally discovered the human being as the total personality involved in the series of more or less total situations" (p. 56).

From the University of Berlin, Lewin (1933) summarized in English his interpretation of "Environmental Forces," which he elaborated for the first edition of this *Manual* (see Chapter 15).

Frank (1928) outlined a theory of personality development viewed as a product of the learning process. More specifically, he attempted

> to sketch the personality as the outcome of the individual's learning how to manage his physiological tensions, under the tutelage of parents and other adults who present him with various tensional problems in their efforts to mold his behavior into the socially sanctioned patterns [p. 705].

Frank (1936) reversed the perspective of 1909 by stating that it is our culture that is "sick" and not fit for healthy children to grow up in. From this article, "Society as the Patient," has been taken the title for one volume of Frank's (1948) collected writings, most of which are quite within the scope of psychodynamics of social development. Among many others who contributed expository writings are to be found Mead (1934) on the meaning of language and communication, Plant (1937) on the interaction of the child and his culture, Cottrell (1942) on situational fields in social psychology, and Sullivan (1947) on psychiatry as a science of interpersonal relations.

4. *The Multi-discipline Approach*. A fourth trend evident since 1900 is the multidiscipline approach to the study and modification of behavior.

Child guidance clinics. The multi-discipline approach was a conspicuous feature of Healy's first clinic, the Juvenile Psychopathic Institute in Chicago. The Commonwealth Fund combined three of the four trends cited above when, in the 1920's, they established their demonstration clinics. They emphasized the study of the individual, the understanding of the child's interaction with his environment, and the multi-discipline approach. Looking back, one can see that it was inevitable that more systematic efforts would be made to integrate the contributions of persons from many disciplines working together on common problems. The American Orthopsychiatric Association, whose members are psychiatrists, psychiatric social workers, and clinical psychologists, was founded in 1924 to fulfill a need for communication among these disciplines. One criterion for membership in this organization, applicable to each of the disciplines, was practical experience in a *teamwork* relationship with members of the other disciplines. In a literal sense, this organization has represented a very productive kind of *social development* among adult professional workers.

The research institutes. Another type of multi-discipline approach is seen in the research institutes of child welfare established under the aegis of the Laura Spelman Rockefeller Foundation in the 1920's. These institutes followed somewhat the organizational pattern of the Child Welfare Research Station established "by the people of Iowa" at the State University of Iowa in 1917. Although most of the staffs of these institutes were psychologists, they had direct or indirect collaboration in research with physicians, pediatricians, dentists, orthodontists, physiologists, nutritionists, psychiatrists, pychoanalysts, sociologists, anthropometrists, anthropologists, nursery school teachers, and parent educators. To facilitate communication among research workers from the various disciplines the Committee on Child Development of the National Research Council fostered the founding of the Society for Research in Child Development in the 1930's.

Trends of the times were reflected in the early research publications from these institutes, several of which established monograph series. As research in any discipline is limited by the refinement or elaboration of method, it is understandable that the early research was concerned mainly with studies of physical growth and studies of mental and motor development. Yardsticks, tape measures, and mental tests were already at hand. The trend of research soon turned, however, to the observation, quantification, and statistical treatment of social interaction, social responses, and social development.[1] This swift expansion of emphasis is seen in the titles of the first monographs to appear from four of these institutes.

The first monograph from the Iowa Child Welfare Research Station was Baldwin's (1921) *The Physical Growth of Children from Birth to Maturity*. In the first monograph from the Institute of Child Welfare, University of Minnesota, J. E. Anderson and Foster (1927) explicitly included the child's environment in the title, *The Young Child and His Parents*. A Study of One Hundred

[1] Harris (1953) closed his review of research in the general field of child psychology with a footnote comment on the current disproportion, as he found it, between the numbers of studies reflecting research interests in personality problems and social influences, on the one hand, and the paucity of studies of intellectual growth and motor skills, on the other. "More than thirty excellent quantitative studies of personality disorganization in children appeared this year but cannot be reviewed—for lack of space. Likewise, the literature utilizing the case approach has been omitted. A striking feature of this review is the dearth of material on motor and intellectual growth and the development of skills as contrasted with the emphasis on social influences on personality" (p. 27).

Cases. From Teachers College, Columbia University, Child Development Monograph No. 1, by Thomas and her associates (1929), was entitled *Some New Techniques for Studying Social Behavior*. Bott (1933) published *Method in Social Studies of Young Children* as Monograph No. 1 in the Child Development Series of the University of Toronto Studies.

A multi-discipline longitudinal research study was begun in 1929 at the Child Guidance Clinic, Institute of Child Welfare, University of California, Berkeley. Macfarlane (1938), director of the study, made an elaborate report of methodology of data collection and organization for this cumulative clinical study of normal children. From this time on, studies of social response, social interaction, social development, not to mention clinical studies and individual case reports of breakdowns in the process of social development, have appeared in such numbers that further documentation here is unimportant.

5. *Contributions by Other Investigators*. Meanwhile, from widely separated parts, studies of social behavior began to appear in the 1920's. In Vienna, a whole series of imaginatively conceived studies inspired by Charlotte Bühler appeared. These studies have been well summarized by Bühler (1933). In Geneva, from La Maison des Petites and the Rousseau Institute, Piaget (1923) published his report on egocentric language and thinking. In Canada, Bridges (1931) published her *Social and Emotional Development of the Preschool Child*. Isaacs (1931) wrote *Contribution à la psychologie sociale des jeunes enfants*, and (1933) a book in English by a similar title. Murchison, with his editorial ear to the ground, founded the *Journal of Social Psychology* in 1930.

6. *Discovery of the Child's Unverbalized Social Defenses*. In addition to the objective, observational studies with their

quantifiable, statistical treatment, there were other research inquiries in the 1930's, with roots deeply sunk in Freudian psychodynamics, that were distinctly of an individual, qualitative nature. Murray's (1938) *Explorations in Personality* is the best example. Although these studies were made on adults, they introduced techniques for inferring human needs and defenses. Frank (1939) collected a wide variety of these newer concepts under the rubric *projective techniques,* a term that was seized upon with almost too much avidity by psychologists. Projective techniques (Bell, 1948; Abt and Bellak, 1950; H. H. Anderson and G. L. Anderson, 1951), as unstructured materials, offer a minimum of obvious or meaningful threat to the subject. Devised to evoke symbolic expressions of attitude, anxiety, and tension, they reveal to the psychologist hitherto concealed hostilities, aggressions, fears, anxieties, and unconscious defenses. These techniques have opened up new and subtle means for diagnosing deficiencies in social development and obstructions to the social communication process.

7. *Psychotherapy with Children.* Psychotherapy, viewed by whatever school or cult, whether regarded as speeding up the growth processes, gaining insight into one's cosmic orientation, learning or relearning, or resolving an obstinate Oedipus, is inseparably related to the problem of social development. In fact, the difficulties in a child's social development or social orientation are usually the symptoms by which a need for psychotherapy is deduced in the first place. Although many books have been written on adult diagnosis and on descriptions of adult disease entities, there were very few books on psychotherapy for adults or children written before 1935. In his excellent treatment of the history of psychiatric therapy, Appel (1944) listed only two books dated prior to 1935 (A. Freud, 1928; and Klein, 1932) which deal

with children. The first issue (1930–1931) of the *American Journal of Orthopsychiatry* reported the symposium, mentioned above, on "The Treatment of Behavior and Personality Problems in Children." The symposium produced the judgment, expressed by Lowrey (1930–1931, p. 51), that, although there were many persons competent to write a book on diagnosis, no one at that time was competent to write a book on treatment. The record has validated Lowrey's judgment of the situation in 1930.

In the 1930's there was much self-examination of what clinicians did. Schilder (1938), who had worked with children and adults, published a book with the unmodified title *Psychotherapy.* Rogers (1939) wrote *The Clinical Treatment of the Problem Child,* followed (1942) by *Counseling and Psychotherapy.* Allen (1942) published *Psychotherapy with Children.* In the next 10 years more than a dozen books were produced on specific topics of individual and group psychotherapy with children. It is true that practically everything from depth psychology to doll play and drop-the-handkerchief has in the 1940's been called psychotherapy. It is equally true that significant advances in psychology and psychiatry have been made in the form of more discerning observation and more discriminating interpretation of what happens in the therapeutic process.

Hypotheses, Definitions, and Organization of Concepts

The Process of Science, the Progressive Developing of Conceptual Schemes. It can be seen in the brief presentation of historical trends that a *process of activity has been evolving.* Moreover, this process has certain discernible characteristics that are familiar in other contexts. The discovery of the individual delinquent or of the individuality of reports of religious experience represented a *differentiation* in psychological perceptions. The concept of the whole child in the total situation evolved into a still more differentiated concept of a relationship of interpenetrating attitudes and activities. The multi-discipline approach represented a conscious effort to test hypotheses against wider and wider experience and to achieve a higher degree of organization of all available relevant percepts. The meaning of interpersonal relationships is slowly becoming verbalized; it, too, is in process. Psychologists are fumbling with words trying to describe to each other something which they tentatively and vaguely call *dynamic*. Like the astronomers who had not yet discovered Pluto but who were agreed that "something is out there," psychologists and psychiatrists are unanimously agreed that they are about to get a better perspective on something important in human relations. They may expect that the new perspective will itself evolve into a still newer organization of percepts.

The vagueness of percepts of social behavior, the inconsistencies in interpretation, the contradictions in definitions, the hundreds of studies reporting slightly different segments of human behavior or segments observed from a slightly different point of view—all this may look like a process of confusion. To the extent, however, that it is *process* it satisfies the criteria of vigorous, lusty, scientific growth.

> The history of science is a history of inadequate and incomplete statements, and every new insight makes possible the recognition of the inadequacies of previous propositions and offers a springboard for creating a more adequate formulation. The history of thought is the history of an ever-increasing approximation to the truth. Scientific knowledge is not absolute but "optimal"; it contains the optimum

of truth obtainable in a given historical period [Fromm, 1947, p. 239].

The history of science reveals a struggle to refine observations and to communicate with others. Conant (1947), in attempting to formulate a definition of science, said: "In the early days one sees in clearest light the necessary fumblings of even intellectual giants when they are also pioneers" (p. 18). In fact, for Conant, the very definition of science is in terms of process, of the interweaving of concepts, the mutual stimulation.

> The texture of modern science is the result of the interweaving of the fruitful concepts. The test of a new idea is therefore not only its success in correlating the then-known facts, but much more of its success or failure in stimulating further experimentation or observation which in turn is fruitful. This dynamic quality of science viewed not as a practical undertaking but as development of conceptual schemes seems to me to be close to the heart of the best definition [p. 24].

The Characteristics of Biological Growth.[1] There are two generally recognized aspects of growth that are important both in physiology and psychology. Growth is at once a differentiation (creation of differences) and an integration (organization) of differences. The truth of this observation is perhaps more readily perceived in physiology than in psychology. An illustration from biology will facilitate the definition of a number of terms applicable also to psychological growth.

Figure 1 presents an example of an unfertilized egg living in an environment in which there is a spermatozoon. Each is said to be an individual organism. Each is different from the other in structure and

---

[1] In the preparation of this chapter the writers have drawn and freely adapted materials from H. H. Anderson (1951, 1952—both by permission of the publishers).

function. Each constitutes a part of the environment of the other. It can be said that the presence of the egg makes a difference in the behavior of the spermatozoon and that the presence of the spermatozoon makes a difference in the behavior of the egg. The phenomenon of this process of relating is called the *confronting of differences*. *Confronting of differences* is a relationship (process of relating) in which the behavior or presence of one individual or organism makes a difference in the behavior of the other. Without the egg to fertilize,

FIGURE 1.   A biological illustration of the confronting of differences.

the spermatozoon in due course loses its identity as a spermatozoon; it dies. Likewise, unless it is fertilized, the egg loses its form and its function as an egg; it also disintegrates.

In the confronting of differences, however, there is necessarily a concept of *integrity* as well as *integerness*. There is not only the fact of difference, but there is an *acting* differently. The egg behaves, *acts*, like an egg, and the spermatozoon behaves, *acts*, like a spermatozoon, and each is biologically free to "be itself." In the hypothesis that growth occurs only through the confronting and the free interplay of differences, there is necessarily a concept of the integrity of differences but also of *action* consistent with this biological integrity. *Confronting* of differences is not necessarily *conflict* of differences. Conflict of differences implies an outside attack against the biological integrity of the cell, from which we derive our concepts of rigidity, defense, disunity, disorganization, and disintegration. To the extent that the process of interplay or confronting of differences represents conflict and its concomitant charac-

teristics of rigidity, domination, attack, one-way communication, disunity, defense, disorganization, disintegration, it can represent lower levels of change, but not the process of unity, integration, growth. In contrast with conflict which represents one-way communication, growth, in a very real biological sense, is a process of *two-way communication* between individual cells or organisms.

It was said that Figure 1 presents an example of an unfertilized egg living in an environment in which there is a spermatozoon. From the standpoint of the biological dynamics of this situation it would be equally true (meaningful) to write the sentence two ways, giving preference to neither the spermatozoon nor the egg. Thus Figure 1 presents also an example of a spermatozoon living in an environment in which there is an unfertilized egg. Actually, neither form of the sentence, nor both together, is satisfactory. Figure 1 represents a momentary cross-section of a process of dynamic interplay between these two individual and different organisms which cannot be adequately sketched or verbalized. In the process in which biologists are interested, that is, conception and growth of an individual, the egg and the spermatozoon are each essential. They are each different; but it is not meaningful to say, or to imply, that one is more important than the other.

> There is neither a struggle of the members amongst each other in the organism, nor a struggle of the whole with the members. . . . Only deterioration or imperfect adaptation of the organism makes members stand out abnormally [Goldstein, 1939, p. 423].

It does not seem either necessary or meaningful to say of Figure 1: (1) that the spermatozoon dominates the egg or *vice versa*, or that one is ascendant over the other; (2) that either the egg or the spermatozoon is submissive to the other; (3) that there is anything aggressive or hostile in the behavior of either; or (4) that there is anything in the behavior of either that can meaningfully be said to represent force, coercion, or conflict.[1]

In the process of fertilization (see Figure 2), the egg abandons its structure and its function as an unfertilized egg for a new and emerging structure and a new and emerging function. The spermatozoon also abandons its structure and function as a

FIGURE 2. The "non-coerced" yielding to differences—biological example.

spermatozoon for a new and emerging structure and function. Growth comes about through the *confronting of differences*, the *responding to differences*, and the *abandoning* of the individual's self as it is for a new self in process of emerging.

This one-celled, fertilized egg is different in structure and in function from anything that has ever existed before. It is a *differentiated* and *differentiating* organism. Growth is the creation of differences (see Figure 3). Instead of mere reproduction of the structure and function of the original fertilized egg cell, there appear cells that become, for example, nerve tissue, cells that become muscle tissue, others that become bone tissue, and still others that become glandular tissue. Each of these cells

1 Herein is a difference between concepts of some psychologists and biologists, the difference being a source of confusion mainly to psychologists. There are psychological theories, postulated in various ways, that in nature there is a pervasive conflict; that in human organisms there is an inherent or innate hostility, an aggressive instinct that must be dealt with; and that in human relations one must be either a boot or a doormat, that one is either dominant or submissive. These theories fall short of including the phenomenon of growth as a positive process in nature.

is different from the others and from the parent cell in structure and function. Yet through the chromosomes they are all said to have the same biological heredity. This is that aspect of the process that is called *differentiation:* the *emergence of originals.* In both the physiological family of cells and the psychological society of persons there are an infinite number of problems of individual differences.

Growth comes about also through an *integration* of differences. There is a biological oneness of purpose implied in the act of fertilization. In the fertilization of the egg, the egg's chromosomes unite with the chromosomes of the spermatozoon. There is no perfect or complete integration of differences. So far as is known, the pattern of integration could have been different. It represents a "voluntary" or spontaneous abandoning of a momentary status quo. Growth is process. It cannot be forced or coerced; it develops only under propitious

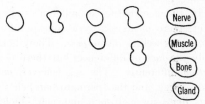

FIGURE 3. Differentiation. "Children are different from their parents and different from each other."

circumstances. It proceeds along a principle of intercommunication and participation of the parts in achieving a more highly differentiated, integrated, organized whole.

As physiological growth tends to achieve an increasing development of individual differences, there is also a continued trend toward an *integration of differences* (see Figure 4). The body lives and grows as a more or less integrated organism. The nerves are not rigid and inflexible but are responsive to the heart, the bones, the muscles. The glands are flexible in their sensitivity to the needs of the other parts of the body. There is, in fact, a common purpose among differences implied in the biologists' discovery that the individual acts as a whole. There is an expenditure of energy by the parts in such a way that the needs of the entire body are satisfied.

Sinnott (1950, 1952) has discussed the thesis that the protoplasmic basis for bi-

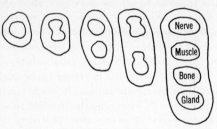

FIGURE 4. Integration of differences. "The child acts as a whole."

ological organization and the basis for psychological behavior are fundamentally the same.

Protoplasm, to be sure, is a complex laboratory of metabolism but let us not forget that it also *builds organisms*. The living machine, unlike any others that we know, grows, develops, and finally reproduces itself. The activities of which it is the seat do not occur at random but are so precisely coordinated that a change in one part is accompanied by specific changes elsewhere. As a result the growing individual does not expand into a homogeneous spherical mass but its growth is more rapid in some dimensions than in others and produces tissues that are differentiated in position and character. "Organism" is a very happy term, for the most significant fact in biology is that protoplasmic systems are *organized*. . . . Organization is the central fact in the life sciences. The autonomy of biology—and I believe the autonomy of psychology also—rests upon this concept.

Organization is evident in various ways. Even in such a loosely integrated body as

a tree the growth in length and in thickness of a branch is related to the development of the whole. The embryonic development of an animal shows still more precisely coordinated growth. As cell divisions follow one another and the various organs and tissues become differentiated all things move in harmony [Sinnott, 1952, pp. 458, 459].

It should be pointed out that in regard to the characteristics of growth or the processes of living matter all things are relative: they are found in degrees. In complex organisms are found cells that do not seem to differentiate but "merely" to proliferate. It is not yet clear whether it is these proliferating cells which ultimately destroy the organism upon which they must depend for their existence or whether the cells are themselves products (not to say victims) of biological disorganization at a higher level. Upon this problem of organization and disorganization Sinnott (1952) has made this further comment:

This organizing, regulatory activity of living stuff is not invariable. It often is upset and may go quite awry. The frequency of tumors, cancers, fasciations, and other "abnormal" growths in animals and plants is ample proof of this. In such cases the cells themselves are often normal and it is only the higher coordinating control that is upset. . . . It must be admitted that this phenomenon (biological organization) still lies, an unexplained, perplexing and challenging fact, at the very heart of biology. It might almost be said that life *is* organization [pp. 459, 460].

In all biological life high differentiation is accompanied by high harmony of the parts. For millions of years biological cells have been "learning" to live harmoniously. Biologists call this evolution. It is a process of the communication between, and the mutual participation of, the parts, of the confronting and free interplay of differences, of the emergence of originals.

The criteria for physiological growth are two: differentiation and integration. They are not found separate in nature and, in fact, are inseparable. *Differentiation* and *integration* of differences are different aspects of one process—growth.

For the growth processes represented in Figures 1 to 4 inclusive, this much appears meaningful: (1) Growth is a non-coerced *abandoning* or *yielding* of a structure and function as they are for a new structure and new function that are in process of emerging. This is also called *differentiation* or *individuation*. Growth cannot be forced or coerced. This non-coerced *yielding* or *differentiation*, is not to be confused with *submission*, a term used to designate a form of behavior or a relationship that is associated with coercion. (2) Growth occurs only through the *confronting* and *free interplay* of differences. (3) The *confronting of differences*, as related to growth, does not mean conflict of differences. Confronting of differences may represent hostility, aggression, or attack, but to this extent it is foreign to a concept of growth. (4) Growth represents a process of *integrating* differences. (5) The process of integration represents a progressive process of change to higher and higher levels of *organization*, or of meaningful relations between the parts. This aspect of growth is not adjustment; it is invention, the emergence of originals, the creation of differences. (6) A concept of meaningful relations between the parts necessitates a concept of intercommunication.

Criteria for Psychological Growth. The criteria for psychological growth are also two. They are differentiation and integration, though other terms have been introduced for the same criteria.

Differentiation, spontaneity, individuation. In all recorded history man has struggled with two problems of social behavior. The first is how to be an individual; how to have ideas of one's own; how to learn from one's own perceptions; how to develop judgment based upon one's own experience; how to think for one's self; how to be original, imaginative, creative, explorative, experimentally minded, resourceful; how to be one's self; how to be spontaneous in one's behavior; how to have the freedom to act on one's own ideas and on one's own value system; how to grow and develop psychologically at one's optimum; and also, within this freedom, how to listen and how to learn from others.

But it happens that in trying "to be one's self" one frequently makes life inconvenient for others. In exercising the freedom to act on one's own ideas one often obstructs the initiative of those about him or encounters inconsistent and conflicting value systems. In attempting to be original, explorative, experimentally minded, it almost inevitably happens that one's behavior conflicts with the needs and plans of others, and with their values, biases, prejudices, misperceptions, expectations, and demands.

Integration, harmony. The second great problem that man has struggled with is the reconciliation of individual differences in desires, purposes, motives, goals, values, and actions. Individuals are different, but they must exercise these differences in such a way that there shall be the greatest harmony in the behavior of men. This second problem, that of discovering, developing, inventing, achieving harmony in human behavior, is thus inseparably linked with the first. If men behaved in such a way that each could approximate his optimum of spontaneity and self-development, that, by definition, would achieve the greatest good for the greatest number. The greatest good for the greatest number implies the approach to some kind of optimum development, some maximum of individuality, for each member of the social group.

In a sense these two problems encompass the whole of human living. Out of the recognized need for spontaneity and harmony have arisen our concepts of law: contracts, torts, equities, rights. Out of the problem of integration of differences, of securing for *all persons* freedom to be themselves, have arisen our systems of ethics. It can well be maintained that the social development of the child is not separate and apart from, but basic to, these epic strivings. Out of failure to clarify and to reconcile the spontaneities of many persons, wars and strife have developed. Delinquency, neuroses, and the behavior problems of children represent errors of perception, distortion of fact, confusions, failures, shortcomings, obstructions to possible and potential social development of the individuals involved.

The perception and reciprocal communication to others of one's needs and desires, the reciprocal interpretation to others of one's judgments and values, and in meeting human needs the mutual discovery of common purposes among differences at the level of action without coercion, threat, or guilt—this is a crude statement of psychological growth; this is social development. Anything less than this represents, by that much less, a lower level of social development; anything more represents by that much more a higher level of social development.

On the criteria of differentiation and integration Murray and Kluckhohn (1948) have given the following elaboration:

Furthermore, no conception of personality could be complete without some reference to the developments that occur, most of which can be adequately described in terms of differentiation and integration. "Differentiation" covers all refinements of discrimination in perception, interpreta-

tion, and conceptualization, as well as detailed specifications in laying out plans and exact directions and timing in action. Mental differentiation is involved in the appreciation of differences, in the intellectual process of analysis, as well as in the isolation and perfection of specialized action systems and abilities, verbal and manual. "Integration" includes the ability to perceive similarities, as well as different kinds of relations between objects and events, to develop a coherent conceptual scheme, to resolve conflicts, to maintain loyalties, to rationalize values, to build a philosophy of life, to coordinate different plans, to think and talk in a logical manner, to organize dynamic systems into a unified whole [pp. 30–31].

Krech and Crutchfield (1948) take the position that not only do the processes of differentiation and integration occur simultaneously but they are aspects of psychological as well as physiological growth. Discussing "higher" levels of stable organization, they stated:

The growth of the human individual—physically, mentally, and psychologically—can be regarded as a process of simultaneous differentiation and integration. In other words, the individual is constantly growing more complex, and at the same time the complexities are becoming better synthesized [p. 67].

Growth of Civilizations. The concepts of differentiation and integration have been used by Toynbee (1939) in the interpretation of *The Growths of Civilizations.* Toynbee has devoted his highly documented Volume III of *A Study of History* to a discussion of the nature and process of the growths of civilizations: the criteria of growth, the relation between growing civilizations and individuals, the interaction between individuals in growing civilizations and problems of arrested growths in civilizations. For Toynbee, growth of civilization is a process of differentiation and integration, the most essential criterion being an increase in self-determination.

Growth is achieved when an individual or a minority or a whole society replies to a challenge by a response which not only answers the particular challenge that has evoked it but also exposes the respondent to a fresh challenge which demands a fresh response on his part. And the process of growth continues, in any given case, so long as this recurrent movement of disturbance and restoration and overbalance and renewed disturbance of equilibrium is maintained. This is the process of growth as we have observed it in a comparative study of a number of cases; but, although the process may be uniform, the experiences of the various parties that undergo the process are not the same. . . . Each successive challenge that any growing civilization undergoes is apt to differentiate the experiences of its constituent individuals and communities . . . and it is evident that the differentiation is cumulative. The longer the series of recurrent Challenge-and-Response-and-Challenge, the greater the progressive differentiation of the parties concerned [p. 377].

Growth is a Positive, Constructive Process. There is nothing in the phenomena of differentiation and integration and of the emergence of originals that can be meaningfully described in terms of domination, submission, aggression, frustration, hostility, mastery, rigidity, compensation, conflict, or even sublimation. Operationally defined, differentiation and integration are proceeding at their maximum under the existing conditions of the organism, of its environment, and of the nature of the interplay between them. Rigidity, submission, mastery, aggression, conflict, hostility, pathology, and disease are terms used to designate conditions, relations, and processes that are low in differentiation, low in integration, or in which the growth proc-

esses are abnormally retarded. The emphasis which psychologists have given to mental disease and to these other associated concepts constitutes a negative approach to the understanding of personality. The very concept of *defense mechanism* implies some answer not only to the question "Defense against what?" but also to "Defense for what?" Defense mechanisms are called into play when trouble arises, when "something is the matter," when the environment has interfered with the positive growth processes of differentiation and integration. Defense mechanisms are used when the person needs to protect his spontaneity, his autonomy, his own differentiating processes, his integrity, his biological and psychological process of growing.

Fromm (1947) refers to growth and productiveness as the "primary potentials" of man, and to defense mechanisms and destructiveness as a secondary "potentiality" that comes into manifest existence only in case of abnormal, pathogenic conditions:

man is not necessarily evil but becomes evil only if the proper conditions for his growth and development are lacking. The evil has no independent existence of its own, it is the absence of the good, the result of the failure to realize life . . . the normal individual possesses in himself the tendency to develop, to grow, and to be productive, and the paralysis of this tendency is in itself a symptom of mental sickness. Mental health, like physical health, is not an aim to which the individual must be forced from the outside but one the incentive for which is in the individual and the suppression of which requires strong environmental forces operating against him [pp. 218–219].

Fromm calls attention to similar views that have been strongly emphasized by Goldstein (1939), Sullivan (1947), and Horney (1937, 1945).

It follows from Goldstein, Sullivan, and Horney, and from many others, that the person is inseparable from the environment and that the understanding of the person is possible only to the extent that we understand also the environment. Mead (Chapter 12) and other anthropologists (Kluckhohn and Murray, 1948) have shown that one must understand the culture in which the person lives. For Cameron and Magaret (1951), the understanding of behavior pathology necessitates an understanding of learning in a social situation, the process of interplay between the individual and his environment. From Murphy's (1949) biosocial viewpoint,

> personality is an interaction of organism and culture, and the situation is consequently part of the personality . . . the interpersonal relations depend on the individuals, but . . . the individuals also depend on the relations [pp. 21–22].

Not only the individual *and* his environment but the *process* of *interacting* must be understood. *This process of interacting is social learning.* A group of nine persons has attempted by group process to formulate their conceptualizing of personality in interaction. The report of their joint efforts has been edited by Parsons and Shild (1951).

Optimum Growth and a Propitious Environment. It has been mentioned that growth, like everything else a psychologist discusses, exists in degrees. Although the units of measurement or of comparison are often crude or even non-existent, growth may be considered as faster or slower, or as more or less. Theoretically, there are limits beyond which a given individual cannot go. Practically speaking, however, it is difficult to say that anyone ever achieves this highest limit. In other words, a person is growing at his optimum, or he is growing at something less than his opti-

mum. It is helpful to postulate a concept of optimum growth, which necessitates also a concept of propitious environment.

One child is differentiating at a more rapid rate than another of the same age. One mother permits or assists her child to emancipate (differentiate) himself from her faster than another mother. The units of comparisons are coarse and crude, but the comparisons are possible and useful.

The concepts of optimum growth and propitious environment are quite acceptable in other biological sciences and can be equally useful to psychologists. No farmer would expect the same crop from a weedy corn field that he would get from a well-tilled field. No farmer expects the same crop of corn from a mountain field several thousand feet above sea level that he would get from a field in Iowa or Illinois. There are good reasons why cotton is not a commercially profitable crop in Minnesota. Given seed from the same stock, environment plays a determining rôle in the growth process.

It is no more correct to say that the cotton crop of Minnesota is characteristic of the "inherent" or "inevitable" or "predetermined" qualities of the seed used than to say that it is a product of cool nights and a short season. The cotton crop of Minnesota would be a product of the dynamic interplay between the plant and the environment. In Minnesota one cannot bring out the "best" there is in cotton no matter how "good" the seed.

Some children, as Ribble (1943), Spitz (1945), and others have reported, are indeed brought up in a chilly climate; other children, as Plant (1937) and Frank (1948) have tried to tell us, are literally scorched. *Man is not only a product of his environment, in a very real sense man is also a victim of his environment.*

What, then, are the elements of the *hypothetical situation in which an individual is approaching his optimum?* How many different characteristics can be expected in a situation where a person is growing at something approximating the optimum of his hereditary potential in an optimum environment?

1. There is a minimum of *psychological rejection, environmental press,* or *domination.* This is consistent with the hypothesis that growth is spontaneous and with the well-demonstrated fact that growth cannot be forced or coerced. A minimum of domination is another way of saying that the setting is one in which there is a maximum of being *accepted as one is.*

2. It follows that with a minimum of environmental press or domination there is a maximum of spontaneity. Since one is accepted as he is, there can be the free expression of any ideas, activities, and impulses that occur to the individual.

3. With free expression, there is the maximum of communication to the environment, making possible a maximum of understanding of the person by the environment.

4. Since there are no threats from the environment, a maximum approximation of "true perception" would be expected. That is, perception would not be distorted by concern for what the percept meant for one's personal security. (One is secure when accepted as he is.) This high quality of perception would facilitate the maximum of understanding of others by the person himself.

5. Since there are no threats from the environment, there is a minimum necessity for repressing into the unconscious, and, therefore, a minimum basis for neurosis.

6. Similarly being accepted as he is, the person has no cause for attacking, dominating, or coercing others. Others would show a maximum of spontaneity, of com-

munication, thus facilitating a "richer" interplay of ideas and activities.

7. Because behavior is "circular" in its effects, as we shall discuss later, the relationship between the person and his environment shows a maximum of harmony, of *working with* others. (To the extent that one's spontaneity is not in harmony with the spontaneity of others, one does not continue to be accepted as he is.)

8. In this relation, the term "conflict with the environment" is meaningless. Projective techniques would elicit only expressive behavior; no defense mechanisms would be found. (Defense mechanisms are elicited by environmental threat.)

9. As for emotional behavior, in this situation the person experiences love, ecstasy, delight, and other positive, constructive, creative, pleasant, and satisfying emotions. In this optimum environment are to be found the "inspired moments," the "insightful" flashes of the Gestaltists. Here is the joy of discovery and the thrill in learning. These are moments in a positive growth relationship with one's environment. They are real in themselves. They are not a sublimation of anything.

10. But, one must now add, there is no perfection except by definition. No one is completely accepted as he is, for that would necessitate complete understanding. All things that psychologists observe are relative. There are, however, many human relationships and many situations that satisfy these criteria to a high degree, in which it is not meaningful to speak of conflict or fear of each other, of aggression or attack, of ascendance or mastery. Rousseau (1925 edition), it seems, had this relation in mind when, writing on the social relation of the sexes, he said:

> But in the harmony which reigns between them, everything tends to the common end, and we do not know which con

tributes the most to it, each follows the impulsion of the other; each obeys and both are masters.

The Place of Value. The concept of a propitious environment may seem to be a departure from the perspective of a scientist. A propitious environment implies direction, goal, choice, and value. It must be remembered, however, that the concepts of growth and development are based on concepts of direction, organization, regulation, and preference. The scientist who studies social development must study all these things, including human choices and human values. The writers wish here to call attention to a recognition of the relation of value to the science of psychology.

Murray and Morgan (1945) freely admitted that attitudes or sentiments are inseparable from a concept of human values.

Hovering in the background of our minds was a half-formulated program for applying psychological methodology to the study of specified human values and so establishing pragmatic grounds for their tentative acceptance or rejection. There is nothing very unusual or revolutionary about this plan, though at first blush it may bear the look of heresy.

Since, by definition, the object of a positive sentiment is a *value* to the possessor of this sentiment, to investigate the one is to investigate the other. Thus ours has been a study of human values as much as it has been a study of sentiments. . . .

Thus, maintaining all the while his rôle as a scientist, the psychologist should eventually be able to provide formulations for a pragmatic system of values.

This conclusion seems to fly in the face of the axiom that science is not concerned with value. Science describes and explains events but it does not pass judgment on them. It says, "This is what happens; take it or leave it." Arguing from this creed, people have concluded that science can be of no service to man in his search for a

satisfactory philosophy. As we see it, however, the exact opposite is true, at least so far as psychological science is concerned [pp. 7–8].[1]

Allport and Vernon (1931), in their *A Study of Values,* developed a test based upon the frames of reference of Spranger (1928). Among other psychologists who have devoted attention to the nature and place of value are Köhler (1938), Wickert (1940), Sherif and Cantril (1945, 1946), Cantril (1949), McClelland (1951), Rokeach (1951), and Grace and Grace (1952).

From Sinnott (1952) the following statement is taken:

Human individuality and personality, the ego itself, is simply one manifestation of the . . . process by which living matter pulls itself together into integrated and organized self-regulating systems. The goal of the organizing process is a *single, whole individual.* Protoplasm always comes in separate packages. Each center of organization has its own psychical unity. Such a living individual maintains its

---

1 One number of the *Journal of Social Issues* for 1949 was devoted to "Social Values and Personality Development." It contained articles by Miller and Hutt (1949) and Hutt and Miller (1949), with commentaries by Titiev (1949) and Mathews (1949). Another number of the same journal was devoted to "Values and the Social Scientist," edited by Benne and Swanson (1950). This number contained a leading article by Geiger (1950) and a symposium of extended commentaries by representatives of the fields of psychology, philosophy, economics, psychoanalysis, education and theology: Ayres (1950), Cattell (1950), Alexander (1950), Wieman (1950), Feigl (1950), Raup (1950), Lippitt (1950), Hobbs (1950), and Churchman (1950).

Still another symposium treating of "Values in Personality Research" was edited by Wolff and Precker (1950) for Symposium No. 1 in *Personality Symposia.* In this number, values were discussed by Josey and Snygg (1950), Klee (1950), Maslow (1950), White (1950), Clark (1950), Auerbach (1950), and Wolff (1950). These authors raised serious question about the neglect of value by persons who think of themselves as scientists.

Tolman (1949, p. 8) made a special point of the place of values in perceptual readiness in animal learning.

identity and endures, even if its material substance is continually changing. The organized pattern of human personality is a surprisingly tough fabric and can survive many vicissitudes. It is a *whole* and must be treated as such.

Even the ancient question of freedom may perhaps be stated in fresh terms in light of the present speculation. It may be interpreted as the translation into action of the regulatory purposes set up in the brain. The purpose and the purposer are one. It is the individual who wills and does, not some agent foreign to it. If this is so, we do what we will, for the desires that arise in us are an essential part of us; and to speak of compulsion here seems meaningless. As Whitehead once said, the psychical is part of the creative advance into novelty. These biological norms that become desires, purposes and ideas may be true "emergents" that actually break new ground in the universe.

It is even possible to look at the vexed question of value from this biological point of view. Values may be said to come from the direction and character of the goals of life, the norms set up in protoplasm and determining the directions toward which an organism moves, either physically or psychically. We may perhaps gain insight on them by studying the cause and orientation of organized living systems. Protoplasm has its preferences, and value judgments are their ultimate expression [pp. 466–467].

That the biological purpose and the purposer are one is a statement very similar to the point of view of Fromm (1947) concerning humanistic ethics: "In authoritarian ethics an authority states what is good for man and lays down the laws and norms of conduct; in humanistic ethics man himself is both the norm giver and the subject of the norms, their formal source or regulative agency and their subject matter" (pp. 8–9). This quotation is only one of many which might be taken from *Man for Himself* to which Fromm (1947) gave the subtitle *An Inquiry into the Psychology of Ethics.* In his book Fromm elaborated his thesis:

problems of ethics cannot be omitted from the study of personality either theoretically or therapeutically. . . . The divorcement of psychology from ethics is of a comparatively recent date. The great humanistic ethical thinkers of the past, on whose works this book is based, were philosophers *and* psychologists; they believed that the understanding of man's nature and the understanding of values and norms for his life were interdependent [p. viii].

Social Development and the Second Law of Thermodynamics

In the past, psychologists, in their development of scientific method, have drawn heavily upon the physical sciences. There has been an attempt to extend the multi-discipline approach in the study of man to a closer integration of the physical and biological sciences. Attempt has been made, for example, to discover the similarities and differences between communication theory in physics and communication theory in physiology, neurology, and psychology. Since social development is based upon communication it is important to review some of the main concepts in these efforts at cross fertilization (intercommunication and integration) of the disciplines. In Figure 5 we have presented diagrammatically a comparison of some of the concepts of the physical and biological sciences.

Physical Matter: The Closed System. The first law of thermodynamics concerns the conservation of energy or the constancy of energy in a closed system. The second law of thermodynamics concerns a quantity of energy which, while remaining constant in a closed system, tends to decrease in quality and never to increase. While

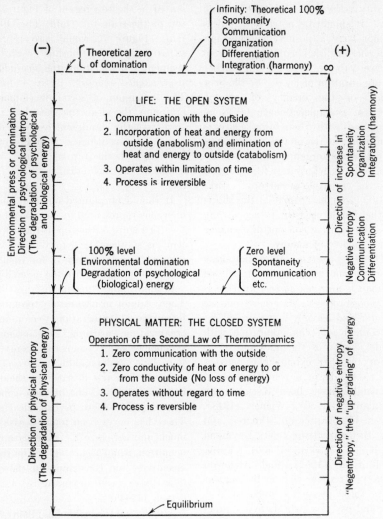

FIGURE 5. Diagrammatic comparison of concepts in the physical and biological sciences.

it appears that no exceptions to the second law have ever been found, physicists have been unable to adapt it consistently to living matter. The closed system in which the law is supposed to operate is a theoretical machine that has no conductivity of heat or communication with the outside. No material enters or leaves it. It operates without friction and without regard to time, and the process within it is reversible. Within this closed system there is no loss of energy, but the free energy changes in quality, ultimately reaching equilibrium. This loss in quality of energy is called *entropy.*

Entropy is a negative concept; it refers to that process in nature wherein energy of high quality is degraded to energy of a lower quality. *Entropy is the degradation of energy.* It should be noted that physicists do not have a positive concept nor a word in the English language to refer to the positive process of achieving higher levels of organization of energy or the "enhancement" of the quality of energy. Physicists, for example, Wiener (1948, p. 18), struggling with their own concepts and attempting to relate the problems of communication and organization in physics and biology, have referred to the positive process as the "negative of entropy." Brillouin (1949, 1950) has proposed the shortening of the double negative to *negentropy* to express the positive concept of a change to a higher quality of energy.

Life: The Open System. While both laws of thermodynamics apply only to closed systems, man is an *open system* and life is an *irreversible* process. Materials from the outside enter and leave a living organism; there is contact and communication with the outside. Some of the questions as to whether or to what extent man behaves according to, beside, or beyond the laws of thermodynamics have been discussed by von Bertalanffy (1950), Wiener (1948), especially in his chapter on "Progress and Entropy," Brillouin (1949, 1950), Raymond (1950), Krech (1950a, 1950b), Frank (1951), Ransom (1952), and Anderson (1952, 1953). It seems that in the current writings of these physicists, biologists, sociologists, and psychologists there is a process of differentiation and of integration in their thinking taking place and that a consistency in their thinking can be illustrated by referring again to Figure 5.

If life is an open system, with energy and stimulation flowing both ways, and communication occurring in two directions, then the most open system, the greatest freedom, the greatest flow of ideas out and in, the maximum of communication with the environment is found as represented in the top region of Figure 5. The top of the scale for "Life: The Open System," Figure 5, would also represent a situation or a relationship in which environmental domination, the *degradation of psychological energy,* is at a minimum. The maximum of social development, the optimum, the ideal, the "healthy" relationship from the standpoint of social development and psychological growth, would also be found at the top of Figure 5. This would be the theoretical optimum environment.

It should be pointed out that for all dimensions represented by the ascending scale (+) in Figure 5, the top of the "Open System" is a "theoretical maximum" which is infinity ∞. In Figure 5, for each dimension that increases with the ascending scale, "optimum" and "maximum" are identical. There cannot in nature be "too much" differentiation, integration, communication, organization, learning, "enhancement" of psychological or biological energy, evolution, love, understanding, or social development. The test in nature is the degradation of energy. None of these concepts is related positively to psychological entropy. There has never been found a case of "too much mother love"; "over-learning," by definition, is not "learning." The resources, incentives, and constraints of the environment have been discussed by J. E. Anderson (1944).

Murray and Kluckhohn (1948), writing about the socializing process, stated that an organism can be "over-socialized." There is no inconsistency or confusion with the term as they elaborated it. Over-socializing, to Murray and Kluckhohn, is the operation of the same process of cultural domination which meets our test of *psychological entropy.* They wrote:

> By definition a highly socialized person is just like the majority, the average. Con-

structive social innovations and intellectual and artistic creations will hardly come from such individuals. Moreover, too great socialization tends to eliminate that spontaneity of response which is of great value in ordinary social intercourse [p. 29].

Any socializing process which tends to level productive energies toward the mean instead of releasing creative energies in the direction of maximum or optimum realization of the individual's potentials is degrading human energy and producing both an individual and a social loss. It is the measure of this individual and social loss which is the measure of psychological entropy. Future research in social development may invent a kind of mathematics of statistical probabilities for the poet's hypothesis "The saddest of these, it might have been."

Psychological Entropy: The Degradation of Energy. In Figure 5, as it is drawn, the degradation of energy would seem to proceed from the top of the figure through both the "Open System" and the "Closed System" in one continuum. Beginning at the top with small degrees of environmental domination (authoritarian relations, psychological rejection, small restrictions on behavior or communication, the "socializing process"), the scale increases downward in domination.

One aspect of the degradation of psychological energy is a diminishing of spontaneity and of two-way communication, which, as mentioned above, can happen only in the "Open System." Authoritarianism and domination, the use of force, threats, and their symbolic forms of shame, blame, and guilt, are a form of one-way communication. Psychologists are studying this "negative concept of the open mind" under such titles as rigidity, ethnocentrism, prejudice, anxiety, the unconscious.

The lowest levels of communication with the outside are to be found near the bottom of the scale for the "Open System." Psychologists and psychiatrists speak of extremely uncommunicative patients as "merely vegetating," or as being psychologically or emotionally "encysted." There is little or no perceptible process of differentiation, growth, or learning in these patients. They are more nearly in a state of psychological atrophy. *Psychological entropy* for them is high; their psychological energy is much degraded. Psychologically, they are living close to the border between life and death. Communication ceases altogether in the "Closed System."

The borderline between the "Open System" and the "Closed System" has so far been crossed by man in only one direction. Movement at this point of Figure 5 is irreversible. Death, the ultimate in degradation of psychological energy, can occur through environmental domination, by overt intent of the environment: by capital punishment or murder. It can occur through slower processes of interacting with the environment: through disease or physical starvation. Infants, according to Spitz (1945) and Spitz and Wolf (1946), have crossed the line through lack of human communication, lack of maternal affection. The second law of thermodynamics, as it is presently formulated by physicists, operates when the individual as a living organism ceases to live, disintegrates, and can be treated as a closed system.

Value in Relating: Psychological Negative Entropy. Figure 5 has a plus sign $(+)$ on the right-hand side of the diagram for the ascending scale and a minus sign $(-)$ for the descending scale on the left-hand side of the diagram. The vertical dimension of the "Open System," Figure 5, represents degrees or levels of relationship between the individual and his environment. A person may be very near the top at one moment, or in one situation, and an instant later the situation (field forces) may have changed so that he is very much lower on the scale. His spontaneity may be very much curtailed. Communication may be reduced even to defensive misrepresentation or false communication. The interpersonal interaction may be slowed. In a very real sense the dominating environment may be effecting a degradation of psychological and biological energy. A given point on the vertical dimension of the "Open System," Figure 5, like Lewin's (Chapter 15) diagrams of field forces, represents a moment in time, a cross-section of interplay, of interacting between an individual and his environment. It is possible with the successive changes in relationships, with additional communication or failure of communication, for an individual to move up or down or to remain indefinitely at one level of relationship, depending on the nature of the relationship, the demands of the environment, the motives of the person, the extent to which he ean or cannot meet his needs, and on his freedom to act. Figure 5 represents direction: not direction of motion, but direction of *value in relating*, the *value to the changing individual which the moment of relating holds for him*. Figure 5 represents direction toward or away from the optimum of self-realization, the optimum growth of the individual. The level of *value in relating* is the psychological analogue of negative entropy. Psychological negative entropy is growth, *social development*, creative experience.

Although from moment to moment there may be movement up or down on Figure 5, "Life: The Open System" is still an "irreversible process," and "time is of the essence." It is not possible for a biological organism to relive any moment in time.

Hypothesis of Equifinality of Growth. It may be mentioned here, and it will be referred to briefly again under psychotherapy, that the fact of movement up and down the scale of Figure 5 illustrates another hypothesis: that of the *equifinality* of growth. Von Bertalanffy (1950) has pointed out that in most physical systems the final state of a process is determined by the initial conditions. Growth, on the contrary, he said, is *equifinal;* it is independent of the initial conditions. The goal of psychotherapy is to help the patient move upward on the scale of relating in Figure 5. As there are many ways to express the goals of therapy, there are many ways of attaining the same goal. In this hypothesis of the *equifinality* of growth lies the hope of the therapist: that therapy can be a speeded-up growth process and that the client can make up for "lost" time. A similar idea has been expressed by Frank (1951, p. 507).

Psychological Entropy and Culture. The concept of psychological entropy as a degradation of energy (with negative entropy as the release of psychological power or energy) is a biological concept of broad application. It represents a functional interplay between an environment and a human being. It holds for infants and for persons of all ages. It would seem to be a test of a propitious environment that could be applied to all cultures. Moreover, it is amenable to measurement in quantifiable units and to prediction in statistical probabilities. The amount of psychological entropy for an individual in a given situation can be a test of, for example, "goodness" of parent-child relations or of a school environment. As a test of culture it can be a "common denominator" or a "standard score" by means of which diverse cultures may be compared.

The application of a concept of entropy would simplify many of the semantic confusions in psychology. For example, ascendance, as defined by Allport (1928–1929), Jack (1934), and Page (1936), contains both dominative behavior (high in entropy) and integrative behavior (low in entropy) (see H. H. Anderson, 1937b). If psychologists employed the test of entropy, they could avoid the confusion shown in current uses of the term dominance. Where dominance is defined as behavior that is not domineering it is low in degradation of energy. But dominant, by implication and by common usage is high in entropy. Other examples of such confusions have been discussed by H. H. Anderson (1940, 1946a) and by Schneirla (1946).

Theory of Probability, "Scientific" Prediction, and Organization. The mathematical basis for the concept of entropy is not different from the mathematics of the theory of probability. Entropy, according to Brillouin (1949, p. 559), "acquires a precise mathematical definition as the logarithm of probability." As entropy increases and energy approaches "equilibrium," probability also increases. Prediction is greatest at the lowest part of Figure 5, and least at the top of the "Open System." Stated the other way, as entropy decreases, that is, as one proceeds upward from the bottom of Figure 5, probability also decreases. Negative entropy, or the enhancement of energy, is today synonymous with the increase of information and the increase of organization in electronic computers, as well as in the higher levels of growth in living organisms.

Socially integrative behavior, the *working with* others, represents a high state of organization. Moreover, it represents the interplay of open minds, the openness to new information, which is one important reason for calling life an "Open System." Conflict, on the other hand, the *working against* others, represents action toward disorganization. Emotional behavior in conflict, such as in fear and anger, is even defined by some psychologists as disorganized behavior. In Figure 5, the degree of organization is highest at the top; it is

lower, in conflict, at the middle portion of the scale; and it is lowest at the bottom, in states of atrophy, disease, and disorganization. Wiener (1948) relates "amount of information" not only to a negative concept of entropy but to a concept of organization.

> The notion of the amount of information attaches itself very naturally to a classical notion in statistical mechanics: that of *entropy.* Just as the amount of information in a system is a measure of its degree of organization, so the entropy of a system is a measure of its degree of disorganization; and the one is simply the negative of the other [p. 18].

If it is true, as it appears to be, that the lowest predictability in statistical mechanics, biology, and psychology is to be found at the highest levels of organization, then the most difficult problems of prediction lie ahead of those psychologists who would study the positive aspects of human behavior: social development. This mathematical and methodological difficulty has already been noted in a number of researches. Two examples will be given. Anderson (1937b, 1939, 1946a) has consistently found that dominative behavior was more reliably *observed and recorded* than integrative behavior. Children, well known to their teachers, were *rated* with high reliability and high validity for dominative behavior (aggression, hostility, conflict), but with much lower reliability and validity for integrative behavior. That is, prediction of conflict and discord was more reliable than prediction of harmony.

Harris, Gough, and Martin (1950) reported similar findings in their study of parent attitudes toward child training practices.

> In reviewing the results—one is impressed with the fact that the negative and less "desirable" aspects of the picture seem to be somewhat better determined. The

authoritarian and rigidity or "fussiness" complexes show a higher degree of interrelationship than do parent-child integration and permissiveness 'attitudes. It is perhaps significant that it was more difficult to locate items which would make satisfactory appraisal of these latter dimensions. The writers are willing to suggest that even though a satisfactory number of items was obtained, the resulting correlation would not be so high as the correlations found between the less socially acceptable attitudes. This phenomenon appears to be an incidental illustration of the fact that less socially acceptable or negative statements in personality or attitude tests make sharper discriminations than do more positively stated or desirable aspects of personality [pp. 179–180].

As psychologists, we should be neither surprised nor dismayed at these findings. They are consistent with and predictable from the theory of probability used in physics and statistical mechanics. The continuum in the theory of probability extends from the virtual "dead certainty" at the state of relatively complete degradation of matter, equilibrium, at the one extreme, to the relatively improbable prediction of the emergence of an original at the highest theoretical integration or organization of matter, at infinity (one chance in infinity), in the "Open System." Learning, at the higher levels, thus becomes the emergence of an original, and social development is a psychology of invention.

There is reason to believe that our present methods and concepts in psychological research are still relatively static and but crudely adaptable for prediction in the dynamic problems of social learning and human interrelating. Since there is a chapter "Methods of Child Psychology" (J. E. Anderson, Chapter 1), the implications of entropy and the theory of probabilities for psychological research methodology and

prediction in social development are mentioned here only in passing.

Levels of Dynamic Human Interacting

The scales represented in "Life: The Open System," Figure 5, can now be subdivided into differentiable levels of human interacting. The six levels presented in Figure 6 have been adapted from H. H. Anderson (1951). The number of levels could be increased or diminished. As research and observation become more refined the number will probably be increased, an increase being in the expected (predictable) direction of further scientific differentiation. The six levels proposed here are related to each other on a continuous scale of dynamic interplay which decreases as domination increases. They therefore offer practical utility in presenting research reports that bear on social development. Brief comments on selected relevant research will follow a description of these levels.

It will be noticed that in Figure 6, as in Figure 5, there is a vertical dimension downward on the left-hand side of the diagram. This dimension is marked with a negative sign (−), because direction on this dimension is toward disintegration, disorganization, and degradation of energy, all proportionately related to environmental domination.

Similarly, there is a vertical dimension upward on the right-hand side of the diagram. This dimension is marked with a positive sign (+), because direction upward in Figure 6 represents an increase in differentiation, organization, integration, communication, understanding, learning, invention, action, social development, growth, all of which in theory are inversely related to environmental domination.

1. *Socially Integrative Behavior.* The first, or top, level in Figure 6 is called

"Socially integrative behavior." Socially integrative behavior is possible in a relationship in which individuals may come closer and closer together in their understandings and in their actions and still remain different. This is obviously an ideal relationship; for purposes of growth, differentiation can be at its highest where a person is accepted as he is.

radation of his energy) for granted. He continues to like his friends; he continues to enjoy their associations; he bears no hostility for the minor inconveniences. He continues to show high spontaneity in his own behavior and to accept a high degree of spontaneity in theirs. Such a relationship is *socially integrative*. It is basically a *working together;* the use of one's own

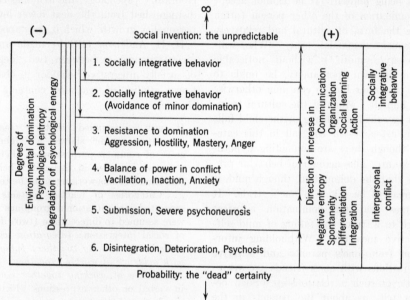

FIGURE 6. Levels of dynamic human interaction.

There is no perfect harmony in human relations. Perfect harmony would require perfect understanding of the desires and purposes of others, as well as of one's self. Since each person cannot be too articulate about his own needs, it would be expecting too much of others to have a perfect understanding of him. At the highest stage of harmony in human relations each person causes some inconvenience to those about him; each person finds his own spontaneity somewhat restricted by the well-meaning behavior of others. Each takes a considerable amount of such inconvenience (deg-

power with others. Each can reveal himself to others and not feel a need to be self-protective. Because each can be essentially himself, each can achieve a high level of communication with and understanding of others. This is not "adjustment"; this is "creative experience" (Follett, 1924), social learning.

In this relationship it is meaningless to speak of conflict, aggression, attack, hostility, fear, or defense mechanisms. Although the socially integrative relationship is an ideal, an increasing number of research studies show that a considerable amount of human behavior can be properly classified at this level.

2. *Socially Integrative Behavior, Avoidance of Minor Domination.* Figure 6 postulates two levels of socially integrative behavior. It happens at one time or another for most persons that one is obliged to live in some proximity to another and finds the other an obstruction to his spontaneity, to his being himself. If he cannot accept the domination of the other person (often taking the form of cultural and relatively impersonal demands: the "What-will-people-say!" motif [1]) without noticeable loss of his own spontaneity, he tends to avoid the other but to continue otherwise to be himself. Much of the cultural training or so-called socializing of the child falls in this category—or *can* fall in this category, though there are conflicting hypotheses extant. This manner of behavior presumes that the domination, though mild, is too great to be taken in one's stride. It presumes that the domination is great enough to warrant the taking of mild self-protective measures. Withholding information from one's parents and selective conversations with one's friends are symptomatic of such a relationship. Such behavior tells us about the persons in the environment as well as about the individual himself.

In these two highest levels of growth in which there are responses to mild domination, the infringement on one's own spontaneity is not great enough to be classified as frustration and to call forth resistance to the other person or to deflect one's energies from his own essential purposes. Behavior still reflects socially integrative relationships. But where one perceives his situation to be such that it seems desirable

1 The theme of such milder degradations of energy that do not really deflect one from his essential purpose was quite effectively set to music in the song "People will say we're in love" in *Oklahoma.*

to withhold information or to be protectively selective in ideas, there is reduced interplay of communication and therefore less understanding. Where such behavior is found, however, it is not meaningful to say that the persons are in conflict; they are not expending energies in opposition to each other. By an adaptation of the concept of just-noticeable differences used in laboratory psychology, the *avoiding* can be distinguished from the next lower level of personality growth, which is resistance.

H. H. Anderson (1946*b*) made an empirical distinction between two "degrees" of socially integrative behavior in observational studies of teachers' contacts with children.

It was . . . assumed that a teacher's integrative contact showed a "higher degree" of common purpose when there was objective evidence in the child's behavior that the child was working with the teacher. . . . Categories of teacher contacts were separated into situational groupings which were assumed to differentiate (two) degrees of social integration: *Integration with no evidence of working together; Integration with evidence of working together.*

Evidence of *working together* consisted in verbal or other expressions which indicated that both teacher and child were pursuing the same goal or were trying to find a common purpose without the *imposition* of goals, desires, or ideas of the one on the other. Thus, in recording the teacher's behavior, this evidence could appear only when the teacher attempted to cooperate with the child in an activity in which he was already engaged or when the child had already given indication that he voluntarily or spontaneously accepted the teacher's ideas or goals as his own. The "acceptance" of the teacher's goals or problems does not include obedience nor conforming under duress [pp. 15–16].

This differentiation of two situational "degrees" of integrative relating was used by J. E. Brewer (1940, 1946) and was subsequently reported by H. H. Anderson (1943, 1946c), Clifton (1943), Reed (1946), and H. H. Anderson and J. E. Brewer (1946). In these studies the data for the two degrees of integrative contacts were reported separately, and their implications for social development were interpreted according to a set of hypotheses. The details of the findings will not be reviewed here.

For the remainder of this chapter these two levels of socially integrative behavior are combined, and no further distinction is made unless explicitly noted. Under socially integrative behavior reports are classified all studies in which the degradation of energy, domination, is at a minimum. Examples are studies of democratic relations in the home, responsibility, rapport, altruism, leadership, sympathy, empathy, needs for affection, cooperation, and friendliness. Studies of group behavior of children in "climates" of democratic leadership are properly classified at this level of relating, but are reviewed by Lewin, Chapter 15. Likewise, studies involving the positive emotions would be classified here, but are reviewed by Jersild, Chapter 14. The test for classifying behavior, or a concept of behavior, at the socially integrative level is that psychological entropy be low, negative entropy high. Fromm's (1947) criterion—and it is a good criterion—would be that "productivity" be high.

3. *Resistance to Domination.* Of the vast proliferation of studies in social development and related areas, by far the greatest number would be classified at this third level of human interrelating (Koshuk, 1941). In these studies the environmental domination—authoritarian restrictions of the parents, the family, and of the complex assortment of cultural institutions—has increased to a point where the concepts of frustration and conflict take on meaning.

Moreover, the individual victim of this domination has sufficient spontaneity to attempt to do something about it himself. He uses his *power against* others.

One tends to resist environmental press or domination when it increases to the extent that it actively interferes with the attainment of one's goals and purposes. This is the meaning of the first part of the frustration-aggression proposition "that the occurrence of aggressive behavior always presupposes the existence of frustration" (Dollard, Doob, Miller, Mowrer, Sears, *et al.*, 1939, p. 1).

Thus this level could be given one or more accessory titles: frustration, aggression, hostility, negativism, mastery, anger, ascendance, dominance. These behaviors and relationships are classified at this third level.

It should be noted that these resistant forms of relating are characterized by a relatively high degree of spontaneity and action. Because of the defensive nature of the relating, the spontaneity and the action are at a lower level than is found in the less restricted interplay of socially integrative behavior. Below the level of resistance, both action and spontaneity are conspicuously lowered. When one is uncertain about the strength of his adversary or when one is certain that it is not safe to resist, the response to frustration may take any one or a combination of the forms of the Freudian defense mechanisms and find a lower level of energy output and action in projection, rationalization, aggressive fantasy, displacement, or other inadequate and unproductive symptoms.

In part because resistant behavior is high in action, but more probably because of its nuisance value to other persons, it is more easily observed, more reliably recorded, and therefore more easily and more frequently studied by psychologists.

4. *Balance of Power in Conflict.* When domination increases still further it reaches a theoretical relationship in which strength of the domination equals the ability of the person to resist. This is not represented by a point on any scale; the power relationship oscillates up and down according to the changes in one's perception of the strength and source of attack and one's estimation of his own resources. This is the *balance of power in conflict.*

Balance of power, whether used as a concept in understanding personality, or in interpreting international diplomacy, has meaning only in relations of conflict, in relations in which *energy is being expended against* others. Balance of power is meaningless in relations where either persons or nations are *working with* each other through socially integrative behavior. At the level of balance of power a person's perceptions tend to become noticeably distorted. He is confused as to the source of the domination, as to its strength, or both. From his perception of his relation to the world about him he cannot know whether to attack (and what to attack) or to run (and where to run). In children we call the hesitant, faltering, indecisive behavior at this level "excessive shyness" or anxiety. In students it is worry and nervousness. It represents a distinguishably greater degree of degradation of psychological energy than does aggression or resistance.

Anger, aggression, hostility, resistance represents a response to a relatively highly differentiated (well-perceived) source of attack or fear. When the fear stimulus, that is, the source and the strength of attack, is undifferentiated, the person is said to be in a state of anxiety or vacillation. At this fourth level, and continuing into the fifth and sixth, clarity of perception, communication, and action are all greatly reduced. A shy child cannot say why he is shy, nor can a student give a reason why

he cannot study or concentrate. The source of anxiety is often a principal diagnostic problem. Some behavior at this level is regarded as neurotic and is scarcely distinguishable from submission. In the behavior of mice and men it may be "behavior without a goal" (Maier, 1949), or behavior in which the means for attaining the goal is vague or unperceived.

5. *Submission, Severe Psychoneurosis.* A still lower level of personality growth is found in expressions of submission to environmental press. Because of high necessity for conformity and obedience, and the consequently low level of action, behavior at this level, as mentioned above, is often scarcely distinguishable from that at the level of *balance of power.* In vacillation at the balance of power there tends to be more spontaneity, more fluctuating moments of aggression when the person confronts his environment, even though he then retreats. In submission there is frustration and tension.

Psychoneurosis is not a clearly defined diagnostic entity. "Psychoneurosis" is found at all four levels of interpersonal conflict (Figure 6). Much psychoneurotic behavior is found under extreme environmental domination. In therapy such patients, with increasing insight and clarified perceptions, usually move up the scale through these levels of relating before they achieve a socially integrative relationship. No attempt will be made to review the increasing volume of diagnostic and therapeutic studies and clinical case reports of human behavior at this level of relating.

6. *Disintegration, Deterioration, Psychosis.* A person who has retreated from reality into one of the several classifications of psychosis is an example of severe degradation of energy. There is so little confronting that he is even said to be "out of contact" with reality. There is often no discernible communication. It is to

this extent meaningless at this level to speak of learning, or of differentiation, integration, or social development. This is the behavior that is found in cases of pathological fears, in persons who have lived in a tremendously oppressive environment. Here are found persons whose perceptions, if communicated at all, are grossly distorted, even delusional. It is not our purpose here to attempt a classification of personality disorders and mental disease, nor to classify at any of these relationship levels persons with organic difficulties. Some of the problems of children at these two lowest levels of social interaction are discussed in Benda's Chapter 18.

Circular Behavior

The Concept of Circular Behavior. The concept of circular behavior is not new. It is found in Shakespeare and in the New Testament. The behavior itself is within us and all about us. Yet circular behavior, as a term, is found in the index of very few books on psychology. Follett (1924) is the first, according to the writers' knowledge, to have extended the concept of circular behavior as a psychological concept to the interaction of human beings.

The Growth Circle. Through the confronting of differences and the free interplay of differences shown in open-minded discussion, Follett observed the solutions to problems which she, as mediator of labor disputes, thought could not have been devised without the participation of all parties to the dispute. Problem solving in social conflict, for Follett, was not a psychology of adjustment, but a psychology of invention. *Creative Experience,* the title of her book, was the outcome of a circular process of interacting, of the interweaving of experiences. The emergence of originals represented an integration of differences. The free interaction of minds in disagreement was creative. It was not a sequence of stimulus-response behaviors, but a process; the response was not just to a stimulus, but a response to a relating. This circular behavior was creative, inventive; it was a growth circle:

any psychology of integration, of whatever school, shows us that kind of relation which creates. The psychology of the specific response did not give us the creating relation; the doctrine of circular response involved in the theory of integration gives us creative experience [p. 116].

This appears to be the essence of a dynamic psychology. This is circular behavior in the direction of growth. This is the productive release of energy. The hypothesis of the growth circle is: *integrative behavior in one person tends to induce integrative behavior in others.*

The Vicious Circle. Follett found another kind of circular behavior in persons who could not integrate their activities in a creative direction. This behavior was domination, the use of *power over* others instead of, as in integration, the use of *power with* others. The hypothesis of the vicious circle is: *domination in one person tends to incite domination in others.*

It has been explained above that the situations of life (psychological fields) which constitute the areas of psychological interaction research are not discretely arranged according to the levels of relating diagrammed in Figure 6. One may find himself generally at one level, or he may find both expected and unexpected shifts from one level to another. It is usually possible to find examples of both kinds of circular behavior in any given social situation.

In Figure 6 the *growth circle* behavior is classified at the level of "Socially integrative behavior." The *vicious circle* behavior represents conflict and is placed at the level of "Resistance." When domination becomes so great that human interaction is largely suspended (as in the "Balance of power") or suppressed (as in "Submission") it is classified below the level of "Resistance" in Figure 6. When interaction is so reduced as to place the relating at one of the three lowest levels of Figure 6 it is not meaningful to speak of circular behavior.

The growth circle relationship, the use of socially integrative behavior in the family, school, industry, or anywhere, is a means of "cutting the vicious circle." The use of *rapport* in the clinical situation (G. L. Anderson, 1951) is a means of cutting the vicious circle. Similarly, psychotherapy, which is basically a socially integrative relationship, is also a means of cutting the vicious circle. Consistent with the emphasis placed in psychology upon negative concepts and on things that disturb us, there are many more references in the psychological literature to the vicious circle than to the growth circle.

Circular Behavior in Research. That domination incites domination was a hypothesis consistent with the interpretation that Wickman (1928) gave to some of the data in his study of teachers' attitudes toward children's behavior. Wickman reported that teachers "met aggression with aggression." Wickman's research was not a study of behavior but of attitudes toward behavior.

Observational Studies, Children. In 1935 H. H. Anderson (1937a, 1937b) undertook a study to determine whether dominative and integrative behavior of preschool children could be defined in such a way as to be reliably observed and recorded, and, if so, to test the hypotheses about circular behavior in the recorded behavior of preschool children.

The method was observational (see page 1205 below). The data were recorded items of behavior. The subjects were pre-school children. Two groups lived in an orphanage and constituted a nursery school and a control group of non-nursery school children. Children were taken in pairs to an experimental playroom where they were permitted to play for 5 minutes by themselves, their behavior being observed by the experimenters through a one-way-vision screen.

Each nursery school child was paired at random with five nursery school children from which pairings each child obtained a frequency score for dominative behavior and a frequency score for integrative behavior. The same was true for each control group child. In addition, each nursery school child was paired with five control group children. From these cross pairings, each child received frequency scores for dominative and for integrative behavior.

The Vicious Circle. It was found that the nursery school children in the orphanage were more dominating than were the control group children. In the cross pairings, however, the high domination scores of the nursery school children decreased and the lower domination scores of the control group increased—so much so, that in the cross pairings the domination scores of the nursery school children were actually lower than those of the control group.

Girls in the orphanage were not only more dominating than the boys but almost twice as dominating when paired with girls as they were when paired with boys. In both cases the differences were significant. Boys, on the other hand, became about 25 per cent more dominating when paired with girls than they were when paired with boys. In the cross pairings of the sexes the boys rose to a domination score higher than that of the girls.

Moreover, the correlation between the high domination scores and low domination scores in 513 pairings yielded a coefficient of .68.

As reported above, three different analyses of the data gave consistent support to the hypothesis that *domination incites domination:* (1) the cross pairings of the nursery school and control group children, (2) the cross pairings of the boys and girls, and (3) the correlation of .68 for domination scores in the pairings.

The Growth Circle. Analyses were made of integration scores. In the comparison of the homogeneous and cross pairings of orphanage nursery school and control groups none of the differences between mean integration scores was significant. Nevertheless, the dynamic tendencies, though smaller than for domination, were consistent. The higher integrative group, when cross paired, reduced its mean integration scores, and the lower integration group, when cross paired, showed an increase.

In the sex comparisons of integrative behavior there were no differences between boys and girls.

The coefficient of correlation between high integration scores and low integration scores in 514 pairings was .82.

Thus, two separate analyses of the data were consistent with the hypothesis that *integration in one child induces integration in the companion.*

Furthermore, *domination and integration were shown to be psychologically different* and, in this experimental situation, dynamically unrelated. When domination was correlated with integration the coefficients were both low, though negative in sign: −.07 for the child's own scores, −.10 for the domination and integration of the respective companions. These coefficients were based on 1030 pairings.

Two years later the methods of this same study were repeated (H. H. Anderson, 1939) with kindergarten children from quite different socio-economic backgrounds.

This study gave consistent support to the hypotheses of the growth circle and the vicious circle.

With the kindergarten children the boys were more dominating than the girls. But even with this sex reversal (of the previous findings with orphanage children) in the cross pairings of kindergarten boys and girls the high mean domination score of the boys dropped and the low mean domination score of the girls increased, the differences in both cases approaching statistical reliability.

On the basis of differences which they reported to be unreliable but to show a high internal consistency, Muste and Sharpe (1947) reported the same circular trend of aggression in the cross pairings of boys and girls:

> boys are more aggressive when paired with boys and less aggressive when paired with girls. While girls are more aggressive when paired with boys than when paired with girls . . . the sex differences are shown to be consistent in (the two) different schools [p. 22].

Correlations from H. H. Anderson (1939) related to the hypotheses of two kinds of circular behavior are given in Tables 1 and 2. They support the hypotheses consistently and significantly.

One other bit of evidence in this study, whose bearing on circular behavior was not pointed out in the original report, is the relation between the teacher's contacts with the child in the schoolroom and the child's

TABLE 1

CHILD'S DOMINATION CORRELATED WITH
COMPANION'S DOMINATION SCORES

Subjects	Number	r
School X	63	.85 ± .02
School Y	24	.82 ± .05
Preschool (previously reported)	513	.68 ± .02

TABLE 2

CHILD'S INTEGRATION CORRELATED WITH
COMPANION'S INTEGRATION SCORES

Subjects	Number	r
School X	63	.65 ± .05
School Y	24	.72 ± .07
Preschool (previously reported)	514	.82 ± .01

behavior with a companion in the experimental play situation. The teachers had much higher frequencies of dominative than of integrative contacts with the children. On the basis of low but positive and reliable coefficients of correlation there was some tendency for the child who was most dominated in the schoolroom to be most dominating of his companion in the experimental play situation (H. H. Anderson, 1939, p. 375).

Observational Studies, Children and Adults. H. M. Brewer (H. M. Brewer and H. H. Anderson, 1945) undertook an investigation whose purpose was, in part, to study the nature and degree of relationship between the children's behavior and the teacher's dominative and socially integrative contacts. Her subjects were 32 children in a kindergarten taught by a head teacher and an assistant.

The positive coefficient of .57 between teacher's domination initiated by the teacher and teacher's domination initiated by the child indicated that those children who tended to receive highest frequencies of teacher-initiated domination tended to be highest in encountering domination when they themselves approached the teacher.

When the total *domination* initiated by the teacher was correlated with *integrative* contacts initiated by the teacher, the coefficient of .21 indicated virtually a zero relationship.

The systematic behavior pattern of the teachers shown by the coefficients of .57 and .21 would contribute no "solution" to personality problems of the children. The failure to use integrative behavior in a systematic way with those children who have been more dominated (by the teacher) than others, would mean that the teacher was failing to "cut the vicious circle" of domination and resistance. The teachers would thus be failing to use systematically the most effective technique for giving the misbehaving children status in the room and making them feel that they belonged, and that they had a part to play and a contribution to make. This interpretation was supported consistently in the correlations between the teachers' contacts and the children's behavior.

By way of summary, it was reported

that these kindergarten teachers had higher mean frequencies of dominative than integrative contacts; that, among the contacts initiated by the teacher, two out of three were dominative; that, on the other hand, among teacher contacts which resulted from the child's initiative six out of seven were integrative. It was revealed, however, that these teachers were meeting aggression with aggression; that they were systematically inciting resistance and not systematically cutting the vicious circle [p. 156].

J. E. Brewer (1940, 1946), with revised and improved observational methods, made records of the behavior of teachers and children in two second grade rooms in the same elementary school building. There was no systematic factor in selecting the children for one room or the other: the children had been assigned by lot in the first grade and had been promoted as rooms. One teacher was found to be consistently more integrative (democratic) and less dominative; the other was consistently more dominative (authoritarian). The differences were large and statistically reliable.

The children with the more integrative teacher showed significantly higher frequencies of behavior in a number of categories representing spontaneity and initiative and in twelve categories of social contributions to others. All these were consistent with the hypothesis that *integration in the teacher induces integrative behavior in the child.*

The children with the more dominating teacher showed significantly higher frequencies of behavior defined as non-conforming to teacher domination, which supported directly the hypothesis that *domination incites resistance.* In addition, J. E. Brewer found that the children with the more dominating teacher had significantly higher frequencies recorded as conforming, looking up at seat work, "undetermined" child-child contacts (including whispering), and playing with "foreign objects," most of which represent the degradation of energy in the schoolroom. These data supported a quite logical and legitimate extension of the hypothesis that domination incites resistance.

If it is a pedagogical objective for a teacher to reduce the conflict and increase the harmony in her schoolroom, then the study showed that teacher 2D was defeating her own purpose. Both the analysis of data for mean frequencies and the correlations between teacher contacts and child behavior showed that the more dominating teacher, 2D, was not cutting the vicious circle. Her domination maintained the conflict, at the same time stifling the initiative and spontaneity of the children. And her infrequent integrative contacts were unsystematically used and ineffective [J. E. Brewer, 1946, p. 125].

Reed (1946) used the methods of J. E. Brewer in a follow-up study. Reed's subjects were Brewer's two rooms of children 1 year later with new teachers in the third grade, and the same two second grade

teachers 1 year later with new groups of children. Teachers and rooms were designated, 2C, 2D, 3C, and 3D. Teacher 2C was the more integrative, and teacher 2D the more dominative.

Reed found virtually the same differences between the second grade teachers and practically the same differences in the behavior of the new rooms of second grade children. She found a trend of fairly high correlations in the behavior of the second grade teachers from year to year. On the contrary she found practically a zero relationship between the behavior of the children in the second grade and that of the same children 1 year later with different teachers in the third grade. Her conclusion was that there was a tendency toward constancy in the behavior trends of the adults, and great flexibility and responsiveness in the children. These findings have some bearing on the difficult problem of "causation" in a dynamic field of interrelating.

> Coefficients show that the teacher did not take direct issue with those children by meeting the child's aggression toward other children with aggression toward the child himself. Here again teacher 2C was cutting the vicious circle [p. 82].

Of teacher 2D, Reed reported:

> Teacher 2D had no reliable coefficients of correlation between *domination in conflict* and any other type of teacher contact. . . . *Domination in conflict* had no reliable negative coefficients of correlation with any category of child behavior. It had reliable positive relations with N, *dominates other children,* and M, *nonconforming.* This follows out the assumption that domination produces domination or resistance [pp. 91–92].

Reed presented other data to show the existence of the vicious circle and several kinds of evidence that one teacher was cutting the vicious circle; the other teacher was not.

In still another study H. H. Anderson and J. E. Brewer (1946) discussed in even more detail the cautions necessary in interpreting a circular or antecedent relation in coefficients of correlation. They made consecutive studies from fall to winter to see what changes in psychological interplay might be found after the teachers had been with their children approximately 5 months. They reported in summary that in *group contacts* there was no evidence that either teacher was reducing conflict in the room by "cutting the vicious circle" of domination. The report for teachers' *contacts with individual children* was somewhat different:

> Coefficients of correlation showed that in both the fall and winter samplings teacher C was, through her individual contacts, "cutting the vicious circle" of domination; while in both fall and winter samplings teacher D was not. In respect to the child behavior *dominating other children* neither teacher was doing anything systematically to reduce the conflict by *working with* those children who were most in conflict with each other [p. 151].

The studies cited above involved both an experimental free play situation and group behavior of children and teachers in their natural habitat: the schoolroom.

Another type of approach to group behavior is the series of studies of autocracy and democracy in experimentally induced social "climates." Although these studies are reviewed in Chapter 15, they are mentioned here for their evidence on circular behavior. These studies, first reported in a preliminary note by Lewin and Lippitt (1938), followed by Lewin, Lippitt, and White (1939), Lippitt (1939, 1940), were summarized by Lippitt and White (1943).

The "democratic climate" is the productive relation of socially integrative behavior which in the group is circular and self-renewing. There is mutual acceptance of each other and a *working with* each other. One quotation from Lippitt and White (1943) gives some of the characteristics of their concept of morale, which, in turn, is primarily a characteristic of the democratic relationship:

> the somewhat vague term "morale" will be used with a single and relatively definite meaning: it will mean *spontaneous cohesion* in a group. "Cohesion" here means "hanging together" in every respect . . . working together for common goals, thinking in terms of "we" rather than "I," showing friendliness rather than hostility toward other group members, etc. "Spontaneous" here means that the cohesion is a result of attitudes which the group feels to be its own rather than induced by the leader and dependent upon his continued physical or psychological presence in the group.
>
> If this definition is adopted, it can be seen without hesitation that morale was decidedly higher in our democratic groups than in our laissez-faire groups, or in either type of reaction to autocracy [p. 499].

It appears that in the "laissez-faire" climate there was also a considerable amount of domination which produced frustration which, in turn, was interpreted (Lippitt and White, 1943) as a considerable source of "group disruption" and was called by them a vicious circle:

> The vicious circle of frustration-aggression-frustration. . . . In the running accounts of the laissez-faire meetings there was evident a vicious circle involving frustration which led to aggression, and aggression which led, in turn, to mutual frustration. Both the psychological tension which resulted from frustration and the idleness which resulted from the absence of any organized, constructive group activity were apparently conducive to a large amount of

more or less good-natured bickering and competitive horseplay. This aggression, then, tended to "frustrate" the persons who were attacked, especially if these persons were sincerely attempting to start some constructive work. Thus, the work-minded boys who wanted to exercise their "freedom" to do constructive work found it almost impossible to do so. Mutual interference proved to be a highly effective disrupting force [p. 503].

The operation of the vicious circle was also reported by Bishop (1951) in her observational study of "Mother-Child Interaction and the Social Behavior of Children." Bishop suggested the operation of a "circular causation" in her data and pointed out cautions in interpreting causation. Her findings are interpreted in relation to both the vicious circle and the growth circle.

Specific control on the part of the mother showed positive correlations with the same behavior pattern in the child and with the various measures of child resistance and non-cooperation. . . . These data would seem to indicate that those mothers who tended to show a fairly high degree of specificity of control over their children had children who similarly tended to be specific in their control over the mother and who also tended to be resistant and non-cooperative.

For the growth circle:

Conversely, a positive correlation existed between suggesting and structurizing behavior by the mother and the various measures of wholehearted cooperation, together with the use of the suggesting types of behavior by the child. . . . It would appear that those mothers who employ less forcible types of control are less likely to instigate non-cooperation and aggressive behavior in their children. The child whose individuality, opinions, and abilities are recognized whenever possible may feel less necessity for asserting his independence

in negative responses. There is also an indication that the child reflects in his own behavior the type of control which his mother has used in guiding his behavior [pp. 19–20].

The studies reported above represent recorded observations of actual behavior. Other studies report circular behavior based on attitudes, symbolism, fantasy, and ratings of behavior.

Circular Behavior in Symbolism, Fantasy, and Ratings. Hollenberg and Sperry (1951) studied antecedents of aggression and effects of frustration in the doll play of nursery school children. The antecedents were ratings of frustration and punishment for aggression at home made by intensive interviews with mothers. They reported: "1. Children who are severely frustrated by their mothers at home tend to be more aggressive in doll play than children who are mildly frustrated." They pointed out that their numbers were small, that the findings were in the predicted direction, but that the differences were not statistically reliable. "2. Children who are highly punished for aggression at home tend to be *more* aggressive in doll play than children who are mildly punished" (p. 43). The differences were in the consistent direction, but again not significant.

At the second grade level, H. A. Grace and Lohmann (1952) used incomplete stories involving parent-child conflict in the home. The outcome of the stories was scored according to four categories in a priority rank, and with the indicated percentages of total outcomes. Since emo-

	Per Cent of Outcomes
1. Emotional outburst, physical or verbal attack on parent, or threat to withdraw affection	12.7
2. Constructive	21.5
3. Active opposition	41.9
4. Simple compliance	23.8

tional outbursts and active opposition were both defined in terms of resistance to frustration, or to domination, the findings showed the sum of the percentages for these first and third categories to be 54.6 per cent responding according to the hypothesis of the vicious circle. It should be noted that one might draw the inference that those children showing constructive outcomes (21.5 per cent) had the pattern of "cutting the vicious circle." The remainder, 23.8 per cent, would be classified as showing a pattern of submissive relationships in parent-child conflict.

Graham, Charwat, Honig, and Weltz (1951) investigated aggression as a function of the attack and the attacker. They utilized 50 incomplete statements which indicated the nature (5 kinds) of an aggressive act and the individual (parent, authority, sibling, friend, inferior) who had committed it. The 106 adolescent subjects completed the statements according to what they thought an individual who had been attacked in this way would do. The responses were scored in two categories, as aggressive or non-aggressive, and according to the degree of aggressiveness shown. Only the aggressive responses were reported. The authors found that both the frequency of the aggressive responses and the degree of aggressiveness were a direct function of the degree of aggressiveness with which the attack had been made. They pointed out the similarity between the findings of their paper-and-pencil study and a laboratory study by McClelland and Apicella (1945) in which the strength of aggression seemed to depend on the degree of blocking. That is, the number of aggressive responses increased significantly when the examiner during a frustration procedure increased the intensity of derogatory remarks made to the subject.

With quite a different medium Child, Potter, and Levine (1946) studied stories in children's textbooks in relation to personality development. They reported that the treatment of dominant behavior was such as to teach children that in order to influence the behavior of those around him it is more useful to be helpful than to be aggressive. This would be the growth circle kind of relating. But in situations of aggression the stories in these books did not teach the integrative, problem-solving relationships. The teaching was more at the level of ambiguous, ambivalent, indecisive relations or evasions of the problem.

An extensive series of investigations of the effects of parental behavior on the social development of children has combined the Fels Parent Behavior Rating Scales (Champney, 1941a, 1941b) and a rating scale of children's actual behavior as observed in the nursery school or school situation (Baldwin, 1946, 1947, 1948, 1949). By a "syndrome analysis" of the behavior rating scales, three fundamental and several minor syndromes of parental behavior were revealed by Baldwin, Kalhorn, and Breese (1945). The three most important syndromes were democracy, indulgence, and acceptance.

Baldwin (1949) reported that democracy in the home was by far the most important of the three factors in accounting for the variability of the nursery school behavior. The variables reflected three sorts of consequences of democracy: (1) higher rating on active, socially outgoing behavior, "the hostile and domineering kinds of activity as well as the friendly kinds"; (2) children in a favored position in their groups, "aggression and bossing are on the whole successful, and they are not likely to have inferior status in the group"; (3) high rating on activities demanding intellectual curiosity, originality, constructiveness. These findings, except for the high rating on hostile and domineering behavior and successful bossing, are consistent with the expectations of the outcome of a democratic or socially integrative home atmosphere. If one assumes, as we do, that spontaneity is innate, while harmony must be learned, this inconsistency can be accounted for by a "time lag" in learning to behave harmoniously. In fact, Baldwin, Kalhorn, and Breese (1945) found that the children from democratic homes had actually made up for the time lag:

> By the time the child from the *democratic* home has become of school age his social development has progressed markedly. He is popular and a leader, not so much because he is aggressive and dominant as because he is bright enough to have ideas and is friendly and good natured. Throughout all of his development the child from the *democratic* home seems emotionally secure, serene, and unexcitable. He has a close attachment to his parents and is able to adjust well to his teacher [p. 69].

The effects of indulgence were found to be generally opposite to those of democracy, and the children from the rejecting homes appeared to demonstrate the expected outcomes of the vicious circle relationships.

> The actively and repressively rejected children are marked throughout their development by a highly emotional non-conformist attitude. They rebel against the pressures and restrictions of their environment. Intellectually they are average but their use of their intellectual abilities is below par in terms of originality and creativity [p. 70].

Baldwin, Kalhorn, and Breese (1949) produced a detailed manual for the use of the Fels Parent Behavior Rating Scales, together with data on the reliability of the scale when used by trained raters. Roff (1949) published a factorial study of the intercorrelations of the thirty original rating variables from which he extracted seven factors.

Other Applications of the Concept of Circular Behavior. In the psychological literature one finds other references—rather casual references, for the most part —to circular behavior as such, again with more examples of the vicious circle. Writers have referred to the circular nature of punishment: that it tends to incite resistance or rebellion, or to drive the child into a still lower level of behavior. Healy (1925) noted this in delinquency. Discussing the psychology of the situation he mentioned as an extraordinarily serviceable concept concerning delinquency and delinquents: *"Circular response:* what the delinquent does to society when society does things to him, and, after that, what society does in return, and how he 'gets back' at it" (p. 52).

Referring to punishment, Lewin (1935) said that punishment necessarily created a situation which is an expression of domination inciting resistance. "Thus the threat of punishment creates necessarily a situation in which child and adult stand over against each other as enemies" (p. 142).

That punishment as a form of domination defeats one's purposes with both mice and men is also supported by Maier's (1949) research. If growth, learning, differentiation, integration, invention, problem-solving, or constructive and cooperative behavior are desirable objectives, then domination produces something decidedly less than growth at its optimum. From Maier:

> Constructive and cooperative behavior is characteristic of the individual in a motivated state. This behavior disappears under frustration, a condition in which the individual is likely to become a target for punishment. If it is true that punishment increases frustration, society finds itself in

the position of punishing individuals who have the least chance of benefiting from it; instead, the very condition that should be corrected is aggravated [p. 204].

One must be cautious in generalizing for the behavior of humans from experiments with animals. Nevertheless, in connection with a concept of "pressure of the environment," of domination, and of the numerous instances from the studies above where teachers were found by the use of domination to be "defeating their own purposes," it is not amiss to cite an experimental investigation of punishment by Estes (1944). At the conclusion of his study, in which he used albino rats, Estes discussed "Punishment in the Practical Control of Behavior."

> Probably the most important practical implication of the present study is the demonstration that a response cannot be eliminated from an organism's repertoire more rapidly with the aid of punishment than without it. In fact, severe punishment may have precisely the opposite effect. A response can be permanently weakened only by a sufficient number of unreinforced elicitations and this process of extinction cannot proceed while a response is suppressed as a result of punishment. The punished response continues to exist in the organ's repertoire with most of its original latent strength. While it is suppressed, the response is not only protected from extinction, but it also may become a source of conflict [p. 37].

Dollard, Doob, Miller, Mowrer, and Sears, and their collaborators (1939) rejected Freud's death-instinct hypothesis that aggression is the expression of the death instinct directed outward and stated: "The basic hypothesis which has been presented is that aggression is always a consequence of frustration" (p. 27). While the experiments were made largely with adults, subsequent work has shown their basic hypothesis equally applicable to children.

That this hypothesis was not an old fashioned stimulus-response concept but a dynamic concept of circular behavior was specifically stated: "Obviously this vicious circle—frustration, aggression, interference with aggression, more frustration—tends to be repeated as long as successive acts of aggression suffer interference" (p. 40). For these writers, too, the tendency toward aggression besides being expressed in overt behavior might take several forms such as displacement, or aggression toward "innocent bystanders." Other factors, which they discussed, need to be taken into account such as the strength of aggression, the amount of frustration, whether aggression is directed at the object of the frustration or at others, whether it is vigorous and undisguised or subtle and roundabout. It is not clear that catharsis or tension reduction through aggression constitutes a cutting of the vicious circle, or, as Maier and others might put it, freeing the person from his domination-induced fixation.

Mowrer and Kluckhohn (1944) have since used the concept of domination inciting domination and have called it a vicious circle even when the response represents a displacement on a succeeding generation:

> But because of the harshness with which their own infantile tendencies were subdued, many adults in our culture feel impelled to be equally harsh with their children. . . . Acts which are only a phase of the infant's development and merely part of their exploration of reality are damned as "naughty" and treated as if they were manifestations of innate depravity which must be eliminated at once. A vicious circle is thus set up [p. 93].

Jackson and Todd (1948) used the term "vicious circle" precisely as it has been used above. They even have a chapter entitled "Breaking the Vicious Circle," from which the following quotation is taken:

The child's conflicts, unhappiness, and neurotic attitudes provoke negative, intolerant, or anxious reactions on the part of his immediate environment, with repercussions on a wider scale, spreading in concentric circles as the child becomes older and forms contacts with larger groups of individuals. Early in the process a vicious circle is formed: certain attitudes on the part of the child's environment become established which lead to the aggravation of the child's symptoms, and are, of course, confirmed by this turn of events. The more "difficult" the child grows, the greater becomes the pressure of the environment, and the fewer the prospects of modification in the desired direction. The task of the therapist is to break this vicious circle by producing a change in attitude, first in the child, and then through the child in the parent, or whenever possible, by more direct means, in the parents themselves. Once this has been done, a way is open to possibilities of further development and creative adjustment, until finally a "virtuous" circle has been established and a hopeful, positive atmosphere replaces the former atmosphere of hopeless resignation or of sullen revolt [p. 38].

Newcomb (1950) used the concept of the vicious circle under the heading "Toward the Reduction of Hostility."

To those interested in the reduction of hostility and conflict among groups, many passages in this chapter may have seemed rather discouraging. We have pointed to circular relationships and vicious circles which may seem to suggest that a relationship of conflict, once begun between two groups, can proceed only from bad to worse. Such, however, is not the fact. There is nothing fatalistic or inevitable about the processes by which hostile attitudes are so often expressed. Such circular processes are not necessarily irreversible. There are forms of interaction which reduce the feeling that an outgroup represents a shared threat, as well as those which increase it [p. 604].

Then, without mentioning specifically that cutting the vicious circle is itself a circular process in the direction of social integration, Newcomb explained what he meant by the phrase "going to the roots of the matter" under the topics: "Reducing Personal Susceptibility to Threat Orientation," "Reducing Barriers to Communication," and "Changing Group Norms through Joint Participation." These activities are in the direction of greater communication, greater understanding, and working together in a newly discovered common purpose.

To the degree that people become involved in some shared interest or in the solution to some common problem, they are perceiving not only the objects of common interest but *also one another* in a common frame of reference. And if this occurs among members of the groups prejudiced against each other, the previous divergent norms which each had attributed to the other tend to give way to the shared norms demanded by the common activity. . . . The one essential condition for this kind of interaction, according to present evidence, is sufficient concern over some common problem among some members of both groups to result in joint participation among them [pp. 614–615].

A point of view expressing somewhat more optimism and confidence in the social value of circular behavior is found in Bowlby (1949). Bowlby discussed the use of the concept of circular behavior in psychiatric and analytic child guidance, extended the principle to family interaction, and, consistent with Bion (1948), Bion and Rickman (1943), and Jaques (1947, 1948, 1950), to interaction in group relations and group psychotherapy in industry: "The vicious circle may be broken at any point, the virtuous circle may be promoted at any point." Jaques called the process "social therapy." Social development has been extended to the community and to industry, and society is now becoming the patient.

A chief ill of society, according to Fromm (1947), continues to be a pervading authoritarianism. But Fromm, too, had an optimistic perspective in which civilization has a chance of saving itself:

> Just as the person who has become sterile and destructive is increasingly paralyzed and caught, as it were, in a *vicious circle*, a person who is aware of his own powers and uses them productively gains in strength, faith, and happiness, and is less and less in danger of being alienated from himself; he has created, as we might say, a "virtuous circle." The experience of joy and happiness is not only, as we have shown, the *result* of productive living but also its *stimulus* [p. 230].

Frank (1951) has reminded us again that we do not even have a language to communicate to each other our ideas about the dynamics of human interacting. Frank sees circular behavior as a positive process of growth through the confronting, communicating, interweaving of differences:

> We need a conception of *trans-actions* which are dynamic circular processes occurring in a field [p. 508].

> Today we are beginning to formulate a dynamic conception of organization which, as in embryology, is in terms of field theory. In field theory what we call "parts" are not to be conceived as separate, independent, randomly self-acting entities. The "parts" are what we have selected for observation within a dynamic organized complex; these so-called "parts" are continually acting, reacting, interacting, *transacting*, by a reciprocal circular process as shown in organic functioning. By their dynamic, circular activity the "parts" create and maintain the "whole" which reciprocally organizes and governs the activities of the "parts" and thereby gives rise to that organized "whole," with its dynamic

circular relations to the environing field. This dynamic circular activity of "parts-whole" in a field is what we call "organization," which is not an entity or a superior power or force or something imposed upon parts in a dominance-submission relationship, but what arises from this circular process of the "whole" and its "parts."

> We cannot pick out one of these "parts" in an organized "whole" and endow it with causal potency as a self-acting agent, forgetting that this "part" and its activity is significant only as a participant in the "whole" which patterns its activity. Thus, in the living organism, every cell, tissue, and organ is engaged in a continuous process of functioning that creates and maintains the intact organism which, in turn, governs what each cell, tissue, and organ does in its specialized functioning, to maintain the living organism as a self-repairing, self-regulating organism [pp. 509–510].

> This circular process, of putting the meaning, the stimulus value if you wish, into situations, into people, and then responding to them in terms of what they mean to that individual, does not involve any mysterious subjective entities or psychic operations. It appears as an extension, a refinement, of the basic processes that have been operating for ages but have reached in man a greater complexity and sensitivity not otherwise observable and operate as highly idiomatic processes [p. 513].

Socially Integrative Behavior

The studies involving socially integrative behavior reported above have been cited for their bearing on the circularity of interaction in the direction of growth. There are other studies which bear on socially integrative behavior, the highest level of social development. Because of their methods or the scope of the specific problem they may contribute less directly to an understanding of circular behavior. Still other publications are attempts to define or refine hypotheses or inferences concerning social development.

Infancy. Many researches have been made in an effort to show the influence of early experiences on later development. On the influence of nursing experience, including breast vs. bottle feeding, length of breast feeding, self-demand vs. scheduled feeding, and weaning, studies have been reported by Levy (1939, 1943), Rogerson and Rogerson (1939), Peterson and Spano (1941), Escalona (1945), Trainham (1945), Aldrich (1947), Kluckhohn (1947), Leighton and Kluckhohn (1947), Moloney (1947), and Klatskin (1952).

Studies of thumb and finger sucking have been reported by Levy (1928, 1934, 1937), Roberts (1944), Davis and Havighurst (1946), Simsarian (1947), and Klackenberg (1949).

Ribble (1938, 1939, 1941, 1943, 1944), Goldfarb (1944, 1945), Spitz and Wolf (1946), and Fischer (1952) have given emphasis to the importance of "mothering." Pinneau (1950), in a special review of Ribble's publications, reported insufficient evidence to support her contentions.

Sphincter control has been a subject of interest to Gorer (1943) and Fries (1946).

Restraint of motion has been studied experimentally by Dennis (1938, 1940) and discussed by Levy (1944) and Greenacre (1944), who have also given summaries of the literature.

Vincent (1951) in a bibliographical survey reported a trend away from dogmatism in infant-care ideas concerning the breast vs. artificial feeding controversy and infant-care disciplines. Senn (1947) edited the proceedings of a conference on the problems of early infancy. The World Federation for Mental Health held a conference on "Mental Health and Infant Behavior" at Chichester, England, reported briefly by Staniland (1952); a fuller report was announced for later publication.

Material from child development and animal studies relating early experience to mental health is found in conference proceedings edited by Scott (1951). Ross (1951) made a study of sucking deprivation in puppies and confirmed the earlier study by Levy (1934). Social behavior in animal infancy has been reviewed by Cruikshank in Chapter 3.

The research and theorizing on the importance of infancy have been critically examined in a scholarly review by Orlansky (1949), whose definite, if negative, conclusions in regard to the effect of certain features of infant care upon personality represent a perceptible trend:

We conclude that the rigidity of character structuring during the first year or two of life has been exaggerated by many authorities, and that the events of childhood and later years are of importance in reinforcing or changing the character structure tentatively formed during infancy. Or one may substitute Horney's (1939, p. 152) formulation: ". . . the sum total of childhood experiences brings about a certain character structure, or rather starts its development. With some persons this development essentially stops at the age of five. With some it stops in adolescence, with others around thirty, with a few it goes on until old age."

In short, it is contended that personality is not the resultant of instinctual infantile libidinal drives mechanically channeled by parental disciplines, but rather that it is a dynamic product of the interaction of a unique organism undergoing maturation and a unique physical and social environment. This view is in substantial agreement with the position which Horney (1939, p. 70) and Fromm (1941, p. 286), among others, have advocated [p. 39].

Emotional Behavior. Since emotional development is reviewed by Jersild in Chapter 14, only a word will be mentioned here concerning its relation to social development.

It is no accident nor oversight that psychologists have failed to report any "neutral" emotional experiences. Emotions have been no "fence straddling" experiences so far as the psychological and organic "welfare" of the individual is concerned: they have been either highly organized, top-level growth experiences, or they have been highly disorganized, disrupting experiences. As we have repeatedly remarked, because of the ease with which one observes calamity in nature and the difficulty in perceiving concord, most of the psychological writings on emotions have dealt with disorganizing experiences.

Bridges (1931) divided the emotions genetically into *delight* and *distress*. Similarly, Thompson (1952) twenty years later discussed "two quite different types of emotional behavior: the *pleasant,* or *integrative,* and the *unpleasant,* or *disintegrative*" (p. 288). Leeper (1948) has outlined a motivational theory of emotions to replace emotion as disorganized response.

It is to be noted that the distinction between *delight* and *distress, pleasant* and *unpleasant, integrative* and *disintegrative* is made precisely at the division on the diagram in Figure 6 between the *growth circle* and the *vicious circle,* and between *socially integrative behavior* and *resistance to domination.* This is the limen where interpersonal conflict becomes meaningful. The consistency which psychologists have shown in these distinctions is a further validation of the arrangement of levels of human interacting shown in Figure 6.

The integrative emotions represent a high level of *working with* the environment in a common purpose, high communication, high security, high spontaneity, high acceptance, high sense of achievement, satisfaction and happiness, high productivity, or approximations of these levels.

Thus, for example, studies in sympathy (Murphy, 1937) and efforts to describe, identify, or measure empathy (Dymond, 1948, 1949, 1950; Cottrell and Dymond, 1950; Kerr and Speroff, 1951; Speroff, 1953) would be classified as studies in psychologically integrative emotions. Hastorf and Bender (1952) have added a word of caution concerning the attempt to measure empathic ability.

Love, in its broadest sense, is not different from socially integrative behavior. It is that socially integrative relationship that has the greatest acceptance, communication, understanding, harmony, interaction, creativity, and the *least* degree of psychological entropy, the *least* degradation of energy. Defined in this way, love of mankind should pervade the earth like the air we breathe,—perhaps *could* pervade the earth in this way. If it did, there would be so much understanding as not to admit a need for special inquiry or interpretation of human behavior by psychologists.

In the past 50 years, however, although much has been written about psychological rejection, no one has prepared a bibliography of studies on "wanted babies." Psychologists have reified the negative. Problem-solving is a "substitute" for anger, and bibliographers are intrigued by "anaclitic depression." Instead of hate being the incapacity to love, love is the absence of hate. In Old Testament theology it was the devil against the angels; in orthodox Freudian theory it is "Love vs. Hate." Love, organization, communication, integration are basic in nature, and everything else, including hate, anger, and the other forms of disorganized interrelating are lesser levels of interaction. In war, conflict, strife, anger, and hate "nobody wins." In love and integrative relating nobody loses.

Popularity, Friendships, and Choice of Companions. Studies of popularity, friendship, and choice of companions represent positive approaches to the study of integrative, harmonious relating. Low scores in these studies usually represent lower spontaneity, lower social communication, lower understanding, lower productivity, lower interacting.

Wellman (1926) made one of the earlier studies of children's choice of companions. Other investigations such as Green's (1933) had the negative approach in a study of quarrels as well as in the study of friendships. Koch (1933) used a paired comparison method to determine degree of acceptability or popularity of preschool children. Lippitt (1941), using methods similar to those of Koch, obtained comparable findings. Social compliance and quick adaptation to the nursery school procedures seemed most highly related to judgments of popularity. These results were confirmed by Northway (1943), which probably indicates a stereotype in nursery school "culture" as much as a constancy in children as such.

Bonney (1943, 1944, 1946, 1947) has used sociometric techniques to discover the socially successful child, his social acceptability, and popularity. Other studies have been reported on friendship fluctuations and social status by Horrocks and Thompson (1946), Thompson and Horrocks (1947), Austin and Thompson (1948), and Horrocks and Buker (1951).

Frenkel-Brunswik and Potashin (1944) reviewed sociometric and pre-sociometric (pre-Moreno, 1934) literature on friendship and social acceptance among children. They presented a bibliography of fifty items on interpersonal relations among children.

Friendliness, Cooperation, and Integrative Behavior. Although psychologists and teachers have shown low reliability and low validity in observing or rating the positive, constructive interactions, kindergarten children, according to Hanfmann (1935), had no difficulty in either their perceptions or their preferences. When asked by the teacher with whom they liked best to play, they were able to distinguish the *objective leader* and the *social leader*, and eight of ten children expressed their preferences for these two "leaders" from the two who dominated them by destructiveness and social isolation. Eight of the ten children expressed their preferences for the two children whose behavior was described by Hanfmann as "taking turns," "joint enterprise," "skill in social relationships," "joint play."

Another comparison between adults and children needs further study. Teachers in the ordinary classroom situation in kindergarten and the elementary school grades were consistently more dominative than integrative in studies by H. H. Anderson (1939, 1946c), H. M. Brewer and H. H. Anderson (1945), J. E. Brewer (1946), Reed (1946), and H. H. Anderson and J. E. Brewer (1946). Clifton (1943) found some exceptions in second grade teachers. Research workers have not found comparable integration-domination or friendliness-unfriendliness ratios in the free play of children. Children are more friendly than unfriendly by our current measures. Mengert (1931), H. H. Anderson (1937a, 1937b, 1939), McFarland (1938), Jersild and Fite (1939) found children definitely higher in integration and friendliness and lower in domination and unfriendliness. Jersild (1947) called attention to this relative incidence of hostile and friendly forms of behavior in children's social relationships. He cited unpublished findings of observations by McKinnon (1940) which showed that for children in a relatively free play school situation friendly comments and contacts outnumbered hostile criticisms and unfriendly contacts in the ratio of about three to one.

Other investigations in which an interest is shown in integrative behavior are illustrated by studies of leadership (Parten, 1932, 1933), altruism (Turner, 1948), the studies mentioned above on democratic climates in homes (Baldwin, Kalhorn, and Breese, 1945, 1949; Baldwin, 1949) and in experimental groups (Lewin, Lippitt, and White, 1939).

Leadership. Leadership is properly a concept that belongs with socially integrative, productive, harmonious human relationships. There is confusion in the definitions of leadership. It would seem that there should be a difference between a person who can elicit the voluntary cooperation of others at a high level of performance and the person who by force or threat or by other means of degradation of psychological energy secures conformity. The concept of leadership would be much simplified and the studies would be more comparable with each other if domination or psychological entropy were eliminated from the qualities of leadership.

Responsibility. Discussing social responsibility as a goal of psychotherapy, Anderson (1946*d*) pointed out that there are two criteria for responsible behavior: spontaneity and harmony, which are the two criteria for growth. Responsibility which is spontaneous from within is often confused with a concept of legal liability which is enforced from without. In responsibility the person himself discovers or helps to define what it takes to live in harmony with others. Responsible behavior is of the very essence of *social learning.* Liability, on the the other hand, covers the behavior of the person for whom harmony in human relations has no meaning. Legal liability is a defined minimum framework of relating within which society has agreed to live harmoniously.

The Vineland Social Maturity Scale (Doll, 1936, 1940) is an instrument designed to assess the child's development in social responsibility for certain developmental tasks which involve others and for regulating the satisfaction of his needs in a way that is harmonious with those about him.

Gough, McClosky, and Meehl (1952) have constructed a personality scale for social responsibility. In their working definition they have included by implication the criteria of both spontaneity and harmony. Responsibility for them is behavior or relating that would be classified as highly integrative.

Social Learning

Since there is a chapter on learning (Munn, Chapter 7), the reader is referred there for general references to learning theory and to such specific application of it as can be made to the life and growth of the child, including his social development. Only brief mention will be made here to a few studies whose findings have some bearing on social learning.

We have said above that responsible behavior is of the very essence of social learning. This follows from the assumption that in personality growth spontaneity is innate while harmony must be learned.

We have discussed a view widely held that the individual cannot be separated from his environment. It is this dynamic process of interacting between the person and his environment that is social learning. Social learning is therefore a function of the environment as well as of the person. The characteristics of the "democratic" home atmospheres reported by Baldwin, Kalhorn, and Breese (1945) and by Baldwin (1949) and the characteristics of certain schoolrooms found by J. E. Brewer (1946) and Reed (1946) represent situations in which the environment facilitated social learning. The various measures of the behavior of the children from these respective home and school situations confirmed the assumption. In a general way these studies have shown situations in which the demands of the environment were reasonably satisfactorily tempered to the needs and capacities of the child. Demands of the environment, school or home routines, were explained and made meaningful in a way that inspired mutual confidence and general working together for common purposes.

Research in an orphanage (H. H. Anderson, 1937b), reported above (also pages 1190–1192), has further bearing on social learning. In the fall of 1934 an experimental nursery school was established in an orphanage. Children were matched for certain criteria and placed in a nursery school and a control group. The control group children continued to spend all day in the cottages, their activities for the most part consisting in sitting on chairs in a circle in the living room "being good." The nursery school children, on the other hand, left the cottages during the day, had plenty of play materials, and were in charge of trained nursery school teachers who encouraged the children to play. After 8 months the two groups of children were observed for dominative and integrative social contacts. No significant differences between groups in integrative contacts were found. In dominative behavior, however, the orphanage nursery school children used significantly more dominative contacts than the control children. How could one explain the findings that nursery school children were more dominating than matched non-nursery school children?

The explanation given was not that the children had "poor" teachers or that the nursery school was a "bad" influence on the children. The explanation was that in total social contacts there was more interaction among the children who had gone 8 months to nursery school than among those who had remained in the cottages all day. The hypothesis was that spontaneity is a "good" thing even if it is expressed in "misbehavior."

If harmony with others must be learned then it seems that children who have been greatly dominated and who are then transferred to a less dominating environment, move up through the levels of relating, illustrated in Figure 6, as a *process of social learning.*

The orphanage nursery school children started at a very low level of spontaneity; they had been very much dominated, and they were tractable and submissive.

The teachers reported that for weeks the nursery school children came each day and simply sat and stared as though they did not believe they *could* play with the toys. After several months the teachers noticed a change. A child would come to the teacher, point to anything, a doorknob, or the plaster wall, and say: "Tell me a story about that." After 8 months in the nursery school the children were found to be more aggressive in a dominating way than their paired companions. The interpretation offered now is that the nursery school children moved from a level of social atrophy and submission, through a process of relating in which they were confused, anxious, indecisive,—where they were not oppressed, but where they behaved as though they did not understand the nature or degree of threat, the balance of *power over* them. As their perceptions increased they became more communicative; their own powers and energies were released, and they became more spontaneous. But they had not had sufficient opportunity (time, experience) to develop perceptual readiness for social learning.

Similar findings have been reported by Lewin, Lippitt, and White (1939). They found a bi-modal distribution of aggression in autocratic groups and asked: "Why is the reaction to autocracy sometimes very aggressive, with much rebellion or persecution of scapegoats and sometimes very non-aggressive?" They offered evidence that both the aggressive and the non-aggressive boys were frustrated.

In terms of the levels of dynamic interplay diagrammed above in Figure 6, the highly aggressive behavior was at the level of "Resistance," the vicious circle. The non-aggressive boys were under stronger domination, greater threat, and were behaving as one would expect at the level of "Balance of Power," or at the still lower level of "Submission."

When these boys were transferred from a highly autocratic group (say, level of "submission") to a democratic group, what happened?

If they behaved like the orphanage nursery school children who were transferred from a highly rejecting to a highly accepting environment, they would show after transfer more spontaneity; they would give some symptoms of anxiety; or their greater spontaneity would take the form of aggression, hostility, disturbance of others.

Lewin, Lippitt, and White reported that there were first of all sudden outbursts of aggression which occurred on the days of transition from a repressed, autocratic atmosphere to a much freer atmosphere of democracy or laissez-faire.

> The boys behaved just as if they had previously been in a state of bottled-up tension, which could not show itself overtly as long as the repressive influence of the autocrat was felt but which burst out unmistakably when that pressure was removed [p. 283].

Baldwin (1949) and Baldwin, Kalhorn, and Breese (1945) found that nursery school children from democratic homes showed the behavior expected at the integrative level, except that they showed hostile and domineering activity as well as the friendly kinds. Is this inconsistency to be explained by unknown environmental circumstances which activate a vicious circle, or as possibly a "time lag" in social learning? By the time that the children were of school age, they had apparently made up the time lag, as quoted previously in this chapter.

Chittenden (1942) undertook to give social training to the most dominative children in a nursery school. Her program was designed to decrease domination and to increase problem-solving and cooperation in social conflicts. On retests after the training program the children showed a significant decrease in dominative behavior although their increase in cooperative behavior was not statistically significant. To the extent of the reduction of dominative behavior, the children were giving significantly fewer reinforcements to the operation of the vicious circle in their interacting with their friends. This may not be a cutting of the vicious circle, but it is a slowing up of the action in the use of *power against* others.

Muste and Sharpe (1947) regarded social learning in small children from a point of view similar to that of teachers who speak of "reading readiness" and similar to that of Tolman (1949) who has spoken of "perceptual readiness" in the learning of animals and in human social learning. Writing on the significance of trends of aggressive behavior with relation to age, Muste and Sharpe said:

> The younger children within the nursery school age range tend to have only brief

contacts with other children, to spend much time in parallel play, and to direct many of their social responses toward adults. Because they are so involved with the interest in sensory experience and independent investigation, there are fewer opportunities for aggressive behavior. As children grow older their exploration is increasingly in the social field. They spend more time in social interchange and their contacts with others are more complex. With the increased vitality of social interchange there is an increase in the frequency of aggression [p. 16].

. . . Many of the aggressive incidents of these young children seem not to have the quality of deliberate attacks upon others. The young child is not able to perceive a situation except from his own point of view and his behavior is initiated by drives toward his own ends. He has his own objectives in mind and seeks to fulfill his own desires or interests, taking no heed of the objectives of others. The inhibition of activities for the satisfaction of one's own need because they may mean discomfort for others requires a higher level of social consciousness and a greater ability to project one's thinking beyond the boundaries of self than many of them have attained. The two children who had the lowest aggression scores also had the lowest scores in social participation [p. 17].

Psychotherapy and Levels of Interacting

There are many different ways of stating the goals of therapy. Our purpose here is merely to indicate the relation of therapy to the levels of human interacting shown above in Figure 6.

A person whose behavior and whose relations with his environment would classify him at the socially integrative level in Figure 6 has no need for a therapist. He already finds life stimulating and satisfying. He is accepted by others, he can "be himself." He is flexible, not rigid. He can learn by new experience. He is free to change. He has a minimum of repressed experiences and lives largely at a conscious level. He occasionally experiences the joy of discovery. His emotions tend to be more on the positive side. Not being threatened or "rejected," he has little use for defense mechanisms. His perceptions, undistorted by personal fears and anxieties, are highly valid. He lives at a high reality level. It must be remembered that all things are relative, that there is no perfection under Heaven except by definition, and that a given person can only approximate the conditions listed above. Persons who approximate even some of these conditions do not need or seek a therapist. It is, in fact, the goal of therapy to achieve these relationships.

Persons who do need a therapist are found in one or the other of the lower growth levels which are grouped under "Interpersonal conflict" in Figure 6. Those who live at the level of "Resistance to domination" still have sufficient spontaneity to be hostile and aggressive. Occasionally one has sufficient spontaneity to seek a therapist. Persons in the lowest level of growth in Figure 6 usually do not seek therapy but are brought by someone else.

In one sense, the task of the therapist is to take a patient at whatever growth level he happens to find him and help the patient move up into a higher level. To do this is therapy. The ultimate goal is to attain the socially integrative relationship. But therapy can be good therapy and still fall short of that goal.

In another sense, it is the task of the therapist to help the patient increase the validity of his perceptions and thus improve his insight. This could be another way of saying that the patient moves from a lower growth level to a higher level. There is some evidence to justify the hypothesis, at least for functional disorders, that the validity of perception is inversely related to the strength of environmental domination. The validity of perception and the quality of insight decrease as psychological entropy increases. Therapy moves the patient away from the state of low interaction into a situation of high negative entropy.

As there are many ways to express the goals of therapy, there are many ways of attaining the same goal. This is consistent with von Bertalanffy's (1950) concept of *equifinality*. As mentioned above, von Bertalanffy has pointed out that in most physical systems the final state of a process is determined by the initial conditions. Growth on the contrary, he said, is equifinal: it is independent of the initial conditions. In this hypothesis of the equifinality of growth lies the hope of the therapist: that therapy can be a speeded-up growth process, and that the client can make up for lost time.

There is some evidence to show that, consistent with the equifinality of growth, a patient starting at the lowest level of growth tends to move through the successive levels of interrelating and into hostility and aggression before he can attain the upper levels of harmony. A plausible explanation for this is that while spontaneity is innate and can only be suppressed or facilitated, harmony must be learned. A person under heavy environmental domination who has submitted to the domination is low in spontaneity. As the therapist helps the patient to become released from his present or past domination (his neurosis or his fixation), the new and growing spontaneity takes the form of behavior apparently without regard for other persons. The patient has up to this moment depended on someone else to make decisions and to do his social thinking for him. He has not *learned* to evaluate by himself the desires and purposes of others.

More important, he has not learned the meaning of the vicious circle which his own new spontaneous behavior can set up. He has not learned that his new spontaneity will meet resistance to the extent that it is out of harmony with others. Patients in therapy often seem to increase in confusion and in causing trouble to others before they can learn how to act spontaneously and at the same time harmoniously.

It is not sufficient to say that therapy is a cutting of the vicious circle. This is a negative statement. Therapy is a positive process; it is a growth process, social development.

Beyond the release of energy in spontaneity, therapy is a process of social learning in an environment propitious for optimum growth. Conflict, by definition, is disintegrating. Therapy is a restoration of integrative processes.

Commenting on a forthcoming volume French (1952) said:

> In a psychoanalytic treatment we try to help a patient find solutions for unresolved conflicts. By studying this process we hope to get a more vivid picture, not only of the disintegrating effect of conflict, but also of the process of restoration of a more normal integrative pattern under favoring circumstances [p. 240].

A Broadening Concept of Social Responsibility and Social Development

Several other kinds of studies are emerging. Barker and Wright (1949, 1951) and Barker, Wright, Nall, and Schoggen (1950) have reported studies of psychological ecology and the problem of psychosocial development. A community approach by an interdisciplinary team studying the *constructive* elements in the community has been described by Bronfenbrenner and Devereux (1952). Projects in which a community or an industrial group studies its own problems and, through group participation, plans action in developing answers represent an enlarging scope of the concepts of social development and social responsibility. Examples of such studies are those reported by Bion and Rickman (1943), Bion (1948), Bowlby (1949), Lippitt (1949), and Jaques (1950). Follett (1922, 1924) presented the theoretical structure and suggestions for a plan of action for such positive approaches to creative, inventive problem-solving in industrial and international relations.

Bibliography

Abt, L. E., and L. Bellak. 1950. *Projective psychology.* New York: Knopf. Pp. xii + 485 + xiv.

Adler, A. 1907. *Organ inferiority.* New York: Moffat Yard.

——. 1909. *The neurotic constitution.* New York: Moffat Yard.

——. 1923. *Practice and theory of individual psychology.* New York: Harcourt, Brace.

Aldrich, C. A. 1947. The advisability of breast feeding. *J. Amer. Med. Assoc., 135,* 915–916.

Alexander, F. 1950. Values and science. *J. Soc. Issues, 6,* 28–32.

Allen, F. H. 1942. *Psychotherapy with children.* New York: Norton.

Allport, G. W. 1928–1929. A test for ascendance-submission. *J. Abnorm. Soc. Psychol., 23,* 118–136.

——. 1937. *Personality.* New York: Holt.

Allport, G. W., and P. E. Vernon. 1931. *A study of values.* Boston: Houghton Mifflin.

Anderson, G. L. 1951. Qualitative aspects of the Stanford-Binet. Chapter 20 in H. H. Anderson and G. L. Anderson (Eds.), *An introduction to projective techniques,* pp. 581–603. New York: Prentice-Hall.

Anderson, H. H. 1929. *Les cliniques psychologiques pour l'enfance aux États-unis et l'oeuvre du Dr. Healy.* Neuchatel et Paris: Delachaux et Niestlé.

——. 1937a. An experimental study of dominative and integrative behavior in children of preschool age. *J. Soc. Psychol., 8,* 335–345.

——. 1937b. Domination and integration in the social behavior of young children in an experimental play situation. *Genet. Psychol. Monogr., 19,* 341–408.

Anderson, H. H. 1939. Domination and social integration in the behavior of kindergarten children and teachers. *Genet. Psychol. Monogr., 21,* 287–385.

——. 1940. An examination of the concepts of domination and integration in relation to dominance and ascendance. *Psychol. Rev., 47,* 21–37.

——. 1943. *Shorter observational procedures for recording teacher contacts.* (Unpublished manuscript.)

——. 1946a. Socially integrative behavior. *J. Abnorm. Soc. Psychol., 41,* 379–384.

——. 1946b. A revised method for recording teachers' dominative and socially integrative behavior in the schoolroom. Chapter 1 in H. H. Anderson and J. E. Brewer, Studies of teachers' classroom personalities, II. Effects of teachers' dominative and integrative contacts on children's classroom behavior. *Appl. Psychol. Monogr., 8,* 15–32.

——. 1946c. Dominative and socially integrative behavior at the fourth and sixth grade levels. Chapter 3 in H. H. Anderson and J. E. Brewer, Studies of teachers' classroom personalities, II. Effects of teachers' dominative and integrative contacts on children's classroom behavior. *Appl. Psychol. Monogr., 8,* 88–122.

——. 1946d. Directive and nondirective psychotherapy: The role of the therapist. *Amer. J. Orthopsychiat., 16,* 608–614.

——. 1951. Human behavior in personality growth. Chapter 1 in H. H. Anderson and G. L. Anderson (Eds.), *An introduction to projective techniques,* pp. 3–25. New York: Prentice-Hall.

——. 1952. Circular behavior. Chapter 7 in W. Wolff and J. A. Precker (Eds.), *Success is psychotherapy,* pp. 163–190. *Personality Monogr.,* No. 3. New York: Grune & Stratton.

——. 1953. *Psychological entropy: The degradation of energy.* (Unpublished paper.)

Anderson, H. H., and G. L. Anderson (Eds.). 1951. *An introduction to projective techniques.* New York: Prentice-Hall.

Anderson, H. H., and J. E. Brewer. 1946. Consecutive studies from fall to winter of teachers' dominative and socially integrative contacts and related changes in the children's classroom behavior. Chapter 3 in H. H. Anderson, J. E. Brewer, and M. F. Reed, Studies of teachers' classroom personalities, III. Follow-up studies of the effects of dominative and integrative contacts on children's behavior. *Appl. Psychol. Monogr., 11,* 101–156.

Anderson, J. E. 1944. Freedom and constraint or potentiality and environment. *Psychol. Bull., 41,* 1–29.

Anderson, J. E., and J. C. Foster. 1927. *The young child and his parents. A study of one hundred cases. Inst. Child Welfare Monogr. Ser.,* No. 1. Minneapolis: University of Minnesota Press.

Appel, K. E. 1944. Psychiatric therapy. In J. McV. Hunt (Ed.), *Personality and the behavior disorders,* Vol. 2, pp. 1107–1163. New York: Ronald.

Auerbach, J. G. 1950. Value changes in therapy. *Personality Symposia*, No. 1, 63–67. New York: Grune & Stratton.

Austin, M. C., and G. G. Thompson. 1948. Children's friendships: A study of the basis on which children select and reject their best friends. *J. Educ. Psychol.*, *39*, 101–116.

Ayres, C. E. 1950. The values of social scientists. *J. Soc. Issues*, *6*, 17–20.

Baldwin, A. L. 1946. Differences in parent behavior toward three- and nine-year-old children. *J. Personal.*, *15*, 143–165.

——. 1947. Changes in parent behavior during pregnancy: An experiment in longitudinal analysis. *Child Develpm.*, *18*, 29–39.

——. 1948. Socialization and the parent-child relationship. *Child Develpm.*, *19*, 127–136.

——. 1949. The effect of home environment on nursery school behavior. *Child Develpm.*, *20*, 49–62.

Baldwin, A. L., J. Kalhorn, and F. H. Breese. 1945. Patterns of parent behavior. *Psychol. Monogr.*, *58*, No. 268, 1–75.

——. 1949. The appraisal of parent behavior. *Psychol. Monogr.*, *63*, No. 299, vii + 85.

Baldwin, B. T. 1921. *The physical growth of children from birth to maturity*. *Univ. Iowa Stud., Stud. Child Welfare*, *1*, No. 1. Pp. 411.

Barker, R. G., and H. F. Wright. 1949. Psychological ecology and the problem of psychosocial development. *Child Develpm.*, *20*, 131–143.

——. 1951. *One boy's day: A specimen record of behavior*. New York: Harper. Pp. 435.

Barker, R. G., H. F. Wright, J. Nall, and P. Schoggen. 1950. There is no class bias in our school. *Progressive Educ.*, *27*, 106–110.

Bell, J. E. 1948. *Projective techniques*. New York: Longmans, Green.

Benne, K. D., and G. E. Swanson (Eds.). 1950. Values and the social scientist. *J. Soc. Issues*, *6*, 1–82.

Bertalanffy, L. von. 1950. The theory of open systems in physics and biology. *Science*, *111*, 23–29.

Binet, A. 1898. La mésure en psychologie individuelle. *Rev. philosophique*, *46*, 2d Sem., 113–123.

——. 1902. *L'étude experimentale de l'intelligence*. Paris: Alfred Costes.

Bion, W. R. 1948. Experiences in groups. *Human Rel.*, *1*, No. 3.

Bion, W. R., and J. Rickman. 1943. Intra-group tensions in therapy: Their study as a task of the group. *Lancet*, November.

Bishop, B. M. 1951. Mother-child interaction and the social behavior of children. *Psychol. Monogr.*, *65*, Whole No. 328, v + 34.

Bonney, M. E. 1943. Personality traits of socially successful and socially unsuccessful children. *J. Educ. Psychol.*, *34*, 449–472.

——. 1944. Relationships between social success, family size, socioeconomic background and intelligence among school children in grades three to five. *Sociometry*, *7*, 26–39.

Bonney, M. E. 1946. A sociometric study of the relationship of some factors to mutual friendships on the elementary, secondary and college levels. *Sociometry*, *9*, 21–47.

——. 1947. Popular and unpopular children, a sociometric study. *Sociometry Monogr.*, No. 9. Pp. 81.

Bott, H. M. 1933. *Method in social studies of young children*. *Univ. Toronto Stud.*, *Child Develpm. Ser.*, No. *1*. Toronto: The University Toronto Press. Pp. 110.

Bowlby, J. 1949. The study and reduction of group tensions in the family. *Human Rel.*, *2*, 123–128.

Brewer, H. M., and H. H. Anderson. 1945. The measurement of the behavior of kindergarten children in relation to the teachers' dominative and socially integrative contacts. Chapter 3 in H. H. Anderson and H. M. Brewer, Studies of teachers' classroom personalities, I. Dominative and socially integrative behavior of kindergarten teachers. *Appl. Psychol. Monogr.*, *6*, 109–152.

Brewer, J. E. 1940. *The measurement of the behavior of second grade children in relation to the teachers' dominative and socially integrative contacts*. Ph.D. thesis. University of Illinois Library. Urbana. Pp. 104.

——. 1946. The measurement of the behavior of second grade children in relation to the teachers' dominative and socially integrative contacts. Chapter 2 in H. H. Anderson and J. E. Brewer, Studies of teachers' classroom personalities, II. Effects of teachers' dominative and integrative contacts on children's classroom behavior. *Appl. Psychol. Monogr.*, *8*, 33–122.

Bridges, K. M. B. 1931. *Social and emotional development of the preschool child*. London: Kegan Paul. Pp. x + 277.

Brillouin, L. 1949. Life, thermodynamics, and cybernetics. *Amer. Scientist*, *37*, 554–568.

——. 1950. Thermodynamics and information theory. *Amer. Scientist*, *38*, 594–599.

Bronfenbrenner, U., and E. C. Devereux. 1952. Interdisciplinary planning for team research on constructive community behavior. The Springdale project. *Human Rel.*, *5*, 187–203.

Bühler, C. 1933. Social behavior in children. In C. Murchison (Ed.), *A handbook of child psychology*. Pp. 374–416. (2nd ed.) Worcester: Clark University Press.

Cameron, N., and A. Magaret. 1951. *Behavior pathology*. Boston: Houghton Mifflin. Pp. xvi + 645.

Cantril, H. 1949. Toward a scientific morality. *J. Psychol.*, *27*, 363–376.

Cattell, R. B. 1950. The scientific ethics of "beyond." *J. Soc. Issues*, *6*, 21–27.

Champney, H. 1941a. The measurement of parent behavior. *Child Develpm.*, *12*, 131–166.

——. 1941b. The variables of parent behavior. *J. Abnorm. Soc. Psychol.*, *36*, 525–542.

Child, I. L., E. H. Potter, and E. M. Levine. 1946. Children's textbooks and personality development:

An exploration in the social psychology of education. *Psychol. Monogr., 60*, No. 3, 1–54.

Chittenden, G. E. 1942. An experimental study in measuring and modifying assertive behavior in young children. *Monogr. Soc. Research Child Develpm., 7*, 1–87.

Churchman, C. W. 1950. When do we start value research? *J. Soc. Issues, 6*, 61–63.

Clark, W. H. 1950. Psychology of religious values. *Personality Symposia*, No. 1, 45–62. New York: Grune & Stratton.

Clifton, D. E. 1943. *Dominative and socially integrative behavior of twenty-five second grade teachers.* Ph.D. thesis. University of Illinois Library, Urbana.

Conant, J. B. 1947. *On understanding science. An historical approach.* New Haven: Yale University Press. Pp. 145.

Cottrell, L. S., Jr. 1942. The analysis of situational fields in social psychology. *Amer. Sociol. Rev., 7*, 370–382.

Cottrell, L. S., Jr., and R. F. Dymond. 1950. The empathic responses: A neglected field for research. *Psychiatry, 12*, 355–359.

Darwin, C. 1877. A biographical sketch of an infant. *Mind, 2*, 285–294.

Davis, A., and R. J. Havighurst. 1946. Social class and color differences in child rearing. *Amer. Sociol. Rev., 11*, 698–710.

Dennis, W. 1938. Infant development under conditions of restricted practice and of minimum social stimulation. A preliminary report. *J. Genet. Psychol., 53*, 149–158.

——. 1940. Infant reaction to restraint. *Trans. N. Y. Acad. Sci., 2*, 202–218.

Doll, E. A. 1936. The Vineland social maturity scale: Revised, condensed manual of directions. *Publ. Training School Vineland, N. J., Dept. Research*, Ser. No. 3.

——. 1940. Annotated bibliography on the Vineland social maturity scale. *J. Consult. Psychol., 4*, 123–132.

Dollard, J., L. W. Doob, N. E. Miller, O. H. Mowrer, R. R. Sears, *et al.* 1939. *Frustration and aggression.* New Haven: Yale University Press.

Dymond, R. F. 1948. A preliminary investigation of the relation of insight and empathy. *J. Consult. Psychol., 12*, 228–233.

——. 1949. A scale for the measurement of empathic ability. *J. Consult. Psychol., 13*, 127–133.

——. 1950. Personality and empathy. *J. Consult. Psychol., 14*, 343–350.

Escalona, S. K. 1945. Feeding disturbances in very young children. *Amer. J. Orthopsychiat., 15*, 76–80.

Estes, W. K. 1944. An experimental study of punishment. *Psychol. Monogr., 57*.

Feigl, H. 1950. The difference between knowledge and valuation. *J. Soc. Issues, 6*, 39–44.

Fischer, L. K. 1952. Hospitalism in six-month-old infants. *Amer. J. Orthopsychiat., 22*, 522–533.

Follett, M. P. 1922. *The new state.* Longmans, Green.

Follett, M. P. 1924. *Creative experience.* New York: Longmans, Green.

Frank, L. K. 1928. The management of tensions. *Amer. J. Sociol., 33*, 705–736.

——. 1936. Society as the patient. *Am. J. Sociol., 42*, 335–344.

——. 1939. Projective methods for the study of personality. *J. Psychol., 8*, 389–413.

——. 1948. *Society as the patient.* New Brunswick: Rutgers University Press. Pp. xiv + 395.

——. 1951. Symposium on genetic psychology: 4. Genetic psychology and its prospects. *Amer. J. Orthopsychiat., 21*, 506–522.

French, T. M. 1952. *The integration of behaviors:* Vol. 1, *Basic postulates.* Chicago: University of Chicago Press.

Frenkel-Brunswik, E., and R. Potashin. 1944. A survey of sociometric and pre-sociometric literature on friendship and social acceptance among children. *Sociometry, 7*, 422–431.

Freud, A. 1928. Introduction to the technique of child analysis. *Nerv. Ment. Dis. Monogr.*, No. 48.

——. 1951. Symposium on genetic psychology 2. The contribution of psychoanalysis to genetic psychology. *Amer. J. Orthopsychiat., 21*, 476–497.

Freud, S. 1896. The aetiology of hysteria. (Trans. by C. M. Baines.) In *Collected papers.* Vol. 1. London: International Psychoanalytical Press.

——. 1900. The interpretation of dreams. In *The basic writings of Sigmund Freud.* (Trans. and ed. by A. A. Brill.) New York: Modern Library, 1938.

——. 1904. On the psychopathology of everyday life. In *The basic writings of Sigmund Freud.* (Trans. and ed. by A. A. Brill.) New York: Modern Library, 1938.

——. 1910. The origin and development of psychoanalysis (five lectures delivered at Clark University). (Trans. Harry W. Chase.) *Amer. J. Psychol., 21*, 181–218.

Fries, M. E. 1944. Psychosomatic relationships between mother and infant. *Psychosom. Med., 6*, 159–162.

——. 1946. The child's ego development and the training of adults in his development. *Psychoanalytic study of the child, 2*, pp. 85–112. New York: International Universities Press.

——. 1947. Diagnosing the child's adjustment through age level tests. *Psa. Rev., 34*, 1–31.

Fries, M. E., and B. Lewi. 1938. Interrelated factors in development. (A study of pregnancy, labor, delivery, lying-in period, and childhood.) *Amer. J. Orthopsychiat., 8*, 726–752.

Fromm, E. 1941. *Escape from freedom.* New York: Farrar & Rinehart.

——. 1947. *Man for himself. An inquiry into the psychology of ethics.* New York: Rinehart.

Geiger, G. 1950. Values and social science. *J. Soc. Issues, 6*, 8–16.

Goldfarb, W. 1944. Effects of early institutional care on adolescent personality—Rorschach data. *Amer. J. Orthopsychiat., 14*, 441–447.

Goldfarb, W. 1945. Effects of psychological deprivation in infancy and subsequent stimulation. *Amer. J. Psychiat.*, *102*, 18–33.

Goldstein, K. 1939. *The organism*. New York: American Book.

Gorer, G. 1943. Themes in Japanese culture. *Trans. N. Y. Acad. Sci.*, *2*, 106–124.

Gough, H. G., H. McClosky, and P. E. Meehl. 1952. A personality scale for social responsibility. *J. Abnorm. Soc. Psychol.*, *47*, 73–80.

Grace, G. L., and H. A. Grace. 1952. The relationship between verbal and behavioral measures of values. *J. Educ. Research*, *46*, 123–131.

Grace, H. A., and J. J. Lohmann. 1952. Children's reactions to stories depicting parent-child conflict situations. *Child Develpm.*, *23*, 61–74.

Graham, F. K., W. A. Charwat, A. S. Honig, and P. C. Weltz. 1951. Aggression as a function of the attack and the attacker. *J. Abnorm. Soc. Psychol.*, *46*, 512–520.

Green, E. H. 1933. Friendships and quarrels among preschool children. *Child Develpm.*, *4*, 237–252.

Greenacre, P. 1944. Infants' reactions to restraint. *Amer. J. Orthopsychiat.*, *14*, 204–218.

Hanfmann, E. 1935. Social structure of a group of kindergarten children. *Amer. J. Orthopsychiat.*, *5*, 407–410.

Harris, D. B. 1953. Child psychology. Chapter in *Annual review of psychology*, pp. 1–30. Stanford: Annual Reviews.

Harris, D. B., H. G. Gough, and W. E. Martin. 1950. Children's ethnic attitudes: II. Relationship to parental beliefs concerning child training. *Child Develpm.*, *21*, 169–181.

Hastorf, A. H., and I. E. Bender. 1952. A caution respecting the measurement of empathic ability. *J. Abnorm. Soc. Psychol.*, *47*, No. 2 Supp., 574–576.

Healy, W. 1915a. *The individual delinquent*. Boston: Little, Brown.

——. 1915b. *Honesty*. New York: Bobbs-Merrill.

——. 1925. The psychology of the situation: A fundamental for understanding and treatment of delinquency and crime. In J. Adams *et al.*, *The child, the clinic, and the court*, pp. 37–52. New York: New Republic.

Hobbs, N. 1950. Some reflections on empirical investigations of ethics. *J. Soc. Issues*, *6*, 56–60.

Hollenberg, E., and M. Sperry. 1951. Some antecedents of aggression and effects of frustration in doll play. *Personality*, *1*, 32–43.

Horney, K. 1937. *The neurotic personality of our time*. New York: Norton.

——. 1939. *New ways in psychoanalysis*. New York: Norton.

——. 1945. *Our inner conflicts*. New York: Norton. Pp. 250.

Horrocks, J. E., and M. E. Buker. 1951. A study of friendship fluctuations of preadolescents. *J. Genet. Psychol.*, *78*, 131–144.

Horrocks, J. E., and G. G. Thompson. 1946. A study of the friendship fluctuations of rural boys and girls. *J. Genet. Psychol.*, *69*, 189–198.

Hutt, M. L., and D. R. Miller. 1949. Value interiorization and democratic education. *J. Soc. Issues*, *5*, 31–43.

Isaacs, S. 1931. Contribution à la psychologie sociale des jeunes enfants. *J. de psychol.*, *28*, 372–387.

——. 1933. *Social development in young children: A study of beginnings*. New York: Harcourt, Brace. Pp. 480.

Jack, L. M. 1934. An experimental study of ascendant behavior in preschool children. In L. M. Jack, E. M. Manwell, I. G. Mengert, and others, *Behavior of the preschool child*. *Univ. Iowa Stud., Stud. Child Welfare*, *9*, 9–65.

Jackson, L., and K. M. Todd. 1948. *Child treatment and the therapy of play*. (2nd ed.) London: Methuen. Pp. 115.

James, W. 1902. *The varieties of religious experience*. New York: Longmans, Green.

Jaques, E. (issue Ed.) 1947. Social therapy. *J. Soc. Issues*, *3*, 1–68.

——. 1948. Interpretive group discussion as a method of facilitating social change. *Human Rel.*, *1*, No. 4.

——. 1950. Studies in the social development of an industrial community (The Glacier Project). I. Collaborative group methods in a wage negotiation. *Human Rel.*, *3*, 223–249.

Jersild, A. T. 1946. Emotional development. In L. Carmichael (Ed.), *Manual of Child Psychology*, pp. 752–790. New York: Wiley.

——. 1947. *Child psychology*. (3rd ed.) New York: Prentice-Hall.

Jersild, A. T., and M. D. Fite. 1939. *The influence of nursery school experience on children's social adjustment*. New York: Bur. Pub., Teachers College, Columbia University.

Josey, C. C., and D. Snygg. 1950. The place of psychology in the development of values. *Personality Symposia*, No. 1, 1–6. New York: Grune & Stratton.

Jung, C. G. 1916. *Collected papers on analytical psychology*. (Trans. by C. E. Long.) London: Baillière, Tindall.

——. 1923. *Psychological types*. London: Routledge.

Kerr, W. A., and B. J. Speroff. 1951. *The empathy test*. Chicago: Psychometric Affiliates.

Klackenberg, G. 1949. Thumbsucking: Frequency and etiology. *Pediat.*, *4*, 418–424.

Klatskin, E. H. 1952. Shifts in child care practices in three social classes under an infant care program of flexible methodology. *Amer. J. Orthopsychiat.*, *22*, 52–61.

Klee, J. B. 1950. Experience and selection. *Personality Symposia*, No. 1, 7–10. New York: Grune & Stratton.

Klein, M. 1932. *The psychoanalysis of children*. London: Hogarth.

Kluckhohn, C. 1947. Some aspects of Navaho infancy and early childhood. *Psychoanal. Soc. Sci.*, *1*, 37–86.

Kluckhohn, C., and H. A. Murray (Eds.). 1948. *Personality in nature, society, and culture*. New York: Knopf. Pp. xxi + 561 + x.

Koch, H. 1933. Popularity in preschool children. *Child Develpm.*, *4*, 164-175.

Köhler, W. 1938. *The place of value in a world of facts.* New York: Liveright.

Koshuk, R. P. 1941. Social influences affecting the behavior of young children. *Monogr. Soc. Res. Child Develpm.*, *6*, No. 2.

Krech, D. 1950a. Dynamic systems, psychological fields, and hypothetical constructs. *Psychol. Rev.*, *57*, 283-290.

———. 1950b. Dynamic systems as open neurological systems. *Psychol. Rev.*, *57*, 345-361.

Krech, D., and R. S. Crutchfield. 1948. *Theory and problems of social psychology.* New York: McGraw-Hill.

Leeper, R. W. 1948. A motivational theory of emotion to replace "emotion as disorganized response." *Psychol. Rev.*, *55*, 5-21.

Leighton, D., and C. Kluckhohn. 1947. *Children of the people.* Cambridge: Harvard University Press.

Levy, D. M. 1928. Finger sucking and accessory movements in early infancy. *Amer. J. Psychiat.*, *7*, 881-918.

———. 1934. Experiments on the sucking reflex and social behavior of dogs. *Amer. J. Orthopsychiat.*, *4*, 203-224.

———. 1937. Thumb or fingersucking from the psychiatric angle. *Child Develpm.*, *8*, 99-101.

———. 1939. Maternal overprotection. *Psychiatry, 2*, 99-128.

———. 1943. *Maternal overprotection.* New York: Columbia University Press.

———. 1944. On the problem of movement restraint. *Amer. J. Orthopsychiat.*, *14*, 644-671.

Lewin, K. 1933. Environmental forces. Chapter 14 in C. Murchison (Ed.), *Handbook of child psychology*, pp. 590-625. (2nd ed.) Worcester: Clark University Press.

———. 1935. *A dynamic theory of personality.* New York: McGraw-Hill.

Lewin, K., and R. Lippitt. 1938. An experimental approach to the study of autocracy and democracy: A preliminary note. *Sociometry, 1*, 292-300.

Lewin, K., R. Lippitt, and R. K. White. 1939. Patterns of aggressive behavior in experimentally created "social climates." *J. Soc. Psychol., 10*, 271-299.

Lippitt, R. 1939. Field theory and experiment in social psychology: Autocratic and democratic group atmospheres. *Amer. J. Sociol., 45*, 26-49.

———. 1940. An experimental study of the effect of democratic and authoritarian group atmospheres. *Univ. Iowa Stud., Stud. Child Welfare, 16*, 3, 43-195.

———. 1949. *Training in community relations.* New York: Harper.

———. 1950. Action-research and the values of the social scientist. *J. Soc. Issues, 6*, 50-55.

Lippitt, R., and R. K. White. 1943. The "social climate" of children's groups. Chapter 28, in R. G. Barker, J. S. Kounin, and H. F. Wright (Eds.), *Child behavior and development*, pp. 485-508. New York: McGraw-Hill.

Lippitt, Rosemary. 1941. Popularity among preschool children. *Child Develpm., 12*, 305-332.

Lowrey, L. G. (Chairman.) 1930-1931. Symposium: The treatment of behavior and personality problems in children. *Amer. J. Orthopsychiat., 1*, 3-60.

McClelland, D. C. 1951. *Personality.* New York: William Sloane.

McClelland, D. C., and F. S. Apicella. 1945. A functional classification of verbal reactions to experimentally induced failure. *J. Abnorm. Soc. Psychol., 40*, 376-390.

McFarland, M. B. 1938. Relationships between young sisters as revealed by their overt responses. *Child Develpm. Monogr.*, No. 24.

McKinnon, K. 1940. Consistency and change in personality, and behavior manifestations—as observed in a group of 16 children during a five year period. (Unpublished manuscript.) Teachers College, Columbia University, New York.

Macfarlane, J. W. 1938. *Studies in child guidance. I. Methodology of data collection and organization. Monogr. Soc. Res. Child Develpm.*, III, 6. Washington: National Research Council. Pp. vii + 254.

Maier, N. R. F. 1949. *Frustration: The study of behavior without a goal.* New York: McGraw-Hill.

Maslow, A. H. 1950. Self-actualizing people: A study of psychological health. *Personality Symposia*, No. 1, 11-34. New York: Grune & Stratton.

Mathews, W. M. 1949. Social values and research in child development. *J. Soc. Issues, 5*, 47-49.

Mead, G. H. 1934. In C. W. Morris (Ed.), *Mind, self and society.* Chicago: University of Chicago Press.

Mengert, I. G. 1931. A preliminary study of the reactions of two-year-old children to each other when paired in a semi-controlled situation. *J. Genet. Psychol., 39*, 393-398.

Miller, D. R., and M. L. Hutt. 1949. Value interiorization and personality development. *J. Soc. Issues, 5*, 2-30.

Moloney, J. C. 1947. The Cornelian Corner and its rationale. In M. J. E. Senn (Ed.), *Problems of early infancy.* New York: Josiah Macy, Jr., Foundation.

Moreno, J. L. 1934. *Who shall survive? A new approach to the problem of human interrelations.* Washington: Nervous and Mental Disease Publishing.

Mowrer, O. H., and C. Kluckhohn. 1944. Dynamic theory of personality. Chapter 3 in J. McV. Hunt (Ed.), *Personality and the behavior disorders*, Vol. 1, pp. 69-135. New York: Ronald.

Murphy, G. 1949. The relationships of culture and personality. In S. S. Sargent and M. W. Smith (Eds.), *Culture and personality*, pp. 13-30. New York: Viking Fund.

Murphy, L. B. 1937. *Social behavior and child personality. An exploratory study of some roots of sympathy.* New York: Columbia University Press.

———. 1944. Childhood experience in relation to personality development. Chapter 21 in J. McV.

Hunt (Ed.), *Personality and the behavior disorders,* Vol. 2, pp. 652–690. New York: Ronald.

Murray, H. A., and C. Kluckhohn. 1948. Outline of a conception of personality. Chapter 1 in C. Kluckhohn and H. A. Murray (Eds.), *Personality in nature, society, and culture.* New York: Knopf.

Murray, H. A., and C. D. Morgan. 1945. A clinical study of sentiments: I, II. *Genet. Psychol. Monogr., 32,* 3–149 and 153–311.

Murray, H. A., and others. 1938. *Explorations in personality.* New York: Oxford University Press.

Muste, M. J., and D. F. Sharpe. 1947. Some influential factors in the determination of aggressive behavior in preschool children. *Child Develpm., 18,* 11–28.

Newcomb, T. M. 1950. *Social psychology.* New York: Dryden.

Northway, M. L. 1943. Social relationships among preschool children: Abstracts and interpretations of three studies. *Sociometry, 6,* 429–433.

Orlansky, H. 1949. Infant care and personality. *Psychol. Bull., 46,* 1–48.

Page, M. L. 1936. The modification of ascendant behavior in preschool children. *Univ. Iowa Stud., Stud. Child Welfare, 12.* Pp. 69.

Parsons, T., and E. A. Shild (Eds.). 1951. *Toward a general theory of action.* Cambridge: Harvard University Press. Pp. 496.

Parten, M. B. 1932. Social participation among preschool children. *J. Abnorm. Soc. Psychol., 27,* 243–270.

———. 1933. Leadership among preschool children. *J. Abnorm. Soc. Psychol., 27,* 430–441.

Peterson, C. H., and F. Spano. 1941. Breast feeding, maternal rejection and child personality. *Character & Pers., 10,* 62–66.

Piaget, J. 1923. Le langage et la pensée chez l'enfant. Neuchatel et Paris: Delachaux et Niestlé. Pp. 318. *The language and thought of the child.* (Trans. by M. Warden.) New York: Harcourt, Brace; London: Kegan Paul, 1926. Pp. xxiii + 246.

Pinneau, S. R. 1950. A critique on the articles by Margaret Ribble. *Child Develpm., 21,* 203–228.

Plant, J. S. 1937. *Personality and the cultural pattern.* New York: Commonwealth Fund.

Preyer, W. 1882. *Die Seele des Kindes.* (5th ed., 1900.) Leipzig: Fernau.

———. 1888, 1889. *The mind of the child.* Part 1, The senses and the will; Part 2, The development of the intellect. (Trans. by H. W. Brown.) New York: Appleton.

Ransom, D. 1952. Science on the march: Psychobiological periodic table of chemical elements. *Sci. Mon., 74,* 358–365.

Raup, R. B. 1950. Choice and decision in social intelligence. *J. Soc. Issues, 6,* 45–49.

Raymond, R. C. 1950. Communication, entropy, and life. *Amer. Scientist, 38,* 273–278.

Reed, M. F. 1946. Consecutive studies of the schoolroom behavior of children in relation to the teachers' dominative and socially integrative contacts. Chapter 1 in H. H. Anderson, J. E. Brewer,

and M. F. Reed. Studies of teachers' classroom personalities, III. Follow-up studies of the effects of dominative and integrative contacts on children's behavior. *Appl. Psychol. Monogr., 11,* 15–100.

Ribble, M. A. 1938. Clinical studies of instinctive reactions in newborn babies. *Amer. J. Psychiat., 95,* 145–160.

———. 1939. Significance of infantile sucking for psychic development. *J. Nerv. Ment. Dis., 90,* 455–463.

———. 1941. Disorganizing factors of infant personality. *Amer. J. Psychiat., 98,* 459–463.

———. 1943. *The rights of infants.* New York: Columbia University Press.

———. 1944. Infantile experience in relation to personality development. Chapter 20 in J. McV. Hunt (Ed.), *Personality and the behavior disorders,* Vol. 1, pp. 621–651. New York: Ronald.

Roberts, E. 1944. Thumb and finger sucking in relation to feeding in early infancy. *Amer. J. Dis. Child., 68,* 7–8.

Roff, M. 1949. A factorial study of the Fels Parent Behavior Scales. *Child Develpm., 20,* 29–45.

Rogers, C. R. 1939. *The clinical treatment of the problem child.* Cambridge: Riverside.

———. 1942. *Counseling and psychotherapy.* Boston: Houghton Mifflin.

Rogerson, B. C. F., and C. H. Rogerson. 1939. Feeding in infancy and subsequent psychological difficulties. *J. Ment. Sci., 85,* 1163–1182.

Rokeach, M. 1951. Toward the scientific evaluation of social attitudes and ideologies. *J. Psychol., 31,* 97–104.

Ross, S. 1951. Sucking behavior in neonate dogs. *J. Abnorm. Soc. Psychol., 46,* 142–149.

Rousseau, J-J. 1925 ed. *Emile.* New York: Dutton.

Schilder, P. 1938. *Psychotherapy.* New York: Norton.

Schneirla, T. C. 1946. Problems in the biopsychology of social organization. *J. Abnorm. Soc. Psychol., 41,* 385–402.

Scott, J. P. (Ed.). 1951. Minutes of the conference on the effects of early experience on mental health. September 6–9. Roscoe B. Jackson Memorial Laboratory, Bar Harbor, Me. Pp. 45.

Scupin, E., and G. Scupin. 1907. *Bübis erste kindheit.* Leipzig: Grieben.

Sears, R. R. 1943. Survey of objective studies of psychoanalytic concepts. *Soc. Sci. Res. Coun. Bull. 51.* New York.

———. 1944. Experimental analysis of psychoanalytic phenomena. In J. McV. Hunt (Ed.), *Personality and the behavior disorders,* Vol. 1, pp. 306–332. New York: Ronald.

Senn, M. J. E. (Ed.). 1947. Symposium: Problems of early infancy. New York: Josiah Macy, Jr., Foundation.

Sherif, M., and H. Cantril. 1945. The psychology of "attitudes." Part I. *Psychol. Rev., 52,* 295–319.

———. 1946. The psychology of "attitudes." Part II. *Psychol. Rev., 53,* 1–24.

Shinn, M. W. 1893–1899. Notes on the development of a child. *Univ. Calif. Publ., 1,* 1–178 and 179–424.

Shinn, M. W. 1900. *Biography of a baby.* Boston: Houghton Mifflin.

Simsarian, F. P. 1947. Case histories of five thumb-sucking children breast fed on unscheduled regimes, without limitation of nursing time. *Child Develpm., 18,* 180–184.

Sinnott, E. W. 1950. *Cell and psyche.* Chapel Hill: University of North Carolina Press.

——. 1952. The biology of purpose. *Amer. J. Orthopsychiat., 22,* 457–468.

Speroff, B. J. 1953. Empathy and role-reversal as factors in industrial harmony. *J. Soc. Psychol., 37,* 117–120.

Spitz, R. A. 1945. Hospitalism. An inquiry into the genesis of psychiatric conditions in early childhood. *Psychoanalytic Study of the Child,* Vol. I. New York: International Universities Press.

Spitz, R. A., and K. M. Wolf. 1946. Anaclitic depression. An inquiry into the genesis of psychiatric conditions in early childhood. *Psychoanalytic Study of the Child,* Vol. II. New York: International Universities Press.

Spranger, E. 1928. *Types of men.* (Trans. by J. W. Pigors.) Halle (Saale). Germany: Niemeyer.

Staniland, A. 1952. The Chichester seminar on mental health and infant development. *Bull. World Fed. Ment. Health, 4,* 168–171.

Stern, C., and W. Stern. 1907. Die Kindersprache: Eine Psychologische und Sprachtheoretische. Untersuchung. *Monogr. seel. Entwick. Kindes,* Vol. 1. Leipzig: Barth. Pp. 394. (3d ed., 1922. Pp. xii + 434.)

——. 1909. Erinnerung, Aussage und Lüge in der ersten Kindheit. *Monogr. seel. Entwick. Kindes,* Vol. 2. Leipzig: Barth. Pp. x + 160.

Sullivan, H. S. 1947. *Conceptions of modern psychiatry.* Washington: William Alanson White Psychiatric Foundation.

Thomas, D. S., and associates. 1929. *Some new techniques for studying social behavior. Child Develpm. Monogr.,* No. 1. New York: Bur. Publ. Teachers College, Columbia University.

Thompson, G. G. 1952. *Child psychology.* Boston: Houghton Mifflin. Pp. xxxiii + 667.

Thompson, G. G., and J. E. Horrocks. 1947. A study of the friendship fluctuations of urban boys and girls. *J. Genet. Psychol., 70,* 53–63.

Titiev, M. 1949. Cultural adjustment and the interiorization of social values. *J. Soc. Issues, 5,* 44–46.

Tolman, E. C. 1949. The psychology of social learning. *J. Soc. Issues, 5,* Supp. 3, 3–18.

Toynbee, A. J. 1939. *A study of history.* Vol. III. *The growths of civilization.* London: Oxford University Press. Pp. vi + 551.

Trainham, G. 1945. Case history of the first thirteen months of life of a pair of twins breast fed on a self-demand schedule. *Psychosom. Med., 7,* 176.

Turner, W. D. 1948. Altruism and its measurement in children. *J. Abnorm. Soc. Psychol., 43,* 502–516.

Vincent, C. E. 1951. Trends in infant care ideas. *Child Develpm., 22,* 199–209.

Wellman, B. L. 1926. The school child's choice of companions. *J. Educ. Research, 14,* 126–132.

White, R. K. 1950. Verbal data and "self-evident" values. *Personality Symposia,* No. 1, 35–44. New York: Grune & Stratton.

Wickert, F. R. 1940. The interrelationships of some general and specific preferences. *J. Soc. Psychol., 11,* 275–302.

Wickman, E. K. 1928. *Children's behavior and teachers' attitudes.* New York: Commonwealth Fund. Pp. 247.

Wieman, H. N. 1950. Science in service of values. *J. Soc. Issues, 6,* 33–38.

Wiener, N. 1948. *Cybernetics, or control and communication in the animal and the machine.* New York: Wiley. Pp. 194.

Wolff, W. 1950. One plus one = ? An inquiry into methodology, perception, and values. *Personality Symposia,* No. 1, 68–74. New York: Grune & Stratton.

Wolff, W., and J. A. Precker (Eds.) 1950. Values in personality research. *Personality Symposia,* No. 1, 1–74. New York: Grune & Stratton.

INDEX

McGinnis, J. M., 233, 286, 392, 393, 395, 398, 406, 455
McGranahan, D. V., 492, 493, 515, 522, 624
McGrath, M. C., 960, 969
McGraw, M. B., 51, 57, 217, 218, 249, 250, 251, 257,
  258, 259, 261, 275, 276, 279, 286, 388, 432, 455,
  624, 846, 914, 924, 969
McGuire, C., 25, 55
McHale, K., 314, 331
McHugh, G., 682, 693
McIlroy, A. L., 124, 180
McIntosh, D. M., 644, 693
McIntyre, G. A., 1071, 1109
McKee, P., 624
McKelvey, R. K., 200, 212
McKillop, A. S., 855, 914
McKinnon, K., 1203, 1213
McLendon, P. A., 224, 289
McNattin, R. F., 103, 177
McNeil, 1096, 1109
McNemar, O., 1064
McNemar, Q., 29, 40, 44, 48, 50, 57, 471, 473, 476,
  490, 675, 681, 693, 1046, 1060, 1068, 1074, 1109,
  1113
McPhee, C., 775, 780
Mead, C. D., 525, 579, 599, 624
Mead, G., 836, 915, 1165, 1213
Mead, M., 700, 704, 731, 735, 736, 737, 738, 739, 741,
  742, 743, 744, 745, 746, 747, 749, 750, 753, 756,
  757, 758, 759, 761, 762, 764, 766, 767, 768, 769,
  775, 776, 780, 812, 830, 918, 919, 969, 1175
Meader, C. L., 492, 493, 625
Mean menstruation age, 115
Meaning, 520, 526
  as criterion of word, 528
  first sound with, 523
  of word judged by place in child's activity, 523
  symbolic, 521
Measurements, in primitive society, 745
  of vocabulary, 528ff
Measures of language development, interrelationships
  of, 574–576
  correlations of, with chronological age and mental
    age, 575
Measuring instruments, contamination in, 38
  development of, 33–38
  reliability of, 37f
    heterogeneity in, 37f
    homogeneity in, 37f
  scaling of, 36
  standardization of, 36
  validity of, 34f
Mechanical ability, 467
Mechanical factors in embryological development, 74ff
Medawar, P. B., 299, 331
Medulla, stimulation of, and breathing in human fetus,
  133
Meehl, P. E., 1204, 1212
Meek, L. H., 417, 418, 422, 455
Meeker, M., 59
Megalocephaly, 1135
Meier, G. W., 199, 212
Meier, J., 776
Meigs, M. F., 20, 57

Meigs, M. M., 856, 913
Meine, F. J., 1084, 1109
Mekeel, S., 742, 745, 776, 780
Melcher, R. T., 404, 455
Mellone, M. A., 1069, 1109
Melton, A. W., 45, 57
Meltzer, H., 856, 885, 915, 1101, 1109
Membranes, fetal, 78–79
Memorizing, studies in, 415–418
  techniques, relative efficacy of, 418–422
  transfer of improvement in, 423–425
Memory, 407–430
  comparison of, in humans and in animals, 196–198
  delayed reaction, studies in, 408–412
  in fetal life, 170
  in young animals, 196–199
  of early emotional experiences, 857–858
  selective recall in, 857–858
Memory-span, studies in, 412–415
  test, 374
Mena, R., 776
Menarche, and behavior tendencies, 1100
  See also Menstruation and Puberty
Mendel, 462
Mengert, I. G., 497, 539, 574, 580, 598, 630, 1111, 1203,
  1213
Meningeal fibrosis, 1136
Meningitis serosa, 1135
Menino, C., 321, 332
Menninger, K. A., 915
Menninger Foundation, 975
Mensh, I. N., 1060
Menstruation, 309
  age, 115
  age differences in first, 712–713
  as criterion of puberty, 712–713
  onset of, in relation to body build, 309
  problems in decreasing average age of first, 713
  See also Menarche and Puberty
Mental abilities, 468
  primary, 469
  sex differences and, 1067–1075
  studies of, and interclass migration, 649
Mental ability, 631
  individual differences in, 631
  nature of, 631–632
Mental age, 470–471, 473, 665f
  as related to environmental factors, 647
  differentiation and, 966
  velocity of satiation and, 953
Mental defects, 465
  diagnosis of, 465ff
  theories of causation, 465–466
Mental defectives, 599
  and delayed speech, 599
  and normal speech, 599
  and speech correction, 599, 602
  classes of, 460
  family history of, 462
  proportion of among institutionalized delinquents,
    462
  See also Feeble-minded children; Inadequate child;
    and Mental deficiency